THE STATESMAN'S YEAR-BOOK

1971–1972

Man hat behauptet, die Welt werde durch Zahlen regiert:
das aber weiss ich, dass die Zahlen uns belehren, ob sie gut
oder schlecht regiert werde. GOETHE

THE
STATESMAN'S
YEAR-BOOK

STATISTICAL AND HISTORICAL ANNUAL

OF THE STATES OF THE WORLD

FOR THE YEAR

1971-1972

EDITED BY

JOHN PAXTON

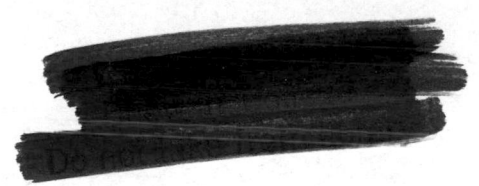

MACMILLAN

ST MARTIN'S PRESS

© Macmillan London Ltd 1971

First published in 1864
108th edition 1971

Published by
MACMILLAN LONDON LTD
Little Essex Street London WC2R 3LF
and also at Bombay Calcutta and Madras
Macmillan South Africa (Publishers) Pty Ltd Johannesburg
The Macmillan Company of Australia Pty Ltd Melbourne
The Macmillan Company of Canada Ltd Toronto
St Martin's Press Inc New York
Gill and Macmillan Ltd Dublin

Printed in Great Britain by
RICHARD CLAY (THE CHAUCER PRESS) LTD
Bungay, Suffolk

Library of Congress Catalog No. 4–3776

SBN 333 11304 7

PREFACE

Several changes in the names of countries are recorded in this, the 108th edition, of The Statesman's Year-Book. Muscat and Oman becomes 'Oman'. Rumania is now 'Romania' (in the 1864 edition it was Roumania) and Cambodia is indexed as 'Khmer Republic'. As is usual revisions and amendments appear on nearly every one of the 1,500 pages.

The editor would like to thank all the officials, government departments and members of the diplomatic services of almost every country, as well as numerous international organizations and individual friends who have contributed to this edition. He was particularly grateful to those who wrote giving constructive and informed criticism. Not all the valid suggestions could be incorporated in this volume but the information will be used in the editor's planning for future editions.

J.P.

The Statesman's Year-Book Office,
Macmillan London Ltd,
Little Essex Street,
London, WC2R 3LF

WEIGHTS AND MEASURES

On 1 Jan. 1960 following an agreement between the standards laboratories of Great Britain, Canada, Australia, New Zealand, South Africa and the USA, an international yard and an international pound (avoirdupois) came into existence. 1 yard = 91·44 centimetres; 1 lb. = 453·59237 grammes. The abbreviation 'm.' signifies 'million(s)'.

LENGTH		DRY MEASURE	
Centimetre	0·394 inch	Litre	0·91 quart
Metre	1·094 yards	Hectolitre	2·75 bushels
Kilometre	0·621 mile		

		WEIGHT—AVOIRDUPOIS	
		Gramme	15·42 grains
LIQUID MEASURE		Kilogramme	2·205 pounds
Litre	1·76 pints	Quintal (= 100 kg)	220·46 pounds
Hectolitre	22 gallons	Metric ton (= 1,000 kg)	{0·984 long ton / 1·102 short tons

SURFACE MEASURE		WEIGHT—TROY	
Square metre	10·76 sq. feet	Gramme	15·43 grains
Hectare	2·47 acres	Kilogramme	{32·15 ounces / 2·68 pounds
Square kilometre	0·386 sq. mile		

BRITISH WEIGHTS AND MEASURES

LENGTH		WEIGHT	
1 foot	0·305 metre	1 ounce (= 437·2 grains)	28·350 grammes
1 yard	0·914 metre	1 lb. (= 7,000 grains)	453·6 grammes
1 mile (= 1,760 yds)	1·609 kilometres	1 cwt. (= 112 lb.)	50·802 kilogrammes
		1 long ton (= 2,240 lb.)	1·016 metric tons
		1 short ton (= 2,000 lb.)	0·907 metric ton

SURFACE MEASURE		LIQUID MEASURE	
1 sq. foot	9·290 sq. decimetres	1 pint	0·568 litre
1 sq. yard	0·836 sq. metre	1 gallon	4·546 litres
1 acre	0·405 hectare	1 quarter	2·909 hectolitres
1 sq. mile	2·590 sq. kilometres		

CONTENTS

Comparative Statistical Tables

Part I: International Organizations

vii

Part II: The Commonwealth

Part III: The United States of America

Part IV

MAPS

Earthquakes

Regional Migration in Western Europe

WHEAT

Countries	Area (1,000 hectares)					Production (1,000 metric tons)				
	Average 1948–52	1966	1967	1968	1969	Average 1948–52	1966	1967	1968	1969
Algeria	1,597	1,482	1,998	2,253	2,150	996	630	1,266	1,534	1,100
Argentina	4,487	5,214	5,812	5,837	5,191	5,175	6,247	7,320	5,740	7,020
Australia [1]	4,620	8,427	9,081	10,845	9,470	5,161	12,699	7,547	14,804	10,834
Bulgaria [1,2]	1,432	1,142	1,064	1,060	1,039	1,776	3,193	3,254	2,549	2,569
Canada	10,507	12,016	12,189	11,907	10,104	13,443	22,516	16,137	17,686	18,623
Chile [1]	777	780	719	700	743	928	1,346	1,204	1,220	1,214
China (Mainland) [1]	23,049 [3]	·	·	·	·	15,913 [3]	25,700	28,000	27,000	28,500
Czechoslovakia [2]	785	889	927	998	1,051	1,493	2,247	2,516	3,153	3,257
France	4,264	3,992	3,929	4,090	4,034	7,791	11,297	14,288	14,985	14,459
Germany (West) [2]	1,020	1,389	1,414	1,464	1,494	2,669	4,533	5,819	6,198	6,000
Greece	878	1,132	1,051	1,100	1,083	894	2,020	1,936	1,561	1,701
Hungary [1,4]	1,385	1,082	1,167	1,331	1,324	1,909	2,349	3,022	3,360	3,586
India	9,290	12,656	12,838	14,998	15,948	6,087	10,424	11,393	16,540	18,652
Iran	2,085 [3]	4,400	4,400*	4,800*	4,600*	1,879	3,964	4,000*	4,977	4,000
Iraq	936	1,737	1,842	2,010	2,089	448	826	860	1,371	1,189
Italy	4,705	4,274	4,012	4,280	4,218	7,170	9,400	9,596	9,665	9,585
Japan [1]	745	421	367	322	287	1,375	1,024	997	1,012	758
Morocco	1,287	1,640	1,770	1,930	1,953	786	1,000	1,310	2,556	1,469
Pakistan [1]	4,218	5,210	5,417	6,061	6,277	3,685	3,951	4,393	6,477	6,711
Poland [1]	1,464	1,654	1,722	1,844	1,965	1,833	3,556	3,857	4,567	4,710
Portugal	689	523	586	614	563	499	312	637	748	452
Romania [1]	2,728 [3]	3,034	2,913	2,817	2,760	2,778 [3]	5,065	5,820	4,848	4,349
S. Africa, Republic of	928	1,030*	1,234*	1,250	1,270	555	567	1,089	1,270	1,328
Spain [2]	4,162	4,191	4,263	3,960	3,802	3,625	4,881	5,654	5,315	4,629
Tunisia	917	845*	815*	833	800	452	349	330	383	350
Turkey [2]	4,770	8,069	8,112	8,352	8,743	4,770	9,715	10,110	9,603	10,593
USSR [1]	42,633 [5]	69,958	67,026	67,231	66,426	35,759 [5]	100,499	77,419	93,393	79,917
UAR [1]	605	542	523	594	523	1,111	1,465	1,299	1,518	1,269
UK	881	906	933	978	833	2,397	3,475	3,903	3,469	3,364
USA	27,756	20,180	23,781	22,363	19,245	31,065	35,699	41,432	42,898	39,704
Yugoslavia [2]	1,821	1,833	1,883	2,012	2,021	2,171	4,603	4,823	4,363	4,882
World total	173,284	218,155	222,119	227,315	221,165	171,151	309,806	298,852	332,539	315,359

* Unofficial figures. [1] Sown area. [2] Includes spelt. [3] Average of 4 years. [4] Field crops and other crops. [5] Average of 3 years.

xiii

RYE

Countries	Area (1,000 hectares)					Production (1,000 metric tons)				
	Average 1948–52	1966	1967	1968	1969	Average 1948–52	1966	1967	1968	1969
Argentina	717	420	565	604	528	526	270	352	360	377
Austria	230	144	139	142	147	343	363	377	413	440
Belgium	86	29	26	26	22	221	76	90	87	73
Bulgaria [1]	226	41	31	24	24	240	56	38	24	29
Canada	571	294	277	275	375	469	437	304	331	419
Czechoslovakia [2]	638	395	319	337	276	1,110	790	689	769	687
Denmark	155	46	37	38	38	365	137	118	131	126
Finland	133	93	96	72	74	201	119	163	134	134
France	496	198	175	163	154	573	357	344	327	309
Germany (East)	1,293	771	746	735	690	2,516	1,642	1,986	1,936	1,544
Germany (West)	1,388	1,019	974	962	872	3,066	2,693	3,159	3,186	2,886
Hungary [1,3]	592	229	209	192	186	732	251	230	240	239
Italy	97	46	46	42	38	123	83	82	75	71
Netherlands	176	74	73	75	62	455	190	239	239	207
Poland [1]	5,063	4,304	4,271	4,263	4,174	6,374	7,661	7,645	8,438	8,166
Portugal	270	282	239	239	236	162	145	175	199	167
Romania [1]	184 [4]	91	62	43	42	177 [4]	100	71	48	47
Spain	622	384	398	366	353	482	353	336	364	345
Sweden	128	39	61	69	72	258	85	197	210	184
Turkey	493	732	735	690	685	500	850	900	820	817
USSR	23,592 [5]	13,583	12,418	12,269	9,237	17,961 [5]	13,146	12,986	14,120	10,945
USA [1]	686	516	433	410	540	524	706	614	594	798
Yugoslavia	269	141	138	132	124	248	176	171	138	135
World total	38,628	24,040	22,641	22,330	19,089	36,967	30,880	31,464	33,365	29,299

[1] Sown area.   [2] Includes mixture of wheat and rye.   [3] Field crops and other crops.   [4] Average of 4 years.   [5] 1950.

BARLEY

Countries	Area (1,000 hectares)					Production (1,000 metric tons)				
	Average 1948–52	1966	1967	1968	1969	Average 1948–52	1966	1967	1968	1969
Algeria	1,166	394	558	720	607	808	130	340	538	465
Argentina	540	411	496	539	457	656	438	588	556	570
Australia [1]	455	1,011	1,057	1,341	1,578	531	1,397	835	1,646	1,789
Bulgaria [1]	240	416	387	402	412	332	1,064	985	807	905
Canada	2,845	3,019	3,284	3,576	3,859	4,245	6,558	5,414	7,084	8,238
Czechoslovakia	606	687	708	710	779	1,046	1,608	1,936	2,113	2,499
Denmark	495	1,112	1,170	1,254	1,305	1,709	4,159	4,382	5,047	5,255
France	954	2,642	2,818	2,781	2,859	1,534	7,421	9,874	9,139	9,452
Germany (East)	259	521	553	595	642	593	1,525	1,927	2,121	2,067
Germany (West)	586	1,288	1,308	1,330	1,387	1,402	3,869	4,734	4,974	5,130
Hungary [1,2]	454	491	450	387	382	654	919	939	906	909
India	3,128	2,633	2,825	3,375	2,758	2,384	2,377	2,348	3,504	2,424
Iran	757	1,000	1,761	867	900	767	935	607	811	864
Iraq	934	1,169	1,087	1,218	1,218	722	832	855	931	1,250
Japan [1]	984	388	352	316	283	2,020	1,105	1,032	1,021	812
Korea, South [1]	624	961	961	977	942	846*	2,018	1,916	2,084	2,066
Mexico	222	233	224	251	240	160	233	175	180	250
Morocco	2,023	1,794	1,835	2,135	2,062	1,481	612	1,322	3,217	2,044
Peru [1]	181	178	185	180*	185	208	154	172	170*	174
Poland [1]	836	679	645	628	759	1,061	1,398	1,394	1,478	1,948
Romania [1]	506 [3]	246	257	292	308	412 [3]	483	531	590	544
Spain	1,557	1,338	1,500	1,923	2,170	1,909	2,006	2,576	3,441	3,969
Syria	369	336	646	631	626	321	203	590	512	627
Tunisia	590	377	335	365	345	218	80	70	130	80
Turkey	1,972	2,710	2,725	2,730	2,687	2,270 [4]	3,800	3,800	3,560	3,740
USSR [1]	8,565 [4]	19,395	19,125	19,353	22,500	6,354 [4]	27,879	24,662	28,904	32,733
UK	818	2,481	2,439	2,401	2,413	2,061	8,724	9,215	8,271	8,664
USA	4,095	4,131	3,715	3,930	3,858	5,843	8,562	8,121	9,211	9,222
Yugoslavia	321	394	343	312	300	323	713	606	451	459
World total	52,412	70,641	71,278	74,163	77,702	59,323	116,522	118,751	130,352	136,940

* Unofficial figures.   [1] Sown area.   [2] Field crops and other crops.   [3] Average of 4 years.   [4] 1950.

OATS

Countries	Area (1,000 hectares)					Production (1,000 metric tons)				
	Average 1948–52	1966	1967	1968	1969	Average 1948–52	1966	1967	1968	1969
Argentina	634	412	516	443	327	743	540	690	490	425
Australia	842	1,723	1,368	1,567	1,821	560	1,943	719	1,710	1,452
Austria	203	126	124	119	102	274	325	336	324	288
Belgium	174	91	96	86	84	483	293	361	315	283
Canada	4,531	3,207	3,009	3,058	3,098	6,220	5,778	4,691	5,591	5,728
China (Mainland)	2,020					1,540				
Czechoslovakia [2]	609	388	435	407	401	961	746	968	869	969
Denmark	291	234	243	218	205	922	864	904	863	765
Finland	435	479	455	489	524	718	881	940	1,064	1,235
France	2,355	1,094	1,040	949	851	3,392	2,578	2,821	2,528	2,309
Germany (East)	545	261	270	256	272	1,188	703	845	864	841
Germany (West)	1,133	777	808	821	860	2,523	2,340	2,718	2,893	2,976
Hungary [1, 3]	180	73	62	57	52	216	86	97	71	86
Irish Republic	276	98	96	88	77	616	283	294	286	251
Italy	469	359	358	323	312	495	477	556	390	491
Netherlands	142	99	88	76	82	419	357	365	318	322
Poland [1]	1,710	1,380	1,405	1,365	1,367	2,238	2,594	2,768	2,831	3,063
Portugal	302	218	226	224	207	124	63	111	129	79
Romania [1]	507 [4]	138	127	132	131	369 [4]	170	163	114	137
Spain	623	469	486	508	493	519	442	492	539	547
Sweden	494	461	455	484	479	804	1,154	1,396	1,584	1,129
Turkey	307	400	390	365	351	326	510	510	450	468
USSR [1]	16,152 [5]	7,162	8,688	8,998	9,348	13,005 [5]	9,199	11,581	11,639	13,090
UK	1,249	366	409	380	382	2,852	1,120	1,386	1,224	1,308
USA	15,266	7,228	6,482	7,095	7,256	18,970	11,631	11,456	13,634	13,790
World total	54,022	30,815	31,308	32,204	32,719	61,720	48,530	50,748	54,205	55,496

[1] Sown area. [2] Includes mixture of oats and barley. [3] Field crops and other crops. [4] Average of 4 years. [5] 1950.

MAIZE

Countries	Area (1,000 hectares)					Production (1,000 metric tons)				
	Average 1948–52	1966	1967	1968	1969	Average 1948–52	1966	1967	1968	1969
Argentina	1,741	3,275	3,451	3,378	3,576	2,839	7,040	8,510	6,560	6,900
Brazil	4,632	8,703	9,274	9,584	9,654	5,841	11,371	12,824	12,814	12,693
Bulgaria	737	574	567	557	578	720	2,207	1,971	1,768	2,415
China (Mainland)	9,570*	...	...	...	...	14,082[1]	...	...	...	...
Colombia	731	846	790	693	...	753	850	850	880	796
France	332	964	1,016	1,024	1,186	452	4,340	4,152	5,390	5,734
Ghana	142[2]	381	295	272	275	168[2]	402	343	301	305
Greece	245	139	133	149	150	225	275	313	342	400
Hungary	1,174	1,253	1,257	1,276	1,273	2,081	3,958	3,580	3,814	4,820
India	3,349	5,074	5,583	5,716	5,862	2,165	3,717	6,269	5,701	5,674
Indonesia	2,020[2]	3,778	2,547	3,220	2,384	1,535[2]	2,874	2,369	3,166	2,271
Italy	1,253	988	1,017	967	1,000	2,306	3,510	3,860	3,991	4,506
Mexico	4,101	8,287	7,612	7,675	7,700	3,090	9,038	8,596	8,978	8,496
Morocco	518	440	460	630	465	302	190	310	382	414
Pakistan	394	557	611	620	652	384	590	795	629	670
Peru	191	355	362	316	360	275	581	591	532	602
Philippines	969	2,158	2,248	2,256	2,420	695	1,490	1,619	1,732	2,008
Portugal	489	473	436	438	427	421	565	577	548	553
Rhodesia	403[3]	380	400	400	...	309	952	1,000	950	...
Romania	3,089[3]	3,288	3,221	3,344	3,293	2,495[3]	8,022	6,858	7,105	7,676
S. Africa, Republic of	3,228	4,360	4,400	5,480	...	2,629	5,056	9,762	5,316	5,339
Spain	334	482	478	523	494	520	1,162	1,195	1,473	1,507
Turkey	599	655	675	655	659	747	1,000	1,050	1,000	1,000
USSR [4]	4,385[3]	3,229	3,485	3,350	4,167	5,751[3]	8,416	9,163	8,828	11,954
UAR	660	662	624	653	623	1,378	2,376	2,163	2,297	2,396
USA	29,856	23,040	24,506	22,614	22,095	74,308	104,585	120,911	111,594	116,401
Venezuela	310	467	616	626	641	303	557	633	661	670
Yugoslavia	2,294	2,500	2,510	2,460	2,397	3,078	7,980	7,200	6,810	7,821
World total	88,116	103,133	105,339	104,884	105,969	139,851	241,424	264,433	251,351	265,015

* Unofficial figures.   [1] 1952.   [2] Average of 3 years.   [3] Average of 4 years.   [4] For dry grain only.

RICE (Paddy)

Countries	Area (1,000 hectares)					Production (1,000 metric tons)				
	Average 1948-52	1966	1967	1968	1969	Average 1948-52	1966	1967	1968	1969
Brazil	1,845	4,005	4,291	4,459	4,621	2,921	5,802	6,792	6,652	6,394
Burma	3,757	4,516	4,706	4,763	4,678	5,481	6,636	7,770	8,023	7,985
Cambodia	1,679 [1]	2,182	2,020	2,324	2,427	1,635 [1]	2,376	2,457	3,251	2,503
Ceylon	336	520	539	562	530	479	955	1,146	1,347	1,374
China (Mainland)	26,819 [2]	...	...	...	...	58,188 [2]	88,000	92,000	91,000	...
India	30,092	35,251	36,437	36,966	37,680	33,383	45,657	56,418	59,642	60,645
Indonesia	5,876 [1]	7,691	7,516	8,013	8,209	9,441 [1]	14,009	13,670	15,249	16,197
Iran	220	280	261	312	...	424	1,050	1,083	1,054	1,110
Iraq	174	111	141	143	140	203	182	308	325	284
Italy	149	132	144	156	169	723	621	745	639	862
Japan	2,996	3,254	3,263	3,280	3,274	12,736	16,552	18,770	18,769	18,186
Korea, South	934	1,231	1,235	1,151	1,220	3,385 *	5,297	4,869	4,318	5,528
Madagascar	615	770	850	996	1,150	829	1,360	1,700	1,762	1,785
Malaysia	415	553	542	632	683	631	1,234	1,201	1,438	1,605
Mexico	96	157	173	139	185	173	383	417	347	525
Pakistan	9,003	10,480	11,309	11,297	11,883	12,399	16,410	19,005	20,065	21,584
Philippines	2,350	3,096	3,166	3,332	3,113	2,767	4,094	4,561	4,445	5,233
Sierra Leone	316 [2]	327	350	60	310	274 [2]	434	468	426	417
Spain	58	59	60	60	65	280	375	366	362	...
Taiwan	762	789	787	790	787	1,771	3,117	3,162	3,299	3,041
Thailand	5,211	7,353	6,400	6,940	...	6,846	13,500	11,198	12,410	13,410
USSR	139 [3]	248	281	312	328	202 [3]	712	895	1,063	1,107
UAR	256	355	452	506	500	971	1,678	2,278	2,586	2,557
USA	752	796	797	952	861	1,925	3,856	4,054	4,721	4,120
Vietnam, North	...	...	...	...	...	...	...	...	4,920 *	...
Vietnam, South	1,760 [4]	2,295	2,296	2,394	2,430	2,395 [4]	4,336	4,688	4,366	5,115
World total	102,584	126,278	129,055	131,904	135,033	167,336	254,950	277,071	285,156	295,436

* Unofficial figures. [1] Average of 3 years. [2] Average of 4 years. [3] 1950. [4] Average of 2 years.

MILLET

Countries	Area (1,000 hectares)					Production (1,000 metric tons)				
	Average 1948–52	1966	1967	1968	1969	Average 1948–52	1966	1967	1968	1969
Argentina	177	163	188	210	197	146	186	224	229	196
Australia	7	26	21	26	..	7	32	21	26	..
Burma	199 [1]	145	133	218	241	70	41	26	55	66
Ceylon	38	36	24	22	24	18	20	15	14	19
Ghana	175 [2]	161	156	140	162	99 [2]	79	93	73	91
India	16,605	19,139	19,956	1,9036	20,009	6,064	7,587	8,976	7,254	9,176
Japan	113	18	14	11	8	127	28	22	20	14
Korea, South	191	98	87	79	62	60	59	42	79	61
Pakistan	918	837	914	736	631	342	371	414	330	302
Poland	60 [2]	22	21	19	23	61 [2]	27	27	25	28
Rhodesia [3]	297 [4]	390	390	390	..	92 [4]	220	220	220	..
Sudan	352	548	610	603	635	181	253	369	267	427
Turkey	74	45	42	40	39	78	60	55	53	56
USSR	3,767 [5]	3,252	3,802	3,050	3,376	1,705 [5]	3,101	3,218	2,660	3,289
World total	29,046	32,183	33,587	31,519	33,470	12,348	17,455	18,878	16,289	19,589

[1] Average of 2 years.   [2] Average of 3 years.   [3] On farms and estates.   [4] 1949.   [5] 1950.

SORGHUM

Countries	Area (1,000 hectares)					Production (1,000 metric tons)				
	Average 1948–52	1966	1967	1968	1969	Average 1948–52	1966	1967	1968	1969
Argentine	77	1,123	1,033	1,266	1,456	73	2,386	1,618	2,033	2,616
Australia	57	203	187	236	212	75	319	288	431	299
Cameroun [5]	654	329	580	500	458	371	390	388	350	339
Congo (K.) [5]	90 [1]	45	39	39	...	56 [1]	40	35	35	...
El Salvador	96 [1]	107	104	114	...	115 [1]	115	108	124	107
Ethiopia [2, 5]	3,397 [3]	3,560	3,703	3,935	3,484	1,727	2,356	2,444	2,564	2,628
Ghana	134 [3]	204	145	151	145	79 [3]	127	98	83	98
Guinea [4, 5]	228	260	260	260	...	93	150*	155*	150	...
Honduras	57	59	60	68	...	47	44*	53	66	69
India	15,894	18,054	18,423	18,731	18,605	5,981	9,224	10,048	9,804	9,721
Mali [4, 5]	1,268	876	959	910	1,390	682	837	865	757	795
Morocco	165	90	89	90	...	81	36	58	80	41
Pakistan	505	559	585	474	491	239	277	291	262	283
Rhodesia	136	75	75	70	...	48 [1]	60	58	55	...
Rwanda	95	130	130	129	126	106	135*	140*	123	126
Senegal [4, 5]	782	1,009	1,171	1,036	...	308	428	661	454	610
S. Africa, Republic of	283	373	488	260	...	180	336	844	207	232
South Arabia [5]	35	45	45	50	...	16 [1]	50	52	52	...
Syria [5]	93	28	39	41	25	65	15	40	37	21
Togo [4, 5]	175	282	318	417	...	92	113	126	193	160
UAR	191	217	220	224	199	518	859	881	906	813
USA	3,087	5,185	6,070	5,663	5,473	3,897	18,162	19,202	18,789	18,982
Upper Volta	782	1,000	1,312	831	...	352	540	604	530	...
World total	65,230	75,178	78,043	76,926	78,067	35,492	67,164	70,668	68,804	71,602

[1] Average of 4 years. [2] Includes teff. [3] Average of 3 years. [4] Includes fonio. [5] Unspecified millet and sorghum.
* Unofficial figures.

CENTRIFUGAL RAW SUGAR

(in 1,000 metric tons; year beginning March)

Countries	Average 1948–52	1965–66	1966–67	1967–68	1968–69	1969–70	1970–71
Argentina	638	1,310	1,040	785	936	978	974 *
Australia [1]	913	1,985	2,380	2,372	2,768	2,214	2,530
Barbados [2]	168	175	204	162	142	156	160 *
Brazil [3]	1,649	4,746	4,297	4,376	4,353	4,453	5,400 *
Canada	122	139	154	141	135	134	110 *
China (Mainland)	367	2,250 *	2,420 *	2,500 *	2,700 *	3,000 *	3,150 *
Cuba	5,786	4,455	6,229	5,315	4,724 *	8,533 *	5,750 *
Czechoslovakia	697	717 *	836 *	822 *	861	716 *	763 *
Dominican Rep. [4]	552	691	819	668 *	864	1,043 *	1,180 *
France	1,085	2,381	1,810	1,729	2,382	2,672	2,603 *
Fiji [1]	122	316	308	296	400	304	391 *
Germany (East)	700	527	553	554	495 *	440 *	489 *
Germany (West)	823	1,562	1,913	2,060	1,994	2,019	2,036 *
Guyana	218	294	349	322	370	351	320 *
India [5]	1,316	3,840	2,347	2,421	3,869	4,620 *	4,402 *
Indonesia [6]	287	775	605	659	603	731	750 *
Italy [7]	598	1,238	1,361	1,661	1,296	1,406	1,209 *
Jamaica	279	508	456	452	389	377	400 *
Mauritius [6]	443	664	562	638	597	669	579
Mexico	733	2,102	2,444 *	2,299 *	2,565 *	2,363 *	2,383 *
Pakistan [5]	55	514	476	395	506	782 *	770 *
Peru [4]	496	891	731 *	752 *	633 *	750 *	750 *
Philippines	827	1,402	1,560	1,593	1,597	1,885	2,207 *
Poland	871	1,472	1,684	1,913	1,706	1,527	1,649 *
Puerto Rico	1,157	801	742	586	439	417 *	454 *
S Africa, Rep. of	555	909	1,628	1,822	1,505	1,622	1,550 *
Spain [7]	315	564	617 *	598	702	802 *	904 *
Sweden	285	199	229	260	293	185	243 *
Taiwan	619	1,010	771	862	758	748 *	734 *
Trinidad	151	214	204	247	244	221	256 *
USSR	2,700	9,196 *	8,966 *	10,433 *	10,125 *	8,853 *	9,290 *
UAR	196	366	363	379	461 *	491 *	515 *
UK	626	936	935	963	974	938	978 *
USA [8]	2,785	4,731	4,787	4,793	5,380	5,065	5,408
World total	32,320	62,771	64,848	66,409	68,503	73,060	72,865

[1] 94° net titre.   [2] Includes the sugar equivalent of fancy molasses.   [3] Years June–May.
[4] Calendar year referring to the second part of the split year.   [5] Includes sugar (raw value) refined from gur.   [6] Tel quel.   [7] Years July–June.   [8] Includes Hawaii.
* Unofficial figures.

CRUDE PETROLEUM[1]

(in 1,000 metric tons)

	1950	1960	1968	1969	1970 [2]
North America					
Canada [3]	3,800	27,480	56,947	62,059	69,500
USA [3]	285,200	384,080	502,767	510,411	534,000
Mexico	10,296	14,125	20,014	21,000	..
Caribbean					
Trinidad	2,980	6,075	9,467	8,125	7,000
Colombia	4,850	8,100	9,188	10,660	11,000
Venezuela	78,140	148,690	187,144	187,413	193,000
South America					
Brazil	40	4,050	7,797	8,340	1,650
Ecuador	360	390	238	206	220
Peru	2,050	2,680	3,650	3,325	2,800
Bolivia	80	450	1,898	1,806	1,500
Chile	80	990	1,749	1,742	1,650
Argentina	3,460	9,160	17,947	18,132	20,000
Middle East					
Turkey	30	350	3,103	3,599	3,550
Iraq	6,650	47,480	73,848	74,700	75,600
Iran	32,260	52,065	141,791	168,235	190,000
Saudi Arabia	26,620	61,090	140,998	148,839	175,500
Kuwait	17,290	81,860	122,085	129,549	138,000
Kuwait neutral zone	—	7,270	22,827	23,502	27,000
Bahrain	1,560	2,250	3,768	3,795	3,800
Qatar	1,640	8,210	16,363	17,341	17,000
Abu Dhabi	—	—	24,006	28,761	32,800
Dubai	—	—	—	523	4,200
Oman	—	—	12,068	16,069	16,400
Syria	—	—	833	3,200	4,500
UAR	2,370	3,600	11,495 [4]	15,466 [4]	23,500
Israel	—	130	109	99	85
Far East					
India	315	440	5,773	6,723	6,800
Pakistan	250	360	512	484	500
Burma	125	530	729	990	1,000
Indonesia	6,450	20,560	29,712	39,650	45,000
Brunei and Sarawak	4,340	4,690	6,180	6,550	7,400
Japan	350	510	781	786	800
China (Taiwan)	—	—	60	82	95

[1] Crude oil and natural gas liquids.
[2] Provisional estimates.
[3] 1968–70 figures for Canada and US refer to all hydrocarbon liquids and are therefore not strictly comparable with earlier compilations which list only crude oil proper.
[4] Including the Sinai fields, now occupied by Israel. Production, 1970, 4·5m. metric tons (1969 and 1968, 2·5m.).

CRUDE PETROLEUM (*contd.*)

(in 1,000 metric tons)

	1950	1960	1968	1969	1970[1]
Europe					
Austria	1,600	2,440	2,724	2,768	2,800
Germany (West)	1,120	5,560	7,982	7,876	7,535
Netherlands	700	1,920	2,147	2,022	1,930
UK	40	90	76	77	80
France	120	2,260	2,688	2,497	2,350
Italy	8	1,990	1,506	1,479	1,400
Spain	—	—	108	191	200
Africa (excluding UAR)					
Morocco	100	90	89	58	40
Algeria	80	8,630	42,145	43,824	46,400
Tunisia	—	—	3,173	3,708	4,100
Libya	—	—	124,524	149,084	159,000
Gabon and Congo (Br.)	—	850	4,684	5,077	5,350
Angola	—	70	752	2,434	4,300
Nigeria	—	880	7,298	26,627	53,000
Oceania					
Australia	—	—	1,767	2,010	8,350
Communist countries					
USSR	37,500	148,000	309,150	328,648	353,000
Romania	4,100	11,500	13,285	13,246	13,350
Yugoslavia	110	1,040	2,494	2,689	2,900
Hungary	500	1,215	1,807	1,754	1,950
Poland	175	195	475	438	430
Albania	395	600	1,100	1,200	1,400
Bulgaria	—	200	475	325	330
Czechoslovakia	50	140	205	210	210
Germany (East)	—	—	60	60	60
China[2]	110	5,500	9,800	14,000	19,000
Estimated total World Production[3]	538,470	1,090,680	1,976,324	2,134,531	2,334,000

[1] Provisional estimate.

[2] Until 1962 shale oil and oil from coal amounted yearly to an additional 1·7m. tons. From 1963 the figures include shale and coal-based oil.

[3] Estimates differ widely because of conversion difficulties of barrels to metric tons. Thus, for instance, for crude petroleum of specific gravity, at 60° F., of 0·78 (corresponding to American Petroleum Institute gravity rating of 49·91), there are 8·08 bbls to a metric ton. At the other end of the scale, for crude petroleum of specific gravity 0·98 (API rating, 12·89), there are only 6·43 bbls to a metric ton. Middle East crude petroleum has an average conversion rate of approximately 7·5 bbls to a metric ton. Excluding small-scale production in Cuba, Mongolia, New Zealand and Thailand.

TERRITORIAL SEA LIMITS

	Territorial sea	Exclusive fishing zone
Albania	12 miles	—
Algeria	12 miles	—
Argentina	200 miles	—
Australia	3 miles	12 miles
Belgium	3 miles	12 miles
Brazil	200 miles	—
Bulgaria	12 miles	—
Burma	—	—
Cambodia	5 miles	—
Cameroun	6 miles	—
Canada	12 miles	12 miles
Ceylon	6 miles	—
Chile	50 km	200 miles
China (Taiwan)	3 miles	—
Colombia	3 miles	12 miles
Congo (Brazzaville)	3 miles	—
Costa Rica	In accordance with international law	200 miles
Cuba	3 miles	—
Cyprus	12 miles	—
Dahomey	12 miles	—
Denmark (including Faroe Islands and Greenland)	3 miles	3–12 miles
Dominican Republic	3 miles	—
Ecuador	200 miles	—
El Salvador	200 miles	—
Ethiopa	12 miles	—
Finland	4 miles	—
France	3 miles	12 miles
Gabon	25 miles	—
Gambia	12 miles	—
Germany (West)	In accordance with international law	12 miles
Ghana	12 miles	—
Greece	6 miles	—
Guatemala	12 miles	—
Guinea	130 miles	—
Guyana	3 miles	—
Haiti	6 miles	—
Honduras	12 miles	—
Iceland	—	12 miles
India	12 miles	—
Indonesia	12 miles	—
Iran	12 miles	—
Iraq	12 miles	—
Irish Republic	3 miles	12 miles
Israel	6 miles	—
Italy	6 miles	—
Ivory Coast	6 miles	12 miles
Jamaica	3 miles	—
Japan	3 miles	—
Jordan	3 miles	—
Kenya	3 miles	—
Korea (South)	—	20–200 miles
Kuwait	12 miles	—
Lebanon	—	6 miles
Liberia	3 miles	—

TERRITORIAL SEA LIMITS (*contd.*)

	Territorial sea	Exclusive fishing zone
Libya	12 miles	—
Madagascar	12 miles	—
Maldive, Republic of	6 miles	—
Malta	3 miles	—
Malaysia	3 miles	—
Mauritania	12 miles	—
Mauritius	12 miles	—
Mexico	9 miles	12 miles
Monaco	3 miles	12 miles
Morocco	—	12 miles
Netherlands	3 miles	12 miles
New Zealand	3 miles	12 miles
Nicaragua	—	200 miles
Nigeria	12 miles	12 miles
Norway	4 miles	12 miles
Pakistan	12 miles	—
Panama	200 miles	—
Peru	—	200 miles
Poland	3 miles	12 miles
Portugal	—	12 miles
Romania	12 miles	—
Saudi Arabia	12 miles	—
Senegal	6 miles	12 miles
Sierra Leone	12 miles	—
Somalia	6 miles	—
South Africa, Republic of	6 miles	12 miles
Spain	6 miles	12 miles
Sudan	—	12 miles
Sweden	4 miles	12 miles
Syria	12 miles	—
Tanzania	12 miles	—
Thailand	12 miles	—
Togo	12 miles	—
Trinidad and Tobago	12 miles	—
Tunisia	6 miles	12 miles
Turkey	6 miles	12 miles
USSR	12 miles	—
UAR	12 miles	—
UK	3 miles	12 miles
USA	3 miles	12 miles
Uruguay	200 miles	—
Venezuela	12 miles	—
Vietnam (South)	3 miles	—
Yugoslavia	10 miles	—

The table above, reproduced from the relevant sections of the FAO survey, shows: (*a*) the territorial sea limit, and (*b*) the limit of the exclusive fishing zone claimed by the country concerned.

Notes:

(*a*) An extension of Cameroun's territorial sea limit from 6 to 18 nautical miles was approved by its Assembly in Oct. 1967; it will not take effect until promulgated by the President.

(*b*) Congo (K.) has not yet enacted any legislation on this subject, and so therefore does not appear in the table.

(*c*) Denmark's exclusive fishing zone is drawn 12 miles from the base-lines in the North Sea, the Skagerrak and the Kattegat, and 3 miles elsewhere. In the case of the Faroe Islands and Greenland it is 12 miles.

(*d*) The territorial sea of the Philippines is determined by straight base-lines joining appropriate points of the outermost islands forming the Philippine archipelago.

ADDENDA

UGANDA. *High Commissioner in London:* Maj. Eli Lukakamwa.

FINLAND. Ministerial changes. *Justice:* Nikko Laaksonen (SDP). *Traffic:* Kalervo Haapasalo (SDP). *Trade and Industry:* Arne Berner (Lib.), Olavi Salonen (SDP). *Social Affairs:* Pekka Kuusi (SDP), Katri-Helena Eskelinen (Centre).

NORTHERN IRELAND. *Prime Minister and Minister of Home Affairs:* Right Hon. A. B. D. Faulkner. *Agriculture:* Right Hon. H. W. West. *Commerce:* Right Hon. R. J. Bailie. *Development:* Right Hon. R. H. Bradford. *Community Relations:* Right Hon. D. W. Bleakley.

HAITI. Jean-Claude Duvalier took office as President on 22 April 1971 following the death of his father, Dr François Duvalier.

UAR, SYRIA AND LIBYA. A decision was taken on 18 April 1971 to form a Federation of Arab Republics. Sudan withdrew from the proposed union a few days before this agreement was reached.

PART I

INTERNATIONAL ORGANIZATIONS

THE UNITED NATIONS

The United Nations is an association of states which have pledged themselves, through signing the Charter, to maintain international peace and security and to co-operate in establishing political, economic and social conditions under which this task can be securely achieved. Nothing contained in the Charter authorizes the organization to intervene in matters which are essentially within the domestic jurisdiction of any state.

The United Nations Charter originated from proposals agreed upon at discussions held at Dumbarton Oaks (Washington, D.C.) between the USSR, US and UK from 21 Aug. to 28 Sept., and between US, UK and China from 29 Sept. to 7 Oct. 1944. These proposals were laid before the United Nations Conference on International Organization, held at San Francisco from 25 April to 26 June 1945, and (after amendments had been made to the original proposals) the Charter of the United Nations was signed on 26 June 1945 by the delegates of 50 countries. Ratification of all the signatures had been received by 31 Dec. 1945. (For the complete text of the Charter see THE STATESMAN'S YEAR-BOOK, 1946, pp. xxi–xxxii.)

The United Nations formally came into existence on 24 Oct. 1945, with the deposit of the requisite number of ratifications of the Charter with the US Department of State. The official languages of the United Nations are Chinese, English, French, Russian and Spanish; the working languages are English, French and (in the General Assembly) Spanish and Russian.

The headquarters of the United Nations is in New York City, USA.

Membership. Membership is open to all peace-loving states whose admission will be effected by the General Assembly upon recommendation of the Security Council.

The table on pp. 11–13 shows the member states of the United Nations and their participation in the Related Agencies, and those non-member states which have been admitted to certain Related Agencies.

The Principal Organs of the United Nations are: 1. The General Assembly. 2. The Security Council. 3. The Economic and Social Council. 4. The Trusteeship Council. 5. The International Court of Justice. 6. The Secretariat.

1. THE GENERAL ASSEMBLY consists of all the members of the United Nations. Each member is entitled to be represented at its meetings by 5 delegates and 5 alternate delegates, but has only 1 vote. The General Assembly meets regularly once a year, commencing on the third Tuesday in Sept.; the session normally lasts until mid-December and is resumed for some weeks in the new year if this is required. Special sessions may be convoked by the Secretary-General if requested by the Security Council, by a majority of the members of the United Nations or by 1 member concurred with by the majority of the members. The General Assembly elects its President for each session.

The first regular session was held in London from 10 Jan. to 14 Feb. and in New York from 23 Oct. to 16 Dec. 1946.

Special sessions have been held, on Palestine, in 1947, 1948, 1963 and 1967; emergency sessions on the Middle East and on Hungary in 1956, on Lebanon in 1958, on the Congo in 1960, on South West Africa and the Middle East in 1967.

The work of the General Assembly is divided between 6 Main Committees and the Special Political Committee, on each of which every member has the right to be represented by 1 delegate. I. Political Security. II. Economic and Financial.

3

III. Social, Humanitarian and Cultural. IV. Trust and Non-Self-Governing Territories. V. Administrative and Budgetary. VI. Legal.

In addition there is a General Committee charged with the task of co-ordinating the proceedings of the Assembly and its Committees; and a Credentials Committee which verifies the credentials of the delegates. The General Committee consists of 25 members, comprising the President of the General Assembly, its 17 Vice-Presidents and the Chairmen of the 7 Main Committees. The Credentials Committee consists of 9 members, elected at the beginning of each session of the General Assembly. The Assembly has 2 standing committees—an Advisory Committee on Administrative and Budgetary Questions, and a Committee on Contributions. The General Assembly establishes subsidiary and *ad hoc* bodies when necessary to deal with specific matters. These include: Special Committee on Peace-keeping Operations (33 members), Commission on Human Rights (32 members), Advisory Committee on the UN Emergency Force (7 members), Commission for the unification and rehabilitation of Korea (7 members), Committee on the peaceful uses of outer space (28 members), Conciliation Commission for Palestine (3 members), Conference of the Committee on Disarmament (26 members), International Law Commission (25 members), Scientific Committee on the effects of atomic radiation (15 members), Special Committee on the implementation of the declaration on the granting of independence to colonial countries and peoples (24 members), Special Committee on the policies of Apartheid of the Government of the Republic of South Africa (11 members), UN High Commissioner for Refugees, UN Relief and Works Agency for Palestine Refugees in the Near East, Peace Observation Commission (14 members), UN Commission on International Trade Law (29 members) and Committee on the Peaceful Uses of Sea-bed and Ocean Floor Beyond the Limits of National Jurisdiction (42 members), Preparatory Committee on the Human Environment Conference, Stockholm, 1972 (27 members), Preparatory Committee on the Second Development Decade (27 members).

The General Assembly may discuss any matters within the scope of the Charter, and, with the exception of any situation or dispute on the agenda of the Security Council, may make recommendations on any such questions or matters. For decisions on important questions a two-thirds majority is required, on other questions a simple majority of members present and voting. In addition, the Assembly at its fifth session, in 1950, decided that if the Security Council, because of lack of unanimity of the permament members, fails to exercise its primary responsibility for the maintenance of international peace and security in any case where there appears to be a threat to the peace, breach of the peace or act of aggression, the General Assembly shall consider the matter immediately with a view to making appropriate recommendations to members for collective measures, including in the case of a breach of the peace or act of aggression the use of armed force when necessary, to maintain or restore international peace and security.

The General Assembly receives and considers reports from the other organs of the United Nations, including the Security Council. The Secretary-General makes an annual report to it on the work of the Organization.

2. THE SECURITY COUNCIL consists of 15 members, each of which has 1 representative and 1 vote. There are 5 permanent and 10 non-permanent members elected for a 2-year term by a two-thirds majority of the General Assembly. Retiring members are not eligible for immediate re-election. Any other member of the United Nations will be invited to participate without vote in the discussion of questions specially affecting its interests.

The Security Council bears the primary responsibility for the maintenance of peace and security. It is also responsible for the functions of the UN in trust territories classed as 'strategic areas'. Decisions on procedural questions are made by an affirmative vote of 9 members. On all other matters the affirmative vote of 9 members must include the concurring votes of all permanent members (in practice, however, an abstention by a permanent member is not considered a veto), subject to the provision that when the Security Council is considering methods for the peaceful settlement of a dispute, parties to the dispute abstain from voting.

For the maintenance of international peace and security the Security Council can, in accordance with special agreements to be concluded, call on armed forces, assistance and facilities of the member states. It is assisted by a Military Staff Committee consisting of the Chiefs of Staff of the permanent members of the Security Council or their representatives.

The Presidency of the Security Council is held for 1 month in rotation by the member states in the English alphabetical order of their names.

The Security Council functions continuously. Its members are permanently represented at the seat of the organization, but it may meet at any place that will best facilitate its work.

The Council has 2 standing committees, of Experts and on the Admission of New Members. In addition, from time to time, it establishes *ad hoc* committees and commissions such as the Truce Supervision Organization in Palestine. It has also appointed a Representative for India and Pakistan.

Permanent Members: China, France, USSR, UK, USA.
Non-Permanent Members: Argentina, Belgium, Italy, Japan, Somalia (until 31 Dec. 1972); Poland, Burundi, Sierra Leone, Nicaragua, Syria (until 31 Dec. 1971).

3. THE ECONOMIC AND SOCIAL COUNCIL is responsible under the General Assembly for carrying out the functions of the United Nations with regard to international economic, social, cultural, educational, health and related matters. By Jan. 1963, 14 specialized inter-governmental agencies working in these fields had been brought into relationship with the United Nations. The Economic and Social Council may also make arrangements for consultation with international non-governmental organizations and, after consultation with the member concerned, with national organizations; by Dec. 1965, 141 non-governmental organizations had been granted consultative status and a further 219 were on the register.

The Economic and Social Council consists of 1 delegate each of 27 Member States elected by a two-thirds majority of the General Assembly. Nine are elected each year for a 3-year term. Retiring members are eligible for immediate re-election. Each member has 1 vote. Decisions are made by a majority of the members present and voting.

The Council nominally holds 2 sessions a year, and special sessions may be held if required. The President is elected for 1 year and is eligible for immediate re-election.

The Economic and Social Council has the following commissions:

Regional Economic Commissions: ECE (Economic Commission for Europe); ECAFE (Economic Commission for Asia and the Far East. Bangkok); ECLA (Economic Commission for Latin America. Santiago, Chile); ECA (Economic Commission for Africa. Addis Ababa). These Commissions have been established to enable the nations of the major regions of the world to co-operate on common problems and also to produce economic information.

(1) Six functional Statistical Commissions; with subcommission on Statistical Sampling. (2) Commission on Human Rights; with subcommission on Prevention of Discrimination and Protection of Minorities; (3) Social Development Commission; (4) Commission on the Status of Women; (5) Commission on Narcotic Drugs; (6) Population Commission; (7–10) Four regional Economic Commissions for Europe, Asia and the Far East, Latin America, Africa.

The Economic and Social Council has the following standing committees: The Economic Committee, Social Committee, Co-ordination Committee, Committee on Non-Governmental Organizations, Interim Committee on Programme of Conferences, Committee for Industrial Development, Advisory Committee on the Application of Science and Technology to Development, Committee on Housing, Building and Planning.

Other special bodies are the Permanent Central Opium Board, the Drug Supervisory Body, the Interim Co-ordinating Committee for International Commodity Arrangements and the Administrative Committee on Co-ordination to ensure (1) the most effective implementation of the agreements entered into between the United Nations and the specialized agencies and (2) co-ordination of activities.

Membership: Indonesia, Jamaica, Norway, Pakistan, Sudan, USSR, UK, Uruguay, Yugoslavia (until 31 Dec. 1971); Peru, Brazil, Ghana, Kenya, Tunisia, France, Italy, Greece, Ceylon (until 31 Dec. 1972); Congo (K.), Haiti, Hungary, Lebanon, Madagascar, Malaysia, New Zealand, Niger, USA (until 31 Dec. 1973).

4. THE TRUSTEESHIP COUNCIL. The Charter provides for an international trusteeship system to safeguard the interests of the inhabitants of territories which are not yet fully self-governing and which may be placed thereunder by individual trusteeship agreements. These are called trust territories. By 1968 all, except 2, trust territories had become independent or joined independent countries.

The Trusteeship Council consists of the 2 members administering trust territories: Australia, USA; the permanent members of the Security Council that are not administering trust territories: China, France, USSR and UK; and any other members elected for 3-year terms by the General Assembly. Elected member: Liberia (until 31 Dec. 1968). Decisions of the Council are made by a majority of the members present and voting, each member having 1 vote. The Council holds one regular session each year, and special sessions if required.

5. THE INTERNATIONAL COURT OF JUSTICE was created by an international treaty, the Statute of the Court, which forms an integral part of the United Nations Charter. All members of the United Nations are *ipso facto* parties to the Statute of the Court.

The Court is composed of independent judges, elected regardless of their nationality, who possess the qualifications required in their countries for appointment to the highest judicial offices, or are jurisconsuls of recognized competence in international law. There are 15 judges, no 2 of whom may be nationals of the same state. They are elected by the Security Council and the General Assembly of the United Nations sitting independently. Candidates are chosen from a list of persons nominated by the national groups in the Permanent Court of Arbitration established by the Hague Conventions of 1899 and 1907. In the case of members of the United Nations not represented in the Permanent Court of Arbitration, candidates are nominated by national groups appointed for the purpose by their governments. The judges are elected for a 9-year term and are eligible for immediate re-election. When engaged on business of the Court, they enjoy diplomatic privileges and immunities.

The Court elects its own President and Vice-Presidents for 3 years and remains permanently in session, except for judicial vacations. The full court of 15 judges normally sits, but a quorum of 9 judges is sufficient to constitute the Court. It may form chambers of 3 or more judges for dealing with particular categories of cases, and forms annually a chamber of 5 judges to hear and determine, at the request of the parties, cases by summary procedures.

Competence and Jurisdiction. Only states may be parties in cases before the Court, which is open to the states parties to its Statute. The conditions under which the Court will be open to other states are laid down by the Security Council. The Court exercises its jurisdiction in all cases which the parties refer to it and in all matters provided for in the Charter, or in treaties and conventions in force. Disputes concerning the jurisdiction of the Court are settled by the Court's own decision.

The Court may apply in its decision: (*a*) international conventions; (*b*) international custom; (*c*) the general principles of law recognized by civilized nations; and (*d*) as subsidiary means for the determination of the rules of law, judicial decisions and the teachings of highly qualified publicists. If the parties agree, the Court may decide a case *ex aequo et bono*. The Court may also give an advisory opinion on any legal question to any organ of the United Nations or its agencies.

Procedure. The official languages of the Court are French and English. At the request of any party the Court will authorize the use of another language by this party. All questions are decided by a majority of the judges present. If the votes are equal, the President has a casting vote. The judgment is final and without appeal, but a revision may be applied for within 10 years from the date of the judgment on the ground of a new decisive factor. Unless otherwise decided by the Court, each party bears its own costs.

Judges. The judges of the Court, elected by the Security Council and the General Assembly, are as follows: (1) To serve until 5 Feb. 1973: André Gros (France), Luis Padilla Nervo (Mexico), Sir Zafrulla Khan (Pakistan), Isaac Forster (Senegal), Sir Gerald Fitzmaurice (UK). (2) To serve until 5 Feb. 1976: Fouad Ammoun (Lebanon), Cesar Bengzon (Philippines), Sture Petren (Sweden), Manfred Lachs (Poland), Charles D. Onyeama (Nigeria). (3) To serve until 5 Feb. 1979: Frederico de Castro (Spain), Louis Ignacio-Pinto (Dahomey), C. Dillard (USA), Eduardo Jiménez de Aréchaga (Uruguay), Platon D. Morozov (USSR).

'National' Judges. If there is no judge on the bench of the nationality of the parties to the dispute, each party has the right to choose a judge. Such judges shall take part in the decision on terms of complete equality with their colleagues.

The Court has its seat at The Hague, but may sit and exercise its functions elsewhere whenever it considers this desirable. The expenses of the Court are borne by the United Nations.

Registrar: Stanislas Aquarone (Australia).

Year-Book of the International Court of Justice. The Hague, 1950 ff.

6. THE SECRETARIAT is composed of the Secretary-General, who is the chief administrative officer of the organization, and an international staff appointed by him under regulations established by the General Assembly. However, the Secretary-General, the High Commissioner for Refugees and the Managing Director of the Fund are appointed by the General Assembly. The first Secretary-General was Trygve Lie (Norway), 1946–53; the second, Dag Hammarskjöld (Sweden), 1953–61.

The Secretary-General acts as chief administrative officer in all meetings of the General Assembly, the Security Council, the Economic and Social Council and the Trusteeship Council.

Secretary-General: U Thant (Burma), appointed Acting Secretary-General in Nov. 1961; unanimously elected Secretary-General on 30 Nov. 1962; re-appointed on 2 Dec. 1966 (until 31 Dec. 1971).

The Secretary-General is assisted by 11 Under-Secretaries-General and 5 Assistant Secretaries-General.

The UN DEVELOPMENT PROGRAMME, created on 22 Nov. 1965, is an amalgamation of the programme of Technical Assistance and the Special Fund. *Administrator:* Paul G. Hoffman (USA) and *Deputy Administrator:* C. V. Narasimhan (India).

The UN CONFERENCE ON TRADE AND DEVELOPMENT was established by the General Assembly on 30 Dec. 1964. It comprises those states which are members of the UN, its specialized agencies or the International Atomic Energy Agency. Its permanent organ, the Trade and Development Board (55 members), meets twice a year. Its 4 subsidiary organs meet annually: these are the Committees on Commodities, Manufactures, Shipping, and Invisibles and Financing Related to Trade. *Secretary-General:* Manrel Perez Guerrero (Venezuela, March 1969–31 March 1972). *Headquarters:* Geneva, Switzerland.

The UN DEVELOPMENT ORGANIZATION (UNIDO) has worked as an autonomous body with the UN to promote industrialization and co-ordinate activities undertaken by the UN family in this field since 1967. Principal body is the 45-member Industrial Development Board, which formulates UNIDO's policy and its programme of activities. UNIDO tries to help the urgent need of developing countries to accelerate their promotional and operational activities and supports them by relevant studies and research. *Executive Director:* Ibrahim H. Abdel-Rahman. *Headquarters:* Rathausplatz 2, Vienna, Austria.

THE OFFICE OF THE UNITED NATIONS HIGH COMMISSIONER FOR REFUGEES (UNHCR) was established by the UN General Assembly with effect from 1 Jan. 1951, originally for 3 years. In view of the persistence of the refugee problem, the Office's lifetime has since been extended for several 5-year periods, most recently until 31 Dec. 1973. The UNHCR's task is to provide legal protection and, when needed, material assistance to refugees, and to seek permanent solutions to refugee problems on a purely social, humanitarian and non-political basis. Its statute covers existing as well as future refugees. Only those refugees who are the direct concern of other UN Offices (such as the Palestine refugees, who are the concern of UNRWA) and those who are displaced inside the borders of their own countries as a result of civil wars or other disturbances, or have the nationality of the country granting them asylum are not the High Commissioner's responsibility. The High Commissioner's concern is exclusively with the circumstances of the refugees in the countries which grant them asylum, rather than with the causation of their plight.

Throughout 1970, world conditions continued to generate new refugees. Nevertheless, UNHCR has not only managed to clear up the last remnants of the legacy of 'old refugees' left by its predecessors but also to find rapid and durable solutions to the multitude of refugee problems which are constantly arising. On the whole there has been marked progress in international refugee work, with increasing recognition of the rights and status of refugees, as well as of the principle that no refugee should be returned to his country of origin against his will. Moreover, there is increasingly general acceptance of the fact that the granting of asylum is a humanitarian action which in no way should be considered as an unfriendly act by neighbouring states.

The basic legal instruments which define and codify the refugees' rights and status are the Convention of 28 July 1951, subsequently widened in scope by a Protocol relating to the Status of Refugees, which came into force on 4 Oct. 1967. Up to the end of 1970, 60 states were parties to the Convention, and 43 had acceded to the Protocol. The important Convention, governing the specific aspects of refugee problems in Africa, was unanimously adopted during a summit meeting of the Organization of African Unity (OAU), held at Addis Ababa in Sept. 1969 is not yet in force but many of the African states already act in the spirit of the Convention. Moreover, 26 African states are parties to the 1951 Convention and/or the 1967 Protocol.

The High Commissioner is elected by and reports to the UN General Assembly. The debate on his latest report culminated in a resolution, endorsing the 'humanitarian and constructive' work of UNHCR (9 Dec. 1970) which, for the third successive year in UNHCR's history, was adopted by acclamation, without dissent or abstention. The UN Secretary-General's recommendation that the present High Commissioner's term of office be extended for a further 5 years (1969–73) was adopted by the General Assembly by acclamation on 15 Nov. 1968.

UNHCR programmes (directed by a 31-member committee with executive as well as advisory functions) are designed to clear up residual problems left by former refugee waves, and to solve as rapidly as possible any new refugee problems that arise. They are financed exclusively through voluntary contributions, primarily from governments, and so conceived as to provide the basic starting-point for wider action. Today, some 86 Governments contribute to the programme. The programme target set for 1971 was $6·6m.

When UNHCR was established refugee problems of concern to the Office were essentially those of European refugees in Europe. Since 1957, however, the epicentre of refugee problems of concern to UNHCR has moved from Europe to the other continents, primarily to Africa.

In 1970, the total number of refugees of concern to UNHCR was in the region of 2·5m. Of these refugees, over 1m. are located in Africa, and some 160,000 in Asia, primarily Tibetans in Nepál and India (60,000) and Chinese in Macao (80,000). Some 1,415,000 are refugees of European origin, residing either in Europe (750,000) or in various countries overseas (665,000), including North and Latin America, Australasia, the Middle and the Far East. Only a fraction of them, however, still required material aid from UNHCR.

The overwhelming majority of refugees of concern to UNHCR who require not only protection but also material aid to become self-supporting again are the approximately 1m. refugees in Africa, a special feature of the situation being not only the spreading of the refugee problem on that continent, but also the inter-change of refugees between neighbouring countries. Most of these refugees are located in Botswana, Burundi, the Central African Republic, Congo (K.) Ethiopia, Senegal, Sudan, Tanzania, Uganda and Zambia. For the majority of these refugees, local integration through the creation of new rural communities has become the most practical solution.

Towards the end of 1970, moreover, the Governments of Gabon, the Ivory Coast and Nigeria jointly invited the UNHCR's 'good offices' and technical assistance in facilitating the return home, by way of an airlift, of some 5,000 Nigerian children evacuated during the civil war.

UNHCR is one of the smallest UN bodies, with a total staff of some 100 officers and 200 secretaries and clerks at headquarters and in the field. The High Commissioner has over 40 delegates and correspondents engaged in the implementation of the UNHCR material assistance programme in more than 50 countries, in addition to their responsibilities in the field of international protection.

In 1971, the Office of the United Nations High Commissioner for Refugees (UNHCR) will observe the 20th anniversary of its foundation. The year 1971 will also mark the 50 years which have elapsed since international assistance to refugees was first organized by Fridtjof Nansen, the League of Nations' first High Commissioner for Refugees; and the 20th anniversary of the signing, in Geneva, of the (1951) Convention relating to the Status of Refugees.

Headquarters: Palais des Nations, Geneva, Switzerland.
UK Office: 14 Stratford Place, London, W1.
High Commissioner: Prince Sadruddin Aga Khan (Iran).

UNHCR Reports. Geneva, 1966 ff.
UNHCR Bulletin. Geneva, 1968 ff.
Forty Years of International Assistance to Refugees. Geneva, 1962
The Red Cross and the Refugees. Geneva, 1963

The United Nations Relief and Works Agency for Palestine Refugees in the Near East (UNRWA) was established by the General Assembly in Dec. 1949. It is supported by private contributions and by governmental pledges made each year at the General Assembly. UNRWA's operations, direct relief, long-term rehabilitation and vocational training, cover the Gaza Strip, Jordan, Lebanon and Syria, where over 1m. refugees were living before the war of June 1967.

Headquarters: Museitbeh Quarter, Beirut, Lebanon.
Commissioner-General: Laurence Michelmore (USA).

The Children's Fund (UNICEF), established by the General Assembly on 11 Dec. 1946, functions under the supervision of the Economic and Social Council. It assists child health, nutrition and welfare programmes in 116 countries and territories. Its work is financed through voluntary contributions from governments and donations from the public. Income 1970: $59·4m.

Headquarters: United Nations Headquarters, New York City.
Executive Director: Henry R. Labouisse (USA).

The Budget of the United Nations. The financial year coincides with the calendar year; accountancy is in US$. Budget for 1971, $192,149,300.

Membership and percentage scale of contributions to UN budget, 1971–73:

Afghánistán	0·04	Greece	0·29	Niger	0·04
Albania	0·04	Guatemala	0·05	Nigeria	0·12
Algeria	0·09	Guinea	0·04	Norway	0·43
Argentina	0·85	Guyana	0·04	Pakistan	0·34
Australia	1·47	Haiti	0·04	Panama	0·04
Austria	0·55	Honduras	0·04	Paraguay	0·04
Barbados	0·04	Hungary	0·48	Peru	0·10
Belgium	1·05	Iceland	0·04	Philippines	0·31
Bolivia	0·04	India	1·55	Poland	1·41
Botswana	0·04	Indonesia	0·28	Portugal	0·16
Brazil	0·80	Iran	0·22	Romania	0·36
Bulgaria	0·18	Iraq	0·07	Rwanda	0·04
Burma	0·05	Irish Republic	0·15	Saudi Arabia	0·07
Burundi	0·04	Israel	0·20	Senegal	0·04
Byelorussia	0·50	Italy	3·24	Sierra Leone	0·04
Cambodia	0·04	Ivory Coast	0·04	Singapore	0·05
Cameroun	0·04	Jamaica	0·04	Somalia	0·04
Canada	3·08	Japan	5·40	South Africa, Rep. of	0·54
Central African Rep.	0·04	Jordan	0·04	Southern Yemen	0·04
Ceylon	0·05	Kenya	0·04	Spain	1·04
Chad	0·04	Kuwait	0·08	Sudan	0·05
Chile	0·20	Laos	0·04	Sweden	1·25
China	4·00	Lebanon	0·05	Syria	0·04
Colombia	0·19	Lesotho	0·04	Tanzania	0·04
Congo (Br.)	0·04	Liberia	0·04	Thailand	0·13
Congo (K.)	0·05	Libya	0·07	Togo	0·04
Costa Rica	0·04	Luxembourg	0·05	Trinidad	0·04
Cuba	0·16	Madagascar	0·04	Tunisia	0·04
Cyprus	0·04	Malawi	0·04	Turkey	0·35
Czechoslovakia	0·90	Malaysia	0·10	Uganda	0·04
Dahomey	0·04	Maldive, Republic of	0·04	Ukraine	1·87
Denmark	0·62	Mali	0·04	USSR	14·18
Dominican Republic	0·04	Malta	0·04	UAR	0·18
Ecuador	0·04	Mauritania	0·04	UK	5·90
El Salvador	0·04	Mexico	0·88	USA	31·52
Equatorial Guinea	0·04	Mongolia	0·04	Upper Volta	0·04
Ethiopia	0·04	Morocco	0·09	Uruguay	0·07
Finland	0·45	Nepál	0·04	Venezuela	0·41
France	6·00	Netherlands	1·18	Yemen	0·04
Gabon	0·04	New Zealand	0·32	Yugoslavia	0·38
Gambia	0·04	Nicaragua	0·04	Zambia	0·04
Ghana	0·08				

Eight non-member States participate in certain activities of the United Nations, such as regional economic commissions, the International Court of Justice, UNCTAD, UNIDO or the international control of narcotic drugs. They contribute to the expenses of such activities on the basis of the following percentages: West Germany (6·8); Holy See (0·04); Liechtenstein (0·04); Monaco (0·04); Korea (0·11); Vietnam (0·07); San Marino (0·04); Switzerland (0·84).

BOOKS OF REFERENCE

Yearbook of the United Nations. New York, 1947 ff. Annual
United Nations Chronicle. Monthly
Monthly Bulletin of Statistics
General Assembly: Official Records; Resolutions
Reports of the Secretary-General of the United Nations on the Work of the Organization. 1946 ff.
Documents of the United Nations Conference on International Organization, San Francisco, 1945. 16 vols.
Charter of the United Nations and Statute of the International Court of Justice. Text in English, French, Chinese, Russian and Spanish.
Repertory of Practice of UN's Organs. 5 vols. New York, 1955
Official Records of the Security Council, the Economic and Social Council, Trusteeship Council and the Disarmament Commission
Demographic Yearbook, 1948 ff. New York, 1969
Everyman's United Nations. 7th ed. New York, 1958 ff. Annual
Statistical Yearbook. New York, 1947 ff.
Yearbook of International Statistics. New York, 1950 ff.
World Economic Survey. New York, 1947 ff.
Economic Survey of Asia and the Far East. New York, 1946 ff.
Economic Survey of Latin Americs. New York, 1948 ff.
Economic Survey of Europe. New York, 1948 ff.
Economic Survey of Africa. New York, 1960 ff.
Bailey, S. D., *The General Assembly.* London, 1960
Boyd, A., *United Nations: Piety, Myth and Truth.* Harmondsworth, 1962
Condre, A. W., and Foote, W., *The Quest for Peace.* New York, 1965

Foote, W., *Dag Hammarskjold—Servant of Peace.* London, 1962.
Gross E., *United Nations—Structure for Peace.* London, 1962
Lie, Trygve, *In the Cause of Peace.* London, 1954
Nicholas, H. G., *The United Nations as a Political Institution.* OUP, 1959
Richards, J. H., *International Economic Institutions.* London, 1970
Savage, K., *The Story of the United Nations.* London, 1962
Thant, U, *Towards world peace.* New York, 1964
Walters, F. P., *A History of the League of Nations.* 2 vols. London, 1952
Witthauer, K., *Die Bevölkerung der Erde: Verteilung und Dynamik.* Gotha, 1958
Her Majesty's Stationery Office. *Sectional List 23* (currently revised) and *International Organizations Publications* contain a full list of publications on UN and Specialized Agencies, issued by HMSO.

London Information Centre. 14–15 Stratford Place, W.1.

AGENCIES IN RELATIONSHIP WITH THE UN

(as in 1971)

	IAEA	ILO	FAO	UNESCO	WHO	BANK & FUND	ICAO	UPU	ITU	WMO	IFC	IMCO	GATT
Afghánistán	*	*	*	*	*	*	*	*	*	*	*	—	—
Albania	*	—	—	*	*	—	—	*	*	*	*	—	—
Algeria	*	*	*	*	*	*	*	*	*	*	*	—	—
Argentina	*	*	*	*	*	*	*	*	*	*	*	*	*
Australia	*	*	*	*	*	*	*	*	*	*	*	—	*
Austria	*	*	*	*	*	*	*	*	*	*	*	—	*
Barbados	—	*	*	*	*	—	*	*	*	*	*	*	*
Belgium	*	*	*	*	*	*	*	*	*	*	*	*	—
Bolivia	*	—	*	—	*	*	*	*	*	*	*	—	—
Botzwana	—	—	*	—	—	*	—	*	*	*	—	—	—
Brazil	*	*	*	*	*	*	*	*	*	*	*	*	*
Bulgaria	*	*	*	*	*	—	*	*	*	*	—	—	—
Burma	*	*	*	*	*	*	*	*	*	*	*	*	*
Burundi	—	*	*	*	*	—	*	*	*	*	—	—	*
Byelorussia	*	*	—	*	*	—	—	*	*	*	—	—	—
Cambodia (Khmer Republic)	*	*	*	*	*	*	*	*	*	*	—	*	—
Cameroun	*	*	*	*	*	*	*	*	*	*	—	*	*
Canada	*	*	*	*	*	*	*	*	*	*	*	*	*
Central African Rep.	—	*	*	*	*	*	*	*	*	*	—	—	*
Ceylon	*	*	*	*	*	*	*	*	*	*	*	—	*
Chad	—	*	*	*	*	*	*	*	*	*	—	—	*
Chile	*	*	*	*	*	*	*	*	*	*	*	—	—
China (Taiwan)	*	*	—	*	*	*	*	*	*	*	*	*	—
Colombia	*	*	*	*	*	*	*	*	*	*	—	—	*
Congo (Br.)	—	*	*	*	*	*	*	*	*	*	—	—	*
Congo (K.)	*	*	*	*	*	*	*	*	*	*	*	—	—
Costa Rica	*	*	*	*	*	*	*	*	*	*	*	—	—
Cuba	*	*	*	*	*	—	*	*	*	*	*	—	*
Cyprus	*	*	*	*	*	*	*	*	*	*	*	—	*
Czechoslovakia	*	*	*	*	*	—	*	*	*	*	—	*	*
Dahomey	—	*	*	*	*	*	*	*	*	*	*	*	*
Denmark	*	*	*	*	*	*	*	*	*	*	*	*	*
Dominican Rep.	*	*	*	*	*	*	*	*	*	*	*	*	—
Ecuador	*	*	*	*	*	*	*	*	*	*	*	—	—
El Salvador	*	*	*	*	*	*	*	*	*	*	*	—	—
Equatorial Guinea	—	—	—	—	—	*	—	—	—	—	—	—	—
Ethiopia	*	*	*	*	*	*	*	*	*	*	*	—	—
Fiji	—	—	—	—	—	—	—	—	—	—	—	—	—

FAO has also 2 associate members: Bahrain and Qatar.
UNESCO also has 3 associate members: Bahrain, British Eastern Caribbean Group, Qatar.
WHO has 3 associate members: Bahrain, Qatar, Rhodesia.
UPU members also include: French Overseas Territories; Netherlands Antilles and Surinam; Portuguese Overseas Provinces; Spanish territories in Africa; UK overseas territories; USA territories; Bhután.
ITU members also include French Overseas Territories; Portuguese Overseas Provinces; Spanish territories in Africa; UK protectorates and overseas territories; US territories; Rhodesia.
WMO members also include British Caribbean Territories; French Polynesia; French Somaliland; Hong Kong; Mauritius; Netherlands Antilles and Surinam; New Caledonia; Portuguese East and West Africa; Spanish territories in Africa; Rhodesia.
GATT also includes Rhodesia. Acceded provisionally, Tunisia, UAR.
IMCO has 1 associate member; Hong Kong.

	IAEA	ILO	FAO	UNESCO	WHO	BANK & FUND	ICAO	UPU	ITU	WMO	IFC	IMCO	GATT
Finland	*	*	*	*	*	*	*	*	*	*	*	*	*
France	*	*	*	*	*	*	*	*	*	*	—	—	*
Gabon	—	*	*	*	*	*	—	*	*	*	—	—	*
Gambia	—	—	*	—	—	*	—	—	—	—	—	—	*
German (West)	*	*	*	*	*	*	*	*	*	*	*	*	*
Ghana	*	*	*	*	*	*	*	*	*	*	*	*	*
Greece	*	*	*	*	*	*	*	*	*	*	*	—	—
Guatemala	*	*	*	*	*	*	*	*	*	*	*	—	—
Guinea	—	*	*	*	*	*	*	*	*	*	*	—	—
Guyana	—	*	*	*	*	*	*	*	*	*	*	—	*
Haiti	*	*	*	*	*	*	*	*	*	*	*	—	*
Holy See	*	—	—	*	—	—	—	*	—	—	—	—	—
Honduras	—	*	*	*	*	*	*	*	*	*	*	*	—
Hungary	*	*	*	*	*	—	—	*	*	*	*	—	—
Iceland	*	*	*	*	*	*	*	*	*	*	—	*	—
India	*	*	*	*	*	*	*	*	*	*	*	*	*
Indonesia	*	*	*	*	*	*	*	*	*	*	*	*	—
Iran	*	*	*	*	*	*	*	*	*	*	*	*	—
Iraq	*	*	*	*	*	*	*	*	*	*	*	—	—
Irish Rep.	*	*	*	*	*	*	*	*	*	*	*	*	*
Israel	*	*	*	*	*	*	*	*	*	*	*	*	*
Italy	*	*	*	*	*	*	*	*	*	*	*	*	*
Ivory Coast	*	*	*	*	*	*	*	*	*	*	*	*	*
Jamaica	*	*	*	*	*	*	*	*	*	*	*	—	*
Japan	*	*	*	*	*	*	*	*	*	*	*	*	*
Jordan	*	*	*	*	*	*	*	*	*	*	*	—	—
Kenya	*	*	*	*	*	*	*	*	*	*	*	—	*
Korea, Rep. of	*	—	*	*	*	*	*	*	*	*	*	*	*
Kuwait	*	*	*	*	*	*	*	*	*	*	*	*	—
Laos	—	*	*	*	*	*	*	*	*	*	*	—	—
Lebanon	*	*	*	*	*	*	*	*	*	*	*	*	—
Lesotho	—	*	*	*	*	*	—	*	*	*	—	*	—
Liberia	*	*	*	*	*	*	*	*	*	*	—	*	—
Libya	*	*	*	*	*	*	*	*	*	*	—	—	—
Liechtenstein	*	—	—	—	—	—	—	*	*	*	—	—	—
Luxembourg	*	*	*	*	*	*	*	*	*	*	—	*	*
Madagascar	*	*	*	*	*	*	*	*	*	*	*	—	*
Malawi	—	*	*	*	*	*	*	*	*	*	—	—	—
Malaysia	—	*	*	*	*	*	*	*	*	*	—	*	—
Maldive Is.	—	—	—	—	*	—	—	*	*	—	—	*	—
Mali	*	*	*	*	*	*	*	*	*	*	*	—	—
Malta	—	*	*	*	*	—	*	*	*	*	—	*	*
Mauritania	—	*	*	*	*	*	*	*	*	*	—	—	*
Mauritius	—	*	*	*	*	*	—	—	—	*	—	—	*
Mexico	*	*	*	*	*	*	*	*	*	*	*	*	—
Monaco	*	—	—	—	*	—	—	*	*	—	—	—	—
Mongolia	—	—	—	*	*	*	—	—	*	*	—	—	—
Nauru	*	*	*	*	*	*	*	*	*	*	*	*	—
Morocco	—	—	—	—	—	—	—	—	—	*	—	—	—
Nepál	—	*	*	*	*	*	*	*	*	*	*	*	—
Netherlands	*	*	*	*	*	*	*	*	*	*	*	*	*
New Zealand	*	*	*	*	*	*	*	*	*	*	*	*	*
Nicaragua	—	*	*	*	*	*	*	*	*	*	*	—	*
Niger	—	*	*	*	*	*	*	*	*	*	—	—	*
Nigeria	*	*	*	*	*	*	*	*	*	*	*	*	*
Norway	*	*	*	*	*	*	*	*	*	*	*	*	*
Pakistan	*	*	*	*	*	*	*	*	*	*	*	*	*
Panama	*	*	*	*	*	*	*	*	*	*	*	—	—
Paraguay	*	*	*	*	*	*	*	*	*	*	*	—	—
Peru	*	*	*	*	*	*	*	*	*	*	*	*	*
Philippines	*	*	*	*	*	*	*	*	*	*	*	*	*
Poland	*	*	*	*	*	—	*	*	*	*	—	*	*
Portugal	*	*	*	*	*	*	*	*	*	*	*	—	*
Romania	*	*	*	*	*	—	*	*	*	*	—	*	*
Rwanda	—	*	*	*	*	*	—	*	*	*	—	—	—
San Marino	—	—	—	—	—	—	—	*	—	—	—	—	—
Saudi Arabia	*	—	*	*	*	*	*	*	*	*	*	—	—
Senegal	*	*	*	*	*	*	*	*	*	*	*	*	*
Sierra Leone	*	*	*	*	*	*	*	*	*	*	*	—	*
Singapore	*	*	—	*	*	*	*	*	*	*	*	*	—
Somalia	—	*	*	*	*	*	*	*	*	*	*	—	—
South Africa, Rep. of	*	—	—	—	—	*	*	*	*	*	*	*	*

See notes on p. 11.

	IAEA	ILO	FAO	UNESCO	WHO	BANK & FUND	ICAO	UPU	ITU	WMO	IFC	IMCO	GATT
Southern Yemen	—	*	*	—	*	*	—	*	*	*	—	—	—
Spain	*	*	*	*	*	*	*	*	*	*	*	*	*
Sudan	*	*	*	*	*	*	*	*	*	*	*	—	—
Swaziland	—	—	—	—	—	*	—	*	*	*	—	—	—
Sweden	*	*	*	*	*	*	*	*	*	*	*	*	*
Switzerland	*	*	*	*	*	*	—	*	*	*	—	*	*
Syria	*	*	*	*	*	*	*	*	*	*	*	*	—
Tanzania	—	*	*	*	*	*	*	*	*	*	*	—	*
Thailand	*	*	*	*	*	*	*	*	*	*	*	*	—
Togo	—	*	*	*	*	*	*	*	*	*	*	—	*
Trinidad	—	*	*	*	*	*	*	*	*	*	*	—	*
Tunisia	*	*	*	*	*	*	*	*	*	*	*	*	—
Turkey	*	*	*	*	*	*	*	*	*	*	*	*	*
Uganda	*	*	*	*	*	*	*	*	*	*	*	—	*
Ukraine	*	*	—	*	*	—	—	*	*	*	—	—	—
USSR	*	*	—	*	*	—	—	*	*	*	—	*	—
UAR	*	*	*	*	*	*	*	*	*	*	*	*	*
UK	*	*	*	*	*	*	*	*	*	*	*	*	*
USA	*	*	*	*	*	*	*	*	*	*	*	*	*
Upper Volta	—	*	*	*	*	*	*	*	*	*	*	—	*
Uruguay	*	*	*	*	*	*	*	*	*	*	*	—	—
Venezuela	*	*	*	*	*	*	*	*	*	*	*	—	—
Vietnam	*	*	*	*	*	*	*	*	*	*	*	—	—
Western Samoa	—	—	—	—	*	—	—	—	—	—	—	—	—
Yemen	—	*	*	*	*	—	*	*	*	—	—	—	—
Yugoslavia	*	*	*	*	*	*	*	*	*	*	—	*	*
Zambia	—	*	*	*	*	*	*	*	*	*	*	—	—

See notes on p. 11.

1. INTERNATIONAL ATOMIC ENERGY AGENCY (IAEA)

Origin. The International Atomic Energy Agency came into existence on 29 July 1957. Its statute had been approved on 26 Oct. 1956, at an international conference held at UN Headquarters, New York. A relationship agreement links it with the United Nations.

Functions. (1) To accelerate and enlarge the contribution of atomic energy to peace, health and prosperity throughout the world, and (2) to ensure that assistance provided by it or at its request or under its supervision or control is not used in such a way as to further any military purpose.

The IAEA gives advice and technical assistance to member states (103 as of Jan. 1970) on nuclear power development, including its application in water desalination, on health and safety, and on radioactive waste management. It promotes the use of radiation and radioisotopes in medicine, agriculture, industry and hydrology through expert services, training courses and fellowships, research contracts, scientific meetings and publications. Since 1958 the Agency has provided the services of more than 1,000 experts, 3,000 fellowships, equipment worth over $4m. and research contracts worth more than $6m. The IAEA has research laboratories in Austria and Monaco. At Trieste, the International Centre for Theoretical Physics was established in 1964 which is now operated jointly by UNESCO and IAEA. The Agency's safeguards system to prevent the diversion of nuclear materials to military use now covers 10 nuclear power stations, 68 other reactors, 4 conversion plants, fabrication plants and fuel reprocessing plants, 74 other activities in 32 states.

Total budget for 1970, $14,837,000; estimate for, 1971 $17,029,000.

Organization. The Statute provides for an annual General Conference, a Board of Governors of 25 members and a staff headed by a Director-General.

Director-General: Sigvard Eklund (Sweden).
Headquarters: Kärntnerring 11–13, A1010 Vienna I, Austria.

2. INTERNATIONAL LABOUR ORGANIZATION (ILO)

Origin. The ILO, established in 1919 as an autonomous part of the League of Nations, is an intergovernmental agency with a tripartite structure, in which representatives of governments, employers and workers participate. It seeks through international action to improve labour conditions, raise living standards and promote economic and social stability. In 1946 the ILO was recognized by the United Nations as a specialized agency. In 1969 it was awarded the Nobel Peace Prize. In 1971 it numbered 121 members.

Functions. One of the ILO'S principal functions is the formulation of international standards in the form of International Labour Conventions and Recommendations. Member countries are required to submit Conventions to their competent national authorities with a view to ratification. If a country ratifies a Convention it agrees to bring its laws into line with its terms and to report periodically how these regulations are being applied. A total of 3,695 ratifications of 134 Conventions had been deposited by the end of 1970. Machinery is available to ascertain whether Conventions thus ratified are effectively applied.

Recommendations do not require ratification, but member states are obliged to consider them with a view to giving effect to their provisions by legislation or other action. By the end of 1970 the International Labour Conference had adopted 142 recommendations.

Organization. The ILO consists of the International Labour Conference, the Governing Body and the International Labour Office.

The Conference is the supreme deliberative organ of the ILO; it meets annually at Geneva. National delegations are composed of 2 government delegates, 1 employers' delegate and 1 workers' delegate.

The Governing Body, elected by the Conference, is the executive council. It is composed of 24 government members, 12 workers' members and 12 employers' members.

Ten governments hold permanent seats on the Governing Body because of their industrial importance, namely, Canada, China, France, Germany (West), India, Italy, Japan, USSR, UK and USA. The remaining 14 government seats were, at the end of 1970, held by Brazil, Central African Republic, Colombia, Czechoslovakia, Ecuador, Indonesia, Kenya, Libya, Nigeria, Romania, Syria, Upper Volta, Uruguay and Vietnam.

The Office serves as secretariat, operational headquarters, research centre and publishing house.

The ILO budget for 1970–71was $62·9m.

Activities. In addition to its research and advisory activities, the ILO extends technical co-operation to governments under its regular budget and under the UN Development Programme and Funds-in-Trust in the fields of human resources development (including vocational training), development of social institutions, small-scale industries, rural development, social security, industrial safety and hygiene, productivity, etc. Technical co-operation also includes information to governments and organizations on request, advisory missions and a fellowship programme. A total of $24·9m. was spent on technical co-operation projects in 1969 ($20·8m. in 1968). This was allocated as follows: Africa, $10m.; the Americas, $4·3m.; Asia, $5·1m.; Europe, $3·3m.; Middle East, $1·3m.; interregional projects, $0·9m.

Major emphasis is being given during the UN Second Development Decade to the ILO's World Employment Programme, launched in 1969 with the purpose of stimulating national and international efforts to increase the volume of productive employment, and so to counter the problem of rising unemployment in developing countries. The first national study to be completed under the Programme was carried out in 1970 in Colombia. Further national studies are being planned for Ceylon and for several East African countries in 1971.

In 1960 the ILO established in Geneva the International Institute for Labour Studies. The Institute specializes in advanced education and research on social and labour policy. It brings together for group study experienced persons from all parts of the world—government administrators, trade-union officials, industrial experts, management, university and other specialists.

A training institution was opened by the ILO in Turin, Italy, in 1965—the International Centre for Advanced Technical and Vocational Training. The Centre provides opportunities for technical, vocational and management development training for individuals who have advanced beyond the facilities available in their own countries. Many courses are geared particularly to the needs of developing countries. ILO celebrated its 50th anniversary in 1969 and was awarded the Nobel Prize.

Headquarters: 154, rue de Lausanne, CH-1211 Geneva 22, Switzerland.

Director-General: Wilfred Jenks (UK).

Chairman of the Governing Body: Simeon Olujimi Koku (Nigeria).

London Office: 40 Piccadilly, W1.

There are also branch and area offices in Algiers, Beirut, Bonn, Buenos Aires, Cairo, Dakar, Dar es Salaam, Djakarta, New Delhi, Islamabad, Istanbul, Lagos, Lusaka, Manila, Mexico City, Moscow, Ottawa, Paris, Port-of-Spain, Rio de Janeiro, Rome, San José (Costa Rica), Taipeh, Tokyo, Washington and Yaoundé. There are regional offices in Addis Ababa (for Africa), Bangkok (for Asia) and Lima (for the Americas).

Publications. Regular periodicals in English, French and Spanish include the *International Labour Review* (monthly); *Legislative Series* (bimonthly); *Bulletin of Labour Statistics* (quarterly); *Official Bulletin* (quarterly); the *Year Book of Labour Statistics*; *ILO Panorama* (bimonthly); a series of studies and reports; *Towards Full Employment: A Programme for Colombia.* Geneva, 1970.

3. FOOD AND AGRICULTURE ORGANIZATION OF THE UNITED NATIONS (FAO)

Origin. The UN Conference on Food and Agriculture in May 1943, at Hot Springs, Virginia, set up an Interim Commission in Washington in July 1943 to plan the Organization, which came into being on 16 Oct. 1945.

Functions. FAO gives international support to national programmes to increase the efficiency of agriculture, forestry and fisheries, and to improve the conditions of the people working in these industries.

FAO keeps world food and agricultural conditions under continuous review and supplies member governments with facts and figures, appraisals and forecasts relating to trends in the world agricultural situation and on production, trade and consumption. In 1969 it issued a provisional Indicative World Plan for Agricultural Development—an analysis of the main problems which will face world agriculture up to 1985, together with suggestions for their solution through national and international action. It provides secretariat services for the exchange of information and for co-operative action in its fields of concern. About 2,100 experts are assigned to field projects in the developing countries. Through co-operative arrangements with private and public lending institutions, including the World Bank, it helps to mobilize capital backing for programmes of development. With the UN, FAO shares control of the World Food Programme, which uses supplies of food pledged by members of the two organizations for such purposes as paying workers on development programmes, supporting settlers on new lands while they wait to harvest their first crops and assisting institutional feeding programmes for mothers, children and students. Through the Freedom from Hunger Campaign, which is conducted by 90 national committees, it is arousing concern over the gravity and extent of the world food situation and mobilizing public support for governmental and non-governmental programmes to improve the situation. Administers, in collaboration with UN, the World Food Programme (WFP) providing food for economic development and relief.

Organization. FAO's programme and overall policy are approved by a Conference (composed of one representative of each of the 119 member nations) and more detailed supervision is given by a Council (consisting of 34 nations elected by the Conference). The work of the Organization is carried out by an international staff led by a Director-General.

Budget for 1971: $39·73m.

Headquarters: Viale delle Terme di Caracalla, Rome, Italy.
Director-General: Mr A. H. Boerma (Netherlands).

FAO publications include: Catalogue of Publications 1945–66 and supplements; *The State of Food and Agriculture* (annual), 1947 ff.; *Third World Food Survey,* Rome, 1963; *Animal Health Yearbook* (annual), 1957 ff.; *Production Yearbook* (annual), 1947 ff.; *Trade Yearbook* (annual), 147 ff.; *An Annual Review of World Production Consumption and Trade of Fertilizers,* 1951 ff.; *FAO Commodity Review* (annual), 1961 ff.; *Yearbook of Forest Products Statistics* (annual), 1947 ff.; *Yearbook of Fishery Statistics* (in two volumes: *Catches and Landings* and *Fishery Commodities*) (annual), 1947 ff.; *Ceres* (monthly).

4. UNITED NATIONS EDUCATIONAL, SCIENTIFIC AND CULTURAL ORGANIZATION (UNESCO)

Origin. A Conference for the establishment of an Educational, Scientific and Cultural Organization of the United Nations was convened by the Government of the UK in association with the Government of France, and met in London, 1–16 Nov. 1945. UNESCO came into being on 4 Nov. 1946.

Functions. The purpose of UNESCO is to contribute to peace and security by promoting collaboration among the nations through education, science and culture in order to further universal respect for justice, for the rule of law and for the human rights and fundamental freedoms which are affirmed for the peoples of the world, without distinction of race, sex, language or religion, by the Charter of the United Nations. The UNESCO budget for 1969 was $42,095,750.

Activities. The education programme has three main objectives: the extension of education; the improvement of education; and education for living in a world community.

To train teachers specialized in the techniques of fundamental education. UNESCO is helping to establish regional and national training centres. A centre for Latin America was opened in Mexico in 1951, one for the Arab States was set up in Egypt in 1953. UNESCO seeks to promote the progressive application of the right to free and compulsory education for all and to improve the quality of education everywhere.

In the natural sciences, UNESCO seeks to promote international scientific co-operation, such as the International Hydrological Decade which began in 1965. It encourages scientific research designed to improve the living conditions of mankind. Science co-operation offices have been set up in Montevideo, Cairo, New Delhi and Jakarta.

In its mass communication work, UNESCO endeavours, by disseminating information, carrying out research and providing advice, to increase the scope and quality of press, film and radio services throughout the world.

Organization. The organs of UNESCO are a General Conference (composed of representatives from each member state), an Executive Board (consisting of 30 government representatives elected by the General Conference) and a Secretariat. UNESCO had 125 members and 3 associate members in 1969.

National commissions act as liaison groups between UNESCO and the educational, scientific and cultural life of their own countries.

Budget for 1971: $49·24m.

Headquarters: UNESCO House, 9 Place de Fontenoy, Paris (7ème).
Director-General: René Maheu (France).

Periodicals. Museum (quarterly, English and French); *International Social Science Journal* (quarterly, English and French); *Impact of Science on Society* (quarterly, English and French); *Unesco Courier* (monthly, English, French and Spanish); *Fundamental and Adult Education Bulletin* (quarterly, English, French and Spanish); *Copyright Bulletin* (twice-yearly, English and French); *Unesco Chronicle* (monthly, English, French and Spanish); *Unesco Bulletin for Libraries* (monthly, English, French and Spanish).

5. WORLD HEALTH ORGANIZATION (WHO)

Origin. An International Conference, convened by the UN Economic and Social Council, to consider a single health organization resulted in the adoption on

22 July 1946 of the constitution of the World Health Organization. This constitution came into force on 7 April 1948.

Structure. The principal organs of WHO are the World Health Assembly, the Executive Board and the Secretariat. Each of the 128 member states and the 3 Associate Members (1970) has the right to be represented at the Assembly, which meets annually usually in Geneva, Switzerland. The 24-member Executive Board is composed of technically qualified health experts designated by as many member states elected by the Assembly. The Secretariat consists of technical and administrative staff headed by a Director-General. WHO activities have been progressively decentralized and regional organizations have been established in Africa (regional office, Brazzaville), South-East Asia (New Delhi), Europe (Copenhagen), Eastern Mediterranean (Alexandria) and Western Pacific (Manila). The Pan American Sanitary Bureau serves as the Regional Office of WHO for the Americas (Washington).

Functions. WHO's objective, as stated in the first article of the Constitution is 'the attainment by all peoples of the highest possible level of health'. As the directing and co-ordinating authority on international health it establishes and maintains collaboration with the UN, specialized agencies, government health administrations, professional and other groups concerned with health. The Constitution also directs WHO to assist governments to strengthen their health services, to stimulate and advance work to eradicate diseases, to promote maternal and child health, mental health, medical research and the prevention of accidents; to improve standards of teaching and training in the health professions, and of nutrition, housing, sanitation, working conditions and other aspects of environmental health. The Organization also is empowered to propose conventions, agreements and regulations and make recommendations about international health matters; to revise the international nomenclature of diseases, causes of death and public health practices; to develop, establish and promote international standards concerning foods, biological pharmaceutical and similar substances.

Methods of work. Country projects, undertaken only on the request of the government concerned, are organized and administered through the 6 regional offices of the Organization. World-wide technical services are made available by headquarters. Expert committees chosen from the 43 advisory panels of experts meet to advise the Director-General on a given subject. Scientific groups and consultative meetings are called for similar purposes. To further the education of all levels of health personnel of all categories, seminars, technical conferences and training courses are organized and advisors, consultants and lecturers are provided. WHO awards fellowships for study to nationals of member countries (the cumulative total reached 36,000 by the end of 1970).

Activities. In communicable diseases WHO is sponsoring world-wide campaigns to eradicate both malaria and smallpox. In malaria, WHO's role is to help plan national campaigns, provide expert advice, stimulate research, organize training programmes and pilot projects and co-ordinate the world programme. By the end of 1969, of the 1,800m. people living in originally malarious areas in 145 countries of the world, 39% then were in areas where malaria had been eradicated and a further 40% in areas where eradication programmes were in progress. Smallpox cases in the world have declined steadily since 1967 when the intensified global smallpox eradication campaign was undertaken. In 1969 there were 53,814 cases, and in 1970, not more than 30,000 cases were reported, the lowest figure in history.

WHO has assisted member countries to build up their health services in one form or another, including the planning and organization of public health laboratories. It promotes national environmental health programmes and advises on soil, water, air and food pollution. The Organization is also assisting a number of countries in the development of suitable systems of health care in relation to popular trends, including the development of services for family planning.

WHO also has programmes in non-communicable diseases, such as cardiovascular diseases and cancer, in which research figures prominently. Work in cancer is carried out both at the International Agency for Research on Cancer at Lyons in the field of environmental biology, and in Geneva, where WHO concentrates on clinical studies, classification and cancer control services. The medical research programme of WHO is based on a world-wide network of reference centres. A number of countries are being helped to develop an effective organization of mental health services. In pharmacology and toxicology work is geared to ensuring the availability of effective and safe drugs. In its studies and programmes the Organization considers both the quality of foods and their safety particularly where food additives are concerned. Education and training of staff remains a top priority matter, including the preparation of nurses for teaching and administrative roles.

Headquarters: Avenue Appia, 1211 Geneva 27. *Regional Offices:* Alexandria, Brazzaville, Copenhagen, Manila, New Delhi, Washington.

Director-General: Dr Marcolino Gomes Candau (Brazil).

Basic Documents. 21st ed., 1970 (English, French, Russian, Spanish)
Handbook of Resolutions and Decisions. 10th ed., 1969 (English, French, Russian, Spanish)
Official Records, 1947 ff. (English, French, Russian, Spanish; 175 vols. to date)
WHO Chronicle (monthly from 1947; Chinese, English, French, Russian and Spanish)
Bulletin of WHO (quarterly, 1947–51; monthly, from 1952; English, French, Russian)
International Digest of Health Legislation (quarterly, from 1948; English and French)
World Health, the Magazine of WHO. 1957 ff. (10 issues a year; English, French, German, Portuguese, Russian, Spanish, Japanese, Hindi)
WHO Technical Report Series, 1950 ff. (English, French, Russian, Spanish)
WHO Monograph Series, 1951 ff. (English, French, Russian, Spanish)
Public Health Papers, 1959 ff. (English, French, Russian, Spanish)
World Health Statistics Annual (from 1939; English, French and Russian)
World Health Statistics Report (monthly, from June 1947; English and French)
Weekly Epidemiological Record (from 1926; English and French)
Publication of the WHO, 1947–57; a bibliography (1958).—*1958–62* (1965).—*1963–67* (1969)
World Directories:
    Dental Schools, 1963 (1967); *Medical Schools* (1963).—*1967 Supplement* (1969); *Post-Basic and Post-Graduate Schools of Nursing* (1965); *Schools of Pharmacy, 1963* (1966); *Schools of Public Health, 1965* (1968); *Venereal Disease Treatment Centres at Ports* (1961); *Veterinary Schools, 1964* (1968)
Medical Research Programme of WHO (1969; English, French, Russian, Spanish)
Specifications for the Quality Control of Pharmaceutical Preparations International Pharmacopeioa (2nd ed., 1967; English, French, Russian, Spanish)
Manual of the International Statistical Classification of Diseases, Injuries and Causes of Death. 8th rev. (1967; English, French, Russian, Spanish)
The First Ten Years of the World Health Organization (1958; English, French, Russian, Spanish)
The Second Ten Years of the World Health Organization, 1958–1967 (1968; English, French, Spanish)

6. INTERNATIONAL MONETARY FUND (FUND)

The International Monetary Fund was established on 27 Dec. 1945 as an independent international organization; its relationship with the UN is defined in an agreement of mutual co-operation which came into force on 15 Nov. 1947. The total of all quotas of the 117 members was $28,433m. at 31 Dec. 1970, when the Fund held $4,934·8m. in the form of gold and $24,485·97m. in the form of national currencies.

In Jan. 1962 the Fund provided for up to $6,000m. in supplementary resources when it approved an arrangement whereby 10 industrial countries (Belgium, Canada, France, West Germany, Italy, Japan, Netherlands, Sweden, UK, USA) will stand ready to lend to the Fund if this is necessary to forestall or cope with an impairement of the international payments system. These arrangements have been extended until Oct. 1975. They were used to finance the drawings made by the UK in 1964, 1965, 1968 and 1969, and by France in 1969 and 1970. The amount still available under the arrangements as of 31 Dec. 1970 was $5,415·8m.

Purposes. To promote international monetary co-operation and exchange stability, to assist in the removal of exchange restrictions and to assist in establishing a multilateral system of payments. The Fund seeks to facilitate expansion of world trade as a means of promoting high levels of employment and income, and of developing the productive resources of its members.

Activities. Each member of the Fund undertakes to establish and maintain an agreed par value (in terms of gold or of the US dollar) for its currency, and to consult the Fund on any change in excess of 10% of the initial parity. The Fund works towards the removal of restrictions on current exchange transactions, and is consulted by its members on major changes in their foreign-exchange practices. The Fund makes its foreign exchange resources available, under proper safeguards, to its members to meet short-term or medium-term payments difficulties. The Fund also supplements, as and when needed, the existing reserve assets of participants in the Special Drawing Account. The first allocation of special drawing rights was made on 1 Jan. 1970, in a total amount equivalent to $3,414·4m. Preparations were completed for the second allocation, to be made on 1 Jan. 1971, in a total amount equivalent to approximately $3,000m.

Organization. The highest authority in the Fund is exercised by the Board of Governors on which each member government is represented. The Governors assemble once a year to review the Fund's work.

The Executive Directors are responsible for the general operations of the Fund. At present, 6 of them are appointed and the other 14 are elected by member countries not represented by appointed Directors. Voting power in these elections is governed by the amount of each nation's subscription quota. Each appointed Director has voting power proportionate to the quota of the government he represents. Each elected Director casts all the votes of the countries which elected him.

The Managing Director is selected by the Executive Directors; he presides as chairman at their meetings, but may not vote except in case of a tie. His term is for 5 years, but may be terminated at the discretion of the Executive Directors. He is responsible for the ordinary business of the Fund, under general control of the Executive Directors, and supervises a staff of 1,176.

Headquarters: 19th & H St. NW, Washington, D.C., 20431. Offices in Paris and Geneva.

Managing Director: Pierre-Paul Schweitzer (France).

Publications. Summary Proceedings of Annual Meetings of the Board of Governors.—Annual Report of the Executive Directors.— Financial Statement (quarterly).—*Schedule of Par Values (see* pp. 19–21).—*International Financial Statistics* (monthly).—*International Financial News Survey* (weekly).—*Balance of Payments Yearbook.* Washington, 1949 ff.—*IMF Staff Papers* (three times a year). Washington, from Feb. 1950.—*Annual Report on Exchange Restrictions.* Washington, 1950 ff.—*Finance and Development.* Washington, from June 1964 (quarterly).—*Direction of Trade* (monthly).

SCHEDULE OF PAR VALUES. The Fund Agreement requires that 'the par value of the currency of each member shall be expressed in terms of gold as a common denominator or in terms of the US$ of the weight and fineness in effect on 1 July 1944'.
The following table records the par values at 15 Oct. 1970.
Par values have not yet been agreed with the Fund for the following countries: Algeria, Barbados, Cambodia, Cameroun, Central African Republic, Chad, Congo (K.), Dahomey, Equatorial Guinea, Gabon, Guinea, Indonesia, Ivory Coast, Korea, Laos, Madagascar, Mali, Mauritania, Mauritius, Niger, Senegal, Southern Yemen, Togo, Upper Volta, Vietnam, Yemen.

CURRENCIES OF METROPOLITAN AREAS

Country	Currency	Grammes of fine gold per currency unit	Currency units per troy oz. of fine gold	Currency units per US$	US cents per currency unit
Afghánistán	Afghani	0·019 748 2	1,575·000	45·000	2·222 22
Australia	Dollar	0·995 310	31·250	0·892 857	112·000
Austria	Schilling	0·034 179 6	910·000	26·000	3·846 15
Belgium	Franc	0·017 773 4	1,750·000	50·000	2·000
Botswana	Rand	1·244 14	25·000	0·714 28 6	140·000
Burma	Kyat	0·186 621	166·667	4·761 9	21·000
Burundi	Franc	0·010 156 2	3,062·500	87·500	1·142 86

Country	Currency	Grammes of fine gold per currency unit	Currency units per troy oz. of fine gold	Currency units per $US	US cents per currency unit
Canada	Dollar	0·822 021	37·837 8	1·081 08	92·500
Ceylon	Rupee	0·149 297	208·333	5·952 37	16·800
China	Dollar	0·222 216 8	1,400·000	40·000	2·500
Congo (K.)	Zaïre	1·777 34	17·500	0·500	200·000
Costa Rica	Colón	0·134 139	231·875	6·625	15·094 3
Cyprus	Pound	2·132 81	14·583 3	0·416 667	240·000
Denmark	Krone	0·118 489	262·500	7·500	13·333 3
Dominican Repub.	Peso	0·888 671	35·000	1·000	100·000
Ecuador	Sucre	0·035 546 8	875·000	25·000	4·000
El Salvador	Colón	0·355 468	87·500	2·500	40·000
Ethiopia	Dollar	0·355 468	87·500	2·500	40·000
Finland	Markka	0·211 590	146·999	4·199 97	23·809 7
France	Franc	0·160 000	192·397	5·554 19	18·004 4
Gambia	Pound	2·132 81	14·583 3	0·416 667	240·000
Germany (West)	Mark	0·242 806	128·100	3·660	27·322 4
Ghana	New Cedi	0·870 897	35·714 3	1·020 41	98·000
Greece	Drachma	0·029 622 4	1,050·000	30·000	3·333 33
Guatemala	Quetzal	0·888 671	35·000	1·000	100·000
Guyana	Dollar	0·444 335	70·000	2·000	50·000
Haiti	Gourde	0·177 734	175·000	5·000	20·000
Honduras	Lempira	0·444 335	70·000	2·000	50·000
Iceland	Króna	0·010 095 5	3,080·000	88·000	1·136 36
India	Rupee	0·118 489	265·200	7·500	13·333 33
Iran	Rial	0·011 731 6	2,651·250	75·750	1·320 13
Iraq	Dinar	2·488 28	12·500	0·357 143	280·000
Irish Republic	Pound	2·132 81	14·583 3	0·416 667	240·000
Israel	Pound	0·253 906	122·500	3·500	28·571 4
Italy	Lira	0·001 421 87	21,875·000	625·000	0·160
Jamaica	Dollar	1·066 41	29·166 7	0·833 333	120·000
Japan	Yen	0·002 468 53	12·600	360·000	0·277 778
Jordan	Dinar	2·488 28	12·500	0·357 143	280·000
Kenya	Shilling	0·124 414	250·000	7·142 86	14·000
Kuwait	Dinar	2·488 28	12·500	0·357 143	280·000
Lebanon	Pound	0·405 512	76·701 8	2·191 48	45·631 3
Lesotho	Rand	1·244 14	25·000	0·714 286	140·000
Liberia	Dollar	0·888 671	35·000	1·000	100·000
Libya	Pound	2·488 28	12·500	0·357 143	280·000
Luxembourg	Franc	0·017 733 4	1,750·000	50·000	2·000
Malawi	Pound	2·132 81	14·583 3	0·416 667	240·000
Malaysia	Dollar	0·290 299	107·143	3·061 22	32·666 7
Malta	Pound	2·132 81	14·583 3	0·416667	240·000
Mexico	Peso	0·071 093 7	437·500	12·500	8·000
Morocco	Dirham	0·175 61	177·117	5·060 49	19·760 9
Nepál	Rupee	0·087 77	354·375	10·125	9·876 54
Netherlands	Guilder	0·245 489	126·700	3·620	27·624 3
New Zealand	Dollar	0·995 310	31·250	0·892 857	112·000
Nicaragua	Córdoba	0·126 953	245·000	7·000	14·285 7
Nigeria	Pound	2·488 28	12·500	0·357 143	280·000
Norway	Krone	0·124 414	250·000	7·142 86	14·000
Pakistan	Rupee	0·186 621	166·667	4·761 9	21·000
Panama	Balboa	0·888 671	35·000	1·000	100·000
Philippine Repub.	Peso	0·227 864	136·500	3·900	25·641
Portugal	Escudo	0·030 910 3	1,006·250	28·750	3·478 26
Rwanda	Franc	0·008 886 71	3,500·000	100·000	1·000
Saudi Arabia	Rial	0·197 482	157·500	4·500	22·222 2
Sierra Leone	Leone	1·066 41	29·166 7	0·833 333	120·000
Singapore	Dollar	0·290 299	107·143	3·061 22	32·666 7
Somalia	Shilling	0·124 414	250·000	7·142 86	14·000
Sth. Africa, Rep. of	Rand	1·244 14	25·000	0·714 286	140·000
Spain	Peseta	0·012 695 3	2,450·000	70·000	1·428 57
Sudan	Pound	2·551 87	12·188 5	0·348 242	287·156
Swaziland	Rand	1·244 14	25·000	0·714 286	140·000
Sweden	Krona	0·171 783	181·062	5·173 21	19·330 4
Syria	Pound	0·405 512	76·701 8	2·191 48	45·631 3
Tanzania	Shilling	0·124 414	250·000	7·142 86	14·000
Thailand	Baht	0·042 724 5	728·000	20·800	4·807 69
Trinidad & Tobago	Dollar	0·444 335	70·000	2·000	50·000
Tunisia	Dinar	1·692 71	18·375	0·525	190·476
Turkey	Lira	0·059 244 7	525·000	15·000	6·666 67
Uganda	Shilling	0·124 414	250·000	7·142 86	14·000
UAR	Pound	2·551 87	12·188 5	0·348 242	287·156
UK	Pound	2·132 81	14·583 3	0·416 667	240·000
USA	Dollar	0·888 671	35·000	1·000	100·000
Uruguay	Peso	0·120 091	259·000	7·400	13·513 5
Venezuela	Bolívar	0·265 275	117·250	3·350	29·850 7
Yugoslavia	Dinar	0·071 093 7	437·500	12·500	8·000
Zambia	Kwacha	1·244 14	25·000	0·714 286	140·000

CURRENCIES OF NON-METROPOLITAN AREAS

Member and non-metropolitan areas	Currency and relation to metropolitan unit	Grammes of fine gold per currency unit	Currency units per troy oz. of fine gold	Currency units per US$	US cents per currency unit
FRANCE					
French Guiana Guadeloupe Martinique	Franc (Parity with French franc)	0·160 000	194·397	5·554 19	18·004 4
Comoro Is. Réunion St Pierre and Miquelon	CFA Franc (= 0·02 French franc)	0·003 2	9,719·84	277·710	0·360 088
Polynesia N. Caledonia Wallis & Futuna	CFP Franc (= 0·055 French franc)	0·008 8	3,534·49	100·985	0·990 243
N. Hebrides	CFP franc, New Hebrides (=0·061875 French franc)	0·009 9	3,141·77	89·764 7	1·114 02
Afars & Issas	Djibouti Franc	0·004 145 07	7,503·73	214·392	0·466 435
NETHERLANDS					
Netherlands Antilles, Surinam	Guilder (= 1·919 555 Netherlands guilders)	0·471 230	66·004 9	1·885 85	53,026 4
UK					
Gibraltar (Gibraltar £) and Falkland Is. (Falkland £) are at parity with UK £ sterling.					
Bahamas	B. Dollar (2·400 00 per £ sterling)	0·888 671	35·000	1·000	100·000
Leeward Is. Windward Is.	East Caribbean Dollar (4·80 per £ sterling)	0·444 335	70·000	2·000	50·000
Bahrain	B. Dinar (1·142 86 per £ sterling)	1·866 21	16·666 7	0·476 190	210·000
Bermuda	B. Dollar (2·40 per £ sterling)	0·888 671	35·000	1·000	100·000
British Honduras	Br. Honduras $ (4·00 per £ sterling)	0·533 203	58·333 3	1·666 67	60·000
Seychelles	Rupee (13·3 per £ sterling)	0·159 961	194·444	5·555 55	18·000
Hong Kong	Hong Kong $ (14·545 5 per £ sterling)	0·146 631	212·121	6·060 61	16·500
Brunei	Brunei $ (7·346 93 per £ sterling)	0·290 299	107·143	3·061 22	32·666 7
Rhodesia	Rhodesia £ (0·857 143 per £ sterling)	2·488 28	12·500	0·357 143	280·000
Qatar Dubai	Qatar Dubai Riyal (11·428 per £ sterling)	0·186 621	166·667	4·761 90	21·000

7. INTERNATIONAL BANK FOR RECONSTRUCTION AND DEVELOPMENT

Conceived at the Bretton Woods Conference, July 1944, the Bank began operations in June 1946. Its purpose is to provide and facilitate international investment for increasing production, raising living standards and helping to bring a better balance in world trade.

The Bank obtains its funds from the capital subscribed by member countries, from the sale of bonds, from sales of parts of its loans, and from repayments and net earnings. The subscribed capital of the Bank amounted to $23,066m. at 31 Dec. 1969. Ten per cent of this amount is paid-in while the remainder is subject to call if needed to meet the Bank's obligations. Borrowing in the market had reached $8,069m. net by 31 Dec. 1969, of which $4,303m. was outstanding. In addition, the Bank has sold portions of loans from its portfolio worth $2,343m.

By 31 Dec. 1969 the Bank had made 657 loans totalling $13,115m. in 88 of its 112 member countries or their territories. This total includes early Bank loans totalling $497m. for post-war reconstruction in western Europe. The balance has been distributed as follows: Electric power, $4,426m.; transportation, $3,993m.; communications, $193m.; agriculture, $1,234m.; industry, $1,974m.; general development, $552m.; water supply, $109m.; education, $98m.; project preparation, $900,000; International Finance Corporation (IFC), $200m. In order to eliminate wasteful overlapping of development assistance and to ensure that the funds available are used to the best possible effect, the Bank has organized consortia or consultative groups of aid-giving nations for the following countries: Colombia, India, Korea, Malaysia, Morocco, Nigeria, Pakistan, Peru, the Sudan, Thailand, Tunisia and East Africa (Kenya, Uganda, Tanzania). The Bank furnishes a wide variety of technical assistance services. It acts as executing agency for a number of pre-investment surveys financed by the UN Development Programme. Permanent missions have been established in East and West Africa to help in the preparation of agricultural and transportation projects. The Bank helps member countries to identify and prepare projects in the fields of agriculture and education by drawing on the expertise of the FAO and UNESCO through its co-operative agreements with these two organizations. The Bank maintains a staff college, the Economic Development Institute in Washington, D.C., for senior officials of the member countries.

The Bank itself is self-supporting; its net earnings for the fiscal year ending 30 June 1969 amounted to $171m. In addition, the Bank had reserves of $1,326m.

To help nations whose borrowing capacity is limited by foreign-exchange stringency, member countries of the Bank established the INTERNATIONAL DEVELOPMENT ASSOCIATION (IDA) in 1960. IDA grants development credits on a long-term, interest-free basis. By 31 Dec. 1969 IDA had extended 178 credits to 51 countries, totalling $2,292m. IDA's primary lending resources have been the subscriptions and supplementary contributions of member countries, chiefly its 18 wealthiest. In addition, it has negotiated interest-free loans from Switzerland. The World Bank has made grants to IDA out of its net income; the Association also has a small flow of net income of its own.

Headquarters: 1818 H St., Washington, D.C., 20433. *European office:* 4 avenue d'Iéna, Paris (16), France. *London office:* New Zealand House, SW1. *President:* Robert S. McNamara (USA).

Publications. Annual Reports. 1946 ff.—Summary Proceedings of Annual Meetings. 1947 ff.— The World Bank Group. 1969.—The World Bank Atlas. 1967.—The World Bank, IDA and IFC, Policies and Operations. 1969.

8. INTERNATIONAL FINANCE CORPORATION (IFC)

The Corporation, an affiliate of the World Bank, was established in July 1956. Paid-in capital at the end of 1969 was $107m., subscribed by 92 member countries. In addition, it has reserves of $54m. IFC supplements the activities of the World Bank by encouraging the growth of productive private enterprises in less developed member countries. Chiefly, IFC makes investments in the form of subscriptions to the share capital of privately owned companies, or long-term loans, or both. The Corporation will help finance new ventures, and it will also assist established enterprises to expand, improve or diversify their operations.

At 31 Dec. 1969 IFC has made commitments, amounting to $377m., in 40 countries. The total amount of loans and equity which IFC had sold or agreed to sell to other investors as of that date was $96·5m. Standby and underwriting commitments totalled $26·1m.

Administrative expenses for 1969–70: $5·36m.

President: Robert S. McNamara (USA).
Executive Vice-President: William S. Gand (USA).

Publications. Proceedings of Annual Meeting. 1956 ff.—Annual Reports. 1956 ff.—General Policies. 1970.

9. INTERNATIONAL CIVIL AVIATION ORGANIZATION (ICAO)

Origin. The Convention providing for the establishment of the International Civil Aviation Organization was drawn up by the International Civil Aviation

Conference held in Chicago from 1 Nov. to 7 Dec. 1944. A Provisional International Civil Aviation Organization (PICAO) operated from 6 June 1945 until the formal establishment of ICAO on 4 April 1947.

The Convention on International Civil Aviation superseded the provisions of the Paris Convention of 1919, which established the International Commission for Air Navigation (ICAN), and the Pan American Convention on Air Navigation drawn up at Havana in 1928.

Functions. It assists international civil aviation by establishing technical standards for safety and efficiency of air navigation and promoting simpler procedures at borders; develops regional plans for ground facilities and services needed for international flying; disseminates air-transport statistics and prepares studies on aviation economics; fosters the development of air law conventions. As part of the UN Development Programme it provides technical assistance to States in developing civil aviation programmes.

Organization. The principal organs of ICAO are an Assembly, consisting of all members of the Organization, and a Council, which is comprised of 27 states elected by the Assembly, for 3 years, and meets in virtually continuous session. In electing these states, the Assembly must give adequate representation to: (1) those member states of major importance in air transport; (2) those member states not otherwise included which make the largest contribution to the provision of facilities for the international civil air navigation; (3) those member states not otherwise included whose election will ensure that all major geographical areas of the world are represented. The main subsidiary bodies are: the Air Navigation Commission, composed of 12 members elected by the Council; Air Transport Committee, open to council members; and the Legal Committee, on which all members of ICAO may be represented.

Budget for 1971: $8·51m.

Headquarters: International Aviation Building, 1080 University St., Montreal, 101, Quebec, Canada.

Secretary-General: Dr Assad Kotaite (Lebanon).

ICAO Bulletin (published 12 times per year; with list of all ICAO publications)

10. UNIVERSAL POSTAL UNION (UPU)

Origin. The UPU was established on 1 July 1875, when the Universal Postal Convention adopted by the Postal Congress of Berne on 9 Oct. 1874 came into force. The UPU was known at first as the General Postal Union, its name being changed at the Congress of Paris in 1878.

Functions. The aim of the UPU is to assure the organization and perfection of the various postal services and to promote, in this field, the development of international collaboration. To this end, the members of UPU are united in a single postal territory for the reciprocal exchange of correspondence.

Organization. The UPU is composed of a Universal Postal Congress, which usually meets every 5 years, a permanent Executive Council, a consultative Committee, which consists of 27 members elected on a geographical basis by each Congress, and an International Bureau, which functions as the permanent secretariat.

Since 1 July 1948 the Union has been governed by the revised Convention adopted by the twelfth Congress in Paris on 5 July 1947.

Budget for 1971: $2·16m.

Headquarters: Schosshaldenstrasse 46, 3000, Berne, Switzerland.

Director-General: Dr Michel Rahi (UAR).

Publications. *Universal Postal Convention: Paris, 5 July, 1948.* (Cmd. 7435.).—*The Postal Union* (monthly, Arabic, Chinese, English, French, Spanish, Russian).—*The UPU: its foundation and development.* Bern, 1959.

B

11. INTERNATIONAL TELECOMMUNICATION UNION (ITU)

Origin. The International Telegraph Union, founded in Paris in 1865, and the International Radiotelegraph Union, founded in Berlin in 1906, were merged by the Madrid Convention of 1932 to form the International Telecommunication Union. ITU came into being on 1 Jan. 1934. The ITU has been governed since 1 Jan. 1949 by the revised International Telecommunication Convention adopted on 2 Oct. 1947.

Functions. The ITU: (1) allocates radio frequencies and registers radio-frequency assignments; (2) seeks to establish the lowest rates possible, consistent with efficient service and taking into account the necessity for keeping the independent financial administration of telecommunication on a sound basis; (3) promotes the adoption of measures for ensuring the safety of life through telecommunication; and (4) makes studies and recommendations and collects and publishes information for the benefit of its members.

Organization. The ITU consists of the Plenipotentiary Conference, Administrative Conferences, the Administrative Council of 25 members, the General Secretariat, the International Frequency Registration Board, and 3 international consultative committees (radio, telephone, telegraph).
  Budget for 1971: $8·2m.

Headquarters: Place des Nations, Geneva, Switzerland.
Deputy Secretary-General: Mohamed Mili (Tunisia).

Publications. *International Convention on Telecommunications, 1947.* (Cmd. 8124.) HMSO, 1950.—*International Telecommunication Convention, 1959.* (Cmd. 1075.) HMSO, 1960.—*ITU Bulletin* (monthly).

12. WORLD METEOROLOGICAL ORGANIZATION (WMO)

Origin. A Conference of Directors of the International Meteorological Organization (set up in 1878), meeting in Washington in 1947, adopted a Convention creating the World Meteorological Organization. The WMO Convention became effective on 23 March 1950, and WMO was formally established on 19 March 1951, when the first session of its Congress was convened in Paris. An agreement to bring WMO into relationship with the United Nations was approved by this Congress and came into force on 21 Dec. 1951 with its approval by the General Assembly of the United Nations.

Functions. (1) To promote international co-operation in the field of meteorology and the quick exchange of weather data; (2) to establish world-wide networks of meteorological stations and facilitate the publication and standardization of their observations; (3) to further the application of meteorology to human activities; and (4) to encourage research and training in the field of meteorology.

Organization. WMO consists of a World Meteorological Congress, an Executive Committee, regional meteorological associations and technical commissions set up by the Congress, and a permanent secretariat. The organization is headed by a President and 3 Vice-Presidents.
  Budget for 1971: $4·2m.

Headquarters: 41 Avenue Giuseppe Motta, Geneva, Switzerland.
Secretary-General: David A. Davies (UK).

Publications. *WMO Bulletin.* 1952 ff.—*Meteorological Services of the World.* 1959.

13. INTER-GOVERNMENTAL MARITIME CONSULTATIVE ORGANIZATION (IMCO)

Origin. IMCO was established as a specialized agency of the UN by a convention drawn up at the UN Maritime Conference held at Geneva in Feb./March 1948. The Convention became effective on 17 March 1958 when it had been ratified by 21 countries, including 7 with at least 1m. gross tons of shipping each. IMCO started operations in Jan. 1959.

Functions. To facilitate co-operation among governments on technical matters affecting merchant shipping, especially concerning safety at sea; to encourage abolition of discriminatory and restrictive practices affecting merchant shipping. IMCO is responsible for convening international maritime conferences and for drafting international maritime conventions.

Organization. IMCO had 72 members in 1971. The Assembly, composed of all member states, normally meets every 2 years. The Council of 18 member states acts as governing body between Assembly sessions. The 16-member Maritime Safety Committee deals with all technical questions. It can establish specialized sub-committees to deal with specific problems. The Secretariat is composed of international civil servants.

IMCO is depositary authority for the International Convention for the Safety of Life at Sea, 1960, and the Regulations for Preventing Collisions at Sea, 1948 and 1960; the International Convention for the Prevention of Pollution of the Sea by Oil, 1954, as amended in 1962; the Convention on Facilitation of International Maritime Traffic, 1965; the International Convention on Load Lines, 1966; the International Convention on Tonnage Measurement of Ships, 1969; the International Convention relating to Intervention on the High Seas in cases of Oil Pollution Casualties 1969; the International Convention on Civil Liability for Oil Pollution Damage, 1969.

Headquarters: 101 Piccadilly, London, W1V OAE.
Secretary-General: Colin Goad (UK).
Deputy Secretary-General: Jean Quéguiner (France).
Secretary, Maritime Safety Committee: Vsevolod Nadeinski (USSR).

IMCO, what it is, what it does. 1968

14. GENERAL AGREEMENT ON TARIFFS AND TRADE (GATT)

Origin. In 1946 the Economic and Social Council of the United Nations established a Preparatory Committee to draw up a draft of an international trade charter. This charter—known as the Havana Charter—was complete in 1948, but was laid aside when it became evident that it would not be ratified by the USA. The member countries of the Preparatory Committee in 1947 concluded a General Agreement on Tariffs and Trade. The Agreement entered into force on 1 Jan. 1948, there being 23 contracting parties. The number of contracting parties had by Oct. 1970 reached 78 (plus countries participating under various other arrangements).

Functions. The GATT may be described as a multilateral treaty, which lays down a common code of conduct in international trade, provides machinery for reducing and stabilizing tariffs and the opportunity for regular consultation on trade problems. A key provision of GATT is a guarantee of most-favoured-nation treatment. The reduction of tariff barriers is provided for through multilateral tariff negotiations. The resulting tariff schedules are 'bound', *i.e.*, cannot normally be increased; they are appended to the Agreement and form an integral part of it. The use of quantitative restrictions on imports is forbidden in principle, but there are certain exceptions, notably balance-of-payments difficulties. Since 1947 there have been 6 major tariff conferences, culminating in the Kennedy Round of Trade Negotiations, 1964–67.

Flexibility has been the keynote in the application of GATT rules. Exceptions to the basic provisions are embodied in the Agreement itself. In addition, individual members may be temporarily allowed to digress from the common rules after waivers have been defined and safeguards instituted. Thus a system has been evolved of international consultation and the settlement of grievances, and a body of decisions and recommendations has come into existence. The regular sessions of the Contracting Parties and their subsidiary bodies have become the recognized forum for the discussion of many aspects of commercial policy.

Since the publication of the Haberler Report (1958) much of the work of GATT has been focused on the need for developing countries to increase their export earnings and to reduce or eliminate barriers facing their exports. Additional GATT articles setting out the objectives and commitments of GATT members as regards trade and development were adopted in 1965. In May 1964 the International Trade Centre was established to provide developing countries with information on export markets and marketing and help them to develop the techniques of export promotion and to train the personnel required to apply them. Since 1968 the Centre has been operated jointly by GATT and UNCTAD (UN Conference on Trade and Development).

Following the successful conclusion of the Kennedy Round of trade negotiations in June 1967 a programme was established in Nov. 1967, looking towards the further liberalization of trade; specifically in the tariff and non-tariff field, in trade in agricultural products and as regards the trade problems of developing countries.

Budget for 1971: $4m.

Director-General: Olivier Long (Switzerland).
Headquarters: Villa le Bocage, Palais des Nations, Geneva, Switzerland.

Publications. Basic Instruments and Selected Documents. 4 vols and 17 supplements 1952–70.— *International Trade [i.e.,* annual review], 1952 ff. Annually, from 1953.—*GATT, what it is, what it does* (1969).—*GATT Activities,* 1969–70.

WORLD COUNCIL OF CHURCHES

The World Council of Churches was formally constituted on 23 Aug. 1948, at Amsterdam, by an assembly representing 147 churches from 44 countries. The second assembly was held at Evanston, Illinois, in Aug. 1954, when delegates attended from 163 member churches. The third assembly was held at New Delhi, India, in Nov.–Dec. 1961, with delegates representing 197 churches in 84 countries. The fourth assembly took place in July 1968 in Uppsala, Sweden, when 704 delegates were present from over 230 member churches.

The basis of membership states: 'The World Council of Churches is a fellowship of Churches which confess the Lord Jesus Christ as God and Saviour according to the Scriptures and therefore seek to fulfil together their common calling to the glory of the one God, Father, Son and Holy Spirit.' Membership is open to Churches which express their agreement with this basis and satisfy such criteria as the Assembly or Central Committee may prescribe. Today 239 Churches of Protestant, Anglican, Orthodox and Old Catholic Confessions belong to this fellowship.

The movements which joined together to form the World Council were:

(a) *Co-operation in oversea missionary work* by the non-Roman Catholic Churches. The World Missionary Conference held in Edinburgh, Scotland, in 1910 was followed in 1921 by the establishment of the *International Missionary Council.* In 1961 this Council became the Commission and Division of World Mission and Evangelism of the World Council.

(b) *The Faith and Order Movement* was founded through the initiative of Charles Brent, Bishop of the Protestant Episcopal Church of the USA in the Philippines. This movement has held world conferences at Lausanne in 1927, Edinburgh in 1937, Lund in 1952 and Montreal in 1963.

(c) *The Life and Work Movement* was founded largely under the leadership of Archbishop Nathan Söderblom of Uppsala. World conferences were held in Stockholm in 1925, at Oxford in 1937 and in Geneva in 1966. The Department on Church and Society promotes common Christian study and action on social, political and economic problems of the present time.

On 13 May 1938 at Utrecht a provisional committee was appointed to prepare for the formation of a World Council of Churches. It was under the chairmanship of William Temple, then Archbishop of York.

Organization. The Fourth Assembly at Uppsala, Sweden, in July 1968, appointed a new Central Committee (increasing the number of members from 100 to 120), an Honorary President and 6 Presidents (see below).

The work of the Council is carried on in 3 Divisions; and among those sections directly linked to the General Secretariat, are: (a) Secretariat of the Commission on Faith and Order; (b) Department on Church and Society; (c) Commission of the Churches on International Affairs (CCIA); (d) World Council–Roman Catholic Joint Committee on Society, Development and Peace; (e) Programme to Combat Racism.

The structure of the World Council is still under review. At 31 Jan. 1971 this was as follows:

1. *General Secretariat* (Dr Eugene Carson Blake): Secretariat of the Commission on Faith and Order (Dr Lukas Vischer); Department on Church and Society (Rev. Paul Abrecht); World Council of Churches–Roman Catholic Joint Committee on Society, Development and Peace (Fr George Dunne, SJ); Programme to Combat Racism (Dr Baldwin Sjollema).

2. *Division of World Mission and Evangelism* (Rev. Philip Potter): Theological Education Fund (Rev. Dr J. F. Hopewell); Christian Literature Fund (Mr Charles Richards); Christian Medical Commission (Mr James McGilvray); Department on Studies in Mission and Evangelism (Rev. Steven Mackie).

3. *Division of Ecumenical Action* (Rev. Ernst Lange): Ecumenical Institute (Prof. Nikos A. Nissiotis); Department on Co-operation of Men and Women in Church, Family and Society (Rev. Leslie C. Clements); Youth Department (Rev. Oscar L. Bolioli); Department of the Laity (Mr Ralph C. Young); Office of Education (Dr W. B. Kennedy).

4. *Division of Inter-Church Aid, Refugee and World Service* (Rev. Alan A. Brash, OBE., Director): Refugee Programme (Mr M. Christopher King).

5. *Department of Finance and Administration* (Mr Frank Northam).

6. *Department of Communication* (Dr Albert H. van den Heuvel).

7. *Commission of the Churches on International Affairs* (L. J. Niilus, Director).

The Assembly has no legislative power or authority over the member churches, so that all its acts are of an advisory nature, depending for their implementation on the member churches' acceptance.

The British Council of Churches, which is an associated national council of the World Council, acts as agent for the WCC in the United Kingdom (10 Eaton Gate, London, SW1).

The officers of the World Council are as follows:

PRESIDIUM. *Hon. President:* The Rev. Dr W. A. Visser 't Hooft. *Presidents:* His Holiness Patriarch German of Serbia (Yugoslavia), The Rt Rev. Bishop Hanns Lilje (Germany), The Rev. Dr Ernest A. Payne, CH (UK), The Rev. Dr John Coventry Smith (USA) and the Rt Rev. Bishop A. H. Zulu (South Africa).

CENTRAL COMMITTEE. *Chairman:* Mr M. M. Thomas (India). *Vice-Chairmen:* His Eminence Metropolitan Meliton of Chalcedon (Turkey); Miss Pauline M. Webb (UK).

GENERAL SECRETARY: Dr Eugene Carson Blake. ASSISTANT GENERAL SECRETARY: The Rev. Jens J. Thomsen.

Office: 150 route de Ferney, 1211 Geneva 20, Switzerland.

MEMBER CHURCHES. The following is a list of the Member Churches:

Argentina. Iglesia Evangelica del Rio de la Plata.
Australasia. Methodist Church of Australasia.
Australia. Church of England in Australia; Congregational Union of Australia; Federal Conference of Churches of Christ in Australia; Presbyterian Church of Australia.
Austria. Evangelische Kirche AB in Oesterreich; Altkatholische Kirche Österreichs.
Belgium. Église Réformée de Belgique; Église Protestante de Belgique.
Brazil. Episcopal Church; Igreja Evangélica Pentecostal; Igreja Metodista do Brasil; Evangelical Church of Lutheran Confession.
Bulgaria. Bulgarian Orthodox Church.
Burma. Burma Baptist Convention.
Cameroons. Evangelical Church; Presbyterian Church; Presbyterian Church in West Cameroon; Union des Églises Baptistes du Cameroun.
Canada. Anglican Church of Canada; Churches of Christ (Disciples); Presbyterian Church in Canada; United Church of Canada; Yearly Meeting of the Society of Friends.

Central Africa. Church of the [Anglican] Province of Central Africa; Evangelical Lutheran Church.
Ceylon. Methodist Church in Ceylon.
Chile. Evangelical Lutheran Church; Pentecostal Church of Chile.
China. China Baptist Council; Chung Hua Chi-Tu Chiao-Hui (Church of Christ in China); Chung Hua Sheng Kung Hui (Anglican Church in China); Hua Pei Kung Li Hui (Congregational Church).
Congo (Br.). Eglise Evangélique du Congo.
Congo (K.). Church of Christ on Earth by the Prophet Simon Kimbangua; Eglise du Christ au Congo (Disciples); Eglise Evangélique de Manianga-Matadi.
Cyprus. Church of Cyprus.
Czechoslovakia. Českobratska Čirkev Evangelická (Evangelical Church of Czech Brethren); Czechoslovak Church; Evangelická Čikev A. V. na Slovensku (Evangelical Church in Slovakia, Augsburg Confession); Orthodox Church; Ref. Čirkev na Slovensku (Reformed Church in Slovakia); Slezka Čirkev Evangelicka AV (Evangelical Church of Augsburg Confession in Silesia).
Denmark. Baptist Union of Denmark; Evangelisklutherske Folkekirke.
East Africa. Church of the [Anglican] Province of East Africa; Presbyterian Church; Methodist Church in Kenya.
Egypt. Coptic Evangelical Church; Coptic Orthodox Church; Greek Orthodox Patriarchate of Alexandria.
Ethiopia. Ethiopian Orthodox Church.
Finland. Suomen Evankelis-Lutherilainen Kirko.
France. Église de la Confession d'Augsbourg d'Alsace et de Lorraine; Église Évangélique Luthérienne de France; Église Réformée d'Alsace et de Lorraine; Église Réformée de France.
Germany. Altkatholische Kirche in Deutschland; Evangelische Brüder-Unität; Evangelische Kirche in Deutschland; Vereinigung der DeutschenMennonitengemeinden.
Ghana. Evangelical Church; Methodist Church; Presbyterian Church.
Greece. Church of Greece; Greek Evangelical Church.
Holland. Algemene Doopsgezinde Societeit (General Mennonite Society); Evangelisch Lutherse Kerk; Netherlandse Hervormde Kerk; Oud-Katholieke Kerk (Old Catholic Church); Remonstrantse Broederschap.
Hong Kong. The Church of Christ in China, Hong Kong Council.
Hungary. A Magyarországi Evangélikus Egyház (Lutheran Church of Hungary); A Magyarországi Református Egyház (Reformed Church of Hungary); Baptist Church.
Iceland. Evangelical Lutheran Church.
India. Church of India, Pakistan, Burma and Ceylon; Church of South India; Federation of Evangelical Lutheran Churches in India; Mar Thoma Syrian Church of Malabar; Orthodox Syrian Church of the East; Samawesam of Telugu Baptist Churches; United Church of Northern India.
Indonesia. Geredja Kalimantan Evangelis (Church of Kalimantan); Geredja Keristen di Sulawesi Tengah (Toradja Church); Geradja Kristen Djawiwetan (East Java Church); Geredja Kristen Indonesia (Indonesia Christian Church); Geredja Masehi Indjili di Minahasa (Church of Minahasa); Geredia Masehi Indjili di Timor (Protestant Church of Timor); Huria Kristen Batak Protestant (Protestant Batak Church); Geradja Keristen di Djawa Tengah (Christian Churches in Central Java); Geredja Protestan Maluku (Church of the Moluccas); Geredja Protestan di Indonesia; Geredja Gereformeerd di Indonesia; Geredja Kristen Pasundan (Sundanese Christian Church); Karo Batak Protestant Church of Kabandjahe, Sumatra.
Iran. Synod of the Evangelical Presbyterian Church of Iran.
Italy. Chiesa Evangelica Metodista d'Italia; Chiesa Evangelica Valdese.
Japan. Nippo Kirisuto Kyodan (Church of Christ); Nipon Sei Ko Kwai (Anglican Church in Japan).
Jerusalem. Greek Orthodox Patriarchate.
Korea. Korean Methodist Church; Presbyterian Church in the Republic of Korea; Presbyterian Church.
Lebanon. Armenian Apostolic Church; Union of Armenian Evangelical Churches.
Madagascar. Eglise de Jésus Christ à Madagascar; Malagasy Lutheran Church.
Mexico. Iglesia Métodista de Mexico.
New Zealand. Associated Churches of Christ in New Zealand; Baptist Union of New Zealand; Church of the Province of New Zealand; Congregational Union of New Zealand; Methodist Church of New Zealand; Presbyterian Church of New Zealand.
Norway. Norske Kirke.
Pacific. Congregational Christian Church in Samoa; Église Évangélique en Nouvelle-Calédonie et aux îles Loyauté; Presbyterian Church of New Hebrides; Église Évangélique de Polynésie Française.
Pakistan. United Presbyterian Church of Pakistan.
Philippine Islands. United Church of Christ in the Philippines; Philippine Independent Church of Poland; Evangelical Church of the Augsburg Confession; Old Catholic Mariavite Church; Orthodox Church of Poland; Polish Catholic Church.
Romania. Evangelical Synodal Presbyterial Church of the Augsburg Confession; Evangelical Church, Augsburg Confession; Romanian Orthodox Church; Reformed Church.
Southern Africa. Bantu Presbyterian Church of South Africa; Church of the Province of South Africa (Anglican); Evangelical Lutheran Church in Southern Africa (S.E. Region); Evangelical Lutheran Church in Southern Africa (Transvaal Region); Methodist Church of South Africa; Moravian Church in South Africa; Moravian Church (Eastern Province) in South Africa; Presbyterian Church of Southern Africa; United Congregational Church of Southern Africa.
Spain. Iglesia Evangelica Española.
Sweden. Svenska Kyrkan; Svenska Missionsförbundet (Swedish Mission Covenant).
Switzerland. Christkatholische Kirche der Schweiz (Old Catholic Church); Fédération des Églises Protestantes de la Suisse.
Syria. Greek Orthodox Patriarchate of Antioch; Evangelical Synod of Syria and Lebanon; Syrian Orthodox Patriarchate of Antioch and all the East.

Taiwan. Tai-oan Ki-tok Tiu-lo Kau-hoe (Presbyterian Church in Taiwan).
Tanzania. Evangelical Lutheran Church.
Thailand. Church of Christ in Thailand.
Turkey. Oecumenical Patriarchate of Constantinople.
Uganda. The Church of Uganda, Rwanda and Burundi.
USSR. Armenian Apostolic Church; Estonian Evangelical Lutheran Church; Evangelical Lutheran Church of Latvia; Georgian Orthodox Church USSR; Orthodox Church of Russia Patriarchate of Moscow); Union of Evangelical Christian Baptists of USSR.
UK and Eire. Baptist Union of Great Britain and Ireland; Churches of Christ in Great Britain and Ireland; Church of England; Church of Ireland; Church of Scotland; Church in Wales; Congregational Church in England and Wales; Congregational Union of Scotland; Episcopal Church in Scotland; Methodist Church; Methodist Church in Ireland; Moravian Church in Great Britain and Ireland; Presbyterian Church of England; Presbyterian Church in Ireland; Presbyterian Church of Wales; United Free Church of Scotland.
USA. African Methodist Episcopal Church; African Methodist Episcopal Zion Church; American Baptist Convention; American Lutheran Church; Antiochian Orthodox Christian Diocese; Christian Methodist Episcopal Church; Church of the Brethren; Evangelical United Brethren Church; The Church of the East (Assyrian); Hungarian Reformed Church in America; International Convention of Christian Churches; Lutheran Church in America; Methodist Church; Moravian Church in America; National Baptist Convention of America; National Baptist Convention of USA, Inc.; Orthodox Church in America; Polish National Catholic Church of America; Presbyterian Church in the US; Protestant Episcopal Church; Reformed Church in America; The Religious Society of Friends; Friends United Meeting; Friends General Conference; Romanian Orthodox Episcopate in America; Seventh Day Baptist General Conference; United Church of Christ; United Presbyterian Church in the USA.
West Africa. Church of the Province of West Africa (Anglican); Église Évangélique du Gabon; Methodist Church of Nigeria; Presbyterian Church of Nigeria; Église Évangélique du Togo; The Methodist Church of Sierra Leone.
West Indies. Anglican Church of the West Indies; Moravian Church in Jamaica; Presbyterian Church of Jamaica; Presbyterian Church in Trinidad; United Church of Jamaica and Grand Cayman.
Yugoslavia. Reformed Christian Church of Yugoslavia; Serbian Orthodox Church; Slovak Evangelical Church of the Augsburg Confession.
Zambia. United Church.
Churches not classified nationally. Eesti Ev. Luth. Usu Kiriku (Estonian Evangelical Lutheran Church); Lietuvos Ev. Reformatu Baznycia (Lithuanian Reformed Church); Salvation Army.
Associated Churches: Korean Christian Church (Japan); Union of Protestant Churches (Netherlands Antilles); Lusitanian Church (Portugal); Spanish Reformed Episcopal Church; Bengal Orissa–Bihar–Baptist Convention, India; Evangelical Presbyterian Church of Portugal; Evangelical Presbyterian Church in Rio Muni; Church of Christ in the Upper Nile, Sudan. Eglise Protestante Africaine (Cameroun); Methodist Church of Cuba; Presbyterian Reformed Church in Cuba; United Evangelical Lutheran Church of Argentina; Presbytery of Liberia.

BOOKS OF REFERENCE

Official Reports: The First [. . . etc.] *Assembly* (London, 1948, 1955, 1962, Geneva, 1968)
New Delhi to Uppsala, 1961–68. Geneva, 1968
Official reports of the Faith and Order Conferences at Lausanne 1927, Edinburgh 1937, Lund 1952, Montreal 1963
Official reports of the Life and Work Conferences at Stockholm 1925 and Oxford 1937; Conference on Church and Contemporary Society 1966
Minutes of the Central Committee. Geneva, 1949 to date
Fey, H. E., *The Ecumenical Advance, 1948–68.* London, 1970
Goodall, N.. *The Ecumenical Movement.* 3rd ed. OUP, 1966
Coxill, H. W. (ed.), *World Christian Handbook.* 5th ed. London, 1968

INTERNATIONAL TRADE UNIONISM

International trade-union co-operation is organized through the three major 'Internationals', the democratic International Confederation of Free Trade Unions (ICFTU), the Communist-directed World Federation of Trade Unions (WFTU) and the World Confederation of Labour (WCL). In addition, federations of specific trades or industries protect their special interests by organizing on an international level and are associated to a varying degree with their corresponding 'Internationals'. The International Trade Secretariats (ITS) are completely autonomous but seek to co-ordinate their policies and activities with those of the ICFTU; the Christian Trade Internationals (TIs) are very closely integrated with the WCL; the Trade Union Internationals (TUIs) are completely subservient to WFTU.

History. The first general trade-union International, the International Federation of Trade Unions (IFTU), was set up in 1913, but no real achievement was possible until its post-war reconstitution in 1919. Some trade-union movements, seeking to implement the social precepts of the Christian faith, established the International Federation of Christian Trade Unions (IFCTU) in 1920. The name was changed to the World Confederation of Labour in 1968, although no major ideological changes were made.

During the Second World War moves to establish universal trade unionism resulted in the formation of the World Federation of Trade Unions (WFTU) in 1945. The Christian trade unions refused to join the new association and reconstituted the IFCTU. Attempts by the Communists to impose their own ideology within the WFTU led to the eventual secession of the democratic elements, which reconstituted themselves in the ICFTU in 1949.

INTERNATIONAL CONFEDERATION OF FREE TRADE UNIONS

The first congress of ICFTU was held in London in Dec. 1949. The constitution as amended provides for co-operation with the United Nations and the International Labour Organization and for regional organizations to promote free trade unionism, especially in under-developed countries.

Organization. The Congress meets every 3 years. It elects the Executive Board of 29 members nominated on an area basis for a 3-year period; the Board meets at least twice a year. Various committees cover policy *vis-à-vis* the European Economic Community, problems connected with Atomic Energy and also the administration of the International Solidarity Fund. There are joint ICFTU–ITS Committees for co-ordinating activities and also for women workers' problems. Headquarters: 37–41, rue Montagne aux Herbes Potagères, Brussels 1, Belgium.

General Secretary: Harm Buiter.

Regional organizations exist in Europe, office in Brussels; America, office in Mexico City; Asia, office in New Delhi; Africa, office in Lagos.

Membership. The total membership in 1970 was about 50m. The biggest groups were the British Trades Union Congress (9·1m.), the West-German Deutscher Gewerkschaftsbund (6·5m.), the Federation of Indonesian Islamic Trade Unions (2·75m.), the Confederazione Italiana Sindacati Lavoratori (2·4m.), the Confederación de Trabajadores de Mexico (2m.), the Swedish Landsorganisationen (1·6m.), the Canadian Labour Congress (1·6m.), the Österreichischer Gewerkschaftsbund (1·5m.), the Indian National Trade Union Congress (1·5m.), and the French Confédération Générale du Travail Force Ouvrière (500,000).

The American Federation of Labor and Congress of Industrial Organizations disaffiliated in Feb. 1969.

Publications (in 4 languages). *Free Labour World* (monthly); *ICFTU Bulletin* (bi-monthly); *Press and Radio Service* (weekly); *International Trade Union News* (fortnightly).

THE WORLD FEDERATION OF TRADE UNIONS

The WFTU formally came into existence on 3 Oct. 1945, representing trade-union organizations in more than 50 countries of the world, both Communist and non-Communist, excluding Germany and Japan, as well as a number of lesser and colonial territories. Representation from the USA was limited to the Congress of Industrial Organizations, as the American Federation of Labor declined to participate.

In Jan. 1949 the British, USA and Netherlands trade unions withdrew from WFTU, which had come under complete Communist control; and by June 1951 all non-Communist trade-unions, including the Yugoslavian Federation, had left WFTU.

Organization. The Congress meets every 4 years. In between, the General Council, of 134 members (including deputies), is the governing body, meeting (in theory) at least once a year. The Bureau controls the activities of WFTU between meetings of the General Council; it consists of the President, the General Secretary and members from different continents, the total number being decided at each Congress. The Bureau is elected by the General Council.

General Secretary: Pierre Gensous (France).

Membership. In Oct. 1969 a total membership of 150m. was claimed. The biggest groups are the Soviet All-Union Central Council of Trade Unions (86m.), the East-German Free German Trade Union Federation (7·3m.), the Polish Central Council of Trade Unions (6·9m.), the Czechoslovak Central Council of Trade Unions (5·4m.), the Italian General Confederation of Labour (CGIL, 3·5m.), the Romanian General Confederation of Labour (3·2m.), the Hungarian Central Council of Trade Unions (2·8m.) and the French Confederation of Labour (CGT, 2m.); the General Federation of Iraqi Trades Unions was affiliated in 1967.

Publications. World Trade Union Movement (monthly, in 11 languages); *Trade Union Press* fortnightly, in 6 languages).

WORLD CONFEDERATION OF LABOUR

The first congress of IFCTU, as it was then called, met in 1920; but a large proportion of its 3·4m. members were in Italy and Germany, where affiliated unions were suppressed by the Fascist and Nazi regimes, and in 1940 IFCTU went out of existence. It was reconstituted in 1945, and declined to merge with WFTU and, later, with ICFTU. The policy of IFCTU, and subsequently the WCL, is based on the papal encyclicals *Rerum novarum* (1891) and *Quadragesimo anno* (1931), but the Federation claims also some Protestant, Buddhist and Moslem members.

Organization. The Christian International is organized on a federative basis, leaving wide discretion to the autonomy of its constituent unions. Its governing body is the Congress, which meets every 3 years. The General Council, meeting at least once a year, is composed according to the proportion of membership of the Congress. The Executive Committee, elected by Congress, consists of at least 12 members; it appoints the Secretary-General for an indefinite period. Headquarters: 26, rue Juste Lipse, Brussels 4, Belgium.

Secretary-General: Jean Bruck (Belgium).

There are regional organizations in Europe (office in Brussels), Latin America (office in Caracas), Africa (office in Bathurst, Gambia) and Asia (office in Manila). There is also a liaison centre in Montreal.

Membership. A total membership of over 12m. was claimed. The biggest groups are the French Democratic Confederation of Labour (700,000) the Confederation of Christian Trade Unions of Belgium (1m.), the Netherlands Catholic Workers' Movement (426,000), the Vietnamese Confederation of Labour (750,000).

Publication. Labor (bi-monthly, in 3 languages).

WORLD INTELLECTUAL PROPERTY ORGANIZATION (WIPO)

Origin. The Convention establishing WIPO was signed at Stockholm in 1967 by 51 countries, and entered into force in April 1970.

Functions. The objectives of WIPO are to promote the protection of intellectual property throughout the world through co-operation among States and, where appropriate, in collaboration with any other international organization, and to ensure administrative co-operation among the Unions established by various Conventions for the protection of intellectual property. The Convention provides expressly for the encouragement of the conclusion of international agreements designed to promote the protection of intellectual property, and for the provision of legal-technical assistance at the request of States.

Intellectual property includes the rights relating to: literary, artistic and scientific works; performances of performing artists, phonograms and broadcasts; inventions in all fields of human endeavour; scientific discoveries; industrial designs; trademarks, service marks and commercial names and designations; protection against unfair competition and all other rights resulting from intellectual activity in the industrial, scientific, literary or artistic fields.

Among its other functions, WIPO performs the administrative tasks of the Unions, assembles and disseminates information concerning the protection of intellectual property, carries out and promotes studies in this field, publishes the results of such studies, and maintains services, including registration and publication services, facilitating the international protection of intellectual property.

The Unions for which WIPO performs the administrative tasks are those established by the International (Paris) Convention for the Protection of Industrial Property, by various Special Agreements made within the framework of the Paris Convention and by the International (Berne) Convention for the Protection of Literary and Artistic Works. The Special Agreements referred to above are: Madrid Agreement for the Repression of False or Deceptive Indications of Source on Goods, Madrid Agreement concerning the International Registration of Marks, The Hague Agreement concerning the International Deposit of Industrial Designs, Nice Agreement concerning the International Classification of Goods and Services for the Purposes of the Registration of Marks, Lisbon Agreement for the Protection of Appellations of Origin and their International Registration, Locarno Agreement Establishing an International Classification for Industrial Designs.

WIPO also provides the Secretariat for ICIREPAT (Paris Union Committee for International Co-operation in Information Retrieval among Patent Offices). The objective of ICIREPAT is to promote international co-operation in the field of the storage and retrieval of technical information needed in connexion with the searching or examination of applications for patents, inventors' certificates, or other similar industrial property rights. 'Storage and retrieval of technical information' are understood in their widest sense and include all supporting operations and all activities facilitating them, including in particular: abstracting, indexing, classification, translation, standardization of the form of documents and of search tools, processing of documents, communication and exchange of documents.

So far as its administrative functions are concerned, WIPO is a continuation of the United International Bureaux for the Protection of Intellectual Property (BIRPI), which, under the supervisory authority of the Government of the Swiss Confederation, has provided the International Bureau of each Union since the end of the 19th century. As long as there are States members of the Paris or Berne Unions which have not become members of WIPO, the International Bureau and the Director-General of WIPO function as BIRPI, and its Director, respectively.

Membership in WIPO is open to any State which is a member of any of the Unions and to other States which are members of the organizations of the United Nations system, are party to the Statute of the International Court of Justice, or are invited to join by the General Assembly of WIPO. Membership of the Unions is open to any State. The total combined membership of the Unions and of WIPO on 31 Dec. 1970, including 2 States not members of either of the Unions, was 85 States, or 86 States if East Germany is regarded as a member; the States disagree on this question. The WIPO Convention permits States which are members of any of the Unions but have not become party to the Convention to exercise, if they so desire, for 5 years from the date of entry into force of the Convention, the same rights as if they had become party to it.

WIPO member States and States which have notified their desire to exercise the same rights: Algeria, Argentina, Belgium, Brazil, Bulgaria, Byelorussia, Cameroun, Canada, Chad, Cuba, Czechoslovakia, Dahomey, Denmark, Finland, France, Gabon, Germany (East) disputed: see above, Germany (West), Greece, Hungary, Irish Republic, Israel, Italy, Ivory Coast, Japan, Luxembourg, Malawi, Malta, Morocco, Netherlands, Niger, Norway, Poland, Portugal, Romania, Senegal, South Africa, Spain, Sweden, Switzerland, Syria, Thailand, Tunisia, Turkey, Ukraine, USSR, UAR, UK, USA, Upper Volta, Vatican, Yugoslavia (51 or 52 States).

Paris Union: Algeria, Argentina, Australia, Austria, Belgium, Brazil, Bulgaria, Cameroun, Canada, Central African Republic, Ceylon, Chad, Congo (Br.), Cuba, Cyprus, Czechoslovakia, Dahomey, Denmark, Dominican Republic, Finland, France, Gabon, Germany (East) disputed, Germany (West), Greece, Haiti, Hungary, Iceland, Indonesia, Iran, Irish Republic, Israel, Italy, Ivory Coast, Japan, Kenya, Lebanon, Liechtenstein, Luxembourg, Madagascar, Malawi, Malta, Mauritania, Mexico, Monaco, Morocco, Netherlands, New Zealand, Niger, Nigeria, Norway, Philippines, Poland, Portugal, Rhodesia, Romania, SanMarino, Senegal, South Africa, Spain, Sweden, Switzerland, Syria, Tanzania, Togo, Trinidad and Tobago, Tunisia, Turkey, Uganda, USSR, UAR,UK, USA, Upper Volta, Uruguay, Vatican, Viet-Nam, Yugoslavia, Zambia.(78 or 79 States.)

Berne Union: Argentina, Australia, Austria, Belgium, Brazil, Bulgaria, Cameroun, Canada, Ceylon, Chile, Congo (Br.), Congo (K.), Cyprus, Czechoslovakia, Dahomey, Denmark, Finland, France, Gabon, Germany (East), disputed, Germany (West), Greece, Hungary, Iceland, India, Irish Republic, Israel, Italy, Ivory Coast, Japan, Lebanon, Liechtenstein, Luxembourg, Madagascar, Mali, Malta, Mexico, Monaco, Morocco, Netherlands, New Zealand, Niger, Norway, Pakistan, Philippines, Poland, Portugal, Romania, Senegal, South Africa, Spain, Sweden, Switzerland, Thailand, Tunisia, Turkey, UK, Uruguay, Vatican, Yugoslavia. (59 or 60 States.)

Organization. The bodies of WIPO are: The *General Assembly*, consisting of all States members of WIPO which are members of any of the Unions. Among its other functions, the General Assembly appoints and gives instructions to the Director-General, reviews and approves his reports and adopts the triennial budget of expenses common to the Unions. The *Conference*, consisting of all States members of WIPO whether or not they are members of any of the Unions. Among its other functions, the Conference adopts its triennial budget and establishes the triennial programme of legal-technical assistance. The *Co-ordination Committee*, consisting of the States members of WIPO which are members of the Executive Committees of the Paris or Berne Unions. Among its other functions, the Co-ordination Committee establishes the annual budgets and programmes on the basis of the triennial budgets adopted by the General Assembly and the Conference.

In addition, the Paris au Berne Unions have Assemblies and Executive Committees, with functions similar to those of the WIPO bodies in respect of the triennial and annual budgets and programmes of the Unions. Each Union holds conferences at irregular intervals to revise its Convention.

The Director-General is also the Secretary-General of the International Union for the Protection of New Varieties of Plants (UPOV) whose Headquarters are at the same address (see below under UPOV).

Planning. The legal-technical assistance programme of WIPO is intended to assist developing countries in the improvement of their intellectual property systems in order to support their national and regional plans for economic development. The methods used include expert advice on the modernization of laws and on the building of appropriate governmental institutions, including the training of staff, together with the stimulation of industrial research and development activities by assisting in the flow of scientific and technical information.

The International Bureau of WIPO will act also as the International Bureau of the Patent Co-operation Treaty (PCT), which was signed by 35 countries in 1970 but is not expected to enter into force for a few years. The PCT contains provisions relating to technical assistance on a larger scale than that likely to be provided for in the WIPO programme, and calls for the conclusion of agreements between the International Bureau and international financing organizations concerned with development. Before the entry into force of the PCT, an Interim Committee, consisting of all signatory countries, has been authorized to put the technical assistance programme into effect.

Principal publications. Industrial Property (monthly, in English and French).—*Copyright* (monthly, in English and French).—*La Propriedad Intelectual* (quarterly, in Spanish).—*Les Marques internationales* (monthly, in French).—*Manuals and Brochures of Conventions and Agreements.*— *Collections of Laws and Treaties.*—*Model Laws for Developing Countries on Inventions, on Marks, Trade Names and Acts of Unfair Competition and on Designs* (in English, French and Spanish).— *Guide to the Application of the Paris Convention, by Professor G. H. C. Bodenhausen* (in English, French and German).

Director: G. H. C. Bodenhausen (Netherlands).
Headquarters: 32, chemin des Colombettes, 1211 Geneva 20, Switzerland.

The Director of WIPO is also the Secretary-General of the International Union for the Protection of New Varieties of Plants (UPOV) whose headquarters are at the same address.

Origin. The Convention establishing UPOV was signed in Paris in 1961 and entered into force in 1968. UPOV began its operation in Oct. 1969 upon the appointment of its first Secretary-General.

Functions. The purpose of the Convention for the Protection of New Plant Varieties is to recognize and secure to the breeder of a new plant variety certain rights in the member States, in particular to ensure that he receives a fair remuneration for his work. The effect of the rights of the breeder is that his prior authorization shall be necessary for the production of propagating material of his protected variety for the purpose of sale. Before protection is granted the new variety is subject to examination for novelty (distinctness from other varieties), stability and homogeneity and must have received a denomination. In some cases (regarding certain species) the Convention provides for national treatment of breeders belonging to the member States. In other cases (regarding other species) protection is granted to breeders from other member States on the basis of reciprocity concerning the species in question. UPOV assists member States in the promotion of international co-operation concerning the examination of new plant varieties and the naming of such varieties.

Principal publications. Industrial Property (monthly, in English and French).—*Copyright* (monthly, in English and French).—*La Propiedad Intelectual* (quarterly, in Spanish).—*Les Marques internationales* (monthly, in French).—*Manuals and Brochures of Conventions and Agreements.* —*Collections of Laws and Treaties.*—*Model Laws for Developing Countries on Inventions and on Marks, Trade Names and Acts of Unfair Competition.*

EUROPEAN ORGANIZATIONS

	OECD	NATO	WEU	C of E	ECSC, EEC, Euratom	EFTA	Warsaw Pact	Comecon
Albania	—	—	—	—	—	—	*	*[1]
Austria	*	—	—	*	—	*	—	—
Belgium	*	*	*	*	*	—	—	—
Bulgaria	—	—	—	—	—	—	*	*
Cyprus	—	—	—	*	—	—	—	—
Czechoslovakia	—	—	—	—	—	—	*	*
Denmark	*	*	—	*	—	*	—	—
Finland	—	—	—	—	—	o	—	—
France	*	*	*	*	*	—	—	—
Germany, East	—	—	—	—	—	—	*	*
Germany, West	*	*	*	*	*	—	—	—
Greece	*	*	—	o	—	—	—	—
Hungary	—	—	—	—	—	—	*	*
Iceland	*	*	—	*	—	*	—	—
Irish Republic	*	—	—	*	—	*	—	—
Italy	*	*	*	*	*	—	—	—
Luxembourg	*	*	*	*	*	—	—	—
Malta	—	—	—	*	—	—	—	—
Netherlands	*	*	*	*	*	—	—	—
Norway	*	*	—	*	—	*	—	—

	OECD	NATO	WEU	C of E	ECSC, EEC, Euratom	EFTA	Warsaw Pact	Comecon
Poland	—	—	—	—	—	—	*	*
Portugal	*	*	—	—	—	*	—	—
Romania	—	—	—	—	—	—	*	*
Spain	*	—	—	—	—	—	—	—
Sweden	*	—	—	*	—	*	—	—
Switzerland	*	—	—	*	—	*	—	—
Turkey	*	*	—	*	o	—	—	—
USSR	—	—	—	—	—	—	*	*
UK	*	*	*	*	*	*	—	—
Yugoslavia	o	—	—	—	—	—	—	—
Canada	*	*	—	—	—	—	—	—
Mongolia	—	—	—	—	—	—	—	*
USA	*	*	—	—	—	—	—	—

* = member. o = associate. — = non-member. [1] Resigned in Dec. 1962.

Eighteen African states including Madagascar are associates of the EEC, as are Kenya, Uganda and Tanzania.

ORGANIZATION FOR ECONOMIC CO-OPERATION AND DEVELOPMENT (OECD)

On 30 Sept. 1961 the Organization for European Economic Co-operation (OEEC), after a history of 14 years (*see* THE STATESMAN'S YEAR-BOOK, 1961, p. 32), was replaced by the Organization for Economic Co-operation and Development. The change of title marks the Organization's altered status and functions: with the accession of Canada and USA as full members it ceased to be a purely European body; while at the same time it added development aid to the list of its other activities. The member countries are now Austria, Belgium, Canada, Denmark, Finland, France, West Germany, Greece, Iceland, Irish Republic, Italy, Japan, Luxembourg, the Netherlands, Norway, Portugal, Spain, Sweden, Switzerland Turkey, UK and USA. Australia and Yugoslavia participate in certain of the Organization's activities and have been given special status for these associations.

Chairman of the Council (ministerial): William P. Rogers (USA).
Chairman of the Council (official level): The Secretary-General.
Chairman of the Executive Committee. Belgium.
Secretary-General: Emile Van Lennep (Netherlands).
Headquarters: Château de la Muette, 2, rue André Pascal, Paris (16e).

The aims of the reconstituted Organization, as defined in the convention signed on 14 Dec. 1960, are as follows: (*a*) to achieve the highest sustainable economic growth and employment and a rising standard of living in member countries, while maintaining financial stability, and thus to contribute to the development of the world economy; (*b*) to contribute to sound economic expansion in member as well as non-member countries in the process of economic development; and (*c*) to contribute to the expansion of world trade on a multilateral, non-discriminatory basis in accordance with international obligations. Responsibility for the achievement of these aims has been vested in the Economic Policy Committee, the Development Aid Committee and the Trade Committee. The second of these is made up of representatives of all the 16 principal capital-exporting member countries, together with the Commission of the European Communities. Other committees deal with economic and development review; the environment; technical co-operation; payments; invisible transactions; insurance; fiscal matters; agriculture; fisheries; education; science policy; manpower and social affairs; energy, industry, gas, tourism, maritime transport, etc. Two of the purely European aspects of OEEC have been retained: the European Nuclear Energy Agency and the European Monetary Agreement with its Board of Management.

An OECD Development Centre began work in 1963. In 1968 a Centre for Educational Research and Innovation was set up.

At a meeting of the Council, at Ministerial level, in May 1970 a collective growth target for the period 1970–80 of 65% was set and the qualitative aspects of growth were stressed. The co-ordination of environmental activities and of member countries' economic policies, and the improvement of volumes and terms of development assistance were given high priority among the activities of the Organization.

Convention on the Organisation for Economic Co-operation and Development. 1960
The OECD Observer. Bi-monthly, from 1962
The OECD Economic Outlook. 1966 ff.
OEEC/OECD Economic Surveys of Member Countries. 1954 ff.
European Nuclear Energy Annual Report. 1959 ff.
The Flow of Financial Resources to Countries in course of Economic Development. 1960 ff.
Development Assistance Efforts and Policies. 1962 ff.
Aubrey, H. G., *Atlantic ecnomoic cooperation: the OECD.* New York, 1967

NORTH ATLANTIC TREATY ORGANIZATION (NATO)

On 28 April 1948 the Canadian Secretary of State for External Affairs broached the idea of a 'security league' of the free nations, in extension of the Brussels Treaty of 17 March 1948. The United States Senate, on 11 June, recommended 'the association of the United States with such regional and other collective arrangements as are based on continuous self-help and mutual aid, and as affect its national security'. Detailed proposals were subsequently worked out between the Brussels Treaty powers, the USA and Canada.

On 4 April 1949 the foreign ministers of Belgium, Canada, Denmark, France, Iceland, Italy, Luxembourg, the Netherlands, Norway, Portugal, the UK and the USA met in Washington and signed a treaty, the main clauses of which read as follows:

ARTICLE 1. The parties undertake, as set forth in the Charter of the United Nations, to settle any international disputes in which they may be involved by peaceful means in such a manner that international peace and security and justice are not endangered, and to refrain in their international relations from the threat or use of force in any manner inconsistent with the purposes of the United Nations.

ARTICLE 2. The parties will contribute toward the further development of peaceful and friendly international relations by strengthening their free institutions, by bringing about a better understanding of the principles upon which these institutions are founded, and by promoting conditions of stability and well-being. They will seek to eliminate conflict in their international economic policies and will encourage economic collaboration between any or all of them.

ARTICLE 3. In order more effectively to achieve the objectives of this treaty, the parties, separately and jointly, by means of continuous and effective self-help and mutual aid, will maintain and develop their individual and collective capacity to resist armed attack.

ARTICLE 4. The parties will consult together whenever, in the opinion of any of them, the territorial integrity, political independence, or security of any of the parties is threatened.

ARTICLE 5. The parties agree that an armed attack against one or more of them in Europe or North America shall be considered an attack against them all and consequently they agree that, if such an armed attack occurs, each of them, in exercise of the right of individual or collective self-defence recognized by article 51 of the Charter of the United Nations, will assist the party or parties so attacked by taking forthwith, individually and in concert with the other parties, such action as it deems necessary, including the use of armed force, to restore and maintain the security of the North Atlantic area. Any such armed attack and all measures taken as a result thereof shall immediately be reported to the Security Council. Such measures shall be terminated when the Security Council has taken the measures necessary to restore and maintain international peace and security.

ARTICLE 6. For the purpose of Article 5 an armed attack on one or more of the parties is deemed to include an armed attack (i) on the territory of any of the parties in Europe or North America, on the Algerian Departments of France,* on the territory of Turkey or on the islands under the jurisdiction of any of the parties in the North Atlantic area north of the Tropic of Cancer; (ii) on the forces, vessels or aircraft of any of the parties, when in or over these territories or any other area in Europe in which occupation forces of any of the parties were stationed on the date when the treaty entered into force or the Mediterranean Sea or the North Atlantic area north of the Tropic of Cancer.†

* The relevant clauses of the treaty have become inapplicable to the Republic of Algeria as from 3 July 1962.
† This Article was modified as a result of the accession of Greece and Turkey to the treaty.

ARTICLE 8. Each party declares that none of the international engagements now in force between it and any other of the parties or any third state is in conflict with the provisions of this treaty, and undertakes not to enter into any international engagement in conflict with this treaty.

ARTICLE 10. The parties may, by unanimous agreement, invite any other European state in a position to further the principles of this treaty and to contribute to the security of the North Atlantic area to accede to this treaty. Any state so invited may become a party to the treaty by depositing its instrument of accession with the government of the United States of America. The government of the United States of America will inform each of the parties of the deposit of each such instrument of accession.

ARTICLE 12. After the treaty has been in force for 10 years, or at any time thereafter, the parties shall, if any of them so requests, consult together for the purpose of reviewing the treaty, having regard for the factors then affecting peace and security in the North Atlantic area, including the development of universal as well as regional arrangements under the Charter of the United Nations for the maintenance of international peace and security.

ARTICLE 13. After the treaty has been in force for 20 years, any party may cease to be a party one year after its notice of denunciation has been given to the government of the United States of America, which will inform the governments of the other parties of the deposit of each notice of denunciation.

The treaty came into force on 24 Aug. 1949. Greece and Turkey were admitted as parties to the treaty in 1951 (effective Feb. 1952), the Federal Republic of Germany in Oct. 1954 (effective 5 May 1955).

As reorganized by the Council at its session in Lisbon in Feb. 1952, the structure of NATO is as follows:

The *Council*, the principal body of the organization, 'charged with the responsibility of considering all matters concerning the implementation of the provisions of the Treaty', incorporates the Council and the Defence Committee originally envisaged. The Council is a Council of Governments, on which NATO nations are normally represented by their Minister for Foreign Affairs and/or the Minister of Defence, or by other competent Ministers, especially those responsible for financial and economic affairs. The Council normally meets at ministerial level two or three times a year.

Each member government appoints a *Permanent Representative* to represent it on the Council when its ministerial representatives are not present. Each Permanent Representative also heads a national delegation of advisers and experts. The Permanent Representatives meet once or twice a week and can be called together at short notice at any time.

In carrying out its role, the Council is assisted by a number of committees, some of a permanent nature, some temporary. Like the Council, the membership of each committee is made up of national representatives. They study questions submitted to them by the Council for recommendation. The work of the Committees has a direct hearing on the activities of the International Secretariat.

The Political Committee, charged with preparing the political agenda for the Council, dates from 1957 as does the Economic Committee, which studies and reports to the Council on economic issues of special interest to the Alliance. In 1963 a Defence Planning Committee was established as the civilian co-ordinating body for the defence plans of member countries. Since France's withdrawal from NATO military organizations, this Committee is composed of the Permanent Representatives of the 14 countries which take part in NATO's integrated common defence. Like the Council, it also meets at ministerial level. And at the Ministerial meeting in Dec. 1966 two bodies for nuclear planning were established: the Nuclear Defence Affairs Committee and a Nuclear Planning Group of 7–8 members.

Among other important Committees are: the Science Committee and the Infrastructure Committee, whose varied tasks are directly linked to fundamental and applied research; the Senior Civil Emergency Planning Committee; the Committee for European Airspace Co-ordination; the Committee for Pipelines; the Committee for Information and Cultural Relations; and the Civil and Military Budget Committees, who carefully supervise the expenditures of NATO funds for the maintenance of the International Secretariat and military headquarters. In Nov. 1969 the Council established a Committee on the Challenges of Modern Society to consider problems of the human environment. This new Committee examines methods of improving the exchange of views and experience among the Allied countries in the task of creating a better environment for their societies.

More recently, the old Armaments Committee has been replaced by the Conference of National Armaments Directors.

Headquarters: 1110 Brussels, Belgium.
Secretary-General: Manlio Brosio (Italy), appointed May 1964.

The Secretary-General takes the chair at all Council meetings, except at the opening and closing of Ministerial sessions, when he gives way to the Council President. The office of President is held annually by the Foreign Minister of one of the Treaty countries.

The *Military Committee* is composed of the Chiefs of Staff or their representatives of all the member countries except France, which in 1966 withdrew from the Military Committee while remaining a member of the Council. (Iceland, having no military establishment, may be represented by a civilian.) It meets at Chiefs of Staff level two or three times a year as required, but remains in permanent session at the level of military representatives and is assisted by an integrated *international military staff*. It provides general policy guidance of a military nature to the Council.

In Dec. 1950 the Council approved the establishment of an integrated force for the defence of Western Europe under a Supreme Headquarters Allied Powers, Europe (SHAPE). General Eisenhower was the first Supreme Allied Commander Europe (SACEUR); he was succeeded by Generals Ridgway (1 June 1952), Alfred M. Gruenther (11 July 1953), Lauris Norstad (20 Nov. 1956), Lyman L. Lemnitzer (1 Jan. 1963) and Andrew J. Goodpaster (1 July 1969); Deputies: Field-Marshal Lord Montgomery, 1950–58; Gen. Sir Richard Gale, 1958–60; Gen. Sir Hugh Stockwell, GCB, KBE, DSO, 1960–63; Marshal of the Royal Air Force Sir Thomas Pike, GCB, CBE, DFC, 1964–67; Gen. Sir Robert Bray, KCB, CBE, DSO, 1967–70; Gen. Sir Desmond Fitzpatrick, DSO, MBE, MC, 1970–.

The *European Command* covers the land area from the North Cape to the Mediterranean and from the Atlantic to the eastern border of Turkey, excluding the UK and Portugal, the defence of which does not fall under any one major NATO Command.

The *Atlantic Command* extends from the North Pole to the Tropic of Cancer and from the coastal waters of North America to those of Europe and Africa, but excludes the Channel and the British Isles. The Supreme Allied Commander Atlantic (SACLANT), Adm. Charles K. Duncan (USN), is an operational rather than an administrative commander, and, unlike SACEUR, has no forces permanently attached to his command.

The *Channel Command* covers the English Channel and the southern North Sea. The Allied C.-in-C. Channel is Admiral Sir William O'Brien.

The *Canada–US Regional Planning Group*, which covers the North American area, develops and recommends to the Military Committee plans for the defence of this area. It meets alternately in Washington and Ottawa.

The NATO Handbook.—NATO: Facts and Figures.—The NATO Letter (bi-monthly).—*Aspects of NATO.—NATO Pocket Guide.—Why NATO pamphlet.—NATO Maps*

WESTERN EUROPEAN UNION

On 17 March 1948 a 50-year treaty 'for collaboration in economic, social and cultural matters and for collective self-defence' was signed in Brussels by the Foreign Ministers of the UK, France, the Netherlands, Belgium and Luxembourg. (*See* THE STATESMAN'S YEAR-BOOK, 1954, pp. 32 f.)

On 20 Dec. 1950 the Western Union defence organization was merged with the North Atlantic Treaty command.

After the rejection by France of the European Defence Community on 30 Aug. 1954 a conference was held in London from 28 Sept. to 3 Oct. 1954, attended by Belgium, Canada, France, Federal Germany, Italy, the Netherlands, Luxembourg, the UK and the USA, at which it was decided to invite the Federal Republic of Germany and Italy to accede to the Brussels Treaty, to end the occupation of Western Germany and to invite the latter to accede to the North Atlantic Treaty; the Federal Republic agreed that it would voluntarily limit its arms production, and provision was made for the setting up of an agency to control the armaments of the 7 Brussels Treaty powers; the UK undertook not to withdraw from the Continent her 4 divisions and the Tactical Air Force assigned to the Supreme Allied Commander against the wishes of a majority, *i.e.*, 4, of the Brussels Treaty powers, except in the event of an acute overseas emergency.

At a Conference of Ministers held in Paris from 20 to 23 Oct. 1954 these decisions were put into effect. The Union was formally inaugurated on 6 May 1955.

The *Council of WEU* consists of the Foreign Ministers of the 7 powers or their representatives. An *Assembly*, composed of the WEU delegates to the Consultative Assembly of the Council of Europe, meets twice a year, usually in Paris. An *Agency for the Control of Armaments* and a *Standing Armaments Committee* have been set up in Paris. The social and cultural activities were transferred to the Council of Europe on 1 June 1960.

After the breakdown of the negotiations for Britain's entry into the Common Market in 1963 (*see* p. 42) the 6 EEC countries proposed to the UK that the WEU Council (the Six and the UK) should meet every 3 months 'to take stock of the political and economic situation in Europe'. The UK welcomed this proposal, and regular meetings have been held ever since. While political consultation continues, discussion of the economic situation has been suspended since June 1970 when negotiations for the enlargement of the EEC began.

Headquarters: 9 Grosvenor Place, London, SW1.
Secretary-General: Georges Heisbourg.

COUNCIL OF EUROPE

In 1948 the 'Congress of Europe', bringing together at The Hague nearly 1,000 influential Europeans from 26 countries, called for the creation of a united Europe, including a European Assembly. This proposal, examined first by the Ministerial Council of the Brussels Treaty Organization, then by a conference of ambassadors, was at the origin of the Council of Europe. The Statute of the Council was signed at London on 5 May 1949 and came into force 2 months later. The founder members were Belgium, Denmark, France, the Irish Republic, Italy, Luxembourg, the Netherlands, Norway, Sweden and the United Kingdom. Turkey and Greece joined in 1949, Iceland in 1950, the Federal Republic of Germany in 1951 (having been an associate since 1950), Austria in 1956, Cyprus in 1961, Switzerland in 1963, Malta in 1965.

Membership is limited to European States which 'accept the principles of the rule of law and of the enjoyment by all persons within [their] jurisdiction of human rights and fundamental freedoms'. The Statute provides for both withdrawal (Art. 7) and suspension (Arts. 8 and 9). Greece withdrew from the Council in Dec. 1969.

Structure. Under the Statute two organs were set up: an inter-governmental *Committee of* (Foreign) *Ministers* with powers of decision and of recommendation to governments, and an inter-parliamentary deliberative body, the *Consultative Assembly*—both of which are served by the Secretariat. In addition, a large number of committees of experts have been established, two of them, the Council for Cultural Co-operation and the Committee on Legal Co-operation, having a measure of autonomy; on municipal matters the Committee of Ministers receives recommendations from the European Local Authorities Conference.

The Committee of Ministers meet usually twice a year, their deputies 10 times a year.

The Consultative Assembly normally consists of 140 persons elected or appointed by their national parliaments (Austria 6, Belgium 7, Cyprus 3, Denmark 5, France 18, Germany 18, Iceland 3, Irish Republic 4, Italy 18, Luxembourg 3, Malta 3, Netherlands 7, Norway 5, Sweden 6, Switzerland 6, Turkey 10, UK 18); it meets for 3 week-long sessions every year. For domestic reasons Cyprus is not at present represented in the Assembly. The work of the Assembly is prepared by parliamentary committees.

The *Joint Committee*, consisting of the Committee of Ministers and representatives of the Assembly, harmonizes relations between the two organs.

Under the European Convention of 1950 a special structure has been established for the protection of human rights. A *European Commission* investigates alleged violations of the Convention submitted to it either by States or, in some cases, by individuals. Its findings can then be examined by the *European Court of Human Rights* (set up in 1959), whose obligatory jurisdiction has been recognized by 11 States, or by the Committee of Ministers, empowered to take binding decisions by two-thirds majority vote.

For questions of national refugees and over-population, a Special Representative has been appointed, responsible to the governments collectively.

Aims and Achievements. Art. 1 of the Statute states that the Council's aim is 'to achieve a greater unity between its members for the purpose of safeguarding and realising the ideals and principles which are their common heritage and facilitating their economic and social progress'; 'this aim shall be pursued . . . by discussion of questions of common concern and by agreements and common action'. The only limitation is provided by Art. 1 (*d*), which excludes 'matters relating to national defence'.

It has been the task of the Assembly to propose action to bring European countries closer together, to keep under constant review the progress made and to voice the views of European public opinion on the main political and economic questions of the day. The Ministers' role is to translate the Assembly's recommendations into action, particularly as regards lowering the barriers between the European countries, harmonizing their legislation or introducing where possible common European laws, abolishing discrimination on grounds of nationality and undertaking certain tasks on a joint European basis.

In May 1966 the Committee of Ministers approved a programme, designed to streamline the activities of the Council of Europe. It comprises projects for co-operation between member governments in economic, legal, social, public health, environmental, and educational and scientific matters; and is to be reviewed every year.

Over 70 conventions have been concluded, covering such matters as social security, patents, extradition, medical treatment, training of nurses, equivalence of degrees and diplomas, innkeepers' liability, compulsory motor insurance, the protection of television broadcasts, adoption of children, transportation of animals and *au pair* replacement. A *Social Charter* sets out the social and economic rights which all member governments agree to guarantee to their citizens.

The official languages are English and French.

Chairman of the Committee of Ministers: (held in rotation).
President of the Consultative Assembly: Olivier Reverdin (Switzerland).
President of the European Court of Human Rights: Henri Rolin (Belgium).
President of the European Commission of Human Rights: Max Sørensen (Denmark).
Secretary-General: Lujo Tončić-Sorinj (Austria).
Headquarters: Maison de l'Europe, Strasbourg, France.

European Yearbook. The Hague, from 1955
Forward in Europe. Strasbourg, from 1959, 5 times a year
Manual of the Council of Europe. London, 1970.
Nova, F., *Contemporary European Governments.* Dublin, 1965
P.E.P., *European Organisations.* 2nd ed. London, 1966
Robertson, A. H., *The Council of Europe.* 2nd ed. London, 1961.—*European Institutions.* 2nd ed.
London, 1966

EUROPEAN COMMUNITIES

Six countries of western Europe—Belgium, France, Federal Germany, Italy,
Luxembourg and the Netherlands—have established 3 communities with the
aims of gradually integrating their economies and of moving towards political
unity: the European Coal and Steel Community (ECSC), the European Economic Community (EEC) and the European Atomic Energy Community
(EAEC or Euratom).

Up to 1 July 1967 the 3 communities, though legally separate under their constituent treaties, had some institutions in common. On that date they merged
their 3 executives in one Commission of the European Communities and also
their 3 councils. This was the first step towards the complete merger of the
3 communities under a new single treaty.

The COMMISSION consists of 9 members appointed by the member states to
serve for 4 years, the President and 3 Vice-Presidents serve for 2 years, but
who act independently in the interests of the Community as a whole. Its task is
the implementation of the Treaties, and in this it has the right of both initiative
and execution: it proposes to the Council of Ministers the methods by which
the aims of the Treaties can be achieved, and is then responsible for carrying
them through.

President: Franco Maria Malfatti.
Address: 200, rue de la Loi, Brussels, 4.

The COUNCIL OF MINISTERS consists of Ministers from the 6 national governments and represents the national as opposed to the Community interests. It is
the body which has the power of decision in the Community. Under the Treaties
many of its decisions are taken to be by qualified majority vote; since the 'Luxembourg Compromise' of 1966 majority voting has been used for minor matters
only.

Address: 2 rue Ravenstein, Brussels, 1.

The EUROPEAN PARLIAMENT consists of 142 members delegated by the 6
national Parliaments. The EEC Treaty provides for the direct election of its
members, and arrangements for this are now under discussion between the
Council and the Parliament. It has to be consulted over the annual budgets of
the 3 Communities and a wide range of other matters. It can dismiss the
Commission on a motion of censure approved by a two-thirds majority. As
part of the decision in 1970 to provide the Community with its own independent financial resources, the Parliament has been given more control over the
administrative budget consisting of non-mandatory expenditure, *i.e.*, expenditure
not arising directly from the Treaty or from regulations made under it. The
budgetary power of the Parliament will be reviewed in 1972.

President: Mario Scelba.
Address: Centre Européan du Kirchberg, Luxembourg.

Annuaire—Manue. de l'Assemblée Parlementaire Européenne. Annual, from 1959

The COURT OF JUSTICE is composed of 7 judges, is responsible for the adjudica-
tion of disputes arising out of the application of the treaties, and its findings are
enforceable in all member countries.

President: Robert Lecourt.
Address: 12, rue de la Côte-d'Eich, Luxembourg.

Receuil de la Jurisprudence de la Cour. From 1954
Bebr, G., *Judicial Control of the European Communities.* London, 1962

The ECONOMIC AND SOCIAL COMMITTEE, common to the EEC and Euratom, has an advisory role and consists of 101 representatives, employers, trade unions, consumers, etc. The CONSULTATIVE COMMITTEE, of 50 members, performs a similar role for the ECSC.

EUROPEAN ECONOMIC COMMUNITY
(E.E.C. or COMMON MARKET)

The EEC came into being on 1 Jan. 1958, based on the treaty signed in Rome on 25 March 1957, by Belgium, France, Germany, Luxembourg, Italy and the Netherlands.

The *Customs Union.* The Treaty required the achievement of a complete customs union between the 6 countries over a transitional period of 12 to 15 years. This was achieved 18 months ahead of the 12-year schedule when, on 1 July 1968, customs duties on trade between the Six were removed. The last alignment on the common external tariff was also made at the same time; it is based upon the average of the national tariffs, less a reduction of 20% on some items negotiated in the Dillon Round tariff-cut talks in GATT and the first two-fifths of the tariff cuts agreed under the Kennedy Round. Free movement of workers was also introduced in July 1968, and substantial progress has been achieved in introducing free movement of capital and the free supply of services throughout the Community.

The *Economic Union.* Greatest progress has been made in the field of agriculture, where the basic features of a common policy were adopted in Jan. 1962. The aims are greater efficiency in production, stable market conditions, a fair return for the farmers and reasonable prices for consumers. The two essential principles are common price levels and the replacement of the present national systems of protection by a Community system whose most characteristic feature is a system of variable levies on imports of certain farm products. The common marketing arrangements for all major items were operative by July 1968. Management committees of national experts advise the Commission on the various products. A European Guidance and Guarantee Fund has also been established to finance the common policy. In Dec. 1968 the Commission put forward proposals for a major reform of agriculture, aiming at retiring or retraining 5m. farmers by 1980, taking much land out of cultivation and reorganizing the structure of farming into larger units. An initial problem to be overcome was the over-production of wheat, sugar and butter owing to the fixing of intervention prices too high. In 1971–74 an independent revenue system for the Community will be phased in, ultimately comprising 90% of all food-import levies, 90% of import duties and the product of up to a 1% point of the common value-added tax system.

Much work has been done on common transport and foreign trade policies and the co-ordination of financial, commercial, economic and social policies. The Treaty forbids agreements or practices which restrict, prevent or distort free competition, and firms now have to submit such agreements to the Commission, except in cases where Community regulations have exempted certain types of agreement.

At the Hague 'summit' of Dec. 1969 the Six agreed to move towards an economic and monetary union, and also to intensify their scientific co-operation.

External Relations. Britain, Ireland, Norway and Denmark applied for membership in 1961, but negotiations were broken off at the insistence of France in Jan. 1963.

Following exploratory talks with the 6 governments, Britain formally applied for membership on 10 May 1967, as did the Irish Republic (10 May), Denmark (11 May) and Norway (24 July). On 26 July Sweden requested participation on terms compatible with her neutrality status.

On the request by the Council of Ministers, the Commission drew up an 'opinion' on the applications (published in Oct. 1967), which recommended the opening of negotiations. This was favoured by 5 members states, with France opposed. On 18 Dec. 1967 the Council agreed to disagree on the 4 applications which, however, remain on the Council's agenda. After the retirement of President de Gaulle, and particularly after The Hague 'summit' meeting of the Six, the way to negotiations was open, and these began in July 1970.

Greece and Turkey are associated with the Community, with a view to eventual full membership when their economies have become strong enough to allow them to compete on the Community market. Since the Greek *coup d'état* in April 1967 the Association Agreement has been 'frozen' and no further steps towards a customs union taken. An Association Agreement with Malta was signed in Dec. 1970.

Association of 18 African ex-colonies, now fully sovereign and independent, was renewed for a further 5 years by a convention signed at Yaoundé in 1963. This gives them free entry into the EEC market and provides access to a special European Development Fund—additional to national aid—to which the Six allotted nearly $1,400m. for the years 1958–69. The Convention, renewed in 1969, for the years 1970–75, provided for another $1,000m. in aid grants and loans. An Association Agreement has been signed with Nigeria, but so far has not come into force. Trade agreements with Israel, Lebanon and Iran are in operation. Kenya, Uganda and Tanzania have negotiated an Association Agreement with the Community, and trading agreements have been negotiated with Tunisia, Morocco, Spain and Yugoslavia. Negotiations are taking place with Egypt, Japan and Argentina.

From 1 Jan. 1973 all commercial agreements are to be negotiated on a common basis; until then nationally negotiated agreements are subject to Council approval.

In the Kennedy-Round negotiations in GATT the Commission negotiated for the Community as a whole and the member governments did not appear as such.

As a first step towards the creation of a political union, the Six agreed, in 1970, to hold twice-yearly consultations on foreign policy; the first meeting of foreign ministers was held in Nov. 1970.

General Report on the activities of the Community (annual, from 1958).—*Bulletin of the EEC* (monthly).—*Bulletin Général de Statistiques* (monthly). *Statistique Mensuelle du Commerce Extérieur* (monthly).—*Graphiques et Notes Rapidos sur la conjoncture de la Communauté* (monthly, from 1959)

European Community (monthly), obtainable from European Community Information Service, 23 Chesham St., London, SW1.

Broad, R., and Jarrett, R., *Community Europe: a short guide to the Common Market*. London, 1967
Calmann, J. (ed.), *The Rome Treaty: The Common Market explained*. London, 1967
Camps, M., *Britain and the European Community, 1955–63*. Princeton Univ. Press, 1964.—*What Kind of Europe?* OUP, 1965.—*European Unification in the Sixties*. New York, 1967
Mayre, R., *The Recovery of Europe*. London, 1970
Walsh, A. E., and Paxton, J., *Trade in the Common Market Countries*. London, 1965.—*The Structure and Development of the Common Market*. London, New York, 1968.—*Trade and Industrial Resources of the Common Market and EFTA Countries*. London, 1970

EUROPEAN COAL AND STEEL COMMUNITY

The ECSC came into being on 10 Aug. 1952 following the ratification of a treaty signed in Paris on 18 April 1951. The original suggestion for it was made in the Schuman Plan on 9 May 1950, which proposed the pooling of Franco-German coal and steel production in a Community open to other western European countries as a first step towards a United States of Europe. (*See* map in THE STATESMAN'S YEAR-BOOK, 1958.)

Until 1 July 1967 the *High Authority* was the executive body of the ECSC and consisted of 8 members appointed by the 6 governments plus one co-opted member. After the merger of the Executives its power passed to the single European Commission which is now responsible for the execution of the ECSC Treaty.

The Common Market for Coal and Steel. A common market for coal, iron ore and scrap was established on 10 Feb. 1953, for steel on 1 May 1953 and for special steels on 1 Aug. 1954. A harmonized external tariff on steel is now at around 9%. Rules for fair competition have been established; currency restrictions, the dual-pricing system (under which prices for export and home-consumed coal and steel varied) and discriminatory transport rates based upon nationality have been abolished within the Community.

To meet the changing circumstances in the two industries, and especially to ensure that the contraction of the coal industry occurs without social or economic dislocation, the High Authority had by April 1970 granted readaption aid to 408,100 workers, most of them coalminers, at a cost of $155m., matched by an equivalent amount from the governments; it had also spent $112m. on research.

A Common Energy Policy. Of the various forms of energy, coal falls within the competence of the ECSC, nuclear energy within that of Euratom, and all others with that of the EEC. The first effective steps towards a common energy policy for the Community was taken when a Protocol of Agreement on Energy was signed by the 3 Communities in April 1964. In Dec. 1968 the single commission published guidelines for a common energy policy.

External Relations. An Association Agreement was concluded with the UK in 1954.

General Report of the High Authority (annual, from 1953).—*Bulletin Statistique* (bi-monthly from 1952).—*Investment Report* (annual, from 1956).—*Financial Report* (annual, from 1956).—*Journal Officiel de la CECA* (1952–58).—*Journal Officiel des Communautés Européennes* (from 1958).— *European Community* (monthly, from 1963)

Diebold, W., *The Schuman Plan; a study in Economic Co-operation, 1950–59.* New York, 1959
Lister, L., *Europe's Coal and Steel Community.* New York, 1960
Meade, J. E. (ed.), *Case Studies in European Economic Union.* Oxford, 1962
Schuman, R., *Pour l'Europe.* Paris, 1963

EUROPEAN ATOMIC ENERGY COMMUNITY (EURATOM)

Euratom came into being on 1 Jan. 1958 following the ratification of a treaty signed in Rome on 25 March 1957. Its task is to promote a common effort between its 6 members in the development of nuclear energy for peaceful purposes. It is in no way concerned with the military uses of nuclear energy; indeed, the member governments are forbidden under the Treaty to use nuclear materials obtained from or through the Community in national military programmes.

The execution of the treaty now rests with the *European Commission*, which is advised by a *Scientific and Technical Committee* (20 members) and the *Economic and Social Committee* (101 members). Major decisions are taken by the *Council of Ministers*, which is common also to the EEC.

Euratom supplements and co-ordinates research undertaken by the member states, pools scientific information and promotes the training of scientists and technicians. It promotes research (*a*) through its own research centres at Ispra, Italy (concentrating on the Orgel heavy-water reactor), at Geel, Belgium (the Central Nuclear Measurements Bureau), at Karlsruhe, Germany (the European Transuranium Institute) and at Petten, Netherlands (a general-purpose research establishment); (*b*) by contracting specific tasks to national centres or firms, and by 'association contracts' under which it contributes finance and personnel to joint teams; (*c*) by joining international projects such as the European Nuclear Energy Agency project at Winfrith Heath, England (the Dragon reactor).

Euratom has its own large Information and Documentation Centre, has set up a radioisotope information bureau and has worked out a Community policy on ownership of patents resulting from nuclear research. It has laid down basic standards for health protection throughout the Community, and worked out an insurance convention for large-scale atomic risks.

A common market for all nuclear materials and equipment came into force, and external tariffs were suspended, on 1 Jan. 1959. The budget of Euratom for research and investment was $59m. in 1971.

International Links. A co-operation agreement with the UK, signed in Feb. 1959, ensures close collaboration with the UK Atomic Energy Authority and it was renewed for 2 years in Feb. 1969. An agreement was signed with the US Atomic Energy Commission in Nov. 1958 and widened in 1964.

General Report on the Activities of the Community (annual, from 1958).—*Euratom Bulletin* quarterly, from Jan. 1962)

EUROPEAN FREE TRADE ASSOCIATION

The EFTA has 8 full members: Austria, Denmark, Iceland, Norway, Portugal, Sweden, Switzerland and UK, and one associate member, Finland. The Stockholm Convention establishing the Association entered into force on 3 May 1960, and Finland became associated on 27 March 1961. Iceland joined EFTA on 1 March 1970 and was immediately granted duty free entry for industrial goods exported to EFTA countries, while being given 10 years in which to abolish her own existing protective duties.

The Association was set up with two main aims: to achieve free trade in industrial products between member countries and to work towards a wider settlement for Western Europe as a whole.

The first objective was achieved on 31 Dec. 1966, when virtually all inter-EFTA tariffs were removed. This was 3 years earlier than originally planned. Finland removed her remaining EFTA tariffs a year later on 31 Dec. 1967.

The achievement of free trade made EFTA the world's first completed free-trade area, and intra-EFTA trade more than doubled in the period 1959–68.

Work towards the achievement of the second objective was renewed in 1970 when three EFTA members, Denmark, Norway and UK, presented application for full membership of the EEC. All other EFTA members have expressed an interest in some form of special trading arrangement with an enlarged EEC.

Area tariff treatment applies to those industrial products which are of EFTA origin, and these are traded freely between member countries. Each EFTA country remains free, however, to impose its own rates of duty on products entering from outside the EFTA area.

Generally, agricultural products do not come under the provisions for free trade, but bilateral agreements have been negotiated to increase trade in these products (including one between UK and Denmark).

The operation of the Convention is the responsibility of a Council assisted by a small secretariat. Each EFTA country holds the chairmanship of the Council for 6 months.

Secretary-General: Sir John Coulson, KCMG.
Headquarters: 9–11 Rue de Varembé, 1211 Geneva 20, Switzerland.

Convention establishing the European Free Trade Association (new ed. 1970).—EFTA (1966)

COLOMBO PLAN

At meetings held during 1950 in Colombo, Sydney and London Commonwealth Ministers published on 28 Nov. 1950 the 'Colombo Plan for Co-operative Economic Development in South and South-East Asia'. The plan came into force on 1 July 1951 and was successively extended beyond the original date of 30 June 1957 and now continues until 1976.

The plan represents the co-operative effort of both developed and developing countries to further the economies and raise living standards in South and South-East Asia.

In 1970 the members were: Afghánistán, Australia, Bhután, Burma, Cambodia, Canada, Ceylon, India, Indonesia, Iran, Japan, Korea, Laos, Malaysia, Maldive Islands, Nepál, New Zealand, Pakistan, Philippines, Singapore, Thailand, UK, USA and Vietnam.

The annual meetings of the Consultative Committee are also attended by observers from the Asian Development Bank, the International Labour Organization, International Bank for Reconstruction and Development, the Economic Commission for Asia and the Far East and the United Nations Development Programme, the Asian Productivity Organization and (from 1966) the Commonwealth Secretariat.

Technical Co-operation. The Colombo Plan has no permanent secretariat. A small Bureau, set up in Colombo in 1951, operates under the supervision of a Council for Technical Co-operation in South and South-East Asia, representing member governments. An information unit has been attached to the Bureau since 1953. The Council publishes its own annual report.

During 1969, 964 experts were assigned to countries of the region, and 6,681 training places were provided. Most training is given outside the region, but the Bureau has increasingly urged members to make more use of training facilities available within the region, by adequate arrangements for the exchange of students.

External Aid. The net flow of aid to countries of the region provided by Australia, Canada, Japan, UK and USA during 1969 was US$2,365m. In addition, there is substantial private investment from countries outside the region. In 1969 UK aid amounted to £68·1m., bringing the total since 1950 to £637m. Of the total expenditure in 1969, £3·6m. was on technical assistance, bringing the total of such expenditure since 1950 to £27m. UK private investment (excluding oil and portfolio) the area is estimated to have been about £17·7m. in 1968.

The Colombo Plan (Cmd. 8080). HMSO, 1950; reprinted 1952.—*Annual Report.* HMSO, 1952 to date.—*Report of the Council for Technical Co-operation.* HMSO, 1954 to date
Reports of the Council for Technical Co-operation. HMSO annually until 1966–67 followed by the Colombo Plan Bureau, Ceylon, 1967–68 and 1969–70.

SOUTH-EAST ASIA COLLECTIVE DEFENCE TREATY

On 8 Sept. 1954 Australia, France, New Zealand, Pakistan, the Philippines, Thailand, the UK and the USA signed at Manila a pact, which established a collective defence system in South-East Asia.

The treaty (printed in THE STATESMAN'S YEAR-BOOK 1964–65, p. 44) provides for the peaceful settlement of disputes, collective defence against aggression, the strengthening of free institutions by economic and technical co-operation, and action to meet common danger on invitation of the government concerned. Within the framework of the United Nations the treaty area is defined as the general area of South-East Asia including the entire territories of the Asian parties and the general area of the South-West Pacific not including the Pacific area north of 21° 30′ N. lat. The duration of the treaty is indefinite, but any party may withdraw one year after it has given notice.

To the treaty text was added the following 'understanding' of the USA:

The United States of America in executing the present treaty does so with the understanding that its recognition of the effect of aggression and armed attack and its agreement with reference thereto . . . apply only to Communist aggression, but affirms that in the event of other aggression or armed attack it will consult under the provisions of article 4 (2).

[This paragraph states that 'If in the opinion of any of the parties the inviolability or the integrity of the territory or the sovereignty or political independence of any party in the treaty area or of any other state or territory [which the parties by unanimous agreement may designate] is threatened in any way other than by armed attack or is affected or threatened by any fact or situation which might endanger the peace of the area, the parties shall consult immediately . . .']

A protocol to the treaty states:

The parties to the South-East Asia collective defence treaty unanimously designate for the purposes of [defence against aggression] the States of Cambodia and Laos and the free territory under the jurisdiction of the State of Vietnam.

The parties further agree that the above-mentioned States and territory shall be eligible in respect of the economic measures contemplated.

A joint statement by Thailand and the USA, 6 March 1962, states that the treaty obligation of the USA does not depend upon the prior agreement of all other parties to the treaty; a majority of the members have accepted this view.

The 8 nations also issued a declaration of principles, the Pacific Charter (see THE STATESMAN'S YEAR-BOOK 1964–65, p. 45).

Structure of Seato. The *Council*, consisting of the Foreign Ministers of the 8 member countries, sets the broad policy of the organization. It meets usually once a year in the several capitals.

Military Advisers are named by each nation, and the group meets usually twice a year. They are officers at chief-of-staff or theatre-commander level, responsible to the Council.

Council Representatives meet usually once a month in Bangkok. Composed of 7 ambassadors to Thailand and a special Thai representative, they carry on the overall political direction of SEATO affairs.

Military Advisers' Representatives are assigned to SEATO Headquarters by their respective governments to represent national views on matters affecting the work of the Military Planning Office.

The *Military Planning Office*, composed of officers assigned by the 8 member nations, has to prepare military plans in the light of changing or anticipated conditions. Military exercises are staged each year to give the defence forces of the member nations training in combined operations.

The *Permanent Working Group*, composed of senior staff members of the Council Representatives, carries out preparatory work on proposals and policy.

The *Secretary-General* is the spokesman for SEATO, and directs its civil activities, which include economic, cultural and research programmes.

Defence. In 1970 the Office of the Special Assistant was renamed Office for 'Counter-subversion and Counter-insurgency' (OCS) and reorganized to take account of the greater emphasis which SEATO now places on counter-subversion and counter-insurgency work.

Economic and Social Projects. The SEATO Graduate School of Engineering, established in Bangkok in 1959, became an independent institution in 1967 called 'The Asian Institute of Technology'. It offers advanced courses in hydraulic, structural, public health and highway engineering to qualified students of Asia. Enrolment (1967), 110 students.

Skilled labour schools have been established in Pakistan, the Philippines and Thailand to train workers for newly developing industries.

Medical research is carried on at the Medical Research Laboratory and the Clinical Research Centre in Bangkok, and the Cholera Research Laboratory in Dacca, East Pakistan.

The Cultural Relations programme provides undergraduate and postgraduate scholarships, research fellowships and exchange professorships.

A Regional Community Development Centre and a Tribal Research Centre have been established in northern Thailand. A meteorological telecommunications system has been installed between Bangkok and Manila.

Secretary-General: Lieut.-Gen. Jesus Vargas.

South-East Asia Collective Defence Treaty (Cmnd. 265). HMSO, 1957; reprinted 1961
Modelski, G. (ed.), *Seato: six studies.* Austral. National Univ., 1962

On 7 Aug. 1967 Indonesia, Thailand, the Philippines, Malaysia and Singapore formed the **Association of South-East Asian Nations** (ASEAN), to promote active collaboration and mutual assistance in matters of common interest in the economic, social, cultural, technical, scientific and administrative fields.

CENTRAL TREATY
ORGANIZATION (CENTO)

A pact of mutual defence was signed in Baghdad by Turkey and Iraq on 24 Feb. 1955. It was joined by the UK (4 April), Pakistan (23 Sept.) and Iran (3 Nov.). The USA became a full member of the economic and counter-subversion committees in April 1956, of the military committee in March 1957 and of the scientific council in May 1961, and is represented at the council meetings by observers. Bilateral defence agreements between the USA and Turkey, Iran and Pakistan were signed in Ankara on 5 March 1959.

Iraq ceased to participate in the activities of the Pact countries after the revolution in July 1958 and formally withdrew on 24 March 1959.

Headquarters was transferred from Baghdad to Ankara in Oct. 1958. On 21 Aug. 1959 the name of the organization was changed from Baghdad Pact to Central Treaty Organization (CENTO).

Secretary-General: Turgut Menemencioğlu (Turkey).

The main clauses of the Pact may be summarized as follows:

1. Consistent with Art. 51 of the UN Charter, the contracting parties will co-operate for their security and defence. This co-operation may form the subject of special agreements.
3. The contracting parties undertake to refrain from any interference in each other's internal affairs. They will settle any dispute between themselves in a peaceful way in accordance with UN Charter.
4. The contracting parties declare that the dispositions of the Pact are not in contradiction with any of the international obligations contracted by either of them with any third state. They undertake not to enter into any international obligations incompatible with the Pact.
5. The pact is open for accession to any State concerned with the security and peace of this region, and which is recognized by Turkey and Iraq.
7. This Pact remains in force for a period of 5 years, renewable for other 5-year periods. Any party may withdraw by notifying the other parties 6 months before the expiration of any of the above-mentioned periods.

The economic development programmes include:

Road Links: Pakistan–Iran road link joining Karachi, Lasbella, Quetta, Zahedan and Kerman in progress. Pakistan–Iran road link joining Lasbella, Pishin and Bandar Abbas in progress. Turkey–Iran road link joining Bağişli, Rezaiyeh and Tabriz–Tehran main road at Zanjan completed. Turkey–Iran road link joining Cizre, Hakkari and Bağişli under construction.

Rail Links: Turkey–Iran rail link (including a ferry across Lake Van) joining Muş, Tatvan, Khoy and Sharafkhaneh under construction. Muş–Tatvan section completed 1964; remainder scheduled for completion in 1971. Pakistan–Iran rail link joining Bad to Zahedan and Quetta under construction.

Port Development: Development of the ports of Trabzon and Iskenderun; Trabzon project completed in 1963. First stage of Iskenderun project finished in 1969.

Airway: CENTO Airway; US and UK have contributed considerable amounts towards improved navigational and other aids for regional air traffic. Now virtually completed.

Telecommunications: High-frequency radio telecommunication links between London and key regional stations, *i.e.*, Istanbul, Ankara, Tehrán, Karachi and Dacca. First stage completed in 1964; in full operation 1968. Ankara–Tehrán–Karachi microwave links project involving 88 relay stations and 13 air navigation stations, opened 1965, completed 1966. Tehrán Control Centre opened 1969.

In addition, research is being undertaken into health, science, agriculture and mineral development. Technical assistance is also undertaken and an industrial development officer was appointed in 1970.

ORGANIZATION OF AMERICAN STATES

On 14 April 1890 representatives of the American republics, meeting in Washington at the First International Conference of American States, established an 'International Union of the American Republics' and, as its central office, a 'Commercial Bureau of American Republics', which later became the Pan American Union. This international organization's object was to foster mutual understanding and co-operation among the nations of the western hemisphere. Since that time, successive inter-American conferences have greatly broadened the scope of work of the Organization.

This led to the adoption on 30 April 1948 by the Ninth International Conference of American States, at Bogotá, Colombia, of the Charter of the Organization of American States. This co-ordinated the work of all the former independent official entities in the inter-American system and defined their mutual relationships. The purpose of the OAS is to achieve an order of peace and justice, promote American solidarity, strengthen collaboration among the member states and defend their sovereignty, territorial integrity and independence. The OAS is a regional agency of the United Nations.

Membership is on a basis of absolute equality. Each country has one vote in the Council of the Organization and its organs. The member countries are: Argentina, Barbados (admitted on 15 Nov. 1967), Bolivia, Brazil, Chile, Colombia, Costa Rica, Cuba, Dominican Republic, Ecuador, El Salvador, Guatemala, Haiti, Honduras, Jamaica (admitted on 20 Aug. 1969), Mexico, Nicaragua, Panama, Paraguay, Peru, Trinidad and Tobago (admitted on 17 March 1967), USA, Uruguay, Venezuela. Two years have to elapse for ratification of a withdrawal of membership.

Without neglecting its responsibilities in the area of peace and security, the OAS has been concerned increasingly in recent years with programmes to promote Latin American economic and social development. The OAS currently provides specialized training for about 3,000 Latin Americans each year in a wide variety of development-related fields. It also sends some 70 missions per year in response to requests from member governments for advisory services.

On 27 Feb. 1967 the Third Special Inter-American Conference in Buenos Aires approved the Protocol of Amendment to the Charter of the OAS, which contained new standards for inter-American co-operation and a number of structural changes in the Organization.

On 14 April 1967 the Declaration of the Presidents of America, signed in Punta del Este, Uruguay, expressed the commitment of the American chiefs of state to promote Latin American economic integration; to join in efforts to increase substantially Latin American foreign-trade earnings; to modernize the living conditions of the rural population and raise agricultural productivity; and to expand programmes in education, science, technology and health.

On 24 Sept. 1967 the Twelfth Meeting of Consultation condemned the present government of Cuba 'for its repeated acts of aggression and intervention against Venezuela and for its persistent policy of intervention in the internal affairs of

Bolivia and of other American states' and appealed to non-member states to co-operate in the trade embargo against Cuba.

On 22 Feb. 1968, in the Resolution of Maracay, the Inter-American Cultural Council launched new regional programmes for educational development and for scientific and technological development.

On 27 Feb. 1970, by ratification of more than the mandatory two-thirds of the OAS member states, the Protocol of Buenos Aires, modifying the 1948 Charter, entered into effect.

Under the amended Charter, the OAS accomplishes its purposes by means of:

(a) The *General Assembly*, which takes the place of the Inter-American Conference and meets annually in various countries of the member states.

(b) The *Meeting of Consultation of Ministers of Foreign Affairs*, held to consider problems of an urgent nature and of common interest. It is assisted by an *Advisory Defence Committee*, composed of the highest military authorities in the member countries and meeting whenever it is considered advisable to study questions of collective self-defence.

(c) Three councils of equal rank: the *Permanent Council*, which replaces the old OAS Council; the *Inter-American Economic and Social Council*; and the *Inter-American Council for Education, Science and Culture*. Functions are to direct and co-ordinate work in the areas of their competence and render the governments such specialized services as they may request. Each council is composed of 1 representative from each member state, appointed by his government.

(d) The *Inter-American Juridical Committee*, taking the place of the Inter-American Council of Jurists, acts as an advisory body to the OAS on juridical matters and promotes the development and codification of international law. Eleven jurists, elected every 4 years by the General Assembly, represent all the American States.

(e) The *Inter-American Commission on Human Rights* oversees the observance and protection of human rights and serves as a consultative organ of the OAS. Six members represent all the OAS member states.

(f) The *General Secretariat*, formerly the Pan American Union, the central and permanent organ of the OAS.

(g) The *Specialized Conferences*, meeting to deal with special technical matters or to develop specific aspects of inter-American co-operation.

(h) The *Specialized Organizations*, intergovernmental organizations established by multilateral agreements to discharge specific functions in their respective fields of action, such as women's affairs, agriculture, child welfare, Indian affairs, geography and history, and health.

Secretary-General: Galo Plaza (Ecuador).
Assistant Secretary-General: M. Rafael Urquía (El Salvador).
Assistant Secretaries: Walter Sedwitz (USA), *Economic and Social Affairs*; Rodolfo Martínez (Argentina), *Education, Science and Culture*; Stuart Portner (USA), *Management*; João Gonçalves de Souza (Brazil), *Technical Co-operation*.

Departmental Directors. Economic Affairs: Nicholas A. Barletta (Panama). *Social Affairs:* Theo Crevenna (USA). *Legal Affairs:* Francisco V. Garcia Amador (Cuba). *Cultural Affairs:* Borceló J. Malagón (Mexico). *Information and Public Affairs:* Raúl Nass (Venezuela). *Statistics:* Tulo H. Montenegro (Brazil). *Administrative Affairs:* Reinaldo C. Santós (USA). *Scientific Affairs:* Jesse Perkinson (USA). *Educational Affairs:* Francisco Céspedes (Panama).

Office Directors—Secretariat of the Inter-American Conference, the Meeting of Consultation and the Council of the Organization: Santiago Ortiz (USA). *Financial Services:* (Vacant). *Publication Services:* John A. McAdams (USA).

The Secretary-General and the Assistant Secretary-General are elected by the Council of the Organization for 5-year terms. The Secretary-General appoints the Department Directors as well as the lesser personnel of the Union. The Council approves the annual budget for the Organization, which is financed by quotas contributed by the member governments.

General Secretariat: Washington, D.C. 20006, USA.

Books of Reference

Publications of the OAS General Secretariat include:

Charter of the Organization of American States. 1948.—*As amended by the Protocol of Buenos Aires in 1967*
Americas. Illustrated monthly, from 1948 (Spanish, Portuguese and English edition)
Organization of American States, a Handbook. Rev. ed. 1971
Organization of American States. Directory. Monthly, from 1951
The Organization of American States and the United Nations. 3rd ed. 1955
Report on the Tenth Inter-American Conference, Caracas 1954. 1955
Inter-American Review of Bibliography. Quarterly, from 1951
Bibliography of Selected Statistical Sources of the American Nations. 1955–57
Annual Report of the Secretary-General
Inter-American Status of Treaties and Conventions. 1969
The Alliance for Progress. From 1962
Human Rights in the American States. 1960
Report of Inter-American Peace Committee to Council of OAS. 1963
Economic Survey of Latin America, 1962. 1964
The OAS Chronicle. Bi-monthly from Aug. 1965

Publications on Latin America (*see also* the bibliographical notes appended to each country):

Revenue, Expenditure and Public Debts of the Latin American Republics. Division of Financial Information, US Department of Commerce. Annual
Fortnightly [from July 1960 also *Quarterly*] *Review of Business and Economic Conditions in South and Central America.* Bank of London and South America. London, 1935–66; restyled *B.O.L.S.A. Review,* from Jan. 1967
Boundaries of the Latin American Republics: An Annotated List of Documents, 1493–1943. Department of State, Office of the Geographer. Washington, 1944
Latin America: an introduction to the basic books in English. 2nd. ed. Hispanic & Luso-Brazilian Councils, London, 1966
Statistical Abstract of Latin America. 6th ed. Univ. of California, 1963
Baerresen, D. W., and others, *Latin American Trade Patterns.* Washington, D.C., 1965
Bailey, H. M., and Nasatir, A. P., *Latin America: the Development of its Civilization.* London, 1960
Benham, F., and Holley, H. A., *The Economy of Latin America.* London, 1960
Burgin, M. (ed.), *Handbook of Latin American Studies.* Gainesville, Fla., 1935 ff.
Calvert, P., *Latin America: Internal Conflict and International Peace,* London, 1969
Davies, H. (ed.), *The South American Handbook.* London, 1924 to date
Ferguson, J. M., *Latin America: the balance of race redressed.* OUP, 1961
Gunther, J., *Inside South America.* New York, 1967
Hirschman, Albert O., *Latin American Issues:* [11] *essays and comments.* New York, 1961
Humphreys, R. A., *Latin American History: a guide to the literature in English.* London, 1958
James, P. E., *Latin America.* 3rd ed. New York, 1959
Karnes, T. L., *The Future of Union: Central America 1824–1960.* Univ. of N. Carolina, Chapel Hill, 1961
Kurzman, D., *The revolution of the damned.* New York, 1965
Manger, W., *Pan America in Crisis.* New York, 1961
Munro, D. G., *The Latin American Republics; a history.* London, 1961
Nehemkis, P., *Latin America: Myth and reality.* New York, 1964
Pendle, G., *A History of Latin America.* Rev. ed. Harmondsworth, 1967
Plaza, G., *The Organization of American States: Instrument for Hemispheric Development.* Washington, 1969
Steward, J. H. (ed.), *Handbook of the South American Indian.* 7 vols. Washington, 1946–59
Szulc, T., *Winds of revolution.* New York, 1965
Thomas, A. V. W. and A. J., *The Organization of American States.* Southern Methodist Univ. Press, 1963
Tovar, A., *Catálogo de las lenguas de América del Sur.* Buenos Aires, 1961
Ureña, P. H., *A concise history of Latin American culture.* London, 1966
Worcester, D. E., and Schaeffer, W. G., *The Growth and Culture of Latin America.* OUP, 1956

LATIN AMERICAN ECONOMIC GROUPINGS

The Economic Commission for Latin America, an organ of the United Nations, with headquarters in Santiago, Chile, has facilitated the co-operation of two groups of countries concerning production, tariffs and trade.

Latin American Free Trade Association was concluded in Montevideo on 18 Feb. 1961 by Argentina, Brazil, Chile, Mexico, Paraguay, Peru and Uruguay. Colombia

(3 Oct. 1961), Ecuador (20 Oct. 1961) and Venezuela (1 Sept. 1966) have joined the ALALC/LAFTA Treaty. The permanent secretariat is at Montevideo.

Central American Common Market (ODECA). On 13 Dec. 1960, at Managua, El Salvador, Guatemala, Honduras and Nicaragua concluded a general treaty on Central American integration; a protocol on the equalization of import duties and charges; and an agreement establishing the Central American Bank for Economic Integration. Costa Rica acceded in 1962 and in Sept. 1963 ratified the charter of the Banco Centroamericano de Integración Económica (in Tegucigalpa), whose capital was thereupon increased to US$20m.

The San Salvador Charter, signed on 14 Dec. 1962, expanded these provisions, envisaging permanent political, economic, educational, defence, etc., councils. The permanent secretariat is at Guatemala City.

Total intra-ODECA trade increased from US$8·6m. in 1960 to US$176m. in 1966. Total USA investments in the area are about $400m.

ALALC. *Boletín del Centro de Estadiscas Nacionales.* Montevideo, from April 1964 (quarterly)
British Bulletin of Publications on Latin America, the West Indies, Portugal and Spain. London, from June 1949 (half-yearly)
Libre Comercio. Revista oficial de la Asociación de Empresarios participantes de la ALALO. Montevideo. from June 1964 (monthly)
Furtado, C., *Economic Development of Latin America.* London, 1970
Committee on Latin America (COLA), *Latin American Economic and Social Serials.* London, 1969
Dell, S., *A Latin American Common Market.* OUP, 1966
UN Economic Commission for Latin America, *The Latin American Economy in 1967.* Washington, 1968
Wionczek, M. S. (ed.), *Latin American Economic Integration—Experiences and Prospects.* New York and London, 1966

THE ARAB LEAGUE

Origin. The formation of the League of Arab States in 1945 was largely inspired by the Arab awakening of the 19th century. This movement sought to recreate and reinregrate the Arab community which, though for 400 years a part of the Ottoman Empire, had preserved its identity as a separate national group held together by memories of a common past, a common religion and a common language, as well as by the consciousness of being part of a common cultural heritage. The leaders of the Arab movement in the 19th century and of the Arab revolt against Turkey in the First World War sought to achieve these aims through secession from the Ottoman Empire into a united and independent Arab state comprising all the Arab countries in Asia. However, the 1919 peace settlement divided the Arab world in Asia (with the exception of Saudi Arabia and the Yemen) into British and French spheres of influence and established in them a number of separate states and administrations (Syria, Lebanon, Iraq, Jordan and Palestine) under temporary mandatory control.

By 1943, however, all these countries, with the exception of Palestine, had substantially achieved their independence. An Arab conference therefore met in Alexandria in the autumn of 1944; it formulated the 'Alexandria Protocol', which delineated the outlines of the Arab League. It was found that neither a unitary state nor a federation could be achieved, but only a league of sovereign states. A covenant, establishing such a league, was signed in Cairo on 22 March 1945 by the representatives of Egypt, Iraq, Saudi Arabia, Syria, Lebanon, Jordan and Yemen. Libya joined the League in March 1953; the Sudan in Jan. 1956; Tunisia and Morocco in Oct. 1958; Kuwait in July 1961; Algeria on 16 Aug. 1962.

An annex to the Covenant provides for the co-operation with Arab countries outside the League, in the Arabian Peninsula and North Africa.

Organization. The machinery of the League consists of a Council, a number of Special Committees and a Permanent Secretariat. On the Council each state has one vote. The Council may meet in any of the Arab capitals. Its functions include mediation in any dispute between any of the League states or a League state and a country outside the League. The Council has a Political Committee consisting of the Foreign Ministers of the Arab states.

The Permanent Secretariat of the League, under a Secretary-General (with the status of ambassador), has its seat in Cairo.

The League considers itself a regional organization within the framework of the United Nations at which its secretary-general is an observer.

Secretary-General: Abdul Khaliq Hassouna, a former Egyptian Minister for Foreign Affairs (elected 14 Sept. 1952, re-elected in 1957 and 1962, for 5-year periods).

Arab Common Market. The Arab Common Market came into operation on 1 Jan. 1965. The agreement, reached in April 1964 and open to all the Arab League states, has been signed by Iraq, Jordan, Syria and UAR. The agreement provides for the abolition of customs duties on agricultural products and natural resources within 5 years, by reducing tariffs at an annual rate of 20%. Customs duties on industrial products are to be reduced by 10% annually. The agreement also provides for the free movement of capital and labour between member countries, the establishment of common external tariffs, the co-ordination of economical development and the framing of a common foreign economic policy.

BOOKS OF REFERENCE

Atlas of the Arab World and the Middle East. London and New York, 1960
Oxford Regional Economic Atlas: The Middle East and North Africa. OUP, 1960
Glubb, Sir John, *Britain and the Arabs.* London, 1956.
Macdonald, R. W., *The League of Arab States.* Princeton Univ. Press, 1965
Nuseibeh, H. Z., *The Ideas of Arab Nationalism.* Cornell Univ. Press, 1956

ORGANIZATION OF AFRICAN UNITY

On 25 May 1963 the heads of state or government of 30 African countries, at a conference in Addis Ababa, signed a charter establishing an 'Organization of African Unity' (*Organisation de l'Unité Africaine*).

Its chief objects are the furtherance of African unity and solidarity; the co-ordination of the political, economic, cultural, health, scientific and defence policies; the elimination of colonialism in Africa; and the common defence of the independence of the member states.

The organs of the Organization are: (1) the conference of the heads of state or government; (2) the council of foreign ministers; (3) the secretariat-general; (4) a commission of mediation, conciliation and arbitration. In addition to the African languages, French and English are recognized as official languages.

DANUBE COMMISSION

The convention, signed at Belgrade on 18 Aug.1948 by Bulgaria, Czechoslovakia, Hungary, Rumania, Ukraine, USSR and Yugoslavia, supersedes the Paris convention of 1921, on which the European Commission of the Danube (1856–1948) was eventually based. The Belgrade convention reaffirms free navigation on the Danube from Regensburg to Izmail, open to nationals, merchant vessels and trade of all countries, on a footing of equality.

In 1959 Austria and in 1963 West Germany acceded to the convention and joined the commission (West Germany as an associate member). USA, UK and France have refused to sign the convention because it does not safeguard their former rights. Headquarters of the commission was in 1949 transferred from Belgrade to Budapest.

EARTHQUAKES

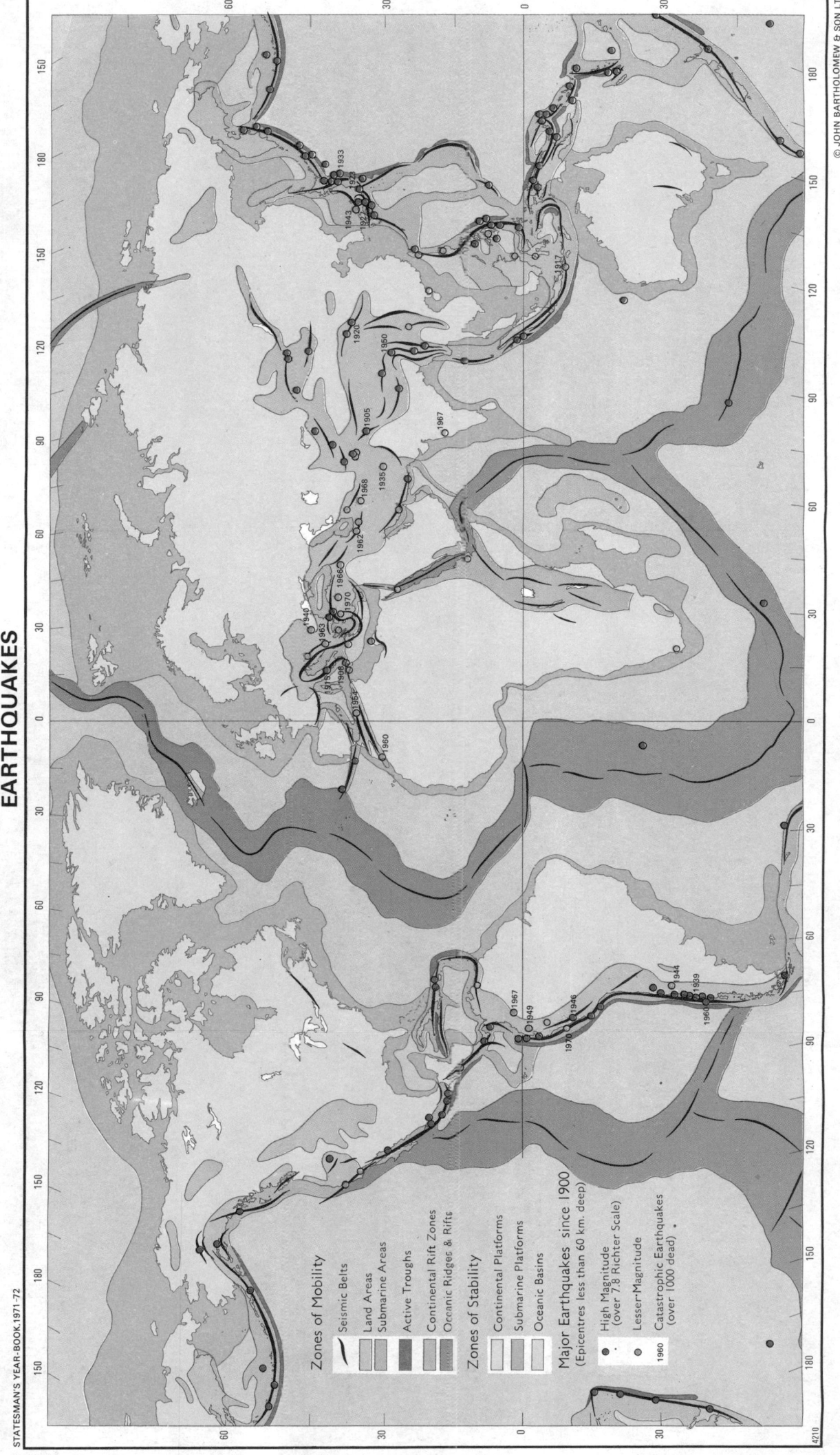

Zones of Mobility

Seismic Belts
Land Areas
Submarine Areas
Active Troughs
Continental Rift Zones
Oceanic Ridges & Rifts

Zones of Stability

Continental Platforms
Submarine Platforms
Oceanic Basins

Major Earthquakes since 1900
(Epicentres less than 60 km. deep)

High Magnitude
(over 7.8 Richter Scale)

Lesser Magnitude

1960 Catastrophic Earthquakes
(over 1000 dead)

1:110,000,000

PART II

THE COMMONWEALTH

THE COMMONWEALTH

REIGNING QUEEN, HEAD OF THE COMMONWEALTH

Elizabeth II Alexandra Mary, born 21 April 1926 daughter of King George VI and Queen Elizabeth; married on 20 Nov. 1947 Lieut. Philip Mountbatten (formerly Prince Philip of Greece), created Duke of Edinburgh, Earl of Merioneth and Baron Greenwich on the same day and created Prince Philip, Duke of Edinburgh, 22 Feb. 1957; succeeded to the crown on the death of her father, on 6 Feb. 1952. Offspring: *Charles* Philip Arthur George, Prince of Wales, born 14 Nov. 1948 (Heir Apparent); Princess *Anne* Elizabeth Alice Louise, born 15 Aug. 1950; Prince *Andrew* Albert Christian Edward, born 19 Feb. 1960; Prince *Edward* Antony Richard Louis, born 10 March 1964.

The Queen Mother: Queen Elizabeth, born 4 Aug. 1900, daughter of the 14th Earl of Strathmore and Kinghorne; married the Duke of York, afterwards King George VI, on 26 April 1923.

Sister of the Queen: Princess Margaret Rose, born 21 Aug. 1930; married Antony Armstrong-Jones (created Earl of Snowdon, 3 Oct. 1961) on 6 May 1960. Offspring: *David* Albert Charles (Viscount Linley), born 3 Nov. 1961; Lady Sarah Frances Elizabeth Armstrong-Jones, born 1 May 1964.

Living Uncles of the Queen: Prince *Edward* Albert, created Duke of Windsor 12 Dec. 1936, born 23 June 1894; married Mrs Wallis Warfield on 3 June 1937. Reigned as Edward VIII from 20 Jan. 1936 to 10 Dec. 1936.

Prince *Henry* William, born 31 March 1900; created Duke of Gloucester, Earl of Ulster and Baron Culloden, on 31 March 1928; married Lady Alice Montagu-Douglas-Scott (born 25 Dec. 1901), 6 Nov. 1935. Offspring: *William* Henry Andrew Frederick, born 18 Dec. 1941; *Richard* Alexander Walter George, born 26 Aug. 1944.

Children of the late Duke of Kent (died 25 Aug. 1942): Edward George Nicholas Patrick, Duke of Kent, born 9 Oct. 1935; married Katharine Worsley on 8 June 1961 (offspring: George Philip Nicholas, Earl of St Andrews, born 26 June 1962; Lady Helen Windsor, born 28 April 1964; Lord Nicholas Charles Edward Jonathan Windsor, born 25 July 1970). Alexandra Helen Elizabeth Olga Christabel, born 25 Dec. 1936; married 24 April 1963, Angus Ogilvy (offspring: James Robert Bruce, born 29 Feb. 1964; Marina Victoria Alexandra, born 31 July 1966). Michael George Charles Franklin, born 4 July 1942.

Children of the late Princess Royal (died 28 March 1965): George Henry Hubert, 7th Earl of Harewood, born 7 Feb. 1923; married Marion Stein on 29 Sept. 1949; divorced on 6 April 1967; remarried Patricia Tuckwell on 31 July 1967 (offspring: David Henry George, Viscount Lascelles, born 21 Oct. 1950; James Edward Lascelles, born 5 Oct. 1953; Robert Jeremy Hugh Lascelles, born 14 Feb. 1955; Mark Hubert Lascelles, born 5 July 1964); Gerald David Lascelles, born 21 Aug. 1924; married Angela Dowding on 15 July 1952 (offspring: Henry Ulick Lascelles, born 19 May 1953).

The Queen's legal title rests on the statute of 12 and 13 Will. III, c. 3, by which the succession to the Crown of Great Britain and Ireland was settled on the Princess Sophia of Hanover and the 'heirs of her body being Protestants'. By proclamation of 17 July 1917 the royal family became known as the House and Family of Windsor. On 8 Feb. 1960 the Queen issued a declaration varying her confirmatory declaration of 9 April 1952 to the effect that while the Queen and her children should continue to be known as the House of Windsor, her descendants, other than descendants entitled to the style of Royal Highness and the title of Prince or Princess, and female descendants who marry and their descendants should bear the name of Mountbatten-Windsor. Under the Abdication Act of 1936, the issue, if any, of King Edward VIII, or the descendants of that issue, have no right, title or interest in or to the succession to the Throne, and the Royal Marriages Act, 1772, ceased to apply to King Edward VIII after his abdication. The titles of Queen Elizabeth II are: In the United Kingdom, the Associated States, and the Dependent Territories: 'Elizabeth the Second, by the Grace of God, of the United Kingdom of Great Britain and Northern Ireland and of Her other Realms and Territories Queen, Head of the Commonwealth, Defender of the Faith'. In Canada, Australia and New Zealand: 'Elizabeth the Second, by the Grace of God of the United Kingdom, [name of country] and Her other Realms and Territories Queen, Head of the Commonwealth, Defender of the Faith'. In Ceylon, Mauritius, Fiji and Sierra Leone, 'Elizabeth the Second, Queen of [name of country] and of Her other Realms and Territories, Head of the Commonwealth'. In Trinidad and Tobago, Malta, Guyana and Barbados 'Elizabeth the Second, by the Grace of God, Queen of [name of country] and of Her other Realms and Territorities, Head of the Commonwealth'. In Jamaica, 'Elizabeth the Second, by the Grace of God, of Jamaica and of her other Realms and Territories, Queen, Head of the Commonwealth'. In The Gambia, 'Elizabeth the Second, Queen of The Gambia, and all Her other Realms and Territories, Head of the Commonwealth'. In India, Pakistan, Malaysia, Cyprus, Ghana, Nigeria, Uganda, Zambia, Tanzania, Kenya, Singapore, Malawi, Botswana, Lesotho, Swaziland and Nauru: 'Head of the Commonwealth'.

By letters patent of 30 Nov. 1917 the titles of Royal Highness and Prince or Princess are restricted to the Sovereign's children, the children of the Sovereign's sons and the eldest living son of the eldest son of the Prince of Wales.

Provision is made for the support of the royal household by the settlement of the Civil List soon after the beginning of each reign. (For historical details, *see* THE STATESMAN'S YEAR-BOOK, 1908, p. 5, and 1935, p. 4.) According to the Civil List Act of 1 Aug. 1952, the Civil List of the Queen, after the usual surrender of hereditary revenues, was fixed at £475,000, of which £60,000 is appropriated to the privy purse of the Queen, £185,000 for which £60,000 is appropriated to the privy purse of the Queen, £185,000 for salaries of the royal household, £121,800 for household expenses, £13,200 for alms and bounty and £95,000 as supplementary provision. The Acts also provides for £40,000 a year to the Duke of Edinburgh.

The Civil List Acts of 1910, 1937 and 1952 provide for an annuity of £70,000 to Queen Elizabeth (the Queen Mother); £35,000 to the Duke of Gloucester; £15,000 to the Princess Margaret.

Sovereigns of Great Britain, from the Restoration (with dates of accession):

House of Stewart		George III	25 Oct. 1760
Charles II	29 May 1660	George IV	29 Jan. 1820
James II	6 Feb. 1685	William IV	26 June 1830
		Victoria	20 June 1837
House of Stewart-Orange			
William and Mary	13 Feb. 1689	*House of Saxe-Coburg and Gotha*	
William III	28 Dec. 1694	Edward VII	22 Jan. 1901
House of Stewart		*House of Windsor*	
Anne	19 March 1702	George V	6 May 1910
House of Hanover		Edward VIII	20 Jan. 1936
George I	1 Aug. 1714	George VI	11 Dec. 1936
George II	11 June 1727	Elizabeth II	6 Feb. 1952

THE COMMONWEALTH

CONSTITUTION. The Commonwealth is a free association of the United Kingdom, Canada, Australia, New Zealand, India, Pakistan, Ceylon, Ghana, Nigeria, Cyprus, Sierra Leone, Jamaica, Trinidad and Tobago, Uganda, Kenya, Malaysia, Tanzania, Malawi, Malta, Zambia, The Gambia, Singapore, Guyana, Botswana, Lesotho, Barbados, Mauritius, Swaziland, Tonga, Western Samoa, Nauru and their dependent territories.

Up to July 1925 the affairs of all the British Empire, apart from the United Kingdom and India, were dealt with by the Colonial Office. From that month a new secretaryship of state, for Dominion Affairs, became responsible for the relations between the United Kingdom and all the independent members of the Commonwealth.

In July 1947 the designations of the Secretary of State for Dominion Affairs and the Dominions Office were altered to 'Secretary of State for Commonwealth Relations' and 'Commonwealth Relations Office'. The following month, on the independence of India and Pakistan, the India Office ceased to exist and the staff were transferred to the Commonwealth Relations Office, which then became responsible for relations with India and Pakistan.

The Colonial Office was merged with the Commonwealth Relations Office on 1 Aug. 1966 to form the Commonwealth Office, and the post of Secretary of State for Commonwealth Relations became Secretary of State for Commonwealth Affairs. The post of Secretary of State for the Colonies was retained until 6 Jan. 1967. The Commonwealth Office was merged with the Foreign Office on 17 Oct. 1968.

The Secretary of State for Foreign and Commonwealth Affairs is now responsible for relations with the independent members of the Commonwealth, Nauru and the Associated States, for the administration of the UK dependent territories, and for relations with the protected states of Brunei and Tonga in addition to his responsibilities for relations with foreign countries.

On 18 April 1949, when the Republic of Ireland Act 1948 came into force, Southern Ireland ceased to be a member of the Commonwealth.

MEMBER STATES. The Imperial Conference of 1926 defined Great Britain and the Dominions, as they were then called, as 'autonomous communities within the British Empire, equal in status, in no way subordinate one to another in any aspect of their domestic or foreign affairs, though united by a common allegiance to the Crown, and freely associated as members of the British Commonwealth of Nations'. On 11 Dec. 1931 the Statute of Westminster, which by legal enactment recognized the status of the Dominions as defined in 1926, became law. Each of the Dominions, which then included Canada, Australia, New Zealand, South Africa and Newfoundland (which in 1949 became a Canadian Province) had signified approval of the provisions of the Statute.

India and Pakistan became independent on 15 Aug. 1947; Ceylon on 4 Feb. 1948; Ghana (formerly the Gold Coast) on 6 March 1957; the Federation of Malaya on 31 Aug. 1957 (renamed the Federation of Malaysia on 16 Sept. 1963, including from that date North Borneo, Sarawak and Singapore until 9 Aug. 1965 when Singapore became a separate independent state); Nigeria on 1 Oct. 1960; Cyprus on 16 Aug. 1960; Sierra Leone on 27 April 1961; Tanganyika on 9 Dec. 1961 (renamed United Republic of Tanzania on 25 April 1964 when she joined with Zanzibar, which had become independent on 10 Dec. 1963); Jamaica on 6 Aug. 1962; Trinidad and Tobago on 31 Aug. 1962; Uganda on 9 Oct. 1962; Western Samoa on 28 Aug. 1970; Kenya on 12 Dec. 1963; Malawi (formerly Nyasaland) on 6 July 1964; Malta on 21 Sept. 1964; Zambia (formerly Northern Rhodesia) on 24 Oct. 1964; The Gambia on 18 Feb. 1965; Guyana (formerly British Guiana) on 26 May 1966; Botswana (formerly Bechuanaland) on 30 Sept. 1966; Lesotho (formerly Basutoland) on 4 Oct. 1966; Barbados on 30 Nov. 1966; Mauritius on 12 March 1968; Swaziland on 6 Sept. 1968; Nauru on 31 Jan. 1968; Tonga on 4 June 1970; Fiji on 10 Oct. 1970. All became members of the Commonwealth on independence, except Cyprus and Western Samoa which joined on 13 March 1961 and 28 Aug. 1970 respectively.

India became a republic on 26 Jan. 1950, Pakistan on 23 March 1956, Ghana on 1 July 1960, Cyprus on 16 Aug. 1960, Tanganyika on 9 Dec. 1962, Nigeria on 1 Oct. 1963, Uganda on 9 Oct. 1963, Tanzania (on the unification of Tanganyika and Zanzibar) on 26 April 1964, Singapore on 9 Aug. 1965, Malawi on 6 July 1966, Botswana on 30 Sept. 1966, Nauru on 31 Jan. 1968, Guyana on 23 Feb. 1970 and The Gambia on 24 April 1970. They accept the Queen as the symbol of the free association of its independent member nations and as such Head of the Commonwealth.

On 4 Jan. 1948 Burma became an independent republic outside the Commonwealth.

South Africa withdrew from the Commonwealth on becoming a republic on 31 May 1961.

To cater for the special circumstances of Nauru, a 'special membership' of the Commonwealth has been devised in close consultation with the independent Government of Nauru.

Nauru has the right to participate in all functional activities of the Commonwealth and to receive appropriate documentation in relation to them as well as the right to participate in non-Governmental Commonwealth organizations. Nauru is not represented at meetings of Commonwealth Heads of Government, but may attend Commonwealth meetings at ministerial or official level in such fields as education, medical co-operation, finance and other functional and technical areas as the Nauruan Government desires. It is eligible for Commonwealth technical assistance.

ASSOCIATED STATES. The Caribbean islands of Antigua, St Christopher–Nevis–Anguilla, Dominica, Grenada and St Lucia entered into a new form of association with Britain in Feb. 1967. St Vincent became an associated state on 27 Oct. 1969. Each has control of its internal affairs, with the right to amend its own constitution (including the power to end the associated status and declare itself independent). Britain continues to be responsible for external affairs and defence.

DEPENDENT TERRITORIES. Territories dependent on the United Kingdom comprise dependent territories (properly so-called), protectorates and protected states. A dependent territory is a territory belonging by settlement, conquest or annexation to the British Crown. A protectorate is a territory not formally annexed but in which, by treaty, grant and other lawful means the Crown has power and jurisdiction. A protected state is a territory under a ruler which enjoys Her Majesty's protection, over whose foreign affairs she exercises control, but in respect of whose internal affairs she does not exercise jurisdiction.

United Kingdom dependencies administered through the Foreign and Commonwealth Office comprise, in the Far East: Brunei (protected state), Hong Kong (dependent territory); in the Indian Ocean: British Indian Ocean Territory, Seychelles (dependent territories); in the Mediterranean: Gibraltar (dependent territory); in the Atlantic Ocean: Falkland Islands and St Helena (both dependent territories with dependencies); in the Caribbean: Bahamas, Bermuda, British Honduras, British Virgin Islands, Cayman Islands, Turks and Caicos Islands, Montserrat (dependent territories); in the Western Pacific: Pitcairn (dependent territory), British Solomon Islands (protectorate), Gilbert and Ellice Islands (dependent territory), New Hebrides (Anglo-French Condominium).

While constitutional responsibility to Parliament for the government of the colonial territories rests with the Secretary of State for Foreign and Commonwealth Affairs, the actual administration is carried out by the various territorial governments.

Commonwealth Secretariat. In the communiqué issued at the end of the Commonwealth Prime Ministers' Conference in July 1964, instructions were given for the preparation of proposals for the establishment of a Commonwealth Secretariat. These proposals were approved at the Commonwealth Prime Ministers' Conference in June 1965, and the first Secretary-General, Arnold Smith (Canada), took up his duties on 17 Aug. 1965.

BOOKS OF REFERENCE

Year-Book of the Commonwealth. HMSO, 1970
The Cambridge History of the British Empire. 8 vols. CUP, 1929 ff.
Economic Survey of the Colonial Territories. 7 vols. HMSO, 1952 ff.
Bradley, K. (ed.), *The Living Commonwealth.* London, 1961
Burns, Sir Alan, *In Defence of Colonies.* London, 1957
Casey, Lord, *The Future of the Commonwealth.* London, 1963
Crick, W. F. (ed.), *Commonwealth Banking Systems.* OUP, 1965
Hailey, Lord, *An African Survey.* Rev. ed. Oxford, 1957.—*Native Administration in the British African Territories.* 5 vols. HMSO, 1951 ff.
Jeffries, Sir C., *The Colonial Office.* London, 1956
Keeton, G. W. (ed.), *The British Commonwealth: its laws and constitutions.* 9 vols. London, 1951 ff.
Kuczynski, R. R., *Demographic Survey of the British Colonial Empire.* 3 vols. London, New York, Toronto, 1948–53
Mansergh, N., *The Commonwealth Experience.* London, 1969
Maxwell, W. H. and L. F., *A Legal Bibliography of the British Commonwealth of Nations.* 2nd ed. London, 1956
Patterson, A. D., *Handbook of Commonwealth Organizations.* London, 1965
Wade, E. C. S., and Phillips, G. G., *Constitutional Law: an outline of the law and practice of the constitution, including central and local government and the constitutional relations of the British Commonwealth and Empire.* 7th ed. London, 1965
Walker, P. Gordon, *The Commonwealth.* London, 1962
Wheare, K. C., *The Statute of Westminster and Dominion Status.* 5th ed. Oxford, 1953.—*Constitutional Structure of the Commonwealth.* Oxford, 1960
Wiseman, V. H., *The Cabinet in the Commonwealth.* London, 1958

GREAT BRITAIN AND NORTHERN IRELAND

CONSTITUTION AND GOVERNMENT

The supreme legislative power is vested in Parliament, which in its present form, as divided into two Houses of Legislature, the Lords and the Commons, dates from the middle of the 14th century.

Parliament is summoned by the writ of the sovereign issued out of Chancery, by advice of the Privy Council, at least 20 days previous to its assembling. Every session must end with a prorogation, and all Bills which have not been passed during the session then lapse. A dissolution may occur by the will of the sovereign, or, as is most usual, during the recess, by proclamation, or finally by lapse of time, the statutory limit of the duration of any Parliament being 5 years.

Under the Parliament Acts 1911 (1 and 2 Geo. V, ch. 13) and 1949 (12, 13 and 24 Geo. VI, ch. 103), all Money Bills (so certified by the Speaker of the House or Commons), if not passed by the House of Lords without amendment, may become law without their concurrence on the royal assent being signified. Public Bills, other than Money Bills or a Bill extending the maximum duration of Parliament, if passed by the House of Commons in 2 successive sessions, whether of the same Parliament or not, and rejected each time, or not passed, by the House of Lords, may become law without their concurrence on the royal assent being signified, provided that 1 year has elapsed between the second reading in the first session of the House of Commons and the third reading in the second session. All Bills coming under this Act must reach the House of Lords at least 1 month before the end of the session.

The House of Lords consists of: (1) hereditary peers and peeresses sitting by virtue of creation or descent, other than those who have disclaimed their titles for life under the provisions of the Peerage Act, 1963; (2) life peers being (*a*) 16 Lords of Appeal (active and retired), under the Appellate Jurisdiction Act, 1876, as amended; (*b*) (Jan. 1971) 195 life peers and peeresses under the Life Peerages Act, 1958: (3) 2 archbishops and 24 bishops (as long as they hold their sees). The full House consists of about 1,080, of whom about 100 are not in receipt of a writ of summons, and the average attendance is about 250; in 1970–71, 186 peers were in receipt of leave of absence.

The House of Commons consists of members representing county and borough constituencies. Persons under 21 years of age, Clergymen of the Church of England, Ministers of the Church of Scotland, Roman Catholic clergymen, civil servants, members of the regular armed forces, policemen and most judicial officers are disqualified from sitting in the House of Commons. No English or Scottish peer can be elected to the House of Commons unless he has disclaimed his title for life under the Peerage Act, 1963, but Irish peers and holders of courtesy titles are eligible. Under the Parliament (Qualification of Women) Act, 1918, women are also eligible.

In Aug. 1911 provision was first made for the payment of a salary of £400 per annum to members, other than those already in receipt of salaries as officers of the House, as Ministers or as officers of Her Majesty's household. As from Oct. 1964 the salaries of members are £3,250 per annum, with income-tax relief on expenses incurred in the course of parliamentary duties. A secretarial allowance of £500 came into effect in Oct. 1969. Members of the House of Lords are only entitled to recover expenses incurred for the purpose of attendance at sittings of the House, within a maximum of £6·50. for each day of attendance.

The Representation of the People Act, 1948, abolished the business premises and University franchises, and the only persons entitled to vote at Parliamentary elections are those registered as residents or as service voters. No person may vote in more than one constituency at a general election. Persons may apply on certain grounds to vote by post or by proxy.

All persons over 17 years old and not subject to any legal incapacity to vote and who are either British subjects or citizens of the Irish Republic are entitled to be included in the register of electors for the constituency containing the address at which they were residing on the qualifying date for the register and are entitled to vote at elections held during the period for which the register remains in force. The current register was published on 15 Feb. 1970.

Members of the armed forces, Crown servants employed abroad, and the wives accompanying their husbands, are entitled, if otherwise qualified, to be registered as 'service voters' provided they make a 'service declaration'. To be effective for a particular register, the declaration must be made on or before the qualifying date for that register.

The Representation of the People Act, 1969, abolished the occupier's qualification for voting in Local Government elections.

The Act of 1948 effected a redistribution of the constituencies in the United Kingdom. The number of constituencies in Great Britain must be not substantially greater or less than 613, in Scotland not less than 71, in Wales not less than 35 and in Northern Ireland 12. Every constituency returns a single member.

The House of Commons (Redistribution of Seats) Acts, 1944, 1949 and 1958, provided for the setting up of Boundary Commissions for England, Wales, Scotland and Northern Ireland. The Commissions are required to make general reports at intervals of not less than 3 and not more than 7 years and to submit reports from time to time with respect to the area comprised in any particular constituency or constituencies where some change appears necessary. Any changes giving effect to reports of the Commissions are to be made by Orders in Council laid before Parliament for approval by resolution of each House. The electorate of the United Kingdom and Northern Ireland in the register used at the election of 18 June 1970 numbered 39,384,364, of whom 32,769,792 were in England, 1,960,521 in Wales, 3,636,651 in Scotland and 1,017,400 in Northern Ireland.

The following is a table of the duration of Parliaments called since the accession of King Edward VII.

Reign	When met	When dissolved	Duration (years and days)	
Edward VII	13 Feb. 1906	10 Jan. 1910	3	328
Edward VII and George V	15 Feb. 1910	28 Nov. 1910	0	287
George V	31 Jan. 1911	25 Nov. 1918	7	301
,,	4 Feb. 1919	26 Oct. 1922	3	269

Reign	When met	When dissolved	Duration (years and days)	
George V	20 Nov. 1922	16 Nov. 1923	0	362
,,	8 Jan. 1924	9 Oct. 1924	0	276
,,	2 Dec. 1924	10 May 1929	4	161
,,	25 June 1929	7 Oct. 1931	2	75
,,	3 Nov. 1931	25 Oct. 1935	3	358
George V, Edward VIII and George VI	26 Nov. 1935	15 June 1945	9	205
George VI	1 Aug 1945	3 Feb. 1950	4	188
,,	1 Mar. 1950	5 Oct. 1951	1	219
George VI and Elizabeth II	31 Oct. 1951	6 May 1955	3	188
Elizabeth II	7 June 1955	18 Sept. 1959	4	105
,,	20 Oct. 1959	25 Sept. 1964	4	341
,,	27 Oct. 1964	10 Mar. 1966	1	134
,,	18 Apr. 1966	29 May 1970	4	81
,,	29 June 1970	—	—	—

The executive government is vested nominally in the Crown, but practically in a committee of Ministers, called the Cabinet, which is dependent on the support of a majority in the House of Commons.

The head of the Ministry is the Prime Minister, a position first constitutionally recognized, and special precedence accorded to the holder, in 1905. His colleagues in the Ministry are appointed on his recommendation, and he dispenses the greater portion of the patronage of the Crown.

Heads of the Administrations since 1908 (C. = Conservative, L = Liberal, Lab. = Labour, Nat. — National, Coal. = Coalition, Care. = Caretaker):

H. H. Asquith (L.)	8 Apr. 1908	N. Chamberlain (Nat.)	28 May 1937
H. H. Asquith (Coal.)	25 May 1915	W. S. Churchill (Coal.)	10 May 1940
D. Lloyd George (Coal.)	7 Dec. 1916	W. S. Churchill (Care.)	23 May 1945
A. Bonar Law (C.)	23 Oct. 1922	C. R. Attlee (Lab.)	26 July 1945
S. Baldwin (C.)	22 May 1923	W. S. Churchill (C.)	26 Oct. 1951
J. R. MacDonald (Lab.)	22 Jan. 1924	Sir Anthony Eden (C.)	6 Apr. 1955
S. Baldwin (C.)	4 Nov. 1924	H. Macmillan (C.)	10 Jan. 1957
J. R. MacDonald (Lab.)	5 June 1929	Sir Alec Douglas-Home (C.)	18 Oct. 1963
J. R. MacDonald (Nat.)	25 Aug. 1931	H. Wilson (Lab.)	16 Oct. 1964
S. Baldwin (Nat.)	7 June 1935	E. Heath (C.)	19 June 1970

In April 1971 the Government consisted of the following members:

(a) MEMBERS OF THE CABINET

1. *Prime Minister and First Lord of the Treasury and Minister for the Civil Service:* Right Hon, Edward Heath, MBE, MP, born 1916. (Salary £14,000 per annum.)

2. *Secretary of State for the Home Department:* Right Hon. Reginald Maudling, MP, born 1917. (£8,500.)

3. *Secretary of State for Foreign and Commonwealth Affairs:* Right Hon. Sir Alec Douglas-Home, KT, MP, born 1903. (£8,500.)

4. *Lord Chancellor:* Right Hon. The Lord Hailsham of St Marylebone, born 1907. (£14,500.)

5. *Chancellor of the Exchequer:* Right Hon. Anthony Barber, TD, MP, born 1920. (£8,500).

6. *Lord President of the Council and Leader of the House of Commons:* Right Hon. William Whitelaw, MC, MP, born 1918. (£8,500.)

7. *Secretary of State for Defence:* Right Hon. The Lord Carrington, KCMG, MC, born 1919. (£8,500.)

8. *Secretary of State for Social Services:* Right Hon. Sir Keith Joseph, Bt. MP, born, 1918. (£8,500.)

9. *Chancellor of the Duchy of Lancaster:* Right Hon. Geoffrey Rippon, QC, MP, born 1924. (£8,500.)

10. *Secretary of State and Secretary of State for Employment:* Right Hon. Robert Carr, MP, born 1916. (£8,500.)

11. *Secretary of State for Education and Science:* Right Hon. Margaret Thatcher, MP, born 1925. (£8,500).

12. *Secretary of State for Scotland:* Right Hon. Gordon Campbell, MC, MP, born 1921. (£8,500.)

13. *Lord Privy Seal and Leader of the House of Lords:* Right Hon. The Earl Jellicoe, DSO, MC, born 1918. (£8,500.)

14. *Secretary of State for the Environment:* Right Hon. Peter Walker, MBE, MP, born 1932. (£8,500.)

15. *Secretary of State for Wales:* Right Hon. Peter Thomas, QC, MP, born 1920. (£8,500.)

16. *Minister of Agriculture, Fisheries and Food:* Right Hon. James Prior, MP, born 1927. (£8,500.)

17. *Secretary of State for Trade and Industry and President of the Board of Trade:* Right Hon. John Davies, MBE, MP, born 1916. (£8,500.)

(b) MINISTERS NOT IN THE CABINET

18. *Minister of Posts and Telecommunications:* Right Hon. Christopher Chataway, MP, born 1931. (£8,500.)

19. *Paymaster-General:* Right Hon. The Viscount Eccles, KCVO, born 1904. (£7,625.)

20. *Minister for Trade:* Right Hon. Michael Noble, MP, born 1913. (£5,625.)

21. *Minister Aerospace:* Right Hon. Frederick Corfield, MP, born 1915. (£8,500).

22. *Minister of Overseas Development:* Right Hon. Richard Wood, MP, born 1920. (£8,500.)

23. *Minister of Housing and Construction:* Right Hon. Julian Amery, MP, born 1919. (£8,500.)

24. *Minister for Transport Industries:* Right Hon. John Peyton, MP, born 1919. (£8,500.)

25. *Minister for Local Government and Development:* Graham Page, MBE, MP, born 1911. (£5,625.)

26. *Minister for Industry:* Sir John Eden, MP, born 1925. (£5,625.)

27. *Minister of State, Home Office:* Richard Sharples, OBE, MC, MP, born 1916. (£5,625.)

28. *Minister of State, Home Office:* The Lord Windlesham, born 1932. (£5,625.)

29. *Minister of State for Foreign and Commonwealth Affairs:* Right Hon. Joseph Godber, MP, born 1914. (£7,625.)

30. *Chief Secretary of the Treasury:* Maurice Macmillan, MP, born 1921. (£7,625.)

31. *Parliamentary Secretary, Treasury (Chief Whip):* Right Hon. Francis Pym, MC, MP, born 1922. (£5,625.)

32. *Financial Secretary, Treasury:* Patrick Jenkin, MP, born 1926. (£5,625.)

33. *Minister of State, Treasury:* Terence Higgins, MP, born 1928. (£5,625.)

34. *Minister of State, Defence:* The Lord Balniel, MP, born 1927. (£7,625.)

35. *Minister of State for Defence Procurement:* Ian Gilmour, born 1927. (£7,625.)

36. *Minister of State, Department of Health and Social Security:* The Lord Aberdare, born 1919. (£5,625.)

37. *Minister of State, Department of Employment:* Paul Bryan, DSO, MC, MP, born 1913. (£5,625.)

38. *Minister of State, Scottish Office:* The Baroness Tweedsmuir of Belhelvie, born 1915. (£5,625.)

39. *Minister of State, Welsh Office:* David Gibson-Watt, MC, MP, born 1918. (£5,625.)

40. *Minister without Portfolio:* Right Hon. The Lord Drumalbyn, born 1908. (£5,625.)

(c) LAW OFFICERS

41. *Attorney-General:* Right Hon. Sir Peter Rawlinson, QC, MP, born 1919. (£13,000.)

42. *Lord Advocate:* Right Hon. Norman Wylie, QC, MP, born 1923. (£8,000.)

43. *Solicitor-General:* Sir Geoffrey Howe, QC, MP, born 1926. (£9,000.)

44. *Solicitor-General for Scotland:* Daniel Brand, QC, born 1924. (£5,625.)

Leader of the Opposition in the House of Commons: Right Hon. Harold Wilson, OBE, MP, born 1916. (£4,500.)

Leader of the Opposition in the House of Lords: Right Hon. The Lord Shackleton, OBE, born 1911. (£2,000.)

The constitution of the House of Commons after the general election held on 18 June 1970 was as follows: Conservative, 330; Labour, 287; Liberal, 6; Others, 6; Speaker, 1; total, 630. The numbers of votes cast were, Conservative, 13,144,692 (46% of poll); Labour, 12,179,166 (43%); Liberals, 2,117,638 (7·5%); Others, 903,311 (3·2%).

By the end of April 1971 the number of seats held by the political parties in Parliament remained unchanged.

Butler, D. E., and Freeman, J., *British Political Facts 1900–1968*. London, 1969
Butler, D. E., and Pinto-Duschinsky, M., *The British General Election of 1970*. London, 1971
Craig, F. W. S. *British Parliamentary Election Statistics 1918–1968*. Glasgow, 1968
Ford, P. and G., *A Guide to Parliamentary Papers*. New ed. OUP, 1956
Gordon Walker, P., *The Cabinet*. London, 1970
Jennings, Sir I., *Cabinet Government*. 3rd ed. CUP, 1959.—*The British Constitution*. 5th ed. CUP, 1966.—*Parliament*. 2nd ed. CUP, 1957.—*Party Politics*. 3 vols. CUP, 1960–62
Jones, J. M., *British Nationality Law*. Rev. ed. London, 1955
King, A., *The British Prime Minister*. London, 1969
McKenzie, R. T., *British Political Parties*. 2nd ed. London, 1963
Mackintosh, J. P., *The British Cabinet*. London, 1962
May, Sir T. E., *Treatise on the Law, Privileges, Proceedings and Usage of Parliament*. 18th ed. London, 1971
Mitchell, B. R., and Boehm, K. H., *British Parliamentary Elections, 1950–64*. CUP, 1966
Taylor, E., *The House of Commons at Work*. 7th ed. London, 1967
Wilding, N., and Laundy, P., *An Encyclopaedia of Parliament*. 2nd ed. London, 1961
Young, R., *The British Parliament*. London, 1962

Local Government

England and Wales. Local Administration is carried out by four different types of bodies, namely: (i) local branches of some central ministries, such as the Ministry of Social Security; (ii) local sub-managements of nationalized industries (coal, electricity, gas, public transport and the post office); (iii) specialist authorities such as the police and water conservation; and (iv) the system of *local government* described below. The phrase 'local government' has come to mean that part of the local administration conducted through elected councils.

Local Government—Outside London. There are six types of councils, namely parish, rural district, urban district, municipal borough, administrative county and county borough councils. Councillors are elected by their local electors for 3 years. In boroughs such elections are held annually by thirds. In counties and parishes they are elected triennially *en bloc*. In districts it is possible to have one system or the other. In addition, the councillors of counties and boroughs elect aldermen. Their number is one-third of the number of councillors; they hold office for 6 years, half retiring at 3-yearly intervals. Otherwise they have the same rights as councillors. The president of a borough council is called the mayor, or in a few famous or large places the lord mayor. The others are called chairmen. They are elected annually by their councils.

There are 79 county boroughs with populations ranging between about 1·1m. and 33,000. These are surrounded by the administrative counties but are not part of them. Within the 45 counties there are 227 boroughs and 449 urban districts; their populations vary from 120,000 to 500; save where several of them are clustered together they are embedded in, but are not part of the 409 rural districts, which cover 90% of the areas of most counties, and have populations of between 106,000 and 1,500. Every rural district is divided into parishes. There are 10,500 of them. Their populations vary from nil to 34,000, and only the 7,500 larger ones have parish councils.

A council has only those specific powers which have been conferred expressly upon it by Act of Parliament, and no more. The relationship between the different types of authority is therefore one of specialization, depending upon the powers deemed by parliament to be appropriate to its type, and not upon any hierarchical principle; each authority is free within the definition of its own powers to make what decisions its likes. The larger do not supervise the smaller, but in certain cases (mostly planning) there is a right of appeal to the government, which can also publicly inquire into complaints. Moreover, government sanction is required to borrow money and, in some cases, to sell land.

Councils are kept within the law by a system of public audit and in the last resort can be restrained from overstepping their powers by the courts.

Disregarding a few exceptions (such as the unclassified roads maintained by urban districts and municipal boroughs) the totality of Local Government functions may be classified into parish, rural district and county functions. In urban districts and boroughs (which contain no parishes) the council exercises the combined functions of the parish and the rural district. In county boroughs (which contain neither districts nor parishes) the council will exercise the functions of county, district and parish. The following is the threefold classification suggested above: *Parish functions.* Allotments, burial and cremation, halls and meeting places, facilities for exercise and recreation, public lighting, footpaths. *Rural District functions.* Aerodromes, civic restaurants, entertainment, housing, markets, refuse and sewerage. *County functions.* Welfare of children, old people, the physically handicapped and the infirm; primary, secondary and further educations; animal diseases, fire, inspection of food, drugs, weights and measures and shops, public health, highways (other than trunk and motor ways), libraries, vehicle registration, smallholdings and most important of all land-use planning. County Councils frequently delegate functions or parts of them to district and non-country borough councils.

Finance. The councils have since the Second World War been financed in roughly equal proportions by treasury grants, loans, rents and rates, though the grant element tends to rise. Grants and loans are wholly controlled by the government, which partly controls rents. The rate is the only local tax: it is levied on the annual value of property other than agricultural land. The total expenditure of the councils in 1968–69 was £5,920m., of which £1,597m. was on capital account.

The system has been criticized since 1943, and 3 commissions have investigated it with a view to reforms.

Greater London. Since 1965 the Metropolitan area, with a population of 7·76m., has had a Greater London Council (GLC) and has been subdivided into 32 London Boroughs. The 12 most central boroughs together with the ancient City of London form the Inner London Education Authority. In the outer 20 boroughs the borough is the education authority. The other functions listed above are differently divided between the GLC and the boroughs, in particular, the GLC deals with large-scale planning, major roads, ambulance and fire services, refuse disposal, major sewerage, land drainage and Thames flood prevention. The GLC and the boroughs all have housing functions, the boroughs being generally limited to operations in their own areas with the GLC operating over the whole of London and even wider by arrangement with expanding towns; the City is in most respects independent of the surrounding system, and has an ancient constitution and has powers respecting sanitation, police, bridges, justice, etc., in the City of London.

Scotland. A Local Government Act was passed for Scotland in 1889. The powers of local administration in counties formerly exercised by the Commissioners of Supply, the Justices and Road Trustees were either wholly or in part transferred to county councils, which took over their duties and responsibilities in 1890. By the Local Government (Scotland) Act, 1894, a local government board for

Scotland was constituted, and a parish council was established in every parish to take the place of the parochial boards. Their principal function was the administration of the poor laws, and in addition they exercised powers similar to those of the parish councils in England. There were 869 civil parishes in 1921. The Scottish Board of Health Act, 1919, transferred the powers and duties of the Local Government Board to the newly constituted Scottish Board of Health. The Reorganization of Offices (Scotland) Act, 1928, established the Department of the Secretary of Scotland, including the Department of Health for Scotland, which took the place of the Scottish Board of Health. In June 1962 the Scottish Development Department took over responsibility for local government affairs, and the Scottish Home and Health Department responsibility for social services, e.g., health, police and fire services.

Each burgh has a town council consisting of a provost or lord provost, bailies and councillors. The provost is the head of the Scottish municipality and holds office for 3 years. Bailies are selected by the councillors from among their own number; they act as magistrates and sit as such in police courts. There are in Scotland three principal kinds of burghs, numbering altogether 201: (1) royal burghs, i.e., burghs created by a charter of the Crown; (2) parliamentary burghs, which possess statutory constitutions almost identical with those of the royal burghs; (3) police burghs, constituted under a general Police Act. Burghs are classified according to functions as counties of cities (4), other large burghs (21) and small burghs (176). All burghs have town councils and their administration is regulated by the Burgh Police (Scotland), Town Councils (Scotland) and Local Government (Scotland) Acts or corresponding local Acts. The Local Government (Scotland) Act, 1929, abolished parish councils and transferred poor law and certain other functions to county councils and large burghs (with a population of 20,000 or more). The Act established elected district councils for the landward parts of counties. These councils have certain local powers, such as the acquisition of ground for public recreation, and can requisition for expenditure to a limited extent. The Social Work (Scotland) Act 1968 placed a general duty on county councils and large burghs to promote the social welfare of the people in their areas by making available advice, guidance and assistance and providing the necessary facilities, including residential and other accommodation. It also brought together in one statute the various duties and responsibilities of local authorities in relation to the care and social support of children, the elderly, the ill and the mentally or physically handicapped and others needing help.

The Local Government (Scotland) Act, 1947, consolidated with amendments the enactments relating to authorities for the purpose of local government in Scotland.

The total number of local government electors in Scotland was 3,659,244 in 1970.

Local Government in England. Cmnd 4584. HMSO, 1971
Report of the Royal Commission on Local Government in England. HMSO, 1969
Griffith, J. A. G., *Central Departments and Local Government.* London, 1966
Hart, W. O., *Introduction to the Law of Local Government and Administration.* 8th ed. London, 1968
Jackson, R., *The Machinery of Local Government in England and Wales.* London, 1966
Jackson, W. B., *The Structure of Local Government in England and Wales.* 5th ed. London, 1966
Smellie, K. B. S., *A History of Local Government.* 4th ed. London, 1968
Wiseman, H. V., *Local Government in England, 1958–69.* London, 1970

AREA AND POPULATION

Area (in sq. miles) and population at the census taken 23 April 1961:

Divisions	Area	Males	Females	Total
England	50,331	21,012,069	22,448,456	43,460,525
Wales (incl. Monmouthshire)	8,016	1,291,764	1,352,259	2,644,023
Scotland [2]	30,405	2,484,170	2,694,320	5,178,490
Isle of Man [2]	211	22,060	26,091	48,151
Channel Islands [2]	75	50,090	54,288	104,378
	89,038 [1]	24,860,153	26,575,414	51,435,567

[1] 230,609 sq. km.   [2] Preliminary figures.

Population at the 4 previous decennial censuses:

Divisions	1911	1921	1931	1951
England	33,649,571	35,230,225	37,359,045	41,159,213
Wales	2,420,921	2,656,474	2,158,374	2,598,675
Scotland	4,760,904	4,882,497	4,842,980	5,096,415
Isle of Man	52,016	60,284	49,308	55,253
Channel Islands	96,899	90,230	93,205	102,806
Army, Navy and Merchant Seamen abroad	145,729	256,811	434,532	—
Total	41,126,040	43,176,521	44,937,444	—

In 1961 in Wales and Monmouthshire 26,223 persons 3 years of age and upwards were able to speak Welsh only, and 629,779 able to speak Welsh and English: these totals represent 26% of the total population. In Scotland in 1961, 974 persons could speak Gaelic only, and 80,004 could speak Gaelic and English, totalling 1·5% of the population.

At the census of 1961, in England and Wales, there were 14,702,823 private families, occupying 14,647,922 dwellings.

The age distribution in 1967 of the population of England and Wales and Scotland was as follows (in 1,000):

Age-group	England and Wales	Scotland	Great Britain
Under 5	4,174	478	4,652
5 and under 10	3,747	462	4,209
10 ,, 15	3,284	411	3,695
15 ,, 20	3,549	404	3,953
20 ,, 25	3,552	374	3,926
25 ,, 35	5,914	603	6,517
35 ,, 45	6,102	625	6,727
45 ,, 55	6,203	629	6,832
55 ,, 65	5,812	603	6,415
65 ,, 70	2,220	229	2,449
70 ,, 75	1,652	166	1,818
75 ,, 85	1,808	171	1,979
85 and upwards	374	32	406
Total	48,391	5,187	53,577

At 30 June 1967 the estimated age distribution of the population of England and Wales was: between 0 and 14, 5,744,700 males, 5,406,400 females; 15 and under 70, 16,475,100 males, 16·88m. females; aged 70 and over, 1,342,500 males, 2,491,100 females.

Estimated total home population of Great Britain at 30 June:

	England and Wales [1]	Scotland [2]	Total of Great Britain
1967	48,390,800	5,186,600	53,577,400
1968	48,593,000	5,193,400	53,786,400
1969	48,826,800	5,194,700	54,021,500
1970	48,987,700	..	..

[1] The home population of England and Wales is the population of all types, actually in the country.
[2] Excluding merchant seamen overseas.

England and Wales

The census population of England and Wales 1801 to 1961:

Date of enumeration	Population	Pop. per sq. mile	Date of enumeration	Population	Pop. per sq. mile
1801	8,892,536	152	1881	25,974,439	445
1811	10,164,256	174	1891	29,002,525	497
1821	12,000,236	206	1901	32,527,843	558
1831	13,896,797	238	1911	36,070,492	618
1841	15,914,148	273	1921	37,886,699	649
1851	17,927,609	307	1931	39,952,377	685
1861	20,066,224	344	1951	43,757,888	750
1871	22,712,266	389	1961	46,104,548	791

There is only one other major country in Europe, Netherlands (population density 893 persons per sq. mile), which is more crowded than England and Wales.

Area (land and inland water) and population of the administrative counties and county boroughs in 1931, 1951 and 1961 (provisional figures) (for areas of administrative counties, etc., 1931, see THE STATESMAN'S YEAR-BOOK, 1950, p. 51):

	Area, 1961, including county boroughs [2]	Census population [1] Counties, including county boroughs		
		1931	1951	1961
ENGLAND				
Bedfordshire	302,940	220,525	311,937	380,837
Berkshire	463,830	311,453	403,141	504,154
Buckinghamshire	479,406	271,586	386,291	488,233
Cambridgeshire	315,166	140,004	166,887	190,384
Isle of Ely	239,950	77,698	89,049	89,180
Cheshire	649,519	1,087,655	1,258,507	1,368,979
Cornwall	868,256	317,968	345,442	342,301
Cumberland	973,147	263,151	285,338	294,303
Derbyshire	643,572	757,374	826,437	877,620
Devonshire	1,671,613	732,968	797,738	823,751
Dorsetshire	623,744	239,352	291,323	313,460
Durham	649,440	1,486,175	1,463,868	1,515,643
Essex	978,056	1,755,459	2,044,964	2,288,058
Gloucestershire	804,933	786,000	939,433	1,001,706
Hampshire	962,191	1,014,316	1,197,170	1,336,794
Isle of Wight	94,141	88,454	95,625	95,752
Herefordshire	538,924	111,767	127,159	130,928
Hertfordshire	404,526	401,206	609,775	832,901
Huntingdonshire	233,985	56,206	69,302	79,924
Kent	975,926	1,219,273	1,564,324	1,701,851
Lancashire	1,201,850	5,039,455	5,117,853	5,129,416
Leicestershire	532,389	541,861	631,077	682,568
Lincolnshire—				
The parts of Holland	267,847	92,330	101,555	103,327
The parts of Kesteven	462,100	110,060	129,785	134,842
The parts of Lindsey	974,438	422,199	474,482	505,427
London	74,898	4,397,003	3,347,956	3,200,484
Middlesex	148,687	1,638,728	2,269,315	2,234,543
Norfolk	1,314,332	504,940	548,062	561,071
Northamptonshire	585,149	309,474	359,690	398,005
Soke of Peterborough	53,463	51,839	63,791	74,758
Northumberland	1,292,040	756,782	798,424	821,243
Nottinghamshire	540,017	712,731	841,211	902,988
Oxfordshire	479,178	209,621	275,808	309,452
Rutlandshire	97,273	17,401	20,537	23,504
Shropshire	861,801	244,156	289,802	297,466
Somerset	1,032,325	475,142	551,453	599,046
Staffordshire	738,258	1,431,359	1,619,697	1,733,519
Suffolk, East	557,354	294,977	321,909	343,056
Suffolk, West	390,917	106,137	120,652	128,918
Surrey	461,833	1,180,878	1,602,509	1,731,042
Sussex, East	527,210	544,547	618,516	665,904
Sussex, West	405,348	222,995	322,792	411,613
Warwickshire	628,972	1,535,007	1,861,670	2,025,476
Westmorland	504,917	65,408	67,392	67,180
Wiltshire	860,611	303,373	386,692	422,985
Worcestershire	447,943	420,056	524,783	569,957
Yorkshire, East Riding	750,384	482,936	510,904	527,292
Yorkshire, North Riding	1,361,795	469,375	525,481	554,102
Yorkshire, West Riding	1,785,760	3,352,555	3,586,274	3,644,582
Total	32,212,352	37,794,003	41,159,213	43,460,525
WALES				
Anglesey	176,694	49,029	50,660	51,705
Breconshire	469,281	57,775	56,508	55,185
Caernarvonshire	364,108	120,829	124,140	121,767
Cardiganshire	443,189	55,184	53,278	53,648
Carmarthenshire	588,472	179,100	172,034	168,008
Denbighshire	427,977	157,648	170,726	174,151
Flintshire	163,707	112,889	145,279	150,082
Glamorganshire	523,244	1,225,177	1,202,581	1,229,728
Merionethshire	422,372	43,201	41,465	38,310
Monmouthshire	346,781	434,958	425,115	444,679
Montgomeryshire	510,110	48,473	45,990	44,165
Pembrokeshire	393,007	87,206	90,906	94,124
Radnorshire	301,165	21,323	19,993	18,471
Total Wales (13 counties)	5,130,107	2,158,374	2,598,675	2,644,023
Total—England and Wales	37,342,460	39,952,377	43,757,888	46,104,548

[1] The 1931 and 1951 populations refer to the area constituted at the 1931 and 1951 census.
[2] In statute acres.

The area and population of the county boroughs (C.B.) and the more important other boroughs, with populations of over 80,000, are given in the following table:

	Area in statute acres, 1961	Census population 1951	Census population 1961	Estimated population [1] June 1970
ENGLAND				
Aldridge-Brownhills	—	—	—	88,070
Barnsley (C.B.)	7,817	75,630	74,704	74 470
Barrow-in-Furness (C.B.)	11,002	67,476	64,927	63,510
Basildon	—	—	—	126,180
Bath (C.B.)	6,278	79,294	80,901	84,810
Birkenhead (C.B.)	8,616	142,501	141,813	141,410
Birmingham (C.B.)	51,147	1,112,685	1,107,187	1,084,180
Blackburn (C.B.)	8,088	111,218	106,242	100,010
Blackpool (C.B.)	8,609	147,194	153,185	150,000
Bolton (C.B.)	15,280	167,167	160,789	152,010
Bootle (C.B.)	3,057	74,977	82,773	79,780
Bournemouth (C.B.)	11,448	144,845	154,296	147,540
Bradford (C.B.)	25,525	292,403	295,922	291,960
Brighton (C.B.)	14,347	158,068	163,159	162,070
Bristol (C.B.)	26,350	442,994	437,048	426,370
Burnley (C.B.)	4,686	84,987	80,559	76,610
Burton-upon-Trent (C.B.)	4,219	49,167	50,751	50,600
Bury (C.B.)	7,433	58,838	60,149	67,880
Cambridge	10,060	81,500	95,527	100,010
Canterbury (C.B.)	4,798	27,795	30,415	33,150
Carlisle (C.B.)	6,092	67,798	71,101	71,410
Chester (C.B.)	4,660	48,237	59,268	61,490
Coventry (C.B.)	19,140	258,242	305,521	335,230
Darlington (C.B.)	6,469	84,886	84,184	84,340
Derby (C.B.)	8,116	141,267	132,408	220,130
Dewsbury (C.B.)	6,720	53,487	52,963	51,840
Doncaster (C.B.)	8,371	82,054	86,322	83,590
Dudley (C.B.)	4,328	64,463	62,965	182,420
Eastbourne (C.B.)	10,957	57,821	60,918	70,130
Exeter (C.B.)	9,035	75,513	80,321	93,340
Gateshead (C.B.)	4,560	115,039	103,261	100,060
Gillingham	8,315	70,676	72,910	90,900
Gloucester (C.B.)	5,294	67,280	69,773	90,110
Great Yarmouth (C.B.)	3,689	51,105	52,970	50,180
Grimsby (C.B.)	5,882	94,557	96,712	96,020
Halifax (C.B.)	14,080	98,404	96,120	93,220
Hastings (C.B.)	7,323	65,522	66,478	74,000
Havant and Waterloo	—	—	—	109,000
Huddersfield (C.B.)	14,080	129,026	130,652	129,840
Ipswich (C.B.)	9,957	107,418	117,395	121,930
Kingston upon Hull (C.B.)	14,421	299,105	303,261	290,270
Leeds (C.B.)	40,615	505,880	510,676	502,320
Leicester (C.B.)	16,985	285,181	273,470	276,690
Lincoln (C.B.)	7,518	70,333	77,077	74,760
Liverpool (C.B.)	27,810	788,659	745,750	667,000
Luton (C.B.)	8,773	110,381	131,583	161,410
Manchester (C.B.)	27,255	703,082	661,791	590,000
Newcastle upon Tyne (C.B.)	11,094	291,724	269,678	236,730
Northampton (C.B.)	6,201	104,432	105,421	122,790
Norwich (C.B.)	8,141	121,236	120,096	120,140
Nottingham (C.B.)	18,370	307,850	311,899	300,580
Oldham (C.B.)	6,392	121,266	115,346	108,080
Oxford (C.B.)	8,785	98,747	106,291	109,330
Plymouth (C.B.)	13,140	208,012	204,409	256,600
Poole	15,760	83,007	92,111	104,640
Portsmouth (C.B.)	9,249	233,545	215,077	211,790
Preston (C.B.)	6,357	121,367	113,341	100,140
Reading (C.B.)	9,105	114,196	119,937	127,310
Rochdale (C.B.)	9,556	88,429	85,787	87,720
Rotherham (C.B.)	9,255	82,341	85,478	86,360
St Helens (C.B.)	8,865	112,521	108,674	102,900
Salford (C.B.)	5,203	178,194	155,090	135,530
Sheffield (C.B.)	39,586	512,850	494,344	525,230
Slough	6,202	66,471	80,781	93,570
Solihull (C.B.)	20,189	67,979	95,977	111,050
Southampton (C.B.)	11,543	178,343	204,822	209,660
Southend-on-Sea (C.B.)	10,284	151,806	165,093	164,770
Southport (C.B.)	9,652	84,039	82,004	83,000
South Shields (C.B.)	4,676	106,598	109,521	104,600
Stockport (C.B.)	8,440	141,650	142,543	139,330
Stoke-on-Trent (C.B.)	21,209	275,115	265,306	270,800

[1] Home population.

	Area in statute acres, 1961	Census population 1951	Census population 1961	Estimated population [1] June 1970
ENGLAND—continued				
Sunderland (C.B.)	8,575	181,524	186,686	217,630
Sutton Coldfield	13,978	47,957	72,165	82,010
Swindon	6,359	69,028	91,739	98,110
Teesside (C.B.) [2]	—	—	—	411,200
Thurrock	40,552	82,106	114,263	127,870
Torbay [2] (C.B.)	—	—	—	104,000
Tynemouth (C.B.)	4,679	66,564	70,091	71,680
Wakefield (C.B.)	5,799	60,371	61,268	59,450
Wallasey (C.B.)	5,913	101,369	103,209	100,470
Walsall (C.B.)	8,780	114,535	118,498	184,430
Warley (C.B.) [3]	9,500	—	—	166,790
Warrington (C.B.)	4,520	80,735	75,964	70,300
West Bromwich (C.B.)	7,180	87,981	96,041	173,010
West Hartlepool (C.B.)	4,679	72,662	77,035	98,080
Wigan (C.B.)	5,083	84,560	78,690	79,300
Wolverhampton (C.B.)	9,126	162,672	150,825	263,580
Worcester (C.B.)	6,114	62,069	65,923	71,920
Worthing	—	—	—	84,130
York (C.B.)	6,933	105,415	104,392	107,150
WALES				
Cardiff (C.B.)	15,085	243,632	256,582	284,010
Merthyr Tydfil (C.B.)	17,760	61,142	59,039	56,130
Newport (Monmouth) (C.B.)	7,693	106,420	108,123	111,780
Rhondda	23,886	111,389	100,287	94,000
Swansea (C.B.)	21,600	160,988	167,322	170,870

[1] Home population.   [2] New authority, created 1968.   [3] New authority, created 1966.

The following table shows the distribution of the urban and rural population of England and Wales in 1931, 1951 and 1961.

	England and Wales	Population Urban districts [1]	Population Rural districts [1]	Percentage Urban [1]	Percentage Rural [1]
1931	39,952,377	31,951,918	8,000,459	80·0	20·0
1951	43,757,888	35,335,721	8,422,167	80·8	19·2
1961	46,071,604	36,838,442	9,233,162	80·0	20·0

As existing at each census.

Conurbations. These are aggregates of local-authority areas with high population densities. In June 1970 there were 7 in England and Wales, with a population of 16,373,220 (33·4% of total population). Excluding the London conurbation, their populations were: Tyneside, 835,030; W. Yorks., 1,725,470: S.E. Lancs., 2,429,420; Merseyside, 1,330,950; W. Midlands, 2,440,070; S.E. Wales, 1,942,750.

The municipal and parliamentary City of London, coinciding with the registration City of London, has an area of 677 acres. The registration County of London (the London for purposes of the census, the registration of births, deaths and marriages, and for poor law purposes), coinciding with the former administrative county, has an area of 74,898 acres, and nearly coincides with the collective area of the London parliamentary boroughs. The population of registration London, of the 'Outer Ring', and of 'Greater London' (the area covered by the City and Metropolitan police) at the dates of the census, was:

	1921	1931	1941	1961
Registration London	4,484,523	4,397,003	3,347,982	3,200,484
'Outer Ring'	3,003,859	3,818,670	5,000,041	4,982,066
'Greater London' [1]	7,488,382	8,215,673	8,348,023	8,182,550

[1] Area 461,885 acres (1961).

In June 1970 the estimated population of the Greater London conurbation was 7,612,280.

Greater London Boroughs. Estimated population in June 1970:

Barking	166,060	Croydon	327,180	Haringey	238,410
Barnet	313,080	Ealing	294,820	Harrow	206,060
Bexley	215,140	Enfield	262,690	Havering	252,130
Brent	278,500	Greenwich	226,130	Hillingdon	235,780
Bromley	301,820	Hackney	233,490	Hounslow	204,380
Camden	223,150	Hammersmith	187,980	Islington	227,340

C

Kensington and		Merton	181,460	Southwark	166,480
Chelsea	203,730	Newham	247,170	Sutton	182,260
Kingston upon		Redbridge	242,840	Waltham Forest	235,040
Thames	142,690	Richmond-on-		Wandsworth	317,410
Lambeth	321,260	Thames	174,550	Westminster	234,430
Lewisham	279,350	Tower Hamlets	284,690		

Census of England and Wales, 1961. HMSO, 1961–65
Royal Commission on Local Government in Greater London, Report. HMSO, 1960 (Cmnd. 1164)

Scotland

Area 29,796 sq. miles, including its islands, 186 in number, but excluding inland water 609 sq. miles.

Population (including military in the barracks and seamen on board vessels in the harbours) at the dates of each census:

Date of enumeration	Population	Pop. per sq. mile	Date of enumeration	Population	Pop. per sq. mile
1811	1,805,864	60	1891	4,025,647	135
1821	2,091,521	70	1901	4,472,103	150
1831	2,364,386	79	1911	4,760,904	160
1841	2,620,184	88	1921	4,882,497	164
1851	2,888,742	97	1931	4,842,980	163
1861	3,062,294	100	1951	5,096,415	171
1871	3,360,018	113	1961	5,179,344	174
1881	3,735,573	125			

The 1961 population included 2,484,170 males, 2,694,320 females.

The number of married persons in 1951 was 2,247,855 (1,112,007 males and 1,135,848 females), and widowed, 346,111 (96,391 males and 249,721 females).

There are 33 civil counties, as follows:

	Area in statute acres (1931)	Census population 1931	Census population 1951	Census population 1961	Estimated population [1] June 1967
1. Aberdeen	1,261,521	300,436	308,008	321,783	317,731
2. Angus	559,037	270,190	274,876	278,399	276,761
3. Argyll	1,999,472	63,050	63,361	59,390	58,525
4. Ayr	724,523	285,217	321,237	342,822	349,283
5. Banff	403,053	54,907	50,148	46,454	44,501
6. Berwick	292,535	26,612	25,086	22,437	21,304
7. Bute	139,658	18,823	19,283	15,170	12,832
8. Caithness	438,833	25,656	22,710	27,370	28,285
9. Clackmannan	34,927	31,948	37,532	41,394	42,932
10. Dumfries	686,302	81,220	85,660	88,440	87,809
11. Dunbarton	157,433	146,723	164,269	184,559	215,765
12. East Lothian	170,971	47,338	52,258	52,677	54,173
13. Fife	322,844	276,368	306,778	320,692	323,057
14. Inverness	2,695,094	82,108	84,930	83,480	84,333
15. Kincardine	244,482	39,865	47,403	48,810	25,451
16. Kinross	52,410	7,454	7,418	6,702	6,290
17. Kirkcudbright	575,832	30,168	30,725	28,870	28,569
18. Lanark	562,821	1,587,663	1,614,363	1,626,424	1,563,086
19. Midlothian	234,325	526,296	565,735	580,329	590,894
20. Moray	304,931	40,805	48,218	49,170	51,802
21. Nairn	104,252	8,294	8,719	8,423	8,176
22. Orkney	240,847	22,077	21,255	18,747	17,878
23. Peebles	222,240	15,051	15,232	14,156	13,502
24. Perth	1,595,802	120,793	128,029	127,056	124,963
25. Renfrew	153,332	287,991	324,660	338,872	356,840
26. Ross and Cromarty	1,977,248	62,799	60,508	57,642	56,914
27. Roxburgh	426,028	45,685	45,557	43,183	42,648
28. Selkirk	170,793	22,711	21,729	21,052	20,311
29. Shetland (Zetland)	352,319	21,421	19,352	17,812	17,231
30. Stirling	288,842	166,447	187,527	194,878	199,799
31. Sutherland	1,297,914	16,101	13,670	13,507	13,137
32. West Lothian (Linlithgow)	76,861	81,431	88,577	92,768	103,630
33. Wigtown	311,984	29,331	31,620	29,124	28,188
Total Scotland	19,070,466	4,842,980	5,096,415	5,179,344	5,186,600

[1] Home population.

In 1961 the population of cities, large and small burghs was 3,645,584 (70·4% of the total). In 1951 the total was 3,592,383 (70·5%; figures are adjusted to refer to boundaries altered since 1951).

The birthplaces of the 1951 population were: Scotland, 4,695,829; England. 222,162; Wales, 9,632; Northern Ireland, 43,354; Irish Republic, 45,126; Commonwealth, 28,810; foreign countries, 49,446 (including 28,950 aliens).

Burghs	Census population 1951	1961	Estimated population June 1967	Burghs	Census population 1951	1961	Estimated population June 1967
Glasgow	1,079,000	1,055,017	960,527	Kirkcaldy	51,800	52,390	52,102
Edinburgh	470,800	468,361	467,986	Clydebank	44,638	49,651	50,474
Dundee	181,800	182,978	182,284	Dunfermline	44,719	47,151	51,742
Aberdeen	186,900	185,390	182,117	Kilmarnock	42,123	47,509	47,722
Paisley	97,200	95,750	95,527	Ayr	42,377	45,276	46,747
Motherwell	73,100	72,794	75,609	Hamilton	40,174	41,928	45,917
Greenock	78,400	74,560	71,876	Perth	40,487	41,196	41,360
Coatbridge	54,300	53,825	53,241	Falkirk	37,535	38,044	37,718

The population of the Central Clydeside conurbation in June 1967 was 1,764,428.

In 1967 the estimated age distribution of the population in Scotland was: between 0 and 14+, 691,950 males, 658,357 females; 15 and over, 1,796,750 males, 2,039,543 females.

Isle of Man and Channel Islands

Islands	Area in statute acres, 1951	Census population 1931	1951	1961[1]
Isle of Man	141,263	49,308	55,253	48,151
Jersey	28,717	50,462	57,310	57,200
Guernsey, Herm and Jethou	16,068	40,643 ⎫		
Alderney	1,962	1,521 ⎬	45,496	47,178
Sark, Brechou and Lihou	1,386	579 ⎭		
Total	189,396	142,513	158,059	152,529

[1] Provisional.

VITAL STATISTICS for calendar years:

England and Wales

	Estimated home population at 30 June[1]	Total live births	Illegitimate live births	Deaths	Marriages	Divorces, annulments and dissolutions
1966	48,985,300	849,823	67,056	563,624	384,497	39,067
1967	48,300,800	832,164	69,928	542,516	386,052	43,093
1978	48,593,000	819,272	69,806	576,754	407,495	45,794
1969	48,826,800	797,538	67,041	579,378	396,746	51,310
1970	48,987,700	783,000[2]	..	573,777[2]	..	..

[1] Estimated home population includes alien military personnel within England and Wales and excludes seamen abroad.
[2] Provisional estimates based on numbers registered.

In 1969 the proportion of male to female births was 1,058 male to 1,000 female and the live birth rate was 16·3 and the death rate 11·9 per 1,000 of the population; infant mortality rate, 18 per 1,000 of live births. The average age of marriage was 27·2 years for males and 24·8 years for females.

Scotland

	Estimated home population at 30 June[1]	Total births	Illegitimate births	Deaths	Marriages	Divorces, annulments and dissolutions
1966	5,190,800	96,536	6,160	63,689	41,851	3,576
1967	5,186,600	96,221	6,663	59,523	42,116	3,038
1968	5,187,500	94,786	6,998	63,311	43,696	4,803
1969	5,194,700	90,290	6,733	63,821	43,294	4,246

[1] Includes merchant navy at home and forces stationed in Scotland.

In 1969 the proportion of male to female births was 1,069 male to 1,000 female; the live birth rate was 17·4 and the death rate 12·3 per 1,000 of the population.

Emigration and Immigration

In the years 1815–52 the total number of emigrants from the UK was 3,463,592. Up to 1852 the emigration returns made no distinction between British subjects and foreigners. From 1853 to 1938 inclusive, the number of emigrants of British origin, to places out of Europe, was 16,710,072. The following table gives a selection of migration statistics based on the International Passenger Survey, 1969. This sample survey conducted by the Central Office of Information for the Board of Trade covers passenger movements on all the principal air and sea routes of the UK, except those to and from the Irish Republic.

By country of last or intended residence	Into UK (1,000)	Out from UK (1,000)	Balance (1,000)
Commonwealth	119	184	−65
Australia	26	97	−71
India, Pakistan, Ceylon	32	10	+22
West Indies	10	9	+ 1
Canada	13	34	+21
Other	38	34	+ 4
Foreign	87	109	−22
USA	20	23	− 3
W. Europe	45	47	− 2
Other	21	39	−18
By age			
−15	35	68	−33
15–64	164	218	−54
65+	6	7	− 1
Total	206	293	−87

RELIGION

The Church of England is the originating church of the Anglican Communion, which parallels in its fellowship of autonomous churches the evolution of British influence beyond the seas from colonies to dominions and independent nations. There is no terrestrial head of the Anglican Communion; the Archbishop of Canterbury presides as *primus inter pares* at the decennial meetings of the bishops of the Anglican Communion at the Lambeth Conference.

The Anglican churches, in addition to the Church of England, comprise the churches and provinces in communion with the see of Canterbury which are situated in Wales; Ireland; Scotland; United States of America; Canada; Australia; New Zealand; West Indies; Brazil; South Africa; Central Africa; West and East Africa; Jerusalem and the Middle East; Burma, Ceylon; Japan and China.

In addition to the dioceses included within the Provinces of Canterbury and York, the Church of England includes a number of dioceses overseas over which the Archibishop of Canterbury exercises metropolitan jurisdiction, while Church of England chaplaincies in North and Central Europe are under the jurisdiction of the Bishop of London.

England and Wales. The Established Church of England, which baptizes some two-thirds of the children born in England (*i.e.*, excluding Wales but including the Isle of Man and the Channel Islands), is Protestant Episcopal. Civil disabilities on account of religion do not attach to any class of British subject. Under the Welsh Church Acts, 1914 and 1919, the Church in Wales and Monmouthshire was disestablished as from 31 March 1920, and Wales was formed into a separate Province.

The Queen is, under God, the supreme governor of the Church of England, with the right, regulated by statute, to nominate to the vacant archbishoprics and bishoprics. The Queen, on the advice of the First Lord of the Treasury, also appoints to such deaneries, prebendaries and canonries as are in the gift of the

Crown, while a large number of livings and also some canonries are in the gift of the Lord Chancellor.

There are 2 archbishops (at the head of the 2 Provinces of Canterbury and York) 141 bishops and 92 suffragan and assistant bishops in England. Each archbishop has also his own particular diocese, wherein he exercises episcopal, as in his Province he exercises metropolitan, jurisdiction. In the Church are 36 deans (including Westminster, Windsor and other Peculiars), 109 archdeacons and 14 provosts of parish church cathedrals. There is an Assembly, called 'the General Synod, in England, consisting of a House of Bishops, a House of Clergy and a House of Laity, which has power to frame legisation regarding Church matters. The first two Houses consist of the members of the Convocations of Canterbury and York, each of which consists of the diocesan bishops (forming an Upper House), deans, provosts, and archdeacons, and a certain number of proctors elected as the representatives of the inferior clergy, together with, in the case of Canterbury Convocation, representatives of the Universities of Oxford, Cambridge and London and the chaplains in the Forces (forming the Lower House). The House of Laity is elected by the lay members of the Deanery Synods. Parochial affairs are managed by annual parochial church meetings and parochial church councils. Every measure passed by the General Synod must be submitted to the Ecclesiastical Committee, consisting of 15 members of the House of Lords nominated by the Lord Chancellor and 15 members of the House of Commons nominated by the Speaker. This committee reports on each measure to Parliament, and the measure receives the Royal Assent and becomes law if each House of Parliament resolves that the measure be presented to the Queen.

At 31 Dec. 1969 there were 14,514 ecclesiastical parishes, inclusive of the Isle of Man and the Channel Islands, but excluding Wales. These parishes do not, in many cases, coincide with civil parishes. Owing to the shortage of clergymen, although each parish has its church, not every one nowadays can have its own incumbent or minister; so that in the least populated areas one or more parishes may be served by a clergymen, who must be in priest's orders, and in these cases he holds the parishes in plurality. At 31 Dec. 1969, of the total of 11,162 parochial livings there were 1,264 vacant; there were 9,898 incumbents. In addition there were 3,347 assistant curates working in the parishes.

Private persons possess the right of presentation to over 2,000 benefices; the patronage of the others belongs mainly to the Queen, the bishops and cathedrals, the Lord Chancellor, and the universities of Oxford and Cambridge. In 1969 there were 12,105 benefices. In addition to the 13,245 parochial incumbents and assistant curates, there were (1969) 2,253 non-parochial clergyman serving in the Armed Services, universities, colleges, schools, prisons, hospitals and homes, having a total of about 2,700 non-parochial churches or chapels and other places of worship in use.

According to a revised estimate, the income of the Church of England for 1966-67 was about £68m., made up as to £34m. for cathedrals, parochial church councils and extra-parochial churches; £21m. administered by the Church Commissioners; £3m. by the Church of England Pensions Board, the Central Board of Finance and the 43 diocesan boards of finance. The remainder goes directly into the accounts of the missionary societies, theological colleges and many central and diocesan church societies.

The membership of the Church at 30 June 1968 was estimated to be 27,756,000 baptized members, of whom 9·69m. were confirmed.

Of the 41,613 churches and chapels registered for the solemnization of marriages at 30 June 1967, 17,058 belonged to the Established Church and the Church in Wales and 24,555 to other religious denominations. Of the 386,052 marriages celebrated in 1967 (407,822 in 1968), 44·9% were in the Established Church and the Church in Wales, 21% in churches or chapels of other denominations and 34·1% were civil marriages in a Registrar's Office.

Roman Catholics in England and Wales were estimated at 4m. in 1965. There were 5 archbishops and 14 bishops, (1966) 7,707 clergy and about 2,900 churches and chapels.

The Unitarians have about 330 places of worship, the Catholic Apostolic Church over 80, the New Jerusalem Church about 75. The Salvation Army, a religious body with a quasi-military organization, carries on both spiritual and social work at home and abroad, and had, in British Territory, 1968, 2,659 officers, 940 corps, 31 Red Shield Centres and 51 Red Shield Mobile Units. There were also 38 eventide homes, 13 maternity homes, 2 maternity hospitals, 46 hostels for men, 14 hostels for women and girls, and 9 approved and training schools.

The following is a summary of statistics of certain churches in England and Wales, Channel Islands and Isle of Man:

Denomination	Full members	Ministers in charge	Local and lay preachers
Methodist	759,128	4,167	20,244
Independent Methodist	6,581	224	—
Wesleyan Reform Union	4,874	24	256
Congregational Union	181,101	1,683	—
Baptist	275,062	2,084	—
Presbyterian	65,066	315	—
Calvinistic Methodist Church of Wales	110,155	368	—
Moravian	2,773	40	—
Society of Friends	20,857	—	—

There are about 450,000 Jews in the UK with about 240 synagogues.

Scotland. The Church of Scotland (established in 1560 at the Reformation and re-established in 1688 as part of the Revolution Settlement) is Presbyterian, the ministers all being of equal rank. There is in each parish a kirk session, consisting of the minister and of several laymen called elders. There are presbyteries (formed by groups of parishes), meeting frequently throughout the year, and these are again grouped in synods, which meet half-yearly and can be appealed to against the decisions of the presbyteries. The supreme court is the General Assembly, which now consists of 1,362 members, half clerical and half lay, chosen by the different presbyteries. It meets annually in May (under the presidency of a Moderator appointed by the Assembly, the Sovereign being present or represented by a Lord High Commissioner, appointed by the Queen on the nomination of the Government of the day), and sits usually for 8 days. Any matters not decided during this period may be left to a Commission which sits at stated intervals until the meeting of the next General Assembly.

On 2 Oct. 1929 the Church of Scotland and the United Free Church of Scotland were reunited under the name of The Church of Scotland, and the two bodies met in General Assembly in Edinburgh as one. The united Church had, in Scotland, on 31 Dec. 1969, 2,124 congregations, 1,178,334 members, besides adherents; 33,734 teachers and 241,522 scholars in attendance in Sunday schools. The Church courts are the General Assembly, 12 synods, 59 presbyteries in Scotland, 1 in England and 3 on the Continent, in addition to overseas presbyteries. Income in 1969 was £10,113,439. There are divinity faculties in 4 Scottish universities of Edinburgh, Glasgow, Aberdeen and St Andrews, with 55 professors and lecturers who are mostly ministers of the Church of Scotland.

The Episcopal Church of Scotland is in full communion with the Church of England and is a Province of the Anglican Church. As at 31 Dec. 1969 it had 7 bishoprics, 363 churches and missions, 288 clergy and 90,066 members, of whom 50,967 were communicants.

There are in Scotland some small outstanding Presbyterian bodies and also Baptists, Congregationalists, Methodists and Unitarians.

The Roman Catholic Church had in Scotland (1970) 2 archbishops and 6 bishops, 1,279 clergy, about 450 churches, chapels and stations, and 809,680 adherents.

The proportion of marriages in Scotland according to the rites of the various Churches in 1969 was: Church of Scotland, 48·6%; Roman Catholic, 15·9%; Episcopal, 2%; United Free, 0·6%; others, 5%; civil, 27·9%.

Facts and Figures about the Church of England. Church Information Office, London, 1962
Davies, H., *The English Free Churches*. 2nd ed. London, 1963
Mayfield, G., *The Church of England: its members and its business*. 2nd ed. OUP, 1963
Moorman, J. R. H., *A History of the Church of England*. London, 1953

EDUCATION

State System of Education

England and Wales

There are three stages in the English and Welsh system: primary, secondary and further (including higher) education. The years of compulsory schooling are from 5 to 15 (from 1972–73 the minimum leaving age will be 16). The transition from primary to secondary school is made between 10½ and 12 years. No fees are payable in any publicly maintained school (but it is open to parents, if they choose, to pay for their children to attend other schools). The third stage, which is voluntary, includes universities, colleges of education and the technical colleges, as well as adult education and the youth service: financial assistance is generally available to students at all universities and colleges.

There are about 28,500 primary and secondary schools maintained by the education authorities. They have a pupil population approaching 8·5m.

Primary Education. Children under 5 may be provided for in nursery schools or in nursery classes attached to infant schools. There were fewer than 500 maintained nursery schools or departments in Jan. 1970; they accommodated on average about 50 children each.

About half of the primary schools take the complete age-range from 5 to 11. About a quarter take infants only, up to about 7 years; most of the rest take juniors only, 7–11 years. The great majority of all of these schools take boys and girls. More than a half had between 100 and 300 children each; most of the remainder smaller than this.

Rather more than 2,000 of these primary schools are in Wales. In those primary schools (and some secondary schools) which are in the predominantly Welsh-speaking areas the main language of instruction is Welsh. There are also 'Welsh' or, more accurately, bilingual schools in mainly English-speaking parts of Wales.

Secondary Education. There is approximately 1 secondary school for every 4 primary schools, over half of them taking between 300 and 600 children.

In most areas pupils are selected at 11 for grammar schools on the basis of ability. Those who are not selected attend secondary modern. In a growing number of areas, however, there is no selection and comprehensive schools are provided for pupils of all ability. Still the biggest group of schools at present is the modern schools, which provide a general education up to the minimum school-leaving age, though pupils can—and increasingly do—stay on beyond that age. There are nearly 3,000 of these schools, and they have nearly 1·3m. pupils—two-thirds of them in mixed schools. The next group in size comprises the grammar schools, which provide a mainly academic course for pupils from age 11 to 18. There are nearly 1,100, with a roll approaching 605,000; two-thirds are for boys or girls only. There are also a number of technical schools, the academic equals of grammar schools but specializing in technical studies, and various combinations of grammar, technical and modern schools. There are nearly 1,200 fully comprehensive schools with nearly 950,000 pupils.

With the development of comprehensive education some authorities have extended the age of transfer to secondary education from 11 to 12 or 13. In these cases middle schools are provided with the age ranges 8–12, 9–13 or 10–13. There are about 300 middle schools at present.

In Jan. 1970 there were 8,546,744 full-time and 50,707 part-time pupils, aged between 2 and 19, on the registers of primary and secondary schools maintained by local education authorities.

Direct-Grant Grammar Schools. These schools receive grants direct from the Department of Education and Science and are independent of local education authorities. They charge fees, but must offer 25% of their places each year, free of charge, to pupils who have previously attended grant-aided primary schools for at least 2 years. These free places are usually offered through the agency of the local education authority, in which case the authority pays the fees. The school governors must also, if requested by the local education authority, put at the authority's disposal a further 25% of places for pupils who need not have attended a grant-aided school. Tuition fees for the remaining places are payable by parents, but relief may be claimed in certain circumstances. On 1 Jan. 1970 there were 118,659 pupils in 176 direct-grant grammar schools.

Special Schools. Special educational treatment is provided for children who are deaf, partially hearing, blind, partially sighted, physically handicapped, educationally sub-normal, epileptic, delicate, maladjusted or suffering from speech defects not due to deafness. The educationally sub-normal are the largest category in this group. Some handicapped children attend ordinary schools. Others attend maintained special schools: there are at present over 800 of these, catering (in Jan. 1970) for nearly 79,000 pupils, approximately 60% boys, including about 3,000 in schools in hospitals for children receiving medical treatment as in-patients. (Local education authorities also send pupils to 'non-maintained' and independent special schools and pay the fees.) The particular function of special schools is to provide a regime to overcome the learning difficulties of handicapped children and to educate them to become as far as possible self-reliant and respon-sible adults. To this end these schools have a more generous staffing ratio and provide physiotherapy, speech therapy and other medical treatment as well as special teaching facilities. About two-thirds of the maintained special schools are day schools. For children with severe handicaps, for whom day special schools cannot cater, and for children who live out of reach of a suitable day school, free boarding education is provided. Attendance is compulsory from 5 to 16, but some special schools (including a few for children of high intellectual ability) keep pupils longer. Some establishments provide the physically handicapped or blind school leaver with a period of further education, pre-vocational training and assessment for employment. (Some pre-vocational or vocational training is also given by the Department of Employment and Productivity and by voluntary bodies, and in some cases, where necessary, special arrangements are made for handicapped pupils in normal maintained further education establishments.) In addition to the provision in special schools, authorities make special arrange-ments for educating children at home, in small groups or in hospitals when there is no special school. In Jan. 1970 over 3,800 pupils were being educated in this way.

Ancillary Services. Local education authorities must make available free medical and dental inspection and treatment for children attending maintained schools in their area. Many authorities provide child-guidance clinics, and speech therapy is an important part of school health provision.

Every local education authority is required to make meals available to pupils attending maintained schools as far as is reasonably practicable, and most main-tained schools now have facilities for school dinners. Part of the cost is borne by the parents but a pupil may receive a dinner free if the parents' income after certain allowances is below a national scale laid down by the Department of Education and Science.

One-third of a pint of milk should be made available daily free of charge to pupils attending maintained primary and special schools, but the Government intend to introduce a Bill to discontinue the supply of free milk to pupils at the end of the summer term after they reach the age of 7 (except for pupils in special schools and those who in the opinion of the school medical officer have a medical requirement). Milk may also be provided to similar pupils at independent schools at the discretion of local education authorities.

In primary and secondary schools (including nursery and special schools) maintained by local education authorities 67·9% of pupils present took dinners on a day in autumn 1970 and 91·2% of eligible pupils present took milk. For

1970–71 the estimated cost of school meals was £98·5m. and of milk was £13·5m.

Children below the age of 8 with 2 miles or more to travel to school must be provided with free transport by the local education authority, while older children with 3 miles or more to travel get similar provision. Where public transport exists, authorities may make use of it by paying the children's fares.

Further Education. In Nov. 1969 there were about 700 institutions providing day courses of further education, including 524 technical colleges and 8 polytechnics, 125 colleges of art, 4 national colleges and 45 agricultural institutes. These establishments offer courses ranging from short-hand instruction to degree-level and post-graduate work, and cater for full-time, part-time (many of them apprentices) and sandwich students (whose periods of study at college alternate with periods of practical training in industry). Students attending these colleges numbered 261,225 full-time (including 33,540 sandwich students) and 1,468,778 part-time; students released by their employers numbered 645,272.

There were in addition about 6,900 evening institutes, which provide mainly recreational courses and were attended by 1,352,552 students.

The further education system includes a sector of higher education which complements the universities and colleges of education, and which meets the needs of part-time as well as full-time and sandwich students. Courses leading to degrees, professional qualifications and other qualifications at all levels of higher education are provided in a wide range of disciplines. Full-time higher education within the further education system is now mainly concentrated in the new polytechnics, which were formed from existing colleges already extensively engaged in higher education, but many part-time and some full-time courses are offered by other further education establishments. In Jan. 1971, 27 of the 30 polytechnics originally proposed had been established and formally designated.

Education at institutions of further education is not free, but fees are generally low, and are remitted for most students under the age of 18 by the local authority. Students on degree-level courses receive grants on the same scale as university students.

Awards to Students. The Education Act 1962 placed the main responsibility on local education authorities for making awards to students taking first-degree courses at universities in England and Wales. In 1969, 46,504 awards were taken up, and there was a total of 140,292 awards current at universities on 31 Dec. 1969.

The State Scholarship scheme continues to run down, and in 1969 the number had declined to 47. Up to 30 Mature State Scholarships are still awarded annually by the Department of Education and Science.

842 State Studentships (for postgraduate studies in the humanities) were taken up at universities in 1969.

Teachers. In order to qualify for work in maintained schools, most teachers take a course of training at a college of education. Graduates and holders of some specialist qualifications obtained before 31 Dec. 1969 are at present regarded as qualified to teach without training, but anyone obtaining these qualifications from 1 Jan. 1970 will be obliged to take a training course before being appointed for the first time to a primary school, and from 1 Jan. 1974 before first appointment to a secondary school.

Some 164 colleges provide 3-year and other courses for intending teachers. The majority are known as general colleges and are concerned with most subjects taught in schools, but a few are concerned only with the training of women specialist teachers of physical education or housecraft. About two-thirds of the colleges are maintained by local education authorities, and the remainder by voluntary bodies which are usually associated with a religious denomination. At Oct. 1970 there were about 111,000 students in the colleges.

There are also art teacher-training centres for specialist teachers of art, university departments of education for graduates and colleges of education (technical) for people wishing to work mainly in further education. All of these offer one-year courses. Some colleges of education offer one-year courses for graduates.

On 1 Jan. 1970, 334,400 full-time teachers (138,095 men and 196,305 women) were employed by local education authorities in maintained schools.

Finance. Total current and capital expenditure on education in England and Wales from public funds (excluding university education and loan charges) is estimated at £1,813m. for 1970–71, as compared with £1,720m. for 1969–70.

Scotland

Primary Education. In 1968–69 there were 2,587 schools with primary departments and the number on the registers was 622,647. In addition, there were 100 nursery schools, and nursery classes attached to 66 primary schools, with a total enrolment of 9,290 pupils.

In Dec. 1969, 21,885 recognized certificated teachers were employed in primary schools or departments.

Secondary Education. In 1968–69 secondary schools numbered 616, 89 providing Scottish Certificate of Education courses only, 328 providing Scottish Certificate of Education and non-certificate courses, and 199 providing non-certificate courses only. The number of pupils was 307,185. The number of teachers in secondary departments in Dec. 1969 was 18,909.

Teacher-Training. In Nov. 1969 there were 12,573 students, including 1,816 graduates, in 10 colleges of education, training to be qualified teachers.

Special and Approved Schools. In 1969 there were 32 residential special schools, 72 day special schools and 64 junior occupational centres; special classes were attached to 68 ordinary schools. The total number of handicapped children under instruction was 12,073, of which 9,403 were mentally handicapped, 1,125 were physically handicapped, 367 were blind or partially blind and 787 were deaf or partially deaf, and 391 were otherwise handicapped. At 31 March 1969 there were 27 approved schools with a total enrolment of 1,685.

Further Education. Centres for further education numbered, 1,386 in 1968–69 with a total enrolment of 318,366 students. The number of students enrolled at the 13 central institutions was 13,119 (7,162 full-time and 5,957 part-time), including those within the administrative sphere of the Department of Agriculture and Fisheries for Scotland.

Finance. Total expenditure on education during 1968–69 was £171m. (excluding university education and loan charges).

Independent Schools

Outside the state system of education there were in England and Wales 2,775 independent schools in Jan. 1970, ranging from large 'public' schools to small local ones catering for a handful of children; there were 413,788 pupils in these schools. In Scotland there were 111 independent schools, with a total of 17,315 pupils in 1969. Fees are charged by all these schools, which receive no grant from public funds. All independent schools are open to inspection by HM Inspectors, and just over one-half are recognized as efficient by the Department. The term 'public schools' refers to independent schools in membership of the Headmasters' Conference, Governing Bodies Association or the Governing Bodies of Girls' Schools Association. Qualifications under which a school may be represented at the Headmasters' Conference include the measure of independence enjoyed by the governing body and the amount of advanced courses undertaken. Some of these schools are for boarders only, but the majority include non-resident 'day-pupils'.

The earliest of the schools were founded by, and attached to, the medieval churches. Many were founded as 'grammar' (classical) schools in the 16th century, receiving charters from the reigning sovereign. Reformed mainly in the middle of the 19th century, these schools now provide the highest form of English pre-university education. Among the most well-known independent schools are Eton College, founded in 1440 by Henry VI, with 1,195 boys; Winchester College, 1394, founded by William of Wykeham, Bishop of Winchester, 530 boys; Harrow

School, founded in 1560 as a grammar school by John Lyon, a yeoman, 681 boys; Charterhouse, 1611, 615 boys. Among the earliest foundations are King's School, Canterbury, founded 600; King's School, Rochester, 604; St Peter's, York, 627.

University Education

In *England* there are 33 degree-giving universities. In addition there are the University of Manchester Institute of Science and Technology; and the London and Manchester Business Schools. Seven new universities have been established since 1961.

The Open University received its charter on 1 June 1969 and is an independent, self-governing institution, awarding its own degrees. It is financed by the Government through the Department of Education and Science and by the receipt of students fees.

At present the university offers undergraduate courses leading to the award of the BA degree. Tuition is by means of correspondence, broadcasts on radio and television. No formal entry qualifications are required and students are normally over 21. Places were offered to 25,000 students in Jan. 1971 for the first Arts, Mathematics, Science and Social Sciences foundation courses. Educational Studies and Technology courses start in 1972. In Jan. 1971 the full-time staff was over 700.

In *Wales* there is one university, the University of Wales, with colleges at Aberystwyth, Bangor, Cardiff and Swansea. The Welsh National School of Medicine is a school of the University, and the University of Wales Institute of Science and Technology became a constituent college in Nov. 1967. St David's College, Lampeter, will also be incorporated in the University.

In *Scotland* there are 8 universities, Aberdeen, Dundee, Edinburgh, Stirling, Strathclyde, Heriot-Watt, Glasgow and St Andrews. The Carnegie Trust, founded in 1901 with a capital of £2m., has an annual income of £100,000, of which half is devoted to the equipment and expansion of the Scottish universities and half to assisting students.

All these universities and colleges are independent, self-governing institutions, although they receive substantial aid from the state through the University Grants Committee. This is a committee appointed by the Secretary of State for Education and Science designed to advise the Government on the needs of the universities, and to prepare plans for future development. The members are drawn from education and industry. The local education authorities have no responsibility for universities.

All universities charge fees, but financial help is available to students from several sources. The universities themselves provide scholarships of various kinds, the Department of Education and Science offers a number of scholarships for mature students every year and all local education authorities have a system of awards to help suitable students to attend university. Most of the undergraduate awards to UK students made by local education authorities are offered on the results of the General Certificate of Education. The amount of aid given generally depends upon the parents' means. About 98% of the students at the English and Welsh universities are in receipt of some form of financial assistance.

Awards known as state studentships are offered on a competitive basis by the Department from among candidates considered by the universities to be qualified for post-graduate studies in the humanities; similar awards, tenable at universities or technical colleges, are offered by the Research Councils to students studying science, mathematics and technology at the post-graduate level.

The following table gives the approximate number of professors, lecturers, etc., and students (full-time and sandwich courses) for 1969–70.

University or college	Students	Staff	University or college	Students	Staff
England—			England (contd.)—		
Aston	2,909	398	Brunel	1,690	217
Bath	1,958	255	Cambridge	10,367	1,212
Birmingham	6,594	1,226	City	2,414	292
Bradford	3,312	379	Durham	3,363	396
Bristol	6,207	857	East Anglia	2,451	282

University or college	Students	Staffs	University or college	Students	Staff
England (contd.)—			*England* (contd.)		
Essex	1,691	205	Surrey	2,349	286
Exeter	3,279	371	Sussex	3,682	519
Hull	3,835	471	Warwick	1,793	239
Keele	1,817	281	York	2,187	270
Kent	2,172	269			
Lancaster	2,333	317	*Wales*—		
Leeds	8,814	1,239	Aberystwyth U.C.	2,401	334
Leicester	3,256	350	Bangor U.C.	2,382	360
Liverpool	6,553	916	Cardiff U.C.	3,304	411
London Business School	96	56	St. David's Lampeter	306	41
London	31,687	6,329	Swansea U.C.	3,410	458
Loughborough	2,364	249	Welsh Nat. School of		
Manchester Business			Medicine	354	78
School	79	56	Univ. of Wales Institute of		
Manchester University	8,129	1,357	Science and Technology	1,788	227
Univ. of Manchester					
Inst. of Science and			*Scotland*—		
Technology	3,272	481	Aberdeen	5,267	639
Newcastle	5,612	938	Dundee	2,424	408
Nottingham	5,081	681	Edinburgh	9,200	1,310
Oxford	10,834	1,489	Glasgow	7,814	1,279
Reading	4,854	747	Heriot-Watt	2,461	237
Salford	3,375	448	St Andrews	2,378	272
Sheffield	5,629	716	Stirling	605	125
Southampton	4,321	496	Strathclyde	5,053	692

At most of the universities and university colleges women students are admitted on equal terms with men. Number of women students: England, 46,298; Wales, 4,438; Scotland, 11,001. There are, however, colleges exclusively for female students at Oxford and Cambridge. Numbers of students at institutions receiving aid from the University Grants Committee: England, 170,359; Wales, 13,945; Scotland, 35,202; total, 219,506.

THE BRITISH COUNCIL

The British Council was established in Nov. 1934 and incorporated by Royal Charter in 1940. Its principal purposes are the promotion of a wider knowledge of Britain and the English language abroad and the development of closer cultural relations between Britain and other countries.

The Council's funds come mainly from parliamentary grants, which in 1970–71 amounted to £13,473,000. Of this sum, £8·5m. came from the Foreign and Commonwealth Office vote, £4·9m. from the Overseas Development Administration, £1,000 from the Board of Trade and £2,000 from the Department of Education and Science. With Council earnings and donations estimated at £1·1m., the total budget for 1970–71 was £14·62m. The Council administered the expenditure of an additional £7·7m. as agent for Departments of State and for international organizations.

The Council is governed by an Executive Committee consisting of the Chairman, 20 other elected members and 8 members nominated by Ministers. There are advisory committees for Scotland and Wales, and also advisory committees or panels for the main branches of the Council's work. In Feb. 1971 the Council had staff in 76 countries.

The Council is normally the body designated by the British Government to carry out bilateral cultural agreements, including that with the Soviet Union. The Council's work broadly divides into English language teaching and other educational work, the promotion of wider use and availability of British books and periodicals, the development of personal contacts and the exchange of information, especially in the fields of education, medicine, science, technology and the arts.

In the field of English language teaching, its main task is to advise and assist educational authorities overseas, particularly in the training of teachers. It maintains an English Teaching Information Centre in London which collects and disseminates information about methods of English teaching and about relevant research. It recruits British teachers for service overseas. It organizes training courses in Britain and abroad for overseas teachers of English. It assists in producing English-by-television programmes overseas and, in co-operation with the BBC, English language teaching films for showing overseas.

The Council runs or assists about 200 libraries in some 70 countries with stocks of 2·25m. volumes, makes grants to assist public library development, mainly in East and West Africa, and arranges touring exhibitions of new British books and periodicals (168 exhibitions in 1969–70).

The Council arranges short advisory tours overseas by British experts. It is also the overseas administrative arm of 3 of the 4 member-societies of the British Volunteer Programme. It awards scholarships and bursaries and arranges study programmes for over 12,000 visitors a year.

In Britain the Council administers the programmes of award schemes for overseas students, meets many students on arrival from overseas, and provides an accommodation service and a programme of educational and recreational courses and visits, mainly for students from overseas for whom it has a special responsibility. The Council runs some 25 offices and centres in Britain, mainly in university cities, for these purposes.

The sciences, including medicine, technology and agriculture, form a growing area of Council work. Specialist departments and libraries in London and scientifically qualified officers overseas help to develop scientific contacts, provide information and advise on training in Britain and the provision of experts overseas. Assistance is given in the expansion and reshaping to local needs of the teaching of science in the schools in the developing countries of the Commonwealth.

In the field of the arts the British Council presents overseas the best in British theatre, ballet and music; mounts exhibitions of British painting and sculpture; sponsors recordings of music and literature; and provides information on British composers, dramatists and writers.

The Council publishes the following periodicals: *British Medical Bulletin*, *British Medical Book List* and *British Book News*. Other publications produced include the series *Writers and their Work*, a number of booklets such as *The Novel Today*, *Drama in Britain*, *Higher Education in the United Kingdom* and *How to Live in Britain*. The Council edits *Scientific and Learned Societies of Great Britain*.

Chairman: (Vacant).
Director-General: The Hon. Sir John Henniker, KCMG, CVO, MC.
Headquarters: 65 Davies St., London, W1Y 2AA.

JUSTICE

England and Wales

The legal system of England and Wales, divided into civil and criminal courts has at the head of the superior courts, as the ultimate court of appeal, the House of Lords, which hears each year a number of appeals in civil matters, including a certain number from Scotland and Northern Ireland, as well as some appeals in criminal cases. In order that civil cases may go from the Court of Appeal to the House of Lords, it is necessary to obtain the leave of either the Court of Appeal or the House itself, although in certain cases an appeal may lie direct to the House of Lords from the decision of the High Court. An appeal can be brought from a decision of the Court of Appeal or the Divisional Court of the Queen's Bench Division of the High Court in a criminal case provided that the Court is satisfied that a point of law 'of general public importance' is involved, and either the Court or the House of Lords is of the opinion that it is desirable in the public interest that a further appeal should be brought. As a judicial body, the House of Lords consists of the Lord Chancellor, the Lords of Appeal in Ordinary, commonly called Law Courts, and such other members of the House as hold or have held high judicial office. The final court of appeal for certain of the Commonwealth countries is the Judicial Committee of the Privy Council which, in addition to Privy Counsellors who are or have been in High Judicial Office in the UK, includes others who are or have been Chief Justices or Judges of the Superior Courts of Commonwealth countries.

Civil Law. The main courts of original civil jurisdiction are the county courts for less valuable cases, and the High Court for the more important hearings.

There are nearly 400 county courts located throughout the country, grouped in districts, and each presided over by a paid judge (or, in some cases, 2 or 3 Judges). They have a general jurisdiction (subject to certain rights of transfer to the High Court given to defendants) to determine all actions founded on contract or tort involving sums of not more than £750. Certain matters, such as action of libel and slander, are entirely reserved for the High Court. In addition, certain designated county courts have jurisdiction in matrimonial proceedings. Divorce proceedings may now be commenced in these courts and, subject to being transferred to the High Court upon become defended, may be determined in the county court.

The High Court has both appellate and original jurisdiction, covering virtually all civil causes not determined in the county court. The judges of the High Court are attached to one of its 3 divisions: Chancery; Queen's Bench; and Probate, Divorce and Admiralty; each with its separate field of jurisdiction. There are 72 such judges, called puisne judges. For the hearing of cases of first instance, the High Court judges sit singly. Apellate jurisdiction is usually exercised by courts consisting of 3 (sometimes 2) judges, though in certain circumstances a judge sitting alone may hear the appeal.

The Restrictive Practices Court was set up in 1956 under the Restrictive Trade Practices Act, and is responsible for deciding whether a restrictive trade agreement is in the public interest. It is presided over by a judge, but laymen sit on the bench also.

The Court of Appeal (Civil Division) hears the more important appeals in civil actions. It includes the Lord Chancellor and the heads of the other 2 divisions (Queen's Bench and Probate) of the High Court, but effectively the head of the Civil Division is the Master of the Rolls, aided by 14 Lords Justices of Appeal sitting in 2 or 3 divisions.

Civil proceedings are instituted by the aggrieved person, but, as they are a private matter, they are frequently settled by the parties to a dispute through their solicitors before the matter actually comes to court. In some cases, at the instance of either party, a jury may sit to decide questions of fact and award of damages.

Criminal Law. At the base of the system of criminal courts are the lay magistrates who, outside the larger towns, try the great proportion of minor offenders (over 98% of all criminal cases) as well as undertaking an increasing proportion of civil work. Most of these magistrates' courts consist of 2 to 7 lay magistrates who are unpaid and need not possess legal qualifications (though they undergo a course of training), though they do have the assistance on points of law of a profesional clerk to the justices. In central London and large cities there exist stipendiary magistrates, paid for their duties. These are professional lawyers and usually sit alone. Exercising summary jurisdiction in petty sessions, justices have power to pass sentences of imprisonment up to, in general, 6 months, and to impose fines up to, in general, £400. One of their most important functions is to examine accused persons charged with graver offences and to determine whether they should be committed for trial at Assizes or Quarter Sessions. The justices also deal with traffic offences and breaches of such statutes as those dealing with food and drugs, hours of work, etc. There are some 19,000 justices who are appointed to the Commission of the Peace by the Lord Chancellor; he is assisted by advisory committees. Women are eligible to act as justices, and the number on the Commission of the Peace is estimated to be about 6,000.

Specially qualified justices sit in juvenile courts to hear cases involving young persons under 17 years of age charged with criminal offences (other than homicide) or brought before the court as being in need of care and protection. These courts normally sit with 3 magistrates, including 1 woman, and are accommodated separately from other courts.

Above these magistrates' courts are courts of Quarter Sessions, sitting at least 4 times a year. In the counties these courts consist of lay magistrates presided over by a legally qualified chairman. The Chairman and Deputy Chairmen of these courts normally serve part-time. The courts in London, Durham, Cheshire, Kent and Lancashire are exceptional in that they have a whole-time Chairman, and some of them have one or more whole-time Deputy Chairmen. In the larger boroughs these courts are presided over by a Recorder, who is a barrister specially appointed to act in this capacity. These courts have a more extensive original jurisdiction than magistrates' courts and have certain powers to hear appeals from the magistrates' courts.

Assize courts are branches of the High Court presided over by High Court judges and sitting in certain large towns. Their responsibility is to try the most serious offences and cases presenting special difficulties. Special criminal courts, called Crown Courts, sit in Liverpool and Manchester, presided over by whole-time Recorders and acting both as Quarter Sessions for these cities and Assizes for South Lancashire. In London the Central Criminal Court sits at the Old Bailey, acting as the Assizes for Greater London, presided over by salaried judicial officers.

Appeals from magistrates' courts go either to a Divisional Court of the High Court (when a point of law alone is involved) or to Quarter Sessions who may entertain an appeal against conviction or sentence. Appeals from other courts of criminal jurisdiction go to the Court of Appeal (Criminal Division). Appeals on questions of law go by right, and appeals on other matters by leave. The Lord Chief Justice and the other judges of the High Court may sit with the Master of the Rolls and the Lords Justices to constitute this Court.

There remains as a last resort the invocation of the royal prerogative exercised on the advice of the Home Secretary. In 1965 the death penalty was abolished for murder.

All contested criminal trials, except those which come before courts of summary jurisdiction, are tried by a judge and a jury, consisting of 12 members, completely independent of the judiciary. The composition of the jury may be challenged if cause can be shown for objection to any juror, and, in a limited number of instances, by the defendant without showing cause. The judge is responsible for sentences given to convicted offenders, but the jury decides whether the accused is guilty or not. If, after at least 2 hours of deliberation, a jury is unable to reach a unanimous verdict it may, provided that in a full jury of 12 at least 10 of its members are agreed, bring in a majority verdict. The failure of a jury to agree on a unanimous verdict or to bring in a majority verdict involves the retrial of the case before a new jury.

Military Courts. Offences by military personnel against the system of military law created under the powers of the Army Act, Air Force Act or Naval Discipline Act are dealt with by courts-martial. Appeals lie to a Courts-Martial Appeals Court, and from that court an appeal may lie to the House of Lords.

The Personnel of the Law. All judicial officers except the Lord Chancellor are independent of Parliament and the Executive. Most of them are appointed by the Crown on the advice of Ministers and hold office until retiring age or, in some cases, for a fixed term of years. The legal profession is divided; barristers, who advise on legal problems and conduct cases in court, usually act for the public only through solicitors, who deal directly with the legal business brought to them by the public. Higher judicial appointments are made from barristers of long standing.

Aid is provided for persons who are unable through lack of means to pay for legal assistance in civil or criminal proceedings. Under the provisions of the Legal Aid and Advice Act, 1949, a person of poor or moderate means may be provided with the services of solicitor and counsel in most civil proceedings, and proceedings before the Lands Tribunal either without charge or, if his means allow, on payment of a contribution. In 1969-70 there were 206,629 applications for legal aid under the Act. The cost of legal aid in civil cases is met from (*a*) contributions from assisted persons; (*b*) costs recovered from opposed parties; (*c*) a grant from the Exchequer. The cost of such legal aid to the State in the year 1969-70 was £10·05m. Under Part IV of the Criminal Justice Act 1967 a court dealing with criminal proceedings has discretion to order legal aid to be given if it appears that the defendant (or appellant) requires financial assistance in meeting the costs of legal representation for his defence, and that it is in the interests of justice for him to be granted legal aid. (Persons on murder charges, in need of financial assistance for legal representation, must be granted legal aid.) The costs of legal aid in criminal proceedings are paid by the central government, but since 1 Oct. 1968, courts have had the power to require legally aided persons to contribute towards the cost of legal aid given to them. The cost of legal aid in criminal proceedings in 1969–70 was approximately £5,729,000.

Under the Parliamentary Commissioner Act, passed 22 March 1967, M.P.s may refer to the Parliamentary Commissioner complaints received from the public regarding improper or inequitable administration in most spheres of central government affairs. Generally, other available remedies (such as legal action) must be exhausted before a complaint can be investigated. If a complaint is found to require a remedy the Parliamentary Commissioner makes a report to Parliament.

The authorized strength of the police force in England and Wales in Dec. 1969 was 103,667 men and 4,267 women: the actual strength (including Metropolitan Police additionals) was 87,391 men and 3,486 women. In addition, there were 230 whole-time auxiliaries of the First Police Reserve and 39,110 special constables (including 1,968 women). Total police net expenditure (estimated) in England and Wales for 1967–68 was £225,557,962 (£240,751,654 for 1968–69).

Jackson, R. M., *The Machinery of Justice in England*. 5th ed. London, 1967

Scotland

The High Court of Justiciary is the supreme criminal court in Scotland and has jurisdiction in all cases of crime committed in any part of Scotland, unless expressly excluded by statute. It consists of the Lord Justice-General, the Lord Justice-Clerk and 16 other judges, who are the same judges as of the Court of Session, the Scottish supreme civil court. The Court, which is presided over by the Lord Justice-General, whom falling, the Lord Justice-Clerk, exercises an appellate jurisdiction as well as one of first instance, and sits as business requires in Edinburgh as a Court of Appeal (the *quorum* being 3 judges) and also there and on circuit at various towns throughout the country for the trial of criminal cases. The decisions of the Court in either case are not subject to review by the House of Lords. One judge sitting with a jury of 15 persons can, and usually does, try cases, but 2 or more (with a jury) may do so in important or complex cases. It has a privative jurisdiction over cases of treason, murder, rape, deforcement of messengers and breach of duty by magistrates. It also, in practice, is the only court which tries cases of incest, sodomy and other serious or aggravated crimes against person or property and generally those cases in which a sentence greater than imprisonment for 2 years may be imposed either under statute or common law. Moreover, the Court has inherent power to try and to punish all acts which are plainly criminal though previously unknown and not dealt with by any statute.

The appellate jurisdiction of the High Court of Justiciary extends to all cases tried on indictment, whether in the High Court or the Sheriff Court, and persons so convicted may appeal to the Court on any ground involving a question of law alone, or apply for leave to appeal, on any question of fact or of mixed law and fact, or on any other sufficient ground, and also against sentence unless it is one fixed by law. It is also a court of review from courts of summary criminal jurisdiction, and on the final determination of any summary prosecution either party may appeal to the Court by way of stated case on questions of law, procedure, etc., but not on questions of fact. A further or complementary form of process of review which can be resorted to by convicted persons in these courts is by Bill of Suspension (and Liberation), but it is of strictly limited application. A prosecutor in these courts may also bring under review a decision in law, prior to final judgment of the case, by way of Bill of Advocation, but this process is infrequently resorted to, The Court also hears appeals under the Courts-Martial (Appeals) Act 1951.

The Sheriff Court has an inherent universal criminal jurisdiction (as well as an extensive civil one) limited in general to crimes and offences committed within a sheriffdom (*i.e.*, a county or a combination of counties), which has, however, been curtailed by statute or practice under which the High Court of Justiciary has exclusive jurisdiction in relation to the crimes above-mentioned. This Court is presided over by a Sheriff-Principal or a Sheriff-Substitute, and when trying cases on indictment sits with a jury of 15 persons. His power of awarding punishment involving imprisonment is restricted to 2 years in the maximum, but he may under certain statutory powers remit the prisoner to the High Court for sentence. The Sheriff also exercises a wide summary criminal jurisdiction and when doing so sits without a jury; and he has concurrent jurisdiction with every other court within his sheriffdom in regard to all offences competent for trial in summary courts. The great majority of offences which come before the courts are of a minor nature and, as such, are disposed of in the Sheriff Courts. In cases indicted for trial in the High Court of Justiciary the Pleading, or First Diet, is always held in the Sheriff Court and, in these cases, the Sheriff may dispose of any objection of a preliminary nature, whether to the citation or relevancy or otherwise. or may refrain from doing so. In either case the Sheriff's decision can be reviewed by the High Court at the Second, or Trial, Diet.

Burgh Magistrates (Police Courts) and Justice of the Peace Courts have jurisdiction in petty cases occurring within the burgh, or county, and in minor offences under various statutes.

The Court of Session, presided over by the Lord President (the Lord Justice-General in criminal cases), and divided into an Inner House comprising 2 divisions of 4 judges each, and an Outer House comprising 10 single judges, exercises the highest civil jurisdiction in Scotland, with the House of Lords as a court of appeal.

The police forces in Scotland at the end of 1968 had an authorized establishment of 11,091 (including 417 women); the strength was 9,842 men and 384 women. Whole-time 'additional' policemen numbered 70, and there were 4,916 part-time special constables. The estimated expenditure on police, borne by the Government, was £10,331,000 for 1967–68.

CIVIL JUDICIAL STATISTICS

ENGLAND AND WALES	1967	1968	1969
Appellate Courts			
Judicial Committee of the Privy Council	40	37	33
House of Lords	34	52	48
Court of Appeal	834	948	948
High Court of Justice (appeals and special cases from inferior courts)	792	776	747
Courts of First Instance			
High Court of Justice:			
Chancery Division	19,781	21,361	24,954
Queen's Bench Division	166,481	166,991	208,716
Probate, Divorce and Admiralty Division	51,785	55,838	62,036
County courts	1,617,648	1,515,844	1,643,274
Other courts	22,532	30,115	29,698
SCOTLAND			
House of Lords (Appeals from Court of Sessions)	16	12	15
Court of Session—General Department	9,592	10,875	10,918
Sheriff's Ordinary Court	34,161	34,247	38,384
Sheriff's Small Debt Court	160,981	155,680	162,868
Justice of Peace Small Debt Court	1,650	1,470	1,018

CRIMINAL STATISTICS

ENGLAND AND WALES	1967	1968	1969[1]
Indictable offences—			
Number of persons against	261,169	277,718	329,702
Number of persons found guilty at Magistrates' Courts	216,623	229,932	271,637
Number of persons found guilty at Assizes and Quarter Sessions	25,585	27,395	32,433
Non-indictable offences—			
Number of persons proceeded against	1,402,708	1,387,724	1,372,584
Number of persons found guilty	1,337,445	1,319,541	1,302,658

[1] Theft Act 1968 came into force 1 Jan. 1969.

ENGLAND AND WALES (contd.)	1967	1968	1969 [2]
Juveniles (included above) [1]—			
Number of persons found guilty of indictable offences	61,818	64,371	72,445
Number of persons found guilty of non-indictable offences	52,319	53,166	47,483
Number of persons found guilty of indictable or non-indictable offences at Magistrates' Courts	113,302	116,586	118,724
Number of persons found guilty at Assizes or Quarter Sessions	835	951	1,204
SCOTLAND			
Crimes—			
Proceedings taken	39,005	39,096	41,775
Disposed of summarily	36,112	36,439	39,132
Miscellaneous offences—			
Proceedings taken	176,247	166,376	173,006
Juveniles [1]—			
Crimes—charges proved without finding of guilt	3,699	3,416	5,707
Found guilty	8,491	8,402	9,606

[1] Young persons under 17 years of age.   [2] Theft Act 1968 came into force 1 Jan. 1969.

Daily average population in prisons, borstals and detention centres (1969) in England and Wales was 34,667 (convicted, 31,736; untried, 2,499, and 432 non-criminal prisoners); in Scotland (1969), 4,834 (convicted, 4,267; untried, 567).

NATIONAL INSURANCE

The National Insurance Act, 1946, came into operation on 5 July 1948, repealing the existing schemes of health, pensions and unemployment insurance. This Act, along with later legislation, was consolidated as the National Insurance Act, 1965.

This Act applies in general to all persons in Great Britain who are over school-leaving age, and divides contributors into three classes, *i.e.*: (a) employed persons who work under contract of service or are paid apprentices; (b) self-employed persons; (c) non-employed or insured persons not in one of the other two classes,

From April 1961 a measure of graduated contributions and additions to retirement pensions related to employees' earnings has been introduced into national insurance. Members of an occupational pensions scheme can, subject to certain conditions, be contracted out of part of the graduated pension scheme. From Oct. 1966 a scheme, also financed from graduated contributions, was introduced for the payment of earnings-related supplements to sickness and unemployment benefits and widows' supplementary allowances. The main rates of combined weekly contributions payable are as follows:

		Flat-rate Contributions			
		Men		Women	
		Age 18 or over	Age under 18	Age 18 or over	Age under 18
		£	£	£	£
Class 1: Employees *not* contracted out	Employee	0·88	0·57	0·75	0·48
	Employer	3·25	1·82	2·00	1·33
	Total	4·23	2·39	2·75	1·81

Graduated national insurance contributions range from ½p a week by employees earning just over £9 a week, to £0·82 a week by those earning £30 a week or more. The employer pays an equal amount.

Class 1: Employees contracted out	Employee	1·00	—	0·83	—
	Employer	3·47	—	2·08	—
	Total	4·47	—	2·91	—

In addition, a graduated contribution ranging from ½p to 43p is payable by employees. The employer pays an equal amount.

	Ordinary Flat-rate Contributions			
Class 2: Self-employed people	1·24	0·70	1·03	0·60
Class 3: Non-employed people	0·99	0·56	0·78	0·46

The weekly flat-rate contributions shown above include for employees in Class 1, the industrial injuries contributions, and for all Classes the National Health Service contributions, as well as the employer's redundancy contributions and selective employment tax.

Contributions for a man are payable up to the age of 65. If, at that age, he retires from work, he pays no more contributions. If he continues working contributions are payable to the age of 70. If he works after age 70 he is liable for Industrial Injuries contribution only, but the employer remains liable for his share of the full contribution. Comparable ages for women are 60 and 65.

Benefits. The benefits are: (1) Unemployment benefit; (2) Sickness benefit; (3) Maternity benefit; (4) Widow's benefit; (5) Guardian's allowance; (6) Child's special allowance; (7) Retirement pension; (8) Death grant.

Employed persons qualify for all the benefits; self-employed qualify for all except unemployment; non-employed qualify for all except unemployment, sickness and maternity allowance. Qualification for any benefit depends upon the fulfilment of the appropriate contribution and other conditions laid down in the Act and Regulations.

Sickness and Unemployment Benefit. The normal rate is £5 a week plus £3·10 a week for an adult dependant, plus £1·55 for the first child below the family-allowance age limit, 65p for the second child and 55p for each subsequent child in addition to any family allowances due. An earnings-related supplement may be paid from the 13th to 168th day of a period of interruption of employment to a person aged 18 or over and under minimum pension age (65 for men, 60 for women) who is entitled to flat-rate sickness and unemployment benefit and who has reckonable earnings of at least £450 in the relevant, usually the last complete, income-tax year.

Maternity Benefit. For a confinement a woman may receive a maternity grant of £25 and, where 2 or more children are born at the confinement, a further grant of £25 for each additional child who is alive 12 hours after its birth. If the woman has been gainfully employed or self-employed, and has been paying full national insurance contributions, she may receive a maternity allowance of £5 a week normally payable for 18 weeks commencing 11 weeks before the expected week of confinement, provided she does not work during this period. Maternity allowance may be increased in certain circumstances in respect of dependants in the same way as sickness and unemployment benefits.

Widow's Benefit. On her husband's death a widow normally qualifies for 26 weeks for an allowance of £7 a week for herself plus allowances for children below the family allowance age at the following rates: £2·45 for the first, £1·55 for the second and £1·45 for each other child (in addition to family allowances). A supplementary allowance based on her late husband's earnings may also be paid. At the end of the 26 weeks she receives a widowed mother's allowance of £5 for herself, and the allowances for the qualifying children continue at the same rate as for the first 26 weeks of widowhood. She may also receive her allowance at the personal rate of £5 a week if she has living with her a son or daughter who is under 19.

A widow who is 40 or over when this allowance ceases (or, if there are no children under the age limit, when the widow's allowance ceases) qualifies for a widow's pension. If at that time she is 50 or over (40 if the husband died before 4 Feb. 1957) the full standard rate of pension payable is £5 a week. If she is between 40 and 50 there is a scale of pension, depending on age at the time of entitlement, varying from 30% of the full pension for a woman at 40 to the full pension for a woman aged 50. The pension does not increase as the widow grows older but remains at the rate for the age when awarded.

Child's Special Allowance. An allowance may be payable for the children of divorced parents where the father has died. It is payable to the mother if she has not remarried and her former husband was contributing, or legally liable to contribute, at least 25p a week towards the children's support in cash or kind or if she took reasonable steps to enforce maintenance. It is similar to the allowances for widow's children and is payable at the same rates together with family allowances.

Guardian's Allowance. A person who has in his family a child below the family-allowances age limits may be entitled to a guardian's allowance of £2·45 a week if both the parents of the child are dead and at least one of them was insured under the National Insurance Acts. When the child is illegitimate, or the parents were divorced, or one parent is missing, or serving a long sentence of imprisonment, the allowance may, in certain circumstances, be paid on the death of one parent only.

Retirement Pension. In order to receive a retirement pension, men between 65 and 70, and women between 60 and 65 must have retired from regular employment. This does not apply to women who are widowed or divorced when over 60, who can receive the pension on the termination of their marriage. The standard rates are £5 a week for a man or a woman on his or her own insurance, and £3·10 for a married woman through her husband's insurance. An increase of £3·10 a week may be payable for a dependent wife if she does not earn more than £3·10 a week. In addition, £1·55 a week may be payable for the first child of the family under the age limits, 65p for the second child and 55p for each subsequent child, in addition to any family allowances. In certain circumstances an increase of £3·10 a week may be payable for a woman having care of the pensioner's children. In addition, a man who has paid graduated contributions receives 2½p per week for every £7·50 of graduated contributions paid, and a woman 2½p per week for every £9 paid. If, after being awarded a retirement pension, a man under 70 or a woman under 65 earns more than £7·50 in a calendar week the pension for the next pension week, including any increase for dependants, will be reduced by 5p for every 10p earned between £7·50 and £9·50 and by 5p for every 5p earned over £9·50. If retirement is postponed after minimum pension age increments of flat rate pension of 5p a week can be earned for every 9 contributions which are paid for weeks of employment or self-employment between the ages of 65 and 70 for a man (60 and 65 for a woman). These increments are added to the pension when a person eventually retires or reaches the age of 70 (65 for a woman) whichever is the earlier. At age 70 (65) the pension for which a person has qualified may be paid in full whether a person continues in work or not irrespective of the amount of earnings.

Old Persons' Pensions. Under the National Insurance (Old persons' and widows' pensions and attendance allowance) Act 1970 a pension is provided as of right to these elderly people who have no state pension because they were over pensionable age when the National Insurance scheme started on 5 July 1948 and were not insured under earlier schemes. Subject only to a simple residence test, pensions are payable to these people and to less elderly wives, widows and former wives of men who are entitled to this benefit or who would have been entitled if they had survived. A married woman gets £1·85 and all other persons £3 a week. People who qualified for contributory pensions under pre-1948 schemes and who are now entitled to a pension at low rates have this 'topped up' to £3 or £1·85.

Death Grant. This is a lump sum paid on the death of an insured person or his close relative. The normal amount of the payment is: For an adult, £30; for a child aged 6 but under 18, £22·50; for a child aged 3 but under 6, £15; for a child under 3, £9. For the death of a person who was within 10 years of pensionable age on 5 July 1948 (*i.e.*, a man over 55 and a woman over 50 on that date) only half the standard amount is payable. No grant is payable for the death of a person over pensionable age on 5 July 1948.

Payment. Unemployment benefit is paid through the Employment Exchanges, retirement pensions and widows' benefits are generally paid through Post Offices by order books; other payments through local Social Security Offices by a giro order.

NATIONAL INSURANCE (INDUSTRIAL INJURIES) ACT, 1965

The Industrial Injuries Act, which also came into operation on 5 July 1948, with its later amending Acts, was consolidated as the National Insurance (Industrial Injuries) Act, 1965. This Act provides a system of insurance against 'personal injury by accident arising out of and in the course of employment' and against certain prescribed diseases and injuries due to the nature of the employment. It takes the place of the Workmen's Compensation Acts and covers broadly the persons who are insured as employed persons under the National Insurance Act. The cost of the contribution is included in the employed person's National Insurance stamp, but there are no contribution conditions for the payment of benefit. Three types of benefit are provided:

(1) *Injury benefit*, payable during incapacity for work for a maximum of 26 weeks from the date of the accident or the development of the prescribed disease. The rate of this benefit is £7·75 a week, plus earnings-related supplement where there is underlying title to sickness benefit, with increases of £3·10 for 1 adult dependant and £1·55 for the first child under the age limits, 65p for the second child and 55p for each subsequent child in addition to any family allowances due. If the insured person is under 18 years of age and is not entitled to a dependant's increase benefit will be payable at a reduced rate—£5·25 for a person between 17 and 18 and £4·50 for a person under 17. For children under the school-leaving age in part-time employment, the rate is £1·55.

(2) *Disablement benefit*. This is payable where, as the result of an industrial accident or prescribed disease, there is a loss of faculty after injury benefit ceases to be payable. The loss of faculty will be assessed at a percentage by comparison with a person of the same age and sex whose condition is normal. If the assessment is 20%, or more, benefit will be a pension varying according to the assessment, from £1·70 a week to £8·40 a week. If the assessment is under 20% benefit will normally be a gratuity of an amount not exceeding £550. Increases of benefit may be payable where a disablement causes special hardship, *i.e.*, it prevents the beneficiary from undertaking his regular job and one of a similar status, or unemployability; where there is a need for constant attendance; where there is exceptionally severe disablement and the need for constant attention is likely to be permanent or where the beneficiary is in hospital for treatment for his injury. In the case of an unemployable pensioner, or a pensioner receiving hospital treatment, an increase of £3·10 for an adult dependant and £1·55 for the first child under the age limits, 65p for the second child and 55p for each subsequent child in addition to any family allowance due, will be payable. Pensions for persons under 18 are reduced similarly to injury benefit.

(3) *Death benefit*. On the death of a person as the result of an industrial accident or a prescribed disease, certain dependants may qualify for benefit. Benefit for a widow is a pension normally of £7 weekly for the first 26 weeks and thereafter £5·55, depending on such factors as age, entitlement to a child's allowance and permanent incapacity for self-support. If the conditions for pension at the higher rate are not satisfied the widow may receive a pension of £1·50 a week. Children's allowances are payable to the widow, or other person, caring for children of the deceased. For widows, these allowances are usually at the rate of £2·45 a week for the eldest or only child, £1·55 for the second and £1·45 for any subsequent children; for other persons, the rate is £1·55 for the first child and 65p for the second child and 55p for each subsequent child. A pension of £1 is payable to a woman having care of a child of the deceased. Benefit for widows, parents and certain other relatives takes the form of pensions, allowances or gratuities according to the relationship to, and degree of maintenance by, the deceased.

WAR PENSIONS

The number of beneficiaries in receipt of war (1914–18) pensions or allowances in payment as at 31 Dec. 1970 was 128,610. The number of beneficiaries in receipt of war (1939–45) pensions or allowances in payment as at 31 Dec. 1970 was 396,650. The estimated expenditure for both wars for 1970–71 is £122,360,000. The expenditure is exclusive of administrative expenses.

NATIONAL INSURANCE FUND

At 1 April 1969 the combined balances of the National Insurance Fund and the National Insurance (Reserve) Fund amounted to £1,229,820,347. Income to the

National Insurance Fund during the period 1 April 1969 to 31 March 1970, consisting of contributions from insured persons and employers, payments from the Exchequer and interest on investments, etc., was £2,364,845,871. Payments of benefit in respect of unemployment were £127,116,825; sickness, £382,680,179; maternity, £38m.; widows, £162m.; guardian's allowance, £600,000; child's special allowances, £60,000; retirement pension, £1,626,895,038; death grants, £11,896,191. Included in those figures are the following estimated amounts of earnings-related supplement; unemployment benefit, £21m.; sickness benefit. £59·25m.; widow's benefit, £5·8m.; graduated retirement benefit, £10m. The combined balance at 31 March 1970 was £1,039,631,913.

Industrial Injuries Fund. At 1 April 1969 there was a balance of £343,505,157. Income during the period 1 April 1969 to 31 March 1970, consisting of contributions from insured persons and employers, payments from the Exchequer and interest on investments, etc., amounted to £119,831,487. Benefits for injury totalled £33,381,335; for disablement, £60,579,409; for deaths, £8·5m. Administrative and other payments cost £15,176,665. There was a balance at 31 March 1970 of £345,699,235.

FAMILY ALLOWANCES

Family allowances are cash payments, for the benefit of the family as a whole, to families with more than one child below the age limits. The weekly allowance in April 1971 was 90p for the second such child and £1 for each younger child. The age limits are 15 for children who leave school at that age, 16 for certain handicapped children and 19 for those who are receiving full-time education at a school, college or university, or are apprentices with low earnings.

SUPPLEMENTARY BENEFIT

Supplementary Benefit. Under the Ministry of Social Security Act, 1966, the Supplementary Benefits Commission is responsible for the award of financial assistance to any persons in Great Britain aged 16 years or over (excluding persons at school or college or anyone directly involved in a trade dispute) who are not in full-time remunerative work and who are without resources, or whose resources (including national insurance benefits) need to be supplemented in order to meet their requirements. A person who is excluded from benefit may, nevertheless, receive payments to meet urgent need. The general standards by reference to which supplementary benefit is granted are determined by statutory regulations approved by Parliament. Persons who are dissatisfied with the amount of benefit granted to them may appeal to one of the local Appeal Tribunal established under the Act.

During the financial year 1968–69 net payments on supplementary benefit amounted to £429m.

Newman, T. S., *Digest of British Social Insurance.* London. 1947 (and supplements, to date)

NATIONAL HEALTH

The National Health Service in England and Wales started on 5 July 1948 under the National Health Service Act, 1946. There is a separate Act for Scotland and also one for Northern Ireland, where the Health Services are run on similar lines to those in England and Wales.

The National Health Service, which is available to every man, woman and child, is a charge on the national income in the same way as the armed forces and other facilities. Every person normally resident in this country is entitled to use any complete part of the services, and no insurance qualification is necessary.

Most of the cost of running the service is met from the national exchequer, *i.e.*, from taxes, and about half the expenses of the local health services are met from local rates.

Since Sept. 1957 there has been a weekly National Health Service contribution which is now 24p for men (employee 16p, employer 8p). Women, persons under 18, self-employed and non-employed persons pay a smaller contribution. For convenience this contribution is collected with the National Insurance contribution in a single combined weekly stamp, and for 1969–70 is estimated to be £159m. (£163m. in 1968–69). Eligibility for treatment under the National Health Service does not in any way depend on the payment of contributions.

Organization. England is divided into 14 hospital regions, each with its own Regional Hospital Board, which administers the hospital and specialist services in the area. The chairmen and members of the boards are appointed by the Secretary of State for Social Services. Teaching Hospitals have their own boards of governors whose chairmen and members are similarly appointed. The Secretary of State for Wales is directly responsible for the administration of the Health Services in Wales and he appoints the chairman and members of the Welsh Hospital Board. Under the powers of the Health Services and Public Health Act 1968, some hospitals providing clinical teaching facilities are designated university hospitals. These are similiar to teaching hospitals except that their administration remains under their Regional Hospital Boards.

Services. The main branches into which the National Health Service is broadly divided are: hospital and specialist services, general medical and dental services, pharmaceutical services and ophthalmic services; local authority health services. All these services are frce of charge except for such things as prescriptions, spectacles, dentures and dental treatment, amenity beds in hospitals and for some of the local authority services, for which a charge is made.

The total cost of the Health and Welfare Services (England and Wales) is estimated at £1,887m. for 1970–71 (£1,768m. in 1969–70) and the estimated net expenditure by the Exchequer (except for the Local Health and Welfare Services, where the rates and the Exchequer grants amounted to £254m.) in 1970–71 is £1,373m.

The number of abortion notifications received in 1970 under the provisions of the Abortion Act, 1967, was 83,851. Of these, 39,532 (47·1%) were to single women, 36,532 (47·1%) were to married women, 7,387 (8·8%) were to widowed, divorced or separated women. The remaining 134 (0·2%) were to women who did not state their marital status.

WELFARE

ACCOMMODATION AND WELFARE UNDER PART III OF THE NATIONAL
ASSISTANCE ACT, 1948

The number of persons in residential and temporary accommodation provided by local authorities was as follows:

England and Wales (31 Dec.)	Residential accommodation Adults and Children	Temporary accommodation Adults	Temporary accommodation Children	Total Adults and Children
1967	106,838	5,641	9,933	122,412
1968	110,079	6,889	11,960	128,928
1969	107,977	7,669	13,151	128,797
Scotland	*Adults*	*Adults*		*Adults*
1967	7,589	190		7,779
1968	7,784	227		8,011
1969	8,284	216		8,500

England and Wales. Expenditure and income relating to accommodation and welfare services undertaken (in £ sterling):

Year ended 31 March	Expenditure [1] (including loan charges)	Specific income Government grants	Specific income Other specific income	Balance of expenditure not met out of specific income
1967	69,299,000	14,000	22,975,000	46,310,000
1968	82,030,000	18,000	24,786,000	57,226,000
1969	88,905,000	..	25,747,000	63,158,000

[1] By local authorities.

Scotland. The total local authority expenditure for 1968–69 in respect of residential accommodation and welfare services under the National Assistance Act, 1948, was £7,805,000 (ordinary expenditure, £6,876,451, exclusive of loan charges, and capital expenditure, £928,549) and the income received, including contributions from other local authorities, was £2·9m.

FINANCE

Revenue and expenditure for years ending 31 March, in £ sterling:

Revenue	Estimated in the Budgets	Actual receipts into the Exchequer	More (+) or less (−) than estimates
1967	10,519,000,000	10,279,000,000	−240,000,000
1968	11,093,000,000	11,177,000,000	+ 84,000,000
1969	12,875,000,000	13,363,000,000	+488,000,000
1970	15,008,000,000	15,266,000,000	+258,000,000
1971	16,124,000,000	15,841,000,000	−282,000,000

The Budget estimate of ordinary revenue for 1971–72 is £16,762m.

Expenditure	Budget and supplementary estimates	Actual payments out of the Exchequer	More (+) or less (−) than estimates
1967	9,472,000,000	9,541,000,000	+ 69,000,000
1968	10,359,000,000	10,878,000,000	+519,000,000
1969	11,489,000,000	11,615,000,000	+126,000,000
1970	12,551,000,000	12,882,000,000	−271,000,000
1971	13,526,000,000	14,084,000,000	+558,000,000

The Budget estimate of ordinary expenditure for 1971–72 is £14,446m.

The imperial revenue in detail for 1970–71 and the expenditure, are given below, as is the budget estimate for 1971–72 (in £1m.):

Sources of revenue	Net receipts 1970–71	Budget estimate 1971–72
Inland Revenue:		
Income tax	5,725	6,491
Surtax	240	360
Corporation tax	1,600	1,620
Capital Gains tax	140	165
Death duties	360	375
Stamp duties	115	108
Other	5	1
Total Inland Revenue	8,185	9,120
Customs and Excise:		
Tobacco	1,145	1,100
Purchase tax	1,280	1,495
Oil	1,390	1,460
Spirits, beer and wine	930	1,000
Betting and gaming	130	145
Other revenue duties	10	10
Protective duties	255	265
Import deposits	−420	−116
Total Customs and Excise	4,720	5,359
Motor Vehicle duties	423	440
Selective Employment tax (gross)	1,985	1,298
Total taxation	15,313	16,217
Miscellaneous receipts:		
Broadcasting receiving licences	101	120
Interest and dividends	97	105
Other	330	320
Total	15,841[1]	16,762

[1] It was estimated that, as a result of the postal strike, £250m. of receipts due 1970–71 would not be received until 1971–72.

The following are the branches of expenditure and the issues out of the Exchequer for year ended 31 March 1971 and the estimates for 1971–72 (in £1m.):

Supply Services

Defence	Net expenditure 1970–71	Estimates 1971–72
Defence	2,085	2,185
Department of Trade and Industry	5	5
Ministry of Aviation Supply	216	216
Department of Environment	174	206
Total Defence	2,480	2,545

Civil supply:		
Government and Finance	216	216
Commonwealth and Foreign	317	312
Home and Justice	301	334
Trade, Industry and Employment	2,352	2,394
Agriculture	422	441
Environmental Services	3,373	3,643
Social Services	3,187	3,388
Education and Science	523	564
Museums, Galleries and the Arts	24	25
Other Public Departments and Common Governmental Services	213	240
Miscellaneous	12	6
Total Civil Supply	10,970	11,604
Supplementary provision		−278
Total Supply Services	13,450	13,871

Consolidated Fund Standing Services

Payment to the National Loans Funds in respect of service of the National Debt	327	225
Northern Ireland—share of reserved taxes, etc.	277	320
Other services	30	30
Total	14,084	14,446

Gross National Product

	1946	1950	1960	1968	1969
Expenditure (£1m.)					
Consumers' expenditure	7,273	9,400	16,933	27,113	28,618
Public authorities' current expenditure on goods and services	2,282	2,123	4,248	7,705	8,118
Gross domestic fixed capital formation	925	1,700	4,120	7,889	7,927
Value of physical increase in stocks and work in progress	−126	−210	594	210	294
Total domestic expenditure at market prices	10,354	13,013	25,895	42,917	44,957
Exports and property income from abroad	1,775	3,807	6,309	10,669	11,986
Less Imports and property income paid abroad	−2,083	−3,492	−6,483	−10,713	−11,318
Less Taxes on expenditure	−1,573	−2,065	−3,391	−6,944	−7,868
Subsidies	384	474	487	890	844
Gross national product at factor cost	8,855	11,737	22,817	36,819	38,601
Factor incomes (£1m.)					
Income from employment	5,758	7,627	15,174	25,334	27,174
Income from self-employment[1]	1,126	1,389	2,014	2,919	3,009
Gross trading profits of companies[1,2]	1,476	2,126	3,736	5,024	4,948
Gross trading surplus of public corporations[1]	20	196	539	1,372	1,461
Gross trading surplus of other public enterprises[1]	86	139	179	108	114
Rent[3]	429	539	1,244	2,379	2,601
Total domestic income before providing for depreciation and stock appreciation	8,895	12,016	22,886	37,136	39,307
Less Stock appreciation	−125	−650	−135	−634	−815
Residual error	—	−25	−165	—	−342
Gross domestic product at factor cost	8,770	11,341	22,586	36,502	38,150
Net property income from abroad	85	396	231	317	451
Gross national product	8,855	11,737	22,817	36,819	38,601
Capital consumption	..	953	1,933	3,378	−3,694
National income	..	10,784	20,884	33·441	34,907

[1] Before providing for depreciation and stock appreciation.
[2] Selective employment tax is included on a cash basis and refunds or premium are allowed for when they are received.　　　　[3] Before providing for depreciation.

National Economic Development Council. The NEDC (Neddy), which first met in 1962, is the national forum for economic consultation between government, management and unions. The 20-member council, with the Chancellor of the Exchequer in the chair, includes leading representatives of the government, CBI and TUC besides chairmen of nationalized industries and independent members. Discussions at the monthly council meetings are normally based on papers, presented by the participating parties, which deal primarily with questions of long-term national economic performance and prospects for both government and industry, besides seeking to agree on ways of improving industrial efficiency through consultation. Council meetings are held in private to encourage the frank exchange of views between members, and the discussions are summarized at a press conference taken by the Director-General of NEDC following each meeting. The Economic Development Committees (Little Neddies), like the NEDC, bring together representatives of management and unions, and officials from government, who use this neutral meeting place to study the efficiency and prospects of individual industries. The National Economic Development Office (NEDO) provides the professional staff for the NEDC and the EDCs.

Taxation

Income Tax. The gross amount of income brought under the review of the Inland Revenue Department in the year ended 5 April 1939 in Great Britain and Northern Ireland, was £4,158,111,482; in 1965–66 it was estimated to be approximately £31,842m. The income on which tax was chargeable in 1938–39, after allowing for exemptions and reliefs, was £1,482,564,496, and the estimated amount for 1965–66 was £11,500m. The tax is mainly on the income of individuals, and is imposed, for each year of assessment ending 5 April, at a standard rate supplemented in the case of individuals by the surtax (*see below*). The rates and principal allowances for recent years have been as follows:

Standard rate. 1955–59 8s. 6d., 1959–65 7s. 9d., 1965–71 8s. 3d., 1971–72 7s. 9d. in the £.

Earned income allowance. 1952–57 two-ninths of the first £2,025 of earned income (max. £450); 1957–65 two-ninths of the first £4,005 of earned income (max. £890) and one-ninth of the next £5,940 (max. £660). For 1955–68 the two-ninths allowance was given on investment income also where the total income did not exceed £450. In 1971 earned income relief was increased to 15% of the excess over £4,005 without limit.

Personal allowance (married). 1963–65 £320, 1965–69 £340, 1969–70 £375, 1970–71 £465. A married woman received a separate single personal allowance on her earned income. An additional personal allowance of £100 for all single (including divorced and separated) women who were entitled to child allowance for a young child resident with them, was introduced in 1970–71. From 1972–73 a married couple will be able to elect that the wife should be taxed as a single person.

Personal allowance (single). 1963–65 £200, 1965–69, £220, 1969–70 £255, 1970–71 £325.

Each child. 1955–57 £100; 1957–63 £100 for a child not over 11, £125 for a child between 11 and 16, and £150 for a child aged 16 and over continuing further education. In 1963 these rates were increased to £115, £140 and £165 and in 1969 the rates were reduced by £42 for each child for whom family allowance is due. An increase of £40 for each child was made in 1971.

Reduced rates on taxable income. 1955–59, £60 at 2s. 3d., £150 at 4s. 9d., £150 at 6s. 9d.; 1959–63, £60 at 1s. 9d., £150 at 4s. 3d., £150 at 6s. 3d.; 1963–69, £100 at 4s., £200 at 6s.; 1969–70, £260 at 6s.; 1970–71, reduced rate abolished. A separate reduced rate relief is allowed on a married woman's earned income.

Surtax. Surtax is payable by individuals whose total income from all sources, after making certain deductions referred to below, exceeds £2,500. The rates are on a graduated scale, those for 1952–71 rising from 2s. in the £ at £2,500 (although where surtaxable income slightly exceeds £2,500 the surtax will be limited to 40% of the excess), to 10s. in the £ on the layer of income exceeding £30,000.

In general, the definition of net income chargeable to surtax follows that used for income tax, but certain exceptions and deductions allowable for income tax are not allowed for surtax, and vice versa. For 1956–57 and subsequent years the amount by which certain personal allowances exceed the single allowance (£140) is allowed as a deduction from total income. As from 1961–62 the earned income relief applicable to income tax applied to surtax, and the starting level for earned income was £4,000 and was raised to £5,700 in 1970–71.

Corporation Tax. Corporation Tax applies, with certain exceptions, to trades or businesses carried on by bodies corporate or by unincorporated societies or other bodies and this tax came into force from April 1966 replacing Profits Tax. The rate of this tax for 1966–67 was 40%; 1967–69, 42½%, and for 1969–71, 45%; but in Oct. 1970 this was reduced to 42½% for financial year 1969–70 and reduced again to 40% in 1970–71.

Capital Gains Tax. Gains resulting from the disposal of capital assets (other than British Government and Government guaranteed securities and certain exempted forms of property such as a private car and personal residences) are taxed under the Finance Act 1965. In 1970–71 exemption was granted for all gains made in a financial year which in total did not exceed £500.

Selective Employment Tax. Employers pay an employment tax on each employee at the rate of £1·20 for men and 60p for women. Reduced rates apply to employees under 18. Refunds of this tax are paid to industries engaged in manufacturing activities and to registered charities and additional sums are paid to manufacturers in Development Areas. In 1970 the production of plays for public performance became exempt from the scope of Selective Employment Tax.

It was announced in April 1971 that Selective Employment Tax and Purchase Tax would be abolished in 1973–74 and would be replaced by Value Added Tax.

National Debt

Borrowing by the State on the security of taxes was practised in Norman times but the National Debt really dates from the time of William III. The acknowledged debt in 1689 was about £664,000, on which the annual charge for interest and management was £40,000. At various subsequent dates the amounts (in £1m.) were as follows (including the Irish debt throughout):

		Debt[1]	Annual charge[2]	Annuities only
1756	Beginning of Seven Years' War	75	2·8	0·2
1763	End ,, ,, ,, ,,	133	5·0	0·5
1775	Beginning of American War	127	4·7	0·5
1784	End ,, ,, ,,	243	9·5	1·4

[1] These amounts do not include the capital value of terminable annuities.
[2] Including annuities.

		Gross debt[1]	Annual charge[2]	Total interest[3]
1793	Begining of French Wars		9·7	..
1815	End ,, ,, ,,		32·6	
1817	Consolidation of English and Irish Exchequers		31·6	..
1854	Beginning of Crimean War	802	27·4	..
1857	End ,, ,, ,,	837	28·6	..
1899	Beginning of Boer War	635	23·2	..
1903	End ,, ,, ,,	798	27·0	..
1914	Beginning of First World War	708	24·5	..
1939	Beginning of Second World War	8,301	230·0	..
1946	End ,, ,, ,, ,,	23,774	490·3	0·5
1965–66		31,340[5]	..	1,100·3[4]
1966–67		31,986[5]	..	1,198·0[4]
1967–68		34,194[5]	..	1,321·1
1968–69		34,000[5]	..	1,309·9
1969–70		33,079	..	1,411·6

[1] Including terminable annuities.
[2] Including interest met from revenue, management and sinking fund.
[3] Interest included in National Debt services.
[4] Met from receipts under various Acts: £397m. 1963–64, £406m. 1964–65, £471m. 1965–66, £555m. 1966–67 and £671m. in 1967–68. [5] Net debt.

On 31 March 1970 the net national debt amounted to £33,079,397,075 including National Savings Certificates, £1,926,079,217; Premium Savings Bonds,

£765,595,066; Defence Bonds, £83,603,450; National Development Bonds, £417,905,004; British Savings Bonds, £321,870,123.

Advances to Allied Governments (Second World War), outstanding at 31 March 1970, amounted to: Poland, £47·5m; Czechoslovakia, £19,747,398; China, £12,237,395; totals, £79,484,793. Post-war liabilities of Austria outstanding at 31 March 1970 totalled £1·78m. Amounts due from other overseas governments under agreements, etc., £404,917. Amount due, at 31 March 1970, from Rhodesia in respect of payments made under guarantee to the International Bank of Reconstruction and Development (excluding occrued interest) £11·1m.

Local Taxation

The amount of rates collected by local authorities in 1970–71 in England and Wales is estimated to have been £1,754m. (£1,591m. in 1969–70); in Scotland (1969–70) £183m.

Under the Local Government Act 1966,'the Government gives general financial assistance to local authorities by means of rate support grants. These grants contain: (i) the needs element which is payable to county, county borough and London borough councils. (40% of the total grants for inner London is payable to the Greater London Council who, through the Inner London Education Authority, administer education in inner London.) Needs elements have been fixed at total amounts of £1,607m. for 1971–72 and £1,694m. for 1972–73; (ii) the resources element which is payable to county councils and rating authorities who qualify by reason of a deficiency in rateable resources per head of population. Total grants have been prescribed at £280m. for 1971–72 and £290m. for 1972–73; (iii) the domestic element, which compensates rating authorities for loss of rate income in reducing rates to domestic dwellings (£0·9½ in 1971–72 and £0·10½ in 1972–73). Total grants have been fixed at £117m. for 1971–72 and £132m. for 1972–73.

Grants are also payable on revenue expenditure for specific services, including police and housing improvement; and capital expenditure on certain services also attracts capital grant, e.g., on principal roads, rural water and sewerage coast protection.

In Scotland, from 16 May 1967, under the Local Government (Scotland) Act 1966, the rate support grant replaced General grant, Exchequer equalization grant and certain specific grants, in particular grants in aid of school milk and meals, and some highway grants. The aggregate and the amounts of the three component parts of the rate support grants for the local authority years 1971–72 and 1972–73, the 2 years of the grant third period, as prescribed by the Rate Support Grant, (Scotland) Order, 1971, as £251·2m. (£265·73m.); need element, £176·92m. (£186·45m.); resources element £58·97m. (£62·15m.), and £15·31m. (£17·13m.) domestic element. The domestic element is given towards the cost of reducing the rates payable on domestic properties as required by the 1966 Act (£0·11 in the £ in 1971–72, taking account of revaluation in that year), and payments under Part V of the Local Government Act, 1948, amounted in 1970–71 to £4,754,365. As in England and Wales, capital and revenue grants are also payable on expenditure for certain specific services.

Local authority loan debt at 31 March 1968 amounted to £11,415m. The Public Works Loan Board provided £3,837m., and £1,251m. was represented by quoted Stock Exchange securities other than bonds. (Negotiable bonds amounted to £258m.)

The rateable value on which rates were leviable in England and Wales immediately prior to the revaluation which took effect from 1 April 1963 was £756,164,511. The rateable value at 1 April 1968 was £2,313,678,100. In Scotland the effective rateable value was £150,238,806 in 1969–70.

In England and Wales the average amount of the rates collected per £ of rateable value was £0·34 in 1913–14; and estimated to be £0·60 for 1967–68 and £0·62½ for 1968–69. In Scotland the estimated average amount per £ of rateable value of the rates, inclusive of water rates, in 1969–70 was £1·22.

The rateable value of the Greater London Council was £673,855,535 on 1 April 1970. The net debt of the Greater London Council on 31 March 1971 was estimated to be £883,366,000. The education service of the Inner London Education Authority is estimated to cost £175m. and £85·75m. has been provided for housing and other loans in 1971–62.

Local Government Financial Statistics. HMSO (annual)

DEFENCE

All important problems of defence policy are considered by the Defence and Oversea Policy Committee presided over by the Prime Minister, and consisting of certain Ministers of the Government, among whom are the Secretary of State for Defence, the Foreign and Commonwealth Secretary and the Home Secretary. The Secretary of State for Defence is responsible for carrying out this Committee's decisions relating to defence, after endorsement as necessary by the Cabinet.

The complete re-organization of the 3 Service Departments (Admiralty, War Office and Air Ministry) under the Secretary of State for Defence took place in 1964. A Defence Council was also established under the Secretary of State to exercise the powers of command and administrative control previously exercised by the separate service councils, which became subordinate to it. Further re-organization, on 6 Jan. 1967, reduced the status of the administrative heads of the 3 Services from Ministers to Under-Secretaries of State, while creating 2 new posts: Minister of Defence (Administration) and Minister of Defence (Equipment). Further reorganization of these 2 posts later reduced them to that of a single Minister of State for Defence. The present membership of the Defence Council consists of the Secretary of State for Defence, the Minister of State, the 3 Service Under-Secretaries of State, the Chiefs of Defence, Naval, General and Air Staffs, the Chief Adviser (Projects and Research), the Chief Adviser (Personnel and Logistics) and the Permanent Under-Secretary of State.

Logistics Services. Since the inception of a unified Ministry of Defence in 1964, progress has been made in the rationalization of the logistics services of the Royal Navy, the Army and the Royal Air Force. Airfield construction for all Services is now the responsibility of the Army's Royal Engineers; the Air Force Department is responsible for accommodation stores for maintenance and for the initial furnishing of new buildings; the Army Department is the single management authority for the design, development, procurement and inspection of clothing other than certain specialized clothing; the Navy Department is responsible for ration policy, provisioning, procurement, storing and distribution of food to main depots and to Army forward supply depots in BAOR; the Air Force Department is responsible for the procurement of petrol, oil, lubricants and solid fuel on behalf of all three Services, and the Army Department has responsibility for research and development, procurement, storage and distribution of vehicles, repair of vehicles and provision, storage and distribution of spare parts. The Army Department is also responsible for the procurement of small arms and ancillaries for all Services. It has been agreed that the supply of Naval air stores will be integrated with those of the RAF when the RN ceases front-line fixed-wing flying in the early seventies. A study of the rationalization of water transport is in progress. Considerable savings in money and in Service and civilian manpower have already been realized and are expected to continue.

Service Strengths at 1 April 1971 (estimate); all ranks, males and females: Royal Navy and Royal Marines, 84,600; Army, 185,300; Royal Air Force, 111,700; Total, 381,600.

Defence Budget Estimates: 1970–71, £2,280m.; 1971–72, £2,545m.

Royal Navy

The Royal Navy is a permanent establishment, governed by the Admiralty Board of the Defence Council. The Secretary of State for Defence is Chairman of the Admiralty Board; the Minister of State for Defence is Vice-Chairman. The members of the Admiralty Board and their responsibilities are as follows: The Parliamentary Under-Secretary of State for Defence for the Royal Navy; The Chief of the Naval Staff and First Sea Lord (professional head of the Royal Navy), assisted by the Vice-Chief of the Naval Staff; The Chief of Naval Personnel and Second Sea Lord, responsible for the manning of the Fleet; The Controller of the Navy (formerly also Third Sea Lord), responsible for research and development, design, production, inspection, repair and maintenance of ships, their weapons and equipment; The Chief of Fleet Support, known until 1968 as Chief of Naval Supplies and Transport and Vice-Controller (formerly also Fourth Sea Lord), responsible for the provision of naval armament, victualling and medical stores and fuels, and for the movement of transport of persons and material, and superintending Dockyard organization and maintenance of the Fleet; and The Chief Scientist (Royal Navy), responsible for superintending the conduct of all research and development and the deployment of scientific effort. The post of Second Permanent Under-Secretary of State (Royal Navy) (formerly Permanent Secretary) lapsed in 1968 (he was Civil Service head, responsible for general co-ordination of the Admiralty Board business, the interior economy of the Navy department, Navy contracts and the administration of civil staff, and accounting officer for Navy Votes responsible for the control of expenditure and adviser to the Admiralty Board on financial questions). Thus the office of Samuel Pepys, of which the last holder was the 33rd, passed into history. The Deputy Under-Secretary of State (Navy) is the Board Member now responsible for some of these functions. Financial and staff control is vested in the Second Permanent Under-Secretary for Administration and the Second Permanent Under-Secretary for Equipment.

The following is a summary of the more important units:

Category	Completed by the end of								
	1962	1963	1964	1965	1966	1967	1968	1969	1970
Aircraft carriers	7 [1]	7 [1]	7 [1]	7 [1]	7 [1]	6 [1]	6 [1]	5 [1]	5 [2]
Submarines	49	47	48	44	46	44	40	35	34
Cruisers	5	5	5	5	4	3	3	3	3
Destroyers	27	26	26	24	22	22	18	15	11
Frigates	75	70	74	65	68	70	68	64	64

[1] Includes 2 commando carriers.   [2] Includes 3 commando carriers.

There are also 2 assault ships, 8 depot, repair and maintenance ships, 1 ice patrol ship, 4 fast patrol boats, 3 seaward patrol craft, 13 surveying vessels, 48 coastal minesweepers, 3 inshore minesweepers, 1 minelayer, 20 boom defence vessels, 200 auxiliaries and 100 service craft. In the following table the principal surface warships are grouped in classes, in descending order of modernity.

Completed	Name	Standard displacement Tons	Armour		Principal armament	Shaft horsepower	Speed Knots
			Belt In.	Turrets In.			

Aircraft Carriers

| 1955 | Ark Royal [2] | 43,060 | ? | — | 4 'Seacat' | 152,000 | 31·5 |
| 1951 | Eagle [1] | 43,000 | ? | — | 8 4·5-in.; 6 'Seacat' | 152,000 | 31·5 |

[1] Rebuilt Dec. 1959–Jan. 1964.   [2] Rebuilt Feb. 1967–70.

The aircraft carrier *Victorious* was scheduled for disposal in Nov. 1967, decommissioned on 13 March 1968 to await disposal and left Portsmouth for breaking up at Faslane on 11 July 1969. The aircraft carrier *Centaur* used from 1965 to 1970 as an accommodation ship for aircraft carriers and commando carriers refitting, was officially declared for disposal in Feb. 1971.

Commando Carriers

1959	Hermes [2]	23,900	—	—	2 'Seacat'	78,000	28·0
1954	Albion [1] ⎱	23,300	—	—	Light AA	78,000	28·0
1954	Bulwark [1] ⎰						

[1] Converted from fixed wing aircraft carriers into commando carriers 1959–62.
[2] Began conversion from fixed wing aircraft carrier to commando carrier in 1971.

Cruisers

1961	Blake [1] ⎱				⎧ 2 6-in.; 2 3-in. ⎫		
1960	Lion [3]	9,550	4	2	⎨ 4 6-in.; 6 3-in. ⎬	80,000	31·5
1959	Tiger [2] ⎰				⎩ 2 6-in.; 2 3-in. ⎭		

[1] Converted into a helicopter carrier.   [2] Being converted into a helicopter carrier.
[3] Not now to be converted into a helicopter carrer (reconstruction rescinded in Oct. 1970).

The cruiser *Belfast* was reclassified as a harbour accommodation ship in June 1966 but ceased to act in this capacity in Feb. 1971.

The cruisers *Ceylon* and *Newfoundland* were sold to Peru in Dec. and Nov. 1959 respectively. *Birmingham* was scrapped in 1960; *Jamaica* and *Superb* were scrapped in 1961; *Kenya* and *Swiftsure* in 1962; *Bermuda* and *Mauritius* in 1965. *Sheffield* was towed to the shipbreakers in Jan. 1967; *Gambia* in 1968.

Submarines are of the following classes: 'Resolution', 4; 'Valiant', 3; 'Dreadnought', 1; 'Oberon', 13; 'Porpoise', 8; 'A', 5. Surface displacements range from 1,385 to 7,500 tons.

The first nuclear-powered fleet submarine, *Dreadnought*, was commissioned on 17 April 1963; and the first nuclear powered ballistic missile submarine, *Resolution*, was accepted in Oct. 1967.

The destroyers of the Royal Navy are of the following classes: 'County', 8; later 'Battle',1; 'C', 2. Standard displacements range from 2,106 to 5,440 tons.

Frigates are of the following classes: 'Leander', 24; 'Tribal', 7; 'Rothesay', 9; 'Leopard', 4; 'Salisbury', 4; 'Whitby', 5; 'Blackwood', 8; 'Type 15', 4. Displacements range from 1,180 to 2,550 tons.

Ships under construction or on order include 6 nuclear powered submarines, 2 guided missile armed destroyers and 6 frigates.

The 'Type 82' guided missile armed destroyer *Bristol*, larger than the 'County' class, was launched on 30 June 1969 and the first 'Type 42', *Sheffield*, was laid down on 15 Jan. 1970.

The Navy estimates for 1959–60, £370·7m.; 1960–61, £397·5m.; 1961–62, £413·2m.; 1962–63, £422,273,000; 1963–64, £439,951,000; 1964–65, £496,015,000; 1965–66, £544,188,000; 1966–67, £597,129,000; 1967–68, £648,043,000; 1968–69, £668,743,000; 1969–70, £642,043,000; 1970–71, £659,378,500.

For 1959–60 the total personnel of officers and ratings provided for was (in 1,000) 106; 1960–61, 102; 1961–64, 100; 1964–65, 103; 1965–66, 104; 1966–67, 103; 1967–68, 100·5; 1968–69, 98: 1969–70, 95·5; 1970–71, 86·6; 1971–72, 83·1 (forecast).

Blackman, R. V. B. (ed.), *Jane's Fighting Ships*. 73rd ed. London, 1970–71
Blackman, R. V. B., *The World's Warships*. London, 1969

Army

Control of the British Army is vested in the Defence Council and is exercised through the Army Board, which consists of 7 civilian and 5 military members. The Secretary of State for Defence is Chairman of the Army Board, with the Minister of State for Defence and the Parliamentary Under-Secretary of State for Defence for the Army as Vice-Chairman. Other civilian members are the Second Permanent Under-Secretary of State (Administration), the Second Permanent Under Secretary of State (Equipment), who attend as appropriate, the Chief Scientist (Army) and the Deputy Under-Secretary of State (Army).

The Military members of the Army Board are the Chief of the General Staff, the Adjutant-General, the Quartermaster-General, the Master-General of the Ordnance and the Vice-Chief of the General Staff. The Chief of the General Staff is the professional head of his Service and the professional adviser to Ministers on the Army aspects of military problems. He is responsible for the fighting efficiency of his Service; for the consideration of all Army aspects of policy planning; for Army advice on the conduct of operations; and for the issuing of such single Service operational orders as may be appropriate resulting from defence policy decisions. The Chief of the General Staff is a member of the Chiefs of Staff Committee which is collectively responsible to HM Government for professional advice on strategy and military operations and on the military implication of defence policy. This advice is tendered to the Secretary of State for Defence by the Chairman of the Chiefs of Staff Committee, the Chief of the Defence Staff. In exercise of his General Staff responsibilities the Chief of the General Staff is assisted by the Vice-Chief of the General Staff. The Adjutant-General is responsible for raising and organizing the personnel of the Regular Army and the Reserves, and for the well-being of soldiers and their families. He also deals with personnel problems of the T & AVR and Cadets. Management involves recruiting, manning, personnel administration, individual training, the release and recall of reserves, discipline and the administration of military law, medical services, education, leave, welfare and other personal services. The Quartermaster-General is responsible for the feeding and quartering of the Army; all military movement, the issue and repair of equipment and vehicles; the supply of ammunition; the provision of stores; upkeep and operation of military ports, railways and inland water transport; supply and delivery of petroleum products; provision and operation of transport; barrack services; canteen services; mail; military labour and civil labour in overseas theatres; salvage; fire service; veterinary and remount service; certain services for the RAF in an overseas theatre. Corps controlled by the Quartermaster-General for these purposes include: Royal Engineers (engineers stores and postal services), Royal Corps of Transport, Royal Army Ordnance Corps, Army Catering Corps, Royal Electrical and Mechanical Engineers, Royal Pioneer Corps, Royal Army Veterinary Corps. The Master-General of the Ordnance is responsible for the research, development and production of all arms, vehicles and equipment for the Army, with the exception of aircraft, guided and nuclear weapons, and electronic equipment, for which the Ministry of Aviation Supply is responsible. The Chief Scientist (Army) is the professional head of the Army Department Scientific Staff and is responsible for the Army Department Research Programme. He is further responsible for furnishing scientific advice to the Army Board and for seeing that the technical facilities needed at the Army Department Research and Development Establishments are available and for ensuring that scientific information is properly disseminated and appreciated. He and his staff form part of the Defence Scientific Staff under the Chief Adviser (Projects and Research) when the problems with which they deal are of a Defence and not a single Service character. The Deputy Under-Secretary of State (Army) is Secretary of the Army Board. He is responsible for the general co-ordination of Army Board business and, under the Permanent Under-Secretary of State and the 2 Second Permanent Under-Secretaries of State, for providing it with financial and administrative guidance.

There are 3 major Army geographic Commands in England. These are: Northern (York), Southern (Hounslow) and Western (Chester) Commands. There is also Headquarters Scotland (Edinburgh) and Headquarters Northern Ireland (Lisburn). Each is commanded by a lieut.-general. The 3 geographic Commands in England have 3 or more districts commanded by maj.-generals, and Headquarters Scotland has 2 areas each commanded by a brigadier. In addition there is a major functional Command, Army Strategic Command, whose Headquarters commands the majority of the field force Army units. All 4 Commands are to be abolished as part of a major re-organization of the Army Command Structure in the UK. A new Headquarters, HQ United Kingdom Land Forces, will open on 1 April 1972 and will command districts directly. The number of districts will be reduced from 12 to 10. There are 3 major overseas Commands: Near East Land Forces, Far East Land Forces and the British Army of the Rhine. There are also garrisons in the Persian Gulf, Malta, Gibraltar and British Honduras.

The strength of the Regular Army (less the Brigade of Gurkhas, locally enlisted personnel and junior soldiers) on 1 Jan. 1971 was 158,000 men and 5,500 women. The citizen force is the Territorial and Army Volunteer Reserve, formed on 1 April 1967 to replace the Territorial Army and the Army Emergency Reserve. There are also reserves of men who have completed active service in the Regular Army, or in National Service with a reserve liability.

The Territorial and Army Volunteer Reserve has an establishment of about 74,000. Its role is to provide a national reserve for employment on specific tasks at home and overseas and to meet the unexpected when required; and, in particular, to complete the Army Order of Battle of NATO committed forces and to provide certain units for the support of NATO Headquarters, to assist in maintaining a secure UK base in support of forces deployed on the Continent of Europe and to provide a framework for any future expansion of the Reserves. All T & AVR units, with the exception of a small number of miscellaneous units, may be called out by a Queen's Order when warlike operations are in preparation or in progress.

Men who enlist into the Regular Army do so for 22 years. A man who enlists for 22 years has the right to transfer to the reserve at the end of 3, 6 or 9 years or to terminate his service after 12 years or any succeeding period of 3 years from the 12-year point. Men who waive their right to leave at the 3 and 6 years points receive the benefit of higher rates of pay. Women serve in both the Regular

Army and the T & AVR in the Queen Alexandra's Royal Army Nursing Corps and the Women's Royal Army Corps, the latter's employments including communications, motor transport, clerical and catering duties. Some officers of the Women's Royal Army Corps are employed on the staffs of military headquarters.

Fortescue, J. W., *History of the British Army*. 14 vols. London, 1899–1930
Sheppard, E. W., *Short History of the British Army*. 4th ed. London, 1950

Royal Air Force

In May 1912 the Royal Flying Corps first came into existence with military and naval wings, of which the latter became the independent Royal Naval Air Service in July 1914. On 2 Jan. 1918 an Air Ministry was formed, and on 1 April 1918 the Royal Flying Corps and the Royal Naval Air Service were amalgamated, under the Air Ministry, as the Royal Air Force. In 1937 the units based on aircraft-carriers and naval shore stations again passed to the operational and administrative control of the Admiralty, as the Fleet Air Arm. In 1964 control of the Royal Air Force became a responsibility of the unified Ministry of Defence.

The Royal Air Force is administered by the Air Force Board, of which the Secretary of State for Defence is Chairman. The Ministers of Defence for Administration and Equipment are Vice-Chairmen. Other members of the Board are the Under-Secretary of State for Defence for the Royal Air Force, who normally acts as Chairman on behalf of the Secretary of State, the Chief of the Air Staff, who is assisted by the Vice-Chief of the Air Staff and the Deputy Chief of the Air Staff, the Air Member for Personnel, the Air Member for Supply and Organization, the Chief Scientist (Royal Air Force) and the Deputy Under-Secretary of State (Air.) The Royal Air Force is organized into commands:

Home Commands. Strike, Air Support, Training and Maintenance Command. The Air Training Corps and the Air Sections of the Combined Cadet Force are under the control of Training Command.

Overseas Commands. The Near East Air Force (HQ Cyprus); Air Forces Gulf (Bahrain); the Far East Air Force (Changi); Royal Air Force Germany (2nd Tactical Air Force).

The RAF College, which trains general-duties and engineering cadets for permanent commissions is at Cranwell. The RAF Staff College is at Bracknell. The RAF College of Air Warfare is at Manby. The RAF apprenticeship scheme started in 1922 at Halton. The estimated strength on 1 April 1970, including WRAF and boys, was 112,200.

Current equipment of Strike Command includes 5 home-based squadrons of Mk. 2 Vulcan 4-jet medium bombers, 2 capable of carrying Blue Steel 'stand-off' missiles, supported by Victor flight-refuelling tankers; Buccaneer low-level strike and maritime attack aircraft; Shackleton and Nimrod maritime reconnaissance aircraft; Lightning and Phantom supersonic all-weather fighters, armed with air-to-air missiles; and Bloodhound surface-to-air missiles. The Command has NATO commitments, but is available for overseas reinforcement. It incorporates No. 90 (Signals) Group and reconnaissance squadrons of Victor BSR. Mk. 2 and Canberra aircraft. Squadrons of RAF Germany, under SACEUR, have Harrier vertical take-off strike aircraft, Phantom and Lightning all-weather fighters, Buccaneer strike aircraft, Canberra tactical bombers, Wessex helicopters and Bloodhound surface-to-air missiles. The Harriers, Phantoms, transport aircraft and helicopters of No. 38 Group, Air Support Command, are at the disposal of SACEUR. Air Support Command's equipment includes VC10 and Comet jets, turboprop Britannia, Belfast, Hercules, Argosy and Andover transports, and smaller aircraft and helicopters, including Basset light communications aircraft. This Command also administers the RAF Regiment, with Rapier and Tigercat missiles for airfield defence. The Near East Air Force has 2 squadrons of Vulcan Mk. 2 medium bombers, Lightning fighters, Canberra reconnaissance aircraft, Shackleton maritime reconnaissance aircraft, Argosy transports, helicopters and Bloodhound surface-to-air missiles, and has to support CENTO. Air Forces Gulf is equipped with Hunter ground attack fighters, tactical transport squadrons and helicopters. The Far East Air Force has Lightnings, Shackletons, Hercules transports and helicopters and Bloodhound surrace-to-air missiles, and has a commitment to SEATO. Current plans entail major reductions of strength in the Gulf area and Far East. Training Command utilizes Chipmunk primary trainers, Jet Provost basic trainers, Gnat and Varsity advanced trainers, twin-jet Dominies and Varsities for navigation and aircrew training, and a variety of other types, including Sioux and Whirlwind helicopters. New types in production for the RAF include Jaguar strike and advanced training aircraft and SA-330 Puma assault helicopters.

The net total of Ministry of Defence (Air) estimates for 1969–70 is £590·68m. and for 1970–71 is £593·34m.

The Royal Air Force, 1939–45. Vol. I, II, III. HMSO, 1953–54
Taylor, J. W. R. *Pictorial History of the R.A.F.* Vols. I, II, III. London, 1968–70
Taylor, J. W. R. (ed.), *Jane's All the World's Aircraft.* London. Annual from 1909
Taylor, J. W. R., *Military Aircraft of the World.* London, 1971
Thetford, O., *Aircraft of the Royal Air Force since 1918.* London, 1971

AGRICULTURE

General distribution of the surface, in acres (1970):

Divisions	Total land surface	Rough grazing land	Permanent pasture	Arable land
England	32,030,000	3,116,000	8,059,000	13,167,000
Wales and Monmouth	5,100,000	1,554,000	1,826,000	738,000
Scotland	19,071,000	11,328,000	1,018,000	3,140,000
Isle of Man	141,000	45,000	24,000	54,000

Distribution of the cultivated area in Great Britain (in acres):

| | England and Wales | | Scotland | |
	1969	1970	1969	1970
Corn crops [1]	7,779,871	7,855,692	1,143,528 [5]	1,128,999 [5]
Green crops [2]	2,062,249	2,076,386	325,882	320,938
Hops	16,735	17,493	—	—
Small fruit	33,350 [3]	33,145 [3]	10,412	10,842
Orchards	156,598	153,725	384 [6]	.
Bare fallow	402,309	232,310	11,726	9,006
Clover and rotation grasses	3,567,584 [4]	3,537,803 [4]	1,711,331	1,670,658
Permanent pasture	9,919,498	9,885,465	1,094,705	1,018,435
Total	23,937,038	23,790,479	4,297,584	4,158,878

[1] Includes wheat, barley, oats, mixed corn and rye, for threshing.
[2] Green crops include beans, potatoes, turnips and swedes, mangolds, sugar-beet, cabbage, etc., for fodder, vegetables, and all other crops.
[3] Includes acreage of small fruit in orchards.   [4] Including lucerne.
[5] Excludes rye for threshing.
[6] The land beneath the trees is also accounted for as grass, bare fallow, small fruit or other crops.

The number of workers employed in agriculture in Great Britain was, in June 1970, 400,000 (300,300 males, 99,700 females), and in June 1969, 402,300 (326,200 males, 77,000 females).

In 1970, in the UK, land under the plough amounted to 17·8m. acres (crops and fallow, 12·1m. acres; temporary grassland (including lucerne), 5·7m. acres). Permanent grassland amounted to 12·2m. acres.

Principal crops in the UK as at June in each year:

	Wheat	Barley	Oats	Beans	Potatoes	Fodder crops [2]	Man-gold [1]	Sugar-beet
	Acreage (1,000 acres)							
1966	2,238	6,130	907	103 [3]	669	301	42	446
1967	2,305	6,027	1,012	140	708	289	36	457
1968	2,417	5,933	945	229	691	269	31	465
1969	2,059	5,962	945	220	614	261	26	457
1970	2,495	5,542	929	189	669	248	24	463
	Total produce (1,000 tons)							
1966	3,420	8,586	1,102	121 [3]	6,476	5,770	1,041	6,495
1967	3,841	9,069	1,364	170	7,087	5,768	897	6,775
1968	3,414	8,140	1,205	221	6,763	5,429	803	7,006
1969	3,311	8,527	1,287	232	6,117	5,461	611	5,939
1970 [4]	4,108	7,378	1,214	157	7,364	5,561	571	6,311

[1] Fodder crops.   [2] Turnips and swedes for stock-feeding, including fodder beet.
[3] Includes peas.   [4] Provisional.

Livestock in the UK as at June in each year (in 1,000):

	1966	1967	1968	1969	1970
Cattle	12,206	12,342	12,151	12,374	12,581
Sheep	29,957	28,885	28,004	26,604	26,080
Pigs	7,333	7,107	7,387	7,783	8,049
Poultry	118,940	125,624	127,459	126,514	139,513

FISHERIES

Quantity (in tons) and value (in £) of fish of British taking landed in Great Britain (excluding salmon and sea-trout):

Quantity	1966	1967	1968	1969	1970[1]
England and Wales	496,053	514,058	520,595	532,475	505,331
Scotland	400,305	327,524	329,708	350,936	390,599
G.B. (excluding shell-fish)	896,358	841,582	850,303	883,411	895,930
Value					
England and Wales	39,214,077	38,185,474	38,142,882	40,769,262	45,918,821
Scotland	18,767,491	18,558,831	18,918,521	18,975,552	23,287,428
G.B. (excluding shell-fish)	57,981,568	56,744,305	57,061,403	59,744,814	69,206,249
Value of shell-fish	3,481,274	3,757,269	4,604,647	5,663,595	6,278,987

[1] Provisional figures.

FUEL AND POWER

Fuel. The Number of National Coal Board mines producing coal on 27 March 1970 was 299, and there were also (Sept. 1970) 211 licensed mines. Statistics of the coalmining industry (including licensed mines) for recent years are as follows:

	1966–67[1]	1967–68[1]	1968–69[1]	1969–70[1]
Saleable output of coal:				
Total deep-mined (1,000 tons)	165,900	163,800[2]	154,000	140,800
Opencast (1,000 tons)	7,100	7,100	6,600	6,600
Average weekly number of wage-earners on colliery books				
All workers (NCB only)	419,400	391,900	336,300	305,100
Underground workers (NCB only)	331,400	309,100	226,000	240,000
Coal exports:				
Total (1,000 tons)	2,461	1,961	3,066	3,500

[1] 12-month period ending March.   [2] Includes licensed mines—1·02m. tons.

Total stocks of coal on 27 March 1970 amounted to 24·35m. tons (9·92 tons distributed, 14·43m. tons undistributed). Operating profits made by the NCB for the year ended 28 March 1970 amounted to £8·8m. (collieries, £11·8m. loss; opencast, £7·3m. profit). Interest payable to the Department of Trade and Industry, £37m.

Production of coke (including coke breeze) amounted in 1969–70 to 4·42m. tons.

There were no imports of coal or coke by the NCB in 1969–70; exports, 1969–70, amounted to 4m. tons, valued at £20m. (3·4m. tons valued at £16m. in 1968–69).

In 1969–70 inland consumption (1,000 tons) of coal at home is estimated to have been 158,936, some of the principal users being: Power stations, 75,988; domestic, 20,989; coke ovens, 25,413; gas works, 6,001; chemicals and allied trades, 4,262; collieries, 1,994; paper industry, 2,730; cement industry, 4,251; engineering and other metal trades, 1,759; food, drink and tobacco industry, 1,530; other industrial users (including iron and steel, railways, textiles, bricks, pottery and glass), 3,965.

Petroleum. Production 1970, 1,000 tons (1969 in brackets): Throughput of crude process and shale oil, 100,298 (90,251); output of refinery fuel, 5,928 (5,546); aviation and motor spirits, 22,151 (19,170); kerosine, 5,747 (5,366); diesel oil, 22,151 (19,170); fuel oil, 42,170 (37,661); lubricating oils, 1,298 (1,183); bitumen, 1,881 (1,695).

Gas. The British gas industry passed into public ownership of 1 May 1949 and was vested in the body forming the Gas Council, which consists of a Chairman, Deputy Chairman and up to 5 full-time members, and the Chairmen of the 12 Area Gas Boards, all of whom are appointed by the Secretary of State for Trade and Industry.

The duties and powers of the Council and of the 12 Area Boards are set out in the Gas Act 1948, the Gas Act 1960, the Electricity and Gas Act 1963, the Gas Act 1965 and the Gas and Electricity Act 1968. The duties and powers of the Council can be briefly summarized as follows: (i) to advise the Minister of Power on matters affecting the gas industry; (ii) to assist the Area Boards in carrying out their duties; (iii) to promote and assist the co-ordinated development of gas supplies in Great Britain; (iv) to manufacture and get or acquire gas and to supply it to the 12 Area Boards; (v) to supply gas direct to consumers subject to the consent of the Minister; (vi) to raise the capital required by the Council itself and by the Area Boards; (vii) to conduct or arrange for research into matters affecting gas supply: (viii) to negotiate the terms and conditions of employment of persons employed by the Council and by the Area Boards. The principal duty of each Area Board is to develop an efficient and economical system of gas supply in its area and to satisfy, so far as it is economic to do so, all reasonable demands for gas in its area.

Gas manufactured (1m. therms), 1969–70: Coal gas, 427; oil gas, 1,747; other gases, 46. Gas purchased reflected the tremendous increase in the use of natural gas (especially from the North Sea reserves) which increased to 2,895m. therms, about half of total supply. Other purchases (refinery gas, LPG and coke-oven gas) totalled 829m. therms, and total gas available reached the record level of 5,744m. therms. Gas sales increased by more than 12% over the year 1968–69 and have increased by more than two-thirds over the past 7 years. In 1969–70 coal used for gas production was 5·9m. tons; quantity of oil used, 4·6m. tons. Gas sales for 1969–70 amounted to £498m. Total number of consumers at 31 March 1970 was 13,346,800, of whom 12,734,000 were domestic. Total number employed at 31 March 1970 was 119,475.

Electricity. The electricity industry was invested in the British Electricity Authority on 1 April 1948. Following the re-organization of the electricity supply industry after the passing of the Electricity Act, 1957, the statutory bodies comprising the electricity service in England and Wales are the Electricity Council, the Central Electricity Generating Board and the 12 Area Electricity Boards.

The Electricity Council has functioned from Jan. 1958 as the central council for the supply industry in England and Wales for consultation on, and formulation of, general policy; its main functions are to advise the Secretary of State for Trade and Industry on all matters affecting the supply industry, and to promote and assist the maintenance and development by the Central Electricity Generating Board and the Area Boards known collectively as Electricity Boards) of an efficient, co-ordinated and economical system of electricity supply. The Council can also perform services for the Boards, and, in addition, has certain specific functions, particularly in matters of finance, research and industrial relations.

The Central Electricity Generating Board is responsible for the generation and bulk supply of electricity to the 12 Area Boards in England and Wales. It therefore plans the provision of new generating and transmission capacity, including the siting and construction of new generating stations, both conventional and nuclear, and is responsible for the operation and maintenance of generating stations and the main transmission systems.

Area Electricity Boards. Each of the 12 Area Electricity Boards acquires bulk supplies of electricity from the Generating Board and is responsible for distribution networks and sales of electricity to its Area consumers. Thus distribution and utilization of electricity, and also the contracting and sale of appliances side of the industry, are their responsibilities.

The number of power stations owned by the Generating Board in England and Wales on 31 March 1970 was 193 with a total output capacity of 46,857 mw.

Total number of consumers on 31 March 1969 was 18,087,011 (on 31 March 1970, 18,271,086).

Electricity supplied in England and Wales in 1969–70 amounted to 180,718m. units. Revenue from sales of electricity in 1969–70 was £1,328m. Coal used for electricity generation in 1969–70 amounted to 69m. tons (68·6m. tons in 1968–69). Total fuel (coal equivalent) used in 1968–69 amounted to 86m. tons and in 1969–70 to 90·2m. tons. In 1960 the Government announced a revised programme of 5,000 mw × 3 of nuclear generating power by 1968. In April 1964 it announced the Second Nuclear Power Programme, which planned for a capacity of 5,000 mw × 3 of nuclear generating power being commissioned in England and Wales between 1970 and 1975 (subsequently raised to 8,000 mw × 3). At the beginning of 1971, 7 commercial nuclear power stations were in operation and 5 more under construction.

The number of persons employed by the Generating Board, the Electricity Council and the Area Boards at the end of March 1970 was 196,962.

METALS

The UK is the fifth largest steel producing country in the world.

Output in recent years was as follows (in 1,000 tons):

	Iron ore	Pig-iron	Crude steel	Home consumption [1]
1967	12,739	15,153	23,895	21,292
1968	13,715	16,432	25,862	22,744
1969	12,104	16,390	26,422	23,900
1970	11,828	17,393	27,883	..

[1] Finished steel (ingot equivalent).

In 1970 imports of iron ore amounted to 19·87m. tons valued at £106m. (compared with 18·17m. tons in 1969 valued at £87·5m.). Exports of finished steel products were 3·7m. tons in 1970 and were valued at £300·5m. (compared with 3·6m. tons in 1969 valued at £250·7m.).

Iron Castings. Production of iron castings was 3·76m. tons in 1969 and 1970. At the end of 1970 the number of persons employed in the production of iron castings was some 101,000.

Capital Expenditure. Capital expenditure in 1970 in the iron and steel industry (including iron foundries) is estimated to have been about £135m. (compared with £93m. in 1969).

The industry is divided between the 'public sector' and the 'private sector'. The former consists of the British Steel Corporation which was established on 22 March 1967 under the Iron and Steel Act 1967. This Act brought into public ownership the 14 major steel producers who together accounted for over 90% of the UK output of crude steel. These companies, including nearly 200 subsidiaries, of which some 50 were overseas subsidiaries, vested in the Corporation on 28 July 1967. The creation of the Corporation represented a massive merger, resulting in the second largest steel business in the free world and one of the world's largest industrial undertakings. It produces and sells steel and other products with an annual value of over £1,350m. and employs some 260,000 people. The Act left a substantial part of the British iron and steel industry in private ownership accounting for a turnover of approximately a third of the total for the whole industry at that time with particular strengths in finished steels and in the high value special steels such as alloy, stainless, high speed and tool steels.

The private sector of the steel industry has formed the British Independent Steel Producers Association (BISPA), 109 members, to protect and represent its interest to the Corporation and the Government, and to ensure that liaison continues between the public and private sectors in areas of mutual interest, such as research, standards and statistics.

Production of non-ferrous metals in 1969 (in 1,000 tons): Refined copper, 195·1 (194·6 in 1968); refined lead, 139·4 (141·4 in 1968); tin metal, 28·3 (27·7 in 1968); virgin aluminium, 33·3 (37·6 in 1968); slab zinc, 151 (130·7 in 1968).

INDUSTRIAL PRODUCTION

Statistics of a cross-section of industrial production are as follows:

	1968	1969	1970
Sulphuric acid (1,000 tons)	3,282	3,235	3,200
Synthetic resins (1,000 tons)	1,238	1,309	1,329
Agricultural machinery (value £1m.)	57	67	..
Commercial motor vehicles (no. 1,000)	409	466	457
Cotton single yarn (1m. lb.)	304	292	268
Wool tops (1m. lb.)	213	203	175
Woollen yarn (1m. lb.)	325	314	286
Man-made fibres (rayon, nylon, etc.) (1m. lb.)	1,189	1,221	1,320
Plywood (1,000 cu. ft)	1,105	1,019	..
Newsprint (1,000 tons)	724	777	744

Engineering. In 1970 the number (in 1,000) of passenger cars produced amounted to 1,641 (1,717 in 1969); aircraft production in 1969 was 500 (1968: 278).

Electrical Goods. Production (in 1,000) for 1969 (1968 in brackets): Radio sets and radiograms, 1,420 (1,736); gramophone records, 106,354 (98,551); television sets, 1,902 (1,963); domestic washing machines, 829 (884).

Textile Manufacturers. Production for 1969 (1968 in brackets): Woven cloth, cotton (1m. yd), 723 (731); man-made fibres (1m. lb), 1,221 (1,189); woven woollen and mixture fabrics (1m. sq. yd), deliveries, 286 (295).

Construction. Total value (in £1m.) of constructional work by all agencies in 1969 was 4,697 (4,569 in 1968), including new housing, 1,179. Value of industrial buildings for private developers completed in 1969 was £510m. New work (other than housing) for public authorities was valued at £1,046m.

Census of Production. Reports for 1963. 130 parts. HMSO, 1968
Pollard, S., *The Development of the British Economy, 1914–1950.* London, 1962
Smith, Wilfred, *An Economic Geography of Great Britain.* 2nd ed. London, 1953
Stamp, L. D., *The Land of Britain: Its Use and Misuse.* 3rd ed. London, 1962
Statistical Summary of the Mineral Industry. HMSO, annual
Worswick, G. D. N., and Ady, P. H. (ed.), *The British Economy, 1945–50.* OUP, 1952.—*The British Economy in the Nineteen-Fifties.* OUP, 1962

LABOUR AND EMPLOYMENT

The distribution of total man-power in Great Britain was at June 1970 (in 1,000): Total working population, 25,044 (16,023 males, 9,021 females). Total employed in armed forces and women's services, 372. Total engaged in civil employment, 24,148, including agriculture and fishing, 372; mining and quarrying, 415; manufacturing industries, 8,727; national and local government service, 1,391; transport and communications, 1,567; building and civil engineering, 1,322; distributive trades, 2,651; finance, professional, scientific and miscellaneous services, 5,012.

The total number of registered unions was 328 in 1969 with a membership of over 8m. Income (1969) £38,280,000 from members and £7,502,000 from other sources.

In 1970 there were 150 unions affiliated to the Trade Union Congress with a total membership of 9,402,170 (including about 2,168,268 women). The General Council is elected by Congress and is composed of 39 members (37 representing 19 trade groups and 2 representing women workers). The membership and number of unions in each trade group included: Transport (other than railways), 1,656,804 (9); engineering, founding and vehicle building, 1,465,691 (13); mining and quarrying, 321,940 (3); building, woodworking, 380,536 (9); railways, 290,111 (3).

The following table is a statistical summary relating to trade disputes for recent years:

	No. of stoppages		No. of workers involved		Working days lost through stoppages	
	1968	1969	1968	1969	1969	1970
Mining and quarrying	227	193	30,000	145,000	1,041,000	1,091,000
Metals, engineering, shipbuilding and vehicles	1,103	1,430	1,911,000	750,000	3,739,000	4,548,000
Textiles and clothing	69	96	16,000	28,000	140,000	384,000
Construction	276	285	47,000	44,000	278,000	237,000
Transport and communications	342	540	145,000	393,000	786,000	1,304,000
Total (including those not specified)	2,378	3,116	2,256,000	1,656,000	6,846,000	10,970,000

The average annual numbers (in 1,000) of registered unemployed in Great Britain were 1970, 603·4 (males, 514·1; females, 89·3); 1969, 559·5 (males, 475·9; females, 183·4). Wholly unemployed (including casuals), 1968, 549·5 (males, 460·7; females, 88·8); 1967, 520·9 (males, 420·7; females, 100·2).

Allen, V. L., *Trade Unions and the Government*. London, 1960
The Trade Union Situation in the United Kingdom. Intern. Labour Organization, Geneva, 1961

COMMERCE

Value of the imports and exports of merchandise (excluding bullion and specie and foreign merchandise transhipped under bond) of the UK for 5 recent years (in £1,000):

	Total imports	Exports of British produce	Exports of foreign and colonial produce	Total exports
1966	5,946,787	5,046,950	194,371	5,241,321
1967	6,434,118	5,028,760	184,780	5,213,540
1968	7,890,126	6,182,565	219,628	6,402,193
1969[1]	8,315,141	7,039,346	258,662	7,298,008
1970[1]	9,051,466	..	..	8,062,750

[1] Provisional.

The value of goods imported is generally taken to be that at the port and time of entry, including all incidental expenses (cost, insurance and freight) up to the landing on the quay. For goods consigned for sale, the market value in this country is required and recorded in the returns. For exports, the value at the port of shipment (including the charges of delivering the goods on board) is taken. Imports are entered as from the country whence the goods were consigned to the UK, which may, or may not, be the country whence the goods were last shipped. Exports are credited to the country of ultimate destination as declared by the exporters.

For details of imports and exports for 1968 and 1969, *see* pp. 109–11.

Trade according to countries for 1969 and 1970 (in £1,000):

	Imports of merchandise from		Exports of merchandise to		
			British produce		Foreign and colonial produce
Countries	1969[1]	1970[1]	1969[1]	1970[1, 2]	1969[1]
Foreign countries:					
Europe and Colonies—					
Soviet Union	197,155	220,054	96,403	102,103	757
Finland	173,608	195,005	99,079	128,901	2,285
Sweden	332,805	371,047	294,766	364,065	6,446
Norway	179,656	198,637	140,781	173,834	3,872
Iceland	6,774	8,951	5,891	9,284	174
Denmark and Faroe Islands	246,118	276,249	192,650	221,149	3,735
Poland	57,001	63,025	54,175	59,695	894
Germany (East)	14,620	16,082	12,131	16,901	624
Germany (West)	466,129	548,934	366,498	502,903	47,485
Netherlands	409,140	459,102	278,929	377,767	16,052
Netherlands Antilles	13,062	13,137	6,448	8,260	126
Surinam	410	718	2,671	3,135	27
Belgium	182,603	192,503	280,844	288,620	7,383
Luxembourg	4,657	4,306	2,020	5,653	673

[1] Provisional figures.   [2] Total exports.

| | Imports of merchandise from | | Exports of merchandise to | | Foreign and colonial produce |
| | | | British produce | | |
Countries	1969[1]	1970[1]	1969[1]	1970[1], [2]	1969[1]
Foreign countries:					
Europe and Colonies (contd.)—					
France	324,448	368,243	290,954	339,329	21,136
Terr. of the Afars and the Issas	108	29	2,035	1,353	8
French West India Islands	12	54	773	1,257	8
Switzerland and Liechtenstein	174,462	198,839	167,716	209,298	16,025
Portugal	75,907	85,630	74,850	86,776	1,298
Azores	426	227	302	557	11
Maderia	336	516	905	1,307	8
Angola	3,639	8,920	11,101	13,819	86
Moçambique	4,019	5,859	11,597	13,131	143
Spain	98,774	108,490	115,254	123,169	3,403
Canary Islands	16,225	18,034	15,715	19,526	438
Spanish North Africa	4	—	500	498	3
Italy	222,920	249,176	190,994	239,663	18,667
Austria	64,123	79,596	69,356	90,706	1,892
Hungary	9,408	10,629	12,744	18,995	579
Czechoslovakia	21,508	22,774	17,654	20,376	530
Yugoslavia	24,799	21,725	31,251	45,608	528
Albania	7	2	113	167	—
Greece	16,626	19,604	57,945	57,239	1,006
Bulgaria	7,333	8,307	4,936	11,118	128
Romania	24,970	23,188	28,637	29,077	423
Turkey	15,658	15,609	33,890	35,932	1,091
EEC	1,609,896	1,822,264	1,410,239	1,753,835	111,395
EFTA	1,247,443	1,411,861	1,041,379	1,283,535	35,573
Africa—					
Sudan	7,301	7,624	21,558	18,181	191
UAR	9,302	10,852	15,036	18,724	493
Ethiopia	1,950	1,963	4,813	4,834	165
Libya	151,557	166,876	42,465	24,346	685
Congo (K.)	22,834	18,872	11,229	12,033	215
South Africa, Republic of	302,322	258,266	285,797	332,896	5,083
S.W. Africa	26,429	26,052	1,615	1,883	24
Liberia	8,693	11,972	13,655	13,628	219
Morocco	15,690	16,250	12,617	12,609	263
Tunisia	2,835	2,487	3,488	4,306	32
Rwanda	373	974	328	261	1
Burundi	974	2,081	199	275	—
Mali	231	318	65	284	—
Senegal	1,783	2,109	1,454	1,503	80
Algeria	22,073	21,166	8,719	16,774	780
Cameroun	2,247	2,081	3,696	3,728	295
Mauritania	9,338	8,586	1,720	1,234	138
Ivory Coast	10,107	9,637	2,944	3,122	46
Asia—					
Israel	39,304	45,079	101,086	96,157	1,697
Syria	1,235	489	7,128	5,995	55
Lebanon	3,995	3,124	20,874	23,013	508
Jordan	202	217	16,410	12,266	62
Saudi Arabia	86,796	104,231	56,161	35,249	808
Kuwait	171,982	165,397	40,888	36,224	630
Iraq	31,119	18,729	21,332	23,774	571
Iran	73,768	76,054	70,844	66,335	783
Afghánistán	7,265	6,433	1,963	1,697	51
Burma	3,055	4,274	6,760	6,346	162
Thailand	5,705	5,509	30,758	32,112	218
Indonesia	6,599	7,273	8,793	11,840	86
China	37,727	33,538	51,802	44,586	2,688
Japan	104,453	134,414	124,678	147,841	3,947
Korea (South)	4,099	6,239	12,042	11,393	109
Phillippines	4,333	7,480	27,911	25,087	258
America—					
USA	1,222,708	1,170,234	862,793	932,736	34,284
Puerto Rico	3,343	3,004	6,749	8,139	87
Cuba	5,410	5,702	13,053	20,559	179
Haiti	178	144	812	976	4
Dominican Republic	685	1,144	2,835	3,552	26

[1] Provisional figures. [2] Total exports.

Countries	Imports of merchandise from		Exports of merchandise to		Foreign and colonial produce
			British produce		
	1969[1]	1970[1]	1969[1]	1970[1], [2]	1969[1]
Foreign countries:					
America (contd.)—					
Mexico	14,525	6,343	29,170	34,170	760
Guatemala	799	859	3,505	4,150	40
Honduras (not British)	347	260	1,282	1,506	11
El Salvador	172	340	1,768	2,338	12
Nicaragua	996	821	2,939	2,724	14
Costa Rica	365	367	5,748	4,745	28
Colombia	7,481	8,904	12,173	12,942	72
Panama	2,699	1,839	7,575	8,765	171
Venezuela	56,653	50,825	31,035	33,706	620
Ecuador	399	588	4,136	7,027	18
Peru	13,903	15,197	11,569	9,905	227
Chile	72,145	64,860	17,248	20,519	326
Brazil	50,716	62,784	43,235	60,769	430
Uruguay	13,119	8,556	4,709	6,401	133
Bolivia	34,212	28,460	2,584	2,201	25
Argentina	78,740	65,598	46,189	44,065	754
Paraguay	2,122	2,271	2,412	2,210	38
Total (including those not specified above)	6,384,227	6,893,311	5,475,748	6,367,320	232,351
Commonwealth countries:					
In Europe—					
Gibraltar	532	680	5,032	5,739	285
Malta	5,382	5,760	23,027	25,695	768
Cyprus	18,943	20,432	25,641	26,088	583
In Africa—					
West Africa:					
Gambia	2,024	4,139	2,521	2,110	67
Sierra Leone	36,165	31,448	13406	12,530	168
Ghana	43,304	38,948	36,746	38,380	729
Nigeria, Federation of	104,489	123,874	77,904	114,385	1,227
South Africa:					
Rhodesia	68	49	810	503	6
Malawi	10,658	12,135	7,568	7,983	55
Zambia	105,519	101,384	34,454	37,866	621
Botswana	833	3,133	346	426	1
Swaziland	9,830	9,411	134	353	—
Lesotho	1	1	88	67	—
East Africa:					
Tanzania	23,954	23,963	17,985	19,583	132
Kenya	25,706	27,064	49,242	52,822	712
Uganda	17,466	17,652	10,058	9,960	52
Mauritius	21,379	22,495	4,813	5,899	28
Seychelles	137	51	1,306	1,302	137
St Helena	60	53	696	768	84
In Asia—					
Bahrain	2,072	1,554	12,454	24,340	314
Qatar	24,743	30,581	5,815	7,430	32
India	107,064	106,044	65,528	72,900	916
Pakistan	39,720	35,332	53,187	49,249	548
Malaysia	33,549	46,596	46,628	60,426	761
Singapore	30,600	33,546	49,465	62,518	937
Ceylon	33,101	36,558	29,094	18,508	145
Hong Kong	125,359	128,394	87,134	99,516	1,528
In Oceania—					
Australia	237,443	260,084	318,164	346,094	3,197
Papua and New Guinea	7,013	8,240	3,092	3,005	32
New Zealand	216,159	203,558	120,230	129,285	1,100
Western Samoa	71	90	293	323	—
Nauru	336	—	1,231	63	1
Fiji Islands	11,727	10,206	5,836	6,083	44
Other Pacific Islands (Brit.)	1,558	431	1,150	1,315	10

[1] Provisional figures   [2] Total exports

	Imports of merchandise from		Exports of merchandise to		Foreign and colonial produce
			British produce		
Countries	1969[1]	1970[1]	1969[1]	1970[1, 2]	1969[1]
Commonwealth countries:					
In America—					
Canada	504,858	682,732	300,633	288,123	8,069
Bermuda	11,216	15,882	9,814	11,093	228
Bahamas	1,978	2,752	13,446	11,073	419
Jamaica	26,174	27,480	34,878	38,203	736
Leeward Islands	1,327	1,922	5,268	6,337	97
Windward Islands	12,727	9,473	6,356	9,735	117
Barbados	6,680	6,836	9,283	11,973	171
Trinidad and Tobago	21,688	19,309	24,866	28,131	402
British Honduras	2,281	2,347	3,016	3,597	67
Guyana	13,182	12,550	13,163	14,903	221
Falkland Islands	937	604	397	451	12
Total, Commonwealth countries (including those not specified above)	1,930,914	2,158,155	1,563,598	1,695,430	26,311
Irish Republic	293,635	341,255	316,549	381,209	13,097
Grand Total	8,315,141	4,051,466	7,039,346	8,062,750	258,662

[1] Provisional figures.   [2] Total exports

Imports and exports for 1969 and 1970 (Great Britain and Northern Ireland) (in £1,000):

Import values c.i.f. Export values f.o.b.	Total imports		Domestic exports	
	1969	1970	1969	1970
0. Food and Live Animals				
Live animals (excluding zoo animals, dogs and cats)	53,865	56,488	28,841	32,629
Meat and meat preparations	432,497	438,201	15,849	21,260
Dairy products and eggs	184,050	185,524	13,630	14,441
Fish and fish preparations	69,960	74,247	14,127	20,839
Cereals and cereal preparations	251,907	281,427	25,735	33,721
Fruit and vegetables	358,295	379,908	17,776	22,179
Sugar, sugar preparations, honey	112,514	117,479	27,982	30,734
Coffee, tea, cocoa, spices	182,657	209,690	20,736	41,568
Feeding stuff for animals	81,383	88,219	9,469	11,418
Miscellaneous food preparations	23,143	31,421	17,327	20,545
Total of Section 0	1,750,269	1,862,604	191,471	249,335
1. Beverages and Tobacco				
Beverages	69,201	79,049	190,034	224,911
Tobacco and tobacco manufactures	114,550	110,348	34,853	40,097
Total of Section 1	183,751	189,397	224,886	265,008
2. Crude Materials, Inedible, except Fuels				
Hides, skins and furskins, undressed	78,147	70,161	9,719	53,061
Oil seeds, oil nuts and oil kernels	38,509	41,745	407	1,126
Crude rubber (including synthetic and reclaimed)	60,878	57,693	19,114	23,105
Wood and cork	217,518	238,818	882	2,109
Pulp and waste paper	165,445	197,948	2,300	2,987
Textile fibres and their waste	210,873	183,940	99,021	96,377
Crude fertilizers and crude minerals (excluding fuels)	63,109	65,340	36,923	47,820
Metalliferous ores and metal scrap	291,214	346,575	17,958	26,394
Crude animal and vegetable materials, not elsewhere specified	55,437	60,936	5,072	10,552
Total of Section 2	1,181,130	1,263,157	191,395	263,533

Import values c.i.f. Export values f.o.b.	Total imports		Domestic exports	
	1969	*1970*	*1969*	*1970*
3. *Mineral Fuels, Lubricants and* *Related Materials*				
Coal, coke and briquettes	1,252	3,416	25,062	29,081
Petroleum and petroleum products	889,581	925,375	145,693	176,341
Gas, natural and manufactured; electric energy	19,433	16,951	680	1,439
Total of Section 3	910,266	945,742	171,435	206,861
4. *Animal and Vegetable Oils* *and Fats*	73,137	100,675	8,319	9,285
5. *Chemicals*				
Chemical elements and compounds	202,282	237,807	166,493	210,340
Dyeing, tanning and colouring materials	27,817	33,389	76,235	81,477
Medicinal and pharmaceutical products	25,453	33,724	117,692	139,751
Essential oils and perfume; toilet and cleansing preparations	21,987	23,310	60,685	67,021
Fertilizers, manufactured	24,237	23,088	5,375	4,785
Plastic materials	92,727	110,863	128,381	143,747
Total of Section 5	463,029	542,793	685,036	786,100
6. *Manufactured Goods Classified* *Chiefly by Material*				
Leather and dressed furs	37,419	32,484	45,784	50,651
Rubber	24,647	27,619	72,432	92,667
Wood and cork (excluding furniture)	90,108	108,530	7,156	11,197
Paper, paperboard	203,636	231,145	78,596	89,228
Textile yarn, fabrics	238,670	256,394	347,136	396,832
Non-metallic mineral manufactures	386,881	382,338	454,148	390,318
Iron and steel	173,887	222,475	284,999	347,887
Non-ferrous metals	608,880	608,677	312,046	350,571
Manufactures of metal, not elsewhere specified	75,835	97,037	214,568	260,449
Total of Section 6	1,839,962	1,966,699	1,816,865	1,989,801
7. *Machinery and Transport* *Equipment*				
Machinery, other than electric	681,080	855,737	1,417,338	1,642,376
Electrical machinery, apparatus	266,366	342,236	465,642	579,052
Transport equipment	371,711	298,525	1,071,176	1,079,789
Total of Section 7	1,319,127	1,496,499	2,954,356	3,301,218
8. *Miscellaneous Manufactured* *Articles*				
Sanitary, plumbing, heating and lighting fixtures	7,608	10,016	17,299	20,809
Furniture	13,488	15,618	23,213	25,328
Travel goods, handbags and similar articles	5,300	5,735	4,142	4,435
Clothing	124,513	129,431	107,510	123,116
Footwear	35,501	40,574	33,528	35,511
Scientific instruments; watches and clocks	115,279	141,508	179,091	208,591
Miscellaneous manufactured articles, not elsewhere specified	212,864	231,033	271,206	313,064
Total of Section 8	514,513	573,915	635,989	730,852
9. *Commodities and Transactions not* *Classified According to Kind*				
Post parcels	44,177	51,926	108,901	159,556
Animals, not elsewhere specified	1,631	860	784	448
Total of Section 9	79,918	109,985	159,593	260,758
Total of all classes	8,315,141	9,051,466	7,039,346	8,062,750

COMMUNICATIONS

Shipping

The total gross tonnage (1,000 tons) of merchant vessels (500 gross tons and over) on the UK register (excluding foreign-owned vessels on bareboat charter or requisition) was, on 30 Dec. 1970, 24,061 (non-tankers, 12,211; tankers, 11,849). The total number of ships was 1,977.

At 31 Dec. 1970 the effective strength of the British Merchant Navy (excluding Asiatic seamen signed on in Asia) was 99,649.

At 31 Dec. 1970 the world total of shipping under construction (excluding ships of less than 100 tons gross) amounted to 21,510,420 tons, of which 7·7% was building in the UK, aggregating 146 vessels of 1,649,441 tons (5 steamers, 301,300 tons; 141 motorships, 1,348,241 tons). Tankers under construction in the UK numbered 15 (458,680 tons) out of a world construction total of 210 (9·4m. tons).

The world oil tanker fleet at 30 June 1970 numbered 4,903 vessels of 87·8m. gross tons, of which the UK owned the third largest fleet of 11·3m. tons. Ships launched in 1970 in the UK aggregated 1,237,134 tons (5·7% of the world total); the UK lies in fourth place after Japan (48·3%), Sweden (7·89%) and West Germany (7·78%)). Laid up tonnage on 1 Jan. 1971 included 4 ships (126,180 gross tons) registered in the UK out of a world total of 38 ships (398,551 gross tons).

The total net tonnage of entrances at ports of the UK with cargoes during 1970 was 126·6m. (including 49·8m. tons, Commonwealth); total clearances were 68,600,000 net tons (including 32·8m. tons, Commonwealth). Of the foreign tonnage, 76·8m. tons entered: Norway had 14·1m.; Liberia, 13·2m.; Netherlands, 6·9m.; Sweden, 5·54m.; France, 6·2m.; Denmark, 3·2m.; USA, 2·8m.; Panama, 2·2m.

The total net tonnage of Commonwealth and foreign vessels employed in the coasting trade that arrived at ports in the UK with cargo in 1970 was 43·2m. (44·2m. in 1969); departures amounted to 41·3m. (41·6m. in 1969).

Bird, J., *The Major Seaports of the United Kingdom*. London, 1963
Rees, H., *British Ports and Shipping*. London, 1958
Thornton, R. H., *British Shipping*. 2nd ed. CUP, 1958

Inland Waterways

There are approximately 2,500 miles of navigable canals and locked river navigations in Great Britain. Of these, the British Waterways Board are responsible for some 300 miles of commercial waterways (maintained for freight traffic) and some 1,100 miles of cruising waterways (maintained for pleasure crusing, fishing and amenity). The Board are also responsible for a further 600 miles of canals, mostly no longer navigable, whose future is being considered in conjunction with local authorities. The Board's gross receipts for the year 1969 were £4·8m. The total traffic on their waterways was 6·7m. tons.

The most important of the river navigations and canals under other authorities include the rivers Thames, Great Ouse, Nene and Yorkshire Ouse, the Norfolk Broads and the Manchester Ship Canal.

Manchester, one of the leading ports in the UK, was opened to maritime traffic in 1894 by the construction of the Manchester Ship Canal, which is 35½ miles in length and owned and operated by the Manchester Ship Canal Company. The entrance lock is 80 ft wide and the maximum width of other locks within the canal is 65 ft. Ships up to 28 ft 10 in. fresh-water draught can navigate to Ince Oil Berth; between Ince Oil Berth and Manchester the maximum draught is 26 ft 6 in. in fresh water.

The Port of Manchester includes the Queen Elizabeth II Oil Dock at Eastham (separate entrance lock 100 ft wide), the oil docks at Stanlow and a considerable number of public and private wharves and installations along the canal, as well as the terminal docks at Manchester. Total sea-borne and barge traffic in 1969 amounted to 16,484,764 tons; tolls, dues, etc., £11,626,170; in 1968, 16,451,318 tons, £11,729,435. The total issued capital of the Company at 31 Dec. 1969 was £22,204,795. Operating surplus in 1969 was £2·42m. (1968, £2·36m.).

British Waterways, Recreation and Amenity. (Cmd 3401.) HMSO, 1967
Edwards, L. A., *Inland Waterways of Great Britain and Northern Ireland.* 3rd ed. London, 1962
Hadfield, C., *British Canals.* Rev. ed. Newton Abbot, 1966

Railways and Highways

Under the provisions of the Transport Act, 1947, the 4 main-line railways, together with their associated lines, docks, steamships and hotels, the London Passenger Transport Board and the major canal undertakings, passed on 1 Jan. 1948 into the ownership of the British Transport Commission, as the instrument of the State.

The Transport Act, 1962, dissolved the Commission and created in its stead separate Boards for British Railways, London Transport, British Transport Docks and British Waterways. The new Boards assumed their responsibilities as from 1 Jan. 1963. Other main provisions of the Act reconstructed the finances of the Boards and gave them a greater measure of commercial freedom.

The Transport Act, 1968, set up 3 new state-owned transport organizations. The National Freight Corporation inherited the road haulage subsidiaries of the THC, British Rail sundries division, now National Carriers Ltd, and 51 % of BR's freightliner company. The National Bus Company acquired the assets of 65 companies, mainly concerned with road passenger transport in England and Wales, including those companies operated by the THC. The Scottish Transport Group acquired the assets of the THC's road passenger transport companies in Scotland, including ships, ferry services and British Railways domestic Scottish shipping services. These new organizations assumed their responsibilities on 1 Jan. 1969.

On 1 Jan. 1970, the responsibility for the London Transport Board was transferred to the Greater London Council and renamed London Transport Executive. The LTB Country Bus services and Green Line services were transferred at the same time to the National Bus Company and renamed London Country Buses.

Gross receipts in 1969 for these Boards were: British Railways Board, £611m.; London Transport Board, £111m.; British Transport Docks Board, £29·6m.; Transport Holding Company, £1m.; National Bus Company, £142·2m.; National Freight Corporation, £180m., and British Waterways Board, £1·9m.

Railways. The nationalized railway system, known as 'British Rail', together with British Transport Hotels Ltd, British Rail Engineering Ltd, British Rail Hovercraft Ltd and Shipping and International Services 'Sealink' are owned and managed by a public authority, the British Railways Board. The Board is required to direct its affairs in such a way as to ensure that standards of public service and safety are maintained while at the same time keeping within the financial contraints of the 1968 Transport Act.

The British Railways Board has a mainly non-executive role in order to give greater emphasis to overall corporate planning, policy making and the longer-term direction at each of its businesses while still ensuring that they are effectively managed.

Each subsidiary activity, other than British Rail, has a subsidiary board, chaired by a members of the main Board to direct that business.

The management of each business is delegated to a chief executive for that business. The Chief Executive (Railways) is supported by an advisory body known as the Railway Management Group comprising 6 executive directors for

Freight, Passenger, System and Operations, Finance, Personnel and Planning at headquarters and 5 regional General Managers, *Eastern, London Midland, Scottish, Southern* and *Western.* Each General Manager is assisted by a Regional Railway Board, but there is no longer any statutory obligation upon the Railways Board to retain these bodies.

The Transport Act, 1968, reduced the railways commencing debt from £1,562m. to £300m. The Act also enables the Secretary of State for the Environment to make grants towards the cost of unremunerative but socially necessary passenger services, and tapering grants up to 1973 towards the cost of surplus track and signalling equipment. These is no provision for the extension of deficit grants beyond 1968.

In 1970 the total freight traffic amounted to 199m. tons, comprising coal and coke 112m. tons, iron and steel 40m. tons and other freight, excluding carryings for Freightliners Ltd and National Carriers Ltd, for which tonnage figures are not available, 47m. tons. Passenger journeys amounted to 824m. Rolling stock (standard gauge) at the end of 1970 included 4,449 locomotives, 18,678 passenger-carrying vehicles (including Pullman carriages), 6,508 luggage and parcel vans and 370,917 freight vehicles. At the end of the year 11,799 (standard gauge) route miles were open to traffic.

The London Transport Board, in Nov. 1970, had 237 route miles of railway open for traffic and also operated over 17 miles of track owned by British Rail. Number of vehicles owned: Railways, 4,311 (including 2,981 electric motor vehicles); buses 6,591. Total number of miles run in passenger service (1969) was 422m. miles. The number of passengers carried in 1969 was: Railways, 676m.; red buses, 1,589m. Average takings per passenger journey (1969) were: Railways, £0·80, road services, £0·03.

Road Transport. Motor vehicles for which licences were current under the Vehicles (Excise) Act, 1962, numbered, at 30 Sept. 1969, 14·75m., including 11·23m. cars, 1·13m. mopeds, scooters and motor cycles, 101,600 public transport vehicles (including taxis) and 1·57m. goods vehicles. New vehicle registrations in 1969 numbered 1,401,836.

Road casualties in Great Britain numbered in 1968, 349,208 (63,962 under 15 years), including 6,810 killed; in 1969, 353,194 (62,656 under 15), including 7,383 killed.

Highways. The Secretary of State for the Environment is the highway authority for all trunk roads in England; for trunk roads in Wales and Scotland, the relevant Secretary of State is highway authority. For principal and other roads in England and Wales the highway authority may be a county council, county borough council, municipal borough council or urban district council (or in London the Greater London Council or a London borough council).

The Secretary of State for the Environment also possesses powers to provide, or to confirm schemes made by local highway authorities for the provision of special roads reserved for certain categories of traffic. Where the Secretary of State provides a special road it has trunk road status. The special roads at present under construction or in use are designed for limited classes of motor traffic only and are generally referred to as motorways.

Over 1,000 miles of motorway are planned to form a network carrying through traffic at relatively high speeds between important centres of trade and industry; at 4 Nov. 1970, 747·4 miles were open to traffic in Great Britain and a further 304·6 miles were under construction.

During 1967 and 1968 the, then, Ministry of Transport after consultations with the County Councils' Association, established 6 Road Construction Units to undertake the design, and supervise the construction of, major trunk road schemes in England including trunk and road motorways. The pattern of participation of county councils in each of the units is as follows (as at 1 April 1968):

Unit	Participating counties
North West	Lancashire, Cheshire
North East	Durham, Yorkshire (W. Riding)
Midland	Derbyshire, Staffordshire, Warwickshire
South West	Devon, Gloucestershire, Somerset
South East	Hampshire, Kent, Surrey
Eastern	Bedfordshire, Buckinghamshire, Essex, Hertfordshire

The construction and improvement of trunk roads in Wales and the smaller schemes in England (generally those costing under £1m.) are carried out by local authorities as agents of the Secretary of State for the Environment or Secretary of State for Wales, who bear the full cost of the work. These agent authorities are also responsible for the maintenance of all trunk roads.

The Department of Environment pays 75% of the cost of approved schemes for the construction or improvement of principal roads. The construction and improvement of non-principal roads, and the maintenance of all local authority roads, are financially aided through the Rate Support Grant, which is a non-specific grant to local authorities.

The public highways in Great Britain at 1 April 1970 (Scotland, 16 May 1970), excluding mileages of unsurfaced roads (green lanes), had a total length of 207,665 miles (England, 157,454 miles; Wales, 20,910; Scotland, 29,301), of which 8,350 were all-purpose trunk roads, 660 were motorways, 20,224 were principal roads and 178,431 were other roads including green lanes.

Civil Aviation

The British Overseas Airways Corporation (BOAC) was set up under the British Overseas Airways Act 1939 and British European Airways (BEA) was established under the Civil Aviation Act 1946. In addition to the 2 nationalized corporations, there are about 20 independent air transport operators.

BOAC is engaged on long-haul operations. Its scheduled services link Britain with Europe, the Middle East, the Far East, Australasia, Africa and North and South America. It co-operates closely with airlines of several other Commonwealth countries and has financial interests in companies operating local and regional services adjacent to its main routes as well. BEA operates a network of short-haul services to over 80 places in Britain, Europe, North Africa and the Middle East. BEA also has a financial interest in several associated companies both in Britain and abroad, most of which collaborate in providing local services.

The 2 State Córporations had a statutory monopoly up to 1961, although there was an arrangement by which independent operators could provide services as private companies associated with the Corporations. The Civil Aviation (Licensing) Act 1960 established a new independent licensing authority, the Air Transport Licensing Board, and placed the independent airlines on an equal footing with the 2 Corporations for licensing purposes. There has since been a significant expansion by independent operators who have carried increasing numbers of passengers and volumes of freight on a network of scheduled and non-scheduled domestic and international services. In addition to the public transport operators there are a number of companies engaged in miscellaneous aviation activities such as crop-spraying, aerial survey and photography, and flying instruction.

The provisional operating and traffic statistics of the UK airways corporations and the independent operators on scheduled services during the calendar year 1969 (and 1968) are as follows: Aircraft miles flown, 168,031,000 (153,839,000); revenue passengers carried, 13·22m. (12·18m.); freight carried, 319,461 short tons (304,452); mail carried, 22,897 short tons (24,098).

Traffic between the UK airports and places abroad in 1969 (and 1968) included 311,100 (317,300) commercial transport aircraft movements, and 18·69m. (15·89m.) passengers were carried.

There were 2,578 civil aircraft with current certificates of airworthiness registered in the UK at 31 Dec. 1970.

Posts and Telecommunications

Number of post offices at 31 March 1970 was 24,650; number of letter boxes including those at post offices, over 101,400; staff employed, 430,297.

	1966–67 (1m.)	1967–68 (1m.)	1968–69 (1m.)	1969–70 (1m.)
Correspondence (incl. registered items) posted	11,400	11,500	11,300	11,400
Parcels handled	222	217	212	208
Telegrams handled	31	31	29	30
Telex: Inland (units)	204	230	246	259
Overseas (minutes)	65	74	88	105

Weight (lb.) of air-mail traffic (all services) dispatched abroad: Letters, printed papers, etc., 1969, 19,227,000; 1970, 20,755,000; parcels, 1969, 9,652,000; 1970, 10,773,000.

In 1969–70 the total value of money orders, including COD trade charge orders, was £211·2m.; postal orders, £565·8m.

On 31 March 1970 the London Telecommunications Region had 384 local exchanges, 88 auto-manual and automatic trunk exchanges, 11,907 call offices and 3,905,782 telephone stations. In the provinces there were 5,754 local exchanges, 293 auto-manual and automatic trunk exchanges, 63,444 call offices and 10,053,044 telephone stations. For telephone private wires that accrued revenue in 1969–70 amounted to £23,534,000.

The number of sound broadcast receiving licences issued during the year ended 31 March 1970 was 2·2m. and the figure for combined sound and television broadcast receiving licences was 15·7m., including 300,000 for colour.

The approximate surpluses of income over expenditure (after charging interest on capital) are as follows for years ended 31 March (in £1,000 sterling); 1966, 40,155; 1967, 44,339; 1968, 39,328; 1969, 46,500; 1970, 36,203.

Broadcasting

Radio and television services in Great Britain are controlled by the British Broadcasting Corporation and (in the case of the commercial television network) by the Independent Television Authority. These are public corporations, established by Royal Charter and the Television Act 1964, respectively, until July 1976. Both corporations are independent of the Government in their day-to-day operations.

MONEY AND BANKING

Sterling. The monetary unit of Great Britain is the pound sterling. A gold standard was adopted in 1816, the sovereign or twenty-shilling piece weighing 7·98805 grammes 0·916⅔ fine. Currency notes for £1 and 10s. were first issued by the Treasury in 1914, replacing the circulation of sovereigns. The issue of £1 and 10s. notes was taken over by the Bank of England in 1928. The issue of 10s. notes ceased on the issue of the 50p coin in 1969.

Following the post-war fluctuations in the value of the pound, Great Britain returned to the Gold Standard in 1925 with the pound fixed at the pre-war parity of US$4.8666. But the world financial crisis of 1931 forced the country off the Gold Standard again, and in the following year the Exchange Equalization Account was set up for the purpose of checking undue fluctuations in the exchange value of the pound. With the relative stability of the pound which followed, a 'Sterling Bloc' emerged consisting of most Empire countries and those others who voluntarily pegged their currencies to the pound.

The Bloc was superseded at the outbreak of the Second World War by the 'Sterling Area'. The pound was then fixed at $4.03 and remained at that rate until Sept. 1949, when it was devalued to $2.80. On 18 Nov. 1967 it was further devalued to $2.40.

The Sterling Area, referred to in the Exchange Control Act 1947 as the 'Scheduled Territories', now comprises the British Commonwealth (except Canada and Rhodesia), the Irish Republic, British Trust Territories, British Protectorates and Protected States, Iceland, the Hashemite Kingdom of Jordan, Kuwait, Libya, South Africa, and SW Africa, Southern Yemen and Western Samoa.

Coinage. The sovereign (£1) weighs 123·27447 grains, or 7·98805 grammes, 0·916⅔ (or eleven-twelfths) fine, and consequently it contains 113·00159 grains or 7·32238 grammes of fine gold. The shilling (20s. = £1) weighs 87·27 grains, or 5·6552 grammes, and down to 1920 was 0·925 (or thirty-seven-fortieths) fine, thus containing 80·727 grains, or 5·231 grammes, of fine silver, but under the Coinage Act, 1920, the fineness was reduced to 0·500 (one-half). The Coinage Act, 1946, however, provides for the replacement of silver coinage by coins of cupro-nickel of the same weight. An exception was made in regard to Maundy coins, which, by the Act, reverted to a fineness of 0·925. Bronze coins consist of a mixture of copper, tin and zinc. The penny (12d. = 1s.) weighs 145·83 grains, or 9·45 grammes. Threepenny pieces of nickel-brass were issued for the first time in 1937 (standard weight of each coin is 105 grains, or 6·804 grammes); they are legal tender up to 2s. The standard of value is gold. According to the Coinage Act, 1870, silver is legal tender up to 40s. (and according to the Coinage Act, 1946, cupro-nickel to the same amount); bronze (pennies up to 12d. The 50p seven-sided cupro-nickel coin (the shape being known as an equilateral curve heptagon) which was first issued in Oct. 1969, to replace the 10s. note is legal tender for amounts up to £10. The Decimal Currency Act, 1969, increased the legal tender limits of cupro-nickel coins to £5 (except for the 50p) and of bronze and nickel-brass coins to 4s. (20p) with effect from 15 Feb. 1971—the official date for the change-over to the decimal system (£1 = 100 new pence or 100p). 10p and 5p coins made under the provisions of the Decimal Currency Act, 1967, were put into general circulation nearly 3 years before the decimal change-over date and are identical in weight, size and value with with florins and shillings respectively.

The specifications of the decimals coins are: cupro-nickel 50p (13·5 grammes), 10p (11·31), 5p (5·66); bronze 2p (7·13), 1p (3·56), ½p (1·78).

The value of money issued in 1969 was, cupro-nickel £127·3m., bronze and nickel-brass £1·5m. In addition, 888,000 sets of decimal coins were issued consisting of 10p, 5p, 2p, 1p and ½p. During 1969 the Royal Mint in London struck 1,288,353,535 coins and a further 1,397,209,559 coins were struck in South Wales. By about 1973 most of the functions of the present Mint in London will have been transferred to Llantrisant in Wales.

UK coins produced in 1969 totalled 2,374·81m., as follows, in millions: 50p 164·1, 10p 398·1, 5p 82·7, 2p 415, 1p 565·3, ½p 391, sixpences, 92·2, threepences 47, pennies 219·4,

It is estimated that the following coins were in circulation in the UK in Dec. 1969, in millions: 50p 158, half-crowns 189, florins 592, 10p 485, shillings 996, 5p 91, sixpences 1,927, threepences 897 and pennies 2,185.

Bank-notes. The Bank of England issues notes in denominations of £1, £5 £10 and £20 for the amount of the fiduciary note issue. Under the provisions of the Currency and Bank Notes Act, 1954, which came into force on 22 Feb. 1954, the amount of the fiduciary note issue was fixed at £1,575m., but this figure might be altered by direction of HM Treasury and after representations made by the Bank of England.

All Bank of England notes are legal tender in England and Wales, and notes of denominations less than £5 are legal tender in Scotland and Northern Ireland. The banks in Scotland and Northern Ireland have certain note-issuing powers. The average circulations of such notes were £160m. (Scotland—4 weeks ended 29

D

Dec. 1970) and £20m. (Northern Ireland—4 weeks ended 21 Nov. 1970); these notes are widely accepted in their area of origin but are not legal tender in any part of the UK.

The total amount of notes issued for the week as at 30 Dec. 1970 was £3,700m., of which £3,666,358,059 were in the hands of other banks and the public and £33,641,941 in the Banking Department of the Bank of England.

Banking. The Bank of England, Threadneedle Street, London, is the Government's banker and the 'banker's bank'. It has the sole right of note issue in England and Wales, manages the National Debt and administers the Exchange Control regulations. The Bank operates under royal charters of 1694 and 1946. The capital stock has, since 1 March 1946, been held by the Treasury. The holders of Bank stock were given £58,212,000 3% Treasury stock in exchange.

The statutory return is published weekly. End-December figures for the past 5 years are as follows (in £1m.):

	Notes in circulation	Notes and coin in Banking Department	Public deposits (government)	Other deposits [1]
1966	3,063	38	29	523
1967	3,206	45	16	623
1968	3,367	34	13	657
1969	3,430	73	13	603
1970	3,666	35	17	779

[1] Including Special Deposits.

The fiduciary note issue was £3,700m. at 30 Dec. 1970. All the profits of the note issue are passed on to the National Loans Fund.

Official holdings (Exchange Equalization Account) of gold and convertible currencies at 31 Dec. 1969 amounted to £1,053m.

Debit bank clearings (excluding provincial clearings) for 1969, £700m.; 1968, £600m. Credit clearings for 1969, £14m.; 1968, £12m.

The following statistics relate to the London clearing banks for the years 1970 and 1969. As a result of several amalgamations during this period the number of clearing banks was reduced to 6. (Averages of mid-monthly figures in £1m.) Deposits, etc., 10,151 (10,610 in 1969); cash in hand and balances with the Bank of England, 826 (879); money at call and short notice, 1,467 (1,451); Treasury Bills discounted, 207 (294); other bills discounted, 714 (568); investments, 1,115 (1,201); advances, 5,624 (5,328).

Total net profits from the operations of clearing bank groups in 1970 amounted to £124m., of which £50m. in gross dividends, £74m. transferred to reserves. The full figures incorporate a number of changes in accounting practice from previous years and, for the first time, contain details of true profits and reserves.

Most commercial banking business in Britain is conducted by clearing banks. Industrial and overseas trading business is handled primarily by the merchant banks, who also deal with such matters as the issue of shares to the public for new companies and act as registrars for public companies.

Trustee Savings Banks. Trustee Savings Banks started in Scotland in 1810. They are managed by Boards of Trustees who receive no payment for their services. The Banks have no shareholders or proprietors, they are under the supervision of the National Debt Commissioners, and subject to regular inspection by the Trustee Savings Banks Inspection Committee, a statutory body.

There are 75 independent Trustee Savings Banks in the British Isles, with a total of 1,505 offices. The total of active accounts in all Departments on 20 Nov. 1970 was 12,533,561. Funds managed by the Banks at that date totalled £2,790,288,718, made up as follows: Ordinary Department (including current accounts), £1,064,180,407; Special Investment Department, £1,474,392,077; Government Stock Department, £197,497,913 (face value), SAYE contracts, £6,630,871 and combined surplus funds, £47,587,450. In addition, the value of units in the TSB Unit Trust, held for depositors on 20 Sept. 1970, was £15,230,168.

National Savings Bank. Statistics for 1967 and 1968:

	Total 1967	England and Wales	Scotland	Northern Ireland[2]	Total
		1968			
Accounts open at 31 Dec.[1]	21,574,094	19,916,435	1,018,792	319,490	21,254,717
Amounts—	£1,000	£1,000	£1,000	£1,000	£1,000
Received	505,644	456,407	17,728	5,036	479,171
Interest credited	40,760	37,101	1,473	571	39,145
Paid	613,515	572,286	21,530	6,712	600,528
Due to depositors at 31 Dec.[3]	1,672,679	1,506,641	60,521	23,305	1,590,467
Average amount due to each depositor in active acounts	£77 7s. 2d.	£75 9s. 4d.	£59 3s. 9d.	£72 13s. 3d.	£74 12s. 11d.

[1] Excluding accounts with balances of less than £1 which have been inactive for 5 years or more. The average balance of these accounts is 3s. 2·04d.
[2] Including accounts opened prior to 1923 in territory which is now the Irish Republic.
[3] The amount due to depositors in ordinary accounts on 1 Jan. 1970 was approximately £1,499,737,000 and in investment accounts £243,820,000.
The receipts and payments include purchases and sales of Government Stock for investors on the Post Office Register, but the amount shown as due to depositors is exclusive of the stocks held. The latter amounted to £974·2m. at the end of 1967, and £921m. at the end of 1968.

There were 572,046 Post Office Savings Bank Investment Accounts open at 31 Dec. 1969. At that date, £243·8m. was due to depositors, to each of whom an average of £426 13s. was due.

Bank of England Quarterly Bulletin. Bank of England
Bank of England Annual Report. Bank of England
Central Statistical Office, Financial Statistics. HMSO (monthly)
Report of the Committee on the Working of the Monetary System. HMSO, 1959
Clapham, Sir J. H., *The Bank of England: a History.* 2 vols. CUP, 1944
Craig, J., *The Mint.* Cambridge, 1953
Horne, H. O., *History of Savings Banks.* London, 1947

BOOKS OF REFERENCE CONCERNING GREAT BRITAIN

The annual and other publications of the various Public Departments, and the Reports, etc. of Royal Commissions and Parliamentary Committees. (These may be obtained from HM Stationery Office.)

Allen, G. C., *British Industries and their Organization.* 4th ed. London, 1959
Bickmore, D. P., and Shaw, M. A. (ed.), *The Atlas of Great Britain and Northern Ireland.* OUP, 1963
Burn, D., *The Structure of British Industry.* 2 vols. CUP, 1958
Central Statistical Office. *Annual Abstract of Statistics,* HMSO.—*Monthly Digest of Statistics,* HMSO
Central Office of Information. *Britain: An Official Handbook.* HMSO, 1971
Demangeon, A., *The British Isles.* 3rd ed. London, 1952
History of the Second World War. HMSO, 1949 ff.
Kendall, M. G. (ed.), *The Source and Nature of the Statistics of the United Kingdom.* 2 vols. London, 1952–1957
Mitchell, B. R., *Abstract of British Historical Statistics.* OUP, 1962
Mitchell, J. (ed.), *Great Britain: geographical essays.* CUP, 1962
Oxford History of England. 15 vols. OUP. 1936 ff.
Stamp, L. D., and Beaver, S. H., *The British Isles: a geographic and economic survey.* 4th ed., London, 1954
Woodward, Sir E. L., and Butler, R., *Documents on British Foreign Policy, 1919–39.* HMSO, 1957 ff.

Scotland

Scottish Council (Development and Industry). *Inquiry into the Scottish Economy, 1960–61.* Edinburgh, 1961.
Scottish Home Dept. *Digest of Scottish Statistics.* HMSO (bi-annual).—*Scottish Administration: a handbook.* Rev. ed. HMSO, 1950
Cairncross, A. K. (ed.), *The Scottish Economy.* Cambridge, 1954
Darling, F. F. (ed.), *West Highland Survey.* Oxford, 1955
Meikle, H. W. (ed.), *Scotland: a description of Scotland and Scottish life.* London, 1947
Oakley, C. A. (ed.), *Scottish industry.* Edinburgh, 1953
Rait, Sir R., and Pryde, G. S., *Scotland.* 2nd ed. London, 1954

Wales

Wales and Monmouthshire: report . . . for the year ended 30 June 1956. (Cmd. 9887.) HMSO, 1956
The Council for Wales and Monmouthshire: third memorandum. (Cmd. 53.) HMSO, 1957
Digest of Welsh Statistics. HMSO (annual)
Thomas, B. (ed.), *The Welsh Economy.* Cardiff, 1962
Williams, D., *A History of Modern Wales.* London, 1951

NORTHERN IRELAND

CONSTITUTION AND GOVERNMENT. Under the Government of Ireland Act, 1920, as amended by the Irish Free State (Consequential Provisions) Act, 1922, a separate parliament and executive government were established for Northern Ireland, which comprises the counties of Antrim, Armagh, Down, Fermanagh, Londonderry and Tyrone, and the boroughs of Belfast and Londonderry. The Parliament consists of a Senate of 2 *ex-officio* and 24 elected persons and a House of Commons of 52 elected members. The Parliament has power to legislate for its own area, except in regard to (1) matters of Imperial concern (the Crown, making of peace or war, military, naval and air forces, treaties, titles of honour, treason, naturalization, domicile, external trade, submarine cables, wireless telegraphy, aerial navigation, lighthouses, etc., coinage, etc., trade marks, etc.), and (2) certain matters 'reserved' to the UK Parliament (postal service, post office and trustee savings banks, designs for stamps). The executive power is vested in the Governor on behalf of H.M. the Queen: he holds office for 6 years and is advised by ministers responsible to Parliament. Senators, who are elected by members of the House of Commons on a proportional representation basis, hold office for a fixed term of years: the House of Commons continues for 5 years, unless sooner dissolved. The qualifications for membership of the Parliament are similar to those for membership of the UK House of Commons. In 1928 the franchise was conferred upon women upon the same terms as it had hitherto been enjoyed by men; and in 1929 the system of proportional representation (under which the Parliaments which met in 1921 and in 1925 had been elected) was abolished, and parliamentary representation was based upon single-member constituentscie.

Northern Ireland returns 12 members to the UK House of Commons.

Two Acts of the UK Parliament, passed in 1928 and 1932, modified certain restrictions placed on the powers of the Northern Irish Parliament by the Act of 1920. The legislative and administrative powers relating to Railways, Fisheries and the Contagious Diseases of Animals were transferred to the Parliament and Government of Northern Ireland as from 1 April 1926.

The UK Government's Land Purchase Scheme has been completed, the Land Purchase Commission for Northern Ireland being wound up on 1 April 1937, and the general subject-matter of the Acts relating to land purchase has ceased to be 'reserved' by the Act of 1920. Four further Acts passed by the UK Parliament extended the jurisdiction of the Northern Ireland Parliament and removed minor constitutional difficulties which had tended to hinder the full and free exercise by the Parliament of Northern Ireland of its general legislative power. An Act of 1945 related to criminal law and procedure. A 1947 Act conferred power to deal with schemes extending athwart the land frontier and with transport services, health services and publicly-owned property. By a 1955 Act the local Parliament was empowered to deal with the administration and distribution of estates of deceased persons, and with the appointment, jurisdiction, etc., of coroners. An Act of 1962 amended the law concerning the administration of justice in Northern Ireland and enlarged the legislative power of the Northern Ireland Parliament with respect to other miscellaneous matters.

The Northern Ireland Parliament met for the first time in June 1921.

State of parties in July 1970: 34 Unionists, 3 Independent Unionists, 2 Protestant Unionists, 5 Nationalists, 2 Northern Ireland Labour, 2 Republican Labour, 4 Independents.

Members of the Senate (except those in receipt of salaries as members of the Government or as officers of the Senate) receive £2 5s. *per diem* in respect of expenses for attendance at meetings of the Senate, Select Committees of the Senate, and Joint Committees of the Senate and House of Commons. Members of the House of Commons (including members of the Government) receive £300 per annum in respect of expenses. Senators and members (except those in receipt of salaries as members of the Government or as officers of either House) also receive a salary of £600 and £1,450 per annum respectively.

Governor: The Lord Grey of Naunton, GCMG, KCVO, OBE. Assumed office 3 Dec. 1968.

The Cabinet, all the members of which belong to the Ulster Unionist Party, was, in Sept. 1970, composed as follows:

Prime Minister: Maj. the Right Hon. J. D. Chichester-Clark.
Minister in and Leader of the Senate: Senator the Right Hon. J. L. O. Andrews.
Minister of Finance: Right Hon. H. V. Kirk.
Minister of Home Affairs: Maj. the Right Hon. J. D. Chichester-Clark.
Minister of Health and Social Services: Right Hon. W. K. Fitzsimmons.
Minister of Education: Capt. the Right Hon. W. J. Long.
Minister of Agriculture: Right Hon. Phelim O'Neill.
Minister of Commerce: Right Hon. Roy Bradford.
Minister of Development: Right Hon. A. B. D. Faulkner.
Minister of Community Relations: Right Hon. Dr Robert Simpson.
Minister of State at the Ministry of Development: Right Hon. N. O. Minford.
Minister and Leader of the House: Right Hon. John Dobson.
Minister of State at the Ministry of Home Affairs: Right Hon. J. D. Taylor.

The Attorney-General, who is not in the Cabinet, is the Right Hon. Basil Kelly, QC.

The Prime Minister receives a salary of £5,750 per annum, a Minister being head of a department, £4,250; any other Minister, £3,500; in addition, they receive expenses allowances.

The usual channel of communication between the Government of Northern Ireland and the UK Government is the Home Office.

Agent of the Government of Northern Ireland in Great Britain: H. E. Jones, CBE (11 Berkeley St., W1).

LOCAL GOVERNMENT. Northern Ireland has 66 principal local authorities. There is 1 county borough council and 6 county councils. The counties are divided into districts and there are 9 borough councils, 24 urban district councils and 26 rural district councils. In County Fermanagh there are no district councils and the county council is the local authority for the whole county. In addition, the functions of an urban district council are exercised by Craigavon Development Commission in Craigavon Urban District, while Londonderry Development Commission exercises the functions of a county borough council in Londonderry County Borough and of an urban district council in the former Londonderry Rural District.

The pattern of services provided is broadly similar to that in Great Britain with the exceptions that police, civil defence and (except in Belfast) fire services are centrally administered.

County Councils are responsible for education, health and welfare and, in the rural districts, for rating, planning, roads (except trunk roads) and tourist development. Borough and Urban District Councils are responsible for rating, planning, roads (except trunk roads), housing, water and sewerage, parks, markets and tourist development. Rural District Councils are primarily housing and sanitary authorities. The County Borough of Belfast has all the powers of a County and District Council and additional powers under its own local acts.

A Review Body appointed by the Minister of Development, which reported in June 1970, has made recommendations for the future administration of local government services consequent on the decision of the Government to centralize local housing functions. No decision has yet been taken on the Review Body's recommendations.

TOWN AND COUNTRY PLANNING. The Northern Ireland Development Programme, 1970–75, broadly endorses the Government's existing regional strategy of concentrating development in a number of growth towns outside the main urban centre of Belfast, the further expansion of which will continue to be controlled.

In the west and other areas outside Greater Belfast (this covers an area of some 20 miles in radius from the city of Belfast) Londonderry and Ballymena are designated as centres of accelerated industrial growth together with 8 key centres—Newry, the Coleraine Triangle, Larne, Dungannon, Omagh, Enniskillen, Strabane and Downpatrick. In the Greater Belfast Area there will be an urgent acceleration of housing redevelopment in Belfast City, some specific outward adjustments of the Stopline (proposed in 1963 by Sir Robert Matthew to limit the growth of the Belfast Urban Area) for public authority housing and industry; together with 'overspill' arrangements to facilitate population movement to Craigavon, Antrim and the inner growth centres of Bangor, Newtownwards and Carrickfergus.

Craigavon, Antrim/Ballymena and Londonderry have been designated for development under the New Towns Act (N.I.) 1965 and Development Commissions appointed to promote and co-ordinate the implementation of the published Area Plans. Area Plans have also been published for the Belfast Urban Area and for the Coleraine–Portrush–Portstewart Triangle. Plans for other areas of the Province are at various stages of preparation.

The protection of the visual amenities and areas of natural history in the Ulster countryside was strengthened by the Amenity Lands Act (N.I.) 1965 under which the Ministry of Development is advised by the Ulster Countryside Committee on the establishment of National Parks, the designation of Areas of Outstanding Natural Beauty and the acquisition of amenity areas, and by the Nature Reserves Committee on the creation and management of Nature Reserves and Areas of Scientific Interest. Seven Areas of Outstanding Natural Beauty have been designated and 3 areas have been recommended for designation as National Parks. Four amenity areas have been acquired and are being developed. Negotiations are proceeding for the acquisition of a number of other such areas. On the recommendation of the Nature Reserves Committee, 26 sites have been notified as Areas of Scientific Interest, and negotiations are in hand for the declaration of over 20 nature reserves.

AREA AND POPULATION. Area (revised by the Ordnance Survey Department) and population at the census of 9 Oct. 1966, were as follows:

Counties and county boroughs	Area in sq. miles	Males	Females	Total
Antrim	1,175·78	153,689	160,302	313,991
Armagh	512·35	61,914	63,250	125,164
Belfast C.B.	28·21	187,634	210,771	398,405
Down	952·21	139,721	146,910	286,631
Fermanagh	714·67	25,703	24,183	49,886
Londonderry	813·83	59,714	59,250	118,964
Londonderry C.B.	4·03	26,595	29,099	55,694
Tyrone	1,260·81	68,914	67,126	136,040
Northern Ireland	5,461·89[1]	723,884	760,891	1,484,775

[1] 12,574·7 sq. km.

VITAL STATISTICS for calendar years:

	Marriages	Divorces	Births	Deaths
1967	10,924	206	33,415	14,671
1968	11,240	257	33,173	15,933
1969	11,587	240	32,428	16,338

RELIGION. The religious professions at the census of 1961 were: Roman Catholics, 497,547; Presbyterians, 413,113; Church of Ireland, 344,800 (including Church of England and Episcopal Church of Scotland); Methodists, 71,865; others and not stated, 97,717.

EDUCATION. The following are the statistics for 1969–70:

Universities. The Queen's University of Belfast (founded in 1849 as a college of the Queen's University of Ireland and reconstituted a separate university in 1908) had 80 professors, 122 readers and senior lecturers, 460 lecturers and tutors and 6,528 students.

The New University of Ulster at Coleraine, which admitted its first students in Oct. 1968, had 13 professors, 23 readers and senior lecturers, 76 lecturers and tutors and 902 full-time students. Magee University College, Londonderry (founded 1865), had 5 professors, 9 lecturers and 223 students; the College is now associated with the New University of Ulster.

Secondary Education. 81 grammar schools with 50,818 pupils and 2,679 full-time teachers; 168 secondary (intermediate) schools with 80,876 pupils and 4,121 full-time teachers; 17 technical intermediate schools with 905 pupils.

Primary Education. 1,256 primary schools with 208,002 pupils and 7,136 teachers; 22 nursery schools with 861 pupils and 32 teachers.

Further Education. 31 institutions of further education embracing 146 centres with 1,256 full-time and 1,401 part-time teachers and an enrolment of 11,748 full-time, 11,913 part-time day and about 40,000 evening students.

Special Educational Treatment. 24 special schools, including hospital schools, with 2,148 pupils and 195 teachers.

Teachers. There were 15,469 full-time teachers (6,414 men and 9,055 women) in grant-aided schools and institutions of further education. The minimum general teacher-training course is of 3 years' duration and there were 2,726 students (906 men and 1,820 women) in training, these included students following teacher-training courses at university establishments.

Expenditure. Expenditure on education for 1970–71 is estimated at £59,297,000 (Ministry of Education) and £14,344,000 (local education authorities). Substantial grants are made to all types of recognized voluntary schools.

HEALTH SERVICES. The comprehensive health service is similar to that in Great Britain. The general medical, dental, pharmaceutical and supplementary eye services are administered by the Northern Ireland General Health Services Board, while hospital and specialist services and accommodation (including hospital services for the mentally ill and subnormal) are provided by the Northern Ireland Hospitals Authority on behalf of the Ministry of Health and Social Services.

County and County Borough Councils provide personal health and welfare services on a similar basis to those in Great Britain. Environmental health and sanitary services are largely the responsibility of boroughs and district councils.

HOUSING. At 31 March 1970 a total of 178,813 post-war dwellings had been built in Northern Ireland. Of this number, approximately 67,127 were built by Local Authorities for letting, 828 by Development Commission and 42,821 by the Northern Ireland Housing Trust, a statutory body set up to complement the efforts of Local Authorities. Subsidies are payable annually for 60 years on these houses; they are reviewed quarterly to take account of changes in rates of interest and in building costs. The subsidies are payable in the proportion of three to one by the Exchequer and the rates respectively; in the case of the Housing Trust and also of housing associations (which have built a small number of houses for letting) the full subsidy is provided by the Exchequer.

Lump-sum subsidies are payable in respect of houses for letting or owner occupation, and to farmers for new farmhouses or the improvement of existing farmhouses. Grants are also available towards the cost of improving houses built before 1946 and the conversion of houses or buildings into dwelling or hostel accommodation. Financial assistance is also available towards providing basic amenities in local authority houses built in 1946–60.

In slum clearance and redevelopment work the Housing Trust works in conjunction with local authorities and the expenditure is grant-aided by the Government. A Bill was presented to Parliament in June 1970 to establish a Northern Ireland Housing Executive and an advisory Northern Ireland Housing Council which would take over the existing housing functions of local authorities and the Northern Ireland Housing Trust.

WATER SUPPLY AND SEWERAGE. Local sanitary authorities are responsible for these services. There are 11 Joint Water Boards and 1 Sewage Disposal Joint Board. The largest water authority is the Belfast City and District Water Commissioners, who are a directly elected body. Government grants can be given to assist local authorities; up to 31 March 1970 grants amounting to £32m. have been paid towards expenditure amounting to £64m.

SOCIAL SECURITY. The social security schemes in Northern Ireland are similar to those in force in Great Britain.

The national insurance and industrial injuries schemes operate as a single system throughout the United Kingdom. The National Insurance Joint Authority and the Industrial Injuries Joint Authority (consisting in each case of the Secretary of State for Social Services and the Minister of Health and Social Services for Northern Ireland) co-ordinate the schemes and make such financial adjustments as may be necessary. There are comprehensive reciprocal agreements with the Isle of Man, and agreements covering reciprocity in respect of most benefits have been made by the Government of the UK, applying to the schemes in both Great Britain and Northern Ireland, with Australia, Belgium, Canada, Cyprus, Denmark, Finland, France, Germany (West), Guernsey, Irish Republic, Israel, Italy, Jersey, Luxembourg, Malta, the Netherlands, New Zealand, Norway, Sweden, Switzerland, Turkey and Yugoslavia. There are also limited agreements with Bermuda and USA.

NATIONAL INSURANCE. The total number of contributors is about 610,000. During the year ended 31 March 1970 the average number of persons in receipt of sickness benefit was 43,000 and in receipt of unemployment benefit was 22,000. Widow's benefits were in payment to about 17,000 women and retirement pensions to about 153,000 persons. Receipts, including an item related to the financial adjustments mentioned above, of the Northern Ireland National Insurance Fund in the year ended 31 March 1970 were £66,674,000 and payments, £67·47m. During the year £5m., which is not included in the above-mentioned receipts, was transferred to the National Insurance Fund from the National Insurance Reserve Fund. The combined balance of these Funds at 31 March 1970 was £25·26m.

INDUSTRIAL INJURIES INSURANCE. About 542,000 persons are covered by the scheme, and the contributions they pay and the benefits to which they may be entitled are the same as in Great Britain. Accidents in respect of which claims to benefit are made occur at the rate of about 290 a week. Receipts of the Northern Ireland Industrial Injuries Fund in the year ended 31 March 1970 were £2,821,000, and payments, £2·36m.

FAMILY ALLOWANCES. The number of families in receipt of allowances is about 135,000, and the cost of the allowances in the year ended 31 March 1970 was £15·1m.

SUPPLEMENTARY BENEFITS. Persons in receipt of supplementary benefits numbered 99,800 at 31 March 1970. These benefits cost £18·77m. in the financial year ended 31 March 1970.

JUSTICE. The superior courts in Northern Ireland comprise the Supreme Court of Judicature and the Court of Criminal Appeal. All matters relating to these courts are under the jurisdiction of the Parliament of the UK and the judges of the superior courts are appointed by the Crown on the advice of the Lord Chancellor.

Inferior courts come under the jurisdiction of the Parliament of Northern Ireland and comprise the County Courts and the Magistrates' Courts (Petty Sessions). The County Courts deal with criminal matters and with civil disputes, where the sum at issue does not exceed £300. They also act as appellate courts from the decisions in Petty Sessions. The Petty Sessions are held regularly in 76 Petty Sessions districts and are presided over by Resident Magistrates, who are permanent judicial officers and normally sit alone. In Juvenile Courts, however, the Resident Magistrate is assisted by two lay members, one of whom must be a woman.

POLICE. The police force consists of the Royal Ulster Constabulary, supported by the Royal Ulster Special Constabulary Reserve, a part-time force.

FINANCE. There are two main sources of revenue: reserved tax revenue levied and collected by the UK Government, and transferred tax revenue imposed by the Northern Ireland Government. Reserved revenue includes the Inland Revenue taxes (income tax, surtax, etc.) and Customs and Excise Duties on goods. Transferred revenue comprises selective employment tax, estate duty, motor-vehicle duties, stamp duty and betting duty.

The Government of Northern Ireland also raises money for capital purposes by means of Stock Issue, Ulster Savings Certificates, Ulster Development Bonds and borrowing from the United Kingdom Government.

The Public Income of the Northern Ireland Exchequer for the past 5 years was as follows (in £ sterling):

	1966–67	1967–68	1968–69	1969–70	1970–71
Reserved tax revenue	157,315,000	176,148,000	199,818,000	231,067,567	247,380,000
Transferred tax revenue	21,658,856	32,753,817	45,615,849	56,322,570	59,795,000
Other	34,539,425	37,717,766	55,152,707	58,937,674	69,631,000
Total public income	213,513,281	246,619,583	300,586,556	346,327,811	376,806,000

The Public Expenditure of Northern Ireland comprises expenditure on supply services, the cost of certain reserved services (inland revenue and customs and excise departments, etc.) and a contribution towards the cost of imperial services (national debt charges, military, naval and air force services, etc.). The following table shows expenditure over the past 5 years (in £ sterling):

	1966–67	1967–68	1968–69	1969–70	1970–71
Supply services	184,007,159	221,084,986	260,199,039	303,115,175	339,138,070
Cost of reserved services	2,679,000	2,860,000	2,971,000	3,206,000	3,483,000
Imperial contribution	3,500,000	2,000,000	2,000,000	2,000,000	1,000,000
Other	23,277,474	20,610,374	35,292,425	37,853,983	33,100,000
Total public expenditure	213,463,633	246,555,360	300,462,464	346,175,158	376,721,070

The public debt at 31 March 1969 was as follows: Northern Ireland 6% Exchequer Stock 1977, £7m.; Northern Ireland 6¼% Exchequer Stock 1974, £12m.; Northern Ireland 6½% Exchequer Stock 1979–80, £15m; Northern Ireland 7% Exchequer Stock 1982–84, £20m.; Ulster Savings Certificates, £40,159,836; Ulster Development Bonds, £11,288,773; borrowing from UK Government, £149,263,378; borrowing from Northern Ireland Government funds, £62,164,900; borrowing from bank, £2·05m.; total, £318,926,887.

The Northern Ireland Government lends to local authorities and other public bodies for public utility services. The amount of principal outstanding at 31 March 1970 for these loans was £248,598,189.

AGRICULTURE. Estimated gross output in 1968–69:

	Quantity (1,000)	Value (£1m.)		Quantity (1,000)	Value (£1m.)
Fat cattle ⎫	487	38·1	Grass seed	3	0·2
Calves ⎪	28	1·0	Hay and		
Store cattle ⎬ head	19	1·1	straw ⎫	9	0·1
Sheep ⎪	542	3·7	Fruit ⎬ tons	30	1·3
Pigs ⎪	1,584	27·0	Vegetables ⎪	41	1·3
Poultry ⎭	15,557	3·6	Mushrooms ⎭	4	1·1
Eggs (1,000 dozen):			Sundry	—	2·2
for consumption	141,225	20·3			
for hatching	2,905	0·9	Total all items	—	133·1
Wool (lb.)	3,262	0·6			
Milk (gallons)	161,800	22·5	Total gross agri-		+1·8
Potatoes ⎫	343	5·4	cultural output		
Oats ⎪ tons	13	0·4	(adjusted)	—	134·9
Barley ⎬	86	2·1			
Wheat ⎭	2	0·1			

Acreage (in 1,000) of crops (provisional for 1970):

	1969	1970		1969	1970
Oats	57·7	45·5	Fruit	7·5	7·3
Barley	135·6	125·9	Rotation and permanent		
Other cereals and pulses	14·0	18·9	grass	1,792·1	1,805·3
Potatoes	42·8	46·7			
Turnips and kale[1]	1·8	1·7		2,056·3	2,056·4
Vegetables	3·1	3·3			
Other crops	1·7	1·8			

[1] Stock feeding only.

Livestock (1,000) at June cenus (1970 provisional):

	1969	1970		1969	1970
Dairy cows	205	210	Total sheep	935	973
Beef cows	191	220	Breeding sows	113	119
Total cattle	1,243	1,330	Total pigs	1,033	1,087
Breeding ewes	466	479	Total poultry	12,942	13,195

MINING. The output of minerals (in 1,000 tons) during 1969 was: Basalt and igneous rock, 8,134; chalk, 729; clay, 448; diatomite, 2; granite, 22; grit and conglomerate, 1,892; limestone, 1,572; sand and gravel, 2,700; sandstone, 27, and other minerals (coal, fireclay, rocksalt, flint and perlite), 219.

MANUFACTURES. Northern Ireland is an important and expanding industrial region, and about 223,000 people are employed in manufacturing industry, building and construction. The manufacture of linen and the shipbuilding industry had long been predominant, but many new industries have been established, and a wide diversification of activity has resulted. The textile industry has been widened by the introduction of man-made fibres, although linen remains the most important of the textile industries. (Exports of Northern Ireland linen goods (including yarn and thread) to countries outside the UK were valued at £14m. in 1968.) The textile and clothing industries together give employment to about 68,000 people. About 50,000 people are employed in engineering, shipbuilding and the production of aircraft. The engineering industries include also the manufacture of textile machinery, turbines, dust-collecting and air-conditioning plant, tea-estate machinery, oilfield equipment, data processing equipment, automobile and aero-engine components, and sound reproduction equipment.

The Government offers special encouragement towards the establishment of new and the expansion of existing industry, including substantial grants towards capital investment and the provision of government-built factories at a low rent or on repayment terms. By June 1970 the establishment of 270 new firms and over 230 schemes of expansion by existing firms since 1945 had been assisted, giving employment to over 76,000 additional workers.

ELECTRICITY. In 1967 the Northern Ireland Joint Electricity Authority was set up by statute, with headquarters and control centre at Castlereagh, near Belfast. It co-ordinates the generation of electricity at power stations owned by the participating undertakings, viz., the Electricity Board for Northern Ireland, Belfast Corporation and Londonderry Corporation. The electricity is acquired at cost by the Authority and resold to the undertakings at a common tariff.

The installed capacity of the system is 1,204 mw. This includes the first two 120-mw. sets of the new Ballylumford 'B' power station near Larne, which commenced operation in 1968. The capacity of the new station is planned to reach 960,000 mw. by 1974. The total sales of electricity in Northern Ireland in the year ended 31 March 1970 amounted to 3,437m. units supplied to a total of 451,566 consumers.

COMMERCE. Northern Ireland has a substantial export trade with countries overseas, but as a large part of it is routed through Great Britain, separate details are not available. The main markets outside the UK are USA, Norway, Canada, the Irish Republic, Australia, West Germany, Pakistan, Sudan and the Netherlands.

Imports and exports, including trade with Great Britain (in £1m. sterling), for calendar years:

	1962	1963	1964	1965	1966	1967	1968	1969
Imports	414	438	470	513	523	552	660	728
Exports	360	386	423	461	478	507	596	669

¹ Provisional.

In 1968, 74% of the total imports (by value) came from Great Britain or from foreign countries *via* Great Britain; 9% from the Irish Republic. Of the exports 87% (by value) went to Great Britain or to foreign countries *via* Great Britain; 6% to the Irish Republic.

Principal imports in 1968 (including imports from Great Britain) were valued at: Machinery £106·8m.; transport equipment, £88m.; tobacco and manufactures, £39·9m.; cereals and preparations, £29·4m.; coal, £20m.; textiles, £75·9m.; clothing and footwear, £16·1m.; metals and metal manufactures, £51·8m.; yarns, £14·4m.; chemicals, £24·7m.; paper and manufactures, £17·9m.; petroleum and products, £21·8m.; fruit and vegetables, £18·1m.

Principal exports in 1968 (including exports to Great Britain) were valued at: Machinery, £77·1m.; clothing and footwear, £50·3m.; live animals, £18·9m.; meat and meat preparations, £42·8m.; transport equipment, £36·2m.; textiles, £133·3m.; yarns, £24·5m.; dairy produce and eggs, £30·8m.

ROADS. Under the Roads Act (Northern Ireland), 1948, the Government set up a trunk roads system and took on full financial responsibility for the improvement and maintenance of the main traffic routes of Northern Ireland. Under the Special Roads Act (Northern Ireland) 1963 provision was made for the construction of motorways by the Ministry of Development or by other road authorities. At 1 April 1970 the total mileage of roads was 14,109, graded for administrative purposes as follows: Motorway, 47 miles; all-purpose trunk, 332 miles; Class I, 1,012 miles; Class II, 1,733 miles; Class III, 2,876 miles; unclassified, 8,109 miles.

The Councils of County Boroughs, Boroughs and Urban Districts are the road authorities for all roads (other than trunk roads) in their areas. The cost of upkeep of such roads is chargeable to them. For roads (other than trunk roads) situated in rural areas the County Councils are the road authorities. The cost of upkeep of these roads is chargeable to all the rural districts in the county, except that the cost of upkeep of an unclassified road is chargeable only to the rural district or districts in which the road is situated.

A Road Fund to which are credited motor-vehicle duties and drivers' licence fees, and out of which are paid grants to local authorities for the maintenance, improvement and reconstruction of public roads (other than trunk roads), is administered by the Ministry of Development. The net income of the Fund for the year ended 31 March 1970 was £8,827,000, and grants amounting to £8,014,000 were paid to local authorities.

ROAD AND RAIL. The Northern Ireland Transport Holding Company was established under the Transport Act (Northern Ireland) 1967 with overall responsibility for the financing but not the operation of bus and train services. A subsidiary of the Holding Company, Ulsterbus Ltd, operates most of the road passenger services (apart from Belfast City services). The services in the Belfast Area are provided by the Belfast Corporation. A few privately owned bus undertakings operate services in certain rural areas. Another subsidiary of the Holding Company, Northern Ireland Railways Company Ltd, operates all rail services.

A private-enterprise system under licence is in operation for the carriage of goods by road for reward. Approximately 1,400 operators and 3,900 vehicles have been licensed; the biggest single operator is Northern Ireland Carriers Ltd, owned jointly by the Northern Ireland Holding Company and the National Freight Corporation.

The number of motor vehicles licensed at 30 Sept. 1969 was 369,000, including private cars, 276,000; motor cycles, 16,000; goods vehicles, 41,000; agricultural vehicles, 26,000.

SHIPPING. Services operate from Belfast, Larne, Coleraine, Newry, Londonderry and Warrenpoint. In 1969 the net tonnage of shipping using these ports was about 11m. tons. Conventional cargo services have given way in many cases to container, unit load and drive on/drive off services. The latter type of service now operates between Larne and (i) Preston, (ii) Ardrossan and (iii) Stranraer; between Belfast and (i) Liverpool, (ii) Ardrossan, (iii) Preston, (iv) Heysham; between Londonderry and Preston; between Newry and Preston and between Warrenpoint and Garston.

AVIATION. Scheduled passenger and freight services operate between Belfast airport and airports throughout Great Britain including 2 separate services to airports in the London area. Scheduled transatlantic services operate *via* both Shannon and Prestwick. In 1969, 1·03m. passengers and 25,000 metric tons of freight and mail were handled at Belfast airport. The Government has embarked on a programme of expansion of the Belfast airport to international standards, including a major runway extension to be completed in 1972.

BOOKS OF REFERENCE

The annual and other publications of the various Departments and the Reports, etc., of Parliamentary Committees may be obtained from H.M. Stationery Office, Belfast.

Ulster Year Book 1969. Belfast, HMSO, 1969
Census of Population Reports, Northern Ireland. Belfast, HMSO
Digest of Statistics. Belfast, HMSO (bi-annual)
Northern Ireland Economic Report. Belfast, HMSO (annual)
Who Makes What in Northern Ireland: a trade directory. Belfast, HMSO, 1968
Reports on the Census of Production of Northern Ireland. Belfast, HMSO (annual)
Higher Education in Northern Ireland. Belfast, HMSO, 1965
Economic Development in Northern Ireland. Belfast, HMSO, 1965
Beckett, J. C., and Glasscock, R. E. (ed.), *Belfast: origin and growth of an industrial city.* BBC, 1967
Blake, J. W., *Northern Ireland in the Second World War.* Belfast, HMSO, 1956
Isles, K. S., and Cuthbert, N., *An Economic Survey of Northern Ireland.* Belfast, HMSO, 1957
Quekett, Sir A. S., *The Constitution of Northern Ireland.* 3 pts. Belfast, 1928–47
Shearman, Hugh, *Northern Ireland. Its People, Resources, History and Government.* Belfast HMSO, 1968.—*How Northern Ireland is Governed.* Belfast, HMSO, 1963

ISLE OF MAN

Constitution and Government. The Isle of Man is administered in accordance with its own laws by the Court of Tynwald, consisting of the Governor, appointed by the Crown; the Legislative Council, composed of the Lord Bishop of Sodor and Man, the First Deemster, the Attorney-General and 7 members selected by the House of Keys, total 11 members, including the Governor; and the House of Keys, a representative assembly of 24 members chosen on adult suffrage with 6 months' residence for 5 years by the 6 'sheadings' or local sub-divisions, and the 4 municipalities. The island is not bound by Acts of the Imperial Parliament unless specially mentioned in them.

Flag: Red, with 3 steel-coloured legs armoured and spurred (knees and spurs, yellow) in the centre.

The elections to the House of Keys, Dec. 1966, resulted in the return of 22 Independents and 2 Labour. Number of voters, 39,946.

An Executive Council to act with the Governor on all matters of government was set up under the Isle of Man Constitution Act, 1961. It consists at present of 5 members of the House of Keys and 2 of the Legislative Council.

Lieut.-Governor: Sir Peter Stallard, KCMG, CVO, MBE (term of office began 7 Sept. 1966).
Government Secretary: W. B. Kennaugh.

Area and Population. Area, 227 sq. miles (572 sq. km); population, 50,423 (census, 1966). The principal towns are Douglas (population, 19,517), Ramsey (3,880), Peel (2,739), Castletown (2,378). Vital statistics, 1969: Births, 760;

deaths, 905; marriages, 424. The number of Manx-speaking people was 165 in 1961 (355 in 1951), all of whom are bilingual.

Education. In Jan. 1967 there were 33 primary schools. The enrolled pupils numbered 4,562. The net expenditure on education for 1969–70 amounted to £1,308,348; in addition, capital grants of £183,983 were made for school buildings. There are 6 secondary schools, 4 provided by the Education Board (2,869 registered pupils), 1 direct grant school for girls (267 registered pupils), 1 independent public school for boys (353 registered pupils), 1 college of further education (58 full- and 1,888 part-time and evening pupils), 1 domestic science college (39 full- and 334 part-time pupils).

Police. The police force numbered 111 all ranks in 1970.

Finance. Revenue is derived from customs duties and from income tax. In 1969–70 the total revenue amounted to £10,138,624; expenditure to £7,964,901. In addition, capital expenditure, mainly out of borrowings, amounted to £696,968.

Agriculture. The principal agricultural produce of the island consists of oats, wheat, barley, turnips and potatoes, and grasses. The total area under crops in 1969 was 77,720 acres and of rough grazings, 44,911 acres. The total area under cereals was 10,874 acres, including 5,106 under oats, 477 under wheat and 4,808 under barley or bere. There were also 2,658 acres under turnips and swedes, 1,347 under potatoes, 6,467 under hay and 32,603 under grass, following rotational cropping. Livestock in 1969: 503 horses, 32,073 cattle, 113,269 sheep and 3,810 pigs.

Communications. The registered shipping (1967) comprised 15 vessels of 24,353 net tons. The railways (70 miles) are run by a consortium. There are 500 miles of roads. Several road races for motor cycles and bicycles take place annually. Number of vehicles (31 March 1970): 18,849 cars and trucks, 933 taxis and buses, 1,679 motor cycles and scooters, 1,444 tractors.

Birch, J. W., *The Isle of Man: a study in economic geography*. CUP, 1963
Kinvig, R. H. *History of the Isle of Man*. Oxford 1945
Mais, S. B. P., *Isle of Man*. London, 1954
Stenning, E. H., *Portrait of the Isle of Man*, London, 1958

CHANNEL ISLANDS

Area. The Channel Islands are situated off the north-west coast of France and are the only portions of the 'Duchy of Normandy' now belonging to the Crown of England, to which they have been attached since the Conquest. They consist of Jersey (28,717 acres), Guernsey (15,654 acres) and the following dependencies of Guernsey—Alderney (1,962), Brechou (74), Great Sark (1,035), Little Sark (239), Herm (320), Jethou (44) and Lihou (38), a total of 48,083 acres, or 75 sq. miles (194 sq. km).

The climate is mild. Total rainfall (1969), Jersey, 33·95 in.; Guernsey, 32·04 in. Temperature registered (1969): highest, Jersey, 91°; Guernsey, 84°; lowest, Jersey, 23°; Guernsey, 27°.

Constitution. The Lieut.-Governors and Cs.-in-C. of Jersey and Guernsey are the personal representatives of the Sovereign, the Commanders of the Armed Forces of the Crown and the channel of communication between H.M. Government in the UK and the insular governments. They are appointed by the Crown and have a voice but no vote in the Assemblies of the States (the insular legislatures). The Secretaries to the Lieut. Governors are their staff officers.

The Bailiffs are appointed by the Crown and are Presidents both of the Assembly of the States and of the Royal Courts of Jersey and Guernsey. They have in the States a casting vote.

Language. The official languages are French and English, but English is gradually supplanting French. The language commonly used is English, but in the country districts of Jersey and Guernsey and throughout Sark some people also speak a Norman-French dialect; that of Alderney has died out.

Church. Jersey and Guernsey each constitutes a deanery within the diocese of Winchester. The rectories (12 in Jersey; 10 in Guernsey) are in the gift of the Crown. The Roman Catholic and various Noncomformist Churches are represented.

Justice. Justice is administered by the Royal Courts of Jersey and Guernsey, each of which consists of the Bailiff and 12 Jurats, the latter being elected by an electoral college. There is an appeal from the Royal Courts to the Courts of Appeal of Jersey and of Guernsey. A final appeal lies to the Privy Council in certain cases. A stipendiary magistrate in each, Jersey and Guernsey, deals with minor civil and criminal cases.

Trade. From 1958 the trade of the Channel Islands with the UK has been regarded as internal trade.

Communications. Passenger and cargo steam services between Jersey, Guernsey and England are maintained by British Railways; between Guernsey, Jersey and England and St Malo by the Commodore Shipping Co.; between Guernsey, Jersey, Alderney and France by Condor Ltd (hydrofoil), and between Guernsey and Alderney and Guernsey and Sark by local companies.

Scheduled air services are maintained by BEA, British Islands Airways, Cambrian Airways, Channel Airways and other companies between the Islands and airports in the United Kingdom, Eire and France. During the summer months these services are greatly increased, both in the number of airports served and in the frequency of flights.

Omnibus services operate in all parts of Jersey and Guernsey.

Postal and overseas telephone and telegraph services are maintained by the respective Postal Administration of each island. The local telephone services are maintained by the insular authorities. There were, in 1969, 16,570 subscribers in Jersey and 14,181 in Guernsey.

There is an independent television station in Jersey.

Lempiere, R., *Portrait of the Channel Islands*. London, 1970
Lockley, R. M., *The Channel Islands*. London, 1968
Myhill, H., *Introducing the Channel Islands*. London, 1964
Uttley, J., *The Story of the Channel Islands*. London, 1966

JERSEY

Constitution. The States consist of 12 senators (elected for 6 years, 6 retiring every third year), 12 Constables (triennial) and 28 Deputies (triennial), all elected on universal suffrage by the people.

The island legislature is 'The States of Jersey'. The States comprises the Bailiff, the Lieut.-Governor, 12 Senators, the Constables of the 12 parishes of the island, 28 Deputies, the Dean of Jersey, the Attorney-General and the Solicitor-General. They all have the right to speak in the Assembly, but only the 52 elected members (the Senators, Constables and Deputies) have the right to vote; the Bailiff has a casting vote. General elections for Senators and Deputies are held every third year. Except in specific instances, enactments passed by the States require the sanction of the Queen-in-Council. The Lieut.-Governor has the power of veto on certain forms of legislation.

Lieut.-Governor and C.-in-C. of Jersey: Air Chief Marshal Sir John Davis, GCB, OBE.

Secretary and ADC to the Lieut.-Governor: Lieut.-Cdr O. M. B. de Las Casas, OBE, RN (Retd).

Bailiff of Jersey and President of the States: Sir Robert Le Masurier, DSC.

Population (1969), 72,400. In the year ended 31 Dec 1969 there were 1,067 births and 849 deaths. The town is St Helier on the south coast.

Education (1969). There are 2 public schools, namely, Victoria College for boys (625 pupils) and the Jersey College for Girls (510 pupils); 4,820 pupils attend the States primary schools, 2,260 the States secondary schools and 2,005 attend private schools. The Institute of Further Education provides facilities for technical instruction, domestic science and evening classes and recreational courses in adult education.

Finance (year ending 31 Dec. 1969). Revenue, £13,071,992; expenditure, £10,143,901; public debt, £5,115,048. The standard rate of income tax is 4s. in the pound. No super-tax or death duties are levied. Parochial rates of moderate amount are payable by owners and occupiers.

On 12 July 1963 the States began issuing bank-notes in denominations of £5, £1 and 10s.

Commerce (1969). Principal imports: Food, £8,649,430; machinery and transport equipment, £9,181,377; beverages and tobacco, £3,142,328; fuel, £1,872,547; chemicals, £2,316,141. Principal exports: Potatoes, £3,177,977; tomatoes, £2,185,001; cattle, £53,327.

Shipping. Number of commercial ships entering St Helier (1969), 3,155. All vessels arriving in Jersey from outside Jersey waters report at St Helier or Gorey on first arrival. There is a harbour of minor importance at St Aubin. Ships registered in Jersey (excluding fishing boats), 1969: Motor, 19; steam, 0; yachts, 753 (of 15 ft and over); dumb barges, 1. Passengers arrived (and departed) in 1969, 238,711 (and 233,743).

Aviation. The Jersey airport is situated at St Peter. It covers approximately 322 acres. Number of aircraft (1969), 24,768; passengers, 543,745 arrivals, 540,796 departures.

Balleine, G. R., *Biographical Dictionary of Jersey.* London, 1948.—*A History of the Island of Jersey.* London, 1950.—*The Bailiwick of Jersey.* 3rd ed. London, 1970
Le Maistre, F., *Dictionnaire Jersiais-Français.* Jersey, 1966

STATES OF JERSEY LIBRARY. Royal Square, St Helier. *Librarian:* J. K. Antill, FLA.

GUERNSEY

Constitution. The government of the island is conducted by committees appointed by the States.

The States of Deliberation, the parliament of Guernsey, is composed of the following members: The Bailiff, who is President *ex officio;* 12 Conseillers; H.M. Procureur and H.M. Comptroller (Law Officers of the Crown), who have a voice but no vote; 33 People's Deputies elected by popular franchise; 10 Douzaine Representatives elected by their Parochial Douzaines; 2 representatives of the States of Alderney. The Lieut.-Governor has no power of veto.

The States of Election, an electoral college, elects the Jurats and Conseillers. It is composed of the following members: The Bailiff (President *ex officio*); the 12 Jurats or 'Jurés-Justiciers'; the 12 Conseillers; the 10 Rectors; H.M. Procureur and H.M. Comptroller; the 33 People's Deputies; 34 Douzaine Representatives; and (for the election of Conseillers) 4 representatives of the States of Alderney.

Since Jan. 1949 all legislative powers and functions (with minor exceptions) formerly exercised by the Royal Court have been vested in the States of Deliberation. Projets de Loi (Bills) require the sanction of the Queen-in-Council.

Lieut.-Governor and C.-in-C. of Guernsey and its Dependencies: Vice-Adm. Sir Charles Mills, KCB, CBE, DSC.

Secretary and ADC to the Lieut.-Governor: Capt. M. H. T. Mellish, OBE.

Bailiff of Guernsey and President of the States: Sir William Arnold, CBE.

Population. Estimated population at 30 June 1969 was 46,343. Births during 1969 were 837; deaths, 643. The town is St Peter Port.

Education. There are 2 public schools in the island: Elizabeth College, founded by Queen Elizabeth in 1563, for boys, and the Ladies' College, for girls. The States grammar schools provide for education up to University entrance requirements, and there are numerous modern secondary and primary schools. The total number of school children is 8,772. Facilities are available for the study of art, domestic science and many other subjects of a technical nature. There is also a convent school with boarding facilities for girls.

Finance (year ending 31 Dec. 1969). Revenue, £6,113,148 (including £160,574 for Alderney); expenditure, £7,649,193 (including £198,492 for Alderney); States' funded debt less sinking fund provisions, £2,830,050; note and coin issue, £1,490,361. The standard rate of income tax is 4s. in the pound. States and parochial rates are very moderate. No supertax or death-duties are levied.

Commerce (1969). Principal imports: Coal, 44,536 tons; petrol and oils, 48·76m. gallons. Principal exports: Tomatoes, 51,503 tons net; flowers and fern, 9,412 tons; stone, 59,959 tons.

Shipping. The principal harbour is that of St Peter Port, and there is a harbour at St Sampson's (used mainly for commercial shipping). In 1969 the number of ship tons net entering and leaving Guernsey was 1,824,686. 90,947 passengers arrived from places outside the Channel Islands. Ships registered in Guernsey at 31 Dec. 1969 numbered 102 (sail, 6; yachts, 96).

Aviation. The airport in Guernsey, situated at La Villiaze, has a landing area of approximately 124 acres and a tarmac runway of 4,800 ft. In 1969, 144,593 passengers arrived from places outside the Channel Islands.

Alderney. Population (30 June 1969), 1,513. The island has an airport. The constitution of the island (reformed 1949) provides for its own popularly elected President and States (9 members), and its own Court. The town is St Anne.

> *President of the States:* G·W.Baron
> *Clerk of the States:* P. W. Radice, MA, ICS (Retd).
> *Clerk of the Court:* G. N. P. Crombie, MA, LLB.

Sark. Population (30 June 1969), 577. The constitution is a mixture of feudal and popular government with its Chief Pleas (parliament), consisting of 40 tenants and 12 popularly elected deputies, presided over by the Seneschal. The head of the island is the Seigneur (at present La Dame). Sark has no income tax. Motor vehicles, except tractors, are not allowed.

> *La Dame de Sercq:* Dame Sibyl Hathaway, DBE.
> *Seneschal:* B. G. Jones.

Carteret, A. R. de, *The Story of Sark*. London, 1956
Clark, L., *Sark Discovered*. London, 1956
Durand, R., *Guernsey, Present and Past*. Guernsey, 1933.—*Guernsey under German Rule*. London 1946
A Short History of and Guide to Alderney. New ed. Guernsey, 1968
Hathaway, Sybil, *Dame of Sark: an autobiography*. London, 1961
Le Huray, C. P., *The Bailiwick of Guernsey*. London, 1952
Wood, A. and M. S., *Islands in Danger*. 2nd ed. London, 1957

THE COMMONWEALTH OF THE BAHAMAS

Area and Population. The Commonwealth of the Bahamas consists of more than 30 inhabited and many uninhabited cays and rocks off the S.E. coast of Florida. They are the surface protuberances of two oceanic banks, the Little Bahama Bank and the Great Bahama Bank. Of the group, about 700 areas might be classified as islands: the rest only as rocks. Land area, 5,386¼ sq. miles (13,950 sq. km). The total rainfall (New Providence) in 1969 was 54·52 in.; highest in June (20·35 in.). Average winter temperature, 69·9° F. (21·1° C); average summer temperature, 82·8° F. (28·2° C.).

Principal islands with census population in 1963: New Providence (80,907, containing capital, Nassau), Abaco (6,490), Harbour Island (997), Grand Bahama (8,230), Cat Island (3,131), Long Island (4,176), Mayaguana (707), Eleuthera (7,247), Exuma (3,440), San Salvador or Watling's Island (968), Acklin's Island (1,217), Crooked Island (766), Inagua (1,240), Andros (7,461), Bimini (1,652), Spanish Wells (849), Ragged Island (371).

Total estimated population, 1969, 166,200 (males, 82,374; females, 83,826). Vital statistics, 1968: Births, 4,093; deaths, 1,023 (excluding still-births).

Constitution and Government. Internal self-government with cabinet responsibility was introduced on 7 Jan. 1964. There are a Senate of 16 members and a House of Assembly of 38 elected members. Nine senators are appointed by the Governor on the advice of the Premier, 4 on the advice of the Leader of the Opposition and 3 at the Governor's discretion. The General Assembly Elections Act, 1959, as amended provides for universal adult suffrage. Persons of 18 years and over who hold Bahamian status are eligible to register and vote. The normal life of the House is 5 years, but it may be dissolved at any time by the Governor.

At the elections of 10 April 1968 the Progressive Liberal Party obtained 29 seats; the United Bahamian Party won 7 seats; Labour 1 seat; 1 independent.

Governor and C.-in-C.: The Hon. Sir Francis Cumming-Bruce, KCMG (also Governor of the Turks and Caicos Islands).
Prime Minister and Minister of External Affairs: Lynden O. Pindling.

Education (1969). Education is compulsory between the ages of 5 and 14. There are 169 state-maintained infant and primary schools with a total roll of 25,911; 10 government secondary and grammar schools with a total roll of 12,422 pupils; and 83 denominational and private schools (infant, primary and secondary) with a total roll of 14,124 pupils. Government expenditure B$15,316,317.

Cinemas (1969). There are 18 cinemas and 2 drive-ins.

Newspapers (1969). There are 2 daily newspapers in Nassau with a combined circulation of 108,555 per week.

Justice (1969). 18,522 cases (traffic, 9,930; criminal, 4,692; civil, 3,900) were dealt with in the magistrates' court, and 877 (criminal, 86; civil, 791) in the Supreme Court. The strength of the police force was 79 officers and 947 other ranks.

Finance. CURRENCY. A decimal system of currency was introduced in 1966 with the Bahamian $ equalling 41p. sterling or US cents 98. Notes: $0·50, 1, 3, 5, 10, 20, 50, 100; coins: 1, 5, 10, 15, 25, 50 cents, $1, 2, 5. Sterling currency has been withdrawn. American and Canadian currency is generally accepted. Bank of England notes are not accepted, except at the banks from travellers from the UK.

BUDGET (1969). Revenue, B$84·5m. (1970 est., B$97·6m.); estimated expenditure, B$81·35m. (1970 est., B$97·05m.). Public debt (1967), B$31,682,924. The tourist industry is the chief source of income (1,332,396 visitors in 1969).

Commerce. The principal exports in 1969 were cement, alcoholic beverages, pulpwood, crawfish and salt, which is extracted from brine by solar radiation.

Imports and exports (excluding bullion and specie) for 6 calendar years (in £; from 1966 in B$):

	Imports	Exports		Imports	Exports
1964	35,669,627	5,588,211	1967	160,863,283	32,270,861
1965	37,431,175	6,656,653	1968	179,987,251	51,781,802
1966	137,975,638	22,780,582	1969	302,278,440	54,325,928

Imports (excluding specie) (1969) from USA were valued at B$206,005,890; from UK, B$25,905,017; from Canada, B$13,457,475. Principal imports were: Food, drink and tobacco (B$61,682,664); raw materials and articles mainly unmanufactured (B$6,110,302); articles wholly or mainly manufactured (B$1,129,758); animals not for food (B$43,741).

Principal exports were: Pulpwood (B$1,653,974), crawfish (B$677,211) alcoholic spirits (B$3,676,599); cement (B$1,727,685); used motor cars (B$1,500,067).

Trade with U.K., in £1,000 sterling (British Board of Trade returns):

	1965	1966	1967	1968	1969	1970
Imports to UK	506	904	990	1,841	1,978	2,752
Exports from UK	5,309	6,812	7,735	10,623	13,446 ⎫	
Re-exports from UK	194	184	186	282	419 ⎭	11,073

Shipping. In 1969, 2,954 vessels tons entered and 2,861 vessels cleared at Nassau.

Roads. There are more than 230 miles of paved roads in New Providence, 130 miles of good roads on Eleuthera and 152 miles on Grand Bahama. The other major islands also have motorable roads. In 1969, 55,713 motor vehicles were registered. There are no railroads.

Power. Electricity for lighting and power is available in New Providence, Grand Bahama and the Out Islands. Total units generated in New Providence in 1969, 247·6m. kwh. Total number of consumers, 29,089.

Telecommunications. In the island of New Providence an automatic telephone system of the latest type is in operation, together with an extensive system of underground cables. The total number of telephones in use at 31 Dec. 1969 was 35,513. 132 radio-telephone channels provide service *via* the USA to any part of the world. All the important islands are connected with Nassau by means of radio-telegraphy, and in most cases radio-telephony is also available. Connexion through Nassau to the UK, the USA, Canada and Central America can be provided. Radio-teletype to Bermuda and Florida and ship–shore radio-telephone services are also available. Radio-teletype service is provided from Nassau to Freeport and West End in Grand Bahama. The Bahamas broadcasting station operates on 1,540 and 1,240 kilocycles.

Aviation. Nassau international airport is located on the island of New Providence, about 10 miles from the city of Nassau. Scheduled flights—BOAC: daily from New York (twice daily from Dec. to April); twice weekly from Bermuda; once weekly from Jamaica. PANAM: daily from New York; four times daily from Miami. Air Canada: daily from Toronto, Montreal and Jamaica. Eastern Airlines: daily from Tampa, West Palm Beach and Fort Lauderdale; 3 times daily from Miami; once weekly from Jacksonville *via* West End, Grand Bahama. There are numerous domestic schedules to the Out Islands. Colony Airlines and Out Island Airways provide commercial and charter services to the Out Islands and Florida. There are 55 airstrips on the various Out Islands and numerous water alighting areas. During 1969, 970,000 passengers landed at Nassau and Freeport.

Banking. The Royal Bank of Canada, the Bank of Nova Scotia, Barclays Bank DCO, The Canadian Imperial Bank of Commerce, the Bank of London and Montreal, The Chase Manhattan Bank, The First National City Bank of New York, E. D. Sassoon Banking Co., Butlers Bank, Commonwealth Industrial Bank, International Bank of Washington and the Mercantile Bank of the Bahamas have branches in Nassau. The Royal Bank of Canada, Bank of Nova Scotia and Barclays Bank DCO have branches on several other islands.

Post office savings bank, 30 June 1969, depositors, 28,813; balance due, B$2,727,708.

BOOKS OF REFERENCE
Annual Report, 1968–69. HMSO, 1969
Craton, M. A., *A History of the Bahamas.* London, 1962
LIBRARY. Nassau Public Library.

BERMUDA

History. The Spaniards visited the islands in 1515, but, according to a 17th-century French cartographer, they were discovered in 1503 by Juan Bermudez, after whom they were named. No settlement was made, and they were uninhabited until a party of colonists under Sir George Somers was wrecked there in 1609. A company was formed for the 'Plantation of the Somers' Islands', as they were called at first, and in 1684 the Crown took over the government.

Area and Population. Bermuda consists of a group of some 300 small islands about 20 inhabited), situated in the western Atlantic (32° 18′ N. lat., 64° 46′ W. long.); the nearest point of the mainland, about 570 miles distant, is Cape Hatteras, N.C., and 690 miles from New York; noted for its climate and scenery; a favourite resort for Americans.

The area is 20·59 sq. miles (53·3 sq. km), of which 2·3 sq. miles were leased in 1941 for 99 years to the US Government for naval and air bases. The civil population (*i.e.,* excluding British and American military, naval and air force personnel) at 30 June 1969 was estimated at 50,927.

Chief town, Hamilton; population, about 3,000.

In 1969 there were 934 live births, 490 marriages and 372 deaths; infantile mortality rate was 26·77.

Constitution and Government. Bermuda is a colony with representative government. Under the constitution of 8 June 1968 the Governor, appointed by the Crown, is normally bound to accept the advice of the Executive Council in matters other than external affairs, defence, internal security and the police, for which he retains special responsibility. The Executive Council is appointed from among members of the bicameral legislature, on the recommendation of the Government Leader. The Legislative Council, of whom one or two members may serve on Executive Council, consists of 11 members; 5 are appointed in the discretion of the Governor, 4 on the recommendation of the Government Leader and 2 on the recommendation of the Opposition Leader. The 40 members of the House of Assembly are elected 2 from each of 20 constituencies under full universal, adult suffrage. The general election on 22 May 1968 resulted in the return of 30 members of the United Bermuda Party and 10 members of the Progressive Labour Party.

Governor: The Rt. Hon. Lord Martonmere, PC, KCMG.
Government Leader: Sir Henry Tucker, CBE, JP.

Education. Education is compulsory between the ages of 5 and 16, and government assistance is given by the payment of grants, and, where necessary, of school fees. Free elementary education was introduced on 1 May 1949. In 1969, 7 aided and 35 maintained schools, with 13,805 pupils, received government grants. There is a school for handicapped children (43 pupils) 3 special schools (221 pupils). There are also 2 private schools.

Cinemas (1969). There are 4 cinemas with a seating capacity of 2,260.

Justice. There are 4 magistrates' courts, a supreme court and a court of appeal. The police had a strength of 274 in 1969.

Finance. CURRENCY. Decimal currency based on a Bermuda dollar of 100 cents was introduced on 6 Feb. 1970 (£1 = 2·4 Bermuda dollars). The Bermuda

Monetary Authority issues notes in denominations of $50, $20, $10, $5, and $1, and coins in values of 50c, 25c, 10c, 5c and 1c.

BUDGET. Revenue and expenditure (in £ sterling) for calendar years until 1969 and in $B for years ending 31 May from 1970–71:

	1966	1967	1968	1969	1970–71[1]
Revenue	7,643,518	8,071,866	10,691,565	11,788,392	35,510,920
Expenditure	7,250,439	8,647,615	9,944,788	11,308,457	35,753,292

[1] Estimates.

Expenditure was earmarked as follows (actual for 1966–69, estimated for 1970):

	1966	1967	1968	1969	1970[1]
Agriculture and fisheries	223,109	275,061	300,745	345,195	1,421,979
Tourism and trade development	857,022	970,522	1,168,307	1,171,027	3,197,399
Education	1,155,733	1,313,496	2,238,437	2,603,269	7,454,658
Hospital grant	338,000	435,000	525,700	587,825	1,968,000
Police	507,579	566,500	640,587	653,170	2,142,059
Prisons	228,437	249,556	278,636	281,752	791,463
Post office	259,364	316,259	396,128	426,625	1,284,726
Health and welfare	320,843	688,038	792,335	869,414	3,000,536
Public transportation	306,848	380,908	418,587	403,451	1,403,627
Public works	598,112	765,216	956,060	1,309,173	4,924,783
Civil aviation	172,904	186,225	227,471	429,538	1,130,893

[1] In Bermuda dollars.

Chief sources of revenue in 1969 were: Customs, £6,768,246; stamp duties, £855,478; vehicles and drivers' licences, £485,526; omnibus services, £429,943; land tax, £665,805; companies tax, £387,350.
Public debt, as at 31 Dec. 1969, £221,000.

Production. The chief products are pharmaceutics, concentrated essences, plants, bananas, citrus fruit, lilies, potatoes and other kitchen-garden vegetables. In 1969, 740 acres were under cultivation.

TOURISM. In 1969, 370,290 tourists visited Bermuda. Tourism contributed about £27·5m. to the economy in 1969.

Trade Unions. Legislation providing for trade unions was enacted in Oct. 1946, and there are 6 trade unions (Amalgamated Union of Teachers, 444 members; Industrial Union, 2,783; Civil Service Association, 446; Hotel Employers Council, 24; Electricity Supply, 148; Musicians and Artists, 285).

Commerce. Imports and exports[1] (in £ sterling) for 6 calendar years:

	1964	1965	1966	1967	1968	1969[1]
Imports	20,987,925	20,942,177	23,665,281	24,697,462	30,449,458	35,625,940
Exports	726,928	945,723	723,680	558,778	784,284	1,086,180

[1] Excluding imports into and exports from free port.

The visible adverse balance of trade is more than compensated for by invisible exports, including tourism.

Imports in 1969 from USA, £15,417,498; UK, £8,051,721; Canada, £3,561,416; Netherlands West Indies, £976,262; West Germany, £757,181; New Zealand, £733,506; Commonwealth Caribbean territories, £732,480; France, £688,884. Exports in 1969 to UK, £173,596; Canada, £113,654; USA, £65,255.

In 1969 the principal imports were electrical supplies (£2·14m.), cotton clothing (£1·4m.), fresh beef (£1·5m.); the principal local exports, concentrated essences (£991,629).

Total trade between Bermuda and UK, in £1,000 sterling (British Board of Trade returns):

	1965	1966	1967	1968	1969	1970
Imports to UK	4,342	5,590	6,989	9,829	11,216	15,882
Exports from UK	4,750	5,631	5,696	7,220	9,814 }	11,093
Re-exports from UK	153	157	168	195	228 }	

Shipping. The registered shipping consisted (1967) of 9 steam vessels of 91,635 tons net, 31 sailing vessels of 3,298 tons net and 82 motor vessels of 135,207 tons net. In 1969 the gross tonnage of vessels entered and cleared was 5,952,035 tons.

Roads. In 1948 the railway service was discontinued and a government-operated bus service introduced.

Between 1908 and Aug. 1946 the use of motor vehicles, with the exception of ambulances, fire engines and other essential services, was prohibited. With the passing of the Motor Car Act in 1946, the use of motor vehicles, subject to certain limitations on size and horse-power, became lawful. In 1969, 10,061 private cars, 611 public passenger vehicles, 1,659 lorries and trucks, 23,347 auto-cycles and 796 miscellaneous motor vehicles were registered.

Post (1970). There are 12 post offices. The telephone company is privately owned and operates about 28,094 telephones. Cables connect the islands with the USA, Halifax (N.S.) and Tortola, providing connexion with the world.

Radio and television broadcasting is commercial.

Aviation. BOAC, PANAM, Eastern Airlines and Northeast Airlines maintain regular services between Bermuda and the USA. BOAC also have regular flights through Bermuda linking London with Mexico and the Caribbean. Air Canada Airlines call at Bermuda on their service between Canada, Barbados, Antigua and Trinidad; they also operate services between Bermuda, Toronto, Montreal and Halifax. Qantas calls at Bermuda between Sydney and London *via* Bahamas, Mexico, Tahiti and Fiji. Aircraft entered and cleared in 1969, 6,175, carrying 847,260 passengers.

Banking. There are 4 banks, the Bank of Bermuda, Ltd, the Bank of N. T. Butterfield and Son, Ltd, the Bermuda National Bank, Ltd, and the Bermuda Provident Bank, Ltd. Post office savings bank deposits at the end of 1969 totalled £266,411 to the credit of 8,174 depositors.

Weights and Measures are British, except that US instead of Imperial fluid measures are used.

BOOKS OF REFERENCE

Annual Report, 1967. HMSO, 1968
Bermuda Historical Quarterly 1944 ff.
Baron, S., *Your guide to Bermuda.* London, 1965
Bell, E. Y., *Beautiful Bermuda.* 10th ed. New York and Bermuda, 1947
Dyer, H. T., *The Next 20 Years; A Report on the Development Plans for Bermuda.* Hamilton, 1963
Zuill, W. E. S., *Bermuda Today.* New York, 1958

NATIONAL LIBRARY. The Bermuda Library, Hamilton. *Head Librarian:* Mrs M. Skiffington.

BRITISH HONDURAS

HISTORY. The early settlement of the territory was probably effected by British woodcutters about 1638; from that date to 1798, in spite of armed opposition from the Spaniards, settlers held their own and prospered. In 1780 the Home Government appointed a superintendent, and in 1862 the settlement was declared a colony, subordinate to Jamaica. It became an independent colony in 1884. The proposed new name of the colony is Belize.

CONSTITUTION AND GOVERNMENT. Under the constitution, which came into force on 1 Jan. 1964, British Honduras has a 2-chamber legislature, with a ministerial system and cabinet responsibility. The House of Representatives consists of 18 members elected by universal suffrage. The Senate consists of 8 members, 5 of whom are appointed on the advice of the Premier, 2 on the advice of the Leader of the Opposition and 1 by the Governor.

Elections held on 5 Dec. 1969 gave the People's United Party 17 and the National Independence Party 1 seat.

The Governor retains reserve powers in respect of defence, external affairs, internal security, the safeguarding of conditions of service of public officers, and over finance 'so long as the Government of British Honduras is in receipt of budgetary aid from the British Government'.

Governor and C.-in-C.: Sir John Paul, GCMG, OBE, MC.
Premier and Minister of Finance and Development: George Price.

AREA AND POPULATION. Area, 8,867 sq. miles (22,963 sq. km).

Population, census 1970, 119,645. Voters on the roll numbered 29,863 in 1968. In 1967 the birth rate per 1,000 was 42·1 and the death rate 7; infantile mortality 59·9 per 1,000 births; there were 680 marriages and 16 divorces.

Main city, Belize City; population, census 1970, 39,257. Following the severe hurricane which struck the territory on 31 Oct. 1961 the capital Belmopan has been moved to a new site 50 miles inland; construction began in Jan. 1967 and it became the seat of government on 3 Aug. 1970.

Police. The police force contained (1966) 9 officers, 6 inspectors, 330 n.c.o.s and constables and 10 women constables.

EDUCATION. In 1969, 2 government, 161 grant-aided and 11 private primary schools had a total enrolment of 27,419 pupils; 18 secondary schools, 2,642 pupils; a government technical high school, 267 pupils; a government junior college, 250 pupils. All aided schools, except the government technical high school, are under the management of Christian bodies. The inter-denominational teachers' college has absorbed 3 formerly separate teacher-training institutions; in Oct. 1969 it had 130 students.

CINEMAS (1965). There were 10 cinemas with seating capacity of 4,937.

NEWSPAPERS (1969). There was 1 daily newspaper with a combined circulation of 6,000 and 4 weekly.

FINANCE. Currency. The British Honduras dollar equals 25p. sterling and US cents 60. There was (31 Dec. 1965) a paper currency of $4,785,965 in government notes and a subsidiary mixed metal coinage of 1-, 5-, 10-, 25- and 50-cent pieces whose issues amount to $600,782.

Budget. Revenue and expenditure (in $BH) for calendar years:

	1965	1966	1967[1]	1968	1969[1]	1970[1]
Revenue	9,301,650	11,967,899	18,700,653	24,419,578	..	26,459,678
Expenditure	9,763,453	14,505,481	18,628,942	25,171,728	27,928,754	26,482,551

[1] Estimates.

Colonial Development and Welfare grants amounted to $BH9·9m. in 1970.

Debt, 31 Dec. 1968, $8,815,108; sinking fund, $1,410,989.

AGRICULTURE. The main agricultural export is sugar, followed by citrus fruit, chiefly grapefruit and oranges, whole, canned, juice and concentrates. Sugar production in 1969–70 was 67,300 tons. The total acreage under citrus for export was 8,664 in 1965.

FORESTRY. 2,964 sq. miles, 49% of the total land area, are under forests which include mahogany, cedar, Santa Maria, pine and rosewood, and many secondary hardwoods of known or probable market value, as well as woods suitable for pulp production. Exports of forest produce in 1965 amounted to $BH5,803,803 (33·2% of the total exports).

FISHERIES. Food and game fish are plentiful, and domestic consumption is heavy. The main items exported in 1967 were lobsters (Spiny) whole and tails, 316,600 lb., valued at $BH405,759, fresh and dried fish, 305,500 lb., valued at

$BH75,448; conchs (1966), 135,844 lb., valued at $35,263. Turtles—Hawksbill, Loggerhead and Green—are plentiful but as yet are not exported.

A development finance corporation with an authorized capital of $BH4m. was set up in 1961 to provide medium- and long-term credit for agriculture, forestry, tourism and other industries and in 1973 has a paid-up share capital of $BH318,000.

LABOUR. The labour market alternates between full employment, often accompanied by local shortages in the citrus and sugar-cane harvesting (Jan.–July), and under-employment during the wet season (Aug.–Dec.), aggravated by the seasonal nature of the major industries.

In March 1967 (the peak period of employment) full-time paid workers numbered 14,997, of whom agriculture, fishery and forestry accounted for 4,225, mining and quarrying for 29, manufacturing for 2,743, construction for 1,314, gas, water, electricity and sanitary services for 216, commerce for 1,502, transport and communications for 589, services for 4,268.

In 1965 there were 8 trade unions registered with a reported membership of 3,657.

COMMERCE. In 1967 total imports amounted to $36,951,914, of which $9·3m. was for machinery and transport equipment; $9·44m. for food; $7·39m. for manufactured goods; $3·81m. for miscellaneous manufactures; $2·29m. for mineral fuel, lubricants, etc. Total domestic exports, $16·35m. The principal domestic exports were: Timber, $1·18m.; sugar, $8·03m.; citrus, $3·47m. Total exports, 1967, $20·51m.

Total trade between British Honduras and UK (British Board of Trade returns in £1,000 sterling):

	1965	1966	1967	1968	1969	1970
Imports to UK	2,080	2,199	2,302	2,175	2,281	2,347
Exports from UK	2,666	3,347	2,661	2,791	3,016 ⎱	3,593
Re-exports from UK	51	56	40	58	67 ⎰	

SHIPPING (1967). Tonnage entered, 631,117 net tons. Registered shipping, 29 sailing vessels, 223 net tons, 45 motor vessels, 1,062 net tons and 2 others, 235 net tons.

POST. Telephone lines connect Belize City with Corozal Town and Consejo on the coast, Orange Walk Town on New River, San Antonio on the Rio Hondo and other stations in the north, San Ignacio and Benque Viejo Towns in the west, Stann Creek and Punta Gorda Towns and other points in the south. Number of telephones (1969), 2,111. The government-operated telecommunication services were taken over by Cable and Wireless Ltd in 1962, which installed an automatic telephone service in 1963 and also operates a radio-telephone service. There are 6 post offices and 44 rural sub-post offices.

AVIATION. In 1968, 41,347 passengers and 4,204,232 lb. of freight arrived and departed on international flights.

BANKING. The Royal Bank of Canada took over the business of the local bank in 1912; it has 4 branches. There are 6 government savings banks; depositors, about 13,500; deposits, $2,330,469 on 31 Dec. 1968.

Barclays Bank DCO have 5 branches and Bank of Nova Scotia have 2 branches.

BOOKS OF REFERENCE

Annual Report, 1962–63. Government Printer, Belize City, 1965
Abstract of Statistics 1962. Government Printer, Belize City, 1963
UN Economic Report, 1963. Ministry of Finance and Development, 1964
Anderson, A. H., *Brief Sketch of the British Honduras.* 7th ed. Belize, 1958
Bianchi, W. J., *Belize: the controversy between Guatemala and Great Britain.* New York, 1959
Gregg, A. R., *British Honduras.* HMSO, 1969
Romney, D. H. (ed.), *Land in British Honduras.* HMSO, 1959
Waddell, D. A. G., *British Honduras: a historical and contemporary survey.* OUP, 1961

BRUNEI

HISTORY. The Sultanate of Brunei was a powerful state in the early 16th century, with authority over the whole of the island of Borneo and some parts of the Sulu Islands and the Philippines. At the end of the 16th century its power had begun to decline and various cessions were made to Great Britain, the Rajah of Sarawak and the British North Borneo Company in the 19th century to combat piracy and anarchy. By the middle of the 19th century the State had been reduced to its present limits.

In 1847 the Sultan of Brunei entered into a treaty with Great Britain for the furtherance of commercial relations and the suppression of piracy, and in 1888, by a further treaty, the State was placed under the protection of Great Britain. Brunei was the only former British dependency inhabited by a Malay people that did not join the Federation of Malaysia in 1963.

AREA AND POPULATION. Brunei, on the north-west coast of Borneo, is bounded on all sides by Sarawak territory, which splits the State into two separate parts. Area, about 2,226 sq. miles (5,800 sq. km), with a coastline of about 100 miles. Estimated population in mid-1969 was 130,000 (revised). The capital is Brunei Town (population, 34,000, including the Kampong Ayer), 9 miles from the mouth of Brunei River. The climate is of tropical marine type, hot and moist, with cool nights.

CONSTITUTION AND GOVERNMENT. On 29 Sept. 1959 the Sultan promulgated a constitution. There is a Privy Council, an Executive and a Legislative Council. On 6 Jan. 1965 the constitution was amended to provide for general elections to the Legislative Council; at the same time the Executive Council was renamed Council of Ministers. The Legislative Council is presided by a Speaker and consists of 6 *ex-officio* members, 5 nominated members and 10 elected members. The Council of Ministers is presided by the Sultan and consists of 6 *ex-officio* members, the High Commissioner and 4 other members, all of whom are members of the Legislative Council. The Mentri Besar, who is one of the *ex-officio* members of the Legislative Council and the Council of Ministers, is responsible to the Sultan for the exercise of executive authority in the State.

The official language is Malay, but English may be used for all official purposes. The official religion is Islam.

Sultan of Brunei: The 28th Sultan abdicated on 4 Oct. 1967 in favour of his son, who was installed on the 5th as Sultan Hassanal Bolkiah Muizzaddin Waddaulah, DK, PSPNB, PSNB, PSLJ, SPMB, PANB, CMG, DK (Kelantan), DK (Johore), and was crowned on 1 Aug. 1968.

Her Majesty's High Commissioner: A. R. Adair, CVO, MBE.
Mentri Besar: Pengiran Setia Negara Haji Mohd. Yusuf bin Pengiran Haji Abdul Rahim, DK, SPMB, DSNB, POAS, PHBS, CBE, PJK.

EDUCATION (1970). Free education in the Malay language is provided in government primary schools (15,719 pupils) and 6 government secondary schools (4,487 pupils). Free education in English was provided in 10 government preparatory schools (4,928 pupils) and 5 government secondary schools (3,278 pupils). Teacher-training was provided in one government teachers' college, in both Malay and English, for 177 post-LCE and post-GCE O Level students and for 103 Malay probationer primary teachers. Seven unassisted Mission schools provided education in English at kindergarten, primary and secondary level for a total of 5,744 pupils; 8 assisted Chinese schools provided education in Chinese at the same three levels for a total of 5,232 pupils. One private kindergarten and primary school, administered by the Brunei Shell Petroleum Company, provided education in either English or Dutch for a total of 23 pupils, and there was also one private secondary school (41 pupils), and one private vocational school administered by the Brunei Shell Petroleum Company (119 artisan-trainees).

Recurrent expenditure on education in 1969 was $17·5m.; capital expenditure, $19·3m.

POLICE. Establishment provides for 958 officers and men. In addition, there is a small auxiliary force mostly employed on static guard duties.

INDUSTRY. Brunei depends primarily on its oil industry, which employs one-tenth of the entire working population. Other important products are rubber, padi, jelutong, firewood and sago. Native industries include boat-building, cloth weaving and the manufacture of brass- and silverware. Most of the interior is under forest, containing large potential supplies of serviceable timber.

The Seria oilfield, discovered in 1929, has passed its peak production. The oilfield extends offshore and many wells have been drilled from jetties extending out to sea. Further search for new sources of oil is being conducted in the off-shore areas. Part of the oil produced is refined at Lutong, where a large refinery, destroyed during the War, has been rebuilt.

A National Development Plan designed to strengthen, improve and further develop the economic, social and cultural life of the people of the State has been implemented by Government.

FINANCE. Currency. The currency is the Brunei Dollar with a par value of £0·13 or US cents 32·67.

Budget. The estimated revenue was $190,529,229 in 1968 and $236,193,542 in 1969; estimated expenditure was $168m. in 1968 and $214m. in 1969. The main sources of revenue were: Customs $7,013,000; income tax, $90,208,300; mining rents and oil royalties, $30,737,880; interest, etc., $54,852,840. The main heads of expenditure were: Public works recurrent, $13,886,742; medical and health, $7,978 365; education, $16,761,845; Royal Brunei Malay Regiment, $19,917,487.

COMMERCE. In 1969 imports totalled $221,112,473; exports, $270,139,966.

Total trade with UK (British Board of Trade returns, in £1,000 sterling):

	1965	1966	1967	1968	1969	1970
Imports to UK	47	16	60	114	54	49
Exports from UK	1,181	1,560	2,083	2,053	2,585 }	2,882
Re-exports from UK	24	6	3	21	65 }	

COMMUNICATIONS. The State has about 733 miles of road, of which 262 miles are bituminous surfaced. The main road connects Brunei Town with Kuala Belait and Seria. Considerable work is being undertaken for development of secondary roads. The number of motor vehicles (1970) was 14,405.

There were 7 post offices and a telephone network (5,046 telephones) linking the main centres. A central wireless station at Brunei is in direct communication with Singapore, Sarawak and Sabah; 3 subsidiary stations at Kuala Belait, Seria and Temburong serve internal traffic.

Regular shipping services operate from Singapore, Hong Kong, and from ports in Sarawak and Sabah to Brunei Town. The Straits Steamship Company carry passengers in some of their ships operating between Singapore and Brunei Town. The Government of Brunei operates a passenger ferry service between Brunei Town and Labuan, Sabah 6 days a week.

Malaysia Singapore Airlines is the only major airline now operating into Brunei until such time when the new international airport is completed in 1971–72. Apart from other smaller operators, MSA provides daily services linking Sarawak. Brunei and Sabah and West Malaysia and Singapore. At present passengers travelling abroad will have to proceed to Kota Kinabalu for connecting flights. MSA also operates in the rural areas with their Britten Norman Islander aircraft, The Malaysia Air Charter Ltd and other smaller operators provide various chartered services both in Brunei and East Malaysia.

FALKLAND ISLANDS AND DEPENDENCIES

AREA AND POPULATION. The Crown Colony is situated in the South Atlantic Ocean about 480 miles north-east of Cape Horn. The numerous islands cover 4,700 sq. miles. The main East Falkland Island, 2,610 sq. miles; the West Falkland, 2,090 sq. miles, including the adjacent small islands. The Dependency of South Georgia lies 800 miles south-east of the Falklands, has an area of 1,450 sq. miles; the South Sandwich group, 470 miles south-east of South Georgia, has an area of 130 sq. miles.

The population of the Falkland Islands on 31 Dec. 1969 was 2,098. The only town is Stanley, in East Falkland, with a population of just over 1,100. The population of South Georgia varies with the season, but the resident population on 31 Dec. 1969 was 11 (males). The South Shetlands are uninhabited.

South Georgia, once a base for whaling and sealing operations, is now occupied only by members of the British Antarctic Survey at the base at King Edward Point.

The population of the Falkland Islands and Dependencies is white and almost exclusively of British birth or descent.

CONSTITUTION AND GOVERNMENT. The Colony is administered by a Governor, assisted by an Executive Council consisting of the Colonial Secretary and Colonial Treasurer, both *ex officio*; 2 members elected by the Legislature and 2 appointed members; and a Legislative Council composed of the Colonial Secretary and Colonial Treasurer, both *ex officio*, 2 elected members representing Stanley, one elected member from the East Falkland and one from the West Falkland and 2 nominated independent members.

Governor and Commander-in-Chief: Ernest Gordon Lewis, OBE.
Colonial Secretary: John Ashley Jones, OBE.

EDUCATION. Education is compulsory between the ages of 5 and 15 years. In 1969 there were 2 government schools in Stanley, with 208 pupils; in the country districts 16 travelling and other teachers instructed 114 pupils. There is a boarding school at Darwin, East Falkland, with 48 pupils.

FINANCE. Currency. The Falkland £ is at parity with the £ sterling.

Budget. Revenue and expenditure (in £ sterling) for fiscal years ending 30 June:

	1964–65	1965–66	1966–67	1967–68	1968–69	1969–70[1]
Revenue	406,500	410,000	380,000	474,000	407,000	427,000
Expenditure	342,000	365,500	392,000	419,000	465,000	480,000

[1] Estimates.

Chief sources of revenue (1968–69): Customs, £48,300; internal revenue, £110,662; investment, £31,146; posts and telecommunications, £101,194. These figures do not include details of revenue of the development budget.

SHEEP FARMING. The whole acreage of the Colony is divided into large sheep runs. Wool is the principal product, but hides are exported. In 1968 there were 573,867 sheep, 10,792 cattle and 3,507 horses in the islands.

DEVELOPMENT. A comprehensive development scheme has provided extra concrete roads in Stanley, improved education facilities throughout the Colony, radio telephone services to many countries, including the UK, New Zealand and Australia and telex and telecommunication facilities. The British Science Research Council and European Space Research Organization both maintain telemetry tracking stations in Stanley.

TRADE. Total imports in 1968 amounted to £598,839 and exports to £841,671.

COMMUNICATIONS. There are no made-up roads in the islands beyond the immediate vicinity of Stanley. There is a small internal air service. Communication between Stanley and the outside world is effected principally through Montevideo, to which port a service is maintained by a steamship belonging to the Falkland Islands Company, Ltd, and by charter vessel to the UK. Communication with the Colony, the Dependencies and the British Antarctic Territory is kept up by the Royal Research Ships *John Biscoe* and charter vessels.

In 1969 the total tonnage of shipping entered and cleared was 51,396 in the Falkland Islands, and in South Georgia (1968) a tonnage of 20,043.

BANKING. On 30 June 1969 the government savings bank held a balance of £1,139,420 belonging to 1,986 depositors. Some banking facilities are also offered by Lloyds Bank and Hambros Bank.

WILD LIFE. The Falkland Islands and South Georgia are noted for their outstanding wild life, including penguin and seal. Two Nature Reserves have been declared and 7 Bird Sanctuaries gazetted. The brown trout introduced between 1947 and 1952 can now be found in nearly all the rivers.

BOOKS OF REFERENCE

Annual Report, 1967–68. HMSO, 1969
Falkland Islands Journal. Stanley, from 1967

GIBRALTAR

HISTORY. The Rock of Gibraltar was settled by Moors in 711; they named it after their chief Jabal Tariq, 'the Mountain of Tarik'. In 1462 it was taken by the Spaniards, from Granada. It was captured by Admiral Sir George Rooke on 24 July 1704, and ceded to Great Britain by the Treaty of Utrecht, 1713. The cession was confirmed by the treaties of Paris (1763) and Versailles (1783).

On 10 Sept. 1967, in pursuance of a United Nations resolution on the de colonization of Gibraltar, a referendum was held in Gibraltar in order to ascertain whether the people of Gibraltar believed that their interests lay in retaining their link with Britain or in passing under Spanish sovereignty. Out of a total electorate of 12,762, 12,138 voted to retain the British connexion, while 44 voted for Spain.

GOVERNMENT. Following a Constitutional Conference held in July 1968, a new Constitution was introduced in 1969. The Legislative and City Councils were merged to produce an enlarged legislature known as the Gibraltar House of Assembly. Executive authority is exercised by the Governor, who is also Commander-in-Chief. The Governor, while retaining certain reserved powers, is normally required to act in accordance with the advice of the Gibraltar Council, which consists of 5 elected and 4 *ex-officio* members (the Deputy Governor, the Deputy Fortress Commander, the Attorney-General and the Financial and Development Secretary). The elected members of the Gibraltar Council are appointed by the Governor after consultation with the Chief Minister and are styled Ministers. Matters of domestic concern are devolved to Ministers, with Britain responsible for other matters, including external affairs, defence and internal security. There is a Council of Ministers presided over by the Chief Minister.

The House of Assembly consists of a Speaker appointed by the Governor, 15 elected and 2 *ex-officio* members (the Attorney-General and the Financial and Development Secretary).

A Mayor of Gibraltar is elected from among the members of the Assembly by the elected members of the Assembly.

Governor and C.-in-C.: Adm. of the Fleet Sir Varyl Begg, GCB, DSO, DSC.
Chief Minister: Maj. Robert J. Peliza.

AREA AND POPULATION. Area, 2½ sq. miles (6·5 sq. km). Total population, including port and harbour (census, 3 Oct. 1961), 24,075 (11,061 males; 13,014 females). Estimated population, end of 1968, 26,007. The population are mostly of Genoese, Portuguese and Maltese descent.
Vital statistics (1968): Births, 542; marriages, 548; deaths, 216.

RELIGION. Religion of civil population mostly Roman Catholic; 1 Anglican and 1 Roman Catholic cathedral and 2 Anglican and 6 Roman Catholic churches; 1 Presbyterian and 1 Methodist churches and 4 synagogues; annual subsidy to each communion, £500.

EDUCATION. Education is provided for children between ages 5 and 15 years. There were, in 1968, 15 primary, 7 secondary, 1 commercial schools and 1 technical college. Total number of schoolchildren was 5,072, including those in private schools.

JUSTICE. The judicial system is based on the English system. There is a Supreme Court, presided over by the Chief Justice, a court of first instance and a magistrates' court.

FINANCE. Currency. The legal currency consists of Gibraltar Government notes and UK coins. The amount of local currency notes in circulation at the end of 1968 was £1,632,446.

Budget and Trade. Revenue and expenditure, and imports and exports (in £ sterling):

	1965	1966	1967	1968	1969[1]
Revenue	1,848,407	2,103,496	2,493,106	2,493,106	2,396,930
Expenditure	2,018,265	1,987,806	2,400,465	2,400,465	2,410,762
Imports	9,224,896	9,195,027	10,230,377	10,230,377	—
Exports	3,083,038	2,811,428	2,425,763	2,425,763	—

[1] Estimates.

Britain and the Commonwealth provide the bulk of the imports, but fresh vegetables, fruit and fish come mainly from Morocco, Portugal and the Netherlands. Exports of local produce are negligible. Gibraltar depends largely on tourism, the entrepôt trade and the provision of supplies to visiting ships.

INDUSTRY. There are a number of relatively small industrial concerns engaged in the assembly of watches, bottling of beer and mineral waters, etc., mainly for local consumption. There is a small but important commercial ship-repair yard. Tourism is of increasing importance.

LABOUR. The insured labour force on 31 Dec. 1968 consisted of 9,998 males and 2,117 females. The males included about 4,800 Spanish frontier workers who later, in June 1969, were prevented by the Spanish authorities from entering Gibraltar, as had been done with Spanish women workers in 1966. Measures which had been taken previously against the possibility of such a withdrawal worked well, and not very much disruption was occasioned to the day-to-day life of Gibraltar. Some industries, particularly construction, were more affected than others, and these are now in a period of readjustment. Nearly one-half of the insured labour force is employed by the UK departments or the Gibraltar government.
A considerable proportion of the workers are organized in one or other of the 28 registered trade unions, of which the Transport and General Workers Union has the largest membership; 10 of these are local branches of parent associations in the UK.

SHIPPING. Gibraltar is a naval and air base of great strategic importance. There is a deep Admiralty harbour of 440 acres. Vessels called in 1968, 3,332, net tonnage, 12,175,369.

POST. An automatic telephone system exists in the town, and there is world-wide communication *via* the cable and/or wireless circuits of Cable & Wireless Ltd. Air-mails arrive by BEA daily. A direct air-mail service between Gibraltar and Tangier is run by Gibraltar Airways, Ltd. Surface mails arrive direct and through France and Spain.

BANKING. There are 6 banks, including a branch of Barclays Bank DCO. Government savings bank, with 16,470 depositors, had £1,398,604 deposits at the end of 1968.

BOOKS OF REFERENCE

Annual Report on Gibraltar, 1966. London, 1966
Gibraltar Directory and Guide Book. Gibraltar, 1961
Howes, H. W., *The Story of Gibraltar.* London, 1946

HONG KONG

HISTORY. The Crown Colony of Hong Kong was ceded by China to Great Britain in Jan. 1841; the cession was confirmed by the treaty of Nanking in Aug. 1842, and the charter bears date 5 April 1843. Since then Hong Kong has been under British administration, with the exception of the period from 25 Dec. 1941 to 30 Aug. 1945, when it was occupied by the Japanese.

CONSTITUTION AND GOVERNMENT. The administration is in the hands of a Governor, aided by an Executive Council, composed of the Commander, British Forces, the Colonial Secretary, the Attorney-General, the Secretary for Home Affairs, the Financial Secretary (who are members *ex officio*) and such other members, both official and unofficial, as may be appointed by the Governor. In 1970 there were, in addition to the 5 *ex-officio* members, 1 nominated official and 8 nominated unofficial members, 4 of whom were Chinese, 1 Portuguese and 3 British. There is also a Legislative Council, presided over by the Governor, and consisting of not more than 12 official members (including 4 *ex-officio* members, namely the Colonial Secretary, the Attorney-General, the Secretary for Home Affairs and the Financial Secretary) and not more than 13 unofficial members. In 1970 there were 12 official and 13 unofficial members, 11 of whom were Chinese, 2 British.

Governor and C.-in-C.: Sir David Trench, GCMG, MC.
Commander British Forces: Lieut.-Gen. Sir Basil Eugster, KCB, KCVO, CBE, DSO, MC.
Colonial Secretary: Sir Hugh Norman-Walker, KCMG, OBE.

AREA AND POPULATION. Victoria, the colonial capital, situated on Hong Kong island, is 20 miles east of the mouth of the Pearl River and 91 miles south-east of Canton. The area of the island is 29 sq. miles. It is separated from the mainland by a fine natural harbour. On the opposite side is the peninsula of Kowloon (3½ sq. miles), which, with Stonecutters Island (¼ sq. mile), was added to the colony by the Convention of Peking, 1860. By a further convention, signed at Peking on 9 June 1898, 365½ sq. miles, consisting of all the immediately adjacent mainland and numerous islands in the vicinity, were leased to Great Britain by China for 99 years. This area is known as the New Territories. Total area of colony, 398¼ sq. miles (1,012 sq. km), a large part of it being steep and unproductive hillside. Shortage of land suitable for development for housing and industry, is a serious problem. Since 1945, the government has reclaimed about 1,865 acres from the sea, principally from the sea fronts of Victoria and Kowloon, fronting the harbour. Two rapidly developing new towns constructed partly on reclamation at Kwun Tong and Tsuen Wan Kwai Chung have large textile, enamel and rubber factories, iron works, etc. Two more new towns are planned in the New Territories at Castle Peak and Sha Tin. There is extensive development and redevelopment of Crown land for all purposes.

The climate is sub-tropical, the winter being cool and dry and the summer hot and humid. The average rainfall is 85·39 in., May to Sept. being the wettest months. A serious problem is the provision of storage of the summer rainfall to meet the water requirements, particularly during the dry winter months. With the completion of the Plover Cove reservoir (37,000m. gallons capacity) the Colony's storage capacity was increased to 54,000m. gallons distributed in 17 reservoirs, supplemented by 15,000m. gallons annually purchased from China.

In Jan. 1970 the population was 4,039,000. During the war years the population of Hong Kong fluctuated sharply. In Sept. 1945, at the end of the Japanese occupation, it was about 600,000. In the spring of 1950 it was estimated at 2·36m. Since 1956 the net annual increase has been between 92,000 and 180,000. Of the present population 39% are under 15 years of age. All but 2% of the population was born in Hong Kong and China.

EDUCATION. Education is not compulsory, but all schools have to be registered with the Education Department and, unless specially exempted, are inspected and required to comply with regulations as to staff, buildings, numbers of pupils and health.

In March 1970 there were 134,858 pupils in kindergarten (all private), 746,429 (525,548)[1] in primary schools including special afternoon classes, 254,593 (68,126) in secondary schools, 62,722 (34,329) in post-secondary colleges, in institutions offering technical, adult and other further education, and in special schools. In all, there were 2,764 schools and 39,548 teachers.

[1] The figures shown in brackets are for government and aided schools.

Northcote College of Education had 407 students (including 249 women), Grantham College of Education, 340 (including 234 women) and Sir Robert Black College of Education, 419 (including 313 women).

The University of Hong Kong had 3,034 students (2,203 men, 831 women) and 355 full-time teachers. The Chinese University of Hong Kong, inaugurated in Oct. 1963, had 2,239 students (1,315 men, 924 women), and 324 full-time teachers.

CINEMAS. In 1970 there were 104 cinemas with a seating capacity of 122,287; of these 35 are on Hong Kong Island, 48 in Kowloon and 21 in the New Territories.

NEWSPAPERS. In 1970 there were 72 daily or weekly newspapers, including 4 English-language papers; the remaining ones are almost all in Chinese.

BROADCASTING. There is a government broadcasting station, Radio Hong Kong, with daily transmissions in English and 4 Chinese dialects. Wireless licences were abolished as from 1 March 1967. Rediffusion (HK) Ltd operates a commercial broadcasting service in English and Chinese to which, at the end of 1968, there were 35,000 loudspeakers connected. Rediffusion also operates a television service. The Hong Kong Commercial Broadcasting Co. Ltd transmits daily in English and 2 Chinese dialects.

TELEVISION. Hong Kong Television Broadcasting Ltd transmits commercial wireless television in English and Chinese.

JUSTICE. There is a supreme court, having original, bankruptcy and companies winding-up, criminal, probate, divorce, admiralty and prize jurisdiction, and a court of appeal. There are also 3 district courts and 9 magistracies, most containing several courts. The district courts, apart from hearing civil cases where the claim does not amount to more than HK$10,000, also have jurisdiction over certain criminal matters. A tenancy tribunal hears cases covering disputes between landlord and tenant, etc.

Police. The police force numbered, in 1970, 12,149, composed of 1,128 gazetted and inspectorate officers, 9,966 Cantonese, 376 Shantung, 129 Pakistanis, 10 Portuguese rank and file and a women's section of 22 inspectorate and 518 rank and file.

FINANCE. Currency. The unit of currency is the Hong Kong dollar. From 1935 to 1967 its value has been maintained at approximately £0·06. In Nov. 1967 the Hong Kong dollar was revalued in terms of sterling at £0·07. Bank-notes (of denominations of $5 upwards) are issued by the Hongkong and Shanghai Banking Corporation, the Chartered Bank and the Mercantile Bank Ltd. Their combined note issue was, in June 1970, $2,188,771,000. Subsidiary currency consisting of $1, 50-cent, 10-cent, 5-cent nickel-alloy coins and 1-cent notes is issued by the Hong Kong Government and in June 1970 totalled $163,983,549.

Budget. The public revenue and expenditure for the financial years ending 31 March were as follows (in HK$):

	1967–68	1968–69	1969–70	1970–71
Revenue	1,899,527,499	2,081,118,425	2.480,657,388	2,584,204,000
Expenditure	1,766,022,040	1,872,974,955	2,032,183,388	2,393,081,220

The revenue is derived chiefly from rates, licences, duties on liquor, tobacco and hydrocarbon oils, and a tax on earnings and profits.

The outstanding public debt as at 31 March 1970 totalled $63,343,545; consisting of $45,889,000 3½% Rehabilitation Loan redeemable 1973–78 by a sinking fund which stood at $28,729,345 on 31 March 1970 and a loan from the UK Government for Kai Tak airport development amounting to $17,454,545.

DEFENCE. Formed on 1 May 1949, the part-time Hong Kong Auxiliary Air Force has 4 Auster AOP liaison aircraft and 3 Alouette III helicopters, mainly for internal security and air-sea rescue duties. There are 7 fixed-wing and 6 helicopter pilots. The RAF assists with training and maintenance.

INDUSTRY. Hong Kong has established itself as a modern industrial complex, following external developments that imposed severe restrictions upon the entrepôt trade on which Hong Kong had lived and prospered for 100 years. Whereas in 1954 there were only 2,600 factories in operation, by June 1970, 15,899 registered factories employed 577,978 people. Industry depends almost entirely on exports, over 90% of all industrial production being exported.

The largest sector is the textile industry, which accounts for half of all Hong Kong's domestic exports and employs two-fifths of the industrial work force. Electronics, wigs, synthetics and wool are examples of recent industrial diversification, while the plastic, electrical, metalware and footwear industries continue to be significant. Heavy industry includes shipbuilding and ship repairing, iron foundries and mills rolling steel bars and rounds. Agriculture, fishing and some mining are the main primary industries.

TOURISM. Tourists spent an estimated HK$1,317m. in the Colony in 1969. During the year tourists totalled 765,213, including overseas Chinese visitors.

COMMERCE. Hong Kong's magnificent sheltered deep-water harbour is well situated in relation to the growing markets of Japan, the Philippines, Indonesia, Malaysia and Thailand. The Colony's prosperity was originally founded on the entrepôt trade; it still accounts for 20% by value of total exports. With the main emphasis on industrial production and exports, Hong Kong has modernized and expanded port facilities and improved export services, including an ocean terminal capable of berthing the largest liner afloat.

Hong Kong maintains a policy of free enterprise and free trade. Duties are levied only on tobacco, hydrocarbon oils, alcoholic liquors (including proprietary medicines and toilet preparations containing more than 2% of proof spirit), table waters and methyl alcohol, whether imported into or manufactured in the Colony for local consumption. All imports (apart from foodstuffs, which are subject to a flat charge of HK$2.00 per shipment) and exports are subject to an 0·05% *ad valorem* charge.

Hong Kong has a free exchange market except for transactions which might damage the sterling area. Foreign merchants may remit profits or repatriate capital. Import and export controls are kept to the minimum, consistent with strategic requirements and the protection of sterling. Merchants and manufacturers from abroad are encouraged to establish themselves in the Colony without discrimination.

The total value of imports in 1968 was HK$12,472m.; in 1969, HK$14,893m.; of exports, HK$8,428m. in 1968, and HK$10,518m. in 1969.

In 1969 the main importing countries were Japan (23%), China (18%), USA (13%) and UK (8%); the chief items being foodstuffs (19%), textiles (17%) and machinery and transport equipment (15%). The main export markets were USA (42%), UK (14%) and the EEC countries (10%); clothing and textiles accounted for 47% of the total exports.

The adverse balance on visible trade is offset by a favourable balance from exchange, shipping and insurance transactions, an inflow of capital, ship repairing, a flourishing tourist industry, remittances from overseas Chinese, etc.

Imports from the Commonwealth countries (HK$2,544m. in 1969 and HK$2,399m. in 1968) amounted to 17% and 19% of total imports in 1969 and 1968 respectively (17·2% in 1938), and exports to the Commonwealth countries (HK$2,864m. and HK$2,587m.) were 27% and 31% of all exports from Hong Kong (16·3% in 1938).

The trade of Hong Kong and UK (British Board of Trade returns in £1,000 sterling) is given as follows:

	1965	1966	1967	1968	1969	1970
Imports to UK	70,221	80,564	89,531	115,267	125,359	128,394
Exports from UK	65,004	64,912	61,038	76,332	87,134 }	99,516
Re-exports from UK	570	740	1,383	1,527	1,528 }	

ROAD AND RAILWAY. In 1970 the Colony had 593 miles of roads, distributed as follows: Hong Kong Island, 201; Kowloon and New Kowloon, 171, and New Territories, 221.

There is an electric tramway of 19½ miles, and a cable tramway connecting the Peak district with the lower levels in Victoria. A railway, 22 miles in length 4 ft 2½ in. gauge, owned by the Government, runs between Kowloon and the Chinese frontier. It forms a direct overland communication with Canton, Hankow and Shanghai, but since Oct. 1949 all through passenger traffic has been suspended.

SHIPPING. The total vessels entering and clearing the Colony and engaged in foreign trade during the year ending 31 March 1970 amounted to 13,781 ocean-going vessels of 45,129,873 net tons. Launches and junks engaging in local trade, totalled 26,073 vessels of 3,352,134 net tons. 438 vessels (698,133 net tons) were registered in Hong Kong as British ships on 31 March 1970.

AVIATION. Hong Kong airport, Kai Tak, is situated on the north shore of Kowloon Bay. It is regularly used by 28 airlines and many charter airlines which provide frequent services throughout the Far East to Europe, North America, Africa, Australia and New Zealand. The Colony, with its modern runway, is an important link on the main air routes of the Far East. BOAC operates 16 services per week, 9 to London, 5 to USA and 2 to Sydney. Cathay Pacific Airway Ltd, provides 110 flights a week on Far East routes. In 1969–70, 40,318 aircraft arrived and departed on international flights, carrying 1·97m. passengers, 3,440 metric tons of mail and 52,511 metric tons of freight.

POST AND TELECOMMUNICATIONS. There were 59 post offices in 1970; postal revenue (1969–70) totalled $143,651,882; expenditure, $80,705,868.

Telephone routes of Hong Kong Telephone Co. Ltd on 30 June 1970 comprised 1,806,912 wire miles (828,691 circuit miles), carried in 3,367 miles of cable and 12,441 miles of wire distribution. Telephones numbered 538,549. Cable and Wireless Ltd, operate the external communications and also provide for marine, meteorological and aeronautical communications. Facilities have been augmented by the addition of a satellite earth station and computerized message switching system.

BANKING. There are 70 incorporated banks in Hong Kong, including 51 authorized to deal in foreign exchange. Deposits at the end of June 1970 totalled $13,650,383,000, a record figure.

WEIGHTS AND MEASURES. The *Tael* (*leung*) $= 1\frac{1}{3}$ oz. avoirdupois; the *Picul* (*taam*) $= 133\frac{1}{3}$ lb. (often taken as $\frac{1}{17}$ of a ton); the *Catty* (*kan*) $= 1\frac{1}{3}$ lb. avoirdupois; the *Chek* (Chinese foot) $= 14\frac{5}{8}$ in. (but varying from $11\frac{1}{2}$ to $14\frac{5}{8}$ in. according to the custom of various trades, the commonest equivalent being 14·14 in.); the *Tsuen* (Chinese inch) $= \frac{1}{10}$ of a *Chek*, the *Cheung* $= 10$ *Chek*; the *Lei* (Chinese mile) $= 707$–744 yd.

Besides the above weights and measures of China, those of Great Britain are in general use.

BOOKS OF REFERENCE

STATISTICAL INFORMATION. The Census and Statistics Department is responsible for the preparation and collation of Government statistics. These statistics are published mainly in the Special Supplement No. 4 to the *Hong Kong Government Gazette* at the end of each month; the Special Supplement are also available in a collected annual edition. The Department publish monthly trade statistics and economic indicators. The Commerce and Industry Department issues an annual review of overseas trade. Statistical information is also published in the annual reports of Government departments. Full details of all Government publications are obtainable from the Government Printer, North Point, Hong Kong. The Trade Development Council issues a monthly *Hong Kong Enterprise*.

Hong Kong Report for the Year 1967. Hong Kong Government Press, 1967
Hong Kong Bibliography. Hong Kong Government Press, 1965
Hong Kong Trade Directory. London, 1964
Endacott, G. B., *A History of Hong Kong.* OUP, 1958.—*Government and people in Hong Kong, 1841–1962. A constitutional history.* OUP, 1965
Szcepanik, F. F., *The Economic Growth of Hong Kong.* OUP, 1958
Tregear, T. R., *Land Use in Hong Kong,* Hong Kong Univ. Press, 1958.—*Hong Kong Gazetteer.* Hong Kong Univ. Press, 1958.—*The Development of Hong Kong as told in Maps.* Hong Kong Univ. Press, 1959

PITCAIRN ISLAND

Pitcairn Island (1·75 sq. miles; 4·6 sq. km) is situated in the Pacific Ocean, nearly equidistant from New Zealand and Panama (25° 04′ S. lat., 130° 06′ W. long.). It was discovered by Carteret in 1767, but remained uninhabited until 1790, when it was occupied by 10 mutineers of HMS *Bounty*, with 12 women and 6 men from Tahiti. Nothing was known of their existence until the island was visited in 1808. In 1856 the population having become too large for the island's resources, the inhabitants (194 in number) were, at their own request, removed to Norfolk Island; but 43 of them returned in 1859–64. The population has been declining and on 31 Dec. 1969 it was approximately 80.

Pitcairn was brought within the jurisdiction of the High Commissioner for the Western Pacific in 1898 and transferred to the Governor of Fiji in 1952.

The Local Government Ordinance of 1964 constitutes a Council of 10 members, of whom 4 are elected, 5 are nominated (3 by the 4 elected members and 2 by the Governor) and the Island Secretary is an *ex officio* member. The Island Magistrate, who is elected triennially, presides over the Council; other members hold office for only 1 year. Liaison between Governor and Council is through a Commissioner in the British South Pacific Office in Suva, Fiji.

Fruit, vegetables and curios are sold to passing ships; flour, sugar and other foodstuffs are imported.

The uninhabited islands of Henderson (12 sq. miles), Ducie (2½ sq. miles) and Oeno (2 sq. miles) were annexed in 1902, and are included in the Pitcairn group.

Governor: Sir Arthur Galsworthy, KCMG.
Island Magistrate: Pervis Young (elected Dec. 1969).

A Guide to Pitcairn. British South Pacific Office, Suva, Fiji, 1963, revised ed. 1969
Ross, A. S. C., and Moverly, A. W., *The Pitcairnese Language.* London, 1964

ST HELENA

GOVERNMENT. The Government of St Helena is administered by a Governor, with the aid of a Legislative Council consisting of the Governor, 2 *ex-officio* members (the Government Secretary and the Treasurer) and 12 elected members. Committees of the Legislative Council are responsible for the general oversight of the activities of government departments and have, in addition, statutory and administrative functions.

The Governor is also assisted by an Executive Council consisting of the 2 *ex-officio* members and the chairmen of the Council committees.

Governor and C.-in-C.: Sir Dermod Art Murphy, CMG, OBE.
Government Secretary: I. C. Rose.

AREA AND POPULATION. St Helena, of volcanic origin, is 1,200 miles from the west coast of Africa. Area, 47 sq. miles (121·7 sq. km), with a cultivable area of 8,000 acres (3,580 hectares). The port of the island is Jamestown.

Population (1969), 4,829. Births (living), 159; deaths, 45; marriages, 31; divorces, nil. There are 5 Anglican churches and 4 Baptist chapels.

EDUCATION. Eleven primary and 1 secondary schools controlled by the Government had 1,105 pupils in 1969.

JUSTICE. Police force, 21; cases dealt with by police magistrate, 80 in 1969.

FINANCE AND TRADE, for calendar years, in £ sterling:

	1966	1967	1968	1969	1970
Revenue[1]	517,068	513,717	607,843	515,422	471,537
Expenditure[1]	509,849	493,616	555,296	547,312	519,392
Exports[2]	50,000	19,000	14,710	7,509	..
Imports[2]	395,000	410,000	375,790	460,960	..

[1] Including imperial grants (1966, £194,911; 1967, £215,706; 1968, £235,545; 1969, £257,000; 1970. £279,000).
[2] Excluding government stores.

The revenue from customs was, in 1966, £46,839; 1967, £48,651; 1968, £48,300; 1969, 51,095; 1970, £48,000.

The colony's assets at 31 Dec. 1969 exceeded the liabilities by £86,672.

The principal exports were flax fibre, tow, rope and twine; they totalled 1,189 tons in 1960; 925·75 tons in 1961; 1,305 tons in 1962; 1,016 tons in 1963; 1,410 tons in 1964; 860 tons in 1965. The flax mills closed in 1966.

Total trade between Ascension and St Helena and UK (British Board of Trade returns, in £1,000 sterling):

	1964	1965	1966	1967	1968	1969	1970
Imports to UK	48	68	58	16	135	60	53
Exports from UK	362	688	1,169	667	924	696 }	768
Re-exports from UK	40	48	92	46	65	84 }	

COMMUNICATIONS. The number of merchant vessels that called in 1969 was 41; total tonnage entered and cleared was 171,901. There are 47·7 miles of all-weather motor roads.

The Cable and Wireless Ltd cable connects St Helena with Cape Town and Ascension Island. There is a telephone service with 80 miles of wire and 120 telephones.

BANKING. Savings-bank deposits on 31 Dec. 1969, £368,877, belonging to 2,015 depositors.

Ascension is a small island of volcanic origin, of 34 sq. miles (88 sq. km), 700 miles north-west of St Helena. In Nov. 1922 the administration was transferred from the Admiralty to the Colonial Office and annexed to the colony of St Helena. There are 10 acres under cultivation providing vegetables and fruit. Population, 31 Dec. 1946, was 292; 1956, 416; 1960, 429; 1969, St. Helenians 739, others 700.

The island is the resort of sea turtles, which come to lay their eggs in the sand annually between Jan. and May. Rabbits, wild goats and partridges are more or less numerous on the island, which is, besides, the breeding ground of the sooty tern or 'wideawake', these birds coming in vast numbers to lay their eggs every eighth month.

Cable and Wireless Ltd own and operate a cable station, connecting the island with St Helena, Sierra Leone, St Vincent, Rio de Janeiro and Buenos Aires. There is an airstrip (Miracle Mile) near the settlement of Georgetown.

Administrator: Brig. H. W. D. McDonald, DSO.

Tristan da Cunha, a small group of islands in the Atlantic, half-way between the Cape and South America, in 37° 6′ S. lat., 12° 1′ W. long. Besides Tristan da Cunha and Gough Island, there are Inaccessible and Nightingale Islands, the former 2 and the latter 1 mile long, and a number of rocks. As from 12 Jan. 1938 the 4 islands have become dependencies of St Helena.

Tristan consists of a volcano rising to a height of 6,760 ft, with a circumference at its base of 21 miles. The volcano, believed to be extinct, erupted unexpectedly early in Oct. 1961. The whole population was evacuated without loss and settled temporarily in the United Kingdom. In 1963 they returned to Tristan.

Before that disaster occurred the habitable area was a small plateau on the north-west side of about 12 sq. miles, 100 ft above sea-level. Only about 30 acres was under cultivation, three-quarters of it for potatoes. There were apple and peach trees; bullocks, sheep and geese were reared, and fish are plentiful.

The island is extremely lonely, but the community was growing. In 1880 it numbered 109, in 1969, 271. The original inhabitants were shipwrecked sailors and soldiers who remained behind when the garrison from St Helena was withdrawn in 1817.

At the end of April 1942 Tristan da Cunha was commissioned as HMS *Atlantic Isle*, and became an important meteorological and radio station. In Jan. 1949 a South African company commenced crawfishing operations. An Administrator was appointed at the end of 1948 and a body of basic law brought into operation. The Island Council, which was set up in 1932, consists of 6 nominated and 15 elected members under the chairmanship of the Administrator, with the Society for the Propagation of the Gospel in Foreign Parts' missionary and the company manager as *ex-officio* members. Women's affairs are discussed by the Island Women's Council, which presents them for consideration to the general council.

Administrator: J. I. H. Fleming.

BOOKS OF REFERENCE

Annual Report, 1962–63. HMSO, 1965
Blakeston, O., Isle of St Helena. London, 1957
Booy, D. M., Rock of Exile: a narrative of Tristan da Cunha. London, 1957
Holdgate, M., Mountains in the Sea. London, 1958
Munch, P. A., Sociology of Tristan da Cunha. Oslo, 1945
Stonehouse, B., Wideawake Island [Ascension]. London, 1960

SEYCHELLES

HISTORY. The islands were first colonized by the French in the middle of the 18th century, in order to establish plantations of spices to compete with the Dutch monopoly. They were captured by the English in 1794 and incorporated as a dependency of Mauritius in 1814. In 1888 the office of administrator was created, with an Executive Council and a Legislative Council. In 1897 the Administrator was given full powers as Governor, and in Nov. 1903 he was raised to the rank of Governor with the Seychelles archipelago becoming a separate colony.

British Indian Ocean Territory, a new colony created in 1965, consists of the Chagos Archipelago (formerly a dependency of Mauritius), Aldabra, Farquhar and Des Roches.

CONSTITUTION AND GOVERNMENT. A new Constitution was introduced in Nov. 1970 immediately following a general election. The Legislative Assembly consists of 15 elected members, 3 *ex-officio* members and a Speaker. In the election, the Seychelles Democratic Party obtained 10 seats and the Seychelles Peoples United Party 5 seats.

Governor and C.-in-C.: Sir Bruce Greatbatch, CMG, CVO, MBE, concurrently Commissioner of the British Indian Ocean Territory.
Chief Minister: J. R. Mancham.

AREA AND POPULATION. Seychelles and its Dependencies consist of 84 islands and islets with a total estimated area of about 107 sq. miles (277 sq. km). The principal island is Mahé (57 sq. miles), smaller islands of the group being Praslin, Silhouette, La Digue, Curieuse and Félicité. Among dependent islands are the Amirantes, Assumption Island, Astove Island, Cosmoledo Island, Providence Island, Coetivy Island and Platte Island.

The capital is Victoria on Mahé, which has a good harbour (population 13,000). The population, in mid-1970, was 53,000.

Vital statistics (1969): Births, 1,715; deaths, 561; marriages, 277.

EDUCATION. There are 16 pre-primary schools, 2 organized kindergarten schools, 35 primary schools, 11 junior secondary schools, 2 secondary grammar schools, 4 vocational schools and 1 teacher-training college.

In Dec. 1969 there were 4,290 boys and 4,479 girls in primary schools, 999 boys and 1,093 girls in junior secondary and secondary grammar schools and 160 children in kindergarten schools. Twelve students were undergoing further education and training in the UK under the Commonwealth Teacher Bursary Scheme.

JUSTICE. In 1969, 2,053 criminal cases were brought before the courts. The police force numbered 313 all ranks and 77 special constabulary.

FINANCE. Currency. The Seychelles rupee equals £0·03. or US cents 18.

Budget, in rupees, for calendar years:

	1965	1966	1967	1968	1969
Local revenue	8,932,444	9,981,870	12,073,914	14,663.004	20,440,531
Recurrent expenditure	9,929,250	9,657,469	13,492,143	17,605,308	25,641,037
Grant-in-aid	1,174,763	900,000	2,466,667	4,460,000	1,693,334

Chief items of revenue 1969: Customs and harbours, Rs 7,873,000; direct taxes, Rs 3,870,310; fees and fines, Rs 2,150,517; post office, Rs 1,399,750; government property, Rs 1,297,910.

Chief items of expenditure, 1969: Medical, Rs 434,205; education, Rs 3,045,217; agriculture, Rs 1,688,690; police, Rs 1,480,260; public works (recurrent), Rs 1,254,560.

PRODUCTION. Chief products, coconuts, cinnamon, vanilla beans, coir, salted fish, tortoiseshell and other marine products, and patchouli. Food crop production and tea are being encouraged. On some islands guano deposits are worked. Fishing is actively pursued, both for local supply and export of salted fish to East Africa, Ceylon and Ghana. Re-afforestation is progressing. Melittomma, the major pest of the coconut, is being eradicated.

COMMERCE. Total trade, in rupees, for calendar years:

	1964	1965	1966	1967	1968
Imports	15,724,845	18,672,040	19,955,802	24,595,360	33,875.243
Exports	8,661,651	9,629,559	8,610,140	10,517,737	16,195,767

Principal imports (1968): Rice, 4,047 tons, Rs 3,993,725; sugar, 1,611 tons, Rs 795,776; cotton piece-goods, 823,584 yd, Rs 1,972,413; flour, 1,396 tons, Rs 856,521; motor cars and cycles, Rs 2,037,321; motor spirit, 11,750,998 litres, Rs 4,529,813; cigarettes, 11,140,465, Rs 253,523; wines, 153,973 litres, Rs 321,072; beer, 910,133 litres, Rs 1,684,766.

Principal exports (1969): Copra, 5,980 tons, Rs 5,843,465; cinnamon bark, 1,414 tons, Rs 6,279,622; cinnamon leaf oil, 12,060 tons, Rs 280,441; vanilla, 203 kg, Rs 7,155; patchouli leaf oil, 0·62 ton, Rs 23,328; salted fish, 20,061 kg, Rs 21,602.

Imports (1968) from UK, Rs 9,448,887; Iran, Rs 4,417,796; Kenya, Rs 2,927,572; Hong Kong, Rs 2,892,615; South Africa, Rs 2,158,825; Burma, Rs 2,156,866; India, Rs 2,067,314; Netherlands, Rs 1,698,900; Australia, Rs 1,526,201; Thailand, Rs 942,213; Japan, Rs 886,365; Singapore, Rs 711,920.

Exports (1968) to India, Rs 5,901,838; Israel, Rs 1,280,029; UK, Rs 1,101,253; South Africa, Rs 479,240; West Germany, Rs 435,359; France, Rs 424,426; Mauritius, Rs 364,645; Netherlands, Rs 342,959.

TOURISM. The tourist industry is in its embryo stage, but considerable development is expected once the airport on Mahé is completed. Work on this project, financed by the British Government, started in early 1969, and completion is anticipated mid-1971. Visitors in 1968 numbered 744.

COMMUNICATIONS. Shipping (1969) entered and cleared, 66,713 tons, mainly British, exclusive of coasters trading between Mahé and the dependencies. The British-India vessels now call at Victoria, Mahé, each way during their sailings to and from Mombasa, Bombay and Durban. In addition, occasional cargo boats run directly from London (Brocklebank Line), Singapore (Royal Interocean Line), Australia (Australian Red Sea Line), Durban (Unicorn Line) and from Mombasa (Southern Line). Some of these vessels carry passengers. The BIOT (British Indian Ocean Territory) vessel travels to and from Mombasa and occasionally visits the outlying islands.

There is a good system of tarmac (56 miles) and earth roads (30 miles) in Mahé; extensive road-making is being undertaken. There is direct telegraphic communication with Mauritius, Aden and Colombo and a radio-telephone link with Nairobi and London. Telephones in 1967 numbered 570.

BANKING. Barclays Bank DCO and Standard Bank have branches in Victoria, Mahé.

BOOKS OF REFERENCE

Report on the Seychelles, 1967–68. HMSO, 1968
Population Census 1960.—Agricultural Census 1960. Government Printer, Seychelles, 1961
Benedict, B., *People of the Seychelles.* HMSO, 1966
Webb, A. W. T., *Story of Seychelles.* Government Printer, 1965

WESTERN PACIFIC HIGH COMMISSION

The office of High Commissioner in, over and for the Western Pacific Islands was created by the Western Pacific Order in Council 1877. Until 1952 the Governor of Fiji was concurrently High Commissioner for the Western Pacific with headquarters at Suva. In that year the transfer was made to Honiara in the British Solomon Islands Protectorate and a separate High Commissioner appointed.

High Commissioner for the Western Pacific: Sir Michael Gass, KCMG.
Chief Secretary: T. Russell, CBE.

The jurisdiction of the High Commissioner extends over all islands in the Western Pacific not being within the limits of the territories administered by the Commonwealth of Australia and New Zealand or the Governor of Fiji, and not being within the jurisdiction of any other civilized power. The Pacific Order in Council, 1893, extended the High Commissioner's jurisdiction to foreigners and (in most cases) to natives residing in British settlements or protectorates within the limits of the Order. Under the provisions of the New Hebrides Order in Council, 1922, the jurisdiction of the High Commissioner extends also to the New Hebrides, the Banks Islands and Torres Islands.

The expenses of the High Commission are met from the funds of the Gilbert and Ellice Islands Colony and the British Solomon Islands Protectorate, but a contribution is paid from UK funds for work in connexion with the New Hebrides.

The principal groups under the High Commissioner are: (1) The Gilbert and Ellice Islands Colony; (2) The British Solomon Islands Protectorate, and (3) The Anglo-French Condominium of the New Hebrides. There is a Resident Commissioner at Tarawa in the Gilbert and Ellice Islands and one in Vila in the New Hebrides.

JUSTICE. The High Court of the Western Pacific constituted by the Western Pacific (Courts) Order in Council, 1961, consists of a Chief Justice and a puisne judge. The Chief Justice lives in Honiara, the puisne judge in Vila in the New Hebrides. The Court is a Superior Court of Record and possesses all the jurisdiction which is vested in Her Majesty's High Court of Justice in England. Magistrates' courts with both civil and criminal jurisdiction were established in 1962.

PLANNING. Economic development is accorded high priority in all three territories which make up the Western Pacific High Commission. The British Solomon Islands 6th Development Plan at present under preparation will lay emphasis on the development of the major industries, copra and timber, and on the establishment of new secondary industries in cattle breeding and oil palms. There will also be considerable investment in the extension of secondary education and in communications. In the Gilbert and Ellice Islands, the 1970–72 Development Plan aims at a major replanting programme to increase copra production and allocates substantial funds to extend secondary education and provide employment by the enlargement of the marine training school for seamen. In the New Hebrides, the final draft of the 1971–75 Development Plan envisages substantial expenditure on the extension of the Agricultural Department, a survey of the meat industry and heavy investment in communications (airstrips, roads and the telephone network) and in the development of the tourist industry.

CURRENCY. Currency in use throughout the Western Pacific High Commission is the Australian dollar. In the Condominium of the New Hebrides the French Pacific franc is used side by side with Australian currency.

TRADE. Trade of British Pacific Islands with UK (British Board of Trade returns, in £1,000 sterling):

	1965	1966	1967	1968	1969	1970
Imports to UK	1,307	1,245	1,128	1,692	1,558	431
Exports from UK	1,134	981	1,365	1,315	1,150 ⎱	1,315
Re-exports from UK	10	13	10	9	10 ⎰	

BOOKS OF REFERENCE

South Pacific Commission. *Agreement of 6 Feb., 1947, and Extension of 7 Nov., 1951.* HMSO, 1952
Among Those Present. The Official Story of the Pacific Islands War. HMSO. 1946
Belshaw, C. S., *Island Administration in the South West Pacific.* London, 1950
Fox, C. E., *Lord of the Southern Isles.* London, 1958
Leckie, R., *Challenge for the Pacific.* London, 1966
Luke, Sir Harry, *The Islands of the South Pacific.* London, 1962
Morrell, W. P., *Britain in the Pacific Islands.* OUP, 1960
Robson, R. W. (ed.), *The Pacific Islands Year Book.* Sydney, Pacific Publications Ltd
Scarr, D., *Fragments of Empire: a History of the Western Pacific High Commission.* Canberra, 1967
Taylor, C. R. H., *A Pacific Bibliography.* 2nd ed. OUP, 1965

GILBERT AND ELLICE ISLANDS COLONY

HISTORY. The Gilbert and Ellice Islands were proclaimed a protectorate in 1892 and annexed (at the request of the native governments) as the Gilbert and Ellice Islands Colony on 10 Nov. 1915 (effective on 12 Jan. 1916).

GOVERNMENT. The Colony comes under the jurisdiction of the High Commissioner for the Western Pacific, who is represented by a Resident Commissioner, with headquarters at Bairiki, Tarawa.

The Gilbert and Ellice Islands Order, 1967, established a Governing Council and a House of Representatives, both of which are presided over by the Resident Commissioner. The former comprises 2 *ex-officio* (Assistant Resident Commissioner and the Attorney-General), not more than 3 appointed and 5 elected members, one of whom is the Chief Elected Member. The Council has legislative as well as executive functions.

The House of Representatives has 2 *ex-officio* members (Assistant Resident Commissioner and the Attorney-General); up to 5 official members appointed by the Resident Commissioner and 23 members elected by universal adult suffrage. It elects 5 of its own members to the Governing Council and advises the Council on proposed legislation and other public matters referred to it by the Council or raised by individual members of the House.

The Colony is divided into 18 electoral districts, of which 5 return 2 members and 13 return 1 member to the House of Representatives. A General Election under the new Constitution was held at the end of 1967, the intention being that one should normally be held every 2 years. The life of the present House has been extended, pending the result of discussions on further constitutional change.

A form of local government was to be found on each of the islands as early as 1915, but it is only recently that a unified form of island administration has been created by the Local Government Ordinance of 1966. Under its provision Island Councils have been set up on each of 24 islands in the Gilbert and Ellice Islands, each being elected by the adult population of the island. They are empowered to enact bye-laws and are responsible for providing social services on the islands. They also prepare yearly estimates of revenue and expenditure. An Island President acts as Chairman and an Island Executive Office as full-time Secretary to the Council.

The Colony comes within the jurisdiction of the High Court of the Western Pacific, with right of appeal to the Fiji Court of Appeal. Island Courts, under legislation of 1965, are now capable of jurisdiction over all the races, both in civil and criminal fields, subject to review by the Senior Magistrate. Lands Courts deal with land litigation.

Resident Commissioner: Sir John Field, KBE, CMG.

AREA AND POPULATION. The Colony comprises 4 groups of atolls together with the adjacent Ocean Island. Total population at 5 Dec. 1968 was 53,517.

Ocean Island is situated at 0° 52′ S. lat., 169° 35′ E. long. and is approximately 2 sq. miles in area. Population (Dec. 1968) 2,192, including 160 Europeans and 26 Chinese. This island was annexed and included in the Colony (at that time a protectorate) by a proclamation of 28 Nov. 1900.

The **Gilbert Islands** between 4° N. and 3° S. lat. and 172° and 177° E. long. comprise Makin, Butaritari, Marakei, Abaiang, Tarawa (headquarters of the colony and Gilbert Islands district), Maiana, Abemama, Kuria, Aranuka, Nonouti, Tabiteuea, Beru, Nikunau, Onotoa, Tamana and Arorae. Population (Dec. 1968) 44,206, including about 300 Europeans; area approximately 102 sq. miles (260 sq. km). The Gilbertese are classed as Micronesians.

The **Ellice Islands** between 5° 30′ and 11° S. lat. and 176° and 180° E. long. comprise Nanumea, Nanumanga, Niutao, Nui, Vaitupu, Nukufetau, Funafuti (Ellice Islands district headquarters), Nukulaelae and Niulakita. Population (Dec. 1968) 6,332. Area approximately 9½ sq. miles (24 sq. km). The Ellice Islanders are a Polynesian race; their language is also known as Ellice.

The **Phœnix Islands** between 3° and 5° S. lat. and 170° and 175° W. long. comprise the islands of Canton, Enderbury, Birnie, McKean, Phœnix, Hull, Sydney and Gardner. Area approximately 11 sq. miles (28 sq. km).

The Phœnix Islands were included in the Colony by an Order in Council of 18 March 1937. In March 1938 the USA claimed sovereignty over Canton and Enderbury. On 6 April 1939 the UK and US Governments agreed, without prejudice to their respective claims, to exercise joint control over the 2 islands for a period of 50 years. Canton used to be an international airport on the trans-Pacific route between Fiji and Honolulu, but, with the use of long-range jet aircraft, is no longer serviced by scheduled flights and is now uninhabited.

The southern Phœnix Islands of Hull, Sydney and Gardner were colonized by Gilbertese between 1938 and 1940, but due to long droughts permanent settlement on them ceased between 1955 and 1964. Enderbury, Phœnix, Birnie and McKean Islands are also uninhabited. The Phœnix Islands are now administered by the District Commissioner, Gilbert Islands.

The **Line Islands** between 4° 40′ and 2° N. lat. and 160° 20′ and 157° W. long. comprise Fanning, Washington and Christmas Islands. Fanning Island: population (Dec. 1968) 376, including 2 Europeans; area approximately 13 sq. miles (33 sq. km). Washington Island: population (Dec. 1968) 437; area approximately 5 sq. miles (13 sq. km). Christmas Island (headquarters of the Line Islands district): population (Dec. 1968) 367; area approximately 139 sq. miles (359 sq. km). Fanning and Washington Islands were annexed in 1889 and a repeating station for the Pacific cable was established on Fanning; they were included in the Colony in 1916. Both islands are worked as copra plantations by Fanning Island Plantations, Ltd, using Gilbertese labour. The Cable & Wireless Station at Fanning Island closed early in 1964, after operating for 62 years. Christmas Island was discovered by Capt. Cook in 1777, annexed by Great Britain in 1888 and included in the Colony in 1919. It is reputed to be the largest atoll in the world. The island is worked as a copra plantation by the Government.

The following 5 Line Islands do not form part of the Colony but are administered directly by the High Commissioner for the Western Pacific. **Starbuck Island,** 5° 35′ S. lat., 155° 52′ W. long.; area 1 sq. mile, uninhabited. **Malden Island,** 4° S. lat., 155° W. long.; area 35 sq. miles (90 sq. km), containing deposits of guano of doubtful value, uninhabited. **Flint Island,** 11° 26′ S. lat., 151° 48′ W. long, and **Caroline Island,** 10° S. lat., 150° 14′ W. long., were, in 1951, leased to commercial interests in Tahiti. **Vostock Island,** 10° 06′ S. lat., 152° 23′ W. long., uninhabited.

CLIMATE. The rainfall varies considerably. In normal years the annual rainfall ranges from 40 in. in the vicinity of the equator to about 100 in. in the North Gilbert Islands and 120 in. in the Ellice Islands. The Southern and Central Gilbert Islands and Ocean Island are subject to periodic droughts. The temperature varies between 80° and 90° F. (27–32° C.) by day and drops to a minimum of 70° F. (21° C.) at night.

EDUCATION (1970). The Government maintains a co-educational boarding school, the King George V and Elaine Bernacchi School at Tarawa, with 165 boys and 96 girls, 33 primary schools, with a total of 4,259 pupils. Primary aided schools had 8,841 pupils; primary unaided schools, 786 pupils. The Government also maintains a teachers' training college with (1969) 59 students.

A number of islanders are being sent to various overseas countries for secondary and further education, expenses being met by the Colony, UK, Australian and New Zealand Governments and other aid sources.

There are 254 village schools throughout the Gilbert and Ellice groups run by the Congregational Council for World Mission, the Mission of the Sacred Heart, the Seventh Day Adventists Mission, the Church of God of South Carolina Mission and the Bahai Mission. Grants-in-aid to local government and Mission schools amounted to $A88,036 for the year 1969.

WELFARE. Government maintains free medical and other services. There are few towns, and the people are almost without exception landed proprietors, thus eliminating child vagrancy and housing problems to a large extent, except in the Tarawa urban area. Destitution is almost unknown.

POLICE. The Colony has a police force of 139 under a Chief Police Officer. Detachments are stationed at colony and district headquarters and some outer islands.

FINANCE. Revenue for the calendar year 1969 amounted to $A4,688,855; principal items: customs duties, $A689,300; direct taxation, $A210,000; taxation on phosphate, $A2,567,460. Expenditure in 1969 amounted to $A4,237,118. Currency is Australian.

PLANNING. A Development Plan 1970–72 has been published which identifies trends in income and expenditure to 1985 and defines the strategy of planning and investment until 1972.

AGRICULTURE. The land is basically coral reefs upon which coral sand has built up, and then been enriched by humus from rotting vegetation and flotsam which has drifted ashore. The principal tree is the coconut, which grows prolifically on all the islands except some of the Phœnix Islands. Other food-bearing trees are the pandanus palm and the breadfruit. As the amount of soil is negligible, the only vegetable which grows in any quantity is a coarse calladium (alocasia) with the local name 'babai', which is cultivated most laboriously in deep pits. There is also a little taro cultivated in the Ellice group. Pigs and fowls are kept throughout the Colony, and there is an abundance of fish.

Copra production is mainly in the hands of the individual landowner, who collects the coconut products from the trees on his own land.

TRADE. The principal imports are rice, flour, cotton piece-goods, tobacco and manufactured articles such as bicycles. The value of imports for 1969 amounted to $A2,769,632. Exports are almost exclusively phosphate and copra. The British Phosphate Commissioners exported 555,000 tons in 1969, valued at $A6,106,100. Copra exports amounted to 7,825 tons in 1969, valued at $A1,199,243.

COMMUNICATIONS. Fiji Airways operates a weekly service Nadi–Funafuti–Tarawa–Nauru. An internal air service from Tarawa to 3 outer islands started in 1969.

Report on the Gilbert and Ellice Islands, 1968. HMSO, 1969
Exchange of Notes between HM Government in the United Kingdom and the United States Government regarding the Administration of the Islands of Canton and Enderbury. (Cmd. 5989.) London, 1939
Grimble, Sir Arthur, *A Pattern of Islands.* London, 1953.—*Return to the Islands.* London, 1957
Kennedy, D. G., *Handbook of the Languages of the Ellice Islands.* Suva, 1945

BRITISH SOLOMON ISLANDS PROTECTORATE

The Solomon Islands were discovered in 1568 by Alvaro de Mendana, on a voyage of discovery from Peru; 200 years passed before European contact was again made with the Solomons. The British Solomon Islands Protectorate lies within the area 5° to 12° 30′ S. lat. and 155° 30′ to 169° 45′ E. long. The group includes the main islands of Guadalcanal, Malaita, San Cristobal, New Georgia, Santa Isabel and Choiseul; the smaller Florida and Russell groups; the Shortland, Mono (or Treasury), Vella Lavella, Kolombangara, Ranongga, Gizo and Rendova Islands; to the east, Santa Cruz, Tikopia, the Reef and Duff groups; Rennell and Bellona in the south; Ontong Java or Lord Howe to the north; and innumerable smaller islands.

The four first-named were placed under British protection in 1893; the other islands were added in 1898 and 1899. The land area of the Protectorate is estimated at 11,500 sq. miles (29,785 sq. km). The larger islands are mountainous and forest-clad, with flood-prone rivers of considerable energy potential. Guadalcanal has the largest land area and the greatest amount of flat coastal plain, but Malaita is the most populous (estimated 51,000 inhabitants). The estimated population of the Protectorate in 1969 was: Europeans, 1,990; Chinese, 700; Polynesians, 5,550; Micronesians, 2,040; Melanesians, 141,500; others, 360; total, 152,000. Census 1970 (provisional), 161,524.

The capital, Honiara, on Guadalcanal, is the largest urban area, with an estimated population in 1970 of 11,389. Rainfall at Honiara (which lies in a rain shadow) is 90 in. per annum; elsewhere as high as 300 in.; the average is 120–140 in.

CONSTITUTION. There is a newly formed Governing Council, made up of 17 elected, 3 *ex-officio* and 6 official members, which meets two times a year. Under a revised constitution, direct elections were held in 1967.

Local government councils, elected by universal adult suffrage, operate throughout the Protectorate and are responsible for certain local projects and administrative matters; revenue is raised by an annual tax and fines levied for minor offences tried in the native courts.

EDUCATION. Primary education is largely in the hands of the churches. Government gives aid to scheduled schools in the form of salary subsidies, boarding and equipment grants. In 1969 there were 400 registered schools including 7 secondary schools with together 22,393 pupils. There are 2 teacher-training colleges, and a technical institute, which is made up of schools of marine training, agriculture survey and draughting and commence. Overseas scholarships were awarded in 1969 to 110 students, for university, medical, higher technical and post-primary studies.

CURRENCY. The medium of exchange is Australian decimal currency introduced in February 1966. ($A1 = 46½p. stlg.) The estimated amount of currency in circulation at the end of December 1969 was $A3,642,329.

BUDGET. The budget for the calendar year 1970 balanced at $A9,692,800 (including colonial development and welfare funds, $A2,851,730. UK grant-in-aid $2,314,660). The Fifth Development Plan has provided $A8·4m. for development projects from 1968 to 1970.

PRODUCTION. Coconuts, tropical roots, cocoa, rice and sorghum are grown. Copra is the main cash crop, with rice second and cocoa third. The rapid development and success of rice crops grown on the Guadalcanal Plains could make the Protectorate self-supporting in the supply of rice within a year. Timber is being developed; the value of timber exported in 1969 was $A2·47m. Most timber exports went to Japan.

COMMERCE. The main imports are agricultural machinery and tractors, petrol and petroleum products, rice, meat, motor vehicles and flour. Exports comprise copra (23,463 tons in 1969), timber (7,335,169 cu. ft), marine shell, cocoa, sorghum, navy biscuits and crocodile skins. In 1969 total imports amounted to $A8,543,654. Exports were valued at $A6,306,798, and re-exports at $A168,572. Australia supplied 43·8% of the imports, UK 18·7% in 1968, and of the exports, 44·1% went to UK, 40·3% to Japan, 13% to Australia.

COMMUNICATIONS. Regular flights from Fiji and Australia (*via* Papua, New Guinea) provide the main communication link; shipping services are maintained with Australia, New Zealand, UK and the Far East. An internal airline and innumerable small ships provide inter-island transport. Number of telephones (Dec. 1969), 1,067.

Annual Report, 1969. Honiara, 1970
Pacific Islands Year Book and Who's Who. Sydney, 1968
Fox, C. E., *Story of the Solomons.* Taroaniara, 1967
Horton, D. C., *The Happy Isles.* London, 1965

NEW HEBRIDES CONDOMINIUM
Nouvelles Hébrides

The New Hebrides group lies roughly 500 miles west of Fiji and 250 miles north-east of New Caledonia. The group is administered for some purposes jointly, for others unilaterally, as provided for by Anglo-French Convention of 27 Feb. 1906, ratified 20 Oct. 1906. and a protocol signed at London on 6 Aug. 1914 and ratified on 18 March 1922. The interests of British, French and New Hebrideans, respectively, are protected; the conditions of land-holding in the islands fixed, and the regulation of the recruitment of native labour provided for. Within the islands Great Britain and France are represented by High Commissioners who delegate their powers to Resident Commissioners stationed in the group.

British Resident Commissioner: C. H. Allan, CMG, OBE.
French Resident Commissioner: R. Langlois.

AREA AND POPULATION. The estimated land area is 5,700 sq. miles (14,760 sq. km). The larger islands of the group are: Espiritu Santo, Malekula, Epi, Pentecost, Aoba, Maewa, Paama, Ambrym, Efate, Erromanga, Tanna and Aneityum. There are 3 active volcanoes, on Tanna, Ambrym and Lopevi, respectively. Earth tremors are of common occurrence. Rainfall at Vila averages 80 in. per annum.

The first complete census was taken in 1967. The total population was found to be 77,982, of whom 72,237 were New Hebrideans, 1,631 were British Resortissants and 3,840 were French Resortissants.

HEALTH. Pulmonary complaints and helminthic infections but especially malaria are important causes of death among the natives. The tuberculin sensitivity survey, begun in 1961, is now being conducted by the World Health Organization.

French Government hospitals and medical aid posts are established at Vila, Santo and Malekula and staffed by French national medical officers. The British Government established a new hospital on Tanna in 1967; subsidizes mission hospitals in Efate, Aoba, Tongoa, Epi, Santo and Pentecost, and maintains its own rural clinics in the Banks, Pentecost, Paama, Malekula, Maewa, Emau and North Efate. The British Government is going to build a new central hospital in Vila in 1971. British and French national medical officers comprise a Condominium Medical Service providing preventive measures and free medical attention to the native population. The joint administration subsidizes the work of the mission medical services.

EDUCATION. The Condominium Government has no education service but makes an annual subsidy (1970: $A102,500) to each national administration for education. The British Administration finances small multi-racial primary schools at Vila and Santo and a secondary school (opened in 1966), and makes grants to Mission voluntary agencies who conduct primary schools throughout the group. The French Government has some primary schools, a secondary school and assists French Missions. The training of teachers is being concentrated at the British central teacher-training college near Vila which opened in March 1962. The British Administration sponsors New Hebridean students taking tertiary courses overseas.

FINANCE. The Condominium budget for 1969 balanced at $A2,859,107. British National Service revenue 1969–70 (estimate) balanced expenditure at $A2,266,788. French National Service estimates, 1969, envisaged revenue and expenditure balancing at $A3,442,314. Australian decimal currency was introduced in 1966. It and the New Hebrides franc are the currencies in use.

JUSTICE. There are Condominium and English and French national courts.

DEVELOPMENT. A local development plan, financed from local revenues, provides for a large number of minor schemes. A joint plan of economic development, financed from Colonial Development and Welfare funds and the French FIDES, is being implemented as part of a continuing process. Many schemes for the development of roads, agriculture, civil aviation, telecommunications, surveys and special studies have been completed, while others are still under way, including the construction of a deep-water wharf at Vila.

PRODUCTION. The main commercial crops are copra, cocoa and coffee. Yams, taro, manioc and bananas are grown for local native consumption. A large number of cattle are reared on plantations and a beef industry is developing rapidly.

Prospecting licences for more than 900 areas have been issued. The manganese mine, established at Forari on Efate by the Compagnie Française des Phosphates de l'Océanie, closed in 1968 but was reopened in 1970 by Southland Mining of Australia. Timber (Kauri pine) is exploited on Aneityum and a forestry industry is established on Erromanga. There are no manufacturing industries.

Subsistence fishing is done by the New Hebridians, and a plant for freezing of tuna and bonito commenced operation in 1957. This plant, which is sited on Santo, freezes and packages for export to Japan and elsewhere, fish caught by Japanese and other vessels under contract to the British company running the plant.

COMMERCE. In 1968 imports totalled $A8,447,178 and exports $A9,704,314. 40·05% of total imports came from Australia, 14·67% from France, 3·10% from UK.

Principal imports were foodstuffs, beer, wine, spirits, tobacco and cigarettes, cement, timber, corrugated iron, clothing, machinery including motor vehicles, pharmaceutical products and petroleum products. Principal exports were copra ($5,184,414), sintered manganese ore ($1,406,276), fish (frozen) ($2,229,478), cocoa ($499,032), meat (canned) ($102,768), meat (frozen) ($50,152), coffee ($56,664) and sandalwood ($23,510).

SHIPPING. Shipping services link the New Hebrides with Australia, UK and Europe, USA/Canada, South America, North Africa, West Indies, Formosa,

China, Japan, New Guinea, Hong Kong, Singapore, New Zealand, Tahiti, New Caledonia, Fiji and the B.S.I.P. Small vessels give a frequent inter-islands service. In 1968, 251 vessels of 403,389 net tons entered and left New Hebrides; 58 of them (162,060 tons) were French, 86 (89,910 tons) British, 52 (84,105 tons) Japanese.

ROADS. The Public Works Department maintains limited roads on Efate, Santo, Tanna and Malekula. There are, in addition, tracks usable by motor vehicles on some of the other islands.

AVIATION. Fiji Airways Ltd operates a service three time a week; Suva, Vila, Santo, Honiara and return to Suva, where regular services to Australia, New Zealand, USA and Britain are provided by Qantas, BOAC and other carriers. Union de Transports Aériens provides a twice-weekly air service to and from New Caledonia, whence there are regular services to Australia, New Zealand and Tahiti. A local airline, Air Melanesiae, provides air services throughout the group. There are 2 international airports and 10 local aerodromes on various islands.

TELECOMMUNICATION. Telegraphic communication is by direct wireless contact with Suva, Honiara, Noumea and Sydney, and there is an internal network of teleradio stations. There is also a radio-telephone service with Honiara, Noumea, Suva and Sydney, from where the service can be extended to USA, Europe, etc. Air radio facilities are provided. Marine coast station facilities are available at Vila and Santo.

In 1966 Radio Vila began a twice-daily news broadcast.

BANKING. There are branches of the Bank of Indo-China at Vila and Santo and savings bank agencies of the Commonwealth Bank of Australia at Vila, Santo, Tanna and Aoba. The Bank of Australia and New Zealand opened a branch at Vila in 1969.

Annual Report, 1963–64. HMSO, 1966

WEST INDIES

The West Indies federation, established on 3 Jan. 1958, was dissolved in Feb. 1962 after Jamaica and Trinidad had opted out of it.

In 1967 new constitutional arrangements were made for 'the West Indies Associated States'. Antigua, St Kitts–Nevis–Anguilla (on 27 Feb.), Dominica, St Lucia (on 1 March), Grenada (on 3 March) and St Vincent (on 1 June) were given self-government in association with Britain which retains powers and responsibilities for defence and external affairs.

The following common institutions have been maintained after the dissolution of the federation:

EDUCATION. The University College of the West Indies, situated at Mona, Jamaica, was affiliated to London University, but became independent in April 1962. It received a Royal Charter in 1949 and has faculties of Medicine, Arts, Natural Sciences and a Department of Education. The former Imperial College of Tropical Agriculture in Trinidad is the faculty of Agriculture and Engineering; a College of Arts and Science has been added.

JUSTICE. The British Caribbean Court of Appeal has replaced the Federal Supreme Court. It has exclusive original jurisdiction and an appellate jurisdiction and can hear and determine appeals from British Guiana and British Virgin Islands by agreement. The Court, which travels between the territories, consists of a Chief Justice and 5 justices.

TRADE. The **Caribbean Free Trade Area** (CARIFTA) was established between Antigua, Barbados, Guyana, and Trinidad and Tobago on 1 May 1968; it was joined by Dominica, Grenada, St. Kitts–Nevis–Anguilla, St Lucia and St Vincent on 1 July, and by Jamaica and Montserrat on 1 Aug.

SHIPPING. The West Indies Shipping Corporation continues to provide a regular shipping service for passengers and cargo, the West Indies Shipping Corporation Act 1961 continuing with adaptation to be part of the law of the territories, including Jamaica and Trinidad and Tobago.

The West Indies Meteorological Service continues on a completely reorganized basis. It also serves Guyana, British Honduras and British Virgin Islands.

TELECOMMUNICATIONS. The territories are linked by cable, radio-telegraph and radio-telephone. Cable & Wireless (West Indies) Ltd have installed a multi-channel tropospheric scatter-link between Trinidad and Barbados and a network of VHF circuits covering the other territories.

CURRENCY. After Trinidad and British Guiana had withdrawn from the British Caribbean Currency Board, Barbados, the Leeward Islands (Antigua, St Kitts–Nevis–Anguilla, Montserrat), and the Windward Island (St Vincent, St Lucia, Dominica) united under the East Caribbean Currency Authority to issue new currency notes of $1, 5, 20 and 100, with effect from 6 Oct. 1965.

On 1 April 1965, $69,860,809 notes and $5,824,343 coins were in circulation; demonetized government notes outstanding totalled $292,550. The liability for Trinidad and Tobago Government demonetized notes outstanding at 14 Dec. 1964 has been assumed by the Central Bank of Trinidad and Tobago and is therefore not included in the circulation for which the British Caribbean Currency Board is liable.

BOOKS OF REFERENCE

A survey of economic potential and capital needs of the Leeward Islands, Windward Islands and Barbados. HMSO, 1963
The West Indies and Caribbean Year Book. London, annual
Aspinall, Sir Algernon, *The Pocket Guide to the West Indies.* 10th ed. London, 1954
Aycarst, X., *The British West Indies: the search for self-government.* London, 1960
Burns, Sir Alan, *History of the British West Indies.* London, 1954
Mordecai, J., *The West Indies.* London, 1968
Parry, J. H., and Sherlock, P. M., *A Short History of the West Indies.* London, 1956
Proudfoot, M., *Britain and the United States in the Caribbean.* London, 1954

Leeward and Windward Islands

Ministerial government was introduced in most of the Leeward and Windward Islands in 1956 and in Montserrat in 1960. A new constitution for the 7 federated territories of the Leeward and Windward Islands was introduced 1 Jan. 1960. The two posts of Governor were abolished. The Administrators of the territories are now appointed by HM the Queen.

Each Legislative Council (except that of Montserrat where the Administrator presides) is presided over by a Speaker elected from among members of the Council or from outside. Subject to the variations set out in brackets, the Council comprises 10 elected members (Dominica 11, St Vincent 9, Montserrat 7), 2 nominated members (Montserrat 1) and the Principal Law Officer *ex officio* (Montserrat: also the Financial Secretary).

Each Executive Council consists of a Chief Minister, 3 other Ministers (Montserrat 2) and 1 other member appointed by the Administrator on the advice of the Chief Minister from the unofficials of the Legislative Council, and the Principal Law Officer *ex officio* (Montserrat: also the Financial Secretary). The Chief Minister is appointed by the Administrator from the elected members of the Legislative Council. The other Ministers are appointed by the Administrator on the advice of the Chief Minister.

The Governors were formerly responsible for the Public Service; this responsibility has now devolved upon the Administrator acting after consultation with his local advisory Public Service Commission.

There are a single Judicial and Legal Service Commission and a single Police Service Commission.

There are 2 separate police forces in the Leewards: one for St Kitts–Nevis–

Anguilla and the other for Antigua–Montserrat–Virgin Islands. There is a police force in each territory of the Windward Islands.

Report by the Leeward and Windward Islands Constitutional Conference, 1961. (Cmd 1434)

Leeward Islands. The group, which lies to the north of the Windward group, and south-east of Puerto Rico, consists of the 4 territories of Antigua (with Barbuda and Redonda), St Christopher–Nevis–Anguilla, Montserrat and the Virgin Islands.

The chief products are sugar and molasses (Antigua and St Kitts), cotton (Antigua, Montserrat, St Kitts–Nevis), limes and fruits, vegetables, cotton seed (Montserrat), salt (Anguilla and St Kitts) and livestock, fish, vegetables, fruit and charcoal (Virgin Islands).

Leeward Islands: an Economic Survey. Barclays Bank, London, 1960
Harris, D. R., *Plants, animals and man in the outer Leeward Islands.* Univ. of California Press, 1965

Antigua. Area, 108 sq. miles (280 sq. km); the islands of Barbuda (62 sq. miles, 160 sq. km) and Redonda (1 sq. mile) are dependencies; population in 1963 was 61,664. Chief town, St. John's, 13,000. In 1963 the birth rate per 1,000 was 30·3, the death rate 7·4; there were 203 marriages.

In Nov. 1940 sites near Parham were leased to the USA as military and naval bases; in Dec. 1960, 900 acres including Coolidge airfield were released; 300 acres are being retained for 17 years.

Governor: Sir Wilfred Jacobs, QC.
Chief Minister: V. C. Bird.

EDUCATION. There are 34 government primary schools, 9 non-assisted primary schools, 3 government secondary schools, 2 grant-aided and 4 non-assisted secondary schools. In 1965 government schools had 360 teachers and 17,058 pupils.

FINANCE AND TRADE. Revenue (1964), $10,439,996 (including colonial development and welfare); expenditure, $9,962,746. The budget for 1965 showed a surplus of $1,675. Public debt (1964), $3,423,388. Imports (1965), $32·42m.; exports, $2·47m. Chief products are sugar (21,160 tons from 12,676 acres in 1964) and cotton (99,059 lb. in 1965). Tourism is of increasing importance (1958, 12,781 visitors; 1967, 59,174).

Total trade of Antigua, St Christopher and Montserrat with UK (British Board of Trade returns, in £1,000 sterling):

	1966[1]	1967[1]	1968[1]	1969[1]	1970[1]
Imports to UK	2,326	2,042	1,670	1,327	1,922
Exports from UK	5,187	3,264	4,460	5,268 ⎫	6,337
Re-exports from UK	77	65	78	97 ⎭	

[1] Includes also the British Virgin Islands.

SHIPPING. The island is generally flat with low hills rising in the south-west. There are numerous sheltered harbours, but they are too shallow for steamships. Passenger steamers from Europe, Canada and the USA call at ports.

POST. Telephone lines, 720 miles; 1,405 telephones. Air-mail services connect the colony with Barbados, Trinidad, the Windward Islands, Jamaica and Puerto Rico, UK, Canada and USA.

BANKING. In government savings bank, 6,861 depositors on 31 Dec. 1964, $714,823 deposits. Barclays Bank DCO, the Royal Bank of Canada, the Imperial Bank of Canada and the Bank of Nova Scotia have branches at St John's. The Antigua Co-operative Bank was opened in Jan. 1965.

Biennial Report, 1961–62. HMSO, 1962
LIBRARY. Public Library, St John's. *Librarian:* Mrs Phyllis Meyers.

St Christopher (St Kitts), Nevis and Anguilla. AREA AND POPULATION. The area is 153 sq. miles (396 sq. km): St Kitts, 68; Nevis, 50; Anguilla, 35. Population, 1966, 57,617; St Kitts 37,150; Nevis, 15,072; Anguilla, 5,395. Chief town of St Kitts, Basseterre (population, 15,897); of Nevis, Charlestown (population, 1,530).

CONSTITUTION AND GOVERNMENT. In Feb. 1967 the colonial status was replaced by an 'association' with Britain, giving the islands full internal self-government, while Britain remains responsible for defence and foreign affairs. There is an elected House of Assembly and a Cabinet system of Government. The Premier is the head of the Government and presides at Cabinet meetings.

Governor: Sir Fred Phillips, CVO.
Premier: R. L. Bradshaw.

EDUCATION (1966). There were 37 government primary and senior schools (16,487 pupils), 2 denominational (aided) and 7 private (unaided) elementary schools (927 pupils); and 4 government and 1 private unaided secondary schools (1,538 pupils). Government expenditure on education in 1966 was $1,267,197.

FINANCE. In 1965 actual revenue was $6,820,617; actual expenditure $6,530,756; public debt (at 31 Dec. 1963), $4,495,714. Estimates, 1966: revenue, $7,890,782; expenditure, $8,023,284.

TRADE. Imports, 1966, $15,817,508; exports, $8,614,875. Chief exports were: Sugar ($7,599,641), molasses ($207,791), cotton ($178,328) and salt ($168,170).

POST. There were 875 telephones on 1 Jan. 1968 in St Kitts.

BANKING. The savings bank at 31 Dec. 1965 had 5,715 depositors, $1,342,879 deposits. There is a branch of Barclays Bank DCO, of the Royal Bank of Canada and of the Bank of America at Basseterre, a sub-branch of Barclays Bank at Charlestown and a branch of the Swiss bank in Anguilla. Local banks are the St Kitts Industrial Bank in Basseterre and the Nevis Co-operative Banking Co. Ltd in Nevis.

Biennial Report, 1957–58. HMSO, 1961
LIBRARY. Public Library, Basseterre. *Librarian:* Miss E. Byron.

SOMBRERO is a small island in the Leeward Islands group, attached to the Colony of St Kitts–Nevis–Anguilla; area, 2 sq. miles. Phosphate of lime exists in limited quantities. There is a Board of Trade lighthouse.

Montserrat. Area, 39·5 sq. miles (101 sq. km). Population, 1968, 14,689. Chief town, Plymouth, 4,000 inhabitants.

GOVERNMENT. The Executive Council is composed of 4 unofficial members (the Chief Minister, 2 other Ministers and a member without portfolio) and 2 official members (Attorney-General and Financial Secretary). The Legislative Council consists of 7 elected, 1 nominated and 2 official members (the Attorney-General and Financial Secretary). Both Councils are presided over by the Administrator.

Administrator: D. R. Gibbs, CMG, CVO, DSO.
Chief Minister: W. H. Bramble.

JUSTICE. There are 2 magistrates' courts, at Plymouth and Cudjoe Head. Strength of the police force (1968), 2 officers and 54 other ranks.

EDUCATION. There are 13 government elementary, 1 government secondary, 1 grant-aided denominational elementary, 1 unaided denominational elementary schools, 2 preparatory private schools for children between the ages of 5 and 12 and 2 private kindergarten schools. In 1968, 2,618 children were enrolled in the primary schools, with 111 teachers; 263 in the secondary school, with 21 teachers.

FINANCE AND TRADE. In 1969 the budget estimates balanced at $4,037,180 (including grant-in-aid). Imports in 1967 totalled $6,923,900; exports, $320,239. Chief imports were manufactured goods ($1,250,533), food and beverages ($1,434,405); the main supplying countries were UK ($2·2m.), USA ($1·42m.) and Canada ($826,703). Chief exports in 1967 were fruit and vegetables ($45,189), and Sea Island cotton ($2,320).

SHIPPING. In 1968, 465 vessels arrived, landing 22,912 and loading 639 tons of cargo.

TOURISM. In 1968, 7,125 tourists arrived in Montserrat.

POST. A modern automatic telephone system, catering for 2,000 subscribers was installed by Cable & Wireless (West Indies) Ltd in 1967, under a 20-year agreement. By the end of 1969 subscribers numbered 604.

AVIATION. At the modernized Blackburne airport 1,775 aircraft landed in 1968, disembarking 12,406 passengers and 88·2 tons of cargo.

Biennial Report, 1965–66. HMSO, 1968

LIBRARY. Public Library, Plymouth. *Librarian:* Mrs S. Taylor.

The British Virgin Islands form the eastern extremity of the Greater Antilles and, exclusive of small rocks and reefs, number 36, of which 16 are inhabited. The largest are Tortola (1969 population, 9,730), Virgin Gorda, Anegada and Jost Van Dyke. Total area about 59 sq. miles (130 sq. km); population (1970), 10,840. Road Town, on the south-east of Tortola, is a port of entry; population, approximately 3,500.

CONSTITUTION AND GOVERNMENT. The Administrator is responsible for defence and internal security, external affairs, the public service, the courts and finance. The Executive Council consists of the Administrator, 2 *ex-officio* members and 3 ministers from the legislature. The Legislative Council consists of 2 official members, 1 nominated member and 7 elected members; the Speaker is elected from outside the Council.

Administrator: D. G. Cudmore, OBE.

EDUCATION. There are 2 government elementary, 12 denominational elementary, 2 private primary and 1 government secondary schools. In 1969 there were altogether 100 teachers and 2,617 pupils.

FINANCE AND TRADE. In 1969 revenue was $2,960,334; expenditure, $3,672,358 (both inclusive of grant-in-aid and Colonial Development and Welfare funds); imports, $8,099,208; exports, $49,754; imports from the UK, $529,349.

In 1969 the UK gave financial aid of $786,000, raising the total aid since 1955 to about $2·97m. The revised development plan concentrates on improvements of roads, electricity, water supply, airfields and waterfront reclamation, as well as social services.

The chief products are livestock (including poultry), fish, fruit and vegetables. The export trade is carried on almost entirely with the Virgin Islands of the USA. The main industry is tourism. The currency of the islands is the US dollar.

Barclays Bank DCO, the Virgin Islands National Bank, the Bank of Nova Scotia and the Chase Manhattan Bank have branches in the islands.

Biennial Report, 1963 and 1964. HMSO, 1965
Report of Constitutional Commissioner, 1965. HMSO, 1965

LIBRARY. Public Library, Road Town. *Librarian:* Miss Verna Penn.

Windward Islands

The group consists of Grenada, St Vincent, the Grenadines (half under St Vincent, half under Grenada), St Lucia and Dominica, and form the eastern barrier to the Caribbean Sea between Martinique and Trinidad.

Total trade with UK (British Board of Trade returns, in £1,000 sterling):

	1965	1966	1967	1968	1969	1970
Imports to UK	13,033	10,625	10,084	10,845	12,727	9,473
Exports from UK	4,475	4,899	5,113	4,926	6,536 ⎫	
Re-exports from UK	55	74	82	86	117 ⎬	9,735

Windward Islands: an Economic Survey. Barclays Bank, London, 1960

E

Grenada. AREA AND POPULATION. 133 sq. miles (344 sq. km); population, census 1960, 88,677; estimated population 1969, 104,579. St George's, the capital, had 8,600 inhabitants. The largest of the Grenadines attached to Grenada is Carriacou, area 6,500 acres; population 1969, 8,179.

Vital statistics (1969): Births, 2,757; deaths, 768; infant deaths, 110; marriages, 299.

The general elections on 24 Aug. 1967 were won by the United Labour Party.

Governor: Dr Hilda Louisa Bynoe, DBE.

Premier: Eric M. Gairy.

EDUCATION. There were (1969) 12 government and 45 government-aided primary schools, with 29,883 pupils and average attendance 24,993; and 11 secondary schools (2 boys, 3 girls, 6 co-educational) with 2,912 pupils. There were also 26 housecraft and handicraft centres and departments.

FINANCE. The 1969 estimates balanced at $21,309,540 (1969: $26,735,388) including $2,243,630 ($2,848,300) Colonial Development and Welfare grant. Public debt at 31 Dec. 1969 was $13,676,676.

AGRICULTURE. The principal crops grown are: Cocoa (15,000 acres), nutmegs (6,500 acres), bananas (7,500 acres), coconuts (3,000 acres), citrus (1,200 acres) and sugar-cane (1,100 acres), in addition to small scattered cultivation of cotton, cloves, cinnamon and coffee.

TRADE. Total value of imports 1968, $26,346,011; exports, $9,962,319. Chief exports 1968: Cocoa beans (3·9m. lb.), $2,312,399; nutmegs (2·9m. lb.), $2,548,599; mace (362,254 lb.), $721,644; bananas (2,070,659 stems), $3,864,122. Chief imports 1968: Flour (11·5m. lb.), $1,170,188; motor cars (306), $804,220; fertilisers (6,175 tons), $756,018.

Value of imports 1968: From UK $8,649,326; Canada, $2,682,468; USA, $2,682,468. Value of exports 1968: To UK, $6,222,385; USA, $480,948; Canada, $267,139.

TOURISM. In 1969, 29,627 (1968: 23,164) visitors were registered, spending an estimated $22·9m. in 1969.

SHIPPING. Total shipping for 1968 was 798 motor and steamships and 553 sailing and auxiliary vessels, with a total net tonnage of 1,154,262 and 21,012 respectively.

ROADS. The scheduled road mileage is 577, of which 377 have an oiled surface and 210 are graded as third- and fourth-class roads.

AVIATION. International Aeradio Ltd control by radio all plane movements within this area, and keep Pearls Airport in contact with St George's, on official airways business.

POST. The telephone system, owned by the Grenada Government, is operated and maintained by Cable & Wireless (West Indies) Ltd. The system is completely automatic, and in Sept. 1969 served 1,623 subscribers.

Cable & Wireless (West Indies) Ltd operates a VHF radio system (telephone and telegraph) to Trinidad and Barbados, from where connexion is made to all principal West Indian islands and all other parts of the world.

Windward Islands Broadcasting Service is government owned and operated.

BANKING. At 31 Dec. 1969, depositors in the Government Savings Bank had balances totalling $851,143.

In 1969 there were 6 Commercial Banks in Grenada, including Barclays Bank DCO, Royal Bank of Canada, Bank of Nova Scotia, Canadian Imperial Bank of Commerce and the Grenada Co-operative Bank. The Grenada Agricultural Bank was established in 1965 to encourage agricultural development.

Biennial Report 1965 and 1966. HMSO, 1967

LIBRARY: Public Library, St George's. *Librarian:* Mrs Sheila Buckmire.

St Vincent. Area, 150·3 sq. miles (389 sq. km); population, census of 7 April 1960, 79,948. Capital, Kingstown, population, 20,440. Vital statistics (1966): Live births, 3,771; still births, 60; deaths, 832; marriages, 220.

Administrator: Hywell George, CMG, OBE.
Chief Minister: R. Milton Cato.

EDUCATION (1967). Fifty-eight primary schools; pupils on roll, 26,992, average attendance, 21,036. Expenditure on primary education, $1,287,750. There is also a secondary school for boys (348 pupils) and one for girls (376 pupils). Expenditure on secondary education, including subsidy to 7 private secondary schools and cost of evening classes, $236,679.

JUSTICE (1967). There were 2,945 convictions in the 3 magistrates' courts. Strength of police force, 205 (including 4 officers).

FINANCE. Revenue, 1967, $8,319,170 ($621,577 from colonial development and welfare funds and $35,242 from overseas service aid); expenditure, $8,812,053 ($897,907 on colonial development and welfare schemes and $40,411 on overseas service aid). The 1968 estimates balanced at $10,607,355 ($2·22m. from grant-in-aid; $2,263,652 on development and welfare). Public debt at end of 1967, $1,749,642.

PRODUCTION. The estimated alienated area is about 47,000 of the total acreage of 85,120. 34,000 acres are under forest and woodland; of these about 5,000 acres are used for grazing; 3,000 are considered potentially productive for agriculture and 5,000 for forestry. About 14,000 acres are considered unsuitable for either agriculture or forestry and approximately 6,000 acres are built on roads, rivers, etc. Of the total alienated area, 34,000 acres are considered arable land, of which 20,000 acres are under temporary crops, 4,000 acres under temporary meadows, 300 acres devoted to market-garden crops with temporary fallow and all other arable land making up a further 9,700 acres. About 2,000 acres are under permanent meadow, of which 750 are cultivated.

Bananas, arrowroot flour, copra, cotton, sweet potatoes, yams, tannias and other starchy roots, nutmegs and mace and small amounts of peanuts are produced. The Territory is largely self-supporting in vegetables. St Vincent is renowned for its arrowroot and long staple Sea Island cotton, the finest there is.

Land ownership: Crown, 38,000 acres; planters, 17,000 acres; small farmers, 25,500 acres; settlements, 6,000 acres.

The electricity system is owned and operated by the St Vincent Electricity Services (CDC). The system consists of 3 power stations: Colonarie Hydro (716 kw.); Kingston Diesel (1,460 kw.) and Richmond Hydro (1,100 kw.), which are linked by 11,000-volt transmission lines covering the island from Richmond through Kingstown to Georgetown. Current is supplied at 400 volts 3-phase, 50 cycles for industrial purposes and 230 volts single phase for domestic purposes. There are 6,250 consumers.

LABOUR. There are 6 registered trade unions: Federal Industrial and Agricultural Workers Union, the St Vincent Union of Teachers, the Civil Service Association, the Secondary School Teachers' Association, the Commercial, Technical and Allied Workers' Union, and the St Vincent Employers' Federation.

TRADE (1967). Imports, $15,808,406; exports, $6,319,979. Value of imports from the UK, $4,949,670; of exports to the UK, $3,574,973 (plus bullion and specie).

Principal exports:

	$BWI				$BWI
Sea Island cotton			Bananas	2,173,572 stems	3,102,001
(white lint)	24,026 lb.	29,267	Sweet potatoes	5,344,596 lb.	160,339
Arrowroot starch	4,543,815 lb.	995,820	Nutmegs	150,705 lb.	122,105
Copra	5,431,841 lb.	873,075	Mace	26,245 lb.	39,369

COMMUNICATIONS. There are 166 miles of all-weather roads, 196 miles of motorable roads and 202 miles of tracks.

Besides the postal service, there is a telephone system with 1,200 miles of line and 760 subscribers, and a radio-telephone service to Bequia in the Grenadines.

Shipping (1966): (a) 316 sailing vessels and schooners of 10,217 NRT entered, while 312 of 9,674 NRT cleared. (b) 398 steamships of 729,228 NRT entered the territory; of these 185 of 242,515 tons were British. (c) 379 steamships of 687,516 NRT cleared, 167 of 290,826 tons being British. (d) 34 tankers of 19,089 NRT entered and 39 of 23,230 NRT cleared. A deep-water harbour at Kingstown was completed in 1964.

Scheduled services are operated daily by LIAT and thrice weekly by Caribair. Passengers are able to travel daily through the chain of islands stretching as far north as San Juan, Puerto Rico and south to Trinidad. Connexions to the USA, Canada, South America and Europe are possible via Barbados, Antigua and Trinidad.

BANKING. There are branches of Barclays Bank DCO, the Royal Bank of Canada and the Canadian Imperial Bank of Commerce at Kingstown.

Biennial Report, 1964–65. HMSO, 1966

LIBRARY. St Vincent Public Library, Kingstown. *Librarian:* Mrs Lorna Small.

St Lucia.

Area, 238 sq. miles (616 sq. km); population (1965) 100,000. The capital is Castries (population, 40,000). Vital statistics (1964): Births, 4,187; deaths, 746.

The USA in Sept. 1964 gave up all the remaining leased lands, including a large hospital and 2 airstrips.

Governor: Sir Frederick Clarke.

Chief Minister: J. G. M. Compton.

EDUCATION (31 Dec. 1965). Fifty-eight primary schools (51 Roman Catholic, 3 Anglican, 3 Methodist, 1 government), with 23,120 pupils on roll; government expenditure, 1965, $1,587,617. Primary education is free and compulsory by law, but the legislation is not enforced. There are 3 secondary schools (2 Roman Catholic, 1 government) with 939 pupils; government grants to the Roman Catholic secondary schools totalled $135,000 in 1966.

JUSTICE. The island is divided into 2 judicial districts, and there are 9 magistrates' courts. Appeals lie with the Court of Appeal of the Windward and Leeward Islands, subject to exceptions and conditions as may be enacted by the St Lucia legislature.

In 1964 the Supreme Court dealt with 79 civil and 39 criminal cases.

Police establishment in 1965 was 5 officers, 5 inspectors and 320 others.

FINANCE. Estimated revenue in 1966 (including colonial development and welfare schemes and overseas aid scheme) was $10·2m.; estimated expenditure, $9·4m. Parliamentary grant-in-aid of administration ceased in 1964 after 16 years.

Public debt, 31 Dec. 1964, $5,856,367.

AGRICULTURE. Bananas, cocoa, copra and coconut oil are the chief products.

TOURISM. The total number of visitors during 1964 was 17,716; their estimated expenditure was $1,577,000.

TRADE. Value of imports (1966), $28,379,884; of exports, $12,108,770, including coconut oil, cocoa beans, copra and bananas. Main items of imports were artificial silk and cotton piece-goods, cement, plastic goods, iron and steel products, hardware, motor vehicles, agricultural machinery, fertilizers, wheat flour, codfish and rice.

SHIPPING. Registered fleet (31 Dec. 1964): 14 motor vessels (1,278 gross tons) and 11 sailing vessels (932 gross tons). In 1964, 1,629 vessels of 1,609,156 gross tons entered Castries and Vieux Fort.

ROADS. The island has 418 miles of main and secondary roads.

POST. There are 1,030 miles of telephone line, of which 212 miles are trunk and 818 branch lines; number of telephones, 2,233.

AVIATION. The island is served on a scheduled basis by British West Indies Airways and Leeward Islands Air Transport.

BANKING. There are Barclays Bank DCO with a branch and 2 agencies, the Royal Bank of Canada and the Nova Scotia Bank with a branch each, the St Lucia Co-operative Bank and the Government Savings Bank.

The Government Savings Bank (end of 1964), 4,172 depositors, $518,015 deposits.

Biennial Report, 1963–64. HMSO, 1965

LIBRARY. The Central Library, Castries. *Librarian:* Mrs Mary Prescod.

Dominica. Area, 289·5 sq. miles (728 sq. km). Census population, 1960, 59,916, estimate, 1967, 70,177. Chief town, Roseau (population, about 12,200). Dominica contains a Carib settlement with a population of about 400, nearly all of whom are of mixed Negro blood.

Governor: Sir Louis Colls-Lartigue, OBE.
Premier and Minister of Finance: E. O. LeBlanc.

CONSTITUTION. On 1 March 1967 Dominica received a new constitution on becoming an associate state of Britain.

The House of Assembly has 11 elected and 3 nominated members, one nominated on the advice of the Leader of the Opposition. The Speaker is elected from among the members of the House or from outside. The Cabinet is presided over by the Premier and consists of 4 other Ministers and the Attorney-General (official member). The Premier is appointed by the Governor from the elected members of the House of Assembly. The other Ministers are appointed by the Governor on the advice of the Premier.

JUSTICE. There are 3 magistrates' courts. They dealt with 502 civil and 1,830 criminal cases in 1968. The police force consists of 4 officers and 169 other ranks.

FINANCE. Revenue, 1968, $10,519,917 (including $1,298,941 from development and welfare fund, $1·7m. grant-in-aid and $37,587 overseas aid scheme); expenditure, $10,053,484 (including $1,597,603 from development and welfare fund); public debt, $2,177,742.

TRADE (1968). Imports, $20,212,755 c.i.f.; exports $12,413,121. Chief products: fruit juice, bananas, essential oils, cocoa, coconuts, copra, vanilla, fruit and fruit preparations, and rum. Exports (1968) of copra, 334 long tons ($127,763); cocoa, 111 long tons ($117,281); bananas, 4,152,254 stems ($9,387,402).

POST. Telephone lines, 824 miles; number of telephones, 836 (1969).

BANKING. Savings bank (1968), 1,739 depositors, with $291,061 deposits. There are branches of Barclays Bank DCO, Royal Bank of Canada and Dominica Co-operative Bank in Roseau, a branch of Barclays at Portsmouth and an agency of Barclays at Marigot.

Biennial Report, 1963–65. HMSO, 1967

LIBRARY. Public Library, Roseau. *Librarian:* Mrs R. Riviere.

CAYMAN, TURKS AND CAICOS ISLANDS

These two groups of islands were administered by the Governor of Jamaica until 1962; after Jamaica became independent, they were placed under the British Colonial Office.

CAYMAN ISLANDS consist of Grand Cayman, Little Cayman and Cayman Brac. Situated in the Caribbean Sea, about 200 miles NW of Jamaica, the islands were discovered by Columbus on 10 May 1503.

Area and Population. Area, 100 sq. miles (260 sq. km). Census population of 1960, 7,616, excluding 1,187 persons absent on census night, mostly seamen.

Grand Cayman (population 6,345), 22 miles long, 4–8 miles broad; capital: Georgetown (population 2,400). Little Cayman, 10 miles long, 1 mile broad. Cayman Brac, 12 miles long and 1¼ miles wide. Total population of the lesser islands, 1,271. Vital statistics (1969): Births, 272; marriages, 70; deaths, 46. Principal occupations are seafaring, turtle fishing, shark fishing, rope-making and the tourist industry. There are 9 government primary schools with 1,250 pupils, 5 private elementary and 3 private secondary schools.

Constitution and Government. The Legislative Assembly consists of the Administrator, not less than 2 nor more than 3 official members, not less than 2 nor more than 3 nominated members and 12 elected members.

The Executive Council consists of 2 official members appointed from among the official members of the Legislative Assembly, 1 nominated member appointed from among the nominated members of the Assembly and 2 elected members elected by the nominated and elected members of the Assembly from among the elected members of the Assembly.

Administrator: A. C. E. Long, CMG, CBE.

Finance. Revenue 1969, J$1,533,738; expenditure, J$1,467,136. Public debt (31 Dec. 1969), J$770,620; reserve fund, J$124,102.

Trade. Exports, 1969, totalled J$8,754; principal items were rope, turtle and shark skin. Imports (1969), J$5,846,984; principally foodstuffs, textiles and building materials.

Shipping. Motor vessels ply regularly between the Cayman Islands, Jamaica and Florida. Shipping registered at Georgetown, 44 vessels of 10,639 net tons (1968).

Aviation. British West Indian Airways operate regular air services between Kingston (Jamaica), Grand Cayman and Miami (Florida). Lineas Aereas Costarricenses operates regular services between Costa Rica, Panama, Grand Cayman and Miami. Cayman Airways provide regular services between Grand Cayman, Cayman Brac and Kingston.

Banking. The Royal Bank of Canada and the Canadian Imperial Bank of Commerce each has a branch at Georgetown. Barclays Bank DCO has branches at Georgetown and Stake Bay.

Biennial Report, 1964–65. HMSO, 1967

THE TURKS AND CAICOS ISLANDS. Area and Population. The Turks and Caicos Islands are geographically a portion of the Bahamas, of which they form the two south-eastern groups. There are upwards of 30 small cays; area 166 sq. miles (430 sq. km). Only 6 are inhabited; the largest, Grand Caicos, is 30 miles long by 2 to 3 miles broad. The seat of government is at Grand Turk, 7 miles long by 1½ broad; 2,000 inhabitants. Population (1960 census), 5,668, of whom 5,315 were of African descent and 77 of European descent.

Vital statistics (1967): Births, 137; marriages, 26; deaths, 27.

Constitution and Government. The constitution provides for an Administrator and a State Council. The State Council consists of a Speaker, 3 official members not less than 2 or more than 3 nominated members and 9 elected members. The normal life of the State Council is 5 years.

On 5 Nov. 1965 the Governor of the Bahamas became also Governor of the Turks and Caicos Islands.

Administrator: R. E. Wainwright, CMG.

Education. Education is free in the 14 government schools between the ages of 7 and 14. Average number on rolls in 1968, 1,665; average attendance, 1,601.

Finance. Actual revenue in 1968 was £512,168 (including £224,000 grant-in-aid and £123,641 colonial development and welfare schemes); expenditure, £532,173.

Trade (1968). Total imports, £442,793; total exports, £63,133. Principal imports were food, drink and tobacco (£93,205) and manufactured articles (£144,308). Principal exports: Salt, 2,504 tons (£3,796); conchs, 187,000 (£597); conch shell, 71,000 (£592); crawfish, 174,860 lb. (£58,115). The most important industry used to be salt raking; it is now limited to Salt Cay.

A tourist industry is rapidly developing and will become the major industry of the islands within two or three years.

Shipping. Registered shipping (1968), 151 vessels of 2,715 tons.

Aviation. There is a 5,500-ft paved airfield on Grand Turk under the control of the US Air Force on which civilian aircraft can land. On South Caicos there is a 6,000-ft paved airstrip. There are other small unpaved airstrips on three other islands. There is an internal air service throughout the islands and a thrice-weekly air service from Nassau.

Banking. Savings bank deposits (1968), £128,580; depositors, 1,689. There is a branch of Barclays Bank DCO in Grand Turk.

Biennial Report, 1965–66. HMSO, 1967

CANADA

HISTORY. The territories which now constitute Canada came under British power at various times by settlement, conquest or cession. Nova Scotia was occupied in 1628 by settlement at Port Royal, was ceded back to France in 1632 and was finally ceded by France in 1713, by the Treaty of Utrecht; the Hudson's Bay Company's charter, conferring rights over all the territory draining into Hudson Bay, was granted in 1670; Canada, with all its dependencies, including New Brunswick and Prince Edward Island, was formally ceded to Great Britain by France in 1763; Vancouver Island was acknowledged to be British by the Oregon Boundary Treaty of 1846, and British Columbia was established as a separate colony in 1858. As originally constituted, Canada was composed of the provinces of Upper and Lower Canada (now Ontario and Quebec), Nova Scotia and New Brunswick. They were united under the provisions of an Act of the Imperial Parliament known as 'The British North America Act, 1867', which came into operation on 1 July 1867 by royal proclamation. The Act provides that the constitution of Canada shall be 'similar in principle to that of the United Kingdom'; that the executive authority shall be vested in the Sovereign, and carried on in his name by a Governor-General and Privy Council; and that the legislative power shall be exercised by a Parliament of two Houses, called the 'Senate' and the 'House of Commons'. The present position of Canada in the British Commonwealth of Nations was defined at the Imperial Conference of 1926 (*see* p. 55).

On 30 June 1931 the House of Commons approved the enactment of the Statute of Westminster emancipating the Provinces as well as the Dominion from the operation of the Colonial Laws Validity Act, and thus removing what legal limitations existed as regards Canada's legislative autonomy. The statute received the royal assent on 12 Dec. 1931.

Provision was made in the British North America Act for the admission of British Columbia, Prince Edward Island, the Northwest Territories and Newfoundland into the Union. In 1869 Rupert's Land, or the Northwest Territories, was purchased from the Hudson's Bay Company; the province of Manitoba was erected from this territory and admitted into the confederation on 15 July 1870. On 20 July 1871 the province of British Columbia was admitted, and Prince Edward Island on 1 July 1873. The provinces of Alberta and Saskatchewan were formed from the provisional districts of Alberta, Athabaska, Assiniboia and Saskatchewan, and admitted on 1 Sept. 1905. Newfoundland formally joined Canada as its tenth province on 31 March 1949.

In Feb. 1931 Norway formally recognized the Canadian title to the Sverdrup group of Arctic islands. Canada thus holds sovereignty in the whole Arctic sector north of the Canadian mainland.

CONSTITUTION AND GOVERNMENT. The members of the Senate are appointed until age 75 by summons of the Governor-General under the Great Seal of Canada. Members appointed before 2 June 1965 may remain in office for life. The Senate consists of 102 senators, namely, 24 from Ontario, 24 from Quebec, 10 from Nova Scotia, 10 from New Brunswick, 4 from Prince Edward Island, 6 from Manitoba, 6 from British Columbia, 6 from Alberta, 6 from Saskatchewan and 6 from Newfoundland. Each senator must be at least 30 years of age, a born or naturalized British subject, and must reside in, and be possessed of property, real or personal, to the value of $4,000 within the province for which he is appointed. The House of Commons is elected by the people, for 5 years, unless sooner dissolved. Women have the vote and are eligible. From 1867 to the election of 1945 representation was based on Quebec having 65 seats and the other provinces the same proportion of 65 which their population had to the population of Quebec. In the General Election of 1949 readjustments were based on the population of all the provinces taken as a whole and, generally speaking, this format for representation has prevailed in all subsequent elections, with readjustments made after each decennial census.

The twenty-eighth Parliament, elected on 25 June 1968, comprises 264 members and the provincial and territorial representation are: Ontario, 88; Quebec, 74; Nova Scotia, 11; New Brunswick, 10; Manitoba, 13; British Columbia, 23; Prince Edward Island, 4; Saskatchewan, 13; Alberta, 19; Newfoundland, 7; Yukon Territory, 1; Northwest Territories, 1.

State of parties in the Senate (Jan. 1971): Liberals, 62; Progressive Conservatives, 23; Independent, 5; vacant, 11; total 102.

State of the parties in the House of Commons (Jan. 1971): Liberals, 152; Progressive Conservatives, 72; Social Credit Rally, 13; New Democratic Party, 23; Independent, 1; vacant, 3; total, 264.

The following is a list of Governors-General of Canada:

Viscount Monck	1867–1868	Duke of Devonshire	1916–1921
Lord Lisgar	1868–1872	Viscount Byng of Vimy	1921–1926
Earl of Dufferin	1872–1878	Viscount Willingdon	1926–1931
Marquess of Lorne	1878–1883	Earl of Bessborough	1931–1935
Marquess of Lansdowne	1883–1888	Lord Tweedsmuir	1935–1940
Lord Stanley of Preston	1888–1893	Earl of Athlone	1940–1946
Earl of Aberdeen	1893–1898	Field-Marshal Viscount Alex-	
Earl of Minto	1898–1904	ander of Tunis	1946–1952
Earl Grey	1904–1911	Vincent Massey	1952–1959
HRH the Duke of Connaught	1911–1916	Georges Philias Vanier	1959–1967

Governor-General: The Rt Hon. Roland Michener (sworn in April 1967).

The office and appointment of the Governor-General are regulated by letters patent, signed by the King on 8 Sept. 1947, which came into force on 1 Oct. 1947. He is assisted in his functions, under the provisions of the Act of 1867, by a Privy Council composed of Cabinet Ministers.

The following is the list of the Liberal Cabinet in Jan. 1971, in order of precedence, which in Canada attaches generally rather to the person than to the office:

Prime Minister: Rt Hon. Pierre Elliott Trudeau.
Minister without Portfolio and Leader of the Government in the Senate: Paul Joseph Martin.

Secretary of State for External Affairs: Mitchell Sharp.
Public Works: Arthur Laing.
President of the Queen's Privy Council: Allen Joseph MacEachen.
President of the Treasury Board: Charles Mills Drury.
Finance: Edgar John Benson.
Industry, Trade and Commerce: Jean-Luc Pépin.
Regional Economic Expansion: Jean Marchand.
Energy, Mines and Resources: John James Greene.
Without Portfolio (Postmaster General): Joseph Julien Jean-Pierre Côté.
Justice and Attorney-General: John Napier Turner.
Indian Affairs and Northern Development: Joseph Jacques Jean Chrétien.
Labour: Bryce S. Mackasey.
National Defence: Donald S. Macdonald.
National Health and Welfare: John C. Munro.
Secretary of State of Canada: Gérard Pelletier.
Fisheries and Forestry: Jack Davis.
Agriculture: H. A. Olson.
Veterans Affairs: Jean-Eudes Dubé.
Consumer and Corporate Affairs: Ronald Basford.
Transport: Donald Jamieson.
Communications: Eric Kierans.
Supply and Services and Receiver-General: James Richardson.
Without Portfolio: Robert Andras; Robert Stanbury.
Manpower and Immigration: Otto E. Long.
National Revenue: Herb Gray.
Solicitor-General: Jean-Pierre Goyer.

The sessional allowance of members of the Senate and House of Commons is $12,000 per annum. Senators receive an additional annual tax-free expense allowance of $3,000 and members of Parliament $6,000; the Leader of the Government in the Senate $10,000 and the Opposition Leader in the Senate $6,000. The remuneration of the Prime Minister is $25,000, a cabinet minister and Leader of the Opposition $15,000, a minister without portfolio $7,500, in addition to the sessional and expense allowances they receive as members of Parliament. Each minister and the Leader of the Opposition is also entitled to a $2,000 motor vehicle allowance. The Speakers of the Senate and the House of Commons receive, besides the sessional and expense allowances, a salary of $9,000 per annum and a motor vehicle allowance of $1,000. An allowance of $4,000 is given to the leader of a party with 12 or more members in the House of Commons, other than the Prime Minister and Leader of the Opposition, and to the chief Government and Opposition whips. Parliamentary Secretaries receive an additional annual allowance of $4,000.

An Act to provide retiring allowances, on a contributory basis, to members of the House of Commons was given the Royal Assent on 4 July 1952. This Act was amended in July 1963; a member can now opt for a reduced retiring allowance in favour of an additional allowance for the widow; and provision has been made for retiring allowance for former Prime Ministers and their widows.

The Canadian Parliamentary Guide. Annual. Ottawa
Report of the Royal Commission on Dominion–Provincial Relations, Canada 1867–1939. 3 vols.
    Ottawa, 1940
Bissonnette, B., *Essai sur constitution du Canada.* Montreal, 1963
Cheffins, R. I., *The Constitutional Process in Canada.* Toronto, 1969.
Clokie, H. McD., *Canadian Government and Politics.* New rev. ed. Toronto, 1950
Corry, J. A., *Democratic Government and Politics.* 3rd ed. Toronto, 1959
Dawson, R. M., *Democratic Government in Canada.* Rev. ed. Toronto, 1957
Dawson, R. M. (ed.), *The Government of Canada.* 3rd ed. Toronto, 1957
Eayrs, J. G., *The Art of the Possible: government and foreign policy in Canada.* Toronto, 1961
Eggleston, W., *Road to Nationhood: A Chronicle of Dominion–Provincial Relations.* Toronto,
    1946.—*Canada at Work.* Montreal, 1953
Hodgetts, J. E., *Canadian Public Administration.* Toronto, 1960
Kennedy, W. F. M., *Statutes, Treaties and Documents of the Canadian Constitution, 1713–1929.*
    Toronto, 1930

Kunz, F, A, *The Modern Senate of Canada, 1925–63.* Toronto, 1965
Lamontagne, M., *Le Fédéralisme canadien.* Quebec, 1954
Laskin, B., *Canadian Constitution Laws.* 2nd ed. Toronto, 1960
Lower, A. R. M. (and others), *Evolving Canadian Federation.* Duke Univ. Press, Durham, NC, 1958
McWhinney, E., *Comparative Federation; States' rights and national power.* Toronto, 1962
Martin, C. B., *Foundations of Canadian Nationhood.* Toronto, 1955
Olmsted, R. A., *Decisions of the Judicial Committee of the Privy Council Relating to the British North America Act, 1867, and the Canadian Constitution, 1867–1954.* Ottawa, Queens' Printer, 1954
Ricker, J. C., *How Are we Governed?* Toronto, 1961
Saywell, J. T., *The Office of Lieutenant-Governor.* Toronto, 1957
Trudeau, P. E., *Federalism and the French Canadians.* London, 1968
Varcoe, F. P., *The Distribution of Legislative Power in Canada.* Toronto, 1954
Ward, N., *The Public Purse: a study in Canadian democracy.* Toronto, 1962
Willms, A. (ed,), *Public Administration in Canada.* Toronto, 1862.

DIPLOMATIC REPRESENTATIVES

Country	Canadian representative	Foreign representative
Afghánistán	C. J. Small	Abudullah Malikyar
Algeria	James A. Roberts	Tayeb Seddikioui[2]
Argentina	A. P. Bissonet	Constantino Ramos
Australia[1]	Arthur Redpath Menzies	David Williamson McNicol
Austria	N. F. H. Berlis	Eduard Schiller
Barbados[1]	G. A. Rau	C. B. Williams, OBE
Belgium	J. C. Langley	Louis G. Delhaye
Bolivia	Pierre Charpentier	Julio Sanjines-Goytia
Botswana[1]	H. H. Carter	Linchwe II Molefhi Kgafela
Brazil	Christian Hardy	Frank de Mendança Moscoso
Britain[1]	Charles S. A. Ritchie	Peter T. Hayneur, CMG, CVO
Bulgaria	Bruce M. Williams	Kiril Chterev
Burma	John G. Hadwen	Thakin Chan Tun
Burundi	Marc Baudouin	Nsanga Térence
Cameroun	Roger Rousseau	Joseph N. Owono
Central African Republic	Roger Rousseau	Roger L.G. Guèrillot
Ceylon[1]	R. M. Macdonnell	P. H. William de Silva
Chad	Roger Rousseau	—
Chile	G. B. Summers	Fausto Soto
China	John M. Frazer[2]	Hsu Chung-fu[2]
Colombia	S. A. Freifeld	Luis Ernesto Ordoñez Castillo
Congo (Br.)	—	Jean Mombouli[2]
Congo (K.)	Marc Baudouin	Joseph Ndanu
Costa Rica	D. W. Munro	D. R. Alberto Zuniga-Tristan
Cuba	K. C. Brown	Jose Fernandez de Cossio
Cyprus[1]	C. E. McGaughey	Zenon Rossides
Czechoslovakia	T. B. B. Wainman-Wood	Bretislav Matonoka
Dahomey	D. B. Hicks	—
Denmark	Max H. Wershof	A. Bogh Andersen
Dominican Republic	D. S. McPhail	Virgilio A. Sanchez
Ecuador	John H. Cleveland	Arturo Bustamante Lecaro[2]
El Salvador	S. A. Freifeld	—
Ethiopia	C. J. Woodsworth	Ato Dawit Abdou
Finland	Frank G. Hooton	Holger Lennart Sumelius
France	Léo Cadieux, QC	Pierre Siraud
Gabon	Roger Rousséau	G. R. Bouckat-Bou.-Nziengui
Gambia[1]	G. G. Riddell	—

[1] High Commissioner.   [2] Chargé d'Affaires.   No figure = Ambassador.

Country	Canadian representative	Foreign representative
Germany (West)	Gordon G. Crean	Dietrich, Baron von Mirbach
Ghana[1]	D. B. Hicks	Maj. Seth K. Anthony
Greece	Michel Gauvin	Aristide N. Pilavachi
Guatemala	Saul F. Rae	Julio A. Wunderlick
Guinea	G. G. Riddell	Fadiala Keita
Guyana[1]	J. A. Stiles	Rahman Baccus Gajraj
Haiti	K. C. Brown	Philippe Cantave
Honduras	D. W. Munro	—
Hungary[2]	T. B. B. Wainman-Wood	Gyula Baranyi
Iceland	G. K. Grande	Magnus Vignir Magnusson
India[1]	James George	Ashok B. Bhadkamkar
Indonesia	W. T. Delworth	Rear-Adm. R. Darmo Bandoro
Iran	C. C. Eberts	Mohsen Merat Esfandiary
Iraq	C. C. Eberts	—
Irish Republic	J. J. McCardle	Joseph Francis Shields
Israel	C. E. McGaughey	Ephraim Evron
Italy	Benjamin Rogers	Paulo Pansa Cedronio
Ivory Coast	Georges Charpentier	Timothée N. Ahoua
Jamaica[1]	Victor C. Moore	V. C. Smith
Japan	H. O. Moran	Shinyichi Kondo
Jordan	Jacques Gignac	Cherif A. Hamid Sharaf
Kenya[1]	J. M. Cook	—
Korea (South)	H. O. Moran	Pil Shik Chin
Kuwait	C. C. Eberts	Talat Al-Ghoussein
Lebanon	Jacques Gignac	Dr Alif Gébara
Lesotho[1]	H. H. Carter	Mothusi Thamsanga Mashologu
Liberia	—	S. Edward Peal
Libya	D'Iberville Fortier	
Luxembourg	J. C. Langley	Jean Wagner
Malagasy Republic	Charles J. Woodsworth	Blaise Rabetafika
Malaysia[1]	John G. Hadwen	H. M. A. Zakaria
Mali	G. G. Riddell	Seydon Traore
Malta[1]	Benjamin Rogers	Arvid Pardo
Mauritania	G. G. Riddell	Sid'Amed Ould Taya
Mauritius[1]	J. A. Irwin	Guy Girald Balancy, CBE
Mexico	Saul F. Rae	E. Rafael Urdaneta
Morocco	J. E. G. Hardy	
Nepál	James George	K. S. Sharwa
Netherlands	A. J. Pick	Theodorus Hendrikus Bot
New Zealand[1]	J. A. Dougan	Dean J. Eyre
Nicaragua	D. W. Munro	Dr Guillermo Sevilla-Sacasa
Niger	George Charpentier	Georges Condat
Nigeria[1]	A. S. McGill	Edward O. Enahoro
Norway	G. K. Grande	Torfinn Oftedal
Pakistan[1]	C. J. Small	M. S. Shaikh
Panama	D. W. Munro	—
Paraguay	A. P. Bissonnet	—
Peru	Pierre Charpentier	Salvador Agusto de Sousa Sampayo
Poland	Pamela A. McDougall	Marian Stradowski
Portugal	Michel Gauvin	Dr Alfredo Lencastre da Veiga
Romania	Bruce M. Williams	Bucur Schiopu
Rwanda	Marc Baudouin	Etienre Munyeshuti
Senegal	G. G. Riddell	Cheikh Ibrahima Fall
Sierre Leone[1]	A. S. McGill	John Akar, MBE
Singapore[1]	John G. Hadwen	T. T. B. Koh
Somalia	Charles J. Woodsworth	Abdulrahim Abby Farah

[1] High Commissioner. [2] Chargé d'Affaires. No figure = Ambassador.

Country	Canadian representative	Foreign representative
South Africa, Republic of	H. H. Carter	Matthya Izak Botha
Spain	J. E. G. Hardy	Juan José Rovina
Sudan	Thomas L. Carter	Sayed Fakhreddine Mohamed
Swaziland[1]	H. H. Carter	Dr Samuel Thornton Msind- azwe Sukati
Sweden	Blanche M. Meagher	Carl Ake Malmaeus
Switzerland	James A. Roberts	Erwin Bernath
Syria	Jacques Gignac	—
Tanzania[1]	John A. Irwin	Abbas Kleist Sykes
Thailand	G. E. Cox	Anand Panyarachun
Togo	D. B. Hicks	Alexandre J. Ohin, MD
Trinidad and Tobago[1]	G. A. Rau	Matthew Ramcharam
Tunisia	D'Iberville Fortier	Abdel-Assiz Hamzaoui
Turkey	Klaus Goldschlag	Gen. Irfan Tansel
Uganda[1]	J. M. Cook	Erifasi Otema Allimadi
USSR	R. A. D. Ford	Boris P. Miroshnichenko
UAR	Thomas L. Carter	Mohamed Choucri
USA	Marcel Cadieux	Adolph W. Schmidt
Upper Volta	Georges Charpentier	Paul Tensoré Rouamba
Uruguay	A. P. Bissonnet	Hector Luisi, OBE
Vatican	J. E. Robbins	Most Rev. Guido del Mestri[3]
Venezuela	D. S. McPhail	Wolfgang Larrazabal
Yugoslavia	Bruce M. Williams	Dr Tode Curuvija
Zambia[1]	John A. Irwin	V. J. Mwaanga

[1] High Commissioner. [2] Chargé d'Affaires. [3] Pro-Nuncio. No figure = Ambassador.

AREA AND POPULATION. The following is the population of the area now included in Canada:

1851	2,436,297	1901	5,371,315	1951	14,009,429
1861	3,229,633	1911	7,206,643	1961	18,238,247
1871	3,689,257	1921	8,787,949	1968 (est.)	20,744,000
1881	4,324,810	1931	10,376,786[1]	1969 (est.)	21,061,000
1891	4,833,239	1941	11,506,655[1]	1960 (est.)	21,377,000

[1] Excluding population of Newfoundland: 289,588 in 1935, and 321,819 in 1945.

Estimated population, 1 Oct. 1970, was 21,489,000.

Areas of the provinces, etc. (in sq. miles) and population at recent censuses:

Province	Land area	Fresh water area	Total land and fresh water area	Population, 1956	Population, 1961	Population, 1966
Newfoundland	143,045	13,140	156,185	415,074	457,853	493,396
Prince Edward Island	2,184	—	2,184	99,285	104,629	108,535
Nova Scotia	20,402	1,023	21,425	694,717	737,007	756,039
New Brunswick	27,835	519	28,354	554,616	597,936	616,788
Quebec	523,860	71,000	594,860	4,628,378	5,259,211	5,780,845
Ontario	344,092	68,490	412,582	5,404,933	6,236,092	6,960,870
Manitoba	211,775	39,225	251,000	850,040	921,686	963,066
Saskatchewan	220,182	31,518	251,700	880,665	925,181	955,344
Alberta	248,800	6,485	255,285	1,123,116	1,331,944	1,463,203
British Columbia	359,279	6,976	366,255	1,398,464	1,629,082	1,873,674
Yukon	205,346	1,730	207,076	12,190	14,628	14,382
Northwest Territories	1,253,438	51,465	1,304,903	19,313	22,998	28,738
Total	3,560,238[1]	291,571[2]	3,851,809	16,080,791	18,238,247	20,014,880

[1] 9,221,001 sq. km. [2] 755,168 sq. km.

Of the total population in 1961, 15,393,984 were Canadian born, 1,017,602 other British born and 1,826,661 foreign born, 283,908 of the latter being USA born.

The population born outside Canada in the provinces was in the following ratio (%): Newfoundland, 1·37; Prince Edward Island, 2·86; Nova Scotia, 4·64; New Brunswick, 3·89; Quebec, 7·39; Ontario, 21·7; Manitoba, 18·44; Saskatchewan, 16·15; Alberta, 21·68; British Columbia, 25·97.

In 1961, figures for the population, according to origin, were:

British Isles		Polish	323,517	Belgian	61,382
English	4,195,175	Hebrew	173,344	Chinese	58,197
Scottish	1,902,302	Indian and Eskimo	220,121	Austrian	106,535
Irish	1,753,351	Italian	450,351	Romanian	43,805
Other	145,841	Norwegian	148,681	Icelandic	30,623
		Swedish	121,757	Japanese	29,157
Total, British	7,996,669	Russian	119,168	Yugoslav	68,587
		Czech and Slovak	73,061	Negro	32,127
French	5,540,346	Hungarian	126,220	Greek	56,475
German	1,049,599	Finnish	59,436	Lithuanian	27,629
Ukrainian	473,337	Danish	85,473	Not stated	210,382
Netherlands	429,679				

The native Indian population numbered 237,490 in 1969 and the Eskimo population was estimated at 16,000.

Populations of cities (proper) and census metropolitan area, 1966 census:

	City proper	Metropolitan area		City proper	Metropolitan area
Montreal	1,222,255	2,436,817	Halifax	86,792	198,193
Toronto	664,584	2,158,496	Sudbury	84,888	117,075
Vancouver	410,375	892,286	St John's	79,884	101,161
Edmonton	376,925	401,299	Oshawa	78,082	100,255
Calgary	330,575	330,575	Sherbrooke	75,690	79,667
Hamilton	298,121	449,116	Sault Ste Marie	74,594	74,594
Ottawa	290,741	494,535	Brantford	59,854	62,036
Winnipeg	257,005	508,759	Trois-Rivières	57,540	94,476
London	194,416	207,396	Victoria	57,453	173,455
Windsor	192,544	211,697	Niagara Falls	56,891	60,768
Quebec	166,984	413,397	Peterborough	56,177	56,177
Regina	131,127	131,127	Sarnia	54,552	66,713
Saskatoon	115,892	115,892	Saint John	51,567	101,192
Kitchener	93,255	192,275	Guelph	51,377	51,377

The total 'urban' population of Canada in 1961 was 12,971,927, against 14,726,759 in 1966.

While the registration of births, marriages and deaths is under provincial control, the statistics are compiled on a uniform system by the Dominion Bureau of Statistics

The following table gives the results for 1968:

	Living births		Marriages		Deaths	
Province	Number	Per 1,000 population	Number	Per 1,000 population	Number	Per 1,000 population
Newfoundland	12,820	25·3	4,242	8·4	3,123	6·2
Prince Edward Island	2,105	19·1	750	6·8	990	9·0
Nova Scotia	13,774	18·1	6,284	8·3	6,610	8·7
New Brunswick	11,607	18·6	5,389	8·6	4,905	7·9
Quebec	96,622	16·3	46,004	7·8	39,537	6·7
Ontario	126,257	17·3	62,109	8·5	55,552	7·6
Manitoba	17,424	17·9	8,291	8·5	7,878	8·1
Saskatchewan	18,197	19·0	7,747	8·1	7,498	7·8
Alberta	30,149	19·8	13,640	8·9	9,963	6·5
British Columbia	33,687	16·8	16,914	8·4	16,828	8·4
Yukon Territory	370	24·7	170	11·3	84	5·6
Northwest Territories	1,298	41·9	226	7·3	228	7·4
Total	364,310	17·6	171,766	8·3	153,196	7·4

Immigrant arrivals by country of last permanent residence:

Country	1965	1966	1967	1968	1969
England	28,820	43,561	43,481	28,623	24,556
Northern Ireland	1,934	2,400	2,644	1,477	1,491
Scotland	8,363	16,077	14,953	7,302	5,426
Wales	682	1,192	1,263	449	490
Lesser isles	58	61	79	38	14
Total, British Isles	39,857	63,291	62,420	37,889	31,977

Country	1965	1966	1967	1968	1969
Austria	1,472	2,313	2,745	8,125	..
Australia	2,150	3,329	4,967	3,710	..
China	4,352	4,094	6,409	8,382	..
France	5,225	7,872	10,122	8,184	..
Germany	8,927	9,263	11,779	8,966	..
Greece	5,642	7,174	10,650	7,739	..
India	2,241	2,233	3,966	3,229	..
Irish Republic	861	1,774	2,181	1,545	..
Israel	822	1,488	2,345	1,497	..
Italy	26,398	31,625	30,055	19,774	10,383
Jamaica	1,214	1,407	3,459	2,885	4,124
Netherlands	2,619	3,749	4,401	3,264	2,494
Philippines	1,502	2,639	2,994	2,678	3,001
Poland	1,975	1,678	1,470	1,092	859
Portugal	5,734	7,930	9,500	7,738	7,182
Switzerland	2,169	2,982	3,738	3,529	..
UAR	1,378	1,854	1,728	1,915	2,307
USA	15,143	17,514	19,038	20,422	22,785
Yugoslavia	1,230	1,502	2,089	4,660	4,053
Total, all countries	146,758	194,743	222,876	183,974	161,531

Blishen, B. R. (ed.), *Canadian Society: sociological perspectives.* 3rd ed. Toronto, 1965
Brunet, M., *La présence anglaise et les Canadiens.* Montreal, 1958
Card, B. Y., *Trends and Change in Canadian Society: their challenge to Canadian Youth.* Toronto, 1968
Clark, S. D., *Urbanism and the Changing Canadian Society.* 2nd ed. Toronto, 1970.—*The Developing Canadian Community.* 2nd ed. Toronto, 1968
Cowan, H. I., *British Emigration to British North America, the first hundred years.* Rev. ed. Toronto, 1961
Dawe, A., *Profiles of a Nation: Canadian Themes and Styles.* Toronto, 1970
Garigue, P., *La Vie familiale des Canadiens français.* Montreal, 1962
Geliner, J., and Smerek, J., *The Czechs and Slovaks in Canada.* Toronto, 1968
Iglauer, E., *The New People: The Eskimo's Journey in our Time.* New York, 1966
Jenness, D., *The Indians of Canada.* 5th ed. Ottawa, 1960
Kosa, J., *Land of Choice: the Hungarians in Canada.* Toronto, 1957
Park, J., *The Culture of Contempary Canada.* Toronto, 1970
Porter, J., *The Vertical Mosaic.* Toronto, 1965
Richmond, A. H., *Post-war Immigration in Canada.* Toronto, 1967
Rosenberg, S. E., *The Jewish Commmnity in Canada:* A History. Toronto, 1970
Wade, M., *The French Canadians, 1760–1967.* 2 vols. 2nd ed. Toronto and London, 1968

RELIGION. Membership of the leading denominations in 1961:

Province	Roman Catholic	United Church of Canada	Anglican Church of Canada	Presbyterian	Baptist
Newfoundland	163,618	97,886	130,688	2,510	693
Prince Edward Island	48,256	27,395	6,085	12,744	5,942
Nova Scotia	260,104	163,633	133,247	41,063	101,093
New Brunswick	310,607	85,710	68,165	13,546	94,070
Quebec	4,635,610	154,938	193,849	55,955	15,174
Ontario	1,873,110	1,640,564	1,117,862	491,436	250,343
Manitoba	210,871	269,975	127,487	29,661	17,247
Saskatchewan	242,888	296,253	94,593	25,080	16,184
Alberta	298,741	418,927	156,630	55,337	42,430
British Columbia	285,184	504,317	367,096	90,093	49,481
Yukon	3,981	2,519	4,516	823	710
Northwest Territories	9,856	1,891	8,850	310	186
Total Canada	8,342,826	3,664,008	2,409,068	818,558	593,553

Other denominations: Lutheran, 662,744; Greek Orthodox, 239,766; Ukrainian (Greek) Catholic, 189,653; Mennonite, 152,452; Pentecostal, 143,877; Jewish, 254,368; other, 767,374.

Boon, T. C. B., *The Anglican Church from the Bay to the Rockies.* Toronto, 1962
Walsh, H. H.. *The Christian Church in Canada.* Toronto, 1956
Wilson, D. J., *The Church Grows in Canada.* Toronto, 1966

EDUCATION. By the British North America Act each provincial government is responsible for its education system. While each system differs from the others in particulars, the general plan is similar for all provinces. Separate elementary and secondary schools for minority groups, mainly Roman Catholic, are found in most provinces. Though administration of the schools in Newfoundland has a denominational basis, they are not exclusive and a number are non-denominational. In general, education is free to the end of the secondary level. The principal sources of revenue are provincial government grants and direct taxation for school purposes. Except in Quebec the number of private schools is small; their enrolment was 3 % of the total in elementary and secondary grades.

The federal government operates schools for Indians and Eskimos with an enrolment in 1968–69 of 35,874. An additional 33,635 attend non-federal schools.

In 1969–70, 299,889 full-time regular students were enrolled in 61 degree-granting institutions, other than purely theological institutions, and 150 affiliated or independent colleges. Some 166,123 enrolled in arts and science, 25,733 in engineering, 17,870 in commerce and business administration, 8,746 in medicine, 6,661 in law 31,176 in education, and the remainder in more than 30 other faculties. Another 125,000 or more students were enrolled in part-time courses.

The following statistics give information, for 1969–70 (expenditure 1967-68), about all elementary and secondary schools, public, federal and private:

Province	Schools	Teachers	Pupils	Expenditure ($1,000)
Newfoundland	897	6,389	160,782	47,772
Prince Edward Island	268	1,489	29,764	11,066
Nova Scotia	757	10,166	216,205	87,626
New Brunswick	628	7,890	174,850	69,921
Quebec	4,175	75,485	1,592,820	830,750
Ontario	5,245	92,731	2,037,929	1,282,390
Manitoba	879	11,870	259,863	118,089
Saskatchewan	1,117	11,874	255,368	153,585
Alberta	1,313	20,372	422,738	264,193
British Columbia	1,658	22,085	529,091	284,593
Yukon and Northwest Territories	94	775	14,074	20,153
National Defence (overseas)	18	501	7,916	10,000
Total	17,047	261,627	5,701,400	3,180,138

CINEMAS (1968). There were 1,148 cinemas with a seating capacity of 649,344 and 261 drive-in theatres with a capacity of 106,231 cars.

NEWSPAPERS (1970). There were 120 daily newspapers, of which 102 are in English, 12 in French and 6 in other languages.

Canadian Universities and Colleges. 7th ed. Ottawa 1960 (both in English and French)
Craik, W. A., *History of Canadian Journalism.* 2 vols. Toronto, 1959
Harris, R. S., and Trembley, A., *A Bibliography of Higher Education in Canada.* Toronto and Quebec, 1960
Harrison, J. F. C., *Learning and Living, 1790–1960; a study in the history of the English adult education movement.* Toronto, 1961
Irving, J. A., *Mass Media in Canada.* Toronto, 1962
Katz, Joseph, *Elementary Education in Canada.* Toronto, 1961
Reeves, A. W. (ed.), *The Canadian School Principal.* Toronto, 1962
Sissons, C. B., *Church and State in Canadian Education.* Toronto, 1959
Thompson, W. P., *Graduate Education in the Sciences.* Toronto, 1963

JUSTICE.

There is a Supreme Court in Ottawa, having appellate, civil and criminal jurisdiction in and throughout Canada. There is an Exchequer Court, which is also a Court of Admiralty. There is a Superior Court in each province and county courts, with limited jurisdiction, in most of the provinces, all the judges in these courts being appointed by the Governor-General. Police magistrates and justices of the peace are appointed by the provincial governments. Police force, *see* p. 186.

For the year ended 31 Dec. 1967, 45,703 adults were convicted of 86,689 indictable offences; total offences punishable on summary conviction amounted to 2,395,466. The number of juvenile adjudged delinquents was, in 1967, 18,248.

Canadian Legal and Directory. Annual. Toronto
Anger, W. H., *Summary of Canadian Commercial Law.* 18th ed. Toronto, 1958
Gosse, R., *The Law on Competition in Canada.* Toronto, 1962
Houlden, L. W., *Bankruptcy Law of Canada.* Toronto, 1960
Jaffary, S. K., *Sentencing of Adults in Canada.* Toronto, 1963
Jameson, I. M. B., *Canadian Estate Tax.* Toronto, 1960

McRuer, J. D., *The Evolution of the Judicial Process*. Toronto, 1957
McWhinney, E., *Canadian Jurisprudence: civil law and common law*. Toronto, 1958
O'Connor, A. R. M., *An Analysis of and a Guide to the New Criminal Code*. Toronto, 1955
Rosenbluth, G., *Canadian Anticombines Administration, 1952–1960*. Toronto, 1963
Williamson, J. P., *Securities Regulation in Canada*. Toronto, 1960

SOCIAL WELFARE. During 1965 a compulsory, wage-related contributory programme of old-age, disability and survivors insurance was introduced. Known as the Canada Pension Plan, it provides a basic level of security for all Canadians. It covers virtually all working Canadians from age 18 with pension available at age 65. The plan, which became operative on 1 Jan. 1966, called for contributions on earnings between $600 and $5,000. The $5,000 ceiling was applied during the first 2 years and was subject to upward adjustment if there were increases in the Consumer Price Index (maximum adjustment per year is 2%). In 1971 this maximum was $5,400. Pensions will also be increased annually, by the same rate, as measured by the Consumer Price Index. The Act makes provision for a province to establish and operate its own provincial pension plan provided certain requirements are met. The Province of Quebec enacted similar legislation to establish the Quebec Pension Plan, which also commenced 1 Jan. 1966.

Existing Federal programmes of family allowances and old-age security will continue. Family allowances are paid at a rate of $6 a month for children under 10 and $8 for those aged 10–16. Legislation enacted in 1964 provided for payment of $10 a month in respect of children 16 and 17 attending full-time educational or training courses.

The Canada Pension Plan makes certain amendments to the Old Age Security Act. Commencing in 1971, $80 a month is payable at age 65 to persons meeting the residence test. Provision is made also for annual adjustments of the pension in line with increases in the Consumer Price Index. An amendment to the residence test permits eligibility of persons proving 40 years of residence in Canada since age 18.

Canada has a national system of unemployment insurance with compulsory coverage of persons under a contract of service unless specifically excepted. The National Employment Service, formerly operated by the Department of Labour, was transferred to the new Department of Manpower and Immigration in Oct. 1966 and became the key operational agency in the manpower field. Both employers and employees contribute to unemployment insurance. The federal government contributes one-fifth of the combined employer–employee contribution and pays administrative costs. From 1 July 1941 to 31 March 1970 employers and employees contributed $5,756m., to which the federal government added $1,151m.; benefit payments amounted to $6,804m.

The Canada Assistance Plan, a comprehensive public assistance measure to complement provisions of the Canada Pension Plan, received Royal Assent in July 1966. It provides a single administrative framework for federal sharing with the provinces of assistance and welfare services. It is designed to replace the 4 existing programmes of unemployment assistance, old age assistance, blind person's allowances and disabled person's allowances, but the provinces have the option of continuing the separate administration of the programme.

The Federal Hospital Insurance and Diagnostic Services Act 1957 provides for a system of federal grants-in-aid to the provinces to help meet the cost of specified hospital services.

Provincial legislation provides for compensation to a workman for injury by accident. Other provincial welfare programmes include general assistance and social allowances, mothers' allowances, services for the aged and child care. In most provinces responsibility for a number of programmes is shared by the provinces and their municipalities.

Clark, R. M., *Economic Security for the Aged in the United States and Canada*. 2 vols. Dept. of National Health and Welfare. Ottawa, 1959
Mercer, W. M., *Canadian Handbook of Pension and Welfare Plans*. 2nd ed. Toronto, 1959
Oliver, M. K. (ed.), *Social Purpose for Canada*. Toronto, 1961

FINANCE. Currency. The denominations of money in the currency of Canada are dollars and cents. The cent is one-hundredth part of a dollar. Subsidiary coins of the denominations of 1, 5, 10, 25 and 50 cents and $1 are in use. The monetary standard is gold of 900 millesimal fineness (23·22 grains of pure gold equal to 1 gold dollar). The Currency Act provides for gold coins in the denominations of $5, $10 and $20, which are legal tender. The British and US gold coins are also legal tender, at the par rate of exchange. The legal equivalent of the British sovereign is $4.86⅔.

The Bank of Canada has the sole right to issue paper money for circulation in Canada. Restrictions introduced by the 1944 revisions of the Bank Act cancelled the right of chartered banks to issue or re-issue notes after 1 Jan. 1945; and in Jan. 1950 the chartered banks' liability for such of their notes as then remained outstanding was transferred to the Bank of Canada in return for payment of a like sum to the Bank of Canada. On 31 May 1970 the Canadian dollar which was stabilized at 92·50 US cents was allowed to fluctuate. The value of the US$ in Canadian funds was 102·1 cents in Dec. 1970.

The Bank of Canada issues notes, which are legal tender, in denominations of $1, $2, $5, $10, $20, $50, $100, $500 and $1,000. Under the terms of the Bank of Canada Act, the bank is required to sell gold in bars of 400 oz. to any person tendering legal tender. This obligation is at the present time suspended by Order-in-Council. The exportation of gold from Canada is prohibited except by licence issued by the Minister of Finance to the Bank of Canada or a chartered bank.

The Ottawa Mint was established in 1908 as a branch of the Royal Mint, in pursuance of the Ottawa Mint Act, 1901. In Dec. 1931 control of the Mint was passed over to the Canadian Government, and since that time has operated as the Royal Canadian Mint. The Mint issues silver, nickel, bronze and steel coins for circulation in Canada. In 1967, in celebration of Canada's Centennial of Confederation, a $20 gold piece was minted, the first gold coin struck since 1919. In 1935, on the occasion of His Majesty's Silver Jubilee, the Royal Canadian Mint issued the first Canadian silver dollars. Commemorative dollars were also issued in 1939 on the occasion of the visit of King George VI and Queen Elizabeth to Canada; in 1949, when Newfoundland became the tenth Province of Canada; in 1958, the one-hundredth anniversary of the establishment of the Colony of British Columbia; in 1964, the centennial of the Charlottetown and Quebec Conferences which paved the way to confederation. The silver dollar bearing the design of the canoe manned by an Indian and a Voyageur has been issued in the years 1935–38, 1945–48, 1950–57, 1959–63, and 1965 and 1966. For centennial year the Canada goose replaced the usual canoe design on the silver dollar. Because of a world-wide shortage of silver, the Government, in Aug. 1967, authorized the Mint to change the metal content of the 25-cent and 10-cent coins. Commencing in Sept. 1968, the 10-cent, 25-cent, 50-cent and $1 coins were minted in pure nickel. No silver dollars have been minted since 1967.

Gold refining is one of the principal activities of the Mint. In 1969, 2,146,506 troy oz. of fine gold were received for treatment, and 2,089,226 troy oz. of bullion were issued. Coin issued: Bronze, $3,300,505; nickel, $41,704,879.

Budget. Budgetary revenue and expenditure of the Government of Canada for years ended 31 March (in Canadian $):

	1965–66	1966–67	1967–68	1968–69	1969–70
Revenue	7,695,820,204	8,358,178,383	9,029,305,904	10,162,843,413	12,312,812,713
Expenditure	7,734,795,525	8,779,680,996	9,824,080,573	10,738,956,256	11,937,601,593

Budgetary revenue, 1969–70 (in Canadian $):

Income tax, personal	4,085,120,802	Estate tax	100,630,908
Income tax, corporation	2,611,961,028	Other tax revenue	248,762,146
Sales and other excise taxes	2,095,322,916	Post office, net revenue	354,752,869
Excise duties	518,844,479	Return on investments	860,028,750
Customs import duties	818,282,786	Other non-tax revenue	142,606,029

Details of budgetary expenditure, year ended 31 March 1970 (in Canadian $):

Agriculture	383,833,688	Industry, Trade and Commerce	263,736,936
Atomic Energy	74,885,613	Justice	19,661,561
Auditor-General	2,865,748	Labour	155,519,032
Canadian Broadcasting Corporation	166,000,000	Manpower and Immigration	439,510,592
		National Defence	1,789,508,003
Central Mortgage and Housing Corporation	43,590,285	National Health and Welfare	1,957,028,538
		National Research Council	121,651,855
Communications (including Post Office)	353,944,314	National Revenue	144,583,159
		Parliament	22,988,752
Consumer and Corporate Affairs	16,697,483	Privy Council	11,256,175
		Public Works	288,244,032
Dominion Bureau of Statistics	32,393,197	Regional Economic Expansion	236,060,698
Energy, Mines and Resources	120,853,553	Secretary of State	387,497,162
External Affairs	242,225,671	Solicitor-General	184,084,217
Finance	2,849,590,304	Supply and Services	80,820,561
Fisheries and Forestry	76,866,896	Transport	467,342,612
Governor-General and Lieutenant-Governors	1,124,040	Treasury Board	269,443,206
		Veterans Affairs	422,359,151
Indian Affairs and Northern Development	311,434,559		

On 31 March 1970 the net debt was $16,960,626,870.

Foreign Debts. The following amounts (in $1m.) were outstanding on 31 March 1970 on loans to national governments: Belgium, 16·1; China 49·4 (inactive); France, 66·9; Greece, 6·5 (inactive); Netherlands, 32·1; Romania 24·3 (inactive). On the same date, under the Financial Agreement Act between Britain and Canada, the amount outstanding was $1,038m.

Canadian Fiscal Facts; principal statistics of Canadian public finance. Canadian Tax Foundation Toronto, 1957; suppl. 1958

Ferns, H. H., *Mathematics of Canadian Finance.* Toronto, 1963

Fullerton, D. H., *The Bond Market in Canada.* Toronto, 1962

Perry, J. H., *Taxation in Canada.* 3rd ed. rev. Toronto, 1961.—*Taxes, Tariffs and Subsidies,* Toronto, 1955

Robinson, A. J., (ed.), *Public Finance, Selected Readings.* Toronto, 1968

DEFENCE. The control and management of all matters relating to national defence, the Canadian Armed Forces (which were constituted as a single service on 1 Feb. 1968), and the Defence Research Board are the responsibility of the Minister of National Defence.

Effective 1 Aug. 1964, the Headquarters of the Royal Canadian Navy, the Canadian Army and the Royal Canadian Air Force were integrated to form a single Canadian Forces Headquarters (CFHQ) under a single Chief of Defence Staff, who provides military advice to the Minister of National Defence and controls and administers the Canadian Forces through CFHQ. CFHQ is organized in 4 functional branches headed by the Vice-Chief of Defence Staff, the Chief of Personnel, the Chief of Technical Services and the Comptroller General. The civilian administration of the Department is organized under the Deputy Minister.

COMMAND STRUCTURE. The Canadian forces are organized on a functional basis to reflect the major commitments assigned by the Government. All forces devoted to a primary mission are grouped under a single commander who is assigned sufficient resources to discharge his responsibilities. Specifically, the Canadian forces are formed into 7 major entities reporting to the Chief of the Defence Staff. These are as follows:

1. *Mobile Command* provides units trained and equipped to support the United Nations or other peacekeeping operations; provides ground forces, including tactical air support, for the protection of Canadian territory; maintains combat formations in Canada for support of overseas commitments. It is comprised of 3 infantry brigade groups in Canada; the United Nations force in Cyprus; one RCAF reconnaissance squadron; one transport helicopter platoon. Two of the brigade groups in Canada are being reorganized and will be provided with airportable equipment. New support aircraft being delivered to Mobile Command include 115 CF-5 supersonic fighter-bombers, 50 CUH-1N twin-engined helicopters and 74 OH-58A Kiowa light observation helicopters.

Fourth Canadian Infantry Brigade Group (4 CIBG) is the Canadian contribution to NATO ground forces in Europe. It also contains a surface-to-surface missile (Honest John) battery in addition to the normal field artillery regiment.

2. *Maritime Command.* All maritime sea and air forces on the Atlantic and Pacific coasts have been placed under the Commander, Maritime Command, with headquarters in Halifax, Nova Scotia. The Maritime Commander (Pacific), who is the Deputy Commander, has his headquarters in Esquimalt, British Columbia. Maritime Command is to defend Canada against attack from the sea; provide anti-submarine defence in support of NATO; conduct search and rescue operations on the east and west coast; provide sea transport in support of Mobile Command. Composition of the maritime forces includes 22 destroyer-escorts, 2 supply ships; 4 submarines, 6 small support and training vessels; 4 air squadrons of CP-107 Argus maritime reconnaissance aircraft and 6 naval air squadrons. Sea King helicopters are operated from destroyers.

3. *No. 1 Air Division* is the Canadian contribution to the strike-reconnaissance forces available to the Supreme Allied Commander Europe (SACEUR). The division is operationally responsible to the Fourth Allied Tactical Air Force (4 ATAF) and had originally 6 squadrons equipped with CF-104 Super Starfighters located at airfields in Germany. This force is being reduced to 3 squadrons (2 strike, 1 reconnaissance) as No. 1 Canadian Air Group of Mobile Command.

4. *Air Defence Command* participates with the USA in the air defence of North America through NORAD. The forces assigned to Air Defence Command are 3 CF-101B Voodoo all-weather interceptor squadrons, 2 Bomarc surface-to-air missile (SAM) squadrons, one semi-automatic ground environment (SAGE) control centre and 2 trans-continental radar lines. Operational control is exercised by HQ NORAD.

5. *Air Transport Command* supplies air transport to Canadian forces everywhere; conducts search and rescue operations in most of Ontario and Quebec. The command comprises 4 squadrons operating short-range, long-range and troop-carrying aircraft; including C-130 Hercules, CC-115 Buffalo, CC-109 Cosmopolitan, Fan Jet Falcon, C-47, and CC-137 (Boeing 707-320C). Two of the 4CC-137s are equipped as flight refuelling tankers.

6. *Training Command* provides training for the forces and conducts search and rescue operations in the Prairie Provinces. The Canadian Services Colleges (Royal Military College, Royal Roads and Collège militaire royal de Saint-Jean), the Staff Colleges and medical–dental training are under the direct control of CFHQ. While operational training in land–air warfare is the responsibility of Mobile Command, basic parachute training and basic fixed-wing or helicopter pilot training are a Training Command responsibility.

7. *Canadian Forces Communications System* (*CFCS*) provides fixed communications networks for the forces and a national communications system for survival operations (civil defence). CFCS commands all fixed communications installations in Canada.

8. *Reserve and Survival Organization.* Command and administration of the army reserves is effected through 5 Regional and 7 District Headquarters, responsible to the Deputy Chief of Reserves through the appropriate functional commanders. The reserves provide aid to the civil power, emergency forces for the national survival and a training force to support the regular forces.

Canadian Armed Forces expenditures amounted to $1,693,309,501 in 1967–68 and $1,695,871,969 in 1966–67. Estimates for 1969–70 and for the next 2 fiscal years were fixed at $1,800m. Strength of the Regular Forces in Oct. 1969 was 95,019, comprised of RCN, 17,555; Canadian Army, 36,255; RCAF, 42,100.

NAVY. In Dec. 1970 the Fleet included 4 submarines, 20 destroyer escorts, 6 coastal minesweepers, 2 escort maintenance ships, 4 patrol craft, 6 oceanographic research vessels, 4 gate vessels, 3 22,000-ton operational support ships, a diving depot ship (*ex*-frigate), 3 supply vessels, 2 oilers, 10 tenders and 28 tugs.

Four destroyer helicopter carriers are being built in Canada. The aircraft carrier *Bonaventure* (ex-*Powerful*) paid off on 1 April 1970 and was scrapped.

Thirty Canadian warships are allocated to the NATO naval forces under control of the Supreme Allied Commander, Atlantic (SACLANT).

In 1970 the naval personnel strength of Maritime Command was 14,770 officers and men.

The Navy estimates amounted to $300m. in 1967–68; $283·2m. in 1968–69; $359·7m. in 1969–70; $360m. in 1970–71 (Maritime Command).

POLICE FORCES. The police forces of Canada are organized in three groups: (1) the federal force, which is the Royal Canadian Mounted Police; (2) provincial police forces—the Provinces of Ontario and Quebec have their own provincial police forces, but all other provinces engage the services of the Royal Canadian Mounted Police to perform parallel functions within their borders, and (3) municipal police forces—each urban centre of reasonable size maintains its own police force or engages the services of the provincial police, under contract, to attend to police matters. In addition, the Canadian National Railways, the Canadian Pacific Railway Company and the National Harbours Board have their own police forces.

ROYAL CANADIAN MOUNTED POLICE. It was organized in 1873 as the North West Mounted Police, to provide police protection in the unsettled portions of the north-west. In 1904 the title 'Royal' was given to the force. In 1920 the Dominion Police was amalgamated with it and the name was changed to the Royal Canadian Mounted Police. The headquarters was moved from Regina to Ottawa, and the force may now be called upon to perform duties in any portion of Canada. In 1928 the Royal Canadian Mounted Police absorbed the Saskatchewan Provincial Police, and in 1932 the Provincial Police Forces of Alberta, Manitoba, New Brunswick, Nova Scotia and Prince Edward Island. During 1932 the Force also assumed the administration of the Preventive Service Branch of the Department of National Revenue. In Aug. 1950 the Royal Canadian Mounted Police absorbed the Newfoundland Rangers and selected members of the Newfoundland Constabulary whose duties are outside the City of St John's. The British Columbia Provincial Police were also absorbed by the Royal Canadian Mounted Police in 1950. The Force is under the jurisdiction of the Solicitor-General of Canada.

The term of engagement in the Royal Canadian Mounted Police is 5 years. Recruits are trained at Regina, Sask., and Ottawa, Ont.

In March 1970 the Force had a total strength of 9,925, including marine and special constables. It maintained 2,894 motor vehicles. 38 police service dogs and 122 horses.

The Force has 12 divisions actively engaged in law enforcement, one Headquarters Division and 3 training divisions. In addition it maintains a Marine Division and Air Division with headquarters at Ottawa. The Marine Division also has establishments at Halifax, N.S. and Esquimalt, B.C. and is comprised of 60 ships and boats which operate on the east and west coasts, the Great Lakes and the St Lawrence River. The Air Division has stations throughout Canada and maintains 22 aircraft.

Canada's Army in Korea. Dept. of National Defence. Ottawa, 1956
Dornbusch, C. E., *The Canadian Army 1855–1958; regimental histories.* Cornwallville, N.Y., 1959
Eayrs, J., *In Defence of Canada.* 2 vols. Toronto, 1965
Feasby, W. R. (ed.), *Official History of the Canadian Medical Services, 1939–45.* 2 vols. Dept. of National Defence. Ottawa, 1953–56
Goodspeed, D. J., *A History of the Defence Research Board of Canada.* Defence Research Board, Ottawa, 1958
Roberts, L., *There Shall Be Wings; a history of the Royal Canadian Air Force.* Toronto, 1960
Schull, J., *The Far Distant Ships: an official account of Canadian naval operations in the Second World War.* Ottawa, Queen's Printer, 1952
Stacey, C. P., *Six Years of War: Official History of the Canadian Army.* 3 vols. Ottawa, Queen's Printer, 1955–60
Stanley, G. F. G., *Canada's Soldiers; the military history of an unmilitary people.* Rev. ed. Toronto, 1960
Swettenham, J., *Canada and the First World War.* Toronto, 1970
Tucker, G. N., *The Naval Service of Canada: its official history.* 2 vols. Ottawa, Queen's Printer, 1952

AGRICULTURE. Though the manufacturing industries now predominate, agriculture is very important to the Canadian economy. It contributes between 9 and 12% of the net value of production and in 1969 accounted for 12% of the value of commodities exported. It is estimated that about 48% of the total land area is forested; according to the census of 1966, 272,070 sq. miles (less than 8% of the total land area) is classed as occupied agricultural land. Grain growing, dairy farming, fruit farming, ranching and fur farming are all carried on successfully. The following table shows the estimated value of agricultural production for 1969, in $1,000 Canadian:

Field crops	2,278,534[1]	Poultry meat	255,071	Vegetables	82,164
Livestock on farms	2,789,861	Eggs	202,735	Fruits	87,034[1]
Milk production	742,763	Poultry	158,175	Maple products	9,047
Butter, creamery	244,997	Tobacco	162,925	Honey	8,817

[1] Revised figures for 1968.

Number of occupied farms (census of 1966) was 430,522.

IRRIGATION. Large-scale irrigation in Canada began with the passing of the North West Irrigation Act, 1894. With the transfer of the natural resources in 1931, the administration of water rights, excepting international streams, became a provincial responsibility. The Prairie Farm Rehabilitation Act, 1935, marked the beginning of a new phase whereby the Dominion Government was to undertake construction of large irrigation works, to provide assistance for individual projects, as well as to conduct surveys and prepare plans. About 1·5m. acres have been or are being developed out of a potentially irrigable 3m. acres.

Irrigation projects are in operation in Alberta with an irrigable area of about 1m. acres, when completed; the St Mary, Belly and Waterton Rivers Project irrigates about 510,000 acres. A total of 216,000 acres of land are irrigated in British Columbia, mainly for the growing of small fruits and vegetables and for dairying. Construction of the South Saskatchewan River project began in 1959; it is to irrigate 500,000 acres. Other projects are being developed in Manitoba (Wilson Creek, Assiniboine dam, etc.).

FIELD CROPS. In 1968, 66,252,000 acres were under principal field crops with an estimated total value of $2,278,534,000. The most valuable field crops are wheat, tame hay, oats, barley, potatoes, corn for grain, flaxseed, mixed grains, rapeseed, fodder corn, soybeans and sugar-beet. The estimated acreage and yield of the principal field crops, by provinces, in 1969 were:

	Wheat		Tame hay		Oats	
	1,000	1,000	1,000	1,000	1,000	1,000
Provinces	acres	bu.	acres	tons	acres	bu.
Prince Edward Island	3	92	175	354	71	4,089
Nova Scotia	3	138	207	381	24	1,248
New Brunswick	4	122	229	412	69	3,167
Quebec	29	754	3,300	7,029	975	38,415
Ontario	369	14,570	3,150	8,631	810	42,768
Manitoba	2,500	64,000	1,000	1,900	1,530	69,000
Saskatchewan	16,600	461,000	1,200	1,670	2,100	107,000
Alberta	5,300	140,000	2,900	4,000	2,000	102,000
British Columbia	160	3,600	445	1,200	76	3,700
Total Canada	24,968	684,276	12,606	25,577	7,655	371,387

	Barley		Potatoes		Corn for grain	
	1,000	1,000	1,000	1,000	1,000	1,000
Provinces	acres	bu.	acres	cwt.	acres	bu.
Prince Edward Island	20	1,054	53	10,494	—	—
Nova Scotia	7	304	4	691	—	—
New Brunswick	10	409	62	11,786	—	—
Quebec	24	866	68	7,698	45	3,483
Ontario	315	15,750	46	8,531	930	69,843
Manitoba	1,200	42,000	29	3,800	3	64
Saskatchewan	2,700	109,000	7	573	—	—
Alberta	5,100	204,000	27	4,500	—	—
British Columbia	160	5,000	10	2,150	—	—
Total Canada	9,535	378,383	306	50,223	978	73,390

Provinces	Flaxseed		Mixed grains		Rapeseed	
	1,000 acres	1,000 bu.	1,000 acres	1,000 bu.	1,000 acres	1,000 bu.
Prince Edward Island	—	—	60	3,528	—	—
Nova Scotia	—	—	13	651	—	—
New Brunswick	—	—	9	417	—	—
Quebec	17	192	94	3,752	—	—
Ontario	3	46	855	50,018	—	—
Manitoba	1,100	11,200	190	7,100	196	3,500
Saskatchewan	770	11,300	135	5,600	1,000	19,600
Alberta	550	8,000	380	16,000	816	14,000
British Columbia	1	10	6	280	—	—
Total Canada	2,441	30,748	1,740	87,346	2,012	37,100

Provinces	Fodder corn		Soybeans		Sugar-beet	
	1,000 acres	1,000 tons	1,000 acres	1,000 bu.	1,000 acres	1,000 bu.
Prince Edward Island	—	—	—	—	—	—
Nova Scotia	—	—	—	—	—	—
New Brunswick	—	—	—	—	—	—
Quebec	93	1,086	—	—	9	158
Ontario	550	6,985	322	7,664	..	..
Manitoba	23	157	—	—	31	343
Saskatchewan	5	20	—	—	—	—
Alberta	—	—	—	—	39	577
British Columbia	11	211	—	—	—	—
Total Canada	682	8,459	322	7,664	79	1,078

LIVESTOCK. In parts of Saskatchewan and Alberta stockraising is still carried on as a primary industry, but the livestock of the Dominion at large is mainly a subsidiary of mixed farming. The following table shows the numbers of livestock (in 1,000) by provinces in 1970:

Provinces	Horses	Milch cows	Other cattle	Sheep and lambs	Swine	Poultry
Prince Edward Island	4	36	83	10	112	357
Nova Scotia	5	47	93	40	72	3,273
New Brunswick	5	41	82	24	54	1,674
Quebec	43	1,046	899	98	1,185	26,321
Ontario	68	870	2,292	247	2,145	33,887
Manitoba	30	118	1,002	47	884	9,657
Saskatchewan	65	115	2,271	126	985	7,466
Alberta	80	198	3,337	247	1,600	11,220
British Columbia	26	80	450	59	49	8,800
Total 1970	325	2,551	10,519	898	7,086	102,649
Total 1969	341	2,584	9,883	883	6,090	92,473

Net production of farm eggs in 1961, 430·4m. doz. ($153·39m.); 1962, 433·7m. doz. ($152,497,000); 1963, 417·2m. doz. ($160,178,000); 1964, 435·6m. doz. ($142,472,000); 1965, 431·3m. doz. ($156,604,000); 1966, 416·8m. doz. ($178,427,000); 1967, 442·1m. doz. ($155·9m.); 1968, 452·9m. doz. ($171·4m.); 1969, 471·2m. doz. ($202·7m.).

Wool production (in 1m. lb.), 1960, 7·8; 1961, 7·5; 1962, 7·2; 1963, 6·8; 1964, 6·3; 1965, 5·8; 1966, 5; 1967, 3·8; 1968, 3·5; 1969, 3·5.

DAIRYING. The dairy industry has shown a marked tendency towards centralization; the number of establishments decreased between 1961 and 1969 from 1,710 to 1,037 (almost 40%), whereas employment, wages, revenues, etc., have remained constant Production, 1969: Creamery butter, 349·8m. lb.; factory cheese, 206·6m. lb.; milk, 18,696m. lb.

FRUIT FARMING. The value of fruit production by provinces in 1968 was (in $1,000): Ontario, 36,282; British Columbia, 31,562; Quebec, 13,018; Nova Scotia, 4,078; New Brunswick, 1,609; Prince Edward Island, 337; Newfoundland, 148. Total apple production in Canada in 1968 was 20,081,000 bu.

TOBACCO. The production in 1969 of tobacco, which is practically confined to Ontario and Quebec, was estimated at 247m. lb. from 132,752 acres and valued at $163m.

FORESTRY. The total area of land covered by forests is estimated at 1,710,788 sq. miles, of which 57% is capable of producing merchantable timber.

Lumber production (in 1,000 bd ft) 1963, 9,489,025; 1964, 10,424,525; 1965, 10,166,874; 1966, 10,007,790; 1967, 9,962,480; 1968, 10,754,523.

The gross value of lumber production (including all saw-mill products) in 1968 was $1,179,513,000. Pulp production rose to a record 16·8m. tons in 1968 and 15·9m. tons in 1967. In the same years newsprint production amounted to 8,204,000 tons (8,108,000 tons in 1967) and was valued at $1,015,794,000 ($998,832,000 in 1967).

FISHERIES. During 1969, landings in Canadian commercial fisheries reached 2,731·6m. lb. The landed value was $183m. and the estimated market value exceeded $381m. The landed value of principal fish in 1969 was (in $1,000): Salmon, 30,109; cod, 22,891; lobster, 29,443; scallops, 12,058; herring (including sardines), 11,420; halibut, 15,871; redfish,5,883.

MINING. Ontario, Alberta, Quebec, British Columbia and Saskatchewan are the chief mining provinces. The total value of the mineral produced in 1969 was $4,690,642,200. The principal minerals produced in 1969 were as follows:

Metallics	Quantity	Value ($)
Copper (lb.)	1,116,455,909	574,193,275
Nickel (lb.)	426,650,432	482,412,858
Iron ore (tons)	40,000,640	431,930,310
Zinc (lb.)	2,392,581,968	364,390,237
Lead (lb.)	630,063,880	95,391,671
Gold (troy oz.)	2,502,169	94,331,773
Silver (troy oz.)	43,092,976	83,169,443
Molybdenum (lb.)	30,291,644	52,623,117
Uranium, U_3O_8 (lb.)	7,709,547	49,665,506
Total metallics	..	2,320,947,545
Non-metallics		
Asbestos (tons)	1,596,450	196,759,000
Potash, K_2O (tons)	3,146,160	67,119,877
Sulphur, elemental (tons)	2,984,937	62,986,315
Salt (tons)	4,247,170	29,424,420
Titanium dioxide	..	29,066,600
Gypsum (tons)	6,871,971	13,433,102
Total non-metallics	..	447,088,679
Fuels		
Petroleum, crude (bbls)	407,498,677	1,010,230,132
Natural gas (1,000 cu. ft)	1,985,280,751	263,564,593
Natural gas, by-products (bbls)	66,106,853	135,566,258
Coal (tons)	10,635,098	52,038,954
Total fuels	..	1,461,399,937
Structural materials		
Cement (tons)	8,543,622	171,257,887
Sand and gravel (tons)	204,060,000	130,650,000
Stone (tons)	70,069,100	88,194,500
Clay products (bricks, tiles, etc.)	..	50,995,351
Lime (tons)	1,718,155	20,108,301
Total structural materials	..	461,206,039

Value (in Canadian $) of mineral production by provinces:

Provinces	1968	1969	Provinces	1968	1969
Newfoundland	309,711,994	239,093,692	Saskatchewan	357,173,719	347,652,483
Pr. Ed. Island	976,742	1,050,000	Alberta	1,091,749,049	1,193,279,802
Nova Scotia	56,927,553	54,175,233	British Columbia	389,311,009	422,765,745
New Brunswick	88,451,436	98,393,595	Yukon Territory	21,365,555	37,655,800
Quebec	728,783,871	720,067,082	N.W. Territories	115,636,016	116,456,132
Ontario	1,355,628,670	1,214,456,935			
Manitoba	209,625,533	245,595,701	Total	4,725,341,147	4,690,642,200

With the discovery of large oilfields in Alberta, the production of petroleum became a major Canadian industry. The Interprovincial Pipeline, Canada's longest oil pipeline, has a right-of-way length of 2,025 miles from the Redwater oilfields in the Edmonton area to Port Credit, Ontario, near Toronto, and includes a 95-mile lateral line to Buffalo, New York. The total pipeline mileage in the right-of-way was 4,680 miles at the end of 1969. It serves 19 refineries in Canada and 17 in the USA. Another pipeline, Trans Mountain, extends from Edmonton to Vancouver, with a right-of-way length of 780 miles and a total pipe mileage of 930 miles. Eight refineries, 5 in Canada and 3 in Washington State, are served by the pipeline. At the end of 1969 Canada's oil pipeline system had 14,832 miles of line in operation. Net oil deliveries in 1969 were 678,888,399 bbls. The Trans-Canada natural gas line is the longest in the world (3,638 miles in 1969). It brings natural gas from the Alberta–Saskatchewan border across the prairies, through northern Ontario to Toronto, then eastward to Montreal. Natural gas pipeline mileage totalled about 54,942 miles in 1969. Net deliveries of natural gas into the pipelines in 1969 was 1,642,288·5m. cu. ft.

MANUFACTURES. Statistics for 1968, for the 20 leading industries:

Industry	Em-ployees	Salaries and wages ($1,000)	Cost of materials ($1,000)	Value of shipments of goods of own manufacture ($1,000)
Motor vehicle manufacturers	39,113	349,509	2,195,259	2,935,721
Pulp and paper mills	73,498	552,162	1,183,007	2,446,874
Slaughtering and meat processors	30,541	190,975	1,448,572	1,772,506
Petroleum refining	9,091	80,010	1,315,863	1,621,887
Iron and steel mills	44,634	323,573	630,974	1,367,087
Motor-vehicle parts and accessories manu- facturers	39,454	280,666	667,993	1,193,805
Dairy factories	39,841	160,943	874,206	1,184,638
Sawmills and planing mills	48,031	264,538	634,164	1,179,572
Miscellaneous machinery and equipment manufacturers	47,810	313,711	489,930	1,008,012
Smelting and refining	34,719	250,948	382,435	932,585
Manufacturers of industrial chemicals	20,365	157,258	342,555	846,952
Metal stamping, pressing and coating in- dustry	29,555	185,161	418,087	771,323
Miscellaneous food manufacturers	15,882	91,598	384,480	676,825
Communications equipment manufacturers	43,117	248,880	285,718	674,468
Aircraft and parts manufacturers	35,143	257,734	293,962	653,899
Commercial printing	38,437	239,714	244,987	624,142
Publishing and printing	34,113	219,774	131,713	537,863
Feed manufacturers	9,258	48,410	397,698	513,297
Fruit and vegetable canners and preservers	19,343	90,073	302,015	509,986
Bakeries	32,341	153,634	214,669	484,135

FUR TRADE. In 1968–69 (year ended 30 June), 3,920,332 wild-life pelts valued at $18,663,153, were taken. Beaver furs led in total value, followed by seals, muskrat, mink, squirrel, fox and lynx. The most important animals raised on fur farms are mink, chinchilla, fox and nutria. The value of pelts from fur farms in 1968 was $22,925,933, of which mink accounted for $22,689,586 (99%). There were, in 1968, 2,585 fur farms, of which 1,395 reported chinchilla and 1,147 mink.

WATER POWER. Canada is richly endowed with water-power resources; on 31 Dec. 1968 the estimated undeveloped water-power resources was 63,783,000 kw. available 50% of the time. The installed capacity was 35,908,000 kw., of which 69% was hydro power and 31% thermal. Utilities accounted for 85% of the generating capacity and 82% of the net generation in 1968. The total net electric energy generated in 1968 was 175,374·38m. kwh. In 1968 gross revenue from 6,512,556 customers was $1,472,567,000. A treaty signed in Washington 17 Jan. 1961 provides for the joint development of Columbia River basin by Canada and the US. The treaty will run for 60 years. The US has the option to build the Libby Dam on the Kootenay in northern Montana within 5 years of ratification. Canada will build 3 dams, at Arrow Lake, Mica Creek and Duncan Lake.

Canadian Mines Handbook. Annual. Toronto, from 1931
Caves, R. E., and Holton, R. H., *The Canadian Economy: Prospect and Retrospect*. Harvard Univ. Press, 1959
Currie, A. W., *Economic Geography of Canada*. Toronto, 1949.—*Canadian Economic Development*. Toronto, 1951
Hanson, E. J., *Dynamic Decade*. Toronto, 1958
Innis, H. A., *The Fur Trade in Canada*. Rev. ed. Toronto Univ. Press, 1956.—*The Cod Fisheries*. Rev. ed. Toronto, 1954
LeBourdais, D. M., *Metals and Men: the story of Canadian mining*. Toronto, 1957.—*Canada and the Atomic Revolution*. Toronto, 1959
Lougheed, W. F., *Secondary Manufacturing Industry in the Canadian Economy*. Toronto, 1961
Main, O. W., *The Canadian Nickel Industry*. Toronto, 1955
Robinson, J. L., *Resources of the Canadian Shield*. Toronto, 1969.
Scott, Anthony, *Natural Resources: the economics of conservation*. Toronto, 1955
Stovel, J. A., *Canada in the World Economy*. Harvard Univ. Press, 1959
Strange, H. G. L., *A Short History of Prairie Agriculture*. Winnipeg, 1954
Wilson, G. W., and others, *Canada: An Appraisal of its needs and resources*. Toronto, 1965.

LABOUR. In Oct. 1969 the industrial distribution of the employed was estimated as follows (in 1,000): Manufacturing, 1,829; service, 1,961; trade 1,280; agriculture, 548; other primary industries, 208; construction, 505; transportation and other utilities, 685; finance, insurance and real estate, 365; public administration, 447; total employed, 7,828; unemployed, 314.

About 34% of Canada's non-agricultural paid workers belong to trade unions, which had 2·17m. members in Jan. 1969. Almost 75% of the organized workers are members of unions affiliated with the Canadian Labour Congress, and over 10% are in affiliates of another central body, the Confederation of National Trade Unions. More than 1·4m. of the union members were in international unions, which have branches both in Canada and the United States and in most cases belong to central labour organizations in both countries.

It is generally established by legislation, both federal and provincial, that a trade union to which the majority of employees in a unit suitable for collective bargaining belong, is given certain rights and duties. An employer is required to meet and negotiate with such a trade union to determine wage-rates and other working conditions of his employees. The employer, the trade union and the employees affected are bound by the resulting agreement. If an impasse is reached in negotiation conciliation services provided by the appropriate government are available. Generally, work stoppages may not take place until an established conciliation procedure has been carried out and are prohibited while an agreement is in effect. Nearly half the workers affected by collective agreements are in the manufacturing industry.

Freedom of association is a civil right in Canada, and under common law workers are at liberty to join unions and participate in their activities. This right has also been guaranteed by statutes which make it an offence to interfere with freedom of association.

Certain specific minimum standards in regard to working conditions are set by law, for the most part by provincial labour legislation. Minimum wages, maximum hours of work or an overtime rate of pay after a specified number of hours, minimum weekly rest periods and annual vacations with pay are established for the majority of workers.

Workmen injured in the course of employment or disabled by industrial disease are required to receive compensation under workmen's compensation laws which apply to most employees except agricultural workers. Benefits during the period of disability for work are set by law at a proportion (now 75%) of the workman's average earnings, subject to a maximum established in each province. Benefits (which also include monthly allowances to dependants in the case of the death of a workman caused by an accident or disease arising out of his employment) are paid out of an accident fund administered by a government board in each province. The fund is made up of contributions from employers according to an annual assessment rate, varying from a few cents to several dollars per $100 of payroll according to the hazards of the industry.

Dept. of Labour, *Working Conditions in Canadian Inudstry.* Annual, Ottawa.
Cameron, J. C., *The Status of Trade Unions in Canada.* Kingston, 1960
Carrothers, A. W. R., *Labour Arbitration in Canada.* Toronto, 1961
Crysler, A. C., *Handbook on Canadian Labour Law.* Toronto, 1957
Jamieson, S., *Industrial Relations in Canada.* Toronto, 1957
Woods, H. D., *Labour Policy and Labour Economics in Canada.* Toronto, 1962

COMMERCE. In the past the custom tariff of Canada has been protective, with a preferential tariff in favour of the UK, the Dominions, a number of the Crown Colonies, and the Irish and South African Republics. At the Imperial Economic Conference of 1932, held in Ottawa, the UK developed further the policy of preferential tariffs to the Dominions, and on the part of the latter there was a general lowering of the existing tariffs against certain lines of UK manufacturers. Canada is one of the signatories of the General Agreement on Tariffs and Trade (GATT) and of the Kennedy Round agreements.

Imports for home consumption and domestic exports (in $1,000 Canadian) for calendar years (merchandise only):

	Imports	Exports		Imports	Exports
1960	5,482,695	5,255,575	1965	8,633,430	8,522,953
1962	6,257,776	6,178,523	1966	9,866,841	10,070,766
1963	6,558,209	6,798,529	1967	11,075,199	11,120,674
1964	7,489,707	8,094,360	1968	12,357,982	13,250,960

Exports (domestic) by principal countries in 1969 (in $1,000 Canadian):

Australia	163,258		Belgium and Luxembourg	116,232
Bahamas	15,213		Bolivia	2,086
Bahrain	86		Brazil	50,246
Barbados	8,762		Burma	1,469
Bermuda	9,060		Cameroun Republic	853
Britain	1,096,480		Chile	22,837
British Honduras	1,720		China	122,418
British Oceania	72		Colombia	18,778
Ceylon	3,153		Congo (K.)	1,394
Cyprus	494		Costa Rica	3,190
Falkland Islands	13		Cuba	40,739
Fiji	873		Czechoslovakia	3,770
Gambia	148		Dahomey	826
Ghana	5,100		Denmark	15,010
Guyana	8,395		Dominican Republic	6,163
Hong Kong	17,678		Ecuador	2,596
India	95,552		El Salvador	4,907
Irish Republic	13,949		Ethiopia	257
Jamaica	40,481		Finland	7,177
Kenya	2,375		France	124,708
Leeward and Windward Islands	10,396		French Africa	2,216
Malaysia	15,524		French Oceania	715
Malawi	294		French West Indies	641
Malta and Gozo	1,951		Gabon	1,000
Mauritius and Dependencies	199		Germany, East	1,846
New Zealand	36,976		Germany, West	277,382
Nigeria	4,169		Greece	10,265
Pakistan	22,142		Guatemala	3,845
Qatar	158		Haiti, Republic of	3,694
Rhodesia	2		Honduras, Republic of	1,098
Sierra Leone	538		Hungary	2,882
Singapore	4,822		Iceland	385
South Africa, Republic of	78,513		Indonesia	2,948
Tanzania	637		Iran	5,225
Trinidad and Tobago	19,492		Iraq	2,792
Trucial States	4,169		Israel	16,975
Uganda	839		Italy	133,671
Zambia	1,504		Ivory Coast	651
			Japan	624,837
Total, Commonwealth and			Jordan	645
preferential countries	1,685,338		Korea, South	15,331
			Kuwait	1,706
Afghánistán	91		Lebanon	3,524
Albania	3,655		Liberia	1,340
Algeria	2,948		Libya	2,364
Angola	386		Mauritania	606
Argentina	62,315		Mexico	72,873
Austria	9,067		Morocco	1,463

Moçambique	3,006	Sweden	41,278
Netherlands	184,966	Switzerland	34,239
Netherlands Antilles	3,149	Syria	910
Nicaragua	2,430	Taiwan	12,631
Norway	103,645	Thailand	8,539
Panama	6,499	Tunisia	2,584
Paraguay	348	Turkey	18,912
Peru	26,234	USSR	9,071
Philippines	32,328	UAR	2,942
Poland	6,554	USA	10,215,400
Portugal	7,039	US Oceania	1,734
Portuguese Africa	269	US Virgin Islands	1,046
Puerto Rico	36,976	Uruguay	3,351
Romania	1,221	Venezuela	92,902
Saudi Arabia	3,618	Vietnam	2,135
Spain	55,908	Yugoslavia	8,023
St Pierre and Miquelon	4,997		
Sudan	499	Total, foreign countries	12,756,218
Surinam	1,383		

Imports (for consumption) by principal countries in 1969 (in $1,000 Canadian):

Australia	96,285	Germany, East	3,481
Bahamas	4,495	Germany, West	354,714
Barbados	1,497	Greece	4,335
Bermuda	268	Guatemala	4,949
Britain	790,974	Guinea	101
British Honduras	2,526	Haiti	692
Ceylon	9,279	Honduras	12,645
Cyprus	298	Hungary	9,184
Fiji	5,681	Iceland	34
Ghana	5,623	Indonesia	284
Guyana	31,050	Iran	30.177
Hong Kong	72,942	Iraq	8,838
India	40,905	Israel	15,066
Irish Republic	11,101	Italy	141,117
Jamaica	45,978	Ivory Coast	4,710
Kenya	5,623	Japan	495,704
Leeward and Windward Islands	2,464	Korea, South	12,192
Malawi	538	Kuwait	6,072
Malaysia	32,824	Lebanon	853
Malta and Gozo	1,458	Liberia	928
Mauritius and Dependencies	14,130	Libya	8,873
New Zealand	41,182	Malagasy Republic	122
Nigeria	22,202	Mexico	64,067
Pakistan	7,064	Morocco	447
Singapore	21,967	Moçambique	903
South Africa, Republic of	45,944	Netherlands	78,679
Tanzania	3,829	Netherlands Antilles	50,395
Trinidad and Tobago	17,742	Nicaragua	1,953
Trucial States	14,923	Norway	44,895
Uganda	6,657	Panama	13,513
Yemen	404	Paraguay	1,100
		Peru	2,835
Total, Commonwealth and		Philippines	4,486
preferential countries	1,362,890	Poland	12,408
		Portugal	13,648
Algeria	43	Puerto Rico	5,098
Angola	6,175	Romania	7,142
Argentina	8,644	Saudi Arabia	26.751
Austria	38,878	Spain	28,714
Belgium–Luxembourg	60,936	Sudan	305
Brazil	42,128	Surinam	8,135
Bulgaria	1,315	Sweden	84,505
Burma	55	Switzerland	83,926
Chile	3,273	Taiwan	42,456
China	27,421	Thailand	995
Colombia	14,565	Tunisia	19
Congo (K.)	1,341	Turkey	3,646
Costa Rica	8,706	USSR	12,302
Cuba	7,759	UAR	1,144
Czechoslovakia	30,046	USA	10,312,631
Denmark	32,392	Uruguay	313
Dominican Republic	603	Venezuela	345,596
Ecuador	8,542	Yugoslavia	5,632
El Salvador	2,093		
Finland	12,610	Total, foreign countries	12,838,737
France	153,712		
French Oceania	2,842		

Leading imports into Canada in 1969 (in $1m. Canadian):

Motor vehicles and parts	3,646	Wearing apparel and accessories	248
Machinery, except farm	1,442	Printed matter	234
Aircraft and parts	401	Other petroleum and coal products	224
Petroleum, crude	393	Plastic materials	203
Steel, all types	461	Tractors and parts	194
Communications equipment	394	Aluminium	188
Electrical equipment	325	Farm equipment	157
Scientific equipment	321	Wood lumber and plywood	148
Textile fabrics	261	Cotton (fabric, thread and yarn)	133
Fruit and fruit products	250	Meat and meat preparations	123

Principal exports (Canadian produce) in 1969 (in $1m. Canadian):

Motor vehicles and parts	3,503	Aircraft and parts	325
Newsprint paper	1,126	Iron and steel (including alloys)	301
Wheat	473	Machinery, except farm	369
Lumber	701	Fish	252
Wood pulp and similar pulp	753	Communication equipment	200
Copper and alloys	535	Asbestos unmanufactured	216
Nickel and alloys	451	Zinc, ores and alloys	179
Aluminum, including alloys	494	Farm machinery	180
Petroleum, crude	526	Whisky	189
Iron ores and concentrates	333	Natural gas	176

The following figures (in £1,000 sterling) are from the British Board of Trade returns:

	1966	1967	1968	1969	1970
Imports to UK	424,954	455,946	512,770	504,858	682,732
Exports from UK	215,337	213,455	259,140	300,633⎱	288,123
Re-exports from UK	8,209	6,857	7,104	8,069⎰	

Royal Commission on Canada's Economic Prospects. Report. Ottawa, 1957
Brewis, T. N., *Canadian Economic Policy*. Toronto, 1961
Cockfield, Brown & Co., *Canada's Economic Future: digests of 127 submissions to the Royal Commission on Canada's Economic Prospects*. Toronto, 1957
Arnold, J. R., *Practical Exporting and Importing in Canada*. Toronto, 1961
Easterbrook, W. T., *Canadian Economic History*. Toronto, 1956
Litvak, I., and Mallen, B., *Marketing in Canada: Recent Readings*, Toronto, 1964
Mahatoo, W. H., *Marketing Research in Canada*. Toronto, 1968
Newman, D., and Newman, J. P., *Canadian Business Handbook*. Toronto, 1964
Officer, L. H. (ed.), *Canadian Economic Problems and Policies*. Toronto, 1970
Shea, A. A., *Canada 1980*. Toronto, 1960
Wilkinson, B. W., *Canada's International Trade: An Analysis of Recent Trends and patterns*. Toronto, 1968,

SHIPPING. The registered shipping on 1 Jan. 1969, including vessels for inland navigation, totalled 26,964 with a gross tonnage of 3,714,028. The sea-going and coasting vessels that entered Canadian ports during the year ending 31 Dec. 1968 were as follows: Foreign service vessels, 26,740 of 102,140,678 tons. Coasting service vessels, 88,847 of 90,613,696 tons.

The major canals in Canada are those of the St Lawrence–Great Lakes waterway with their 7 locks, providing navigation for vessels of 25·75-ft draught from Montreal to Lake Ontario; the Welland Canal by-passing the Niagara River between Lake Ontario and Lake Erie with its 8 locks; and the Sault Ste Marie Canal and lock between Lake Huron and Lake Superior. These 16 locks overcome a drop of 582 ft from the head of the lakes to Montreal. The St Lawrence Seaway was opened to navigation on 25 April 1959 (*see* map in THE STATESMAN'S YEAR-BOOK, 1957). The value of fixed assets administered by the National Harbours Board was $404,558,351 at 31 Dec. 1969. In 1969, 19,710 vessels passed through the Canadian canals, carrying 97,357,234 tons of freight, chiefly grain iron ore and coal.

COAST GUARD. The Canadian Coast Guard (formed in 1962) is responsible to the Minister of Transport. In 1970 it comprised the arctic patrol vessel (helicopter carrier and icebreaker) *Labrador*; 2 weather-ships; 9 heavy and 9 light icebreakers; a special arctic service ship; a cable repair ship; 9 supply vessels (former landing craft); and 114 other vessels.

RAILWAYS. The total first maintrack mileage of railways in Canada on 31 Dec. 1969 was 43.613. The total mileage, including second maintrack, yardtrack and sidings, was 59,114.

Canada has 2 great trans-continental systems: the Canadian National Railways, a government-owned body which operates 22,903 miles of the total first maintrack, and the Canadian Pacific Railway Company, a joint-stock corporation with first maintrack totalling 16,597 miles (31 Dec. 1969).

Selected statistics of Canadian railways for 1969: Passengers carried, 23·7m.; revenue freight, 94·7m. ton-miles; freight revenue, $1,325m.; total railway operating revenues, $1,581m.

URBAN TRANSIT. In 1968 urban transit systems (motor bus, trolley coach, street car and subway operations) operated 8,583 vehicles and carried 1,055,636,787 initial revenue fare passengers over 257,674,340 vehicle-miles for an operating revenue of $222,563,348. Operating expenses totalled $230,055,914. Total assets were $340,413,655 and long-term debt was $182,677,670. The 32 municipal transit systems had a net operating deficit of $7,865,563, while the 50 privately operated systems reporting declared a net operating revenue of $372,997.

ROADS. The total highway mileage in Canada in 1968 was 475,982. Of this total 340,138 miles were surfaced and 135,844 miles improved and other earth roads. Expenditure (1968) on roads, bridges, ferries, etc., reached a total of $1,350,841,000. Provincial governments supplied $1,064,755,000, with the remainder contributed by federal, municipal and other sources. Federal expenditures were chiefly devoted towards the upkeep of national-park roadways and nationally owned bridges and ferries, although for the 'Mackenzie Highway' from Grimshaw, Alberta, to Hay River, N.W.T., the federal government paid about 68% of the total cost. In general, however, highways are provincially controlled and maintained, and the responsibility of assisting municipalities and townships falls directly on the provinces.

The Alaska Highway is part of the Canadian highway system. For the Trans-Canada Highway *see* map in THE STATESMAN'S YEAR-BOOK, 1962.

Registered motor vehicles totalled 8,254,160 in 1969; they included 6,433,283 passenger cars and taxis, 1,682,515 commercial vehicles and 138,362 motor cycles.

AVIATION. The branch of the Director of Civil Aviation is under the jurisdiction of the Assistant Deputy Prime Minister, Air Services, Department of Transport, and is responsible for the administration of the air regulations, aircraft registration, airmen licensing, etc.

Landings and take-off controlled by the Department of Transport's 51 towers totalled 4,488,000 in 1969.

In 1969 Canadian airlines carried 10,264,000 passengers, flying 9,484m. revenue-passenger-miles and 315·6m. ton-miles of freight. Operating revenue was $702·7m.; operating expenditure, $665·6m.

POST. On 31 March 1970 there were 9,575 post offices. There were also 5,221 rural mail delivery routes servicing 731,544 households. Gross revenue was $404·1m.; gross expenditure, $497m. for the fiscal year 1969–70.

There were 568,418 miles of telegraph wire in Canada in 1967 and 13,241 nautical miles of external cable landed in Canada. There were 48·11m. miles of telephone wire and 8,818,000 telephones on 31 Dec. 1968 (42·1 per 100 population).

WIRELESS COMMUNICATIONS. There were 312 standard broadcast band stations operating in Canada in April 1970, of which 44 were Canadian Broadcasting Corporation stations and 278 were privately owned stations. In addition, there were 22 short-wave stations, 16 of which were CBC and 6 privately owned, together with 6 CBC and 71 privately owned frequency-modulation stations. Of the 360 television stations, 111 were owned by the CBC and 249 privately owned. Radio and television licence fees were abolished in 1953.

Wireless 'beam' stations are operated at Montreal for direct communications with Great Britain and Australia, and a station at Louisburg, N.S., provides a long-distance service to ships.

Boggs, W. S., *The Postage Stamps and Postal History of Canada*. 2 vols. Kalamazoo, Mich., 1945–46
Canadian Ports and Shipping Directory, including the St Lawrence Seaway system and the United States ports on the Great Lakes. 18th ed. Gardenvale, Quebec, 1962
Chevrier, L., *The St Lawrence Seaway*. London, 1959
Currie, A. W., *Economics of Canadian Transportation*. 2nd ed. Toronto, 1959.—*The Grand Trunk Railway of Canada*. Toronto, 1957
Ellis, F. H., *Canada's Flying Heratage*. Toronto, 1961
Hills, T. L., *The St Lawrence Seaway*. London, 1959
Stevens, G. R., *Canadian National Railways*. 2 vols. Toronto, 1960
Willoughby, William R., *The St Lawrence Waterway: a study in politics and diplomacy*. Univ. of Wisconsin Press, 1960

BANKING. Commercial banks in Canada are known as chartered banks and are incorporated under the terms of the Bank Act, which imposes strict conditions as to capital, notes in circulation, returns to the Dominion Government, types of lending operations and other matters. In Sept. 1970 there were in operation 9 chartered banks incorporated under the provisions of the Bank Act, with 6,127 branches and sub-agencies in Canada and 270 branches and sub-agencies in other countries. The Bank Act is subject to revision by Parliament every 10 years; latest revision 1967. Bank charters expire every 10 years and are renewed at each decennial revision of the Bank Act. The chartered banks make detailed monthly and yearly returns to the Minister of Finance and are subject to periodic inspection by the Inspector-General of Banks, an official appointed by the Government.

The following are some particulars of the 9 chartered banks at 30 Sept. 1970: Capital paid up, $305·7m.; rest account, $1,202·2m.; Canadian currency deposits, $28,041·8m.; foreign currency deposits, $12,992·2m.; liabilities to the public, $43,298·2m.; total assets, $44,806·2m. Cheques cashed at the clearing-house centres of Canada for 1969 amounted to $735,404m.

The deposits in the Quebec savings banks, incorporated under a special Dominion Act, amounted to $527,979,571 on 31 Oct. 1970.

The Bank of Canada Act, passed on 3 July 1934, provided for the establishment of a central bank for the Dominion. This bank commenced operations on 11 March 1935 with a paid-up capital of $5m. By reason of certain changes introduced into the composition of stockholders of the bank (for which *see* THE STATESMAN'S YEAR-BOOK, 1944, pp. 322–23), the Minister of Finance on behalf of the Dominion of Canada is the sole registered owner of the capital stock of the bank. The revised Bank Act, which came into force on 1 May 1967, requires the chartered banks, beginning Feb. 1968, to maintain a statutory cash ratio of 12% on demand deposits and 4% on other deposits, in the form of reserves with and notes of the Bank of Canada. A secondary reserve of 7% in treasury bills, government bonds, etc., is also required. All gold held in Canada by the chartered banks was transferred to the Bank of Canada along with the gold held by the Government as reserve against Dominion notes outstanding at the time of the commencement of operations of the Bank of Canada. The liability of the Dominion notes outstanding at the commencement of business of the Bank of Canada was assumed by the bank. The following are some of the particulars of the Bank of Canada as at 31 Dec. 1970: Notes in circulation ,$3,632m.; chartered bank deposits, $1,176m.; total liabilities, $5,404m.; investments, $4,796m.

In Aug. 1944 the Industrial Development Bank, a subsidiary of the Bank of Canada, was set up for the purpose of providing credit in the post-war period to small industrial establishments. The statement of assets and liabilities of the Industrial Bank for the fiscal year ended 30 Sept. 1969 showed outstanding loans and investments of $416·3m. The authorized, issued and paid-up capital at this date amounted to $71·7m.

Binhammer, H. H., *Money, Banking and the Canadian Financial System*. Toronto, 1968
Boreham, G. F., and others, *Money and Banking: analysis and policy in a Canadian context*. Toronto, 1969
Cairns, James P. (ed.), *Canadian Banking and Monetary Policy: recent readings*. Toronto, 1965
O'Brien, J. H. and Lerner, G., *Canadian Money and Banking*. 2nd ed. Toronto, 1969

WEIGHTS AND MEASURES. The legal weights and measures are the Imperial yard, pound avoirdupois, gallon and bushel; but the hundredweight is declared to be 100 lb. and the ton 2,000 lb. avoirdupois, as in the USA.

BOOKS OF REFERENCE

STATISTICAL INFORMATION. The Dominion Bureau of Statistics, Ottawa, has been the official central statistical organization for Canada since 1918. The Bureau, which reports to Parliament through the Minister of Industry, Trade and Commerce, serves as the statistical agency for Federal Goverment Departments; co-ordinates the statistics of the Provincial Goverments along national lines; and channels all Canadian statistical data to internal organizations. *Dominion Statistician:* Walter E. Duffet.

Publications of the Dominion Bureau of Statistics are classified as periodical (issued more frequently than once a year), annual, biennial and occasional publications. The occasional publications frequently supplement the annual reports and usually contain historical information. A complete list is contained in the 1968 edition of the Dominion Bureau of Statistics catalogue and supplements, available on request. Official publications include:

The Canada Year Book. Annual, from 1905
Canada, Official Handbook. Annual, from 1930
Atlas of Canada. Dept. of Mines and Technical Surveys. Geographical Branch. Ottawa, 1958
Canadian Statistical Review. Monthly, with weekly supplements, from 1948
Canadiana; a list of publications of Canadian interest. National Library, Ottawa. Monthly, with annual cumulation. 1951 ff.
Tenth Decennial Census of Canada, 1961. Ottawa, 1962

NON-OFFICIAL PUBLICATIONS

Cambridge History of the British Empire, Vol. VI, Canada and Newfoundland. Cambridge, 1930
Canadian Annual Review. Annual, from 1960
Canadian Dictionary: French–English. Toronto, 1970
Canadian Who's Who. 11th ed. Toronto, 1969
National Reference Book on Canadian Business Personalities. 11th ed. Montreal, 1969
Angus, H. F., *Canada and the Far East, 1940–53.* Toronto, 1953
Brebner, J. B., *North Atlantic Triangle: The Interplay of Canada, the United States and Great Britain.* New York, 1958
Brown, G. W. (ed.), *Dictionary of Canadian Biography*, Vol. I. Univ. of Toronto Press, 1966
Bruchési, Jean, *L'Histoire du Canada*. 6th ed. Montreal, 1951.—*Canada, réalités d'hier et d'aujourd' hui*. Montreal, 1954.—*Le Canada*. Paris, 1952
Brunet, M., and others, *Histoire du Canada par les textes*. Montreal, 1952
Camu, P., Weeks, E. P., and Sametz, Z. W., *Economic Geography of Canada*. London, 1965
Careless, J. M. S., *Canada, A Story of Challenge*. Rev. ed. Toronto, 1963
Creighton, Donald G., *Dominion of the North: A History of Canada*. New ed. Toronto, 1957.—*The Empire of the St Lawrence*. Toronto, 1956.—*Canada's First Century*. Toronto, 1970
Dictionnaire canadien; français–anglais–français. Toronto, 1962
Encyclopedia Canadiana. 10 vols. Rev. ed. Ottawa, 1967
Fortin, J.-A., *Biographies canadiennes-françaises*. 16th ed. Montreal, 1952
Garneau, F. X., *Histoire du Canada*. 8th ed. Montreal, 1944–45
Glazebrook, G. P. de T., *A History of Canadian External Relations*. Toronto, 1950
Keenleyside, H. L., *Canada and the United States*. Rev. ed. New York, 1952
Kerr, D. G. G., *Historical Atlas of Canada*. Toronto, 1960
Lefebvre, F. J., *Le Canada, l'Amerique-geographique, historique, biographique, litéraire; supplement du Larousse canadien complet*. Montreal, 1954
Lower, A. R. M., *Colony to Nation: a history of Canada*. 4th ed. Toronto, 1964
McInnis, E., *Canada: A Political and Social History*. Rev. ed. Toronto, 1959
MacLennan, Hugh, *Seven Rivers of Canada: the Mackenzie, the St Lawrence, the Ottawa, the Red, the Saskatchewan, the Fraser, the St John*. Toronto, 1961
Putnam, D. F., *Canadian Regions. A Geography of Canada*. 2nd ed. Toronto, 1954
Robinson, J. L., and J., *Geography of Canada*. Toronto, 1951
Ross, M. M., *Our Sense of Identity; a book of Canadian essays*. Toronto, 1954
Sandwell, B. R., *La Nation canadienne*. Monaco, 1954
Tanghe, R., *Bibliography of Canadian Bibliographies*. Toronto, 1962
Urquhart, M. C., and Buckley, K. A. H. (ed.), *Historical Statistics of Canada*. Toronto, 1965
Wilson, G. W., and others, *Canada: an appraisal of its need and resources*. New York, 1965

NATIONAL LIBRARY. The National Library of Canada. Ottawa, Ontario. *Librarian:* J. Guy Sylvestre.

CANADIAN PROVINCES

The 10 provinces have each a separate parliament and administration, with a Lieut.-Governor, appointed by the Governor-General in Council at the head of the executive. They have full powers to regulate their own local affairs and dispose of their revenues, provided only they do not interfere with the action and policy of the central administration. Among the subjects assigned exclusively to the provincial legislatures are: the amendment of the provincial constitution, except as regards the office of the Lieut.-Governor; property and civil rights; direct taxation for revenue purposes; borrowing; management and sale of crown lands; provincial hospitals, reformatories, etc.; shop, saloon, tavern, auctioneer and other licences for local or provincial purposes; local works and undertakings, except lines of ships, railways, canals, telegraphs, etc., extending beyond the province or connecting with other provinces, and excepting also such works as the Dominion Parliament declares are for the general good; marriages, administration of justice within the province; education. Quebec has 2 legislative chambers and other provinces 1 chamber. The Northwest Territories and the Yukon Territory are governed by commissioners, appointed by the Governor-in-Council, assisted by councils.

LOCAL GOVERNMENT. Under the terms of the British North America Act the provinces are given full powers over local government. All local government institutions are, therefore, supervised by the provinces, and are incorporated and function under provincial acts.

The acts under which municipalities operate vary from province to province. A municipal corporation is usually administered by an elected council headed by a mayor or reeve, whose powers to administer affairs and to raise funds by taxation and other methods are set forth in provincial laws, as is the scope of its obligations to, and on behalf of, the citizens. Similarly, the types of municipal corporations, their official designations and the requirements for their incorporation vary between provinces. The following table sets out the classifications as at 1 Jan. 1968.

Province	Metropolitan corporations	Cities	Towns	Villages	Other local municipalities	Counties and regional municipalities	Total incorporated municipalities
Newfoundland	—	2	63	—	99	—	164
Prince Edward Island	—	1	7	22	—	—	30
Nova Scotia	—	3	39	—	24	—	66
New Brunswick	—	6	21	87	—	—	114
Quebec	1	66	184	302	1,099	74	1,726
Ontario	1	38[1]	152	155	580	38	964
Manitoba	1	9	36	40	128	—	214
Saskatchewan	—	11	130	358	304	—	803
Alberta	—	10	100	167	95	—	372
British Columbia	—	31	13	56	40	—	165
Yukon Territory	—	2	—	—	1	—	3
Northwest Territories	—	—	3	1	—	—	4
Total	3	179	748	1,188	2,370	112	4,625

[1] The 5 boroughs of Metropolitan Toronto are included with 'Cities'.

Britain, H. L., *Local Government in Canada*. Toronto, 1951
Crawford, K. G., *Canadian Municipal Government*. Toronto, 1954
Plunkett, T. J., *Municipal Organization in Canada*. Montreal, 1955
Rogers, I. M., *The Law of Canadian Municipal Corporations*. Toronto, 1959
Rowat, D. C., *Your Local Government; a sketch of the municipal system in Canada*. Toronto, 1962

NEWFOUNDLAND

HISTORY. Newfoundland was discovered by John Cabot 24 June 1497, and was soon frequented in the summer months by the Portuguese, Spanish and French for its fisheries. It was formally occupied in Aug. 1583 by Sir Humphrey Gilbert on behalf of the English Crown, but various attempts to colonize the island remained unsuccessful. Although British sovereignty was recognized in 1713 by the Treaty of Utrecht, disputes over fishing rights with the French were not finally settled till 1904.

By the Anglo-French Convention of 1904, France renounced her exclusive fishing rights along part of the coast, granted under the Treaty of Utrecht, but retained sovereignty of the off-shore islands of St Pierre and Miquelon.

In Jan. 1941 three sites in Newfoundland were leased to the USA for naval or military bases; only the naval station at Argentia is still active.

CONSTITUTION AND GOVERNMENT. Until 1832 Newfoundland was ruled by the Governor under instructions from the Colonial Office. In that year a Legislature was brought into existence, but the Governor and his Executive Council were not responsible to it. Under the constitution of 1855, which lasted until its suspension in 1934, the government was administered by the Governor appointed by the Crown with an Executive Council responsible to the House of Assembly of 27 elected members and a Legislative Council of 24 members nominated for life by the Governor in Council. Women were enfranchised in 1925. At the Imperial Conference of 1917 Newfoundland was constituted as a Dominion.

In 1933 the financial situation had become so critical that the Government of Newfoundland asked the Government of the UK to appoint a Royal Commission to investigate conditions. On the strength of their recommendations, the parliamentary form of government was suspended and Government by Commission was inaugurated on 16 Feb. 1934.

A National Convention, elected in 1946, made, in 1948, recommendations to H.M. Government in Great Britain as to the possible forms of future government to be submitted to the people at a national referendum. Two referenda were held. In the first referendum (June 1948) the three forms of government submitted to the people were: commission of government for 5 years, confederation with Canada and responsible government as it existed in 1933. No one form of government received a clear majority of the votes polled, and commission of government, receiving the fewest votes, was eliminated. In the second referendum (July 1948) confederation with Canada received 78,408 and responsible government 71,464 votes.

In the Canadian Senate on 18 Feb. 1949 Royal assent was given to the terms of union of Newfoundland with Canada, and on 23 March 1949, in the House of Lords, London, Royal assent was given to an amendment to the British North America Act made necessary by the inclusion of Newfoundland as the tenth Province of Canada.

Under the terms of union of Newfoundland with Canada, which was signed at Ottawa on 11 Dec. 1948, the constitution of the Legislature of Newfoundland as it existed immediately prior to 16 Feb. 1934 shall, subject to the terms of the British North America Acts, 1867 to 1946, continue as the constitution of the Legislature of the Province of Newfoundland until altered under the authority of the said Acts.

The Constitution of the Legislature of Newfoundland in so far as it relates to the Legislative Council shall not continue, but the Legislature of the Province of Newfoundland may at any time re-establish the Legislative Council or establish a new Legislative Council. The franchise was in 1965 extended to all male and female residents who have attained the age of 19 years and are otherwise qualified as electors.

A Redistribution Act was passed in 1962, constituting 41 electoral districts and 42 members of the Legislature who receive $8,500 per annum.

The general election held on 8 Sept. 1966 returned 39 Liberals and 3 Progressive-Conservatives.

The Province is represented by 6 members in the Senate and by 7 members in the House of Commons of Canada.

Lieut-Governor: E. John A. Harnum (assumed office 2 April 1969).

The Liberal Executive Council was, in Sept. 1970, composed as follows:

Premier: J. R. Smallwood.

President of the Council: L. R. Curtis, QC. *Labour:* W. J. Keough. *Finance:* E. S. Jones. *Municipal Affairs and Housing:* E. N. Dawe. *Public Works:* J. R. Chalker. *Economic Development, Supply and Services:* J. A. Nolan. *Justice:* L. R. Curtis, QC. *Mines, Agriculture and Resources:* W. R. Callahan. *Fisheries:* Vacant (acting E. W. Winsor). *Highways:* H. E. Starkes. *Education and Youth:* Dr F. W. Rowe. *Labrador Affairs:* E. W. Winsor. *Provincial Affairs:* Dr G A. Frecker. *Social Services and Rehabilitation:* S. A. Neary. *Health:* E. M. Roberts. *Community and Social Development:* W. N. Rowe. *Without Portfolio:* P. J. Lewis, QC; G. I. Hill.

Agent-General in London: H. Watson Jamer (60 Trafalgar Sq., WC2).

AREA AND POPULATION. Area, 156,185 sq. miles (383,300 sq. km). The coastline is extremely irregular. Bays, fiords and inlets are numerous and there are many good harbours with deep water close to shore. The coast is rugged with bold rocky cliffs from 200 to 400 ft high; in the Bay of Islands some of the islands rise 500 ft, with the adjacent shore 1,000 ft above tide level. The interior is a plateau of moderate elevation and the chief relief features trend north-east and south-west. Long Range, the most notable of these, begins at Cape Ray and extends north-east for 200 miles; the highest peak reaching 2,673 ft. Approximately one-third of the area is covered by water. Grand Lake, the largest body of water, has an area of about 200 sq. miles. The principal rivers flow towards the north-east. On the borders of the lakes and water-courses good land is generally found, particularly in the valleys of the Terra Nova River, the Gander River, the Exploits River and the Humber River, which are also heavily timbered.

Census population, 1966, was 493,396; estimate (1970), 517,000.

The capital of Newfoundland is the City of St John's (101,161, metropolitan area). The only other city is Corner Brook (27,116); important towns are Wabana (7,884), Grand Falls (7,451), Gander (7,183), Windsor (6,692), Stephenville (5,910), Channel-Port aux Basques (5,692), Carbonear (4,584), Bonavista (4,192).

Vital statistics, *see* pp. 178–80.

Religion, *see* p. 180.

EDUCATION. The number of schools in 1969–70 was 945. The enrolment was 159,235; teachers numbered 6,320. The Memorial University, offering courses in arts, science, engineering and education, had 5,199 full-time students. Total expenditure for education by the Government in 1968–69 was $76,004,079.

FINANCE. Budget[1] in Canadian $1,000 for fiscal years ended 31 March:

	1965–66	1966–67	1967–68	1968–69	1969–70[2]	1970–71[3]
Gross revenue	141,460	165,370	221,338	251,910	272,879	302,583
Gross expenditure	134,425	165,038	216,099	254,900	272,345	302,235

[1] Current amount only.   [2] Subject to audit.   [3] Estimates.

Public debenture debt as at 31 March 1970 was $347m.; sinking fund, $54m.

AGRICULTURE. The estimated value of agricultural products, including livestock, in 1969–70, was $17·5m.

FISHERIES. The principal fish landings are cod, flounder, greysole, plaice, Greenland turbot, perch, lobster, salmon and herring. In 1969 some 8,300 men were employed by the industry and there were 17,770 full- and part-time fishermen. Thirty-four freezing plants and 25 saltfish plants were in operation. The production of fresh and frozen fish products was 153·7m. lb. There were 386 large, 3 sei, 50 minke, and 56 pothead whales caught and processed in 1969.

The total catch in 1969 was 1,009m. lb. valued at $30·8m., of which the main items were: Cod, 329·7m. lb. ($11·5m.); flatfish, 174·9m. lb. ($6·9m.); perch, 70·4m. lb. ($1·7m.); lobster, 3·8m. lb. ($2·5m.); salmon, 3·2m. lb. ($1·4m.). In addition, there were 369·4m. lb. of herring landed.

The seal fishery in 1969 was prosecuted by 6 large licensed and 18 small licensed vessels with 363 men. The number of pelts landed by 24 vessels and 2,240 landsmen totalled 118,072 valued at $817,856.

FORESTRY. The forest economy in the Province is dependent in the main on the operation of two pulp and paper companies which, in 1969, produced 617,716 tons of newsprint. Sawlog operations and miscellaneous cuttings, conducted in Crown Land limits with 1,090 saw-mills, cut 27·5m. f.b.m. Total value of forest production for 1969 was $90m.

MINING. The mineral resources are vast. Large deposits of iron ore, with an ore reserve of over 3,000m. tons at Ruth, Carol and Wabush Lakes, Labrador, are being developed. Fifteen mines are in various stages of production and development; 4 iron ore, 1 limestone, 1 lead, zinc and copper, 2 fluorspar, 1 asbestos and 3 copper, 1 pyrophyllite, 1 quartz and 1 gypsum.

Production in 1969: Iron ore, 14·7m. long tons ($179m.); copper, 19,389 short tons ($20m.); zinc, 33,905 tons ($10·3m.); asbestos, 55,500 short tons ($10·1m.); fluorspar ($3m.); lead, 21,094 tons ($6·4m.); silver, 963,100 troy oz. ($1·9m.).

INDUSTRY. A large number of new industries have been established under government sponsorship. They include an oil refinery, a cement and a gypsum plant, an asbestos mill, a magnesia plant, etc.

Production of newsprint in 1969 was 606,522 tons; value of exports, $87·2m. The mill at Corner Brook, the largest integrated mill in the world, has a daily production of 1,100 tons of newsprint and the mill at Grand Falls a daily production capacity of 830 tons of newsprint.

ELECTRICITY. There are 22 hydro-electric power plants within the Island part of the Province with 1,028,239 h.p. turbine installation. The Newfoundland and Labrador Power Commission has installed five 100,000-h.p. turbines at Bay D'Espoir on the south coast. There are also 40,000 h.p. of conventional oil-fired thermal plant in utility service on the Island and the Newfoundland and Labrador Power Commission has a 2-unit 400,000 h.p. oil-fired steam electric generating station under construction and scheduled for completion in March 1971 at Holyrood, near St John's. Also in service are 40,000 h.p. of gas turbine emergency service plant in 2 units. Churchill Falls Labrador Corporation has under construction at Churchill Falls in Labrador an 11-unit 7m. h.p. generating plant. First unit service is scheduled for 1972 with the last unit scheduled for 1976. This project will result in the shutdown of the 400,000-h.p. Twin Falls Power Company plant on the Unknown River in Labrador. The Iron Ore Company of Canada also operates a 30,000-h.p. hydro plant at Menihek Lake to serve its mining load in the area. On the Island, the rural electricity authority operates approximately 35,000 h.p. of diesel-driven generating plant. This capacity is spread over some 55 small stations.

TRADE UNIONS. There are 137 unions representing 38,500 members of the American Federation of Labor, the Congress of Industrial Organizations, the Canadian Labor Congress and local independent unions (1,500).

SHIPPING. On 31 Dec. 1970 ships registered in Newfoundland consisted of 29 sailing vessels of gross tonnage 2,790; 12 steam vessels of 17,944 gross tons and 1,022 motor vessels of 135,639 gross tons.

RAILWAYS. In 1970 there were 1,085 miles of railway, of which the Canadian National Railways operated 704 (3ft 6in.), the Quebec North Shore and Labrador Railway 357 (4ft 8½in.) and the Grand Falls Central Railway 26.

POST. There were 517 post offices open in 1970, 46 post and telegraph offices, and 129 telegraph and telephone offices. Telephone connexions in the province numbered 100,655.

Labrador, the most northerly district of the Province of Newfoundland, extends from Blanc Sablon at the north-east entrance of the Straits of Belle Isle to Cape Chidley at the eastern entrance of Hudson's Strait. In March 1927 the Privy Council decided the boundary between Canada and Newfoundland in Labrador. The area now under the jurisdiction of Newfoundland is approximately 110,000 sq. miles (285,000 sq. km). The population (1966 census) is 21,157.

Little is known about the geology of the country; exploratory work is being undertaken both by government and private bodies. The prevailing formation on the coast is granite, gneiss or mica slate, above which, in some places, are beds of old sandstone and a stratum of secondary limestone. The secondary rocks disappear towards the interior. At the headwaters of the Hamilton River the geological formations are structurally similar to the iron-ore bearing area of Lake Superior.

In 1954 the Iron Ore Company of Canada began shipping iron ore from a deposit 365 miles north of Seven Islands. The deposit stretching across the Newfoundland–Labrador boundary contains in excess of 400m. tons of 51% iron. The railway line built by the Company connects the deposit with a major stock-piling and shipping installation at Seven Islands. Up to 13m. tons a year have been shipped from this area.

Further development has taken place farther south in the area around Wabush Lake both by the Iron Ore Company and by Wabush Mines (operated by Pickands Mather of Cleveland). A railway line from Mile 224 some 30 miles to Wabush Lake serves both deposits, which are estimated in excess of several thousand million tons of 36% iron ore. In 1962 the first shipment of iron-ore concentrates, up-graded to 67% iron, began moving out of the Iron Ore Company mines and concentrator at Labrador City on the western side of Wabush Lake. Production began at the rate of 6m. tons of concentrate a year, and a plant which pelletizes 5·5m. tons of this concentrate began production in 1963. Across the lake the Wabush Mines project is scheduled for production of some 6m. tons of concentrate a year in early 1965.

To serve both iron-ore operations at Wabush Lake and the towns of Labrador City on the western side of the lake and the city of Wabush on the eastern side of the lake, the British Newfoundland Corporation, through its associated company Twin Falls Corporation, has built and put into operation a hydro-electric development at Twin Falls, Labrador, which is part of the Churchill Falls (formerly Hamilton Falls) watershed; the capacity of the installation is 240,000 h.p. BRINCO also holds a lease of the Churchill Falls watershed.

Between Churchill Falls and the coast of Labrador there exists one of the largest stands of virgin pulpwood timber in North America. In one area around Goose airport 50m. cords of standing timber have been estimated.

The Moravian Missions have maintained, over the past 190 years, mission stations in Northern Labrador at Makkovik, Hopedale and Nain. The Hebron Station was closed in 1959 and the Eskimo population was resettled at Nain, Hopedale and Nakkovik. The Moravian Mission has extended its operations to include Happy Valley and North West River. Happy Valley is a town with an approximate population of 6,000. The International Grenfell Association operates hospitals at Happy Valley and North West River and nursing stations at Nakkovik, Hopedale, Nain, Cartwright, Mary's Harbour and Forteau.

In the months that the coast is ice-free, from June to Nov., the Canadian National Railways operates a scheduled service every 10 days along the coast. The Government of Canada operates an international airport at Goose Bay, located at the south-west extremity of Hamilton Inlet. A second airport is at Wabush.

The Churchill Falls is now being harnessed with expectancy of power going on stream in 1972.

BOOKS OF REFERENCE

Blackburn, R. H. (ed.), *Encyclopaedia of Canada: Newfoundland supplement*. Toronto, 1949
Bruet, E., *Le Labrador et le Nouveau-Québec*. Paris, 1949
Horwood, H., *Newfoundland*. Toronto, 1969
Loture, R. de, *Histoire de la grande pêche de Terre-Neuve*. Paris, 1949
Perlin, A. B., *The Story of Newfoundland, 1497–1959*. St John's, 1959
Tanner, V., *Outlines of Geography. Life and Customs of Newfoundland–Labrador*. 2 vols. Helsinki, 1944, and Toronto, 1947
Taylor, T. G., *Newfoundland: A Study of Settlement*. Toronto, 1946

PRINCE EDWARD ISLAND

HISTORY. The island was discovered by Sebastian Cabot in 1497; it was first settled by the French, but was taken from them in 1758. It was annexed to Nova Scotia in 1763, and constituted a separate colony in 1769. Prince Edward Island entered the Confederation on 1 July 1873.

CONSTITUTION AND GOVERNMENT. The provincial government is administered by a Lieut.-Governor and a Legislative Assembly of 32 members, who are elected for 5 years. Women can also be elected to the assembly. At the elections in May/July 1966 the Liberals gained 17 and the Progressive Conservatives 15 seats.

Lieut.-Governor: J. George MacKay (sworn in 6 Oct. 1969).

The members of the Liberal Executive Council are as follows (Dec. 1969):

Premier, Minister of Development: Alexander B. Campbell.
Minister of Education and Justice, President of the Executive Council, Attorney and Advocate General: Gordon L. Bennett. *Tourist Development:* Dr M. Lorne Bonnell. *Health and Municipal Affairs:* Bruce L. Stewart. *Public Works and Highways:* George J. Ferguson. *Agriculture and Forestry:* Daniel J. MacDonald. *Finance and Provincial Secretary:* T. Earle Hickey. *Labour, Industry, Commerce and Fisheries:* Bruce L. Stewart. *Community Services:* Robert Schurman. *Without Portfolio:* Robert E. Campbell.

Agent-General in London: H. Watson Jamer (40 Trafalgar Sq., WC2).

LOCAL GOVERNMENT. The Village Service Act, 1954, provides for the incorporation of villages. The city of Charlottetown and the town of Summerside have been incorporated under Special Acts. The Town Act, 1951, provides for the incorporation of all towns.

AREA AND POPULATION. The province, which is the smallest in Canada, lies in the Gulf of St Lawrence, and is separated from the mainland of New Brunswick and Nova Scotia by Northumberland Strait. The area of the island is 2,184 sq. miles (5,656 sq. km). Total population (census, 1966), 108,535; estimate, June 1970, 110,000. Population of the principal cities (1966): Charlottetown (capital), 18,427; Summerside, 10,042.

Vital Statistics, *see* pp. 178–80.
Religion, *see* p. 180.

EDUCATION (1969–70). There were 268 schools, 1,486 teachers, 29,614 pupils; exclusive of 1 Roman Catholic convent school at Charlottetown, with

70 pupils. There is 1 university, the University of Prince Edward Island (1,566 full-time students), and a college of applied art and technology (107 students), both in Charlottetown. Total expenditure on education in the year ending 31 March 1970 was $16,273,753.

FINANCE. Revenue and expenditure (in Canadian $) for 6 financial years ending 31 March:

	1965–66	1966–67	1967–68	1968–69	1969–70	1970–71
Revenue	35,308,165	39,267,180	48,871,418	55,803,047	69,066,170	83,166,904
Expenditure	40,621,311	51,042,428	53,817,531	61,202,293	69,825,691	84,559,763

[1] Estimates.

Total sinking funds on 31 March 1970 amounted to $13,586,991; total liabilities of the province to $108,306,212.

AGRICULTURE. The farm land occupied is about 927,000 acres out of a total of 1,397,750 acres. Field crops in 1969 covered about 385,000 acres, and were valued at $30·3m. The land in natural forest covers 813 sq. miles, and in pasture 152,000 acres. For particulars of agricultural production and livestock, *see under* CANADA.

FISHERIES. The fisheries of the province in 1969 had a landed value of $8,776,627. The bulk of the value is derived from lobster (about 59% in 1969); but a fast expanding dragger fishery is developing a growing industry in the production of frozen fillets and of meal and oil by-products. The famous 'Malpeque' oyster abounds in Malpeque Bay where 3,118 acres are under scientific cultivation.

INDUSTRY. Industrial establishments produced goods to a shipment value of $51,659,000 in 1969. Electric power is supplied to over 90% of the population. The tourist industry was estimated at $17·05m. in 1969.

COMMERCE. The trade of Prince Edward Island is chiefly with the other provinces of Canada, and with the north-eastern and southern USA and South America, where seed potatoes are shipped to.

COMMUNICATIONS. The province has a total of 3,355 miles of road, including 1,604 miles of paved highway. Rail service is provided over 283 miles of track within the province and connects with the national railways system *via* New Brunswick. A ferry service provides rail and highway communication with New Brunswick by means of 4 large ferries, 2 of which are powerful icebreakers. Another ferry service employing 2 ferries for highway traffic operates between the province and Nova Scotia throughout the season of open navigation. Air service for passengers, mail and cargo is scheduled to provide 6 flights daily in each direction between the province and various points in eastern Canada. A daily bus service operates between various centres in the province as well as to Nova Scotia and New Brunswick.

In 1969 there were 32,355 telephones.

BOOKS OF REFERENCE

Clark, A. H., *Three Centuries and the Island.* Toronto, 1959
MacKinnon, F., *The Government of Prince Edward Island.* Toronto, 1951

NOVA SCOTIA

HISTORY. The first permanent settlement was made by the French early in the 17th century, and the province was called Acadia until finally ceded to the British by the Treaty of Utrecht in 1713.

CONSTITUTION AND GOVERNMENT. Under the British North America Act of 1867 the legislature of Nova Scotia may exclusively make laws in relation to local matters, including direct taxation within the province, education and the administration of justice. The legislature of Nova Scotia consists of a Lieut.-Governor, appointed and paid by the federal government, and holding office for 5 years, and a House of Assembly of 46 members, chosen by popular vote not more than every 5 years. The province is represented in the Canadian Senate by 10 members, and in the House of Commons by 11.

The franchise and eligibility to the legislature are granted to every person, male or female, if of age (19 years), a British subject or Canadian citizen, and a resident for 1 year in the province and 2 months before the date of the writ of election in the county or electoral district of which the polling district forms part, and it not by law otherwise disqualified. State of parties in Dec. 1970: 23 Liberals, 21 Progressive Conservatives, 2 New Democrats.

Lieut.-Governor: Victor deB. Oland (assumed office 22 July 1968).

The members of the Liberal Ministry are as follows:

Premier and Chairman N. S. Power Commision: G. A. Regan, QC.
Minister of Finance and Economics, Education: P. M. Nicholson, QC. *Highways, Public Works:* A. G. Brown. *Lands and Forests, Fisheries:* B. Comeau. Agriculture and Marketing, *Municipal Affairs and in charge of Liquor Control:* J. W. Gillis. *Public Welfare, Mines and Minister under Water Act:* A. E. Sullivan. *Provincial Secretary, Trade and Industry:* R. F. Fiske. *Attorney-General, Labour:* L. L. Pace. *Public Health, in charge of Housing Development and Human Rights Acts:* D. S. MacNutt.

Agent-General in London: Charles Richardson (60 Trafalgar Sq., WC2N 5EA).

LOCAL GOVERNMENT. The main divisions of the province for governmental purposes are the 3 cities, the 38 towns and the 24 rural municipalities, each governed by a council and a mayor or warden. The cities have independent charters, and the various towns take their powers from and are limited by The Towns Act, and the various municipalities take their powers from and are limited by The Municipal Act as revised in 1967. The majority of municipalities comprise one county, but 6 counties are divided into 2 municipalities each. In no case do the boundaries of any municipality overlap county lines. The 18 counties as such have no administrative functions.

Any city (of which there are 3) or incorporated town (of which there are 38) that lies within the boundaries of a municipality is excluded from any jurisdiction by the municipal council and has its own government.

AREA AND POPULATION. The area of the province is 21,842 sq. miles (55,000 sq. km), of which 20,401 sq. miles are land area, 1,024 sq. miles freshwater area and 417 sq. miles salt-water area (the Bras d'Or lakes). The population (census 1966) was 756,039; estimate (1970) 767,000.

Population of the principal cities and towns (census 1966): Halifax, 86,792; Dartmouth, 58,745; Sydney, 32,767; Glace Bay, 23,516; Truro, 13,007; Amherst, 10,551; New Glasgow, 10,489; Sydney Mines, 9,171; Yarmouth, 8,319.

Vital statistics, *see* pp. 178–80.
Religion, *see* p. 180.

EDUCATION. Public education in Nova Scotia is free, compulsory and undenominational through elementary and high school. Attendance is compulsory to the age of 14 in rural areas and 16 in urban areas. In addition to over 800 public schools there are the Halifax School for the Blind and the Interprovincial School for the Education of the Deaf; the Nova Scotia School for Boys; the Maritime Home for Girls, and the Nova Scotia Training School for mentally deficient children. The province has 14 universities and colleges, of which the largest is Dalhousie University in Halifax. The Nova Scotia Agricultural College and the Nova Scotia Teachers College are located at Truro. The Nova Scotia Technical College at Halifax grants degrees in engineering and architecture.

The Department of Education operates through its Vocational Education Division 2 institutes of technology, 13 regional vocational schools, vocational evening schools, coalmining schools, a land survey institute, a marine engineering school, a marine navigation school, a correspondence study service, a service for the vocational rehabilitation of the physically handicapped and classes for unemployed persons.

The Adult Education Division of the Department of Education, in co-operation with the local authorities, organizes and supports evening classes in elementary and secondary education and non-vocational subjects and vocational evening classes in non-vocational schools. The Provincial Department of Labour conducts apprenticeship classes. Short courses for fishermen and farmers are conducted by the Departments of Fisheries and Agriculture, respectively.

Total expenditure on public education for the year 1968–69 was $102,570,857, of which 64·1% was borne by the provincial government. In 1968–69, 8,981 classrooms operated in 737 school sections, with 9,320 teachers and 211,533 pupils, of whom 50,823 were in junior high school and 33,814 in senior high school grades.

JUSTICE. There is a Supreme Court which is a Court of common law and equity possessing original and appellate jurisdiction in civil and in criminal cases. The Supreme Court consists of an appeal division of 3 judges and a trial division of 6 judges. There are also county courts, family courts, probate courts, magistrates' courts, municipal and justices' courts. Bodies, sometimes referred to as courts, are established for the revision of assessment rolls, voters' lists and like purposes. Juvenile courts throughout the Province have power to try boys and girls under the age of 16 years.

For the year ending 31 March 1970 there were 7,724 admissions to provincial jails (3,669 under sentence, 4,055 on remand). The Adult Probation Service handled 1,962 cases during 1969.

FINANCE. The revenue is raised from federal subsidies granted under the British North America Act and under the Federal Provincial Fiscal Arrangements Act; and from royalties on coal and minerals, special fees on incorporated companies, partnerships, automobiles and other statutory fees, a tax on gasoline, theatre tickets, lands and forests, telephones and the sale of liquor as well as a health services tax.

The Federal-Provincial Fiscal Arrangements Act 1967 provides for a reduction of individual income taxes by reducing the federal tax payable by 28% in 1967. Federal corporation income taxes were reduced by 10% of taxable income. Nova Scotia levies personal and corporate income taxes to the exact amount of the federal reduction. Provision is made for equalization and stabilization grants applicable as well as certain guarantees. The Federal Government continues to pay those provinces not levying succession duties 75% of the federal estate tax yields.

Revenue, expenditure and debt (in Canadian $) for fiscal years ending 31 March:

	1966–67	1967–68	1968–69	1969–70	1970–71[2]
Revenue	168,132,118	221,641,885	255,784,101	322,618,644	353,416.210
Expenditure[1]	159,410,048	203,111,792	245,131,862	302,616,572	337,609,990
Funded debt	454,210,000	580,136,000	701,142,000	806,749,000	..

[1] Not including sinking-fund instalments. [2] Estimates.

Sinking-fund investments totalled $119,044,527 (31 March 1970). Revenue producing assets: Advances to Nova Scotia Power Commission, $54,386,231; to Industrial Estates Ltd, $56,417,623; to Deuterium of Canada Ltd, $109m.; others, including balance at credit of province with federal government, $140,653,477.

AGRICULTURE. Dairying, poultry and egg production, livestock and fruit growing are the most important branches. Farm cash receipts for 1969 were estimated at $63m., with an additional $10m. going to persons on farms as income in kind.

Cash receipts from sale of dairy products was $16·8m., with total milk production of 346m. lb.

Approved hatcheries produced 6·8m. chicks in 1969. During the year 5·6m. chicks were placed for broiler production and 1·2m. for egg production. Production of dressed poultry was about 21·6m. lb. Egg production was 20·9m. dozen.

The main 1969 fruit crops were apples, 3m. bu.; blueberries, 9·3m. lb.; and strawberries, 2·4m. quarts.

Use of ground limestone as a soil conditioner amounted to 71,308 tons in 1968. Sales of mixed fertilizer and materials totalled 33,942 short tons.

The 138 co-operatives in the province had a membership of 33,000, total assets of $24·8m. and sales of $61·5m. in 1968.

FORESTRY. The estimated forest area of Nova Scotia is 16,300 sq. miles, of which about 25% is owned by the Province. The principal trees are spruce, balsam fir, hemlock, pine, larch, birch, oak, maple, poplar and ash. Beech, once an important hardwood species, has almost disappeared. The gross value of all forest products in 1967 was about $100m.

FISHERIES. The fisheries of the province in 1969 had a landed value of $56,414,000, including scallop fishery, $10,145,000, and lobster fishery, $14,833,000. There are about 5,300 employees in the fish processing industry; the value of shipment of goods was $90·58m.

MINING. Principal minerals in 1969 were: Coal, 2,627,869 tons, valued at $21,584,192; gypsum, 5,211,548 tons, valued at $ . . ; salt, 424,656 tons, valued at $4,614,969; barite, 120,400 tons, valued at $1,100,000. Total value of mineral production in 1969 was about $54m.

INDUSTRY. The number of manufacturing establishments was 931 in 1966; the number of employees was 33,025; wages, $152m.; value of shipments in 1969 was $719·4m. Steel, oil, fish products, pulp and paper processing are the leading industries.

TRADE UNIONS. The majority of unions are affiliated with the Canadian Labour Congress. The most important independent organizations are District 26, of the United Mine Workers of America, the Brotherhood of Locomotive Engineers and the Teamsters. In 1969 there were 457 local unions in Nova Scotia with a membership of 59,925.

COMMUNICATIONS. The province is covered with a network of railways, 1,750 miles in extent. There were, in 1970, 15,385 miles of highways; 2,064 trunk (2,043 paved), 13,321 county (4,713 paved) highways. The figures are exclusive of highways within cities and towns.

There is a direct air service to major Canadian and USA cities, London and Bermuda.

Ferry services connect Nova Scotia with Newfoundland, Prince Edward Island, New Brunswick and Maine.

BOOKS OF REFERENCE

Proceedings and Transactions of the Nova Scotia Historical Society and Nova Scotia Institute of Science

Beck, Murray, *The Government of Nova Scotia.* Toronto, 1957.—*Joseph Howe, The Voice of Nova Scotia.* 1964

Brebner, John B. *New England's Outpost.* New York, 1927

Campell, G. C., *The History of Nova Scotia.* Toronto, 1968

Saunders, J. A., *Studies in the Economy of the Maritime Provinces.* London, 1939

Ward, L. R., *Nova Scotia: The Land of Co-operation.* New York, 1942

NEW BRUNSWICK

HISTORY. Touched by Jacques Cartier in 1534, New Brunswick was first explored by Samuel de Champlain in 1604. It was ceded by the French in the Treaty of Utrecht in 1713 and became a permanent British possession in 1763. It was separated from Nova Scotia and became a province in June 1784, as a result of the great influx of United Empire Loyalists. Responsible government came into being in 1848, and consisted of an executive council, a legislative council (later abolished) and a House of Assembly.

CONSTITUTION AND GOVERNMENT. The government is vested in a Lieut.-Governor and a Legislative Assembly of 58 members on a constituency basis. A simultaneous translation system is used in the assembly. Any Canadian subject of full age and 12 months residence is entitled to vote. As a result of the provincial election held on 23 Oct. 1967 and subsequent by-elections, the Assembly is composed of 31 Liberals and 27 Progressive Conservatives. The province has 10 members in the Canadian Senate and 10 members in the federal House of Commons.

Lieut.-Governor: Wallace S. Bird (appointed 1 Feb. 1968).

The members of the Liberal Ministry are as follows (July 1969):

Premier: Louis J. Robichaud, PC, QC.
Agriculture: J. A. Levesque. *Education:* W. W. Meldrum, QC. *Finance:* L. G. DesBrisay. *Fisheries:* Ernest Richard. *Health and Welfare:* Norbert Thériault. *Labour:* H. H. Williamson. *Municipal Affairs:* B. Fernand Nadeau. *Natural Resources:* W. R. Duffie. *Provincial Secretary:* J. E. LeBlanc. *Public Works (Buildings):* Raymond Doucett. *Public Works (Highways):* A. F. Richard. *Youth:* Louis J. Robichaud. *Justice:* Bernard Jean, QC. *Economic Growth:* R. J. Higgins. *Without Portfolio and Chairman of the New Brunswick Power Commission:* H. Graham Crocker.

Deputy Minister in London: John A Paterson.

LOCAL GOVERNMENT. Under the reforms introduced in 1967 the province has assumed complete administrative and financial responsibility for education, health, welfare and administration of justice. Local government is now restricted to provision of services of a strictly local nature. Under the new municipal structure, units include existing and new cities, towns and villages. Counties have disappeared as municipal units. Areas with limited populations have become local service districts. The former local improvement districts have become towns, villages or local service districts depending on their size.

AREA AND POPULATION. The area of the province is 28,354 sq. miles (72,000 sq. km), of which 27,835 sq. miles are land area. The population (census 1966) was 616,788; rural population, 260,816; villages classed as non-rural, 83,852. Census population of urban centres: Saint John, 100,192; Moncton, 69,711; Fredericton (capital), 38,521; Bathurst, 18,256; Edmundston, 17,586; Campbellton, 15,856.

Vital statistics, *see* p. 178–80.
Religion, *see* p. 180.

EDUCATION. Public education is free and non-sectarian. There are 4 universities. The University of New Brunswick at Fredericton (founded 13 Dec. 1785 by the Loyalists, elevated to university status in 1823, reorganized as the University of New Brunswick in 1859) had 4,555 students at the main campus and 513 at a subsidiary campus in Saint John (Dec. 1969); Mount Allison University at Sackville had 1,330 students; the University of Moncton at Moncton,

1,418 students; St Thomas University at Fredericton, 785 students. Colleges affiliated with the University of Moncton had 1,847 students.

There were, as of 30 June 1969, 173,931 pupils and 7,833 teachers using 5,984 classrooms in 685 school buildings (Grades 1–12). Large new regional schools are absorbing numbers of small country schools; the number of school districts has been lowered from 377 to 33.

FINANCE. The ordinary budget (in Canadian $) is shown as follows (financial years ended 31 March):

	1965	1966	1967	1968	1969
Gross revenue	134,701,316	156,357,149	183,337,173	258,849,238	308,953,629
Gross expenditure	132,252,653	146,437,988	180,682,671	263,859,945	322,047,299

Funded debt outstanding (exclusive of Treasury bills) as of 31 March 1969 was $446·2m. Sinking funds held by Province at 31 March 1969, $82·9m.

AGRICULTURE. The total area under field crops in 1967 was estimated at 434,500 acres, exclusive of pasture land (200,000 acres) and the acreage for blueberries, strawberries and orchards. Mixed farming is common throughout the province. Dairy farming is centred around the larger urban areas, and is located mainly along the Saint John River Valley and in the south-eastern sections of the province. For particulars of agricultural production and livestock, *see under* CANADA. Agricultural income is about $70m. annually.

FORESTRY. New Brunswick contains some 13·5m. acres of productive forest lands, of which 7·3m. acres is Crown-owned. The value of forest production is about $225m. annually. The woodpulp and paper-producing mills account for over $160m. Seventy large saw-mills (sawing over 1m. bd ft per year) together with some 175 smaller mills combine to produce over $65m. worth of lumber each year. The combined employment in wood-using plants is over 6,300 men.

FISHING. Commercial fishing is one of the most important basic industries of the province. Over 50 commercial species of fish and shellfish are landed. More than 5,800 fishermen and 4,000 plant workers are employed; the gross yearly income of the fishermen is over $16m., and the total market value of fish products is approximately $60m. The province created a separate Department of Fisheries in 1963 which provides research and development, technical and training facilities and assistance in financing and marketing. Under its sponsorship large steel trawlers have been constructed for offshore operations, and new processing plants have been built by private enterprise.

MINING. A considerable variety of minerals exist in the province, such as lead, copper, tin, tungsten, molybdenum, antimony, manganese, iron, bituminous coal, gypsum, salt, glauberite, oil shale, diatomite, oil and gas. Large reserves of lead–zinc–copper have been located in the north-eastern section of the province, and this has resulted in the construction of two concentrators, a smelter and port facilities at Belledune near the city of Bathurst. Among others in production are mines owned by Consolidated Mining and Smelting Company of Canada and Heath Steele Mines Ltd.

Quantities of good limestone exist in the southern part of the province and are quarried for lime, the pulp industry and as a fertilizing agent. Various granites are quarried and manufactured at St Stephen and Hampstead. Natural gas and oil are produced near Moncton.

INDUSTRY. In 1969 there were about 800 manufacturing establishments, employing about 30,000 persons. Pulp and paper is the most important industry, followed by mining and food processing, especially fish curing and packing. Other manufacturing includes electronics, stoves and furnaces, footwear and clothing, oil refining, brewing and shipbuilding. New Brunswick's location, with harbours open throughout the year, makes it ideal for exporting.

The tourist industry is of growing importance, as New Brunswick abounds with natural attractions and opportunities for recreation.

ELECTRICITY. Hydro-electric and thermal power plants of the New Brunswick Electric Power Commission had a combined capacity of 1m. kw. in July 1969. This includes the first half of the 600,000-kw. Mataquac hydro-electric development near Fredericton.

ROADS. The province had, on 31 March 1969, 13,231 miles of highway, including 8,035 miles of gravel roads, 3,233 miles of bituminized gravel roads and 1,910 miles of paved roads. Passenger vehicles, 31 Dec. 1968, numbered 157,481; commercial vehicles, 39,377, and motor cycles, 3,554.

POST. On 30 June 1969 the New Brunswick Telephone Co. Ltd had 211,604 telephones in service.

BOOKS OF REFERENCE

INDUSTRIAL INFORMATION. Dept. of Economic Growth, Fredericton.

New Brunswick and Its People. Fredericton, 1962
New Brunswick, An Economic Profile. Fredericton,1968
Department of Economic Growth, *Annual Report.* Fredericton, 1968

QUEBEC—QUÉBEC

HISTORY. Quebec was formerly known as New France or Canada from 1535 to 1763; as the province of Quebec from 1763 to 1790; as Lower Canada from 1791 to 1846; as Canada East from 1846 to 1867, and when, by the union of the four original provinces, the Confederation of the Dominion of Canada was formed, it again became known as the province of Quebec (Québec).

The Quebec Act, passed by the British Parliament in 1774, guaranteed to the people of the newly conquerered French territory in North America security in their religion and language, their customs and tenures, under their own civil laws.

CONSTITUTION AND GOVERNMENT. There is a Legislative Assembly consisting of 108 members, elected in 108 electoral districts for 5 years. There were, in Oct. 1969, 57 Union Nationale, 48 Liberals and 3 Independents.

Lieut.-Governor: The Hon. Hughes Lapointe, QC, PC (sworn in 22 Feb. 1966).

The members of the Executive Council as in Nov. 1970, are as follows:

Prime Minister: Robert Bourassa.

Labour and Manpower: Jean Cournoyer. *Roads and Public Works:* Bernard Pinard. *Trade, Commerce and Intergovernmental Affairs:* Gérard D. Levesque. *Tourism, Fish and Game:* Claire Kirkland-Casgarin. *Finance:* Raymond Garneau. *Health, Family and Social Welfare:* Claude Castonguay. *Justice:* Jerôme Choqnette. *Financial Institutions, Companies and Co-operatives:* William Tetly. *Education:* Guy Saint-Pierre. *Civil Service:* Raymond Garneau. *Municipal Affairs:* Maurice Tessier. *Revenue:* Gerald Harvey. *Agriculture and Colonization:* Norman Toupin. *Natural Resources:* Gilles Massé. *Lands and Forests:* Kevin Drummond. *Transport:* Georges-E. Tremblay. *Culture and Immigration:* François Cloutier. *Communications:* Jean-Paul L'Allier. *Without Portfolio:* Oswald Parent; Gérald Harvey; Victor C. Goldbloom; Claude Simard; Robert Quenneville.

Agent-General in London: Guy Roberge, QC (Quebec House, W1).
Agent-General in New York: Charles Chartier (17 West 50th St., Rockefeller Centre).
General-delegate in Paris: Jean Chapdelaine (66 Pergolèse, Paris XVIᵉ).

AREA AND POPULATION. The area of Quebec (as amended by the Labrador Boundary Award) is 594,860 sq. miles (1,540,668 sq. km), of which 523,860 sq. miles is land area and 71,000 sq. miles water. Of this extent, 351,780 sq. miles represent the Territory of Ungava, annexed in 1912 under the Quebec Boundaries Extension Act. The population (census 1966) was 5,780,845; estimate, Jan. 1970, 6,004,000.

Principal cities (1969 est.): Quebec (capital), 174,782; Montreal, 1·46m; Laval, 220,442; Trois-Rivières, 63,350; Sherbrooke, 78,427; Verdun, 90,402; Hull, 61,039.

Vital statistics, see pp. 178–80.

Religion, see p. 180.

EDUCATION. The province has 7 universities: 3 Protestant universities, McGill (Montreal) founded in 1821, Bishop (Lennoxville) founded in 1845 and the Sir George William's College (Montreal) granted a charter in 1848; 3 Catholic universities: Laval (Quebec) founded in 1852, Montreal University, opened in 1876 as a branch of Laval and errected independently in 1920, Sherbrooke University founded in 1954 and University of Quebec founded in 1968. In 1969–70 there were 56,200 full-time university students and 4,300 teachers.

In 1969–70, in kindergartens, there were 108,200 pupils and 2,700 teachers; in elementary schools, 942,800 (34,900); in secondary schools, 608,800 (22,500).

FINANCE. Ordinary revenue and expenditure (in Canadian $1,000) for fiscal years ending 31 March:

	1965–66	1966–67	1967–68	1968–69 [1]	1969–70 [1]
Revenue	1,601,624	1,899,560	2,314,670	2,279,281	3,007,300
Expenditure	1,571,879	1,838,172	2,217,662	2,397,964	3,060,500

[1] Estimates.

The total funded debt at 31 March 1969 was $2,335,546,102, the net bonded debt was $1,549,080,929.

AGRICULTURE. In 1969 the total area of the principal field crops was 4,677,000 acres. The yield of the principal crops was (in 1,000):

Crops	Yield	Crops	Yield
Tame hay [1]	7,029 tons	Fodder corn	1,086 tons
Oats	38,415 bu.	Flaxseed	197 tons
Potatoes	7,029 cwt	Barley	866 bu.
Mixed grains	3,752 bu.	Buckwheat	290 bu.

[1] Including clover and alfalfa.

The farm cash receipts from farming operations in 1969 amounted to $678,094,000. The principal items being: Livestock and products, $567,038,000; crops, $60·2m.; forest and maple products, $11m.; dairy supplements payments, $38·2m.

FORESTRY. Forests cover an area of 378,125 sq. miles. About 220,625 sq. miles are classified as productive forests, of which 77,805 sq. miles are Provincial crown land and 25,114 sq. miles are privately owned. Quebec leads the Canadian provinces in pulpwood production, having nearly half of the Canadian estimated total.

In 1969 production of sawn lumber was 1,738·2m. f.b.m.; wood-pulp, 6,482,000 tons; paper and paperboard, 5,738,000 tons; pulpwood, 5,906,000 cunits (100 cu. ft of solid wood).

FISHERY. The principal fish are cod, herring, mackerel, lobster and salmon. Total catch of sea fish, 1969, 2,114,000 lb, valued at $8,,613,900.

MINING (1969). The value of the mineral production was $721,865,484. Chief minerals: Copper, $162,476,885; iron ore, $109,405,064; zinc, $59,678,030; gold, $27,805,786.

The second major iron-ore development in northern Quebec is, like the one at Knob Lake which gave birth to Schefferville, based on the Quebec–Labrador Trough which extends from Lac Jeannine to the northern tip of Ungava peninsula. The port of Seven Islands and the railway connecting it with Schefferville allow easy shipment to the furnaces and steel mills of Canada, the USA and Europe. The setting-up of a steel industry is being explored.

Non-metallic minerals produced include: Asbestos ($154·4m.; 90% of Canadian production), titanium ($24·6m.), industrial lime, dolomite and brucite, quartz and pyrite. Among the building materials produced were: Cement, $47,377,602; sand and gravel, $18m.; lime, $4,759,680; stone, $37,825,000.

INDUSTRY. In 1967 there were 10,772 industrial establishments in the province; employees, 524,646; salaries and wages, $2,739·28m.; cost of materials, $5,935,243,000; value of shipments, $10,966·4m. Among the leading industries are pulp and paper, non-ferrous metal smelting and refining, chemical products, cotton yarn and cloth, men's and women's clothing, railway rolling stock, ship, building, brass and copper products, electrical apparatus, butter and cheese slaughtering and meat packing, cigars and cigarettes, machinery, boots and shoes.

ELECTRICITY. Water power is one of the most important natural resources of the province of Quebec. Its turbine installation represents about 48% of the aggregate of Canada. At the end of 1967 the installed generating capacity was 11,621,000 kwh. The Quebec Hydro-Electric Commission has completed the hydro-electric power scheme on the Manicouagan River, capable of producing 1·4m. h.p. Production, 1969, was 65,377m. kwh.; energy sold to final consumer, 40,204m. kwh.

EXTERNAL TRADE. In 1969 the value of Canadian exports through Quebec customs ports was $3,421,285,000; value of imports, $3,495,876,000.

COMMUNICATIONS (1967). Quebec had 5,360 miles of railway. Excluding cities, there were 45,994 miles of roads in the province, of which 36,363 were improved; 40,030 miles are maintained in winter. There were (1969) 1,517,397 registered passenger cars and 736,259 other motor vehicles. Telephones numbered 1,319,000. There were 16 television and 61 radio stations.

Quebec has an international airport (Dorval, Montreal) and 100 landing strips.

BOOKS OF REFERENCE

STATISTICAL INFORMATION   The Quebec Bureau of Statistics (Department of Industry and Commerce, Parliament Buildings, Quebec) was established in 1912. Its most important publication is the *Quebec Yearbook* (formerly *Quebec Statistical Year Book*; annually since 1914). Other annual publications include a *Directory of Manufactures*, a *Municipal Guide* and *Répertoire des publications gouvernementales du Québec*.

Atlas du Québec: L'Agriculture. Ministère de l'Industrie et du Commerce, Quebec, 1966
Baudoin, L., *Le Droit civil de la province de Québec*. Montreal, 1953
Blanchard, R., *Le Canada-français*. Paris, 1959
Brunet, M., *Canadiens et Canadians*. Montreal and Paris 1960.
The Economy of Quebec. Econ. Research Corporation Inc., Montreal, 1959
Ouellet, F., *Histoire de la Chambre de Commerce de Québec, 1809–1959*. Québec, 1959.
Raynauld, A., *Croissance et structure économiques de la province de Québec*. Québec, 1961
Wade, F. M., *The French Canadians, 1760–1945*. Toronto, 1955.—*Canadian Dualism: studies of French–English relations*. Quebec–Toronto, 1960

ONTARIO

CONSTITUTION AND GOVERNMENT. The provincial government is administered by a Lieut.-Governor, a cabinet and one chamber elected by a general franchise for a period of 5 years. Women have the vote and can be elected to the chamber.

After the election on 17 Oct. 1967 the provincial legislature was composed as follows: Progressive Conservatives, 69; Liberals, 28; New Democratic Party, 20; Liberal–Labor, 1; total, 117.

Lieut.-Governor: Hon. W. Ross Macdonald, PC, CD, QC (appointed 4 July 1968).

The members of the Executive Council in Jan. 1969 were as follows (all Progressive Conservatives):

Prime Minister and President of the Council: Dr John P. Robarts, QC. *Without Portfolio:* Fernand Guindon. *Tourism and Information:* James A. C. Auld. *Labour:* Dalton A. Bales, QC. *Lands and Forests:* René Brunelle. *Public Works:* J. R. Simonett. *Education and University Affairs:* William G. Davis, QC. *Health:* Thomas L. Wells. *Highways:* George E. Gomme. *Correctional Services:* Allan Grossman. *Transport:* Irwin Haskett. *Treasurer of Ontario and Minister of Economics:* C. S. MacNaughton. *Trade and Development:* Stanley J. Randall. *Financial and Commercial Affairs:* A. B. R. Lawrence, QC. *Energy and Resources Management:* G. A. Kerr. *Municipal Affairs:* W. Darcy McKeough. *Agriculture and Food:* William A. Stewart. *Provincial Secretary and Minister of Citizenship:* Robert Welch, QC. *Justice and Attorney-General:* A. A. Wishart, QC. *Social and Family Services:* John Yaremko, QC. *Mines:* Alan F. Lawrence, QC.

Senior Trade and Industry Counsellor in London: W. T. Thompson (Ontario House, 13 Charles II St., SW1).

LOCAL GOVERNMENT. Local government in Ontario is divided into two branches, one pertaining to municipal institutions and the other to education. The present system of municipal institutions was established on 1 Jan. 1850; its scope and functions have been considerably enlarged.

For general municipal and local government purposes, Ontario is divided into counties (or unions of counties), cities, towns, villages and townships. The cities function independently of the county units, as also do 6 towns which have been separated from the counties for municipal purposes. Every town, village and township which lies within the confines of a county functions for certain specific purposes through the county, but otherwise as a separate unit.

The municipalities have control over all local affairs and undertakings, including the construction and upkeep of roads and streets, other than main traffic arteries, provision of utility services, provision and administration of police forces, fire departments, sanitation services and social welfare services. The annual expenditures for municipal purposes are provided in part by grants received from the Province, but the bulk of the money required is provided by direct taxation imposed upon real property and, in a limited way, upon what is known as business assessment. The council of each municipality also imposes and collects from the taxpayers such moneys as the local educational authority may require.

Each unit of municipal government is governed by a council elected by popular vote. A city council is composed of a mayor and aldermen; a town council of a mayor, reeve (or reeves) and councillors; a village and a township council of a reeve (or reeves) and councillors. A township council is composed of 5 members, including the reeve and the deputy reeve, if any. The councils in cities, towns and villages vary in number of members, but none of them exceeds 25.

The county council is composed of the reeve and deputy reeve (if any) of each town, village and township within the county boundaries. The only exceptions from that rule are the cities and the 6 separated towns referred to above. The principal functions of a county council are related to construction and maintenance of such traffic arteries as have been included in the county road system, the provision of court houses and jails, homes for the aged and child welfare institutions.

No municipality in Ontario may incur long-term debts without the sanction of the tribunal created by the Provincial Legislature and known as the Ontario Municipal Board. Debenture obligations incurred by municipalities for utility undertakings (water-works and electric light and power systems) are discharged ordinarily out of revenues derived from the sale of utility services and do not fall upon the ratepayer.

With respect to education, municipal councils have no jurisdiction, except as to the provision of moneys. Responsibility for provision of school premises, their operation and maintenance and the supply of teachers is in the hands of the local education authority, which is an elected body. In cities and towns education falls under the control of one local authority. The smaller urban communities and the townships usually have separate authorities for elementary and secondary education.

The conduct of municipal institutions comes under the guidance of the Provincial Department of Municipal Affairs. The principal functions of the department are of an advisory nature, but it does exercise a limited control with respect to matters relating to municipal audits and other specific situations. Education comes under the guidance and control of the Provincial Department of Education, which deals with the training of teachers and formulation of the curriculum.

There are considerable areas in the northernmost parts of Ontario where as yet there is little or no settlement of population. In such areas no municipal organization exists, and control for all purposes over such areas remains in the hands of the provincial government.

AREA AND POPULATION. The total area is 412,582 sq. miles (1·55 sq. km), of which 344,092 sq. miles is land area and 68,490 sq. miles fresh water. The province extends 1,000 miles from east to west and 1,050 miles from south to north. About 82% of this area lies south of the isotherm of 60° F. (16° C.) mean July temperature, which is generally considered the northern limit for the economic production of cereals.

The province is bordered by Quebec on the east and Manitoba on the west. The southern boundary has a fresh-water shoreline of 2,362 miles on the Great Lakes; its northern limits have a salt-water shoreline of 680 miles.

The population of the province (estimate, 1 June 1969) was 7,345,000. Census population of the principal cities (1966): Toronto (provincial capital), 664,584 (city), 2,158,496 (metropolitan area); Hamilton, 298,121 (city), 449,116 (metropolitan area); Ottawa (federal capital), 290,742 (city), 384,397 (metropolitan area); Windsor, 192,544 (city), 211,697 (metropolitan area); London, 194,416 (city), 207,396 (metropolitan area); Kitchener, 93,255 (city), 192,275 (metropolitan area); Sudbury, 84,888 (city), 117,075 (metropolitan area).

Vital statistics, *see* pp. 178–80.

Religion, *see* p. 180.

EDUCATION. There is a complete provincial system of elementary and secondary schools. In 1969 publicly controlled elementary and secondary schools had 2,369,796 pupils enrolled. There are several private schools. In 1965 Ontario established Colleges of Applied Arts and Technology; by the end of 1969 full-time enrolment in 20 colleges was 24,742 and part-time enrolment 34,978. An educational television branch was created in 1966 to produce programmes for in-school viewing in both English and French.

The University of Toronto, founded in 1827, had an enrolment of 19,975 (1968–69). Other universities are Queen's at Kingston, Western Ontario at London, McMaster at Hamilton, The University of Windsor at Windsor, Ottawa and Carleton at Ottawa, Waterloo and Waterloo Lutheran at Waterloo, Laurentian at Sudbury, The University of Guelph at Guelph, York at Toronto, Brock at St Catharines, Lakehead at Port Arthur and Trent at Peterborough. All of them receive provincial grants. The net general expenditure of the Provincial Department of Education and University Affairs for the fiscal year ending 31 March 1970 is estimated at $1,333·7m.

FINANCE. The net general revenue and expenditure and the net capital debt (in Canadian $1,000) for years ending 31 March were as follows:

	1965–66	1966–67	1967–68	1968–69	1969–70
Revenue	1,444,246	1,811,269	2,157,952	2,604,386	3.292,000
Expenditure	1,456,198	1,791,129	2,264,700	2,745,370	3.266,500
Capital debt	1,380,505	1,343,700	1,450,500	1,591,500	1,566,000

[1] Estimates (including 8 months' actual revenue and expenditure).

Net general revenue equals net ordinary revenue and net capital receipts from physical assets. Net general expenditure equals net ordinary expenditure including provision for sinking fund and net capital expenditure on physical assets.

AGRICULTURE. In 1969, 7,679,000 acres were under field crops (including tobacco). The net cash income from the sale of farm products was: 1964, $300·73m.; 1965, $340,543,000; 1966, $467,762,000; 1967, $388,787,000; 1968, $398·753,000; 1969, $446,193,000.

FORESTRY (1968). The total area of productive forested land is 164,471·8 sq. miles, comprising: softwoods, 75,460·9; hardwoods, 21,379·7; mixed woods, 55,098·4; reproducing forests, 12,532·8. The growing stock equals 150,683m. cu. ft. The estimated value of shipments by forest products is: 1963, $137m.; 1964, $140m.; 1965, $152m.

MINING (1969). The value of mineral production (in $1m.) of major metals was: Nickel, 330·9; copper, 235·5; iron ore, 126·1; gold, 45·5; uranium, 38·8. The value of structural materials was $191·4m. The total value of mineral production was estimated at $1,355·6m. Ontario's mining industry in 1969 accounted for 26% of Canada's $4,690·6m. total.

INDUSTRY (1967). Ontario is Canada's most heavily industrialized province. In 1967, 71% of value added in commodity-producing industries was accounted for by manufacturing. Construction was next with 13·8%.
In 1967, 13,076 manufacturing establishments employed 818,105 persons. Total salaries and wages paid, $4,821·4m.; selling-value of factory shipments, $20,259·7m.
The leading manufacturing industries are motor vehicles, iron and steel, motor vehicle parts and accessories, slaughtering and meat packing, pulp and paper, chemicals, industrial petroleum refining, miscellaneous machinery and equipment, and dairy.

ELECTRICITY (1969). The Hydro-Electric Power Commission of Ontario recorded for the calendar year a dependable peak capacity of 11,242,000 kw. and a net energy output generated and purchased of 62,448m. kwh.

EXTERNAL TRADE. In 1969 Ontario exported over 40% of Canada's total foreign trade.

ROADS. There were in 1969 13,131·5 miles of highways (excluding roads), of which 10,407·5 miles were surfaced. Motor licences (in 1969–70) numbered 2,953,789, of which 2,308,743 were passenger cars.

RAILWAYS. As of 31 Dec. 1966 there were 9,965 miles of railway, most of which was operated by Canadian National Railways, the Canadian Pacific Railway and Ontario Northland Railway. The Turbo non-stop service Montreal–Toronto is the fastest train in North America.

COMMUNICATIONS (1969). Telephone service is provided by 61 independent systems (165,500 telephones) and the Bell Telephone Co. (3,618,752 telephones).

F

BOOKS OF REFERENCE

STATISTICAL INFORMATION. Publications of the Ontario Department of Treasury and Economics include: *Ontario Statistical Review* (annual), *Ontario Economic Review* (bimonthly), *Population Statistics for Ontario*; Special Regional Economic Surveys: *Mid-Western Ontario Region, 1965*; *Lake Erie Region, 1965*; *Northeastern Ontario Region, 1966: Niagara. 1966*; *Lake St. Clair Region, 1967*; *Lake Ontario Region, 1968*; *Design for Development, 1961*; *The Toronto Centre Region, 1969*; *The Midwestern Ontario Region, 1969*

MANITOBA

CONSTITUTION AND GOVERNMENT. Manitoba was known as the Red River Settlement before its entry into the Dominion in 1870. The provincial government is administered by a Lieut.-Governor and a legislative assembly of 57 members elected for 5 years. Women were enfranchised in 1916. The Electoral Division Act, 1955, created 57 single-member constituencies and abolished the transferable vote. The Electoral Divisions Act, 1969, created 29 rural electoral divisions, and 28 urban electoral divisions. The province is represented by 6 members in the Senate and 13 in the House of Commons of Canada. The Crown lands and other natural resources were transferred from the Dominion Government to the province as from 15 July 1930.

Lieut.-Governor: William John McKeag (sworn in 2 Sept. 1970).

State of parties in Legislative Assembly (elected 25 June 1969): New Democratic Party, 28; Conservative, 22; Liberals, 4; Social Credit, 1; independent, 2. The members of the New Democratic Ministry are as follows (Jan. 1971):

Premier and President of the Executive Council, Minister of Provincial–Dominion Relations, Minister charged with the administration of the Manitoba Development Act: Edward R. Streyer.
Finance: Saul M. Cherniack, QC. *Public Works and Highways:* Joseph P. Borowski. *Attorney-General:* Alvin H. Mackling, QC. *Health and Social Development:* Rene Toupin. *Tourism, Recreation and Cultural Affairs:* Peter Burtniak. *Labour:* A. R. Paulley. *Municipal Affairs:* Howard R. Pawley. *Industry and Commerce:* Leonard S. Evans. *Mines and Natural Resources and Commissioner of Northern Affairs:* Sidney Green, QC. *Youth and Education:* Saul A. Miller. *Agriculture:* Samuel Uskiw. *Consumer, Corporate and Internal Services:* Ben Hanuschak. *Without Portfolio:* Russell Doern.

LOCAL GOVERNMENT. The Municipal Act, R.S.M. 1954, *c.* 173, applies to all incorporated rural municipalities, villages, towns and cities, except cities with special charters (Winnipeg, St Boniface, and in some respects Brandon, St James, Portage la Prairie and East and West Kildonan).

Rural municipalities are incorporated under the Municipal Boundaries Act.

A locality containing over 500 inhabitants and a taxable assessment of over $300,000 may be incorporated as a village corporation. No village so incorporated shall occupy an area of more than 640 acres, unless its population exceeds 2,000.

A locality containing over 1,500 inhabitants may be incorporated as a town corporation. No town incorporated after the passing of the Municipal Act, the population of which does not exceed 2,000, shall occupy an area of more than 640 acres. If the population exceeds 2,000 the limits may be increased in the proportion of 160 acres for every additional 1,000 inhabitants. Public parks are excluded in calculating area.

A town containing over 10,000 inhabitants may be erected into a city.

Upon petition from 50% of the householders in a locality which is not included within the limits of a municipality, it may be incorporated as a municipal district. Localities which do not qualify under the provisions of the Municipal Act, Municipal Boundaries Act or Local Government Districts Act, or if they desire special power or privileges, may be incorporated by special act of the legislature.

AREA AND POPULATION. The area of the province is 251,000 sq. miles (652,218 sq. km), of which 211,775 sq. miles are land and 39,255 sq. miles water. In 1912 its boundaries were extended to the shores of Hudson Bay.

The population (June 1970 estimate) was 981,000, of which the rural population (1966 estimate) was 338,323. Population of the principal cities (1966 census): Winnipeg (capital), 257,005 (metropolitan area (1969), 524,000); St Boniface, 43,214; St James, 35,685; Brandon, 29,981; St Vital, 29,528; East Kildonan, 28,796; West Kildonan, 22,240; Transcona, 19,761; Thompson (1969 estimate), 20,000; Portage la Prairie, 13,012; Flin Flon, 10,201.

Vital statistics, see pp. 178–80.

Religion, see p. 180.

EDUCATION. Education is municipally controlled, as in all the provinces, and is supported by local taxation and government grants. The University of Manitoba, founded in 1877 in Winnipeg, had (in 1970–71) 12,273 regular students in all courses. The University of Brandon had 1,150 and the University of Winnipeg had 2,390 students enrolled. There were (1970–71), 11,579 teachers teaching 180,386 elementary pupils and 65,162 secondary pupils. In 1970–71, $163m. was spent on education.

FINANCE. Revenue and expenditure (current account) for fiscal years ending 31 March (in Canadian $):

	1965–66	1966–67	1967–68	1968–69	1969–70[1]	1970–71[1]
Revenue	210,708,638	292,332,222	346,526,123	357,331,901	398,929,099	448,868,819
Expenditure	195,441,973	291,641,200	345,564,761	355,931,623	398,400,000	448,000,000

[1] Estimates.

The figures from 1966 are on the reporting basis of gross presentation, replacing the net presentation of prior years.

AGRICULTURE. Rich farmland is the main primary resource, although the area of Manitoba in farms is only approximately 14% of the total land area. Commercial farming is confined to the southern part of Manitoba, while the northern three-fifths contain the rich mineral deposits of the Pre-Cambrian Shield. The total value of agricultural products in Manitoba in 1970 was $443m., of which $207m. came from livestock and $232m. from crops.

FORESTRY. About 60% of the land area is wooded, of which 55,700 sq. miles is productive forest land. Value of forest production in fiscal year 1969–70 was $25m.

FUR TRADE. Value of fur pelts taken during 1968–69 from the wild was valued at $2·7m.; from ranch-bred animals, $3·1m.

FISHERIES. From 39,225 sq. miles of rivers and lakes covering Manitoba 18,919,182 lb. of edible fish were caught in 1969–70; market value $3·4m. Whitefish, sauger, pickerel, pike, trout and perch are the principal varieties caught.

MINING. Total value of minerals in 1970 was $325m. Principal minerals mined are nickel, zinc, copper, lead and silver. Selenium, tellurium and cadmium are recovered as by-products from base-metal operations. The International Nickel Co. of Canada mines came into production in 1961. The Thompson complex is producing 170m. lb. of nickel annually. New deposits of zinc, copper and nickel have been discovered in the northern area. A reserve of tantalum and lithium is also being exploited in the south-eastern area of Manitoba. Potential reserves of chromium, gold, bentonite, potash, caesium, kaolin and lithium also occur. The most important non-metallic minerals are cement, sand and gravel, building stone and quartz. Oil production in 1970 was estimated at $15m.

INDUSTRY. Manufacturing, the largest industry in the province, encompasses almost every major industrial activity in Canada. Gross value of factory shipments was estimated at $1,210m. in 1970. The manufacturing industry is comprised of over 1,500 plants employing 50,000 persons and paying $285m. in salaries and wages. Due to the agricultural base of the province, the food and beverage group of industries is by far the largest, accounting for approximately 40% of the total value. The next largest industries are metal fabricating and machinery, which account for approximately 15% of the manufacturing shipments. Clothing represents about 6%, while primary metals, paper and allied products, printing and publishing and transportation equipment each account for approximately 5% of the total value of factory shipments.

TOURISM. In 1970 Canadian, American and foreign tourists contributed about $135m. to the province's economy.

ELECTRICITY. The total generating capacity of Manitoba's power stations is 1·36m. kw. Construction is well under way on Phase One of the $400m. Nelson River Power Development which will almost double Manitoba's present capacity by 1971.

TRADE. Products grown and manufactured in Manitoba find readily available markets in other areas of Canada, in the USA, particularly the Upper Midwest Region, and in foreign countries. Export shipments for Manitoba in 1969 are estimated at $415m. Of these, approximately 6% originate from raw materials, 46% from wheat and unmilled grains and 46% from manufactured products.

COMMUNICATIONS. In the year 1970 the province had 4,900 miles of railway, not including industrial track, yards and sidings. Highways and roads had a total mileage of 11,300. A total of 34 licensed commercial air carriers operate from bases in Manitoba handling more than 18m. lb. of air freight each year. Nearly 96% of the province's 433,598 telephones are now dial-operated.

BOOKS OF REFERENCE

STATISTICAL INFORMATION. Inquiries may be addressed to the Deputy Minister, Department of Industry and Commerce, Room 310, Legislative Building, Winnipeg.

The Department of Industry and Commerce publishes: *Manitoba Trade Directory. Industry and Commerce Bulletin.*—Weir, T. R., *Economic Atlas of Manitoba.* 1960
The Department of Agriculture publishes: *Year Book of Manitoba's Agriculture*
Ninth Census of Canada: Manitoba. Ottawa, 1961

SASKATCHEWAN

HISTORY. Saskatchewan derives its name from its major river system, which the Cree Indians called 'Kis-is-ska-tche-wan', meaning 'swift flowing'. It officially became a province when it joined the Confederation on 1 Sept. 1905.

In 1670 King Charles II granted to Prince Rupert and his friends a charter covering exclusive trading rights in 'all the land drained by streams finding their outlet in the Hudson Bay'. This included what is now Saskatchewan. The trading company was first known as The Governor and Company of Adventurers of England; later as the Hudson's Bay Company. In 1869 the North West Territories was formed, and this included Saskatchewan. In 1882 the District of Saskatchewan was formed. By 1885 the North-West Mounted Police had been inaugurated, with headquarters in Regina (now the capital), and the Canadian Pacific Railway's transcontinental line had been completed, bringing a stream of immigrants to southern Saskatchewan. The Hudson's Bay Company surrendered its claim to territory in return for cash and land around the existing trading posts. Legislative government was introduced.

CONSTITUTION AND GOVERNMENT. The provincial government is vested in a Lieut.-Governor, an Executive Council and a Legislative Assembly, elected for 5 years. Women were given the franchise in 1916 and are also eligible for election to the legislature. State of parties in Dec. 1970: Liberals, 34; New Democratic Party, 24; 1 vacant.

Lieut.-Governor: S. Worobetz, MC.

The Liberal Ministry in Dec. 1970 was composed as follows:

Premier and President of the Council: W. Ross Thatcher, P.C.
Attorney-General Provincial Secretary and Co-operatives: D. V. Heald, QC.
Provincial Treasurer and Deputy Premier: D. G. Steuart. *Mineral Resources:* A. C. Cameron. *Public Health and Telephones:* G. B. Grant. *Highways and Transportation:* D. Boldt. *Agriculture:* D. T. McFarlane. *Public Works:* L. P. Coderre. *Education:* J. C. McIsaac, DVM. *Welfare:* C. P. MacDonald. *Municipal Affairs, Indian and Metis:* A. R. Guy. *Industry and Commerce:* C. L. B. Estey, QC. *Natural Resources:* J. R. Barrie. *Labour:* D. G. MacLennan.

Agent-General in London: F. H. Larson, 28 Chester St., SW1.

LOCAL GOVERNMENT. The organization of a city requires a minimum population of 5,000 persons; that of a town, 500; that of a village, 100 people. No requirements as to population exist for the rural municipality and the local improvement district.

Cities, towns, villages and rural municipalities are governed by elected councils, which consist of a mayor and 6–20 aldermen in a city; a mayor and 6 councillors in a town; a mayor and 2 other members in a village; a reeve and a councillor for each division in a rural municipality (usually 6). Local improvement districts are administered by the Department of Municipal Affairs.

AREA AND POPULATION. Saskatchewan is bounded on the west by Alberta, on the east by Manitoba, to the north by the Northwest Territories; to the south it is bordered by the US states of Montana and North Dakota. The area of the province is 251,700 sq. miles (652,000 sq. km), of which 220,182 sq. miles is land area and 31,518 sq. miles is water. The population (1970 estimate) was 942,000. Population of principal cities (1970 estimate): Regina (capital), 143,000; Saskatoon, 129,266; Moose Jaw, 33,500; Prince Albert, 28,000; Swift Current, 15,250; Yorkton, 14,200; North Battleford, 12,375; Estevan, 9,800; Weyburn, 9,200; Lloydminster, 7,777; Melville, 5,700.

Vital statistics, *see* pp. 178–80.
Religion, *see* p. 180.

EDUCATION. The University of Saskatchewan was established at Saskatoon on 3 April 1907. In 1970–71 it had about 10,600 (day-time) degree students and 817 full-time teaching staff at Saskatoon and over 5,400 students and 341 faculty members at Regina campus. The Saskatchewan public education system in 1969 consisted of 647 school districts serving 171,624 elementary pupils, 76,887 high-school students and 1,682 students enrolled in special classes. In addition, 3 provincial technical and trade schools provided training for approximately 9,000 students. There are also 35 Roman Catholic separate school districts and 3 separate high-school districts and 1 Protestant separate school district.

FINANCE. Budget and net assets (years ending 31 March) in Canadian $1,000:

	1965–66	1966–67	1967–68	1968–69	1969–70 [1]
Budgetary revenue	254,416	284,108	311,596	344,633	362,275
Budgetary expenditure	243,860	283,932	311,340	344,156	362,145
Net assets	52,190	52,736	53,388	54,199	54,711

[1] Preliminary.

NATURAL RESOURCES AND INDUSTRY. Agriculture used to dominate the history and economics of Saskatchewan, but the 'prairie province' is now a rapidly developing mining and manufacturing area. It is a major supplier of oil; has the world's largest deposits of potash; is the only source of helium in the 'free world' outside the USA, which limits production to internal use; and net value of non-agricultural production account for 51·5% of the provincial economy.

AGRICULTURE. Saskatchewan produces normally about two-thirds of Canada's wheat. Wheat production in 1970, was 210m. bu. from 8m. acres; oats, 110m. bu. from 1·95m. acres; barley, 142m. bu. from 3·3m. acres; rye, 11·5m. bu. from 535,000 acres; rape seed, 36m. bu. from 2m. acres; flax, 24·8m. bu. from 1·5m. acres. Livestock (June 1970): Cattle, 2·2m.; swine, 508,000; sheep, 118,000; poultry. 5·65m. Cash income from the sale of farm products in 1969 was estimated at $722m., of which 69% was from grain, the remainder from livestock and livestock products. In all, there are 70,000 commercial farms in the province, each being a holding having agricultural sales of $2,500 or more.

The South Saskatchewan River irrigation project, whose main feature is the Gardiner Dam, was completed in 1967. It will ultimately provide for an area of 200,000 acres of irrigated cultivation in Central Saskatchewan. Currently, 40,000 acres are under development.

FORESTRY. Half of Saskatchewan's area is forested, but only 42,000 sq. miles are of commercial value at present. Forest products valued at $31·2m. were produced in 1968–69. The province's first pulp-mill, at Prince Albert, went into production in 1968; its daily capacity is 1,000 tons of high-grade kraft pulp.

FUR PRODUCTION. In 1968–69 wild fur production was estimated at $1·81m. Ranch-raised fur production amounted to $1·08m.

FISHING. The market value of the 1966–69 commercial fish catch of 11m. lb. was $2·8m.

MINING. The 1969 mineral production was valued at $358m., including (in $1,000): Crude oil, 201,546; natural gas, 7,210; coal, 3,618; gold, 1,427; silver, 1,229; copper, 18,526; zinc, 7,499; cadmium, 290; selenium, 289; tellurium, 28; uranium, 10,915; potash, 67,120; salt, 1,829; sodium sulphate, 8,389; sulphur, 905.

INDUSTRY. In 1968 Saskatchewan had 756 manufacturing establishments. Total labour force (1969), 350,000. The net value of non-agricultural production was $792m. Manufacturing accounted for $174m., construction for $246m.

ELECTRICITY. The Saskatchewan Power Corporation generated 5,100m. kwh. in 1970.

TOURISM. An estimated 1·5m. tourists spent $90m. in 1970.

COMMUNICATIONS (1969). There were approximately 8,690 miles of main railway track in operation. There were 10,400 miles of provincial highways, 116,000 miles of municipal, local and rural roads; 2,600 miles of resources development roads. Motor vehicles registered totalled 472,250. Bus services are provided by 2 major lines.

Saskatchewan has 2 major airports, 176 airports and landing strips.

There were 995 post offices, 20 sound broadcasting stations and 7 television stations. 362,000 telephones were connected to the Saskatchewan Telecommunications system.

BOOKS OF REFERENCE

Tourist and industrial publications, descriptive of the Government's programme, are obtainable from the Department of Industry and Commerce; other government publications from Government Information Services (Legislative Building, Regina).

Saskatchewan Resources Conference 1964. Proceedings. Dept. of Industry and Commerce, Regina, 1965
Archer and Derby, *The Story of a Province.* Toronto, 1955
McCourt, E. A., *Saskatchewan.* Toronto, 1968
Morton, A. S. (ed. C. King), *Saskatchewan, the Making of a University.* Toronto, 1959
Wright, J. F. C., *Saskatchewan, the history of a province.* Toronto, 1955

ALBERTA

HISTORY. The southern half of the province of Alberta was part of Rupert's land which was granted by royal charter in 1670 to the Hudson's Bay Company. The intervention by the North West Company in the fur trade after 1783 led to the establishment of trading posts. In 1869 Rupert's land was transferred from the Hudson's Bay Company (which had absorbed its rival in 1821) to the new Dominion, and in the following year this land was combined with the former Crown land of the North Western Territories to form the Northwest Territories.

In 1882 'Alberta' first appeared as a provisional 'district', consisting of the southern half of the present province. In 1905 the Athabasca district to the north was added when provincial status was granted to Alberta.

Three parties have held office: the Liberals 1905–21; the United Farmers 1921–35, and Social Credit since 1935. The stable political climate created by these parties has eased Alberta's transition from an agrarian to an industrial society.

CONSTITUTION AND GOVERNMENT. The constitution of Alberta is contained in the British North America Act of 1867, and amending Acts; also in the Alberta Act of 1905, passed by the Parliament of the Dominion of Canada, which created the province out of the then Northwest Territories. All the provisions of the British North America Act, except those with respect to school lands and the public domain, were made to apply to Alberta as they apply to the older provinces of Canada. On 1 Oct. 1930 the natural resources were transferred from the Dominion to provincial government control. The province is represented by 6 members in the Senate and 19 in the House of Commons of Canada.

The executive is vested nominally in the Lieut.-Governor, who is appointed by the federal government, but actually in the Executive Council or the Cabinet of the legislature. Legislative power is vested in the Assembly in the name of the Queen.

Members of the Legislative Assembly are elected by the universal vote of adults over the age of 19 years.

There are 65 members in the legislature (elected 23 May 1967): 55 Social Credit, 10 Progressive Conservative.

Lieut.-Governor: His Honour J. W. Grant MacEwan (sworn in, 6 Jan. 1966).

The members of the Ministry (all Social Credit Party) are as follows:

Premier, President of Council: H. E. Strom.

Public Health: J. D. Henderson. *Highways, Transport, and Youth:* G. E. Taylor. *Labour and Telephones:* R. Reierson. *Agriculture:* H. A. Ruste. *Provincial Treasurer:* A. O. Aalborg. *Mines and Minerals:* A. R. Patrick. *Provincial Secretary:* A. Holowach. *Education:* R. C. Clarke. *Attorney-General:* E. H. Gerhart. *Public Works:* A. W. Ludwig. *Social Development:* R. A. Speaker. *Municipal Affairs:* F. C. Colborne. *Lands and Forests:* Dr J. D. Ross. *Industry and Tourism:* R. Ratzlaff. *Without Portfolio:* A. O. Fimrite, Mrs E. S. Wilson.

LOCAL GOVERNMENT. The local government units are City, Town, Village, Summer Village, County and Municipal District.

There are 10 cities in Alberta, namely: Edmonton, Calgary, Lethbridge, Wetaskiwin, Red Deer, Medicine Hat, Drumheller, Camrose, Lloydminster and Grande Prairie. These cities operate under the Municipal Government Act. The governing body consists of a mayor and a council of from 6 to 20 members. A city can be incorporated by order of the Lieut.-Governor-in-Council. A population of 10,000 is required.

There are no limits of area specified in the statutes for any of the different local government units. The population requirement for a Town as specified in the Municipal Government Act is 1,000 people, and the area at incorporation is that of the original village.

A Village must contain 75 separate and occupied dwellings. The Municipal Government Act requires each dwelling to have been occupied continuously for a period of at least 6 months. A Summer Village must contain 50 separate dwellings.

A rural County area is an area incorporated through an order of the Lieut.-Governor-in-Council under the provisions of the County Act. One board of councillors deal with both municipal and school affairs.

A rural Municipal District is an area which has been incorporated under the Municipal Government Act. In Municipal Districts separate boards control municipal and school affairs.

Areas not incorporated as counties or Municipal Districts are termed Improvement Districts or Special Areas. Sparsely populated, such districts are administered and taxed by the Department of Municipal Affairs of the provincial government. There are no requirements as to the minimum number of residents of a County or Municipal District.

AREA AND POPULATION. The area of the province is 255,285 sq. miles; 248,800 sq. miles being land area and 6,485 sq. miles water area. The estimated population (June 1970) was 1·6m.; the urban population, centres of 1,000 or over, was estimated at 1,131,000 and the rural at 462,000. Population of the principal cities (1970): Edmonton, 422,418 (metropolitan area, 450,000); Calgary, 385,436; Lethbridge, 39,552; Red Deer, 26,907, and Medicine Hat, 25,713.

Vital statistics, see pp. 178–80.

Religion, see p. 180.

EDUCATION. Schools of all grades are included under the term of public school. The same board of trustees control the schools from kindergarten to university entrance. All public schools are supported by property taxes collected by municipal authorities; all such taxes are supplemented by government grants. In June 1969 there were 1,400 schools in operation containing 15,516 classrooms with 401,587 pupils and 20,687 teachers. The University of Alberta (in Edmonton), organized in 1907, had, in 1969–70, 24,793 students and 3,481 teachers. The University of Calgary, formerly part of the University of Alberta and autonomous from April 1966, had in 1969–70, 13,215 students and 1,323 teachers. The University of Lethbridge, organized in 1966, 1969–70, had 2,275 students and 142 teachers.

JUSTICE. The Supreme Judicial authority of the Province is the Supreme Court, which consists of the Appellate and Trial divisions. Judges of the Supreme Court are appointed by the Dominion Government and hold office until retirement at the age of 75. There are courts of lesser jurisdiction in both civil and criminal matters. District courts have full jurisdiction over civil proceedings in which the claims do not exceed $2,000. A Provincial Court which has jurisdiction in civil matters up to $500 is presided over by provincially appointed magistrates. Juvenile Courts have power to try boys 16 and under and girls 18 years of age and under for offences against the Juvenile Delinquents Act.

The jurisdiction of all criminal courts in Alberta is enacted in the provisions of the Criminal Code. The system of procedure in civil and criminal cases conforms as nearly as possible to the English system.

FINANCE. The revenue of the province is derived from provincial sources, mainly natural resources and taxes, which contribute 81% of total revenue; and from federal sources, subsidies and cost-sharing payments, which contribute 19%. The fiscal year ends 31 March.

	1966–67	1967–68	1968–69	1969–70	1970–71[1]
Revenue	613,138,370	766,952,024	945,954,756	952,957,858	1,033,168,000
Expenditure	681,975,911	834,428,491	914,859,263	981,856,790	1,146,012,000

[1] Estimates.

The net funded debt of the province on 31 March 1970 amounted to $37,320,713, and the unfunded debt to $43,054,473; total public debt, $80,375,186.

AGRICULTURE. Of the surveyed area of the province (about 85m. acres. approximately 70m. acres may be classed as capable of agricultural development) Up to the present, however, only one-third of this area has been brought under cultivation.

For particulars of agricultural production and livestock, *see under* CANADA. Farmers' total gross income in 1969 was $886,612,000. Licensed grain elevators have a total capacity of 141,504,750 bu., including grain housed in temporary annexes and terminal elevators.

FORESTRY. Alberta has an estimated net merchantable volume of 48,700m. cu. ft of timber, 25,700m. cu. ft of hardwood and 23,000m. of softwood. In 1969, 440m. bd ft of timber were produced; the value of forest produce was $32·9m.

FISHERIES. The lakes of the province abound in whitefish, pickerel, pike and tullibee, but the industry needs better fishing and marketing methods. Value of fish marketed in 1969 was $1·6m.

MINING. Latest available estimates place Alberta's minable coal reserves at about 48,000m. tons. 'Recoverable' reserves, based on present mining methods and the economies of extraction of coal, have been placed at 24,000m. tons, of which 20,000m. tons are minable. The output in 1969 was 4·4m. tons valued at $13·5m. By 1971, Alberta producers will be exporting 4·4m. tons of coking coal to Japan. Natural gas is found in abundance in numerous localities. In 1969, 1,271,559m. cu. ft valued at $200·4m. were sold.

In the same year 326m. bbls of crude oil and condensate were produced with a gross sales value of $837·9m. Alberta produced 70% of Canada's oil output.

Immense deposits of oil sands which contain over 700,000m. bbls of crude oil now are being mined in the McMurray district in northern Alberta.

Value of total mineral production in 1969, $1,193m.

INDUSTRY. The leading manufacturing industries are: meat packing, oil refining, industrial chemicals and plastics, iron and steel products, flour and feed milling, dairy products, wood-pulp milling and printing and publishing. There were in 1968 approximately 1,850 manufacturing establishments, in which were employed about 49,000 persons, who earned in salaries and wages about $274m.

Manufacturing shipments had a total value of $1,649m. in 1968. Chief among these shipments were: food and beverages, $682m.; primary metal, $134m.; metal fabricating, $103m.; petroleum and coal products, $154m.; chemical and chemical products, $110m.

COMMUNICATIONS. In 1969 there were 85,814 miles of roads and highways, including 61,830 miles gravelled and 5,330 miles pavement.

In March 1969 there were 781,522 motor vehicles registered, including 503,925 passenger cars, 215,434 public and commercial vehicles, 86,214 trailers and 16,370 motor cycles.

On the same date the length of main railway lines was 6,081 miles. Alberta's modern telephone system is owned and operated by the provincial government, except in the city of Edmonton and most rural lines. There were 707,121 telephones in service by March 1969.

BOOKS OF REFERENCE

STATISTICAL INFORMATION. The Alberta Bureau of Statistics (Dept. of Industry and Tourism, Edmonton), which was established in 1939, collects, compiles and distributes information relative to Alberta. *Director:* D. I. Istvanffy. Among its publications are: *Alberta Industry and Resources.* 1970.—*Alberta Trade Index.* 1967.—*Annual Review of Business Conditions*

Hardy, W. G., *Alberta Golden Jubilee Anthology.* Toronto, 1955
Horan, J. W., '*West, nor'west': A History of Alberta.* Edmonton, 1945
Kroetsch, R., *Alberta.* Toronto, 1968
Macpherson, C. B., *Democracy in Alberta.* 2nd ed. Toronto, 1962
Nesbitt, L. D., *Tides in the West* [history of the Alberta Wheat Pool]. Saskatoon, 1962

BRITISH COLUMBIA

CONSTITUTION AND GOVERNMENT. British Columbia (then known as New Caledonia) originally formed part of the Hudson's Bay Company's concession. In 1849 Vancouver Island and in 1858 British Columbia were constituted Crown Colonies; in 1866 the two colonies amalgamated. The British North America Act of 1867 provided for eventual admission into Canadian Confederation, and on 20 July 1871 British Columbia became the sixth Province of the Dominion.

British Columbia has a unicameral legislature of 55 elected members. Government policy is determined by the Executive Council responsible to the Legislature. The Lieutenant-Governor is appointed by the Governor-General of Canada, usually for a term of 5 years, and is the head of the executive government of the Province.

Lieut.-Governor: The Hon. John Robert Nicholson, PC, OBE, QC, LLD.

The Legislative Assembly is elected for a maximum term of 5 years. Every male or female Canadian Citizen 19 years and over, having resided a minimum of 6 months in the Province, duly registered, is entitled to vote. Representation of the parties as of Sept. 1969: Social Credit, 38; New Democratic Party, 12; Liberal, 5; total, 55.

The Province is represented in the Federal Parliament by 23 members in the House of Commons, and 6 Senators.

The Executive Council was in Sept. 1969 composed as follows:

Premier, President of the Council, and Minister of Finance: William Andrew Cecil Bennett, PC, LLD, D.Pol.Sc.
Provincial Secretary and Minister of Highways: Wesley Drewett Black. *Minister of Health Services and Hospital Insurance:* Ralph Raymond Loffmark, QC. *Attorney-General and Minister of Labour:* Leslie Raymond Peterson, QC. *Lands, Forests, and Water Resources:* Ray Gillis Williston. *Agriculture:* Cyril Morley Shelford. *Mines and Petroleum Resources and Commercial Transport:* Francis Xavier Richter. *Education:* Donald Leslie Brothers, QC. *Industrial Development, Trade and Commerce:* Waldo McTavish Skillings. *Municipal Affairs:* Daniel Robert John Campbell. *Public Works:* William Neelands Chant. *Recreation and Conservation and Travel Industry:* William Kenneth Kiernan. *Social Welfare:* Philip Arthur Gaglardi. *Without Portfolio:* Isabel Pearl Dawson, Patricia Jane Jordan, Grace McCarthy.

Agent-General in London: Rear-Adm. M. G. Stirling, CD (British Columbia House, 1 Regent St., London, SW1).
Commissioner for Trade and Tourism in USA: (vacant) (British Columbia House, 599 Market St., San Francisco, Cal. 94105 and 8833 Sunset Blvd., Los Angeles, Cal. 90069).

LOCAL GOVERNMENT. Vancouver City was incorporated by statute and operates under the provisions of the Vancouver Charter of 1953 and amendments.

This is the only incorporated area in British Columbia not operating under the provisions of the Municipal Act. Under this Act municipalities are divided into the following classes: (a) a village with a population between 500 and 2,500, governed by a council consisting of a mayor and 4 aldermen; (b) a town with a population between 2,500 and 5,000, governed by a council consisting of a mayor and 4 aldermen; (c) a city where the population exceeds 5,000 governed by a council consisting of a mayor and 6 or 8 aldermen depending on population; (d) a district where the area exceeds 2,000 acres and the average density is less than 2 persons per acre, governed by a council consisting of a mayor and 6 or 8 aldermen depending on population.

There are two other forms of local government: the regional district covering a number of areas both incorporated and unincorporated, governed by a board of directors; and the improvement district governed by a board of 3 trustees.

Revenue for municipal services is derived mainly from real-property taxation, although additional revenue is derived from licence fees, business taxes, fines, public utility projects and grants-in-aid from the Provincial Government.

AREA AND POPULATION. British Columbia has an area of 366,255 sq. miles. The capital is Victoria. The Province is bordered westerly by the Pacific Ocean and Alaska Panhandle, northerly by the Yukon and Northwest Territories, easterly by the Province of Alberta and southerly by the USA along the 49th parallel. A chain of islands, the largest of which are Vancouver Island and the Queen Charlotte Islands, affords protection to the mainland coast.

The June 1970 population estimate was 2·07m.

The principal cities and their populations are as follows: Metropolitan Victoria, 182,000 (1968); Metropolitan Vancouver, 955,000 (1968). 1966 Census Populations: New Westminster, 38,013; North Vancouver, 26,851; Kamloops, 24,000; Prince George, 24,471; Port Alberni, 18,538; Kelowna, 17,006; Penticton, 15,330; Nanaimo, 15,188; Prince Rupert, 14,677; Dawson Creek, 12,392; Trail, 11,600; Vernon, 11,423.

EDUCATION (1967-68). Education, free up to Grade XII levels, is financed jointly from municipal and provincial government revenues. Attendance is compulsory from the age of 6 to 15. There were 467,326 pupils enrolled in public schools and instructed by 18,889 teachers.

Higher education is provided at the University of British Columbia at Vancouver (1908)—20,088 students; the University of Victoria (1963)—4,726 students; Simon Fraser University (1965), Burnaby—5,500 students; Notre Dame University (1963), Nelson—574 students; Selkirk College (1966), Castlegar —508 students; Vancouver City College (1964)—3,700 students; Okanagan Regional College (1968)—1,410 students.

HEALTH. The Government operates a hospital insurance scheme giving universal coverage after a qualifying period of three months' residence in the Province. The Province has come under a national medicare scheme which is partially subsidized by the Provincial Government and partially by the Federal Government.

FINANCE. Current provincial revenue and expenditure, including all capital expenditures, in Canadian $ for fiscal years ending 31 March:

	1966–67	1967–68	1968–69	1969–70[1]
Revenue	731,622,517	810,165,114	963,793,618	1,024,482,415
Expenditure	695,569,587	780,806,564	924,962,668	1,024,072,425

[1] Estimate.

The main sources of current revenue are the sales and gasoline taxes, natural resources taxes or royalties, licences and privileges; and contributions from government enterprises.

The main items of expenditure in 1968–69 are as follows: Education, $264,657,672; highways, $130·37m.; health and welfare, $327,141,995; general government, $118·34m.; natural resources, $59·45m.

AGRICULTURE. Only 6·5m. acres or 2·8% of the total land area is arable or potentially arable. Farm cash receipts, in 1969, reached $211m.

FISHERIES. In 1969 fish landings were valued at $40m. and totalled 362m. lb in 1968.

FORESTRY. About 60% of British Columbia's land is forest land, with 118m. acres bearing commercial forest. 93% of the forest area is owned or administered by the Provincial Government. The total cut from forests in 1969 was 1,830m. cu. ft. During 1968, $1,375m. worth of wood and wood products were reported.

MINING. Copper, molybdenum, lead and zinc are the most important minerals produced. The 1969 total value of mineral production was estimated at $460·0m. Total value of fuels produced in 1969 was $95·9m.

POWER. Electric power consumption in 1969 totalled an estimated 26,300m. gwh.

INDUSTRY. The selling value of factory shipments from all manufacturing industries reached $3,860·0m.

TRADE. Exports through British Columbia customs ports during 1969 totalled $2,300m. in value, while imports amounted to $1,100m.

Principal export commodity groups: Fish products, $56m.; forest products, $765·8m.; metal refinery and mine products, $351·4m.; coal, crude petroleum and natural gas, $292·7m.; grain and cereal products, $387m. About 40% of exports through British Columbia customs ports are products from other provinces, primarily grains, potash and fuels from the Prairie Provinces. USA is the largest market for products exported through British Columbia customs ports ($947·6m. in 1969) followed by Japan ($515·2m.); the UK ($211·6m.).

RAILWAYS. The Province is served by two transcontinental railways, the Canadian Pacific Railway and the Canadian National Railway. British Columbia is also served by the publicly owned Pacific Great Eastern Railway, the Railway Freight Service of the B. C. Hydro and Power Authority, the Northern Alberta Railways Company and the Great Northern Railway. Their combined route-mileage totals 4,290 miles. In addition, 4 American railways interchange with Canadian railways at southern border points or connect by railway barge.

ROADS. At 31 March 1969 there were 27,518 miles of highway in the Province.

SHIPPING. The major ports are Vancouver, New Westminster, Victoria, Nanaimo and Prince Rupert. The volume of coastwise shipping, in 1968, was 20m. tons.

The British Columbia Ferries connect Vancouver Island with the Mainland and also provide service to other coastal points. Service by other ferry systems is also provided between Vancouver Island and the USA. The Alaska State Ferries connect Prince Rupert with centres in Alaska.

AVIATION. International airports are located at Vancouver and Victoria. Daily interprovincial and intraprovincial flights serve all main population centres. Small public and private airstrips are located throughout the Province.

POST. The British Columbia Telephone Company in 1968 had 960,728, telephones in service. There are 9 television systems and 54 radio stations in the Province.

BANKING. Bank debits ($1,000): 1966, $38,057,010; 1967, $41,281,302; 1968, $46,638,961; 1969 (estimate), $58,765,000.

BOOKS OF REFERENCE

STATISTICAL INFORMATION. The Economics and Statistics Branch (Department of Industrial Development, Trade and Commerce, Hon. Waldo M. Skillings—Minister, Parliament Buildings, Victoria, B.C.), which was established in 1937, collects, compiles and distributes information relative to the Province. *Director:* J. R. Meredith.

Publications include *Monthly Bulletin of Business Activity; Summary of Economic Activity* (annual); *Manufacturers' Directory; Facts and Statistics* (annual); *Regional and Industrial Studies.*

Department of Finance, *British Columbia Financial and Economic Review.* Victoria, B.C. (annual)
Forestry Handbook for British Columbia. B.C. University Forestry Club, Vancouver, 1959
Fifteenth British Columbia Natural Resources Conference, *Inventory of the Natural Resources of British Columbia.* 1964
Haigh-Brown, R. L., *Living Land, an account of the Natural Resources of British Columbia.* Toronto, 1961

YUKON TERRITORY

CONSTITUTION AND GOVERNMENT. The Yukon Territory was constituted a separate territory in June 1898. It is governed by a Commissioner (appointed) and a Legislative Council of 7 members who are elected for a 3-year term of office. The seat of government is at Whitehorse.

Commissioner: James Smith (appointed 7 Nov. 1966).

The legislative authority of council includes direct taxation, education, marriage, property and civil rights, territorial civil service, municipalities and generally all matters of local or private nature. All other major administration, particularly that which requires the spending of large sums of money, is federally controlled.

AREA AND POPULATION. The area of the Territory is 207,076 sq. miles (536,000 sq. km), of which 1,730 sq. miles is water. The population reached it, peak in 1901 with 27,219. The census population in 1966 was 14,382 (85% Whites, 14% Indians and less than 1% Eskimos). The estimated population (1970) following a recent mining boom, is 20,000. Principal centres are Whitehorse (capital), 7,500; Watson Lake, 1,115; Dawson City, 500; Mayo, 500.

Vital statistics, *see* pp. 178–80.
Religion, *see* p. 180.

EDUCATION (1969–70). The Territory had 22 schools with 220 full-time and 1 part-time teachers and 4,461 pupils. The Yukon Vocational and Technical Centre has 216 day-school pupils with 17 instructors. The Adult Education Night School programme had an enrolment of about 800 and the number of courses was about 40.

FINANCE. The territorial revenue and expenditure (in Canadian $) for fiscal years ended 31 March was:

	1966–67	1967–68	1968–69	1969–70
Revenue	10,890,668	13,525,463	..	25,102,802
Expenditure	12,103,111	13,923,457	..	27,266,786

MINING. Mining is now and is expected to remain the main industry. Silver, gold, lead, zinc, cadmium and copper are the chief minerals. Production figures (preliminary) for year ending March 1969 were: Gold, 26,305 oz. ($991,700); silver, 2,990,056 oz. ($5,770,808); lead, 30·8m. lb. ($4,663,120); zinc, 34·15m. lb.

($4,201,045); cadmium, 70,000 lb. ($243,000); copper, 15,718,700 lb. ($8,084,127); asbestos, 88,000 tons ($12,701,400).

In July 1970 oil and gas exploration permits had been issued covering 29,855,363 acres and 50 leases covering 161,509 acres.

FORESTRY. The principal forest trees are white spruce, jack-pine, balsam, poplar and birch. In 1969–70, 12,058,470 bd ft measure of lumber, 650,583 linear ft of round timber and 6,084 cords of fuelwood were cut.

GAME AND FURS. The country abounds with big game, such as moose, caribou, mountain sheep and bear. The fur yield for the year ended Feb. 1969 totalled 56,558 pelts, valued at $81,235 to the trapper. Squirrel, muskrat, beaver and lynx constituted the greatest portion of the catch.

SHIPPING. The Yukon River, 1,979 miles long, of which 1,777 are navigable (570 within Yukon Territory), formerly offered water communication from the end of the railway at Whitehorse to Dawson, but after the construction of an all-weather highway to Dawson there is now only a barge service from Dawson down-river and up the Porcupine River to Old Crow.

ROADS. The Alaska Highway and its side roads connect the Yukon's main cities with Alaska and the provinces and with adjacent mining centres. A road serves the Cassiar Asbestos–Clinton Creek mining field north-west of Dawson City. A road connecting the new mining communities of Ross River and Faro with Carmacks has been completed. Total mileage of all roads is 2,332 (including the Alaska Highway and the Yukon portion of the Haines Road). The federal Department of Public Works maintains the Alaska Highway with connexions from Whitehorse to Mayo, Dawson City and Fairbanks, Alaska.

RAILWAYS. The 111-mile White Pass and Yukon Railway connects White-horse with year-round ocean shipping at Skagway, Alaska. A study is being undertaken to extend it from Whitehorse to Carmacks.

AVIATION. Commercial airlines provide passenger and express services every day between Whitehorse and Vancouver or Edmonton where they connect with transcontinental and international lines. Other services extend from Whitehorse to Mayo and Dawson, Fairbanks and Juneau, Alaska, and from Dawson to Old Crow and Inuvik, NWT. There is also a scheduled flight to Watson Lake as well as numerous smaller commercial bush plane operations.

TELECOMMUNICATIONS. There were 16 post offices in 1970; revenue, $269,317. A 600-telephone voice channel micro-wave system is operated by Canadian National Telecommunications which interconnects with Alaska, the provinces of Canada and the USA. A landline telephone system now connects Dawson, Mayo, Carmacks and way points with Whitehorse and the provinces. CNT is also constructing a 300-channel micro-wave system which will connect Whitehorse with Inuvik, NWT. The Canadian Broadcasting Corporation has studios at Whitehorse and 13 relay transmitters at Dawson, Mayo, Elsa, Watson Lake and other areas. CBC also serves Dawson, Watson Lake, Elsa, Clinton Creek and Fort Nelson, BC, with relayed television and this is being expanded to other areas.

BOOKS OF REFERENCE

Publications of the Department of Northern Affairs and National Resources, Ottawa: *The Yukon Act, Chapter 53, Statutes of Canada, 1953,* as amended.—*Mining in the North.* 1962. *The Yukon Today.* 1968.
Annual Report of the Commissioner. 1968.
McCourt, E., *The Yukon and Northwest Territories.* Toronto, 1969

THE NORTHWEST TERRITORIES

CONSTITUTION AND GOVERNMENT. The Northwest Territories comprises all that portion of Canada lying north of the 60th parallel of N. lat. except those portions within the Yukon Territory and the Provinces of Quebec and Newfoundland: it also includes the islands in Hudson Bay, James Bay and Ungava Bay except those within the Provinces of Manitoba, Ontario and Quebec.

The Northwest Territories is governed by a Commissioner and a Council. The Council is composed of 12 members, 5 appointed by the Governor-General-in-Council and 7 elected for a 3-year term of office. The seat of government was transferred from Ottawa to Yellowknife when it was named territorial capital on 18 Jan. 1967.

Commissioner: S. M. Hodgson. *Deputy Commissioner:* J. H. Parker.

Legislative powers are exercised by the Commissioner-in-Council on such matters as taxation within the Territories in order to raise revenue, maintenance or municipal institutions, administration of justice, licences, solemnization of marriages, education, public health, property, civil rights and generally all matters of a local nature.

The administration is carried on by the staff of the Territorial Government in the Mackenzie District and by the staff of the Department of Indian Affairs and Northern Development in the Keewatin and Franklin Districts. On 1 April 1970 the Territorial Government assumed responsibility for the administration of the Keewatin and Franklin Districts as well.

The Royal Canadian Mounted Police are designated as Sub-Registrars of Vital Statistics in most settlements.

AREA AND POPULATION. The total area of the Territories is 1,304,903 sq. miles (3,379,700 sq. km), divided into 3 districts, namely, Mackenzie (527,490 sq. miles), Keewatin (228,160 sq. miles) and Franklin (549,253 sq. miles). The population at the census of 1966 was 25,995, about two-thirds of whom were Indians or Eskimos. Main centres (census 1966): Yellowknife (3,741), Fort Smith (2,120), Inuvik (2,040), Hay River (2,002), Frobisher Bay (1,631), Fort Simpson (712).

EDUCATION (1968–69). The Department of Indian Affairs and Northern Development operated 55 schools with 580 teachers. In addition, one public school district operated at Yellowknife, and Roman Catholic separate school districts at Yellowknife and Hay River. The total enrolment was 8,293, of whom 3,092 were Eskimos and 1,569 Indians. Eight federal pupil residences accommodate a total of 1,280 pupils, and 20 family-type units each accommodate 8–12 pupils. Free correspondence courses are available to any pupil in a settlement where appropriate instruction is not available. Vocational training courses are also provided, including a pre-vocational school at Fort Churchill, Manitoba, for pupils living in the Arctic District. The Northwest Territories Council provides also outright grants and/or interest-free loans for university students from the Territories.

HEALTH AND WELFARE (1967). There were 10 hospitals in the Territories, 6 operated by missions, 1 by a locally elected hospital board at Yellowknife, 2 by the federal government and 1 by a private company. Nineteen nursing stations, 8 health stations and 6 health centres were in operation. Physicians, nurses, dentists, a radiologist and an X-ray technician accompanied the Government's Eastern Arctic supply ship to treat the sick and to conduct physical examinations, surveys and X-rays and administer preventive inoculations.

Welfare services are provided by professional social workers. Facilities include 5 children's receiving homes, 1 home for the aged and 5 transit centres.

MINING. Mineral production for the year 1967 was valued at $114,261,438, of which gold accounted for $13,690,981; silver, $2,495,441; lead, $37·1m.; zinc, $57m.; cadmium, $2·8m.; copper, $215,016.

Yellowknife continues to be the centre of goldmining activity.

As of 1 Sept. 1968, 4,659 permits for oil and gas exploration were held for 221,425,684 acres, of which 88,518,063 acres are on the mainland, 122,726,839 acres in the arctic islands and 10,180,782 acres on the arctic coast.

Crude oil, discovered in 1920, is produced and refined at Norman Wells on the Mackenzie River; production, 1968, 753,592 bbls valued at $875,654.

TRAPPING AND GAME. Fur produced during the 1967–68 season was valued at $826,523 from 354,051 pelts. More than 3,000 reindeer are maintained in the Mackenzie Delta region. A herd of some 12,000 buffalo is protected in Wood Buffalo National Park. Barren ground caribou are increasing, due to more effective management techniques.

FISHERIES. Commercial fishing, principally on Great Slave Lake, in 1968 produced about 2,067 tons of fish, principally whitefish and lake trout.

FORESTRY. The principal trees are white spruce, jack-pine, balsam, poplar and birch. In 1968–69, 2,736,062 bd ft measure of lumber, 128,555 linear ft of round timber and 4,052 cords of fuelwood were cut.

CO-OPERATIVES. There are 14 co-operatives and 2 credit unions in the Mackenzie District and 13 co-ops in the Arctic District. They are active in fisheries, retail stores, bakeries, print shops, provision of housing, contracting for services, etc. Their sales in 1968 were estimated to be $1·5m.

SHIPPING. A direct inland-water transportation route for about 1,700 miles is provided by the Mackenzie River and its tributaries, the Athabasca and Slave rivers. Subsidiary routes on Lake Athabasca, Great Slave and Great Bear River and Lake total more than 800 miles.

ROADS. The Mackenzie Route connects Grimshaw, Alta., with Hay River, Pine Point, Fort Smith, Fort Providence, Rae and Yellowknife. An all-weather road east from Yellowknife towards Mackay Lake and the Mackenzie Highway extension to Fort Simpson are under construction. A road has been opened between Pine Point and Fort Resolution.

RAILWAYS. Construction began on the 438-mile Great Slave Railway in Feb. 1962. This line links the south shore of Great Slave Lake to the southern network, with a spur to major base metal deposits at Pine Point. It was opened for traffic in May 1965.

AVIATION (1969). Seventeen airports are operated by the Department of Transport and there are 45 unlicensed aerodromes. Regular mail, passenger and express services are maintained throughout the Territories. A seaplane base is operated by the Department of Transport and there are 27 licensed private seaplane bases. Scheduled services join major points with centres in southern Canada.

POST (1968). There were 51 post offices. The CBC northern service operated radio stations at Yellowknife, Inuvik, Frobisher Bay and a television station in Yellowknife. Telephone communication has been established between southern Canada and Fort Smith, Hay River and Yellowknife in the Mackenzie District and Frobisher Bay on Baffin Island. Canadian National Telecommunications has established a telephone and telegraph service from Hay River to Inuvik. High-frequency telephone service is also available throughout the eastern Northwest Territories.

BOOKS OF REFERENCE

Annual Report of the Department of Indian Affairs and Northern Development, 1966–67
Annual Report of the Commissioner of the Northwest Territories, 1966–67
Dawson, C. A., The New North-West. Toronto, 1947
MacKay, D., The Honorable Company. Toronto, 1949
Wilson, C., North of 55°. Toronto, 1954

THE COMMONWEALTH OF AUSTRALIA

HISTORY. On 1 Jan. 1901 New South Wales, Victoria, Queensland, South Australia, Western Australia and Tasmania were federated under the name of the 'Commonwealth of Australia', the designation of 'colonies' being at the same time changed into that of 'states'—except in the case of Northern Territory, which was transferred from South Australia to the Commonwealth as a 'territory' on 1 Jan. 1911.

In 1911 the Commonwealth acquired from the State of New South Wales the Canberra site for the Australian capital. Building operations were begun in 1923 and Parliament was opened at Canberra on 9 May 1927 by HRH the Duke of York (afterwards King George VI). A further area at Jervis Bay was acquired in 1915.

Territories under the administration of the Commonwealth, but not included in it, comprise Papua (1 Sept. 1906), Norfolk Island, the trusteeship territory of New Guinea, the territory of Ashmore and Cartier Islands, and the Australian Antarctic Territory (24 Aug. 1936), comprising all the islands and territory other than Adélie Land, situated south of 60° S. lat. and between 160° and 45° E. long.

The British Government transferred sovereignty in the Heard Island and McDonald Islands to the Australian Government on 26 Dec. 1947. Cocos (Keeling) Islands on 23 Nov. 1955 and Christmas Island on 1 Oct. 1958 were also transferred to Australian jurisdiction.

CONSTITUTION AND GOVERNMENT

Federal Government. Legislative power in the Commonwealth is vested in a Federal Parliament, consisting of the Queen, represented by a Governor-General, a Senate and a House of Representatives. Under the terms of the constitution there must be a session of parliament at least once a year.

The Senate comprises 60 senators (10 for each State voting as one electorate) chosen for 6 years. In general, the Senate is renewed to the extent of one-half every 3 years, but in case of prolonged disagreement with the House of Representatives, it, together with the House of Representatives, may be dissolved, and an entirely new Senate elected. The House of Representatives consists, as nearly as may be, of twice as many members as there are senators, the numbers chosen in the several States being in proportion to population as shown by the latest statistics, but not less than 5 for any original State. The numerical size of the House after the election in 1969 was 125, including the members for Northern Territory and the Australian Capital Territory. The Northern Territory has been represented by one member in the House of Representatives since 1922, and the Australian Capital Territory by one member since 1949. The member for the Australian Capital Territory was given full voting rights as from the Parliament elected in Nov. 1966. The member for the Northern Territory was given full voting rights in 1968. The House of Representatives continues for 3 years from the date of its first meeting, unless sooner dissolved. Every senator or member of the House of Representatives must be a British subject, be of full age, possess electoral qualifications and have resided for 3 years within Australia. The franchise for both chambers is the same and is based on universal adult (male and female) suffrage. Compulsory voting was introduced in 1925. If a member of a State parliament wishes to be a candidate in a federal election, he must first resign his State seat.

Formally, executive power in the Commonwealth is vested in the Governor-General, who is advised by an Executive Council. This is presided over by the Governor-General, and its members hold office at his pleasure. All Ministers of State are *ex-officio* members of the Executive Council. Meetings are formal and official in character, and a record of proceedings is kept by the secretary or clerk. At Executive Council meetings the decisions of the Cabinet are (where necessary) given legal form, appointments made, resignations accepted, proclamations issued, and regulations and the like enacted.

The policy of a ministry is, in practice, determined by the Ministers of State meeting without the Governor-General under the chairmanship of the Prime Minister. This group, known as the Cabinet, does not form part of the legal mechanism of government; its meetings are private and deliberative; the actual ministers of the day are alone present; no records of the meetings are made public, and the decisions taken have, in themselves, no legal effect.

In Jan. 1956 the composition of the Ministry was assimilated to the system prevailing in the UK. It now consists of a Cabinet including a limited number of Ministers, and a group of Ministers not in the Cabinet who can be invited to attend Cabinet meetings whenever matters affecting their departments are being considered.

The legislative powers of the Federal Parliament embrace commerce, shipping, etc.; finance, banking, currency, etc.; defence; external affairs; postal, telegraph and like services; census and statistics; weights and measures; copyright; railways; conciliation and arbitration in industrial disputes extending beyond the limits of any one State; social services (an amendment to the constitution in 1946 specifying, in addition to the existing provision for invalid and old-age pensions, the provision of maternity allowances, widows' pensions, child endowment, unemployment, pharmaceutical, sickness and hospital benefits, medical and dental services, etc.). The Senate may not originate or amend money bills; and disagreement with the House of Representatives may result in dissolution or, in the last resort, a joint sitting of the two Houses. No religion may be established by the Commonwealth. The Federal Parliament has limited and enumerated powers, the several State parliaments retaining the residuary power of government over their respective territories. If a State law is inconsistent with a Commonwealth law the latter prevails.

The constitution also provides for the admission or creation of new States. Proposed laws for the alteration of the constitution must be submitted to the electors, and they can be enacted only if approved by a majority of the States and by a majority of all the electors voting.

The 27th Parliament was elected on 25 Oct. 1969.

House of Representatives: Liberal Party, 46; Country Party, 20 (Government Coalition); Australian Labor Party, 59 (Opposition); total 125.

Senate (as at 1 Jan 1971): Liberal Party, 21; Country Party, 5 (Government Coalition); Australian Labor Party, 26 (Opposition); Australian Democratic Labour Party, 5; Independent, 3.

Governor-General: The Rt Hon. Sir Paul Hasluck, GCMG, GCVO (from April 1969).

The following is a list of Governors-General of the Commonwealth:

Earl of Hopetoun	1901–02	Lord Gowrie	1936–45
Lord Tennyson	1902–04	HRH the Duke of Gloucester	1945–47
Lord Northcote	1904–08	Sir William McKell	1947–53
Earl of Dudley	1908–11	Viscount Slim	1953–60
Lord Denman	1911–14	Viscount Dunrossil	1960–61
Viscount Novar	1914–20	Viscount De Lisle	1961–65
Lord Forster	1920–25	Lord Casey	1965–69
Lord Stonehaven	1925–31	Sir Paul Hasluck	1969–
Sir Isaac Isaacs	1931–36		

The Liberal–Country Party Ministry (reconstituted 21 March 1971) is as follows the State from which each member comes is added in brackets):

Ministers in the Cabinet:

Prime Minister: Rt Hon William McMahon MP (NSW).

Deputy Prime Minister and Minister for Trade and Industry: Hon. J. D. Anthony, MP (NSW).

Foreign Affairs: Hon. L. H. E. Bury, MP (NSW).

Primary Industry: Hon. I. M Sinclair, MP (NSW).

Postmaster-General and Vice-President of the Executive Council: Hon. Sir Alan Hulme, MP (Q).

Treasurer: Hon. B. M. Snedden, QC, MP (NSW).
Shipping and Transport: Hon. P. J. Nixon, MP (V).
Supply and Leader of the Government in the Senate: Senator the Hon. Sir Kenneth Anderson (NSW).
Defence: Rt. Hon. J. G. Gorton, MP (V).
National Development: Hon. R. W. C. Swartz, MBE, ED, MP (Q).
Labour and National Service and Leader of the House: Hon. Phillip Lynch, MP (V).
Education and Science: D. E. Fairbairn, QC, MP (NSW).
Attorney-General: Hon. N. H. Bowen, QC, MP (NSW).

Other Ministers:

External Territories: C. E. Barnes, MP (Q).
Health: Senator I. J. Greenwood (V).
Housing: Hon. K. M. K. Cairns, MP (Q).
Social Services and, under the Prime Minister, in Charge of Aboriginal Affairs: W. C. Wentworth, MP (NSW).
Works and, under the Minister for Trade and Industry, in Charge of Tourist Activities: Senator R. C. Wright (TAS).
Civil Aviation: Senator the Hon. Robert Cotton, MP (NSW)
Customs and Excise: Hon. D. A. Chipp, MP (V).
Air: Senator the Hon. T. Drake-Brockman, DFC, MP (WA).
Interior: Hon. J. D. Hunt, MP (NSW).
Repatriation: R. McN. Holten, MP (V).
Army and Minister Assisting the Prime Minister: Hon. Andrew Peacock, MP (V).
Navy: Hon. M. G. MacKay, MP (NSW).

The Acts of the Parliament of the Commonwealth of Australia passed from 1901 to 1950. 6 vols. Sydney, 1952–55. Annual supplement, 1951 to date
Parliamentary Handbook of the Commonwealth of Australia. Canberra, 1915 to date
Commonwealth of Australia Directory [until 1960: *Federal Guide*]. *Prime Minister's Department.* Canberra, 1924 to date
Crisp, L. F., *Australian National Government.* Melbourne and London, 1965
Davies, A. S., *Australian Democracy.* 2nd ed. Melbourne, 1964
Davis, S. R., *Government of the Australian States,* London, 1960
Else-Mitchell, R., *Essays on the Australian constitution.* 2nd ed. Sydney, 1961
Hughes, C. A., and Graham, B. D., *Handbook of Australian government and politics.* Canberra, 1968
Joske, P. E., *Australian federal government.* Sydney, 1967
Odgers, J. R., *Australian Senate Practice.* 3rd ed. Canberra, 1967
Paton, Sir George (ed.), *The Commonwealth of Australia: its Laws and Constitution.* London, 1952
Sawer, G., *Australian Federal Politics and Law 1901–1949.* 2 vols. Melbourne, 1956–63.— *Australian Government To-day.* 9th ed. Melbourne, 1967
Spann, R. N. (ed.), *Public Administration in Australia.* 2nd ed. Sydney, 1960
Wynes, W. A., *Executive and Judicial Powers in Australia.* 3rd ed. Sydney, 1962

State Government. In each of the 6 States (New South Wales, Victoria, Queensland, South Australia, Western Australia, Tasmania) there is a State government whose constitution, powers and laws continue, subject to changes embodied in the constitution of the Commonwealth and subsequent alterations and agreements, as they were before federation. The system of government is the same as that described above for the Commonwealth—*i.e.,* the sovereign, her representative (in this case a governor), an upper and lower house of parliament (except in Queensland, where the upper house was abolished in 1922), a cabinet led by the premier and an executive council. Among the more important functions of the State governments are those relating to education, health, hospitals and charities, law, order and public safety, business undertakings such as railways and tramways, and public utilities such as water supply and sewerage. In the domains of education, hospitals, justice, the police, penal establishments, and railway and tramway operation, State government activity predominates. Care of the public health and recreative facilities are shared with local government authorities and the Commonwealth government, social services other than those referred to above are now primarily the concern of the Commonwealth government, and the operation of public utilities is shared with local and semi-government authorities. Other activities of State government pertain to lands and surveys, agriculture, forestry and public works, including roads (the latter shared with local and semi-government authorities).

Deakin, A., *The Federal Story*. Melbourne. 1944

Local Government. The system of municipal government is broadly the same throughout the Commonwealth, although local government legislation is a State matter.

Each State is sub-divided into areas known variously as municipalities, cities, boroughs, towns, shires or district councils, totalling about 900. Within these areas the management of road, street and bridge construction, health, sanitary and garbage services, water supply and sewerage, and electric light and gas undertakings, hospitals, fire brigades, tramways and omnibus services and harbours is the duty of elected aldermen and councillors. The scope of their duties, however, differs considerably, for in all States the State government, either directly or through semi-governmental authorities, also carries out these types of services. In some instances, *e.g.*, in New South Wales, a number of local government authorities combine to conduct a public undertaking such as the supply of water or electricity.

DIPLOMATIC REPRESENTATIVES

Country	British Commonwealth and foreign representatives	Australian representatives
Afghánistán	—	F. H. Stuart
Argentina	J. I. Gomez-Errazuriz	H. W. Bullock
Austria	Dr Franz Pein	A. M. Morris, OBE
Belgium	Jan Naaykens	O. L. Davis, OBE
Brazil	A. Pinto de Ulyssea	Miss J. H. Barnett[3]
Britain[1]	Sir Charles Hepburn Johnston, KCMG	Sir Alexander Downer, KBE
Burma	U Nyo Tun	W. P. J. Handmer
Cambodia	Nay Valentin	G. B. Feakes
Canada[1]	A. R. Menzies	D. W. McNicol, CBE
Ceylon[1]	J. Siriwardere	H. D. White
Chile	Julio H. Riethmuller	N. St. C. Deschamps
China (Taiwan)	Dr Sampson Shen	H. A. Dunn
Denmark	E. Blytgen-Petersen	E. H. Hanfield (*Consul*)
Ethiopia	—	J. V. R. Hearder[3]
Fiji[2]	R. N. Nair	R. N. Birch
Finland	Tuure Mentula	R. A. Peachey
France	A. Favereau	A. P. Renouf, OBE
Germany (West)	Dr Heinz Voigt	Sir Ronald Walker, CBE
Ghana[1]	H. V. H. Sekyi	J. M. McMillan
Greece	B. Tsamissis	H. Gilchrist
India[1]	A. M. Thomas	Patrick Shaw, CBE
Indonesia	Sujitno Sukirno	G. A. Jockel, OBE
Iran	—	F. B. Hall
Irish Republic	Francis Coffey	Lieut.-Col. R. Honner, DSO, MC
Israel	Moshe Erell	M.L. Johnston
Italy	Dr Mario Majoli	M. R. Booker,
Japan	Shizuo Saito	Gordon Freeth
Kenya[1]	—	J. V. R. Hearder[4]
Korea	Choong Sik Min	A. H. Loomes, OBE
Laos	Tianethone Chantharasy[3]	P. C. J. Curtis
Lebanon	Samira El-Daher[3]	H. N. Truscott
Luxembourg	—	O. L. Davis, OBE

[1] High Commissioner.　　[2] Commissioner.　　[3] Chargé d'Affaires ad interim.
[4] Acting　　No figure = Ambassador.

Country	British Commonwealth and foreign representatives	Australian representatives
Malaysia[1]	Dato Donald Stephens	J. R. Rowland
Malta[1]	Joseph M. Dingle	Sir Hubert Opperman, OBE
Mauritius	—	W. G. A. Landale
Mexico	Dr R. Molina-Pasquel	D. McCarthy, MBE
Nepál	Prakash C. Thakur	Patrick Shaw, CBE
Netherlands	W. G. Zeylstra	Dr L. D. Thomson, MVO
New Zealand[1]	A. J. Yendell	Sir Edwin Hicks, CBE
Nigeria[1]	—	P. N. Hutton
Norway	Arnt. J. Jakobsen	
Pakistan[1]	Dr M. A. Malik	F. H. Stuart
Peru	Juan Patricio Gallagher	H. W. Bullock
Philippines	M. Ezpeleta	J. C. Ingram
Portugal	Dr Carlos A. E. Wemans	K. T. Kelly
Romania	I. Gheorghiu	R. R. Fernandez
Singapore[1]	P. S. Raman	N. F. Parkinson
South Africa	K. Uys	T. W. Cutts
Spain	J. R. Parellada	L. J. Lawrey
Sweden	Per Anger	R. A. Peachey
Switzerland	Dr Max Koenig	A. M. Morris, OBE
Tanzania[1]	—	W. G. A. Landale
Thailand	Prasong Bunchoem	T. K. Critchley, CBE
Turkey	M. Baydur	Vice-Adm. Sir Alan McNicoll, KBE, CB, GM
Uganda[1]	—	J. V. R. Hearder[3]
USSR	N. N. Mesiatsev	F. J. Blakeney, CBE
UAR	K. A. R. El-Ayouty	B. C. Hill
United Nations	—	Sir Laurence McIntyre, CBE
USA	Walter L. Rice	Sir James Plimsoll, CBE
Uruguay	Carlos Calamet[2]	H. W. Bullock
Vietnam	Tran Kim Phuong	R. L. Harry, CBE
Yugoslavia	G. Sekulovski	R. R. Fernandez

[1] High Commissioner.   [2] Chargé d'Affaires ad interim.
[3] Acting   No figure = Ambassador.

AREA AND POPULATION. Area and estimated population[1] on 30 June 1970:

States and Territories (capitals in brackets)	Area (sq. miles)	Males	Females	Total	Per 100 sq. miles
New South Wales (Sydney)	309,433	2,293,700	2,273.300	4,567,000	1,476
Victoria (Melbourne)	87,884	1,729,500	1,714,300	3,443,800	3,919
Queensland (Brisbane)	667,000	911.500	887.800	1,799,200	270
South Australia (Adelaide)	380,070	585,800	578.900	1,164,700	306
Western Australia (Perth)	975,920	498.700	481.300	980,000	100
Tasmania (Hobart)	26,383	198,100	194,300	392,500	1,488
Northern Territory (Darwin)	520,280	38.500	32.900	71,400	14
Aust. Cap. Terr. (Canberra)	939	68,700	64,400	133,100	14,175
Total	2,967,909[2]	6,324,500	6,227,200	12,551,700	423

[1] Includes Aborigines, who numbered 57,722 in 1954, 75,309 in 1961 and 80,207 in 1966.
[2] 7,686,900 sq. km.

Population of major cities and towns; 30 June 1969:

Urban centre	State	Persons	City	State	Persons
Sydney	NSW	2,712,610	Launceston	Tas.	62,390
Melbourne	Vic.	2,372,700	Townsville	Qld.	66,400
Adelaide	SA	808,600	Ballarat	Vic.	41,890
Brisbane	Qld.	833,400	Gold Coast	Qld.	60,500
Perth	WA	625,500	Toowoomba	Qld.	59,200
Newcastle	NSW	342,950	Rockhampton	Qld.	47,600
Wollongong	NSW	196,330	Bendigo	Vic.	31,520
Hobart	Tas.	147,830	Broken Hill	NSW	30,420
Geelong	Vic.	117,340	Greater Darwin	NT	30,200
Canberra	ACT	134,600	Whyalle	SA	28,900

The number of occupied dwellings in Australia (at 1966 census) was 3,185,656, distributed as follows: New South Wales, 1,189,539; Victoria, 888,984; Queensland, 449,169; South Australia, 302,314; Western Australia, 224,663; Tasmania, 99,366; Northern Territory, 8,067; Australian Capital Territory, 23,554. There were also 263,873 unoccupied dwellings. New houses numbered 81,096 in 1965–66; 81,960 in 1966–67; 85,756 in 1967–68; 91,546 in 1968–69; 97,524 in 1969–70.

VITAL STATISTICS for 1969:

States and Territories	Marriages	Divorces[1]	Births	Deaths	Infant mortality[2]
New South Wales	41,286	5,139	86,036	40,665	18·9
Victoria	30,860	2,235	71,035	28,976	15·0
Queensland	15,669	1,243	36,576	15,786	18·9
South Australia	10,599	970	21,977	9,337	15·8
Western Australia	8,993	873	20,754	7,350	21·8
Tasmania	3,532	331	8,445	3,309	16·5
Northern Territory	413	44	2,274	485	45·3
Aust. Cap. Terr.	1,118	144	3,079	588	18·8
Total	112,470	10,979	250,176	106,496	17·92

[1] Includes nullities of marriages and judicial separations.　　　　[2] Rate per 1,000 live births.

The birth rate in 1969 was 20; rate of marriages, 9; rate of mortality, 9 per 1,000 of mean population.

Overseas arrivals during 1969 numbered 898,858 and departures 769,812. Of these 248,591 were long-term and permanent arrivals and 108,260 were long-term and permanent departures. Of these 183,416 came to Australia intending to settle. There were 33,631 Australian residents departing permanently.

Bureau of Census and Statistics, *Demography Bulletin*. Canberra, 1911 to date
First report on the progress and assimilation of migrant children in Australia. Commonwealth Immigration Advisory Council. Canberra, 1960
Appleyard. R. T., *British emigration to Australia*. Canberra, 1964
Borrie, W. D., *Australia's population structure and growth*. 2nd ed. Melbourne, 1965
Coleman, P. (ed.), *Australian Civilization: a symposium*. Melbourne, 1962
Conference on Immigration Research. *The Study of Immigrants in Australia*. Canberra, 1960
Elkin, A. P., *The Australian Aborigines*. 5th ed. Sydney, 1961
Price, C. A., *Southern Europeans in Australia*. Melbourne, 1963
Zubrzycki, J., *Immigrants in Australia*. Melbourne, 1960.—*Statistical supplement*. Canberra, 1960

RELIGION. Under the constitution the Commonwealth cannot make any law to establish any religion, to impose any religious observance or to prohibit the free exercise of any religion, nor can it require a religious test as qualification for office or public trust under the Commonwealth. The figures in the table refer to those religions with the largest number of adherents at the census of 1966. The census question on religion was not obligatory, however.

Religion	Persons	Religion	Persons
Christian		Non-Christian	
Baptist	165,487	Hebrew	63,271
Brethren	15,516	Other	13,112
Catholic, Roman[1]	1,103,969		
Catholic[1]	1,932,161	Total Non-Christian	76,383
Churches of Christ	102,545		
Church of England	3,877,473	Indefinite	36,050
Congregational	76,588	No Religion	94,091
Orthodox	255,493	No Reply	1,138,900
Lutheran	177,324		
Methodist	1,124,310	Grand Total	11,550,462
Presbyterian	1,043,570		
Salvation Army	56,501		
Seventh-day Adventist	37,617		
Protestant (undefined)	105,223		
Other (including Christian undefined)	131,261		
Total Christian	10,205,038		

[1] As stated in individual census schedules.

EDUCATION. The provision of education is mainly the responsibility of State governments. However, a Commonwealth Department, known as the Department of Education and Science, was created in Dec. 1966. It absorbed the

Commonwealth Office of Education and is concerned with grants for educational purposes, e.g., for universities through the Australian Universities Commission, for Colleges of Advanced Education through the Commonwealth Advisory Committee on Advanced Education, for science buildings and libraries in secondary and technical schools, for building teacher's colleges, for per capita grants to independent schools, and with providing financial assistance to students who are undergoing secondary and tertiary training through a number of scholarships. A total of 23,499 scholars received Commonwealth Scholarships in 1969—Commonwealth University Scholarships' Scheme, 8,948; Commonwealth Advanced Education Scholarship Scheme, 1,541; Commonwealth Post-graduate Awards Scheme, 650; Commonwealth Secondary Scholarship Scheme, 9,910, and Commonwealth Technical Scholarship Scheme, 2,450. In addition, the Minister for Education and Science is responsible for the Commonwealth Scientific and Industrial Research Organization.

Primary and secondary education is undertaken by the State (government) schools and the 'private' (non-government) schools. The latter include the denominational schools, the most numerous being those of the Roman Catholics. The following is a summary for 1969 of primary and secondary school education:

States and Territories	Schools Government	Schools Non-government	Teachers[1] Government schools	Teachers[1] Non-government schools	Pupils[2] Government schools	Pupils[2] Non-government schools	Net expenditure on government schools[3]
NSW	2,483	794	33,139	8,254	744,766	220,787	199,521
Victoria	2,235	572	26,448	6,931	572,125	189,432	146,019
Queensland	1,248	342	11,519	3,096	291,939	89,048	66,843
S. Australia	656	171	9,488	1,524	226,091	36,669	55,191
W. Australia	573	196	6,472	1,550	168,195	41,053	44,084
Tasmania	295	67	3,552	633	78,339	14,740	20,634
North. Terr.	75	14	549	78	12,293	2,691	2,820
Aust. Cap. Terr.	41	20	974	363	22,862	8,681	6,092
Total	7,606	2,176	92,141	22,429	2,116,610	603,121	541,204

[1] Full-time teachers plus the full-time equivalent of part-time teaching.
[2] Enrolment first week in August.
[3] 1968–69. In $A1,000. Excludes capital expenditure.

Total expenditure on education in Australia in 1968–69 was estimated at $A1,115m., of which $A884m. was current expenditure. Direct expenditure on education by public authorities was $A943m., including $A47m. by Commonwealth authorities. In addition, the Commonwealth spent $A34m. on scholarships and other grants to persons and non-government organizations, and $A107m. in grants to the States for specific educational purposes. Total direct expenditure by State and local government authorities amounted to $A807m., and a further $A28m. was paid in scholarships, etc.

In 1969 there were 14 universities in Australia: 5 in New South Wales, 3 in Victoria, 2 in South Australia, 1 each in Queensland, Western Australia and Tasmania; and the Australian National University in Canberra. At 30 June 1969 full-time teaching staff numbered 7,009; student enrolment was 109,662, of whom 68,348 were full-time.

Technical education is provided for in 232 colleges of advanced education, senior technical schools and technical colleges; students numbered 388,824 in 1968.

CINEMAS (1969). There were 974 cinemas including 230 drive-in cinemas, with a total seating capacity of about 471,000.

NEWSPAPERS (1969). There were 2 national newspapers (average daily circulation 165,000) and 15 metropolitan daily newspapers in Australia with a combined daily circulation of 3·8m. Of these, 3 papers published in Melbourne accounted for 1·3m. and 4 published in Sydney for 1·3m.

Australian Universities Commission, *Fourth Report*. Canberra, 1969
Austin, A. G., *Australian Education, 1788–1900*. Melbourne, 1961
Connell, W. F. (and others), *The foundations of education*. 2nd ed. Sydney, 1967

First Report of the Commonwealth Advisory Committee on Advanced Education. June 1966
Report of the Committee on the Future of Tertiary Education in Australia. Aug. 1964
Review of Education in Australia, 1955-62. Australian Council for Educational Research, 1964

SOCIAL WELFARE. The National Welfare Fund finances all Commonwealth social and health benefits except repatriation and a few minor benefits. Total expenditure from the Fund during 1969-70 was $A1,341 8m.

The following summarizes the rates and conditions of the major benefits provided. For expenditure on these benefits during 1969-70, *see* table on p. 241.

Age pensions—are paid to men 65 years of age and over, and to women 60 years of age and over, who have lived in Australia for at least 10 years, and *invalid pensions* to persons 16 years of age and over, who have lived at least 5 years in Australia and who are permanently incapacitated for work or permanently blind. There is a means test. 'Means as assessed' of $A520 and $A442 (each) per annum are allowed without reduction of pensions for 'standard rate' and 'married rate' pensions respectively. From 8 Oct. 1970 the maximum 'standard rate' payable is $A15.50 a week and the maximum 'married rate' $A27.50 ($A13.75 each) a week. There are additional allowances in respect of permanent incapacitation, dependent spouse, dependent children, etc.

Maternity allowance—is paid without means test in respect of every child born (alive or dead) in Australia. The rates are $A30 where there are no other children under 16 years; $A32 where there are one or two other children under 16; $A35 where there are three or more other children under 16; in addition $A10 is paid for each additional child born at a birth.

Child endowment—is paid without means test. For children under 16 years, the rates payable per week are: 50c. for the first or only child in a family, $A1 for the second child, $A1.50 for the third and then cumulative increases of 25c. for the fourth and subsequent children, making $A1.75 for the fourth, $A2 for the fifth and so on. For full-time student children, aged 16 to 21 years, the rate is $A1.50 a week. $A1.50 is also payable for each child under 16 years or full-time student child, 16 to 21 years, in an approved institution.

Widows' pensions—from 29 Sept. 1970 payment of $A15.50 per week is made to widows maintaining children under 16 years of age (a mother's allowance of $A4 a week—$A6 a week if caring for a child under 6 years of age—with an allowance for each child in her custody is also paid). For widows 50 years of age and over who are not maintaining children, and for widows under 50 years for a period of not more than 26 weeks (in cases of pregnancy, until the birth of the child) following the death of the husband, the rate payable is $A13.75 a week. Supplementary assistance of $A2 a week under certain conditions is also available to widow pensioners. All widows' pensions are subject to a means test.

Unemployment and sickness benefits—are paid to persons between the ages of 16 and 65 (males) and 16 and 60 (females) who have suffered a loss of income through unemployment or sickness and are not in receipt of an invalid, etc., pension or tuberculosis allowance. Claimants must have resided in Australia for the 12 months preceding the claim or intend to reside permanently in Australia. The claimant must be unemployed (not due to direct participation in a strike), registered for employment with the Commonwealth Employment Service and not in receipt of income beyond a certain level.

Hospital benefits—$A2 per day is paid for each qualified patient insured with a registered benefit organization, 80c. per day for all uninsured patients in public and approved private hospitals, $A2 per day for each qualified patient in an approved nursing home, whether the patient is insured or not, and $A5 per day for persons covered by the pensioner medical service. From 1 Jan. 1969 a supplementary benefit of $A3 a day is payable for nursing-home patients who are medically classified as in need of and receiving intensive care.

Medical benefits—the Commonwealth Government subsidizes the payment of medical expenses of members of registered organizations.

Pensioners' medical service—provides free medical service and pharmaceutical benefits to eligible pensioners and their dependants.

Pharmaceutical benefits—a comprehensive range of drugs and medicinal preparations is available. In general, a fee of 50c. is charged for each prescription.

Tuberculosis campaign—this provides for diagnosis, treatment, after-care and allowances to sufferers and their dependants. The Commonwealth Government meets approved additional maintenance costs and provides all capital money required.

Service pensions—are paid, subject to a means test, to (a) aged ex-members of the forces, (b) ex-members of the forces who are permanently unemployable and to their dependants, (c) ex-members of the forces suffering from tuberculosis and to their dependants.

War pensions—are not subject to a means test and may be paid to ex-service men and women who have incurred incapacity as a result of war service, and their dependants. Expenditure on war pensions during 1969–70 was $A183·45m. and on service pensions $A39·91m.

The total numbers of pensions, etc., in force at 30 June 1970 were: Age and invalid pensions, 912,773; child endowment (number of endowed children), 4,079,378; widows' pensions, 86,921; unemployment, etc., 25,993; war pensions, 585,307; and service pensions, 74,420. Maternity allowances (number granted during 1969–70), 251,904.

Department of Territories, *Progress Towards Assimilation*. Canberra, 1958
Bilton, J., *The Royal Flying Doctor Service of Australia*. Sydney, 1961
Kewley, T. H., *Social security in Australia*. Sydney University Press, 1965
Scott, D., *Leisure: a social enquiry into leisure activities and needs in an Australian housing estate*. Melbourne, 1962
Stoller, A. (ed.), *The Family Today*. Melbourne, 1962.—*Growing Old: problems of old age in the Australian community*. Melbourne, 1960
Stubbs, J., *The hidden people; poverty in Australia*. Melbourne, 1966

JUSTICE. The judicial power of the Commonwealth is vested in the High Court of Australia (the federal supreme Court), in the federal Courts created by Parliament (the Federal Court of Bankruptcy and the Commonwealth Industrial Court) and in the State Courts invested by Parliament with federal jurisdiction.

High Court. The High Court consists of a Chief Justice and 6 other Justices, appointed by the Governor-General in Council. The Constitution confers on the High Court original jurisdiction, *inter alia*, in all matters arising under treaties or affecting consuls or other foreign representatives, matters between the States of the Commonwealth, matters to which the Commonwealth is a party and matters between residents of different States. Parliament may make laws conferring original jurisdiction on the High Court, *inter alia*, in matters arising under the Constitution or under any laws made by Parliament. It has in fact conferred jurisdiction on the High Court in matters arising under the Constitution and in matters arising under certain laws made by Parliament.

The High Court may hear and determine appeals from its own Justices exercising original jurisdiction, from any other federal Court, from a Court exercising federal jurisdiction and from the Supreme Courts of the States. It also has jurisdiction to hear and determine appeals from the Supreme Courts of the Territories. No appeal from the High Court to the Privy Council is permitted on questions as to the limits *inter se* of the constitutional powers of the States or the Commonwealth and the States except on the certificate of the High Court. Appeal from the High Court to the Privy Council by special leave of the Privy Council is possible in matters of non-federal jurisdiction.

Other Federal Courts. Two other federal courts, which have been created to exercise special jurisdiction, are the Commonwealth Industrial Court (*see below*) and the Federal Court of Bankruptcy. The Federal Court of Bankruptcy consists of a Judge appointed by the Governor-General in Council. The State Supreme

Courts have also been invested with federal jurisdiction in bankruptcy. Legislation was introduced in 1968 preparatory to the absorption of these two federal courts in a new federal court of wider jurisdiction. This legislation has not been proceeded with.

State Courts. The general federal jurisdiction of the State Courts extends, subject to certain restrictions and exceptions, to all matters in which the High Court has jurisdiction or in which jurisdiction may be conferred upon it. In matters of non-federal jurisdiction appeal is still possible, as a matter of law, from the State Courts direct to the Privy Council.

Industrial Tribunals. The chief industrial tribunals of the Commonwealth are at present the Industrial Court, constituted by judges, and the Conciliation and Arbitration Commission, constituted by presidential members (with the status of judges) and commissioners. The Industrial Court deals with questions of law, the judicial interpretation of awards, imposition of penalties, etc. The Commission's functions include settling industrial disputes, making awards, determining the standard hours of work, wage fixation, etc.

Australian Digest of Reported Decisions of the Australian Courts and of Australian Appeals to the Privy Council. 1st ed. Sydney, Law Book Co. 1934—Supplements 1934–1963 2nd ed. 1963 ff.
Baalman, J., *Outline of Law in Australia.* 3rd ed. Sydney, 1969
Benjafield, D. G., and Whitmore, H., *Principles of Australian Administrative Law.* 3rd ed. Sydney, 1966
Cowen, Z., *Federal Jurisdiction in Australia.* Melbourne, 1959
Fleming, J. G., *The Law of Torts.* 3rd ed. Sydney, 1965
Gunn, J. A. L., *Australian Income Tax Law and Practice.* 9th ed. by F. C. Bock and E. F. Mannix, Sydney, 1969, and *Butterworths' Taxation Service* to date
Howard, C., *Australian Criminal Law.* Sydney, 1965
Joske, P. E., *Matrimonial Causes and Marriage and Pratice of in Australia and New Zealand.* 2 vols. 5th ed. Sydney, 1969
Mills, C. P., and Sorrell, G. H., *Federal Industrial Laws.* (*Nolan and Cohen.*) 4th ed. Sydney, 1968
O'Connell, D. P. (ed.), *International Law in Australia.* Sydney, 1966
Paterson, W. E., and Ednie, H. H., *Australian Company Law.* Sydney, 1962, and *Butterworth's Company Service* to date
Wynes, A., *Legislative, Executive and Judicial Powers in Australia.* 4th ed. Sydney, 1970
Yorston, R. K., and Fortescue, E. E., *Australian Mercantile Law.* 13th ed. Sydney, 1965

MONEY. On 14 Feb. 1966 Australia adopted a system of decimal currency. The new currency unit, the dollar ($) divided into 100 cents, is equal to 10s. in the £ s. d. system. The transition period ended on 31 July 1967. Decimal system notes have been issued in denominations of $1, 2, 5, 10 and 20. Coins have been issued in denominations of 50, 20, 10, 5 and 2 cents and 1 cent.

Australian notes, issued by the note-issue department of the Reserve Bank, are legal tender throughout Australia. The total value of notes in circulation on 24 June 1970 was $A1,215·5m., of which $A1,050·3m. were held by the public. Coins are issued by the Commonwealth Treasury and distributed by the Reserve Bank. The aggregate net issue of pre-decimal coins at 30 June 1970 was $A52·4m. and decimal coins $A111·8m.

The Royal Australian Mint at Canberra went into production in 1965 to mint the coins of the new decimal currency. The Melbourne mint ceased production of Commonwealth coins on 30 June 1968 and the Perth mint ceased production on 30 Sept. 1968.

FINANCE. Commonwealth. In 1929, under a financial agreement between the Commonwealth and States, approved by a referendum, the Commonwealth took over all State debts existing on 30 June 1927 and agreed to pay $A15,169,824 a year for 58 years towards the interest charges thereon, and to make substantial contributions towards a sinking fund to extinguish existing debts in 58 years and future debts in 53 years. The Commonwealth Government arranges all borrowing for both Commonwealth and States through a loan council consisting of representatives of Commonwealth and State governments. Since 1942 the Commonwealth Government alone has levied taxes on incomes. In return for vacating this field of taxation, the States are reimbursed by a grant from the Commonwealth out of revenue received. All figures in the following table are in $A1,000 (for years ending 30 June).

	1966–67	1967–68	1968–69	1969–70
Revenue:				
Customs	275,095	312,258	346,281	413,573
Excise	806,423	855,255	902,428	939,295
Sales tax	380,695	416,726	494,114	568,691
Estate duty	41,534	54,717	60,726	71,332
Income taxes	2,729,832	3,036,695	3,418,768	4,055,523
Pay-roll tax	172,232	184,416	205,568	230,469
Gift duty	7,659	8,543	9,376	8,553
All other [1]	814,251	891,870	648,505	691,314
Total revenue	5,227,721	5,760,480	6,085,765	6,978,750
Expenditure:				
From revenue	5,227,721	5,760,480	6,085,765	6,978,750
From loans	478,563	683,074	279,027	499,556
Total expenditure	5,706,284	6,443,554	6,364,792	7,478,306
Including:				
Defence services [2]	957,936	1,115,434	1,164,697	1,103,060
War and Repatriation services: [3]				
From loans	5,936 [3]	5,212 [3]	4,294 [3]	3,386 [3]
From revenue	321,404	318,466	347,705	366,799
Age and invalid pensions	481,840	513,984	558,587	641,982
Maternity allowances	7,294	7,349	7,960	8,000
Child endowment	199,282	187,920	193,263	220,143
Widows' pensions	56,438	61,061	69,080	81,753
Unemployment, sickness and special benefits	19,044	18,832	16,830	18,592
Hospital and nursing home benefits	67,398	74,749	85,942	111,381
Medical benefits	58,192	62,547	66,468	76,087
Commonwealth rehabilitation service	1,844	1,944	2,260	2,758
Pharmaceutical benefits	101,281	105,134	118,373	136,718
Loan consolidation and investment reserve ..	227,655	312,761	226,765	578,425
Payments to States:				
From revenue	1,220,026	1,354,062	1,458,276	1,659,186
From loan [4]	120,000	122,840	126,000	132,230

[1] Includes unrequired balances of Trust Accounts, 1966–67, $8,322,000; 1967–68, $22,674,000; 1968–69, $66,137,000; 1969–70, $63,242,000.
[2] Includes capital works and services.
[3] Gross expenditure (repayments amounting to $6,507,000 in 1966–67, $5,156,000 in 1967–68, $5,644,000 in 1968–69 and $4,682,000 in 1969–70 included).
[4] Advances to States for housing.

The estimated receipts of Consolidated Revenue Fund for 1970–71 amount to $A7,722m. and the expenditure (adjusted to exclude defence, war and repatriation services and payments to the Loan Consolidation and Investment Reserve) $A5,578m. The estimated defence (excluding payments financed under credit arrangements with USA), war and repatriation expenditure is $A1,509m.

The following table shows Government securities on issue on account of Commonwealth and States, at 30 June 1970:

Currency in which repayable	Commonwealth	States	Total
Australian Dollars ($A1,000)	2,818,633	8,806,095	11,624,728
Sterling (£Stg.1,000)	69,917	164,685	234,601
United States Dollars (US$1,000)	687,199	149,829	837,028
Canadian Dollars (Can.$1,000)	24,792	12,154	36,946
Swiss Francs (Sw.F.1,000)	249,604	50,296	299,900
Netherlands Guilders (fl.1,000)	5,719	26,281	32,000
Deutsche Marks (DM 1,000)	938,740	—	938,740
Total ($A1,000 equivalents) [1]	3,884,914	9,320,061	13,204,976

[1] Converted at rate of exchange ruling at 30 June 1970.

The annual interest payable, was $A634·5m., an average rate of 4·8%. The amount of interest payable in sterling amounted to £11·4m., in US dollars to $43·78m., in Swiss francs to Sw.Fr.15·84m., in Canadian dollars to $1·86m., in Netherlands guilders to fl.1·6m. and in Deutsche Marks to DM 61·08m.

The average rate of interest on internal debt at 30 June 1930, 1940 and 1970 was 5·27%, 3·62% and 4·74% respectively.

Debt per head of population at 30 June 1970 was $A1,051·11, while the annual interest charge amounted to $A50.50 per head.

States. The following tables present a summary of the revenue and expenditure of the States during 1969–70, showing, under general headings, the main sources of income and items of expenditure (in $A1,000):

State revenue (Preliminary)	Taxation	Business under- takings	Common- wealth payments[1]	Lands and other	Total
New South Wales	234,676	304,537	403,344	134.152	1,076,709
Victoria	191,829	138,839	301.222	95,010	726,900
Queensland	69,613	105,903	205.593	59,965	441,074
South Australia	56,453	71,744	138,571	57,056	323,824
Western Australia	50,865	66,663	141,483	59,178	318,189
Tasmania	19,065	262	72,116	32,276	123,719
Total	622,501	687,948	1,262,329	437,637	3,010,415

[1] Includes special grants and payments under the States Grants Acts.

State expenditure (Preliminary)	Debt charges	From revenue Business under- takings	Administra- tion, works and social services	Total	From loan —Net ex- penditure on works
New South Wales	135,730	256,597	695.655	1,087,982	192,156
Victoria	154,460	125,178	462.644	742,282	154,777
Queensland	69,773	103,950	270,895	444,618	86,158
South Australia	77,686	54,539	188,679	320,904	82,263
Western Australia	51,427	79,466	188,008	318,901	59,347
Tasmania	36,690	2,196	82,018	120,904	44,970
Total	525,766	621,926	1,887,899	3,035,591	619,671

The aggregate revenue and expenditure (excluding loan) of Commonwealth and States combined during 1969–70 was respectively $A8,695·36m. and $A8,720,539,000. Aggregate net loan expenditure on works was $A763,209,000.

Finance (5 parts), Bureau of Census and Statistics. Canberra, 1907–1962/63
Australian National Accounts. Bureau of Census and Statistics. 1953–54 to date
Public Authority Finance, 1963–64 to 1967–68. Bureau of Census and Statistics, 1970
Commonwealth Finance. Bureau of Census and Statistics. 1962–63 to date
State, Territory and Local Government Authorities' Finance and Government Securities. Bureau of Census and Statistics. 1962–63 to date
National Income and Expenditure. Department of the Treasury. Canberra, 1946 to date
Australia's *Committee of Economic Enquiry*. Report. Canberra, 1965
Treasury Information Bulletin (and Supplements). Canberra Treasury Dept., 1956 to date (quarterly)
Arndt, H. W. (ed.), *The Australian Economy*. Melbourne, 1963
Campbell, W. J., *Australian State Public Finance*. Sydney, 1954
Karmel, P. H., *The Structure of the Australian Economy*. Melbourne, 1962
Maxwell, J. A., *Commonwealth–State Financial Arrangements in Australia*. Melbourne University Press
Ratchford, B. U., *Public Expenditure in Australia*. Durham, N.C., 1959

DEFENCE. Army. Subject to the overall authority of the Minister for the Army, the Military Board is charged with the control and administration of all matters relating to the Australian Military Forces. Command and control is exercised through Army Headquarters and commands geographically related to States—Northern Command, Eastern Command, Southern Command, Central Command, Western Command, Tasmania Command, Northern Territory Command and Papua and New Guinea Command.

Since 1957, the basis of the readiness of the Army has been with emphasis on south-east Asia as an area of primary strategic importance to Australia. The strength of the Regular Army, including National Servicemen, was 44,533 at the end of June 1970. The field force organization has been expanded with emphasis on a substantial increase in the combat element and high-priority logistic units, to meet the present requirement for 'cold' and limited warfare with light, air-portable formations. In addition, the Pacific Islands Regiment of 2 battalions and supporting units, with a total Pacific Islander strength of 2,434, is capable of further expansion.

Compulsory selective service to increase the numbers in the Regular Army applies to young men in their 20th year. The number inducted at present is 8,400 a year. Recruits serve 2 years full time, followed by 3 years in the Reserve. They are liable for overseas service. A volunteer Regular Army Emergency Reserve of 822 former Regular Army members has been formed and can be called out, as desired, by the Governor-General. The strength of the Citizen Military Forces is 31,397 and the strength of School Cadets 41,380.

Currently there are about 8,500 Australian Army personnel serving overseas in Malaysia and Vietnam.

Training for commissioned rank in the Regular Army is carried out at the Royal Military College, the Officer Cadet School and the Officer Training Unit. The Royal Military College was established in the Australian Capital Territory in 1911 to train young men from Australia and New Zealand for commissioned rank in the Regular Armies of the two countries. The college accepts young men between the ages of 17 and 20 years who have qualified to enter university. The course is 4 years, and includes both military instruction and academic studies. The college has entered into an affiliation with the University of New South Wales whereby the university has established a Faculty of Military Studies in the college. The faculty is responsible for presenting courses leading to the award of the university's degrees of Bachelor of Arts in Military Studies (B.A.(Mil.)) and Bachelor of Science in Military Studies (B.Sc.(Mil.)). The B.Sc.(Mil.) caters for both the applied science and engineering courses. The Officer Cadet School was established at Portsea, Victoria, in 1952. The school accepts young men between the ages of 19 and 23 years for normal entry and 19 and 25 years for special entry. The duration of the course is about 11 months. The Officer Training Unit was established at Scheyville in 1965 to train selected National Service trainees for commissioned rank in the Regular Army Supplement. The duration of the course is 21 weeks. Direct entry officers are also trained at the Officer Training Unit.

High staff and command training of Army officers is, in the main, carried out at the Australian Staff College, Queenscliff, Victoria. The curriculum is closely co-ordinated with those of the staff colleges of Britain and other countries of the Commonwealth of Nations. A system of exchange of instructors and students promotes mutual understanding and a common doctrine.

Expenditure on Army capital equipment, was $A53m. in 1967–68, $A64m. in 1968–69 and $50·6m. in 1969–70

Navy. The overall control of the Royal Australian Navy is vested in the Naval Board, which consists of the Minister for the Navy and 4 Naval Members (First Naval Member and Chief of Naval Staff; Second Naval Member and Chief of Naval Personnel; Third Naval Member and Chief of Naval Technical Services; Fourth Naval Member and Chief of Supply), and the Secretary, Department of the Navy. Headquarters of the Naval Board and the Department of the Navy are in Canberra. The operation and administration of the Fleet is the responsibility of the Flag Officer Commanding H.M. Australian Fleet.

Aircraft carriers of the Royal Australian Navy:

Completed	Name	Standard displacement, tons	Principal armament	Shaft-horse-power	Speed, knots
1955	Melbourne (ex-Majestic)	16,000	12 40-mm AA	40,000	24
1949	Sydney (ex-Terrible)[1]	12,569	4 40-mm AA	40,000	24

[1] Converted to a fast military transport in 1961.

There are also 4 British-built 'Oberon' class submarines, *Onslow*, *Otway*, *Ovens* and *Oxley* (completed in 1967–69), 3 US-built 'Charles F. Adams' class guided-missile destroyers, *Brisbane*, *Hobart* and *Perth* (completed in 1965–68).

4 destroyers (3 'Daring',[1] 1 'Battle' class), 8 destroyer escorts or fast anti-submarine frigates (6 type 12, 2 type 15), 3 oceanographic research ships, 2 minehunters, 4 minesweepers, a destroyer tender, 20 patrol craft, 1 survey ship, 1 small survey ship, 1 fleet tanker and 10 servicing craft. One destroyer escort is being built in Australia.

[1] Including *Duchess*, on loan from the Royal Navy.

Naval dockyards exist at Garden Island, Sydney, and Williamstown, Victoria. Naval shipbuilding is carried out at Williamstown, at Cockatoo Dock and Engineering Company, Sydney, or by private contract. The main repair base and store depots are at Sydney.

The main training establishments are HMAS *Cerberus* in Victoria, HMAS *Watson*, HMAS *Penguin* and HMAS *Nirimba* at Sydney, HMAS *Albatross* (Naval Air Station) at Nowra, NSW, and HMAS *Creswell* (Royal Australian Naval College) at Jervis Bay, ACT. Training for junior recruits is carried out at HMAS *Leeuwin* in Fremantle, WA. Reserve training is conducted in naval establishments in all capital cities.

The Fleet Air Arm was established in 1948 as an integral part of the Navy. In June 1970 it had 70 aircraft and 1,661 officers and sailors. Its operational aircraft consist of Skyhawk jet fighters, Tracker anti-submarine aircraft and Westland Wessex anti-submarine helicopters. There is a squadron of 5 Bell Iroquois helicopters for search and rescue, training and communication duties; and 1 Westland Scout helicopter for oceanographical survey duties.

The serving strength at 30 June 1970 totalled 17,304 officers and sailors.

Navy estimates, 1969–70, totalled $A241·14m.; 1970–71, $A243·01m., including $A15·81m. and $A26·12m., respectively for USA logistics under credit arrangement.

Air Force. The Royal Australian Air Force was established as a separate service on 31 March 1921. The Department of Air exercises governmental and financial control. The controlling body is the Air Board, which consists of the Chief of the Air Staff, Air Member for Personnel, Air Member for Technical Services, Air Member for Supply and Equipment and the Secretary Department of Air. The Air Board is responsible to the Minister for Air and determines all policy matters of major importance.

Operational Command with Headquarters near Sydney is responsible for operations, while Support Command with Headquarters in Melbourne is responsible for recruitment, training, supply and maintenance.

Flying establishment comprises 16 squadrons of which 2 are equipped with F-4E Phantom aircraft as an interim measure until F-111C 'swing wing' strike/reconnaissance aircraft become available. Of the others 1 is equipped with Canberra bombers, 4 with missile-armed Mirage III-O Mach-2 fighters, 1 with Orion maritime reconnaissance bombers, 1 with Neptune reconnaissance aircraft and 2 with Iroquois helicopters. There are 5 transport squadrons, 2 with Hercules turboprop transports, 2 with Caribou STOL transports and a special transport squadron equipped with BAC One-Eleven, Fan Jet Falcon and HS748 aircraft. Training aircraft include Aermacchi MB 326H jets used for 'all-through' pilot training and HS748 aircraft used for navigation and air electronics training. An order for 12 Boeing-Vertol CH-47C medium-lift helicopters was announced in 1970.

As part of Australia's contribution to the Commonwealth Strategic Reserve, 2 Mirage squadrons with supporting units are based in Malaysia and Singapore. One Canberra, 1 Caribou and an Iroquois squadron are operating in South Vietnam.

At 1 July 1970 the strength of the RAAF was as follows: Permanent Air Force, 22,642; Citizen Air Force, 841; General Reserve, 8,536; Emergency Force, 668.

Long, G. (ed.), *Australia in the War of 1939–45*. 22 vols. Canberra, 1952 ff.
Millar, T. B., *Australia's Defence*. Melbourne Univ. Press, 1965

AGRICULTURE. At 30 June 1969, 609m. acres, representing 32·1% of the total area of Australia, were either unoccupied or occupied by the Crown; only 9·4% had been actually alienated (178m. acres); 2·5% (48m. acres) was in process of alienation, and 56·1% (1,065m. acres) was held under the various forms of leases and licenses.

Area and yield of the principal crops in 1968–69:

Crops	Total acreage (1,000 acres)	Total yield (1,000 bushels)
Wheat (grain)	26.799	543,950
Oats (grain)	3,872	94,250
Barley (grain)	3,314	72,588
Maize (grain)	176	6,826
		(1,000 tons)
Hay	3,955	7,330
Potatoes (ordinary)	113	798
Sugar-cane (for crushing)	568	18,413
Vineyards	127[1]	545
		(1,000 gallons)
Wine made	..	51,936
Orchards and fruit gardens	310	..

[1] Bearing area.

The following summary shows the production and net value of the most important items or classes of production, classified by States:

Production, 1968–69	NSW	Vic.	Q'ld	SA	WA	Tas.	Australia
Area of crops (1,000 acres)	15,570	7,910	5,449	7,704	9,812	476	46,940[1]
Production of wheat (1,000 bu.)	215,119	90,728	42,000	83,160	112,450	410	543,950[1]
Total wool production (1m. lb.)	673·5	364·3	247·0	238·1	375·7	47·0	1,947·8[1]
Factory butter (1,000 lb.)	52,172	280,206	43,083	14,507	13,937	35,315	439,220
Factory cheese (1,000 lb.)	12,201	75,256	17,871	42,218	4,458	12,834	164,838
All meat (tons, carcass weight)	487,269	497,413	428,120	108,380	149,470	57,412	1,749,002[1]
Production of minerals[2] (net value $A1m.)	239·5	4·9	133·2	56·3	100·0	33·0	701·6[1]
Total primary production (net value $A1m.)	1,158·1	788·2	754·8	346·1	522·8	119·4	3,737·0[1]

[1] Includes Northern Territory and Australian Capital Territory.
[2] Mining and quarrying 1968.

Livestock (in 1,000) at 31 March 1969:

	NSW	Vic.	Q'ld	SA	WA	Tas.	N. Terr.[1]	ACT	Australia
Horses[2]	146	55	182	16	35	7	38	1	479
Cattle	4,864	3,878	7,668	865	1,546	586	1,185	14	20,606
Sheep	68,153	30,185	20,324	18,392	32,901	4,395	7	246	174.602
Pigs	690	422	535	288	220	95	2	..	2,253

[1] At 30 June.   [2] At 31 March 1967.

MINING. The mineral output was valued at the mine as follows (in $A1,000)[1]

Mineral	1967	1968	Mineral	1967	1968
Copper[2]	72,515	92,396	Zinc[2]	29,354	30,398
Gold[2]	24,456	23,525	Black coal	160,099	188,785
Iron ore	82,994	131.482	Brown coal	20,686	21,555
Lead[2]	73,654	89,705			
Rutile	19,615	21.528	Total (value of mining		
Tungsten	4,509	5,514	and quarrying)	696,701	850,736

[1] The values in this table include the value of materials used in process of production, whereas those in preceding and subsequent tables exclude these values to show net value.
[2] Value of all minerals containing the metal shown as the principal content.

Gold production (fine oz.) in 1963, 1,023,970; 1964, 963,834; 1965, 877,643; 1966, 916,985; 1967, 805,336; 1968, 781,782; 1969, 699,194.

Black coal (1,000 tons) mined in 1963, 24,856; 1964, 27,401; 1965, 31,439; 1966, 33,334; 1967, 34,707; 1968, 40,183; 1969, 45,403.

INDUSTRY. Statistics of the manufacturing industries in Australia in 1967–68: Number of establishments,[1] 62,954; workers employed,[2] 1,331,147; salaries and wages paid,[3] $A3,666m.; value of plant and machinery, land and buildings, $A9,265m.; value of materials and fuel and power used, $A9,663m.; value of production, $A7,431m.; value of output, $A17,094m.

[1] Employing 4 or more persons and using non-manual power.
[2] Including working proprietors.   [3] Excluding amounts drawn by working proprietors.

Estimated net value (in $A1,000) of the products of Australia:

Products	1964–65	1965–66	1966–67	1967–68	1968–69
Agriculture	975,164	857,913	1,209,003	899,425	1,212 684
Pastoral	1,194,438	1,159,500	1,181,848	1,044,436	1,191 279
Dairy, poultry, bees	415,771	416,003	445,123	439,263	450 641
Trapping, forestry, fisheries	159,166	166,588	165,468	174,543	180,784
Mining and quarrying[1]	400,119	443,853	514,534	568,065	701,627
Manufacturing	5,896,754	6,251,861	6,877,001	7,430,853	..
Total	9,041,410	9,295,720	10,392,980	10,556,568	..

[1] At 31 Dec. of first year shown.

TOURISM. During 1969, 299,889 overseas visitors arrived in Australia intending to stay for less than 12 months, spending an estimated $A119m.

Bureau of Census and Statistics, Canberra: *Rural Industries*. 1962–63 to date.—*Non-rural Primary Industries*. 1965–66 and 1966–67.—*Value of Production*. 1964–65 to date.—*Manufacturing Industry*.1963–64 to date.—*Manufacturing Commodities*. 1963–64 and 1964–65.—*Building and Construction*. 1964–65 to date
Quarterly Review of Agricultural Economics. Bureau of Agricultural Economics. Canberra, 1948 to date
Atlas of Australian Resources. Department of National Development. Canberra, 1953–60
Developments in Australian Manufacturing Industry. Department of Trade. Melbourne, 1954/55 to date (annual)
Survey of Manufacturing Industry in Australia. Department of Trade. Melbourne, 1956 to date
The Australian Mineral Industry Review. Department of National Development—Bureau of Mineral Resources, Geology and Geophysics. Canberra, 1948 to date
Australian Economy. Department of the Treasury. Canberra, 1956 to date
The Australian Wheat Growing Industry. Department of Primary Industry. Canberra, 1960
Report of the Dairy Industry Committee of Enquiry. Department of Primary Industry. Canberra, 1960
Report of the Wool Marketing Committee of Enquiry. Department of Primary Industry. Canberra, 1962
Andrews, J., *Australia's Resources and Their Utilisation*. 5th ed. Sydney, 1957
Australasian Institute of Mining and Metallurgy. *Proceedings: new series*. Melbourne, 1912 to date
Barnard, J. A. (ed.), *The Simple Fleece: studies in the Australian wool industry*. Melbourne, 1962
Beattie, W. A., *A Survey of the Beef-cattle Industry of Australia*. Melbourne, 1956
Davidson, F. G., *The Industrialisation of Australia*. 3rd ed. Melbourne, 1962
Diesendorp, W. (ed.), *The Snowy Mountains Scheme*. Sydney, 1961
Drane, N. T. (ed.), *The Australian Dairy Industry*. Melbourne, 1961
James, W., *Wine in Australia*. 3rd ed. Melbourne, 1962
O'Loghlen, F. (ed.), *Cattle Country: an illustrated survey of the beef cattle industry*. Sydney, 1960
Roughley, T. C., *Fish and Fisheries of Australia*. Rev. ed. Sydney, 1961
Shann, E. O. G., *An Economic History of Australia*. London, 1948
Shaw, A. G. L., *Economic Development of Australia*. 4th ed. Melbourne, 1960
Wadham, Sir Samuel, Kent Wilson, R., and Wood, J., *Land Utilisation in Australia*. 3rd ed. Melbourne, 1957

LABOUR AND EMPLOYMENT. The majority of wage and salary earners in Australia have their minimum wages and conditions of work prescribed in awards of industrial arbitration authorities established under federal and State legislation. However, in some States, some conditions of work (*e.g.*, normal weekly hours of work, long-service leave, annual leave) are set down in State legislation. Practically all employees in Australia have a standard working week of 40 hours or less; paid annual leave of at least 3 weeks; and paid long-service leave (*i.e.*, leave granted to workers who remain with one employer over an extended period of time) of at least 13 weeks after 15 years continuous service.

In addition to the minimum rates of pay for a standard working week prescribed in awards of industrial arbitration authorities, many wage-earners are in receipt of over-award pay and payments for overtime. At the end of Oct. 1969 it was estimated that the average weekly earnings of adult males (other than managerial, professional and higher supervisory staff) in full-time private employment was $A74 and average weekly hours 43·6.

Employees in all States are covered by workers' compensation legislation which provides for compensation for work injuries.

During 1969 industrial disputes involving stoppages of work of 10 man-days or more accounted for 1,958,000 working days lost. In these disputes 1,285,000 workers were involved. Over 68% of the working days lost in 1969 were due to disputes which lasted 3 days or less.

The following table shows estimates (in 1,000) of the civilian wage and salary earners in Australia classified by industry (excluding employees in agriculture and private domestic service):

Industry	June 1967	June 1968	June 1969	June 1970
Mining and quarrying	54·9	58·0	62·8	69·2
Manufacturing	1,283·1	1,310·0	1,344·6	1,377·0
Electricity, gas, water and sanitary services	108·2	110·7	112·1	113·4
Building and construction	338·0	349·5	358·9	368·2
Transport and storage	226·8	232·2	237·1	245·3
Communication	108·1	111·2	113·0	117·0
Finance and property	177·7	185·1	195·6	208·8
Commerce	673·2	689·2	707·0	730·8
Public authority activities	166·2	173·4	182·1	192·3
Health, hospitals, etc.	189·0	198·1	208·6	222·3
Education	194·2	208·1	221·5	235·1
Amusement, hotels, personal service	215·7	228·6	241·9	261·5
Total (including other groups)	3,902·3	4,029·8	4,171·7	4,341·8

The following table shows the number of unemployed persons, of job vacancies which employers registered with the Commonwealth Employment Service and of persons in receipt of unemployment benefit:

	June 1966	June 1967	June 1968	June 1969	June 1970
Registered unemployed	59,020	68,491	65,253	54,866	51,515
Registered job vacancies	33,021	29,335	28,722	34,996	39,865
Unemployment benefit recipients	19,058	23,394	21,275	15,910	13,043

Trade Unions. At the end of 1969 there were 309 trade unions in existence in Australia with a reported membership of 2,239,100. Over 50% of wage and salary earners were estimated to be members of unions. In 1969, 202 unions (109,300 members) reported membership of less than 2,000, and 33 unions (1,617,100 members) reported membership of 20,000 or more. Many of the larger trade unions are affiliated with central labour organizations, the oldest being the Australian Council of Trade Unions formed in 1927. Other central labour organizations have as affiliates Public Service associations, and salaried and professional associations.

Labour Report. Bureau of Census and Statistics. Canberra, 1913 to date
Foenander, O. de R., *Better Employment Relations and Other Essays in Labour.* Sydney, 1954.—*Industrial Conciliation and Arbitration in Australia.* Sydney, 1959.—*Trade Unionism in Australia.* Sydney, 1962.—*Shop Stewards and Shop Committees.* Melbourne Univ. Press, 1965
Isaac, J. E., *Trends in Australian Industrial Relations.* Melbourne, 1962
O'Dea, R., *Industrial Relations in Australia.* Sydney, 1965
Periman, M., *Judges in Industry.* Melbourne, 1954
Portus, J. H., *The Development of Australian Trade Union Law.* Melbourne, 1958
Sykes, E. I., *Strike Law in Australia.* Sydney, 1960
Walker, K. F., *Industrial Relations in Australia.* Cambridge, Mass., 1956

COMMERCE. Throughout Australia there are uniform customs duties, and trade between the States is free. For 1969–70 the gross revenue collected from customs duties amounted to $A452,367,000, and from excise to $A946·3m. The total net revenue from customs and excise for 1969–70 after allowing for drawbacks and credit to Commonwealth Government departments for duty paid, was $A1,352·9m.

Value of the total imports and exports for years ending 30 June, in $A1,000 (f.o.b.):

		Exports (excluding ships' and aircraft stores)		
		Australian		
	Imports	Produce	Re-exports	Total
1967–68	3,264.473	2,935.156	109.519	3,044.675
1968–69	3,468.505	3,245.079	129.185	3,374.263
1969–70	3,884.052	3,960.283	171.335	4,131.618

The Australian customs tariff provides for preferences to goods produced in and shipped from certain specified countries such as UK, Canada, New Zealand and Ireland. Preferences occur as a result of reciprocal trade agreements between Australia and these countries. Australia also has bilateral agreements with a number of other countries guaranteeing reciprocal treatment in matters of trade. The Australia–New Zealand free-trade agreement came into force on 1 Jan. 1966 in certain scheduled goods. In addition, Australia is a signatory to the multilateral General Agreement on Tariffs and Trade (GATT).

Principal commodities exported and imported (in $A1,000, f.o.b.) in 1969–70:

	Exports	Imports		Exports	Imports
Live animals	7,358	4,355	Plastic materials	6,802	91,161
Meat	417,909	2,288	Chemical materials and		
Dairy products	102.254	5,757	products, n.e.s.	23,537	49,726
Fish	39.281	33,368	Leather manufactures, n.e.s.	5,652	7,332
Cereals	432,019	4,747	Rubber manufactures, n.e.s.	12,127	41,995
Fruit and vegetables	94,102	23,855	Wood and cork manufac-		
Sugar, etc., and honey	121,848	3,004	tures (except furniture)	2,559	15,391
Coffee, tea, etc.	4,240	51,396	Paper and paperboard	12,080	107,799
Food for animals	12,406	6,882	Textile yarn, fabrics, etc.	18,909	287,324
Miscellaneous food	3,500	4,199	Non-metallic mineral manu-		
Beverages	7,623	16,469	factures, n.e.s.	27,042	78,267
Tobacco	2,982	31,975	Iron and steel	135,707	95,286
Hides, skins, etc.	89,922	1,664	Non-ferrous metals	283,771	24,515
Oil-seeds, nuts, kernels	1.094	9,897	Manufactures of metal,		
Crude rubber	806	30.111	n.e.s.	42,466	94,650
Wood, timber and cork	4,397	53,077	Machinery (except electric)	89,804	708.828
Pulp and waste paper	411	36,550	Electric machinery	36,927	251,367
Textile fibres and their			Transport equipment	153,071	567,535
waste	768,802	33,815	Sanitary, etc., fixtures and		
Crude fertilizers and			fittings	1,769	5,664
minerals	9,524	60,989	Furniture	1,355	5,463
Metalliferous ores and			Travel goods and handbags	293	5,740
metal scrap	506,428	7,877	Clothing	9,030	34,385
Crude animal and vegetable			Footwear, gaiters, etc.	761	15,481
materials, n.e.s.	14,636	13,265	Professional and scientific		
Coal, coke and briquettes	172,582	804	instruments; photo-		
Petroleum and products	27,722	254,278	graphic and optical		
Petroleum gases	193	45	goods, watches and		
Animal oils and fats	24,836	893	clocks	20,106	120,711
Fixed vegetable oils and			Miscellaneous manufac-		
fats	100	12,532	tured articles, n.e.s.	23,765	162,179
Animal and vegetable oils			Commodities and trans-		
and fats	913	2,174	actions of merchandise		
Chemicals	94,141	117,454	trade, not elsewhere		
Mineral tar, crude chemi-			classified	88,143	123,611
cals from coal, etc.	256	2,162			
Dyeing, tanning and colour-			Total merchandise trade	3,994,203	3,825,448
ing materials	8,472	22,364			
Medicinal and pharma-			Commodities and trans-		
ceutical products	18,383	54,157	actions not included in		
Essential oils and perfumes,			merchandise trade	137,415	58,604
etc.	6,104	16,505			
Fertilizers, manufactured	844	7,209	Total recorded trade	4,131,618	3,884,052
Explosives and pyrotechnic					
products	2,436	4,922			

Total trade (in $A1,000, f.o.b.) with the more important countries, according to origin (imports) and consignment (exports):

	Imports		Exports	
From or to	1968–69	1969–70	1968–69	1969–70
Belgium–Luxembourg	20,140	29,120	43,784	42,863
Canada	153,085	151,031	67,611	112,773
Ceylon	15,184	11,321	15,083	14,718

From or to	Imports		Exports	
	1968–69	1969–70	1968–69	1969–70
China (Mainland)	29,651	32,082	67,214	125.815
France	63,442	70,059	112,526	114.640
Germany (West)	201,544	258,275	104,550	115,625
Hong Kong	41,075	54,022	70,973	84,706
India	32,196	31,839	32,017	40.237
Indonesia	59,956	48,882	20,665	35,266
Iran	13,464	12,658	7,164	14,794
Italy	78,962	77,378	106,726	105,961
Japan	414,676	481,203	822,101	1,021,319
Kuwait	41,611	45,661	8,197	9,084
Malaysia	30,022	34,922	63,670	68,525
Netherlands	50,084	59,981	53,759	70,995
New Zealand	74,734	86,435	158,846	198,872
Pakistan	17,068	18,953	6,905	16,394
Papua–New Guinea	21,130	21,631	105,832	147,298
Saudi Arabia	43,558	42,099	8,923	10,385
Singapore	12,496	14,031	63,325	98.469
Sweden	50,588	59.136	8,707	9,635
Switzerland	47,826	62,258	2,911	3,456
USSR	2,039	3,475	40,289	51,438
UK	747,155	845,344	424,836	489,427
USA	883,068	965,071	480,001	556,607

Imports and exports for particular States, 1969–70 ($A1,000, f.o.b.):

States, etc.	Imports	Exports	States, etc.	Imports	Exports
New South Wales	1,707,445	1,158,757	Tasmania	46,886	143,331
Victoria	1,347,053	912,576	Northern Territory	39,829	49,725
Queensland	297,051	773,519	Aust. Cap. Terr.	2,267	1,571
South Australia	201,223	417,091			
Western Australia	242,299	675,027	Total	3,884,052	4,131,618

In this table the value of goods sent from one state to another for transhipment abroad has been included in the State from which the goods were finally dispatched.

Total trade between UK and Australia according to the British Board of Trade returns (in £1,000 sterling):

	1966	1967	1968	1969	1970
Imports to UK	207,931	173,771	210,792	237,443	260,084
Exports from UK	255,465	253,866	316,646	318,164	346,094
Re-exports from UK	2,513	2,427	2,785	3,197	

Overseas Trade. Bureau of Census and Statistics. Canberra, 1906 to date

SHIPPING. As at 30 June 1969 the Australian merchant marine (vessels of 200 tons gross and over) consisted of 127 coastal vessels of 875,107 tons gross and 13 overseas vessels of 68,491 tons gross.

Entrance and clearance of vessels (with cargo and in ballast) engaged in overseas trade:

	Entrances		Clearances	
	No.	Net tons	No.	Net tons
1967–68	3,972	30,108,746	4,013	30,278,225
1968–69	4,390	36,419,361	4,360	36,158,982

The following summary shows shipping activity by States, 1968–69:

Particulars		NSW	Vic.	Q'ld	SA	WA	Tas.	NT	Aust.
Entrances of overseas vessels:									
Number		1,282	446	1,060	311	1,095	81	115	4,390
Net tonnage (1,000 tons)		11,249	2,892	6,920	3,040	11,064	580	675	36,420
Overseas cargo:									
Discharged (1,000 tons)	weight	9,610	8,724	3,102	2,604	4,761	243	254	29,298
	meas.	2,085	1,969	382	408	295	47	28	5,214
Loaded (1,000 tons)	weight	14,400	2,057	11,256	3,377	21,148	1,593	1,125	54,956
	meas.	597	663	145	151	263	233	2	2,054
Interstate cargo:									
Shipped (1,000 tons)	weight	3,915	1,331	929	6,163	5,211	805	157	18,511
	meas.	153	868	32	9	61	807	2	1,932

RAILWAYS. Government railways for the year ended 30 June 1969:

System	Route-miles open	Revenue train-miles run 1,000	Passenger-journeys,[1] 1,000	Goods and livestock carried,[1] 1,000 tons	Gross earnings,[2] $A1,000	Working expenses, $A1,000
State:						
New South Wales	6,061	38,201	248,469	31,871	228,560	205,164
Victoria	4,176	19,689	144,866	11,316	100,502	111,216
Queensland	5,824	17,109	28,165	12,975	102,452	91,427
South Australia	2,460	6,176	14,423	5,003	30,300	36,154[3]
Western Australia	3,826	7,901	10,170	8,934	49,364	49,947[3]
Tasmania	500	1,197	1,045	1,242	6,947	9,089[3]
Commonwealth:						
Trans-Australian	1,108	2,341	196	881	16,232 ⎫	
Central Australia	818	961	23	2,394	7,045 ⎪	24,614[3,4]
North Australia	317	241	..	879	1,851 ⎬	
Aust. Cap. Terr.	5	16	79	247	243 ⎭	
Total	25,095	93,832	447,437	75,742	543,496	527,611

[1] Intersystem traffic is included in the total for each system over which it passes.
[2] Excluding government grants.   [3] Includes provision of reserves for depreciation.
[4] Not available separately.

The State railway gauges are: New South Wales, 4 ft 8½ in.; Victoria, 5 ft 3 in. (202 miles, 4 ft 8½ in. and 9 miles, 2 ft 6 in.); Queensland, 3 ft 6 in. (69 miles, 4 ft 8½ in., and 30 miles, 2 ft); South Australia, 5 ft 3 in. for 1,631 miles (the rest 3 ft 6 in.); West Australia, 3 ft. 6 in., and Tasmania, 3 ft 6 in. Of the Commonwealth lines, the gauge of the Trans-Australian and Australian Capital Territory is 4 ft 8½ in., for the Central Australia, 3 ft 6 in. for 601 miles and 4 ft 8½ in. for 217 miles and for North Australia, 3 ft 6 in. Under various Commonwealth–State standardization agreements Brisbane, Sydney and Melbourne are already linked by a standard 4 ft 8½ in. gauge line and Sydney is linked with Perth, *via* Broken Hill to Port Pirie (South Australia), from Port Pirie to Kalgoorlie (Western Australia) and from Kalgoorlie to Perth. The overall length of the Sydney–Perth railway is 2,461 miles. The terminus of the North Australia railway is at Birdum (317 miles from Darwin), while the Central Australia railway extends as far north as Alice Springs (3 ft 6 in. gauge from Maree to Alice Springs).

ROADS. The length of roads in Australia for general traffic is about 560,000 miles, of which approximately 112,000 is sealed, 141,000 of macadam and similar composition, and 307,000 of cleared or natural surface or formed only.

At 31 Dec. 1969, 4,739,512 motor vehicles, including 3,676,241 cars and station wagons, 949,587 utilities, panel vans, trucks and omnibuses, and 113,684 motor cycles, were registered in Australia. The revenue derived from registration fees and motor tax for the year 1968–69 was $A143·3m., drivers' and riders' licences, $A16·2m., and miscellaneous, $A67·9m. New vehicles registered in 1969–70 numbered 409,282 cars and station wagons, 89,718 utilities, panel vans, trucks and omnibuses and 27,270 motor cycles.

AVIATION. Civil flying in the Commonwealth and Territories is subject to legislative control by the Commonwealth Government. The administration of the Air Navigation Act and Regulations is a function of the Civil Aviation Department under the Minister of Civil Aviation. The permanent head of the department is the Director-General of Civil Aviation.

Operations of regular internal air services in Australia include flights of all Australian-owned airlines, except Qantas Airways, within the Commonwealth. During 1968–69 hours flown numbered 244,606. The total mileage flown was 60·3m. Paying passengers carried numbered 5,184,828; weight of goods carried was 89,947 short tons, and gross weight of mails was 9,876 short tons.

During 1968–69 hours flown by Australian regular oversea services numbered 74,757; miles flown, 33·6m.; paying passengers, 642,524; freight, 18,537 short tons; mail, 2,862 short tons.

Expenditure by the Commonwealth Government on civil aviation for the year 1969–70 was $A107·1m. (including $A41·5m. on capital works).

At 30 June 1969 there were 383 licensed land aerodromes, 108 governmental land aerodromes and 13 water aerodromes in Australia, excluding Papua and New Guinea.

POST AND TELEGRAPHS. Business, year ended 30 June 1969. Number of post offices, 7,324. Earnings: Postal, $A154·9m.; telecommunications, $A412·3m.; total, $A567·2m. Working expenses: Postal, $A155·9m.; telecommunications, $A314·5m.; total $A470·4m. Interest: Postal, $A7·7m.; telecommunications, $A81·1m.

At 30 June 1969, 6,230 telephone exchanges with 2,511,000 services and 3,599,000 instruments, were in operation.

Wireless broadcasting stations are in operation in all State capitals and in other regional areas throughout Australia. The National Broadcasting Service is provided by the Australian Broadcasting Commission, which at 30 June 1969 operated 71 medium-wave and 8 high-frequency stations and 9 high-frequency stations for overseas services. In addition, 114 medium-wave commercial broadcasting stations were operating.

The Overseas Telecommunications Commission, established in Aug. 1946, is responsible for all overseas services by cable, radio, telephone, including radio telephone services with ships at sea.

Television services are conducted in each State and the Australian Capital Territory by the National Television Service and by the Commercial Television Service. There were 39 national television stations and 45 commercial television stations in operation at 30 June 1969.

At 30 June 1969 there were in force 2,630,212 broadcast and 2,649,457 television licences, including 2,189,683 combined licences; combined licences were introduced on 1 April 1965. Revenue in 1968–69 was $A45·1m. from all licences.

Australian Transport. Sydney, Institute of Transport, 1937 to date (quarterly)
Bureau of Census and Statistics, *Transport and Communication.* Canberra, 1906 to date
Brogden, S., *Australia's Two Airline Policy.* Melbourne, 1968
Brogden, S., *The History of Australian Aviation.* Melbourne, 1960

BANKING. The banking system in Australia comprises:

(*a*) The Reserve Bank of Australia. This is the central bank which in addition to its central banking business (including the note-issue department) provides special financing facilities through the rural credits department for the processing, manufacture and marketing of primary produce.

(*b*) Seven major trading banks: (i) The Commonwealth Trading Bank of Australia; (ii) 6 private trading banks: the Australia and New Zealand Banking Group Ltd, The Bank of Adelaide, the Bank of New South Wales, The Commercial Bank of Australia Ltd, The Commercial Banking Company of Sydney Ltd and The National Bank of Australasia Ltd. The Australia and New Zealand Banking Group Ltd, incorporated in the UK, assumed ownership of 2 banks (the Australia and New Zealand Bank Ltd and The English, Scottish and Australian Bank Ltd) and as from 1 Oct. 1970 has conducted their combined banking business.

(*c*) Other trading banks: (i) 3 State Government banks—The Rural Bank of New South Wales, the State Bank of South Australia, and the Rural and Industries Bank of Western Australia; (ii) one joint stock bank—The Bank of Queensland Ltd, formerly The Brisbane Permanent Building and Banking Co. Ltd, which has specialized business in one district only; (iii) branches of 3 overseas banks—the Bank of New Zealand, the Banque Nationale de Paris and the Bank of China, which are mainly concerned with financing trade, etc., between Australia and overseas countries.

(*d*) The Commonwealth Development Bank of Australia.

(e) Savings Banks.

(f) The Australian Resources Development Bank Ltd opened on 29 March 1968. Its main objective is to assist Australian enterprises in the development of Australia's natural resources, through direct loans and equity investment or by refinancing loans made by trading banks. The bank is jointly owned by the 7 major Australian trading banks. At end June 1970 the total of capital and loan funds raised since the bank's inception is almost $A168m., following the inception of the Australia and New Zealand Banking Group Ltd.

The Reserve Bank's functions and responsibilities derive from the Reserve Bank Act 1959 and the Banking Act 1959, which came into effect in 1960. They had their origins, however, in the development of the central banking role of the Commonwealth Bank, which was established in 1911 as a Government savings and trading bank.

Control of the Australian note issue was transferred from the Commonwealth Treasury to a Notes Board in 1920 and, in 1924, to the Bank. The Commonwealth Bank Act 1945 formally constituted the Bank as a central bank, and these powers were carried through into the 1959 Act establishing the Reserve Bank.

The Acts of 1959 provided for: (i) the separation of the central bank from the Commonwealth group of banking institutions and its reconstitution as the Reserve Bank of Australia; (ii) the establishment of an entirely separate Commonwealth Banking Corporation, with responsibilities for the non-central-banking elements that had developed from within the original Commonwealth Bank—namely the Commonwealth Trading Bank, the Commonwealth Savings Bank and the Commonwealth Development Bank, the latter being basically an amalgamation of the Mortgage Bank and Industrial Finance Department of the Commonwealth Bank.

At 30 June 1970 the capital of the Reserve Bank totalled $A49,428,000 and reserve funds (including a special reserve for IMF special drawing rights) $A110,717,439. The capital was distributed as follows: Central banking business, $A40m.; rural credits department, $A9,428,000. Reserve funds held were: Central banking business, $A101,658,892; rural credits department, $A9,059,000. Profits for the year ended 30 June 1970 (including all departments) amounted to $A47,073,000.

Particulars as at 30 June 1970 for the banks under the control of the Commonwealth Banking Corporation: Commonwealth Trading Bank, capital, $A14,858,000; reserve fund, $A19,278,000; profits for the year, $A4,624,000. Commonwealth Development Bank, capital, $A61,714,000; reserve fund, $A29,253,000; profits for the year, $A2,069,000. Commonwealth Savings Bank, reserve fund, $A38·87m.; profits for the year, $A3,024,000.

At 30 June 1970 the 14 trading banks operating in Australia provided full banking facilities at 4,797 branches and 1,580 agencies all over Australia.

The average deposits in Australia with all trading banks (under (b) and (c) above) for June 1970 amounted to $A7,098,945,000, the average of advances made by the banks to $A4,902,598,000; the average of total assets was $A7,960,477,000.

At 30 June 1970, 13 savings banks were operating in Australia. These are the Commonwealth Savings Bank with branches throughout Australia; 7 private savings banks being wholly owned subsidiaries of the 7 private trading banks and operating, with certain exceptions, in all States and Territories; the State Savings Banks in Victoria and South Australia; the Rural and Industries Bank of Western Australia, and 2 Trustee Savings Banks in Tasmania. At 30 June 1970 these savings banks provided savings facilities at 5,483 branches and 15,414 agencies throughout Australia. At end of June they held deposits in Australia amounting to $A7,104,693,000.

In 1970 there were 46 companies registered under the Life Insurance Acts, 1945–1965, transacting life insurance business in Australia; in addition there were 2 state government institutions. During 1969–70 premium receipts were $700·2m. and claims, etc., paid were $332·75m.

The following table is a summary of banking and insurance business (in $A1,000) in the several States of the Commonwealth:

Particulars	NSW	Vic.	Q'ld.	SA	WA	Tas.	Australia (excl. Terri- tories)
All trading banks:[1]							
Fixed deposits	1,296,060	847,627	407,602	201,648	236,705	53,235	3,082,636
Current deposits	1,689,536	1,098,061	509,652	221,762	295,929	79,403	3,968,437
Advances	2,172,077	1,217,152	580,311	390,932	347,729	82,457	4,871,816
Savings bank deposits[2]	2,400,821	2,386,761	875,580	733,099	431,877	199,790	7,104,693
Life insurance:[3]							
New policies issued (value)							
Ordinary	919,378	851,321	436,453	290,979	316,911	93,895	3,375,127
Superannuation	200,521	580,029	106,278	81,600	71,024	26,726	1,802,497
Industrial	69,501	50,059	22,600	15,394	13,004	3,955	177,304
Policies existing[3] (value)							
Ordinary	4,949,396	4,790,724	2,707,511	1,701,702	1,517,315	538,348	18,069,986
Superannuation	681,238	2,212,742	432,134	363,771	273,355	135,183	6,776,917
Industrial	443,580	341,247	148,965	105,041	78,368	23,686	1,153,335

[1] Weekly averages for June 1970.   [2] At 30 June 1970.
[3] Year ended 30 June 1970.

Banking and Currency. Bureau of Census and Statistics, 1962–63 to date
Insurance and Other Private Finance. Bureau of Census and Statistics, 1962–63 to date
Treasury Information Bulletin. Department of the Treasury. Canberra, 1956 to date (quarterly)
Reserve Bank of Australia. *Statistical Bulletin*. Sydney, 1937 to date
Arndt, H. W., and Harris, C. P., *The Australian Trading Banks*. 3rd ed. Melbourne, 1965
Gifford, J. L. K., Wood, J. V., and Reitsma, A. J., *Australian Banking*. 4th ed. Brisbane, 1960

BOOKS OF REFERENCE

STATISTICAL INFORMATION. The Commonwealth Bureau of Census and Statistics (Treasury Building, Canberra, A.C.T., 2600) was established in 1906. All the activities of the Bureau are covered by the Census and Statistics Act, which confers authority to collect information and contains secrecy provisions to ensure that individual particulars obtained are not divulged. Under the provisions of the Statistics (Arrangements with States) Act which became law on 12 May 1956, the statistical services of all the States have been integrated with the Commonwealth Bureau. An outline of the development of statistics in Australia is published in the *Official Year Book*, No. 51, 1965. Acting Commonwealth Statistician: J. P. O'Neill.

The principal publications of the Bureau are:

Official Year Book of the Commonwealth of Australia. 1907 to date
Pocket Compendium of Australian Statistics. 1913 to date
Quarterly Summary of Australian Statistics. Dec. 1917 to date
Monthly Review of Business Statistics. Oct. 1937 to date
Digest of Current Statistics. Aug. 1959 to date

Special Publications:

Census—Detailed Tables and Statistician's Report. 1911–61.—*1966 Preliminary Tables*
Australian Life Tables. 1881–90 to 1960–62
Australian Balance of Payments. 1928–29 to 1951–52

Annual printed bulletins are listed under specified subjects.

OTHER OFFICIAL PUBLICATIONS

Atlas of Australian Resources. Dept. of National Development, Melbourne, 1955 ff.
Climatological Atlas of Australia. Bureau of Meteorology. Melbourne, 1940
Norfolk Island—Annual Report. Government of New South Wales and Commonwealth of Australia. From 1896
Cocos (Keeling) Islands—Annual Report. Department of External Territories, Canberra. From 1955
Christmas Island—Annual Report. Department of External Territories, Canberra. From 1958
Australian books; select list of works about or published in Australia. National Library of Australia. Canberra, 1934 to date
Australian national bibliography. Canberra, 1936 to date
Historical Records of Australia. 34 vols. National Library, Canberra, 1914–25
Australia: official handbook. Dept. of the Interior, Canberra, 1961 to date
Current Notes on International Affairs. Dept. of Foreign Affairs, Canberra, 1936 to date

NON-OFFICIAL PUBLICATIONS

Australian Quarterly: a Quarterly Review of Australian Affairs. Sydney, 1929 to date
Australian National Travel Association. *Australian Tourist Guide*. Melbourne, 1960
Barnes, V. S. (ed.), *The modern encyclopædia of Australia and New Zealand*. Sydney, 1965
Casey, R. G., Lord, *Friends and Neighbours*. Melbourne, 1954

Chisholm, A. H. (ed.), *Australian Encyclopædia*. 10 vols. Sydney, 1962
Clark, C. M. H. (ed.), *Select Documents in Australian History, 1788–1900*. 2 vols. Sydney, 1950–55
Eggleston, Sir Frederic, *Reflections on Australian Foreign Policy*. Melbourne, 1957
Ferguson, Sir John, *Bibliography of Australia, 1784–1850*. 4 vols. Sydney, 1941–55; vol. 5 (1851–1900), Part 1, 1963. Parts 2 and 3 in preparation
Greenwood, G. (ed.), *Australia, a political and social history*. 3rd ed. Sydney, 1960.—(ed.), *Australia in World Affairs, 1950–55*. Melbourne, 1957
Hancock, Sir Keith. *Australia*. Brisbane, 1961
Laseron, C. F., *The Face of Australia*. 2nd ed. Sydney, 1961
Menzies, Sir Robert, *Speech is of Time*. London, 1958
Moore, T. I. (ed.), *A Book of Australia*. London, 1961
Noble, N. S. (ed.), *The Australian Environment*. 3rd ed. Melbourne, 1960
Pike, D., *Australia—the quiet continent*. CUP, 1961
Ratcliffe, F. N., *Flying Fox and Drifting Sand*. Sydney, 1963
Serle, P., *Dictionary of Australian Biography*. 2 vols. Sydney, 1949
Spate, O. H. K., *Australia*. London, 1968
Taylor, T. G., *Australia: A Study of Warm Environments and their Effect on British Settlement*. 7th ed. London, 1959
Who's Who in Australia. Melbourne, 1906 to date
NATIONAL LIBRARY. The National Library, Canberra, A.C.T. *Librarian:* A. P. Fleming, OBE.

AUSTRALIAN TERRITORIES
THE NORTHERN TERRITORY

GOVERNMENT. The Northern Territory, after forming part of New South Wales, was annexed on 6 July 1863 to South Australia and in 1901 entered the Commonwealth as a corporate part of South Australia. The Commonwealth Constitution Act of 1900 made provision for the surrender to the Commonwealth of any territory by any state, and under this provision an agreement was entered into on 7 Dec. 1907 for the transfer of the Northern Territory to the Commonwealth, and it formally passed under the control of the Commonwealth Government on 1 Jan. 1911.

On 1 Feb. 1927 the Northern Territory was divided for administrative purposes into two parts, North Australia and Central Australia, the dividing line being the 20th parallel of S. lat. Each part was under a Government Resident, with headquarters at Darwin and Alice Springs respectively. This division was effected under the authority of the Northern Australia Act, 1926, which also provided for a North Australia Commission, the powers of which extended to matters relating to the development of North Australia, and also to the administration of Crown lands throughout North Australia and Central Australia. The Northern Australia Act, 1926, was repealed as from 12 June 1931 by the Northern Territory (Administration) Act, 1931. The North Australia Commission was abolished, and the whole of the Northern Territory was again placed under the control of an Administrator. The Administrator administers the Territory on behalf of the Commonwealth; his residence is at Darwin.

The Legislative Council for the Northern Territory was set up by an amendment to the Northern Territory (Administration) Act in 1947. The Council was reconstituted in 1959 by a further amendment to the Act to consist of the Administrator, 6 official members, 3 appointed non-official members and 8 elected members. In 1965 an amendment provided for the withdrawal of the Administrator and the election of a Council President from among the elected members. The council was again reconstituted in 1968 to consist of 6 official and 11 elected members with effect from the elections for the Council held in Oct. 1968.

All Ordinances passed by the Council are presented to the Administrator for assent. The Administrator must reserve certain Ordinances for the Governor-General's pleasure. Others he may assent to, withhold assent, reserve for the Governor-General's pleasure or return to the Council with amendments that he recommends. The Governor-General may assent to an Ordinance, withhold assent to whole or part of an Ordinance, or return it to the Administrator with amendments he recommends. He may also disallow in whole or part any Ordinance the Administrator has assented to. All Ordinances must be laid before each House of Parliament.

An Administrator's Council was set up in 1959 to advise the Administrator on any matter referred to it by the Administrator or in accordance with any Ordinance. The Council consists of the Administrator and 2 official and 3 elected members of the Legislative Council.

The Northern Territory elects a member to the House of Representatives who has full voting rights. Prior to 1968 the member had been able to vote only on matters relating solely to the Northern Territory. Between 1922 and 1936 the Northern Territory member had no vote.

Administrator: F. C. Chaney, CBE, AFC.

AREA AND POPULATION. The Northern Territory is bounded by the 26th parallel of S. lat. and 129° and 138° E. long. Its total area is 520,280 sq. miles (332,979,000 acres). On 30 June 1969 the area alienated under freehold tenure was 318,000 acres; 185,923,800 acres were held under leasehold and 7·97m. acres under licences, etc.; 61,123,800 acres were reserved for Aborigines, public requirements, etc.; and 77,643,500 acres were unoccupied and unreserved. Land rents collected for the year 1969–70 amounted to $A507,375. The coastline is about 1,040 miles in length, the principal port being Darwin. The greater part of the interior consists of a tableland rising gradually from the coast to a height of about 2,300 ft. On this tableland there are large areas of excellent pasturage. The southern part of the Territory is generally sandy and has a small rainfall, but water may be obtained by means of sub-artesian bores. The climate is tropical, but varies considerably over the whole Territory. In the coastal region, there are two main climatic divisions—the wet season, Nov. to April, and the dry season, May to Oct. Farther south the climate is of a continental type, showing a great variation between the hottest and coldest months.

The census population, excluding full-blood Aborigines, was as follows:

	Europeans	Total		Europeans	Total
1881	667	3,451	1947	9,116	10,868
1901	782	4,811	1954	14,031	16,469
1911	1,418	3,310	1961	23,599	27,095
1921	2,458	3,867	1966	33,784	37,433
1933	3,306	4,850			

The census population, including Aborigines, was 56,504 as at 30 June 1966; the population of Darwin urban area was 21,671.

The estimated total population of the Northern Territory at 30 June 1970 was 71,300.

FINANCE. The revenue and expenditure (in $A1,000) for years ended 30 June cover the transactions of the Commonwealth Consolidated Revenue Fund relating to the Northern Territory and were as follows:

	1965–66	1966–67	1967–68	1968–69	1969–70
Revenue	6.434	7,273	9,663	11,060	12.449
Expenditure	45,991	58,445	63,215	69,350	87,164

The chief sources of revenue for 1969–70 were: Electricity supply, $A4,202,000; rents and rates, $A2,318,000. The chief items of expenditure (excluding interest, loans, etc.) were: Aboriginal affairs (including capital expenditure), $A14,772,000; public health, etc., $A7,625,000, and educational services, $A3·71m. (excluding special schools for Aboriginal children). Capital expenditure (excluding business undertakings) amounted to $A37,607,000.

PASTORAL INDUSTRY. The beef cattle industry is the main form of rural activity, the cattle population being over 1m. head. The Government provides veterinary and extension services to pastoralists. A range lands research institute is operating at Alice Springs. Three abattoirs are operating, 2 of which are for exports. Value of production in 1968–69 was approximately $A20·1m.

Livestock (30 June 1969): 1,162,000 cattle, 39,000 horses, 10,000 sheep, 2,000 pigs.

AGRICULTURE. In 1952 the Government established an experimental farm at Katherine to test the economics of a dry farming system, on a commercial scale, in which peanuts and grain sorghum would be grown in rotation with pastures for cattle fattening. The Government is also trying out experiments with drought-resisting grasses, fodder crops, cattle fattening on grains, crop residues, natural and improved pastures, phosphate supplements and rice.

In 1965 responsibility for applied rice research was taken over by the Administration.

In 1956 an experimental farm was established at Berrimah near Darwin to conduct investigations into fruit and vegetables, fodder crops and pastures. Fruit and vegetables are produced near Darwin and at Alice Springs.

Since 1964 pilot schemes have been conducted on the Marrakai land system about 60 miles south of Darwin, to test the fattening and breeding of cattle and the improving of pastures.

FORESTRY. A new forest development programme has been approved for the 5 years from July 1970. It continues development begun under earlier programmes including softwood planting at the rate of 1,000 acres per year, research, conservation and management of native forest resources, and the introduction of suitable additional tree species in both arid and high rainfall areas. The possibility of the establishment of a wood chip export industry based on the eucalypt forests of the higher rainfall areas is under consideration.

FISHING. In 1968, 3 joint Australian–Japanese companies, using foreign ships and crews for an initial period, and 4 Australian companies were approved to commence prawning operations in waters off the Northern Territory. All 7 companies are required to build shore processing plants by the end of 1972. Already processing has commenced at 2 plants built in Darwin and at plants established at Katherine and Groot Eylandt. Two more plants at Darwin and 1 at Gove have yet to be established.

During 1969, the first full season of fishing, about 5m. lb. heads off weight of prawns, valued at approximately $A5m, were landed in the Northern Territory. Most of the catch was exported to Japan. Prior to this development the principal commercial fishing was based on catching the giant perch (*barramundi*). A pearl culture farm is operating at Port Essington.

MINING. The mining industry is the Northern Territory's main industry in terms of value of production, and accounts for more than 40% of the gross value of production of all primary and secondary industries. Manganese, copper, iron ore and gold are the most valuable minerals produced. Other minerals produced include silver, lead, zinc, bismuth, tin and uranium. Mining activity is increasing, and value of production in 1969–70 rose by some 9% to some $A40m. over the value of production in 1968–69. Large deposits of bauxite are being developed in the Gove area of Arnhem Land where a bauxite/alumina operation costing in excess of $A300m. is being established. Plans are proceeding for the construction of an alumina plant which will have a capacity of at least 500,000 tons of alumina per annum by the end of 1972. Large deposits of manganese ore are being mined at Groote Eylandt in the Gulf of Carpentaria. Total shipments in 1969–70 were approximately 625,000 tons, and an expansion programme to raise capacity to 1m. tons a year by 1974 is under way. Manganese ore is currently the Territory's main mineral product in terms of value of production, and large tonnages are exported to Japan, Europe and the US. Shipments of iron ore from Frances Creek commenced in June 1967 and from Mount Bundey in July 1968. Shipments in 1969–70 totalled about 1,028,000 tons. The value of export contracts from Frances Creek and Mount Bundey ore are estimated at about $A75m. and $A11m. respectively. A new copper mine which will more than double production of copper from the area to over 18,000 tons per annum is being developed near Tennant Creek. Large lead and zinc deposits are being investigated near Borroloola in the McArthur River area. In the Rum Jungle area exploration is proceeding on lead/zinc mineralization at Woodcutters. Large rich discoveries of uranium ore have recently been made in the area of Western Arnhem Land border.

Mine and quarry production in the Territory in 1968–69 was valued at $A36,869,000, principally manganese, $A13·09m.; copper, $A7,838,000; iron ore, $A7,168,000, and gold, $A4,241,000. The value of mine production will increase greatly when production of alumina commences at Gove in about 1972.

The search for oil in the Territory is continuing, with the main areas of interest in the Amadeus Basin of Central Australia and in the offshore areas of the Bonaparte Gulf Basin and in the Ashmore and Cartier Islands area. Large reserves of natural gas have been discovered at Mereenie and Palm Valley near Alice Springs.

INDUSTRY. In 1967–68 the value of factory production, from 188 factories, was $A9·7m. More than 1,500 persons were employed in these factories.

TOURISM is the Territory's third most important industry; the number of visitors rose from 18,000 in 1962–63 to 73,000 in 1969–70 spending about $A19m.

COMMERCE. The two main items are cattle and minerals. Value in $A1,000:

	1964–65	1965–66	1966–67	1967–68	1968–69
Cattle	8,021	13,037	12,726	17,146	20,646
Minerals[1]	10,912	13,206	20,534	27,862	36,869

[1] Excluding uranium.

SHIPPING. Regular freight shipping services connect Darwin with Western Australia, the eastern States and overseas.

ROADS. The two sealed highways Darwin–Alice Springs (Stuart Highway, 956 miles) and Tennant Creek–Mount Isa (Barkly Highway, 403 miles) are the principal arteries of the Northern Territory; 1,140 miles of other high standard roads have been completed, about 470 miles are under construction.

RAILWAYS. Lines connect Darwin with Birdum (317 miles) and Adelaide with Alice Springs.

AVIATION. Darwin is the first port of arrival in Australia for many aircraft from Europe and Asia. There are regular inland services connecting Darwin with all the State capitals and many inland towns.

Territory of Ashmore and Cartier Islands. By United Kingdom Order in Council of 23 July 1931, Ashmore Islands (known as Middle, East and West Islands) and Cartier Island, situated in the Indian Ocean, some 200 miles off the north-west coast of Australia, were placed under the authority of the Commonwealth.

Under the Ashmore and Cartier Islands Acceptance Act, 1933, the islands were accepted by the Commonwealth under the name of the Territory of Ashmore and Cartier Islands, and the effective date was proclaimed by the Governor-General to be 10 May 1934. It was the intention that the Territory should be administered by the State of Western Australia, but owing to administrative difficulties the Territory was annexed to and deemed to form part of the Northern Territory of Australia (by amendment to the Act in 1938) and all the laws of the Northern Territory, as far as they are applicable, apply to the Territory of Ashmore and Cartier Islands. The islands are uninhabited.

An automatic weather station on West Ashmore Island (completed in Sept. 1962) supplies the Commonwealth Meteorological Bureau with regular reports.

Periodic visits are made to the islands by ships of the Royal Australian Navy, and aircraft of the Royal Australian Air Force make aerial surveys of the islands and neighbouring waters.

BOOKS OF REFERENCE

The Northern Territory: Annual Report. Dept. of Territories. Canberra, from 1911
Australian Territories. Dept. of Territories. Canberra, 1960 to date

Northern Territory Statistical Summary. Bureau of Census and Statistics. Canberra, from 1960
Prospects of Agriculture in the Northern Territory. Dept. of Territories. Canberra, 1961
Northern Territory Scientific Liaison Conference, Darwin 1961, Conference Papers. Melbourne, 1961
Holmes, J. M., Australia's Open North. Sydney, 1963
Lockwood, D. W., Fair Dinkum. London, 1960
Polisheck, N., Life on the Daly River. London, 1961

AUSTRALIAN CAPITAL TERRITORY

GOVERNMENT. The area, now the Australian Capital Territory, was first visited by white men in 1820 and settlement commenced in 1824. Until its selection as the seat of government it was a quiet pastoral and agricultural community.

The constitution of the Commonwealth provided (Sec. 125) that the seat of government should be selected by parliament and that it should be within New South Wales but at least 100 miles from Sydney. The present area was surrendered by New South Wales and vested in the Commonwealth from 1 Jan. 1911. In 1915 an additional 28 sq. miles at Jervis Bay was transferred from New South Wales to the Commonwealth. In 1911 an international competition was held for the city plan. The plan chosen was that of W. Burley Griffin, of Chicago. Construction was delayed by the First World War, and it was not until 1927 that, with the transfer of parliament and certain departments, Canberra became in fact the seat of government. Most departments now have their headquarters in Canberra.

The general administration of the Territory is in the hands of the Minister for the Interior, but certain specific services are undertaken by the Department of Education and Science, the Department of Health, the Department of Works and the Attorney-General. The Minister is advised on matters of local concern by an advisory council, consisting of 4 nominated, 8 elected members and 1 observer.

In 1958 the Commonwealth Government established the National Capital Development Commission as the statutory body charged with the responsibility of planning, developing and constructing Canberra.

The Australian Capital Territory Representation Act, 1948–66, provided for the representation of residents of the Territory by one elected member in the House of Representatives.

AREA AND POPULATION. The area of the Australian Capital Territory is 939 sq. miles (including Jervis Bay area). The population at 30 June 1970 was 133,000. Previous census population:

	Males	Females	Total		Males	Females	Total
1911	992	722	1,714	1954	16,229	14,086	30,315
1921	1,567	1,005	2,572	1961	30,858	27,970	58,828
1933	4,805	4,142	8,947	1966	49,991	46,041	96,032
1947	9,092	7,813	16,905				

(Figures before 1961 exclude particulars of full-blood Aboriginals.

EDUCATION. State education in the Australian Capital Territory is the responsibility of the Department of Education and Science. The curriculum is that of the NSW Department of Education, which also supplies the teachers. There are 37 government primary and infants' schools, including 1 in the Jervis Bay area, with a total enrolment (Aug. 1970) of 16,803 pupils. Secondary education is provided at 10 high schools with an enrolment, at Aug. 1970, of 8,226 pupils. Pre-school education is provided at 49 centres with a total enrolment of 3,128 (Aug. 1970). There are also 22 denominational schools, 6 of which provide secondary education; total enrolment (Aug. 1970) 9,181. The Canberra Technical College with an enrolment of nearly 7,000 at Aug. 1970 provides training for apprentices and journeymen and also offers commercial and special courses.

The Canberra School of Music, opened in 1965, had 680 students in 1970.
The Australian National University is situated in Canberra (see p. 237).

FINANCE. The revenue and expenditure of the Australian Capital Territory cover the transactions of the Commonwealth Consolidated Revenue Fund relating to the Territory.

Revenue and expenditure ($A1,000) for years ended 30 June:

	Revenue	Capital works	Expenditure Other services	Total
1968	18,884	57,339	25,514	82,853
1969	25,098	59,898	30,523	90,421
1970	29,478	63,794	33,162	96,956

The chief sources of revenue in 1969–70 were: Rent and rates, $A9·27m.; premiums on lease sales, $A7·94m., and housing, $A6·98m. The main capital works expenditures were: Roads, bridges, water supply and sewerage, $A9·58m.; housing, $A8·37m., and land development, $A9·96m.

PRODUCTION. The Territory is predominantly pastoral. Livestock, 31 March 1970: 755 horses, 15,188 cattle, 241,294 sheep. A considerable amount of re-afforestation (mostly pine) has been undertaken, the total area of plantations at 31 Dec. 1969 being 30,745 acres. There is no secondary industry of any importance.

BOOKS OF REFERENCE

A.C.T. Statistical Summary. Bureau of Census and Statistics. From 1960
National Capital Development Commission, Canberra, *The Future Canberra.* 1965
Borrie, W. D., and others, *Canberra: the next decade.* Canberra, 1963
Wigmore, L., *The Long View: a history of Australia's national capital.* Melbourne, 1963

Norfolk Island. 29° 04′ S. lat., 167° 57′ E. long., area 8,528 acres (3,451 hectares), population, 30 June 1969, 1,377. The island was formerly part of the colony of New South Wales and then of Van Diemen's Land. It has been a distinct settlement since 1856, under the jurisdiction of the state of New South Wales; and finally by the passage of the Norfolk Island Act 1913, it was accepted as a Territory of the Commonwealth Government. Norfolk Island Council consists of the Administrator and 8 elected members. The Council may consider and advise the Administrator on any matter affecting the peace, order and government of the territory, and is consulted on legislative and financial matters.

The island is very picturesque and has a delightful climate. It supplies its own beef and is especially suitable for the cultivation of citrus fruits, bananas, vegetables and beans for seed. Tourism is the major industry. The island has many links with Australia's early penal days and the descendants of the *Bounty* mutineers are residents. In 1968–69 the imports ($A1·6m. from Australia) totalled $A2·6m. and exports $A300,000. A programme of forestry development is being carried out.

Administrator: R. N. Dalkin, DFC.

PAPUA AND NEW GUINEA

The Papua and New Guinea Act 1949–1968 provides for the administration of the UN Australian Trust Territory of New Guinea in an administrative union with the Territory of Papua, in accordance with Art. 5 of the New Guinea Trusteeship Agreement, under the title of the Territory of Papua and New Guinea. The Act, which is administered by the Minister of State for External Territories, provides for the appointment of an Administrator to administer the government of the Territory on behalf of the Commonwealth of Australia.

The first House of Assembly was inaugurated in 1964 and replaced the previous Legislative Council. The second House, elected in 1968, consists of 94 members (69 from open electorates, 10 official, 15 from regional electorates where candidates must have certain educational qualifications). The House has power to make ordinances for peace, order and good government, subject to the assent of the Administrator or, in certain cases, of the Governor-General of Australia. The Governor-General may also disallow an ordinance and all ordinances must be laid before the Commonwealth Parliament.

In 1968 the Papua and New Guinea Act was amended to provide for the Administrator's Council to become the Administrator's Executive Council, deciding major matters of Territory policy. In June 1968 it had its first meetings. It consists of the Administrator, the 7 ministerial members, 3 official members, and a twelfth councillor who is an elected MHA nominated by the Administrator. From Aug. 1970, ministerial office holders have been responsible for day to day running of their departments. In addition (subject to the Administrator's Executive Council) they exercise full authority in a substantial number of specific matters. The Commonwealth Government has retained authority in defence, external affairs, trade, the judiciary, major development projects and non-specific matters.

The seat of the administration is at Port Moresby.

Administrator: L. W. Johnson.

Trade between Papua and New Guinea and UK (British Board of Trade returns, in £1,000 sterling):

	1965	1966	1967	1968	1969	1970
Imports to UK	6,630	5,976	5,318	7,709	7,013	8,240
Exports from UK	2,049	1,598	1,513	2,178	3,092 ⎱	3,005
Re-exports from UK	24	15	16	64	32 ⎰	

I. PAPUA

HISTORY. To prevent that portion of the island of New Guinea not claimed by the Netherlands from passing into the hands of a foreign power, the Government of Queensland annexed it in 1883. This step was not sanctioned by the Imperial Government, but on 6 Nov. 1884 a British Protectorate was proclaimed over the southern portion of the eastern half of New Guinea, and in 1887 Queensland, New South Wales and Victoria undertook to defray the cost of administration, and the territory was annexed to the Crown the following year. The Federal Government took over the control in 1901; the political transfer was completed by the Papua Act of the Federal Parliament in Nov. 1905, and on 1 Sept. 1906 a proclamation was issued by the Governor-General of Australia declaring that British New Guinea was to be known henceforth as the Territory of Papua.

AREA AND POPULATION. Papua comprises the south-eastern part of the island of New Guinea, together with the Trobriand, Woodlark, D'Entrecasteaux and Louisiade groups of islands, and lies between 5° and 12° S. lat., and 141° and 155° E. long. Area 86,100 sq. miles, of which 83,325 comprise the mainland and 2,775 the islands. On 30 June 1966 the non-indigenous census population was 14,377; the indigenous census population was 591,959. The estimated indigenous population for 30 June 1969 was 609,784, comprising Central, 115,059; Gulf, 67,369; Milne Bay, 104,578; Northern, 56,934; Southern Highlands, 200,904; and Western, 64,940. The main towns (census, 1966) are Port Moresby 41,848 (76% indigenes), Daru 3,663 (94%), Popondetta 2,139 (86%) and Samarai 2,201 (77%).

ADMINISTRATION. For administrative purposes the Territory is divided into 6 districts (Southern Highlands, Western, Gulf, Central, Northern, Milne Bay), each in charge of a District Commissioner, assisted by a Deputy District Commissioner, District Officers, Assistant District Officers and patrol officers.

By 30 June 1970, 52 native local government councils had been established in which some 539,109 people are represented by 1,323 councillors.

EDUCATION. During 1969 about 68,900 indigenous students attended administration and mission schools. The University of Papua and New Guinea opened in 1966.

AGRICULTURE. At 30 June 1969, 405,000 acres of land had been leased, of which 300,000 acres were for agricultural purposes, the principal crops being coconuts, cocoa, coffee and rubber. A preferential tariff is granted by the Commonwealth on certain produce from Papua. Freehold alienation of land is prohibited, but leases may be obtained at low rentals for long terms. Indigenous sago is plentiful in the western district of the Territory, and there are considerable numbers of native-owned coconut trees. Timber production is expanding and fishing is carried on. Surveys are being made for pelagic fisheries potential.

FORESTRY. Timber production is of growing importance for both local consumption and export. In 1968–69, about 31·5m. superfeet of logs were harvested.

FISHERIES. Prawn fishing is rapidly becoming the main source of income from marine fisheries. Giant perch is taken in commercial quantities on the south coast. A small export trade in crayfish has been developed. Three pearl culture enterprises have been started in Papua. There is also a small export trade in marine shell.

FINANCE. Currency. The currency and its legal tender are the same as in the Commonwealth of Australia.

Budget. Local revenue is mainly from income tax and customs duties.

Years ended 30 June	Total revenue ($A1,000)	Expenditure from revenue ($A1,000)	Imports (f.o.b.) ($A1,000)	Exports (f.o.b.) ($A1,000)
1967	43,406	43,286	49,952	8,838
1968	49,468	48,543	60,388	11,346
1969	51,627	51,470	56,035	11,429

MINING. Gold used to be the main mineral product, but it is no longer important. Deposits containing gold, copper, lead and zinc on Misima Island are being investigated. Oil companies have spent nearly $A100m. in search for oil, but no commercial deposits have yet been found. Several wells of natural gas have been discovered.

INDUSTRY. Secondary and service industries are expanding for the local market. Industries at Port Moresby include the manufacture of paint, gases, concrete, twist tobacco, brewing, boat-building, furniture and the assembly of electrical appliances.

LABOUR. In 1968 about 35,400 indigenous wage-earners were in regular employment; the proportion of skilled and semi-skilled workmen is increasing through education in technical schools and apprenticeship schemes.

TRADE. The chief imports are foodstuffs, chemicals, manufactured goods, machinery and transport equipment. Exports in 1968–69 included copra (16,627 tons, $A2·6m.) and rubber (5,736 tons, $A2,276).

SHIPPING. There are regular shipping services between Australia and Territory ports, and also services to Europe and Asia. Small coastal vessels run between the various territory ports. There is also a connecting service to North America through the New Hebrides and New Caledonia. Overseas and inter-territory vessels cleared from Papua ports in 1968–69 totalled 719,000 net tons. Cargo discharged from overseas was 287,346 tons; cargo loaded for overseas was 41,070 tons.

AVIATION. Frequent air services operate to and from Australia, and there is a twice-weekly flight from Sydney through Port Moresby to Manila and Hong Kong. A twice-weekly service is maintained from the Territory to Honiara in the British Solomons. An air service is maintained between Madang and Djajapura in West Irian.

TELECOMMUNICATIONS. There are wireless telegraph stations at Port Moresby, Kerema, Daru and Samarai. Telephones numbered 8,006 on 30 June 1968.

Broadcasting. The Australian Broadcasting Commission operates 2 short-wave stations and 1 medium-wave station from Port Moresby. The Administration Broadcasting Service operates short-wave stations at Daru, Kerema and Samarai.

BANKING. Four Australian commercial banks also operate in Papua and New Guinea. These are the Australia and New Zealand Bank Ltd, the Bank of New South Wales, Commonwealth Banking Corporation and The National Bank of Australasia Ltd, all of whom offer trading and savings facilities. The Commonwealth Development Bank of Australia conducts business through branches of the Commonwealth Banking Corporation.

The Reserve Bank of Australia also operates in Papua and New Guinea. A Papua and New Guinea Division of the Bank has been established to develop central banking there. Apart from normal central banking activities, it also undertakes some broader responsibilities relating to the growth of banking and financial institutions and the use of money by Papuans and New Guineans.

In addition to the Australian banks operating in Papua and New Guinea, there is one local bank, the Papua and New Guinea Development Bank, which commenced business on 6 July 1967. Its function is to provide longer-term development finance with particular attention to the needs of small-scale enterprises. To finance its activities the Bank has received $10·2m. in capital allocations through the Territory Budget, and further capital will be provided in this manner as the need arises. It is also permitted to borrow funds and to issue debentures or other securities. At 30 June 1970 advances approved totalled $A14·1m.

II. NEW GUINEA

The Territory of New Guinea has an area of 92,160 sq miles (238,694 sq. km), extending from the Equator to 8° S. lat., and from 141° E. long. to 156° E. long. An Australian force occupied the Territory in 1914. Under a mandate from the League of Nations on 9 May 1921 the Australian Government established its civil administration and after the Second World War placed the Territory under the trusteeship system established under the Charter of the United Nations. The trusteeship agreement for the Territory, under which the Government of Australia is the sole administering authority, was approved by the General Assembly of the United Nations on 13 Dec. 1946.

ADMINISTRATION. For administrative purposes the Territory is divided into 12 districts (Morobe, Madang, East Sepik, West Sepik, Chimbu, Eastern Highlands, Western Highlands, Manus, East New Britain, West New Britain, New Ireland and Bougainville) each administered by a District Commissioner, assisted by a Deputy District Commissioner, District Officers, Assistant District Officers and Patrol Officers.

By 30 June 1970, 93 native local government councils had been established in which 1,511,123 people are represented by 2,808 councillors.

POPULATION. The non-indigenous population at census, 30 June 1966, was 20,292 and the indigenous population, 1,558,358. Estimate (1969) 1·7m.

EDUCATION. About 159,864 indigenous students are attending 385 administration and 892 mission schools.

AGRICULTURE. At 30 June 1969, 478,794 acres of land had been leased, including 316,830 for agriculture and 89,034 for pastoral purposes. Coconuts, coffee and cocoa are the main crops. Rice, passionfruit, tea, pyrethrum and peanuts are grown on a smaller scale. An oil-palm industry is being established. Tropical fruits grow abundantly. The staple food of the natives includes sweet potatoes, yams, taro, sago and bananas. There is extensive grassland, and a beef-cattle industry is being developed.

INDUSTRY. As well as industries processing primary products, industries catering for the local markets are expanding. The centres of growth are at Lae, Madang and Rabaul. Industries include the manufacture of cigarettes, twist tobacco, wire products, paint, drums, boat building, car batteries, tyre retreading, glass bottles, packaging material and beer; pyrethrum, copra, plywood and pulped fruit are produced for export.

FORESTRY. Timber production is important for both local consumption and export. During 1968–69 about 136·6m. superfeet of logs were harvested for conversion to sawn timber, production of plywood or for export. Plywood and veneer are produced at a modern factory at Bulolo and veneer is also produced at Lae. In 1968–69, 168·1m. superfeet of veneer and 36m. superfeet of plywood was produced.

FISHING. A small quantity of marine shell is exported, valued at $A39,000 in 1968–69, otherwise fishing is carried on for local consumption, but surveys of pelagic fisheries potential are being made.

LABOUR. In 1968 about 80,000 indigenous wage-earners were in regular employment; the proportion of skilled and semi-skilled workmen is increasing through education in technical schools and apprenticeship schemes.

MINING. Gold and silver are the only minerals produced in quantity. Major copper deposits in the Kieta subdistrict of Bougainville have proven reserves of about 960m. tons. Production of copper concentrates for export is expected to begin in 1972. The total value of mineral production in 1969–70 was $A824,000.

FINANCE AND TRADE. Receipts (in $A) during the years ended 30 June:

Source	1967	1968	1969[1]	1970
Customs	9,037,489	10,436,419	11,677,355	17,235,693
Licences	397,337	460,789	519,451	580,514
Stamp duties	172,305	268,797	281,032	426,535
Postal	1,352,838	1,660,593	2,037,296	2,493,834
Land revenue	442,934	384,485	438,105	556,364
Mining receipts	25,437	25,733	45,386	63,626
Fees and fines	131,345	152,119	177,410	233,561
Health revenue	182,982	184,674	210,011	292,890
Forestry	484,082	546,810	470,317	560,366
Agriculture	673,402	896,045	881,394	685,285
Direct taxation	5,647,243	6,759,963	6,778,734	8,556,250
Public utilities	240,341	316,386	414,385	506,026
Miscellaneous	3,942,340	4,289,004	4,962,441	7,978,911
Total internal revenue	22,730,075	26,381,817	28,893,317	40,169,856
Territory Loans	4,052,831	5,588,345	4,818,327	10,504,453
International Loans	—	—	34,389	1,383,814
Grant by Commonwealth Government of Australia[1]	49,979,402	54,453,853	64,269,499	71,419,907
Total receipts	76,762,308	86,424,014	98,015,532	135,890,799

[1] The annual grants by the Government of the Commonwealth of Australia are made to the Territory of Papua and New Guinea, and these amounts have been allocated to New Guinea.

G

Imports (in $A1,000) during the years ended 30 June:

	1967	1968	1969	1970[1]
Food	15,509	19,311	21,104	14,284
Beverages and tobacco	2,495	2,870	3,242	2,326
Crude materials	243	280	251	152
Mineral fuels, lubricants and related materials	2,870	3,598	4,030	2,662
Animal and vegetable oils and fats	77	94	102	67
Chemicals	4,301	4,952	6,026	3,965
Manufactured goods classified chiefly by material	14,643	14,966	16,646	13,301
Machinery and transport equipment	23,480	21,675	25,545	19,252
Miscellaneous manufactured articles	9,611	10,697	11,301	8,021
Miscellaneous transactions and commodities, not elsewhere specified	2,783	4,680	4,289	2,687
Total	76,012	83,123	92,536	66,717
Outside packages	98	1,122	1,393	849
Total imports	76,109	84,244	93,929	67,566

[1] Preliminary.

Exports for years ended 30 June (value in $A1,000):

	1967		1968		1969		1970[3]	
Commodity	Quantity	Value	Quantity	Value	Quantity	Value	Quantity	Value
Cocoa beans (tons)	21,094	9,336	23,717	11,641	27,066	15,900	16,294	4,311
Coconut (copra oil) (tons)	23,181	5,181	24,097	6,875	20,563	5,772	21,900	5,864
Coffee beans (tons)	12,765	10,095	18,246	14,306	19,858	15,523	10,698	8,712
Copra (tons)	59,013	7,911	61,400	11,143	77,115	12,216	71,738	11,749
Copra oilcake and meal (tons)	13,149	659	10,450	530	11,250	589	11,910	725
Crocodile skins	—	392	—	235	—	157	—	378
Gold	—	913	—	823	—	836	—	945
Passionfruit juice and pulp (tons)	133	112	247	202	126	103	167	174
Peanuts (tons)	1,644	526	1,376	430	1,573	469	1,533	527
Plywood (1,000 sq. ft)[1]	21,430	2,040	25,043	2,264	24,484	2,252	17,784	1,903
Pyrethrum extract (1,000 lb.)	57	390	60	417	45	313	5	89
Rubber (tons)	17	6	—	—	—	—	38	15
Shell,Trochus and other (tons)	372	76	829	66	224	39	152	30
Tea (tons)	4	3	38	42	284	297	11	11
Timber, logs (1,000 superft)	40,018	1,371	44,166	1,635	29,571	1,069	26,511	877
Timber, sawn (1,000 superft)	5,120	884	9,089	1,013	8,541	1,159	5,134	807
Veneer sheets (1,000 sq. ft)[2]	8,830	84	14,779	120	16,334	221	5,793	83
Other produce	..	282	..	638	..	1,500	..	231
Total Territory produce	..	40,262	..	52,382	..	58,424	..	37,431
Total re-exports	..	4,120	..	6,523	..	5,948	..	3,458
Total all exports	..	44,382	..	58,905	..	64,372	..	40,889

[1] Plywood unit is face area $\times \frac{3}{16}$ in. [2] Veneer unit is face area $\times \frac{1}{16}$ in.
[3] Preliminary.

SHIPPING. Inter-island trade is carried on by small vessels. There are regular shipping services from Australia to the main ports of the Territory and also services to Europe and Asia. There is also a connecting service to North America through the New Hebrides and New Caledonia.

Overseas and inter-territory vessels cleared from New Guinea ports in 1968–69 totalled 1,613,000 net tons. Cargo discharged from overseas was 493,473 tons; cargo loaded for overseas was 272,626 tons.

AVIATION. There are regular air services to and from Australia *via* Papua while internal air services connect many places in the Territory. There is also a weekly service with Honiara in the British Solomons. An air service is also maintained between Madang and Djajapura in West Irian.

TELECOMMUNICATIONS. External wireless telegraph communication is through the Overseas Telecommunication Commission's stations at Lae and Rabaul, and an internal telegraph service is operated by the Administration. The

Seacom cable provides international communication from Madang, with relay links to Lae and Port Moresby. Telephones numbered 6,880 at 30 June 1968.

Broadcasting. The Australian Broadcasting Commission operates a medium-wave station at Rabaul. The Administration Broadcasting service operates short-wave stations at Rabaul, Wewak, Goroka, Mount Hagan and Kieta.

1. New Guinea Mainland. This region, the northern section of south-east New Guinea, lies between 2° 35′ and 8° S. lat. and 141° and 148° E. long. The area, including Manam, Karkar, Long, Bagabag, Schouten, Kairiru (D'Urville) and some smaller islands, is 69,095 sq. miles. The native population at 30 June 1969 was approx. 1·42m. The coastline is very little broken, and there are few good harbours. There are high ranges running parallel with the coastal plain, which is from 50 to 150 miles wide and broken with steep spurs in some places extending to the actual coastline. The ranges in the interior have not been completely explored, but some of their summits are known to attain over 14,500 ft. The principal rivers are the Sepik, which is navigable for about 300 miles, the Ramu and the Markham. The climate is hot and the rainfall high. There were 67 missionary societies at work in 1966; some of these missions have plantations, saw-mills, etc.

The 7 administrative districts are Morobe, Eastern Highlands, Chimbu, Western Highlands, West Sepik, East Sepik and Madang. The main towns are: Lae, 16,546 (81% indigenes); Madang, 8,837 (84%); Wewak, 8,945 (90%); Goroka, 4,826 (81%); Mount Hagen, 3,314 (83%); and Bulolo, 2,725 (82%).

2. New Guinea Islands. The archipelago comprises 4 main islands and some 100 smaller islands. There are 5 administrative districts: East New Britain, West New Britain, New Ireland, Manus and Bougainville. The indigenous population as at 30 June 1969 was 281,712. The main towns (census, 1966) are Rabaul, 10,561 (66% indigenes); Lorengau, 2,446 (86%); Kavieng, 2,142 (80%).

New Britain, the largest island of this group, has a mean breadth of 50 miles and a length of 300 miles. The native population (including adjacent small islands) was 135,689 at 30 June 1969. A mountain chain traverses the entire length of the island, and in the centre consists of several irregular ranges. There are several active volcanoes. The highest known peak is the Father, about 7,500 ft high, which is an active volcano. The island has very fine harbours; the principal town is Rabaul. The chief export products are copra, cocoa and timber. An oil palm industry is being established on the north coast. Non-indigenous census population at 30 June 1966 was 5,349.

New Ireland, the second in size and importance, is situated north of New Britain, from which it is separated by St George's Channel. The chief town is Kavieng, at the north-west extremity of the island. The only other town is Namatanai on the south-east coast. The island has a long range of mountains running through it. It is of older formation than New Britain, and does not show any signs of recent volcanic activity. The principal harbour is Nusa Bay on the north coast, on which Kavieng, the seat of the local administration, is situated. The native population at 30 June 1969 was 48,774, including adjacent islands; non-indigenous census population was 964. The soil is reasonably fertile. The chief industry is coconut growing. There are numerous plantations around the coast near Kavieng. Smaller islands include Tabar, Lihir, Tanga, Feni, Nissan (Green Island), Nuguria, Mussau and Emirau Groups.

The Solomon Islands. The portion of the Solomon Islands within the area of the Territory of New Guinea consists of Bougainville, Buka and adjacent islands, including Kilinailau (Carteret Island), Taku (Mortlock) and Nukumanu (Tasman) Islands. Bougainville has an area of 4,100 sq. miles, and the native census population in 1969 was 72,661, including Buka, which has an area of 190 sq. miles; non-indigenous census population was 728. Smaller islands have a total area of 30 sq. miles. The islands are very mountainous. Of the several volcanic cones, Bagana (in the Crown Prince range) and Balbi are the only active volcanoes. The principal harbours are Kieta, situated on the east coast of Bougainville, and Raua and Tinputz on the north-east coast of Bougainville. There is a good harbour on the west side of Buka, named Carola Hafen. Bananas, coconuts, taro, sweet potatoes and cocoa are grown by the indigenous population.

The Admiralty Islands are the most important of the small groups. The chief island is Manus; the chief town is Lorengau on its north-east coast. The native census population of the group at 30 June 1969 was 21,588; non-indigenous census population was 447. Coconuts are the chief cultivated crop, and marine shell is taken for commercial purposes.

BOOKS OF REFERENCE

The Territory of Papua. Annual Report. Commonwealth of Australia. 1906–1940–41 and from 1945–46
The Territory of New Guinea. Annual Report. Commonwealth of Australia. 1914–1940–41 and from 1946–47
Report on New Guinea. UN visiting missions to . . . Nauru and New Guinea. New York, 1962
International Bank, *The economic development of the territory of Papua and New Guinea.* Johns Hopkins Press and CUP, 1965
Bettison, D. G., and others, *Independence of Papua–New Guinea.* Sydney, 1962.—*The Papua–New Guinea Elections 1964.* Canberra, 1966
Essal, B., *Papua and New Guinea.* Melbourne, 1961
Hasluck, P. M. C., *The Economic Development of Papua–New Guinea.* Canberra, 1962
Robson, R. W. (ed.), *Handbook of Papua and New Guinea.* Rev. ed. Sydney, 1961
Ryan, J., *The Hot Land.* London, 1970
Simpson, C., *Plumes and Arrows Inside New Guinea.* Sydney, 1962
Wilkes, J. (ed.), *New Guinea and Australia.* Austral Inst. of Political Science, 1959

Heard and McDonald Islands. These islands, about 2,500 miles south-west of Fremantle, were transferred from UK to Australian control as from 26 Dec. 1947. Heard Island is about 27 miles long and 13 miles wide; Shag Island is about 5 miles north of Heard. The McDonald Islands are 26 miles to the west of Heard. The laws of the Australian Capital Territory were declared to be in force in the Territory by the Heard and McDonald Islands Act, 1953.

AUSTRALIAN ANTARCTIC TERRITORY

An Imperial Order in Council of 7 Feb. 1933 placed under Australian authority all the islands and territories other than Adélie Land situated south of 60° S. lat. and lying between 160° E. long. and 45° E. long. The Order came into force with a Proclamation issued by the Governor-General on 24 Aug. 1936 after the passage of the Australian Antarctic Territory Acceptance Act 1933. The boundaries of Adélie Land were definitively fixed by a French Decree of 1 April 1938 as the islands and territories south of 60° S. lat. lying between 136° E. long. and 142° E. long. The Australian Antarctic Territory Act 1954 declared that the laws in force in the Australian Capital Territory are, so far as they are applicable and are not inconsistent with any ordinance made under the Act, in force in the Australian Antarctic Territory.

On 13 Feb. 1954 the Australian National Antarctic Research Expeditions (ANARE) established a base on MacRobertson Land at lat. 67° 36′ S. and long. 62° 53′ E. The base was named Mawson in honour of the late Sir Douglas Mawson. Meteorological and other scientific research is conducted at Mawson, which is the centre for coastal and inland survey expeditions.

A second Australian scientific research station was established on the coast of Princess Elizabeth Land on 13 Jan. 1957 at lat. 68° 34′ 36″ S. and long. 77° 58′ 36″ E. The station was named Davis in honour of Capt. John King Davis, Mawson's second-in-command on 2 expeditions. The station was temporarily closed down in Jan. 1965 and re-opened in Feb. 1969.

In Feb. 1959 the Australian Government accepted from the US Government custody of Wilkes Station, which was established by the US on 16 Jan.

1957 on the Budd Coast of Wilkes Land, at lat. 66° 15′ S. and long. 110° 32′ E. The station was named in honour of Lieut. Charles Wilkes, who commanded the 1838–40 US expedition to the area, and was closed in Feb. 1969. Operations were transferred to the new station, Casey. Construction commenced on Casey station in Jan. 1965 and was continued, mainly during summer visits, until Feb. 1969, when it was opened. The station, specially designed to withstand blizzard winds and prevent inundation by snow, is situated 1·5 miles south of Wilkes Land at lat. 66° 17′ S. and long. 110° 32′ E. It was named after Lord Casey, Governor-General of Australia 1965–69. ANARE have also operated a station, since March 1948, at Macquarie Island, about 850 miles south-east of Hobart. Macquarie Island is a dependency of the State of Tasmania.

On 1 Dec. 1959 Australia signed the Antarctic Treaty with Argentine, Belgium, Chile, France, Japan, New Zealand, Norway, South Africa, the USSR, the UK and the USA. Poland, Czechoslovakia and Denmark have subsequently acceded to the Treaty. The Treaty reserves the Antarctic area south of 60° S. lat. for peaceful purposes, provides for international co-operation in scientific investigation and research, and preserves, for the duration of the Treaty, the *status quo* with regard to territorial sovereignty, rights and claims. The Treaty entered into force on 23 June 1961. Since then the Antarctic Treaty powers have held several consultative meetings.

Cocos (Keeling) Islands. The Cocos (Keeling) Islands, 2 separate atolls comprising some 27 small coral islands with a total area of about 5½ sq. miles, are situated in the Indian Ocean in 12° 05′ S. lat. and 96° 53′ E. long. They lie some 1,720 miles north-west of Perth and 2,290 miles west of Darwin, while Colombo is 1,400 miles to the north-west of the group.

The islands were discovered in 1609 by Capt. William Keeling of the East India Company. The islands were uninhabited until 1826, when the first settlement was established on the main atoll by an Englishman, Alexander Hare, who left the islands in 1831. In the meantime a second settlement was formed on the main atoll by John Clunies-Ross, a Scottish seaman and adventurer, who landed with several boat-loads of Malay seamen. In 1857 the islands were annexed to the Crown; in 1878 responsibility was transferred from the Colonial Office to the Government of Ceylon, and in 1886 to the Government of the Straits Settlement. By indenture in 1886 Queen Victoria granted the land comprised in the islands to George Clunies-Ross and his heirs in perpetuity (with certain rights reserved to the Crown). The head of the family had semi-official status as resident magistrate and representative of the Government. In 1903 the islands were incorporated in the Settlement of Singapore and in 1942–46 temporarily placed under the Governor of Ceylon. In 1946 a Resident Administrator, responsible to the Governor of Singapore, was appointed.

On 23 Nov. 1955 the Cocos Islands were placed under the authority of the Commonwealth of Australia, which accepted them under the Cocos (Keeling) Islands Act, 1955, as the Territory of Cocos (Keeling) Islands.

The main islands are West Island (the largest, about 6 miles from north to south), on which is an aerodrome and most of the European community; Home Island, the headquarters of the Clunies-Ross Estate; Direction Island, the Department of Civil Aviation's marine base; South Island and Horsburgh. North Keeling Island, which forms part of the Territory, lies about 15 miles to the north of the group and has no inhabitants. Main settlements are on West Island and Home Island.

An airport is established on West Island under the control of the Department of Civil Aviation. Until April 1967 it was a re-fuelling point for aircraft on the service between Australia and South Africa.

The population of the Territory at 30 June 1970 was 611, including 128 Europeans. The Cocos Islanders reside on Home Island.

The group of atolls is low-lying, flat and thickly covered by coconut palms, and surrounds a lagoon in which ships drawing up to 23 ft may be anchored, but which is extremely difficult for navigation.

The climate is equable and pleasant, being usually under the influence of the south-east trade winds for about three-quarters of the year. However, the winds vary at times, and meteorological reports from the Territory are particularly valuable to those engaged in forecasting for the eastern Indian Ocean. The temperature varies between 70° and 80° F., the rainfall is moderate and there are occasional violent storms.

Responsibility for the administration of the Territory rests with the Minister of State for External Territories, whose Official Representative is in charge of the local administration. The laws of the Colony of Singapore which were in force in the islands immediately before the transfer have, with certain exceptions, been continued in force. They can be amended, repealed or substituted by ordinances made by the Governor-General of Australia.

Official Representative: C. W. Suthern.

Christmas Island is in the Indian Ocean, lat. 10° 25′ 22″ S., long. 105° 39′ 59″ E. It lies 224 miles S., 8° E. of Java Head, and 259 miles N. 79° E. from Cocos Islands, 815 miles from Singapore and 1,630 miles from Fremantle. Area about 52 sq. miles (135 sq. km). The climate is healthy. The island was formally annexed on 6 June 1888, placed under the administration of the Governor of the Straits Settlements in 1889, and incorporated with the Settlement of Singapore in 1900. Sovereignty was transfered to the Commonwealth of Australia on 1 Oct. 1958. The population on 30 June 1970 was 3,361.

The legislative, judicial and administrative systems are regulated by the Christmas Island Act, 1958–66, which is administered by the Minister of State for External Territories with an Administrator, responsible for the local administration. The laws of Singapore which were in force before the transfer have been continued but can be amended, repealed or substituted by ordinances made by the Governor-General of Australia.

Extraction and export of rock phosphate and phosphate dust is the island's only industry. In Dec. 1948 Australia and New Zealand bought the lease rights of the Christmas Island Phosphate Co. and set up the Christmas Island Phosphate Commission, for which the British Phosphate Commissioners act as managing agents. The export of phosphate rock during 1968–69 was 1,130,250 tons, which is shipped to Australia and New Zealand; in addition, about 98,000 tons of phosphate dust was shipped to Singapore and Malaysia and 5,700 tons to Australia.

There is direct radio communication with Australia and Singapore. No air service is available to or from the island.

At 30 June 1969 there were 851 pupils at primary and secondary schools. There is also a technical training centre.

Medical, dental and hospital services are provided free of charge by the British Phosphate Commission.

Administrator: J. S. White.

NEW SOUTH WALES

HISTORY. New South Wales became a British possession in 1770; the first settlement was established at Port Jackson in 1788; a partially elective Council was established in 1843, and responsible government in 1856. New South Wales federated with the other Australian states to form the Commonwealth of Australia in 1901.

CONSTITUTION AND GOVERNMENT. The legislative power is vested in a Parliament of the two Houses, the Legislative Council and the Legislative Assembly.

The Legislative Council consists of 60 members. At triennial elections 15 members are elected for a term of 12 years at joint sittings of both Houses of Parliament. The President has an annual salary of $A7,710; the Chairman of

Committees, $A5,005; the Leader of the Opposition, $A5,850; the Deputy Leader of the Opposition and Government and Opposition Whips, $A3,245 each. These also receive annual expense and special allowances: the President, $A2,865; the Leader of the Opposition, $A2,395; the others, $2,045 each. Other members who are not Ministers receive an annual salary of $A2,395, an annual expense allowance of $A1,690 and a daily attendance allowance of $A10 if they live outside the metropolitan area.

The Legislative Assembly has 94 members elected for a period of 3 years. Voting is compulsory. British subjects above 21 years of age, having resided 6 months in the Commonwealth, 3 months in the State and 1 month in any one electoral district, are eligible for enrolment as electors. Women were enfranchised in 1902.

The Speaker of the Legislative Assembly receives a salary of $A12,925; the Leader of the Opposition, $A13,630; the Chairman of Committees, $A9,420; the Deputy Leader of the Opposition and Government and Opposition Whips, $A9,400 each. The Speaker also receives an expense allowance of $A1,175; the Leader of the Opposition, $A1,880; the Chairman of Committees, $A590, the Deputy Leader of the Opposition and Government and Opposition Whips, $A470 each; and the Country Party Whip, $A425. Members who are not Ministers receive an annual salary of $A8,035. All members receive an annual electoral allowance ranging from $A1,945 to $A2,880 according to the location of their constituencies.

The Legislative Assembly, elected on 24 Feb. 1968, consisted in Oct. 1970 of the following parties: Liberal and Country Party, 52; Labour, 40; Independent, 2.

The executive is in the hands of a Governor, appointed by the Crown, and an Executive Council consisting of members of the Cabinet. Ministers receive the following annual salaries: Premier, $A18,215; Deputy Premier, $A16,075; Vice-President of the Executive Council and 15 other Ministers, $A15,040 each. Ministers also receive an expense allowance (Premier, $A4,700; Deputy Premier, $A2,115; other Ministers, $A1,880 each). In addition, Ministers who are members of the Legislative Assembly receive an electoral allowance ranging from $A1,945 to $A2,880 according to the location of their constituency. The Leader and Deputy Leader of the Government in the Legislative Council also receive a special allowance of, respectively, $A1,410 and $A355 per annum.

Governor: Sir Roden Cutler, VC, KCMG, KCVO, CBE (sworn in 20 Jan. 1966).

The Liberal–Country Party Cabinet, in Oct. 1970, was constituted as follows

Premier and Treasurer: R. W. Askin, MLA.
Deputy Premier, Minister for Education and for Science: C. B. Cutler, MLA.
Minister for Labour and Industry, Chief Secretary, and Minister for Tourism: E. A. Willis, MLA.
Decentralization and Development, Vice-President of the Executive Council: J. B. M. Fuller, MLC.
Public Works: Davies Hughes, MLA.
Attorney-General: K. M. McCaw, MLA.
Local Government and Highways: P. H. Morton, MLA.
Transport: M. A. Morris, MLA.
Lands: T. L. Lewis, MLA.
Conservation: J. G. Beale, MLA.
Agriculture: G. R. Crawford, DCM, MLA.
Housing and Co-operative Societies: S. T. Stephens, MLA.
Justice: J. C. Maddison, MLA.
Health: A. H. Jago, MLA.
Mines: W. C. Fife, MLA.
Child Welfare and Social Welfare: F. M. Hewitt, MLC.
Assistant Ministers: J. L. Waddy, OBE, DFC, MLA; G. F. Freudenstein, MLA.

Agent-General in London: J. E. Pagan, CMG, MBE (56–57 Strand, WC2).

LOCAL GOVERNMENT. A system of local government extends over most of the State, including the whole of the Eastern and Central land divisions and more than two-thirds of the sparsely populated Western division. There are 92 municipalities, and 133 corporate bodies called shires. A number of the municipalities and shires have combined to form 53 county councils, which administer electricity or water supply undertakings or render other services of common benefit.

AREA AND POPULATION. New South Wales is situated between the 28th and 38th parallels of S. lat. and 141st and 154th meridians of E. long., and comprises 309,433 sq. miles (801,400 sq. km), inclusive of Lord Howe Island (6 sq. miles) but exclusive of the Australian Capital Territory (911 sq. miles at Canberra and 28 sq. miles at Jervis Bay).

Census population (excluding full-blood aborigines):

	Males	Females	Persons	Population per sq. mile	Average annual increase % since previous census
1881	410,211	339,614	749,825	2·42	4·07
1891	609,666	517,471	1,127,137	3·63	4·16
1901	710,264	645,091	1,355,355	4·37	1·86
1911	857,698	789,036	1,646,734	5·32	1·97
1921	1,071,501	1,028,870	2,100,371	6·79	2·46
1933	1,318,471	1,282,376	2,600,847	8·41	1·76
1947	1,492,211	1,492,627	2,984,838	9·65	0·99
1954	1,720,860	1,702,669	3,423,529	11·06	1·98
1961	1,972,909	1,944,104	3,917,013	12·66	1·94
1966	2,124,462	2,109,360	4,233,822	13·68	1·57

At 30 June 1969 the population of Sydney (Statistical Division) was 2,646,800; Newcastle (Statistical District), 338,920; Wollongong (Statistical District), 187,910. Population of principal country towns: Broken Hill, 30,320; Wagga Wagga, 27,180; Albury, 26,210; Tamworth, 22,480; Orange, 21,970; Goulburn, 21,090; Lismore, 20,040; Bathurst, 17,330; Blue Mountains (part not in Sydney S.D.), 16,820; Grafton, 16,150; Dubbo, 15,970; Armidale, 15,890; Queanbeyan, 13,330; Lithgow, 12,710; Taree, 10,910.

VITAL STATISTICS for calendar years:

	Live births	Marriages	Divorces	Deaths (excluding still-births)	Infantile mortality per 1,000 live births	Estimated net migration
1967	78,841	37,077	4,555	39,613	18·4	34.300
1968	81,696	39,213	4,880	41.803	18·7	42,100
1969	86,036	41,286	5,123	40,665	18·9	55,800

The annual rates per 1,000 of the population in 1969 were: Births, 19·21; deaths, 9·08; marriages, 9·22.

RELIGION. There is no established church in New South Wales, and freedom of worship is accorded to all.

The following table shows the statistics of the religious denominations in New South Wales at the census, and of ministers of religion registered for the celebration of marriages, in 1966:

Denomination	Ministers	Adherents	Denomination	Ministers	Adherents
Church of England	850	1,622,066	Churches of Christ	54	96,606
Roman Catholic	1,453	1,174,779[1]	Orthodox	40	13,940
Presbyterian	341	353,084	Seventh Day Adventist	125	14,437
Methodist	378	305,733			
Baptist	226	55,773	Hebrew	21	25,913
Congregational	80	23,017	Others	204	501,087[2]
Lutheran	42	30,019			
Salvation Army	163	17,368	Total	3,977	4,233,822

[1] Includes 728,481 'Catholics undefined'.
[2] Includes 33,196 'no religion' and 382,477 'religion not stated' (this is not a compulsory question in the census schedule).

EDUCATION. The State maintains a system of national education, and attendance at school is compulsory from 6 to 15 years of age. In all State schools education is free. Private schools are subject to State inspection.

In Aug. 1969 there were 2,524 State schools, comprising 1,952 primary schools, 177 combined primary and secondary schools, 304 secondary schools and 91 special-purpose schools. In Aug. 1969 the effective enrolment was 767,628 children, comprising 511,495 receiving primary instruction and 256,133 receiving secondary instruction. There were, in 1969, 33,278 full-time teachers and 10,165 student teachers in training.

In Aug. 1969 there were 814 private schools with 8,010 full-time teachers and an effective enrolment of 229,468 pupils, of which 656 were Roman Catholic schools, having 5,943 teachers and 196,737 scholars. Church of England schools numbered 37 with 920 teachers and 15,201 scholars; other denominational schools, 41; teachers, 626; pupils, 10,953; undenominational schools, 80; teachers, 521, and scholars, 6,577.

The University of Sydney, founded in 1850, in 1969 had 16,085 students (including 5,304 women). There are 5 denominational colleges, and an undenominational college for women, affiliated to the university. The principal government training college for teachers is situated in the university grounds.

The University of New England at Armidale, previously affiliated with the University of Sydney, was incorporated on 1 Feb. 1954, and in 1969 had 5,154 students (including 1,626 women).

The New South Wales University of Technology, renamed in 1958 the University of New South Wales, was established by the State Government in 1949. Enrolments in 1969 numbered 15,920 (including 2,880 women). The University of Newcastle, previously affiliated with the University of New South Wales, was granted autonomy from 1 Jan. 1965, and in 1969 had 2,836 students (including 733 women). The Macquarie University in Sydney, established on 12 June 1964, in 1969 had 3,455 students (including 1,179 women).

Post-school technical education is provided at State-technical institutes and colleges, principally in the evening. Students enrolled in 1969 totalled 170,698 (including 23,335 correspondence students).

State government expenditure (including loan expenditure) on education in 1969–70 was $A344,131,240.

JUSTICE. Legal processes may be carried on in Lower or Magistrates Courts, or in the Higher Courts presided over by judges. There is also an appellate jurisdiction. Prisoners charged with the more serious crimes must be tried before the Supreme Court.

Children's Courts have been established with the object of removing children as far as possible from the atmosphere of a public court. There are also a number of tribunals exercising special jurisdiction, e.g., the Industrial Commission and the Workers' Compensation Commission.

In 1969 there were 727,923 convictions (mainly for drunkenness, minor traffic offences, etc.) before magistrates at Courts of Petty Sessions and Children's Courts and 3,609 distinct persons were convicted at the Higher Courts. On 30 June 1969 there were 3,327 convicted prisoners in gaol.

SOCIAL WELFARE. The Commonwealth Government makes provision for social benefits, such as age and invalid pensions, widows' pensions, child endowment, health benefits, maternity allowances, and unemployment and sickness benefits.

The number of age and invalid pensions current in New South Wales on 30 June 1970 was: Age, 292,889 (males, 85,403; females, 207,486); invalid, 55,450 (males, 30,875; females, 24,575). The annual liability at 30 June 1970 was $A209,780,428 for age pensions and $A45,353,386 for invalid pensions.

Commonwealth widows' pensions current in New South Wales at 30 June 1970 numbered 32,034, and the annual liability was $A31,584,563.

At 30 June 1970 endowed children under 16 years numbered 1,339,149 (including 5,819 in institutions) and endowed 'student' children (full-time students between 16 and 21 years) numbered 81,673. The annual liability as at 30 June 1970 was $A70,510,986.

During the year 1969–70, 86,526 maternity allowances amounting to $A2,741,107 were paid in New South Wales.

Unemployment, sickness and special benefits commenced on 1 July 1945. During the year 1969–70 claims totalling $A6,041,718 were paid in New South Wales. At 30 June 1970 unemployment benefit was being paid to 3,804 persons, and sickness and special benefits to 4,851 persons.

To relieve distress caused by unemployment and other causes, social welfare bureaux are conducted in various districts under the supervision of welfare officers, who are assisted by medical officers and nurses. Food, clothing, medical and dental treatment, etc., is provided for necessitous persons.

LABOUR. Two systems of industrial arbitration and conciliation for the adjustment of industrial relations between employers and employees are in operation—the State system, which operates within the territorial limits of the State, and the Commonwealth system, which applies to industrial disputes extending to other parts of the Commonwealth.

The industrial tribunals are authorized to fix minimum rates of wages and other conditions of employment. Their awards may be enforced by law, as may be industrial agreements between employers and organizations of employees, when registered.

The principal State tribunal is the Industrial Commission, constituted by judges. The Commission is empowered to exercise all the arbitration and conciliation powers conferred on subsidiary tribunals, and has in addition authority to determine any widely defined 'industrial matter', to adjudicate in case of illegal strikes and lockouts, etc., to investigate union ballots when irregularities are alleged and to hear appeals from subsidiary tribunals. Subsidiary tribunals are Conciliation Committees for various industries, each having an equal number representing employers and employees and a Conciliation Commissioner as chairman.

The chief industrial tribunals of the Commonwealth are the Industrial Court, constituted by judges, and the Conciliation and Arbitration Commission, constituted by presidential members, commissioners and conciliators (*see* p. 240).

The rates of wages prescribed by State awards and agreements consist of a basic wage (which applies to an unskilled worker) and margins added for skill, etc. The margins are assessed separately for each industry and vary widely. In Sept. 1970 the State basic wage was $A36.90 for adult males and $A28.30 for females. Separate specification of basic wage, margin and other elements of award wage rates under Commonwealth awards was discontinued and a total wage for each award classification was introduced from July 1967.

A standard working week of 40 hours is prescribed for employees in most industries. Overtime is permitted under prescribed conditions.

Registration of trade unions is effected under the New South Wales Trade Union Act, 1881–1959, which follows substantially the Trade Union Acts of 1871 and 1876 of England. Registration confers a quasi-corporate existence with power to hold property, to sue and be sued, etc., and the various classes of employees covered by the union are required to be prescribed by the constitution of the union. For the purpose of bringing an industry under the review of the State industrial tribunals, or participating in proceedings relating to disputes before Commonwealth tribunals, employees and employers must be registered as industrial unions, under State or Commonwealth industrial legislation respectively.

FINANCE. State revenue and expenditure (in $A1,000) for financial years ending 30 June:

Service	1966–67	1967–68	1968–69	1969–70
Revenue				
Governmental	572.813	615,503	684.595	771,843
Business undertakings	262,522	276,124	285,698	308,087
Total[1]	830,685	888,077	966,743	1,076,381
Working Expenditure				
Governmental	498,759	530,803	590,703	672,133
Business undertakings	229,747	243,621	258,644	274,552
Debt Charges	109,976	116,743	124,533	137,352
Total	833,832	887,618	970,330	1,080,782

[1] Net of inter-fund transfers.

Government revenue in 1969–70 included (in $A1,000) receipts from the Commonwealth of 404,410; namely, towards interest on State debt, 5,835; general financial assistance, 337,893; hospitals, etc., benefits, 13,933; other purposes, 6,749 (incl. 21 for drought relief). State taxes, in $A1,000 (including taxes paid direct to special funds), totalled 344,264, including probate duty, 55,460; stamp duty, 108,990; land tax, 32,550; motor taxation, 76,773; racing, betting, etc., taxes, 54.072, and liquor licences, 16,445. Revenue of business undertakings (in $A1,000) comprised railways, 250,488; omnibuses, 32,559, and harbour services, 25,000. Provision for debt redemption included in debt charges was 18,172 in 1966–67, 19,163 in 1967–68, 20,342 in 1968–69, and 21,985 in 1969–70.

In terms of the financial agreement between Commonwealth and States, the Commonwealth has assumed responsibility for debts of the Australian States, and contributes towards the interest thereon and sinking funds established for redemption of the debts. Loans for the States are raised by the Commonwealth in accordance with decisions of the Australian Loan Council.

The public debt of New South Wales at 30 June 1970 (oversea loans converted to Australian currency equivalent at current rates of exchange) comprised the following (in $A1,000): Repayable in Australia, 2,824,216; in London, 190,538; in New York, 55,345; in Canada, 3,158; in Switzerland, 3,233; in Netherlands, 2,049. Interest payments in 1969–70 amounted (in $A1,000) to 149,010, of which 12,862 was in respect of the external debt. The Commonwealth contributed 5,834 towards the interest. Contributions to the sinking fund for New South Wales debt, 35,667, included 7,723 contributed by the Commonwealth, and the cost of securities redeemed in the year was 45,821.

Since the institution of the sinking fund in 1928 contributions have totalled $A519·34m. ($A114·86m by Commonwealth), and redemptions at cost $A518,263,000.

LAND SETTLEMENT. The total area of land alienated or in process of alienation from the Crown on 30 June 1969 was 66,561,739 acres, exclusive of the Australian Capital Territory; 100,445,400 acres (including 71,441,242 acres in the Western Division) were held under perpetual lease from the Crown; 13,571,797 acres under the Crown leasehold tenures, and the total area of land neither alienated nor leased (including roads, reserves for public purposes, etc.) was 17,458,184 acres.

RURAL INDUSTRIES. The area under cultivation in New South Wales during 3 years (ended 31 March) and the principal crops produced were as follows:

	1967	1968	1969
Acres under cultivation	12,053,000	12,846,000	15,257,713
Value (farm) of all crops	$A427m.	$A262m.	$A418m.

Principle crops	Acreage	Produce	Acreage	Produce	Acreage	Produce
Wheat { Grain (bu.)	7,135,000	202,501,000	8,214,905	87,323,000	9,959104	215,119,000
Hay (long tons)	102,710	162,978	120,539	99,038	126.518	182,698
Maize Grain (bu.)	49,001	2,469,897	51,569	2,320,372	48,341	2,253,993
Barley { Grain (bu.)	384,824	3,926,640	376,480	4,834,143	486,351	11,187,761
Hay (long tons)	2,643	4,201	3,681	2,808	3,825	5,252
Oats { Grain (bu.)	1,362,607	40,904,490	907,252	8,234,788	1,184,751	27,453,874
Hay (long tons)	129,059	208,266	104,869	96,210	155,254	251,396
Potatoes (long tons)	23,594	126,183	24,334	122,795	29,236	160,823
Lucerne (hay) (long tons)	269,094	595,673	231,849	427,769	250,268	546,002
Tobacco (cwt)	1,794	19,046	1,831	18,529	2,190	22,148
Rice (bu.)	66,511	11,243,049	75,874	11,584,595	78.602	12,719,298
Cotton (lb.)	30,104	79,159,424	53,474	170,064,281	59,769	173,759,192

In 1968–69, 22,174 acres of sugar-cane were cut for crushing, the yield being 997,813 long tons. The total area under grapes was 24,394 (including 3,841 not bearing) acres; the production of table grapes was 7,470 long tons; of wine (1967–68), 8,349,774 gallons; of sultanas, raisins and currants, 193,779 cwt.

In 1968–69 the production of citrus fruit, principally oranges, was 6,580,869 bu. from 2,746,724 bearing trees; of other orchard fruit, 6,479,075 bu. from 3,029,606 bearing trees. In addition, there were 19,434 acres of banana plantations, the yield from 18,124 acres being 3,694,722 bu., and there were 1,006 acres of passion fruit, pineapples, berries, etc.

At 31 March 1969 the State had 68·1m. sheep and lambs, 4,864,409 cattle, and 690,226 pigs. The production of wool in 1968–69 was 673·62m. lb. (greasy). In the year ended 30 June 1969 production of butter was 52,172,000 lb.: cheese, 9,320,830 lb., and bacon and ham, 33,033,728 lb.

FORESTRY. The estimated forest area of Crown and private lands is 23,977,211 acres. The total area of State forests amounts to 7m. acres, and 1,055,808 acres have been set apart as timber reserves.

The revenue from royalties, licences, etc., amounted in the year ended June 1969 to $A6,409,019.

There were 685 saw-mills in the year ended 30 June 1968, the employees numbered 8,105, the value of plant and machinery was $A10,820,291, and land and buildings $A13,420,237. The value of production from forestry in 1967–68 was $A37·32m.

MINING. The value of output in 1969 of the mining and quarrying industries of New South Wales was $A360,521,428 and total employment was 24,311 persons. The two principal classes of mining were coalmining, which employed 13,227 persons and produced 33·44m. long tons of coal valued at $A169,530,310, and silver–lead–zinc mining, which employed 4,943 persons and produced minerals valued at $A89,482,658. The following table shows the mine production of metals, *i.e.*, gross contents of metallic minerals produced) in calendar years:

	1966	1967	1968	1969
Antimony (long tons)	971	930	842	905
Cadmium (long tons)	1,005	1,079	1,007	1,249
Cobalt (long tons)	84	100	113	135
Copper (long tons)	9,242	11,392	12,279	15,290
Gold (fine oz.)	9,078	10,716	8,668	10,564
Lead (long tons)	283,044	282,173	249,488	280,363
Silver (fine oz.)	10,544,370	10,714,149	9,520,917	10,749,280
Sulphur (long tons)	210,312	223,338	203,231	247,026
Tin (long tons)	1,367	1,569	1,448	1,520
Titanium (long tons TiO$_2$)	209,140	210,523	215,392	236,844
Zinc (long tons)	275,191	298,672	280,219	343,480

The estimated gross value of recorded production from the primary industries in 1968–69 was as follows (in $A1,000): Agriculture, 542,184; pastoral, 445,340; dairying and farmyard, 233,103; forestry, fisheries and trapping, 50,110; mining (including the output of quarries), 300,005; total primary, 1,570,741.

SECONDARY INDUSTRY. Establishments employing 4 or more hands, or using power other than manual, supply annual returns of factory operations. Development since 1938–39 is shown in the following table:

	Establish-ments (No.)	Persons employed (No.)	Salaries and wages ($A1,000)	Motive power installed (1,000 h.p.)	Materials, fuel used ($A1,000)	Value of production ($A1,000)
1938–39	9,464	228,781	89,213	1,792	256,306	180,532
1948–49	16,087	378,380	293,071	2,649	717,051	502,398
1958–59	22,684	449,518	826,029	5,740	2,294,274	1,610,630
1966–67	24,849	524,054	1,399,746	10,710	3,704,247	2,938,227
1967–68	24,884	531,185	1,498,067	11,627	3,965,534	3,130,982

Approximately 30% of the work force in New South Wales is employed in factories.

Large iron and steel works, with subsidiary factories, are in operation in proximity to the coalfields, at Newcastle and Port Kembla. The products include iron and steel of various grades, pipes, boilers, steel wire and wire netting, copper wire, copper and brass cables, and tinplate.

Statistics of the main classes of secondary industry in 1967–68 were:

	Establish-ments (No.)	Persons employed (No.)	Salaries and wages ($A1,000)	Motive power installed (1,000 h.p.)	Value of produc-tion ($A1,000)
Chemicals, paints, oils, etc.	638	27,318	88,894	504	338,540
Industrial metals, machines, etc.	11,692	267,936	801,962	2,141	1,413,051
Clothing (except knitted)	3,157	44,418	82,053	34	152,973
Food, drink, tobacco	2,319	44,357	117,308	346	317,550
Woodwork and furniture	2,717	29,434	75,150	255	139,092
Paper, printing	1,292	36,222	107,501	193	234,570
Total (incl. all others)	24,834	531,185	1,498,067	11,627	3,130,982

Some of the principal articles manufactured in 1969–70 were:

Article	Quan-tity	Article	Quan-tity
Beer and stout (1,000 galls)	133,941	Gas (town) (1,000 therms)	133,929
Flour (1,000 short tons)	554	Steel ingots (1,000 long tons)	5,691
Footwear (1,000 prs)	8,408		
Cloth: cotton, wool, rayon, synthetic (1,000 sq. yd)	59,946	Cars, etc.[1] (1,000)	126
Pig-iron (1,000 long tons)	4,307	T.V. receiving sets (1,000)	205
Refrigerators (domestic)	134,216	Electricity (1m. kwh.)	20,874

[1] Finished and partly finished motor vehicles, excluding trucks.

COMMERCE. The external commerce of New South Wales, exclusive of interstate trade, is included in the statement of the commerce of the Commonwealth (*see* pp. 245–46). The oversea commerce of the State is given in $A1,000 ending 30 June:

	Imports	Exports[1]		Imports	Exports[1]
1964–65	1,277,405	803,734	1967–68	1,405,331	943,182
1965–66	1,257,603	781,206	1968–69	1,500,559	1,010.488
1966–67	1,323,597	878,446	1969–70	1,708,939	1,158,757

[1] Includes non-Australian produce ($A171m. in 1969–70).

The main exports of Australian produce are wool (19·4%), wheat (14·7%), coal (9·3%), iron and steel (6·8%) and meat (5·8%). Principal imports are machinery and equipment (23·7%), transport equipment (9·4%), chemicals, paints, etc. (7%) and textiles.

Principal destination of all exports from New South Wales are Japan (18·4%),

EEC countries (10·8%), USA (9·2%), UK (9%), New Zealand (8·9%) and Papua–New Guinea (8·9%). Major sources of supply are USA (25·5%), UK (20·7%), EEC countries (12·5%), Japan (11·3%) and Canada (3·8%).

SHIPPING. The vessels engaged in the interstate and oversea trade which entered the ports of New South Wales in 1968–69 numbered 4,039; net tonnage, 24,455,580; the clearances were 4,812 vessels, 24,362,499 tons. Sydney Harbour is the principal port of Australia. The number of vessels, coastal, interstate and oversea, which entered in 1969–70 was 3,896; net tonnage, 16·24m.

RAILWAYS. On 30 June 1969, 6,061 miles of government railway were open. The earnings in 1969–70 were $A245m.; the working expenses, $A210m.; the number of passengers carried, 251,578,000. Also open for traffic are 203 miles of Victorian Government railways which extend over the border; 85 miles of private railways (mainly in mining districts) and 6 miles of Commonwealth-owned track.

ROADS. There are 122,745 miles of roads and streets in New South Wales, comprising 533 miles cement concrete, 1,484 miles bituminous concrete, 31,477 miles other bitumen surface, 41,659 miles gravel or stone, 28,169 miles formed only, 6,524 miles cleared only, 19,900 miles natural surface. The bridge across Sydney Harbour is the largest arch bridge in the world.

The principal omnibus services in Sydney and Newcastle are the property of the Government. The conversion of metropolitan government tramway services to omnibus operation was completed in 1961.

The number of registered motor vehicles (excluding tractors and trailers) on 31 May 1970 was 1,702,759, including 1,105,311 cars, 230,172 station wagons, 128,228 utilities, 68,056 vans, 114,803 trucks, 7,277 buses and 48,842 motor cycles.

AVIATION. Sydney is the major airport in New South Wales and Australia's principal international air terminal. During the year ended 31 Dec. 1969 aircraft movements at Sydney totalled 82,951. Passengers handled numbered 3,159,672 on domestic services and 734,727 on international services. Freight handled on domestic and international services was 46,320 short tons and 25,455 short tons respectively.

BANKING. There were 12 trading banks operating in New South Wales at 30 June 1970, including the Commonwealth Trading Bank and Rural Bank (Government banks), 2 foreign banks and 1 New Zealand bank. The trading bank business is transacted chiefly by the Commonwealth Trading Bank and 7 private banks, of which 5 have their head offices in Australia and 2 in London. At 30 June 1970 the 12 banks operated 1,786 branches and 360 agencies in New South Wales.

The weekly average amount of deposits held in New South Wales by the 12 banks was $A2,985·6m. in June 1970, consisting of $A1,502,685,000 bearing interest and $A1,482,912,000 not bearing interest. Bank advances, overdrafts, bills discounted, etc., amounted to $A2,172,077,000. A statement of other assets and liabilities of the banks in New South Wales is of little significance, as banking business is conducted on an Australia-wide basis.

Savings bank deposits at the end of June 1970 amounted to $A2,400,821,000, representing $A526 per head of population.

Lord Howe Island, 31° 33′ 4″ S., 159° 4′ 26″ E., a dependency of New South Wales, situated about 436 miles north-east of Sydney; area, 4,088 acres (1,656 hectares), of which only about 300 acres are arable; population (30 June 1969), 280. The island, which was discovered in 1788, is of volcanic origin. Mount Gower, the highest point, reaches a height of 2,840 ft (852 metres).

A Board at Sydney and an elected Island Committee manage the affairs of the island and supervise the Kentia palm-seed industry.

BOOKS OF REFERENCE

STATISTICAL INFORMATION. The NSW Government Statistician's Office was established in 1886, and in 1957 was integrated with the Commonwealth Bureau of Census and Statistics. *Deputy Commonwealth Statistician and Government Statistician of NSW:* R. G. Walker. Its principal publications are:

Official Year-Book of New South Wales (1886/87–1900/01 under the title *Wealth and Progress of NSW*): latest full issue, 1969: separate sections, 1969
New South Wales Statistical Register. Published annually since 1858; latest issue of separate sections, 1968–69 and 1969
New South Wales Pocket Year-Book. Published since 1913 · latest issue, 1971
New South Wales Statistical Bulletin (quarterly). Published since 1905 (except 1943–48
Monthly Summary of Business Statistics. Published since May 1931
New South Wales Dept. of Tourist Activities, *Facts about New South Wales.* Sydney, 1970
State Planning Authority, *Sydney Region: Prelude to a Plan.* Sydney, 1967.
State Planning Authority, *Sydney Region: Outline Plan.* Sydney, 1968
Sydney City Council, *The City of Sydney: Official Guide.* Sydney, 1966

STATE LIBRARY. The Public Library of NSW, Macquarie St., Sydney. *Principal Librarian:* G. D. Richardson, MA.

VICTORIA

CONSTITUTION AND GOVERNMENT. Victoria, formerly a portion of New South Wales, was, in 1851, proclaimed a separate colony, with a partially elective Legislative Council. In 1855 responsible government was conferred, the legislative power being vested in a parliament of two Houses, the Legislative Council and the Legislative Assembly. At present the Council consists of 36 members who are elected for 6 years, one-half retiring every third year. The Assembly consists of 73 members, elected for 3 years from the date of its first meeting unless sooner dissolved by the Governor. Members and electors of both Houses must be adult natural born or naturalized British subjects. Women are fully enfranchised. No property qualification is required, but ministers of religion and judges may not be members of either House. Single voting (one elector one vote) and compulsory preferential voting apply to Council and Assembly elections. Enrolment of Council and Assembly electors is compulsory. The Council may not initiate or amend money bills, but may suggest amendments in such bills other than amendments which would increase any charge. Any Minister, with the consent of the House of which he is not a member, may sit and speak in that House to explain a bill relating to the department administered by him, but may not vote in that House. A bill shall not become law unless passed by both Houses, except that, in the event of a continued disagreement between the two Houses as to a bill passed by the Assembly, other than certain constitutional bills, the Governor having dissolved the Assembly may subsequently dissolve the Council, and if the disagreement still continues he may convene a joint sitting of the members of the Council and the Assembly; if at such joint sitting the bill in dispute is passed by an absolute majority of all members it shall become law.

Private members of both Houses receive reimbursement of expenses ($A7,750 per annum), additional allowances rising from $A2,000 (metropolitan constituencies) to $A3,100 (outer country), and a living-away-from-home allowance of $A14 for each day of attendance for each member (not being a responsible Minister).

Members holding the following offices receive the salaries and allowances specified: The President of the Council, $A11,875 salary and $A800 expense allowance; the Speaker of the Assembly, $A11,875 salary and $A800 expense allowance; the Chairman of Committees of the Council, $A9,450 salary and $A300 expense allowance; the Chairman of Committees of the Assembly, $A9,450 salary and $A300 expense allowance; the Leader of the Opposition in the Assembly, $A13,250 salary and $A1,550 expense allowance; the Deputy Leader of the Opposition in the Assembly, $A9,700 salary and $A350 expense allowance; the Leader of any recognized party (other than the Opposition) consisting of at least 14 members of Parliament, of which party no member is a responsible Minister, $A9,700 salary and $A475 expense allowance; a member of either House who is the Parliamentary Secretary of the Cabinet, $A9,700 salary and $A475 expense allowance; the Government Whip in the Assembly, $A8,425 salary; the Whip of any recognized Party which consists of at least 14 members of Parliament, of which Party no member is a responsible Minister, $A8,150 salary. All members have free passes over the Victorian Railways; country members are also entitled to certain allowances for air travel.

The Legislative Assembly, elected on 30 May 1970, is composed as follows: Liberal Party, 42; Labor Party, 22; Country Party, 8; Independent Labor, 1.

Governor: Maj.-Gen. Sir Rohan Delacombe, KCMG, KCVO, KBE, CB, DSO.

In the exercise of the executive power the Governor is advised by a Cabinet of responsible Ministers. The Constitution Act Amendment Act provides that the number of responsible Ministers shall not at any one time exceed 15, of whom 5 may sit in the Legislative Council. No responsible Minister may hold office for more than 3 months unless he is or becomes a member of the Council or the Assembly.

Responsible Ministers receive the following amounts: The Premier, $A19,000 salary and $A3,750 expense allowance and, if he represents an electorate outside the metropolitan area and maintains an additional place of residence within the latter, an allowance of $A1,150; the Deputy Premier, $A15,500 salary and $A1,800 expense allowance; 13 other responsible Ministers $A13,250 salary and $A1,550 expense allowance. Each responsible Minister receives, when travelling on business of the State, a travelling allowance. Members of Committees receive attendance fees and certain travelling expenses when on Committee duties.

The Liberal Party Government (first appointed 7 June 1955) is as follows:

Premier and Treasurer: Sir Henry Bolte, KCMG, MP.
Chief Secretary: Sir Arthur Rylah, KBE, CMG, ED, MP.
Housing, Forests and Aboriginal Affairs: E. R. Meagher, MBE, ED, MP.
Agriculture: G. L. Chandler, CMG, MLC.
Education: L. H. S. Thompson, MP.
Public Works: M. Byrne, MLC.
Health: J. F. Rossiter, MP.
Attorney-General and Immigration: G. O. Reid, MP.
Transport: V. F. Wilcox, MP.
Local Government: R. J. Hamer, ED, MLC.
Lands, Soldier Settlement, and Conservation: W. A. Borthwick, MP.
Labour and Industry and Asst. Minister of Education: J. A. Rafferty, MP.
State Development and Tourism: V. O. Dickie, MLC.
Fuel and Power and Mines: J. C. M. Balfour, MP.
Water Supply: I. W. Smith, MP.

Agent-General in Great Britain: Sir Murray V. Porter (Victoria House, Melbourne Place, WC2).

LOCAL GOVERNMENT. With the exception of Yallourn Works area (8,653 acres) and the unincorporated areas of French Island (41,600 acres), Lady Julia Percy Island (653 acres), the Bass Strait Islands and Gippsland Lakes (82,886 acres) and Tower Hill (1,459 acres), the State is divided (as at 30 June 1969) into 210 municipal districts, namely 60 cities, 5 towns, 8 boroughs and 137 shires. The constitution of cities, towns and boroughs is based on statutory requirements concerning population and rate revenue, with the net annual value of rateable property as an additional requirement for boroughs. For shires, the basis derives from the rate revenue and the net annual value of rateable property; rate revenue must be at least $A60,000 with rateable property of a net annual value of at least $A400,000.

AREA AND POPULATION. The State has an area of 87,884 sq. miles (227,600 sq. km). It is divided into 37 counties, varying in area from 920 to 5,933 sq. miles.

The census population (exclusive of full-blood aboriginals) was:

Date of census enumeration	Population Males	Population Females	Population Total	On previous census Numerical increase	On previous census Increase %
3 April 1881	451,623	409,943	861,566	131,368	17·99
5 April 1891	598,222	541,866	1,140,088	278,522	32·33
31 March 1901	603,720	597,350	1,201,070	60,982	5·35
3 April 1911	655,591	659,960	1,315,551	114,481	9·53
4 April 1921	754,724	776,556	1,531,280	215,729	16·40
30 June 1933	903,244	917,017	1,820,261	288,981	18·87
30 June 1947	1,013,867	1,040,834	2,054,701	234,440	12·88
30 June 1954	1,231,099	1,221,242	2,452,341	397,640	19·35
30 June 1961	1,474,395	1,455,718	2,930,113	477,772	19·48
30 June 1966	1,613,904	1,605,622	3,219,526	289,413	9·88

The average density is 36·6 persons per sq. mile.

The population of Melbourne metropolitan area (capital city) on 30 June 1966 was 2,110,168, or 65·5% of the population of the State. The population of urban Geelong was 105,059; urban Ballarat, 56,290; urban Bendigo, 42,208. Other urban centres: Moe-Yallourn, 23,198; Shepparton, 17,506; Warrnambool, 17,499; Morwell, 16,610; Wangaratta, 15,175; Traralgon, 14,079; Mildura, 12,931; Horsham, 10,562; Hamilton, 10,054; Dromana-Sorrento, 9,935; Colac, 9,498; Sale, 8,640; Ararat, 8,233; Werribee, 8,228; Benalla, 8,224; Bairnsdale, 7,785; Maryborough, 7,707; Swan Hill, 7,381; Mornington-Balcombe, 7,349; Castlemaine, 7,103.

VITAL STATISTICS for calendar years:

	Births	Marriages	Divorces	Deaths	Oversea arrivals	Oversea departures
1967	65,485	28,004	2,039	28,373	95,852	60,393
1968	70,228	29,724	2,515	29,967	82,452	58,956
1969	71,035	30,860	2,220	28,976	79,955	60,600

The annual rates per 1,000 of the population in 1969 were: Marriages, 9·11; births, 20·97; deaths, 8·55; infant deaths, 15 per 1,000 births.

RELIGION. There is no State Church in Victoria, and no State assistance has been given to religion since 1875. At the date of the 1966 census the following were the enumerated numbers of each of the principal religions: Catholic, Roman,[1] 253,947; Catholic,[1] 635,548; Church of England, 923,078; Methodist, 279,300; Presbyterian, 387,108; Protestant (undefined), 44,456; other Christian, 289,664; Hebrew, 31,058; other non-Christians, 4,190; Indefinite, 9,478; no religion, 27,965; no reply, 333,734.

[1] So described on individual census schedules.

EDUCATION. Education establishments in Victoria consist of 3 universities, established under special Acts and opened in 1855, 1961 and 1967; Colleges of Advanced Education; State schools (primary, primary-secondary, secondary and junior technical, senior technical schools or colleges, and registered schools).

The University of Melbourne, founded in 1853, had, in 1969, 14,498 students (including 4,443 females) and 951 teaching and research staff. Affiliated with the university are 9 denominational colleges, 2 undenominational colleges and 2 halls of residence.

Monash University, founded in 1958 in an eastern suburb of Melbourne, had, in 1969, 9,542 students (including 2,956 females) and 682 teaching and research staff.

La Trobe University, founded in 1964 in a northern suburb of Melbourne, had 2,052 students (including 768 females) and 174 teaching and research staff in 1969.

Primary education of children of the ages of 6 to 15 years inclusive is free, secular and compulsory. At 1 Aug. 1969 there were 1,848 State primary schools with 12,791 full-time and 354 part-time teachers and an enrolment of 348,868 pupils; 53 State primary-secondary schools had 756 full-time and 73 part-time teachers and an enrolment of 15,609 pupils. There were also 334 State secondary schools, comprising post-primary schools, girls' schools, junior technical schools and high schools with 11,347 full-time and 2,636 part-time teachers and an enrolment of 207,648 pupils. There were also 83 senior technical schools, attached to which were the junior technical schools included above in secondary schools, with 74,948 senior students excluding those tertiary students enrolled at colleges affiliated with the Victoria Institute of Colleges. The total cost to the State of public instruction, including grants to the universities, was $A272m. in 1968–69.

Registered Schools. There were at 1 Aug. 1969, 572 registered schools, excluding commercial colleges, with 6,530 full-time and 1,477 part-time teachers and 189,452 pupils enrolled. Of these schools, 479 were connected with the Roman Catholic community; some were under the control of the Church of England, the Presbyterian, Methodist and other Churches, while a few were managed by private persons or companies.

SOCIAL SERVICES. Victoria was the first State of the Commonwealth to make a statutory provision for the payment of Age Pensions. The Act providing for the payment of such pensions came into operation on 18 Jan. 1901, and continued until 1 July 1909, when the Commonwealth Invalid and Old Age Pension Act came into force. The Social Services Consolidation Act, which came into operation on 1 July 1947, repealed the various legislative enactments relating to age (previously old-age) and invalid pensions, maternity allowances, child endowment, and unemployment and sickness benefits and, while following in general the Acts repealed, considerably liberalized many of their provisions: it has since been amended. On 30 June 1970 there were 206,608 age and 29,753 invalid pensioners in Victoria, and the amount paid in pensions, including payments to wives of invalid pensioners, during 1969–70 was $A163·35m.

The number of war pensions (members of the forces and their dependants) payable in Victoria on 30 June 1970 was 159,268, and the number of service pensions was 18,307. The amount paid in war and service pensions by the Commonwealth Government during 1969–70 was $A61·06m.

During the year ended 30 June 1970 maternity allowance was granted to 70,259 mothers in the State, the total amount paid in allowances during the year being $A2·3m.

Under the Commonwealth *Unemployment and Sickness Benefit Act* 1944, there were 6,682 persons receiving benefits at June 1970 (excluding migrants in accommodation centres), and the amount paid in benefits totalled $A4·82m. in the year ended 30 June 1970.

The number of widow's pensions in force in Victoria at 30 June 1970 was 23,318, and the total amount paid in allowances during that year was $A21·7m.

The number of child endowments in force in Victoria at 30 June 1970 was 553,168, representing 1,142,296 endowable children (including students). In addition, endowment was being paid in respect of 5,526 children who were being maintained in approved institutions. The total amount paid in endowment in Victoria during the year ended 30 June 1970 was $A62·42m.

STATE HOUSING. The Housing Acts, as amended in 1954, provide for the appointment of a Housing Commission of 3 full-time members as the housing authority of the State. The Housing Commission was established in March 1938, and its activities are now spread throughout the whole State. Since its inception to 30 June 1970, 314 'estates', including 173 in the country, have been developed by the commission and 66,801 dwelling units provided thereon. In addition, 3,150 dwellings were under construction. About 43% of the units built in 1969–70 were located in country towns, particularly where decentralized industries have been established. The capital works expenditure of the commission was $A524m. up to 30 June 1970. Rental charges for the year 1969–70 were $A18,062,000, against which $A1,596,780 was allowed in rent rebates to tenants on low incomes, including pensioners.

JUSTICE. There is a Supreme Court with a Chief Justice and 16 puisne judges. There are courts of general and petty sessions, county courts, courts of mines, court of licensing and children's courts.

Criminal statistics for 1969: 292,358 convictions (including some 175,000 for driving and traffic offences) in magistrates' courts; 1,790 convicted persons in higher (judges') courts.

There are 13 gaols in Victoria. At 30 June 1969 there were confined in these prisons, 2,281 males and 49 females.

FINANCE. The consolidated revenue and expenditure (in $A1,000) of the State in the years shown (ended 30 June) were:

	1965–66	1966–67	1967–68	1968–69	1969–70	1970–71[1]
Revenue	508,554	559,596	601,328	664,183	726,900	802,848
Expenditure	516,639	559,596	604,122	666,644	742,282	810,953

[1] Estimates.

The principal items of state consolidated revenue (in $A1,000) during 1968–69 were: Taxation, 433,166 (including Commonwealth reimbursement, 250,563, but excluding 72,418 paid to special funds); railways, 100,329; other Commonwealth payments, 14,944, and water supply, sewerage, etc. (including interest), 14,482. The principal heads of expenditure were: Interest and public debt charges (including railways), 119,514; railways, 104,322; education, 207,354; health, hospitals and charities, 93,732.

The amount raised by taxation (exclusive of taxes collected by Commonwealth or paid to special funds but inclusive of Commonwealth reimbursements under the uniform taxation scheme), as shown in the above paragraph, was approximately $A129.08 per head of population.

The public debt of Victoria (in $A1m.) on 30 June 1969 was 2,254. An amount of 2,618 has been expended from loan funds. Of this amount 472 was spent on railways; 398 on waterworks; 111 on land settlement; 120 on soldier settlement; 70 on roads and bridges; 259 on electricity supply; 443 on universities, schools and colleges; 100 on other public buildings; 54 on forestry; 237 on hospitals; 41 on housing; 65 on revenue deficits; 248 on all other purposes.

LAND SETTLEMENT. Of the total area of Victoria (56,245,760 acres), 34,296,461 acres at the end of 1968 were either alienated or in process of alienation. The remainder (21,949,299) constituted crown land as follows: State forests, timber, water and other reserves, 7,244,900; roads, 1,707,565; water frontages, river-beds, lakes, unsold land in cities, etc., 3,844,606; perpetual leases, 142,788; other leases and licences, 10,966; occupied under grazing leases or unoccupied, 8,998,474. Rural holdings in 1968–69 numbered 71,056.

AGRICULTURE. The following table shows the area under the principal crops and the produce of each for 3 seasons (in 1,000 units):

Season	Total cultivation	Wheat		Oats		Barley		Potatoes		Hay	
	Acres	Acres	Bushels	Acres	Bushels	Acres	Bushels	Acres	Tons	Acres	Tons
1966–67	9,168	3,138	70,896	1,079	31,248	228	5,420	37	225	1,558	2,982
1967–68	8,459	3,224	28,317	723	6,859	305	2,709	40	216	1,165	1,556
1968–69	10,377	3,984	90,728	991	30,230	409	8,885	40	300	1,847	3,635

In 1968–69 there were 48,970 acres of vines, yielding 6,241,000 gallons of wine, 40,583 tons of dried fruit and 6,939 tons of table grapes. Green fodder covered 91,764 acres, and orchards and vegetables, including potatoes and onions, occupied 167,241 acres.

At March 1969 there were in the State 3,877,826 head of cattle, 30,184,874 sheep and 421,655 pigs. The wool produced in the season 1968–69 amounted to 364m. lb., valued at $A156m. The quantity of butter produced in 1968–69 was 280·21m. lb.

The gross value of Victorian primary production (in rural and non-rural) 1968–69 was $A1,025m.

MINING. The recorded production of certain metals and minerals raised in Victoria for the year 1968 was: Gold, 11,069 fine oz., value $A431,417; coal, black, 26,314 tons, value $A209,434; coal, brown, 23m. tons, value $A21·6m.

MANUFACTURERS. The total number of factories in 1967–68 was 18,030. 72·7% of the factories, and 82·4% of the persons employed in factories are in the Melbourne Statistical Division. Persons employed (including working proprietors) numbered 449,945 (316,108 males, 133,837 females). Working proprietors numbered 12,025 (9,544 males, 2,481 females). Salaries and wages paid to persons employed (excluding working proprietors) was $A1,244m.; land, buildings, machinery and plant were valued at $A2,685m. The value of materials used (including containers, tools replaced and repairs) was $A2,813m., the value of power, fuel and light used (including water and lubricating oil) was $A143m., and value added by manufacture, $A2,395m.

The number of persons employed in the largest classes of industry were: Industrial metals, machines, conveyances, 192,073; clothing, 49,027; food, drink and tobacco, 44,143; textiles, 43,077; paper, printing, bookbinding, 30,991.

TRADE UNIONS. There were 152 trade unions with a total membership of 550,800 operating in Victoria in 1969.

ELECTRICAL ENERGY. The State Electricity Commission of Victoria, the largest electricity supply authority in Australia, produces over 99% of the electricity generated in the State available for public supply; its supply network serves over 99% of the population and some New South Wales municipalities and irrigation settlements bordering the river Murray. The total installed capacity of the Commission's system at 30 June 1970 was 3,545,815 kw., including Victoria's share of about one-third (610,000 kw. at 30 June 1970) of the Snowy Mountains hydro-electric scheme and its half share (25,000 kw.) of the output of the Hume hydro-electric station (shared with New South Wales). Power generated in 1969–70 totalled 13,454m. kwh. Thermal stations at Hazelwood, Yallourn, Morwell, Melbourne (3), Geelong, Ballarat and Red Cliffs had an installed capacity of 2,587,300 kw. Burning raw brown coal on site on the coalfields, the Latrobe Valley power stations (2,137,500 kw. inclusive of Yallourn briquette works) produced over 87% of Victoria's electricity. Hazelwood, a new coal field power station under construction, had a capacity of 1·4m. kw. at 30 June 1970; it will be 1·6m. kw. on completion in 1971. Excluding Snowy and Hume, the installed hydro-electric capacity totalled 334,515 kw. at 30 June 1970, with Kiewa (3 stations totalling 183,600 kw.) as the chief undertaking.

COMMERCE. The commerce of Victoria, exclusive of inter-state trade, is included in the statement of the commerce of the Commonwealth of Australia *see* pp. 245–46.

The total value of the oversea imports and exports of Victoria, including bullion and specie but excluding inter-state trade, was as follows (in $A1,000):

	1964–65	1965–66	1966–67	1967–68	1968–69	1969–70
Imports	1,026.834	1,017,360	1,072,514	1,130,741	1,182,705	1,347,053
Exports	723,046	768,063	801,168	685,755	707,579	912,596

The chief exports in 1968–69 were: Wool, meat, wheat, butter, fruits, hides and skins, milk products, motor vehicles and parts, flour, oats, cheese, tallow and malt.

RAILWAYS. All the railways are the property of the State and are under the management of 3 commissioners appointed by the Government.

At 30 June 1969, 4,190 miles of government railway were open. Gross capital expenditure to this date was $A471,040,116. During the year 1968–69 the gross revenue amounted to $A100,590,879 and the total working expenses to $A111,344,202. 144,865,905 passengers, 11,031,425 tons of freight and 278,491 tons of livestock were carried.

ROADS. At 30 June 1969 there were 100,708 miles of road open for general traffic consisting of 213 miles cement concrete, 30,113 miles of bituminous seal, 29,158 miles of waterbound macadam, gravel, etc., 20,792 miles formed, but not paved, and 20,432 miles not formed. The number of registered motor vehicles (other than tractors) at 30 June 1969 was 1,254,638.

AVIATION. During the year ended 30 June 1969 there were 52,484 aircraft movements at Essendon. Passengers totalled 2·3m. on domestic flights (international, 51,816). Freight handled, 48,532 short tons, domestic flights (719 international).

BANKING. On 30 June 1970 there were 4·69m. operative accounts (excluding school bank accounts) in savings banks in Victoria. The total credit due to depositors amounted to $A2,387m., made up of State Savings Bank, $A1,163m.; Commonwealth Savings Bank, $A537m.; private savings banks, $A686m.

The weekly average of deposits and advances of trading banks operating in Victoria during June 1970 were as follows: Deposits, not bearing interest, $A951m.; deposits, bearing interest, $A995m.; total deposits, $A1,946m.; loans, advances, and bills discounted, $A1,217m. The weekly average of debits to customers' accounts (excluding debits to Commonwealth and State Government accounts at City branches in State capitals) for the same period totalled $A1,540m.

BOOKS OF REFERENCE

STATISTICAL INFORMATION. The Commonwealth Bureau of Census and Statistics (Commonwealth Banks Building, corner of Elizabeth and Flinders Streets, Melbourne, 3000). *Deputy Commonwealth Statistician and Government Statist:* V. H. Arnold, FIA.

Victorian Year Book. (Annually since 1873)
Victorian Pocket Year Book. (Annually since 1956)

Victorian Statistical Register. (Annually from 1854 to 1916)
Quarterly Abstract of Statistics. (Feb. 1947–March 1958)
Victorian Monthly Statistical Review (from Jan. 1960)

Victoria: The First Century. Official History of Victoria. Melbourne, 1934
Leeper, G. W. (ed.), *Introducing Victoria.* Melbourne, 1955
Pratt. A., *The Centenary History of Victoria.* Melbourne, 1934
Saunders, D. (ed.), *Historic Buildings of Victoria.* Melbourne, 1966

STATE LIBRARY. The State Library of Victoria, Swanston St,, Melbourne, 3000. *Chief Librarian:* K. A. R. Horn, BA, Mus.B(NZ), Dip.NZLS.

QUEENSLAND

CONSTITUTION AND GOVERNMENT. Queensland, formerly a portion of New South Wales, was formed into a separate colony in 1859, and responsible government was conferred. The power of making laws and imposing taxes is vested in a Parliament of one House—the Legislative Assembly, which comprises 78 members, returned from 3 electoral zones for 3 years, elected for single-member constituencies at compulsory ballot. Members are entitled to $A7,560 per annum, with individual electorate allowances for travelling, postage, etc., of from $A1,245 to $A2,970.

At the general election of 17 May 1969 there were 945,583 persons registered as qualified to vote under the Elections Acts Amendment Act 1959. This provides for male and female adult franchise, qualified by 6 months' residence in the Commonwealth and 3 months in the electoral district.

The Legislative Assembly, following the elections of 17 May 1969, was composed of the following parties: Country, 26; Liberal, 19; Australian Labor, 31; Democratic Labor, 1; North Queensland Labor, 1; total, 78.

Governor of Queensland: Sir Alan James Mansfield, KCMG, KCVO (appointed Jan. 1966).

The Executive Council of Ministers, from 4 Sept. 1969, consists of the following members:

Premier and Minister for State Development: Johannes Bjelke-Petersen (Country).
Treasurer: Gordon William Wesley Chalk (Liberal).
Mines and Main Roads: Ronald Ernest Camm (Country).
Justice and Attorney-General: Peter Roylance Delamothe (Liberal).
Education and Cultural Activities: Alan Roy Fletcher (Country).
Primary Industries: John Alfred Row (Country).
Health: Seymour Douglas Tooth (Liberal).
Labour and Tourism: John Desmond Herbert (Liberal).
Transport: William Edward Knox (Liberal).
Industrial Development: Frederick Alexander Campbell (Liberal).
Lands: Victor Bruce Sullivan (Country).
Works and Housing: Allen Maxwell Hodges (Country).
Conservation, Marine and Aboriginal Affairs: Neville Thomas Eric Hewitt (Country).
Local Government and Electricity: Wallace Alexander Ramsay Rae (Country).

Each Minister has a salary of $A12,415; the Premier receives $A15,795, the Deputy Premier, $A13,540, and the Leader of the Opposition, $A10,720.

Agent-General in London: Colin H. Curtis (392 Strand, WC2).

LOCAL GOVERNMENT. Provision is made for local government by the subdivision of the State into cities, towns and shires. These are under the management of aldermen or councillors, who are elected by adult suffrage for a 3-year period and are charged with the control of all matters of a parochial nature, such as sanitary and health services, domestic water supplies, and roads and bridges within their allotted areas. Rates are levied on the unimproved capital value of land. Shires for the most part are purely rural districts.

The number and area of these subdivisions, together with the receipts and expenditure (including receipts and expenditure from loans) for the year ended 30 June 1968, were:

	No.	Area in sq. miles	Receipts,[1] $A1,000	Expenditure,[1] $A1,000	Rateable values, $A1,000
City of Brisbane	1	385	98.711	101.657	418,901
Other cities	14	16,329[2]	43,435	42.291	299,359
Towns	5	68	5 949	5.329	16,098
Shires	111	649,196	72,134	68,613	541,242
Total	131	665,978	220,229	217,890	1,275,600

[1] These columns include receipts from loans and loan subsidies of $A56·96m.; expenditures from loans and loan subsidies of $A53·4m.; and the operating receipts and expenditures of business undertakings (principally water supply, electricity and transport) which were $A68·31m. and $A68·9m. respectively.
[2] From 30 May 1968 the shire of Mount Isa (15,917 sq. miles) was raised to the status of a city.

AREA AND POPULATION. Queensland comprises the whole northeastern portion of the Australian continent, including the adjacent islands in the Pacific Ocean and in the Gulf of Carpentaria. Estimated area 667,000 sq. miles (1,727,500 sq. km) with a seaboard of 3,236 miles.

The increase in the population as shown by the censuses since 1901 has been as follows:

	Population at census date			Intercensal increase	
Year	Males	Females	Total	Numerical	Rate per annum (%)
1901	277,003	221,126	498,129	—	—
1911	329,506	276,307	605,813	107,684	1·98
1921	398,969	357,003	755,972	150,159	2·24
1933	497,217	450,317	947,534	191,562	1·86
1947	567,471	538,944	1,106,415	158,881	1·11
1954	676,252	642,007	1,318,259	211,844	2·53
1961	774,579	744,249	1,518,828	200,569	2·04
1966	843,897	819,788	1,663,685	144,857	1·84

Of the total population of 1,663,685 (exclusive of Aborigines) recorded at the census of 30 June 1966, 1,461,829 persons were born in Australia; 7,608 in New Zealand; 106,112 in the British Isles; 68,193 in other parts of Europe; 19,943 elsewhere.

VITAL STATISTICS (including Aborigines) for calendar years:

	Total births	Marriages	Divorces	Deaths
1967	34,692	13,634	1,083	14,736
1968	35,190	14,860	1,140	16,078
1969	36,576	15,669	1,243	15,786

The annual rates per 1,000 population in 1969 were: Marriages, 8·9; births, 20·7; deaths, 8·9. The infant death rate was 18·9 per 1,000 births.

Brisbane, the capital, had on 30 June 1969 a population of 833,400 (Statistical Division). The populations of the other chief towns at the same date were: Townsville, 66,400; Gold Coast, 60,500; Toowoomba, 59,200; Rockhampton, 47,600; Cairns, 27,850; Bundaberg, 27,100; Mackay (including N. Mackay), 26,750; Maryborough, 20,000; Mount Isa, 19,800; Gladstone, 12,500; Gympie, 11,400; Warwick, 10,200.

RELIGION. There is no State Church. Membership, census 1966: Church of England, 522,540; Roman Catholic, 166,558; Catholic (not further defined), 259,111; Presbyterian, 188,492; Methodist, 179,591; Lutheran, 40,237; Baptist, 26,032; Orthodox, 13,896; Congregational, 9,949; other Christian, 66,063; Jews, 1,629; all others (including not stated and no religion), 189,587.

EDUCATION. Education is compulsory between the ages of 6 and 15 years. Education is free in State primary and high schools. The public expenditure on education for 1968–69, net of certain receipts, was $A104·5m. At Aug. 1969 there were 1,145 State primary schools (including 17 native schools administered by the Department of Aboriginal and Island Affairs, 23 special schools and 1 correspondence school), with 7,460 teachers (including sewing mistresses), and enrolment of 210,595 scholars. Secondary education was provided during 1969 by 103 State high schools and 123 secondary departments attached to State primary schools, with 4,060 teachers, the enrolment being 83,591 scholars, and by 8 subsidized grammar schools (4 for boys, 3 for girls, 1 mixed), with 202 teachers and an enrolment of 4,026 secondary and 82 primary pupils. There were, in addition, 334 other, mostly church, schools, with 3,334 teachers and an enrolment of 84,940 children.

In 1969, tertiary level course enrolments at colleges of advanced education and technical colleges were 3,981 full-time and 1,690 part-time. Non-tertiary level course enrolments at these establishments and rural training schools numbered 1,454 full-time and 26,221 part-time, including correspondence and apprenticeship students. The Queensland University (established in 1911, in Brisbane) had, at July 1969, 160 professors, associate professors and readers; 495 senior lecturers and lecturers; 273 assistant lecturers, demonstrators, tutors and teaching fellows. There were 15,773 students (including 854 at Townsville University College). There are 6 denominational and 3 undenominational residential colleges attached to the university, and a hall of residence and 5 affiliated colleges at Townsville.

JUSTICE. Justice is administered by a Supreme Court, district courts, magistrates' courts and children's courts. The Supreme Court comprises a Chief Justice, a senior puisne judge and 11 puisne judges; the district court, 12 district court judges. Stipendiary magistrates preside over the lower courts, except in the smaller centres, where justices of the peace officiate. A parole board may recommend prisoners for release.

The total number of persons convicted of serious offences by the superior courts in 1968–69 was 1,610; the summary convictions in lower courts (including cases of bail estreated) numbered 90,620. There were, at 30 June 1969, 4 prisons, 2 gaols for short-term prisoners and 2 prison farms conducted on the honour system, with 1,095 male and 39 female prisoners. The total police force, including 22 women police and 11 native trackers, was 3,190 at 30 June 1969.

SOCIAL WELFARE. Public hospitals are maintained by State and Commonwealth Government endowment, supplemented by fees from patients not in public wards. Medical and hospital benefit schemes, subsidized by the Commonwealth Government, are operated by approved organizations to provide voluntary insurance against medical and hospital expenses. Welfare institutions for aged people, and for orphans and the blind, deaf and dumb, and homes for other handicapped persons are also maintained or assisted by the State. A maternal and child welfare service is provided throughout the State. Age, invalid, widows' and war pensions, maternity allowances, child endowment, and unemployment and sickness benefits are paid by the Commonwealth. Age pensioners in the State at 30 June 1969 numbered 110,989; invalid pensioners, 21,370; war pensioners, 91,541 (including dependants). Maternity allowance was paid to 35,790 mothers during 1968–69.

There were 12,030 widows' pensions current at 30 June 1969, and at the same date child endowment was being paid to 240,099 families in respect of 553,216 children under 16 years. In addition, 16,923 families received endowment for 18,456 student children aged 16–21.

HOUSING. In 1969–70, 17,189 new dwellings (including 2,436 flats) were completed and 4,234 were being built at 30 June 1970. The Queensland Housing Commission, financed by State and Commonwealth loans, builds dwellings for sale and for rental (in 1969–70, 1,652 houses). Building and co-operative housing societies are assisted by State and Commonwealth loans.

FINANCE. Revenue and expenditure of the Consolidated Revenue Fund of Queensland during 5 years ending 30 June (in $A1,000):

	1966–67	1967–68	1968–69	1969–70	1970–71[1]
Revenue	323,781	376,987	387,866	441,074	486,958
Expenditure	323,523	376,017	388,777	444,618	489,445

[1] Estimate.

Net government receipts of consolidated revenue and trust funds, excluding as far as possible transfers between funds, in 1968–69 were $A698·5m., including: Taxation (including Commonwealth reimbursement), $A253·3m.; railways, $A98·7m.; Commonwealth grants, $A81·9m. Net expenditure from these funds was $A694m., including: Development and maintenance of State resources, $A218·5m.; education, $A 100·2m.; railways, $A93·6m.; public debt charges, $A86m.; health, $A68·3m.; law and order, $A31·8m.; general administration, $A23·8m. Loan expenditure amounted to $A92·4m.

Revenue and expenditure of Commonwealth departments on account of Queensland are not included.

The gross public debt of the State amounted, on 30 June 1969, to $A1,148·82m. The debt was domiciled as follows (in $A1,000): Australia, 1,090,887; UK, 45,250; USA, 7,105; Switzerland, 1,305; Canada, 668; Netherlands, 609; other European countries, 2,996. The annual interest charge on the public debt at 30 June 1969 was $A55·38m.

LAND SETTLEMENT. Of the total area of the State, 26,949,000 acres had been alienated at 31 Dec. 1969; in process of alienation, under deferred payment system, were 25·99m. acres, leaving 373·94m. acres still the property of the Crown, or 87·6% of the total area. A large proportion of the area is leased for pastoral purposes (243·4m. acres at 31 Dec. 1969), besides 78·6m. acres in grazing selections and 13·3m. acres under occupation licence. Perpetual leases amounted to 5,495,000 acres.

In the western portion of the State water is comparatively easily found by sinking artesian bores. At 30 June 1969, 3,117 such bores had been drilled, of which 2,079 were flowing.

RURAL INDUSTRIES. Livestock on farms and stations at 31 March 1970 numbered 172,768 horses, 7,514,917 cattle, 16,445,833 sheep and 479,586 pigs. The wool production (greasy) was, in 1968–69, 247,005,000 lb., valued at $A108·06m. The total area under crops during 1968–69 was 5,404,487 acres. 401,448 acres were irrigated in 1968–69, the principal crops so watered being sugar-cane, fodder crops, vegetables, cereals, tobacco, cotton and fruit.

	Acres		Yield[1]	
Crop	1967–68	1968–69	1967–68	1968–69
Sugar-cane, crushed	530,828	546,306	15,717,789 tons	17,414,966 tons
Wheat	1,476,589	1,788,583	27,416,757 bushels	41,999,539 bushels
Maize	147,732	120,200	4,777,848 „	3,670,047 „
Sorghum	382,192	436,479	8,938,816 „	11,800,389 „
Barley	342,468	426,953	8,964,544 „	12,869,310 „
Oats	30,772	55,042	450,086 bushels	1,119,084 bushels
Potatoes	17,348	18,516	106,429 tons	122,990 tons
Pumpkins[3]	11,962	12,810	38,158 „	41,728 „
Tomatoes	5,757	5,903	1,219,495 bushels	1,324,172 bushels
Peanuts	61,373	78,454	67,447,221 lb.	37,266,918 lb.
Cotton (raw)	11,629	12,140	6,684,876 „	8,343,840 „
Tobacco	12,472	13,837	15,021,456 „	19,516,744 „
Apples[3]	9,735	10,587	1,070,950 bushels	2,042,736 bushels
Grapes[3]	3,071	3,178	11,658,067 lb.	13,858,090 lb.
Citrus[3]	4,958	5,487	1,394,216 bushels	1,427,564 bushels
Bananas[3]	4,711	4,798	883,236 „	992,862 „
Pineapples[3]	10,267	10,567	6,767,309 „	6,323,661 „
Green fodder	1,336,857	1,405,622	..	..
Hay (all kinds)	111,226	105,572	283,776 tons	260,200 tons

[1] Tons = long tons of 2.240 lb.   [2] For human consumption only.   [3] Bearing area only.

Total value of all crops, 1968–69, $A363,704,000; 1967–68, $A308,922,000.

FORESTRY. A considerable area consists of natural forest, eucalyptus, pine and cabinet woods being the timbers mostly in evidence; a large quantity of ornamental woods are utilized by cabinet makers. The amount of native timber sawn in 1967–68 was (in 1,000 sup. ft): Softwoods, 58,544; hardwoods, brushwoods and scrubwoods, 135,044; total value, $A29,152,118. The plywood industry is important; 93,185,000 sq. ft of plywood were produced, the value being set down at $A8,877,379. In addition, 387·58m. sq. ft of veneers was produced, of which 212·94m. sq. ft, valued at $A3,868,164, was for sale; the rest was used locally to produce plywood, etc. Most of the veneer came from cabinet woods of the north. Forest and timber reservations total 9,013,000 acres (30 June 1969); areas for national parks, 2,369,000 acres. The State Forest Service had planted 150,700 acres for reforestation and had treated 847,200 acres for natural regeneration by June 1969. Thinnings from State reforestation areas are used for hardboard and paper pulp.

MINING. Principal minerals produced during 1968 were: Copper, 68,871 long tons; coal, 6,551,799 long tons; lead, 115,959 long tons; zinc, 84,062 long tons; silver, 9,603,000 oz.; tin, 1,230 long tons; gold, 82,854 fine oz.; bauxite, 3,256,995 long tons; mineral sands concentrates, 191,379 long tons. The 743 mines employed 11,060 workers and had a value of output, at the mine, of $A185,755,000. The chief mines are Mount Isa (copper, lead, zinc, silver), Weipa (bauxite), Mount Morgan (copper, gold), Moreton, Callide, Moura and Blackwater (coal).

Oil was discovered at Moonie in southern Queensland in 1961. A pipeline has been laid from Moonie to Brisbane, where refineries are operating. Large natural gas reserves have been proved in southern and central Queensland and a pipeline has been laid from Roma to Brisbane. Natural gas was first supplied to consumers in March 1969.

INDUSTRY. Approximately one-third of the secondary production of the State is from works processing primary products, the most important being sugar-mills, meat works, butter factories and saw-mills. There are 31 cane-crushing mills, 2 oil refineries, 1 alumina refinery, 2 sugar refineries, 45 meat works (including bacon factories) producing largely for export, 43 butter factories and many saw-mills and plywood and veneer mills. Other industries include engineering works, railway workshops, shipbuilding, copper and oil refining, rubber, cement, woollen mills, cardboard and building board manufacture, ammonia and fertilizer works and the production of various items of food, clothing and vehicles, chiefly for local use. In 1967–68 there were 6,099 factories, employing 98,027 males and 22,825 females, and making goods worth $A1,722·25m. The value of production (value added in manufacture) was $A626·7m. In addition, there were 43 electricity stations and 12 gasworks.

The gross value of Queensland primary production (in $A1,000) during 1968–69 amounted to 1,023,788, which included agriculture, 363,704; dairying and pigraising, 64,267; pastoral, 340,021; poultry and bee-keeping, 23,822; mining, 203,933; forestry, 18,411; fisheries, 8,089; trapping, 1,542. Manufacturing, including production of light, heat and power, was $A657,853,000 (net value) in 1967–68.

ELECTRICITY. The State Electricity Commission, established in 1938 and under a single Commissioner since 1948, co-ordinates the electricity industry in Queensland. In 1967–68, 14 generating stations were operated by local authorities, 16 by regional boards, 7 by the Southern and 5 by the Northern Electric Authority of Queensland and 1 by a private concern. Electricity generated by the principal stations in the year ended 30 June 1968 was 4,920m. kwh; estimate for 1968–69, 5,402m. kwh. Natural gas is being used for electric generation at Roma. Black coal was used to generate 86% of the power; hydro-electric stations generated 14%.

LABOUR. Industrial wages and conditions are controlled partly by Commonwealth and partly by State authorities. A State Industrial Commission is empowered to determine all industrial matters in relation to employers and employees, and to fix minimum wage-rates and other conditions of employment. An Industrial Court hears appeals and decides points of industrial law. The Commonwealth Industrial Court and Conciliation and Arbitration Commission are superior within their jurisdictions. In Queensland most employees (66%) work under State awards; 23% under Commonwealth awards.

Rates of wages for each occupation are prescribed by these courts. The minimum weighted average award wage for adult males was $A52.18 and for adult females $A37.94, at 30 June 1970, while average weekly earnings (including overtime, etc.) were $A70.70 per employed male unit. (Average earnings are calculated on a unit basis, as earnings are not available separately for males and females.) A standard working week of 40 hours is prescribed for most awards.

Unions both of employees and employers must be registered with the State or Commonwealth Commission. There were 76 employees' and 36 employers' unions registered with the State Commission at 31 Dec. 1969, the former comprising 286,964 and the latter 40,402 members.

COMMERCE. The overseas commerce of Queensland is included in the statement of the commerce of the Commonwealth of Australia (*see* pp. 245–46).

Total value of the direct overseas imports and exports of Queensland (in £A1,000 until 1964–65 and $A1,000 from 1965–66 f.o.b. port of shipment for both imports and exports):

	1964–65	1965–66	1966–67	1967–68	1968–69	1969–70[1]
Imports	99,758	201,483	193,677	227,022	288,600	297,051
Exports	244,111	462,597	499,968	562,938	677,459	773,521

[1] Preliminary.

In 1968–69 interstate exports totalled $A495·5m. and imports $A859·02m. The chief exports overseas are minerals, meat (preserved or frozen), sugar, wool, wheat, hides and skins. Principal imports are machinery, crude petroleum, chemicals, motor vehicles, textiles, paper and paper board, and iron and steel.

Chief sources of imports in 1968–69 were USA ($A91·56m.), UK ($A45·7m.), Japan ($A37·41m.); exports went chiefly to USA ($A183·98m.), Japan ($A180·47m.), UK ($A111·25m.)

RAILWAYS. Practically all the railways are owned by the State Government. Total mileage was 5,824 at 30 June 1969. In 1968–69, 28,165,000 passengers and 12·98m. tons of goods and livestock were carried.

ROADS. At 30 June 1969 there were 118.891 miles of road; of these, 78,736 miles were formed roads, of which 37,875 miles were surfaced with concrete, bitumen or macadam.

At 30 June 1970 motor vehicles registered in Queensland totalled 688,675, comprising 501,709 cars and station wagons, 100,891 vans, 3,373 buses, 62,669 trucks and 20,033 motor cycles.

SHIPPING. In 1968–69, 3,226 vessels totalling 16·6m. net tons entered Queensland ports. Cargo discharged was 4·14m. tons and cargo shipped was 12·36m. tons.

AVIATION. Queensland is well served with a network of air services, with overseas and interstate connexions. Subsidiary companies provide planes for taxi and charter work, and the Flying Doctor Service operates throughout western Queensland.

BROADCASTING. At 30 June 1970, 43 broadcasting and 18 television stations were in operation throughout Queensland. Listeners' licences totalled 384,591 and viewers' licences, 372,610.

BANKING. There were 10 trading banks operating in Queensland at 30 June 1969, including the Commonwealth Trading Bank of Australia, the 7 larger Australian trading banks, a Queensland bank with head office in Brisbane and the Banque Nationale de Paris. The Commonwealth Trading Bank had 110 branches and 63 agencies; the private banks had 599 branches and 209 agencies in the State. Queensland deposits of all banks, including the Commonwealth Trading Bank of Australia, amounted to $A871·81m.; and loans, advances and bills discounted in Queensland were $A534·28m. At 30 June 1969 savings bank business was conducted in Queensland by 8 banks, the Commonwealth Savings bank with 153 branches and 1,549 agencies, and 7 private banks with 597 branches and 1,035 agencies. Depositors' balances amounted to $A819m. in 1,906,503 accounts.

BOOKS OF REFERENCE

STATISTICAL INFORMATION. The Statistical Office (320–330 Adelaide St., Brisbane) was set up in 1859. Deputy Commonwealth Statistician: A. W. Mumme. A Queensland Official Year Book was issued in 1901, the annual ABC of Queensland Statistics from 1905 to 1936 with exception of 1918 and 1922. Present publications include: Queensland Year Book. Annual, from 1937 (omitting 1942, 1943, 1944).—Queensland Pocket Year Book. Annual, from 1950.—Statistics of Queensland. Annual, from 1859.—Monthly Summary of Queensland Statistics. From Jan. 1961

Australian and New Zealand Association for the Advancement of Science, Introducing Queensland. Brisbane, 1961
Queensland Department of Agriculture and Stock, The Queensland Agricultural and Pastoral Handbook. 2 vols. Brisbane, 1962
Australian Sugar Year Book. Brisbane, from 1941
Bolton, G. C., A thousand miles away! a history of North Queensland to 1920. Brisbane, 1963
Cilento, R., and Lack, C., Triumph in the Tropics. Brisbane, 1959
Greenwood, G., and Laverty, J., Brisbane 1859–1959. Sydney, 1959
Greenwood, R. H., Queensland, City, Coast and Country. London, 1959
Lack, C., Queensland, Daughter of the Sun. Brisbane, 1959.—Three Decades of Queensland Political History. Brisbane, 1962

STATE LIBRARY. The Public Library of Queensland, William St., Brisbane. State Librarian: J. L. Stapleton.

SOUTH AUSTRALIA

CONSTITUTION AND GOVERNMENT. South Australia was formed into a British province by letters patent of Feb. 1836, and a partially elective Legislative Council was established in 1851. The present constitution bears date 24 Oct. 1856. It vests the legislative power in an elected Parliament, consisting of a Legislative Council and a House of Assembly. The former is composed of 20 members. Every 3 years half the members retire, and their places are supplied by members elected from each of the 5 districts into which the State is divided for this purpose. The qualifications of an elector are, to be a resident of the State, a natural born or naturalized British subject and 21 years of age, and (for the Legislative Council) certain property or war service qualifications. By the Constitution Act Amendment Act, 1894, the franchise was extended to women, who voted for the first time at the general election of 25 April 1896. The qualifications for election as a member of the House of Assembly are the same as for an elector, but a candidate for the Legislative Council must have attained the age of 30 and be a resident in the State for 3 years. Judges and ministers of religion are ineligible for election to either House.

The House of Assembly consists of 47 members elected for 3 years, representing single electorates. Election of members of both Houses takes place by preferential secret ballot. Voting for the House of Assembly is compulsory.

The House of Assembly, elected on 30 May 1970, consists of the following members: Australian Labor Party, 27; Liberal and Country League, 20; The Legislative Council consists of 16 Liberal and Country League and 4 Labor members.

Each member of Parliament receives $A7,500 per annum with allowances of $A1,400–2,200 depending on distance, a free pass over government railways and superannuation rights. Electors enrolled (May 1970) numbered 635,533 for the House of Assembly and 261,565 for the Legislative Council.

The executive power is vested in a Governor appointed by the Crown and an Executive Council, consisting of the Governor and the Ministers of the Crown. The Governor has the power to dissolve the House of Assembly but not the Legislative Council unless that Chamber has twice consecutively with an election intervening defeated the same or substantially the same Bill passed in the House of Assembly by an absolute majority.

Governor: Maj.-Gen. Sir James Harrison, KCMG, CB, CBE (sworn in 4 Dec. 1968).

The Australian Labor Party Ministry, announced 2 June 1970 is as follows:

Premier, Treasurer, Minister of Development and Mines: Donald Allan Dunstan, QC, MP. *Deputy Premier, Minister of Works and Marine:* James Desmond Corcoran, MP. *Chief Secretary and Minister of Health:* Albert James Shard, MLC. *Minister of Education:* Hugh Richard Hudson, MP. *Attorney-General, Minister of Social Welfare and Aboriginal Affairs:* Leonard James King, QC, MP. *Minister of Roads, Transport and Local Government:* Geoffrey Thomas Virgo, MP. *Minister of Agriculture and Forests:* Thomas Mannix Casey, MLC. *Minister of Conservation and Minister Assisting the Premier:* Glenn Raymond Broomhill, MP. *Minister of Labour and Industry:* David Hugh Mckee, MP. *Minister of Lands, Repatriation and Irrigation:* Alfred Francis Kneebone, MLC.

The provision for the payment of Ministers is $A113,100. They are jointly and individually responsible to the legislature for all their official acts, as in the UK.

Agent-General in London: R. C. Taylor (50 Strand, WC2).

LOCAL GOVERNMENT. The closely settled part of the State (mainly near the sea-coast and the river Murray) is incorporated into local government areas, and subdivided into district councils (rural areas only), municipal corporations (mainly metropolitan, but including larger country towns) and cities (more densely populated areas with a qualification of 15,000 residents in the metropolitan area, and 10,000 in the country). The main functions of councils are the construction and maintenance of roads and bridges, and the administration of the Health and Building Acts.

The number and area of the subdivisions, together with revenue expenditure and rateable values (in $A1,000) for the year ended 30 June 1968, were:

	No.	Area (sq. miles)	Roads and bridges	Health and recreation	All other	Assessed values
City of Adelaide	1	6	1,316	981	2,196	18,348
Remainder of Adelaide statistical division	30	890	8,813	3,613	6,807	98,564
Other municipal corporations and district councils	111	56,960	11,384	1,788	5,435	56,798
Total	142	57,856	21,513	6,382	14,438	173,711

The improved capital value of all property in local government areas is approximately 20 times the above assessed values.

AREA AND POPULATION. The total area of South Australia is 380,070 sq. miles (984,300 sq. km). The settled part is divided into counties and hundreds. There are 49 counties proclaimed, covering 56m. acres, of which 48·2m. acres are occupied. Outside this area there are extensive pastoral districts, covering 187m. acres, 115m. of which are under pastoral leases.

Census population (exclusive of aboriginals):

	Population				Population		
	Males	Females	Total		Males	Females	Total
1891	161,920	153,292	315,212	1933	290,962	289,987	580,949
1901	180,485	177,861	358,346	1947	320,031	326,042	646,073
1911	207,358	201,200	408,558	1961	490,225	479,115	969,340
1921	248,267	246,893	495,160	1966	548,530	543,345	1,091,875

Population, 31 Dec. 1969, 1,155,300; population of the city of Adelaide and suburbs, 757,900.

The number of Aboriginals (persons of 50% or more of Aboriginal blood) in the State at the census of 30 June 1966 was 5,505; the nomadic proportion is decreasing.

VITAL STATISTICS for calendar years:

	Births	Marriages	Divorces	Deaths
1967	20,386	9,434	929	9,071
1968	21,207	9,652	915	9,916
1969	21,977	10,599	963	9,337

The infant mortality rate in 1969 was 15·78 per 1,000 live births.

RELIGION. No state aid is given for religious purposes.

At the census of 1966 the religious distribution of the population was as follows: Church of England, 286,154; Methodist, 227,483; Roman Catholic and Catholic (so described), 220,576; Lutheran, 59,281; Presbyterian, 42,687; other Christians, 131,760; non-Christian, 2,340; indefinite, 3,501; no religion, 8,372; no reply, 109,721.

EDUCATION. Education is secular and is compulsory to the age of 15. Primary, secondary and technical education at government schools is free. In 1968 there were 688 government schools, comprising 519 primary, 55 predominantly primary (with some secondary pupils), 59 high, 30 technical high and 25 part-time and technical education centres. There were 226,811 full-time and 46,962 part-time pupils. There are an Institute of Technology; an agricultural college; 5 training colleges for teachers; and 2 universities which are substantially subsidized by the Government. Most of the 171 private schools and colleges are associated with religious denominations (36,413 pupils). There are also 125 free kindergartens.

JUSTICE. There is a Supreme Court, a court of vice-admiralty and over 100 local courts and courts of summary jurisdiction. Circuit courts are held at several places. Bankruptcy jurisdiction is administered by the State Court of Insolvency at Adelaide which is invested with jurisdiction by the Federal Bankruptcy Act. During 1969 there were 659 sequestrations and schemes under the Bankruptcy Act; 712 convictions for felonies and misdemeanours in the higher courts and 105,966 in the magistrates' courts. The total number of persons in gaols on 30 June 1969 was 884.

SOCIAL WELFARE. Age, Invalidity, War, etc., Pensions are paid by the Commonwealth Government. The number of pensioners in South Australia at 30 June 1969 was: War and service, 62,968; age, 66,331; invalid, 10,285. There are schemes for maternity allowances, childhood endowment, widows, unemployment and sickness and hospital and pharmaceutical benefits. The total amount paid during 1968–69 was $A126,581,000.

LABOUR. Two systems of industrial arbitration and conciliation for the adjustment of industrial relations between employers and employees are in operation—the State system, which operates when industrial disputes are confined to the territorial limits of the State, and the Commonwealth system, which applies when disputes involve other parts of the Commonwealth as well as South Australia.

The industrial tribunals are authorized to fix minimum rates of wages and other conditions of employment, and their awards may be enforced by law. Industrial agreements between employers and organizations of employees, when registered, may be enforced in the same manner as awards.

State industrial legislation was substantially changed by the Industrial Code Amendment Act, 1966. The Industrial Code now provides for an Industrial Court, consisting of a President with power to deal only with matters of law, an Industrial Commission and a number of conciliation committees.

The Industrial Commission consists of the President of the Industrial Court and 2 commissioners appointed by the Governor, one associated with the interests of employers, the other with trade union affairs. The Commission is constituted by the President and the 2 commissioners (Full Bench) or by any one of them, and has power to deal with any industrial matter outside the jurisdiction of the conciliation committees.

Conciliation Committees consist of an equal number of employer and employee representatives with one of the commissioners as chairman, and are set up on the recommendation of the Commission. They have power to make awards determining any industrial matter in respect of the industry or industries for which they have been formed. Important matters in dispute before these Committees can be dealt with by the Full Bench of the Commission. The code also includes provision for appeals against any decision by a Commissioner or conciliation committee, such appeals being heard by the commission constituted by the President, the Commissioner not involved in the matter and the Industrial Registrar.

The Full Bench of the Industrial Commission has power to declare the 'living wage' to be paid to adult male and female employees.

The first declaration of the 'living wage' ('a sum sufficient for the normal and reasonable needs of the average employee') by the then Board of Industry, on 15 July 1921, fixed the wage at $A7.95. The present living wage (last adjusted in Jan. 1971) is $A37.85 per week.

The Industrial Code was amended in 1950 to provide that the Governor may by proclamation fix the living wage, if the Minister of Industry is satisfied that the proclamation is desirable in order to avoid unjustifiable differences between the Commonwealth basic wage and the State living wage and the President of the Court recommends it. The living wages since 1950 have been fixed by proclamation.

FINANCE. Revenue and expenditure (in $A1,000) for years ended 30 June:

	1965	1966	1967	1968	1969	1970	1971[1]
Revenue	220,182	236,816	258,823	274,544	298,355	38,498	371,864
Expenditure	224,802	243,650	258,717	277,404	297,895	35,578	376,760

[1] Estimates.

The public debt of the State amounted, on 30 June 1970, to $A1,210,489,000, representing $A1,039 per head of the population.

AGRICULTURE. Of the total area of South Australia (243,244,800 acres), 17m. acres were alienated or in process of alienation under systems of deferred payments, 77m. acres were unoccupied, 150m. acres were held under lease; 14m. acres were under cultivation, on 31 Dec. 1969.

Soil Conservation. Under the direction of special officers in the Department of Agriculture, determined efforts are made to deal with the problems of erosion and soil conservation. Included in the programme are the planting of cereal rye, perennial rye and other grasses to check sand drifts; contour-furrowing and contour banking; contour planting with vines and fruit trees and several water-diversion schemes.

Irrigation. In 1968–69, 112,494 acres were under irrigated culture, being used as follows: Vineyards, 31,108; orchards, 32,570; vegetables, 14,414; green forage, 6,412, and other crops, 27,990. These figures are exclusive of 61,417 acres of irrigated pasture land. Most of these areas are along the river Murray.

Gross value of production (in $A1,000), 1968–69: Crops, 220,464; pastoral, 36,070; dairying, 39,016; fisheries and game, poultry, forestry, bees, 29,861. Total gross value, 425,411; local value (i.e., less marketing costs), 385,169; net value (i.e., less materials used), 308,776.

Chief crops	1967–68		1968–69	
	Acres	Quantities	Acres	Quantities
Wheat	2,864,200	26,898,900 bu.	3,748,400	83,160,500 bu.
Barley	1,156,600	12,379,500 ,,	1,412,300	9,550,700 ,,
Oats	524,900	3,298,905 ,,	515,600	11,895,500 ,,
Hay	429,000	418,046 tons	614,800	985,184 tons
Vines	..	30,055,000 galls.[1]	..	36,230,000 galls.[1]

[1] Of wine.

Fruit culture is extensively carried on, and in 1968–69, 146,267 cwt of dried fruit and 8m. bushels of fresh fruit were produced. Other products, in addition to all kinds of root crops and vegetables, are grass seeds, eucalyptus oil, olive oil and chicory. Livestock, March 1970: 1,026,000 cattle, 19,747,000 sheep and 351,000 pigs. In 1968–69, 233·1m. lb. of wool and 103m. gallons of milk were produced.

MINING. The value of minerals produced in 1969 was $A98,526,000. The principal minerals produced are iron, pyrite, gypsum, salt, opals, talc, clays, limestone, dolomite and sub-bituminous coal.

INDUSTRY. Dissection of 1967–68 statistics according to the main classes of industry is given in the folowing table:

Classification	Establishments (No.)	Persons employed (No.)	Salaries and wages paid ($A1,000)	Value of output ($A1,000)	Value of production[1] ($A1,000)
Industrial metals, machines, etc.	3,294	72,643	209,538	838,189	359,761
Textiles and textile goods	64	2,829	6,444	23,392	10,911
Clothing	511	5,162	8,564	25,629	15,160
Food, drink, tobacco	697	12,264	29,242	202,549	67,904
Saw-milling, joinery, etc.	442	5,546	12,794	50,895	23,126
Paper, printing	202	5,724	15,440	61,523	32,818
Chemicals, dyes, paints	109	3,253	10,039	106,828	38,710
All factories	6,255	121,417	330,060	1,475,328	631,104

[1] I.e., value added to materials by treatment.

Machinery, land, buildings, etc., were valued at $A813·1m. in 1968. Practically all forms of secondary industry are to be found, the most important being smelting, motor-body building, shipbuilding, saw-milling and the manufacture of household appliances, agricultural machinery, industrial chemicals and chemical fertilizers.

The marked increase in secondary industries in the State is indicated by the increase of factory workers from 43,371 in 1939 to 121,417 in 1968.

COMMERCE. The commerce of South Australia, exclusive of inter-state trade, is comprised in the statement of the commerce of Australia given under the heading of the Commonwealth, see pp. 245–46.

Overseas imports and exports in $A1,000 (year ending 30 June):

	1964–65	1965–66	1966–67	1967–68	1968–69	1969–70
Imports	204,856	198,156	196,771	215,619	231,956	201,223
Exports	302,242	296,276	325,170	282,767	300,934	417,030

Principal exports in 1969–70 were (in $A,1,000): Wool, 81,797 (208m. lb.); lead, 44,961; wheat, 55,944 (41·3m. bu.); barley, 6,133 (9·6m. bu.); concentrates and ores, 65,038; skins and hides, 8,337; meats, 16,538; machinery and transport equipment, 34,748; fruit (fresh and dried), 3,892; flour, 3,519; wine, 1,866.

Principal imports in 1969–70 were (in $A1,000): Machinery, non-electric, 37,728; transport equipment, 34,473; electrical machinery and appliances, 15,578; textile yarn and fabrics, 10,910; wood, timber and cork, 7,389; iron and steel, 15,133; petrol and products, 21,285; crude fertilizers and crude minerals, 6,681; non-metallic mineral manufactures, 5,808.

In 1969–70 the leading suppliers of imports were (in $A1m.), USA (43·27) UK (43·25), Japan (21·67), Saudi Arabia (19·03); main exports went to Japan (79·31), UK (71·01), USA (39·25), China, mainland (35·03), New Zealand (13·68).

RAILWAYS. There were (1969) 3,831 miles of railway, including the South Australian portion of the Transcontinental Railway from Port Pirie in South Australia to Kalgoorlie in Western Australia, which, in connexion with various State lines, completes a through rail connexion between Brisbane on the north-east coast and Fremantle on the west coast. It also includes the South Australian portion of the Commonwealth Railway from Whyalla to the Northern Territory and private railways from Knob to Port Augusta and Coffin Bay to Port Lincoln. In the year ending 30 June 1969 the State-controlled sections carried 14,423,386 passengers and 5m. tons of freight.

ROADS. At 30 June 1970 there were 8,156 miles of proclaimed main roads and 67,135 miles of district roads, totalling 75,291 miles. Lengths of road classified by surface were as follows: Bitumen or concrete, 9,484 miles; gravel or crushed stone, 18,703 miles; formed only, 7,637 miles; unformed, 39,467 miles. Costs of construction and maintenance are shared by the State and federal governments and by the councils of the local areas. Motor vehicles registered at 30 June 1970 include 368,554 cars, 88,440 commercial vehicles and 13,971 cycles.

SHIPPING. There are several good harbours, of which Port Adelaide is the principal one. In 1968–69, 1,371 vessels (exceeding 200 net tons) of 7,981,421 tons entered South Australian ports direct from interstate or overseas.

AVIATION. For the year ended 30 June 1969 there were 937,016 passengers and 15,449 short tons of freight at Adelaide, South Australia's principal airport. On 30 June 1969 there were 9 government and 20 licensed aerodromes, and 16 scheduled services in South Australia.

POST. Postal, telephone and telegraph facilities are afforded at 897 offices. Telephone services connected totalled 239,452 on 30 June 1970; on 30 June 1969 there were 16 wireless and 8 television stations; 302,519 wireless listeners' and 292,359 televiewers' licences were current (both include combined licences).

BANKING. There were 8 trading banks at 30 June 1970, including the Commonwealth and State Government Banks. In June quarter, 1970, their average deposits were $A437,436,000 and average advances $A385,307,000.

The 8 savings banks on 30 June 1970 had deposits amounting to $A733·10m. or $A629 per head of population.

BOOKS OF REFERENCE

STATISTICAL INFORMATION. The State branch of the Commonwealth Bureau of Census and Statistics is in Prudential Building, 195 North Terrace, Adelaide (GPO Box 1433J). *Deputy Commonwealth Statistician:* D. L. J. Aitchison. Although the first printed statistical publication was the *Statistics of South Australia, 1854* with the title altered to *Statistical Register* in 1859, there is a written volume for each year back to 1838. These contain simple records of trade, demography, production, etc. and were prepared only for the use of the Colonial office; one copy was retained in the State.

The publications of the State branch include the *South Australian Year Book*, the *Pocket Year Book of South Australia* and the *Statistical Register* (annual), a printed *Quarterly Abstract* and a duplicated *Monthly Summary of Statistics*, a duplicated quarterly bulletin of building constructions, duplicated quarterly bulletins of trade statistics and approximately 20 special duplicated bulletins issued each year as particulars of various sections of statistics become available.

Best, R. J. (ed.), *Introducing South Australia.* Cambridge, 1959
Centenary History of South Australia. Royal Geographical Society of Australasia. Adelaide, 1936
Finlayson, H. H., *The Red Centre: Man and Beast in the Heart of Australia.* 2nd ed. Sydney, 1952
Madigan, C. T.. *Central Australia.* 2nd ed. Melbourne, 1944

STATE LIBRARY. The State Library of S.A., North Terrace, Adelaide. *State Librarian:* R. K. Olding, B. Ec., F.L.A.A.

WESTERN AUSTRALIA

HISTORY. In 1791 Vancouver, in the *Discovery*, took formal possession of the country about King George Sound. In 1826 the Government of New South Wales sent 20 convicts and a detachment of soldiers to King George Sound and formed a settlement then called Frederickstown. In 1827 Captain (afterwards Sir) James Stirling surveyed the coast from King George Sound to the Swan River, and in May 1829 Captain (afterwards Sir) Charles Fremantle took possession of the territory. In June 1829 Captain Stirling, newly appointed Lieut.-Governor, founded the colony now known as the State of Western Australia. On 1 Jan. 1901 Western Australia became one of the 6 federated States within the Commonwealth of Australia.

CONSTITUTION AND GOVERNMENT. In 1870 partially representative government was instituted, and in 1890 the administration was vested in the Governor, a Legislative Council and a Legislative Assembly. The Legislative Council was, in the first instance, nominated by the Governor, but it was provided that in the event of the population of the colony reaching 60,000, it should be elective. In 1893 this limit of population being reached, the Colonial Parliament amended the constitution accordingly.

The Legislative Council consists of 30 members, 2 members representing each of the 15 electoral provinces. Each member is elected for a term of 6 years, one-half of the members retiring every 3 years.

There are 51 members of the Legislative Assembly, each member representing one of the 51 electoral districts of the State. Members are elected for the duration of the Parliament, normally 3 years. The qualifications applying to candidates and electors are identical for the Legislative Council and the Legislative Assembly. A candidate must have resided in Western Australia for a minimum of 12 months, be at least 21 years of age and free from legal incapacity, be a British subject, and be enrolled, or qualified for enrolment, as an elector. A judge of the Supreme Court, the Sheriff of Western Australia, a minister of religion, an undischarged bankrupt or a debtor against whose estate there is a subsisting order in bankruptcy may not be elected to Parliament. No person may hold office as a member of the Legislative Assembly and the Legislative Council at the same time. An elector must be at least 18 years of age, be a British subject free from legal incapacity, must have resided in the Commonwealth of Australia for 6 and in Western Australia for 3 months continuously and in the electoral district for which he claims enrolment for a continuous period of 1 month immediately preceding the date of his claim. Enrolment is compulsory for all qualified persons except Aboriginal natives of Australia, who are entitled but not required to enrol. Voting at elections is on the preferential system and is compulsory for all enrolled persons.

Ordinary members of the legislature are paid a salary of $A7,500 a year, with additional allowances, ranging from $A1,600 to $A3,300 according to location of electorate. Members are entitled to free travel on Western Australian government railways and, by arrangement, once every year on government railways in other States. All members of Parliament contribute to superannuation benefits.

The Premier receives a salary, including electorate allowance, of $A18,700 the Deputy Premier $A15,400, the Leader of the Government in the Legislative Council $A14,800, and all other Ministers $A13,400–14,500 according to location of electorate.

The Legislative Assembly, elected on 23 March 1968, is composed as follows: Australian Labor Party, 23; Liberal Party, 19; Country Party, 9. The Legislative Council, one-half of which was elected on the same day, is composed of 10 Australian Labor Party, 12 Liberal Party, 8 Country Party.

Governor: Maj.-Gen. Sir Douglas Kendrew, KCMG, CB, CBE, DSO (sworn in 25 Oct. 1963).

The Liberal–Country Party Cabinet was, in Sept. 1970, constituted as follows:

Premier, Treasurer and Minister for Tourists: Sir David Brand, KCMG, MLA
Deputy Premier, Minister for Agriculture and Electricity: Crawford David Nalder, MLA.
Industrial Development and the North-West: Charles Walter Michael Court, OBE, MLA.
Education and Native Welfare: Edgar Henry Mead Lewis, MLA.
Mines and Justice and Leader of the Government in the Legislative Council: Arthur Frederick Griffith, MLC.
Lands, Forests and Immigration: William Stewart Bovell, MLA.
Works and Water Supplies: Ross Hutchison, DFC, MLA.
Local Government, Town Planning and Child Welfare: Leslie Arthur Logan, MLC.
Chief Secretary and Minister for Police and Traffic: James Frederick Craig, MLA.
Housing and Labour: Desmond Henry O'Neil, MLA.
Transport and Railways: Raymond James O'Connor, MLA.
Health and Fisheries and Fauna: Graham Charles MacKinnon, MLC.

Agent-General in London: G. P. Wild, MBE (Western Australia House, Strand, WC2).

LOCAL GOVERNMENT. At 30 June 1970 all land in Western Australia (except King's Park, a public reserve of about 1,000 acres in Perth) was incorporated within the district of a city, town or shire. Including the lord-mayoralty of Perth there were 6 cities (all in the metropolitan area), 10 towns and 124 shires. The executive body in each of these districts is normally an elective council, presided over by a mayor (city and town) or a president (shire), but in certain circumstances it may be a commissioner appointed by the Governor. Their functions include road construction and repair, the provision of parks and recreation grounds, the administration of building controls and local services such as health and, in country districts, traffic. Finance is derived largely from rates levied on property owners as well as charges for services and government grants (mainly for road construction).

AREA AND POPULATION. Western Australia lies between 113° 09′ and 129° E. long. and 13° 44′ and 35° 08′ S. lat.; its area is 975,920 sq. miles (2,526,933 sq. km.).

The enumerated population at each census from 1901 was as follows[1]:

	Males	Females	Total		Males	Females	Total
1901	112,875	71,249	184,124	1947	258,076	244,404	502,480
1911	161,565	120,549	282,114	1954	330,358	309,413	639,771
1921	177,278	155,454	332,732	1961	380,740	366,010	746,750
1933	233,937	204,915	438,852	1966	432,569	415,531	848,100

[1] Until 1961 the figures exclude persons with more than one-half Aboriginal blood.

Of the census population in 1966, 637,882 were born in Australia. Married persons numbered 368,292 (185,239 males and 183,053 females); widowers, 7,652; widows, 30,134; divorced, 3,741 males and 3,774 females; never married, 224,525 males and 187,035 females. The number of males under 21 was 180,202, and of females 171,055.

Perth, the capital, had an estimated population of 635,500 at 30 June 1969. This includes the City of Perth (central city and suburbs) with a population of 97,000 and the chief port of the State, the City of Fremantle, with a population of 26,000.

Principal towns outside the metropolitan area, with estimated population at 30 June 1969: Kalgoorlie-Boulder, 20,900; Bunbury, 16,900; Geraldton, 14,100; Albany, 12,300; Collie, 7,600; Northam, 7,650; Narrogin, 5,000.

VITAL STATISTICS for calendar years [1]:

	Births	Ex-nuptial births	Marriages	Divorces	Deaths
1967	18,023	1,944	7,430	726	6,779
1968	19,541	2,013	8,086	812	7,468
1969	20,754	2,230	8,993	873	7,350

[1] Including Aborigines.

RELIGION. There is no State Church, and freedom of worship is accorded to all. At the census, 30 June 1966, the principal denominations were: Church of England, 316,153; Roman Catholic, 114,541; Catholic (not further defined), 99,118; Methodist, 80,840; Presbyterian, 44,055; Churches of Christ, 11,496; Orthodox, 11,835; Baptist, 10,720; Congregational, 8,375; Lutheran, 5,153; Salvation Army, 4,922; Seventh-day Adventist, 4,357; other Christian, 19,642; Hebrew, 2,996; all other, including not stated and no religion, 102,470.

EDUCATION. School attendance is compulsory from the age of 6 until the end of the year in which the child attains 15 years. Pre-school education is provided by a kindergarten system partly financed from government subsidy. Government primary and secondary schools are free, but fees are charged at non-government schools. In 1969 there were 573 government schools with 168,195 pupils and 405 non-government schools with 50,244 pupils.

Technical education is available at The Western Australian Institute of Technology (opened in 1966, autonomous in 1967); and the Perth Technical College and a number of other technical colleges, schools and centres, which are staffed and controlled by the Education Department.

In 1970 the full-time teaching staff of the University of Western Australia was 455 and the number of students enrolled was 7,782.

State Government expenditure from consolidated revenue on education, including financial assistance to the University, during the year ended 30 June 1969, amounted to $A56,351,963.

JUSTICE. In Western Australia justice is administered by a Supreme Court, consisting of a Chief Justice and 6 puisne judges, a district court comprising a chairman of judges and 3 district court judges and magistrates' courts exercising both civil and criminal jurisdiction. The lower courts are presided over by justices of the peace, except in the more important centres, where the court is constituted by a stipendiary magistrate. There are special magistrates' courts for juvenile offenders.

Offences against law[1]	1965	1966	1967	1968	1969
Charges[2]	68,821	68,184	76,458	86,836	93,157
Lower Court convictions[3]	65,542	64,756	72,798	81,892	85,956
Higher Court convictions[4]	312	302	358	510	518

[1] Including offences by Aborigines.
[2] In the case of concurrent offences each offence is included.
[3] Includes convictions for traffic offences: 35,428 in 1965; 33,905 in 1966; 36,468 in 1967; 43,929 in 1968; 43,428 in 1969. In addition, small fines were imposed for minor traffic offences as follows: 1965, 49,590; 1966, 63,560; 1967, 64,055; 1968, 83,146; 1969, 116,820.
[4] Distinct persons convicted.

The total number of admissions to prison for penal imprisonment in the year ended 30 June 1969 was 6,183. Inmates at 30 June 1969 numbered 1,146 males and 68 females.

SOCIAL WELFARE. At 30 June 1970 there were 5 geriatric hospitals and 47 general hospitals maintained wholly by public funds, while 2 geriatric and 63 general hospitals were assisted therefrom. In addition, there are numerous private hospitals. Government mental health services comprise 3 mental hospitals, 8 clinics, 4 rehabilitation units, 2 units concerned with the mentally deficient and 7 after-care hostels.

Child Welfare Department institutional facilities include 2 reception homes for the temporary care and assessment of children, a secure remand and assessment centre, a secure training centre for delinquent boys and 4 hostels for working teenage boys or girls. The Department also runs a training centre, in a farm-like setting, for less delinquent boys who do not require placement in a closed institution.

In Feb. 1970 the Department opened a new treatment and rehabilitation centre for girls.

Some 17 institutions caring for children are financed partly from private sources and partly from Government funds, and all but 2 are conducted by religious organizations. In addition, 13 country missions are Government sub-sidized to care for native wards.

Through the Department, the State Government makes financial assistance available to people in necessitous circumstances, in many cases supplementing social-service pension income provided by the Commonwealth Government.

At 30 June 1970, 1,113 families were receiving assistance.

The Department of Native Welfare is administered in accordance with the Native Welfare Act, 1963. Welfare activity is organized through 25 district offices within the State. There are in existence throughout the State 25 hostels which cater for the accommodation of Aboriginal school children and working youths living away from home. Of these, 12 are located in the metropolitan area, where an additional hostel is used for the accommodation of transient medical cases.

Also active within the State are 35 church mission establishments which provide accommodation and training for Aboriginal people.

Aborigines throughout the State are afforded the same educational, hospital and medical facilities provided for the general community.

Age, Invalid, Widows' and War and Service Pensions are paid by the Commonwealth Government. The number of pensioners in Western Australia at 30 June 1970 was: Age, 56,017; invalid, 7,933; widows, 6,086; and war and service pensioners and dependants, 55,776.

LABOUR. The Industrial Arbitration Act Amendment Act (No. 2), 1963, which came into operation on 1 Feb. 1964, abolished the Court of Arbitration and established The Western Australian Industrial Commission and the Western Australian Industrial Appeal Court.

The commission consists of a chief industrial commissioner and 3 other commissioners. A commissioner sitting or acting alone constitutes the commission and may exercise all its powers and jurisdiction. The commission in court session is constituted by not less than 3 commissioners sitting or acting together; in addition to other functions, it hears and determines appeals from decisions of a single commissioner.

Working conditions in the State are governed by decisions of the commission, which is also empowered to declare a State basic wage, subject to regular review, and to determine wage rates, including a minimum wage, for all awards under the jurisdiction. Basic wage rates which came into operation on 26 Oct. 1970 are $A38.45 for males and $A29.40 for females.

The Western Australian Industrial Appeal Court consists of 3 judges, one of whom is president of the court. An appeal lies to the court from any decision of the commission or the commission in court session, but only on the ground that such decision is erroneous in law or in excess of jurisdiction.

Under the Act associations of employees and of employers may be registered and the Act confers upon these associations the right of approaching the commission in connexion with industrial disputes. There were 100 employees' and 13 employers' bodies registered at 30 June 1970; the former comprising 137,556 and the latter 1,830 members.

FINANCE. The revenue and expenditure (in $A) of Western Australia in years ended 30 June, are given as follows:

	1968	1969	1970	1971[1]
Revenue	250,737,839	275,081,341	318,188,778	
Expenditure	249,909,203	276,136,959	318,900,637	

[1] Estimates.

Main items of revenue in 1969–70: Railways ($A57,199,647), taxation ($A50,864,578), lands, timber and mining ($A23,633,366), public utilities other than railways ($A5,721,720), from Commonwealth Funds ($A141,326,221). Western Australia had a net loan liability of $A886,596,676 on 30 June 1970, the charge for the year being $A51,918,299.

LAND SETTLEMENT. Up to 31 Dec. 1969, of the entire area of the State (624,588,800 acres) 34,311,549 acres had been alienated; on that date 14,169,579 acres were in process of alienation; the area alienated and in process of alienation thus amounting to 48,481,128 acres. There were in force leases comprising an area of 248,872,406 acres, of which 238,589,805 acres were pastoral, 3,738,887 acres were timber, 107,570 acres mining leases, 34,620 acres Miners' Homestead leases and 6,401,524 for reserves, residential lots, special and perpetual leases.

AGRICULTURE.

Crop	1968–69		1969–70	
	Acres	Production	Acres	Production
Wheat (bu.)	7,295,094	112,450,000	6,788,177	66,700,000
Oats (bu.)	1,092,469	22,941,897	1,139,430	15,463,313
Barley (bu.)	552,810	9,187,114	900,187	12,058,055
Hay (tons)	341,176	501,377	..	..
Potatoes (tons)	6,588	74,435	..	..
Apples (bu.)	15,165	2,870,187	..	2,623,350
Pears (bu.)	978	191,351	..	222,787
Oranges (bu.)	4,506	550,962	..	..
Currants and raisins (tons, dried)	..	1,870	..	1,070

Irrigation has been established by the Government along the south-western coastal plain and in the north of the State. Reservoirs with an aggregate capacity of 90,307m. gallons provided water for 5 main irrigation districts of a total area of 44,503 acres in 1968–69. Dairying and stockraising activities account for about 72% of the area irrigated throughout the irrigation regions, and cotton growing, vegetable growing (including potatoes), fruit cultivation and experimental crops for the remaining 28%.

The livestock at 31 March 1970 consisted of 1,681,084 cattle, 33,633,957 sheep and 250,051 pigs.

The wool clip in 1969–70 was 330m. lb.; the exports for 1969–70, greasy wool, 264,966,207 lb.; degreased wool, 27,676,301 lb.

FORESTRY. The area of State forests and timber reserves at 30 June 1970 was 6,990,058 acres; the approximate number of superfeet of sawn timber was (1968–69) 188m., principally Jarrah and Karri hardwoods.

MINING. Gold was first obtained in Western Australia in 1885. The sensational gold-finds at Coolgardie and Kalgoorlie in 1892 and 1893 gave an impetus to Western Australian goldmining, which, in a short time, placed this State at the head of all the Australian States as regards gold output. The aggregate output to the end of Dec. 1968 was 67,255,479 fine oz., valued at $A1,064,309,844. At 31 Dec. 1968 there were in force 1,032 goldmining leases, representing an area of 19,299 acres; men, employed in the mines, 3,662, viz. 1,961 above and 1,701 underground; refinery production of gold, 1968, 511,703 fine oz., value $A16,785,723.

Large-scale mining of iron ore, principally for export overseas, commenced in 1966 and in that year total production was 6,106,105 tons, value $A33,771,718; in 1968 production was 18,827,593 tons, value $A131,939,262.

The total value of mining and quarrying to the State in 1967 was $A157,545,261; in 1968, $A223,819,005. Principal minerals in 1968, other than gold and iron ore, were: Petroleum, 10,776,534 bbls, value $A31,036,418; coal, 1,087,379 tons, value $A4,816,725; manganese ore, 150,338 tons, value $A3,135,445; pyritic ore, 32,879 tons, value $A420,825; mineral beach sands, 567,054 tons, value $A6,585,848; tin ore and concentrates, 895 tons, value $A1,658,241. In addition, 36,880 tons of nickel concentrates and 1,607,988 tons of bauxite were produced in 1968.

INDUSTRY. There were, for the year ended 30 June 1968, a total of 5,404 industrial establishments in the State, employing either machinery or at least 4 workers. The average number of persons employed by them over the year was 67,335. The gross output of these establishments for the year was computed at $A887,372,060, while the net production, *i.e.*, the value added in the course of manufacture, was $A388,256,986.

The estimated gross value of Western Australian primary production during 1968–69 was as follows: Agricultural, $A218,642,787; pastoral and trapping, $A211,990,734; mining and quarrying, $A223,819,005; dairy, poultry and bee-farming, $A38,801,373; forestry and fisheries, $A37,181,912.

HOUSING. The State Housing Commission was established in Jan. 1947 to replace the Workers' Homes Board created in 1912. The objects of the Commission are 'the improvement of existing housing conditions' and 'the provision of adequate and suitable housing accommodation for persons of limited means and certain other persons not otherwise adequately housed'. The Commission provided 1,863 new dwelling units for sale and for rental in 1968–69. During the same period 12,840 new houses and 3,491 new flats were completed throughout the State.

COMMERCE. The external commerce of Western Australia, exclusive of interstate trade, is comprised in the statement of the commerce of Australia given under the heading of the Commonwealth, *see* pp. 245–46.

The total value of the imports and exports, including interstate trade in 5 years (30 June) is, in $A, as follows:

	1965–66	1966–67	1967–68	1968–69	1969–70
Imports	578,744,158	634,242,049	734,031,213	765,844,996	
Exports[1]	434,023,447	537,354,970	599,764,941	696,257,549	

[1] Excluding ships' stores.

Principal exports (in $A) for 1968–69: Wool, 160,500,862; wheat, 77,987,299; iron ore, 151,796,859; petroleum and petroleum products, 47,338,354; gold bullion, 12,701,223; crayfish tails, 17,133,230; beef and veal, 16,939,123; oats,

9,133,790; timber, 5,067,834; hides and skins, 6,013,101; apples, 5,781,211; flour, 2,432,718.

Principal imports in 1968–69 (in $A): Machinery, 161,813,960; transport equipment, 111,096,912; textiles and apparel, 77,131,260; iron and steel, 51,590,764; petroleum and petroleum products, 38,528,037; chemicals, 63,849,106; food, 56,949,981; rubber and rubber manufactures, 18,148,933; beverages and tobacco, 19,637,964.

The chief countries exporting to Western Australia were (in $A): UK, 40,859,600; USA, 37,945,847; Japan, 27,826,406; Kuwait, 12,397,446; West Germany, 10,207,712; Canada, 7,699,522. Western Australian exports (in $A) went chiefly to: Japan, 226,648,650; USA, 66,274,567; UK, 37,604,831; Chinese mainland, 29,856,307; West Germany, 25,964,483; France, 20,196,847.

SHIPPING. The sea-borne trade of Western Australia is concentrated on the port of Fremantle. In 1968–69, the number, net tonnage of vessels entering and cargo shipped at major ports were as follows: Port of Fremantle, 1,390 vessels of 8·93m. net tonnage, 5m. cargo tonnage shipped; Dampier, 271 vessels of 3·73m. net tonnage, 11·4m. cargo tonnage shipped; Port Hedland, 307 vessels of 2·09m net tonnage, 5·66m. cargo tonnage shipped; Yampi, 165 vessels of 1·29m. net tonnage, 2·85m. cargo tonnage shipped.

ROADS. At 30 June 1967 there were 82,745 miles of prepared and formed roads in Western Australia, namely, 13,806 miles of bituminous surface, 23,193 other constructed surfaces and 45,746 formed but not metalled or otherwise prepared. In addition, there are approximately 26,362 miles unprepared except for clearing which are used for general traffic. New motor vehicles registered in Western Australia during the year ended 31 Dec. 1969 were 50,484.

RAILWAYS. At 30 June 1969 the State had 3,826 miles of State government railway and 454 miles of Commonwealth line, the latter being the western portion of the Trans-Australian line (Kalgoorlie–Port Pirie), which links the State railway system to those of the other States of the Commonwealth. In addition, mining companies operate 518 miles of private railways for the transport of ore to ports on the north-west coast.

AVIATION. Two interstate airlines, one of which is owned and operated by the Commonwealth Government, connect Perth with the other State capitals by a daily service. A route to Darwin (NT) is flown by another airline, which also maintains regular communications with inland centres and ports around the coast. Perth Airport is an important Australian international airport.

POST. Postal, telephone and telegraph facilities are afforded at 765 offices. Telephones connected totalled 256,303 at 30 June 1970. There are 30 wireless broadcasting and 11 television stations; and 37,700 listeners', 38,713 viewers' and 158,979 combined receiving licences were current at 30 June 1970.

MONEY AND BANKING. A branch of the Royal Mint was opened at Perth in 1899. To 31 Dec. 1969 production of coins was: Gold (minting discontinued in Sept. 1931), $A213,503,070; silver, $A131,600 (minting discontinued in 1946); bronze, $A11,145,036 (minting discontinued in 1968); and of bullion: gold, $A267,646,145; silver, $A6,590,240.

There are 10 trading banks in Western Australia including the Commonwealth Trading Bank and The Rural and Industries Bank of Western Australia. In June quarter, 1970, the average of customers' balances was $A554m. and average advances $A349·7m.

At 30 June 1970, the 9 savings banks held deposits of $A431,877,000 in 1,096,466 accounts.

BOOKS OF REFERENCE

STATISTICAL INFORMATION. The State Government Statistician's Office was established in 1897 and now functions as the Western Australian Office of the Commonwealth Bureau of Census and Statistics (1–3 St George's Tce, Perth). *Deputy Commonwealth Statistician and Government Statistician:* F. W. Sayer. Its principal publications are: *Statistical Register of Western Australia* (annual, from 1896 to 1967–68). *Statistics of Western Australia* (annual, from 1968–69). *Western Australian Year Book* (new series, from 1957). *Western Australian Pocket Year Book* (from 1919). *Quarterly Statistical Abstract* (from 1917). *Abstract of Statistics of Local Government Areas* (annual, from 1960).

Crowley, F. K., *A Short History of Western Australia.* Melbourne, 1959.—*Australia's Western Third.* London, 1960

Crowley, F. K., and De Garis, B. K., *A Short History of Western Australia.* Melbourne, 1969

Gentilli, J., *Atlas of Western Australian Agriculture.* Perth, 1941

Kerr, Alex, *The South-West Region of Western Australia.* Perth, 1965.—*Australia's North-West.* Perth, 1967

Stephenson, G., and Hepburn, J. A., *Plan for the Metropolitan Region: Perth and Fremantle.* Perth, 1955

STATE LIBRARY. The State Library of Western Australia, Perth. *State Librarian:* F. A. Sharr, BA, FLA.

TASMANIA

HISTORY. Abel Janzoon Tasman discovered Van Diemen's Land (Tasmania) on 24 Nov. 1642. The island became a British settlement in 1803 as a dependency of New South Wales; in 1825 its connexion with New South Wales was terminated; in 1851 a partially elective Legislative Council was established, and in 1856 responsible government came into operation. On 1 Jan. 1901 Tasmania was federated with the other Australian states into the Commonwealth of Australia.

CONSTITUTION AND GOVERNMENT. Parliament consists of the Governor, the Legislative Council and the House of Assembly. The Council has 19 members, elected by adults with 6 months' residence. Members sit for 6 years, 3 retiring annually and 4 every sixth year. There is no power to dissolve the Council. Vacancies are filled by by-elections. The House of Assembly has 35 members, elected for 5 years by adults with 6 months' residence in the State. Members of both Houses are paid a salary of $A7,200, plus an electorate allowance, according to the division represented. The annual amounts vary from $A650 (Queenborough) to $A1,475 (Russell) in the Council and from $A1,100 (Denison) to $A2,500 (Wilmot) in the Assembly. Women received the right to vote in 1903. Proportional representation was adopted in 1907, the method now being the single transferable vote in 7-member constituencies. Casual vacancies in the House of Assembly are determined by a transfer of the preference of the vacating member's ballot papers to consenting candidates who were unsuccessful at the last general election.

A Minister must have a seat in one of the two Houses; all of the present Ministers are in the House of Assembly.

In addition to the salary paid to Ministers as members of either House, the following allowances are payable: Premier, in conjunction with a ministerial office, $A8,800 plus entertainment allowance $A900; Deputy Premier, in conjunction with a ministerial office, $A6,200; Ministers, $A5,000; Leader of the Opposition, $A4,300. Holders of these offices receive only 75% of electorate allowance.

At the election on 10 May 1969 for the House of Assembly 17 Labor, 17 Liberal and 1 Centre Party members were returned. The Liberal and Centre Parties formed a coalition government. The Legislative Council is predominantly independent without formal party allegiance; 2 members are Labor-endorsed.

Governor: Lieut.-Gen. Sir Edric Bastyan, KCMG, KCVO, KBE, CB.

The Cabinet led by W. A. Bethune is composed as follows:

Premier, Treasurer, Minister in Charge of Hydro-Electric Commission: W. A. Bethune.
Deputy Premier and Chief Secretary, Tourism: K. O. Lyons. *Education:* R. Mather. *Lands and Works and Local Government:* W. G. Barker. *Agriculture and Forests:* E. N. Beattie. *Attorney-General, Police and Licensing:* E. M. Bingham. *Development, Housing, Fisheries:* D. F. Clark. *Health, Road Safety:* N. D. Abbott. *Transport, Racing and Gaming, Mines:* L. H. Bessell.

Agent-General in London: R. R. Neville.
Official Secretary: R. J. Garrad, OBE (458/9 Strand, WC2).

LOCAL GOVERNMENT. For the purposes of local government, the State is divided into 49 municipal areas comprising the cities of Hobart, Launceston and Glenorchy and 46 municipalities. The cities and municipalities are managed by elected aldermen and councillors respectively with reference to local matters such as sanitation and health services, domestic water supplies and roads and bridges within each particular area. The chief source of revenue is rates, derived from capital values and levied on owners of property. A government-appointed commission recommended reduction to 20 municipal areas, but appeals have delayed implementation. The Government has now decided to reconstitute the commission with wider terms of reference.

AREA AND POPULATION. Area (including islands) 26,383 sq. miles (68,300 sq. km) or about 16,885,000 acres, of which 16,032,000 acres form the area of the main island. The population at 8 consecutive censuses was:

	Population	Increase % per annum		Population	Increase % per annum
1901	172,475	1·64	1947	257,078	0·87
1911	191,211	1·04	1954	308,752	2·65
1921	213,780	1·12	1961	350,340	1·82
1933	227,599	0·52	1966	371,435	1·18

The census population on 30 June 1966 consisted of 187,390 males and 184,045 females; 5·1% were natives of the British Isles, 3·5% natives of other European countries and 90·7% natives of Australia and New Zealand, almost exclusively of European ancestry. The last Tasmanian Aboriginal died in 1876.

Census population (30 June 1966): Hobart metropolitan area, 119,469 (estimate 30 June 1970, 127,260), includes Hobart City, 53,257 (52,900); Launceston urban area, 60,456 (62,500), includes Launceston City, 37,217 (36,620).

VITAL STATISTICS for calendar years:

	Marriages	Divorces	Births	Deaths	Natural increase
1967	3,213	248	7,547	3,228	4,319
1968	3,426	303	8,317	3,284	5.033
1969	3,532	331	8,445	3,309	5,136

RELIGION. There is no State Church. At the census of 1966 the following numbers of adherents of the principal religions were recorded:

Church of England	166,023	Churches of Christ	2,701
Roman Catholic	71,089	Other religions	18,128
Methodist	43,084	Not stated[1]	40,623
Presbyterian	17,498		
Baptist	7,759	Total	371,435
Congregational	4,530		

[1] Includes 2,275 whose religion was indefinite and 2,020 who stated 'no religion'.

EDUCATION. Education is controlled by the State and is free, secular and compulsory between the ages of 6 and 16. At 1 Aug. 1970 government schools had a total enrolment of 77,447 pupils, including 26,895 at secondary level; private schools had a total enrolment of 14,399 pupils, including 6,302 at secondary level.

The University of Tasmania, established 1890, had 202 full-time teachers with 3,119 students in 1970. University expenditure in 1969 (exclusive of capital expenditure) was $A4·7m.

JUSTICE. The Supreme Court of Tasmania, with civil, criminal, ecclesiastical, admiralty and matrimonial jurisdiction, established by Royal Charter on 13 Oct. 1823, is a superior court of record, with both original and appellate jurisdiction, and consists of a Chief Justice and 4 puisne judges. There are also inferior civil courts with limited jurisdiction, licensing courts, mining courts, courts of petty sessions and coroners' courts.

During the year 1969, 26,515 persons were summarily convicted in lower courts (14,378 for traffic offences) and 747 persons were committed for trial in the Supreme Court. The total police force on 30 June 1969 was 721. There was one gaol, with 356 inmates at the end of June 1969.

SOCIAL WELFARE. Old Age, Invalid, War Service and Widows' Pensions are paid by the Commonwealth Government. The number of pensioners in Tasmania on 30 June 1970 was: Age, 23,915; invalid, 4,051; war, 23,807; widows, 2,958. Benefit payments in Tasmania during 1968–69 for all Commonwealth social and health services totalled $A36·2m. (excluding pensions to ex-servicemen and women, $A8·7m.).

LABOUR. The Commonwealth Industrial Court (judicial powers) and Commonwealth Conciliation and Arbitration Commission (arbitral powers) have jurisdiction over federal unions, *i.e.*, with interstate membership. The Arbitration Commission hears national wage cases annually, the metal trades award being the test case; in June 1967 it abolished the concept of the basic wage and made an award in terms of total wage; in June 1969 it adopted the principle of equal pay for equal work for females.

Most Tasmanian employees not covered by federal awards operate under State Wages Boards established for the various trades by resolution of Parliament or proclamation of the Governor. Each Board consists of a Chairman appointed by the Governor with equal representation of employers and employees. The Boards have authority over minimum rates for wages or piece work, number of working hours for which the wage is payable, conditions of apprenticeship, annual leave and adjustment of wage and piece-work rates. Wages Boards follow to a large extent the wage rates fixed by the Conciliation and Arbitration Commission; in July 1967, Oct. 1968 and Dec. 1969 they followed the quantum of increase fixed by the Commonwealth Commission but did not abolish the basic wage concept.

FINANCE. The revenue is derived chiefly from taxation (motor, land, stamp and death duties), and from grants and reimbursements from the Commonwealth. Customs, excise, sales and income tax are in the hands of the Commonwealth, which makes certain grants to Tasmania and contributes a fixed amount per annum towards interest on the State's public debt. Principal Commonwealth grants taken into revenue amounted to $A71·04m. in 1969–70.

Budgets, in $A1,000, for financial years ending 30 June:

	1964–65	1965–66	1966–67	1967–68	1968–69	1969–70
Revenue	74,846	83,564	92,676	100,563	107,846	120,528
Expenditure	76,465	85,585	93,248	102,413	111,540	122,375

The public debt at current exchange rates amounted to $A643·8m. at 30 June 1970.

In 1969–70 State taxation receipts amounted to $A19·1m., of which motor vehicles provided $A4·8m.; death duties, $A3·3m.; other stamp duties, $A6·3m.; land tax, $A2·6m. The earlier Commonwealth tax reimbursement grant has been replaced by the financial assistance grant which amounted to $A46·3m. in 1969–70 (included in 'principal grants' above).

PRIMARY INDUSTRIES. The estimated gross value of recorded production from primary industries in 1968–69 was (in $A1,000): Agriculture, 44,599; pastoral, 39,117; dairying, 27,713; poultry and bees, 5,996; forestry, 15,885; fisheries and trapping, 5,233; mining, 50,622; total gross value, 189,165.

AGRICULTURE. The area occupied by the 10,384 holdings in 1968–69 totalled 6,591,402 acres, of which 489,069 were devoted to crops. The following table shows the area and production of the principal crops:

Crop	1966–67		1967–68		1968–69	
	Acres	Production	Acres	Production	Acres	Production
Wheat (bu.)	12,747	385,243	12,018	316,288	17,394	410,263
Barley (bu.)	21,057	771,750	24,051	884,222	26,214	884,067
Oats (bu.)	35,909	947,960	35,371	1,013,665	31,434	582,910
Peas (Blue) (bu.)	4,372	111,658	4,262	93,336	3,355	79,359
Green peas, ex-shell (1,000 lb.)	15,304	56,790	14,944	54,005	14,110	54,401
Potatoes (tons)	10,278	73,300	10,960	79,058	11,461	72,120
Hay (tons)	203,181	436,907	178,838	309,099	210,563	494,227
Apples (Bearing) (bu.)	18,540	6,301,000	14,945	7,943,000	14,487	7,138,000
Hops (Bearing) (lb.) (dry)	1,446	2,091,415	1,502	3,005,000	1,521	3,488,000

Livestock at 31 March 1969: Sheep, 4·4m.; cattle, 585,718; pigs, 95,363. Wool produced during 1968–69 was 47m. lb., valued at $A21·18m. In 1968–69, butter production was 15,764 tons; cheese, 5,728 tons.

The net value of rural production during 1968–69 was $A68·94m.

FORESTRY. Indigenous forests cover a considerable part of the State, and the saw-milling industry is very important. Production of sawn timber in 1968–69 was 175m. superfeet. Newsprint and paper are produced from native hardwoods, principally eucalypts.

MINING. The assayed content of principal metallic minerals contained in locally produced concentrates for 1968 was: Zinc, 48,146 tons; iron, 494,526 tons; copper, 16,601 tons; lead, 14,913 tons; tin, 3,103 tons; gold, 36,498 fine oz.; silver, 1,748,606 fine oz. Coal production (1968), 90,930 tons.

MANUFACTURES. The most important manufactures for export are refined metals, newsprint and other paper manufactures, pigments, woollen goods, fruit pulp and jam, confectionery, butter, preserved and dried vegetables, sawn timber, iron ore pellets and processed fish products. The electrolytic-zinc works at Risdon near Hobart treat large quantities of local and imported ore, and produce zinc, sulphuric acid, superphosphate, sulphate of ammonia, cadmium and other by-products. At George Town, large-scale plants produce refined aluminium and manganese alloys. During 1971 the first of 3 proposed woodchip plants commenced exporting to Japan and have export contracts valued at about $A350m. In 1967–68 the number of industrial establishments was 1,797; number of employees, 35,178; value of output, $A445·08m.; salaries and wages paid $A96·24m., excluding amounts drawn by working proprietors; cost of materials used, $A203·08m.; value of production, $A198·02m.; value of plant and machinery, $A184·68m.; value of land and buildings, $A263·36m.

POWER. Tasmania has plentiful supplies of hydro-electric power because of assured rainfall and high level water storages (natural and artificial). The Hydro-Electric Commission, Tasmania's sole commercial supplier of electricity, has been surveying water power resources of the State for many years and it is estimated that about 3m. kw. can be economically developed. In 1969 over 1,015,600 kw. of generating plant was in commission with a peak loading of 735,500 kw. and average load factor of 72%. A recently completed 120,000 kw. oil-fired thermal power station together with present construction will bring generating plant capacity to 1·6m. kw. by 1975. The major construction project is the Gordon River scheme involving the construction of Australia's largest artificial water storage (11·8m. acre ft) and one of the nation's largest dams. Water will be carried from the Lake Gordon storage by a near vertical shaft to the power station 610 ft underground, which is designed to be operated by remote control from Hobart, 100 miles away. Generator capacity of the Gordon River (Stage 1) scheme is 240,000 kw.

TOURISM. In the year ended 31 March 1969 an estimated 104,000 tourists visited Tasmania and contributed some $A10m. to the gross income of the State. The tourist industry is expected to develop rapidly in the coming decade and various government measures have been aimed at promoting the industry.

COMMERCE. Commerce by sea and air in $A1m. for years ending 30 June:

	1964–65	1965–66	1966–67	1967–68	1968–69
Imports	227·5	257·4	281·1	285·2	300 0
Exports	306·5	330·4	339·5	337·5	393·4

In 1968–69 imports by sea and air from other Australian States totalled $A262·4m.; from the UK, $A8·7m.; from Japan, $A5·7m.; from USA, $A5·6m.; from other countries, $A17·5m. Exports to other Australian States amounted to $A291·3m.; to Japan, $A24·4m.; to the UK, $A17·3m.; to USA, $A16·2m.; to other countries, $A44·2m.

Principal imports, 1968–69, in $A1m.: Clothing, 13·5; tobacco, cigarettes, etc., 13·7; machinery, 34·6; new motor vehicles, 25·9. Principal exports: Fresh fruit, 13·4; refined copper and zinc, 42·8; preserved vegetables, 14·3; greasy wool, 18·6; woollen manufactures, 27·6; timber, 15·3; iron ore 17·1, and confectionery, aluminium, newsprint and fine papers, wood-pulp for paper making and Portland cement.

ROADS. The road mileage is about 13,642, consisting of a classified road system of 2,300 miles maintained by the State Department of Public Works, and the remainder maintained by local government authorities, the Forestry Commission and the Hydro-Electric Commission. Motor vehicles registered at 31 Dec. 1969 comprised 117,000 cars, 34,000 commercial vehicles and 2,900 motor cycles.

SHIPPING. The most important development has been the introduction of roll-on roll-off ferries and freighters, allowing door-to-door delivery between Tasmanian and mainland ports.

For railways, posts and telegraphs, see COMMONWEALTH OF AUSTRALIA, pp. 250–51.

AVIATION. Regular daily passenger and freight air services connect the south, north and north-west of the State with the mainland of Australia. Statistics of regular air transport services for the year 1968–69 are as follows: Miles flown, 4·8m.; passengers carried, 480,202; freight carried, 17,526 short tons; mail carried, 358 short tons.

BANKING. Trading bank activity in Tasmania is divided between 6 private banks and the Commonwealth Bank of Australia. For the month of June 1970 liabilities represented by depositors' balances averaged $A132·6m. and assets represented by advances, $A82·5m. The 9 savings banks operating in Tasmania are the Commonwealth Savings Bank, 2 trustee savings banks and 6 private savings banks operated by trading banks. At 30 June 1970 total savings bank deposits were $A199·8m. or approximately $A511 per head of population.

Tasmanian Islands. Three inhabited Tasmanian islands (Bruny, King and Flinders) are organized as municipalities. Nearly 1,000 miles south-east lies Macquarie Island, part of the State, and used only as an Australian research base and meteorological station.

BOOKS OF REFERENCE

STATISTICAL INFORMATION. The State Government Statistical Office (Kirksway House, Kirksway Pl., Hobart), established in 1877, became in 1924 the Tasmanian Office of the Commonwealth Bureau of Census and Statistics, but continues to serve State statistical needs as required. *Deputy Commonwealth Statistician and Government Statistician:* R. Lakin.

Main publications: *Statistics of the State of Tasmania.* Annual (from 1822).—*Pocket Year Book of Tasmania.* Annual (from 1913).—*Tasmanian Year Book.* Annual (from 1967).—*Monthly Summary of Statistics* (from July 1945)
Clark, C. I., *The Parliament of Tasmania.* Hobart, 1947
Davies, J. L. (ed.), *Atlas of Tasmania.* Hobart, 1965
Green, F. C. (ed.), *A Century of Responsible Government.* Hobart, 1956
Walch's *Tasmanian Almanac.* Hobart and London. Annual
Wettenhall, R. L., *A Guide to Tasmanian Government Administration.* Hobart, 1968
STATE LIBRARY. The State Library of Tasmania, Hobart. *Librarian:* A. E. Browning, B.Ec. FLA, ALAA.

NEW ZEALAND

HISTORY. The first European to discover New Zealand was Tasman in 1642. The coast was explored by Capt. Cook in 1769. From about 1800 onwards, New Zealand became a resort for whalers and traders, chiefly from Australia. By the Treaty of Waitangi, in 1840, between Governor William Hobson and the representatives of the Maori race, the Maori chiefs ceded the sovereignty to the British Crown and the islands became a British colony. Then followed a steady stream of British settlers.

The Maoris are a branch of the Polynesian race, having emigrated from the eastern Pacific before and during the 14th century. Between 1845 and 1848, and between 1860 and 1870, misunderstandings over land led to war, but peace was permanently established in 1871, and the development of New Zealand has been marked by racial harmony and integration.

CONSTITUTION AND GOVERNMENT. Definition was given the status of New Zealand by the (Imperial) Statute of Westminster of Dec. 1931, which had received the antecedent approval of the New Zealand Parliament in July 1931. The Governor-General's assent was given to the Statute of Westminster Adoption Bill on 25 Nov. 1947.

The powers, duties and responsibilities of the Governor-General and the Executive Council under the present system of responsible government are set out in Royal Letters Patent and Instructions thereunder of 11 May 1917, published in the *New Zealand Gazette* of 24 April 1919. In the execution of the powers vested in him the Governor-General must be guided by the advice of the Executive Council.

The following is a list of Governors-General, the title prior to June 1917 being Governor:

Earl of Liverpool	1917–20	Lord Freyberg, VC	1946–52
Viscount Jellicoe	1920–24	Lord Norrie	1952–57
Sir Charles Fergusson, Bt	1924–30	Viscount Cobham	1957–62
Lord Bledisloe	1930–35	Sir Bernard Fergusson	1962–67
Viscount Galway	1935–41	Sir Arthur Porritt, Bt	1967–
Sir Cyril Newall	1941–46		

Parliament consists of the House of Representatives, the former Legislative Council having been abolished since 1 Jan. 1951.

The statute law on elections and the life of Parliament is contained in the Electoral Act, 1956. In 1969 the voting age was reduced from 21 to 20 years.

The House of Representatives consists of 84 members, including 4 Maoris, elected by the people for 3 years. The 4 Maori electoral districts cover the whole country and adult Maoris of half-blood or more are the electors. A half-caste Maori is entitled to register either for a European or a Maori electoral district. Women's suffrage was instituted in 1893; women became eligible as members of the House of Representatives in 1919. The House in 1970 included 4 women members.

During Parliamentary sittings the proceedings of the House are broadcast regularly on sound radio.

House of Representatives as composed in 1970: National Party, 44; Labour, 40; total 84.

The Executive Council was composed as follows in June 1970:

Governor-General and C.-in-C.: Sir Arthur Porritt, Bt, GCMG, KCVO, CBE (assumed office 1 Dec. 1967).

Prime Minister, Minister of Foreign Affairs, Minister in charge of the State Services, including Security Intelligence Service, of the Legislative and of the Audit Departments: Sir Keith Holyoake, GCMG, CH, PC.

Deputy Prime Minister, Minister of Labour, Minister of Overseas Trade, Attorney-General, Minister of Immigration: J. R. Marshall, PC.

Minister of Industries, Mines and Commerce: N. L. Shelton.

Minister of Education and Science: B. E. Talboys.

Minister of Housing, Minister in charge of the State Advances Corporation, of the Public Trust Office, of the Government Life Insurance Office, of the State Insurance Office, and of the Earthquake and War Damage Commission: J. Rae.

Minister of Agriculture: D. J. Carter.

Minister of Health, Minister of Social Security, Minister for the Welfare of Women and Children, Minister in charge of the Child Welfare Division: D. N. McKay.

Minister of Internal Affairs, Minister of Local Government, Minister of Civil Defence: D. C. Seath.

Minister of Works, Minister of Electricity: P. B. Allen.

Postmaster-General, Minister of Marine and Fisheries, Minister in charge of the Government Printing Office: A. McCready.

Minister of Transport, Minister of Railways, J. B. Gordon.

Minister of Lands, Minister of Forests, Minister in charge of the Valuation Department, Minister of Maori and Island Affairs: Duncan MacIntyre.

Minister of Defence, Minister in charge of War Pensions and of Rehabilitation, Minister of Police: D. S. Thomson.

Minister of Customs, Associate Minister of Industries and Commerce: L. R. Adams-Schneider.

Minister of Finance, Minister in charge of the Department of Statistics, Minister in charge of Friendly Societies: R. D. Muldoon.

Minister of Tourism, Minister in charge of Publicity, Minister of Broadcasting: H. J. Walker.

Minister of Justice, Associate Minister of Labour and Immigration: D. J. Riddiford.

Associate Minister of Finance: H. E. L. Pickering.

The Prime Minister (provided with residence) has a salary of NZ$17,000 plus a tax-free expense allowance of $4,000 per annum; Ministers with portfolio, $11,250 plus a tax-free expense allowance of $1,500 (Minister of Foreign Affairs $1,750) per annum; Ministers without portfolio, $8,650 plus a tax-free expense allowance of $1,275 per annum; Parliamentary Under-Secretaries, $8,450 plus an expense allowance of $1,275 per annum. In addition, Ministers and Parliamentary Under-Secretaries not provided with residence at the seat of Government receive $600 per annum house allowance. An allowance of $12 per day while travelling within New Zealand on public service is payable to Ministers.

The Speaker of the House of Representatives receives $10,000 plus an expense allowance of $1,300 per annum in addition to his electorate allowance, and residential quarters in Parliament House, and the Leader of the Opposition $10,500 plus expense allowance of $1,500 per annum.

Members are paid $6,100 per annum, plus an expense allowance varying from $1,340 to $2,400 according to the area of electorate represented.

There is a compulsory contributory superannuation scheme for members; retiring allowances are payable to a member after 9 years' service and the attainment of 50 years of age.

Dollimore, H. N., *The Parliament of New Zealand and Parliament House.* 2nd ed. Wellington, 1964
Milne, R. S., *Political Parties in New Zealand.* OUP, 1966
Polaschek, R. J., *Government Administration in New Zealand.* London, 1958
Scott, K. J., *The New Zealand Constitution.* OUP, 1962

LOCAL GOVERNMENT. For purposes of local government New Zealand is divided into counties, boroughs and town districts. Some counties are subdivided into ridings. There are also numerous other local authorities created for specific functions, such as electric-power districts, river (*i.e.*, river protection) districts, gas districts, pest destruction districts, etc.

DIPLOMATIC REPRESENTATIVES

Country	New Zealand representative	Overseas representative
Argentina	—	J. I. Gomez Errazuriz
Australia[1]	J. L. Hazlett	Sir Edwin Hicks, CBE
Austria[2]	—	Dr Franz Pein[4]
Belgium	M. Norrish	Andre Domus
Brazil	—	Mrs Margarida Nogueira[4]
Britain[1]	Sir Denis Blundell, KBE	Sir Arthur Galsworthy, KCMG
Burma	—	U Nyo Tun[4]
Canada[1]	Dean Eyre	R. M. Macdonnell
Ceylon[1]	B. S. Lendrum	N. J. L. Jansz, MBE[4]
China	—	Konsin C. Shah
Czechoslovakia	—	Jaroslav Matouš[3]
Denmark	—	P. A. von der Hude
Finland	—	Tuure Mentula[4]
France	O. P. Gabites	Christian de Nicolay
Germany, West	B. D. Zohrab	Kurt Luedde-Neurath
Greece	D. N. Hull	B. L. Tsamissis[4]
India[1]	B. S. Lendrum	P. S. Nasker
Indonesia	R. L. G. Challis	Air Vice-Marshal Sujitno Sukirno
Irish Republic	Sir Denis Blundell, KBE	Frank Coffey
Israel	—	S. Pratt[4]
Italy[1]	A. D. McIntosh, CMG	Giulio Carnevali
Japan	—	Kenichiro Yoshida
Korea (South)	—	Choong Sik Min[4]
Laos	I. L. G. Stewart	O. Souyannavong[5]
Malaysia[1]	R. L. Hutchens	Lim Taik Choon
Nepál	B. S. Lendrum	Prakash Chand Thakur[6]
Netherlands[2]	R. R. Cunninghame	H. M. van Walt van Praag
Norway	—	Arnt-Jakob Jakobsen[4]
Pakistan[1]	—	M. Aslam Malik[4]
Philippines[2]	W. G. Thorp	Mariano Ezpeleta[4]
Romania	—	Josif Gheorgiu[6]
Singapore[1]	J. H. Weir	K. M. Byrne
Spain	—	J. R. Parellada
Sweden	—	C. G. Béve
Switzerland	Miss H. N. Hampton	Max Corti
Thailand	I. L. G. Stewart	Prasong Bunchoem[4]
USSR	—	A. I. Ivantsov
UAR	—	K. El Ayonti[4]
USA	F. H. Corner	Kenneth Franzhein II
Vietnam (South)	P. K. Edmonds	Tran Kim Phuong[4]
Western Samoa[1]	R. B. Taylor	

[1] High Commissioner.   [2] Minister.   [3] Chargé d'Affaires.
[4] Resident in Australia.   [5] Resident in Saigon.   [6] Resident in Tokyo.
No figure = Ambassador.

There are in Wellington consuls-general of Yugoslavia, South Africa, Poland, Bulgaria, Chile (Auckland) and Mexico (Auckland); honorary representatives of Ecuador, Finland, Norway, Panama (Auckland), Peru (Auckland), Portugal, Turkey (Auckland), Venezuela (Auckland).

AREA AND POPULATION. There are two principal islands, the North and South Islands, besides Stewart Island, Chatham Islands and small outlying islands, as well as the territories overseas (*see* pp. 324 ff.).

New Zealand (*i.e.*, North, South and Stewart Islands) extends over 1,100 miles from north to south. Area, excluding territories overseas, 103,736 sq. miles; North Island, 44,281 sq. miles; South Island, 58,093 sq. miles; Stewart Island, 670 sq. miles; Chatham Islands, 372 sq. miles; minor islands, 320 sq. miles. Total, 66,390,700 acres. Census population, exclusive of territories overseas:

	Total population	Average annual increase %		Total population	Average annual increase %
1858	115,462	—	1916[1]	1,149,225	1·50
1874	344,984	—	1921	1,271,664	2·27
1878	458,007	7·33	1926	1,408,139	2·06
1881	534,030	5·10	1936	1,573,810	1·13
1886	620,451	3·05	1945[1]	1,702,298	0·83
1891	668,632	1·50	1951[1]	1,939,472	2·37
1896	743,207	2·13	1956[1]	2,174,062	2·31
1901[1]	815,853	1·89	1961[1]	2,414,984	2·12
1906	936,304	2·75	1966[1]	2,676,919	2·10
1911	1,058,308	2·52			

[1] Excluding members of the Armed Forces overseas.

The census of New Zealand is quinquennial, but the census falling in 1931 was abandoned as an act of national economy, and owing to war conditions the census due in 1941 was not taken until 25 Sept. 1945.

The areas and populations of statistical areas (with principal centres) at 1 April 1970 were as follows[1]:

Statistical Area[2]	Sq. miles	Total population
Northland (Whangarei)	4,880	95,400
Central Auckland (Auckland)	2,150	673,852
South Auckland—Bay of Plenty (Hamilton)	14,187	415,900
East Coast (Gisborne)	4,200	47,400
Hawke's Bay (Napier, Hastings)	4,260	131,900
Taranaki (New Plymouth)	3,750	101,900
Wellington (Wellington)	10,870	551,200
Total, North Island	*44,297*	*2,017,552*
Marlborough (Blenheim)	4,220	30,600
Nelson (Nelson)	6,910	68,700
Westland (Greymouth)	6,010	23,800
Canterbury (Christchurch)	16,769	390,962
Otago (Dunedin)	14,070	182,600
Southland (Invercargill)	11,460	106,600
Total, South Island	*59,439*	*803,262*
Total, New Zealand	103,736[3]	2,820,814

[1] For statistical purposes, the 9 provincial districts have now been replaced by 13 statistical areas. For the population of the territories overseas *see* pp. 322 ff.
[2] Listed from north to south.   [3] 268,680 sq. km.

Maori population: 1896, 42,113; 1936, 82,326; 1945, 98,744; 1951, 115,676; 1961, 171,553; 1966, 201,159; 31 March 1970 (estimated), 227,090.

The estimated population of the urban areas and cities at 1 April 1970 was as follows:

	Urban area	City proper		Urban area	City proper
Auckland	603,500	152,300	Rotorua	37,300	29,300
Christchurch	260,200	166,100	Tauranga	35,300	26,800
Wellington	179,300	134,900	Whangarei	32,600	30,600
Hutt	122,000	59,400	Gisborne	29,500	26,500
Dunedin	110,100	81,300	Timaru	28,600	28,000
Hamilton	71,900	71,600	Nelson	28,700	28,300
Palmerston North	52,700	51,000	Manukau	96,000[1]	
Invercargill	49,300	46,700	Lower Hutt	59,400[2]	
Napier	41,500	38,200	Takapuna	24,200[1]	
Hastings	41,000	29,100	Porirua	28,500[3]	
Wanganui	38,800	36,600	Papatoetoe	22,000[1]	
New Plymouth	36,700	33,100	Upper Hutt	20,300[2]	

[1] Included in Auckland Urban Area.   [2] Included in Hutt Urban Area.
[3] Included in Wellington Urban Area. *Note:* Wellington and Hutt urban areas may be regarded as a single centre with a combined population of 301,300.

VITAL STATISTICS for calendar years:

	Total live births	Ex-nuptial births	Deaths	Marriages	Divorces (decrees absolute)
1967	61,169	7,783	23,007	23,515	2,047
1968	62,284	8,094	24,464	24,057	2,172
1969	62,564	8,127	24,161	24,971	..

Birth rate, 1969, 22·5 per 1,000; death rate, 8·68 per 1,000; marriage rate, 8·97 per 1,000; infant mortality, 16·89 per 1,000 live births (total).

EXTERNAL MIGRATION (exclusive of crews and through passengers) for years ended 31 March:

	Arrivals	Departures		Arrivals	Departures
1965	190,291	178,300	1968	259,381	267,471
1966	219,939	207,918	1969	255,736	266,584
1967	250.406	235,971	1970	293,406	295,465

Population, Migration and Building. Dept. of Statistics, Wellington, 1969

RELIGION. No direct state aid is given to any form of religion. For the Church of England the country is divided into 7 dioceses, with a separate bishopric (Aotearoa) for the Maoris. The dioceses of Melanesia and Polynesia also form part of the Province of New Zealand. The Bishop of Waiapu is Primate and Archbishop of New Zealand.

The Presbyterian Church is divided into 23 presbyteries and the Maori Synod. The Moderator is elected annually. The Methodist Church is divided into 10 districts; the President is elected annually.

The Roman Catholic Church is divided into 4 dioceses, with the Archbishop of Wellington as Metropolitan Archbishop.

Religious denomination	Number of clergy (Jan. 1969)	Number of adherents	
		1961 census	1966 census
Church of England	692	835,434	901,701
Presbyterian	608	539,459	582,976
Roman Catholic (including 'Catholic' undefined)	894	364,098	425,280
Methodist	364	173,838	186,260
Baptist	192	40,886	46,748
Brethren	85	25,764	23,139
Ratana	142	23,126	27,570
Protestant (undefined)	—	45,100	46,090
Salvation Army	190	15,454	17,737
Church of Christ	48	10,485	10,301
Latter-Day Saints (Mormon)	120	17,978	25,564
Congregationalist	39	9,377	12,101
Seventh-Day Adventist	41	8,220	9,551
Ringatu	66	5,377	5,605
Christian (undefined)	—	12,130	21,548
Christian Scientist	—	3,719	1,161
Jehovah's Witnesses	39	5,944	7,455
Freethinkers	—	3,359	5,474
Hebrew	5	4,006	4,104
Lutheran	14	4,817	5,730
Other bodies[1]	341	30,956	47,893
Unspecified	—	13,916	19,300
Object to state	—	204,056	210,851
No religion (so returned)	—	17,486	32,780
Total	3,880	2,414,984	2,676,919

[1] Including the Society of Friends with 790 members in 1961 and 887 in 1966.

EDUCATION. New Zealand has 6 universities, the University of Auckland, University of Waikato (at Hamilton), Victoria University of Wellington, Massey University (at Palmerston North), the University of Canterbury (at Christchurch) and the University of Otago (at Dunedin). There is, in addition, Lincoln College near Christchurch, a university college of agriculture, which is a constituent college of the University of Canterbury. The number of students in 1969 was 31,542. There were 9 teachers' training colleges with 6,912 students in July 1969.

H

At 1 July 1969 there were 204 state secondary schools with 8,251 full-time teachers and 150,562 pupils. There were also 66 district high schools with 5,311 scholars in the secondary division. At 1 July 1969, 98,208 part-time pupils attended technical classes, including 1,248 receiving part-time tuition from the correspondence school, and 14,165 receiving part-time instruction from the technical correspondence school. At 1 July 1969, 518 full-time pupils received tuition from the secondary department of the correspondence school. There were 116 registered private secondary schools with 1,290 teachers and 27,910 pupils.

At the end of 1969 there were 2,200 state primary schools (including intermediate schools and departments), with 450,850 pupils; the number of teachers was 17,110. A correspondence school for children in remote areas and those otherwise unable to attend school had 1,062 primary pupils and 31 teachers. There were 344 registered primary private schools, with 1,659 teachers and 52,407 pupils.

Education is compulsory between the ages of 6 and 15. Children aged 3 and 4 years may enrol at the 293 free kindergartens maintained by Free Kindergarten Associations, which receive government assistance. There are also 520 play centres offering free educational facilities. In July 1969 there were 22,933 and 15,042 children on the rolls respectively.

There are 28 occupation centres for intellectually handicapped children; 6 cerebral palsy schools; 34 hospital classes, 216 special classes for backward children, 102 speech clinics, 7 health camp schools, 4 classes for partially sighted, 12 remedial clinics, 5 classes for physically handicapped or delicate children; 2 schools for the deaf and 1 private school for deaf children; 16 classes for the deaf; a school for the blind; a residential school for severely disturbed or maladjusted children; 9 classes for maladjusted children; 2 special schools for mentally backward children and 18 psychological centres employing 69 professional officers.

Total expenditure out of government funds in 1969–70 upon education was NZ$209·1m.

ORGANIZATIONAL CONTROL. The universities and the affiliated agricultural colleges are autonomous bodies. Most secondary schools are controlled by their own boards. Virtually all state primary schools are controlled by the district education board: there are 10 education districts. The Department of Education exercises certain defined functions in connexion with the general supervision of the education provided in state primary and secondary schools and disburses the government grants payable to controlling authorities for the running of those schools. Education in state schools is free for children under 19 years of age. Private schools are regularly visited by state school inspectors.

CINEMAS. There were in 1969, 312 cinemas with a seating capacity of 178,722.

NEWSPAPERS. There were, in April 1968, 41 daily newspapers (9 morning and 32 evening) with a combined circulation of 1,044,000. Eight of these newspapers (2 each in Auckland, Wellington, Christchurch and Dunedin) had a circulation of 727,500.

Report of the Minister of Education ('E.1. Report'). Annually. Wellington, Government Printer
NZ Commission on Education, Report . . . Wellington, 1962
NZ Committee on Universities, Report . . . Wellington, 1960
Parkyn, G. W. (ed.), The Administration of Education in New Zealand. Wellington, 1954.—Success and Failure at University. Wellington, 1959
Thom, A. H., The District High Schools of New Zealand. Wellington, 1950
Watson, J. E., Intermediate Schooling in New Zealand. Wellington, 1964

JUSTICE. The judiciary consists of the Chief Justice, 3 judges of the Court of Appeal and 12 Supreme Court judges, 2 judges of the Court of Arbitration and one judge each for the Courts of Compensation and Land Valuation.

At the end of 1969 the gaols and Borstal institutions contained 2,047 prisoners, 1,960 males and 87 females. In 1969, 10,654 persons were received into all penal institutions.

The death penalty for murder was replaced by life imprisonment in 1961.

The Criminal Injuries Act, 1963, which came into force on 1 Jan. 1964, provided for the compensation of persons injured by certain criminal acts and of the dependants of persons killed by such acts.

Police. The police in New Zealand are a national body maintained wholly by the central government. The total strength at 31 March 1970 was 3,119, the proportion of police to population being 1 to 904. The total cost of police services for the year 1969–70 was NZ$14·9m., equivalent to $5.30 per head of population.

Ombudsman. This office (currently held by Sir Guy Powles, KBE, CMG) was created in 1962. His principal function is to investigate complaints from members of the public relating to administrative decisions of government departments and related organizations.

From 1 Oct. 1962 to 31 March 1970, 5,257 complaints were received, 464 of which were held to be justified and were rectified by the department or organization concerned. No complaint of actual malpractice has been found justified.

SOCIAL SECURITY. New Zealand's record for progressive legislation reaches back to 1898, when it was second only to Denmark in introducing non-contributory old-age pensions.

The present system is based on the Social Security Act 1938, which came into operation from 1 April 1939. In a comprehensive scheme it provides for retirement, unemployment, widowhood, invalidity and sickness, as well as hospital and other medical care. Since 1 April 1969 the scheme has been financed from general taxation. Previously there was a special social security tax on virtually all income of individuals and companies in excess of $4 a week which met approximately three-quarters of the cost of the scheme, the balance being met from general taxation.

At 2 Sept. 1970 the current weekly rates of age, widows', invalids', miners' and superannuation benefits were as follows:

Unmarried persons	$14.75
Unmarried under 20 (invalids benefit only)	$12.75
Married persons (each)	$13.50
Married man with dependent wife (age, invalids' and miners' benefit only)	$27.00

For sickness and unemployment benefits the rates were:

Unmarried persons under 20	$11.75
Unmarried over 20	$14.75
Married persons	$13.50
Married man with dependent wife	$27.00

There are additional payments for dependent children.

All benefits except superannuation and family allowances are subject to an income test.

Family Benefit. A family benefit of $1.50 a week is payable for each dependent child, irrespective of the parent's income.

Unemployment Benefit. The payment is subject to the conditions that the applicant is unemployed, has taken reasonable steps to find work and is capable and willing to undertake suitable employment.

Age Benefit. The usual qualifying age is 60 years for both men and women, but the benefit may be granted to an unmarried woman between 55 and 60 years of age who is unable to engage in regular employment. The standard income test applies. Where the wife of a man receiving age benefit is not eligible herself, the husband can receive the benefit at double the rate for the married person.

Superannuation Benefit. The qualifying age for both men and women is 65 years. For a married couple to both receive the benefit each must qualify independently. There is no income test, but a superannuation benefit is not payable in addition to any other benefit except a family benefit.

Sickness Benefit. Payment is subject to medical evidence of incapacity of a person who has suffered a loss of weekly earnings as a result. In no case may the rate of benefit exceed the amount of weekly earnings lost. The standard income test applies.

Other benefits include emergency benefits and supplementary assistance for those who are in need but who either do not qualify for one of the standard benefits or who have special needs or commitments for which a benefit at the standard rate is insufficient.

Medical, Hospital and Related Benefits. In addition to monetary benefits, medical, hospital and other related benefits are also provided under the Social Security scheme. These consist mainly of the payment of certain prescribed fees for medical attention by private practitioners, free treatment in public and mental hospitals, certain prescribed fees for treatment in private hospitals, maternity benefits (including ante-natal and post-natal treatment and services of doctors and nurses at confinements), pharmaceutical benefits (medicines, drugs, etc., prescribed by medical practitioners), etc. There are also benefits in connection with dental services up to the age of 16, X-ray diagnosis, massage, home-nursing, artificial aids, etc.

Pensions (including economic pensions). Provision is made for the payment of pensions and allowances, on certain conditions, to members or dependants of disabled, deceased or missing members, of the New Zealand Forces who served in the South African War, the two World Wars, the Korean War, to members of the New Zealand Mercantile Marine during the Second World War, or in connexion with any emergency whether arising out of the obligations undertaken by New Zealand in the Charter of the United Nations or otherwise. Members of the Emergency Reserve Corps and Civil Defence Organization are also provided for. Principal rates are: War pensions (mercantile marine and emergency reserve corps pensions on similar lines) are payable to widows at a rate of $8.70 a week, together with a mother's allowance of $8.25 a week, increased by $1 a week for the second and each additional child, in addition to the normal child allowance of $1.50 per week for each child. The rate for total disablement is $11.80 plus up to $11.25 a week for a dependent wife if the husband is unable to maintain her. These rates may be increased by an amount not exceeding $7 per week if the pensioner is suffering from total blindness, two or more serious disabilities or one extremely severe disability.

An 'economic pension' is defined as a supplementary pension granted on economic grounds and is additional to any pension payable as of right in respect of death or disablement. The maximum weekly rates are $12 to a married person (if unmarried, $13.25) or the widow or dependent widowed mother of a member.

War veterans' allowances are $637 a year plus an equal amount to a wife, increased by $78 each at age 65, subject to income qualifications.

Social Security Benefits and War Pensions (as at 31 March 1970):

Benefits	Number in force	Annual value (NZ$1,000)	Total payments 1969–70 (NZ$1,000)
SOCIAL SECURITY:			
Monetary—			
Superannuation	142,867	93,336	88,819
Age	98,905	69,022	67,003
Widows	15,663	14,473	13,742
Orphans	315	150	150
Family	408,397	72,318	72,318
Invalids	8,342	6,441	6,093
Miners	98	90	99
Unemployment	983	1,465	1,465
Sickness	5,876	6,073	6,073
Emergency	5,266	4,025	4,025
Supplementary Assistance	12,887	..	2,703
Advances (house repairs and maintenance)	..	..	54
Family (capitalization)	..	..	10,696
Total	699,599	..	262,491

Benefits SOCIAL SECURITY (contd.):	Number in force	Annual value (NZ$1,000)	Total payment 1969–70 (NZ$1,000)
Medical—			
Medical	..	..	9,695
Hospital	..	..	5,487
Maternity	..	..	2,956
Pharmaceutical	..	..	27,308
Supplementary	..	..	7,628
Total	..	..	53,074
WAR PENSION, ETC.:			
First World War	8,836	6,322	6,303
Second World War	24,254	9,087	9,434
South African War	6	..	4
War veterans' allowances	12,032	..	14,195
Mercantile Marine	25	..	10
Emergency Reserve Corps.	8	..	6
K Force	255	83	54
Total	45,416	..	30,006
Sundry Pensions and Annuities	990	..	332
Grand total	46,406	..	30,338

Reciprocity with Other Countries. There are reciprocal arrangements between New Zealand and Australia in respect of age, invalids', widows', family, unemployment and sickness benefits, and between New Zealand and Great Britain and between New Zealand and Northern Ireland in respect of family, age, superannuation, widows', orphans', invalids', sickness and unemployment benefits.

NATIONAL INCOME. Some of the more important national income aggregates for the last 4 years are given in the following tables (in NZ$1m.):

Year ended 31 March	Private income	Public authority trading income	National income at factor cost (national income)	National income at market prices	Gross national product
1967	3,578	147	3,357	3,619	3,919
1968	3,683	168	3,457	3,753	4,074
1969	3,909	188	3,683	4,008	4,354
1970	4,276	207	4,034	4,386	4,757

The source of private income for the last 4 years ended 31 March was as follows (in NZ$1m.):

	1967	1968	1969	1970
Salary and wage payments	2,041	2,128	2,246	2,490
Pay and allowances, Armed Forces	39	42	43	45
Social security benefits and pensions	252	270	278	299
Rental value, owner occupier houses	119	129	136	150
Other personal income:				
Farming	298	289	300	292
Manufacturing and commerce	213	207	214	227
Professional and other services	97	101	109	118
Changes due to income stabilization measures	−19	−15	−8	−5
Interests, rent	74	76	80	83

FINANCE. Currency. Decimal currency was introduced on 10 July 1967. The monetary unit is the New Zealand dollar, divided into 100 cents. On 21 Nov. 1967 New Zealand devalued its currency by 19·45% in relation to the US dollar, bringing the NZ dollar to parity with the Australian dollar. At IMF par value, the NZ dollar became worth £0·4667 sterling.

Budget. The following tables of revenue and expenditure relate to the Consolidated Revenue Account, which covers the ordinary revenue and expenditure of the general government—*i.e.,* apart from capital items, commercial and special undertakings, advances, etc. Revenue in the Account (in NZ$1m.) was as follows:

Year ended 31 March	Customs and excise	Sales tax	Income tax and social security tax	Other taxes	Trading profits and departmental receipts	Interest	Total
1967	126·7	78·9	664·4	48·6	66·4	66·3	1,051·3
1968	141·6	75·4	672·8	59·7	66·5	76·0	1,091·9
1969	154·1	82·8	691·6	63·6	64·7	84·1	1,140·9
1970	156·2	97·6	779·2	69·1	73·3	89·9	1,265·4

Expenditure from the Consolidated Revenue Account was as follows (in NZ$1m.):

Year ended 31 March	Debt services	Social services[1]	Industrial development	Defence	General administration and finance	Total (including other)
1967	144·6	571·5	60·0	88·6	79·9	1,050·6
1968	170·4	608·5	63·2	87·1	61·6	1,095·3
1969	149·8	644·0	67·5	85·3	61·8	1,146·9
1970	185·2	707·0	81·5	89·7	65·3	1,275·1

[1] Includes education, health, and social security.

Taxation receipts in 1969–70 for all purposes amounted to $1,181,251,000, giving an average of $423 per head of mean population. Included in the total taxation is $78,836,000 National Roads Fund taxation. The estimate for 1970–71 is $1,308m., the total being inclusive of an estimated $84m. of National Roads Fund taxation.

The gross public debt at 31 March 1970 was $2,877m., of which $2,260m. was held in New Zealand, $341·6m. in London and Europe, $107·5m. in USA and $76·8m. with the World Bank. The gross annual interest charge on the public debt at 31 March 1970 was $143,958,000.

DEFENCE. The control and co-ordination of defence activities is obtained through the Ministry of Defence, the establishment of which was approved by Government in Nov. 1962. This is a unitary department combining not only all joint-Service functions but also the former Departments of Army, Navy and Air. The Ministry acts as a co-ordinating defence authority to advise the Government on defence policy, planning and expenditure. The Secretary of Defence, in addition to his function as head of the Ministry, is responsible for co-ordinating the business of the Ministry as a whole and for the co-ordination of long-term financial planning. The principal military adviser to the Minister is the Chief of the Defence Staff, who is also the convenor and chairman of the Chiefs of Staff Committee, which comprises the Chief of the Defence Staff and the Chiefs of the Naval, General and Air Staffs.

The major corporate body within the Ministry of Defence is the Defence Council, which consists of the Minister as Chairman, the Secretary of Defence and the Chief of the Defence Staff as deputy chairmen and the Chiefs of Staff of the 3 services, and may co-opt officers of other departments. Subject to the control of the Minister of Defence, the Defence Council is responsible for the administration and command of the Defence Forces and for advising the Minister on important matters of defence policy.

Army. The Army Board consists of the Minister of Defence as chairman, the Chief of the General Staff, Adjutant-General, Quartermaster-General, Deputy Secretary of Defence (Army) and a senior Territorial Officer.

The New Zealand Army is organized into the Static Support Force of regular personnel; the Field Force containing a combat brigade group and a logistic support force with regular and integrated regular and territorial units; a Combat Reserve Brigade manned mainly by Territorials; the Cadet Corps.

New Zealand contributes to military operations in South Vietnam 2 regular infantry companies, an artillery battery and a medical team. A Regular Force battalion is stationed in Malaysia as part of the Commonwealth Strategic Reserve. There is also an engineer road construction team in Thailand.

Regular personnel, on 31 March 1970, totalled 5,782 all ranks; territorial personnel totalled 11,169; the cadet corps totalled 10,637 cadets.

Navy. The Royal New Zealand Navy is administered by the New Zealand Naval Board. This board consists of: (*a*) The Minister of Defence (as Chairman of the Board); (*b*) First Naval Member (the Chief of Naval Staff); (*c*) Second Naval Member (for Personnel); (*d*) Third Naval Member (for Technical Services); (*e*) The Deputy Secretary of Defence (Navy).

The RNZN ships include 4 frigates, 1 surveying vessel (*ex*-frigate), 2 escort minesweepers, 9 seaward patrol craft, 1 antarctic support ship and 2 tenders.

Personnel, on 31 March 1970, totalled 2,975 officers and ratings and 2,378 in the naval reserve.

Air Force. The Royal New Zealand Air Force is organized on a two-group basis, comprising Operations Group and Training Group, both of which are responsible to an Air Headquarters. The superior agency of the Air Headquarters is an Air Board, comprising the Minister of Defence (chairman), the Chief of Air Staff, Air Member for Personnel, Air Member for Supply and a Deputy Secretary of Defence (Air).

The Operations Group has the responsibility for the operational functions of the RNZAF and has its headquarters at Auckland. A Training Group with headquarters at Wigram (Christchurch) is responsible for all RNZAF training. Ten A-4K Skyhawk attack aircraft supported by 4 TA-4K trainers, equip No. 75 Squadron at Ohakea. Other operational units include 1 maritime reconnaissance squadron of P-3B Orions, 1 battlefield support squadron equipped with Bristol Freighters, Austers, Iroquois and Sioux helicopters, 1 long-range transport squadron with C-130 Hercules aircraft, 1 Bristol Freighter transport squadron based in Singapore and 1 communications squadron flying C-47s and Devons. Training types include Airtourers, Harvards and Vampires.

The strength on 31 March 1970 was about 4,475 regular personnel and 1,850 non-regular personnel.

PLANNING. A series of 'key sector' conferences were held between 1953 and 1964 to plan the development of housing, industry, exports and agriculture. Long-term economic projections were used as the basis from planning targets for sector production for up to a decade ahead. The experiences gained from these conferences resulted in the National Development Conference held in May 1969. Among the major targets adopted by the conference were an increase in real GNP of 4½% per annum; an increase in exports of 6·6% per annum; and an increase in the proportion of GNP used for investment. Major expansions are planned for tourism, forestry and agriculture. The National Development Council, representing both Government and the private sector, is continuing the work of the conference.

Major industrial developments in recent years have included the establishment of a large-scale timber, pulp and paper industry and an oil refinery. Electricity generating capacity has been doubled in 10 years. An iron and steel industry using New Zealand iron sands is being developed, as is an aluminium smelter using cheap hydro-electric power. Natural gas deposits are being commercially exploited.

AGRICULTURE. Two-thirds of the surface of New Zealand is suitable for agriculture and grazing. The total area under cultivation at 31 Jan. 1968 was 22,721,340 acres (including residential area and domestic orchards). There were 20,149,653 acres of sown pasture, including areas sown with crops, and 1,102,142 acres of timber plantations. The area of Crown lands (other than reserves) leased under various tenures at 31 March 1970 was 14,908,142 acres.

The largest freehold estates are held in the South Island. The extent of occupied holdings of or over 10 acres as at 31 Jan. 1960 (exclusive of holdings within borough boundaries) was as follows:

Size of holdings (acres)	Number	Acres	Size of holdings (acres)	Number	Acres
10– 19	4,549	61,808	2,000– 4,999	2,021	6,091,356
20– 49	7,172	237,958	5,000– 9,999	551	3,755,107
50– 99	12,353	918,596	10,000–19,999	264	3,839,876
100– 149	11,068	1,343,984	20,000–29,999	84	2,031,858
150– 199	7,316	1,274,528	30,000–49,999	61	2,298,538
200– 319	10,687	2,692,109	50,000 and over	53	4,871,885
320– 639	12,109	5,470,835			
640– 999	4,659	3,683,904	Total	76,928	44,018,897
1,000–1,999	3,981	5,446,555			

The acreage and produce for each of the principal crops are given as follows (area and yield for threshing only, not including that grown for chaff, hay, silage, etc.):

	Wheat			Oats			Barley		
Crop years	Acres	1,000 bushels	Average per acre	Acres	1,000 bushels	Average per acre	Acres	1,000 bushels	Average per acre
1968	313,000	16,253	51·93	34,000	2,467	72·56	155,000	9,674	62·41
1969	321,000	16,779	52·27	39,000	2,874	73·69	157,000	10,254	55·69
1970[1]	260,000	10,221	39·31	50,000	3,042	60·84	131,000	7,296	55·69

[1] Estimate.

Private air companies are carrying out such aerial work as top-dressing, spraying and crop-dusting, seed-sowing, rabbit poisoning, aerial photography and surveying, and dropping supplies to deer cullers and dropping fencing materials in remote areas. The main aerial activity was top-dressing, statistics for the year ended March 1970 being: Hours flown, 115,732; fertilizer distributed, 924,000 tons.

Livestock in 1969: 8,604,874 cattle (including 2,304,000 milch cows), 59,937,000 sheep and 553,388 pigs. Total meat produced in the year ended 30 Sept. 1969 was 1,014,100 tons (including 344,200 tons of beef and 357,100 tons of lamb). Total liquid milk produced in the year ended 31 May 1970 was 1,301·8m. gallons; of this, 1,157·7m. were used for butter and cheese making.

Production of wool for the 12 months ended 30 June 1969, 735m. lb. (greasy basis); exports of all wool in the year ended 30 June 1970, was 579·8m. lb.

Primary Production in New Zealand. Dept. of Agriculture, Wellington, 1962
Farm Production. Dept. of Statistics, Wellington, 1968
National Resources Survey. West Coast Region: Bay of Plenty Region: Northland Region: Nelson Region. Ministry of Works, Wellington, 1959, 1962
Evans, B. L., *A History of Agricultural Production and Marketing.* Palmerston North, 1969
Hadfield, J. W., *Arable farmcrops of New Zealand.* Wellington, 1952
Levy, Sir Bruce, *Grasslands of New Zealand.* Wellington, 1955
Poole, A. L., *Forestry in New Zealand: the Shaping of Policy.* London, 1969

MANUFACTURES. Statistics of the principal manufactories (excluding mines and quarries):

Production year	Persons engaged	Salaries and wages paid (NZ$1,000)	Cost of materials (NZ$1,000)	Value of production (NZ$1,000)	Net output (net value added) (NZ$1,000)
1965–66	222,851	455,030	1,416,403	2,374,447	709,211
1966–67	229,302	492,730	1,466,347	2,483,742	741,407
1967–68	225,738	495,878	1,492,863	2,538,349	756,657

The following is a statement of the value of the products (including repairs) of the principal industries for the year 1967–68 (in NZ$1,000):

Manufactures, works, etc.	Value of products	Manufactories, works, etc.	Value of products
Meat freezing and preserving	396,146	Sheet-metal working	54,039
Ham and bacon curing	20,906	Basic metal industries	29,669
Butter and cheese	180,994	Machinery (including agricultural)	124,608
Other milk products	56,845	Metal products	56,088
Wool-scouring	35,850	Electrical machinery	56,577
Saw-milling (excl. logging) planing, etc.	84,802	Printing and publishing (newspapers)	47,126
Lime-crushing and cement	17,028	Job and general printing	45,243
Grain-milling	18,550	Motor-body building	11,622
Biscuit	11,214	Motor and cycle repairs	133,446
Confectionery	19,740	Motor vehicle assembly	86,872
Fruit and vegetable preserving	31,263	Rubber ware	36,518
Brewing and malting	32,110	Furniture and fixtures	38,315
Tobacco and cigarettes	20,050	Footwear (other than rubber)	26,438
Paint and varnish	16,620	Woollen-mills	23,445
Chemical fertilizers	41,859	Hosiery and knitted goods	34,295
Joinery and wood products	50,361	Clothing manufacture	93,594
Paper bags and cartons	38,117	Petroleum and coal products	62,391

Ward, R. G. and M. W. (ed.), *New Zealand's Industrial Potential*. Auckland, 1960
Industrial Production. Dept. of Statistics, Wellington, 1970

MINING. New Zealand's production of minerals in 1969 included 10,400 fine oz. of gold, 2,129 tons of diatomite earth, 5,630 tons of bentonite, 256,263 tons of clay for bricks, tiles, etc., 9,889 tons of potters' clays, 1,167 tons of iron ore, 1,010,194 tons of limestone for agriculture and 112,136 tons of limestone for industry, 1,470,342 tons of limestone, marl, etc., for cement, 19,001 tons of pumice, 76,991 tons of serpentine, 105,787 tons of silica sand. Mineral fuel production amounted to 2,326,607 tons of coal, 105,570 gallons of crude petroleum and 2,336,100 cu. ft of natural gas. Mineral production for the year was valued at $47,684,353.

The resources of natural gas discovered in 1961 in the Taranaki area of the North Island are now being developed and pipelines are being laid to Auckland and Wellington for household supply.

ELECTRICITY. The general policy of the Government in regard to electric power is to supply power in bulk, leaving the reticulation and retail supply in the hands of local authorities. Originally these consisted of cities, boroughs, etc., but, to facilitate the extension of electric supply into country areas, Electric Power Boards were created, and these now embrace most of the country. Some Power Boards operate small generating stations. Practically all stations rely on water-power, but there are 3 steam-powered stations, 2 coal-fired with a capacity of 420,000 kw., the other geothermal-operated with a present capacity of 192,420 kw. which could ultimately be raised to 250,000–280,000 kw.

Principal statistics for 4 years ended 31 March are:

	1966	1967	1968	1969
Number of establishments	97	97	98	98
Total motive power (1,000 b.h.p.)	3,462	3,639	4,043	4,280
Generators (capacity) AC (1,000 kw.)	2,522	2,650	2,927	3,138
Units generated (1m. kwh.)	10,578	11,317	11,605	12,185
Revenue ($1,000)	161,630	174,031	194,925	221,438
Expenditure:				
Operating ($1,000)	82,080	86,294	94,943	107,940
Management, etc. ($1,000)	10,370	11,515	12,877	14,148
Capital charges ($1,000)	50,348	55,077	65,396	72,308
Capital outlay:				
During year ($1,000)	84,804	111,899	99,978	73,652
To date ($1,000)	918,794	1,030,693	1,130,671	1,204,322

TOURISM. The country has a growing tourist industry, and the number of visitors has trebled in the last 8 years. In the year ended 31 March 1970, 241,110 travellers visited New Zealand (including 118,706 tourists), compared with 220,685 (including 100,341 tourists) in 1968–69.

LABOUR. In Dec. 1969 there were 359 industrial unions of workers with a total of 366,436 members.

The industrial distribution of the labour force as estimated in April 1970 was: Primary industries, 143,800; manufacturing, 303,600; construction, 86,000; commerce, 189,500; transport and communication, 96,200; services, 72,800; administration and professions, 185,500; armed forces, 11,900; unemployed, 1,400; total labour force, 1,090,700.

All employees are entitled to workers' compensation benefits.

Unions of workers and employers are registered under the Conciliation and Arbitration Act 1954. A union of workers can compel employers to negotiate with it in a Conciliation Council and, if no agreement is reached, to secure a decision from the Court of Arbitration in the form of an award governing wages, hours and working conditions.

Woods, N. S., *Industrial Conciliation and Arbitration in New Zealand*. Wellington, 1963

COMMERCE. Trade (excluding specie and bullion) in NZ$1,000 for 12 months ended 30 June:

	Total merchandise imported (c.d.v.)[2]	Exports of domestic produce	Re-exports	Total merchandise exported (f.o.b.)
1966–67	753,206	717,623	9,601	727,224
1967–68	617,392	804,637	15,838	820,475
1968–69	1,006,022	968,878	20,219	989,097
1969–70[1]	849,644	1,064,774	22,251	1,087,026

[1] Provisional figures. [2] Current domestic value in country of export.

The principal imports for the 12 months ended 30 June 1970:

Articles of import	Quantity (in 1,000)	Value (NZ$1,000) (c.d.v.)
Fruit and vegetables	..	12,766
Wheat	553 bu.	717
Sugar (raw)	2,745 cwt	9,123
Tea	16,835 lb.	4,621
Alcoholic beverages (including wines)	..	4,427
Tobacco	..	4,322
Textile fibres	..	7,517
Clothing and footwear	..	4,515
Textiles, yarns, fabrics, etc.	..	88,097
Petroleum and petroleum products	..	58,952
Iron and steel	9,945 cwt	74,921
Non-ferrous metals	..	42,442
Electrical machinery	..	55,298
Agricultural machinery	..	21,615
Other machinery (excluding electric)	..	107,671
Transport equipment (excluding motor cars)	..	72,399
Motor cars	62 no.	61,611
Other metal manufactures (excluding machinery	..	31,354
Raw rubber and rubber goods (including tyres)	..	15,014
Paper (printing and other)	..	10,928
Fertilizers	..	17,179
Chemical elements and compounds	..	31,484
Medicinal and pharmaceutical products	..	23,127
Timber	..	4,866
Printed matter	..	19,841
Plastic materials	..	26,309

The principal exports of New Zealand produce for the 12 months ended 30 June 1970 were:

Articles of export	Quantity (in 1,000)	Value (NZ$1,000)	Articles of export	Quantity (in 1,000)	Value (NZ$1,000)
Butter	3,896 cwt	109,695	Meats, canned	7,585 lb:	3,219
Cheese	1,783 cwt	44,343	Sausage casings	7.649 hanks	13,495
Edible tallow	4 tons	630	Milk and cream	..	34,228
Inedible tallow	67 tons	8,382	Apples	118,177 lb.	8,724
Fish	152 cwt	14,299	Hides and skins	..	48,779
Meats, frozen:			Seeds (grass and		
Pork	1,511 lb.	597	clover)	175 centals	3,576
Edible offals	81,610 lb.	22.033	Frozen and canned vegetables	..	6,245
Other	8,347 lb.	4,498	ned vegetables	..	6,245
Beef	369,773 lb.	143,277	Casein	1,220 cwt	25,753
Veal	22,220 lb.	11,014	Wool	668,731 lb.	204,465
Lamb	707,480 lb.	154,952	Newsprint	2,392 cwt	15,848
Mutton	261,903 lb.	28,249	Pulp	82 tons	7,286

The following table shows the trade with different countries (in NZ$1,000):

Countries	Imports c.d.v. from 1968	1969	1970	Exports and re-exports f.o.b. to 1968	1969	1970
Australia	132,871	158,329	197,144	57,765	74,282	36,997
Bahrain	390	1,659	3,672	..	8	29
Belgium and Luxembourg	2,753	4,183	4,442	11,462	19,304	21,307
British West Indies	381	382	416	10,589	9,900	11,583
Canada	29,501	30,448	37,4º2	10,528	16,383	45,225
Ceylon	4,405	4,937	4,401	765	1,242	2,049
China	2,842	4,984	4,366	5,717	3,683	4,086
Czechoslovakia	1,330	1,483	1,800	946	1,014	2,776
Denmark	1,862	1,862	2,434	1,684	1,825	2,456
Fiji	659	2,496	959	5,753	7,638	8,822
France and Monaco	5,186	6,670	7,534	26,510	36,781	28,732
Germany (West)	21,077	33,807	36,822	21,033	28,734	29,564
Ghana	2,042	1,069	2,702	125	118	140
Hong Kong	12,997	13,722	17,872	2,557	3,673	4,581
India	5,848	8,882	8,509	1,015	1,962	1,357
Indonesia	659	1,058	1,596	23	75	780
Iran	9,769	10,152	11,390	199	311	1,318
Italy and San Marino	8,370	11,145	11,914	15,548	21,591	23,720
Japan	51,359	64,594	78,115	68,186	88,001	106,870
Malaysia	4,700[1]	6,621	6,434[1]	6,763[1]	6,319	7,264[1]
Nauru	4,097	6,136	6,317	368	369	359
Netherlands and Antilles	6,798	8,472	9,672	11,006	14,173	16,667
Norway	1,035	1,518	1,367	800	1,326	1,197
Panama (incl. Canal Zone)	..	..	..	520	798	925
Peru	18	26	40	3,987	2,310	4,127
Philippines	195	268	242	5,979	7,031	6,479
Poland	82	308	430	1,346	2,103	3,129
Portugal	496	651	684	1,898	1,499	1,804
Saudi Arabia	3,612	4,973	5,041	49	70	108
Singapore	1,823	3,038	3,060	6,061	8,424	8,731
South Africa	2,344	3,941	3,941	1,959	2,472	3,183
Sweden	8,120	9,390	7,299	1,963	2,493	2,590
Switzerland	6,361	9,281	9,382	1,009	1,035	2,162
UK	187,878	243,483	278,610	352,039	382,749	385,718
USSR	284	728	646	5,839	11,669	16,934
USA	68,304	99,655	123,166	138,240	169,802	166,066
Venezuela	841	2	..	101	295	430
Western Samoa	1,395	1,257	1,441	1,528	1,946	3,399

[1] Excluding Singapore.

According to the British Board of Trade returns, the total trade between UK and New Zealand was as follows (in £1,000 sterling):

	1966	1967	1968	1969	1970
Imports to UK	186,978	185,894	196,602	216,159	203,558
Exports from UK	126,334	99,366	102,957	120,230 }	129,285
Re-exports from UK	1,282	621	828	1,100 }	

SHIPPING. At the end of 1969 the registered vessels were 36 steamships, 589 motor vessels, 64 other vessels (sailing ships, barges, etc.); total, 689 vessels of 99,881 net tons.

Shipping inwards and outwards (excluding coastwise shipping):

	Vessels inwards With cargo No.	Tons	In ballast No.	Tons	Vessels outwards With cargo No.	Tons	In ballast No.	Tons
1967	788	4,179,566	244	1,657,999	730	3,149,429	327	2,736,951
1968	817	4,326,337	377	2,319,229	879	3,455,199	316	3,107,462
1969	839	4,467,277	391	2,466,944	940	3,891,073	290	2,995,700

RAILWAYS. On 31 March 1970 there were 3,063 miles of 3 ft 6 in. gauge railway open for traffic. Operating earnings from government railways, 1969–70, $83,194,012; operating expenses, $79,835,943. In 1969–70 the tonnage of goods (including livestock) carried was 11,592,946, and passengers numbered 21,031,381. In addition, the railways road motor-services carried 22,175,000 passengers. Two rail/road ferries maintain a regular service between the North and South Islands and 2 more vessels are on order.

The total revenue (including road motor and other subsidiary services) amounted to $99,728,906, and total expenditure $96,001,871 in 1969–70.

ROADS. Total mileage of formed roads in New Zealand at 31 March 1969 was 58,265. There were 9,483 bridges of over 25 ft in length with a total length of 880,683 ft at 31 March 1968. The network of State highways, which from 1 April 1960 replaced the system of State and main highways, comprised, at 31 March 1969, 7,239 miles, including the principal arterial traffic routes.

Total expenditure on roads, streets and bridges by the central government and local authorities combined for the financial year 1969–70 amounted to $108,312,863.

At 31 March 1970 motor vehicles licensed numbered 1,174,078, of which 871,864 were cars, 4,737 omnibuses and contract vehicles, 171,477 goods service vehicles. Included in the remaining number were 29,285 motor cycles, 18,826 power cycles and 77,889 vehicles exempt from paying fees. Licensed road goods-services for the year ended 31 March 1969 recorded a total vehicle mileage of 330m. Total revenue amounted to $153·1m. The road passenger services vehicle miles amounted to 83,324,000, and passengers carried totalled 171,148,000. Total passenger revenue amounted to $27,288,670.

AVIATION. Domestic scheduled passenger services are mainly operated by the New Zealand National Airways Corporation. A private company operates an inter-island freight service under contract to the New Zealand Railways Department. International services are operated to and from New Zealand by a state-owned company, Air New Zealand Ltd, and by a number of overseas companies. Non-scheduled services are run by the main companies and also by a number of small operators and aero clubs.

Domestic scheduled services during the 12 months ended March 1970: Passengers carried, 1,478,785; mail, 1,859 tons; freight, 67,034 tons. International services: Passengers carried, 487,194; mail, 1,358,697 kg; freight, 11,247,836 kg.

POST. Receipts of the Post Office for year ended 31 March 1970 were $119,499,423; total expenditure was $117,086,940. Personnel numbered 31,773 (including 4,861 temporary and casual).

The telegraph and telephone systems are operated by the Post Office. At 31 March 1970 there were 802,805 telephone subscribers and 1,202,590 telephones. The telegraph and telephone receipts for the year 1969–70 were $82,793,216.

From 1 April 1962 the New Zealand Broadcasting Corporation took over from the Government the control and operation of radio and television services. Nearly 80% of New Zealand households have TV sets. There are 47 medium-wave broadcasting stations and 2 short-wave transmitters. Some commercial material is broadcast by both sound and TV services. Number of radio and TV receiving licences at 31 March 1970 was 801,206.

BANKING. The Reserve Bank is the sole note-issuing authority. Six denominations of Reserve Bank notes are issued: NZ$1, 2, 5, 10, 20, 100.

The New Zealand banking system comprises a central bank—the Reserve Bank of New Zealand—5 commercial or trading banks and 19 savings banks (including the post office savings bank). The trading banks have operated savings-bank facilities from 1 Oct. 1964.

The Reserve Bank was set up with £500,000 publicly subscribed shares in 1934; in 1936 these shares were purchased by the Government and the bank became a state-owned institution. The primary functions of the Bank are to act as the central bank, to advise the Government on matters relating to monetary policy, banking and overseas exchange, and to give effect to the monetary policy of the Government. In 1960 the Bank's statutory powers of credit regulation were extended to the regulation and control on behalf of the Government, of money, banking, credit, currency interest rates and the transfer of money to and from New Zealand, and particularly the control of trading-bank credit. Final authority to determine the London–New Zealand exchange rates has been transferred to the Minister of Finance subject to consultation with the Bank.

Of the 5 trading banks 2 are primarily Australian concerns, 2 have their head office in London and the Bank of New Zealand has been state owned since 1 Nov. 1945.

At the end of March 1970 the amount on deposit at trading banks was $851·4m., while advances amounted to $685m. The daily average bank-note circulation in March 1970 was $147·8m.

The number of accounts with the post office savings bank at 31 March 1970 was 2,701.000; amount deposited during year, $586·5m.; withdrawn, $561·8m.; total amount to credit of depositors at end of year, $922·02m. At 31 March 1970, $435·69m. was on deposit in 13 Trustee Savings Banks to the credit of 1,238,000 depositors. The amount to the credit of 663,000 depositors with savings accounts in the trading banks was $326·8m. at 31 March 1970. The post office school savings scheme is operated by 2,370 schools, deposits totalling $4·05m. as at 31 March 1970.

MINOR ISLANDS

The minor islands (total area, 320 sq. miles, 775 sq. km) included within the geographical boundaries of New Zealand are the following: Kermadec Islands, Three Kings Islands, Auckland Islands, Campbell Island, Antipodes Islands, Bounty Islands, Snares Islands, Solander Island. With the exception of Raoul Island in the Kermadec Group (population, 9) and Campbell Island (population, 9) none of these islands is inhabited.

The **Kermadec Islands,** which were annexed to New Zealand in 1887, have no separate administration and all New Zealand laws apply to them. Situation, 29° 10′ to 31° 30′ S. lat., 177° 45′ to 179° W. long., 600 miles N.N.E. of New Zealand. Area, 13 sq. miles (33·5 sq. km). The largest of the group is Raoul or Sunday Island, 20 miles in circuit, while Macauley Island is 3 miles in circuit.

A meteorological station and an aeradio station have been established on Raoul Island, the official staff of 9 being the only inhabitants.

TERRITORIES OVERSEAS

Territories Overseas coming within the jurisdiction of New Zealand consist of Niue Island, the Tokelau Islands and the Ross Dependency.

Niue Island is one of the Cook Islands, but has been under separate administration since 1903. There is a Resident Commissioner and an Island Assembly, and legislative measures apply as in the case of the Cook Islands. Distance from Auckland, New Zealand, 1,343 miles; from Rarotonga, 580 miles. Area, 100 sq. miles; circumference, 40 miles; height above sea-level, 220 ft. Population at 31 March 1970 was 5,302. During 1968 live births registered numbered 194, deaths 44.

Revenue, 1968–69, $809,453 (excluding grants from New Zealand, $900,000); expenditure, $1,766,969. Exports, 1968, $56,832; imports, $693,323.

There were 10 government schools with 1,848 pupils in 1969. There is a wireless station at Alofi, the port of the island. Telephones in use at 31 March 1969 numbered 172. The most important products of the island are copra, kumaras and bananas.

Resident Commissioner: S. D. Wilson.

Tokelau Islands. Situated some 300 miles to the north of Western Samoa between 8° and 10° S. lat., and between 171° and 173° W. long., are the 3 atoll islands of Atafu, Nukunonu and Fakaofo of the Tokelau (Union) group. Formerly part of the Gilbert and Ellice Islands Colony, the group was transferred to the jurisdiction of New Zealand on 11 Feb. 1926, the administration being carried out by the Administrator in Apia, Western Samoa. By legislation enacted in 1948, the Tokelau Islands were declared part of New Zealand as from 1 Jan. 1949. The area of the group is 4 sq. miles; the population at 25 Sept. 1969 was 1,745.

Ross Dependency. By Imperial Order in Council, dated 30 July 1923, the territories between 160° E. long. and 150° W. long. and south of 60° S. lat. were brought within the jurisdiction of the New Zealand Government. The region was named the Ross Dependency. From time to time laws for the Dependency have been made by regulations promulgated by the Governor-General of New Zealand.

The mainland area is estimated at 160,000 sq. miles and is completely ice-covered. In Jan. 1957 a New Zealand expedition under Sir Edmund Hillary established a base in the Dependency. In Jan. 1958 Sir Edmund Hillary and 4 other New Zealanders reached the South Pole. Survey parties explored and mapped a large part of the Dependency in 1957–59. On 15 April 1958 the Government set up the Ross Dependency Research Committee to co-ordinate and supervise New Zealand activity beyond the conclusion of the International Geophysical Year. Occupation and exploration of the Territory have continued since.

SELF-GOVERNING TERRITORY OVERSEAS

The **Cook Islands**, which lie between 8° and 23° S. lat., and 156° and 167° W. long., were proclaimed a British protectorate in 1888, and on 11 June 1901 were annexed and proclaimed part of New Zealand. The islands within the territory fall roughly into two groups—the scattered islands towards the north (Northern group) and the islands towards the south known as the Lower group.

Area and Population. The names of the islands with their populations as at 1 Sept. 1966 were as follows:

Lower Group—	Population	Northern Group—	Population
Rarotonga	9,971	Nassau	167
Mangaia	2,002	Palmerston (Avarau)	86
Atiu	1,327	Penrhyn (Tongareva)	545
Aitutaki	2,579	Manihiki (Humphrey)	584
Mauke (Parry I.)	671	Rakahanga (Reirson)	323
Mitiaro	293	Pukapuka (Danger)	684
Manuae and Te au-o-tu	15	Suwarrow (Anchorage)	Nil
		Total	19,247

Total area of the Cook Islands, excluding Niue, is about 93 sq. miles (241 sq. km). Rarotonga is 20 miles in circumference; Atiu, 20 miles; Aitutaki, 14·5 miles. Total population (1968) 20,938.

In 1966, 823 live births and 168 deaths were registered.

Constitution and Government. The Cook Islands Constitution Act 1964, which provides for the establishment of internal self-government in the Cook Islands, came into force on 4 Aug. 1965.

The Act establishes the Cook Islands as fully self-governing but linked to New Zealand by a common Head of State, the Queen, and a common citizenship, that of New Zealand. It provides for a ministerial system of government with a Cabinet consisting of a Premier and up to 5 other Ministers. The Resident Commissioner became the High Commissioner of the Cook Islands, who exercises the dual functions of representative of the Queen and of the New Zealand Government. New Zealand continues to be responsible for the external affairs and defence of the Cook Islands, subject to consultation between the New Zealand Prime Minister and the Premier. The changed status of the Islands does not affect the consideration of subsidies or the right of free entry into New Zealand for exports from the group.

High Commissioner: L. J. Davis.

Health. All Cook Islanders receive free medical and surgical treatment in their villages, the hospital and the tuberculosis sanatorium. Cook Island Maori patients in the hospital and the sanatorium and all schoolchildren receive free dental treatment.

Education. Twenty-four primary schools are established in the various islands. There are also 6 Roman Catholic missionary schools and a Seventh Day Adventist mission school. Post-primary education is provided for by 4 government and 2 mission schools on Rarotonga. The instruction given in government schools is similar to that of the New Zealand state schools, but with a special syllabus suited to the requirements of the people. Regular instruction is given in the Maori language in all classes, while during the first 2 years all instruction is in the vernacular, English being taught only as a subject. Numbers of pupils on the rolls (31 March 1967): Government schools, 5,116; Roman Catholic and Seventh Day Adventist, 380.

Finance. Revenue is derived chiefly from customs duties which follow the New Zealand customs tariff, income tax and stamp sales, and for the financial year 1965–66 amounted to $1,582,130 (excluding grants from New Zealand of $1,743,000, mainly for medical and educational purposes); expenditure, $3,229,860.

Commerce. Imports during 1967 were valued at $2,991,000, and exports at $1·78m. Chief exports were citrus fruits ($157,000), fruit juice ($906,000), manufactured goods (apparel) ($395,000), copra ($101,000), pearl shell ($19,000) and tomatoes ($31,000).

Communications. Wireless stations are maintained at all the permanently inhabited islands. A monthly passenger-cargo shipping service and a weekly air service are provided between New Zealand and Rarotonga.

Buck, P. H., *Vikings of the Sunrise.* New York. 1938.—*The Coming of the Maori.* Wellington. 1950
Ross, A. (ed.) *New Zealand's Record in the Pacific Islands in the Twentieth Century*, Auckland, 1969

BOOKS OF REFERENCE

STATISTICAL INFORMATION. The central statistical office for New Zealand is the Department of Statistics (Wellington, C1). *Government Statistician:* J. P. Lewin, MA, LLB, Dip. Jour.
    The beginning of a statistical service may be seen in the early 'Blue books' prepared annually from 1840 onwards under the direction of the Colonial Secretary, and designed primarily for the information of the Colonial Office in England. A permanent statistical authority was created in 1858. The Department of Statistics functions under the Statistics Act 1955 and reports to Parliament through the minister in charge of the Department, who is usually also the Minister of Finance. A comprehensive statistical service has been developed to meet national requirements, and close control is maintained with the United Nations Statistical Office and other international statistical organizations; through the Conference of Asian Statisticians assistance is being given with the development of statistics in the region.
    The oldest publications consist of (*a*) census results from 1858 onwards and (*b*) annual volumes of statistics (first published 1858 but covering years back to 1853). Main current publications:

New Zealand Official Yearbook. Annual, from 1893
Local Authority Statistics of New Zealand. Annual, from 1926
Catalogue of New Zealand Statistics. 1966
Statistical Reports of New Zealand. Annual
Monthly Abstract of Statistics. From 1914
Pocket Digest of Statistics. Annual, 1927–31, 1938 ff.

Parliamentary Reports of Government Departments. Annual
Pacific Islands Yearbook. Sydney, 1968
Dictionary of New Zealand Biography. 2 vols. Wellington, 1940

Encyclopaedia of New Zealand. 3 vols. Wellington, 1966
Money and Banking in New Zealand. Wellington, 1963
National Bibliography. Wellington, 1968
New Zealand Financial System. Wellington, 1966
Oxford New Zealand Encyclopaedia. London, 1965
Department of Maori Affairs, *The Maori today.* Wellington, 1964
Baker, J. V. T., *The New Zealand People at War; War Economy.* Wellington, 1965
Best, Elsdon, *The Maori as he was.* Wellington, 1952
Bright, T. N., *Banking Law and Practice in New Zealand.* 2nd ed. Wellington, 1969
Condliffe, J. B., *The Economic Outlook for New Zealand.* Wellington, 1969
Firth, R., *Economics of the New Zealand Maori.* Wellington, Government Printer, 1959
Hall, D. O. W., *Portrait of New Zealand.* 3rd ed. Wellington, 1961
Holcroft, M. H., *New Zealand.* Wellington, 1968
Institute of Public Administration, *Administration in New Zealand's Multi-racial Society.* Wellington, 1968
McLintock, A. H. (ed.), *A Descriptive Atlas of New Zealand.* Wellington, Government Printer, 1959
Milne, R. S., *Bureaucracy in New Zealand.* London, 1957
Morrell, W. P., and Hall, D. O. W., *A History of New Zealand Life.* Christchurch and London, 1957
Neale, E. P., *Guide to New Zealand Official Statistics.* 3rd ed. Auckland, 1955
Oliver, W. H., *The Story of New Zealand.* London, 1963
Petersen, G. C., *Who's Who in New Zealand.* 9th ed. Wellington, 1968
Polaschek, R. J. (ed.), *Local Government in New Zealand.* Wellington, 1956.—*Government Administration in New Zealand.* Wellington, 1958
Robson, J. L. (ed.), *New Zealand: the Development of its Laws and Constitution.* 2nd ed. London, 1967
Rowe, J. W. and M. A., *New Zealand.* London, 1967
Sinclair, K., *A History of New Zealand.* Penguin, 1959
Sutch, W. B. *The Quest for Security in New Zealand, 1840 to 1966.* Wellington, 1966—*Poverty and Progress in New Zealand.* 2nd ed. Wellington, 1968
Watters, R. F. (ed.), *Land and Society in New Zealand.* Wellington, 1965
Weststrate, C., *Portrait of a Modern Mixed Economy.* Wellington, 1959
Wise's New Zealand Guide. 4th ed. Dunedin, 1969

INDIA

Bharat

CONSTITUTION. On 26 Jan. 1950 India became a sovereign democratic republic. India's relations with the British Commonwealth of Nations were defined at the London conference of Prime Ministers on 27 April 1949. Unanimous agreement was reached to the effect that the Republic of India remains a full member of the Commonwealth and accepts the Queen as 'the symbol of the free association of its independent member nations and, as such, the head of the Commonwealth'. This agreement was ratified by the Constituent Assembly of India on 17 May 1949.

The constitution was passed by the Constituent Assembly on 26 Nov. 1949 and came into force on 26 Jan. 1950. It has since been amended 22 times.

India is a Union of States and comprises 17 States and 10 Union territories. Each State is administered by a Governor appointed by the President for a term of 5 years while each Union territory is administered by the President through an administrator appointed by him.

The capital is New Delhi.

PRESIDENCY. The head of the Union is the President in whom all executive power is vested, to be exercised on the advice of ministers responsible to Parliament. He is elected by an electoral college consisting of all the elected members of Parliament and of the various state legislative assemblies. He holds office for 5 years and is eligible for re-election. He can be removed from office by impeachment for violation of the constitution. There is also a Vice-President who is *ex-officio* chairman of the Upper House of Parliament.

CENTRAL LEGISLATURE. The Parliament for the Union consists of the President, the Council of States (*Rajya Sabha*) and the House of the People (*Lok Sabha*). The Council of States, or the Upper House, consists of not more than 250 members; in 1967 there were 228 elected members and 12 members nominated by the President. The election to this house is indirect; the representatives of each

State are elected by the elected members of the Legislative Assembly of that State. The Council of States is a permanent body not liable to dissolution, but one-third of the members retire every second year. The House of the People, or the Lower House, consists of not more than 500 members, directly elected on the basis of adult suffrage from territorial constituencies in the States, and not more than 25 members to represent the Union territories, chosen in such manner as Parliament may by law provide; in Dec. 1967 there were 520 elected members and 3 members nominated by the President.

The House of the People unless sooner dissolved continues for a period of 5 years from the date appointed for its first meeting.

STATE LEGISLATURES. For every State there is a legislature which consists of the Governor, and (a) 2 Houses, a Legislative Assembly and a Legislative Council, in the States of Andhra Pradesh, Jammu and Kashmir, Madhya Pradesh, Maharashtra, Mysore, Tamil Nadu and Uttar Pradesh, and (b) 1 House, a Legislative Assembly, in the other States. Every Legislative Assembly, unless sooner dissolved, continues for 5 years from the date appointed for its first meeting. Every State Legislative Council is a permanent body and is not subject to dissolution, but one-third of the members retire every year. Parliament can, however, abolish an existing Legislative Council or create a new one, if the proposal is supported by a resolution of the Legislative Assembly concerned. The Legislative Council of West Bengal has been abolished. Legislative Councils have not less than 40 members, ten-twelfths elected and the rest nominated by the Governor. Legislative Assemblies have between 60 and 500 directly elected members.

LEGISLATION. The various subjects of legislation are enumerated in three lists in the seventh schedule to the constitution. List I, the Union List, consists of 97 subjects (including defence, foreign affairs, communications, currency and coinage, banking and customs) with respect to which the Union Parliament has exclusive power to make laws; the State legislature has exclusive power to make laws with respect to the 66 subjects in list II, the State List—these include police and public order, agriculture and irrigation, education, public health and local government; the powers to make laws with respect to the 47 subjects (including economic and social planning, legal questions and labour and price control) in list III, the Concurrent List, are held by both Union and State governments, though the former prevails. But Parliament may legislate with respect to any subject in the State List in circumstances when the subject assumes national importance or during emergencies.

Other provisions deal with the administrative relations between the Union and the States, interstate trade and commerce, distribution of revenues between the States and the Union, official language, etc.

FUNDAMENTAL RIGHTS. Two chapters of the constitution deal with fundamental rights and 'Directive Principles of State Policy'. 'Untouchability' is abolished, and its practice in any form is punishable. The fundamental rights can be enforced through the ordinary courts of law and through the Supreme Court of the Union. The directive principles cannot be enforced through the courts of law; they are nevertheless fundamental in the governance of the country.

CITIZENSHIP. Under the Constitution, every person who was on the 26 Jan. 1950, domiciled in India and (a) was born in India or (b) either of whose parents was born in India or (c) who has been ordinarily resident in the territory of India for not less than five years immediately preceding that date became a citizen of India. Special provision is made for migrants from Pakistan and for Indians resident abroad. Under the Citizenship Act, 1955, which supplemented the provisions of the Constitution, Indian citizenship is acquired by birth, by descent, by registration and by naturalization. The Act also provides for loss of citizenship by renunciation, termination and deprivation. The right to vote is granted to every person who is a citizen of India and who is not less than 21 years of age on a fixed date and is not otherwise disqualified.

Parliament. Parliament and the state legislatures are organized according to the following schedule (figures show distribution of seats on 20 April 1968):

| | Parliament | | State Legislatures | |
	House of the People (Lok Sabha)	Council of States (Rajya Sabha)	Legislative Assemblies (Vidhan Sabhas)	Legislative Councils (Vidhan Parishads)
States:				
Andhra Pradesh	41	18	287	90
Assam	14	7	126	—
Bihar	53	22	318	96
Gujarat	24	11	168	—
Haryana[1]	9	5	81	—
Kerala	19	9	133	—
Madhya Pradesh	37	16	296	90
Maharashtra	45	19	270	78
Mysore	27	12	216	63
Nagaland	1	1	46	—
Orissa	20	10	140	—
Punjab	13	7	104	40
Rajasthan	23	10	184	—
Tamil Nadu	39	18	234	63
Uttar Pradesh	85	34	425	108
West Bengal	40	16	280	—[4]
Jammu and Kashmir	6	4	75[3]	36
Union Territories:				
Andaman and Nicobar Islands	1	—	—	—
Chandigarh[1]	1	—	—	—
Dadra and Nagar Haveli	1	—	—	—
Delhi	7	3	—	—
Goa, Daman and Diu	2	—	30	—
Himachal Pradesh	6	3	60	—
Laccadive, etc. Islands	1	—	—	—
Manipur	2	1	30	—
Pondicherry	1	1	30	—
Tripura	2	—	30	—
Total	523[2]	228	3,563	739

[1] Created 1966.
[2] Includes also 2 nominated members to represent Anglo-Indians and 1 nominated member to represent the North East Frontier Agency.
[3] Excludes 25 seats for Pakistan-occupied areas of the State which are in abeyance.
[4] The Legislative Council of West Bengal has been abolished by the West Bengal Legislative Council Abolitions Act, 1969 with effect from 1 Aug. 1969.

The number of seats allotted to scheduled castes and scheduled tribes in the House of the People is 77 and 37 respectively. Out of the 3,563 seats allotted to the Legislative Assemblies, 503 are reserved for scheduled castes and 262 for scheduled tribes.

Composition by party of the House of the People in March 1971: Congress, 350; Communists, 48; Swatanta, 8; Jan Sangh, 22; Telengana Separatist Movement, 10; Dravida Munnetra Kazhagam, 22; Samyuktha Socialists, 3; other groups and Independents, 44; vacant, 4.

Total number of votes cast at the 1967 election was 150m. (126m. in 1962).

National flag: Deep saffron, white, dark green (horizontal); with Asoka's wheel in navy blue in the centre of the white band.

National anthem: Jana-gana-mana (words by Rabindranath Tagore).

Indian Independence Act, 1947. (Ch. 30.) London, 1947
The Constitution of India (modified up to 15 Apr. 1967). Delhi, 1967
Austin, G., *The Indian Constitution.* OUP, 1966
Bagga, S. N., *Constitution of India.* Allahabad, 1963
Basu, D. D., *Commentary on the Constitution of India.* 3rd ed. 2 vols. Calcutta, 1956
Erdman, H. L., *The Swatantra Party and Indian Conservatism.* CUP, 1967
Maheshwar, S., *The General Election in India.* Allahabad, 1963
Menon, V. P., *Transfer of Power in India.* Bombay, 1957
More, S. S., *Practice and Procedure of Indian Parliament.* Bombay, 1960
Morris-Jones, W. H., *Parliament in India.* London, 1957.—*The Government and Politics of India.* London, 1964
Mukherjea, A. R., *Parliamentary Procedure in India.* OUP, 1958
Pylee, M. V., *Constitutional Government in India.* 2nd ed. Bombay, 1965
Rao, K. V., *Parliamentary Democracy of India.* 2nd ed. Calcutta, 1965

Rau, B. N., *India's Constitution in the Making*. Bombay and London, 1961
Seervai, H. M., *Constitutional Law of India*. Bombay, 1967
Sinha, S., *Indian Independence in Perspective*. London, 1965

Language. The constitution provides that the official language of the Union shall be Hindi in the Devanagari script. It was originally provided that English should continue to be used for all official purposes until 1965. But the Official Languages Act 1963 provides that, after the expiry of this period of 15 years from the coming into force of the constitution, English might continue to be used, in addition to Hindi, for all official purposes of the Union for which it was being used immediately before that day, and for the transaction of business in Parliament. The Official Languages Amendment Act, 1967, provides that bilingualism shall continue; central government officers will choose their medium for official business. Translations will be provided for them until they attain a working knowledge of Hindi.

The following 15 languages are included in the Eighth Schedule to the Constitution: Assamese, Bengali, Gujarati, Hindi, Kannada, Kashmiri, Malayalam, Marathi, Oriya, Punjabi, Sanskrit, Sindhi, Tamil, Telugu, Urdu.

The total number of mother tongues (including 103 non-Indian languages) returned in the 1961 Census was 1,652. Hindi or Urdu languages (grouped under each) are spoken by 30.40% and 5.31% of the population respectively.

Fallon, S. W., *A New English–Hindustani Dictionary*. Lahore, 1941
Ferozsons English–Urdu, Urdu–English Dictionary. 2 vols. 4th ed. Lahore, 1961
Grierson, Sir G. A., *Linguistic Survey of India*. 11 vols. (in 19 parts). Delhi, 1903–28
Mehta, B. N., and B. B., *Modern Gujarati–English Dictionary*. 2 vols. Baroda, 1925
Mitra, S. C., *Student's Bengali–English Dictionary*. 2nd ed. Calcutta, 1923
Scholberg, H. C., *Concise Grammar of the Hindi Language*. 3rd ed. London, 1955
University of Madras, *Tamil Lexicon*. 7 vols. Madras, 1924–39
Vyas, V. G., and Patel, S. G., *Standard English–Gujarati Dictionary*. 2 vols. Bombay, 1923

GOVERNMENT.

President of the Republic: V. V. Giri (assumed office 24 Aug. 1969).
Vice-President: G. S. Pathak (assumed office 31 Aug. 1969).

There is a Council of Ministers to aid and advise the President of the Republic in the exercise of his functions; this comprises Ministers who are members of the Cabinet, Ministers of State who are not members of the Cabinet and Deputy Ministers. A Minister who for any period of 6 consecutive months is not a member of either House of Parliament ceases to be a Minister at the expiration of that period. The Prime Minister is appointed by the President; other Ministers are appointed by the President on the Prime Minister's advice.

The salary of each Minister is Rs 27,000 per annum, and that of each Deputy Minister is Rs 21,000 per annum. Each Minister is entitled to the free use of a furnished residence throughout his term of office. At the administrative head of each Ministry is a Secretary of the Government.

Following is the composition of the Cabinet and the portfolios as on 1 Nov. 1970:

Prime Minister, Atomic Energy, Planning and Home Affairs: Mrs Indira Gandhi.
Industrial Development, Company Affairs and Internal Trade: Fakhruddin Ali Ahmed.
Finance: Y. B. Chavan.
Labour and Rehabilitation: D. Sanjivayya.
Food and Agriculture: F. A. Ahmed.
Law and Social Welfare: K. Hanumanthaiya.
Steel and Heavy Engineering: B. R. Bhagat.
Education and Youth Services: Dr V. K. R. V. Rao.
Railways: G. L. Nanda.
Petrochemicals, Mines and Metals: Dr T. Sen.
Information, Broadcasting and Communications: S. N. Sinha.
External Affairs: S. S. Singh.
Tourism and Civil Aviation: Dr Karan Singh.
Defence: Jagjivan Ram.

Health, Family Planning, Works, Housing and Urban Development: K. K. Shah.
Foreign Trade: L. N. Mishra.
Supply: R. K. Khadilkar.

There are 21 Ministers of State and 17 Deputy Ministers.

DIPLOMATIC REPRESENTATIVES

Country	Indian representative	Foreign representative
Afghánistán	A. N. Mehta	Ataollah Nasser-Zia
Albania[2]	I. J. Bahadur Singh	—
Algeria	M. Yunus	Ali Lakhdari
Argentina	B. K. Sanyal	—
Australia[1]	A. M. Thomas	P. Shaw
Austria	V. C. Trivedi	Dr J. Nestor
Barbados[1]	L. N. Ray	—
Belgium	B. R. Patel	C. Kerremans
Bolivia	S. V. Patel	Dr G. Q. Galdo
Brazil	S. V. Patel	W. do Amaral Murtinho
Britain[1]	Appa B. Pant	Sir Morrice James
Bulgaria	Dr. G. Singh	N. Beltchev
Burma	B. Prasad	U. Hla Maw
Cambodia	Dr S. Gupta	Nong Kimny
Cameroun	S. G. Ramachandran	—
Canada[1]	A. B. Bhadkamkar	James George
Ceylon[1]	Y. K. Puri	—
Chile	K. L. Mehta	Julio Barrenechea
China	B. C. Mishra[3]	Huang Ming-Ta[3]
Colombia	K. L. Mehta	J. V. Iragorri[3]
Congo (K.)	S. S. Alirajpur	M. F. Ipoto
Cuba	B. K. Massand	J. E. Valdes
Cyprus[1]	A. K. Dar	—
Czechoslovakia	S. H. Desai	R. Dvorak
Dahomey	S. G. Ramachandran	—
Denmark	M. R. Thadani	H. A. Biering
Ethiopia	O. V. Alagesan	T. Abay[3]
Finland	C. J. Starcey	F. W. Schreck
France	D. N. Chatterjee	J. Vyau de Lagarde
Gambia[1]	G. J. Malik	—
Germany (West)	K. Chand	G. Diel
Ghana[1]	A. S. Mehta	P. K. Owusu-Ansah
Greece	R. Jaipal	J. Yannakakis
Guinea	P. Shunker	—
Guyana[1]	D. Hejmadi	—
Hungary	C. B. Muthama	Dr P. Kos
Indonesia	N. B. Menon	Mohammad Razif
Iran	M. A. Rahman	M. Reza Amirteymour
Iraq	Mahboob Ahmed	S. K. Hindawi
Irish Republic	A. G. Meneses	V. Iremonger
Italy	J. K. Atal	Dr M. de Strobel di fratta e Campocigno
Ivory Coast	G. J. Malik	—
Jamaica[1]	L. N. Ray	—
Japan	V. H. Coelho	A. Uyama
Jordan	A. K. Dar	A. Nashashibi
Kenya[1]	A. Singh	L. P. Odero
Kuwait	S. K. Chowdhry	E. A. R. Al-Essa
Laos	A. S. Gonsalves	—

[1] High Commissioner.   [2] Minister-Envoy.   [3] Chargé d'Affaires.
No figure = Ambassador.

Country	Indian representative	Foreign representative
Lebanon	A. K. Dar	M. Fathallah
Liberia	A. S. Mehta	—
Libya	I. J. Bahadur Singh	—
Luxembourg	B. R. Patel	—
Madagascar	—	—
Malawi[1]	M. M. Khurana	—
Malaysia[1]	K. C. Nair	Raja Aznam bin Raja Haji Ahmad
Maldives	Y. K. Puri	—
Mali	P. Shunker	—
Malta[1]	J. K. Atal	—
Mauritania	G. J. Malik	—
Mexico	B. K. Massand	C. Gutierrez Macias
Mongolia	D. P. Dhar	T. Demiddavag
Morocco	G. Singh	A. Lamrani
Nepál	R. Bahadur	B. Bahadur Pande
Netherlands	J. N. Dhamija	F. Calkoen
New Zealand[1]	P. S. Naskar	B. S. Lendrum
Nigeria[1]	S. G. Ramachandran	J. N. Ukegbu
Norway	J. K. Ganju	Haakon Nord
Pakistan[1]	B. K. Acharya	S. Hyder
Panama	B. K. Massand	—
Paraguay	B. K. Sanyal	N. de B. Flecha Torres
Peru	K. L. Mehta	E. Sarmiento Calmet
Philippines	C. D. Rao	L. M. Guerrero
Poland	V. M. M. Nair	R. Spasowski
Romania	S. Than	P. Tanasie
Saudi Arabia	T. T. P. Abdullah	Sheikh Anes Youssef Yassin
Senegal	G. J. Malik	—
Sierra Leone[1]	A. S. Mehta	—
Singapore[1]	P. Bhatia	P. Coomaraswamy
Somalia	M. Lal	—
Spain	S. R. Shah	G. Nadal
South Yemen	S. H. Desai	—
Sudan	K. L. Dalal	H. L. El-Amin
Sweden	P. R. S. Mani	Gunnar Heckscher
Switzerland	Azim Hussain	Dr A. Lindt
Syria	K. A. Kidwai	M. Al-Kassar
Tanzania[1]	V. C. Vijaya Raghavan	S. Chale
Thailand	P. K. Banerji	HH Prince Prem Purachatra
Togo	S. G. Ramachandran	—
Trinidad & Tobago[1]	L. N. Ray	—
Tunisia	G. Singh	—
Turkey	U. S. Bajpai	M. Dikerdem
Uganda[1]	R. R. Sinha	G. W. Kinuka
UAR	I. J. Bahadur Singh	M. Amin Hilmy II
USSR	D. P. Dhar	N. M. Pegov
USA	L. K. Jha	K. B. Keating
Upper Volta	G. J. Malik	—
Uruguay	B. K. Sanyal	A. Urioste
Vatican	Azim Hussain	Mgr M.-J. le Mieux[3]
Venezuela	S. V. Patel	Dr P. Abreu
Yemen	I. J. Bahadur Singh	A. K. M. Othman[2]
Yugoslavia	R. Jaipal	D. S. Komar
Zambia[1]	J. C. Kakar	—

[1] High Commissioner.   [2] Chargé d'Affaires.   [3] Internuncio.
No figure = Ambassador.

LOCAL GOVERNMENT. There were in 1970, 29 municipal corporations, 1,449 municipalities, 323 town area committees, 177 notified area committees and 62 cantonment boards. The municipal bodies have the care of the roads, water supply, drainage, sanitation, medical relief, vaccination and education. Their main sources of revenue are taxes on the annual rental value of land and buildings, octroi and terminal, vehicle and other taxes. The municipal councils enact their own bye-laws and frame their budgets, which in the case of municipal bodies other than corporations generally require the sanction of the State government. All municipal councils are elected on the principle of adult franchise.

For rural areas there is a 3-tier system of *panchayats* at village, block and district level. In March 1967, 3,493 *panchayat samitis* (block level) and 250 zila *parishads* (district level) were functioning. These provide for primary and secondary education, construct and maintain roads other than highways, and manage public health services. By 31 March 1967, 212,492 village *panchayats* had been established covering about 554,979 villages with a population of about 350m. The whole of the rural population of India was covered by village *panchayats* except in Bihar and Maharashtra, where 99% of the population was covered, and in Orissa (94%), Andaman, and Nicobar Islands (95%), Manipur (63%) and Tripura (81%). Elected by the entire adult population, village *panchayats* are responsible for civic amenities, sanitation, provision of medical facilities and management of community assets.

Statistical Abstract of India. Annual. Delhi
Organisation of the Government of India. Institute of Public Administration. Bombay, 1958
Chanda, A., *Indian Administration.* London, 1958
Khera, S. S., *District Administration in India.* London, 1964
Potter, D. C., *Government in rural India.* London School of Economics, 1964
Roy, N. C., *The Civil Service in India.* 2nd ed. Calcutta, 1960
Santhanam, K., *Union–State Relations in India.* London, 1961
Sharma, B. M., *The Republic of India.* London, 1967

AREA AND POPULATION. The area of the Indian Union (excluding Jammu and Kashmir) is 1,178,995 sq. miles (3,053,597 sq. km). Its population according to the 1961 census was 439,235,082 (including Sikkim but excluding the Pakistan-occupied area of Jammu and Kashmir); this represents an increase of 21·64% since 1951. Sex ratio was 941 females per 1,000 males (946 in 1951); density of population, 373 per sq. mile (287 in 1951). Government estimate of population, mid-1967, was 509,175,997.

Vital statistics based on registrations 1962: Birth rate, 20·8 per 1,000 population (1961 : 21); death rate, 8·8 (9·3); infant mortality (incomplete area coverage), 81 per 1,000 live births (83). But many births and deaths go unregistered. Data from certain areas of better registration and field studies suggest that the 1961 birth rate was about 42 per 1,000 population, the death rate 23 per 1,000 and infant mortality (1960) 134 per 1,000 live births.

Marriages and divorces are not registered. The minimum age for a civil marriage is 18 for women and 21 for men; for a sacramental marriage, 14 for girls and 18 for youths.

The leading details of the census of 1 March 1951 and of 1 March 1961 are:

Name of State	Land area in sq. miles (1961)	Population 1951[1]	1961
States			
Andhra Pradesh	106,286	31,115,259	35,983,447
Assam	47,091	8,830,732	11,872,772
Bihar	67,196	38,783,778	46,455,610
Gujarat	72,245	16,262,657	20,633,350
Jammu and Kashmir[2]		3,253,852	3,560,976
Kerala	15,002	13,549,118	16,903,715
Madhya Pradesh	171,217	26,071,637	32,372,408
Maharashtra	118,717	32,002,564	39,553,718
Mysore	74,210	19,401,956	23,586,772
Nagaland	6,366	212,975	369,200
Orissa	60,164	14,645,946	17,548,846
Punjab[11]	47,205	16,134,890	20,306,812
Rajasthan	132,152	15,970,774	20,155,602
Tamil Nadu	50,331	30,119,047	33,686,953
Uttar Pradesh	113,654	63,215,742	73,746,401
West Bengal	33,829	26,302,386	34,926,279

Name of State	Land area in sq. miles (1961)	Population 1951[1]	1961
Union Territories			
Andaman and Nicobar Islands	3,215	30,971	63,548
Delhi	573	1,744,072	2,658,612
Himachal Pradesh	10,885	1,109,466	1,351,144
Laccadive, Minicoy and Amindivi Islands	11	21,035	24,108
Manipur	8,628	577,635	780,037
Tripura	4,036	639,029	1,142,005
Dadra and Nagar Haveli	189	41,532[3]	57,963[4]
Goa, Daman and Diu	1,426	637,591[5]	626,978[5]
North Eastern Frontier Agency	31,438	—[6]	336,558[7]
Pondicherry	185	317,253[8]	369,079
Grand total	1,178,995[12]	361,129,622[9]	439,235,082[10]

[1] Figures adjusted to 1961 land area.
[2] Population of the area in Indian occupation (53,065 sq. miles); the 1951 figure is arithmetic mean of 1941/1961 populations.   [3] 1950 Portuguese census.   [4] 1962 census.
[5] 1960 Portuguese census.   [6] Census not taken.   [7] Provisional.   [8] 1948 French census.
[9] Includes Sikkim (137,725 persons in 1951 census) but excludes NEFA (*see* note 6).
[10] Includes Sikkim (162,189 in 1961 census) but excludes the Pakistan-occupied area of Jammu and Kashmir.
[11] By the creation of Haryana (1966) Punjab has lost c. 7m. people to the new state, 89,000 to the new Union territory of Chandigarh and a further 1·5m. to Himachal Pradesh.
[12] Total area does not include Jammu and Kashmir.

Registered foreigners on 31 Dec. 1962 numbered 59,774 (excluding Commonwealth nationals). Of these, 10,627 were Chinese and 14,988 were Tibetans.

The number of persons of Indian origin resident outside India is not accurately known, but with Pakistanis the total may be about 5m. Guyana had about 325,000 in 1965, Ceylon 852,000 in 1960, Fiji 235,000 in 1965, Kenya 188,000 in 1966, Malaya 696,000 (excluding Pakistanis) in 1959, Burma 500,000 in 1964 (in 1947: 1m.), Mauritius 493,000 in 1964, Singapore 124,000 in 1957, South Africa 500,000 in 1961, Trinidad and Tobago 302,000 in 1960 and the UK 170,000 in 1958.

Cities[1] (with states in brackets) having more than 100,000 population at the 1961 census were:

Agra (U.P.)	462,029	Gorakhpur (U.P.)	180,255	Nagercoil (T.N.)	106,207
Ahmedabad (Guj.)	1,149,918	Guntur (A.P.)	187,122	Nagpur (Mah.)	643,659
Ahmednagar (Mah.)	119,020	Gwalior (M.P.)	300,587	Nasik (Mah.)	131,103
Ajmer (Raj.)	231,240	Howrah (W.B.)	512,598	Nellore (A.P.)	106,776
Akola (Mah.)	115,760	Hubli (Mys.)	171,326	Patiala (Pun.)	125,234
Aligarh (U.P.)	185,020	Hyderabad (A.P.)	1,118,553	Patna (Bih.)	363,700
Allahabad (U.P.)	411,955	Indore (M.P.)	394,941	Poona (Mah.)	597,562
Allepey (Ker.)	138,834	Jabalpur (M.P.)	295,375	Raipur (M.P.)	139,792
Ambala (Pun.)	105,543	Jaipur (Raj.)	403,444	Rajahmundry (A.P.)	130,002
Amravati (Mah.)	137,875	Jammu (J. & K.)	102,738	Rajkot (Guj.)	193,498
Amritsar (Pun.)	376,295	Jamnagar (Guj.)	139,652	Rampur (U.P.)	135,407
Asansol (W.B.)	103,405	Jamshedpur (Bih.)	291,791	Ranchi (Bih.)	122,416
Bally (W.B.)	101,159	Jhansi (U.P.)	140,217	Saharanpur (U.P.)	185,213
Bandar (A.P.)	101,417	Jodhpur (Raj.)	224,760	Salem (T.N.)	249,145
Bangalore (Mys.)	905,134	Jullundur (Pun.)	222,569	Shahjahanpur (U.P.)	110,432
Baranagar (W.B.)	107,837	Kakinada (A.P.)	122,865	Sholapur (Mah.)	337,583
Bareilly (U.P.)	254,409	Kamarhati (W.B.)	125,457	South Dum Dum	
Baroda (Guj.)	295,144	Kanpur (U.P.)	895,106	(W.B.)	111,284
Belgaum (Mys.)	127,885	Kharagpur (W.B.)	147,253	South Suburban	
Bhagalpur (Bih.)	143,850	Kozhikode (Ker.)	192,521	(W.B.)	185,811
Bhatpara (W.B.)	147,630	Kolar Gold Fields		Srinagar (J. & K.)	285,257
Bhavnagar (Guj.)	171,039	(Mys.)	146,811	Surat (Guj.)	288,026
Bhopal (M.P.)	185,374	Kolhapur (Mah.)	187,442	Thana (Mah.)	101,107
Bikaner (Raj.)	150,634	Kotah (Raj.)	120,345	Thanjavur (T.N.)	111,099
Bombay (Mah.)	4,152,056	Kurnool (A.P.)	100,815	Tiruchirapalli (T.N.)	249,862
Burdwan (W.B.)	108,224	Ludhiana (Pun.)	244,032	Trivandrum (Ker.)	239,815
Calcutta (W.B.)	2,927,289	Lucknow (U.P.)	595,440	Tuticorin (T.N.)	124,230
Coimbatore (T.N.)	286,305	Madras (T.N.)	1,729,141	Udaipur (Raj.)	111,139
Cuttack (Ori.)	146,303	Madurai (T.N.)	424,810	Ujjain (M.P.)	144,161
Darbhanga (Bih.)	103,016	Malegaon (Mah.)	121,408	Ulhasnagar (Mah.)	107,760
Dehra Dun (U.P.)	126,918	Mangalore (Mys.)	142,669	Varanasi (U.P.)	471,258
Delhi	2,061,758	Mathura (U.P.)	116,959	Vellore (T.N.)	113,742
Eluru (A.P.)	108,321	Meerut (U.P.)	200,470	Vijayawada (A.P.)	230,397
Ernakulam (Ker.)	117,253	Mirzapur (U.P.)	100,097	Visakhapatnam	
Garden Reach (W.B.)	130,770	Moradabad (U.P.)	180,100	(A.P.)	182,002
Gauhati (Ass.)	100,707	Muzaffarpur (Bih.)	109,048	Warangal (A.P.)	156,106
Gaya (Bih.)	151,105	Mysore (Mys.)	253,865		

[1] Area of the municipality or other single local-government body, not 'town groups' as listed in the census report.

Report of the Officials of the Government of India and the People's Republic of China on the Boundary Question. New Delhi, Ministry of External Affairs, 1961
1961 Census: Final general totals. 1962
Census of India, 1951 and 1961: Reports and Papers, Decennial series. (All published by Government of India.)
Annual Report on the Working of Indian Migration. Government of India, from 1956
Report of the Commissioner for Scheduled Castes and Scheduled Tribes. Government of India. Annual
Public Health. Report of the Public Health Commission with the Government of India. Annual
Agarwala, S. N., *India's Population.* London, 1960
Chandrasekhar, S., *Infant Mortality in India, 1901–55.* London, 1959
Coale, A. J., and Hoover, E. M., *Population Growth and Economic Development in Low Income Countries.* Princeton, 1958
Gyan Chand, *Some Aspects of the Population Problem in India.* Patna, 1956
Hutton, J. H., *Caste in India.* 3rd ed. Bombay, 1961
Mamoria, C. B., *India's Population Problem.* Allahabad, 1961
Mayer, A. C., *Caste and Kinship in Central India.* London. 1960
Misra, B. B., *The Indian Middle Classes.* R. Inst. of Int. Affairs, 1961
Sovani, N. V., *Urbanization and Urban India.* London, 1966
Turner, R. (ed.), *India's Urban Future.* Univ. of California Press and CUP, 1962

RELIGION. The principal religions in 1961 (census) were: Hindus, 366,526,866. Sikhs, 7,845,915; Jains, 2,027,281; Buddhists, 3,256,036 (180,823 in 1951). Moslems, 46,940,799; Christians, 10,728,086.

The Church of South India was inaugurated in 1947 by the union of the Methodist Church and the South India United Church (Presbyterian and Congregationalist) with the Church of India (Anglican) dioceses of Madras, Travancore, Tinnevelly and Dornakal; it had (1966) about 420,000 members.

Sundkler, B., *Church of South India.* London, 1954

EDUCATION. LITERACY. According to the 1961 census the literacy percentage in the country (excluding age-group, 0–5) was 24 (16·6 in 1951), of which the figure for men was 34·5 (24·9) and for women 13 (7·9). Government estimates (1969) give 33% literacy.

EDUCATIONAL ORGANIZATION. In the states the general control over education rests with the state government. In the union territories education is under the direct control of the central government. The authority of the Government is delegated to universities, boards of secondary and/or intermediate education, local bodies, etc.

The Union Government is responsible for the collection and dissemination of educational information for the whole country and for co-ordinating facilities and standards. It is also responsible for developing and promoting the Hindi language alongside other Indian languages. These obligations are discharged by the central Ministry of Education and Youth Services through its various programmes and through the agency of such bodies as the University Grants Commission, the Council of Scientific and Industrial Research, the National Council of Educational Research and Training and the Central Hindi Directorate. The Union Government also subsidizes the State Governments for developing their educational programmes. It also controls 5 universities (Aligarh, Banaras, Delhi, Visva-Bharati and Jawaharlal Nehru), 18 public schools, including the Lawrence schools at Sanawar and Lovedale, and institutions of national importance, such as the Delhi College of Engineering, Central Institute of Education (Delhi) and the 5 Indian Institutes of Technology.

SCHOOL EDUCATION. The school system in India can be divided into four stages: pre-primary, primary, middle and high. The latter two combined together constitute the secondary stage.

There are as yet not many pre-primary schools in India.

Education is imparted either at independent primary (or junior basic) schools or primary classes attached to middle or high schools. The period of instruction in this stage varies from 4 to 5 years and the medium of instruction is the mother tongue of the child or the regional language. Legislation for compulsory and free primary education has been passed by almost all state governments but it is not practicable to enforce compulsion and attendance is more often ensured by incentive.

The period for the middle stage varies from 2 to 4 years and instruction is given in middle classes of high schools or middle schools, the latter having, generally, primary classes attached to them. At this stage English is taught as a compulsory subject.

The high-school extends from 2 to 4 years. Education is given in higher classes of high schools, which have middle or primary (or both) departments attached. English is generally taught as a compulsory subject. The medium of instruction is mostly the mother tongue or the regional language.

The eventual pattern is to be 8 years elementary (basic) education, 3 or 4 years secondary education with diversified courses, 3 years university education.

There are, in addition, schools for professional subjects such as teachers' training, engineering, technology, medicine, agriculture, etc., and special schools for students of the fine arts, and for adult education generally, and for the physically and mentally handicapped, etc.

HIGHER EDUCATION. Higher education is given in arts, science or professional colleges, universities and all-India educational or research institutions. In 1968 there were 74 universities, 9 institutions of national importance and 10 institutions deemed as universities. For details see the sections 'Education' under each state.

Grants are paid through the University Grants Commission to the central universities on cent per cent basis for their maintenance and development and to state universities on a sharing basis for their development projects only. During 1967–68 the University Grants Commission sanctioned grants of Rs 14·80 crores.

TECHNICAL EDUCATION. The number of institutions awarding degrees in engineering and technology in 1968–69 was 138 (in 1947: 38), and those awarding diplomas in engineering and technology numbered 284 (in 1947: 53); the former are able to admit about 25,000, the latter about 48,000, students. For the training of high-level engineers and technologists 5 Institutes of Technology have been established. During 1968–69 their total enrolment was 9,688.

STUDENTS AND TRAINEES ABROAD. There were nearly 14,000 students and trainees abroad on 1 Jan. 1968, 9,640 in USA and 1,830 in Britain (engineering and technology, 5,345; science, 2,188; arts, 2,044; medicine, 978; agriculture, 406; commerce, 342; education, 235).

EDUCATIONAL STATISTICS for the year ending 31 March 1966 (provisional):

Type of recognized institution	No. of institutions	No. of students on rolls
Higher education		
Universities	63	
Institutions deemed as universities	9	
Institutions of national importance	9	
Research institutions	40	1,968,000
Boards of education	25	
Professional and technical colleges	2,690	
Arts and science colleges	1,970	
Colleges for special education	1,232	
Primary and secondary education		
Pre-primary	3,277	230,764
Primary	388,618	36,240,169
Secondary	102,755	28.667,965
Vocational and technical	3,264	280,787
Special and other education	220,182	1,775,224

Expenditure (on recognized institutions) 1965–66 (in Rs crores):

From government funds	412·41	From endowments and	
From local body funds	32·73	other sources	40·07
From university funds	6·42		
From fees	94·70	Total	586·33

University Development in India: a statistical report, 1961–62. New Delhi, 1962
Mudaliar, A. L., *Education in India*. London, 1960
Rawat, P. L., *History of Indian education*. 4th ed. Agra, 1965
Vakil, K. S. and Natarajan, S., *Education in India*. 3rd ed. Bombay, 1966

CINEMAS. In 1965 there were 5,350 permanent cinemas and 1,450 touring cinemas.

NEWSPAPERS. In Dec. 1967 the total number of newspapers and periodicals was 9,315. Of this, 1,452 were published in Maharashtra, 1,050 in West Bengal, 1,406 in Uttar Pradesh and 1,016 in Delhi. Papers in 8 principal languages had a circulation of 17,763,000; English papers had a circulation of 5,156,000; Hindi, 3,773,000; Tamil, 2,377,000.

Annual Report of the Registrar of Newspapers for India. New Delhi
Natarajan, S., *History of the press in India.* London, 1962

BROADCASTING. There were (1968) 36 principal radio stations in India and 22 auxiliary centres; on 31 Dec. 1967, 7,579,468 receiver licences were in force and 70% of the population had medium-wave coverage; nearly all had 2nd-grade short-wave coverage. The television service was started at Delhi, 15 Sept. 1959. There were (1968) 6,200 television receivers in Delhi, used mainly for communal viewing in clubs and for teaching in schools.

HEALTH. Health programmes are primarily the responsibility of the state governments. The Union Government has sponsored and supported major schemes for disease prevention and control which are implemented nationally. These include the prevention and control of malaria, filaria, tuberculosis, leprosy, venereal diseases, smallpox, trachoma and cancer. There are also Union Government schemes in connexion with water supply and sanitation, and with nutrition. The Nutrition Advisory Committee of the Indian Council of Medical Research sponsors schemes for research and advises the Government. The National Nutrition Advisory Committee is to formulate a national nutrition policy and recommend measures for improving national standards.

Medical relief and service is primarily the responsibility of the states. By 1965–66 the number of medical institutions was 14,600. In 1968 there were 251,200 hospital beds. There were 4,928 primary health centres, 96,000 active doctors, 55,000 nurses, 48,000 pharmacists. Medical education is also a state responsibility, but there is a co-ordinating Central Health Educational Bureau.

Family planning is centrally sponsored and locally implemented. The goal is to reduce the birth-rate from the present 40 per 1,000 to 25 per 1,000 by 1976, and to do so by means of education in family planning methods.

JUSTICE. All courts form a single hierarchy, with the Supreme Court at the head, which constitutes the highest court of appeal. Immediately below it are the high courts and subordinate courts in each state. Every court in this chain, subject to the usual pecuniary and local limits, administers the whole law of the country, whether made by Parliament or by the state legislatures.

The Supreme Court of India is the highest court in respect of constitutional matters. The states of Andhra Pradesh, Assam (in common with Nagaland), Bihar, Gujarat, Haryana, Jammu and Kashmir, Kerala, Madhya Pradesh, Maharashtra, Mysore, Orissa, Punjab (in common with the state of Haryana and the Union Territory of Chandigarh), Rajasthan, Tamil Nadu, Uttar Pradesh and West Bengal have each a High Court. There are Courts of Judicial Commissioners, which are in status equivalent to High Courts, in the Union Territories of Manipur, Tripura and Goa. There is a separate High Court for Delhi, which has a bench at Simla for Himachal Pradesh. For the Andaman and Nicobar Islands the Calcutta High Court, for Pondicherry the High Court of Madras, and for the Laccadive, Minicoy and Aminidivi Islands the High Court of Kerala are the highest judicial authorities; in Dadra and Nagar Haveli the Appellate Court is the highest civil and criminal court. Below the High Court each state is divided into a number of districts under the jurisdiction of district judges who preside over civil courts and courts of sessions. There are a number of judicial authorities subordinate to the district civil courts. On the criminal side magistrates of various classes act under the general supervision of the district magistrate.

The judiciary has been completely separated from the executive (Art. 50 of the Constitution) in Gujarat, Haryana, Kerala, Maharashtra, Mysore, Orissa, Punjab and Tamil Nadu. It has also been separated over large areas of Andhra Pradesh, Bihar, Madhya Pradesh and Uttar Pradesh, and in some of the districts of Assam and Rajasthan. The Union Territories (Separation of Judicial and

Executive Functions) Act, 1969, was enforced in the Union territory of Delhi on 2 Oct. 1969.

Police. The states control their own police force through the state Home Ministers. The Home Minister of the central government co-ordinates the work of the states and controls the Central Bureau of Investigation, the Central Detective Training School, the Central Forensic Laboratory, the Central Fingerprint Laboratory as well as the National Police Academy at Mount Abu (Rajasthan) where the Indian Police Service is trained. The Indian Police Service, about 1,659 strong, is recruited by competitive examination of university graduates and provides all senior officers for the state police forces.

The cities of Calcutta, Madras, Bombay and Hyderabad have separate police organizations.

Total sanctioned strength of police was 640,244 in 1968.

Sarkar, P. C., *Civil Laws of India and Pakistan.* 2 vols. Calcutta, 1953.—*Criminal Laws of India and Pakistan.* 2nd ed. 2 vols. Calcutta, 1956
Setalvad, M. C., *The Common Law of India.* London, 1960
Sharma, S. R. *Supreme Court in the Indian Constitution.* Delhi, 1959

FINANCE. Currency. A decimal system of coinage was introduced in 1957. The Indian *rupee* is divided into 100 *paise* (until 1964 officially described as *naye paise*), the decimal coins being 1, 2, 5, 10, 25 and 50 *paise* (or *naye paise*) and rupee.

On 6 June 1966 the rupee was devalued by 36·5%, 21 rupees being the equivalent of £1 sterling. On the devaluation of the £ in Nov. 1967, the £ became equivalent to Rs 18.

The paper currency consists of: (1) Reserve Bank notes in denominations of Rs 2, 5, 10, 100, 1,000, 5,000 and 10,000; and (2) Government of India currency notes of denominations of Re 1 (issued in 1917), Rs 2½, 5, 10, 20, 50 and 100. Re 1 notes of a different type, issued since 1940, are deemed to be included in the expression 'rupee coin' for purposes of the Reserve Bank of India Act, 1934. Bank and Government notes bearing the king's effigy and other earlier issues have ceased to be legal tender, 28 Oct. 1957, except at the issue department of the Reserve Bank, government treasuries and sub-treasuries, and agency branches of the State Bank of India and its subsidiaries.

According to the Reserve Bank of India, the total value of currency in circulation in 1969–70 was Rs 4,006 crores (of which Rs 3,799 crores were in notes).

Value of pure nickel, cupro-nickel, nickel-brass and bronze money minted at the Alipore, Hyderabad and Bombay Mints (year ended 31 March): 1960, Rs 3,96,92,700; 1961, Rs 5,62,89,100; 1962, Rs, 8,79,60,720; 1963, Rs 10,58,67,000; 1964, Rs 9,54,00,400.

100,000 rupees are called 1 lakh and are written thus: Rs 1,00,000; 100 lakhs are called 1 crore and are written thus: Rs 100,00,000. A lakh of rupees at the exchange rate of Rs 18 = £1 is equivalent to £5,555.

Budget. Revenue and expenditure (on revenue account) of the central government[1] for years ending 31 March, in crores of rupees:

	1965–66	1966–67	1967–68[2]	1968–69[2]	1969–70[2]	1970–71[3]
Revenue	2,320·39	2,872·70	2,545	3,027	3,587·15	4,036·78
Expenditure	2,000·63	2,731·06	2,458	2,896	2,976·42	3,152·18

Under the Constitution (Part XII and 7th Schedule), the power to raise funds has been divided between the central government and the states. By and large, the sources of revenue are mutually exclusive. Certain taxes are levied by the Union for the sake of uniformity and distributed to the states. The Finance Commission (Art. 280 of the Constitution) advises the President on the distribution of the taxes which are distributable between the centre and the states, and on the principles on which grants should be made out of Union revenues to the states. The main sources of central revenue are: customs duties; those excise duties levied by the central government; corporation, income and wealth taxes; estate and succession duties on non-agricultural assets and property, and revenues from the railways and Posts and Telegraphs. The main heads of revenue in the states are: taxes and duties levied by the state governments (including land revenues and agricultural income tax); civil administration and civil works; state undertakings; taxes shared with the centre; and grants received from the centre.

[1] Excluding states' share of excise duties and other taxes.   [2] Revised.
[3] Budget estimates.

Important items of revenue and expenditure charged to revenue of the central government for 1970–71 (estimates), in crores of rupees:

Revenue		Expenditure	
Customs	465·00	Civil administration	189·70
Union excise duties	1,814·40	Debt Services	597·48
Corporation tax	342·00	Social and developmental	
Taxes on income	438·00	services	319·85
Debt services	611·27	Defence services (net)	1,017·84
Currency and Mint	98·07	Contributions and adjustments	10·77

The following table shows the revenue and expenditure (on revenue account) of the states,[1] in crores of rupees:

	Revenue			Expenditure		
	1968–69 (revised)	1969–70 (budget)	1970–71 (budget)	1968–69 (revised)	1969–70 (budget)	1970–71 (budget)
Andhra Pradesh	173·59	243·73	265·96	162·35	201·97	266·43
Assam	88·27	94·03	111·03	91·25	99·27	110·69
Bihar	156·41	168·83	234·90	142·27	171·25	236·17
Gujarat	144·74	153·63	193·12	102·79	128·82	188·94
Haryana	63·47	66·30	92·44	59·79	67·53	90·60
Jammu and Kashmir	46·76	47·35	67·20	47·98	56·54	65·26
Kerala	127·61	130·72	144·47	131·12	140·85	157·95
Madhya Pradesh	164·87	179·47	220·43	166·81	198·76	212·39
Maharashtra	336·89	346·76	432·82	260·11	306·82	426·25
Mysore	165·59	175·27	233·47	153·81	172·96	248·95
Nagaland	18·56[2]	30·00	33·93	19·03[2]	35·69	33·93
Orissa	102·11	98·26	126·36	104·84	100·51	143·46
Punjab	110·45	110·38	154·39	98·63	111·73	134·96
Rajasthan	119·79	133·63	168·64	139·62	149·48	188·07
Tamil Nadu	247·95	229·24	288·04	186·45	202·21	296·98
Uttar Pradesh	306·78	299·41	455·25	305·14	342·49	413·80
West Bengal	210·34	222·84	279·31	230·41	226·63	285·42
Total	2,584·18	2,729·85	3,497·83	2,402·40	2,623·51	3,500·25

[1] Figures are as published by the Reserve Bank of India.
[2] Budget figure.
Revenue figures for Gujarat exclude transfers from Revenue Reserve Funds.

Debt. On 31 March 1969 the interest-bearing obligations of the Government of India were estimated to amount to Rs 13,158 crores, of which total obligations in India were Rs 6,931·85 crores; external public debt included USA, Rs 3,266·17 crores; UK (Government), Rs 638·38 crores; West Germany, Rs 405·69 crores; USSR, Rs 369 crores; International Bank, Rs 268·89 crores; IDA, 589·10 crores.

Bhargava, R. N., *Indian Public Finance*. London, 1962
Chelliah, R. J., *Fiscal Policy in Underdeveloped Countries, with Special Reference to India*. London, 1960
Misra, B. R., *Indian Federal Finance*. Rev. ed. Bombay, 1960
National Council of Applied Economic Research, *Management of Public Debt in India*. New Delhi, 1965
Premchand, A., *Control of Public Expenditure in India*. New Delhi, 1963
Sadeque, A., *Indian and Pakistan Currency*. Dacca, 1965

DEFENCE. The Supreme Command of the Armed Forces vests in the President of the Indian Republic. Policy is decided at different levels by a number of committees, including the Defence Committee of the Cabinet presided over by the Prime Minister and the Defence Minister's Committee. Administrative and operational control rests in the respective Service Headquarters, under the control of the Ministry of Defence.

The Ministry of Defence is the central agency for formulating defence policy and for co-ordinating the work of the three services. Among the organizations directly administered by the Ministry are the Research and Development Organization, the Production Organization, the National Defence College, the National Cadet Corps and the Directorate-General of Armed Forces Medical Services.

The Research and Development Organization (headed by the Scientific Adviser to the Minister) has under it about 30 research establishments. The Production

Organization controls 7 public-sector undertakings and 24 ordnance factories; the total value of production in 1966–67 was estimated at Rs 150 crores.

The National Defence College, New Delhi, was established in 1960 on the pattern of the Imperial Defence College (UK): the 1-year course is for officers of the rank of brigadier or equivalent and for senior civil servants. The Defence Services Staff College, Wellington, trains officers of the three Services for higher command for staff appointments. There is an Armed Forces Medical College at Poona.

The National Defence Academy, Khadakvasla, gives a 3-year basic training course to officer cadets of the three Services prior to advanced training at the respective Service establishments.

The Defence budget estimates for 1970–71 totalled Rs 1,241·96 crores, divided as follows: Revenue expenditure, Rs 1,052·08 crores; capital expenditure, Rs 139·20 crores.

Army. The Army Headquarters functioning directly under the Chief of the Army Staff is divided into the following main branches: General Staff Branch; Adjutant-General's Branch; Quartermaster-General's Branch; Master-General of Ordnance Branch; Engineer-in-Chief's Branch; Military Secretary's Branch.

The Army is organized into 4 commands—eastern, central, western and southern—each divided into areas, which in turn are subdivided into sub-areas.

Recruitment of permanent commissioned officers is through the Indian Military Academy, Dehra Dun. It conducts courses for ex-National Defence Academy, National Cadet Corps and direct-entry cadets, and for serving personnel and technical graduates.

The Territorial Army came into being in Sept. 1949, its role being to: (1) relieve the regular Army of static duties and, if required, support civil power; (2) provide anti-aircraft units, and (3) if and when called upon, provide units for the regular Army. The Territorial Army is composed of practically all arms of the Services.

The authorized strength of the Army is 828,000, that of the Territorial Army, 50,000.

Navy. Since 26 Jan. 1950 the former Royal Indian Navy, which traced its history in an unbroken line from the foundation in 1613 of the East India Company's Marine, has been known as 'Indian Navy', and the ships referred to as 'INS' instead of 'HMIS'

Principal ships of the Indian Navy:

Completed	Name	Standard displacement Tons	Armour Belts in.	Armour Turrets in.	Principal armament	Shaft horsepower	Speed Knots
			Aircraft Carrier				
1961	Vikrant (*ex*-Hercules)	16,000	—	—	15 40 mm. AA	40,000	24·5
			Cruisers				
1940	Mysore (*ex*-Nigeria)	8,700	3–4½	2	9 6-in.; 8 4-in.	72,500	31·5
1933	Delhi (*ex*-Achilles)	7,114	2–4	1	6 6-in.; 8 4-in.	72,000	32

In Jan. 1957 the unfinished aircraft-carrier *Hercules* was acquired from the Government of the UK, large-scale reconstruction and modernization being carried out in Belfast. She was commissioned on 4 March 1961 and renamed *Vikrant*. The cruiser *Mysore* (*ex*-HMS *Nigeria*) was purchased from Great Britain in 1957.

The fleet also includes 4 submarines, a submarine depot ship, 3 destroyers (*Rajput* [ex-HMS *Rotherham*], *Rana* [ex-HMS *Raider*], *Ranjit* [ex-HMS *Redoubt*]), 2 anti-submarine frigates, 3 smaller anti-submarine frigates, 3 anti-aircraft frigates (all 8 completed in Great Britain, 1958–60), 6 frigates (including 3 'Hunt' class small escort destroyers acquired from Great Britain, 1953), 5 new Soviet-built escorts, 1 ocean minesweeper, 4 coastal minesweepers acquired from Great Britain in 1956, 2 inshore minesweepers acquired from Great Britain in 1955, 6 motor torpedo-boats, 6 patrol craft, 9 seaward defence boats, 4 motor launches, a tank landing ship, 3 tank landing craft, an ocean tug, 4 surveying vessels, a repair ship, 2 Avcat tankers and 3 small oilers.

Three general-purpose frigates of the British 'Leander' class are being built in India and 3 more are projected. Submarines have been acquired from the USSR.

At the naval base at Cochin, the Fleet Requirement Unit of the Naval Aviation Station, INAS *Garuda*, has been developed. At present this unit is equipped with Firefly target tugs and Vampire aircraft which work with the ships and training schools of the Navy. Sea Hawk fighters and Alizé anti-submarine aircraft have also been acquired for the aircraft carrier.

Naval personnel in 1970 comprised 24,000 officers and sailors.

Air Force. The Indian Air Force Act was passed in 1932, and the first flight was formed in 1933.

The Air Headquarters, under the Chief of Air Staff, consists of 4 main branches, viz., Air Staff, Administration, Policy and Plans, and Maintenance. Units of the IAF are organized into 5 commands—Eastern, Western, Central, Training, Maintenance.

It is proposed to build up first-line strength of the Air Force to 45 squadrons, largely by both direct purchase and licence-production of aircraft.

Air defence units include squadrons of Gnat fighters, MiG-21F/FLs and many batteries of surface-to-air missiles. Initial delivery of MiG-21s from the Soviet Union has been followed by large-scale licence production in India. There are squadrons of Sukhoi Su-7s, Hunter F56s, Mystère IVAs and Hindustan HF-24 Marut supersonic fighter-bombers.

The transport force includes An-12s, jet-boosted C-119Gs, C-47s, HS 748s, Caribou, Il-14s, Otters, Tu-124s and smaller aircraft and helicopters for VIP and other duties. Helicopter units have Mi-4s and Alouette IIIs; main training types are the Hindustan HT-2, T-6G, Vampire T.55, Hunter T.66 and MiG-21UTI, with the Hindustan HJT-16 in early production for 'all-through' jet training.

Elementary flying training is provided at the IAF Flying College, Jodhpur, and advanced flying training at the IAF Station, Hyderabad. The IAF Technical College, Jalahalli, imparts technical training, while the IAF Administrative College, Coimbatore, trains officers of the ground duty branch. There are also land–air warfare, flying instructors' and medical schools.

Pannikar, K. M., *Problems of Indian Defence*. London, 1960
Singh, R., *Aspects of Indian defence*. Calcutta, 1965
Sridharan, K., *A maritime history of India*. Delhi, 1965

PLANNING. The third five-year plan ended in March 1966 and 3 annual plans, as periods of stabilization, led up to the beginning of the fourth plan in April 1969. The formal fourth plan document was presented by the Prime Minister on 18 May 1970. The fourth plan stresses agriculture and land usage, and manufacturing industries.

Outlay is set at Rs 24,882 crores, of which Rs 8,980 crores is for the private sector and Rs 15,902 crores for the public sector, including Rs 8,871 crores for central and centrally-sponsored schemes, Rs 6,606 crores for state schemes and Rs 425 crores for union territories. Central help to states is 60% on basis of population, 10% on *per capita* income (if below the national average), 10% on tax effort related to *per capita* income and 10% towards commitment in major irrigation and development schemes. The remaining 10% is for distribution to assist with local problems. States now have more initiative in forming their development programmes.

Priority is given to expanding elementary education and facilities for backward areas and for educating girls.

Most help is allocated to the manufacture of fertilizers, metals, petroleum products and machinery. At present imports meet 60% of fertilizer needs, 65% of alloy and special steel, 74% of copper, 64% of crude oil and 30% of machinery. Targets for home production by 1974 and production 1968–69 (in metric tons):

	Target 1974	Production 1968–69
Ingot steel	9·8m.	6·5m.
Alloy and special steel	220,000	43,000
Aluminium	220,000	125,000
Machine tools	Rs 65 crores (value)	Rs 20 crores (value
Refinery products	26m.	15·4m.
Plastics	225,000	58,100

The plan provides for 151m. hectares of sown land by 1980–81 (137m. hectares in 1967). Irrigated land should increase to 58m. hectares. Gujarat has received IDA credit for Rs 260·50m. as a 50-year loan towards the Kadana Dam project. In March 1970 Haryana and Uttar Pradesh agreed to build a joint dam with 2 canals at Kishan in the Dehra Dun hills; Haryana pays two-thirds of the estimated cost of Rs 180 crores. The plan aims at 12·9m. metric tons annual foodgrain production by 1974.

It is estimated that demand for consumer goods will rise by 4% per annum. An increase of 9% in industrial output and 5% in agricultural output is needed.

Objective is a net installed capacity of 23m. kw., which will allow for obsolete plant to be taken out of service. Outlay is Rs 210 crores for continuing generating schemes, including Rs 120 crores for nuclear generation.

An overall growth rate of 5·5% is considered feasible.

AGRICULTURE. The chief industry of India has always been agriculture. About 70% of the people are dependent on the land for their living. The 1961 census showed that of a working population of 188,675,500, there were 131,142,816 engaged in agriculture; 99,621,175 of these were farmers, and 31,521,641 labourers. A National Sample Survey in 1961 showed 6·95m. rural households, 72% possessing operational holdings. There were 4·89 m. of such holdings with an average size between 2·4 and 26·3 hectares.

Agricultural commodities account for 40–45% by value of Indian exports, while agricultural commodities, machinery and fertilizers account for about 25–30% of imports. Tea accounts for 45–50% of agricultural exports.

An increase in food production of at least 2% per annum is necessary to keep pace with the rising population. In the first five-year plan (1950–51 to 1955–56) agriculture was given a more dominant part than industry and this, plus a series of good monsoons, produced a satisfactory increase in production. In the second five-year plan (1955–56 to 1960–61) less stress was laid on agricultural expansion, and import of foodstuffs was increased, though largely paid for by foreign aid. Even so, during the decade 1951–61 the rate of growth of agricultural production was ahead of the rate of growth of population; while population increased 21·5%, agricultural production increased by 39·1% (foodgrains by 35%, non-foodgrains by 47·3%). In the third five-year plan (1961–62 to 1965–66) a production target of 100m. tons of foodgrains was set, an increase of 22% over the 82m.-ton food-grain harvest of 1960–61. There was no increase in foodgrain production in the first 3 years of the third Plan: 82·7m. tons in 1961–62, 78·4m. tons in 1962–63, 80·2m. tons in 1963–64; a rise to 89m. tons in 1964–65 and a severe setback because of the unprecedented drought in 1965–66, with a harvest of only 72·3m. tons. The harvest in 1966–67 rose to 75·9m. tons and the estimate for 1967–68 was about 93·5m. tons.

The Indian Council for Agricultural Research, which was established in 1929 and which became fully autonomous in Jan. 1966, co-ordinates agricultural research and education in the Union. The more important central research institutes are the Indian Agricultural Research Institute (New Delhi), the Indian Veterinary Research Institute (Izatnagar), the National Dairy Research Institute (Karnal), the Central Rice Institute (Cuttack), the Central Potato Research Institute (Simla), the Indian Forest Research Institute and College (Dehra Dun), the Central Marine Fisheries Research Station (Mandapam), the Central Island Fisheries Research Station (Barrackpore), the Central Fisheries Technological Research Stations (Cochin and Ernakulam) and the Rubber Research Institute (Kottayam). Besides, there are 9 Central Commodity Committees which carry on research and development on cotton, wheat, lac, jute, sugar-cane, tobacco, oil-seeds, coconuts and arecanuts. The directorate of economics and statistics of the

Ministry of Food and Agriculture is responsible for statistical publications, including the monthly *Agricultural Situation in India*.

Land Tenure. There are three main systems of land tenure: *ryotwari* tenure, where the individual holders, usually peasant proprietors, are responsible for the payment of land revenues; *zamindari* tenure, where one or more persons own large estates and are responsible for payment (in this system there may be a number of intermediary holders); and *mahalwari* tenure, where village communities jointly hold an estate and are jointly and severally responsible for payment.

The following table shows, in 1,000 hectares, according to states and territories, the net area and the classification of areas of India that were in 1962–63 cultivated, and uncultivated, and the areas under forests and irrigation:

State or Territory	Total geographical area according to Surveyor-General of India	Net area according to village papers for which returns exist	Forests	Net area irrigated[1]	Cultivated		Uncultivated	
					Net area actually sown	Fallow lands	Not available for cultivation	Other uncultivated land excl. fallow lands[2]
Andhra Pradesh	27,467	27,474	6,117	3,182	11,644	2,861	1,869	4,983
Assam	21,989	13,284	3,525	612	2,331	294	727	6,407
Bihar	17,404	17,329	3,708	1,985	8,344	2,046	1,410	1,821
Gujarat	18,706	18,315	1,110	750	9,563	715	499	6,428
Kerala	3,886	3,859	1,056	336	2,009	87	214	493
Madhya Pradesh	44,344	44,066	14,349	1,021	16,353	2,016	2,002	9,346
Madras (Tamil Nadu)	12,984	13,015	1,868	2,507	6,096	1,486	1,361	2,204
Maharashtra	30,754	30,770	5,428	1,126	18,012	2,321	709	4,300
Mysore	19,215	18,811	2,689	941	10,396	1,257	852	3,617
Orissa	15,582	15,540	3,566	977	5,844	1,035	1,143	3,952
Punjab	12,195	12,535	370	3,267	7,584	463	739	3,103
Rajasthan	34,227	33,986	852	1,859	13,821	4,681	1,142	13,490
Uttar Pradesh	29,385	29,409	3,724	5,282	17,268	1,440	1,938	5,039
West Bengal	8,787	8,852	1,102	1,351	5,436	382	—[4]	1,932
Jammu and Kashmir[3]	22,280	4,873	3,128	272	698	104	274	669
Delhi	148	148	2	36	87	6	31	19
Himachal Pradesh	2,817	2,819	940	40	276	17	76	1,510
Manipur	2,235	2,199	602	68	166	—	27	1,404
Tripura	1,045	1,066	636	14	227	11	37	155
Andaman and Nicobar Islands	833	675	647		9	—	2	15
Laccadive, Minicoy and Amindivi Islands	3	3			3	—		—[5]
All India	326,287	299,912	55,448	25,663	136,244	21,225	15,065	71,930

[1] Net irrigated area in Assam is for 1953–54, in Gujarat, Orissa and Andaman and Nicobar for 1961–62 and in West Bengal for 1958–59.
[2] Includes permanent pastures and other grazing lands, and land under miscellaneous tree crops not included in net area sown.
[3] All figures, except those in first column, exclude Pakistan occupied area.
[4] Included under 'Forests'.
[5] Less than 200 hectares.

Agrarian reform, initiated in the first Five-Year Plan, being undertaken by the state governments includes: (1) The abolition of intermediaries under *zamindari* tenure. Formerly the *zamindari* system prevailed in about 43% of the country, but by 1958 it had been abolished, usually in favour of *ryotwari* tenure, in all except about 5%. The total amount payable in compensation had been estimated at Rs 570 crores, payable in cash in some states and in transferable bonds in others; up to 31 Dec. 1966 about Rs 300 crores had been paid. (2) Tenancy legislation designed to scale down rents to $\frac{1}{4}$–$\frac{1}{3}$ of the value of the produce, to give permanent rights to tenants (subject to the landlord's right to resume a minimum holding for his personal cultivation), and to enable tenants to acquire ownership of their holdings (subject to the landlord's right of resumption for personal cultivation) on payment of compensation over a number of years. (3) Fixing of ceilings on existing holdings and on future acquisition, following a census of land holdings. Ceilings vary widely in different states according to local conditions; e.g., on existing holdings, 22$\frac{3}{4}$ acres in Jammu and Kashmir, 50 acres in the plains of Assam, 18–216 acres in the Telingana area of Andhra Pradesh and the Hyderabad area of Mysore and 25 acres in West Bengal. (4) The consolidation of holdings in community project areas (45·3m. acres had been consolidated by 31 March 1965, mainly in the Punjab, Madhya Pradesh and Uttar Pradesh) and the prevention of fragmentation of holdings by reform of inheritance laws. (5) Promotion of farming by co-operative village management (*see* pp. 346–47).

Further changes in the traditional forms of land tenure are being made by the *Bhoodan* movement, which began in 1951 and which seeks voluntary donation of one-sixth of owner's land for distribution among the landless; by Oct. 1965 about 4·2m. acres had been donated, of which about 1·1m. acres had been distributed. This has now widened into the *Grandan* movement, whose object is the donation of entire villages so that the land may belong to the village community as a whole; by Oct. 1965, 11,370 villages had been donated.

Agricultural Production. The total cropped area in 1962–63 was 156·7m. hectares Area (in 1,000 hectares) and production (in 1,000 metric tons) of principal crops for 3 years:

Crops	1965–66[1]		1966–67[1]		1967–68	
	Area sown	Yield	Area sown	Yield	Area sown	Yield
Rice	35,077	30,614	35,598	30,440	36,722	37,838
Jowar and Bajra	28,609	11,090	30,459	13,447	31,169	15,239
Maize	4,683	4,632	5,061	4,991	5,577	6,275
Wheat	12,798	10,720	13,135	11,528	14,916	16,567
Total cereals	90,192	62,247	94,206	66,126	98,818	73,351
Total foodgrains[2]	111,642	72,264	116,464	73,317	121,484	85,587
Groundnuts[3]	7,171	4,022	7,251	4,485	7,553	5,731
Rape and mustard	2,891	1,268	2,995	1,245	3,204	1,482
Total oilseeds	14,638	6,096	14,852	6,489	15,483	8,166
Sugar-cane[4]	2,749	11,830	2,329	9,494	2,037	9,959
Cotton[5]	7,827	4,708	7,834	4,931	8,047	5,562
Jute[5]	748	4,485	797	5,358	885	6,369

[1] Final estimate. [2] Cereals and pulses. [3] Nuts in shell. [4] Raw sugar or gur.
[5] 1,000 bales of 180 kg.

One of the most important industries connected with agriculture is the tea industry, the average number of persons employed daily being 923,459 in 1958; by value tea accounts for about 25% of all India's exports; in 1963, 65% of the production was exported. The area under tea (in 1,000 hectares), and production (in 1,000 metric tons) in 1963–64 were as follows: Assam, 164 (170); West Bengal, 83 (83); Kerala 40 (42); Madras, 33 (44); total (including other states and territories), 334 (346). Production in 1967 was 379,442 metric tons from 345,000 hectares. In 1968, 401·5m. kg was produced, 200·8m. kg of it being exported, to the value of Rs 156·51 crores.

The production of coffee (1967) was 75,627 metric tons (Mysore, 42,343 and Kerala, 16,564 metric tons).

Production of natural rubber (1963–64) was 36,300 metric tons (Kerala, 33,800 metric tons), from 152,000 hectares (Kerala, 145,000 hectares).

Production of wool, 1963, was 75m. lb. (greasy basis); 1964 (preliminary), 78m. lb.

LIVESTOCK, census 1961: Cattle, 175·7m.; buffaloes, 51·1m.; sheep, 40·3m.; goats, 60·8m.; horses, 1·4m.; poultry, 116·9m.; compared with 155m. cattle, 39m. sheep, 47m. goats, 1·5m. horses and 73·5m. poultry in 1951.

Opium. By international agreement the poppy is cultivated under licence, and all raw opium is sold to the central government. Opium, other than for wholly medical use, is available only to registered addicts, of whom there were about 432,000 in 1958. Production, 1961–62:

	Area (hectares)	Licensed cultivators	Raw opium (kg)
Uttar Pradesh	15,311	82,756	274,626
Madhya Pradesh	15,610	46,710	376,538
Rajasthan	14,511	55,576	318,215
Total	45,432	185,042	969,420

FORESTRY. The lands under the control of the state forest departments are classified as 'reserved forests' (forests intended to be permanently maintained for the supply of timber, etc., or for the protection of water supply, etc.), 'protected forests' and 'unclassed' forest land. The following table shows the extent of the forests and their composition (1964–65):

	Sq. km.		1,000 cu. metres
Total forest area	752,982	Timber produced	19,211
Area with commercial		Timber	5,926
produce	590,064	Roundwood	513
Coniferous	46,144	Pulp and matchwood	12
Sal	97,818	Fuel	12,574
Teak	91,222	Charcoal	186
Other broadleaved	517,798		

Total value of production was Rs 5,856·3 lakhs, including Rs 1,585·9 lakhs from bamboos, canes, gums, resins and other minor products. In 1970 forests occupied 21·8% of the land area, and gave a return of Rs 2·60 per acre.

Mamoria, C. B., *Agricultural problems of India.* 5th ed. Allahabad, 1966.

IRRIGATION. The net area of 27·5m. hectares (1966–67) under irrigation exceeds that of any other country except China, and equals about 19% of the total area under cultivation. The length of canals is about 67,500 miles. Irrigation projects have formed an important part of all three Five-Year Plans. Between 1950–51 and 1964–65 the total irrigated area increased by about 5·4m. hectares.

MINERALS. Production (1966) in metric tons: Barytes, 51,663; bauxite, 750,000; china clay, 644,000; chromite ore, 77,656; coal, 67,974,000; copper ore, 480,863; feldspar, 26,004; gold, 3,740 kg; gypsum, 1,292,556; iron ore, 19,802,350; lead, 5,151; magnesite, 231,923; manganese ore, 1,604,885; mica, crude, 22,052; crude petroleum, 5m. (est.); phosphate-rock (apatite), 16,275; salt, 4·5m.; sillimanite, 10,286; kyanite, 63,670; silver, 1,220 kg; titanium (ilmenite), 30,167; zinc, 8,900. Total value of mineral production, 1966, Rs 247·7 crores, of which coal accounted for Rs 178 crores. Total value, 1968: Rs 3,703m., of which fuels accounted for Rs 2,985m. Bihar produced 32·33% of total value. West Bengal 18·23% and Madhya Pradesh 13·32%.

In 1964 about 667,425 persons were employed in about 3,200 working mines (mainly coal, mica, manganese ore, iron ore and gypsum).

Production of processed minerals (metric tons, 1966): Aluminium, 83,282; pig-iron and ferro-alloys, 7,239,505; steel ingots and castings, 6·53m.; ammonium sulphate, 86,388; refined petroleum products, 11m.

The figures in this section exclude Goa which produced 6·5m. metric tons of iron ore, 16,669 metric tons manganese ore and 55,942 metric tons ferruginous manganese ore in 1966.

INDUSTRIES. The most important indigenous industry, after agriculture, is the weaving of cotton cloth. Other important indigenous industries are silk-rearing and weaving, shawl and carpet weaving, wood-carving and metal-working.

Indian Government industrial policy aims to further a socialist pattern of society. Railways, air transport, armaments and atomic energy are government monopolies. In a number of industries (including the manufacture of iron and steel and mineral oils, shipbuilding and the mining of coal, iron and manganese ores, gypsum, gold and diamonds) new units are set up only by the state. In a further group of industries (road transport, manufacture of chemicals such as drugs, dyestuffs, plastics and fertilizers) the state established new undertakings, but private enterprise may develop either on its own or with state backing, which may take the form of loans or purchase of equity capital. Under the Industries (Development and Regulation) Act, 1951, as amended, industrial undertakings are required to be licensed; 162 industries are within the scope of the Act. The Government are authorized to examine the working of any undertaking, to issue directions to it and to take over its control if this be deemed necessary. A Central Advisory Council has been set up consisting of representatives of industry, labour, consumers and primary producers. There are 16 Development Councils for individual industries. The *Annual Survey of Industry*, 1962, reported:

	No. of factories registered	No. of factories reporting	Productive capital (Rs lakhs)	No. of persons employed	Gross output ex-factory value (Rs lakhs)	Value added by manufacture net of industrial services (Rs lakhs)
Grain mill products	460	451	1,539	34,185	10,833	642
Sugar factories and refineries	236	235	13,824	126,947	21,786	4,437
Miscellaneous food preparations	1,253	1,229	15,192	218,860	40,444	6,251
Tobacco manufactures	339	332	2,908	95,692	9,377	2,055
Spinning, weaving and finishing of textiles	1,107	1,083	50,574	1,142,292	106,449	32,987
Manufacture of textiles, n.e.s.	995	989	1,777	76,503	5,653	721
Pulp, paper and paper board	109	106	8,765	50,400	7,720	2,173
Printing, publishing and allied industries	353	347	4,537	86,055	6,700	2,704
Basic industrial chemicals incl. fertilizers	141	141	19,063	52,518	14,525	4,215
Miscellaneous chemical products	283	282	8,618	65,535	16,151	5,175
Petroleum refineries	8	8	9,050	5,423	4,519	1,635
Cement	34	33	6,571	28,717	7,238	1,863
Iron and steel basic industries	454	443	84,888	258,563	41,220	8,711
Machinery, except electrical	503	494	10,921	119,643	12,949	4,521
Electrical machinery, apparatus, etc.	273	271	11,447	98,407	13,716	3,905
Rail and road equipment	125	117	8,182	164,172	10,892	4,186
Motor vehicles	91	89	6,998	58,388	14,030	4,120

For 1965 the *Survey* gives (provisionally): 13,459 factories each employing 50 or more workers with power and 100 or more without. Total employment 39·53 lakhs, earning Rs 941 crores. The 12,963 reporting factories had Rs 1,687 crores value added by manufacture.

In the cotton industry the number of spindles in 650 mills on 1 June 1969 was 17·52m. and of looms, about 207,000. The production of yarn in 1967 was 891m. kg and of cloth, 3,744m. metres (mill cloth accounts for about 58% of total production of 6,640m. metres, the balance being produced by hand loom and small industries). In 1970 there were 759,000 workers in the mills and 10m. handloom weavers. The value of their output for the year was Rs 800 crores. In 1966 the jute industry had a total of 71,948 looms. Production, 1967, was 1·15m. metric tons.

POWER statistics:

Year	Steam	Diesel	Hydro	Total	Energy generated (1m. kw.)
		Installed capacity of plant at 31 March (1,000 kw.)			
1951 (31 Dec.)	1,097	163	573	1,835	5,860
1964	2,699	354	3,167	6,220	25,510
1970	5,975	420	5,487	11,883	41,195

In 1968, 2,601 towns and 57,372 villages had electric power in the States, and 59 towns and 3,168 villages in the Union Territories. The capacity for use in industry was 1·2m. kw.

COMPANIES. The total number of companies limited by shares at work in India, 31 March 1969 was 28,954, aggregate paid-up capital was Rs 3,772 crores. There were 6,226 public limited companies with an aggregate paid-up capital of Rs 1,664 crores, and 22,728 private limited companies (Rs 2,108 crores).

During 1969–70, 1,510 new limited companies were registered in the Indian Union under the Companies Act 1956 with a total authorized capital of Rs 273 crores; 104 were public limited companies (Rs 132 crores) and 1,406 were private limited companies (Rs 141 crores). Of the new companies, 43 had an authorized capital of Rs 1 crore and above, and 36 of between Rs 50 lakhs and Rs 1 crore; 23 were government companies (*i.e.*, companies in which Government owns at least 51% of share capital). During 1969–70, 227 companies with an aggregate paid-up capital of Rs 799 lakhs went into liquidation and 296 companies (Rs 76 lakhs) were struck off the register.

On 31 March 1969 there were 282 government companies at work with a total paid-up capital of Rs 1,790 crores; 81 were public limited companies and 201 were private limited companies.

On 31 March 1969, 561 companies incorporated elsewhere were reported to have a place of business in India; of these 351 were of UK and 84 of USA origin.

Department of Company Affairs, Govt. of India. *Joint Stock Companies in India.* New Delhi. Quarterly

CO-OPERATIVE MOVEMENT. On 30 June 1964 there were in the Indian Union 356,410 co-operative societies of all types with a membership of 45,289,219, and working capital of 2,099·46 crores. There were 21 state co-operative banks; these advanced loans of Rs 317·88 crores during the year 1963–64. The central co-operative banks (including banking unions) numbered 372, with a membership of 365,009; total advances were Rs 529·14 crores, and working capital Rs 460·32 crores. The number of agricultural primary credit societies (which constitute the base of the co-operative credit structure of the country) was 209,622, with a membership of 23,728,000 and a working capital of Rs 440·39 crores. Non-agricultural primary credit societies numbered 13,323, with a membership of 5,677,000 and a working capital of Rs 220 crores. There were 18 central land mortgage banks (membership, 432,933; working capital, Rs 114·13 crores) and 583 primary land mortgage banks, the majority of which were in Mysore, Andhra Pradesh and Madras (membership, 1,278,316; working capital. Rs 74·08 crores).

Following the recommendations (1954) of a committee appointed by the Reserve Bank of India, the co-operative movement was extended from its chief function of providing credit to include marketing, processing, warehousing, etc. On 30 June 1964 non-credit societies included 3,166 primary marketing societies, 9,269 primary sugar-cane supply societies, 70 sugar factories, 5,942 milk supply societies, 5,850 farming societies, 1,499 irrigation societies, 2,932 fishermen's societies, 12,733 primary weavers' societies, 151 cotton ginning and pressing societies, 47 spinning mills, 8,467 other processing societies and 25,065 other industrial societies; there were 9,900 primary consumers' stores and 9,886 housing societies.

The position of co-operative credit societies in the states, 30 June 1965, was:

State	No. of societies	Membership (in 1,000)	Total working capital (Rs lakhs)
Andhra Pradesh	20,477	2,902	1,47,26
Assam	5,453	376	16,68
Bihar	19,605	1,693	30,64
Gujarat	9,418	1,905	2,04,26
Jammu and Kashmir	1,307	285	6,19
Kerala	2,900	1,503	52,16
Madhya Pradesh	18,128	1,701	1,44,65
Madras (Tamil Nadu)	12,844	5,456	2,36,24
Maharashtra	23,698	4,971	4,52,79
Mysore	11,033	2,350	1,30,01
Orissa	5,833	1,256	41,02
Punjab	22,217	2,024	97,53
Rajasthan	13,378	1,041	39,26
Uttar Pradesh	40,950	5,411	1,86,95
West Bengal	14,339	1,870	97,77
Delhi	878	131	8,32
Other territories	1,996	279	6,39
Total	224,454	35,154	18,98,12

Planning Commission. *The Third Five Year Plan.* Delhi, 1961.—*The New India: Progress through Democracy.* New York, 1958
Council of Scientific and Industrial Research. *The Wealth of India: a dictionary of Indian raw materials and industrial products.* New Delhi, 1948–. In progress
Indian Agricultural Atlas. Delhi, 1958
Indian Labour Guide. Monthly. Delhi
Agricultural Situation in India. Monthly. Delhi
Co-operative Movement in India, Statistical Statements Relating to. Annual. Reserve Bank of India, Bombay
Arakerl, H. R. (and others), *Soil Management in India.* London, 1959
Brown, J. C., *India's Mineral Wealth.* 3rd ed. OUP, 1955
Dantwala, M. L., *India's Food Problem.* London, 1961
Das, N., *Industrial Enterprise in India.* 3rd ed. Bombay, 1961
Dube, R. N., *The Economic Geography of the Indian Republic.* Allahabad, 1954
Ghose, B. C., *Industrial Organization.* 2nd ed. OUP, 1959
Ghosh, A., *Indian Economy, its Nature and Problems.* 7th ed. Calcutta, 1963
Hanson, A. H., *The Process of Planning: a study of India's five-year plans, 1950–64.* OUP, 1966
Hough, E. M., *Co-operative Movement in India.* 4th ed. OUP, 1959
Karnik, V. B., *Indian Trade Unions.* 2nd ed. Bombay, 1966
Kulkarni, K. R., *Agricultural Marketing In India.* 2nd ed. Bombay, 1956
Kust, M. J., *Foreign Enterprise in India.* Bombay, 1964
Neale, W. C., *Economic Change in Rural India.* Yale Univ. Press, 1962
Pant, S. C., *Indian Labour Problems.* Allahabad, 1965
Rangnekar, D. K., *Poverty and Capital Development in India.* OUP, 1958
Rao, R., *Surveys of Indian Industries.* 2 vols. OUP, 1957–59
Rao, V. K. R. V., and Narain, D. *Foreign Aid and India's Economic Development.* London, 1963
Sharma, T. R. and Singh Chauhan, S. D., *Indian industries.* 2nd ed. Agra, 1965
Sharma, V. S., *Sahayoga, or Indian Co-operation.* Hoshiarpur, 1964
Singh, B., *Next Step in Village India.* London, 1961
Sinha, S. P., *Food in India: an analysis of the prospects of self-sufficiency by 1975–76.* OUP, 1962.—*Indian agriculture.* Allahabad, 1965
Srinivas, M. N., *India's Villages.* 2nd ed. London, 1961
Stebbing, E. P., *The Forests of India.* 3 vols. London, 1922–26
Thorner, D., *Agricultural Co-operatives in India.* Bombay, 1964
Turner, R. (ed.), *India's Urban Future.* California Univ. Press, 1961
Venkatasubbiah, H., *Indian Economy Since Independence.* 2nd ed. London, 1961
Ward, B., *India and the West.* London, 1961.—*The Plan under Pressure.* London, 1963

COMMERCE. The external trade of India (excluding land-borne trade with Tibet, Sikkim and Bhután) was as follows (in 1,000 rupees):

	Imports		Exports and Re-exports	
	Merchandise[1]	Treasure	Merchandise	Treasure
1965–66	1,394,04,89	13,34,25	809,54,96	2,85,99
April and May 1966[2]	227,05,88	54,31	126,55,91	62,01
June 1966–March 1967[2]	1,647,61,41	9,24,00	967,22,28	1,79,64
1967–68	1,986,38,00	6,67,45	1,198,69,00	51,22
1968–69	1,785,84,00	90,58[3]	1,353,48,00	81,78[3]

[1] Excludes certain consignments of foodgrains and stores awaiting adjustment.
[2] Pre- and post-devaluation periods.
[3] Provisional

The distribution of commerce by countries and areas was as follows in the year ended 31 March 1970 (in 1,000 rupees):

Countries	Exports to	Imports from		Exports to	Imports from
Afghánistán	11,26,85	11,59,10	Népal	27,27,63	14,39,72
Argentina	69,37	26,88	Netherlands	11,15,33	15,67,64
Australia	24,39,77	31,27,56	New Zealand	5,83,51	1,56,64
Belgium	24,73,54	8,09,40	Pakistan, East	14	..
Burma	20,82,62	20,15,45	Pakistan, West	31	..
Canada	26,32,82	73,88,61	Poland	21,28,71	22,46,24
Ceylon	25,63,31	2,85,98	Saudi Arabia	14,99,49	17,49,00
Czechoslovakia	30,07,14	22,97,94	Singapore	13,82,21	1,54,41
Denmark	3,72,74	4,18,53	Sudan	19,84,60	27,22,23
France	21,69,52	23,24,30	Sweden	5,18,20	10,43,38
Germany, East	20,01,67	24,31,78	Switzerland	7,58,58	11,01,86
Germany, West	29,75,58	83,72,98	USSR	176,24,10	170,39,87
Hungary	9,40,30	17,16,98	UAR	34,63,46	21,68,68
Iran	23,98,18	83,42,85	UK	164,24,18	100,38,03
Italy	12,90,81	39,60,16	USA	237,58,21	459,96,34
Japan	179,32,10	66,82,27	Yemen	1,90	140
Kenya	7,73,89	4,52,75	Yugoslavia	33,97,89	6,17,15
Malaysia	8,24,31	8,27,23			

The value (in 1,000 rupees) of the leading articles of merchandise was as follows in the year ended 31 March 1970:

Exports	Value
Fish	30,83,18
Edible nuts and fresh fruits	59,95,38
Coffee	19,61,55
Tea and mate	124,50,29
Spices	34,48,84
Oilseed, oilnuts and oil kernels	8,23,71
Tobacco	32,70,55
Hides and skins, undressed	8,30,57
Wood (unworked)	6,83,25
Wool and other animal hair	4,95,80
Cotton, raw	17,77,27
Cotton waste; shoddy	43,13
Stone, sand and gravel	36,13
Iron ore and concentrates	94,61,57
Iron and steel scrap	8,94,38
Ore and concentrates, non-ferrous base metals	14,71,13
Coal, coke and briquettes	2,05,38
Fixed vegetable oils	4,95,07
Leather	80,53,09
Textile yarn and thread	40,91,71
Textile fabrics (woven) except cotton and jute	10,92,11
Cotton manufactures except yarn, thread and clothing	86,62,69
Jute manufactures except twist and yarn	204,96,60
Floor coverings, tapestries, except cotton and jute	16,27,26
Manufactures of leather or artificial leather	78,09
Imports	
Milk and cream	7,60,29
Wheat, spelt and meslin	184,32,51
Rice	58,24,83
Edible nuts and fresh fruit	34,22,37
Pulp and waste paper	12,47,45
Wool and other animal hair	17,24,34
Cotton, raw	82,78,48
Jute	1,08,06
Vegetable fibres except cotton and jute	5,77,11
Crude fertilizers	8,73,98
Sulphur and unroasted iron pyrites	10,70,45
Petroleum, crude and partly refined	96,32,71
Petroleum products	41,23,98
Animal oils and fats	12,00,56
Fixed vegetable oils	17,23,04
Organic chemicals	51,50,26
Medical and pharmaceutical products	18,26,02
Manufactured fertilizers	67,18,33
Plastic materials	8,31,33
Chemical materials and products	14,12,17
Paper, paperboard and manufactures	23,70,73
Pearls, precious and semi-precious stones	28,43,02
Iron and steel bars, angles, shapes, sections	11,25,13
Iron and steel universals, plates and sheets	46,08,71
Iron and steel tubes, pipes, fittings	10,23,71
Copper	47,38,00
Zinc	8,25,32
Tin	6,29,46
Machinery other than electrical	2,79,21,12
Electrical machinery	63,63,44
Transport equipment	49,85,74

The trade between India and UK (British Board of Trade returns) is as follows (in £1,000 sterling):

	1965	1966	1967	1968	1969	1970
Imports to UK	128,338	119,105	125,700	134,989	107,064	106,044
Exports from UK	114,079	95,405	81,550	71,687	65,528 ⎱	72,900
Re-exports from UK	2,323	1,334	1,717	1,080	916 ⎰	

Annual Statement of the Foreign Trade of India. 2 vols. Calcutta
Monthly Statistics of the Foreign Trade of India. Calcutta
Review of the Trade of India. Annual. Delhi
Indian Trade Journal. Weekly. Calcutta

SHIPPING. In Aug. 1970, 254 ships totalling 2,354,112 GRT were on the Indian Register; of these, 75 ships of 270,895 GRT were engaged in coastal trade, and 179 ships of 2,083,217 GRT in overseas trade. Traffic of major ports, 1968–69, was as follows:

	Ships entered		Imports	Exports
Port	No.	GRT (1,000)	(1m. metric tons)	(1m. metric tons)
Calcutta	1,409	10,316	4·00	4·00
Bombay	2,769	18,630	12·10	4·31
Madras	1,114	9,430	3·02	2·36
Cochin	1,083	8,452	3·78	1·40
Marmagoa	622	6,621	0·37	8·41
Vishakhapatnam	626	7,055	2·69	5·43
Kandla	261	2.152	1·71	0·33
Total	7,884	62,656	27·67	26·24

The shipyard at Vishakhapatnam is capable of building ocean-going vessels of a maximum dead weight tonnage of 15,000. Present capacity is 3 ships of 12,500 DWT each per year. Two more shipyards (at Bombay and Calcutta) can build sea vessels of smaller tonnage. A shipyard is being built at Cochin as a public sector project, with a building dock for ships of 66,000 DWT and a repair dock for ships up to 85,000 DWT. A contract for technical collaboration has been signed with Mitsubishi Heavy Industries, Tokyo.

RAILWAYS. The Indian railway system is government-owned and (under the control of the Railway Board) is divided into 9 zones, with route km as follows at 31 March 1969:

Zone	Headquarters	Broad gauge	Metre gauge	Narrow gauge	Total
Central	Bombay	2.853	238	495	3,586
Eastern	Calcutta	2,494	—	81	2,575
Northern	Delhi	4,286	2,133	162	6,581
North Eastern	Gorakhpur	32	3.053	—	3,085
North East Frontier	Pandu	400	1,801	54	2,255
Southern	Madras	1,442	2,986	98	4,526
South Central	Secunderabad	1,619	1,978	229	3,826
South Eastern	Calcutta	3,308	—	918	4,226
Western	Bombay	1,716	3,777	747	6,240

Passengers carried in 1968–69 were 2,230·39m. (1963–64: 1,892·6m.); freight, 205·04m. (192·3m.) metric tons; this includes freight carried for railway purposes. Railway staff on 31 March 1969 numbered 1,358,857. Total route, 31 March 1969: 60,014·42 km.

Indian Railways pay to the central government a fixed dividend of 4½% on capital-at-charge.

Financial years	Gross traffic receipts (Rs crores)	Working expenses (Rs crores)	Net revenues (Rs crores)	Net surplus or deficit (Rs crores)
1968–69	898·84	636·78	142·81	− 7·86
1969–70[1]	950·55	683·05	145·88	−12·55
1971–72[2]	1,122·00	700·99	189·47	+22·38

[1] Revised estimate. [2] Budget.

Prasad, A., *Indian Railways.* Bombay and London, 1960
Saxena, K. K., *Indian Railways.* Bombay, 1962
Srivatsava, S. K., *Transport Development in India.* 2nd ed. Ghaziabad, 1956

ROADS. In 1969 there were about 941,100 km of roads, of which 317,800 km were metalled. Roads are divided into 5 main administrative classes, namely, national highways, state highways, major district roads, district roads and village roads. The national highways (23,720 km in 1969) connect capitals of states, major ports and foreign highways. During the third Plan the national highway system was linked with the ECAFE (Economic Co-operation Administration Far East) international highway system. The state highways are the main trunk roads of the states, while the major district roads connect subsidiary areas of production and markets with distribution centres, and form the main link between headquarters and neighbouring districts.

There were (31 March 1967) about 1,187,434 motor vehicles in India, comprising 442,217 private cars and jeeps, 37,905 taxis, 280,869 motor cycles and auto-rickshaws, 77,799 public service vehicles, 268,327 goods vehicles and 80,371 miscellaneous vehicles. Total of motor vehicles in 1968 was 1,307,222.

AVIATION. The air transport industry in India was nationalized in 1953 with the formation of two Air Corporations: Air India for operating long-distance international air services, and Indian Airlines Corporation for operating air services within India and to adjacent countries, viz., Burma, Ceylon, Nepál, Pakistan and Afghánistán. Air India operates 15 flights a week to London, 2 of them *via* Moscow, the rest with 14 halts through the Middle East and Europe; other scheduled flights are made to East Africa (Kenya and Uganda), Australia and Fiji (Sydney *via* Singapore and Perth), Indonesia (Jakarta *via* Singapore), the Far East (Tokyo *via* Bangkok and Hong Kong), Kuwait (*via* Bahrain) and Mauritius. Boeing aircraft are in use on these services. In addition, a service to Kuwait (*via* Karachi and Bahrain) is operated with de Haviland Comet aircraft. Caravelle, Viscount, Skymaster, Fokker Friendship, HS-748 and Dakota aircraft are flown by India Airlines Corporation.

In 1968 Indian aircraft flew 60m. km on scheduled services, carrying about 2·1m. passengers and 37·1m. kg of cargo and mail. On non-scheduled services 4·6m. km were flown, about 152,500 passengers and 12·1m. kg of freight were carried.

The Civil Aviation Department maintains and operates 85 aerodromes, including the 4 international airports at Bombay (Santa Cruz), Calcutta (Dum Dum), Delhi (Palam) and Madras.

On 31 Dec. 1968, 258 aircraft held current certificates of airworthiness.

POST. On 31 March 1969 there were 73,085 permanent and 29,392 experimental post offices and 14,594 telegraph offices (including licensed offices). The department at the end of the year was maintaining 407,436 km of line, including cables, and 10,017,827 km of wire, including cable conductors.

The telephone system is in the hands of the Indian Posts and Telegraphs Department. On 31 March 1969 there were 16,002 telephone exchanges (including private and private branch exchanges) and 1,120,357 telephones.

BANKING. The Reserve Bank, the central bank for India, was established in 1934 and started functioning on 1 April 1935 as a shareholder's bank; it became a nationalized institution on 1 Jan. 1949. It has the sole right of issuing currency-notes. The Bank acts as adviser to the government on financial problems and is the banker for central and state governments, commercial banks and some other financial institutions. The Bank manages the rupee public debt of central and state governments. It is the custodian of the country's exchange reserve and supervises repatriation of export proceeds and payments for imports. The Bank gives short-term loans to state governments and scheduled banks and short- and medium-term loans to state co-operative banks and industrial finance institutions. The Bank has extensive powers of regulation of the banking system, directly under the Banking Regulation Act, 1949, and indirectly by the use of variations in bank rate, variation in reserve ratios, selective controls and open market operations. Bank rate was 5% in the financial year 1969–70. For commercial banks there is a progressive increase in the cost of credit made available by the

Reserve Bank, by relating borrowing to the net liquidity position of the borrowing bank; when this is 33% or above, the Reserve Bank charges the bank rate, but for every 1% decrease or fraction thereof in the liquidity ratio of the borrowing bank the rate charged on its excess borrowings is increased by 1% above bank rate. Refinance is at $4\frac{1}{2}$% for banks' credit to exporters and to certain primary co-operative credit societies, and at bank rate for short term lending to small industries and direct lending to agriculturists. The net profit of the Reserve Bank of India for the year ended 30 June 1970 amounted to Rs 75 crores.

The commercial banking system consisted of 73 scheduled banks (*i.e.*, banks which are included in the 2nd schedule to the Reserve Bank Act) and 14 non-scheduled banks on 31 Dec. 1969; total number of offices was 9,051. Total deposits in commercial banks, 31 Dec. 1969, stood at Rs 4,900 crores; in post office savings banks 31 March 1970 deposits were 841 crores. The business of non-scheduled banks forms less than 1% of commercial bank business. Of the 73 scheduled banks, 15 are foreign banks which specialize in financing foreign trade but also compete for domestic business. The largest scheduled bank is the State Bank of India, constituted by nationalizing the Imperial Bank of India in 1955. The State Bank acts as the agent of the Reserve Bank and the subsidiaries of the State Bank act as the agents of the State Bank for transacting government business as well as undertaking commercial functions. An act of Parliament receiving assent on 9 Aug. 1969 nationalized 14 banks with aggregate deposits of not less than Rs 50 crores on 27 June 1969. This brought the share of public sector banks to 83% of deposits and 84% of credit.

Reserve Bank of India: Report on Currency and Finance.—Report on the Trend and Progress of Banking in India.—Report of the Central Board of Directors. Annual. Bombay.
Reserve Bank of India—Functions and working. Reserve Bank of India, 1970
Laud, G. M., *Co-operative Banking in India.* Bombay, 1956
Muranjan, S. K., *Modern Banking in India.* Bombay, 1952
Panandikar, S. G., *Banking in India.* 8th ed. Calcutta, 1956

WEIGHTS AND MEASURES

A complete change to the metric system by Dec. 1966 was envisaged by the Standards of Weights and Measures Act, 1956. The reform has been introduced gradually, through a phased programme, covering different industries, trades, public undertakings and regions.

The use of metric units prescribed under the Standards of Weights and Measures Act, 1956, including the Celsius scale of temperature, has become compulsory in commercial transactions throughout the country. The system has also been adopted in education, general and technical, including engineering and medical courses. The metric system is now being progressively introduced in more complicated fields such as the public works department, printing and stationery, survey and land records, irrigation and power, etc.

Organizations for the enforcement of the weights and measures laws on a uniform basis as a continuing task have been set up both at the centre and in the States, so that a single system of weights and measures prevails in the country. An expert committee is bringing the present laws into line with the recommendations of the International Organization of Legal Metrology (OIML) and the General Conference on Weights and Measures (CGPM).

For weights previously in legal use under the Standards of Weight Act, 1956, *see* THE STATESMAN'S YEAR-BOOK, 1961, p. 171.

CALENDAR

The dates of the Saka era (named after the north Indian dynasty of the first century A.D.) are being used alongside Gregorian dates in issues of the *Gazette of India*, news broadcasts by All-India Radio and government-issued calendars, from 22 March 1957, a date which corresponds with the first day of the year 1879 in the Saka era.

BOOKS OF REFERENCE

Special works relating to States are shown under their separate headings.

The Gazetteer of India. Central Gazetteers Unit. Delhi, 1965
India: a reference annual. Delhi Govt. Print. Annual
Cambridge History of India. 6 vols. CUP, 1922–47. Supp., 1953
The Times of India Directory and Yearbook. Bombay and London. Annual

Handbook for Travellers in India, Pakistan, Burma and Ceylon. 19th ed. by L. F. Rushbrook Williams. London, 1962
Chatterjee, S. P., Indian Climatology. Calcutta, 1956.—(ed.), National Atlas of India (Preliminary [Hindi] edition). Calcutta, 1957
Desai, A. R., The Social Background of Indian Nationalism. Bombay, 1954
Griffiths, P. J., The British Impact on India. London, 1952
Kesavan, B. S. and Kulkarni, V. Y. (eds), The National Bibliography of Indian Literature, 1901–53. New Delhi, 1963 ff.
Kundra, J. C., Indian Foreign Policy, 1947–54. Bombay, 1955
Majumdar, R. C., Raychandhuri, H. C., and Datta, K., An Advanced History of India. 2nd ed. London, 1950
Mitra, H. N., The Indian Annual Register. Calcutta, from 1953
Murty, K. S., Indian Foreign Policy. Calcutta, 1964
Philips, C. H. (ed.), The Evolution of India and Pakistan: select documents. OUP, 1962 ff.—Politics and Society in India. London, 1963
Platt, R. (ed.), India: a compendium. New York, 1962
Poplai, S. L. (ed.), India, 1947–50 [select documents]. 2 vols. Bombay and London, 1959
Smith, V. E., Oxford History of India. 3rd ed. OUP, 1958
Spate, O. H. K., India and Pakistan: a general regional geography. 3rd ed. London, 1968
Sutton, S. C., Guide to the India Office Library [founded in 1801]. HMSO, 1952
Yasdani, C. (ed.), Early History of the Deccan. 2 vols. London, 1960

STATES AND TERRITORIES

The Republic of India is composed of the following 17 States and 10 centrally administered Union Territories:

States	Capital	States	Capital
Andhra Pradesh	Hyderabad	Mysore	Bangalore
Assam	Shillong	Nagaland	Kohima
Bihar	Patna	Orissa	Bhubaneswar
Gujarat	Ahmedabad	Punjab	Chandigarh
Haryana	Chandigarh	Rajasthan	Jaipur
Jammu and Kashmir	Srinagar	Tamil Nadu	Madras
Kerala	Trivandrum	Uttar Pradesh	Lucknow
Madhya Pradesh	Bhopal	West Bengal	Calcutta
Maharashtra	Bombay		

Union Territories

Andaman and Nicobar Islands; Chandigarh; Dadra and Nagar Haveli; Delhi; Goa, Daman and Diu; Himachal Pradesh; Laccadive, Minicoy and Amindivi Islands; Manipur; Pondicherry; Tripura.

States Reorganization. The Constitution, which came into force on 26 Jan. 1950, provided for 9 Part A States (Assam, Bihar, Bombay, Madhya Pradesh, Madras, Orissa, Punjab, Uttar Pradesh and West Bengal) which corresponded to the previous governors' provinces; 8 Part B States (Hyderabad, Jammu and Kashmir, Madhya Bharat, Mysore, Patalia–East Punjab (PEPSU), Rajasthan, Saurashtra and Travancore–Cochin) which corresponded to Indian states or unions of states; 10 Part C States (Ajmer, Bhopal Bilaspur, Coorg, Delhi, Himachal Pradesh, Kutch, Manipur, Tripura and Vindhya Pradesh) which corresponded to the chief commissioners' provinces; and 2 Part D Territories and other areas (Andaman and Nicobar Islands, and Sikkim). Part A States (under governors) and Part B States (under rajpramukhs) had provincial autonomy with a ministry and elected assembly. Part C States (under chief commissioners) were the direct responsibility of the Union government, although Kutch, Manipur and Tripura had legislatures with limited powers. Andhra was formed as a Part A State on its separation from Madras in 1953. Bilaspur was merged with Himachal Pradesh in 1954.

The States Reorganization Act, 1956, abolished the distinction between Parts A, B and C States and established two categories for the units of the Indian union to be called States and Territories. The following were the main territorial changes: the Telugu districts of Hyderabad were merged with Andhra; Mysore absorbed the whole Kannada-speaking area (including Coorg, the greater part of 4 districts of Bombay, 3 districts of Hyderabad and 1 district of Madras); Bhopal, Vindhya Pradesh and Madhya Bharat were merged with Madhya Pradesh, which ceded 8 Marathi-speaking districts to Bombay; the new state of Kerala, comprising the majority of Malayalam-speaking peoples, was formed from Travancore–Cochin with a small area from Madras; Patalia–East Punjab was included in Punjab; Kutch and Saurashtra in Bombay; and Ajmer in Rajasthan; Hyderabad ceased to exist.

On 1 May 1960 Bombay State was divided into two parts: 17 districts (including Saurashtra and Kutch) in the north and west became the new state of Gujarat; the remainder was renamed the state of Maharashtra.

In Aug. 1961 the former Portuguese territories of Dadra and Nagar Haveli became a Union territory. The Portuguese territory of Goa and the smaller territories of Daman and Diu, occupied by India in Dec. 1961, were constituted a Union territory in March 1962. In Aug. 1962 the former French territories of Pondicherry, Karikal, Mahé and Yanaon were formally transferred to India and became a Union territory. In Sept. 1962 the Naga Hills Tuensang Area was constituted a separate state under the name of Nagaland. On 1 Nov. 1966, under the Punjab Reorganization Act 1966, a new state of Haryana and a new Union Territory of Chandigarh were created from parts of Punjab (India); for details, see pp. 358–59 and 382.

Report of the States Reorganization Commission. Government of India. Delhi, 1956
Menon, V. P., The Story of the Integration of the Indian [Princely] States. London, 1956
Santhanam, K., Union–State relations in India. London, 1961

ANDHRA PRADESH

Andhra was constituted a separate state on 1 Oct. 1953, on its partition from Madras, and consisted of the undisputed Telugu-speaking area of that state. To this region was added, on 1 Nov. 1956, the Telangana area of the former Hyderabad State, comprising the districts of Hyderabad, Medak, Nizamabad, Karimnaga, Warangal, Khammam, Nalgonda and Mahbubnaga, parts of the Adilabad district and some taluks of the Raichur Gulbarga and Bidar districts, and some revenue circles of the Nanded district. On 1 April 1960, 326 sq. miles in the Chingleput and Salem districts of Madras were transferred to Andhra Pradesh in exchange for 405 sq. miles from Chittoor district. The district of Ongole was formed by an Ordnance of 2 Feb. 1970.

GOVERNMENT AND CONSTITUTION. Andhra Pradesh has a bicameral legislature. The Legislative Council consists of 90 members: Congress, 67; Communist (Marxists), 3; Swatantra, 3; independents, 7; Communist Party of India, 3; Barateeya Janasangh, 4; National Teachers' Front, 3. The Legislative Assembly has 287 members, of which 215 held Congress seats on 7 Feb. 1970. A regional committee composed of the elected members of Telangana Region is consulted by the Government on matters pertaining to that region.

For administrative purposes there are 20 districts in the state. The capital is Hyderabad.

Governor: K. K. Desai.
Chief Minister: K. Brahmananda Reddi.

AREA AND POPULATION. The state has an area of 275,281 sq. km and a population (1961) of 35·98m., an increase of 15·6% since 1951. The principal language is Telugu. Cities with over 100,000 population (1961 census) see p. 333.

RELIGION. At the 1961 census Hindus numbered 31,814,025; Moslems, 2,715,021; Christians, 1,428,729; Jains, 9,012; Sikhs, 8,563; Buddhists, 6,753.

EDUCATION. In 1961 about 21% of the population were literate (29·7% males, 11·8% females). There were, in 1966, 41,747 recognized educational institutions with (1962) 4,090,285 pupils, namely, 71 pre-primary, 36,690 primary, 339 senior basic, 1,288 middle and 1,435 high schools. Education is free for children up to 14.

Osmania University, Hyderabad (founded in 1918), had (1965–66) 28 day colleges for men, 7 day colleges for women and 13 evening colleges for men; Andhra University, Waltair (1926), had 26 day colleges for men, 7 day colleges for women and 2 evening colleges for men; Sri Venkateswara University, Tirupati (1954), had 14 day colleges for men, 3 day colleges for women and 3 evening colleges for men. The AP Agricultural University was inaugurated at Rajendra Nagar, Hyderabad, in 1964.

JUSTICE. The High Court of Judicature at Hyderabad has a Chief Justice and 19 puisne judges.

FINANCE. The budget estimates for 1968–69 showed total revenue receipts of Rs. 199 crores, and expenditure of Rs 204·67 crores. Receipts included: Contributions and adjustment between central and state governments, Rs 43,78·96 lakhs; taxes on income, Rs 10,96·95 lakhs; state excise, Rs 16,57·31 lakhs; stamps, Rs 6,41·79 lakhs; forests, Rs 5,79·58 lakhs; sales tax, Rs 35,48 lakhs; vehicles taxes, Rs 10,73 lakhs; debt services, Rs 28,37·56 lakhs; civil administration, Rs 11,49·70 lakhs. Expenditure included: Education, Rs 34,08·94 lakhs; public works and improvements, Rs 9,82·25 lakhs; irrigation, embankment, etc., Rs 25,67·47 lakhs; medical, and public health, Rs 17,06·32 lakhs; police, Rs 10,15·09 lakhs; agriculture, Rs 997·60 lakhs; general administration, Rs 12,30·13 lakhs; debt services, Rs 31,33·25 lakhs; extraordinary, including community projects and local development, Rs 4,44·99 lakhs; industries, Rs 1,35·63 lakhs.

AGRICULTURE. There are about 13m. hectares of cultivable land. Production of principal crops, 1968–69: Rice, 4·34m. tons; jowar, maize and bajra, 1·81m. tons; wheat, 3m. tons; total foodgrains, 6·8m. tons.

Livestock (1961 census): Cattle, 12·28m.; buffaloes, 6·97m.; goats, 4·27m.; sheep, 3·37m.

FORESTS. An administration report for 1965–66 estimated that forests occupy about 24% of the total area of the state; value of forest produce, Rs 517·73 lakhs.

IRRIGATION. The Tungabhadra dam, inaugurated in 1953, has been completed, thus irrigating about 336,000 hectares in Andhra Pradesh and Mysore. The Nagarjunasaga project, which incorporates canals and a dam (the tallest masonry dam in the world) on the Krishna River 160 km from Hyderabad, will irrigate over 800,000 hectares on completion of the final phase. The first phase has been completed, and the waters let out for irrigation.

MINERALS (1966–67). Production of principal minerals (in 1,000 metric tons): Manganese, 100; mica, 8; iron ore, 414; limestone, 1,815; coal, 4,277; barytes, 35.

INDUSTRY. In 1965 Andhra Pradesh had 6,073 factories subject to the Factories Act, 1948. There were 12 textile-mills, 12 sugar-mills and 2 paper-mills. Other industries include cement, tanning and glass. There is an oil refinery at Vishakhapatnam, where India's only major shipbuilding yards are situated.

Cottage industry includes the manufacture of carpets, wooden and lacquer toys, brocades, bidriware, filigree and lace-work. The wooden toys of Nirmal and Kondapalli are particularly well known.

POWER. The total installed capacity of the Machkund hydro-electric project (financed jointly with Orissa) is 114,750 kw.

SHIPPING. The chief port is Vishakhapatnam. There are minor ports at Kakinada, Machilipatam, Bheemunipatnam, Narsapur, Krishnapatnam, Vadasevu and Calingapatnam.

RAIL. In 1966 there were 7,334 route km of railway, of which 4,425 km were broad gauge, 3,011 km metre gauge and 60 km narrow gauge.

ROADS. In 1966 there were 370,123 km of roads, including state highways, 14,934 km; national highways, 2,205 km; major district roads, 14,371 km; other district roads, 6,098 km.

ASSAM

Assam first became a British Protectorate at the close of the first Burmese War in 1826. In 1832 Cachar was annexed; in 1835 the Jaintia Hills were included in the East India Company's dominions, and in 1839 Upper Assam was annexed to Bengal. In 1874 Assam was detached from Bengal and made a separate chief commissionership. On the partition of Bengal in 1905, it was united to the Eastern Districts of Bengal under a Lieut.-Governor. From 1912 the chief commissionership of Assam was revived, and in 1921 a governorship was created. On the partition of India almost the whole of the predominantly Muslim district of Sylhet was merged with East Bengal (Pakistan). Dewangiri in North Kamrup was ceded to Bhután in 1951. The Naga Hill district, administered by the Union government since 1957, became part of Nagaland in 1962. In April 1969 the Lok Sabha passed a bill creating the autonomous state of Meghalaya within Assam and comprising the districts of Garo Hills, Khasi Hills and Jaintia.

GOVERNMENT AND CONSTITUTION. Assam has a unicameral legislature of 126 members. The state of the parties in the Legislative Assembly in March 1967 was: Congress, 73; Praja Socialist, 5; Hill Leaders' Conference, 9; Communists, 7; S.S.P., 4; Swatantra, 2; independents, 26. Meghalaya has a Legislative Assembly which sits in Tura.

There are 11 districts (including Meghalaya and excluding NEFA). The Constitution of India (6th Schedule) makes special provision for the administration of the Hill Districts. The capital is Shillong.

Governor: B. K. Nehru.
Chief Minister: Bimala Prasad Chaliha.
Chief Minister of Meghalaya: Capt. W. Sangma.

North East Frontier Agency. The NEFA is administered by the Governor of Assam, acting as the agent of the President, through an Advisor whose status corresponds to that of a Commissioner. It includes the Kameng, Tirap, Subansiri, Siang and Lohit Frontier Divisions, has an area of 81,524 sq. km and an estimated population of 336,558. The integration of the Agency with Assam was agreed upon in March 1963.

AREA AND POPULATION. The area of the state, excluding the NEFA, is 121,973 sq. km. Its population (excluding the NEFA) was 11,872,772 at the 1961 census, an increase of 34% since 1951. Principal towns with population (1961) are: Shillong, 102,398 (urban area); Gauhati, 100,707; Dibrugarh, 58,480; Silchar, 41,062; Nowgong, 38,600. The principal languages are Assamese and Bengali.

RELIGION. At the 1961 census Hindus numbered 7,884,921; Moslems, 2,765,509; Christians, 764,553; Buddhists, 36,513; Sikhs, 9,686; Jains, 9,468.

EDUCATION. The 1961 census showed 27·4% of the population to be literate (males, 37·3%; females, 16%).
In 1961, 19,736 schools for general education had 1,556,952 pupils; 103

schools for professional education had 8,558 pupils; 830 schools for special education had 30,006 students. Primary education is free.

The University of Gauhati (established 1948) is affiliating, teaching and residential. The number of full-time students in the university and its affiliated colleges (1962–63) was 30,351.

JUSTICE. The seat of the High Court is Gauhati. It has a Chief Justice and 3 puisne judges.

FINANCE. The budget estimates for 1968–69 showed total revenue receipts of Rs 90,30·17 lakhs, and expenditure of Rs 91,67·76 lakhs. The receipts included: Contributions and adjustments between central and state governments, Rs 49,98·98 lakhs; taxes on income, Rs 6,87·18 lakhs; state excise, Rs 2,62·66 lakhs; stamps, Rs 1,00·61 lakhs; forests, Rs 3,10·35 lakhs; sales tax, Rs 10,59·72 lakhs; vehicles taxes, Rs 1,63·35 lakhs; debt services, Rs 34·60 lakhs; civil administration, Rs 2,42·66 lakhs. Expenditure included: Education, Rs 17,49·47 lakhs; public works and improvements, Rs 12,27·92 lakhs; irrigation, embankment and electricity, Rs 1,60·71 lakhs; medical, and public health, Rs 6,65·61 lakhs; police, Rs 10,03·63 lakhs; agriculture, Rs 7,09·23 lakhs; general administration, Rs 2,20·93 lakhs; debt services, Rs 12,65·31 lakhs; extraordinary, including community projects and local development, Rs 2,74·42 lakhs; industries, Rs 1,24·32 lakhs.

PRODUCTION. The cultivation and manufacture of tea is the principal industry in Assam. Agriculture employs about 90% of the population. In 1967 the production of tea amounted to 187,567 metric tons, about 50% of India's total.

Production of other principal crops: Rice (1968–69), 2·25m. metric tons; oilseeds (1964–65), 56,000 metric tons; jute (1964–65), 882 bales (of 180 kg).

FORESTRY. There are 16,232 sq. km of reserved forests under the administration of the Forest Department and 29,083 sq. km of unclassed forests; the latter includes 8,744 sq. km under various civil authorities.

OIL. Assam contains important oilfields. Production at the Digboi oil refinery amounted to 114·5m. gallons in 1958 (1948: 67·8m. gallons), all from local sources. Refineries at Gauhati and Barauni went into production in 1962 and 1964 respectively.

INDUSTRY. Sericulture and hand-loom weaving, both silk and cotton, are the most important home industries. There are some coalfields; output in 1968 was 509,000 metric tons.

POWER. In the year April 1966–March 1967 power stations in Assam generated 126m. kwh. of electricity.

COMMUNICATIONS. Lower Assam depends to a considerable extent on water transport. Air transport is increasingly important; daily scheduled flights connect the principal towns with the rest of India. An important road–rail bridge across the Brahmaputra River was completed in 1962.

ROADS. In 1968 there were 20,678 km of road in Assam, of which 2,934 km were national highway.

RAIL. The open length of railways in 1966 was 5,827 km, of which 3,334 km was running track and the rest sidings.

Goswami, P. C., *Economic Development of Assam*. London, 1963
Reid, Sir Robert, *History of the Frontier Areas bordering on Assam*. Shillong, 1942

BIHAR

The state contains the 2 ethnic areas of Bihar and Chota Nagpur. In 1956 certain areas of Purnea and Manbhum districts were transferred to West Bengal.

GOVERNMENT AND CONSTITUTION. Bihar has a bicameral legislature. The Legislative Council consists of 96 members. The Legislative Assembly consists of 318 elected members. The election of Feb. 1970 returned a Congress-led coalition ministry.

For the purposes of administration it is divided into 4 divisions covering 17 districts. The capital is Patna; the hot-weather seat is Ranchi.

Governor: Nityanand Kanungo
Chief Minister: D. Prasad Rai

AREA AND POPULATION. The area of Bihar is 174,038 sq. km and its population (1961 census), 46,455,610, an increase of 19·8% since 1951. Population of principal towns, *see* p. 333.

The official language is Hindi.

RELIGION. At the 1961 census Hindus numbered 39,347,050; Moslems, 5,785,631; Christians, 502,195; Sikhs, 44,413; Jains, 17,598; Buddhists, 2,885.

EDUCATION. At the census of 1961 the proportion of literates was 18·2% (males, 29·8%, females, 6·9%).

There were, 1960–61, 1,541 high, higher secondary and post-basic schools with 523,621 pupils, 4,408 middle and senior basic schools with 812,023 pupils, 37,323 primary and junior basic schools with 2,711,991 pupils, 230 schools for professional education with 32,422 pupils, 8,253 schools for special education with 331,408 pupils and 610 unrecognized institutions of different categories with 43,438 pupils. Education is free for children up to 14.

There are 6 universities: Patna University (founded 1917) with (1962–63) 10,576 full-time students; Bihar University, Muzaffarpur (1952) with 3 constituent colleges, 35 affiliated colleges and (1961–62) 24,121 students; Bhagalpur University (1960); Ranchi University (1960); Darbhanga Sanskrit University (1961); Magadha University, Gaya (1962).

JUSTICE. There is a High Court (constituted in 1916) at Patna with a Chief Justice, 13 puisne judges and 4 additional judges.

Police. The police force is under an inspector-general; there is 1 policeman to 1,852 of the population.

FINANCE. The budget estimates for 1968–69 show total revenue receipts of Rs 1,63,40·27 lakhs and expenditure of Rs 1,60,35·60 lakhs. Receipts included: Contributions and adjustments between central and state governments, Rs 43,62·10 lakhs; taxes on income, Rs 14,58·76 lakhs; state excise, Rs 10,28·56 lakhs; stamps, Rs 7,99·45 lakhs; forests, Rs 3,62·76 lakhs; sales tax, Rs 33,54·55 lakhs; vehicles taxes, Rs 32 lakhs; debt services, Rs 6,23·84 lakhs; civil administration, Rs 16,45·87 lakhs; land revenue, Rs 12,00·00 lakhs. Expenditure included: Education, Rs 27,57·59 lakhs; public works and improvements, Rs 4,51·61 lakhs; irrigation, embankment, etc., Rs 8,19·78 lakhs; medical, and public health, Rs 14,12·43 lakhs; police, Rs 11,90·19 lakhs; agriculture, Rs 17,56·36 lakhs; general administration, Rs 5,33·47 lakhs; debt services, Rs 32,54·66 lakhs; extraordinary, including community projects and local development, Rs 8,35·84 lakhs; industries, Rs 2,37·45 lakhs.

AGRICULTURE. Production, 1968–69: Rice, 5·2m. metric tons; wheat, 1·26m. metric tons; jowar, bajra and maize, 1·03m. metric tons; total foodgrains, 8·87m. metric tons.

Livestock (1961 census): Buffaloes, 3,698,000; other cattle, 16,104,000; sheep, 1,156,000; goats, 8,671,000; horses and ponies, 133,000.

MINING. Bihar is the foremost state for mineral deposits; value of production in 1966 was Rs 94 crores (38% of India total). Coal is the principal mineral, but copper, of which Bihar is the only Indian producer, iron ore, ruby mica, kyanite and bauxite are important. The recently discovered large deposits of pyrites in the Shahabad district are being exploited. Mineral production, 1966, in metric tons: Coal, 31·39m.; mica (crude), 12,106; iron ore, 5·37m.; copper ore, 480,863; kyanite, 63,558; bauxite, 379,858; limestone, 2·8m.

ROADS. In 1959 the state had 1,189 miles of national highway. The total mileage is 13,430 (including 3,410 miles of unmetalled roads). Passenger transport has been nationalized in 7 districts.

SHIPPING. The length of waterways open for navigation is 900 miles.

RAIL. The North Eastern and Eastern railways traverse the province.

Diwaker, R. R. (ed.), *Bihar Through the Ages*. Bombay and London, 1961

GUJARAT

On 1 May 1960, as a result of the Bombay Reorganization Act, 1960, the state of Gujarat was formed from the north and west (predominantly Gujarati-speaking) portion of Bombay State, the remainder being renamed the state of Maharashtra. Gujarat consists of the following districts of the former state of Bombay: Banas Kantha, Mehsana, Sabar Kantha, Ahmedabad, Kaira, Panch Mahals, Baroda, Broach, Surat, Dangs, Amreli, Surendranagar, Rajkot, Jamnagar, Junagadh, Bhavnagar, Kutch, Gandhinagar and Bulsar.

GOVERNMENT AND CONSTITUTION. Gujarat has a unicameral legislature, the Legislative Assembly, which has 168 elected members. The state of the parties in the Assembly, April 1970, was: Congress (O), 85; Congress (R), 7; Swatantra, 54; Praja Socialist, 3; Jan Sangh. 1; Samyuktha Socialist, 1; independents, 16. The Council of Ministers consists of the chief minister, 7 other ministers and 8 deputy ministers.

The capital is Gandhinagar. There are 19 districts.

Governor: Shriman Narayan.
Chief Minister: Hitendra Desai.

AREA AND POPULATION. The area of the state is 187,091 sq. km and the population at the 1961 census was 20,633,350, an increase of 26·8% since 1951. The chief cities, *see* p. 333. Gujarati and Hindi in the Devanagari script are the official languages.

RELIGION. At the 1961 census Hindus numbered 18,356,061; Moslems, 1,745,103; Jains, 409,754; Christians, 91,028; Sikhs, 9,646; Buddhists, 3,185.

EDUCATION. Literacy is 30·5% of the population. Primary education is free for children aged 7–11. In 1968 there were an estimated 22,000 primary schools; nearly all villages with more than 500 people have one. In Jan. 1969 there were 2,010 secondary schools with 630,000 pupils.

In 1968 over 293,236 pupils and students received free education, scholarships or grants; 697 students received loan scholarships.

There are 7 universities in the state. Gujarat University, Ahmedabad, founded in 1949, is teaching and affiliating; it has 4 constituent colleges, 73 affiliated colleges. The Maharaja Sayajirao University of Baroda (1949), is residential and teaching. The Sardar Vallabhnhai Vidyapeeth, Anand (1955) has 8 constituent and affiliated colleges. The 4 newer universities are Saurashtra University at

Rajkot, South Gujarat at Surat, Gujarat Vidyapeeth at Ahmedabad and Gujarat Ayurvedic University at Jamnagar. In 1968 there were altogether 197 affiliated colleges, and the total number of students was 92,000. There were also 14 recognized research institutes.

HEALTH. In 1969 there were 251 primary health centres and 10,703 hospital beds. The annual intake at medical colleges was 655.

JUSTICE. The High Court of Judicature at Ahmedabad has a Chief Justice and 14 puisne judges.

FINANCE. Until 1970 Gujarat was treated as a deficit state. The deficit over this period, estimated at Rs 40 crores, to be made up by the state of Maharashtra. For the first 2 years Rs 12,16 crores was paid out of revenue accruing from the central government, the remainder to be paid in a lump sum and placed in a separate account. In addition, Rs 10 crores to be made available by Maharashtra for the building of a new capital city.

Budget estimates, 1968–69, showed total revenue of Rs 1,64,52·98 lakhs, and expenditure of Rs 1,51,53·03 lakhs. Receipts included: Contributions and adjustments between central and state governments, Rs 40,19·71 lakhs; taxes on income, Rs 7,87·36 lakhs; state excise, Rs 55·40 lakhs; stamps, Rs 4,32·30 lakhs; sales tax, Rs 45,70 lakhs; vehicles taxes, Rs 5,35·30 lakhs; debt services, Rs 14,51·98 lakhs; civil administration, Rs 12,04·22 lakhs; land revenue, Rs 7,32 lakhs. Expenditure included: Education, Rs 27,56·44 lakhs; public works and improvements, Rs 11,39·81 lakhs; irrigation, embankment, etc., Rs 10,19·63 lakhs; medical, and public health, Rs 6,60·74 lakhs; police, Rs 6,95·74 lakhs; agriculture, Rs 5,73·46 lakhs; general administration, Rs 3,78·47 lakhs; debt services, Rs 23,80·17 lakhs; extraordinary, including community projects and local development, Rs 4,15·91 lakhs; industries, Rs 2,19·51 lakhs.

AGRICULTURE. Irrigated area, 1968, was 1,645,887 hectares. (Approximately 12% of total area.) Area and production of principal crops, 1965–66: Rice, 536,200 hectares (255,300 metric tons); jowar, 1,292,100 hectares (338,200 metric tons); maize, 251,100 hectares (228,700 metric tons); groundnuts, 2,065,800 hectares (944,700 metric tons); cotton, 1·75m. hectares (1,425,000 bales of 180 kg); tobacco, 82,400 hectares (75,800 metric tons). Total foodgrains, 4·9m. hectares (2·4m. metric tons). In 1967–68 foodgrain production was 3,262m. metric tons oilseed production was 1,525m. metric tons and cotton production was 1,537m. bales.

Livestock (1961 census): Buffaloes, 2,916,581; other cattle, 6,556,555; sheep, 1,481,033; goats, 2,223,499; horses and ponies, 113,000.

MINERALS. Chief minerals produced in 1968 included salt (2,789,400 metric tons valued at Rs. 3,59·39 lakhs), manganese (2,748 metric tons valued at Rs 1·48 lakhs), limestone and bauxite. Total value of mineral production, 1968, Rs 562 lakhs.

Commercial production from the Ankeleshwar oilfields started in 1960. Output in 1963 was 730,000 tons.

INDUSTRY. Gujarat is one of the 3 most industrialized states. In 1968 there were over 5,000 registered factories employing an estimated 405,000 workers. This figure includes 122 textile mills. There were 13 industrial estates and 600 small industry centres. Principal industries are textiles, general and electrical engineering, vegetable oils, chemicals, soda ash and cement. Large fertilizer and petro-chemical plants are developing. There is an oil refinery at Baroda.

POWER. In 1968 the total generating capacity was 666 Mw of electricity. The 254-Mw power station at Dhuvaran is in course of expansion over a 5-year period. 2,812 towns and villages had electricity in 1968.

I

RAIL. In 1968 the state had 3,412 km metre-gauge railway, 1,141 km narrow gauge and 900 km broad gauge.

ROADS. In 1968 there were 27,947 km of roads. Gujarat State Transport Corporation operated 1,688 routes over 59,877 route km.

SHIPPING. The largest port is Kandla. There are 49 other ports, including Okha, Bedi, Bharnagar, Verawal, Sikka and Porbandar.

AVIATION. Ahmedabad is the main airport. There are 6 services daily between Bombay, Ahmedabad and Delhi. There are 8 other airports.

POST. There are 5,719 post offices, 785 telegraph offices. Ahmedabad has direct dialling telephone connexion with Delhi, Bombay, Poona and Surat, and telex connexions with other cities.

Rushbrook Williams, L. F., *The Black Hills: Kutch in History and Legend.* London, 1958

HARYANA

The state of Haryana, created on 1 Nov. 1966 under the Punjab Reorganization Act, 1966, was formed from the Hindi-speaking parts of the state of Punjab (India). It comprises the districts of Hissar, Mohindergarh, Gurgaon, Rohtak and Karnal; parts of Sangrur and Ambala districts; and part of Kharar tehsil.

CONSTITUTION AND GOVERNMENT. The state has a unicameral legislature with 81 members. After the election of May 1968 Congress held 47 seats, Vishal Haryana 13, independents and others 20. The state shares with Punjab (India) a High Court, a university and certain public services. The capital (shared with Punjab) is Chandigarh (*see* p. 383). There are 7 districts.

Governor: B. N. Chakravati.
Chief Minister: Bansi Lal.

AREA AND POPULATION. The state has an area of 43,869 sq. km and an estimated (1966) population of 7m. The principal language is Hindi.

JUSTICE. Haryana shares the High Court of Punjab and Haryana at Chandigarh which had (1968) a Chief Justice and 16 puisne judges.

FINANCE. Budget estimates for 1968–69 showed a total revenue of Rs 67,98·72 lakhs, and expenditure of Rs 66,35·37 lakhs. Receipts included: Contributions and adjustments between central and state governments, Rs 10,93·01 lakhs; taxes on income, Rs 2,43 lakhs; state excise, Rs 5,47 lakhs; stamps, Rs 2,59·17 lakhs; sales tax, Rs 11,88·74 lakhs; debt services, Rs 10,84·63 lakhs; civil administration, Rs 5,09·81 lakhs. Expenditure included: Education, Rs 12,50·45 lakhs; public works and improvements, Rs 2,60·83 lakhs; irrigation, embankment, etc., Rs 7,20·73 lakhs; medical, and public health, Rs 4,14·79 lakhs; agriculture, Rs 5,09·06 lakhs; debt services, Rs 15,97·68 lakhs.

INDUSTRY. In the year Nov. 1966–Oct. 1967 the state produced 16,734,000 kg of cotton yarn and 33,178,000 metres of cotton cloth.

JAMMU AND KASHMIR[1]

The state of Jammu and Kashmir, which had earlier been under Hindu rulers and Moslem sultans, became part of the Mogul Empire under Akbar from 1586. After a period of Afghan rule from 1756, it was annexed to the Sikh kingdom of the Punjab in 1819. In 1820 Ranjit Singh made over the territory of Jammu to

[1] About 84,000 sq. km of Kashmir is occupied by Pakistan (*see* p. 397).

Gulab Singh. After the decisive battle of Sobraon in 1846 Kashmir also was made over to Gulab Singh under the Treaty of Amritsar. British supremacy was recognized.

On 15 Aug. 1947 the Maharajah, Sir Hari Singh, entered into a standstill agreement with the Government of Pakistan; but he acceded to the Dominion of India, 27 Oct. 1947. The persistent dispute between India and Pakistan was first brought before the United Nations in 1948; hostilities were ended by a ceasefire in 1949, ceasefire line was confirmed by the Tashkent Declaration in Jan. 1966.

GOVERNMENT. The Maharajah's son, Yuvraj Karan Singh, took over as Regent in 1950 and, on the ending of hereditary rule (17 Oct. 1952), was sworn in as Sadar-i-Riyasat. On his father's death (26 April 1961) Yuvraj Karan Singh was recognized as Maharajah by the Indian Government; he decided not to use the title while he was elected head of state.

The permanent Constitution of the state came into force in part on 17 Nov. 1956 and fully on 26 Jan. 1957. There is a bicameral legislature; the Legislative Council has 36 members and the Legislative Assembly has 75. The state of the parties in the Legislative Assembly, after the 1967 elections, was: Congress, 61; National Conference, 8; Jan Sangh, 3; independent, 3. Since the 1967 elections the 6 representatives of Jammu and Kashmir in the central House of the People are directly elected. The Council of Ministers consists of 6 Ministers, 2 Ministers of State and 6 Deputy Ministers.

Kashmir Province has 4 districts and Jammu Province has 6 districts; the frontier district of Ladakh is in the former. Srinagar is the summer and Jammu the winter capital.

Governor: B. Sahay.
Chief Minister: Ghulam Muhammad Sadiq.

AREA AND POPULATION. The area is 222,800 sq. km, of which about 84,000 sq. km is occupied by Pakistan; the population of the territory on the Indian side of the line, 1961 census, was 3,560,976. For the population of Srinagar and Jammu, *see* p. 333. The official language is Urdu; other commonly spoken languages are Kashmiri, Dogri, Balti, Dardi (Pali), Punjab and Bodhi.

RELIGION. The bulk of the population, except in Jammu, are Moslems. At the 1961 census Moslems numbered 2,432,067; Hindus, 1,013,193; Sikhs, 63,069; Buddhists, 48,360; Christians, 2,848; Jains, 1,427.

EDUCATION. The proportion of literates is 11% (17% males, 4·3% females). Education is free. There are approximately 7,000 schools and 60% of children in the 6–11 age-group attend. Jammu and Kashmir University (founded 1948) conducts 21 post-graduate departments and has 39 affiliated colleges (1968). There is a medical college, an engineering college, 2 agricultural colleges and an Ayurvedic college.

HEALTH. In 1968 there were 20 main hospitals and 7 district hospitals, 75 primary health units and centres, 234 clinics and dispensaries, 32 family planning centres. Expenditure on health *per capita* was Rs 9·12 in 1968.

JUSTICE. The High Court, at Srinagar and Jammu, has a Chief Justice and 3 puisne judges. Its status was assimilated to that of the high courts of other states in 1959.

FINANCE. Budget estimates for 1968–69 show total revenue of Rs 49,25·82 lakhs, and expenditure of Rs 54,55·54 lakhs. Receipts included: Contributions and adjustments between central and state governments, Rs 25,42·52 lakhs; taxes on income, Rs 1,02 lakhs; state excise, Rs 1,80 lakhs; forests, Rs 5,00 lakhs; debt services Rs 1,86·67 lakhs. Expenditure included: Education, Rs 8,00·60 lakhs; public works and improvements, Rs 8,97·75 lakhs; irrigation, embankment, etc., Rs 3,28·50 lakhs; medical, and public health, Rs 3,94·64 lakhs; police, Rs 3,41·70 lakhs; agriculture, Rs 3,59·54 lakhs; general administration, Rs 1,32·18 lakhs; debt services, Rs 2,30 lakhs; extraordinary, including community projects and local development, Rs 1,26·31 lakhs.

AGRICULTURE. More than 80% of the population are supported by agriculture. Area and production of principal crops (1966–67): Rice, 224,000 hectares, 272,000 metric tons; maize, 241,000 hectares, 222,000 metric tons; wheat, 160,000 hectares, 112,000 metric tons; oilseeds (rape and mustard and linseed), 39,000 hectares, 3,000 metric tons. The total area under crops (1968) was estimated at 858,731 hectares. Total foodgrains produced, 1968–69, 1·1m. metric tons.

Livestock (1966 census): Cattle, 1,791,000; buffaloes, 428,000; sheep, 1,152,000; goats, 605,000; horses, 66,000, and 1,535,000 poultry.

There were (1966) 131 tractors.

FORESTRY. Forests cover about one-eighth of the area of the state, forming an important source of revenue, besides providing employment to a large section of the population. About 5,000 sq. km of forests yield valuable timber. Most forests yield medicinal drugs.

IRRIGATION. Total irrigated area (1966), 312,000 hectares.

INDUSTRIES. The chief industry is sericulture, which dates back to the 16th century.

ROADS. Kashmir is linked with the railway system of India by the motorable Jammu–Pathankot road. The Jawahir Tunnel, through the Banihal mountain, connects the towns of Srinagar and Jammu, and maintains road communication with the Kashmir Valley during the winter months. In 1967 there were 2,829 km of surfaced highways and 2,473 km of other roads.

AVIATION. Major airports, with daily service from Delhi, are at Srinagar and Jammu. Srinagar airport accommodates jet aircraft and is linked with international routes *via* Delhi and Kábul.

POST. There were 890 post offices in 1967. In 1968 there were 35 telephone exchanges and approximately 6,000 private telephones. There is direct dialling between Srinagar, Jammu and Delhi.

Banzai, P. N. K., *A History of Kashmir.* Delhi, 1962
Birdwood, Lord, *Two Nations and Kasmir.* London, 1956
Gupta, S., *Kashmir: a study in India–Pakistan relations.* London, 1967
Khan, S. M. I., *The Kashmir Saga.* Lahore, 1965
Korbel, J., *Danger in Kasmir.* Rev. ed. Princeton Univ. Press, 1966

KERALA

The state of Kerala, created under the States Reorganization Act, 1956, consists of the previous state of Travancore–Cochin, except for 4 taluks of the Trivandrum district and a part of the Shencottah taluk of Quilon district. It took over the Malabar district (apart from the Laccadive and Minicoy Islands) and the Kasaragod taluk of South Kanara (apart from the Amindivi Islands) from Madras State.

CONSTITUTION. The state has a unicameral legislature of 133 members. The election of 17 Sept. 1970 returned: Congress (R), 30; Communist Party of India, 17; Muslim League, 11; other Congress supporters, 9; Democratic Front parties, 17; Marxist Front parties, 49.

The state has 9 districts. The capital is Trivandrum.

Governor: V. Viswanathan.
Chief Minister: E. M. S. Namboodiripad.

AREA AND POPULATION. The state has an area of 38,855 sq. km. The 1961 census showed a population of 16,903,715, an increase of 24·76% since 1951; density of population was 1,127 per sq. mile (highest of any state). Population of principal cities, see p. 333.

Languages spoken in the state are Malayalam, Tamil and Kannada.

The physical features of the land fall into three well-marked divisions: (1) the hilly tracts undulating from the Western Ghats in the east and marked by long spurs, extensive ravines and dense forests; (2) the cultivated plains intersected by numerous rivers and streams; and (3) the coastal belt with dense coconut plantations and rice fields.

RELIGION. At the 1961 census Hindus numbered 10,282,563; Christians, 3,587,365; Moslems, 3,027,639; Jains, 2,967.

EDUCATION. Kerala is the most literate Indian State—46·8% at the 1961 census (males, 55%; females, 38·9%), twice the national average. Education is free up to the age of 14.

In 1963–64 there was a total of 10,484 educational institutions with a total enrolment of 3,818,436 students; expenditure was Rs 18,45·92 lakhs. Primary schools had 3,263,617 students and high schools, 554,919 students.

Kerala University (established 1937) at Trivandrum, is affiliating and teaching; in 1966 it had 50 affiliated arts and science colleges and 38 affiliated professional colleges; total enrolment, 1966–67, 125,000 full-time students.

JUSTICE. The High Court at Ernakulam has a Chief Justice and 9 puisne judges; the Kerala High Court is the only one in India with a female judge.

FINANCE. Budget estimates for 1968–69 showed total revenue of Rs 1,31,00·46 lakhs, and expenditure of Rs 1,44,68·54 lakhs. Receipts included: Contributions and adjustments between central and state governments, Rs 45,53·94 lakhs; taxes on income, Rs 8,14·54 lakhs; state excise, Rs 9,35·49 lakhs; stamps, Rs 4,52·86 lakhs; forests, Rs 7,14·00 lakhs; sales tax, Rs 27,50·83 lakhs; vehicles taxes, Rs 5,54·67 lakhs; debt services, Rs 6,64·49 lakhs; civil administration, Rs 7,18·12 lakhs; land revenue, Rs 1,80·35 lakhs. Expenditure included: Education, Rs 44,43·94 lakhs; public works and improvements, Rs 6,53·17 lakhs; irrigation, embankment, etc., Rs 2,90·65 lakhs; medical, and public health, Rs 14,14·57 lakhs; police, Rs 5,34·64 lakhs; agriculture, Rs 8,37·41 lakhs; general administration, Rs 2,93·12 lakhs; debt services, Rs 16,08·74 lakhs; extraordinary, including community projects and local development, Rs 3,57·36 lakhs; industries, Rs 1,31·90 lakhs.

AGRICULTURE. The chief agricultural products of the state are rice, tapioca, coconut, arecanut, oilseeds, pepper, sugar-cane, rubber, tea, coffee and cardamom. About 98% of Indian black pepper and about 95% of Indian rubber is produced in Kerala. Area under principal crops, 1963–64 (in 1,000 hectares): Coconut, 545; rice, 805; tapioca, 210; sugar-cane, 9; pepper, 99; cardamom, 29; ginger, 12; cashew, 82; arecanut, 57; coffee, 20; tea, 38; rubber, 143. Production (1963–64) in 1,000 metric tons: Rubber, 33·8; black pepper, 22·4; rice, 1,128·1; sugar-cane (gur), 44; coconut, 3,262; tapioca, 2,523·7; ginger, 11·2; cashew, 92·3; arecanut, 8,522; coffee, 8·5; tea, 41; rubber, 143. Total foodgrains (1968–69), 1·43m. metric tons.

Livestock (1961 census): Buffaloes, 485,089; other cattle, 2,753,165; sheep, 24,000; goats, 1,312,000.

FORESTRY. About a third of the area is comprised of forests, including teak, sandalwood, ebony and black-wood and varieties of softwood.

FISHING. Fishing is a flourishing industry; the annual catch is about 216,000 metric tons.

MINING. Next to Bihar, Kerala possesses the widest variety of economic mineral resources among the Indian States. The beach sands of Kerala contain monazite, ilmenite, rutile, zircon, sillimanite, etc. There are extensive white-clay deposits; other minerals of commercial importance include mica, graphite, limestone, quartz sand and lignite.

INDUSTRIES. Most of the major industrial concerns are either owned or sponsored by the Government. The Government owns 11 industrial concerns and has substantial shares in more than 40 concerns. Among the privately owned factories are the numerous cashew and coir factories. Other important factory industries are rubber, tea, tiles, oil, textiles, ceramics, fertilizers and chemicals, sugar, cement, rayon, glass, matches, pencils, monazite, ilmenite, titanium oxide, rare earths, aluminium, electrical goods, paper, shark-liver oil, etc.

The number of factories registered under the Factories Act 1948 on 31 Dec. 1964 was 2,704; 2,587 of these had average daily employment of 175,855.

Among the cottage industries, coir-spinning and handloom-weaving are the most important ones, forming the means of livelihood of a large section of the people. Other industries are the village oil industry, ivory carving, furniture-making, bell metal, brass and copper ware, leather goods, screw-pines, mat-making, rattan work, bee-keeping, pottery, etc. These have been organized on a co-operative basis.

POWER. The state's power stations generated 1,326,139,000 kwh. of electricity in 1966–67.

SHIPPING. Port Cochin, administered by the central government, is one of India's 6 major ports.

ROADS. In 1966 there were 17,252 km of roads in the state, of which 3,915 km were metalled; national highways, 450 km.

Mankekar, D. R., *The Red Riddle of Kerala*. Bombay, 1966
Pillai, V. R., and Panikar, P. G. K., *Land Reclamation in Kerala*. London, 1965
Woodcock, G., *Kerala*. London, 1968

MADHYA PRADESH

Under the provisions of the States Reorganization Act, 1956, the State of Madhya Pradesh was formed on 1 Nov. 1956. It consists of the 17 Hindi districts of the previous state of that name, the former state of Madhya Bharat (except the Sunel enclave of Mandsaur district), the former states of Bhopal and Vindhya Pradesh and the Sironj subdivision of Kotah district, which was an enclave of Rajasthan in Madhya Pradesh.

For information on the former states, *see* THE STATESMAN'S YEAR-BOOK, 1958, pp. 180–84.

GOVERNMENT AND CONSTITUTION. Madhya Pradesh is one of the 9 states for which the Constitution provides a bicameral legislature, but the Vidhan Parishad or Upper House (to consist of 90 members) has yet to be formed. The Vidhan Sabha or Lower House has 296 elected members. The state of the parties, 4 March 1967, was: Congress, 167; Jan Sangh, 78; Praja Socialist, 9; Samyuktha Socialists, 10; Swatantra, 7; Communist, 1; independents, 24.

For administrative purposes the state has been split into 7 divisions with a Commissioner at the head of each; the headquarters of these are located at Bhopal, Bilaspur, Gwalior, Indore, Jabalpur, Raipur and Rewa. There are 43 districts, each under a Collector, 190 tehsils and 160 municipalities.

The seat of government is at Bhopal.

Governor: K. C. Reddy.
Chief Minister: G. N. Singh.

AREA AND POPULATION. Madhya Pradesh is the largest Indian state in size, with an area of 443,452 sq. km. In respect of population it ranks seventh. Population (1961 census), 32,372,408 (males, 16·6m. and females, 15·8m.), an increase of 24·17% since 1951. Density of population was 189 per sq. mile.

Cities with over 100,000 population, see p. 333.

The number of persons speaking each of the more prevalent languages (1961 census) were: Hindi, 19,965,972; Urdu, 365,969; Marathi, 582,821; Rajasthani, 896,644; Gujrati, 114,000; Sindhi, 128,041.

RELIGION. At the 1961 census Hindus numbered 30,425,798; Sikhs, 65,715; Moslems, 1,317,617; Jains, 247,927; Buddhists, 113,365; Christians, 188,314.

EDUCATION. The 1961 census showed 17·13% of the population to be literate (27·03% males, 6·73% females). Education is free for children aged up to 14.

In 1963–64 there were 39,172 educational institutions with a total enrolment of 3,457,625 students and an expenditure of Rs 26,81 lakhs. Primary schools had 2·3m. pupils and higher secondary schools, 415,000 pupils.

There are 8 universities in Madhya Pradesh: the University of Sagar (established 1946), at Sagar, had 65 affiliated colleges and 22,727 students in 1964–65; Jabalpur University (1957) had 21 affiliated colleges and 12,172 students; Vikram University (1957), at Ujjain, had 39 affiliated colleges and 24,172 students; Indira Kala Sangeet Vishwavidyalaya (1956), at Khairagarh, had 99 students on roll (this university teaches music); Indore University (1964) had 26 affiliated colleges and 11,284 students; Jivagi University (1963), at Gwalior, had 30 affiliated colleges and 16,200 students; Jawaharlal Nehru Krishi University (1964), at Jabalpur, had 8 affiliated colleges and 2,280 students; Ravishankar University (1964), at Raipur, had 45 affiliated colleges and 77 university teaching departments. In 1965–66 there were 143 degree-granting colleges, 120 teacher-training colleges, 25 professional colleges and 23 polytechnics.

JUSTICE. The High Court of Judicature at Jabalpur has a Chief Justice and 15 puisne judges.

FINANCE. Budget estimates for 1968–69 showed total revenue of Rs 1,74,27·70 lakhs, and expenditure of Rs 1,79,94·62 lakhs. Receipts included: Contributions and adjustments between central and state governments, Rs 41,49·91 lakhs; taxes on income, Rs 9,62·99 lakhs; state excise. Rs 14,70 lakhs; stamps. Rs 3,92·70 lakhs; forests, Rs 22,71·01 lakhs; sales tax, Rs 33,07 lakhs; vehicles taxes, Rs 3,41·15 lakhs; debt services, Rs 12,06·51 lakhs; civil administration, Rs 8,46·46 lakhs; land revenue, Rs 8,95·33 lakhs. Expenditure included: Education, Rs 44,13·69 lakhs; public works and improvements, Rs 12,38·49 lakhs; irrigation, embankment, etc., Rs 2,05·59 lakhs; medical, and public health; Rs 16,40·15 lakhs; police, Rs 12,47·70 lakhs; agriculture, Rs 10,83·81 lakhs; general administration, Rs 5,93·26 lakhs; debt services, Rs 29,20·47 lakhs, extraordinary, including community projects and local development, Rs 4,48·56 lakhs; industries, Rs 1,45·30 lakhs.

AGRICULTURE. Agriculture is the mainstay of the state's economy. The Malwa region abounds in rich black cotton soil, the low-lying areas of Gwalior, Bundelkhand and Baghelkhand and the Chhatisgarh plains have a lighter sandy soil, while the Narmada valley is formed of deep rich alluvial deposits. Production of principal crops, 1965–66: Rice, 1,700,552 tons; jowar, 1,313,860 tons; wheat, 1,327,263 tons; pulses, 599,106 tons; groundnuts, 265,321 tons; linseed, 70,281 tons, and cotton, 313,785 bales (of 180 kg). In 1965–66, 16,528,816 hectares were sown, of which 14,938,432 were under food crops, and 976,450 were irrigated. Total foodgrain production (1968–69), 9·46m. metric tons.

Livestock (1965 census): Buffaloes, 5,549,000; other cattle, 22,586,067; sheep, 906,029; goats, 4,614,756; horses and ponies, 145,921.

FORESTRY. Nearly 30% of the state's area is covered by forests. The forests are chiefly of saj, babul, salai, dhavra, tendu, mahua, bamboo, teak, sal, anjan and harra. They are the chief source in India of best-quality teak.

IRRIGATION. Major irrigation projects include the Chambal Valley scheme (started in 1952 with Rajasthan) which will irrigate some 1·1m. acres, and the Tawa project in Hoshangabad district (1958) which will irrigate 780,000 acres.

MINING. The state has extensive mineral deposits. Coal, iron ore and manganese are found in the Chhatisgarh Division, bauxite has been located in Amarkantak, Balaghat, Seoni and elsewhere, while in the Sidhi, Rewa, Panna, Chhatarpur and Tikamgarh Districts, coal, ochre and sillimanite are exploited. In 1966 the output of major minerals was (in metric tons): Coal, 9,788,000; manganese, 322,173; iron ore, 3,964,428; bauxite, 107,915; china clay, 11,283; limestone, 3,756,172; ochre, 16,242; dolomite, 455,629; fireclay, 88,898; quartz and silica, 32,925; corundum, 385; diamonds, 2,113 carats.

INDUSTRY. Industries include cotton textiles (22 mills (1967), with 13,175 looms and 599,573 spindles, employment (1959), 41,907); newsprint (India's only plant in the public sector, with a capacity of 30,000 tons, is located at Nepanagar; in the private sector, Orient Paper Mills at Amlai, Shahdol District, started production in 1966); sugar refining, pottery, carpets, art-silk, rayon, jute, glass and engineering goods. The country's largest cement works is at Kymore, near Katni; this and three others have a total licensed capacity of 1,644,000 tons per year.

The Bhilai steel plant near Durg is one of the 3 major steel mills being built by the central government; production, 1965, included 1·49m. metric tons of pig-iron and 1·27m. metric tons of steel ingots. A new power station at Korba (Bilaspur) with a capacity of 90,000 kw. serves both Bhilai and the Korba coal-field.

The heavy electricals factory was set up by the Government of India at Bhopal during the second-plan period. This is India's first heavy electrical equipment factory and also one of the largest of its type in Asia. This factory took up for the first time in the country the manufacture of a variety of highly complicated equipment required for generation, transmission, distribution and utilization of electric power.

COTTAGE INDUSTRIES. The state is known for its traditional village and home crafts such as Chanderi Saree, toys, pottery, lac work, woodwork and metal utensils. The ancillary industries of dyeing, calico printing and bleaching are centred in areas of textile production.

ROADS. Total length of roads in 1966 was 54,347 km, of which 45,118 km were surfaced. Transport is being gradually nationalized.

MAHARASHTRA

Under the States Reorganization Act, 1956, Bombay State was formed by merging the states of Kutch and Saurashtra and the Marathi-speaking areas of Hyderabad (commonly known as Marathwada) and Madhya Pradesh (also called Vidarbha) in the old state of Bombay, after the transfer from that state of the Kannada-speaking areas of the Belgaum, Bijapur, Kanara and Dharwar districts which were added to the state of Mysore, and the Abu Road taluka of Banaskantha district, which went to the state of Rajasthan.

By the Bombay Reorganization Act, 1960, which came into force 1 May 1960, 17 districts (predominantly Gujarati-speaking) in the north and west of Bombay State became the new state of Gujarat, and the remainder was renamed Maharashtra.

The state of Maharashtra consists of the following districts of the former

Bombay State: Ahmednagar, Akola, Amravati, Aurangabad, Bhandara, Bhir, Buldana, Chanda, Dhulia (West Khandesh), Greater Bombay, Jalgaon (East Khandesh), Kolaba, Kolhapur, Nagpur, Nanded, Nasik, Osmanabad, Parbhani, Poona, Ratnagiri, Sangli, Satara, Sholapur, Thana, Wardha, Yeotmal; certain portions of Thana and Dhulia districts have become part of Gujarat.

GOVERNMENT AND CONSTITUTION. Maharashtra has a bicameral legislature. The Legislative Council has 78 members. The Legislative Assembly has 270 elected members and 1 member nominated by the Governor to represent the Anglo-Indian community. The state of the parties in the Legislative Assembly, 1 Oct. 1970, was: Congress, 204; Sampoorna Maharashtra Samiti, 41; Lokshahi Aghadi, 14; Jansangh, 6; Republican, 2; Independent, 1. The Council of Ministers consists of the Chief Minister, 14 other Ministers, 10 Ministers of State and 5 Deputy Ministers.

The capital is Bombay.

Governor: Ali Yawar Jung.
Chief Minister: V. P. Naik.

AREA AND POPULATION. The state has an area of 306,345 sq. km. The population at the 1961 census was 39,553,718 (an increase of 23·6% since 1951), of whom about 30m. were Marathi-speaking. The area of Greater Bombay (1967) was 105,910 acres and its population (1961 census) 4,152,056; Bombay City had an area of 16,751 acres and a population of 2,771,933. For other principal cities, *see* p. 333.

RELIGION. At the 1961 census Hindus numbered 32,530,901; Moslems, 3,034,332; Buddhists, 2,789,501; Christians, 560,594; Jains, 485,672; Sikhs, 57,617.

EDUCATION. The proportion of literates to the total population, according to the 1961 census, was 29·7% (males, 41·8%; females, 16·7%).

The total number of recognized institutions in 1968–69 was 51,074, with 8,911,377 students. Higher and secondary schools numbered 6,280 with 2,360,423 pupils, and primary schools, 44,794, with 6,505,954 pupils.

Bombay University, founded in 1857, is mainly an affiliating university. It has 63 constituent colleges and 41 post-graduate departments in Bombay with a total (1968–69) of 88,131 students. Colleges in Goa can affiliate to Bombay University. Nagpur University (1923) is both teaching and affiliating. In addition to the 18 post-graduate departments there were (1968–69) 99 affiliated colleges with 66,697 students. Poona University, founded in 1948, is teaching and affiliating; in 1967–68 it had 55 affiliated colleges, 20 post-graduate departments and a total of 45,559 students. The SNDT Women's University had, in 1968–69, 7 constituent colleges and 9 affiliated colleges with a total of 9,168 students. Marathwada University, Aurangabad, was founded in 1958 as a teaching and affiliating body to control colleges in the Marathwada or Marathi-speaking area, previously under Osmania University; in 1968–69 there were 52 affiliated colleges and 10 post-graduate departments. Shiwaji University, Kolhapur, was established in 1963 to control affiliated colleges previously under Poona University. In 1968–69 it had 58 affiliated colleges and 14 post-graduate departments.

JUSTICE. The High Court has a Chief Justice and 26 judges. The seat of the High Court is Bombay, but it has a bench at Nagpur.

FINANCE. Budget estimates, 1970–71, showed total revenue of Rs 4,32,82·00 lakhs; expenditure, Rs 4,26,25·00 lakhs. Receipts included: Contributions and adjustments between central and state governments, Rs 74,48·00 lakhs; taxes on income, Rs 40,45·00 lakhs; stamps, Rs 14,08·00 lakhs; sales tax, Rs 1,35,71·00 lakhs; vehicles taxes, Rs 14,05·00 lakhs. Expenditure included: Education, Rs 83,82·00 lakhs; public works and improvements, Rs 11,21·00 lakhs; irrigation, embankment, etc., Rs 21,16·00 lakhs; medical, and public health, Rs 35,85·00 lakhs; police, Rs 34,93·00 lakhs; agriculture and community development, Rs 24,72·00 lakhs; general administration, Rs 14,81·00 lakhs; debt services, Rs 74,30·00 lakhs; industries, Rs 2,54·00 lakhs.

AGRICULTURE. Area (in 1,000 hectares) and production (in 1,000 metric tons) of principal crops in 1969–70 (final forecast report): Rice, area 1,374 (output 1,415); wheat, area 865 (output 1,391); jowar, area 6,091 (output 3,214); bajri, area 2,037 (output 689); total cereals, area 10,852 (output 5,971); total pulses, area 2,344 (output 846); total foodgrain, area 13,245 (output 7,025); sugar-cane, area 179 (output 245); groundnuts, area 968 (output 629); cotton, area 2,760 (output 1,190 bales of 180 kg).

Livestock (1966 census): Buffaloes, 3,304,119; other cattle, 1,472,446: sheep, 2,203,063; goats, 5,121,237; horses and ponies, 101,004; poultry, 9,901,983.

INDUSTRY. The number of factories on 31 Dec. 1969 was 9,116 employing about 887,174 workers. There were also 18,720 factories (1966–67) registered as small-scale industries.

The textile industry is dominant in production. On 31 Dec. 1969 there were 97 cotton textile (18 spinning and 79 composite) mills with installed capacity of 4·58m. spindles and 77,946 looms, and an average daily employment of about 298,000 workers. There are 17 woollen mills and 2 viscose filament and 2 nylon filament yarn factories. Other industries include sugar and industrial alcohol, chemicals, engineering, food and transport.

RAIL. The total length of railway is about 5,162 km.

ROADS. On 31 March 1969 there were 60,694 km of roads, of which 34,222 km were surfaced. Passenger and freight transport has been nationalized.

SHIPPING. Maharashtra has a coastline of 720 km. Bombay is the major port, and there are 14 minor ports.

STATISTICAL INFORMATION. The Director of Publicity, Sachivalaya, Bombay.
Annual Statistical Abstract (from 1951)
STATE LIBRARY. Central Library, Town Hall, Bombay.

MYSORE

The state of Mysore, constituted under the States Reorganization Act, 1956, brings together the Kannada-speaking people previously distributed in 5 states, and consists of the territories of the old states of Mysore and Coorg, the Bijapur, Kanara and Dharwar districts and the major portion of the Belgaum district in former Bombay, the major portions of the Gulbarga, Raichur and Bidar districts in former Hyderabad, and South Kanara district (apart from the Kasaragod taluk) and the Kollegal taluk of the Coimbatore district in Madras.

GOVERNMENT AND CONSTITUTION. Mysore has a bicameral legislature. The Legislative Council has 63 members. The Legislative Assembly consists of 216 elected members and 1 nominated member. The state of the parties in the Assembly, July 1970, was: Congress, 160; Samyuktha Vidhayakdal (comprising Praja Socialist, Samyuktha Socialist, Jan Sangh, Janatha Paksha, Republican Party of India), 44; Independent, 11; Speaker, 1; vacant, 1.

The state has 19 districts (of which Coorg is one) in 4 divisions: Bangalore, Mysore, Belgaum and Gulbarga. The capital is Bangalore.

Governor: Dharma Veera.
Chief Minister: Veerendra Patil.

AREA AND POPULATION. The area of the state is 191,757 sq. km, and its population (1961 census), 23,586,772, an increase of 21·4% since 1951. Kannada is the language of administration and is spoken by about 60% of the people. Other languages include Telugu (8·7%), Urdu (8·6%), Marathi (4·5%) and Tamil (3·6%). Principal cities, see p. 333.

RELIGION. At the 1961 census Hindus numbered 20,582,853; Moslems, 2,328,376; Christians, 487,587; Jains, 174,366; Buddhists, 9,770; Sikhs, 3,287.

EDUCATION. The proportion of literates to the total population, according to the 1961 census, was 25·3% (males, 36%; females, 14·2%). In 1968–69 the state had 21,716 lower primary schools attended by 1,268,070 pupils, 10,494 higher primary schools with 1,560,687 pupils, 1,833 high schools with 503,361 students and 293 schools for professional and technical education with 128,785 students. Education is free up to pre-university level.

The University of Mysore (founded in 1916) at Mysore has 3 university colleges at Mysore and 101 affiliated colleges; total enrolment, 1967–68, was 54,240. Karnatak University (1950) at Dharwar has 4 constituent colleges and 55 affiliated colleges. Bangalore University (1964) has 46 constituent colleges, the University of Agricultural Sciences, Hebbal, Bangalore, (1964) has 3 constituent colleges. The Indian Institute of Science, Bangalore, is unaffiliated; it conducts diploma courses in engineering, metallurgy and technology.

JUSTICE. The seat of the High Court of Mysore is at Bangalore. It has a Chief Justice and 16 puisne judges.

FINANCE. Budget estimates for 1969–70 showed total revenue of Rs 2,13,25·86 lakhs; expenditure, Rs 2,54,09·51 lakhs. Receipts included: Contributions and adjustments between central and state governments, Rs 56,04·86 lakhs; taxes on income, Rs 21,11·03 lakhs; state excise, Rs 13,90·71 lakhs; stamps, Rs 5,60 lakhs; forests, Rs 11,65·60 lakhs; sales tax, Rs 35,78 lakhs; vehicles taxes, Rs 7,10 lakhs; debt services, Rs 17,41·31 lakhs; land revenue, Rs 5,77·29 lakhs. Expenditure included: Education, Rs 46,06·47 lakhs; public works and improvements, Rs 14,33·46 lakhs; irrigation, embankment, electricity, Rs 18,38·86 lakhs; medical, and public health, Rs 16,57·10 lakhs; police, Rs 8,28·54 lakhs; agriculture, Rs 10,51·13 lakhs; general administration, Rs 4,39·60 lakhs; extraordinary, including community projects and local development, Rs 3,03·24 lakhs; industries, Rs 13,17·55 lakhs.

AGRICULTURE. Agriculture forms the main occupation of more than three-quarters of the population. Physically, the original Mysore divides itself into two regions—the 'maidan' or plain country, comprising roughly the districts of Bangalore, Tumkur, Chitaldrug, Kolar, Bellary, Mandya and Mysore, and the 'malnad' or hill country, comprising the districts of Chickmagalur, Hassan and Shimoga. Rainfall is heavy in the 'malnad' tracts, and in this area there is dense forest. The greater part of the 'maidan' country is cultivated. Coorg district is essentially agricultural.

In 1969–70, 6,796,699 hectares were under foodgrains (production, 4,369,887 metric tons); other crops included groundnuts (474,458 metric tons) and other oilseeds, cotton (413,740 bales of 180 kg), chillies, tobacco (29,600 kg), sugar-cane and rubber. In 1968–69, 1,099,425 hectares were brought under the Japanese method of paddy cultivation. There were then 1,037,323 hectares under cotton, 1,100,779 hectares under oilseeds and 95,305 hectares under sugar-cane.

Livestock (1966 census): Buffaloes, 2,945,997; other cattle, 9,685,981; sheep, 4,747,964; goats, 2,783,682; horses and ponies, 64,874.

FORESTRY. Total forest area in the state (1968) is about 13,582 sq. km, producing sandalwood, bamboo and other timbers, and ivory.

IRRIGATION. About 1,021,790 hectares were irrigated in 1966–67.

MINING. Mysore has India's only sources of gold; production, 1968, 3,588 kg, about 90% of which came from the Kolar Gold Fields and the remainder from those at Hutti; about 30,000 men are employed in the goldfields. Production of other minerals in 1968 included iron ore, 3,362,724 metric tons, and manganese ore, 332,085 metric tons. In 1968, 274 kg of silver were mined.

INDUSTRY. The Mysore Iron and Steel Works is situated at Bhadravarti, while at Bangalore are national undertakings for the manufacture of aircraft, machine tools, light engineering and electronics goods. Other industries include textiles, cement, chemicals, sugar, paper, porcelain and soap. In addition, much of the world's sandalwood is processed in Mysore, the oil being one of the most valuable productions of the state. Sericulture is a most important cottage industry giving employment, directly or indirectly, to perhaps 1m. persons; production in 1969 was about 1,291 tons of silk, nearly half the Indian total.

POWER. In 1969–70 the states' power stations generated 3,325m. kwh. of electricity.

ROADS. In 1969 the state had 63,285 km of roads, of which 37,752 km were asphalted. There were about 420 km of cement concrete roads.

RAIL. In 1969 there were 2,757 km of railway (including 154 km of narrow gauge) in the state.

SHIPPING. Mangalore and Karwar are being developed into deep-water ports for the export of mineral ores.

Learmonth, A. T. A., and Bhat, L. T., *Mysore State*. 2 vols. London, 1961–62
Prakasa Rao, V. L. S., *Towns of Mysore State*. London, 1964

NAGALAND

The territory was constituted by the Union Government in Sept. 1962. It comprises the former Naga Hills district of Assam and the former Tuensang Frontier division of the North-East Frontier Agency; these had been made a Centrally Administered Area in 1957, administered by the President through the Governor of Assam. In Jan. 1961 the area was renamed and given the status of a state of the Indian Union, which was officially inaugurated on 1 Dec. 1963.

For some years a section of the Naga leaders sought independence. Military operations from 1960 and the prospect of self-government within the Indian Union led to a general reconciliation, but rebel activity continued. A 2-month amnesty in mid-1963 had little effect. A 'ceasefire' in Sept. 1964 was followed by talks between a Government of India delegation and rebel leaders, which, however, had proved inconclusive by March 1965. The peace period was extended and has since been observed.

GOVERNMENT AND CONSTITUTION. An Interim Body (Legislative Assembly) of 42 members elected by the Naga people and an Executive Council (Council of Ministers) of 5 members were formed in 1961, and continued until the State Assembly was elected in Jan. 1964. At the second general election, Feb. 1969, a 52-member Assembly was elected, including 12 Tuensang members elected by the Tuensang Regional Council. The Nagaland Cabinet comprises the Chief Minister, 5 Cabinet Ministers, 5 Ministers of State and 6 Deputy Ministers. The Governor has extraordinary powers, which include special responsibility for law and order.

The state has 3 districts (Kohima, Mokokchung and Tuensang). The capital is Kohima.

Governor: B. K. Nehru.
Chief Minister: Hokishe Sema.

AREA AND POPULATION. Nagaland has an area of 16,488 sq. km and a population (1961 census) of 369,200. Towns include Kohima, Mokokchung, Tuensang and Dimapur. The chief tribes in numerical order are: Angami, Ao, Sema, Konyak, Chakhesang, Lotha, Phom, Khiemnungan, Chang, Yimchunger, Zeliang-kuki, Rengma and Sangtam.

RELIGION. At the 1961 census Christians numbered 195,588; Hindus, 34,677. The Naga Baptist Christian Convention had, 1960, 632 churches and a total church membership of 73,500.

EDUCATION. In 1969 there were 2 government and 2 private colleges, 32 government and 1 private high schools, 129 government and 17 private middle schools and 946 lower primary schools, 1 polytechnic, 3 teacher-training schools and 121 adult literary centres. The number of students totalled 92,601.

FINANCE. Budget estimates for 1969–70 show total revenue of Rs 3,000·50 lakhs and expenditure of Rs 3,569·60 lakhs. Receipts included: Statutory grant under the Finance Commission award, Rs 1,083 lakhs; share of central taxes and duties, Rs 1,642 lakhs; grants-in-aid for plan expenditure, Rs 1,771·57 lakhs; loans from the Government of India, Rs 5,41·00 lakhs. Expenditure included: Education, Rs 5,700 lakhs; medical, and public health, Rs 23 lakhs; police, Rs 621·63 lakhs; agriculture, Rs 33 lakhs. Estimates for 1970–71 show receipts of Rs 3,126·18 lakhs, including grants in aid of Rs 617·23 lakhs for Plan projects. Estimated expenditure is Rs. 3,393·61 lakhs.

AGRICULTURE. More than 80% of the people derive their livelihood from agriculture. The Angamis, in Kohima district, practise a fixed agriculture in the shape of terraced slopes, and wet paddy cultivation in the lowlands. In the other two districts there is a traditional form of shifting cultivation (*jhumming*). About 695,000 hectares were under cultivation in 1969. Production of rice (1968–69) was 66,000 metric tons.

Elwin, V., *Nagaland*. Shillong, 1961
Fürer-Haimendorf, C. von, *The naked Nagas*. 2nd ed. Calcutta, 1962

ORISSA

Orissa, ceded to the Mahrattas by Alivardi Khan in 1751, was conquered by the British in 1803. In 1804 a board of 2 commissioners was appointed to administer the province, but in the following year it was designated the district of Cuttack and was placed in charge of a collector, judge and magistrate. In 1823 it was split up into 3 regulation districts of Cuttack, Balasore and Puri, and the nonregulation tributary states which were administered by their own chiefs under the ægis of the British Government. Angul, one of these tributary states, was annexed in 1847, and with the Khondmals, ceded in 1835 by the tributary chief of the Boudh state, constituted a separate non-regulation district. Sambalpur was transferred from the Central Provinces to Orissa in 1905. These districts formed an outlying tract of the Bengal Presidency till 1912, when they were transferred to Bihar, constituting one of its divisions under a commissioner. Orissa was constituted a separate province on 1 April 1936, some portions of the Central Provinces and Madras being transferred to the old Orissa division.

The rulers of 25 Orissa states surrendered all jurisdiction and authority to the Government of India on 1 Jan. 1948, on which date the Provincial Government took over the administration. The administration of 2 states, viz., Saraikella and Kharswan, was transferred to the Government of Bihar in May 1948. By an agreement with the Dominion Government, Mayurbhanj State was finally merged with the province on 1 Jan. 1949. By the States Merger (Governors' Provinces) Order, 1949, the states were completely merged with the state of Orissa on 19 Aug. 1949.

GOVERNMENT AND CONSTITUTION. The Legislative Assembly has 140 elected members. The state of the parties in the Assembly, March 1967, was: Congress, 30; S.S.P., 2; Praja Socialist, 21; Swatantra, 49; Communist, 8; independents and others, 30.

The state consists of 17 districts, of which 4 are linked with other districts for administrative purposes.

The capital is Bhubaneswar (18 miles south of Cuttack).

Governor: S. S. Ansari.
Chief Minister: R. N. Singh Deo.

AREA AND POPULATION. The area of the state is 155,825 sq. km, and its population (1961 census), 17,548,846, an increase of 19·9% since 1951. The second-largest city next to Cuttack (*see* p. 333) is Rourkela, with 90,287 inhabitants. The principal language is Oriya.

RELIGION. There were in 1961: Hindus (including scheduled castes and scheduled tribes), 17,123,194; Moslems, 215,319; Christians, 201,017; Buddhists, 454; Sikhs, 5,030; Jains, 2,295.

EDUCATION. The percentage of literates in the population is 21·7% (males, 34·7%, females, 8·6%).

The total number of recognized schools in 1961–62 was 24,960. The schools for general education included 2,060 secondary schools with 232,364 pupils and 22,856 primary schools with 1,476,000 pupils. The special schools for the students from scheduled tribes numbered 1,266 with a total of 60,000 students in 1961–62.

Utkal University was established in 1943 at Cuttack and moved to Bhubaneswar in 1962; it is both teaching and affiliating. It has 2 university colleges (engineering and law) and 35 affiliated colleges. The total number of full-time students (1962–63) was 17,907.

JUSTICE. The High Court of Judicature at Cuttack has a Chief Justice and 3 puisne judges.

FINANCE. Budget estimates, 1968–69 showed total revenue of Rs 1,23,07·84 lakhs and expenditure of Rs 1,22,18·90 lakhs. Receipts included: Contributions and adjustments between central and state governments, Rs 50,22·46 lakhs; taxes on income, Rs 5,12·66 lakhs; state excise, Rs 3,20·73 lakhs; forests, Rs 5,76 lakhs; sales tax, Rs 13,80 lakhs; vehicles taxes, Rs 2,28·19 lakhs; debt services, Rs 16,10·55 lakhs; civil administration, Rs 6,11·80 lakhs; income from river, irrigation and electricity schemes, Rs 6,16·20 lakhs. Expenditure included: Education, Rs 17,62·06 lakhs; public works and improvements, Rs 9,00·21 lakhs; irrigation, embankment, etc., Rs 16,21·72 lakhs; medical, and public health, Rs 8,53·81 lakhs; police, Rs 5,59·19 lakhs; agriculture, Rs 9,79·45 lakhs; general administration, Rs 3,95·95 lakhs; debt services, Rs 25,21·71 lakhs; extraordinary, including community projects and local development, Rs 3,99·81 lakhs; industries, Rs 1,12·36 lakhs.

AGRICULTURE. The cultivation of rice is the principal occupation of nearly 80% of the population. The area under paddy, 1964–65, was 4·3m. hectares and production amounted to 4·42m. metric tons; only a very small amount of other cereals is grown; production of pulses (1964–65) was 512,000 metric tons from 1·1m. hectares. Production of foodgrains (1964–65) totalled 5,045,000 metric tons from 5·6m. hectares. Jute (415,000 metric tons), cotton, tobacco and sugarcane are also grown. Turmeric is cultivated in the uplands of the districts of Ganjam, Phulbani and Koraput, and is exported.

Livestock (1961 census): Buffaloes, 1,075,000; other cattle, 9·81m.; sheep, 994,000; goats, 2,382,000; horses and ponies, 58,000.

FORESTS. Forests occupy about 42% of the area of the state, the most important species being sal.

FISHERIES. A large fish export trade to Calcutta is catered for by 8 ice factories. There were, in 1962, 116 fishery co-operative societies.

MINING. Production in 1,000 metric tons, 1966, included iron ore, 6,722; manganese ore, 509; coal, 1,184; limestone and dolomite, 2,681. About 36,000 workers are employed in the mines.

INDUSTRY. The steel plant at Rourkela, which is being built by the central government, will have a capacity of 1·8m. tons per annum; 3 blast furnaces and 3 open-hearth furnaces were commissioned, 1959–61; production, 1963, was 893,000 metric tons of pig-iron and 845,000 metric tons of steel ingots. Building on a large coal-based fertilizer plant at Talcher began in Feb. 1970.

There are a modern textile-mill, weaving-mills, a cement factory, 2 paper-mills, 2 cold storage plants, glass factories, a sugar factory, 2 ferro-manganese plants, an aluminium plant, a number of rice-mills, oil- and flour-mills and soap factories.

There are cottage and small-scale industries in the state, *e.g.*, handloom weaving and the manufacture of baskets, wooden articles, hats and nets; silver filigree works of Orissa are specially well known.

POWER. The Hirakud Dam Project on the river Mahanadi (started 1949) will, when completed, irrigate 1·8m. acres and deliver 270,000 kw. The dam (the largest earth dam in the world) was completed in 1957. Hydro-electric power totalling 85,000 kw. is now serving Cuttack, Puri and Dhenkanal districts. The total installed capacity of the Machkund hydro-electric project (financed jointly with Andhra Pradesh) is 114,750 kw.

ROADS. On 31 Dec. 1962 mileage of roads was: National highway, 852; state highway, 1,343; major district roads, 3,540; other district roads, 1,053; municipal roads, about 700.

RAIL. The total mileage of railway in 1963 was 939 miles.

SHIPPING. Paradip was declared a 'minor' port in 1958 and is being developed to handle 2m. tons of traffic. Other ports are at Chandbali and Gopalpur.

PUNJAB (INDIA)

The Punjab was constituted an autonomous province of India in 1937. In 1947, the province was partitioned between India and Pakistan into East and West Punjab respectively, under the Indian Independence Act, 1947, the boundaries being determined under the Radcliffe Award. The name of East Punjab was changed to Punjab (India) under the Constitution of India. On 1 Nov. 1956 the erstwhile states of Punjab and Patiala and East Punjab States Union (PEPSU) were integrated to form the state of Punjab. On 1 Nov. 1966, under the Punjab Reorganization Act, 1966, the state was reconstituted as a Punjabi-speaking state comprising the districts of Gurdaspur (excluding Dalhousie), Amritsar, Kapurthala, Jullundur, Ferozepore, Bhatinda, Patiala and Ludhiana; parts of Sangrur, Hoshiarpur and Ambala districts; and part of Kharar tehsil. The remaining area comprising an area of 18,000 sq. miles and an estimated (1967) population of 8·5m. was shared between the new state of Haryana and the Union Territory of Himachal Pradesh. Also, the existing capital of Chandigarh was made the joint capital of both Punjab and Haryana. The state shares a High Court with Haryana.

GOVERNMENT AND CONSTITUTION. Punjab (India) has a unicameral legislature. The Legislative Council was abolished in Jan. 1970. The state of the parties in the Legislative Assembly of 104 members, March 1969, was: Congress, 38; Akali Dal, 43; Jan Sangh, 8; independents and others, 14.

There are 11 districts. The capital is Chandigarh (*see* p. 383). There are 104 municipalities and 7,827 elected village *panchayats*.

Governor: D. C. Pavate.
Chief Minister: S. P. Singh Badal.

AREA AND POPULATION. The area of the state is 50,376 sq. km, with census (1961) population of 11,135,069. The largest cities, *see* p. 333. The official language is Punjabi.

RELIGION. At the 1961 census Hindus numbered 12,930,045; Sikhs, 6,769,129; Moslems, 393,314; Christians, 149,834; Jains, 48,754; Buddhists, 14,857.

EDUCATION. Compulsory education was introduced in April 1961; at the same time free education was introduced up to 8th class for boys and 9th class for girls as well as various fee concessions.

In 1969–70 there were 7,147 primary schools, 922 middle schools, 890 high and 255 higher secondary schools.

Punjab University was established in 1947 at Chandigarh as an examining, teaching and affiliating body. It is shared with Haryana and Himachal Pradesh. Kurukshetra University, for Indology, was established in 1956; in 1962 Punjabi University was established at Patiala and an agricultural university at Ludhiana. Guru Nanak University has been established at Amritsar to mark the 500th anniversary celebrations for Guru Nanak Dev, first Guru of the Sikhs. Altogether there are 139 affiliated colleges, 110 for arts and science. 17 for teacher training, 4 medical, 2 dental, 2 engineering, and 4 for other studies.

HEALTH. Punjab claims the longest life expectancy (52 years) and lowest death rate (9·35 per 1,000). There are 768 medical institutions, including 117 hospitals, 3 Ayurvedic hospitals, 126 primary health centres and 522 dispensaries.

JUSTICE. The Punjab and Haryana High Court exercises jurisdiction over the states of Punjab and Haryana and the territories of Delhi and Chandigarh. It is located in Chandigarh and has a circuit bench at Delhi. It consists (1970) of a Chief Justice, 11 puisne judges and 7 additional judges.

FINANCE. Budget estimates for 1970–71 show total revenue of Rs 154·39 crores and expenditure, Rs 134·96 crores. Receipts included: Grants-in-aid, Rs 12,17 lakhs; share from central taxes, Rs 16,69 lakhs; other tax revenue, Rs 19,24 lakhs; state excise, Rs 21,51 lakhs; non-tax receipts, Rs 14,68 lakhs; sales tax, Rs 30,30 lakhs; debt services, Rs 27,83 lakhs; land revenue, Rs 2,40 lakhs; social and development services, Rs 4,54 lakhs; multi-purpose irrigation works, Rs 5,03 lakhs. Expenditure included: Scientific and education departments, Rs 30,85 lakhs; multi-purpose irrigation schemes and public works and improvements, Rs 18,77 lakhs; medical, and public health, Rs 11,36 lakhs; police, Rs 7,73 lakhs; agriculture, Rs 7,89 lakhs; community development, Rs 7,83 lakhs; industries, Rs 4,00 lakhs; forests, Rs 113 lakhs.

Expenditure under the third Five-Year Plan was Rs 255·87 crores in the Punjab before reorganization. For the reorganized Punjab the fourth plan provides for an outlay of Rs 293·56 crores.

AGRICULTURE. About 80% of the population depends on agriculture. Agricultural prosperity is mainly due to irrigation. The canal-irrigated area served by Punjab canals rose from 2·21m. hectares in 1950–51 to 3·82m. hectares in 1968–69: total production of foodgrains rose from 1·99m. metric tons to 6·2m. metric tons. Production in 1,000 metric tons (area in 1,000 hectares) in 1968–69: Wheat, 4,491 (2,063); maize, 706 (490); rice, 470 (345); pulses, 263 (411); sugar-cane (gur), 516 (157); cotton, 747,000 bales (of 180 kg) from 392,000 hectares.

Livestock (1966 census): Buffaloes, 2,936,000; other cattle, 3·12m.; sheep and goats, 1,048,000; horses and ponies, 31,000; poultry, 1,648,500.

FORESTRY. In 1969–70 there were 202,195 hectares of forest land, of which 90,255 hectares belonged to the Forest Department.

INDUSTRY. In Jan. 1970 the number of registered factories in the Punjab (India) was 4,780; 4,256 operational factories employed about 109,100 people. The chief manufactures are textiles, sewing machines, sports goods, sugar, starch, fertilizers, bicycles, scientific instruments, electrical goods, machine tools and pine oil. Total production from factories in 1967 was valued at Rs 220·85 crores.

RAIL. The Punjab possesses an extensive system of railway communications, served by the Northern Railway.

ROADS. The total length of metalled roads on 31 March 1968 was 7,000 km. State transport services cover 151,340 route km daily with a fleet of 778 buses carrying a daily average of 1,260,000 passengers. Coverage by private operators is estimated as equalling this.

Darling, M. L., *The Punjab Peasant in Prosperity and Debt*. 4th ed. London, 1949
Mangat Rai, E. N., *Civil Administration in the Punjab*. Cambridge, Mass., 1963
Singh, Khushwant, *A History of the Sikhs*. 2 vols. Princeton and OUP, 1964–67

RAJASTHAN

As a result of the implementation of the States Reorganization Act, 1956, the erstwhile state of Ajmer, Abu Taluka of Bombay State and the Sunel Tappa enclave of the former state of Madhya Bharat were transferred to the state of Rajasthan on 1 Nov. 1956, whereas the Sironj subdivision of Rajasthan was transferred to the state of Madhya Pradesh.

GOVERNMENT AND CONSTITUTION. There is a unicameral legislature, the Legislative Assembly, having 184 elected members. The state of the parties in the Assembly, 13 May 1969, was: Congress, 110; Swatantra, 28; Jan Sangh, 19; Socialists, 7; Communists, 1; Bhartiya Kranti Dal, 11; independents, 5 (including the Speaker); vacant, 3.

The capital is Jaipur. There are 26 districts.

Governor: Hukam Singh.
Chief Minister: Mohan Lal Sukhadia.

AREA AND POPULATION. The area of the state is 342,274 sq. km and its population (1961 census), 20,155,602, an increase of 26% since 1951. The chief cities, see p. 334.

RELIGION. At the 1961 census Hindus numbered 18,132,690; Moslems, 1,314,613; Jains, 409,417; Sikhs, 274,198; Christians, 22,864.

EDUCATION. The proportion of literates to the total population was 15·2% (23·7% males, 5·8% females) at the 1961 census. In 1967–68 about 84% of children of primary school age were receiving education.

In 1967–68 enrolment in 33,164 educational institutions was 2,874,410; primary schools (including nursery schools) had 1·63m. students and higher secondary schools (including junior high secondary schools), 395,000 students. Elementary education is free but not compulsory. The percentage in 1967–68 of children attending school in the age-group 6–11 was 54·5 (40·9 in 1961), in the 11–14 age-group 22·3 (14·4) and in the age-group 14–17 it was 10·6 (6·8).

Rajasthan University, established at Jaipur in 1947, is teaching and affiliating; in 1966 it had 4 university colleges and 65 affiliated colleges with 30,960 students. Jodhpur University (founded 1962) had 5 affiliated colleges; Rajasthan

Agricultural University at Udaipur (1962) had 5 affiliated colleges. There are also 4 agricultural colleges, 1 veterinary and animal science college, 3 engineering colleges, 7 Ayurvedic colleges and 8 polytechnics.

JUSTICE. The seat of the High Court is at Jodhpur. There is a Chief Justice and 10 puisne judges.

HEALTH. In 1968 there were 574 hospitals and dispensaries and over 600 other health and family planning centres. Rajasthan had 1,834 doctors and 6,337 nurses and assistants. There are 5 medical colleges.

FINANCE. Budget estimates for 1968–69 show total revenue of Rs 1,27,77·90 lakhs, and expenditure of Rs 1,41,86·94 lakhs. Receipts included: Contributions and adjustments between central and state governments, Rs 43,80·79 lakhs; taxes on income, Rs 5,92·39 lakhs; state excise, Rs 9,00 lakhs; sales tax, Rs 21,25 lakhs; vehicles taxes, Rs 2,64 lakhs; debt services, Rs 8,67 lakhs; civil administration, Rs 8,83·97 lakhs; land revenue, Rs 10,00 lakhs. Expenditure included: Education, Rs 29,19·47 lakhs; public works and improvements, Rs 10,38·94 lakhs; irrigation, embankment, etc., Rs 8,29·77 lakhs; medical and public health, Rs 15,45·94 lakhs; police, Rs 9,38·71 lakhs; agriculture, Rs 7,28·19 lakhs; general administration, Rs 3,97·53 lakhs; debt services, Rs 33,80·80 lakhs; extraordinary, including community projects and local development, Rs 2,95·81 lakhs; industries, Rs 64·69 lakhs.

AGRICULTURE. Production of principal crops (1,000 metric tons), 1967–68: Jowar, 398; bajra, 1,446; maize, 1,025; wheat, 1,305; barley, 776; pulses (all kinds), 1,529; sugar-cane (gur), 312; total oilseeds, 325; cotton, 135,000 bales (of 180 kg). Total production of foodgrains, 7·42m. metric tons from 13,971,000 hectares. Tractors numbered 4,185 in 1966.

Livestock (1965–66): Buffaloes, 4,222,043; other cattle, 33,253,462; sheep, 8,806,174; goats, 10,323,396; horses and ponies, 63,085; poultry, 864,592.

MINING. The state is rich in minerals. There is a mica belt of about 3,000 sq km; production, 1968, 3,500 metric tons (crude). Gypsum (122,900 metric tons in 1968), limestone and salt are also produced. Total value of mineral production in 1968 was Rs 10,47 lakhs.

INDUSTRY. In 1968 a daily average of 57,988 persons were employed in 1,751 (1,949 in 1965) factories subject to the Factories Act, 1948. Chief manufactures are cotton textiles, cement, glass and sugar.

POWER. The increase of power from 125·05m. kwh. in 1960 to 566m. kwh. in 1967–68 (due particularly to the Bhakra and Chambal projects) enabled over 1,000 additional places to be included in the electrification scheme. The Rana Pratap Sagar Dam and power station were opened in Feb. 1970, as the second stage of the Chambal project.

ROADS. In 1967–68 there were 16,851 km of surfaced and 13,023 km of unsurfaced roads in Rajasthan; there were 1,256 km of national highway. Total road coverage in 1967–68 was 31,130 km. Motor vehicles numbered 71,527 in 1968.

TAMIL NADU

The first trading establishment made by the British in the Madras State was at Peddapali (now Nizampatnam) in 1611 and then at Masulipatnam. In 1639 the English were permitted to make a settlement at the place which is now Madras, and Fort St George was founded. By 1801 the whole of the country from the Northern Circars to Cape Comorin (with the exception of certain French and Danish settlements) had been brought under British rule.

Under the provisions of the States Reorganization Act, 1956, the Malabar district (excluding the islands of Laccadive and Minicoy) and the Kasaragod district taluk of South Kanara were transferred to the new state of Kerala; the South Kanara district (excluding Kasaragod taluk and the Amindivi Islands) and the Kollegal taluk of the Coimbatore district were transferred to the new state of Mysore; and the Laccadive, Amindivi and Minicoy Islands were constituted a separate Territory. Four taluks of the Trivandrum district and the Shencottah taluk of Quilon district were transferred from Travancore–Cochin to the new Madras State. On 1 April 1960, 405 sq. miles from the Chittoor district of Andhra Pradesh were transferred to Madras in exchange for 326 sq. miles from the Chingleput and Salem districts. In Aug. 1968 the state was renamed Tamil Nadu.

GOVERNMENT AND CONSTITUTION. The Governor is aided by a Council of 13 ministers. There is a bicameral legislature; the Legislative Council has 63 members and the Legislative Assembly has 233 members. The state of parties in the Assembly, Nov. 1967, was: Congress, 50; Dravida Munnetra Kazhagam, 138; Swatantra, 20; Communist, 13; Samyuktha Socialist, 2; independents and others, 7.

There are 14 districts. The capital is Madras.

Governor: Ujjal Singh.
Chief Minister: M. Karunanidhi.

AREA AND POPULATION. Area, 130,357 sq. km. Population (1961 census), 33,686,953, an increase of 11·85% since 1951. Official estimate of population (1969), 38,639,400. Tamil is the principal language and has been adopted as the state language with effect from 14 Jan. 1958. The principal towns, see p. 333.

RELIGION. At the 1961 census Hindus numbered 30,297,115; Christians, 1,762,954; Moslems, 1,560,414; Jains, 28,350; Sikhs, 2,576; Buddhists, 777; others, 34,767.

EDUCATION. At the 1961 census 31·4% of the total population was literate (44·5% males; 18·2% females).

Education is free up to pre-university level. In 1966–67 there were 2,440 high schools with a total enrolment of 1,301,579 students. The number of elementary schools was 31,075, and their enrolment, 4,922,453. 4,175 basic schools were attended by 825,585 pupils. Total expenditure on educational institutions, 1965–66, was Rs. 38 crores.

There are 3 universities. Madras University (founded in 1857) is affiliating and teaching. It had (1968) 119 colleges for arts and sciences with 106,571 students. Annamalai University, Annamalainagar (founded 1928) is residential; Madurai University (founded 1966) is an affiliating and teaching university.

JUSTICE. There is a High Court at Madras with a Chief Justice and 13 judges.

Police. The police force in 1967–68 numbered 31,882 for the state, and there was a force of 4,741 for Madras city.

FINANCE. Budget estimates, 1968–69 show total revenue of Rs 2,48,27·41 lakhs and expenditure of Rs 2,47,53·89 lakhs. Receipts included: Contributions and adjustments between central and state governments, Rs 47,20·64 lakhs; taxes on income, Rs 13,98·33 lakhs; sales tax, Rs 65,54·11 lakhs; stamps, Rs 10,34·82 lakhs; vehicles taxes, Rs 17,60·60 lakhs; debt services, Rs 25,93·85 lakhs; civil administration, Rs 19,51·09 lakhs; other taxes, Rs 16,79·76 lakhs. Expenditure included: Education, Rs 56,27·90 lakhs; public works and improvements, Rs 10,60·70 lakhs; irrigation, embankment, etc., Rs 8,56·03 lakhs; medical, and public health, Rs 18,24·97 lakhs; police, Rs 11,53·17 lakhs; agriculture, Rs

17,88·12 lakhs; general administration, Rs 10,44·71 lakhs; debt services, Rs 33,35·92 lakhs.

AGRICULTURE. Agriculture engages 29% of the population. Of the total land area (13·01m. hectares), 7·3m. hectares were cultivated and 2·5m. hectares were irrigated in 1966–67. Area in hectares (and production, in metric tons) of principal crops, 1967–68: Paddy, 2·76m. (4·29m.); millets and other cereals, 1·99m. (1·54m.); sugar-cane, 95,200 (8·3m.); groundnuts, 908,700 (0·8m. in shell); gingelly, 112,750 (36,300); cotton 335,870 (0·3m. bales of 180 kg).

Livestock (1966 census): Buffaloes, 2,753,049; other cattle, 11,009,368; sheep, 6,641,843; goats, 3,796,736; swine, 874,880; horses, ponies, mules, camels, etc., 185,336; poultry, 10,898,862.

FORESTRY. The estimated revenue from forests in 1967–68 was Rs 8,82·79 lakhs. In 1966–67 the forests produced 32,589 cu. metres of timber. Output of sandalwood was 1,730 metric tons.

INDUSTRY. Industry contributed 20·26% to the state income in 1966–67 (1960–61 : 16·02%). Major industries include the Neyveli lignite project, designed to mine 3·5m. tons of lignite per annum; 12 co-operative cotton-spinning mills with 167,456 spindles (1968 production, 8,824,782 kg of yarn worth Rs 7·43 crores); 7 co-operative sugar-mills with crushing capacity of 6,500 metric tons a day. Other industries include coachbuilding, surgical instrument making, brick making, chemicals and engineering.

ELECTRICITY. Production on 31 March 1969 amounted to 5,260m. units. There were 48,595 km of high-tension cable and 104,654 km of low-tension cable. 31,727 villages were supplied with electricity.

TOURISM. In 1968, 16,512 tourists visited the state, 70% of whom came by air and 12% by sea.

ROADS. At the end of 1967 the state had 67,273 km of metalled and unmetalled roads. In 1967 there were 86,240 registered motor vehicles.

RAIL. In 1965 there were 4,955 km of railway.

SHIPPING. Madras is the chief port. Important minor ports are Cuddalore and Nagapattinam. A harbour is under construction at Tuticorin.

STATISTICAL INFORMATION. The Department of Statistics (Fort St George, Madras) was established in 1948 and reorganized in 1953. *Director:* D. S. Rajabushanam, MA. Main publications: *Annual Statistical Abstract; Decennial Statistical Atlas; Season and Crop Report; Quinquennial Wages Census; Quarterly Abstract of Statistics.*

National Council of Applied Economic Research, *Economic Atlas of Madras State.* New Delhi, 1962

UTTAR PRADESH

In 1833 the then Bengal Presidency was divided into two parts, one of which became the Presidency of Agra. In 1836 the Agra area was styled the North-West Province and placed under a Lieut.-Governor. The two provinces of Agra and Oudh were placed, in 1877, under one administrator, styled Lieut.-Governor of the North-West Province and Chief Commissioner of Oudh. In 1902 the name was changed to 'United Provinces of Agra and Oudh', under a Lieut.-Governor, and the Lieut.-Governorship was altered to a Governorship in 1921. In 1935 the name was shortened to 'United Provinces'. On Independence, the states of Rampur, Banaras and Tehri-Garwhal were merged with United Provinces. In 1950 the name of the United Provinces was changed to Uttar Pradesh.

GOVERNMENT AND CONSTITUTION. Uttar Pradesh has had an autonomous system of government since 1937. There is a bicameral legislature. The state was brought under Presidential rule in Oct. 1970. The Legislative Assembly was suspended but not dissolved.

There are 11 administrative divisions, each under a Commissioner, and 54 districts. The number of municipalities (1968) is 142, that of Zila Parishads 51 and that of Antarim Zila Parishads 3. On 23 March 1970 all Zila Parishads were dissolved for 2 years or until their reconstitution.

The capital is Lucknow.

Governor: S. Gopala Reddy.

AREA AND POPULATION. The area of the state is 294,366 sq. km. Population (1961 census), 73,746,401, an increase of 16·7% since 1951. Cities with more than 100,000 population, *see* p. 333. The official language is Hindi.

RELIGION. At the 1961 census Hindus numbered 62,437,313; Moslems, 10,788,089; Sikhs, 283,737; Jains, 122,108; Christians, 101,641; Buddhists, 12,893.

EDUCATION. For secondary education there were, in 1966–67, an estimated 9,250 institutions, with 2,686,093 scholars, and for primary education, 60,752 schools, with 9,306,988 scholars. Compulsory education for boys was in force in 95 municipalities and for girls in 10 municipalities.

Uttar Pradesh has 11 universities: Allahabad University (founded 1887) with 3 university colleges, 6 associated colleges and 6,783 students in 1962–63; Agra University (1927) with 129 affiliated colleges and 48,576 full-time students; the Banaras Hindu University, Varanasi (1916) with 14 constituent colleges, 5 affiliated colleges and 6,905 students; Lucknow University (1921) with 3 university colleges and 14,468 students; Aligarh Muslim University (1920) with 5,151 students; Roorkee University (1948), formerly Thomason College of Civil Engineering (established in 1847) with 1,823 students; Gorakhpur University (1957), with 30 affiliated colleges and 15,771 students; Varanasaya Sanskrit Vishwavidyalaya, Varanasi (1958) with about 1,000 students, and Uttar Pradesh Agriculture University, Phoolbagh (1960) with about 700 students. Kanpur University and Meerut University were founded in 1965. The Indian Institute of Technology, Kanpur (1960), has university status; in 1962–63 there were 288 post-graduate students. In 1966–67 an estimated 39,775 students were studying in the universities and 65,084 in the affiliated colleges.

JUSTICE. The High Court of Judicature at Allahabad (with a bench at Lucknow) has a Chief Justice, 40 puisne judges including additional judges. There are 45 sessions divisions in the state.

FINANCE. Budget estimates, 1968–69, show total revenue of Rs 3,55,63·69 lakhs and expenditure of Rs 3,54,86·53 lakhs. Receipts included: Contributions and adjustments between central and state governments, Rs 92,37·33 lakhs; taxes on income, Rs 22,20·06 lakhs; state excise, Rs 19,99·59 lakhs; forests, Rs 1,55·03 lakhs; sales tax, Rs 39,10·10 lakhs; debt services, Rs 39,13·76 lakhs; civil administration, Rs 22,82·58 lakhs; land revenue, Rs 22,93·24 lakhs. Expenditure included: Education, Rs 29,19·47 lakhs; public works and improvements, Rs 10,38·94 lakhs; irrigation, embankment, etc., Rs 8,29·77 lakhs; medical, and public health, Rs 15,45·94 lakhs; police, Rs 9,38·71 lakhs; agriculture, Rs 7,28·19 lakhs; general administration, Rs 3,97·53 lakhs; debt services, Rs 33,80·80 lakhs; extraordinary, including community projects and local development, Rs 2,95·81 lakhs; industry, Rs 64·69 lakhs.

AGRICULTURE. Agriculture occupies 75% of the population. Production (1967–68) in 1,000 metric tons (area in 1,000 hectares): Rice, 3,078 (4,177); wheat, 5,935 (5,045); pulses (all kinds), 3,207 (5,026); sugar-cane (gur), 4,000 (993); oilseeds (all kinds), 1,585 (3,879). Total foodgrain production, 16,625 (20,053).

INDUSTRY. Sugar and cotton processing are the leading industries. In 1967 there were 72 sugar factories (72,000 workers) and 31 cotton-mills (50,251 workers). At the end of 1966 there were 4,327 registered trade unions.

POWER. The State Electricity Board had, 31 March 1968, an installed capacity of 1,075 Mw. The total length of transmission lines was 78,318 circuit km.

ROADS. There were, 31 March 1968, 81,990 km of roads, of which 28,091 km were metalled. (This excludes forest roads.)

Brass, P. R., *Factional politics in an Indian state: the Congress Party in Uttar Pradesh.* Univ. of California Press, 1965

WEST BENGAL

For the history of Bengal under British rule, from 1633 to 1947, *see* THE STATESMAN'S YEAR-BOOK, 1952, p 183.

Under the terms of the Indian Independence Act, 1947, the Province of Bengal ceased to exist. The Moslem majority districts of East Bengal, consisting of the Chittagong and Dacca Divisions and portions of the Presidency and Rajshahi Divisions, became East Pakistan (*see* p. 399).

GOVERNMENT AND CONSTITUTION. The state of West Bengal came into existence as a result of the Indian Independence Act, 1947. The territory of Cooch-Behar State was merged with West Bengal on 1 Jan. 1950, and the former French possession of Chandernagore became part of the state on 2 Oct. 1954. Under the States Reorganization Act, 1956, certain portions of Bihar State (an area of 3,157 sq. miles with a population of 1,446,385) were transferred to West Bengal.

The state was brought under Presidential rule in March 1970.

The capital is Calcutta.

For administrative purposes there are 2 divisions (Burdwan and Presidency), under which there are 15 districts, excluding Calcutta. The Calcutta Metropolitan Development Authority has been set up to co-ordinate development in the metropolitan area (1,000 sq. km). For the purposes of local self-government there are 15 district boards, 325 *anchalik parishads* (regional boards), 2,926 *anchal* (regional) *panchayats* and 19,662 *gram* (village) *panchayats*. There is no district board in Cooch-Behar district. There are 90 municipalities. The Calcutta Corporation was reconstituted in 1969 with a mayor and deputy mayor, a commissioner, aldermen and standing committees.

Governor: S. S. Dhavan.

AREA AND POPULATION. The total area of West Bengal is 88,563 sq. km. At the 1961 census its population was 34,926,270, an increase of 33% since 1951, the density of population 1,032 per sq. mile. Present estimate of population, 41·1m.; density, 464 per sq. km. Population of chief cities, *see* p. 333. The principal language is Bengali.

RELIGION. At the 1961 census Hindus numbered 27,542,794; Moslems, 6,971,287; Christians, 201,854; Buddhists, 109,205; Sikhs, 34,342; Jains, 26,973.

EDUCATION. In 1970 recognized educational institutions numbered 43,700, with 5,063,797 pupils. There were 34,242 primary and junior basic schools, with 3,524,759 pupils and 5,298 secondary schools, with 1,343,385 pupils. Primary education is free.

The University of Calcutta (founded 1857) is affiliating and teaching; in 1961–62 a total of 97.454 students were enrolled in 6 constituent colleges and 139 affiliated institutions. Visva Bharati, Santiniketan (originally established by Tagore), residential and teaching, had 384 students in 1962–63. The University of Jadavpur, Calcutta (1955), had 3,234 students in 1962–63. Burdwan University was established 15 June 1960 with 31 affiliated colleges previously under the supervision of the University of Calcutta; in 1962–63 there were 21,962 students. Kalyani University was established in 1961.

JUSTICE. The High Court of Judicature at Calcutta has a Chief Justice and 38 puisne judges. The Andaman and Nicobar Islands (*see* pp. 382–83) come under its jurisdiction.

Police. In 1970 the police force numbered 43,643, under an inspector-general. Calcutta has a separate force under a commissioner directly responsible to the Government; its strength is 18,733.

FINANCE. The revised estimates for 1970–71 show total revenue of Rs 2,90,81·26 lakhs and expenditure of Rs 3,11,15·99 lakhs. Receipts included: Contributions and adjustments between central and state governments, Rs 69,65·66 lakhs; taxes on income, Rs 34,24·02 lakhs; state excise, Rs 15,41·36 lakhs; stamps, Rs 7,60·77 lakhs; sales tax, Rs 70,40·00 lakhs; vehicles taxes, Rs 6,94·50 lakhs; debt services, Rs 14,39·57 lakhs; civil administration, Rs 21,28·74 lakhs; land revenue, Rs 6,33·27 lakhs. Expenditure included: Education, Rs 67,81·57 lakhs; public works and improvements, Rs 11,48·38 lakhs; medical, and public health, Rs 27,30·99 lakhs; police, Rs 25,27·79 lakhs; agriculture, Rs 19,54·14 lakhs; general administration, Rs 8,12·50 lakhs; debt services, Rs 55,69·92 lakhs; extraordinary, including community projects and local development, Rs 5,03·43 lakhs; industries, Rs 5,92·99 lakhs.

AGRICULTURE. Area in 1,000 hectares (and production in 1,000 metric tons) of principal crops, 1964–65: Rice, 4,673 (5,763); pulses, 757 (373), and jute, 456 (3,646,000 bales of 180 kg, 60% of India total). Total foodgrain production, 5,577 (6,228). In 1970 the cultivable area *per capita* was 0·12 hectare. Principle food crop was rice, production 6·65m. metric tons.

Livestock (1961 census): 11,464,812 cattle, 948,450 buffaloes, 548,210 sheep, 4,474,028 goats, 24,882 horses and 11,674,758 poultry; tractors numbered 328.

IRRIGATION AND POWER. Important major irrigation and power schemes at present under construction are the Damodar Valley scheme; the Kansabati project; and the Mayurakshi River project. The Canada Dam on the Mayurakshi was opened on 1 Nov. 1955.

INDUSTRY. The jute textile industry in West Bengal employs nearly 297,000 workers. The total number of registered factories, 1968, was 5,714. The coal-mining industry had 220 mines employing 111,000 workers. There are about 297 tea estates which employ about 183,000 workers.

There is a large automobile factory at Uttarpara, and there are aluminium rolling-mills at Belur and Asansol. At Durgapur a major steel plant was completed in 1962. Durgapur has other industries under the state sector—a thermal power plant, coke oven plant, fertilizer factory, alloy steel plant and ophthalmic glass plant. There is a locomotive factory and cable factory at Chittaranjan and Rupnarayanpur. A refinery and fertilizer factory are under construction at Haldia.

ROADS. In March 1958 the length of national highway was 1,281 km and of state roads, 19,150 km (including 8,195 km metalled). On 31 March 1969 the state had 154,623 motor vehicles.

SHIPPING. Calcutta is the chief port: a barrage is being built at Farakka to control the flow of water and to provide a rail and road link between North and South Bengal. A second port is being developed at Haldia, halfway between the present port and the sea, which is intended mainly for bulk cargoes. West Bengal possesses 779 km of navigable canals.

RAIL. The length of railways within the state is 2,908 km.

Chatterjee, S. P., *Bengal in Maps.* Bombay, 1950

UNION TERRITORIES

ANDAMAN AND NICOBAR ISLANDS. The Andaman and Nicobar Islands are administered by the President of the Republic of India acting through a Chief Commissioner and an Advisory Council of 8 members. The seat of administration is at Port Blair, which is connected with Calcutta (1,255 km away) and Madras (1,190 km) by steamer service which calls about every 10 days; there is a bi-weekly air service from Calcutta. There is an Additional Deputy Commissioner at Car Nicobar and an Assistant Commissioner at Nancowrie.

The population (1961 census) was 63,548.

Budget estimates for 1970–71 show total revenue receipts of Rs 2,62·51 lakhs, and total expenditure on revenue account of Rs 9,31·42 lakhs, and total capital expenditure of Rs 6,08·70 lakhs.

Administrator: Shri H. S. Butalia.

The **Andaman Islands** lie in the Bay of Bengal, 193 km from Cape Negrais in Burma, 1,255 from Calcutta and 1,190 from Madras. Five large islands grouped together are called the Great Andamans, and to the south is the island of Little Andaman. There are some 204 islets, the two principal groups being the Ritchie Archipelago and the Labyrinth Islands. The total area is about 6,475 sq km. The Great Andaman group is about 467 km long, at the widest, 51 km broad.

The original inhabitants live in the forests by hunting and fishing; they are of a small Negrito type and their civilization is about that of the Stone Age. Their exact numbers are not known, as they avoid all contact with civilization. The total population of the Andaman Islands (excluding the aborigines) was in 1951, 18,962 (12,734 males and 6,228 females). Under a central government scheme started in 1953, some 4,000 displaced families, mostly from East Pakistan, had been settled in the islands by May 1967.

Japanese forces occupied the Andaman Islands on 23 March 1942. Civil administration of the islands was resumed on 8 Oct. 1945.

From 1857 to March 1942 the islands were used by the Government of India as a penal settlement for life and long-term convicts, but the penal settlement was abolished on re-occupation in Oct. 1945.

The Great Andaman group, densely wooded, contains many valuable trees, both hardwood and softwood. The best known of the hardwoods is the *padauk* or Andaman redwood; *gurjan* is in great demand for the manufacture of plywood. Large quantities of softwood are supplied to match factories. Annually the Forest Department export about 25,000 tons of timber to the mainland. Coconut, coffee and rubber are cultivated. The islands are slowly being made self-sufficient in paddy and rice, and now grow approximately half their annual requirements. The average yield of rice in 1966–67 was 1·24 metric tons per hectare. Total livestock (1961 census) was 38,617. There is a saw-mill at Port Blair and a coconut-oil mill at Dunbar Point. There are about 338 km of black top road in the entire territory.

The islands possess a number of harbours and safe anchorages, notably Port Blair in the south, Port Cornwallis in the north and Elphinstone and Mayabandar in the middle.

The **Nicobar Islands** are situated to the south of the Andamans, 121 km from Little Andaman. The British formally took possession in 1869. There are 19 islands, 7 uninhabited; total area, 1,645 sq. km. The islands are usually divided into 3 sub-groups (southern, central and northern), the chief islands in each being respectively, Great Nicobar, Camotra with Nancowrie and Car Nicobar. There is a fine land-locked harbour between the islands of Camotra and Nancowrie, known as Nancowrie Harbour.

The population numbered, in 1961, 14,563. The coconut and arecanut are the main items of trade, and coconuts are a major item in the people's diet.

The Nicobar Islands were occupied by the Japanese in July 1942; and Car Nicobar was developed as a big supply base. The Japanese built some roads in Car Nicobar and small jetties at Malacca in Car Nicobar, and in the harbour at Nancowrie. The Allies reoccupied the islands on 9 Oct. 1945.

Ministry of Information and Broadcasting. *The Andaman and Nicobar Islands*. Delhi, 1957
Sen, P. K., *The Land and people of the Andamans*. Calcutta, 1962

CHANDIGARH. On 1 Nov. 1966 the city of Chandigarh and a 26-sq.-km area surrounding it was constituted a Union Territory. Population (1967), 89,000. It serves as the joint capital of both Punjab (India) and the new state of Haryana, and is the seat of a High Court and of a university serving both states. The city will ultimately be the capital of just the Punjab; joint status is to last for not more than 5 years from 1970 while a new capital is built for Haryana.

Evenson, N., *Chandigarh*. Berkeley, Cal., 1966

DADRA AND NAGAR HAVELI. By the 10th amendment to the constitution the Portuguese territories of Dadra and Nagar Haveli (area, 490 sq. km; population (1962), 57,963) became a centrally administered Union Territory with effect from 11 Aug. 1961. Formerly for administrative purposes a part of Damão (on the south Gujarat coast), they were separated from it by a 26-km strip of Indian territory. In July 1954 'nationalist volunteers' occupied Dadra and Nagar Haveli and a pro-India administration was formed; this body made a request for incorporation into the Union, 1 June 1961, and has been recognized by the Indian Government as able to exercise an advisory role on the pattern of territorial councils. The Indian Government appointed an Administrator in Oct. 1960. Headquarters are at Silvassa.

The Administrator: Nakul Sen.

JUSTICE. The territory is under the jurisdiction of the Bombay (Maharashtra) High Court. There is a District and Sessions Court at Silvassa.

EDUCATION. Literacy was 9·5% of the population at the 1961 census. In 1970 there were 4 pre-primary schools, 150 primary schools and 4 high schools. Total enrolment was 8,653. During 1969–70 scholarships amounting to Rs 22,919 were awarded to older students.

FINANCE. Budget estimates for 1969–70 show provision of Rs 1,09·81 lakhs, including Rs 4,19·38 lakhs for Plan expenditure.

INDUSTRY. An industrial estate has been set up at Piparia which had 109 registered factories in 1969 for chemical products, engineering, textiles, plastics, fertilizers and other manufactures. Of these, 24 were in production by Feb. 1970.

AGRICULTURE. Farming is the chief occupation, and 16,527 hectares were under crops in 1970. Much of the land is terraced. The major food crop is rice; 365 hectares were under extensive paddy cultivation in 1970. There are veterinary centres and 2 breeding centres to improve strains of cattle and poultry. There are 7 co-operatives covering 32 villages: they received Rs 18,000 in loans and subsidies during 1968–69.

FOREST. About 43% of the total area is forest, mainly of teak and khair.

DELHI. Delhi became a Union Territory on 1 Nov. 1956. It is administered by the Union Minister of Home Affairs with the aid of an Advisory Council (of which he is chairman) composed of Delhi MPs, the Mayor, the Vice-Chancellor of Delhi University, the President of the New Delhi Municipal Committee, the Inspector-General of Police and two Advisers (Chairman, Public Relations Committee, and Chairman, Industrial Advisory Board). The senior executive is the Chief Commissioner.

The municipal corporation, instituted 7 April 1958, has 86 members. The Panchayat Raj system has been introduced into the whole of the rural area.

Lieut.-Governor: A. N. Jha.

AREA AND POPULATION. Delhi has an area of 1,484 sq. km. At the 1961 census its population was 2,658,612 (density per sq. mile, 4,614). In the rural area of Delhi there are 305 villages in 5 community development blocks.

RELIGION. At the 1961 census Hindus numbered 2,234,597; Sikhs, 203,916; Moslems, 155,453; Jains, 29,595; Christians, 29,269; Buddhists, 5,466.

EDUCATION. The proportion of literates to the total population was 52·7% (60·8% males, 42·5% females) at the 1961 census, higher than any other territory or state (national average, 23·7%).

The total number of educational institutions in 1959–60 was 1,287, with an enrolment of 445,399 students and a total expenditure of Rs 8,94 lakhs. Primary schools had 172,406 students and higher secondary schools, 184,005 students.

The University of Delhi was founded in 1922; it has 34 constituent colleges and institutions with, 1962–63, a total of 19,350 students.

FINANCE. Budget estimates 1968–69 show total revenue of Rs 36,30·38 lakhs and expenditure of Rs 37,78·93 lakhs. Biggest source of revenue was sales tax (Rs 19,97·70 lakhs). Biggest item of expenditure was education (Rs 11,78·20 lakhs).

INDUSTRY. The modern city of Delhi and New Delhi is not only the largest commercial centre in northern India but is also an important industrial centre. Since 1947 a large number of industrial concerns have been established; these include factories for the manufacture of watches, razor blades, sports goods and parts for radios, bicycles and station wagons. The number of factories registered under the Factories Act, 1948, was 1,005 in 1960; during the period July–Dec. 1958 average number of workers employed was 59,280. There are also about 8,000 small-scale industrial and cottage establishments employing about 60,000 workers.

An industrial estate was established at Okha, 10 miles south of the city, in 1957; it has 35 light engineering factories.

Some traditional handicrafts, for which Delhi was formerly famous, still flourish; among them are ivory carving, miniature painting, gold and silver jewellery and papier mâché work. The handwoven textiles of Delhi were particularly fine; this craft is being successfully revived.

AGRICULTURE. About 110,000 hectares are cultivated. Animal husbandry is increasing and mixed farms are common. Chief crops in 1964–65, production in 1,000 metric tons (area in 1,000 hectares), were: Wheat, 45 (32); jowar and bajra, 11 (31); pulses, 13 (20); sugar-cane (gur), 1 (4); fruit, vegetables and flowers.

COMMUNICATIONS. Three national highways pass through the city; it is also an important rail junction and served by 2 airports.

There were (1962) 74,826 registered motor vehicles in Delhi including about 2,000 taxis. The city transport service has over 700 buses.

GOA, DAMAN AND DIU. Goa, bounded on the north by Maharashtra and on the east and south by Mysore, has a coastline of 105 km; the coast was captured for Portugal by Afonso de Albuquerque in 1510 and the inland area was added in the 18th century. Daman (Damão) on the Gujarat coast, 70 miles north of Bombay, was seized by the Portuguese in 1531 and ceded to them (1539) by the Shar of Gujarat. The island of Diu, captured in 1534, lies off the south-east coast of Kathiawar (Gujarat); there is a small coastal area. In Dec. 1961 the territories were occupied by India and incorporated into the Indian Union.

The Indian Parliament passed legislation in March 1962 by which Goa, Daman and Diu became a Union Territory with retrospective effect from 20 Dec. 1961. Goa is represented by 2 elected members in the Indian House of the People.

For judicial purposes the territory comes under the High Court of Bombay. The capital is Panjim (Nova Goa).

There is a Legislative Assembly of 32 members. The Maharashtrawadi Gomantak party won the elections of 27 March 1967 and formed the government.

Lieut.-Governor: Nakul Sen.
Chief Minister: Dayanand G. Bandodkar.

AREA AND POPULATION. The area of the territory is 3,693 sq. km, that of Goa itself being about 3,496 sq. km. Population (1960) 626,978. Panjim (population in 1950, 31,950) is the largest town. The languages spoken are Marathi and Portuguese; the dialect Konkani is widely used.

RELIGION. About 62% of the population is Hindu, 36% Christian, 2% Muslim and other communities.

EDUCATION. In 1967–68 the intake in primary and middle schools was 100,000 and in high schools 13,715. Sixteen new primary schools, 48 middle schools and 5 high schools were opened during the year to accommodate this intake. In 1968 there were 5 arts and science colleges affiliated to Bombay University. The Medical College at Panaji had 350 students. There was also a pharmacy college, a commercial college, an engineering college, a polytechnic and an industrial training institute.

HEALTH. There are (1968) 20 hospitals with 1,813 beds, also mobile and specialist clinics.

JUSTICE. The territory comes under the High Court of Bombay.

FINANCE. Budget estimates, 1968–69, show total revenue of Rs 10,56·77 lakhs, expenditure of Rs 10,56·77 lakhs. Contributions and adjustments between central and state governments brought receipts of Rs 5,20·76 lakhs, sales tax brought Rs 1,20 lakhs. Expenditure was highest on education, Rs 2,09·01 lakhs. An estimated Rs 8·62 crores was spent on development during 1967–68.

AGRICULTURE. Agriculture is the main occupation; important crops are rice, maize, sugar-cane, groundnuts, bananas and coconuts.

MINERALS. Resources include manganese ore and iron ore, both of which are exported.

INDUSTRY. Tourism is important, and a provision of Rs 8,35 lakhs has been made for tourist projects in 1968–69. The fishing industry received Rs 35,43 lakhs in government assistance in 1967–68; fish is the territory's staple food. Two industrial estates have been set up.

POWER. Units load capacity in 1967–68 is estimated at 4,100m. kwh. Revenue from the sale of energy generated was Rs 61·4 lakhs. Eleven towns and 48 villages were supplied with electric power.

SHIPPING. The main port is Marmagoa. There is a daily steamer service between Panaji and Bombay, and weekly service between Bombay and Cochin, calling at Marmagoa.

ROADS. In Goa itself a road network has been developed in conjunction with the tourism industry.

RAILWAYS. There is a metre gauge line from the Poona–Bangalore line into Goa. There are no railways on Diu or in Daman.

AVIATION. Bombay–Cochin daily service stops in Goa at Dabolim.

National Council of Applied Economic Research, *Techno-economic Survey of Goa, Daman and Diu.* New Delhi, 1964

HIMACHAL PRADESH. The Union Territory of Himachal Pradesh lies to the north of Uttar Pradesh and to the east of Punjab (India); Tibet is on its eastern boundary.

The territory came into being on 15 April 1948 and comprises 30 former Hill States. The state of Bilaspur was merged with Himachal Pradesh in 1954. On 1 Nov. 1966, under the Punjab Reorganization Act, 1966, certain parts of the state of Punjab (India) were transferred to Himachal Pradesh. These comprise the districts of Simla, Kulu, Kangra, and Lahaul and Spiti; and parts of Hoshiarpur and Ambala districts, with an estimated population (1967) of 1·5m.

The 6 original districts were: Mahasu, Sirmur, Mandi, Chamba, Bilaspur and Kinnaur. The capital is Simla.

There is a unicameral legislature. The Legislative Assembly has 63 seats of which Congress holds 42.

Lieut.-Governor: Lieut.-Gen. K. Bahadur Singh.
Chief Minister: Y. S. Parmar.

AREA AND POPULATION. The area of the territory is 55,658 sq. km and it had a population at the 1961 census of 2,811,731. In 1968 the estimated population was 3,204,271. Principal language is Pahari.

JUSTICE. The state comes under the jurisdiction of the Delhi High Court, which has a bench at Simla.

FINANCE. Total revenue for 1970–71 was (on budget estimates) Rs 47,99·76 lakhs. Expenditure was Rs 57,70·09 lakhs. Receipts included: Contribution and adjustments between central and state governments, Rs 27,35·07 lakhs; forests, Rs 6,60 lakhs. Expenditure included: Education, Rs 11,19·73 lakhs, public works and improvements, Rs 14,03·97 lakhs; agriculture, Rs 2,94·39 lakhs.

AGRICULTURE. Main crops are seed potatoes and fruits such as apples, peaches, apricots, nuts, pomegranates.

Production of maize and wheat (1967–68): 392,758 metric tons of maize from 242,480 hectares, and 268,099 metric tons of wheat from 315,738 hectares.

Livestock (1961 census): Buffaloes, 208,442; other cattle, 1,212,539; sheep, 661,731; goats, 594,770.

Salt is another important item. Handicrafts, which include Pashmina shawls, wool of quality, resin, herbs, musk and skins, are a third source of income.

FORESTRY. Himachal Pradesh forests supply the largest quantities of coniferous timber in northern India. They are the main source of revenue of the Pradesh. The forests also ensure the safety of the catchment areas of the Jamuna, Sutlej, Beas, Ravi and Chenab rivers.

LACCADIVE, MINICOY AND AMINDIVI ISLANDS. The territory consists of a group of 26 islands (10 inhabited), about 300 km off the west coast of Kerala. It was constituted a Union Territory in 1956. The total area of the islands is 27·86 sq. km. The northern portion is called the Amindivis. The remaining islands are called the Laccadives (including Minicoy Island). Minicoy is the largest island, 3·24 sq. km, and is considerably to the south of the other islands. An Advisory Committee associated with the Union Home Minister and an Advisory Council to the Administrator assist in the administration of the islands; these are constituted annually. Population (1961 census), 24,108, nearly all Moslems. The language is Malayalam, but the language in Minicoy is Mahl. There were in 1969–70 one higher secondary school, 4 high schools and 33 nursery/primary/upper primary schools. There are 2 hospitals and 7 primary health centres. The staple products are coconut-husk fibre (coir) coconuts and fish. Headquarters of administration, Kavaratti Island.

Administrator: K. D. Menon.

MANIPUR. Formerly a state under the political control of the Government of India, Manipur, on 15 Aug. 1947, entered into interim arrangements with the Indian Union and the political agency was abolished. The administration was taken over by the Government of India on 15 Oct. 1949 under a merger agreement, and it is centrally administered by the Government of India through a Chief Commissioner. The Legislative Assembly consists of 33 elected members: it was dissolved on 16 Oct. 1969 and Presidential rule introduced. There are 5 districts. Capital, Imphal (population, 1961, 67,717).

Chief Commissioner: Baleswar Prasad.

AREA AND POPULATION. Manipur has an area of 20,793 sq. km and a population (1966) of 940,876. The valley, which is about 1,813 sq. km, is 2,600 ft above sea-level. The hills rise in places to nearly 10,000 ft, but are mostly about 5,000–6,000 ft. The average annual rainfall is 65 in. The hill areas covering nearly 20,800 sq. km are inhabited by various hill tribes who constitute about one-third of the total population of the state. There are about 40 tribes and sub-tribes falling into the two main groups of Nagas and Kukis. A large number of dialects are spoken, while Hindi is gradually becoming prevalent.

EDUCATION. In 1970 there were 2,132 primary schools, 303 middle schools, 123 high schools and 13 colleges. The number enrolled at the schools (provisional) was 230,000.

HEALTH. In 1970 there were 12 hospitals, 59 dispensaries and 12 primary health centres. There are also about 65 specialist centres and clinics.

FINANCE. Revised estimates for 1969–70 show revenue of Rs 1,89·06 lakhs and expenditure on revenue account of Rs 14,41·73 lakhs. Main sources of revenue were land revenue, Rs 35·00 lakhs; sales tax, Rs 26·00 lakhs; electricity, Rs 13·12 lakhs; agriculture, Rs 8·54 lakhs; transport, Rs 55·00 lakhs. Main item of expenditure was education, Rs 3,77·00 lakhs.

PRODUCTION. Rice is the principal crop; production, 1969–70, 232,000 metric tons from 144,000 hectares. Handloom weaving is a popular industry. Many development schemes are in progress under the five-year plans. Under the fourth plan Rs 30·25 crores will be spent on development work.

COMMUNICATIONS. Imphal has air links with Silchar and Calcutta.

PONDICHERRY. Formerly the chief French settlement in India, was founded by the French in 1674, taken by the Dutch in 1693 and restored to the French in 1699. The English took it in 1761, restored it in 1765, re-took it in 1778, restored it a second time in 1785, retook it a third time in 1793 and finally restored it to the French in 1814. Administration was transferred to India on 1 Nov. 1954. A Treaty of Cession (together with Karikal, Mahé and Yanaon) was signed on 28 May 1956; instruments of ratification were signed on 16 Aug. 1962 from which date (by the 14th amendment to the Indian Constitution) Pondicherry, comprising the 4 territories, became a Union Territory.

GOVERNMENT. By the Government of Union Territories Act 1963 Pondicherry is governed by a Lieut.-Governor, appointed by the President, and a Council of Ministers (5) responsible to a Legislative Assembly of 30 members. The state of the parties in the Assembly (Sept. 1970) was: Congress, 10; United Democratic Front, 18; Independents, 2.

Lieut.-Governor: B. D. Jatti.

AREA AND POPULATION. The total area of Pondicherry (with Karikal, Mahé and Yanaon) is 469 sq. km, divided into 16 Communes. Population (1961), 369,079; Pondicherry city had 40,421 inhabitants. The principal languages spoken are French, English, Tamil, Telegu and Malayalam.

EDUCATION. There are 4 university colleges in the territory and 2 for pre-university education. There are 2 French-founded colleges, one of which is still affiliated to the University of Paris; the other is now the Post-Graduate Institute of Medical Education and Research, maintained by the Ministry of Health.

FINANCE. Budget estimates for 1970–71 show revenue receipts of Rs 4,31·86 lakhs and expenditure on revenue account of Rs 7,07·24 lakhs. Main sources of revenue were contributions and adjustments between central and state governments, Rs 2,75·38 lakhs; income from multi-purpose river, irrigation and electricity schemes, Rs 1,50·08 lakhs; state excise, Rs 1,24·45 lakhs; sales tax, Rs 40·00 lakhs. Main items of expenditure were: Education, Rs 1,24·69 lakhs; river, irrigation and electricity schemes, Rs 1,09·10 lakhs; medical, and public health, Rs 99·69 lakhs. Under the third five-year plan, expenditure was Rs 6,03·27 lakhs in the State Sector. During the two subsequent annual plans, Rs 3,32·26 lakhs was spent. The fourth plan provides for an outlay of Rs 12·50 crores.

PRODUCTION. The main food crop is rice (88,600 metric tons in 1969–70); cash crops include groundnuts, coconuts, gingelly, pepper, chillies and sugar-cane. Sugar cane production (1968–69) was 176,000 metric tons. The main industry is cotton textiles (2,465 looms and 121,528 spindles producing cloth worth Rs 8·67 crores in 1970).

TRIPURA. A Hindu state of great antiquity having been ruled by the Maharajahs for 1,300 years before its accession to the Indian Union on 15 Oct. 1947. With the reorganization of states on 1 Sept. 1956 Tripura became a Union Territory.

GOVERNMENT. The Government of Union Territories Act 1963 (effective 1 July 1963) appointed as head of government an Administrator assisted by a small Council of Ministers and a Legislative Assembly of 30 members: Congress, 27; Communists, 3. The territory has 1 district, divided into 10 administrative subdivisions, namely, Sadar, Khowai, Kailasahar, Dharmanagar, Sonamura, Udaipur, Belonia, Kamalpur, Sabroom and Amarpur.

The capital is Agartala (population, 1961, 54,878).

Chief Commissioner: U. N. Sharma.
Chief Minister: Sachindra Lal Singh.

AREA AND POPULATION. It is bounded on the north, west and south by East Pakistan, and on the east by the Lushai Hill Tract of Assam. The major portion of the state is hilly and full of jungles. It has an area of 10,453 sq. km and a population of 1,142,005 (1961 census).

FINANCE. Budget estimates 1968–69 show revenue receipts of Rs 12,76·92 lakhs, of which grants from the central government amounted to Rs 11,36·55 lakhs, and expenditure on revenue account of Rs 14,38·96 lakhs, of which education cost Rs 3,56·56 lakhs and public works, Rs 2,89·59 lakhs.

PRODUCTION. The agricultural wealth of the territory consists of rice, jute, cotton, tea and fruits, while its forests yield timber, firewood and charcoal. Production in 1,000 metric tons (area in 1,000 hectares) in 1964–65: Rice, 190 (219); jute, 60,000 bales of 180 kg (10); cotton, 6,000 bales of 180 kg (6).

PROTECTORATE

SIKKIM. Until the transfer of power in India in Aug. 1947 Sikkim was under British paramountcy. Under a treaty, signed in Gangtok on 5 Dec. 1950, Sikkim continues to be a protectorate of the Government of India, which has special responsibility in respect of her defence, external relations and communications. The ruler is HH Maj.-Gen. Palden Thondup Namgyal, PV, OBE, Chogyal of Sikkim, born 1923, succeeded 2 Dec. 1963.

GOVERNMENT. A retired Indian civil servant assists the Chogyal as head of his administration. There is a Council, on which 18 out of 24 seats are elective; on this council 7 seats are reserved for Bhutias and Lepchas, 7 for Nepalese, 6 for the Chogyal's nominees and 1 seat each for the Sangha (monasteries); the general interests, the Tsongs (a tribal group of Nepalese origin) and the scheduled classes. In the 1967 elections the National Party won 5 seats, the Sikkim National Congress 8 seats and the State Congress 2 seats. Independent candidates hold the 3 reserved seats for the Sangha, the scheduled classes and the Tsongs. Both Congress Parties demand further democratization an obstacle to which is the formulation of safeguards for the Lepcha and Bhutia minorities. In June 1961 Sikkim subjecthood was granted to those who had been resident for 15 years; previously the qualification had been 15 years residence prior to 1951 and possession of landed property. The number of Nepalese eligible to vote has thus been substantially increased.

The capital is Gangtok (population, 1964, 12,000).

Indian Political Officer: N. B. Menon.
Head of the Chogyal's Administration: I. S. Chopra.

AREA AND POPULATION. Area, 7,298 sq. km. Census population (1961), (162,189; about 75% are Nepalese, the remainder are Lepchas and Bhutias. 95·78% of the population is rural.

RELIGION. The state religion is Mahayana Buddhism. Nearly 60% of the population is Hindu.

EDUCATION. Sikkim has 123 government, 58 government-aided and 11 privately managed schools, besides a basic training institute.

WELFARE. Five hospitals, 26 dispensaries, 4 sub-dispensaries, a maternity ward, chest clinic and 2 blocks for TB patients are in use. Medical care and hospital treatment are free.

FINANCE. The annual revenue is about Rs 2·14 crores. The Government of India is financing the third five-year plan (1967–72), involving an outlay of Rs 9 crores. There is also a Government of India grant-in-aid to the Sikkim Mining Corporation.

PRODUCTION. Sikkim produces rice, corn and millet, cardamom, oranges, apples and pineapples. Potatoes are the main cash crop. Forests occupy one-third of Sikkim, but are largely unexploited. There is a distillery at Rangpo and a fruit-preservation factory at Singtam. An ore containing lead, zinc and copper is being mined at Photang by an Indo-Sikkimese venture, the Sikkim Mining Corporation.

ROADS. Sikkim has neither airfields nor railways, but Gangtok is connected to the Indian air terminal and railhead of Siliguri by a motorable road *via* Rangpo. India has been aiding the building of strategic roads such as that between Nathu La and Gangtok and the North Sikkim highway, which has opened up the northern areas.

Coelho, V. H., *Sikkim and Bhutan.* New Delhi, 1970
Olschak, B. C., *Sikkim.* Zürich, 1965

PAKISTAN
Islamic Republic of Pakistan

CONSTITUTION AND GOVERNMENT. Pakistan, on 23 March, 1956, was proclaimed an Islamic republic, after the Constituent Assembly had adopted the draft constitution on 29 Feb. The Republic of Pakistan continues her full membership of the Commonwealth of Nations, accepting the Queen as the symbol of the free association of its independent member nations and, as such, the Head of the Commonwealth.

Pakistan was constituted as a Dominion on 14 Aug. 1947, under the provisions of the Indian Independence Act, 1947, which received the royal assent on 18 July 1947. The Dominion consisted of the following former territories of British India; Balúchistán, East Bengal (including almost the whole of Sylhet, a former district of Assam), North-West Frontier, West Punjab and Sind; and those States which had acceded to Pakistan.

National flag: Dark green with a white vertical bar at the mast, the green portion bearing a white crescent in the centre and a 5-pointed white heraldic star. The white portion is one-quarter of the size of the rectangular flag.

Governors-General of Pakistan: Quaid-I-Azam Mohammed Ali Jinnah (14 Aug. 1947–11 Sept. 1948); Khawaja Nazimuddin (14 Sept. 1948–17 Oct. 1951; took over the premiership after the assassination of Liaquat Ali Khan); Ghulam Mohammad (17 Oct. 1951–6 Aug. 1955); Maj.-Gen. Iskander Mirza (acting from 7 Aug. 1955, elected Provisional President on 5 March 1956).

On 7 Oct. 1958 President Mirza declared martial law in Pakistan, dismissed the central and provincial Governments, abolished all political parties and abrogated the constitution. Mohammed Ayub Khan, the Army Commander-in-Chief, was appointed as chief martial law administrator. Field Marshal Mohammed Ayub Khan, assumed office on 28 Oct. 1958, after Maj.-Gen, Iskander Mirza had handed all powers to him. His authority was confirmed by a ballot in Feb. 1960 when he received 75,283 votes out of a total of 78,720 'basic democracies' entitled to vote; and again in Jan. 1965 when he obtained 49,647 votes against 28,343 votes cast for Miss Fatima Jinnah. He proclaimed a new constitution on 1 March 1962.

On 25 March 1969 President Ayub Khan resigned and handed over power to the army under the leadership of Maj.-Gen. Agha Muhammad Yahya Khan who immediately proclaimed martial law throughout the country, appointing himself chief martial law administrator. The Army Chief of staff and the chiefs of the Navy and Air Force were appointed as deputy martial law administrators and later formed the Council of Administration. A Council of Ministers was also appointed, consisting of 8 civilians. On 29 March 1970 the Legal Framework Order was published, defining a new constitution: Pakistan to be a federal republic with a Moslem Head of State; the National Assembly and Provincial Assemblies to be elected in free and periodical elections, the first of which was to be held in Dec. 1970; the National Assembly to have 313 seats; 300 general members directly elected on adult franchise and 13 seats reserved for women, each of whom to be elected by the general elected members from her Province. Women can also be elected to general seats. Election to the Provincial Assemblies would be on the same basis.

Distribution of seats:

	National Assembly		Provincial Assemblies	
	General	Women	General	Women
East Pakistan	162	7	300	10
Punjab	83	3	180	6
Sind	27	1	60	2
Baluchistan	4	1	20	1
NW Frontier Province	18	1	40	2
Centrally Administered Tribal Areas	7			

At the general election, 7 Dec. 1970, the Awami League led by Shaikh Mujibur Rahman gained 149 seats and the Peoples' Party 94. Martial law continued pending the settlement of differences between East and West.

DIPLOMATIC REPRESENTATIVES

Country	Pakistan representative	Foreign representative
Afghánistán	H. M. Ahson	Nour Ahmed Etemadi
Albania	Hamid Nabat Khan	—
Algeria	Hamid Nawaz	L. Sekkiou
Argentina	K. K. Panni	Dr E. A. Colombo[1]

[1] Chargé d'Affaires.   No figure = Ambassador.

Country	Pakistan representative	Foreign representative
Australia[1]	M. Aslam Malik	L. H. Border, MVO
Austria	Enver Murad	Franz Schlechta
Belgium	Riaz Piracha	J. C. Salmon
Bolivia	Iftikhar Ali	—
Brazil	Iftikhar Ali	Paulo Valladares[3]
Britain[1]	Salman A. Ali	Sir Cyril Pickard, KCMG
Bulgaria	J. K. A. Marker	—
Burma	H. Rahman	Thiri Pyanchi U Than Hla
Cambodia	H. Rahman	—
Cameroun	Dr S. M. Koreshi	—
Canada[1]	M. S. Shaikh	C. E. McGaughey
Central African Republic	H. Nawaz	—
Ceylon[1]	H. K. Panni	H. Fernando
Chad	M. Attaullah	—
Chile[2]	K. K. Panni	—
China	K. M. Kaiser	Ting Kuo-yu
Columbia	Iftikhar Ali	—
Cuba	M. S. A. Baig	R. Cadalso Hernandez[3]
Cyprus[1]	Air Cdre M. Rabb	—
Czechoslovakia	M. A. Alvie	—
Dahomey	Dr S. M. Koreshi	—
Denmark	K. M. Kaiser	F. G. de Dompierre de Jonquieres
Ethiopia[2]	M. A. Rahman	—
Finland	S. A. Ali	A. A. Pakaslahti
France	S. K. Dehlavi	A. Beaulieux
Germany (West)	A. Rahman	G. Scholl
Ghana[1]	Ali Arshad	E. R. T. Madjitey
Greece	J. G. Kharas	A. Matsas
Guinea	Ali Arshad	—
Guyana[1]	M. S. A. Baig	—
Hungary[2]	Enver Murad	—
India[1]	S. Hyder	S. Sen
Indonesia	Maj.-Gen. Sher Ali Khan	—
Iran	Shah Nawaz	Hushang Ansary
Iraq	M. Masood	Abdul Kadir Al-Gaylani
Irish Republic	—	—
Italy	Hamid N. Khan	Luea Dainelli
Jamaica[1]	—	—
Japan	S. M. Murshed	Masayoshi Kakitsubo
Jordan	S. R. Chatari	Hani Hashim
Kenya[1]	R. R. Noore	—
Kuwait	Mazhar Hussein	—
Laos[2]	M. Rabb	Prince Tiao Khampan
Lebanon	Air Cdre M. Rabb	—
Liberia	Ali Arshad	—
Libya	M. Ataullah	—
Luxembourg[2]	S. Osman Ali	—
Malagasy	M. R. Ahmad	—
Malawi[1]	—	—
Malaysia[1]	M. S. Shaikh	Tengku Indra Putra, DK, PMN
Mali	A. Arshad	—
Malta[1]	M. Ataullah	—
Mauri tius	M. R. Ahmad	—
Mexico	Agha Hilaly	Rafael de la Colina

[1] High Commissioner. [2] Envoy. [3] Chargé d'Affaires.
No figure = Ambassador.

Country	Pakistan representative	Foreign representative
Mongolia	S. Mohammed Khan	Dondogyn Tsvegmid
Morocco	Anwar Khan	Rachid El-Khattabi[3]
Nepál	A. R. Khan	Bharat Raj Bhandary[3]
Netherlands	S. M. Hasan	Jonkheer Dr E. V. E. Teixeira de Mattos
New Zealand[1]	M. Aslam Malik	—
Niger	Dr S. M. Koreshi	—
Nigeria[1]	Dr S. M. Koreshi	Alhaji A. R. Mora
Norway	K. M. Kaiser	Egil Ulstein, CVO, DFC
Panama	Clarence O. Boyd[3]	—
Paraguay	Iftikhar Ali	—
Philippines	—	R. S. Busuego
Poland	M. Shafqat	E. Pszczolkowski
Portugal	H. R. Chaudhury	Dr H. Alves Morgado
Romania	J. K. A. Marker	—
Saudi Arabia	Brig. M. Hayat	Ali Mohammed Shadly[3]
Senegal	Ali Arshad	—
Sierra Leone[1]	Ali Arshad	—
Singapore[1]	H. Rahman	—
Somalia	Brig. M. Hayat	—
Spain	Maj.-Gen. S. A. Shah	The Duke of Amalfi
Sudan	M. A Rahman	Sayed Hamid Mohamed El-Amin
Sweden	K. M. Kaiser	Lennart Finnmark
Switzerland	Afzal Iqbal	René Stoudmann
Syria	A. A. Shaikh	Mohammed Said Al-Sabbagh[3]
Tanzania[1]	M. R. Ahmad	—
Thailand	M. H. Junejo	Luang Peekdhip Malakul
Togo	A. Arshad	—
Trinidad[1]	M. S. A. Baig	—
Tunisia	Abdul Ghayur	—
Turkey	Iftikhar Ali	Sinasi Orel
Uganda[1]	R. R. Noore	—
USSR[2]	Salman A. Ali	Alexei E. Nesterenko
UAR	I. A. Akhund	Ahmed Saleh El Zahid[3]
USA	Agha Hilaly	Benjamin H. Oehlert
Uruguay	K. K. Panni	—
Vatican[2]	A. K. Hafizuddin	Mgr Dr X. Zupi
Venezuela	Agha Hilaly	—
Yemen	I. A. Akhund	—
Yugoslavia	J. G. Kharas	Nikola Miličević

[1] High Commissioner. [2] Envoy. [3] Chargé d'Affaires.
No figure = Ambassador.

AREA AND POPULATION. The total area of Pakistan is 365,529 sq. miles (936,720 sq. km); population (census 1961), 93,720,613 (49,308,645 male, 44,411,968 female). These figures include non-Pakistani nationals.

Provinces	Area (sq. miles)	Total	Males	Females
East Pakistan	55,126	50,840,235	26,348,843	24,491,392
West Pakistan	310,403	42,880,378	22,959,802	19,920,576

These figures exclude Jammu and Kashmir, Gilgi and Baltistan, Junagardh, Manavadar and Pakistan enclaves in India.

The population of the principal cities (census of 1961) is:

Chittagong	364,205	Hyderabad	434,537	Lyallpur	425,248	Quetta	106,633
Dacca	556,712	Karachi	1,912,598	Multan	358,201	Rawalpindi	340,175
Gujranwala	196,154	Lahore	1,296,477	Peshawar	218,691	Sialkot	164,346

RELIGION. 88·1% of the population are Moslems, 5·8% Scheduled Caste Hindus, 4·9% Caste Hindus, 0·8% Christians and 0·4% Buddhists.

EDUCATION. In 1961 literacy of the population aged 5 and over was 19·2%; and 15·9% of the total population. In East Pakistan literates totalled 8,955,501 (21·5% of the population); in West Pakistan, 5,380,308 (16·3% of the population). In East Pakistan, Khulna district recorded the highest literacy of 27·2%, closely followed by the districts of Chittagong (26·4%) and Dinajpur (25·9%). Karachi District showed the highest literacy of 38·1% in West Pakistan, followed by 32·4% in Rawalpindi and 25% in Lahore. The lowest percentage of literacy was in Lasbela District (West Pakistan) with 3·4%.

Bengali and Urdu are the national languages; until 1972 English is the official language.

The numbers and types of educational institutions (1965–66):

	Number	Enrolment
Universities	10	27,539
Arts and science colleges	329	67,872
Medical colleges	15	6,112
Law colleges	13	4,923
Engineering colleges	5	2,681
Agricultural colleges	5	1,292
Teacher-training institutions	112	25,717
Primary schools	51,594	6,999,706
Secondary schools	6,956	2,430,580

In 1966–67 the annual intake of technical students increased by 6,290 in technical institutions, 11,014 in industrial and vocational training, 4,168 in commerce and 1,753 in engineering. Present policy stresses vocational and technical education, disseminating a common culture based on the precepts of Islamiat.

NEWSPAPERS AND MAGAZINES numbered 1,667 in 1969: 19 were English language dailies, 83 were vernacular dailies and the rest were periodicals in English and regional languages.

JUSTICE. The Central Judiciary consists of the Supreme Court of Pakistan, which is a court of record and has three-fold jurisdiction, namely, original, appellate and advisory. There are 3 High Courts for West Pakistan in Lahore, Peshawar and Karachi, and one in Dacca for East Pakistan. District and sessions courts are the courts of first instance in each division; they have also some appellate jurisdiction. Criminal cases not being sessions cases are tried by district magistrates and subordinate magistrates. There are subordinate civil courts also.

Jurisdiction of the Judicial Committee of the Privy Council ceased on 30 April 1950.

DEFENCE. A mutual defence assistance agreement between Pakistan and the USA was signed in Karachi on 19 May 1954.

Army. The Pakistan Army is manned entirely by volunteers. It consists of 8 infantry divisions and 2 armoured divisions, 1 independent armoured group, 2 independent brigades and 1 air defence brigade. Total strength, 250,000. General headquarters is at Rawalpindi. The entire officers cadre receives its precommission training in the Military Academy at Kakul.

Navy. The fleet comprises 4 submarines, 1 light cruiser (cadet training ship), 5 destroyers, 2 fast anti-submarine frigates, 1 survey ship, 8 coastal minesweepers, 4 patrol craft, 2 seaward defence motor launches, 2 oilers, 1 water carrier and 4 tugs. Three of the submarines were built in France in 1967–71.

The principal naval bases are Karachi and Chittagong. Naval personnel in 1970 comprised 870 officers and 9,000 ratings.

Air Force. The Pakistan Air Force came into being on 14 Aug. 1947. It has its headquarters at Peshawar. Tactical units include 2 squadrons of B-57B (Canberra) bombers, 1 squadron of Mirage III–EP supersonic fighters, about 6 squadrons of MiG-19 (F-6) supersonic fighter-bombers acquired from China, 1 squadron of F-104A Starfighter interceptors, 6 squadrons of F-86F Sabre and Canadian Sabre 6 fighters, Mirage III-RP and RT-33A jet reconnaissance aircraft and 2 squadrons of C-130B Hercules turboprop transports. Some of the F-86Fs will be replaced by 30 Mirage 5s in 1972. Flying training schools are equipped mainly with T-33 and T-37BZC jet trainers supplied by the USA. Albatross amphibians and H-19 helicopters, plus a small number of Mil Mi-8 helicopters, perform maritime reconnaissance, search and rescue duties. There is a flying college at Risalpur and an apprentices college at Korangi Creek. Total strength in early-1969 was about 250 aircraft and 15,000 all ranks.

FINANCE. Currency. The monetary unit is the Pakistani rupee, the sterling equivalent of which, since Nov. 1967, is about 1s. 9d.; the official rate is Rs 11.42 = £1. Decimal coinage was introduced on 1 Jan. 1961. The rupee, which previously consisted of 64 pice, now consists of 100 paisas, but coins of both types still circulate. The notes are of Rs 100, 10, 5, 2 and Re 1 denominations; the coinage in the old series is silver–nickel of Re 1, ½, ¼, copper–nickel of annas 2, 1, ½, and bronze of 1 pice (¼ anna); and the coinage in the decimal series is half-rupee, quarter-rupee, tenth, twentieth and hundredth of a rupee.

Currency in circulation in July 1969 amounted to Rs 6,683m.

Budget. Ordinary budget for fiscal years, 1 July–30 June, in Rs 1m.:

	1968–69	1969–70	1970–71
Revenue	[6,889·3	7,533·7	8 505·8
Expenditure	5,842·1	6,120·3	6,916·9

PLANNING. All government plans and policies aim primarily at economic self-reliance. The third 5-year plan (1966–70) target was a 6·5% annual growth rate and an expenditure of Rs 52,000m. (30,000m. for the public sector), of which Rs 27,000m. were allocated to East Pakistan. Successive plans have achieved an increase in GNP of 55% between 1959 and 1968; agricultural production increased by 40%, industrial production by 160% and per capita income from Rs 318 to Rs 515. The fourth plan (1970–75) aims at an increasingly self-reliant economy, with less disparity in per capita income and a workable synthesis between economic growth and social justice.

Agriculture has been subsidized at Rs 30 to Rs 40 crores a year, excluding indirect subsidies through price maintenance. During the fourth plan the subsidies policy is to be reviewed and agricultural policy generally to be reconsidered with particular reference to the need for expansion in processing and exporting food surplus; diversification to meet emerging demands for edible oils, sugar, vegetables, poultry, fish, meat and dairy products; extending modern technology and better credit and marketing facilities to small farms; the effects of mechanization on productivity and on rural labour.

In industry the fourth plan is designed to emphasize steel, machinery, chemicals, fertilizers, natural gas, mining, agricultural processing and export industries. Modernizing and making fuller use of existing capacity takes precedence over expansion: any further industrialization is to be largely based on domestic raw materials. Estimated government subsidy to industry is (1970) Rs 50 crores a year, excluding export bonus schemes; fourth plan policy favours reduced protection and increased competition.

AGRICULTURE. Of the surveyed area of 156m. acres, cultivated land accounts for 63m. acres, of which 11m. acres consist of fallow land, so that the net area sown is 52m. acres.

Production, 1968–69 (in 1,000 tons): Rice, 13,165; wheat, 6,605; maize, 619; gram, 574; sugar-cane (gur), 28,921; cotton, 520; tea, 28·1 (from 101,000 acres); jute, 1,050 (from 2m. acres). Production of rice and wheat touched record levels, due both to government development measures and favourable weather. The Mangla Dam scheme has begun the reclamation of 3m. acres of salt-affected land. The Tarbela Dam is now being built and is designed to irrigate a further 1m. acres.

FORESTRY. There are 18,438 sq. miles of reserved and protected forests, of which 8,558 sq. miles are located in East Pakistan, 2,558 in West Punjab, 2,487 in Balúchistán, 2,473 in Sind, 2,250 in the North-West Frontier Province, 85 in Bahawalpur and 27 in Khairpur. East Pakistan forest products consist of timber, bamboos, resin, gum, fibre and honey.

MINING. The quantity (in 1,000 tons) of the chief minerals produced in 1968–69 was as follows: Chromite, 24·9; gypsum, 210; limestone, 2,270; petroleum, 136m. gallons; natural gas, 69·2m. cu. ft.

INDUSTRY. In 1968–69 the production index for manufacturing industries (1959–60 taken as base year) rose from 214·2 in 1965–66 to 274·4. The Chittagong steel mill is now in production and has been expanded. There are 29 jute-mills and 136 textile-mills.

Production 1968–69: Cotton cloth, 745·2m. yd; cotton yarn, 648·2m. lb.; jute goods, 520,000 tons; paper, 82,100 tons; cement, 2·57m. tons.

POWER. The hydro-electric station at Rasul (Punjab) has an installed capacity of 22,000 kw.; the Malakand station (NWFP) has 19,600 kw.; Dargai, 20,000 kw.; Karnafuli, 80,000 kw.; Warsak, 160,000 kw.; Chichokimalian, 12,000 kw.; Shadiwal, 12,000 kw.; Mangla, 300,000 kw.; Renala, 1,000 kw. Further stations are under construction at Sukkur, Hyderabad and Quetta. Total available electrical energy at the end of 1963, 2,881·8m. kwh; total installed capacity, 838,812 kw. Gas pipelines from Sui to Karachi (345 miles) and from Sui to Multan (200 miles) supply natural gas to industry and domestic consumers. Natural gas is now supplied to Dacca from Titas.

Ali, M. (ed.), *A Handbook of Pakistan Economy.* Lahore, 1957
Andrus, J. R., and Mohammed, A. F., *The Economy of Pakistan.* OUP, 1958
Ansari's Trade Directory of Pakistan and Who's Who. Karachi, 1950
Peach, W. N. (ed.), *Basic data of the economy of Pakistan.* Karachi, 1959

COMMERCE. Total value of exports during 1968–69 amounted to Rs 3,253·5m., and the total value of imports to Rs 4,233·1m. The value of the chief articles imported into and exported from Pakistan in 1968–69 was (in Rs 1m.):

Imports		Exports	
Food	412·5	Raw jute	622
Chemicals	474·5	Raw cotton	119
		Cotton manufactures	239
		Jute manufactures	176

Total trade with UK, in £1,000 sterling (British Board of Trade returns):

	1965	1966	1967	1968	1969	1970
Imports to UK	27,345	31,916	32,861	40,435	39,720	35,332
Exports from UK	50,374	52,574	50,771	46,749	53,187	49,249
Re-exports from UK	1,135	560	668	568	548	

RAILWAYS. Pakistan Railways comprises the Western Railway in West Pakistan and the Eastern Railway in East Pakistan. The Western Railway had (1970) a route mileage of 5,383. The Eastern Railway had route mileage of 1,571. Both railways have sections of 5 ft 6 in. gauge, metre gauge and narrow gauge line. Passenger-miles and cargo-tons for the Western and Eastern Railways were respectively 5,932m. and 4,186m., and 2,015m. and 1,057m.

SHIPPING. There are 3 ports in Pakistan: Karachi, Chittagong and Chalna. During the year 1967–68, Karachi handled 3·6m. tons; Chittagong, 2·4m. tons, and Chalna, 1·03m. tons. The National Shipping Corporation has sailings to 25 countries. Its merchant fleet comprises over 60 ocean-going vessels.

ROADS. At the end of 1965 Pakistan had 23,617 miles of roads, of which 1,859 miles were in East Pakistan and 21,758 miles in West Pakistan. The number of motor vehicles on 31 Dec. 1964 totalled 68,443 (excluding those of the armed forces).

AVIATION. Karachi is on the main BOAC, KLM, PANAM, Lufthansa, Swissair and Air France services between the UK and India, Singapore and Sydney. Dacca airport, too, can now operate heavy aircraft.

Two Pakistani airlines are operating: Pakistan International Airlines (founded 1953; the majority of shares is held by the Government), and Pakistan Aviation, Ltd, which provides common technical repair facilities for the other airlines and for the Royal Pakistan Air Force.

POST. Telephones, on 30 June 1967, numbered 139,000; all are government-owned. The number of post offices in 1967 was 12,067; 1,340 of them had telegraph facilities. There were also 93 independent telegraph offices. Television stations in Lahore and Dacca were inaugurated in Dec. 1964 and in Karachi in 1966.

BANKING. A state bank came into operation on 1 July 1948, with an authorized capital of Rs 30m. Total assets at 17 May 1968 amounted to Rs 5,972·5m.

An Agricultural Development Bank was established in Feb. 1961, by the merger of the Agricultural Development Finance Corporation and the Agricultural Bank of Pakistan, with a paid-up share capital of Rs 100m.

WEIGHTS AND MEASURES. The principal units in all the scales of weights are the maund, seer and tola, and the standard weights for each of these are 82·27 lb., 2·057 lb. and 180 grains troy respectively.

The decimal system already used in coinage is to be introduced in weights and measures; details are being worked out.

BOOKS OF REFERENCE

Ahmad, K. S., *A Geography of Pakistan.* OUP, 1964
Anwar, M. R., *Presidential government in Pakistan.* 2nd ed. Lahore, 1964
Birkhead, G. S. (ed.), *Administrative Problems in Pakistan.* Syracuse Univ. Press, 1966
Callard, K., *Pakistan.* London, 1957
Choudhury, G. W., *Democracy in Pakistan.* Univ. of British Columbia, 1963
Department of Films and Publications, *Transport and Communications in Pakistan.* Karachi, 1966
Feldman, H., *Pakistan—an Introduction.* OUP, 1968
Feldman, H., *Revolution in Pakistan: a study of the martial-law administration.* OUP, 1967
Hussain, A., *Pakistan: its ideology and foreign policy.* London, 1966
Jennings, Sir Ivor, *Constitutional Problems in Pakistan.* CUP, 1957
Khalid bin Sayeed, *Pakistan, the Formative Phase.* Karachi, 1961
Office of the Economic Adviser, *Pakistan—basic facts.* Rawalpindi, 1966
Papnek, G. F., *Pakistan's Development—Social Goals and Private Incentives.* OUP, 1968
Qureshi, A. I., *Pakistan: the road to prosperity, 1959–64.* Lahore, 1965
Stephens, I., *Pakistan.* New York, 1963
Suleri, Zia-ud-din Ahmad, *Politicians and Ayub: a survey of Pakistani politics from 1948 to 1964.* Lahore, 1965
Tayyeb, A., *Pakistan: a political geography.* OUP, 1966
Van Vorys, C., *Political Development in Pakistan.* Princeton Univ. Press, 1965
Williams, L. F. R., *The State of Pakistan.* 2nd ed. CUP, 1966

PROVINCES
FEDERAL CAPITAL

On 23 July 1948 the city of Karachi, with 566 sq. miles of its surrounding area and the islands of Manora, Bhit, Baba, Bunkor and Shamspir (Sandspit), were taken over by the Pakistan central government. In 1961 the federal territory was re-incorporated in West Pakistan. The population (1961) was 2,135,000 (1·21m. male, 925,000 female).

In 1959 it was decided to shift the federal capital from Karachi to an area on the Potwar plateau 7 miles from Rawalpindi. It is called 'Islamabad' and became a Centrally Administered Area on 1 July 1970. A number of Ministries have already moved there. The President and some Ministries have their temporary headquarters in Rawalpindi. Dacca is the seat of the National Assembly.

WEST PAKISTAN

West Pakistan comprises the former provinces of the Punjab, the North-West Frontier, Sind and Balúchistán, the states of Bahawalpur and Khairpur, the Balúchistán States Union, the frontier states and the tribal areas of Balúchistán and the north-west. These were merged into a single unit on 14 Oct. 1955. In April 1970 a presidential order dissolved the single unit into 4 provinces: Punjab, Sind, Baluchistan, NW Frontier Province.

Kashmir. Between one-third and one-half of Kashmir is controlled by Pakistan. This area is known as Azad (Free) Kashmir, and is the northern and western portion of the country. There is a President (Mr Justice Abdul Hamid) and a nominated council of ministers. The seat of government is Muzaffarabad.

(For the area on the Indian side of the cease-fire line in Kashmir, *see* pp. 360–62.)

AREA AND POPULATION. The area of West Pakistan, including Karachi, is 310,403 sq. miles (801,408 sq. km). The provincial capitals are Peshawar (NW Frontier Province), Lahore (Punjab), Karachi (Sind) and Quetta (Baluchistan). Census population (1961): 42·88m. (22·96m. male, 19·92m. female). The next census will be held in 1971.

Gen. Atiqur Rahman is Chairman of a Council of Administration of Governors of the 4 provinces.

RELIGION. 97·1% of the population are Moslems, 1·3% Christians, 1·1% Scheduled-caste Hindus and 0·5% Caste Hindus.

EDUCATION. In 1967 there were 32,040 primary schools in West Pakistan, with 2·7m. boys and girls; 7,500 secondary schools with 2·1m. pupils; 300 colleges had 220,000 students.

Total expenditure on education in 1966–67 was Rs 400m.

The official language is English; the main languages spoken in the province are Urdu, Sindhi, Punjabi, Pushto and Baluchi.

There were, in 1959, 87 daily and 335 bi-weekly and weekly newspapers.

FINANCE. The revised budget for 1969–70 showed revenue amounting to Rs 2,180m., and expenditure amounting to Rs. 2,150m. The development budget in 1969–70 provided Rs 1,960m., including agriculture, education and 'works programme'.

AGRICULTURE. The entire area in the north and west is covered by great mountain ranges. The rest of the province consists of a fertile plain watered by 5 big rivers and their tributaries. Agriculture is the occupation of a vast majority of the population, and is dependent almost entirely on the irrigation system based on these rivers. The main crops are wheat, cotton, barley, sugar-cane, millet, rice, maize and fodder crops, while the Quetta and Kalat divisions (formerly Balúchistán) are known for their fruits and dates.

By 1963, 2·3m. acres of land had been resumed from 6,000 landlords, and 1·25m. acres had been distributed to 74,000 tenants.

Agricultural statistics (1968–69), in 1m. acres and 1m. tons:

Produce	Acreage	Production	Produce	Acreage	Production
Rice	3·4	8·1	Cotton	4·3	0·5
Wheat	14·8	4·2	Bajra	1·8	0·3
Gram	2·5	0·5	Maize	1·5	0·6
Sugar-cane	1·4	20·7	Jowar	1·4	0·3

FORESTRY. Forests cover about 5·14m. acres (3% of the land surface).

IRRIGATION. The Indus water treaty of 1960, concluded between India and Pakistan, has created the basis for a large-scale development programme. The Indus Basin Development Fund Agreement has been subscribed by Australia, Canada, Germany, New Zealand, UK and USA and is administered by the International Bank; the works to be constructed call for expenditure of US$1,000m. and are scheduled to be completed by 1973. The main purpose of the treaty is the division of the water power of the Indus and its 5 tributaries between India and Pakistan. After the construction of some 460 miles of canals, the Indus and the 2 western tributaries will serve Pakistan and the entire flow of the 3 eastern tributaries will be released for use in India.

The Lloyd Barrage and Canal Construction Scheme, which consists of a barrage across the river Indus at Sukkur and 7 canals—4 on the left and 3 on the right bank—is designed to provide an assured supply of water to an area of about 1·83m. acres in territory which used to be dependent upon inundation canals. It also brings under irrigation a further area of 3·62m. acres in Sind, the Khairpur state and the Nasirabad tehsil in Balúchistán.

Another barrage across the Indus, 4½ miles north of Kotri, called the Ghulam Muhammad Barrage, was completed in 1955; the fourth and last of the main canals taking off it was opened in 1958. The irrigable area to be served by this scheme is about 2·75m. acres in the Lower Sind area.

The Taunsa barrage on the Indus, 80 miles downstream of Kalabagh, was completed in 1958. It will eventually irrigate 1·4m. acres in the Muzaffargah and Dera Ghazi Khan districts.

The Gudu barrage, 10 miles from Kashmore, serves 2·6m. acres of the rice-growing tracts north of Sukkur; it was completed in 1962.

The former province of the Punjab set up in 1949 the Thal Development Authority to colonize the Thal desert between the Indus and Jhelum rivers. The project envisages the irrigation of some 2m. acres and the establishment of a balanced economy of agriculture, trade and industry.

The Mangla Dam on the Jhelum was inaugurated in Nov. 1967; it will generate 300,000 kw., of hydro-electric power.

Other projects are in varying stages of preparation on the Kurram River, the Upper Jhelum, the Upper and Lower Chenab canals and the Tarbela dam.

The total area dependent on irrigation was 24m. acres in 1961.

MINING. Coal is mined at Sharigh and Harnai on the Sind–Pishin railway and in the Bolan pass, also in Sor Range in the Quetta-Pishin district. Chromite is extracted in the Zhob district near Hindubagh. Limestone is quarried in small quantities. Gypsum is mined in the Sibi district near Spintangi railway station. Natural gas has been found at Sui. Iron ore is being worked in Kalabagh. Oil has been found at Kot Sarang, 70 miles SW of Rawalpindi.

INDUSTRY. Industry employs about 10% of the population. Woollen and other cottage industries, especially cotton weaving (with 17,000 workers), have made great strides. Annual production of cloth is 20m. sq. yd. Industries recently started include sodium silicate, chocolate, tanning, and paint and varnish factories. The cottage industry produces for export lacquered and embroidered articles and glazed pottery. Large quantities of raw hides and skins, wheat and rice are also exported. The population engaged in the fishing industry is about 39,000.

The cotton industry of West Pakistan had (July 1967) an installed capacity of

2,047,000 spindles and 30,000 looms. Eight woollen-mills had an aggregate of 22,760 woollen and 21,832 worsted spindles.

ROADS. There are approximately 42,000 miles of roads, of which 11,000 miles are metalled. In 1966–67 motor vehicles numbered about 57,500.

RAILWAYS. See p. 395.

West Pakistan Year Book. Public Relations Dept., Lahore, from 1956
Caroe, Sir Olaf, *The Pathans.* London, 1958

EAST PAKISTAN

East Pakistan comprises the eastern territories of the partitioned province of Bengal and the former Assam district of Sylhet, with the exception of certain thanas of the Karimganj sub-division. East Pakistan is administratively divided into 4 divisions and 17 districts: (1) Dacca Division—the districts of Dacca, Mymensingh and Faridpur; (2) Chittagong Division—the districts of Chittagong, Comilla, Noakhali, Chittagong Hill Tracts and Sylhet; (3) Rajshahi Division— the districts of Rajshahi, Dinajpur, Rangpur, Bogra and Pabna; (4) Khulna Division—the districts of Kushtia, Jessore, Khulna and Bakarganj. In Nov. 1970 the southern Ganges delta was devastated by a cyclonic tidal wave. The number of dead was estimated as at least 220,000 and the number of dwellings destroyed and damaged as 350,000. Crops and stock were also destroyed.

Governor: Vice Admiral S. M. Ahsan.

AREA AND POPULATION. The area is 55,126 sq. miles (142,797 sq. km); population (1961 census), 50·84m. (26,349,000 male, 24,491,000 female). The capital of the province is Dacca (population, 556,712 in 1961) and its ports are Chittagong and Chalna.

EDUCATION. The compulsory primary education scheme has been replaced by model primary education, and the Government has dissolved the District School Boards and taken over the administration of the schools. There are 3 universities, at Dacca, Rajshahi and Chittagong (founded in Aug. 1964).

The third 5-year plan (1965–69) envisages the spending of Rs 1,400m. on educational projects: 320m. on primary, and 310m. on secondary education.

HEALTH. The province has 6,668 beds in various hospitals, including a mental and 2 tuberculosis hospitals. There are 3 medical colleges and 5 nursing training centres.

FINANCE. The revised budget for 1969–70 showed a revenue of Rs 1,533·4m., expenditure amounting to Rs 1,527·2m., showing a revenue surplus of Rs 186·2m.

AGRICULTURE. East Pakistan is primarily an agricultural area; agriculture employs about 82% of her population. 64% of the total area of the province is under cultivation. The area which can be classified as cultivable waste is about 1·5m. acres. Among food crops, rice is the most important; the average annual production of rice is about 10m. tons (1968–69: 11·1m. tons). Other products in 1968–69 include sugar-cane (7·2m. tons), wheat (92,000 tons), gram (54,000 tons), tea (26,000 tons).

East Pakistan produces about 80% of the world production of raw jute; the area under jute in 1968–69 was about 2·2m. acres and production about 1·6m. tons.

FORESTS. The total area under forests is 8,558 sq. miles, of which 4,600 sq. miles are Reserved Forests. The annual output of timber is nearly 15m. cu. ft.

Among minor forest products, East Pakistan produces 76·5m. stems of bamboos, 415,000 canes, 6,500 maunds of honey annually.

FISHERY. Being bounded on the south by the Bay of Bengal and having numerous rivers, streams, khals and bils, East Pakistan is pre-eminently a fish-producing area and possesses great possibilities for the manufacture of various oils and fish products. The estimated annual production of fresh fish is over 33·2m. maunds (1 maund = 82·2 lb) and that of sea fish is about 70,000 tons.

MINERALS. Oil has been located in the Bay of Bengal.

INDUSTRY. In 1968–69, 1,098 industrial establishments employed 201,000 workers. Out of the existing industries, its 22 textile-mills, 7 sugar factories, 18 match factories, 7 glass works, 178 hosiery factories, a paper-mill, 29 jute-mills, 28 aluminium works and a cement factory are the most prominent. There is also a newsprint factory, a fertilizer factory, a shipyard and a dockyard. Jute factories in 1966–67 had 15,614 looms and produced 403,700 tons, of which 80% was exported. Cotton fabrics totalled 70·6m. yd in 1966–67. Cotton yarn production was 74·3m. lb. Paper production in 1966–67 was 26,500 tons and newsprint production, 36,500 tons.

POWER. Natural gas from Titas is piped to Dacca. Drilling is in progress at other sites where gas is indicated.

SHIPPING. East Pakistan possesses important natural advantages in her navigable channels which give valuable service in carrying produce by cheap water routes. There are 3 principal waterways, the Ganges, Brahmaputra and Maghna. These are freely used by inland steam vessels, which serve areas where railways cannot be economically constructed.

ROADS. The province is backward in the matter of road communications. Since partition the Government have taken up the construction of nearly 2,000 miles of road. Further construction development will provide for a further 6,000 miles of trunk, district and feeder roads. The introduction of helicopter passenger services has opened up the interior and offset to some extent the paucity of roads.

East Pakistan Bureau of Statistics, *Handbook of Economic Indicators of E. Pakistan*, 1965. Dacca, 1966
er-Rashid, H., *East Pakistan: a systematic regional geography.* Lahore,1965

CEYLON
Sri Lanka

HISTORY. According to the Mahawansa chronicle, an Indian prince from the valley of the Ganges, named Vijaya, arrived in the 6th century B.C. and became the first king of the Sinhalese. The monarchical form of government continued until the beginning of the 19th century when the British subjugated the Kandyan Kingdom in the central highlands.

In 1505 the Portuguese formed settlements on the west and south, which were taken from them about the middle of the next century by the Dutch. In 1796 the British Government annexed the foreign settlements to the presidency of Madras. In 1802 Ceylon was constituted a separate colony. Passing through various stages of increasing self-government, Ceylon reached fully responsible status within the British Commonwealth when the Ceylon Independence Act, 1947, came into force on 4 Feb. 1948.

CONSTITUTION AND GOVERNMENT. Parliament consists of the House of Representatives and the Senate. The House of Representatives is composed of 157 members (including 6 women), of whom 151 are elected by universal suffrage, and 6 are nominated. The Senate consists of 30 members, of whom 15 are elected by the House of Representatives and 15 are appointed by the Governor-General. One-third of the Senators retire every third year. The Independence Act includes agreements on defence, external affairs and public officers. The defence agreement provided that the UK and Ceylon would give to each other such military assistance as it may be in their mutual interest to provide. The UK may base such naval and air forces and maintain such land forces in Ceylon as may be required for these purposes, and as may be mutually agreed. The UK naval base at Trincomalee and the air base at Katunayake were taken over by Ceylon on 15 Oct. and 1 Nov. 1957 respectively.

The agreement on external affairs declares the readiness of Ceylon to adopt and follow the resolutions of past imperial conferences; provides that in external affairs generally the two governments will conform to the principles and practice observed by other members of the Commonwealth; provides that Ceylon will enjoy reciprocal rights and benefits enjoyed by the UK, and bear the obligations carried by the UK, which arise out of any valid international instrument which applies to Ceylon.

The public officers agreement protects the positions of specified classes of person holding office in the public service of Ceylon.

The House of Representatives is discussing a new constitution which is to supersede the Ceylon Independence Act, 1947, and the Ceylon (Constitution and Independence) Orders-in-Council, 1947.

Governor-General: William Gopallawa, MBE (sworn in 2 March 1962, after the resignation, on 26 Feb., of Sir Oliver Goonetilleke, GCMG, KCVO, KBE).

The elections held on 27 May 1970 had the following results: 91 Sri Lanka Freedom Party, 19 Lanka Sama Samaja Party, 17 United National Party, 13 Federal Party, 6 Communist Party, 3 Tamil Congress, 2 Independent and others. Six women were elected.

A coalition cabinet was formed, including the Sri Lanka Freedom Party, the Lanka Sama Samaja (Trotskyist) Party and the pro-Moscow Communist Party.

Prime Minister, Defence, External Affairs, Planning, Employment: Mrs. S. D. Bandaranaike. *Irrigation, Power and Highways:* M. Senanayake. *Foreign and External Trade:* T. B. Illangaratne. *Education:* B. Mahmud. *Shipping and Tourism:* P. C. Kalugalle. *Labour:* M. P. de Z. Siriwardene. *Public Administration, Local Government and Home Affairs:* F. R. D. Bandaranaike. *Industries and Scientific Affairs:* T. B Subasingh. *Finance:* Dr N. M. Perera. *Communications:* L. S. Goonewardene. *Plantation Industry:* C. R. de Silva. *Justice:* J. M. Jayamanne. *Agriculture and Lands:* H. S. R. B. Kobbekaduwa. *Fisheries:* G. Rajapekse. *Housing and Construction:* P. G. B. Keuneman. *Post and Telecommunications:* C. Kumarasurier. *Health:* W. P. Ariyadasa. *Information and Broadcasting:* R. S. Perera. *Social Services:* T. B. Tennekoon. *Cultural Affairs:* S. S. Kulatilake. *Parliamentary Affairs and Chief Government Whip:* K. B. Ratnayake.

For purposes of general administration, the island is divided into 22 districts, each presided over by a government agent with assistants. There are 12 municipalities, with 34 urban councils and 79 town councils.

DIPLOMATIC REPRESENTATIVES

Country	Ceylon representative	Foreign representative
Afghánistán	—	Dr A. Popal
Australia[1]	J. Siriwardene	G. N. Upton
Austria[2]	—	Dr Johanna Nestor
Belgium	S. J. Walpita	—

[1] High Commissioner.　　[2] Minister.　　No figure = Ambassador.

Country	Ceylon representative	Foreign representative
Brazil	—	W. do Amaral Martinho
Britain[1]	Dr M. V. P. Peiris, OBE	A. M. Mackintosh, CMG
Bulgaria	—	N. Penev Belchev
Burma	H. O. Wijegoonewardene	U. Hai Maung
Cambodia	—	Iat Bountheng
Canada[1]	—	R. M. MacDonald
China	D. B. R. Gunawardene	I. Karannagoda
Cuba	—	J. E. Valdes[3]
Czechoslovakia	—	P. Pavlic
Denmark[2]	U. M. Jorgenson	H. A. Biering
Finland[2]	—	W. Schreck
France	T. Wijerature	A. Chambon
Germany	S. J. Walpita	F. J. Hoffmann
Ghana[1]	—	W. A. Sare-Brown
Greece	—	J. Tannakis
Hungary[2]	—	Dr P. Kos
India[1]	N. Q. Dias	Y. K. Puri
Indonesia	D. T. E. G. Abeyasinghe	Abdoel Hamid
Iran	—	Dr M. H. M. Faridani
Iraq	—	Abdul Kadir Al-Gaylani
Italy	—	Dr F. Fabbricotti
Japan	H. E. Tennekoon	Y. Yamamoto
Jordan	—	A. El Nashashibi
Laos	—	Phagna Thib Prakhin
Lebanon	C. O. Coorey	—
Malaysia[1]	V. R. M. Karunaratne	Tengku Indra Petra
Maldive Islands	—	Ahmed Hilmy Didi
Mexico	—	C. Gutierrez
Mongolia	—	T. Demiddagra
Nepál	—	S. Bhim Bhadur
Netherlands	—	C. G. Verdouck Huffenagal
New Zealand[1]	—	B. S. Lendrum (Acting)
Norway[2]	—	Haakon Nord
Pakistan[1]	—	A. A. Shaik
Philippines	H. E. Tennekoon	J. R. Calvo
Poland	—	R. Spasowski
Portugal[2]	—	Dr G. M. da Costa Mesquita de Brito[3]
Romania	—	P. Tanasie
Spain	—	G. Nadal
Sudan	C. O. Coorey	A. M. Sid Ahmed
Sweden	R. C. S. Koelmeyer	Professor Gunnar Heckscher
Switzerland	—	F. H. Andres
Thailand	—	HH Prince Prem Pura-chatra
Turkey	—	M. Dikerdem
UAR	C. O. Coorey	K. A. A. Moustafa
USSR	—	V. P. Stepnov
USA	N. T. D. Kankarne	R. Strausz-Hupe
Yugoslavia	—	P. Serbanovic

[1] High Commissioner.   [2] Minister.   [3] Charge d'Affaires.

No figure = Ambassador.

Ceylon has now extended diplomatic recognition to the German Democratic Republic; the Democratic Republic of Vietnam (N. Vietnam); the Provisional Revolutionary Government of the Republic of South Vietnam (Viet Cong); the Democratic People's Republic of Korea (N. Korea). Diplomatic relations with Israel have been suspended.

AREA AND POPULATION. Area (in sq. miles) and census population on 8 July 1963 (based on 10% sample tabulation):

Provinces	Area	Population	Provinces	Area	Population
Western	1,412	2,838,877	North-Central	4,067	393,759
Central	2,155	1,697,018	Uva	3,843	654,105
Southern	2,129	1,430,740	Sabaragamuwa	1,893	1,124,543
Northern	3,353	741,341			
Eastern	3,115	546,474	Total	24,959 [1]	10,582,064
North-Western	2,992	1,155,207			

[1] 64,644 sq. km.

The estimated population of Ceylon in mid-1968 was 11,992,000. Population (in 1,000) according to race and nationality at the 1963 Census: 7,513 Sinhalese, 1,165 Ceylon Tamils, 625 Ceylon Moors, 46 Burghers and Eurasians, 33 Malays, 1,123 Indian Tamils, 57 Indian Moors. Non-nationals of Ceylon totalled 1,012,181.

Vital statistics. 1968: births, 384,178; marriages, 82,223; deaths, 94,903. 1967: births, 369,531; marriages, 76,024; deaths, 87,877.

The urban population is 19% of the total population. The principal towns and their population according to the census of 1963 are: Colombo, 511,644; Jaffna, 94,670; Kandy, 68,202; Galle, 65,236; Negombo, 46,908; Kurunegala, 21,179; Nuwara Eliya, 15,482.

The official language is Sinhala. English is a major second language. The use of Tamil for some official purposes was approved by Parliament in 1966.

RELIGION. Buddhism was introduced from India in the 3rd century B.C., and is the religion of the majority of the inhabitants. There were (1963) 7,003,287 Buddhists, 1,958,394 Hindus, 884,949 Christians, 724,043 Moslems and 11,330 others.

EDUCATION. Education is free from the kindergarten to the university and is imparted in the medium of the mother tongue.

In 1969 there were 9,701 schools with about 100,595 teachers and 2·64m. students from grades I to XII. 19·8% of the current expenditure of Government is on education. Education is now administered in 24 education districts under 14 regional directors of education. The overall control of the education districts is vested in the Ministry of Education.

Only about 40% of the teachers in these schools are trained. This training has been carried on in the university departments of education for graduates and in 24 general training colleges and 2 specialist training colleges for non-graduates. In 1969 there were 6,525 non-graduates and 87 graduates in training.

The University of Ceylon was established in 1942, its nucleus being formed by the Ceylon Medical College founded in 1870 and the Ceylon University College founded in 1921. In 1969 the University had faculties of oriental studies, arts, science, medicine, law, engineering, agriculture and veterinary science with a total of 8,883 students.

Two other universities, Vidyodaya and Vidyalankara, established in 1959, provided courses in languages (Pali, Sinhalese, Sanskrit, English, Hindi), arts (history, geography, economics, mathematics and philosophy), business and public administration, in education and in Buddhist studies. In 1969 the Vidyo-daya University had 2,460 students. The Vidyalankara University had 1,410 students in 1969.

All 3 universities and institutes of higher education have been brought within the ambit of one Higher Education Act which became law in Sept. 1966. The National Council of Higher Education has been established under the Act to co-ordinate the activities of all these institutes.

The Department of Technical Education and Training, which grew out of the Ceylon Technical College, controlled technical and commercial education till Oct. 1966. Now technical education is organized as a section of the Ministry of Education administering the new College of Technology, the Ceylon Technical College (now used mainly for commerce courses), the Institute of Practical Technology at Katubedde and a number of junior technical and trades schools.

CINEMAS (1969). There were 342 cinemas with a seating capacity of 142,480.

NEWSPAPERS (1969). There were 17 daily newspapers with a total circulation of 780,390 and 11 Sunday papers with a total circulation of 966,535.

JUSTICE. The systems of law which obtain in Ceylon are the Roman-Dutch law, the English law, the Tesawalamai, the Moslem law and the Kandyan law.

The Kandyan law applies to the Kandyan Sinhalese in the Central, North-Central, Uva and Sabaragamuwa provinces in respect of all matters relating to inheritance, matrimonial rights and donations. The law of England is observed in most maritime and commercial matters. The law of Tesawalamai is applied to all Tamil inhabitants of Jaffna, in all matters relating to inheritance, marriages, gifts, donations, purchases and sales of land. The Moslem law is applied to all Moslems in respect of succession, donations not involving Fidei Commissa, marriage, divorce and maintenance. These customary and religious laws have been modified in many respects by local enactments.

District courts and Courts of Requests administer justice on the civil side. The Supreme Court exercises only an appellate jurisdiction in civil matters. On the criminal side magistrates' courts, district courts and the Supreme Court exercise an original jurisdiction. The Supreme Court also exercises an appellate jurisdiction in cases decided by magistrates' courts and district courts. A Court of Criminal Appeal exercises an appellate jurisdiction in cases tried by the Supreme Court in its original criminal jurisdiction. Rural courts exercise a criminal and civil jurisdiction in rural areas in respect of petty crimes and civil disputes where the subject matter is valued less than Rs 100. Conciliation Boards were established in 1958; the Minister of Justice may appoint Conciliation Boards in any area and he may appoint the panel of conciliators for them; 232 boards were functioning in Sept. 1968.

Police. The strength of the police service on 31 Dec. 1969 was 11,135.

SOCIAL WELFARE. The activities of the Department of Social Services fall into two main divisions and these, together with the more important sub-divisions grouped under them, are as follows:

SOCIAL ASSISTANCE SERVICES. Public assistance (monthly allowances); casual relief; relief to leprosy and tuberculosis patients and their dependants; relief of widespread distress due to failure of crops, floods, storms, etc., including relief to individual cases of distress among fishermen due to acts of God such as fire, storms and accidents; rehabilitation and resettlement of flood victims; state homes for the aged; grants-in-aid to voluntary agencies and local authorities for the running of charitable and welfare institutions, homes for children, homes for the aged and crèches; services for orthopaedically handicapped persons; services for the deaf and blind; vagrancy and administration of the house of detention.

WORKMEN'S COMPENSATION. The payment of compensation to workmen meeting with accidents in the course of their work is provided for under the Workmen's Compensation Ordinance No. 19 of 1934, as amended in 1957, 1959 and 1966. It was brought into operation in 1935, and has been administered by the Director of Social Services since 1948.

FINANCE. Currency. The Monetary Law (Amendment) Act No. 16 of 1967 provides that the standard monetary unit is the Ceylon rupee having a par value equal to 0·149297 of a grain of fine gold. Following the devaluation of sterling in Nov. 1967, the Ceylon rupee was devalued by 20%.

The Central Bank is the sole authority for the issue of currency in Ceylon and all currency notes and coins issued by the Central Bank are legal tender in Ceylon for the payment of any amount. Currency notes are issued in the denominations of Re 1, Rs 2, 5, 10, 50 and 100. The following coins are legal tender: (1) nickel brass, 10 and 5 cents; (2) cupro-nickel, Re 1, 50 and 25 cents; (3) aluminium, 2 and 1 cent, and copper, ½ cent. The note circulation stood at Rs 1,181·9m. on 31 Dec. 1968. The official rate between Ceylon and the UK is Rs 14·29 to £1.

Budgets in Rs for financial years ending 30 Sept.:

Year	Revenue	Recurrent	Expenditure Capital	Total
1964–65	1,816,814,543	2,175,857,901	394,830,701	2,570,688,602
1965–66	1,877,586,030	1,976,402,408	445,979,115	2,422,381,523
1966–67	1,954,805,869	2,011,752,956	621,662,733	2,633,415,689
1967–68	2,202,063,119	2,320,886,301	710,645,480	3,031,531,781
1968–69	2,338,509,171	2,356,779,828	1,034,004,165	3,390,783,993
1969–70[1]	2,833,922,860	2,882,548,047	1,116,663,109	3,999,211,156

[1] Estimates.

The principal sources of revenue in 1968–69 were (in Rs 1m.): Customs, 754·9; ports, harbour, wharf, warehouse and other dues, 41; excise, 524·1, income tax, 397·1; licences and internal revenue, 46·1; post and telecommunications, 71; railway, 109·7; and electrical department, 72·6.

The principal items of expenditure in 1968–69 (in Rs 1m.): Defence and external affairs, 154·8; state, 346; finance, 627·6; land, irrigation and power, 396·8; home affairs, 69·9; health, 227·2; nationalized services, 50·3; industries and fisheries, 219·5; commerce and trade, 11·2; justice, 29·3; local government, 95·4; agriculture and food, 514·5; education and cultural affairs, 463·1; labour, employment and housing, 14; public works, post and telecommunications, 235·1; communications, 180·4; social services, 32·8.

The net public debt on 30 Sept. 1969 (adjusted following devaluation) was Rs 6,238·9m., consisting of domestic loans (4,901·6m.) and foreign loans (1,337·3m.).

DEFENCE. Army. The Ceylon Army was constituted on 10 Oct. 1949. The Army consists of the Regular Force, the Regular Reserve, the Volunteer Force and the Volunteer Reserve.

Navy. The Royal Ceylon Navy was constituted on 9 Dec. 1950. It comprises a frigate, 27 small patrol boats, a hydrofoil craft and a tug. HMCyS *Gemunu* and HMCyS *Rangalla* are commissioned as shore establishments. Personnel in 1970 numbered 160 officers and 1,820 ratings. Officers and men are sent to the UK for their training. There is also the Royal Ceylon Naval Reserve, a Volunteer Naval Force and a Voluntary Naval Reserve.

Air Force. The Royal Ceylon Air Force was formed on 10 Oct. 1950. Its flying bases are at Katunayake and China Bay, Trincomalee. In 1970 equipment included 8 Jet Provosts (armed), 9 Chipmunk trainers, 4 Heron and 5 Dove light transports (also used for coastal reconnaissance) and 3 Twin Pioneer aircraft and 3 JetRanger, 3 Bell Model 205 and 2 Dragonfly helicopters for internal security operations. Total strength is about 1,000 officers and airmen. There is also a Royal Ceylon Air Force Reserve.

AGRICULTURE. The area of the island is approximately 16,212,480 acres, of which about 4·5m. acres are under cultivation, and about 456,000 acres pasture land. The acreage and production of the main crops in 1969 were as follows: Paddy, 1,709,152 (65m. bu.); tea, 596,514 (484m. lb.); coconuts, 1,152,428 (2,123m. nuts); rubber, 569,518 (333m. lb.).

Livestock in 1969: 1,584,426 cattle, 765,437 buffaloes, 108,313 swine, 542,587 goats and 28,260 sheep.

The Mahaweli Ganga power and irrigation scheme has been inaugurated. Two major diversions, at Polgolla near Kandy and at Bowatenna on the Amban Ganga River, will benefit 120,000 acres of land already cultivated and irrigate an extra 104,000 acres of new land.

FISHERIES. The Government is implementing a programme for the development of fisheries in inland as well as deep-sea waters. Estimated fish landings for 1969 were 2,444,176 cwt.

MINING. Graphite is the chief mineral mined and exported from Ceylon. There were 8 mines working at the end of 1968. The total quantity of graphite exported during 1969 was 224,772 cwt (Rs 8,267,473).

The Ceylon Mineral Sands Corporation is running a plant at Pulmoddai on the NE coast for the recovery of ilmenite; exports in 1969 were 1·63m. cwt. There are several gem pits from which sapphire, ruby, aquamarine, moonstone, topaz, chrysoberyl (cat's eye), zircon, spinel, tourmaline and other semi-precious stones are obtained. There are also deposits of kaolin, iron-ore and glass sand. The miocene limestone of the north is the basis of Ceylon's cement industry.

Manufacture of salt is a government monopoly.

TRADE UNIONS. The registration and control of trade unions are regulated by the Trade Unions Ordinance (Ch. 138 of the Legislative Enactments). As at 30 Sept. 1969 there were 1,230 unions; 799 employees' unions reported a membership of 1,286,012; and 10 employers' unions reported 1,293 members.

COMMERCE. The values of total imports and exports (both including bullion, specie and postal articles; exports, including re-exports and ship's stores) for calendar years (in Rs 1,000):

	1965	1966	1967	1968	1969
Imports	1,474,381	2,028,268	1,738,365	2,173,089	2,543,445
Exports	1,915,916	1,675,959	1,630,864	1,975,135	1,875,220

Principal exports (domestic) in 1969 (in Rs 1,000): Tea, 1,061,143; cocoa, 6,955; cinnamon (quills), 33,822; copra, 26,009; coconut oil, 107,860; plumbago, 8,267; coconut (desiccated), 89,626; arecanuts, 641; rubber, 430,750.

Principal imports in 1969 (in Rs 1,000): Rice 257,219; textiles, 98,533; liquid fuel and gas oil, 156,036; wheat flour, 255,307; fish and fish preparations, 7,073; sugar, 116,821; fertilizers, 78,057; milk products, 44,479; coal, 2,704.

In 1968 the principal sources of imports were (in Rs 1,000): UK, 319,080; China, 245,403; USA, 171,557; India, 152,601; Australia, 125,190; Japan, 116,842; West Germany, 115,073; USSR, 96,868; Thailand, 92,533; Burma, 60,436. The principal countries of destination were: UK, 488,798; China, 194,534; USA, 139,383; Australia, 100,997; South Africa, 98,709; USSR, 94,347; West Germany, 82,587; Canada, 62,213; Japan, 54,551; Netherlands, 45,774.

Of the 443·9m. lb. of black tea in 1969, the following countries received the largest amounts: UK, 131m.; USA, 45·3m.; Australia, 33·9; Iraq, 33·1m.; South Africa, 27·2m.; Libya, 16·7m.; UAR, 15·4m.; Canada, 15m.; New Zealand, 14·7m.; Saudi Arabia, 13·3m.; Kuwait, 11·4m.; Iran, 8·5m.; Syria, 8·1m.; Netherlands, 7·3m.

Trade with UK, according to British Board of Trade returns (in £1,000 sterling):

	1965	1966	1967	1968	1969	1970
Imports to UK	42,277	36,334	39,577	39,886	33,101	36,558
Exports from UK	18,918	23,293	20,577	22,818	24,094 }	18,508
Re-exports from UK	82	104	200	111	145 }	

SHIPPING. In 1969, 2,514 ocean-going merchant vessels totalling 9,895,381 NRT entered and 2,551 vessels of 9,093,843 NRT cleared the ports of Ceylon.

RAILWAYS. There are 932 miles of railway open, 845 miles being 5 ft 6 in. gauge, and 87 miles 2 ft 6 in.

ROADS. There are about 11,700 miles of motorable roads, of which 6,520 are black-topped.

Number of motor vehicles, 31 Dec. 1969, 169,353, including 84,678 private cars and cabs, 31,196 lorries and vans, 9,688 buses and coaches, 14,280 tractors, 8,361 trailers, 18,994 motor cycles, 314 ambulances and hearses.

AVIATION. Air Ceylon Ltd operates internal and international services.

Foreign airlines which operate scheduled services to Ceylon are BOAC, UTA French Airlines, Qantas, Indian Airlines Corporation, Swissair, Aeroflot, TWA and Malaysian Airways; various others operate charter services.

POST. In 1969 there were 278 post offices, 2,159 sub-post offices, 12 receiving offices for postal business. There were 1,302 telegraph offices. There were 60,206 telephones, of which 34,161 were in Colombo. Throughout the Greater Colombo Area inter-dialling facilities are now available between 21 stations.

The Overseas Telecommunication Service operates telegraph and telephone services through submarine cables and/or VHF radio circuits to most parts of the world. Broadcasting is provided by the Ceylon Broadcasting Corporation, which assumed the functions of Radio Ceylon on 5 Jan. 1967.

BANKING. Foreign exchange assets at 1 Jan. 1969 stood at Rs 463m.

The leading banks in Ceylon are: The Bank of Ceylon and the People's Bank (state-managed), The Mercantile Bank Ltd, the State Bank of India, National & Grindlays Bank, the Hongkong and Shanghai Banking Corporation, the Chartered Bank, the Eastern Bank, the Hatton Bank, the Indian Bank, the Habib Bank (Overseas) Ltd and the Indian Overseas Bank Ltd.

The state-owned Ceylon Insurance Corporation has a monopoly of all insurance business. Business completed in 1968 amounted to Rs 84·3m.

The Ceylon Savings Bank had 125,923 depositors, and deposits amounting to Rs 102·4m. on 31 Dec. 1969. The post office savings bank on 31 Dec. 1969 had a balance to depositors' credit of Rs 489·7m. The loans granted by the Ceylon State Mortgage Bank for the year ended 30 Sept. 1969 amounted to Rs 8·3m. (provisional).

WEIGHTS AND MEASURES. The Imperial weights and measures of the UK are established as the standard weights and measures of Ceylon. Local and customary weights and measures are still used in various parts of the country.

BOOKS OF REFERENCE

The Ceylon Year Book
Census Publications from 1871
Collins, Sir C., *Public Administration in Ceylon*. London, 1951
Farmer, B. H., *Pioneer Peasant Colonization in Ceylon*. R. Inst. of Int. Affairs, 1957
Ferguson's *Ceylon Directory*. Annual (from 1858)
Jennings, Sir I., *The Economy of Ceylon*. 2nd ed. OUP, 1952.—*The Constitution of Ceylon*. 3rd ed. London, 1953
Ludowyk, E. F. C., *The Story of Ceylon*. London, 1962
Pakeman, S. A., *Ceylon*. New York, 1964
Pickens, V. L., *Serendipity*. New York, 1964
Ratnasuriya, M. D., and Wijeratne, P. B. F., *Shorter Sinhalese–English Dictionary*. Colombo, 1949
Sievers, A., *Ceylon, eine sozialgeographische Landeskunde*. Wiesbaden, 1964
Snodgrass, D. R., *Ceylon: an export economy in transition*. Homewood, Ill., 1966
Williams, H., *Ceylon*. London, 1963
Wriggins, W. H., *Ceylon: Dilemma of a new nation*. Princeton Univ. Press, 1960

GHANA

HISTORY. The State of Ghana came into existence on 6 March 1957 when the former Colony of the Gold Coast and the Trusteeship Territory of Togoland attained Dominion status. The name of the country recalls a powerful monarchy which from the 4th to the 13th century A.D. ruled the region of the middle Niger.

The Ghana Independence Act received the royal assent on 7 Feb. 1957. The General Assembly of the United Nations in Dec. 1956 approved the termination of British administration in Togoland and the union of Togoland with the Gold Coast on the latter's attainment of independence.

The country was declared a republic within the Commonwealth on 1 July 1960.

National flag: Red, gold, green (horizontal); a black star in the centre.
National anthem: Hail the name of Ghana.

CONSTITUTION AND GOVERNMENT. On 24 Feb. 1966 the army with the co-operation of the police took over the government while Dr Kwame Nkrumah, the then head of state, was in Peking on his way to Hanoi. The

K

'National Liberation Council' dismissed Dr Nkrumah and his ministers, suspended the constitution and parliament, banned the Convention People's Party and all other political parties.

In accordance with the provision of the new Constitution for the Second Republic of Ghana promulgated on 22 Aug. 1969, a 3-man Presidential Commission was established. The Commission, inaugurated on 3 Sept. 1969, was dissolved on 30 June 1970.

On 28 Aug. 1970 Edward Akufo-Ardo was elected President for a 4-year term. He took office on 31 Oct. 1970. The creation of the Council of State which was inaugurated on 9 Oct. 1969 is made up of 12 members.

The Progress Party won 105 of the 140 seats in the National Assembly at general elections held on 29 Aug. 1969. On 3 Sept. 1969 Dr K. A. Busia was appointed Prime Minister. The cabinet in Jan. 1970 was as follows:

Interior: S. D. Dombo. *Defence:* J. K. Lamptey. *Attorney-General:* Victor Owusu. *Foreign Affairs:* William Ofori-Atta. *Works:* S. W. Awuku-Darko. *Housing* and *Town Planning:* Dr W. Bruce-Konuah. *Transport and Communications:* Harona Esseku. *Finance:* J. H. Mensah. *Youth and Rural Development:* A. A. Munufie. *Trade Industries* R. A. Quarshie. *Labour and Co-operatives:* Jatoe Kaleo. *Agriculture:* Dr K. Safo-Adu. *Land and Mineral Resources:* R. R. Amponsah. *Health:* G. D. Ampaw.

REGIONAL ORGANIZATION. Ghana is divided into 9 regions: Eastern, Western, Ashanti, Northern, Volta, Central, Upper, Brong-Ahafo; and the Greater Accra Area. Each region is administered by a Chief Executive.

DIPLOMATIC REPRESENTATIVES

Country	Ghana representative	Foreign representative
Afghánistán	—	Muhammed M. Shafiq
Algeria	Y. A. Osebre	A. Bouchouk
Argentina	—	A. E. Acuna
Australia [1]	J. Owusu-Acheampong	John Mill McMillan
Austria	—	Dr A. Otto
Belgium	—	George Barthelemy
Brazil	E. C. Quist-Therson	Viera de Mello
Britain [1]	A. B. Attafua	Henry S. H. Stanley
Bulgaria	—	D. I. Tchorbadjiev
Canada [1]	Maj. S. K. Anthony, MBE	Douglas B. Hicks
Ceylon [1]	—	M. R. Perera
Congo (K.)	R. E. K. Matanawi	H. E. D. Kaninda
Czechoslovakia	J. T. Afrifa	Josef Zabortský
Dahomey	E. O. K. Dumoga	—
Denmark	Mrs Bertha Amonoo-Neizer	Mrs J. N. G. C. Wright
Ethiopia	H. R. Amonoo	Goytan Petros
France	Dr K. Dsane-Selby	Pierre Authonioz
Germany (West)	F. L. Bartels	Helmut Muller
Hungary	—	Janos Lorinez-Nagy
India [1]	P. K. Omusu-Anshah	Amrik S. Mehta
Israel	Maj.-Gen. S. J. A. Otu	A. Cohen
Italy	H. V. H. Sekyi	Luigi Gasbarri
Ivory Coast	Dr Claude Ennin	Christope M. Koreki
Japan	S. K. Williams	Saburo Kimoto
Kenya [1]	E. K. Otoo	—
Lebanon	O. H. Kwasi Brew	Said El-Hibri
Lesotho	—	P. M. Mabathoana
Liberia	Mrs A. Obetsebi-Lamptey	A. B. Cranshaw
Malaysia	—	Yusof Ariff

[1] High Commissioner.   No figure = Ambassador.

Country	Ghana representative	Foreign representative
Mali	Alhaji Abu Wemah	Mahmoud Ould Aly
Mexico	A. K. Adu	E. Madero
Morocco	J. E. K. Osafo	Mohamed A. El Alaoui
Netherlands	E. P. K. Seddoh	Dr J. M. Vos
Niger	—	Tiecoura Alzouma
Nigeria [1]	Maj.-Gen. N. A. Aferi	V. A. Adegoroye
Norway	—	L. G. Onsager
Pakistan [1]	Maj.-Gen. C. C. Bruce	Ali Arshad
Philippines	—	F. M. Maglaya
Poland	—	Z. Krolak
Romania	—	G. Idson
Saudi Arabia	—	A. A. Mubarak
Senegal	S. K. Odamtten	Andre Colbary
Sierra Leone [1]	E. B. Awooner-Williams	J. C. W. Porter [2]
Spain	—	J. M. T. De Bas
Sweden	—	B. Arvidson
Switzerland	K. B. Asante	F. Schnyder
Togo	S. G. Antor	S. T. Babelene
Tunisia	—	R. B. Baouab
Turkey	—	H. H. Anli
Uganda [1]	A. E. K. Oforti-Atta	L. C. E. Avua
USSR	J. Ownsu-Ansah	V. S. Safronchuk
UAR	K. Owusu-Sekyere	A. A. Al-S. El-Moursi
USA	E. M. Debrah	T. W. McElhiney
Upper Volta	M. Bukari	Victor Kabore
Venezuela	—	Dr A. H. Rovati
Yugoslavia	J. B. Lomotey	Trifum Nikolic

[1] High Commissioner.   [2] Chargé d'Affaires.   No figure = Ambassador.

AREA AND POPULATION. The area of Ghana is 92,100 sq. miles (238,537 sq. km); census population 1970 (prelim.), 8,545,561.

The capital is Accra (population, 1970, 663,880).

Regions	Area (sq. miles)	Population census 1970	Capital	Population census 1970
Eastern	8,750	1,262.882	Koforidua	69.804
Western	9,494	768.312	Sekoni	161.071
Central	3,656	892.593	Cape Coast	71.594
Ashanti	9,700	1,477.397	Kumasi	342.986
Brong-Ahafo	14,900	762.673	Sekondi	61.772
Northern	27,122	728.572	Tamale	98.818
Volta	8,000	947,012	Ho	46.348
Upper	10,478	857.295	Bolgatanga	93.182
Greater Accra	—	848,825	Accra	633,880

Other chief towns (population, census, 1970): Sekondi/Takoradi, 161,071; Asamankese, 101,144; Nsawam, 57,350; Oda, 40,740; Obuasi, 40,001; Winneba, 36,104; Keta, 27,461; Swedru (Agona), 23,843.

Estimated birth rate, between 47 and 52 per 1,000; death rate, about 23 per 1,000.

EDUCATION. In the 1968–69 academic year the combined enrolment in the 2 independent universities—the University of Ghana and the University of Science and Technology—together with the University College of Cape Coast, was 5,035.

The Institute of Adult Education (affiliated to the University of Ghana), established in 1962, had in 1967 an enrolment of 5,599; this institute has established workers' colleges in the principal towns.

Compulsory, fee-free primary and middle school education was introduced in Sept. 1961. Secondary and technical education became free in Sept. 1965. Primary schools in 1969 numbered 7,293; they were attended by 1,016,457 children; 3,200 middle schools had an enrolment of 381,551.

There were 108 secondary schools with 46,512 students, while 4,011 were in training at the 11 government technical institutes. The number of teacher-training colleges was 81, with 18,728 trainees. In 1969 there were 25,000 trained teachers.

From Sept. 1967 pupils began to pay an annual nominal fee of 1·50, 3 and 6 new cedis each in the primary, middle and secondary schools respectively, for the supply of text-books and school materials and this was extended in Sept. 1970 to secondary schools and pupils pay 10 new cedis per annum.

RESEARCH. The West African Inter-Territorial Research Organization with its headquarters in Accra has been abolished, and each country (Ghana, Nigeria, Sierra Leone and Gambia) has taken over the research units within its borders. In Ghana its functions have been taken over by the Ghana Academy of Sciences (established on 23 Jan. 1963) which plans and co-ordinates all activities of the 10 research institutes of Ghana.

NEWSPAPERS. There are 3 daily, 3 bi-weekly and 4 weekly papers, and some 6 magazines.

JUSTICE. The judicial power of Ghana is vested in the Judiciary with the Chief Justice as the Head. It has jurisdiction in all civil and criminal matters, including those relating to the new Constitution of Ghana.

The Courts of Ghana are constituted as follows: (1) *Superior Court of Judicature*, consisting of the Supreme Court of Ghana, the Court of Appeal and the High Court of Justice. (2) *Inferior Courts* embracing the Circuit Courts, the District Courts and such other inferior courts as may be provided by law, *e.g.*, Juvenile Courts.

The Supreme Court. The Supreme Court is the final Court of Appeal in and for Ghana. It has all the powers, authority and jurisdiction vested in any Court established under the Constitution or any other law. It consists of the Chief Justice as President, together with not less than 6 other Justices of the Supreme Court and such other Justices of the Superior Courts as the Chief Justice may request. The Court is duly constituted by not less than 5 Justices.

The Court of Appeal. The Court of Appeal has jurisdiction throughout Ghana to hear and determine appeals from any judgement decree or order of the High Court of Justice and such other appellate jurisdiction as may be conferred upon it. It consists of the Chief Justice, with not less than 5 Justices of the Court of Appeal and such other Justices of the Superior Courts of Judicature as the Chief Justice may request. It is, however, duly constituted by any 3 Justices thereof, the most senior presiding. Divisions of the Appeal Court may be created, subject to the discretion of the Chief Justice.

The High Court of Justice. This Court has jurisdiction in civil and criminal matters as well as those relating to industrial and labour disputes, including administrative complaints. It has supervisory jurisdiction over all inferior and traditional courts, but has no power in a trial for offences involving treason, to convict any person for any offence other than treason. The High Court consists of the Chief Justice, not less than 12 Puisne Judges and such other Judges of the Superior Court as may be requested by the Chief Justice. It is constituted by between 1 Justice (with or without a jury) to 3 Justices for specific offences.

The country has been divided into 7 circuits, and there are 11 Circuit Judges sitting in these courts with original jurisdiction in all criminal cases, except offences where the maximum punishment is death. The original jurisdiction in civil matters is restricted to cases where the subject-matter of the suit is not more than N₵4,000 (or £2,000). District Courts (Grade I and II): sitting throughout the country in the magisterial districts. Juvenile Courts, dealing with persons under the age of 17, have been established in Accra, Cape Coast, Sekondi, Kumasi and Koforidua.

Police. The establishment of the force was (1969) 427 police officers, 1 director of music, 687 inspectors and 17,565 other ranks, distributed over 558 stations.

WELFARE. Medical facilities include 43 government hospitals, 49 health centres, 3 university hospitals, 2 mental hospitals, 4 leprosaria, 6 military hospitals, 1 prison hospital, 42 mission hospitals, 13 mines hospitals and 31 private hospitals. In addition, there are 11 nurses and midwives training schools.

An intensive health post building programme, which began in 1968, is being actively pursued for the development of basic health services. It is expected that when the programme is completed in 1978, there will be about 205 posts and so far 32 are in operation.

FINANCE. Currency. The monetary unit is the New Cedi (N₵), divided into 100 New Pesewas (NP) and equivalent to £0·41 (N₵2.45 to the £) or US$0.98. Notes are issued of 1, 5 and 10 NP; copper coins of ½ and 1 NP, and cupro-nickel coins of 2½, 5, 10 and 20 NP.

Budget. Revenue and expenditure for fiscal years ending 30 June (excluding Ghana Railway and Takoradi Harbour accounts), in N₵1,000:

	1966–67	1967–68	1968–69
Revenue[1]	241,465	300,247	291,177
Expenditure[2]	301,061	344,589	353,591

[1] Excludes redemption of loans.
[2] Excludes contribution to sinking funds, repayment of loans, loans and refunds of revenue.

The main items of expenditure envisaged for 1969–70 were (in N₵1,000): Social services, 132,944; general services, 144,841; economic services, 70,534; community services, 41,687.

PUBLIC DEBT. On 30 June 1969 total public debt was N₵1,083m. of which external debt was N₵503·8m. and internal debt N₵579·2m. The external debt includes suppliers credit amounting to N₵324·8m. (provisional). Sinking Fund in connexion with funded debt was N₵13·2m.

DEFENCE. The Ministry of Defence is responsible for the armed services, the military academy and the workers' brigade. The Military Academy provides a 2-year course for army officers, a 1-year course for later entrants in the flying-training school and a preliminary 6-month course for navy cadets.

Army. The Ghana Army consists of 6 infantry battalions, 1 reconnaissance squadron with armoured cars, and ancillary units. Total strength, about 14,000. There is also a volunteer force which supplies a cadre of reserves.

Navy. The Ghana Navy was formed in 1959. It comprises 2 corvettes, a coastal minesweeper, 2 inshore minesweepers, 2 seaward defence boats, 3 patrol boats, a training ship and a maintenance repair craft. A frigate was built in Britain. Naval personnel (1970): 800 officers and ratings.

Air Force. The Ghana Air Force was formed in 1959, when an Air Force Training School was established at Accra. It has, for training and transport operations, 8 Caribou, 7 Otter and 11 Beaver transports, all built in Canada; 1 HS.125 twin-jet light transport, 3 Heron VIP transports, 7 Chipmunk trainers and 2 Wessex and 3 Whirlwind turbine-engined helicopters built in England; 3 Hughes 300 and 3 H-19 helicopters built in the US; and 5 Italian-built Aermacchi M.B.326 armed jet trainers. There are air bases at Takoradi and Tamale. Aerial survey and crop-spraying for the civil administration are part-duties of the Air Force.

AGRICULTURE. Cocoa is by far the most important crop and covers about 5m. acres. There has been a considerable increase in cocoa yields as a result of the Capsid control and the introduction of improved varieties. Coffee, improved types of oil palm and coconut are being planted on an increased scale and production from these crops is increasing. A start has been made in the planting of Clonal rubber in south-west Ghana. In the south-east coastal belt irrigation works are being constructed and black-clay farming is being tested in the Accra plains.

Of the main foodstuffs in south and central Ghana, maize, rice, cassava, plantain, groundnuts, yam and cocoyam predominate. Tobacco is proving an attractive and very important cash crop in food-crop-producing areas.

In northern Ghana the chief food crops are groundnuts, rice, maize, guinea corn, millet and yams, with tobacco as an important cash crop. Land planning in northern Ghana extends over 4,442 sq. miles of catchment area, and some 4,000 farmers have adopted mixed farming methods using bullocks and ploughs. In 1966, 422,000 long tons of cocoa were produced.

The Department of Agriculture has been abolished. A State Farm Corporation has been created. There were in 1963, 105 state farms (most of them experimental farms taken over from the former Department of Agriculture and the Agriculture Development Corporation) and 35 Workers' Brigade farms with over 20,000 acres under maize, guinea corn, rice, vegetables, tobacco (1966 production, 1·3m. lb. from 7,224 acres) and cotton. The United Ghana Farmers' Council Co-operatives and individual farmers are growing rubber, coffee and other crops to diversify agriculture.

FORESTRY. The total area of closed forest is 31,760 sq. miles, of which 5,851 sq. miles are reserved. The area of savannah (not closed) forests is 60,283 sq. miles, of which 2,496 sq. miles are reserved. Exports (1968) of logs, 20·1m. cu. ft; of sawn timber (1965), 6·2m. cu. ft.

The destruction of unreserved forests by farming is threatening the timber supply for exports. The Protected Timber Lands Act, 1959, as well as further reservation and afforestation try to counteract this trend.

ANIMAL HEALTH. Livestock, 1969: Cattle, 580,253; sheep, 645,529; goats, 569,507; horses (1966), 2,523; pigs, 112,488; poultry, 2·73m. The Central Veterinary Laboratory is located at Pong-Tamale under the Veterinary Research Officer. The efficient control of rinderpest and bovine pleuro-pneumonia, the two main killing diseases of cattle, has made it possible to quadruple the cattle in the past 20 years. The control of imported livestock is effected by 8 quarantine stations along the frontier.

FISHERIES. Fishing is carried on by about 150,000 fishermen with 10,000 canoes operating from open beaches or with 311 motor craft from harbours. The equipping of the canoes with outboard motors is assuming greater importance. The total catch in 1966 was about 56,000 tons.

The Ghana Fishing Corporation has been set up to take over the fisheries division of the former Agricultural Development Corporation.

MINING. In 1967 gold production was 762,600 fine oz. (1968: 727,100); manganese ore, 509,724 short tons (1968: 406,800), and bauxite, 274,650 long tons (1968: 280,200). Construction on the Volta Aluminium Co. smelter at Tema began in 1964 and production started in 1966.

COMMERCE. Total trade, in N₵1,000, for calendar years:

	1965	1966	1967	1968	1969
Imports	320,657	251,209	261,523	314,032	354,391
Exports	226,985	191,394	245,122	338,782	333,264

Principal exports (in N₵1,000)	1964	1965	1966	1967	1968	1969
Cocoa	145,560	148,788	103,057	130,670	185,600	158,327
Timber	29,384	24,689	20,916	22,394	28,616	39,227
Gold	20,615	19,052	10,884	12,695	16,258	24,178
Diamonds	12,241	13,517	10,843	12,636	17,430	13,867
Manganese	8,673	9,571	12,151	9,233	10,546	7,017
Bauxite	1,285	1,315	1,488	1,593	..	..

In 1969 the most important items of imports were food, mineral fuels, chemicals, manufactured goods, machinery and transport equipment.

Total trade (in £1,000 sterling) between Ghana and UK (British Board of Trade returns):

	1966	1967	1968	1969	1970
Imports to UK	18,489	24,118	35,037	43,304	38,948
Exports from UK	30,609	30,373	32,612	36,746 ⎱	38,380
Re-exports from UK	629	613	562	729 ⎰	

West African Common Market. On 4 May 1967, 12 West African countries (Dahomey, Ghana, Ivory Coast, Liberia, Mali, Mauritania, Niger, Nigeria, Senegal, Sierra Leone, Togo and Upper Volta) signed articles of association in Accra, setting up a common market for goods and services among them and eliminating customs and trade barriers.

NATIONAL INCOME. The GNP (in N₵1m.) was 2,035 in 1968 (1967: 1,757).

RAILWAYS. The total railway mileage open on 1 Dec. 1969 was 592, including a link of 51 miles between the Central Province line at Achiasi and the Accra–Kumasi line at Kotoku opened in Feb. 1956. The main line runs from Takoradi to Kumasi, thence to Accra (355 miles); with branches: Takoradi Junction–Sekondi (3 miles), Tarkwa–Prestea (19 miles), Hunni Valley–Kade (99 miles, Central line), Dunkwa–Awaso (46 miles), Achimota–Tema (16 miles), Achiasi–Kotoku (51 miles) and Accra–Accra Beach (2 miles). All are 3 ft 6 in. gauge. During 1968–69 capital expenditure was N₵1·71m., revenue was N₵0·05m. and expenditure (including renewals) N₵10·47m.

ROADS. The total mileage of roads maintained by the Public Works Department in 1967 was 6,238, of which 2,444 miles were bitumen surfaced and 3,794 miles gravel surfaced.

The number of vehicles with valid licences at 31 Dec. 1965 was 52,601. The principal categories were: Cars, 27,425 (including taxis); goods vehicles, 13,911; motor cycles, 3,816; special-purpose vehicles, 2,450.

SHIPPING. The chief port is Takoradi; the 'surf' ports at Accra, Winneba, Cape Coast and Keta ceased to operate when a new harbour was opened on 11 Feb. 1962 at Tema, 17 miles east of Accra. In 1966, 1,478,103 tons of cargo were imported and 1,862,984 tons were exported by 2,034 ships.

AVIATION. There are 4 major aerodromes in Ghana, situated at Accra, Takoradi, Kumasi and Tamale; and 3 airstrips for domestic services. Accra airport is an international airport. The following airlines operate scheduled services: Ghana Airways, BOAC, Air France, Nigerian Airways, Air Mali, United Arab Airlines, KLM, Swissair, BUA and several other companies. Total aircraft movement in 1968 was 34,794.

Ghana Airways, operating domestic, regional and international services, was incorporated in Accra on 4 July 1958. On 14 Feb. 1961 it bought up the 40% share held by BOAC.

POST. There were (31 Dec. 1967) 2,190 miles of telegraph land wire, 20,948 miles of telephone trunks, 181 post offices and 659 postal agencies. There were 359 telephone exchanges and 526 call offices with (1968) 38,225 telephones in use and 29,227 miles of underground and overhead land wires in the exchange areas. There are internal wireless stations at Accra, Kumasi, Bawku, Lawra, Kete-Krachi, Tamale, Yendi, Kpandu and Tumu.

BANKING. The Bank of Ghana was established in Feb. 1957 as the central bank of the country. The Ghana Commercial Bank, also established in Feb.

1957, is the former Bank of the Gold Coast. It is a purely commercial institution and has 100 branches in the country and one in London. Barclays Bank DCO has 58 branches and agencies and the Standard Bank of West Africa Co. has 42 branches.

The Ghana National Investment Bank, opened in June 1963, is a finance-cum-development agency. The former post office savings bank has been transformed into the Ghana Savings Bank.

BOOKS OF REFERENCE

Digest of Statistics. Accra. Quarterly (from May 1953)
Trade Directory of the Republic of Ghana. 5th ed. London, 1967
The Volta River Project. 3 vols. HMSO, 1956
Acquah, L., *Accra Survey.* Univ. of London Press, 1958
Afrifa, A. A., *The Ghana coup 24th February 1966.* London, 1966
Alexander, H. T., *African Tightrope.* London, 1965
Austin, D., *Politics in Ghana, 1946–60.* OUP, 1964
Boateng, E. A., *A Geography of Ghana.* 2nd ed. CUP, 1966
Hilton, T. E., *Ghana Population Atlas.* Edinburgh, 1960
Lystad, R. A., *The Ashanti.* Rutgers Univ. Press, 1958
Manshard, W., *Die geographischen Grundlagen der Wirtschaft Ghanas.* Wiesbaden, 1961
Timothy, B., *Kwame Kkrumah: his rise to power.* London, 1964
Ward, W. E. F., *A History of Ghana.* London, 1959
Wills, J. B. (ed.), *Agriculture and Land Use in Ghana.* OUP, 1962

MALAYSIA

On 16 Sept. 1963 Malaysia came into being, consisting of the Federation of Malaya, the State of Singapore and the colonies of North Borneo (renamed Sabah) and Sarawak. The agreement between the UK and the 4 territories was signed on 9 July (Cmnd. 2094); by it, the UK relinquished sovereignty over Singapore, North Borneo and Sarawak from independence day and extended the 1957 defence agreement with Malaya to apply to Malaysia. Malaysia became automatically a member of the Commonwealth of Nations. *See* map in THE STATESMAN'S YEAR-BOOK, 1964–65.

On 9 Aug. 1965, by a mutual agreement dated 7 Aug. 1965 between Malaysia and Singapore, Singapore seceded from Malaysia to become an independent Sovereign nation.

CONSTITUTION AND GOVERNMENT. The constitution of Malaysia is based on the constitution of the former Federation of Malaya, but includes safeguards for the special interests of Sabah and Sarawak.

The federal capital is Kuala Lumpur. The official language is Malay.

The constitution provides for one of the 9 Rulers of the Malay States to be elected from among themselves to be the Yang di-Pertuan Agong (Supreme Head of the Federation). He holds office for a period of 5 years. The Rulers also elect from among themselves a Deputy Supreme Head of State, also for a period of 5 years.

Supreme Head of State (Yang di-Pertuan Agong): HM Sultan Abdul Halim Mu'adzam Shah ibni Al-Marhum Sultan Badlishah, DUK, DK, DMN, SPMK, Ruler of Kedah (elected 21 Sept. 1970).

Sultan of Pahang: HRH Sultan Abu Bakar Ri'ayatuddin Al-Mu'adzam Shah ibni Al-Marhum Al-Mu'tasim Billah Al-Sultan Abdullah, DK, DMN, acceded 28 May 1933.

Raja of Perlis: HRH Tuanku Syed Putra ibni Al-Marhum Syed Hassan Jamalullail, DK, DKM, DMN, SMN, SPMP, acceded 12 March 1949.

Sultan of Kedah: HRH Sultan Abdul Halim Muadzam Shah ibni Al-Marhum Sultan Badlishah, DUK, DK, DMN, SPMK, acceded 20 Feb. 1959.

Sultan of Johore: HRH Sultan Ismail ibni Al-Marhum Sultan Ibrahim, DK, DMN, SMN, SPMJ, acceded 10 Feb. 1960.

Sultan of Kelantan: HRH Al-Sultan Yahya Petra ibni Al-Marhum Sultan Ibrahim, DK, DMN, SPMK, SJMK, SMN, acceded 17 July 1961.

Sultan of Selangor: HRH Sultan Salahudd inAbdul Aziz Shah ibni Al-Marhum Sultan Hisamuddin 'Alam Shah Al-Haj, DK, DMN, SPMS, acceded 28 June 1961.

Sultan of Perak: HRH Sultan Idris Al-Mutawakkil Alallahi Shah ibni Al-Marhum Sultan Iskandar Shah Kadasallah, DK, DMN, SPMP, acceded 26 Oct. 1963.

Yang di-Pertuan Besar of Negri Sembilan: HRH Tuanku Ja'afar ibni Al-Marhum Tuanku Abdul Rahman, DMN, acceded 8 April, 1968.

Regent of Trengganu: HH Tengku Mahmud ibni Sultan Ismail Nasiruddin Shah, DK, appointed 19 Sept. 1965.

Governor of Malacca: HE Tun Haji Abdul Malek bin Yusuf, SMN, appointed 31 Aug. 1959; re-appointed 31 Aug. 1963 and 31 Aug. 1967.

Governor of Sarawak: HE Tun Abang Haji Openg bin Abang Sapi'ee, SMN, PNBS, appointed 16 Sept. 1963, re-appointed 16 Sept. 1965.

Yang di-Pertua Negara Sabah: HE Tun Pengiran Haji Ahmad Raffae bin Orang Kaya Pengiran Haji Omar, SMN, PDK, appointed 16 Sept. 1965.

Governor of Penang: HE Tun Syed Sheh bin Syed Abdullah Shahabuddin, SMN, appointed 31 Aug. 1967.

Parliament consists of the Yang di-Pertuan Agong and two Majlis (Houses of Parliament), known as the Dewan Negara (Senate) of 58 members and Dewan Ra'ayat (House of Representatives) of 144 members. Malaya has 104, Sabah 16 and Sarawak 24 representatives. Appointment to the Senate is for 6 years. The maximum life of the House of Representatives is 5 years, subject to its dissolution at any time by the Yang di-Pertuan Agong on the advice of his Ministers.

The elections to the House of Representatives, held on 25 April 1964, returned the following members: Alliance Party, 89; Pan-Malayan Islamic Party, 9; People's Progressive Party, 2; Socialist Front, 2; United Democratic Party, 1; People's Action Party, 1.

The last election which was held on 10 May 1969 was not completed due to the disturbances which were followed by the Emergency. The Emergency ended 19 Feb. 1971.

The Cabinet was in Feb. 1971 composed as follows:

Prime Minister, Foreign Affairs and Defence: Tun Abdul Razak, SMN.

Deputy Prime Minister and Home Affairs: Tun Dr Ismail bin Dato Abdul Rahman, SMN. *Finance:* Tun Tan Siew Sin, SSM, JP. *Works, Posts and Telecommunications:* Tun V. T. Sambanthan, SSM. *Health:* Tan Sri Jaji Sardon bin Haji Jubir. *Commerce and Industry:* Mohammed Khir Johari. *Sarawak Affairs:* Tan Sri Temenggong Jugah Anak Barieng, PMN, PDK, PNBS. *Labour:* Tan Sri V. Manickavasagam. *Agriculture and Land:* Tan Sri Mohammed Ghazali bin Haji Jawi. *National and Rural Development:* Abdul Ghafar bin Baba. *Transport:* Dato Ganie Gilong. *Information and Culture:* Dato Hamzah bin Dato Abu Samah. *Welfare Services:* Tan Sri Fatimah binte Haji Hashim. *Attorney General and Justice:* Tan Sri Abdul Kadir bin Yusof. *Education:* Hussein bin Onn. *Minister with Special Duties, attached to Prime Minister's Department, Head of National Unity and General Planning Unit:* Tan Sri Mohammad Ghazali bin Shafie. *Ministers without Portfolio:* Tan Sri Ong Yoke Lin; Lee Siok Yew; Dato Ong Kee Hui.

DIPLOMATIC REPRESENTATIVES

Country	Malaysia representative	Foreign representative
Australia[1]	Tan Sri Donald Stephens, PSM	J. R. Rowland
Austria	Enche A. F. bin Zakaria [2]	Dr Werner Sautter
Belgium	Tan Sri A. H. bin Haji Jumat	Jean Bourgaux
Brazil	Tan Sri Ong Yoke Lin, PMN	L. E. do Nascimento e Silva
Britain	Tan Sri Abdul Jamil Rais, PMN	Sir Michael Walker, KCMG
Burma	Enche A. R. bin Jalal	U Pe Kin
Canada[1]	Enche Zakaria bin Haji Mohd. Ali	J. G. Hadwen
Ceylon[1]	Tengku Indra Putra, DK, PMN	A. C. L. Ratwatte
Denmark	Tan Sri A. H. bin Haji Jumat	—
Ethiopia	Enche Kassin bin Hussein	—
France	Enche Anthony Yeo Keat Seorg [2]	Barthelemy Epinat
Germany (West)	Tan Sri Philip. H. H. Kuok, PSM, SPMJ	Gerhard Fischer
Greece	—	John Yannakakis
India[1]	Raja Aznam bin Raja Haji Ahmad	K. C. Nair
Indonesia	Tan Sri Ya'acob bin Abdul Latiff, PSM, JMN	H. A. Thalib Gelar Depati Santio Bawo
Iran	Enche A. Zainal Abidin	Abdel H. Hamzavi
Italy	Tan Sri Wong Pow Nee, PMN	Dr Enrico Carrara
Japan	Enche Hussain bin Mohd. Osman, JSM, AMN	Taisaku Kojima
Jordan	Enche Kamaruddin Ariff	Dr Khaled Rsheidat [2]
Korea (South)	Enche Toh Chor Keat	Dr Hongkee Karl, PMN
Kuwait	Enche Kamaruddin Ariff	—
Morocco	Enche A. H. bin Pawanchee [2]	Dr Mohammad Saadani
Nepál	—	Gyandndra Bahadur Karki [2]
Netherlands	Tan Sri A. H. bin Haji Jumat	G. J. de Graag
New Zealand[1]	Enche Lim Taik Choon	R. L. Hutchens
Nigeria[1]	Enche T. H. Yogaratnam (Acting)	—
Pakistan[1]	Enche Mohd. S. bin Sheikh Ibrahim	S. Irtizza Hussein
Philippines	Enche Hashim bin Sultan	R. S. Busnego
Saudi Arabia	Enche Kamaruddin Ariff	Hussain Fatanay
Singapore[1]	Tan Sri Jamal bin Abdul Latiff, PSM, DPMT, DPMK, DPMJ, GCCT	Maurice Baker
Sudan	Tuan Haji Khalid bin Awang Osman	—
Sweden	—	Count Axel Lewenhaupt
Switzerland	—	Dr Theo Schmidlin
Thailand	Gen. Tan Sri A. H. Bidin, PMN	Maj.-Gen. Sangkadis Diskul
Turkey	—	Hikmet Hayri Anli
USSR	Tan Sri Zainton Ibrahim bin Ahmad, PSM	V. N. Kuznetsov
UAR	Tuan Haji Khalid bin Awang Osman	Mohd. Khair El-Din Nassar
USA	Tan Sri Ong Yoke Lin, PMN	Jack Whydman
Vietnam (South)	—	Nguyen Duy Quang
Yugoslavia	—	Victor Repic

[1] High Commissioner   [2] Minister.   No figure = Ambassador.

POPULATION. End-1968 estimates gave a total of 8,899,030 for West Malaysia, 622,480 in Sabah and 933,609 in Sarawak.

JUSTICE. The Courts of Judicature Act, 1964, established the Federal Court of Malaysia and 2 High Courts in Malaya and Borneo. The Federal Court consists of the Lord President, the Chief Justices of the High Courts and 3 Federal Judges. Each of the High Courts consists of the respective Chief Justices and Puisne Judges.

FINANCE. Currency. Bank Negara Malaysia (Central Bank of Malaysia) assumed sole currency issuing authority in Malaysia on 12 June 1967. The unit of currency is the Malaysian dollar having a par value equivalent to 0·290299 gramme of fine gold or the equivalent of US$32.6667 cents. Prior to June 1967, currency in Malaysia was issued by the Board of Commissioners of Currency, Malaya and British Borneo, which was also the currency issuing authority in Singapore and Brunei. The Malayan dollar issued by the Board ceased to be legal tender on 16 Jan. 1969. At the time when Malaysia, Singapore and Brunei issued their separate currencies, arrangements were instituted for the free interchangeability of the three currencies in order to minimize any inconvenience which would otherwise arise for residents of one country travelling to the other two countries. The effect of these interchangeability arrangements is that Malaysian notes and coins are accepted at face value in Singapore and Brunei, and Singapore and Brunei notes and coin are accepted at face value in Malaysia.

The unit of currency issued by Bank Negara Malaysia is the Malaysian dollar, which is divided into 100 cents. Currency notes are of denominations of $1, 5, 10, 50 100 and $1,000. Coins are of denominations of 1 cent. 5, 10, 20, 50 cents and $1. The circulation of currency on 31 July 1970 was M$1,019·15m.

In Dec. 1968 the rate of exchange was £1 = M$7.34; US$1 = M$3.06.

Budget. Revenue and expenditure for calendar years, in M$1.000:

	1967	1968	1969[1]	1970[2]
Revenue	1,833,618	1,889,975	2,060,001	2,262,673
Expenditure	1,897,222	1,901,000	1,956,399	2,282,230
Development expenditure	625,190	618,692	804,980	961,181

[1] Revised. [2] Estimates.

DEFENCE. Army. The active army is an all regular force consisting of 6 brigade groups organized in 2 infantry divisions. Each brigade consists of infantry, reconnaissance, artillery, signals, engineers and supported by adequate logistics units. The Army is still at its phase of expansion in view of the heavy responsibility it has to carry in post-1971, as a result of the withdrawal of the British Armed Forces. The total strength is approximately 40,000.

Navy. Command of the Royal Malaysian Navy is exercised by the Chief of the Naval Staff from the integrated Ministry of Defence in Kuala Lumpur. The main naval bases are KD Malaya situated on Singapore Island and KD Sri Labuan on Labuan Island. These establishments are responsible for the operation and administration of the ships, and KD Malaya for the training of personnel.

The ships include 2 frigates, 6 coastal minesweepers, 2 inshore minesweepers, 4 fast patrol boats, 28 patrol craft and 1 survey vessel. The peace-time tasks include fishery protection and anti-piracy patrols. Naval personnel: 4,000 officers and ratings.

Air Force. Formed on 1 June 1958, the Royal Malaysian Air Force is equipped primarily to provide limited air defence and air support for the Army, Navy and Police. Its secondary rôle is to render assistance to Government departments and civilian organizations, especially during periods of national disasters. There are 11 squadrons, of which 8 operate transport aircraft. Equipment includes 10 Commonwealth CA-27 Sabre Mk. 32 jet fighters, 20 Canadair CL-41G Tebuan dual-purpose light jet strike and training aircraft, 8 Herald twin-turboprop transports, 12 Caribou twin-engined STOL transports, 2 Heron and 4 Dove light liaison/communications aircraft, 16 Sikorsky S-61A-4 heavy troop and cargo transport helicopters, 27 Alouette helicopters, 12 piston-engined Provost basic trainers and 2 H.S.125 Merpati twin-jet executive transports.

Volunteer Forces. The Army Volunteer Force (Territorial Army) consists of first-line infantry, signals, engineer and logistics units able to take the field with the active army, and a second-line organization to provide local defence. There is also a small Naval Volunteer Reserve with Headquarters in Penang and Kuala Lumpur. The Royal Malaysian Air Force Volunteer Reserve has both air and ground elements.

Royal Military College. The College, founded in 1953, is now accommodated at Sungei Besi near Kuala Lumpur. It has a Boys' Wing which prepares young Malaysians 'to take their places as officers in the Armed Forces, in the higher divisions of the public service and as leaders in the professional, commercial and industrial life of the country'. The Cadet Wing trains officers for both regular and short service commissions.

PLANNING. The first 5-year plan, 1966–70, envisages an outlay of M$10,500m. It has been the first phase of a 20-year 'perspective plan'.

TRADE. Total trade (in £1,000 sterling) of Malaysia (including Singapore until 1965) with UK (British Board of Trade returns):

	1966	1967	1968	1969	1970
Imports to UK	32,136	28,041	35,682	33,549	46,596
Exports from UK	50,474	43,074	47,850	46,628 }	60,426
Re-exports from UK	389	322	386	761 }	

POST. The Postal Services Department of Malaysia is under the portfolio of the Minister of Works, Posts and Telecommunications and is headed by the Postmaster-General, Malaysia.

BANKING. Thirty-eight banks were operating in 1969; of these 16 were incorporated in Malaysia and 5 in Singapore; 9 banks were incorporated in other countries. Total deposits amounted to M$3,306m. at the end of Dec. 1969.

BOOKS OF REFERENCE

STATISTICAL INFORMATION. The Department of Statistics, Malaysia, Kuala Lumpur, was set up in 1963, taking over from the Department of Statistics, States of Malaya. Chief Statistician: R. Chander. Main publications: *West Malaysia Monthly* and *Annual Statistics of External Trade*; *West Malaysia Statistical Bulletin* (monthly): *Rubber Statistics* (monthly); *Rice Supplement to Bulletin* (annual); *Rubber Statistics Handbook* (annual): *Census of Manufacturing Industries 1963*; *Survey of Manufacturing Industries* (1964); *Population Census Report 1957*; *National Accounts of West Malaysia* (1960–66); *West Malaysia Industrial Classification* (1967); *States of Malaya Employment, Unemployment and Under-employment* (1962); *Malaysia External Trade* (quarterly, from (1965); *Census of Distributive Trade* (1966).

Books about Malaysia. Singapore, National Library, 1965.
The Economic Aspects of Malaysia. Report by the International Bank. Singapore, 1963
Harrison, B., *South-east Asia, a short history.* 3rd ed. London, 1966
Purcell, V., *Malaysia.* London, 1965.—*The Chinese in S.E. Asia.* New ed. OUP, 1965
Wang Gungwu (ed.), *Malaysia.* New York, 1965

STATES OF MALAYA
Negeri Tanah Melayu

CONSTITUTION AND GOVERNMENT. The States of Malaya comprises the 11 States of Johore, Pahang, Negri Sembilan, Selangor, Perak, Kedah, Perlis, Kelantan, Trengganu, Penang and Malacca. On 31 Aug. 1957 the Federation became the 11th sovereign member-state of the Commonwealth of

Nations. For earlier history of the States and Settlements *see* THE STATESMAN'S YEAR-BOOK, 1957, pp. 241 f.

The constitution is based on the agreements reached at the London conference of Jan.–Feb. 1956, between H.M. Government in the UK, the Rulers of the Malay States and the Alliance Party (which at the first federal elections on 27 July 1955 obtained 51 of the 52 elected members), and subsequently worked out by the Constitutional Commission appointed after that conference.

AREA AND POPULATION. The total area of West Malaysia is about 50,806 sq. miles (131,587 sq. km). The federal capital is Kuala Lumpur.

State	Area (sq. miles)	Population (end-1968 estimates)
Johore	7,330	1,352 505
Kedah	3,639	963 945
Kelantan	5,765	703 482
Malacca	637	428 144
Negri Sembilan	2,565	530 782
Pahang	13,886	445,479
Penang	399	778 747
Perak	8,110	1,701,873
Perlis	307	121 867
Selangor	3,166	1,477 535
Trengganu	5,002	394,671
West Malaysia	50,806	8,899 030

Population by races (1968 estimates): 4,488,113 Malays; 3,236,113 Chinese; 982,387 Indians and Pakistani; 191,799 others.

VITAL STATISTICS (1968). Births, 309,501; deaths, 66,638.

RELIGION. More than half the population are Moslems, and Islam is the official religion. In 1969 there were 136,800 Roman Catholic and, in 1962, 124,453 Protestant Christians in West Malaysia.

EDUCATION (1969). The number of schools (fully assisted, partially assisted and private) of all types, of teachers and pupils of both sexes were (as at 31 Jan.) as follows:

	Malay	English	Chinese	Tamil	Total
Schools	2,637	946	1,085	668	5,336
Teachers	26,514	22,541	12,618	3,357	65,030
Pupils	739,664	685,486	402,102	81,092	1,908,344

Upper secondary vocational training is given in 8 secondary trade schools (2,118 pupils), and upper secondary technical education in 3 secondary technical schools (1,668 pupils).

Post-secondary professional education (1969–70) is given at the Technical College, Kuala Lumpur (68 lecturers, 872 students), the College of Agriculture (40 lecturers, 565 students), Ungku Omar Polytechnic, Ipoh (15 lecturers, 277 students), Tunku Abdul Rahman College, Kuala Lumpur (30 lecturers, 794 students), Muslim College, Petaling Jaya (125 lecturers, 2,500 students) University of Penang (4 lecturers, 54 students) and the University of Malaya, Kuala Lumpur (28 professors, 545 lecturers and tutors, 6,672 students).

Primary teachers are trained at the Sultan Idris Training College in Perak (242 students), the Malay Women's Training College in Malacca (174 students), the Kota Bharu Teacher's College (357 students) and 9 Day Training Centres/Colleges (652 students).

Secondary teachers are trained at the Malayan Teacher's College in Penang (315 students), Kuala Lumpur (77 students) and Johore Bahru (174 students), the Language Institute, Kuala Lumpur (180 students), the Specialist Teachers' Training Institute, Kuala Lumpur (219 students), the Technical Teachers' Training College, Kuala Lumpur (207 students), and the Trade Teachers' Training College, Kuantan (90 students).

Further education classes are provided by the Government throughout the country (127 centres, 527 classes, 1,964 teachers and 14,189 students). Adult education, mainly literacy courses, is organized by the Government (16,537 courses/classes, 9,394 teachers and 408,270 students).

HEALTH AND SOCIAL WELFARE. In 1969 Government maintained 59 general and district hospitals with 16,455 beds, 2 institutions with 3,399 beds for the treatment of Hansens' disease, 2 mental institutions with 4,209 beds and 1 institution (293 beds) for tuberculosis treatment. For the care of the rural population there were 2,071 health clinics, 42 main health centres, 169 sub-health clinics, 883 midwives' clinics, 275 static, 209 travelling dispensaries, 450 dental clinics, 43 maternal and child health clinics. The Government also maintains an Institute for Medical Research with 2 branch laboratories at Ipoh, Perak and Penang.

JUSTICE. The Courts Ordinance, 1948, established sessions courts, magistrates' courts and Penghulu's courts. There are also juvenile courts for offenders under the age of 17.

There are 18 penal institutions, including 3 Borstal establishments and 1 open prison camp. There were 15,685 admissions in 1969. There were also 4 detention camps with an average of 294 detainees in 1969.

FINANCE. Revenue and expenditure for calendar years, in M$1,000:

	1967	1968	1969[1]	1970[2]
Revenue	306,044	323,972	320,707	347,546
Expenditure	294,396	326,101	331,384	365,500
Development expenditure[3]	68,167	74,678	89,976	161,673

[1] Revised. [2] Estimates. [3] Excludes federal reimbursements.

AGRICULTURE. Total area under agricultural crops, 1968, 6·8m. acres.

Rice: Production in 1967 and (1968) 659,110 (780,000) tons from 971,240 (1,136,860) acres.

Rubber: Production in 1968 and (1969): 1,034,707 (1,191,532) tons from 4·3m. (4·3m.) acres.

Palms: Production in 1968, 260,687 tons; 1969, 320,755 tons (preliminary) of palm oil; 1968, 58,724 tons; 1969, 73,691 tons (preliminary) of kernels; 1968, 89,755 tons; 1969, 82,646 tons (preliminary) of coconut oil.

Tea: Production of made tea in 1968, 7,645,000 lb.; 1969, 7·69m. lb.

Livestock, 1968 (in 1,000 heads): Oxen, 286; buffaloes, 227; sheep, 36; swine, 692.

FORESTRY (1969). Reserved forests, 13,198 sq. miles; productive, 8,750 sq miles. Production of round timber, 3,633,643 tons of 50 cu. ft and outturn of sawn timber, 1,442,462 tons of 50 cu. ft. Production of plywood and veneer 323·7m. sq. ft (227m. exported).

FISHERIES. Landings in 1968, 339,482 tons; 1969, 292,840 tons. Number of vessels: (1968) 13,160 motor, 6,293 sailing; (1969) 13,576 motor, 5,608 sailing.

MINING. Production (in 1,000 tons): Tin-in-concentrates: 1968, 75·1; 1969, 72·2. Iron ore: 1968, 5,085·3; 1969, 5,151. Bauxite: 1968, 786; 1969, 1,056·1. Ilmenite (exports): 1968, 123·8; 1969, 130·5. Gold: 1968, 1,453; 1969, 3,151 troy oz.

ELECTRICITY. In 1969, 3,156m. kwh. were generated; commerce and industry are the main consumers.

TRADE UNIONS. There were, on 31 Dec. 1968, 260 registered trade unions with 300,183 members.

TOURISM. In 1969, 53,229 foreigners visited Malaya, entering through Kuala Lumpur, Penang and Port Swettenham. Statistical data on visitors arriving from Singapore and Thailand are not available.

COMMERCE. Imports and exports for calendar years in M$1m.:

	1964	1965	1966	1967	1968	1969
Imports	2,521·4	2,608·3	2,632·5	2,585·9	2,771·1	2,820·5
Exports	2,780·9	3,102·9	3,119·5	2,918·8	3,216·7	4,075·6

Chief imports (1969): Food and live animals, $590·8m.; machinery and transport equipment, $642·9m.; manufactured goods, $545·8m.; chemicals, $243·9m.; mineral fuels, $208m.; crude material, inedible, $294·4m.

Chief exports (1969): Rubber, 1,264,900 tons ($1,940m.); tin metal, 89,822 tons ($932m.); iron ore, 5,219,435 tons ($114·8m.); palm oil, 323,372 tons ($141m.); sawn timber, 610,310 tons ($122·5m.); sawn logs, 1,044,456 tons ($85m.).

In 1969 imports came chiefly from Japan ($479·6m.), UK ($387·6m.), Australia ($212·3m.), Singapore ($194·8m.), China ($174·9m.), Thailand ($164·9m.), USA ($160·8m.), Exports went mainly to Japan ($793·3m.), Singapore ($793·2m.), USA ($724·3m.), UK ($252·9m.), USSR ($240m.).

ROADS. In 1968 the Public Works Department maintains 10,518 miles of public road, of which 6 miles is concrete surface, 7,545 miles is bituminous metalled surface, 151 metalled surface waterbound, 1,206 hard surface waterbound, 401 earth surface, 1,209 hard surface bitumen sealed.

At Dec. 1969, 605,362 motor vehicles were registered, including 213,247 private cars; 5,347 buses; 51,375 lorries and vans; 312,686 motor cycles.

RAILWAYS. The Malayan Railway main line runs from Singapore to Butterworth opposite Penang Island. From Bukit Mertajam 8 miles south of Butterworth a branch line connects Malaya with the State Railways of Thailand at the frontier station of Padang Besar. Other branch lines connect the main line with Port Swettenham, Teluk Anson, Port Dickson and Port Weld. The east-coast line, branching off the main line at Gemas, runs for over 300 miles to Tumpat, Kelantan's northernmost coastal town; a short branch line linking Pasir Mas with Sungei Golok makes a second connexion with Thailand. The route mileage in 1970 is 1,036 (metre gauge) and the annual budget is about $77m.

SHIPPING. The major ports of the States of Malaya are Penang, Malacca, Port Swettenham, Tumpat, Dungun, Port Dickson, Teluk Anson and Kuantan. The volume of shipping (vessels of over 75 NRT only) handled at these ports, exclusive of coasting trade, was as follows (in 1,000 NRT).

Ports		Arrivals		Departures	
		Number	Tonnage	Number	Tonnage
Penang	1968	2,054	8,051	2,055	8,181
	1969	2,074	8,190	2,061	8,161
Port Swettenham	1968	2,146	8,378	2,133	9,318
	1969	2,279	8,280	2,292	8,395
Total (all ports)	1968	5,196	21,674	5,172	22,698
	1969	5,169	21,244	5,171	21,281

The total cargo handled in all ports during 1968 was 17,362,000 tons; 1969, 17·81m. tons.

AVIATION (1969). There are 8 aerodromes used by scheduled air services and 22 other landing grounds. Malaysia–Singapore Airlines Ltd provide internal services; Malaysia Air Charter offer charter services. BOAC, Qantas, KLM, Air Ceylon, Cathay Pacific Airways, Thai International, SAS, Air India, Air Vietnam, Japan Airlines and China Airlines operate through Kuala Lumpur and Thai Airways Co. Ltd and Garuda Airways call at Penang. Malaysia–Singapore Airlines also provides services from Kuala Lumpur and Penang to Bangkok, Taipeh, Phnom-Penh, Tokyo and Hong Kong and from Singapore to Djakarta, Sydney and Perth. In 1969 passengers who arrived and departed numbered 651,237; cargo handled, 3·18m. kg, mail handled, 1·06m. kg.

POST. As at 31 Dec. 1968, 238 post offices and 600 postal agencies were operating in West Malaysia, and the cash turnover for the year, excluding savings bank, amounted to $913·5m.

There were 150,382 telephone stations on 1 July 1970. These were connected to 306 telephone exchanges. In 1969, 302,985 wireless licences and 151,017 television licences were issued.

The post office savings bank held a total amount of $256m. due to 1,587,232 depositors at 31 Dec. 1969.

WEIGHTS AND MEASURES. The standard measures are the imperial yard, pound and gallon.

BOOKS OF REFERENCE

Gullick, J. M., *Malaya*. 2nd ed. London, 1965
Jin-Bee, Ooi, *Land, People and Economy in Malaya*. London, 1963
Kennedy, J., *A History of Malaya*. London, 1962
O'Ballance, E., *Malaya: the communist insurgent war, 1948–60*. London, 1966
Ratnam, K. J., *Communalism and the political process in Malaya*. OUP, 1965
Wilkinson, R. J., *Malay–English Dictionary*. 2 vols. New ed. London, 1956
Winstedt, Sir R., *Malaya and its History*. 3rd ed. London, 1953.—*An English–Malay Dictionary*. 3rd ed. Singapore, 1949.—*The Malays: a cultural history*. London, 1959

SABAH

HISTORY. The territory now named Sabah, but until Sept. 1963 known as North Borneo, was in 1877–78 ceded by the Sultans of Brunei and Sulu and various other rulers to a British syndicate, which in 1881 was chartered as the British North Borneo (Chartered) Company. The Company's sovereign rights and assets were transferred to the Crown with effect from 15 July 1946. On that date, the island of Labuan (ceded to Britain in 1846 by the Sultan of Brunei) became part of the new Colony of North Borneo. On 16 Sept. 1963 North Borneo joined the new Federation of Malaysia and became the State of Sabah.

AREA AND POPULATION. Area, about 29,388 sq. miles (80,520 sq. km). with a coastline of about 900 miles. The interior is mountainous, Mount Kinabalu being 13,455 ft (4,175 metres) high. Population (1960 census), 454,421, of whom 306,498 were natives, 104,542 Chinese, 1,896 Europeans and Eurasians and 41,485 others. The native population comprises Kadazans (mainly agricultural), Bajaus and Bruneis (agriculture and fishing), Muruts (hill tribes), Suluks (mostly seafaring) and several smaller tribes.

The island of Labuan, 35 sq. miles (75 sq. km) in area, lying 6 miles off the north-west coast of Borneo, has a fine port, Victoria Harbour.

The principal towns are situated on or near the coast. They include Jesselton (renamed Kota Kinabalu, the capital; 1967 census population, 33,365), Sandakan (33,331), Kudat (4,343), Tawau (17,446) on the mainland and Victoria (4,964) on the island of Labuan.

GOVERNMENT AND CONSTITUTION. The constitution of the State of Sabah provides for a Head of State, called the Yang di-Pertua Negara. The Executive authority is vested in the Yang di-Pertua Negara, who is advised by a State Cabinet in the exercise of his functions.

Head of State: Tun Pengiran Haji Ahmad Raffae bin OKK Pengiran Haji Omar, SMN, PDK.

The Cabinet consists of a Chief Minister and 8 ministers.

Chief Minister: Tun Datu Haji Mustapha bin Datu Harun, SMN, PDK, SIMP, PNBS, SPMJ, KVO, OBE.

Finance: Enche Salleh bin Sulong. *Communications and Works:* Dato Pang Tet Tshung, SPDK. *Agriculture and Fisheries:* Enche Mmmedoha Said bin Keruak, SPDK. *Local Government:* Tuan Habib Abdul Rahman bin Habib Mahmud, ADK, JBS. *Social Welfare:* Enche Payar Juman. *Health:* Enche Wong Lok Khiam, ADK. *Co-ordination:* Dato Haji Mohd. Yassin bin Haji Hashim, PDK, OBE. *Minister without Portfolio:* Dato Khoo Siak Chiew, PDK.

The Legislative Assembly consists of the Speaker, 32 elected members and not more than 6 nominated members.

The official language is English for a period of 10 years after 16 Sept. 1963 and thereafter until the State Legislature otherwise provides. During the same period Sabah representatives may use English in both Houses of the Federal Parliament.

EDUCATION (1969). There are 355 government, 309 grant-aided and 10 non-aided primary schools and 34 government, 39 grant-aided and 11 non-aided secondary schools. Government also maintains 2 trade/vocational schools and 3 teachers' training colleges. Further education classes in Kota Kinabalu, Tuaran, Papar, Labuan, Keningau, Tenom, Beaufort, Sandakan, Tawau and Lahad Datu are being run by the Education Department. Primary education is provided in Malay, Chinese and English. Secondary education is principally in English, although a number of schools conduct classes in Chinese, and 7 Malay medium secondary schools have been established.

In 1969 the enrolment in primary schools was 110,480, of whom 61,786 were boys and 48,694 were girls. There were 26,954 pupils in secondary schools, of whom 16,293 were boys and 10,661 were girls.

HEALTH. The principal diseases are pulmonary tuberculosis and intestinal infestations.

There are 3 general hospitals (795 beds) and 10 cottage hospitals (718 beds). Thirty-eight dispensaries in outlying districts are staffed by senior dressers under the supervision of district medical officers. There is a mental hospital at Sandakan (160 beds). There are maternal and child health centres at Sandakan, Kota Kinabalu, Labuan, Keningau and Tawau. Rural health nurses are being trained in the new rural health training school in Papar.

JUSTICE. When Sabah attained independence on 16 Sept. 1963 the Supreme Court of Sarawak, North Borneo and Brunei was replaced by the High Court in Borneo with 2 registries for Sarawak (at Kuching) and Sabah (at Kota Kinabalu). The Chief Justice of Borneo and the Registrar remain in Kuching the administrative head, while the senior puisne judge and deputy registrar in Kinabalu.

In addition to the High Court, magistrate courts, there are native courts with jurisdiction in cases concerning local native customs. Appeal from native courts lie to administrative officers, with a final appeal to the Native Court of Appeal.

In 1969, 1,158 convictions were obtained in 1,244 cases taken to court.

FINANCE. Budgets for calendar years, in Malaysian $:

Ordinary Budget	1965	1966	1967	1968	1969
Revenue	74,872,177	91,281,067	137,664,445	159,227,974	180,735,123
Expenditure [1]	66,560,159	73,437,112	99,127,772	124,021,484	183,945,909

Development Budget					
Revenue	35,650,270[2]	36,141,191[2]	29,891,007[2]	61,248,846[2]	101,074,684[2]
Expenditure	41,882,227[2]	32,583,458[2]	30,803,040[2]	60,755,755[2]	91,183,661[2]

[1] Includes contributions to Development Budget: 1965, $10m.; 1966, $10m.; 1967, $15m.; 1968, $40m.; 1969, $86m.
[2] Excluding federal accounts on federal subjects in the State.

COMMERCE. The main imports are machinery, tobacco, provisions, petroleum products, metals, rice, textiles and apparel, vehicles, sugar, building material. Statistics for calendar years, in Malaysian $:

	1965	1966	1967	1968	1969
Imports	336,205,190	346,749,884	330,169,884	344,031,434	419,021,708
Exports	304,964,325	358,285,845	409,593,636	433,148,600	521,230,991

The main imports and exports were (in $1m.):

Imports	1955	1960	1967	1968	1969
Rice	6·4	8·4	19·9	16·7	15·5
Provisions	13·0	22·3	36·3	39·1	44·3
Textiles and apparel	5·9	9·2	15·2	15·4	19·1
Tobacco, cigars and cigarettes	4·2	12·8	22·9	16·6	30·0
Sugar	2·5	3·5	4·0	4·7	5·8
Vehicles	2·2	8·1	23·7	25·3	35·6
Machinery	6·9	30·0	56·1	65·7	88·7
Petroleum products	5·0	15·8	23·8	27·2	26·5
Metals	7·5	12·1	23·1	24·9	28·8
Building materials	2·1	2·8	4·9	7·8	10·6

Exports					
Rubber	45·9	49·5	26·3	25·9	41·1
Timber	21·6	90·7	317·3	335·3	375·1
Hemp	2·2	5·2	2·4	2·3	2·1
Fish, fresh, dried and salted	0·4	0·9	7·1	8·0	6·9
Copra (including re-exports)	14·2	40·2	5·3	6·5	7·1
Cocoa beans	—	—	1·6	2·6	3·6
Veneer sheets	—	0·5	0·9	1·1	1·4

TOURISM. From 1966–69 some 30,000 tourists visited Sabah.

SHIPPING (1969). Merchant shipping (men-of-war and government vessels excluded) totalling 12,697,674 gross tons, used the ports, handling 4,796,156 tons of cargo and 85,624 passengers.

RAILWAYS. A metre-gauge railway, 96 miles, runs from Kota Kinabalu on Gaya Bay to Melalap in the interior.

ROADS (1970). There were 1,800 miles of roads, of which 311 miles were bitumen surfaced, 1,019 miles gravel surfaced and 470 miles of earth road. Work is in progress on a network of roads, notably the Kota Kinabalu–Sandakan and Tawau–Lahad Datu road links.

AVIATION. External communications are provided from the international airport at Kota Kinabalu by Cathay Pacific Airways Ltd to Hong Kong and Manila and by Malaysian Airways to Hong Kong, Brunei, Kuching, Singapore and Kuala Lumpur. Internal communications are provided by Malaysia Airways between Kota Kinabalu, Sandakan, Lahad Datu, Tawau, Labuan, Kudat, Ranau, Keningau, Sepulot and Semporna.

The total air traffic handled at Sabah aerodromes during 1969 was 492,269 passengers, 2,920,357 kg freight and 568,484 kg mail.

POST. As at 31 Dec. 1970 there were 17 post offices, 6 mobile post offices and a network of postal agencies. There were 9,574 telephones on 31 Dec. 1968.

BANKING. There are branches of The Chartered Bank at Kota Kinabalu, Sandakan, Tawau, Labuan, Kudat, Tenom and Lahad Datu. The Hongkong and Shanghai Bank has branches at Kota Kinabalu, Sandakan, Labuan, Beaufort, Papar and Tawau. The Hock Hua Bank (S) and the Chung Khiaw Bank have each a branch at Kota Kinabalu and Sandakan. Malayan Banking Ltd has branches at Kota Kinabalu, Tawau and Sandakan. Bank Negara Malaysia and the Overseas Chinese Banking Corporation have each a branch at Kota Kinabalu.

A post office savings bank was introduced in 1968, and has $4·99m. due to 14,740 depositors.

STATISTICAL INFORMATION. The State Information Officer, Kota Kinabalu.

Treconning, K. G., *North Borneo*. HMSO, 1960.

SARAWAK

HISTORY. The Government of part of the present territory was obtained on 24 Sept. 1841 by Sir James Brooke from the Sultan of Brunei. Various accessions were made between 1861 and 1905. In 1888 Sarawak was placed under British protection. On 16 Dec. 1941 Sarawak was occupied by the Japanese. After the liberation the Rajah took over his administration from the British military authorities on 15 April 1946. The Council Negri, on 17 May 1946, authorized the Act of Cession to the British Crown by 19 to 16 votes, and the Rajah ceded Sarawak to the British Crown on 1 July 1946.

On 16 September 1963 Sarawak joined the Federation of Malaysia.

AREA AND POPULATION. The area is about 48,250 sq. miles (121,400 sq. km), with a coastline of 450 miles and many navigable rivers.

Estimated population in mid-1968 was 924,000, including 264,000 Sea Dayaks; 168,000 Malays; 78,000 Land Dayaks; 52,000 Melanaus; 306,000 Chinese; 2,000 Europeans.

The chief towns are the capital, Kuching, about 21 miles inland, on the Sarawak River (estimated population: 70,000), Sibu, 80 miles up the Rejang River, which is navigable by large steamers (estimated population: 40,000), and Miri, the headquarters of the Sarawak Shell Oilfields, Ltd (estimated population: 19,539).

CONSTITUTION AND GOVERNMENT. On 24 Sept. 1941 the Rajah began to rule through a constitution. Since 1855 two bodies, known as the Supreme Council and the Council Negri, had been in existence. By the constitution of 1941 they were given, by the Rajah, powers roughly corresponding to those of a colonial executive council and legislative council respectively. Sarawak has retained a considerable measure of local autonomy in state affairs. The Council Negri or Legislature consists of 48 elected members.

A ministerial system of government was introduced in 1963. The Chief Minister presides over the Supreme Council, which contains no more than 8 other Council Negri members, all of whom are Ministers.

Elections to the Council Negri on 4 July 1970 returned 15 members of the Sarawak Alliance, 12 of the Sarawak United Peoples' Party, 9 of Party Pesaka and 12 of Sarawak National Party.

Political Parties. Since the 1970 elections, Sarawak United People's Party has joined together with Party Bumiputra and Party Pesaka forming Sarawak Coalition Government. One opposition party is Sarawak National Party.

Sarawak has 24 seats in the Malaysia Parliament.

Governor: Tun Tuanku Haji Bujang bin Tuanku Othman, SMN, PSM, OBE.
Chief Minister: Dato Haji Abdul Rahman Ya'kub, PNBS.

Deputy Chief Ministers: Stephen K. T. Yong (*Communications and Works*) and Simon Dembab Maja. *Lands and Mineral Resources:* Simon Dembab Maja. *Welfare:* Abang Ikhwan Zaini, KMN, *Local Government:* Sim Kheng Hong. *Minister of Culture:* Penghulu Abok anak Jalin.

State Secretary: Dato Gerunsin Lembat, PNBS. *State Attorney-General:* Tan Chiaw Thong, PBS. *State Financial Secretary:* T'en Kuen Foh, JMS, PBS, AMN.

The official languages are Malay and English. The continuing use of English as official language in Sarawak will be reviewed in 1973.

RELIGION. There are Church of England, Roman Catholic, American Methodist, Seventh Day Adventist and Borneo Evangelical missions. There is a large Moslem population and many Buddhists.

EDUCATION (1969). All schools (government, missions, local authorities) numbered 1,319 with 187,110 (1968: 176,881) pupils, of whom 35,621 were in secondary classes. There are 3 teacher-training centres.

NEWSPAPERS. There are 2 English, 7 Chinese and 1 Malay daily; 1 Malay and 1 Iban (Sea Dayak) monthly newspapers as well as a weekly news review in Malay and Iban published by government.

JUSTICE (1969). There are 5 prisons and 1 centre of protective custody. There were 1,361 admissions, of whom 404 were sentenced to penal imprisonment and 368 committed on remand or awaiting trial, and 53 paid fines. Daily average prison population was 824.

Police. There is a Royal Malaysia Police, Sarawak Component, with a total establishment of 4,175 regular officers and men.

HEALTH. At the end of 1969 there were 10 government hospitals (1,104 beds), 6 mission hospitals (143 beds) and 42 static and 16 travelling dispensaries, 1 urban health centre, 5 dental clinics, 28 school dental clinics and 73 maternal and child health centres.

FINANCE. Currency. The Malaysian dollar is based on gold, 0·290299 gramme to a dollar, which is on a par of £0·14. Currency in circulation as at 31 Dec 1968 was $41·9m.

Budget. In 1968 actual revenue was $182·12m. (of which State revenue was $95·43m.); actual expenditure, $207·76m. (of which State expenditure was $62·08m.). The revenue is derived from export and custom duties royalty on oil, land revenue, timber royalty, trade licenses, income tax and excise revenue.

The first Malaysian 5-year development plan (1966–70) provides for Sarawak an expenditure of $400m.; of this sum $168m. is to be spent on communications, facilities and transport, $131m. on agriculture and rural development, $86m. on social services.

PRODUCTION. The State produces rubber (exports, 1968, 23,784 net tons, $26,313,574; 1969, 38,729 net tons, $49·9m.), timber (exports, 1968, 1,875,435 tons, $181,065,058; 1969, 1,912,472 tons, $186·5m.), sago (exports, 1968, 35,973 tons, $4,946,401; 1969, 28,692 tons, $3,705,000), pepper (exports, 1968, 22,804 tons, $34,664,294; 1969, 28,632 tons, $52·9m.), and other jungle produce. There are also gold (1968, 2,718 troy oz.; 1969, 2,271 troy oz.) and coal deposits.

COMMERCE. Export of crude oil (Sarawak production), in 1969 was 439,888 tons ($19,535,023). The main import is that of crude oil ($269m. in 1968).

Total import value, 1968, $574·8m.; 1969, $579·7m. Export, 1968, $604·3m.; 1969, $642m.

ROADS. There are no railways. In 1969 there were 1,823 miles of roads, consisting of 306 miles of bitumen surfaced, 1,064 miles of gravel or stone surfaced and 453 miles of earth roads.

SHIPPING. In 1969 Sarawak ports loaded 7·46m. tons (1968: 6·92m. tons) and discharged 6·47m. tons (1968: 6·24m. tons).

POST. There are 46 post offices (including 2 mobile offices) and wireless-telegraph stations and 53 agencies. A telephone system with 60 stations (12,189 telephones) covers the country. There is communication by wireless with Singapore and other Commonwealth countries. The government broadcasting service had, at the end of 1969, 48,973 registered receivers.

BANKING. The post office savings bank had 15,854 depositors at the end of 1969; the amount to their credit was $5,308,000. There are a branch of Bank Negara Malaysia in Kuching, and branches of the Chartered Bank, the Hongkong & Shanghai Bank, the Oversea Chinese Banking Corporation, the Oversea Union Bank and 6 other banks.

BOOKS OF REFERENCE

Sarawak Annual of Statistics. Dept of Statistics, Kuching, 1969
Sarawak Annual External Trade Statistics. Dept. of Statistics, Kuching, 1969
Sarawak-in-Brief. Information Dept., Kuala Lumpur
Dickson, M. G., *Sarawak and its People.* New ed. Kuching, 1962
Geddes, W. R., *The Land Dayaks of Sarawak.* HMSO, 1954
Harrison, T., *World Within: a Borneo story.* London, 1959
Jones, L. W., *Sarawak: Report on the census of population 1960.* Kuching, 1962
MacDonald, M., *Borneo People.* London, 1956
Runciman, S., *The White Rajahs.* CUP, 1960
Scott, N. C., *Sea Dyak Dictionary.* Govt. Printing Office, Kuching, 1956
NATIONAL LIBRARY. The Sarawak Central Library, Kuching.

FEDERATION OF NIGERIA

HISTORY. The Federation comprises a number of areas formerly under separate administrations. Lagos, ceded in Aug. 1861 by King Docemo, was placed under the Governor of Sierra Leone in 1866. In 1874 it was detached, together with the Gold Coast Colony, and formed part of the latter until Jan. 1886, when a separate 'colony and protectorate of Lagos' was constituted. Meanwhile the National African Company had established British interests in the Niger valley, and in July 1886 the company obtained a charter under the name of the Royal Niger Company. This company surrendered its charter to the Crown on 31 Dec. 1899, and on 1 Jan. 1900 the greater part of its territories was formed into the protectorate of Northern Nigeria. Along the coast the Oil Rivers protectorate had been declared in June 1885. This was enlarged and renamed the Niger Coast protectorate in 1893; and on 1 Jan. 1900, on its absorbing the remainder of the territories of the Royal Niger Company, it became the protectorate of Southern Nigeria. In Feb. 1906 Lagos and Southern Nigeria were united into the 'colony and protectorate of Southern Nigeria', and on 1 Jan. 1914 the latter was amalgamated with the protectorate of Northern Nigeria to form the 'colony and protectorate of Nigeria', under a Governor. On 1 Oct. 1954 Nigeria became a federation under a Governor-General.

CONSTITUTION. On 1 Oct. 1960 the Federation of Nigeria became sovereign and independent and a member of the Commonwealth of Nations. On 1 Oct. 1963 Nigeria became a republic.

At the plebiscite held on 11 Feb. 1961 the northern portion of the trusteeship territory of the Cameroons voted to join Nigeria while the southern Cameroons opted for unification with the Cameroun Republic.

The official language is English.

On 15 Jan. 1966 a group of 25 officers staged a military *coup d'état* and murdered the Federal Prime Minister, Sir Abubakar Tafawa Balewa, the Federal Minister of Finance, Chief Festus Okotie-Eboh, the Premier of Northern Nigeria Sir Ahmadu Bello, the Premier of Western Nigeria, Chief S. L. Akintola, the Adjutant-General of the Army, Lieut.-Col. Jack Pam, and other officers. By 17 Jan. Maj.-Gen. Johnson Aguiyi-Ironsi, head of the army, had suppressed the revolt and assumed supreme power.

Gen. Ironsi suspended the constitution and set up a supreme military council. All political parties and tribal associations were abolished. On 24 May the 'regions' were replaced by 'provinces' and the name of the Federation was changed to 'Republic of Nigeria'.

On 29 July 1966 the regime of Gen. Ironsi was overthrown by a military coup, leaders of which accepted Lieut.-Col. Yakubu Gowon as a compromise leader. By decree of 31 Aug. he restored, as from 1 Sept., the federal system of government. The National Military Government was renamed the Federal Military Government, the provinces became again regions and the capital territory of Lagos again the federal territory of Lagos.

On 27 May 1967 the Federal Republic was divided into 12 states, 6 in the former Northern Region, 3 in the former Eastern Region, a new Lagos state, the West and Mid-West.

On 30 May Lieut.-Col. Ojukwu, the Military Governor of the Eastern States, announced secession from the Federal Republic of Nigeria and renamed the region as the Republic of Biafra.

On 9 Aug. the Mid-West State was taken by Col. Ojukwu's forces but recaptured by the federal army later that year. By April 1968 the federal army had reconquered the greater part of the breakaway states. In Jan. 1970 the rebellion had collapsed and Col. Ojukwu fled the country leaving Col. Philip Effiong to surrender to Federal forces.

Head of State: Maj.-Gen. Yakubu Gowon.

DIPLOMATIC REPRESENTATIVES

Country	Nigerian representative	Foreign representative
Algeria	J. D. O. Sokoya	—
Argentina	—	A. E. Acuna
Australia[1]	—	H. D. White
Austria	—	Dr A. K. Otto
Belgium	M. A. Sanusi	André Chaval
Brazil	A. R. Ladipo	P. F. M. Polzin[2]
Britain[1]	Brig. B. A. O. Ogundipe	Sir Leslie Glass, KCMG
Bulgaria	—	Peter Vasiler[2]
Cameroun	Ado Sanusi	H. Alim
Canada[1]	Edward Enahoro	T. P. Malone
Central Africa	—	C. Sevot
Chad	M. K. Bayero	B. Hassane
Congo	E. Ogunsulire	A. Tshilumba-Kabishi
Czechoslovakia	—	Dr J. Vila
Dahomey	F. O. Olufolabi	—
Denmark	—	Troels Munk
Equatorial Guinea	W. Bassey	S. M. E. Besebo
Ethiopia	E. O. Sanu	Ato Araya Ogbagsy
Finland	—	Oli Auero
France	L. O. Harriman	André Roger
Gambia[1]	B. A. T. Balewa	Y. Ben Yaccov
Germany (West)	A. Haastrup	Theodore Axenfeld
Ghana[1]	V. A. Adegoroye	J. O. Akyeampong
Guinea	M. Subairu[2]	S. Ousmane
Hungary	—	Dr Jozsef Miko
India[1]	J. N. Ukegbu	S. G. Ramachandran
Indonesia	—	D. Adjam
Iraq	—	Akira Shigemitsu
Irish Republic	Brig. B. A. O. Ogundipe	Paul J. Keating
Israel	—	—
Italy	J. M. Garba	Dr V. Manfredi
Japan	G. H. Dove-Edwin	Hisaji Hattori
Jordan	—	K. Alsharif
Kenya[1]	I. C. Olisameka	—
Lebanon	—	Bulind Beydoun
Liberia	O. Jolaoso	Edward R. Moore
Libya	—	Mohammed Al-Busari
Mali	A. E. Dehinde	—
Morocco	G. Bukar-Kolo	Ahmed Snoussi
Netherlands	—	Arnout De Waal
Niger	S. Kontagora	B. Issa
Norway	—	Lars Onsager

[1] High Commissioner.   [2] Chargé d'Affaires.   No figure = Ambassador.

Country	Nigerian representative	Foreign representative
Pakistan[1]	Alhaji A. R. Mora	Dr S. M. Koreshi
Philippines	—	Froilan M. Maglaya
Poland	S. Williams	M. Dedo
Saudi Arabia	S. A. Yero	Fond Alkhateeb
Senegal	B. A. T Balewa	Latyr Kamura
Sierra Leone[1]	P. A. Afolabi	A. Mansaray
Spain	J. M. Garba	J. L. Aparicio
Sudan	N. Mohammed	Ahmed El-Sherif El-Habib
Sweden	C. C. Chukwura	L. B. T. Arvidson
Switzerland	S. D. Kolo	Dr F. Real
Syria	—	Dr Zakaria Alsibahy
Thailand	—	Suwit B. Thana
Togo	V. A. Adegoroye	M. Simtekpeati
Turkey	—	Dogan Turkman
Uganda[1]	M. J. Etulk	—
USSR	Lieut.-Col. G. Kurubo	Alexandr I. Romanov
UAR	O. Ahmadu-Suka	Dr A. Khalil
USA	J. T. F. Iyalla	William C. Trueheart
Uruguay	—	Carlos A. Margre[2]
Venezuela	—	L. A. Olavarria
Yugoslavia	—	Milutia Kukolj[2]

[1] High Commissioner. [2] Chargé d'Affaires. No figure = Ambassador.

LOCAL GOVERNMENT. Local government is the main responsibility of a large number of Native Administrations. Throughout the country, in recent years, the influence of British local government institutions has been increasingly marked. The establishment of Native Authorities or Local Government bodies is controlled by legislation enacted on a state basis. The state government has authority to dismiss or suspend Councils which run into difficulties. The composition and duties of such councils and Native Authorities are defined by law together with procedure for election and appointment of members and officers. In general, the aim has been to retain the traditional rulers and their courts within the framework of local government.

AREA AND POPULATION. Area approximately 356,669 sq miles (923,773 sq. km). Census population, Nov. 1963, 55,653,821.

State	Area (in sq. miles)	Population	Density per sq. mile
Western	29,100	9,487,525	326
North-Eastern	103,639	7,793,443	75
Central-Eastern	11,310	7,227,559	639
Kano	16,630	5,774,842	347
North-Western	65,143	5,733,296	88
South-Eastern	11,166	3,622,589	324
North-Central	27,108	4,098,305	151
Benue-Plateau	40,590	4,009,408	99
Mid-Western	14,922	2,535,839	170
Kwara	28,672	2,399,365	84
Rivers	7,008	1,544,314	220
Lagos	1,381	1,443,567	1,045
Total	356,669	55,670,052	156

The populations of the largest towns are estimated as follows: Ibadan, 300,000; Lagos, 600,000; Ogbomosho, 140,000; Kano, 130,000; Oshogbo, 123,000; Ife, 111,000; Iwo, 100,000; Abeokuta, 84,000; Onitsha, 77,000; Ilesha, 72,000; Oyo, 72,000; Port Harcourt, 72,000; Enugu, 63,000; Aba, 58,000; Yerwa-Maiduguri, 57,000; Benin, 54,000; Zaria, 54,000; Katsina, 53,000.

Topography and Climate. A belt of mangrove swamp forest lies along the entire coastline. North of this there is a zone of tropical rain forest and oil-palm bush some 50–100 miles wide. Farther inland the country rises and the vegetation changes to open woodland and savannah. In the extreme north the country is almost desert. There are few mountains except along the eastern boundary and on the northern plateau, where peaks of over 5,000 ft. occur. The Niger, Benue and Cross are the main rivers.

The climate varies with the types of country, but Nigeria lies wholly within the tropics, and temperatures are high. Temperatures of over 100° are common in the north; coast temperatures are seldom over 90°, but the humidity at the coast is much higher than in the north. Most of the rain falls between April and Sept. in the north and between March and Nov. in the south; rainfall varies from under 25 in. a year to 150 in. During the dry-season the 'harmattan' wind, laden with fine particles of dust, blows from the north-east.

Under a convention concluded in May 1964, Nigeria, Niger, Chad and Cameroun will develop the basin of Lake Chad as a single economic region.

RELIGION. The 1963 census figures were: Moslems, 26·2m.; Christians, 19·2m.; others, 10·1m. Northern Nigeria is mainly Moslem; Southern Nigeria is predominantly Christian. The Protestant and Roman Catholic Churches assess their membership at 2·5m. each.

The main Christian missionary societies represent the Roman Catholic, Anglican, Scottish, Methodist and Baptist Churches. In addition, there are several inter-denominational Protestant societies, such as the Sudan Interior Mission, the Sudan United Mission and the Qua Iboe Mission.

EDUCATION. On 1 Oct. 1954 education became the responsibility of the Regional Governments, the Federal Government retaining responsibility for education in Lagos and for those institutions of higher learning which have Nigerian significance, such as the University of Ibadan, King's College and the Man o' War Bay Training Centre. Free education for all primary school-children within the 6–12 year age group was implemented in the Western State in Jan. 1955 and in Lagos and the Eastern State in Jan. 1957.

In 1966 there were more than 3·1m. out of over 5m. children of primary school age at school. The demand for secondary education continues to exceed the number of places available, particularly in Eastern and Western States and in Lagos. There are more than 1,000 secondary schools, including some secondary modern schools. All external examinations of the Universities of London and Cambridge have been taken over by the West African Examination Council.

Teacher-training institutions totalled 266 in 1966. There were also 35 trade centres and vocational training institutes for sub-professional technicians' and tradesmen.

The University of Ibadan was founded in 1948, and was an autonomous University College in special relationship with the University of London. Its graduates were prepared for degrees of the University of London. In 1962 the College was transformed into a full University, awarding its own degrees. In 1966 there were about 3,000 full-time students. A 500-bed teaching hospital was opened in 1957.

The University of Nigeria, opened Oct. 1960, had about 3,000 students in 1966.

The Ahmadu Bello University was opened in Oct. 1962 at Zaria in Northern Nigeria. It had almost 1,000 students in 1966.

The University of Ife, in the Western State, founded in Oct. 1961 and formally opened in 1962, includes the Ibadan branch of the former Nigerian College of Arts, Science and Technology. It had about 1,000 students in 1966.

The University of Lagos, concentrating initially on law, medicine and business administration, was opened in Oct. 1962. It had about 1,000 students in 1966. Total enrolment at Nigerian universities in 1967–68 was 7,058.

CINEMAS (1967). There were 105 cinemas, with a seating capacity of 106,000. Mobile cinemas are used by the Federal and States Information Services.

NEWSPAPERS. There are 49 newspapers and magazines; the highest circulation of a daily is about 120,000. Most of the papers are published in English.

HEALTH. Most tropical diseases are endemic to Nigeria. Blindness, yaws, leprosy, sleeping sickness, worm infections, malaria are major health problems which, however, are yielding to remedial and preventative measures. In co-operation with the World Health Organization river blindness and malaria are being tackled on a large scale, while annual campaigns are undertaken against the danger of smallpox epidemics. Over 33m. people were vaccinated against smallpox in 1968. Dispensaries and travelling dispensaries are found in most parts of the country.

The teaching hospital at Lagos University has 350 beds and a nursing school and a teaching hospital at Ibadan University. Medical courses at Ahmadu Bello University and the University of Ife are planned.

JUSTICE. The highest court is the Federal Supreme Court, which consists of the Chief Justice of the Federation, not less than 3 Federal Judges and the Chief Justice of each State. It has original jurisdiction in any dispute between the Federation and any State or between States; and to hear and determine appeals from any of the High Courts and from any court or tribunal established by Parliament. It may be given powers of advisory jurisdiction by Parliament in respect of the exercise of the prerogative of mercy by the Heads of State of the Federation or the States.

High Courts, presided over by a Chief Justice, are established in most of the states. Magistrates' courts are established throughout the Federation, and customary law courts in Western, Eastern, South Eastern, East Central and Lagos States of Nigeria. In Northern States of Nigeria there are the Sharia Court of Appeal and the Court of Resolution. Moslem Law has been codified in a Penal Code and is applied through alkali courts.

The Advisory Judicial committee has powers of appointment and discipline. The constitutional safeguard of fundamental rights was suspended 15 Feb. 1966.

POLICE. The police has a strength of 24,000.

FINANCE. Currency. Since 1 July 1959 a Nigerian currency has been issued by the Central Bank of Nigeria. The denominations are £5, £1, 10s. and 5s. notes and 2s., 1s., 6d., 3d., 1d. and ½d. coins.

At 31 March 1967 currency in circulation amounted to £N109·7m.

Budget. Central government revenue, expenditure and public debt, in £1,000 sterling for fiscal years ending 31 March:

	1962–63	1963–64	1964–65	1965–66	1966–67[1]	1967–68[1]
Revenue	115,821	124,576	149,567	160,935	169,598	161,100
Expenditure	152,809	169,466	191,971	214,361	221,496	..
Public debt	113,530	136,872	162,710	189,539	243,401	..

[1] Estimates.

In 1967, £N173·15m. was internal debt, £N70·25m. external.

DEFENCE. Army. The Army consists of 5 infantry battalions, 2 armoured-car reconnaissance squadrons, 1 field battery, 1 engineers squadron and 1 signals squadron. Total strength, 9,000.

Navy. The Navy includes the frigate *Nigeria* (completed in the Netherlands in 1965), 6 seaward defence boats, 3 fast patrol boats, 1 landing craft and 2 survey craft. Two corvettes are being built in Britain for delivery in 1971 and 1972. Personnel, 120 officers and 1,600 ratings.

Air Force. The Nigerian Air Force was established in Jan. 1964. Pilots were trained initially in Canada, India and Ethiopia. Subsequently the Air Force was being built up with the aid of a West German mission; 14 Piaggio P.149D piston-engined trainers, 20 Dornier Do 27 liaison aircraft and some twin-engined Do 28s at the training school at Kaduna were supplied in this period. Later equipment includes a small number of MiG-15UTI fighter-trainers and MiG-17 fighter-bombers, Il-28 twin-jet bombers and L-29 Delfin armed jet trainers from Czecho-slovakia. There are also some 10 DC-3 transports converted for bombing and piston-engined Whirlwind helicopters.

PLANNING. The first national development plan ran from 1962 to 1968; the second plan (1968–73) is to be part of a 20-year plan covering the period 1968–88.

AGRICULTURE. Groundnuts, cotton and soybean come mainly or wholly from the north, palm produce, cocoa, timber and rubber from the south. Tobacco is grown in commercial quantities in parts of the Northern and Western States.

Livestock. Estimates of the cattle stock vary from 4m. to 10m. About 1m. head of cattle and 6m. sheep and goats are slaughtered annually.

MINING. There are important tin- and coalmining industries at Jos and Enugu respectively. In 1967 tin production amounted to 12,620 tons; columbite (1967), 1,955 tons; gold (1967), 39 troy oz.; tantalite (1967), 19,304 lb.; coal, 95,000 tons (used mainly in the country); petroleum (1967), 116,519,000 bbls (of 42 gallons).

INDUSTRY. Timber and hides and skins are other major export commodities. Industrial products include soap, cigarettes, beer, margarine, groundnut oil, meat and cake, concentrated fruit juices, soft drinks, canned food, metal containers, plywood, textiles, ceramic products and cement.

POWER. The Electricity Corporation of Nigeria generated 1,064·22m. kwh. in 1965–66. The Niger dams at Kainji were completed in early 1969 (investment of £87m.) and will provide cheap hydro-electricity for rapid industrialization.

COMMERCE. The principal ports are Lagos, Port Harcourt, Sapele, Calabar and Burutu. There is a great deal of internal commerce in local foodstuffs and imported goods moving by rail, lorry and pack animals overland, and by launches, rafts and canoes along an extensive and complex network of inland waterways. Kano is still, as it has been for centuries, the focus of caravan routes linking a territory which stretches from the Sudan on the east to Senegal in the west, with branches northwards across the Sahara.

Imports, exports, re-exports and overseas shipping are shown below:

Merchandise	1963	1964	1965	1966	1967
Total imports (in £1,000)	207,556	253,880	275,322	254,452	223,300
Domestic exports (in £1,000)	184,986	210,462	263,341	279,697	242,800
Re-exports (in £1,000)	4,767	4,188	5,020	5,351	...

	1965		1966	
Principal Imports	Value(£1,000)	Quantity	Value(£1,000)	Quantity
Cotton piece-goods (1,000 sq. yd)	21,418	209,829	8,939	29,540
Fish (tons)	6,673	26,570	6,877	25,396
Salt (tons)	2,443	127,993	1,886	99,838
Machinery	92,414	—	27,576	—
Motor vehicles (number)	17,605	24,292	11,426	18,011
Jute bags (1,000)	4,995	34,781	5,747	32,201
Petroleum oils (1,000 bbls)	69,097	140,117	91,981	152,428

Principal Exports (in 1,000 tons)	1957	1958	1959	1960	1961	1962	1963	1964	1965	1966
Cocoa	135	88	149	154	183	195	175	197	255	190
Palm-oil	166	171	184	183	164	119	126	134	150	143
Palm-kernels	406	441	430	418	410·6	367	398	394	416	394
Groundnuts	302	513	497	332	493·8	530	614	544	512	573
Rubber	40	42	53	57	54·8	59	62	72	68	70
Hides and skins	8	7	8·6	9·5	9·7	..	8	8·3	8·6	8·2
Tin ore	13	7·6	7·5	10·6	10·4	..	9·8	10·6	10·6	11·5
Oil	..	..	..	..	..	..	..	5,783	13,019	18,945

Trade by main countries	Imports (in £1,000)			Exports (in £1,000)		
	1964	1965	1966	1964	1965	1966
UK	78,669	85,054	76,253	80,657	101,465	105,177
USA	28,930	33,083	41,516	14,320	..	..
Japan	30,810	..	..	2,570	..	..
Netherlands and possessions	..	..	..	27,054	31,539	26,105
German	22,508	29,542	27,458	26,902	27,856	27,757

Total trade between UK and Nigeria, according to British Board of Trade returns (in £1,000 sterling):

	1965	1966	1967	1968	1969	1970
Imports to UK	112,619	112,648	78,913	70,266	104,489	123,874
Exports from UK	72,611	65,941	58,450	57,831	77,904 }	114,385
Re-exports from UK	751	780	764	920	1,227 }	

RAILWAYS. There are 2,278 route miles of line of 3 ft 6 in. gauge. The north-western main line runs from Lagos to Kano (700 miles) through Abeokuta, Ibadan, Ilorin, Jebba, Minna, Kaduna and Zaria. From Kano the line continues for a further 142 miles in a north-easterly direction to its terminus at Nguru, while a branch line from Zaria *via* Gusau to Kaura Namoda serves north-western Nigeria; this line is, in addition, linked with Sokoto by a scheduled railway road service from Gusau. The eastern line runs from Port Harcourt deep-water quay on the Bonny River through the thickly populated oil-palm area to Enugu, where it serves the collieries; it then crosses the Benue River and joins the north-western line at Kaduna (569 miles). A branch line of 63 miles from Kafanchan serves the tin-mines at Jos. An extension from Kuru (near Jos) to Maiduguri (400 miles), to serve the area of Bornu, was opened to traffic in Nov. 1964.

In 1968–69 operating receipts were £11·95m. and working expenditure (including depreciation) was £12·81m.

ROADS (1969). There are about 45,000 miles of maintained roads, of which 5,000 miles are tarred.

At 1 Jan. 1965, 27,705 motor cars were registered. Bus services, by private owners, operate in the larger towns and between the main towns in Eastern and Western Nigeria, but the bulk of passenger and goods traffic by road is carried in lorries (mammy wagons). Taxis are available in the large towns.

AVIATION. There is an extensive system of internal and international air routes, serving Europe, South and West Africa. Regular services are operated by Nigerian Airways (WAAC), BOAC, Air France, KLM, SABENA, Swissair, PANAM and other lines. Aircraft arrivals from outside Nigeria in 1961 totalled 3,804, carrying 726 tons of freight. During the year ended 31 March 1962, 60,036 passengers and 924 tons of mail and freight were carried on internal services.

POST. Postal facilities are provided at 1,428 offices and agencies; telegraph, money order and savings bank services are provided at 280 of these. Most internal letter mail is carried by air at normal postage rates. External telegraph services are owned and operated by Nigerian External Telecommunications, Ltd, at Lagos, from which telegraphic communication is maintained with all parts of the world. There were 74,725 telephones in use in 1968, of which 30,760 were in Lagos and 7,568 in Ibadan.

Federal and some state governments have established commercial corporations for sound and television broadcasting, which are widely used in schools.

BANKING. In Aug. 1967 the statutory foreign-exchange cover of the Central Bank was reduced from 40 to 25%, and the percentage of government securities the Bank is permitted to hold was raised from 33½ to 50% of its total liabilities.

The Central Bank of Nigeria, the Standard Bank of Nigeria, Ltd, Barclays Bank of Nigeria, Ltd, the National Bank of Nigeria, the African Continental Bank, the Merchants' Bank, Ltd, the United Bank for Africa, the Bank of America, the Chase Manhattan Bank, the Bank of the North and the Co-operative Bank are the principal banks operating in Nigeria. All banks are required to be registered as Nigerian companies from 1969.

In 1965–66 the post office savings bank had 340,442 depositors holding £2,913,392.

BOOKS OF REFERENCE

National Development Plan, 1962–68. Ministry of Economic Development, 1962
Economic Survey of Nigeria, 1959. Federal Government Printer, Lagos, 1959
Nigeria Digest of Statistics. Lagos, 1951 ff. (quarterly)
Annual Abstract of Statistics. Federal Office of Statistics, Lagos, 1960 ff.
Nigeria Trade Journal. Federal Ministry of Commerce and Industries (quarterly)
Nigeria Handbook of Commerce and Industries, 1962. Ministry of Commerce and Industries
Aboyade, O., *Foundations of an African economy: investment and growth in Nigeria.* New York, 1966
Afolabi Ojo, G. J., *Yoruba Culture.* Univ. of London Press, 1967
Blitz, F. (ed.), *The Politics and Administration of Nigerian Government.* Lagos and London, 1965
Buchanan, K. H., and Pugh, J. C., *Land and People in Nigeria.* Univ. of London Press, 1955
Burns, A. C., *History of Nigeria.* New ed. London, 1963
Elias, T. O., *Nigerian Land Law and Custom.* London, 1951
Mackintosh, J. P., and others, *Nigerian government and politics.* London, 1966
Nwabueze, B. O., *The Machinery of Justice in Nigeria.* London, 1964
Okigbo, P. N. C., *Nigerian public finance.* Northwestern Univ. Press, 1965
Trade Directory of the Federation of Nigeria. 4th ed. London, 1965

CYPRUS
Kypriaki Dimokratia—Kıbrıs Cumhuriyeti

HISTORY. About the middle of the 2nd millennium B.C. Greek colonies were established in Cyprus and later it formed part of the Persian, Roman and Byzantine empires. In 1193 it became a Frankish kingdom, in 1489 a Venetian dependency and in 1571 was conquered by the Turks. They retained possession of it until its cession to England for administrative purposes under a convention concluded with the Sultan at Constantinople, 4 June 1878. On 5 Nov. 1914 the island was annexed by Great Britain and on 1 May 1925 given the status of a Crown Colony.

For the history of Cyprus from 1931 to 1958 *see* THE STATESMAN'S YEAR-BOOK 1958, pp. 237–38, and 1959, p. 236.

On 1 April 1955 the Greek Cypriots embarked on a guerilla struggle against the British. On 19 Feb. 1959, following discussions in Zürich between the Greek and Turkish Foreign Ministers, an agreement was signed in London by the Prime Ministers of Great Britain, Greece and Turkey, and by the representatives of the Greek Cypriots and Turkish Cypriots. This agreement was implemented on 16 Aug. 1960, when Cyprus became an independent republic. By treaties between the Republic of Cyprus, Great Britain, Greece and Turkey both Enosis and partition are precluded; and Britain retains sovereignty over the areas containing her military bases in the island.

When President Makarios proposed some incisive modifications of the Zürich–London agreements, violent clashes between Greek and Turkish Cypriots broke out on 22 Dec. 1963. First, a joint force of British, Greek and Turkish troops and later a UN peace force were sent to Cyprus. A UN mediator on 26 March 1965 submitted proposals for a settlement of the Cyprus problem. These were accepted by Greece and the Greek Cypriots, but rejected by Turkey; thereupon the mediator, Dr Galo Plaza (Ecuador), resigned. The UN General Assembly on 17 Dec. 1965 called upon all states to respect the sovereignty, unity, independence and territorial integrity of Cyprus and to refrain from any intervention.

In June 1968 representatives of the Greek and Turkish Cypriots started talks in Cyprus aiming at finding a solution to the Cyprus problem.

CONSTITUTION AND GOVERNMENT. The legislative power is exercised by the House of Representatives of 50 members, of whom 35 were elected by the Greek community and 15 by the Turkish community. As from Dec. 1963 the Turkish members have ceased to attend.

On 13 Dec. 1959 Archbishop Makarios was elected President of the Republic, having received 144,501 votes (against 71,753 cast for the candidate sponsored by the Left). Dr Fazil Kuchuk was elected Vice-President unopposed; he resigned on 4 Jan. 1964.

In the presidential elections of 25 Feb. 1968 Archbishop Makarios was re-elected President of the Republic, having received 220,911 votes (against 8,577 cast for the opposition candidate and 16,215 abstentions).

The elections held on 5 July 1970 returned 15 Unified party, 9 Akel Party (Communists), 7 Progressive Front, 2 Democratic Centre Union, 2 Independents. The Turks have not participated in the proceedings of the House since Dec. 1963.

On 16 Feb. 1961 the House of Representatives decided by 41 to 9 votes to apply for membership of the Commonwealth. Cyprus was admitted on 13 March.

In Sept. 1970 the Cabinet, from which the Turkish members have withdrawn, was composed as follows:

External Affairs: Spyros Kyprianou. *Interior and Defence:* Epaminondas Komodromos. *Justice:* Georghios Ioannides. *Labour and Social Insurance:* Andreas Mavromatis. *Agriculture and Natural Resources:* Panayotis Toumazis. *Communications and Works:* Nicos Roussos. *Commerce and Industry:* Nicos Dimitriou. *Finance:* Andreas Patsalides. *Education:* Frixos Petrides. *Health:* Michael Glykys.

DIPLOMATIC REPRESENTATIVES

Country	Cyprus representative	Foreign representative
Austria	—	Dr Ludwig Steiner
Belgium[1]	—	A. C. Paternotte de la Vaillée
Brazil	Zenon Rossides	J. Oswaldo de Meira Penna
Britain[1]	C. Ashiotis, MBE	Edward Ramsbotham, CMG
Bulgaria	—	Gatco Gatcev
Canada[1]	Zenon Rossides	J. C. Gordon Brown
China	—	Matthew Tseng-hua Liu
Cuba	—	Luis Reyes
Czechoslovakia[2]	Demos Hadjiniltis	Josef Manis
Denmark[2]	—	Hans Bortelsen
Finland[2]	—	Leo Tuominen
France	—	Jean de Garnier des Garets
Germany (West)	Tassos Panayides	Dr Alexander Török
Greece	N. Kranidiotis	Constantinos Panayotakos
Hungary	—	Imre Hollai
India[1]	—	A. K. Dar
Israel	—	Shaul Bur-Haim
Italy	N. Kranidiotis	Allesandro C. N. Bugnano
Ivory Coast	—	Anoma Kanie
Japan	—	Shusaku Wada
Lebanon	Antis Soteriades	Alexandre Ammoun[3]
Netherlands	—	Adrianos C. Vroom
Norway[2]	—	Kaare Ingstad
Pakistan[1]	—	M. Rabb
Poland	—	Henryk Golanski
Romania	—	Stelian Pereanu
Spain	—	Manuel Valdes Larranaga
Sudan	—	Salah Osman Hashim
Sweden	Costas Ashiotis	Albert Ake Axel Johnson
Switzerland[1]	—	Hans Georg Hess
Syria	Antis Soteriades	Mohammed Jouheir Accad
Turkey	Ahmed Zaim	Erciiment Yavuzalp[3]
USSR	Demos Hadjiniltis	Nikita P. Tolubeyev
UAR	Antis Soteriades	Salah El-Din M. Sharaway
USA	Zenon Rossides	David H. Popper
Yugoslavia	N. Kranidiotis	Ducan Blagojević

[1] High Commissioner.   [2] Minister.   [3] Chargé d'Affaires.   No figure = Ambassador.

AREA AND POPULATION. Area 3,572 sq. miles (9,251 sq. km); about 140 miles is greatest length from east to west, and about 60 miles is greatest breadth from north to south.

Populations by religions:

Religion	1931	1946[1]	1956[1,2]	1960[3]	1969[4]
Greek Orthodox	276,573	361,199	416,986	441,656	485.100
Turkish Moslem	64,238	80,548	92,642	104,942	115.290
Others	7,148	8,367	19,251	26,968	29.610
Total	347,959	450,114	528,879	573,566	630,000

[1] Excluding military and camps.　　[2] Registration.　　[3] Census.
[4] Mid-year estimate; density per sq. mile, 169.

Principal towns with populations (1969 estimate): Nicosia (the capital), 114,000; Limassol, 51,000; Famagusta, 42,000; Larnaca, 21,300; Paphos, 11,800, and Kyrenia, 4,900. There are 6 administrative districts named after these towns.

VITAL STATISTICS. The birth rate in 1969 was 2·6%; the death rate, 0·72%; infantile mortality, 2·67%; marriage rate, 8·3%.

EDUCATION. During the school year 1969–70 there were 553 elementary schools with 2,185 teachers and 70,125 pupils; 83 secondary (including private) schools, of which 10 are technical-vocational and 1 agricultural, with 1,781 teachers and 36,269 students. Figures for Turkish–Cypriot education are not available.

Primary education, for children between the ages of 5½ and 12 years, is free and compulsory. Secondary and technical education, provided for the age-group 13–18 years, is not free or compulsory. The Government meets the teachers' salaries bill for all public schools, and at the same time some 25% of the pupils receive scholarships. Recent statistics show that 77% of the primary school leavers proceed to secondary schools and another 3·1% to 8-grade primary, the latter being free.

Special education is provided for children who are mentally retarded, blind, deaf or delinquents.

Third-level education is given at 2 teachers' training colleges (for primary schools), one for the Greeks and another for the Turks. Other full-time institutions are the Forestry College, the Higher Technical Institute and the School of Nursing and Midwifery. There are also 8 institutes for foreign languages and a number of private post-secondary schools which function on a part-time basis. But the bulk of third-level education is effected at universities abroad, mainly in Greece, Turkey and the UK.

Greek is the language of 80% of the population and Turkish of 18%. English is widely spoken. English and French are compulsory subjects in secondary schools.

Illiteracy is largely confined to older people.

CINEMAS (1969). There are 140 winter cinemas (82,000 seats) and 200 open-air cinemas (122,000 seats).

NEWSPAPERS (1969). There are 1 English, 2 Turkish and 7 Greek daily newspapers and 17 Greek and 2 Turkish weeklies.

SOCIAL SECURITY. The administration of the social-security services in Cyprus is in the hands of the Ministry of Labour and Social Insurance, with the Ministry of Health providing medical services through public clinics and hospitals on a means test, except medical treatment for employment accidents, which is given free to all insured employees and financed by the Social Insurance Scheme.

SOCIAL INSURANCE. The island's Social Insurance Scheme. which covers compulsorily both employees and self-employed persons, provides, in the case of employees, cash benefits for sickness. unemployment, maternity, marriage (females only), old-age, widowhood and death and cash benefits with free medical treatment for employment accidents and occupational diseases. Self-employed are covered for marriage, old-age, widowhood and death. The Scheme is financed by 3 equal weekly contributions from employers, employees and the State.

PNEUMOCONIOSIS COMPENSATION SCHEME. The Pneumoconiosis Compensation Scheme, introduced in 1960, provides for the payment of compensation in cases of disablement or death caused or accelerated by pneumoconiosis accompanied by tuberculosis. For the purpose of this Scheme, the term pneumoconiosis includes silicosis, sidero-silicosis and asbestosis. The Scheme covers all persons employed in mines and quarries as well as in work which exposes those employed in it to the danger of pneumoconiosis.

ANNUAL HOLIDAY SCHEME. An Annual Holidays with Pay Law, introduced in 1967, provides for a minimum of 9 days paid leave to all workers in the island. The law is implemented by means of regular contributions by employers into a fund administered by Government. Employers offering more than 9 days' paid leave by collective agreement or otherwise may be exempted from paying contributions into the fund.

TERMINATION OF EMPLOYMENT SCHEME. A Termination of Employment law also enacted in 1967 provides for the establishment of a Redundancy Fund to which all employers contribute 0·5 % of their pay-roll, for a maximum period of notice of 1 month in case of dismissal, and for compensation up to 1 year's wages payable direct by employers in case of arbitrary dismissal. Claims under both laws are adjudicated by an Arbitration Tribunal.

JUSTICE. Under the Constitution and other legislation in force the following judicial institutions are established: The Supreme Court of the Republic, the Assize Courts, District Courts and Communal and Ecclesiastical Courts.

The Supreme Court is composed of 5–7 judges (at present 6), one of whom is the President. The Supreme Court adjudicates exclusively and finally: on all constitutional and administrative law matters, including any recourse that any law or decision of the House of Representatives or the budget is discriminatory against either of the two Communities; on any conflict of competence between state organs, questions of unconstitutionality of any law or decisions on any question of interpretation of the Constitution in case of ambiguity, as well as recourses for annulment of administrative acts, decisions or omissions. The Supreme Court is the highest appellate court in the Republic and has jurisdiction to hear and determine all appeals from any court. It has exclusive jurisdiction to issue orders in the nature of *habeas corpus, mandamus,* prohibition, *quo warranto* and *certiorari* and in admiralty and matrimonial matters.

There are 6 Assize Courts and 6 District Courts, one for each district. The Assize Courts have unlimited criminal jurisdiction and power to order compensation up to £800. The District Courts exercise original civil and criminal jurisdiction, the extent of which varies with the composition of the Bench. In civil matters (other than those within the original jurisdiction of Supreme Court) a District Court composed of not less than 2 and not more than 3 judges has unlimited jurisdiction. A President or a District Judge sitting alone has jurisdiction up to £500, and is also empowered to deal with any action for the recovery of possession of any immovable property, and certain other specified matters. In criminal matters the jurisdiction of a District Court is exercised by its members sitting singly and is of a summary character. A President or a District Judge sitting alone has power to try any offence punishable with imprisonment up to 3 years, or with a fine up to £500 or with both, and may order compensation up to £500.

Civil disputes relating to personal status of members of the Turkish Community, including matrimonial cases and maintenance, are dealt with by 2 Turkish Communal Courts. There is a communal appellate court to which appeals may be made from the decision of the Courts of first instance.

There is a Greek Orthodox Church tribunal with exclusive jurisdiction in matrimonial causes between members of the Greek Orthodox Church. There is an appellate tribunal of that Church.

FINANCE. Currency. The Cyprus £ is equivalent to the £ sterling; it is divided into 1,000 *mils*. Notes of the following denominations are in circulation: £5, £1, 500 mils. 250 mils. Coins in circulation: Cupro-nickel: 100, 50, 25 mils; bronze: 5 and 3 mils; aluminium: 1 mil.

Budget. Revenue and expenditure for calendar years (in £ sterling):

Ordinary	1965	1966	1967	1968	1969
Revenue	24,456,234	27,054,928	28,838,102	30,963,578	35,726,061
Expenditure[2]	19,732,273	19,926,893	21,497,809	25,738,782	27,881,153
Development					
Expenditure	4,021,059	4,172,323	4,428,923	5,591,292	7,543,761

[1] Estimates.
[2] Includes transfers to Development Fund: 1967: £8m.

Main sources of ordinary revenue in 1969 were: Import duties, £11,615,124; excise duties, £3,999,822; income tax, £5,849,194; other duties, taxes and licences, £3,898,560; rents, royalties and interest, £2,570,234; fees and charges, £3,800,083; post office, £652,531.

Main divisions of ordinary expenditure in 1969 were: Personal emoluments, £12,257,176; pensions and gratuities, £1,194,180; public works, £482,785; commodity subsidies, £1,903,179; subventions and contributions, £2,264,124; public debt charges, £2,012,721.

Development expenditure for 1969 included £1,685,154 for water development, £1,342,395 for agriculture, forests and fisheries, £295,536 for rural development, £1,886,010 for roads, ports and airports, and £519,366 for commerce and industry.

The outstanding public debt as at 31 Dec. 1969 was £12,148,651 and accumulated sinking funds totalled £4,341,630. Outstanding loans as at 31 Dec. 1969 totalled £21,811,788; including £7,883,926 to the Electricity Authority of Cyprus and £2,988,000 to the Cyprus Telecommunications Authority.

DEFENCE. In 1964 compulsory conscription of 6 months was introduced and extended to 24 months in 1967. The National Guard, which was set up in 1964, is a modern and well-equipped force entrusted with the island's defence. The Cyprus Police Force is mainly employed for the maintenance of law and order, the preservation of peace and the prevention and detection of crime. For the performance of all these duties the members of the force are entitled to carry arms.

AGRICULTURE. Chief agricultural products in 1969: Wheat, 80,000 tons; barley, 100,000 tons; olives, 19,000 tons; carobs, 55,000 tons; potatoes, 160,000 tons; grapes, 200,000 tons; wines, including commandaria (1968), 9·3m. gallons; oranges, 105,000 tons; lemons, 23,000 tons; grapefruit, 48,500 tons; melons, 7,000 tons; carrots. 23,000 tons; milk, 60,600 tons; meat 27,650 tons.

Of the island's 2·3m. acres, approximately 1m. are farmed. About 37% of the economically active population are engaged in agriculture.

Livestock in 1969 (in 1,000): Cattle, 40; sheep, 415; goats, 335; pigs, 113.

FORESTRY. During 1969 the Forest Department continued preserving and developing existing forests. Total forest area, 670 sq. miles. In 1969 the chief forest products, valued at £92,949, were 1,297,058 cu. ft of lumber and 416,073 cu. ft of firewood. In 1969 an area of 5,100 donums (approximately 1,370 acres) was reforested.

MINING. The principal minerals exported during 1969 were (in long tons): Iron pyrites, 834,082; cupreous concentrates, 62,780; copper cement, 9,412; asbestos, 18,842; gypsum, 8,882; chromium ores and concentrates, 26,467. Mining provided about 30·7% of all exports in 1969 and 35·6% in 1968. Total value of minerals exported in 1969 was £11m.

INDUSTRY. Cyprus has no heavy industry, but a wide variety of light manufacturing industries. The establishment of a Development Bank in 1963 has given further impetus to industrial activity. Manufacturing industry in 1969 contributed about 11·4% to the gross domestic product and gave employment to 16·9% of the economically active population. The gross domestic product of manufacturing industries in 1969 was estimated at £21m.

Since 1960, £11·4m. has been spent on water dams, water supplies, hydrological research and geophysical surveys. Existing dams have (1969), a capacity of 10,265m. gallons as against 250m. gallons before independence.

TOURISM. Some 118,000 foreign tourists visited Cyprus in 1969.

TRADE UNIONS AND ASSOCIATIONS. Cyprus has trade-union legislation on the lines of the British Trade Union Acts. Registration is compulsory and freedom of association is constitutionally and statutorily guaranteed. At the end of 1968 the trade unions were distributed as follows: Pancyprian Federation of Labour ('old' trade unions), 34,664 members in 17 unions; Cyprus Workers Confederation ('free' labour syndicates), 17,767 members in 40 unions; Pancyprian Federation of Independent Trade Unions, 1,116 members in 7 unions; Cyprus Turkish Trade Unions Federation, 2,591 members in 21 unions; Cyprus Democratic Labour Federation, 1,095 members in 13 unions; Civil Service and other trade unions, 9,880 members in 25 unions.

The 'old' trade unions are affiliated to the World Federation of Trade Unions, the 'free' labour syndicates and the Turkish Federation are affiliated to the International Confederation of Free Trade Unions.

In Dec. 1968 the total number of employers' associations was 15 with a total membership of 593. Most of the employers' associations are members of the Cyprus Employers' Consultative Association, an organization with 232 'direct' members and 10 trade associations consisting of 454 members. The number of persons employed by the above members is 25,013 (18,530 by *direct* members and 6,483 by trade associations).

COMMERCE. The commerce and the shipping, exclusive of coasting trade, for calendar years were (in £ sterling):

	1965	1966	1967	1968	1969
Imports[1]	37,615,571	51,406,712	55,367,591	59,712,404	86,461,463
Exports[2]	20,549,041	25,287,888	29,238,267	29,696,609	40,90 ,699
Bullion imports	95,847	165,491	184,921	207,579	268,665

[1] Excluding Naafi imports of about £1m.–£2m. annually.
[2] Including re-exports and ships stores of about £2m.–£2·5m. annually.

Chief civil imports, 1969 (in £1,000 sterling):

Meat and preparations	1,838	Cereals and cereal preparations	3,164
Sugar	586	Petroleum and petroleum products	5,976
Medicines	1,366	Gas, natural and manufactured	6,365
Egg and dairy products	1,839	Fuel and lubricants	6,365
Textile yarn and fabrics made up	7,842		

Chief domestic exports, 1969 (in £1,000 sterling):

Grapes	1,258	Wine	1,571
Grapefruit	1,709	Distilled alcoholic beverages	1,337
Lemons	1,150	Asbestos	945
Oranges	4,352	Copper cement	2,264
Raisins (including sultanas)	319	Cupreous concentrates	4,370
Potatoes	4,795	Cupreous pyrites	723
Carobs: seed and kibbled	1,229	Iron pyrites	3,172
Carrots	1,308		

In 1969 UK supplied 31·1% of the imports; other parts of the Commonwealth, 2·3; the European countries, 49·9; of the exports, 36·8 went to the UK, 1·2 to other parts of the Commonwealth, 53·4 to the European countries.

Total trade between Cyprus and UK, in £1,000 sterling (British Board of Trade returns):

	1965	1966	1967	1968	1969	1970
Imports to UK	10,515	12,372	14,462	15,899	18,943	20,432
Exports from UK	15,511	16,463	16,394	22,730	25,641 ⎫	26,088
Re-exports from UK	458	451	414	479	583 ⎭	

ROADS. In 1969 the total length of roads was 4,791 miles, of which 2,123 miles were paved and 2,668 miles were earth or gravel roads. The main paved roads which are maintained by the Ministry of Communications and Works (Public Works Department) totalled 1,272 miles. The total of urban streets was 586 miles, of which 429 miles were asphalted. Village roads and streets totalled 2,157 miles, of which 422 miles were paved, the rest being of earth or gravel surface. There were also 776 miles of unpaved forest roads.

SHIPPING. In 1969, 2,802 ships of 4,867,332 net tons entered and 2,795 of 4,852,412 cleared Cyprus ports. Ships under Cyprus registry (1969) numbered 219 of 1,149,330 tons.

AVIATION. Nicosia airport is the only civil airport of the country. During 1969, 350,954 persons travelled and 5·2m. kg of commercial air-freight was handled through the airport.

POST (1969). There were 39 post offices, 32 postal-order agencies, 836 postal agencies and 13 telegraph offices. Wireless licences issued were 112,504 and television licences 33,286.

The Cyprus Telecommunications Authority runs radio-telephone and telegraph services to most parts of the world. A ship-to-shore telephone and telegraph service is also in operation.

BANKING. There is a Central and Issuing Bank exercising monetary functions, and the Cyprus Development Corporation created by the Government as a major source of loan funds for industrial development. Commercial banks carrying on business in Cyprus are: Bank of Cyprus Ltd, Turkish Bank of Nicosia, Banque Populaire de Limassol, Barclays Bank DCO, The Chartered Bank, National Bank of Greece, Turkiye Ish Bankasi, The Co-operative Central Bank, National & Grindlays Bank and Lombard Banking (Cyprus) Ltd.

The Central Bank of Cyprus, established in 1963, is responsible for the issue of currency, the regulation of money supply and credit, administration of the exchange control law and the foreign-exchange reserves of the Republic. The Bank also acts as a banker of the banks operating in Cyprus and of the Government.

At the end of Dec. 1969 total deposits in banks were £113·3m. Advances and loans were £90·1m., as compared to £85m. in 1968. The country's foreign-exchange reserves at the end of Dec. 1968 were £72·1m., and the foreign-exchange coverage of the total liabilities of the Central Bank of Cyprus was 104·1 %.

WEIGHTS AND MEASURES. Cyprus weights and measures follow the standard weights and measures of Great Britain. The metric system may also be lawfully used. In internal trade the following special Cyprus weights and measures are in use: 1 *pic* = $\frac{2}{3}$ yd; 1 *oke* = 2·8 lb.; 1 *kilé* = 8 Imperial gallons. The Cyprus *donum* is approximately $\frac{1}{3}$ acre.

BOOKS OF REFERENCE

STATISTICAL INFORMATION. Statistics and Research Deparment, Nicosia.

Alastos, D., *Cyprus in History*. London, 1955.—*Cyprus Guerilla*. London, 1960
Christodoulou, D., *The Evolution of the Rural Land use Pattern in Cyprus*. Bude, 1960
Emilianides, A., *Histoire de Chypre*. Paris, 1962.—*The Zurich and London Agreements and the Cyprus Republic*. Athens, 1962
Hill, Sir George F., *A History of Cyprus*. 4 vols. Cambridge, 1940–52
Luke, Sir Harry, *Cyprus*. Rev. ed. London, 1965
Politis, J. N., *Chypre*. Paris, 1959
Spyridakis, C., *An Outline of the History of Cyprus*. Nicosia, 1957
The Directory of the Republic of Cyprus [with Trade Index and Who's Who]. London, 1962

SIERRA LEONE

HISTORY. The Colony of Sierra Leone originated in the sale and cession, in 1787, by native chiefs to English settlers, of a piece of land intended as a home for natives of Africa who were waifs in London, and later it was used as a settlement for Africans rescued from slave-ships. The hinterland was declared a British protectorate on 21 Aug. 1896.

CONSTITUTION AND GOVERNMENT. The Constitution embodied in the Sierra Leone (Constitution) Order in Council 1961, came into force at Independence on 27 April 1961 when Sierra Leone became a sovereign and independent member state of the Commonwealth of Nations. Sierra Leone was accordingly admitted to the United Nations as the 100th member.

Under the Constitution, the Queen's Representative is the Governor-General appointed on the advice of the Prime Minister. The Government consists of the Prime Minister appointed by the Governor-General and Ministers appointed by the Governor-General on the advice of the Prime Minister from among members of the House of Representatives.

The House of Representatives consists of a Speaker and not less than 60 members elected from constituencies established by an Electoral Commission.

After the elections held on 17 March 1967 the Governor-General Sir Henry Lightfoot-Boston, GCMG, JP, appointed Siaka Stevens, leader of the All People's Congress, Prime Minister on 21 March. On the same day, however, the Government was overthrown by a military coup under the Army Commander, Brig. David Lansana. On 23 March 1967 there was a counter-coup by senior army and police officers who proclaimed the National Reformation Council on 25 March with Brig. Andrew Juxon-Smith as Chairman, Commissioner of Police L. W. Leigh as Deputy Chairman and 6 others.

On the night of 17-18 April 1968 the National Reformation Council was overthrown by army and police non-commissioned officers, who announced the formation of the Anti-Corruption Revolutionary Movement. The ACRM appointed an Interim Council, but later decided, in concurrence with the elected parliamentarians, that there should be a national government comprising candidates drawn from both political parties, independent candidates and Paramount Chiefs.

On 26 April 1968 constitutional government and civilian rule was restored with the appointment and swearing-in of Siaka Stevens as Prime Minister by the Chief Justice Banja Tejan-Sie, performing the functions of Governor-General.

The Cabinet consists of 20 Ministers from the ruling All Peoples Congress (APC), including 2 Paramount Chiefs as Ministers of State, and 6 Deputy Ministers, with Dr Siaka Stevens as head of the Cabinet.

LOCAL GOVERNMENT. The Provinces are administered through the Department of the Interior and divided into 147 Chiefdoms, each under the control of a Paramount Chief and Council of Elders known as the Tribal Authority, who are responsible for the maintenance of law and order and for the administration of justice (except for serious crimes). 143 of these Chiefdoms have been organized into local government units, empowered to raise and disburse funds for the development of the Chiefdom concerned. In each administrative district there is a fully elective District Council, with a president elected by the members from their number. District Councils have now developed into local government units with funds at their disposal for the development of their districts.

DIPLOMATIC REPRESENTATIVES

Country	Sierra Leone representative	Foreign representative
Belgium	—	G. Barthelemy
Britain[1]	V. S. Kanu	S. J. L. Olver, CMG, MBE

[1] High Commissioner.   No figure = Ambassador.

Country	Sierra Leone representative	Foreign representative
Canada[1]	—	Paul Malone
China	—	Rear-Adm. Lir Hoh-tu
Czechoslovakia	—	Jan Sebik
France	—	Jean Finés
Germany (West)	D. E. Fashole-Luke	Dr W. Seldis
Ghana[1]	—	R. Andani
Guinea	E. E. M'Bayo[2]	M. Toure'[2]
India[1]	—	Amirik S. Mehta
Israel	—	Modechai Lador
Italy	—	A. Capele di Bugnane
Ivory Coast	—	Pierre Kofi
Upper Volta		
Dahomey		
Japan	—	S. Tsurnga
Korea, South	—	Wan Bok Choi
Lebanon	—	F. Solloukh[2]
Liberia	Dr R. E. Chaulker	G. T. Brewer
Madagascar	—	D. A. Ratsimananga
Mali	—	—
Netherlands	—	J. P. Engels
Nigeria[1]	A. B. Mausaray	O. Jolaoso
Pakistan[1]	—	H. M. Ashon
Poland	—	M. Sieczkowski[2]
Spain	—	M. Carbrera[2]
Sweden	—	O. Ripa
Switzerland	—	J. Monnier[2]
USSR	A. P. Genda	Alexander Alexandrov
UAR	C. O. Bright[2]	Abdel Aziz Khairat[2]
USA	J. J. Akar, MBE	Robert G. Miner
Yugoslavia	—	A. Psonack[2]

[1] High Commissioner.   [2] Chargé d'Affaires.   No figure = Ambassador.

AREA AND POPULATION. Sierra Leone is bounded on the north-west, north and north-east by the Republic of Guinea, on the south-east by Liberia and on the south-west by the Atlantic Ocean. The coastline extends from the boundary of the Republic of Guinea to the north of the mouth of the Great Scarcies River to the boundary of Liberia at the mouth of the Mano River, a distance of about 212 miles.

The area of Sierra Leone is 27,925 sq. miles (73,326 sq. km). Population (census April 1963, preliminary), 2,183,000; estimate (1966) 2·49m., of whom about 2,000 are Europeans, 3,000 Asiatics and 30,000 non-native Africans. The capital is Freetown, with 128,000 inhabitants.

Sierra Leone is divided into 3 provinces (Eastern, Southern, Northern) covering 12 districts, each administered by a Resident Minister. The principal peoples are the Limbas and Korankos in the north, the Temnes in the centre, and the Mendis in the south.

EDUCATION (1968–69). There were 914 registered primary schools with a total enrolment of 139,413. Primary education is as yet neither free nor compulsory. School attendance varies considerably in different parts of the country. The western area has about 47% of its primary-school-age children in school, while the percentage is as low as 12% elsewhere.

There were 72 secondary schools with a total enrolment of 25,207 pupils; nine of these schools take the pupils up to university level. Technical education was provided in 2 technical institutes, 2 trade centres and in the technical training establishments of the mining companies. There is also a rural institute.

Teacher-training was carried out in 9 training colleges, 2 of which are government-run, 5 mission-operated; 2 in the western area—Milton Margai Teachers

Training College and the Freetown Teachers College, are autonomous. The number of teachers in training for the teachers certificate was 901.

Fourah Bay College and Njala University College are the 2 constituent colleges of the University of Sierra Leone. They have a total student enrolment of 901 students. The newly formed Institute of Education which is part of the University, is now responsible for teacher education, educational research and curriculum development in the country.

HEALTH. In the western area there are 7 government hospitals (806 beds and 202 cots), including a maternity hospital, a children's hospital and an infectious diseases hospital near Freetown. A mental hospital at Kissy has accommodation for 217 patients. In the provinces there are 13 government hospitals, 4 hospitals associated with mining companies and 6 mission hospitals. There is a school of nursing in Freetown. There are 107 government dispensaries and health and treatment centres. There is also a military hospital (60 beds).

JUSTICE. The Supreme Court has jurisdiction in civil and criminal matters. Subordinate courts are held by magistrates in the various districts. Native Courts apply native law and custom under a criminal and civil jurisdiction. Appeals from the decisions of magistrates' courts are heard by the Supreme Court. Appeals from the decisions of the Supreme Court are heard by the Sierra Leone Court of Appeal. Appeal lies from the Sierra Leone Court of Appeal to the Privy Council.

In 1966, 284 persons were convicted in the Supreme Court.

Police. The police force at 1 Aug. 1968 had an authorized strength of 56 superior police officers, 76 junior police officers and 1,985 other ranks. In the provinces each Chiefdom keeps an additional force known as Chiefdom Police.

A non-pensionable force, known as the Auxiliary Force and consisting of 2 junior police officers and 270 other ranks, are helping the regular force in maintaining law and order in the diamond protected area in the Eastern Province.

FINANCE. Currency. The Bank of Sierra Leone, which was established on 4 Aug. 1964, is responsible for providing the currency in the country. It introduced on 4 Aug. 1964 a decimal currency, the *leone*, equalling 10s. and the *cent* worth £0·06 The paper currency consists of 1, 2 and 5 *leone* notes; the coinage of ½, 1, 5, 10 and 20 *cents*.

The currency is interchangeable with sterling at par. At 31 Dec. 1968 total Sierra Leone notes and coins in circulation was Le. 19,679,354.

Budget. Revenue and expenditure (in £ sterling, from 1965 in leones) for years ending 30 June.

	1964–65	1965–66	1966–67	1967–68	1968–69
Revenue	17,525,908	42,201,797	41,336,354	37,384,358	41,700,000
Expenditure	17,559,813	43,933,759	39,576,124	41,701,151	40,800,000

Estimated ordinary revenue in 1967–68 was Le. 41,716,542; fees, payment for services, etc., Le. 1·31m.; post and telecommunications, Le. 319,266; direct taxes, Le. 10m.; licences, etc., Le. 601,320; reimbursements, royalties and interest, Le. 407,256.

AGRICULTURE. In the western area farming is largely confined to the production of cassava and garden crops, such as maize and vegetables, for local consumption. In the provincial areas the principal products include rice, which is the staple food of the country, and export crops such as palm kernels, cocoa beans, coffee, and ginger. Cattle production is important in the northern part of the country, and most of the poultry, eggs and pork are produced in the western area.

The first agricultural statistical survey showed that in 1965–66 there were 251,000 small holdings cultivating 981,000 acres; large farmers cultivated 22,700 acres. Rice plantations covered 741,600 acres; groundnuts, 49,300 acres; coffee, 77,400 acres.

Livestock (rough estimate): Cattle, 170,000; goats, 1·35m.; sheep, 45,800; chickens, 928,700.

FISHERIES. There has been a gradual expansion of the fishing industry due to the introduction of new fishing techniques and gear. The indigenous canoe fishery for sardines and Bonga (*Ethamalosa fimbriata*) was estimated to have produced 24,000 tons of fish in 1966. The Food and Agricultural Organization is carrying out a 5-year survey of pelagic fish resources along the coastline and continental shelf.

Total catch of fish is still below the demand of the country. In 1966, 184,283 cwt of fish were imported at a value of Le. 1,310,054. Total catch for 1966 was 29,000 tons.

MINING. The chief minerals mined are diamonds, iron ore, bauxite and rutile. These minerals accounted for 89·5% of domestic exports in 1967. Molybdenite and gold are being prospected.

INDUSTRY. Four pioneer oil-mills for the expressing of palm-oil are operated by the Sierra Leone Produce Marketing Board. Government also operates 4 rice-mills, and there are a number of privately owned mills. At Kenema the Government Department of Forest Industries produces sawn timber, joinery products (including prefabricated buildings) and high-class furniture. In addition, there is a smaller privately owned sawmill at Panguma and several small furniture workshops throughout the country. All these products are used internally. Village industries include fishing, fish curing and smoking, weaving and hand methods of expressing palm-oil and cracking palm kernels.

LABOUR. A large proportion of the population was engaged in agriculture and about 120,000 workers in wage-earning employment at the end of 1967, distributed as follows: Government, 31,180; private undertakings, 27,530; statutory boards and corporations, 4,933. The rest are employed in establishments employing fewer than 6 persons which need not submit returns.

The Labour Division has its headquarters in Freetown, offices in Bo, Kenema and Makeni and 7 employment exchanges.

Wages and conditions of employment are regulated by 4 Joint Industrial Councils and 5 Wages Boards, which together cover the majority of wage-earners.

There are 24 registered trade unions (19 workers and 5 employers). The number of persons registered for employment at the end of 1967 was 8,984, excluding maritime, articled and the dock workers who are registered in the Port Labour (Maritime, Articled and Harbour) Pools; registrations in these Pools numbered 7,191.

COMMERCE. Total trade (in £ sterling; from 1964 in *leone*) for calendar years:

	1963	1964	1965	1966	1967	1968
Imports	29,854,699	71,018,594	76,875,000	71,707,000	65,268,000	75,481,995
Exports	25,440,267	67,965,199	63,224,000	59,130,000	50,458,000	75,727,891

In 1965 the principal imports were: Wheat meal and flour, 279,813 cwt, Le. 1,457,987; sugar, 424,760 cwt, Le. 1,795,302; fish, 100,325 cwt, Le. 559,953; milk and cream, 34,253 cwt, Le. 543,450; meat, 3,856 cwt, Le. 203,019; beer, ale, stout and porter, 520,428 gallons, Le. 662,486; tobacco unmanufactured, 24,114 cwt, Le. 997,726; motor spirit, 7,876,813 gallons, Le. 800,204; diesel and gas oil, 41,876,667 gallons, Le. 3,677,988; medicinal and pharmaceutical products, Le. 1,135,879; soap, 73,915 cwt, Le. 529,253; cotton fabrics, 6,100,078 sq. yd, Le. 1,029,786; fabrics of synthetic fibres, 3,430,426 sq. yd, Le. 1,022,758; corrugated-iron sheet, 4,586 tons, Le. 738,546; cement, 27,354 tons, Le. 439,488; motor vehicles, Le. 5,736,093; electrical machinery, Le. 548,605; footwear, Le. 890,113; mining machinery, Le. 1,321,400; radio sets, Le. 287,689.

Principal exports in 1965 were: Palm kernels, 49,274 tons, Le. 5,681,133; coffee (raw), 76,105 cwt, Le. 1,340,765; cocoa, 58,643 cwt, Le. 902,809; piassava, 89,051 cwt, Le 437,000; iron ore, 2,296,812 tons, Le. 10,899,195; diamonds, 1,525,437 carats, Le. 36,959,039; bauxite, 173,472 tons, Le. 578,617.

Of the imports 38% came from UK, 10·2% from Japan, 7·9% from West Germany. Of the exports 78·3% went to UK, 9·8% to Netherlands, 6·9% to West Germany.

Total trade between Sierra Leone and UK (British Board of Trade returns, in £1,000 sterling):

	1965	1966	1967	1968	1969	1970
Imports to UK	27,134	19,514	22,522	34,807	36,165	31,448
Exports from UK	10,290	9,465	8,244	9,851	13,406	12,530
Re-exports from UK	348	374	217	183	168	

RAILWAYS. A government railway, a single line of 2 ft 6 in. gauge, is open from Freetown to Pendembu, near the Liberian frontier (227½ miles). From Bauya Junction, 64½ miles from Freetown, a branch line runs to Makeni (83 miles), but following the government decision to phase out the railway, this line was closed in 1968. Total receipts, 1967–68, Le. 690,513; total ordinary working expenditure, Le. 1,685,905.

The Sierra Leone Development Co. Ltd railway (3 ft 6 in. gauge, 58 miles) is used for the transport of iron ore from Marampa to the port of Pepel.

SHIPPING. During 1968 the total tonnage handled by the port of Freetown was 419,519 tons of cargo and 435,244 tons of bunker fuel; a total of 1,584 vessels called at Freetown during 1967.

Bonthe-Sherbro, 80 miles south of Freetown, is used for the shipment of piassava, palm kernels, rutile and bauxite. Pepel, the terminal loading port for iron ore, lies some 12 miles from Freetown; 81 vessels called in 1967.

ROADS. There are about 4,460 miles of main roads, of which 380 miles are surfaced with bitumen.

Motor vehicles licensed during 1966–67 totalled 14,063 passenger cars, 5,458 buses and trucks and 1,223 motor cycles.

AVIATION. Freetown Airport (Lungi), situated north of Freetown in the Port Loko District, is the only international airport in Sierra Leone and all aircraft entering and leaving the territory must land at Lungi.

The airport is served by Sierra Leone Airways, Ghana/Nigeria Airways, BUA, Union de Transport Aériens, Middle East Airlines, KLM, Air Afrique, United Arab Airlines and Czechoslovakia Airlines. A once weekly non-stop flight from London (Gatwick) to Freetown and vice versa is also provided.

Sierra Leone Airways provide domestic flights daily (except Sundays) from Hastings (14 miles from Freetown) to Gbangatoke, Bo, Kenema, Yengema, twice weekly to Bonthe and occasional flights to Marampa and Port Loko on charter basis.

POST. The Posts and Telecommunications Department maintains a trunk network of radio and overhead telephone and telegraph routes of approximately 3,000 miles linking the western area with the other provinces. Automatic telephone exchanges have been introduced at the provincial centres of Bo, Kenema and Makeni; microwave radio relay link now replaces overhead open wire on main trunk routes. An extension programme to link important mining areas at Koidu and Mokanji to the national network by microwave links is well on the way.

The wired broadcasting relay service was replaced in Jan. 1964 by a transistor radio service. Approximately 20,000 transistor radios purchased under this scheme are now in service. Number of telephones (1970) 8,000. Telegraphic facilities are provided at 58 offices. There are 136 post offices and postal agencies. The number of private wireless-licence holders at 30 June 1969 was 67,316 and 555 television sets were in operation.

BANKING. The Bank of West Africa and Barclays Bank DCO have their headquarters at Freetown; the former has 9 and the latter 10 branches and agencies.

At the end of 1960 there were 72,888 depositors in the 41 branches of the post office savings bank, with £1,589,302 (inclusive of interest) to their credit.

BOOKS OF REFERENCE

Atlas of Sierra Leone. Ed. Survey and Lands Dept. Freetown, 1953
Sierra Leone Studies. Ed. J. D. Hargreaves. Freetown, 1953 ff.
Fyfe, C., A History of Sierra Leone. OUP, 1962.—Fyfe, C., and Jones, E. (ed.), Freetown. Sierra Leone Univ. Press and OUP, 1968
Jack, D. T., Economic Survey of Sierra Leone. Government Printer, Freetown, 1958
Lewis, R., Sierra Leone. HMSO, 1954
Porter, A. T., Creoledom: a study in the development of Freetown society. OUP, 1963
Saylor, R. G., The economic system of Sierra Leone. Duke Univ. Press, 1968

UNITED REPUBLIC OF TANZANIA

On 26 April 1964 Tanganyika, Zanzibar and Pemba combined to form the United Republic of Tanganyika and Zanzibar (named Tanzania on 29 Oct.)

CONSTITUTION AND GOVERNMENT. An 'interim constitution' was approved by parliament on 5 July 1965 and assented to by the President on 8 July 1965.

The country is a one-party state, the Tanganyika African National Union constituting the one party in Tanganyika and the Afro-Shirazi Party in Zanzibar.

The President of the United Republic is head of state and commander-in-chie of the armed forces. The first vice-president is head of the executive in Zanzibar under the title of President of Zanzibar; the second vice-president is also the leader of the National Assembly.

The National Assembly is composed of 107 elected members from the mainland, 10 members appointed (from both Tanganyika and Zanzibar), 15 National Members (elected by the National Assembly after nomination by various national institutions), 20 Regional Commissioners, up to 32 members of the Zanzibar Revolutionary Council and up to 20 other Zanzibar members appointed by the President in agreement with the President of Zanzibar.

The central government was in July 1969 composed as follows:

President of the United Republic and Minister for Foreign Affairs: Dr Julius K. Nyerere (re-elected for 5 years on 30 Sept. 1965 by 2,519,866 against 92,359 votes).

First Vice-President: Shaikh Abeid Amani Karume. Second Vice-President: Rashidi Mfaume Kawawa.

Finance: Amir Jamal. Economic Affairs and Development Planning: Paul Bomani. Agriculture and Co-operatives: Derek Bryceson. Commerce and Industry: A. M. Babu. Regional Administration and Rural Development: P. A. Kisumo. Communications, Labour and Works: Job Lusinde. Lands, Housing and Urban Development: J. W. Kihampa. Education: C. Y. Mgonje. Home Affairs: S. A. Maswanya. Information and Tourism: Hasnu Makame. Health and Social Welfare: L. N. Sijaona. Foreign Affairs: S. Mhando.

Five Ministers of State are attached to the presidential offices.

DIPLOMATIC REPRESENTATIVES

Country	Tanzanian representative	Foreign representative
Algeria	—	Ali Benghenzal
Australia[1]	—	W. G. Landale
Austria	—	E. Gebauer
Belgium	—	E. Nopper
Brazil	—	F. T. de Mesquita
Britain[1]	P. P. Muro	H. Phillips
Bulgaria	—	Veliko Entchen
Burundi	—	Protais Mangona
Canada[1]	A. Sykes	J. A. Irwin
China	R. Wambura	Chung Hsi-tung
Congo (K.)	A. H. Diria	L. G. Eketebi
Cuba	S. A. Salim	A. M. Zorilla
Czechoslovakia	—	R. Rezeh
Denmark	—	Kai Johansen
Ethiopia	F. Rutakyamirwa	Ata Abate Agede
Finland	—	J. Pekuvi
France	A. Faraji	A. Naudi
Germany (East)	—	E. Butzke
Germany (West)	A. B. Nyaki	N. Hebich
Ghana[1]	—	E. L. Nathan
Guinea	S. S. Rashid	Sakko Damon
Hungary	—	M. Bard
India[1]	S. Chale	V. C. Vijaya Raghavan
Indonesia	—	Brig.-Gen. Otto A. Rehman
Israel	—	S. H. Moratt
Italy	—	Dr Vittorio Zadotti
Ivory Coast	—	G. Attoungbre
Japan	—	M. Suma
Korea	R. Wambura	Song Gi Tae
Lesotho	—	P. A. Mabathona
Liberia	—	J. J. Cooper
Mali	—	A. Sangare
Mongolia	—	B. Lotchin
Morocco	—	A. Boumhdi
Netherlands	I. A. Wakil	A. M. E. Brinks
Norway	—	J. Ostern
Pakistan[1]	—	Dr M. O. Chani
Poland	—	J. Witek
Rwanda	—	A. M. Kakenza
Somalia	—	Brig.-Gen. A. Farah
Sudan	W. M. Aryamba	M. O. M. El Awad
Sweden	Chief M. Lukumbuzya	S. F. Hedin
Switzerland	—	L. Mossz
Syria	—	Naim Kaddan
Tunisia	—	S. Abellah
Turkey	—	Sadum Terem
USSR	R. Lukindo	V. Ustinov
UAR	S. Nkigula	M. F. El-Bedewy
USA	G. A. Rutabanzibwa	C. G. Ross
Vietnam (North)	R. S. Wambura	Le Than Tan
Yugoslavia	—	M. Knezovic
Zambia[1]	C. P. Ngaiza	S. V. Mukando

[1] High Commissioner. No figure = Ambassador.

POPULATION. The census of Aug. 1967 gave 12,231,342 for the United Republic, of which 11,876,982 were counted in mainland Tanzania (density per sq. mile, 34·8) and 354,360 in Zanzibar (density per sq. mile, 347·1).

FINANCE. Currency. The monetary unit is the Tanzanian shilling divided into 100 cents. Although it replaced the East African Shilling on 14 June 1966, the latter remained a legal tender until Oct. 1967. The Tanzanian coinage has denomination of 5, 20, 50 Cts. and 1 Sh.; 1 sh. = 14 US cents. Notes and coins in circulation at the end of Feb. 1967 were 409·2m. sh.

Budget. Revenue and expenditure (in Tanzanian Sh.1m.) for financial years ending 30 June:

	1965–66	1966–67	1967–68	1968–69	1969–70[1]
Revenue	891·9	1,017·2	1,123·6	1,257·3	1,498·2
Expenditure	887·7	979·7	1,065·0	1,186·0	1,435·0

[1] Estimate.

Import duties in 1969–70 amounted to 580·5m. sh. and income tax to 335m. sh. The main items of expenditure for the year 1969–70 were communications, transport and labour (278·5m. sh.), education (56·2m. sh.) and agriculture, food and co-operatives (109·9m. sh.). Development expenditure, 1969–70, was estimated at 623m. sh.

Development expenditure, 1967–68, is estimated at 394,893,000 sh.

Total national debt on 30 June 1969 amounted to 1,412·44m. sh.

DEFENCE. The Army consists of 3 battalions in Tanganyika and 1 battalion in Zanzibar. No navy is maintained.

Following withdrawal of West German assistance in 1965, the Air Force was built up with the help of Canada. Equipment supplied from Canada comprises 5 Caribou, 8 Otter and 6 Beaver transport aircraft. About 7 Piaggio P.149D trainers are also in service. Following a new agreement with China, personnel are being trained near Peking and will operate 2 squadrons of MiG-17 jet fighters.

TRADE. There is a uniform customs tariff in Tanzania, Kenya and Uganda, the three countries being united in a customs union since 1949. For details *see* pp. 471–73.

In 1969 the main countries from which goods were imported into Tanzania and exported (not including re-exports) to and from Tanzania were (values in Tanzanian Sh.1m.):

Imports: UK, 378·1; Japan, 130·3; West Germany, 111·5; Iran, 104·2; USA, 82·8; China (mainland), 79·4; Italy, 77·4; Netherlands, 66·3; India, 47·6; France, 45·9.

Exports: UK, 429·1; India, 132·1; USA, 126·4; Zambia, 105·6; Hong Kong, 103·5; Japan, 82; China (mainland), 77·8; West Germany, 68·3; Singapore, 57·7; Netherlands, 48·3; Italy, 47·8; Belgium, 25·2; Canada, 18.

Total trade with UK (British Board of Trade returns, in £1,000 sterling):

	1966	1967	1968	1969	1970
Imports to UK	22,597	24,203	24,433	23,954	23,963
Exports from UK	14,886	14,158	18,510	17,985 }	19,583
Re-exports from UK	140	81	81	132 }	

BANKING. On 14 June 1966 the central bank called the Bank of Tanzania, with a government-owned capital of 20m. sh., began operations.

On 6 Feb. 1967 all commercial banks with the exception of National Co-operative Banks were nationalized all over Tanzania and their interests vested in the National Bank of Commerce on the mainland and the Peoples' Bank in Zanzibar.

TANGANYIKA

HISTORY. German East Africa was occupied by German colonialists from 1884 and placed under the protection of the German Empire in 1891. It was conquered in the First World War and subsequently divided between the British and Belgians. The latter received the territories of Ruanda and Urundi and the British the remainder, except for the Kionga triangle, which went to Portugal. The country was administered as a League of Nations mandate until 1946 and then as a UN trusteeship territory until 9 Dec. 1961.

Tanganyika achieved responsible government in Sept. 1960 and full self-government on 1 May 1961. On 9 Dec. 1961 Tanganyika became a sovereign independent member state of the Commonwealth of Nations. It adopted a republican form of government on 9 Dec. 1962.

AREA AND POPULATION. Tanganyika extends from the Umba River on the north to the Rovuma River on the south, the coastline being some 500 miles long, and includes the adjacent islands (except Zanzibar and Pemba). The northern boundary runs north-west to Lake Victoria at the intersection of the first parallel of southern latitude with the eastern shore. The boundary on the west follows the Kagera River (the eastern frontier of Rwanda), thence the eastern boundary of Burundi to Lake Tanganyika. The western boundary then follows the middle of Lake Tanganyika to its southern end at the Kalambo River 50 miles south of Kasanga, whence it goes south-east to the northern end of Lake Nyasa. It follows the middle of Lake Nyasa, and rather less than half-way down the lake turns east and follows the Rovuma River to the sea. The total area is 362,688 sq. miles (939,936 sq. km), which includes 20,650 sq. miles (53,480 sq. km) of water. Dar es Salaam is the capital and chief port; census population 1967, 372,515.

The country is divided into 17 regions (with capitals of the same name, unless added in brackets), with census population, Aug. 1967:

Coast (Dar es Salaam)	781,267	Mtwara	1,032,896
Arusha	601,515	Mwanza	1,057,695
Dodoma	708,422	Ruvuma (Songea)	392,812
Iringa	683,555	Shinyanga	888,209
Kigoma	470,773	Singida	454,749
Kilimanjaro (Moshi)	650,533	Tabora	552,339
Mara (Musoma)	535,882	Tanga	769,304
Mbeya	955,891	West Lake (Bukoba)	658,079
Morogoro	683,061		

Other towns are Kigoma, the principal port on Lake Tanganyika; Iringa, in the Southern Highlands; Morogoro (Eastern), and Lindi (Mtwara Region).

The mid-1965 estimate of the European population was 17,000; Indians and Pakistani, 86,000; Arabs, 26,000; Africans, 10,046,000.

The African population of Tanganyika is made up of members of more than 100 tribes, each with a distinctive dialect and varying customs. Most of the tribes are of Bantu origin, although there are considerable Hamitic and Nilo-Hamitic intrusions. In 1966 some 13,500 refugees from Rwanda, 800 from Congo and 12,000 from Moçambique were living in Tanganyika.

Swahili is generally spoken and understood throughout Tanzania.

EDUCATION. The educational system has been integrated on non-racial lines. Schools are maintained by the Government, local authorities and voluntary agencies, including missions; most of the latter are wholly or partly financed by Government or local authorities.

In 1970, 850,900 children attended primary schools and 30,700 secondary schools.

Technical and vocational education is provided at 2 government trade schools and at the Dar es Salaam Technical College.

There were, in 1967, 23 teacher-training centres, including the college at Chang'ombe for secondary-school teachers. About 2,500 students are in training, of whom about 1,100 are annually taking up posts.

In 1970, 2,007 Tanzanian students attended the University of East Africa founded in 1963.

FINANCE. The revenue and expenditure, including development-revenue and expenditure, for financial years ended 30 June were (in Sh.1m.):

	1965–66	1966–67	1967–68	1968–69	1969–70
Revenue	1,101·8	1,311·6	1,467·7	1,717·8	2,121·2
Expenditure	1,117·6	1,274·1	1,409·1	1,646·5	2,230·7

The chief actual items of revenue for 1969–70 are (in Sh.1m.): Import and excise duties, 581; export taxes, 5·4; income taxes, 335; licences and other taxes, 50; sales taxes, 155. Chief items of expenditure are (in Sh.1m.): Social services, 471·3; economic services, 1,856·3; general administration, 558·5.

PLANNING. In 1964 the first 5-year plan (1964–69) was approved. The second plan for economic and social development (1969–74) is in progress.

AGRICULTURE AND FORESTRY. Tanganyika has three natural regions—the coast lowlands, the high plateau and the high mountain slopes around Mount Kilimanjaro and other northern peaks and round Rungwe and the Livingstones in the south. In these regions there are high rainfall areas as also in the foothills of the Ulugurus and Usambaras characterized by the presence of tropical rain-forest. The total area of this type is about 4,000 sq. miles and is insignificant in comparison to the 135,000 sq. miles of savannah forest (miombo woodland). By the end of 1961, 45,472 sq. miles had been set aside as forest reserves. The forests contain some good merchantable timbers in varying quantity, among which camphor, podo, mvule and certain African mahoganies are the most important. In addition, valuable hardwoods occur as single trees or in groups widely scattered throughout the savannah forests, the chief being muninga and African blackwood. Mangroves are valuable as a source of tanning bark and also of poles which are carried by Arab dhows to the Persian Gulf.

Exports in 1969 included (in Sh.1m.): Cotton, 235 (70,000 tons); coffee, 235 (49,000 tons); sisal, 160 (169,000 tons); diamonds, 178 (780,000 carats); cashew-nuts, 119 (123,000 tons).

Livestock (1968). 12m. cattle, 2·8m. sheep, 4·1m. goats.

MINERALS. The value of mineral exports in 1968 was 163·5m. sh. Principal exports, 1968, were (in Sh.1m.): Diamonds, 135·4; gold, 4·8; tin, 6·9; salt, 9·6. In 1967 the production of gold was 18,000 troy oz.

POWER. A hydro-electric station on the Pagani River near Tanga is being built; £3m. of its estimated cost of £5·25m. is being provided by the Commonwealth Development Corporation.

ROADS. Motor traffic is possible over 25,000 miles of road during dry season and at almost all times over 21,500 miles.

RAILWAYS, POST AND TELECOMMUNICATIONS. *See* pp. 473–74. There were 29,202 telephones in use at 31 Dec. 1968.

AVIATION. There are 51 aerodromes and landing strips maintained or licensed by Government; of these, one is of International Class C standard and 18 are suitable for Dakotas. The East African Airways Corporation provide regular and frequent services to all the more important towns within the territory and the neighbouring countries of Kenya and Uganda, together with a regular service to the UK, India and Pakistan, Zambia and Malawi. Charter services are operated by 2 companies. In 1966, 162,000 passengers and 2,208m. kg of freight were handled at Dar es Salaam airport.

BANKING. The Tanganyika post office savings banks had, in 1968, 283,500 depositors with a balance of Sh.43·76m.

BOOKS OF REFERENCE

Statistical Abstract, 1965.
Handbook of Tanganyika. 2nd ed. Government Printer, Dar es Salaam, 1958
Atlas of Tanganyika. 3rd ed. Dar es Salaam, 1956
Tanganyika Notes and Records. Tanganyika Society, Dar es Salaam. (Twice yearly, from 1936)
The Economic Development of Tanganyika. Report . . . by the International Bank. Johns Hopkins Univ. Press and OUP, 1961
Chidzero, B. T. G., *Tanganyika and international trusteeship.* OUP, 1961
Taylor, J. C., *The Political Development of Tanganyika.* Stanford Univ. Press, 1963

ZANZIBAR

HISTORY. At the end of the 17th century the inhabitants of Zanzibar drove out the Portuguese with the assistance of the Arabs of Oman. Thereafter an Arab governor from Oman was sent to Zanzibar, but the government of the interior remained in the hands of a local ruler. In 1832 Seyyid Said bin Sultan, ruler of Oman, established his capital at Zanzibar, and thereafter the whole of that island and the island of Pemba together with a large strip of the East African mainland coast came under his effective rule. Seyyid Said died in 1856. Five years later his former African possessions were, under an arbitration award made by Lord Canning (then Governor-General of India), declared to be independent of Oman. In 1887 the Sultan of Zanzibar handed over the administration of his possessions to the north of Vanga on the African continent to the British East Africa Association. These territories eventually passed to the British Government and are now part of Kenya. In 1888 a similar concession was granted to the German East Africa Association of the Sultan's mainland territories between the river Umba and Cape Delgado. In 1890 the German Government bought these territories outright for 4m. marks. In 1892 the administration of the Benadir Ports (which had in 1889 been conceded to the British East Africa Association) was, with the consent of the Sultan, transferred to the Italian Government in consideration of a quarterly payment of Rs 40,000. The Sultan renounced in 1886 in favour of Portugal all claims to the coast to the south of Cape Delgado.

In 1890 the islands of Zanzibar and Pemba were placed under British protection by the Sultan, Seyyid Ali bin Said.

On 24 June 1963 Zanzibar became an internal self-governing state and on 9 Dec. 1963 she became independent. On 24 June 1963 the Legislative Council was replaced by a National Assembly.

On 12 Jan. 1964 the sultanate was overthrown and the sultan sent into exile by a revolt of the Afro-Shirazi Party leaders who established the People's Republic of Zanzibar. The 'interim constitution' of Tanzania provides for a separate executive and legislature in Zanzibar.

AREA AND POPULATION. The island of Zanzibar is situated in 6° S. lat., and is separated from the mainland by a channel 22¼ miles across at its narrowest part. It is the largest coralline island on the African coast, being 50 miles long by 24 broad, and having an area of 640 sq. miles (1,658 sq. km). To the north-east, at a distance of some 25 miles, lies the island of Pemba in 5° S. lat., 42 miles long by 14 broad, having an area of 380 sq. miles (984 sq. km). The average annual rainfall is about 60 in. in Zanzibar and nearly 80 in. in Pemba.

The population of Zanzibar and Pemba, at the 1967 census, was 354,360 (Zanzibar, 190,117; Pemba, 164,243). The African population is composed of the indigenous Watumbatu, Wahadimu and Wapemba, and other Africans comprising at least 50 mainland tribes. The racial composition of the population was as follows in 1958: Indigenous inhabitants, Arabs, Comorians and mainland Africans, 279,935; Asians other than Arabs, 18,334; Europeans, 507; others, 335. Zanzibar town had a population of 57,923.

RELIGION. Most of the residents are Moslems (Sunnis of the Shafi school). There are 3 Christian Missions: the Universities Mission to Central Africa (Church of England), the Mission of the Holy Ghost (Roman Catholic) and the Friends' Industrial Mission (Quakers).

EDUCATION. In 1967 there were 90 primary schools with 39,000 pupils and 12 secondary schools with 1,961 pupils.

JUSTICE. In the cases in which persons subject to the Zanzibar Order-in-council, 1924, are parties, justice is administered by the High Court and the courts subordinate thereto. Subordinate courts are presided over by resident magistrates, administrative officers, Kathis and Mudirs. There are also juvenile courts comprising male and female members selected from panels. Appeals lie to the Court of Appeal for Eastern Africa and thence to the Privy Council.

FINANCE. Revenue and expenditure (in Sh.1m.) for fiscal years ending 30 June:

	1963–64	1964–65	1965–66[1]	1966–67[1]
Revenue	59·66	57·56	63·72	60·66
Expenditure	63·22	56·11	63·32	59·83

[1] Estimates.

AGRICULTURE. Zanzibar provides the greater part of the world's supply of cloves. There are about 80,000 acres under cloves with about 4m. trees; five-sixths of the clove output is produced on Pemba. Cloves and clove oil (distilled from the stems) form more than half Zanzibar's exports.

The coconut industry ranks next in importance. There are about 5·5m. bearing trees in both islands. Chillies, cocoa, limes, other tropical fruits and coil tobacco are also cultivated. The chief food crops are rice, bananas, cassava, pulses, maize and sorghum.

FISHERIES. A Fisheries Development Company, in which the Government has a financial interest, is catching sardines and tuna for export.

MANUFACTURES. Manufactures are principally coir fibre, bags and rope, soap, marine shell, ivory and ebony ornaments, and metalware. Private factories have been taken over by the government.

COMMERCE. Total imports and exports in (Sh.1m.):

	1961	1962	1963	1964	1965	1966
Imports	110	106	108	76	82	90
Exports	72	64	86	74	68	94
Re-exports	16	26	16	16	12	8

The principal articles of import in 1965 (in Sh.1m.) were: Rice, 11·9; wheat, 4·88; sugar, 2·72; khangas, 2·22; fuel, 4·7. Main exports: Cloves, 46; copra, 15·16.

The trade between Zanzibar (and Pemba) and UK has since 1965 been included in that of Tanzania.

SHIPPING. The vessels of many British and foreign steamship companies visit the port. The Zanzibar Government steamers operate services to Pemba and Dar es Salaam, and occasional trips to Mombasa.

Ocean-going shipping in 1962, 456 vessels (2,073,777 NRT); coastwise, 258 vessels (138,063 NRT).

ROADS. There are in Zanzibar 279 miles of tarmac roads and 70 miles of all-weather unsealed roads; in Pemba there are 86 miles of tarmac roads and 184 miles of dry-weather earth roads.

AVIATION. There is an all-weather landing-ground in Zanzibar and a smaller all-weather landing-ground in Pemba.

POST. The Government maintains a telephone system in the town of Zanzibar, which is connected with the district and agricultural stations in the country. A telephone service in the island of Pemba connects the 3 main townships, *i.e.*, Wete, Chake Chake and Mkoani. There are 7 post offices and 1,750 telephones in the two islands. The government savings bank at the end of 1962 had 35,413 depositors, with £514,349 on deposit.

There is cable communication with Europe either *via* Aden or *via* Durban and a wireless telephone communication with the other East African territories.

WEIGHTS. An important local unit of weight is the frasla (or frasila) = 35 lb. av.

BOOKS OF REFERENCE

Lofchie, M. F., *Zanzibar: background to revolution.* Princeton Univ. Press, 1965
Ommanney, F. D., *Isle of Cloves.* London, 1955

WESTERN SAMOA
Samoa i Sisifo

HISTORY. Western Samoa, a former German protectorate (1900 to the First World War), was administered by New Zealand from 1920 to 1961, at first under a League of Nations Mandate and since 1946 under a United Nations Trusteeship Agreement. In May 1961 a plebiscite held under the supervision of the United Nations on the basis of universal adult suffrage voted overwhelmingly in favour of independence as from 1 Jan. 1962, on the basis of the Constitution, which a Constitutional Convention had adopted in Aug. 1960. In Oct. 1961 the General Assembly of the United Nations passed a resolution to terminate the trusteeship agreement as from 1 Jan. 1962, on which date Western Samoa became an independent sovereign state.

Under a treaty of friendship signed on 1 Aug. 1962 New Zealand acts, at the request of Western Samoa, as the official channel of communication between the Samoan Government and other governments and international organizations outside the Pacific islands area. Liaison is maintained by the New Zealand High Commissioner in Apia, who is the only diplomatic representative accredited to the Government of Western Samoa.

AREA AND POPULATION. Western Samoa lies between 13° and 15° S. lat. and 171° and 173° W. long. It comprises the two large islands of Savai'i and Upolu, the small islands of Manono and Apolima, and several uninhabited islets lying off the coast. The total land area is 1,097 sq. miles (2,842 sq. km), of which 662 sq. miles are in Savai'i, and 433 sq. miles in Upolu. The islands are of volcanic origin, and the coasts are surrounded by coral reefs. Rugged mountain ranges form the core of both main islands and rise to 3,608 ft in Upolu and 6,094 ft in Savai'i. The large area laid waste by lava-flows in Savai'i is a primary cause of that island supporting less than one-third of the population of the islands despite its greater size than Upolu.

The population at the census of 21 Nov. 1966 was 131,377 (67,842 males and 63,535 females), of whom 95,218 were in Upola (including Manono and Apolima) and 36,161 in Savai'i. The capital and chief port is Apia in Upolu (population 21,699 on 25 Sept. 1961).

CONSTITUTION AND GOVERNMENT. The Constitution provides for a Head of State known as 'Ao o le Malo', which position from 1 Jan. 1962 was held jointly by the representatives of the two royal lines of Tuiaana/Tuiatua and Malietoa. On the death of HH Tupua Tamasese Mea'ole, CBE, on 5 April 1963, HH Malietoa Tanumafili II CBE, became, as provided by the constitution, the sole Head of State for life. Future Heads of State will be elected by the Le islative Assembly and hold office for 5-year terms.

The executive power is vested in the Head of State, who appoints the Prime Minister and, on the Prime Minister's advice, the 8 Ministers to form the Cabinet which has general direction and control of the executive Government.

Parliament comprises the Head of State and the Legislative Assembly. The Legislative Assembly has 45 members elected from territorial constituencies on a franchise confined to matais or chiefs (of whom there are about 11,000) and 2 members elected on universal adult suffrage from the individual voters roll, which has replaced the old European roll (approximately 1,350 in 1971).

The official languages are English and Samoan.

Head of State: HH Malietoa Tanumafili II, CBE.
Prime Minister: Tupua Tamasese Lealofi IV.

FINANCE. Currency. On 10 July 1966 Western Samoa changed over to decimal currency. The Western Samoa *talā* (dollar) is at parity with the NZ dollar, equally £0·50. Currency in circulation consists of Samoan Treasury notes and coins.

Budget. Revenue and expenditure for calendar years, in $WS:

	1970[1]	1971[1]
Revenue	6,333,565	6,478,156
of which NZ Government grants	120,000	120,000
Expenditure	6,840,650	7,036,611

[1] Estimates.

COMMERCE. In 1967, imports were valued at $WS5,635,235 and exports at $WS3,139,038. Principal exports were copra (7,405 tons; $WS927,966), bananas (94,490 cases; $WS259,564) and cocoa (3,116 tons; $WS,1,461,635). Chief imports in 1967 included meat (28,293 cwt; $WS514,928) and spirits and alcoholic beverages (150,947 gallons; $WS128,983).

Total trade between Western Samoa and UK, in £1,000 sterling (British Board of Trade returns):

	1965	1966	1967	1968	1969	1970
Imports to UK	163	110	270	110	71	90
Exports from UK	233	187	233	253	293	323
Re-exports from UK	1	2	1	2	—	

ROADS (1962). Western Samoa has over 233 miles of main roads, 93 miles of municipal secondary and village roads and 151 miles of plantation roads fit for light traffic. In 1968 there were 799 passenger cars and 524 commercial vehicles.

SHIPPING. There is a regular fortnightly shipping communication from New Zealand and Fiji, connecting also with Japan, UK and USA, as well as direct shipping communication with Japan and UK.

AVIATION. Western Samoa is linked by daily air service with American Samoa, which is on the route of the weekly New Zealand–Tahiti and New Zealand–Honolulu air services, with connexions to Fiji, Australia, USA and Europe. There are also twice-weekly services to and from Fiji and Tonga. Internal services link Upolu and Savai'i .

TELECOMMUNICATIONS. There is a radio communication station at Apia. Radio telephone service connects Western Samoa with American Samoa, Fiji, New Zealand, Australia, Canada, USA and England. Telephone subscribers numbered 1,800 in Jan. 1970.

BANKING. In 1959 the Bank of Western Samoa was established with a capital of $WS500,000, of which $WS275,000 was subscribed by the Bank of New Zealand and $WS225,000 by the Government of Western Samoa. In 1961 the bank became the note-issuing authority of Western Samoa.

BOOKS OF REFERENCE

Statistical Year-Book. 1968
Report on Economic Survey. 1961
The Economy of Western Samoa. 1968
Clare, B. L., *A Review of Social Labour and Economic Conditions in Western Samoa.* Apia, 1962, reprinted 1963.—*The Parliament of Western Samoa.* Rev. cd. Apia, 1964
Fox, J. W. (ed.), *Western Samoa.* Univ. of Auckland, 1963
Milner, G. B., *Samoan–English, English–Samoan Dictionary.* OUP, 1965

JAMAICA

HISTORY. Jamaica was discovered by Columbus in 1494, and was occupied by the Spaniards between 1509 and 1655, when the island was captured by the English; their possession was confirmed by the Treaty of Madrid, 1670. Self-government was introduced in 1944 and gradually extended until Jamaica achieved complete independence within the Commonwealth on 6 Aug. 1962.

AREA AND POPULATION. The area of Jamaica is 4,411 sq. miles (11,525 sq. km). The population at the census of 7 April 1960 was 1,609,803, distributed on the basis of the 14 parishes of the island as follows: Kingston, 123,403; St Andrew, 296,013; St Thomas, 68,725; Portland, 64,510; St Mary, 94,223; St Ann, 114,360; Trelawny, 56,080; St James, 83,003; Hanover, 53,901; Westmoreland, 109,606; St Elizabeth, 116,706; Manchester, 11,788; St Catherine, 153,535; Clarendon, 163,950.

Estimated population, 31 Dec. 1969 was 1,972,130.

Vital statistics (1969): Births, 64,700; deaths, 14,100; infant deaths, 2,200; emigrants to UK (1969), 16,947; returned from UK (1968), 14,691; number of work vouchers issued by UK to Jamaicans, 136.

CONSTITUTION AND GOVERNMENT. A new Constitution was enacted with Independence in Aug. 1962. The Crown is represented by a Governor-General chosen by the Crown on the advice of the Prime Minister. The Governor-General is advised by a Privy Council.

The Legislature comprises two chambers, an elected House and a nominated Senate. The Executive is chosen from both chambers.

The Executive comprises the Prime Minister, who is the leader of the majority party, and Ministers appointed by the Prime Minister. Together they form the Cabinet, which is the highest executive power. An Attorney-General is an elected member of the House and is legal adviser to the Cabinet.

The Senate consists of 21 senators appointed by the Governor-General, 13 on the advice of the Prime Minister, 8 on the advice of the Leader of the Opposition. The House of Representatives (53 members) is elected by universal adult suffrage for a 5-year period. Electors and elected must be Jamaican or Commonwealth citizens resident in Jamaica for at least 12 months before registration. The powers and procedure of Parliament correspond to those of the British Parliament.

The Privy Council consists of 6 members appointed by the Governor-General on the advice of the Prime Minister.

Governor-General: Sir Clifford Campbell, GCMG, GCVO.

The elections to the House of Representatives, held on 21 Feb. 1967, returned 33 members of the Jamaica Labour Party and 20 members of the People's National Party.

Prime Minister: Hugh Shearer, PC.
Trade and Industry: R. C. Lightbourne. *Finance and Planning:* E. P. G. Seaga.
Public Utilities and Housing: Wilton Hill. *Agriculture and Fisheries:* J. P. Gyles.
Health: Dr H. W. Eldemire. *Home Affairs:* R. A. McNeill. *Labour and National Insurance:* L. G. Newland. *Education:* E. L. Allen. *Local Government:* L. A. Lynch. *Communications and Works:* N. C. Lewis. *Youth and Community*

L

Development: Allan Douglas. *Attorney-General and Legal Affairs:* V. B. Grant, QC. *Without Portfolio:* Senator Sir Neville Ashenheim (*Leader of Government Business, Senate*). *Rural Land Development:* W. G. McLaren.

DIPLOMATIC REPRESENTATIVES

Country	Jamaican representative	Foreign representative
Argentina	Keith Johnson	Dr Julio Negre
Barbados[1]	I. de Souza, OBE	—
Britain[1]	Sir Laurence Lindo, CMG	Edward Larmour
Canada[1]	V. H. McFarlane, CBE	Victor C. Moore
China	—	Samuel C. H. Ling
Dominican Rep.	—	Carlos Nouel
France	Sir Laurence Lindo, CMG	Michel Louet
Germany (West)	Sir Laurence Lindo, CMG	Kurt Schmidt
Guyana[1]	I. de Souza, OBE	Winnifred Gaskin
Mexico	Sir Egerton Richardson, CMG	Alejandro Gomez Maganda
Netherlands	—	Michael P. Gorsira
Panama	V. H. McFarlane, CBE	Francisco Quijano
Trinidad[1]	I. de Souza, OBE	A. K. Sabga-Aboud
USA	Sir Egerton Richardson, CMG	Vincent de Roulet
Venezuela	I. de Souza, OBE	Brig.-Gen. Alfredo Monch
Yugoslavia	Kenneth Scott	—

[1] High Commissioner.   No figure = Ambassador.

High Commissioners and ambassadors for the following countries are resident in other territories: Austria, Belgium, Brazil, Chile, Colombia, Ethiopia, Ghana, India, Israel, Italy, Japan, Korea, Lebanon, Pakistan, Switzerland, UAR, Yugoslavia.

RELIGION. There is no established Church. Adherents of the various religious communities at the census of 1960 numbered: Anglican, 317,643; Baptist, 306,037; Church of God, 191,231; Roman Catholic, 115,291; Methodist, 108,858; Presbyterian, 82,698; Seventh Day Adventist, 78,360; Moravian, 52,467; Congregationalist, 22,440; Pentecostal, 14,739; Plymouth Brethren, 14,555; Salvation Army, 10,416; Society of Friends, 3,977; Pocomania, 811; Christian Science, 341; Hindu, 1,181; Jews, 600; others, 14,876; no religion, 183,738; not specified, 89,555.

EDUCATION. Primary and junior secondary education is free to all children between the ages of 6 and 15. At 30 Sept. 1969 there were 767 public primary schools with 387,924 children, 40 junior secondary schools with 33,323, and 40 secondary schools with 22,739 enrolled. There are 2 comprehensive schools, 5 vocational schools, 2 trade training centres, 6 technical high schools, the Jamaica School of Agriculture, and a College of Arts, Science and Technology. There are 7 training colleges, providing 2- and 3-year courses for primary-school teachers. By Sept. 1970, 48 new public primary schools will be built to accommodate 16,500 more pupils of 6–11 years. It is expected that in 1971, 50 junior secondary schools will be completed, providing 18,845 more places to students between the ages of 12 and 15.

Evening institutes for adult education are attached to 29 primary schools.

Degrees in Art, Natural and Social Sciences, Education, Medicine and General Studies are offered at the Mona Campus of the University of the West Indies. The faculties of Engineering and Agriculture are at the St Augustine Campus in Trinidad, and the Law Faculty is at Cave Hill in Barbados.

CINEMAS (1967). There are 55 cinemas with a seating capacity of 50,204, and 1 drive-in cinema for 400 cars.

JUSTICE. The Judicature comprises a supreme court, a court of appeal, resident magistrates' courts, petty sessional courts, coroners' courts and a traffic court. The Chief Justice is head of the judiciary. All prosecutions are initiated by the Director of Public Prosecutions.

Police. The Constabulary Force in 1969 stood at 84 officers and 3,050 other ranks (men and women). There are, in addition, district constables and special constables.

FINANCE. Currency. On 8 Sept. 1969 Jamaica adopted decimal currency, the dollar, divided into 100 cents. The £ sterling is equal to J$2 (US$ = J$0·833). Currency circulation on 31 March 1970 was J$41,120,472 and J$2,229,210 coin.

Budget. Revenue and expenditure for fiscal years ending 31 March (in J$):

	1965–66	1966–67	1967–68	1968–69	1969–70	1970–71[1]
Revenue	131,211,254	136,224,294	155,733,130	182,191,070	212,691,758	249,857,477
Expenditure	129,540,398	141,795,824	163,300,886	186,713,300	212,031,540	168,845,062

[1] Estimates.

The chief heads of recurrent revenue are customs and excise duties, income tax, motor vehicle licences and post office receipts. Capital revenue is derived mainly from royalties.

Public debt at 31 Dec. 1969, J$241·6m.

Remittances from overseas amounted to approximately J$19·1m in 1969.

DEFENCE. The Air Wing of the Jamaica Defence Force was formed in July 1963 and has since been expanded and trained successively by the British Army Air Corps and Canadian Air Force personnel. Equipment for army liaison, search and rescue, police co-operation, survey and transport duties includes a Twin Otter, 2 Bell 47 light helicopters and a Cessna 185 Skywagon.

AGRICULTURE (1969). Production: Sugar, 383,000 tons; rum and other spirits, 3·4m. proof gallons; molasses (1968), 156,051 tons; copra, 17,217 tons. Exportable commodities: Bananas, 151,000 tons; cocoa, 1·5m. tons; coffee, 1·1m. lb.; citrus fruit (fresh), 264,000 pkg., (canned) 23·1m. lb., (juices), 1·8m. gallons; pimento, 3,225 tons; ginger, 614,000 lb.

MINING. Bauxite, ceramic clays, marble, silica and gypsum are commercially valuable. Jamaica has become the world's largest producer of bauxite and alumina. The deposits are worked by a Canadian and 3 American companies. The Canadian company processes bauxite into alumina. In 1968, 6,212,000 tons of bauxite ore and 868,000 tons of alumina were exported. Gypsum production in 1968 was 256,268 tons.

INDUSTRY. By the end of 1968, 181 industries had been established under Industrial Incentives Laws, implemented by the Industrial Development Corporation. From processing only a few agricultural products—sugar, rum, condensed milk, oils and fats, cigars and cigarettes—the island is now producing a wide range of manufactures using both local and imported raw materials. Among the manufactured goods are clothing, footwear, textiles, paints, building materials, including cement, agricultural machinery and toilet articles. An oil refinery is also in operation in Kingston. In 1969 manufacturing and processing contributed J$121·1m. to the total g.n.p.

TOURISM. In 1968, 396,347 tourists (1969: 407,105) stayed in Jamaica, spending about J$73·2m. (1969: J$77·9m.).

ELECTRICITY. The Jamaica Public Service Company is the public supplier of electricity. The bauxite companies, sugar estates and the Caribbean Cement Co. generate their own electricity.

COMMERCE. Value of imports and domestic exports for calendar years (in J$m):

	1965	1966	1967	1968	1969
Imports	206·5	233·7	252·6	320·4	369·4
Domestic exports	153·1	162·9	163·3	183·0	213·4

Principal imports in 1969 (in J$1,000): Manufactured goods, 92,016; food, 59,900; machinery and transport equipment, 116,256; mineral fuels, lubricants, etc., 25,294; chemicals, 28,838.

Principal exports, 1969 (in J$m.): Bauxite and alumina, 118·6; sugar, rum and molasses, 32·9; bananas, 12; citrus, cocoa, coffee, pimento, ginger, 11·6; manufactured goods, 22·8.

In 1968 USA supplied 38·6% of the imports; UK, 20·4%, and Canada, 9·6%; of the domestic exports, 39·2% went to USA, 23·7% to UK and 14·4% to Canada.

Total trade with UK, in £1,000 sterling (British Board of Trade returns):

	1965	1966	1967	1968	1969	1970
Imports to UK	28,045	28,733	28,726	26,172	26,174	27,480
Exports from UK	23,271	23,767	23,188	28,068	34,878 ⎱	38,203
Re-exports from UK	384	535	452	601	736 ⎰	

SHIPPING. Jamaica has 6 first-class and 13 second-class ports. In 1969 the port of Kingston unloaded 1·09m. tons of cargo.

RAILWAYS. There are 205 miles of railway open of 4 ft 8½ in. gauge, operated by the Jamaica Railway Corporation, which also operates 19½ miles (Alcoa Mineral Railway) on behalf of one of the bauxite companies.

ROADS (1968). The island had 2,682 miles of main roads, maintained by the Ministry of Communications and Works or the councils, and in Kingston and St Andrew by the corporation.

AVIATION. In 1969, 12 scheduled commercial international airlines served Jamaica, operating through the international airports at Palisadoes and Montego Bay. Jamaica Air Services and Jamaica Air Taxi operate internal flights. Air Jamaica, originally set up in conjunction with BOAC and BWIA in 1966, became a new company, Air Jamaica (1968) Ltd and is affiliated to Air Canada. In 1969 it began operations as Jamaica's national airline.

TELECOMMUNICATIONS. Post and telecommunications are the responsibility of the Ministry of Communications and Works. At 31 Dec. 1969 there were 309 post offices, 443 postal agencies and 34 sub-agencies.

The Jamaica Telephone Company operates the telephone system. In Jan. 1970 there were 66,643 telephones in use. All telephone exchanges are automatic. Jamaica is linked to USA by a submarine telephone cable.

There are 1 commercial and 1 publicly owned broadcasting stations; the latter also operates a television service.

BANKING. On 1 May 1961 the Bank of Jamaica opened for business as Jamaica's Central Bank. It has the sole right to issue notes and coins in Jamaica, acts as Banker to the Government and to the commercial banks, and administers the island's external reserves and exchange control.

On 29 Feb. 1968 the government savings bank had a balance at credit amounting to £8,410,443.

There are 7 commercial banks in operation, with main offices in Kingston. They are the Bank of Nova Scotia (Jamaica) Ltd., Barclays Bank DCO, the Royal Bank of Canada, the Canadian Imperial Bank of Commerce, the Bank of London and Montreal, the First National City Bank of New York and Jamaica Citizens' Bank.

BOOKS OF REFERENCE

STATISTICAL INFORMATION. The Department of Statistics (93 Hanover St., Kingston) was set up in 1945—the nucleus being the Census Office, which undertook the operations of the 1943 Census of Jamaica and its Dependencies. *Director:* Dexter Rose. Publications of the Bureau include the *Bulletin of Statistics on External Trade* and the *Annual Abstract of Statistics.*

Economic Survey of Jamaica. Ministry of Finance and Planning. Yearly
Guide to Jamaica. Issued by Jamaica Tourist Association. Kingston, from 1937
Handbook of Jamaica. Government Printer, Kingston, yearly from 1886
The Trade Directory of Jamaica. London, 1962
Abrahams, P., *Jamaica: an island mosaic.* HMSO, 1957
Black, C. V., *History of Jamaica.* London, 1965.
Carley, M. M., *Jamacia.* London, 1963
Cassidy, F. G., and Le Page, R. B., *Dictionary of Jamaican English.* CUP, 1966
Delattre, R., *A Guide to Jamaica Reference Material.* Kingston, 1965
Roberts, G. W., *The Population of Jamaica.* CUP, 1957
Bibliography of Jamaica, 1900–1963. Jamaica Library Service, 1963

LIBRARIES: Institute of Jamaica, Kingston. Jamaica Library Service, Kingston. *Director:* Mrs J. Robinson, MBE, FLA.

TRINIDAD AND TOBAGO

HISTORY. Trinidad was discovered by Columbus in 1498 and colonized by the Spaniards in the 16th century. During the French Revolution a large number of French families settled in the island. In 1797, Great Britain being at war with Spain, Trinidad was occupied by the British and ceded to Great Britain by the Treaty of Amiens in 1802. Trinidad and Tobago were joined in 1889.

Under the Bases Agreement concluded between the governments of the UK and the USA on 27 March 1941, and the concomitant Trinidad–US Bases Lease of 22 April 1941, defence bases were leased to the US Government for 99 years. On 8 Dec. 1960 the US agreed to abandon 21,000 acres of leased land; the area retained is for a period of 17 years.

AREA AND POPULATION. Area: Trinidad, 1,864 sq. miles (4,828 sq. km); Tobago, 116 sq. miles (300 sq. km). Population (census 7 April 1960): 827,957 (411,580 males and 416,377 females) (Trinidad, 794,624; Tobago, 33,333). Capital, Port-of-Spain, 93,954; other important towns, San Fernando (39,890), and Arima (10,982). The white population (15,718) is chiefly composed of persons of English, French, Spanish and Portuguese descent. The majority are of African descent (358,588), the balance being made up of Indians (301,946), mixed races (134,748) and Chinese (8,361). English is spoken generally.

Estimated population in mid-1967, 1,010,100 (504,350 males, 505,750 females).

Vital statistics, 1967: Births, 28,460; deaths, 6,780; marriages, 5,479.

CONSTITUTION AND GOVERNMENT. On 31 Aug. 1962 Trinidad and Tobago became an independent member state of the British Commonwealth.

The constitution provides for a bicameral legislature of a Senate and a House of Representatives. The Senate consists of 24 members appointed by the Governor-General, 13 of them on the advice of the Prime Minister, 4 on the advice of the Leader of the Opposition and 7 from religious, economic and social bodies the Prime Minister considers should be represented.

The House of Representatives consists of 36 elected members.

The Cabinet consists of the Prime Minister, appointed by the Governor-General, and other Ministers, including the Attorney-General (15 in 1969).

The elections held on 7 Nov. 1966 gave the People's National Movement 24 seats and the Democratic Labour Party 12 seats.

Governor-General: Sir Solomon Hochoy, GCMG, GCVO, OBE (appointed 31 Aug. 1962).

Prime Minister and Minister of Finance, Planning and Development: Dr Eric E. Williams, PC.

DIPLOMATIC REPRESENTATIVES

Country	Trinidad representative	Foreign representative
Argentina	—	Julio Negre
Belgium	—	Albert Nijs
Brazil	Andrew Rose	A. Bonlitreau Fragasgo
Britain[1]	Donald Grenado	R. C. C. Hunt
Canada[1]	Matthew Rancheron	Gerald Ray
Ethiopia	V. C. McIntyre	—
France	—	Paul de Lehelec
Germany	—	Fritz Gajewski
India[1]	Ashford Sinanan	Lakshmi Narayan Ray
Israel	—	Jacob Duron
Italy	—	Vittorio Codero di Montezemdo
Jamaica[1]	Eric Murray	Ivor de Souza
Japan	—	Shigeru Hirota
Lebanon	—	Antoine Francis
Liberia	—	William B. Fernandez
Netherlands	—	S. D. Emannels
Pakistan[1]	—	M. S. A. Baig
Senegal	—	Cheikh Ibrahim Fall
Sweden	—	Otto Rathsman
Switzerland	—	Walter Bossi
UAR	—	Mohammed Shattie
USA	Sir Ellis Clarke, CMG	J. F. Symington
Venezuela	—	Pearo Liscano Lobo

[1] High Commissioner.   [2] Chargé d'Affaires.   No figure = Ambassador.

RELIGION. According to the census in 1960 there were 175,042 Anglicans (under the Bishop of Trinidad and Tobago), 299,649 Roman Catholics (under the Archbishop of Port-of-Spain), 32,400 Presbyterians, 18,589 Methodists, 18,522 Baptists, 12,632 Seventh Day Adventists, 3,822 Jehovah's Witnesses, 4,031 Pentecostal, 190,403 Hindus, 49,736 Moslems.

EDUCATION. In 1968 there were 463 primary and intermediate schools 103 government, 360 assisted), 130 private (non-assisted) primary schools and 118 secondary schools (21 government, 23 assisted and 74 private).

There were 223,164 pupils on roll in the primary and intermediate schools and 27,094 in the secondary schools (government and assisted); the private primary and secondary schools had 20,130 pupils on roll. Education in government and assisted secondary schools was made free in 1960.

There are also 5 training colleges. Technical and commercial education is provided by 4 government sponsored technical schools.

CINEMAS (1967). There are 70 cinemas and 4 drive-in cinemas.

NEWSPAPERS (1970). There are 2 daily newspapers with an average daily circulation of 84,713 (Sunday, 138,474), and an evening paper (Monday–Friday) with a daily circulation of 43,942.

JUSTICE. The High Court consists of the Chief Justice and not fewer than 10 puisne judges. In criminal cases a judge of the High Court sits with a jury of 12 in cases of treason and murder, and with 9 jurors in other cases. The Court of Appeal consists of the Chief Justice and 3 Justices of Appeal; there is a limited right of appeal from it to the Privy Council. There are 6 High Courts and 28 magistrates' courts.

Police. At the end of 1966 the police force consisted of 591 officers, 7 inspectors and 2,348 other ranks.

FINANCE. Currency. The Trinidad and Tobago dollar of 100 cents equals £0·21. Total circulation of notes was TT$46,912,450 and of coins, TT$2,706,541 as at 31 Dec. 1965.

Budget and Commerce. Statistics of 5 calendar years (in TT$1,000):

	1964	1965²	1966¹	1967¹	1968
Revenue	261,114	256,639	215,800	232,300	
Expenditure	264,615	250,715	214,600	225,000	
Public debt²	214,357	232,559	266,108	298,205	
Customs and excise	58,901	61,883	63,352	61,279	
Imports	730,580	817,031	783,106	725,342	
Exports	699,016	690,458	730,461	765,777	
Ships' stores and bunkers	53,369	43,121	40,818	45,491	

¹ Provisional.   ² Revised.

The principal items of revenue during 1969 were: Customs and excise, $70m.; royalty, $35·1m.; motor vehicle licence fees and duties, $11·9m.; income tax, $111·5m.

Chief imports, 1966	TT$1,000	Chief imports, 1966	TT$1,000
Food	89,726·9	Machinery and transport	
Beverages and tobacco	6,406·7	equipment	102,409·6
Mineral fuels, lubricants, etc.	391,263·6	Manufactured goods	40,757·2
Chemicals	32,814·3		

The principal domestic exports during 1966 were (in TT$1,000): Sugar, 34,742·4; cocoa beans, 4,244·9; petroleum products (including crude petroleum), 579,207·2; natural asphalt, 3,569·8; chemicals, 58,994·6.

The chief countries of origin of imports were: Venezuela (30·2%), UK (16·8%), USA (14%), Saudi Arabia (13·2%). Exports were shipped chiefly to USA (34%), UK (13·5%), Netherlands (6·3%), Sweden (6%), Canada (4·1%).

Trade of Trinidad and Tobago with UK (British Board of Trade returns, in £1,000 sterling):

	1966	1967	1968	1969	1970
Imports to UK	22,057	22,971	22,336	21,688	19,309
Exports from UK	23,368	19,845	23,278	24,866 ⎫	28,131
Re-exports from UK	430	290	409	402 ⎭	

AGRICULTURE. Of the total area of 1,267,236 acres (Trinidad, 1,192,844 acres, and Tobago, 74,392 acres), about half has been alienated. Acres under cultivation and care include (1963): Forest, 694,792; sugar, 84,252; cocoa, 120,000; coconuts, 35,000; citrus, 13,000; tonca beans, 1,735. Sugar production in 1968 was 239,556 (1969: 237,231) tons. The territory is still largely dependent on imported food supplies, especially flour, dairy products, meat, rice and fish. Areas have been irrigated for rice, and soil and forest conservation is practised.

INDUSTRY. Oil production is one of Trinidad's leading industries and an important source of revenue. Commercial production began in 1909; production in 1968 was 67m. bbls; in 1967, 65m. bbls. Trinidad also possesses 2 refineries, with throughput capacity of 14·6m. bbls annually; crude oil is imported from Venezuela and Saudi Arabia and refined in Trinidad. Besides oil, Trinidad's natural resources include the 'Pitch Lake', an important source of asphalt; production, 1966, 157,703 tons.

In 1963 there were 84 workers' and 16 employers' unions with a total membership of 76,844.

TOURISM. In 1969, 98,908 (1968, 91,700) foreigners visited Trinidad and Tobago.

ROADS. There are 2,604 miles of main and local roads. Motor vehicles at the end of 1967 included 45,203 private cars, 7,536 hiring and rented cars, 195 buses, 8,769 goods vehicles, 2,708 tractors and trailers, 1,182 motor cycles.

SHIPPING. In 1966, 5,738 vessels arrived.

AVIATION. The following airlines operate scheduled passenger, mail and freight services: British West Indian Airways, Ltd, Air Canada, PANAM, KLM, Linea Aeropostal Venezolana, Aerolinas Argentinas, Leeward Islands Air Transport, Air France and BOAC.

TELECOMMUNICATIONS. Communication by cable with the UK, Europe, North America and other parts of the world is maintained by Cable and Wireless (West Indies), Ltd; 119 miles of telegraph. Number of post offices (1969), 179; number of telephones, 49,031, of which 29,985 are in Port-of-Spain.

Four wireless stations are maintained by the Trinidad Government and 3 by airline companies. A meteorological station is maintained at Piarco airport.

BANKING. Banks operating: Barclays Bank DCO; Royal Bank of Canada; Canadian Imperial Bank of Commerce; Bank of Nova Scotia; Trinidad Co-operative Bank, Ltd; Bank of London and Montreal; Chase Manhattan Bank; First National City Bank. A Central Bank began operations in Dec. 1964.

Government savings banks are established in 51 offices, with a head office in Port-of-Spain, the amount of deposits at the end of 1967 being $8,715,000 and the total number of depositors (in 1964) 136,997.

Tobago is situated about 21 miles north-east of Trinidad. Main town is Scarborough.

Principal goods shipped from Tobago to Trinidad are copra, cocoa, livestock and poultry, fresh vegetables, coconut oil and coconut fibre.

BOOKS OF REFERENCE

STATISTICAL INFORMATION: The Central Statistical Office, Government of Trinidad and Tobago, 2 Edward St., Port-of-Spain. *Director:* J. Harewood. Publications include *Annual Statistical Digest, Quarterly Economic Report, Annual Overseas Trade Report, Population and Vital Statistics Annual Report.*

Report of the Trinidad and Tobago Independence Conference, 1962. (Cmnd. 1757.). HMSO, 1962
Development Plan for Tobago. HMSO, 1957
Economic Survey of Trinidad and Tobago, 1953–48. Government Printer, Port-of-Spain, 1959
Five Year Development Programme, 1958–1962. Government Printer, Port-of-Spain, 1958
Third Five Year Plan, 1969–73. Government Printer, Port-of-Spain, 1970
Trinidad and Tobago Year Book. Port-of-Spain. Annual (from 1865)
Trade Dictionary of Trinidad and Tobago. 2nd ed. London, 1966
Braithwaite, L., *Social Stratification in Trinidad.* Social & Economic Studies, 2 (Jamaica), 1953
CENTRAL LIBRARY. The Central Library of Trinidad and Tobago, Queen's Park East, Port-of-Spain. *Librarian:* Miss M. Lumsden, FLA.

UGANDA

AREA AND POPULATION. Total area 91,134 sq. miles (236,037 sq. km), including 16,386 sq. miles of swamp and water.

The population of Uganda is 9·53m. (1969 estimate), including some 9,000 Europeans and 88,000 Asians. The majority of the Africans (1,044,000) are Baganda, the tribe from which the country takes its name. In 1966 some 68,000 Tutsi refugees from Rwanda, some 55,000 Sudanese refugees and some 33,000 refugees from the Congo were living in Uganda.

About 3m. Africans speak Bantu languages; there are a few Congo pygmies living near the Semliki River; the rest of the Africans belong to the Hamitic, Nilotic and Sudanese groups. Ki-Swahili is generally understood in trading centres.

The capital is Kampala; population nearly 80,000; greater Kampala, 170,000. The official language is English.

CONSTITUTION AND GOVERNMENT. Uganda became a fully independent member of the Commonwealth on 9 Oct. 1962 after nearly 70 years of British rule. Full sovereign status was granted by the Uganda Independence Act, 1962, and the Constitution is embodied in the Uganda (Independence) Order in

Council, 1962. The post of Governor-General was on 9 Oct. 1963 replaced by that of President as head of state, elected by the National Assembly for a 5-year term.

Uganda became a republic on 8 Sept. 1967. Under the 1967 Constitution, the executive authority is vested in the President. The President is assisted by a Cabinet of Ministers. Unlike the Presidential system in the United States and other countries, in Uganda the President is a Member of the National Assembly, and takes an active part in the Assembly's deliberations.

On 25 Jan. 1971, Dr A. Milton Obote was overthrown by troops led by Gen. Idi Amin.

Military Head of State: Gen. Idi Amin. *Foreign Affairs:* Wanume Kibedi.

National flag: Six horizontal stripes of black, yellow, red (repeated) with a crested emblem on a white orb in the centre.

For administrative purposes Uganda is divided into 4 regions: (1) the Eastern Region, comprising the districts of Bugisu, Bukedi, Busoga, Mbale Township, Sebei and Teso; (2) the Western Region, comprising the districts of Bunyoro, Toro, Ankole and Kigezi; (3) Buganda Region, with islands in Lake Victoria, comprising the districts of Mengo, Masaka and Mubende; and (4) the Northern Region, comprising the districts of Karamoja, Lango, Acholi and West Nile.

DIPLOMATIC REPRESENTATIVES

Country	Uganda representative	Foreign representative
Algeria	—	N. Djoudi
Belgium	—	E. Ritweger de Moor
Britain[1]	Dr S. B. Asea	D. A. Scott, CMG
Canada[1]	M. Lubega	B. Margaret Meagher
China	—	Chen Chih-fang
Czechoslovakia	—	J. Staddler
Ethiopia	—	Ato Getachew Mekasha
France	—	M. Flory
Germany (West)	Leonard Basudde	Dr W. Sarrazin
Ghana[1]	W. Matovu	E. A. Dzima
Hungary	—	János Katona
India[1]	George W. Kamba	K. R. P. Singh
Israel	—	Uriel Lubrani
Italy	—	Marchese Giovanni
Japan	—	Toshio Urabe
Netherlands	—	Dr J. C. van Benskom
Nigeria[1]	—	L. O. Harriman
Norway	—	I. Rindal
Pakistan[1]	—	R. R. Noore
Rwanda	—	A.-M. Kazenga
Sudan	—	H. M. El-Amin
Sweden	—	C. Gustaf Bere
Switzerland	—	Dr H. Karl Frey
USSR	M. Engur	D. F. Safonov
UAR	Paul Muwanga	Gamal Barakat
USA	Erifazi Otema-Alimadi	Henry E. Stebbins
Yugoslavia	—	M. Milge

[1] High Commissioner.   No figure = Ambassador.

EDUCATION. Education is a joint undertaking by the government, local authorities and, to some extent, voluntary agencies. The education system is divided into three sectors, primary, secondary and post-secondary. The primary course covers 7 years. There were 633,546 pupils in grant-aided primary schools in 1966. Education at secondary level falls into 4 categories, namely, secondary schools, which are the grammar type of schools with a course extending over 6 years to Higher School Certificate; technical schools; farm schools; and primary teacher-training colleges. Further education is provided at the Uganda Technical College, the National Teachers' College, the Uganda College of Commerce and Agricultural Colleges. There are also several Departmental Training Schools for training staff for different departments. The Medical Department alone has 8 such schools for training nurses, midwives, Medical Assistants, Health Inspectors, and other medical staff.

University level education is available at Makerere University College and the 2 other constituent Colleges of the University of East Africa; the University College, Nairobi, in Kenya, and the University College, Dar es Salaam, in Tanzania. Uganda students also go to universities and colleges outside East Africa for higher education.

JUSTICE. The High Court of Uganda, presided over by the Chief Justice and 12 puisne judges, exercises original and appellate jurisdiction throughout Uganda. Subordinate courts, presided over by Chief Magistrates and Magistrates of the first, second and third grade, are established in all areas: jurisdiction varies with the grade of Magistrate. Chief and first-grade Magistrates are professionally qualified; second- and third-grade Magistrates are trained to diploma level at the Law School, Entebbe.

Chief Magistrates exercise supervision over and hear appeals from second- and third-grade courts.

The Court of Appeal for Eastern Africa was re-established on 9 Dec. 1962 as the Court of Appeal for Uganda; it hears appeals from the High Court.

A law school has been established at Entebbe to train magistrates in civil and criminal law. The African courts have been integrated with the Central Government Courts so that a unified courts system has been established.

FINANCE. Currency. East African Currency Board notes ceased to be legal tender from 14 Sept. 1967. The exchange rate is 17·14 Uganda shillings = £1.

Budget. The revenue and expenditure (exclusive of loan disbursements) for fiscal years (1 July–30 June) were (in £1,000 sterling):

	1962–63	1963–64	1964–65	1965–66	1966–67[1]	1967–68[1]
Revenue	22,182	27,089	30,748	32,340	768	880
Expenditure	20,020	24,992	31,963	33,455	652	722

[1] Uganda sh. 1m.

In 1965–66 (and estimate 1966–67) income tax amounted to £4·55m. (£7·48m.) and other direct taxation to £30,200 (£1·5m.). Public debt June 1967, £60·97m.

In 1965–66 Uganda contributed £1,503,103 (1966–67 estimate, £1·64m.) to the East Africa Common Services Organization Distributable Pool Fund, from which Uganda received £942,078 (1966–67 estimate, £1m.).

DEFENCE. The army, organized in 4 infantry battalions, has a strength of 5,700.

The air force was formed in 1964 and has undergone rapid expansion with the assistance of Israeli and Czechoslovakian training missions. Current equipment includes 7 MiG-15 jet fighter-bombers, 3 C-47 transports, about 10 L-29 Delfin armed jet trainers, 8 Super Cub primary trainers, 10 Piaggio P 149 piston-engined and 24 Israeli-built Magister jet basic trainers. In addition the Police Air Wing has Twin Otter and 1 Caribou twin-engined STOL transports, Cessna 180 and Piper Aztec light aircraft, and a JetRanger and 2 Scout light helicopters.

AGRICULTURE. Cotton and coffee are the principal exports, the former being grown entirely and the latter very largely by African farmers. Production of cotton in 1969–70 was 468,000 bales (of 400 lb.) which was a record. The 1965–66 coffee crop amounted to 160,000 tons, of which 145,000 tons was *robusta*. Other cash crops produced in 1965–66 were tea (24·7m. lb.), tobacco (6m. lb.), groundnuts (8,400 lb. exported), maize (42,000 lb. exported), castor seed (1,900 tons exported), sisal (320 tons) and sugar (1966, 125,700 tons; 1965, 115,696 tons).

FORESTRY. Exploitable forests consist almost entirely of hardwoods. Internal consumption is rising. During 1964–65 approximately 28,000 tons of sawn timber were produced. About half of the timber exported goes to the United Kingdom and another quarter to Kenya and Tanganyika, from which in return the bulk of the softwood imports are obtained.

FISHERY. With its 13,600 sq. miles of lakes and many rivers, Uganda possesses one of the largest fresh-water fisheries in the world. In 1966 fish production was 80,000 tons with a retail value of £6·5m. Fish farming (especially carp and tilapia) is a growing industry.

MINERALS. With the opening of the Kilembe mine in 1956, copper has become Uganda's most valuable mineral export. In 1966 the principal minerals produced were: Blister copper, 16,041 long tons (£6,995,500) (1967: 14,392 long tons, £5,593,000); cement (1963), 54,282 long tons (£616,101); tin ore, 180·3 long tons (£171,982) (1967: 156·6 long tons, £143,325). Total value of mineral production in 1963 was £4,539,240.

POWER. Industrial expansion is based on hydro-electric power provided by the Owen Falls scheme, which has a capacity of 150,000 kwh.

COMMERCE. Since 1927 Uganda has been united in a customs union with Kenya and Tanzania (see pp. 471–73).

In 1966, £15·5m. of the imports came from the UK, £4·8m. from West Germany, £2·3m. from Japan. The biggest buyers were USA (£17m.), UK (£12·3m.), Japan (£3·3m.).

Total trade between Uganda and UK in £1,000 sterling (British Board of Trade returns):

	1965	1966	1967	1968	1969	1970
Imports to UK	8,651	11,153	13,744	15,190	17,466	17,652
Exports from UK	7,509	8,962	8,069	8,275	10,058⎫	9,960
Re-exports from UK	25	23	39	33	52⎭	

COMMUNICATIONS. Lake, marine, railway and some road services are operated by the East African Railways and Harbours Administration (see pp. 472–73).

Roads. There are 3,876 miles of all-weather roads maintained by the Ministry of Works, of which 796 miles are two-lane bitumenized highways, and some 11,230 miles of other roads, maintained by district governments.

Aviation. Entebbe has a first-class international airport and has direct flights to Europe, Rhodesia, Sudan, Kenya, Tanzania, Congo Republic, Burundi and Rwanda by BOAC, BUA, EAA, Sudan Airways, Air Congo, SABENA, SAS, Alitalia and many charter companies. Entebbe airport was used by 125,029 passengers in 1964. Eleven other government airfields are used for internal communications.

Post. For posts see p. 474. There were 23,368 telephones in use at 1 Jan. 1968.

BANKING. The Bank of Uganda was set upon 16 May 1966; its external assets as at 31 Aug. 1967 were £9m. The Uganda Credit and Savings Bank, set up in 1950, was on 9 Oct. 1965 reconstituted as the Uganda Commercial Bank, with its capital fully owned by the Government.

Barclays Bank DCO has 11 branches and 7 agencies; National & Grindlays Bank Ltd has 12 branches and 12 agencies; the Standard Bank Ltd has 6 branches and 2 agencies; the Bank of Baroda Ltd has 3 branches; the Bank of India Ltd has 2 branches. Other banks operating in Uganda are the Algemene Bank Nederland NV, the Ottoman Bank and the Commercial Bank of Africa.

BOOKS OF REFERENCE

Atlas of Uganda. Dept. of Lands and Surveys. Kampala. 1962
Faller, L. A. (ed.), The King's Men. OUP, 1964
Ingham, K., The Making of Modern Uganda. London, 1957
Ingrams, H., Uganda. HMSO, 1959
Kendall, H., Town Planning in Uganda. London, 1955
Kitching, A. L., and Blackledge, G. R., A Luganda–English and English–Luganda Dictionary. Kampala, 1925
Larimore, A. E., The Alien Town: patterns of settlement in Uganda. Chicago, 1959
Uganda Trade Directory. London, 1966

KENYA

HISTORY. Until Kenya became independent on 12 Dec. 1963, it consisted of the colony and the protectorate. The protectorate comprised the mainland dominions of the Sultan of Zanzibar, viz., a coastal strip of territory 10 miles wide, to the northern branch of the Tana River; also Mau, Kipini and the Island of Lamu, and all adjacent islands between the rivers Umba and Tana. The Sultan on 8 Oct. 1963 ceded the coastal strip to Kenya with effect from 12 Dec. 1963.

The colony and protectorate, formerly known as the East African Protectorate were, on 1 April 1905, transferred from the Foreign Office to the Colonial Office and in Nov. 1906 the protectorate was placed under the control of a governor and C.-in-C. and (except the Sultan of Zanzibar's dominions) was annexed to the Crown as from 23 July 1920 under the name of the Colony of Kenya, thus becoming a Crown Colony. The territories on the coast became the Kenya Protectorate.

A treaty was signed (15 July 1924) with Italy under which Great Britain ceded to Italy the Juba River and a strip from 50 to 100 miles wide on the British side of the river. Cession took place on 29 June 1925. The northern boundary is defined by an agreement with Ethiopia in 1947.

AREA AND POPULATION. The total area of Kenya is 224,960 sq. miles (582,600 sq. km), of which 219,790 sq. miles is land area. According to the 1969 census, the population was 10,942,708, of which 10,771,192 were Africans, 137,037 Asians, 40,593 Europeans, 27,886 Arabs.

On the coast the Arabs and Swahili predominate, farther inland the races speaking Bantu languages, and non-Bantu tribes, such as the Luo, the Nandi and Kipsigis, the Masai, the Somali and the Gallas.

Population of the Provinces (1969): Nyanza, 2·1m.; Central, 1·7m.; Rift Valley, 2·2m.; North Eastern, 0·2m.; Eastern, 1·9m.; Western, 1·3m.; Nairobi district, 0·5m.

Nairobi, the capital, was given a Royal charter on 30 March 1950; the 1969 census showed a population of 509,286, including 19,185 Europeans and 67,189 Asians.

Population of the largest towns: Mombasa, 246,000; Nakuru, 47,800; Kisumu, 30,700; Eldoret, 16,900.

GOVERNMENT. A constitution conferring internal self-government was brought into force on 1 June 1963, and full independence was achieved on 12 Dec. 1963. On 12 Dec. 1964 Kenya became a republic.

President of the Republic: Mzee Jomo Kenyatta. *Vice-President and Minister of Home Affairs:* Daniel Arap Moi.

The House of Representatives and the Senate were in Dec. 1966 amalgamated into one National Assembly.

On 10 Nov. 1964 Kenya became a one-party state of the Kenya African National Union (KANU) when the voluntary dissolution of the Kenya African Democratic Union (KADU) was declared. Later a second party, the Kenya People's Union (KPU) was formed but on 30 Oct. 1969 was proscribed.

The cabinet was composed in Jan. 1971 as follows:

Finance and Economic Development: Mwai Kibaki. *Defence:* J. S. Gichuru. *Agriculture and Animal Husbandry:* J. J. M. Nyagah. *Health:* I. O. Okero. *Local Government:* Dr J. G. Kiano. *Works:* J. Nyamweya. *Power and Communications:* R. G. Ngala. *Labour:* E. N. Mwendwa. *Tourism and Wild Life:* J. L. M. Shako. *Land and Settlement:* J. H. Angaine. *Housing:* P. J. Ngei. *Attorney-General:* C. Njonjo. *Information and Broadcasting:* Dr. Z. Onyonka. *Natural Resources:* Odongo Omamo. *Co-operatives and Social Services:* Masinde Muliro. *Commerce and Industry:* J. Osogo. *Education:* Taita Towett. *Minister of State:* Mbiyu Koinange. *Foreign Affairs:* Dr. N. Mungai.

Administration. The country is divided into the Nairobi Area and 7 provinces over which there are local councils with administrative functions. The provinces are: Coast, Central, Eastern, Rift Valley, Western, Nyanza and North Eastern.

DIPLOMATIC REPRESENTATIVES

Country	Kenya representative	Foreign representative
Algeria	—	Ali Benghezai[2]
Australia[1]	—	J. V. R. Hearder
Austria	—	Dr F. Rader
Belgium	—	Dr H. Nopper
Botswana[1]	—	P. P. M. Makepe
Brazil	—	F. H. de Mesquita
Britain[1]	Ngethe Njoroge	Eric G. Norris, CMG
Bulgaria	—	Lynbomir Zhelyazlov
Burundi	—	Protais Mangona
Canada[1]	—	J. M. Cook
China	—	Wang Hui-min[2]
Congo (K.)	F. M. Hinawy	M. Kisaka
Czechoslovakia	—	M. Lescisin
Denmark	—	Kai Johansen
Ethiopia	P. M. Echaria	Ato Abate Aghide
Finland	—	J. A. Pekuri
France	J. J. Isige[2]	René Millet
Germany (West)	N. N. Muli	Dr J. Ruhfus
Ghana[1]	—	Eric K. Otoo
Greece	—	N. A. Saitas
Guinea	—	Damon Sakho
Hungary	—	Joseph Bajnok
India[1]	S. K. Kimalel	Gurbachen Singh
Iraq	—	Dr Hassan Kittany
Israel	—	Reuven Dafni
Italy	—	Vittorio Zadotti
Ivory Coast	—	Y.A.O.G. Attoungbre
Japan	—	Ryuichi Ando
Korea	—	Yun Young Lim
Kuwait	—	S. M. Al-Sani
Lesotho[1]	—	M. P. Khoali
Liberia	—	Robert F. Okai, Jr
Malawi[1]	—	Joe Kachingwe
Morocco	—	A. M. Hammedi Mostapha
Netherlands	—	Jan Polderman
Nigeria[1]	—	Ignatius C. Olisemeka
Norway	—	S. J. Gjellum
Pakistan[1]	—	M. K. Khan
Poland	—	Dr E. Hachalski
Rwanda	—	A. M. Kagenza

[1] High Commissioner.   [2] Chargé d'Affaires.   No figure = Ambassador.

Country	Kenya representative	Foreign representative
Sudan	—	Mohammed Mirghani
Sweden	J. Muliro	Carl-George Crafoord
Somalia	J. K. Ilako	Hashi Abdulla
Switzerland	—	Dr H. K. Frey
Turkey	—	Sadun Terem
USSR	W. O. Ndisi	D. P. Goryunov
UAR	F. M. Hinwy	N. A. F. Helmy
USA	L. Kibinge	Robinson McIlvaine
Vatican	Dr J. N. Karanja	Archbishop P. Sartorelli
Yugoslavia	—	Ivo Pelicon
Zambia[1]	L. A. Odero	D. K. Konoso

[1] High Commissioner.   No figure = Ambassador.

RELIGION. The indigenous African background is largely influenced by belief in God in Judaic forms, but Christianity is making an important contribution to the life of the whole territory, not only through the educational and medical services of Christian missions, but by the growth of churches under African leadership, and by its impact on the thought and policy of the country. The Roman Catholic Church (about 1·5m. adherents) has been developed mainly by Irish, British, Dutch and Italian missionary bodies and is now organized in 12 dioceses under the archbishop of Nairobi.

The Protestant Churches (about 950,000 adherents) were started mainly by British and American mission societies; most of them are now linked together by the National Christian Council of Kenya. The Church of the Province of Kenya, formerly the Anglican Church Province of East Africa, was inaugurated on 3 Aug. 1970; at the same time the first Archbishop of Kenya was enthroned. The East African Yearly Meeting of Friends (Religious Society of Friends) has 90,000 adherents.

The Arabs on the coast are Moslems, and Islam has spread among some of the African coastal tribes and in the cities. The Asians are Hindus and Moslems, with the exception of the Goans, who are Roman Catholics.

EDUCATION. *Primary* (1970). 6,111 primary schools (5,765 maintained, 179 assisted and 167 unaided), with together 1,360,750 children, of whom 551,240 were girls and 809,510 boys.

Secondary (1970). There were 800 secondary schools (283 maintained, 19 assisted and 498 unaided), with a total enrolment of 134,856, of whom 37,654 are girls and 97,211 are boys.

Technical (1970). The Kenya Polytechnic in Nairobi, with an enrolment of 2,858 students, and Mombasa Technical Institute, with an enrolment of 988 students, of whom 490 are full-time students and 498 part-time students, are the most advanced institutions. There are also schools which had a total enrolment of 4,293 students of whom 1,934 were taking secondary trade courses and 2,359 were taking vocational courses.

Teacher training (1970). 6,776 students were training as primary teachers, 1,268 as secondary teachers and 13 teachers for the deaf.

Higher Education. The University of East Africa, which had 3 constituent Colleges, Makerere University College in Kampala, Uganda, the University College in Nairobi, Kenya, and University College in Dar es Salaam, Tanzania was disbanded in 1970. The University of Nairobi was inaugurated on 10 Dec. 1970. The University of Nairobi is now wholly supported by Kenya Government, and provides courses in arts, science, education, agriculture, medicine, art, architecture, engineering, veterinary, law and domestic science. In 1970 there were some 3,605 Kenya students at college in East Africa and abroad, 1,226 of them at University of Nairobi.

HEALTH. In 1970 beds in hospitals (including mission and non-government hospitals) totalled 13,104. 194 health centres were in operation. Total expenditure of the Ministry of Health in 1969–70 was £4,981,100 on health services. Development expenditure on health services totalled £1,636,850 in 1969–70. Free medical service for all children and adult out-patients was launched in 1965.

JUSTICE. The courts of justice comprise the High Court, established in 1921, with full jurisdiction both civil and criminal over all persons and all matters in Kenya, including Admiralty jurisdiction arising on the high seas and elsewhere, and Subordinate Courts. The High Court has its headquarters at Nairobi and consists of the Chief Justice and 11 puisne judges; it sits continuously at Nairobi, Mombasa, Nakuru and Kisumu; civil and criminal sessions are held regularly at Eldoret, Nyeri, Meru, Kitale, Kisii and Kericho.

The Subordinate Courts are presided over by Senior Resident, Resident or District Magistrates and are established in the main centres of all districts. They sit throughout the year. There are also Moslem Subordinate Courts established in mixed areas where the local population is predominantly Mohammedan; they are presided over by Kadhis and exercise limited jurisdiction in matters governed by Mohammedan law.

FINANCE. Currency, see p. 471.

Budget. Revenue and expenditure (in Kenya £1,000) for fiscal years 1 July–30 June:

	1966–67	1967–68[1]	1968–69	1969–70	1970–71
Net revenue	60,213	69,256	75,507	87,081	93,725
Net expenditure	56,305	63,735	68,868	73,982	81,292
Development revenue	13,598	14,945	15,552	26,827	30,883
Development expenditure	16,856	20,076	25,459	33,076	36,486

[1] Estimates.

Of the revenue in 1968–69, customs and excise accounted for K£33·6m.; income tax, K£22·7m.; other licences, duties and taxes, K£7·6m. Of the 1967–68 development receipts K£167,921 came as grants from UK Government, K£3,172,155 from UK exchequer loans, K£1,471,318 from International Development Association loan, K£607,560 from US–AID loan and K£7,948,000 was raised locally at 6%.

Funded public debt at 30 June 1969 was K£75,111,068.

DEFENCE. The army consists of 3 infantry battalions and a paratroop company; total strength, 4,200.

An air force formed 1 June 1964, has been built up with RAF assistance. Initial equipment, all of Canadian design, consisted of 6 Chipmunk primary trainers, 4 Caribou twin-engined transports and 7 single-engined Beavers for transport, air ambulance, anti-locust spraying and security duties. The first combat unit is equipping with BAC 167 Strikemaster light jet attack aircraft. The Chipmunks will be replaced with 5 Scottish Aviation Bulldog primary trainers in 1972.

AGRICULTURE. As agriculture is possible from sea-level to altitudes of over 9,000 ft, tropical, sub-tropical and temperate crops can be grown and mixed farming can be advocated. Four-fifths of the country is range-land which produces mainly livestock products and wild game which constitutes the major attraction of the country's tourist industry.

The main areas of crop production are the Central, Rift Valley, Western and Nyanza Provinces and parts of Eastern and Coastal Provinces. Coffee, tea, sisal, pyrethrum, maize and wheat are crops of major importance in the Highlands, while coconuts, cashew nuts, cotton, sugar, sisal and maize are the principal crops grown as the lower altitudes. The livestock industry is important, and considerable quantities of corned beef, butter, bacon, ham, and hides and skins are exported.

Groundnuts, simsim, potatoes, beans, essential oils and other miscellaneous crops are grown according to elevation and rainfall. An export trade is developing in mangoes, fresh fruits, flowers and vegetables flown by air to Europe.

FORESTRY. The total area of gazetted forest reserves in Kenya amounts to 16,800 sq. km, of which the greater part is situated between 6,000 and 11,000 ft above sea-level, mostly on Mount Kenya, the Aberdares, Mount Elgon, Tinderet, Londiani, Mau watershed, Elgeyo and Charangani ranges. These forests may be divided into coniferous, broad-leafed or hardwood and bamboo forests. The upper parts of these forests are mainly bamboo, which occurs mostly between altitudes of 8,000 and 10,000 ft and occupies some 10% of the high-altitude forests. Plantations established by 31 Dec. 1969 total 180,560 hectares, of which 90,450 are exotic softwood. In addition 3,100 hectares of pines have been planted for pulpwood. The Forest Department employs about 11,000 men and primary forest industries about 8,000. Water catchment is no longer considered to be the primary role of forests. Revenue from timber royalties, fuel royalties and from exports of forest-based products continues to increase. Exports of forest-based products earned £6,101,240 in 1969. The revenue to the Forest Department from timber royalties and miscellaneous produce amounted to £437,000. In 1969, 4,633 tons of softwood logs and 12,781 tons of hardwood were extracted from forest reserves.

MINING. By mid 1970 over 75% of the area of Kenya had been geologically mapped. A special and 2 ordinary oil-prospecting licences were extant at the end of 1969, together covering 22,250 sq. miles. A joint UN–Kenya Government project is investigating the mineral resources in western Kenya and the exploration and development of mineral deposits is proceeding.

Mineral production during 1969, excluding much building material and manufactured cement, was valued at £2,821,449. The main products were: Cement, 653,091 long tons (£5,464,450); soda ash, 108,476 long tons (£1,142,999); copper, 77 long tons (£40,444); gold (refined), 556,847 grammes (£273,821); limestone and products, 24,904 long tons (£180,672), diatomite, 2,303 long tons (£32,241); carbon dioxide, 761 long tons (£71,635); salt, 42,285 long tons (£398,034); kaolin, 1,472 long tons (£36,225). Other minerals comprised vermiculite, barytes, magnesite, felspar, beryl, aquamarine fluorite, silver, sapphires, galena, guano, wollastrite and corundum.

TOURISM. In 1970, 276,000 overseas visitors travelled to Kenya.

COMMERCE. Since 1949 Kenya has been united in a customs union with Uganda and Tanganyika. In addition to the items listed on pp. 472–73, Kenya in 1965 also exported 18,600 centals of butter and ghee valued at £292,613.

The chief countries of origin in 1969 were: UK, 31·2%; USA, 7·5%; West Germany, 8·2%; Japan, 7·8%. Chief countries of destination: UK, 21·6%; West Germany, 11·4%; USA, 7·3%.

Total trade between Kenya and UK, in £1,000 sterling (British Board of Trade returns):

	1965	1966	1967	1968	1969	1970
Imports to UK	16,187	19,800	19,781	2529,4	25,706	27,064
Exports from UK	34,268	43,384	47,398	46,917	49,242 }	52,822
Re-exports from UK	426	389	556	516	712 }	

ROADS. In Sept. 1970 there were approximately 5,500 km of trunk roads, of which 2,436 km were bitumen surfaced. There were approximately 36,000 km of secondary roads, of which 564 km were bitumen surfaced. Including minor and administration roads there were a total of 42,000 km of public road.

Under the 1965–70 Development Plan contracts have been let for the bitumenization of 71 more miles and the improvement, to a gravel standard, of a further 121 miles of trunk road.

BROADCASTING. The Voice of Kenya operates 2 national services (Swahili–English) from Nairobi and regional services in Kisumu, Nairobi and Mombasa. The television service provides programmes mainly in English and Swahili. A new television station opened in Mombasa in 1970.

BANKING. Banks operating in Kenya: the National & Grindlays Bank, Ltd; the Standard Bank, Ltd; Barclays Bank DCO; Algemene Bank Nederland NV; Bank of India, Ltd; Bank of Baroda, Ltd; Habib Bank (Overseas), Ltd; African Banking Corporation (E.A.), Ltd; Commercial Bank of Africa, Ltd. The Co-operative Bank of Kenya, Ltd; National Bank of Kenya, Ltd.

BOOKS OF REFERENCE

STATISTICAL INFORMATION. *See* p. 474.

Statistical Abstract. Government Printer, Nairobi, 1969
International Bank, *The Economic Development of Kenya.* Johns Hopkins Press, 1963
Standard English–Swahili Dictionary. Ed. Inter-territorial Language Committee of East Africa. 2 vols. London, 1939
Askwith, T. G., *The Story of Kenya's Progress.* E.A. Literature Bureau, rev. ed., 1958
Bolton, K., *Haramble Country: A Guide to Kenya.* London, 1970
Hill, M. F., *Permanent Way, the story of the Kenya and Uganda Railway.* E.A. Railways and Harbours, Nairobi, 1950
Huxley, E., and Perham, M., *Race and Politics in Kenya.* Rev. ed. London, 1956
Mboya, T. J., *Freedom and After.* London, 1963

EAST AFRICAN COMMUNITY

Organization. On 9 Dec. 1961, with the achievement of full independence by Tanganyika, the East Africa High Commission, which had, since 1947, been administering services of an inter-territorial nature for Kenya, Uganda and Tanganyika, was re-organized under the name of the East African Common Services Organization. On 6 June 1967 the heads of state of Kenya, Tanzania and Uganda signed a treaty in Kampala, which transformed and expanded the EACSO into an East African Economic Community and Common Market. This was inaugurated on 1 Dec. 1967.

The Community has its headquarters in Arusha, Tanzania.

Secretary-General: Z. H. K. Bigirwenkya.

There are 5 councils: the Common Market Council, the Communications Council, the Economic Consultative and Planning Council, the Finance Council, and the Research and Social Council. Each of these consists of the 3 East African Ministers plus a varying number of national Ministers (one from each country in the Finance Council, 3 from each country in the other Councils).

To legislate for all Community matters there is an East African Legislative Assembly, with 9 members appointed from each country, together with the East African Ministers and Deputy Ministers, the Secretary-General, the Counsel to the Community and a Chairman.

The 4 Corporations within the Community, that is, the E.A. Railways Corporation; the E.A. Harbours Corporation; the E.A. Posts and Telecommunications Corporation; and the E.A. Airways Corporation, conduct their business according to commercial principles, and are controlled by a Board of Directors.

The treaty also includes a transfer tax system to protect from undue competition young industries in the less-developed member countries in the common market.

The E.A. Development Bank established under the Treaty, gives financial and technical aid to industries within the Community.

Currency. Tanzania introduced its own currency on 14 June 1966, Uganda on 14 Aug. 1966 and Kenya on 14 Sept. 1966 and later replaced the coins of the East African Currency Board by their own issues. The standard coin is the East African shilling of 100 cents (20 shillings = 1 East African £). The paper currency in general use consists of 5, 10, 20, 50 and 100-shilling notes and is freely exchangeable in the 3 countries.

Commerce. Tanzania, Kenya and Uganda form a single trade unit and there is, apart from the transfer tax, virtual freedom of trade between them. Power to legislate fiscally is vested in the territorial governments and the revenue is allocated between them by means of a system of transfer forms. The customs and excise revenue is collected by the E.A. customs and excise departments and income tax revenue is collected by the E.A. tax department, both Common Services, established on 1 Jan. 1949.

Volume of trade (in £1,000, £1 = 20 Kenyan, Tanzanian or Ugandan shillings):

| | Kenya | | Tanzania | | Uganda | | Total East Africa | |
	1968	1969	1968	1969	1968	1969	1968	1969
Net imports:								
Commercial	97,724	116,830	67,260	70,937	40,335	45,462	205,319	233,229
Government	16,934	—	9,324	—	3,460	—	29,718	—
Gold	106	121	1	2	17	42	124	165
Total	114,764	116,951	76,585	70,939	43,812	45,504	235,161	233,394
Domestic exports:								
Excluding gold	57,489	63,117	79,030	83,106	65,471	69,885	201,990	216,108
Gold	306	215	241	236	—	—	547	451
Re-exports	5,140	—	2,070	—	876	—	8,087	—
Total	62,935	63,332	81,341	83,342	66,347	69,885	210,623	216,559

Principal net imports, 1969:

| | Kenya | | Tanzania | | Uganda | |
	Quantity	Value £1,000	Quantity	Value £1,000	Quantity	Value £1,000
Milk and cream, tinned (centals)	41,000	180	200,000	1,145	26,000	147
Rice (centals)	5,000	31	176,000	514	95,000	420
Sugar (centals)	188,000	324	68,000	99	2,000	7
Brandy, gin, gineva, whisky, rum (proof gallons)	..	736	..	466	..	338
Petroleum, crude (tons)	2,034,000	10,168	615,000	2,969	—	—
Aviation spirit (1,000 Imperial gallons)	..	..	..	..	..	..
Motor spirit (1,000 Imperial gallons)	..	..	..	..	..	..
Jet fuel (1,000 Imperial gallons)	..	..	..	..	..	..
Kerosene (1,000 Imperial gallons)	..	..	..	..	..	..
Distillate fuels (1,000 Imperial gallons)	..	..	..	..	..	..
Lubricating oils (1,000 Imperial gallons)	..	..	..	..	..	..
Chemical elements and compounds	..	1,678	..	711	..	482
Paints, varnishes, dyestuffs, etc.	..	692	..	859	..	545
Medicinal and pharmaceutical products	..	2,459	..	1,516	..	1,042
Soap (centals)	55,000	410	24,000	227	8,000	112
Fertilizers (tons)	84,000	2,272	36,000	824	16,000	424
Insecticides, fungicides, disinfectants, etc. (centals)	82,000	1,348	32,000	541	34,000	372
Rubber tyres and tubes (centals)	..	1,603	..	1,253	..	962
Wood and cork manufactures	..	446	..	208	..	101
Paper, paperboard and manufactures thereof	..	5,697	..	1,405	..	1,431
Cotton fabrics (1,000 sq. yd)	17,616	1,923	23,590	2,481	8,331	935
Jute bagging and sacking (1,000 sq. yd)	4,110	387	10,669	890	8,901	774
Fabrics of synthetic fibres, artificial fibre, etc. (1,000 sq. yd)	17,630	2,350	4,683	770	11,008	1,719
Jute bags and sacks (1,000)	4,110	387	10,669	890	8,901	774
Blankets and travelling rugs (1,000)	515	80	579	97	1,121	159
Non-metallic mineral manufactures	..	714	..	728	..	501
Iron and steel:						
Bars, rods, angles, shapes and sections (tons)	33,000	1,481	10,000	633	13,000	631
Universals, plates and sheets (tons)	825,000	3,567	808,000	1,659	722,000	1,285

	Kenya		Tanzania		Uganda	
		Value		*Value*		*Value*
	Quatity	*£1,000*	*Quantity*	*£1,000*	*Quantity*	*£1,000*
Iron and Steel (*contd.*)						
Railway track material (tons)	3,000	170	6,000	324	2,000	92
Tubes, pipes and fittings (tons)	7,000	606	12,000	714	5,000	476
Aluminium, unwrought and simply worked (tons)	1,000	416	3,000	706	2,000	480
Other metals and manufactures of metal	—	4,783	—	3,719	—	3,255
Tractors other than road tractors (number)	1	1,190	1	1,116	..	347
Agricultural machinery and implements	—	717	—	514	—	438
Office machines	—	1,023	—	306	—	245
Sewing machines (number)	..	..	..	..	..	..
Machinery other than electric	..	13,392	..	9,528	..	6,209
Wireless sets and television sets (number)	55,000	476	32,000	248	66	359
Other electrical machinery, etc.	—	5,744	—	3,761	—	3,057
Railway rolling stock	—	954	—	135	—	52
Passenger motor cars (number)	9,000	4,914	3,000	1,735	3,000	1,805
Buses, lorries, trucks, vans, road tractors (number)	5,000	4,979	2,000	4,304	3,000	3,221
Cycles (number)	11,000	99	29,000	298	17,000	165
Other transport equipment	..	..	..	..	..	..
Clothing		1,409		2,104		828
Footwear		271		310		177

Principal domestic exports, 1969:

	Kenya		Tanzania		Uganda	
	Quantity	*Value*	*Quantity*	*Value*	*Quantity*	*Value*
	(1,000)	*(£1,000)*	*(1,000)*	*(£1,000)*	*(1,000)*	*(£1,000)*
Coffee, not roasted (cwt)	1,003	16,337	974	12,853	3,554	38,996
Cotton, raw (centals)	61	761	1,250	11,734	1,166	12,548
Sisal fibre and tow (tons)	35	1,717	169	7,982	—	—
Tea (centals)	724	11,271	167	2,416	349	4,653
Diamonds (carats)	—	—	780	8,877	—	—
Hides, skins, etc. (centals)	144	1,871	151	1,779	88	1,334
Copper, unwrought (centals)	—	—	—	—	16	1,614
Meat and meat preparations (centals)	131	2,595	127	2,362	—	1
Cashew nuts, raw (centals)	9	680	81	5,947	—	—
Feeding stuff for animals (centals)	659	521	1,633	1,716	1,798	2,107
Pyrethrum extract (lb.)	810	2,224	378	1,036	—	—
Oilseeds, oil nut: and oil kernels (centals)	7	349	38	2,248	7	429
Jet fuel (Imperial gallons)	45,539	3,848	10,243	560	—	—
Residual fuel oils (Imperial gallons)	129.447	2,514	27.992	423	—	—
Wattle bark extract (centals)	364	1,144	193	452	—	—
Beans, peas, etc. (centals)	239	529	160	515	10	10
Sodium carbonate (soda ash) (tons)	85	904	—	—	—	—
Cement (tons)	304	1,434	2	21	2	28
Tobacco, unmanufactured (lb.)	1	—	9.947	1,766	4,577	849
Distillate fuels (Imperial gallons)	23,865	901	60,369	2,323	—	—
Cordage, rope, twine of sisal (centals)	71	223	343	1,304	—	—

Communications. *See* map of the roads, railways, ports and airports in THE STATESMAN'S YEAR-BOOK, 1964–65.

Revenue, 1968, from railways, inland waterways and road services, £26·27m.; from harbours, £12·59m. Expenditure (excluding contribution to renewals fund), 1967, on railways, £18·69m.; on harbours, £8·81m.

RAILWAYS. The railways comprise 3,663 route miles of single metre-gauge track. Main lines: Mombasa–Kasese, 1,036 miles; Dar es Salaam–Kigoma, 779 miles; Tanga–Moshi–Arusha, 272 miles. Principal branch lines: Nakuru–Kisumu, 131 miles; Nairobi–Nanyuki, 145 miles; Tororo–Pakwach, 313 miles; Voi–Kahe, 94 miles; Tabora–Mwanza, 236 miles; Mnyusi–Ruvu, 117 miles. Minor branch lines: Gilgil–Thomson's Falls, 48 miles; Rongai–Solai, 27 miles;

Leseru–Kitale, 41 miles; Busembatia–Jinja *via* Mbulamuti, 93 miles; Kisumu–Butere, 43 miles; Port Bell–Kampala, 6 miles; Kilosa–Mikumi, 44 miles; Kaliua–Mpanda, 131 miles; Konza–Magadi, 91 miles. Construction of the Tan–Zam railway linking Dar es Salaam with Kipiri Mposhi, on the Zambian border, began in 1970.

In 1968, 5,196,000 tons of goods and 4,719,000 passengers were carried by the railway.

SHIPPING. The principal harbours are: Mombasa (Kilindini) in Kenya; Tanga, Dar es Salaam and Mtwara in Tanzania. Kilindini has 11 deep-water berths, bulk oil jetty and lighterage quays. There are 3 deep-water berths at Dar es Salaam and 2 at Mtwara.

Steamer services are operated on lakes Victoria and Tanganyika.

ROADS. Road services operate in Uganda over approximately 370 miles connecting Kampala with Masindi, and Pakwach, the railhead on the Nile with Arua. Road services in Tanzania over approximately 2,000 miles serve the Southern Highlands from the Central (Dar es Salaam–Kigoma) line. A railway link between the Tanga and Central lines, completed in 1963, replaces the road services north of the Central line, with the exception of the Arusha–Dodoma passenger service.

AVIATION. East African Airways in 1968 carried 421,989 revenue passengers and flew 448m. passenger-miles. The earned surplus was £466,534. The E.A. directorate of civil aviation, a common service and member of ICAO, is responsible for the safety of all civil aircraft in the E.A. flight information region.

POSTS AND TELECOMMUNICATIONS. The East African Posts and Telecommunications Corporation operates as a self-contained service with its own capital account. Capital assets (1968), £17·4m. The total revenue earned during 1969 was £12·1m.; working expenditure, £9·7m.; capital expenditure, £3·8m. At the end of 1968 there were 924 post offices and 120,065 telephones in use. East African External Communications Ltd operate the overseas telegraph and telephone services and a radio-telephone service.

BOOKS OF REFERENCE

STATISTICAL INFORMATION. The East African Statistical Department is responsible for the collection, analysis and publication of economic statistics relating to East Africa. The department was set up originally as the Statistical Section of the Conference of the East African Governors in 1943 and is situated in Arusha, Tanzania (P.O. Box 1003).

Statistics relating to the individual territories are the responsibility of the appropriate government departments, as follows: TANZANIA: The Government Statistician, Central Statistical Bureau, P.O. Box 796, Dar es Salaam.—UGANDA: The Government Statistician, Ministry of Planning and Economic Development, P.O. Box 13, Entebbe.—KENYA: The Chief Statistician, Ministry of Economic Planning and Development, P.O. Box 30266, Nairobi.

The East African Statistical Department issues a quarterly Economic and Statistical Review, and each territorial office an annual statistical abstract, in addition to other economic and statistical reports.

Annual Report and Accounts, 1968. E. A. Posts and Telecommunications Corp. Kampala, 1969
Hill, M. F., Permanent Way: The Story of the Kenya and Uganda Railway. E. A. Railways and Harbours, 1950
Russell, E. W., The Natural Resources of East Africa. Nairobi, 1962

MALAWI

AREA AND POPULATION. Land area (excluding inland water of Lakes Palombe, Chilwa and Chiuta) 36,324 sq. miles, divided into 3 regions and 22 districts, each administered by a District Commissioner.

Lake Malawi waters belonging to Malawi are 9,250 sq. miles and the whole Lake Malawi (including the waters under Moçambique by an agreement made between the two countries in 1950) is 11,650 sq. miles.

Revised provisional results of the census held in Aug. 1966: 4,020,724 Africans, 11,299 Asians, 7,395 Europeans, 165 undetermined: total 4,039,583 (1,913,262 males, 2,126,321 females). 91·8% of the population live in villages.

The chief settlements are Blantyre–Limbe (declared the city of Blantyre in July 1966) in the Shire Highlands (population 109,461); Zomba, the capital (19,666); Lilongwe (19,425); Cholo (1,164); Salima (2,307); Mzuzu (8,490), and Mlanje (1,225); on Lake Malawi are Fort Johnston (1,467); Nkhota-kota (1,117); Nkhata Bay (1,188), and Karonga (979).

CONSTITUTION AND GOVERNMENT. Malawi formerly Nyasaland (until 1907 British Central Africa) Protectorate, constituted on 15 May 1891, lies along the southern and western shores of Lake Malawi (the third largest lake in Africa).

Nyasaland became a self-governing country on 1 Feb. 1963, and on 6 July 1964 an independent member of the Commonwealth under the name of Malawi. It became a Republic on 6 July 1966. The President of the Republic is also head of Government.

Malawi is one-party state. Parliament is composed of 50 members of the Malawi Congress Party and 5 special nominees.

The Cabinet was in 1 July 1970 composed as follows:

President, Justice, External Affairs, Works and Supplies, Defence and Public Service: Ngwazi Dr H. Kamuzu Banda.

Trade and Industry: J. W. Gwengwe *Transport and Communications:* J. D. Msonthi. *Health and Community Development:* A. M. Nyasulu. *Ministers of State, Office of the President:* A. A. Muwalo, A. B. J. Chiwanda. *Finance, Information and Tourism:* A. K. Banda. *Agriculture and Natural Resources:* R. B. Chidzanja. *Education:* M. M. Lungu. *Labour and Local Government:* R. J. Sembereka. *Ministers of Regions:* M. Q. Y. Chibambo (*Northern*); G. C. Chakuamba (*Southern*); J. T. Kumbweze (*Central*).

DIPLOMATIC REPRESENTATIVES

Country	Malawi representative	Foreign representative
Austria	B. W. Katenga	Dr F. Kudernatsch
Belgium	R. W. Katenga-Kaunda	P. Van Haute
Botswana[1]	—	P. M. Makepe
Britain[1]	R. W. Katenga-Kaunda	W. R. Haydon
China	—	Dr Chin-yung Chao
Denmark	B. W. Katenga	K. Johansen
Ethiopia	V. H. Gondwe	
France		J. Nouvel
Germany (West)	B. W. Katenga	Dr B. Heibach
India[1]	—	M. M. Khurana
Irish Republic	—	R. F. Fitzsimons[3]
Israel	—	S. Ben-Haim
Italy	—	Dr G. Trotta
Japan	—	R. Ando
Kenya[1]	J. Kachingwe	
Korea	—	Yun Young Lim
Netherlands	R. W. Katenga-Kaunda	Jonkheer Dr M. A. Beelaerts van Blokland
Nigeria	—	M. T. Etuk
Norway	B. W. Katenga	S. J. Gjellum
Portugal	R. W. Katenga-Kaunda	Dr V. F. Pereira
South Africa	P. A. Richardson, CBE	Jan F. Wentzel
Sweden	B. W. Katenga	Olof Kaijser
Switzerland	B. W. Katenga	W. C. Burdett
USA	N. W. Mbekeani	Marshall P. Jones
Vatican	R. W. Katenga-Kaunda	—
Zambia[1]	—	R. K. Chinambu

[1] High Commissioner.   [2] Chargé d'Affaires.   [3] Consul.   No figure = Ambassador.

RELIGION. In 1970 the Roman Catholic Church claimed 803,330 members; the Presbyterian Church of Central Africa, 711,000; the Diocese of Malawi (part of the Province of Central Africa of the Anglican Communion), 66,000; Seventh Day Adventist Church, 78,000; Zambezi Evangelical Church (formerly Nyasa Mission), 30,000; Assemblies of God, 6,000; Seventh-Day Baptists (Central Africa conference), 9,000; Churches of Christ, 18,000; African Evangelical Church, 6,000; Assemblies of God, 6,000. No statistics are available for the Baptist Mission of Central Africa, the Church of the Nazarene and the Providence Industrial Mission. Moslems are estimated to number between 500,000 and 1m.

EDUCATION (1967). The Ministry of Education controls all aspects of education.

The number of pupils in the 1,790 primary schools was 286,056; in the 43 secondary schools, 6,539. There were 9,407 teachers. The primary school course is of 8 years duration, followed by a 4-year secondary course. English is taught from the 1st year and becomes the general medium of instruction from the 4th year.

Teacher-training is undertaken in 12 residential colleges, 1 of which is directly controlled by the Ministry; the others receive grants in aid as assisted institutions. Courses last 3 years. Enrolment 1,350. Technical and trade courses are offered in commerce, building, woodwork and mechanical engineering, as well as home craft for girls; 1,904 trainees undertook courses at government and voluntary schools in 1966.

The Malawi University in Limbe was inaugurated on 6 Oct. 1965. It has 5 constituent colleges. In Jan. 1967 there were 177 students taking degree courses and 300 taking diploma courses.

JUSTICE. Justice is administered in the High Court, the magistrates' courts and traditional courts. There are 23 magistrates' courts, 173 traditional courts and 23 local appeal courts.

Appeals from traditional courts are dealt with in the traditional appeal courts and to the High Court. Eventually, however, appeals from traditional courts will not go to the High Court, but will go to the national traditional appeal court. Appeals from magistrates' courts lie to the High Court, and appeals from the High Court to Malawi's Supreme Court of Appeal.

FINANCE. Revenue and expenditure (in £1,000) for calendar years until 1968 and then years ending 31 March:

	1966	1967	1968	1969–70[1]	1970–71[2]
Revenue	17,200	19,323	20,200	26,100	22,700
Expenditure	17,736	19,437	20,000	26,700	22,700

[1] Fifteen months to 31 March 1970. [2] Estimate.

Main revenue items (in £1,000) in 1970–71 are: Indirect taxes, 8,200; direct taxes, 6,200; income from state activity and property, 1,300, and interest and loan redemption, 800.

Main expenditure items (in £1,000) in 1970–71 are: Education, 4,100; public debt charges, 2,700; pensions and gratuities, 1,500; health, 1,500. Public debt, Dec. 1969, was £34·2m., of which £8·6m. was unfunded.

The currency will be decimalized on 15 Feb. 1971. The new unit will be the *kwacha* (dawn) worth 10s., which will be subdivided into 100 *tambala* (cockerels).

DEFENCE. The army consists of a headquarters—a large infantry battalion complete with its own supporting arms and services—and a depot back-up of an engineering workshop and an ordnance depot in Zomba and at Mzuzu. The total strength is 54 officers and 1,050 other ranks.

AGRICULTURE. Malawi is predominantly an agricultural country with over 50% of the population living in rural areas. In 1969 agriculture contributed more than 50% to the GDP, and agricultural produce accounted for over 75% of total exports. Of the total area of 23·25m. acres, 13·1m. could be cultivated and, in 1969, 3·36m. were being cultivated, of which 2·64m. were under maize. Maize is the main subsistance crop and is grown by over 95% of all small-holders. Almost all the surplus crops produced by small-holders are sold to the Farmers Marketing Board. In 1969 the board purchased: Groundnuts, £1·8m.; cotton, £893,800; tobacco, £574,900; maize, £781,000.

Livestock in 1967: Cattle, 464,006; goats, 668,007; sheep, 81,277; pigs, 149,276; poultry, 5m.

POWER. The first and second stages of the Nkula Falls hydro-electric scheme, commissioned in July 1966 and Aug. 1967, have a total capacity of 24 mw. The Electricity Supply Commission also operates stations at Lilongwe, Fort Johnston and Mzuzu. Construction has commenced on the Tedzani hydro-electric scheme, 4 miles downstream from Nkula Falls. The first stage of this scheme consists of two 8-mw. sets. The new scheme should be in commission by March 1973.

COMMERCE. The main items of export in 1967 was unmanufactured tobacco (£4.225,663), tea (£4,490,563), groundnuts (£3,434,300) and raw cotton (£692,249). Malawi's imports included manufactured goods (£10·44m.); machinery and transport equipment (£6,325,000); food and live animals (£1,786,000), and chemicals (£1,883,000).

Trade statistics for calendar years are (in £):

	1966	1967	1968	1969
Imports	27,145,843	25,548,782	29,575,000	30,700,000
Exports	13,834,515	16,615,102	16,928,000	18,300,000

During 1967, 54·8% of the exports went to UK (£9,110,972); 5% to the Netherlands (£834,184); 3·8% to Rhodesia (£634,521); 3·2% to USA (£536,007); 2·3% to Ireland (£465,787); 2·7% to the Republic of South Africa (£456,644); and 2·3% to Zambia (£387,934). 28·3% of the imports came from the UK (£7,235,170); 20·9% from Rhodesia (£5,343,881); 8·4% from Japan (£2,144,313); 7·7% from the Republic of South Africa (£1,965,820); 6·9% from Zambia (£1,767,470); and 2·9% from USA (£712,375).

RAILWAYS. Malawi Railways (289 miles—3 ft 6 in. gauge) operates a main line from Salima to the Moçambique border near Nsanje, from which running powers over the Trans-Zambesia Railway allow access to the port of Beira; a branch opened in 1970 runs eastwards from a point 10 miles south of Balaka to the Moçambique border to give a direct route to the deep-water port of Nacala. The 16-mile section from Nsanje to the border is operated by the Central Africa Railway Co. Ltd.

BANKING. In July 1964 the Reserve Bank of Malawi was set up with a capital of £500,000, to be responsible for the issue of currency and the holding of external reserves and to issue treasury bills and local registered stock on behalf of the Government. Since then, the Reserve Bank has fully assumed the responsibilities of a Central Bank. Barclays Bank DCO and the Standard Bank Ltd have a total of 10 branches and 2 sub-branches in major urban areas and 32 static and 76 mobile agencies in rural areas. The Commercial Bank of Malawi Ltd opened in 1970 and has branches at Limbe and Lilongwe and an agency in Dedza and headquarters at Blantyre.

The Post Office Savings Bank has 158 offices conducting savings business throughout the country, and the New Building Society has agencies in Limbe, Zomba and Lilongwe with its head office in Blantyre. Two finance houses now operate in Malawi, providing longer-term industrial and consumer finance.

BOOKS OF REFERENCE

GENERAL INFORMATION. The Director of Information, Department of Information P.O. Box 494, Biantyre.

Clutton-Brock, G., *Dawn in Nyasaland*. London, 1964
Debenham, F., *Nyasaland*. HMSO, 1964
Gelfand, M., *Lakeside Pioneers. Socio-medical Study of Nyasaland, 1875–1920*. Oxford, 1964
Jones, G., *Britain and Nyasaland*. London, 1964
Pike, J. G., *Malawi, A Political History*. London, 1967
Pike and Rimmington, *Malawi, a Geographical Study*. Oxford, 1965
Read, F. E., *Malawi, Land of Promise*. Govt. Dept. of Information, 1969.—*Malawi, Land of Progress*. Govt. Dept. of Information, 1969
Wishlade, R. L., *Secretarianism in S. Nyasaland*. Oxford, 1965

MALTA

HISTORY. Malta was held in turn by Phoenicians, Greeks, Carthaginians and Romans, and was conquered by Arabs in 870. From 1090 in was joined to Sicily until 1530, when it was handed over to the Knights of St John, who ruled until dispersed by Napoleon in 1798. The Maltese rose in rebellion against the French and the island was subsequently blockaded by the British aided by the Maltese from 1798 to 1800. The Maltese people freely requested the protection of the British Crown in 1802 on condition that their rights and privileges be preserved. The islands were finally annexed to the British Crown by the Treaty of Paris in 1814.

On 17 April 1942, in recognition of the steadfastness and fortitude of the people of Malta during the Second World War, King George VI awarded the George Cross to the island.

AREA AND POPULATION. The area of Malta is 94·9 sq. miles; Gozo, 25·9 sq. miles; Comino, 1·075 sq. miles; total area 121·8 sq. miles (316 sq. km), Population, census 27 Nov. 1967, 314,216; estimate, 31 Dec. 1969, 322,352 (including temporary visitors). Chief town and port, Valletta, population 15,547 (1969).

VITAL STATISTICS, 1969: Births, 5,096; deaths, 3,024; marriages, 2,184; net emigration, 1969, 2,366; gross emigration (including emigrants who later returned), 2,648.

CONSTITUTION AND GOVERNMENT. Malta was granted a measure of self-government (subject to the reservation of certain powers to the Governor) under a constitution introduced by letters patent dated 5 Sept. 1947. On the resignation of the Government led by D. Mintoff on 24 April 1958 and the disturbances that followed, a state of emergency was declared on 30 April 1958, and the direct administration of the island was assumed by the Governor. On 15 April 1959 the state of emergency was brought to an end and the 1947 constitution was replaced by an interim constitution. A new Constitution was introduced by the Malta (Constitution) Order in Council, 1961, under which the island became known as 'the State of Malta'. The UK Government retained responsibility for defence and external affairs.

On 20 Aug. 1962 the Prime Minister made a formal request for independence within the Commonwealth. Following a constitutional conference in July 1963 and further talks in London, a referendum was held in the island in May 1964 to decide on the form of the Independence Constitution. A Malta Independence Bill was passed by the House of Commons and by the Malta Legislative Assembly. The Maltese Parliament also agreed to Malta's applying for Commonwealth membership. Malta became independent on 21 Sept. 1964.

The new Constitution provides for a parliament consisting of Her Majesty and a House of Representatives of 50 elected members and a Cabinet consisting of the Prime Minister and such number of Ministers as may be appointed. The Constitution makes provision for the protection of fundamental rights and freedom of the individual, and ensures that all persons in Malta shall have full freedom of conscience and religious worship.

The defence agreement will enable British forces to remain in Malta for 10 years, and under the financial agreement Britain will provide during the same period capital aid for development and diversification of the economy to a total of £51m.

Maltese and English, and such other language as may be prescribed by Parliament, are the official languages.

Elections were held on 26–28 March 1966. State of parties in Jan. 1970: Nationalist Party, 28; Malta Labour Party, 22.

The Cabinet (Nationalist Party) was sworn in on 7 April 1966.

Governor-General: Sir Maurice Dorman, GCMG, GCVO.

Prime Minister, Minister for Commonwealth and Foreign Affairs, Finance, Customs and Port: Dr G. Borg Olivier.

Public Building and Works: Dr C. Caruana. *Justice and Parliamentary Affairs:* Dr T. Caruana Demajo. *Trade, Industry and Agriculture:* Dr J. Spiteri. *Health:* Dr A. Cachia Zammit. *Education, Culture and Tourism:* Dr P. Borg Olivier. *Labour, Employment and Welfare:* Dr V. Tabone. *Finance, Customs and Port:* Dr G. Felice.

DIPLOMATIC REPRESENTATIVES

Country	Maltese representative	Foreign representative
Australia[1]	J. Mamo Dingli	Sir Hubert Opperman, Kt.
Austria	P. Pullicino, MBE	Dr E. P. Hochleitner[2]
Belgium	G. T. Curmi, OBE	Baron J. van den Bosch
Britain[1]	Dr A. A. Pullicino	Sir Duncan Watson, KCMG
Canada[1]	Dr A. Pardo	Benjamin Rogers
China	—	Shao-Chang Hsu
Czechoslovakia	—	Vladimir Berger
Denmark	—	H. R. Tabor
France	G. T. Curmi, OBE	Phillippe Thiollier
Finland	—	J. Vanamo
Germany (West)	G. T. Curmi, OBE	Y. A. Freiherr von Wendland
Greece	P. Pullicino, MBE	Antoine Pampouras
India[1]	—	Raja J. Atal
Israel	P. Pullicino, MBE	A. E. Najar
Italy	P. Pullicino, MBE	Dr Diego Soro
Japan	—	O. Kataoka
Korea (South)	—	Ei Whan Pai
Libya	L. Ozzard Low	A. Deibani[2]
Luxembourg	G. T. Curmi OBE	—
Netherlands	G. T. Curmi, OBE	Jher H. Van Vredenburch
Norway	—	Dr J. G. Raeder
Pakistan[1]	—	H. N. Khan
Portugal	—	J. H. Themido
Romania	—	Dr I. Ionascu
Spain	G. T. Curmi, OBE	Don Juan Pablo de Lojendio
Sweden	—	B. Eng
Switzerland	P. Pullicino, MBE	J. de Rhan
Tunisia	L. Ozzard Low	—
Turkey	—	A. Axda[2]
USSR	Dr Arvid Pardo	M. Smirnovsky
UAR	L. Ozzard Low	M. K. Mortagi
USA	Dr Arvid Pardo	J. C. Pritzlaff
Vatican	—	Mgr. Giuseppe Mojoli
Yugoslavia	—	S. Prica

[1] High Commissioner.   [2] Chargé d'Affaires.   No figure = Ambassador.

EDUCATION. In 1970 there were 110 primary and infant schools with 31,722 pupils, 30 secondary modern schools with 11,500 pupils, 4 grammar schools for girls with 3,164 students, 2 lyceums with 1,668 boys, 3 secondary technical schools for boys with 2,700 pupils, 2 secondary technical schools for girls with 1,992 pupils. There are also 3 technical institutes with 1,357 students, a College of Arts, Science and Technology (1,450 students), a junior college (460 students) and the Royal University with 1,300 regular students. There were also 80 private schools with 16,538 pupils, a school for the handicapped 281 students and evening classes for 6,000 students.

CINEMAS (1969). There were 40 cinemas with a seating capacity of 30,387.

NEWSPAPERS. There are 4 English and 3 Maltese daily newspapers.

WELFARE. The National Insurance Act, 1956, provides cash benefits for marriage (women only), sickness, unemployment, widowhood, orphanhood, invalidity, old age and industrial injury. An agreement, signed on 26 Oct 1956, established reciprocity in matters of social insurance between Malta and the UK.

The total number of persons in receipt of benefits on 31 Dec. 1969 was 11,884, viz., 984 in receipt of sickness benefit, 710 unemployment benefit, 112 injury benefit, 115 disablement benefit, 93 death benefit, 6,919 old-age pensions, 2,488 widows' pensions, 16 guardian's allowance and 447 invalidity pensions.

The National Assistance Act, 1956, provides for the payment of social assistance and medical assistance, while the Old Age Pensions Act of 1948 provides for the payment of non-contributory old-age pensions to persons over 60 years of age and to blind persons over the age of 14 years.

The number of households in receipt of social assistance and of medical assistance on 31 Dec. 1969 was 4,007 and 4,243 respectively, and the number of old-age pensioners under the Old Age Pensions Act, 1948, was 11,629.

JUSTICE. The number of persons convicted in 1969 of crimes was 1,472; those convicted for contraventions against various laws and regulations numbered 15,558. 91 were committed to prison, 4 male juveniles were committed to St Philip Neri School, 12,397 were awarded fines, 664 released under the provisions of the Probation of Offenders Act, 1957, other penalties amounted to 1,091.

Police. On 31 Dec. 1969 police numbered 46 officers and 1,270 other ranks, including 13 women police.

FINANCE. Currency. Government of Malta currency notes issued under the Currency Notes Ordinance, 1949, and Central Bank of Malta currency notes issued since 7 June 1968 under Central Bank of Malta Act, 1967, together with British coins are the sole legal tender. The amount of local currency notes in circulation on 31 Dec. 1969 was £41,646,000.

Budget. Revenue and expenditure (in £ sterling) for financial years ending 31 March:

	1966–67	1967–68	1968–69	1969–70	1970–71[1]
Revenue	22,726,036	24,379,256	28,783,440	33,576,720	41,893,009
Expenditure	21,113,056	25,483,200	28,136,829	33,524,976	43,343,154

[1] Estimates.

The most important sources of revenue are customs duties, income tax, licences, stamp duties, succession and donation duties, post office, water receipts, land revenue, interest, profit from lotteries and receipts from the Central Bank of Malta.

ECONOMY. Malta's first and second development plans covering the period 1959–69 have been a response to the need to replace the former economic structure, which essentially revolved around military defence expenditure, by aiming chiefly at strengthening the exports of goods and services. The naval dockyard has been converted into a commercial complex, and the establishment of new industries, the fast growing tourist trade and the influx of new settlers have all contributed to a building boom. The long-term objective of the third development plan (1969–74) is to exploit to the fullest extent Malta's economic potential to secure a balanced self-sustained growth at the same time ensuring a high level of employment and a rising standard of living.

AGRICULTURE. The chief products are wheat, barley, potatoes, onions, beans, cumin-seed, vegetables, tomatoes, forages, flowers, and seeds, grapes and other fruits. The total value of agricultural produce during the agricultural year 1967–68 was £8·8m. Area cultivated, 36,100 acres.

Livestock in Sept. 1968: Horses, 1,584; mules, 1,137; donkeys, 1,705; cattle, 9,850; sheep and lambs, 9,034; goats, 20,164; pigs, 23,351; poultry, 729,100; rabbits, 45,604.

FISHERIES. The fishing industry occupied 751 motor and 182 other fishing boats, engaging about 590 persons (full-time) in 1969. The catch in 1969 was 22,760 cwt valued at £320,263 at first sale.

INDUSTRY. The Aids to Industries Scheme, introduced in 1959, provides capital grants and interest-free loans to new industries, as well as income-tax relief and exemption from customs duty. Assisted projects include textile and metal plants, the propagation of flower-seeds and cuttings, and factories producing light engineering goods, polystrene insulating materials, furniture, detergents, paints, ceramic tiles, plastic products, fibre glass, etc. The Malta Development Corporation is responsible for fiscal and financial aids under the Aids to Industry Scheme.

ELECTRICITY. All towns and villages in Malta and Gozo are provided with electric current. The islands obtain their electricity power supplies from 2 interconnected power stations located at Marsa (Malta). The new power/water station with a generating capacity of 25 MW is also equipped with distillation plant capable of also producing fresh water for public consumption at the rate of 1m. gallons per day. Work on the extension of the power/water station and desalination plant is now in progress. The installed capacity will be 115 MW, and the water production capacity 4·5m. gallons per day.

The gross electricity consumption in 1967–68 was 156·55m. kwh.; 1968–69, 173m. kwh.; 1969–70, 191·01m. kwh.

TOURISM. In 1969, 186,084 foreigners visited Malta, spending an estimated £11·5m.

LABOUR. The male working population in 1969 was estimated at 79,090, distributed as follows: Agriculture, 5,080; fishing, 540; service departments, including H.M. Forces, 7,250; private industry, 50,880; government, 15,340. Approximately 21,370 women were in gainful employment. The number of registered unemployed as at 31 Dec. 1969 was 3,813.

There were 51 trade unions registered as at 31 Dec. 1969, with a total membership of 41,200.

COMMERCE. Imports and exports including bullion and specie (in £1,000 sterling):

	1964	1965	1966	1967	1968	1969
Imports	34,594	35,145	38,880	40,509	51,399	61,516
Exports	6,918	8,653	10,755	9,890	14,144	15,957

In 1969 the principle items of imports were: Meat, £2·8m.; dairy products, £1·6m.; cereals, fruits, vegetables, £5·8m.; fuels, £3m.; textiles and clothing,

£7·1m.; machinery, £9·3m.; transport equipment, £4·2m.; beverages and tobacco, £1·6m. Of domestic exports (in £1,000): Potatoes, 526; textile threads and yarns, 1,789; scrap metal, 465; wine, 254; textile fabrics, 502; rubber goods, 1,201; gloves, 323; onions, 80; cigarettes, 144; refined edible oils, 109; clothing, 2,793; paints, 14; detergents, 140; plastics, 381; mattresses and furniture, 134; fuel, £1·4m. (the main item of re-exports).

In 1969, £26·2m. of the imports came from UK, £9·8m. from Italy, £2·2m. from France; £1·9m. from USA; of the re-exports, £2m. went to ships and aircraft stores, £370,000 to UK; of domestic exports, £5·1m. went to UK; £1·5m. to Italy; £501,000 to Canada; £550,000 to Libya; £807,000 to France; £761,000 to West Germany.

SHIPPING. The number of ships registered in Malta on 31 Dec. 1968 was 92, and their tonnage was 57,973 gross tons.

ROADS. Every town and village is served by motor omnibuses. There are ferry services running between Malta and Gozo; cars can be transported on the ferries. Motor vehicles registered during 1969 totalled 51,895, of which 35,158 were passenger cars, 2,031 hire cars, 9,845 commercial vehicles, 623 buses, 3,535 motor cycles and 703 other motor vehicles.

AVIATION. The principal airlines, namely BEA, Malta Airlines, Alitalia and Libyan Arab Airlines, operate scheduled services between Malta and UK, Italy and Libya.

During 1968 there were 6,307 civil aircraft movements at Luqa Airport. 325,298 passengers and 4,364 tons of freight (excluding mail) were handled.

POST. There is a government system of telephones with exchanges at Malta and Gozo. On 31 Dec. 1968 there were 20,383 exchange lines with 32,839 extensions.

BANKING. Commercial banking facilities are provided by Barclays Bank DCO with 30 branches throughout Malta and Gozo, the National Bank of Malta (to which is affiliated Sciclunas Bank) with 23 branches, Tagliaferro Bank Ltd, Lombard Bank (Malta) Ltd and the Bank of Industry, Commerce and Agriculture Ltd.

A government savings bank with 18 branches had on 31 Dec. 1968, 71,433 depositors and £10,867,780 deposits.

BOOKS OF REFERENCE

STATISTICAL INFORMATION. The Central Office of Statistics (1 Windmill Street, Valletta) was set up in 1947. It publishes *Statistical Abstracts of the Maltese Islands*, a quarterly digest of statistics, monthly vital statistics and annual publications on foreign trade, shipping and aviation, education, taxation, agriculture and industry.

Government publications: The Department of Information (24 Merchants Street, Valletta), set up in 1954, publishes *The Malta Government Gazette* (twice weekly), *Ir-Review* (weekly), *Malta Today* (monthly), *Malta in Brief*, etc.

Malta Independence Constitution (Cmnd 2406). HMSO, 1964
Malta Who's Who. Malta, 1969–70
Economic Survey 1969, Malta, 1970
Third Development Plan 1969–74. Malta, 1970
The Malta Year Book, Malta from 1952
Abela, M., *A Developing Economy.* Central Office of Statistics, Malta, 1963
Blouet, Brian, *The Story of Malta.* London, 1967
Busuttil, E. D., *Kalepin Dizzjunarju Malti-Ingliz.* Valletta, 1941
Cassar, P., *Medical History of Malta.* London, 1966
Cremona, J. J., *The Malta Constitution of 1835 and its Historical Background.* Malta, 1959.—
   The Constitutional Developments of Malta under British Rule. Malta University Press, 1963.—
   Human Rights Documentation in Malta. Malta University Press, 1966
Dobie, E., *Malta's Road to Independence.* University of Oklahoma, Norman, USA, 1967
Luke, Sir Harry, *Malta.* 2nd ed. London, 1962
Price, G. A., *Malta and the Maltese: a study in 19th-century migration.* Melbourne, 1954
Smith, Harrison, *Britain in Malta.* 2 vols. Malta, 1954
Trade Directory of Malta. London, 1965

ZAMBIA

HISTORY. By an Order in Council dated 4 May 1911 the two provinces of North-eastern and North-western Rhodesia were amalgamated under the name of Northern Rhodesia, with effect from 17 Aug. 1911.

By an Order in Council dated 20 Feb. 1924, the office of Governor was created, an executive council constituted and provision made for the institution of a legislative council which, since 1945, had an unofficial majority. On 1 April 1924 the British South Africa Company was relieved of the administration of the territory by the Crown.

On 24 Oct. 1964 Northern Rhodesia became the independent Republic of Zambia after 10 months of internal self-government following the dissolution of the Federation of Rhodesia and Nyasaland on 31 Dec. 1963.

AREA AND POPULATION. The area is 290,586 sq. miles (752,262 sq. km). The population at 31 Dec. 1966 consisted of: 3,815,000 Africans; 67,400 Europeans; 11,800 others.

CONSTITUTION AND GOVERNMENT. The Constitution provides for a President, elected in the first instance by the Legislative Assembly, but subsequently at each general election by the electorate. A Vice-President, appointed by the President, leads the Government in the National Assembly. The Assembly consists of 105 elected members, 5 nominated members, including a Cabinet of 18. The National Assembly is presided over by an elected Speaker.

At the elections for the National Assembly held on 19 Dec. 1968 the United National Independence Party obtained 81 seats, the African National Congress 23 and the Independents 1.

President: Dr Kenneth David Kaunda. *Vice-President:* Simon Mwansa Kapwepwe.

The Cabinet, as of Jan. 1969, was composed as follows:

Foreign Affairs: Elijah H. K. Mudenda. *Rural Development:* Reuben Chitandika Kamanga. *Home Affairs:* Alexander Grey Zulu. *Information and Broadcasting:* Sikota Wina. *Labour and Social Services:* Lewis Changufu. *Trade, Industry and Mines:* Justin M. Chimba. *Education:* Wesley Nyirenda. *Transport, Power and Works:* Peter M. Matoka. *Western Province:* Hyden D. Banda. *Central Province:* Mainza M. Chona. *Southern Province:* Alex. K. Shapi. *Luapula Province:* Fwanyanga M. Mulikita. *Eastern Province:* Solomon Kalulu. *Northern Province:* Ackson J. Soko. *North-Western Province:* Robert Makasa. *Barotse Province:* Humphrey Mulemba.

DIPLOMATIC REPRESENTATIVES

Country	Zambia representative	Foreign representative
Austria	—	Dr F. Kudernatsch[3]
Belgium	—	E. Henniquiau[4]
Botswana[1]	J. B. A. Siyomunji	R. N. Mannathoko
Britain[1]	P. W. Matoka	J. L. Pumphrey, CMG
Canada[1]	—	John A. Irwin[5]
Chile	—	Alberto A. Besa
China	P. Lumbi[2]	Chin Li-Chen
Congo (K)	T. J. Kankasa	E. Kashemwa
Czechoslovakia	—	E. Keblusek[2]
Denmark	—	B. Abrahamson[3]
Ethiopia	J. Mutti	A. G. Mekasha

[1] High Commissioner.   [2] Chargé d'Affaires.   [3] Resident in Nairobi.
[4] Resident in Bujumbura.   [5] Resident in Dar es Salaam.   No figure = Ambassador.

Country	Zambia representative	Foreign representative
Finland	—	H. L. Blomstedt[5]
France	—	Baron de Schonen
Germany (West)	I. C. Mupanshya	Karl-Heinz Wever
Guinea	—	C. O. M'Baye
Hungary	—	Dr K. Szabo[4]
India[1]	—	S. Krishnamurti
Italy	—	Dr A. Albini[2]
Israel	—	M. Dagan
Ivory Coast	A. Simbule	—
Japan	—	T. Watanabe[3]
Kenya[1]	H. Soko	—
Lebanon	Chief Mapanza[7]	—
Netherlands	—	Dr M. A. Beelaerts van Blockland
Norway	—	I. R. Rindal[3]
Poland	—	K. Lewandowski[2]
Sweden	—	O. R. Kaijser
Switzerland	—	T. R. Curchod[8]
Tanzania[1]	S. M. Mukando	—
USSR	P. J. F. Lusaka	S. A. Slipchenko
UAR	Chief Mapanza	H. El-Sinbawi
USA	R. Banda	R. C. Good
Vatican	E. Chipimo[6]	Archbishop Alfredo Poledrini
Yugoslavia	—	V. Burzevski

[1] High Commissioner.   [2] Chargé d'Affaires.   [3] Resident in Nairobi.
[4] Resident in Dar es Salaam.   [5] Resident in Addis Ababa.   [6] Resident in London.
[7] Resident in Cairo.   [8] Resident in Kinshasa.   No figure = Ambassador.

PROVINCIAL ADMINISTRATION. The Republic is divided into 8 provinces. Their names, headquarters, area (in sq. miles) and census population in 1966 are as follows:

Province	Headquarters	Area	Population	Province	Headquarters	Area	Population
Western	Ndola	12,096	608,500	Eastern	Chipata	26,682	535,000
Luapula	Mansa	19,524	393,000	Southern	Livingstone	32,928	508,000
Northern	Kasama	51,076	619,000	N.-Western	Solwezi	48,582	229,000
Central	Kabwe	44,900	540,000	Barotse	Mongu	48,798	399,000

The provinces are administered by Cabinet Ministers for the provinces who are responsible for the overall government administration of their respective areas. The Ministers are assisted by a Minister of State and a Permanent Secretary. Each district in all provinces is headed by a District Governor, and these are directly responsible to their respective provincial Ministers.

The seat of Government is at Lusaka. The other important centres are Livingstone, the old capital, Ndola, Luanshya, Mufulira, Kitwe, Bancroft, Kalulushi and Chingola on the Copperbelt; Kabwe, the oldest mining township; Chipata, centre of a tobacco farming area.

Since independence the following towns have been renamed: Abercorn (Mbala), Bancroft (Chililabombwe), Broken Hill (Kabwe), Fort Rosebery (Mansa), Fort Jameson (Chipata).

RELIGION. Freedom of worship is one of the constitutional rights of Zambian citizens. Minority groups, such as the Asian community, are free to practise the religions of Hinduism and Islam, and the views of the leaders of these communities are respected by the Government. The Lumpa Church was banned in 1965 for security reasons, following considerable loss of life, but the Jehovah's Witnesses are allowed to continue their way of life despite the conflict of authority in their views and the views of politicians.

The Christian faith has largely replaced traditional African religion, and the Christian Churches number about 500,000 members and adherents. These are divided almost equally between Roman Catholic and Protestant communities. The Churches, founded mainly from the Western world, are slowly finding their autonomy—as illustrated by the United Church of Zambia (formerly British and French missions) and the Reformed Church of Zambia (formerly South African mission).

There is close co-operation between the Catholic and Protestant churches, and the Protestant churches themselves work in the fields of radio, television, education, medicine, refugee aid, etc., through the Christian Council of Zambia. The United Church and the Anglian Church are holding union discussions, and Roman Catholic, Anglican and United Church leaders meet together for consultation, and together they discuss matters of common concern with the President of Zambia, Dr Kaunda.

EDUCATION. In June 1968 the 2,527 primary schools were attended by 608,893 pupils, of whom 268,965 were girls. 22 unaided primary schools had 3,095 pupils. 109 secondary schools (93 government, 16 private) had 42,388 pupils. Ten teacher-training colleges had 2,160 students. In 1968 the University of Zambia had 706 full-time students, 242 correspondence students and 900 extra-mural students. Government expenditure on education in 1968 was K52,533,000.

JUSTICE. The Judiciary consists of the Court of Appeal, the High Court and 4 classes of magistrates' courts; all have civil and criminal jurisdiction.

The Court of Appeal hears and determines appeals from the High Court. It consists of the Chief Justice, the Justice of Appeal and one of the puisne judges of the High Court appointed *ad hoc*. Its seat is at Lusaka.

The High Court exercises the powers vested in the High Court in England, subject to the High Court ordinance of Zambia. Its sessions are held where occasion requires, mostly at Lusaka and Ndola. All criminal cases tried by subordinate courts are subject to revision by the High Court.

FINANCE. Currency. Decimal currency was introduced on 16 Jan. 1968. The Kwacha (K), corresponding to £0·58 and US$1.40, is divided into 100 ngwee (n). Notes of K20, K10, K2, K1 and 50 ngwee correspond to the old £10, £5, £1, 10s. and 5s. notes. Money circulation at 14 Aug. 1968 was K38,239,808.

Budget. Revenue and expenditure for fiscal years ending 30 June (in £1,000) and from 1968, calendar years (in K):

	1963–64[1]	1964–65[1]	1965–66[1]	1966–67[1]	1968[1]
Revenue: Current	20,074	56,081	84,422	122,956	250,124,000
Capital fund	7,706	5,605	25,823	11,977	161,540,000
Expenditure: Current	21,745	45,291	83,950	82,237	249,790,693
Capital fund	10,179	15,092	25,798	68,272	168,820,270

[1] Estimates.

The public debt at 30 Dec. 1967 was K253·10m. (£126·55m. post-devaluation Zambian £).

DEFENCE. Army. The army consists of 3 infantry battalions, 1 armoured car squadron, 1 battery of howitzers and supporting units. Strength, 3,000.

Air Force. Creation of the Zambian Air Force was assisted initially by an RAF mission. Equipment acquired in this period and still in use includes 4 twin-engined Caribou and 6 single-engined Beaver transports built in Canada, 4 C-47 transports and 2 Chipmunk trainers. Training and expansion of the Air Force has now been taken over by Italy, with initial purchase of Aermacchi M.B.326 jet basic trainers, 8 Siai-Marchetti SF.260M piston-engined trainers and 5 Agusta-Bell 205 helicopters.

DEVELOPMENT. A 4-year development plan (1967–70) envisages government investment of K564m. and private investment of K294m. The present 'copper bound' economy is to be diversified. K500m. is to be allocated to the construction industry, K78·8m. to education (including K29·4m. on secondary education), K52m. on hydro-electric expansion (including K22m. for a dam on the Kafue River), and K48m. on surface links with Tanzania and Malawi. An oil pipeline from Dar-es-Salaam to Ndola, scheduled for completion in late 1969, was completed in Aug. 1968, and is now in operation.

AGRICULTURE. Principal agricultural products (1967–68) are maize (sales, 4,131,000 bags of 200 lb.); tobacco, 14,753,633 lb; groundnuts, 176,972 bags of 183 lb; cotton, 8m. lb.

Livestock (1968). 1,424,900 cattle; 80,000 pigs; 200,000 pigs and goats. Poultry: 3m. day-old chicks; 4·5m. dozen eggs, 2·9m. live and dressed birds.

MINING. The total value of minerals produced in 1967 was K448,223,150:

	Output (1,000 tons)	Value (1,000 K)		Output (1,000 tons)	Value (1,000 K)
Copper (blister)	90·5	56,530	Lead	21·4	2,724
Copper (electrolytic)	588·8	386,452	Manganese	28·0	508
Zinc	49·8	8,386	Cobalt	1,603·9	3,392

POWER. The total installed capacity of hydro and thermal power stations, including Zambia's share of Kariba, South, amounts to 612 Mw. and the energy consumption during 1967 amounted to some 3,101m. kwh., including imports from the Congo.

The hydro stations are located at Mbala, Mansa, Kasama, Mulungushi, Lunsemfwa and Victoria Falls. The thermal stations are located at Chipata, Mongu, Lusaka, Copperbelt mines and the Broken Hill Development Corp.

A contract for the construction of Stage 1 of the Kafue River Gorge hydro-electric scheme has been awarded to a Yugoslav firm, and work began in Aug. 1968. Zambia intends to construct a power house on the north bank of Kariba.

LABOUR. In 1967 there were 37,413 persons in government employment, 35,376 working in agriculture and 50,615 in the mining industry.

COMMERCE. In 1967 imports totalled K306,350,074, exports K467,015,972 and re-exports K2,993,000. The principal imports were machinery and transport equipment (K126,331,094), mineral fuels and lubricants (K31,230,878), chemicals (K20,800,820), manufactured articles (K28,390,700). Principal exports were metals (K448,223,150), tobacco (K3,704,514) and foodstuffs (maize, groundnuts, fish) (K9,701,610).

Principal trade areas were: Sterling area: imports K194,826,176, exports K162,402,604; other African countries: imports K1,459,830, exports K3,869,342; EEC: imports K37,485,148, exports K125,029,614; EFTA (excluding UK): imports K7,720,158, exports K27,434,456; other European countries: imports K2,407,618, exports K11,417,770; Socialist countries: imports K2,051,872, exports K6,593,120; dollar area: imports K36,711,412, exports K23,941,720; non-dollar Latin America: imports K939,938, exports K3,748,110; Asia: imports K19,522,216, exports K102,052,338; Middle East countries: imports K3,225,706, exports K526,898.

RAILWAYS. Zambia Railways are that part of the old Rhodesia Railways north of the Victoria Falls. Route-miles open for traffic, 649 (3 ft 6 in. gauge). Construction of the 1,100-mile Tan–Zam railway, which will give Zambia access to Dar es Salaam, began at the Tanzanian end in 1970.

BANKING. Barclays Bank DCO has 23 branches and 32 agencies; Standard Bank has 17 branches, 30 agencies and 3 mobile agencies; National & Grindleys, 6 branches and 8 agencies; Commercial Bank Zambia Ltd, 5 branches; the post office savings bank has branches throughout the Republic. The Merchant Bank (Zambia) Ltd began business on 1 Sept. 1966, with a capital of K500,000.

The Industrial Development Corporation, a limited company wholly owned by the Government, works for the establishment and management of projects in which the Government is the sole shareholder, and private concerns in which the Government has taken a shareholding.

The Credit Organization of Zambia, formed in Aug. 1967, has taken over the functions formerly performed by the Land and Agricultural Bank of Zambia. It provides loans to farmers, co-operatives, farmers' associations, agricultural societies and such bodies as will further the agricultural industry. It also provides commercial loans to small businessmen.

BOOKS OF REFERENCE

GENERAL INFORMATION. The Director, Zambia Information Services, P.O. Box R/W 20, Lusaka.

This is Zambia. Zambia Information Services, Lusaka, 1968
Laws of Zambia. 13 vols. Govt. Printer, Lusaka
Bancroft, J. A. *Mining in Northern Rhodesia*. British South Africa Co., London, 1961
Gann, L. H., *History of Northern Rhodesia to 1953*. London, 1964
Hall, R., *Zambia*. London, 1965
Hall, R., *Kaunda, Founder of Zambia*. London, 1964
Kaunda, Kenneth D., *Zambia Shall be Free*. London, 1962.—*Humanism in Zambia*. Lusaka, 1967.
—*Zambia's Economic Revolution*. Lusaka, 1968.—*Zambia's Guide for the next Decade*. Lusaka, 1968
Kay, G., *A social geography of Zambia*. London, 1967
Legum, C., *Zambia Independence and Beyond*. London, 1966
Mulford, D. C., *The Northern Rhodesia General Election 1962*. OUP 1964.—*Zambia, the politics of independence 1957–64*. OUP, 1968
Office of National Development and Planning, *First National Development Plan 1966–70*
Central Statistical Office, Lusaka, *Statistical Year-Book, 1967*

THE GAMBIA

HISTORY. The Gambia was discovered by the early Portuguese navigators, but they made no settlement. During the 17th century various companies of merchants obtained trading charters and established a settlement on the river, which, from 1807, was controlled from Sierra Leone; in 1843 it was made an independent Crown Colony; in 1866 it formed part of the West African Settlements, but in Dec. 1888 it again became a separate Crown Colony. The boundaries were delimited only after 1890. The Gambia achieved full internal self-government on 4 Oct. 1963 and became an independent member of the Commonwealth on 18 Feb. 1965.

A referendum was held in Nov. 1965 to decide whether Gambia was to become a republic. With 61,568 votes in favour of a republic and 31,921 against, the referendum failed, as any alteration of the constitution requires a two-thirds majority.

AREA AND POPULATION. Area of Bathurst and environs, 29·4 sq. miles (76·1 sq. km); population (1963), 40,017. In the Provinces (area, 3,948 sq. miles, 9,225·3 sq. km) the settled population (1963) was 275,469, not including temporary immigrants. Total population (census, April 1963), 315,486. The largest tribe is the Mandingo (128,807), followed by the Fulas (42,723), Woloffs (40,805), Jolas (22,046) and Sarahulis (21,318). The capital is Bathurst (27,809 inhabitants, including 412 Europeans).

The rainy season lasts from June to Oct. The total rainfall at Bathurst was 63·15 in. in 1967, but fell to 26·28 in. in 1968.

CONSTITUTION AND GOVERNMENT. Parliament consists of the Governor-General and the House of Representatives. The House consists of a Speaker, Deputy Speaker and 32 elected members; in addition, 4 Chiefs are elected by the Chiefs in Assembly; 4 nominated members are without votes.

Governor-General: Al-Haji Sir Farimang M. Singhateh, GCMG.

At the general election of 26 May 1966, the People's Progressive Party obtained 24 and the opposition 8 seats.

The Cabinet is composed of the Prime Minister and 7 Ministers drawn from the Legislature.

Three special agreements with Senegal, on external affairs, defence and security, and development have been signed.

The Government was in Feb. 1970 composed as follows:

Prime Minister: Sir Dauda Kairaba Jawara.

Finance: S. M. Dibba. *Local Government, Lands and Mines:* Yayo Ceesay. *Education:* Alhaji I. M. Garba-Jahumpa. *Agriculture:* H. O. Semega-Jameh. *Works and Communications:* K. Singhateh. *Health:* (vacant). *External Affairs:* A. D. Camara.

High Commissioner in London: H. R. Monday, CBE.
Ambassador to Senegal: B. O. Semega-Janneh.
British High Commissioner: J. G. W. Ramage.
Deputy Chief of USA Mission: Robert T. Burke.

LOCAL ADMINISTRATION. The Gambia is divided into 35 districts, each traditionally under a Chief, assisted by Village Heads and advisers. These districts are grouped into 6 Area Councils containing a majority of elected members, with the Chiefs of the district as *ex-officio* members. The city of Bathurst is administered by a City Council.

RELIGION. The population is predominantly Moslem. Bathurst is the seat of an Anglican and a Roman Catholic bishop. There are several Methodist mission centres.

EDUCATION (1970). There were 94 primary schools 11 post-primary schools or departments and 6 secondary schools, 4 of which are recognized for School Certificate Examination. The total school enrolment was 20,242 pupils, including over 6,000 girls. The vocational training centre in Bathurst offers courses in carpentry and metalwork. Yundum College provides training for teachers.

NEWSPAPERS. There is an official (three times weekly) and several duplicated newsheets.

RADIO. Radio Gambia, a government station, broadcasts for approximately 6 hours each evening.

FINANCE. Currency. West African currency notes and coins have been replaced by those of the Gambia currency board. Note circulation on 31 Dec. 1968 was £1,896,177 and coins, £134,640.

Budget. Revenue and expenditure for calendar years until 1964 and for years ending 30 June from 1965–66 were as follows (in £1,000 sterling):

	1964	1965[2]	1965–66	1966–67[1]	1967–68[3]
Revenue	1,968	1,461	2,833	3,274	2,500
Expenditure	2,676	1,749	3,260	2,727	2,300

[1] Revised estimates. [2] Jan.–June. [3] Estimates.

On 30 June 1966 public debt was £570,335, and sinking fund, £120,459.

Principal items of revenue (in £1,000) in 1966–67: Customs, 1,831; groundnut sales tax, 220; direct taxes, 263; Currency Board profit, 125; port and harbour, 45; interest, 40. Grant-in-aid from Britain (not included in the estimates), 360. Main items of expenditure (in £1,000) in 1966–67: Personal emoluments, 1,103; pensions and gratuities, 354; transfer to development fund, 50.

AGRICULTURE. Almost all commercial activity centres upon the marketing of groundnuts, which is the only export crop of financial significance. Rice is of growing importance for local consumption.

MINING. Deposits of ilmenite exist on old storm beaches along the Atlantic coast. They were exploited by UK interests from 1956 to 1959, but operations have now ceased. No other workable mineral deposits are known.

TRADE. Chief items of imports in 1967–68 (in £1,000): Rice, 476; wheat, 138; sugar, 239; beverages, 129; cigarettes and tobacco, 412; petroleum products, 266; medical and pharmaceutical products, 152; cotton fabrics, 1,149; other fabrics, 126; bags and sacks, 196; cement, 140; corrugated steel sheets, 184; machinery (except electrical), 363; electric batteries, 74; radio receiving sets, 124; motor vehicles and parts, 639; apparel, 140.

Imports and exports, in £1,000:

	1964[1]	1965[2]	1965–66	1966–67[3]	1967–68[4]
Imports	4,333	2,812	5,814	7,125	..
Exports	3,296	3,892	4,350	6,313	..

[1] Calendar year.   [2] Jan.–June   [3] Revised estimates.   [4] Estimates.

Chief items of exports in 1967–68: Groundnuts, 28,098 tons, £1,576,024; palm kernels, 1,941 tons, £137,334; dried and smoked fish, 341 tons, £13,682; groundnut oil, 24,725 tons, £2,400,401; groundnut cake, 26,149 tons, £1,073,079.

Trade between the Gambia and UK (British Board of Trade returns, in £1,000 sterling):

	1966	1967	1968	1969	1970
Imports to UK	3,149	3,535	3,391	2,024	4,139
Exports from UK	2,391	2,574	2,967	2,521 }	2,110
Re-exports from UK	40	46	56	67 }	

LABOUR. There are 2 large and 2 small trade unions.

SHIPPING. The chief port, Bathurst, which has 2 deep-water wharves, handled 160,514 tons of cargo in 1967–68. Internal communication is maintained by steamers and launches.

ROADS. There are 730 miles of motorable roads, of which 330 miles rank as all-season. Number of licensed motor vehicles (June 1967): 4,148 passenger and commercial vehicles and 705 motor cycles.

AVIATION. Air movements at Yundum Airport in 1967 numbered 1,629, including 1,032 scheduled services.

POST. There are several post offices and agencies; postal facilities are also afforded to all river towns by means of a travelling post office on the government river mail-steamers. Bathurst is connected with St Vincent (Cape Verde islands) and with Sierra Leone by cable. Bathurst is in wireless communication with London and the main centres up river. A trans-Gambia telephone system provides direct communications with Dakar and Ziguinchor. Telephones numbered 1,427 in Sept. 1968. A Telex service was introduced in 1968.

BANKING. There are 2 banks in the Gambia, the Standard Bank of West Africa Ltd and la Banque Internationale pour le Commerce et l'Industrie (BICI). On 1 Jan. 1968 the government savings bank had over 17,028 depositors holding £241,952.

BOOKS OF REFERENCE

The Gambia Independence Act, 1964
The Gambia Independence Order, 1965
Gailey, Jr, H. A., *A History of the Gambia*. London, 1964
Rice, B., *Enter Gambia*. Sydney, 1968

REPUBLIC OF SINGAPORE

CONSTITUTION AND GOVERNMENT. For the early history of the settlement (1819) and colony (1867) *see* THE STATESMAN'S YEAR-BOOK, 1959, pp. 246 f.

By an agreement entered into between the Governments of Malaysia and of the State of Singapore on 7 Aug. 1965, effective on 9 Aug. 1965, Singapore ceased to be one of the 14 states of the Federation of Malaysia and became an independent sovereign state. The separation was ratified by the Constitution and Malaysia (Singapore Amendment) Act of the Malaysian Parliament on 9 Aug. The 2 governments agreed to enter into a treaty on external defence and mutual assistance. The Singapore Government retains its executive authority and legislative powers under its State Constitution and took over the powers of the Malaysian Government under the Malaysian Constitution in Singapore. The sovereignty and jurisdiction of the head of the Malaysian State was transferred to the Singapore Government. Civil servants working in Singapore for the Federal Departments became Singapore civil servants. Singapore citizens ceased to be Malaysian citizens. Singapore accepted responsibility for international agreements entered into by the Malaysian Government on its behalf.

Singapore entered the Commonwealth of Nations on 15 Oct. 1965.

By a constitutional amendment the name of the state was changed to 'Republic of Singapore', the head of state was named 'President of Singapore' and the legislative assembly was renamed 'Parliament'.

Malay, Chinese, Tamil and English are the official languages; English is the language of administration.

President of Singapore: Dr Benjamin Henry Sheares (sworn in 2 Jan. 1971).

Parliament consists of 58 members, elected by secret ballot from single-member constituencies, and is presided over by a Speaker, chosen by Parliament from its own members or from outside the Assembly. In the latter case, the Speaker has no vote. With the customary exception of those serving criminal sentences, all citizens over 21 are eligible to vote irrespective of sex, race, education or property qualification. There is a common roll without communal electorates. Citizenship is automatic by birth; it can also be acquired by registration or by naturalization.

Parliament, elected on 13 April 1968, is composed of 58 People's Action Party members.

The People's Action Party cabinet, sworn in on 16 April 1968, is composed as follows:

Prime Minister: Lee Kuan Yew.

Science and Technology: Dr Toh Chin Chye. *Finance:* Hon Sui Sen. *Foreign Affairs and Labour:* S. Rajaratnam. *Education:* Lim Kim San. *Communications:* Yong Nyuk Lin. *Defence:* Dr Goh Keng Swee. *Culture:* Jek Yeun Thong. *Social Affairs:* Othman Wok. *Law and National Development:* E. W. Barker. *Health:* Chua Sian Chin. *Home Affairs:* Prof. Wong Lin Ken. There are also 7 Ministers of State.

DIPLOMATIC REPRESENTATIVES

Country	Singapore representative	Foreign representative
Australia[1]	P. S. Raman	N. F. Parkinson
Austria	—	Dr Werner Sautter
Belgium	—	Jacques D'Hondt
Brazil	E. S. Monteiro	L. E. do Nascimento e Silva
Bulgaria	—	Stancho Stanchev

[1] High Commissioner.　　　　　　　　No figure = Ambassador.

Country	Singapore representative	Foreign representative
Burma	—	Pe Kin
Cambodia	Chan Keng Howe	Khong R. L. Wongsanith
Canada[1]	T. Koh Thong Bee	J. G. Hadwen
Denmark	—	Leif Donde[2]
France	—	Marcel Flory
Germany (West)	—	Dr Wilhelm Löer
Great Britain[1]	Arumugam Ponnu Rajah	S. Falle
Greece	—	John Yannakis
India[1]	P. Coomaraswamy	Prem Bhatia
Indonesia	Lee Khoon Choy	Soenarso
Israel	—	Hagay Dikan
Italy	—	R. de Cordona
Japan	Dr Ang Kok Peng	Yasuhiko Nara
Malaysia[1]	Maurice Baker	Tan Sri Jamal bin Abdul Latiff
Nepál	P. Coomaraswamy	G. Bahadur Karki
Netherlands	—	R. C. Pekelharing
New Zealand[1]	Kenneth M. Byrne	H. H. Francis
Norway	—	A. S. Slordahl
Pakistan[1]	A. Kajapathy[2]	M. S. Islam
Philippines	Tuan Haji Ya'acab bin Mohamed	C. M. Valdez[2]
Poland	—	Romuald Spasowski
Romania	—	Alexie Marin
Spain	—	C. Fernandez de Henestrosa
Sweden	G. S. R. Wahlgren[3]	E. Virgin
Switzerland	—	J. Etter[2]
Thailand	Ho Rih Hwa	Nibhon Wilairat
Turkey	—	—
USSR	—	I. I. Safronov
UAR	A. Kajapathy[2]	Abdel Hady H. Makhlouf[2]
USA	E. S. Monteiro	C. T. Cross
Yugoslavia	A. Kajapathy[2]	Viktor Repic

[1] High Commissioner. [2] Chargé d'Affaires. [3] Hon. Consul. No figure = Ambassador.

AREA AND POPULATION. The Republic of Singapore consists of Singapore Island itself, with some adjacent islets.

Singapore Island is situated off the southern extremity of the Malay peninsula, to which it is joined by a causeway carrying a road and railway. The straits between the island and the mainland are about three-quarters of a mile wide. The island is some 26 miles in length and 14 miles in breadth, and about 225·6 sq. miles (581·5 sq. km) in area, including the adjacent islets.

Estimated population by race, Dec. 1969: 1,512,000 Chinese, 294,900 Malays, 161,800 Indians and Pakistanis and 64,800 others; total 2,033,500.

Annual Report on the Registration of Births and Deaths, Marriages and Persons. Singapore, Govt. Printer
Population estimates of Singapore. Dept. of Statistics, Singapore, bi-annual

EDUCATION. Statistics of registered institutions for 1970:

Classification	Schools	Enrolment	Teachers
Government schools	266	337,566	12,891
Government-aided schools	236	168,549	5,770
Private schools	62	7,548	317
Total	564	513,663	18,978

On 1 Jan. 1962 the Singapore division of the University of Malaya was constituted as the University of Singapore. There are 7 faculties: arts and social sciences, law, science, medicine, dentistry, engineering and architecture; and 4 schools: accountancy and business administration, education, pharmacy and postgraduate medical studies. It numbered 4,228 students in 1969–70. The

Nanyang University, established in 1956, has 3 Colleges of Arts, Science, Commerce in addition to a Language and Computer Centre. A College of Graduate Studies is being established. There were 2,039 students in 1969–70. The Singapore Polytechnic had 3,256 students in 1969. The Ngee Ann College had 529 students in 1969.

Final report of the Commission of Enquiry into Education. Singapore, Govt. Printer. 1964
150 Years of Education in Singapore. Singapore, Teachers' Training College, 1969

CINEMAS (1969). There were 72 cinemas with a seating capacity of 58,000.

JUSTICE. There is a Supreme Court in Singapore which consists of the High Court, the Court of Appeal and the Court of Criminal Appeal. The Supreme Court is composed of a Chief Justice and 6 Judges. An appeal from the High Court lies to the Court of Appeal in civil matters and to the Court of Criminal Appeal in criminal matters. Further appeal can in certain cases be made to the Judicial Committee of the Privy Council. The High Court has original civil and criminal jurisdiction as well as appellate civil and criminal jurisdiction in respect of appeals from the Subordinate Courts. There are 3 civil district courts, 5 criminal district and magistrates' courts, 7 magistrates' courts, 1 juvenile court and 2 coroners' courts.

FINANCE. Public revenue and expenditure for calendar years until 1968 and then financial years, in Singapore dollars ($1 = £0·13):

	1966	1967	1968	1969–70[1]	1970–71[2]
Revenue	585,174,169	663,041,573	761,000,000	1,146,500,000	1,041,200,000
Expenditure	530,286,958	592,126,866	699,000,000	1,144,100,000	1,040,922,000

[1] Financial year from 1 Jan. 1969 to 31 March 1970. Estimated figure.
[2] Financial year from 1 April 1970 to 31 March 1971. Estimated figure.

DEFENCE. The formation of an Air Defence Command began in 1968, with *ab initio* training on Cessna 172 light aircraft. Delivery of 16 BAC 167 Strikemaster armed jet basic trainers and 4 Alouette III helicopters began in 1969. They have been followed by 12 Hunter jet fighter-bombers 4 Hunter reconnaissance-fighters, 4 two-seat Hunter trainers, 2 Airtourer piston-engined primary trainers built in New Zealand and a Cessna 402 twin-engined communications aircraft. About 60 Bloodhound surface-to-air missiles have been taken over from the RAF.

PLANNING. Gross Domestic Product was $1,968m. in 1959 ($4,833m. in 1969). Total investment amounted to 7·6% of the GDP in 1959 (19% in 1969). Trade promotion and the search for investments were intensified overseas. By 1969 there were Economic Development Board offices in London, Chicago, New York, San Francisco and Stockholm. A trading organization INTRACO was established in 1968 to give added stimulus to exports to world markets and deal with the state trading organizations of socialist countries. Investment was predominantly in the private sector which in 1969 reached $596·1m., an increase of 156% since 1966. 236 pioneer industries employed 35,000 workers and produced goods to the value of $1,226m., 46% of the total value of manufactures. Expansion of trade and industry more than offset the reduction in British military expenditure. Singapore's economic expansion, the strength of its currency and the acceptance in 1968 of the obligation of convertibility under Article VIII of the Articles of Agreement of the International Monetary Fund has encouraged Singapore's growth as a centre of international banking. The Asian Dollar Market inaugurated in Singapore in Nov. 1968, was firmly established during 1969. The Economic Development Board, established in Aug. 1961, is a statutory body to formulate, execute and promote the industrialization programme of the State. It also advises the Government on industrial policy.

Apart from the smaller industrial estates, the Singapore Government, through the Economic Development Board, is developing a 17,000-acre industrial satellite town at Jurong for new and expanding industries.

Industries in Jurong include shipbuilding and those manufacturing steel rods, steel pipes, tyres, chemicals, pharmaceuticals, plywood and veneer, plastics, cement, bricks, cables, textiles and wiremesh. Smaller industrial estates elsewhere in Singapore have light industry factories producing food, paper and miscellaneous consumer goods.

Lim Tay Boh, *The Development of Singapore's Economy*. Singapore, 1960
Ministry of Finance, *Development plan, 1961–64*. Singapore, 1961
Economic Planning Unit, *First development plan, 1961–64; review of progress*. Singapore, Govt. Printer, 1964

FISHERIES. As the prospect of increasing fish production from inshore waters is poor, in 1967 various projects were supplemented to provide the necessary infrastructure of an offshore and deep-sea fishing industry, with the aim of making Singapore self-sufficient in fish as well as a major fishing base in the region.

The Jurong fishing port and fish market began operating on 26 Feb. 1969. A Fishery Training Institute was established at Changi with the assistance of the United Nations Development Programme (Special Fund) to train youths and fishermen in modern fishing techniques. At Changi, too, a Marine Fisheries Research Department is being set up under the sponsorship of the South-east Asian Fisheries Development Centre. The total supply of fresh fish in 1969 was about 50,000 tons.

POWER. Electrical power is generated by 3 stations and part of new Jurong power station, with a total generating capacity of 584 mw. Consumption of electricity in Singapore 1969 was about 1,353 kwh, Work on the new power station in Jurong which is designed for a maximum installed capacity of 480 mw should be completed by 1970–71.

TOURISM. In 1969, 408,709 foreigners visited Singapore, including 49,477 from the UK and 90,883 from USA. Tourists spent an estimated S\$228·1m. in 1969.

COMMERCE. The imports during 1969 amounted to S\$6,243·6m., the exports to S\$4,740·7m. (inclusive of trade with West Malaysia).

In the following table (British Board of Trade returns, in £1,000 sterling) the imports include produce from Borneo, Sarawak and other eastern places, transhipped at Singapore, which is thus entered as the place of export:

	1966	1967	1968	1969	1970
Imports to UK	15,810	17,822	26,384	30,600	33,546
Exports of British produce	39,583	35,769	39,879	49,465 ⎱	62,518
Re-exports	417	438	614	937 ⎰	

SHIPPING. A total of 34,049 vessels of 129·3m. NRT entered into and cleared from Singapore during 1969.

ROADS. Singapore has 1,188 miles of road. On 31 Nov. 1969 motor vehicles registered in Singapore included 129,146 private cars, 30,089 goods vehicles, 7,720 public vehicles, and 98,720 motor cycles and scooters.

RAILWAY. A 16-mile main line runs through Singapore, connecting with the States of Malaya and as far as Bangkok· Branch lines serve the port of Singapore and the industrial estate at Jurong.

POST. In 1969, 42 post offices and 25 postal agencies were in operation. Telephones numbered 136,267 at 31 Dec. 1969.

BANKING. The Central Bank of Malaysia Ordinance, 1958, and the Banking Ordinance, 1958, continued to apply to Singapore until 12 June 1967, when the currencies of Singapore and Malaysia were separated. With the independence of Singapore on 9 Aug. 1965 these 2 ordinances continue to apply until new legislation is passed.

There were 36 commercial banks with 166 banking offices operating in Singapore in 1969. Total deposits amounted to $2,968m. in July 1970.

The amount deposited in the Singapore post office savings bank was $67m.; number of depositors, 498,163 (Aug. 1969).

WEIGHTS AND MEASURES. The standard measures are the Imperial yard; the Imperial pound; the Imperial gallon.

Among the Asian commercial and trading classes, Chinese steel-yards (called 'liteng' and 'daching') of various sizes are generally employed for weighing, purposes. Other local measures are:

Weight and capacity			Length
Chupak	1 quart	2 jengkals	1 hasta
Gantang	1 gallon	2 hastas	1 ela
Tahil	1¼ oz.	2 elas	1 depa (1 fathom or 6 ft)
Kati (16 tahils)	1⅓ lb.	4 sq. depas	1 sq. jemba (144 sq. ft)
Picul (100 katis)	133⅓ lb.	400 sq. jembas	1 sq. orlong (1⅓ acres)
Koyan (40 piculs)	5,333⅓ lb.	1 chhum	1⅛8 in.
		1 chhek	10 chhums (14¾ in.)

BOOKS OF REFERENCE

STATISTICAL INFORMATION. The Department of Statistics (PO Box 3010, Singapore) was established 1 Jan. 1922. Its publications include: *Singapore External Trade Statistics* (quarterly), *Monthly Digest of Statistics*, *Yearbook of Statistics*, *Population estimates of Singapore* (bi-annual). *Chief Statistician:* P. Arumainathan.

The Sabah, Sarawak and Singapore (State Constitutions) Order in Council 1963. Singapore, Govt. Printer, 1963
Singapore. Annual Report. Singapore, Govt. Printer
Singapore. Government Gazette (published weekly with supplement)
Republic of Singapore (Government) Directory. Govt. Printer, annual
Singapore Economic Development Board, *Annual Report*
Laws of the Colony of Singapore. 8 vols., 1955 (and annual supplements)
Hughes, H. (ed.) *Foreign Investment and Industrialisation in Singapore.* Canberra, 1969
Ooi, J. B. (ed.) *Modern Singapore.* Singapore, 1969

See also the bibliography under MALAYA.

NATIONAL LIBRARY. National Library, Stamford Rd, Singapore. *Director:* Mrs Hedwig Anuar.

GUYANA

HISTORY. The territory, including the counties of Demerara, Essequibo and Berbice, named from the 3 rivers, was first partially settled by the Dutch West Indian Company about 1620. The Dutch retained their hold until 1796, when it was captured by the English. It was finally ceded to Great Britain in 1814 and named British Guiana. On 26 May 1966 British Guiana became an independent member of the Commonwealth under the name of Guyana.

AREA AND POPULATION. Guyana is situated on the north-east coast of South America on the Atlantic Ocean, with Surinam on the east, Venezuela on the west and Brazil on the south and west. Area, 83,000 sq. miles (210,000 sq. km). Estimated population (June 1970), 740,196, of whom 377,256 were East Indians and 227,091 Africans. Births (1968), 25,380 (34·7 per 1,000 population); deaths, 5,619 (7·7 per 1,000). The capital, Georgetown, with suburbs, and in 1970 an estimated population of 195,250.

In Nov. 1940 sites on the bank of the Demerara River, about 25 miles from the sea, and at Makouria, about 40 miles up the Essequibo River, were leased to the USA as military bases. The site on the Demerara River is being operated by the Guyana Government as a civil airport. The US Government relinquished its claims to Atkinson on Guyana's attainment of independence. On 1 May 1969 the airport and surrounding area (formerly Atkinson) were renamed Timehri.

CONSTITUTION AND GOVERNMENT. The constitution is based on the agreement reached at the independence conference in London in Nov. 1965. It provides for a unicameral national assembly of 53 elected members. Elections are held under the single-list system of proportional representation, with the whole of the country forming one electoral area and each voter casting his vote for a party list of candidates. The legislature is elected for 4 years unless earlier dissolved. Guyana became a Republic on 23 Feb. 1970.

The elections held on 16 Dec. 1968 gave the People's National Congress 30 seats, the People's Progressive Party 19 seats, the United Force 4 seats.

The P.N.C. with an overall majority formed a 15-member cabinet.

President: Arthur Chung.

The cabinet was on 31 Dec. 1970 composed as follows:

Prime Minister, External Affairs, Economic Development, Public Corporations, Public Service, Community Development: L. F. S. Burnham.
Agriculture and Deputy Prime Minister: Dr P. A. Reid. *Finance:* D. Hoyte. *Trade:* B. Ramsaroop. *Communications:* M. Kasim. *Education:* Miss S. Field Ridley. *Home Affairs:* O. Clarke. *Works, Hydraulics and Supply:* H. Green. *Health:* Dr S. Talbot. *Labour and Social Security:* W. G. Carrington. *Attorney-General and Minister of State:* S. S. Ramphal. *Information and Culture:* Miss S. Field Ridley (acting). *Housing and Reconstruction:* D. Singh. *Mines and Forests:* H. O. Jack. *Local Government:* V. Mingo.

DIPLOMATIC REPRESENTATIVES

Country	Guyana representative	Foreign representative
Brazil	Evan Drayton	Brig.-Gen. Jose Da Cunha Garcia
Britain[1]	John Carter[2]	W. S. Bates
Canada[1]	—	J. Stiles
Germany (West)	—	W. Klingeberg
India[1]	—	D. Hejmadi
USA[3]	R. B. Gajraj	Spencer M. King
Venezuela	Dr Anne Jardim	Dr Ramon Rojas-Cabot

[1] High Commissioner.   [2] Also ambassador to France, Germany (West) and Netherlands.
[3] Also High Commissioner to Canada.   No figure = Ambassador.

EDUCATION (1969). There were 389 schools (including 80 in remote and sparsely populated districts), 158 of which were government schools and 231 received government grants. They had 171,469 pupils and 5,421 teachers. Secondary education was provided for both boys and girls in 31 government-owned, 13 grant-aided and 50 privately owned schools.

The University of Guyana was inaugurated on 1 Oct. 1963; it has faculties of arts, natural science, social science, education and technical studies. There were 1,030 students in Oct. 1969.

CINEMAS (1970). There are 48 cinemas with seating capacity of 37,220.

NEWSPAPERS (1970). There are 3 daily newspapers with a combined circulation of 60,656 and 8 weekly papers with a combined circulation of 140,000.

JUSTICE. The law, both civil and criminal, is based on the common and statute law of England, save that the principles of the Roman–Dutch law have been retained in respect of the registration, conveyance and mortgaging of land.

The Supreme Court of Judicature consists of a Court of Appeal and a High Court. Appeals from the Court of Appeal lie to the Judicial Committee of the Privy Council.

FINANCE. Currency. Accounts are kept in dollars and cents ($ = £0·21). The Bank of Guyana, established in 1965, issues Guyana dollar notes of $1, 5, 10 and 20 and coins of 1-, 5-, 10-, 25- and 50-cent pieces. The face value of Guyana notes in circulation at 31 Dec. 1969 was $39m. British Caribbean currency notes have been withdrawn from circulation.

Budget. Revenue and expenditure for calendar years (in G$1,000):

	1965	1966	1967	1968	1969[1]	1970[2]
Revenue	77,281	85,629	92,864	102,600	112,000	121,000
Expenditure	81,998	84,154	87,904	98,200	110,500	116,400

[1] Revised estimates.   [2] Estimates.

These figures are exclusive of special receipts from the Colonial Development Fund, US grant and the related expenditure.

Chief items of revenue 1969 (in G$1,000): Customs and excise, 59,120; internal revenue, 38,358; fees, fines, etc., 2,755; rents, royalties, etc., 2,349; post, 2,500; debt charges, 17,586. Expenditure: health, 10,328; education, 17,369; social services, 4,684; public works, 10,242; post and telecommunications, 3,114; pensions, 4,222; transport, 2,904.

Public debt, 31 Dec. 1969, was G$240·4m.

DEFENCE. The Guyana army has a strength of more than 1,300, including a women's army corps, and operates 2 Helio H-295 Courier STOL liaison aircraft.

PRODUCTION. Guyana can be divided roughly into 3 regions: (1) A low coastal region varying in width up to about 30 miles and constituting the agricultural area; (2) an intermediate area about 100 miles wide, of slightly higher undulating land containing the chief mineral and forest resources of the country; and (3) a hinterland of several mountain ranges and extensive savannahs. Approximately 87% of the land area is forested, and about 60,000 sq. miles of this is still available for timber exploitation. Only about 20% of the forest area is at present regarded as being reasonably accessible for timber extraction on an economic basis, however. In 1969 this area accounted for the production of 9,374,048 cu. ft of wood and wood products. Large areas of unimproved land in the coastal region, which vary in width up to about 50 miles from the sea, are still available for agricultural and cattle-grazing projects.

AGRICULTURE. Acreage under cultivation, 1969: Sugar-cane, 126,030 (sugar output, 364,465 tons); rice, 279,303 (output, 110,857 tons); coconuts, 46,085; coffee, 3,123; cocoa, 1,967; ground provisions, 8,795; citrus fruit, 5,609; corn, 2,598. Other tropical fruits and vegetables are grown mostly in scattered plantings; they include mangoes, papaws, avocado pears, melons, bananas.

Livestock estimate (1969): Cattle, 256,500; pigs, 80,900; sheep, 98,500; goats, 38,900; poultry, 6·5m.; horses, mules and donkeys, 6,450.

MINING. Placer goldmining commenced in 1884, and was followed by diamond mining in 1887. From 1884 to 1968 the output of gold was 3,414,030 bullion oz. (2,102 oz. in 1969). From 1901 to 1969 the production of diamonds was 3,798,364 metric carats (49,266 in 1868). There are large deposits of bauxite; 4,238,346 long tons and 293,370 tons of alumina were produced in 1969. Fullscale production of manganese began in 1960 and 114,988 wet tons were produced in 1968. The North West Guyana Mining Co. Ltd, operating through the Manganese Mines Ltd, closed operation in Guyana by the end of 1968.

COMMERCE. Imports and exports (in G$) for calendar years:

	1965	1966	1967	1968	1969
Imports	180,130,717	202,006,600	225,291,709	219,310,742	235,832,615
Exports	167,952,468	186,431,000	197,518,632	216,319,640	233,658,722

Chief imports (1969); Machinery, $47,523,314; diesel oil and other fuel oils, 4,575,748 bbls, $12,248,662; motor spirit, 356,005 bbls, $2,161,471; kerosene, 200,797 bbls, $1,746,343; flour, 43,644,977 lb., $4,351,888; tobacco in leaf, 678,579 lb., $1,014,196; cotton fabrics, 12,226,732 sq. yd, $5,195,944; footwear,

195,547 doz. pairs, $4,983,890; dairy products, $8,870,315; beer, 61,201 gallons, $183,994; ale, 8,787 gallons, $36,229; stout, 67,788 gallons, $236,745.

Chief domestic exports (1969): Sugar, 6,998,303 cwt, $83,766,710; rum, 1,444,851 proof gallons, $2,853,787; rice, 164m. lb., $19,669,918; timber, 898,037 cu. ft, $2,476,026; diamonds, .. carats, $3,798,355; bauxite, 2,336,933 tons, $62,616,938; alumina, 296,155 tons, $38,935,643; molasses, 2,093,700 cwt, $4,284,143; shrimps, 9,598,684 lb., $7,622,879.

Imports (exclusive of transhipments), 1969, from UK, 31%; from USA, 21%; from Canada, 8%; exports (exclusive of transhipments) to USA, 25%; to UK, 24%; to Canada, 18%.

SHIPPING. In 1969, 2,257 vessels of 3,329,710 NRT entered and 2,458 of 3,389,354 NRT cleared the ports from Georgetown, New Amsterdam and Kaituma.

Guyana is in direct sea-communication with the UK, France, Netherlands, Canada, USA, the West Indies, and Netherlands and French Guianas. There are 217 nautical miles of river navigation. There are ferry services across the mouths of the Demerara, Berbice and Essequibo rivers, the last providing a link between the West Coast Railway and the islands of Leguan and Wakenaam and the mainland at Adventure, and a number of coastal and river-boat services carrying both passengers and cargo. A number of launch services are operated in the more remote areas by private concerns.

Georgetown harbour, about ½ mile wide and 2½ miles long, has a minimum depth of 24 ft. New Amsterdam harbour is situated at the mouth of the Berbice River; there are wharves for coastal vessels only. Bauxite is loaded on ocean-going freighters at Mackenzie, 67 miles up the Demerara River, and at Everton on the Berbice River, about 10 miles from the mouth of the waterway. The Essequibo River has several timber-loading berths ranging from 20 to 40 ft. Springlands on the Corentyne River is the point of entry and departure of passengers travelling by launch services to and from Surinam. It is also a shipping point for rice and other produce from the Corentyne to Georgetown.

ROADS. There are 370 miles of driving or motor road, 244 miles of forest road from Bartica at the junction of the Essequibo and Mazaruni rivers to the Potaro goldmining district (including branches to the Upper Potaro River at Kangaruma on the route to Kaieteur, to Issano on the Mazaruni River above the long range of falls and rapids and to the Lower Potaro River at a point beneath the large fall of Tumatumari) and 469 miles of trails (including a government cattle trail of 182 miles, from Takama on the Berbice River to Annai on the Rupununi savannah). Motor vehicles, as of 31 Dec. 1969 totalled 35,776, including 12,453 passenger cars, 3,737 lorries and vans, 4,889 tractors and trailers, and 10,387 motor cycles.

RAILWAYS. There are 2 government-owned railways: the East Coast Railway, 60·5 miles of single-line standard gauge 4 ft 8½ in. linking Georgetown and New Amsterdam; and the West Coast Railway, 19 miles of 3 ft 6 in. gauge, linking Georgetown and Parika at the mouth of the Essequibo River.

In addition, there is a short, privately owned railway in the North West District which is operated by the African Manganese Co. for handling manganese ore. The Demerara Bauxite Co. operates a standard-gauge railway of 80 miles from Mackenzie on the Demerara River to Ituni. In March 1967 a bridge (740 ft) across the Demerara River was opened to enable the company to resume mining operations on the west bank of the river.

AVIATION. Guyana Airways Corporation operates scheduled services within the state. Other services in operation: BOAC, PANAM, to and from North, Central and South America twice a week; Air France, to and from Guadeloupe, Paramaribo and Cayenne once a week; British West Indian Airways, Ltd, to and from Trinidad daily, providing direct connexion with New York and London; KLM, to and from Curaçao and Paramaribo twice weekly; Cruzeiro do Sul, to and from Manaos and Boa Vista once a week.

TELECOMMUNICATIONS. The inland public telegraph and radio communication services are operated and maintained by the Telecommunication Corporation, established on 1 March 1967. On 31 Dec. 1969 there were 151 post offices and agencies (including travelling post offices and agencies).

The telephone exchanges had at the end of 1969 a total of 7,261 direct exchange lines with 13,540 telephone instruments. The number of route miles in the coastal and inland areas was 335 miles. 49 land-line stations were maintained at post offices in the coastal area, and 8 telegraph stations in the interior provide communication with the coastal area through a central telegraph office in Georgetown.

Overseas radio-telephone and telegraphic communication are provided by Cable and Wireless (W.I.) Ltd. In Georgetown a central radio station provides facilities for radio communication with 5 branch offices operated in combination with the wireless telegraph stations mentioned above, 14 stations operated by other government departments, 35 stations operated by private concerns (including mining, ranching, timber and other commercial interests) and 12 coastal ships and launches. This system is linked with the telephone system and is available to the general public.

A Tropospheric Scatter System, operated by Cable and Wireless (W.I.) Ltd, was opened on 26 March 1969. It provides for a maximum of 64 channels linking Guyana with the rest of the world *via* Trinidad, the nearest point for connexion in the company's broad band system. The Guyana United Broadcasting Co. Ltd, operates 1 station on a commercial basis. The Government of Guyana established a national broadcasting service on 1 Oct. 1968 which is also operating on a commercial basis.

BANKING. Barclays Bank DCO and the Royal Bank of Canada maintain branches in Berbice, Demerara and Essequibo while the Bank of Baroda (India) has branches in Demerara and Berbice. The Chase Manhattan Bank (USA) and the Bank of Nova Scotia each have a branch in Georgetown. The Guyana National Co-operative Bank opened in Feb. 1970.

As at 31 Dec. 1969 the Bank of Guyana had external assets totalling $40·8m.

BOOKS OF REFERENCE

Daly, P. H., *From Revolution to Republic*. Georgetown, 1970
Daly, Vere T., *A Short History of the Guyanese People*. Georgetown, 1967
Newman, P., *British Guiana—Problem of cohesion in an immigrant society*. OUP, 1964
Report of the British Guiana Commission of Inquiry of the International Commission of Jurists on Racial Problems in the Public Service. Geneva, 1965
Roth, V., *Handbook of Natural Resources of British Guiana*. Georgetown, 1946
Smith, R. T., *British Guiana*. OUP, 1962
Swan, M., *British Guiana*. HMSO, 1957

BOTSWANA

HISTORY. In 1885 the territory was declared to be within the British sphere; in 1889 it was included in the sphere of the British South Africa Company, but was never administered by the company; in 1890 a Resident Commissioner was appointed, and in 1895, on the annexation of the Crown Colony of British Bechuanaland to the Cape of Good Hope, the British Government was in favour of transferring the Protectorate to the BSA Company, but the three major chiefs of the Bakwena, the Bangwaketse and the Bamangwato went to England to protest against this proposal, and agreement was reached that their country should remain a British Protectorate if they ceded a strip of land on the eastern side of the country for railway construction. This railway was built in 1896–97.

On 30 Sept. 1966 the Bechuanaland Protectorate became an independent and sovereign member of the Commonwealth under the name of the Republic of Botswana.

National flag: light blue, white, black.

AREA AND POPULATION. Botswana comprises the territory lying between the Molopo River on the south and the Zambezi on the north, and extending from the Transvaal Province and Rhodesia on the east to South-West Africa on the west. The climate is on the whole sub-tropical and the atmosphere throughout the year is very dry. Area about 222,000 sq. miles (575,000 sq. km); population, according to the census of 1964, is 543,105, including 3,921 Europeans, 3,489 Eurafricans and 382 Asians. The most important tribes are the Bamangwato (201,007), under Chief Leapeetswe Khama; the Bakgatla (32,118), under Chief M. Pilane; the Bakwena (73,088), under Chief Neale Sechele; the Bangwaketse (71,289), under Chief Seepapito IV; the Batawana (42,347), under Chief Letsholathebe; the Bamalete (13,861), under Regent Kelemogile Mokgosi (brother of the late Chief Mokgosi, who died in 1966); the Batlokwa (3,711) under Chief Kgosi Gaborone; the Barolong (10,662), under Chief Kebalepile Montshiwa.

The main business centres are Lobatse (10,000), Gaberone (14,000) and Francistown (13,000). The largest towns are Kanye (37,000), Serowe (37,000), Molepolole (32,000) and Mochudi (19,000).

The seat of government is at Gaborone.

CONSTITUTION AND GOVERNMENT. The constitution of the Republic is based on the constitution which came into effect in March 1965, with some minor alterations.

The executive rests with the President of the Republic who is responsible to the National Assembly.

The National Assembly consists of 36 members (31 elected by universal suffrage, 4 specially elected and the Attorney-General *ex-officio*). The second general election, held on 18 Oct. 1969, returned 24 members of the Democratic Party, 3 People's Party and 3 National Front, Independent.

There is also a House of Chiefs to advise the Government. It consists of the Chiefs of the 8 principal tribes as *ex-officio* members and 4 members elected by and from among the sub-chiefs in 4 districts.

President of the Republic: Sir Seretse Khama, KBE.
Vice-President and Minister of Development Planning: Dr Q. K. J. Masire, JP.
Education, Health and Labour: B. C. Thema, MBE. *Works and Communications:* A. M. Dambe, BEM. *Commerce, Industry and Water Affairs:* M. K. Bogokgo, JP. *External Affairs:* E. S. Masisi. *Health, Labour and Home Affairs:* A. M. Dambe, BEM. *Agriculture:* Tsheko Tsheko, MBE. *Local Government and Lands:* E. M. K. Kgabo, JP. *Finance:* J. G. Hoskins, OBE.

High Commissioner in UK: G. K. T. Chicpe.
British High Commissioner: G. D. Anderson, CMG.
High Commissioner in Zambia: P. P. Makepe.
Ambassasor in USA: Chief Linchwe II.
Deputy Chief of USA Mission: W. Kennedy Cromwell.

LOCAL GOVERNMENT. Local government is carried out by 9 district councils and 3 town councils. Revenue is obtained mainly from local income tax, levied on all inhabitants in the area.

EDUCATION (1969). There were 314 primary and 10 secondary schools and 3 teacher-training colleges. The great majority of the primary schools and the junior secondary schools are controlled, under the Director of Education, by school committees with district-council and mission representatives. Three secondary schools and the homecraft centre are run by missions with Government support; Moeng College by a governing council; the remaining schools by the Government. District-council schools are financed by district-council treasuries and assisted with grants from the Central Government. Enrolment in primary schools in 1969 was 82,377, in secondary schools 3,049, in teacher-training colleges 359. University students abroad numbered 72. Total expenditure on education was R1,995,588 for the year ended 31 March 1967.

In 1964, 21·8 % of the total population were literate in Setswana and 15% in English.

The official languages are English and Tswana.

JUSTICE. The Botswana Court of Appeal succeeded the Court of Appeal for Basutoland, Bechuanaland and Swaziland, which was established in 1954. It has jurisdiction in respect of criminal and civil appeals emanating from the High Court of Botswana. Further appeal lies in certain circumstances to the Judicial Committee of the Privy Council.

The High Court for Botswana succeeded the High Court for Bechuanaland, which was established in 1938. It has jurisdiction in all criminal and civil causes and proceedings. Subordinate courts and African courts are in each of the 12 administrative districts.

Police. The police force consists of 82 officers, 73 n.c.o.s and 597 other ranks.

WELFARE (1969). There are 10 general hospitals, a mental home, 14 health centres and 84 dispensaries (with 1,700 beds). There are 34 registered medical practitioners. Government expenditure on medical services, R776,480 for the year ended 31 March 1967.

FINANCE. Currency. The currency is the South African Rand (R1 = £0·58 sterling).

Budget. Revenue and expenditure (in Rand) for financial years ending 31 March:

	1965–66	1966–67	1967–68	1968–69[1]	1969–70[1]
Revenue	10,987,101	11,621,821	15,025,502	16,053,000	21,404,000
Expenditure	10,104,659	11,881,419	15,699,838	15,903,000	20,394,000

[1] Estimates.

Chief items of revenue, 1968–69: Taxes and duties, R2,253,000; customs and excise, R1,397,000; posts and telegraphs, R607,000; government property, R718,000; licences, R364,000.

Chief items of expenditure, 1967–68: Education, R664,662; medical, R796,220; public works, R1,151,722; veterinary, R797,468; agriculture, R716,644; post and telegraphs, R602,920; development, R3,793,757.

British financial aid granted between 1955 and 1967 amounted to R13,467,100. From 1945 to 1966 British Government aid totalled R41·4m.

Public debt, on 31 March 1968, amounted to R10,536,266.

PRODUCTION. Cattle-rearing and dairying are the chief industries, but the country is more a pastoral than an agricultural one, crops depending entirely upon the rainfall. However, increasing numbers of boreholes are being established where underground supply is adequate. The abattoir at Lobatsi, opened in Oct. 1954, is of great importance to the country's economy. In 1967 the number of cattle was 1,104,722; goats, 716,599; sheep, 218,346; poultry, 119,049.

Production of gold and silver, in 1964, was 142 fine oz. (R3,490); manganese ore, 23,041 short tons (R145,886); asbestos, 1,774 short tons (R219,030).

The National Development Plan 1968–73 envisages a total capital expenditure of R69·3m.

LABOUR. In 1966, 33% of the wage-earners were employed in agriculture, 15% in construction, electricity and water services, 8% in administration, 6% in manufacturing and 3% in mining and quarrying.

COMMERCE. Chief items of import in 1966: Cereals (R3·8m.); sugar (R1·16m.); petroleum products (R1·87m.); iron and steel products (R1·88m.). Chief items of export in 1966: Carcases (R6·9m.), cattle (R792,664), hides and skins (R893,228), abattoir by-products (R767,970), beans (R191,545), canned meat (R669,704), meat extract (R124,674).

In 1969 imports from UK were valued £835,000; exports to UK, £346,000. Botswana is joined to the South African customs system.

COMMUNICATIONS. The telegraph, telephone and railway (394 miles) lines from Cape Town to Rhodesia traverse Botswana. Wireless communication has been established between headquarters at Gaborone and various district offices and police stations. There are 22 post offices and 45 agencies. There were 2,642 telephones and about 5,000 licensed radio sets in 1968.

There are 4,875 miles of roads, of which the Public Works Department maintains 2,753. In 1968 there were 5,101 registered motor vehicles, including 1,325 commercial vehicles and 900 agricultural vehicles.

There are 2 aerodromes, 16 airfields and 10 emergency landing grounds. Regular flights are flown by Botswana Airways Corporation.

BANKING. The Standard Bank of South Africa, Ltd, and Barclays Bank DCO have branches in Francistown, Lobatse, Mahalapye and Gaborone and about 30 agencies.

A government-financed National Development Bank was founded in 1964.

The post office savings bank has deposits of about R370,000 from 7,000 depositors.

BOOKS OF REFERENCE

STATISTICAL INFORMATION. The Chief Information Officer, P.O. Box 51, Gaborone, Botswana, publishes *Facts About Botswana*, the monthly *Kutlwano* and *Daily News*.

Annual Report, 1965. HMSO, 1966
Report of the Economic Survey Mission. HMSO, 1960
Young, B. A., *Bechuanaland.* HMSO, 1966

LESOTHO

HISTORY. Basutoland first received the protection of Britain in 1868 at the request of Moshesh, the first paramount chief. In 1871 the territory was annexed to the Cape Colony, but in 1884 it was restored to the direct control of the British Government through the High Commissioner for South Africa.

On 4 Oct. 1966 Basutoland became an independent and sovereign member of the Commonwealth under the name of the Kingdom of Lesotho.

AREA AND POPULATION. Lesotho is bounded on the west by the Orange Free State, on the north by the Orange Free State and Natal, on the east by Natal and East Griqualand, and on the south by the Cape Province. The altitude varies from 5,000 to 11,000 ft. The climate is dry and rigorous, with extremes of heat and cold both seasonal and diurnal. The temperature varies between 93° F. (34° C.) and 3° F. (−16° C.). The rainfall is variable, the average being about 29 in. per annum.

The area is 11,716 sq. miles (30,340 sq. km). Lesotho is a purely African territory, and the few European residents are government officials, traders, missionaries and artisans. The census taken on 14 April 1966 showed a total population of 969,634 persons (465,784 males, 503,850 females), of whom 97,529 males and 19,744 females were absent.

CONSTITUTION AND GOVERNMENT. On 4 Oct. 1966 the country became the Kingdom of Lesotho, with the Paramount Chief as King.

Parliament consists of the National Assembly (60 members elected by adult suffrage) and a Senate (22 principal chiefs and 11 members nominated by the King). The general election held on 30 April 1965 returned 31 members of the National Party, 25 members of the Congress Party and 4 members of the Marematlou Freedom Party. The elections of 27 Jan. 1970 were declared invalid on 31 Jan. The constitution suspended and a state of emergency declared.

King of Lesotho: Moshoeshoe II.
Prime Minister: Chief Leabua Jonathan. *Deputy Prime Minister:* Chief Sekhonyana Maseribane.

The College of Chiefs settles the recognition and succession of Chiefs and adjudicates cases of inefficiency, criminality and absenteeism among them.

High Commissioner in London: C. M. Molapo.
British High Commissioner: I. B. Watt, CMG.
High Commissioner in Kenya: P. Mabathona.
Ambassador in USA: Mothusi T. Moshologu.

LOCAL GOVERNMENT. The country is divided into 9 districts as follows: Maseru, Qacha's Nek, Mokhotlong, Leribe, Butha-Buthe, Teyateyaneng, Mafeteng, Mohale's Hoek, Quthing. Each district is subdivided into wards, most of which are presided over by hereditary chiefs allied to the Moshoeshoe family.

District councils, established in 1944, were abolished on 17 Jan. 1966; their functions are now excercised by officials appointed by the Ministry of Local Government.

RELIGION. About 70% of the population are Christians, 40% being Roman Catholics.

EDUCATION. Education is largely in the hands of the 3 main missions (Paris Evangelical, Roman Catholic and English Church), under the direction of the Education Department. The total expenditure on all schools in 1968–69 was R2,029,630. The total enrolment in 1,131 primary schools was 167,170; in 27 secondary schools, 3,094; in 7 teacher-training schools, 623. University education is provided at the University of Botswana, Lesotho, Swaziland and at Roma, which opened in 1964 (388 students). Primary education is free at government schools. Bursaries are provided at all stages for secondary, teacher-training and University work. In 1968, 118 Basotho were studying at universities outside Lesotho.

JUSTICE. An appeal court for Lesotho was established at Maseru on 4 Oct. 1966.

Police. The police force on 31 Dec. 1967 had an establishment of 47 officers and 1,109 other ranks.

HEALTH. The government medical staff of the territory consists of 1 Permanent Secretary for Health and chief medical officer, 1 senior medical officer, 25 medical officers, 1 medical officer of health and 6 specialist physicians and surgeons.

There are 10 government hospitals staffed by 122 matrons, sisters and nurses. There is accommodation for 1,000 patients in government hospitals. The new 316-bed Queen Elizabeth II hospital in Maseru was completed in 1957. There are 9 mission hospitals subsidized by the Government with 656 beds. Health centres and mountain dispensaries provide outpatient medical facilities and maternity services to people living in remote areas. The leper settlement 5 miles out of Maseru had 273 patients at the end of 1968.

The principal diseases are venereal diseases, chronic rheumatism, malnutrition, infections of the respiratory tract and dyspepsia. The heaviest toll of lives in children is due to malnutrition, diphtheria, whooping cough and gastro-enteritis. The incidence of nutritional and deficiency diseases is comparatively high and is allied to maize being the staple food. Typhus, plague and smallpox occur only rarely.

FINANCE. Currency. The currency is the South African Rand (R1 = £0·50).

Budget. The financial year ends on 31 March.

	1965–66	1966–67	1967–68	1968–69[1]	1969–70[1]	1970–71[1]
Revenue	10,265,700	9,856,286	11,200,851	11,048,338	11,322,650	11,704,510
Expenditure	8,383,700	9,856,311	11,200,851	10,913,338	10,497,380	11,041,480

[1] Estimates.

The major items of expenditure in 1967–68 were education (R2·2m.), health (R1·1m.) and agricultural co-operatives and marketing (R1m.). Revenue is expected to yield R4·9m., including Lesotho's share of South African customs duties (R1·8m.); R6m. will be contributed by a UK grant-in-aid.

AGRICULTURE. The chief crops are wheat, maize and sorghum; barley, oats, beans, peas and other vegetables are also grown. The land is held in trust for the nation by the King and may not be alienated.

Soil conservation and the improvement of crops and pasture are matters of vital importance. A total area of 1,006,817 acres has been protected against soil erosion by means of terracing, training banks and grass strips. Efforts are being made to secure the general introduction of rotational grazing in the mountain area.

Livestock (1968): Cattle, 442,582; horses, 68,235; donkeys, 42,006; sheep, 1,364,703; goats, 679,344; mules, 29,387.

INDUSTRY. Industrial development is progressing under the National Development Corporation. Diamond production in 1967 was valued at R1,017,623.

COMMERCE. Lesotho, Botswana and Swaziland are members of the South African customs union, by agreement dated 29 June 1910.

Total values of imports and exports into and from Lesotho (in £ sterling):

	1961	1962	1965[1]	1966[1]	1967[1]
Imports	3,059,525	3,131,759	17,335	22,917	23,800
Exports	1,410,309	1,711,797	4,690	4,389	4,168

[1] In R1,000.

Principal imports in 1966 were food, drink and tobacco (R7m.), semi-manu-factures and chemicals (R7m.) and consumer goods (R3·6m); principal exports were wool (R1·86m.), mohair (R943,000) and diamonds (R697,000). Money remitted by workers in South Africa amounted to R4·4m.

In 1969 imports from UK were valued £1,000; exports to UK, £88,000.

RAILWAYS. A railway built by the South African Railways, 1 mile long, connects Maseru with the Bloemfontein–Natal line at Marseilles.

ROADS. There are 91 miles of tarred roads and 530 miles of gravel-surfaced roads along the western border of Lesotho, with outlets to the border ports of exit. Regular motor services of the South African Railways operate between Zastron (OFS) and Quthing, Zastron (OFS) and Mohale's Hoek, and between Fouriesburg (OFS) and Butha Buthe. In addition to the main roads there are 341 miles of by-roads leading to trading stations and missions. Communications into the mountainous interior are by means of bridlepaths suitable only for riding and pack animals, but a mountain road of 80 miles has been constructed, and some parts are accessible by air transport, which is being used increasingly.

AVIATION. There is a scheduled passenger service between Maseru and Jan Smuts Airport, Johannesburg operated jointly by Lesotho National Airways and SAA. There are also 29 airstrips for light aircraft.

POST. There were 1,844 telephones on 1 Jan. 1969.

BANKING. The Standard Bank of South Africa and Barclays Bank DCO have branches at Maseru, Mohale's Hoek and Leribe.

M

BOOKS OF REFERENCE

STATISTICAL INFORMATION. Bureau of Statistics, P.O.B. 455, Maseru, Lesotho.

Lesotho: Report for 1968. Maseru, 1969
Ashton, H., *The Basuto.* 2nd ed. OUP, 1967
Hailey, Lord, *The Republic of South Africa and the High Commission Territories.* OUP, 1963
Spence, J. E., *Lesotho.* OUP, 1968

BARBADOS

Barbados became an independent sovereign state within the Commonwealth on 30 Nov. 1966 and is a member of the United Nations and the Organization of American States.

AREA AND POPULATION. Barbados lies to the east of the Windward Islands. Area 166 sq. miles (430 sq. km). The hot and rainy seasons last from June to December, and the average rainfall is 61 in. per year. At 30 Sept. 1970 the estimated population was 238,000. Births (1969), 5,216; deaths (1969), 1,995. Bridgetown is the principal city; population, 12,400.

CONSTITUTION AND GOVERNMENT. Barbados was occupied by the British in 1627 and during its colonial history never changed hands. Full internal self-government was attained in 1961. The Legislature consists of the Governor-General, a Senate and a House of Assembly. The Senate comprises 21 members appointed by the Governor-General, 12 being appointed on the advice of the Prime Minister, 2 on the advice of the leader of the opposition and 7 in the Governor-General's discretion. The House of Assembly comprises 24 members elected every 5 years. In 1963 the voting age was reduced to 18.

In Oct. 1970 the Democratic Labour Party held 15 seats, the Barbados Labour Party 8 and the Barbados National Party 1.

The Privy Council is appointed by the Governor-General after consultation with the Prime Minister. It consists of 11 members and the Governor-General as chairman. It advises the Governor-General in the exercise of the royal prerogative of mercy and in the exercise of his disciplinary powers over members of the public and police services.

Governor-General: Sir Winston Scott, GCMG.
Prime Minister: Right Hon. Errol Walton Barrow, PC.
British High Commissioner: (vacant)

RELIGION. The majority (*c.* 70%) of the population are Anglicans, the remainder mainly Methodists, Moravians and Roman Catholics.

EDUCATION. On 30 June 1970 children in 117 primary schools numbered 42,216; in 7 comprehensive schools, 9,013; in 10 secondary grammar schools, 5,328. There are 17 government-aided independent schools with 7,259 pupils and a number of independent schools for which no accurate figures are available. As from Jan. 1962 tuition fees were abolished for children at all government secondary schools.

In 1963 Erdiston College became one of the constituent Colleges of the University of the West Indies Institute of Education. The College of Arts and Sciences of the University of the West Indies in Barbados was opened in Sept. 1963. In 1970, 425 students attended. Education at this College is free for Barbadians. A Community College for higher education at pre-university level was opened in 1969. In 1970, 325 students attended the S. J. Prescod Polytechnic which was opened in Nov. 1969 to give training in, among other things, construction, electrical and engineering trades. In 1969–70, 55 government scholars, bursars and exhibitioners were attending universities overseas. Government expenditure on education during 1969–70 was $13,856,656.

CINEMAS. There are 8 cinemas with a seating capacity of 46,675, and 2 drive-in cinemas for 568 cars.

NEWSPAPERS (1970). There is 1 daily newspaper (average daily circulation 23,000). There are 3 weeklies (combined circulation 17,000) and 1 bi-weekly (40,700 circulation).

JUSTICE. Justice is administered by the Supreme Court and by magistrates' courts. All have both civil and criminal jurisdiction. There is a Chief Justice and 3 puisne judges of the Supreme Court and 8 magistrates.

AGRICULTURE. Of the total area of 106,240 acres, about 68,500 acres are arable land. The land is intensely cultivated, and sugar cane occupies 60,000 acres, 50,000 were reaped in 1969. The agricultural sector accounted for 14% of GDP in 1968 (1946, 45%; 1967, 24%). In 1969, 13,154 persons were employed on sugar estates and 1,451 in sugar factories. In 1969, 139,000 tons of sugar were produced. There are 17 sugar factories, 2 syrup plants and 3 rum distilleries in production.

FISHERY. There are about 500 powered boats and many men and women are employed during the flying-fish season. Large numbers of these boats are laid up from July to Oct. The catch in 1969 was estimated at 5·6m. lb. The UN Caribbean Fisheries Development Project has its headquarters in Barbados.

TOURISM. In 1969, 137,630 visitors came to Barbados, including 55,134 from USA, 31,935 from Canada and 12,390 from UK.

INDUSTRIES. Industries operating in Barbados in 1968 numbered about 180 and ranged from the manufacture of processed food to small specialized products, such as plastic products and electronic parts.

FINANCE AND TRADE. The fiscal year runs from 1 April to 31 March; accounts in E. Caribbean dollars (4·8 EC$ = £1).

	1966–67	1967–68	1968–69	1969–70[2]
Revenue	50,956,831	52,094,010	57,010.086	57,767,554
Expenditure	56,118,581	45,515,444	57,122,135	62,061,395
Public debt	52,900,000	50,400,000	57,657,000	61,500,000
Imports[1]	132,595,700	134,311,160	168,024,924	194,553,582
Exports[1]	74,145,600	72,309,480	76,641,943	74,255,165

[1] Exclusive of bullion and specie.   [2] Estimates.

In 1969 the principal imports were: Electrical machinery, apparatus and appliances, $14,140,611; other machinery, $13,692,543; motor vehicles, $5,709,830 paper and paper manufactures, $5,222,701; lumber, $4,874,276; food waste and prepared animal feeds, $3,687,019; milk, $3,521,563; crude petroleum, $3,311,043; flour, $2,697,368; rice, $2,456,625; diesel oil, $2,416,358.

The principal exports in 1969 were: Sugar, $26,982,463; crustaceans and molluscs (mainly shrimp), $7,236,653; rum, $2,938,376; electrical goods, $5,537,352; molasses and syrup, $3,451,325; clothing, $2,741,319.

Total trade with UK in £1,000 sterling (British Board of Trade returns):

	1965	1966	1967	1968	1969	1970
Imports from UK	6,496	6,972	6,123	7,222	6,680	6,836
Exports to UK	5,887	6,714	6,949	7,180	9,283 }	11,973
Re-exports to UK	135	172	113	168	171 }	

SHIPPING. A deep-water harbour opened in 1961 at Bridgetown provides 8 berths for ships 500–600 ft in length, including one specially designed for bulk sugar loading. The number of merchant vessels entering in 1968 was 2,195, of 4,712,000 NRT.

ROADS. There are 840 miles of road open to traffic, of which 722 miles are all-weather roads. On 30 June 1970 there were 22,699 motor vehicles, including 15,918 cars and 229 buses.

AVIATION. There is an international airport at Seawell, Christ Church, Barbados, served by BOAC, BWIA, Air France, Leeward Islands Air Transport, PANAM, Air Canada, Caribair, SAS, Dutch Antillian Airways and Venezuelan Airlines. In 1969, 212,370 passengers arrived and 215,866 departed by air; 51,485 were in transit.

TELEPHONE. In June 1970 there were 18,122 exchange lines and 27,997 stations in service.

BANKING. Six main banks operate in Barbados: Barclays Bank DCO, the Royal Bank of Canada, Canadian Imperial Bank of Commerce, the Bank of Nova Scotia, the Bank of America and the First National City Bank of New York. The Government Savings Bank on 31 Sept. 1970 had 45,250 depositors and deposits of $16,615,000.

Barbados is headquarters for the Caribbean Development Bank and for The Eastern Caribbean Currency Authority. It is a member of the Caribbean Free Trade Area (CARIFTA). The Barbados Development Bank opened on 15 April 1969 and Barbados became a member of the Inter-American Development Bank on 19 March 1969.

BOOKS OF REFERENCE

STATISTICAL INFORMATION. The Barbados Statistical Service (Garrison, St Michael) produces selected monthly statistics and annual abstracts. *Government Statistician:* C. G. Alleyne, AIS.

Barbados Economic Survey, 1969
Barbados Development Plan, 1969–72
Chandler, M. J., *A Guide to Records in Barbados.* University of the West Indies, 1965
Hoyos, F. A., *Barbados, Our Island Home.* London, 1960
Starkey, O. P., *Commercial Geography of Barbados.* Indiana Univ. Press, 1963

LIBRARY. The Barbados Public Library, Bridgetown. *Librarian:* Chalmer St Hill, BA.

NAURU

AREA AND POPULATION. The island is situated 0° 32′ S. lat. and 166° 55′ E. long. Area, 5,263 acres (2,130 hectares). It is an oval-shaped up-heaval coral island of approximately 12 miles in circumference, surrounded by a reef which is exposed at low tide. There is no anchorage. On the seaward side the reef dips abruptly into the deep waters of the Pacific. On the landward side of the reef there is a sandy beach interspersed with coral pinnacles. From the sandy beach the ground rises gradually, forming a fertile section ranging in width from 150 to 300 yd and completely encircling the island. On the inner side of the fertile section there is a coral cliff which rises to a height of 200 ft. Above the cliff there is an extensive plateau bearing phosphate of a high grade, the mining rights of which were vested in the British Phosphate Commissioners until 1 July 1970, subject to the rights of the Nauruan landowners. In July 1970 the Nauru Phosphate Corporation assumed control and management of the enterprise. It is chiefly on the fertile section of land between the sandy beach and the plateau that the Nauruans have established themselves. With the exception of a small fringe round a shallow lagoon, about 1 mile inland, the plateau, which contains the phosphate deposits, has few food-bearing trees and is not settled by the Nauruans.

At 30 June 1970 the population totalled 6,664, of whom 3,407 were Nauruans, and 883 Chinese, 560 Europeans and (1969) 1,824 other Pacific Islanders.

Vital statistics, 1968–69: Births, 229; deaths, 48.

GOVERNMENT. The island was discovered by Capt. Fearn in 1798, annexed by Germany in Oct. 1888, and surrendered to the Australian forces in 1914. It was administered under a mandate, effective from 17 Dec. 1920, conferred on the British Empire and approved by the League of Nations until 1 Nov. 1947, when the United Nations General Assembly approved a trusteeship agreement with the governments of Australia, New Zealand and UK as joint administering authority.

A Legislative Council was established by the Nauru Act, passed by the Australian Parliament in Dec. 1965 and was inaugurated on 31 Jan. 1966. The trusteeship agreement terminated on 31 Jan. 1968, on which day Nauru became an independent republic but having special relationship with the Commonwealth (*see* p. 56). An 18-member Legislative Assembly was elected on 26 Jan. 1968.

President and Minister for Foreign Affairs: Hammer DeRoburt, OBE.

EDUCATION. Attendance at school is compulsory for all children between the ages of 6 and 15 (if European) and 6 and 17 (if Nauruan). In 1970 there were 9 primary schools, 94 teachers and 1,465 pupils and 2 secondary schools with 28 teachers and 368 pupils. Scholarships are available for Nauruan children to receive secondary and higher education and vocational training in Australia.

FINANCE. Revenue and expenditure (in $A) for financial years ending 30 June: 1968–69, revenue, 16,447,858; expenditure, 13,368,774, and 1969–70, revenue, 7·64m.; expenditure, 6,311,279.

The interests in the phosphate deposits were purchased in 1919 from the Pacific Phosphate Company by the governments of the UK, the Commonwealth of Australia and New Zealand, at a cost of £Stg3·5m., and a Board of Commissioners representing the 3 governments was appointed to manage and control the working of the deposits. In May 1967, in Canberra, the British Phosphate Corporation agreed to hand over the phosphate industry to Nauru and on 15 June 1967 agreement was reached that the Nauruans could buy the assets of the B.P.C. for approximately $A20m. over 3 years. Final payment was made on 23 April 1969 and control was handed over on 1 July 1970.

It is estimated that the deposits will be exhausted by the end of the century.

COMMERCE. The export trade consists almost entirely of phosphate shipped to Australia, New Zealand and Japan. Phosphate exported, 1968–69, 2,186,000 tons.

The imports consist almost entirely of food supplies, building construction materials and machinery for the phosphate industry. Value of imports: 1968–69, $A5,224,924. Exports 1968–69, $A24,046,000.

Trade with the UK (British Board of Trade returns, in £1,000 sterling):

	1965	1966	1967	1968	1969	1970
Imports to UK	1,577	1,172	855	783	336 }	—
Exports from UK	119	68	20	37	1,231 }	63

SHIPPING. The Nauru Local Government Council owns 3 ships. These ships ply between Australia, Pacific Islands and Japan. Other shipping coming to the island consists of those under charter to the phosphate industry.

AVIATION. There is an airstrip on the island and Fiji Airways conduct a fortnightly service *via* Tarawa. Air Micronesia operates a fortnightly service through Majuro and Air Nauru a weekly service from Brisbane in Australia and a fortnightly service from Nauru/Tarawa/Nauru.

TELECOMMUNICATIONS. Direct daily schedules are maintained with Sydney (N.S.W.), Suva and Nandi (Fiji), Tarawa, Ocean Island and Port Moresby, and with merchant shipping—both long- and short-wave transmission. A radio-telephone circuit is maintained Mondays to Fridays with Sydney. A separate tele-radio service exists between Nauru and Ocean Island.

BOOKS OF REFERENCE

Report to the General Assembly of the United Nations on the Administration of the Territory of Nauru. 1949 to date
Text of Trusteeship Agreement. (Cmd. 7290; Treaty Series No. 89, 1947)
Territory of Nauru—Annual Report. Dept. of Territories. Canberra, 1920–40 and from 1947–48
Pittman, G. A., *Nauru, the Phosphate Island.* London, 1959

MAURITIUS

HISTORY. Mauritius was known to Arab navigators probably not later than the 10th century. It was probably visited by Malays in the 15th century, and was discovered by the Portuguese between 1507 and 1512, but the Dutch were the first settlers (1598). In 1710 they abandoned the island, which was occupied by the French under the name of Isle de France (1715). The British occupied the island in 1810, and it was formally ceded to Great Britain by the Treaty of Paris, 1814. Mauritius attained independence on 12 March 1968.

AREA AND POPULATION. The island, situated 20° S. Lat., $57\frac{1}{2}$° E. Long., is of volcanic origin. The climate is free from extremes of weather, except for tropical cyclones at times. A very severe cyclone occurred on 27–28 Feb. 1960. Yearly rainfall varies from 30 in. on the north-west coast to 200 in. in the uplands.

Mauritius has an area of about 720 sq. miles (1,843 sq. km). According to the census of 30 June 1962, the population of the island was 681,619 (342,306 males, 339,313 females); that of the dependencies was 19,400. The estimated population at the end of 1969 was 870,000, and the population of Port Louis, the capital with its suburbs, numbered 139,300. Port Louis was granted city status on 25 Aug. 1966.

Vital statistics, 1969: Births, 21,719 (27·2 per 1,000); marriages, 3,882 (9·7 per 1,000); deaths 6,428 (8 per 1,000).

CONSTITUTION AND GOVERNMENT. Mauritius became an independent state and a monarchical member of the British Commonwealth on 12 March 1968 after seven months of internal self-government. The Governor-General is the local representative of HM the Queen, who remains the Head of the State.

In accordance with the Mauritius Independence Order 1968 the Cabinet is presided over by the Prime Minister, who is also the Minister for External Affairs. Each of the other 20 members of the Cabinet is responsible for the administration of specified departments or subjects and is bound by the rule of collective responsibility. There are also 10 Parliamentary Secretaries appointed by the Governor-General on the advice of the Prime Minister.

The Legislative Assembly consists of a Speaker and 62 elected members (3 each for the 20 constituencies of Mauritius and 2 for Rodrigues) and 8 additional seats in order to ensure a fair and adequate representation of each community within the Assembly. General Elections are held every 5 years on the basis of universal adult suffrage.

The Constitution also provides for the Public Service Commission and the Judicial and Legal Service Commission, which have both assumed executive powers for appointments to the Public Service. An Ombudsman assumed office on 2 March 1970. Adequate provision is also made for the protection of fundamental rights and freedoms of the individual.

Governor-General: Sir Arthur Leonard Williams, GCMG (sworn in 3 Sept. 1968).

Prime Minister: Sir Seewoosagur Ramgoolam, Kt.
High Commissioner in London: Dr L. Teelock, CBE.
High Commissioner in New Delhi: R. Ghurburrun.
Ambassador in USA: P. G. Balancy, CBE.
Ambassador in Paris: G. Forget, CBE.

RELIGION. At the 1962 census there were 218,572 Roman Catholics, 7,692 Protestants (Church of England and Church of Scotland). The Hindus numbered 332,851 and the Moslems, 110,332. State aid is granted to the churches and amounted to Rs 828,458 in 1968–69.

EDUCATION. Primary education is free but not compulsory, though under the Education Ordinance of 1957 compulsion may be introduced as circumstances permit. At the end of Oct. 1969 there were 176 government and 55 state-aided schools. Average attendance at government schools was 78,905 (102,902 on roll) and at state-aided primary schools 30,277 (37,951 on roll). There were, in Oct. 1969, 2 state senior primary schools, one for boys and one for girls, and 1 state mixed central school (375 on roll) providing a free 3-year post-primary non-vocational course with emphasis on handicraft and homecraft respectively, 106 unaided primary schools with an enrolment of 2,310, 9 grant-aided and 21 unaided secondary schools with primary sections with an enrolment of 3,327.

For secondary education there were in Oct. 1969, 3 government boys' schools (one of which has technical and commercial streams) and 1 government girls' school with 2,616 pupils, and 13 aided and 124 unaided secondary schools for boys and girls, with a roll of 7,003 and 32,825 respectively.

There are also a government post-secondary Agricultural College (62 full-time and 76 part-time students on the roll) which now forms part of the University of Mauritius, a teachers' training college (668 on roll) and 5 vocational training centres (101 on roll).

Government expenditure on education in 1968–69 was Rs 29·6m., excluding capital expenditure on new buildings and other development work, which cost Rs 1·4m.

NEWSPAPERS. There are 7 French daily papers (with occasional articles in English) with a combined circulation of 66,900 and 3 Chinese daily papers with a combined circulation of 6,600.

FINANCE. Currency. The unit of currency is the Mauritius Rupee, divided into 100 cents; it is equivalent to $7\frac{1}{2}$p. sterling or approximately US cents 18.

The currency consists of: (i) Bank of Mauritius notes of Rs 50, 25, 10 and 5; (ii) Government notes of Rs 25, 10 and 5. These notes are being withdrawn from circulation and ceased to be legal tender on 14 Oct. 1968; (iii) Cupro-nickel coins of one rupee, half rupee, quarter rupee and 10 cents; (iv) Bronze coins of 5 cents, 2 cents and 1 cent.

Notes and coins in circulation as at 30 June 1970 amounted to Rs 88,575,285 and Rs 5,828,271 respectively.

Budget. Revenue and expenditure (in Rs) for years ending 30 June:

	1965–66	1966–67	1967–68	1968–69	1969–70
Revenue	182,175,126	199,293,738	232,452,925	249,025,470	228,019,960
Expenditure	213,943,113	220,996,691	232,282,351	248,631,550	227,339,519

Principal sources of revenue, 1968–69: Direct taxes, Rs 58,323,829; indirect taxes, Rs 126,464,356; receipts from public utilities, Rs 20,979,102; receipts from public services, Rs 6,276,409; interests and royalties, Rs 6,879,793; reimbursement, Rs 6,370,062. Capital expenditure, 1968–69, was Rs 43,370,313; capital receipts, Rs 20,539,236.

On 30 June 1969 the debt of Mauritius was Rs 320,478,476, and the municipal debt of Port Louis was Rs 14,125,320.

DEFENCE. On 30 June 1968 the Mauritius Naval Volunteer Force was disbanded. The Mauritius Police is equipped with arms; its strength (including the Special Force) at 31 Aug. 1970 was 2,064 officers and men (establishment: 2,071). The British Garrison left Mauritius on 30 June 1960 after 150 years of service in the island. It was replaced, for purposes of internal security, by the Special Mobile Force with an authorized establishment of 7 officers, 1 medical officer and 320 other ranks.

AGRICULTURE. The area planted with sugar-cane is 204,631 acres. There were (1969) 22 factories in operation and the amount of sugar produced was 22,924 metric tons of white sugar and 645,748 metric tons of raw sugar. 166,160 metric tons of molasses were also produced.

The main secondary crops are tea (8,096 arpents, yielding 3,066 metric tons of tea), tobacco (609 arpents, yielding 442 metric tons of tobacco), aloe (1,873 arpents, yielding 1,294 metric tons of fibre), potato (1,091 arpents, yielding 5,761 metric tons) and onion (455 arpents, yielding 2,037 metric tons of green onions).

(1 arpent = 1·043 acre or 0·422 hectare)

FORESTRY. The total forest area is estimated at approximately 100,000 acres; if scrub and grazing lands are included the total would probably come to 175,000 acres.

In 1969 sales of forest produce from Crown land totalled about 1·36m. cu. ft, worth Rs 0·26m. Free collections of firewood could not be accurately estimated, nor could the production from private lands.

TOURISM. In 1969, 20,587 tourists visited Mauritius, spending about Rs 21m.

LABOUR. There were on 31 Dec. 1969, 105 registered trade unions, including 14 employers' unions, with a total membership of 40,030.

COMMERCE. Total trade in rupees for calendar years:

	1965	1966	1967	1968	1969
Imports[1]	367,278,798	333,220,569	371,081,146	421,101,157	375,964,388
Exports[2]	313,356,535	337,590,514	306,772,377	354,011,977	365,174,327

[1] Excluding bullion and specie.
[2] Including value of sugar quota certificates.

In 1969, 19·8% of the imports came from UK, 8·3% from South Africa and 7·2% from Australia; 71·3% of the exports went to UK, 17·3% to Canada and 5% to USA.

Sugar exports in 1969, 596,187 metric tons (Rs 326,015,300); 1968, 596,048 metric tons (Rs 320,700,659).

Total Trade between Mauritius and UK, in £1,000 sterling (British Board of Trade returns):

	1965	1966	1967	1968	1969	1970
Imports to UK	22,823	21,302	23,222	24,269	21,739	22,495
Exports from UK	7,338	6,212	5,403	5,882	4,813 ⎫	5,899
Re-exports from UK	87	47	29	33	28 ⎭	

SHIPPING. The registered shipping, as at 31 Dec. 1969, consisted of 8 motor vessels (14,185 NRT). In 1969, 1,496 vessels (109 of which were British) of 2,581,773 NRT entered and 1,489 vessels (106 of which were British) of 2,572,332 NRT cleared Mauritius.

ROADS. There are 9·5 miles of motorway, 351 miles of main roads, 369 miles of urban roads and 380 miles of rural roads. All the main urban and rural roads have a bitumen surface. At 31 Dec. 1969 there were 12,442 cars, including 1,331 for public hire, 693 buses and 2,718 motor cycles. 1,097 vehicles were government-owned. Commercial vehicles comprised 3,405 lorries and vans and 666 haulage tractors.

AVIATION. The airport (Plaisance) is operated and managed by the Government. Air France and Air Mauritius operate jointly a scheduled service thrice weekly between Mauritius and Réunion, whence connexions to Madagascar, Europe and elsewhere can be made. BOAC provide a weekly service between London and Mauritius via Nicosia and Nairobi. Lufthansa operate a weekly service between Frankfurt and Mauritius via Cairo, Entebbe, Nairobi and Dar es Salaam. Qantas operate a schedule service twice weekly and South African Airways weekly between Australia and South Africa, the route being Sydney–Mauritius–Johannesburg. South African Airways also operate a weekly service between Durban and Mauritius with a technical stop at Tananarive. East African Airways operate a weekly service London–Mauritius via Nairobi and Dar es Salaam. Air India operates a weekly service between Bombay and

Mauritius. Zambia Airways provide a weekly service between Lusaka and Mauritius *via* Blantyre and Tananarive. No internal services exist.

TELECOMMUNICATIONS. In Dec. 1969 there were 23 telephone exchanges and 16,793 telephone stations. Communication with other parts of the world is established *via* radio links. A radio-telephone service operates with all East African countries and islands, UK, Irish Republic, Israel, USA, Canada, India, Australia, New Zealand, South Africa, Algeria, Morocco, Tunisia, Hawaii and most European countries.

Television was introduced in Feb. 1965.

BANKING. The Bank of Mauritius was established in 1966, with an authorized capital of Rs 10m., to exercise the function of a central bank. There are 6 commercial banks, the Mauritius Commercial Bank Ltd (established 1838), Barclays Bank DCO, the Bank of Baroda Ltd, The Mercantile Bank Ltd, the Mauritius Co-operative Central Bank Ltd, and the Habib Bank (Overseas) Ltd. Other financial institutions include the Mauritius Housing Corporation, the Development Bank of Mauritius and the post office saving bank.

On 30 June 1970 the post office savings bank held deposits amounting to Rs 27,191,269, belonging to 92,000 depositors.

DEPENDENCIES

RODRIGUES (under a Magistrate and Civil Commissioner) is about 350 miles east of Mauritius, 9½ miles long, 4½ miles broad. Area, 40 sq. miles (103·6 sq. km). Population (census 1962), 18,335; estimated population on 31 Dec. 1969, 23,064 (11,332 males; 11,732 females). Imports, 1968, Rs 8,481,064; 1969, Rs 6,605,388. Exports, 1968, Rs 1,298,845; 1969, Rs 1,466,343. There are 2 government, 5 aided primary and 2 private secondary schools.

LESSER DEPENDENCIES. Agalega, St Brandon Group. St Brandon is 250 miles from Mauritius. Total population of the lesser dependencies, census 1962, 1,062. The main exports (to Mauritius) in 1969 were 195 metric tons of salted fish.

In 1965 the Chagos Archipelago was transferred to the newly created colony of British Indian Ocean Territory (*see* Seychelles).

BOOKS OF REFERENCE

STATISTICAL INFORMATION. The Central Statistical Information Office (Rose Hill, Mauritius) was founded in July 1945. *Director:* J. R. M. Etienne, AIS, FSS. Its main publication is the *Bi-annual Digest of Statistics.*

Barnwell, P. J. and Toussaint, A., *A Short History of Mauritius*. London 1949
Brouard, N. R., *A History of Woods and Forests in Mauritius*. Government Printer, 1963
Central Statistical Office, *Population Census of Mauritius and its Dependencies*. 2 vols. 1962.
Fougere, H., *A Survey of the Fisheries of Mauritius*. Government Printer, 1964
Jessop, A., *A History of the Mauritius Government Railways 1864–1964*. Government Printer, 1964
Leys, Colin, *The Development of a University College of Mauritius*. Government Printer, 1964
Lockwood, J. F., *An Examination of the Possibility of Setting up a University College in Mauritius*. London, 1962
Meade, J. E., *The Economic and Social Structure of Mauritius*. Government Printer, 1960
Ministry of Industry, *Handbook of Commerce and Industry*. Port Louis, 1967
Ministry of Information and Broadcasting, *Mauritius at a Glance*. Mauritius Printing, 1969
Napal, D., *Les constitutions de l'ile Maurice*. Port Louis, 1962
Titmuss, R. and Abel-Smith, B., *Social Politics and Population Growth in Mauritius*. London, 1961
Société de l'Historie de l'Ile Maurice. *Dictionnaire de biographie mauricienne*. Port Louis, 1967
Toussaint, A. and Adolphe, H., *Bibliography of Mauritius (1502–1954)*. Port Louis, 1956
The Census of Industrial Production, 1964. Government Printer, 1965
10 annees de realisations. Ministry of Information and Broadcasting, 1967
Annual Report on Mauritius, 1966. Government Printer, 1967

LIBRARY. The Mauritius Institute Public Library, Port Louis

SWAZILAND

HISTORY. The Swazi migrated into the country to which they have given their name, in the last half of the 18th century. They settled first in what is now southern Swaziland, but moved northwards under their chief, Sobhuza—known also to the Swazi as Somhlolo. Sobhuza died in 1838 and was succeeded by Mswati. The further order of succession has been Mbandzeni and Bhunu, whose son, Sobhuza II, was installed as King of the Swazi nation in 1921 after a long minority.

The independence of the Swazis was guaranteed in the conventions of 1881 and 1884 between the British Government and the Government of the South African Republic. In 1890, soon after the death of Mbandzeni, a provisional government was established representative of the Swazis, the British and the South African Republic Governments. In 1894 the South African Republic was given powers of protection and administration. In 1902, after the conclusion of the Boer War, a special commissioner took charge, and under an order-in-council in 1903 the Governor of the Transvaal administered the territory, through the Special Commissioner.

AREA AND POPULATION. Swaziland is bounded on the north, west and south by the Transvaal Province, and on the east by Portuguese territory and Zululand. The area is 6,705 sq. miles (17,400 sq. km).

The country is divided geographically into 4 longitudinal regions running from north to south; 3 of roughly equal width—Highveld (westernmost), Middleveld, Lowveld—and the Lubombo plateau in the east. The mountainous region on the west rises to an altitude of over 6,000 ft (1,800 metres). The Middleveld is mostly between 1,700 and 3,000 ft, while the Lowveld has an average height of not more than 1,000 ft (300 metres). The whole country is now virtually free from malaria. The Highveld and the Middleveld are well watered. Innumerable small streams unite with the large rivers, notably the Usutu and Komati, which traverse the country from west to east. Except for these the Lowveld is not very well watered. The climate is good except for a few months in summer, when the heat is somewhat excessive in low-lying parts.

Population (census 1966), 374,571 (178,795 males, 195,767 females).

GOVERNMENT AND CONSTITUTION. Swaziland became independent on 6 Sept. 1968.

On 25 April 1967 the British Government gave the country internal self-government. It changed the country's status to that of a protected state with the Ngwenyama, Sobhuza II, recognized as King of Swaziland and head of state. Britain's protection ended at independence, when a constitution similar to the 1967 constitution was brought into force. The general elections (by universal adult franchise) in April 1967 gave the royalist and traditional Imbokodvo National Movement all 24 seats. The Parliament consists of a House of Assembly, with 24 elected and 6 nominated members and the Attorney-General, who has no vote, and a Senate comprising 12 members, 6 of whom are elected by the House of Assembly and 6 appointed by the King. The executive authority is vested in the King and exercised through a Cabinet presided over by the Prime Minister, and consisting of the Prime Minister, the Deputy Prime Minister and up to 8 other ministers.

His Majesty the King: Sobhuza II.

Prime Minister: Prince Makhosini.

High Commissioner in London: Nkomeni Douglas Ntiwane.

British High Commissioner: Peter Gautrey, CVO.

Ambassador to USA and High Commissioner to Canada: Dr S. T. M. Sukati, MBE.

LOCAL GOVERNMENT. In Dec. 1963 the former 6 districts were replaced by the 4 districts of Shiselweni, Lubombo, Manzini and Hhohho. They are administered by District Commissioners. The main urban areas are: Mbabane, the administrative capital (population 14,000); Manzini (16,000); Havelock Mine (4,500); Goedgegun (1,700); Stegi (3,600); Pigg's Peak (1,400), Mhlume (2,200) and Big Bend (2,900).

RELIGION. It is estimated that more than 60% of the population is Christian, but no accurate figures are available. The remainder hold traditional beliefs. A large number of churches and missionary societies are established throughout the country and, in addition to evangelism, are doing important work in the fields of education and medicine. In the larger centres there are churches of several denominations—Protestant, Roman Catholics and others.

EDUCATION. In 1968 there were 389 schools with 62,000 pupils in primary classes and 6,000 in secondary classes. The Swaziland Agricultural College and University Centre at Luyengo was opened in Oct. 1966. The college is associated with the University of Botswana, Lesotho and Swaziland, which is in Lesotho. Technical and vocational training classes are run at the Government's Industrial Training Institute and its Staff Training Institute. The Government also operates a police college.

JUSTICE. The judiciary is headed by the Chief Justice. A High Court having full jurisdiction and subordinate courts presided over by Magistrates and District Officers are in existence. During 1968 there were 6,500 convictions in subordinate courts and 37 convictions in the High Court.

There is a Court of Appeal with a President and 3 Judges. It deals with appeals from the High Court.

There are 14 Swazi courts of first instance, 2 Swazi courts of appeal and a Higher Swazi Court of Appeal. The channel of appeal lies from Swazi Court of first instance to Swazi Court of Appeal, to Higher Swazi Court of Appeal, to the Judicial Commissioner and thence to the High Court of Swaziland.

The police force in 1968 had a strength of 38 senior and 163 subordinate officers and 448 other ranks.

FINANCE. Currency The currency in circulation in Swaziland is that of the Republic of South Africa. In Feb. 1961 the territory followed the South African change to a decimal currency (1 Rand = £0·583 sterling).

Budget Revenue and expenditure (in rands) for financial years ending 31 March:

	1964–65	1965–66	1966–67	1967–68	1968–69[1]	1969–70[1]
Revenue	4,402,720	5,796,008	6,804,800	8,565,700	10,625,000	10,976,200
Expenditure	7,539,180	8,578,621	8,650,300	11,344,600	14,917,400	14,627,600
Grant-in-aid from UK	3,278,000	3,020,000	2,400,000	1,760,400	3,291,800	3,256,600

[1] Estimates.

Chief items of estimated revenue, 1969–70: Customs and excise, R2,713,000; income tax, R4·25m.

The public debt expenditure was estimated at R871,800 in 1969–70.

AGRICULTURE. Some 56% of the country, which covers 4,290,944 acres, is reserved for occupation by the Swazi. The main crops are sugar, citrus and rice, all of which are grown under irrigation, and cotton, maize (the staple product), sorghum, tobacco and pineapples. It is usually necessary to import maize from South Africa. Sugar, first produced in 1958, and wood-pulp and other forest products are the two main agricultural exports (worth R7,779,900 and R8,475,400 respectively in 1968).

Livestock (1967): Cattle, 504,523; goats, 235,275; sheep, 35,778; poultry, 343,825.

MINING. Swaziland produces a large tonnage of iron ore from the Ngwenya mine near Mbabane (2,260,200 short tons worth R11,828,400 in 1968) and asbestos from the Havelock Mine (42,900 short tons worth R6,045,700 in 1968). Coal is mined at Mpaka (106,700 short tons worth R249,000 in 1968). Small quantities of quarry stone, kaolin, barytes and pyrophyllite are also mined. Total mineral production was valued in 1966, R15,475,900; 1967, R17,391,000, 1968, R18,277,300.

A railway has been built from the Ngwenya hæmatite deposits to Goba, in Moçambique, chiefly for the transportation of iron ore. The Swaziland Iron Ore Development Company has entered into a contract to supply Japanese buyers with 14·5m. tons of ore over 10 years; first shipments began in Nov. 1964. The extensive deposits of low-volatile bituminous coal in the Lowveld are being worked to provide coal for the railway, sugar-mills and export.

COMMERCE. By agreement with the Republic of South Africa, Swaziland is united in a customs union with the Republic and receives a *pro rata* share of the customs dues collected.

Total exports in 1968 amounted to R42,105,700. The chief items were: Iron ore, R11,828,400; wood-pulp and other forest products, R8,475,400; sugar, R7,779,900; asbestos, R6,045,700; meat and meat products, R2,270,500; citrus, R1,776,300.

Total trade (in £1,000 sterling) of Lesotho, Botswana and Swaziland (from 1967 only Swaziland) with UK (British Board of Trade returns):

	1965	1966	1967	1968	1969	1970
Imports to UK	8,987	10,562	8,454	7,619	9,830	9,411
Exports from UK	453	307	77	245	1,134 }	383
Re-exports from UK	2	11	—	—	1	

COMMUNICATIONS. There is daily (except Sundays) communication by railway motor-buses between Manzini, Mbabane and Breyten; Manzini, Mankaiana and Piet Retief. There are 101 miles of tarred trunk roads, 930 miles of gravelled main road and 470 miles of branch roads. There are 27 post offices, 2 telephone–telegraph agencies and 4 telephone agencies. There were, in 1969, 4,461 telephones in the country.

Swaziland's railway, constructed in 1962–64, is 139 miles long, starting at Kadake, operated by Moçambique State Railways, and connecting at the Moçambique frontier with an extension to the Moçambique State Railways between Lourenço Marques and Goba.

The country's chief airport is at Matsapa. It is served by Swazi Air and South African Airways, connecting with Johannesburg and Durban, and DETA connecting with Lourenço Marques.

BANKING. Barclays Bank DCO and the Standard Bank Ltd maintain branches at Mbabane and Manzini; sub-branches and agencies are operated in 17 other places. Bank rates are those in force throughout South Africa and are prescribed by the main South African offices of the 2 banks. The Swaziland Credit and Savings Bank, a statutory body, was opened in 1965. It specializes in credit for agriculture and low-cost housing. Its head office is in Mbabane and it has branches or agencies at 3 other places.

BOOKS OF REFERENCE

The Kingdom of Swaziland. Swaziland Government Information Services, 1968
Barker, D., *Swaziland.* HMSO, 1965
Holleman, J. F. (ed.), *Experiment in Swaziland: Sample Survey 1960.* OUP, 1964
Kuper, H., *An African Aristocracy.* New ed. London, 1961.—*The Uniform of Colour.* Johannesburg, 1947.—*The Swazi: An Ethnographical Survey.* London, 1952

TONGA
Friendly Islands

HISTORY. The kingdom of Tonga attained unity under Taufa'ahau Tupou (George I) who became ruler of his native Ha'apai in 1820, of Vava'u in 1833 and of Tongatapu in 1845. By 1860 the kingdom had become converted to Christianity (George himself having been baptized in 1831). In 1862 the king granted freedom to the people from arbitrary rule of minor chiefs and gave them the right to the allocation of land for their own needs. These institutional changes, together with the establishment of a parliament of chiefs, paved the way towards the democratic constitution under which the kingdom is now governed, and provided a background of stability against which Tonga was able to develop her agricultural economy.

The kingdom continued up to 1899 to be a neutral region in accordance with the Declaration of Berlin, 6 April 1886. By the Anglo-German Agreement of 14 Nov. 1899, subsequently accepted by the USA, the Tonga Islands were left under the Protectorate of Great Britain. A protectorate was proclaimed on 18 May 1900, and a British Agent and Consul appointed.

AREA AND POPULATION. The kingdom consists of some 150 islands and islets with a total area of 270 sq. miles (700 sq. km; including inland waters), and lies between 15° and 23° 30' S. lat. and 137° and 177° W. long., its western boundary being the eastern boundary of Fiji. The islands are split up into the following groups reading from north to south: The Niuas, Vava'u, Ha'apai, Kotu, Nomuka, Otu Tolu and Tongatapu. The 3 main groups, both from historical and administrative significance, are Tongatapu in the south, Ha'apai in the centre and Vava'u in the north. The Tongatapu group was discovered by Tasman in 1643. The capital is Nuku'alofa on Tongatapu.

The islands to the east, being mostly of limestone formation, are low lying and with but a few exceptions seldom exceed 100 ft above sea-level. The islands to the west are of a volcanic nature, approximately 11, average between 350 and 3,380 ft in height. After a violent volcanic eruption in Sept. 1946 on the island of Niuafo'ou (Tin Can Island to philatelists, so named because of the method that was used of collecting and delivering mail) the 1,300 inhabitants were evacuated, most of them to Tongatapu and 'Eua, but more than 600 have returned since 1958. It was thought that a new island had been born when an eruption took place on the Metis Shoal on 12 Dec. 1967; during the volcanic activity a small rocky mass reached a maximum elevation of about 50 ft, but by Feb. 1968 the area was once more awash.

The climate is mild and healthy, malaria being unknown. The temperature from May to Nov. rarely exceeds 84° F. in the shade, with a minimum temperature of 52° F. Census population at 30 Nov. 1966, 77,429, including 76,121 Tongans, 402 Europeans, 512 Part-Europeans and 394 others.

CONSTITUTION AND GOVERNMENT. Relations between the UK and Tonga have been governed by the 1900 Treaty of Friendship and Protection and several subsequent revisions. For earlier history of this relationship *see* THE STATESMAN'S YEAR-BOOK, 1970–71. By exchange of letters on 19 May 1970 it was agreed that the UK Government should, as from 4 June 1970, cease to have any responsibility for the external relations of the Kingdom of Tonga. On the same date Tonga became a full member of the Commonwealth. The British High Commissioner in New Zealand was appointed concurrently UK High Commissioner (non-resident) in Tonga while the resident British post became that of Deputy High Commissioner. Tonga is represented in London by a High Commissioner.

King: HM King Taufa'ahau Tupou IV, GCVO, KCMG, KBE, born 4 July 1918, succeeded on 16 Dec. 1965 on the death of his mother, Queen Salote; his coronation took place on 4 July 1967.

Premier: HRH Prince Tu'ipelehake, CBE, younger brother of the King.

The present constitution is almost identical with that granted in 1875 by King George Tupou I. There is a Privy Council, Cabinet, Legislative Assembly and Judiciary. The legislative assembly, which meets annually, is composed of 7 nobles elected by their peers, 7 elected representatives of the people and the Privy Councillors (numbering 8); the King appoints one of the 7 nobles to be the Speaker. The elections are held triennially. In 1960, women voted for the first time.

RELIGION. The Tongans are Christian, the vast majority being adherents of the Wesleyan Church.

EDUCATION. The Tongans enjoy free education, free medical attendance and dental treatment. In 1968 there were 79 government and 42 denominational primary schools, with a total of 16,424 pupils. There are 3 government and 58 mission schools at which post-primary education is provided for both boys and girls, with a total roll of 9,421.

JUSTICE. Now that British extra-territorial jurisdiction has lapsed and British and foreign nationals charged with an offence against the laws of Tonga (the enforcement of which is a responsibility of the Minister of Police) are fully subject to the jurisdiction of the Tongan courts to which they are already subject in all civil matters.

FINANCE. Currency. In 1935 the exchange standard system was adopted, based on Australian currency. There is a government note issue of *pa'anga* (T$) 10, 5, 2, 1 and ½ and coin issue of T$1 and *seniti* 50, 20, 10, 5, 2 and 1. The change-over to decimal currency took place on 3 April 1967; the *pa'anga* being at par with the Australian dollar and the *seniti* with the Australian cent. In April 1963 gold coins were issued in denominations of 1, ½ and ¼ *koula* (1 *koula* = T£20) and in July 1967, Coronation Palladium coins of 1, ½ and ¼ *hau* (1 *hau* = T$100).

Budget. Revenue and expenditure in T$1,000:

	1967–68	1968–69	1969–70[1]
Revenue	2,097	2,608	2,513
Expenditure	2,097	2,398	2,725

[1] Estimate.

PLANNING. A 5-year plan 1965–70 has been successfully completed at a total cost of T$5m. The 1970–75 plan will lay greater stress on economic services.

PRODUCTION. Tongan produce consists almost entirely of copra and bananas. Imports in 1968 were valued at T$5,150,440; exports, T$3,846,340, including copra (7,985 tons), T$1,479,069, and bananas (535,856 cases), T$1,734,744.

COMMUNICATIONS. The Union Steamship Co. of New Zealand maintains a bi-monthly service New Zealand–Fiji–Tonga, and cargo steamers visit the group from time to time for shipments of copra. Shipping cleared at Nuku'alofa in 1968 was 270,376 tons; at Vava'u, 16,583 tons; at Ha'apai, 3,244 tons.

There is an air service 4 times a week between Fiji and Tonga by Fiji Airways and twice a week between Western Samoa and Tonga by Polynesian Airlines.

The kingdom has its own issue of postage stamps. Telephones numbered 895 in 1968.

There are no trading banks.

The weights and measures are the same as in Great Britain.

Deputy British High Commissioner: A. C. Reid, CMG, CVO.

BOOKS OF REFERENCE

Biennial Report, 1962–63. HMSO, 1965
Bain, K. R., *Royal Visit to Tonga: Tonga Government Official Record.* London, 1954—*The Friendly Islanders.* London, 1967
Churchward, C. M., *Tongan Dictionary.* London, 1959
Luke, Sir Harry, *Queen Salote and her Kingdom.* London, 1954
Morrell, W. P., *Britain in the Pacific Islands.* OUP, 1960
Neill, J. S., *Ten Years in Tonga.* London, 1955
Wood, A. H., *A History and Geography of Tonga.* Rev. ed. Nuku'alofa, 1963

FIJI

HISTORY. The Fiji Islands were discovered by Tasman in 1643 and visited by Capt. Cook in 1774, but first recorded in detail by Capt. Bligh after the mutiny of the *Bounty* (1789). In the 19th century the search for sandalwood, in which enormous profits were made, brought many ships. Deserters and shipwrecked men stayed on; fire-arms salvaged from wrecks were used in native wars, new diseases swept the islands, and rum and muskets became regular articles of trade. Tribal wars became bloody and general until Fiji was ceded to Britain on 10 Oct. 1874, after a previous offer of cession had been refused. British administrators produced order out of chaos, and since then there has been steady political, social and economic progress.

Governor-General: Sir Robert Foster, GCMG.
Prime Minister: Ratu Sir Kamisese Mara, KBE.

AREA AND POPULATION. Fiji comprises about 844 islands and islets (about 106 inhabited) lying between 15° and 22° S. lat. and 174° E. and 177° W. long. The largest is Viti Levu, area 4,010 sq. miles; next is Vanua Levu, area 2,137 sq. miles. The island of Rotuma (18 sq. miles), about 12° 30′ S. lat., 178° E. long., was added to the colony in 1881. Total area, 7,055 sq. miles (18,272 sq. km).

A population census is taken every 10 years. In Sept. 1966 it was 476,727, comprising 202,176 Fijians (102,479 males, 99,697 females); 240,960 Indians (122,632 males, 118,328 females); 6,590 Europeans (3,427 males, 3,163 females); 9,687 Part Europeans (4,951 males, 4,736 females); 5,149 Chinese (2,910 males, 2,239 females); 5,797 Rotumans (2,939 males, 2,858 females); 6,095 other Pacific Islanders (3,207 males, 2,888 females); 273 others (202 males, 71 females). Estimated population at 31 Dec. 1969 was 513,717.

Suva, the capital, is on the south coast of Viti Levu; census population (1966), 54,157. Suva was proclaimed a city on 2 Oct. 1953.

Vital Statistics, 1969	Euro-peans	Part Euro-peans	Fijians	Indians	Rotu-mans	Other Pacific Islanders	Chinese	Total
Births	185	251	5,854	8,281	180	173	114	15,038
Marriages	65	57	1,480	2,262	51	29	38	3,982
Deaths	42	38	1,011	1,236	32	21	29	2,409

CONSTITUTION AND GOVERNMENT. Fiji became an independent nation with Dominion status within the Commonwealth on 10 Oct. 1970. This had been agreed at a constitutional conference held in London in April 1970. Elections will be held in 1971 for a House of Representatives of 52 members (12 Fijians, 12 Indians and 3 general members elected on communal rolls and 10 Fijians, 10 Indians and 5 general members on national rolls). On national rolls members of all races vote together. The general roll consists of electors who are not eligible for inclusion on the Fijian and Indian rolls. It was agreed that after the elections a Royal Commission would be set up to recommend the appropriate method of election and representation for the future and the terms of reference would be agreed by the Prime Minister and the Leader of the Opposition. There is also an Upper House, the Senate, of 22 members (8 nominations by the Council of Chiefs, 7 by the Prime Minister, 6 by the Leader of the Opposition and 1 by the Rotuma Council).

LOCAL GOVERNMENT. The Fijian Administration, established in 1876, had jurisdiction over all Fijians. This was increased under the terms of the Fijian Affairs Ordinance 1944, which came into operation on 1 Jan. 1945. As a result of recommendations made by the Burns Commission in 1960, the Fijian Administration underwent substantial modifications in 1966 and 1967. The old administrative units called *tikina* have been abolished, with only the provincial or *yasana* administrative unit remaining.

The Colony is now divided into 14 provinces, each with its own council. Elections to these councils in 90 constituencies were conducted for the first time in 1967 on a full adult franchise amongst Fijians.

The councils have wide powers to make by-laws and draw up their own budget subject to confirmation by the Fijian Affairs Board. Each council has its own treasury and levies rates to raise its revenue. These provincial rates vary from £3 to £6 per annum for every male adult, but those maintaining 5 or more children pay lower rates until their children become taxpayers. A start has been made, however, to change over to a system of land rating based upon the unimproved value of Fijian-owned land. This is considered to be more equitable and related to ability to pay.

These newly elected councils held their inaugural and 1968 budget meetings towards the end of 1967, when the chairman for each of these 14 councils was also elected from among its members. Members were elected for 2 years and new elections were held in 1969.

At the apex of the Fijian Administration is the Great Council of Chiefs presided over by the Minister of Fijian Affairs and Local Government. The Council of Chiefs consists of 14 Fijian members of Legislative Council, 30 representatives, elected by the Provincial Councils, 7 representatives nominated by the Minister for Fijian Affairs and Local Government and not more than 7 representatives nominated by the Governor-General.

Fijian courts are being abolished gradually and merged into the magistrates' court.

The Council of Chiefs advises the Government generally on Fijian affairs.

RELIGION. The 1966 census showed: Methodists, 182,193; Roman Catholics, 43,000; Anglican Church, 6,584; Seventh Day Adventists, 6,149; Presbyterians, 1,019; other Christians, 2,116; Hindus, 191,705; Moslems, 37,116; Sikhs, 3,002; Confucians, 174; others, 460. The Methodist Church lists 153,355 adherents, of whom 37,000 are full members; it has 1,281 congregations, 176 ministers (including those retired), 971 catechists and lay pastors and 7,463 lay preachers. The Anglican Church (Province of New Zealand) has a bishop, 33 priests and 2 deacons with 16 churches and 18 meeting places, 7 schools with 49 teachers and 16 lay preachers. The Catholic Mission has an archbishop and 53 European, 12 Fijian, 1 Rotuman, 1 Indian and 2 Chinese priests, 15 European, 2 Indian and 1 Samoan teaching brothers, 96 churches and chapels, 3 training institutions, 208 catechists and teachers. The Seventh Day Adventists have 87 churches, 37 ordained ministers and 48 schoolteachers.

EDUCATION (1969). There were 685 schools, of which 36 were controlled by the Government. The total enrolment (excluding 48 kindergartens and the medical and agricultural schools) was 124,040, of whom 49,482 were Fijians, 66,157 Indians, 3,472 Europeans, 1,535 Chinese and 3,394 others. There were 4,113 teachers, of whom 3,134 were trained. There are also 3 teacher-training colleges and a medical and agricultural school. Total Government expenditure in 1969 was over $5m. (including $400,000 aid from UK). The South Pacific University at Suva was opened in Feb. 1968.

CINEMAS (1970). There were 24 cinemas with a seating capacity of 10,000.

FINANCE. Currency. Fiji changed to decimal currency on 13 Jan. 1969, with the major unit being $1. The securities forming the investment portion of the Note Security Fund were £F4,806,423 in the investment portion and £F565,311 in the Joint Consolidated Fund at 31 Dec. 1968.

The Fiji dollar is linked to sterling by law at the fixed rate of $F209 = £100 sterling; $F1 = US$1·13.

Budget. The financial year corresponds with the calendar year. All figures are in $ Fijian.

	1965	1966	1967	1968	1969	1970
Revenue	25,159,832	23,172,546	28,366,094	32,325,287	31,715,186	36,843,175
Expenditure	23,311,124	23,074,716	29,065,388	30,731,192	32,135,455	35,666,926

The principal sources of revenue in 1969 were (in $F1,000): Customs and port dues, 17.127; taxes and licences, 11,282; court fees, etc., 2,935; post office, 2,627; interest, 895. The public debt on 31 Dec. 1969 was $F35,789,000.

Estimated capital expenditure on development projects which is in addition to recurrent expenditure is estimated at $F11,356,041 in 1970. Capital expenditure for development is financed by grants from Britain, loans and contributions from recurrent revenue. In 1969 capital expenditure was $F9,899,973.

DEFENCE AND POLICE. The Fiji Military Forces Ordinance, 1949, provides for the maintenance of a small regular force, with territorial units and trained reserves.

There is a police force consisting of Fijians and Indians, with European, Indian and Fijian officers. Strength of police force in 1970, 896.

AGRICULTURE. In 1968 there were under cultivation: Bananas, 10,000 acres; coconuts, 179,000 acres; sugar-cane, 131,000 acres; rice, 25,000 acres; pineapples, 500 acres; cocoa, 5,200 acres; tobacco, 1,000 acres; maize, 4,000 acres; water melons, 800 acres. There were 135,000 cattle, 66,000 goats, 24,000 pigs, 25,000 horses and 390,000 poultry in 1968.

FORESTRY. The total forest area amounts to about 3,600 sq. miles, but only about 30% is commercially productive. The annual planting programme rose from 498 acres in 1960 to 4,813 acres in 1969, when the total area under plantations of mahogany and pine was 30,520 acres.

At the end of 1968, 68 saw-mills were registered. Total log production was 35·3m.; Hoppus super feet yielding 21·7m. super ft of sawn timber.

INDUSTRY. Major industries include 4 large sugar-mills, the goldmines (95,346 fine oz. in 1969) and 3 mills which process copra into coconut oil and coconut meal. There is a great variety of light industries.

TRADE UNIONS. There were 32 trade unions and 32 industrial associations registered at the end of 1969.

COMMERCE. Exports in 1969 included: Sugar, 316,000 tons ($F28,134,000); coconut oil, 17,100 tons ($F3,909m.); gold, 95,000 fine oz. ($F3,361,000); bananas, 6·5m. lb. ($F289,000); coconut meal, 8,000 tons ($384,000).

Total trade (in $F) in calendar years:

	1965	1966	1967	1968	1969
Imports	58,162,038	50,444,000	56,290,778	68,402,000	77,900,000
Exports	42,530,434	38,874,000	42,661,110	49,118,000	43,548,000

Balance of trade deficits in recent years have been more than offset by gross receipts from tourism, amounting to $F20m. in 1969 and substantial inflows of capital.

Imports in 1969 (in $F1,000) from Australia were 19,654; Japan, 11,059; New Zealand, 7,265; USA, 3,690; Hong Kong, 2,804; India, 1,376.

Exports in 1969 (in $F1,000) to UK were 18,419; USA, 8,357; Australia, 5,483; Canada, 4,938; New Zealand, 2,921; Japan, 1,896.

Total trade between Fiji and UK (British Board of Trade returns, in £1,000 sterling):

	1965	1966	1967	1968	1969	1970
Imports to UK	9,446	8,456	9,039	9,118	11,727	10,206
Exports from UK	4,590	3,886	3,506	6,136	5,836 ⎱	6,083
Re-exports from UK	24	26	23	33	44 ⎰	

ROADS. There is a principal highway round Viti Levu, the distance from Suva to Lautoka *via* Ra, Tavua and Ba (King's Road) being 166 miles and *via* Navua and Sigatoka and Nadi (Queen's Road) being 156 miles. Branch roads run 34 miles along the Sigatoka Valley, 18 miles to Nadarivatu and Navai, 5½ miles to Vatukoula Goldfields, 35 miles to Serea and 7 miles to Vunidawa.

On Vanua Levu highways are in the neighbourhood of Labasa (Nasea) and Nasavusavu (Valeci). There are highways, 92 miles south and 36 miles west of Labasa. A highway extends to Buca Bay, 45 miles east of Nasavusavu. Coastal roads connect villages and plantations on parts of the islands of Taveuni and Ovalau.

Total road mileage is 1,439, of which 1,245 are all-weather roads.

RAILWAY. There is a private 2-ft-gauge railway (South Pacific Sugar Mills Railway) of 362 miles from Tavua to Sigatoka serving most of the sugar-cane producing area.

SHIPPING. On 31 July 1970, 113 vessels of 2,914 net tons were registered with the Fiji Marine Board. Suva has 4 slipways of 100, 200, 500 and 1,000 tons, and there are 3 shipbuilding and repair firms.

AVIATION. Fiji provides an essential staging point for long-haul trunk-route aircraft operating between North America, Australia and New Zealand. Under the South Pacific Air Transport Council, which comprises the United Kingdom, Australia, New Zealand and Fiji, the international airport at Nadi has been developed and administered. Four other airports are in use for domestic services.

Long-haul services touching Nadi airport are operated by PANAM (USA, Honolulu, Sydney), Air New Zealand (Auckland, Pago Pago, Honolulu, Los Angeles), Qantas (Sydney, Honolulu, San Francisco; Sydney, Tahiti. Mexico), Union de Transports Aériens (Sydney, Nouméa, Tahiti, Los Angeles), Canadian Pacific Airlines (Vancouver, Honolulu, Auckland, Sydney), Air India (Perth, Sydney), BOAC (Sydney–London and USA–London) and American Airlines (West Coast US–Sydney, Auckland).

Domestic and regional services are operated by Fiji Airways (Tonga, New Hebrides, Solomon Islands, Gilbert and Ellice Islands, Western Samoa) and Polynesian Airlines (Western Samoa).

POST. There are 156 post offices and agencies. Overseas postal communications are excellent. There is a daily air service to the major countries of the world and frequent dispatches by sea to UK, Australia, New Zealand and North America. Overseas telephone and telegram services are available through the Commonwealth cable to most countries except those in the South Pacific, which are served by direct radio circuits. The automatic telex network operates through New Zealand into the international telex system. There are ship-to-shore radio facilities. There were 16,567 telephones in 1970.

BANKING. The Bank of New South Wales has 5 branches and 8 agencies, and the Bank of New Zealand has 5 branches and 5 agencies and the Australia and New Zealand Bank has 2 branches and 3 agencies and the Bank of Baroda has 3 branches and 3 agencies in Fiji.

The post office savings bank had, at the end of 1969, deposits amounting to $F4,717,154 due to 144,852 accounts. The headquarters are at the General Post Office, Suva, and there are 60 branches throughout Fiji.

WEIGHTS AND MEASURES are the same as in the UK.

BOOKS OF REFERENCE

STATISTICAL INFORMATION. A Government Statistical Office was set up in 1950 (Government Buildings, Suva). *Government Statistician:* A. M. Sahib.
Annual Report, 1968. HMSO, 1968
Trade Report. Annual (from 1887 [covering 1883–86]). Suva
Journal of the Fiji Legislative Council. Annual (from 1914 [under different title from 1885]). Suva
Fiji Information. Annually. Suva
Report of Commission of Inquiry into natural resources and population trends in Fiji. Suva, Government Press, 1960
Ashford, J. E., *Social Security in Fiji.* Suva Government Press, 1964
Burns, Sir Alan, *Fiji.* HMSO, 1963
Capell, A., *New Fijian Dictionary.* 2nd ed. Glasgow, 1957
France, P., *The Charter of the Land.* OUP, 1969
Luke, Sir H., *The Islands of the South Pacific.* London, 1962
Roth, G. K., *The Fijian Way of Life.* Melbourne, 1954
Sahlins, M. D., *Moala: culture and nature on a Fijian island.* Univ. of Michigan Press, 1962
Spate, O. H. K., *The Fijian People: economic problems and prospects.* Suva, Government Press, 1959
Ward. R. G., *Land use and population in Fiji.* HMSO, 1965
Watters, R. F., *Koro: Economic Development and Social Change in Fiji.* OUP, 1969

RHODESIA

GOVERNMENT. Prior to Oct. 1923 Southern Rhodesia, like Northern Rhodesia, was under the administration of the British South Africa Company. In Oct. 1922 Southern Rhodesia voted in favour of responsible government. On 12 Sept. 1923 the country was formally annexed to His Majesty's Dominions, and on 1 Oct. 1923 government was established under a governor, assisted by an executive council, and a legislature.

The government proposals for a new constitution were endorsed by 41,949 votes against 21,846 at a referendum on 26 July 1961.

By an Order in Council dated 6 Dec. 1961, Southern Rhodesia was granted the new constitution. Under this the Legislative Assembly consists of 65 members—50 on the upper roll and 15 on the lower roll, thus ensuring African representation. Most of the reserved rights of the UK are replaced by a Declaration of Rights, a Constitutional Council and other safeguards.

After the dissolution of the Federation of Rhodesia and Nyasaland on 31 Dec. 1963 Southern Rhodesia reverted to the status of a self-governing colony within the Commonwealth, but, at the same time, became responsible for several functions of government which hitherto had been exercised by the Federal Government. These included agriculture (European), defence, education (Non-African), external affairs, health services, taxation and other fiscal responsibilities, posts, trade, transport and power.

The Legislative Assembly, elected on 7 May 1965, consisted in Oct. 1968 of 50 Rhodesian Front, 10 United People's Party, 3 independents and 2 Democratic Party.

Ian Smith, Prime Minister from 14 April 1964, had discussions about independence in London with the Prime Ministers, Sir Alec Douglas-Home (7–8 Sept. 1964) and Harold Wilson (4–11 Oct. 1965); and in Salisbury with the Prime Minister, the Commonwealth Secretary and the Attorney-General (25–30 Oct.1965).

On 5 Nov. 1965 Prime Minister Smith declared a state of emergency, overriding normal constitutional safeguards. After abortive appeals by Prime Minister Wilson (10–11 Nov.) the Smith government issued a unilateral declaration of independence on 11 Nov. Thereupon the Governor dismissed Smith and his cabinet. The British Government reasserted its own formal responsibility for Rhodesia, excluded Rhodesia from Commonwealth preference in trade and from the sterling area; and had an enabling bill passed by Parliament on 15 Nov., which gave the Government power to deal with the situation by Orders-in-Council. Effective internal government was nevertheless carried on by the Smith cabinet.

The United Nations Security Council on 20 Nov. called upon all member states to break off economic relations with Rhodesia. Only Portugal and the Republic of South Africa did not impose an embargo, which from 17 Dec. also included oil.

In Sept. 1966 the conference of the Commonwealth Prime Ministers urged the British Government to approach the United Nations with a view to imposing mandatory selective sanctions, unless Rhodesia returned to legality by the end of 1966. From 1 to 3 Dec. Prime Minister Wilson, the Commonwealth Secretary, the Attorney-General, the Governor and the Chief Justice of Rhodesia met Mr Smith and a colleague of his on board HMS *Tiger*. They drafted a 'Working Document' on the procedure for progress towards legal independence on the basis of the 1961 Constitution and the so-called 'six principles'. This statement was approved by the British cabinet on 4 Dec., but rejected by the Smith régime on 5 Dec. As a result the British Government approached the United Nations and on 16 Dec. 1966 the Security Council voted for mandatory sanctions including oil; France and USSR abstained.

Further talks based on the *Tiger* proposals were held between the British and Rhodesian Prime Ministers aboard HMS *Fearless* at Gibraltar on 10–13 Oct. 1968. On 2 March 1970 the Smith régime declared Rhodesia a 'republic' and adopted a new 'constitution'. Parliament was dissolved and elections were announced for 10 April. The British Government stated on 3 March 1970 that 'The purported assumption of a republican status by the régime in Southern Rhodesia is, like the 1965 declaration of independence itself, illegal.'

AREA AND POPULATION. Rhodesia is situated between the northern border of the Transvaal and the Zambezi River and is bordered on the east by Portuguese East Africa and on the west by the republic of Botswana. The area is 150,820 sq. miles (390,622 sq. km). The growth of the population is given in the following table:

	European (census)			Asiatic and Coloured	African total (estimated)	Total population (estimated)
	Males	Females	Total			
1911	15,580	8,026	23,606	2,912	745,000	772,000
1931	27,280	27,630	49,910	4,102	1,076,000	1,130,000
1941	36.615	32,339	68,954	6,521	1,404,000	1,479,000
1951	71,307	64,289	135,596	10,283	2,170,000	2,320,000
1961	111,720	109,784	221,504	17,812	3,618,150[1]	3,857,466
1969[2]	116,140	112,440	228,580	23,870	4,840,000	5,090,000

[1] Actual Census, April–May 1962.   [2] Preliminary results.

Census (1969) population of main urban areas:

	Europeans	Africans	Others
Salisbury	96,420	280,090	8,020
Bulawayo	50,090	187,590	7,910
Umtali	8,340	36,220	1,950
Que Que	3,160	29,250	450
Gwelo	8,390	36,880	760
Gatooma	1,880	18,770	310
Fort Victoria	2,530	8,470	350
Shabani	1,560	14,170	80
Wankie	2,160	17,980	—

VITAL STATISTICS (European):

	1963	1964	1965	1966	1967	1968	1969
Births	4,457	4,017	3,863	3,782	4,031	4,004	4,089
Marriages[1]	2,008	2,046	2,071	2,135	...	...	...
Deaths	1,449	1,306	1,369	1,460	1,512	1,646	1,633
Immigrants	5,093	7,000	11,128	6,418	9,618	11,864	10,929

[1] Including Asians and Coloured.

In 1969 the birth rate was 18 per 1,000, the crude death rate 7 per 1,000 and infant mortality 18 per 1,000 for Europeans. Figures for Africans were estimated as follows: births, 48 per 1,000; deaths, 14 per 1,000.

In 1969, 5,890 Europeans left the country and 10,929 Europeans immigrated.

INTERNAL AFFAIRS. In 1962 the Ministry of Internal Affairs took over all functions performed by the then Department of Native Affairs, except in the field of agriculture which was taken over by the Ministry of Agriculture and the administration of Native Purchase Areas which was taken over by the Ministry of Mines and Lands. The Ministry of Internal Affairs is responsible for district and general government administration and the development of the Tribal Trust Land. The land areas previously known as Native Reserves and Special Native Areas have been reclassified as Tribal Trust Land and are set aside entirely for African occupation. In 1969 the Ministry of Internal Affairs took control of development of African agriculture. On 2 March 1970 the Land Tenure Act came into effect and distribution of land was:

	Acres (in 1m.)
European Area	44·95
African Area	44·95
National Area [1]	6·60

[1] Reservered for Wild Life Conservation and National Parks.

All judicial functions (excluding Native Customary Law civil cases) previously performed by the Department of Native Affairs has been transferred to the Ministry of Justice. The Ministry of Internal Affairs is responsible for the supervision of the Government's policy of community development.

African Councils, formed for communities wanting to become responsible for local government, may be authorized to provide services, facilities and amenities and establish and maintain any undertaking for the benefit of the area. Councils have powers to impose rates on adults in the area in regard to stock or buildings and on the value of any land and grazing right.

There are 76 established African Councils which, in general, meet at monthly intervals.

RELIGION. The largest religious groups are the Anglicans with 86,000 members (36% of the non-African population), the Presbyterians with 29,000 members (12%) and the Roman Catholics with 35,500 (15%). There are no accurate figures for Africans.

EDUCATION. On 1 Jan. 1964 Rhodesia assumed responsibility for all education services which were under the control of the Federal Government. For administrative reasons the educational system of the country was divided between Africans and Non-Africans, and separate ministries were charged with the responsibility for the educational needs of these two groups. At present all educational services are under one ministry.

Total Government expenditure on education for the financial year 1970–71 is estimated at R$34·66m.

African Education. The total enrolment of African pupils for 1970 was 703,729. There were 3,217 primary schools, 97 senior and 11 junior secondary schools, 6 special schools for the physically handicapped, 96 aided farm schools, 469 self-help primary schools, 9 homecraft schools, 60 part-time classes and 122 study groups and 20 teacher-training schools. Approximately 90% of African children between the ages of 6 and 16 receive a minimum of 5 years primary education, and half of them 8 years.

Non-African Education. The total enrolment of Non-African pupils for 1969 was 64,478 in 236 schools.

Higher Education. The University College of Rhodesia provided facilities for higher education under which students could obtain London University degrees and Birmingham medical degrees and in 1970 plans to achieve full university status. In 1970 the total enrolment of students was 937, including 363 Africans.

HEALTH. 123 hospitals, clinics and health centres are operated by the Ministry of Health; 72 hospitals and clinics are operated by medical missions with government grants-in-aid and 32 without government grants. There is one medical practitioner for every 9,300 inhabitants in Rhodesia and there are 3 hospital beds per 1,000 of the population.

SOCIAL WELFARE. The Children's Protection and Adoption Act provides for the establishment of juvenile courts, the protection, welfare and supervision of children and juveniles; the establishment of corrective institutions and the treatment therein; the recognition, registration and inspection of certified institutions for the reception and custody of juveniles; for the adoption of minors and other matters. Administrative procedures make provision for public assistance and certain grants-in-aid.

JUSTICE. The High Court consists of an appellate division and a general division. The appellate division consists of the Chief Justice, the Judge President and at least one other judge of appeal. The general division consists of the Chief Justice and 5 puisne judges. The appellate division considers appeals from the general division and the lower courts; the general division has full jurisdiction, civil and criminal, over all persons and matters within Rhodesia. The Chief Justice is the head of the judiciary of Rhodesia. The Judge President presides over the appellate division in the absence of the Chief Justice. The Courts sit at Salisbury and Bulawayo, and sittings of the general division are held at 3 other principal towns three times a year.

Regional Courts, established in Salisbury and Bulawayo, are intermediate in jurisdiction between the magistrates courts and the High Court, but have no civil jurisdiction. There are 19 principal courts of magistrates and 64 periodical courts presided over by magistrates.

African Courts have jurisdiction over African persons in civil matters which are decided in accordance with African law and custom.

FINANCE. Currency. On 17 Feb. 1970 decimal currency was adopted. The unit of currency is the Rhodesian dollar which is worth 10 Rhodesian shillings.

Budget. Revenue and expenditure (in £1,000 until 1967–68 then R$1,000) for years ending 30 June:

	1965–66	1966–67	1967–68	1968–69	1969–70[1]	1970–71[1]
Revenue	73,982	78,327	82,606	184,065	198,470	158,280
Ordinary expenditure:						
From revenue funds	72,784	73,829	71,421⎫	187,972	206,758	215,715
From loan funds	21,249	26,255	22,769⎭			

[1] Estimate.

Receipts during the year ended 30 June 1969 were (in R$1,000): Income and super tax and undistributed profits tax, 70,167; personal tax, 4,653; customs and excise, 31,659; stamp duties and fees, 3,035; vehicle tax, 4,523; sales tax, 13,286.

Principal items of expenditure from revenue funds were (in R$1,000): Agriculture, 17,396, interest payments, 24,320; African education, 16,347; pensions, 8,539; justice, 1,495; local government and housing, 2,213; posts, 9,001; health, 13,824; treasury, 3,369.

The gross amount of the public debt outstanding in June 1969 was R$595·8m.

DEFENCE. Army. The Rhodesia Army consists of (a) the Regular Force, (b) the territorial force, (c) the Class A and B Reserves, together with the appropriate ancillary units. Control is effected through the Army Headquarters (established in Salisbury and Bulawayo). Attached to each brigade is one regular battalion and also battalions of the territorial force. In addition, there are 6 reserve battalions and an artillery regiment of the territorial force and the various supporting units necessary for an independent command. The Regular Army consists of approximately 3,400 officers and other ranks. The Territorial Force (including the Reserve) totals approximately 8,400.

Air Force. The Rhodesian Air Force (regular) has 1 squadron of Canberra bombers, 2 squadrons of Hunter Mk. 9 and Vampire fighter-bombers, a reconnaissance squadron of T.52 (armed) Provosts, a transport support squadron equipped with Dakota and Aermacchi AL-60 aircraft, and a squadron of Alouette III helicopters. Headquarters RAF and New Sarum RAF station, at which are based the transport and reconnaissance squadrons, are in Salisbury. The fighter and bomber squadrons and the training organization are based at Thornhill, Gwelo. Total strength is about 900 men and 75 aircraft.

NATURAL RESOURCES. The Natural Resources Board, set up in 1941, is the trustee of the natural resources of Rhodesia. The resources are defined as the soil, water and minerals, the animals, bird and fish life; the trees, grasses and other vegetation; the springs, marshes, swamps and public streams; other features the President may proclaim as natural resources such as landscapes and scenery. The principal executive bodies are the Conservation Area Committees of which there were 175 in 1967, covering the whole of the European farming area and about 77% of the African Purchase Areas. In the Tribal Trust Areas the Board had established 9 Tribal Trust Land Committees by 1967.

AGRICULTURE. The most important single food crop in Rhodesia is maize, the staple food of a large proportion of the population; production in 1966 was 6,631,000 bags (of 200 lb.). The livestock industry is second to tobacco as regards its export potential. Dairying forms the foundation of many mixed farms. The annual production of milk is approximately 23m. gallons.

Fish farming is being developed and large catches are taken from Lake Kariba, where a fish freezing plant was completed in 1964.

Sugar is being produced in the Triangle and Hippo Valley estates (2·9m. tons of cane from 59,200 acres in 1966).

The citrus estates of the British South Africa Company, the state-owned deciduous orchards at Inyanga and a scheme for large-scale citrus growing at Hippo Valley form the basis of the citrus fruit industry in Rhodesia. However, many parts of the country between 2,500 and 4,000 ft above sea-level are suitable for citrus culture, and large numbers of deciduous fruit trees planted in the Melsetter and Inyanga areas are coming into production.

In 1966 cotton production was 48·6m. lb. and irrigated wheat production amounted to 98,000 bags (of 200 lb.).

Rhodesia has 7 large tea plantations, 2 of which are in the Inyanga district and 5 in Chipinga; production in 1966 was 2,500 short tons. Other crops grown in substantial quantities include small grains (sorghums and millet), rice, groundnuts, cassava. These crops form the basis of much subsistence farming undertaken by the African population.

Tobacco is the most important single product, amounting to about half the total agricultural output (by value). In 1965 tobacco accounted for £32·6m. out of a total agricultural output of £66·5m. In 1965–66, 201,730 acres yielded 244,291,000 lb. of Virginia-type tobacco.

Livestock (1968): European, 1·64m. cattle; African, 2·5m. cattle.

MINING. The total value of all minerals produced in 1965 was £31,944,113. Output (in 1,000 tons) and value (in £1,000):

	Output			Value		
	1963	1964	1965	1963	1964	1965
Asbestos	142·3	153·4	176·1	5,996·8	6,849	8,525
Gold (1,000 oz.)	566·3	574·4	549·6	7,101·2	7,228	6,895
Chrome ore	412·4	493·3	645·5	1,895·0	2,219	2,624
Coal	3,021·0	3,047·0	3,868·3	3,077·6	3,431	3,872
Copper	18·5	18·3	19·8	3,233·6	4,156	6,283

INDUSTRIES. Manufacturing industries are becoming increasingly important and have been stimulated by the abrogation of the Customs Convention with the Union in 1955 and the substitution of a trade agreement. In 1964 agriculture formed 21·9% and industry 16·9% of the total economy. Industry employed 697,000 Africans and 99,500 Europeans, Coloured and Asians in 1969.

TOURISM. In 1969, 299,697 tourists visited Rhodesia.

LABOUR. In 1969 the monthly average of Non-Africans in employment was 99,500 and of Africans, 697,000. Largest employers of African labour were agriculture (267,300), manufacturing (92,600), construction (41,100), mining (50,400) and domestic service (105,500).

The conditions of service for all workers in all industries other than agriculture and private domestic service are negotiated through the 27 Industrial Councils and the 54 Industrial Boards established under the Industrial Conciliation Act. The training, including full-time technical training, and conditions of employment for apprentices are determined by Apprenticeship Committees established in terms of the Apprenticeship Act. There is a system of national employment exchanges including youth employment and careers advisory services.

Workmen's compensation is by compulsory insurance through a Government established fund. Health and safety in industry is safeguarded through the Factories and Works Act.

COMMERCE. The leading commodities exported from Rhodesia are tobacco, asbestos, copper, clothing, meat, chrome ore, sugar, pig-iron and coal. Statistics (in £ sterling until 1968 and then Rhodesian dollars) for the Federation (1963) and Rhodesia (from 1964):

	1965	1966	1967	1968	1969
Imports	119,789,362	84,707,000	93,526,000	103,524,000	199,426,000
Exports	142,455,000	89,029,000	88,361,000	91,734,000	226,904,000

Total imports of merchandise in 1965 from UK amounted to £36·36m.; from the Republic of South Africa, £27·46m.; from USA, £8·2m. Domestic exports to UK were £31·15m.; to the Republic of South Africa, £12·8m.

Principal exports in 1965: Copper, £6,056,240; tobacco, £46,968,149; asbestos, £10,761,271; chrome ore, £3,809,799; coal, £2,222,679; ferrochrome, £1,690,620; pig-iron, £2,472,537; sugar, £3,482,485; meat, £4,227,722; meat preparations, £2,523,107; clothing, £5,417,452.

Total trade between Rhodesia and UK (in £1,000 sterling; British Board of Trade returns):

	1966	1967	1968	1969	1970
Imports to UK	4,575	147	90	68	49
Exports from UK	2,685	1,041	809	810 }	503
Re-exports from UK	34	2	2	6 }	

COMMUNICATIONS. The Minister of Transport and Power is responsible for the Government's relations with the Rhodesia Railways and with the Air Rhodesia Corporation.

Shipping. Rhodesia outlets to the sea are the Moçambique ports of Beira and Lourenço Marques.

Railways. Rhodesia is served by the Rhodesia Railways, which connect with the South African Railways to give access to the South African ports; with the Moçambique Railways to give access to the ports of Beira and Lourenço Marques; and with the Zambia railway system. The total mileage was 2,037 in June 1968. In 1968–69 Rhodesia Railways carried 11·9m. tons of freight and 2·9m. passengers.

Roads. Main roads connect all the main centres of the country with one another and with adjacent territories, and secondary roads serve rural areas. The total mileage of surfaced roads maintained by the central government was 5,259 and a further 43,248 miles of secondary roads are maintained by local councils in 1969.

Number of motor vehicles excluding military (Oct. 1966) in Rhodesia: Private cars, 109,408; commercial vehicles (excluding farm tractors), 32,515.

Aviation. The Air Rhodesia Corporation, in association with Central African Airways, South African Airways, Air Malawi and DETA, operates regular scheduled services to Malawi, Mauritius, Moçambique and South Africa. In 1969–70 the Corporation flew 153·27m. passenger-miles.

Post. At 1 Jan. 1969 there were 116,973 telephones in Rhodesia; at June 1969 127,738 radio licences and 42,309 combined radio and television licences.

BANKING. The Reserve Bank of Rhodesia is the country's central bank; it became operative when the Bank of Rhodesia and Nyasaland ceased operations on 1 June 1965. It acts as banker to the Government and to the commercial banks and as agent of the Government for important financial operations. It is also the central note-issuing authority and co-ordinates the application of the Government's monetary policy. The British Government dismissed the governor and directors on 3 Dec. 1965 and appointed a new board in London.

The post office savings bank had R$70m. deposits at 30 June 1970.

The leading banks are Barclays Bank DCO, National Overseas & Grindlays Bank, Netherlands Bank of Rhodesia, Standard Bank Ltd.

BOOKS OF REFERENCE

STATISTICAL INFORMATION, The Central Statistical Office, PO Box 8063, Causeway, Salisbury, Rhodesia, originated in 1927 as the Southern Rhodesian Government Statistical Bureau. Ten years later its name was changed to Department of Statistics, and in 1948 it assumed its present title when it took over responsibility for certain Northern Rhodesian and Nyasaland statistics (which it relinquished in Dec. 1963 on the dissolution of the Federation). It publishes *Monthly Digest of Statistics*.

Rhodesia: Documents relating to proposals for a settlement, 1966. (Cmd. 171) HMSO, 1966
Collins, M. O. (ed.), *Rhodesia: its natural resources and economic development.* London, 1966
Cann, L. H., *A history of Southern Rhodesia to 1934.* London, 1965
Gray, R., and Gelfand, L. H., *Huggins of Rhodesia.* London, 1964
Hanna, A. J., *The Story of the Rhodesias and Nyasaland.* 2nd ed. London, 1965
Howarth, D., *The Shadow of the Dam: The Story of Lake Kariba.* London, 1961
Lardner-Burke, D., *Rhodesia: The Story of the Crisis.* London, 1966
Palley, C., *The Constitutional History and Law of Southern Rhodesia, 1888–1965.* OUP, 1966
Rayner, W., *The Tribe and its successors: an account of traditional life and European settlement in Southern Rhodesia,* London, 1962
Wills, A. J., *An Introduction to the history of Central Africa.* 2nd ed. OUP, 1967
Young, K., *Rhodesia and Independence.* London, 1969

REFERENCE LIBRARY. National Archives of Rhodesia. PO Box 8043, Causeway, Salisbury.

PART III

THE UNITED STATES OF AMERICA

UNITED STATES OF AMERICA

GOVERNMENT

The Declaration of Independence of the 13 states of which the American Union then consisted was adopted by Congress on 4 July 1776. On 30 Nov. 1782 Great Britain acknowledged the independence of the USA, and on 3 Sept. 1783 the treaty of peace was concluded and was ratified by the USA on 14 Jan. 1784.

Constitution. The form of government of the USA is based on the constitution of 17 Sept. 1787.

By the constitution the government of the nation is composed of three co-ordinate branches, the executive, the legislative and the judicial.

The National Government has authority in matters of general taxation, treaties and other dealings with foreign Powers, foreign and inter-state commerce, bankruptcy, postal service, coinage, weights and measures, patents and copyright, the armed forces (including, to a certain extent, the militia), and crimes against the USA; it has sole legislative authority over the District of Columbia and the possessions of the US.

The 5th article of the constitution provides that Congress may, on a two-thirds vote of both houses, propose amendments to the constitution, or, on the application of the legislatures of two-thirds of all the states, call a convention for proposing amendments, which in either case shall be valid as part of the constitution when ratified by the legislatures of three-fourths of the several states, or by conventions in three-fourths thereof, whichever mode of ratification may be proposed by Congress. Ten amendments (called collectively 'the Bill of Rights') to the constitution were added 15 Dec. 1791; two in 1795 and 1804; a 13th amendment, 6 Dec. 1865, abolishing slavery; a 14th in 1868, including the important 'due process' clause; a 15th, 3 Feb. 1870, establishing equal voting rights for white and coloured; a 16th, 3 Feb. 1913, authorizing the income tax; a 17th, 8 April 1913, providing for popular election of senators; an 18th, 16 Jan. 1919, prohibiting alcoholic liquors; a 19th, 18 Aug. 1920, establishing woman suffrage; a 20th, 23 Jan. 1933, advancing the date of the President's and Vice-President's inauguration and abolishing the 'lame-duck' sessions of Congress; a 21st, 5 Dec. 1933, repealing the 18th amendment; a 22nd, 26 Feb. 1951, limiting a President's tenure of office to 2 terms, or to 2 terms plus 2 years in the case of a Vice-President who has succeeded to the office of a President; a 23rd, 30 March 1961, granting citizens of the District of Columbia the right to vote in national elections; a 24th, 4 Feb. 1964, banning the use of the poll-tax in federal elections; a 25th, 10 Feb. 1967, dealing with Presidential disability and succession.

National flag: Seven red and 6 white alternating stripes, horizontal; with a blue canton, extending down to the lower edge of the 4th red stripe from the top, and displaying 50 white 5-pointed stars, one for each state. The stars have one point directed vertically upward, and they are arranged in 6 rows of 5 each, alternating with 5 rows of 4 each. On the admission of additional states, stars are added, effective on 4 July following the date of admission. Congress, by law of 22 Dec. 1942, has codified 'existing rules and customs' pertaining to the display of the flag, for civilians.

National anthem: The Star-spangled Banner, 'Oh say, can you see by the dawn's early light' (words by F. S. Key, 1814; tune by J. S. Smith; formally adopted by Congress 3 March 1931).

National motto: 'In God we trust'; formally adopted by Congress 30 July 1956.

Presidency. The executive power is vested in a president, who holds office for 4 years, and is elected, together with a vice-president chosen for the same term, by electors from each state, equal to the whole number of senators and representatives to which the state may be entitled in the Congress. The President must be a natural-born citizen, resident in the country for 14 years, and at least 35 years old.

The presidential election is held every fourth (leap) year on the Tuesday after the first Monday in November. Technically, this is an election of presidential electors, not of a president directly; the electors thus chosen meet and give their votes (for the candidate to whom they are pledged, in some states by law, but in most states by custom and prudent politics) at their respective state capitals on the first Monday after the second Wednesday in December next following their election; and the votes of the electors of all the states are opened and counted in the presence of both Houses of Congress on the sixth day of January. The total electorate vote is one for each senator and representative.

If the successful candidate for President dies before taking office the Vice-President-elect becomes President; if no candidate has a majority or if the successful candidate fails to qualify, then, by the twentieth amendment, the Vice-President acts as President until a president qualifies. The duties of the Presidency, in absence of the President and Vice-President by reason of death, resignation, removal, inability or failure to qualify, devolve upon the Speaker of the House under legislation enacted 18 July 1947. And in case of absence of a Speaker for like reason, the presidential duties devolve upon the President *pro tem.* of the Senate and successively upon those members of the Cabinet in order of precedence, who have the constitutional qualifications for President.

The presidential term, by the 20th amendment to the constitution, begins at noon on 20 Jan. of the inaugural year. This amendment also instals the newly elected Congress in office of 3 Jan. instead of—as formerly—in the following December. The President's salary is $200,000 per year, plus $50,000 to assist in defraying expenses resulting from official duties. Also $40,000 non-taxable for travel and official entertainment. The office of Vice-President carries a salary of $62,500, plus $10,000 allowance for travel.

The President is C.-in-C. of the Army, Navy and Air Force, and of the militia when in the service of the Union. The Vice-President is *ex-officio* President of the Senate, and in the case of 'the removal of the President, or of his death, resignation, or inability to discharge the powers and duties of his office', he becomes the President for the remainder of the term.

President of the United States: Richard Milhous Nixon, of California, born at Yorba Linda, California, 9 Jan. 1913; Lieut.-Cmdr, US Naval Reserve, 1942–46; member, House of Representatives, 1946–51; Senator, 1951–52; Vice-President of the USA, 1952–61; Presidential candidate in 1960 elections. Unsuccessfully stood for Governorship of California in 1962. In legal practice, 1960–68.

At the Presidential election on 5 Nov. 1968 total vote cast, including men and women in the armed services, was 73,186,819, of which Richard M. Nixon (R.) received 31,770,237 (43·4%) (302 electoral college votes), while Hubert H. Humphrey (D.) received 31,270,533 (42·7%) (191 electoral college votes) and George C. Wallace (Ind.) received 9,906,141 (0·4%) (45 electoral college votes); others 239,908. Votes cast represented approximately 60% of the total registered vote.

PRESIDENTS OF THE USA

Name	From state	Term of service	Born	Died
George Washington	Virginia	1789–97	1732	1799
John Adams	Massachusetts	1797–1801	1735	1826
Thomas Jefferson	Virginia	1801–09	1743	1826
James Madison	Virginia	1809–17	1751	1836
James Monroe	Virginia	1817–25	1759	1831
John Quincy Adams	Massachusetts	1825–29	1767	1848

Name	From state	Term of service	Born	Died
Andrew Jackson	Tennessee	1829–37	1767	1845
Martin Van Buren	New York	1837–41	1782	1862
William H. Harrison	Ohio	Mar.–Apr. 1841	1773	1841
John Tyler	Virginia	1841–45	1790	1862
James K. Polk	Tennessee	1845–49	1795	1849
Zachary Taylor	Louisiana	1849–July 1850	1784	1850
Millard Fillmore	New York	1850–53	1800	1874
Franklin Pierce	New Hampshire	1853–57	1804	1869
James Buchanan	Pennsylvania	1857–61	1791	1868
Abraham Lincoln	Illinois	1861–Apr. 1865	1809	1865
Andrew Johnson	Tennessee	1865–69	1808	1875
Ulysses S. Grant	Illinois	1869–77	1822	1885
Rutherford B. Hayes	Ohio	1877–81	1822	1893
James A. Garfield	Ohio	Mar.–Sept. 1881	1831	1881
Chester A. Arthur	New York	1881–85	1830	1886
Grover Cleveland	New York	1885–89	1837	1908
Benjamin Harrison	Indiana	1889–93	1833	1901
Grover Cleveland	New York	1893–97	1837	1908
William McKinley	Ohio	1897–Sept. 1901	1843	1901
Theodore Roosevelt	New York	1901–09	1858	1919
William H. Taft	Ohio	1909–13	1857	1930
Woodrow Wilson	New Jersey	1913–21	1856	1924
Warren Gamaliel Harding	Ohio	1921–Aug. 1923	1865	1923
Calvin Coolidge	Massachusetts	1923–29	1872	1933
Herbert C. Hoover	California	1929–33	1874	1964
Franklin D. Roosevelt	New York	1933–Apr. 1945	1882	1945
Harry S. Truman	Missouri	1945–53	1884	—
Dwight D. Eisenhower	New York	1953–61	1890	1969
John F. Kennedy	Massachusetts	1961–Nov. 1963	1917	1963
Lyndon B. Johnson	Texas	1963–69	1908	—
Richard M. Nixon	California	1969–	1913	—

VICE-PRESIDENTS OF THE USA

Name	From state	Term of service	Born	Died
John Adams	Massachusetts	1789–97	1735	1826
Thomas Jefferson	Virginia	1797–1801	1743	1826
Aaron Burr	New York	1801–05	1756	1836
George Clinton	New York	1805–12[1]	1739	1812
Elbridge Gerry	Massachusetts	1813–14[1]	1744	1814
Daniel D. Tompkins	New York	1817–25	1774	1825
John C. Calhoun	South Carolina	1825–32[1]	1782	1850
Martin Van Buren	New York	1833–37	1782	1862
Richard M. Johnson	Kentucky	1837–41	1780	1850
John Tyler	Virginia	Mar.–Apr. 1841[1]	1790	1862
George M. Dallas	Pennsylvania	1845–49	1792	1864
Millard Fillmore	New York	1849–50[1]	1800	1874
William R. King	Alabama	Mar.–Apr. 1853[1]	1786	1853
John C. Breckinridge	Kentucky	1857–61[1]	1821	1875
Hannibal Hamlin	Maine	1861–65	1809	1891
Andrew Johnson	Tennessee	Mar.–Apr. 1865[1]	1808	1875
Schuyler Colfax	Indiana	1869–73	1823	1885
Henry Wilson	Massachusetts	1873–75[1]	1812	1875
William A. Wheeler	New York	1877–81	1819	1887
Chester A. Arthur	New York	Mar.–Sept. 1881[1]	1830	1886
Thomas A. Hendricks	Indiana	Mar.–Nov. 1885[1]	1819	1885
Levi P. Morton	New York	1889–93	1824	1920
Adlai E. Stevenson	Illinois	1893–97	1835	1914

[1] Position vacant thereafter until commencement of the next presidential term.

Name	From state	Term of service	Born	Died
Garret A. Hobart	New Jersey	1897–99[1]	1844	1899
Theodore Roosevelt	New York	Mar.–Sept. 1901[1]	1858	1919
Charles W. Fairbanks	Indiana	1905–09	1855	1920
James S. Sherman	New York	1909–12[1]	1855	1912
Thomas R. Marshall	Indiana	1913–21	1854	1925
Calvin Coolidge	Massachusetts	1921–Aug. 1923[1]	1872	1933
Charles G. Dawes	Illinois	1925–29	1865	1951
Charles Curtis	Kansas	1929–33	1860	1935
John N. Garner	Texas	1933–41	1868	1967
Henry A. Wallace	Iowa	1941–45	1888	1965
Harry S. Truman	Missouri	1945–Apr. 1945[1]	1884	—
Alben W. Barkley	Kentucky	1949–53	1877	1956
Richard M. Nixon	California	1953–61	1913	—
Lyndon B. Johnson	Texas	1961–Nov. 1963[1]	1908	—
Hubert H. Humphrey	Minnesota	1965–69	1911	—
Spiro T. Agnew	Maryland	1969–	1918	—

[1] Position vacant thereafter until commencement of the next presidential term.

Cabinet. The administrative business of the nation has been traditionally vested in several executive departments, the heads of which, unofficially and *ex officio*, formed the President's Cabinet. Beginning with the Interstate Commerce Commission in 1887, however, an increasing amount of executive business has been entrusted to some 60 so-called independent agencies, such as the Veterans Administration, Atomic Energy Commission, Housing and Home Finance Agency, Tariff Commission, etc.

All heads of departments and of the 60 or more administrative agencies are appointed by the President, but must be confirmed by the Senate.

The Cabinet consists of the following:

1. *Secretary of State* (created 1789). William P. Rogers, of New York; lawyer; Deputy Attorney General, 1952–57; Attorney General, 1957–61; born 1913.

2. *Secretary of the Treasury* (1789). John B. Connally, of Texas; Governor of Texas, 1962–68; born 1917.

3. *Secretary of Defense* (1947). Melvin R. Laird, of Wisconsin; taxation expert and author; born 1922.

4. *Attorney-General* (Department of Justice, 1870). John N. Mitchell, of New York, constitutional lawyer; national campaign manager for Mr Nixon in the 1968 Presidential election; born 1913.

5. *Postmaster-General* (1792). Winston M. Blount, of Alabama; construction firm executive; President of US Chamber of Commerce; born 1921.

6. *Secretary of the Interior* (1849). Rogers C. B. Morton, of Maryland; Congressman; born 1914.

7. *Secretary of Agriculture* (1889). Clifford M. Hardin, of Nebraska; agricultural economist; Chancellor of the University of Nebraska from 1953; born 1915.

8. *Secretary of Commerce* (1903). Maurice H. Stans, of Minnesota; Deputy Postmaster-General, 1955; Budget Director, 1957; born 1908.

9. *Secretary of Labor* (1913). George P. Shultz, of Chicago; Senior staff economist to the Council of Economic Advisers, 1955–56; Dean of Univ. of Chicago Graduate School of Business since 1962; born 1920.

10. *Secretary of Health, Education and Welfare* (1953). Elliot L. Richardson, of Massachusetts; Attorney-General of Massachusetts, 1959–61; Under Secretary of State, 1969–70; born 1920.

11. *Secretary of Housing and Urban Development* (1966). George W. Pomney, of Michigan; industrialist; Governor of Michigan, 1962–68; born 1907.

12. *Secretary of Transportation* (1967). John A. Volpe, of Massachusetts; Massachusetts Commissioner of Public Works, 1953–56; Governor of Massachusetts, 1960–62 and 1964–68; born 1908.

Each of the above Cabinet officers receives an annual salary of $60,000 and holds office during the pleasure of the President; the Postmaster-General alone must be re-appointed and confirmed at the beginning of a president's second term, the others merely continuing in office.

Congress. The legislative power is vested by the Constitution in a Congress, consisting of a Senate and House of Representatives.

Electorate. By amendments of the constitution, disqualification of voters on the ground of race, colour or sex is forbidden. Accordingly, the electorate consists theoretically of all citizens of both sexes over 18 years of age, but the franchise is not universal. There are requirement of residence varying in the several states as to length from 6 months to 2 years and differing requirements as to registration. In 20 states the ability to read (usually an extract from the constitution) is required—in Alaska the ability to read English; in Hawaii, English or Hawaiian; in Louisiana, English or one's native tongue. In Alabama the voter must take an 'anti-Communist oath' and fill out a questionnaire to the satisfaction of the registrars. In some southern states voters are required to give a reasonable explanation of what they read. Estimate of Negroes registered in the 11 southern states of Ala., Ark., Fla., La., Miss., N.C., Okla., S.C., Tex., Tenn. and Va.: 1947, 595,000; 1956, 1,238,000; 1960, 1,414,000; 1970, 3,324,000 (66·3% of Negroes of voting age). At the end of 1968 there were about 6·3m. registered Negro voters in the USA, of whom over 2m. were in southern states. In most states convicts are excluded from the franchise, in some states duellists and fraudulent voters.

Legislation designed to discourage the rise of third parties has been adopted in a few states. In Illinois a new party must present a petition signed by at least 25,000 voters, including at least 200 in each of 50 of the 102 counties.

The method of balloting varies greatly. Seventeen states use different ballots for federal, state and local elections. In Delaware and South Carolina the various political parties furnish their own ballot-papers to the voters as he or she enters the polling-booth.

Senate. The Senate consists of 2 members from each state, chosen by popular vote for 6 years, one-third retiring or seeking re-election every 2 years. Senators must be not less than 30 years of age; must have been citizens of the USA for 9 years, and be residents in the states for which they are chosen. The Senate has complete freedom to initiate legislation, except revenue bills (which must originate in the House of Representatives); it may, however, amend or reject any legislation originating in the lower house. The Senate is also entrusted with the power of giving or withholding its 'advice and consent' to the ratification of all treaties initiated by the President with foreign Powers, a two-thirds majority of senators present being required for approval. (However, it has no control over 'international executive agreements' made by the President with foreign governments; such 'agreements', representing an important but very recent development, cover a wide range and are actually more numerous than formal treaties.) It also has the power of confirming or rejecting major appointments to office made by the President, but it has no direct control over the appointment by the President of 'personal representatives' or 'personal envoys' on missions abroad. Members of the Senate constitute a High Court of Impeachment, with power, by a two-thirds vote, to remove from office and disqualify any civil officer of the USA impeached by the House of Representatives, which has the sole power of impeachment.

The Senate has 16 Standing Committees to which all bills are referred for study revision or rejection. The House of Representatives has 21 such committees. In both Houses each Standing Committee has a chairman and a majority representing the majority party of the whole House; each has numerous sub-committees. The jurisdictions of these Committees correspond largely to those of the appropriate executive departments and agencies. Both Houses also have a few special Committees with limited duration. There are some Joint Committees of both Houses.

House of Representatives. The House of Representatives consists of 435 members elected every second year. The number of each state's representatives is determined by the decennial census, in the absence of specific Congressional legislation affecting the basis. The states, in 1970, had the following representatives:

Alabama	8	Indiana	11	Nebraska	3	South Carolina	6
Alaska	1	Iowa	7	Nevada	1	South Dakota	2
Arizona	3	Kansas	5	New Hampshire	2	Tennessee	9
Arkansas	4	Kentucky	7	New Jersey	15	Texas	23
California	38	Louisiana	8	New Mexico	2	Utah	2
Colorado	4	Maine	2	New York	41	Vermont	1
Connecticut	6	Maryland	8	North Carolina	11	Virginia	10
Delaware	1	Massachusetts	12	North Dakota	2	Washington	7
Florida	12	Michigan	19	Ohio	24	West Virginia	5
Georgia	10	Minnesota	8	Oklahoma	6	Wisconsin	10
Hawaii	2	Mississippi	5	Oregon	2	Wyoming	1
Idaho	2	Missouri	10	Pennsylvania	27		
Illinois	24	Montana	2	Rhode Island	2		

Whilst the average constituency contains between 300,000 and 400,000 population (of which about two-thirds are of voting age), there were, in 1963, 32 districts (7% of the total) with 250,000 or less and 33 with populations exceeding 450,000; the number in each category is likely to be reduced by the decision of the Supreme Court, 17 Feb. 1964, that the federal constitution requires congressional districts within each state to be substantially equal in population. By almost invariable custom the representative lives in the district from which he is elected.

Representatives must be not less than 25 years of age, citizens of the USA for 7 years and residents in the states from which they are chosen. The House also admits a 'resident commissioner' from Puerto Rico, who has the right to speak on any subject and to make motions, but not to vote; he is elected in the same manner as the representatives but for a 4-year term. Each of the two Houses of Congress is sole 'judge of the elections, returns and qualifications of its own members'; and each of the Houses may, with the concurrence of two-thirds, expel a member. The period usually termed 'a Congress' in legislative language continues for 2 years, terminating at noon on 3 Jan.

The salary of a senator or representative, also that of a resident commissioner in Congress, is $42,500 per annum, with tax-free expense allowance and allowances for travelling expenses and for clerical hire. The salary of the Speaker of the House of Representatives is $62,500 per annum, with a taxable allowance of $10,000.

No senator or representative can, during the time for which he is elected, be appointed to any *civil* office under authority of the USA which shall have been created or the emoluments of which shall have been increased during such time; and no person holding *any* office under the USA can be a member of either House during his continuance in office. No religious test may be required as a qualification to any office or public trust under the USA or in any state.

The 91st Congress (1969–71) was constituted (Jan. 1969) as follows: Senate, 57 Democrats, 43 Republicans; House of Representatives, 243 Democrats, 192 Republicans. The House of Representatives had 10 women members and the Senate 2; the House had 6 Negro members. About 68% of the Senate and 56% of the House were lawyers.

Indians. By an Act passed on 2 June 1924 full citizenship was granted to all Indians born in the USA, though those remaining in tribal units were still under special federal jurisdiction. Those remaining in tribal units constitute from one-half to three-fourths of the Indian population. The Indian Reorganization Act of 1934 gave the tribal Indians, at their own option, substantial opportunities for self-government and of self-controlled corporate enterprises empowered to borrow money, buy land, machinery and equipment; these corporations are controlled by democratically elected tribal councils; by 1945 roughly a third of the Indians had taken advantage of this Act. Recently a trend towards releasing Indians from federal supervision has resulted in legislation terminating supervision over specific tribes. Indian lands (1965) amounted to 55,319,000 acres, of which about 71% was tribally owned and 20% in trust allotments, with the remainder owned by the Government. Indian lands are held free of taxes. Indian population under jurisdiction of the Indian Bureau was about 343,000 in 1950; nearly one-half were in the three states of Oklahoma, Arizona and New Mexico. Total Indian population at the 1960 census (the first at which individuals were responsible for their own classification by race) was 523,591, of which Oklahoma, Arizona and New Mexico accounted for 40%.

STATE AND LOCAL GOVERNMENT

The Union comprises 13 original states, 7 states which were admitted without having been previously organized as territories, and 30 states which had been territories—50 states in all. Each state has its own constitution (which the USA guarantees shall be republican in form), deriving its authority, not from Congress, but from the people of the state. Admission of states into the Union has been granted by special Acts of Congress, either (1) in the form of 'enabling Acts' providing for the drafting and ratification of a state constitution by the people, in which case the territory becomes a state as soon as the conditions are fulfilled, or (2) accepting a constitution already framed, and at once granting admission.

Each state is provided with a legislature of two Houses (except Nebraska, which since 1937 has had a single-chamber legislature), a governor and other executive officials, and a judicial system. Both Houses of the legislature are elective, but the senators (having larger electoral districts usually covering 2 or 3 counties compared with the single county or, in some states, the town, which sends one representative to the Lower House) are less numerous than the representatives, while in 37 states their terms are 4 years and in a few the Senate is only partially renewed at each election. Terms of the lower houses are usually shorter; in 45 states, 2 years.

Members of both Houses are paid at the same rate, which varies from $200 per biennium (New Hampshire) to $48,950 per annual session (California) or from $5 (Rhode Island, North Dakota) to $50 (Louisiana) per day during session, plus mileage, etc. In 1962, 327 women—a record number—were serving in the state legislatures, 34 in state senates and 293 in the lower houses. Only 5 states had no women legislators, Alabama, Georgia, Louisiana, Oklahoma and Wisconsin. The trend is towards annual sessions of state legislatures; in 1970, 26 met annually (in 1939, only 4) the other 24 holding biennial sessions, in the odd-numbered years (with 3 exceptions).

The Governor has power to summon an extraordinary session, but not to dissolve or adjourn. The duties of the two Houses are similar, but in many states money bills must be introduced first in the Lower House. The Senate sits as a court for the trial of officials impeached by the other House, and often has power to confirm or reject appointments made by the Governor.

State legislatures are competent to deal with all matters not reserved for the federal government by the federal constitution nor specifically prohibited by the federal or state constitutions. Among their powers are the determination of the qualifications for the right of suffrage, and the control of all elections to public office, including elections of members of Congress and electors of President and Vice-President; the criminal law, both in its enactment and in its execution, with unimportant exceptions, and the administration of prisons; the civil law, including all matters pertaining to the possession and transfer of, and succession to, property; marriage and divorce, and all other civil relations; the chartering and control of all manufacturing, trading, transportation and other corporations, subject only to the right of Congress to regulate commerce passing from one state to another; labour; education; charities; licensing; fisheries within state waters, and game laws (apart from the hunting of migratory birds, which is a federal concern under treaties with Canada and Mexico). Taxes on income were left to the states until 1913, when the 16th amendment authorized the imposition of federal taxes on income without regard to apportionment.

The Governor is chosen by direct vote of the people over the whole state. His term of office varies in the several states from 2 to 4 years, and his salary from $10,000 (Arkansas) to $50,000 (New York). His duty is to see to the faithful administration of the law, and he has command of the military forces of the state. He may recommend measures but does not present bills to the legislature. In some states he presents estimates. In all but one of the states (North Carolina) the Governor has a veto upon legislation, which may, however, be overridden by the two Houses, in some states by a simple majority, in others by a three-fifths or two-thirds majority. In some states the Governor, on his death or resignation, is succeeded by a Lieut.-Governor who was elected at the same time and has been presiding over the state Senate. In several states the Speaker of the Lower House succeeds the Governor.

The chief officials by whom the administration of state affairs is carried on (secretaries, treasurers, members of boards of commissioners, etc.) are usually chosen by the people at the general state elections for terms similar to those for which governors hold office. State employees, Oct. 1968, numbered 2,495,000, earning 1,256·6m. monthly; education accounted for 1·04m. employees (44%). Local government employees numbered 6,864,000, earning $3,495·2m. monthly; 3,792,000 of them were in education.

LOCAL GOVERNMENT

The chief unit of local government is the county, of which there were (1962) 3,043 with definite functions; in addition, Rhode Island has 5 'counties' which have no functions; Alaska does not have 'counties' as such and, since Oct. 1960, there has been no active county government in Connecticut. The counties maintain public order through the sheriff and his deputies, who may, in a crisis, be drawn temporarily from willing citizens; in many states the counties maintain the smaller local highways; other functions are the granting of licences and the apportionment and collection of taxes. In a few states they also manage the schools.

The unit of local government in New England is the rural township, governed directly by the voters, who assemble annually or oftener if necessary, and legislate in local affairs, levy taxes, make appropriations and appoint and instruct the local officials (selectmen, clerk, school-committee, etc.). Townships are grouped to form counties. Where cities exist, the township government is superseded by the city government. On 1 Jan. 1958, 1,533 cities and 17 counties had 'city managers' or 'council-managers' with large executive powers.

Including the 3,043 counties, there were (1963) 18,000 municipalities, 17,142 townships, 34,678 school districts and 18,323 special districts; total, excluding US Government and the 50 state governments, 91,186 units.

The **District of Columbia**, ceded by the State of Maryland for the purposes of government in 1791, is the seat of the US Government. It includes the city of Washington, and embraces a land area of 61 sq. miles. The District has no municipal legislative body, and its citizens have no right to vote either in national or municipal concerns, Congress having sole plenary legislative authority; however, a constitutional amendment conferring the right to vote in national elections passed Congress in 1960 and was ratified 30 March 1961. By an Act of Congress of 1878, its municipal government is administered by 3 commissioners, appointed by the President; for some years there has been considerable agitation for some degree of 'home rule' which would at the same time relieve Congress of much local detail.

The **Commonwealth of Puerto Rico, Guam** and the **Virgin Islands** each have a local legislature, whose acts may be modified or annulled by Congress, though in practice this has seldom been done. The President appoints the Governor and federal judges in Guam and the Virgin Islands. Puerto Rico since its attainment of commonwealth status on 25 July 1952, enjoys practically complete self-government, including the election of its governor and other officials. The conduct of foreign relations, however, is still a federal function and federal bureaus and agencies still operate in the island.

General supervision of territorial administration is exercised by the Office of Territories in the Department of Interior.

The Constitution of the United States of America. Analysis and interpretation. Ed. Edward S. Corwin. Washington, Gov. Printing Office, 1953
Constitutions of the US, National and State. 2 vols. [with subsequent amendments]. Dobbs Ferry, 1962
Anderson, W. and others. *Government in the Fifty States.* Rev. ed. New York, 1960
Bates, F. G., *State Government.* 3rd ed. by Field, Sikes and Stoner. New York, 1949
Binkley, W. E., *American Political Parties.* 4th ed. New York, 1963
Binkley, W. E., and Moos, M. C., *A Grammar of American Politics: The National, State and Local Governments.* 3rd ed. New York, 1957
Cater, D., *Power in Washington.* London, 1964
Corwin, E. S., *The President: Office and Powers. History and Analysis of Practice and Opinion.* 4th ed. New York, 1957
Coyle, D. C., *The United States political system and how it works.* New York, 1954; London, Hansard Society, 1957
Fenno, H. F., *The President's Cabinet . . . Wilson to Eisenhower.* Harvard Univ. Press, 1959
Ferguson, J. H., and McHenry, D. E., *Elements of American Government.* 6th ed. New York, 1963
Griffith, E. S., *The American System of Government.* 4th ed. London, 1965
Hacker, A., *Congressional Districting.* Rev. ed. Washington, D.C., 1964
Kelly, A. H., and Harbison, W. A., *The American Constitution, its origin and development.* 3rd ed. New York, 1963
Key, V. O., *American State Politics.* New York, 1956
MacNeil, N., *Forge of Democracy: the House of Representatives.* New York, 1963
Maddox, R. W., and Fuquay, R. F., *State and Local Government.* New York, 1961; London, 1962
Mayer, G. H., *The Republican Party, 1854–1964.* OUP, 1964
Ogg, F. A., and Ray, P. O., *Introduction to American Government.* 12th ed. New York, 1962.— *Essentials of American National Government.* 9th ed. New York, 1964
Rossiter, C., *Parties and Politics in America.* Ithaca, 1964
Scammon, R. M. (ed.), *America Votes. Handbook of contemporary election statistics.* 5 vols. Pittsburg, 1952–64
Tugwell, R. G., *The Enlargement of the Presidency.* Garden City, N.Y., 1960
White, T. H., *The Making of the President.* New York, 1960,—*The Making of the President 1964.* New York, 1965
Williams, I. G., *The Rise of the Vice-Presidency.* Washington, D.C., 1956

AREA AND POPULATION

PROGRESS AND PRESENT CONDITION

Population of conterminous USA at each census from 1790 to 1950, and for USA including Alaska and Hawaii, 1960. Residents of Puerto Rico, the Philippine Islands, Guam, American Samoa, Virgin Islands of the USA and Panama Canal Zone, and persons in the military and naval service stationed abroad are not included in the figures of this table. Residents of Hawaii and Alaska are excluded prior to 1960. Residents of Indian reservations are excluded prior to 1890.

	White	Negroes	Other races	Total	Decennial increase %
1790	3,172,006 [1]	757,208	—	3,929,214	—
1800	4,306,446	1,002,037	—	5,308,483	35·1
1810	5,862,073	1,377,808	—	7,239,881	36·4
1820	7,866,797	1,771,656	—	9,638,453	33·1
1830	10,537,378	2,328,642	—	12,866,020	33·5
1840	14,195,805	2,873,648	—	17,069,453	32·7
1850	19,553,068	3,638,808	—	23,191,876	35·9
1860	26,922,537	4,441,830	78,954 [2]	31,443,321	35·6

[1] Made up of Anglo-Scottish, 89·1%; German, 5·6%; Dutch, 2·5%; Irish, 1·9%; French, 0·6%.
[2] 34,933 Chinese and 44,021 Indians.

	White	Negroes[1]	Other races[2]	Total	Decennial increase %
1870[3]	33,589,377	4,880,009	88,985	38,558,371	22·6
1870[3]	34,337,292	5,392,172	88,985	39,818,449	26·6
1880	43,402,970	6,580,793	172,020	50,155,783	30·1
1890	55,101,258	7,488,676	357,780	62,947,714	25·5
1900	66,809,196	8,833,994	351,385	75,994,575	20·7
1910	81,731,957	9,827,763	412,546	91,972,266	21·0
1920	94,820,915	10,463,131	426,574	105,710,620	14·9[4]
1930	110,286,740[5]	11,891,143	597,163	122,775,046	16·1[4]
1940	118,214,870	12,865,518	588,887	131,669,275	7·2
1950	134,942,028	15,042,286	713,047	150,697,361	14·5
1960[6]	158,831,732	18,871,831	1,619,612	179,323,175	18·5

[1] Seventeen southern states (including D.C.) in 1900 had 7,922,969 Negroes (89·7% of the total Negro population); in 1920, 8,912,231 (85·2%); in 1940, 9,904,619 (77%); in 1950, 10,225,407 (68%); in 1960, 11,311,607 (59·9%).

[2] 1870: 63,199 Chinese, 55 Japanese and 25,731 Indians; 1880, 105,465 Chinese, 148 Japanese and 66,407 Indians; 1890, 107,488 Chinese, 2,039 Japanese and 248,253 Indians; 1900, 89,863 Chinese, 24,326 Japanese and 237,196 Indians; 1910, 71,531 Chinese, 72,157 Japanese, 265,683 Indians and 3,175 other races; 1920, 61,639 Chinese, 111,010 Japanese, 244,437 Indians and 9,488 other races; 1930, 332,397 Indians, 74,954 Chinese, 138,834 Japanese and 50,978 other races; 1940, 333,969 Indians, 77,504 Chinese, 126,947 Japanese and 50,467 other races; 1950, 343,410 Indians, 141,768 Japanese, 117,629 Chinese, 110,240 other races; 1960, 523,591 Indians, 464,332 Japanese (including 203,455 in Hawaii), 237,292 Chinese (38,197), 176,310 Filipino (69,070), 218,087 other races (114,405).

[3] Enumeration in 1870 incomplete. Figures in italics represent estimated corrected population.

[4] Between the 1910 census (15 April 1910) and the 1920 census (1 Jan. 1920), the period covered was 116½ months (less than a full decade). Adjusting for this, the exact rate of increase for the decade was 15·4%. Similarly correcting for the 123 months between the 1920 and 1930 censuses, the true rate of increase was 15·7%.

[5] Figures for 1930 have been revised to include Mexicans (1,422,533), who were classified with 'Other Races' in the 1930 census reports.

[6] Figures for 1960 strictly comparable with those given for other years (i.e., excluding Alaska and Hawaii) are: White, 158,454,956; Negroes, 18,860,117; other races, 1,149,163; total, 178,464,236; decennial increase, 18·4%.

Total population in 1960 at 179,323,175 comprised 88,331,494 males and 90,991,681 females; 125,268,750 were urban and 54,054,425 were rural. Negroes had 9,113,408 males, and other races, 850,937 males.

Estimated population, including Alaska and Hawaii, and armed forces overseas, on 1 July 1950, 152,271,000; 1955, 165,931,000; 1960, 180,684,000; 1964, 192·12m.; 1965, 194,592,000; 1966, 196·91m.; 1967, 199,114,000; 1968, 201,152,000; 1969, 203,216,000; 1970, census (provisional) 204,765,770.

The age distribution by sex of the total population of the US and outlying areas (including US population abroad, but excluding Trust Territory of the Pacific Islands, and miscellaneous small islands of sovereignty or jurisdiction) at the 1960 census was as follows (in 1,000):

Age-group	Male	Female	Total	Age-group	Male	Female	Total
Under 5	10,615	10,266	20,881	55–59	4,173	4,341	8,513
5–9	9,740	9,416	19,156	60–64	3,446	3,767	7,213
11–14	8,732	8,452	17,184	65–69	2,962	3,354	6,316
15–19	6,869	6,737	13,605	70–74	2,206	2,572	4,778
20–24	5,612	5,674	11,287	75–79	1,372	1,707	3,079
25–29	5,515	5,672	11,186	80–84	671	921	1,592
30–34	6,000	6,224	12,224	85 and over	367	574	941
35–39	6,217	6,515	12,732				
40–44	5,782	6,005	11,786	Total	90,510	92,702	183,212
45–49	5,441	5,589	11,030	Median age			
50–54	4,792	4,917	9,709	(years)	28·3	30·1	29·2

The following table includes population statistics, the year in which each of the original 13 states ratified the constitution, and the year when each of the other states was admitted into the Union. Postal abbreviations for the names of the states are shown in brackets. Land area includes land temporarily or partially covered by water, and lakes, etc., of less than 40 acres. (For census population by states and regions in 1930 and 1940 see THE STATESMAN'S YEAR-BOOK, 1944, pp. 495 and 496.)

Geographic divisions and states		Land area: sq. miles, 1960	Census population 1 April 1950	Census population 1 April 1960	Pop. per sq. mile, 1960
United States		3,548,974	150,697,361	179,323,175	50·5
New England		63,126	9,314,453	10,509,367	166·5
Maine (1820)		31,012	913,774	969,265	31·3
New Hampshire (1788)	(N.H)	9,014	533,242	606,921	67·3
Vermont (1791)	(Vt.)	9,276	377,747	389,881	42·0
Massachusetts (1788)	(Mass.)	7,867	4,690,514	5,148,578	654·5
Rhode Island (1790)	(R.I.)	1,058	791,896	859,488	812·4
Connecticut (1788)	(Conn.)	4,899	2,007,280	2,535,234	517·5
Middle Atlantic		100,467	30,163,533	34,168,452	340·1
New York (1788)	(N.Y.)	47,939	14,830,192	16,782,304	350·1
New Jersey (1787)	(N.J.)	7,521	4,835,329	6,066,782	806·6
Pennsylvania (1787)	(Pa.)	45,007	10,498,012	11,319,366	251·5
East North Central		244,811	30,399,368	36,225,024	148·0
Ohio (1803)		40,972	7,946,627	9,706,397	236·9
Indiana (1816)	(Ind.)	36,185	3,934,224	4,662,498	128·9
Illinois (1818)	(Ill.)	55,930	8,712,176	10,081,158	180·2
Michigan (1837)	(Mich.)	57,019	6,371,766	7,823,194	137·2
Wisconsin (1848)	(Wis.)	54,705	3,434,575	3,951,777	72·2
West North Central		509,674	14,061,394	15,394,115	30·2
Minnesota (1858)	(Minn.)	80,009	2,982,483	3,413,864	42·7
Iowa (1846)		56,032	2,621,073	2,757,537	49·2
Missouri (1821)	(Mo.)	69,138	3,954,653	4,319,813	62·5
North Dakota (1889)	(N.D.)	69,457	619,636	632,446	9·1
South Dakota (1889)	(S.D.)	76,378	652,740	680,514	8·9
Nebraska (1867)	(Nebr.)	76,612	1,325,510	1,411,330	18·4
Kansas (1861)	(Kans.)	82,048	1,905,299	2,178,611	26·6
South Atlantic		267,695	21,182,335	25,971,732	97·0
Delaware (1787)	(Del.)	1,978	318,085	446,292	225·6
Maryland (1788)	(Md.)	9,874	2,343,001	3,100,689	314·0
Dist. of Columbia (1791)	(D.C.)	61	802,178	763,956	12,523·9
Virginia (1788)	(Va.)	39,838	3,318,680	3,966,949	99·6
West Virginia (1863)	(W. Va.)	24,079	2,005,552	1,860,421	77·3
North Carolina (1789)	(N.C.)	49,067	4,061,929	4,556,155	92·9
South Carolina (1788)	(S.C.)	30,272	2,117,027	2,382,594	78·7
Georgia (1788)	(Ga.)	58,274	3,444,578	3,943,116	67·7
Florida (1845)	(Fla.)	54,252	2,771,305	4,951,560	91·3
East South Central		179,908	11,477,181	12,050,126	67·0
Kentucky (1792)	(Ky.)	39,863	2,944,806	3,038,156	76·2
Tennessee (1796)	(Tenn.)	41,762	3,291,718	3,567,089	85·4
Alabama (1819)		51,060	3,061,743	3,266,740	64·0
Mississippi (1817)	(Miss.)	47,223	2,178,914	2,178,141	46·1
West South Central		429,332	14,537,572	16,951,255	39·5
Arkansas (1836)	(Ark.)	52,499	1,909,511	1,786,272	34·0
Louisiana (1812)	(La.)	45,106	2,683,516	3,257,022	72·2
Oklahoma (1907)	(Okla.)	68,887	2,233,351	2,328,284	33·8
Texas (1845)	(Tex.)	262,840	7,711,194	9,579,677	36·4
Mountain		856,951	5,074,998	6,855,060	8·0
Montana (1889)	(Mont.)	145,736	591,024	674,767	4·6
Idaho (1890)		82,708	588,637	667,191	8·1
Wyoming (1890)	(Wyo.)	97,411	290,529	330,066	3·4
Colorado (1876)	(Colo.)	103,884	1,325,089	1,753,947	16·9
New Mexico (1912)	(N. Mex.)	121,510	681,187	951,023	7·8
Arizona (1912)	(Ariz.)	113,575	749,587	1,302,161	11·5
Utah (1896)		82,339	688,862	890,627	10·8
Nevada (1864)	(Nev.)	109,788	160,083	285,278	2·6
Pacific		897,010	15,114,964	21,198,044	23·6
Washington (1889)	(Wash.)	66,709	2,378,963	2,853,214	42·8
Oregon (1859)	(Oreg.)	96,248	1,521,341	1,768,687	18·4
California (1850)	(Calif.)	156,573	10,586,223	15,717,204	100·4

Geographic divisions and states	Land area: sq. miles, 1960	Census population 1 April 1950	Census population 1 April 1960	Pop. per sq. mile, 1960
Pacific (contd.)				
Alaska (1959)	571,065	128,643	226,167	0·4
Hawaii (1960)	6,415	499,794	632,772	98·6
Outlying Territories, 1960	4,914[1]	2,907,436[2]	3,961,834[3]	806·2
Puerto Rico (1898)	3,421	2,210,703	2,349,544	686·8
Virgin Islands (1917)	132	26,665	32,099	243·0
American Samoa (1900)	76	18,937	20,051	264·0
Guam (1898)	209	59,498	67,044	321·0
Panama Canal Zone (1903)	362	52,822	42,122	116·4
US population abroad	—	481,545	1,374,421	—
Grand Total	3,553,888	154,233,234[2]	183,285,009[3]	51·6

[1] Including Midway Islands (2 sq. miles), Wake Island (3 sq. miles), Canton and Enderbury Islands (27 sq. miles), Swan Islands (1 sq. mile), Corn Islands (4 sq. miles), Howland, Baker and Jarvis Islands (3 sq. miles), other islands (6 sq. miles), and Trust Territory of the Pacific Islands (687 sq. miles). Johnston and Sand Islands, Palmyra Island and Kingman Reef, less than 1 sq. mile. The sovereignty of 25 islands in the Pacific (including Canton and Enderbury Islands and Christmas Island) is disputed with the UK or New Zealand; that of 3 islands in the Caribbean with Colombia. Canton and Enderbury are controlled jointly by the USA and Great Britain. Corn Islands are leased from Nicaragua.

[2] Including population of Midway Islands (416), Wake Island (349), Canton and Enderbury Islands (272), Johnston and Sand Islands (46), Swan Islands (36), Corn Islands (1,304) and Trust Territory of the Pacific Islands (54,843).

[3] Including population of Midway Islands (2,356) Wake Island (1,097), Canton and Enderbury Islands (320), Johnston and Sand Islands (156), Swan Islands (28), Corn Islands (1,872) and Trust Territory of the Pacific Islands (70,724).

The 1960 census showed 9,293,992 foreign-born Whites. The 10 countries contributing the largest numbers who were foreign-born were Italy, 1,255,812; Germany, 986,564; Canada, 941,906; United Kingdom, 830,673 (England, Wales and N.I., 526,157; Scotland, 213,026); Poland, 747,250; USSR, 689,462; Mexico, 572,564; Irish Republic, 338,350; Austria, 304,192; Hungary, 244,945; Czechoslovakia, 227,467; Sweden, 214,313.

Median age of foreign-born Whites was 57·8 years, that of native Whites being 28·5 years. The large difference reflects decline in immigration during recent decades.

Increase or decrease of native White, and foreign-born White, population from 1860 to 1950, by decades:

	Native White			Foreign-born White		
	Total	Increase	Per cent. increase	Total	Increase or decrease (−)	Per cent. change
1860	22,825,784	5,513,251	31·8	4,096,753	1,856,218	82·8
1870	28,095,665	5,269,881	23·1	5,493,712	1,396,959	34·1
1880	36,843,291	8,747,626	31·1	6,559,679	1,065,967	19·4
1890	45,979,391	9,018,732[1]	24·5	9,121,867	2,562,188	39·1
1900	56,595,379	10,615,988	23·1	10,213,817	1,091,950	12·0
1910	68,386,412	11,791,033	20·8	13,345,545	3,131,728	30·7
1920	81,108,161	12,721,749	18·6	13,712,754	367,209	2·8
1930	96,303,335	15,195,174	18·7	13,983,405	270,651	2·0
1940	106,795,732	10,492,397	10·9	11,419,138	−2,564,267	−18·3
1950	124,780,860	17,985,128	16·8	10,161,168	−1,257,970	−11·0
1960	149,543,638	24,762,778	19·8	9,293,992	−867,176	−8·5

[1] Exclusive of population specially enumerated in 1890 in Indian Territory and on Indian reservations.

PRINCIPAL CITIES

Cities with	No. of cities[1]			Combined population[1]		
	1910	1950	1960	1910	1950	1960
250,000 or more	19	41	51	15,461,680	34,832,955	39,360,951
100,000–250,000	31	65	81	4,840,458	9,478,662	11,652,426
50,000–100,000	59	126	201	4,178,915	8,930,823	13,835,902
25,000–50,000	119	252	432	4,023,397	8,807,721	14,950,612
25,000 or more	228	484	765	28,504,450	62,050,161	79,799,871

[1] Exclusive of Honolulu (Hawaii) in 1910 and 1950 and San Juan (Puerto Rico) in 1910, 1950 and 1960.

The population of leading cities (with over 100,000 inhabitants) at the censuses of 1950 and 1960 were as follows:

Cities	1 April 1950	1 April 1960	Cities	1 April 1950	1 April 1960
New York, N.Y.	7,891,957	7,781,984	Worcester, Mass.	203,486	186,587
Chicago, Ill.	3,620,962	3,550,404	Austin, Tex.	132,459	186,545
Los Angeles, Calif.	1,970,358	2,479,015	Spokane, Wash.	161,721	181,608
Philadelphia, Pa.	2,071,605	2,002,512	St Petersburg, Fla.	96,738	181,298
Detroit, Mich.	1,849,568	1,670,144	Gary, Ind.	133,911	178,320
Baltimore, Md.	949,708	939,024	Grand Rapids, Mich.	176,515	177,313
Houston, Tex.	596,163	938,219	Springfield, Mass.	162,399	174,463
Cleveland, Ohio	914,808	876,050	Nashville, Tenn.	174,307	170,874
Washington, D.C.	802,178	763,956	Corpus Christi, Tex.	108,287	167,690
St Louis, Mo.	856,796	750,026	Youngstown, Ohio	168,330	166,689
Milwaukee, Wis.	637,392	741,324	Shreveport, La.	127,206	164,372
San Francisco, Calif.	775,357	740,316	Hartford, Conn.	177,397	162,178
Boston, Mass.	801,444	697,197	Fort Wayne, Ind.	133,607	161,776
Dallas, Tex.	434,462	679,684	Bridgeport, Conn.	158,709	156,748
New Orleans, La.	570,445	627,525	Baton Rouge, La.	125,629	152,419
Pittsburg, Pa.	676,806	604,332	New Haven, Conn.	164,443	152,048
San Antonio, Tex.	408,442	587,718	Savannah, Ga.	119,638	149,245
San Diego, Calif.	334,387	573,224	Tacoma, Wash.	143,673	147,979
Seattle, Wash.	467,591	557,087	Jackson, Miss.	98,271	144,422
Buffalo, N.Y.	580,132	532,759	Paterson, N.J.	139,336	143,663
Cincinnati, Ohio	503,998	502,550	Evansville, Ind.	128,636	141,543
Memphis, Tenn.	396,000	497,524	Erie, Pa.	130,803	138,440
Denver, Colo.	415,786	493,887	Amarillo, Tex.	74,246	137,969
Atlanta, Ga.	331,314	487,455	Montgomery, Ala.	106,525	134,393
Minneapolis, Minn.	521,718	482,872	Fresno, Calif.	91,669	133,929
Indianapolis, Ind.	427,173	476,258	South Bend, Ind.	115,911	132,445
Kansas City, Mo.	456,622	475,539	Chattanooga, Tenn.	131,041	130,009
Columbus, Ohio	375,901	471,316	Albany, N.Y.	134,995	129,726
Phoenix, Ariz.	106,818	439,170	Lubbock, Tex.	71,747	128,691
Newark, N.J.	438,776	405,220	Lincoln, Nebr.	98,884	128,521
Louisville, Ky.	369,129	390,639	Madison, Wis.	96,056	126,706
Portland, Oreg.	373,628	372,676	Rockford, Ill.	92,927	126,706
Oakland, Calif.	384,575	367,548	Kansas City, Kans.	129,553	121,901
Fort Worth, Tex.	278,778	356,268	Greensboro, N.C.	74,389	119,574
Long Beach, Calif.	250,767	344,168	Topeka, Kans.	78,791	119,484
Birmingham, Ala.	326,037	340,887	Glendale, Calif.	95,702	119,442
Oklahoma City, Okla.	243,504	324,253	Beaumont, Tex.	94,014	119,175
Rochester, N.Y.	332,488	318,611	Camden, N.J.	124,555	117,159
Toledo, Ohio	303,616	318,003	Columbus, Ga.	79,611	116,779
St Paul, Minn.	311,349	313,411	Pasadena, Calif.	104,577	116,407
Norfolk, Va.	213,513	304,869	Portsmouth, Va.	80,039	114,773
Omaha, Nebr.	251,117	301,598	Trenton, N.J.	128,009	114,167
Honolulu, Hawaii	248,034	294,194	Newport News, Va.	42,358	113,662
Miami, Fla.	249,276	291,688	Canton, Ohio	116,912	113,631
Akron, Ohio	274,605	290,351	Dearborn, Mich.	94,994	112,007
El Paso, Tex.	130,485	276,687	Knoxville, Tenn.	124,769	111,827
Jersey City, N.J.	299,017	276,101	Hammond, Ind.	87,594	111,698
Tampa, Fla.	124,681	274,970	Scranton, Pa.,	125,536	111,443
Dayton, Ohio	243,872	262,332	Berkeley, Calif.	113,805	111,268
Tulsa, Okla.	182,740	261,685	Winston Salem, N.C.	87,811	111,135
Wichita, Kans.	168,279	254,698	Allentown, Pa.	106,756	108,347
Richmond, Va.	230,310	219,958	Little Rock, Ark.	102,213	107,813
Syracuse, N.Y.	220,583	216,038	Lansing, Mich.	92,129	107,807
Tucson, Ariz.	45,454	212,892	Cambridge, Mass.	120,740	107,716
Des Moines, Iowa	177,965	208,982	Elizabeth, N.J.	112,817	107,698
Providence, R.I.	248,674	207,498	Waterbury, Conn.	104,477	107,130
San Jose, Calif.	95,280	204,196	Duluth, Minn.	104,511	106,884
Charlotte, N.C.	134,042	201,564	Anaheim, Calif.	14,556	104,184
Albuquerque, N.M.	96,815	201,189	Peoria, Ill.	111,856	103,162
Jacksonville, Fla.	204,517	201,030	New Bedford, Mass.	109,189	102,477
Flint, Mich.	163,143	196,940	Niagara Falls, N.Y.	90,872	102,394
Mobile, Ala.	129,009	194,856	Wichita Falls, Tex.	68,042	101,724
Sacramento, Calif.	137,572	191,667	Torrance, Calif.	22,241	100,991
Yonkers, N.Y.	152,798	190,634	Utica, N.Y.	101,531	100,410
Salt Lake City, Utah	182,121	189,454	Santa Ana, Calif.	45,533	100,350

VITAL STATISTICS

Vital statistics are based on records of births, deaths, foetal deaths, marriages and divorces filed with registration officials of states and cities. Figures for the US include Alaska beginning with 1959 and Hawaii beginning with 1960.

Annual collection of mortality records from a national death-registration area was inaugurated in 1900. A national birth-registration area was established in 1915. These areas, which at their inception comprised 10 states and the District of Columbia, expanded gradually until 1933, when both the birth- and death-registration areas covered the entire continental US. Marriage and divorce statistics are compiled from reports furnished by state and local officials. Data on annulments are included in the divorce statistics. The marriage-registration area was established in 1957 with 29 states and 4 other areas. The divorce-registration area was established in 1958 with 14 states and 3 other areas. In Jan. 1970 the marriage-registration area included 39 states and 5 other areas, and the divorce-registration area included 28 states and one other area.

	Live births[1]	Deaths[2]	Marriages[3]	Divorces[4]	Maternal deaths[5]	Deaths under 1 year[6]
1900	—	343,217	709,000	55,751	—	—
1910	2,777,000	696,856	948,166	83,045	—	—
1920	2,950,000	1,118,070	1,274,476	170,505	12,058	129,531
1930	2,618,000	1,327,240	1,126,856	195,961	14,836	142,413
1940	2,559,000	1,417,269	1,595,879	264,000	8,876	110,984
1950	3,632,000	1,452,454	1,667,231	385,144	2,960	103,825
1960	4,257,850[7]	1,711,982	1,523,000	393,000	1,579	110,873
1966	3,606,274[7]	1,863,149	1,857,000	499,000	1,049	85,516
1967	3,520,959[8]	1,851,323	1,927,000	533,000	987	79,028
1968	3,501,564	1,930,082	2,059,000[9]	582,000[9]	950[9]	76,263
1969[9]	3,571,000	1,916,000	2,146,000	660,000	980	74,100

[1] Figures through 1959 include adjustment for under-registration (the 1959 registered count was 4,244,796); beginning 1960 figures represent number registered.
[2] Excluding fœtal deaths and deaths among the armed forces overseas.
[3] Estimates for all years.
[4] Includes reported annulments. Estimated for all years except 1930.
[5] Deaths for 1968 (Eighth Revision, International Classification of Diseases, adapted, 1965). Deaths from deliveries and complications of pregnancy, childbirth and the puerperium. Deaths for 1958–67 were classified according to the Seventh Revision of the International Lists of Diseases and Causes of Death, those for 1949–57 according to the Sixth Revision and those for 1939–48, according to the Fifth Revision.
[6] Excluding fœtal deaths.   [7] Based on a 50% sample
[8] Based on a 20–50% sample.   [9] Provisional.

The crude birth rate, based on total live-birth estimates per 1,000 total population, fell from 29·5 in 1915 to 18·4 in 1933; it rose to a peak of 26·6 in 1947—its highest for 25 years. This peak reflects demobilization (1945–46), the record number of marriages that followed, and the high levels of employment and income. The decrease in the following 3 years was moderate. In 1951 the rate moved upward and levelled off in 1957 at about 25 per 1,000 population. Since 1957 the crude birth rate has declined every year to 18·4 live births per 1,000 population in 1966. The crude birth rate for 1968 was 18·4. Estimated number of illegitimate births in 1968 was 339,200, a rate of 96·9 illegitimate births per 1,000 registered live births.

Deaths, excluding fœtal deaths (per 1,000 population), declined from 17·2 in 1900 to 10 in 1946. The death rate has been below 10 per 1,000 since 1947, fluctuating slightly from year to year, mainly under the impact of occurrences of outbreaks of severe respiratory diseases. Since the record low of 9·2 in 1954 the rate has ranged only between 9·3 and 9·6. The rate for 1963 was 9·6, for 1964, 9·4, for 1965, 9·4, for 1966. 9·5, for 1967, 9·4, for 1968, 9·7.

Leading causes of death, 1968, per 100,000 population: Diseases of heart, 372·9; malignant neoplasms, 159·6; vascular lesions affecting central nervous system, 104·8; accidents, 55·8. Suicides in 1968 were 10·7 per 100,000 population; homicides, 7·1.

The marriage rate per 1,000 population for selected years are: 1920, 12; 1932, 7·9; 1946, 16·4; 1951, 10·4; 1961, 8·5; 1963. 8·8; 1964, 9; 1965, 9·3; 1966, 9·5; 1967 9·7; 1968 (provisional), 10·3; 1969 (provisional), 10·6. The divorce rates per 1,000 population for selected years are: 1920, 1·6; 1946, 4·3; 1951 2·5: 1961, 2·3; 1965, 2·5; 1966, 2·5; 1967, 2·6; 1968 (provisional), 2·9; 1869 (provisional) 3·3.

Maternal mortality rates (deaths of mothers from conditions associated with deliveries and complications of pregnancy, childbirth and the puerperium) per 100,000 live births, were 1915–19, 727·9 and thereafter declined: 493·9 for 1935–39; 376 for 1940; 207·2 for 1945; 83·3 for 1950; 52·4 for 1954, and from 1955 to 1967 dropped 40% to 28. The 1967 rate for white women was 19·5 and for all other women 69·5. By state, the average maternal rate for 1965–67 was highest for Mississippi (69·4) and lowest for Vermont (4·2).

The infant mortality rate, 99·9 per 1,000 live births in 1915, fell to 85·8 in 1920; 71·7 in 1925; 64·6 in 1930; 38·3 in 1945; 29·2 in 1950; 26·4 in 1955; 26 in 1960; 24·8 in 1964; 24·7 in 1965; 23·7 in 1966; 22·4 in 1967; 21·8 in 1968. In 1968 the rate for whites was 19·2; for all other, 34·5.

IMMIGRATION

Immigration and the naturalization of aliens are regulated by the Immigration and Nationality Act of 1952 and amendments. On 3 Oct. 1965 the President signed into law amendments to the 1952 Act, which do away with the national origins quota system. Effective 1 Dec. 1965, the new Act provides for a maximum of 170,000 immigration visas annually from the Eastern Hemisphere countries and their dependencies. From 1 July 1968, all national origins quotas were abolished.

In addition to providing an annual numerical limitation of 170.000 immigrants for Eastern Hemisphere countries, and a maximum of 20,000 for any one country, there was also established an annual maximum of 120,000 immigrants to be admitted from independent countries of the Western Hemisphere. Parents, spouses and children of American citizens are designated 'immediate relatives', and are not subject to the numerical limitations. Certain other classes of immigrants are also exempt from these numerical limits. Public Law 89-732, which became effective 2 Nov. 1966, made it possible for qualified Cuban refugees who had lived in the US for 2 years or longer to be adjusted to permanent resident status in the US. By the end of fiscal year 1970, 135,823 had become permanent residents.

During the year ended 30 June 1970, 373,326 aliens became permanent residents of the US either as immigrants from abroad or by means of adjustment of status while in the US. Immigrants subject to numerical limitations numbered 287,283, or 77% of the total. Of the 86,343 immigrants not subject to numerical restrictions, 79,213 were immediate relatives of US citizens.

Immigrant aliens admitted to US for permanent residence, by country or region of birth, years ended 30 June:

Country or region of birth	Immigrants admitted			
	1967	1968	1969	1970
All countries	361,972	454,448	358,579	373,326
Europe	139,514	139,514	120,086	118 106
Austria	1,101	1,249	758	888
Czechoslovakia	1,406	1,678	3,307	4,520
Denmark	1,158	1,307	635	602
France	3,440	3,402	2,024	2,477
Germany	16,041	15,920	9,289	9,684
Greece	14,905	13,047	17,724	16,464
Hungary	2,016	2,063	1,795	1,770
Ireland	2,624	3,004	1,989	1,562
Italy	26,565	23,576	23,617	24,973
Netherlands	2,039	2,245	1,303	1,457
Norway	1,341	1,306	636	539
Poland	5,976	5,995	4,052	3,585
Portugal	13,927	12,212	16,528	13,195
Sweden	1,763	1,666	722	722
UK	24,965	28,586	15,014	14,158
USSR (Europe and Asia)	1,033	1,113	931	912
Yugoslavia	5,879	6,783	8,868	8,575
Other Europe	13,335	14,362	10,894	12,023
North America	140,138	228,060	132,426	129,114
Canada	23,442	27,662	18,582	13,804
Mexico	42,371	43,563	44,623	44,469
Cuba	33,321	99,312	13,751	16,334
Other West Indies	31,952	46,439	45,644	45,069
Central America	8,709	10,675	9,692	9,343
Other North America	343	409	134	95
South America	16,517	21,976	23,928	21,973
Asia	59,233	57,229	73,621	92.816
Africa	4,236	5,078	5,876	8,115
Australia and New Zealand	1,661	1,799	1,878	2,280
Other countries	673	792	764	922

The total number of immigrants admitted from 1820 up to 30 June 1970 was 45,162,638; this included 9,506,084 from UK and Ireland, 6,917,097 from Germany, 5,176.488 from Italy, 4,301,867 from Austria–Hungary, 3,968,708 from Canada, 3,346,815 from USSR, 1,592,592 from Mexico and 1,519,235 from Asia.

Aliens coming to the US for temporary periods of time are classified as non-immigrants. In the year ending 30 June 1970, a total of 4,431,180 non-immigrants came to the US as tourists, students, exchange visitors, aliens in transit and representatives of foreign governments. This is exclusive of multiple entries at land borders and of alien crewmen. Tourists, primarily from Mexico, Canada, the UK and Germany numbered 3,020,359, 27% increase over 1969.

During the year ended 30 June 1970, 16,893 aliens were deported and 303,348 other deportable aliens were required to depart from the US without formal deportation proceedings.

In accordance with the Immigration and Nationality Act, 4,247,377 aliens filed address reports in Jan. 1970: of the 3,719,750 permanent resident aliens who reported, 714,509 were nationals of Mexico, 398,310 of Canada, 298,881 of the UK, 235,842 of Italy, 218,118 of Cuba and 216,593 of Germany. States with the largest alien populations were: California, 981,842; New York, 820,578; Florida, 290,237; Illinois, 263,935; Texas, 257,876, and New Jersey, 232,967.

In the year ended 30 June 1970, 110,399 persons became US citizens through naturalization; this includes 79,761 who were naturalized under the general provision of 5-year residence in the US, 19,922 spouses and children of US citizens, 10,616 military and 100 who were naturalized under other provisions. Of the total, there were 20,888 former nationals of Cuba, 10,067 of Germany, 7,892 of Italy, 7,549 of the UK, 6,340 of Canada, 6,195 of Mexico and 5,469 of the Philippines.

Bogue, D. J., *The Population of the USA.* Glencoe, Ill., 1959
Coale, A. J., and Zelnik, M., *New Estimates of Fertility and Population in the United States.* Princeton Univ. Press, 1963
Divine, R. A., *American Immigration Policy, 1924–52.* Yale Univ. Press, 1957
Hutchinson, E. P., *Immigrants and their Children, 1850–1950.* New York, 1956
Jones, M. A., *American Immigration.* Univ. of Chicago Press, 1960
Okun, B., *Trends in Birth Rates in the US since 1870.* Johns Hopkins Univ. Press, 1958
Thompson Company, J. Walter, *Population and its Distribution.* 8th ed. New York, 1961

RELIGION

The *Yearbook of American Churches for 1970*, published by the National Council of the Churches of Christ in the USA, New York, presents the latest figures available from official statisticians of church bodies. The large majority of the reports are for the calendar year 1968, or a fiscal year ending in 1968. The reports indicate that there were 128,469,636 members in 226 religious bodies of US, in 328,866 local churches. There were 209,913 clergymen having local congregations. The figures for membership represented a gain of 2,024,526 persons over the reports in the previous *Yearbook*. The principal religious bodies (numerically or historically) or groups of religious bodies are shown below:

Denominations	Local churches	Total membership
Summary:		
Protestant bodies	288,539	70,396,454
Roman Catholic Church	23,781	47,873,238
Jewish Congregations[1]	4,700	5,780,000
Eastern Churches	1,352	3,526,068
Old Catholic, Polish National Catholic and Armenian	435	793,876
Buddhists	59	100,000
1969 totals	318,866	128,469,636[2]

[1] Includes Orthodox, Conservative and Reformed bodies.
[2] Care should be taken in interpreting membership statistics for the US Churches. Some statistics are accurately compiled and others are estimates. Also statistics are not always comparable.

Denominations	Local churches	Total membership
Protestant bodies:		
Adventist bodies	3,714	426,632
Assemblies of God	8,510	595,231
Baptist bodies	113,261	25,896,250
Brethren, German Baptist	1,354	238,256
Brethren, River	175	9,473
Christian Churches (Disciples of Christ), International Convention and Churches of Christ	14,464	4,143,263
Church of Christ, Scientist[1]	2,461	. . .
Church of God in Christ	4,500	425,000
Church of the Nazarene	4,652	358,346
Churches of God	9,911	542,990
Churches of the Living God	383	45,922
Churches of the New Jerusalem	70	5,771
Evangelical Free Church of America	517	50,312
Evangelical United Brethren Church[2]	3,970	732,377
Evangelistic Associations	602	74,864
Friends, Religious Society of	1,123	126,982
Latter Day Saints[3]	5,467	2,063,522
Lutheran bodies	17,365	8,999,007
Mennonite bodies	2,002	198,888
Methodist bodies	57,795	13,693,322
Moravian bodies	172	66,742
Pentecostal Assemblies	5,545	458,606
Presbyterian bodies	14,354	4,406,411
Protestant Episcopal Church	7,180	3,420,297
Reformed bodies	1,667	688,814
Salvation Army	1,121	324,911
Spiritualists[4]	297	24,174
Unitarian Universalist Churches[5]	1,135	177,431
United Brethren bodies	356	25,057
United Church of Christ[6]	6,909	2,052,857

[1] For 1936, as reported in Federal Census of Religious Bodies. Figures not included in the totals above. The Church of Christ, Scientist, has a regulation forbidding the publication of statistics of membership.
[2] Represents merger of Evangelical Church and the Church of the United Brethren in 1946.
[3] Of this group, Church of Jesus Christ of Latter-day Saints (parent body) reported 4,413 churches and 1,981,965 members in 1967.
[4] The classification embraces all denominations calling themselves Spiritualists.
[5] Represents merger in 1961 of the American Unitarian Association and the Universalist Church of America.
[6] Represents merger in 1961 of Congregational Christian Churches and the Evangelical Reformed Church.

Yearbook of American Churches. Annual, from 1951. New York
Blanshard, P., American Freedom and Catholic Power. 2nd ed. Boston, 1948
Clark, E. T., The Small Sects in America. Rev. ed. New York, 1949
Johnson, A. W., and Yost, F. H., Separation of Church and State in the United States. Minneapolis and London, 1949
Mead, F. S., Handbook of Denominations in the US. 4th ed. New York, 1965
Moehlman, C. H., The Wall of Separation between Church and State. Boston, 1951
Roemer, T., The Catholic Church in the United States. Rev. ed. New York, 1961
Sperry, W. L., Religion in America. London, 1945
Stokes, A. P., and Pfeffer, L., Church and State in the US. New York, 1964
Sweet, W. W., The Story of Religion in America. 2nd ed. New York, 1950

EDUCATION

Under the system of government in the USA, elementary and secondary education is committed in the main to the several states. Each of the 50 states has a system of free public schools, established by law, with courses covering 12 years. There are 3 structural patterns in common use: the 8–4 plan, meaning 8 elementary grades followed by 4 high school grades; the 6–3–3 plan, or 6 elementary grades followed by a 3-year junior high school and a 3-year senior high school; and the 6–6 plan, 6 elementary grades followed by a 6-year high school. All plans lead to high-school graduation, usually at age 17 or 18. Vocational education is an integral part of secondary education. In addition, all but 5 states have kindergartens and some states have 2-year junior colleges as part of the free public school system. Each state has delegated a large degree of control of the educational programme to local school districts (numbering 19,169), each with a board of education (usually 3 to 9 members) elected locally and serving mostly without pay. The school policies of the local districts must be in accord with the laws and the regulations of their state Departments of Education. Almost every state has compulsory school attendance laws; in 37 states and the District of Columbia children are required to attend school until the age of 16 years; in 7 states until 17 and in 4 states until 18.

The Census Bureau estimates that in April 1960 only 3,055,000 or 2·4% of the 126m. persons who were 14 years of age or older were unable to read and write; in 1930 the percentage was 4·8. In 1940 a new category was established—the 'functionally illiterate', meaning those who had completed fewer than 5 years of elementary schooling; for persons 25 years of age or over this percentage was 5·6 in March 1969 (for the non-white population alone it was 15·2%); it was 1·2 for white and 2·4% for non-whites in the 25–29-year-old group. The Bureau reported that in March 1969 the median years of school completed by all persons 25 years old and over was 12·1, and that 10·7% had completed 4 or more years of college. For the 25–29-year-old group, the median school years completed was 12·6 and 16% had completed 4 or more years of college.

In the autumn of 1969, 7·3m. students (4·4m. men and 2·9m. women) were enrolled in 2,525 colleges and universities; 1·7m. were first-time students. Total enrolment represents a number equal to 31 per 100 persons between the ages of 18 and 24.

Public elementary and secondary school revenue is supplied from county and other local sources (52% in 1967–68), state sources (38·5%) and federal sources (8·8%). The tendency is for the counties and local units to contribute less and for the state and federal sources to contribute more. In 1967–68 the amount, including interest, expended on public elementary and secondary schools was $27,863m., representing an annual cost per pupil of $811. In addition, $4.256m., or $115 per pupil, was expended for capital outlay. Estimated expenditures for private elementary and secondary schools in 1967–68 were $4,400m. In 1967–68 the 2,400 universities and colleges expended $16,825m., of which $10,342m. was spent by institutions under public control. Federal funds for higher education amounted to 19·9% of current income; educational and general income from state governments totalled 24·9%; students contributed in fees 20%, and all other sources 35·2%.

Vocational education below college grade, including the training of teachers to conduct such education, has been federally aided since 1938. During the school year 1968–69 enrolments in the vocational classes were: Agriculture, 850,705; distributive occupations, 563,431; health occupations, 175,101; home economics, 2,449,052; trade and industry, 1,270,859; technical education, 315,311; office occupations, 1,835,124. Federal support funds were $254·7m.

Summary of statistics of schools (public and non-public), teachers and pupils in autumn 1969 (compiled by the US Office of Education):

Schools by level	Number of schools	Teachers	Enrolment
Elementary schools:			
Public	68,456	1,108,000	27,400,000
Non-public	14,396	147,000	4,300,000
Secondary schools:			
Public	26,657	906,000	18,200,000
Non-public	4,153	80,000	1,400,000
Higher education:			
Public	1,060	382,000	5,400,000
Non-public	1,465	192,000	1,900,000
Total	116,187	2,815,000	58,600,000

Most of the non-public elementary and secondary schools are affiliated with religious denominations. Of the children attending non-public schools, 87% are enrolled in Roman Catholic schools, 8% in other church-related schools and 5% in schools which are not affiliated to a religious denomination.

During the school year 1968–69 high-school graduates numbered 2,839,000 (1,408,000 boys and 1,431,000 girls). Institutions of higher education conferred 769,810 bachelor's and first professional degrees for the academic year 1968–69, 447,001 to men and 322,809 to women; 194,414 master's degrees, 121,881 to men and 72,533 to women; and 26,189 doctorates, 22,753 to men and 3,436 to women.

Nearly 135,000 foreign citizens were on American college and university campuses during the academic year 1968–69; 121,400 were students, and 12,100 were scholars engaged in research or teaching. The percentages of students coming from various areas were: Far East, 35; Latin America, 19; Europe, 15; Near and Middle East, 12; North America, 11; Africa, 6; Oceania, 2. There were 11 US institutions enrolling 1,500 or more, the greatest number, 6,146, being at the University of California (all campuses).

School enrolment, Oct. 1968, embraced 74·9% of the 4·1m. who were 5 years old; 98·3% of the 4·2m. aged 6; 99·1% of the 28·9m. aged 7–13 years; 94·3% of the 15m. aged 14–17; 50·4% of the 6·6m. aged 18 and 19; 21·4% of the 14m. aged 20–24 years.

The US Office of Education estimates the total enrolment in the autumn of 1970 at all the country's educational institutions (public and non-public) at 59·2m. (58·7m. in the autumn of 1969); this was 29% of the total population of the USA as of 1 Sept. 1970.

Elementary: Public schools, 27·5m. (27·4m. in 1969); non-public schools, 4·2m. (4·3m.); total, 31·8m. (31·7m.).

Secondary: Public schools, 18·5m. (18·2m.); non-public, 1·4m. (1·4m.); total, 19·6m. (19·6m.).

Higher education: Universities, other 4-year colleges and 2-year institutions of higher education, 7·6m. (7·3m.).

The number of teachers in the public elementary and secondary schools in the autumn of 1970 is estimated at 2m. The average annual salary of the public school teachers was about $8,520 in 1969–70.

All states require at least a bachelor's degree, and 3 states require completion of 5 years of college work for secondary school teachers; 47 states require a bachelor's degree for elementary school teachers, and the other states at least 2 years of college work. Thirty states, the District of Columbia and Puerto Rico require that the applicant for a teaching certificate be a citizen of the US or that he must have filed a declaration of intent. Twenty-five states, the District of Columbia and Puerto Rico require that the applicant subscribe to an oath of allegiance or loyalty to the US and the state.

CINEMAS. Cinemas increased from 17,003 in 1940 to 20,239 in 1950 and decreased to 9,150 (plus 3,502 drive-in cinemas) in 1963.

NEWSPAPERS. Of the daily newspapers being published in the USA in 1966, 324 were morning papers with a circulation (1 Oct.) of 24,806,000, and 1,444 were evening papers with a circulation of 36,592,000. The 578 Sunday papers had a total circulation of 49·3m.

BROADCASTING. On 1 Jan. 1968 there were in the USA and Territories, 7,102 authorized commercial broadcast stations, of which 813 were for television; those on the air numbered 6,513 (television, 634). In June 1967, 94% of households had television sets.

Digest of Educational Statistics. Annual. Office of Education, Washington 25, D.C. (from 1962)
American Junior Colleges. 6th ed. American Council of Education. Washington, 1963
American Universities and Colleges. 9th ed. American Council of Education. Washington, 1964
Ayer's Directory of Newspapers and Periodicals. Annual, from 1880. Philadelphia
Berelson, B., *Graduate Education in the United States.* New York, 1960
De Young, C. A., and Wynn, D. R., *American Education.* 5th ed. New York, 1964
Douglass, H. R., *Secondary Education in the US.* 2nd ed. New York, 1964
French, W. M. *America's Educational Tradition.* Boston, 1964
Good, H. G., *History of American Education.* 2nd ed. New York and London, 1962
Hofstadter, R., and Smith, W., *American Higher Education: a documentary history.* 2 vols. Univ. of Chicago Press, 1962
Mott, F. L., *American Journalism: A History of Newspapers in the United States.* 3rd ed. New York, 1962

JUSTICE

Legal controversies may be decided in two systems of courts: the federal courts, with jurisdiction confined to certain matters enumerated in Article III of the

Constitution, and the state courts, with jurisdiction in all other proceedings. The federal courts have jurisdiction exclusive of the state courts in criminal prosecutions for the violation of federal statutes, in civil cases involving the government, in bankruptcy cases and in admiralty proceedings, and have jurisdiction concurrent with the state courts over suits between parties from different states, and certain suits involving questions of federal law.

The highest court is the Supreme Court of the US, which reviews cases from the lower federal courts and certain cases originating in state courts involving questions of federal law. It is the final arbiter of all questions involving federal statutes and the Constitution; and it has the power to invalidate any federal or state law or executive action which it finds repugnant to the Constitution. This court, consisting of 9 justices who receive salaries of $60,000 a year (the Chief Justice, $62,500), meets from Oct. until June every year and disposes of about 3,380 cases, deciding about 380 on their merits. In the remainder of cases it either summarily affirms lower court decisions or declines to review. A few suits, usually brought by state governments, originate in the Supreme Court, but issues of fact are mostly referred to a master.

The US courts of appeals number 11 (in 10 circuits composed of 3 or more states and 1 circuit for the District of Columbia); the 97 circuit judges receive salaries of $42,500 a year. Any party to a suit in a lower federal court usually has a right of appeal to one of these courts. In addition, there are direct appeals to these courts from many federal administrative agencies. In the year ending 30 June 1970 more than 11,660 appeals were filed in the courts of appeals.

The trial courts in the federal system are the US district courts, of which there are 90 in the 50 states, 1 in the District of Columbia and 1 each in the territories of Puerto Rico, Virgin Islands, Canal Zone and Guam. Each state has at least 1 US district court, and 3 states have 4 apiece. Each district court has from 1 to 27 judgeships. There are 401 US district judges ($40,000 a year), who handle about 87,000 civil cases and 48,000 criminal defendants every year.

In addition to these courts of general jurisdiction, there are special federal courts of limited jurisdiction. The Court of Claims (7 judges at $42,500 a year) decides claims for money damages against the federal government in a wide variety of matters; the Customs Court (9 judges at $40,000 a year) determines controversies concerning the classification and valuation of imported merchandise; and the Court of Customs and Patent Appeals (5 judges at $42,500 a year) hears appeals from the Customs Court, the Tariff Commission and the Patent Office.

The judges of all these courts are appointed by the President with the approval of the Senate; to assure their independence, they hold office during good behaviour and cannot have their salaries reduced. This does not apply to the territorial judges, who hold their offices for a term of years. The judges may retire with full pay at the age of 70 years if they have served a period of 10 years, or at 65 if they have 15 years of service, but they are subject to call for such judicial duties as they are willing to undertake. Only 9 US judges up to 1970 have been involved in impeachment proceedings, of whom 3 district judges and 1 commerce judge were convicted and removed from office.

Of the 87,321 civil cases filed in the district courts in the year ending 30 June 1970, about 39,300 arose under various federal statutes (such as labour, social security, tax, patent, securities, antitrust and civil rights laws); 25,300 involved personal injury or property damage claims; 17,150 dealt with contracts; and 3,300 were actions concerning real property.

Of the 38,102 criminal cases filed in the district courts in the year ending 30 June 1970, about 4,600 were charged with alleged infractions of the immigration laws; 4,600, the transport of stolen motor vehicles; about 3,225, larceny and theft; 3,700, embezzlement and fraud; about 1,350, liquor laws, and 3,500 narcotics laws.

Persons convicted of federal crimes are either fined, released on probation under the supervision of the probation officers of the federal courts, confined in prison for a period of up to 6 months and then put on probation (known as split sentencing) or confined in one of the following institutions: 3 for juvenile and youths; 7 for young adults; 5 for intermediate term adults; 5 for short-term adults; 2 for females; 1 hospital and 8 community service centres. In addition, prisoners are confined in centres operated by the National Institutes of Mental Health. In addition, prisoner drug addicts may be committed to US Public Health Service hospitals for treatment. In 1969–70 about 1,500 of the federal prison population were placed on work release, that is, they were confined in prison at night and permitted to work at gainful employment during the weekdays. Another 278 at any given time were placed in pre-release centres. Prisoners confined in institutions operated by the US Bureau of Prisons for the year ending 30 June 1970, numbered 21,206.

The state courts have jurisdiction over all civil and criminal cases arising under state laws, but decisions of the state courts of last resort as to the validity of treaties or of laws of the United States, or on other questions arising under the Constitution, are subject to review by the Supreme Court of the US. The state court systems are generally similar to the federal system, to the extent that they generally have a number of trial courts and intermediate appellate courts, and a single court of last resort. The highest court in each state is usually called the Supreme Court or Court of Appeals with a Chief Justice and Associate Justices, usually elected but sometimes appointed by the Governor with the advice and consent of the State Senate or other advisory body; they usually hold office for a term of years, but in some instances for life or during good behaviour. Their salaries range from $14,000 to $40,000 a year. The lowest tribunals are usually those of Justices of the Peace; many towns and cities have municipal and police courts, with power to commit for trial in criminal matters and to determine misdemeanours for violation of the municipal ordinances; they frequently try civil cases involving limited amounts.

The Federal Bureau of Investigation estimates the number of major crimes in the US and its possessions as follows:

Crime index classification	1959–61 average	1969	Crime index classification	1959–61 average	1969
Murder	8,670	14,590	Burglary	789,300	1,949,800
Forcible rape	15,860	36,470	Larceny over $50	464,300	1,512,900
Robbery	87,570	297,580	Motor car theft	312,000	871,900
Aggravated assault	129,400	366,420			
			Total	1,807,100	4,989,700

The death penalty is illegal in Alaska, Hawaii, Iowa, Maine, Minnesota, Oregon, West Virginia, Wisconsin and Michigan; in North Dakota it is legal only for treason and first-degree murder committed by a prisoner serving a life sentence for first-degree murder, in Rhode Island only for murder committed by a prisoner serving a life sentence and in Vermont and New York for the murder of a peace officer in the line of duty and for first-degree murder by those who kill while serving a life sentence for murder. The death penalty, although still legal in most states, has fallen into disuse and has been abolished *de facto* in many states.

In 1967 only 2 persons were executed under civil authority; both for murder. No executions in 1968, 1969 and 1970. On 31 Dec. 1969, 524 prisoners were reported under sentence of death.

The total number of civilian executions carried out in the US from 1930 to 1967 was 3,859, including 1,751 white persons (20 women), 2,066 Negroes (12 women) and 42 persons of other races.

Federal 'Political' Crimes. Prosecutions for what may be loosely described as 'political' offences, or crimes directed towards the overthrow by violence of the federal government, which were somewhat numerous in the early 1950s, have declined sharply over the last 15 years and are now exceedingly rare. During the fiscal year 1969–70 the following number of defendants appeared in federal courts: Espionage, none; Subversive Activities Control Act, 1950, none; contempt of Congress, 2.

A Guide to Court Systems. Institute of Judicial Administration. New York, 1960
The United States Courts (88th Congress, 1st Session, House Document No. 180). US Government
  Printing Office, 1967

N

The Challenge of Crime in a Free Society. Report of the President's Commission on Law Enforcement and Administration of Justice. US Government Printing Office, 1967
Hart and Wechsler, *The Federal Courts and the Federal System*. Brooklyn, N.Y., 1953
Hurst, J. Willard, *The Growth of American Law*. New York, 1950
Mayers, L., *The American Legal System*. Rev. ed. New York, 1964
Murphy, W. F., *Congress and the Court*. Univ. of Chicago Press, 1962
Smith, B., *Police Systems in the US*. Rev. ed. New York, 1960
Vanderbilt, A. T., *Minimum Standards of Judicial Administration*. New York, 1949
Warren, Charles, *The Supreme Court in United States History*. 2 vols. Rev. ed. Boston, Mass, 1960

HEALTH AND SOCIAL WELFARE

Admission to the practice of medicine (for both doctors of medicine and doctors of osteopathic medicine) is controlled in each state by examining boards directly representing the profession and acting with authority conferred by state law. Although there are an increasing number of variations, the usual time now required to complete basic training is 8 years beyond the secondary school with an additional year of internship training. Certification as a specialist may require as much as 5 more years of hospital training plus experience in practice. In academic year 1968–69 the 104 US schools (including 5 osteopathic, 8 medical developing 4-year programmes and 3 basic science with 2-year programmes after which the students complete their training in a medical school) graduate 8,486 physicians. About 9% of the total students were women. In 1969 the total estimated number of physicians (MD and DO—in all forms of practice and retired from medical practice) in the US, Puerto Rico and outlying US areas was 339,400. The distribution of physicians throughout the country is uneven, both by state and by urban–rural areas.

In 1968–69 the 52 dental schools graduated 3,433 dentists. Dentists in 1969 numbered 113,600. New York state had 1 to 1,287 population and South Carolina, 1 to 3,988; national average, 1 to 1,287.

In 1968–69 schools of professional nursing numbered 1,870 with 42,176 graduates that year. In 1969 there were an estimated 680,500 professional nurses employed full- or part-time (1 to 296 inhabitants), ranging (in 1966) from 1 per 186 in Connecticut to 1 per 750 in Arkansas.

Number of hospitals listed by the American Hospital Association in 1969 was 7,144, with 1·65m. beds and 30,729,000 admissions during the year; average daily census was 1,346,000. Of the total, 415 hospitals with 170,000 beds were operated by the Federal Government; 2,230 with 819,000 beds by state and local government; 3,650 with 607,000 beds by non-profit organizations (including church groups); 849 with 55,000 beds are proprietary. Chief categories of non-federal hospitals are 5,853 short-term general and special hospitals with 826,000 beds; 509 psychiatric hospitals with 571,000 beds; 107 tuberculosis hospitals with 21,000 beds. Distribution of short-term general hospital facilities among states ranges from 2·31 (Alaska) to 6·16 (N. Dakota) hospital beds per 1,000 population; the national average is 4·17. It was estimated that, on 1 Jan. 1969, more than 91,000 additional beds in general hospitals, 175,000 additional long-term care beds (nursing homes and chronic disease hospitals) and 1,000 tuberculosis beds were needed. Also 228,000 general hospital beds, 244,000 long-term care beds and 9,000 tuberculosis beds are in need of modernization.

Social welfare legislation was chiefly the province of the various states until the adoption of the Social Security Act of 14 Aug. 1935. This as amended provides for a federal system of old-age, survivors and disability insurance; health insurance for the aged; federal state unemployment insurance; and federal grants to states for public assistance (old-age assistance, medical assistance for the aged, aid to families with dependent children, and aid to the permanently and totally disabled) and for maternal and child-health and child-welfare services. The Social Security Administration of the Department of Health, Education and Welfare has responsibility for the only completely federal programme under the Act—old-age, survivors and disability insurance, and health insurance for the aged. The Social and Rehabilitation Service, an agency of the same Department, has federal responsibility for all other programmes except unemployment insurance, which is the responsibility of the Department of Labor, and maternal and child health services, which is the responsibility of Health Services and Mental Health Administration (DHEW).

Since 1966 the Social Security Act provides for protection against the cost of medical care in old age through the two-part programme of health insurance for people 65 and over (Medicare). During the first 4 years of operation 22·6m. in-patient hospital admissions were recorded under the hospital insurance part of the programme. Hospitals were paid $15,700m. for this in-patient care. Under the voluntary medical insurance part of Medicare, $5,700m. was paid on 127·5m. bills for services during the first 4 years.

In Jan. 1970 about 94m. persons were in employment covered by old-age, survivors and disability insurance (including about 650,000 covered jointly by that programme and railroad retirement).

In Jan. 1970, 25·31m. beneficiaries were on the rolls, and the average benefit paid to a retired worker (not counting any paid to his dependants) was $112.

Benefits paid during fiscal year 1969 totalled $26,800m., including $2,500m. paid to disabled workers and their dependants.

Total expenditures for public assistance (including medical assistance) during the calendar year 1969 amounted to $11,547·48m. By Jan. 1970 all states, plus Washington, D.C., Guam, Puerto Rico and the Virgin Islands were making payments under the programme of medical assistance (Medicaid) authorized by 1965 legislation. In March 1970 about 7·86m. persons (adults and children) were receiving payments under aid to families with dependent children (average, $43.30). Average payments of $75.10 were going to 2·07m. old-age assistance recipients. Payments to 80,300 needy blind averaged $100.10, and 830,000 permanently and totally disabled persons received an average of $92.55. The federal government shares in the financing of all these state-administered programmes. General assistance, financed entirely by state and local governments, went to 932,000 persons and averaged $51.95 per person.

During the fiscal year 1969–70 federal appropriations for grants to states were made for maternal and child health services amounting to $50m.; for crippled children's services, $58m., and for child welfare services, $46m. Additional appropriations for grants for research projects relating to maternal and child health and crippled children's services were $5·9m.; research, training and demonstration projects in the field of child welfare, $10·2m.; maternity and infant care projects, $36m.; projects to provide comprehensive health care for school and pre-school children, $38·7m.; and training personnel for health care of mothers and children, $9m.

Burns, E. M., *Social Security and Public Policy*. New York, 1956
Friedlander, W. A., *Introduction to Social Welfare*. 2nd ed. New York, 1961
Gagliardo, D., *American Social Insurance*. Rev. ed. New York, 1955
Grod, F. P., *Public Health Law Manual*. New York, 1965
Schottland, C. A. *The Social Security Program in the US*. New York, 1963
Smillie, W. G., *Public Health Administration in the US*. 3rd ed. New York, 1947

FINANCE

FEDERAL

Since 10 June 1921 a National Annual Budget System and an independent Audit of Government Accounts have been installed.

A new unified comprehensive budget concept was introduced in Jan. 1968 to replace the several budget concepts used in the past. This budget covers all the programmes of federal government, including those financed through trust funds, such as for social security, Medicare and highway construction. Total outlays are divided between an expenditure account and a loan account to distinguish the different economic impact which these two types of transactions have. Receipts of the Government include all income from its sovereign or compulsory powers; income from business-type or market-oriented activities of the Government is offset against outlays.

BUDGET RECEIPTS AND OUTLAYS
(in millions of dollars)

Year ending 30 June	Receipts	Outlays	Surplus (+) or deficit (−)
	Consolidated Cash Statement		
1945	50,162	95,184	− 45,022
1950	40,940	43,147	− 2,207
	Unified Budget		
1955	65,469	68,509	− 3,041
1960	92,492	92,223	+ 269
1965	116,833	118,430	− 1,596
1969	187,792	184,556	+ 3,236
1970	193,844	196,752	− 2,908
1971 [1]	202,183	200,771	+ 1,331

[1] Estimate.

BUDGET RECEIPTS, BY SOURCE
(Fiscal years. In millions of dollars)

Source	1969	1970	1971[1]
Individual income taxes	87,249	90,371	91,000
Corporation income taxes	36,678	32,829	35,000
Social insurance taxes and contributions:			
Employment taxes and contributions	34,236	39,132	42,842
Unemployment insurance	3,328	3,465	3,335
Contributions for other insurance and retirement	2,353	2,699	2,931
Excise taxes	15,222	15,711	17,520
Estate and gift taxes	3,491	3,620	3,600
Customs	2,319	2,430	2,260
Miscellaneous	2,916	3,587	3,614
Total	187,792	193,844	202,103

[1] Estimate.

BUDGET OUTLAYS, BY AGENCY
(Fiscal years. In millions of dollars)

Agency	1969	1970	1971[1]
Agriculture Department	8,330	8,528	7,953
Commerce Department	854	1,027	1,014
Health, Education and Welfare Department	46,594	52,350	59,653
Housing and Urban Development Department	1,529	2,603	3,317
Interior Department	837	1,119	913
Justice Department	515	637	985
Labor Department	3,475	4,358	5,563
Post Office Department	920	1,514	382
State Department	437	447	473
Transportation Department	5,970	6,418	7,048
Treasury Department	16,924	19,491	19,066
Corps of Engineers	1,217	1,164	1,360
Foreign Economic Assistance	1,781	1,606	1,640
Office of Economic Opportunity	1,813	1,801	1,285
Atomic Energy Commission	2,450	2,453	2,411
General Services Administration	425	458	28
National Aeronautics and Space Administration	4,247	3,749	3,400
Veterans Administration	7,669	8,653	8,455
Export-Import Bank	246	219	195
Civil Service Commission	1,682	2,647	3,147
All other civilian agencies	3,095	4,058	4,212
Subtotal civilian agencies	111,010	125,300	132,500
Department of Defense, military and military assistance	78,666	77,831	71,791
Allowances, undistributed	—	—	3,118
Undistributed intrabudgetary transactions:			
Employer share, employee retirement	− 2,018	− 2,243	− 2,366
Interest received by trust funds	− 3,099	− 3,934	− 4,273
Total	184,556	196,752	200,771

[1] Estimate.

FOREIGN AID

The Agency for International Development is, within the US Department of State, responsible for the administration of the economic assistance programmes of the US Government. The AID, established in Nov. 1961, is the successor to the International Co-operation Administration (ICA), the Development Loan Fund (DLF), the Foreign Operation Administration (FOA), the Mutual Security Agency (MSA), the Technical Co-operation Administration (TCA) and the Economic Co-operation Administration (ECA). TCA was originally established to administer the Point IV programme, while ECA administered the European Recovery Programme, the so-called Marshall Plan, named after the then Secretary of State, the late George Marshall.

The Foreign Assistance Act of 1961 affirms the policy of the US Congress to 'make assistance available, upon request, . . . in scope and on a basis of long-range continuity essential to the creation of an environment in which the energies of the peoples of the world can be devoted to constructive purposes . . .'. The programme emphasizes long-term development, self-help efforts on the part of less developed countries, the value of private investment and the assistance to less-developed areas by industrialized countries.

Funds for these non-military programmes are authorized by Part I of the Foreign Assistance Act of 1961. Loans under the Development Loan Fund are made to assist long-range plans and programmes as well as to individual projects of high priority in the development plans of less-developed countries. They are payable in dollars and carry low interest rates and long periods of amortization. Funds appropriated for Technical Co-operation and Development Grants finance the sending of US technicians to less-developed countries, bringing people from those countries to the US for training and for other economic development activities, particularly those for the development of human resources in circumstances where even soft-term loans are not appropriate. Supporting Assistance is furnished to friendly countries and organizations to support or promote economic or political stability.

Funds are authorized and appropriated annually by the Congress. The funds authorized for the fiscal year ending 30 June 1970 totalled $1,878,000m. The most important appropriations were as follows (in $1m.):

Technical Co-operation and Development grants	166·8	Development loans	300·0
		International organizations	105·0
Alliance for Progress (grants and loans for Latin America)	336·5	Supporting assistance	395·0
		Contingency fund	12·5

President Nixon signed the appropriation bill on 9 Feb. 1970, which had been approved by the Senate on 28 Jan. 1970.

From 1 July 1945 to 30 June 1967 the US extended to foreign countries net foreign grants, credits and other assistance (through net accumulation of foreign currency claims for agricultural products sold), totalling $112,882m., after allowing for collections on principal, reverse grants and returns on grants, and the currencies disbursed by the US. Of this, $75,831m. was in economic aid and $37,486m. was in military assistance charged to the foreign appropriations.

NATIONAL DEBT

The gross public debt and guaranteed obligations on 30 June 1968 was $348,100m.

National direct debt excluding guaranteed obligations (in $1,000), and *per capita* debt (in $) on 30 June of the years shown:

	Public debt	Per capita[2]		Public debt	Per capita[2]
1919[1]	25,484,506	243	1962	298,645,042	1,600
1920	24,299,321	228	1963	306,466,243	1,618
1930[1]	16,185,310	132	1964	312,525,891	1,627
1940	48,496,602	367	1965	317,864,225	1,625
1950	257,376,855	1,697	1966	320,369,000	1,662
1960	286,470,603	1,585	1967	326,220,938	1,638

[1] On 31 Aug. 1919 gross debt reached its First World War (1914–18) peak of $26,596,702,000. which was the highest ever reached up to 1934; on 31 Dec. 1930 it had declined to $16,026m., the lowest it has been since the First World War. On 30 Nov. 1941, just preceding Pearl Harbour, debt stood at $61,363,867,932. The highest Second World War debt was $279,764,369,348 on 28 Feb. 1946.

[2] *Per capita* figures, beginning with 1960, have been revised; they are based on the Census Bureau's estimates of the total population of the US, including Alaska and Hawaii.

The permanent statutory debt limit is $285,000m.; a temporary limit of $324,000m. was in effect until 30 June 1965.

STATE AND LOCAL FINANCE

Revenue of the 50 states and all local governments (81,248) from their own sources amounted to $113,001m. in fiscal year 1968–69; in addition they received $19,153m. in revenue from fiscal aid, shared revenues and reimbursements from the federal government, bringing total revenue from all sources to $132,153m. Of the revenue from state and local sources, taxes provided $76.712m., of which property taxes (mainly imposed by local governments) yielded $30,673m. or 40% of all tax revenue; and sales taxes, both general sales taxes and selective excises, provided $26,519m. (35%).

State tax revenue totalled $41,931m. in fiscal year 1969. Largest sources of state tax revenue are general sales taxes (imposed during 1969 by 44 states), motor fuel sales taxes (all states), individual income (38 states), motor vehicle and operators' licences (all states), corporation income (41 states), tobacco products (49 states) and alcoholic beverage sales taxes (all states).

General revenue of local units from own sources in fiscal year 1968–69 totalled $45,861m. In addition they received $26,082m. from state and federal aids. Property taxes provided 40% of total general revenue.

Total expenditures of state and local governments were $131,600m. in 1968–69, of which approximately 65% was for current operation. Education took $47,238m. in current and capital expenditure; highways, $15,417m.; welfare (chiefly public assistance), $12,110m., and health and hospitals, $8,520m. Capital outlays (construction, equipment and land purchases) totalled $28,240m.

Gross debt of state and local governments totalled $133,548m. or $661 per capita at the close of their 1968–69 fiscal year. Total cash and investment assets of state and local governments were $123,177m., about 22% being in cash and the remainder in investments, mainly non-governmental securities.

American Economic Association, *Readings in fiscal policy*. Homewood, Ill., 1955
Brookings Institute and National Bureau of Economic Research, *Role of direct and indirect taxes in the federal revenue system*. Washington, D.C., 1964
National Bureau of Economic Research, *National economic accounts of the US: review, appraisal and recommendations*. 1958
Burkhead, J., *Government budgeting*. New York, 1956
Kimmell, L. H., *Federal budget and fiscal policy, 1789–1958*. Washington and London, 1959
Lewis, W., *Federal Fiscal Policy in the Post-war Recessions*. New York, 1963

NATIONAL DEFENCE

The President is C.-in-C. of the Army, Navy and Air Force.

The National Security Act of 1947 provides for the unification of the Army, Navy and Air Forces under a single Secretary of Defense with cabinet rank. The President is also advised by a National Security Council and the Office of Civil and Defense Mobilization.

The major components of the Department of Defense are the Office of the Secretary of Defense and the Joint Chiefs of Staff, who provide immediate staff assistance and advice to the Secretary; the departments of the Army, Navy and Air Force, each separately organized under a civilian head (not of cabinet rank); and the unified and specified commands.

ARMY

Secretary of the Army: Stanley R. Resor.

Central Administration. The Secretary of the Army is the head of the Department of the Army. Subject to the authority of the President as C.-in-C. and of the Secretary of Defense, he is responsible for all affairs of the Department.

The Secretary of the Army is assisted by the Under Secretary of the Army, 4 Assistant Secretaries of the Army (Financial Management; Installations Logistics; Research and Development; Manpower and Reserve Affairs), the Director of Civil Defense, the General Counsel, an Administrative Assistant, Chief of Legislative Liaison, Chief of Public Information and the Army Staff headed by the Chief of Staff, US Army. The office of the Under Secretary of the

Army includes a Deputy Under Secretary (International Affairs) and Deputy Under Secretary (Operations Research).

The Chief of Staff is the principal military adviser of the Secretary of the Army, and performs his duties under the direction of the Secretary of the Army, except as otherwise prescribed by law, by the President or by the Secretary of Defense. He has supervision of all members and organizations of the Army. The Vice Chief of Staff assists and advises the Chief of Staff.

The Army Staff furnishes professional assistance to the Secretary of the Army. The Army General Staff is the principal element of the Army Staff, and includes the offices of the Chief of Staff, Vice Chief of Staff, Assistant Vice Chief of Staff, Secretary of the General Staff, the 3 Deputy Chiefs of Staff (Military Operations, Personnel and Logistics), the Chief of Research and Development, the Comptroller of the Army, the Chief, Office of Reserve Components, the Assistant Chief of Staff for Intelligence, the Assistant Chief of Staff for Force Development and Assistant Chief of Staff for Communications (Electronics) and Director for Civil Disturbance Planning and Operations, Safeguard System Manager and the Army Reserve Forces Policy Committee. Other elements of the Army Staff are the offices of Judge Advocate General, Inspector General, Chief of Information, Chief National Guard Bureau, Chief Army Reserve, Chief of Military History, Adjutant General, Provost Marshal General, Chief of Chaplains, Chief of Personnel Operations, Surgeon General, Chief US Army Audit Agency, Chief of Engineers and Chief of Support Services.

The Army consists of the Regular Army, the Army National Guard of the US, the Army National Guard in the service of the US and the Army Reserve; and all persons appointed to, enlisted in or conscripted into, the Army without component; and all persons serving under call or conscription, including members of the National Guard of the States, etc., when in the service of the US.

Department of the Army strength, including cadets, was 1,431,837, as of 31 Dec. 1969, comprised, in major combat units, of 16 divisions, also brigades and regiments.

The Continental Army Command has responsibility for all installations of the 5 Continental US Armies and the Military District of Washington, D.C. The headquarters of the Continental US Armies are: First Army, Fort George G. Meade, Md.; Third Army, Fort McPherson, Ga.; Fourth Army, Fort Sam Houston, Texas; Fifth Army, Fort Sheridan, Chicago, Ill.; Sixth Army, Presidio of San Francisco, Cal.

The Commanding General, US Continental Army Command, with headquarters at Fort Monroe, Va., reports directly to the Chief of Staff.

The US Army Combat Developments Command assures the combat effectiveness of the soldier, using the latest scientific methodology and operations research techniques. The US Army Materiel Command is responsible for all Army operations dealing with equipment development, procurement, delivery, supply and maintenance.

Some 46% of the Army is deployed overseas. Headquarters of US Seventh and Eighth Armies are in Europe and Korea respectively.

Operational Commands and Weapons. The larger commands are the army group, the field army and the corps. A typical army group may consist of 2 field armies. A typical field army may consist of 3 corps; combat forces of armour and infantry; air defence artillery (*Nike-Hercules* and *Hawk* missile battalions); field artillery (*Pershing* missile battalions); combat support forces of aviation, engineer and signal elements; and combat service support forces. A typical corps may consist of 2 mechanized infantry divisions, 1 infantry division and 1 armoured division; 1 mechanized infantry brigade; 1 armoured cavalry regiment; corps artillery (105-mm howitzer, 155-mm howitzer, 8-in. howitzer, 175-mm gun, *Honest John* rocket and *Sergeant* missile battalions), air defence group (*Nike-Hercules, Hawk* and *Chaparral/Vulcan* battalions), and a target-acquisition battalion; combat support and combat service support forces.

US Army Divisions have a common base (containing command, aviation, divisional artillery, combat and combat support units) and a varying mixture of 'combat manoeuvre battalions' (usually 10 or 11 in number in 3 brigades) to make up airborne, infantry, armoured, mechanized infantry and airmobile divisions. Divisions can in this way be 'tailored' to fit a variety of strategic or tactical situations. An infantry division (ROAD), with about 15,900 men, may have 8 infantry battalions and 2 armoured battalions; a mechanized infantry division (ROAD), with about 16,000 men, may have 7 mechanized infantry battalions, 3 armoured battalions; an armoured division (ROAD), with about 16,000 men, may have 5 mechanized infantry battalions and 6 armoured battalions; an airborne division, with 13,000 men, may have 9 infantry (airborne) battalions.

Small arms include the M-14, which fires the 7·62 mm NATO cartridge either automatically or semi-automatically, and the M-16, which fires a 5·56-mm cartridge. The standard general-purpose machine-gun is the M-60 (23 lb.; 550 rounds of 7·62-mm per minute). Infantry weapons also include the M-79 grenade launcher and the M203 grenade launcher attachment for the M16A1 rifle, both of which fire a 40-mm grenade up to 400 metres, and the M-72 rocket, a light anti-tank weapon.

Combat vehicles of the US Army are the tank, armoured personnel carrier, armoured reconnaissance airborne assault vehicle and the armoured command and reconnaissance vehicle. The first-line tank is the M60A1 'Patton' with 105-mm main armament. The standard armoured personnel carrier is the M113A1; it carries a mechanized infantry squad. The M-114 command and reconnaissance vehicle is found in armoured cavalry regiments, squadrons and in scout platoons of armoured and mechanized infantry battalions. The M-551 'Sheridan' is an Armoured Reconnaissance Airborne Assault Vehicle in armoured cavalry units and assault units of airborne divisions; it fires both missiles and conventional ammunition.

The approved calibres of artillery are: light, 105-mm howitzer, medium 155-mm howitzer; and heavy, 175-mm gun and 8-in. howitzer. The 4·2-in. mortars and the 81-mm mortar are used by combat manoeuvre elements. The 90-mm, 106-mm recoilless rifles and the *Tow* are the present anti-tank weapons for infantry use. The *Dragon* continues in development. *Chaparral* and *Vulcan*, forward-area air-defence weapons, provides the capability of low-altitude defence against high-performance aircraft.

The Army has two categories of missiles—surface-to-surface field (artillery) and surface-to-air (air defence artillery). Surface-to-surface missiles are: *Honest John*, free flight, rocket equivalent to long-range artillery, nuclear or HE warhead, highly mobile, operational; *Sergeant*, guided, range about 75 miles, nuclear warhead, units activated, operational; *Pershing*, ballistic range about 400 miles operational; *Lance*, guided, storable, liquid propellant, under development. Surface-to-air missiles, for air defence, are: *Nike-Hercules*, guided, field or fixed installation, operational; *Hawk*, homing type, low-altitude, field, operational; *Chaparral*, infra-red homing, low-altitude, forward area, operational; *Redeye*, hand-held, infra-red homing, low-altitude forward area, operational; *Sam-D*, forward area, low-altitude, high-explosive warhead, under development; *Safeguard* and anti-missile system, under development.

The Army has fixed- and rotary-wing aircraft organic to its organizations where their use requires direct control and planning by the unit commander and their immediate and constant availability is essential. The Army has aircraft assigned for the following missions: command and control, reconnaissance and surveillance, fire-power, manoeuvre and mobility, logistics, utility transport and administrative mission support.

Enlistment, Draft, Terms of Service. Terms of service may be 2, 3, 4, 5 or 6 years. All male citizens and all male aliens admitted for permanent residence are required to register at age 18. Men between 18½ and 26 may be drafted by any of the Armed Forces for a period of 24 months' active service. Men eligible for the draft may volunteer for induction to discharge their active service obligations. Men inducted or who enlist incur a 6-year reserve obligation and must serve in the reserve any part of the period not served on active duty.

The Women's Army Corps is composed of volunteers in the Regular and Reserve components of the Army. They are eligible for military duties (other than of a combat nature) in all the Army's occupational areas.

The Army National Guard is a reserve military component with a dual status and role. Enlistment is voluntary. The members are recruited by each state, but are equipped and paid by the federal government. Training is supervised by the active Army (USCONARC), and unit organization parallels that for the active army; training facilities are made available by the USA and each state. As the organized militia of the several states, the District of Columbia and Puerto Rico, the Guard may be called into service for local emergencies by the sovereigns in those jurisdictions; and may be called into federal service by the President to thwart invasion or rebellion or to enforce federal law. In its role as a reserve component of the Army, the Guard is subject to the order of the President in the event of national emergency. Army Guardsmen man 50% of the air-defence missile positions and, together with the Air Guard, provide 100% of the air defence of Hawaii.

The Army Reserve is designed to supply qualified and experienced units and individuals in an emergency. Commanding General, USCONARC, commands the units of the Army Reserve. Members are assigned to one of 3 categories: the Ready, Standby or Retired Reserve. A limited number of Ready Reservists is subject to call by the President in case of national emergency without declaration of war by Congress. The Standby Reserve and the Retired Reserve may be called only after declaration of war or national emergency by Congress.

Army 1968 Green Book. Association of the U.S. Army, Washington, D.C.
The Army Almanac. Dept. of the Army, Washington, D.C.
Dupuy, R. E. and T. N., *Military Heritage of America.* New York, 1956
Forman, S., *West Point.* New York, 1950
ROTCM 145–20, Department of the Army ROTC Manual, *American Military History, 1607–1953.* Washington, 1956

NAVY

Secretary of the Navy: John H. Chafee.

The activities of the Department of the Navy are administered under the authority, direction and control of the Secretary of Defense by the Secretary of the Navy, assisted by an Under Secretary, 4 Assistant Secretaries, the Chief of Naval Operations and Commandant of the Marine Corps.

The 3 principal divisions of the Department of the Navy are:

The Navy Department: Central executive authority of the Department of the Navy composed of staff offices of the Secretary; those dealing with financial management, installations and logistics, man-power and reserves affairs, research and development; the office of the Chief of Naval Operations (comprised of the Vice Chief, Assistant Vice Chief, 6 Deputy Chiefs, 4 Program Directors, 3 Assistant Chiefs and the Naval Inspector General); Headquarters, U.S. Marine Corps; Headquarters; Naval Material Command; Bureau of Naval Personnel; and the Bureau of Medicine and Surgery.

The Operating Forces: Comprised of the Military Sea Transportation Service; U.S. Naval Forces, Europe; Atlantic and Pacific Fleets, including Fleet Marine Forces; operating forces of the Marine Corps; and other Naval forces and commands not otherwise assigned.

The Shore Establishment: Consists of commands dealing with the various systems (air, electronic, facilities engineering, ordnance, ship, supply) as well as communications; weather service; intelligence; naval air training; oceanographic; security; naval reserve training; 15 naval districts; Marine Corps Reserve and Supporting Establishment. Also includes other designated shore activities which are under command or supervision of many of the organizations depicted.

Among major shore activities are 9 shipyards, 41 air stations and facilities, 2 amphibious bases, 2 submarine bases and 14 naval stations. Under an agreement dated 2 Sept. 1940, the British Government granted leases for naval and air bases in Newfoundland, Bermuda, the Bahamas, Jamaica, St Lucia, Trinidad, Antigua and British Guiana; but these are not all now active.

Naval appropriations in recent years have been as follows: 1963, $15,270m.; 1964, $14,490m.; 1965, $14,809m.; 1966, $18,128m.; 1967, $20,709m.; 1968, $21,157m.; 1969, $21,004m.; 1970, $23,211m.; 1971, $21,545m.

The total personnel on duty on 31 July 1970 was 686,859 officers, enlisted men and officer candidates, plus 285,596 officers and enlisted Marines.

The following is a tabulated statement of US vessels existing on 31 Dec.:

Category	1963	1964	1965	1966	1967	1968	1969	1970
Attack aircraft carriers	15	16	16	16	17	17	15	15
Support aircraft carriers	11	11	11	11	11	11	12	12
Helicopter carriers[1]	7	6	8	8	9	9	7	7
Auxiliary aircraft transports	8	8	7	7	5	5	3	2
Aircraft ferry ships	16	15	15	15	15	15	15	13
Communications relay ships	1	1	2	2	2	2	2	2
Command ships	2	2	2	2	2	2	2	2
Nuclear powered submarines	31	50	55	65	73	77	87	93
Submarines (conventional)	144	140	140	137	127	116	89	62
Battleships	4	4	4	4	4	4	4	4
Cruisers	40	41	40	37	35	35	35	32
Frigates (Destroyer leaders)	24	26	30	35	33	33	33	33
Destroyers	358	357	360	350	345	343	294	289
Destroyer minelayers	10	10	10	10	10	10	10	10
Escort ships	274	277	270	264	258	252	225	223
Escort transports	64	55	46	35	23	15	13	11

[1] Rated as Amphibious Assault Ships.

The following table shows the principal surface ships of the US Navy, including all ships expected to be completed up to 1 April 1970 (in the armament column, guns of less than 3-in. calibre are not given):

Com- pleted	Name	Standard displace- ment Tons	Armour Belt In.	Guns In.	Principal armament	Shaft horse- power	Speed Knots
			Attack Aircraft Carriers				
1968	John F. Kennedy	67,000	—	—	Guided missiles (100 aircraft)	280,000	35
1965	America	64,000	—	—	Guided missiles (90 aircraft)	280,000	35
1962	Enterprise	75,700	—	—	100 aircraft	300,000 (nuclear power)	35
1962	Constellation	60,000	—	—	Guided missiles (85 aircraft)		35
1961	Kitty Hawk	60,000	—	—			35
1959	Independence	60,000	—	—		260,000	35
1957	Ranger	60,000	—	—	4 5-in. (80 aircraft)		35
1956	Saratoga	60,000	—	—			35
1955	Forrestal	59,650	—	—			33
1950	Oriskany	33,100	3	—	8 5-in. (75 aircraft)	150,000	33
1947	Coral Sea						
1945	F. D. Roosevelt Midway Bon Homme	51,000	—	—	4 5-in. (80 aircraft)	212,000	33
1944	Richard Hancock	33,100	3	—	4 5-in. (70 aircraft)	150,000	33
			Support Aircraft Carriers [1]				
1946	Kearsarge						
1945	Antietam Bennington						
1944	Randolph Shangri-La Ticonderoga Hornet Intrepid	30,800 to 33,100	3	—	4 5-in. (47 aircraft— more or fewer, according to size and type	150,000	33
1943	Lexington Wasp Yorktown						
1942	Essex						

The 'Essex' class comprised the *Essex, Yorktown, Intrepid, Hornet, Franklin, Lexington, Bunker Hill, Wasp, Ticonderoga, Hancock, Randolph, Bennington, Bon Homme Richard, Shangri-La, Tarawa, Antietam, Boxer, Kearsarge, Lake Champlain, Leyte, Philippine Sea, Princeton, Valley Forge, Oriskany.* (Five were rated as attack aircraft carriers, 11 as anti-submarine warfare aircraft carriers, 5 as auxiliary aircraft transports and 3 as amphibious assault ships.)

[1] *Lake Champlain* was stricken from the Navy List in Dec. 1969.

Com-pleted	Name	Standard displace-ment Tons	Armour Belt In.	Guns In.	Principal armament	Shaft horse-power	Speed Knots

Auxiliary Aircraft Transports (ex-Carriers) [1]

| 1943 | { Monteray [2]
{ San Jacinto | 11,000 | 3 | — | Light AA (45 aircraft) | 100,000 | 32 |

[1] Of the 'Essex' class *Bunker Hill* was converted to electronics laboratory in 1965, *Franklin* was stricken from the Navy List in 1964, *Tarawa* in 1967 and *Leyte* and *Philippine Sea* in 1969.

[2] Sister ship *Cabot* was transferred to Spain as a helicopter carrier on 30 Aug. 1967.

Aircraft Ferry Ships (ex-Escort Carriers)

| 1944–46 | { 9 Commence-
{ ment Bay
{ Class [1] | 11,373 | — | — | { 1 5-in.; Light AA (34
{ aircraft) | 16,000 | 19 |
| 1942–43 | 4 Bogue Class [2] | 9,800 | — | — | 30 aircraft | 8,500 | 18 |

[1] The 'Commencement Bay' class comprises the *Badoeng Strait*, *Commencement Bay*, *Cape Gloucester*, *Kula Gulf*, *Rabaul*, *Point Cruz*, *Rendova*, *Saidor*, *Vella Gulf*.

[2] The 'Bogue' class comprises the *Breton*, *Card*, *Core* and *Croatan*.

Helicopter Carriers (Amphibious Assault Ships)

1970	Inchon						
1968	New Orleans						
1966	Tripoli						
1965	Guam	17,000	—	—	24 helicopters	22,000	30
1963	Guadalcanal						
1962	Okinawa						
1961	Iwojima						

(The Amphibious Assault ship *Thetis Bay*, former Escort Aircraft Carrier, was stricken from the Navy List in 1964 and *Valley Forge*, *Boxer* and *Princeton* in 1969.)

Command Ships

| 1953 | Northampton [1] | 14,700 | 6 | — | 4 5-in.; 8 3-in. | 120,000 | 33 |
| 1947 | Wright [2] | 14,500 | 4 | — | Light AA | 120,000 | 33 |

[1] Originally designed as a heavy cruiser; redesigned as a tactical command ship; reclassified as a command ship in 1961.

[2] Originally built as light fleet aircraft carrier, reclassified as aircraft transport in 1959; reclassified and converted into Command Ship in 1962–63.

Major Communications Relay Ships (ex-Carriers)

| 1946 | Arlington [1] | 14,500 | 4 | — | Light AA | 120,000 | 33 |
| 1945 | Annapolis [2] | 11,373 | — | — | Light AA | 16,000 | 19 |

[1] Former Auxiliary Aircraft Transport *Saipan* (ex-Aircraft Carrier), converted to Major Communications Relay Ship (instead of Command Ship) 1963–64.

[2] Former Aircraft Ferry Ship *Gilbert Islands* (ex-Escort Carrier) converted to Major Communications Relay Ship 1962–64 and renamed.

Battleships

1944	{ Missouri [1] { Wisconsin [1]						
	{ Iowa [1]	45,000	19	18	9 16-in.; 20 5-in.	212,000	33
1943	{ New Jersey [2]						

[1] All laid up in reserve since 1955–58. [2] Reactivated in 1968–69.

Heavy Cruisers

1961	Long Beach	14,200	—	—	{ 1 twin 'Talos' and 2 { twin 'Terrier'; guid- { ed missile launchers; { 2 5-in.	80,000 (nuclear power)	30·5
1949	{ Newport News { Salem	17,000	8	3–5	{ 9 8-in.; 12 5-in.; 16 to 22 { 3-in.	130,000	33
1948	Des Moines						
1946	Albany	13,700	6	3–5	{ 2 twin 'Talos'; 2 twin { 'Terrier'; 2 5-in.	120,000	33
1946	{ Rochester { Oregon City	13,700	6	3–5	9 8-in.; 12 5-in.; 20 3-in.	120,000	33
1945	{ Chicago { Columbus	13,600	6	3–5	{ 2 twin 'Talos'; 2 twin { 'Terrier'; 2 5-in.	120,000	33

Only 5 of the above are active, *i.e.*, *Long Beach*, *Newport News*, *Albany*, *Chicago* and *Columbus*.

Completed	Name	Standard displacement Tons	Armour Belt In.	Guns In.	Principal armament	Shaft horse-power	Speed Knots

Heavy Cruisers (contd.)

Completed	Name	Tons	Belt In.	Guns In.	Principal armament	Shaft horse-power	Speed Knots
1943–46	{9 Baltimore Class}	13,600	6	3–5	9 8-in.; 12 5-in.; 14 3-in.	120,000	33
1943	{Boston Canberra}	13,300	6	3–5	{2 twin 'Terrier', 6 8-in.; 10 5-in.; 8 3-in.}	120,000	33

The 'Baltimore' class comprises the *Baltimore, Pittsburgh, Toledo, Bremerton, Fall River, Helena, Los Angeles, St Paul* and *Quincy.*

The *Boston* and *Canberra* were reclassified as Guided Missile Heavy Cruisers in 1955. The *Albany* was reclassed as a guided-missile cruiser in 1958 when she was decommissioned for conversion, completed by Nov. 1942. The *Chicago* and *Columbus* were reclassed as guided-missile cruisers in 1958–59, when they were scheduled for conversion which was complete in 1964 and 1963, respectively.

Light Cruisers

Completed	Name	Tons	Belt In.	Guns In.	Principal armament	Shaft horse-power	Speed Knots
1949 1948	Roanoke Worcester [1]	14,700	3–6	4	12 6-in.; 24 3-in.	120,000	32
1944–46	6 Galveston Class	10,670	5	3–5	{Twin 'Talos' or 'Terrier'; 3 or 6 6-in.; 2 or 6 5-in.}	100,000	33
1944–45	6 Cleveland Class	10,500	5	3–5	12 6-in.; 12 5-in.	1000,000	33

Galveston, Little Rock, Oklahoma City, Providence, Springfield and *Topeka* (originally of the 'Cleveland' class) were converted into guided-missile cruisers in 1958–60.

The 'Cleveland' class comprises *Amsterdam, Pasadena, Portsmouth* and *Wilkes-Barre* (*Vincennes* was striken from the Navy List in 1966). *Atlanta* of this class, now known as IX-304, is completely converted for support of Pacific experiments.

Of the 'Juneau' class anti-aircraft light cruisers *San Diego, San Juan, Oakland, Reno* and *Juneau* were stricken in 1959, *Fresno* and *Flint* in 1965, and *Tucson* in 1966. The remaining ship, *Spokane*, was converted into a sonar test ship in 1967.

[1] *Fargo* was stricken from the Navy List in 1970 and *Astoria* of the 'Cleveland' class in 1969.

Frigates (*Destroyer Leaders*)

Completed	Name	Tons	Belt In.	Guns In.	Principal armament	Shaft horse-power	Speed Knots
1967	Truxtun	8,200	—	—	{1 twin 'Terrier'; 1 5-in.; 2 3 in.}	{Over 60,000 (nuclear power)}	{Over 30}
1962	Bainbridge	7,600	—	—	2 twin 'Terrier'; 4 3-in.		
1964–67	9 Belknap Class [1]	6,570	—	—	{1 twin 'Terrier'; 1 5-in.; 2 3-in.}	85,000	34
1962–64	9 Leahy Class [2]	5,670	—	—	2 twin 'Terrier'; 4 3-in.	85,000	34
1959–62	10 Coontz Class [3]	4,700	—	—	{1 twin 'Terrier'; 1 5-in.; 4 3-in.}	85,000	34
1954	{Wilkinson Willis A. Lee}	3,675	—	—	2 5-in.	80,000	35
1953	Norfolk [4]	5,600	—	—	8 3-in.	80,000	32

[1] The 'Belknap' class comprises *Belknap, Biddle, Fox, Horne, Josephus Daniels, Jouett, Sterett, Wainwright* and *William H. Standley.*

[2] The 'Leahy' class comprises *Dale, England, Gridley, Halsey, Harry E. Yarnell, Leahy, Reeves, Richmond K. Turner* and *Worden.*

[3] The 'Coontz' class comprises *Coontz, Dahlgren, Dewey, Farragut, King, Luce, Macdonough, Mahan, Preble* and *William V. Pratt.*

[4] Designed as a special anti-submarine cruiser (*Cruiser, Hunter, Killer Ship*); reclassified as a destroyer leader in 1951 and as a frigate in 1955.

In addition to the above named ships there are 93 nuclear-powered submarines, 62 conventional submarines, 289 destroyers, 10 destroyer minelayers, 223 destroyer escorts, 11 destroyer escort transports, 10 escorts, 180 minelayers and minesweepers, 18 patrol vessels, 18 fast patrol boats, 170 amphibious craft, 370 fleet auxiliaries and 1,700 service craft. The US Fleet consists of a total of 3,400 naval vessels, 2,000 of which are operational.

The 1971 New Construction Programme included 4 nuclear-powered attack submarines, 1 nuclear-powered guided missile frigate, 2 amphibious assault ships and 6 destroyers.

The 1970 New Construction Programme included 1 nuclear-powered attack aircraft carrier, 3 nuclear-powered submarines, 1 nuclear-powered guided missile frigate, 2 amphibious assault ships and 3 destroyers.

The 1969 New Construction Programme included 2 nuclear-powered attack submarines, 1 amphibious assault ship, 5 destroyers and 4 fast deployment logistic ships.

By 1973 it is planned that there will be 110 nuclear-powered submarines, including 41 armed with ballistic missiles.

The US Coast Guard operates under the Department of Transportation in time of peace and as a part of the Navy in time of war. It comprises 360 ships including cutters of frigate, corvette and patrol vessel types, powerful icebreakers, and para-military auxiliaries and tenders. Its peace-time duties embrace generally law enforcement upon the sea and navigable waters of US, the maintenance of navigational aids and the saving of life and property. The authorized strength of personnel in the 1967 fiscal year was 34,546 officers and men. An Academy is maintained for the education of cadets for careers as commissioned officers.

Blackman, R. V. B. (ed.), *Jane's Fighting Ships*. 73rd ed. London, 1970–71
Blackman, R. V. B., *The World's Warships*. London, 1969
Howard, J. L., *United States Modern Navy*. London, 1962

AIR FORCE

Secretary of the Air Force: Dr Robert C. Seamans, Jr.

The Department of the Air Force was activated within the Department of Defense on 18 Sept. 1947, coequal with the Army and the Navy under the terms of the National Security Act of 1947. It is headed by a Secretary of the Air Force, assisted by an Under Secretary and 4 Assistant Secretaries (Research and Development, Installation and Logistics, Financial Management, Manpower and Reserve Affairs).

The US Air Force, under the administration of the Department of the Air Force, is commanded by a Chief of Staff, who is a member of the Joint Chiefs of Staff. He is assisted by a Vice Chief of Staff, Assistant Vice Chief of Staff, 5 Deputy Chiefs of Staff and a Comptroller.

The USAF consists of the Regular Air Force, the Air Force Reserve and the Air National Guard. For operational purposes the service is organized into 15 major commands and 6 separate operating agencies. The Aerospace Defense Command is responsible for the air defence of the USA. It is in turn responsible to the North American Air Defense Command (NORAD), a joint agency which has available US and Canadian Air Force, and US Army and Navy air defence units for air defence of North America. The Strategic Air Command, equipped with long-range bombers based both in the USA and overseas, and with intercontinental guided missiles, is maintained primarily for strategic air operations anywhere on the globe. The Tactical Air Command operates fighters, fighter-bombers, tactical bombers and aircraft for photo-reconnaissance and assault airlift. The Military Airlift Command provides worldwide airlift for men and supplies.

The other functional commands, all supporting organizations, are the Air Force Logistics Command, the Air Force Systems Command, the Air Training Command, the Air University, the US Air Force Academy, the Air Force Accounting and Finance Center, the Aeronautical Chart and Information Center, the Air Force Communications Service, the USAF Security Service, Air Force Reserves, Air Force Data Systems Design Center, Air Reserve Personnel Center, and Headquarters Command. The oversea commands are the Pacific Air Forces, the US Air Forces in Europe, the Alaskan Air Command and the USAF Southern Command. These oversea commands are operationally responsible to joint theatre commands normally headed by an officer of a service with primary interests.

Of the fighter-bomber and interceptor aircraft in service, the F-100 Super Sabre, F-101 Voodoo, F-102 Delta Dagger, F-105 Thunderchief, F-106 Delta Dart, F-111 and F-4 Phantom II fly faster than sound in level flight and can carry a variety of armament, including nuclear weapons. Strategic bombers are the B-52 Stratofortress heavy bomber and the FB-111A 'swing-wing' supersonic bomber.

Strategic Air Command also operates SR-71 long-range supersonic reconnaissance aircraft. Tactical bombers include the B-57. Latest transport types are the KC-135 Stratotanker jet tanker-transport, C-141 Starlifter and C-135 Stratolifter jet transports, the very large C-5 Galaxy jet transport and the turboprop-powered C-130 Hercules and C-133 Cargomaster. Intercontinental ballistic missiles in USAF service are Titan II and Minuteman I, II and III.

In mid-1970, the Air Force had more than 1·2m. military and civilian personnel. Total aircraft strength about 14,600.

The total budget appropriated for the Air Force for the 1971 fiscal year will be approximately $22,729m.

The Army Air Forces in World War II. 7 vols. Univ. of Chicago Press, 1948 ff.
Goldberg, A.. *A History of the US Air Force. 1907–57.* New York, 1957
Mondey, D. C. *Pictorial History of the USAF.* London 1971

AGRICULTURE

Agriculture in the USA is characterized by its ability to adapt to widely varying conditions, and still produce an abundance and variety of agricultural products. From colonial times to about 1920 the major increases in farm production were brought about by adding to the number of farms and the amount of land under cultivation. During this period nearly 320m. acres of virgin forest were converted to crop land or pasture, and extensive areas of grass lands were ploughed. Improvident use of soil and water resources was evident in many areas.

During the next 20 years the number of farms reached a plateau of about 6·5m., and the acreage planted to crops held relatively stable around 330m. acres. The major source of increase in farm output arose from the substitution of power-driven machines for horses and mules. Greater emphasis was placed on development and improvement of land, and the need for conservation of basic agricultural resources was recognized. A successful conservation programme, highly co-ordinated and on a national scale—to prevent further erosion, to restore the native fertility of damaged land and to adjust land uses to production capabilities and needs—has been in operation since early in the 1930s.

Following the Second World War the uptrend in farm output has been greatly accelerated by increased production per acre and per farm animal. These increases are associated with a higher degree of mechanization; greater use of lime and fertilizer; improved varieties, including hybrid maize and grain sorghums; more effective control of insects and disease; improved strains of livestock and poultry; and wider use of good husbandry practices, such as nutritionally balanced feeds, use of superior sites and better housing. During this period land included in farms decreased slowly, crop land harvested declined somewhat more rapidly, but the number of farms declined sharply.

Some significant changes during these transitions are:

All land in farms totalled less than 500m. acres in 1870, rose to a peak of over 1,200m. acres in the 1950s and declined to 1,119m. acres in 1970, even with the addition of the new States of Alaska and Hawaii in 1960.

The number of farms declined from 6·35m. in 1940 to 2,895,000 in 1970, as the acreage size of farm nearly doubled. The average size of farms in 1970 was 387 acres, but ranged from 3 to many thousand acres. In 1964, 182,583 farms (244,328 in 1959) were smaller than 10 acres; 637,442 (813,216), 10–49 acres; 542,433 (657,990), 50–99 acres; 824,195 (998,084), 100–219 acres; 615,488 (660,446), 200–499 acres; and 355,723 (336,439), 500 acres or larger. Over 60,000 farms contained at least 2,000 acres in 1964.

Farms operated by owners or part-owners, 1964, were 2,600,147 (82% of all farms); by all tenants, 539,921 (17%); and by hired managers, 17,796 (1%). The proportion of farms operated by tenants is declining, and currently is two-fifths of the peak recorded in 1930. The average size of farms in 1964 was 175 acres for full owners, 682 acres for part-owners, 6,369 acres for hired managers and 268 acres for tenants. Farms with white operators numbered

2,958,310, and non-white operators 199,554. A higher proportion of non-white operators were tenants and operated a significantly smaller acreage than white operators.

Farms also vary widely in degree of specialization and output. About 60% of all farms received over half their farm income from a single enterprise, such as dairying, or from a single crop, such as cotton, wheat, tobacco or fruit. In 1969 (with 1960 figures in parentheses) large-scale, highly mechanized farms with sales of agricultural products totalling over $20,000 per farm made up 19% (9%) of all farms and accounted for 72% (51%) of the value of farm products sold. Farms selling between $2,500 and $20,000 worth of products per farm were 40% (45%) of all farms and sold 25% (43%) of all sales. The remaining 41% (46%) of farms sold less than $2,500 worth of products per farm in 1969, 3% (6%) of total sales. Many farms in this lowest sales class are called part-time or part-retirement farms, on which farm income is less than income from non-farm sources. Some farm operators in every sales category received off-farm income, but operators selling less than $2,500 per year received 55% of the estimated $12,800m. income received by farm families from non-farm sources.

A century ago three-quarters of the total US population was rural, and practically all rural people lived on farms. In April 1969 less than 30% of the population is rural, and the 10·3m. farm residents comprised about 5% of the total population.

Hired farm workers in 1969 averaged about 1·2m., and farm family workers, including operators, about 3·4m. In 1950 there were nearly 10m. farm workers. At that time each farm worker supplied farm products for 15 people; today, over 45 people.

Cash receipts from farm marketings and government payments (in $1m.):

	Crops	Livestock and livestock products	Government payments	Total
1932	1,996	2,752	—	4,748
1945	9,655	12,008	742	22,405
1950	12,356	16,105	283	28,744
1960	15,208	18,946	702	34,856
1967	18,434	24.259	3,079	45,772
1968	18,734	25,484	3,462	47,680
1969	18,790	28,439	3,794	51,023

Realized gross farm income (including government payments), in $1m., was 54,598 in 1969, compared with 51,038 in 1968; net income of farm operators, 16,154 (15,026). Farm-mortgage debt, on 1 Jan. 1970, was estimated at $28,700m.; increase in 1969 was about 6%.

US agricultural exports, fiscal year, totalled: 1963–64, $6,067m.; 1964–65, $6,097m.; 1965–66, $6,677m.; 1966–67 $6,772m.; 1967–68, $6,312m.; 1968–69, $5,741m; 1969–70; $6,646m.

Total area of farm land under irrigation in 1964 was 36,977,580 acres (297,522 farms); in 1959: 33,162,978 acres and 307,783 farms.

Federal income taxes paid by farm people was $15m. in 1941, $1,365m. in 1948, $1,182m. in 1961 and about $1,900m. in 1969. Total taxes levied on farm real estate in 1969 was $2,263m, ($974m. in 1956).

According to census returns and estimates of the Economic Research Service, the acreage and specified values of farms has been as follows (area in 1,000 acres; value in $1,000):

	Farm area [1]	Crop land available for crops [2]	Value, land, bldgs, machinery, livestock	Value of products in preceding year [2]
1910	878,798	431,000	41,089,000	. .
1930	986,771	480,000	57,815,000	9,609,924
1940	1,060,852	467,000	41,829,000	6,681,581
1950	1,158,566	478,000	99,366,000	22,051,129
1959	1,125,508	448,100	164,200,000	30,492,721
1964	1,110,097	434,800	190,500,000	35,305,964

[1] Acreages are for the preceding year except for 1954 and 1959.
[2] Also includes any crop land used only for pasture. Ploughable pasture not in rotation with crops is not included as land available for crops.

The areas and production of the principal crops for 3 years were:

| | 1967 | | | 1968 | | | 1969[1] | | |
| | 1,000 | 1,000 | Yield per | 1,000 | 1,000 | Yield per | 1,000 | 1,000 | Yield per |
Crops	acres	bushels	acre	acres	bushels	acre	acres	bushels	acre
Corn for grain	60,557	4,760,076	78·6	55,808	4,393,273	78·6	54,573	4,577,864	83·9
Wheat	58,771	1,522,382	25·9	55,262	1,576.251	28·5	47,555	1,458.872	30·7
Oats	16,017	789,196	49·3	17,533	939.228	53·6	18,003	949,874	52·8
Barley	9,177	372,898	40·6	9,709	422.959	43·6	9,388	417,156	44·4
Soybeans for beans	39,767	976,060	24·5	41,104	1,103,129	26·8	40,857	1,116,876	27·3
Flaxseed	1,975	20,036	10·1	2,098	27,067	12·9	2,704	36,448	13·5
Rice, rough [2]	1,970	89,379	4,537	2,353	104,075	4,422	2,128	91,303	4,290
Potatoes [2]	1,457	305,334	210	1,378	294,192	214	1,404	307.229	219
Cotton [2]	7,997	7,458	447	10,160	10,948	516	11,094	10,080	436
Tobacco [2]	960	1,967,911	2,050	880	1,710,362	1,943	921	1,802,611	1,958

[1] Preliminary.
[2] Production of rice and potatoes in 1,000 cwt, cotton in 1,000 500-lb. bales, tobacco in lb.; yield per acre for all crops in bushels except rice, cotton and tobacco in lb.; and potatoes in cwt.

Wheat. The chief wheat-growing states (1969) were (estimated yield in 1,000 bu.): Kansas, 305,319; N. Dakota, 203,561; Oklahoma, 118,275; Montana, 96,794; Washington, 95,242; Nebraska, 85,586; Texas, 68,856; Illinois, 48,137; Idaho, 47,982; Colorado, 45,045; South Dakota, 42,915; Ohio, 39,479; Indiana, 35,061; Missouri, 33,120; Oregon, 30,030; Michigan, 25,102; Minnesota, 24,607.

Cotton. In 1969 the 5 western-most states producing cotton (Texas, New Mexico, Arizona, Nevada and California) furnished 50% of the crop. Production, 1969, by state (in 1,000 bales, 500 lb. gross) was: Texas, 2,862; Mississippi, 1,328; California, 1,315; Arkansas, 1,140; Arizona, 634; Louisiana, 483; Alabama, 461; Tennessee, 422; Missouri, 326; Georgia, 282; Oklahoma, 279; S. Carolina, 205; New Mexico, 157; N. Carolina, 100.

Tobacco. Output (1,000 lb.) of the chief tobacco-growing states (91% of the crop) was in 1969; N. Carolina, 715,968; Kentucky, 436,802; S. Carolina, 136,658; Virginia, 134,629; Tennessee, 120,747; Georgia, 97,890.

Livestock. Number of farm animals (in 1,000) on farms on 1 Jan.:

	1930	1940	1950	1960	1969	1970
Horses	13,742	10,444	5,548	3,089	—[1]	—[1]
Mules	5,382	4,034	2,233			
Cattle of all kinds	61,003	68,309	77,963	96,236	109,885	112,330
Milch cows	23,032	24,940	23,853	19,527	14,152	13,875
Sheep and lambs	51,565	52,107	29,826	33,170	21,238	20.422
Swine	55,705	61,165	58,937	59,026	60,632	56,743

[1] Count discontinued in 1961.

Total value of livestock, excluding poultry and, from 1961, horses and mules (in $1m.) on farms in the USA on 1 Jan. was: 1930, 6,061; 1933 (low point of the agricultural depression), 2,733; 1968, 18,322; 1969, 19,714; 1970, 22,897.

In 1969 the production of shorn wool was 165·8m. lb. from 19·6m. sheep (average 1961–65, 230m. lb. from 27·2m. sheep); of pulled wool, 17·1m. lb. (1961–65, 28·3m. lb.).

Hathaway, D. E., *Government and agriculture.* New York, 1963
Haystead, L., and Fite, G. C., *The Agricultural Regions of the USA.* London, 1956
Higbee, E. C., *American agriculture: geography, resources, conservation.* New York, 1958
Mighell, R. L., *American Agriculture, its Structure and Place in the Economy.* New York, 1955
Wilcox, W. W., *Economics of American Agriculture.* 2nd ed. New York, 1960

FORESTS AND FORESTRY

In 1968 the US forest lands, including Alaska and Hawaii, capable of producing timber for commercial use, covered 510,212,500 acres (more than one-fifth of the land area), classified as follows: Saw-timber stands, 226,115,500 acres; pole timber stands, 129,540,300 acres; seedling and sapling stands, 128,182,000 acres; non-stocked and other areas, 26,374,800 acres. Ownership of commercial forest land is distributed as follows: Federal government, 112,746,500 acres; state, county and municipal, 29,219,800 acres; privately owned, 368,246,200 acres, including 140,904,200 acres on farms. Of the live saw-timber stand (2,490,401·3m. bd ft) Douglas fir constitutes 24%; Southern yellow pine, 8%; Western yellow (ponderosa) pine, 10%; other softwoods, 39%; hardwoods, 19%. In 1967 timber cut amounted to 13,258·74m. cu. ft compared to net annual growth of about 17,346·9m. cu. ft. Saw-timber cut amounted to 57,466·9m. bd ft against an annual growth of 53,710·3m. bd ft. The net area of the 154 national forests and other areas in USA and Puerto Rico administered by the US Forest Service, including commercial and non-commercial forest land, was on 30 June 1969, 186,632,152 acres.

Fire takes a heavy annual toll in the forest: total area burned over in 1969 was 6,689,081 acres, of which 15% was unprotected land; 1,163·8m. acres of land are now under organized fire-protection service. The area planted in the year ending 30 June 1969 was 1,457,470 acres, a decrease of 11,154 acres over the previous year.

Timber Trends in the USA. Forest Service, US Dept of Agriculture. 1965 (Forest Resources Report No. 17)
Allen, S. W., *An Introduction to American Forestry.* 3rd ed. New York, 1960

MINING

Total value of minerals produced in US (including Alaska and Hawaii) in 1968 was $24,971m. ($26,928m. in 1969). Details are given in the following tables.

Production statistics of metallic minerals (long tons, 2,240 lb.; short tons, 2,000 lb.):

	1968		1969	
Metallic minerals	Quantity	Value ($1,000)	Quantity	Value ($1,000)
Bauxite (dried equiv.), long tons	1,665,000	23,752	1,843,000	25,725
Copper (recoverable content), short tons	1,204,621	1,008,195	1,544,579	1,468,400
Gold (recoverable content), troy oz.	1,478,292	58,038	1,733,176	71,944
Iron ore (usable),[1] 1,000 long tons, gross	81,934	836,433	89,051	920,203
Lead (recoverable content), short tons	359,156	94,903	509,013	151,635
Molybdenum (content of concentrate), 1,000 lb.	93,245	151,000	103,009	173,819
Silver (recoverable content), 1,000 troy oz.	32,729	70,191	41,906	75,040
Zinc (recoverable content), short tons	529,446	142,950	553,124	161,512
Other metals	—	317,538	—	291,632
Total metals	—	2,703,000	—	3,338,000

[1] Excluding by-product iron sinter.

The two world wars and record levels of industrial production have hastened the depletion of once abundant supplies of metal and US is increasingly an importer. US is wholly or almost wholly dependent upon imports for industrial diamonds, quartz, tin, chromite, nickel, strategic-grade mica and long-fibre asbestos; it imports the bulk of its tantalum, platinum, manganese, mercury, cadmium, tungsten, cobalt and flake graphite, and substantial quantities of antimony, bauxite, arsenic, lead, fluorspar, zinc, gypsum, bismuth and copper.

In 1969 precious metals were mined mainly in Utah, Arizona S. Dakota, Nevada, and Montana (in order of combined output of gold and silver). US output of gold (troy oz.), 1930–39, 314,53,370; 1940–49, 24,171,646; 1950–59, 18,817,241; total 1792–1968, 313,143,938. Output of silver (troy oz.), 1930–39, 466,412,499; 1940–49, 434,656,631; 1950–59, 374,055,521; total 1792–1968, 4,614,518,507.

Statistics of important non-metallic minerals and mineral fuels are:

	1968		1969	
		Value		*Value*
Non-metallic minerals	*Quantity*	*($1,000)*	*Quantity*	*($1,000)*
Boron minerals, short tons	963,000	76,535	1,020,000	81,261
Cement:				
Portland, 1,000 bbls of 376 lb.	388,525	1,227,942	400,883	1,284,600
Masonry, 1,000 bbls of 280 lb.	23,167	66,259	23,253	69,106
Natural and slag, 1,000 bbls of 376 lb.	86	332	..	..
Clays, 1,000 short tons	57,348	246,938	58,694	264,415
Gypsum, 1,000 short tons	10,018	36,775	9,905	38,354
Lime, 1,000 short tons	18,637	249,639	20,209	280,736
Phosphate rock, 1,000 short tons	41,251	250,692	39,725	208,689
Potassium salts, 1,000 short tons (K₂O equivalent)	2,722	75,664	2,804	73,572
Salt (common), 1,000 short tons	41,274	272,275	44,245	287,680
Sand and gravel, 1,000 short tons	917,468	1,020,107	936,906	1,070,302
Stone, 1,000 short tons	819,597	1,317,911	862,895	1,424,694
Sulphur (Frasch-process), 1,000 long tons	6,645	268,146	6,551	176,659
Other non-metallic minerals	—	338,785	—	364,932
Total non-metallic minerals	—	5,448,000	—	5,625,000
Mineral fuels				
Coal: Bituminous and lignite, 1,000 short tons	545,245	2,546,340	560,505	2,795,509
Pennsylvania anthracite,[1] 1,000 short tons	11,461	97,245	10,473	100,769
Gas: Natural gas,[2] 1m. cu. ft	19,322,400	3,168,688	20,698,240	3,455,615
Natural gasoline and cycle products, 1,000 bbls of 42 gallons	199,049	571,679	201,784	603,084
L.P. gases, 1,000 bbls of 42 gallons	351,262	552,335	378,457	498,927
Petroleum (crude), 1,000 bbls of 42 gallons	3,329,042	9,794,826	3,371,751	10,426,680
Other mineral fuels	—	88,887	—	84,416
Total mineral fuels	—	16,820,000	—	17,965,000

[1] Includes a small quantity of anthracite mined in states other than Pennsylvania.
[2] Value at wells.

Minerals Yearbook. Bureau of Mines. Washington, DC. Annual from 1932–33; continuing the *Mineral Resources of the United States* series (1866–1931); from 1963 in 4 vols. (*Metals and Minerals; Fuels; Area Reports; Domestic and International*)

MANUFACTURES

The following table presents general statistics of manufactures as reported at various censuses from 1909 to 1963 and from the Annual Survey of Manufactures for years in which no census was taken. The figures for 1958 and 1963 include data for some establishments previously classified as non-manufacturing. The figures for 1939, but not for earlier years, have been revised to exclude data for establishments classified as non-manufacturing in 1954. The figures for 1909–33 were previously revised by the deduction of data for industries excluded from manufacturing during that period.

The statistics for 1958, 1963 and 1968 relate to all establishments employing 1 or more persons any time during the year; for 1950, 1956–57 and 1959–62, on a representative sample of manufacturing establishments of 1 or more employees; for 1929 through 1939, those reporting products valued at $5,000 or more; and for 1909 and 1919, those reporting products valued at $500 or more. These differences in the minimum size of establishments included in the census affect only very slightly the year-to-year comparability of the figures.

The annual Surveys of Manufactures carry forward the key measures of manufacturing activity which are covered in detail by the Census of Manufactures. The estimate for 1950 is based on reports for approximately 45,000 plants out of a total of more than 260,000 operating manufacturing establishments; those for 1956–57 on about 50,000, and those for 1959–62 and 1964–66 on about 60,000 out of about 300,000. Included are all large plants and representative sample of the much more numerous small plants. The large plants in the surveys account for approximately two-thirds of the total employment in operating manufacturing establishments in the US.

	Number of establishments	Production workers (average for year)	Production workers' wages, total ($1,000)	Value added by manufacture[1] ($1,000)
1909	264,810	6,261,736	3,205,213	8,160,075
1919	270,231	8,464,916	9,664,009	23,841,624
1929	206,663	8,369,705	10,884,919	30,591,435
1933	139,325	5,787,611	4,940,146	14,007,540
1939	173,802	7,808,205	8,997,515	24,487,304
1947	240,807	11,917,884	30,243,971	75,366,527
1950	260,000	11,778,803	34,600,025	89,749,765
1954	286,814	12,372,002	44,590,545	117,032,326
1956	..	13,131,313	52,040,794	144,909,346
1957	..	12,838,889	52,569,022	147,838,425
1958	299,017	11,681,143	49,605,180	141,540,618
1959	..	12,272,622	54,714,135	161,535,816
1960	..	12,209,514	55,555,452	163,998,531
1961	..	11,778,518	54,764,619	164,291,080
1963	306,617	12,232,041	62,093,601	192,103,102
1967	305,680	13,955,300	81,393,600	261,983,800

[1] For the period 1954–67 value added represents adjusted value added and for earlier years unadjusted value added. Unadjusted value is obtained by subtracting cost of materials, supplies and containers, fuel, electricity and contract work from the value of shipments for products manufactured plus receipts for services rendered. Adjusted value added also takes into account value added by merchandizing operations plus net change in finished goods and work-in-process inventories between the beginning and end of the year.

For comparison of broad types of manufacturing, the industries covered by the Census of Manufactures have been divided into 20 general groups according to the *Standard Industrial Classification*. This was revised in 1967; 1958 figures are not therefore strictly comparable.

Code No.	Industry group	Census year	Production workers (average for year)	Production workers' wages total ($1,000)	Value added by manufacture[1] ($1,000)
20.	Food and kindred products	1958	1,152,877	4,548,983	17,685,157
		1963	1,098,116	5,159,376	21,825,516
		1967	1,121,700	6,062,600	26,620,900
21.	Tobacco manufactures	1958	76,306	247,842	1,413,460
		1963	68,579	271,496	1,680,594
		1967	66,200	303,600	2,032,000
22.	Textile mill products	1958	810,490	2,408,291	4,857,638
		1963	775,330	2,768,414	6,122,982
		1967	828,200	3,556,600	8,153,000
23.	Apparel and related products	1958	1,035,295	2,774,182	6,011,667
		1963	1,132,859	3,482,286	7,861,011
		1967	1,200,000	4,340,600	10,064,400
24.	Lumber and wood products	1958	506,381	1,628,556	3,183,131
		1963	497,409	1,943,287	4,020,600
		1967	495,700	2,290,600	4,973,400
25.	Furniture and fixtures	1958	287,987	1,023,404	2,353,700
		1963	314,762	1,289,989	3,068,287
		1967	357,500	1,653,700	4,169,500
26.	Paper and allied products	1958	448,529	2,038,997	5,707,474
		1963	467,795	2,551,148	7,395,677
		1967	507,700	3,205,500	9,756,300
27.	Printing and publishing	1958	530,565	2,595,699	7,939,061
		1963	559,843	3,190,988	10,476,433
		1967	631,600	4,011,300	14,355,100
28.	Chemical and allied products	1958	453,581	2,244,926	12,273,185
		1963	474,141	2,779,938	17,586,138
		1967	541,400	3,555,200	23,550,100
29.	Petroleum and coal products	1958	130,508	758,422	2,518,424
		1963	109,448	745,123	3,713,231
		1967	99,400	786,400	5,425,800
30.	Rubber and plastics products, not elsewhere classified	1958	270,500	1,211,372	3,276,612
		1963	328,785	1,672,376	4,653,953
		1967	410,100	2,312,500	6,799,500
31.	Leather and leather products	1958	310,145	912,256	1,898,007
		1963	290,339	932,096	2,078,572
		1967	293,300	1,147,000	2,626,500
32.	Stone, clay and glass products	1958 [2]	446,221	1,935,737	5,534,559
		1963 [2]	455,818	2,350,233	7,043,987
		1967	469,300	2,784,100	8,333,400

[1] Figures for 1958, 1963 and 1967 represent adjusted value added. For definitions see footnote 1 to previous table.
[2] Includes production of unhardened concrete omitted in previous years.

Code No.	Industry group	Census year	Production workers (average for year)	Production workers' wages, total ($1,000)	Value added by manufacture[1] ($1,000)
33. Primary metal industries		1958	886,594	4,715,957	11,671,341
		1963	922,160	5,933,628	15,261,089
		1967	1,041,500	7,457,300	19,978,200
34. Fabricated metal products		1958	813,212	3,726,691	9,422,856
		1963	843,795	4,483,688	11,791,081
		1967	1,056,900	6,541,600	18,042,600
35. Machinery (except electrical)		1958	949,320	4,647,302	12,392,954
		1963	1,045,075	6,209,341	17,310,599
		1967	1,349,000	9,236,100	27,836,400
36. Electrical machinery		1958	808,621	3,509,746	10,395,369
		1963	1,049,357	5,405,786	17,010,665
		1967	1,323,800	7,607,000	24,487,000
37. Transportation equipment		1958	1,134,769	6,020,390	15,284,706
		1963	1,150,082	7,731,192	22,765,674
		1967	1,336,500	9,918,200	28,173,900
38. Instruments and related products		1958	202,373	921,498	2,906,390
		1963	208,448	1,100,718	3,992,131
		1967	265,900	1,569,000	6,418,400
39. Miscellaneous manufacturing		1958	412.887	1,702,939	4,755,290
		1963	315,017	1,253,518	3,992,131
		1967	344,400	1,552,500	4,599,400

[1] Figures for 1958, 1963 and 1967 represent adjusted value added. For definitions see footnote 1 to previous table, p. 569.

IRON AND STEEL

Output of the iron and steel industries (in net tons of 2,000 lb.), according to figures supplied by the American Iron and Steel Institute, was:

	Furnaces in blast 31 Dec.	Pig-iron (including ferro-alloys)	Raw steel	Steel by method of production[1]			
				Open hearth	Bessemer	Electric[2]	Basic Oxygen
1932[3]	44	9,835,227	15,322,901	13,336,210	1,715,925	270,044	..
1939	195	35,677,097	52,798,714	48,409,800	3,358,916	1,029,067	..
1944[4]	218	62,866,198	89,641,600	80,363,953	5,039,923	4,237,699	..
1950	234	66,400,311	96,336,075	86,262,509	4,534,558	6,039,008	..
1960	114	68,566,384	99,281,601	86,367,506	1,189,196	8,378,743	3,346,156
1967	173	89,472,000	127,213,000	70,690,000	—[5]	15,089,000	41,434.000
1968	154	91,362,000	131.462,000	65,836,000	—[5]	16,814,000	48,812,000
1969	169	97,593,000	141,262,000	60,894,000	—[5]	20,132,000	60,236,000

[1] The sum of these 4 items should equal the total in the preceding column; any difference appearing is due to the very small production of crucible steel, omitted prior to 1950.
[2] Includes crucible production beginning 1950.
[3] Low point of the depression.
[4] Peak year of war production.
[5] Included with open hearth.

Wholesale price index of iron and steel (1957–59 = 100) was: 1939, 38; 1944, 38·5; 1950, 66·9; 1960, 100·6; 1967, 103·5; 1968, 105·5; 1969, 111.

Leading producers of pig-iron (including ferro-alloys) in 1969 were: Pennsylvania, 22·33m. net tons; Ohio, 16·9m.; Indiana, 12,663,000; Illinois, 7,129,000.

Consumption of ore, 1969, was 143,925,000 net tons, of which blast-furnaces took 102,576,000 tons; steel producing furnaces, 3,543,000 tons, and agglomerating plants, 37,806,000 tons.

The iron and steel industry in 1968 employed 415,301 wage-earners (compared with 449,888 in 1960), who worked an average of 38·6 hours per week (46·6 in peak year 1944) and earned an average of $4·566 per hour (compared with the average of $1·17 during 1942 to 1945): total wages were $3,813m. and total salaries for 128,718 employees was $1,518m.

Apparent per capita US consumption of finished steel products, 1968, was 1,070 lb. (941 lb. in 1967).

Adams, W. (ed.), *The Structure of American Industry*. 3rd ed. New York, 1961
Alderfer, E. B., and Michl, H. E., *Economics of American Industry*. 3rd ed. New York, 1957
Fuchs, V. R., *Changes in the Location of Manufacturing since 1929*. Yale Univ. Press, 1962
Glover, J. G. (ed.), *The Development of American Industries*. 4th ed. New York, 1959
Resources for the Future. *Regions, Resources and Economic Growth*. Baltimore, 1960

TENNESSEE VALLEY AUTHORITY

Established by Act of Congress, 1933, the TVA is a multiple-purpose federal agency which carries out its duties in an area embracing some 41,000 sq. miles, in 125 counties (aggregate population, about 4m.) in the 7 Tennessee River Valley states: Tennessee, Kentucky, Mississippi, Alabama, North Carolina, Georgia and Virginia. In addition, 76 counties outside the Valley are served by TVA power distributors. Its 3 directors are appointed by the President, with the consent of the Senate; headquarters are in Knoxville, Tenn. There were 22,800 employees at 30 June 1970.

Under the Act its chief duties are flood control; the maintenance of navigation; generation, transmission and sale of electric power; the development and production of fertilizers and munitions; assistance in forestry development; and related activities in a single unified approach to resource development. There are now 32 major dams and reservoirs (22 built by TVA) controlling the flow of the river. A navigable channel 650 miles long, connecting with the American system of inland waterways, in 1969 carried 3,342m. ton-miles of traffic in iron and steel products, grains, coal, petroleum, chemicals and other products. Flood damages averted by river control exceed $388m.

TVA supplies electric power to 161 local distribution systems serving 2m. customers in an area of 80,000 sq. miles. The TVA power system originated with the water-power development of the Tennessee River, but has become predominantly a thermal system as power requirements have outgrown the region's hydro-electric potential. In fiscal year 1970 the TVA system generated 92,684m. kwh; the same region used 1,500m. kwh in 1933 before TVA operations began. Installed capacity, 1970, was 19,422,480 kw, with another 10·4m. kw under construction or authorized in nuclear, coal-fired, gas-turbine and pumped-storage installations. Residential consumers served by TVA power distributors used an average of 14,560 kwh in fiscal year 1970 at an average rate of about 1 cent per kwh; US averages were 6,810 kwh and 2·1 cents.

Another activity is experimentation in the development and manufacture of mineral fertilizers accompanied by programmes designed to encourage proper fertilizer use in all parts of the country. The TVA works closely with other federal agencies, and with state and local authorities in combating soil erosion, improving forest resources, improving agriculture and to the development of local industries based on natural resources. In the depression year, 1933, the average *per capita* income in the Valley region was $168 compared with the national average of $375; in 1968 the region's *per capita* income had multiplied 14 times to $2,416 while the national average had increased 8 times to $3,421.

Power operations are financially self-supporting from revenues. In fiscal year 1970 power revenues were $479·6m. and net income $74·6m. Power facilities are financed from revenues and the sale of revenue bonds and notes, and TVA is repaying appropriations previously invested in power facilities. In fiscal 1970 TVA paid the US Treasury $15m. as a capital repayment and $57·6m. in dividends on the remaining appropriation investment, making a total of $823m. to date paid to the Treasury from power revenues. Other TVA resource development programmes continue to be financed primarily from appropriations, which amounted to $50·6m. in fiscal year 1970.

Annual Report of the TVA. Knoxville, 1934 to date
Clapp, G. R., *The TVA; an Approach to the Development of a Region*. Univ. of Chicago Press, 1955
Lilienthal, D. E., *TVA; Democracy on the March*. 20th Anniversary ed. New York and London, 1953
Munger, M. E., *Valley of Vision: The TVA Years*. New York, 1969
Tennessee Valley Authority. *A Quality Environment in the Tennessee Valley*, 1969.—*Facts About TVA Operations*. Knoxville, Tennessee, 1969.—*Short History of the TVA*. Knoxville, Tennessee, 1968.—*TVA: the First Twenty Years* (ed. R. C. Martin), Univ. of Tennessee Press, 1956

COMMERCE

The subjoined table gives the total value of the imports and exports of merchandise by yearly average or by year (in $1m.):

	Exports		General		Exports		General
	Total	US mdse.	imports		Total	US mdse.	imports
1941–45	10,051	9,922	3,514	1961–65	24,006	23,707	17,659
1946–50	11,829	11,673	6,659	1967	31,526	31,142	26,733
1951–55	15,333	15,196	10,832	1968	34,092	33,626	33,092
1956–60	19,204	19,029	13,650	1969	37,274	36,770	36,022

For a description of how imports and exports are valued by the US Customs, see *Explanation of Statistics of Foreign Commerce and Navigation of the United States*, Bureau of the Census, US Department of Commerce, Washington, D.C., 1946.

The 'most favoured nation' treatment in commerce between Great Britain and US was agreed to for 4 years by the treaty of 1815, was extended for 10 years by the treaty of 1818, and indefinitely (subject to 12 months' notice) by that of 1827.

Imports and exports of gold and silver bullion and specie in calendar years (in $1,000):

	Gold			Silver		
			Balance			Balance
	Exports	Imports	+ or −	Exports	Imports	+ or −
1932	809,528	363,315	+ 446,213	13,850	19,650	− 5,800
1940	4,995	4,749,467	− 4,744,472	3,674	58,434	− 54,760
1944	959,228	113,836	+ 845,392	126,915	23,373	+ 103,542
1955	7,257	104,592	− 97,335	8,331	72,932	− 64,601
1960	1,647	335,032	− 333,385	25,789	57,438	− 31,649
1965	1,285,097	101,669	+ 1,183,428	54,061	64,769	− 10,708
1966	457,333	42,004	+ 415,329	114,325	78,378	+ 35,947
1967	1,005,199	32,547	+ 972,652	100,710	80,178	+ 20,532
1968	839,160	226,262	+ 612,898	252,148	145,153	+ 106,995
1969	..	227,842	..	103,386	71,247	+ 32,139

The domestic exports of US produce, including military, and the imports for consumption by economic classes for 3 calendar years were (in $1m.):

	Exports (US merchandise)			Imports for consumption		
	1967	1968	1969	1967	1968	1969
Crude materials	3,293	3,467	3,476	3,707	4,012	4,121
Crude foodstuffs	2,595	2,334	2,086	1,981	2,294	2,141
Manufactured foodstuffs	1,596	1,671	1,786	2,518	2,882	3,043
Semi-manufactures	4,489	5,117	5,774	5,592	7,141	6,774
Finished manufactures	19,265	21,609	24,327	13,091	16,987	19,973
Total	31,238	34,199	37,444	26,889	33,226	36,052

Leading exports of US merchandise are listed below for the calendar year 1969: Special Category Type II merchandise is included, but Type I is excluded.[1] The 16 commodity classes accounted for approximately 85% of total exports. Data for major subdivisions of certain classes are also given:

Commodity	$1m.	Commodity	$1m.
Machinery, total	9,865	Plastic materials and resins	590
Industrial machinery	7,188	Automobiles (and parts)	3,788
Power generating machinery,		Aircraft (and parts)	2,389
non-electrical	1,257	Fats, oils and oilseeds	..
Metalworking machinery	343	Soybeans	822
Agricultural machines and tractors	644	Cotton	286
Office machines	1,051	Textiles and apparel	576
Electrical apparatus	2,618	Tobacco and manufactures	695
Telecommunications apparatus	618	Iron and steel-mill products	712
Electrical power machinery and		Nonferrous base metals	347
switchgear	561	Pulp, paper and products	308
Grains and preparations	2,127	Coal	638
Wheat (and flour)	831	Fruits, nuts and vegetables	504
Maize	726	Petroleum and products	434
Chemicals	3,383	Firearms of war and ammunition	746
Chemical elements and compound	1,381		

[1] Type I includes military equipment and a few special types of machine tools. Type II includes certain radio and other electrical apparatus, military motor vehicles and aircraft, explosives, ammunition and small arms.

Chief imports for consumption for the calendar year 1969; the following 30 commodity classes account for approximately 78% of total imports:

Commodity	$1m.	Commodity	$1m.
Petroleum and products	2,560	Sugar	638
Petroleum	1,318	Iron and steel-mill products	1,724
Fuel oil	1,037	Cattle, meat and preparations	958
Non-ferrous base metals	1,535	Beef	467
Copper	487	Automobiles and parts	4,096
Aluminium	264	Fish (and shellfish)	692
Nickel	219	Wood, shaped	324
Bauxite, crude	..	Fruit, nuts and vegetables	662
Tin	189	Alcoholic beverages	648
Pulp, paper and products	1,081	Whisky	502
Newsprint	939	Iron ore and concentrates	403
Wood pulp	499	Wool and other hair	155
Textiles and apparel	2,125	Metal manufactures	..
Clothing	1,106	Diamonds (excl. industrial)	511
Cotton fabrics, woven	174	Rubber (and latex)	280
Machinery, total	4,489	Plywood	..
Electrical apparatus	1,947	Oils and oilseeds	59
Industrial machinery	2,542	Cocoa (and cacao beans)	168
Agricultural machines and tractors	264	Glass and pottery	314
Office machines	371	Footwear	488
Coffee	894	Toys and sports goods	348
Chemicals	1,232	Furs, undressed	94
Chemical elements and compound	645	Scientific/Photographic apparatus	333
Uranium oxide	15	Artworks and antiques	185
Fertilizers	137	Grains and animal feeds	124

Total trade between the United States and the United Kingdom for 5 years (British Board of Trade returns) in £1,000 sterling:

	1966	1967	1968	1969	1970
Imports to UK	720,234	803,038	1,055,949	1,122,708	1,170,234
Exports from UK	621,130	610,259	871,916	862,793 }	932,736
Re-exports from UK	25,625	24,596	30,754	34,284 }	

Imports and exports by continents, areas and selected countries for calendar years (in $1m.):

	General imports		Exports, incl. re-exports[1]	
Area and country	1968	1969	1968	1969
Canada	9,005	10,390	8,072[2]	9,138[2]
20 American Republics	4,288	4,214	4,699[2]	4,869[2]
Western Europe	10,139	10,140	11,132[2]	12,370[2]
Other areas	9,794	11,307	10,732[2]	11,611[2]
	33,226	36,051	34,635[2]	37,988[2]
Western Hemisphere	14,148	15,555	13,411	14,714
Canada	9,008	10,390	8,072	9,138
20 American Republics	4,288	4,214	4,699	4,869
Central American Common Market	343	368	367	353
Costa Rica	88	101	74	77
El Salvador	45	41	61	56
Guatemala	71	76	93	84
Honduras	89	94	75	75
Nicaragua	50	56	62	59
Panama	79	75	136	164
Latin American FTA	3,685	3,577	4,059	4,203
Argentina	190	156	281	378
Brazil	670	616	705	672
Chile	206	151	307	315
Colombia	264	240	319	303
Ecuador	90	81	98	98
Mexico	910	1,029	1,378	1,450
Paraguay	12	12	25	23
Peru	329	313	197	168
Uruguay	22	15	38	31
Dominican Republic	156	165	115	124
Haiti	26	29	24	24
Bolivia	32	23	55	59
Venezuela	950	940	655	708
Bahamas	36	48	165	179

[1] Data exlude exports of commodities classed for security reasons as 'special category' except as indicated.
[2] 'Special category' exports are included in these totals.

Area and Country	General Imports		Exports, incl. re-exports[1]	
	1968	1969	1968	1969
Western Hemisphere (*contd.*):				
Netherlands Antilles	332	392	89	99
Jamaica	138	151	147	175
Trinidad and Tobago	216	232	62	61
Europe				
Western Europe	10,139	10,140	11,132	12,370
OECD Countries	10,033	10,035	11,031	12,274
European Economic Community	5,885	5,800	6,127	6,981
Belgium and Luxembourg	767	684	823	960
France	842	843	1,095	1,195
Germany (West)	2,721	2,603	1,709	2,118
Italy	1,102	1,204	1,121	1,262
Netherlands	453	467	1,380	1,447
Greece	63	58	142	255
Turkey	99	68	267	299
EFTA countries	3,548	3,655	3,877	4,029
Austria	96	115	50	56
Denmark	220	258	207	205
Norway	156	150	156	198
Portugal	88	86	87	78
Sweden	390	355	441	477
Switzerland	438	452	595	605
UK	2,058	2,121	2,289	2,335
Finland	103	120	52	76
Iceland	24	28	13	12
Irish Republic	108	123	87	118
Spain	306	304	517	580
Yugoslavia	103	102	90	86
Soviet bloc	198	196	215	249
Poland	97	98	82	53
USSR	58	52	58	106
Asia[2]	6,911	8,276	7,582	8,265
Near East	355	..	1,046	1,277
Iran	83	87	280	352
Iraq	3	3	15	15
Israel	117	129	279	457
Kuwait	39	30	109	76
Lebanon	11	10	82	90
Saudi Arabia	58	41	187	154
Arabic Peninsula States[3]	30	35	49	39
UAR	32	38	48	67
Japan	4,054	4,888	2,954	3,490
Other Asia	2,855	3,385	4,628	4,776
Ceylon	31	29	28	21
Hong Kong	637	815	304	364
India	312	344	718	517
Indonesia	174	194	167	201
Korea, Republic of	199	291	510	699
Malaysia	240	307	54	52
Singapore	29	55	102	152
Pakistan	64	73	302	195
Philippines	436	423	436	374
Thailand	81	92	186	148
Taiwan (Formosa)	270	388	387	393
Vietnam	2	3	271	285
China[4]	..	..	—	—
Mongolia	2	2	—	—
Oceania	697	828	1,026	998
Australia	488	588	872	855
New Zealand and W. Samoa	187	216	114	99
Africa[5]	1,122	1,045	1,269	1,392
Algeria	5	2	53	64
Ethiopia	46	45	46	22
Libya	90	111	115	134
Morocco	11	9	70	53

[1] See note on previous page.
[2] Includes United Arab Republic.
[3] Excludes Southern Yemen and Bahrain.
[4] Imports from China (including Manchuria) and North Korea, rigidly controlled by the US Treasury, were 1962, $241,000; 1963, $268,000; 1964, $0·5m.; 1965, $0·5m.; 1966, $0·1m.; exports are embargoed.
[5] Excludes United Arab Republic.

Area and Country	General Imports		Exports incl. re-exports [1]	
	1968	1969	1968	1969
Africa (contd.):				
Ghana	78	69	56	62
Liberia	51	60	38	44
Nigeria	36	71	56	72
Kenya	20	16	20	19
Congo (K.)	42	35	51	44
South Africa, Republic of [2]	256	243	456	506

[1] See note on p. 573.
[2] Includes also South-West Africa (Namibia).

Tariffs. The American tariff system has ceased to be an important revenue-raising device. In 1789–91 customs duties (plus the tonnage tax) furnished 99·5% of the government revenue; in 1859, just preceding the Civil War, 92·6%; in 1939 (excluding the tonnage tax), 6·1%; and now provides about 1%.

During the 5-year period 1958–60 annual imports for consumption averaged $13,570m. (as compared with $10,784m. during 1951–55 and $2,440m. during 1936–40. Of 1956–60 imports, 43·1% ($5,843m.) entered duty free and the remainder ($7,727m.) paid duties averaging $882m. or 11·4% of dutiable imports and 6·5% of total imports for consumption. Imports increased from 1955 to 1958, levelled off in 1958, rose again in 1959, levelled off in 1960 and 1961, and rose again in 1962 to 1965.

Per capita exports fell from $41.77 in 1929 (the 'boom year' when American investors lent heavily abroad) to a low of $12.42 in the depression year of 1932, rising to $23.44 in 1939, and to $103.68 in 1947 (including civilian supplies donated abroad); thereafter they stood at: 1950, $65.65; 1955, $91.68; 1960, $111.17; 1963, $120.15; 1964, $134.24; 1965, $137.6; 1966, $149.86 (all years including economic and military aid shipments). *Per capita* imports (for consumption) were as follows: 1929, $35.14; 1932, $10.44; 1939, $17.08; 1947, $38.57; 1950, $56.59; 1955, $67.41; 1960, $80.04; 1963, $88.58; 1964, $95.53; 1965, $107.92; 1966, $127.15.

The average rate of duty actually collected on US dutiable imports has declined markedly since the early 1930s, as a result both of reductions in US import duties by trade agreements and of the great advance in prices. In the depression years of 1930–33 the average rate under the Hawley–Smoot Law was 52·8%. The rate on dutiable goods declined to 37·3% in 1939, then to an average of 28·2% in the 5 years, 1943–47, then to 14·3% in 1948 (the first year the majority of the Geneva concessions were in effect). Rates since have been: an average of 12·1% in 1951–55, an average of 11·4% in 1956–60, 12% in 1961, 12·2% in 1962, 11·7% in 1963 and 11·6% in 1964. In 1949 the average rate of duty on total US imports for consumption—both dutiable and free—was 5·8%; in 1951–55, an average of 5·3%; in 1956–60, an average of 6·3%; in 1961, 7·1%; in 1962, 7·6%; in 1963, 7·3%, and in 1964, 7·2%.

US *Department of Commerce. Bureau of the Census.* Quarterly summary of foreign commerce of the United States
US *Department of Commerce. Bureau of International Commerce.* Overseas Business Reports

NATIONAL INCOME AND PRODUCT

The Office of Business Economics of the Department of Commerce prepares detailed estimates on the national income and product of the United States. The principal estimates are published monthly in *Survey of Current Business*; the complete set of national income and production tables are published in the *Survey* regularly each July, showing data for recent years. *The National Income and Product Accounts of the United States, 1929–1965* (1966) contains the complete set of tables from 1929 through 1965. The conceptual framework and statistical methods, underlying the US accounts were described in *National Income, 1954.* Subsequent limited changes were described in *US Income and Output* (1958), and in *Survey of Current Business* (Aug. 1965).

These latest figures[1] in $1,000m. for various years are as follows:

	1929[2]	1933[3]	1950	1960	1967	1968	1969
I. Gross National Product	103·1	55·6	284·8	503·7	793·9	865·0	931·4
(a) Personal consumption expenditures	77·2	45·8	191·0	325·2	492·1	535·8	577·5
(b) Gross private domestic investment	16·2	1·4	54·1	74·8	116·6	126·5	139·8
(c) Net exports of goods and services	1·1	0·4	1·8	4·0	5·2	2·5	1·9
(d) Government purchases of goods and services	8·5	8·0	37·9	99·6	180·1	200·2	212·2
1. GNP less adjustments not accruing to individuals, such as indirect business taxes and depreciation, equals:							
2. National Income which, minus corporate profit taxes, undistributed corporate profits and contributions for social insurance, plus transfer payments to persons, equals:	86·8	40·3	241·1	414·5	653·6	712·7	769·5
3. Personal income whereof	85·9	470·	227·6	401·0	629·3	688·7	748·9
4. Personal taxes take leaving	2·6	1·5	20·7	50·9	82·9	97·6	117·3
5. Disposable personal income divided into	83·3	45·0	206·9	350·0	546·3	591·2	631·6
(e) Personal outlays[4]	79·1	46·5	193·9	333·0	506·0	550·8	593·9
(f) Personal saving	4·2	−0·9	13·1	17·0	40·4	40·4	37·6
IA. GNP in constant (1958) $s	203·6	141·5	355·3	487·7	675·2	707·2	727·1
(a) Personal consumption expenditures	139·6	112·8	230·5	316·1	430·1	452·3	467·7
(b) Gross private domestic investment	40·4	5·3	69·3	72·4	101·2	105·7	111·3
(c) Net exports of goods and services	1·5	0·0	2·7	4·3	3·6	0·9	0·2
(d) Government purchases of goods and services	22·0	23·3	52·8	94·9	140·2	148·3	147·8
II. National Income composed of	86·8	40·3	241·1	414·5	653·6	712·7	769·5
Compensation of employees	51·1	29·5	154·6	294·2	467·2	514·1	564·2
(g) Salaries and wages	50·4	29·0	146·8	270·8	423·1	464·1	509·0
(h) Supplements	0·7	0·5	7·8	23·4	44·2	49·3	55·1
Proprietors' income	15·1	5·9	37·5	46·2	62·1	64·1	66·8
(i) Farm	6·2	2·6	13·5	12·0	14·8	15·0	16·4
(j) Business and professional	9·0	3·3	24·0	34·2	47·3	49·1	50·5
Personal incomes from rents	5·4	2·0	9·4	15·8	21·1	21·3	22·0
Net interest	4·7	4·1	2·0	8·4	24·4	27·8	30·7
Corporate profits	10·5	−1·2	37·7	49·9	78·7	85·4	85·8
(k) Tax liabilities	1·4	0·5	17·8	23·0	33·2	40·6	42·7
(l) Inventory valuation adjustment	0·5	−2·1	−5·0	0·2	−1·1	−3·3	−5·4
(m) Dividends	5·8	2·0	8·8	13·4	21·4	23·3	24·7
(n) Undistributed profits	2·8	−1·6	16·0	13·2	25·3	24·9	23·9

[1] The inclusion of statistics for Alaska and Hawaii in 1960 does not significantly affect the comparability of the data. The 1965 figures are preliminary.
[2] Peak year between First and Second World Wars.
[3] Low point of the depression.
[4] Includes personal consumption expenditures, interest paid by consumers and personal transfer payments to foreigners.

CONSUMER PRICE INDEX

The Department of Labor compiles an index of retail prices of consumer goods and services bought by wage-earners and clerical workers in 56 cities and urban areas ranging in population from 2,500 upward.

Indexes shown below are published on the 1957–59 = 100 base. The index for 'housing' has several sub-groups; in the table below only that for rent is given.

Average for year or month	All items	Food	Apparel & Upkeep	Housing Total[1]	Rent	Transport	Medical care
1945	62·7	58·4	70·1	67·5	66·1	55·4	57·5
1955	93·3	94·0	95·9	94·1	94·8	89·7	88·6
1960	103·1	101·4	102·2	103·1	103·1	103·8	108·1
1965	109·9	108·8	106·8	108·5	108·9	111·1	122·3
1968	121·2	119·3	120·1	119·1	115·1	119·6	145·0
1969	127·7	125·5	127·1	126·7	118·8	124·2	155·0
1970							
March	133·2	131·6	130·6	133·6	122·3	127·1	161·6
June	135·2	132·7	132·2	135·6	123·4	130·6	164·7
Sept.	136·6	133·3	133·6	137·8	124·6	131·0	167·6
Dec.	138·5	132·8	135·9	140·1	126·6	135·5	169·8

[1] Includes shelter, rent, home ownership, home maintenance and repairs, and household furnishings and operation.

LABOUR

The American trade unions comprise about 190 national and international unions plus a large number of small independent local or single-firm unions. In 1966 total membership was approximately 19·1m., including 1·22m. Canadian workers affiliated with American unions and 105,000 others outside the continental USA. The American Federation of Labor (founded 1881 and taking its name in 1886) and the Congress of Industrial Organizations merged into one organization, named the AFL–CIO, in Dec. 1955, representing 16·2m. workers in 1966.

Four Railroad Brotherhoods (2 members of the AFL–CIO and 2 unaffiliated) covering operating staffs embracing engine-drivers, firemen, conductors and trainmen, had nearly 288,380 in 1966. Unaffiliated or independent unions, inter-state in scope, including those organizing coalminers, teamsters and government workers, had an estimated total membership of about 2·8m.

The Labor–Management Relations (Taft–Hartley) Act, 1947, applicable to industries affecting inter-state commerce, prohibits the closed shop, but permits union shop arrangements except where forbidden by state laws. Statutes regulating, restricting or prohibiting closed shop or other types of union security agreements are in effect in 23 states, of whom 19 ban all types of union security agreements (Alabama, Arizona, Arkansas, Florida, Georgia, Iowa, Kansas, Mississippi, Nebraska, Nevada, North Carolina, North Dakota, South Carolina, South Dakota, Tennessee, Texas, Utah, Virginia and Wyoming); a 20th state, Louisiana, has such an act applicable only to agricultural labourers and workers engaged in processing certain agricultural products; Colorado and Wisconsin ban all-union agreements unless a certain percentage of employees have voted for them; in Hawaii an all-union agreement may be entered into unless a majority of employees votes against it. Thirteen states have acts to prevent industrial disputes between public utilities and their employees by means of compulsory arbitration or seizure; however, a number of these laws have been declared unconstitutional in so far as industries in inter-state commerce are concerned. Laws to restrict or regulate picketing or other strike activities have been enacted in over half the states. About one-half of the states also prohibit certain types of strikes, as 'sit down', jurisdictional or sympathy strikes.

Minimum-wage laws governing private employers are in operation in 39 states the District of Columbia and Puerto Rico. Three additional states have such laws, but they are inoperative since no minimum-wage rate is provided. The laws of 29 states, the District of Columbia and Puerto Rico cover men, women and, usually, minors; in the other states they cover only women and girls, or women and minors. The minimum wage rate under federal law is $1.60 per hour for employees who are engaged in commerce, in the production of goods for commerce or in certain enterprises which are engaged in commerce. A minimum of $1.45 applies to a large number of workers.

A total of 4,595 strikes and lockouts occurred in 1968, involving 2·87m. workers and 49m. idle man-days; the number of idle man-days was 0·28% of the year's total working time of all workers.

There are 3 federal agencies which provide formal machinery for the adjustment of labour disputes: (1) The Federal Mediation and Conciliation Service, now an independent agency, whose mediation services are available 'in any labor dispute in any industry affecting commerce'. Its aim is to prevent and minimize work stoppages. (2) The National Mediation Board (1934) provides much the same facilities for the railroad and air-transport industries pursuant to the Railway Labor Act. (3) The National Railroad Adjustment Board (1934) acts as a board of final appeal for grievances arising over the interpretation of existing collective agreements under the Railway Labor Act; its decisions are binding upon both sides and enforceable by the courts.

The National Labor Relations Act, as amended by the Labor–Management Relations (Taft–Hartley) Act, 1947 (see THE STATESMAN'S YEAR-BOOK, 1955, p. 617), was again amended by the Labor–Management Reporting and Disclosure Act, 1959. This requires extensive reporting and disclosure of certain financial and administrative practices of labour organizations, employers and labour relations consultants. In addition, certain powers are vested in the Secretary of Labor to prevent abuses in the administration of trusteeships by labour organizations, to provide minimum standards and procedures for the election of union officers and to establish rules prescribing minimum standards for determining the adequacy of union procedures for the removal of officers. Other provisions impose a fiduciary responsibility upon union officers and provide for the exclusion of those convicted of certain named felonies from office for specified periods; more stringently regulate secondary boycotts and banning of 'hot' cargo agreements; put limitations upon organizational and recognition picketing and permit States to assert jurisdiction over labour disputes where the National Labor Relations Board declines to act. The Act also contains a 'Bill of Rights' for union members (enforceable directly by them) dealing with such things as equal rights in the nomination and election of union officers, freedom of speech and assembly subject to reasonable union rules, and safeguards against improper disciplinary action.

The Census of Population (1 April 1960) showed that the total labour force was 69,877,481 (55·3% of those 14 years and over); the armed forces accounted for 1,733,402 and the civilian labour force for 68,144,079, of whom 64,639,252 were employed and 3,504,827—or 5·1%—were unemployed. The following table shows employment by industry group and sex of the employed civilian labour force and percentage distribution of the total:

Industry Group	Male	Female	Total	Percentage distribution
Employed (1,000 persons):	43,467	21,172	64,639	100·0
Agriculture, forestry and fisheries	3,932	418	4,350	6·7
Mining	4,284	185	654	1·0
Construction			3,816	5·9
Manufacturing:				
Durable goods	8,101	1,727	9,829	15·2
Non-durable (including not specified)	5,011	2,674	7,684	11·9
Transportation, communication and other public utilities	3,687	771	4,458	6·9
Wholesale and retail trade	7,398	4,395	11,793	18·2
Finance, insurance and real estate	1,464	1,230	2,695	4·2
Business and repair services	1,270	341	1,611	2·5
Personal services	1,083	2,776	3,858	6·0
Entertainment and recreation services	346	157	503	0·8
Professional and related services	3,019	4,559	7,578	11·7
Public administration	2,289	914	3,203	5·0
Industry not reported	1,583	1,025	2,608	4·0

The Bureau of Labor Statistics estimated the average total labour force (including armed forces) during 1968 at 82,272,000; of the civilian labour force (78,737,000), 2,817,000 persons (3·6%) were unemployed; 3,817,000 were working in agriculture and 72,103,000 in non-agricultural industries. The Bureau estimated that an average of 19·74m. persons were employed in manufacturing, 4,111,000 in trade and 12,202,000 in civilian government services.

Bureau of Labor Statistics, US Dept. of Labor. *Directory of National and International Labor Unions in the US.* 1965.—*Brief History of the American Labor Movement.* 1964.—*Handbook of Labor Statistics.* 1969

Commons, J. R. (ed.), *History of Labor in the United States*. 4 vols. New York, 1918–36
Hardman, J. B. S., and Neufeld, M. S. (ed.), *The House of Labor; Internal Operation of American Unions*. New York, 1951
Lebergott, S., *Manpower in Economic Growth: the American record since 1800*. New York and London, 1963
Millis, H. A., and Brown, E. C., *From the Wagner Act to Taft–Hartley*. Chicago, 1950
Raybeck, J. G., *A History of American Labor*. New York, 1959
Peterson, F., *American Labor Unions*. Rev. ed. New York and London, 1963
Taft, P., *The Structure and Government of Labor Unions*. Harvard Univ. Press, 1954.—*Organized Labor in American History*. New York, 1964

COMMUNICATIONS

SHIPPING

On 31 Dec. 1969 the US merchant marine included 1,937 sea-going vessels of 1,000 gross tons or over, with aggregate dead-weight tonnage of 24·56m. This included 305 tankers of 7,594,000 dead-weight tons.

On 31 Dec. 1969 US merchant ocean-going vessels were employed as follows: Active, 933 of 15·28m. dead-weight tons, of which 405 of 5·72m. tons were in foreign trade, 247 of 5,613,000 tons in domestic trade and 281 of 3·96m. tons in other US agency operations. Inactive vessels totalled 1,004 of 9,279,000 dead-weight tons, of which 45 of 618,000 tons were temporarily inactive; 57 of 627,000 dead-weight tons privately owned were laid up and 902 of 8,034,000 tons were in the Maritime Administration's reserve fleet. Of the total vessels in the US fleet, 931 of 15,453,000 dead-weight tons were privately owned. US exports and imports carried on dry cargo and tanker vessels in the year 1969 totalled 428m. long tons, of which 21m. long tons or 4·8% were carried in US flag vessels.

ROADS

On 1 Jan. 1968 the total US highway mileage, including rural and urban roads, amounted to 3,684,085 miles, of which, 2,869,883 miles were surfaced roads. The total mileage cited includes 292,382 miles of rural roads under control of the states, 2,737,022 miles of local roads, 175,272 miles of federal park and forest roads, and 479,409 miles of municipal roads and streets. Expenditures for construction and maintenance amounted to $14,537m. in 1969.

By the end of 1969, toll roads, financed by private capital through bond issues and administered by state toll authorities, totalled 4,500 miles (including some under construction) compared with 344 miles in 1940. Additional toll-road programmes contemplated at present will add approximately 3,370 miles to the toll-road network.

Motor vehicles registered in the calendar year 1969 were (US Bureau of Public Roads) 105,096,603, including 86,861,334 automobiles, 364,282 buses and 17,870,987 trucks.

Road haulage of goods by motor lorries and trucks in 1969 used 17,870,987 vehicles (250,048 in 1916). The industry (1969) employed 8·83m. workers, or 1 out of every 7 employed in the USA.

Inter-city trucks (private and for hire) averaged 404,000m. revenue net ton-miles in 1969. Of the 364,282 buses in service in 1969, 273,973 were school buses (including some church, industrial, etc., buses). The 22,500 buses in inter-city service operated a total of 1·2m. bus-miles and earned a total of $840·8m. in 1969.

There were 56,400 deaths in road accidents in 1969.

RAILWAYS

Railway history in the USA commences in 1828, but the first railway to convey both freight and passengers in regular service (between Baltimore and Ellicott's Mills, Md., 13 miles) dates from 24 May 1830. Mileage rose to 52,922 miles in 1870; to 167,191 miles in 1890, and to a peak of 266,381 miles in 1916, falling thereafter to 261,871 in 1925; 246,739 in 1940 and 222,164 in 1969 (these include some duplication under trackage rights and some mileage operated in Canada by US companies). The ordinary gauge is 4 ft 8½ in. (about 99·6% of total mileage). The USA has about 29% of the world's railway mileage.

The following table, based on the figures of the Interstate Commerce Commission, shows some railway statistics for 4 calendar years:

	1960	1967	1968	1969[1]
Classes I and II Railroads:				
Mileage owned (first main tracks)	223,779	206,785	205,603	178,099
Revenue freight originated (1m. short tons)	1,421	1,498	1,515	1,473
Freight ton-mileage (1m. ton-miles)	591,550	727,075	750,468	767,841
Passengers carried (1,000)	488,019	304,028	301,372	295,701
Passenger-miles (1m.)	31,790	15,264	13,164	12,159
Operating revenues ($1m.)	9,587	10,582	11,062	11,450
Operating expenses ($1m.)	7,135	8,359	8,724	9,067
Net railway operating income ($1m.)	1,055	690	694	655
Net income after fixed charges ($1m.)	855	368	623	464
Class I Railroads:				
Locomotives in service	40,949	27,687	27,376	27,033
Steam locomotives	25,640	21	21	21
Freight-train cars (excluding caboose cars)	1,721,269	1,477,166	1,453,883	1,434,824
Passenger-train cars	57,146	17,589	14,619	12,426
Average number of employees	1,220,784	610,191	590,536	578,277
Average wage per week ($1)	72.59	155.48	166.42	178.35

[1] Class I only.

AVIATION

In civil aviation there were, on 31 Dec. 1969, 720,028 certified pilots (299,491 private) and 190,749 registered civil aircraft (133,814 active).

Airports on 31 Dec. 1969: Air carrier, 817; general aviation, 10,233; total conventional land-based, 9,909. There were also, 1 Jan. 1969, 430 seaplane bases and 711 heliports.

Data of the Civil Aeronautics Board indicate that in 1969 the US domestic certified air carriers flew 1,919,673,000 revenue miles, with 154,407,000 revenue passengers; revenue passenger-miles in scheduled domestic operations, 95,946m. American-flag air carriers in scheduled international and territorial air transport operations flew 465,215,000 revenue aircraft-miles (17·49m. revenue passengers) and 29,468m. revenue passenger-miles.

Association of American Railroads. Bureau of Railway Economics. *Statistics of railroads in the United States.* Washington, Annual.—*A review of railroad operations.* Washington, Annual
Barger, H., *The Transportation Industries, 1889–1946.* New York, 1951
Civil Aeronautics Board. *Handbook of Airline Statistics.* Washington, Biennial
Landon, C. E., *Transportation: principles, practices, problems.* New York, 1951
Lewis, R. G., *Handbook of American Railroads.* 2nd ed. New York, 1956
Locklin, D. P., *Economics of Transportation.* 5th ed. Homewood, Ill., 1960
Maritime Administration, US Dept. of Commerce. *Employment Report.* Washington, Quarterly
Nelson, J. C., *Railroad transportation and public policy.* Washington and London, 1959
Van Metre, T. W., *Transportation in the US.* 2nd ed. Brooklyn, 1950
Westmeyer, R. E., *Economics of Transportation.* New York, 1952

POSTS AND TELEGRAPHS

The telephone business is largely in the hands of the American Telephone and Telegraph Company and its telephone operating subsidiaries, which together are known as the Bell Telephone System. There are, however, many hundreds of smaller telephone companies having no common ownership affiliation with the Bell companies, but which connect with them for universal service, countrywide and worldwide. The message telegraph service is in the hands of The Western Union Telegraph Company, but it competes with the telephone industry in providing other record communication services such as telex and private leased line.

The number of telephones in service in the USA has increased in the period since the close of the Second World War much more proportionately than has the population. Among principal reasons there may be cited the facts that an increasingly high percentage of families have telephones installed in their homes, and extension phones associated with the main home telephones have become increasingly common. In marked contrast, the number of public telegrams handled has shown a decreasing trend. Telegrams have lost favour due to shifts in user preference to the air mail and to the telephone. The telex networks of both the telephone industry and the telegraph company have also found broad acceptance in place of telegrams for business purposes. The following table contains key data items on a comparative basis for the domestic telephone and message telegram services:

	1945	1950	1960	1969
All telephone systems:				
Total telephones	27,946,000	43,131,000	74,342,000	115,201,000
Bell Telephone System:				
Total telephones	22,445,500	35,343,400	60,735,100	92,691,000
Average daily telephone calls	90,548,000	140,782,000	219,093,000	348,717.000
Local[1]	85,877,000	134,870,000	209,373,000	328,662,000
Long distance[1]	4,671,000	5,912,000	9,720,000	20,055.000
Total plant ($1,000)	5,702,057	10,101,522	24,072,499	15,778,037
Total operating revenues ($1,000)	1,934,348	3,271,029	7,958,125	735,856
Employees, number	387,300	523,251	580,405	
Western Union Telegraph System:				
Public telegrams for year	193,848,000	153,054,000	102,931,000	53,383,000
Total plant ($1,000)	357,784	294,451	398,023	968.401
Revenue from public telegrams ($1,000)	132,725	132,281	160,746	134,289
Total operating revenues ($1,000)	182,048	177,994	262,365	391,338
Employees, number	63,446	40,482	32,655	25,164

[1] Figures are adjusted to a basis of 1 Jan. 1970 for changes in classification between local and long-distance calls due to enlargement of local calling areas.

International communication services, providing overseas connexions with all parts of the world, are furnished principally by the American Telephone and Telegraph Company and three telegraph companies. The old-type telegraph-only-transmission-capability ocean cables have all been abandoned in favour of using telegraph circuits derived from voice channels in the newer telephone ocean cables which have also made inroads on the use of high-frequency radio. More recently, transoceanic radio service by microwave radio relay through miniaturized equipment housed in satellites in equatorial orbit has been available not only for telephone and telegraph services but for television transmission as well.

International overseas telegrams, inbound to and outbound from the continental US, numbered 19·4m. in 1969, which is a growth of 41·1% since 1950. This service has tended to level off in volume in recent years. It has lost ground to the air-mail and, in addition, in more recent years to the telex and telephone services. For the US and its possessions the volume of international telephone overseas calls has grown enormously with the availability of the excellent voice-transmission qualities provided in the telephone ocean cables and in the satellite radio relays. Whereas, international telephone calls were 990,000 in 1955, the last year in which there was no cable service available, there were 11·3m. such calls in 1969.

Postal business for the years ended 30 June included the following items:

	1960	1968	1969	1970
Number of post offices, on 30 June	35,238	32,626	32,260	32,002
Postal revenue ($1,000)[1]	3,277,000	5,101,983	5,660,112	6,472,738
Postal expenses ($1,000)[2]	3,874,000	6,249,027	6,680,972	7,982,552

[1] Beginning 1963, revenues include operating reimbursements and are stated without deduction for certain costs previously deducted as being financed by revenue.
[2] Beginning 1963, expenses are stated on the basis of accrued expense rather than appropriation obligations.

BANKING

On 30 June 1970 there were 14,167 domestic banks doing a general deposit business with the public and having aggregate deposits of $502,658m. Of these, 4,637 with deposits of $254,261m. were national banks operating under charters granted by the federal government; the remaining banks, including trust companies and savings banks, were organized under the laws of the various states. Of the total number, 5,803 were members of the Federal Reserve System, namely, all the 4,637 national banks and 1,166 state banks admitted to membership.

The Federal Reserve System, established under an Act of 1913, comprises the Board of 7 Governors, the 12 regional Federal Reserve Banks with their 24 branches, 5,803 member banks, the Federal Open Market Committee and the Federal Advisory Council. The Board of Governors, appointed by the President with the consent of the Senate, determine monetary, credit and operating policies. Each Governor holds office for 14 years, one Governor's term expiring every 2 years. No two may come from the same Federal Reserve District. The Board supervises the Reserve Banks and the issue and retirement of Federal Reserve notes; it appoints 3 of the 9 directors of each Reserve Bank; it passes on the admission of state banks to the System and has power to correct unsound conditions in State member banks or violations of banking law by them, including, if necessary, disciplinary action to remove officers and directors for unsafe or unsound banking practices or for continuous violations of banking laws; and it has power to control the expansion of bank holding companies and to require divestment of their non-banking interests. The Board and 5 representatives of the Reserve Banks constitute the Federal Open Market Committee, which directs the purchase and sale principally of Government obligations, made by the Reserve Banks to influence the general credit conditions of the country. The Board also influences credit conditions through powers to set member-bank reserve requirements, to approve discount rates at Federal Reserve Banks, and to fix margin requirements on stock-market credit.

The 12 Reserve Banks (one for each district) implement Federal Reserve policies, chiefly through their dealings with member banks, which, although outnumbered by non-member banks, hold about 80% of the country's total commercial banking resources. The Reserve Banks hold bank reserves, advance funds to member banks, provide currency for circulation, act as fiscal agent for the Government and afford nation-wide cheque-clearing and fund transfer arrangements. They may issue notes, fully secured; discount paper for member banks; increase or reduce the country's supply of reserve funds by buying or selling Government securities and other obligations at the direction of the Federal Open Market Committee. Their capital stock is held by the member banks, but it carries no voting rights except in the election of directors.

Every member bank is required to subscribe to stock in the Reserve Bank of its district in an amount equal to 6% of its paid-up capital and surplus. Only one-half of the par value of the stock is paid in, the other half remaining subject to call by the Board of Governors. However, no call has been made for the second half of the subscription. The reserve balances which member banks must carry with Reserve Banks are based on the volume of their net demand and time deposits. The Board of Governors has the power to alter these requirements within limits. The Board of Governors also has authority to limit the rate of interest payable by member banks on time and savings deposits. Under provisions of the Defense Production Act of 1950 the Board of Governors prescribes regulations under which the Federal Reserve Banks act as fiscal agents of certain Government departments and agencies in guaranteeing loans made by banks and other private financing institutions to finance contracts for the procurement of materials or services which the guaranteeing agencies consider necessary for the national defence.

Under the President's programme to reduce the deficit in the nation's balance of payments, the Board of Governors administers a foreign credit restraint programme for the nation's privately owned financial institutions.

Under the Credit Control Act of 1969 the President is empowered to authorize the Board of Governors to institute credit controls when necessary to curb inflation.

Under the provisions of the Truth in Lending Act of 1968 the Board of Governors is required to prescribe regulations to assure a meaningful disclosure by lenders of credit terms so that consumers will be able to compare more readily the various credit terms available and avoid the uninformed use of credit.

The Federal Advisory Council consists of 12 members (one from each district); it meets in Washington four times a year (or oftener) to advise the Board of Governors on general business and financial conditions.

Banks which participate in the federal deposit insurance fund have their deposits insured against loss up to $20,000 for each depositor. The fund is administered by the Federal Deposit Insurance Corporation established in 1933; it obtains resources through annual assessments on participating banks.

All members of the Federal Reserve System are required to insure their deposits through the Corporation, and non-member banks may apply and qualify for insurance. On 30 June 1970, 13,478 commercial banks with deposits of $431,093,539,000 were members of the insurance fund. This insurance also covered 330 mutual savings banks with deposits of $60,193,707,000. There were 359 uninsured banks comprising 193 commercial banks and trust companies (including 1 non-deposit state bank that is non-insured) with deposits of $2,279,875,000 and 166 mutual savings banks with deposits of $19,091,134,000.

There are also banks which operate solely in the field of agricultural credits under the Farm Credit Administration, and Federal Home Loan Banks to make advances to financial associations and institutions upon the security of home mortgages.

US Board of Governors of the Federal Reserve System. *The Federal Reserve System: Purposes and Functions.* 5th ed. revised, 1963.—*Federal Reserve Bulletin.* Monthly.—*Annual Report.—The Federal Reserve Act, as amended to 5 Nov. 1966.* 1967
Chandler, L. V., *Economics of Money and Banking.* 5th ed. New York, 1969
Clifford, A. J., *The Independence of the Federal Reserve System.* Philadelphia, 1965
Friedman and Swartz, *A Monetary History of the United States, 1867–1960,* National Bureau of Economic Research, New York, 1963
Prochnow, H. V., *The Federal Reserve System.* New York, 1960
Robinson, R. I. (ed.), *Financial Institutions.* 3rd ed. Homewood, Ill., 1960
Studenski, P., and Krooss, H. E., *Financial History of the US.* 2nd ed. New York, 1963
Trescott, P. B., *Financing American Enterprise: the story of commercial banking.* New York, 1963

CURRENCY

Prior to the banking crisis that occurred early in 1933, the monetary system had been on the gold standard for more than 50 years. An Act of 14 March 1900 required the Secretary of the Treasury to maintain at a parity with gold all forms of money issued by the USA. For a description of these, *see* THE STATESMAN'S YEAR-BOOK, 1934, p. 491.

The old gold dollar had a par value of 49·32*d.*, or $4·8666 to the £ sterling; it contained 25·8 grains (or 1·6718 grammes) of gold 0·900 fine. Under existing statutes the Government is still under obligation to maintain parity between gold and all forms of currency. By the Act of 12 May 1933 the President of the USA was given authority to reduce the gold content of the dollar by not more than 50% and by the Gold Reserve Act of 30 Jan. 1934 the minimum reduction which he could make was fixed at 40%; on 31 Jan. 1934 he fixed its value at 59·06%, or 15$\frac{5}{21}$ grains of gold 0·900 fine. This was equal to a price for gold of $35 a fine oz. (old price, $20·67183). The President's power to alter the gold content of the dollar to 50% of its value, which was extended by Congress in 1937, 1939 and 1941, was not again extended in 1943.

At the time of the banking crisis in March 1933 gold payments by banks and the Treasury were suspended by the Government, and an embargo was placed on gold exports. Steps were taken to withdraw from circulation all gold coin and gold certificates.

Currency in the USA for many years has comprised several varieties. Prior to May 1933 the legal tender qualities of the classes varied, but in that month all types of currency were made equally legal tender.

Only two of the eight kinds of notes outstanding are now significant: Federal Reserve notes in denominations of $1, $5, $10, $20, $50 and $100; and US notes in denominations of $100. The issue of (*a*) $500, $1,000, $5,000, $10,000 and Federal Reserve notes of (*b*) silver certificates and of (*c*) $5 and $2 US notes was discontinued recently, although they are still in general circulation. The following issues were stopped many years ago and are in process of retirement: (1) Federal Reserve Bank notes; (2) National Bank notes; (3) Treasury notes of 1890; (4) fractional currency.

Federal Reserve notes are obligations of the USA and a first lien on the assets of the Federal Reserve Banks through which they are issued. Each of the 12 banks issues them against the security of an equal volume of collateral.

Gold coins (of the old weight and fineness) were $20, $10, $5 and $2½ pieces called *double eagles, eagles, half-eagles* and *quarter-eagles*. The old eagle weighed 258 grains or 16·7181 grammes 0·900 fine, and therefore contained 232·2 grains or 15·0463 grammes of fine gold. Except for collector's holdings, these are no longer in circulation. The stock of gold bullion held by the Treasury on 30 June 1970 was 340m. fine oz., valued at $11,889m.; stock of silver bullion was 63·2m fine oz. (excluding 165m. fine oz. held for defence stockpile. Estimated stock of domestic coin was $6,362m., of which $485m. were standard silver dollars and the remainder silver and other subsidiary coin.

The silver dollar weighs 412·5 grains or 26·7296 grammes 0·900 fine, and contains 371·25 grains or 24·0566 grammes of fine silver. Subsidiary, 0·900 fine, silver coins contain 347·22 grains of fine silver per dollar. These are the half-dollar, quarter-dollar and dime (one-tenth). Minor coins currently issued are the cupro-nickel 5-cent piece and the bronze 1-cent piece. Pursuant to the Coinage Act of 1965, Congress authorized the minting and issuance of new silver clad half-dollars containing 40% silver and cupro-nickel quarter-dollars and dimes containing no silver.

WEIGHTS AND MEASURES

British weights and measures are usually employed, but the old Winchester bushel and wine gallon are used instead of the new or imperial standards: *Wine gallon* = 0·83268 Imperial gallon; *Bushel* = 0·9690 Imperial bushel. Instead of the British cwt of 112 lb., one of 100 lb. is used; the *short* or *net ton* contains 2,000 lb.; the *long* or *gross ton*, 2,240 lb.

DIPLOMATIC REPRESENTATIVES

OF THE UNITED STATES IN GREAT BRITAIN (Grosvenor Sq., W1)

Ambassador: Walter H. Annenberg (accredited 30 April 1969).

Ministers: Joseph N. Greene; Stanley M. Cleveland (*Economic and Commercial*).

Counsellors: William H. Brubeck (*Political*); Jack A. Herfurt (*Consular*); William E. Weld (*Public Affairs*); William J. Galloway, Peter J. Skoufis (*Administration*); Archie M. Andrews (*Commercial*); Stephen H. Rogers (*Economic Affairs*).

First Secretaries: Alan G. James; Dudley W. Miller; James T. Pettus (*Public Affairs*); Jack A. Sulser; Gordon D. King; William J. Ford, John J. Ingersoll (*Economic*); James E. Kiley (*Consular*); John P. Mulligan (*Commercial*); John B. McGrath (*Economic*).

Service Attachés: Rear-Adm. Fillmore B. Gilkeson (*Defence, Navy, Navy-Air*), Col. John M. Cutler (*Air*); Col. Thomas C. Finneran (*Army*).

Attachés: David L. Hume (*Agricultural*); George H. White (*Financial*); Robin W. Winks (*Cultural*); William L. R. Rice (*Atomic Energy*); Robert J. Murray (*Politico-Military Affairs*); Irwin S. Lippe (*Labour*); Henry T. Snowdon (*Civil Air*); Dr Alan G. Mencher (*Scientific*).

There are Consuls-General in Belfast, Edinburgh, Liverpool and London.

OF GREAT BRITAIN IN THE USA (3100 Massachusetts Ave., Washington, D.C., 20008)

Ambassador: The Earl of Cromer, PC, MBE.

Ministers: G. E. Millard, CMG, CVO; D. C. Tebbit, CMG (*Commercial*); D. Mitchell, CB, CVO (*Economic*); W. H. Stephens, CB (*Defence Research and Development*); T. A. K. Elliott, CMG (*Head of Chancery*).

Counsellors: W. R. Lythgo, OBE (*Consul-General*); J. J. Watson (*Labour*); B. W. Meyneu (*Commercial*); E. Bolland; M. P. J. Lynch (*Overseas Development*); P. G. Hudson (*Civil Air*); J. R. Steele (*Shipping*); Dr J. M. Lock (*Scientific*);

A. H. B. Hermann; C. M. Rose, CMG; W. M. Drower, MBE; J. F. Gough; B. Russel-Jones; E. F. C. Stanford (*Defence Supply*); J. D. Taylor, CMG, OBE; D. P. M. S. Cape; B. Hutchinson; R. H. Willmott; K. J. Uffen (*Economic*).

First Secretaries: D. H. Mather, MBE, H. B. Walker (*Commercial*); D. A. Burns (*Information*); M. K. Molloy; H. V. Richardson; Miss J. F. Veasey, MBE (*Consul*); B. L. Crowe; Λ. J. Clift; A. R. Thomas; W. N. Hewson.

Service Attachés: Air Marshal Sir John Lapsley, KBE, CB, DFC, AFC (*Defence*); Rear-Adm. C. C. H. Dunlop, CBE (*Navy*); Air Cdre C. W. Coulthard, AFC (*Air*).

There are Consuls-General in Atlanta (Ga), Boston (Mass.), Chicago (Ill.), Cleveland, Detroit (Mich.), Houston, Los Angeles, New York, Philadelphia (Pa.), San Francisco (Cal.), Seattle, Washington (D.C.) and Consuls in Anchorage (Alaska), Denver, Honolulu, Kansas City, Miami, New Orleans (La.), Portland (Oreg.), St Louis, St Paul-Minneapolis.

BOOKS OF REFERENCE
I. STATISTICAL INFORMATION

Within the federal government of the USA, responsibilities for the collection, compilation, analysis and publication of statistics are decentralized among a number of agencies, with specified responsibilities for general-purpose statistics in particular areas. In addition, most agencies of the Government collect statistical data as a by-product of their administrative or operating responsibilities in specific fields. Responsibility for co-ordinating the decentralized statistical activities rests in the Office of Statistical Standards, Bureau of the Budget, Washington 25, D.C., as a part of the Executive Office of the President. This Office reviews all proposed collections of statistical data to avoid duplication or overlapping; promotes the use of improved statistical techniques; develops standard definitions and classifications so that the data collected by different agencies are comparable; serves as liaison between federal agencies and international organizations and as an information centre on government statistical programmes. The Division does not itself collect or publish statistics.

The major general-purpose statistical agencies and their principal areas of responsibility are:

(1) Bureau of the Census in the Department of Commerce (A. Ross Eckler, Director). Decennial censuses of population and housing and quinquennial censuses of agriculture, manufactures and business; current statistics on population and the labour force, manufacturing activity and commodity production, retail and wholesale trade and services, foreign trade, and state and local government finances and operations.

(2) Bureau of Labor Statistics in the Department of Labor (Geoffrey H. Moore, Commissioner), Current statistics on employment, earnings, man-hours, labour turnover, industrial accidents, work stoppages, wage rates; collective bargaining agreements; construction; industrial productivity; wholesale prices, retail prices and urban consumers' price indexes; income and expenditures of urban families.

(3) Statistical Reporting Service and Economic Research Service in the Department of Agriculture. Statistics on crop and livestock production and inventories; crop forecasts; food processing and food consumption; farm population, labour and wages; farm management; farm ownership values, transfers, taxation and finance; prices farmers pay and receive; farm income; accidents; studies of land and water uses.

(4) National Center for Health Statistics in the Public Health Service, Department of Health, Education and Welfare (Theodore D. Woolsey, Chief). Current statistics on births, deaths, marriages and divorce.

(5) Bureau of Mines in the Department of the Interior (John F. O'Leary, Director). Statistics on production, consumption and stocks of metals and minerals, and on injuries in mineral industries.

Other agencies in which statistics are an important by-product of regulatory or other administrative functions include: Social Security Administration in the Department of Health, Education and Welfare; Internal Revenue Service in the Treasury Department; Federal Power Commission; Federal Trade Commission; Interstate Commerce Commission, and the Securities and Exchange Commission.

Among the more important statistical publications of a fairly general nature are:

Statistical Abstract of the United States, published by the Bureau of the Census, Department or Commerce. Annual. Important summary statistics on the industrial, social, political and economic organization of the USA, with a representative selection from most of the important statistical publications. *Survey of Current Business,* published by the Office of Business Economics, Department of Commerce. Monthly. Interpretative text and charts reviewing business trends, etc.; official estimates of national income. *Economic Indicators,* prepared by the Council of Economic Advisers and published by the Congressional Joint Committee on the Economic Report. Monthly. Tables and charts presenting current data on the total output of the economy; prices; employment and wages; production and business activity; purchasing power; money, banking and federal finance. *Monthly Labor Review,* published by the Bureau of Labor Statistics, Department of Labor. *Federal Reserve Bulletin,* published by the Board of Governors of the Federal Reserve System. Monthly. Current data on money and banking and selected other economic series. Federal Reserve indexes of industrial production, etc.; international financial statistics. *Treasury Bulletin,* published by the Office of the Secretary, Department of the Treasury. Monthly. Current coverage of federal fiscal statistics; international capital movements. *Minerals Yearbook*, published by the Bureau of Mines, Department of the Interior. Annual. *Agricultural Statistics*, published by the Department of Agriculture. Annual. *Crops and Markets*, published by the Bureau of Agricultural Economics in the Department of Agriculture. Monthly. Crop report and market statistics. *Foreign Agriculture*, published by the Office of Foreign Agriculture Service, Department of Agriculture. Monthly. Foreign agricultural production, foreign government policies relating to agriculture and international trade in agricultural products. *Vital Statistics of the United States*, published by the Public Health Service, US Department of Health, Education and Welfare. Monthly and Annual. Natality and mortality data tabulated by place of occurrence, with supplemental tables for Puerto Rico and the Virgin Islands; and tabulated by place of residence.

An annotated bibliography of about 100 periodical statistical publications is included in *Statistical Services of the United States Government*, a pamphlet issued by the Division of Statistical Standards, Bureau of the Budget, describing the general organization of the statistical system of the USA and the principal types of economic statistics.

II. Other Offical Publications

Guide to the Study of the United States of America. General Reference and Bibliography Division, Library of Congress. 1960.

Historical Statistics of the United States, colonial times to 1957: a statistical abstract supplement. Washington, 1960.—*Continuation to 1962 and revisions*. 1965

United States Government Manual. Washington. Annual.

The official publications of the USA are issued by the US Government Printing Office and are distributed by the Superintendent of Documents, who issued in 1940 a cumulative *Catalog of the Public Documents of the . . . Congress and of All the Departments of the Government of the United States*. This *Catalog* is kept up to date by *United States Government Publications, Monthly Catalog* with annual index and supplemented by *Price Lists*. Each *Price List* is devoted to a special subject or type of material, *e.g.*, *American History* or *Census*. Useful guides are Schmeckebier, L. F., and Eastin, R. B. (eds.), *Government Publications and their Use*. 2nd ed., Washington D.C., 1961; Boyd, A. M., *United States Government Publications*. 3rd ed. New York, 1949, and Leidy, W. P., *Popular Guide to Government Publications*. 2nd ed. New York and London, 1963.

Treaties and other International Acts of the United States of America (Edited by Hunter Miller), 8 vols. Washington, 1929–48. This edition stops in 1863. It may be supplemented by *Treaties, Conventions . . . Between the US and other Powers, 1776–1937* (Edited by William M. Malloy and others). 4 vols. 1909–38. A new Treaty Series, *US Treaties and other International Agreements* was started in 1950.

Writings on American History. Washington, annual from 1902 (except 1904–5 and 1941–47).

III. Non-Official Publications

A. Handbooks

National Historical Publications Commission. *Guide to Archives and Manuscripts in the United States*, ed. P. M. Hamer. Yale Univ. Press, 1961

Adams, J. T. (ed.), *Dictionary of American History*. 2nd ed. 7 vols. New York, 1942

Dictionary of American Biography, ed. A. Johnson and D. Malone. 23 vols. New York, 1929–64.— *Concise Dictionary of American Biography*. New York, 1964

Current Biography. New York, annual from 1940; monthly supplements

Alsberg, H. G. (ed.), *The American Guide*. New York, 1955

Handlin, O., and others, *Harvard Guide to American History*. Cambridge, Mass., 1954

Kreutz, B., and Fleming, E., *Introducing America*. London, 1963

Lord, C. L., and E. H., *Historical Atlas of the US*. Rev. ed. New York, 1953

Who's Who in America. Chicago, 1899–1900 to date; monthly Supplement. 1940 to date

B. General History

Barck, Jr, O. T., and Blake, N. M., *Since 1900: a History of the United States*. 4th ed. New York, 1965

Bellot, H. H., *America History and American Historians*. London, 1952

Billington, R. A., *Westward Expansion*. 2nd ed. New York, 1960

Carman, H. J., and others, *A History of the American people*. Rev. ed. 2 vols. New York, 1961

Clark, T. D., *Frontier America: the story of the westward movement*. New York, 1959

Commager, H. S. (ed.), *Documents of American History*. 8th ed. New York, 1966

Faulkner, H. U., *American Political and Social History*. 7th ed. New York, 1957

Hicks, J. D., *The American Nation, a history of the United States from 1865*. 4th ed. Boston, 1963

Link, A. S., and Catton, W. B., *American epoch: a history of the United States since the 1890s*. 3rd ed. New York, 1967

Morison, S. E., *The Oxford History of the American People*. OUP, 1968

Morison, S. E., with H. S. Commager, *The Growth of the American Republic*. 2 vols. 5th ed. OUP, 1962–63

Parkes, H. B., *The United States of American, a History*. 3rd ed. New York, 1968

Savelle, M., *A Short History of American Civilization*. New York, 1957

Scammon, R. N. (ed.), *American Votes: a handbook of contemporary American election statistics*. Washington, D.C., 1956 to date (biennial)

Schlesinger, A. M., *The Rise of Modern America, 1865–1951*. 4th ed. New York, 1951.—*The Age of Roosevelt*. 4 vols. New York and London, 1957–62.—*A thousand days: John F. Kennedy in the White House*. New York and London, 1965

Thistlewaite, F., *The Great Experiment: An introduction to the History of the American people*. CUP, 1955

Wish, H., *Society and Thought in America*. 2 vols. OUP, 1962

C. Minorities

Bennett, M. T., *American immigration policies: a history.* Washington, D.C., 1963
Brown, F. J. (ed.), *One America: the history, contributions and present problems of our racial and national minorities.* 3rd ed. New York, 1952
Burma, J. H., *Spanish-speaking Groups in the US.* Duke University Press, 1954
Burns, W. H., *The Voices of Negro Protest in America.* OUP, 1963
Frazier, E. F., *The Negro in the United States.* Rev. ed. New York, 1957
McNickle, D., *The Indian Tribes of the United States.* OUP, 1962
McWilliams, Carey, *Brothers Under the Skin: A Study of the Position o Racial Minorities in Continental United States and the Possessions.* Rev. ed. New York, 1951
Rose, A. and C., *America Divided: Minority Group Relations in the United States.* New York, 1949
Sklare, M., *The Jews: social patterns of an American group.* Glencoe, Ill., 1958
Wissler, Clark, *Indians of the United States.* New York, 1946

D. Economic History

The Economic History of the United States. 9 vols. New York, 1946 ff.
Bining, A. C., and Cochran, T. C., *The Rise of American Economic Life.* 4th ed. New York, 1963
Dorfman, J., *The Economic Mind in American Civilization.* 5 vols. New York, 1946–59
Fainsod, M., and Gordon, L., *Government and the American Economy.* 3rd ed. New York, 1959
Faulkner, H. U., *American Economic History.* 8th ed. New York, 1960
Friedman, M., and Schwartz, A. J., *A monetary history of the United States, 1867–1960.* New York, 1963
Jones, P. d'A., *America's Wealth.* London, 1963
Landsberg, H. H., and others, *Resources in America's future: patterns of requirements and availabilities, 1960–2000.* Washington, D.C., 1963
Mund, V. A., *Government and Business.* 4th ed. New York, 1965

E. Foreign Relations

American Foreign Policy Library, ed. Sumner Wells (Harvard Univ. Press); E. A. Speiser, *The US and the Near East* (rev. ed. 1950); C. Brinton, *The US and Britain* (rev. ed. 1948); J. K. Fairbank, *The US and China* (rev. ed. 1958); V. M. Dean, *The US and Russia* (1948); D. Perkins, *The US and the Caribbean* (rev. ed., 1967); A. P. Whitaker, *The US and South America* (1948); D. C. McKay, *The US and France* (1951); E. O. Reischauer, *The US and Japan* (rev. ed., 1957); W. N. Brown, *The US and India and Pakistan* (1953); H. S. Hughes, *The US and Italy* (1953); H. F. Cline, *The US and Mexico* (1953); L. V. Thomas and R. N. Frye, *The US and Turkey and Iran* (1951); F. D. Scott, *The US and Scandinavia* (1950); A. P. Whitaker, *The US and Argentina* (1954); R. L. Wolff, *The Balkans in Our Time* (1956); C. H. Grattan, *The US and the SW Pacific* (1961)
Documents on American Foreign Relations. Princeton, from 1948. Annual
The United States in World Affairs. 1931 ff. Council on Foreign Relations. New York, from 1932. Annual
Bartlett, R. J. (ed.), *The Record of American Diplomacy: Documents and Readings in the History of American Foreign Relations.* 4th ed. New York, 1964
Beloff, M., *The United States and the Unity of Europe.* London, 1963
Bemis, S. F., *Diplomatic History of the US.* 4th ed. New York, 1955.—*Short History of American Foreign Policy and Diplomacy.* Rev. ed. New York, 1959.—*The United States as a World Power: a diplomatic history.* Rev. ed. New York, 1955
DeConde, A., *The American Secretary of State.* London, 1963
Graebner, N. A. (ed.), *An Uncertain Tradition: American Secretaries of State in the 20th Century,* New York, 1961.—*Cold War Diplomacy: American Foreign Policy, 1945–60.* Princeton, 1962
Hyde, L. K., *The United States and the United Nations.* New York, 1960
Lary, H. B., *Problems of the United States as world trader and banker.* New York, 1963
Leopold, R. W., *The Growth of American Foreign Policy: a history.* New York, 1962
McCamy, J. L., *Conduct of the new diplomacy.* New York, 1964
Pratt, J. W., *A History of United States Foreign Policy.* New York, 1955
Rostow, W. W., *The United States in the World Arena: an essay in recent history.* New York, 1960
Smith, R. F., *The United States and Cuba: business and diplomacy, 1917–1960.* New York, 1962
Spanier, J. W., *American Foreign Policy Since World War II.* 2nd ed. London, 1962
Stuart, Graham H., *American Diplomatic and Consular Practice.* 2nd ed. New York, 1952.—*Latin America and the United States.* 5th ed. New York, 1955
Wilcox, F. C., and Kalijarvi, T. V., *Recent American Foreign Policy: basic documents, 1941–51.* New York, 1952
Williams, W. A. (ed.), *The Shaping of American Diplomacy: readings and documents in American foreign relations. 1750–1955.* 2 vols. Chicago, 1956

F. National Character

Brogan, D. W., *USA: An Outline of the Country, Its People and Institutions.* 2nd ed. Oxford, 1947
Coan, O. W., *America in Fiction, an annotated list of novels.* 5th ed. Stanford Univ. Press, 1967
Commager, H. S., *The American Mind.* Yale Univ. Press, 1950
Curti, M. B., *The Growth of American Thought.* 3rd ed. New York, 1964
Degler, C. N., *Out of our past: the forces that shaped modern America.* New York, 1959
Gabriel, R. H., *The Course of American Democratic Thought.* 2nd ed. New York, 1956
Hertzler, J. O., *American Social Institutions: a sociological analysis.* Boston, 1961
Lerner, M., *America as a Civilization: Life and Thought in the United States Today.* 2 vols. New York, 1961
Riesman, D., with R. Denny and N. Glazer, *The Lonely Crowd: A Study of the Changing American Character.* New York, 1950
Rossiter, C. L., *Conservation in America.* 2nd ed. New York, 1962
Wish, H., *Society and Thought in America.* 2nd ed. 2 vols. New York [1962].—*Contemporary America.* 3rd ed. New York, 1961

NATIONAL LIBRARY. The Library of Congress. Washington 25, D.C. *Librarian:* Lawrence Quincy Mumford, AB, MA, BS.

STATES AND TERRITORIES

For information as to State and Local Government, see under UNITED STATES, *p.* 537 *and p.* 538.

Against the names of the Governors and the Secretaries of State, (D.) *stands for Democrat and* (R.) *for Republican.*

Figures for the revenues and expenditures of the various states are those of the Federal Bureau of the Census unless otherwise stated, which takes the original state figures and arranges them on a common pattern so that those of one state can be compared with those of any other.

Official publications of the various states and insular possessions are listed in the *Monthly Check-List of State Publications*, issued by the Library of Congress since 1910. Their character and contents are discussed in J. K. Wilcox's *Manual on the Use of State Publications* (1940). Of great importance bibliographically are the publications of the Historical Records Survey and the American Imprints Inventory, which record local archives, official publications and state imprints. These publications supplement those of state historical societies which usually publish journals and monographs on state and local history. An outstanding source of statistical data is the material issued by the various state planning boards and commissions, to which should be added the annual *Governmental Finances* issued by the US Bureau of the Census.

The Book of the States. Biennial. Chicago, Council of State Governments, 1953 ff.
County and City Data Book. Dept. of Commerce, 1967

Regionalism

Bogue, D. J., and Beale, C. L., *Economic Areas of the United States.* New York, 1961
Odum, H. W., *American Regionalism, a cultural–historical approach to national integration.* New York, 1938
Jensen, M. (ed.) *Regionalism in America.* Univ. of Wisconsin Press, 1965
Visher, S. S. *Climatic Atlas of the USA.* Harvard Univ. Press, 1954

A. North-East

Black, J. D., *The Rural Economy of New England.* Harvard Univ. Press, 1950
Gottman, J., *Megalopolis, the Urbanized North-eastern Seaboard of the US.* New York, 1964
Harris, S. E., *The Economics of New England.* Harvard Univ. Press, 1952
Webster, C. M., *Town Meeting Country.* New York, 1945

B. The South

Cash, W. J., *The Mind of the South.* New York, 1960
Clark, T. D., *The Emerging South.* New York, 1961
Clement, E., *A History of the Old South.* New York, 1949
Ezell, J. S., *The South since 1865.* New York and London, 1963
Heseltine, W. B., and Smiley, D. L., *The South in American History.* 2nd ed. Englewood Cliffs, 1960
Hoover, C. B., *Economic Resources and Policies of the South.* New York, 1951
Sindler, A. P. (ed.), *Change in the Contemporary South.* Duke Univ. Press, 1963
Stephenson, W. H., and Coulter, E. M. (ed.), *A History of the South.* 10 vols. Louisiana State Univ. Press, 1947–67.
Vance, R. B., and Danilevsky, N., *All These People; the nation's human resources in the South.* Univ. of N. Carolina Press, 1945

C. The Middle West

Atherton, L. E., *Main Street on the Middle Border.* Indiana Univ. Press, 1954
Lynd, R. S. and H. M., *Middletown: a study in contemporary American culture.* New York and London, 1929.—*Middletown in Transition: a study in cultural conflicts.* New York and London, 1937
Nye, R. B., *Midwestern Progressive Politics, 1870–1958.* Michigan State Univ. Press, 1959

D. The West

Fogelson, R. U., *The Fragmented Metropolis: Los Angeles, 1850–1930.* Harvard Univ. Press, 1967
Freeman, O. W., and Martin, H. H., *The Pacific Northwest: an overall appreciation.* 2nd ed. 1954
Fuller, G. W., *History of the Pacific Northwest.* 2nd ed. New York, 1938
Garnsey, M. E., *America's New Frontier, the Mountain West.* New York, 1950
Hafen, L. R. R., and Rister, C. C., *Western America . . . beyond the Mississippi.* 2nd ed. New York, 1950
Johansen, D. O., and Gates, C. M., *Empire of the Columbia: a history of the Pacific North-West.* New York, 1957
Parrish, P. H. *Before the Covered Wagon.* Portland, Oreg., 1931
Quiett, G. C., *They Built the West, an epic of rails and cities.* New York and London, 1934
Scott, H. W., *History of the Oregon Country.* 6 vols. Cambridge, Mass, 1924
West, R. B., *Rocky Mountain Cities.* New York, 1949
Winther, O. O., *The Great Northwest: a history.* 2nd ed., rev. New York, 1950
Young, E., *West of the Rockies.* London, 1949

ALABAMA

GOVERNMENT. Alabama, settled in 1699 as part of the French Province of Louisiana, and ceded to the British in 1763, was organized as a Territory, 1817, and admitted into the Union on 14 Dec. 1819. The present constitution dates from 1901; it has had 282 amendments. The legislature consists of a Senate of 35 members and a House of Representatives of 106 members, all elected for 4 years. The Governor and Lieut.-Governor are elected for 4 years.

The state is represented in Congress by 2 senators and 8 representatives. Applicants for registration must take an 'anti-communist oath' and fill out a questionnaire to the satisfaction of the registrars. In 12 of the 67 counties Negroes constitute 50% or more of the population. In the 1968 presidential election Nixon polled 138,300 votes, Humphrey 140,056 and Wallace 691,430.

Montgomery is the capital.

Governor: George C. Wallace (D.), 1971–75 ($25,000).
Lieut.-Governor: Jere Beasley.
Secretary of State: Mabel S. Amos (D.) ($15,000).

AREA AND POPULATION. Area, 51,609 sq. miles, including 549 sq. miles of inland water. Census population, 1 April 1960, 3,266,740, an increase of 6·7% over that of 1950. Estimated population, 1 July 1969, 3·6m. Births, 1967, 64,083 (18 per 1,000 population); deaths, 31,740 (8·9); infant deaths, 1,727 (26·9 per 1,000 live births); marriages, 41,732 (11·9); divorces, 11,964 (3·4).

Population in 4 census years (with distribution by sex, 1960) was:

	White	Negro	Indian	Asiatic	Total	Per sq. mile
1910	1,228,832	908,282	909	70	2,138,093	41·4
1930	1,700,844	944,834	465	105	2,646,248	51·3
1950	2,079,591	979,617	928	669	3,061,743	59·3
1960	2,283,609	980,271	1,276	915	3,266,740	63·3
Male	1,124,061	466,206	All others 1,442		1,591,709	—
Female	1,159,548	514,065	All others 1,418		1,675,031	—

Of the total population in 1960, 1,791,721 (54·8%) were urban (43·8% in 1950). Those 21 years or older numbered 1,834,378; 65 years or older, 261,147. Foreign-born whites numbered 14,000 in 1960.

The large cities (1970) were: Birmingham, 356,000(urbanized area, 780,000); Mobile, 238,000; Montgomery (capital), 172,000; Huntsville, 161,000; Tuscaloosa, 81,200; Gadsden, 70,000.

RELIGION. Chief religious bodies (in 1968) are: Negro Baptists (500,000), Southern Baptists (802,793), Methodist (North Alabama Conference, 199,855 in 1967; West Florida Conference, 129,175), Roman Catholic (140,000), Presbyterian (41,780), Episcopalian (33,393 in 1967).

EDUCATION. In 1967–68 the 1,662 public elementary and high schools required 32,929 teachers to teach 860,295 pupils enrolled in grades 1–12. The 27 state-supported colleges had 54,549 students and 4,031 faculty members. During the regular session (1967–68) only, Alabama College, Auburn University, the University of Alabama and the University of South Alabama enrolled 23,740 resident students; the 4 state colleges, at Florence, Jacksonville, Livingston and Troy, 9,646 resident students; the 2 Negro colleges, at Normal and Montgomery, 3,646 resident students.

WELFARE. In 28 counties the state controls the sale of alcoholic beverage, while 39 counties remain 'bone dry'. In June 1969 there were 114,174 recipients of old-age assistance, receiving an average of $76.50 a month, including $14.67 for vendor payments for medical care; 25,707 families with 105,421 dependent children, $64.12 per family; 16,959 permanently and totally disabled, $59.44; 1,938 blind, $74.91.

In 1968 there were 137 hospitals (15,150 beds) licensed by the State Board of Health. In 1968 hospitals for mental diseases had 10,378 beds.

The prison population on 31 July 1969 was 4,263.

In 1967 there were no executions; from 1930 to 1967 there were 135 executions (electrocution): 25 whites and 80 Negroes for murder, 2 whites and 20 Negroes for rape, 1 white and 5 Negroes for armed robbery and 2 Negroes for burglary.

The transportation system is now integrated. Marriage between white and coloured persons is prohibited.

FINANCE. The general revenue for the fiscal year ending 30 Sept. 1969 was $967m. ($572m. from taxation and $293m. from federal aid); general expenditure was $983m., of which education took $388m.; highways, $166m., and public welfare, $154m.

The net long-term debt on 30 Sept. 1968 amounted to $542,281,000.

Estimated *per capita* income (1969) was $2,567.

AGRICULTURE. Alabama is largely an agricultural state; the number of farms in 1964 was 92,530, covering 15,225,797 acres; average farm had 164·5 acres and was valued at $20,552. In 1964, 59,455 farms were less than 100 acres; 2,141 more than 1,000 acres. Proportion of farms operated by tenants in 1959 was 27·5% (in 1964: 21%).

Area of national forest lands on 30 June 1968, 631,315 acres.

Cash income, 1966, from crops, $182·3m.; livestock, $465m. Chief crops (1967) are cotton (197,000 bales of 500 lb.); maize (37·8m. bu.); soybeans (12·9m. bu.). On 1 Jan. 1968 the livestock included 166,000 milch cows, 1,915,000 all cattle, 7,500 sheep and 902,000 swine. In 1967 broilers added $136·3m. to gross farm income. Layers on Alabama farms produced 2,645m. eggs valued at $85·1m. in 1967.

MINING. Production of principal minerals (1969): Coal, 12,042,949 short tons; petroleum (1966), 8,030,046 bbls; Portland cement (1965), 14·09m. bbls. Total mineral output was valued at $246m.

INDUSTRY. In 1968, 4,549 manufacturing establishments employed 305,900 production workers, earning $1,158m.; value added by manufacture was $3,644m. in 1966. Pig-iron, 1966, amounted ot 4·4m. short tons.

TOURISM is rapidly expanding. In 1969 out-of-state visitors spent $310m. touring the state. Total receipts of tourism amounted to $1,046m.

COMMUNICATIONS. The only port is Mobile, with a large ocean-going trade; imports (1968), 5,808,015 short tons; exports, 2,316,626 short tons. The 9-ft channel of the Tennessee River traverses North Alabama for 200 miles; the Warrior–Tombigbee Waterway (476 miles) connects the Birmingham industrial area with Mobile and also with the Gulf Intracoastal Waterway; the Chatta-hoochee River 9-ft channel extends from the Gulf to Phenix City (Alabama). In 1967 the railways had a length of 4,579 miles. In 1969 the state had 120 airports (90 public, 30 private). Paved roads of all classes in 1969 totalled 36,189 miles; total highways, 67,648 miles.

BOOKS OF REFERENCE

Alabama Official and Statistical Register. Montgomery. Quadrennial
Alabama Encyclopædia. Vol. I. Northport, 1965
Economic Abstract of Alabama. Bureau of Business Research, Univ. of Alabama, 1963
The Deep South in Transformation: a Symposium. Univ. of Alabama Press, 1964
Farmer H., *The Legislative Process in Alabama*. Univ. of Alabama, 1949

ALASKA

GOVERNMENT. Discovered in 1741 by Vitus Bering, its first settlement, on Kodiak Island, was in 1784. The area known as Russian America with its capital (1806) at Sitka was ruled by a Russo-American fur company and vaguely claimed as a Russian colony. Alaska was purchased by the United States from Russia under the treaty of 30 March 1867 for $7·2m. It was not organized until 1884, when it became a 'district' governed by the code of the state of Oregon. By Act of Congress approved 24 Aug. 1912 Alaska became an incorporated Territory; its first legislature in 1913 granted votes to women, 7 years in advance of the Constitutional Amendment.

Alaska officially became the 49th state of the Union on 3 Jan. 1959. It has the largest area of any state, being more than twice the size of Texas.

An important provision of the Enabling Act is that the state has the right to select 103·55m. acres of vacant and unappropriated public lands in order to establish 'a tax basis'; it can open these lands to prospectors for minerals, and the state is to derive the principal advantage in all gains resulting from the discovery of minerals. In addition, certain federally administered lands reserved for conservation of fisheries and wild life have been transferred to the state. Special provision is made for federal control of land for defence in areas of high strategic importance.

The constitution of Alaska was adopted by public vote, 24 April 1956. The state legislature consists of a Senate of 20 members (elected for 4 years) and a House of Representatives of 40 members (elected for 2 years). The state sends 2 senators and 1 representative to Congress. The franchise may be exercised by all citizens over 19 years of age.

The capital since 1906 has been at Juneau.

In the 1968 presidential election Nixon polled 37,600 votes, Humphrey 35,411 and Wallace 10,024.

Governor: Keith H. Miller (R.), 1966–70 ($32,000).
Secretary of State: Robert Ward (R.) ($28,500).

AREA AND POPULATION. The gross area (land and water) is 586,400 sq. miles: the land area is 571,065 sq. miles, of which 98·8% was in federal ownership in 1961. Census population, 1 April 1970, was 297,000, including military personnel, an increase of 30% over 1960. Births, 1969, were 6,824 (23·6 per 1,000 population); deaths, 1,300 (4·6); infant deaths, 138 (29·4 per 1,000 live births); marriages, 3,168 (10·8); divorces, 1,516 (5·2).

Census population: 1880, 33,426; 1900, 63,592; 1910, 64,356; 1940, 72,526; 1950, 128,643; 1960, 226,167; 1970, 297,000.

The white population in 1960 numbered 174,546 (101,194 males and 73,352 females); Indians, Aleuts and Eskimos, 48,522; Negroes, 6,771; Japanese, Chinese and Filipino, 1,769.

The largest town is Anchorage, which had a 1970 census population of 46,137; other towns are Fairbanks, 14,336; Juneau, capital, 13,338; Ketchikan, 6,703. Metropolitan area populations (1970), Anchorage, 123,631; Fairbanks, 41,987; Ketchikan, 9,473. There are altogether 28 incorporated boroughs and cities with an assessed valuation, 1969, of $2,086m.

RELIGION. In Alaska are many religious missions representing the Russian Orthodox, Roman Catholic, Episcopalian, Presbyterian, Methodist and other denominations.

EDUCATION. During 1969 there were 100 rural schools (5,326 pupils), 29 incorporated district schools (56,527), 7 military-base schools (9,440). The Bureau of Indian Affairs schools had 6,796 pupils attending schools in the state with an additional 881 students attending BIA high schools in other states. The University of Alaska (founded in 1922) had (1969) 2,225 students. Alaska

Methodist University had (1969) 790 students and Sheldon Jackson Junior College 195 students.

WELFARE. Old-age assistance was established under the Federal Social Security Act, and 1,617 persons received an average of $96.45 per month in 1969; aid to dependent children funds covered 8,334 persons; dependent children received an average of $66.29 per month; 89 blind persons received an average of $133.66 per month.

In 1969 there were 32 hospitals, with 1,925 beds, recognized by the American Hospital Association; there were 2 mental hospitals with 225 beds.

Alaska is the only state where women, by legislative Act, are guaranteed equal pay for equal work.

There is no death penalty in Alaska.

FINANCE. General revenue for the year ended 30 June 1969 (Alaska Department of Revenue figures) was $198·4m. ($112·4m. from taxation, $86·1m. from federal sources). General expenditure was $177·5m. (including $58m. for education, $56m. for highways and $21·5m. for public welfare).

Net long-term debt on 30 June 1969 was $105m.

Per capita income (1969) was $4,512.

AGRICULTURE. In some parts of the state the climate during the brief spring and summer (about 100 days in major areas and 152 days in the south-eastern coastal area) is not unsuitable for agricultural operations, thanks to the long hours of sunlight, but Alaska is a food-importing area. In 1964, 1,959,440 acres were classified as agriculture land, 90% of this was unimproved pasture primarily government leases for grazing of sheep and beef cattle in south-west Alaska. In 1967, 17,425 acres, less than 1% of total was actual land from which crops were harvested. Deeded or privately owned lands were estimated at 62,000 acres. In 1969 there were 310 farms (382 in 1964) with a total cultivated acreage of 16,895. Total value of land and buildings in 1960 was $15,826,500. In 1960 there were 750 horses. In 1969 there were 3,000 milch cows, 1,100 hogs and 27,000 sheep and lambs; tractors (1960) numbered 607. Farm production in 1969 was valued at $4,574,000 (milk, $1·94m.; grain crops, $862,000; potatoes, $378,000; vegetables, $164,000).

There were 31,000 reindeer in western Alaska in 1969, owned by individual Eskimo herders with the exception of 750 at Nome owned by the government.

FORESTRY. In south-eastern Alaska timber fringes the shore of the mainland and all the islands extending inland to a depth of 5 miles. The state's enormous forests could produce an estimated annual sustained yield of 1,500m. bd ft of lumber, nearly three times Alaska's record 1969 cut. Alaska has 2 national forests: the Tongass of 16·8m. acres and the Chugach of 4·81m. acres. A total of 591m. bd ft was cut from national forests in 1969. The value of timber products (1969) amounted to $101·2m. Alaska has 2 large pulp-mills at Ketchikan and Sitka. A third mill is planned for the Juneau area which will have a capacity of 550 tons daily.

FISHERIES. The catch for 1968 was 476·6m. lb. of fish and shellfish having a wholesale market value of $217·5m. This compares with 365·5m. lb. in 1969 with a value of $126·7m. Salmon remains the highest per unit value species, with a catch in 1968 of 301·8m. lb. valued at $123·9m.

MINING. Commercial production of crude petroleum began in 1959 and by 1961 had become the most important mineral by value. Production: 1961, 6,327,000 bbls (of 42 gallons); 1965, 11m. bbls; 1969, 74m. bbls. Oil comes from the Swanson River field and several Cook Inlet fields. The state of Alaska ranked 8th in oil production and 1st in oil production per well. Other minerals (1969): Natural gas, 49,424m. cu. ft; sand and gravel, 13,542 short tons; bituminous coal, 278,000 short tons; gold 16m. troy oz. Total value of mineral production, 1969, $244·8m. (of which petroleum accounted for $210·4m.). By 1961, 603,415 acres of the state had been leased for oil and natural gas exploration.

Alaska receives 90% of all royalties (12·5%) from oil, gas and coal production on federal lands and the full 12·5% royalty for production in state lands. Direct revenue to the state from the petroleum industry was in excess of $900m. in 1969. In 1969, the state conducted a major competitive lease sale for the Arctic coastal region where reserves are estimated to be as large as 50,000m. bbls.

LABOUR. Total employed civilian labour force (1969) averaged 107,900.

SHIPPING. Regular shipping services to and from the US are furnished by 2 steamship lines and several barge lines operating out of Seattle and other Pacific coast ports. Two Canadian companies also furnish a regular service from Vancouver, B.C.

A 490-mile ferry system for motor cars and passengers (the 'Marine Highway') operates from Seattle, Washington and Prince Rupert (British Columbia) to Juneau, Haines (for access to the Alaska Highway) and Skagway. A second system extends throughout the south-central region of Alaska linking the Cook Inlet area with Kodiak Island.

RAILWAYS. There is a railway of 111 miles from Skagway to the town of Whitehorse, in the Canadian Yukon region. The government-owned Alaska Railroad runs from Seward to Fairbanks, a distance of 471 miles.

ROADS. Alaska's highway and road system, 1969, totalled 7,123 miles, of which 3,498 miles were primary roads connecting the major cities; secondary roads totalled 3,624 miles. Registered motor vehicles, 1968, 133,301.

The Alaska Highway extends 1,523 miles from Dawson Creek, British Columbia, to Fairbanks, Alaska. It was built by the US Army in 1942, at a cost of $138m. The greater portion of it, because it lies in Canada, is maintained by the Canadian Government.

AVIATION. In 1969 the state had 668 airports, of which 53 were publicly owned. Passengers by air to and from Alaska (1967) numbered 654,037.

BOOKS OF REFERENCE

STATISTICAL INFORMATION. Department of Economic Development, Pouch EE, Juneau.

Alaskan Earthquake, preliminary report. Civil Defense Office (Army), Washington, 1964
Adams, B., *The Last Frontier.* New York, 1961
Gruening, E., *The State of Alaska.* New York, 1954
Hulley, Clarence C., *Alaska, 1741–1953.* Portland, Oregon, 1953
Look North. Department of Economic Development, Juneau, 1970
Rogers, G. W., *Alaska in Transition: the south-east region.* Johns Hopkins Univ. Press, 1960.—*The Future of Alaska.* Johns Hopkins Univ. Press, 1962
Rogers, G. W., and Cooley, R. L., *Alaska's Population and Economy, Regional Growth, Development and Future Outlook.* 2 vols. Juneau, 1962

STATE LIBRARY, Pouch G, Juneau. *Librarian:* Richard Engen.—Alaska Historical Library, Pouch G, Juneau. *Librarian:* Phyllis Nottingham.

ARIZONA

GOVERNMENT. Arizona was settled in 1752, organized as a Territory in 1863 and became a state on 14 Feb. 1912. The state constitution (1910, with now 65 amendments) placed the government under direct control of the people through the Initiative, Referendum and the Recall. The state Senate consists of 30 members and the House of Representatives of 60, all elected for 2 years. Arizona sends to Congress 2 senators and 3 representatives. In the 1968 presidential election Nixon polled 216,431 votes, Humphrey 136,143 and Wallace 35,357.

The state capital is Phoenix. The state is divided into 14 counties.

Governor: John R. (Jack) Williams (D.), 1971–74 ($27,500).
Secretary of State: Wesley Bolin (D.) ($17,000).

AREA AND POPULATION. Area, 113,909 sq. miles, including 346·6 sq. miles of inland water. Of the total area (72,688,000 acres) 32,578,158 were owned by the federal government in 1968, including 19,650,490 acres held by the Office of Indian Affairs. Census population on 1 April 1970 was 1,302,161, an increase of 73·7% over 1960. Estimated population, 1970, 1·75m. Births, 1969, 34,113 (19·8 per 1,000 population); deaths, 13,958 (8·1); infant deaths, 728 (21·3 per 1,000 live births); marriages, 18,012 (10·4); divorces, 11,918 (6·9).

Population in 4 census years (with distribution by sex, 1960):

	White	Negro	Indian	Chinese	Japanese	Total	Per sq. mile
1910	171,468	2,009	29,201	1,305	371	204,354	1·8
1930	378,551	10,749	43,726	1,110	879	435,573	3·8
1950	654,511	25,974	65,761	1,951	780	749,587	6·6
1960	1,169,517	43,403	83,387	2,937	1,501	1,302,161	11·3
Male	587,872	22,252	All others	44,804		654,928	—
Female	581,645	21,151		44,437		647,233	—

Of the total population in 1960, 970,616 (74·5%) were urban (55·5% in 1950); 441,889 were 21 years of age or older; foreign-born whites numbered 67,829.

The 1960 census population of Phoenix was 439,170 (urbanized area, 552,043); Tucson, 212,892 (227,433); Mesa, 33,773; Tempe, 24,897; Yuma, 23,974.

RELIGION. The leading religious bodies are Roman Catholics and Mormons (Latter Day Saints); others include Methodists, Presbyterians, Baptists and Episcopalians. No recent statistics of membership are available.

EDUCATION. School attendance is compulsory between the ages of 8 and 16 years, and instruction is free for pupils from 6 to 21 years of age. The enrolled pupils in autumn 1969 in the elementary schools were 330,843 and public high schools had 129,282 pupils. Teachers for both elementary and high schools totalled 18,518. The total expenditure (including capital expenditure) for public schools, 1969, was $321,292,174. In 1969–70 teachers' salaries (elementary) averaged $8,435 and (secondary) $9,390. The state maintains 3 universities at Tucson, Tempe and Flagstaff and 11 junior colleges.

WELFARE. Old-age assistance (maximum $80 a month) is given, with federal aid, to needy citizens 65 years of age or older. In June 1970, 12,726 old persons were receiving an average of $63.23 per person; 43,699 families, $65.57 per recipient; 593 blind, $72.02; 6,104 totally disabled, $65.57.

In 1969 there were 68 hospitals reported by the State Department of Health; capacity 9,193 beds. Resident patients in mental hospitals on 30 June 1969 numbered 1,141.

Marriage is forbidden between white and coloured persons.

A 'right-to-work' amendment to the constitution, adopted 5 Nov. 1946, makes illegal any concessions to trade-union demands for a 'closed shop'.

The Arizona state prison 30 June 1970 held 1,600 men and 72 women. There were no executions in 1968; from 1930 to 1968 there were 38 executions (lethal gas) all for murder, and all men (28 whites, 10 Negro).

FINANCE. General revenues, year ending 30 June 1970 (US Census Bureau figures), were $575m. (taxation, $365m. and federal aid, $129m.); general expenditures, $541m. (education, $291m.; highways, $121m., and public welfare, $50m).

Net long-term debt 30 June 1967, was $45,697,000.

Per capita income (1969) was $3,336.

AGRICULTURE. Arizona, despite its dry climate, is well suited for agriculture along the water-courses and where irrigation is practised on a large scale from great reservoirs constructed by the US as well as by the state government and private interests. Irrigated area, 1969, 1·2m. acres. The wide pasture lands are favourable for the rearing of cattle and sheep, but numbers are either stationary or declining compared with 1920.

In 1970 Arizona contained 5,970 farms and ranches with 1·2m. acres of crop land, out of a total farm and pastoral area of 43·3m. acres (55·3% of the land area); value (1964) of farm lands and buildings, $2,139m. Farming is highly commercialized (4,572 commercial farms, 1964) and mechanized, and concentrated (1969) largely on cotton (2,670 cotton farms) picked by machines and by Indians, Mexicans and migratory workers. The average farm (1969) was 7,233 acres, valued at $57 per acre.

Area under cotton (1970), 273,000 acres; 'an estimated 540,000 bales of short staple and 37,000 bales of Egyptian cotton were harvested.

Cash income, 1969, from crops, $316,508,000; from livestock, $327,344,000. Most important cereals are grain sorghums and barley; other crops include oranges, grapefruit and lettuce. On 1 Jan. 1970 there were, 1,302,000 all cattle, 54,000 milch cows, 508,000 sheep and 61,000 swine. The wool clip in 1969 amounted to 3·57m. lb.; mohair production was 288,000 lb. from 72,000 goats.

The national forests in the state had an area (1969) of 11·36m. acres.

MINING. The mining industries of the state are important, but less so than agriculture and manufacturing. By value much the most important mineral produced is copper; production (1969) was 790·35m. short tons; gold (100,300 troy oz.) and silver (6·07m. troy oz.) are both largely recovered from copper ore. Other minerals include sand and gravel (14·3m. short tons), zinc (8,960 short tons) and lead (200 short tons). Total value of minerals mined in 1969 was $850,527,000.

INDUSTRY. Manufacturing establishments (numbering 1,300 in 1969) had 57,200 production workers, earning $733m.; value added by manufacture, $2,000m.

TOURISM. In 1969 total estimated tourist business in the state was $500m.

COMMUNICATIONS. Airports, 1969, numbered 207, of which 100 were general. There were (1969) 5,498 miles of municipal roads and 17,827 miles of rural roads, of which 4,204 miles were surfaced.

BOOKS OF REFERENCE

Arizona Statistical Review. 24th ed. Valley National Bank, Phoenix, 1969
Federal Writers' Project. Arizona: The Grand Canyon State. 4th ed. New York, 1966
Cross, J. L., ed., Arizona, its People and Resources. Tucson, 1960
Goff, J. S., Arizona Civilization. 2nd ed. Cove Creek, 1970
Mason, B. B., and Hink, H., Constitutional Government of Arizona. 2nd ed. Tempe, 1965
Morey, R. D., Politics and Legislation: the office of Governor in Arizona. Tucson, 1965
Wyllys, R. K., Arizona: the History of a Frontier State. Phoenix, 1951

STATE LIBRARY. Department of Library and Archives, Capitol, Phoenix 85007. Director: Mrs Marguerite B. Cooley.

ARKANSAS

GOVERNMENT. Arkansas was settled in 1686, made a Territory in 1819 and admitted into the Union on 15 June 1836. The name is Indian, and means 'the people down stream'. The constitution, which dates from 1874, has been amended 59 times. The General Assembly consists of a Senate of 35 members, elected for 4 years, partially renewed every 2 years, and a House of Representatives of 100 members elected for 2 years. The sessions are biennial and usually limited to 60 days. The Governor and Lieut.-Governor are elected for 2 years. The state is represented in Congress by 2 senators and 4 representatives. As from 1 March 1965 payment of a poll tax as a form of registration for state election voting was abolished. In 5 counties Negroes constitute 50% or more of the population.

In the 1968 presidential election Nixon polled 189,062 votes, Humphrey 184,901 and Wallace 235,627.

The state is divided into 75 counties; the capital is Little Rock.

Governor: Dale L. Bumpers (D.) (1971–72) ($10,000).
Lieut.-Governor: Dr Bob C. Riley (D.) ($2,500).
Secretary of State: Kelly Bryant (D.) ($5,000).

AREA AND POPULATION. Area, 53,104 sq. miles (608 sq. miles being inland water). Census population (preliminary) on 1 April 1970 was 1,886,210, an increase of 5·6% from that of 1960. Births, 1969, were 33,337 (16·7 per 1,000 population); deaths, 20,947 (10·5); infant deaths, 767 (23·2 per 1,000 live births); marriages, 21,598 (10·8); divorces, 8,755 (4·4).

Population in 4 census years (with distribution by sex, 1960) was:

	White	Negro	Indian	Asiatic	Total	Per sq. mile
1910	1,131,026	442,891	460	72	1,574,449	30·0
1930	1,375,315	478,463	408	296	1,854,482	35·2
1950	1,481,507	426,639	533	832	1,909,511	36·3
1960	1,466,084	482,578	580	996	1,786,272	34·0
Male	690,762	187,336	All others 889		878,987	—
Female	704,941	201,451	All others 893		907,285	—

Of the total population in 1960, 765,303 persons (43%) were urban (33% in 1950); 1,041,364 were 21 years of age or older. Foreign-born whites numbered 7,017.

Little Rock (capital) had a population of 128,880 in 1970; Fort Smith, 61,549; North Little Rock, 59,014; Pine Bluff, 55,597; Hot Springs, 35,319; Fayetteville, 31,080; Jonesboro, 26,934; West Memphis, 25,796. The Little Rock–North Little Rock standard metropolitan statistical area (Pulaski–Salina counties), 315,375 in 1970.

RELIGION. The most numerous religious bodies in the state are Baptist (Negro Baptists with 150,664 members in 1936), Southern Baptists (78,825), Methodist (114,924), Roman Catholic and Disciples of Christ. Total membership, all denominations, 570,219.

EDUCATION. In the autumn of 1968 elementary schools had 250,011 enrolled pupils and 9,534 classroom teachers; secondary schools, 203,303 pupils and 10,125 teachers. Average salaries of teachers in elementary and secondary schools, 1968, was $6,155. Expenditure on public schools in 1968 was $247·7m.

An educational TV network began operating in 1966 with a full 12-hour-day telecasting and plans to provide the entire state with educational television.

Higher education is provided at the University of Arkansas at Fayetteville and Little Rock, Arkansas State University at Jonesboro, 6 state colleges, 11 private or church colleges and 2 junior colleges. Total enrolment in institutions of higher education, 1968–69, was 46,429. Expenditure on state institutions of higher education, 1968–69, was $66m.

WELFARE. During 1968–69, 61,159 persons were drawing old-age assistance at an average amount of $69.87 per month and 2,459 persons were drawing medical assistance for the aged, $161.45; 9,780 families (29,960 children), $87.85 per family; 1,817 blind persons, $81.15; 11,317 totally and permanently disabled, $94.19.

There were 91 hospitals (with 11,758 beds) listed by the American Hospital Association in 1967; resident patients in mental hospitals, 1966, numbered 2,298.

State prisons on 31 Dec. 1967 had 1,651 inmates (84 per 100,000 population). In 1965–68 there were no executions; from 1930 to 1964 there were 118 executions (electrocution) including 25 whites, 73 Negroes and 1 Indian for murder and 2 whites and 17 Negroes for rape.

FINANCE. The state's general revenue for the fiscal year ending 30 June 1969 (US Census Bureau figures) was $562·7m., of which taxation furnished $317·6m.

and federal aid, $194·4m. General expenditure was $552·3m., of which education took $222·5m.; highways, $138·6m., and public welfare, $87·8m.

Net long-term debt on 30 June 1969 was $93·3m.

Per capita income (1969) was $2,488 (second lowest in USA).

AGRICULTURE. Arkansas is an agricultural state. In 1964, 79,898 farms had a total area of 16·6m. acres; average farm was of 207·4 acres valued (land and buildings) at $36,734. Tenant-farmers were 13,907 (17%). About 6·09m. acres are being more intensely farmed; in 1964 the irrigated area (974,297 acres) included 426,890 acres of rice. Land erosion is serious. Some 12·2 acres (36% of the total) are considered to have lost one-fourth of their top soil, and require drastic curative treatment; 3·3m. acres (10%) require preventive treatment.

The largest source of income is broiler production (415m. in 1969, ranking second in USA); soybeans (production, 86·7m. bu., ranks fourth); cotton production (fourth); cattle and calves (twenty-fourth); rice (first); and eggs (third). Cash farm income (1969) was $1,038·9m.; from crops, $504·9m., and $534m. from livestock.

Livestock on 1 Jan. 1970 included 1,805,000 all cattle, 157,000 milch cows, 8,000 sheep and 288,000 swine.

MINING. In 1968 crude petroleum amounted to 19·5m. bbls; LP-gases, 1·4m. bbls, and natural gas, 156,627m. cu. ft. Arkansas produces over 95% of the country's supply of bauxite for aluminium; production 1968, 1·58m. long tons dried bauxite equivalent. The state has a large coal area; 211,000 short tons were mined in 1968 compared with an annual average of 1·5m. in 1946–50. Total mineral output in 1968 was valued at $198·7m.

INDUSTRY. In 1969 total employment averaged 698,000 (62,300 farm, 168,000 manufacturing 104,600 commerce, 101,400 government and 262,100 other industries). The census of manufactures, 1967, showed 2,911 manufacturing establishments employing 120,600 production workers, earning $496·3m.; value added by manufacture, $1,524·3m. In 1969 the most important manufacturing group was the metalworking industries employing 48,700 workers, 29% of total manufacturing employment.

COMMUNICATIONS. In 1967 there were in the state 3,611 miles of commercial railway. Six commercial airlines serve the state; there were, in 1968, 130 airports (64 public-owned and 66 private). State-maintained highways (1967) total 12,885 miles; local highways, 56,192 miles; federal highways, 1,887 miles; municipal roads, 8,247 miles. In 1969 there were 962,872 registered motor vehicles.

BOOKS OF REFERENCE

Arkansas Handbook. Arkansas History Commission. Little Rock. Biennial
Federal Writers' Project. *Arkansas: A Guide to the State.* New York, 1941
Fletcher, J. G., *Arkansas.* Univ. of N. Carolina, Chapel Hill, 1947
Shannon, K. (ed.), *Arkansas Almanac.* Little Rock, 1954

CALIFORNIA

GOVERNMENT. California, first settled in July 1769, was from its discovery down to 1846 politically associated with Mexico. On 7 July 1846 the American flag was hoisted at Monterey, and a proclamation was issued declaring California to be a portion of the US, and on 2 Feb. 1848, by the treaty of Guadalupe–Hidalgo, the territory was formally ceded by Mexico to the US, and was admitted to the Union 9 Sept. 1850 as the thirty-first state, with boundaries as at present.

The present constitution dates from 4 July 1879; it has had 340 amendments.

The Senate is composed of 40 members elected for 4 years—half being elected each 2 years—and the Assembly, of 80 members, elected for 2 years. Sessions are held annually. The Governor and Lieut.-Governor are elected for 4 years.

California is represented in Congress by 2 senators and 38 representatives.

In the 1968 presidential election Nixon polled 3,409,554 votes, Humphrey 3,187,364 votes and Wallace 482,162 votes.
The capital is Sacramento. The state is divided into 58 counties.

Governor: Ronald Reagan (R.), 1971–74 ($44,100).
Lieut.-Governor: Robert H. Finch (R.) ($22,050).
Secretary of State: Frank M. Jordan (R.) ($21,500).

AREA AND POPULATION. Area, 158,693 sq. miles (2,120 sq. miles being inland water). In 1965 the federal government owned 45m. acres (44·9% of the land area); 471,000 acres were under jurisdiction of the Bureau of Indian Affairs, of which 465,000 acres were allotted to tribes. Public lands, vacant on 30 June 1964, totalled 14,922,000 acres, practically all either mountains or deserts.

Census population, 1 April 1960, 15,717,204, an increase of 48·5% over 1950, leading all states in numbers gained (5,130,981). Estimated population, 1 July 1968, 19,782,000, making California the most populous state of the USA (New York: 18,258,000). Births in 1967, 340,661 (17·8 per 1,000 population); marriages, 147,378 (7·7); deaths, 159,610 (8·3); infant deaths (1966), 1,165 (26·7 per 1,000 live births); divorces (1965), 69,926 (3·8).

Population in 4 census years (with distribution by sex, 1960) was:

	White	Negro	Japanese	Chinese	Total (incl. all others)	Per sq. mile
1910	2,259,672	21,645	41,356	36,248	2,377,549	15·3
1930	5,408,260	81,048	97,456	37,361	5,677,251	36·2
1950	9,915,173	462,172	84,956	58,324	10,586,223	67·5
1960	14,455,230	883,861	157,317	95,600	15,717,204	100·4
Male	7,193,094	436,881	All others	206,732	7,836,707	—
Female	7,262,136	446,980		171,381	7,880,497	—

On the 1960 population 13,573,155 persons (86·4%) were urban (71% in 1940). The largest county, Los Angeles, had (1965 estimate) 6,878,200. Those 21 years old or older numbered 9·66m.; foreign-born whites were 1,221,713.

The largest cities with 1960 census population are:

Los Angeles	2,479,015	Burbank	90,155	San Leandro	65,962
San Francisco	742,855	Norwalk	88,739	Inglewood	63,390
San Diego	573,224	Stockton	86,321	Alameda	61,316
Oakland	367,548	Riverside	84,332	Vallejo	60,877
Long Beach	344,168	Garden Grove	84,238	Santa Clara	58,880
San José	204,196	Santa Monica	83,249	Santa Barbara	58,768
Sacramento	191,667	Downey	82,505	Bakersfield	56,848
Fresno	133,929	Arden-Arcade	73,352	Fullerton	56,180
Glendale	119,442	Hayward	72,700	Alhambra	54,807
Pasadena	116,407	Richmond	71,854	South Gate	53,831
Berkeley	111,268	Compton	71,812	Sunnyvale	52,898
Torrance	100,991	San Mateo	69,870	Palo Alto	52,287
Santa Ana	100,350	Pomona	67,157	West Covina	50,645
San Bernardino	91,922	Lakewood	67,126		

Urbanized areas (1960 census): Los Angeles–Long Beach, 6,488,791; San Francisco–Oakland, 2,430,663; San Diego, 836,175; San José, 602,805; Sacramento, 451,920; Fresno, 213,444; San Bernardino–Riverside, 577,531.

RELIGION. The Roman Catholic Church, with 2,483,411 adherents in 1954, is much stronger than any other single church; next are the Jewish congregations with an estimated 431,471 members, Methodists (113,241, 1936 figure), Presbyterians and Baptists.

EDUCATION. Full-time attendance at school is compulsory for children from 8 to 16 years of age for a minimum of 170 days per annum, and part-time attendance is required from 16 to 18 years. In the autumn of 1967 there were 2,849,000 pupils enrolled in elementary schools and 1,617,000 pupils in secondary schools. Elementary schools (1967) had 101,540 classroom teachers (average salary, 1968, $8,550) and secondary schools, 70,560 teachers ($9,450). Estimated expenditure on public schools, 1968, was $4,008m.

The University of California (1868) has colleges for resident instruction and research at Berkeley, Los Angeles, San Francisco and 8 other centres; in 1964–65 there were at all centres 6,500 faculty members and 71,267 resident students. Stanford University, near Palo Alto, was founded in 1885 by Mr and Mrs Leland Stanford in memory of their son and opened in 1891; in 1963 it had 1,107 faculty members and 9,212 students. The University of Southern California at Los Angeles (Methodist) had 1,422 faculty members and 17,819 full-time students. The California Institute of Technology at Pasadena had 520 instructors and 1,259 students. In all there are 179 institutions of higher education, in which 667,902 students were enrolled in autumn 1964. State expenditure, 1966, totalled $1,668,083.

WELFARE. San Francisco leads all American cities in racial equality. In the public schools whites are teaching Negroes, Negro teachers teaching whites and Asiatic teachers teaching both. There are Acts which declare illegal and void all marriages of white persons with Negroes, mulattoes, Mongolians and members of the Malay race, but in 1948 the State Supreme Court held that an Act forbidding Negro–white marriages was unconstitutional.

Old-age assistance has been established for those 65 years or older who have been citizens and residents of the state for 15 years, and have real-property assets not exceeding $3,500 or personal property not exceeding $1,200. In June 1965, 270,293 aged persons were receiving an average of $111.21 per month; 27,353 aged persons were receiving medical assistance ($348.85 per month); 12,220 blind persons, $138.05 per month; 126,643 families with 382,595 children, $182.35 per month per family; 59,905 totally disabled, $118.26 per month.

In 1966 there were 638 hospitals listed by the American Hospital Association; capacity, 140,020 beds. On 30 June 1964 state hospitals for the mentally retarded had 15,320 patients and state hospitals for the mentally ill had 47,389 patients.

State prisons, 31 Dec. 1966, had 27,467 inmates (139 per 100,000 population). In 1964–66 there were no executions; from 1930 to 1963 there were 291 executions (lethal gas); 279 were for murder, 6 for kidnapping and 6 for aggravated assault (by prisoners under life sentence).

FINANCE. For the year ending 30 June 1967 (US Census Bureau figures) general revenues were $6,178m. (taxation, $3,485m., and federal aid, $2,062m.); general expenditures were $6,770m. ($2,145m. for education, $1,106m. for highways and $1,451m. for public welfare).

The net long-term state debt was $1,587,326,000 on 30 June 1963.

Per capita personal income (1968) was $4,012.

AGRICULTURE. Extending 700 miles from north to south, and intersected by several ranges of mountains, California has almost every variety of climate, from the very wet to the very dry, and from the temperate to the semi-tropical. Of the total surface area (100,313,600 acres), estimates show 10·4m. acres to be seriously eroded, 46·3m. acres moderately affected and 43·7m. with little or no erosion.

In 1964 there were 81,000 farms, comprising 36·9m. acres; the average farm was of 458 acres. The state leads in value of farm products, cotton, fruit, poultry and vegetables being particularly important; commercial farms annually selling produce valued at $40,000 or more numbered 16,117 in 1964, many more than any other state. Cash income, 1967, from crops, $2,370m.; from livestock and poultry, $1,491m. Cattle, dairy produce, cotton, hay, grapes and tomatoes (in that order) are the main sources of farm income.

Production of cotton, 1967, was 1,035,000 bales (500 lb. gross); other field crops included sugar-beet (4m. short tons, leading all states). Cereal crops include winter wheat, barley and rough rice, 14·7m. cwt in 1964. Principal tree crops include wine, table and raisin grapes (1964: 3,155,000 tons—90% of US total); peaches (1,198,000 tons); apricots (208,000 tons); plums (116,000 tons); prunes, pears, apples and cherries. Citrus fruit crops (1963–64) were: Oranges, 32m. boxes; lemons, 17·3m. boxes; grapefruit, 4·2m. boxes.

o

On 1 Jan. 1968 the farm animals were: 857,000 milch cows, 4,927,000 all cattle, 1,535,000 sheep and 182,000 swine.

FORESTRY. Total forest area in 1965 was 42,541,000 acres, of which 17,317,000 acres was commercial forest. California ranks second to Oregon in lumber production, mainly softwoods; total annual cut is about 5,500m. bd ft. National forest area in 1965 was 19,969,292 acres.

FISHERY. California ranks first as a fishing state (by value of fish caught). The catch in 1966 was 584m. lb., valued at $82m.; leading species were yellowfin tuna and albacore.

MINING (1967). California is one of the three most important petroleum-producing states of the Union (Texas and Louisiana being the other two); the output was 359m. bbls. Outputs of natural gas was 681,080m. cu. ft; of natural gasoline, 583·3m. gallons and of LP-gases, 366·6m. gallons. Gold output was 40,574 troy oz.; gypsum, 1,241,000 short tons; mercury, 16,385 flasks (of 76 lb.) —70% of US total; tungsten, lead, chromite, zinc, copper and iron ore are also produced. The estimated value of all the minerals produced was $1,696,233,000, of which petroleum accounted for $829·1m.

INDUSTRY. In 1965, 32,201 manufacturing establishments employed 1,406,000 production workers earning $5·57m.; value added by manufacture $18,858,000. The petroleum products industry ranks second to Texas. Transportation equipment (423,800 employees, 1966) and food products (166,600) are leading industries. Aircraft, electrical machinery and equipment, and missile engineering are important.

COMMUNICATIONS. The chief ports are San Francisco and Los Angeles. Total mileage of railways, 31 Dec. 1964, was 7,516 miles. In 1965 California had 37,457 miles of municipal roads and 118,550 miles of rural roads (75,661 miles surfaced). In 1965 it had 8,371,000 registered motor cars and 1,484,000 trucks, buses and public vehicles, leading all states in all items by a wide margin. Airports, 1967, numbered 684, including 241 public.

BOOKS OF REFERENCE

California Statistical Abstract. 7th ed. Economic Development Agency, Sacramento, 1966
Arnold, R. K. (ed.), *The California Economy 1947–1980.* Menlo Park, 1961
Crouch, W. W., and others, *California Government and Politics.* 2nd ed. New York, 1960
Roney, D., *The California Citizen.* Houston, 1955
Turner, H. A., and Veig, J. A., *The government and politics of California.* 2nd ed. New York, 1964
Zierer, C. M. (ed.), *California and the Southwest.* New York, 1956

STATE LIBRARY. The California State Library, Library-Courts Bldg, Sacramento 95814.

COLORADO

GOVERNMENT. Colorado was first settled in 1858, made a Territory in 1861 and admitted into the Union on 1 Aug. 1876; the constitution adopted at that time is still in effect with (1967) 73 amendments. The General Assembly consists of a Senate of 35 members elected for 4 years, one-half retiring every 2 years, and of a House of Representatives of 65 members elected for 2 years. Sessions are annual, beginning 1951. The Governor, Lieut.-Governor, Attorney-General and Secretary of State are elected for 4 years. Qualified as electors are all citizens, male and female (except criminals and insane), 21 years of age, who have resided in the state for 12 months immediately preceding the election. The state is divided into 63 counties. The state sends to Congress 2 senators and 4 representatives.

In the 1968 presidential election Nixon polled 409,345 votes, Humphrey 335,174 and Wallace 59,357.

The capital is Denver.

Governor: John A. Love (R.), 1971–74 ($20,000).
Lieut.-Governor: Mark Hogan (D.) ($4,800).
Secretary of State: Byron A. Anderson (R.) ($10,000).

AREA AND POPULATION. Area, 104,247 sq. miles (450 sq. miles being inland water). Federal lands, 1967, 24,201,000 acres (36·4% of the land area).

Census population, 1 April 1960, was 1,753,947, an increase of 428,859 or 32·4% since 1950. Estimated population, 1 July 1968, 2,048,000. Births, 1967, were 35,166 (17·4 per 1,000 population); deaths, 16,321 (8·1); infant deaths, 805 (22·9 per 1,000 live births); marriages, 21,845 (10·8); divorces (1965), 6,700 (3·3).

Population in 4 census years (with distribution by sex, 1960) was:

	White	Negro	Indian	Asiatic	Total	Per sq. mile
1910	783,415	11,453	1,482	2,674	799,024	7·7
1930	1,018,793	11,828	1,395	3,775	1,035,791	10·0
1950	1,296,653	20,177	1,567	5,870	1,325,089	12·7
1960	1,700,700	39,992	4,288	8,967	1,753,947	16·7
Male	843,875	20,060	2,253	4,579	870,467	—
Female	857,125	19,932	2,035	4,388	883,480	—

Of the total population in 1960, 1,292,790 (73·7%) were urban (62·7% in 1950); those 21 years or older were 1,104,808; foreign-born whites numbered 56,789. Denver, the capital, had an estimated population, 1968, of 491,000 (urbanized area, 1,125,000). Other cities with 1968 population: Colorado Springs, 118,500; Pueblo, 104,000; Aurora, 69,000; Boulder, 60,000; Fort Collins, 40,000; Arvada, 38,000; Englewood, 36,000; Greeley, 33,000; Grand Junction, 23,000.

RELIGION. In 1967 the Roman Catholic Church had 377,000 members; the 12 leading Protestant Churches (out of 100 in the state) totalled 370,000 members; the Jewish community had 24,000 members. Buddhism is among other religions represented.

EDUCATION. In 1967–68 the school districts had 502,550 pupils and 24,981 teachers and administrators; total instructional salaries averaged $7,201. Enrol ments in universities and larger colleges, 1968–69 were: US Air Force Academy (Colorado Springs), 3,000 students; University of Colorado (Boulder), 17,400; University of Colorado (Extension Division and Denver Department of Medicine), 9,200; Colorado State University (Fort Collins), 15,185; University of Denver (Denver), 8,595; Colorado School of Mines (Golden), 1,630; Colorado State College (Greeley), 8,447; Southern Colorado State College (Pueblo), 5,672; Western State College (Gunnison), 3,000; Adams State College (Alamosa), 2,750; Metropolitan State College (Denver), 4,385; Colorado College (Colorado Springs), 1,610.

WELFARE. A constitutional amendment, adopted 1956, provides for minimum old age pensions of $100 per month, which may be raised on a cost-of-living basis ($124 for March 1968); for a $5m. stabilization fund and for a $10m. medical and health fund for pensioners. Old-age assistance is available to citizens 60 years of age and resident for stated periods, with assets not exceeding $1,000 (excluding home ownership). In June 1968, 38,904 persons were drawing an average of $77.45 per month.

Under the medical fund, 36,000 pensioners received medical care during fiscal year 1967–68. Approved hospitals, 1967, numbered 92 with 15,788 beds. In 1967, 6 hospitals for mental diseases had 8,062 patients (399 per 100,000 population).

State prisons during 1967–68 averaged 2,784 inmates (129 per 100,000 population). In 1967 there was 1 execution; since 1930 executions (by lethal gas) numbered 47, including 41 whites, 5 Negroes and 1 other; all were for murder.

Colorado has a Civil Rights Act (1935) forbidding places of public accommodation to discriminate against any persons on the grounds of race, religion, colour or nationality. No religious test may be applied to teachers or students in the public schools, 'nor shall any distinction or classification of pupils be made on account of race or colour'. In 1957 the General Assembly prohibited discrimination in employment of persons in private industry and in 1959 adopted the Fair Housing Act to discourage discrimination in housing. A 1957 Act permits marriages between white persons and Negroes or mulattoes.

FINANCE. The state's general revenue for the year ending 30 June 1968 was $640,036,000, of which taxation and other revenue furnished $410,056,000 and federal grants $229·98m. General expenditures were $626,966,496, of which education took $202,113,794; highways, $123m., and health, welfare and rehabilitation, $132,297,242.

The state has no general debt. The net long-term debt (in revenue bond) on 30 June 1968 was $129·41m.

Per capita personal income (1969) was $3,568.

AGRICULTURE. Farms in 1964 numbered 29,797, with a total area of 38,257,577 acres (57·5% of the land area); 4,725,684 acres were harvested crop land; value of land and buildings, $2,753,034,221; average farm, 1,284 acres valued at $93,393; commercial farms numbered 26,152. Cash income, 1967, from crops, $195m.; from livestock, $612·5m. Important farm industry (3,524 farms) is the growing of sugar-beet on some 127,700 acres (1967); in 1964, 18,316 farms had 2,690,008 acres under irrigation.

Production of principal crops in 1968: Maize, 21,335,000 bu.; wheat, 40,812,000 bu.; barley, 9·5m. bu.; potatoes, 10·9m. bags (of 100 lb.); sugar-beet, 2·8m. tons; oats, rye, dry beans, sorghums and broomcorn are grown, as well as fruit.

On 1 Jan. 1968 the number of farm animals was: 106,000 milch cows, 3,021,000 all cattle, 1,384,000 sheep, 210,000 swine. The wool clip in 1967 yielded 11·34m. lb. of wool from 1·27m. fleeces.

MINING. Colorado has a variety of mineral resources. Estimates (1959) of recoverable coal are 40,387m. tons, ranking the state as seventh among the US. Coal production, 1967, 5·44m. tons. The world's largest molybdenum mine is at Climax; output since 1914 has been about 72% of the country's cumulative total. Output, 1966, was 57,289,000 lb. valued at $88,851,000. In 1967 the gold output was 21,181 oz.; silver, 1,818,000 oz.; copper, 3,993 short tons; lead, 21,923 short tons; zinc, 54,442 short tons; petroleum, 33,905,000 bbls; natural gas, 116,857m. cu. ft; natural gas liquids, 71·54m. gallons. Oil shale reserves are estimated at 1,259,000m. bbls. Uranium ore production, 1967, was 2,537,000 lb., valued at $20·29m. Total mineral output in 1967 was valued at $346,235,000.

INDUSTRY. The 2,453 manufacturers (1963 US census) had 93,722 employees, who earned $596,011,000; value added by manufacture was $1,193,838,000. Wholesale trade had 3,720 establishments with 34,095 employees, who earned $195,419,000; total value of wholesale sales was $3,623·19m. Retail trade had 17,294 establishments with 94,208 employees, who earned $315·47m.; total value of retail sales was $2,648,618,000. Service industries had 12,988 establishments with 34,709 employees, who earned $120,431,000; total value of receipts of service industries was $438,223,000.

TOURISM. During 1966–67 visitors to Colorado totalled 7,425,716, including 412,600 for ski-ing. Tourist expenditures, $577,178,732.

COMMUNICATIONS. In 1967 there were in the state 3,444 miles of main-track railway. There were (1967) 177 airports, including 64 for general use. The state highway system included, 1968, 8,926 miles of highway, of which 8,363 miles are hard-surfaced. County roads totalled 66,662, and city streets, 5,835 miles. Total road mileage, 81,423. It has 55 mountain peaks over 14,000 ft high, 27 of which rank among the 50 highest in the US.

BOOKS OF REFERENCE

Colorado Year-Book. 27th ed., 1965–68. State Planning Commission. Denver, 1968
Hafen, L. R. R., *The Colorado Story.* Denver, 1953

STATE LIBRARY. Colorado State Library, State Capitol, Denver, 80203. *State Librarian:* Gordon
Bennett.

CONNECTICUT

GOVERNMENT. Connecticut was first settled in 1635 and has been an
organized commonwealth since 1637. In 1639 a written constitution was adopted
which, it is claimed, was the first in the history of the world formed under the
concept of a social compact. This constitution was confirmed by a charter from
Charles II in 1662, and replaced in 1818 by a state constitution, framed that year
by a constitutional convention.

The 1818 Constitution was revised in June 1953 effective 1 Jan. 1955. On
30 Dec. 1965 a new constitution went into effect, having been framed by a constitutional convention in the summer of 1965 and approved by the voters in
Dec. 1965.

The 1965 Constitution provides for 30 to 50 members of the Senate (instead of
24 to 36) and for 125 to 225 members of the House of Representatives, to be
elected from assembly districts, rather than 2 or 1 from each town, as in the
former constitution. The convention has added a new provision for a 3-day
session following each regular or special session, solely to reconsider bills vetoed
by the Governor.

The General Assembly consists of a Senate of 36 members and a House of
Representatives of 177 members. Members of each House are elected for the
term of 2 years (annual salary $3,250; expenses $750, and travel expenses).
Legislative sessions are annual. The Governor and Lieut.-Governor are elected
for 4 years. All citizens (with necessary exceptions and the usual residential requirements) have the right of suffrage.

Connecticut is one of the original 13 states of the Union. The state is represented in Congress by 2 senators and 6 representatives.

In the 1968 presidential election Nixon polled 549,002 votes, Humphrey
615,991 and Wallace 75,993.

The state capital is Hartford.

Governor: Thomas Meskill (R.), 1971–75 ($35,000).
Lieut.-Governor: T. Clark Hull (R) ($10,000).
Secretary of State: Mrs. Gloria Schaeffer (D.) ($15,000).

AREA AND POPULATION. Area, 5,000 sq. miles (110 sq. miles being inland water). Census population, 1 April 1970, 3,032,317, an increase of 496,983
or 19·6% since 1960. Births (1968) were 48,327 (16·3 per 1,000 population);
deaths, 26,688 (9); infant deaths, 934 (19·2 per 1,000 live births); marriages,
24,263 (16·4); divorces, 5,363 (3·6).

Population in 4 census years (with distribution by sex, 1960) was:

	White	Negro	Indian	Asiatic	Total	Per sq. mile
1910	1,098,897	15,174	152	533	1,114,756	231·3
1930	1,576,700	29,354	162	687	1,606,903	328·0
1950	1,952,329	53,472	333	1,146	2,007,280	409·7
1960	2,423,816	107,449	923	3,046	2,535,234	517·5
Male	1,189,653	52,394	456	1,726	1,244,229	—
Female	1,234,169	55,055	467	1,220	1,291,005	—

In 1960 foreign-born whites numbered 271,253. Of the total population,
1,985,567 persons (78·3%) were urban (77·6% in 1950); households, 752,736.
Those 21 years old or older numbered 1,985,567; foreign-born whites, 271,253.

The chief cities and towns, with census population 1 April 1970, are:

Hartford	158,017	East Hartford	57,583	Manchester	47,994
Bridgeport	156,542	Fairfield	56,487	Enfield	46,189
New Haven	137,707	Meriden	55,959	Norwich	41,433
Stamford	108,798	Bristol	55,487	Groton	38,523
Waterbury	108,033	West Haven	52,851	Wallingford	36,924
New Britain	83,441	Milford	50,858	New London	35,714
Norwalk	79,113	Danbury	50,781	Torrington	31,952
West Hartford	68,031	Stratford	49,775	Middletown	31,630
Greenwich	59,755	Hamden	49,357		

Larger urbanized areas, 1970 census: Hartford, 657,104; Bridgeport, 385,746; New Haven, 348,424; Stamford, 204,888; Waterbury, 206,625.

RELIGION. The leading religious denominations (1969) in the state are the Roman Catholic (1,272,473 members), United Churches of Christ (140,733), Protestant Episcopal (139,330), Jewish (103,730), Greek Orthodox (60,000), Methodist (55,932), Baptist (23,223), Presbyterian (12,802).

EDUCATION. Elementary instruction is free for all children between the ages of 4 and 16 years, and compulsory for all children between the ages of 7 and 16 years. In 1968–69 the 872 public elementary schools had 369,558 enrolled pupils; the 102 junior high schools had 92,292 pupils; the 15 vocational technical state schools, 532 teachers and 8,212 pupils. Expenditure of the state Board of Education for grants-in-aid, 1968–69, was $140,831,867; local expenditure, $462,968,551. Average salary of teachers in public schools, $8,517.

Connecticut has 47 colleges, 4 state teachers' colleges and 8 regional community colleges. The University of Connecticut at Storrs, founded 1881, had 1,042 faculty and 18,670 students in 1969. Yale University, New Haven, founded in 1701, had 791 faculty and 9,341 students. Wesleyan University, Middletown, founded 1831, had 247 faculty and 1,714 students. Trinity College, Hartford, founded 1823, had 131 faculty and 1,875 students. Connecticut College for Women, New London, founded 1915, had 145 faculty and 1,695 students. The University of Hartford had 233 faculty and 8,863 students. The regional community colleges (2-year course) had 12,339 students.

WELFARE. Disbursements during the year ending 30 June 1969 amounted to $8,113,902 for old-age assistance, and medical aid to the aged, $30,671,713. In June 1970, 8,015 old people were receiving $90.93 monthly; 23,617 families were receiving $235.29 per family on aid to dependent children; 242 blind, $99.34; 6,792 totally disabled, $117.53.

Hospitals listed by the American Hospital Association, 1969, numbered 65 (including 5 federal) with 24,356 beds, and an average daily census, 21,166. Average daily census of the 11 state psychiatric hospitals was 10,261. In July 1970 the state controlled 4 hospitals for the mentally retarded, 1 institution for the deaf and 3 chronic disease hospitals.

In 1970 there was no execution; since 1930 there have been 22 executions (19 by electrocution, 3 by hanging), including 19 whites and 3 Negroes, all for murder. The 6 community correctional centres, 1 Jan. 1970, had 1,261 inmates; 5 correctional institutions had 1,203 inmates.

The Civil Rights Act makes it a punishable offence to discriminate against any person or persons 'on account of alienage, colour or race' and to hold up to ridicule any persons 'on account of creed, religion, colour, denomination, nationality or race'. Places of public resort are forbidden to discriminate. Insurance companies are forbidden to charge higher premiums to persons 'wholly or partially of African descent'. Schools must be open to all 'without discrimination on account of race or colour'.

FINANCE. For the year ending 30 June 1970 (state government figures) general revenues were $669,623,493 (taxation, $787,341,023, and federal aid,

$84,466,462); general expenditures were $787,341,023 (education, $261,770,339; highways, $200,988,146, and public welfare, $196,747,269).

The total net long-term debt on 30 June 1970 was $1,850,315,000.

Per capita income, 1968, was $4,256 (highest in US).

AGRICULTURE. In 1968 the state had 6,068 farms with a total area of 186,850 acres (60% of the total land area); average farm was of 118·9 acres, valued at $561 per acre. Of the farms, 4,148 were commercial and 1,920 were residential or part-time. Total cash income, 1968, was $162m., including $66m. from crops and $96m. from livestock and products (mainly from dairy products and poultry). Principal crops are tobacco, hay, oats, maize, potatoes, apples, peaches, pears, vegetables and small fruit.

Livestock (1 Jan. 1969): 124,000 all cattle (value $13,592,000), 5,000 sheep ($47,000), 10,000 swine ($523,000) and 10·3m. poultry ($7·38m.).

MINING. The state has some mineral resources: sheet mica, sand, gravel, clays and stone; total production in 1969 was valued at $21,346,000.

FORESTRY. The state had (1970) 132,767 acres of state forest land, which is about 4·1% of the total land area.

INDUSTRY. Manufacturing establishments (numbering 5,608 in 1969) employed 465,260 production workers in Sept. 1969, who earned average weekly wages of $139.26; value added by manufacture, (1967), $6,510m. Average total non-agricultural employment in 1969 was 1,173,360.

COMMUNICATIONS. On 30 June 1970 there were 694 miles of railway track. In 1970 there were 66 airports (28 commercial, including 4 state-owned, and 20 heliports). The state (1970) maintains 3,914 miles of highways, all surfaced. Motor vehicles registered 1 July 1970 numbered 1,853,918 (licences issued 1969, 1,104,174).

BOOKS OF REFERENCE

Organization and Functions of the Connecticut State Government. Dept. of Finance and Control, Hartford, 1964
The Register and Manual of Connecticut. Secretary of State. Hartford. Annual
Bingham, H. J., *History of Connecticut.* 4 vols. New York, 1962
Hoyt, J. B., *The Connecticut Story.* New Haven, 1961
Van Dusen, A. E., *Connecticut: a fully illustrated history.* New York, 1961

STATE LIBRARY. Connecticut State Library, Capitol Avenue, Hartford, 06015. *State Librarian:* Walter T. Brahm.
Connecticut in Focus. Hamden, 1970

DELAWARE

GOVERNMENT. Delaware, permanently settled in 1638, is one of the original 13 states of the Union, and the first one to ratify the Federal Constitution. The present constitution (the fourth) dates from 1897, and has had 51 amendments; it was not ratified by the electorate but promulgated by the Constitutional Convention. The General Assembly consists of a Senate of 19 members elected for 4 years and a House of Representatives of 39 members elected for 2 years. The Governor and Lieut.-Governor are elected for 4 years.

With necessary exceptions, all adult citizens, registered as voters, who have resided in the state 1 year, and complied with local residential requirements, have the right to vote; those who have attained the age of 21 since 1900 must be able to read English and to write their names. Citizens resident for 3 months or over may vote for President and Vice President only.

Delaware is represented in Congress by 2 senators and 1 representative, elected by the voters of the whole state.

In the 1968 presidential election Nixon polled 96,714 votes, Humphrey 89,194 and Wallace 28,459.

The state capital is Dover. Delaware is divided into 3 counties.

Governor: Russell W. Peterson (R.), 1966–73 ($35,000).
Lieut.-Governor: Eugene D. Bookhammer (R.) ($9,000).
Secretary of State: Gene Bunting (R.) ($21,000) (appointed by the Governor).

AREA AND POPULATION. Area 2,399 sq. miles (437 sq. miles being inland water). Census population, 1 April 1960, was 446,292, an increase of 128,207 or 40·3% since 1950. Census preliminary, April 1970, 542,979. Births in 1969, 10,124 (18·56 per 1,000 population); deaths, 5,004 (9·1); infant deaths, 217 (21·5 per 1,000 live births); marriages, 3,992 (7·5); divorces, 1,055 (2·9).

Population in 4 census years (with distribution by sex, 1960) was:

	White	Negro	Indian	Asiatic	Total	Per sq. mile
1910	171,102	31,181	5	34	202,322	103·0
1930	205,718	32,602	5	55	238,380	120·5
1950	273,878	43,598	—	87	266,505	134·7
1960	384,327	60,688	597	410	446,292	224·0
Male	190,186	30,311	All others 639		221,136	—
Female	194,141	30,377	All others 658		225,156	—

Of the total population in 1960, 292,994 (65·7%) were urban (62·6% in 1950); households, 158,582. Those 18 years old or older numbered 283,253; foreign-born whites, 14,307.

The 1970 census figures show Wilmington with population of 79,978; Newark, 21,351; Dover, 17,165; Elsmere, 8,234; Milford, 5,374; New Castle, 4,870.

RELIGION. No recent statistics concerning church affiliation are available.

EDUCATION. The state has free public schools and compulsory school attendance. In Sept. 1970 the elementary and secondary public schools had 132,745 enrolled pupils and 5,430 classroom teachers. Appropriations for public schools, 1969, was $77,165,679. Average salary of classroom teachers, 1969, was $8,703. The state supports the University of Delaware (1834), Newark, with, in Sept, 1970, 616 professors and 15,600 students, and State College, Dover (1892) with 96 full-time instructors and 1,669 students.

WELFARE. Old-age assistance (maximum now $75 per month) was established in 1931 for citizens 65 years of age or older who have been residents of the state for 1 year and who have no relatives to care for them without undue sacrifice. On 30 June 1970, 2,282 persons were drawing an average of $75.15 per month. Provisions are also made for the care of 5,701 families totalling 21,561 persons ($34.50 per person), for 1,336 totally disabled ($110.90 monthly), general assistance, 2,545 families totalling 5,302 persons ($29.48 per person) and (Dec. 1963) 292 blind people ($78.97). The total public assistance caseload was 12,604 assisting 32,275 persons, at a cost of $1,492,471 in June 1970.

In 1964 there were 16 hospitals (5,582 beds) listed by the American Hospital Association. In June 1967 patients in mental hospitals numbered 1,150.

State prisons, 1967 had daily average of 644 inmates. The death penalty was illegal from 2 April 1958 to 18 Dec. 1961. Executions since 1930 (by hanging) have totalled 12 (none in 1967).

FINANCE. For the year ending 30 June 1969 general receipts was $387·53m., of which taxes furnished $170·73m. and federal grants $49m.; General expenditure was $366·04m. (education $121·2m.; highways, $36·6m.; health and public welfare, $47·6m.).

On 30 June 1969 the net long-term debt was $338,145,861.

Per capita income (1969) was $4,013.

AGRICULTURE. Delaware is mainly an industrial state, but 60·3% of the land area is in farms (763,000 acres), which in 1959 numbered 5,203; average farm was of 146·4 acres and valued (land and buildings) at $32,554. Commercial farms numbered 3,887.

Cash income, 1963, from crops and livestock (chiefly poultry), $114·1m. The chief cereals are maize and wheat.

MINING. The mineral resources of Delaware are not extensive, consisting chiefly of clay products, stone, sand and gravel. Value of mineral production in 1966 was $1,980,000.

INDUSTRY. In 1962, manufacturing establishments (numbering 547 in 1958) employed 29,000 production workers, earning $145m.; value added by manufacture was $542m.

COMMUNICATIONS. In 1970 the state had 293 miles of railway. In 1970 Delaware had 23 airports, of which 11 were for general use. The state in 1970 maintained 4,372 miles of surfaced highways including 597 miles of primary roads.

BOOKS OF REFERENCE

INFORMATION. Public Archives Commission, Hall of Records, Dover. *State Archivist:* Leon de Valinger, Jr.

State Manual, containing Official List of Officers, Commissions and County Officers. Secretary of State, Dover. Annual
The Delaware Economy, 1939–58. Bureau of Economic & Business Research, Univ. of Delaware, 1961
Dolan, P., *The Government and Administration of Delaware.* New York, 1956
Federal Writers' Project. *Delaware: A Guide to the First State.* Rev. ed. New York, 1955

DISTRICT OF COLUMBIA

GOVERNMENT. The District of Columbia, organized in 1790, is the seat of the Government of the US, for which the land was ceded by the state of Maryland to the US as a site for the national capital. It was established under Acts of Congress in 1790 and 1791. Congress first met in it in 1800 and federal authority over it became vested in 1801.

Local government, from 1 July 1878 until Aug. 1967, was that of a municipal corporation administered by a board of 3 commissioners, of whom 2 were appointed from civil life by the President, and confirmed by the Senate, for a term of 3 years each. The other commissioner was detailed by the President from the Engineer Corps of the Army. Reorganization Plan No. 3 of 1967 submitted by the President to Congress on 1 June 1967 abolished the Commission form of government and instituted a new Mayor Council form of government. The mayor, with the title of Commissioner, is appointed by the President with the advice and consent of the Senate. The term of the first Commissioner expires on 1 Feb. 1969 and thereafter appointments are for 4 years. The 9 member city council is also appointed by the President. They are appointed with a view to achieving community representation. Congress alone enacts legislation and appropriates money for the municipal expenses. A proposal to grant local self-government has been discussed by Congress in 1950 and 1951, and legislation to that end was passed by the House and Senate, but no law has been enacted.

The 23rd amendment to the federal constitution (1961) conferred the right to vote in national elections; in the 1968 presidential election Nixon polled 31,012 votes, Humphrey 139,566. (Wallace not on ballot.)

Executive Secretary to the Commissioner: F. E. Ropshaw.

AREA AND POPULATION. The area of the District of Columbia is 69·245 sq. miles, 8 sq. miles being inland water. The federal government on 30 June 1968 owned 13,314 acres (43·3% of the land area).

Census population, 1 April 1960, was 763,956, a decrease of 4·8% from that of 1950. Estimated population, 1 July, 1967 820,000. Of the 1960 population 509,000 were 21 years old or older; 33,540 were foreign-born. Population, 1960, of the urbanized area Washington, DC.–Md–Va. was 1,808,423; of the metropolitan statistical area (1968 estimate), 2·8m. Births, 1965, in the District were 30,021 (21·9 per 1,000 population); resident deaths, 8,914 (11·1); infant deaths, 611 (34·7 per 1,000 live births); marriages, 9,162 (11·4); divorces, 1,214 (1·5).

Population in 4 census years (with distribution by sex, 1960) was:

	White	Negro	Indian	Chinese and Japanese	Total	Per sq. mile
1910	236,128	94,446	68	427	331,069	5,517·8
1930	353,981	132,068	40	780	486,869	7,981·5
1950	517,865	280,803	330	2,178	802,178	13,150·5
1960	345,263	411,737	587	3,532	763,956	12,523·9

	White	Negro		Total	
Male	158,124	196,257	All others 3,790	358,171	—
Female	187,139	215,480	All others 3,166	405,785	—

RELIGION. Churches in Washington, D.C., 1964, numbered 526, including 459 Protestant churches (both white and Negro denominations); 42 Roman Catholic churches, 15 Jewish synagogues, 8 Eastern Orthodox churches and 2 Islamic congregations. 56% of the metropolitan area population have religious affiliation; 30% with the Protestant churches, 22% Roman Catholic, 3% Jewish, 1% Eastern Orthodox and Islamic.

EDUCATION. In 1966, 145 public elementary, junior and senior high, and special schools had 145,460 pupils; teachers numbered 5,784. Segregation was abolished in 1954.

Higher education is given in Georgetown University, founded in 1795 by the Jesuit Order, with (1964) 1,392 faculty and 7,461 students; George Washington University, non-sectarian, founded in 1821, 500 faculty and 11,965 students; Howard University, founded in 1867, 855 faculty and 9,401 students; Catholic University of America, founded in 1884, with 739 faculty and 6,050 students; American University (Methodist) with 270 faculty and 11,243 students.

WELFARE. In Jan. 1968 old-age assistance was being paid to 2,346 persons, receiving an average of $74.45 per month; aid to 198 blind persons $89.04, aid to 5,515 families ($38.23 per 25,527 recipients per month) for dependent children, and aid to 4,299 permanently and totally disabled, $88.74. In 1967 over $18m. was spent on public assistance payments, an increase of 23% on 1966.

Since 1958 there have been no executions; from 1930 to 1957 there were 40 executions (electrocution) including 3 whites for murder and 35 Negroes for murder and 2 for rape. On 31 Dec. 1965 the District's 5 prisons had 1,604 inmates (200 per 100,000 population).

FINANCE. The District's revenues are derived from a tax on real and personal property, sales taxes, taxes on corporations and companies, licences for conducting various businesses and from federal payments.

Annual appropriations for the District of Columbia stood in the fiscal year 1968, as follows: General fund, $445,108,000; highway fund, $36·47m.; metropolitan area sanitary sewage works fund, $11,133,000; water fund $13,381,000; grand total, $518,868,264.

The District of Columbia has no bonded debt not covered by its accumulated sinking fund.

INDUSTRY. The District has few industries, with products mainly for local consumption. In 1966, 614 manufacturing establishments had 20,532 (1963: 19,700) production workers, earning $162m. (1963: $135m.); value added by manufacture in 1962: $245m.

COMMUNICATIONS. Within the District are 340 miles of bus routes. The District has 2 general airports; across the Potomac River in Arlington, Va., is National Airport, and in Chantilly, Va., is Dulles International Airport. A rapid rail transit system including a town subway system has been approved by Congress.

BOOKS OF REFERENCE

Reports of the Commissioners of the District of Colombia. Annual. Washington
Federal Writers' Project. *Washington, D.C.: A Guide to the Nation's Capital.* New York, 1942
National Capital Park and Planning Commission. *Monographs on Washington, Present and Future.* Washington, D.C., 1950
Rutherford, G. W. *Administration problems in a metropolitan area: the national capital region.* Chicago, 1952

FLORIDA

GOVERNMENT. White men, likely Spaniards but possibly English, saw Florida for the first time in the period 1497–1512. Juan Ponce de Leon sighted Florida on 27 March 1513. Going ashore between 2 and 8 April in the vicinity of what is now St Augustine, he named the land 'Pascua Florida' because his landing was 'in the time of the Feast of Flowers'. The first permanent settlement in the entire US was made at St Augustine, 8 Sept. 1565. It was claimed by Spain until 1763, then ceded to England; back to Spain in 1783, and to the US in 1821. Florida became a Territory in 1821 and was admitted into the Union on 3 March 1845. The 1968 Legislaturer evised the constitution of 1885. The state legislature consists of a Senate of 48 members, elected for 4 years, and House of Representatives with 119 members elected for 2 years. Sessions are held annually, and are limited to 60 days. The Governor is elected for 4 years, but in 1964 a 2-year term (1965–67) was inserted in order to change election dates to midway between presidential elections. Two senators and 12 representatives are elected to Congress.

In the 1968 presidential election Nixon polled 886,804 votes, Humphrey 676,794 and Wallace 624,207.

The state capital is Tallahassee. The state is divided into 67 counties.

Governor: Reuben Askew (D.), 1971–74 ($36,000).
Lieut.-Governor: Ray C. Osborne (R.), 1969–71 ($34,000).
Secretary of State: Tom Adams (D.) ($34,000).

AREA AND POPULATION. Area, 58,560 sq. miles, including 4,308 sq. miles of inland water. Census population, 1 April 1960, was 4,951,560, an increase of 78·7% since 1950—largest per cent increase of any state. Estimated population, 1 July 1968, 6·2m. Births in 1968 were 100,971 (16·3 per 1,000 population); deaths, 68,710 (11·1); infant deaths, 2,433 (24·1 per 1,000 live births); marriages, 62,673 (10·1); divorces, 31,655 (5·1).

Population in 4 federal census years (with distribution by sex, 1960) was:

	White	Negro	Indian	Asiatic	Total	Per sq. mile
1910	443,634	308,669	74	242	752,619	13·7
1930	1,035,390	431,828	587	406	1,468,211	27·1
1950	2,166,051	603,101	1,011	1,142	2,771,305	51·1
1960	4,063,881	880,186	2,504	4,990	4,951,560	84·6
Male	2,000,593	432,107	All others 4,083		2,436,783	—
Female	2,063,288	448.079	All others 3,410		2,514,777	—

Of the population in 1960, 3,661,383 (73·9%) were urban (65·5% in 1950); 3,087,699 were 21 years of age or over; 255,071 were foreign-born whites.

The largest cities in the state (1960 census) are: Miami, 291,688 (urbanized area, 852,705); Tampa, 274,970 (301,790); Jacksonville, 201,030 (372,569);

St Petersburg, 181,298 (324,842); Orlando, 88,135; Fort Lauderdale, 83,648; Hialeah, 66,972; Miami Beach, 63,145; Pensacola, 56,752; West Palm Beach, 56,208; Tallahassee, 48,174; Lakeland, 41,350; Daytona Beach, 37,395; Hollywood, 35,237; Coral Gables, 34,793; Clearwater, 34,653; Sarasota, 34,083; Key West, 33,956.

RELIGION. In 1960, 30·3% of the population were members of 6 churches: Baptists (455,175), Roman Catholics (466,028), Methodists (223,151), Presbyterians (105,834) and Episcopalians (83,656). Jews numbered 159,337.

EDUCATION. Attendance at school is compulsory between the ages of 7 and 16.

In 1968 the public elementary and high schools had 57,172 teachers with 1,329,137 enrolled pupils. State expenditure on public schools was $569·3m. The state maintains 31 junior colleges with a total enrolment of 103,000.

There are 7 universities in the state system, namely the University of Florida at Gainesville (founded 1905) with 19,849 students and 1,178 instructors, the Florida State University (founded at Tallahassee in 1857) with 16,301 students and 1,100 instructors, the University of South Florida at Tampa (founded 1960) with 11,943 students and 607 instructors, Florida A. & M. University (for Negroes) at Tallahassee (founded 1887) with 3,947 students and 274 instructors, Florida Atlantic University at Boca Raton with 4,348 students and 274 instructors, the University of West Florida at Pensacola with 2,499 students and 176 instructors, and the Florida Technological University at Orlando with 1,499 students and 97 instructors.

WELFARE. Florida in 1935 established a system of old-age assistance (maximum now $70 per month) for those citizens who are infirm or 65 years of age. In 1967, 79,030 persons were drawing an average of $50 per month. Aid to 2,587 blind averaged $64; aid to dependent children averaged $60; aid to the disabled averaged $61.

Hospitals listed by the American Hospital Association, 1966, numbered 179 with 39,053 beds; state and county mental hospitals had an average daily census of 10,023 patients in 1966.

In 1968 there were no executions; from 1930 to 1968 there were 168 executions (electrocution), including 57 whites and 73 Negroes for murder, 1 white and 36 Negroes for rape and 1 white for kidnapping. State prisons, 18 Aug. 1968, had 8,412 inmates (133 per 100,000 population).

FINANCE. There is no state income tax on individuals or companies. For the year ending 30 June 1968 the state had a general revenue of $2,518,728,889, of which taxation furnished, $1,052,700,220 and federal aid $325,784,008. General expenditure was $2,458,311,683, of which education took $569,327,309; public welfare, $183,376,360, and highways, $345,276,944.

Net long-term debt, 30 June 1968, amounted to $824m.

Per capita personal income (1969) was $3,427.

AGRICULTURE. In 1964, 40,541 farms had a total acreage of 15,410,541; average farm was 380·1 acres valued (land and buildings) at $109,732. Non-whites operated 2,383 farms. Cash income, 1968, from crops, $865m., and from livestock, $353m. Production of grapefruit, 32·9m. boxes in 1968, and oranges, 100·5m. boxes. Other crops are tobacco (25·5m. lb. 1967); sugar-cane (6m. tons, 1967); maize, oats and peanuts. On 1 Jan. 1968 the state had 1,877,000 cattle, including 241,000 milch cows and 299,000 swine.

The national forests area in June 1967 was 1,076,000 acres.

FISHERIES. Florida has extensive fisheries for oysters, shrimp, red snappers, mullet, turtles and sponges, of which Florida has almost a monopoly. Catch (1968), 181m. lb. valued at $32·9m.

MINING. Chief mineral is phosphate rock, of which marketable production in 1968 was 27·5m. long tons, leading all states. Total value of mineral production, 1968, $319m.

INDUSTRY. In 1967 there were 8,000 manufacturers. They employed, in 1967, 292,600 persons who earned $1,400m.; value added by manufacture (1967), $3,000m. The metalworking, lumber, chemical, woodpulp, food-processing and aero-space industries are important.

TOURISM. During 1968 over 26m. persons visited Florida, of whom Florida counts approximately 20m. as tourists. They spend over $5,508m. annually in Florida, making tourism the biggest industry in the state.

COMMUNICATIONS. In 1968 there were 4,800 miles of railway. The state (1967) maintained 16,304 miles of highways; counties, 47,068 miles. In 1967 Florida had 281 airports, including 6 seaplane bases.

BOOKS OF REFERENCE

Florida Tourist Study. Florida Development Commission, Tallahassee. Annual
Report. Florida Secretary of State. Tallahassee. Biennial
Report of the Comptroller. Tallahassee. Annual
Dimensions. Bureau of Business and Economic Research, Univ. of Florida, Gainesville. Monthly
Cowles, F., *What to Look for in Florida.* Tampa, 1964
Morris, Allen, *The Florida Handbook.* Tallahassee, 1969–70. Biennial
Raisz, E. J., and others, *Atlas of Florida.* Univ. of Florida Press, 1963

STATE LIBRARY. Supreme Court Building, Tallahassee. *Librarian:* F. William Summers.

GEORGIA

GOVERNMENT. Georgia (so named from George II) was founded in 1733 as the 13th original colony; she became the 4th original state. A new constitution was adopted on 7 Aug. 1945; there have been 84 general amendments. The General Assembly, consists of a Senate of 54 members and a House of Representatives of 205 members, both elected for 2 years. The Governor and Lieut.-Governor are elected for 4 years. Legislative sessions are annual, beginning the 2nd Monday in Jan. and lasting for 40 days.

Georgia was the first state to extend the franchise to all citizens 18 years old and above. The state is represented in Congress by 2 senators and 10 representatives.

Registered voters, 1968, numbered 2,362,784. At the 1968 presidential election Nixon polled 380,111 votes, Humphrey 334,439 and Wallace 535,550.

The state capital is Atlanta. Georgia is divided into 159 counties.

Governor: Jimmy Carter (D.) 1971–74 ($42,500).
Lieut.-Governor: George T. Smith (D.) ($20,000).
Secretary of State: Ben W. Fortson, Jr (D.), ($22,500).

AREA AND POPULATION. Area, 58,876 sq. miles, of which 602 sq. miles are inland water. Census population, 1 April 1960, was 3,943,116, an increase of 14·5% since 1950. Estimated population, 1 Jan. 1970, 4,672,593. Births, 1965, were 94,336 (21·6 per 1,000 population); deaths, 38,104 (8·7); infant deaths, 2,734 (29 per 1,000 live births); marriages, 55,537 (12·7); divorces and annulments, 12,043 (2·8).

Population in 4 census years (with distribution by sex, 1960) was:

	White	Negro	Indian	Asiatic	Total	Per sq. mile
1910	1,431,802	1,176,987	95	237	2,609,121	44·4
1930	1,837,021	1,071,125	43	317	2,908,506	49·7
1950	2,380,577	1,062,762	333	—	3,444,578	58·9
1960	2,817,223	1,122,596	749	2,004	3,943,116	67·7
Male	1,391,735	532,509	All others	1,669	1,925,913	—
Female	1,425,488	590,087		1,628	2,017,203	—

Of the 1960 population, 2,182,117 (55·3%) were urban (34·4% in 1940); those 21 years of age and over numbered 2,231,000; foreign-born whites, 23,888.

The largest cities are: Atlanta (capital), with population, 1960 census, of 487,455 (urbanized area, 768,125); Savannah, 149,245 (169,887); Columbus, 116,779 (158,382); Augusta, 70,626; Macon, 69,764; Albany, 55,890; Rome, 32,226; Athens, 31,355.

RELIGION. Baptists predominate, having more than half of the religious membership of the state. Negro Baptists had 596,648 adherents at the latest estimate. Southern Baptists numbered 844,000 in 1959; White Methodists, 348,315; Negro Methodists (4 groups), 211,740; Catholics (1964), 72,342. Total membership, all denominations, is estimated at 2,475,600.

EDUCATION. Since 1945 education has been compulsory; tuition is free for pupils between the ages of 6 and 18 years. At the end of the 1967–68 school year the 482 high schools, 94 junior high schools, 1,276 elementary schools and 51 combination junior high and elementary schools had 1,174,414 pupils and 45,883 teachers and principals. Teachers' salaries averaged $6,600 in 1968–69. Integration in public schools is now an accepted practice.

The University of Georgia (Athens) was founded in 1785 and was the first chartered State University in the US. Other institutions of higher learning include Georgia Institute of Technology (Atlanta), Emory University (Atlanta), Agnes Scott College (Decatur), Georgia College (Milledgeville), Georgia State University (Atlanta) and Mercer University (Macon). The Atlanta University Center, devoted primarily to Negro education, includes Clark College and Morris Brown College, co-educational, Morehouse, a liberal arts college for men, Inter-denominational Theological Center, a co-educational theological school, and Spelman College, the first liberal arts college for Negro women in the US. Wesleyan College near Macon is the oldest chartered women's college in the US. Total enrolment, Sept. 1969, was 109,400 in 49 institutions of higher education.

WELFARE. In Aug. 1968, 88,605 persons were receiving old-age assistance of an average $51.88 per month; 30,648 families were receiving as aid to dependent children an average of $97.50 per family; aid to the blind went to 3,105 persons (averaging $62.80 monthly); aid to 29,583 totally and permanently disabled persons was $55.80 monthly.

Hospitals licensed by the Georgia Health Department, 1 July 1968, numbered 205 with 31,393 beds.

State prisons, 31 July 1968, had 8,517 inmates. Since' 1965 there have been no executions. From 1930 to 1964 there were 368 executions (electrocution), including 65 white and 236 Negroes for murder, 3 white and 58 Negroes for rape and 6 Negroes for armed robbery.

Under a Local Option Act, the sale of alcoholic beverages (not including malt beverages and light wines) is prohibited in more than half the counties.

FINANCE. For the fiscal year ending 30 June 1966 general revenue was $942,415,432 ($585,583,839 from taxes and $268,567,999 in federal aid); general expenditure was $927,210,078.

On 30 June 1963 net long-term debt was $453,505,000.

Estimated *per capita* personal income (1969) was $2,743.

AGRICULTURE. In 1964, 83,366 farms had an area of 17·9m. acres; average farm was of 215 acres valued (land and buildings) at $30,500. For 1967, cotton output was 230,000 bales (of 500 lb.) (valued at $31·9m.). Other crops, 1967, included tobacco, 148·5m. lb. ($100·9m.); corn, 88·9m. bu. ($48·4m.); peanuts, 975m. lb. ($111·6m.); peaches, 3m. bu.; pecans, 48·4m. lb. Cash income, from crops (1968), $415m., and from livestock, $624m.

The national forest area in 1968 was 796,719 acres.

On 1 Jan. 1966 farm animals included 1,554,000 cattle, including 185,000 cows, 9,000 sheep and 1,277,000 swine.

MINING. Georgia is the leading producer of kaolin, of granite and marble (crushed and dimension) and of crushed slate. The state ranks second in production of fuller's earth and bauxite. Iron-ore (usable) production in 1967 was 267,000 short tons. Mineral products, 1968, had a record value (for the 12th successive year) of $163m.

INDUSTRY. In 1968 the state had approximately 6,000 manufacturing establishments employing 424,315 workers, who (in 1967) earned approximately $2,100m.; the value added by manufacture was $4,572m. in 1966.

COMMUNICATIONS. The principal port is Savannah; there were, 1966, 5,705 miles of railways; airports (1967) numbered 131. Total road mileage (1969) was 97,732 (city, county and state); primary roads totalled 17,587 miles. Motor vehicles registered, 1969, numbered 2,628,491.

BOOKS OF REFERENCE

Georgia Statistical Abstract. Univ. of Georgia, Athens. Annual
Official Register. Dept. of Archives and History. Atlanta. Irregular
Gosnell, C. B., and Anderson, C. D., *The government and administration of Georgia.* New York, 1956
Range, W., *A Century of Georgia Agriculture.* Univ. of Georgia, Athens, 1954
Rowland, A. R., *A bibliography of the writings on Georgia history.* Hamden, Conn., 1966
Saye, A. B., *A Constitutional History of Georgia, 1732–1945.* Univ. of Georgia, Athens, 1948

STATE LIBRARY. Judicial Building, Capital Sq., Atlanta. *State Librarian:* John D. M. Folger.

HAWAII

GOVERNMENT. The Hawaiian Islands, formerly known as the Sandwich Islands, were discovered by Capt. James Cook in Aug. 1778. The islands formed during the greater part of the 19th century an independent kingdom, but in 1893 the reigning Queen, Liliuokalani (died 11 Nov. 1917), was deposed and a provisional government formed; in 1894 a Republic was proclaimed, and in accordance with the request of the people of Hawaii expressed through the Legislature of the Republic, and a resolution of the US Congress of 6 July 1898 (signed 7 July by President McKinley), the islands were on 12 Aug. 1898 formally annexed to the US. On 14 June 1900 the islands were constituted as a Territory of Hawaii.

Statehood was granted to Hawaii on 11 and 12 March 1959. The constitution took effect on 21 Aug. 1959.

The Legislature consists of a Senate of 25 members elected for 4 years, and a House of Representatives of 51 members elected for 2 years. The constitution provides for annual meetings of the legislature with 60-day regular sessions. The Governor and Lieut.-Governor are elected for 4 years. The registered voters, 1967, numbered 274,174.

The state sends to Congress 2 senators and 2 representatives.

In the 1968 presidential election Nixon polled 91,425 votes, Humphrey 141,324 and Wallace 3,469.

Governor: John A. Burns (D.), 1971–74 ($38,182).
Lieut.-Governor: Thomas P. Gill (D.), 1966–70 ($32,455).

AREA AND POPULATION. The Hawaiian Islands lie in the North Pacific Ocean, between 18° 50′ and 28° 15′ N. lat. and 154° 40′ and 178° 15′ W. long., about 2,090 nautical miles south-west of San Francisco. There are more than 20 islands in the group, of which 7 are inhabited. The land and inland water area of the state is 6,424 sq. miles, with census population, 1 April 1960, of 632,772, an increase of 132,978 or 26·6% since 1950; density was 98·6 per sq. mile. Estimated civilian population, 1 Jan. 1968, 792,444.

The principal islands are Hawaii, 4,021 sq. miles (population, 1960, 61,332); Maui, 728 (35,717); Oahu, 598 (500,409); Kauai, 551 (27,922); Molokai, 259

(5,023); Lanai, 141 (2,115); Niihau, 72 (254); Kahoolawe, 45 (0). The capital, Honolulu, on the island of Oahu, had a population in 1960 of 294,194 and Hilo, on the island of Hawaii, 25,966.

Figures for racial groups, 1960, are: 202,230 Caucasians, 4,943 Negroes, 472 Indians, 203,455 Japanese, 38,197 Chinese, 69,070 Filipinos, 114,405 all others. Of the total, approximately 89% were citizens of the US.

Inter-marriage between the races is popular. Of the 14,690 persons married in the calendar year 1967, 33·5% married a wife or husband of a different race. Births, 1967, were 14,765 (19·4 per 1,000 civilian population); deaths, 3,921 (4·9); infant deaths, 250 (16·9 per 1,000 live births); marriages, 7,345 (9·7); divorces, 1,451 (1·9).

RELIGION. The residents of Hawaii are mainly Christians, though there are many Buddhists. There are about 500 churches in the state, 62 of which are Roman Catholic. Roman Catholics number about 200,000, Mormons about 16,000, Congregationalists about 12,000.

EDUCATION. Education is free, and compulsory for children between the ages of 6 and 18. The language in the schools is English. In 1968–69 there were 210 public schools (enrolment, 171,872 with 7,892 teachers) and 101 private schools (33,385 pupils) ranging from kindergarten through the 12th grade. The expenditure for public instruction in 1968–69 was $171,637,212. The University of Hawaii, founded in 1907, had 17,781 day students and 1,264 full-time faculty members in 1968–69.

WELFARE. During 1967–68 the Department of Social Services spent $37,928,446 (excluding administrative costs); the federal government met 40% of this fund. In 1967 there were 32 non-military hospitals (5,408 beds) listed by the Department of Health. During 1967–68 an average of 1,807 persons per month received old-age assistance ($80.24); 74 blind persons received a monthly average of $100.69; aid to 1,500 disabled cases, $107.38 monthly; aid to 4,659 families with 21,125 dependent children, $187.62 per family; 819 children received welfare foster care at an average of $99.50; 3,655 persons received medical payments for the aged ($126.45). Other medical assistance payments totalled $995,990. Prison population, 31 Dec. 1967, 437.

There is no capital punishment in Hawaii.

FINANCE. Revenue is derived mainly from taxation of sales and gross receipts, real property, corporate and personal income, and inheritance taxes, licences, public land sales and leases. For the year ending 30 June 1968, the federal internal revenue collections were $440,237,000; state general fund receipts amounted to $331,859,563; special fund receipts, $86,243,401; and federal grants, $104,557,113. State general fund expenditures were $330,904,923, and special fund, $85,548,264 (education, $171,637,212; highways, $36,222,695; public welfare, $77,316,899; figures include both special and general funds).

Net long-term debt, 30 June 1968, amounted to $176·9m.

Estimated *per capita* personal income (1969) was $3,882.

AGRICULTURE. Farming is highly commercialized, aiming at export to the American market, and highly mechanized. In 1964 there were 4,864 farms with an acreage of 2,354,454. Of the total farms, 88 were under managers, 3,659 were farmed by their owners and 1,117 by tenants. The average farm was of 484·1 acres.

Sugar and pineapples are the staple industries, while coffee, molasses, hides, bananas and fresh flowers are also exported. For the calendar year 1967 sugar-cane was planted on 239,800 acres; production, 1967, 1·2m. short tons of sugar. Production is mainly by 25 companies (which jointly own a large refinery in California) and some 759 independent planters. Cane is allowed to grow from 18 to 22 months. The pineapple pack for the crop year ending 31 May 1966 was 28,035,755 cases of canned fruit and juices. Coffee crop for the year ended 30

June 1967 was 6·2m. lb. In 1967 animal products had an estimated total value of $37·4m. But sugar and pineapple marketings, at $324m., were over 63% of the total agricultural income.

The forest reserves aggregate 928,000 acres; state lands, 1·5m. acres. Land held by the federal government aggregated 233,000 acres in 1963.

Hawaii's mainland dollar earnings, 1967, were $1,856m. with a favourable balance of $59m.

MINING. Total value of mineral production, 1967, amounted to $16·94m. Cement shipped from plants amounted to 1,395,000 bbls (valued at $7·4m.); pumice, 290,000 short tons; value of pumice, used for road construction, and stone totalled $0·7m.

INDUSTRY. In 1967 manufacturing establishments (numbering 603) employed 15,173 production workers who earned an estimated $135m.; value added by manufacture was estimated at $310m.

TOURISM. Tourism is an outstanding factor in Hawaii's economy. Tourist arrivals numbered 109,798 in 1955, and reached 1,001,810 in 1967. Tourist expenditures, totalling $55m. in 1955, contributed $400m. to the state's economy in 1966.

TRADE. In 1967 imports of newsprint, fertilizer, lumber, feed, crude oil and other products from foreign countries such as Arabia, Indonesia and Japan amounted to $125m. Exports, primarily food and manufactures, amounted to $373m. About 87% of Hawaii's overseas trade is with the mainland USA.

COMMUNICATIONS. *Shipping.* Several lines of steamers connect the islands with the mainland of US, Canada, Australia, the Philippines, China and Japan. In 1967–68, 1,774 overseas vessels entered (with 2,445,000 tons) and cleared (with 1,930,818 tons) the port of Honolulu. A barge navigation company provides communication between the islands.

Roads. In Dec. 1967 there were 338,420 passenger motor cars, and a total of 2,975 miles of highways (including 1,085 miles of federally assisted highways and federal highways in national parks).

Aviation. Ten scheduled and 2 non-scheduled airlines connect Hawaii with US, British Columbia, the Antipodes and the Orient. In 1967–68 passengers overseas numbered 2,931,792, and there were 1,748,963 passengers between the islands. Five scheduled and 2 irregular air carriers operate between the islands. There are 12 commercial airports.

Post. There were 352,196 telephones at 1 Jan. 1968.

BOOKS OF REFERENCE

Government in Hawaii. Tax Foundation of Hawaii. Honolulu, 1969
Guide to Government in Hawaii. 3rd ed. Legislative Reference Bureau, University of Hawaii, Honolulu, 1966
All About Hawaii: Thrum's Hawaiian Annual and Standard Guide. Honolulu, 1875 to date
Current Hawaiiana (quarterly bibliography). Hawaii Library Association, Honolulu
Allen, G. E., *Hawaii's war years.* 2 vols. Hawaii Univ. Press, 1950–52
Catton, M. M. L., *Social service in Hawaii.* Palo Alto, 1959
Day, A. Grove, *Hawaii and its People.* New York, 1955.—and Stroven, C., *A Hawaiian Reader.* New York, 1961
Fodor, E., ed., *Hawaii, 1965.* New York, 1965
Fuchs, L. E., *Hawaii Pono: a social history.* New York, 1961
Kamins, Robert M., *Hawaii's Revised Tax System.* Honolulu, 1957
Kuykendall, R. S., and Day, A. G., *Hawaii, a History.* Rev. ed. New Jersey, 1961
Lind, A. W., *Hawaii's People.* Honolulu, 1955
Mann, A. F., *Hawaii: the fiftieth state: government and economy.* Honolulu, 1960
Pukui, M. K., and Elbert, S. H., *Hawaiian–English Dictionary.* Honolulu, 1957
Smith, Bradford, *Yankees in Paradise: the New England Impact on Hawaii.* Philadelphia, 1956

IDAHO

GOVERNMENT. Idaho was first permanently settled in 1860, although there was a mission for Indians in 1836 and a Mormon settlement in 1855. It was organized as a Territory in 1863 and admitted into the Union as a state on 3 July 1890. The constitution then adopted is still in force; it has had 79 amendments. A new constitutional study is under revision. The Legislature consists of a Senate of 35 members and a House of Representatives of 70 members, all the legislators being elected for 2 years. Annual sessions last for 60 days and 30 days for extraordinary sessions. The Governor, Lieut.-Governor and Secretary of State are elected for 4 years. Voters are citizens, over the age of 21 years, who have resided in the state over 6 months. The state is represented in Congress by 2 senators and 2 representatives.

In the 1968 presidential election Nixon polled 165,369 votes, Humphrey 89,273 and Wallace 36,541.

The state is divided into 44 counties. The capital is Boise.

Governor: Cecil Andrus (D.), 1971–74 ($30,000).
Lieut.-Governor: Jack M. Murphy (R.), 1967–71 ($7,000).
Secretary of State: Pete Cenarrusa (R.), 1967–71 ($17,000).

AREA AND POPULATION. Area, 83,557 sq. miles, of which 849 sq. miles are inland water. In 1970 the federal government owned 33,979,389 acres (63% of the state area). Census population, 1 April 1970, 698,350, an increase of 4·7% since 1960.

Births, 1968, 12,668 (17·9 per 1,000 population); deaths, 5,798 (7·9); infant deaths, 226 (50 per 1,000 live births); marriages, 11,283; divorces (1967), 3,183 (4·4).

Population in 4 census years (with distribution by sex, 1960) was:

	White	Negro	Indian	Asiatic	Total	Per sq. mile
1910	319,221	651	3,488	2,234	325,594	3·9
1930	438,840	668	3,638	1,886	445,032	5·4
1950	581,395	1,050	3,800	2,392	588,637	7·1
1960	657,383	1,502	5,231	2,958	667,191	8·1
Male	333,298	808	All others 4,315		338,421	—
Female	324,085	694	All others 3,991		328,770	—

Of the total 1960 population, 317,097 (57·50%) were urban (33·7% in 1940). Those 21 years of age or older were 372,484; foreign-born whites numbered 14,779.

The largest cities are Boise (capital) with 1970 census population of 73,330; Pocatello, 38,826; Idaho Falls, 35,318; Twin Falls, 21,337; Nampa, 20,035.

RELIGION. The leading religious denomination is the Church of Jesus Christ of Latter Day Saints (Mormon Church), with 180,103 adherents in 1968; Roman Catholics had 51,000; Methodists, 18,719; Lutherans, 4,500; Episcopalians, 4,941, and Presbyterians, 13,926.

EDUCATION. In 1969–70 public elementary schools (grades 1 to 6) had 92,322 pupils and 3,808 classroom teachers; secondary schools had 87,551 pupils and 4,159 classroom teachers. Average salary, 1969, of elementary and secondary classroom teachers, $7,034. Total expenditure on public schools (1969–70) was $78·8m. The University of Idaho, founded at Moscow in 1889, had 410 professors in 1968–69 and 6,441 students. There are 9 other institutions of higher education, 4 of which are public institutions, with a total enrolment (1969–70) of 20,301.

WELFARE. Old-age assistance is granted to needy persons 65 years of age. In June 1969, 3,246 persons were drawing an average of $64.94 per month; 3,488 families with 9,312 children were drawing an average of $177.28;

108 blind persons, $78.83; 2,843 persons permanently and totally disabled, $76·06.

In 1970, 50 hospitals (4,232 beds) were listed by the American Hospitals Association. In 1968 there were 627 patients in mental hospitals and 672 in institutions for the metally retarded.

The death penalty is legal for first degree murder, but has been used sparingly. Since 1926 only 3 men (white) have been executed, by hanging (2 in 1951 and 1 in 1957). The state prison, 1 Aug. 1970, had 395 inmates.

FINANCE. For the year ending 30 June 1970 (State Auditor's Office) general revenues were $343·77m. (taxation, $141·6m., and federal aid, $68·9m.) and general expenditures were $26·5m (education, $55m.; highways, $60·4m., and public welfare, $26·5m.).

Per capita personal income (1969) was $2,051.

AGRICULTURE. Agriculture is the leading industry, although a great part of the state is naturally arid. Extensive irrigation works have been carried out, bringing an estimated 3·5m. acres under irrigation; 83 reservoirs have a total capacity of 10·4m. acre-ft, 7·3m. acre-ft of which is primarily used for irrigation.

In 1970 there were 29,108 farms with a total area of 15,301,001 acres (29% of the land area); average farm had 515·9 acres with land and buildings valued at $68,178.

As of 30 June 1970 there were 52 soil conservation districts, managed by local farmers and ranchers, embracing 50·35m. acres, of which 38,947 acres (exclusive of federal lands and urban areas) are in farms and ranch operating units.

Cash income, 1969, from major crops and livestock, $621m. The most important crop is potatoes—leading all states; in 1968 the production amounted to 88m. bu. Other crops are wheat (71m. cwt, 1968), sugar-beet (39m. short tons), alfalfa (3·1m. tons, 1965), oats, barley, field peas, dry beans, apples, prunes and hops. On 1 Jan. 1966 the number of sheep was 1,987,000; milch cows, 254,000; all cattle, 1,589,000; swine, 116,000.

FORESTRY. In 1970 a total of 21,815,000 acres (almost 40% of the state's area) was in forests; 63% of this was in commercial production. The volume of sawtimber in commercial forests was 126,801m. bd ft; of growing stock, 26,514 cu. ft. The value of forest products is about $221m. *per annum*, of which $83m. is added by process. Ownership of commercial forests is 75% federal, 6% state, 19% private. Approximately 13,400 workers are involved in forestry.

MINING. Production of the most important minerals (1969): Lead, 69,942 short tons, ranking second in US; silver, 18·66m. troy oz.—50% of US total; zinc, 58,157 short tons, ranking second in US. Other minerals produced included phosphate rock, cobalt and antimony, columbium–tantalum, copper, gold, mercury, nickel, rare-earth metals, tungsten, thorium barite and clays. Beryllium ore has recently been discovered. Value of total mineral output was $126m.

INDUSTRY. In 1970 there were about 1,151 manufacturing establishments and they employed 39,500 production workers; value added by manufacture was $600m.

COMMUNICATIONS. The state had (1970) 3,073 miles of railways operated by 8 companies. There were, 1970, 267 airports. Water transportation is provided from the Pacific to Lewiston, by way of the Columbia and Snake rivers, a distance of 480 miles. The state maintained in 1970, 4,929 miles of roads of the total of 54,759 miles of public roads. In 1969, 528,310 automobiles were registered.

BOOKS OF REFERENCE

Biennial Report. Secretary of State. Boise
Idaho Industrial Opportunity. 2nd ed. Dept. of Commerce & Development, Boise, 1967
Idaho's Yesterdays. State Historical Society, Quarterly
Brosnan, C. J., *History of the State of Idaho.* 3rd ed. New York, 1948
Martin and Barber, *Idaho in the Pacific Northwest.* Boise, 1956

ILLINOIS

GOVERNMENT. Illinois was first discovered by Joliet and Marquette, two French explorers, in 1673, and settled in 1720. In 1763 the country was ceded by the French to the British. In 1783 Great Britain recognized the title of the US to Illinois, which was organized as a Territory in 1809 and admitted into the Union on 3 Dec. 1818. The present constitution dates from 1870; 14 amendments have been adopted. The General Assembly consists of a Senate of 58 members elected for 4 years (about half of whom retire every 2 years), and a House of Representatives of 177 members elected for 2 years. Sessions are biennial. The Governor, Lieut.-Governor and Secretary of State are elected for 4 years. Electors are citizens 21 years of age, having the usual residential qualifications.

The state is divided into senatorial and representative districts, in each of which 1 senator and 3 representatives are chosen; for the election of the latter each elector has 3 votes, of which he may cast 1 for each of 3 candidates or 1½ for each of 2, or all 3 for 1 candidate.

Illinois is represented in Congress by 2 senators and 24 representatives.

In the 1968 presidential election Nixon polled 2,174,774 votes, Humphrey 2,039,814 and Wallace 390,958.

The capital is Springfield. The state has 102 counties.

Governor: Richard B. Ogilivie (R.), 1969–73 ($45,000).
Lieut.-Governor: Paul Simon (D.), 1969–73 ($25,000).
Secretary of State: Paul Powell (D.), 1969–73 ($30,000).

AREA AND POPULATION. Area, 56,400 sq. miles, of which 470 sq. miles are inland water. Census population, 1 April 1960, 10,081,158, an increase of 15·7% since 1950. Estimated population, 1 July 1967, 10·8m. Births in 1967 were 195,644 (18 per 1,000 population); deaths, 110,030 (10·2); infant deaths, 4,611 (23·6 per 1,000 live births); marriages, 105,295 (9·7); divorces, 28,657 (2·6).

Population in 4 census years (with distribution by sex, 1960) was:

	White	Negro	Indian	All others	Total	Per sq. mile
1910	5,526,962	109,049	188	2,392	5,638,591	100·6
1930	7,295,267	328,972	469	5,946	7,630,654	136·4
1950	8,064,058	645,980	1,443	18,695	8,712,176	155·8
1960	9,010,252	1,037,470	4,704	28,732	10,081,158	180·3
Male	4,435,687	498,884	2,445	15,850	4,952,866	—
Female	4,574,565	538,586	2,259	12,882	5,128,292	—

Of the total population in 1960, 8,140,315 persons (80·7%) were urban (77·6% in 1950); 6,280,637 were 21 years of age or older; foreign-born whites numbered 673,029.

The most populous cities with population (1960 census, unless otherwise indicated), are:

Chicago	3,550,404	Aurora	63,715	Alton	43,047
Rockford (1964)	132,109	Oak Park	61,093	Moline	42,705
Peoria	103,162	Waukegan	55,719	Danville	41,856
Springfield (cap.)	83,271	Berwyn	54,224	Elmhurst (1963)	40,329
East St Louis	81,712	Rock Island	51,863	Granite City	40,073
Evanston	79,283	Des Plaines (1965)	50,789	Pax Ridge (1964)	39,065
Decatur	78,004	Champaign	49,583	Bloomington (1965)	37,791
Cicero	69,130	Elgin	49,447	Belleville	37,264
Skokie (1964)	67,865	Oaklawn (1965)	49,084	Galesburg	37,243
Joliet	66,780	Quincy	43,793	Chicago Heights	34,331

Standard Metropolitan Statistical Area population (1960 census): Chicago, 6,220,913; St Louis, Mo.–Ill., 2,060,103; Davenport–Rock Island–Moline, Iowa–Ill., 319,375; Peoria, 313,412; Rockford, 230,091.

RELIGION. Among the larger religious denominations are: Roman Catholic (1966), 3,303,681; Methodist (1966), 485,000; Jewish (1966), 283,625; United Presbyterian Church, USA (1967), 214,300; Lutheran Church in America (1967), 226,562; Lutheran Church, Missouri Synod (1967), 244,918; Disciples of Christ (1964), 101,940; American Baptist (1967), 113,148. The Illinois Council of Churches comprised 11 Protestant denominations with an estimated member-ship of approximately 1·33m. in 1967.

EDUCATION. Education is free and compulsory for children between 7 and 16 years of age. In 1968–69 there were 1,283 school districts, of which 692 were elementary (kindergarten through 8th grade), 201 were secondary (grades 9–12) and 390 were unit districts (kindergarten through 12th grade). Elementary enrolments (1967) were 1,425,000 pupils with 56,700 teachers; secondary enrol-ments, 777,000 pupils with 40,200 teachers. Enrolment (fall 1967) in non-public schools was 462,100 elementary and 119,100 secondary. Teachers' salaries, 1967, averaged $7,400. Total estimated expenditure on public schools, 1966–67, $1,412m. Total enrolment in institutions of higher education (fall 1966) was 323,522.

Colleges and universities with over 2,000 students:

Founded	Name	Place	Control	Fall 1967 Enrolment
1851	Northwestern University	Evanston	Methodist	17,356
1857	Illinois State University	Normal	Public	11,440
1867	University of Illinois	Urbana	Public	47,974
1869	Chicago State College[1]	Chicago	Public	4,992
1869	Southern Illinois University	Carbondale	Public	28,388
1870	Loyola University	Chicago	Roman Catholic	12,651
1871	Elmhurst College	Elmhurst	Un. Ch. of Christ	2,685
1890	University of Chicago	Chicago	Non-Sect.	10,464
1895	Eastern Illinois University	Charleston	Public	6,491
1895	Northern Illinois University	DeKalb	Public	18,057
1897	Bradley University	Peoria	Non-Sect.	6,333
1898	DePaul University	Chicago	Roman Catholic	9,627
1899	Western Illinois University	Macomb	Public	8,360
1940	Illinois Institute of Technology[2]	Chicago	Non-Sect.	8,471
1945	Roosevelt University	Chicago	Non-Sect.	6,410
1961	Northeastern Illinois State College[3]	Chicago	Public	6,139

[1] Formerly Illinois Teachers College (South).
[2] Illinois Institute of Technology formed in 1940 by merger of two older technical schools.
[3] Formerly Illinois Teachers College (North).

WELFARE. In June 1968, 63,598 persons were drawing old age assistance (averaging $112.51 per month); 315,463 were drawing aid to dependent children (averaging $55.73 per month); 2,072 persons in blind assistance (averaging $114.27), and 40,494 persons in assistance to the disabled (averaging $153.90).

In 1967 hospitals listed by the American Hospital Association numbered 320, with 105,656 beds. In 1967 state schools for the mentally retarded had 9,504 residents, and state hospitals for the mentally ill 24,714 residents.

In 1966 there was no execution; since 1930 there have been 90 executions (electrocution), including 58 white men, 1 white woman and 31 Negro men, all for murder. In April 1968 the total average daily prison population was 8,394 for all institutions.

A Civil Rights Act (1941) bans all forms of discrimination by places of public accommodation, including inns, restaurants, retail stores, railroads, aeroplanes, buses, etc., against persons on account of 'class, creed, religion, sect, denomina-tion or nationality'; another section similarly mentions 'race or colour'. The Fair Employment Practices Act of 1961, as amended, prohibits discrimination in employment based on race, colour, religion, national origin or ancestry, by employers, employment agencies, labour organizations and others.

FINANCE. For the year ending 30 June 1967 (US Census Bureau figures) general revenues were \$2,398m. (taxation, \$1,450,326,000 and federal aid, \$527,322,000) and general expenditures were \$2,456m. (education, \$900·11m.; highways, \$476,331,000, and public welfare, \$392,336,000).

Total net long-term debt, 1 July 1967, was \$1,210,229,000.

Per capita personal income (1969) was \$4,310.

AGRICULTURE. In 1968, 131,000 farms had an area of 29·9m. acres; the average farm was 228 acres.

Cash receipts, 1967, from crops, \$1,327m. (third in the US); from livestock and livestock products, \$1,278m. (fourth in the US). Illinois is a large producer of high-yielding hybrid maize. Output, 1967, was 1,091·5m. bu. (first in the US). Other crops were, in 1967, wheat, 76·6m. bu.; oats, 44·7m. bu.; potatoes, hay, barley, rye and buckwheat are also grown. Output of soybeans, 184·2m. bu. in 1967 (first in the US). On 1 Jan. 1967 there were 346,000 milch cows, 3,413,000 all cattle, 402,000 sheep and 6,772,000 swine. The wool clip in 1967 was 2,854,000 lb.

FORESTRY. National forest area under the US Forest Service administration, 1967, 220,183 acres.

MINING. The chief mineral product is coal; 77 mines had an output (1967) of 64,814,771 tons. Mineral production in 1967 also included: Crude petroleum, 60m. bbls; fluorspar, 210,207 short tons; lead, 2,384 short tons. Total value of mineral products, 1967, was \$636·8m.

INDUSTRY. In 1963, 18,135 manufacturing establishments employed 1,210,977 workers, earning \$7,555m.; value added by manufacture was \$14,557,060. Largest industry was machinery (excluding electrical). Pig-iron production in 1964 was 5,672,000 short tons; steel (1961), 8,395,000 short tons.

BUSINESS. In 1963, 92,069 retail establishments with total sales of \$15,190,141m. employed 63,997 persons; 18,690 wholesale establishments with total sales of \$29,135,150m. employed 216,186 in the workweek ended nearest 15 Nov.; 61,710 service establishments with total receipts of \$3,346,031m. employed 25,575 persons. In May 1968 there were 4,237,300 employees on non-agricultural payrolls. The average weekly earnings of production workers in manufacturing was \$131.70.

In 1967 the seaport of Chicago handled exports of 3,180m. short tons valued at \$314,373m. and imports of 2,701m. short tons valued at \$261,209m.

COMMUNICATIONS. There were, 1965, 10,956 miles of railway. In 1967 there were 126 certified airports, 57 heliports and 482 restricted landing areas. In 1967 there were 4,209,860 automobiles, 592,753 trucks and buses, 289,761 trailers and 93,904 motor cycles registered in the state. In 1966 there were 13,068 miles of state administered rural roads and 89,438 miles of locally administered rural roads.

In Dec. 1965 there were 5,823,000 telephones in the state.

BOOKS OF REFERENCE

Blue Book of the State of Illinois. Edited by Secretary of State. Springfield. Biennial
Federal Writers' Project. *Illinois: A Descriptive and Historical Guide.* Rev. ed. Chicago, 1947
Angle, Paul M., and Beyer, R. L., *A Handbook of Illinois History* (published by the Illinois State Historical Society). Springfield, 1943
Pease, T. C., *The Story of Illinois.* 3rd ed. Chicago, 1965

STATE LIBRARY. The Illinois State Library. Centennial Building, Springfield. *State Librarian:* Paul Powell, Secretary of State.

INDIANA

GOVERNMENT. Indiana, first settled in 1732–33, was made a Territory in 1800 and admitted into the Union on 11 Dec. 1816. The present constitution (the second) dates from 1851; it has had (as of 1971) 25 amendments. The General Assembly consists of a Senate of 50 members elected for 4 years, and a House of Representatives of 100 members elected for 2 years. Sessions are held biennially. The Governor and Lieut.-Governor are elected for 4 years. The state is represented in Congress by 2 senators and 11 representatives.

In the 1968 presidential election Nixon polled 1,067,885 votes, Humphrey 806,659 and Wallace 243,108.

The state capital is Indianapolis. The state is divided into 92 counties and 1,008 townships.

Governor: Edgar D. Whitcomb (R.), 1969–73 ($25,000 plus $6,000 expenses).
Lieut.-Governor: Richard E. Folz (R.) (1969–73) ($16,500).
Secretary of State: Larry Conrad (D.) (1970–72) ($16,500).

AREA AND POPULATION. Area, 36,291 sq. miles, of which 106 sq. miles are inland water. Census population (preliminary), 1 April 1970, was 5,143,422, an increase of 480,924 or 10·3% since 1960. In 1969 births were 91,666 (17·8 per 1,000 population); deaths, 48,750 (9·5); infant deaths, 1,859 (22·4 per 1,000 live births); marriages, 57,867 (11·2); divorces, 23,317 (4·5).

Population in 4 census years (with distribution by sex, 1960) was:

	White	Negro	Indian	Asiatic	Total	Per sq. mile
1910	2,639,961	60,320	279	316	2,700,876	74·9
1930	3,125,778	111,982	285	458	3,238,503	89·4
1950	3,758,512	174,168	438	1,106	3,934,224	108·7
1960	4,388,554	269,275	948	2,447	4,662,498	128·9
Male	2,165,509	130,725	All others	2,504	2,298,738	—
Female	2,223,045	138,550	All others	2,165	2,363,760	—

Of the total in 1960, 2,910,149 (62·4%) were urban (59·9% in 1950); 2,777,924 were 21 years of age or older; foreign-born whites numbered 90,972.

The largest cities with population (census 1970, preliminary) are: Indianapolis (capital), 742,613; Fort Wayne, 175,083; Gary, 174,132; Evansville, 137,997; South Bend, 122,797; Hammond, 107,108; Anderson, 69,923; Terre Haute, 69,247; Muncie, 68,066; East Chicago, 46,470; Lafayette, 44,668; Richmond, 43,800; Kokomo, 43,359; Elkhart, 42,455.

RELIGION. Religious denominations, in 1957, included: Methodist bodies (358,540), Roman Catholic (466,705), Disciples of Christ (194,941), Baptist bodies (122,578), Evangelical United Brethren (84,292), Presbyterian churches (95,048), Society of Friends (23,759). Total, all denominations, 1,715,289.

EDUCATION. School attendance is compulsory from 7 to 16 years of age. In autumn 1969 public elementary schools, kindergarten to grade 6, had 601,241 pupils and 24,275 teachers; public secondary schools, grades 7 to 12, had 532,402 pupils and 23,908 teachers. Teachers' salaries, 1970, averaged $8,574. Total expenditure for public schools, 1968–69, $965m.

The principal institutions for higher education are:

Begun	Institution	Control	Professors 1969	Students (full-time, 1969)
1824	Indiana University, Bloomington	State	2,517	56,578
1837	De Pauw University, Greencastle	Methodist	192	2,370
1842	University of Notre Dame	RC	614	7,526
1850	Butler University, Indianapolis	—	240	4,300
1859	Valparaiso University, Valparaiso	Evangelical Lutheran Church	303	4,244
1870	Indiana State University, Terre Haute	State	866	13,311
1874	Purdue University, Lafayette	State	2,353	36,750
1898	Ball State University, Muncie	State	579	14,446

WELFARE. Old-age assistance (maximum $80 per month plus medical expenses) is available for those American citizens 65 years of age or older. In Jan.–June 1969 an average of 17,977 persons were drawing (for old-age assistance) an average of $42.41 per month ($126.78 including direct medical aid); 43,844 dependent children from 14,121 families were receiving $132.76 per family per month ($174.74); 711 crippled children were receiving care through hospitals, clinics and foster homes; 1,481 blind persons were receiving an average of $56.34 ($126.43). Hospitals listed by the American Hospital Association (1970) numbered 136 (38,306 beds). In 1970, 12 state mental hospitals had 15,846 patients enrolled (11,442 present).

In 1963–70 there were no executions; since 1930 there were 41 executions (electrocution), namely 31 whites and 10 Negroes for murder. State correctional institutions, Aug. 1970, had 6,202 inmates (excluding juveniles).

The Civil Rights Act of 1885 forbids places of public accommodation to bar any persons on grounds not applicable to all citizens alike; no citizen may be disqualified for jury service 'on account of race or colour'. An Act of 1947 makes it an offence to spread religious or racial hatred. In 1961 an Act was passed 'to provide all . . . citizens equal opportunity for education, employment and access to public conveniences and accommodations' and creating a Civil Rights Commission.

FINANCE. In the fiscal year ending 30 June 1969 (US Census Bureau figures) general revenues were $1,448,647,000 ($881·7m. from taxes and $319,001,000 from federal aid). General expenditures were $1,451·73m. ($740,893,000 for education, $333,463,000 for highways and $71,367,000 for public welfare).

On 30 June 1969 net long-term debt amounted to $527·39m.; this was owed by subsidiary units, not by the state as such.

Per capita personal income (1969) was $3,691.

AGRICULTURE. Indiana is largely agricultural, about 77·5% of its total area being in farms. In 1969, 98,000 farms had 17·4m. acres (average, 178·5 acres). Cash income, 1969, from crops, $670·5m.; from livestock and products, $816·6m.

The chief crops (1969) were maize (446·02m. bu.), oats (19,706,000 bu.), soybeans (104,896,000 bu.), popcorn (114m. lb.), rye, barley, hay (alfalfa, clover, timothy), lespedeza seed, clover seed, apples, strawberries, tomatoes, watermelons and tobacco.

The livestock on 1 Jan. 1970 included 1,918,000 all cattle, 270,000 milch cows, 266,000 sheep and lambs, 4,499,000 swine, 18,167,000 chickens. In 1969 the wool clip yielded 1,921,000 lb. of wool from 247,000 sheep.

FORESTRY. The national forests area, 30 June 1969, was 149,065 acres; 12 state forests (1969) totalled 139,455 acres.

MINING (1968). The state has important coalfields and provided 83% of all building limestone used in US, and produced more face veneer than all the other states combined. In 1968 the output of coal was 18·49m. short tons; cement, 14·77m. bbls (of 376 lb.); petroleum, 8,692,000 bbls (of 42 gallons); stone, 26·31m. short tons. The total mineral output was valued at $235·4m.

INDUSTRY. Manufacturing establishments, numbering 6,920 in 1967, employed 543,600 production workers, earning $3,453·5m.; value added by manufacture was $10,308·7m. The steel industry is the third largest in the country. Production of pig-iron, 1968, was 12·48m. short tons. Refinery production, 1968, included 87·6m. bbls of petrol.

COMMUNICATIONS. In 1968 there were 6,807 miles of main railway. Of airports, 1970, 131 were publicly owned and 1 was military. In 1969 there were 703 miles of interstate highways; 157 miles, toll road; 10,329 miles, other state highways; 79,490 miles, county roads and city streets. Motor vehicles registered, 1969, 3,113,227.

BOOKS OF REFERENCE

The Indiana Year Book. Indianapolis
Statistical Report. State Board of Accounts. Indianapolis. Annual
Indiana State Chamber of Commerce. *Here is Your Indiana Government.* 13th ed. Indianapolis, 1967–68
Martin, J. B., *Indiana: an interpretation.* New York, 1947
STATE LIBRARY. Indiana State Library, 140 North Senate, Indianapolis 46204. *Director:* Miss Marcelle Foote.

IOWA

GOVERNMENT. Iowa, first settled in 1788, was made a Territory in 1838 and admitted into the Union on 28 Dec. 1846. The constitution of 1857 still exists; it has had 24 amendments. The General Assembly comprises a Senate of 59 and a House of Representatives of 124 members, meeting annually for an unlimited session. Senators are elected for 4 years, half retiring every second year; representatives for 2 years. The Governor and Lieut.-Governor are elected for 2 years. The state is represented in Congress by 2 senators and 7 representatives. Iowa is divided into 99 counties; the capital is Des Moines.

In the 1968 presidential election Nixon polled 619,106 votes, Humphrey 476,699 and Wallace 66,422.

Governor: Robert Ray (R.), 1971–74 ($30,000, plus $5,000 expenses).
Lieut.-Governor: Roger W. Jepsen (R.) ($80 per day).
Secretary of State: Melvin D. Synhorst (R.) ($18,000).

AREA AND POPULATION. Area, 56,290 sq. miles, including 258 sq. miles of inland water. Census population, 1 April 1960, 2,757,537, a decrease of 5·2% since 1950. Census (preliminary) population, 1 July 1970, 2·79m. Births, 1969, were 46,235 (17·2 per 1,000 population); deaths, 29,346 (10·7); infant death, 894 (18·9 per 1,000 live births); marriages, 24,686 (9); divorces, 6,923 (2·5).

Population in 4 census years (with distribution by sex, 1960) was:

	White	Negro	Indian	Asiatic	Total	Per sq. mile
1870	1,188,207	5,762	48	3	1,194,020	21·5
1930	2,452,677	17,380	660	222	2,470,939	44·1
1950	2,599,546	19,692	1,084	620	2,621,073	46·8
1960	2,729,286	25,354	1,708	1,022	2,757,537	49·2
Male	1,344,933	12,373	All others 1,741		1,359,047	—
Female	1,383,776	12,981	All others 1,733		1,398,490	—

At the census of 1960, 1,462,512 persons (53%) were urban (47·7% in 1950); 1,664,371 were 21 years of age or older; foreign-born whites numbered 55,422.

The largest cities in the state, with their census population in 1960, are: Des Moines (capital), 208,982 (urbanized area, 241,115); Cedar Rapids, 92,035; Sioux City, 89,159; Davenport, 88,981; Waterloo, 71,755; Dubuque, 56,606; Council Bluffs, 54,361; Ottumwa, 33,871; Clinton, 33,589; Iowa City, 33,443; Burlington, 32,430; Mason City, 30,642; Fort Dodge, 28,399.

RELIGION. Chief religious bodies in 1936 were: Roman Catholic (294,833 members), Methodist Episcopal (204,047), Lutheran (61,682), Disciples of Christ (60,973). Total, all denominations, 1,086,989. In 1951 the Society of Friends had 8,261 members.

EDUCATION. School attendance is compulsory for 24 consecutive weeks annually during school age (7–16). In 1969–70 of the 885,715 persons between the ages of 5 and 21 years, 659,882 were attending public schools; 79,031 pupils were enrolled in private and parochial schools. One non-high school district had 20 elementary pupils, 453 high school districts had 458,009 elementary and 191,705 secondary pupils. Teachers (1969–70) numbered 32,393 (includes area college teachers) with average salary of $8,075. Total expenditure on public schools in 1968–69 was $468,407,870. Leading institutions for higher education (1969–70) were:

Founded	Institution	Control	Professors and instructors	Students (full-time)
1847	University of Iowa, Iowa City	State	ʳ 797	20,604
1847	Grinnell College, Grinnell	Congregational	128	1,245
1852	Wartburg College, Waverly	—	93	1,374
1853	Cornell College, Mount Vernon	Methodist	91	933
1858	Iowa State University, Ames	State	1,695	19,620
1876	Univ. of Northern Iowa, Cedar Falls	State	417	8,419
1881	Drake University, Des Moines	Private	276	4,889
1881	Coe College, Cedar Rapids	Presbyterian	83	1,500
1894	Morningside College, Sioux City	Methodist	76	1,277

WELFARE. Iowa has a Civil Rights Act (1939) which makes it a misdemeanour for any place of public accommodation to deprive any person of 'full and equal enjoyment' of the facilities it offers the public.

Old-age assistance was established in 1934 for citizens 65 years of age or older; in Sept. 1970, 23,336 persons were drawing an average of $122.85 per month. Aid to dependent children, established 1944, was received by 19,800 families ($190.75 per family) representing 71,839 persons; aid to disabled was paid to 3,120 persons (average, $142.35); 1,172 recipients of aid to the blind averaged $122.70.

In 1969, the state had 147 hospitals (21,724 beds). On 30 June 1970 hospitals for mental diseases had 1,160 patients.

There is now no capital punishment in Iowa. State prisons, 30 June 1970, had 1,808 inmates.

FINANCE. For the year ending 30 June 1970 (State Comptroller's figures) general revenues were $1,221·4m. (taxation, $597·1m. and federal aid, $216·8m.). General expenditures were $1,202·98m. (education, $207·4m.; highways, $185·1m., and public welfare, $156·8m.).

On 30 June 1970 the net long-term debt was $9·1m.

Per capita personal income (1969) was $3,549.

AGRICULTURE. Iowa is the wealthiest of the agricultural states, partly because nearly the whole area (95·5%) is arable and included in farms. It has escaped large-scale commercial farming; in 1964 only 592 farms exceeded 1,000 acres. The average farm (in 1969) was 241 acres; in 1964, 43,050 farms were between 100 and 180 acres. Tenant-farmers owned (1969) 52·5% of the farm area.

In 1968, 147,000 farms had 34·5m. acres of farm land; in 1960, 154,329 farms were commercial farms, of which 125,137 had gross sales of more than $5,000; 91·7% of all farms had telephones and (1968) the number of tractors on farms was 284,922. About 9% of land in farms has suffered severe erosion.

The national forests area in 1969 was 360 acres.

Cash farm income (1969) was $3,788m. (second to California); from livestock, $2,858m. (leading all states), and from crops, $930m. Production of maize in 1969 was 922,768,000 bu. and of oats, 92m. bu. Commercial meat production in 1969 totalled a record 5,804·36m. lb. On 1 Jan. 1970 totals included swine, 13·95m. (leading all states); milch cows, 568,000; all cattle, 7,478,000 (second only to Texas), and sheep and lambs, 869,000. The wool clip (1969) yielded 6·15m. lb. of wool from 771,000 sheep.

MINING. The leading products by value are cement (14·6m. bbls in 1969) and stone (26·5m. short tons). Coalfields produced 902,911 tons in 1969. The value of mineral products, 1969, was $114·4m.

INDUSTRY. In 1969 manufacturing establishments (numbering 3,998) employed 164,500 production workers, with average weekly earnings of $137.96; value added by manufacture was $3,652·6m. in 1969.

COMMUNICATIONS. The state, 1969, had 11,234 miles of Class I railway, 245 miles of Class II railway and 34 miles of electric railway. On 1 Jan. 1970 the number of miles of state-maintained road was 110,386 miles; county maintained road, 90,375 miles, and municipal road, 11,533 miles. Airports (1970) numbered 230, including 122 municipal and 108 private and commercial.

BOOKS OF REFERENCE

City and Community Measurement: a statistical reference for 20 Iowa cities. 7th ed. City Council, Sioux City, 1965
Official Register. Secretary of State. Des Moines. Biennial
Federal Writer's Project. *Iowa: A Guide to the Hawkeye State.* New York, 1949
Petersen, W. J., *Iowa History Reference Guide.* Iowa City, 1952
Ross, R. M., *The government and administration of Iowa.* New York, 1957

IOWA STATE LAW LIBRARY, Des Moines 50319. *Librarian:* Geraldine Dunham.

KANSAS

GOVERNMENT. Kansas, first settled in 1727, was made a Territory (along with part of Colorado) in 1854, and was admitted into the Union with its present area on 29 Jan. 1861. That year saw the adoption of the present constitution; it has had 54 amendments. The Legislature includes a Senate of 40 members, elected for 4 years, and a House of Representatives of 125 members, elected for 2 years. Sessions are annual. The Governor and Lieut.-Governor are elected for 2 years. The right to vote is (with the usual exceptions) possessed by all citizens. The state is represented in Congress by 2 senators and 5 representatives.

The state was the first (of 42 states) to establish in 1933 a Legislative Council of 10 senators and 15 representatives to sit continuously between sessions for the study of legislative problems.

In the 1968 presidential election Nixon polled 478,674 votes, Humphrey 302,996 and Wallace 88,921.

The capital is Topeka. The state is divided into 105 counties.

Governor: Robert B Docking (D.), 1971–73 ($20,000).
Lieut.-Governor: James H. DeCoursey (R.) ($8,000).
Secretary of State: Elwill M. Shanahan (R.) ($12,650).

AREA AND POPULATION. Area, 82,264 sq. miles, including 216 sq. miles of inland water. Census population, 1 April 1960, 2,178,611, an increase of 14·3% since 1950; population, 1 Jan. 1969, as reported by county assessors, 2,287,302.

Provisional vital statistics, 1969: Births, 35,637 (15 per 1,000 population); deaths, 22,445 (9·8); infant deaths, 667 (20·1 per 1,000 live births); marriages, 22,395 (9·6); divorces, 8,020 (3·1).

Population in 4 federal census years (with distribution by sex, 1960) was:

	White	Negro	Indian	Asiatic	Total	Per sq. mile
1870	346,377	17,108	914	—	364,399	4·5
1930	1,811,997	66,344	2,454	204	1,880,999	22·9
1950	1,828,961	73,158	2,381	431	1,905,299	23·2
1960	2,078,666	91,445	5,069	2,271	2,178,611	26·3
Male	1,031,409	45,743	All others	4,225	1,081,377	—
Female	1,047,257	45,702		4,275	1,097,234	—

Of the total population in 1960, 1,328,741 were urban (61% compared with 52·1% in 1950). Households were 672,907. Those 21 years of age or older numbered 1,321,835; foreign-born whites numbered 31,098.

1969 estimates gave Wichita a population of 282,989; Kansas City, 169,978; Topeka (capital), 136,407; Hutchinson, 41,119; Salina, 39,013; Lawrence, 32,832; Leavenworth, 28,213; Manhattan, 24,796.

RELIGION. The most numerous religious bodies are Roman Catholic, with 157,292 adherents in 1936, Methodists (140,792), and Disciples of Christ (65,740). Total membership, all denominations, was 691,438.

EDUCATION. In 1968–69 the 330 organized school districts had, for grades 1 to 12, 521,947 enrolled pupils and 25,380 teachers for all 4 or more teacher schools. Teachers' salaries averaged $7,217.

Kansas has 6 state supported institutions of higher education: the University of Kansas, Lawrence, founded in 1865; Kansas State University of Agriculture and Applied Science, Manhattan (1863); Kansas State Teachers' College, Emporia (1865); Kansas State College of Pittsburg, Pittsburg (1903); Fort Hays State College, Hays (1901) and Wichita State University (1964), an associate of the University of Kansas. There is one municipal university, Washburn University, Topeka (1944).

WELFARE. In April 1970, 101,036 persons received assistance under programmes of aid to the aged, blind or disabled, aid to dependent children, general assistance, and medical assistance. Total payments amounted to $9,151,293. In 1969 the state had 165 hospitals (19,900 beds) listed by the American Hospital Association; psychiatric hospitals had an average daily census of 4,317.

There were 2,042 sentenced prisoners in state institutions, Dec. 1969. The death penalty (by hanging) for murder was abolished in 1907 and restored in 1935; there were no executions in 1968; total executions 1934 to 1968 have been 15 (all for murder).

For the various Civil Rights Acts forbidding racial or political discrimination, see THE STATESMAN'S YEAR-BOOK, 1955, p. 666. The 1965 Kansas Act against Discrimination declared that it is the policy of the state to eliminate and prevent discrimination in all employment relations, and to eliminate and prevent discrimination, segregation or separation in all places of public accommodations covered by the Act.

FINANCE. For the year ending 30 June 1969 (US Census Bureau figures) general revenue was $662,586,000, of which taxation furnished $385,077,000 and federal aid $170,205,000. General expenditures were $643,898,000 ($279·34m. for education, $131,743,000 for highways and $89,596,000 for public welfare).

Total net long-term debt, 30 June 1969, amounted to $236·4m.

Per capita personal income (1969) was $3,488.

AGRICULTURE. Kansas is pre-eminently agricultural, but sometimes suffers from lack of rainfall in the west. In 1969, 88,000 farms had an area of 50m. acres; average farm was 568 acres, value of lands and buildings (1959) $48,084; in 1959, 10,070 farms had 1,000 acres or more and 10,562 farms had 49 acres or less. The national grassland area, 30 June 1968, was 107,708 acres.

Cash income, 1969, from crops was $571·28m.; from livestock and products, $1,132·74m.; from government payments, $234·23m.

Kansas is a great wheat-producing state. Its output in 1969 was 305·3m. bu. Other crops in 1969 (in bushels) were maize, 91·5m.; grain sorghums, 182·9m.; soybeans, 19·6m.; oats, 6·08m.; barley, 6·11m.; rye, 1·12m. The state has an extensive livestock industry, comprising, on 1 Jan. 1970, 224,000 milch cows, 6,016,000 all cattle, 378,000 sheep and lambs and 1,643,000 swine. Wool clip (1969), 2,944,000 lb. from 352,000 sheep.

MINING. Production (1969, estimated): Coal, 1·31m. short tons; petroleum, 88·71m. bbls (of 42 gallons); natural gas, 888,038m. cu. ft; natural gas liquids, 27·15m. bbls (of 42 gallons); lead 395 short tons; zinc, 1,900 short tons. Total value of mineral products, $605m.

INDUSTRY. In 1967 there were 2,564 manufacturing establishments, 107,000 production workers earned $655m.; value added by manufacture was $2,108m. The slaughtering industry, manufacture of transportation equipment and petroleum refining are important.

COMMUNICATIONS. There were 7,864 miles of railway in 1968. There were 272 airports in 1969, of which 119 were public and 163 were private. The state maintained, 1969, 10,144 miles of highway.

BOOKS OF REFERENCE

Annual Economic Report of the Governor. Topeka
Directory of State Officers, Boards and Commissioners and Interesting Facts concerning Kansas. Topeka. Biennial
Drury, J. W., *The Government of Kansas.* Lawrence, Univ. of Kansas, 1970
Hornbaker, Allison L., *The Kansas mineral industry, 1967.* Lawrence, Univ. of Kansas, State Geological Survey, 1968
Howes, C. C., *This Place Called Kansas.* Univ. of Oklahoma, Norman, Okla., 1952
Zornow, W. F., *Kansas: a history of the Jayhawk State.* Norman, Okla., 1957

STATE LIBRARY. Kansas State Library, Topeka. *State Librarian:* Denny Stephens.

KENTUCKY

GOVERNMENT. Kentucky, first settled in 1765, was originally part of Virginia; it was admitted into the Union on 1 June 1792 and its first legislature met on 4 June. The constitution dates from 1891; there had been 3 preceding it. The 1891 constitution was promulgated by convention and provides that amendments be submitted to the electorate for ratification. The General Assembly consists of a Senate of 38 members elected for 4 years, one-half retiring every 2 years, and a House of Representatives of 100 members elected for 2 years. Sessions are biennial. The Governor and Lieut.-Governor are elected for 4 years. All citizens are (with necessary exceptions) qualified as electors; the voting age was in 1955 reduced from 21 to 18 years. There is no official state register of voters maintained, hence the size of the electorate is unknown; there were 1,042,636 voters in the presidential election of 1968; Nixon polled 462,411 votes, Humphrey 397,541 and Wallace 193,098.

The state is represented in Congress by 2 senators and 7 representatives.
The capital is Frankfort. The state is divided into 120 counties.

Governor: Louie B. Nunn (R.), 1967–71 ($30,000).
Lieut.-Governor: Wendell H. Ford (D.), 1967–71 ($20,000).
Secretary of State: Leila F. Begley (R.) ($18,000).

AREA AND POPULATION. Area, 40,395 sq. miles, of which 532 sq. miles are water. Census population, 1970, 3,160,555, an increase of 4% since 1960. Births in 1968, 56,435 (17·7 per 1,000 population); deaths, 32,958 (10·3); infant deaths, 1,232 (21·8 per 1,000 live births); marriages, 32,499 (10·2); divorces, 6,854 (2).

Population in 4 census years (with distribution by sex, 1960) was:

	White	Negro	Indian	Asiatic	Total	Per sq. mile
1910	2,027,951	261,656	234	64	2,289,905	57·0
1930	2,388,452	226,040	22	75	2,614,589	65·2
1950	2,742,090	201,921	234	561	2,944,806	73·9
1960	2,820,083	215,949	391	1,298	3,038,156	75·6
Male	1,401,904	105,547	All others	997	1,508,488	—
Female	1,418,179	110,402	All others	1,127	1,529,708	—

Of the total population in 1960, 1,353,215 (44·5%) were urban (36·8% in 1950). Those 21 years old or older numbered 1,763,644; foreign-born whites numbered 15,726.

The principal cities, with census population in 1970 are: Louisville, 356,982 (urbanized area, 819,057); Lexington, 107,944; Covington, 52,016; Owensboro, 49,751; Paducah, 31,100; Ashland, 28,278; Newport, 25,900; Frankfort (capital), 20,054.

RELIGION. The chief religious denominations in 1960 were: Baptists (Southern and National), with 650,000 members, Roman Catholic (225,000), Methodists (220,000) and Disciples of Christ (136,500). Total, all denominations, about 1,345,000.

EDUCATION. Attendance at school between the ages of 7 and 15 years (inclusive) is compulsory, the normal term being 9½ months. In 1969–70, 17,978 teachers were employed in public elementary and 10,434 in secondary schools, in which 504,137 and 199,575 pupils enrolled respectively. Expenditure on elementary and high school education in 1969–70 was $446·7m.; teachers' salaries (1969) averaged $7,220 in elementary and $7,880 in secondary schools.

The state has 7 universities, 15 senior colleges, 17 junior colleges and 14 community colleges, with a total of 91,258 students. Of these universities and colleges, 22 are state-supported, and the remainder are supported privately. The largest of the institutions of higher learning are (1969): University of Kentucky, with 26,308 students, 1,240 teachers; University of Louisville, 9,057 students, 340 teachers; Western Kentucky University, 11,069 students, 518 teachers; Eastern Kentucky University, 9,664 students, 462 teachers; Murray State University, 7,255 students, 397 teachers; Morehead State University, 6,460 students, 333 teachers. Three of the several privately endowed colleges of standing are Berea College, Berea; Centre College, Danville, and Bellarmine–Ursuline College, Louisville.

WELFARE. In Oct. 1970, a total of 220,560 persons received financial assistance; 63,198 of these persons were 65 years of age or over and received an average monthly payment of $54.73; 2,109 needy blind persons received an average monthly payment of $74.11; and 17,099 permanently and totally disabled persons aged 18–64 received an average of $73.84. The remaining 138,154 (99,434 children and 38,720 adults) were members of 37,295 families who received an average of $113.20 per family. From Dec. 1970, persons residing in personal care homes receive $164, $149 or $139 depending upon classification of the home.

In addition to money payments, medical care services are available to all grant recipients as well as an additional 90,800 persons eligible for medical care only. During an average month, approximately 42% of those eligible utilize the programme. The average monthly cost for those receiving services is approximately $36.

In 1968 the state had 127 general hospitals (12,236 beds), 8 hospitals for mental diseases (5,514 beds), 8 tuberculosis hospitals (1,099 beds) and 4 children's hospitals (354 beds).

There are 3 penal institutions for men, and a reformatory for women. Juvenile offenders are placed in custody of the Department of Child Welfare, which maintains 6 institutions and 3 forestry camps.

In 1969–70 the prisons had an average of 2,791 inmates. There has been no execution since 1962. Total executions, 1911–62, were 162, including 76 whites and 86 Negroes; 144 were for murder, 13 for rape, 5 for armed robbery.

FINANCE. For the fiscal year ending 30 June 1970 general revenues were $917·1m. (federal grants, $221·3m., and taxes, $695·8m.) and general expenditures, $1,179m. (education, $477·3m.; public welfare, $260·2m.; highways, $312·8m.).

The total net long-term debt on 30 June 1968 was $1,119·5m.

Per capita personal income (1969) was $2,850.

AGRICULTURE. In 1969, 130,000 farms had an area of 16·9m. acres. The average farm was 130 acres.

Cash income, 1968, from crops, $379·61m., and from livestock, $445,201,000. The chief crop is tobacco: production, in 1968, 413·95m. lb., ranking second to N. Carolina in US. Other principal crops include corn, hay, soybeans, wheat, lespedeza seed, fescue seed, popcorn, barley, peaches and apples.

Soil erosion has been severe on 11,724,735 acres (45·6% of the total) and moderate on 12,613,103 acres (40·1%).

The Watershed Conservancy District Law, 1958 (the first of its kind in the US), allows funds to be raised to secure easements and rights of way, and to maintain the improvement works financed by the federal government: 46 watershed conservancy districts have been organized.

Stock-raising is important in Kentucky, which has long been famous for its horses. The livestock on 1 Jan. 1969 included 400,000 milch cows, 2,748,000 all cattle, 112,000 sheep, 1,361,000 swine and (1960) 155,000 horses and mules.

FORESTRY. National forests area, 1968, 535,255 acres. Total commercial forest land, 1968, 11,712,800 acres; almost 93% is owned by 243,000 individuals.

MINING (1968). The principal mineral product of Kentucky is coal, 98·7m. tons mined. Output of petroleum, 14·08m. bbls (of 42 gallons); natural gas, 93,100m. cu. ft; fluorspar, 29,000 short tons; clay, 1·1 short tons. Total value of mineral products produced in 1968 was $526,037,000.

INDUSTRY. In 1969 the state's 3,000 manufacturing plants had 247,000 production workers earning $1,695m.; value added by manufacture (1967) was $3,638m. The leading manufacturing industries (by census groups) are electrical equipment, apparel, foods, machinery (except electrical), fabricated metal products, chemicals, tobacco.

COMMUNICATIONS. In 1969 there were 3,838 miles of railway. There is an increasing amount of barge traffic on 1,374 miles of navigable rivers. There were 58 airports in 1969, of which 51 were public (7 commercial), 4 private and 3 military. In 1969 the state controlled 24,833 miles of road; local, 40,669 miles, and municipal authorities, 3,995 miles. There were, 1968, 1,671,044 motor vehicle registrations (excluding motor cycles).

BOOKS OF REFERENCE

Deskbook of Kentucky Economic Statistics. 7th ed. Department of Commerce, Frankfort, 1968
Directory for the Use of Courts, State and County Officials and General Assembly of the State of Kentucky. Frankfort. Biennial
Federal Writers' Project, *Kentucky: A Guide to the Bluegrass State.* Rev. ed. New York, 1954
Coleman, J. W., *A Bibliography of Kentucky History.* Univ. of Kentucky, Lexington, 1949
Schwendeman, J. R., *Geography of Kentucky.* Oklahoma City, 1958

LOUISIANA

GOVERNMENT. Louisiana was first settled in 1699. That part lying east of the Mississippi River was organized in 1804 as the Territory of New Orleans, and admitted into the Union on 30 April 1812. The section west of the river was added very shortly thereafter. The present constitution dates from 1921; it has had 439 amendments.

The Legislature consists of a Senate of 39 members and a House of Representatives of 105 members, both chosen for 4 years. Sessions are annual; a fiscal session is held in odd years. The Governor and Lieut.-Governor are elected for 4 years. A Governor may serve a second consecutive term. Qualified electors are (with the usual exceptions) all registered citizens with the usual residential qualifications.

In the 1968 presidential election Nixon polled 257,535 voters, Humphrey 309,615 and Wallace 530,300.

The state sends to Congress 2 senators and 8 representatives. Louisiana is divided into 64 parishes (corresponding with the counties of other states).

The capital is Baton Rouge.

Governor: John J. McKeithen (D.), 1968–72 ($28,374).
Lieut.-Governor: C. C. Aycock (D.) ($24,329).
Secretary of State: Wade O. Martin, Jr (D.) ($26,529).

AREA AND POPULATION. Area, 48,523 sq. miles, including 3,417 sq. miles of inland water. Census population, 1 April 1960, 3,257,022, an increase of 21·4% since 1950. Estimated population, 31 March 1969, 3,714,658. Births, 1968, 73,834 (20·1 per 1,000 population); deaths, 34,137 (9); infant deaths, 1,868 (26·4 per 1,000 live births); marriages, 31,639 (9); divorces, 3,130.

Population in 4 census years (with distribution by sex, 1960) was:

	White	Negro	Indian	Asiatic	Total	Per sq. mile
1910	941,086	713,874	780	648	1,656,388	36·5
1930	1,322,712	776,326	1,536	1,019	2,101,593	46·5
1950	1,796,683	882,428	409	3,996	2,683,516	59·4
1960	2,211,715	1,039,207	3,587	2,004	3,257,022	72·2
Male	1,090,306	498,758	All others	3,190	1,592,254	—
Female	1,121,409	540,449		2,190	1,664,768	—

Of the 1960 total, 2,060,606 (63·3%) were urban (54·8% in 1950); those 21 years of age or older were 1,803,805; foreign-born whites numbered 28,668.

The largest cities with their 1960 census population and (in parentheses) 1969 estimated population are: New Orleans, 627,525 (690,521); Shreveport, 164,372 (185,257); Baton Rouge (capital), 152,419 (173,560); Lake Charles, 63,392 (72,990); Monroe, 52,219 (61,070); Lafayette, 40,400 (49,691); Alexandria, 40,279 (46,291); Bossier City, 32,776 (39,305). Population of major urbanized areas (1960 census) was: New Orleans, 845,237; Shreveport, 208,583; Baton Rouge, 193,485.

RELIGION. The Roman Catholic Church is the largest denomination in Louisiana, with 1,231,378 white and Negro members in 1964. The leading Protestant Churches are Baptist, with 430,557 white members; Methodist, 123,155; Episcopal, 28,095, and Presbyterian, 32,123.

EDUCATION. Attendance in elementary schools was, until 1956, compulsory between the ages of 7 and 15, both inclusive; but in 1956 the Legislature exempted any school faced with desegregation by court order, and the constitution was amended, giving the Legislature sole control over segregation. In 1960 token integration was enforced in 2 New Orleans primary schools. In 1967–68 there were 1,029 public elementary and high schools for whites which had 23,209 teachers and 525,813 pupils; for Negroes there were 468 public schools (13,110 Negro teachers) with 337,225 pupils. In 1967–68 instructional staff had an average salary of $6,979. There are 10 four-year-endowed colleges and universities and 27 state trade schools. Total expenditure on elementary and secondary schools (1967–68), $421,917,357. Superior instruction is given in the Louisiana State University (founded 1860), with, 1968, 1,968 professors and 25,079 students. Tulane University (1835) in New Orleans had 2,045 professors and 8,325 students in 1968. This university has state support to the extent of the remission of certain taxes. The Roman Catholic Loyola University (1911) at New Orleans had 364 professors and 4,334 students in 1968. Dillard University in New Orleans (with 944 students and 67 professors) and Southern University in Baton Rouge (with 7,250 students and 399 professors) are for Negroes.

WELFARE. In June 1969, 120,049 persons were receiving old-age assistance to an average of $69.49 per month; 40,933 families with dependent children were receiving an average of $103.04 per month; 2,425 blind persons, $76.87 per month; 22,044 totally disabled persons, $53.72.

In 1968 the state had 165 accredited hospitals and clinics (22,265 beds); 3 mental hospitals cared for 17,712 patients.

Prisons, on 30 June 1968, had 4,300 inmates.

In 1968 there was no execution; total executions by electrocution since 1930 were 135 (30 whites and 105 Negroes—including 17 Negroes for rape).

Statutes require the separation of whites and Negroes in all educational institutions, mental hospitals and penal institutions. Children may not be adopted save by persons of the same race. Marriage is prohibited between any white or Indian persons and any coloured person.

FINANCE. For the fiscal year ending 30 June 1968 (Louisiana Division Administration figures) general revenues were $1,346,959,985 (taxation, $969,455,546, and federal aid, $377,504,439); general expenditures were $1,315,914,680 (education, $507,853,157; highways, $223,990,555, and public welfare, $239,772,291).

Per capita personal income (1969) was $2,780.

AGRICULTURE. The state is divided into two parts, the uplands and the alluvial and swamp regions of the coast. A delta occupies about one-third of the total area. Manufacturing is the leading industry, but agriculture is important. In 1964, 62,466 farms had an area of 10,411,045 acres; average farm had 166·7 acres and was valued at $40,859; 31,890 farms (51·1%) were less than 50 acres; tenant-farmers numbered 12,151 (32·5%).

Cash income, 1968, from crops, $435m.; from livestock, $201m. Production of sugar-cane was 7·6m. tons in 1968; sugar-cane syrup, 1,881m. gallons; rice, 22m. bags (of 100 lb.); maize, 5·8m. bu.; sweet potatoes, 4·2m. cwt; soybeans, 37m. bu.; pecans, 17,000m. lb.; cotton, 540,000 bales (of 500 lb.); strawberries, 11·7m. lb. On 1 Jan. 1969 the state contained 198,000 milch cows, 1·72m. all cattle, 26,000 sheep and 196,000 swine.

FORESTRY. Forests, 16m. acres, represent 56% of the state's area. Income from forest production and manufacturing enterprises totalled $740m. in 1960. In 1968 pulpwood cut, 2,301,515 cords; sawtimber cut, 1,054,267,609 bd ft.

MINING. Louisiana is second only to Texas as a petroleum-producing state. The yield in 1968 of crude petroleum, including condensate petroleum, was 817m. bbls; natural gas, 6·4m. cu. ft. Rich sulphur mines are found in the state, and wells for the extraction of sulphur by means of hot water and compressed air are in operation; output, 1968, 4,073,000 long tons. Output of salt (1968) was 10·98m. short tons. Total mineral output in 1968 was valued at $4,300m. ranking second in the US.

INDUSTRY. The manufacturing industries are chiefly those associated with petroleum, chemicals, lumber, food, paper. In 1968 manufacturing establishments employed 176,431 workers, who earned $1,236,860,160; value added by manufacture (1967) was $2,728m.

COMMUNICATIONS. The state has ample facilities for traffic, having besides more than 49,000 miles of public roads, the Mississippi and other waterways, with 7,500 miles of navigable water. In 1968 the railways in the state had a length of 4,316 miles on main-line railways. There were, 1968, 161 commercial and military airports. New Orleans is the second largest seaport of the US, handling some 10% of the national total. In 1968, 1,314,226 automobiles were registered in the state.

BOOKS OF REFERENCE

Louisiana: history and government. Legislative Council, Baton Rouge, 1964
Havard, W. C., *Government of Louisiana*. Baton Rouge, 1959
Landry, S. O. (ed.), *Louisiana Almanac and Fact Book*. New Orleans, 1952
Smith, T. L., and Hitt, H. L., *The People of Louisiana*. Baton Rouge, 1952
Scroggs, W. O., *The Story of Louisiana*. 4th ed. Indianapolis, 1953

MAINE

GOVERNMENT. After a first attempt in 1607, Maine was settled in 1623. From 1652 to 1820 it was part of Massachusetts and was admitted into the Union on 15 March 1820. The constitution of 1820 is still in force, but it has been amended 89 times. In 1951 and 1955 the Legislature approved recodifications of the constitution as arranged by the Chief Justice under special authority.

The Legislature consists of the Senate with 32 members and the House of Representatives with 151 members, both Houses being elected simultaneously for 2 years. Apart from these legislators and the Governor (elected for 4 years), no other state officers are elected. An Executive Council of 7, which meets at the call of the Governor, has effective powers of approval or veto in many matters. The Justices of the Supreme Judicial Court give their opinion upon important questions of law and upon solemn occasions when required by the Governor, Council, Senate or House of Representatives. The suffrage is possessed by all citizens, 21 years of age, who can read English and write their own names; persons under guardianship for reasons of mental illness have no vote. Indians residing on tribal reservations and otherwise qualified have the vote in all county, state and national elections, but retain the right to elect their own tribal representative to the legislature.

In the 1968 presidential election Nixon polled 169,254 votes, Humphrey 217,312 and Wallace 6,370.

The state sends to Congress 2 senators and 2 representatives.

The capital is Augusta. The state is divided into 16 counties.

Governor: Kenneth M. Curtis (D.), 1971–74 ($20,000).
Secretary of State: Joseph T. Edgar (R.), 1969–71 ($15,000).

AREA AND POPULATION. Area, 33,215 sq. miles, of which 2,282 are inland waters. Of the state's total area (21,257,600 acres), about 17·2m. acres (87%) are in timber and wood lots. Census population, 1 April 1960, 969,265, an increase of 6·1% since 1950. Estimated population, 1 Jan. 1969, 1,004,000. In 1968, live births numbered 16,854 (17·2 per 1,000 population); deaths, 11,097 (11·3); marriages, 10,179 (10·4); divorces, 3,091 (3·2); infant deaths, 359 (21·3 per 1,000 live births).

Population for 4 census years (with distribution by sex, 1960):

	White	Negro	Indian	Asiatic	Total	Per sq. mile
1910	739,995	1,363	892	121	742,371	24·8
1930	795,185	1,096	1,012	130	797,423	25·7
1950	910,846	1,221	1,522	185	913,774	29·4
1960	963,291	3,318	1,879	597	969,265	31·3
Male	475,682	2,045	All others 1,327		479,054	—
Female	487,609	1,273	All others 1,329		490,211	—

The urban population was 514,000 or 51·9% of the total (51·3% in 1960); those 21 years or older numbered 575,000, foreign-born whites, 59,523.

The largest city in the state is Portland with a census population of 72,566 in 1960. Other cities (with population in 1960) are: Lewiston, 40,804; Bangor, 38,912; Auburn, 24,449; South Portland, 22,788; Augusta (capital), 21,680; Biddeford, 19,255; Waterville, 18,695.

RELIGION. The largest religious bodies are: Roman Catholic (270,283 members), Baptists (36,808 members) and Congregationalists (40,750 members), and other Christian Churches (34,066 members).

EDUCATION. Education is free for pupils from 5 to 21 years of age, and compulsory from 7 to 17. In 1968–69 the 801 public elementary schools had 7,145 teachers and 170,101 enrolled pupils. The 161 public secondary schools had 3,472 teachers and 63,034 pupils. In 1968–69 there were 87 private elementary schools with 687 teachers and 16,309 pupils, and 41 private secondary schools with 707 teachers and 9,065 pupils. Public school teachers' salaries, 1968–69, averaged $7,288. Total public expenditure on public elementary and secondary education in 1967–68, $113,862,391.

The State University of Maine, founded in 1865, had (1968–69) 853 professors and teachers and 13,756 students at Augusta, Orono and Portland and 5 other locations; Bowdoin College, founded in 1794 at Brunswick, had 119 professors and 960 students; Bates College at Lewiston, 74 professors and 985 students, Colby College at Waterville, 133 professors and 1,608 students, and Nasson College at Springvale, 67 professors and 909 students.

WELFARE. Aid to the aged, blind or disabled (maximum $115 per month, excluding hospital and nursing-home care) is granted to needy persons age 16 or over. In April 1969, 10,114 aged persons (out of 112,000 aged 65 or over) were receiving assistance at an average of $59.05 per month; 212 were receiving blind assistance ($84.16) and 3,156 disabled under the age of 65 were receiving assistance ($87.14). Aid to families with dependent children was being granted to 7,737 families (20,237 children) who received an average of $109.20 per family. Payments under Medical Assistance Programme April 1969 totalled $912,068. Child welfare services include basic child protective services, foster home placements, adoptions; services in divorce cases and licensing of foster homes.

In June 1969 the state had 66 non-federal hospitals (7,560 beds); 61 acute general hospitals (4,350 beds); 4 hospitals for mental diseases (3,122 beds), and 1 hospital for tuberculosis control (88 beds).

The state's penal system on 30 June 1969 held 556 men and 52 women (61 per 100,000 population); reform schools (juvenile training centres) had 249 boys and 126 girls. There is no capital punishment. Inmates serving life sentences are eligible for parole consideration after 30 years, less remission for good conduct.

FINANCE. For the financial year ending 30 June 1968 total general revenue was $249,913,000 and expenditure was $168,877,000.

Total net long-term debt on 30 June 1968 was $168,877,000.

Per capita personal income (1969) was $3,039.

AGRICULTURE. In 1964, 12,875 farms occupied 2,590,022 acres, of which 894,206 acres were crop land; the average farm was 201·2 acres, with land and buildings valued at $19,979. All farms were owner-operated except 274 operated by tenants and 127 by managers. Commercial farms, 1968 (ones with annual gross sale of product of $2,500 or more) numbered 5,500 with a total acreage of 1,665,000; of this total there were 57 corporation farms with a total of 92,000 acres.

Cash income, 1968, $8,209·81m. Maine is a large producer of potatoes (about one-eighth of the country's total); output in 1968 was 39·9m. cwt. Other crops include sugar-beet, sweet corn, peas and beans, oats, hay, apples and blueberries. On 1 Jan. 1969 the farm animals included 76,000 milch cows, 147,000 all cattle, 17,000 sheep, 9,000 swine.

FORESTRY. Lumber, wood turnings and pulp are important. In 1968 the cut of softwood was 451m. bd ft; hardwood, 188m. bd ft, and pulpwood, 2,798,465 cords. Spruce and fir, white pine, hemlock, white and yellow birch, sugar maple, northern white cedar, beech and red oak are the most important species cut. There are 17,169,000 acres of commercial forest (98% in private ownership). National forests comprise 50,000 acres; other federal, 16,000 acres; state forests, 64,000 acres; municipal, 75,000 acres.

Wood products industries are of economic importance in two-fifths of the state's communities. There are about 800 wood-using plants in the state.

FISHERIES. In 1968, 218,730,096 lb. of fish and shellfish (valued at $25,613,569 were landed; the catch included 20,501,732 lb. of lobsters (valued at $14,931,671). 1,637,415 cases (100 cans per case) of sardines were packed.

MINING. Minerals include sand and gravel, 11,866,000 short tons in 1968; granite, 1·2m. short tons; cement (Portland and masonry) and fire clay, copper, feldspar, peat, silver and zinc, $8·5m. Mineral output, 1968, was valued at $17·81m.

INDUSTRY. In 1968, 2,054 manufacturing establishments reported 120,726 production workers, earning $664·4m., gross value of production, $2,277·2m. Leading industry is paper with 50 plants, 17,036 workers and output valued at $610m. (26·9% of the state's total manufactures). In 1968 income from tourism exceeded $400m.

COMMUNICATIONS. On 31 Dec. 1968 there were 2,490 miles of railway tracks operated (main tracks, 1,756 miles). In 1968 there were 21,309 miles of roads, of which 3,877 miles were state highways and 7,608 miles state-aided. Commercially licensed airports, 1969, numbered 37, of which 26 were municipal (including 3 international), 3 county and 1 state; there were 2 military airports, 77 private landing strips, 13 licensed commercial seaplane bases (1 municipal) and 27 registered non-commercial seaplane bases. In 1968, 489,701 automobiles were registered.

BOOKS OF REFERENCE

Maine Register, State Year-Book and Legislative Manual. Portland. Annual
Rich, L., State of Maine. New York, 1964
Rowe, W. H., Maritime History of Maine. New York, 1948
Starkey, G., Maine: Its History, Resources and Government. 1947

MARYLAND

GOVERNMENT. Maryland, first settled in 1634, was one of the 13 original states. The present constitution dates from 1867; it has had 125 amendments. The General Assembly consists of a Senate of 43, and a House of Delegates of 142 members, both elected for 4 years. Voters are citizens who have the usual residential qualifications.

At the 1968 presidential election Nixon polled 517,995 votes, Humphrey 538,310 and Wallace 178,734.

Maryland sends to Congress 2 senators and 8 representatives.

The state capital is Annapolis. The state is divided into 23 counties and Baltimore City.

Governor: Marvin Mandel (D.), 1971–73 ($25,000).
Lieut.-Governor: Blair Lee, III (D.), 1971 ($24,000).
Secretary of State: Fred L. Wineland.

AREA AND POPULATION. Area, 10,577 sq. miles, of which 703 sq. miles are inland water; in addition, water area under Maryland jurisdiction in Chesapeake Bay amounts to 2,373 sq. miles. Census population, 1 April 1960, 3,100,689. an increase since 1950 of 757,688 or 32·3%. Estimated population, 1 July 1970, 3,914,000. In 1968 births were 68,407 (18·2 per 1,000 population); deaths, 32,596 (8·9); infant deaths, 1,473 (21·5 per 1,000 live births); marriages, 51,145 (..); divorces, 8,151.

Population for 4 federal censuses (with distribution by sex, 1960) was:

	White	Negro	Indian	Asiatic	Total	Per sq. mile
1920	1,204,737	244,479	32	413	1,449,661	145·8
1930	1,354,226	276,379	50	871	1,631,526	165·0
1950	1,954,975	385,972	314	1,084	2,343,001	237·1
1960	2,573,919	518,410	1,538	5,700	3,100,689	314·0
Male	1,273,444	255,316	All others 4,440		1,533,200	—
Female	1,300,475	263,094		3,920	1,567,489	—

Of the total population in 1960, 2,254,000 persons (72·7%) were urban (69% in 1950); those 21 years old or older numbered 1,845,067; foreign-born whites, 89,975.

The largest city in the state (containing 23% of the population of the state) is Baltimore, with 899,500 in 1969; population of metropolitan areas around Baltimore and Washington, D.C., was 3.258,200. Maryland residents in the Washington, D.C., metropolitan area total more than 1m.; Annapolis (capital), 32,000.

RELIGION. Maryland was the first US state to give religious freedom to all who came within its borders. Present religious affiliations of the population are approximately: Protestant, 32%; Roman Catholic, 24%; Jewish, 10%; remaining 34% is non-related and other faiths.

EDUCATION. Education is compulsory from 6 to 16 years of age. In Sept. 1969 the public elementary schools (including kindergartens and secondary schools) had 891,981 pupils. Teachers in the elementary schools numbered 22,368; secondary schools had 21,948 teachers. Average salary of principals and teachers in elementary and secondary schools (1969–70) was $9,885. Current expenditure by local school boards on education, 1968–69, was $647·6m., of which the state's contribution was $213,853,000.

In 1969 there were 31 degree-granting 4-year institutions and 18 2-year colleges. The largest two were the University of Maryland system, with 48,203 students (Sept. 1969) and Johns Hopkins University with 9,983 students (Sept. 1969).

SOCIAL SERVICES. Under the supervision of the State Department of Public Welfare, local social service departments administer public assistance for needy persons. In June 1970, 8,338 persons were receiving old-age assistance, with an average of $58·56 per month; 7,573 families were receiving general public assistance, with an average of $85.75; 355 needy blind, $89·26; 15,984 persons permanently and totally disabled, $79.05; 36,708 families, $158.86 per family, in respect of 105,768 dependent children; foster care of 10,456 children; nursing home care for 1,551 persons with an average of $311.73 per month.

In July 1970, 70 hospitals (26,635 beds) were licensed by the State Department of Health.

The Maryland State Department of Health, organized in 1874, performs its functions through its central office, 23 county health departments and the Baltimore City Health Department. The state legislature appropriated $138,637,037 for 1971, which included $8,987,382 from the federal government and $12,638,941 from the local governments. From the appropriation $8,803,099 was for operating expenses of 3 chronic disease-rehabilitation hospitals with 1,063 beds, and $3,755,468 for operating expenses of 2 tuberculosis hospitals with 565 beds.

During 1970 Maryland's programme of medical care for indigent and medically indigent patients covered an average of 277,699 persons. The programme, which covers inpatient and outpatient hospital services, laboratory services, skilled nursing home care, physician services, pharmacy services, dental services and home health services, cost $74·18m.

Prisons on 30 June 1970 had 5,613 men and 130 women; the total equalled 149 per 100,000 population, a high rate, which may be explained by the fact that Maryland incarcerates domestic relations law violators in state prisons; state prisons also receive a considerable number of persons committed for misdemeanours by magistrates' courts of the counties as well as from Baltimore's court system.

There was no execution in fiscal year 1970; since 1930 there have been 68 executions (by lethal gas since 1957; earlier by hanging)—7 whites and 37 Negroes for murder, and 6 whites and 18 Negroes for rape. Last execution was June 1961.

Maryland's prison system has conducted a work-release programme for selected prisoners since 1963.

In accordance with the 1950 Supreme Court decisions declaring segregation unconstitutional, the University of Maryland and other public and private colleges admitted Negro students in Sept. 1956. Elementary and secondary schools accept the ruling, and gradual integration is under way in all counties under different methods.

FINANCE. For the fiscal year ending 30 June 1970 (US Census Bureau figures) general revenues were $835,456,970 ($803,734,937 from taxation, $153,317,252 from federal receipts). General expenditures, $778,296,795, including $540,434,391 for education and $143,660,145 for public welfare; special fund expenditures, $449,423,645 for highways.

Total long-term state debt, 30 June 1969, was $562,181,000.

Per capita personal income (1969) was $4,095.

AGRICULTURE. Agriculture is an important industry in the state. In 1970 there were approximately 17,900 farms with an area of 3·2m. acres (51% of the land area); about 84% of the farms were owner operated.

Farm animals, 1 Jan. 1970, were: Milch cows, 182,000; all cattle, 426,000; swine, 192,000; sheep and lambs, 20,000; chickens (not broilers), 2,029,000. The most important crops, 1969, were: Maize, 39m. bu.; soybeans, 6·8m. bu.; tobacco, 30m. lb., and hay, 665,000 tons.

Cash receipts from farm marketings, 1969, were $389m.; from livestock and livestock products, $265m., and crops, $124m. Dairy products and broilers accounted for 51·7% of cash receipts in 1969.

MINING. Value of mineral production, 1969, was $80·7m. Sand and gravel (12·5m. short tons) and stone (14·9m. short tons) account for over 51·1% of the total value. Stone is the leading mineral commodity by value followed by Portland cement, sand and gravel and coal. Output of coal was 1·4m. short tons, valued at $5·7m. Natural gas is produced from 2 fields in Garrett County; 980m. cu. ft in 1969. A third gas field in the same county has recently been converted to gas storage.

INDUSTRY. In 1969 Maryland manufactories had 205,700 production workers earning $1,210m.; value added by manufacture was $3,791m. Chief industries are food and kindred products, primary metal products, transportation equipment, chemicals and products, electrical and other machinery.

TOURISM. Tourism is one of the state's leading industries. In 1969 tourists spent over $300m.

COMMUNICATIONS. The state highway department maintained, 1 Jan. 1970, 5,154 miles of highways, of which 70 miles were toll roads. The 23 counties maintained 15,415 miles of highways, and the 159 municipalities (including the city of Baltimore) maintained 3,663 miles of streets and alleys. Total mileage, 1 Jan. 1970, of public highways, streets and alleys, 24,232 miles. In 1969, 1,860,884 automobiles were registered. Railways, in 1968, had 1,122 miles of line. There were, 1969, 43 commercially licensed airports. In 1970 Baltimore was the fourth largest US seaport in foreign waterborne trade.

BOOKS OF REFERENCE

STATISTICAL INFORMATION. Division of Economic Development, Maryland Department of Economic and Community Development, Annapolis, 21401. *Director:* William A. Pate.

Maryland Manual: A Compendium of Legal, Historical and Statistical Information relating to the State of Maryland. Annapolis. Biennial

STATE LIBRARY. Maryland State Library, Annapolis. *Director:* Nelson J. Molter.

MASSACHUSETTS

GOVERNMENT. The first permanent settlement within the borders of the present state was made at Plymouth in Dec. 1620, by the Pilgrims from Holland, who were separatists from the English Church, and formed the nucleus of the Plymouth Colony. In 1628 another company of Puritans settled at Salem, forming eventually the Massachusetts Bay Colony. In 1630 Boston was settled. In the struggle which ended in the separation of the American colonies from the mother country, Massachusetts took the foremost part, and in 1780 adopted its present constitution (89 amendments since adopted) and on 6 Feb. 1788 became the sixth state to ratify the US constitution.

The legislative body, styled the General Court of the Commonwealth of Massachusetts, meets annually, and consists of the Senate with 40 members, elected biennially, and the House of Representatives of 240 members, elected for 2 years in 175 districts, each of which returns 1, 2 or 3 representatives according to the number of legal voters. The Governor and Lieut.-Governor are elected for 4 years. The state sends 2 senators and 12 representatives to Congress.

At the 1968 presidential election Nixon polled 766,844 votes, Humphrey 1,469,218 and Wallace 87,088.

Electors are all adult citizens, with the usual residential qualifications, who can read and write the English language; excluded are paupers and those under guardianship.

The capital is Boston. The state has 14 counties, 39 cities and 312 towns.

Governor: Francis W. Sargent (R.), 1971–74 (salary, $35,000).
Lieut.-Governor:
Secretary of the Commonwealth: John F. X. Davoren (D.) ($20,000).

AREA AND POPULATION. Area, 8,257 sq. miles, 390 sq. miles being inland water (the state government puts the area at 8,093 sq. miles, including 254 sq. miles of water). The census population 1 April 1960 was 5,149,317, an increase of 458,803 or 8·9% since 1950; population estimate, 1 July 1967, 5,403,000. Births, 1967, were 100,925 (18·6 per 1,000 population); deaths, 59,116 (10·9 per 1,000); infant deaths (1966), 2,070 (20·5 per 1,000 live births); marriages, 40,977 (7·6); divorces (1965), 7,848 (1·5).

Population at 4 federal census years (with distribution by sex, 1960):

	White	Negro	Indian	Asiatic	Total	Per sq. mile
1910	3,324,926	38,055	688	2,747	3,366,416	418·8
1930	4,192,992	52,365	874	3,383	4,249,614	537·4
1950	4,611,503	73,171	5,840		4,690,514	596·2
1960	5,023,144	111,842	13,592		5,148,578	654·5
Male	2,423,947	54,748	All others	7,540	2,486,235	—
Female	2,599,197	57,094		6,052	2,662,343	—

Of the total population in 1960, 4,302,530 persons (83·6%) were urban (84·4% in 1950); those 21 years old or older numbered 3,245,066; foreign-born whites, 564,556.

In 1965 (State census) the population of the principal cities was:

Boston (capital)	616,326	Lynn	92,653	Lawrence	69,070
Worcester	180,341	Newton	88,514	Medford	60,429
Springfield	165,520	Quincy	87,158	Chicopee	58,377
New Bedford	100,176	Lowell	86,535	Waltham	57,134
Fall River	98,053	Somerville	86,332	Pittsfield	56,511
Cambridge	92,677	Brockton	83,499	Malden	56,142

Large urbanized areas, 1960 census: Boston, 2,413,236; Springfield–Chicopee–Holyoke (Mass.–Conn.), 449,777; Worcester, 225,446.

RELIGION. The principal religious bodies are the Roman Catholics with 2,864,332 members in 1966; Jewish Congregations, 226,000; Methodists, 94,810; Episcopalians, 102,822; Unitarians, 35,931. Total membership, all denominations, was 3,639,198.

EDUCATION. School attendance is compulsory for children from 7 to 16 years of age (except in certain instances). Children are excused attendance at school for religious instruction (outside school) for periods not exceeding one hour per week, but no public funds may be expended in connexion with this. In 1968 total expenditure on public schools was estimated at $711m. including $74m. capital outlay. In 1968 public elementary schools had 27,794 classroom teachers ($7,530) and 630,973 pupils; the secondary schools had 22,437 classroom teachers ($7,793) and 481,488 pupils.

Within the state there are 117 degree-granting institutions of higher learning (including 43 colleges and universities) with about 20,000 staff members and 252,683 students (Sept. 1967). Some leading institutions (1967) are:

Year opened	Name and location of universities and colleges	Faculty members	Students
1636	Harvard University, Cambridge[1,2]	2,151	13,909
1793	Williams College, Williamstown[1]	143	1,288
1821	Amherst College, Amherst[1]	131	1,227
1837	Mount Holyoke College, South Hadley[3]	139	1,719
1843	College of the Holy Cross, Worcester[1]	166	2,246
1852	Tufts University, Medford[4]	367	4,919
1861	Mass. Institute of Technology, Cambridge[5]	912	7,567
1863	Boston College (RC), Chestnut Hill[5]	498	9,568
1865	Worcester Polytechnic Institute, Worcester[1]	139	1,694
1867	University of Massachusetts, Amherst[5]	949	13,679
1869	Boston University, Boston[5]	969	21,936
1870	Wellesley College, Wellesley[3]	170	1,775
1871	Smith College, Northampton[3]	248	2,338
1879	Radcliffe College, Cambridge[3]	82	1,282
1885	Springfield College, Springfield[5]	102	1,956
1887	Clark University, Worcester[5]	118	1,527
1898	Northeastern University, Boston[5]	459	31,737
1902	Simmons College, Boston[3]	129	2,067
1947	Merrimac College, North Andover[5]	102	1,770
1948	Brandeis University, Waltham[5]	333	2,549

[1] For men only.   [2] Women graduate students admitted.
[3] For women only.   [4] Includes Jackson College for women.
[5] Co-educational.   [6] Included in Harvard.

WELFARE. In 1967 the state had 202 hospitals (with 64,051 beds) listed by the American Hospital Association; average daily census, 55,601. On 31 June 1968, 21,126 patients were in public and private mental hospitals (excluding those under Veterans Administration) and 7,687 patients were in institutions for the mentally retarded.

Old-age assistance (no maximum) is payable to those citizens 65 years of age or older; in Sept. 1968, 48,644 were drawing an average of $87.61 per month; medical assistance, 214,756, an average of $76.35 per month; aid to families with dependent children, 43,009 families (115,851 children), $223.33 per family; disability assistance, 14,932, $103.21.

On 31 Dec. 1966 state penal institutions held 2,579 inmates (38·1 per 100,000 population). In 1965–67 there were no executions; since 1930 there have been 27 (25 whites and 2 Negroes), all for first-degree murder.

In 1946 the state adopted a 'Fair Employment Practice Act' designed to enforce, the thesis that 'the right to work without discrimination because of race, colour, religious creed, national origin or ancestry is hereby declared to be a right and privilege of the inhabitants of the commonwealth'.

FINANCE. For the fiscal year ending 30 June 1967 (US Census Bureau figures) the general revenue of the state was $1,455·5m. ($953·9m. from taxes and $320·9m. from federal aid); general expenditures, $1,392·9m. ($325·9m. for education, $180m. for highways and $270·9m. for public welfare).

The net long-term debt on 30 June 1967 amounted to $1,686·3m.

Per capita personal income (1969) was $4,138.

AGRICULTURE. On 1 Jan. 1968 there were 7,000 farms (11,179 in 1959), with an area of 800,000 acres. Commercial farms (1967) numbered 5,649, of which 3,134 had gross sales over $10,000; 2,515 under $10,000.

Cash income, 1967, totalled $156m.; dairy, $54,115,000; greenhouse and nursery, $25,317,000; poultry, $25,043,000; vegetables, $13·02m.; tobacco, $10,619,000; cranberries, $8,736,000; fruit, $5,948,000; potatoes, $3,065,000; all other, $10,185,000.

Principal 1968 crops include cranberries, 655,000 bbls; apples, 2·3m. bu.; potatoes, 1,008,000 cwt, and tobacco, 3·8m. lb. On 1 Jan. 1968 farms in the state had 80,000 milch cows, 125,000 all cattle, 92,000 swine, 10,000 sheep, 23,000 turkeys and 2·9m. chickens.

FORESTRY. The national forests area in 1968 was nil.

FISHERIES. The 1967 catch amounted to 316m. lb. valued at $33·2m.

MINING. There is little mining within the state. Total mineral output in 1968 was valued at $41·8m.

INDUSTRY. In 1967, 10,550 manufacturing establishments employed 699,841 production workers, who earned an annual $4,559m.; value (1965) added by manufacture was $7,327m. The 5 most important manufacturing groups, based on employment, were electrical machinery, machinery (except electrical), apparel, leather and leather products, and fabricated metal products.

COMMUNICATIONS. In 1967 there were 1,410 miles of railway. There were (1968) 193 air facilities, of which 23 were publicly owned commercial airports, 13 privately owned commercial airports, 4 military air bases, 1 military seaplane base, 2 state-owned commercial airports, 15 private restricted landing areas, 33 private restricted heliports, 5 private commercial seaplane bases and 18 private restricted seaplane bases. The state has 29 deep-water harbours, the largest of which is Boston (imports (1966), 7,111,054 short tons). In Jan. 1968 the state had 27,084 miles of road (state maintained 2,640 miles; local and municipal, 24,444 miles). The state (1967) registered 2,253,316 motor vehicles.

BOOKS OF REFERENCE

Fact Book. Dept. of Commerce and Development. Boston, Mass., 1967
Manual for the General Court. By Clerk of the Senate and Clerk of the House of Representatives. Boston, Mass. Biennial
This is your Massachusetts Government. Arlington, Mass, 1967

MICHIGAN

GOVERNMENT. Michigan, first settled by Marquette at Sault Ste Marie in 1668, became the Territory of Michigan in 1805, with its boundaries greatly enlarged in 1818 and 1834; it was admitted into the Union with its present boundaries on 26 Jan. 1837. The present constitution was adopted April 1963 and became effective on 1 Jan. 1964. The Senate consists of 38 members, who were elected for 4 years from 1966, and the House of Representatives of 110 members, elected for 2 years. The Governor and Lieut.-Governor, formerly elected for 2 years, were elected for 4 years from 1966. Electors are all citizens over 21 years of age meeting the usual residential requirements. The state sends to Congress 2 senators and 19 representatives.

At the 1968 presidential election Nixon polled 1,370,665 votes, Humphrey 1,593,082 and Wallace 331,968.

The capital is Lansing. The state is organized in 83 counties.

Governor: William G. Milliken (R.), 1971–74 ($45,000).
Lieut.-Governor: James H. Brickley (R.), 1971–4 ($25,000).
Secretary of State: Richard H. Austin (D.), ($30,000).

AREA AND POPULATION. Area, 58,216 sq. miles, of which 56,818 sq. miles are land area, 1,398 sq. miles are inland water; in addition the Great Lakes area amounts to 38,459 sq. miles. Census population, 1 April 1970, 8,937,196, an increase of 1,114,002 or 14·2% since 1960. In 1968 births were 158,644 (18·3 per 1,000 population); deaths, 76,529 (8·8); infant deaths, 2,064 (13 per 1,000 live births); marriages, 88,916 (20·5); divorces, 25,400 (5·9).

Population of 4 federal census years (with distribution by sex, 1960):

	White	Negro	Indian	Asiatic	Total	Per sq. mile
1910	2,785,247	17,115	7,519	292	2,810,173	48·9
1930	4,663,507	169,453	7,080	2,285	4,842,325	84·9
1950	5,917,825	442,296	7,000	4,645	6,371,766	111·7
1960	7,085,865	717,581	9,701	10,047	7,823,194	137·2
Male	3,520,422	352,142	4,898	5,406	3,882,868	—
Female	3,565,443	365,439	4,803	4,641	3,940,326	—

Of the total population in 1960, 5,739,132 persons (73·4%) were urban (70·7% in 1950). Those 21 years old or older numbered 4,580,295; foreign-born whites, 521,546.

Population of the chief cities (census of 1 April 1960) was:

Detroit	1,492,507	Ann Arbor	98,414	Dearborn Heights	80,040
Grand Rapids	193,878	Saginaw	90,603	Taylor	69,668
Flint	193,574	St Clair Shores	86,378	Southfield	68,844
Warren	179,196	Westland	86,291	Roseville	60,505
Lansing (capital)	129,021	Pontiac	84,951	Wyoming	56,196
Dearborn	112,007	Kalamazoo	84,444	SterlingHeights	55,721
Livonia	109,746	Royal Oak	84,081	Lincoln Park	52,979

Larger urbanized areas, 1970 census: Detroit, 4,136,517; Grand Rapids, 535,702; Flint, 493,402; Lansing, 373,474.

RELIGION. Leading religious bodies are the Roman Catholics, with 2,383,399 members in 1970; Methodists, 297,761 (1970), excluding Free or Wesleyan Methodists; Lutheran, 474,578 (1970).

EDUCATION. Education is compulsory for children from 6 to 16 years of age. The operating expenditure for graded and ungraded public schools for the fiscal year ending 30 June 1969, was $1,391,736,281; total, including capital and debt expenditures, $1,882,751,133. In 1969 there were 648 school districts (elementary and secondary schools) with 2,122,915 pupils and 87,487 teachers. Teachers' salaries average $9,134.

In the fall of 1970 the 13 public 4-year institutions reported 215,466 students and the 48 non-public institutions reported 51,434 students. During fiscal year 1969–70 the public 4-year colleges had operating budgets totalling $252,300,000 by state appropriations. State appropriations for capital outlay expenditures were $31,000,000. The public community colleges had $39,300,000 from State appropriations. For 1969–70 the community colleges were appropriated $9·3m. by the State for capital-outlay projects. In 1971 there will be 29 community colleges operating in Michigan with 126,647 students.

WELFARE. Old-age assistance is provided for persons 65 years of age or older who have resided in Michigan for one year before application; assets must not exceed various limits. In 1969–70 assistance for the aged averaged $73.78 monthly to 37,603 persons; aid to 190,025 dependent children in 64,696 families, $206.76 per family; aid to 1,409 blind residents, $96.55; aid to 24,938 permanently and totally disabled persons, $96.97 per month.

On 1 Aug. 1969 the state had 251 hospitals (71,415 beds) listed by the American Hospital Association; 28 psychiatric hospitals had 31,030 beds.

In 1957 a programme came into force which provided for free medical care and hospitalization of certain categories of persons. On 1 Oct., 1966 this programme was superseded by a more comprehensive programme called 'Medicaid' which, with federal support, disbursed, in 1967–68, $153m. to 375,000 persons.

The 1963 Constitution provides that no person shall be denied the equal protection of the law; nor shall any person be denied the enjoyment of his civil or political rights or be discriminated against in the exercise thereof because of religion, race, colour or national origin. A Civil Rights Commission was established, and its powers and duties were implemented by legislation in the extra session of 1963. Earlier statutory enactments guaranteeing civil rights in specific areas are as follows. An Act of 1885, last amended in 1956, orders all places of public accommodation and resort, etc., to furnish equal accommodations without discrimination. An Act of 1941, as last amended, forbids the Civil Service in counties with population exceeding 1m. to discriminate against employees or applicants on the ground of political, racial or religious opinions or affiliations. An Act of 1881 incorporated into the school code of 1955 forbids any discrimination in school facilities. An Act of 1893 incorporated in the insurance code of

1956 prohibits insurance companies from discriminating between white and coloured persons.

In 1951 the legislature restored the unique one-man grand jury system abandoned in 1949.

FINANCE. For the year ending 30 June 1969 the general revenue was $2,874·6m. (taxation, $2,198·5m., and federal aid, $475·2m.); general expenditures, $2,765·1m. (education, $1,188·8m.; highways, etc. $424·4m., and public welfare, $494·1m.).

Total net long-term debt on 30 June 1967 was $946,040.

Per capita personal income (1968) was $3,692.

AGRICULTURE. The state, formerly agricultural, is now chiefly industrial. In 1970 it contained 85,000 farms with a total area of 13m. acres; the average farm was 152 acres valued at $45,345. In 1964 commercial farms numbered 60,187 (98,214 in 1954).

Cash income, 1969, from crops, $384,500,000; from livestock and products, $489,100,000. Principal crops are maize (production, 1969, 96·22m. bu.), hay (3·21m. tons), oats (26·1m. bu.), winter wheat (25·12m. bu.), sugar-beet (1·5m. tons), potatoes (8·8m. cwt), soybeans (11·82m. bu.), dry field beans (8·12m. cwt), and fruit. On 1 Jan, 1970 there were in the state 248,000 sheep, 499,000 milch cows, 1,468,000 all cattle, 691,000 swine, 7·8m. chickens and 107,000 turkey breeder hens. In 1969 the wool clip yielded 2,017,000 lb. of wool from 240,000 sheep.

FORESTRY. The area of national forest land (1 July 1969) was 4,308,682 acres; state forests, 3,752,169 acres; state parks and sites, 131,366 acres; state game area, 249,873 acres; recreation areas, 71,651 acres.

MINING. Most important minerals by value of production are iron ore, cement and natural salines. Output (1969): Iron ore, 14,552,412 long tons ($176,333,574); Portland cement, 31,790,617 bbls ($103,897,422); natural salines, 1,026,048 tons ($89,418,312); copper, 149,952.283 lb ($71,278,318); sand and gravel, 58,092,000 tons ($58,968,000); salt, 4,818,871 tons ($45,960,647), petroleum, 12,212,882 bbls ($37,615,677); stone, 22,037,680 tons ($27,120,834); lime, 1,589,206 tons ($20,372,155); natural gas, 36,162,173m. cu. ft ($9,293,678); natural gas liquids, 99,102,618 gallons ($5,946,157); and silver, 744,290 oz. ($1,332,778). Mineral output in 1969 was valued at $659,445,343.

INDUSTRY. Transport equipment manufacturing is the most important industry. In 1969 it had 398,300 employees. Total labour force (1970) 3·61m.

COMMUNICATIONS. On 1 Jan. 1970 there were 5,533 miles of railway. Airports, 1970, numbered 168 licensed airports, 121 emergency airports, 2 licensed seaplane bases, 3 emergency seaplane bases and 2 licensed heliports. State trunkline mileage (31 July 1970) totalled 9,222, all hard surfaced. Motor vehicle registrations, 30 June 1970, 5,262,833.

BOOKS OF REFERENCE

Michigan Department of Economic Development. *Publications.* Lansing
Michigan Manual. Dept. of State Lansing. Biennial
Bureau of Business and Economic Research, Michigan State University. *Michigan Statistical Abstract.* East Lansing, 1970
Davis, C. M. (ed.), *Readings in the geography of Michigan.* Ann Arbor, 1964
Dunbar, W. F., *Michigan: a history of the Wolverine State.* Grand Rapids, 1970
Lewis, F. Everett. *State Local Government in Michigan.* Lansing, 1966
Milliken, W. G., *Economic Report of the Governor 1970.* Lansing, 1970
BUREAU OF LIBRARY SERVICES. Michigan Department of Education, Lansing 48913. *State Librarian:* Francis X. Scannell.

MINNESOTA

GOVERNMENT. Minnesota, first explored in the 17th century and first settled in the 20 years following the establishment of Fort Snelling (1819), was made a Territory in 1849 (with parts of North and South Dakota), and was admitted into the Union, with its present boundaries, on 11 May 1858. The present consitution dates from 1858; it has had 92 amendments. The Legislature consists of a Senate of 67 members, elected for 4 years, and a House of Representatives of 135 members, elected for 2 years. The Governor and Lieut.-Governor are elected for 4 years. The state sends to Congress 2 senators and 8 representatives.

In the 1968 presidential election Nixon polled 658,643 votes, Humphrey 857,738 and Wallace 68,931.

The capital is St Paul. There are 87 counties, few containing less than 400 sq. miles, the largest being 6,092 sq. miles.

Governor: Wendell R. Anderson (D.), 1971–74 ($27,500).
Lieut.-Governor: James B. Goetz (R.), 1967–71 ($9,600).
Secretary of State: Joseph L. Donovan (DFL.) 1967–71 ($20,500).

AREA AND POPULATION. Area, 84,068 sq. miles, of which 4,059 sq. miles are inland water. Census population, 1 April 1960, 3,413,864, an increase of 14·5% since 1950. Estimated population, 1 July 1969, 3·7m. Births in 1968, 64,000 (17·7 per 1,000 population); deaths, 34,000 (9·3); infant deaths (1966), 1,295 (19·6 per 1,000 live births); marriages, 30,367 (8·3); divorces (1966), 5,507 (1·5).

Population in 4 census years (with distribution by sex, 1960) was:

	White	Negro	Indian	Asiatic	Total	Per sq. mile
1910	2,059,227	7,084	9,053	344	2,075,708	25·7
1930	2,542,599	9,445	11,077	832	2,563,953	32·0
1950	2,953,697	14,022	12,533	2,231	2,982,483	37·3
1960	3,371,603	22,263	15,496	3,642	3,413,864	42·7
Male	1,671,493	11,217	All others	10,252	1,692,962	—
Female	1,700,110	11,046		9,746	1,720,902	—

Of the 1960 population, 2,122,566 persons (62·2%) were urban (54·5% in 1950). Those 21 years of age or older numbered 2,001,455; foreign-born whites, 141,655.

The largest cities are Minneapolis, with a population, 1966 estimate, of 475,110; St Paul (capital), 318,353 (Minneapolis–St Paul urbanized area, 1,724,609); Duluth, 107,349 (Duluth–Superior, 263,142); Bloomington (1965), 66,542; St Louis Park (1965), 48,021.

RELIGION. The chief religious bodies are: Lutheran with 1,020,572 members in 1964; Roman Catholic, 944,222; Methodist, 189,734. Total membership of all denominations, 2,666,681.

EDUCATION. In 1967–68, 1,826 public elementary schools had 18,167 teachers and 483,392 enrolled pupils; 1,619 public secondary schools had 22,200 teachers and 391,590 pupils. In 1968 the 43,604 teachers has an average salary of $7,605. The total public school expenditure (1967–68) was $758,955,494, of which $262,852,242 came from state funds. The University of Minnesota at Minneapolis–St Paul, chartered in 1851 and opened in 1869, had a total enrolment in 1968–69 of 47,534 students and 4,857 academic staff. The 17 state junior colleges had a total enrolment of 15,681. Other main private colleges are: Hamline University, at St Paul, founded in 1854 (1,227 students); St John's University, at Collegeville (1,521); Carleton College (1,482) and St Olaf College (2,562), at Northfield, Macalester (1,971), St Catherine's (1,300) and St Thomas (2,344).

WELFARE. In June 1969, 23,098 persons were receiving in old-age assistance an average of $64.29 per month; 19,563 persons were provided an average of $101.16 in maintenance relief. 21,814 adults received an average of $212.70 in medical assistance. 17,700 families with 49,050 dependent children were provided an average of $194.29 per family per month. 806 blind persons, $80.23 per month. 8,772 disabled persons, $84.14 per month. In 1969 the state had 227 hospitals with 25,787 beds (*U.S. Statistical Abstract*). In June 1969 hospitals for mental diseases had 3,842 patients. Hospitals for mentally defective, 4,550.

In 1957 a Community Mental Health Act authorized mental health centres in local communities with grants from the state to be matched by local funds; in 1968–69, 23 centres served 11,852 persons.

A Civil Rights Act (1927) forbids places of public resort to exclude persons 'on account of race or colour' and another section forbids insurance companies to discriminate 'between persons of the same class on account of race'. Contractors on public works may have their contracts cancelled if 'in the hiring of common or skilled labour' they are found to have discriminated on the grounds of 'race, creed or colour'.

The state's penal reformatory system on 31 June 1969 held 2,440 men and women. There is no death penalty in Minnesota.

FINANCE. General revenues for the year ending 30 June 1968 (US Census Bureau figures) were $1,472m. (taxation, $815m., and federal aid, $349m.); general expenditures, $1,358m. (education, $549m.; highways, $261m., and public welfare, $129m.).

The state's four principal trust funds (derived from royalties from state-owned iron-mines, special tax on iron ore, and sales of land and of timber) on 30 June 1964 totalled $265,308,835.

Net long-term debt, 30 June 1968, was $288,727,000.

Per capita personal income (1968) was $3,341.

AGRICULTURE. Although industry has assumed first position, Minnesota is still an important agricultural state. In 1969 it contained 130,000 farms with a total area of 32·2m. acres (63% of the land area); the average farm was of 248 acres. Average value of land and buildings (1964) $39,075. Commercial farms in 1964 numbered 110,874; 15·5% of the farms were operated by tenant-farmers.

Cash income, 1968, from crops, $524·3m.; from livestock, $1,288·4m. In 1968 Minnesota ranked first in creamery butter, oats, non-fat dried milk, turkeys and sweet corn, and second in milch cows, milk and sweet clover-seed. Other important products are flaxseed, maize, hay, cheese, soybeans and green peas. On 1 Jan. 1968 the farm animals included 4·08m. all cattle, 1,925,000 milch cows, 568,000 sheep, 2,867,000 swine, 12,766,000 chickens and 907,000 turkeys (but production, 1967, 16·76m.). In 1968 the wool clip amounted to 3,869,000 lb. of wool from 477,000 sheep.

FORESTRY. Forests of commercial timber cover 17·1m. acres, of which the national forest area, 1968, was 2·8m. acres and state forest area 3·3m. acres; value of forest products, 1968, was $342·3m.

MINING. The mining of iron ores on the Mesabi, Vermilion and Cuyuna ranges has changed dramatically since the passage of a Taconite Amendment in 1964. Since then new capital investment in taconite facilities has reached approximately $500m., bringing the total investment in the taconite industry to over $1,000m. Taconite made up 58% of Minnesota's iron-ore shipments in 1968. Shipments of usable iron ore from mines in 1968 amounted to 51·3m. long tons valued at $508·81m.; of manganiferous ore, 171·3m. long tons (value undisclosed). Total mineral output in 1968 was valued at $567·43m.

INDUSTRY. The 1967 US Dept. of Commerce showed 5,241 manufacturing establishments employing 195,000 production workers, who earned $1,148m.; value added by manufacture was (1969 estimate), $4,806m.

TOURISM. Estimates for 1969 give approximately 5m. tourists (55% from outside the state), with a total expenditure of $750m.

COMMUNICATIONS. There are 12 Class I railroads operating, with mainline mileage of 8,031 (total track miles, 11,992). The state highway system covered 11,509 miles non-municipal rural trunk highways in 1969; total highway mileage, 126,879. Airports in 1969 numbered 265 (124 municipal, 141 private). In 1969, 2,298,352 automobiles were registered.

BOOKS OF REFERENCE

STATISTICAL INFORMATION. Current information is obtainable from the Department of Economic Development (State Capitol, St Paul 55101); non-current material from the Reference Library, Minnesota Historical Society, St Paul 55101.

Legislative Manual. Secretary of State. St Paul. Biennial
Profile of the State of Minnesota. Dept. of Econ. Dev., 1967
Blegen, T. C., *Minnesota: a history of the state.* Minnesota Univ. Press, 1963
Borchert, J., *The changing geography of Minnesota.* Minnesota Univ. Press, 1959
Minnesota Agriculture Statistics. Dept. of Agric., St Paul. Annual

MISSISSIPPI

GOVERNMENT. Mississippi, settled in 1716, was organized as a Territory in 1798 and admitted into the Union on 10 Dec. 1817. In 1804 and in 1812 its boundaries were extended, but in March 1817 a part was taken to form the new Territory of Alabama, leaving the boundaries substantially as at present. The present constitution was adopted in 1890 without ratification by the electorate; it has since had 48 amendments.

The Legislature consists of a Senate (52 members) and a House of Representatives (122 members), both elected for 4 years, as are also the Governor and Lieut.-Governor. Electors are all citizens who have resided in the state 1 year, in the county 1 year, in the election district 6 months next before the election and have been registered according to law. In 1960 in 31 of the 82 counties Negroes constituted 49% or more of the population; Tunica County, with 79% Negro, had the highest percentage of any county in the US. Of the 1,170,522 potential voters in 1960, 529,262 were registered; 298,171 voted in the 1960 presidential elections. In the 1968 presidential election Nixon polled 88,516 votes, Humphrey 150,644 and Wallace 415,349.

The state is represented in Congress by 2 senators and 4 representatives.

The capital is Jackson; there are 82 counties.

Governor: John Bell Williams (D.), 1968–72 ($25,000).
Lieut.-Governor: Charles L. Sullivan (D.) ($4,500 per regular session).
Secretary of State: Heber Ladner (D.) ($16,500).

AREA AND POPULATION. Area 47,716 sq. miles, 493 sq. miles being inland water. Census (preliminary) population, 1 April 1970, 2,158,872, a decrease of 19,269 or 0·9% since 1960. Estimated population, 1 July 1968, 2,342,000. Births, 1969, were 47,138 (19·7 per 1,000 population); deaths, 23,419 (9·8); infant deaths, 1,476 (34·6 per 1,000 live births—highest rate in US excluding Puerto Rico); marriages, 25,956 (10·1); divorces (1968), 7,020 (2·5).

Population of 4 federal census years (with distribution by sex, 1960):

	White	Negro	Indian	Asiatic	Total	Per sq. mile
1910	786,111	1,009,487	1,253	263	1,797,114	38·8
1930	998,077	1,009,718	1,458	568	2,009,821	42·4
1950	1,188,632	986,494	2,502	1,286	2,178,914	46·1
1960	1,257,546	915,743	3,119	1,481	2,178,141	46·1
Male	625,011	440,494	All others	2,428	1,067,933	—
Female	632,535	475,249		2,424	1,110,208	—

Of the population in 1960, 820,805 persons (37·7%) were urban (10·8% in 1940). Those 18 years old or older numbered 1,273,465; foreign-born whites, 7,125.

The largest cities (estimates 1965) are Jackson, 167,000 (urbanized area, 174,300); Meridian, 52,100; Biloxi, 48,300; Greenville, 46,500; Hattiesburg, 38,100; Gulfport, 35,900; Vicksburg, 31,400; Laurel, 28,700; Columbus, 28,000; Natchez, 26,100.

RELIGION. Southern Baptists (1970), 183,026 members; Methodists (1969), 184,219; Roman Catholics (1969), 82,383; Negro Baptists–National Baptists (1969), 375,000, and Negro Methodists (1970), 33,902.

The number of churches relative to the population is the highest in the US (one church per 289 persons; national average, 814).

EDUCATION. Attendance at school was compulsory until repealed by the Legislature in 1956. The elementary and secondary schools in 1969–70 had 593,091 pupils and 22,936 classroom teachers; private elementary and high schools had 46,981 pupils. In 1969–70 teachers' average salary was $5,798 (lowest of any state). The expenditure (state and local) for elementary and secondary education in 1969–70 was $478 per child in average daily attendance.

There are 17 universities and colleges, of which 8 are state-supported. The University of Mississippi, at Oxford (1844), had 1970–71, 410 instructors and 6,641 students; Mississippi State University, Starkville, 487 instructors and 8,730 students; Mississippi State College for Women, at Columbus, 132 instructors and 2,650 students; University of Southern Mississippi, Hattiesburg, 412 instructors and 7,901 students; Jackson State College, Jackson, 200 instructors and 4,800 students; Delta State College, Cleveland, 149 instructors and 3,000 students; Alcorn College, Lorman, 123 instructors and 2,300 students; Mississippi Valley State College, Itta Bena, 115 instructors and 2,000 students. State operational expenditure, 1969–70, for higher education was $26,128,660.

Junior colleges had (1969–70) 27,526 full-time students and 1,139 instructors. The state appropriation for junior colleges, 1969–70, was $6·19m.

WELFARE. In July 1970, 73,534 persons were receiving old-age assistance amounting to an average of $50.59 per month; 31,636 families with 99,951 dependent children were receiving an average of $46.81 monthly per family; 2,123 blind persons, $59.61 monthly; 21,930 permanently and totally disabled persons, $59.20 per month. A total of 1,825 medical vendor payments in the amount of $13,178 were paid to private hospitals and 2,267 payments in the amount of $392,279 were paid to nursing homes for aged, blind, and permanently and totally disabled persons.

In 1969 the state had 122 acute general hospitals (9,855 beds) listed by the Mississippi Commission on Hospital Care. In 1969, 6 hospitals with facilities for care of the mentally ill had 6,286 beds.

In 1970 there were no executions; from 1955 to 1970 executions (by gas-chamber or in early years by electrocution) totalled 31 (7 whites and 14 Negroes for murder, 9 Negroes for rape and 1 Negro for armed robbery). On 31 Aug. 1970 the state prisons had 1,715 inmates.

FINANCE. For the fiscal year ending 30 June 1970 (US Census Bureau figures) the general revenues were $963,369,792 (taxation, $479,765,486 and federal aid, $243,670,045) and general expenditures were $924,178,184 ($239,934,261 for education, $129,696,059 for highways and $105,170,557 for public welfare).

On 30 June 1970 the total net long-term debt was $420,163,000.

Per capita personal income (1969) was $2,192 (lowest in US).

AGRICULTURE. Agriculture is the leading industry of the state which offers a semi-tropical climate and a rich productive soil. In 1964 farms in the state numbered 109,141 with an area of 17,751,607 acres. Average size of farm was 162·6 acres (valued at $24,322). This compares with an average farm size of

95·9 acres (valued at $7,053) 10 years earlier. Farm owners (including full owners and part owners) numbered 83,099 in 1964; tenant farmers numbered 25,634 or 23·5% of all farm operators.

Cash income from all crops and livestock during 1969 was $940,857,000 Cash income from crops was $325·74m. The chief product is cotton. In 1969, 1,328,000 bales were produced, with cash receipts from cotton lint and cottonseed totalling $137,601,000, ranking third in the US, following Texas and California. Yield per acre of cotton has risen from an average of 187 lb. during 1911–15 to a record high for the state of 732 lb. in 1964. Other important crops include soybeans, with a total of 2,404,000 acres planted in 1970 and income of $128,854,000. As a source of farm income, rice, corn, hay, peanuts, pecans, sweet potatoes, other vegetables and forest products continue to be highly important. The state usually leads in production of tung oil nuts.

On 1 Jan. 1970 there were 2,487,000 head of cattle and calves on Mississippi farms (fifteenth nationally). Cows and heifers 2 years old and over kept for milk totalled 224,000; beef-type cows and heifers 2 years old and over 1,273,000 (ninth nationally); sheep and lambs, 17,000 head, and hogs and pigs, 527,000 head. In 1969 cash income from livestock and products totalled $481,509,000. Of this total, $177·7m. was credited to cattle and calves. Cash income from poultry and eggs totalled $199·59m.; dairy products, $60m.

In 1969 farmers received a total of $133,611,000 in government payments. Total cash receipts from farming (cash receipts from farm marketings plus government payments) amounted to $940·86m.

In 1970 there were 80 soil-conservation districts covering 25,200,831 acres.

FORESTRY. In 1969 income from forestry amounted to over $1,188·3m.; output of logs, lumber, etc., 1,276·9m. bd ft; pulpwood, 4,073,157 cords; distillate wood, 35,087 tons; turpentine gum, 8,258 bbls. There are about 16,891,900 acres of forest (55·8% of the state's area). National forests area, 1969, 1,118,800 acres.

MINING. Petroleum and natural gas account for about 90% (by value) of mineral production. Output of petroleum, 1969, was 64,283,095 bbls and of natural gas 166,712,204m. cu. ft. There are 5 oil refineries. Value of oil and gas products sold 1970 was approximately $222m.

INDUSTRY. In 1969 the 2,228 manufacturing establishments employed 181,982 production workers, earning $980,012,015.

COMMUNICATIONS. The state in 1969 had 3,667 miles of railway and maintained (1970) 9,892 miles of highways, of which 9,322 miles were paved. In July 1970, 812,204 cars were registered.

There were 69 public airports in 1970.

BOOKS OF REFERENCE

Mississippi Official and Statistical Register. Secretary of State. Jackson. Biennial
Bettersworth, J. K., *Mississippi: a history*. Rev. ed. Austin, Tex., 1964
Highsaw, R. B., and Fortenberry, C. N., *The Government and Administration of Mississippi*. New York, 1954
Silver, J. W., *Mississippi: the Closed Society*. New York, 1964
Wilber, G. L., and Bryant, E. S., *Illustrative Projections of Mississippi Population, 1960 to 1985*. State College, 1964

MISSISSIPPI LIBRARY COMMISSION. 405 Woolfolk Building, Jackson. *Reference Librarian:* Mrs Willie Dee Gharst.

MISSOURI

GOVERNMENT. Missouri, first settled in 1735 at Ste Genevieve, was made a Territory on 1 Oct. 1812, and admitted to the Union on 10 Aug. 1821. In 1837 its boundaries were extended to their present limits. A new constitution, the sixth, was adopted on 27 Feb. 1945; it has been amended 21 times. The General Assembly consists of a Senate of 34 members elected for 4 years, and a House of Representatives of 163 members elected for 2 years. The Governor and Lieut.-Governor are elected for 4 years. Missouri sends to Congress 2 senators and 10 representatives.

Voters (with the usual exceptions) are all citizens and those adult aliens who, within a prescribed period, have applied for citizenship. No record is kept of the qualified voters. In the 1968 presidential election Nixon polled 811,932, Humphrey 791,444 and Wallace 206,126.

Jefferson City is the state capital. The state is divided into 114 counties and the city of St Louis.

Governor: Warren E. Hearnes (D.), 1969–73 ($37,500).
Lieut.-Governor: William S. Morris (D.) ($16,000).
Secretary of State: James C. Kirkpatrick (D.) ($20,000).

AREA AND POPULATION. Area, 69,686 sq. miles, 548 sq. miles being water. Census population, 1 April 1960, 4,319,813, an increase since 1950 of 9·2%. Population, 31 Dec. 1968 (state estimate), 4,517,738. Births, 1968, were 72,571; deaths, 50,717; infant deaths, 1,530; marriages, 46,055; divorces, 16,198.

Population of 4 federal census years (with distribution by sex, 1960):

	White	Negro	Indian	Asiatic	Total	Per sq. mile
1910	3,134,932	157,452	313	638	3,293,335	47·9
1930	3,403,876	223,840	578	1,073	3,629,367	52·4
1950	3,655,593	297,088	547	1,046	3,954,653	57·1
1960	3,922,967	390,853	1,723	3,146	4,319,813	62·5
Male	1,918,378	186,742	All others 3,159		2,108,279	—
Female	2,004,589	204,111	2,834		2,211,534	—

Of the total population in 1960, 2,876,557 persons (66·6%) were urban (61·5% in 1940). Those 21 years of age or older numbered 2,695,614; foreign-born whites, 75,492.

The largest cities, with population, 1960 census, are:

St Louis	750,026	Joplin	38,958	Jefferson City	28,228
Kansas City	475,539	Florissant	38,166	Cape Girardeau	24,947
Springfield	95,865	Columbia	36,650	Sedalia	23,874
St Joseph	79,673	Kirkwood	29,421	Overland	22,763
Independence	62,328	Webster Groves	28,990	Hannibal	20,028
University City	51,249				

Urbanized areas, 1960 census: St Louis, 1,667,693; Kansas City, 921,121.

RELIGION. Chief religious bodies are Catholic, with 748,894 members in 1966, Southern Baptists (494,593), Southern Methodists (262,892), Missouri Association of Christian Churches (98,310) and Lutheran (1963: 162,009). Total membership, all denominations, about 2m. in 1960.

EDUCATION. School attendance is compulsory for children from 6 to 16 years for the full term. In the 1967–68 school year, public schools (kindergarten through grade 12) had 1,031,010 pupils and 45,076 teachers. Total expenditure for public schools in 1967–68, $697·6m. Teachers' salaries, 1967–68, averaged $6,929. Institutions for higher instruction include (Sept. 1968) the University of Missouri, founded in 1839 with campuses at Columbia, Rolla, St Louis and Kansas City, with 1,571 accredited teachers and 38,243 students, Washington University at St Louis, founded in 1857, with 854 teachers and 7,500 students, and St Louis University (1818), with 730 teachers and 8,347 students. Six state colleges had 1,501 teachers and 34,602 students. Two former junior colleges have become 4-year colleges with the local junior college district financing the first 2 years and the state financing the third and fourth years. These 2 schools schools are not listed with the other state colleges.

P

WELFARE. In Sept. 1969 the state was paying old-age assistance to 95,142 persons, who received an average of $76.52 per month. The state had 140 hospitals (23,230 beds) licensed by the Missouri Division of Health (exclusive of state and federal hospitals). On 30 Sept. 1969 there were 14,274 long-term patients in 5 state mental hospitals; 413 patients in 3 short-term mental centres.

State prisons in 1969 had an average of 3,400 inmates. There have been no executions since 1965; since 1930 executions (by lethal gas) have totalled 40, including 31 for murder, 6 for rape and 3 for kidnapping.

The State Board of Mediation has jurisdiction in labour disputes involving only public utilities. The Prevailing Wage Law (1959) provides that no less than the local hourly rate of wages for work of a similar character shall be paid to any workmen employed by or on behalf of any public body engaged in public works. The Industrial Commission has authority to make inspections of records to determine that the prevailing wages fixed by commission action have been paid by any contractor or subcontractor constructing public works, and has authority to institute actions for penalties described in the Act.

FINANCE. For the year ending 30 June 1968 (U.S. Census Bureau figures) general revenues were $1,077m. (taxes, $657m., and federal aid $319m.); general expenditures were $1,111m. (education, $439m.; highways, $227m., and public welfare, $167m.).

Total net long-term debt, 30 June 1968, was $132m.

Per capita personal income (1968) was $3,257.

AGRICULTURE. In 1969 there were 145,000 farms in Missouri covering 33·4m. acres. The average size of farms is 230 acres. The 1968 acreage of corn harvested for grain was 2·96m. acres; soybeans for beans, 3·6m. acres, and wheat, 1·3m. acres. Cash receipts, 1968, from crops, $440·8m.

Cash receipts from farming, 1967, $1,460m. Production of principal crops, 1968: Corn, 245·5m. bu.; soybeans, 100·6m. bu.; wheat, 42·2m. bu.; sorghum grain, 14·3m. bu.; oats, 11·3m. bu. The 1968 pig crop for Missouri totalled 7,404,000 head. Cattle and calves on Missouri farms 1 Jan. 1969 totalled a record high of 4,748,000. Cash receipts from livestock, 1968, was $932·7m.

FORESTRY. Forest land area, 1966, 14,977,000 acres.

MINING. Production of Portland cement in 1968 totalled 19·6m. bbls (valued at $69·4m.). Production of other principal minerals, 1968: Lead, 210,800 short tons; barite, 314,000 short tons; lime, 1·67m. short tons; clays, 2·65m. short tons; coal, 3·1m. short tons; stone, 37·2m. short tons; sand and gravel, 10·8m. short tons; iron ore, 1·98m. long tons; crude petroleum, 72,000 bbls. Total value of mineral production, 1968, $276,771,000.

INDUSTRY. Missouri's largest manufacturing industries in terms of employment for 1969 were the manufacture of transport equipment and food and kindred products. Other large industries are electrical equipment and supplies, apparel and related products and machinery. In 1969 there was a total of 415,000 production workers employed, earning $3,102m.; value added by manufacture was $5,801m. in 1966.

COMMUNICATIONS. The state has 15 first-class railroads operating a total of 7,035 miles of main-line track and a total rail mileage of 10,896 miles. Waterways include 545 miles of navigable 9-ft channel on the Mississippi River, 7-ft navigable channel from St Louis to Kansas City on the Missouri River and 6·5-ft navigable channel north of Kansas City; a 9-ft channel on the Missouri River from St Louis to Omaha, Neb., is nearing completion; 10 barge lines operate on these waterways. Federal and state highways, July 1969, totalled 32,000 miles. For the fiscal year ending 30 June 1969 there were 1,840,143 automobiles licensed in the state.

In July 1969 there were 271 airports, of which 199 were open to the public. There were 2 heliports and 4 seaplane bases.

BOOKS OF REFERENCE

Official Manual, Secretary of State, Jefferson City. Biennial
Data for Missouri Counties, Extension Division, University of Missouri, Columbia, 1954
Karsch, R. F., *Political Parties, Elections and the General Assembly in Missouri*. Columbia, 1964
Annual Survey of Manufactures—1965, 1966, U.S. Dept. of Commerce, Bureau of the Census
Missouri Mineral Industry News—August 1968, Missouri Geological Survey and Water Resources, Rolla
State Government Finances in 1968, U.S. Dept. of Commerce, Bureau of the Census
Missouri Farm Facts—1969, Missouri Dept. of Agriculture, Jefferson City

STATE LIBRARY. Missouri State Library, Dawson Building, Jefferson City. *State Librarian:* Charles O'Halloran.

MONTANA

GOVERNMENT. Montana, first settled in 1809, was made a Territory (out of portions of Idaho and Dakota Territories) in 1864 and was admitted into the Union on 8 Nov. 1889. It still has the constitution adopted at that time with some 35 amendments. The Senate consists of 55 senators, elected for 4 years, one half at each biennial election. The 104 members of the House of Representatives are elected for 2 years. The Governor and Lieut.-Governor are elected for 4 years. Montana sends to Congress 2 senators and 2 representatives.

In the 1968 presidential election Nixon polled 136,853 votes, Humphrey 114,117 and Wallace 20,015.

The capital is Helena. The state is divided into 56 counties.

Governor: Forrest Anderson (D.), 1969–73 ($23,250).
Lieut.-Governor: Thomas L. Judge (D.).
Secretary of State: Frank Murray (D.) ($10,500).

AREA AND POPULATION. Area, 147,138 sq. miles, including 1,402 sq. miles of water, of which the federal government, 1964, owned 27,646,000 acres or 29·6%. US Bureau of Indian Affairs administered 5,372,000 acres, of which 1·67m. were allotted to tribes. Census population, 1 April 1960, 674,767, an increase of 14·2% since 1950. Estimated population, 1 July 1966, 702,000. Births, 1967, were 12,087 (17·2 per 1,000 population); deaths, 6,549 (9·3); infant deaths (1967), 290 (24 per 1,000 live births); marriages, 5,563 (7·9); divorces (1967), 2,361 (3·4).

Population in 4 census years (with distribution by sex, 1960) was:

	White	Negro	Indian	Asiatic	Total	Per sq. mile
1910	360,580	1,834	10,745	2,870	376,053	2·6
1930	519,898	1,256	14,798	1,239	537,606	3·7
1950	572,038	1,232	16,606	—	591,024	4·1
1960	650,738	1,467	21,181	1,082	674,767	4·6
Male	331,374	864	10,793	541	343,743	—
Female	319,364	603	10,388	541	331,024	—

Of the total population in 1960, 338,457 persons (50·2%) were urban (43·7% in 1950). There were 103·8 males for every 100 females (national average, 97·1). Persons 18 years of age or older numbered 414,359; foreign-born whites, 29,905. Households, 1960, 202,240.

The largest cities are Great Falls, with estimated population of 58,500 in 1962; Billings, 55,000; Butte, 27,500; Missoula, 27,090; Helena (capital), 21,800; Bozeman, 13,361; Anaconda, 12,054.

RELIGION. The leading religious bodies are (1967): Roman Catholic with 151,065 members; Lutheran, 75,744; Methodist. 26,832.

EDUCATION. 171,806 pupils were enrolled in public elementary and secondary schools, 1 Oct. 1967, and 20,074 in private and parochial schools in 1964–65. Indian pupils (of at least one fourth degree), in 1965–66, numbered 7,535. Public elementary school teachers (5,000), 1 Oct. 1967, had an average salary of $5,725; secondary school teachers (2,760), $6,550. Total estimated expenditure on public school education, 1967–68, was $116m.; expenditure per pupil was $527. The University of Montana consists of the Montana State University, at Bozeman (1967: 6,966 full-time students), the University of Montana, at Missoula, founded in 1895 (6,360), the College of Mineral Science and Technology at Butte (618 students) and 3 colleges of education (5,938 students).

WELFARE. In June 1968, 3,683 persons were receiving in old-age assistance an average of $64.01 per month; 2,653 families (7,601 dependent children), $138.31 per family; 157 blind persons, $79.48; 1,565 totally disabled, $77.33.

In 1966 the state had 64 hospitals (3,424 beds) listed by the Montana State Board of Health. In 1966 hospitals for mental disease had 3,062 patients.

In Dec. 1967 the Montana state prison held 520 men and 15 women. In 1966 there were no executions; total since 1930 (all by hanging) was 6, 4 whites and 2 Negroes, for murder.

FINANCE. General revenues for the year ending 30 June 1967 were $288,955,736 ($83,278,198 from federal aid); general expenditures were $283,267,614 ($72,382,371 for education, $78,855,829 for highways and $12,758,200 for public welfare).

Total net long-term debt on 1 July 1967 was $66,887,000.

Per capita personal income (1969) was $3,124.

AGRICULTURE. In 1967 there were 27,600 farms and ranches (50,564 in 1935) with an area of 67·1m. acres (47,511,868 acres in 1935); average value (land and buildings), $115,000 ($13,720 in 1945). Large-scale farming predominates; in 1964, 12,932 farms (the highest, except that of Texas, of any of the states) were of 1,000 acres or over. Commercial farms numbered 22,593 which sold produce valued in excess of $382m. Irrigated area, 1964, totalled 1,893,260 acres (in 10,843 farms) or 18% of total crop land harvested.

The chief crops are wheat, amounting in 1967 to 119,136,000 bu., ranking fourth in US; barley, 37m. bu., ranking third, sugar-beet, hay, potatoes, alfalfa, mustard seed, oats, dry beans, flax seed and cherries. Cash income, 1967, from crops, $220·8m.; from livestock, $267·2m. On 1 Jan. 1968 there were 51,000 milch cows, 2,984,000 all cattle, 149,000 swine. The wool clip in 1967 was 11,277,000 lb. from 1,092,000 head of sheep.

FORESTRY. Eleven national forests had an area (1966) of 16,675,100 acres.

MINING (1966). Output of crude petroleum, 35·38m. bbls; copper, 128,061 short tons (ranking third in US); sand and gravel, 13,816,000 short tons; phosphate rock, undisclosed; silver, 5·32m. troy oz. (fourth in US); gold, 25,009 troy oz.; zinc, 29,120 short tons; manganese (content of ores), undisclosed; natural gas, 30,685m. cu. ft; coal, 419,000 short tons. Value of total mineral production, $245,268,000, with copper ($92·64m.) the most important commodity.

INDUSTRY. In 1967 manufacturing establishments numbering 971 had 23,237 production workers, earning $148·1m.; value added by manufacture was (1966) $315m. Electric power generated in 1965 was 6,600m. kwh., of which 6,144m. was hydro-electric.

COMMUNICATIONS. In Dec. 1967 there were 4,979 miles of railway in the state. There were 447 airports in 1968, of which 122 were publicly owned. State-maintained highway mileage (Dec. 1967) was 6,567, local, 63,878. The state maintains inter-state highways, 1,216 miles, and primary highways, 4,873 miles; the counties maintain secondary roads, 5,758 miles. In 1967, 521,191 automobiles were registered.

BOOKS OF REFERENCE

Montana Agricultural Statistics. Dept. of Agriculture, Labor and Industry. Helena. Biennial, from 1946
Montana Business Quarterly. Montana State Univ. From 1963
Montana: A State Guide-Book. New York, 1949
Montana Almanac. Montana State Univ. Annual, from 1957
Hamilton, J. McL., *From Wilderness to Statehood: a history of Montana, 1805–1900.* Portland, Ore., 1957
Toole, K. R., *Montana, an uncommon land.* Univ. of Oklahoma Press, 1959

NEBRASKA

GOVERNMENT. The Nebraska region was first reached by white men from Mexico under the Spanish general Coronado in 1541. It was ceded by France to Spain in 1763, retroceded to France in 1801, and sold by Napoleon to the US as part of the Louisiana Purchase in 1803. Its first settlement was in 1847, and on 30 May 1854 it became a Territory and on 1 March 1867 a state. In 1882 it annexed a small part of Dakota Territory, and in 1908 it received another small tract from South Dakota.

The present constitution was adopted in 1875; it has been amended 126 times. By an amendment adopted in Nov. 1934 Nebraska has a single-chambered legislature (elected for 4 years) of 49 members—the only state in the Union to have one. The Governor and Lieut.-Governor are elected for 4 years. Amendments adopted in 1912 and 1920 provide for legislation through the initiative and referendum and permit cities of more than 5,000 inhabitants to frame their own charters. A 'right-to-work' amendment adopted 5 Nov. 1946 makes illegal the 'closed shop' demands of trade unions. Nebraska is represented in Congress by 2 senators and 3 representatives.

In the 1968 presidential election Nixon polled 321,163 votes, Humphrey 170,784 and Wallace 44,904.

The capital is Lincoln. The state has 93 counties.

Governor: James Exan (D.), 1971–74 ($18,000).
Lieut. Governor: John E. Everroud (R.) ($6,000).
Secretary of State: Frank Marsh (R.) ($12,500).

AREA AND POPULATION. Area, 77,227 sq. miles, of which 615 sq. miles are water. Census population, 1 April 1960, 1,411,330, an increase of 6·5% since 1950. Preliminary census population (1970), 1,468,101. Births, 1968, were 24,236 (16·8 per 1,000 population); deaths, 15,017 (10·4); infant deaths (1966), 463 (18·6 per 1,000 live births); marriages, 14,287 (9·9); divorces, 2,940 (2).

Population in 4 census years (with distribution by sex, 1960) was:

	White	Negro	Indian	Asiatic	Total	Per sq. mile
1910	1,180,293	7,689	3,502	730	1,192,214	15·5
1920	1,279,219	13,242	2,888	1,023	1,296,372	16·9
1950	1,301,328	19,234	3,954	821	1,325,510	17·3
1960	1,374,764	29,262	5,545	1,195	1,411,330	18·3
Male	681,603	14,651	All others	3,772	700,026	—
Female	693,161	14,611		3,532	711,304	—

Of the total population in 1960, 766,000 persons (53·6%) were urban (46·9% in 1950); 858,000 were 21 years of age or older; foreign-born whites numbered 39,682. The largest cities in the state are: Omaha, with a census population, 1970, of 327,789; Lincoln (capital), 145,092; Grand Island, 30,917; Hastings, 23,233; Fremont, 22,922; Bellevue, 21,539; North Platte, 19,292; Kearney, 18,855; Norfolk, 16,111.

The Bureau of Indian Affairs, as of 30 June 1967, administered 62,292 acres, of which 14,094 acres were allotted to tribal control.

RELIGION. The Roman Catholics had 290,000 members in 1967; Protestant Churches, 571,000; Jews, 15,000 members. Total, all denominations, 876,000 (unofficial figures).

EDUCATION. School attendance is compulsory for children from 7 to 16 years of age. Public elementary schools, autumn 1969, had 231,690 enrolled pupils; secondary schools, 96,717 pupils. Teachers' salaries, 1967, averaged $5,643 in elementary and $6,553 in secondary schools. Estimated public school expenditure for year enging 30 June 1968 was $175m. Total enrolment in 29 institutions of higher education, autumn 1968, was 60,950 students. The largest institutions were (1968):

Opened	Institution	Teachers	Students
1867	Peru State College, Peru (State)	53	1,600
1869	Univ. of Nebraska, Lincoln (State)	1,532	18,452
1878	Creighton Univ., Omaha (RC)	630	4,180
1883	Midland Lutheran College, Fremont (Lutheran)	51	900
1887	Nebraska Wesleyan Univ. (Methodist)	104	1,458
1891	Union College, Lincoln (Seventh-Day Adventist)	95	1,113
1894	Concordia Teachers College, Seward (Lutheran)	98	1,407
1905	Kearney State College, Kearney (State)	205	5,400
1908	Univ. of Nebraska, Omaha	314	10,780
1910	Wayne State College, Wayne (State)	133	3,068
1911	Chadron State College, Chadron (State)	76	200

The state holds 1·61m. acres of land as a permanent endowment of her schools. The permanent public school endowment fund in June 1968 was $35m.

WELFARE. The administration of public welfare is the responsibility of the County Divisions of Welfare with policy-forming, regulatory, advisory and supervisory functions performed by the State Department of Public Welfare. In April 1968 public welfare provided financial aid and/or services as follows: for 12,138 individuals who were aged, blind or disabled, with an average maintenance payment of $61.11; for 6,123 families with dependent children, with an average payment of $147.81 per family; for 20,462 individuals who had medical needs with an average payment of $103.70 per individual; for 1,629 children in need of child welfare services; for 2,894 children who were in need of crippled children's services and medical care. The amount of aid is based on need in accordance with State assistance standards; the programme of aid to families with dependent children is limited to a maximum maintenance payment of $110.00 for one child plus $30.00 for each additional child. General assistance is the full responsibility of the county of residence.

In 1968 the state had 130 hospitals. Patients in mental hospitals numbered 3,864 on 30 June 1969.

A 'Civil Rights Act' (1929) forbids discrimination against any 'persons' by 'inns, restaurants, public conveyances, barber shops, theatres and other places of amusement'. The state university is forbidden to discriminate between students 'because of age, sex, color or nationality'. An Act of 1941 declares it to be 'the policy of this state' that no trade union should discriminate, in collective bargaining, 'against any person because of his race or color'.

The state's prisons had, 30 June 1969, 1,400 inmates (95·4 per 100,000 population). There have been no executions after 1962. From 1930 to 1962 Nebraska had only 4 executions (electrocution), 3 white men and 1 American Indian, all for murder.

FINANCE. For the fiscal year ending 30 June 1968 (US Census Bureau figures) the state's revenues were $381·4m. (taxation, $193·9m. and federal aid, $109·7m.); general expenditures were $345·6m. ($109m. for education, $92m. for highways and $44·9m. for public welfare).

The state has a bonded indebtedness limit of $100,000.

Per capita personal income (1968) was $3,239.

AGRICULTURE. Nebraska is one of the most important agricultural states. In 1969 it contained approximately 74,000 farms, with a total area of 48·2m. acres. The average farm was 651 acres.

In 1969, 3·8m. acres were irrigated (1,171,369 acres in 1954). In 1969, 34,117 irrigation wells were registered.

Cash income from crops (1968), $774·7m., and from livestock, $1,273·3m. Principal crops, with estimated 1969 yield: Maize, 433m. bu. (ranking fourth in US); wheat, 85·6m. bu.; sorghums for grain, 114m. bu.; oats, 23·8m. bu.; rye, 2·7m. bu., and potatoes, 2·1m. tons. About 1,640 farms grow sugar-beet for 4 factories; output 1969, 1·67m. short tons. On 1 Jan. 1969 the state contained 6·33m. all cattle (ranking third in US), 222,000 milch cows, 393,000 sheep and 3·23m. swine.

FORESTRY. The area of national forest, 1968, was 349,543 acres.

MINING. The total output of minerals, 1968, was valued at $74,837,000, petroleum (13·2m. bbls) being the most important.

INDUSTRY. In 1967, 1,608 manufacturing establishments had 58,700 production workers, earning $327m.; value added by manufacture (1965), $870m. The chief industry is meat-packing, mainly at South Omaha, employing (1957) 11,718 (9,411 production workers) and value added was $128·3m.

COMMUNICATIONS. In 1968 there were 7,900 miles of railway. Airports (1968) numbered 262, of which 81 were publicly owned. The state-maintained highway system embraced 9,657 miles in 1968; local roads, 93,807 miles; federal, 483 miles. In 1969, 673,945 automobiles were registered.

BOOKS OF REFERENCE

Nebraska Statistical Handbook, 1970. Nebraska Dept. of Econ. Development, Lincoln
Nebraska Blue-Book. Legislative Council. Lincoln. Biennial
Olson, J. C., *History of Nebraska.* Univ. of Nebraska Press, 1955

STATE LIBRARY. State Law Library, State House, Lincoln. *Librarian:* George H. Turner.

NEVADA

GOVERNMENT. Nevada, first settled in 1851, when it was a part of the Territory of Utah (created 1850), was made a Territory in 1861, enlarged in 1862 by an addition from Utah Territory and admitted into the Union on 31 Oct. 1864 as the 36th state. In 1866 and 1867 the area of the state was significantly enlarged at the expense of the Territories of Utah and Arizona. The constitution adopted in 1864 is still in force, with over 60 amendments. The Legislature meets biennially (and in special sessions) and consists of a Senate of 20 members elected for 4 years, half their number retiring every 2 years, and an Assembly of 40 members elected for 2 years. The Governor, Lieut.-Governor and Attorney-General are elected for 4 years. Qualified electors are all citizens with the usual residential qualification. Nevada is represented in Congress by 2 senators and 1 representative. A Supreme Court of 5 members is elected for 4 years on a non-partisan ballot.

In the 1968 presidential election Nixon polled 73,188 votes, Humphrey 60,598 and Wallace 20,432.

The state capital is Carson City (population, 5,163 in 1960, the smallest capital city in the country). There are 17 counties, 16 incorporated cities and towns and one city-county (Carson City).

Governor: Mike O'Callaghan (D.), 1971–74 ($25,000).
Lieut.-Governor: Ed Fike (R.) ($4,500).
Secretary of State: John Koontz (D.) ($15,000).

AREA AND POPULATION. Area 110,540 sq. miles, 752 sq. miles being water. The federal government in 1966 owned 60,971,262 acres, or 86·8% of the land area. Vacant public lands, 1967, 46,520,477 acres. The Bureau of Indian Affairs controlled, 1967, 1·35m. acres, of which 1,259,465 acres have been assigned to Indian tribes.

Census population on 1 April 1960 285,278, an increase of 125,195 or 78·2% since 1950. Population, 1 July 1969, 457,000. Births, 1968, were 8,456 (18·8 per 1,000 population); deaths, 3,724 (8·3); infant deaths, 220 (30·3 per 1,000 live births); marriages, 90,756 (202·1 per 1,000 population, largest of any state— national average 9·4); divorces, 10,104 (22·5).

Population in 4 census years (with distribution by sex, 1960) was:

	White	Negro	Indian	Asiatic and all other	Total	Per sq. mile
1910	74,276	513	5,240	1,846	81,875	0·7
1930	84,515	516	4,871	1,156	91,058	0·8
1950	149,908	4,302	5,025	848	160,083	1·5
1960	263,443	13,484	6,681	1,670	285,278	2·6
Male	136,298	6,900	3,338	985	147,521	—
Female	127,145	6,584	3,343	685	137,757	—

Of the total population in 1960, 200,704 persons (70·4%) were urban (57·2% in 1950). Native whites numbered 251,268; foreign-born whites, 12,343. Japanese numbered 544; Chinese, 572; other races, 554; those 18 years of age or older, 185,743.

The largest cities are Las Vegas, with population (1960 census) of 64,405 (urbanized area, 89,427); Reno, 51,470 (70,189); North Las Vegas, 18,422; Sparks, 16,618; Henderson, 12,525, and Elko. 6,298. Clark County (Las Vegas, North Las Vegas and Henderson) and Washoe County (Reno and Sparks) together had 74·3% of the total state population in 1960.

RELIGION. Roman Catholics are the most numerous religious group, followed by members of the Church of Jesus Christ of Latter day Saints (Mormons) and various Protestant churches. In 1952, there were 27,530 Catholics, 16,427 Mormons, 4,518 Episcopalians and 3,111 Methodists out of a total of 60,165 church members.

EDUCATION. School attendance is compulsory for children from 7 to 17 years of age. In 1968–69 the 171 public elementary schools, including kindergartens, had 2,579 classroom teachers and 69,484 pupils; 69 secondary public schools, including junior high and high schools had a first month enrolment of 46,517, with 1,922 secondary regular classroom teachers. Regular elementary classroom teachers received an average salary of $8,157; regular secondary classroom teachers, $8,470; 232 special education teachers (for handicapped pupils) in elementary grades had an average salary of $8,788; 128 vocational teachers averaged $8,494. There were 5,543 students in parochial and private schools at fall 1967. The University of Nevada, Reno, had, in fall 1969, 332 instructors and 6,163 students, and University of Nevada, Las Vegas, 172 instructors and 4,113 students. Technical institutes connected with each institution and a community college in Elko offer 2-year courses of a technical nature.

WELFARE. Old-age assistance is granted to all 65 years of age or older who are in need, and have assets not over $750 ($1,500 for married couples); fiscal year 1968–69, 2,617 persons received average of $74.1 per month; 169 blind, $96.45; 8,607 dependent children in families receiving payments averaging $30.51 per person. Nevada is the only state without aid to the permanently and totally disabled. On 31 Oct. 1967 the state had 21 hospitals (2,518 beds) exclusive of 4 restricted federal units.

Prohibition of marriage between persons of different race was repealed by statute in 1959.

A 1965 Civil Rights Act makes it illegal for persons operating public accommodations, employers of 15 or more employees, labour unions, and employment agencies to discriminate on the basis of race, colour, religion or national origin; a Commission on Equal Rights of Citizens is charged with enforcing the law.

In 1968 there was no execution; since 1924 executions (by lethal gas—the first state to adopt this method, in 1921) have numbered 31.

Prison population, 31 July 1969, was 659.

FINANCE. For the fiscal year ending 30 June 1969 state general fund revenues were $76·64m., excluding federal receipts; general expenditures were $75·57m. Highways and education followed by health and welfare received the largest appropriations.

State bonded indebtedness on 30 June 1969, was $9·5m. The state has no income taxes or inheritance tax. The sales and use tax and gaming taxes are the largest revenue producers.

Per capita personal income (1969) was $4,359.

AGRICULTURE. In 1969, 2,100 farms had a farm area of 8·8m. acres (9·2m. in 1960). Farms averaged 4,190 acres. Area under irrigation (1964) was 824,511 acres compared with 542,976 acres in 1959.

Farm income, 1968, from crops, livestock and government payments, $52·9m. Cattle, dairy products, hay and sheep are the principal commodities in order of cash receipts, 1968. On 1 Jan. 1969 there were 15,000 milch cows, 591,000 all cattle, 231,000 sheep and 10,000 swine. In 1968 the wool clip yielded 2·09m. lb. of wool.

FORESTRY. The area of national forests (1967) under US Forest Service administration was 5,062,932 acres.

MINING. Production, 1968, in order of value was: Copper, 72,870 short tons; gold, 343,000 troy oz.; sand and gravel, 6·2m. short tons. Other minerals are gypsum, iron ore, mercury and stone. Value of mineral output for 1968, $114,034,000.

INDUSTRY. The principal industries are tourism and legalized gambling, mining and smelting, livestock and irrigated agriculture, chemical manufacturing, and lumber processing. The report of the 1963 Census of Manufacturers indicates 283 establishments; the 1967 Census reports 7,000 workers, earning $47m.; value added by manufacture was $123m.

COMMUNICATIONS. In 1966 there were 1,644 miles of main-line railway. Highway mileage (federal, state and local) totalled 47,562 in 1969, of which 14,926 miles were surfaced; motor vehicle registrations in 1968 numbered 335,463. There were (31 Dec. 1967) 89 civil and military airports (896 active civil aircraft registered); 7 scheduled airlines operated.

BOOKS OF REFERENCE

Handbook of the Nevada Legislature, 55th Session, 1969. Legislative Counsel Bureau. Carson City
Legislative Manual, State of Nevada, 55th Session, 1969. Legislative Counsel Bureau. Carson City
Political History of Nevada. Secretary of State. Carson City, 1965
Financing State and Local Government in Nevada. Legislative Counsel Bureau. Carson City, 1960
Study of General Fund Revenues of the State of Nevada. Legislative Counsel Bureau. Carson City, 1966
Bushnell, E., *The Nevada Constitution: origin and growth.* Univ. of Nevada Press, 2nd ed., 1968
Hulse, James W., *The Nevada Adventure, A History.* Univ. of Nevada Press, 2nd ed., 1969
Mack, E. M., and Sawyer, B. W., *Here is Nevada: a history of the State.* Sparks, Nevada, 1965
Rusco, E. R., *Voting Behavior in Nevada.* Univ. of Nevada Press, 1966

STATE LIBRARY. Nevada State Library, Carson City. *State Librarian:* Mildred J. Heyer.

NEW HAMPSHIRE

GOVERNMENT. New Hampshire, first settled in 1623, is one of the 13 original states of the Union. While the present constitution dates from 1784, it was extensively revised in 1792 when the state joined the Union. Since 1775 there have been 15 state conventions with 46 amendments adopted to amend the constitution. The Legislature consists of a Senate of 30 members, elected for 2 years, and a House of Representatives, restricted to between 375 and 400 members, elected for 2 years. The Governor and 5 administrative officers called 'Councillors' are also elected for 2 years. Electors must be adult citizens, able to read and write, duly registered and not paupers or under sentence for crime. New Hampshire sends to the Federal Congress 2 senators and 2 representatives.

In the 1968 presidential election Nixon polled 154,903 votes, Humphrey 130,589 and Wallace 11,173.

The capital is Concord. The state is divided into 10 counties.

Governor: Walter R. Peterson (R.), 1971–73 ($30,000).
Secretary of State: Robert L. Stark (R.).

AREA AND POPULATION. Area, 9,304 sq. miles, of which 312 sq. miles are inland water. Census population, 1 April 1970, 737,681, an increase of 21·5% since 1960. Births, 1969, were 12,336 (18·4 per 1,000 population); deaths, 7,430 (10·8); infant deaths, 240 (0·4 per 1,000 live births); marriages, 10,236 (..); divorces, 2,253 (..).

Population at 4 federal censuses (with distribution by sex, 1960) was:

	White	Negro	Indian	Asiatic	Total	Per sq. mile
1910	429,906	564	34	68	430,572	47·7
1930	464,351	790	64	88	465,293	51·6
1950	532,275	731	74	162	533,242	59·1
1960	604,334	1,903	135	549	606,921	65·2
Male	296,662	1,098	69	278	298,107	—
Female	307,672	805	66	271	308,814	—

Native whites, 1960, were 559,765; foreign-born whites, 44,772. 353,776 (58·3%) were urban (57·5% in 1950); those 21 years of age or older numbered 372,725.

The largest city of the state is Manchester, with a 1970 census population of 87,754. Other cities are: Nashua, 55,820; Concord (capital), 30,022; Dover, 20,850; Portsmouth, 25,717; Keene, 20,467; Rochester, 17,938; Berlin, 15,256; Claremont, 14,221; Laconia, 14,888; Lebanon, 9,725; Somersworth, 9,026; Franklin, 7,292.

RELIGION. The Roman Catholic Church, with 261,444 adherents in 1968, is the largest single body. Protestants number over 350,000 adherents. The largest Protestant churches, 1966, were Congregational (36,944 members), Episcopal (20,960 baptized members in 1964), Methodist (9,031) and United Baptist Convention of N.H. (14,448).

EDUCATION. School attendance is compulsory for children from 6 to 14 years of age during the whole school term, or to 16 if their district provides a high school. Employed illiterate minors between 16 and 21 years of age must attend evening or special classes, if provided by the district. In 1970–71 the 374 public elementary schools (4,002 full-time classroom teachers) enrolled 94,624 pupils and the 98 public secondary schools (3,428 full-time classroom teachers) 64,132 pupils. In 1969–70, 92 private and parochial elementary schools had 22,084 registered pupils and 41 secondary schools, 7,890. Public school salaries, 1969–70, averaged $8,297. Total expenditure on public schools in 1969–70 was estimated at $132,953,237.

Total enrolment, 1968–69, in 29 institutions of higher education was 24,718 students. Dartmouth College, at Hanover, founded in 1769, had 373 instructors and 3,743 students; the University of New Hampshire, at Durham, founded in 1866, had 580 instructors and 8,424 students.

WELFARE. The Division of Welfare handles public assistance for (1) aged citizens 65 years or over, (2) needy aged aliens, (3) needy blind persons, (4) needy citizens between 18 and 64 years inclusive, who are permanently and totally disabled, (5) needy children under 21 years, (6) Medicaid and the medically needy not eligible for a monthly grant. Maximum grants are $115 per month in the adult category.

In June 1969, 4,150 persons were receiving old-age assistance of $11.669 per month, 1,914 families, $179.84 in respect of 5,744 children; 233 blind, $116.42; 752 permanently and totally disabled, $104.09.

In 1969 the state had 30 hospitals (3,100 beds). In 1966–67 mental hospitals had 2,226 patients, and there were 1,010 persons in institutions for the mentally retarded.

The state prison held 196 persons on 1 Aug. 1969. Since 1930 there has been only one execution (by hanging)—a white man, for murder, in 1939.

FINANCE. The state government's general revenue for the fiscal year ending 30 June 1968 (US Census Bureau figures) was $151·5m. ($72m. from taxes and $42m. from federal grants); general expenditures, $126·5m. ($21·6m. for education, $42m. for highways and $16·8m. for public welfare).

Net long-term debt of state, 30 June 1968, was $121·9m.

Per capita personal income (1969) was $3,474.

AGRICULTURE. In 1970, 3,300 farms had a total acreage of 740,000 acres, of which 140,000 acres were harvested crop land; average farm was 211 acres with average land value at $358 per acre. Commercial farms in 1968 numbered about 1,500 with 600,000 acres of crop land. The US Soil Survey estimates that the state has 164,167 acres of excellent soil, 486,615 acres of fair soil, 530,630 of poor soil and 3,843,798 of non-arable soil. Only 636,195 acres (11% of the total area) show moderate erosion.

Cash income, 1968, from dairy products, crops and livestock, $64m. The chief field crops are hay and vegetables; the chief fruit crop is apples. On 1 Jan. 1969 animals on farms were 43,000 milch cows, 74,000 all cattle, 5,600 sheep, 13,000 swine, 2·14m. poultry, 12,000 turkeys and about 20,000 horses.

FORESTRY. In 1968 commercial forest land totalled 4,907,400 acres; national forest, 591,909 acres; state forests had parks, 72,353 acres; forest industry ownership, 793,400 acres.

MINING. Minerals are little worked; total value of mineral output, 1968, $9·2m., over 98% from sand and gravel, stone, and clay for building and highway construction.

INDUSTRY. In 1968, 1,191 manufacturing establishments employed 99,074 persons who earned $586m.; 47% of manufacturing employment is accounted for in durable goods. Principal industries are leather products, electrical machinery, machinery non-electrical and textiles. In 1967, 794 wholesale establishments had gross sales of $505·3m.; 7,045 retail establishments had gross sales of $881·8m.

COMMUNICATIONS. In 1969 the length of railway in the state was 826 miles. There were 40 airports in 1966, of which 14 were public. On 1 Jan. 1969 the length of state highways was 4,359 miles, of which the state maintained 4,141 miles and municipalities 218 miles. The length of town roads, urban and rural, totalled 8,956 miles. Motor vehicles registered, 1968, numbered 412,292.

BOOKS OF REFERENCE

Morrison, L. S. *The Government of New Hampshire.* Concord, 1952
N.H. Register. State Year Book and Legislative Manual. Portland, Maine, 1965
Squires, J. D., *Granite State of the United States.* New York, 1956

NEW JERSEY

GOVERNMENT. New Jersey, first settled in the early 1600s, is one of the 13 original states in the Union. The legislative power is vested in a Senate and a General Assembly, the members of which are chosen by the people, all citizens (with necessary exceptions) 21 years of age, with the usual residential qualifications, having the right of suffrage. The present constitution, ratified by the voters on 4 Nov. 1947, has been amended 10 times. The Constitutional Convention proposed, and the people adopted in 1966, a new plan providing for a 40-member Senate and an 80-member General Assembly. This plan, as modified by the courts and implemented by the Apportionment Commission, provides for 15 Senate districts, each composed of 1, 2 or 3 whole counties, among which the 40 senators are apportioned on the basis of population. The senators are elected from these Senate districts, except that in the multi-member Senate districts composed of more than one county they are elected one from each sub-district (Assembly district). The Governor is elected for 4 years.

The state sends to Congress 2 senators and 15 representatives.

In the 1968 presidential election Nixon polled 1,316,467 votes, Humphrey 1,262,750 and Wallace 262,187.

The capital is Trenton. The state is divided into 21 counties, which are subdivided into cities, towns, boroughs, villages and townships.

Governor: Richard J. Hughes (D.), 1966–70 ($35,000).
Secretary of State: Robert J. Burkhardt ($18,000).

AREA AND POPULATION. Area (US Bureau of Census), 7,532 sq. miles (304 sq. miles being inland water). Census population, 1 April 1960, 6,066,782, an increase of 25·5% since 1950. Estimated population, 1 July 1967, 7,078,400.

Births, 1967, were 113,014 (16·4 per 1,000 population); deaths, 64,238 (9·3); infant deaths, 2,578 (22·2 per 1,000 live births); marriages, 49,132 (6·9); divorces (1966), 7,974.

Population at 4 federal censuses (with distribution by sex, 1960) was:

	White	Negro	Indian	Asiatic	All other	Total	Per sq. mile
1910	2,445,894	89,760	168	1,345	—	2,537,167	337·7
1930	3,829,663	208,828	213	2,630	122	4,041,334	537·3
1950	4,511,585	318,565	621	3,601	956	4,835,329	642·8
1960	5,539,003	514,875	1,699	8,778	2,427	6,066,782	739·5
Male	2,717,512	247,933	839	4,373	1,334	2,971,991	—
Female	2,821,491	266,942	860	4,405	1,093	3,094,791	—

Of the population in 1960, 5,374,369 persons (88·6%, the highest percentage of any state) were urban (86·6% in 1950); 3,921,630 were 20 years of age or older.

Census population of the larger cities and towns in 1960 was:

Newark	405,220	Bayonne	74,215	Plainfield	45,330
Jersey City	276,101	Atlantic City	59,544	Montclair	43,129
Paterson	143,663	Irvington	59,379	Woodbridge[1]	78,846
Camden	117,159	Passaic	53,963	Hamilton[1]	65,035
Trenton (capital)	114,167	Union City	52,180	Union[1]	51,499
Elizabeth	107,698	Bloomfield	51,867	Edison[1]	44,799
Clifton	82,084	Hoboken	48,441	North Bergen[1]	42,387
East Orange	77,259				

[1] Urban townships.

Largest urbanized areas (1960) were: New York–N.E. New Jersey, 14,114,927 (including Newark, Jersey City, Paterson, Clifton and Passaic); Trenton, 242,401.

RELIGION. The Roman Catholic population of New Jersey in 1967 was 2,911,962. No official Protestant or Jewish figures are available, but estimates place membership at 1m. and (1966) 363,265 respectively.

EDUCATION. Elementary instruction is compulsory for all from 7 to 16 years of age and free to all from 5 to 20 years of age. On 30 Sept. 1967 public elementary and secondary schools had 1,368,000 enrolled pupils; 6 teachers' colleges had 40,846 students. The total cost of public schools, 1967–68, $1,094m. Average salary of all 71,881 elementary and secondary classroom teachers in public schools was $7,647.

Princeton University (founded in 1746) had, in 1967–68, 873 professors and instructors and 4,650 undergraduate students; Rutgers, the State University (founded as Queen's College, 1766) had 24,755 students and 2,684 instructors; Fairleigh Dickinson (1941) at Rutherford, Teaneck and Madison and Edward Williams College at Hackensack had 19,002 students and 1,231 instructors; Stevens Institute of Technology (1870) at Hoboken had 187 professors and instructors and 2,500 students. Fairleigh Dickinson opened a graduate centre for English studies at Wroxton, England, in 1965.

WELFARE. Old-age assistance was revised in 1943 to provide aid for all persons 65 years of age or older, without means of support, who have resided in the state for one year preceding application. The monthly grant is limited only by the need of the applicant as determined by a standard budget. Number of recipients, July 1967, 14,596, drawing an average of $63.01 monthly; 34,107 families (103,697 children) received $58.57 monthly per child; 904 blind, $94.50; 9,077 totally disabled, $106.26.

The state's welfare system (in Dec. 1967) cared for 24,061 in institutions for the mentally deficient and epileptics, 1,014 in tuberculosis sanitoria, 383 in veterans' homes and 576 in training schools for juvenile delinquents. Also under care of the state's welfare agencies were 111,728 dependent children and 928 visually handicapped.

In 1968 the state had 128 hospitals (42,032 beds), listed by the New Jersey Hospital Association.

State prisons on 31 July 1968 had 5,741 inmates. In 1967 there were no executions; since 1930 executions (by electrocution) have totalled 74, including 47 whites, 25 Negroes and 2 other races, all for murder.

The constitution of New Jersey forbids discrimination against any person on account of 'religious principles, race, color, ancestry or national origin'. The state has had, since 1945, a 'fair employment act', *i.e.*, a Civil Rights statute forbidding any employer, public or private (with 6 or more employees), to discriminate against any applicant for work (or to discharge any employee) on the grounds of 'race, creed, color, national origin or ancestry'. Trade unions may not bar Negroes from membership.

FINANCE. For the year ending 30 June 1967 (US Census Bureau figures) general revenues were $1,347·8m. (taxation, $833,964,000 and federal aid, $287,627,000); general expenditures were $1,414,073,000 (education, $428,414,000, highways, $259,543,000, and public welfare, $129,277,000).

Total net long-term debt, 30 June 1968, was $1,192,117,000.

Per capita personal income (1969) was $.4,278

AGRICULTURE. Livestock raising, market-gardening, fruit-growing, horticulture and forestry are pursued. In 1967, 9,500 farms had a total area of 1·04m. acres; average farm had 114 acres valued, land and buildings, at $756 per acre, highest in US. In 1963 full owners had 10,500 farms (72%); tenant-farmers, at 1,000, were 7% of the total (23% in 1920).

Cash income, 1967, from crops, $129·4m., and livestock, $13m.

Leading crops are maize (855,000 cwt in 1967); white potatoes (4·16m. cwt); sweet potatoes (610,000 cwt); peaches (50m. lb.); cranberries (175,000 cwt), and apples (111·3m. lb.). Dairy and market-garden produce contribute principally to cash farm receipts.

Farm animals on 1 Jan. 1967 included 86,000 milch cows, 147,000 all cattle, 92,000 sheep and 128,000 swine.

MINING. The chief minerals are stone and sand and gravel; others are clay products, iron ore and magnesium compounds. New Jersey is a leading producer of glass sand, moulding sand, trap rock and of green sand, used in water-softening. Total value of mineral products, 1967, was $72·75m.

INDUSTRY. In 1964 the 14,906 manufacturing establishments employed 829,176 production workers, receiving $5,112m. in wages; value added by manu-facture, $9,980m. The principal industries are: Smelting and refining non-ferrous metals; petroleum refining; chemicals; motor vehicles and supplies; meat-packing (wholesale); shipbuilding and repairing, and paints, varnishes and lacquers. Refinery output of petrol in 1962 was 71·3m. bbls.

COMMUNICATIONS. In 1966, 21 railways had 1,818 miles of track. There were 138 airports in 1967, of which 16 were publicly owned. In 1967 there were 33,186 miles of roads (municipal, 16,116 miles; state, 2,057 miles; local, 15,291 miles; toll, 358; interstate, 364 miles.

BOOKS OF REFERENCE

Manual of the Legislature of New Jersey. Trenton. Annual
Dept. of Conservation and Economic Development, *County Summary*. Trenton, 1966
Economy of New Jersey. Rutgers Univ. Press, 1958
Boyd, J. P. (ed.), *Fundamentals and Constitutions of New Jersey, 1664–1954*. New York, 1964
Cunningham, J. T., *This is New Jersey*. Rutgers Univ., New Brunswick, 1953
Rich, B. M., *The Government and Administration of New Jersey*. New York, 1957

STATE LIBRARY. 185 W. State Street, Trenton, N.J. 08625. *Director:* Roger H. McDonough.

NEW MEXICO

GOVERNMENT. From the time of its first settlement in 1598 until 1771 New Mexico was the Spanish kings 'Kingdom of New Mexico'. In 1771 it was annexed to the northern provinces of New Spain. When New Spain won its independence in 1821, it took the name of Republic of Mexico and established New Mexico as its northernmost department. When the war between the US and Mexico was concluded on 2 Feb. 1848 New Mexico was recognized as be-longing to the US, and on 9 Sept. 1850 it was made a Territory. Part of the Territory was assigned to Texas; later Utah was formed into a separate Territory; in 1861 another part was transferred to Colorado, and in 1863 Arizona was dis-joined, leaving to New Mexico its present area. New Mexico became a state in Jan. 1912. The constitution of 1912 is still in force with 55 amendments. The state Legislature, which meets annually, consists of 43 members of the Senate, elected for 4 years, and 70 members of the House of Representatives, elected for 2 years. The Governor and Lieut.-Governor are elected for 2 years. The state sends to Congress 2 senators and 2 representatives.

In the 1968 presidential election Nixon polled 169,692 votes, Humphrey 130,081 and Wallace 27,508.

The state capital is Santa Fé. For local government the state is divided into 32 counties.

Governor: Bruce King (D.), 1970–72 ($17,500).
Lieut.-Governor: Robert Mondragon (R.), 1970–72.
Secretary of State: Betty Fiorina (D.), ($10,000).

AREA AND POPULATION. Area, 121,666 sq. miles (156 sq. miles being water). Public lands, administered by federal agencies (1960) amounted to 27·1m. acres or 34·9% of the total area. Department of Defense held 3m. acres; Agriculture, 9·2m.; Interior, 14·8m.; Bureau of Indian Affairs, 6·5m. acres. The State of New Mexico held 11·4m. acres; 32·8m. acres were privately owned.

Census population, 1 April 1970, 1,014,979, an increase of 63,956 or 6·7% since 1960. Vital statistics, 1969: Births, 21,493 (19·8 per 1,000 population); deaths, 7,241 (6·9); infant deaths, 511 (25·5 per 1,000 live births); marriages, 10,698; divorces, 3,477.

The population in 4 census years (with distribution by sex, 1970) was:

	White	Negro	Indian	Asiatic	Total	Per sq. mile
1910	304,594	1,628	20,573	506	327,301	2·7
1950	630,211	8,408	41,901	667	681,187	5·6
1960	875,763	17,063	56,255	1,942	951,023	7·8
1970	914,910	19,537	72,703	2,214	1,014,729	..
Male	451,649	9,822	..	..	500,295	..
Female	463,261	9,715	..	..	514,684	..

Native whites, 1960, were 798,558; foreign-born whites, 20,584. Of the 1960 total, 625,174 persons (65·6%) were urban (50·2% in 1950); 500,675 were 21 years of age or older.

Before 1930 New Mexico was largely a Spanish-speaking state. (Both Spanish and English are official languages.) In 1940 about 49·1% of the population were of Spanish or Mexican extraction, but since 1945 an influx of population from other states has reduced the percentage to an estimated 33%. While most Spanish people have adapted themselves to an increasingly commercial and industrial economy, a minority of rural people of Spanish and Mexican descent, particularly in the north of the state, have been forced by economic necessity to emigrate to industrial urban areas where they have experienced difficulty in economic and social adjustment.

The largest cities are Albuquerque, with population (census 1970) 243,751 (urbanized area, 297,445); Santa Fé (capital), 41,167; Las Cruces, 37,857; Roswell, 33,908; Hobbs, 26,025; Carlsbad, 21,297.

RELIGION. A survey (1967) by the National Council of the Churches of Christ shows 300,609 Roman Catholics (68% of total church membership) and 139,920 Protestants. Total, all denominations, 441,774.

EDUCATION. Elementary education is free, and compulsory between 6 and 17 years of age. In 1968–69 the 89 school districts had an estimated enrolment of 273,746 students in public elementary and secondary schools. In 1968–69, 97 private and parochial schools had 17,712 pupils, of whom 12,431 were in 52 Roman Catholic schools. In 1968–69, 11,218 teachers were receiving an average salary of $7,297. Public school expenditure, 1969, was $115·8m.

For higher education (1970–71). New Mexico State University, at Las Cruces, 536 professors and instructors, 8,155 students; the Highlands University, at Las Vegas, 125 instructors, 2,479 students; New Mexico Western University, at Silver City, 67 instructors, 1,425 students; Eastern New Mexico University, at Portales, 190 instructors, 4,275 students; New Mexico Institute of Mining and Technology, at Socorro, 90 instructors, 873 students; the University of New Mexico, at Albuquerque, with 904 professors and 18,061 students, and the University of Albuquerque, at Albuquerque, 89 instructors, 2,015 students.

WELFARE. In April 1970, 9,425 persons were receiving old-age assistance, (average $55.02 per month); 384 persons were receiving aid to the blind (average $73.95 per month); aid to 40,092 dependent children in 14,515 families averaged $121.60 per family. The state's net expenditure, 1969, for public assistance was $45m.

In 1969 the state had 54 hospitals (4,692 beds).

The number of state penitentiary prisoners, average population 1969, was 872. The death penalty (by electrocution) has been imposed on 11 persons since 1930, 9 whites and 2 Negroes, all for murder. The last 2 executions were in 1967.

Since 1949 the denial of employment by reason of race, colour, religion, national origin or ancestry has been forbidden. A law of 1955 prohibits discrimination in public places because of race or colour.

FINANCE. For the year ending 30 June 1969 (US Census Bureau figures) general revenues were $543,028,000 ($237,432,000 from taxation and $161·19m.

from federal grants); general expenditures, $459,416,000 (education, $241m.; highways, $80·5m., and public welfare, $57m.).

Long-term debt on 30 June 1969 was $109,793,000.

Per capita personal income (1969) was $2,897.

AGRICULTURE. New Mexico produces cereals, vegetables, fruit and cotton. Dry farming and irrigation have proved profitable in periods of high prices. There were 13,800 farms and ranches covering 48·3m. acres; average farm (or ranch) was valued (land and buildings) at $117,042 in 1964; 4,046 farms were of 1,000 acres and over.

Cash income, 1969, from crops, $91·5m., and from livestock and products, $298·9m. Principal crops are cotton (165,000 bales from 147,000 acres in 1969), hay (1,063,000 tons), wheat (5·1m. bu.) and grain sorghums (16·9m. bu.). The farm animals on 1 Jan. 1970 included 55,000 milch cows, 1,386,000 all cattle, 834,000 sheep and 48,000 swine. National forest area (1966) covered 9·9m. acres.

Of the total surface area (77,588,536 acres), 60% was severely eroded in 1939 and only 26% without apparent erosion; mountains, etc., covered 13·5% of the rest.

MINING. New Mexico is the country's largest domestic source of uranium with about 65% of total reserves. Production of recoverable U_3O_8 was 12·2m. lb. in 1969. Production of other important minerals, 1969: Petroleum, 128m. bbls; natural gas, 1,210,520m. cu. ft; potassium salts, 2·4m. short tons K_2O (equivalent 83% of US total); natural gas liquids, 34·4m. bbls (of 42 gallons); copper, 122,500 short tons; zinc, 24,220 short tons. The value of the total mineral output in 1969 was $966·3m. An average of 17,288 persons were employed in the mining industry in 1969.

INDUSTRY. Average monthly employment during 1969 was 345,419. A total of 20,254 were employed in manufacturing, 20,751 in agriculture and 85,054 in government. At the 1967 Census of Manufactures, 10,564 production workers earned $55m. during the year; value added by manufacture was $185m.

COMMUNICATIONS. In 1968 there were 2,225 miles of railway. There were 121 airports in 1970. The state, 1969, had 67,632 miles of road (12,857 paved), of which the state maintained 12,457 miles. Motor vehicle registrations, 1969, 667,844.

BOOKS OF REFERENCE

Writers' Program. *New Mexico: A Guide to the Colorful State*. Rev. ed. New York, 1953
New Mexico Business (monthly; annual review in March issue). Bureau of Business Research, Univ. of N.M., Albuquerque
Donnelly, T. C., *The Government of New Mexico*. Univ. of N.M. Press, Albuquerque, 1953
Edgel, R. L., and Wollman, N., *Patterns of New Mexico State Finance*. Bureau of Business Research, Univ. of N.M., Albuquerque, 1950.—and Ximenes, V. T., *Income and Employment in New Mexico, 1949–1959*. Bureau of Business Research, Univ. of N.M., Albuquerque, 1961
Fitzpatrick, G., and Sinclair, J. L., *Profile of a State, New Mexico*. Albuquerque, 1964

NEW YORK STATE

GOVERNMENT. From 1609 to 1664 the region now called New York was claimed by the Dutch; then it came under the rule of the English, who governed the country till the outbreak of the War of Independence. On 20 April 1777 New York adopted a constitution which transformed the colony into an independent state; on 26 July 1788 it ratified the constitution of the US, becoming one of the 13 original states. New York dropped its claim to Vermont after the latter was admitted to the Union in 1791. With the annexation of a small area from Massachusetts in 1853, New York assumed its present boundaries.

The present constitution dates from 1894; a later constitutional convention, 1938, is now legally considered merely to have amended the 1894 constitution, which has now had 93 amendments. The Constitutional Convention of 1967 (4 April through 26 Sept.) was composed of 186 delegates who proposed a new state constitution; however this was rejected by the registered voters on 7 Nov. 1967. The Senate consists of 57 members, and the Assembly of 150 members, both elected every 2 years. The Governor and Lieut.-Governor are elected for 4 years. The right of suffrage resides in every adult who has been a citizen for 90 days, and has the usual residential qualifications; new voters must establish, by certificates or test, that they have had at least an elementary education.

The state is represented in Congress by 2 senators and 41 representatives.

In the 1968 presidential election Humphrey polled 3,378,470 votes, Nixon 3,007,932 and Wallace 358,864.

The state capital is Albany. For local government the state is divided into 62 counties, 5 of which constitute the city of New York. New York leads in state parks and recreation areas, covering 4,502,000 acres in 1969.

Governor: Nelson Rockefeller (R.), 1971–74 ($50,000).
Lieut.-Governor: Malcolm Wilson (R.) ($30,000).
Secretary of State: John P. Lomenzo (R.) ($34,765).

Cities are in 3 classes, the first class having each 175,000 or more inhabitants and the third under 50,000. Each is incorporated by charter, under special legislation. The government of New York City is vested in the mayor (John Lindsay), elected for 4 years, and a city council, whose president is elected for 4 years and members for 2 years. The council has 25 members, each elected from a state senatorial district wholly within the city. The mayor appoints all the heads of departments, except the comptroller, who is elected. Each of the 5 city boroughs (Manhattan, Bronx, Brooklyn, Queens and Richmond) has a president, elected for 4 years. Each of these boroughs is also a county, bearing the same name except Manhattan borough, which, as a county, is called New York, and Brooklyn, which is Kings County.

AREA AND POPULATION. Area, 49,576 sq. miles (1,647 sq. miles being water). Census population, 1 April 1960, 16,782,304, an increase of 13·2% since 1950. Estimated population, 1 July 1968, 18,190,283. Births in 1967 were 307,863 (16·8 per 1,000 population); deaths, 186,911 (10·2); infant deaths, 6,799 (22·1 per 1,000 live births); marriages (1968), 155,335; divorces, 14,454.

Population in 4 census years (with distribution by sex, 1960) was:

	White	Negro	Indian	Asiatic	Total	Per sq. mile
1910	8,966,845	134,191	6,046	6,532	9,113,614	191·2
1930	12,143,191	412,814	6,973	15,088	12,588,066	262·6
1950	13,872,095	918,191	10,640	29,266	14,830,192	309·3
1960	15,287,071	1,417,511	16,491	51,678	16,782,304	350·1
Male	7,421,364	657,534	All others	44,341	8,123,239	—
Female	7,865,707	759,977		33,381	8,659,065	—

Of the Asiatics in 1960, 37,573 were Chinese and 8,702 Japanese. 14,331,925 or 85·4% were urban (85·5% in 1950); those 21 years of age or older numbered 10,880,592; foreign-born whites numbered 2,181,868. Aliens registered in Jan. 1969 numbered 740,639 or 18% of the US total of aliens.

The population of New York City, by boroughs, census of 1 April 1960 (with 1968 estimates in brackets), was: Manhattan, 1,698,281 (1·7m.); Bronx, 1,424,815 (1·47m.); Brooklyn, 2,627,319 (2·6m.); Queens, 1,809,578 (1·99m.); Richmond, 221,991 (280,000); total, 7,781,984 (8·1m.). The New York metropolitan statistical area had, in 1960, 10,694,633 while the larger New York–NE New Jersey urbanized area had 14,114,927.

Estimated population of other large cities and towns 1 July 1968 was:

Buffalo	459,127	Rome	49,654	*Unincorporated towns*[1]	
Rochester	291,070	White Plains	49,388	Cheektowaga NW	84,322
Syracuse	208,309	Elmira	41,686	Hicksville	53,000
Yonkers	207,247	Valley Stream	40,219	Eggertsville	52,000
Albany (capital)	122,670	Jamestown	39,791	East Meadow	47,500
Utica	96,701	Hempstead	39,474	Elmont	36,500
Niagara Falls	85,246	Freeport	38,838	Massapequa	36,000
New Rochelle	73,504	N. Tonawanda	36,036	Oceanside	34,000
Mount Vernon	70,150	Poughkeepsie	35,462	Wantagh	34,000
Schenectady	69,584	Auburn	32,953	Franklin Square	33,000
Binghamton	66,572	Watertown	31,584	Tonawanda	21,946
Troy	62,244	Newburgh	26,337		

[1] Estimates 1965.

Other large urbanized areas, July 1968 (New York State estimates): Buffalo, 1·32m.; Rochester, 828,000; Albany–Schenectady–Troy, 690,000.

RELIGION. The chief churches are Roman Catholic, with 6,583,055 members in 1968, Jewish congregations (2,520,155) and Protestant Episcopal (416,082). Total membership of all Protestant denominations, 1953, was 1,594,000.

EDUCATION. Education is compulsory between the ages of 7 and 16. In autumn 1968 the public elementary schools (grades kindergarten to 6) enrolled 1,925,104 children, public secondary schools (grades 7 to 12) had 1,472,574 pupils; classroom teachers numbered 170,147 in public schools. Total expenditure on public schools in 1967–68 was estimated at $3,621m. Teachers' salaries, 1968, averaged $9,168.

The State's educational system, including public and private schools and secondary institutions, universities, colleges, libraries, museums, etc., constitutes (by legislative act) the 'University of the State of New York', which is governed by a Board of Regents consisting of 15 members appointed by the Legislature. Within the framework of this 'University' was established in 1948 a 'State University' which controls 70 colleges and educational centres, 68 of which conduct classes, and supervises 36 locally operated community colleges. The 'State University' is governed by a Board of 15 Trustees, appointed by the Governor with the consent and advice of the Senate.

Higher education in the State is conducted in 212 institutions (422,066 full-time students), of which 138 are under private control and 74 under public control.

In 1967–68 the 204 institutions of higher education in the state had a total of 47,000 faculty members, and 644,757 full-time students. Among the larger were:

Founded	Name and place	Professors	Students
1754	Columbia University, New York	3,911	15,960
1795	Union University, Schenectady and Albany	119	1,303
1824	Rensselaer Polytechnic Institute, Troy	626	4,957
1831	New York University, New York	5,149	42,000
1846	Colgate University, Hamilton	160	1,739
1846	Fordham University, Catholic, New York	555	6,255
1846	University of Buffalo at Buffalo,	740	17,164
1847	University of the City of New York, New York[1]	8,500	134,000
1848	Rochester, University of, Rochester	1,700	7,557
1849	Syracuse University, Syracuse	1,223	22,348
1854	Polytechnic Institute of Brooklyn	394	5,094
1856	St Lawrence University, Canton	132	1,849
1857	Cooper Union Institute of Technology, New York	171	1,230
1861	Vassar College, Poughkeepsie	175	1,741
1863	Manhattan College, New York	225	4,452
1865	Cornell University, Ithaca	2,276	13,912

[1] Includes the City College of New York, Brooklyn College, Hunter College and Queen's College.

The Saratoga Performing Arts Centre (5,100 seats), a non-profit, tax-exempt organization, which opened in 1966, is the summer residence of the New York City Ballet and the Philadelphia Orchestra—two groups which present special educational programmes for students and teachers.

WELFARE. Old-age assistance provides relief for any person 65 years of age or older who is a resident of the state on the date of application. Number of recipients in May 1969, 83,272, drawing an average of $98.11 per month; medical assistance went to 1,268,547 persons who received $69.76; aid to dependent children included 259,880 families, with 726,078 children, grants averaging $239.03 per family; 3,461 blind, $117.50; 58,456 disabled, $103.6 per month.

In 1966 the state had 440 hospitals (210,038 beds) listed by the American Hospital Association. On 31 Dec. 1964 mental hospitals had 87,887 resident patients and institutions for the mentally retarded had 24,149 resident patients.

In 1945 New York adopted a 'Law against Discrimination' applicable to all employers, public or private, trade unions and employment agencies making it an offence under the police powers of the state to discriminate, in matters of employment, against any persons on account of 'race, creed, colour or national origin'. Enforcement is placed with a 'State Commission against Discrimination', which must first try persuasion and, that failing, may issue 'cease and desist orders', which the courts will enforce. The State Constitution declares that no person shall be subject to discrimination in his civil rights 'because of race, colour, creed or religion', but leaves it to the legislature to define 'civil rights'.

On 31 July 1969, 13,304 persons were in state prisons.

In 1963–67 there were no executions. Total executions (by electrocution) from 1930 to 1962 were 329 (234 whites, 90 Negroes, 5 other races; all for murder except 2 for kidnapping).

In 1966 murders reported in New York were 879; other crimes, 437,257. Police strength in Dec. 1966 was 35,720 (in cities with population of 25,000 and over).

FINANCE. The state's general revenues for the year ending 31 March 1965 (US Census Bureau figures) were $3,912,700 ($2,862·2m. from taxes, $672·1m. from federal aid); general expenditures were $3,985·3m. ($1,595·8m. for education, $519·6m. for highways, $554·2m. for public welfare). In 1965 individual income tax (the state's, not the federal government's), at $1,135m., and corporation income tax, at $527·8m., led all states.

The net long-term debt, 31 March 1962, was $2,597,896,000.

Per capita personal income ($4,421 in 1969) ranked third in USA.

The assessed valuation in 1963–64 of taxable real property in New York City was $28,557m. General revenue of New York City (1961–62) was $2,727m. and general expenditure, $2,597m.

AGRICULTURE. New York has large agricultural interests. In 1967 it had 66,510 farms, with a total area of 12·4m. acres; average farm was 189·6 acres.

Cash income, 1968, from crops, $294m. and from livestock and livestock products, $748m. Dairying, with 31,195 farms, 1964, is the leading type of farming providing $557m. (54%) of farm cash receipts. Field crops comprise maize, winter wheat, oats and hay. New York ranks second in US in the production of apples, grapes, tart cherries and maple syrup. Other products are peaches, pears, plums, strawberries, raspberries, cabbage, onions, potatoes, maple sugar. Estimated farm animals 1 Jan. 1969 included 1,849,000 cattle, 103,000 sheep, 86,000 swine and 13·75m. chickens.

MINING (1967). Production of principal minerals: Sand and gravel (43·5m. short tons), salt (5·3m. short tons), zinc (70,555 short tons), petroleum (1,972,000 bbls), lead (1,653 short tons), stone (33·4m. short tons). The state is a leading producer of titanium concentrate, talc, abrasive garnet, wollastonite and emery. Quarry products include trap rock, slate, marble, limestone and sandstone. The value of mineral output in 1967 was $299·32m.

INDUSTRY. In 1965 manufacturing establishments (numbering 40,160 in 1963) employed 1,836,900 production workers. The estimated 1968 weekly earnings of 1,891,600 workers engaged in industry and manufacturing averaged

$126.40. Leading industries were women's clothing, printing and publishing, newspapers and periodicals, books and commercial printing, men's clothing, electrical machinery, leather products, bread and other bakery products.

COMMUNICATIONS. In New York State there were in 1966, 7,647 miles of railways. There were 371 airports as of 31 Dec. 1966. The canals of the state, combined in 1918 in what is called the Improved Canal System, have a length of 524 miles, of which the Erie or Barge canal has 340 miles. In 1966 the Barge canal carried 3·1m. tons of freight. There were (1967) 102,292 miles of municipal and rural roads; of rural roads (85,396 miles), 14,207 were state maintained. The New York State Thruway extends 559 miles from New York City to Buffalo and thence to the Pennsylvania State line, and is the longest toll highway in the world; in 1967 gross receipts from tolls amounted to $86,705,916. The North-way, a 175-mile toll-free highway, has been completed as a connecting road from the Thruway at Albany to the Canadian border at Champlain, Quebec. Motor vehicle registrations (excluding municipally owned and exempt buses and ambulances) in 1968 were 6,688,601.

BOOKS OF REFERENCE

Annual Summary of Business Statistics, 1956–64. Dept. of Commerce. Albany, 1965
Basic Statistics for Counties and Metropolitan Areas of New York State. Dept. of Commerce, Albany. 1967
Manual for the Use of the Legislature. Secretary of State. Albany
Caldwell, L. K., *The Government and Administration of New York.* New York, 1954
Ellis, D. M., *Short History of New York State.* Cornell Univ. Press, 1958
Hepburn, A., *Complete guide to New York City.* New York, 1964
Nevins, A., and Krout, J. A. (ed.), *The Greater City: New York, 1898–1948.* New York and London, 1949
Thompson, J. H. (ed.), *Geography of New York State.* Syracuse Univ. Press, 1966
Vernon, R., *Metropolis 1985: an interpretation of the New York metropolitan region study.* Harvard Univ. Press, 1960
Wheeler, Alfred H., and Kolevzow, Edward R., *New York State: Its History and Constitution.* New York, 1950

STATE LIBRARY. The New York State Library, Albany 1. *State Librarian and Assistant Commissioner for Libraries:* John A. Humphry.

NORTH CAROLINA

GOVERNMENT. North Carolina, first settled in 1585 by Sir Walter Raleigh and permanently settled in 1663, was one of the 13 original states of the Union. The present constitution dates from 1876 (though largely based on that of 1868); it has had 134 amendments. The General Assembly consists of a Senate of 50 members and a House of Representatives of 120 members, elected for 2 years. The Governor and Lieut.-Governor are elected for 4 years. The Governor may not succeed himself and has no veto. All registered citizens with the usual residential qualifications have a vote.

The state is represented in Congress by 2 senators and 11 representatives.

In the presidential election of 1968 Nixon polled 627,192 votes, Humphrey 464,113 and Wallace 496,188.

The capital is Raleigh.

Governor: Robert W. Scott (D.), 1965–69 ($35,000).
Lieut.-Governor: H. P. (Pat) Taylor (D.).
Secretary of State: Thad Eure (D.) ($22,500).

AREA AND POPULATION. Area, 52,712 sq. miles, of which 3,645 sq. miles are inland water. Census population, 1 April 1960, 4,556,155, an increase of 12·2% since 1950. Estimated population, 1 July 1968, 4,963,895.

Births, 1968, were 92,632 (18·7 per 1,000 population); marriages, 47,989 (9·7); deaths, 44,282 (8·9); infant deaths, 2,433 (26·3 per 1,000 live births); divorces, 12,385 (2·5).

Population in 4 census years (with distribution by sex, 1960):

	White	Negro	Indian	Asiatic	Total	Per sq. mile
1910	1,500,511	697,843	7,851	82	2,206,287	45·3
1930	2,234,958	918,647	16,579	92	3,170,276	64·5
1950	2,983,121	1,047,353	3,742	—	4,061,929	82·7
1960	3,399,285	1,116,021	38,129	2,012	4,556,155	92·2
Male	1,684,797	541,995	All others 20,277		2,247,069	—
Female	1,714,488	574,026	All others 20,572		2,309,086	—

Of the total population in 1960, 1,801,921 persons (39·5%) were urban (33·7% in 1950); 2,556,884 were 21 years old or older; foreign-born whites numbered 20,041.

Cities (with census population in 1960) are: Charlotte, 201,564 (urbanized ares, 209,551); Greensboro, 119,574 (123,334); Winston-Salem, 111,135 (128,176); Raleigh (capital), 93,931; Durham, 78,302; High Point, 62,063; Asheville, 60,192; Fayetteville, 47,106; Wilmington, 44,013; Gastonia, 37,276.

RELIGION. Leading denominations are the Baptists (1,005,833 members in 1968), Methodists (479,397, Presbyterians (153,672). There were approximately 60,000 members of the Roman Catholic Church in 1968. Total estimate of all denominations in 1968 was 2·69m.

EDUCATION. School attendance is compulsory between 7 and 16. Integration of Negro pupils and teachers into formerly all-white schools is being carried out under freedom of choice plans in compliance with the federal Civil Rights Act 1965 and in nearly all school units.

Public school enrolment, 1968–69, was 1,220,636; 867,244 attended 1,868 elementary schools, 353,392 attended 674 high schools. Instructional staff, 1968–69, consisted of 50,393 classroom teachers, 1,993 principals and 566 supervisors, a total of 52,954; average salary for classroom teachers (1968–69) was $6,852, of which $6,445 was paid from state funds. Estimated total current expenditure for public schools, 1968–69, $575m., including $410m. from state, $90m. from local and $75m. from federal sources.

In fall 1968 state-supported colleges and universities included 13 two-year community colleges with 7,170 students; 7 four-year colleges with 7,323 students; 5 senior institutions (granting master's degrees) with 26,034 students; and the University of North Carolina with 4 campuses: the University of North Carolina at Chapel Hill (founded 1789) with 1,170 teachers and 16,233 students; North Carolina State University at Raleigh (1887) with 1,130 teachers and 11,964 students; University of North Carolina at Greensboro (1891) with 334 teachers and 5,889 students; and the University of North Carolina at Charlotte (1946) with 121 teachers and 2,351 students. Total enrolment in state-supported institutions of higher-learning, fall 1968, was 79,076.

There are 42 private and church-related institutions of higher learning: 14 two-year junior colleges enrolled 9,143 students; 28 senior colleges, 37,554 students; Duke University, 7,320 students (fall 1968). In addition, 1,066 students were enrolled in 4 theological colleges.

WELFARE. Old-age assistance was being received in June 1969 by 38,052 persons receiving an average (not including medical care) of $70.85 per month; aid to families with dependent children received by 114,626 recipients averaged $28.66 per person monthly; 11,851 blind, $78.84; 25,246 totally disabled, $74.79. In March 1969 the state had 167 hospitals (31,356 beds).

In 1968 there was no execution; total executions (by lethal gas) since 1930 were 263, including 59 whites, 199 Negroes and 5 other races.

Prison population, 30 June 1969, was 9,906.

FINANCE. General revenue for the year ending 30 June 1968 (US Census Bureau figures) was $1,351·2m. ($901·5m. from taxation and $297·8m. from federal aid). General expenditure was $1,324·9m. (education, $694m.; highways, $273·6m.; public welfare, $104·6m.).

On 30 June 1969 the net total long-term debt amounted to $480·79m. *Per capita* personal income (1969) was $2,890.

AGRICULTURE. In 1969 there were 163,000 farms in North Carolina (a number exceeded only by Texas) covering 16·1m. acres; average size of farms was 99 acres (lowest of any state) and average value (1964), $24,906.

Income is primarily from tobacco, poultry, cattle, swine, maize, cotton, peanuts and soybeans. Cash income, 1968, from crops from $733,554,000 and from livestock and products, $505,066,000.

North Carolina leads in production of tobacco (667,375,000 lb., 1968). Production of maize, 1968, was 80·88m. bu.; cotton, 123,000 bales (of 500 lb.); peanuts, 346·5m. lb.; soybeans, 16,038,000 bu. Also grown extensively are wheat, oats, barley, sweet potatoes, hay, peaches and apples. On 1 Jan. 1969 farms had 211,000 milch cows, 1m. all cattle, 1·47m. swine and 20,000 sheep. Production of commercial broilers, 1968, amounted to 262,872,000 (fourth highest in US).

FORESTRY. North Carolina is the largest lumber-producing state in the South and the fifth largest in the US. Timber, covering 20m. acres in 1968, provided approximately $1,800m. income in forest industries and products. The area of forest lands in public ownership in 1968 was 1·74m. acres.

FISHERIES. Food-fish catch, 1968, amounted to 33m. lb.; menhaden (used for oils and fish meal) catch was 167m. lb. Total fish catch, 1968, was valued at $9·7m., including $2m. for menhaden.

MINING. Mineral production in 1968 was valued at $83m., a new record. Principal minerals mined were stone, sand and gravel, phosphate rock, feldspar, lithium minerals, clays, talc and pyrophyllite. North Carolina ranked first in the production of mica, feldspar and lithium minerals. It is also the leading producer of bricks. In 1968 North Carolina manufactured 860m. bricks valued at $25·4m. or 12% of the total US production.

INDUSTRY. North Carolina's 8,000 industrial establishments in 1969 had 697,000 production workers. Value added by manufacture (1969 estimate) was $7,226m. The leading industries are textile goods (leading all states), manufacture of cigarettes (over 62% of the US production, leading all states), electrical machinery, processing of some 50 food crops and the manufacture of furniture and bricks (leading all states in both). Total receipts of all travel-serving industries was $1,400m. in 1969.

COMMUNICATIONS. The state in 1969 contained 4,408 miles of railway, almost wholly diesel-powered. The state was the first to undertake the maintenance of all highways; she maintained, 1969, nearly 74,000 miles of highways, more than any other state; 46,887 miles were paved. In 1968, 2,898,420 automobiles were registered.

Airports in 1969 numbered 168, of which 55 publicly owned.

BOOKS OF REFERENCE

North Carolina Manual. Secretary of State. Raleigh. Biennial
North Carolina: A Guide to the Old North State. Univ. of N.C., Chapel Hill, 1955
North Carolina Report. First Union National Bank, Charlotte, 1967
Corbitt, D. L., *The Formation of the North Carolina Counties.* Raleigh 1969
Hobbs, S. H., *North Carolina: an economic and social profile.* Univ. of N.C., Chapel Hill, 1958
Lefler, H. T., and Newsome, A. R., *North Carolina: the history of a Southern State.* Univ. of N.C. Chapel Hill, 1963
Powell, W. S., *The North Carolina Gazetteer.* Univ. of N.C., Chapel Hill, 1968
Thornton, M. L., *Bibliography of North Carolina, 1589–1956.* Univ. of N.C., Chapel Hill, 1958
Lonsdale, R. E., *Atlas of North Carolina.* Univ. of N.C., Chapel Hill and OUP, 1967

STATE LIBRARY. North Carolina State Library, Raleigh. *State Librarian:* Philip S. Ogilvie

NORTH DAKOTA

GOVERNMENT. North Dakota, first settled around 1800, was admitted into the Union, with boundaries as at present, on 2 Nov. 1889; previously it had formed part of the Dakota Territory, established 2 March 1861. The present constitution dates from 1889; it has had 73 amendments. The Legislative Assembly consists of a Senate of 49 members elected for 4 years, and a House of Representatives of 98 members elected for 2 years. The Governor and Lieut.-Governor are elected for 4 years. Qualified electors are (with necessary exceptions) all citizens and civilized Indians. The state sends to Congress 2 senators elected by the voters of the entire state and 1 representative elected from each of the state's two congressional districts.

In the 1968 presidential election Nixon polled 138,667 votes, Humphrey 94,769 and Wallace 14,244.

The capital is Bismarck. The state has 53 organized counties.

Governor: William L. Guy (D.), 1969–73 ($18,000 plus $4,000 expenses).
Lieut.-Governor: Richard Larson (R.) ($2,000 plus $2,000 expenses).
Secretary of State: Ben Meier (R.) ($11,000 plus $3,000 expenses).

AREA AND POPULATION. Area, 70,665 sq. miles, 1,385 sq. miles being water. The Federal Bureau of Indian Affairs administered (1964) 865,000 acres, of which 133,000 acres were assigned to tribes. Census population, 1 April 1970, 617,761, a decrease of 14,685 or 2·3% since 1960. Births in 1969 were 10,798 (17·5 per 1,000 population); deaths, 5,595 (9·1); infant deaths 179 (16·6 per 1,000 live births); marriages, 5,339 (8·7); divorces, 893 (1·4).

Population at 4 census years (with distribution by sex, 1960) was:

	White	Negro	Indian	Asiatic	Total	Per sq. mile
1910	569,855	617	6,486	98	577,166	8·2
1930	566,370	377	8,617	194	680,845	9·7
1950	608,448	257	10,766	165	619,636	8·8
1960	619,538	777	11,736	274	632,446	9·1
Male	316,637	492	All others 6,079		323,208	—
Female	302,901	285	All others 6,052		309,238	—

Of the total population in 1970, 273,442 (44·3%) were urban (35·1% in 1960); those 21 years old or older numbered 374,024.

The largest cities are Fargo with population (census), 1970, of 53,365; Grand Forks, 39,008; Bismarck (capital), 34,703, and Minot, 32,290.

RELIGION. The leading religious denominations are the Roman Catholics, with 173,548 members in 1965; Combined Lutherans, 224,721; Methodists, 20,640; Presbyterians, 14,579.

EDUCATION. School attendance is compulsory between the ages of 7 and 16, or until the 17th birthday if the eighth grade has not been completed. In Sept. 1970 the public elementary schools had 4,746 classroom teachers and 103,234 pupils; secondary schools, 2,951 teachers and 47,260 pupils. Average salary of teachers, 1967, was $5,008 in elementary and $6,085 in secondary schools. State expenditure on public schools, 1967 $106m.

The university at Grand Forks, founded in 1883, had (1968) 386 instructors and 7,398 students; the state university of agriculture and applied science, at Fargo, 482 instructors and 6,228 students. Total enrolment in the 9 institutions of higher education, 1968, 24,000.

WELFARE. Old-age assistance is provided for all needy persons who are 65 years of age or older. In 1969, 4,027 aged were drawing an average of $78.27 monthly; 2,478 families with 7,456 dependent children, $186.44. An average of 303 cases received $78.57 monthly in general assistance and an average of 6,411 cases received $132.96 in medical assistance.

In 1966 the state had 109 hospitals (8,498 beds) listed by the American Hospital Association.

The state penitentiary, on 31 Jan. 1968, held 181 inmates (27·8 per 100,000 population). There is no death penalty except for treason, and for murder committed by a murderer in prison.

FINANCE. General revenue of state and local government for the year ending 30 June 1967 was $352m. and general expenditures, $360m., taxation provided $50·6m. and federal aid, $19·8m.; education took $838·9m.; highways, $22m.; and public welfare, $23m.

Total net long-term debt (state and local government) on 30 June 1967, $211m.

Per capita personal income (1969) was $3,011.

AGRICULTURE. Agriculture is the chief pursuit of the North Dakota population. In 1964 there were 48,836 farms (61,943 in 1954) with an area of 42,717,360 acres (41,876,924 in 1954); the average farm was of 874·7 acres valued at $58,450. Farm-tenants, 1964, operated 7,848 of the farms and full owners, 17,821 farms. Large-scale farming is growing; in 1940, 6,405 farms exceeded 1,000 acres, and in 1964, 13,208 farms.

Cash income, 1969, from crops, $475·7m., and from livestock, $296m. North Dakota leads in the production of barley and wheat. Other important products are flaxseed, potatoes, hay, oats and maize. The state has also an active livestock industry, chiefly cattle raising. On 1 Jan. 1970 the farm animals were: 163,000 milch cows, 2,066,000 all cattle, 377,000 sheep and 315,000 swine. The wool clip yielded (1969), 2·95m. lb. of wool from 301,000 sheep.

FORESTRY. National forest area, 1968, 1,105,000 acres.

MINING. The mineral resources of North Dakota consist chiefly of oil which was discovered in 1951. Production of crude petroleum in 1969 was 25·15m. bbls; of natural gas, 52,181m. cu. ft. Output (1969) of lignite coal was 5,001,828 short tons. Total value of mineral output, 1969, $92·1m.

COMMUNICATIONS. In 1969 there were 5,194 miles of railway in the state. The state highway department maintained, in 1968, 6,626 miles of highway; local authorities, 98,515 miles, and municipal, 2,021 miles. Airports in 1969 numbered 307, of which 102 were publicly owned. Motor registrations in 1968 numbered 420,253.

BOOKS OF REFERENCE

North Dakota Growth Indicators, 1970. 8th ed. Business and Industrial Development Dept. Bismarck, 1970

North Dakota Industrial Location Facts. Business and Industrial Development Dept. Bismarck, 1971

North Dakota Blue Book. Secretary of State. Bismarck, 1961

Federal Writers' Project. *North Dakota: A Guide to the Northern State.* 2nd ed. OUP, New York, 1950

OHIO

GOVERNMENT. Ohio, first settled in 1788, unofficially entered the Union on 19 Feb. 1803; entrance was made official, retroactive to 1 March 1803, on 8 Aug. 1953. The question of a general revision of the constitution drafted by an elected convention is submitted to the people every 20 years. The constitution of 1851 had 88 amendments by 1967.

In the 108th General Assembly the Senate consisted of 33 members and the House of Representatives of 99 members. The Senate is elected for 4 years, half each 2 years; the House is elected for 2 years; the Governor, Lieut.-Governor and Secretary of State for 4 years. Qualified as electors are (with necessary exceptions) all citizens 21 years of age who have the usual residential qualifications. Ohio sends 2 senators and 24 representatives to Congress.

In the 1968 presidential election Nixon polled 1,782,734, Humphrey 1,691,505 and Wallace 465,917.

The capital (since 1816) is Columbus. Ohio is divided into 88 counties.

Governor: John J. Gilligan (D.), 1971–74 ($40,000).
Lieut.-Governor: John W. Brown (R.), 1971–74 ($17,000).
Secretary of State: Ted W. Brown (R.), 1971–74 ($25,000).

AREA AND POPULATION. Area, 41,222 sq. miles, of which 250 sq. miles are inland water. Census population, 1 April 1960, 9,706,397, an increase of 1,759,770 or 22·1% since 1950. Estimated population, 1 July 1967, 10,749,221. In 1967 births numbered 185,204 (17·2 per 1,000 population); deaths, 98,041 (9·1); infant deaths, 3,824 (20·6 per 1,000 live births); marriages, 82,991 (7·7); divorces and annulments, 27,611 (2·4).

Population at 4 census years (with distribution by sex, 1960) was:

	White	Negro	Indian	Asiatic	Total	Per sq. mile
1910	4,654,897	111,452	127	645	4,767,121	117·0
1930	6,335,173	309,304	435	1,785	6,646,697	161·6
1950	7,428,222	513,072	1,146	3,528	7,946,627	193·8
1960	8,909,698	786,097	1,910	8,692	9,706,397	236·9
Male	4,376,126	382,627	949	4,516	4,764,228	—
Female	4,533,572	403,470	951	4,176	4,942,169	—

Of the total population in 1960, 7,123,162 persons (73·4%) lived in urban areas (70·2% in 1950). Those 21 years old or older numbered 5,839,311; 65 years or over, 897,124. Foreign-born whites numbered 390,950.

Estimated population of chief cities on 1 July 1967 was:

Cleveland	824,058	Euclid	73,407	East Cleveland	40,875
Columbus	548,105	Lakewood	72,774	Marion	39,265
Cincinnati	500,562	Kettering	68,507	Zanesville	38,850
Toledo	392,733	Warren	65,574	Upper Arlington	38,827
Akron	299,341	Cleveland Heights	62,520	Shaker Heights	38,087
Dayton	267,712	Lima	56,904	Findlay	35,675
Youngstown	164,763	Elyria	53,478	Maple Heights	35,368
Canton	118,321	Cuyahoga Falls	52,478	Barberton	35,298
Parma	95,905	Mansfield	52,145	Steubenville	34,878
Springfield	85,427	Middletown	49,685	Sandusky	34,426
Hamilton	80,163	Newark	46,513	Lancaster	34,415
Lorain	80,122	Garfield Heights	44,829	Norwood	34,382

Urbanized areas, 1960 census: Cleveland, 1,784,991; Cincinnati, 993,568; Columbus (the capital), 616,743; Toledo, 438,283; Akron, 458,253; Dayton, 501,644; Youngstown–Warren, 372,748; Canton, 213,574.

RELIGION. Many religious faiths are represented, including (but not limited to) the Baptist, Jewish, Lutheran, Methodist, Presbyterian and Roman Catholic.

EDUCATION. School attendance during full term is compulsory for children from 6 to 18 years of age. In 1966–67 public elementary schools had 46,965 teachers and 1,484,148 enrolled pupils; junior high schools had 9,402 teachers and 228,567 pupils; high schools had 36,006 teachers and 623,454 pupils. Teachers' salaries averaged $6,482. Expenditure on public schools for 1965–66 was $990·8m., and on higher education for 1964–65, $225·73m. The state's 77 universities and colleges had a total enrolment (1967–68) of 316,877 resident students; the following had 7,000 or more students, spring 1970:

Founded	Institutions	Full-time teachers	Full-time students
1804	Ohio University, Athens (State)	1,006	17,800
1809	Miami University, Oxford (State)	648	11,580
1826	Case Western Reserve University, Cleveland (Private)	1,600	5,300
1850	University of Dayton (Roman Catholic)	630	7,468
1870	University of Akron (State)	228	8,156
1872	Ohio State University, Columbus (State)	1,587	49,000
1872	University of Toledo (State)	560	15,200
1874	University of Cincinnati (Municipal)	1,378	18,378
1908	Youngstown University (State)	689	14,728
1910	Bowling Green State University (State)	924	11,611
1912	Kent State University (State)	1,006	20,150

WELFARE. Public assistance is administered through 5 basic programmes: aid for the aged, aid to dependent children, aid for the disabled, aid to the blind and general relief. Total public assistance expenditures during the year ending 30 June 1968 were $279,530,346. The number of persons receiving public assistance averaged 381,016 per month, of whom 64,833 were aged 65 years or more, 2,876 were blind, 22,766 were disabled and 195,575 were children under 18 years. Of the total fiscal year 1968 expenditure, $85·8m. was used to provide medical care to all recipients. Under the aid to dependent children programme $92·6m. provided assistance to an average of 164,277 children per month in 55,169 families.

In 1963 the state had 268 hospitals (81,927 beds) listed by the American Hospital Association. Hospitals for mental diseases had 30,466 patients on 30 June 1968 (283 per 100,000 population).

A Civil Rights Act (1933) forbids inns, restaurants, theatres, retail stores and all other places of public resort to discriminate against citizens on grounds of 'colour or race'; none may be denied the right to serve on juries on the grounds of 'colour or race'; insurance companies are forbidden to discriminate between 'white persons and coloured, wholly or partially of African descent'.

A state Civil Rights Commission (created 1959) has general administrative powers to prevent discrimination because of race, colour, religion, national origin or ancestry in employment, labour organization membership, use of public accommodations and in obtaining 'commercial housing' or 'personal residence'. Ohio has no *de jure* segregation in the public schools.

The state's penal and reformatory system, 30 June 1968, held 10,403 inmates. In 1967 there were no executions; total executions (by electrocution) since 1930 were 170, all for murder. There have been no executions since 1963.

FINANCE. For the year ending 30 June 1967 (US Census Bureau figures) revenue was $2,255·6m. (taxation, $1,038·5m.; federal aid, $459·6m.; liquor stores revenue (net), $54m.) and general expenditure was $2,223·5m. (education, $433·7m.; highways, $480·8m.; public welfare, $264·8m.).

The net long-term debt of the state on 30 June 1967 was $691·3m.

Per capita personal income (1969) was $3,779.

AGRICULTURE. Ohio is extensively devoted to agriculture. In 1967, 118,000 farms covered 17·8m. acres; average farm was about 151 acres valued at $52,400. Commercial farms (1964) numbered 78,416 and residential farms, 28,378. Tenant-farmers operated 14% of all farms (26·3% in 1940).

Cash income, 1967, from crops and livestock and products, $1,234,297,000. The most important crops in 1967 were: Maize (256m. bu.), wheat (51·5m. bu.), oats (24·4m. bu.), soybeans (50·2m. bu.). The wool clip in 1967 yielded 6,106,000 lb. from 692,000 sheep. On 1 Jan. 1968 the livestock on Ohio farms was: 535,000 milch cows, 2·07m. all cattle, 2·34m. swine, 775,000 sheep and 13·1m. chickens.

FORESTRY. National forest area, 1966, 115,127 acres; state forest area, 167,985 acres.

MINING. Ohio has extensive mineral resources, of which coal is the most important by value; output (1967) 45·9m. short tons. Production of other minerals, 1967: Sand and gravel, 41·7m. short tons; limestone, 44·7m. short tons; sandstone, 2·16m. short tons; salt, 5·45m. short tons; crude petroleum, 9·9m. bbls; natural gas, 42,500m. cu. ft; clay, 2·7m. short tons; shale, 1·93m. short tons; gypsum, 0·35m. short tons; peat, 0·01m. short tons. Total value of minerals listed, 1967, $395m.

INDUSTRY. In 1966, 12,437 manufacturing establishments employed 1·3m. workers. The value added by manufacture in 1962 was $14,580m. The largest industry was manufacturing of machinery with 196,974 workers.

COMMUNICATIONS. The state (1967) maintained 18,666 miles of highway, all hard surfaced. Total miles of highway maintained by all government agencies (1967), 107,754. The railroads had 8,267 miles of track. Ohio had (1968) 445 airports and airfields, of which 235 are licensed by the state. In 1968 Ohio had a total of 5,007 licensed aeroplanes, of which 2,200 were owned by business corporations.

BOOKS OF REFERENCE

Official Roster: Federal State, County Officers and Department Information. Secretary of State, Columbus. Biennial
Statistical Abstract of Ohio, 1960. Dept of Industrial and Economic Development. Columbus, 1960
Aumann, F. R., and Walker, H., *The Government and Administration of Ohio.* New York, 1956
Rose, A. H., *Ohio Government, State and Local.* Saint Louis, 1953
Rosebloom, E. H., and Weisenburger, F. P., *A History of Ohio.* State Arch. and Hist. Soc., Columbus, 1953

OKLAHOMA

GOVERNMENT. An unorganized area in the centre of the present state was thrown open to white settlers on 22 April 1889. The Territory of Oklahoma, organized in 1890 to include this area and other sections, was opened to white settlements by runs or lotteries during the next decade. In 1893 the Territory was enlarged by the addition of the Cherokee Outlet, which fixed part of the present northern boundary. On 16 Nov. 1907 Oklahoma was combined with the remaining part of the Indian Territory and admitted as a state with boundaries substantially as now. The present constitution, dating from 1907, provides for amendment by initiation petition and legislative referendum; it has had 67 amendments.

The Legislature consists of a Senate of 48 members, who are elected for 4 years, and a House of Representatives elected for 2 years and consisting of 99 members. The Governor and Lieut.-Governor are elected for 4 years. Electors are (with necessary exceptions) all citizens 21 years or older, with the usual residential qualifications. Indians are qualified as voters.

The state is represented in Congress by 2 senators and 6 representatives.

In the 1968 presidential election Nixon polled 442,693 votes, Humphrey 297,243 and Wallace 197,167.

The capital is Oklahoma City. The state has 77 counties.

Governor: David Hall (R.), 1971–75 ($35,000).
Lieut.-Governor: George Nigh (D.) ($8,000).
Secretary of State: John Rogers (D.) ($15,000).

AREA AND POPULATION. Area 69,919 sq. miles, of which 1,100 sq. miles are water. Census population, 1 April 1960, 2,328,284, an increase of 94,933 or 4·3% since 1950. Census (preliminary), 1 April 1970, 2,498,378. Births, 1968, were 40,973 (16·3 per 1,000 population); deaths, 25,709 (10·2); infant deaths 821 (20 per 1,000 live births); marriages, 37,369 (14·8); divorces, including annulments, 14,367 (5·7).

The population at 4 federal censuses (with distribution by sex, 1960) was:

	White	Negro	Indian	Asiatic	Total	Per sq. mile
1910	1,444,531	137,612	74,825	187	1,657,155	23·9
1930	2,130,778	172,198	92,725	339	2,396,040	34·6
1950	2,032,526	145,503	53,769	534	2,233,351	32·4
1960	2,107,900	153,084	68,689	1,414	2,328,284	33·8
Male	1,041,202	73,388	All others 33,261		1,147,851	—
Female	1,066,698	79,696	All others 34,039		1,180,433	—

In 1960, 1,465,000 (62·9%) were urban (51% in 1950). Those 21 years of age or older numbered 1,416,000; 65 years or older, 249,000. Foreign-born whites numbered 18,623. In 1964 the US Bureau of Indian Affairs administered 1,634,000 acres, of which 58,000 acres were allotted to tribes.

The most important cities (with population, 1970) are Oklahoma City (capital), 363,225; Tulsa, 328,219; Lawton, 69,069; Norman, 50,500; Enid, 43,557; Midwest City 36,015.

RELIGION. The chief religious bodies in 1968 were Southern Baptists, 529,079; Roman Catholics, 112,127; United Methodists, 299,358; Disciples of Christ (1967), 88,284.

EDUCATION. Oklahoma statutes used to require separate educational facilities for whites and Negroes. The 17 May 1954 US Supreme Court decision radically altered the state public-school system; by Sept. 1960 all public school districts were integrated. In 1949 the legislature enacted a law by which Negroes are admitted to institutions of higher education.

In the autumn of 1968 there were 342,779 pupils enrolled in elementary schools (kindergarten through grade 6) and 261,238 pupils in secondary schools; 27,634 teachers at elementary schools and secondary schools had average salaries of $6,853. Total expenditure on public schools (1967–68), $258·9m.

The University of Oklahoma (founded at Norman in 1899) had 883 full-time professors and 18,489 enrolled students in autumn 1970; Oklahoma State University of Agriculture and Applied Science (founded in 1890 at Stillwater) had 785 full-time professors and 21,035 students. There are 18 other institutions of higher learning in the state system at the senior level and 17 junior colleges.

WELFARE. Public assistance, June 1969, was being drawn by 195,831 persons, receiving an average of $52.65. This includes old age assistance, aid to families with dependent children, AFDC emergency, aid to the blind and aid to the disabled. Medical payments were made to 47,105 persons, and averaged $65.91 per person. Nursing-home service was provided for 15,563 persons at an average of $200.46 per person. Non-technical medical care was provided for 3,187 persons at an average of $83.04 per person. A total of $783,259 was spent for vocational rehabilitation.

In 1968 there were 140 hospitals (14,485 beds) listed by the American Hospital Association. On 31 Dec. 1968 hospitals for mental diseases had 6,978 patients; institutions for mentally retarded had 2,260 patients in 1969.

Penal institutions, 31 Dec. 1967, held 2,783 inmates.

The death penalty may be imposed for murder. In 1966 there was one execution; since 1915 there have been 83 (52 whites, 27 Negroes, 4 other races) executions by electrocution.

FINANCE. General revenue for the year ending 30 June 1968 (US Census Bureau figures) was $866·4m. (taxation, $533m.; federal aid, $313·3m.), and general expenditure, $850m. (education, $317·9m.; highways, $164·6m.; public welfare, $250·8m.).

Total net long-term debt, 30 June 1968, was $557,735,000.

Per capita personal income (1969) was $2,860.

AGRICULTURE. Agriculture is the largest industry. In 1967 the state had 93,000 farms with a total area of 37m. acres; average farm was 401 acres with a value, land and buildings, of $31,141; there were 56,936 commercial farms. Owners and part owners operated 75,410 farms and tenants 18,852 farms (19·9%). Large-scale commercial farming is predominant; 5,907 farms exceeded 1,000 acres; 5,425 farms sold products valued at $20,000 or more. On the other hand, small-scale farming also exists; 14,103 farms were of less than 50 acres, and, of the commercial farms, 8,215 sold products valued at less than $2,500.

Soil erosion is serious. The conservation and development of the renewable natural resources of the state has received close attention by local, county and state governments during the past 20 years. All of the land in the state is within the boundaries of one of the 87 soil and water conservation districts. Of the total surface (44·5m. acres), 28m. acres are being operated under a basic conservation plan prepared by the conservation district with assistance from the Soil Conservation Service. Only 7% of the land received damage from wind erosion during the past year. With improved technology, equipment and crop residue management, farmers are able to control wind erosion. 34% of all the upstream flood prevention reservoirs built in the US have been built in Oklahoma. In addition to these, 824 reservoirs have been built on the Washita River Watershed and 6 on Double Creek. 17m. acres are within the boundaries of 118 watersheds which have asked for assistance under this programme.

The largest change in land use in 1969 was the shifting of 51,000 acres of cropland to grass. This is a continuation of a trend of the last 20 years.

Cash income from crops, 1968, was $266·6m. and from livestock products, $576·5m. The most important crop, by value, is wheat; output, 1966, 132,916,000 bu.—third highest in US. Other crops included cotton (365,000 bales) grain sorghums (22·42m. bu.) and broom corn, of which the state is a leading producer. On 1 Jan. 1969 the stock included 166,000 milch cows, 4·7m. all cattle, 136,000 sheep and lambs and 386,000 swine.

FORESTRY. National forest area, 1967, 459,000 acres, of which 285,000 acres were under forest service administration.

MINING. In the US Oklahoma ranks fourth as a petroleum producer. Producing oilwells, 31 Dec. 1965, 80,947. In 1966, 225m. bbls of crude petroleum were produced; natural gas liquids (1966), 1,562m. gallons; natural gas (1966), 1,351,225m. cu. ft; coal (1966), 843,000 short tons. The total mineral output in 1966 was valued at $997·4m. (of which petroleum accounted for $654m.).

INDUSTRY. Petroleum refining is the chief industry; production, 1968, included 222,484,000 bbls of petrol. In 1967, 2,608 manufacturing establishments had 103,000 production workers; value added by manufacture, $1,274m.

COMMUNICATIONS. The state, 1 Jan. 1969, maintained 11,915 miles of highway; the counties, 82,708 miles; municipalities, 13,280 miles. In 1970, 301 miles of turnpikes were maintained by the Oklahoma Turnpike Authority. In 1969 Oklahoma had 5,551 miles of railway. Airports, 1969, numbered 228, of which 115 were publicly owned. Motor car registrations, 1968, 1,709,761.

BOOKS OF REFERENCE

Directory of Oklahoma Airports. Oklahoma Aeronautics Commission
Directory, State of Oklahoma. State Election Board, Oklahoma City
Chronicles of Oklahoma. State Historical Society, Oklahoma City (from 1921)
OKIE Facts. Oklahoma Industrial Development and Park Department, Oklahoma City, 1970
Oklahoma Data Book, 1968. Bureau of Business Research, Univ. of Oklahoma, Norman, 1968
Dale, E. E., and Wardell, M. L., *History of Oklahoma.* New York, 1948
Debo, Angie, *Oklahoma.* Norman, 1950
McReynolds, Edwin C., *Oklahoma: A History of the Sooner State.* Univ. of Oklahoma, Norman, 1954
Strain, J. E., *Outline of Oklahoma Government.* Norman, 1969

STATE LIBRARY. Oklahoma Dept. of Libraries, 109 State Capitol, Oklahoma City 73105. *State Librarian and State Archivist:* Ralph H. Funk

OREGON

GOVERNMENT. First settled in 1811 by the Pacific Fur Company at Astoria, a provisional government in Oregon was formed on 5 July 1834; a Territorial government was organized, 14 Aug. 1848, and on 14 Feb. 1859 Oregon was admitted to the Union. The present constitution dates from that time; some 80 items in it have been amended. The Legislative Assembly consists of a Senate of 30 members, elected for 4 years (half their number retiring every 2 years), and a House of 60 representatives, elected for 2 years. The Governor is elected for 4 years. The constitution reserves to the voters the rights of initiative and referendum and recall. In Nov. 1912 suffrage was extended to women.

The state sends to Congress 2 senators and 4 representatives.

In the 1968 presidential election Nixon polled 386,039 votes, Humphrey 344,571 and Wallace 47,337.

The capital is Salem. There are 36 counties in the state.

Governor: Tom McCall (R.), 1971–75 ($28,000 plus $1,000 monthly for expenses).
Secretary of State: Clay Myers (R.), 1968–73 ($24,000).

AREA AND POPULATION. Area, 96,981 sq. miles, 733 sq. miles being inland water. The federal government owned (1968) 32,176,516 acres (52·2% of the state area). Census (preliminary) population, 1 April 1970, 2,056,171, an increase of 287,484 or 16·3% since 1960. In 1969 resident births numbered 33,834 (16·3 per 1,000 population); deaths, 19,548 (9·4); infant deaths (deaths within the first year of life), 592 (17·5 per 1,000 live births); marriages, 16,874 (8·1), and divorces, 8,643 (4·2). Four maternal deaths took place in 1969.

Population at 4 federal censuses (with distribution by sex, 1960) was:

	White	Negro	Indian	Asiatic	Total	Per sq. mile
1910	655,090	1,492	5,090	11,093	672,765	7·0
1930	938,598	2,234	4,776	8,179	953,786	9·9
1950	1,497,128	11,529	5,820	6,864	1,521,341	15·8
1960	1,732,037	18,133	8,026	9,120	1,768,687	18·4
Male	861,040	9,141	All others	9,770	879,951	—
Female	870,997	8,992		8,747	888,736	—

Of the total population in 1960, 1,100,122 persons (62·2%) were urban (53·9% in 1950). Those 21 years and older were 1,073,431; 65 years and older, 183,653. Foreign-born whites numbered 68,009.

The US Bureau of Indian Affairs (area headquarters in Portland) administers (1970) 667,415 acres, of which 499,440 acres are held by the US in trust for Indian tribes, and 167,975 acres for individual Indians.

The largest towns, according to the preliminary 1970 census figures, 1 April 1970, are: Portland, 375,161; Eugene, 77,284; Salem (the capital), 63,309; Corvallis, 34,798; Medford, 29,950; Springfield, 24,666; Beaverton, 17,976; Albany, 17,944; Milwaukee, 15,990.

RELIGION. The chief religious bodies (1967) are Catholic, 142,173; Baptist, 66,318; Lutheran, 60,374; Methodist, 53,731, and Presbyterian, 49,028. Total membership, all denominations, 567,735 in 1967.

EDUCATION. School attendance is compulsory from 7 to 18 years of age if the twelfth year of school has not been completed; those between the ages of 16 and 18 years, if legally employed, must attend part-time or evening schools. On 30 June 1970 the 1,002 public elementary schools, 98 junior high schools and 226 standard senior high schools had 25,749 administrators and teachers and 460,371 average daily membership; net enrolment was 498,336 (excluding transfers between districts), of whom 157,844 were high-school pupils. Average salary for all classroom teachers, 1969–70, was $8,814. Total expenditure on elementary and secondary education (1969–70) was $378,205,070.

Leading state-supported institutions of higher education (1969–70) included:

	Teachers	Students
University of Oregon, Eugene	896	15,316
University of Oregon Medical School, Portland	140	922
University of Oregon Dental School, Portland	75	414
Oregon State University, Corvallis	902	15,507
Oregon College of Education, Monmouth	201	3,940
Southern Oregon College, Ashland	215	4,646
Eastern Oregon College, La Grande	96	1,724
Portland State University, Portland	555	11,256
Oregon Technical Institute, Klamath Falls	118	1,481

State supported institutions of higher education had a total enrolment of 55,206 during the autumn term of 1970–71. In addition, there were over 12,000 students enrolled in evening classes and correspondence study.

Largest of privately endowed universities are the University of Portland with, 1970–71, 131 professors and 1,958 students; Willamette University, Salem, 135 professors and 1,713 students; Lewis and Clark College, Portland, 130 professors and 2,188 students; Linfield College, McMinnville, 78 professors and 1,063 students, and Reed College, Portland, 136 professors and 1,303 students.

NEWSPAPERS. In 1970 there were 21 daily newspapers with a circulation of 653,491, and 98 other newspapers with a circulation of 298,118.

WELFARE. Old-age assistance is provided for all needy persons 65 years or older who meet certain eligibility requirements. As of June 1970, 8,008 aged persons were drawing an average of $57.17 per month; 8,926, including aged, mentally ill, retarded or tuberculous, received medical care.

The June 1970 average payment, apart from medical care, was $45.87 for the 86,701 persons in 22,837 families with dependent children; $102.62 for 592 blind persons; $74.01 for 7,458 disabled persons, and $66.96 for 2,450 general assistance cases. Total medical costs in June 1970 were $3,686,994.

A system of unemployment benefit payments, financed by employers, with administrative allotments made through a federal agency, started 2 Jan. 1938, and covers about 44,800 employers with average employment in 1969 of 569,630. By 30 June 1970, $662·4m. had been paid into the trust fund and about $600·3m. paid out in benefits which range from $20 to $55 weekly and up to $1,430 per year. About 27,700 state employees, 33,700 school employees and 10,900 political subdivision employees are participants in the public employees retirement programme. The same employees are covered under the federal old-age, survivors and disability insurance programme. Approximately 13,800 retired public employees are receiving monthly benefit cheques.

In Sept. 1970 there were 117 licensed hospitals (12,813 beds); the 3 state hospitals for mental illness had a daily average of 1,838 patients; 3 separate units for the mentally retarded and an average of 2,814 residents in July 1970.

The Oregon state penitentiary at Salem, June 1969, held an average of 1,346 males and 63 females; the institution for first offenders, 442 persons. Since 1930 there have been 19 executions (lethal gas), for murder. Capital punishment was abolished in 1964.

The sterilization law, originally passed in 1917, was amended in 1967. The amendments changed the number of persons on the Board from 15 to 7 and provided that the Public Defender would automatically represent all persons examined. The bases on which a person would be subject to examination by the Board are: (a) if such person would be likely to procreate children having an inherited tendency to mental retardation or mental illness, or (b) if such person would be likely to procreate children who would become neglected or dependent because of the person's inability by reason of mental illness or mental retardation to provide adequate care. Up to 1 July 1970, 912 men and 1,610 women have been sterilized.

FINANCE. General revenues for the fiscal year ending 30 June 1970 were $1,199,456,505 (taxation, $483,612,825 and federal aid, $275,023,627); general expenditures, $1,066,847,342 (education, $337,074,283; highways, $144,814,496; public welfare, $95,343,823).

On 1 May 1970 the outstanding bonded debt was $668,902,000.

Per capita personal income (1969) was $3,573.

AGRICULTURE. Oregon, which has an area of 61,572,480 acres, is divided by the Cascade Range into two distinct zones as to climate. West of the Cascade Range there is a good rainfall and almost every variety of crop common to the temperate zone is grown; east of the Range stock-raising and wheat-growing are the principal industries and irrigation is needed for row crops and fruits.

There are numerous irrigation districts, and in 1964, 15,869 farms, covering 1,606,947 acres, used irrigation water.

Oregon farms are decreasing in number and increasing in size. There were, in 1964, 39,757 farms with an acreage of 20,509,302 (33·3% of the land area), including 5,281,935 acres of total crop land; average farm size in 1964 was 515·9 acres valued at $59,079 (including buildings), commercial farms numbered 21,505, of which 5,372 sold produce valued at $20,000 or more. In 1964, 4,041 farms (10%) were under 10 acres, 17,858 (45%) were under 50 acres and 3,134 farms exceeded 1,000 acres.

Cash receipts from crops in 1968 amounted to $270·8m., and from livestock and products, $242m. Principal crops are hay, wheat, potatoes, pears, snap beans, strawberries, ryegrass seed, barley and peppermint.

Livestock, 1 Jan. 1969: Milch cows, 204,000; all cattle, 1,577,000; sheep and lambs, 569,000; swine, 117,000.

Federal and state land for grazing cattle and sheep, 19·2m. acres. In 1968 the wool clip yielded 4,334,000 lb. from 537,000 sheep; mohair clip, in 1967, 48,000 lb. from 11,000 goats.

FISHERIES. All food and shellfish landings in the calendar year 1969 amounted to 85,546,028 lb., including salmon, 10,549,116 lb.; tuna, 29,827,549 lb.; crabs, 9,783,998 lb.; bottom fish, 23,243,151 lb.; shrimp, 10,268,433 lb.; shad, 553,229 lb.

FORESTRY. Forest products manufacturing ranks as Oregon's leading industry, with saw-mills, plywood, and pulp and paper-mills contributing almost $1,500m., or about 60% of the state's economy. Some 30m. acres of forest land, nearly half the land area of the state, provides recreational areas, watersheds and an annual harvest of about 8,500m. bd ft. Oregon has been the leading lumber producing state since 1938, and its forest-oriented tourist trade is mounting rapidly. The state's 536,000m. bd ft of sawtimber is capable of sustaining indefinitely a wood-based sector in the economy of about the present size. In Oregon forests stand more than one-fifth of the country's current sawtimber supply. She now supplies nearly one-fourth of the softwood lumber, over half of the plywood and more than one-fourth of the hardboard produced in the US. About 85,134 workers have full-time jobs in this industry that provides an annual payroll of nearly $571m.

MINING. Oregon's mineral resources include gold, silver, copper, lead, mercury, chromite, sand and gravel, stone, clays, lime, silica, diatomite, expansible shale, scoria, pumice and uranium. Oregon is the only state producing nickel in the US. Value of mineral products, 1969, was $60m.

INDUSTRY. During Oct.–Dec. 1969, 4,662 manufacturing establishments reported to the Employment Division, average annual employment, 1969, 182,627 with pay of $1,388,973,728; value added by manufacture (1966 census), $2,038m.

TOURISM. In 1969, 2,847,100 out-of-state cars visited Oregon; the total 1969 income from tourism was estimated to be $326,435,000.

POWER. Four privately owned utilities, 11 municipally owned utilities, 16 co-operatives and 4 utility districts provide electricity in the state. The privately owned companies serve 80% of the electricity. Private utilities generated 7,778,565,000 kwh. of hydro-electric power in 1969.

A federal agency, the Bonneville Power Administration, also markets electric power from 26 federal dams in the Pacific Northwest to 155 public and private utilities and large industrial plants. The dams, which are operated by the Army Corps of Engineers or the Bureau of Reclamation, have a total generating capacity of 9,036,150 kw. Five more dams are under construction, with a total capacity of 6,723,000 kw. The Bonneville transmission network now covers the states of Oregon, Washington, Idaho, Western Montana, and parts of California, Nevada, Utah and Wyoming.

COMMUNICATIONS. The state maintains (1970) 7,533 miles of primary and secondary highways, almost all surfaced; counties maintain 27,958 miles; there were 43,023 miles in national parks and federal reservations. Registered motor vehicles, 1 Jan. 1970, totalled 1,473,817. The state had (1969) 19 railways with a total mileage of 4,992. There were 246 airports in 1970.

Portland is a major seaport for large ocean-going vessels and is 101 miles inland from the mouth of the Columbia River.

In 1970 there were 99 commercial radio stations and 11 educational radio stations. There were 13 commercial television stations and 2 educational television stations.

BOOKS OF REFERENCE

Oregon Blue Book. Issued by the Secretary of State. Salem. Biennial
Oregon State University. *Atlas of the Pacific Northwest Resources and Development*, ed. by R. M. Highsmith. 4th ed. Corvallis, 1968
Oregon University, Bureau of Business and Economic Research. *Oregon Economic Statistics.* Eugene. Annual
Oregon University, Bureau of Municipal Research and Service. *Community Planning in Oregon.* Eugene, 1967
Oregon University, Bureau of Municipal Research and Service. *Issues in the Community.* Eugene, 1967
Federal Writers' Project. *Oregon: End of the Trail.* Rev. ed. Portland, 1951
Baldwin, E., *Geology of Oregon.* 2nd ed. Eugene, 1964
Berry, J., *Profile of Oregon churches.* Portland, 1963
Brooks, J. E., *Oregon Almanac and Book of Facts.* Portland, 1961
Corning, H. M. (ed.), *Dictionary of Oregon History.* New York, 1956
Dicken, S. N., *Oregon Geography.* 4th ed. Eugene, 1965
Friedman, R., *Oregon for the curious.* Portland, 1965
McArthur, L. A., *Oregon Geographic Names.* 3rd ed., rev. and enlarged. Portland, 1952

STATE LIBRARY. The Oregon State Library, Salem. *Librarian:* Eloise Ebert.

PENNSYLVANIA

GOVERNMENT. Pennsylvania, first settled in 1682, is one of the 13 original states in the Union. The present constitution dates from 1874; 67 amendments have been adopted. The General Assembly consists of a Senate of 50 members chosen for 4 years, one-half being elected biennially, and a House of Representatives of 203 members chosen for 2 years. The Governor and Lieut. Governor are elected for 4 years. Every citizen 21 years of age, with the usual residential qualifications, may vote. The state sends to Congress 2 senators and 27 representatives.

In the 1968 presidential election Nixon polled 2,090,017 votes, Humphrey 2,259,403 and Wallace 387,582.

The state capital is Harrisburg. The state is organized in counties (numbering 67), cities, boroughs, townships and school districts.

Governor: Milton J. Shapp (D.) 1971–75 ($45,000).
Lieut.-Governor: Raymond J. Broderick (R.) ($32,500).

AREA AND POPULATION. Area, 45,333 sq. miles, of which 390 sq. miles are inland water. Census population, 1 April 1960, 11,319,366, an increase of 821,354 or 7·8% since 1950. Estimated population, 1 July 1968, 11,755,000. Births, 1967, 195,869 (16·8 per 1,000 population); deaths, 126,820 (10·9); infant deaths, 4,323 (22·1 per 1,000 live births); marriages, 81,337 (7); divorces (1966), 16,940 (1·5).

Population at 4 census years (with distribution by sex, 1960) was:

	White	Negro	Indian	All others	Total	Per sq. mile
1910	7,467,713	193,919	1,503	1,976	7,665,111	171·0
1930	9,196,007	431,257	523	3,563	9,631,350	213·8
1950	9,853,848	638,485	1,141	4,538	10,498,012	233·1
1960	10,454,004	852,750	2,122	10,490	11,319,366	251·5
Male	5,093,879	409,322	1,051	5,599	5,509,851	—
Female	5,360,125	443,428	1,071	4,891	5,809,515	—

Of the total population in 1960, 8,102,051 persons (71·6%) were urban (70·5% in 1950); 7,100,482 were 21 years of age or older; foreign-born whites numbered 596,118.

The population of the larger cities and townships, 1968 estimate, was:

Philadelphia	2,085,400	Harrisburg (cap.)	75,800	Lancaster	53,300
Pittsburgh	531,500	Bethlehem	71,400	McKeesport	45,800
Erie	146.800	Altoona	71,000	Johnstown	43,600
Allentown	109,300	Chester	63,300	New Castle	44,200
Scranton	106,100	Wilkes-Barre	58,800	Williamsport	41,800
Reading	95,900	York	57,300		

Larger urbanized areas, 1960 census: Philadelphia, 3,635,228; Pittsburgh, 1,804,400; Allentown–Bethlehem, 256,016; Wilkes-Barre, 233,932; Harrisburg, 209,501; Scranton, 210,676.

RELIGION. The chief religious bodies in 1967 were the Roman Catholic, with 3,648,725 members; Protestant, 2·7m. (communicants); and Jewish, 452,000. The 5 largest Protestant denominations (by communicants) were: Lutheran Church in America, 600,146; Methodist, 541,612; United Presbyterian Church in the USA, 530,976; United Church of Christ, 262,490; Evangelical United Brethren, 205,031.

EDUCATION. School attendance is compulsory for children 8–17 years of age. In 1968–69 (estimated figures) the public kindergartens and elementary schools had 50,234 classroom teachers (average salary, $7,821) and 1,257,226 pupils; secondary schools had 50,625 classroom teachers (average salary, $7,997) and 1,049,724 pupils. Non-public schools had 570,220 elementary pupils and 139,785 secondary pupils in 1968–69.

Leading senior academic institutions (autumn, 1968) included:

Founded	Institutions	Faculty [1]	Students [2]
1740	University of Pennsylvania, Philadelphia non-sect.)	4,452	17,707
1787	University of Pittsburgh (non-sect.)	2,784	27,602
1832	Lafayette College, Easton (Presbyterian)	147	2,043
1842	Villanova College (R.C.)	579	8,150
1846	Bucknell University (Baptist)	231	2,807
1851	St Joseph's College, Philadelphia	284	6,699
1852	California State College	288	5,808
1855	Pennsylvania State University, University Park	3,132	47,520
1855	Millersville State College	272	4,688
1863	LaSalle College, Philadelphia	352	6,182
1866	Lehigh University, Bethlehem (non-sect.)	568	4,938
1871	West Chester State College	383	7,751
1875	Indiana University of Pennsylvania	456	9,117
1878	Duquesne University, Pittsburgh (R.C.)	565	7,338
1884	Temple University, Philadelphia (non-sec.)	2,426	34,030
1885	Bryn Mawr College	183	1,311
1888	University of Scranton (R.C.)	164	2,963
1891	Drexel Institute of Technology, Philadelphia	535	9,366
1900	Carnegie–Mellon University, Pittsburgh	683	5,203

[1] Includes full- and part-time. [2] Total enrolments.

WELFARE. During June 1968 the average number of cases receiving public assistance and the average grant per case were: Old-age assistance, 42,242, $71.44; aid to dependent children, 70,074, $168.12; state blind pensions, 7,774, $74.32; state-federal blind pensions, 9,323, $107.39; aid to disabled, 25,470, $74.11; general assistance, 31,956, $79.57.

The number of persons for whom payments were made for medical assistance during the month of June 1968 was 86,732—49,814 assistance persons and 36,918 non-assistance persons. Payments for medical assistance during the month totalled $14,122,429—$4,445,999 for assistance persons and $9,676,430 for non-assistance persons. Under the medical assistance programme payments are made for inpatient hospital care, hospital home care, nursing care in home, care in public institutions (nursing homes, mental institutions and geriatric centres), physician's services, dental services, clinic services, prescribed drugs and ambulance services. During June 1968, $6,486,313 was paid for inpatient hospital care, $6,588,827 for care in public institutions and $1,047,289 for all other services.

On 30 June 1968 the state had 321 hospitals (177,254 beds) listed by the American Hospital Association; 13 hospitals (9,071 beds) were federal; 38 (47,905 beds) were psychiatric—of these, 20 were state-owned and had 33,171 patients (285 per 100,000 population).

No executions took place in 1963–68; since 1930 there have been 149 executions (electrocution), all for murder.

Prison population, on 31 Dec. 1967, was 11,371.

FINANCE. Total revenues for the year 1967 were $3,635·4m.; general expenditure, $3,193·7m. (education, $1,046·1m.; highways, $634·8m.; public welfare, $323·5m.).

On 30 June 1967 total net long-term debt amounted to $2,119,334,000.

Per capita personal income (1969) was estimated at $3,664.

AGRICULTURE. Agriculture, market-gardening, fruit-growing, horticulture and forestry are pursued within the state. In 1968 there were 82,000 farms with a total farm area (1964) of 11·5m. acres (4,676,000 acres in crops); the average farm was 131 acres valued at $30,300. Cash income, 1966, from crops, $235m., and from livestock and products, $657·6m.

Pennsylvania ranks high in the production of cigar leaf tobacco (42m. lb., 1966) and mushrooms (113m. lb., value $37·7m., 1968). Other crops are winter wheat (1,025,000 bu.), oats (882,000 bu.), maize (3,549,000 bu.) and potatoes (200,000 cwt). On 1 Jan. 1969 there were on farms: 1,799,000 cattle and calves, including 815,000 milch cows, 170,000 sheep, 506,000 swine. Wool clip, 1963, was 1,487,000 lb. Milk production, 1967, was 6,856m. lb. valued at $385m., and eggs numbered 3,165m. valued at $91·24m. Pennsylvania is also a major fruit producing state: in 1964 apples totalled 11m. bu.; peaches, 2·8m. bu.; cherries, 18,900 tons, and grapes, 38,200 tons.

FORESTRY. In 1968 national forest lands totalled 470,862 acres; state forests, 1,909,892 acres; state parks, 337,091 acres; state game land, 1,051,674 acres; game land leased but not owned by the state, 4,364,280 acres.

MINING. Pennsylvania is almost the sole producer of anthracite coal; its output reached a peak of 100,445,299 short tons in 1917 with a labour-force of 156,148 men. Production in 1967 was 11,332,441 tons with 7,828. Output of bituminous coal, 79,101,385 tons with a labour force of 23,811 men; crude petroleum, 4,442,945 bbls; natural gas (1966), 90,914m. cu. ft. Total value of mineral production, 1966, was $903·4m., ranking fifth in the USA.

INDUSTRY. Pennsylvania leads in the production of iron and steel. Output of steel, 1966, 32·1m. net tons and of pig-iron (1963), 17,692,867 net tons.

In 1967, 18,164 manufacturing establishments employed 1,495,671 production workers (wages, $9,296,364); value added by manufacture was $18,517,343,000.

COMMUNICATIONS. In 1969, 48 railways operated within the state with a line mileage of 8,693. Trade at Delaware river ports (1967, short tons) imports, 46m., exports, 2·97m. There were (1968) 162 commercial and municipal airports, 1 military and 307 private airports. Regularly scheduled airlines operating in the state numbered 16. All highways and roads in the state (federal, local and state combined) totalled (1 July 1968) 113,321 miles. Registered motor vehicles (31 May 1967) numbered 5,670,168 (including 4,722,740 passenger cars). Broadcasting stations comprised (1969) 29 television stations and 195 radio stations, of which 26 are exclusively FM and 63 are AM–FM stations.

BOOKS OF REFERENCE

Pennsylvania Manual. Dept. of Property and Supplies, Division of Documents. Harrisburg. Biennial
Pennsylvania's Regions, A Survey of the Commonwealth. State Planning Board. Harrisburg, 1967
Pennsylvania Statistical Abstract. Dept. of Internal Affairs. Harrisburg. Annual

Branning, R. L., *Annotated Bibliography of Pennsylvania State Government*. Dept. of Political Science, University of Pitsburgh, 1959
Carstens, A. H., *What to See in Pennsylvania*. 2nd ed. Cresco, 1965
Cooke, E. F., and Janosik, G. E., *Pennsylvania Politics*. Rev. ed. New York, 1965
Deatrick, E. S., *Pennsylvania Citizen*. New Brunswick, NJ, 1958
Mulkearn, L., and Pugh, E. V., *Traveller's Guide to Historic Western Pennsylvania*. Rev. ed. Pittsburgh, 1957
Sigafoos, R. A., *Guide to Public Affairs Research in Pennsylvania*. University Park, Pa., 1959
Stevens, S. K., *Pennsylvania: birthplace of a nation*. New York, 1964
Tanger, J., Alderfer, H. F., and McGeary, M. N., *Pennsylvania Government, State and Local*. 3rd ed. State College, Pa., 1960
Wallace, P. A. W., *Pennsylvania: seed of a nation*. New York, 1962
Wilkinson, N. B., *Bibliography of Pennsylvania History*. Pa. Historical & Museum Commission. Harrisburg, 1957

RHODE ISLAND

GOVERNMENT. The earliest settlers in the region which now forms the state of Rhode Island were colonists from Massachusetts who had been driven forth on account of their non-acceptance of the prevailing religious beliefs. The first of the settlements was made in 1636, settlers of every creed being welcomed. In 1647 a patent was granted for the government of the settlements, and on 8 July 1663 a charter was executed recognizing the settlers as forming a body corporate and politic by the name of the 'English Colony of Rhode Island and Providence Plantations, in New England, in America'. On 29 May 1790 the state accepted the federal constitution and entered the Union as the last of the 13 original states. The present constitution dates from 1843; it has had 36 amendments. The General Assembly consists (1970) of a Senate of 50 members and a House of Representatives of 100 members, both elected for 2 years, as are also the Governor and Lieut.-Governor. Every citizen, 21 years of age, who has resided in the state for 1 year, and is duly registered, is qualified to vote.

Rhode Island sends to Congress 2 senators and 2 representatives.

At the 1968 presidential election Nixon polled 122,359 votes, Humphrey 246,518 and Wallace 14,967.

The capital is Providence. The state has 5 counties (unique in having no political functions) and 39 cities and towns.

Governor: Frank Licht (D.), 1971–73 ($30,000).
Lieut.-Governor: J. Joseph Garrahy (D.), 1971–73 ($12,000).
Secretary of State: August P. LaFrance (D.), 1971–73 ($18,000).

AREA AND POPULATION. Area, 1,214 sq. miles, of which 165 sq. miles are inland water. Census population (preliminary), 1 April 1970, 922.461, an increase of 7·3% since 1965. State census population, 1 Oct. 1965, 892,709, an increase of 3·9% since 1960 (white, 867,265; Negro, 22,852).

Births, 1969, were 15,872 (17·2 per 1,000 population); deaths (excluding foetal deaths), 9,283 (10·1); infant deaths, 306 (19 per 1,000 live births); marriages, 7,528 (8·2); divorces, 1,911 (2·1).

Population of 4 census years (with distribution by sex, 1960) was:

	White	Negro	Indian	Asiatic	Total	Per sq. mile
1910	532,492	9,529	284	305	542,610	508·5
1930	677,026	9,913	318	240	687,497	649·3
1950	777,015	13,903	978		791,896	748·5
1960	838,712	18,332	932	1,190	859,488	812·4
Male	411,265	9,228	All others 1,352		421,845	—
Female	427,447	9,104	All others 1,092		437,643	—

Of the total population in 1960, 742,897 persons (86·4%) were urban (84·3% in 1950); 545,885 were 21 years of age or older; foreign-born whites numbered 84,667.

The chief cities and their population (census, preliminary, 1970) are Providence 176,920; Warwick, 82,985; Pawtucket, 76,213; Cranston, 73,633; East Providence, 47,615; Woonsocket, 46,465; Newport, 33,866; Cumberland (town), 26,453; North Kingstown (town), 24,955; Central Falls, 18,428. The Providence–Pawtucket–Warwick Standard Metropolitan Statistical Area had a population of 860,717 in 1965.

RELIGION. Chief religious bodies are (estimated figures Aug. 1970): Roman Catholic with 587,685 members; Protestant Episcopal (baptized persons), 48,437; Baptist, 22,221; Congregational, 12,193; Methodist, 10,000; Jewish, 24,000.

EDUCATION. The school census of 1969 showed 324,099 persons under 21 years of age; at the 1960 census approximately 80% were attending school. In 1968–69 the 298 public elementary schools had 4,792 teachers and average membership of 98,498 pupils; about 42,000 pupils were enrolled in private and parochial schools. The 79 senior and junior high schools had 4,328 teachers and 72,444 pupils. Teachers' salaries (1970) averaged $8,088. Local expenditure, for schools (including evening schools) in 1968–69 totalled $118·9m.

There are 16 institutions of higher learning in the state, including 3 junior colleges. The state maintains Rhode Island College, at Providence, with 345 faculty members and 3,200 full-time students (1970), and the University of Rhode Island, at South Kingstown, with over 695 faculty members and over 9,000 students (including graduate students). Brown University, at Providence, founded in 1764, is now non-sectarian; in 1970 it had 1,100 instructors and 5,571 full-time students, including students at Pembroke College, the womens' division. Providence College, at Providence, founded in 1917 by the Order o Preachers (Dominican), had (1970) 189 professors and 2,285 students. The largest of the other colleges are Bryant College, in Providence, with 100 faculty and over 2,000 students, and the Rhode Island School of Design, in Providence, with about 100 faculty and 1,300 students.

WELFARE. In July 1970 old-age assistance was being granted to 3,879 persons who received an average of $54.24 per month; aid to dependent children, 29,007 children in 10,675 families (39,682 persons), $54.62 per month; aid to permanently and totally disabled, 3,983 persons, $89.42 per month; aid to blind, 115 persons, $81.33 per month; general assistance, 9,750 persons, $36.69 per month.

In 1970 the state had 25 hospitals (approx. 9,000 beds), including 4 mental hospitals.

The state's penal institutions, Aug. 1970, had 470 inmates (50 per 100,000 population).

The death penalty is illegal, except that it is mandatory in the case of murder committed by a prisoner serving a life sentence.

FINANCE. For the fiscal year ending 30 June 1969 (US Census Bureau figures) general revenues were $323·8m. (taxation, $200·1m., and federal aid, $82·7m.); general expenditures were $344m. (education, $72·5m.; highways, $64·7m., and public welfare, $67·7m.).

Total net long-term debt on 30 June 1969 was $288·7m.

Per capita personal income (1969) was $3,858.

AGRICULTURE. While Rhode Island is predominantly a manufacturing state, agriculture contributed to the general cash income $20·5m. in 1969. In 1964 it had 1,115 farms with an area of 105,135 acres (20% of the total land area), of which 45,395 acres were crop land; the average farm was 94·3 acres, valued (land and buildings) at $47,255.

FISHERIES. The number of commercial fishermen in the state in 1960 (US census) was 502; value of all fish landed in 1969, $7·9m.

MINING. The small mineral output, mostly stone, sand and gravel, was valued (1969) at $3·7m.

INDUSTRY. Total civilian employment in 1969 was 377,500, of which 127,100 was manufacturing, 217,100 non-manufacturing and 33,300 farm, household and self-employed. Manufacturing firms totalled 2,936 with payroll of $821·9m.; average weekly earnings for production workers in manufacturing, $107·64; value added by manufacture (1967), $1,357m. Principal industries are metals and machinery, textiles and jewellery–silverware.

COMMUNICATIONS. In 1969, 4 railways operated 161 line-miles (345 track-miles). Of the 12 airports in 1969, 5 were state-owned, 5 privately owned and 2 federally owned. Theodore Francis Green airport at Warwick, near Providence, is served by 6 airlines, and handled 783,693 passengers and 22·4m. lb. of freight in 1969. The state had (1 Jan. 1970) 5,133 miles of road, of which 1,042 were state-owned. In 1969, 466,000 motor vehicles were registered. Waterborne freight through the Port of Providence (1969) totalled 8·5m. tons. There are 22 radio stations and 3 television stations in the state.

BOOKS OF REFERENCE

Rhode Island Manual. Prepared by the Secretary of State. Providence
An Introduction to the Economy of Rhode Island. Issue by the Rhode Island Development Council. Providence, 1953
Providence Journal Almanac: A Reference Book for Rhode Islanders. Providence. Annual
Rhode Island Basic Economic Statistics. Rhode Island Development Council. Providence, 1970

STATE LIBRARY. Rhode Island State Library, State House, Providence 02908. *State Librarian* Elliott E. Andrews.

SOUTH CAROLINA

GOVERNMENT. South Carolina, first settled permanently in 1670, was one of the 13 original states of the Union. The present constitution dates from 1895, when it went into force without ratification by the electorate; it has had 251 amendments. The General Assembly consists of a Senate of 46 members, elected for 4 years (half retiring biennially), and a House of Representatives of 124 members, elected for 2 years. The Governor and Lieut.-Governor are elected for 4 years. Only registered citizens have the right to vote. At the 1968 presidential election Nixon polled 260,558, Humphrey 196,889 and Wallace 211,754. South Carolina sends to Congress 2 senators and 6 representatives.

The capital is Columbia.

Governor: John C. West (D.), 1971–75 ($25,000).
Secretary of State: O. Frank Thornton (D.) ($15,000).

AREA AND POPULATION. Area 31,055 sq. miles, of which 783 sq. miles are inland water. Census population, 1 April 1960, 2,382,594, an increase of 12·5% since 1950. Estimated population (US Bureau of the Census estimate), 1 July 1968, 2,599,000. Births, 1968, were 49,158 (18·4 per 1,000 population); deaths, 23,411 (8·7); infant deaths, 1,341 (27·3 per 1,000 live births); marriages, 54,943 (20·1); divorces, 4,518 (1·2).

The population in 4 census years (with distribution by sex, 1960) was:

	White	Negro	Indian	Asiatic	Total	Per sq. mile
1910	679,161	835,843	331	65	1,515,400	49·7
1930	944,049	793,681	959	76	1,738,765	56·8
1950	1,293,405	822,077	554	—	2,117,927	69·9
1960	1,551,022	829,291	1,098	946	2,382,594	78·7
Male	775,754	398,931	All others 1,133		1,175,818	—
Female	775,268	430,360	All others 1,148		1,206,776	—

Of the total population in 1960, 981,386 persons (41·2%) were urban (36·7% in 1950); those 21 years old or older numbered 1,266,251; foreign-born, 11,140. Estimated populations of large towns as of 31 Dec. 1967 (with those of associated metropolitan areas): Charleston, 80,900 (313,300); Columbia (capital), 102,500 (310,700); Greenville, 80,900 (288,300); Spartanburg, 46,900 (164,200); Anderson, 34,100 (102,300).

RELIGION. The chief religious bodies are the Southern Baptists, with 520,524 members in 1962; Methodists, 185,000, and Presbyterians, 82,000.

EDUCATION. Desegregation is gradually being introduced in the state's educational system. In 1966–67 the total public-school enrolment was 662,046; there were 390,993 white pupils and 271,053 Negro pupils. The total number of teachers, 1968, was 25,447, average salary was $5,440 in elementary and $5,875 in secondary schools. Total expenditure for public education (1967) was $298m.

For higher education the state operates the University of South Carolina, founded at Columbia in 1801, with, 1966–67, 12,988 enrolled students; Clemson University, founded in 1893, with 6,054 students; Citadel College, at Charleston, with 2,182 students; Winthrop College for girls, Rock Hill, with 3,180 students; Medical College of S. Carolina, at Charleston, with 753 students, and S. Carolina State College (for Negroes), at Orangeburg, with 2,010 students.

There are also 107 private elementary and high schools with total enrolment of (1966–67) 24,018 pupils, and 35 state, private and denominational colleges and junior colleges with enrolment of 47,201 students.

WELFARE. Old-age assistance was being granted in Dec. 1966 to 22,927 persons, who received an average of $56.93 per month; 6,439 families (20,287 dependent children) received $65.09 monthly; 1,886 blind, $65.55; 9,300 totally disabled, $58.27. In 1963 the state had 79 hospitals (19,733 beds) listed by the American Hospital Association.

On 31 Dec. 1967 state prisons held 2,248 inmates.

In 1968 there were no executions; from 1930 to 1968 executions (by electrocution) numbered 162, 30 whites (including 1 woman) and 90 Negroes (1 woman) for murder and 5 whites and 37 Negroes for rape.

FINANCE. For the fiscal year ending 30 June 1969 (US Census Bureau figures) general revenues were $688m. (taxes, $529m., and federal aid, $159m.); general expenditures were $559m. (education, $313m.; highways, $144m., and public welfare, $101m.).

On 30 June 1969 the net long-term debt was $326,896,000.

Per capita personal income (1969) was $2,607.

AGRICULTURE. The 1970 census of agriculture showed 53,000 farms covering a farm area of 8·4m. acres and a cropland area of 2·31m. acres. The average farm was of 158 acres. Of the 33,883 commercial farms, there were 1,056 of 1,000 acres or more. Tenant-farmers operated 24·1% of all farms; tenants numbered 12,412.

Cash receipts from farm marketing in 1967 amounted to $276m. for crops and $138m. for livestock. Chief crops are tobacco (accounting for 22% of cash receipts in 1966), cotton (10%), soybeans (13%), vegetables (5%), peaches (6%); livestock accounted for 35% of cash receipts. Production, 1969: Tobacco, 137m. lb.; cotton (1967), 179m. bales (of 500 lb.); peaches, 338m. lb. Livestock on farms, 1 Jan. 1969: 76,000 milch cows, 623,000 all cattle, 1,700 sheep and 471,000 swine.

FORESTRY. The forest industry is important; state and private forest land (1968), 12·05m. acres. National forests, 1968, amounted to 587,221 acres.

MINING. Non-metallic minerals are of chief importance; value of mineral output in 1969 was $53·2m., chiefly from cement, kaolin, clay, stone, sand and gravel, vermiculite, baryte and kyanite. Commodities of minor importance produced include scrap mica, lime pyrite, feldspar, dimension stone and peat. Potentially economic reserves of phosphate and heavy minerals exist.

INDUSTRY. Industry, long ahead of agriculture in economic return, has moved ahead also in total employment in recent years. 339,200 workers were employed in manufacturing industries in 1969, earning $2,000m.; value added by manufacture was $2,987m. in 1966. About 66,400 persons were employed in agriculture in 1969.

COMMUNICATIONS. In 1968 the length of railway in the state was 3,300 miles. There were, 1968, 100 airports. Total highway mileage in the combined highway system in 1969 was 35,882 miles. Motor vehicle registration numbered 1·38m. in 1970.

The state had 3 deep-water ports.

BOOKS OF REFERENCE

General Statistics on South Carolina, 1968. State Development Board, Columbia, 1968
Legislative Manual and Reference Book of South Carolina. Columbia. Annual
Report . . . to the General Assembly. Secretary of State. Columbia. Annual
Reports of the South Carolina State Development Board. Columbia. Annual
Wallace, D. D., *South Carolina, a short history, 1520–1948.* Univ. of North Carolina, Chapel Hill, 1951

STATE LIBRARY. South Carolina State Library, State House, Columbia. *State Librarian:* Mrs Joan R. Faunt.

SOUTH DAKOTA

GOVERNMENT. South Dakota was first visited in 1743 when Verendrye planted a lead plate (discovered in 1913) on the site of Fort Pierre, claiming the region for the French crown. Beginning with a trading post in 1794, it was settled from 1857 to 1861 when Dakota Territory was organized. It was admitted into the Union on 2 Nov. 1889. The constitution adopted in 1889 is still in force with 74 amendments.

Voters are all citizens 21 years of age or older who have complied with certain residential qualifications. The people reserve the right of the initiative and referendum. The Senate has 35 members, and the House of Representatives 75 members, all elected for 2 years, as are also the Governor and Lieut.-Governor The state sends 2 senators and 2 representatives to Congress.

In the 1968 presidential election Nixon polled 149,843 votes, Humphrey 118,023 and Wallace 13,400.

The capital is Pierre (population, 1960, 10,088) The state is divided into 64 organized counties and 3 unorganized, *i.e.*, with no local functions.

Governor: Frank Farrar (R.), 1969–71 ($18,000).
Lieut.-Governor: James Abdnor (R.) ($2,400 per biennium).
Secretary of State: Alma Larson (R.) ($13,000).

AREA AND POPULATION. Area, 77,047 sq. miles, of which 669 sq. miles are water. Area administered by the Bureau of Indian Affairs, 1964, covered 4·94m. acres (10% of the state), of which 1,972,000 acres were held by tribes. The federal government, 1964, owned 3,409,000 acres or 7% of the total.

Census population, 1 April 1960, 680,514, an increase of 4·3% since 1950. Estimated population, 1 Jan. 1970, 724,000. Births, 1967, were 11,424 (17·8 per 1,000 population); deaths, 6,349 (9·2); infant deaths, 252; marriages, 9,051 (11·2); divorces, 1,090.

Population in 4 federal censuses (with distribution by sex, 1960) was:

	White	Negro	Indian	Asiatic	Total	Per sq. mile
1910	563,771	817	19,137	163	583,888	7·6
1930	669,453	646	21,833	101	692,849	9·0
1950	628,504	727	23,344	165	652,720	8·5
1960	653,098	1,114	25,794	336	680,514	8·9
Male	330,434	667	All others 13,170		344,271	—
Female	322,664	447	All others 13,132		336,243	—

Of the total population in 1960, 267,180 persons (39·3%) were urban (33·2% in 1950); 391,597 were 21 years of age or older; foreign-born whites numbered 18,333.

Population of the chief cities (census of 1960) was: Sioux Falls, 65,466; Rapid City, 42,399; Aberdeen, 23,073; Huron, 14,180; Watertown, 14,077; Mitchell, 12,555.

RELIGION. The chief religious bodies are (1968): Lutherans with 171,456 members, Roman Catholics (142,692), Methodist (78,000), Congregational (19,087), Presbyterian (19,922), Baptist (19,000) and Episcopal (18,325).

EDUCATION. Elementary and secondary education are free from 6 to 21 years of age. Between the ages of 8 and 16, attendance is compulsory. In 1969, 184,401 pupils were attending elementary and high (including parochial) schools (10,100 classroom teachers). Teachers' salaries (1969) in elementary schools averaged $5,050; in secondary schools, $6,300. Total expenditure on public schools (1968), $98·5m.

The School of Mines at Rapid City, established 1885, had, autumn 1968, 118 instructors and 1,718 students; the State College, at Brookings, 412 instructors and 5,666 students; the University of South Dakota, founded at Vermillion in 1882, 238 instructors and 4,174 students. Seven private colleges had 310 instructors and 5,413 students; 4 State Colleges had 351 instructors and 7,287 students. The Government maintains Indian schools on its reservations and 2 outside at Flandreau and Pierre.

WELFARE. In 1968–69, 4,724 persons received as old-age assistance $3,488,010; 114 blind persons received $1,117,332; 1,366 permanently and totally disabled, $1,071,571; 14,214 dependent children, $7,658,811.

In 1968 the state had 65 hospitals (3,506 beds) listed by the South Dakota Health Department.

State prisons had, on 1 July 1969, 448 inmates (66 per 100,000 population). The death penalty was illegal from 1915 to 1938; since 1938, one person has been executed, in 1949 (by electrocution), for murder.

FINANCE. For the fiscal year ending 30 June 1969 (US Census Bureau figures) general revenues were $217m. and general expenditures, $200m. Taxes furnished $68m. and federal grants, $83m.; education took $64m.; highways, $68m., and public welfare, $27m.

The state has no debt.

Per capita personal income (1969) was $3,051.

AGRICULTURE. In 1968, 47,500 farms had an acreage of 45m. with a total value of $3,097m.; the average farm had 945 acres. Farm units are large; in 1959 there were only 2,544 farms of 50 acres or less, compared with 9,515 exceeding 1,000 acres. Of the 49,688 commercial farms, 1,164 sold produce valued at $40,000 or over.

Cash income, 1968, from crops, $205m. and from livestock, $153m. South Dakota ranks first in the US as producer of sweet clover and blue grass and second in rye, flax and wild hay. The leading crops (1968) are maize (103m. bu.), wheat (46,115,000 bu.), oats (101·9m. bu.), and barley (12·7m. bu.). The farm livestock on 1 Jan. 1969 included 4,366,000 cattle, 1,266,000 sheep, 1·68m. swine. Milk production, 1968, was 1·64m. lb. and egg production, 1,121m. The wool clip in 1968 amounted to 11·1m. lb. There are 104,000 bee colonies.

FORESTRY. National forest area, 1968, 1,047,792 acres.

MINING. The mineral products include gold (593,900 troy oz. from the Home-stake mine in 1968, leading all states, almost 40% of US total), sand and gravel (14m. short tons, 1968), silver (116,000 troy oz., 1968), iron ore, uranium, feldspar and gypsum. Mineral products, 1968, were valued at $58·5m., of which gold accounts for $22·7m.

INDUSTRY. Chief manufacturing industries are meat-packing and electronic components. In 1969 manufacturing establishments numbered 925 and had 16,300 production workers, who earned $74m.; value added by manufacture was $172m.

COMMUNICATIONS. In 1968 the railways were 3,935 miles in length. In 1969 total road mileage was 83,941. Approved airports, 1968, numbered 77; approved private landing strips, 99. Registered passenger cars numbered 281,429 in 1969; trucks, 115,700; trailers, 34,600.

BOOKS OF REFERENCE

South Dakota Historical Collections. 1902–68
South Dakota Economic and Business Abstract, 1939–1962. Business Research Bureau, University of S. Dakota. Vermillion, 1963
South Dakota Legislative Manual. Department of Finance. Pierre, S.D. Biennial
Schell, H. S., History of South Dakota. Lincoln, Neb., 1961
White, H. L. and B., Who's Who for South Dakota. Pierre, S.D., 1956

TENNESSEE

GOVERNMENT. Tennessee, first settled in 1757, was admitted into the Union on 1 June 1796. The state has operated under 3 constitutions, the last of which was adopted in 1870 and since amended 10 times (first in 1953). Voters at an election may authorize the calling of a convention limited to altering or abolishing one or more specified sections of the constitution. The General Assembly consists of a Senate of 33 members and a House of Representatives of 99 members, both elected for 2 years. No clergyman of any denomination is eligible to either House. Qualified as electors are all citizens (with the usual residential and age (21) qualifications). Tennessee sends to Congress 2 senators and 9 representatives.

In the 1968 presidential election Nixon polled 472,592 votes, Humphrey 351,233 and Wallace 424,792.

For the Tennessee Valley Authority see p. 571.

The capital is Nashville. The state is divided into 95 counties.

Governor: Winfield Dunn (D.), 1970–74 ($18,500).
Secretary of State: Joe C. Carr (D.), ($15,000).

AREA AND POPULATION. Area, 42,244 sq. miles (482 sq. miles water). Census population, 1 April 1960, 3,567,089, an increase of 275,371 or 8·4% since 1950. Estimated population, 1 July 1967, 3·89m. Provisional vital statistics, 1965: Births, 74,673 (20·3 per 1,000 population); deaths, 36,274 (10); infant deaths, 2,070 (28·9 per 1,000 live births); marriages, 39,507 (9·9); divorces, 9,634 (2·4).

Population in 4 census years (with distribution by sex, 1960) was:

	White	Negro	Indian	Asiatic	Total	Per sq. mile
1910	1,711,432	473,088	216	53	2,184,789	52·4
1930	2,138,644	477,646	161	105	2,616,556	62·4
1950	2,760,257	530,603	339	334	3,291,718	78·8
1960	2,977,753	586,876	638	1,243	3,567,089	85·4
Male	1,459,508	279,935	All others	1,247	1,740,690	—
Female	1,518,245	306,941		1,213	1,826,399	—

Of the population in 1960, 1,864,828 persons (52·3%) were urban (44·1% in 1950); those 21 years of age or older numbered 2,092,891.

The cities, with population, 1966 estimate, are: Memphis, 527,492; Nashville (capital), 250,887; Chattanooga, 130,090; Knoxville, 179,973; Jackson, 38,476; Johnson City, 34,053; Kingsport (1964), 33,334; Oak Ridge, 29,696. Urbanized areas, 1960 census: Memphis, 544,505; Nashville, 346,729; Chattanooga, 205,143; Knoxville, 172,734.

RELIGION. The leading religious bodies are the Southern Baptists, with 679,053 members in 1956; Methodists, about 400,000; Negro Baptists, 250,000.

EDUCATION. School attendance has been compulsory since 1925 and the employment of children under 16 years of age in workshops, factories or mines is illegal.

The legislature in 1925 passed an Act prohibiting 'the teaching of the evolution theory in all the universities, normal schools and all other public schools of Tennessee which are supported in whole or in part by the public funds of the state'. This was largely ignored and it was repealed in 1967. In 1967–68 there were 1,934 public schools with 36,593 teachers (whose average salary was $6,146) and a net enrolment of 906,937 pupils. Total expenditure for operating public schools (grades 1 through 12) in 1967–68, $473,714,095. Tennessee has 48 accredited colleges and universities with a total enrolment of 105,000 in 1966–67. The universities include the University of Tennessee, Knoxville (founded 1794), with 1,598 faculty and 26,589 students in 1966–67; Vanderbilt University, Nashville (1873), Agricultural and Industrial State University (1912) and the University of Chattanooga (1886).

WELFARE. Old-age assistance was granted 1967–68 to 49,431 persons, who received an average of $71.87 per month; 1,814 blind persons, $69.86 per month; 17,470 totally disabled persons, $70.11 per month; 24,126 families with dependent children, $108.98 per month.

In 1965 the state had 128 hospitals (25,291 beds) listed by the American Hospital Association; 7,588 patients were in mental hospitals and 2,097 patients in institutions for mentally retarded.

There has been no execution since 1960; since 1930 there have been 22 whites and 44 Negroes executed (by electrocution) for murder and 5 whites and 22 Negroes for rape.

Prison population, 31 Dec. 1965, 3,213.

The law prohibiting the inter-marriage of white and Negro was declared unconstitutional by the U.S. Supreme Court in June 1967.

FINANCE. For the year ending 30 June 1967 US Census Bureau figures) general revenue was $820,657,000 (taxation, $521,112,000 and federal aid, $247,752,000); general expenditure, $833,716,000 (education, $309,716,000; highways, $201,792,000; public welfare, $100,248,000).

Total net long-term debt on 30 June 1966 amounted to $176·19m.

Per capita personal income (1969) was $2,810.

AGRICULTURE. In 1967, 140,000 farms covered 15·4m. acres. The average farm was of 110 acres (only a few states had a smaller average) valued (1965), land and buildings, at $21,088. In 1965, 54,060 farms (40%) were under 50 acres, while 847 farms had 1,000 acres or over; commercial farms numbered 76,352.

Cash income (1967) from crops was $242·61m.; from livestock (1 Jan. 1968), $358,696,000. The cotton crop for 1967 yielded 145,000 bales, the smallest crop for 100 years. The tobacco crop (1967), all types, was valued at $74·7m.

On 1 Jan. 1967 the domestic animals included 395,000 milch cows, 2,285,000 all cattle, 75,000 sheep, 996,000 swine and 6m. chickens excluding broilers.

FORESTRY. Forests occupy 13,432,000 acres (52% of total land area). The forest industry and industries dependent on it employ about 40,000 workers, earning $150m. per year. Cut of sawtimber, 1963: softwood, 2,590m. bd ft and hardwood, 12,760m. bd ft. National forest area (1966) 601,000 acres.

MINING. Coalfields cover about 5,000 sq. miles; output in 1967 was 6·83m. short tons. In 1967 Tennessee led the states in the production of zinc (113,065 short tons), ball clay and pyrite and was the third largest producer of phosphate rock (2,992,000 long tons) and dimension marble. Other mineral products are copper (14,600 short tons), mica, cement, sand and gravel, limestone. Total value of mineral products in 1967 was $189,572,000.

INDUSTRY. The manufacturing industries include iron and steel working, but the most important products are chemicals, including synthetic fibres and allied products, and knit goods. In 1963, 4,718 manufacturing establishments employed 269,000 production workers, who received wages of $1,044m.; value added by manufactures was $3,344m.

TOURISM. More than 23m. out-of-state tourists visit Tennessee each year. Tourist-serving industries have annual gross receipts totalling $25·2m. and employ some 73,000 persons.

COMMUNICATIONS. The state had (1968) 3,339 miles of railway and (1965), 74,317 miles of surfaced highways; total highways covered, 77,182 miles. The state is served by 115 intra-state bus companies and 11 major airlines. Airports, 1965, numbered 71, of which 44 were municipally owned. Motor-vehicle registrations, 1967, totalled 1,842,275.

BOOKS OF REFERENCE

Tennessee Blue Book, 1965–66. Secretary of State. Nashville
Tennessee Agricultural Statistics Annual Summary. Tennessee Crop Reporting Service
STATE LIBRARY. State Library and Archives, Nashville. *Librarian:* Dr William T. Alderson. *State Historian:* Dr Robert White.

TEXAS

GOVERNMENT. In 1836 Texas declared its independence of Mexico, and after maintaining an independent existence, as the Republic of Texas, for 10 years, it was on 29 Dec. 1845 received as a state into the American Union. The state's first settlement dates from 1686. The present constitution dates from 1876; it has been amended 15 times. The Legislature consists of a Senate of 31 members elected for 4 years (half their number retiring every 2 years), and a House of Representatives of 150 members elected for 2 years.

The Governor and Lieut.-Governor are elected for 2 years. Qualified electors are all citizens with the usual residential qualifications. Texas sends to Congress 2 senators and 23 representatives.

In the 1968 presidential election Nixon polled 1,227,844 votes, Humphrey 1,266,804 and Wallace 584,269.

The capital is Austin. The state has 254 counties.

Governor: Preston Smith (D.), 1971–73 ($55,000).
Lieut.-Governor: Ben Barnes (D.), 1971–73 ($4,800).
Secretary of State: Martin Dies (D.), 1971–73 ($26,000).

AREA AND POPULATION. Area, 267,339 sq. miles (including 4,369 sq. miles of inland water). Census population, 1 April 1960, 9,579,677, an increase of 24·2% since 1950. Estimated population, 1 July 1969, 11,187,000. Vital statistics for 1968 (provisional): Births, 206,000 (18·7 per 1,000 population); deaths, 91,000 (8·3); infant deaths, 4,552 (22 per 1,000 live births); marriages, 135,528 (12·3); divorces (1966), 43,046 (4).

Population for 4 census years (with distribution by sex, 1960) was:

	White	Negro	Indian	Asiatic	Total	Per sq. mile
1910	3,204,848	690,049	702	943	3,896,542	14·8
1930	4,967,172	854,964	1,001	1,578	5,824,715	22·1
1950	6,726,534	977,458	2,736	3,392	7,711,194	29·3
1960	8,374,831	1,187,125	5,750	9,848	9,579,677	36·5
Male	4,159,510	576,463	3,016	4,768	4,744,981	—
Female	4,215,321	610,662	2,734	4,080	4,834,696	—

Of the population in 1960, 7,187,470 persons (75%) were urban (62·7% in 1950); households numbered 2,777,646 (of 3·36 persons). Those 21 years old and older were 5,534,277. Foreign-born whites numbered 292,241. A census report, 1960, showed 1,417,810 persons with Spanish surnames, of whom 1,219,617 were natives of the state.

The largest cities, with census population in 1960, are:

Houston	938,219	Amarillo	137,969	Galveston	67,175
Dallas	679,684	Lubbock	128,691	Port Arthur	66,676
San Antonio	587,718	Beaumont	119,175	Midland	62,625
Fort Worth	356,268	Wichita Falls	101,724	Laredo	60,175
El Paso	276,687	Waco	97,808	San Angelo	58,815
Austin (capital)	186,545	Abilene	90,368	Pasadena	58,737
Corpus Christi	167,690	Odessa	80,338	Tyler	51,230

Larger urbanized areas, 1966 estimate: Houston, 1·74m.; Dallas, 1,352,000; San Antonio, 832,000; Fort Worth, 638,000.

RELIGION. The largest religious bodies (1967) are the Roman Catholics (with 1,269,524 members), Baptists (1,732,238), Methodists (807,870), Churches of Christ (280,000), Lutherans (167,432), Presbyterians (184,933) and Episcopalians (130,773).

EDUCATION. In 1960 persons 25 years of age or older who reported no school years completed numbered 204,045 (4·1% of that age group), of whom 172,335 were whites and 31,710 were non-whites; of persons between the ages of 5 and 24, 2,269,120 (67%) were attending school. School attendance is compulsory for children from 7 to 17 years of age. In 1965–66 all of the public schools had either desegregated or were under a plan in which they had started desegregation. The estimated total enrolment is 2,559,280, of which approximately 355,000 pupils are Negro.

In autumn 1968 public elementary schools (kindergarten through grade 8) had 1,509,000 enrolled pupils and 60,461 classroom teachers; secondary schools, 1,195,000 enrolled pupils and 53,204 classroom teachers. Teachers' salaries, 1969, estimate, averaged $6,619. Estimated total public school expenditure, 1969, $1,582m.

The state maintains 114 institutions of higher learning with an estimated enrolment, Sept. 1969, of 399,599 students. The largest institutions, with faculty numbers and student enrolment, were:

Founded	Institutions	Control	Professors	Students
1845	Baylor University, Waco	Baptist	826	6,346
1852	St Mary's University, San Antonio	R.C.	188	4,278
1869	Trinity University, San Antonio	Presb.	200	2,641
1873	Texas Christian University, Fort Worth	Christian	522	6,463
1876	Texas A. and M. Univ., College Station	State	777	13,944
1876	Prairie View Agr. and Mech. Coll., Prairie View	State	178	3,967
1883	University of Texas, Austin	State	1,810	35,730
1891	Hardin-Simmons University, Abilene	Baptist	127	1,705
1895	University of Texas, Arlington	State	486	13,869
1901	North Texas State University, Denton	State	762	15,024
1903	Texas Woman's University, Denton	State	260	5,325
1906	Abilene Christian College, Abilene	Church of Christ	164	3,110
1911	Southern Methodist University, Dallas	Methodist	525	9,769
1912	William Marsh Rice University, Houston	—	325	3,173
1913	University of Texas, El Paso	State	292	10,503
1923	Texas Technological College, Lubbock	State	1,057	19,490
1924	College of Arts and Industries, Kingsville	State	291	7,253
1934	University of Houston, Houston	State	980	24,383
1947	Texas Southern University, Houston	State	225	4,737

WELFARE. Old-age assistance was being granted in Aug. 1969 to 229,377 persons, who received an average of $59.48 per month; aid was given to 4,074 blind persons ($71.77 per month), to 38,084 families with 130,027 dependent children (average per family, $83.91), and to 21,107 permanently and totally disabled persons ($59.07).

In 1969, the state had 570 hospitals (73,641 beds) listed by the American Hospital Association; on 31 Dec. 1966 mental hospitals had 16,094 resident patients and institutions for the mentally retarded, 10,395 resident patients.

The prison system, Oct. 1969, held 12,645 men and women. In 1968 no persons were executed. Total executions from 1930 through 1968 have been 297,210 for murder, 84 (including 71 Negroes) for rape and 3 for armed robbery.

Texas has adopted 11 laws governing the activities of trade unions. An Act of 1955 forbids the state's payment of unemployment compensation to workers engaged in certain types of strikes.

FINANCE. In the fiscal year ending 31 Aug. 1969 (US Census Bureau figures) general revenues were $3,890,017,185; general expenditures, $2,514,507,766 (education, $1,066,323,525; welfare, $399,528,945; highways, $557,018,971). Net long-term debt, 31 Aug. 1969, was $532,190,042.

Texas is unique in the large revenue derived from the severance tax (*i.e.*, tax on the removal of oil, natural gas and sulphur from the soil or waters of the state) which in the 1968–69 fiscal year yielded $224,725,236; tax on motor fuels yielded $267,821,210; cigarette and tobacco taxes and licences $139,962,334; sales tax, $438,524,669.

Per capita personal income (1969) was $3,254.

AGRICULTURE. Texas is one of the most important agricultural states of the Union. In 1959 (census) it had 227,071 farms (205,109 in 1964) covering 143,217,559 acres (141,714,031 acres in 1964); average farm was of 630·7 (690·9 in 1964) acres valued, land and buildings, at $51,787 ($79,625 in 1964). Large-scale commercial farms, highly mechanized, dominate in Texas; farms of 1,000 acres or more numbered 20,852 in 1964, a number far exceeding that of any other state; 26,426 farms sold produce valued at $20,000 or more. But small-scale farming persists; in 1964, 38,471 farms were under 50 acres.

Soil erosion is serious in some parts. For some 97,297,000 acres drastic curative treatment has been indicated and for 51,164,000 acres, preventive treatment. In 1966 there were 183 soil-conservation districts embracing an area of 166·57m. acres, of which 144,366,000 acres were in farms and ranches.

Texas leads in production of cotton (3,475,000 bales from 4,125m. acres in 1968, preliminary); yield was 404 lb. per acre compared with the average of 511 lb. for all cotton states. It also occasionally leads in pecans (38m. lb., 1967, preliminary) and always in grain sorghum (341m. bu., 1968, preliminary). Other important crops, 1967 (preliminary), were maize (19m. bu.), winter wheat (84·2m. bu.), oats and barley (7·96m. bu.), rough rice (27·5m. bags), peanuts (333·5m. lb.), vegetables, oranges (1,800m. boxes), grapefruit (2,800m. boxes), and peaches, potatoes, sweet potatoes.

Cash income, 1968, from crops was $1,244m.; from livestock, $1,462·9m.; total was third highest in US.

The state has a very great livestock industry, leading in the number of all cattle, 11,521,000 on 1 Jan. 1969, and sheep, 3,949,000; it also had 374,000 milch cows, and 943,000 swine. The wool clip in 1967 amounted to 36,998,000 lb.; mohair, 25,514,000 lb. (practically the total US production).

FORESTRY. National forests area under forest service administration (1967), 1,834,000 acres.

MINING. Texas leads all states by a wide margin in the production of crude petroleum and related minerals. In 1969 Texas had 44·97% of proved US petroleum reserves. Production, 1968: Crude petroleum, 1,087,825,044 bbls; natural gas, 8,612,972,196m. cu. ft; natural gasoline, 100,761,445 bbls; butane and propane gases, 122,338,519 bbls; cement, 32,277,000 bbls (of 376 lb.); salt, 8,534,000 short tons. Total value of mineral fuel products (excluding asphalt and coal, undisclosed), 1967, was $5,406m. (highest of all states). Other minerals include carbon black (4·43m. cu. ft in 1967), helium (335·9m. cu. ft in 1967), crude gypsum (984,000 short tons in 1967), granite and sandstone.

Total value of mineral products in 1967, $5,406m., leading all states.

INDUSTRY. The 1965 survey of manufactures showed manufacturing establishments numbering 11,580 employing 398,026 production workers earning $2,056,917; value added by manufactures was $8,611m. Chemical industries along the Gulf Coast, such as the production of synthetic rubber and of primary magnesium (from sea-water), are increasingly important. Steel plants, on 1 Jan. 1959, had a capacity of 2,381,000 net tons of ingots and steel for castings.

COMMUNICATIONS. The state maintained (31 Oct. 1969) 66,280 miles of roads; local roads, 136,916; municipal, 37,352. The railways (1966) had a total mileage of 20,504 miles, of which 14,444 miles were main lines. The port of Houston, connected by the Houston Ship Channel (50 miles long) with the Gulf of Mexico, is the largest inland cotton market of the world. Public airports, Nov. 1969, numbered 238; in addition, there were 443 private airports, of which 267 are open to the public. Motor registration in 1968, 6·9m.

BOOKS OF REFERENCE

Texas Almanac. Dallas. Biennial
MacCorkle, S. A., and Smith, D., *Texas Government.* 5th ed. New York, 1964
Patterson, C. P., and others, *State and Local Government in Texas.* New York, 1948
Richardson, R. N., *Texas, the Lone Star State.* 2nd ed. New York, 1958
Webb, W. P. (ed.), *The Handbook of Texas.* State Hist. Ass., Austin, 1952

LEGISLATIVE REFERENCE LIBRARY. Box 12488, Capitol Station, Austin, Texas 78811. *Director:* James R. Sanders.

UTAH

GOVERNMENT. Utah, which had been acquired by the US during the Mexican war, was, in 1847, settled by Mormons, and on 9 Sept. 1850, organized as a Territory. It was admitted as a state into the Union on 4 Jan. 1896 with boundaries as at present and adopted its present constitution at that time (now with 33 amendments). It sends to Congress 2 senators and 2 representatives.

The Legislature consists of a Senate (in part renewed every 2 years) of 28 members, elected for 4 years, and of a House of Representatives of 69 members elected for 2 years. The Governor is elected for 4 years. The constitution provides for the initiative and referendum. Electors are all citizens, who, not being insane or criminal, have the usual residential qualifications.

The capital is Salt Lake City. There are 29 counties in the state.

In the 1968 presidential election Nixon polled 238,728 votes, Humphrey 156,665 and Wallace 26,906.

Governor: Calvin L. Rampton (D.), 1969–73 ($18,000).
Secretary of State: Clyde L. Miller (R.) ($13,000).

AREA AND POPULATION. Area, 84,916 sq. miles, of which 2,577 sq. miles are water. The federal government (1966) owned 34,876,975 acres or 67·2% of the area of the state. The area of unappropriated and unreserved lands was 23,268,250 acres. The Bureau of Indian Affairs in 1964 administered 2,116,000 acres, of which 2,093,033 acres were allotted to Indian tribes.

Census population, 1 April 1960, 890,627, an increase of 29·3% since 1940. Estimated population, 1969, 1,068,000. Births in 1967 were 23,722 (22·9 per 1,000 population); deaths, 7,077 (7·1); infant deaths (1966), 434 (19·9 per 1,000 live births); marriages (1968), 11,558 (9·5); divorces (1968), 3,390 (2·7).

Population at 4 federal censuses (with distribution by sex, 1960) was:

	White	Negro	Indian	Asiatic	Total	Per sq. mile
1910	366,583	1,144	3,123	2,501	373,351	4·5
1930	499,967	1,108	2,869	3,903	507,847	6·2
1950	676,909	2,729	4,201	—	688,862	8·4
1960	873,828	4,148	6,961	5,207	890,627	10·8
Male	436,198	2,182	All others	6,544	444,924	—
Female	437,630	1,966		6,107	445,703	—

Of the total in 1960, 667,158 persons (74·9%) were urban (63·3% in 1950); 467,817 were 21 years of age or older; foreign-born whites numbered 30,524.

The largest cities are Salt Lake City (capital), with a population (census, 1960) of 189,454 (urbanized area, 445,900); Ogden, 124,000; Provo, 43,800; and Logan, 25,000.

RELIGION. Latter-day Saints (Mormons) form about 63% of the church membership of the state, with approximately 816,447 members in 1968; their church is a substantial property-owner. There were (1965) about 53,000 Catholics. Most Protestant denominations are represented.

EDUCATION. School attendance is compulsory for children from 6 to 18 years of age. There are 40 school districts. Teachers' salaries, 1968–69, averaged $7,644. There were (autumn 1969) 302,394 pupils in public elementary and secondary schools. In 1969–70 estimated public school expenditure was $176·6m.

The University of Utah (1850) (17,656 full-time students in 1969) is in Salt Lake City; the Utah State University (1890) (12,798 students in 1968) in Logan has 2 branch colleges. The Mormon Church maintains the Brigham Young University at Provo (1875) with 24,144 students. Other colleges include: Westminster College, Salt Lake City, 833 students; Weber State College, Ogden, 18,220; College of Southern Utah, Cedar City, 1,714; College of Eastern Utah, Price, 684; Snow College, Ephraim, 779; Dixie State College, St George, 1,182.

WELFARE. The state department of public welfare provided assistance to an average of 42,986 persons per month during the year 1968–69; 5,741 persons received old-age assistance at an average of $96.89 per month; 29,223 persons, aid to dependent children, $50.08; 156 persons, aid to the blind, $112.19; 5,069 persons, aid to the disabled, $119.07; 1,518 persons, general assistance, $72.05; 1,279 persons, foster care, $69.16. Total expenditure of the department for assistance, welfare and administration, 1968–69, was $41,960,083.

In 1966, the state has 40 hospitals (4,610 beds) listed by the American Hospital Association.

The number of inmates of the state prison on 20 Jan. 1970 was 483. There was no execution in 1969; since 1930 total executions have been 13 (12 by shooting, 1 by hanging—the condemned man has choice), all whites, and all for murder.

FINANCE. For the year ending 30 June 1969 (US Census Bureau figures) general revenue was $384·7m. while general expenditures were $384·7m. ($205·9m. for education, $85·1m. for highways and $54·8m. for health and welfare).

The net long-term debt on 30 June 1969 amounted to $58·7m.

Per capita personal income (1969) was $2,994.

AGRICULTURE. In 1969 Utah had 14,500 farms with a total area of 13·3m. acres (only 25% of the total land area), of which 1,062,246 acres were crop land harvested and 945,405 were crop land for pasture, fallow, etc.; 15,700 farms (88·2% of all farms) had 1,061,383 acres using irrigation; the average farm was of 887 acres.

Of the total surface area (52,696,960 acres), 9% is severely eroded and only 9·4% is free from erosion; the balance is moderately eroded.

Cash income, 1969, from crops, $45·8m. and from livestock, $151·7m. The chief crops are wheat, hay, sugar-beet, potatoes, barley and alfalfa seed. On

1 Jan. 1969 the number of animals was: Milch cows, 400,000; all cattle, 785,000; sheep, 1,053,000; swine, 52,000. The wool clip (1968) yielded 10,197,000 lb. of wool from 1,013,000 sheep.

FORESTRY. Area of national forests, 1969, was 9,088,986 acres, of which 7·97m. acres were under forest service administration.

MINING (1966). Production of principal minerals: Copper (recoverable), 265,383 short tons; gold, 438,736 troy oz.; petroleum, 24,112,000 bbls; coal, 4,635,000 short tons; iron ore, 1,956,000 long tons; uranium ore, 236,860 short tons; lead (recoverable), 64,124 short tons; silver, 7,755,000 troy oz.; zinc (recoverable), 37,323 short tons. Total value of mineral production, $444·3m.

INDUSTRY. In 1965 the 1,175 manufacturing establishments had 33,286 production workers, who earned $199m.; value added by manufacture was (1964) $716m. The steel industry ranks fourth in the production of steel plates; its capacity, 1961, was about 2·3m. short tons of ingots and steel for castings.

COMMUNICATIONS. On 1 July 1968 the state had 1,725 miles of railways. There were 74 airports (43 municipal, 25 private, 6 commercial) in 1968. The state, 31 Dec. 1968, maintained 6,246 miles of highway; the counties, 19,551 miles; the federal government, 6,223 miles; municipalities, 3,589 miles. In 1968 there were 588,464 motors registered.

BOOKS OF REFERENCE

Compiled Digest of Administrative Reports. Secretary of State. Salt Lake City. Annual
Statistical Abstract of Government in Utah. Utah Foundation. Salt Lake City. Annual
A Statistical Abstract of Utah's Economy. Bureau of Economic and Business Research, University of Utah, 1964
Writers' Program. *A Guide to the State.* New York, 1954
Arrington, L., *Great Basin Kingdom: an economic history of the Latter-Day Saints, 1830–1900.* Cambridge, Mass., 1958
Nelson, E., *Utah's Economic Patterns.* Salt Lake City, 1956

VERMONT

GOVERNMENT. Vermont, first settled in 1724, was admitted into the Union as the fourteenth state on 4 March 1791. The first constitution was adopted by convention at Windsor, 2 July 1777, and established an independent state government; in 1793 a new constitution was adopted which, with amendments, is still in force. Amendments are proposed by two-thirds vote of the Senate each decennium, and must be accepted by two sessions of the Legislature; they are then submitted to popular vote. The state Legislature, consisting of a Senate of 30 members and a House of Representatives of 150 members (both elected for 2 years), meets in Jan. in odd-numbered years. The Governor and Lieut.-Governor are elected for 2 years. Electors are all citizens who possess certain residential qualifications and have taken the freeman's oath set forth in the constitution.

The state is divided into 14 counties; there are 246 towns and cities. The state sends to Congress 2 senators and 1 representative, who are elected by the voters of the entire state.

In the 1968 presidential election Nixon polled 85,142 votes, Humphrey 70,255 and Wallace 5,104.

The capital is Montpelier (8,609, census of 1970).

Governor: Deane C. Davis (R.), 1971–72 ($25,000).
Lieut.-Governor: Thomas L. Hayes (R.) ($12,000).
Secretary of State: Richard C. Thomas (R.) ($13,000).

Q

AREA AND POPULATION. Area, 9,267 sq. miles, of which 333 sq. miles are inland water. Census population, 1 April 1970, 444,330, an increase of 14% since 1960. Births, 1969, were 7,708 (18·2 per 1,000 population); deaths, 4,484 (10·7); infant deaths (1967), 165 (21·6 per 1,000 live births); marriages, 4,496; divorces, 769.

Population at 4 census years (with distribution by sex, 1960) was:

	White	Negro	Indian	Asiatic	Total	Per sq. mile
1910	354,298	1,621	26	11	355,956	39·0
1930	358,966	568	36	41	359,611	38·8
1950	377,188	443	30	48	377,747	40·7
1960	389,092	519	57	172	389,881	42·0
Male	191,321	289	All others 133		191,743	—
Female	197,771	230	All others 137		198,138	—

Of the population in 1970, 142,889 persons (32·2%) were urban (38·5% in 1960); those 21 years of age or older (1960), 230,645; there were (1960) 23,218 foreign-born whites. Households numbered 110,732. The largest cities are Burlington, with a population in 1970 of 38,633; Rutland, 19,293; Barre, 10,209.

RELIGION. The principal denominations are Roman Catholic (with 142,465 members in 1970), United Church of Christ (26,749 in 1970), United Methodist (22,699 in 1970), Protestant Episcopal (13,301 in 1970), Baptist (8,000 in 1970) and Unitarian-Universalist (2,054 in 1970).

EDUCATION. School attendance during the full school term is compulsory for children from 7 to 16 years of age, or to have completed the 10th grade. In 1970–71 the 355 public elementary schools had 66,431 enrolled pupils; the 68 public high schools had 37,788 pupils; the 23 parochial schools had 7,686 pupils, and the 3 teachers' colleges had (1967–68) 1,948 pupils. Full-time teachers for public elementary and secondary schools numbered 5,966. Teachers' salaries for 1970–71 averaged $8,246. The University of Vermont (1791) had, 1969–70, 6,420 students; Middlebury College (1800), 1,570 students; Norwich University (1834), 1,325 students; St Michael's College, Winooski, 1,420 students. Total expenditure for education, 1969–70, was an estimated $90m., exclusive of capital outlay.

WELFARE. Old-age assistance was being granted in Dec. 1970 to 4,346 persons, drawing an average of $79.10 per month; aid to needy families with children was being granted to 15,207 persons including 10,645 children, drawing an average of $60.22 per month; aid to the blind was being granted to 106 persons, drawing an average of $107.92; and aid to the permanently and totally disabled was being granted to 2,120 persons, drawing an average of $107.65; medical assistance was being granted for approximately 15,312 persons with an average benefit of $60.22.

In July 1968 the state had 21 general hospitals (1,809 beds), 2 mental hospitals (1,698 beds) and 1 T.B. hospital (50 beds).

On 31 Dec. 1966 the state prison had 126 inmates and the house of correction, 105 inmates. There is no capital punishment in Vermont.

FINANCE. The general revenue for the year ending 30 June 1970 (US Census Bureau figures) was $210·51m. ($96,071,000 from taxation and $64·19m. from federal aid) while general expenditure was $243,001,000 (education, $70·24m.; highways, $72·92m., and public welfare, $35·1m.).

Total net long-term debt, 1 July 1970, was $87,429,000.

Per capita personal income (1969) was $3,267.

AGRICULTURE. Agriculture is an important occupation within the state. In 1964 the state contained 9,247 farms with a total area of 2,524,371 acres, of which 878,164 acres were crop land; the average farm was of 273 acres valued, land and buildings, at $30,341. Cash income, 1968, from livestock and products, $127·8m.; from crops, $13·4m. The chief agricultural crops are hay, apples and potatoes. Vermont leads in maple products, of which the output, 1968, was 285,000 gallons of syrup valued at $1·5m.

On 1 Jan. 1966 Vermont had 253,000 milch cows, 367,000 all cattle, 6,000 sheep and 8,000 swine.

FORESTRY. In 1969 there was cut 107m. bd ft hardwood and 56m. bd ft softwood. In addition, 66,539 cords of softwood pulpwood and boltwood and 48,528 cords of hardwood pulpwood and boltwood were produced, and the equivalent of 18,371 cords of softwood and 20,223 cords of hardwood chipped from mill waste.

National forests area (1969), 232,991 acres. There are 33 state forests and 36 state parks with a total acreage of 118,760.

MINING. Stone, chiefly granite, marble and slate, is the leading mineral produced in Vermont, contributing about 71 % of the total value of mineral products. Other products include asbestos, talc, lime, clay, light aggregate, peat, sand and gravel. Total value of mineral products, 1970, $20,042,000.

INDUSTRY. In 1969, 794 manufacturing establishments employed 43,750 production workers who earned $306m.; value added by manufacture was $522m.

COMMUNICATIONS. There were, in 1968, 727 miles of main line railway. There were (1968) 20 airports, of which 4 were state operated, 4 municipally owned and 12 privately owned. The state maintained (1967) 2,302 miles of paved and gravelled state highways and aided towns and cities in the maintenance of 2,480 miles of state aid highways and 9,141 miles of town highways. Motor vehicle registrations, 1967, 223,053.

BOOKS OF REFERENCE

Legislative Directory. Secretary of State. Montpelier. Biennial
Vermont Year-book, formerly *Walton's Register*. Chester, Annual

STATE LIBRARY. Vermont State Library, Montpelier. *State Librarian:* James Igre.

VIRGINIA

GOVERNMENT. The first English Charter for settlements in America was that granted by James I in 1606 for the planting of colonies in Virginia. The state was one of the 13 original states in the Union. Virginia lost just over one-third of its area when West Virginia was admitted into the Union (1863). The present constitution dates from 1902; it has had 87 amendments.

The General Assembly consists of a Senate of 40 members, elected for 4 years, and a House of Delegates of 100 members, elected for 2 years. The Governor and Lieut.-Governor are elected for 4 years. Qualified as electors are (with few exceptions) all citizens 21 years of age, fulfilling certain residential qualifications, who have registered. The state sends to Congress 2 senators and 10 representatives.

In the 1968 presidential election Nixon polled 590,319 votes, Humphrey 442,387 and Wallace 320,272.

The state capital is Richmond; the state contains 96 counties and 35 independent cities.

Governor: A. Linwood Holton (R.), 1970–74 ($35,000).
Lieut.-Governor: J. Sargent Reynolds (D.).
Secretary of the Commonwealth: Cynthia Newman (D.) ($11,500).

AREA AND POPULATION. Area, 39,841 sq. miles, including 976 sq. miles of inland water. Census population, 1 April 1960, 3,966,949, an increase of 648,269 or 19·5% since 1950. Estimated population, 1 July 1969, 4,781,475. In 1969 there were 83,420 births (17·5 per 1,000 population); 39,084 deaths (8·2); 1,849 infant deaths (22·2 per 1,000 live births); 52,575 marriages (11·1), and 11,417 divorces (2·4).

Population for 4 federal census years (with distribution by sex, 1960) was:

	White	Negro	Indian	Asiatic	Total	Per sq. mile
1910	1,389,809	671,096	539	168	2,061,612	51·2
1930	1,770,441	650,165	779	466	2,421,851	60·7
1950	2,581,555	734,211	1,056	758	3,318,680	83·2
1960	3,142,443	816,258	2,155	4,725	3,966,949	99·6
Male	1,571,139	403,858	All others	4,375	1,979,372	—
Female	1,571,304	412,400		3,873	1,987,577	—

Of the total population in 1960, 2,204,913 persons (55·6%) were urban (47% in 1950); those 21 years of age or older numbered 2,312,887; foreign-born whites, 44,605.

The population (census of 1960) of the principal cities was: Norfolk, 304,869 (urbanized area, Norfolk–Portsmouth (1969), 681,521); Richmond, 219,958 (1969: 540,856); Portsmouth, 114,773; Newport News, 113,662 (Newport News–Hampton (1969), 301,200); Roanoke, 97,110; Alexandria, 91,023; Hampton, 89,258; Lynchburg, 54,790; Danville, 46,577; Petersburg, 36,750; Charlottesville, 29,427.

RELIGION. The principal churches are the Baptists, Methodists, Protestant Episcopal and Presbyterian.

EDUCATION. Elementary and secondary instruction is free, and for ages 6–17 attendance is compulsory. No child under 12 may be employed in any mining or manufacturing work.

In 1968–69 the 167 school districts had, in primary schools, 708,212 pupils and 28,725 teachers and in public high schools, 433,377 pupils and 19,870 teachers. Teachers' salaries (1969) averaged $7,328. Total expenditure on education, 1968–69, was $748,488,181. The more important institutions for higher education (1968) were:

Founded	Name and place of college	Staff	Students
1693	William and Mary College, Williamsburg (State)	420	4,635
1749	Washington and Lee University, Lexington	118	1,391
1776	Hampden-Sydney College, Hampden-Sydney (Pres.)	49	607
1819	University of Virginia, Charlottesville (State)	1,015	9,000
1832	Randolph-Macon College, Ashland (Methodist)	67	860
1832	University of Richmond, Richmond (Baptist)	296	4,296
1838	Virginia Commonwealth University, Richmond	1,800	12,300
1839	Virginia Military Institute, Lexington (State)	115	1,143
1865	Virginia Union University, Richmond (Coloured; Bapt.)	95	1,280
1872	Virginia Polytechnic Institute, Blacksburg (State)	970	9,568
1882	Virginia State College, Petersburg	233	2,579
1892	Randolph-Macon Woman's College, Lynchburg	86	866

WELFARE. In 1938 Virginia established a system of old-age assistance under the Federal Security Act; in June 1970, 13,011 persons were drawing an average grant of $61.89; aid to permanently and totally disabled, 7,998 persons, average grant $74.60; aid to dependent children, 98,424 persons, average grant $42.62; general relief, 5,139 cases, average grant $76.80.

In 1968 the state had 130 hospitals (38,275 beds) listed by the American Hospital Association.

Marriage between white and 'non-white' persons is prohibited.

There was no execution in 1969; executions (by electrocution) since 1930 totalled 95, including 17 whites and 58 Negroes for murder and 20 Negroes for rape. Prison population, 31 Dec. 1967, 4,033.

FINANCE. General revenue for the year ending 30 June 1970 was $1,779,865,600 (taxation, $889,489,483, and federal aid, $317,985,015); general expenditures,

$1,709,171,598 ($736,868,103 for education, $351,437,600 for highways and $163,532,916 for public welfare).

Total net long-term debt, 30 June 1969, amounted to $81,371,876.

Per capita personal income (1969) was $3,294.

AGRICULTURE. In 1959 there were 97,623 farms in Virginia with an area of 13,126,000 acres, of which 4,426,000 acres were crop land; average farm had 134·5 acres and was valued at $18,242. Commercial farms numbered 49,517. Moderate erosion affects 15,031,149 acres (59·2% of the total area).

Income, 1969, from crops, $240m., and from livestock and livestock products, $316m. The chief crops are tobacco (118·2m. lb. in 1969), corn, wheat, oats, potatoes, sweet potatoes, peanuts (255·2m. lb.) and apples.

Animals on farms on 1 Jan. 1970 included 370,000 milch cows, 1·43m. all cattle, 189,000 sheep and 618,000 swine.

FORESTRY. National forests, 1969, covered 3·23m. acres.

MINING (1969). Coal is the most important mineral, with output of 35,651,536 short tons. Lead and zinc ores (738,076 short tons), stone, sand and gravel, lime and titanium ore are also produced. Total mineral output was valued (1968) at $296m.

INDUSTRY. The manufacture of cigars and cigarettes and of rayon and allied products and the building of ships lead in value of products. In 1967, 4,950 manufacturing establishments employed 269,000 production workers earning $1,299m.; value added by manufacture was $4,084m.

COMMUNICATIONS. In 1968 there were 3,951 miles of state-owned railways. There were, in 1969, 161 airports, of which 46 were publicly owned. The state highways system, 30 June 1968, had 49,776 miles of highways, of which 7,721 miles were primary roads. Motor registrations, 1969, 2·16m.

BOOKS OF REFERENCE

Statistical Abstract of Virginia. Charlottesville, 1966
Gottmann, J., *Virginias in our Century.* Charlottesville, 1969
STATE LIBRARY. Virginia State Library, Richmond 23219. *State Librarian:* Randolph W. Church.

WASHINGTON

GOVERNMENT. Washington, formerly part of Oregon, was created a Territory in 1853, and was admitted into the Union as a state on 11 Nov. 1889. Its settlement dates from 1811. The constitution, adopted in 1889, has had 54 amendments. The Legislature consists of a Senate of 49 members elected for 4 years, half their number retiring every 2 years, and a House of Representatives of 99 members, elected for 2 years. The Governor and Lieut.-Governor are elected for 4 years. The state sends 2 senators and 7 representatives to Congress.

Qualified as voters are (with some exceptions) all citizens 21 years of age, having the usual residential qualifications.

In the 1968 presidential election Nixon polled 588,510 votes, Humphrey 616,037 and Wallace 85,131.

The capital is Olympia (population, 1970, 22,413). The state contains 39 counties.

Governor: Daniel Jackson Evans (R.), 1969–73 ($32,500).

Lieut.-Governor: John A. Cherburg (D.), 1969–73 ($10,000).

Secretary of State: A. Ludlow Kramer (R.), 1969–73 ($15,000).

AREA AND POPULATION. Area, 68,192 sq. miles, of which 1,529 sq. miles are inland water. Lands owned by the federal government, 1969, were 12·57m. acres or 29·4% of the total area. Census population, 1 April 1970, 3,341,399, an increase of 488,185 or 19·5% since 1960. Estimated population, 1 April 1969, 3,417,330. Births, 1967, were 54,875 (17·1 per 1,000 population); deaths, 29,302 (9·1); infant deaths, 1,050 (19·1 per 1,000 live births); marriages, 38,477 (12·5); divorces and annulments, 12,836.

Population in 4 federal census years (with distribution by sex, 1960) was:

	White	Negro	Indian	Asiatic	Total	Per sq. mile
1910	1,109,111	6,058	10,997	15,824	1,141,990	17·1
1930	1,521,661	6,840	11,253	23,642	1,563,396	23·3
1950	2,316,496	30,691	13,816	17,690	2,378,963	35·6
1960	2,751,675	48,738	12,076	29,253	2,853,214	42·8
Male	1,381,261	26,000	All others 27,776		1,435,037	—
Female	1,370,414	22,738	25,025		1,418,177	—

Of the total population in 1960, 1,943,249 persons (68·1%) were urban (63·2% in 1950); 1,717,597 were 21 years of age or older. Foreign-born whites numbered 164,782; Japanese numbered 16,652.

There are 22 Indian reservations, the largest being the Yakima, which contains 1,092,964 acres. The US Bureau of Indian Affairs administers (1968) 2,471,026 acres, of which 1,862,475 acres are owned by the various tribes, and 608,551 acres by individual Indians. Total Indian population living in or near reservation in 1968, 15,592.

Leading cities are Seattle, with a population (1970) of 516,909; Spokane, 168,654; Tacoma, 151,061; Bellevue, 57,751; Everett, 51,926; Yakima, 45,050; Vancouver, 40,083; Bellingham, 39,797; Bremerton,32,138; Longview, 28,319; Renton, 24,716; Richland, 23,008; Walla Walla, 22,986. Urbanized areas (1960 census): Seattle, 864,109; Spokane, 226,938; Tacoma, 214,930.

RELIGION. Chief religious bodies (1968) are the Roman Catholic (409,007), Lutheran (195,026), Methodist (134,179), Presbyterian (113,044), Baptist (81,504), Latter day Saints (68,095), Episcopalian (58,383), Congregationalist (33,489), Disciples of Christ (33,132).

EDUCATION. Education is given free to all children between the ages of 6 and 21 years, and is compulsory for children from 8 to 16 years of age. In Oct. 1969 the 1,114 elementary schools had 15,358 classroom teachers and 394,852 pupils, 199 junior high schools, 38 middle schools and 297 high schools had 14,402 classroom teachers and 369,357 pupils. In 1969–70 the average salary of teaching staff was $9,833. The total expenditure on public elementary and secondary schools for the school year 1969–70 was $658·2m. In Oct. 1969 an estimated 250 private and parochial elementary and secondary schools had 51,425 elementary and high school pupils.

The University of Washington, founded 1861, at Seattle, had 1970–71, approximately 1,700 teachers and 33,202 students; Seattle University (largest private—Roman Catholic—university in the state), 3,400 students, and Washington State University at Pullman, founded 1890, for science and agriculture, had 14,510 students. Three state colleges had 22,868 students. Evergreen State College is scheduled to open near Olympia in 1971. Twenty-five community colleges had a total enrolment of 61,000 students. Ten accredited private colleges and universities had a total enrolment of 19,791 students.

WELFARE. Old-age assistance is provided for persons 65 years of age or older without adequate resources (and not in need of continuing home care) who are residents of the state. In June 1970, 23,062 persons were drawing an average of $64.78 per month; aid to 124,894 dependents in 35,631 families averaged $20.113 per family monthly; to 498 blind persons, $87.51 per person monthly; to 17,227 totally disabled, $90.85 monthly. 7,654 persons, under foster care, received payments of $98.61 per person.

On 30 June 1969 the 3 state hospitals for mental illness had a daily average of 3,086 patients; schools for handicapped children, 4,490 residents. In 1968–9 the unemployment insurance system covered 65,318 employers with average employment of 816,472. Unemployment in 1969 averaged 61,700 (5·8% of labour force). Benefits to some 105,259 beneficiaries ranged from $17 to $42 per week and averaged (1968–69) $34.09.

The average daily adult population in state prisons for 1968–69 was 2,646. Since 1963 there have been no executions; total 1930–63 (by hanging) was 47, including 40 whites, 5 Negroes and 2 other races, all for murder, except 1 white for kidnapping.

In 1969 the state had 128 hospitals (18,677 beds) listed by the American Hospital Association.

FINANCE. For the year ending 30 June 1969 (US Census Bureau figures) the state's general revenue was $1,471,254,000 ($980,715,000 from taxes and $302,804,000 from federal aid); general expenditure was $1,286,754,000 (education, $691,094,000; highways, $275,269,000 and public welfare, $195,324,000).

Total net long-term debt on 30 June 1968 was $676m.

Per capita personal income (1969) was $3,835.

ECONOMIC ACTIVITY. Traditionally the state's economy has been based on agriculture, forestry, fishing and mining. However, manufacturing, led by the aircraft and aerospace industry, has steadily increased since the Second World War and, by 1964, had become the state's leading primary industry.

AGRICULTURE. Agriculture is constantly growing in value because of more intensive and diversified farming and will be further aided as the 1m.-acre Columbia Basin Irrigation Project proceeds. Irrigated land in farms (1964) amounted to 1,149,842 acres.

In 1964 there were 45,574 farms with an acreage of 19,052,538, of which 4,423,400 acres were harvested crop land; average farm was of 418·1 acres with a value of $65,609; 4,604 farms had less than 10 acres and 3,767 farms had 1,000 acres and over. Realized net income per farm in 1968 was $7,020 compared with a national average of $4,841.

Value of farm production 1968, from crops was $477,498,000; from speciality products, $47·8m., and from livestock, $284·37m. Wheat, the leading farm commodity in Washington, was valued at $120m. Milk production was second at $111·7m. Washington also led as a producer of apples (512,500 tons), hops, late summer potatoes, spearmint and dry field peas. Other large crops are green peas (for processing), wheat (108·9m. bu.), hops (28·2m. lb.), barley, rye, maize, sugar-beet (1,628,000 tons), pears, peaches, prunes, apricots, strawberries, cranberries, asparagus, alfalfa seed and grapes.

On 1 Jan. 1969 animals on farms included 308,000 milch cows, 1,286,000 all cattle, 130,000 sheep and 80,000 swine. The wool clip in 1969 amounted to 1,383,000 lb.

FORESTRY. From the early 1900s to about 1940 the state ranked first in annual bd ft of lumber, but is now third to Oregon and California, producing 10% of the nation's lumber (3,554m. bd ft in 1967). The state is the largest producer of woodpulp (over 10% of US total) and second to Oregon in production of plywood (15% of national total). Timber harvested in 1968 was 7,003·8m. bd ft. The national forest lands of the state had (1968) an area of 9,710,815 acres.

FISHING. Washington ranks second only to Alaska in the catch of salmon and halibut, and in the production of canned salmon. Value of sea products in 1968 was $20,773.737 catch value, $43,789,694 processed value. Total weight of fish caught, 126,099,977 lb., including salmon, 43,789,694 lb.; halibut, 12,359,856 lb.; oysters, 6,474,966 lb.; other shellfish, 12,218,216 lb., and bottom fish, 44,505,237 lb.

MINING (1968). Production of principal minerals: Sand and gravel, 31·4m. short tons; stone, 14·33m. short tons; zinc, 13,884 short tons; coal, 178,000 short tons; lead, 5,655 short tons; clays, 140,000 short tons; peat, 40,440 short tons. Uranium ore is also mined but production figures are not disclosed. Total mineral output in 1968 was valued at $81m.

INDUSTRY. In 1966, 171,352 production workers earned $1,109·63m.; value added by manufacture was $3,289,275,000. Aircraft and aerospace manufacture, shipbuilding, machinery, metals, chemicals, lumber and wood products, pulp and paper, and food processing are the major manufacturing industries.

With about 20% of potential water-power resources of US, the state is first in developed and potential hydro-electricity. Abundance of electric power has made Washington the leading producer of primary aluminium; production of 6 plants, 1970, was 775,419 short tons.

COMMUNICATIONS. The railways had, in 1967, 4,936 miles. There were in 1970, 235 airports (101 publicly owned). The state (1970) maintained 6,892 miles of highway; the counties, 39,568 miles; municipalities, 9,578 miles. Motor vehicle registrations (1969), 2,088,000.

BOOKS OF REFERENCE

Washington State Research Council. *Handbook: a compendium of statistical and explanatory information about state and local government in Washington*, 3rd ed. Olympia, 1968
Avery, M. W., *Washington, a History of the Evergreen State.* Univ. of Wash. Press, 1965.—*Government of Washington State.* Univ. of Wash. Press, 1966
Ogden, Jr, D. M., and Bone, H. A., *Washington Politics.* New York Univ. Press, 1960
Webster. D. H., and others, *Washington state government: administrative organization and functions.* Univ. of Wash. Press, 1962

STATE LIBRARY. Washington State Library, Olympia. *State Librarian:* Maryan E. Reynolds.

WEST VIRGINIA

GOVERNMENT. In 1862, after the state of Virginia had seceded from the Union, the electors of the western portion ratified an ordinance providing for the formation of a new state, which was admitted into the Union by presidential proclamation on 20 June 1863, under the name of West Virginia. Its constitution was adopted by the voters almost unanimously on 26 March 1863; the present one was adopted in 1872; it has had 36 amendments.

The Legislature consists of the Senate of 32 members elected for a term of 4 years, one-half being elected biennially, and the House of Delegates of 100 members, elected biennially. The Governor is elected for 4 years. Voters are all citizens (with the usual exceptions) 21 years of age and meeting certain residential requirements.

In the 1968 presidential election Nixon polled 307,555 votes, Humphrey 374,091.

The state sends to Congress 2 senators and 5 representatives.

The state capital is Charleston. There are 55 counties.

Governor: Arch Alfred Moore, Jr (R.), 1969–73 ($25,000).
Secretary of State: John D. Rockefeller, IV (D.) ($17,000).

AREA AND POPULATION. Area, 24,282 sq. miles, of which 102 sq. miles are water. Census population, 1 April 1960, 1,860,421, a decrease of 7·2% since 1950. Estimated population, 1 July 1968, 1,805,000. Births, 1967, 29,301 (16·3 per 1,000 population); deaths, 19,257 (10·7); infant deaths, 750 (25·6 per 1,000 live births); marriages, 14,330 (7·9); divorces (1967), 3,985 (2·2).

Population in 4 federal census years (with distribution by sex, 1960) was:

	White	Negro	Indian	Asiatic	Total	Per sq. mile
1910	1,156,817	64,173	36	93	1,221,119	50·8
1930	1,614,191	114,893	18	103	1,729,205	71·8
1950	1,890,282	114,867	160	243	2,005,552	83·3
1960	1,770,133	89,378	181	419	1,860,421	77·3
Male	871,178	43,369	All others 488		915,035	—
Female	898,955	46,009	All others 422		945,386	—

Of the total population in 1960, 711,101 (38·2%) were urban (34·6% in 1950); those 21 years of age or older numbered 1,083,000. Foreign-born whites, 1960, were 23,483.

The 1960 census population of the principal cities was: Charleston, 85,796 (urbanized area, 169,500); Huntington, 83,627 (urbanized area, Huntington–Ashland (W. Va.–Ky–Ohio), 165,732); Wheeling, 53,400; Parkersburg, 44,797; Weirton, 28,201; Clarksburg, 28,112; Fairmont, 27,477; Morgantown, 22,487.

The 1967 estimated population of the principal cities was: Charleston, 103,000 (urbanized area, 246,900); Huntington, 81,200 (urbanized area, Huntington–Ashland (W.Va.–Ky–Ohio), 259,500); Wheeling, 49,200; Parkersburg, 47,200; Weirton, 30,600; Fairmont, 27,700; Clarksburg, 25,800; Morgantown, 25,400.

RELIGION. Chief denominations in 1969 were United Methodists (220,000 members); Baptists (119,514 members); and Roman Catholics (89,000). Estimated total membership, all denominations, 600,000.

EDUCATION. Public school education is free for all from 6 to 21 years of age, and school attendance is compulsory for all between the ages of 7 and 16 (school term, 200 days—180–185 days of actual teaching). The public schools are non-sectarian. During school year 1968–69 elementary schools had 9,208 instructional personnel and 222,740 pupils enrolled; secondary schools, 8,804 and 189,846 respectively. Average annual salary of total instructional personnel, 1968–69, was $6,509. Total current expenditures for public schools, $213,514,266.

Leading institutions of higher education in 1969:

Founded		Full-time Staff	Full-time Students
1837	Marshall University, Huntington	358	6,150
1837	West Liberty State College, West Liberty	147	2,880
1867	Fairmont State College, Fairmont	168	2,972
1868	West Virginia University. Morgantown	1,360	15,308
1872	Concord College, Athens	99	1,734
1872	Glenville State College, Glenville	102	1,507
1872	Shepherd College, Shepherdstown	75	1,253
1891	West Virginia State College, Institute	147	2,008
1895	West Virginia Institute of Technology, Montgomery	141	2,271
1895	Bluefield State College, Bluefield	68	1,365
1901	Potomac State College of West Virginia Univ., Keyser	44	754

In addition to the universities and state-supported schools, there are 15 denominational and private institutions of higher education and 13 business colleges.

WELFARE. Since 1936 West Virginia has provided a system of public assistance, state and federally financed. In March 1970 cases of old-age assistance numbered 12,922 (average grant, $72.75 per month); aid to 21,822 families with 26,185 dependent children ($69.51); aid to 563 blind ($70.39); aid to 8,337 totally and permanently disabled ($65.40).

There are 14 charitable, penal and correctional institutions. In 1965 the State Legislature abolished capital punishment. State prisons had, on 30 Aug. 1968, 1,139 inmates.

In 1969 the state had 78 hospitals (8,228 beds) and 44 long-term-care facilities (2,858 beds). Twelve mental hospitals, 5 psychiatric units in general hospitals and 1 tuberculosis hospital had 4,645 beds.

All statutes requiring racial segregation in West Virginia have been eliminated. After a United States Supreme Court decision in June 1967 voided all state and local anti-miscegenation laws, West Virginia's Attorney-General issued a formal opinion that West Virginia's anti-miscegenation law is unconstitutional and invalid. Effective on 1 July 1967, the West Virginia Human Rights Act prohibits discrimination in employment and places of public accommodations based on race, religion, colour, national origin or ancestry. Discrimination in these areas has lessened, but discrimination in housing and real property continues to be a major problem for which legislative remedies have been proposed.

FINANCE. Total revenues for the year ending 30 June 1968 (State Auditor's figures) were $654,349,827 ($458,413,421 from general taxes and licences and $195,936,406 from federal funds); general expenditures were $625,972,959 (education, $223,261,567; highways, $192,774,525; public welfare, $121,808,319; all other governmental costs, including capital outlay, $88,128,548).

Total net long-term debt was $278,322,000 on 30 June 1968.

Estimated *per capita* personal income (1969) was $2,610.

AGRICULTURE. In 1969 the state had 30,000 farms with an area of 5·1m. acres; average size of farm was 176 acres and valued at $16,600. Livestock farming predominates.

Cash income, 1968, from crops was $24·85m. and from livestock and products, $75·42m. Total acreage of field crops and hay harvested, 1968, was 728,150 acres, chief field crops being hay and corn. Apples (4·8m. bu., 1968) and peaches (450,000 bu.) are important fruit crops. Livestock on farms, 1 Jan. 1969, included 461,000 cattle, of which 72,000 were milch cows; sheep, 170,000; hogs, 71,000; chickens, 1,733,000; turkeys, 83,000. Production, 1968, included 1·28m. farm chickens, 1,509,000 turkeys, 16·46m. broilers, 329m. eggs.

FORESTRY. State forests, 1 Oct. 1968, covered 77,069 acres; national forests, 907,647 acres; 74% of the state is woodland.

MINING. West Virginia leads all states in the production of coal; 55% of the state is underlain with mineable coal; 139,315,720 short tons of coal were produced in 1969; coke (oven and bee-hive), 43,200 short tons. Petroleum output has declined from an annual average, 1921–25, of 6,575,000 bbls to 3,104,000 bbls in 1969; natural gas production for 1969 was 231·76m. cu. ft. Lime, salt, sand and gravel, sandstone and limestone are also produced. The total value of mineral output in 1967 was $891·8m.

INDUSTRY. In Sept. 1969, 13,191 manufacturing firms were covered by unemployment insurance; average employment, 1967, 133,515 who earned $908,738,168. There were 107 firms producing metals and metal products (primary and fabricated metals, mostly steel); these employed 33,512 workers who received $268,786,646. The chemical process industry consists of 55 firms employing 25,804 workers with wages and salaries of $222,892,004.

There are approximately 1,200 different industrial installations in West Virginia using nuclear materials and devices. This includes 50 businesses and industries; 105 colleges and other state institutions; and 1,045 in health and medical fields. West Virginia University has pioneered research in wood plastic combinations (WPC). This is a process where wood is impregnated with a monomer (liquid plastic) and bombarded with gamma-rays to polymerize the plastic; thereby creating a 'super hard wood'.

COMMUNICATIONS. In 1969 the state had 3,798 miles of railway, all operated by diesel or electric trains. There were, in 1969, 20 licensed and 5 privately owned airports and 1 heliport. Total highways, 32,968 miles (state system of rural roads and highways, 31,020 miles; municipal streets, 669 miles; national parks, state parks and forests, 1,195 miles; West Virginia Turnpike, 87 miles). Registered motor vehicles, fiscal year ending 30 June 1969, numbered 829,221.

BOOKS OF REFERENCE

West Virginia Blue Book. Legislature. Charleston. Annual, since 1916
West Virginia Statistical Handbook, 1965. Bureau of Business Research. W. Va. Univ., Morgantown, 1964
Bibliography of West Virginia. 2 parts. Dept. of Archives and History. Charleston, 1939
West Virginia History. Dept. of Archives and History. Charleston. Quarterly, from 1939
Writers' Program. *West Virginia: A Guide to the Mountain State*. New York, 1948
Comett, Elizabeth, and Summers, F. P., *The Thirty-Fifth State*. Morgantown, 1966
Conley, P., and Stutler, B. B., *West Virginia Yesterday and Today*. Charleston, 1966
Davis, C. J., and others, *West Virginia State and Local Government*. West Virginia Univ. Bureau for Government Research, 1963
Moore, G. E., *A Banner in the Hills: West Virginia's Statehood*. New York, 1963
Sutton, Felix, *West Virginia*. New York, 1968
Carpenter, Allan, *West Virginia*. Childrens Press, Chicago, 1968

STATE LIBRARY. Dept. of Archives and History, Charleston. Director: Dr James L. Hupp.

WISCONSIN

GOVERNMENT. Wisconsin was settled in 1670 by French traders and missionaries. Originally a part of New France, it was surrendered to the British in 1763 and in 1783, when ceded to the US, became part of the North-west Territory. It was then contained successively in the Territories of Indiana, Illinois and Michigan. In 1836 it became part of the Territory of Wisconsin, which also included the present states of Iowa, Minnesota and parts of the Dakotas. It was admitted into the Union with its present boundaries on 29 May 1848. Its constitution, which dates from 1848, has 92 amendments affecting 52 sections. The legislative power is vested in a Senate of 33 members (1971 term: 12 Democrats and 20 Republicans), elected for 4 years, one-half elected alternately, and an Assembly of 100 members (1971 term: 67 Democrats and 33 Republicans), all elected simultaneously for 2 years. The Governor and Lieut.-Governor are elected for 4 years. All 6 constitutional officers will serve 4-year terms.

Wisconsin has universal suffrage for all citizens over 21 years of age; but, as there is no official list of voters, the size of the electorate is unknown; 1,350,189 voted for Governor in 1970. Wisconsin is represented in Congress by 2 senators and 10 representatives.

In the 1968 presidential election Nixon polled 809,997 votes, Humphrey 748,804 and Wallace 127,835.

The capital is Madison. The state has 72 counties.

Governor: Patrick J. Lucey (D.), 1971–75 ($25,000).
Lieut.-Governor: Martin J. Schreiber (D.), 1971–75 ($15,000).
Secretary of State: Robert C. Zimmerman (R.), 1971–75 ($13,500).

AREA AND POPULATION. Area, 56,154 sq. miles, including 1,439 sq. miles of inland water, but excluding any part of the Great Lakes. Revised census population, 1 April 1960, 3,952,765, an increase of 15·1% since 1950. Census (preliminary), 1 April 1970, 4,366,766. Births in 1969 were 74,324 (17·2 per 1,000 population); deaths, 41,072 (9·5); infant deaths, 1,281 (17·3 per 1,000 live births); marriages, 34,402 (8); divorces and annulments, 7,832 (1·8).

Population in 4 census years (with distribution by sex, 1960) was:

	White	Negro	Indian	Asiatic	Total	Per sq. mile
1910	2,320,555	2,900	10,142	263	2,333,860	42.2
1930	2,916,255	10,739	11,548	464	2,939,006	53.7
1950	3,392,690	28,182	12,196	1,507	3,434,575	62.8
1960[1]	3,858,903	74,546	14,297	4,031	3,951,777	72.2
Male	1,918,199	36,917	7,195	2,201	1,964,512	—
Female	1,940,704	37,629	7,102	1,830	1,987,265	—

[1] 1960 figures are unrevised.

Of the total population in 1960, 2,522,179 persons (63·8%) were urban (57·9% in 1950); 2,354,489 were 21 years old or older. Foreign-born whites numbered 170,609.

Population of the larger cities, 1970 census (preliminary), was as follows:

Milwaukee	709,537	Appleton	56,673	Fond du Lac	35,330
Madison	170,073	Oshkosh	52,460	Beloit	35,256
Racine	94,720	La Crosse	51,448	Manitowoc	33,180
Green Bay	87,239	Sheboygan	47,957	Wausau	32,395
Kenosha	78,063	Janesville	44,173	Brookfield	31,990
West Allis	71,511	Eau Claire	41 892	Menominee Falls	31,377
Wauwatosa	58,668	Waukesha	39,645	Superior	31,297

Population of larger urbanized areas, 1960 census: Milwaukee, 1,393,260; Madison, 287,501; Duluth–Superior (Minn.–Wis.), 261,936; Racine, 171,218; Green Bay, 157,299.

RELIGION. Wisconsin church affiliation, as a percentage of the 1960 population, was estimated in Jan. 1967 at 35·9% Protestant, 32·9% Catholic, 30·3% unaffiliated and all others 0·9%.

EDUCATION. All children between the ages of 7 and 18 are required to attend school full-time to the end of the school term in which they become 18 years of age. In 1969–70 the public elementary schools had 576,078 pupils and 25,424 teachers; high schools had 402,986 pupils and 21,525 teachers. Elementary school teachers' salaries, 1969–70, averaged $8,750; high school teachers, $9,200. Expenditure per pupil (excluding debt services and capital outlay) was $833 in 1969–70. The 9 state universities had, in 1968–69, 3,350 teachers and 58,200 students.

In 1969–70 vocational-technical schools had a total enrolment of 206,026, requiring 2,460 full-time teachers and 7,150 part-time teachers; 174,701 students were in state-aided classes and the remainder in classes supported entirely by local funds.

The University of Wisconsin, established in 1848, had, in 1970–71, 3,769 full-time professors and instructors, 500 part-time teachers and 1,484 (full-time equivalent) teaching and research graduate assistants. There were, during the first half-year, 67,874 students enrolled (34,388 at Madison, 20,822 at the University of Wisconsin–Milwaukee, 4,171 at the Green Bay complex, 4,102 at the Parkside complex and 4,391 at 7 freshman–sophomore centres).

The Wisconsin State University System, comprised of 9 state universities and 4 branch campuses had enrolled 64,214 students for 1970–71.

The total expenditure, 1968–69, for all public education was $1,224m., of which that on elementary and high schools amounted to $774·5m.

The state maintains an educational broadcasting and television service.

WELFARE. Old-age assistance (established in 1925) providing a monthly grant with no maximum, plus medical and burial expenses, is available to persons, 65 years old and over, satisfying requirements as to need. In July 1970, 18,400 persons were drawing an average of $100 per month in addition to benefits under an expanded medical assistance programme.

Aid to dependent children was established in 1913, available to mothers caring for their dependent minor children in their own homes; 22,942 families constituting 80,739 persons received an average of $204 per family in July 1970; 5,383 children in 3,504 foster homes received an average of $101 per child per month; 686 blind persons received an average of $88, and 6,999 totally disabled persons received $91 per month. Medicare in 1969–70 cost $144·3m.

In 1969 the state had 164 general and allied special hospitals (22,639 beds), 48 mental hospitals (17,630 beds) and 12 tuberculosis sanatoria (328 beds) and 511 nursing homes and homes for aged (40,291 beds). Patients in state and county mental hospitals and institutions for the mentally retarded on1 June 1970 numbered 13,733 (318 per 100,000 population).

The state's penal, reformatory and correctional system on 1 July 1970 held 3,443 men and 333 women in the 9 institutions for adult and juvenile offenders; the probation and parole system was supervising 7,867 men and 1,319 women. Wisconsin does not impose a death penalty.

FINANCE. For the year ending 30 June 1970 (Wisconsin Bureau of Finance figures) total revenue for all funds was $2,535,050,554 ($1,240,242,216 from taxation and $357,091,947 from federal aid). General expenditure from all funds was $2,278,578,176 ($751,008,874 for education, $268,950,168 for highways, $370,761,530 for health and social services).

Per capita personal income (1969) was $3,632.

AGRICULTURE. The total number of farms has declined in the last 35 years, but farms have become larger and more productive. There were 112,000 farms with a total acreage of 20·4m. acres and an average size of 182 acres in 1970, compared with 145,000 farms with a total acreage of 22·6m. acres and an average of 156 acres in 1958.

Cash income from products sold by Wisconsin farms in 1969 of $1,525m. was the highest on record, and included $1,313m. from livestock and livestock products and $212m. from crops. The volume of all crops harvested in the state in 1969 was the second highest on record.

Wisconsin ranked first among the states in 1969 in the number of milk cows, milk production, output of American, both Brick and Munster, Limburger, Italian and Blue Mold cheese. Production of all cheese accounted for 43·6% of the nation's total. The state also ranked first in both bulk sweetened whole and skim condensed milk and bulk unsweetened skim condensed milk as well as powdered whey, malted milk powder and dry whole milk. Firsts in the crop list included the tons of corn for silage, all hay, beets for canning and green peas for processing. Production for the principal field crops in 1969 included: Corn for grain, 140m. bu.; corn for silage, 10·5m. tons; oats, 103m. bu.; all hay, 11m. tons. Other crops of importance were more than 12m. cwt. of potatoes, 13m. lb. of tobacco, 746,000 bbls of cranberries, nearly 2m. cwt. of cabbage, over 1m. cwt. of carrots, and the processing crops of 423,750 tons of sweet corn, 134,300 tons of green peas and 95,350 tons of snap beans.

FORESTRY. In July 1968 national forests comprised 1·5m. acres; state forests, 400,000 acres, and county forests, 2·4m. acres. Wisconsin has an estimated 15·5m. acres of forest lands (about 45% of land area). Lumbering, a major industry in early times, remains so, but now under controlled cutting practices.

MINING. Sand and gravel, stone and zinc are the chief mineral products. Mineral production in 1969 was valued at $80m. This value included $35·4m. for sand and gravel and $27·6m. for stone. Production of zinc ore was valued at $6·7m., and lead ore worth approximately $328,000 was recovered as a hy-product. The first taconite plant in Wisconsin began operation in Dec. 1969 and is now producing 750,000 tons of iron ore concentrates annually. Exploration for copper is taking place in northern Wisconsin.

MANUFACTURING. Wisconsin has much heavy industry, particularly in the Milwaukee area. In 1967 the state ranked eleventh in value added by manufacture; machinery was the major industrial group, followed by food processing, electrical machinery, paper manufacturing, fabricated metals and transportation equipment. In 1967 manufacturing establishments had a total employment of 514,200 earning $3,589m.; value added by manufacture, $7,062m.

ELECTRICITY. There were, Jan. 1970, 95 hydro-electric power plants (20 of them municipal) operated by public utilities with a total installed capacity of 412,013 kw.; output, 1969, was 2,036m. kwh. Fuel burning plants numbered 72 (24 municipal); total installed capacity, 4,990,677 kw.; total output (1969), 21,444,151m. kwh.

TOURISM. The tourist-vacation industry ranks among the first three in economic importance. Approximately $1,500m. is spent annually by tourists, 60% of this amount by non-residents. The decline of lumbering and mining in the northern section of the state has increased dependency on the recreation industry.

COMMUNICATIONS. With the opening of the St Lawrence Seaway in 1959, 14 Wisconsin ports became accessible to ocean-going vessels. Green Bay, Kenosha, Manitowoc, Marinette, Milwaukee, Sheboygan, Sturgeon Bay and Superior (one of the world's largest iron-ore and grain ports) have developed foreign waterborne commerce.

On 1 Jan. 1970 the state had 5,980 road miles of railway. There were, in 1970, 90 publicly operated airports. Twenty-four airports were served by 10 scheduled airlines. The state had on 1 Jan. 1970, 102,284 miles of highway. 63% of all roads in the state have a bituminous (or similar) surface. There are 11,889 miles of state trunk roads and 19,567 miles of county trunk roads.

In the year ending 30 June 1970 Wisconsin registered 1,755,804 private motor cars.

BOOKS OF REFERENCE

Wis. Dept. of Administration, Bureau of State Planning. *Wisconsin Statistical Abstract.* Madison, 1969
Wis. Dept. of Local Affairs and Development Div. of Econ. Development. *Wisconsin Facts for Industry.* Madison, 1968
Wis. Historical Society: *Dictionary of Wisconsin Biography.* Madison, 1960
Wis. Legislative Reference Bureau: *Wisconsin Blue Book.* Madison. Biennial
Wis. Natural Resources Committee of State Agencies: *The Natural Resources of Wisconsin.* Madison 1964
Austin, H. R., *The Wisconsin Story.* 5th ed. Milwaukee, 1964

STATE INFORMATION AGENCY. Legislative Reference Bureau, State Capitol, Madison, Wis. 53702. *Chief:* H. Rupert Theobald.

WYOMING

GOVERNMENT. Wyoming, first settled in 1834, was admitted into the Union on 10 July 1890. The constitution, drafted that year, has since had 30 amendments. The Legislature consists of a Senate of 30 members elected for 4 years, and a House of Representatives of 61 members elected for 2 years. The Governor is elected for 4 years.

The state sends to Congress 2 senators and 1 representative, elected by the voters of the entire state. The suffrage extends to all citizens, male and female, who can read, and who have the usual residential qualifications.

In the 1968 presidential election Nixon polled 70,927 votes, Humphrey 45,173 and Wallace 11,105.

The capital is Cheyenne. The state contains 23 counties.

Governor: Stanley K. Hathaway (R.), 1971–75 ($20,000).
Secretary of State: Mrs Thyra Thomson (R.) ($15,000).

AREA AND POPULATION. Area 97,914 sq. miles, of which 503 sq. miles are water. The Yellowstone National Park occupies about 2,221,773 acres; the Grand Teton National Park has 310,350 acres. The federal government in 1970 owned 30m. acres (48·12% of the total area of the state). The Federal Bureau of Indian Affairs in 1970 administered 1,886,556 acres, of which 1,647,420 acres were allotted to tribes.

Census population, 1 April 1960, 330,066, an increase of 13·6% since 1950. Population (preliminary), 1 July 1970, 332,416. Births in 1969 were 5,870 (18·3 per 1,000 population); deaths, 2,942 (9·1); infant deaths, 147 (25 per 1,000 live births); marriages, 4,629 (14·4); divorces, 1,711 (8·5); annulments, 11.

Population in 4 census years (with distribution by sex, 1960) was:

	White	Negro	Indian	Asiatic	Total	Per sq. mile
1910	140,318	2,235	1,486	1,926	145,965	1·5
1930	221,241	1,250	1,845	1,229	225,565	2·3
1950	284,009	2,557	3,237	726	290,529	3·0
1960	322,922	2,183	4,020	805	330,066	3·4
Male	165,349	1,142	All others 2,524		169,015	—
Female	157,573	1,041	All others 2,437		161,051	—

Of the total population in 1960, 187,551 persons (56·8%) were urban (37·3% in 1940). Persons over 21 years of age numbered 190,305; foreign-born whites, 9,376.

The largest towns are Cheyenne (capital), with census population in 1960 of 43,505; Casper, 38,930; Laramie, 17,520; Sheridan, 11,651, and Rock Springs, 10,371.

RELIGION. Chief religious bodies are the Roman Catholic (with 45,000 members in 1970), Mormon (27,406 in 1970) and Protestant churches (49,217 in 1956). There were 5,400 members of the Eastern Orthodox Church in 1970.

EDUCATION. In 1969–70 public elementary and secondary schools had 86,440 pupils. Enrolment in the parochial elementary and secondary schools was 2,758. Approximately 5,000 public school teachers earned an average of $8,604 in 1969–70. The average total expenditure per pupil for 1968–69 was $721.

The University of Wyoming, founded at Laramie in 1887, had in 1969–70, 7,203 students (full-time). There are 2-year colleges at Casper, Riverton, Torrington, Cheyenne, Powell, Rock Springs and Sheridan.

WELFARE. Old-age assistance (maximum $104 a month for a single person and $178 for husband and wife) is provided for needy American citizens 65 years of age or older who are residents of the state and county at the time of application; payments bridge the difference between a standard personal or household budget and actual income. In June 1970, 1,578 persons were drawing an average of $60.95 per month; 1,623 recipients for families with dependent children averaged $151.24 monthly per family; aid to 34 blind averaged $69.18 monthly, and aid to 904 permanently and totally disabled cases averaged $69.18 monthly. (Payments exclude medical care.)

In 1970 the state had 31 hospitals (2,013 beds); the psychiatric hospital had an average daily census of 475 patients (July 1970).

State penal institutions in July 1970 held 361 inmates. Since 1930 the state has had only 8 executions (by lethal gas), 7 whites and 1 Negro, all for murder.

FINANCE. In the fiscal year ending 1 July 1970 (State Auditor figures) general revenues were $211,611,573 (taxation, $126,966,944, and federal aid, $84,644,629); general expenditures were $191,475,062.

Total net long-term debt, 30 June 1970, was $51·09m.

Per capita personal income (1970) was $3,190.

AGRICULTURE. Wyoming is semi-arid, and agriculture is carried on by irrigation and by 'dry farming'. In 1969 there were 8,600 farms and ranches with a total area of 37m. acres; average size was 4,302 acres.

Cash receipts, 1969, from crops was $36·27m.; from livestock and products, $188,404,000. Principal crops (1969) are hay (1·68m. tons), wheat (4·88m. bu.), sugar-beet (1·23m. tons), maize (1·7m. bu.), oats (3,478,000 bu.), barley (5·92m. bu.) and dry edible beans (459,000 cwt). The wool clip (1969) yielded 17,456,000 lb. of wool. Animals on farms on 1 Jan. 1970 included 20,000 milch cows, 1·48m. all cattle, 1,934,000 sheep and lambs (ranking second in US) and 29,000 swine.

The state has the largest elk and pronghorn antelope herds in the world, 11 fish hatcheries and numerous wild game. Receipts from hunters and fishermen in 1965, $99m.

MINING. Wyoming is largely an oil-producing state. In 1969 the output of petroleum was 156,767,255 bbls; natural gas, 330,924,000m. cu. ft. Other mining (1969): Coal, 4,605,995 short tons; bentonite, 2,103,735 tons; trona, 4,064,464 tons; uranium, 1,481,048 tons; iron ore, 2,118,282 tons; other minerals mined include cement, clay, feldspar, gypsum, limestone, phosphate, sand and gravel, and marble. Value of mineral products in 1969 was $616·7m.

INDUSTRY. In 1969 there were 360 industrial establishments having 7,275 production workers who earned $49,260,704. There were 566 mining establishments with 11,822 employees who earned $106m. New industrial investment totalled 105m. in 1969. A large portion of the manufacturing in the state is natural resource oriented, with oil being the largest. Oil refineries produced 1,245,000m. gallons of gasoline in 1969 with approximately an equal amount of oil by-products.

COMMUNICATIONS. The railways, 1970, had a length of 2,131 mainline miles. There were in Oct. 1968, 39 municipal airports and 131 private airstrips. The state highway system (1969) comprised 5,841 miles; local roads, 22,121 miles; federal, 12,524 miles. There were (1969) 286,619 registered motor vehicles.

BOOKS OF REFERENCE

Official Directory. Secretary of State. Cheyenne. Biennial
Wyoming Statistical Abstract, 1967. Division of Business and Economic Research, Univ. of Wyoming, Laramie
Davis, T. S., *A Study of Wyoming People.* Laramie, 1965
Larsen, T. A., *History of Wyoming.* Denver, 1965
Trachsel, H. H., and Wase, R. M., *The Government and Administration of Wyoming.* New York, 1953

STATE LIBRARY. Wyoming State Library, Supreme Court and State Library Building, Cheyenne. *State Librarian:* William H. Williams.

OUTLYING TERRITORIES

Non-Self-Governing Territories: Summaries of Information Transmitted to the Secretary-General of the United Nations. Annual
Coulter, J. W., *The Pacific Dependencies of the United States.* New York, 1957
Perkins, W. T., *The United States and its Dependencies.* Leiden, 1962
Pratt, J. W., *America's Colonial Experiment: How the United States Gained, Governed and in Part Gave Away a Colonial Empire.* New York, 1950
Wiens, H. J., *Pacific Island Bastions of the US.* New York and London, 1962

COMMONWEALTH OF PUERTO RICO

GOVERNMENT. Puerto Rico, by the treaty of 10 Dec. 1898 (ratified 11 April 1899), was ceded by Spain to the US. The name was changed from Porto Rico to Puerto Rico by an Act of Congress approved 17 May 1932. Its territorial constitution was determined by the 'Organic Act' of Congress (2 March 1917) known as the 'Jones Act', which ruled until 25 July 1952, when the present constitution of the Commonwealth of Puerto Rico was proclaimed. Puerto Rico has representative government, the franchise being restricted to citizens 21 years of age or over, residence (1 year) and such additional qualifications as may be prescribed by the Legislature of Puerto Rico, but no property qualification may be imposed. Women were enfranchised in 1932 (with a literacy test) and fully in 1936. Puerto Ricans do not vote in the US presidential elections, though individuals living on the mainland are free to do so subject to the local electoral laws. The executive power resides in a Governor, elected directly by the people every 4 years. Eight heads of departments form the Governor's advisory council, also designated as his Council of Secretaries. The legislative functions are vested in a Senate, composed of 27 members (2 from each of the 8 senatorial districts and 11 senators at large), and the House of Representatives, composed of 51 members (1 from each of the 40 representative districts and 11 elected at large). To give proportional representation to the minority parties, 5 additional senators and 13 representatives at large are serving. Puerto Rico sends to Congress a Resident Commissioner to the US, elected by the people for a term of 4 years. But he has no vote in Congress, and under the doctrine of 'no taxation without representation' Puerto Rico is not subject to US taxes, including income tax. Males, however, are subject to conscription.

On 27 Nov. 1953 President Eisenhower sent a message to the General Assembly of the UN stating 'if at any time the Legislative Assembly of Puerto Rico adopts a resolution in favour of more complete or even absolute independence' he 'will immediately thereafter recommend to Congress that such independence be granted'.

For an account of the constitutional developments prior to 1952, see THE STATESMAN'S YEAR-BOOK, 1952, p. 742. The new constitution was drafted by a Puerto Rican Constituent Assembly and approved by the electorate at a referendum on 3 March 1952. It was then submitted to Congress, which struck out Section 20 of Article 11 covering the 'right to work' and the 'right to an adequate standard of living'; the remainder was passed and proclaimed by the Governor on 25 July 1952.

At the election on 6 Nov. 1968 the New Progressive Party, headed by Luis A. Ferré, polled 389,706 votes (44·6% of the total); the Independence Party (full independence by constitutional means), 24,746; Republican Statehood party (advocates of US statehood and affiliated with the Republican Party on the mainland), 4,032; Popular Democratic Party, 366,884 (42%); El Partido del Pueblo, 87,770.

Governor: Luis A. Ferré (New Progressive), 1969–73 ($20,000).

AREA AND POPULATION. The island has a land area of 3,435 sq. miles (8,891 sq. km) and a population, according to the census of 1970 (preliminary), of 2,689,932, an increase of 340,388 or 14·5% over 1960; density (1960) was 687 per sq. mile. Males (1960 census) numbered 1,126,764; females, 1,186,780. 79·7% of the population (1,762,411) were white in 1950. Of the population in 1960 about 400,000 were bilingual, Spanish being the mother tongue and (with English) one of the two official languages. Rural population (1960), 1,310,243 (55·8%).

Vital statistics (1969): Births, 70,679 (25·5 per 1,000 population); deaths, 17,016 (6·2%); deaths under 1 year, 1,868 (26·4 per 1,000 live births).

Chief towns (1970 census) are: San Juan, 444,952; Bayamon, 146,363; Ponce, 125,926; Carolina, 94,635; Mayagüez, 69,485; Caguas, 62,807.

The Puerto Rican island of Vieques, 10 miles to the east, has an area of 51·7 sq. miles and 7,210 inhabitants. The island of Culebra, with 573 inhabitants, between Puerto Rico and St Thomas, has a good harbour.

EDUCATION. Education was made compulsory in 1899, but in 1964–65, 3·3% of the children still had no access to schooling. The percentage of illiteracy in 1960 was 12·4% of those 10 years of age or older. Total enrolment in public schools, 1968–69, was 720,313, enrolment of secondary standard being (1967–68) 221,687. Accredited private schools had, in 1968–69, 81,049 pupils. All instruction below senior high school standard is given in Spanish only.

The University of Puerto Rico, in Río Piedras, 7 miles from San Juan, had 34,411 students in 1968–69. The Catholic University of Puerto Rico had 5,012 students in 1965–66. Higher education is also available in the Inter-American University of Puerto Rico (7,578 students in 1965–66), the Sacred Heart College (445) and the Puerto Rico Junior College (1,717).

CINEMAS (1965). Cinemas numbered 160, with annual attendance of 9m.

NEWSPAPERS (1969). There were 4 newspapers, of which 2 had a circulation of 164,300.

JUSTICE. The Commonwealth judiciary system is headed by a Supreme Court of 9 members, appointed by the Governor, and consists of a Superior Tribunal with 9 sections and 40 superior judges, a District Tribunal with 37 sections and 72 district judges, and 55 justices of the peace, all appointed by the Governor. The police force (1968) consisted of 6,224 men and women.

FINANCE. Receipts and disbursements (US$) in central government fund (apart from special funds) for the year ending 30 June 1969 were:

Balance, 1 July 1968	167,006,053	Disbursements, 1968–69	924,456,790
Receipts, 1968–69	961,013,994	Transfers to other funds	262
Transfers from other funds	342,465	Balance, 1 July 1969	203,905,460
To	1,128,362,512	Total	1,128,362,512

Receipts and disbursements of special funds (US$):

Balance, 1 July 1968	353,176,512	Disbursements, 1968–69	429,264,322
Receipts, 1968–69	451,778,677	Transfers to other funds	342,465
Transfers from other funds	263	Balance, 1 July 1969	375,384,666
Total	804,955,452	Total	804,955,452

Assessed value of property, 30 June 1968, was $3,209m., and bonded indebtedness, $404m.

The US administers and finances the postal service and maintains air and naval bases. US payments in Puerto Rico, including direct expenditures (mainly military), grants-in-aid and other payments to individuals and to business totalled: 1961–62, $212·2m.; 1962–63, $231·4m.; 1963–64, $257·6m.; 1964–65, $267·8m.; 1965–66, $329m.; 1966–67, $340·7m.; 1967–68, $375·6m.

AGRICULTURE. In 1961 there were 63 'proportional profit' farms of from 277 to 1,662 acres (mostly sugar-cane). The land had been bought from the big corporations by the Land Authority.

Production of raw sugar, 96 degree basis, for the 1969 crop year, was 482,894 short tons.

MINING. Production (1969): Cement, 8·98m. bbls (of 376 lb.), value, $27·8m.; sand and gravel, 16·79m. short tons, value $25·2m.; stone, 7,415,000 short tons, value $13·64m. Total value of mineral production in 1969 was $66·61m.

COMMERCE. In 1968–69 imports amounted to $2,262,663,836, of which $1,764,977,168 came from US; exports were valued at $1,606,469,679, of which $1,395,822,308 went to US.

In 1967–68 the US took: Sugar, 799,506,394 lb. ($68,482,254); tobacco leaf, 14,557,049 lb. ($34,149,910); rum, 4,653,427 proof gallons ($21,817,404.

Puerto Rico is not permitted to levy taxes on imports.

Trade between Puerto Rico and UK (British Board of Trade returns, in £1,000 sterling):

	1965	1966	1967	1968	1969	1970
Imports to UK	878	2,683	3,241	4,240	3,343	3,004
Exports from UK	4,736	3,799	3,355	6,111	6,749 }	8,139
Re-exports from UK	42	39	48	76	87 }	

BANKING. Fifteen banks on 30 June 1968 had total deposits of $1,830m. (including those of the Commonwealth, $113m.), and debits of $1,715m. Bank loans were $1,372m.

COMMUNICATIONS. In fiscal year 1968–69, 5,682 American and foreign vessels of 27,346,625 gross tons entered and cleared Puerto Rico.

The Department of Public Works had under maintenance in June 1968, 3,619 miles of paved road. Motor vehicles registered 30 June 1968, 470,000. On 25 Sept. 1967 there were 63 broadcasting stations and 11 television companies. There were (1969) 281,074 telephones.

There is a British consul at San Juan.

BOOKS OF REFERENCE

STATISTICAL INFORMATION. The Bureau of Economics and Statistics of the Puerto Rico Planning Board publishes: (a) a semi-annual and annual *Economic Report to the Governor*; (b) 3 reports devoted to national income and balance of payments; (c) *Statistical Yearbook* (since 1940–41); (d) *External Trade Statistics* (annual report); (e) *Current Business Statistics* (quarterly); (f) *Historical Series* (since 1958). In addition, there are annual reports by various Departments.

Annual Reports. Governor of Puerto Rico. Washington

Anderson, R. W., *Party politics in Puerto Rico*. Stanford Univ. Press, 1965

Bird, A., *Bibliografía Puertorriqueña, 1930–45*. Social Science Research Centre, Univ. of Puerto Rico. 2 vols. 1946–47

Hanson, E. P., *Transformation: the story of modern Puerto Rico*. New York, 1955

Hill, R. (cd.), *Family and Population control: a Puerto Rican experiment*. Univ. of N. Carolina Press, 1959

Jones, C. F., and Pico, R. (ed.), *Symposium on the Geography of Puerto Rico*. Univ. of P.R. Press, 1955

Tumin, M. M., and Feldman, A. S., *Social Class and Social Change in Puerto Rico*. Princeton Univ. Press, 1961

COMMONWEALTH LIBRARY. Univ. of Puerto Rico Library, Rio Piedras. *Librarian:* José Lázaro.

VIRGIN ISLANDS OF THE UNITED STATES

GOVERNMENT. The Virgin Islands of the United States, formerly known as the Danish West Indies, were purchased by the United States from Denmark for $25m. in a treaty ratified by both nations and proclaimed 31 March 1917. Their value was wholly strategic, inasmuch as they commanded the Anegada Passage from the Atlantic Ocean to the Caribbean Sea and the approach to the Panama Canal. Although the inhabitants were made US citizens in 1927, the islands are, constitutionally, an 'unincorporated territory'.

The Organic Act of 22 July 1954 gives the US Department of the Interior full jurisdiction; some limited legislative powers are given to a single-chambered legislature, composed of 15 senators elected for 2 years (11 represent 3 legislative districts; 4 are elected by all voters).

The Governor is appointed by the President, with the consent of the Senate, for an indefinite term. In 1970 the Islanders will elect a Governor for the first time.

Governor: Melvin H. Evans ($25,890).
Government Secretary: David E. Maas ($22,526).
Comptroller: Howard L. Ross ($20,400).

For administration, there are 13 executive departments, 12 of which are under commissioners and the other, the Department of Law, under an Attorney-General.

The franchise is vested in residents who are citizens of the United States, 21 years of age or over. In 1968 there were 16,887 voters, of whom 13,692 participated in the local elections that year. They do not participate in the US presidential election and have no representative in Congress.

The capital is Charlotte Amalie, on St Thomas Island.

AREA AND POPULATION. The Virgin Islands group, lying about 40 miles due east of Puerto Rico, comprises the islands of St Thomas (32 sq. miles), St Croix (82 sq. miles), St John (19 sq. miles) and about 50 small islets or cays, mostly uninhabited. The total area of the 3 principal islands is 133 sq. miles (344·5 sq. km), of which the US Government owns 9,599 acres (10%).

The Virgin Islands are in the midst of a population explosion. The population, according to the census (preliminary) of 1 April 1970, was 63,200, an increase of 31,101 or 96·9% since 1960; density was 243 per sq. mile. Population had slowly declined since 1835, when it stood at 43,000, but began to recover in the 1940s. Of the 1960 population, males numbered 15,930 and females, 16,169. Whites numbered 5,373; Negroes, 20,634; mixed and other races, 6,092. Estimated population as at 31 Dec. 1968, was 62,802. Births, 1966, were 1,956 (38·5 per

1,000 population); deaths, 388 (7·6); infant deaths, 60 (30·7 per 1,000 live births); marriages, 641 (12·6 per 1,000 population); divorces, 293 (5·8).

The 1960 population of St Thomas was 16,201; St Croix, 14,973; St John, 925. There is one city, Charlotte Amalie, on St Thomas, with a population (1960) of 12,740, and 2 towns, both on Croix, Christiansted with 5,088 (in 1960) and Frederiksted with 1,925 (in 1950).

RELIGION. There are churches of the Protestant, Roman Catholic and Jewish faiths in St Thomas and St Croix.

EDUCATION. Education is compulsory between the ages of 5½ and 16 years, inclusive. In 1969 there were 22 public schools (ranging from kindergarten to high schools); enrolment (1966–67) was 10,594; the school budget was $7,287,929. In 1969 the College of the Virgin Islands had 430 full-time and over 1,000 part-time students.

FINANCE. Under the 1954 Organic Act finances are provided partly from local revenues—customs, federal income tax, real and personal property tax, trade tax, excise tax, pilotage fees, etc.—and partly from Federal Matching Funds, being the excise taxes collected by the federal government on such Virgin Islands products transported to the mainland as are liable. The US Government provides a separate fund to be expended for emergency purposes and essential public works. Total revenue for fiscal year ending 30 June 1969 including federal income taxes, Matching Funds and the federal grant-in-aid, $70,492,569, and expenditure totalled $59,576,266.

AGRICULTURE. The population census of 1960 showed 315 farms in St Croix, 128 in St Thomas and 58 in St John, a total of 501. The average farm is of 87·9 acres; total value of land and buildings, $64,289,529. With the phasing out of the sugar-cane industry in St Croix, and the accelerated construction activities carried on in all three islands, the number of farms has decreased, but the value of land and buildings has increased to $193m. Sugar has been terminated as a commercial crop and over 4,000 acres of prime land will be utilized for food crops.

INDUSTRY AND TOURISM. St Thomas, once an important commercial shipping centre, now is an important port of call for pleasure cruises. In 1968–69 there were 1,107,000 tourists spending approximately $100m. It is also the key to a steadily increasing import–export trade, serving the freeport tourist shopping and local manufacturing industries. Four desalting plants, which also generate electric power, can produce 4·78m. gallons of fresh water per day.

The Virgin Islands National Park covers more than half the island of St John. Tourism is the important business in St John. A few small manufacturing concerns have been established; a new clinic and a public housing project are planned.

The Virgin Islands offer liberal tax exemptions to persons, firms or companies prepared to invest $15,000 in new industries or in the promotion of tourism.

COMMERCE. Exports, 1968, totalled $153,782,838 and imports $260,160,366.

Trade between the US Virgin Islands and UK (British Board of Trade returns, in £1,000 sterling):

	1965	1966	1967	1968	1969	1970
Imports to UK	4	1	5,317	5,134	3,294	787
Exports from UK	1,068	964	1,014	1,282	1,686 }	2,050
Re-exports from UK	37	30	36	100	76 }	

COMMUNICATIONS. There is a daily air-mail and passenger service between St Thomas and St Croix, and a daily boat service—mail and passengers—between St Thomas and St John.

All three Virgin Islands have a dial telephone system. Marine cables have been installed, to make possible direct dialling to Puerto Rico and the mainland. Worldwide radio telegraph service is also available.

The islands are served by 3 radio stations, 2 television stations and 6 newspapers, 3 of them dailies.

The Virgin Islands have approximately 316 miles of roads, and 19,651 motor vehicles were registered in 1969.

MONEY AND BANKING. United States currency became legal tender on 1 July 1934. Banks are the Virgin Islands National Bank; the Chase Manhattan Bank; the Bank of Nova Scotia; the St Croix Savings Bank; the First Federal Savings and Loan Association of Puerto Rico; Barclays Bank DCO; Bank of America; First National City Bank and Virgin Islands Title and Trust Co. Assets (1969) totalled $723,779,152.

There is a British Vice-Consul at St Thomas.

BOOKS OF REFERENCE

Evans, L. H., *The Virgin Islands: From Naval Base to New Deal*. Ann Arbor, Mich., 1945
Jarvis, J. A., *The Virgin Islands and Their People*. Philadelphia, 1944
McGuire, J. W., *Geographic Dictionary of the Virgin Islands of the United States*. US Coast and Geodetic Survey. Special Publication No. 103. Washington, 1925
Reid, C. F., *Bibliography of the Virgin Islands of the United States*. New York, 1941

GUAM

Guam is the largest and most southern island of the Marianas Archipelago, in 13° 26′ N. lat., 144° 43′ E. long. Magellan is said to have discovered the island in 1521; it was ceded by Spain to the US by the Treaty of Paris (10 Dec. 1898). The island was captured by the Japanese on 10 Dec. 1941, and retaken by American forces 21 July–10 Aug. 1944. Guam is of great strategic importance; substantial naval and air force personnel occupy about one-third of the usable land. Its constitutional status is that of an 'unincorporated territory' of the US.

GOVERNMENT. In 1949 the President transferred the administration of the island from the Navy Department (who held it from 1899) to the Interior Department. The transfer was completed by 1 Aug. 1950, on the passage of the Organic Act, which conferred full citizenship on the Guamanians, who had previously been 'nationals' of the US.

Governor: Carlos Garcia Camacho (R.) ($35,495), appointed 1 July 1969.

The Governor and his staff constitute the executive arm of the government. The Legislature is unicameral. The latter's powers are similar to those of an American state legislature. Following the general election of Nov. 1968, the Democratic Party held all 21 seats. Guam will elect its own Governor in Nov. 1970. All adults 18 years of age or over, including women, are enfranchised.

AREA AND POPULATION. The length is 30 miles, the breadth from 4 to 8½ miles, and the area about 209 sq. miles (450 sq. km). Agaña, the seat of government is about 8 miles from the anchorage in Apia Harbour. The census (preliminary) on 1 April 1970 showed a population of 86,926, an increase of 19,882 or 29·7% since 1960; those of Guamanian ancestry numbered about 30,000; density was 321 per sq. mile. On 1 Jan. 1969 there were 61,283 residents, while transient residents connected with the military were estimated at 38,500. The Malay strain is predominant. The native language is Chamorro; English is the official language and is taught in all schools.

On 15 Sept. 1962 a Presidential Executive Order of 1941 was revoked, which had required all persons entering Guam to undergo security investigation by the Navy. Entry of US citizens is now unrestricted; foreign nationals are subject to normal regulations. The port is now open to foreign vessels.

RELIGION. About 95% of the Guamanians are Roman Catholics; others are Baptists, Episcopalians, Bahais, Lutherans, Mormons, Presbyterians, Jehovah's Witnesses and members of the Church of Christ and Seventh Day Adventists.

EDUCATION. Elementary education is compulsory. There were, Sept. 1969, 21 elementary schools, 1 school for handicapped children, 5 junior high schools, 2 senior high schools and 1 vocational-technical school for high school students and adults. A total of 1,000 classroom teachers and a total enrolment of 20,500 students. Budget of the school system, 1969–70, was $15,132,000. The Catholic school system also operates 3 senior high schools, 4 junior high and 5 elementary schools with 6,000 students. The Seventh Day Adventist Guam Mission Academy operates a school from grades 1 through 12, serving over 100 students. St John's Episcopal Preparatory School furnished education for 245 students between kindergarten and the 9th grade. The University of Guam (an accredited institution) had approximately 2,000 students, 1968–69.

NEWSPAPERS. There is 1 daily newspaper and 4 weekly publications (all of which are of military or religious interest only).

JUSTICE. The Organic Act established a District Court with jurisdiction in matters arising under both federal and territorial law; the judge is appointed by the President subject to Senate approval. Misdemeanours are under the jurisdiction of the 'Island court' and the police court. The Spanish law was superseded in 1933 by 5 civil codes based upon California law.

AGRICULTURE. The major products of the island are maize, sweet potatoes, taro, cassava, bananas, and citrus and truck crops, including breadfruit, coconuts and sugar-cane. In 1966–67, 864 full-time and part-time farmers each held 500 acres under cultivation. Livestock included 655 carabao, 6,500 cattle, 1,000 goats, 7,000 hogs, 88 horses and 60,325 laying-hens. Commercial production of fruit and vegetables amounted to 2·23m. lb. ($404,919) in 1968–69; fish caught, 343,000 lb. ($171,750); egg production, 1·3m. dozen.

TRADE. Guam is the only American territory which is completely 'free trade'; excise duties are levied only upon imports of tobacco, liquid fuel and liquor. In the year ending 30 June 1969 imports were valued at $57,779,503. Exports were valued at $1,154,475.

TOURISM. Tourism is developing. From 1,900 visitors in 1964 to approximately 30,000 in 1969. Tourists spent $210,000 in 1964, $3m. in 1968.

COMMUNICATIONS. Three commercial airlines (PANAM, TWA and Continental Air Micronesia) handle air traffic between Guam, US, Japan, Okinawa, Trust Territory of the Pacific Islands and the Philippines.

There are 183 miles of paved and 47 miles of improved roads.

Overseas telephone and radio dispatch facilities are available. On 1 Jan. 1967 there were 18,456 telephones.

There is a commercial radio station and a television station on the island.

BOOKS OF REFERENCE

Report (Annual) of the Governor of Guam to the US Department of Interior
Beardsley, C., Guam past and present. Rutland, Vt, 1964
Carano, P., and Sanchez, P. C., Complete history of Guam. Rutland, Vt, 1964
Thompson, Laura, Guam and its People. 3rd ed. New York, 1947

AMERICAN SAMOA

The Samoan Islands were first visited by Europeans in the 18th century; the first recorded visit was in 1722. On 14 July 1889 a treaty between the USA, Germany and Great Britain proclaimed the Samoan islands neutral territory, under a 4-power government consisting of the 3 treaty powers and the local native government. By the Tripartite Treaty of 7 Nov. 1899, ratified 19 Feb. 1900, Great Britain and Germany renounced in favour of the US all rights over the islands of the Samoan group east of 171° long. west of Greenwich, the islands to the west of that meridian being assigned to Germany (now the Independent State of Western Samoa, see p. 505). The islands of Tutuila and Aunu'u were ceded to the US by their High Chiefs on 17 April 1900, and the islands of the Manu'a group on 16 July 1904. Congress accepted the islands under a Joint Resolution approved 20 Feb. 1929. Swain's Island, 210 miles north-north-west of the Samoan Islands, was annexed in 1925 and is administered as an integral part of American Samoa.

GOVERNMENT. American Samoa is constitutionally an unorganized un-incorporated territory of the US administered under the Department of the Interior. Its indigenous inhabitants are US nationals and are classified locally as citizens of American Samoa with certain privileges under local laws not granted to non-indigenous persons. Polynesian customs (not inconsistent with US laws) are respected.

The harbour at Pago Pago, which nearly bisects the island of Tutuila, is the only good harbour for large vessels in Samoa. Utulei is the seat of the Government.

The islands are organized in 14 counties grouped in 3 districts; these counties and districts correspond to the traditional political units. On 25 Feb. 1948 a bicameral legislature was established, at the request of the Samoans, to have advisory legislative functions. With the adoption of the Revised Constitution of American Samoa, effective 1 July 1967, the legislature was vested with limited law-making authority. The lower house, or House of Representatives, is composed of 20 members elected by universal adult suffrage. The upper house, or Senate, is composed of 18 members elected, in the traditional Samoan manner, in meetings of the chiefs.

Governor: John M. Haydon.

AREA AND POPULATION. The total area of American Samoa is 76·1 sq. miles (197 sq. km); population, 1970, 27,769, nearly all Polynesians or part-Polynesians. The island of Tutuila, 80 miles from Apia, has an area of 53 sq. miles, with a population (1970) of 25,557 (including the island of Aunu'u). Ta'u has an area of 15 sq. miles, and the other islands (Ofu and Olosega) of the Manu'a group have an area of about 3·5 sq. miles with a population of 2,138 in 1970. Swain's Island, circular in shape, has an area of 0·9 sq. mile and a population, 1970, of 74. Rose Island (uninhabited) is 0·4 sq. mile in area.

EDUCATION. Education is compulsory between the ages of 6 and 18. The Government (1970–71) maintains 25 consolidated elementary schools, 4 senior high schools with technical departments and 1 community college. Total enrolment (1970), 8,515. Six private schools had 1,790 students. The public schools employed 422 teachers; the private schools, 51. The new consolidated elementary schools were completed in July 1967 and learning is based on tele-vision methods. Samoa operates one of the most extensive educational television systems in the world.

HEALTH. The Medical Services Department provides the only medical and dental care in American Samoa. It operates a general hospital (154 beds), 3 dis-pensaries on Tutuila and 2 dispensaries in the Manu'a group. A $3·5m. tropical medical centre was completed and placed in service in 1968.

JUSTICE. Judicial power is vested in a High Court. Fifty-nine district courts, traffic courts and small claims court are heard without record and appeals therefrom are tried, *de novo*, in the trial division of the High Court. The trial division also has original jurisdiction of all criminal and civil cases. The probate division has jusridiction of estates, guardianships, trusts and other matters. The land and title division decides cases relating to disputes involving communal land and Matai title court rules on questions and controversy over family titles. The appellate division hears appeals from trial, land and title and probate divisions as well as having original jurisdiction in selected matters. The appellate court is the court of last resort. Two stateside judges sit with 5 Samoan judges permanently. In addition there are 9 temporary judges or assessors who sit occasionally on cases involving Samoan customs.

FINANCE. The chief sources of revenue are annual federal grants from the US Congress, and local revenues from individual and corporate income taxes, import duties, sale of utilities, rents and leases and liquor sales. During the fiscal year ended 30 June 1970 the government operated under a direct federal appropriation of $439,000 and a federal grant-in-aid of $7,908,000. Receipts from local sources were in excess of $5m.

In 1969-70 American Samoa exported goods valued at $36,735,000 and imported goods valued at $15,713,000. Chief exports are canned tuna, copra, pandanus mats and handicrafts. Mats woven from laufala leaves (for floor and wall coverings) are being exported in increasing quantities.

PLANNING. In 1970 American Samoa's first formal economic planning and development office was established. Its aim is to encourage local development in line with long-range plans in order to increase living standards and hasten stronger self-government for the territory.

AGRICULTURE. There are virtually no public lands in American Samoa. Nearly all the land is owned by Samoans and, with a few exceptions, cannot be sold except to persons having at least one-half Samoan blood. Of the 48,640 acres of land area, 11,000 acres are suitable for tropical crops, 1,000 acres for most temperate vegetables, 8,000 acres only to such crops as coconut and cacao with good conservation practice, 5,000 acres to controlled forestation and about 22,500 to indigenous and introduced forest with strict conservation measures; 1,000 acres are roads, building sites and villages. Principal crops are copra, taro, breadfruit, yams, bananas, coconuts, arrowroot, oranges and papayas. Principal livestock are poultry, swine and cattle.

COMMUNICATIONS. There are about 38 miles of paved roads and 5 miles of secondary roads. There are 28 miles of secondary unpaved roads maintained mainly on Tutuila. A commercial radiogram service is available to all parts of the world through 3 principal trunks, Hawaii, Fiji and Western Samoa. Commercial phone services are operated for 15 hours on weekdays and 8 on Saturdays and Sundays to US, Hawaii, Canada, Alaska, Tokyo and other points. Service to Western Samoa is available for 8 hours daily and to Tonga for limited hours. Number of telephones (Nov. 1970), 3,500.

Scheduled air services now provide 7 flights a week from the continental US (*via* Honolulu and Tahiti), and a weekly service from New Zealand (*via* Fiji); Polynesian Airlines operate twice-daily services between American Samoa and Western Samoa. By sea, there is a twice-monthly service from New Zealand; ships provide regular service between US, South Pacific ports and Japan.

BANKING. A branch of the Bank of Hawaii offers all commercial banking services. The Development Bank of American Samoa is concerned primarily with guaranteeing loans to financial institutions which will stimulate development of the local economy.

Report of the Governor to the Secretary of the Interior. Annual

TRUST TERRITORY OF THE PACIFIC ISLANDS

Under the Treaty of Versailles (1919) Japan was appointed mandatory to the former German possessions north of the Equator. In 1946 the US agreed to administer the former Japanese-mandated islands of the Caroline, Marshall and Mariana groups (except Guam) as a Trusteeship for the United Nations; the trusteeship agreement was approved by the Security Council 27 April 1947 and came into effect on 18 July 1947. In 1951 all the islands passed under the care of the US Department of the Interior, but in 1953 responsibility for civil administration of the Northern Marianas (except Rota) was transferred back to the Department of the Navy. On 7 May 1962 Saipan and the islands of the Northern Marianas were transferred back to the Secretary of the Interior, so that the whole area is now under one administration.

The Trust Territory extends from 1° to 20° N. lat. and from 130° to 172° E. long. The area is generally known as Micronesia, or 'land of the small islands'; 2,141 atolls and islands (of which 96 are inhabited) cover less than 700 sq. miles (1,813 sq. km) in some 3m. sq. miles (8m. sq. km) of ocean.

The population of the 6 administrative districts as of 30 June 1969 was: Truk, 27,453; Ponape, 20,093; Marshall Islands, 19,328; Palau, 12,291; Mariana Islands, 11,827; Yap, 7,017; total, 98,009. The administrative centre is Saipan, Mariana Islands. Nine different languages are spoken, each with variations; English is used in the schools and is the official language.

Law and order is maintained by the armed, uniformed and trained 'Insular Constabulary' in each district; the local district community court judges, sheriffs and deputy sheriffs are all Micronesians. Local customs are respected in law and practice. Forty-five of the 102 municipalities have been chartered. Elected councils function in all districts. Membership in some of these includes hereditary leaders as well as elected representatives, although the trend is towards all-elective bodies.

The bicameral Congress of Micronesia, a Senate and House of Representatives, was established in 1964. Regular sessions are held annually in July. Secretarial Order 2882, as amended, has made provision for an organizational session in January of odd-numbered years.

High Commissioner: Edward E. Johnston.

Living standards are being improved through the introduction of higher standards of subsistence and exportable agricultural and marine products.

There are approximately 493 Peace Corps Volunteers in the Territory working in education, public health and community development.

In 1969 there were 209 public and private elementary schools (28,078 pupils), 22 public and private high schools (4,630 pupils), 445 students were attending institutions of higher education abroad.

The public health system, which includes 6 district and 3 large field hospitals and 139 dispensaries, is carried on by a staff consisting chiefly of trained Micronesian medical and dental officers and assistants under senior US medical officers. There is a school of nursing in the Mariana Islands.

Trade (1969). Major imports were food, $5·7m.; beverages, $870,000; and building materials, $1·6m. Total imports were $13·9m., of which $6·7m. were from US and $4·8m. from Japan. Major exports were copra, $2·2m.; scrap metal, $900,000. Total exports were $2·8m., of which $2·3 to Japan.

Report on the Administration of the Trust Territory of the Pacific Islands by the United States to the United Nations. Annual
Basic Information. High Commissioner's Office, Saipan, Mariana Islands
Nathan Associates. *Economic Development Plan for Micronesia .* Washington, D.C., 1968

PACIFIC ISLANDS UNDER
U.S. CONTROL

Administration. Under Article 3 of the Japanese peace treaty (effective 28 April 1952) the United States has 'the right to exercise any and all powers of administration, legislation and jurisdiction' over the Ryukyu Islands (south of 29° N. lat.) including the Daito Islands, the Bonin Islands and Marcus Island, Rosario Island, the Volcano Islands and the island of Parece Vela. The treaty provides that Japan will concur in any proposal of the USA to the United Nations to place these territories under its trusteeship system, with the US as the sole administering authority. No such proposal has been made by the US, which has in the meantime recognized that residual sovereignty of the islands rests with Japan.

In 1953 the Amami–Oshima group (the northernmost group of the Ryukyus) was returned to Japan. The Bonin Islands, Marcus Island, Rosario Island, the Volcano Islands and the island of Parece Vela were returned to Japan in 1968.

The **Ryukyu Islands** extend some 500 miles south-west of Japan between Kyushu and Formosa. The islands total 848 sq. miles with a population (Oct. 1965 census) of 934,176. The repatriation of about 140,000 persons from Japan and elsewhere raised the population from 590,027 in 1944 to 698,827 in 1950.

Responsibility for administration has, by Executive Order, been assigned to the Secretary of Defense and delegated to the Department of the Army. Powers are exercised by a civil administration, headed by a high commissioner who is an active-duty member of the US armed forces; his senior assistant (the Civil Administrator) is a civilian. The local government includes a 32-member unicameral legislature, elected for a 3-year term; a chief executive; and a system of both lower and appellate courts. The first public election of a chief executive, formerly elected by the legislature was held on 10 Nov. 1968. Acts of the legislature are subject to the veto of either the chief executive or high commissioner; the latter rarely exercises this function. The strength of the parties in the legislature as of Nov. 1968 was: Okinawa Liberal Democratic Party, 17; Okinawa Socialist Masses Party, 8; Okinawa Peoples Party, 3; Independent, 2; Okinawa Socialist Party, 2.

The largest and most important island is Okinawa (area, 454 sq. miles); population (1965) 758,777. Naha City, the capital and headquarters of local government, has a population of 257,177; other large towns are Koza (55,923), Gushikawa (35,453), Ginowan (34,573), Itoman (34,065) and Nago (19,601).

High Commissioner: Lieut.-Gen. James B. Lampert.
Civil Administrator: Robert A. Fearey.
Chief Executive: Chobyo Yara.

In April 1968 the Ryukyu Islands had 334 primary schools, including 93 kindergartens (155,128 pupils), 155 junior high schools (77,756), 37 senior high schools (53,412), 4 vocational schools (1,067), 4 special schools (819), 3 universities (6,309) and 5 junior colleges (1,937).

The economy of the islands is affected favourably by the presence of the US forces. About 9% of the local labour force is employed by the US forces, their contractors and American personnel. In 1967 only 32% of the population were engaged in agriculture, compared with about 74% before the Second World War. Chief crops are sugar-cane, pineapples, fresh vegetables, rice, sweet potatoes and tobacco. Fishing is increasing in importance, the catch for 1967–68 was 33,447 metric tons. The major industry is the processing of sugar-cane. Exports in fiscal year 1968 totalled $87·7m.; imports totalled $373·7m. There are 46,923 telephone subscribers. US currency is the sole legal tender.

US Civil Administration of the Ryukyu Islands. *Civil Affairs Activities in the Ryukyu Islands.*
  Semi-annual 1955–62, annual since 1963
The Ryukyu Islands: A Reference List of Books and Articles. Hoover Institution, Stanford, Calif.,
  1954
Kerr, G. H., *Okinawa, The History of An Island People.* Rutland, Vt., and Tokyo, 1958

The **Daito Islands** (area 17·03 sq. miles; population (Oct. 1965), 3,896) form the
easternmost group of the Ryukyus, about 200 miles east of Okinawa.

The Daito Islands. Rutland, Vt., and Tokyo, 1958

PART IV

PART IV

AFGHÁNISTÁN

Doulat i Pádsháhí ye Afghánistán

REIGNING KING. Mohammed Záhir Sháh, born at Kábul in 1914; married on 7 Nov. 1931 to his cousin, Homaira, daughter of Sirdar Ahmed Sháh Khan; succeeded his father, Mohammed Nádir Sháh, who was assassinated on 8 Nov. 1933. Surviving offspring, 5 sons and 2 daughters. The heir apparent is Prince Ahmad Sháh (born 1934).

AREA AND POPULATION. Afghánistán is situated between parallels 29° and 38° 35′ N. lat., and 60° 50′ and 71° 50′ E. long., with a long narrow strip extending to 75° E. long. (Wákhán). For the boundaries, see THE STATESMAN'S YEAR-BOOK, 1925, pp. 654–55. A new boundary agreement with the Soviet Union was signed in Moscow in June 1946; a joint commission completed the demarcation in Sept. 1948. A border treaty with China was signed in 1963; the frontier was demarcated in 1964.

The area is 250,000 sq. miles (657,500 sq. km). Population, according to the latest Afghan estimate, is 13·6m., of which some 2·5m. are nomadic tribes. This estimate would mean a population density equal to that of USA and twice as large as that of Iran. More cautious estimates arrive at about 10m.

A census conducted in Kábul in 1965 showed a population of 435,000. Estimates of population of other municipalities are: Kandahár, 115,000; Herát, 62,000; Gardez, 46,000; Jalálábád, 44,000; Mazár-i-Sharif, 40,000.

GOVERNMENT. Under a new constitution (ratified by the *Loe Jirga* (Grand National Assembly) in Sept. 1964), which took effect in Oct. 1965, Afghánistán became a parliamentary democracy in which legislative authority rests with a National Assembly of 2 houses. The legislative, executive and judicial branches of government are separate. Certain powers, such as the appointment of the Prime Minister and judges of the Supreme Court, rest with the King, who has become a constitutional monarch. This Constitution replaced that which had been in force since 1933.

Prime Minister and Minister of Foreign Affairs: Nur Ahmad Etemadi.
First Deputy Prime Minister: Abdullah Yaftali. *Second Deputy Prime Minister and Minister of Education:* Abdul Qayum. *National Defence:* Khan Muhammad. *Interior:* Muhammad Bashir Ludin. *Justice:* Abdul Satar Sirat. *Planning:* Abdul Wahid Sarabi. *Finance:* Muhammad Aman. *Commerce:* Muhammad Akbar Omar. *Public Works:* Muhammad Yakub Lali. *Information and Culture:* (Vacant). *Communications:* Muhammad Azim Gran. *Public Health:* Ibrahim Majid Seraj. *Mines and Industries:* Amanullah Mansouri. *Agriculture and Irrigation:* Abdul Hakim. *Without Portfolio:* Mrs Shafiqa Ziyaie, Ghulam Ali Ayeen.

There are 29 provinces, each under a governor. These are (with their centres in brackets): Kábul (Kábul); Kapisa (Tagao); Parwan (Charikar); Wardak (Maidan); Logar (Baraki Rajan); Nangarhar (Jalálábád); Paktya (Gardez); Kattawaz and Urgun (Urgun), temporarily linked with Paktya; Ghazni (Ghazni); Zabul (Kalat); Kandahár (Kandahár); Uruzgan (Uruzgan); Bamian (Bamian); Helmand (Lashkargah); Faráh (Faráh); Nimrooz (Zaranj); Ghor (Chakcharan); Herát (Herát); Badghis (Qala-i-Nau); Faryab (Maimana); Jouzjan (Shiberghan); Balkh (Mazar-i-Sharif); Samangan (Haibak); Kunduz (Kunduz); Takhar (Taleqan); Badakhshán (Faizabad); Baghlan and Pul-i-Khumri (Baghlan); Laghman (Metarlam); Kunar (Chaghasarai).

National flag: Black, red, green (vertical); with a white device in the centre.

The official languages are Pushtu, called the national language in the Constitution, and Dari (Persian).

RELIGION. The predominant religion is Islam, mostly of the Sunni sect, though there is a minority of about 1m. Shiah Moslems.

EDUCATION. The number of elementary schools is rapidly increasing, but secondary schools exist only in Kábul and provincial capitals. Both elementary and secondary education are free. There are several teacher-training institutions in Kábul and a few elsewhere; UNESCO is supporting a 30-year expansion programme. Technical, art, commercial and medical schools exist for higher education. The Kábul University was founded in 1932 and has 9 faculties (medicine, science, agriculture, engineering, law and political science, letters, economics, theology, pharmacology). The University of Nangarhar in Jalálábád, founded in 1963, has at present only a faculty of medicine. A Polytechnic in Kábul was completed in 1968.

In 1963 the Prime Minister stated that illiteracy was over 90%.

CINEMAS. There are 16 cinemas in the country.

JUSTICE. Until 1965 Afghánistán was ruled on the basis of Shariat or Islamic law. The new Constitution, however, provided for the creation of a legal code and for a new structure of courts. This consists of a lower court in each *wuluswal* (sub-province), and a court of appeal in each province, with a Supreme Court in Kábul.

FINANCE. Currency. The monetary system is on the silver standard. The unit is the *afgháni*, weighing 10 grammes of silver 0·900 fine, which is subdivided into 100 *puls*. Following the granting of a stand-by credit of US$6·7m. by the International Monetary Fund, the official rate of exchange was brought in line with the unofficial bazaar-rate. Rates of exchange now fluctuate round Afs. 180 = £1; Afs. 45 = US$1.

Budget. The revenue and expenditure for years ending 20 March (in 1m. afghánis):

	1966	1967	1968	1969	1970
Revenue	4,710	4,988	4,879	5,354	6,796
Expenditure	4,622	4,934	5,133	5,979	7,419

Development expenditure financed by foreign aid is excluded. Main sources of revenue in 1968–69 were: Taxation, Afs. 361m.; import duties, Afs. 1,567m.; monopoly and government enterprises, Afs. 1,078m.; natural gas exports, Afs. 428m. Main items of expenditure were: Defence, Afs. 1,300m.; education, Afs. 646m.; development, Afs. 1,950m.; foreign debt, Afs. 612m.

DEFENCE. Army. The Army is based on selective conscription with a regular cadre of officers and n.c.o.s. An agreed figure of conscripts is chosen in each province under local arrangements. A proportion of conscripts is drafted into the Labour Corps (employed mainly on public works). Call-up begins at the age of 20, and is for 2 years (1 year for conscript officers). Reserve liability is up to the age of 42. There is a reserve of officers.

The peace strength of the Army is about 75,000–80,000. It is organized in 3 corps (Kábul, Kandahár, Gardez) and 3 other divisions. There is also a general reserve (Kábul) and a Royal Bodyguard of brigade strength. Equipment is almost entirely Russian and includes T-54 tanks and surface-to-air missiles. Transport is mainly mechanized. A large proportion of the population, especially in the south and east, is naturally warlike and would represent a useful reserve in case of invasion.

The Army has the following training establishments: a military academy (formed 1932), a school for each principal arm, a technical school, a n.c.o.s school and a military high school (Kábul), which takes boys from the age of 10, and from which the regular element in the armed forces is mainly drawn. Selected officers receive training abroad, chiefly in USSR but also in Turkey; a few go to USA, UK and France.

Air Force. The Air Force, which is Russian-equipped, has about 250 aircraft and 6,000 officers and men. There are 2 squadrons of supersonic MiG-21 fighters (about 30 aircraft), 4 or 5 squadrons of MiG-17s (about 70 aircraft), 3 bomber squadrons each with about 15 twin-jet Il-28s, a transport wing with about 25 piston-engined Il-14s, 20 Mi-4 helicopters and 1 or 2 turboprop Il-18s, and Yak-11, Yak-18 and MiG-15UTI trainers. The main fighter station is Bagram, with facilities for the largest jet airliners and bombers. A Russian-built bomber station was completed at Shindand in 1963. There is a training station at Mazar-i-Sharif and an air academy at Sherpur with about 400 cadets. Large numbers of 'Guideline' surface-to-air missiles are operational in Afghánistán.

Gendarmerie. The gendarmerie, about 21,000 strong, is administered by the Ministry of Internal Affairs.

PLANNING. The first two 5-year plans ran 1956–61 and 1962–67; the third plan (1967–72) envisages expenditures of Afs. 33,000m. compared with actual expenditures of 25,000m. during the second plan.

AGRICULTURE. Although the greater part of Afghánistán is more or less mountainous and a good deal of the country is too dry and rocky for successful cultivation, there are many fertile plains and valleys, which, with the assistance of irrigation from small rivers or wells, yield very satisfactory crops of fruit, vegetables and cereals. It is estimated that there are 14m. hectares of cultivable land in the country, of which 7,844,000 hectares are being cultivated (5·34m. hectares of this being irrigated land). Afghánistán is virtually self-supporting in foodstuffs. The castor-oil plant, madder and the asafœtida plant abound. Fruit forms a staple food (with bread) of many people throughout the year, both in the fresh and preserved state, and in the latter condition is exported in great quantities. The fat-tailed sheep furnish the principal meat diet, and the grease of the tail is a substitute for butter. Wool (annual production, about 10,000 tons, of which about 7,000 tons are exported) and skins provide material for warm apparel and one of the more important articles of export. Persian lamb-skins (Karakuls) are one of the chief exports.

Cotton production, 1967–68, was estimated at 55,000 tons.

MINING. Mineral resources are scattered and little developed. Coal is mined at Karkar in Pul-i-Khumri, Ishpushta near Doshi, north of Kábul and Dara-i-Suf south of Mazar (total production, 1967–68, 151,000 tons). Natural gas is found in northern Afghánistán around Shiberghan and Sar-i-Pol; this is now being piped to the USSR, and 57,700m. cu. metres are to be supplied by 1985. Rich, but as yet unexploited, deposits of iron ore exist in the Hajigak hills about 100 miles west of Kábul; beryllium has been found in the Kunar valley and barite in Bamian province. Other deposits include gold; silver (now unexploited, in the Panjshir valley); lapis lazuli (in Badakhshán); asbestos; mica; sulphur (near Maimana); chrome (in the Logar valley and near Herát); and copper (in the north).

INDUSTRY. At Kábul there are factories for the manufacture of cotton and woollen textiles, leather, boots, marble-ware, furniture, glass, bicycles, prefabricated houses and plastics. A large machine shop has been constructed and equipped by the Russians, with a capability of manufacturing motor spares. There is a wool factory and a cotton ginning plant at Kandahár; a small cotton factory at Jabal-us-Seráj and a larger one at Pul-i-Khumri. A new cotton-seed oil extraction plant has been built in Lashkargah by a British firm which also has a contract for the construction of 4 factories in the north which will be operative in 1970. Germans have built and equipped a large modern cotton textile factory at Gulbahar, and another has been built and equipped by the Chinese at Bagram. A large cotton plant is under construction in the north at Balkh.

An ordnance factory manufactures arms and ammunition, boots and clothing, etc. for the Army. There is a beet sugar plant at Baghlan (equipped with British machinery) and a fruit-canning factory in Kandahár. Hydro-electric plants have been constructed at Sarobi, Nangarhar, Naghlu and Mahipar; more hydro and thermal plants are under construction.

Industrial and commercial enterprises are financed partly by the private sector and partly on public account. The largest private investor is the Afghan National Bank (*Bánk-i-Milli*) with interests ranging from textile factories to agricultural processing industries. Government agencies, such as the Ministry of Mines and Industries and the Ministry of Commerce, are actively engaged in the establishment of new industrial enterprises, many of which are assisted by long-term foreign loans. Industries include hydro-electric projects, cement, coalmining, cotton textiles, small vehicle assembly plants, fruit canning, carpet making, leather tanning, footwear manufacture, sugar manufacture, preparation of hides and skins, and building. Most of these are relatively small and, with the exception of hides and skins, carpets and fruits, do not meet domestic requirements. The Government encourages foreign investment in Afghan industries; a new domestic and foreign productive investment law was introduced in 1967, under which about 100 new industries have been established. The Ministry of Planning is responsible for general policy and for co-ordinating the establishment of new industries.

Aid in long-term credits and grants to Afghánistán from the Soviet Union has now reached a total of some US$500m., that from the USA US $370·8m. and that from West Germany US$86m. Long-term credit agreements were signed between the UK and Afghánistán in 1964 (for the modernization of the Baghlan sugar factory), in 1965 (for the construction of the Lashkargah oil extraction plant) and in 1966 for the supply of lorry and bus chassis. A UN technical assistance mission has been active in Afghánistán since 1950.

COMMERCE. Trade is supervised by the Government through the Ministries of Commerce and Finance and the Da Afghánistán Bánk. The Association of Afghan Chambers of Commerce works in close liaison with the Ministry of Commerce. Afghánistán follows liberal trading policies so far as the balance-of-payments position will allow. The Government monopoly controls the import of petrol and oil, sugar, cigarettes and tobacco, motor vehicles and consignment goods from bi-lateral trading countries. Bi-lateral trade agreements exist between Afghánistán and the USSR, Czechoslovakia, Poland, China, India and Pakistan. These agreements are reviewed annually. Transit agreements have been reached with Pakistan (Karachi being the most important port for the transit of Afghan imports and exports), the USSR, Turkey and Iran.

The Afghan Insurance Company, with a 49% British interest was founded in 1964.

In the year ended 20 March 1969 Afghan imports (c.i.f.), including loan and grant imports, totalled Afs. 9,267m. and exports (f.o.b.) Afs. 5,348m.

Afghánistán's largest customers during this period were USSR, USA, UK, India, Pakistan, West Germany and Czechoslovakia, and the largest suppliers were USSR, UK, India, Japan, West Germany and Pakistan. Main export commodities were karakul skins (US$8·32m.), raw cotton (US$5·88m.), dried fruit and nuts (US$18·96m.), fresh fruit (US$8m.) and natural gas (US$9·03m.). Main items imported were petroleum products (US$3·09m.), textiles (US$9·18m., tea (US$9·48m.).

Total trade between Afghánistán and UK (in £1,000 sterling, British Board of Trade returns):

	1966	1967	1968	1969	1970
Imports to UK	6,364	3,016	5,222	7,265	6,433
Exports from UK	1,262	957	1,028	1,963}	1,697
Re-exports from UK	4	15	24	31}	

ROADS. There are now over 2,000 km of asphalted road. The Americans have asphalted the Kandahár–Chaman and Kábul–Torkham roads. The Russians have constructed a road and tunnel through the Salang pass (over 11,000 ft), which was opened in Sept. 1964 and cuts 120 miles off the old road from Kábul to the north; they have continued this road to Kunduz and Sherkhan Bandar (Qizil Qala) on the Oxus. In addition, the Americans in 1966 completed the road between Kábul and Kandahár and the Russians have constructed a concrete road between Kandahár and Herát. In 1968 the Americans completed an asphalt road from Herát to the Iranian frontier at Islam Qala. With Soviet assistance a metalled road from Pul-i-Khumri to Mazar-i-Sharif and Shiberghan was completed in 1969.

RAILWAYS. There are no railways in the country but, under the terms of the Tehran agreement of 1963, Pakistani railways may be extended into Afghánistán at Torkham and/or Chaman.

SHIPPING. There are practically no navigable rivers in Afghánistán, and timber is the only article of commerce conveyed by water, floated down the Kunar and Kábul rivers from Chitral on rafts. A port has been built at Qizil Qala on the Oxus; barge traffic is increasing on the Oxus.

AVIATION. On 29 June 1956 Afghánistán signed an agreement with the USA for the development of civil aviation, including the construction of the international airport at Kandahár, comprising a loan of $5m. and a grant of $9·56m. Kábul airport has been expanded with Russian assistance. New runways at Kábul and Kandahár airports have been completed. Provincial all-weather airports have been constructed at Herát, Qunduz, Jalálábád and Mazar.

Ariana Afghan Airlines (a national airline) operates regular services to Tehran, Beirut, Istanbul, Frankfurt, London, Peshawar, Karachi, New Delhi, Tashkent and Moscow, and to the major provincial aiports.

Bakhtar Afghan Airlines (the domestic national airline) began operations on 8 Feb. 1968 and regularly serves the remoter airfields at Bamian, Chakcharan, Lashkargah, Faizabad, Khost, Maimana, Neemroz and Taleqan.

POST. Telephones, installed in most of the large towns, numbered 10,795 in 1969. There is telegraphic communication between all the larger towns and between Kábul and Kandahár and Peshawar and Chaman. A wireless installation connects Kábul with Europe, Bombay, the Far East, America and other parts of the world. Kábul Radio broadcasts in Pushtu, Persian, Urdu, English, French, Russian and German. The telecommunication system is being expanded slowly, mainly with German assistance.

BANKING. The Afghan State Bank (*da Afghánistán Bánk*) is the largest of the 3 main banks and also undertakes the functions of a central bank, holding the exclusive right of note issue. Total assets of the 3 main banks on 21 Sept. 1967 were: da Afghánistán Bánk, Afs. 28,074·4m.; Pashtany Tejaraty Bánk, Afs. 1,070·46m.; Bánk-i-Milli, Afs. 1,410·29m.

WEIGHTS AND MEASURES. Weights and measures used in Kábul are: Weights: 1 *khurd* = 0·244 lb.; 1 *pao* = 0·974 lb.; 1 *charak* = 3·896 lb.; 1 *seer* = 16 lb.; 1 *kharwár* = 1,280 lb. or 16 maunds of 80 lb. each. Long measure: 1 yd or *gaz* = 40 in. The metric system is in common use by the bigger cloth merchants in Kábul. Square measures: 1 *jaríb* = 60 × 60 kábuli yd or ½ acre; 1 *kulbá* = 40 jaríbs (area in which 2½ kharwárs of seed can be sown); 1 jaríb yd = 29 in.

Local weights and measures are in use at Kandahár, Herát and Jalálábád.

DIPLOMATIC REPRESENTATIVES

Afghánistán maintains embassies in:

China (also for Mongolia)   Germany West (also for Switzerland)
Czechoslovakia (also for Hungary) India (also for Burma, Nepál and
France (also for Austria and Belgium) Malaysia)

Indonesia	USSR (also for Finland, Rumania and
Iran	Sweden)
Iraq	UAR (also for Greece, Lebanon,
Italy (also for Spain)	Sudan and Ghana)
Japan	UK (also for Netherlands and Algeria)
Pakistan (also for Ceylon and Thailand)	USA (also for Brazil, Mexico and
Poland	Argentina)
Saudi Arabia (also for Jordan)	Yugoslavia (also for Bulgaria)
Turkey	

OF AFGHÁNISTÁN IN GREAT BRITAIN (31 Princes Gate, SW7)

Ambassador: (Vacant).
First Secretary: Abdul Ali Sulaiman (*Chargé d'Affaires ad int.*)

OF GREAT BRITAIN IN AFGHÁNISTÁN

Ambassador: P. L. Carter, CMG.
First Secretary: T. H. Gillson.
Oriental Secretary: J. R. James.

OF AFGHÁNISTÁN IN THE USA (2341 Wyoming Ave. NW,
Washington, D.C., 20008)

Ambassador: Abdullah Malikyar.
First Secretary: Mohammad S. Daneshjo.

OF THE USA IN AFGHÁNISTÁN

Ambassador: Robert G. Neumann.
Deputy Chief of Mission: Lowell B. Laingen. *Heads of Sections:* Charles W. Naas (*Political*); David H. Cohn (*Economic*); James W. Kelly (*Administrative*). *Service Attachés:* Col. Richard R. McTaggart (*Army*), Lieut.-Col. Raymond F. Kayea (*Air*).

BOOKS OF REFERENCE

The Kabul Times Annual, 1970
Fraser-Tytler, Sir W. K., *Afghanistan.* Rev. ed. OUP, 1967
Gilbertson, G. W., *Pakkhto Idiom Dictionary.* 2 vols. London, 1932
Griffiths, J. C., *Afghanistan.* New York, 1967
Humlum, J., *La Géographie de l'Afghanistan.* Copenhagen, 1959
Klimburg, M., *Afghanistan.* Vienna, 1966
Mele, P. F., *Afghanistan.* Florence, 1966
Watkins, M. B., *Afghanistan, land in transition.* New York, 1964
Wilber, D. N. (ed.), *Afghanistan.* 2nd ed. New Haven, 1962.—(ed.), *Afghanistan, a bibliography.* 2nd ed. New Haven, 1963

ALBANIA
Republika Popullore e Shqipërisë

HISTORY. After the death of George Kastriota—popularly known as Skanderbeg—in 1467 Albania passed under nominal or actual Turkish suzerainty until 1912. The independence of Albania was proclaimed at Vlonë (Valona) on 28 Nov. 1912, and the London conference of ambassadors, decided upon its frontiers and nominated as its ruler Prince William of Wied, who arrived at Durrës (Durazzo) on 7 March 1914, but on 3 Sept. 1914 left the country, which fell into a state of anarchy. By the secret Pact of London of 26 April 1915 provision was made for the partition of Albania; but this arrangement was repudiated by Italy on 3 June 1917, when the Italian C.-in-C. in Albania proclaimed at Gijrokastër (Argyrocastro) the independence of Albania. In Jan. 1925 the country was proclaimed a republic and on 1 Sept. 1928 a monarchy. Ahmed Beg Zogu, President of the Republic since 31 Jan. 1925, reigned as King Zog till April 1939, when, on the occupation of the country by the Italians, he fled to

England. After the liberation he was formally deposed *in absentia*, on 2 Jan. 1946. During the years 1939–44 the country was overrun by Italians and Germans. The official Albanian date of the liberation is 29 Nov. 1944.

On 10 Nov. 1945 the British, US and USSR Governments recognized the Provisional Government under Gen. Enver Hoxha, on the understanding that it would hold free elections. The elections of 2 Dec. 1945 resulted in a Communist-controlled assembly, which on 11 Jan. 1946 proclaimed Albania a republic.

In 1946 Great Britain and the USA broke off relations with Albania and vetoed its admission to the United Nations. Albania was finally admitted on 15 Dec. 1955, the USA abstaining from voting.

Because of Albania's Stalinist and pro-Chinese attitudes diplomatic relations with USSR were broken off in 1961.

CONSTITUTION AND GOVERNMENT. The political structure derives from the Constitution of 1946 as amended in 1950, 1955, 1960 and 1963. The supreme legislative body is the single-chamber People's Assembly, which meets twice a year, and delegates its day-to-day functions to a Presidium composed of a chairman, 3 deputy chairmen, a secretary and 10 members. Election of deputies to the People's Assembly is by universal suffrage (at 18 years); each deputy represents 8,000 voters.

The government consists of a prime minister (Chairman of the Council of Ministers), 3 deputy prime ministers, 13 ministers and 2 chairmen of commissions.

Effective rule is exercised by the Albanian Labour (*i.e.*, Communist) Party, founded 8 Nov. 1941, whose governing body is the Politburo.

At its 5th Congress (1966) the Party had 63,326 full and 3,310 candidate members.

Titular Head of State: Chairman of the Presidium of the People's Assembly: Haxhi Lleshi, elected July 1953. In March 1971 the chief Party and Government posts were filled as follows: The 11 full members of the Politburo:

First Secretary of the Central Committee of the Party: Enver Hoxha. *Chairman of the Council of Ministers* (*Prime Minister*): Mehmet Shehu. *Deputy-Chairmen of the Council of Ministers:* Beqir Balluku (*Minister of Defence*), Shafer Spahiu and Adil Çarçani. *Secretaries of the Central Committee:* Hysni Kapo, Ramiz Alija, Spiro Koleka (*Chairman, State Planning Commission*); Manush Myftiu; Gogo Nushi; Mrs Rita Marko. The 5 candidate members: Kadri Hazbiu (*Minister of the Interior*); Koço Theodhosi (*Minister of Industry*); Petrit Dume (*Chief of Staff*); Abdyl Këllezi; Pilo Peristeri. Not in the Politburo: *Foreign Minister:* Nesti Nase. *Minister of Foreign Trade:* Kico Ngjela. *Minister of Agriculture:* Pirro Dodbiba.

In the Sept. 1970 elections it was claimed that 100% of the electorate voted unanimously for 264 deputies on the single list of the Albanian Democratic Front.

LOCAL GOVERNMENT is carried out by People's Councils at village, *lokalitet*, town and district level. Councillors are elected for 3 years.

National flag: Red, with a black double-headed eagle and a red, gold-edged 5-pointed star above it. *Mercantile flag:* red, black, red (horizontal).

National anthem: Rreth Flamurit te per bashkuar (The flag that united us in the struggle).

AREA AND POPULATION. The area of the country is 28,748 sq. km (11,101 sq. miles). By the peace treaty Italy restored the island of Sazan (Saseno) to Albania. At the census of 2 Oct. 1960 the population was 1,626,315 (51·3% males, 30·9% urban). Population in 1967, 1,964,730 (males, 1,009,865; urban population, 33·3%; density, 68 per sq. km). Estimate for 1968: 2,019,000. The capital is Tirana (1967 population (in 1,000), 169); other large towns are Durrës

(Durrsi, Durazzo) (53), Shkodër (Shkodra, Scutari) (50), Vlonë (Vlona, Vlorë, Vlora, Valona) (50), Korçe (Korça, Koritza) (46), Elbasan (39), Berat (24), Fier (20), Kavajë (18), Lushnjë (17), Gjirokastër (Argyrocastro) (15), Qytet Stalin (formerly Kuçovë) (13).

There is a small Greek minority (2·4% in 1960).

Vital statistics, 1967 (per 1,000): Births, 35·3; deaths, 8·4; marriages, 8·6; divorces, 0·7. Natural increase, 26·9. Life expectancy in 1960 was 69·4 years (38·3 years in 1938).

The country is administratively divided into 26 districts (*rreth*, pl. *rrethët*)(*see* map in THE STATESMAN'S YEAR-BOOK, 1962. N.B. The district of Ersekë has been renamed Kolonjë). Districts are subdivided into *lokaliteteve*.

Districts	Area (sq. km)	Population (1967)	Districts	Area (sq. km)	Population (1967)
Berat	1,066	104,390	Lushnjë	711	81,595
Dibrë	1,569	93,812	Mat	1,028	45,340
Durrës	861	155,780	Mirditë	698	22,465
Elbasan	1,505	130,430	Përmet	950	30,340
Fier	1,189	24,095	Pogradec	725	42,775
Gramsh	699	49,170	Pukë	969	27,568
Gjirokastër	1,137	18,865	Sarandë	1,097	58,135
Kolonjë	804	18,685	Skrapar	702	23,035
Korcë	2,181	159,115	Shkodër	2,533	150,350
Krujë	612	55,525	Tepelenë	817	30,850
Kukës	1,564	58,880	Tirana	1,186	241,900
Lezhë	472	33,225	Tropojë	1,043	25,570
Librazhd	1,013	42,730	Vlonë	1,609	119,995

The districts are for the greater part named after their capitals; exceptions: Tropojë, chief town, Bajram Curri; Mat, Burrel; Mirditë, Rrëshen; Skrapar, Çorovodë.

The Albanian language is divided into two dialects—Gheg, north of the river Shkumbi, and Tosk in the south. Many places therefore have two forms of name: Vlonë (Gheg), Vlorë (Tosk), etc., and many are known also by an Italian name, *e.g.*, Valona. Since 1945 the official language has been based on Tosk.

RELIGION. For details of the situation before 1967 *see* THE STATESMAN'S YEAR-BOOK, 1969–70. In 1967 the Government closed 2,169 mosques and churches and claimed that Albania was the first atheist state in the world. The population was distributed according to the following estimates: Moslems, 1·2m.; Orthodox Christians (the Orthodox Church of Albania), 300,000; Roman Catholics, 200,000.

EDUCATION. Primary education is free and compulsory in primary schools (7–11 years), and '8-year' schools (11–14 years). Secondary education is available in '12-year' (general), technical-professional or lower vocational schools. There were, in 1967–68, 417 kindergartens with 26,021 pupils and 1,172 teachers; 2,629 primary schools with 268,542 pupils and 8,666 teachers; 871 8-year secondary schools with 177,086 pupils and 7,179 teachers, 61 12-year secondary schools with 19,929 pupils, 913 teachers; and 8 institutes of higher education, with 12,800 students and 959 teachers, including a university in Tirana (founded 1957), a polytechnic, an agricultural college, a medical school, 5 teachers' training colleges and an institute of science. In 1967–68 there were 382 teachers and, in 1970–71, 7,300 full-time students at Tirana University.

CINEMAS. There were 95 cinemas with an attendance of 7·8m. in 1967.

NEWSPAPERS. In 1967 there were 19 newspapers with an annual circulation of 45·5m. The Party-Government paper is *Zëri i Popullit* (Voice of the People).

SOCIAL WELFARE. In 1967 there were 181 hospitals and health centres with 11,813 beds (including 102 general hospitals with 7,519 beds), and 900 doctors.

JUSTICE is administered by People's Courts. In 1952 a new penal code was introduced, modelled on Soviet law, but with severer penalties (41 offences carry the death penalty). Minors (14–18 years) are criminally responsible, but may not receive the death penalty. In Sept. 1966 the Ministry of Justice was incorporated into the Ministry of the Interior. In 1968 tribunals were set up in towns and villages to try minor crimes which had previously been dealt with by district courts.

FINANCE. Currency. The monetary unit is the *lek* of 100 *qintars*. It replaced the Albanian gold franc (*franc ar*) in July 1947. In Aug. 1965 a new *lek* was introduced: 10 old *leks* = 1 new *lek*. Official rates of exchange: £1 = 12 *leks*; US\$1 = 5 *leks*; 1 rouble = 5·55 *leks*. Tourist rates: £1 = 30 *leks*; US\$1 = 12·5 *leks*.

Budget. Budget figures for 1968: Revenue, 40,250m. leks; expenditure, 39,850m. leks. 1967 revenue 36,468m. leks; expenditure, 36,202m. leks.

Financial aid by the USSR up to 1960 is estimated to have been 948m. old roubles. Chinese aid by 1966 (some £168m.) had not made good the withdrawal of Soviet aid. Chinese aid is continuing: in 1966 Albania obtained a loan worth some US\$125m. to help finance the 1966–70 plan.

DEFENCE. Albania did not participate in meetings of the Warsaw Pact countries after 1962 and withdrew from it in Sept. 1968 in protest against the invasion of Czechoslovakia. Military ties with China have been strengthened.

Ranks were abolished in March 1966 and political commissars re-introduced.

Army. Army service is 2 years. Strength in 1969, 30,000 in 6 brigades, armoured with about 100 T-34 tanks. Security police ('SSSh') had a strength of 12,500, divided into 4 security battalions, and 5 battalions of frontier-guards.

Navy. The Navy consists of 4 submarines, 2 fleet minesweepers, 4 patrol vessels, 6 inshore minesweepers, 12 motor torpedo-boats, 2 armoured gunboats, 2 landing craft, a degaussing ship, 2 oilers, 16 district patrol craft and 10 small auxiliaries. Navy personnel, 3,000. Service is 3 years. There is a naval base at Vlorë.

Air Force. The Air Force, controlled by the Army, has about 65 combat aircraft and 5,000 officers and men. There is 1 interceptor squadron of Chinese-built MiG 19s; 3 of the 5 ground attack squadrons have Chinese-built MiG-17s, the others fly MiG-15s. Transport and training types include 3 Il-14s, An-2 biplanes, Mi-4 helicopters, Yak-11s, Yak-18s and MiG-15UTIs.

PLANNING. The first 5-year plan covered 1951–55; the second, 1956–60. The third (1961–65) failed to reach all its targets owing to the 'imperialist-revisionist blockade', increased defence commitments and shortfalls in agriculture, and it was followed by an emergency plan for 1966. The fourth 5-year plan covered 1966–70. It was announced that targets had been met after only 4 years and 7 months. Continuing Chinese economic assistance is a *sine qua non* of Albania's development. The fifth 5-year plan is running from 1971 to 1975. Emphasis is laid on industrial expansion, especially in the oil, mining and chemical industries.

AGRICULTURE. The country for the greater part is rugged, wild and mountainous, the exceptions being along the Adriatic littoral and the Korçë (Koritsa) Basin, which are fertile. In 1967 arable land comprised 555,800 hectares and pasture 675,600 hectares. 80·5% of cultivated land is held by state farms and 18·1% by co-operatives. In 1970, 283,200 hectares were irrigated.

Land is held by the State (largely forests and non-agricultural), state farms (in 1967 holding 110,700 hectares of arable land), co-operatives (in 1967, 1,208 with 442,000 hectares); and privately. The size of private plots was reduced by 50–60% in May 1967. There are also 250 'local agricultural enterprises' holding 10,800 hectares of arable land. Tractors in 1967 numbered 9,049 (in 15-h.p. units).

The yield of the main crops in 1965 was (in 1,000 metric tons): Grain, 326;

cotton, 23; tobacco, 14; potatoes, 21; in 1964: sugar-beet, 135; in 1963: maize, 192; wheat, 60; rye, 5·2; barley, 3; oats, 11; fruits, 44·8; rice, 9·1.

Livestock, 1964: Cattle, 427,100; sheep, 1,682,200; goats, 1,199,300; pigs, 146,600; (1963) horses and mules, 122,100; poultry, 1·69m.

FORESTRY. 47% of the territory of Albania is forest land, of which 38% is oak forest, 26% elm and 18% pine and birch. Timber reserves reach 44·5m. cu. metres. In 1967 forests covered 1,242,100 hectares; 6,784 hectares were afforested, 10,000 hectares improved in 1967.

FISHERIES. The catch in 1964 was 3,600 metric tons.

MINING. The mineral wealth of Albania is considerable but is only recently being developed. In 1970 there were 7 coal, 7 chromium and 6 copper mines. Ferro-nickel ores are mined and output is increasing. In 1969 extensive coal deposits were discovered at Valias, near Tirana. There is no bituminous coal. Salt is extracted near Vlonë and bitumen mined at Selenicë.

INDUSTRY. All industry is nationalized right down to the smallest artisan workshop. Output is small, and the principal industries are agricultural product processing, textile and cement. With Chinese assistance chemical and engineering industries are being built up. An iron and steel works is being built in Elbasan with a smelting capacity of 800,000 tons.

OIL. Oil is produced chiefly at Qytet Stalin. Refining capacity in 1970 was over 1m. metric tons. Some 1·3m. metric tons of crude were produced in 1970, and 250,000 metric tons of refined products in 1969. A pipeline connects Qytet Stalin with the port of Vlonë.

POWER. There are 6 hydro-electric power plants: the Lenin plant near Tirana; the Karl-Marx plant on the Mati River, the Friedrich Engels plant at Shkopeti; in addition to the Stalin plant at Bistrice, a second plant opened there in 1966; and a new plant opened at Fier in 1968. Electric power production in 1965 was 341·9m. kwh.

PRODUCTION (in metric tons):

Chrome ore, 1965	310,800	Timber (cu. metres), 1963	468,000
Copper ore, 1963	143,839	Beer (hectolitres), 1964	109,000
Iron ore, 1963	259,052	Cheese, 1964	4,500
Bitumen, 1964	242,000	Cotton fabrics (1,000 metres),	
Brown coal, 1965	350,000	1965	28,200
Crude oil, 1965	824,800	Woollen fabrics (1,000 metres),	
Lignite, 1959	300,000	1963	1,278
Cement, 1965	133,600	Shoes (1,000 pairs), 1965	1,136
Olive oil, 1963	3,411		
Sugar, 1963	11,593		

LABOUR. In 1967, 312,370 persons worked in the socialist sector of the national economy, of whom 105,301 were employed in industry, 40,060 in building and 64,356 in agriculture. 248,000 women were employed in 1967. Wages are controlled so that minimum wages do not fall below one-third of maximum.

COMMERCE. In 1966, 70% of Albania's trade was with China, 24% with other communist countries (nothing to USSR) and 6% with western Europe. Better trade relations with Yugoslavia were established in 1970.

In 1964 exports totalled US$59·9m., imports US$98·1m. Albania's balance of trade deficit amounted to 1,910m. leks (1964).

In 1967 trade agreements were signed with France and Italy. Aid agreements were signed with China in Oct. 1970.

Total trade between Albania and UK (according to British Board of Trade returns) was as follows (in £1,000 sterling):

	1965	1966	1967	1968	1969	1970
Imports to UK	13	15	12	100	7	2
Exports from UK	100	16	383	83	113 }	167
Re-exports from UK	1	—	—	—	—	

RAILWAYS. All railways, except the short narrow-gauge line Selenicë–Vlonë, have been built since 1947. Total length, in 1964, was 151 km. They comprise the lines Durrës–Tirana, Durrës–Kavajë–Pegin–Elbasan, Vlonë–Memaliaj and Vlonë–Milot. A railway is being built from Elbasan to the iron mines at Pishkash. Goods carried in 1967 amounted to 1,993,000 metric tons; passengers, 4m.

ROADS. There were, in 1960, 3,100 km of roads suitable for motor traffic. The mountain districts of the north are still mostly inaccessible for wheeled vehicles, and communications are still by means of pack ponies or donkeys. Registered motor vehicles in 1960: Cars, 1,900; lorries and buses, 3,400. Road traffic carried 8·6m. passengers in 1967; goods carried, 6·6m. metric tons.

SHIPPING. The ports are Shëngjin (San Giovanni di Medua), Durrës (Durazzo), Vlonë (Valona) and Sarandë (Santi Quaranta). 421,000 metric tons of freight were carried in 1967. Albania has ocean-going ships capable of reaching Shanghai.

AVIATION. East German, Yugoslav, Hungarian and Czechoslovak airlines connect Tirana with Budapest, Prague, Belgrade, Titograd, Bari and Rome.

POST. Number of post and telegraph offices (1967), 240; telephones (1963), 10,150. There are 17 broadcasting stations, including Tirana and Korçë. Radio receiving sets (1967), 104,873; television sets, 1,200. A television broadcasting system is being installed with French help.

BANKING. The National Bank of Albania was founded in 1925 with Italian aid. In 1964 savings deposits amounted to 1,671m. leks. In 1970 the Agricultural Bank was set up as a credit institution for agricultural co-operatives.

DIPLOMATIC RELATIONS. Albania maintains diplomatic relations with Comunist countries except USSR and also with Austria, Belgium (ambassador resident in Belgrade), Central African Republic, Denmark, Ethiopia, Finland (at legation level), France, Italy, Netherlands, Switzerland and Turkey.

BOOKS OF REFERENCE

Vjetari Statistikor (Statistical Yearbook). Tirana, annually, from 1959 (with supplement of captions in English)
Constitution of the People's Republic of Albania. Tirana, 1964
Frasheri, K., *History of Albania.* Tirana, 1964
Griffith, W. E., *Albania and the Sino-Soviet Rift.* Cambridge (Mass.), 1963
Hamm, H., *Albania–China's beachhead in Europe.* Cologne, 1962 [in German]; London, 1963
Mann, S. E., *An Historical Albanian–English Dictionary.* London, 1948.—*An English–Albanian Dictionary.* CUP, 1957
Pano, N. C., *The People's Republic of Albania.* Baltimore, 1968
Skendl, S. (ed.), *Albania.* New York, 1956; London, 1957

ALGERIA

El Djemhouria, El Djazaïria Demokratia Echaabia—
République Algérienne Démocratique et Populaire

LIBERATION. On 1 Nov. 1954 the National Liberation Front (FLN), founded on 5 Aug. 1951, went over to open warfare against the French administration and armed forces. In Sept. 1958 a free Algerian government was formed in Cairo with Ferhat Abbas as provisional president.

A referendum was held in Metropolitan France and Algeria on 6–8 Jan. 1961 to decide on Algerian self-determination as proposed by President de Gaulle.

His proposals were approved by 15,200,073 against 4,996,474 votes in Metropolitan France, and by 1,749,969 against 767,546 votes in Algeria. In Metropolitan France 20·2m. out of 27·2m. registered voters went to the polls; in Algeria 2·5m. out of 4·5m. registered voters.

Long delayed by the terrorism, in Metropolitan France as well as Algeria, of a secret organization (OAS) led by anti-Gaullist officers, a cease-fire agreement was concluded between the French Government and the representatives of the Algerian Nationalists on 18 March 1962; but OAS terror acts continued for some months. On 7 April a provisional executive of 12 members was set up, under the chairmanship of Abderrhaman Farès.

On 8 April 1962 a referendum in Metropolitan France approved the Algerian settlement with 17,505,473 (90·7%) against 1,794,553 (9·3%) and 1,102,477 invalid votes; 6,580,772 voters abstained. On 1 July 1962, 5,975,581 Algerians voted in favour of, 16,534 against the settlement.

CONSTITUTION AND GOVERNMENT. On 3 July 1962 President de Gaulle proclaimed Algeria independent and handed over sovereign power.

On 25 Sept. the National Assembly met and elected Ferhat Abbas President of the Republic and Ben Bella Prime Minister.

A national referundum held on 15 Sept. 1963 elected Ben Bella, the only candidate, as President of the new Democratic People's Republic of Algeria.

The Government was overthrown by a junta of army officers which, on 19 June 1965, established a Revolutionary Council under Col. Houari Boumédienne.

The Government, formed on 10 July 1965, included the following Ministers (but some of them—*e.g.*, Agriculture and Information—may have been dismissed in Nov. 1967):

Prime Minister and Minister of Defence: Houari Boumédienne.
Minister of State: Rabah Bitat. *Foreign Affairs:* Abdelaziz Bouteflika. *Interior:* Ahmed Medeghri. *Finance and Planning:* Cherif Belkacem. *Agriculture and Agrarian Reform:* Tayebi Larbi. *Information:* Mumammad Benyahia. *Justice:* Muhammad Bedjaoud. *Education:* Admed Taleb. *Health:* Tedjini Haddam. *Ex-servicemen:* Boualem Ben Hamouda. *Industry and Energy:* Belaid Abdessalam. *Posts and Telecommunications:* Abdel Kader Zaibek. *Public Works:* Lamine Khene. *Commerce:* Layachi Yaker. *Labour:* Mazoudi Mohaud Said. *Tourism:* Abdelaziz Maaoui. *Youth and Sports:* Abdelkrim Ben Mahmoud. *Religious Affairs:* Ahmed Saadouni.

The official language is Arabic, French being the principal foreign language.

AREA AND POPULATION. Algeria (295,033 sq. km, 113,883 sq. miles) is divided into 15 departments, Sahara (2,171,800 sq. km. 838,315 sq. miles) included. Population (census 1966) 12,102,000; estimate (1969) 13·2m.

The Algerian departments are subdivided into 76 *arrondissements*, which include 634 communes; the Saharan departments (Saoura, Oasis) are divided into 5 *arrondissements*, and 47 *communes*.

Area and population (1966):

Departments	Area (sq. km)	Population (1,000)	Departments	Area (sq. km)	Population (1,000)
Algiers	3,393	1,648·2	Annaba[2]	25,367	950·0
Grand Kabylia	5,806	807·4	Sétif	17,405	1,237·9
El Asnam[1]	12,257	789·6	Aurès	38,494	765·0
Titteri	50,331	809·1	Saïda	60,114	236·9
Oran	16,438	958·4	Oasis	1,301,561	505·5
Tlemcen	8,100	444·1	Saoura	779,797	211·0
Mostaganem	11,432	778·8			
Tiaret	25,997	362·0	Total	2,466,833	10,453·6
Constantine	19,899	1,513·7			

[1] Formerly Orléansville.   [2] Formerly Bône.

The chief towns with estimated population (1967) are: Algiers, 943,000; Oran, 325,000; Constantine, 255,000; Annaba, 165,000; Sidi-Bel-Abbès, 101,000; Sétif, 98,000; Blida, 87,000; Skikda, 85,000; Tlemcen, 80,000; Mostaganem, 64,000; Bougie, 63,000; Colomb-Béchar, 27,000.

RELIGION. The overwhelming part of the population are Moslems. The Roman Catholic Church has an archbishop and 2 bishops, with some 400 officiating clergymen. Jews number about 150,000. There are 13 Protestant pastors and 6 Jewish rabbis sharing in government grants.

EDUCATION 1964–65). Primary schools had 1·4m. (1·8m., 1970) pupils and 29,000 teachers; secondary schools had 82,000 pupils and 3,400 teachers. The University of Algiers had 6,888 students and 455 teachers. A new university in Oran opened in 1967. 2,000 Algerians were studying abroad.

NEWSPAPERS (1970). There are 8 daily newspapers with a combined circulation of 185,000.

HEALTH (1966). There were 148 general and 13 specialized hospitals with together 42,722 beds; in 1962 there were 1,200 doctors, 449 dentists, 708 pharmacists and 622 midwives. The Sahara departments had 15 hospitals (892 beds) in 1960.

JUSTICE. There are appeal courts at Algiers, Constantine and Oran; and in the *arrondissements* are 17 courts of first instance. There are also commercial courts and justices of the peace with extensive powers. Criminal justice is organized as in France. The Supreme Court is at the same time Council of State and High Court of Appeal.

FINANCE. Currency. The Algerian *dinar* (DA) is at par with the new French franc. There are in circulation bank-notes of DA 5, 10, 50 and 100 and coins of 1, 2, 5, 20 and 50 centimes and DA 1. Money in circulation in Dec. 1968, 3,713m. DA.

Budget. The budget (including extraordinary budget) was as follows in calendar years (in 1m. DA):

	1967	1968	1969	1970	1971
Revenue	..	2,940	3,020	..	7,500
Expenditure	3,332	3,539	3,890	4,400	4,900

The revenue (in 1m. DA) in 1969 includes 830 from direct tax; 325 from customs duty; 1,125 from indirect tax. Main items of expenditures: Administration, 989; economic services, 581; social services, 1,666.

DEFENCE. Army. The Army in 1966 had a strength of 45,000 men, organized in 1 motorized division, 4 artillery battalions and a number of infantry battalions. Equipment includes Soviet T-34 and T-54 tanks.

Navy. Two old coastal minesweepers were presented to Algeria by Egypt at the end of 1962 to form the nucleus of the Algerian navy, but one was wrecked. Six coastal escorts, 9 missile boats, 8 torpedo boats, 2 minesweepers and 1 trawler have since been acquired from the USSR.

The French naval base of Mers el Kebir was taken over by the Algerian army and navy in Feb. 1968.

Air Force. Five MiG-15 jet-fighters were delivered in 1962 as the nucleus of an Algerian Air Force. Since then many more aircraft of Soviet design have followed, and the Air Force now has about 130 combat aircraft and 2,000 personnel. Training and technical assistance are given by the United Arab Republic and Soviet Union. There are 3 squadrons (each 12 aircraft) of supersonic MiG-21Fs, 3 squadrons (each 16 aircraft) of MiG-17 and MiG-15 fighter-bombers, 2 squadrons (each 12 aircraft) of Il-28 twin-jet bombers, 2 squadrons of piston-engined Il-14 and turboprop An-12 transports, an Mi-4 helicopter wing and training units equipped with Yak-11s, CM.170 Magisters (28) and MiG-15UTIs. Two SA330 Puma assault helicopters have been acquired from France. Surface-to-air missile units have Soviet-built 'Guidelines'.

AGRICULTURE. There exists a small area of highly fertile plains and valleys near the coast, mainly owned by self-management committees and some Europeans, which is cultivated scientifically, and where profitable returns are obtained from vineyards, cereals, etc., but the greater part of Algeria is of limited value for agricultural purposes. In the northern portion the mountains are generally better adapted to grazing and forestry than agriculture, and a large portion of the native population is quite poor. In spite of the many excellent roads built by the Government, a considerable area of the mountainous region is without adequate means of communication and is accessible only with difficulty. There were an estimated 16·7m. hectares of agricultural land in 1969, of which 6·2m. hectares were arable; 370,000 hectares under vine and 9·6m. hectares pastures and brushlands. The chief crops in 1969 were (in 1,000 metric tons): Wheat, 1,920; barley, 538; wine, 1,200; olive oil, 18; citrus fruit, 420, and dates, 180.

Thirteen barrages with a capacity of 822m. cu. metres of water, in 1958, irrigated 155,000 hectares.

Livestock, 1963: 135,000 horses, 175,000 mules, 290,000 asses, 800,000 cattle (1970), 5m. sheep (1965), 1·9m. goats (1965), 70,000 pigs and 140,000 camels. The wool clip in 1960 was 5,900 metric tons.

FORESTRY. In 1956 the acreage of state forests was 3·07m. hectares. The greater part is mere brushwood, but there are very large areas covered with cork-oak trees, Aleppo pine, evergreen oak and cedar. The dwarf-palm is grown on the plains, alfa on the table-land. Timber is cut for firewood, also for industrial purposes, for railway sleepers, telegraph poles, etc., and for bark for tanning. Considerable portions of the forest area are also leased for tillage, or for pasturage for cattle and sheep.

FISHERIES. There are extensive fisheries for sardines, anchovies, sprats, tunny fish, etc., and also shell fish. In 1963, 568 boats and 4,000 fishermen were employed in fishing. Fish taken in 1963 amounted to 4,000 tons of white and shell fish and 13,000 tons of blue fish (sardines, anchovy, etc.).

MINING. Algeria possesses deposits of iron, zinc, lead, mercury, copper and antimony. Kaolin, marble and onyx, salt (110,000 tons in 1957) and coal are also found. Mineral output in 1965 (in 1,000 metric tons): Iron ore, 2,998; coal, 17; zinc, 420; phosphates, 420·7; lead, 7.

Two large oilfields went into production in 1957 around Edjélé and Hassi Messaoud and in 1959 at El Gassi. In 1960 about 200 wells were productive. Natural gas was discovered at Djebel Berga in 1954 and at Hassi-R'Mel in 1956. Oil pipelines from Edjélé to Skirra (Tunisia) and from Hassi Messaoud to Bougie, and a gas pipeline from Hassi Messaoud *via* Hassi-R'Mel to Mostaganem–Oran–Algiers, have been completed. Oil production in 1967, 38·37m. tons; 1968, 42·9m. tons; 1969, 45m. tons.

A national company for the distribution and transport of hydrocarbons was set up in Jan. 1964.

Production of natural gas in 1969 was 2,556m. cu. metres.

ELECTRICITY. Production of energy in 1969 totalled 1,477m. kwh., and in 1968, 1,035m. kwh.

COMMERCE. The foreign trade of Algeria was as follows (in 1m. DA):

	1967	1968	1969
Imports	3,154	3,889	4,466
Exports	3,572	3,703	4,273

In 1963 France supplied 76% of the imports and took 73% of the exports. Crude oil accounted for over 60% of the exports.

Total trade between UK and Algeria (British Board of Trade returns, in £1,000 sterling):

	1965	1966	1967	1968	1969	1970
Imports to UK	18,007	22,681	15,556	21,157	22,073	21,166
Exports from UK	6,888	3,095	3,002	4,548	8,719 ⎱	16,774
Re-exports from UK	224	209	164	246	780 ⎰	

SHIPPING. In 1968, 43m. tons of goods were handled at Algerian ports.

In 1960 the Algerian merchant fleet consisted of 21 vessels over 2,000 tons, and 925 below 1,500 tons, with a total tonnage of 72,953.

A state shipping line, Compagnie Nationale Algérienne de Navigation, was formed in Jan. 1964 and possesses 6 vessels and also charters others.

ROADS. There were in 1969, 18,200 km of roads, 8,900 of which are in the Sahara departments. Work began in 1969 on the Algerian section (240 miles) of the Trans-Sahara highway. Motor vehicles in 1968 included 115,192 passenger cars and 68,000 commercial vehicles.

RAILWAYS. In 1970 there were 4,100 km of railway open for traffic, of which 2,720 km are of standard gauge (299 km electrified) and 1,380 km of narrow gauge.

AVIATION. There are 65 airfields controlled by government and 135 owned by petroleum companies. In 1963 Air Algeria carried 350,000 passengers, 4,300 tons of goods and 1,600 tons of mail. Air Algeria serves the main Algerian cities, and an international network comprises all important French cities, Geneva, Zürich, Tunis, Casablanca, Cairo, Sofia, Belgrade and Moscow.

Algeria is also served by Swissair, Royal Air Maroc, United Arab Airline, Tunis Air and Air France.

POST. There were, in 1959, 900 post offices, including 381 postal agencies; number of telephones (1969), 156,038, of which 63,035 were in Algiers and 13,436 in Oran. In 1967 there were some 700,000 radio receivers and 100,000 TV licences issued.

Post office savings accounts on 31 Dec. 1958 numbered 196,000, with a total balance of 4,382,000m. francs.

BANKING. The Banque Centrale d'Algérie is the government emission bank. Other banks operating in Algeria are Banque National d'Algérie, Crédit Populaire d'Algérie, Banque Exterieure d'Algérie, Caisse Algérienne de Developpement, Compagnie Algérienne de Crédit et de Banque (the only private bank).

WEIGHTS AND MEASURES. The metric system is in use.

DIPLOMATIC REPRESENTATIVES

Algeria maintains embassies in:

Argentina
Belgium (also for Netherlands and Luxembourg)
Brazil
Bulgaria
Canada
China

Congo (B.)
Cuba
Czechoslovakia
France
Germany (West)
Ghana
Guinea

India	Spain
Indonesia	Sweden (also for Finland, Iceland and
Iraq	Norway)
Italy	Switzerland
Ivory Coast	Syria
Japan	Tanzania
Jordan	Tunisia
Kuwait	USSR
Lebanon	UAR
Libya	UK
Mali	USA
Morocco	Yemen
Pakistan	Yugoslavia
Saudi Arabia	

The USA embassy was closed on 6 June 1967.

OF ALGERIA IN GREAT BRITAIN (6 Hyde Park Gate, SW 7)

Ambassador: (Vacant). *Chargé d'Affaires a.i.:* A. Yadi.

OF GREAT BRITAIN IN ALGERIA

Ambassador: C. M. LeQuesne, CMG.
First Secretaries: J. R. Johnson, S. Relton (*Commercial*).

BOOKS OF REFERENCE

STATISTICAL INFORMATION. The Service de Statistique Générale (12, rue Bab-Azoun, Alger) publishes the annual *Statistique Générale de l'Algérie, Documents statistiques sur le commerce de l'Algérie* (from 1902). *Tableaux de l'économie algérienne* (1960).

Cornet, P., *Le Pétrole Saharien.* Paris, 1961
Gordon, D. C., *The Passing of French Algeria.* OUP, 1965
Le Rumeur, G., *Le Sahara avant le pétrole.* Paris, 1961
Thé, B. de, *Essai de bibliographie du Sahara Français.* Paris, 1961
Verlaque, C., *Le Sahara pétrolier.* Paris, 1964
Verlet, B., *Sahara.* Paris, 1960
Verneuil, H., *Sahara.* Paris, 1960

ANDORRA

Les Vallées d'Andorre—Valls d'Andorra

The co-principality of Andorra is situated in the eastern Pyrenees. The country consists of gorges, narrow valleys and defiles, surrounded by high mountain peaks varying between 1,880 and 3,000 metres. Its maximum length is 30 km and its width 20 km; it has an area of 465 sq. km (190 sq. miles) and a population of about 18,000, scattered in 6 villages. Catalan is the language spoken.

The political status of Andorra was regulated by the *Paréage* of 1278 which placed Andorra under the joint suzerainty of the Comte de Foix and of the Bishop of Urgel. The rights vested in the house of Foix passed by marriage to that of Béarn and, on the accession of Henri IV, to the French crown. The sovereignty is exercised jointly by the President of the French Republic and the Bishop of Urgel. The co-princes are represented in Andorra by the 'Viguier de France' and the 'Viguier Episcopal'. Each co-prince has set up a Permanent Delegation for Andorran affairs; the Prefect of the Eastern Pyrenees is the French Permanent Delegate.

The valleys pay every second year a due of 960 francs to France and 460 pesetas to the bishop.

National flag: Blue, yellow, red (vertical).

A 'General Council of the Valleys' submits motions and proposals to the Permanent Delegations. Its 24 members are elected for 4 years; half of the council is renewed every 2 years. The council nominates a First Syndic (*Syndic Procureur Général*) and a Second Syndic from outside its members.

Judicial power is exercised in civil matters in the first instance, according to the plaintiff's choice, by either the *Bayle Français* or the *Bayle Episcopal*, who are nominated by the respective co-princes. The judge of appeal is appointed alternately by each co-prince; the third instance (*Tercera Sala*) is either the supreme court of Andorra at Perpignan or the ecclesiastical court of the Bishop at Urgel. Criminal justice is administered by the *Tribunal des Corts*, consisting of the 2 Viguiers and the judge of appeal.

During the summer tourism is the main industry of the principality.

A good road connects the Spanish and French frontiers by way of Sant Julià, Andorre-la-Vieille, les Escaldes, Encamp, Canillo and Soldeu: it crosses the Col d'Envalira (2,400 metres). Another road connects Andorre-la-Vieille with Ordino. French and Spanish currency are both in use.

Exports from the UK (British Board of Trade returns, in £1,000 sterling): 1965, 40; 1966, 30; 1967, 37; 1968, ..; 1969, ... Imports to the UK: 1965, below 1; 1966, 3; 1967–68, 1; 1969, ... Re-exports: 1965, 1; 1966, below 1; 1967, 1; 1968, 1; 1969, ...

British Consul-General: H. T. Kennedy, OBE, (resident in Barcelona).

BOOKS OF REFERENCE

Brutails, *La Coutume d'Andorre.* Paris, 1904
Corts Peyret, J., *Geografia e Historia de Andorra.* Barcelona, 1945
Llobet, S., *El medio y la vida en Andorra.* Barcelona, 1947
Vidal y Guitart, J. M., *Instituciones politicas y sociales de Andorra.* Madrid, 1949

ARGENTINA
República Argentina

HISTORY. In 1515 Juan Díaz de Solís discovered the Río de La Plata. In 1534 Pedro de Mendoza was sent by the King of Spain to take charge of the 'Gobernación y Capitanía de las tierras del Río de La Plata', and in Feb. 1536 he founded the city of the 'Puerto de Santa María del Buen Aire'. In 1810 the population rose against Spanish rule, and in 1816 Argentina proclaimed its independence. Civil wars and anarchy followed until, in 1853, stable government was established.

CONSTITUTION AND GOVERNMENT. Until 16 March 1949 the Constitution of the Argentine Republic was that of 1853, with modifications of 1860, 1866 and 1898. On the date mentioned a new constitution drafted by the Perón government and passed by the Constitutional Convention elected 5 Dec. 1948 came into force giving the Government great powers over the national economy. At a National Constituent Assembly held in Sante Fé Sept.–Nov. 1957 it was decided to revert to the 1853 constitution as amended up to 1898; thereafter the President and Vice-President were to be elected through electoral colleges by popular vote for 6-year terms. The President was not to be immediately re-elected. The Vice-President was to preside over the Senate. The President would be Commander-in-Chief of the Armed Services and would make appointments to all civil services and Judicial Offices. The President would be responsible with the Cabinet for the Executive. Both President and Vice-President must be Roman Catholic and of Argentine birth.

The National Congress consisted of a Senate and House of Deputies: the

Senate with 2 representatives from the Capital and each province (with a total of 46 seats), elected by popular vote for 9 years (one-third retiring every 3 years). The House of Deputies was to have 192 seats, each deputy being elected for 4 years and half the seats renewable each 2 years. The 2 Chambers meet annually from 30 Sept. to 2 May. Since 1912 voting has been free, secret and obligatory. Women were enfranchised on 9 Sept. 1947; beginning with the presidential election on 11 Nov. 1951, all women 18 years of age or older must vote. Equal suffrage was confirmed by a revisionary law of Aug. 1961.

The military leaders supported by the Navy and Air Force staged a coup d'état on 27 June 1966, and the temporary Revolutionary Junta of the Commanders-in-Chief of the three Armed Services deposed Dr Illia and his Government elected in 1963. The provincial governors were dismissed and the national and provincial legislatures dissolved, as were all political parties. A former Commander-in-Chief of the Army, Lieut.-Gen. Onganía, was appointed President and the Junta dissolved. The previous Constitution remained in force in so far as it was consistent with the statutes and objectives of the Revolution.

In Aug. 1967 a law was promulgated decreeing the registration of communists and excluding them from holding any public office, any position in employers' and workers' trade unions, and any teaching post in state and private schools.

The following is a list of Presidents from 1946 onwards:

Gen. Juan Domingo Perón, 4 June 1946–22 Sept. 1955. (Deposed.)
Gen. Eduardo Lonardi, 23 Sept.–13 Nov. 1955. (Deposed.)
Gen. Pedro Aramburu, 13 Nov. 1955–30 April 1958.
Dr Arturo Frondizi, 23 Feb. 1958–29 March 1962. (Deposed.)

Dr José Maria Guido, 29 March 1962–12 Oct. 1963.
Dr Arturo Illia, 12 Oct. 1963–June 1966. (Deposed.)
Gen. Juan Carlos Onganía. 29 June 1966–June 1970. (Deposed.)

President of the Republic: Brig.-Gen. Robert Marcelo Levingston, assumed power on 18 June 1970.

The Cabinet, appointed by the President, consists of 5 ministers (Interior, Foreign Affairs and Worship, Economy and Labour, Defence, Social Welfare). The Minister of the Interior has 4 Secretaries responsible to him: Government, Culture and Education, Justice and Communications. The Minister of Economy and Labour has 7: Agriculture and Livestock, Finance, Industry and Commerce, Labour, Public Works, and Transport. The Minister of Social Welfare has 4: Housing, Health, Social Security and Community Assistance.

The Secretaryships of State for War, Navy and Air Force have been assumed by the commanders-in-chief of the Services.

National flag: Sky-blue, white and sky-blue (equal, horizontal); with a rising sun on the white band.

National anthem: Oid, mortales, el grito sagrado Libertad (words by V. López y Planes, 1813; tune by J. Blas Parera).

LOCAL GOVERNMENT. From 1958 until the June 1966 Revolution apart from the period March 1962 to Oct. 1963, the governors were elected for terms of either 3 or 4 years. The Provinces elected their own Legislature and have control over their own internal affairs. After the Revolution of June 1966 the governors were appointed by the President and are responsible to him.

Ravignani, Emilio, *Asambleas Constituyentes Argentinas.* 6 vols. Buenos Aires, 1939
Rivarola, R., *La Constitucion Argentina y sus Principios de Etica Política.* Rosario, 1944

AREA AND POPULATION. The Argentine Republic consists of 22 provinces, 1 federal district, and the National Territories of Tierra del Fuego, the Antarctic and the South Atlantic Islands (census of 1960 and census of 1970) as follows:

Provinces	Area: sq. km, 1960	Population: census, 1960 (1,000)	Population: census, 1970[3] (1,000)	Pop. per sq. km, 1965
Litoral				
Federal Capital (Buenos Aires)	200	3,040	2,972	17,061·0
Buenos Aires (La Plata)	307,804	7,139	8,733	24·2
Corrientes	88,199	559	564	6·75
Entre Ríos (Paraná)	76,216	825	812	11·7
Chaco (Resistencia)	99,633	559	567	6·3
Santa Fé	133,007	1,928	2,136	15·7
Formosa	72,066	189	234	2·8
Misiones (Posadas)	29,801	415	443	14·9
Norte				
Jujuy	53,219	253	302	5·1
Salta	154,775	435	510	3·0
Santiago del Estero	135,254	489	495	3·9
Tucumán	22,524	818	766	39·2
Centro				
Córdoba	168,766	1,829	2,060	11·8
La Pampa (Santa Rosa)	143,440	161	172	1·2
San Luis	76,748	180	183	2·5
Andina				
Catamarca	99,818	179	172	1·9
La Rioja	92,331	133	136	1·6
Mendoza	150,839	869	973	6·25
San Juan	86,137	370	384	4·65
Neuquén	94,078	116	155	1·4
Patagonia				
Chubut (Rawson)	224,686	151	190	0·73
Río Negro (Viedma)	203,013	203	263	1·1
Santa Cruz (R. Gallegos)	243,943	55	84	0·16
Tierra del Fuego (Ushuaia)	20,912	7	13	0·38
Grand total	2,777,815[1]	20,900[2]	..	8·3

[1] Total area claimed was 2,808,602 sq. km (1,084,120 sq. miles).
[2] The official census including the 'Antarctic Sector', and stated to comprise the 'Malvinas' (Falklands), South Orcadas (Orkneys), South Georgias, South Sandwich Islands and the 'sovereign territories of Argentina in the Antarctic'; pop. 3,300.
[3] Provisional.

Estimated registered voters, 31 Dec. 1966, were 6·37m. men and 6·31m. women; total, 12·68m. In 1961 the urban population, *i.e.*, in communities of 2,000 or more inhabitants, was 61·4% of the total; 8 cities of 100,000 or more inhabitants accounted for 39·3% of the total.

The population is overwhelmingly European in origin (principally from Italy and Spain) with little mixture with the aborigines. The dwindling Indian population is estimated at from 20,000 to 30,000. Immigration was, under the Perón Constitution, restricted to white persons, exception being made for the relatives of non-white persons (Japanese, etc.) already resident. An agreement signed in Buenos Aires on 19 Oct. 1964 provided for immigration of French subjects formerly resident in North Africa.

Movement of population:

	Births	Deaths	Immigrants	Emigrants
1964	496,256	193,141	905,644	878,385
1965	481,814	196,467	966,081	939,571
1966	479,396	194,450	967,700	959,200
1967	480,459	195,224	1,038,000	1,008,900
1968	..	..	1,136,900	1,116,400

The population of the capital, Buenos Aires (census 1960), was 2,966,816; and, in 1,000: Rosario, 672; Córdoba, 589; La Plata, 330; Mar del Plata, 320; Tucumán, 287; Santa Fé, 260; Paraná, 174; Bahía Blanca, 150; Mendoza, 104.

Canals, S., *Poblaciones indígenas de la Argentina*. Buenos Aires, 1953
Serrano, A., *Los aborígenes argentinos*. Buenos Aires, 1947

RELIGION. The Roman Catholic religion is supported by the State.
In 1888, civil marriage was established in the republic. Divorce was made legal in Dec. 1954 but ceased to be so by a decree of 1 March 1956.

R

The Department of Worship is under the Ministry of Foreign Affairs. The tax exemption enjoyed by some religious establishments has been derogated. There are at present 2 Cardinal-Archbishops, 11 Archbishops and 46 bishops. The clergy has 10 seminaries. On 10 Oct. 1966 Argentina returned to the Vatican the right to appoint bishops and archbishops, who had been nominated by the Argentine Government since 1853.

EDUCATION. Education is free (subsidized by the central and provincial governments), secular and compulsory for children from 6 to 14 years of age. In 1968 the 25,609 primary schools had 3,480,534 pupils and 180,423 teachers. In 1968, 3,906 secondary, normal and special schools had 887,236 pupils and 122,394 teachers, and (1952) 1,132 incorporated secondary schools had 153,926 pupils. Of the 12·68m. registered voters in Argentina on 31 Dec. 1966, 9·1% were illiterate.

There are national universities at Córdoba (founded 1613), with, 1966, 47,000 students; Buenos Aires (1821), with 81,000 students; La Plata (1897), with 57,000 students; Tucumán (1914), with 8,000 students; the National University of the Litoral, in Santa Fé, with branches in Rosario (1920), and in Corrientes (1920), with 15,000 students; the National University of Cuyo, with 14,700 students, and that of the North-East, with 4,300 students. In 1956 the Technological Institute in Bahía Blanca was raised to the status of 'Universidad del Sur'; (1968) 7,000 students. Since 29 July 1966 these formerly autonomous institutions are under the authority of the Ministry of Education.

CINEMAS (1966). Cinemas number 2,158, with seating capacity of 1·1m.

NEWSPAPERS (1966). Daily newspapers numbered over 400, with an aggregate daily circulation of 3,250,000; 75% of this was shared by the dailies of Buenos Aires.

Ygabone, A. D., *El problema educacional en la Patagonia*. Buenos Aires, 1948
Zuretti, J. C., *Compendio de la historia de la educación general y argentina*. Buenos Aires, 1948

WELFARE. Free medical attention is obtainable from public hospitals. Many trade unions provide medical, dental and maternity services for their members and dependants. Welfare services are scanty in places distant from urban centres. A Ministry of Social Welfare was set up in 1966.

JUSTICE. Justice is administered by federal and provincial courts. The former deal only with cases of a national character, or in which different provinces or inhabitants of different provinces are parties. The chief federal court is the Supreme Court, with 5 judges at Buenos Aires. Other federal courts are the appeal courts, at Buenos Aires, Bahía Blanca, La Plata, Córdoba, Mendoza, Tucumán and Resistencia. Each province has its own judicial system, with a Supreme Court (generally so designated) and several minor chambers. Trial by jury is established by the Constitution for criminal cases, but never practised, except occasionally in the provinces of Buenos Aires and Córdoba.

A new code of civil and commercial procedures came into force on 1 Feb. 1968.

The police force is centralized under the Federal Security Council.

FINANCE. Currency. The monetary system is on a gold-exchange standard, the unit for foreign transactions being, nominally, the *peso oro* (gold peso) and for domestic transactions, the *peso moneda nacional* (paper peso), legal tender for all domestic debts.

The gold peso weighs 1·6129 grammes of gold 0·900 fine; it is divided into 100 *centavos*, but gold is not in circulation. Circulation consists chiefly of paper notes (issued since 1897) ranging from 10,000 down to 50 pesos. The coins actually circulating, 1968, were steel–nickel, 25, 10, 5, 1 peso and 50 centavos. The government is considering (1969) the possibility of introducing a 'new peso', equivalent to 100 of the present units of currency. It has been officially stated that the change will begin gradually from Jan. 1970, to allow time for the consolidation of monetary stability and the design of new notes.

Due to constant inflation, the international value of the peso has fallen steadily.

In Oct. 1955 it was 18 to US$1; in Dec. 1965 it was officially 189 to US$1. The buying and selling of foreign exchange is now controlled, and with certain minor exceptions may only be through authorized institutions. In Sept. 1969 the rate of exchange was officially 350 to US$1 and 835·40 to £1 (selling).

Monetary circulation, 622,200m. pesos on 31 Dec. 1967. Gold and foreign-exchange reserves were equal to US$331·5m. on 30 April 1967.

Budget. The financial year commences on 1 Nov. Budget estimates of total ordinary receipts and expenditures in 1m. paper pesos:

	1964	1965	1966	1967	1968	1969
Revenue	205,925	293,921	338,656	524,510	639,870	977,300
Expenditure	298,128	359,423	480,100	620,500	688,400	1,020,500

Proposed government expenditure for 1968 includes: Education, 152,000m.; social welfare, 43,300m.; defence, 152,300m.; economic development, 372,700m.; public debt service, 66,600m.

Total foreign investments at 31 Dec. 1959 were estimated at US$1,991m. including USA, 31·1% and UK, 20%. Further important investments in chemicals, motor vehicles, oil refineries and the manufacture of machinery have taken place since then, totalling over US$286m.

The national foreign debt in Sept. 1969 totalled about US$545m.

DEFENCE. Army. The Army is a National Militia, service in which is compulsory for all citizens from their 20th to their 45th year. Naturalized citizens are exempt for a period of 10 years. For the first 10 years the men belong to the 'active' Army, or first line. After completing 10 years in the first line the men pass to the National Guard, and serve in it for another 10 years, finishing their service with 5 years in the Territorial Guard; the latter is mobilized only in case of war. The period of continuous service, or training in the ranks with the permanent forces, is for 1 year for the Army or Air Force, and 2 years for the Navy. The reservists can be called out for training periodically.

The territory of the republic is divided into 5 military districts for administrative purposes. The Army is organized in 4 army corps; it consists of 6 infantry brigades, 2 mountain brigades, 1 airborne brigade, 2 mechanized brigades and 10 artillery regiments.

In 1965 the army was 80,000 strong, of whom 60,000 were National Service men and the remainder, an officer corps of 5,000 and 15,000 n.c.o.s, all of whom were career regulars.

The trained reserve numbers about 250,000, of whom 200,00 belong to the National Guard and 50,000 to the Territorial Guard. The territorial reserve numbers 100,000 men.

Navy. Principal ships of the Argentine Navy:

Completed	Name	Standard displacement Tons	Armour Belt In.	Armour Guns In.	Principal armament	Torpedo tubes	Shaft horsepower	Speed Knots
			Aircraft Carriers					
1946	Independencia[1]	14,000	—	—	⎱ 21 planes	—	40,000	24·0
1945	Veinicinco de Mayo[2]	15,892	—	—	⎰ (capacity); light A.A.			
			Cruisers					
1939	⎱ General Belgrano[3]	10,800 ⎱	4	3–5	15 6-in., 8 5-in.	—	100,000	32·5
	⎰ Nueve de Julio[3]	10,500 ⎰						
1939	La Argentina	6,000	3	2	9 6-in.	6	54,000	30·0

[1] Ex-*Warrior*, purchased from the UK in 1958.
[2] Ex-*Karel Doorman*, purchased from the Netherlands in 1968, ex-*Venerable*, purchased from UK in 1948.
[3] Ex-*Phoenix* and ex-*Boise*, purchased from the USA in 1951.

There are also 2 submarines, 9 destroyers, 3 frigates, 2 corvettes, 2 torpedo boats, 4 coastal minesweepers, 2 minehunters, 9 patrol vessels, 3 patrol craft, 3 survey ships, 2 training ships, 5 transports, 5 oilers, 6 landing ships, 25 landing craft, 1 icebreaker, 1 salvage vessel and 15 tugs.

The active personnel of the Navy comprises about 2,300 officers and 31,000 men (including about 11,000 conscripts), who have to serve 2 years. There is a corps of coast artillery of 450 men, a naval school and a school of mechanics.

The Naval Aviation Service, formed on 17 Oct. 1919, has some 2,000 personnel, in 4 wings. Aircraft include a small number of jet-powered Grumman Panthers and Aermacchi M.B326 light attack aircraft, 6 P-2H Neptune and 6 S-2A Tracker anti-submarine aircraft, navalized Harvard trainers, and 45 North American armed T-28s bought from France, of which only the last 3 types can be launched from Argentine aircraft carriers with existing equipment; various training, transport and general purpose aircraft, including helicopters.

Air Force. The Air Force, founded on 10 Aug. 1912 and autonomous since 4 Jan. 1945, includes an Air Operation Command responsible for all flight operations, a Personnel Command responsible for training units and a Supply Command. The operational units form 5 air brigades, each with up to 3 groups of approximate squadron strength operating from a single base. There is a Military Aviation College at Córdoba; the main flying school is at El Palomar. Equipment includes 10 Canberra twin-jet bombers and 2 Canberra trainers acquired from the UK in 1970, about 30 Paris light jet combat, liaison and training aircraft of French design, 20 US-built F-86F Sabre jet-fighters, 48 A-4B Skyhawk strike aircraft supplied by USA, some obsolescent British-built Meteor F4 jet fighter-bombers and 14 Hughes OH-6A/Model 500 helicopters. The Meteors are being replaced by 12 Mirage IIIE fighter-bombers and 2 Mirage IIID trainers ordered from France in 1970. The remaining aircraft are mostly transports, including turboprop C-130E Hercules, F.27 Friendships, Twin Otters and Guarani IIs built in the national aircraft factory at Córdoba, piston-engined DC-6s, C-54s and C-47s, and multi-purpose twin-engined Huanquero utility transport/trainers. The Huanqueros were built in the Córdoba factory, which also assembled Mentor trainers of US design. A counter-insurgency group is equipped with Iroquois helicopters. The Air Force also operates a twin-jet Fokker F.28 as the Presidential transport. Total strength of the Air Force is about 15,000 personnel and 375 aircraft.

AGRICULTURE. Argentina has an area of about 670,251,000 acres, of which about 41% is pasture land, 32% woodland and 11% (73·73m. acres) cultivated. It was estimated (1966) that 30m. hectares were cultivated by the country's 110,600 tractors.

Argentina's wealth is based on agriculture and livestock. With 51·47m. cattle she ranks fourth (eclipsed by India, 160m.; USA, 96m., and USSR, 70m.), but as an exporter of raw meat (excluding Denmark's exceptional trade in bacon) she has long led the world (pre-war average, 662,000 metric tons). In 1965 exports amounted to 483,300 metric tons carcase weight (1966: 455,038 tons) out of a total production of 2·09m. tons.

The livestock estimate (1967) showed: Cattle, 54·9m.; sheep, 46m.; pigs, 3·5m.; horses (1960), 4,846,500. The Province of Buenos Aires has 38% of the cattle. Wool production, 1968–69, was estimated at 180,000 tons. Exports in the wool year ending 30 Sept. 1968, 159,700 tons. Butter production (1965), 42,300 tons; cheese, 151,300 metric tons; 22,000 metric tons of casein were exported.

Wheat production usually exceeds 6m. metric tons, ahead of Australia but well behind Canada and US. Other cereals and linseed are also important.

Crop statistics with area (in 1,000 hectares) and production (in 1,000 metric tons) are shown as follows:

	1967–68		1968–69		1969–70	
	Area	Output	Area	Output	Area	Output
Wheat	6,613	7,320	6,680	5,740	6,239	7,020
Linseed	711	385	889	510	952	640
Maize	4,473	6,560	4,595	6,860	4,666	9,440
Oats	1,193	690	1,299	490	1,129	425
Barley	882	588	1,011	556	945	570
Rye	2,286	352	2,500	360	2,489	377
Sunflower seed	1,194	940	1,354	876	1,443	1,100
Sugar-cane	193	9,500	201	10,680	..	..

The total grain and meat exports, in metric tons:

	Wheat	Maize	Barley	Meat
1967	2,059,712	4,317,000	65,115	550,451
1968	2,421,120	2,892,400	181,628	409,191
1969	2,344,278	4,023,964	208,454	580,623

Argentina's meat exports are calculated in terms of actual weight; not 'carcase weight', as is the international practice.

Cotton, potatoes, vine, tobacco, citrus fruit, olives, rice, soya and yerba maté (Paraguayan tea) are also cultivated. There are 36 cane-sugar mills and 1 beet-sugar factory. Potato harvest, 1965–66, amounted to 1,356,600 metric tons. The area under tobacco, 1965–66, was 62,300 hectares; output (1964–65), 52,500 metric tons. Production of yerba maté, 1965, was 117,000 metric tons. Production of cotton in 1965–66 amounted to 90,200 metric tons of fibre (133,200 tons in 1963–64) and (1964–65) 266m. tons of seed; cotton fibre exports, 1965, were worth US$1,402,000.

Before the Second World War the country was the largest grower and shipper of linseed (flaxseed), but, preferring to convert it into oil, virtually no linseed was exported from 1946 until April 1950, when it was resumed. Exports, 1965, were valued US$49,758,000. Sunflower seed, first grown by Russian immigrants in 1900, now furnishes the country's most popular edible oil. Production of tung oils, 1965, 174,500 metric tons. There are more than 10m. olive trees, of which 48% are in Mendoza. Production in 1964 was 10,304 tons. 58,660 tons of groundnut oil were produced in 1964 (mainly in Córdoba). Argentina's 20 quebracho extract factories produced 109,000 tons of extract in 1965; exports, 1964, 104,000 metric tons. Argentina is the world's largest source of tannin. Woodpulp is produced from 28 factories having about 191,000 tons total capacity; actual output keeps about 25% below this level.

Flour-milling ranks second to refrigeration. In 1964–65 Argentine mills produced 2,259,400 tons of flour.

FISHERIES. The Banco de la Nación has outlined a plan to increase fish production from 121,000 in 1963 to 200,000 tons a year. 6,636 tons of fish-meal were produced in 1963, compared with 903 tons in 1961. On 5 Jan. 1968 a government decree extended Argentina's territorial waters to 200 miles offshore. Fishing by foreign vessels inside this limit up to 12 miles from the coast would be granted.

MINING. Mining is of mainly local importance. Since 1954 it has been under state control. Argentina produced 472,300 tons of washed coal in 1968 (Río Turbio, with reserves of 300m. tons). Gold (500 fine oz., 1963), silver (1,318,150 fine oz. in 1962) and copper are worked in Catamarca, where there are also 2 tin-mines, and gold and copper in San Juan, La Rioja and the south-western territories. Iron ore (225,736 metric tons in 1967), tungsten (1,800 short tons of ore in 1962), beryllium (268,623 metric tons in 1967), mica (45 short tons in 1958), lead (42,726 tons in 1967), barites (13,800 short tons in 1963), zinc (54,408 short tons in 1967), manganese (11,000 short tons in 1963) and limestone are produced. Crude oil production in 1968 was 19·95m. cu. metres.

INDUSTRY. On 30 July 1954 a census showed 621,329 firms, of which 181,763 (employing 1,536,530 men and women) were in manufacturing and mining, 417,423 (employing 1,230,466) were in commerce and 22,143 (employing 163,916) were in construction. Of the total employed in this non-agricultural sector, 2,355,546 were men and 565,366 (19%) were women.

The National Development Plan, 1965–69, was abandoned and another is at present (1970) in preparation.

Cotton yarn produced in 1967 amounted to 83,000 tons. Cement output, 1968, was 4·2m. metric tons. 1965 production of pig-iron was 662,500 tons;

crude steel (1968), 1·55m. tons; finished rolled products, 1,843,000 tons. Electric power production, 1968, was 13,496,559 kwh.

TOURISM. In 1966, 323,159 tourists visited Argentina, contributing about US$52·3m. to the economy.

TRADE UNIONS. According to the 1965 national census of workers' associations there are 502 trade unions with a total of nearly 1,764,700 paying members. Of these unions 240 are connected with manufacturing industries, 5 with construction, 36 with gas, water, electricity and sanitary services, 70 with commerce, 62 with transport, storage and communications and 117 with other services. The majority of these unions are affiliated to the General Confederation of Labour. The economically active population was estimated at the end of 1964 to total 8,422,700, of which 6,623,700 were males and 1,799,000 females. The main groups are agriculture and fishing (19%), manufacturing industries (20%), commerce (12%) and other services (28%).

Legal status which confers authority to negotiate wage agreements and other privileges is granted by the Secretary of Labour (Ministry of Economy and Labour) to one union in each industry or activity. The minimum wage law provides for a twice-yearly adjustment of the minimum wage to take account of cost-of-living changes. On 1 May 1966 the minimum monthly wage for a family consisting of a man, wife and 2 children were fixed at 22,500 pesos and that for a single man at 15,750 pesos.

The Trade Union Law was revised by decree in 1966. Political activity within the unions is prohibited, finances are placed under government supervision and all strikes must be decided by a two-thirds majority obtained by secret ballot.

COMMERCE. The control of imports by permits and quotas was abolished on 30 Dec. 1958. Exchange controls were re-imposed in April 1964.

Import values include charges for carriage, insurance and freight; export values are on a f.o.b. basis. Real values of foreign trade (in US$1m.), exclusive of coin and bullion:

	1962	1963	1964	1965	1966	1967	1968	1969
Imports	1,356·5	978·0	1,077·2	1,199	1,124	1,096	1,169	1,576
Exports	1,216·0	1,365·1	1,410·4	1,493	1,593	1,465	1,368	1,612

Principal imports, 1969	US$1m.	Principal exports, 1969	US$1m.
Vegetable products	87·3	Animals and animal products	359·9
Mineral products	133·9	Vegetable products	508·9
Chemical products	184·6	Animal and vegetable oils	87·1
Paper manufactures	104·1	Food, drink, tobacco	253·6
Wood manufactures	79·3	Mineral products	13·5
Base metals	320·8	Chemical products	57·0
Machinery and electrical equipment	368·3	Hides and skins	103·7
Transport equipment	100·5	Textiles	104·4

Trade by countries in market values (in US$1m.):

Imports from	1968	1969	Exports to	1968	1969
Brazil	138·5	174·5	Brazil	129·1	130·1
France	41·1	51·3	Belgium	60·1	55·6
Germany (West)	127·5	173·7	France	45·3	60·9
Italy	74·1	105·9	Germany (West)	66·5	73·5
Japan	41·6	65·1	Italy	197·5	229·6
Netherlands West Indies	20·3	32·5	Japan	29·1	72·1
UK	78·7	92·8	Netherlands	135·9	169·3
USA	269·9	345·7	UK	105·0	155·3
Venezuela	35·0	38·4	USA	157·3	140·2

Total trade (British Board of Trade returns) between Argentina and UK (in £1,000 sterling):

	1965	1966	1967	1968	1969	1970
Imports to UK	71,464	70,578	72,136	51,686	78,740	65,598
Exports from UK	26,843	23,150	24,859	33,503	46,189 }	44,065
Re-exports from UK	655	198	419	334	754 }	

COMMUNICATIONS. From 1 Nov. 1948 all land, sea, river and air transport was under the control of the Ministry of Transport.

SHIPPING. The merchant fleet, 31 Dec. 1954 (registered with Lloyds), consisted of 400 vessels (over 100 gross tons) of 1,070,995 gross tons; the tanker fleet had 56 vessels of 340,421 gross tons. The total was 1·02m. GRT in Dec. 1966.

The state-owned ocean and river fleet (1963) included 216 vessels of over 1,000 GRT which totalled 1,200,061 GRT.

RAILWAYS. On 1 March 1948 Argentina became the owner of her entire railway system, consisting of 18 different railways with a total length of 42,193 km. (Sole exception was a railway, 900 km of metre-gauge line, belonging to the Province of Buenos Aires, not nationalized until 20 Aug. 1951.) The amalgamation brought together 7 government railways (mostly small) with 8,347 miles (and some 12% of the aggregate revenue), 3 French-owned railways (2,660 miles and 7% of the revenue) and 8 British-owned railways (15,561 miles and 80% of the revenue). Legal formalities were completed on 5 May 1949. For details see THE STATESMAN'S YEAR-BOOK, 1949, p. 746. The present system comprises 6 railways with a total route-mileage of 24,573 (metre, 4 ft 8½ in. and 5 ft 6 in. gauges).

Goods traffic on the railways had declined since 1945 (total, 1958, 28·4m. tons; 1964, 21·3m.; 1968, 19·8m.), but passenger traffic rose from 188m. in 1942–43 to 579m. in 1954–55 and was 481m. in 1968.

ROADS. In 1969, 587,186 miles of national and provincial highways were open and 14% were metalled. The 4 main roads constituting Argentina's portion of the Pan-American Highway were opened to traffic in 1942. Motor vehicles are produced at some 11,000 per month, and in 1968 there were on the roads 1·5m. cars and (1964) 553,450 lorries and buses.

AVIATION. Commercial airlines flew a total of 50,995,500 km in 1968, carrying 2,122,000 passengers and 33·4m. tons of freight, of which air-mail was 1,608 tons. Lines operating international flights to and from Buenos Aires include BUA, Aerolíneas Argentinas, Air France, Iberia, Alitalia, KLM, Swissair, SAS, Canadian Pacific Airlines, Lufthansa and PANAM.

POST. In 1949 the telephone service was nationalized; instruments numbered 1,599,861 (1968), of which 768,615 were in Buenos Aires (Federal District). Privately owned exchanges operated 122,005 instruments. There were, in 1945, 4,382 post offices. There are (1964) 90 broadcasting stations and 10 television stations with 5·2m. viewers. Cable service to other Latin-American countries and US is provided by All-America Cables.

BANKING. A law promulgated 25 March 1946 nationalized the Central Bank (established in 1935), originally as an autonomous institution, but later, in Oct. 1949, placed under the Minister of Finance, who became president. Six decree-laws of Oct. 1957 have brought back a greater elasticity to the structure, especially as regards the deposits and loans of the private banks, which have regained their autonomy. The Central Bank continues the normal functions of a national institution.

On 31 July 1948 there were 44 banks, each with capital of 1m. paper pesos or over (including the Banco de la Nación, with 36% of the total assets of the banking system), consisting of 9 provincial banks, 25 domestic banks and 10 foreign banks, all of which are shareholders in the Central Bank. The Banco de la Nación (founded in 1891) has 306 branches and agencies, including one at Asunción, Paraguay. There are 5 Stock Exchanges.

WEIGHTS AND MEASURES. Since 1 Jan. 1887 the use of the metric system has been compulsory.

DIPLOMATIC REPRESENTATIVES

Argentina maintains embassies in:

Algeria (also for Libya)	Honduras	Pakistan
Australia	Hungary	Panama
Austria	India (also for Ceylon	Paraguay
Belgium (also for Luxem-	and Nepál)	Peru
bourg)	Indonesia	Philippines
Bolivia	Iran (also for Afgháni-	Poland
Brazil	stán)	Portugal
Bulgaria	Irish Republic	Romania
Cambodia	Israel	South Africa, Rep. of
Canada	Italy (also for Cyprus)	Spain
Chile	Jamaica	Sweden
China	Japan	Switzerland
Colombia	Lebanon (also for Jor-	Syria
Costa Rica	dan, Kuwait, Saudi	Thailand (also for Cam-
Czechoslovakia	Arabia)	bodia)
Denmark	Liberia	Trinidad and Tobago
Dominican Republic	Malaysia	Turkey
Ecuador	Mexico	USSR
El Salvador	Morocco (also for	UAR (also for Sudan)
Finland	Tunisia)	UK
France	Netherlands	USA
Germany (West)	New Zealand	Uruguay
Greece	Nigeria (also for Ghana)	Vatican (also for Malta)
Guatemala	Nicaragua	Venezuela
Haiti	Norway	Yugoslavia

OF ARGENTINA IN GREAT BRITAIN (9 Wilton Crescent, SW1)

Ambassador: Gen. Gustavo Martinez-Zuviria.

Ministers: Juan Carlos Marcelinos Beltramino; Leonardo A. Vartalitis; José Alberto del Carril.

Service Attachés: Cdre Francisco Cabrera (*Air and Army*), Rear-Adm. C. R. Perralta (*Navy*).

Counsellors: Enrique Jorge Ros; Edgardo E. Perez-Colman; Ramiro P. Arias; Santos Nestor Martinez.

There is a consular representative at London.

OF GREAT BRITAIN IN ARGENTINA

Ambassador: R. M. Hadow, CMG.

Minister: J. L. Taylor (*Commercial*). *Counsellor:* T. Peters, CMG (*Consul-General*).

Service Attachés: Capt. J. Hood, RN (*Navy*); Group Capt. J. F. C. Melrose, DFC (*Air*); Col. G. W. Croker, MBE, MC (*Defence and Army*).

First Secretaries: R. W. Whitney (*Head of Chancery*); H. Fletcher (*Information*); P. Voller (*Commercial*); A. J. Sims; G. J. Garrett.

There are Consuls at Rosario, La Plata and Córdoba,and there are Vice-Consuls at Cipoletti, Comodoro Rivadavia, Puerto Deseado, Río Gallegos, Río Grande (Tierra del Fuego), Salta, Santa Cruz and Trelew.

OF ARGENTINA IN THE USA (1600 New Hampshire Ave. NW, Washington, DC., 20009)

Ambassador: Pedro E. Real.

Ministers: Carlos de Posada, L. H. Forkin (*Financial*), Carlos Bochert. *Minister-Counsellor:* Rafael M. Vazquez.

Counsellors: Carlos A. Massa, Mario Alberto Campora. *Service Attachés:* Maj.-Gen. Ezequiel A. Martinez (*Air*), Brig.-Gen. Lewis A. Betty (*Army*), Capt. Juan D. Valero (*Navy*).

OF THE USA IN ARGENTINA

Ambassador: John Davis Lodge.
Deputy Chief of Mission: Mitton Barall. *Heads of Sections:* Herbert B. Thompson (*Political*); Joel W. Biller (*Economic*); Emil Castro (*Commercial*); Robert A. Bishton (*Consular*); James F. Magdanz (*Administrative*). *Service Attachés:* Col. Gordon M. Johnson (*Air*), Col. William A. Gresham (*Army*), Capt. Raymond E. Ford (*Navy*).

There is a Consul at Córdoba.

BOOKS OF REFERENCE

Boletin del comercio exterior Argentino y estadisticas económicas retrospectivas. Annual
Anuario de comercio exterior de la República Argentina. Annual
Economic Review, Banco de la Nación. Buenos Aires
Síntesis Estadística Mensual. Dirección General de Estadistica. Buenos Aires, 1947 ff.
Boletín Internacional de Bibliografía Argentina. Ministry of Foreign Relations. Buenos Aires. Monthly
Geografía de la República Argentino. Ed. by the Sociedad Argentina de Estudios Geográficos. 7 vols. Buenos Aires, 1945–53.
Argentine Economic Policy. Buenos Aires, 1967
Bridges, E. L., *Uttermost Part of the Earth* [*Tierra del Fuego*]. New York, 1949
Daus, F. A., *Geografía de la Argentina.* 2 vols. Buenos Aires, 1946–53
Ferns, H. S., *Britain and Argentina in the 19th century.* OUP, 1960
Ferrer, A., *Argentina.* New York, 1969
Pendle, G., *Argentina.* R. Inst. of Int. Affairs. 3rd augmented ed., 1963
Romero, José Luis, *A History of Argentine political thought.* Stanford and O.U.P. 1963
Santillán, Diego A. de (ed.), *Gran Enciclopedia Argentina.* 9 vols. 1956–64
Scobie, J. R., *Argentina, A city and a nation.* New York and OUP, 1964
Tornquist, Ernesto, & Co. Ltd., *Business Conditions in Argentina.* Buenos Aires, from 1916; monthly from Jan. 1968

AUSTRIA

Republik Österreich

CONSTITUTION AND GOVERNMENT. Austria recovered its sovereignty and independence on 27 July 1955 by the coming into force of the Austrian State Treaty between the United Kingdom, the United States of America, the Soviet Union and France on the one part and the Republic of Austria on the other part (signed on 15 May).

On 12 March 1938 Austria was forcibly absorbed in the German Reich until it was liberated by the American, British, French and Soviet armies in spring 1945. Already in the Moscow Declaration of Oct. 1943, Great Britain, the USA and the USSR had resolved upon the re-establishment of a free and independent Austria.

On 27 April 1945 Dr Karl Renner set up a provisional government which restored the Republic of Austria in the spirit of the Constitution of 1920/29, and was recognized by the Four-Power Allied Control Council on 20 Oct. 1945. The last occupation forces left Austria in Oct. 1955.

President of the Republic: Franz Jonas, former Lord Mayor of Vienna, elected on 23 May 1965 by 2,324,474 votes against 2,206,992 cast for Dr Alfons Gorbach, former Federal Chancellor.

On 1 March 1970 the elections were held for the National Assembly, which returned 81 Socialists (74 at the elections of 6 March 1966), 78 People's Party (85), 6 Freedom Party (8).

The government of the Socialist Party which was formed in April 1970 was composed as follows:

Chancellor: Dr Bruno Kreisky.
Vice-Chancellor and Social Welfare: Ing. Rudolf Häuser. *Foreign Affairs:* Dr Rudolf Kirchschläger. *Interior:* Otto Rösch. *Agriculture and Forestry:* Ing. Dr Oskar Weihs. *Transport:* Erwin Frühbauer. *Justice:* Dr Christian Broda. *Finance:* Dr Hannes Androsch. *Education and the Arts:* Leopold Gratz. *Trade, Commerce and Industry:* Dr Josef Staribacher. *Defence:* Karl Lütgendorf. *Construction and Technology:* Josef Moser. *Science and Research:* Dr Hertha Firnberg.

National flag: Red, white, red (horizontal).
National anthem: Land der Berge, Land am Strome (words by Paula Preradovic; tune by W. A. Mozart).

The official language is German.

LOCAL GOVERNMENT. The Republic of Austria comprises 9 provinces (Vienna, Lower Austria, Upper Austria, Salzburg, Styria, Carinthia, Tirol, Vorarlberg, Burgenland). There is in every province an elected Provincial Assembly.

Every commune has a Council, which chooses one of its number to be head of the Commune (burgomaster) and a committee for the administration and execution of its resolutions.

Adamovich, L., *Grundris des österreichischen Verfassungsrechts.* 8th ed. Vienna 1953
Gsteu, H., *Länderkunde Österreichs.* Wien, 1948

AREA AND POPULATION. For the boundaries of Austria according to the Treaty of St Germain, signed in Sept. 1919, *see* THE STATESMAN'S YEAR-BOOK, 1920, pp. 674–75.

Provinces	Area, sq. km	Population (census 21 March 1961)	Percentage of population	Population per sq. km
Vienna (Wien)	415	1,627,566	23·0	3,962
Lower Austria (Niederösterreich)	19,170	1,374,012	19·4	72
Burgenland	3,965	271,001	3·8	68
Upper Austria (Oberösterreich)	11,978	1,131,623	16·0	94
Salzburg	7,155	347,292	4·9	49
Styria (Steiermark)	16,384	1,137,865	16·1	69
Carinthia (Kärnten)	9,533	495,226	7·0	52
Tirol	12,648	462,899	6·6	37
Vorarlberg	2,601	226,323	3·2	87
Total	83,849[1]	7,073,807	100·0	84

[1] 32,366 sq. miles.

VITAL STATISTICS for calendar years:

	Live births	Still births	Deaths[1]	Marriages	Divorces	Emigration Austrians	Others
1966	128,158	1,448	91,036	55,684	8,643	1,190	3,305
1967	127,069	1,368	95,438	56,065	8,880	1,160	4,469
1968	125,792	1,359	95,679	56,001	9,705	1,372	11,353

[1] Excluding still births.

The population of the principal towns (excluding Vienna), according to the census of 21 March 1961 was as follows:

Graz	237,080	St Pölten	40,112	Dornbirn	28,075	Krems a.d.D.	21,046
Linz	195,978	Steyr	38,306	Kapfenberg	23,894	Feldkirch	17,343
Salzburg	108,114	Leoben	36,257	Klosterneu-		Mödling	17,274
Innsbruck	100,695	Wiener		burg	22,787	Bruck an	
Klagenfurt	69,218	Neustadt	33,845	Baden	22,484	der Mur	16,087
Wels	41,060	Villach	32,971	Bregenz	21,428	Traun	16,026

In the case of conurbations, the towns proper had the following populations: Innsbruck, 28,560; Wels, 37,687; St Pölten, 26,417; Leoben, 13,099; Kapfenberg, 5,132; Dornbirn, 27,971; Klosterneuburg, 13,532; Krems, 14,141; Bruck, 11,516; Traun, 6,260.

RELIGION. In 1961 there were 6,295,075 Roman Catholics (88·99%), 438,663 Protestants (6·2%), 70,087 others (0·99%), 266,009 without religious allegiance (3·76%) and 3,973 (0·06%) unknown. The Roman Catholic Church has 2 archbishoprics and 7 bishoprics.

EDUCATION (1969–70). There were in Austria 5,216 elementary and special schools with 41,721 teachers and 916,290 pupils. Of all kinds of secondary schools there were 476 with 186,643 pupils.

There were also 40 commercial academies with 9,429 students and 1,627 teachers. There were 73 schools of technical and industrial training (including schools of hotel management and catering) with 2,756 teachers and 17,096 pupils; 14 schools of women's professions (secondary level) with 848 teachers and 2,394 pupils; 4 training colleges of social workers with 143 pupils. In 1968–69, 76 trade schools had 683 teachers and 16,162 pupils.

Austria has 4 universities maintained by the State, viz., Vienna (2,142 teachers, 18,506 students), Graz 867 teachers, 6,687 students), Innsbruck (806 teachers, 6,130 students) and Salzburg (377 teachers, 2,528 students). There are also 2 technical universities at Vienna (681 teachers, 6,480 students) and Graz (408 teachers, 3,675 students), a mining college at Leoben (150 teachers, 635 students), an agricultural college at Vienna (202 teachers, 1,260 students), a veterinary college at Vienna (151 teachers, 447 students) and commercial colleges at Vienna (166 teachers, 3,671 students) and Linz (146 teachers and 1,382 students).

There are also an academy of fine arts at Vienna (74 teachers, 464 students); an academy of applied arts at Vienna (112 teachers, 527 students); 3 academies of music and dramatic art at Vienna (293 teachers, 400 students), Salzburg (127 teachers, 471 students) and Graz (156 teachers, 497 students).

CINEMAS (1968). There were 1,152 cinemas with a seating capacity of 114,044.

NEWSPAPERS (1970). There were 30 daily newspapers (7 of them in Vienna) with a combined circulation of 2m.

JUSTICE. The Supreme Court of Justice (*Oberster Gerichtshof*) in Vienna is the highest court in the land. Besides there are 4 higher provincial courts (*Oberlandesgerichte*), 18 provincial and district courts (*Landes- und Kreisgerichte*) and 229 local courts (*Bezirksgerichte*).

FINANCE. Currency. The Austrian unit of currency is the *schilling* of 100 *groschen*. The rate of exchange is £1 = 61·6 *schillings*, US$1 = 25·8 *schillings*.

Budget. The budget for calendar years provided revenue and expenditure (ordinary and extraordinary) as follows (in 1m. schillings):

	1965	1966	1967	1968	1969	1970	1971
Revenue	66,795	68,250	74,400	77,787	85,863	92,248	101,574
Expenditure	66,795	68,237	78,000	82,737	93,480	101,223	111,118

DEFENCE. The supreme command is vested in the Federal President; operational control is exercised by the Minister of Defence.

The army is organized in 3 groups: I (Vienna), 3 brigades; II (Graz), 2 brigades; III (Salzburg), 2 brigades. Strength (1968–69), 2,200 officers, 12,000 other ranks (including 6,000 long-term volunteers) and 33,000 soldiers under conscription.

The air force consists of a Flying Corps, a Signal Corps and an Anti-Aircraft Corps. Equipment includes 40 Saab-105Oe jet light attack and training aircraft, 2 Sikorsky S-65 heavy-duty helicopters, 2 Short Skyvan light STOL transports, and an operational helicopter group equipped with Agusta–Bell 204Bs and JetRangers, Alouette II and Alouette III. Other types in service include 20 Cessna O-1 Bird Dogs operated for Army support, 20 Swedish-built Saab Safir piston-engined basic trainers, and 11 French Magister jet trainers. Total strength in Jan. 1970 was 79 fixed-wing aircraft, 64 helicopters and about 6,000 personnel.

AGRICULTURE. In 1968 the total area sown amounted to 1,549,512 hectares. The chief products (area in hectares, yield in metric tons) were as follows:

	1967		1968		1969	
	Area	*Yield*	*Area*	*Yield*	*Area*	*Yield*
Wheat	316,319	1,045,402	305,595	1,044,709	286,100	950,228
Rye	138,651	377,150	142,229	413,298	147,100	439,896
Barley	231,702	772,210	238,396	769,979	273,800	433,706
Oats	123,789	335,691	118,880	324,063	101,800	288,263
Potatoes	133,833	3,048,976	130,243	3,473,076	112,600	2,940,545

Production of raw sugar in 1949, 66,700; 1955, 219,300; 1960, 308,000; 1965, 216,171; 1966, 327,773; 1967, 276,432; 1968, 269,310; 1969, 321,446 metric tons.

Livestock (Dec. 1969): Cattle, 2,417,930; pigs, 3,196,474; sheep, 121,190; goats, 69,399; horses, 52,642; poultry, 11,542,843.

FORESTRY. Felled timber, in cu. metres: 1960, 10,015,925; 1962, 9,638,062; 1964, 9,936,176; 1965, 10,398,058; 1966, 10,024,175; 1967, 10,680,293; 1968, 9,635,001; 1969, 10,468,800.

Land- und forstwirtschaftliche Betriebszählung 1960. 10 vols. Vienna, Statistisches Zentralamt, 1960–64

MINING. The mineral production (in metric tons) was as follows:

	1968	1969		1968	1969
Lignite	4,176,732	3,840,743	Pig-iron	2,473,815	2,815,536
Anthracite	—	—	Raw steel	3,467,482	3,926,316
Iron ore	3,482,100	3,982,000	Rolled steel	2,521,565	2,760,753
Lead and zinc ore[1]	199,505	204,638			
Copper ore[1]	179,379	182,993	Electric current		
Raw magnesite[1]	1,546,682	1,608,421	(m. kwh.)[2]		22,219

[1] Including recovery from slag.   [2] Total generation.

Austria is one of the world's largest sources of high-grade graphite. Production, which averaged 20,000 metric tons yearly from 1929 to 1944, dropped to 246 in 1946, but rose to 18,685 in 1956, 88,036 in 1960 and 102,237 in 1964, and fell again to 79,539 in 1966, 32,000 in 1967, 25,468 in 1968 and 25,825 in 1969.

The commercial production of petroleum began in the early 1930s. Production of crude oil (in metric tons): 1960, 2,448,391; 1965, 2,854,000; 1966, 2,757,113; 1967, 2,689,910; 1968, 2,724,347; 1969, 2,758,240.

Granigg, B., *Die Bodenschätze Österreichs.* Vienna, 1947

INDUSTRY. On 26 July 1946 the Austrian parliament passed a government bill, nationalizing some 70 industrial concerns. As from 17 Sept. 1946 ownership of the three largest commercial banks, most oil-producing and refining companies and the principal firms in the following industries devolved upon the Austrian state: River navigation; coal extraction; non-ferrous mining and refining; iron-ore mining; pig-iron and steel production; manufacture of iron and steel products, including structural material, machinery, railroad equipment and repairs, and shipbuilding; electrical machinery and appliances. Six companies supplying electric power were nationalized in accordance with a law of 26 March 1947.

In 1968 the percentage of the production of nationalized industries in relation to total production was as follows: Copper ore, lead–zinc ore, chemical fertilizers, 100%; pig-iron, 99·9%; iron ore, 100%; raw steel, 95·3%; coal, 90·4%; rolled steel, 95·5%; electrical energy, 82·8%; aluminium, 87·1%.

Tourism is an important industry. In 1969, 21,036 hotels and boarding-houses had a total of 470,261 beds available; 7,841,568 foreigners visited Austria; of these, 433,303 came from the UK and 553,369 from the USA.

Österreichs Industrie 1962 und 1963. Vienna, Statistisches Zentralamt, 1964
Österreichs verstaatliche Industrie. Vienna, Statistisches Zentralamt, 1953
Fremdenverkehr in Österreich. Vienna, Statistisches Zentralamt, from 1952/53

COMMERCE. Excluded from the Austrian customs territory are the 2 Austrian communes of Jungholz and Mittelberg which, because of their isolated location on the Bavarian slope of the Alps, have been united in a customs union with Germany since 1868 and 1890 respectively.

Imports and exports are as follows (excluding precious metal):

	Imports			Exports		
	1967	1968	1969	1967	1968	1969
Quantity (1,000 metric tons)	16,015	18,567	9,660	7,869	8,299	9.002
Value (m. sch.)	60,045	64,925	73,460	47,013	51,704	62,723

The total trade between UK and Austria (British Board of Trade returns) was as follows (in £1,000 sterling):

	1966	1967	1968	1969	1970
Imports to UK	27,799	41,681	58,461	64,123	79,596
Exports from UK	40,784	38,605	50,949	69,356 ⎱	90,706
Re-exports from UK	1,787	1,844	2,018	1,892 ⎰	

Statistik des Aussenhandels [from 1964: *Der Aussenhandel*] *Österreichs.* Vienna, Statistisches Zentralamt. Annually 1949–50; quarterly from 1951

SHIPPING. Austria has no sea frontiers, but the Danube is an important waterway. Goods traffic (in metric tons): 6,545,087 in 1966; 5,508,503 in 1967; 7,201,481 in 1968; 6,402,377 in 1969. Coal and coke and, from 1956, mineral oil products comprise in bulk almost two-thirds of these cargoes. The Danube Steamship Co. (DDSG) is the main Austrian shipping company.

RAILWAYS. Austrian railways have been nationalized since before the First World War. Length of track (1970), 5,908 km, of which 2,414 km were electrified. Nine private railways have a total length of 590 km. Passengers in 1969 numbered 158m.

ROADS. On 1 Jan. 1969 federal roads had a total length of 9,258 km, 442 km autobahn; provincial roads, 22,391 km. On 31 Dec. 1969 there were registered 2,208,896 motor vehicles, including 1,124,183 passenger cars, 112,958 lorries, 230,920 tractors and 81,468 trailers.

AVIATION. Austria has 6 airports in Vienna (Schwechat), Linz, Salzburg, Graz, Klagenfurt and Innsbruck. In 1969, 44,378 aircraft arrived and departed at Austrian airports on scheduled flights.

POST. All postal, telegraph and telephone services are run by the State. On 31 Dec. 1969 there were 1,334,000 direct telephone connexions.

The broadcasting stations served 2,043,837 registered listeners in 1969. Television was inaugurated in autumn 1955; there were 1,276,797 registered viewers at 31 Dec. 1969.

BANKING. The National Bank of Austria, opened on 2 Jan. 1923, was taken over by the German Reichsbank on 17 March 1938. It was re-established on 3 July 1945. Its first weekly balance-sheet (7 Oct. 1946) showed assets and liabilities of 12,560·66m. schillings, including foreign exchange of 8·95m. schillings and a circulation of 5,133·15m. schillings. At 31 Dec. 1969 foreign exchange and gold amounted to 35,465m. and note circulation to 34,121m. schillings.

WEIGHTS AND MEASURES. The metric system of weights and measures is in use.

DIPLOMATIC REPRESENTATIVES

Austria maintains embassies in:

Afghánistán	Australia
Algeria	Belgium
Argentina (also Minister in Paraguay and Uruguay)	Brazil
	Bulgaria

Canada
Chile (also in Peru and Minister in Bolivia)
Colombia (also Minister in Ecuador, Haiti, Panama)
Denmark (also in Iceland)
Ethiopia
Finland
France
Germany (West)
Greece (also in Cyprus)
Hungary
India (also Minister in Ceylon and Nepál)
Indonesia (also in Cambodia)
Iran (also Minister in Afghánistán)
Iraq
Irish Republic
Israel
Italy (also for San Marino)
Japan (also in Korea and Taiwan)
Kenya (also in Malawi, Tanzania, Uganda, Zambia)
Lebanon (also in Kuwait and Syria and Minister in Jordan)
Luxembourg
Mexico (also in Costa Rica and Minister in Cuba, El Salvador, Guatemala, Honduras, Nicaragua, Panama)

Morocco
Netherlands
New Zealand
Nigeria (also in Liberia)
Norway
Pakistan (also in Burma)
Peru
Poland
Portugal
Romania
Saudi Arabia
Senegal
Republic of South Africa
Spain
Sweden
Switzerland
Thailand (also Malaysia, Laos, Philippines, Singapore and Minister in Vietnam)
Tunisia (also Libya)
Turkey
USSR (also in Mongolia)
UAR (also Minister in Somalia, Sudan, Yemen)
UK
USA
Vatican
Venezuela (also Dominican Republic)
Yugoslavia (also Minister in Albania)

Austria maintains a legation in Czechoslovakia.

OF AUSTRIA IN GREAT BRITAIN (18 Belgrave Sq., SW1)
Ambassador: Dr Wilfried Platzer, GCVO (accredited 12 Nov. 1970).
Counsellors: Dr Erich Hochleitner (*Consul-General*); Dr Alfred Missong.
Defence Attaché: Col. Hans Buttlar-Elberberg, CVO.
There are consular representatives at Birmingham and Edinburgh.

OF GREAT BRITAIN IN AUSTRIA
Ambassador: Sir Peter Wilkinson, KCMG, DSO, OBE.
Counsellors: F. H. Jackson, OBE; P. H. Scott (*Commercial*).
First Secretaries: The Hon. E. H. B. Gibbs (*Head of Chancery*); E. E. Key, MVO (*Information*); S. Rosdol, OBE; P. G. F. Bryant (*Commercial*); E. J. Sharland; Dr W. Rhode, MBE.
Defence, Military and Air Attaché: Lieut.-Col. K. L. Todd.
There are Consuls at Innsbruck and Vienna.

OF AUSTRIA IN THE USA (2343 Massachussetts Ave. NW, Washington, D.C., 20008)
Ambassador: Dr Karl Gruber.
Counsellors: Dr Hans Rudofsky; Dr Kurt Krejci (*Press Attaché*); Wolfgang Seutter-Loetzen. *Military and Air Attaché:* Brig.-Gen. Ferdinand Foltin.

OF THE USA IN AUSTRIA
Ambassador: John P. Humes.
Deputy Chief of Mission: Rollie H. White, Jr. *Heads of Sections:* M. Emmett B. Ford, Jr (*Political*); Anthony Geber (*Economic*); Joseph Rand (*Commercial*); Roy C. Nelson (*Administration*). *Army Attaché:* Col. C. P. Keiser, Jr. *Air Attaché:* Lieut.-Col. Andrew C. Iaderosa.

BOOKS OF REFERENCE

STATISTICAL INFORMATION. The Austrian Central Statistical Office was founded in 1863
Address: Neue Burg, Heldenplatz, Vienna. *President:* Dr Lother Bosse. Main publications:

Statistisches Handbuch für die Republik Österreich. New Series from 1950
Statistische Nachrichten. Monthly
Beiträge zur österreichischen Statistik (100 vols.)
Ergebnisse der nichtlandwirtschaftlichen Betriebszählung, 1 Sept. 1954. 1958
Ergebnisse der Volkszählung vom 21 März 1961. 1961–65.
Ergebnisse der Häuser- und Wohnungszählung vom 21 März 1961. 1962–64
Kennst Du Österreich? 2nd ed. 1966

Bobek, H. (ed.), *Atlas der Republik Österreich.* 3 vols. Vienna, 1961 ff.
Goldinger, W., *Geschichte der Republik Österreich.* Vienna, 1962
Mikoletzky, H. L., *Österreichische Zeitgeschichte.* Vienna, 1962
Scheidl, L. G., and Lechleitner, H., *Österreich–Land, Volk, Wirtschaft.* Vienna, 1967
Zöllner, E., *Geschichte Österreichs.* Vienna, 1961

NATIONAL LIBRARY. Österreichische Nationalbibliothek, Vienna. *Librarian:* Dr Rudolf Fiedler.

BELGIUM

Royaume de Belgique—Koninkrijk België

HISTORY. The kingdom of Belgium formed itself into an independent state
in 1830, having from 1815 been part of the Netherlands. The secession was
decreed on 4 Oct. 1830 by a provisional government, established in consequence
of a revolution which broke out at Brussels, on 25 Aug. 1830. A National Congress elected Prince Leopold of Saxe-Coburg King of the Belgians on 4 June
1831; he ascended the throne 21 July 1831.

By the Treaty of London, 15 Nov. 1831, the neutrality of Belgium was
guaranteed by Austria, Russia, Great Britain and Prussia. It was not until after
the signing of the Treaty of London, 19 April 1839, which established peace
between King Leopold I and the King of the Netherlands, that all the states of
Europe recognized the kingdom of Belgium. In the Treaty of Versailles (28 June
1919) it is stated that as the treaties of 1839 'no longer conform to the requirements of the situation', these are abrogated and will be replaced by other treaties.

KING. Baudouin, born 7 Sept. 1930, succeeded his father, Leopold III, on
17 July 1951, when he took the oath on the constitution before the two Chambers;
married on 15 Dec. 1960 to Fabiola de Mora y Aragón, daughter of the Conde de
Mora and Marqués de Casa Riera.

Father of the King. Leopold III, born 3 Nov. 1901, son of the late King Albert
(died 17 Feb. 1934) and of Queen Elisabeth, Duchess of Bavaria (died 23 Nov.
1965); married (1) on 4 Nov. 1926 to Princess Astrid of Sweden, died 29 Aug.
1935, and (2) on 11 Sept. (civil marriage, 6 Dec.) 1941, to Mlle Marie Lilian
Baels, Princess de Rethy, daughter of Hendrik Baels, formerly Minister of
Agriculture. Leopold III succeeded to the throne on 23 Feb. 1934; on 20 Sept.
1944 parliament elected Prince Charles, Count of Flanders, Leopold's brother,
as Regent of the Kingdom. The Regency ended on 22 July 1950; but King Leopold delegated his powers to Prince Baudouin on 11 Aug. 1950, and abdicated
on 16 July 1951.

Brother and Sister of the King. (1) Josephine Charlotte, Princess of Belgium, born
11 Oct. 1927; married to Prince Jean of Luxembourg, 9 April 1953; (2) Albert,
Prince of Liège, born 6 June 1934; married to Paola Ruffo di Calabria, 2 July
1959; *offspring:* Prince Philippe, born 15 April 1960; Princess Astrid, born 5 June
1962; Prince Laurent, born 19 Oct. 1963. *Half-brother and half-sisters of the
King.* Prince Alexandre, born 18 July 1942; Princess Marie Christine, born
6 Feb. 1951; Princess Maria-Esmeralda, born 30 Sept. 1956.

Uncle and Aunt of the King. (1) Prince Charles, Count of Flanders, born 10 Oct. 1903. (2) Princess Marie-José, born 4 Aug. 1906, married to Prince Umberto (King Umberto II of Italy in 1946) on 8 Jan. 1930.

BELGIAN SOVEREIGNS

Leopold I	1831–65		Leopold III	1934–44, 1950–51
Leopold II	1865–1909		Regency	1944–50
Albert	1909–34		Baudouin	1951–

CONSTITUTION AND GOVERNMENT. According to the constitution of 1831, Belgium is a constitutional, representative and hereditary monarchy. The legislative power is vested in the King, the Senate and the Chamber of Representatives. The royal succession is in direct male line in the order of primogeniture. By marriage without the King's consent, however, the right of succession is forfeited, but may be restored by the King with the consent of the two Chambers. No act of the King can have effect unless countersigned by one of his Ministers, who thus becomes responsible for it. The King convokes, prorogues and dissolves the Chambers. In default of male heirs, the King may nominate his successor with the consent of the Chambers. If the successor be under 18 years of age the two Chambers meet together for the purpose of nominating a regent during the minority.

National flag: Black, yellow, red (vertical).

National anthem: Après des siècles d'esclavage (La Brabançonne; words by Jenneval, 1830; tune by F. van Campenhout, 1830).

Both French and Dutch are official languages.

Those sections of the Belgian Constitution which regulate the organization of the legislative power were revised in Oct. 1921. For both Senate and Chamber all elections are held on the principle of universal suffrage.

The Senate consists of members elected for 4 years, partly directly and partly indirectly. The number elected directly is equal to half the number of members of the Chamber of Representatives. The constituent body is similar to that which elects deputies to the Chamber; the minimum age of electors is 21 years, and the minimum length of residence required is 6 months. Women were given the suffrage at parliamentary elections on 24 March 1948. In the direct elections of members both of the Senate and Chamber of Representatives the principle of proportional representation was introduced by law of 29 Dec. 1899.

Senators are elected indirectly by the provincial councils, on the basis of 1 for 200,000 inhabitants. Every addition of 125,000 inhabitants gives the right to 1 senator more. Each provincial council elects at least 3 senators. There are at present 48 provincial senators. No one, during 2 years preceding the election, must have been a member of the council appointing him. Senators are elected by the Senate itself in the proportion of half the preceding category. The senators belonging to these two latter categories are also elected by the method of proportional representation. All senators must be at least 40 years of age. They receive 425,000 francs per annum. Sons of the King, or failing these, Belgian princes of the reigning branch of the royal family, are by right senators at the age of 18, but have no voice in the deliberations till the age of 25 years; this prerogative is hardly ever used.

The members of the Chamber of Representatives are elected directly by the electoral body. Their number, at present 212 (law of 3 April 1965), is proportional to the population, and cannot exceed one for every 40,000 inhabitants. They sit for 4 years. Deputies must be not less than 25 years of age, and resident in Belgium. Each deputy has an annual allowance of 425,000 francs. Senator and deputies have also free railway passes.

The Senate and Chamber meet annually in October and must sit for at least 40 days; but the King has the power of convoking extraordinary sessions and of dissolving them either simultaneously or separately. In the latter case a new election must take place within 40 days and a meeting of the chambers within 2 months. An adjournment cannot be made for a period exceeding 1 month without the consent of the Chambers.

Parties in the Senate, elected 31 March 1968: Christian Social, 64; Socialist, 54, Freedom and Progress, 37; Front Democrate francophone and Rassemblement Wallon, 17; Flemish People's Union, 14; Communist, 2.

Parties in the Chamber elected 31 March 1968: Christian Social, 69 (previously 77); Socialists, 59 (64); Freedom and Progress, 47 (48); Flemish People's Union, 20 (12); Front Democrate francophone and Rassemblement Wallon, 12 (5); Communist, 5 (6).

The Liberal Party, founded in June 1846, on 8 Oct. 1961 changed its name to that of Party of Freedom and Progress.

The Executive Government (Christian Social and Socialist), formed on 17 June 1968, is composed as follows:

Prime Minister: Gaston Eyskens (CS). *Deputy Prime Minister and Budget:* André Cools (S). *Minister without Portfolio in charge of Scientific Policy and Programmes:* Théo Lefévre (CS). *Foreign Affairs:* Pierre Harmel (CS). *Development Aid:* Raymond Scheyven (CS). *Foreign Trade:* Hendrik Fayat (S). *Defence:* Paul Willem Segers (CS). *Finance:* Baron Jean Snoy et d'Oppuers (CS). *Economic Affairs:* Edmond Leburton (S). *Public Works:* Joseph de Saeger (CS). *Transport:* Alfred Bertrand (CS). *Post and Telegraphs:* Edward Anseele (S). *Interior:* Lucien Harmegnies (S). *Civil Service:* René Pêtre (CS). *Justice:* Alphons Vranckx (S). *Education (Dutch):* Pierre Vermeylen (S). *Education (French):* Abel Dubois (S). *Culture (French):* Albert Parisis (CS). *Culture (Dutch):* Frans van Mechelen (CS). *Relations between Dutch- and French-speaking Communities:* Leo Tindemans (CS), *Agriculture:* Charles Héger (CS), *Middle Class:* Charles Hanin (CS). *Labour and Employment:* Louis Major (S). *Social Security:* Placide de Paepe (CS). *Public Health:* Louis Namèche (S). *Family Affairs and Housing:* Gustave Breyne (S). There are also 2 Secretaries of State.

LOCAL GOVERNMENT. The 9 provinces and 2,379 communes of Belgium have a large measure of autonomous government. According to the law of 15 April 1920, changed by the law of 1 July 1969, all Belgians over 18 years of age without distinction of sex, who have been domiciled for at least 6 months, have the right to vote in communal elections. Proportional representation is applied to the communal elections, and communal councils are to be renewed every 6 years. In each commune there is a college composed of the burgomaster as the president and a certain number of aldermen.

De Seyn, *Dictionnaire historique et géographique des communes belges.* 2 vols. Brussels 1934

AREA AND POPULATION. Belgium has an area of 30,513 sq. km (11,778 sq. miles). The Belgium exclave of Baarle-Hertog in the Netherlands has an area of 7 sq. km, and a population (31 Dec. 1969) of 1,112 males and 1,073 females.

By an agreement signed on 23 Sept. 1956 the frontier with Germany was slightly readjusted.

Census	Population	Increase % per annum	Census	Population	Increase % per annum
1900	6,693,548	1·03	1930	8,092,004	0·84
1910	7,423,784	1·09	1947	8,512,195	0·36
1920	7,465,782	0·06	1961	9,189,741	0·52

Provinces	Provincial capitals	Area (hectares)	Estimated population (31 Dec.)		
			1966	*1967*	*1969*
Antwerp (Anvers)	Antwerp	286,058	1,518,464	1,523,266	1,529,826
Brabant	Brussels	336,928	2,148,513	2,157,281	2,166,327
Flanders {West	Bruges	313,233	1,042,586	1,046,825	1,052,052
{East	Ghent	297,722	1,305,717	1,308,319	1,310,638
Hainaut	Mons	379,821	1,331,677	1,332,536	1,331,810
Liège	Liège	387,583	1,019,105	1,017,736	1,016,131
Limbourg	Hasselt	242,172	638,593	644,166	650.338
Luxembourg	Arlon	441,796	219,368	219,312	219,369
Namur	Namur	366,025	381,578	382,469	338,618
Total		3,051,338	9,605,601	9,631,910	9,660,154

In 1969 there were 4,729,643 males and 4,930,511 females. Foreigners numbered 694,447 on 31 Dec. 1969.

VITAL STATISTICS for calendar years:

	Births	Deaths	Marriages	Divorces	Immigration	Emigration
1967	145,899	114,509	68,295	5,414	63,713	40,392
1968	141,242	121,275	69,270	6,158	57,122	44,348
1969	140,834	119,375	72,204	6,588	55,243	47,520

Illegitimate births in 1968, 3,770; of the total births, including still-born (141,984), 72,947 were boys, 69,037 girls).

The most important towns, with estimated population on 31 Dec. 1969:

Brussels and suburbs[1]	1,073,111	Merksem	40,019
Antwerp (Anvers)	230,184	Hasselt	39,549
Ghent (Gand)	151.614	Turnhout	37,927
Liège (Luik)	148,599	Mouscron (Moeskroen)	37,483
Deurne	79,106	Verviers	34,402
Mechelen (Malines)	65,823	Vilvoorde (Vilvorde)	34,158
Oostende (Ostende)	56,954	Tournai (Doornik)	33,625
Genk	57,375	Leuven (Louvain)	32,419
Brugge (Bruges)	51,463	Hoboken	33,278
Berchem	50.767	Namur (Namen)	32,352
Borgerhout	48,766	Herstal	29,711
St Niklaas (St Nicolas)	48,968	Lokeren	26,651
Aalst (Alost)	46.616	Lier (Lierre)	28,370
Kortrijk (Courtrai)	45,138	Jumet	27,977
Wilryck	43,382	Mons (Bergen)	27,704
Seraing	40,617	Ronse (Renaix)	25,127
Roeselare (Roulers)	40,484	Charleroi	23,911

[1] The suburbs comprise 18 distinct communes, viz., Anderlecht, Etterbeek, Forest Ixelles, Jette, Koekelberg, Molenbeek St Jean, St Gilles, St Josse-ten-Noode, Schaerbeek, Uccle, Woluwe-St Lambert, Auderghem, Watermael-Boitsfort, Woluwe-St Pierre, Berchem, Ste Agathe, Evere and Ganshoren.

RELIGION. Of the inhabitants professing a religion the majority are Roman Catholic, but no inquiry as to the profession of faith is now made at the censuses. There are, however, statistics concerning the clergy, and according to these there were in 1969: Roman Catholic higher clergy, 128; inferior clergy, 6,863; Protestant pastors, 50; Anglican Church, 9 chaplains; Jews (rabbis and ministers), 22. The State does not interfere in any way with the internal affairs of any church. There is full religious liberty, and part of the income of the ministers of all denominations is paid by the State.

There are 8 Roman Catholic dioceses subdivided into 261 deaneries.

Estimated number of Protestants, 24,000; of Jews, 35,000.

The Protestant (Evangelical) Church is under a synod. There is also a Central Jewish Consistory, a Central Committee of the Anglican Church and a Free Protestant Church.

EDUCATION. On 8 Nov. 1962/2 Aug. 1963 a linguistic frontier was fixed between the Flemish-speaking, French-speaking and German-speaking parts of Belgium. In the north, Flemish is recognized as the official language, in the south, French, and along the eastern border, German. The city and *arrondissement* of Brussels are bilingual. After some territorial readjustments made on 31 Dec. 1969 the percentage of the population in the Flemish, French, German and bilingual regions was 56, 32·3, 0·6, 11·1. (*See* map in THE STATESMAN'S YEAR-BOOK, 1967–68.)

Higher Education (1969–70). There are universities at Louvain (founded 7 Sept 1426; with branch at Courtrai, 24.604 students), Brussels (10,588 students), Ghent (since Oct. 1930 Flemish; 11,093 students) and Liège (8,189 students), the two latter being state institutions. There are also several state agricultural institutes, viz., a state veterinary school at Cureghem (240 students) and 2 state agricultural institutes (at Gembloux with 440 students). The Polytechnic at

Mons had 483 students; there are also 7 commercial colleges, the University Centre at Antwerp being a state institution (1,913 students). The total number of students in university colleges, faculties and institutes was 69,634.

There are 5 royal academies of fine arts and 5 royal conservatoires at Brussels, Liège, Ghent, Antwerp and Mons.

Secondary Education (1967–68). 1,143 middle schools and (1964) 2,564 technical schools had a total of 380,101 pupils in the general classes and 337,164 in the technical classes.

Elementary Education (1967–68). There were 8,819 primary schools, with 1,002,611 pupils (516,218 boys, 486,393 girls) and 5,327 infant schools, with 459,467 pupils.

Normal Schools (1967–68). There were 56 for training secondary teachers (4,761 students); 99 for training elementary teachers (14,925 students), technical normal schools with 2,934 students and 45 normal infant schools, with 5,566 students.

Each commune must have at least one primary school. The cost of primary instruction devolves on the State.

CINEMAS (1968). There were 811 cinemas, with a seating capacity of 417,641.

NEWSPAPERS (1969). There are 45 daily newspapers (some with additional regional and local editions), of which 29 are in French, 15 in Flemish and 1 in German.

SOCIAL WELFARE. Social security is based on the law of Dec. 1944. It applies to all workers subject to an employment contract, and is administered by the Central National Office of Social Security (ONSS), which collects from employers and employees all contributions referring to family allowances, health insurance, old age insurance, holidays and unemployment. These sums are distributed by the Central Office to the various institutions concerned with these benefits. Insurance against unemployment is organized through a common fund, which also undertakes to retrain the unemployed for another employment while providing for their families. Since 1944 further laws have increased allowances, made fresh provisions for housing (1945), injuries while working, professional illnesses, etc. (1948).

Apart from private charity, the poor are assisted by the communes through the agency of the *Commissions d'assistance publique*. Provisions of a national character have been made for looking after war orphans and men disabled in the war. Certain other establishments, either state or provincial, provide for the needs of deaf-mutes and the blind, and of children who are placed under the control of the courts. Provision is also made for repressing begging and providing shelter for the homeless.

In 1969 there were 14,922 physicians (including 492 dentists), 1,702 other dentists, 6,533 pharmacists and 3,615 midwives. Hospital beds numbered 44,437.

JUSTICE. Judges are appointed for life. There is a court of cassation, 3 courts of appeal, and assize courts for political and criminal cases. There are 26 judicial districts, each with a court of first instance. In each of the 236 cantons is a justice and judge of the peace. There are, besides, various special tribunals. There is trial by jury in assize courts.

FINANCE. Currency. The *franc*, containing 0·01777 gramme of fine gold, is the unit of currency.

No gold has been minted since 1882 (save only 5m. francs struck in 1914). New silver coins of 100 francs have been issued since 15 Oct. 1948.

The official rate of exchange in Dec. 1969 was US$1 = 49.68 francs; £1 = 119.11 francs.

Budget. Revenue and expenditure for calendar years (in 1m. francs):

	1966	1967	1968[1]	1969[1]	1970[2]
Receipts					
Ordinary	201,175	222,923	239,509	267,492	290,480
War	51	60	—	—	—
Extraordinary	21,699	21,913	29,805	28,549	2,015
Total	222,925	244,983	269,314	296,041	292,495
Expenditure					
Ordinary	199,013	225.515	247,443	268,388	290,365
Extraordinary	30,605	29,874	35,729	36,337	40,275
Total	229,618	255,389	283,172	304,725	330,640

[1] Provisional. [2] Budget estimates.

On 30 June 1970 the Belgian public debt consisted of (in 1m. francs): Internal debt consolidated, 408,500; short and middle terms, 89,800; at sight, 49,900. External debt, 61,400. Total, 609,600.

DEFENCE. A military and technical agreement signed by Belgium and the Netherlands on 10 May 1948 provides for standardization of equipment, co-ordination of training methods and contacts between the staffs of the military colleges.

Army. According to the Military Law of 30 April 1962, the Belgian Army is recruited by annual calls to the colours and by voluntary enlistments.

Compulsory service lasts 12 months for private soldiers, 15 months for voluntary reserve officers and for the paracommando regiment. Duration of military obligation is 15 years (regular army and reserve).

The Army comprises as major units 2 mechanized divisions, 2 reserve brigades and 1 paracommando regiment. Total strength, 70,000.

Navy. The naval forces include 7 ocean minesweepers, 2 support ships, 9 coastal minesweepers, 12 inshore minesweepers, 2 research ships, 7 river patrol boats, 13 tugs and harbour craft. Naval personnel in 1970 totalled 330 officers and 4,500 ratings.

Air Force. The Air Force comprises 10 operational squadrons. These are organized into 1 all-weather fighter wing (2 squadrons) of F-104G Starfighters; 2 fighter-bomber wings assigned to NATO, with 2 squadrons of F-104G Starfighters and 2 squadrons of F-84F Thunderstreaks; 1 squadron of RF-84F Thunderflash photo-reconnaissance aircraft; and 1 wing (3 squadrons) equipped with C-119G, DC-6 and C-47 transports. Replacement of the F-84F and RF-84F aircraft with Mirage 5Bs began in July 1970. Two wings (4 squadrons) have Nike surface-to-air missiles. Total strength is about 21,000 personnel and 400 aircraft, including Siai-Marchetti SF260M, Magister and T-33A trainers and second-line aircraft. Lightplanes and light helicopters are operated by the Army.

AGRICULTURE. Of the total area of 3,051,338 hectares, there were, in 1969, 1,609.901 hectares under cultivation, of which 477,253 were under cereals, 23,463 (1968: 19,959) vegetables, 108,801 industrial plants, 85,591 root crops, 803,629 pastures and meadows.

Chief	Area in hectares			Produce in metric tons		
crops	1967	1968	1969	1967	1968	1969
Wheat	197,176	202,544	198.647	828,168	839,334	753,816
Barley	153,049	152,948	155.214	622,619	574,441	555.249
Oats	95,818	87,208	87,360	361,363	314,821	280,752
Rye	26,350	27,182	22,448	90,105	86,982	69 739
Potatoes	54,381	54,874	50.292	1,943,492	1,566,180	1,252.604
Beet (sugar)	77,847	89,568	89,994	3,615,118	4,107,588	4.216.531
Beet (fodder)	36,043	33,587	34,784	3,534,011	3,303,446	3,141,531
Tobacco	506	569	611	1,556	1,837	1,785

On 1 Dec. 1969 there were 75,884 horses, 2,712,951 cattle (including 1,066,389 milch cows), 84,782 sheep, 2,767 goats and 3,093,968 pigs.

FORESTRY. In 1961 the forest area covered 21·8% of the land surface. In 1969, 2,565,000 cu. metres of timber were felled.

FISHERIES. The total quantity of fish landed amounted to 49,958 tons valued at 820·9m. francs in 1969. The fishing fleet had a total tonnage of 29,468 gross tons at 31 Dec. 1969.

MINING. Output (in metric tons) for 5 calendar years:

	1965	1966	1967	1968	1969
Coal	19,786,000	17.499,000	16,435,000	14,806,000	13,200,000
Briquettes	1,074,289	972,000	869,000	823,000	793,000
Coke	7,333,723	6,961,000	6,857,000	7,243,000	7,249,000
Cast iron	8,366,063	8,229,663	8,902,000	10,370,505	11,211,074
Wrought steel	9,168,574	8,916,677	9,716,000	11,572,670	12,836,978
Finished steel	6,713,743	6,867.635	7,511,000	8,669,743	9,829,314

INDUSTRY. In 1969 there were 22 sugar factories, output 219,472 metric tons of raw sugar; 6 sugar refineries, output 237.331 metric tons; 13 distilleries, output 361,117 hectolitres of potable and industrial alcohol; 242 breweries, output 12,478,043 hectolitres of beer; margarine factories, output, 131,731 metric tons; match factories, output, 55,880m. matches.

Six trusts control the greater part of Belgian industry: the Société Générale (founded in 1822) owns about 40% of coal, 50% of steel, 65% of non-ferrous metals and 35% of electricity; Brufina-Confinindus operates in steel, coal, electricity and heavy engineering; the Groupe Solvay rules the chemical industry; the Groupe Copée has interests in steel and coal; Empain controls tramways and electrical equipment; the Banque Lambert owns petroleum firms and their accessories.

POWER. The production of electricity (1m. kwh.) amounted to 21,518 in 1966; 22,603·2 in 1967; 25,060 in 1968; 27,630 in 1969; that of gas (in 1m. cu. metres) to 2,933 in 1966; 3,209 in 1967; 3,127·3 in 1968; 2,511 in 1969.

Baudhuin, Fernand, *Histoire économique de la Belgique, 1914–39.* Brussels. 1944. *L'économie belge sous l'occupation 1940–44.* Brussels, 1943
Buttgenbach, H., *Les Minéraux de Belgique et du Congo Belge.* Liège, 1947
Marione, E., *Les sociétés d'économie mixte en Belgique.* Brussels, 1947
Sabbe, E., *Histoire de l'industrie linière en Belgique.* Brussels, 1945
Van Houtte, J. A., *Esquisse d'une histoire économique de la Belgique.* Louvain, 1943

COMMERCE. By the convention concluded at Brussels on 25 July 1921 between Belgium and Luxembourg and ratified on 5 March 1922 an economic union was formed by the two countries, and the customs frontier between them was abolished on 1 May 1922. Dissolved in Aug. 1940, the union was re-established on 1 May 1945.

On 14 March 1947, in execution of an agreement signed in London on 5 Sept. 1944, there was concluded a customs union between Belgium and Luxembourg, on the one hand, and the Netherlands, on the other. The union came into force on 1 Jan. 1948, and is now known as the Benelux Customs Union. A joint tariff has been adopted and import duties are no longer levied at the Netherlands frontier, but import licences may still be required. A full economic union of the three countries came into operation on 1 Nov. 1960.

BENELUX INFORMATION is supplied by the Secrétariat Général de l'Union Douanière Néerlando-Belgo-Luxembourgeoise, 170, Rue de la Loi, Brussels. It publishes *Benelux. Bulletin Trimestriel de Statistique; Statistisch Kwartaalbericht* (1955 ff.).

Imports and exports for 6 calendar years (in 1,000 Belgian francs):

	Imports	Exports		Imports	Exports
1960	197,854,439	188,771,893	1967	358,795,195	351,621,205
1965	318,678,300	319,083,187	1968	416,669,687	408,199,855
1966	358,700,767	341,450,263	1969	499,432,334	503,251,293

Trade by principal countries (in 1,000 Belgian francs):

	Imports from			Exports to		
	1967	1968	1969	1967	1968	1969
France	53,150,283	63,561,893	79.445.412	62,267,458	75,759,615	105,759,883
USA	29,492,717	34,456,359	38,323,321	29,400,311	38,506,545	34,754,287
UK	25,106,306	30,110,721	34,753,215	16,634,867	17,846,163	20.242,543
Netherlands	54,049,146	60,770,089	71,224,990	75,450,238	85,301,661	97,383,997
Germany (West)	75,949,496	86,564,326	115,891,423	69,651,621	85,475,640	115,233,093
Germany (East)	1,374,533	1,469,775	1,786.992	1,249,293	742,243	754,893
Argentina	4,159,302	3,745,734	3,977,247	427,967	559,307	947,892
Italy	16,164,577	17,938,272	20,133,797	14,082,988	15,456,881	21,618,031
Switzerland	4,721,142	5,386,083	6,525,362	7,738,708	8,154,758	10,281,246
Congo (K.)	12,775,158	16,260,548	21,409,011	2,544,324	3,479,474	4,472,647
Denmark	2,240,786	2,494,420	2,081.913	4,072,746	3,960,281	5,460,802
USSR	2,973,647	3,302,107	2,936.393	2,013,817	2,371,024	2,551,066
India	1,518,270	1,983,164	2,142.097	1,987,796	1,769,612	2,043,817
Rep. of S. Africa.	3,865,917	4,346,245	4,893.661	1,591,814	1,884,051	1,855,778
Canada	4,531,847	5,376,806	5,210,566	2,586,921	2,602,700	2,816,880
Brazil	1,702,463	2,426,243	3,467.919	1,531,953	1,580,885	1,619,165
Australia	2,873,638	2,814,184	3,454,939	1,202,162	1,055,707	1,154,680

The total trade between UK and Belgium (in £1,000 sterling) was as follows (British Board of Trade returns):

	1966	1967	1968	1969	1970
Imports to UK	128,794	143,081	169,687	182,603	192,503
Exports from UK	180,797	177,553	233,846	280,844 ⎱	288,620
Re-exports from UK	5,203	4,955	6,915	7,383 ⎰	

Principal Belgian–Luxembourg exports to the UK in 1969: Textiles (38,291 metric tons; 2,329m. francs); metals (152,700 metric tons; 1,375m. francs); chemical and pharmaceutical products (282,386 metric tons; 1,294m. francs); precious stones and manufactures thereof (471 metric tons; 4,277m. francs).

Principal Belgian–Luxembourg imports from the UK in 1969: Machinery and electrical apparatus (61,307 metric tons; 5,189m. francs); vehicles, chiefly motor cars, and aircraft (116,613 metric tons; 4,437m. francs); textiles (20,780 metric tons; 1,362m. francs); precious stones (98 metric tons; 14,085m. francs); base metals and manufactures thereof (106,214 metric tons; 1,869m. francs).

SHIPPING.[1] On 31 Dec. 1969 the Belgian merchant fleet was composed of 97 vessels of 958,696 tons. There were 25 shipping companies, of which the most important were the Compagnie Maritime Belge, with 23 ships, and the Belgian Fruit Lines, SA, with 6 ships.

The navigation at the port of Antwerp in 1969 was as follows: Number of vessles entered, 17,885; tonnage, 65,523,537. Number of vessels cleared, 17,900; tonnage, 65,596,032.

The total length of navigable waterways (rivers and canals) is 1,571·6 km.

[1] Belgian shipping returns are given in the official 'Moorsom tons', which may be converted into net tons by deducting 19·85% from the Moorsom total.

ROADS. The total length of the roads in Belgium on 31 Dec. 1967 was as follows: State roads, 10,528 km; provincial roads, 1,249 km. The majority of roads are metalled.

Number of motor vehicles in Belgium, 1 Aug. 1969, 2,161,475, including 1,920.638 passenger cars, 14,965 buses, 205.831 lorries, 39,700 non-agricultural tractors, 77,902 agricultural tractors, 63,580 motor cycles and 21,279 special vehicles.

RAILWAYS. The main Belgian lines were a State enterprise from their inception in 1834. In 1926 the 'Société Nationale des Chemins de Fer Belges' (SNCB) was formed to take over the railways. The State is sole holder of the ordinary shares of SNCB, which carry the majority vote at General Meetings. The State also retains a control over fares, freight rates, borrowing and the construction of new lines, and appoints the Board of the company. The length of railway operated on 31 Dec. 1969 was 4,263 km of main lines. Revenue (1969), 22,703m. francs; expenditure, 21,617m. francs.

AVIATION. The national Belgian airline SABENA (Sociéte anonyme belge d'exploitation de la navigation aérienne) was set up in 1923. Its capital is 750m. francs. In addition to its European network, SABENA operates different routes to the Congo *via* Tripoli, Rome, Geneva, Lisbon, Frankfurt, Cairo, Beirut. Athens and Casablanca, with through connexions to South Africa; and services to New York, Israel, Lagos and Abidjan. In 1969 its airfleet comprised 41 aircraft, 2 helicopters and 20 training machines. In 1969 SABENA flew 46·33m. km, carrying 1,256,052 revenue passengers, 169,912,000 ton-km of freight and 7,797,000 ton/km of mail.

POST. On 31 Dec. 1968 there were 1,817 post offices. The gross revenue of the post office in the year 1968 amounted to 5,173m. francs.

A régie of telegraphs and telephones for running the services on business lines was created in 1930. Telegraph offices for dispatching and receiving wires numbered 108; for dispatching only, 1,007. Receipts for 1969 were 1,121,781,790 francs; expenditure, 1,149,864,614 francs.

In 1969 the telephone service comprised 576 exchanges, connecting 3,733 public telephone stations and 1,277,845 subscribers. Number of telephones, 31 Dec. 1969, 1,914,155. Receipts in 1969, 9,502,537,000 francs; expenditure, 8,877·36m. francs.

BANKING. The bank of issue in Belgium is the National Bank, instituted in 1850. It is the cashier of the State, and is authorized to carry on the usual banking operations. The note circulation on 31 Dec. 1969 amounted to 183,002m. francs. The articles of association of the National Bank of Belgium were modified on 13 Sept. 1948 so as to strengthen public control.

The activities of all deposit banks (on 9 May 1969) are controlled, from the point of view of their safety, by the Commission bancaire, instituted by law in 1935, and in view of their monetary policy aspects, by the National Bank of Belgium. There is also a network of important 'public sector financial intermediaries' mainly specialized in middle- and long-term loans to industry, agriculture and commerce.

The savings banks are mainly operated by the Caisse Générale d'Epargne et de Retraite and by the private savings banks. The Caisse Générale d'Epargne et de Retraite is an autonomous institution with legally regulated functions; operating under the supervision of the Minister of Finance. It co operates with the Belgian postal service, thus obviating any need of a postal-savings system. The savings deposits of the Caisse d'Epargne amounted to 154,034m. francs on 31 Dec. 1969. The private savings banks, whose liabilities expressed in savings accounts and bonds amounted to 115,708m. francs on 31 Dec. 1969, are controlled by the 'Office Central de la petite Epargne'.

DIPLOMATIC REPRESENTATIVES

Belgium maintains embassies in:

Algeria	Chad	Finland
Argentina	Chile	France
Australia	Colombia	Gabon
Austria	Congo (Br.)	Gambia
Barbados	Congo (K.)	Germany (West)
Bolivia	Costa Rica	Ghana
Botswana	Cuba	Greece
Brazil	Cyprus	Guatemala
Bulgaria	Czechoslovakia	Guinea
Burma	Dahomey	Haiti
Burundi	Denmark	Honduras
Cameroun	Dominican Republic	Hungary
Canada	Ecuador	India
Central African Republic	El Salvador	Indonesia
Ceylon	Ethiopia	Iran

Iraq	Morocco	Swaziland
Irish Republic	Nepál	Sweden
Israel	Netherlands	Switzerland
Italy	New Zealand	Syria
Ivory Coast	Nicaragua	Tanzania
Jamaica	Niger	Thailand
Japan	Nigeria	Togo
Jordan	Norway	Trinidad and Tobago
Kenya	Pakistan	Tunisia
Korea (South)	Panama	Turkey
Kuwait	Paraguay	Uganda
Laos	Peru	USSR
Lebanon	Philippines	UAR
Lesotho	Poland	UK
Liberia	Portugal	USA
Libya	Romania	Upper Volta
Luxembourg	Rwanda	Uruguay
Madagascar	Saudi Arabia	Vatican
Malawi	Senegal	Venezuela
Malaysia	Singapore	Vietnam (South)
Mali	Somalia	Yugoslavia
Malta	South Africa, Rep. of	Zambia
Mauritania	Spain	
Mexico	Sudan	

Belgium maintains legations in Afghánistán, Cambodia, Sierra Leone.

OF BELGIUM IN GREAT BRITAIN (103 Eaton Sq., SW1)

Ambassador: Baron Jean van den Bosch (accredited 31 Jan. 1966).

Minister-Counsellor: S. Frey. *Counsellors:* Pierre L. J. Van Coppenolle (*Commercial*); C. Raulier; Yves Vercauteren; J. Bousse. *Service Attaché:* Lieut.-Col. Robert Charles Close. *First Secretary:* P. Berghs. *Shipping Counsellor:* Baron Ph. de Gerlache de Gomery, MVO.

There are consular representatives at Aberdeen, Belfast, Birmingham, Bradford, Bristol, Cardiff, Dover, Dundee, Edinburgh, Fowey, Guernsey, Glasgow, Grimsby, Harwich, Hull, Liverpool, Lowestoft, Manchester, Middlesbrough, Milford Haven, Newcastle upon Tyne, Newlyn–Penzance, Plymouth, Portsmouth, St Helier, Sheffield, Southampton, Sunderland, Swansea, Tees-side, West Hartlepool.

OF GREAT BRITAIN IN BELGIUM

Ambassador: Sir John Beith, KCMG.

Counsellors: C. T. E. Ewart-Biggs, OBE (*Head of Chancery*); G. F. Hiller, CMG, DSO (*Commercial*), G. R. Bide (*Economic*). *First Secretaries:* T. H. Gee; J. Doorbar, OBE (*Commercial*); F. J. Bradshaw (*Consul*); A. E. Heath (*Information*); J. S. Vigors (*Labour*); P. L. Morgan, P. M. S. Corley (*Commercial*). *Service Attachés:* Brig. A. I. Hulton, MBE (*Defence, Army and Navy*), Group Capt. E. S. Chandler, AFC (*Air*, resides at The Hague).

There is a Consul-General at Antwerp and Consuls at Brussels, Ghent, Liège and Ostend.

OF BELGIUM IN THE USA (3330 Garfield St. NW, Washington, D.C., 20008)

Ambassador: W. Loridan.

Minister: H. Dehennin (*Economic*).

Counsellors: Andre Rahir; Louis Groven (*Scientific*); T. Lansloot. *Military, Naval and Air Attaché:* Maj.-Gen. van der Heyden.

OF THE USA IN BELGIUM

Ambassador: John S. D. Eisenhower.

Deputy Chief of Mission: Louis C. Boochever. *Heads of Sections:* George Moffitt, Jr *(Political);* Edwin Crowley *(Economic);* Jerome R. Lavallee *(Commercial);* Ralph Scarritt *(Administration). Service Attachés:* Col. Alfred J. Millard *(Army),* Cdr Joseph C. McCoy *(Navy),* Lieut.-Col. David W. Turner *(Air).*

There is a Consul-General in Antwerp and a Consul in Brussels.

BOOKS OF REFERENCE

STATISTICAL INFORMATION. The Institut National de Statistique (44 rue de Louvain, Brussels) was set up on 24 Jan. 1831, under the designation of Bureau de Statistique Générale; after several changes, it received its present name on 2 May 1946. *Director-General:* Dr A. Dufrasne. *Main publications:*

Bulletin du Commerce Extérieur
Bulletin de Statistique. Monthly
Annuaire Statistique de la Belgique (from 1870).—*Annuaire statistique de poche* (from 1965)
Annuaire Agricole. 1946 ff.
Recensement général de la population au 31 déc. 1961. 10 vols.
Recensement de l'agriculture au 15 mai 1959. 8 vols.

Almanach royal officiel. Annual. Brussels
L'économie belge. Ministère des Affaires Economiques. Annual (from 1947)
Dussart, F., and Contreras, R.. *Géographie de la Belgique et du Congo.* Brussels, 1947
Meynaud, J. (ed.), *La Décision politique en Belgique.* Paris, 1965
Raeymaker, O. de, *Belgie's international Beleid, 1919–39.* Brussels, 1945
Van Kalken, Frans, *Histoire de Belgique.* Brussels, 1944.—*Entre deux guerres: Esquises de la vie politique en Belgique de 1918–1940.* Brussels, 1945

BHUTÁN
Druk-yul

HISTORY. In 1774 the East India Company concluded a treaty with the ruler of Bhután, but repeated outrages on British subjects committed by the Bhután hillmen led from time to time to punitive measures, usually ending in the temporary or permanent annexation of various *duars* or submontane tracts with passes leading to the hills. Under a treaty signed in Nov. 1865 the Bhután Government was granted an annual subsidy. By an amending treaty concluded in Jan. 1910 the British Government undertook to exercise no interference in the internal affairs of Bhután, and the Bhután Government agreed to be guided by the advice of the British Government in regard to its external relations.

The Government of India concluded a fresh treaty with Bhután on 8 Aug. 1949. Under this treaty the Government of Bhután continues to be guided by the Government of India in regard to its external relations, and the Government of India have undertaken not to interfere in the internal administration of Bhután. The subsidy paid to Bhután has been increased to Rs 500,000, and the Government of India agreed to retrocede to Bhután an area of about 32 sq. miles in the territory known as Dewangiri, which was annexed in 1865.

AREA AND POPULATION. Bhután is situated in the eastern Himalayas, between 26° 45' and 28° N. lat. and between 89° and 92° E. long., bordered on the north and east by Tibet and India, on the west by Sikkim and on the south by India. Extreme length from east to west 190 miles; extreme breadth 90 miles. Area about 18,000 sq. miles (46,600 sq. km); population estimated at approximately 1m. (1970). The capital is at Thimphu. The official language is Dzongkha, akin to Tibetan.

GOVERNMENT. The form of government in Bhután, which existed from the middle of the 16th century until 1907, consisted of a dual control by the clergy and the laity as represented by Dharma and Deb Rájás. In 1907 the Tongsa Penlop (the governor of the province of Tongsa in eastern Bhután), Sir Ugyen Wangchuk, GCIE, KCSI, was elected as the first hereditary Maharaja of Bhután. He was succeeded by his son, Sir Jigme Wangchuk, KCSI, KCIE (1926–52), and his grandson, Jigme Dorji Wangchuk, who was installed as Maharaja on 27 Oct. 1952. His Bhutanese title is Druk Gyalpo, and he is now addressed as King of Bhutan. From Oct. 1969 the absolute monarchy was changed to a form of 'democratic monarchy'. The powers of removal and selection of the King having been given to the National Assembly (*Tsongdu*). The monarch can be removed by a two-third vote of the Assembly members at any time. A vote of confidence in the King, by a two-thirds majority, is required every 3 years. New monarchs would be appointed by the Assembly from the line of succession of members of the Royal family. The National Assembly was made sovereign with the right to outvote any Government bills or proposals of the King.

District administration is based on Dzongs (literal meaning fort). A Dzong contains administrative offices and also the monastery.

RELIGION. The majority of the people are Mahayana Buddhists of the Druk Kargue or 'Red hat' sect. Tashi-Cho Dzong, the chief monastery in Bhután, contains over 1,000 priests.

DEFENCE. Bhután has an army of about 4,000 men, trained by Indian officers.

PRODUCTION. The chief products are rice, Indian corn, millet, lac, wax, handloom cloth, musk, elephants, ponies and yaks. Extensive and valuable forests abound. Large deposits of limestone and gypsum have been found. Surveys for hydro-electric power are being carried out.

PLANNING. The Government of Bhután has drawn up three 5-year development plans (1961–65, 1966–70, 1971–76), with the active co-operation and financial support of the Government of India. Educational facilities are being expanded and medical facilities are being provided. Forest and mineral wealth is to be exploited. About 800 miles of new roads are to be built.

COMMERCE. Trade with India is considerable. Bhután imported from the UK in 1966 goods valued at £11,000; nil in 1967 and 1968.

DIPLOMATIC RELATIONS. The Government of Bhután has a trade commissioner at Calcutta. The Government of India is represented in Bhután by a Special Officer of India located at Thimphu.

BOOKS OF REFERENCE

Karan, P. P., *Bhutan: a physical and cultural geography*. Univ. of Kentucky Press, 1967
Karan, P. P., and Jenkins, W. M., *The Himalayan Kingdoms*. Princeton Univ. Press, 1963
Ronaldshay, the Earl of, *Lands of the Thunderbolt*. 2nd ed. London, 1931

BOLIVIA
República de Bolivia

CONSTITUTION AND GOVERNMENT. The Republic of Bolivia was proclaimed on 6 Aug. 1825; its first constitution was adopted on 19 Nov. 1826.

La Paz is the actual capital and seat of the Government, but Sucre is the legal capital and the seat of the judiciary.

National flag: Red, yellow, green (horizontal).
National anthem: Bolivianos, el hado propicio (words by I. de Sanjinés; tune by B. Vincenti).

The following is a list of presidents since 1931 and the dates on which they took office:

Dr Daniel Salamanca, 5 March 1931 (resigned Nov. 1934).

Luis Tejada Sorzano, 27 Nov. 1934 (deposed 17 May 1936).

Col. José David Toro, 17 May 1936 (deposed 13 July 1937).

Lieut.-Gen. German Busch, 13 July 1937 (committed suicide 23 Aug. 1939).

Gen. Carlos Quintanilla (provisional), 23 Aug. 1939–12 March 1940.

Gen. Enrique Peñaranda, 12 March 1940 (deposed 20 Dec. 1943).

Maj. Gualberto Villaroel, 20 Dec. 1943 (deposed and lynched 21 July 1946).

Dr Néstor Guillén (27 July–14 Aug. 1946, provisional).

Chief Justice Monje Gutiérrez (15 Aug. 1946–9 March 1947).

Dr Enrique Hertzog (10 March 1947–23 Oct. 1949).

Dr Mamerto Urriolagoitia (24 Oct. 1949–15 May 1951).

Gen. Hugo Ballivián Rojas (15 May 1951–8 April 1952).

Dr Víctor Paz Estenssoro (16 April 1952–6 Aug. 1956).

Dr Hernán Siles Zuazo (6 Aug. 1956–6 Aug. 1960).

Dr Víctor Paz Estenssoro (6 Aug. 1960–4 Nov. 1964, deposed).

Gen. René Barrientos Ortuño, 4 Nov. 1964–26 May 1965 (Head of Military Junta).

Gen. René Barrientos Ortuño and Gen. Alfredo Ovando Candia (joint Presidents), 26 May 1965–Jan. 1966.

Gen. Alfredo Ovando Candia, Jan. 1966–6 Aug. 1966.

Gen. René Barrientos Ortuño (Constitutional President killed in air accident), 6 Aug. 1966–27 April 1969.

Dr Luis Adolfo Siles Salinas (deposed), 27 April 1969–26 Sept. 1969.

Gen. Alfredo Ovando Candia, 26 Sept. 1969–6 Oct. 1969.

President. On 4 Nov. 1964 Dr Víctor Paz Estenssoro fled the country. The government was replaced by a military *junta* headed by Gen. René Barrientos Ortuño, previously Vice-President. Gen. Alfredo Ovando Candia, formerly Commander-in-Chief of the armed forces, was appointed Co-President on 26 May 1965 and became sole President when Gen. Barrientos resigned in Jan. 1966. The latter was named Constitutional President after the 3 July elections, in which his coalition party, the Bolivian Revolution Front, gained 18 of the 27 Senate seats and the 82 of the 102 Chamber seats; he was inducted on 6 Aug. 1966. Gen. Barrientos was killed in a helicopter accident on 27 April 1969, and in accordance with the constitution was succeeded by the Vice-President, Dr Luis Adolfo Siles Salinas. On 26 Sept. 1969, by mandate of the armed forces, the constitutional government was overthrown and Gen. Alfredo Ovando Candia appointed President. On 7 Oct. 1970 Gen. Juan José Torres proclaimed himself President after an abortive military *coup* had overthrown President Alfredo Ovando Candia.

The Cabinet consists of the President and 15 Ministers of State.

Minister of Foreign Affairs: Gen. Emilio Molina Pizarro.

The republic is divided into 9 departments, established in Jan. 1826, with 98 provinces administered by sub-prefects, and 1,272 cantons administered by corregidores. The supreme authority in each department is vested in a prefect appointed by the President.

AREA AND POPULATION. Bolivia is a landlocked state with an area of some 424,160 sq. miles (1,098,580 sq. km). In the series of disastrous wars in the 19th and early 20th centuries its territorial losses to each of 5 neighbouring nations reduced its area from an estimated 1·16m. sq. miles.

Until 1884, when Bolivia was defeated by Chile, she had a strip bordering on the Pacific which contains extensive nitrate beds and at that time the port of Cobija (which no longer exists). She lost this area to Chile; but in Sept. 1953 Chile declared Arica a free port and, although it is no longer a free port for Bolivian imports, Bolivia still has certain privileges.

The following table shows the area and population of the departments (the capitals of each are given in brackets):

Departments	Area (sq. km)	Census Aug.– Sept. 1950	Estimated 1971	Per sq. km 1971
La Paz (La Paz)	133,985	948,446	1,590,000	11·87
Cochabamba (Cochabamba)	55,631	490,475	822,000	14·78
Potosí (Potosí)	118,218	534,399	896,000	7·58
Santa Cruz (Santa Cruz)	370,621	286,145	479,800	1·29
Chuquisaca (Sucre)	51,524	282,980	474,000	9·21
Tarija (Tarija)	37,623	126,752	212,600	5·65
Oruro (Oruro)	53,588	210,260	352.600	6·58
Beni (Trinidad)	213,564	119,770	200,900	0·94
Pando (Cobija)	63,827	19,804	33,200	0·52
Total	1,098,581	3,019,031[1]	5,062,500	4·61

[1] An official estimate allowing for under-enumeration; the total actually recorded was 2,704,165.

A report prepared in 1967 on behalf of the International Labour Office gives the following forecast: 1970, 4,931,000; 1975, 5,634,000. The Ministry of Planning estimated economically active population in 1967 at 1·81m., of whom 1,205,000 were employed in agriculture and fishing, 145,000 in industrial manufacture, 140,000 in construction, 110,000 in commerce and finance, 77,000 in central and local government, 48,000 in mining and 50,000 in transport.

Population (estimated, 1970) of the principal towns: La Paz, 562,000; Cochabamba, 149,900; Santa Cruz, 124,900; Oruro, 119,700; Potosí, 96,800; Sucre, 84,900; Tarija, 35,700; Trinidad, 22,800; Cobija, 4,500.

Crude birth rate, 1968, 42 per 1,000 population; crude death rate, 17; crude marriage rate (1958), 4; infantile mortality, 140 per 1,000 live births.

The language of the educated classes is Spanish, that of the majority of Indians, Aymará (25·2%) or Quechua (34·4%).

RELIGION. The Roman Catholic is the recognized religion of the state; the free exercise of other forms of worship is permitted. The Catholic Church is under a cardinal (in Sucre), an archbishop (in La Paz), 6 bishops (Cochabamba, Santa Cruz, Oruro, Potosí, Riberalta and Tarija) and vicars apostolic (titular bishops resident in Cueva, Trinidad, San Ignacio de Velasco, Riberalta and Rurrenabaque). Protestants numbered 43,135 in 1962.

By a law of 11 Oct. 1911 all marriages must be celebrated by the civil authorities. Divorce is permitted by a law enacted on 15 April 1932.

EDUCATION. Primary instruction is free and obligatory between the ages of 6 and 14 years. Estimates for 1968 show 977,765 children between 6 and 14 years, of whom 581,994 attend school. All illiterates between 15 and 50 years are obliged to attend literacy classes. This meant in 1965 some 66·9%, according to the Minister, who attributed the increase in absolute numbers to the increase in population.

At Sucre, Oruro, Potosí, Cochambamba, Santa Cruz, Tarija, Trinidad and La Paz are universities; La Paz is the most important of them while the San Francisco Xavier University at Sucre is one of the oldest in America, having been founded in 1624.

CINEMAS (1970). Cinemas numbered 90, with seating capacity of about 42,500.

NEWSPAPERS (1968). There were 12 daily newspapers with an aggregate daily circulation of about 103,000.

JUSTICE. Justice is administered by the Supreme Court, superior district courts (of 5 or 7 judges) and courts of local justice. The Supreme Court, with headquarters at Sucre, is divided into two sections, civil and criminal, of 5 justices each, with the Chief Justice presiding over both. Members of the Supreme Court are chosen on a two-thirds vote of Congress. They nominate the district judges and largely administer the judiciary budget.

FINANCE. Currency. On 1 Jan. 1963 the *Boliviano* (equalling US$11,865) was replaced by a new currency unit, the *peso boliviano* ($b.) at the rate of Bs1,000 = $b.1. Current exchange rates are $b.11.86 = US$1 and $b.28.45 = £1.

Money in circulation at the end of Aug. 1969 totalled 1,279·1m. *pesos bolivianos.*

Budget. The foreign-exchange revenue is derived mainly from sales of tin and other non-ferrous metals (furnishing about 86% of export revenue in 1967), but oil and gas are of increasing importance. Revenue and expenditures in 1m. *pesos bolivianos* balanced as follows: 1964, 545·5; 1965, 764·3; 1966, 742·8; 1967, 860·4; 1968, 1,224·7; 1969, 1,265·3.

The above shows the Central Government budget, but only since 1966 a consolidated budget has been issued which includes all State entities.

Some items of expenditure proposed in the 1969 budget were: Education, 18%; transport and roads, 9%. Aid from USA in 1968 was about $30·6m.

The external debt amounted to $404m. in 1970.

DEFENCE. Bolivia is divided into 8 military districts, with divisional headquarters in Viacha, Oruro, Villa Montes, Camiri, Roboré, Riberalta, Santa Cruz, Cochabamba; regional HQ are located at La Paz, Sucre, Tarija, Potosí, Trinidad and Cobija.

The law of 1943 provided for a permanent force of 15,000 men, including the police force and the frontier carabineers, but the standing army in 1969 numbered over 17,000 men. Military service is compulsory for all males from the 19th to the 49th year. The army consists of 2 infantry brigades, 1 motorized regiment, 5 artillery regiments, a paratroop regiment (CITE) and 2 ranger battalions specially trained in anti-guerilla warfare.

The Bolivian Air Force, established in 1923, is organized into 4 groups, and comprises staff, bomber, fighter, transport, training, reconnaissance, maintenance and supply commands. Its small combat force consists of about 10 modernized Cavalier F-51D Mustang piston-engined fighters supplied under MAP and a few T-28 armed trainers, plus 12 Hughes 500M armed light observation helicopters for counter-insurgency operations. Other types in service include T-6 basic trainers, C-47 transports with which a military airline service is operated, a presidential C-54 and some light aircraft. Personnel strength is about 2,200.

PLANNING. A Development Plan (1962–71) is backed by technical and financial aid from the USA Government, the World Bank, the Inter-American Development Bank, the United Nations and several European countries including the UK.

AGRICULTURE. The extensive and still largely undeveloped region east of the Andes comprises about three-quarters of the entire area of the country, and since the agrarian reform of 1952 sugar-cane, rice and cotton have been grown in this *Oriente* in increasing abundance, reaching self-sufficiency in all these products. Output in metric tons in 1969 was: Refined sugar, 108,600 (1968); rice, 58,300; coffee, 9,900; maize, 390,000; potatoes, 671,200; wheat, 52,200, and cotton (lint), 4,400.

In 1966 there were some 827,730 head of cattle, mostly in the Santa Cruz and Beni departments; some are exported to Peru. The public lands of the state have an area of about 245,000 sq. miles, of which 104,000 sq. miles are reserved for special colonization. The National Agrarian Reform Service reported in Nov. 1969 that since May 1965 it had distributed 5·5m. hectares of land in 323,046 properties.

A colony of Jewish refugees was established in 1940 at Buena Tierra, 60 miles east of La Paz and, more recently, Japanese and Okinawan settlements in the region of Santa Cruz. The Bolivian Development Corporation has a programme for relief of over-population on the barren altiplano and in 1964 resettled 1,217 families in tropical areas. Its target was another 8,000 families by the end of 1966.

FORESTRY. Tropical forests with woods ranging from the 'iron tree' to the light *palo de balsa* are beginning to be exploited. In 1962 the Forestry Service announced proved reserves of 46·3m. hectares, plus a similar amount available for immediate development.

In 1968, 9,882 tons of wood and cross-ties were exported. Rubber exports in 1968 totalled 1,768 tons.

MINING. Mining is the most important industry. Bolivia in 1967 produced 15·9% of the tin output of the non-communist world and was second to Malaysia in the production of this metal. Tin mines are at altitudes of from 12,000 to 18,000 ft, where few except native Indians can stand the conditions; transport is costly. Bolivian tin is extracted by shaft-mining, frequently very deep; the ore yields only 3·5% or less of tin and is very refractory; tin is exported in concentrates called *barrilla*, through Pacific ports for refining, much of it in the UK. A twin dredger has been installed by Grace & Co. to exploit alluvial deposits and another dredge is operated by COMSUR. Total tin production in 1969 was 30,220 tons.

A decree of 31 Oct. 1952 nationalized the mining companies of the Patiño, Hochschild and Aramayo groups, which were responsible for about 60% of Bolivia's mineral output. Provisional compensation proposed was: Patiño, $7·5m.; Hochschild, $9·25m.; Aramayo, $4,976,324. Agreements were concluded during 1953 for the gradual payment of compensation on a sliding scale based on prices received for Bolivian tin abroad, but a final settlement has still to be negotiated. The state industry is being run by the Corporación Minera de Bolivia (COMIBOL). This state body has been receiving financial aid since 1961 from the USA and West Germany and the Inter-American Development Bank under a programme (Operación Triangular) for the rehabilitation of the state mines. COMIBOL produced 63% of tin exports in 1968, valued US$58·3m. In 1965 COMIBOL balanced its books for the first time in many years, and despite lower prices in 1966 and 1967 showed an operating profit in both years. Such marked improvement coincides with strong measures against the Miners' Union in May 1965, the new and efficient administration, and some decrease in political interference. COMIBOL employs about 23,000 in mining and administrative capacities.

Alluvial gold deposits in the Alto Beni region are being exploited mainly by USA companies. Co-operative mines at Tipuani produce over 100 kg of gold per month.

There are petroleum and natural gas deposits in the Santa-Cruz–Camiri areas. A pipeline for crude oil connects Caranda (Santa Cruz) with the Pacific coast at Arica (Chile) and a pipeline for natural gas is under construction from Santa Cruz to the Argentine border. Bolivia is virtually self-sufficient in petroleum products. All production, refining and internal distribution is now in the hands of Yacimientos Petroliferos Fiscales Bolivianos (the State Petroleum Organization), the Bolivian Gulf Oil Company having been nationalized on 17 Oct. 1969. Total production of crude oil in 1969 amounted to 2·34m. cu. metres. Production of refined products was as follows (in cu. metres): Petrol, 293,500; paraffin, 118,000; diesel oil, 97,300; fuel oil, 152,000.

INDUSTRY. There are few industrial establishments (1,518 in 1965) and the country relies on imports for the supply of many consumer goods. However, as a result of a new investment law passed in 1965, industrial activity is increasing.

The following table shows the value of some industrial products in 1966 and 1967 (1,000 pesos bolivianos):

Commodity	1966	1967	Commodity	1966	1967
Food and drink	306,911	318,922	Pharmaceuticals	29,178	30,578
Textiles	170,708	174,976	Tobacco and cigarettes	51,673	53,998
Leather and shoes	85,033	88,349	Electricity	55,271	62,500

POWER. Electric power production is expanding. Installed capacity was estimated at 250,600 kw. at the end of 1969. Consumption during 1969 amounted to 705·6m. kwh. Hydro-electric production amounted to 584·6m. kwh.

COMMERCE. The value of imports and exports in US$1,000 has been as follows:

	1964	1965	1966	1967	1968
Imports	107,000	121,500	138,400	151,000	152,800
Exports	113,800	131,836	150,000	166,300	170,600

Tin ore has fallen to about 60% of Bolivia's exports. Total exports, 1969, of minerals, in concentrates, ingots or solder, were valued at US$160·6m., of which tin, 28,867 tons (US$97·4m.); wolfram, 2,305 tons (US$11m.); lead, 5,248 tons (US$6·7m.); copper, 7,926 tons (US$10·7m.); zinc, 26,380 tons (US$7·7m.); antimony, 9,091 tons (US$9·9m.); silver, 195 fine tons (US$11·5m.); gold, 1,494 kg (US$1·6m.); bismuth, 645 tons (US$2·4m.); sulphur, 36,096 tons (US$1·6m.). Large deposits of salt are found near Lake Poopó and in the south of Bolivia.

Bolivia having no seaport, imports and exports pass chiefly through the ports of Arica and Antofagasta in Chile, Mollendo-Matarani in Peru, through La Quiaca on the Bolivian–Argentine border and through river-ports on the rivers flowing into the Amazon. The chief imports are lard, flour, cooking oil, iron and steel products, mining machinery, motor vehicles, pharmaceuticals, paper products and textiles. In 1969 imports (in £1,000) were 24,667 from USA; West Germany, 8,370; Japan, 7,647; UK, 2,609; Netherlands, 1,807.

Import and export licensing, and price subsidies and controls were abolished on 15 Dec. 1956; but in 1963 a measure of import control was reimposed.

Total trade between UK and Bolivia (British Board of Trade returns) for 5 years (in £1,000 sterling):

	1966	1967	1968	1969	1970
Imports to UK	22,338	23,795	26,336	34,212	28,460
Exports from UK	1,712	1,684	2,223	2,584⎫	2,201
Re-exports from UK	41	10	33	25⎭	

SHIPPING. Traffic on Lake Titicaca between Guaqui and Puno is carried on by the steamers of the Peruvian Corporation. About 12,000 miles of rivers, in 4 main systems (Beni, Pilcomayo, Titicaca–Desaguadero, Mamoré), are open to navigation by light-draught vessels.

ROADS. A motor highway, 312 miles long, was completed in Dec. 1953 (with the aid of a $28·7m. loan (plus $4·7m. for asphalting) from the Export-Import Bank) from Cochabamba to the lowland farming region of Santa Cruz. Economically this road, laboriously constructed through a most difficult section of the Andes, is Bolivia's most important, for it assists towards the abolition of costly food imports. A further relief paved road, 135 miles long, was constructed in 1967 to broaden this development. Of other main highways (unmetalled) there is one from La Paz through Guaqui into Peru, another from La Paz, via Oruro, Potosí, Tarija and Bermejo, into Argentina, with branches to Cochabamba, Sucre and Camiri, passable throughout the year except at the height of the rainy season, and others from Villazón to Villa Montes via Tarija, passable during the dry season. The asphalting of the road from La Paz to Oruro has begun, with 27 miles completed, and 2 important roads are under construction, linking Cochabamba with the Chapare and Ichilo areas and with Santa Cruz and the Mamoré river system. The total length of the road system is about 18,312 km (1968). Motor vehicles registered in 1970, 52,624.

RAILWAYS. The total length of railway open in 1970 was 3,524 km. On 1 Nov. 1964 the State Railway Authority was set up to run all lines in the Western system except the Guaqui–La Paz Railway (owned by the Peruvian Corporation); and also the Corumbá–Santa Cruz line, which until 1964 was administered by a Brazilian–Bolivian Mixed Commission. The new 500-km line Santa Cruz–Yacuiba is administered by an Argentine–Bolivian Mixed Commission. Access to the Pacific is by lines to Antofagasta—of which the Chilean section is owned by the Antofagasta (Chili) and Bolivia Railway Co.—and Arica, and to Mollendo in Peru *via* Guaqui and Arequipa. The Bolivian and Peruvian sections are separated by Lake Titicaca (12,506 ft) which is crossed by steamer. Another railway from Santa Cruz to Trinidad Beni is being built.

AVIATION. The national airline is Lloyd Aéreo Boliviano; in 1969 a total of 13,404 hours were flown, carrying 315,351 passengers and 33,692 metric tons of freight. The airline runs regular services between La Paz and Lima, São Paulo, Buenos Aires, Salta and Arica as well as many internal services. Braniff International Airways runs regular flights between La Paz, Lima, Buenos Aires, Santiago and Asunción, linking Bolivia (*via* Lima) to the USA. Lufthansa Iberia and APSA (Peruvian Airlines) link Bolivia with Europe. Aerolíneas Argentinas also provide regular services through La Paz.

POST. In Bolivia there were, in 1969, 418 post offices, of these, 205 provided telegraph and telephone services together with a further 245 offices for telegraph and telephone service only. There is telephone service in the towns of La Paz, Cochabamba, Oruro, Sucre, Potosí and Santa Cruz, with 27,500 telephones. There are about 40 broadcasting stations, of which 7 are state-owned.

BANKING. The Banco Central de Bolivia was established in 1911 as Banco de la Nacion Boliviana and re-organized in 1928. The Bank was nationalized in 1939. In 1945 the Banco Central de Bolivia was divided into two independent departments, the Banking Department and the Monetary Department. The latter has the sole power of note issue and must maintain a legal reserve equal to the amount of notes in circulation; 50% of such reserve must be in gold and foreign exchange and 50% in securities. At 31 Dec. 1968 the Bank's gross gold and foreign exchange reserves amounted to US$46·2m. and Bolivia's net gold and international reserves stood at US$32·4m. The country also has a stand-by agreement of up to US$20m. with the International Monetary Fund.

There are Argentine, Brazilian, Peruvian, USA and domestic banks.

WEIGHTS AND MEASURES. The metric system of weights and measures is used by the administration and prescribed by law, but the old Spanish system is also employed.

DIPLOMATIC REPRESENTATIVES

Bolivia maintains resident diplomatic missions in:

Argentina	Germany (West)	Peru	Uruguay
Brazil	Israel	Spain	Vatican
Colombia	Italy	USSR	Venezuela
Ecuador	Mexico	UK	Yugoslavia
France	Paraguay	USA	

OF BOLIVIA IN GREAT BRITAIN (106 Eaton Sq., SW1)
Ambassador: Gen. Juan Lechin Suarez (accredited 5 Feb. 1970).
Minister-Counsellor: Dr Carlos Hanhart.

There is a consulate at the London Embassy, honorary consulates at Birmingham, Cardiff, Hull, Liverpool and Manchester, and an honorary vice-consulate at Glasgow.

OF GREAT BRITAIN IN BOLIVIA
Ambassador: R. W. Bailey, CMG.
First Secretaries: B. R. Pridham (*Head of Chancery and Consul*); P. A. McLean (*Commercial*). *Defence Attaché:* Group Capt. G. D. Fuller (resides at Lima).

There is also an honorary Consul at Cochabamba.

OF BOLIVIA IN THE USA (Suite 212, 1145–19th St. NW,
Washington, D.C. 20036)

Ambassador: (Vacant).
Minister-Counsellor: Antonio Céspedes Toro (*Chargé d'Affaires*). *Defence Attachés:* Col. René Bernal Escalante (*Army and Navy*).

OF THE USA IN BOLIVIA

Ambassador: Ernest V. Siracusa.
Deputy Chief of Mission: Malcolm Barnebey.
Heads of Sections: Arthur Shankel (*Political*); Gordon Daniels (*Economic*);
Dirk Teller (*Commercial*); Edward W. Coy (*AID*); Allen C. Hansen (*USIA*).
Service Attachés: Col. S. L. Ross (*Defence and Air*), Lieut.-Col. William A.
Crenshaw (*Army*).

BOOKS OF REFERENCE

There is a weekly official gazette.

Anuario Geográfico y Estadístico de la República de Bolivia
Anuario del Comercia Exterior de Bolivia
Boletín Mensual de Información Estadística
Constitución Política del Estado. La Paz, 1961
Barton, J. D., *A Short History of Bolivia.* La Paz, 1968
Fain, O., *Bolivie.* Paris, 1955
Osborne, H., *Bolivia: a land divided.* R. Inst. of Int. Affairs, 3rd ed. 1964.—*Indians of the Andes.*
  London, 1952
Pardo Valle, N., *Poligrafia de Bolivia.* La Paz, 1966
Zondag, *The Bolivian Economy, 1952–65.* New York, 1966

BRAZIL

Brasil

HISTORY. Brazil was discovered on 22 April 1500 by the Portuguese Admiral
Pedro Alvares Cabral, and thus became a Portuguese settlement; in 1815 the
colony was declared 'a kingdom', and on 13 May 1822 Dom Pedro, eldest
surviving son of King João of Portugal, was chosen 'Perpetual Defender' of
Brazil by a National Congress. He proclaimed the independence of the country
on 7 Sept. 1822, and was chosen 'Constitutional Emperor and Perpetual
Defender' on 12 Oct. 1822.

CONSTITUTION AND GOVERNMENT. On 15 Nov. 1889 Dom Pedro
II (1825–91) was dethroned by a revolution, and Brazil declared a republic.
Presidents since the establishment of the republic:

Marshal Deodoro da Fonseca, 15 Nov. 1889–
  23 Nov. 1891 (resigned).
Marshal Floriano Peixoto (Acting), 23 Nov.
  1891–15 Nov. 1894.
Dr Prudente de Moraes Barros, 15 Nov. 1894–
  15 Nov. 1898.
Dr Manuel Ferraz de Campos Salles, 15 Nov.
  1898–15 Nov. 1902.
Dr Francisco da Paula Rodrigues Alves, 15
  Nov. 1902–15 Nov. 1906.
Dr Affonso Penna, 15 Nov. 1906–14 June
  1909 (died).
Dr Nilo Peçanha (Acting), 14 June 1909–15
  Nov. 1910.
Marshal Hermes da Fonseca, 15 Nov. 1910–
  15 Nov. 1914.

Dr Wenceslau Braz, 15 Nov. 1914–15 Nov.
  1918.
Dr Francisco de Paula Rodrigues Alves.[1]
Dr Delphim Moreira (Acting), 15 Nov. 1918–
  28 July 1919.
Dr Epitácio da Silva Pessoa, 28 July 1919–
  15 Nov. 1922.
Dr Arthur Bernardes, 15 Nov. 1922–15 Nov.
  1926.
Dr Washington Luiz Pereira de Souza, 15
  Nov. 1926–25 Oct. 1930 (deposed).
Dr Getúlio Dornelles Vargas, 26 Oct. 1930–
  29 Oct. 1945 (resigned).
Dr José Linhares (Provisional President), 30
  Oct. 1945–31 Jan. 1946.

[1] Owing to illness did not take office; died 16 Jan. 1919.

Gen. Eurico Gaspar Dutra, 31 Jan. 1946–31 Jan. 1951.
Dr Getúlio Dornelles Vargas, 31 Jan. 1951– died 24 Aug. 1954.
Dr João Café Filho, 24 Aug. 1954–8 Nov. 1955 (resigned).
Carlos Coimbra da Luz (Acting), 8 Nov. 1955–11 Nov. 1955 (deposed).
Nereu Ramos (Acting), 11 Nov. 1955–31 Jan. 1956.

Juscelino Kubitschek, 31 Jan. 1956–31 Jan. 1961.
Jânio da Silva Quadros, 31 Jan. 1961–25 Aug. 1961 (resigned).
João Belchior Marques Goulart, 7 Sept. 1961–31 March 1964 (deposed).
Marshal Humberto de A. Castelo Branco, 15 April 1964–15 March 1967.
Marshal Artur da Costa e Silva, 15 March 1967–30 Oct. 1969 (resigned).

On 24 Jan. 1967 both houses of Congress in joint session approved the new constitution and press law which came into force on 15 March. An amendment to the constitution, which came into force on 30 Oct. 1969, was issued on 17 Oct. The present constitution provides for the indirect election of the President and Vice-President by an electoral college, comprising the members of Congress and delegates from the state legislatures; it grants powers to the President to issue decree-laws on matters connected with the economy and national security; it gives the President authority to intervene in any of the 22 states without consultation with Congress and the right to declare a state of siege and to rule by decree. President and Vice-President are elected for a 5-year term and are not immediately re-eligible. The Senate is elected for 8 years, the Chamber of Deputies for 4 years.

The name of the country is changed from 'United States of Brazil' to 'Brazil'.

Freedom of speech and press are not absolute: war propaganda, the teaching of 'subversive doctrines' and the dissemination of race or class prejudices are banned, as also are political parties opposed to democracy, the existing multi-party system or to 'fundamental human rights' which include the right to own private property. The Supreme Electoral Court on 7 May 1947 declared the Communist Party illegal.

The Institutional Act No. 5 issued on 13 Dec. 1968 was incorporated into the new constitution through an amendment on 17th Oct. 1969. This gives the President power to cancel citizens' political rights for periods of 10 years. The Congress renewed its sessions on 22 Oct. 1969 and elections were held on 15 Nov. 1970.

Voting is compulsory for men and women between the ages of 18 and 65 and optional for persons over 65. Enlisted men and illiterates (who comprise about 40% of the adult population) may not vote.

President of the Republic: Gen. Emílio Garrastazu Médici, assumed office 30 Oct. 1969. *Vice-President:* Adm. Augusto H. R. Grünewald.
Minister of Foreign Affairs: Mário Gibson Barbosa.

There are Secretaries of State at the head of the following Ministries: Finance; Justice; Interior; Foreign Affairs; Transport; Communications; Agriculture; Labour and Social Welfare; Education and Culture; Health; Industry and Commerce; Mines and Power; Planning and General Co-ordination; and the Ministries of Army, Marine and Air.

National flag: Green, with yellow lozenge enclosing a blue sphere, with 22 white stars, of which 5 form the southern cross, and the motto *Ordem e Progresso*.
National anthem: Ouviram do Ipiranga (words by J. O. Duque Estrada; tune by F. M. da Silva).

LOCAL GOVERNMENT. Brazil consists of 22 states, 4 federal territories (Rondônia, Roraima, Amapá, Fernando de Noronha) and 1 federal district. Each state has its distinct administrative, legislative and judicial authorities, its own constitution and laws, which must, however, agree with the constitutional principles of the Union. The states may unite or split or form new states. Taxes on interstate commerce, levied by individual states, are prohibited. The governors and members of the legislatures are elected, but magistrates are appointed and are not removable from office save by judicial sentence.

AREA AND POPULATION. Population as at 1 Sept. 1960 (census) and 1 Sept. 1970 (census, provisional figures):

State and capital	Area (sq. km)	Census 1960	Census 1970
North	3,581,180	2,601,519	..
Rondônia[1] (Pôrto Velho[2])	243,044	70,783	95,311
Acre (Rio Branco)	152,589	160,208	203,900
Amazonas[3] (Manaus)	1,564,445	721,215	714,803
Roraima (Boa Vista[2])	230,104	29,489	40,855
Pará (Bélem)[4]	1,250,722	1,550,935	1,984,745
Amapá (Macapá[2])	140,276	68,889	116,481
North-east	1,548,672	22,428,873	..
Maranhão (São Luis)	328,663	2,492,139	2,883,221
Piaui (Teresina)[7]	250,934	1,263,368	1,735,568
Ceará (Fortaleza)[7]	150,630	3,337,856	4,440,286
Rio Grande do Norte (Natal)	53,015	1,157,258	1,603,094
Paraíba (João Pessoa)	56,372	2,018,023	2,383,518
Pernambuco (Recife)	98,281	4,136,900	5,208,011
Alagoas (Maceió)	27,731	1,271,062	1,606,165
Fernando de Noronha[5], [6]	26	1,389	1,239
Sergipe (Aracajú)	21,994	760,273	900,119
Bahia (Salvador)	561,026	5,990,605	7,420,906
South-East:[8]	924,934	31,056,432	..
Minas Gerais (Belo Horizonte)	587,172	9,798,880	11,279,872
Espírito Santo[9] (Vitória)	45,597	1,188,665	1,597,389
Rio de Janeiro (Niterói)	42,912	3,402,728	4,694,089
Guanabara (Rio de Janeiro)	1,356	3,307,163	4,296,782
São Paulo (São Paulo)	247,898	12,974,699	17,716,186
South	577,723	11,873,495	..
Paraná (Curitiba)	199,554	4,277,763	6,741,520
Santa Catarina (Florianópolis)	95,985	2,146,909	2,911,479
Rio Grande do Sul (Pôrto Alegre)	282,184	5,448,823	6,652,618
Central West	1,879,455	3,006,866	..
Mato Grosso (Cuiabá)	1,231,549	910,262	1,475,117
Goiás (Goiânia)	642,092	1,954,862	2,989,414
Distrito Federal (Brasília)	5,814	141,742	544,862
Total	8,511,965[10]	70,967,185	92,237,570

[1] The name 'Território Federal do Guaporé' was changed to 'Território Federal de Rondônia' on 17 Feb. 1956.
[2] Raised to the status of territorial capitals in 1943; previously, Pôrto Velho and Boa Vista belonged to the state of Amazonas and Macapá to the state of Pará.
[3] Excluding 2,680 sq. km in dispute with the state of Pará.
[4] Includes an area of 2,680 sq. km to be demarcated between states of Amazonas and Pará.
[5] Including 8 sq. km of islets.
[6] Territory created in 1942.
[7] A region of 2,614 sq. km is to be delimited between the states of Piauí and Ceará.
[8] Including 10,153 sq. km and population figures of 160,072 and 384,297 respectively for 1950 and 1960 corresponding to the Região da Serra dos Aimorés, territory in dispute between Minas Gerais and Espírito Santo and subsequently separated from both. Dispute settled 1963.
[9] Including the islands of Trindade and Martim Vaz.
[10] 3,286,000 sq. miles.

Census population 1 Sept. 1970, 92·24m.

Density of census population, 1960, was about 9 per sq. km.

The 1950 census showed 25,885,001 males and 26,059,396 females; also 32,027,661 whites (61·7%), 5,692,657 Negroes (11%), 13,786,742 mulattoes (26·5%), 329,082 Asiatics and 108,255 unknown. The urban and suburban population comprised 36·2% in 1950 and 45·1% in 1960.

The language is Portuguese.

The new capital, Brasília, was inaugurated 21 April 1960. The federal district (5,814 sq. km) was detached from the west-central state of Goiás, about 1,000 km north-west of Rio de Janeiro.

In 1970 the census population of the principal cities was: São Paulo, 5,901,533; Rio de Janeiro, 4,296,782; Recife, 1,078,819; Belo Horizonte, 1,232,708; Pôrto Alegre, 885,567; Salvador, 1,000,647; Fortaleza, 842,231; Belém, 642,514; Brasília, 544,862; Goiânia 388,926; Niterói, 324,367; Manaus, 249,797; Natal, 270,124; Maceió, 269,415; São Luis, 267,321; João Pessoa, 221,484.

The number of immigrants, between 1820 and 1953 was over 5m., but it is estimated that only one-half remained. Immigrants in recent years have numbered:

	1966	1967	1968	1969
Portuguese	2,708	3,838	3,917	1,933
Japanese	937	1,070	597	496
Spanish	469	572	743	568
Italian	643	747	738	477
Others	3,418	5,125	6,526	3,139
Total	8,175	11,352	12,521	6,613

Pierson, D., *Negroes in Brazil*. Chicago, 1942.—*Survey of Literature on Brazil of Sociological Significance*. Cambridge, Mass., 1945
Ramos, A., *The Negro in Brazil*. Washington, 1939.—*Las Poblaciones del Brazil*. Mexico City, 1945

RELIGION. The population is overwhelmingly Roman Catholic (93% at the census, 1950). In 1889 connexion between Church and State was abolished; it was restored by the 1934 constitution, but again abolished in 1946. In 1964 there were 31 ecclesiastical provinces and archdioceses, and 123 dioceses with 5,289 parishes. In 1967 Protestants numbered 7·9m., including 2·1m. Lutherans, 1·1m. Baptists, 550,000 Presbyterians, 500,000 Methodists.

EDUCATION. Elementary education is compulsory. In 1960 (census) there were 31,565,718 persons 5 years of age or over who could read and write; this was 53·57% of that age group; 51·1% of the literates were men.

There were, in 1968, 134,909 primary school units with 11,943,506 pupils; and (1968) 12,801 intermediary courses (secondary, commercial, industrial, agricultural and normal-school) with (1968) 3,205,699 pupils; and (1968) 1,712 higher schools with 278,295 pupils.

The Government undertakes to provide, in part, for higher or university instruction, but some institutions are maintained by the states, and some by private associations, while primary schools are chiefly maintained and supervised, either by the states or by the municipalities and private initiative. There are 24 official universities, including the University of Rio de Janeiro (founded on 7 Sept. 1920), the University of Bahia (founded in 1946), the University of Recife (1946), the University of Paraná (1946), the Rural University (1948, State of Rio de Janeiro), the University of São Paulo (1934), the University of Minas Gerais (1927), the University of Rio Grande do Sul (1934) and the University of Brasília (1960). There are also 10 Catholic universities in Rio de Janeiro (1946), São Paulo (1946), Rio Grande do Sul (1948), Pernambuco (1951), Minas Gerais (1958), Bahia, Paraná, Campinas, Petrópolis and Pelotas. Students in 1968 totalled 278,295.

The School of Public Administration in Rio de Janeiro, founded in 1952, trains civil servants for all Latin-American countries; in 1964 students totalled 272.

CINEMAS (1970). Cinemas numbered 3,079, with seating capacity of about 2m.

NEWSPAPERS (1968). There were 250 daily newspapers with a daily circulation of 1·01m. Foreigners and corporations (except political parties) are not allowed to own or control newspapers or wireless stations. The press law of 1967 prohibits anonymous journalism and the publication of material defamatory to the armed forces and other public institutions.

HEALTH. In 1968 there were 506 government and 2,891 private hospitals, and 39,754 physicians.

JUSTICE. There is a supreme federal Court of Justice at Brasília. It has 11 judges; all are appointed by the President with the approval of the Senate. There are also federal courts in each state and the Federal District and in the Territories, as well as 'electoral courts' to protect the elections, and labour tribunals. Justice is administered in the states in accordance with state law, by state courts, but in Brasília federal justice is administered. Judges are appointed for life. There are also 3,074 magistrates and 5,634 justices of the peace. There is no divorce, but there is a form of judicial separation. The death penalty was re-introduced in Sept. 1969.

FINANCE. Currency. On 15 May 1970 the cruzeiro (Cr$) became the monetary unit, equivalent to 1 new cruzeiro; it is divided into 100 centavos. The exchange rate is US$1 = Cr$4·92; £1 = Cr$11·82.

Budget. Receipts and expenditures for the federal government (excluding states, Federal District and municipalities) for calendar years have been as follows in 1m. cruzeiros (paper):

	1965[1]	1966[1]	1967[1]	1968[1,2]	1969[1,3]	1970[1,3]
Revenue	3,137,960	4,680,000	6,610,000	11,098	13,058	16,830
Expenditure	3,774,963	4,720,000	6,943,000	13,591	14,229	19,703

[1] Estimates. [2] NCr$1m. [3] Cr$1m.

Chief items of revenue were estimated in 1970 as follows (in 1,000 Cr$): Taxes, 15,851,948 (of which income tax, 3·5m.); government property, 43,035. Principal items of expenditure: Finance, 425,542; communication, 296,491; army, 1,645,476; education, 1,293,189; navy, 827,199; aviation, 947,904; transport, 3,742,881.

The foreign debt (including states and municipalities) of Brazil on 31 Dec 1969 amounted to £4,345,000, US$5,958,000. Internal funded federal and states debt, 31 Dec. 1969, was 4,856,866m. cruzeiros. Foreign aid (largely US) in 1966 was US$433·2m.

The *Superintendência da Moeda e do Crédito* (now, *Banco Central da República do Brasil*) registered US direct investments, 31 Dec. 1960, at $28,024m. The Bank of England (1955) placed the par value of Brazilian investments held by residents in the UK in 1953 (thus excluding securities repatriated by Brazilians) at £40m. (in 1938, £164m.) on which interest and dividends received, 1953, were, £1·2m. (in 1938, £1·6m.).

DEFENCE. Army. Under the constitution military service is compulsory for every Brazilian man from 21 years of age to 45. The terms of service are 9 years (from the 21st to the 30th years of age) in the Army 'first line' (1 in the ranks, the rest in the reserve) and 14 years (from the 30th to the 45th years of age) in the army 'second line' (7 in the 'second line' and 7 in the reserve of the same). The men in the Territorial Army also have an annual training of 2 to 4 weeks. The army is organized in 7 infantry divisions, 4 mechanized divisions, 1 armoured and 1 airborne division; total strength, 120,000 men.

In 1948 the US sent an Army, Navy and Air Force mission to Brazil to establish a college there for training senior officers in combined operations. In May 1953 the National Congress ratified the agreement for US military assistance, signed on 15 March 1952.

Navy. The principal ships of the Brazilian Navy are as follows:

Completed	Name	Standard displacement Tons	Armour Belt In.	Armour Guns In.	Principal armament	Torpedo tubes	Shaft horse-power	Speed Knots
					Aircraft Carrier			
1945	Minas Gerais[1]	15,890	—	—	10 40-mm. AA	—	40,000	24

[1] Ex-*Vengeance*, purchased from Great Britain in 1956.

					Cruisers			
1939	Tamandaré[1]	10,000	5 }		3–5 15 6-in.; 8 5-in.	—	100,000	32½
1938	Barroso[1]	9,700	4 }					

[1] Ex-*St Louis* and ex-*Philadelphia*, purchased from USA in 1951.

There are also 2 submarines, 12 destroyers, 5 frigates (destroyer escorts), 10 corvettes, 2 coastal minesweepers, 3 seaward defence boats, 2 river monitors, 4 transports, 4 oilers, a repair ship, 6 survey ships and 3 tugs.

Naval bases are at Rio de Janeiro, Belém, Natal, Recife, Salvador, with a river base at Ladario. Aircraft obtained from the USA for service on the carriers include 4 Sikorsky SH-3D and 5 SH-34J helicopters and 12 S-2A Tracker anti-submarine aircraft, the latter being operated by the Air Force. Three Wasp light anti-submarine helicopters were obtained from Britain in 1965, and have been followed by 7 turbine-powered Whirlwind Srs. 3s and 6 American-built Fairchild Hiller FH 1100 light observation helicopters.

The active personnel is 3,800 officers and 36,800 men, including marines.

Air Force. The Air Force, formed in 1918, has been independent of the Army and Navy since 1941. Air defence is organized in 6 zones. The operational units comprise 3 fighter groups of armed AT-33 jet aircraft, which are being replaced by 12 Mirage IIIE fighters and 4 Mirage IIIB trainers ordered in 1970, 1 light bomber group with modernized piston-engined B-26K Invaders and a counter-insurgency squadron with UH-1D Iroquois and armed JetRanger helicopters. There is a maritime reconnaissance squadron with P2V-5 Neptunes, an air/sea rescue group with SA-16 Albatross amphibians and UH-1D Iroquois helicopters, and an anti-submarine warfare carrier group of S-2A Trackers. Equipment of the transport units is predominantly American, including 1 transport group of C-130E Hercules, 1 transport group of DC-6s, 1 transport group of C-47s, 1 transport group of CA-10 Catalina amphibians, and 2 troop-carrier transport groups of C-119s and DHC-5 Buffalos. The VIP transport group has 2 BAC One-Elevens, Viscounts, HS 748s, 6 HS 125 twin-jet light transports and JetRanger helicopters. Equipment of second-line units includes T-6, locally-built Aerotec T-23 Uirapuru piston-engined primary trainers and Super Magister and armed T-37C (jet) basic trainers. Aircraft currently being delivered include 112 Aermacchi MB. 326G armed jet trainers, licence-built in Brazil, and C-95 Bandeirante twin-turboprop light transports, Neiva Universal piston-engined basic trainers and C-42/L-42 Regente light transport/AOP aircraft of local design.

AGRICULTURE. 51·39% of Brazil's population is rural, and 89% of her foreign exchange derives from agricultural exports; yet large quantities of food are still imported. Production (in metric tons):

	1968	1969[1]		1968	1969[1]
Beans	2,419,677	2,199,974	Potatoes	1,606,473	1,506,500
Cocoa	149,338	211,162	Sweet potatoes	2,120,450	2,175,143
Coffee	2,115,404	2,567,014	Rice	6,652,388	6,394,285
Cotton, raw	1,999,465	2,110,775	Sisal	328,276	311,110
Jute	51,206	48,718	Soya	654,476	1,056,607
Maize	12,813,638	12,693,435	Sugar-cane	76,610,500	75,247,090
Mandioca	29,203,229	30,073,943	Wheat	856,170	1,373,691
Oranges	2,717,346	2,896,811			

[1] Provisional

The 4 states of São Paulo, Paraná, Espírito Santo and Minas Gerais are the principal districts for coffee-growing. Large plantations or fazendas with more than 100,000 trees are the rule. Output, 1969, from 2,570,899 hectares, 2,567,014 metric tons; exports, 1,121,375 metric tons. Between 1962 and 1966 about 1,650m. coffee trees were destroyed.

Export of cocoa was nationalized in May 1943, but in 1952 reverted to private enterprise. Bahia furnishes 90% of the output; in 1969 total output was 211,162 metric tons from 437,637 hectares. Two crops a year are grown. The US takes one-half of the crop. Castor-bean output usually exceeds 250,000 metric tons; output, 1969, 378,398 metric tons. The plant grows wild.

Tobacco output was 250,224 metric tons in 1969 (258,019 in 1968), of which 48,169 metric tons (38,627 in 1968) were exported.

Sugar production, 1969, was 4,216,010 metric tons (1968: 4·2m.). Exports, 1969, 1,392,761 metric tons; 1968, 1·24m.

Brazil now ranks second only to the US in production of oranges (estimate, 1969, 2,896,811 metric tons). Output of bananas, 1969, estimate, 9,266,480 metric tons. Cotton lint and seed, estimate 1970, 2,426,963 metric tons. Exports of cotton, 1968, 274,441 metric tons. Brazil formerly furnished only 10% of her own requirements in wheat (average output, 1934–38, 144,000 metric tons); output, 1969, 1,373,691 metric tons; imports, however, remain heavy, 2,355,559 metric tons in 1969. Rice is important; output (rough rice), 1969, was 6,394,285 metric tons.

Rubber is another natural product of the country, chiefly in the states of Acre, Amazonas and Pará. Output, 1968, 32,184 metric tons (gross weight); peak reached in 1912 (when rubber realized US$3 a lb.) was 42,510 gross tons. Output of tyres in local factories has risen from 421,765 units (tyres and tubes) in 1940 to 11,053,053 in 1968. Brazilian consumption of rubber for all purposes in 1969 was 124,318 metric tons. Brazil is the chief source of carnaúba wax, used for electric insulation and gramophone records, exporting 13,415 tons in 1969. Caroá fibre is grown as a substitute for Indian jute; production, 1969, 1,088 metric tons. Jute output, 1969, 48,718 metric tons. Plantations of tung trees established in 1930 (4m. trees in 1946) are beginning to yield tung oils in commercial quantities; output of tung, estimate, 1969, 13,969 metric tons.

Livestock. Brazil now ranks ahead of Argentina as livestock producer; numbers (in 1,000), 1969, showed 95,008 cattle, 65,734 sheep, 24,333 sheep, 14,744 goats, 9,116 horses, 2,992 asses and 4,818 mules. In 1968, 8·7m. cattle, 10·6m. swine, 2·2m. sheep and lambs, 1·9m. goats, 33m. poultry and 32,000 rabbits were slaughtered for meat; total was barely sufficient for domestic needs.

FISHERIES. The fishing industry totalled a fleet of 146,645 vessels in 1965; the catch in 1968 was 500,387 metric tons.

In 1966 the sovereignty over territorial waters, including fishing rights, was extended to 12 miles.

MINING. Brazil is the only source of high-grade quartz crystal in commercial quantities; exports in 1969, 3,826 metric tons. It is an important source of industrial diamonds (exports, 1969, 4,389 grammes); the second largest western producer of chrome ore (reserves of 4m. tons; output, 1967, 15,025; 1968, 17,032 metric tons); fifth in the output of mica (483 tons in 1968); third in zirconium, 328 tons (1968); she is the largest producer of beryllium, output (1968) 744 metric tons; graphite (1968), 22,000 metric tons, titanium ore (1967), 284 tons and magnesite (1968), 137,820 metric tons. Along the coasts of the states of Rio de Janeiro, Espírito Santo and Bahia are found monazite sands containing thorium; reserves are estimated at 100,000 tons. Manganese ores of high content are important (reserves in the Amapá region alone are estimated at 10m. metric tons); exports, 1969, 860,619 metric tons. Exports of tungsten ore and concentrates, 1968, totalled 670 metric tons; in 1967, 420 metric tons. Mine production of lead, (1967) 295,706, (1968) 320,553 metric tons. Asbestos production, (1967) 337,813, (1968) 345,442 metric tons. Coal deposits exist in Rio Grande do Sul, Santa Catarina, Paraná and São Paulo. Total reserves are estimated at 5,000m. tons; output (1969), 5·13m. metric tons.

Iron is found chiefly in Minas Gerais, notably the Cauê Peak at Itabira. The Government is now opening up what is believed to be one of the richest iron-ore deposits in the world, with estimated reserves of 35,000m. tons, of which half rival the Swedish ores in iron content (about 68·5%) and have lower silica and phosphorus contents. Total output of iron ore, 1967, mainly from the Cia. Vale do Rio Doce mine at Itabira, was 22,297,562 (1968: 25,123,213) metric tons. The National Iron and Steel Co. at Volta Redonda, State of Rio de Janeiro, furnishes a substantial part of Brazil's steel requirements. Brazil's total output included: Pig-iron, (1969) 3,717,190, (1968) 3,368,953 metric tons; ingots castings, (1969) 4,924,532, (1968) 4,453,187 metric tons.

Production of aluminium was started in Minas Gerais in 1945; output of bauxite, 1968, 313,748 metric tons. Exports of barytes, 1969, was 18,292 metric tons. Cement output, 1969, was 7,823,487 (1968: 7,280,654) metric tons. Output of phosphate rock, 1968, was 648,793 metric tons, plus 582,703 metric tons of apatite.

Gold is found in practically every state, though large-scale mining is confined to a single mine in Minas Gerais; the production in 1968 was 5,555 kg. Silver output, 1968, 14,296 kg. Salt output (1969), 1,629,507 metric tons. Diamond districts are Diamantine Grão Mogol, Chapada Diamantina, Bagagem, Goiás and Mato Grosso; output in 1966 was 5,460 grammes.

INDUSTRY. The most important manufacturing industry in Brazil is cotton weaving, which employs about 16% of all industrial workers; nearly 50% of the factories are in São Paulo and another 28% in Guanabara and Minas Gerais. The 423 mills, 1950, had 3·3m. spindles (27% modern) and 100,000 looms (7% automatic). Output of cotton textiles, 1969, was 1,170m. metres of cloth. Exports of cotton piece-goods, 1969, were 3,040 metric tons. Rayon yarn output, 1965, was 50,538 metric tons. In all, about 650 textile-mills are working. Local production and assembly of vehicles, including automobiles (236,893 in 1969) and tractors (9,471 in 1969), steadily increasing.

Brazil's potential capacity for electric power production is estimated at 55m. kw., one of the largest in the world. Only 7·6m. kw. had been developed by 1968. Consumption, 1969, 34·2m. Mw. Of the total capital invested in industrial concerns (US$1,779,786,350), 49% was foreign-owned. The entire petroleum industry, including production, importation and refining, was placed under federal control in April 1938; there are, 1968, 12 refineries. The country imports substantial amounts (13,370,636 metric tons in 1969) to supplement its total production. Crude oil output, 1969, 8·4m. tons; 1968, 7·7m. tons; 1967, 7m. tons.

A big paper-mill, reported to be the largest pulp-and-paper mill in South America, is at Monte Alegre, Paraná. Brazil's output of paper, 1969, was 849,192 metric tons.

COMMERCE. In 1957 Brazil modernized her 20-year-old tariff (at present duties are levied mainly on volume and not on values) in order to protect her infant industries and to increase government revenue. Her present tariffs furnish 12% of the Government's revenue (*see* under GATT). She ratified the Treaty of Montevideo on 3 Feb. 1961 (*see* LAFTA).

Imports and exports for calendar years in 1,000 cruzeiros; since 1966, 1,000 new cruzeiros:

	1965	1966	1967	1968	1969
Imports	1,929,646,739	3,264,773	4,291,939	6,826,201	8,981.592
Exports	2,214,843,187	3,813,540	4,265,501	6,177,932	9,214.225

Converted into US$1m., these trade figures were:

	1964	1965	1966	1967	1968	1969
Imports	1,263·5	1,096·4	1,496·2	1,667·4	2,131·9	8.918,992
Exports	1,429·8	1,519·5	1,741·4	1,654·0	1,881·3	9.214,225

Exports in 1969, 30·3m. metric tons; 1968, 23·5m. metric tons. Imports in 1969, 24·6m. metric tons; 1968, 23·6m. metric tons.

Principal imports in 1969 were (in US$1m.): Fuel and lubricants, 164; machinery and vehicles, 404; chemicals, 177; wheat, 92; metals and metal manufactures, 167.

Principal exports in 1969 were (in US$1m.): Coffee, 813; iron ore, 149; cotton, 195; sugar, 115; pinewood, 72.

Of exports in (US$1m.) in 1969, USA took 609·7; West Germany, 200·1; Argentina, 170·9; Italy, 164·4; Netherlands, 135·1; UK, 99·2; France, 99·1; Japan, 105·3. Of 1969 imports, USA furnished 613·2; West Germany, 259·5; Argentina, 133·5; UK, 81·9; Japan, 94·5.

Total trade between UK and Brazil (according to British Board of Trade returns, in £1,000 sterling):

	1965	1966	1967	1968	1969	1970
Imports to UK	28,054	31,545	26,553	37,852	50,716	62,784
Exports from UK	10,652	16,906	19,624	44,048	43,235 ⎫	60,769
Re-exports from UK	112	210	271	609	430 ⎭	

SHIPPING. Inland waterways, mostly rivers, are open to navigation over some 21,944 miles. Rio de Janeiro and Santos are the 2 leading ports; there are 13 other large ports. Bolivia and Paraguay have been given free ports at Santos. During 1969, 6,145 vessels with tonnage of 33·5m. entered the ports of Rio de Janeiro and Santos.

The Lloyd Brasileiro is owned and operated by the Government; its fleet comprised (1965) 57 vessels of 313,800 gross tons. Brazilian shipping, 31 Dec. 1965 (registered with Lloyds), amounted to 435 vessels (over 100 gross tons) of 1,401,985 gross tons. Petrobrás, the government oil monopoly, took over the government tanker fleet of 26 vessels in 1958; total tanker fleet in 1965 was 65 vessels of 574,000 gross tons.

RAILWAYS. Railway history in Brazil begins in 1854. In 1966 the total length of railways was 31,961 km. In 1966–67 about 6,600 km of uneconomic lines were closed. The state-owned Central Brazil Railway (2,888 km) joins up the railways of Brazil with those of Uruguay, Argentina and Paraguay, and is being electrified. Four Anglo-Brazilian railways have a length of 3,165·5 miles; 3 of the 4 were purchased in 1949 by the Brazilian Government for £14,235,000. Brazilian railways today operate over tracks of 5 different gauges and handle annually only 50m. metric tons of merchandise needing transport. The railways, in 1969, transported 355,780,000 passengers, 65,253,000 tons of freight and 783,000 metric tons of animals.

ROADS. There are (1969) 1,089,452 km of highways. In 1968 Brazil had 2,599,168 motor vehicles, including 1,469,643 passengercars, 588,120 lorries and 55,018 buses. 352,192 motor vehicles of all types were produced in 1969.

AVIATION. Twenty-five companies (20 foreign) furnish air-mail and passenger services. In 1969 passengers numbered 2,862,000; freight carried amounted to 34,226 metric tons; mail, 3,215 metric tons.

POST. Of the telegraph system of the country, about half, including all inter-state lines, is under control of the Government. There are 2,379 telegraph offices. Telephone instruments in use, 1 Jan. 1969, were 1,560,701. In 1968 there were 990 broadcasting and 40 television stations.

BANKING. The Bank of Brazil (founded in 1808 and reorganized in 1906, with an authorized capital of NCr$60m. from 1967) is not a central bank of issue but a closely controlled commercial bank; it had 684 branches in 1969 throughout the republic (and branches in Asunción, Montevideo, La Paz, Santiago, Cruz de la Sierra and Buenos Aires). On 31 Dec. 1969 deposits were Cr$13,008·1m.

On 31 Dec. 1964 the Banco Central da República do Brasil was founded.

The country's note circulation, 31 Dec. 1969 was 6,398m. cruzeiros. Since Sept. 1939 gold and dollar supply has risen from US$40m. to US$420m., of which the government's gold was $288m. in May 1961.

Banking institutions numbered 192, with 7,656 agencies in Dec. 1969. All banks (including the Bank of Brazil) had on 31 Dec. 1968 deposits of Cr$31,123·7m. and loans of 23,838·2m. On 31 Dec. 1969 all the domestic and foreign-owned banks had total assets of Cr$113,520·6m.

WEIGHTS AND MEASURES. The metric system has been in use in all official departments since 1862. It was made compulsory in 1872, but the ancient measures are still partly employed in remote districts. They are: *libra* = 1·012 lb. avoirdupois; *arroba* = 32·98 lb.; *quintal* = 129·54 lb.; *alqueire* (of Rio) = 1 Imperial bushel, or 40 litres; *oitava* = 55·34 grains.

DIPLOMATIC REPRESENTATIVES

Brazil maintains embassies in:

Afghánistán	Germany (West)	Paraguay
Argentina	Greece	Peru
Austria	Guatemala	Poland
Belgium	Haiti	Portugal
Bolivia	Honduras	Spain
Canada	India	Thailand
Chile	Indonesia	Tunisia
China	Israel	Turkey
Colombia	Italy	USSR
Costa Rica	Japan	UAR
Czechoslovakia	Korea (South)	UK
Denmark	Lebanon	USA
Dominican Republic	Mexico	Uruguay
Ecuador	Netherlands	Vatican
El Salvador	Nicaragua	Venezuela
Ethiopia	Norway	Vietnam (South)
Finland	Pakistan	Yugoslavia
France	Panama	

Brazil maintains legations in:

Australia	Hungary	Sweden
Bulgaria	Iran	Switzerland
Cambodia	South Africa, Republic of	

OF BRAZIL IN GREAT BRITAIN (32 Green St., W1)

Ambassador: Sérgio Corrêa Affonso da Costa, GCVO.
Minister-Counsellor: Francisco de Assis Grieco.
Naval and Army Attaché: Capt. Fernando E. C. Ribeiro. *Air Attaché:* Col. Durval de Almeida Luz. *First Secretaries:* Ronaldo Costa; Otavio Rainho da Silva Neves; Marcos C. de Azambuja; Paulo C. de Oliveira Pires do Rio; José O. R. de Almeida; Hélcio T. Pires.

There are consular representatives at Cardiff, Glasgow, Liverpool, London, Newcastle upon Tyne and Southampton.

OF GREAT BRITAIN IN BRAZIL

Ambassador: Sir David Hunt, KCMG, OBE.
Minister: J. C. Petersen, CMG (*Commercial*).
Counsellors: E. H. Van Maurik, OBE; A. Brooke-Turner.
Service Attachés: Col. P. B. Winstanley, MC (*Defence and Military*), Capt. J. C. Brandt, RN (*Naval and Air*).
First Secretaries: R. L. Joseph (*Information*); B. O. White (*Head of Chancery*); W. G. E. Beckmann, OBE (*Consul*); R. A. Wellington, DSO, DFC; M. F. Daly (*Commercial*).

There are a Consul-General at Sâo Paulo, Consuls at Belém, Pôrto Alegre, Recife, Santos and Vice-Consuls in 7 other towns.

OF BRAZIL IN THE USA (3007 Whitehaven St. NW.
Washington, D.C., 20008)

Ambassador: (Vacant).
Minister-Counsellor: Celso Diniz. *Counsellors:* Henique A. de A. Mesquita, Sergio de C. W. Vleira.
First Secretaries: Marcel D. C. Hasslocher; Amaury Bler, Alberto V. da C. e Silva; Marcos H. C. Cortes, Sergio S. de Noronha. *Service Attachés:* Gen. Eduardo d'Avila Mello (*Army*), Rear-Adm. Roberto Ferreira T. de Freitas *Navy*), Brig.-Gen. Coars Alfonso Dellamora (*Air*).

OF THE USA IN BRAZIL

Ambassador: (Vacant).
Deputy Chief of Mission: Clarence A. Boonstra. *Heads of Sections:* Herbert
W. Baker (*Labour*); Kenneth E. Albright (*Political*); Edmund L. Andrews
(*Economic*) Morris Allen (*Commercial*); Donald B. Wallace, Jr (*Consular*); John
E. Crawford (*Administrative*). *Service Attachés:* Col. Henry D. Rauchenstein
(*Air*), Col. Arthur S. Moura (*Army*), Capt. Edward O. Dietrich (*Navy*).

There are consular representatives at Belém, Brasília, Manaus, São Luís, Belo
Horizonte, Curitiba, Pôrto Alegre, Recife, Salvador, São Paulo.

BOOKS OF REFERENCE

Anuário Estatístico do Brasil. Conselho Nacional de Estatística, Rio de Janeiro
Atlas do Brasil. Conselho Nacional de Geografia. 2nd ed. Rio de Janeiro, 1959
Brazil Up to Date. Conselho Nacional de Estatística, Rio de Janeiro, 1955
Bulletin of the British Chamber of Commerce in Brazil. Rio de Janeiro. Monthly
Who's Who in Latin America. Part VI: Brazil. Stanford, 1948
Azevedo, Aroldo de, *Geografia do Brasil.* 2 vols. Rio, 1960
Azevedo, Fernando de, *Brazilian Culture.* New York, 1950
Banco do Brasil, *Boletin Trimestral.* Brasilia, D.F. From 1966
Calogeras, João Pandiá, *A History of Brazil.* Chapel Hill, North Carolina, 1939
Camacho, J. A., *Brazil.* R. Inst. of Int. Affairs. 2nd ed. 1954
Castro, J. de, *Géographie de la faim.* Paris, 1949
Delgado de Carvalho, C. M., *Historia diplomatica do Brazil.* Rio, 1961
Freyre, G., *Brazil: An Interpretation.* New York, 1945.—*The Masters and the Slaves.* London, 1946
Furtado, C., *The Economic Growth of Brazil.* Univ. of California Press and CUP, 1963
Hill, L. F. (ed.), *Brazil.* Univ. of California Press and London, 1948
Le Lannou, M., *Le Brésil.* Paris, 1955
Leff, N. H., *Economic Policy-Making and Development in Brazil, 1947–64.* New York and London, 1968
Marshall, A., *Brazil.* London, 1966
Moraes, R. Borba de, *Bibliographia Brasiliana (1504–1900).* 2 vols. 1958
Rodrigues, J. H., *The Brazilians.* Univ. of Texas, 1968
Skidmore, T. E., *Politics in Brazil, 1930–1964.* OUP, 1967
Smith, T. Lynn, *Brazil: People and Institutions.* Rev. ed. Baton Rouge, 1954.—(Ed.) *Brasil: Portrait of Half a Continent.* Gainesville, Fla., 1951
Tendler, J., *Electric Power in Brazil: Entrepreneurship in the Public Sector.* OUP, 1969
Wagley, C., *An Introduction to Brazil.* Columbia Univ. Press, 1963

NATIONAL LIBRARY. Biblioteca Nacional Avenida Rio Branco 219–39, Rio de Janeiro, G.B.
Director: Dr Adonias Filho.

BULGARIA
Narodna Republika Bulgaria

HISTORY. The Principality of Bulgaria and the Autonomous Province of
Eastern Rumelia, both under Turkish suzerainty, were constituted by the Treaty
of Berlin, 13 July 1878. In 1885 Rumelia was reunited with Bulgaria. On 22
Sept. (5 Oct.) 1908 Bulgaria declared her independence of Turkey. *Rulers:*
Prince Alexander I of Battenberg, 1879–86; Prince (after 1908, Tsar) Ferdinand,
1887–1918 (abdicated); Tsar Boris III, 1918–43; Tsar Simeon II, lost his
throne as a result of the referendum held on 8 Sept. 1946. 3,801,160 votes were
cast in favour of a republic, 197,176 votes in favour of the monarchy; 119,168
voting papers were invalid.

Bulgaria, on 1 March 1941, signed the Three Power Pact, and on 25 Nov. 1941
the Anti-Comintern Pact. On 26 Aug. 1944 Bulgaria asked Great Britain and the
USA for an armistice. The USSR formally declared war on Bulgaria on 5 Sept.
1944. The new Bulgarian Government of the Fatherland Front, which was
established on 9 Sept., immediately asked the Soviet Government for an armistice,
which was signed on 28 Oct. 1944 by representatives of the Soviet Union, Great
Britain and the USA. The peace treaty was signed in Paris on 10 Feb. 1947.

CONSTITUTION AND GOVERNMENT. The Bulgarian People's Republic was proclaimed by the National Assembly on 15 Sept. 1946.

The constitution of 4 Dec. 1947, last amended in 1961, provides for a single-chamber National Assembly. The highest organ of the state is a collective body called the Presidium, which consists of a chairman, 2 deputy-chairmen, a secretary and 15 members; it is elected by the National Assembly. Supreme power is vested in the National Assembly, which consists of deputies elected by direct, secret and universal suffrage (everybody over the age of 18 being eligible to vote and hold office). One deputy is elected per 20,000 of the population. The Legislature's term is 4 years; it is to meet at least twice every year. The National Assembly also elects the ministers and the Presidium who are responsible to it.

A general election was held on 27 Oct. 1946. The Fatherland Front, composed of the Workers (Communist), Agrarian, Socialist and Zveno Parties, and non-party independents, obtained 366 seats (277 of which went to the Communists) and the opposition 99. On 26 Aug. 1947 the oppositional Agrarian Union was dissolved; its leader, Nikola Petkov, was sentenced to death and hanged on 23 Sept. The Socialist Party was merged with the Workers' Party in Aug. 1948, and the Zveno Party dissolved itself.

The Fatherland Front was transformed, in Feb. 1948, into a unified mass organization with individual memberships. Inside the Fatherland Front, there remain two political parties, the Bulgarian Communist Party and the Bulgarian People's Agrarian Union.

On 31 Dec. 1969 the membership of the Communist Party was 672,075: Young Communist League, 1,161,000; Agrarian Union, 120,000; Fatherland Front, 3,762,537.

At the elections of 27 Feb. 1966, 99·63% of the electorate voted, and 98·85% of the votes were cast for the 416 candidates of the Fatherland Front; there were no other candidates. The list comprised 280 Communists, 100 Agrarians, 17 Young Communists and 19 non-affiliated. The elections due in 1970 were postponed.

Head of State: Georgi Traikov (*Chairman of the Presidium of the National Assembly, Secretary of the Agrarian Union*), elected 23 April 1964, on the death of Dimitŭr Ganev, re-elected 27 Feb. 1966.

The highest policy-making and executive body of the Bulgarian Communist Party is its Politburo, consisting of 11 full members and 6 candidate-members. The Politburo is elected by and from the Central Committee.

The Politburo was in March 1970 composed as follows: FULL MEMBERS: Todor Zhivkov (*1st Secretary, Central Committee, Chairman of the Council of Ministers, i.e., Prime Minister*), Boyan Bŭlgaranov, Gen. Ivan Mihailov (*Deputy Chairman, Council of Ministers*), Stanko Todorov (*Secretary, Central Committee*), Boris Velchev (*Secretary, Central Committee*), Zhivko Zhivkov (*1st Deputy Chairman, Council of Ministers, Chairman, Committee for Economic Co-odination*), Ivan Popov (*Chairman, State Committee for Science and Technical Progress*), Pencho Kubadinski (*Deputy Chairman, Council of Ministers, Minister for Building and Architecture*), Tano Tsolov (*Deputy Chairman, Council of Ministers; Chairman, State Planning Commission*), Tsola Dragoicheva, Todor Pavlov. CANDIDATE MEMBERS: Lŭchezar Avramov (*Deputy Chairman, Council of Ministers, Minister of Foreign Trade*), Angel Tsanev, Kostadin Giaurov, Krŭstiu Trichkov, Ivan Abadzhiev, Peko Takov (*Minister of Internal Trade*).

Important Ministers not in the Politburo are: Ivan Bashev (*Foreign Affairs*), Gen. Dobri Dzhurov (*Defence*), Lieut.-Gen. Angel Solakov (*Interior and State Security*).

In May 1967 a second 20-year treaty of friendship, co-operation and mutual assistance with the Soviet Union was signed. A commercial and cultural agreement with Yugoslavia was signed in Belgrade on 15 Dec. 1962.

Soviet citizens residing in Bulgaria have equal rights with Bulgarian citizens.

National flag: White, green, crimson (horizontal), with the coat of arms of the Republic in the canton.

National anthem: Mila Rodino (Dear Fatherland); folk-song, declared the national anthem in 1964.

LOCAL GOVERNMENT. People's Councils at province, region, town and village level are elected for terms of 3 years, to deal with all economic, social and cultural problems of their area. They also supervise the management of state and publicly owned enterprises on their territory. The Council's executive organs are Permanent Committees. In 1968 the Permanent Committees had a total membership of 51,278.

AREA AND POPULATION. On 8 Sept. 1940 by the treaty of Craiova, Romania ceded to Bulgaria the Southern Dobrudja, fixing the new frontier on the 1912 line.

In April 1941 Bulgaria occupied the Yugoslav part of Macedonia, and the Greek districts of Western Thrace, Eastern Macedonia, Florina and Castoria. The peace treaty of 1947 restored the frontiers as on 1 Jan. 1941.

The area of Bulgaria is 110,911·5 sq. km (42,823 sq. miles).

The country is divided into 28 provinces (okrŭg, plur. okrŭzi) each administered by a People's Council: Blagoevgrad, Burgas, Gabrovo, Khaskovo, Kiustendil, Kurdzhali, Lovech, Mihailovgrad, Pazardzhik, Pernik, Pleven, Plovdiv, Razgrad, Russe, Shumen, Silistra, Sliven, Smolyan, Sofia Province, Sofia Town, Stara Zagora, Tolbuhin, Tŭrgovishte, Varna, Veliko Tŭrnovo, Vidin, Vratsa and Yambol. In 1969 there were 188 urban and 973 rural communes.

The population at the census of 1 Dec. 1965 was 8,227,866 (males, 4,114,167; urban, 3,822,824). Population on 1 Jan. 1970 was 8,467,300 (52% urban). Population density, 76·3 per sq. km.

National minorities are estimated to total 1·2m. The language estimates are: Bulgarian 88%, Turkish 8·6%. The remainder include Gipsies, Jews, Romanians and Armenians. Regular repatriation of Turks have been made.

Population of principal towns in 1970: Sofia, 868,200; Plovdiv, 247,500; Varna, 219,000; Ruse, 149,600; Burgas, 131,700; Stara Zagora, 109,100; (1969) Pleven, 89,814; Pernik, 79,335; Sliven, 77,458; Shumen, 68,124; Yambol, 67,971; Gabrovo, 67,887; Khaskovo, 63,670; Tolbuhin, 61,440; Pazardzhik, 59,532; Dimitrovgrad, 44,302.

Vital statistics, 1969: Live births, 143,060; deaths, 80,183; marriages, 73,660; divorces, 9,361; crude birth rate, 16·9 per 1,000 population; crude death rate, 9·5; growth rate, 7·8.

Expectation of life was 70·66 years in 1967.

RELIGION. 'The traditional church of the Bulgarian people' (as it is officially described), is that of the Eastern Orthodox Church. It was disestablished under the 1947 Constitution. On 10 May 1953 the Bulgarian Patriarchate was revived and Metropolitan Kiril was elected the first Bulgarian Patriarch since 1393. The seat of the Patriarch is at Sofia. There are 11 dioceses, each under a Metropolitan, 12 bishops and 2,000 priests.

Freedom of conscience and belief is 'guaranteed'; the use of religion and religious institutions for propaganda against the Government is punishable. The State provides 17% of Church funds.

Churches may not maintain schools or colleges, except theological seminaries, or organize youth movements.

According to a Bulgarian Academy of Sciences survey in 1962, 35·5% of the population were religious (26·7% of the population Orthodox and 6·7% Moslems). In 1971 there were some 50,000 Roman Catholics with 50 churches and 60 priests, and 20,000 Protestants with 150 churches and 260 priests. Moslems are under a Grand Mufti and 6 regional mufti boards. There were 1,180 mosques in 1970.

EDUCATION. Education is free, and compulsory for children between the ages of 7 and 16. It was announced in 1969 that the school starting age would eventually be lowered to 6 and secondary schooling made compulsory. Complete literacy is claimed. Schools are classified according to which years of schooling they offer: Elementary (1–4), primary (1–7), preparatory (5–7), secondary (8–11), complete secondary (1–11).

Educational statistics for 1968–69: 8,180 kindergartens (323,839 children, 17,569 teachers); 1,468 elementary schools; 2,902 primary schools; 98 preparatory schools; 135 secondary schools; 138 complete secondary schools. Numbers of teachers and pupils: School years 1 to 4, 20,398 and 544,025; 5 to 7, 28,257 and 535,226; 8 to 11, 6,665 and 107,915. There were also 332 vocational-technical schools (7,409 teachers, 109,708 students), 254 technical colleges (9,296 teachers, 157,099 students), 17 post-secondary institutions (570 teachers, 9,776 students) and 26 institutes of higher education (6,248 teachers, 80,248 students). The Kliment of Ohrid University in Sofia (founded 1889) had 13,036 students in 1968.

The Academy of Sciences (founded 1869) and other research bodies had 144 institutes in 1969.

CINEMAS AND THEATRES (1969). There are 32 theatres, 8 puppet theatres, 6 opera houses and 3,104 cinemas. 249 films were made, of which 15 were full-length.

NEWSPAPERS AND BOOKS. In 1968 there were 17 dailies with a circulation of 1·79m. The Party newspaper is *Rabotnicheskoto Delo* ('The Workers' Cause') with a circulation of 700,000. There were 714 other newspapers (including factory papers), and 737 periodicals (including bulletins). 3,579 book titles were published.

SOCIAL WELFARE. Retirement and disablement pensions and temporary sick pay are calculated as a percentage of previous wages (respectively 55–92%, 35–100%, 69–90%) and according to the nature of the employment.

Family allowances for children under 16: 5 leva for 1 child, 20 leva for 2 children and 55 leva for 3 children.

In 1969, 1·64m. persons received pensions including 474,000 old-age pensions.

All medical services are free. In 1969 there were 1,198 hospitals with 54,543 beds, and 15,338 doctors. There are 3,125 dentists.

JUSTICE. The constitution of 1947 provides for the election (and recall) of the judges by the people and, for the Supreme Court, by the National Assembly. The lower courts include laymen ('assessors') as well as jurists. There are a Supreme Court, 28 provincial (including Sofia) courts and 103 people's courts.

In June 1961 'Comrades' Courts' were set up for the trial of minor offenders by their fellow-workers.

New Family and Penal Codes were approved by the National Assembly in April 1968. The maximum term of imprisonment is now 15 years except for murder which is punishable by a minimum of 20 years' imprisonment.

The Prosecutor General, elected by the National Assembly for 5 years and subordinate to it alone, exercises supreme control over the correct observance of the law by all government bodies, officials and citizens. He appoints and discharges all Prosecutors of every grade. Prosecutors are independent of judges and Government.

FINANCE. Currency. The unit of currency is the *lev* (pl. *leva*) divided into 100 *stotinki* (sing. *stotinka*). It has been linked to the Soviet rouble since May 1952. A new *lev*, equalling 10 old leva, was introduced on 1 Jan. 1962. The parity (clearing value) is 1 rouble = 1·30 leva. The official rate of exchange is £1 = 2·81 leva; US$1 = 1·17 leva; 100 Swiss francs = 26·90 leva. Rate of exchange for non-commercial transactions: £1 = 4·80 leva; US$1 = 2 leva; 100 Swiss francs = 46 leva.

Budget. The revenue and expenditure of Bulgaria for calendar years were as follows (in 1m. leva):

	1964	1965	1966	1967	1968	1969	1970 [1]
Revenue	3,909	3,132	3,702	4,078	4,420	5,052	5,235
Expenditure	3,908	3,121	3,691	4,063	4,480	5,041	5,225

[1] Estimates.

Of the 1969 revenue 3,870m. leva came from the national economy and 1,182m. from other sources. 1969 expenditure was: Investments, 2,632m. leva; social and education, 1,451m.; administration, 102m.

A trade and debt agreement concluded with the UK on 22 Sept. 1955 provides for Bulgarian payments of £400,000 in settlement of UK claims for expropriated property rights and interests; the payments are to be made in annual instalments of 5% from the sterling proceeds of Bulgarian exports to the UK, with effect from 31 March 1956.

An agreement of 1963 settled outstanding financial questions between Bulgaria and USA.

DEFENCE. For the (abortive) restrictions imposed by the peace treaty of 1947, *see* THE STATESMAN'S YEAR-BOOK 1957, p. 853. There is a compulsory service of 2 years in the Army (3 years in the Navy and Air Force).

Army. In Oct. 1966 the Army had a strength of 125,000 men, organized in 8 motorized and 3 tank divisions. There are 3 Army Commands (Military Regions), Sofia, Plovdiv, Sliven. Tanks, mainly T-34s and some T-54s and T-55s, numbered 2,500. Security police numbered 45,000 (5 brigades of border guards, 8 regiments of security forces).

Navy. The Navy consists of 2 *ex*-Soviet submarines, 2 *ex*-Soviet escorts, 8 patrol vessels, 8 motor torpedo-boats, 2 fleet minesweepers, 4 inshore mine-sweepers, 22 minesweeping boats, 10 landing craft, a training vessel and a tug. Personnel, 1969, was 7,000.

Air Force. The large tactical Air Force has about 250 Soviet-built combat aircraft and more than 20,000 personnel. There are estimated to be 6 interceptor squadrons of MiG-19s, 6 interceptor squadrons of MiG-17s (some re-equipping with MiG-21s), 6 ground-attack squadrons of MiG-17s, 3 reconnaissance squadrons of MiG-17s, about 20 transport aircraft and 40 Mi-4 helicopters. Soviet-built 'Guideline' surface-to-air missiles have also been supplied to Bulgaria.

PLANNING. State economic planning started in 1947. After 1964 there was a limited decentralization in planning, culminating in the economic reform of 1 Jan. 1969. Some local planning, profitability and consumer demand have been admitted, although central price regulation has been retained. The economy has been reconstructed into large trusts for each industry, each responsible for its own foreign trade.

For the first four 5-year plans *see* previous volumes of THE STATEMAN'S YEAR-BOOK. In the fifth 5-year plan, 1966–70, emphasis was laid on the expansion of heavy industry. The sixth 5-year plan is running from 1971 to 1975.

AGRICULTURE. Cultivated agricultural land covers 6,022,000 hectares, of which 4,799,000 hectares are arable.

Collectivization was completed by 1958. The United Central Co-operative Union co-ordinates the activities of collective farms and consumer co-operatives. Size of private plots (maximum, 0·5 hectare; in mountainous areas, 1 hectare) is based on the number of members of a household, and their use restricted mainly to production of fodder. The total area of private plots in 1969 was 613,400 hectares. There were, in 1970, 795 co-operative farms, with a total of 3·29m. hectares of arable land, and 159 state farms with 642,600 arable hectares. There were 66 machine-tractor stations. 90,277 tractors (in 15-h.p. units) were in use and 16,610 combine harvesters. It was announced in 1970 that agricultural industrial complexes (agrotowns) would be set up incorporating state farms. A start has been made in the Dobrudzha plain.

In 1969, 26 irrigation systems and 93 dams irrigated 973,100 hectares.

Yield in 1969 (in 1,000 metric tons): Wheat, 2,569; rye, 29; maize, 2,371; barley, 918; oats, 78; sunflower seed, 545; unginned cotton, 41; tobacco, 95;

sugar-beet, 1,628; tomatoes, 726; potatoes, 349; grapes, 1,285. Bulgaria is the world's principal supplier of attar of roses; annual production, 1,200 kg. Production in 1,000 metric tons (1969) of sugar, 316; meat, 257; butter, 15.

Livestock (1970): 181,555 horses, 299,311 asses, 1·26m. cattle, including 574,782 milch cows, 9·2m. sheep, 350,202 goats, 1·97m. pigs and 29·59m. poultry.

FORESTRY. The forest area in 1969 was 7·8m. acres, of which 1·7m. acres were coniferous, 4·3m. cu. metres of round and hewn timber were produced in 1965.

FISHERIES. The catch of sea fish was 57,876 metric tons in 1968.

MINING. Ore production in 1,000 metric tons, 1968: Iron, 870; copper, 168; bauxite, 1,956; lead, 862; zinc, 636; manganese, 71. Further deposits of manganese ore were discovered in the Dobrudzha Plain in 1970. 21·7m. metric tons of lignite and 400,000 metric tons of hard coal were mined in 1968. 126 tons of salt were extracted.

OIL. Oil was discovered in 1951 near Tulenovo, in the Balchik district on the Black Sea. Production started in 1954. Crude oil is also extracted in an offshore area 100 km north of Varna. Crude oil production in 1969 was 325,000 tons. Good-quality oil was struck at Dolni Dubnik near Pleven in 1962, where a refinery with a capacity of 7m. tons per annum was completed in 1970. The Burgas oil refinery started operations in 1963. It has an annual capacity of 5m. tons.

INDUSTRY. All industry was nationalized in 1947.

In 1969 total hydro-electric generating capacity was 811,000 kw., and annual production averages 2,440m. kwh. Remaining capacity is provided by a number of thermo-electric stations: Maritsa-East had a generating capacity of 650,000 kw. in 1966. An atomic power station is being built with Soviet aid at Kozlodni on the Danube to be operational by 1974 with a capacity of 800,000 kw.

The Kremikovtsi iron and steel combine has an annual capacity of 1·62m. tons of pig-iron, 2·4m. tons of steel and 2m. tons of rolled products.

The electronics and shipbuilding industries are being developed.

Industrial production	1960	1965	1966	1967	1968	1969
Electricity (1m. kwh.)	4,657	10,244	11,763	13,631	15,451	17,228
Iron ore (1,000 metric tons)	415	1,800	2,613	2,498	2,645	2,688
Crude steel (1,000 metric tons)	253	588	699	1,239	1,761	1,515
Pig-iron (1,000 metric tons)	..	547	720	992	1,109	1,134
Lead (1,000 metric tons)	40	93	93	97	93	95
Zinc (1,000 metric tons)	16	66	77	74	75	76
Cement (1,000 metric tons)	1,586	2,681	2,851	3,358	3,512	3,551
Sulphuric acid (1,000 metric tons)	123	318	353	360	472	498

In 1969 there were also produced (in 1,000 metric tons): Coke, 795; rolled steel, 1,208; nitrogenous fertilizers, 792; phosphorous fertilizers, 394; calcinated soda, 270; cotton fabrics, 335m. metres; silk fabrics, 21m. metres.

LABOUR. Trade unions had 2,486,988 members on 31 Dec. 1969, comprising 95% of all industrial and office workers. The phased introduction of a 42½-hour 5-day working week commenced in 1968 and is scheduled for completion by 1971. Average monthly wage in 1969: 117 leva. In 1970 the legal minimum wage was fixed at 60 leva per month.

COMMERCE. Foreign trade is controlled by the Ministry of Foreign Trade. Bulgarian trade has developed as follows (in 1m. leva):

	1964	1965	1966	1967	1968	1969
Imports	1,243·0	1,377·9	1,729·6	1,839·1	2,085·3	2,046·7
Exports	1,146·2	1,375·9	1,526·4	1,706·1	1,889·7	2,099·5

Main exports are food products, tobacco, non-ferrous metals, cast iron, leather articles, textiles and (to Communist countries) machinery.

Trade by countries in 1969 (in 1m. leva):

	Imports from	Exports to		Imports from	Exports to
Albania	7·1	3·8	Greece	14·3	12·2
Austria	35·6	23·7	Hungary	37·9	35·8
China	2·3	2·6	Italy	64·9	57·4
Cuba	29·9	26·6	Poland	95·6	76·1
Czechoslovakia	92·5	118·7	Romania	18·4	35·9
France	29·1	25·1	USSR	1,139·3	1,146·2
Germany, East	178·5	174·4	UK	23·1	34·2
Germany, West	53·2	63·4	Yugoslavia	21·0	29·3

80% of Bulgaria's trade is with Communist countries (55% with USSR). Ten agreements with USSR signed in 1969 and 1970 envisage the co-ordination of the Soviet and Bulgarian 5-year plans for 1971–75 in the spirit of 'socialist internationalism'. Bulgaria will import oil, natural gas (a pipeline will be built from Siberia, crossing Romania), steel, cellulose and timber, and export food products, clothing and electronic components. Italy is Bulgaria's biggest non-Communist trading partner.

Total trade between UK and Bulgaria (British Board of Trade returns, in £1,000 sterling):

	1965	1966	1967	1968	1969	1970
Imports to UK	5,383	6,176	6,294	7,471	7,333	8,307
Exports from UK	3,847	7,413	6,137	4,022	4,936⎱	11,118
Re-exports from UK	42	64	74	44	123⎰	

The first British–Bulgarian long-term trade agreement was signed in 1970, replacing all previous aggreements. This increases import quotas for Bulgaria and envisages an expansion in trade.

SHIPPING. Ports, shipping and shipbuilding are controlled by the Bulgarian United Shipping and Shipbuilding Corporation. The mercantile marine in 1969 possessed 22 passenger vessels and 112 cargo vessels and tankers with a total loading capacity of 846,260 deadweight tons. Burgas is a fishing and oil-port, open to tankers of 20,000 tons. Varna is the other important port; its shipyards were re-equipped in 1969. In 1969, 689,000 passengers and 15·7m. metric tons of cargo were carried.

ROADS. In 1969 there were 30,062 km of roads, including 2,327 km of motor roads. 110m. tons of freight and 923m. passengers were carried.

RAILWAYS. In 1969 Bulgaria had 6,013 km of railway, including 712 km electrified. 44% of trains were hauled by steam. 10·5m. passengers and 63m. tons of freight were carried.

AVIATION. BALKAN (Bulgarian Airline) operates internal flights from Sofia (airport: Vrazhdebna) to Burgas, Khaskovo, Plovdiv, Russe, Stara Zagora, Turnovo and Varna, and international flights to Algiers, Amsterdam, Baghdad, Beirut, Belgrade, Berlin, Bucharest, Budapest, Cairo, Copenhagen, Damascus, Frankfurt, Istanbul, Khartoum, London, Moscow, Nicosia, Paris, Prague, Tunis, Vienna, Warsaw and Zürich. In 1969 BALKAN had 157 planes and carried 921,000 passengers and 4,659 metric tons of freight. BEA opened a service from, London to Sofia in 1970.

POST (1969). There were 2,327 post offices, 414,113 telephones, 23 broadcasting stations and 2 television stations with 4 transmitters. Bulgaria participates in the East European TV link 'Intervision'. Radio receiving sets, 2,270,600; television sets, 829,383.

S

BANKING. In Dec. 1947 all banks were nationalized and the National Bank gained complete autonomy, freeing it from any responsibility for state debts. In 1969 the banking system was reorganized. The National Bank was renamed the Central Bank and made responsible for issuing currency. The Industrial Bank, the Agricultural and Trade Bank and the Foreign Trade Bank handle credit and business in their respective fields. The former Investments Bank was merged with the then National Bank in 1967 and its deposits transferred to the State Savings Bank. The former Marine Trade Bank was merged with the Foreign Trade Bank in 1969.

In 1969, 8·34m. depositors had savings totalling 2,725m. leva. The State Savings Bank has advanced personal loans up to 500 leva at 3·5% interest to some 500,000 users. Interest on deposits is 3%.

WEIGHTS AND MEASURES. The metric system is in general use. On 1 April 1916 the Gregorian calendar came into force in Bulgaria.

DIPLOMATIC REPRESENTATIVES

Bulgaria maintains embassies in:

Afghánistán	Greece	Pakistan
Albania	Guinea	Poland
Algeria	Hungary	Romania
Argentina	India	Sudan
Austria	Indonesia	Sweden
Belgium	Iran	Switzerland
Canada	Iraq	Syria
Chile	Italy	Tanzania
China	Japan	Tunisia
Cuba	Kenya	Turkey
Cyprus	Korea (North)	USSR
Czechoslovakia	Kuwait	UAR
Denmark	Lebanon	UK
Ethiopia	Libya	USA
Finland	Mali	Uruguay
France	Mongolia	Vietnam (North)
Germany (East)	Morocco	Yugoslavia
Ghana	Netherlands	

Bulgaria also maintains diplomatic relations at ambassadorial level with:

Burma	Ivory Coast	Peru
Cambodia	Jordan	Senegal
Central African Republic	Laos	Sierra Leone
Ceylon	Luxemburg	Somalia
Congo (K.)	Mauritania	Southern Yemen
Congo (Br.)	Nepál	Uganda
Dahomey	Nigeria	Upper Volta
Iceland	Norway	Yemen

Bulgaria also maintains a legation in Brazil and diplomatic relations with Burundi, Malaysia, Singapore and Zambia.

OF BULGARIA IN GREAT BRITAIN (12 Queen's Gate Gdns, SW7)

Ambassador: Mitko Grigorov (accredited 18 Dec. 1969).

Counsellors: Moritz Assa (*Commercial*); Ivan Moutafchiev. *Military, Naval and Air Attaché:* Col. Dimitŭr Simov.

OF GREAT BRITAIN IN BULGARIA

Ambassador: D. A. Logan, CMG.

First Secretaries: S. W. Martin (*Consul*); W. F. B. Price (*Commercial*). *Service Attaché:* Lieut.-Col. J. Talbot.

OF BULGARIA IN THE USA (2100–16th St. NW, Washington, D.C., 20009)
Minister: Dr Lyuben Gerasimov.
Counsellors: Baruch Greenberg; Philip B. Ishpekov (*Commercial*); Toshko Vantchev (*Agricultural*). *Service Attaché:* Col. Gantcho Gantchev.

OF THE USA IN BULGARIA
Ambassador: Horace G. Torbert, Jr.
Deputy Head of Mission: Robert B. Houston, Jr. *Heads of Sections:* Richard Dwyer (*Economic*); Gerald Engle (*Consular*); Ernest Huehle (*Administrative*). *Service Attachés:* Col. Paul G. Skowronek (*Army*), Lieut.-Col. John C. Osborne (*Air*).

BOOKS OF REFERENCE

Kratka Bŭlgarska Entsiklopediya (Short Bulgarian Encyclopaedia). 5 vols. Sofia, 1963–69
Statisticheski Godishnik (Statistical Yearbook). Sofia from 1956
Guide Book to Bulgaria. Sofia, 1965
Social and Economic Development of Bulgaria, 1944–1964. Sofia, 1964
Brown, J. F., *Bulgaria under Communist Rule.* London, 1970
Chakalov, G. (ed.), *Bŭlgaro-angliiski rechnik* (Bulgarian–English Dictionary). Sofia, 1961
The Nagel Encyclopaedia–Guide to Bulgaria. London, 1968
Pundeff, M. V., *Bulgaria: a Bibliographic Guide.* Library of Congress, 1965.
Rusinov, S., *Bulgaria: Land, Economy, Culture.* Sofia, 1965
Todorov, N., and others. *Bulgaria: Historical and Geographical Outline.* Sofia, 1965

BURMA
Pyi-Daung-Su Myanma-Nainggan

HISTORY. The Union of Burma came formally into existence on 4 Jan. 1948. On this day Sir Hubert Rance, the last British Governor, handed over authority to Sao Shwe Thaike, the first President of the Burmese Republic, and Parliament ratified the treaty with Great Britain providing for the independence of Burma as a country not within His Britannic Majesty's dominions and not entitled to His Britannic Majesty's protection. This treaty was signed in London on 17 Oct. 1947 and enacted by the British Parliament on 10 Dec. 1947.

For the history of Burma's connexion with Great Britain *see* THE STATESMAN'S YEAR-BOOK, 1950, p. 836.

AREA AND POPULATION. The total area of the Union is 261,789 sq. miles (678,000 sq. km). Some small rectifications of the border with China were agreed upon in 1960 and with Pakistan in 1964. The population in 1970 was estimated at 27·58m. The leading towns are: Rangoon, the capital (1970), 1,758,731; Mandalay (1969), over 360,000; and Moulmein (mid-1966), 156,968.

The Burmese belong to the Tibeto-Chinese (or Tibeto-Burman) family.

CONSTITUTION. From Independence Day until 1962 Burma was a parliamentary democracy, having 2 houses, the Chamber of Deputies and the Chamber of Nationalities. The latter comprised 125 members, 62 of whom represented the central unit, 63 the states and special areas. The Chamber of Deputies had twice as many members. Both were elected for 4 years. The Head of State was the President, elected for a 5-year term, by both Chambers of Parliament in joint session.

On 29 Oct. 1958 Gen. Ne Win, the Army Chief of Staff, became prime minister of a caretaker government. The elections to the lower house, held in Feb. 1960, gave the Pyidaungsu (Union) Party, led by U Nu, 161 out of 250 seats. On 2 March 1962 Gen. Ne Win overthrew the government of U Nu and replaced it by a Revolutionary Council. Parliament and the state councils were dissolved; the latter were reformed as 'state supreme councils' under appointed chairmen.

The Revolutionary Council is still the supreme body, but it had 'conferred on its Chairman all legislative, judicial and executive powers with effect from 2 March 1962'. Laws are promulgated by Gen. Ne Win in his own name. His judicial functions are delegated to the courts (and to special tribunals). His executive functions are normally exercised through the council of ministers, usually called the Revolutionary Government.

Members of the Revolutionary Government in Dec. 1968:

Chairman, Council of Ministers, and Defence: Gen. Ne Win.
Finance, Revenue and National Planning: Brig. San Yu. *Co-operatives and Trade:* Col. Maung Lwin. *Foreign Affairs, Education and Health:* Col. Hla Han. *Home Affairs, Immigration and National Registration, Democratization of Local Administration and Local Bodies, Religious Affairs and Judicial Affairs:* Col. Kyaw Soe. *Information, Culture, Relief, Resettlement and National Solidarity, Social Welfare:* Brig. Thaung Dan. *Mines:* Cdre Thaung Tin. *Public Works and Housing:* Brig. Sein Win. *Agriculture, Forests and Land Nationalization:* Col. Thaung Kyi. *Industry and Labour:* Col. Maung Shwe.

All Ministers except Cdre Thaung Tin are members of the Revolutionary Council.

Chairmen of State Supreme Councils: U Tun Aye (Shan), U Ding Ratan (*Kachin*), Dr Saw Hla Tun (*Karen*), U A Mya Lay (*Kayah*), U San Kho Lian (*Chin Affairs*).

National flag: Red, with a canton of dark blue; in the canton, a 5-pointed large white star with 5 smaller stars between the points.

Language. The official language is Burmese; the use of English is permitted.

RELIGION. The Revolutionary Government, having repealed the amendment of 1961 which made Buddhism the state religion, recognizes 'the right of everyone freely to profess and practice his religion'.

EDUCATION. After the attainment of independence the Government has adopted a centralized system of control of schools which are graded as primary, middle and high school. The medium of instruction in all schools is Burmese; English is taught as a compulsory second language in secondary schools.

Education is free in the primary, junior secondary and vocational schools; fees are charged in senior secondary schools and universities.

In 1969–70 there were 556 state high schools with 133,278 pupils, 1,117 state middle schools with 559,012 pupils and 16,559 state primary schools with 3,328,000 pupils; the total teaching staff was 87,140.

On 1 April 1965 the Government nationalized 129 of the 883 registered private schools, including all the major high schools.

The Higher Education Law 1964 has decentralized the University of Rangoon. Beside the Arts and Science University, there are independent degree-giving institutes of engineering, education, medicine, agriculture, economics and commerce, and veterinary sciences. In 1969–70 students numbered 45,876. The University of Mandalay (with 3,000 students) has been similarly decentralized. A foreign-languages institute in Rangoon has 1,709 students learning French, German, Russian, Japanese, Chinese and English.

There are intermediate colleges at Taunggyi, Magwe and Myitkyina, and degree colleges at Moulmein and Bassein, and several technical and agricultural institutes at higher and middle level, 3,696 middle and primary school teachers were being trained in 12 training colleges in 1968–69.

CINEMAS (1968). There were about 422 cinemas.

JUSTICE. The Chief Court has supervision over all courts in the Union. It is presided over by the Chief Judge and 6 other judges, and has superseded the Supreme Court and the High Court, whose powers and functions it exercises by authority of a directive from the Revolutionary Council effective from 1 April 1962. District courts operate unchanged under the Revolutionary Government, together with district army courts.

FINANCE. Currency. The currency unit is now the *kyat* (formerly the Burma rupee) divided into 100 *pyas*; the *kyat* equals £0·09. (US$1 = K.4·8).

Currency in circulation in May 1970 was valued at K.2,175m.

On 17 May 1964 the Government demonetized 50 and 100 *kyat* notes, and K.40 crores were withdrawn from circulation. The largest denomination is the K.20 note.

Budget. The budget estimates (in K. lakhs) for fiscal years 1 Oct.–30 Sept. were as follows:

	1965–66	1966–67	1967–68	1968–69	1969 70	1970–71
Revenue	14,293	11,363	9,253	8,116	8,907	8,841
Expenditure	14,134	11,333	9,195	8,416	9,019	9,359

The largest items, in 1968–69, of revenue were customs (K.2,099·9 lakhs) and income tax (K.5,669·2 lakhs); of expenditure, defence and police (K.1,093 lakhs) and education (K.2,740 lakhs).

The internal public debt was K.12,256 crores at the end of June 1970.

In Dec. 1957 Burma received a USA loan of $5·4m. to reclaim land in the delta, and in 1960 a £30m. loan from China to set up specified projects. Loans have also been made by the Agency for International Development, Japan and West Germany.

DEFENCE. Army. The strength of the Army is approximately 130,000. The Army is organized into 5 major commands, 2 infantry brigades and the Arakan force. Three operational divisions are directly under the Ministry of Defence.

Navy. The Navy includes 1 frigate, 1 escort minesweeper, 2 patrol vessels, 5 motor torpedo-boats, 4 support gunboats (*ex*-landing craft), 13 motor gunboats, 21 river gunboats, 1 transport and 9 landing craft. Personnel in 1970: 300 officers and 5,900 ratings, including reserves.

Air Force. The Air Force is intended primarily for internal security duties. Its primary combat force comprises about 14 T33A jet fighter/trainers supplied under MAP. Training is done with T-33s and piston-engined Provosts, which also carry light armament for security operations. Transport and second-line units are equipped with C-47, Otter and Beech D18 aircraft, and Japanese-built Bell 47 (H-13), Kawasaki-Boeing 107, HH-43B Huskie and Alouette III helicopters. The Air Force had, in 1969, 330 officers and 6,300 men and 151 aircraft.

PLANNING. The 4-year national economic plan (1966/67–1969/70) envisages an average annual rate of growth of 8%; priority is given to investment in agriculture and in industries using agricultural raw materials.

In 1968 168 industrial concerns in Rangoon and Mandalay were nationalized.

FORESTRY. The area of reserved forests in 1969–70 was 34,868 sq. miles. On 1 June 1948 the Government took over one-third of the concessions held by European and indigenous lessees. On 1 Feb. 1949 the European lessees surrendered their concessions. The takeover payments amounted to K.73·54 lakhs.

Teak extracted in 1966–67, 303,000 tons (K.755 lakhs); 1967–68, 300,000 tons (K.855 lakhs); 1968–69 estimates, 318,000 tons (K.919 lakhs). Hardwood, 1966–67, 907,000 tons (K.642 lakhs); 1967–68, 950,000 tons (K.819 lakhs); 1968–69 estimates, 996,000 tons (K.858 lakhs). 900 elephants are at work on extraction.

AGRICULTURE. By the end of 1958, 3,346,911 acres had been distributed among peasant proprietors under the Land Nationalization Scheme. The Revolutionary Government has given top priority to the development of agriculture.

Acreage (1,000) and production (1,000 metric tons) of principal crops:

	1967–68		1968–69		1969–70	
	Acreage	*Production*	*Acreage*	*Production*	*Acreage*	*Production*
Rice, rough	12,193	7,647	12,402	7,896	11,543	7,859
Maize	460	43	416	..	352	..
Pulses	1,616	248	1,751	264	1,478	269
Sesamum	2,051	106	2,037	82	1,641	100
Sugar-cane	146	1,342	162	128	98	1,291
Cotton	526	49	389	32	294	34
Groundnuts	1,259	365	1,151	392	1,472	437

Paddy crop in 1965–66 was 7·93m. tons; in 1966–67, 6·53m. tons; in 1967–68, 8·1m. tons; in 1968–69 (estimate), 8·17m. tons.

Livestock (1969–70): Oxen, 3,557,518; buffaloes, 516,949m.

In 1969–70 the area irrigated by government-controlled irrigation works was 2,017,646 acres; in 1968–69, 2,009,000 acres.

MINING. Production in 1969–70: Crude oil, 210m. gallons; silver, 740,000 oz.; zinc, 7,200 tons; copper matte, 160 tons; refined lead, 8,500 tons; nickel speiss, 80 tons; antimony, 230 tons; lead ore, 800 tons; tin, 637 tons; tungsten, 246 tons; tin tungsten, 274 tons; tin tungsten-scheelite, 420 tons.

POWER. In 1969–70 the total installed capacity of power plants was 253,430 kw.; total units generated, 491m. kwh.

TRADE UNIONS. Labour disputes are dealt with by the government labour sub-committees.

COMMERCE. All foreign trade is handled by the government trading organizations.

Imports and exports (in K. lakhs) for the fiscal years 1 Oct.–30 Sept.:

	1964–65	1965–66	1966–67	1967–68	1968–69[1]
Imports	14,129	8,037	6,918	10,635	10,200
Exports	10,788	9,218	6,577	5,347	7,899

[1] Estimates.

Exports of milled rice and rice products. K2,353 lakhs. Exports of raw rubber amounted to 7,000 tons and raw cotton exports to 6,000 tons in 1965–66.

Trade between Burma and UK (British Board of Trade returns) in £1,000 sterling:

	1965	1966	1967	1968	1969	1970
Imports to UK	6,173	5,199	3,234	3,826	3,055	4,274
Exports from UK	7,909	8,110	6,375	7,718	6,760 }	6,346
Re-exports from UK	134	224	92	231	162 }	

RAILWAYS. The Burma Railway system is entirely of metre gauge (3 ft 3⅜ in.) and its main lines run from Rangoon to Prome (161 miles) to the north-west and Rangoon to Mandalay (386 miles) towards the north, extending to Myitkyina farther north (723 miles from Rangoon). Branch lines extend from Letpadan to Tharrawaw (24 miles) on the west, the delta lines from Henzada to Bassein (82 miles) and Henzada to Kyangin (65 miles). In the Tenasserim Division, the lines are Pegu to Martaban (122 miles)—for Moulmein by bridge—and the Moulmein South to Ye (89 miles), and from Nyaungleb into Madauk (11 miles). Then there are the branch lines from Pyinmana to Kyeeni (163 miles), from Thazi to Myingyan (70 miles), from Mandalay to Madaya (17 miles) and from Ywataung to Alon (71 miles). The Northern and Southern Shan States hill sections connect with the main lines at Myohaung and Thazi. The Ava bridge across the Irrawaddy at Sagaing permits through traffic from Rangoon to Myitkyina (723 miles).

In 1969–70 the railway carried 511,500,000 ton-mileage and 1,224·72m. passenger-mileage.

ROADS. Burma has 2,452 miles of arterial highways and 5,734 miles of other roads in 1969–70.

SHIPPING. Burma has 60 miles of navigable canals. The Irrawaddy is navigable up to Myitkyina, 900 miles from the sea, and its tributary, the Chindwin, is navigable for 390 miles. The Irrawaddy delta has nearly 2,000 miles of navigable water. The Salween, the Attaran and the G'yne provide about 250 miles of navigable waters around Moulmein. The Inland Water Transport Board runs services from Bhamo to Myitkyina. The Burma Five Star Line Ltd operates coastal steamer services to the major ports in Burma, India, East Pakistan, Malaya, Japan and Europe.

The port of Rangoon in 1967–68 handled 2,523,000 tons of seaborne trade.

AVIATION. Union of Burma Airways started its internal service in Sept. 1948 and its external service in Nov. 1950. International services were in 1963 maintained between Rangoon and Bangkok and Calcutta. There were, in 1964, 43 civil aerodromes and landing grounds. In 1969–70 the total ton-mileage was 1,942,000 and the passenger-mileage, 73·65m.

POST. There were 1,039 post offices in 1969. Number of telephones was 25,941 in 1970, of which about 14,700 are in Rangoon.

There are 281 telegraph offices, and the internal system of communication is chiefly by wireless. Radio telephone or direct wireless telegraph links exist with most Asian countries, USA, USSR, UK, Denmark and Switzerland.

BANKING. All Banks in Burma have been nationalized and with effect from 1 Nov. 1969 amalgamated to form the People's Bank of the Union of Burma, in accordance with the provisions of the People's Bank Law of 1967.

The new Bank incorporates the functions of the Foreign Exchange Control Department, the Industrial Development Bank, the Union Insurance Board, Savings and Securities Department and the People's Loan Company. In effect, however, the work of the separate agencies carries on in the same way as before, although their individual titles have been merged into a single identity.

The State Commercial Bank, which is responsible for all transactions involving foreign exchange, was later incorporated in Feb. 1970 and was restyled The People's Bank of the Union of Burma (Foreign Department). This department handles all letters of credit, Bills of Exchange, foreign remittances, travellers cheques and foreign currencies, etc.

DIPLOMATIC REPRESENTATIVES

Burma maintains embassies in:

Afghánistán	Hungary	Poland
Australia	India	Romania
Cambodia	Indonesia	Thailand
Canada	Israel	UAR
Ceylon	Italy	UK
China	Japan	USA
Czechoslovakia	Laos	USSR
France	Malaysia	Yugoslavia
Germany (West)	Pakistan	

OF BURMA IN GREAT BRITAIN (19A Charles St., W1)

Ambassador: U. Chit Myaing (accredited 11 March 1971).
First Secretary: U Maung Maung Gyi. *Service Attaché:* Capt. Chit Ko Ko.

OF GREAT BRITAIN IN BURMA

Ambassador: E. G. Willan, CMG.
First Secretaries: A. B. P. Smart (*Head of Chancery*); R. J. Dowle; W. B. J. Dobbs (*Commercial*).

Service Attachés: Lieut.-Col. C. D. Darroch; MBE (*Defence and Army*), Cdr J. M. B. Walkey (*Navy*, resides in Bangkok), Wing Cdr P. A. Knapton, DFC (*Air*, resides in Bangkok).
Civil Air Counsellor: G. McD. Wilson (resides in Hong Kong).

OF BURMA IN THE USA (2300 S St. NW, Washington, D.C., 20008)

Ambassador: U San Maung.
Counsellor: U Win. *Service Attaché:* Col. Tin Tut.

OF THE USA IN BURMA

Ambassador: Arthur W. Hummel, Jr.
Deputy Chief of Mission: B. A. Fleck. *Heads of Sections:* R. J. Martens (*Political*); Miss M. Crane (*Administrative*); J. B. Amstutz (*Economic*); G. E. Martin (*Consular*); K. White (*AID*).
Service Attachés: Col. Ardrie W. Summers (*Defence and Army*), Cdr John Chadwick (*Navy*), Lieut.-Col. M. J. Walsh (*Air*).

There is a Consul at Mandalay.

BOOKS OF REFERENCE

STATISTICAL INFORMATION. A Central Statistical Office is organized as a department of the Ministry of National Planning.

Burma: Treaty between the Government of the United Kingdom and the Provisional Government of Burma. (Treaty Series No. 16, 1948.) HMSO, 1948
Cornyn, W. S., and Musgrave, J. K., *Burmese Glossary.* New York, 1958
Furnivall, J. S., *A Governance of modern Burma.* New York, 1960
Lehman, F. K., *The structure of Chin society.* University of Illinois Press, 1963
Smith, D. E., *Religion and politics in Burma.* Princeton Univ. Press, 1965
Stewart, J. A., and Dunn, C. W., *Burmese–English Dictionary.* London, 1940 ff.
Tinker, H., *The Union of Burma.* OUP, 1957
Trager, F. N., *Burma: from Kingdom to Republic.* London, 1966
Woodman, D., *The Making of Burma.* London, 1962

BURUNDI

History. Tradition recounts the establishment of a Tutsi kingdom under successive Mwamis as early as the 16th century. German military occupation in 1890 incorporated the territory into German East Africa. From 1919 Burundi formed part of Ruanda-Urundi administered by the Belgians, first as a League of Nations mandate and then as a United Nations trust territory. Elections supervised by the United Nations in Sept. 1961 resulted in a large majority for the Unité et Progrès National party (UPRONA). Internal self-government was granted on 1 Jan. 1962, followed by independence on 1 July 1962. An agreement, signed with Rwanda under United Nations auspices at Addis Ababa in April 1962, provided for a monetary and customs union. This union and all organizations operated jointly by the two governments were dissolved by 30 Sept. 1964.

On 15 Jan. 1965 Prime Minister Ngendandumwe was assassinated. Following an abortive coup d'état in Oct. tribal fighting occurred with heavy loss of life and 76 alleged plotters, including virtually all the leading Bahutu politicians, were executed after closed trials.

On 8 July 1966 Prince Charles deposed his father Mwami Mwambutsa IV, suspended the constitution and made Capt. Michel Micombero Prime Minister. On 1 Sept. Prince Charles was enthroned as Mwami Ntare V. On 28 Nov., while the Mwami was attending a Head of States Conference in Kinshasa (Congo), Micombero declared Burundi a republic with himself as president.

Area and Population. Burundi extends from lat. $2\frac{1}{2}°$ to $4\frac{1}{2}°$ S. and long. 29° to 31° E., and has an area of 27,834 sq. km (10,747 sq. miles). It lies astride the main Nile–Congo dividing crest (6,000–7,000 ft) bounded on the west by the narrow plain of the Ruzizi River and Lake Tanganyika (2,534 ft). The interior is a broken plateau at an average height of about 5,000 ft, sloping eastwards down to Tanzania and the valley of the Maragarazi River. The southernmost tributary of the Nile system, the Luvironza, rises in the south of the country.

The Ruzizi plain has an average temperature of 23° C. (73° F.), the Nile–Congo crest of 17·3° C. (63° F.), the central plateau of 20° C. (68° F.). The long dry season lasts from June to August, the long rainy season from February to May. The annual rainfall at Bujumbura is 31 in., on the Nile–Congo crest 57 in.

The population at the last census in 1959 was 2,213,280; but is now probably over 3·5m. There are three ethnic groups—Hutu (Bantu, forming the great majority): Tutsi (Nilotic, less than 15%); Twa (pygmoids, less than 1%). There are some 3,500 Europeans and 1,500 Asians. In 1968 some 54,000 Tutsi refugees from Rwanda and about 20,000 Congolese refugees were living in Burundi.

Bujumbura, the capital, has about 100,000 inhabitants. Kitega (10,000 inhabitants) was formerly the royal residence.

Government. Burundi is a republic and a one-party (Uprona) state. There is as yet no constitution. The President, whose term of office is 7 years, governs through a Council of Ministers and the Political Bureau of the Party.

President of the Republic: Col. Michel Micombero (born 1940, assumed office 1966).

The administrative divisions are: 8 provinces, each under a military governor (Bujumbura, Bubanza, Muramvya, Ngozi, Gitega, Muhinga, Ruyigi and Bururi); 18 arrondissements; and 181 communes.

Flag: White diagonal cross on green and red quarters, with a circular white panel in the centre with 3 scarlet 5-point stars arranged in a triangular pattern therein.

Religion. The population is predominantly Roman Catholic; there is a Roman Catholic archbishop and 3 bishops. The Anglican Missions under a bishop fall within the archdiocese of Uganda.

Education. In 1967–68 the number of children in primary schools was 170,000, 5,800 pupils were receiving secondary education and 1,337 were receiving craft and technical training. The university of Bujumbura has over 120 students.

The local language is Kirundi, a Bantu language. French is also an official language. Kiswahili is spoken in the commercial centres.

Currency. The currency is administered by the Bank of the Republic of Burundi. The rate is 210 Burundi francs = £1.

Finance. The 1970 budget was 2,080m. Burundi francs, and this included a credit of 322m. Burundi francs for settlement of certain debts.

Defence. The national army totals 2,600 men approx., including a 900-strong *Gendarmerie* or *Force Territoriale*. Officer strength is about 100, including 30 Belgian advisers.

Economy. Economic and technical assistance is provided substantially by Belgium and to a smaller degree by the European Economic Community and the United Nations.

Agriculture. The main economic activity of the country is subsistence agriculture, which accounts for well over half of the gross national product. Beans, kassava, maize, sweet potatoes, groundnuts, peas, sorghum and bananas are grown according to the climate and the region.

The main cash crop is coffee, particularly arabica. A coffee board (OCIBU) manages the grading and export of the crop. The 1969 crop was 14,500 tons, provisional for 1970, 20,000 tons (a record). Cotton is also grown (7,426 tons in 1968). Plantations of good-quality tea are being developed (90 tons in 1968).

Cattle play an important traditional role, and there are about 590,000 head in the country. The quality is poor, but efforts are being made to improve it. There are some 640,000 goats and sheep and 15,000 pigs.

Fisheries. There is a small commercial fishing industry on Lake Tanganyika producing 12,000 tons annually. Under the World Food Programme, a development scheme anticipates a catch of 20,000 tons by 1972.

Mining. There is some incipient mining activity; principal products are basthenaesite, cassiterite, kaolin and gold. Total mineral exports, 487 tons (1967).

Industry. Industrial development is rudimentary. In Bujumbura there are plants for the processing of coffee and by-products of cotton, a brewery, cement works, a textile factory, a soap factory, a shoe factory and small metal workshops.

Commerce. The total value of exports in 1969 was 1,235·4m. Burundi francs and of imports, 1,652·1m. Burundi francs. Sources of imports in 1966 were Belgium–Luxembourg (29%), Japan (13·5%), West Germany (7·5%), Tanzania (6%) USA (6%), UK (5%) and Congo (K.) (3·5%). Principal imports were cottons and cotton goods, motor vehicles, synthetics textiles, flour and petrol products. Main exports in 1969 (in Burundi francs 1m.) were coffee (931·4), raw cotton (114·1); 90% of the coffee is bought by USA.

Trade of Burundi with the UK was as follows (in £1,000 sterling, British Board of Trade returns):

	1965	1966	1967	1968	1969	1970
Imports to UK	2,100	222	1,169	1,996	974	2,081
Exports from UK	159	155	135	340	199 ⎫	275
Re-exports from UK	1	—	1	—	— ⎬	

Communications. There is a comprehensive interior road network connecting with Rwanda, the Congo and Tanzania. But only 25 miles are macadamized; and travelling can be difficult in the rainy season. There are lake services from Bujumbura to Kigoma (Tanzania). The main route for exports and imports is *via* Kigoma, and thence by rail to Dar es Salaam.

Bujumbura has an airport of international standard and there are regular services to Europe, the Congo and East Africa.

British Ambassador: P. H. G. Wright, CMG, OBE (resident in Kinshasa).
Ambassador in London: Laurent Nzeyimana (resident in Brussels).
Ambassador in Washington: Terence Nsanze.
USA Ambassador: Thomas P. Melady.

BOOK OF REFERENCE

Ruanda-Urundi [Engl. ed.]. Office of Information for the Congo, Brussels, 1960
Lemarchand, R., *Rwanda and Burundi*. London

CAMBODIA

HISTORY. The recorded history of Cambodia starts at the beginning of the Christian era with the Kingdom of Fou-Nan, whose territories at one time included parts of Thailand, Malaya, Cochin-China and Laos. The religious, cultural and administrative inspirations of this state came from India. The

Kingdom was absorbed at the end of the 6th century by the Khmers, under whose monarchs was built, between the 9th and 13th centuries, the splendid complex of shrines and temples at Angkor. Attacked on either side by the Vietnamese and the Thai from the 15th century on, Cambodia was saved from annihilation by the establishment of a French protectorate in 1863. Thailand eventually recognized the protectorate and renounced all claims to suzerainty in exchange for Cambodia's north-western provinces of Battambang and Siem Reap, which were, however, returned under a Franco-Thai convention of 1907, confirmed in the Franco-Thai treaty of 1937. In 1904 the province of Stung Treng, formerly administered as part of Laos, was attached to Cambodia.

A nationalist movement began in the 1930s, and anti-French feeling strengthened in 1940–41, when the French submitted to Japanese demands for bases in Cambodia and allowed Thailand to annex Cambodian territory. On 9 March 1945 the Japanese suppressed the French administration and the treaties between France and Cambodia were denounced by King Norodom Sihanouk, who proclaimed Cambodia's independence. British troops occupied Phnom Penh in Oct. 1945, and the re-establishment of French authority was followed by a Franco-Cambodian *modus vivendi* of 7 Jan. 1946, which promised a constitution embodying a constitutional monarchy. Elections for a National Consultative Assembly were held on 1 Sept. 1946 and a Franco-Thai agreement of 17 Nov. 1946 ensured the return to Cambodia of the provinces annexed by Thailand in 1941.

In 1949 Cambodia was granted independence as an Associate State of the French Union. The transfer of the French military powers to the Cambodian government on 9 Nov. 1953 is considered in Cambodia as the attainment of sovereign independence. In Jan. 1955 Cambodia became financially and economically independent, both of France and the other two former Associate States of French Indo-China, Vietnam and Laos.

Anti-French guerilla bands had operated in the jungle from 1945, the most important being a nationalist group known as the Khmer Issarak led by Son Ngoe Thanh, the former Japanese puppet premier. By 1953 Communist bands drawn from the Vietnamese minority and controlled by the Vietminh were active, and in 1954 regular Vietminh forces invaded Cambodia. Fighting came to an end with the conclusion on 21 July 1954, at the Geneva Conference, of the agreement on Cambodia. This ensured the withdrawal of French and Vietminh troops, and most of the Khmer Issarak bands then surrendered. The International Control Commission composed of Canadian and Polish representatives with an Indian chairman and responsible for the implementation of the Geneva Agreements was withdrawn in Dec. 1969 at the request of Prince Sihanouk.

Prince Sihanouk was deposed in March 1970 and the country was subsequently invaded by the Communist Vietnamese. On 9 Oct. 1970 Cambodia became a Republic as the Khmer Republic.

GOVERNMENT. On 6 May 1947 King Sihanouk, who succeeded on 26 April 1941, promulgated a constitution providing for parliamentary government. This did not function well, and in June 1952 the King assumed the premiership. In Jan. 1953 he dissolved parliament and replaced it by a Consultative Assembly. In Feb. 1955 King Sihanouk held a national referendum to decide whether he had successfully completed his mission in leading Cambodia to independence; the referendum was overwhelmingly affirmative. In March he abdicated and was succeeded jointly by his parents, King Norodom Suramarit and Queen Kossamak. Prince Sihanouk then formed a political movement, the Popular Socialist Community (known as the Sangkum), to implement the reforms to the 1947 constitution. The terms of the Geneva Agreement calling for free elections for all Cambodian citizens, including former resistance elements, were implemented on 11 Sept. 1955, when Prince Sihanouk's movement won all 91 seats in the National Assembly. This movement under Prince Sihanouk's leadership has continued to dominate Cambodian politics. It again obtained all seats at the elections of 23 March 1958, 10 June 1962 and, although there were no officially sponsored candidates, 11 Sept. 1966.

After the death on 3 April 1960 of King Norodom Suramarit a council of regency held interim office until 20 June when Prince Sihanouk became head of state without becoming king. He was deposed on 18 March 1970 by a constitutional vote of the National Assembly withdrawing his powers. The country was subsequently invaded by the Communist Vietnamese, who under the régime of Prince Sihanouk had established sanctuaries in Cambodia for their operations in South Vietnam.

Head of State: Cheng Heng. *Prime Minister:* Gen. Lon Nol.

AREA AND POPULATION. Cambodia has an area about 181,000 sq. km (71,000 sq. miles), divided into 17 provinces: Kompong Thom (population 322,000), Kompong Cham (820,000), Battambang (551,860), Kampot (337,879), Siem Reap (313,000), Kompong Chhang (273,000), Kompong Speu (307,000), Takeo (467,000), Kratié (136,000), Stung Treng (136,000), Svay Rieng (287,000), Prey Veng (492,000), Pursat (180,000), Kandal (population, excluding Phnom Penh, 706,000), Ratanakiri (49,400), Mondolkiri (14,300), Koh Kong (38,700).

The total population of 6·3m. (1968) includes an estimated 200,000 Vietnamese, 400,000 Chinese, 85,000 Chams and 4,000 Europeans. In the uplands and in the north-east live various groups of hillmen, known as Khmer-Loeu.

The chief towns are Phnom Penh, the capital (population 600,000), located at the junction of the Mekong and Tonle Sap rivers, Battambang (population 40,000), Kompong Cham (population 30,000) and Kampot (13,000).

Cambodian (Khmer) is the official language; the secondary language is French.

RELIGION. The majority of Cambodians practise Theravada Buddhism. There are about 54,000 Roman Catholics in Cambodia, mostly Vietnamese and Europeans.

EDUCATION (1968). There were 5,028 primary schools (998,000 pupils), 213 secondary schools (107,000 pupils) and 9 universities (14,560 students).

FINANCE. Currency. Under the Paris agreements of 29 Dec. 1954, between the Associate States and France, the parity of the Cambodian *piastre* (henceforth to be known as a *riel*) is to be maintained for the time being at 10 francs = 1 riel. On 31 Dec. 1954 the quadripartite Institut d'Emission ceased operations and a new Cambodian National Bank became responsible for the issue of currency. In Nov. 1955 Vietnamese and Laotian bank-notes ceased to be legal tender in Cambodia.

The rates of exchange are £1 = 133 riels; US$1 = 50 riels.

Budget. In 1969 total government revenue was estimated at 6,250m. riels and total expenditure at 7,565m. riels.

DEFENCE. The armed forces consisted in Jan. 1970 of about 49,000 officers and men in the 3 services. These forces are now considerably expanded to meet the invasion of Cambodia.

Army. The Army has 9 training centres, 1 armoured regiment, 2 parachute battalions, 55 infantry battalions and various auxiliary support companies. Strength (1969), 34,000.

Navy. The Navy, officially founded on 20 April 1954, includes 2 patrol vessels, 2 torpedo boats presented by Yugoslavia, 1 support gunboat (*ex*-landing ship), 4 landing craft, 3 seaward patrol craft and about 30 small craft. Personnel in 1970: Navy, 1,350 officers and men; Marine Corps, 150 officers and men.

Air Force. The Air Force, founded on 1 April 1954, continues to receive aircraft from both eastern and western sources. In recent years, it has re-equipped with about 20 MiG-15 and MiG-17 fighters, supplied by China, 30 Skyraider attack bombers delivered by France, and about 15 T-28D light attack aircraft from USA.

Other equipment includes Magister and T-37B jet trainers, Cessna L-19 observation aircraft, C-47, An-2, Beaver and Il-14 transport aircraft, and S-58, Alouette and Mi-4 helicopters. Strength, about 2,500 men.

AGRICULTURE. The overwhelming majority of the population is engaged in agriculture, fishing and forestry. Of the country's total area of 44m. acres, about 20m. are cultivable and over 20m. are forest land. Some 4m. acres are cultivated, well over half being devoted to rice production. The system of small holdings provides the farmers with a subsistence-level existence; only a small part of the production is marketed.

A crop of about 2·3m. metric tons of paddy were produced in 1968–69. Rubber production in 1968 amounted to 49,000 metric tons.

Other products are maize (154,000 metric tons in 1967–68), and, in order of value, livestock, timber, pepper, haricot beans, soybeans and fish.

FORESTRY. Much of Cambodia's surface is covered by potentially valuable forests, 3·8m. hectares of which are reserved by the government to be awarded to concessionaires, and are not at present worked to an appreciable extent. The remainder is available for exploitation by the local residents, and as a result some areas are over-exploited and conservation is not practised. There are substantial reserves of pitch pine.

FISHERIES. Cambodia has the greatest fresh-water fish resources in South-East Asia. The 1967–68 catch was 84,000 tons, a drastic drop from earlier years that results from over-fishing, silting and the destruction of plant-life.

MINING. A phosphate factory, jointly controlled by the state and private interests, was set up in 1966 near a deposit of an estimated 350,000 tons. Another deposit of about the same size is earmarked for exploitation. High-grade iron-ore deposits (possibly as much as 2·5m. tons) exist in Northern Cambodia, but are not exploited commercially because of transportation difficulties; some experimental quarrying has recently been undertaken by Chinese technicians. Some small-scale gold panning (6,687 troy oz. in 1963) and gem (mainly zircon) mining is carried out by primitive methods.

INDUSTRY. Cambodian industry is developing, and now includes a motor-vehicle assembly plant, 3 cigarette manufacturing concerns, a modern match factory and several metal fabricating concerns. In the state sector, a distillery, a saw-mill, textile, fish canning, plywood, paper, cement, sugar sack, tyre, pottery and glassware factories, a cotton-ginnery and a rice-mill are operative. In the private sector there are about 3,200 manufacturing enterprises, producing a wide range of goods; most of them are small family concerns. Factories are under construction to make tiles, cartridges and more textiles. An oil refinery at Kompong Som came into production in 1969 and supplies all Cambodia's fuel requirements.

COMMERCE. Principal imports by order of value (1968) were metals and machinery (including motor vehicles), mineral products, textiles and foodstuffs.

Principal exports by order of value in 1968 were rice, rubber and maize. France is the main purchaser of Cambodian rubber. Most of Cambodia's trade with the sterling area is with Hong Kong and Singapore.

Total trade with UK, in £1,000 sterling (British Board of Trade returns):

	1964	1965	1966	1967	1969	1970
Imports to UK	241	208	692	657	651	328
Exports from UK	1,386	1,359	1,494	1,470	1,538 ⎫	1,067
Re-exports from UK	—	4	3	4	3 ⎭	

ROADS. Cambodia had, in 1961, 2,179 km of asphalt roads (including the 'Khmer–American Friendship Highway' from outside Phnom Penh to close to Kompong Som, built under the United States aid programme and opened in July 1959), 1,369 km of macadamized roads, and about 1,647 km of improved dirt roads. These have been steadily extended.

RAILWAYS. A line of 385 km (1-metre gauge) links Phnom Penh to Poipet (Thai frontier). In 1967 traffic amounted to 145m. passenger-km and 45m. ton-km. Work was completed during 1969 on a line Phnom Penh–Kompong Som *via* Takeo and Kampot. Total length, 561 km.

SHIPPING. The port of Phnom Penh can be reached by the Mekong (through Vietnam) by ships of between 3,000 and 4,000 tons. In 1968, 561 ocean-going vessels imported 308,576 tons of cargo at Phnom Penh and exported 144,543 tons.

A new ocean port has been built under the French aid programme at Kompong Som (formerly Sihanoukville) on the Gulf of Siam and is being increasingly used by long-distance shipping. In 1968, 380,066 tons were imported and 358,081 tons were exported in 325 vessels (247 in 1967).

AVIATION. Pochentong airport, 10 km from Phnom Penh, gives direct services to Colombo, New Delhi, Bombay, Karachi, Athens, Nouméa, Tōkyō, Vientiane, Saigon, Bangkok, Djakarta, Rangoon, Hong Kong, Singapore, Rome and Paris. The airport accepts aircraft up to the Boeing 707.

The airport at Siemreap can now take DC 6s and Boeings. There is a number of fair-weather landing strips for light aircraft elsewhere.

POST. There were 58 post offices functioning in 1968. There are telephone exchanges in all the main towns; number of telephones in 1968, 6,325. Phnom Penh has a direct telephone link with Hong Kong, Paris and Tokyo; and is linked by teletype with Hong Kong, Osaka, Paris and Saigon. Hong Kong is by far the most important link for both systems. There is an International Telex network in Phnom Penh and direct telephone and telegraphic links with Singapore.

BANKING. By 30 June 1964 all private banks, domestic and foreign, had to close down; their functions were taken over by government banks.

The National Bank showed, as at 30 June 1968, gold and foreign exchange assets of 2,726m. riels. Note circulation was 6,047m. riels at 31 Dec. 1968.

DIPLOMATIC REPRESENTATIVES

Cambodia maintains embassies in:

Australia	Indonesia	USSR
Burma	Japan	UK
Czechoslovakia	Laos	USA
France	Philippines	
India	Singapore	

OF CAMBODIA IN GREAT BRITAIN (26 Townsend Road, NW8)

Ambassador: Samreth Soth. *Counsellor:* Chhnom Chhiet. *First Secretary:* So Yandara.

OF GREAT BRITAIN IN CAMBODIA

Ambassador: A. J. Williams.

First Secretaries: J. A. Davidson (*Head of Chancery*); A. J. Johnstone (*Commercial and Consul*).

Service Attachés: Lieut.-Col. I. A. C. Bruce (*Defence and Military*), Wing Cdr P. A. Knapton, DFC (*Air*, resident in Bangkok). *Counsellor:* G. McD. Wilson (*Civil Air*, resident in Hong Kong).

BOOKS OF REFERENCE

Annuaire Statistique Retrospectif du Cambodge. Vol. I, 1937–57; vol. II, 1958–60. Ministry of Planning, Phnôm-Penh

Indo-China: Geographical Appreciation. Department of Mines and Technical Surveys. Ottawa, 1953
Armstrong, J. P., *Sihanouk Speaks.* New York, 1964
Herz, M. F., *A Short History of Cambodia.* New York and London, 1958
McDonald, M., *Angkor.* London, 1958
Smith, R. M., *Cambodian Foreign Policy.* Cornell Univ. Press, 1965

CHILE

República de Chile

HISTORY. The Republic of Chile threw off allegiance to the crown of Spain, constituting a national government on 18 Sept. 1810, finally freeing itself from Spanish rule in 1818.

CONSTITUTION AND GOVERNMENT. By the constitution of 18 Sept. 1925 legislative power is vested in the National Congress, consisting of the Senate and the Chamber of Deputies, both of which are elected by direct popular vote. The Senate consists of 50 members, elected for 8 years, who represent 10 provincial groups, each of which elects 5 senators. One-half of the Senate is renewable every 4 years. The Chamber of Deputies consists of members elected for 4 years by departments or groups of departments, 1 member for every 30,000 inhabitants or fraction over 15,000. There are 150 in the Congress elected 1964. The Belgian system of proportional representation prevails. Electors are all citizens of 18 years of age or over. Women were fully enfranchised in Jan. 1949. Congress sits from 21 May (Navy Day) to 18 Sept. (Independence Day), excluding extraordinary sessions.

The President is elected for 6 years, by direct popular vote, but is not eligible for re-election; he must be Chilean-born and over 30 years of age. Normally there is no Vice-President, but the President may appoint one temporarily, when ill or out of the country. He has a modified veto; a bill which he has vetoed may, by a two-thirds vote of the members of both Chambers (a majority of the members being present), be sustained and become law.

The validity of all elections of president, deputies and senators is determined by a special body called *Tribunal Calificador,* consisting of 5 members chosen by lot from past-presidents or vice-presidents of the Chamber and Senate, members of the Supreme Court, of the Court of Appeal of the city where Congress meets.

The capital is Santiago, founded on 12 Feb. 1541.

National flag: Two horizontal bands, white, red, with a white star on blue square in top sixth next to staff.

National anthem: Dulce patria, recibe los votos (words by E. Lillo, 1847; tune by Ramón Carnicer, 1828).

The following is a list of the presidents since 1927:

Gen. Carlos Ibáñez (Acting, then elected), 6 May 1927–26 July 1931 (resigned).
Pedro Opazo (Acting), 26–27 July 1931 (resigned).
Juan Esteban Montero (Acting), 27 July–18 Aug. 1931 (resigned).
Manuel Trucco (Acting), 18 Aug.–15 Nov. 1931.
Juan Esteban Montero, 15 Nov. 1931–4 June 1932 (deposed).
Socialist Junta (Carlos Dávila, Col. Marmaduke Grove, Gen. Arturo Puga), 4 June–8 July 1932.
Carlos Dávila (Acting), 8 July–13 Sept. 1932 (deposed).
Gen. Bartolomé Blanche (Acting), 13 Sept.–1 Oct. 1932 (resigned).
Abraham Oyanedel (Acting), 1 Oct.–24 Dec. 1932.

Arturo Alessandri, 24 Dec. 1932–24 Dec. 1938.
Pedro Aguirre Cerda, 24 Dec. 1938–25 Nov. 1941 (died).
Geronimo Méndez (succeeded as Vice-President), 25 Nov. 1941–1 April 1942.
Juan Antonio Rios, 1 April 1942–27 June 1946 (died).
Alfredo Duhalde (Acting), 27 June–3 Aug. 1946 (resigned).
Vice-Admiral Vicente Merino Bielech (Acting), 3 Aug.–3 Nov. 1946.
Gabriel González Videla, 3 Nov. 1946– 3 Nov. 1952.
Carlos Ibáñez del Campo, 3 Nov. 1952–3 Nov. 1958.
Jorge Alessandri Rodriguez, 3 Nov. 1958–3 Nov. 1964.
Eduardo Frei Montalva, 3 Nov. 1964–3 Nov. 1970.

President of the Republic: Dr Salvador Allende Gossens, from 3 Nov. 1970 until Nov. 1976.

The President is assisted by 14 Ministers of State, who constitute a Cabinet and are responsible to him; they must not be members of Congress.

Minister of Foreign Affairs: Clodomiro Almeyda Medina.

3,539,747 voters were registered for the 4 Sept. 1970 elections; votes cast being (provisional): Salvador Allende Gossens (Unidad Popular) 1,075,616; Jorge Alessandri (Independent) 1,036,278; Radomiro Tomic (Christian Democrat) 824,849; blank and invalid, 26,000; total, 2,962,743.

LOCAL GOVERNMENT. For the purposes of local government the republic is divided into provinces, presided over by *Intendentes*, and the provinces into departments, with *Gobernadores* as chief officers, appointed by the President. The departments constitute one or more municipal districts, each with a council or municipality of 5 to 15 members, elected for 3 years. Foreign residents may vote in municipal elections; in April 1950, 5,678 foreigners were on the electoral registers.

AREA AND POPULATION. Chile is divided into 25 provinces. All provinces except 3 extend from the Pacific to the international boundary, while the inter-provincial boundaries in most cases now follow watersheds instead of rivers, thus confining within one province the waters of a single system and avoiding jurisdictional disputes.

Many islands to the north, west and south belong to Chile, including Easter Island (Isla de Pascua; 63·9 sq. miles), discovered in 1722. The coastline is about 2,485 miles in length; the average width of the country, 110 miles. Area, 741,767 sq. km or 286,397 sq. miles.

In 1940 Chile declared, and in each subsequent year has reaffirmed, its ownership of the sector of the Antarctic lying between 53° and 90° W. long.; and asserted that the British claim to the sector between the meridians 20° and 90° W. long. overlapped the Chilean by 27°. Three Chilean bases were established in Antarctica in 1947, 1948 and 1951. A law promulgated 21 July 1955 put the Intendente of the Province of Magallanes in charge of the 'Chilean Antarctic Territory'.

Three thinly-settled southern provinces of Magallanes, Chiloé and Aysén and the northern province of Arica are known as 'free zones', for the severe restrictions on imports prevailing elsewhere are modified in respect of those areas.

The total population at the census of 29 Nov. 1960 was 7,374,115. Density per sq. km, 1959, was 10·1; average annual increase, 2·5%. Estimated population in 1969 was 9·67m.

The areas of the provinces and their populations in 1960 are as follows:

Provinces	Area: sq. km	Population June 1970	Provinces	Area: sq. km	Population June 1970
Aconcagua	10,204	168,339	Llanquihue	18,407	219,655
Antofagasta	123,063	309,330	Magallanes	135,418	92,838
Arauco	5,756	114,887	Malleco	14,277	202,136
Atacama	79,883	196,744	Maule	5,626	102,449
Aysén	88,984	56,520	Ñuble	14,211	352,490
Bío-Bío	11,248	211,991	O'Higgins	7,112	326,544
Cautín	17,370	471,928	Osorno	9,083	183,716
Chiloé	23,446	112,427	Santiago	17,422	3,408,695
Colchagua	8,431	195,639	Talca	9,640	261,972
Concepción	5,701	737,199	Tarapacá	55,287	178,572
Coquimbo	39,889	406,070	Valdivia	20,934	317,844
Curicó	5,737	133,740	Valparaíso	4,818	806,237
Linares	9,820	212,138			

Vital statistics (1967): Revised birth rate 28·45 per 1,000 population; death rate, 9·5; marriage rate, 7·14; infantile mortality rate, 99.7 per 1,000 live births.

The great majority of the population is mixed or *mestizo*, due to the free inter-marriage between the early Spaniards and women of indigenous tribes; language and culture remain of European origin. The indigenous inhabitants are of three branches: The *Fuegians*, mostly nomadic, living in or near Tierra del Fuego; the *Araucanians* (130,747) in the valleys or on the western slopes of the Andes; the *Changos*, who inhabit the northern coast region and work as labourers.

The 3 leading cities, with estimated population in Dec. 1966, are: Santiago 2,566,000 (Greater Santiago, 3·12m. at 30 June 1970); Valparaíso, 296,000; Concepción, 178,000. Other towns, with estimated population 1966, are: Temuco, 109,000; Viña del Mar, 168,800; Osorno, 71,000; Chillán, 82,200; Antofagasta, 120,000; Talcahuano, 139,000; Valdivia, 89,500; Talca, 84,000; Iquique, 63,600. Punta Arenas, on the Straits of Magellan, with a population of 67,600, is the southernmost city in the world. The Antarctic Territory proper is now stated to be 1·25m. sq. km, with a population (1961) of 202.

There are 4 zones in Chile—the arid 'desert' zone in the north, which for many years furnished the world's entire supply of natural nitrate of soda, 90% of its iodine and 18% of copper consumed; the agricultural 'Mediterranean' zone in the centre; the 'forest' zone to the south; and the 'Atlantic' zone in the extreme south, barren on the Pacific side, but with rich sheltered pampa on the Atlantic side.

RELIGION. The Roman Catholic religion was disestablished in 1925; it remains, however, a national Church in a state wherein 89·5% of the population are Catholics. There are 1 cardinal-archbishop, 5 archbishops, 23 bishops and 2 vicars apostolic. Latest estimates show 6·7m. Roman Catholics, 880,500 Protestants and 30,000 Jews.

EDUCATION. Education is free and, since 1928, compulsory for all children between the ages of 7 and 15. In 1958 the public primary schools had 752,274 pupils; secondary schools had an enrolment of 164,019.

An educational crash programme began in 1965, with special emphasis on vocational and technical training. The primary curriculum was in 1966 extended to 7 years.

University education is provided in the state university (founded in 1842), the Catholic University at Santiago (1888), the University of Concepción (1919), the Catholic University at Valparaíso (1928), the Universidad Técnica Federico Santa María at Valparaíso (1949), the Universidad Técnica del Estado (1952), Universidad Austral, Valdivia (1954) and Universidad del Norte, Antofagasta (1957) with a total student population of 22,000 in 1957–58.

CINEMAS (1970). Cinemas numbered 382 with seating capacity of 304,891; 56 of them are in Santiago.

NEWSPAPERS (1970). There were 48 daily newspapers with an aggregate daily circulation of about 550,000.

JUSTICE. There are a High Court of Justice in the capital, 10 courts of appeal distributed over the republic, tribunals of first instance in the departmental capitals and second-class judges in the sub-delegations. The police force had (1969) about 23,000 officers and men; it is organized and regulated by the President of the republic.

FINANCE. Currency. The old monetary unit was the gold *peso*, containing 0·183057 gramme of fine gold with, originally, a par value of £0·2½ gold or 12·7 cents US$ gold (or 20·6 cents new US). From Dec. 1959 onwards the rate (used to value the gold stock) has been 1·049 escudos (1,049 pesos) to the dollar. For customs purposes imports and exports are still valued in the old £0·2½ gold peso.

In Jan. 1960 a system came into force based on the *escudo* (equivalent of 1,000 pesos), the *centésimo* (10 pesos) and the *milésimo* (1 peso). New notes have replaced the old peso notes, and new escudo coins of 10, 5, 2 *centésimos* and 1 *centésimo* have been issued.

Budget. Revenue and expenditure were as follows (1,000 escudos):

	1965	1966	1967[1]	1968[1]	1969[1]	1970[1]
Revenue	3,253,900	5,271,600	5,277,000	7,557,000	10,605,000	17,465,000
Expenditure	3,981,200	5,942,900	7,052,000	7,947,000	11,337,000	17,250,000

[1] Estimate.

Since 1957 the estimates have consisted of a local currency budget (as above) plus a foreign-exchange budget (in US$1m.). The 1970 expenditures envisaged E.5,739m. for defence, E.1,388m. for education, E.775m. for agriculture, E.1,028m. for development and reconstruction, E.781m. for housing and E.1,063m. for public health. The national development corporation (CORFO) had a total budget on local currencies of E.1,157m. and on foreign currencies of US$14·5m. for 1969.

Foreign bonds outstanding at 31 Dec. 1968 were £8·2m., US$46·8m., Sw.Fr. 44·3m. nominal value. Total foreign debt at 31 Dec. 1966 amounted to the equivalent of US$1,988m. and at 31 Dec. 1967 to US$2,090m.

DEFENCE. Chile on 9 April 1952 signed the Military Assistance pact with the US, promising access to raw materials and armed support in defence of the Western Hemisphere.

Army. The Chilean Army is a national militia in which all able-bodied citizens are obliged to serve. Liability extends from the 20th to the 45th year, inclusive. In many cases exemption can easily be obtained, as the supply exceeds the number that can adequately be trained. The annual intake has varied up to 20,000. Recruits are called up in their 20th year, and are trained for 12 months. After this training they pass into the reserve, which is estimated at 300,000.

The Army is organized in 6 infantry brigades, 4 horse and 2 motorized cavalry regiments and 8 artillery regiments. Total strength, 23,000 men.

Navy. The principal ships of the Chilean Navy are as follows:

Completed	Name	Standard displacement Tons	Armour Belt In.	Armour Guns In.	Principal armament	Torpedo tubes	Shaft horse-power	Speed Knots
			Cruisers					
1938	Prat[1]	10,000	4	3–5	15 6-in.	—	100,000	32·5
	O'Higgins[1]	9,700			8 5-in.			

[1] Ex-*Nashville* and ex-*Brooklyn*, purchased from USA in 1951.

There are also 2 submarines, 4 destroyers, 4 escort destroyers, 4 torpedo boats, 3 patrol vessels, 6 landing craft, 1 helicopter support ship, 1 survey ship, 2 transports, 1 training ship, 1 antarctic patrol ship, 2 oilers and 3 tugs. Two modern destroyers were built in Britain, *Almirante Williams* and *Almirante Riveros*, commissioned in 1960 and 1962 respectively.

Naval personnel in 1970 totalled 1,000 officers and 14,000 men, including marines and coastal artillery.

Air Force. Following the purchase of 19 Hunter fighter-bombers and 3 Hunter 2-seat trainers from Britain, the Chilean Air Force has distributed these aircraft and its older F-80C Shooting Star jet fighters and T-33As to form 3 combat groups. There is also a light bomber group of B-26 Invaders. Transport units have 3 DC-6 piston-engined transports supplied under MAP, C-47s, 8 Canadian-built turboprop Twin Otters, 9 Beechcraft 99As, a twin-turboprop HS 748 for presidential and VIP use, and smaller types. Training types in service include the T-34, T-37B, T-33 and Vampire. Albatross amphibians are used for maritime patrol and, with helicopters, for air/sea rescue. Total strength is about 8,000 personnel and 230 aircraft.

AGRICULTURE. Agriculture and forestry contribute one-ninth of the national product, although one-third of the population take part in it. Total area of land being exploited (census of 1965) was 30·6m. hectares; 14·7% for agri-culture, 32·9% for pasture, 19% for forest; 33·4% is desert or unproductive.

Chile has to import annually about two-thirds of the foodstuffs needed, a quarter of the total imports.

Some principal crops and exports were as follows:

Crop	Area sown, 1,000 hectares		Production, 1,000 metric tons
	1966–67	1967–68	1966–67
Wheat	719	718	1,204
Oats	68	68	1,152
Barley	50	50	1,175
Maize	92	92	3,622
Rice	..	33	..
Potatoes	77	77	7,166
Beans	68	68	895
Lentils	7	7	39
Peas	9	11	89
Onions	4	6	1,040

There were in 1955 over 300 large farms, each with more than 12,250 acres, while 500,000 peasants live on less than 4 acres per family. As a result of the Agrarian Reform Bill the CORA (Corporación de la Reforma Agraria) had by May 1968 expropriated 645 farms totalling 1,248,647 hectares and 266 settlements had been formed for 8,921 families, incorporating 1,036,168 hectares of land.

In the Magallanes pampa region and Tierra del Fuego there are about 3m. high-grade sheep (chiefly Romney Marsh and Corriedales). Output of wool is about 11,000 metric tons; exports in 1967, 5,636 metric tons, valued at US$5,172,000.

FORESTRY. According to the Forestry Institute (census 1966) there were 277,944 hectares of artificial forests from Maule to Cautin, the most important species being the pine (*pinus radiata*) which covers 260,685 hectares. Eucalyptus covers 12,943 hectares, poplars 956 hectares. The volume of all species reaches 62m. cu. metres, of which 60m. correspond to pine. There were also 32,550 sq. km of native forest, divided into the following species: Araucaria, Coigüe, Valdiviano, Roble-Raulí, Chilote, Lenga, Alerce and Ciprés.

Production during 1964–65 amounted to 178m. ft of sawn timber. Exports in 1967 were valued at US$2·9m.

Paper production in 1968 was 147,295 metric tons.

FISHERIES. Chile's catch of fish in 1967 was 969,000 metric tons, excluding shell fish, 83,800 tons. Exports of seafood in 1967 were US$27·9m., of which fishmeal accounted for 12·1m.

MINING. The wealth of the country consists chiefly in its minerals, especially in the northern provinces of Atacama and Tarapacá.

Copper is the most important source of foreign exchange (about 80% of exports) and Government revenues (over 30%). Reserves represent 40% of the world total. Production in 1969 amounted to 686,827 metric tons. In 1966 proceeds returned to Chile by the large mining companies equalled US$363·8m., and by the medium- and small-sized companies, $205·2m. On 20 Oct. 1966 the Government became the majority shareholder of the Compañía Minera El Teniente and in July 1969 of the Anaconda Company.

Nitrate of soda is found in the Atacama desert. Once Chile's principal export, production was 782,000 metric tons in 1969 (exports 1967, 0·67m. tons). Iodine is a by-product: 1967 exports totalled 2,276 metric tons. The use of solar evapora-tion as a means of reducing costs has developed the production of potassium salts as an additional by-product.

Iron ore, of which high-grade deposits estimated at over 1,000m. tons exist in the province of Atacama and Coquimbo, has overtaken nitrate as Chile's second mineral. Production in 1969 was 11·63m. metric tons.

Coal reserves exceed 2,000m. tons, partially low in thermal unit. Net 1969 production was 1·7m. metric tons. Petroleum was discovered in 1945 in Magallanes with annual output 2·12m. cu. metres in 1969. This state-owned industry is developing fast, an important by-product being liquefied gas (267,857m. cu. metres in 1968), which covered home requirements and left 29,000 cu. metres for export to Argentina and Brazil.

In 1969 other minerals include gold, of which the major part is from copper production (1,796 kg), silver (87,330 kg), molybdenum (4,630 metric tons, pure), zinc (1,067 metric tons), manganese (23,687 metric tons), salt (1·66m. metric tons), sulphur (112,500 metric tons) and lead (751 metric tons).

INDUSTRY. A nationally-owned steel plant has been established at Huachipato, near Concepción. Output, 1967, 596,170 (1968: 525,878) metric tons of pig-iron; this is to be doubled by 1972–73.

The textile industry consumes 70% of the wool clip of the country, or about 14,000 metric tons. In 1968 Chile produced 1,814 metric tons of rayon products and 1,965 metric tons of rayon fibre.

ELECTRICITY. In 1968 production was 6,793m. kwh., of which public utilities owned 64%, mines 19% and an American company 17%.

TOURISM. There were 155,219 foreign visitors in 1967.

LABOUR. In 1962 the 'economically active' numbered 2,356,000 (including 518,200 women). Professional and 'white-collar' workers numbered 488,500; agriculture employed 632,100; manufacturing, 524,500; mining, 57,300, and transport, 77,700. A National Health Service covers some 2·5m. employees throughout the country, and there are plans to extend it to a further 1·5m.

Trade unions began in the middle 1880s. The legal minimum monthly wage in Santiago for 1969 was fixed at E.427·50, against 373·34 for 1968.

COMMERCE. Imports and exports in US$1m.:

	1964	1965	1966	1967	1968	1969
Imports	608·7	603·6	755·3	726·6	661·0	..
Exports	625·7	687·8	877·5	913·0	893·0	1,061

In 1967 imports (in US$m.) from US were valued at 257·9; West Germany, 91·5; Argentina, 77·1; UK, 48·6; Venezuela, 42·7; Mexico, 23·4. Exports to US were valued at 168·4; Netherlands, 124·4; UK, 123·9; Japan, 108; West Germany, 71; Argentina, 39·8.

In 1967 the principal imports were (in US$1m.): Machinery, 195·5; chemical products, 65·3; railway and transport equipment, 97·3; petroleum products, 68·3. The principal exports in 1967 were (in US$1m.): Copper, 691; iron ore, 88·6; chemical products, 27·3; paper and pulp, 23·3.

Total trade between Chile and UK for 5 years (British Board of Trade returns, in £1,000 sterling):

	1966	1967	1968	1969	1970
Imports to UK	44,240	46,554	56,511	72,145	64,860
Exports from UK	10,725	13,174	14,673	17,248 ⎱	20,519
Re-exports from UK	298	201	374	326 ⎰	

SHIPPING. The mercantile marine had, in 1966, 49 ships of over 100 tons, totally 332,755 GRT and owned by 9 companies. Valparaíso is the chief port. The free ports of Magallanes, Chiloé and Aysén serve the southern provinces. Tonnage handled in all Chilean ports was 22·9m. tons in 1964.

There are 2,185 km of navigable rivers.

ROADS. In 1961 there were in Chile 56,976 km of highways, of which 2,442 first-class paved, 21,840 second class and 31,694 earth. There were in 1968, 130,225 automobiles, 111,721 goods vehicles and 12,614 buses.

RAILWAYS. The total length of railway lines is 7,697 km; of these private railway lines, principally British-owned, amount to 2,607 km. Electrification of the railways is proceeding. A railway from Salta in north-western Argentina to Antofagasta was opened in Dec. 1953.

AVIATION. There were, 1958, 8 customs airports, 11 military airports, 20 civilian airports, 89 landing grounds and 13 seaplane bases. Chile is served by 15 commercial air companies (2 Chilean). There are 4 international airports. In 1959, 193,936 passengers were carried into and out of Chile on international services; 209,500 passengers were carried and 176m. passenger-km were flown on internal routes. In 1960, 7·5m. ton-km of freight and 254m. ton-km of mail were carried by the national airline, LAN, and they carried 388,000 passengers 429·9m. passenger-km.

POST. There are 1,147 post offices and agencies. The length of telegraph lines in 1962 was 44,000 km; there were 603 telegraph offices. In 1968 there were 294,712 telephones in use, all (except 2,500) under private companies, of which the largest is American-owned; Santiago had 166,513 telephones.

A chain of wireless stations along the coast for shore-to-ship transmission is operated by the Navy. At the end of 1963 there were some 120 commercial broadcasting stations. Three television stations are operated by the Universities and there is a national television station. On 9 Aug. 1968 the satellite station at Longaví was inaugurated to cover transmissions (including colour) from USA and Europe.

BANKING. On 31 May 1969 the Central Bank had gold and foreign exchange reserves equal to US$79·1m. compared with US$111m. on 30 June 1968. Notes in circulation and deposits in currency were E°.7,995m. at 31 Dec. 1968; total deposits in the commercial banks stood at E°3,444m. and in the state bank at E°.1,826m. on 31 Dec. 1968.

From 1 Oct. 1966 commercial banks must maintain minimum cash reserves of 40% of the daily average of all sight and term deposits in local currency between 24 Dec. 1965 and 10 Jan. 1966. Higher reserves are obligatory in excess of that level.

Inflation is still severe: the official cost of living index rose 33·3% in 1959, 22·7% in 1962, 45·4% in 1963, 38·4% in 1964, 25·9% in 1965, 17% in 1966, 21·9% in 1967, 27·9% in 1968 and 29·3% in 1969.

WEIGHTS AND MEASURES. The metric system has been legally established in Chile since 1865, but the old Spanish weights and measures are still in use to some extent.

DIPLOMATIC REPRESENTATIVES

Chile maintains embassies in:

Algeria	Germany (West)	Philippines
Argentina	Guatemala	Poland
Australia	Honduras	Portugal
Austria	Hungary	Romania
Barbados	India	Spain
Belgium	Israel	Sweden
Brazil	Italy	Switzerland
Bulgaria	Jamaica	Syria
Canada	Japan	Trinidad
Colombia	Jordan	Turkey
Costa Rica	Lebanon	USSR
Cuba	Luxembourg	UAR
Czechoslovakia	Mexico	UK
Denmark	Netherlands	USA
Dominican Republic	Nicaragua	Uruguay
Ecuador	Norway	Vatican
El Salvador	Panama	Venezuela
Finland	Paraguay	Yugoslavia
France	Peru	Zambia

OF CHILE IN GREAT BRITAIN (3 Hamilton Place, W1)
Ambassador: Alvaro Bunster (accredited 31 March 1971.
Minister-Counsellors: Jorge Berguño; Alejandro Jara. *Service Attachés:*
Rear-Adm. C. Chubretovkh (*Navy*), Wing Cdr Juan Soler, MVO (*Air*). *Civil
Air Attaché:* Rear-Adm. Calixto Rogers.

There are consular representatives at Birmingham, Glasgow, Liverpool,
London and Southampton.

OF GREAT BRITAIN IN CHILE
Ambassador and Consul-General: D. H. T. Hildyard, CMG, DFC.
First Secretaries: G. R. Lee (*Head of Chancery*); W. R. McQuillan; A. S.
Dyer, OBE; L. Borax, OBE (*Consul*); R. P. H. Davies (*Cultural*).
Defence Attaché: Capt. F. G. Thatcher, RN.

There are also consular representatives at Antofagasta, Arica, Concepción,
Coquimbo, Iquique, Punta Arenas and Valparaíso.

OF CHILE IN THE USA (1736 Massachusetts Ave. NW,
Washington, D.C., 20036)
Ambassador: Domingo Santa Maria.
Minister-Counsellor: Manuel Sanchez. *Service Attachés:* Rear-Adm. Victor
Bunster (*Navy*), Maj.-Gen. Ernesto Baeza (*Army*), Col. Gerardo Lopez (*Air*).

OF THE USA IN CHILE
Ambassador: Edward M. Korry.
Deputy Chief of Mission: H. W. Shlaudeman. *Heads of Sections:* John E.
Karkashian (*Political*); Deane R. Hinton (*Economic and AID*); L. Lane
(*Consular*); Manuel Martinez (*Administrative*). *Service Attachés:* Capt. Olyce T.
Knight (*Navy*), Col. Paul M. Wimert, Jr (*Army*), Col. Lester T. Hanser (*Air*).

There are consular representatives at Concepción and Valparaíso.

BOOKS OF REFERENCE

STATISTICAL INFORMATION. The Dirección General de Estadística (Cienfuegos 210, Casilla
1317, Santiago), was founded 17 Sept. 1847. *Director General:* Luis Cárcamo Cantin. Principal
publications: *Anuario Estadística* and the bi-monthly *Estadística Chilena.*
    Other sources are: *Geografía Económica,* by the Corporación de Fomento de la Production, and
Boletín Mensual, by the Banco Central de Chile.

Butland, G. J., *Chile: An Outline of its Geography, Economics and Politics.* 3rd ed. R. Inst. of Int.
    Affairs, 1956.—*The human geography of southern Chile.* London, 1957
Chile y Gran Bretaña. HMSO, 1960
Empresa Periodística, *Diccionario biográfico de Chile.* 8th ed. Santiago, 1952
Gil, F. G., *The political system of Chile.* Boston, 1966
Luke, Sir Harry, *Easter Island* (Geogr. Journal 120, 1954)
Pinochet de la Barra, O., *La Antárctica Chilena.* Santiago de Chile, 1948
Subercaseaux, B., *Chile: A Geographical Extravaganza.* New York, 1943

CHINA
Chung-Hua Jen-Min Kung-Ho Kuo
—People's Republic of China

CONSTITUTION AND GOVERNMENT. In the course of 1949 the
Communists obtained full control of the mainland of China, and in 1950 also
over most islands off the coast, including Hainan.
    On 21 Sept. 1949 the 'Chinese People's Political Consultative Conference' met
in Peking, convened by the Chinese Communist Party. The Conference adopted
a 'Common Programme' of 60 articles and the 'Organic Law of the Central
People's Government' (31 articles). Both became the basis of the Constitution
adopted on 20 Sept. 1954 by the First National People's Congress, the supreme

legislative body. The Consultative Conference (of about 1,200 members in Dec. 1964) continues to exist as an advisory body. A new draft constitution is under consideration.

The Conference elected Mao Tse-tung as Chairman of the Republic; he proclaimed the establishment of the People's Republic of China on 1 Oct. 1949 (now the national day). In 1959 Mao relinquished the position of Chairman of the Republic in favour of Liu Shao-ch'i.

The 1954 Constitution consists of 106 articles. The most important are:

Art. 3. The People's Republic of China is a unified, multi-national State. All the nationalities are equal . . . have freedom to use and develop their spoken and written languages, and to preserve or reform their habits and customs.

Regional autonomy shall be applied in areas entirely or largely inhabited by national minorities. National autonomous areas are inalienable parts of the People's Republic of China.

Art. 6. The state sector of the economy is a socialist sector, owned by the whole people. It is the leading force in the national economy and the material basis for the socialist reconstruction carried out by the state. All mineral resources and waters, as well as forests, undeveloped land and other resources which the state owns by law, are the property of the whole people.

Art 7. The co-operative sector of the economy is either socialist, when collectively owned by the working masses, or semi-socialist, when in part collectively owned by the working masses. Partial collective ownership by the working masses is a transitional form through which individual peasants, individual craftsmen and other individual working people pass to collective ownership by the working masses . . .

The state protects the right of the peasants to own land and other means of production (*Art*. 8), of craftsmen and other non-agricultural individual working people to own means of production (*Art*. 9), of capitalists to own means of production and other capital (*Art*. 10), but, 'the policy of the State towards the rich peasant economy is to restrict and gradually eliminate it' (*Art*. 8) and 'the policy of the state towards capitalist industry and trade is to utilize, to restrict and to reform them. The state gradually replaces capitalist ownership by ownership by the people' (*Art*. 10).

The National People's Congress is the highest organ of state authority (*Art*. 21) and the sole legislative authority in the country (*Art*. 22). It is composed of deputies elected by provinces, autonomous regions, municipalities directly under the central authority, the armed forces and Chinese resident abroad (*Art*. 23).

According to the Electoral Law, as amended on 8 Dec. 1963, the provinces and autonomous regions elect 1 deputy for every 400,000 persons, but at least 10 deputies from each province; cities directly under the central authority, industrial cities and industrial districts with populations of 200,000–300,000 elect 1 deputy for every 50,000 persons; the national minorities, 300 deputies; the armed forces, 120; the overseas Chinese, 30 deputies ('to be elected from among the returned overseas Chinese'). The Third Congress, elected in Sept. 1964, consists of 3,040 deputies, compared with 1,226 before the revision of the electoral law.

The National People's Congress is elected for 4 years and meets at least once a year. It can amend the Constitution with a two-thirds majority vote of all the deputies, enacts laws with an absolute majority vote, elects and has power to remove from office the highest state dignitaries, decides on the national economic plan, on questions of war and peace, etc. The Standing Committee is the permanent body of the Congress, convenes it, conducts the elections, interprets the laws, adopts decrees, supervises the work of the Government, etc. (*Art*. 25–38).

Art. 47–52 deal with the central government—the State Council, otherwise known as the Central People's Government. *Art*. 53–66 deal with local government. There are 3 main administrative levels: (1) Provinces, autonomous regions and municipalities directly under the central authority; (2) *chou*, counties, autonomous counties, cities; (3) *hsiang*, autonomous *hsiang*, and towns. On each level, there are people's congresses and people's councils. *Art*. 67–72 deal with self-government of national minorities in national autonomous areas. *Art.* 73–84 deal with the judicial system. (*See below* JUSTICE.)

For further details *see* THE STATESMAN'S YEAR-BOOK, 1957, pp. 877–79.

State emblem: 5 stars above Peking's Gate of Heavenly Peace, surrounded by a border of ears of grain entwined with drapings, which form a knot in the centre of a cogwheel at the base; the colours are red and gold.

National flag: Red, with 5 stars.

National anthem: The March of the Volunteers (words by Tien Han; tune by Nieh Erh).

The head of State is designated 'Chairman of the People's Republic of China'. There are 2 Vice-Chairmen.

The *State Council* consists of the Premier, Deputy-Premiers, Ministers, Chairmen of Commissions and a Secretary-General. Immediately under the Premier there are 6 central offices to supervise and co-ordinate the work of the ministries and commissions. In recent years there have been 40 ministries and 9 commissions, some of them being headed by Deputy-Premiers.

The Standing Committee of the National People's Congress consists of a Chairman, a number of Deputy-Chairmen, members and a Secretary-General.

In mid-1966 a 'Great Proletarian Cultural Revolution' was launched by Mao to eradicate 'revisionism' in the Party, government and the community generally. The Cultural Revolution has entailed the denunciation of numerous officials of the Communist Party and of State organs at all levels. A meeting of the Central Committee in Oct. 1968 decided to dismiss Liu Shao-ch'i, Chairman of the Republic since 1959, from all his posts and to expel him from the Party. More than half of the 15 Deputy Premiers have been criticized and have ceased to make public appearances. Tung Pi-wu, Vice-Chairman of the Republic, has assumed certain of the functions of the Head of State in an acting capacity. The Cultural Revolution can be taken to have terminated by April 1969, when the Communist Party held its long-delayed 9th National Congress (the 8th Congress was held in two sessions, in 1956 and 1958). It adopted a new Party Constitution and formed a new Central Committee, comprising 170 full and 109 alternate members. Mao Tse-tung was re-elected Chairman of the Party and of its Central Committee, with Lin Piao (*Minister of Defence*) as the sole Vice-Chairman. Lin Piao was also formally designated Mao's eventual successor.

A new Politburo of 21 full and 4 alternate members was chosen by the Central Committee. The full members are: Mao Tse-tung; Lin Piao; Ch'en Po-ta; Chou En-lai (*Premier*); K'ang Sheng (these five constituting the Politburo's Standing Committee); Chang Ch'un-ch'iao; Ch'en Hsi-lien; Chiang Ch'ing (Mme Mao); Ch'iu Hui-tso; Chu Teh; Hsieh Fu-chih; Hsü Shih-yu; Huang Yung-sheng; Li Hsien-nien; Li Tso-p'eng; Liu Po-ch'eng; Tung Pi-wu; Wu Fa-hsien; Yao Wen-yüan; Yeh Chien-ying and Yeh Ch'ün (Mme Lin).

Party membership was officially claimed as 17m. in 1962.

AREA AND POPULATION. China is composed of 22 provinces (this figure includes Taiwan), 5 autonomous regions originally entirely or largely inhabited by national minorities (owing to the immigration of Han Chinese the original nationality is often outnumbered, *e.g.*, by 10 to 1 in Inner Mongolia), namely Inner Mongolia, Sinkiang–Uighur, Kwangsi–Chuang, Ninghsia-Hui, Tibet (and Chamdo area) and 3 centrally controlled municipalities (Peking, Shanghai, Tientsin). The capital is Peking.

See map in THE STATESMAN'S YEAR-BOOK, 1968–69.

The total area is estimated at 9,597,000 sq. km (3,704,400 sq. miles).

Population at the last census (1953): 601,938,035. This figure was arrived at as follows: Direct census, 574,205,940; Taiwan ('yet to be liberated'), 7,591,298; Chinese resident or studying abroad, 11,743,000; Chinese 'in remote border regions', 8,397,477. Urban population, 77·3m. (13·3%); rural population,

505·3m. (86·7%). In 1966 the population was officially claimed to be over 700m. Western estimates vary from 730m. (UN, 1968) to 746m. However, figures published by the provincial Revolutionary Committees in 1968 suggested a total of only 700m. Estimated birth and death rates for 1970 per 1,000: 32, 17; natural increase, 1·5%. In 1970 the birth control campaign was renewed. Women may legally marry at 18 and men at 22, but the recommended ages are 25 (women) and 30 (men). The term 'Han' is used to distinguish racial Chinese from other Chinese citizens. Some 6% of the population are non-Han. Urban population was estimated at 150m. in 1967, but enforced migration to rural areas since may have lowered this figure to 130m.

The number of Chinese outside China and Taiwan was estimated at 16·34m. in mid-1962, including 3·8m. in Thailand, 3·2m. in Hong Kong, 2·5m. in Indonesia, 2·5m. in Malaya, 1·25m. in Singapore, 237,000 in USA, 52,000 in Canada and 12,000 in the UK.

The official 'National Language' is based on the Chinese of Peking. There are a number of widely divergent dialects, but the Communist government (like its precedessor) is promoting its general use. The ideographic writing system is uniform throughout the country. A knowledge of 4,000 characters is sufficient for general reading. Common characters have been simplified, and in 1958 a 26-letter Roman alphabet was officially adopted to help in the task of learning the characters.

From 1949 to 1955 the country was divided into 6 'great administrative regions' for government and Party purposes. This system was terminated in 1955, but in 1961 was revived for Party organizational purposes. The table below shows the Provinces, Autonomous Regions and Special Municipalities grouped regionally. The cities shown in brackets are the seats of the Regional Bureaux of the Party.

	Area (in 1,000 sq. km)	Census 1953 (in 1,000)	Figures made public in 1967–70 (in 1m.)	Capital
North-Eastern Region (Shenyang)				
Heilungkiang	463·6	11,897	25	Harbin
Kirin	187·0	11,290	20	Changchun
Liaoning	150·0	18,545	28	Shenyang[1]
Northern Region (Peking)				
Hopei	202·7	35,985	43	Shihchiachuang
Inner Mongolia (Aut. Region)	1,177·5	6,100	13	Huhehot[2]
Peking (municipality)	7·1	2,768	7	—
Shansi	157·1	14,314	18	Taiyuan
Eastern Region (Shanghai)				
Shantung	153·3	48,877	57	Tsinan
Kiangsi	164·8	16,773	23	Nanchang
Kiangsu	102·2	41,252	47	Nanking
Shanghai (municipality)	5·8	6,204	10	—
Anhwei	139·9	30,344	35	Hofei
Chekiang	101·8	22,866	31	Hangchow
Fukien	123·1	13,143	18	Foochow
Taiwan[3]	36·0	7,591	13	Taipei
Central-Southern Region (Wuhan)				
Honan	167·0	44,215	50	Chengchow
Hupei	187·5	27,790	32	Wuhan
Hunan	210·5	33,227	38	Changsha
Kwantung	231·4	34,770	40	Canton[4]
Kwangsi-Chuang (Aut. Region)	220·4	19,561	24	Nanning
South-Western Region (Chungking)				
Szechwan	569·0	62,304[5]	70	Chengtu
Kweichow	174·0	15,037	20	Kweiyang
Yunnan	436·2	17,473	23	Kunming
Tibet (Aut. Region)	1,221·6	1,273	1	Lhasa

[1] Formerly Mukden.
[2] Formerly Kweisui.
[3] Regarded by the Peking regime as part of China.
[4] Now called Kwangchow.
[5] Plus most of the then 3·4m. population of the former province Sikang, incorporated Aug. 1955 in Szechwan province, except the area to the west of Yangtse River (Chamdo) which was united with Tibet.

	Area (in 1,000 sq. km)	Census 1953 (in 1,000)	Population Figures made public in 1967–70 (in 1m.)	Capital
North-Western Region (Sian)				
Shensi	195·8	15,881	21	Sian
Kansu	366·5⎫	12,928	⎧13	Lanchow
Ningsia-Hui (Aut. Region)	66·4⎭		⎩ 2	Yinchuan[1]
Chinghai	721·0	1,677	2	Sining
Sinkiang-Uighur (Aut. Region)	1,646·8	4,874	8	Urumchi[2]

[1] Formerly Ningsia. [2] Formerly Tihwa.

Municipalities under direct control of the central government, with estimated population in 1968: Peking, 7m.; Tientsin, 4m.; Shanghai, (1970), 10m.

Other large towns, with population at the end of 1957: Shenyang, 2,411,000[1]; Wuhan (the former 3 towns: Hankow, Wuchang and Hanyang), 2,146,000; Chungking, 2,121,000; Canton, 1·84m.[1]; Harbin, 1,552,000[1]; Lü-ta (formerly Port Arthur–Dairen, afterwards Lushun-Talien), 1,508,000[1]; Nanking, 1,419,000; Sian, 1·31m.[1]; Tsingtao, 1,121,000; Chengtu, 1,107,000; Taiyuan, 1·02m.; Fushun, 985,000[1]; Changchun, 975,000[1]; Ashan, 805,000; Tangshan, 800,000.

[1] Western estimates, 1965: Shenyang, 4m.; Canton, 3m.; Harbin, 1·6m.; Lü-ta, 3·6m.; Sian, 1·5m.; Fushun, 1m.; Changchun, 1·8m.

Manchuria, a term not used by the Chinese, is roughly identical with the 3 provinces of the N.E. Region.

Tibet. For events before the revolt of 1959 *see* previous issues of THE STATES-MAN'S YEAR-BOOK under TIBET. After the revolt was suppressed the Preparatory Committee for the Autonomous Region of Tibet (set up 1955) took over the functions of local government, led by its Vice-Chairman, the Panchen Lama, in the absence of its Chairman, the Dalai Lama, who had fled to India in 1959. In Dec. 1964 both the Dalai and Panchen Lamas were removed from their posts. On 9 Sept. 1965 Tibet became an Autonomous Region. 301 delegates were elected to the first People's Congress, of whom 226 were Tibetans. In 1970 the population was reported to be 1·3m. The number of Chinese now in Tibet is at least 500,000. 85,000 Tibetans live in exile (mainly in India). Chinese efforts to modernize Tibet include irrigation (increased by 30%), road-building and the establishment of light industry: some 60 factories have been set up making textiles, cement, matches, paper and chemicals, and there are now 26,000 Tibetan industrial workers.

Organized Buddhism has been suppressed. Education has been secularized and made free and compulsory. In 1965 there were 1,682 primary and 7 secondary schools with some 60,000 pupils. In 1965 there were also 15 hospitals and 149 clinics.

The Dalai Lama, *My Land and My People* (ed. D. Howarth). London, 1962
Ginsburgs, G., and Mathos, M., *Communist China and Tibet*. The Hague, 1964
International Commission of Jurists, *Tibet and the Chinese People's Republic: Reports*. Geneva, 1960, 1964
Jäschke, H. A., *A Tibetan–English Dictionary*. London. 1934
Rahul, R., *The Government and Politics of Tibet*. New Delhi, 1969
Richardson, H. E., *Tibet and its History*. OUP, 1962
Shakabpa, T. W. D., *Tibet: a political history*. Yale UP, 1967

RELIGION. Confucianism, Buddhism and Taoism have long been established. Confucianism has no ecclesiastical organization and appears rather as a philosophy of ethics and government. It has usually dominated the governmental administration from 136 B.C. to A.D. 1905. Buddhism and Taoism present a very gorgeous ceremonial, Taoism—of Chinese origin—having copied Buddhist ceremonial soon after the arrival of Buddhism 1,900 years ago. Buddhism in return adopted many Taoist magical beliefs and practices. It is no longer possible to estimate the number of adherents to these faiths.

Ceremonies of reverence to ancestors have been observed by the whole population regardless of philosophical or religious beliefs.

Moslems are found in every province of China, being most numerous in the Ninghsia–Hui Autonomous Region, Yunnan, Shensi, Kansu, Hopei, Honan, Shantung, Szechwan, Sinkiang and Shansi. The total is estimated at 2–5% of the population.

Roman Catholicism has had a footing in China for more than 3 centuries; in 1949 it had about 3m. adherents. In 1957 the Chinese Roman Catholics, under the Archbishop of Shenyang, declared their independence of Rome.

Protestant Missions date from 1807. Attached to Protestant Missions in 1934 were 19 colleges of university standing and 267 middle schools. In 1949 Protestant Chinese numbered about 700,000. By Sept. 1952 all foreign Christian foundations had lost their identity in a reorganized university system.

Places of worship were closed during the Cultural Revolution.

EDUCATION. In 1959 there were 90m. pupils in elementary schools, 12·9m. in secondary and secondary technical schools. In 1965 there were 1·5m. students in institutes of higher education. There were some 2·6m. primary teachers in 1964.

The 'new-policy' educational system distinguishes full-time, part-study and part-work, and spare-time institutions. Full-time primary and secondary education takes 6 years each; college education, 4–6 years; secondary technical education, 3–4 years. During the Cultural Revolution educational institutes were closed. An uneven return to schools and universities began in 1968 and continues; courses are being shortened, and more emphasis is to be laid on political instruction and practical work.

The Academy of Sciences had in 1964 some 20 provincial branches.

Institutes of higher learning included in 1961: 61 universities, 271 engineering colleges, 113 colleges of agriculture and forestry, 174 teacher-training colleges and 142 medical schools. Some 170,000 students (one-third technical) graduated in 1962.

Among the universities are the following: People's University of China, Peking (founded 1912 by Dr Sun Yat-sen; reorganized 1950; about 3,000 students); Peking University, Peking (1898, enlarged 1945; about 10,000 students); Amoy University, Fukien (1921 and 1937); Futan University, Shanghai (1905); Inner Mongolia University, Huhehot; Lanchow University, Lanchow (Kansu Prov.); Nankai University, Tientsin (1919); Nanking University, Nanking (1888 and 1928); People's University of North-East China, Changchun (Kirin Prov.); North-West University, Sian (Shensi Prov.); Shantung University, Tsingtao (1926); Sun Yat-sen University, Canton (founded 1924 by Dr Sun Yat-sen); Szechwan University, Chengtu (1931); Wuhan University, Wuhan (Hupeh Prov.; 1905 and 1928); Yunnan University, Kunming. In 1958 a university of science and technology was set up by the Academy of Sciences.

CINEMAS numbered 1,386 in 1958.

NEWSPAPERS. The Government newspaper is *Jen Min Jih Pao (or Ren Min Rih Bao.)*

SOCIAL WELFARE. In 1959 workers' insurance covered some 16m. people.

In 1959 there were about 2·16m. doctors and trained medical personnel. Hospitals and sanatoria had about 440,000 beds.

JUSTICE. Justice is administered by 'people's courts' which are divided into some 30 higher, 200 intermediate and 2,000 fundamental courts, and headed by the Supreme People's Court. The latter is accountable to the National People's Congress and not only tries cases and hears appeals, but supervises the work of the people's courts; it has been responsible for judicial administration since the abolition of the Ministry of Justice in 1959.

People's courts are composed of a president, vice-presidents and judges. Elected 'people's assessors' take part in trials alongside judges. Fundamental courts may establish 'people's tribunals' to try civil and minor criminal cases, and 'people's conciliation committees' are charged with settling disputes.

There are also special military courts.

The Procuracy has supervisory powers over the observance of law. It consists of the Supreme People's Procuratorate and local and special procuratorates. The Chief Procurator is elected by the National People's Congress for 4 years.

FINANCE. Currency. The unit of currency is the *yuan* which is divided into 10 *chiao*, the *chiao* into 10 *fen*. On 1 March 1955 new bank-notes were issued; old PBY10,000 = PBY1. The official rate of exchange is £1 = PBY5·9; US$1 = PBY2·46; Hong Kong $1 = PBY0·427; 1 rouble = PBY2·222 (non-commercial, 1 rouble = PBY1·29).

From 1 Dec. 1957 the People's Bank has issued small aluminium coins of 1, 2 and 5 *fen* (= 0·01, 0·02, 0·05 *yuan*) and also a new 10-*yuan* note.

Budget. The latest budget published was that for 1960 which balanced at PBY70,020m. For details *see* previous issues of THE STATESMAN'S YEAR-BOOK. A large budgetary surplus was offically announced for 1970.

It was announced in April 1969 that all national bonds had been redeemed and China no longer had any internal or external debts.

China's gold reserves are estimated to be US$2,250m.

DEFENCE. China is divided into 13 military regions. One field army is assigned to each region, and the military commander also commands the air, naval and civilian militia forces assigned to the region. Conscription was introduced in Feb. 1955. Service begins at the age of 18 and lasts 4 years in the Army, 5 years in the Air Force and 6 years in the Navy.

Formal gradations in military ranks were abolished in 1965; ranks are designated by function.

The Chinese have conducted 10 nuclear weapon tests between Oct. 1964 and Sept. 1969, and launched satellites in April 1970 and March 1971.

Army. The Army consists of 138 divisions, including 20 artillery, 5 armoured, 3 cavalry and 2 airborne divisions. Only a small proportion of the conscript potential, about 700,000 per annum, are called up to serve 3 years. Total strength at the end of 1969 was between 2·5m. and 2·6m.

The security forces, including the armed police, number some 300,000.

The People's Militia has a strength of some 10m., mainly ex-servicemen.

Navy. Present strength comprises 33 submarines, 4 destroyers, 19 frigates and escorts, 10 missile boats, 24 patrol vessels, 160 motor gunboats, 27 minesweepers, 180 motor torpedo boats, 22 coastal and river defence vessels, 70 landing ships and landing craft, 35 auxiliaries and 375 service craft.

Active personnel (1970): 140,000 officers and men, including 28,000 marines and 16,000 naval airmen.

Main naval bases: Tsingtao, Lu Shen (North Sea Fleet); Shanghai, Chou Shan (East Sea Fleet); Whampao, Tsamkong (South Sea Fleet).

Air Force. In 1970 the Air Force was estimated at 2,500 front-line aircraft, organized in 40–50 regiments of jet-fighters and several regiments of tactical bombers, plus reconnaissance, transport and helicopter units. Each regiment is made up of 3 squadrons, and 3 regiments form a division.

Equipment is Russian in design and includes MiG-21, MiG-19, MiG-17 and MiG-15 fighters, about 150 Il-28 jet-bombers and 12 Tu-4 (B-29) piston-engined long-range bombers, Il-14 and An-2 piston-engined transports, and Mi-1 and Mi-4 helicopters. Small numbers of Chinese-built copies of the Soviet Tu-16 twin-jet strategic bomber were reported to be entering service in 1970. The MiG fighters and An-2 transports have been manufactured in quantity in China, under licence, and other types have been assembled there.

Total strength (1970) about 100,000 men.

PRODUCTION. No official statistics have been issued since 1960, and figures for 1958 and 1959 were exaggerated.

PLANNING. The first 5-year plan ran from 1953 to 1957. The second 5-year plan envisaged further expansion of industry, especially of heavy industry, as well as of agriculture, but ran into difficulties attributed to natural calamities, administrative failures (the collapse of the 'Great Leap Forward') and to the withdrawal of Soviet aid. By 1961 long-term planning gave way to annual plans directed towards the recovery of agriculture, while in industry emphasis was given to retrenchment and priority for those sectors serving agriculture. It was announced that a third 5-year plan started in 1966, but planning appeared to continue on a yearly basis. It was again announced in 1971 that a new 5-year plan had started. Priority is given to agriculture and local industry.

AGRICULTURE. China remains essentially an agricultural country. Intensive agriculture and horticulture have been practised for millennia. Present-day policy aims to avert the traditional threats from floods and droughts by soil conservancy, afforestation, irrigation and drainage projects, and to increase the 'high stable yields' areas by introducing fertilizers, pesticides and improved crops. Crop priorities: food grains; raw materials for industry (especially cotton); crops for export (especially oil seeds). Among livestock, priority is given to pig production.

In 1950 the land belonging to the feudal nobility and to monasteries and other institutions was confiscated by the State. By the end of 1952 land reform and by the end of 1958 the socialization of agriculture was declared to be complete.

By the end of 1958 the peasant population of some 500m. had been organized into roughly 24,000 'communes', each consisting of a number of villages and 5,000–10,000 families. The commune took over the local government function at the village (*hsiang*) level and assumed responsibility for management, production, trade, welfare, organization of the local militia, etc. Centralized authority was discharged down through the production 'brigade' to the production 'team' at ground level. Since 1958 some modifications have been made in the commune system, and the number of communes raised to 74,000 by reducing their size. Small private plots are permitted.

In 1964 there were 110m. hectares of arable land. In 1965 there were in use 100,000 tractors (in terms of 15-h.p. units).

Agricultural production (in 1m. metric tons) has been as follows (with the sown area (in 1m. hectares) in parenthesis): Total grain, 1955, 174·8 (118·4); 1959, 167·6 (109·1); 1963, 163,179·1 (118·5); rice, 1955, 78 (29·9); 1959, 80·2 (29·7); 1963, 78·4 (28·2); wheat, 1955, 23 (26·7); 1959, 24·3 (24·3); 1963, 21·8 (24·2); potatoes, 1955, 18·9 (10·1); 1959, 21·6 (12·7); 1963, 24·3 (13·3).

Latest Western estimates in metric tons: (1969) total grain, 195–200m.; (1968) cottonseed, 2·9m.; soybeans, 10·67m.; wheat, 27m.; (1967) apples, 360,000; jute, 460,000; pears, 880,000; rice, 92m.; sugar-beet, 4·7m.; sugar-cane, 26m.; tea, 158,800; tobacco, 850,000.

Livestock. Official claim for 1959: Cattle, 65·43m.; horses, 7·6m.; sheep and goats, 112·53m.; pigs, 180m. FAO estimates: (1967) sheep, 69·7m.; (1968) cattle, 62·9m.; pigs, 213m.

FORESTRY. The chief forested areas are in Heilungkiang, Szechwan and Yunnan. The most important tree is the tung (*Jatropha Curcas* (L.), from which oil is produced: it grows chiefly in Szechwan. Tung-oil production amounted to 115,000 metric tons in 1948–49. Timber output in 1957 was 27·87m.; 1958, 35m.; 1959, 41·2m.

The most important timber product is teak. In 1957, 3·96m. hectares were afforested.

MINING. *Coal.* Most of the provinces contain coal; the entire coal resources of China are estimated at 262,941m. metric tons. By 1957, 31 collieries with an annual output of more than 1m. tons each were to be developed; the 'big five' were to produce by 1957: Kailuan, 9·68m.; Fushun, 9·3m.; Fushin, 8·45m.; Hainan, 6·85m.; Tatung, 6·45m. Coal and lignite production was estimated at between 300m. and 400m. metric tons in 1970.

Iron. Iron ores are abundant in the anthracite field of Shansi, in Hopei, in Shantung and other provinces, and iron (found in conjunction with coal) is worked in Manchuria. 300m. tons of ore are estimated to be in Shansi; the principal iron-ore reserves total about 19,840m. tons. The Tayeh iron deposits, near Wuhan, are among the richest in the world. Estimated output of iron ore in 1967, 30m. metric tons. The biggest steel bases are at Anshan (in Manchuria) with a capacity of 6m. tons, Wuhan and Paotow (Inner Mongolia) (capacity 1·5m. tons).

Oil and natural gas. China has made rapid progress in oil extraction and refining. The largest oilfields are at Taching, Yumen and Karamai. Refining capacity is estimated at 12m. tons yer annum. Crude oil reserves exceed 5,000m. tons. Output (in metric tons) of oil was 400,000 in 1954; in 1958, 2·23m.; in 1959, 3·7m.; in 1960, 5·5m. (including crude petroleum, crude shale oil, oil from coal carbonization and synthetic crude oil from coal). Crude oil production was estimated at 12m. metric tons in 1969. Natural gas production was estimated at 1,000m. cu. metres for 1967.

Tin. Tin ore is plentiful in Yunnan, where the tin-mining industry has long existed; production of tin in 1964, 25,000 metric tons. Tin production was estimated at 20,000 metric tons in 1967.

Tungsten. China is the world's principal producer of tungsten, producing an estimated 20,000 metric tons in 1964. Mining from wolfram (tungsten ore) is carried on in Hunan, Kwangtung and Yunnan.

Estimated production of other minerals in 1967 (in metric tons): antimony (of which China is one of the largest producers), 12,000; phosphate rock, 1m.; salt, 13,000; sulphur, 120,000; asbestos, 170,000; bauxite, 350,000; copper, 90,000; lead, 90,000; manganese, 700,000; zinc, 90,000. Other minerals produced: barite, bismuth, gold, graphite, gypsum, mercury, molybdenum, silver.

INDUSTRY. 'Cottage' industry is very old in the economy and persists into the 20th century. Modern industrial development began with the manufacture of cotton textiles, and the establishment of some silk filatures, steel plants, flour-mills and match factories. The first 5-year plan gave priority to the development of heavy industry, but since the withdrawal of Soviet aid and the failure of the 'Great Leap Forward' a more modest emphasis has been placed on it. Expanding sectors of manufacture are: steel, chemicals, cement, agricultural implements, plastics and lorries.

In 1970 a policy of establishing small-scale local industries was introduced.

Industrial production claimed for 1959, in 1m. metric tons: Coal, 347·8; pig-iron, 20·5; cement, 12·27; paper, 1·7; timber, 41·2m. cu. metres; chemical fertilizers, 1,300 metric tons (1963 output (official) was 1,638 metric tons); electricity (1960), 55,000m. kwh.; cotton yarn, 8·2m. bales; textile fabrics (in 1m. metres): cotton, 7,500; woollen, 23·59; silk, over 190.

Western estimates for 1969 in metric tons: Steel, 11m.; pig-iron, 14m.; aluminium, 90,000; chemical fertilizers, 8·5m.; cement, 11m..

ELECTRICITY. China has a large hydro-electric potential. Estimated output in 1965, 36,000–40,000 kwh.

COMMERCE. Foreign trade is conducted through national corporations under the Ministry of Foreign Trade. In some countries with which China is not in diplomatic relations trade is handled by offices of the China Council for the Promotion of International Trade, a non-governmental body in which the corporations are represented.

Imports include grain, cotton, rubber, fertilizers, metals and machinery; exports: agricultural products, textiles and minerals.

Estimated total trade for 1968: Imports, US$1,900m.; exports, US$1,760.

Owing to the Soviet–Chinese dissensions, trade between the two countries declined (to 51m. roubles in 1969. *Cf.* 5,129m. roubles in 1957) and 75–80% of China's trade is now with non-Communist countries. However, a Sino-Soviet trade agreement was signed in Nov. 1970. Japan is China's biggest trading partner (total trade, 1969, US$550m.), UK fourth after Hong Kong and West Germany.

Total trade between UK and China (British Board of Trade returns, in £1,000 sterling):

	1966	1967	1968	1969	1970
Imports to UK	33,787	29,626	34,274	32,727	33,538
Exports from UK	31,995	37,976	28,505	51,802 }	44,586
Re-exports from UK	1,506	813	595	2,688 }	

More than 95% of UK imports from China are free of quota restrictions.

In Dec. 1969 the USA partially lifted its 19-year-old embargo on trade with communist China.

COMMUNICATIONS. Map of the principal roads, all railways and airlines will be found in THE STATESMAN'S YEAR-BOOK, 1956.

SHIPPING. Shipping in 1969: 237 ships totalling 791,893 GRT.

The Bureau of Navigation has regional centres at Tientsin, Shanghai, Tsingtao, Lü-ta (Dairen) and Canton.

Inland waterways total about 150,000 km, of which 40,000 are navigable for steamers. In 1959 inland and coastwise shipping carried 230m. tons of freight.

ROADS. According to an official report there were almost 300,000 km of 'predominantly all-weather' roads and 500,000 km of 'secondary' roads in 1969. Highways are well graded but mostly unmetalled. In 1969 there were some 409,000 lorries, 60,000 cars and 30,000 buses.

In 1959 road haulage carried 155m. tons of freight.

RAILWAYS. Chinese railway history begins in 1876, when the Wusung (Shanghai) line was opened. According to official statistics from Peking, there were, on 1 July 1950, 21,740 km of railway lines in service. It is probable that some 35,000 km are now open to traffic.

The principal railways are:

(1) The great north–south trunk lines: (*a*) Peking–Canton Railway (over 2,300 km), *via* Chengchow–Wuhan–Chuchow–Hengyang.

(*b*) Tientsin–Shanghai Railway (1,500 km), *via* Pukow and Nanking.

(*c*) Paochi–Chungking Railway, *via* Chengtu (1,174 km). A further line connects Chungking with the east–west route from Hengyang to the Vietnam border, and a route is under construction from Kweiyang to Kunming, connecting there with the Yünnan Railway to the Vietnam border.

(2) Great east–west trunk lines: (*a*) Lung–Hai Railway; Lienyun–Hsuchow–Chengchow (on the Peking–Canton line)–Sian–Paochi (on the great north–south trunk line)–Tienshui–Lanchow (1,500 km). (*b*) Lanchow–Sinkiang Railway: Lanchow–Yumen–Hami–Turfan–Urumchi (1,800 km); an extension Urumchi–Aktogai is planned to link with the Soviet railway system. (*c*) Shanghai–Yuyikuan (Vietnam border) *via* Hangchow, Nanchang, Hengyang (on the Peking–Canton line), Kweilin, Liuchow and Nanning. (*d*) Peking–Lanchow *via* Tsining (from which a branch connects with the lines through Mongolia to the Trans-Siberian Railway), Tatung (from which a branch serves the province of Shansi), Paotow and Yinchuan (Ninghsia).

Branches link coastal areas (*e.g.*, Fukien province) and smaller inland centres with the main parts of the system. Surveys have been made for a new 500-km railway, linking the trunk line with the oilfield of Karamai in Sinkiang.

(3) The Manchurian system: (a) Chinese Eastern (Changchun) Railway (2,370 km), from Manchouli on the Soviet border through northern Inner Mongolia and Manchuria via Tsitsihar, Harbin and Mutankiang to the Soviet border near Vladivostok. (b) South Manchuria Railway (705 km, 1120 km with branches), Changchun–Shenyang (formerly Mukden)–Dairen. (c) Peking–Shenyang Railway, with branches in Manchuria (854 km, 1,350 km with branches).

Branches give connexions with outlying parts of Manchuria and Inner Mongolia as well as international links with Korean railways. Chinese railways are all constructed to the standard gauge except for some 600 km of metre gauge in Yünnan. The trans-Mongolian line, which was constructed to the Russian gauge, was converted to standard in 1965. Trunk routes are being converted from single to double track. The mountainous section of route between Paochi and Chengtu is worked by electric traction.

In 1959 the railways carried 542m. tons of freight.

AVIATION. In 1966 there were some 20 interior air routes, connecting Peking with all important cities. In 1959 Chinese aircraft carried 1·63m. ton-km of freight.

China maintains air services to some communist countries and Burma, France, Cambodia, Indonesia and Pakistan operate services to China.

Soviet airlines operate a weekly flight from Moscow to Peking via Irkutsk.

POST. China has a fairly well-developed telegraph service. Telegraphs connect all the principal cities in the country, and there are lines to all the neighbouring countries. Wireless telegraph stations have been installed at 673 centres. Telephones in use in 1951, 255,000.

Number of post offices of all kinds in 1958 was 67,000.

In 1964 there were some 7m. radio receivers. In 1965 there were 12 main television stations and 30,000 receivers.

BANKING. Banking is controlled by the People's Bank which has 34,000 branches. It is both the bank of issue and the principal commercial bank. It is also the major instrument of economic policy through which financial enterprises are controlled or supervised by the government.

There are some specialized banks: the Agricultural Bank, set up in 1963 to deal with state investments and agricultural loans; the Construction Bank (1954), and the Bank of China for Foreign Exchange, which has branches abroad.

WEIGHTS AND MEASURES. The government is promoting the use of the metric system, but throughout the country many local variants of the old Chinese weights and measures are still in use. In July 1959 some old measures were assigned fixed metric equivalents, e.g., 1 shih chin (catty) = 500 grammes (or 1·1 lb.); 1 li (Chinese mile) = 0·5 km; 1 chih (foot) = ⅓ metre (or 1·1 ft); 1 mou = 6·66 ares (or ⅙ acre). For the old units see THE STATESMAN'S YEAR-BOOK, 1954, pp. 877–88.

DIPLOMATIC REPRESENTATIVES

China maintains diplomatic relations with:

Afghánistán	Czechoslovakia	Iraq
Albania	Denmark	Kuwait
Algeria	Ethiopia	Kenya
Bulgaria	Finland	Korea (North)
Burma	France	Laos
Canada	Germany (East)	Mali
Ceylon	Guinea	Mauritania
Chile	Hungary	Mongolia
Congo (Br.)	India	Morocco
Cuba	Italy	Nepál

CHINA

Netherlands	Sudan	UAR
Norway	Sweden	UK
Pakistan	Switzerland	Vietnam (North)
Poland	Syria	Yemen
Romania	Tanzania	Yugoslavia
Somalia	Uganda	Zambia
Southern Yemen	USSR	

OF CHINA IN GREAT BRITAIN (49 Portland Place, W1)
Chargé d'Affaires ad interim: Pei Chien-tsang.
Counsellor: Chang Tsien-hua (*Commercial*).
First Secretaries: Liu Keng-yuan; Li Wen-cheng.

OF GREAT BRITAIN IN CHINA
Chargé d'Affaires en titre: J. B. Denson, OBE.
First Secretaries: J. N. Allan; J. D. Laughton (*Commercial*).

BOOKS OF REFERENCE

The China Quarterly. London, from 1960
Asia Research Center. *The Great Cultural Revolution in China.* Rutland, Vermont, 1968
Barnett, A. D., *Cadres, Bureaucracy and Political Power in Communist China.* Columbia U.P., 1967.—*China after Mao.* Princeton U.P., 1967
Berton, P., and Wu, F., *Contemporary China: a research guide.* Stanford U.P., 1967
Blaustein, A. P. (ed.), *Fundamental Legal Documents of Communist China.* South Hackensack, N.J., 1962
Boorman, H. L., and Howard, R. C. (eds.), *Biographical Dictionary of Republican China.* 5 vols. Columbia U.P. 1967 ff.
Buchanan, K., *The Chinese People and the Chinese Earth.* London, 1966
Chang Chi-yun, *National Atlas of China.* National War College, Taiwan, 1959–62
Chen, N., *The Economy of Mainland China, 1949–63.* Berkeley, 1963.—*Chinese Economic Statistics.* Edinburgh. 1967
Chen, N., and Galenson, W., *The Chinese Economy under Communism.* Edinburgh, 1969.
Chiang Kai-shek, *Soviet Russia in China.* London, 1957
Constitution of the People's Republic of China adopted on September 20 1954. Peking, 1961
Donnithorne, A., *China's Economic System.* London, 1967
Eckstein, A., *Communist China's Economic Growth and Foreign Trade.* New York, 1966
Eckstein, A., and others (eds.), *Economic Trends in Communist China.* Edinburgh, 1968.
Esmein, J., *La Révolution culturelle chinoise.* Paris, 1970
Fan, K. (ed.), *The Chinese Cultural Revolution: selected documents.* New York, 1968
Gittings, J., *The Role of the Chinese Army.* OUP, 1967
Gray, J., *Modern China's Search for a Political Form.* OUP, 1969
Gray, J., and Cavendish, P. (eds.), *Chinese Communism in Crisis.* London, 1968
Han Suyin, *China in the Year 2001.* New York, 1967
Hermann, A., *An Historical Atlas of China.* Chicago, 1966
Ho, P.-T., and Tsou, T. (eds), *China in Crisis.* 3 vols. Chicago, 1968
Houn, F. W., *A Short History of Chinese Communism.* Englewood Cliffs, N.J., 1967
Hsü, I. C. Y., *The Rise of Modern China.* OUP, 1970
Latourette, K. S., *The Chinese, their History and Culture.* 4th ed. New York, 1965
Leng, S.-C., *Justice in Communist China.* New York, 1967
Li, D. J. (ed.), *The Essence of Chinese Civilization.* Princeton, 1967
McAleavy, H., *Modern History of China.* London, 1967
MacFarquhar, R. (ed.), *China under Mao.* Massachusetts Institute of Technology, 1966
Mao Tse-tung, Selected works. 4 vols. London, 1954–56.—Vol. 2 of 2nd ed., Peking, 1965.—*Quotations from Chairman Mao Tse-tung.* Peking, 1966.—*On Revolution and War.* New York, 1969
Mathews, R. H., *Chinese–English Dictionary.* Cambridge, Mass., 1943–47
Miyashita, T., *The Currency and Financial System of Mainland China.* Tokyo, 1966
Nagel's Encyclopaedia-Guide: China. London, 1968
Needham, J., *Science and Civilization in China.* 7 vols. CUP, 1954 ff.—*Within the Four Seas.* London, 1969
Richman, B. M., *Industrial Society in Communist China.* New York, 1969
Robinson, J., *The Cultural Revolution in China.* Harmondsworth, 1969
Schram, S., *Mao Tse-tung.* Harmondsworth, 1966.—*The Political Thought of Mao Tse-tung.* New York, 1969
Schurmann, F., *Ideology and Organization in Communist China.* Univ. of California Press, 1966
Schurmann, F., and Schell, O. (eds.), *The China Reader.* 3 vols. New York, 1967
Smith, D. H., *Chinese Religions.* London, 1968
Snow, E., *The Other Side of the River: Red China Today.* London, 1963—*Red Star over China.* Rev. ed. London. 1968
Tregear, T. R., *An Economic Geography of China.* London, 1970
Tsien, T.-H. (ed.), *La République Populaire de Chine: droit constitutionnel et institutions.* Paris, 1970
Tuan, Y.-F., *China* ('World's Landscapes Series'). London, 1970

Waller, D. J., *The Government and Politics of Communist China.* London, 1970
Watson, F., *The Frontiers of China.* London, 1966
Who's Who in Communist China. Hong Kong, 1966
Wu Yuan-li, *The Economy of Communist China.* London, 1965

TAIWAN

The island of Taiwan (Formosa) was ceded to Japan by China by the Treaty of Shimonoseki on 8 May 1895. After the Second World War the island surrendered to Gen. Chiang Kai-shek in Sept. 1945 and was formally returned to China on 25 Oct. 1945. It is controlled by the remnants of the Nationalist Government under Chiang Kai-shek, who, on 1 March 1950, resumed the presidency of the 'Republic of China', and was re-elected for his fourth 6-year presidential term in March 1966. He is concurrently leader of the Kuomintang (Nationalist Party). There are 2 other parties: the Young China Party and the China Democratic Socialist Party.

The National Assembly of the Republic of China was elected in 1947. It has 1,435 members. The highest legislative body is the Legislative Yuan (Council) elected in 1948 and now with 442 members. Terms of office in both bodies have been extended indefinitely. There is also a Provincial Assembly of 71 members elected in April 1968.

State emblem: A 12-pointed white sun in a blue sky.
National flag: The state emblem in the upper left canton of a crimson flag.
National anthem: 'San Min Chu I', words by Dr Sun Yat-sen; tune by Cheng Mao-yun.

By a treaty of 1 Dec. 1954 the USA is pledged to protect Taiwan and the offshore islands.

Prime Minister and Vice-President: Dr Yen Chia-kan. *Vice-Premier:* Chiang Ching-kuo (eldest son of the President). *Foreign Minister:* Wei T'ao-ming. *Minister of National Defence:* Gen. Huang Chieh. *Deputy Minister:* Adm. Ma Chi-chuang. *Minister of the Interior:* Hsu Ching-chung. *Minister of Finance:* K. T. Li. *Governor of Taiwan:* Gen. Chen Ta-ching.

AREA AND POPULATION. The island has an area of 13,885 sq. miles (35,961 sq. km). Population (March 1970), 14·42m. (7·5m. males, 6·9m. females), of whom some 2m. are mainland Chinese who came with the Nationalist Government. There are also some 200,000 aborigines. Population density: 370 per sq. km.

In 1969 the birth rate was 2·84%; the death rate, 0·55%; rate of growth, 2·34% per annum (3·25% in 1960).

Taiwan is divided into a special municipality (Taipei, the capital, population 1·7m. in 1969), 4 municipalities (Kaohsiung, Keelung, Taichung, Tainan) and 16 counties (*hsien*): Changhua, Chiayi, Hsinchu, Hualien, Ilan, Kaohsiung, Miaoli, Nantou, Penghu, Pinghung, Taichung, Tainan, Taipei, Taitung, Taoyuan, Yunlin.

EDUCATION. Since 1968 there has been free compulsory education for 9 years (6–15). In that year the curriculum was modernized to give more emphasis to science while retaining the traditional basis of Confucian ethics. There were, in 1969–70, 2,242 primary schools with 57,415 teachers and 2,411,725 pupils; 837 secondary schools with 39,357 teachers and 1,024,298 pupils; 91 institutes of higher learning, including 9 universities, with 9,456 teachers and 184,215 students. 98% of children of school age were attending classes.

CINEMAS (1968). Cinemas numbered 1,600.

NEWSPAPERS (1969). There were 31 daily papers and 1,322 periodicals.

SOCIAL WELFARE. In 1969 there were 29,918 registered medical personnel, including 10,133 doctors and 2,614 'herb doctors', and 1,090 public medical institutions, including 27 general hospitals, 601 health centres and 413 mobile medical units.

FINANCE. Currency. On the return of Taiwan to Chinese sovereignty, the existing currency was converted into notes of the Bank of Taiwan. Taiwan dollars were linked to Chinese national currency at a fixed rate of exchange. When the Gold Yuan entered upon its last phase in early 1949, the Taiwan currency was detached and linked to the US$. Exchange rates: £1 = NT$96; US$1 = NT$40.

Budget. The financial year ends 30 June. There are 2 budgets, the national together with a special defence budget (partly secret) and the provincial (*i.e.*, for Taiwan proper). For 1968–69 revenue was NT$44,480m. and expenditure, NT$42,019m.

DEFENCE. Army The Army, which embodies the remnants of the forces which escaped to Taiwan with Chiang Kai-shek at the end of the civil war in 1949, now numbers about 400,000. It has been reorganized, re-equipped and trained by the USA. There is a conscription system for 2 years and reserve liability. Strong garrisons (about 80,000 men) are maintained on the Pescadores and the offshore islands of Quemoy and Matsu.

Navy. In 1970 the Nationalists had 10 destroyers, 17 frigates, 4 escort vessels, 1 destroyer escort transport, 2 fleet minesweepers, 15 coastal minesweepers, 1 minelayer, 21 submarine chasers, 1 gunboat, 36 landing ships, 38 landing craft, 50 coastal craft, 8 support ships, 6 transports and 5 oilers. Active personnel: 35,000 naval officers and ratings; 27,000 marine officers and men.

Air Force. The Nationalist Air Force is equipped with aircraft of US design, many supplied under military aid programmes. It has squadrons of F-104G Starfighters, F-5 supersonic fighters, a squadron of F-86D all-weather fighters, and a fighter-bomber wing equipped with F-100 Super Sabre fighters. F-5s and F-100s are replacing the few F-86F Sabres still continuing in service. Reconnaissance units operate RB-57, U-2, RF-101 Voodoo and RF-104G Starfighter jet aircraft, while the transport squadron are equipped with C-119s, C-123 Providers, C-47s and C-46D Commandos. Search and rescue units operate Catalina and Albatross amphibians, and there are helicopter and large training elements. Total strength is estimated at 85,000 personnel and about 15 combat squadrons.

Each wing has a front-line complement of about 75 aircraft, but the total effective fighting strength is probably no more than 380 aircraft. There are, however, elements of the USAF on Taiwan, equipped with jet-fighters and tactical missiles.

PLANNING. Taiwan is predominantly agricultural. Government policy is to 'develop industry through agriculture and expand agriculture through industry'. Regional planning is carried out through a series of 4-year plans, of which the fifth (1969–72) sets the target rate for annual economic growth at 7%. Emphasis is on heavy industry; there is some restriction of private spending. A large steel mill and 2 petro-chemical centres are to be built.

AGRICULTURE. In 1969, 2·2m. persons worked in agriculture. The cultivated area was 914,900 hectares in 1969, of which 537,400 hectares were paddy fields. Production in 1,000 metric tons, in 1968 (and 1969): Rice, 2,518 (2,322); tea, 24·4 (26·2); bananas, 645·5 (585·5); pineapples, 311·3 (325); sugar, 846·6 (763); sweet potatoes, 3,445 (3,702); wheat, 17·1 (9·5); soybeans, 73 (67); peanuts, 106·5 (100·8); cotton, 2·1 (1·6); jute, 13·3 (17·7).

Livestock (1969): Cattle, 315,038; pigs, 3m.; goats, 169,382.

FORESTRY. The total area of forests is 2·3m. hectares. Timber production in 1969 was 1,063,563 cu. metres.

FISHING. The fleet comprised 27,348 vessels in 1969; the catch was 560,871 metric tons.

MINING. There are reserves of coal (240m. metric tons), gold (7·7m. tons), copper (7·1m. tons) and sulphur (2·5m. tons). Coal production was 4·6m. metric tons in 1969. Reserves of oil are estimated at 3m. kilolitres, and of natural gas at 27,200m. cu. metres.

INDUSTRY. Output (in metric tons) in 1968 (and 1969): Steel, 418,311 (512,116); pig-iron, 75,630 (78,490); aluminium, 20,020 (22,108); shipbuilding, 79,183 (117,329); sugar, 847 (736); cement, 4m. (4m.); fertilizers, 1,244,331 (1,467,470); paper, 238,194 (272,626); cotton fabrics, 371m. metres (416m.).

In 1969, 5,060m. litres of crude oil were refined; the main refinery at Kaohsiung has an annual capacity of 1m. tons.

Output of electricity in 1969 was 11,119m. kwh.; total generating capacity was 2·2m. kw. A nuclear power station is due for completion by 1975.

In 1969 the non-agricultural labour force numbered 2·7m., of whom 577,000 were employed in the manufacturing industries.

COMMERCE. Principal exports: textiles, bananas, chemicals, metals, machinery, sugar. Total trade, in US$m.:

	1963	1964	1965	1966	1967	1968	1969
Imports	230·0	410·4	556·4	603·1	847	1,026	1,205
Exports	357·5	463·1	487·9	569·4	675	842	1,111

Total trade between UK and Taiwan (British Board of Trade returns, in £1,000 sterling):

	1965	1966	1967	1968	1969	1970
Imports to UK	1,338	1,632	1,964	3,040	3,979	5,869
Exports from UK	1,738	2,162	2,225	3,561	4,694 }	6,630
Re-exports from UK	19	25	50	22	36 }	

RAILWAYS. Total route length in 1969 was 4,400 km, of which a large proportion is owned by the Taiwan Sugar Corporation and other concerns. Taiwan railways have various gauges, ranging from 3 ft 6 in. to 2 ft. Freight traffic amounted to 27·2m. tons and passenger traffic to 145m. passengers in 1969.

ROADS. In 1969 there were 16,933 km of roads. 731,719 motor vehicles were registered in 1969 including 39,620 passenger cars, 7,315 buses, 35,425 trucks and 629,358 motor cycles. 582m. passengers and 31·6m. tons of freight were transported (excluding urban buses).

SHIPPING. The merchant marine in 1969 comprised 4,030 vessels over 20 GRT, totalling 1,365,770 GRT; it included 12 passenger ships and 357 freighters. Ocean-going freight-traffic was 7·32m. metric tons.

Taiwan has 3 international ports, Keelung in the north, Kaohsiung in the south and Hualien on the east coast.

AVIATION. There is an international airport at Taipei. China Airlines (CAL), Far Eastern Transport (FAT) and Civil Air Transport (CAT) operate internal flights and international services to Bangkok, Hong Kong, Kuala Lumpur, Manila, Osaka, Saigon, Seoul, Singapore and Tōkyō.

POST. In 1969 there were 7,757 postal establishments. Number of telephones (1968), 230,229. In 1968 there were 1·41m. radio receivers and 199,593 TV receivers. There are 2 TV networks, one state-owned.

BANKING. The Bank of Taiwan is the largest commercial bank and the fiscal agent of the Government. Other banking institutions include the China Development Corporation and the Bank of Communications.

DIPLOMATIC REPRESENTATIVES

Taiwan maintains diplomatic relations with:

Argentina	Haiti	Panama
Australia	Honduras	Paraguay
Barbados	Iran	Peru
Belgium	Ivory Coast	Philippines
Bolivia	Jamaica	Portugal
Botswana	Japan	Rwanda
Brazil	Jordan	Saudi Arabia
Cameroun	Korea (South)	Senegal
Central African Republic	Kuwait	Sierra Leone
Chad	Lebanon	Spain
Colombia	Lesotho	Swaziland
Congo (K.)	Liberia	Thailand
Costa Rica	Libya	Togo
Cyprus	Luxembourg	Turkey
Dahomey	Malagasy Republic	USA
Dominican Republic	Malawi	Upper Volta
Ecuador	Maldive Islands	Uruguay
El Salvador	Malta	Vatican
Gabon	Mexico	Venezuela
Gambia	New Zealand	Vietnam (South)
Greece	Nicaragua	
Guatemala	Niger	

OF NATIONALIST CHINA IN THE USA (2311 Massachusetts Ave. NW, Washington, D.C., 20008)

Ambassador: Chow Shu-kai.

Ministers: Shih-ying Woo; Martin Wong (*Economic*). *Minister-Counsellors:* I-cheng Loh (*Information*); Dr Nai-wei Chang (*Cultural*). *Counsellors:* Heng-li Chen; Richard Ling-hsun Jen (*Press*); Shan-chung Lee. *First Secretaries:* Kuan-hua Tuanmu; Ellen Ai-ling Woo; Ru-Tseng Lin. *Service Attachés:* Maj.-Gen. Chieh-lin Sun (*Army*), Capt. Hsi-ling Wang (*Navy*), Col. Pang-liang Lo, (*Air*).

TO THE USA IN TAIWAN

Ambassador: Walter P. McConaughy.

Deputy Chief of Mission: Oscar V. Armstrong. *Heads of Sections:* David Dean (*Political*); William N. Morell, Jr (*Economic*); Richard G. Smith (*Commercial*); Paul M. Miller (*Consular*); William E. Beauchamp (*Administration*); Malcolm G. Cook (*AID*), *Service Attachés:* Col. Benjamin C. Warren (*Defence and Air*), Capt. Robert E. Bodamer (*Navy*), Col. Eric C. Orme (*Army*).

There is a British Consul in Tamsui and a British Vice-Consul in Taipeh.

BOOKS OF REFERENCE

Taiwan Statistical Data Book. Taipei, annual
China Yearbook. Taipei, annual
Goddard, W. G., *Formosa: a Study in Chinese History.* London, 1966
Kerr, G. H., *Formosa Betrayed.* London, 1966
Mancall, M. (ed.), *Formosa Today.* New York, 1964

COLOMBIA
República de Colombia

HISTORY. The Vice-royalty of New Granada gained its independence of Spain in 1819, and was officially constituted 17 Dec. 1819, together with the present territories of Panama, Venezuela and Ecuador, as the state of 'Greater Colombia', which continued for about 12 years. It then split up into Venezuela, Ecuador and the republic of New Granada in 1830. The constitution of 22 May 1858 changed New Granada into a confederation of 8 states, under the name of Confederación Granadina. Under the constitution of 8 May 1963 the country was renamed 'Estados Unidos de Colombia', which were 9 in number. The revolution of 1885 led the National Council of Bogotá, composed of 2 delegates from each state, to promulgate the constitution of 5 Aug. 1886, forming the Republic of Colombia, which abolished the sovereignty of the states, converting them into departments, with governors appointed by the President of the Republic, though they retained some of their old rights, such as the management of their own finances. A decree of May 1928 abolished their right to borrow abroad without the sanction of the central government.

CONSTITUTION AND GOVERNMENT. The legislative power rests with a Congress of 2 houses, the Senate, of 106 members, and the House of Representatives, of 204 members, both elected for 4 years. In 1968 a congressional committee unanimously approved a constitutional amendment providing for progressive reductions in the membership of Congress to 90 senators and 162 representatives by 1974. Congress meets annually at Bogotá on 20 July. Women were given the vote, which is now open to citizens of either sex, over 21 years of age, on 25 Aug. 1954.

In the elections in mid-March 1968 the Liberal–Conservative alliance obtained 144 seats and the National Popular Alliance 42 seats in the lower house.

The President is elected by direct vote of the people for a term of 4 years, and is not eligible for re-election until 4 years afterwards. Congress elects, for a term of 2 years, one substitute to occupy the presidency in the event of a vacancy during a presidential term. There are 13 Ministries. The Governors of Departments and the Mayor of Bogotá are nominated by the national government.

A National Economic Council, functioning since May 1935, went through several transformations, becoming in 1954 a Directorate of Planning.

National flag: Yellow, blue, red (horizontal).
National anthem: Oh! Gloria inmarcesible (words by R. Núñez; tune by O. Síndici).

The following is a list of presidents since 1945:

Dr Alberto Lleras Camargo, 7 Aug. 1945–7 Aug. 1946.
Dr Mariano Ospina Pérez, 7 Aug. 1946–7 Aug. 1950.
Dr Laureano Gómez, 7 Aug. 1950–13 June 1953.
Gen. Gustavo Rojas Pinilla, 13 June 1953–10 May 1957.

Military Junta, Maj.-Gen. Gabriel París and 4 others, 10 May 1957–7 Aug. 1958.
Dr Alberto Lleras Camargo (Lib.), 7 Aug. 1958–7 Aug. 1962.
Dr Guillermo León Valencia (Cons.), 7 Aug. 1962–7 Aug. 1966.
Dr Carlos Lleras Restrepo (Lib.), 7 Aug. 1966–7 Aug. 1970.

President: Dr Misael Pastrana Borrero, heading a dual administration composed of Conservatives and Liberals. He obtained 43% of the votes cast in the election on 19 April 1970 and took office on 7 Aug. 1970 until 1974.

Minister of Foreign Affairs: Dr Alfredo Vásquez Carrizosa (C.).

Gibson, W. M., *The Constitutions of Colombia.* Durham, N.C. 1948, and London, 1949

AREA AND POPULATION. The estimated area of the Republic as given to the United Nations is 1,138,914 sq. km (456,535 sq. miles). It lies between lat. 12° 30′ N. and 4° 30′ S., and between long. 67° and 79° W. of Greenwich. It has a coastline of about 2,900 km, of which 1,600 km are on the Caribbean Sea and 1,300 km on the Pacific Ocean. The area (as estimated by the census bureau) and population of the 20 departments, 3 intendencies and 5 commissaries, according to the census of 15 July 1964, were as follows (the capitals in brackets):

	Area (sq. km)	Population, 1964 Total	Per sq. km
Departments			
Antioquia (Medellín)	62,870	2,477,299	39·40
Atlántico (Barranquilla)	3,270	717,406	219·40
Bolívar (Cartagena)	26,392	693,759	26·29
Boyacá (Tunja M.E.)	67,750	1,058,152	15·62
Caldas (Manizales)	11,245	1,150,127	102·28
Cauca (Popayán)	30,495	607,197	19·91
Córdoba (Monteria)	25,175	585,714	23·27
Cundinamarca (Bogotá D.E.)	23,960	2,819,524	117·59
Chocó (Quibdó)	47,205	181,863	3·85
Huila (Neiva)	19,990	416,289	20·82
La Guajira (Riohacha)	20,180	147,140	7·29
Magdalena (Santa Marta)	46,695	789,410	16·91
Meta (Villavicencio)	85,770	165,530	1·93
Nariño (Pasto)	31,045	705,611	22·73
Norte de Santander (Cúcuta)	20,815	534,486	25·68
Quindío[1] (Armenia)	1,825	305,745	167·53
Santander (Bucaramanga)	30,950	1,001,213	32·35
Sucre[2] (Sincelejo)	10,523	312,588	29·71
Tolima (Ibagué)	23,325	841,424	36·07
Valle del Cauca (Cali)	21,245	1,733,053	81·57
Intendencies			
Arauca (Arauca)	23,490	24,148	1·03
Caquetá (Florencia)	90,185	103,718	1·15
San Andrés y Providencia (San Andrés)	44	16,731	380·25
Commissaries			
Amazonas (Leticia)	121,240	12,962	0·11
Guainía (Puerto Inírida)	78,065	3,602	0·05
Putumayo (Mocoa)	25,570	56,284	2·20
Vaupés (Mitú)	90,625	13,403	0·15
Vichada (Puerto Carreño)	98,970	10,130	0·10
Total	1,138,914	17,484,508	15·36

[1] Formerly part of Caldas.   [2] Formerly part of Bolívar.

In Dec. 1966, the department of Risaralda (capital, Pereira) was cut out of Caldas.

Estimated population in July 1970 was 21·16m.

Of the total population in 1964, 52% were urban (38% in 1951); density (1964), 15·36 per sq. km. The bulk of the population lives at altitudes of from 4,000 to 9,000 ft above sea-level. It is divided broadly into: 68% mestizo, 20% white, 7% Indio and 5% Negro.

In 1968 births were 31·4 per 1,000; deaths, 8·5; marriages, 4·2; infant mortality rate (1966), 80 per 1,000 live births. There is a small net emigration every year.

The capital, Bogotá (population of Special District, 1970, 2,512,000), lies 8,661 ft above the sea. The chief commercial towns, with their population in 1970, are: Medellín, an industrial coffee and mining centre (1,089,000); Cali, an industrial and sugar centre (917,600); Barranquilla, international airport and river- and sea-port (640,800); Cartagena, an industrial port with the oil-pipe terminal (318,800); Manizales (283,500); Bucaramanga, tobacco and coffee centre (315,400); Cúcuta, coffee and industrial centre (229,200); Buenaventura, chief port on the Pacific coast (98,000); Santa Marta, on the Caribbean, and terminus of the Ferrocarril del Atlántico (149,000); Pasto (130,000); Ibagué (204,600).

The language spoken is Spanish.

RELIGION. The religion is Roman Catholic, with the Cardinal Archbishop of Bogotá as Primate of Colombia and 7 other archbishops in Cartagena,

Manizales, Medellín, Pamplona, Popayán, Cali and Tunja, 26 bishops, 1,546 parishes and 4,020 priests. Other forms of religion are permitted so long as their exercise is 'not contrary to Christian morals or to the law'; but since 1953 the 90,000 Protestants have complained of police prosecutions and religious disorders.

EDUCATION. Primary education is free but not compulsory, and facilities are limited.

On 31 Dec. 1966, 26,172 public and private primary and secondary schools had 89,096 teachers and 2,728,776 pupils; 1,146 kindergartens, with 2,390 teachers and 49,704 pupils; 194 night schools, with 1,476 teachers and 12,926 pupils; 356 teachers' training schools, with 4,908 instructors and 66,010 pupils; 508 commercial schools, with 4,908 teachers and 66,010 pupils; 119 industrial schools, with 1,187 teachers and 21,397 pupils; 26 art schools, with 284 teachers and 4,603 pupils, and 62 agricultural schools, with 412 teachers and 4,772 students.

Besides the National University in Bogotá (founded 1572), there are 29 more in the capital (including Javeriana, Libre and Andes) and elsewhere, notably Medellín, Cali, Manizales, Popayán. Cartagena, Bucaramanga and Barranquilla. These 22 universities, in 1968, had 8,918 teachers and 62,844 students.

Of the population over 7 years of age in July 1964, the National Department of Statistics estimated that 27·1% were illiterate; intensive efforts to build new schools and to reduce illiteracy are being made.

CINEMAS (1967). 905 cinemas reported attendance of 85,416,957, paying 302,611,718 pesos.

NEWSPAPERS (1965). There were 39 daily newspapers, with daily circulation totalling 1,979,714. There were 388 periodical publications.

HEALTH. In 1967 there were 641 hospitals and clinics with together 39,117 beds.

JUSTICE. The Supreme Court, at Bogotá, of 20 members, is divided into 3 chambers—civil cassation (6), criminal cassation (8), labour cassation (6). Each of the 61 judicial districts has a superior court with various sub-dependent tribunals of lower juridical grade.

Communism was outlawed by government decree on 5 March 1956.

FINANCE. Currency. On 1 Dec. 1966 the Monetary Council fixed a buying rate of 16·25 pesos per US$ in exchange operations previously negotiated on the free exchange market, where it had stood at 16·39–16·42. In March 1967 the Colombian Government imposed regulations for the entire foreign exchange sector, and established a dual currency market: the free rate of the market for 'exchange certificates', which are negotiable through the commercial banks, registered an average of $13.51 for purchases and $13.53 for sales for transactions in March, and the capital market exchange rate was fixed at $16.25 for purchases and $16.30 for sales. The International Monetary Fund continues to treat as the official rate the peso = 51·282 cents US. When Colombia joined the IMF on 18 Dec. 1946 the peso's rate was 57·143 cents US.

Coins include 50, 20 and 10 centavos (90% steel and 10% nickel) and 5, 2 and 1 centavos of various combinations of copper–nickel–bronze–steel. There are also notes representing 1, 5, 10, 20, 50, 100 and 500 gold pesos.

Budget. Ordinary revenue and expenditure for calendar years in 1m. paper pesos:

	1965	1966	1967	1968	1969
Revenue	5,827	8,407	6,439	11,176	14,914
Expenditure	5,808	7,789	6,439	11,176	14,914

The 1968 budget provides 2,306m. pesos for investments and 1,318m. pesos for the public debt service.

The International Bank for Reconstruction and Development has made 11 loans to Colombia aggregating $111·2m., including $47·3m. for highways and $40·9 for the Atlantic Railway.

On 30 June 1970 the public debt of the central government was 19,050m. pesos, compared with (1969) 15,446m. pesos.

DEFENCE. On 17 April 1952 Colombia signed the Military Assistance pact with the USA.

Army. Military service is compulsory between the years of 18 and 30. Service with the colours is for one year. From 30 to 45 years of age the citizens are on the reserved lists, classified in 1st, 2nd and 3rd classes, with the obligation of presenting themselves on being called up. The permanent Army consists of infantry, artillery, cavalry, engineers, motorized troops and the usual services. The peace effective is 50,000 men; the war effective is about 300,000 men. Number of national police, about 35,000.

Colombia was the only Latin American country participating in the Korean war, with a regiment of 1,000 men (three times relieved).

Navy. Colombia has 2 destroyers built in Sweden in 1958; 1 destroyer acquired from the USA in 1961; 4 destroyer escort transports; 5 small transports; 5 oilers; 5 river gunboats; 3 tenders; 8 coastguard vessels; 14 patrol motor launches and 13 tugs. Personnel, 700 officers and 6,500 men. The Navy has also a battalion of marines with 800 officers and men. There are American and British Naval Missions.

Air Force. Formed in 1922, the Air Force has been independent of the Army and Navy since 1943, when its re-organization began with US assistance. In 1970 it had about 175 aircraft, including a combat group of Canadian-built Sabre jet fighters and MAP-supplied F-86F Sabre jet fighter-bombers, a bomber group of B-26 piston-engined bombers, a transport group equipped with 2 C-130s, C-47s and a small number of C-54s, Otter, Beaver and Porter light transports, and a maritime reconnaissance and rescue unit with Catalina flying-boats and helicopters. An order for Mirage supersonic fighters was placed in late 1970. Second-line and support units are also being re-equipped; 30 Cessna T-41D primary trainer/light transports were delivered in 1968 and were followed by 10 T-37C jet advanced trainers to supplement T-33A armed jet trainers already in service. Total strength is about 6,000 personnel.

AGRICULTURE. Very little of the country is under cultivation, but much of the soil is fertile and is coming into use as roads improve. The range of climate and crops is extraordinary; the agricultural colleges have different courses for 'cold-climate farming' and 'warm climate farming'. Some 6m. acres are described as arable, 96m. pasture and 148m. forest; about 15,000 tractors were in use in 1961.

By the end of 1966 the Colombian Institute of Agrarian Reform had resettled 50,000 families on 1·6m. hectares under the plan begun in 1962.

Colombia is the second largest producer of coffee and ranks first in the output of mild coffee, demand for which is unaffected by over-production in Brazil. Crops are grown by smallholders, and are picked all the year round. Coffee output exceeds 7m. bags (of 60 kg). Exports in 1967 were 6·09m. bags. Export of bananas, in 1967, were 325,581,603.

Cotton output, 1967, was 228,229 metric tons, of which 30,011 metric tons were exported.

Rice, for domestic consumption, is increasingly important; output, 1966, 621,077 metric tons (321,642, hectares). Sugar plantations now cover 422,094 hectares. Unrefined brown sugar, known as panela, is consumed locally; output, 1966, of refined sugar, 107,194 tons; 176,465 metric tons of crude sugar were exported, mainly to USA. Output (in metric tons) of maize in 1966 was

939,689 (1,009,519 hectares); other important crops are potatoes, 762,446 (121,653 hectares); yuca, 1,625,286 (234,716 hectares); wheat, 93,304 (114,603 hectares); barley, 61,956 (53,493 hectares), and tobacco, 48,119 (48,263 hectares). Edible oils, lentils and chickpeas were specially imported in 1966; to counteract the sharp rise in the cost of living.

The rubber tree grows wild, and its cultivation has begun; output is a few hundred tons. Fibres are being exploited, notably the 'fique' fibre, which furnishes all the country's requirements for sacks and cordage; output about 12,000 tons. Tolú balsam is cultivated, and copaiba trees are tapped but are not cultivated. Tanning is an important industry, 12m. sq. ft of hides being exported in 1965.

Livestock in 1968 was estimated at 17·7m. cattle, 2·5m. pigs, 1·1m. horses, mules and asses, 835,700 sheep, 31·4m. poultry.

FISHERY. In Sept. 1963 a *Sección de Caza y Pesca* was set up in the Ministry of Agriculture. It extended territorial waters to 200 nautical miles. The principal finance companies founded a development company with over 20m. pesos in Aug. 1966 (*Consorcio Pesquero Colombiano*).

MINING. Colombia is rich in minerals; gold is found chiefly in Antioquia and moderately in Cauca, Caldas, Tolima, Nariño and Chocó; output in 1969, 217,875 fine oz., highest in South America. Foreign concessions produce about 60% of the gold.

Other minerals are silver (98,764 troy oz. in 1968), copper, lead, mercury, manganese, emeralds and platinum (first discovered in Colombia in 1735 and the largest deposit in the world); export of platinum, 1967, 14,214 troy oz. The working of the government-controlled emerald mines has been resumed; the stones are cut in the workshops of the Banco de la República. The chief mines are those of Muzo and Chivor.

The Government holds the monopoly, which is leased to the Banco de la República, for extracting salts from the outstanding Zipaquirá mines (several hundred feet in depth and several hundred square miles in area) and for evaporating many sea salt pans; salt production in 1968 was 317,348 metric tons of land salt from the Zipaquirá mines and 159,125 tons of sea salt from Manaure and Galerazamba on the Caribe coast. Colombia's coal reserves are estimated at 13,200m. metric tons; production (1968) 3·3m. short tons.

Petroleum production in 1969 was 84m. bbls (of 42 gallons), of which about one-quarter were refined in the country, chiefly at Barrancabermeja; fuel oil, 15·9m. bbls; gas oil (ACPM), 5·3m. bbls; gasoline, 12·9m. bbls; propane gas, 123,700 tons. Investments in the petroleum industry (1951) amounted to $257·44m., of which America holds 85% and British about 15%. In 1957 oil companies in the country paid 27·3m. pesos in royalties and 2·6m. in taxes.

INDUSTRY. Value of industrial output (located mainly in the Departments of Antioquia, Cundinamarca and Valle) by 299,508 production workers in 11,797 establishments in 1966 was 33,846m. pesos. There are 69 reassembly plants, apart from the motor industry. At the end of 1965 the 101 firms with more than 50% US control equalled an investment of US$510m.; they employed over 29,000 Colombians.

POWER. Capacity of electric power (1967) is: 1,164,305 kw. from hydro-electric stations, 516,485 kw. from thermal stations. Electric power produced in 1968, 6,038m. kwh. There is increasing utilization of natural gas.

In Oct. 1954 the Department of Valle del Cauca established a local power corporation closely modelled on the Tennessee Valley Authority.

TRADE UNIONS. The Left-wing Colombian Federation of Labour (CTC) had, in 1947, 109,000 members out of a total of 165,000 organized workers. In 1946 there were established an association of trade unions, *Unión de Traba-jadores Colombianos*. In May 1963, 8·6% of the 449,000 workmen in Bogotá were unemployed.

COMMERCE. For the 'Charter of Quito' trading agreement in 1948 between Colombia, Ecuador, Panama and Venezuela, see THE STATESMAN'S YEAR-BOOK, 1956, p. 882. Colombia's entry into the Latin American Free Trade Area (ALALC) was ratified on 29 Sept. 1961. A fresh impulse to this effort was given by the Bases for an Immediate Action Programme under the 'Charter of Bogotá' signed by Colombia, Chile, Ecuador, Peru and Venezuela on 16 Aug. 1966.

Imports (c.i.f. values) and exports (f.o.b. values) (excluding export tax) for calendar years (in US$1m.):

	1963	1964	1965	1966	1967	1968	1969
Imports	506·0	586·3	453·5	674·1	496·9	..	607·5
Exports[1]	446·7	548·1	537·0	496·9	509·9	..	685·3

[1] Excluding export tax.

Trade by principal countries, in US$1m.:

	Imports (c.i.f.)[1]		Exports (f.o.b.)[1]	
	1966	1967	1966	1967
Belgium–Luxembourg	7·0	3·9	7·2	10·2
Canada	17·2	14·7	7·2	7·1
France	9·8	5·1	2·4	4·6
Germany (West)	75·0	51·4	69·1	68·2
Italy	12·5	8·8	4·6	3·6
Japan	22·3	19·3	6·4	5·8
Netherlands	20·6	11·1	21·8	37·6
Spain	12·8	21·7	25·2	22·5
Sweden	10·6	9·7	18·1	16·5
Switzerland	15·8	12·2	1·3	1·1
UK	35·7	33·4	20·1	20·5
USA	323·1	224·5	219·0	218·0

[1] Excluding bullion and specie.

Important articles of export in 1969 (in US$1m.) were coffee (343·9), petroleum (56·7), bananas (19·7), fuel-oil (15·7), sugar (14·7), tobacco (7·3). Colombia has bilateral trade agreements with Bulgaria, Denmark, East Germany, Finland, Hungary, Poland, Romania, Spain, USSR, Yugoslavia, the *Federacion Nacional de Cafeteros* financing import credits for up to 2 years at 12% p.a. The chief imports are machinery, vehicles, tractors, metals and manufacturers, rubber, chemical products, wheat, fertilizers and wool.

Total trade between UK and Colombia for 5 years (British Board of Trade returns, in £1,000 sterling).

	1965	1966	1967	1968	1969	1970
Imports to UK	9,042	10,147	9,755	8,975	7,481	8,904
Exports from UK	7,089	15,595	8,411	12,133	12,173 }	12,942
Re-exports from UK	103	64	40	56	72 }	

SHIPPING. Venezuela, Colombia and Ecuador formed the Greater Colombia Merchant Marine (*Flota Mercante Grancolombiana*) on 8 June 1946, with head-quarters in Bogotá and sectional boards in Caracas and Quito. The corporation had an authorized capital of US$20m., of which Venezuela and Colombia subscribed 45% each and Ecuador 10%. Venezuela withdrew from the group in 1953. The *Flota* calls at 103 American, European and Asian ports. Its capital was 135m. pesos in 1965.

Vessels entering Colombian ports in 1969 had a net registered tonnage of 11,695,952. The Colombian merchant fleet in 1969 owned 23 vessels of 187,906 net tons, and leased 20 of 164,360 net tons; in 1965 it carried 1·9m. metric tons. At present a cargo ship of 11,685 tons is being built in Spain.

In 1964–67, 450m. pesos are to be spent on the modernization of the ports.

The Magdalena River is subject to drought, and navigation is always impeded during the dry season, but it is an important artery of passenger and goods traffic. The river is navigable for 900 miles; steamers ascend to La Dorada, 592 miles from Barranquilla. In 1967 they carried 4,104 passengers and 2,321,209 metric tons of cargo.

ROADS. Owing to the mountainous character of the country, the construction of arterial roads and railways is costly and difficult. The overhead ropeway connecting Mariquita with Manizales is the longest in the world (72 km); it carried 2,630 metric tons of freight in 1965. Total length of highways, 45,000 km in 1967, of which 7,200 paved. Of the 2,300-mile Simón Bolívar highway, which runs from Caracas in Venezuela to Guayaquil in Ecuador, the Colombian portion is complete. Buenaventura and Cali are linked by a highway (Carreterra al Mar). Motor vehicles numbered 256,823, of which 158,786 were passenger cars and 98,037 lorries on 30 June 1967.

RAILWAYS. There are 5 divisions of the State Railway, with a total length of 3,483 km in 1969 and a gauge of 3 ft. The Pacific Railway connects Bogotá with the port of Buenaventura. The Atlantic line from Bogotá to Sta. Marta was opened in July 1961. Total railway traffic, 1967, was 4·8m. passengers and 3,168,963 tons of freight. Nationalization of all railways was decided upon in Jan. 1954.

AVIATION. In civil aviation Colombia ranks perhaps second, after Brazil, among South American countries. There are 426 landing grounds of all kinds. In 1967 the national airlines carried 2,770,390 passengers and 116,626 tons of cargo. In Sept. 1954 the Government bought all its airfields from Avianca, the leading airline.

POST. The length of telephone lines in service is 705,852 km (Bogotá only); instruments in use, 1 Jan. 1968, 515,000, of which 181,426 in Bogotá; 514,500 are under government operation. The cable company is government-owned. There are 223 broadcasting stations. Television was established in 1954. Bogotá is now the centre of a wide repeater network.

BANKING. On 23 July 1923 the Banco de la República was inaugurated as a semi-official central bank, with the exclusive privilege of issuing bank-notes in Colombia; its charter, in 1951, was extended to 1973. Its note issues must be covered by a reserve in gold of foreign exchange of 25% of their value. Gold stock has risen from US$5m., at the start, to $147m. in Jan. 1947, falling rapidly thereafter to $66m. in May 1951, when publication (of the gold figure, separately from foreign exchange) ceased. On 30 Sept. 1967 the Central Bank had gold and foreign exchange valued at US$148·7m.; money supply, 31 Dec. 1966, 11,130m. pesos.

There are 26 domestic commercial banks of importance and 5 foreign banks (English, Canadian, American, French and Franco-Italian); but a high percentage of all commercial bank deposits are with the 4 largest domestic banks, which have branches throughout the country. In Nov. 1950 they were permitted to accept savings deposits, hitherto a government monopoly.

WEIGHTS AND MEASURES. The metric system was introduced in 1857, but in ordinary commerce Spanish weights and measures are generally used; according to new definitions by the Ministry of Development, *e.g.*, *botella* (750 grammes), *galón* (5 *botellas*), *vara* (70 cm), *arroba* (25 lb., of 500 grammes; 4 *arrobas* = 1 quintal).

DIPLOMATIC REPRESENTATIVES

Colombia maintains embassies in:

Argentina	Costa Rica	Guatemala
Belgium	Dominican Republic	Honduras
Bolivia	Ecuador	India
Brazil	El Salvador	Italy
Canada	France	Japan
Chile	Germany (West)	Lebanon

Mexico	Peru	UK
Netherlands	Portugal	USA
Nicaragua	Spain	Uruguay
Panama	Sweden	Vatican
Paraguay	Switzerland	Venezuela

Colombia maintains legations in:

| Austria | Haiti | UAR |
| Denmark | Norway | |

OF COLOMBIA IN GREAT BRITAIN (3 Hans Crescent, SW1)

Ambassador: Dr Camilo de Brigard.
Counsellors: Dr Lucio Gori; Dr José Maria de Guzman; Dr Juan Martinez-Villa. *First Secretary:* Señorita Ninón Millan.

There are consular representatives at Liverpool and London.

OF GREAT BRITAIN IN COLOMBIA

Ambassador: T. E. Rogers, CMG, MBE.
First Secretaries: K. E. H. Morris (*Head of Chancery*); R. G. Marlow (*Commercial*).

There are also consular representatives at Barranquilla, Cali and Medellín.

OF COLOMBIA IN THE USA (2118 Leroy Pl. NW, Washington, D.C., 20008)

Ambassdor: Dr Douglas Botero-Boshell.
Minister: Dr Eduardo Gaitan-Duran. *Counsellor:* Carlos Mejia-Eder. *Service Attachés:* Brig.-Gen. Alberto Camacho-Leyva (*Army*), Capt. Roberto Reyes (*Navy*), Col. Raul A. Paredes (*Air*). *Commercial Attaché* Andrés Uribe.

OF THE USA IN COLOMBIA

Ambassador: Leonard J. Saccio.
Deputy Chief of Mission: Robert A. Stevenson. *Heads of Sections:* Earl H. Lubensky (*Political*); Brewster R. Hemenway (*Economic*); Thomas K. Brewer (*Commercial*); Richard E. Ginnold (*Labour*); George R. Phelan, Jr (*Consular*); Earle M. Welsh, Jr (*Administrative*); Marvin Weissman (*AID*).
Service Attachés: Col. Harry F. Lowman, Jr (*Defence and Army*), Lieut.-Col. Jean W. McLaughlin (*Air*).

There are Consuls at Barranquilla, Cali, Medellín and a consular agent at Buenaventura.

BOOKS OF REFERENCE

Anuario General de Estadística de Colombia. Bogotá. Annual
Anuario de Comercio Exterior de Colombia. Annual
Anuario Estadístico Bogatá D.E. Annual
Boletín Mensual de Estadística. Monthly
Economía y Estadística. Occasional
Informe Financiero del Contralor General. Annual
Informe del Gerente de la Caja de Crédito Agrario, Industrial y Minero. Annual
Memorias (13) de los Ministros al Congreso Nacional. Annual
Charry Lara, Alberto, *Desarrollo histórico de la Estadística nacional en Colombia.* Nat. Dept. of Statistics, Bogotá, 1954.—*El país en cifras.* 1964
Galbraith, W. O., *Colombia, a general survey,* 2nd revd. edn. OUP, 1966
Lebret, R. P. L. J., *Estudio sobre las condiciones del desarrollo de Colombia. Informe de una Misión.* Bogotá, 1960
McGreevey, W. P., *An Economic History of Colombia, 1845–1930,* CUP, 1970
Wurfel, S. W., *Foreign enterprise in Colombia: laws and policies.* Univ. of N. Carolina Press, 1965

CONGO

République Démocratique du Congo

HISTORY. Until the middle of the 19th century the territory drained by the Congo River was practically unknown. When Stanley reached the mouth of the Congo in 1877, King Leopold II of the Belgians recognized the immense possibilities of the Congo Basin and took the lead in exploring and exploiting it. The Berlin Conference of 1884–85 recognized King Leopold II as the sovereign head of the Congo Free State.

The annexation of the state to Belgium was provided for by treaty of 28 Nov. 1907, which was approved by the chambers of the Belgian Legislature in Aug. and Sept. and by the King on 18 Oct. 1908. The law of 18 Oct. 1908, called the Colonial Charter (last amended in 1959), provided for the government of the Belgian Congo, until the country became independent on 30 June 1960.

The departure of the Belgian administrators, teachers, doctors, etc., on the day of independence left a vacuum which speedily resulted in complete chaos. Neither Joseph Kasavubu, the leader of the Abako Party, who on 24 June 1960 had been elected head of state, nor Patrice Lumumba, leader of the Congo National Movement, who was the prime minister of an all-party coalition government, could establish his authority. Personal, tribal and regional rivalries led to the breakaway of Katanga province under premier Moïse Tshombe. Lumumba found his main support in the Oriental and Kivu provinces. Early in July the Force Publique mutinied and removed all Belgian officers. Lumumba called for intervention by the United Nations as well as the USSR. The Secretary-General dispatched a military force of about 20,000, composed of contingents of African and Asian countries. Lumumba was kidnapped by Katanga tribesmen and, in early Feb. 1961, murdered; his place was taken by Antoine Gizenga, who set up a government in Stanleyville.

On 15 Aug. 1961 the United Nations recognized the government of Cyrille Adoula as the central government. United Nations forces, chiefly Irish and Ethiopians, in mid-September invaded Katanga.

On 15 Jan. 1962 the forces of Gizenga in Stanleyville surrendered to those of the central government, and on 16 Jan. Adoula dismissed Gizenga. United Nations forces, chiefly Ethiopians and Indians, again invaded Katanga in Dec. 1962 and by the the the end of Jan. 1963 had occupied all key towns; Tshombe left the country. The U.N. troops left the Congo by 30 June 1964.

The Gizenga faction started a fresh rebellion and after the capture of Albertville (19 June) and Stanleyville (5 Aug.) proclaimed a People's Republic on 7 Sept. 1964. Government troops, Belgian paratroopers and a mercenary contingent captured Stanleyville on 24 Nov. after the rebels had massacred thousands of black and white civilians. The last rebel strongholds were captured at the end of April 1965·

AREA AND POPULATION. The boundaries of the Congo colony were defined by the neutrality declarations of Aug. 1885 and Dec. 1894, and by treaties with Germany, Great Britain, France and Portugal.

On 22 July 1927 Belgium ceded to Portugal territory in the extreme south-west portion of the Belgian Congo, having an area of 3,500 sq. km, in return for a cession by Portugal of an area in the estuary of the Congo, near Matadi, of 3 sq. km. Belgium further undertook the construction of a railway to link up with the Portuguese railway, starting at Lobito; this railway was opened on 1 July 1931.

The area of the republic is estimated at 2,345,409 sq. km (895,348 sq. miles). The population is composed of 3 ethnical groups: Negroes (Bantu, Sudanese, Nilotics), Pygmies and Hamites (in the east). In the census (1970) the population was 21,637,876.

In 1966 some 300,000 refugees from Angola, some 24,000 Tutsi refugees from Rwanda and 24,000 refugees from the Sudan were living in the Congo.

On 2 May 1966 the main cities were renamed: Kinshasa (Léopoldville), Mbandaka (Coquilhatville), Bandundu (Banningville), Kisangani (Stanleyville), Lubumbashi (Elisabethville), Kalemie (Albertville). The capital is Kinshasa.

The country is divided into the following provinces (with population as in 1967): Kinshasa city (1,225,720), Bandundu (2·1m.), Equateur (1,700,638), Kasai West (1,600,182), Kasai East (1,717,779), Kivu (2,168,533), Kongo Central (1,067,105), Katanga (1,853,089), Orientale (2·4m.). (*See* map in THE STATESMAN'S YEAR-BOOK, 1966–67.)

The most important languages are: Kiswahili or Kingwana in the east, Tshiluba or Kiluba in the south, Lingala along the Congo River and Kikongo in the Lower-Congo.

CONSTITUTION. On 30 Sept. 1963 President Kasavubu dissolved parliament, suspended the constitution of Oct. 1962 (*see* THE STATESMAN'S YEAR-BOOK, 1963, p. 914) and (on 1 Oct.) granted Prime Minister Adoula full legislative powers until elections were held and a new constitution had been approved. Tshombe, who returned to the Congo in June 1964, was appointed prime minister on 10 July.

Elections were held in April 1965, but those held in constituencies in which irregularities were proved, were annulled by the Appeal Court.

President Kasavubu dismissed the Tshombe government on 13 Oct. 1965, but the new government under Evariste Kimba, set up on 18 Oct., failed to win the confidence of Parliament on 14 Nov. On 25 Nov. President Kasavubu was deposed by Gen. Joseph Mobutu, the Army Commander-in-Chief, who cancelled the presidential elections due in 1966. The new regime, with Gen. Mobutu as President of the Republic and Minister of Defence, was approved by Parliament on 28 Nov. On 26 Oct. 1966, President Mobutu assumed the office of prime minister and minister of defence. A new Constitution, approved in a national referendum by over 90% of the voters in June 1967, established a Presidential regime in which the President of the Republic is also head of the executive. On 25 July 1969 a National Security Council of 8 members, consisting of the President and the Ministers of Foreign Affairs, Internal Affairs, Defence and Justice, the C.-in-C. of the Army, the Inspector-General of Police and the Security Chief, was established 'to assist the Head of State in ensuring the internal and external security of the State'.

National flag: A yellow star on a blue background crossed by a red band with a narrow yellow stripe on either side.

RELIGION. There were, on 31 Dec. 1958, 10,284 missionaries, of whom 7,436 (including 1,532 natives) were Roman Catholic and 2,848 (including 1,195 natives) Protestant. Numerous missionaries were massacred in 1964.

Roman Catholics in 1962 numbered 5·3m.; Protestants, 1·1m.; Moslems about 115,000 and Jews, 1,520.

EDUCATION. In 1966–67 there were 9,168 primary schools with 2,193,200 pupils, exclusive of nursery schools. There were 878 secondary schools—general, commercial, technical and professional, with a total of 140,620 pupils. Secondary education comprises an initial 2-year orientation cycle, followed by either a 2- or 4-year cycle, during which pupils specialize in literary, scientific, commercial studies, etc.

1,726 students were attending 16 establishments of higher education, apart from universities: 7 advanced teacher-training colleges (Ecoles Normales Moyennes), the National School of Administration, the Institute of Building and Public Works, the National Institute of Mines, the Academy of Fine Arts, the Higher Institute of Commerce, the Higher Institute of Physical Education, the Institute of Social Training, the Institute of Medical Training and the National Institute of Political Studies.

In the 3 universities there was a total enrolment of 2,925 students; 1,837 at Lovanium University in Kinshasa, 902 at the Official University of the Congo in

Lubumbashi and 186 at the Free University of the Congo in Kisangani and Luluabourg.

JUSTICE. On 31 Dec. 1958 there were 26 district courts, 25 magistrates' courts, 139 police courts, 6 courts of first instance, 2 courts of appeal (at Kinshasa and Lubumbashi) and 1,552 native courts.

FINANCE. Currency. The currency unit, introduced on 23 June 1967, is the *zaire*, divided into 100 *makuta*. Each *likuta* (plural *makuta*) is divided into 100 *sengi*. Bank-notes are issued in the following denominations: 5 and 1 zaire, 50, 20 and 10 makuta (0·5 zaire = 1 US$; 1·2 zaire = £1 sterling).

Budget. Estimated revenue and expenditure (in 1m. francs until 1967 then in 1m. *zaires*) for calendar years:

	1965	1966	1967	1968	1969	1970	1971
Revenue	38,000	57,200	59,900	125	181	215	...
Expenditure	60,000	62,500	59,900	125	181	300	285

DEFENCE. Army. The Army is organized in 7 brigade groups totalling approximately 35,000 men. It consists of 12 infantry battalions, 3 parachute battalions (of which one is non-effective following the mercenary revolt of 1967), 4 commando battalions and a number of miscellaneous gendarmerie, training and support units. Following the disbandment of No. 5 Mercenary Commando in May 1967 and the mutiny of No. 6 Mercenary Commando in July 1967 there are now no mercenary forces in the Army.

Air Force. As the result of assistance received from the USA, Italy and elsewhere, the Congolese Air Force has more than 125 aircraft, organized in 2 groups. The *1er Groupement Aérien* is believed to consist of a squadron of 4 C-54s, a squadron of 12 C-47s, a squadron equipped with 6 Doves, 3 Beech 18s and 2 Herons, 2 squadrons with a total of 24 T-6G armed piston-engined trainers, a squadron of 8 Alouette III rescue helicopters, a squadron of 12 Piaggio P.148 trainers, a squadron of 8 T-6 trainers and 2 logistic support squadrons. The *2eme Groupement Aérien Tactique* has a combat wing comprising a squadron of 16 T-28D armed trainers, a squadron of 9 B-26K twin-engined bombers and a support wing made up of a squadron equipped with 6 C-46 and 4 Caribou transports, a rescue squadron of 7 Bell helicopters and a communications squadron with 2 Do 27s, 1 Do 28 and 2 Austers. Delivery of an initial batch of 17 Aermacchi MB.326GB armed jet trainers began in late 1969, followed by 12 Siai-Marchetti SF-260M piston-engined basic trainers; eventually aircraft of these types are expected to replace T-6Gs and T-28Ds now in service. Latest order is for 7 SA.330 Puma assault helicopters. Foreign mercenaries, including Cuban exiles, fly many of the combat aircraft.

AGRICULTURE. The plantations (in hectares) cultivated by Europeans comprised, in 1959, 135,182 of palm, 83,816 of coffee, 368,382 of cotton, 47,937 of rubber, 4,605 of tea and 17,338 of cocoa.

Chief agricultural exports in 1967 (in metric tons): Cassava, 7m.; cotton 9,000; coffee, 60,000; rubber, 30,000; bananas and plantains, 1·55m.; palm-oil 155,000; ground-nuts, 113,000.

In 1959 European-owned cattle (mainly in the provinces of Katanga, Kasaï, Orientale and Kongo Central) numbered 482,525 head; sheep, 19,900; pigs, 49,888; African-owned cattle (mainly in the provinces of Kivu and Orientale), 552,524; sheep, 621,156; goats, 2,135,425; pigs, 318,528.

MINING. Mining flourishes, the chief minerals being copper, diamonds (12·4m. carats in 1966), gold, silver, tin, cobalt, uranium, radium, germanium, zinc and iron. The most important mines in the Congo are the coppermines near Kipushi, Musonoie and Ruwe (production 1969, 362,000 metric tons).

Two oil pipelines connect Matadi with Kinshasa.

On 24 Dec. 1966 the property of the Union Minière du Haut Katanga was seized by the Government as the Union Minière refused to transfer its headquarters from Brussels to Kinshasa. On 31 Dec. a new company, Société Générale Congolaise de Minerais, was created, in which the Congolese Government holds 60% of the shares.

COMMERCE. Imports in 1965 totalled 60,000m. Congo francs, exports totalled 49,503m. Congo francs (1,104,152 metric tons). More than half of the exports (by value) consisted of copper (278,014 metric tons). Other important metals were (in metric tons): Manganese ores (311,188); zinc ores (89,650); raw zinc (51,927); cobalt (8,536); cassiterite (5,142); tin (1,279); gold (1·4); diamonds (12,583,000 carats).

Of the 1965 exports, 74·2% went to the EEC countries, including 41·3% to Belgium–Luxembourg; 13·2% to the UK; 4·1% to USA; 3·6% to South Africa.

Total trade between the Congo and UK (British Board of Trade returns, in £1,000 sterling):

	1965	1966	1967	1968	1969	1970
Imports to UK	11,825	10,172	11,566	17,714	22,834	18,872
Exports from UK	3,428	4,834	6,963	8,006	11,229 ⎱	12,033
Re-exports from UK	35	119	48	94	215 ⎰	

SHIPPING. The Congo and its tributaries are navigable over 13,744 km. Regular traffic has been established between Kinshasa and Kisangani as well as Port Francqui, on the Lualaba (*i.e.*, the Congo River above Kisangani), on some tributaries and on the lakes.

At the port of Matadi, the most important harbour, the imports in 1959 amounted to 503,973 metric tons and the exports to 758,627 metric tons. Imports at Lobito were 82,565 metric tons, and exports, 449,249 metric tons; imports at the oil port of Ango-Ango, 333,259 metric tons, and exports, 28,433 metric tons; imports at Boma, 47,345 metric tons, and exports, 133,703 metric tons.

ROADS. There were (31 Dec. 1958) 145,213 km of roads, of which 33,787 km are main roads. Number of passenger motor cars, 1958, was 35,000; lorries, 21,858; tractors, 619; buses, 489; motor cycles, 3,546.

RAILWAYS. The total length of public railways on 1 Jan. 1970 was 5,795 km. In 1960, 1,996,377 passengers were carried.

AVIATION. There are 5 international, 36 principal, 34 secondary, 75 local and 78 emergency aerodromes. A regular air service, operated by the Belgian company SABENA, flies between Kinshasa and Brussels, and between Kinshasa–Entebbe–Nairobi–Dar es Salaam, Lubumbashi–Salisbury–Johannesburg. Air Congo serves the line Kinshasa–Lagos. Interior routes are operated by the Congo Network.

POST. In 1958 there were 335 post offices. The Congo is included in the Universal Postal Union and in the African Postal Union. Length of telegraph lines, 2,459 km. There were 15 broadcasting stations, 161 stations of wireless telegraphy and 206 telegraph offices; telephones numbered 21,919 in 1969.

BANKING. On 24 Feb. 1961 the Banque Centrale du Congo Belge et du Ruanda-Urundi was superseded by the Banque Nationale du Congo.

Other banks operating are the Banque Nationale du Congo, the Banque Belge d'Afrique, the Société Congolaise de Banque, the Crédit Congolais. There is also a savings bank, the Caisse d'Epargne de la République du Congo.

WEIGHTS AND MEASURES. The metric system was introduced by law on 17 Aug. 1910.

T

DIPLOMATIC REPRESENTATIVES

The Congo Republic maintains embassies in:

Belgium	Italy	Tanzania
Burundi	Ivory Coast	Tunisia
Canada	Liberia	Uganda
Central African Republic	Netherlands	UAR
Ethiopia	Nigeria	UK
France	Senegal	USA
Germany (West)	Spain	Yugoslavia
Greece	Sudan	Zambia
Israel	Switzerland	

OF THE CONGO IN GREAT BRITAIN (26 Chesham Place, SW1)

Ambassador: Gervais Bahizi.
Minister-Counsellor: Joseph Kalume.
Military Attaché: Lieut.-Col. Joseph Mudiayi.

OF GREAT BRITAIN IN THE CONGO

Ambassador and Consul-General: P. H. G. Wright, CMG, OBE.
Counsellor: W. E. H. Whyte. *Defence Attaché:* Col. J. C. Davis. *First
Secretaries:* G. W. Baker, OBE (*Head of Chancery*); A. L. Kettles (*Consul*);
A. J. C. E. Rellie; T. H. Steggle (*Commercial*)

There is a Consul-General at Lubumbashi.

OF THE CONGO IN THE USA (1,800 New Hampshire Ave. NW, Washington, D.C., 20009)

Ambassador: Pierre Ileka. *Counsellor:* Jean-Jacques Kudiwu. *Defence
Attaché:* Col. Valentin H. Okito.

OF THE USA IN THE CONGO

Ambassador: Sheldon B. Vance.
Deputy Chief of Mission: Bayard King. *Heads of Sections:* Charles C.
Flowerree (*Political*); Lucien Heichler (*Economic*); Anthony S. Dalsimer (*Commercial*); E. Mark Linton (*Consular*); Gregory E. Kryza (*Administrative*); Donald
S. Brown (*AID*).
Defence Attaché: Col. Candler R. Wiselogle.

There are Consuls at Bukavu, Kisangani and Lubumbashi.

BOOKS OF REFERENCE

Atlas général du Congo. Brussels, Académie royale
Cornevin, R., *Histoire de Congo.* Paris, 1963
Ganshof van der Meersch, W. J., *Fin de la souveraineté belge au Congo.* Brussels and The Hague, 1965
Gérard-Libois, J., *Sécession au Katanga.* Brussels, 1963
Leclercq, C., *L'O.N.U. et l'affaire du Congo.* Paris, 1965
Lemarchand, R., *Political awakening in the Belgian Congo.* California UP and CUP, 1965
Martelli, G., *Experiment in World Government: the UN Operation in the Congo 1960–64,* London, 1967
Stengers, J., *Combien le Congo a-t-il coûté à la Belgique?* Académie royale des sciences coloniales, Brussels, 1957
Young, C., *Politics in the Congo: decolonization and independence.* Princeton UP and OUP, 1965

COSTA RICA
República de Costa Rica

HISTORY. The republic of Costa Rica (the 'Rich Coast') has been independent since 1821, although it formed, from 1824 to 1838, part of the Confederation of Central America.

AREA AND POPULATION. The area is estimated at 50,900 sq. km (19,653 sq. miles). The population at the census of 1 April 1963 was 1,336,274, compared with 800,875 shown in the 1950 census.

Official estimate of population for 12 July 1969 (1·68m.) was as follows:

Province		Central Cantons	
San José	603,000	San José	203,148
Alajuela	304,363	Alajuela	79,019
Cartago	195,334	Cartago	57,226
Heredia	103,967	Heredia	38,218
Guanacaste	186,103	Liberia	24,793
Puntarenas	206,663	Puntarenas	69,427
Limón	85,740	Limón	49,822

VITAL STATISTICS for calendar years:

	Marriages	Births	Deaths	Immigration	Emigration
1966	8,684	62,963	11,379	143,092	142,094
1967	8,923	61,963	11,214	154,033	155,151
1968	9,624	59,213	10,653	165,809	164,500

Crude birth rate, 1968, was 36·2 per 1,000 population; crude death rate, 6·5; infantile death rate, 59·7 per 1,000 live births; crude marriage rate, 6 per 1,000 population. Males exceeded females by 7,083.

The population of European descent, many of them of pure Spanish blood, dwell mostly around the capital of the republic, San José, and in the principal towns of the provinces. Limón, on the Caribbean coast, and Puntarenas, on the Pacific coast, are the chief commercial ports. The United Fruit Company, who in 1941 abandoned their banana plantations on the Atlantic coast in favour of large new plantations on the Pacific coast, have constructed ports at Quepos and Golfito. The Standard Fruit Co. and others have cleared land since 1958 in the Atlantic coast area and now have 2,325 acres producing some 4·2m. stems a year. There are some 15,000 West Indians, mostly in Limón province. The indigenous Indian population is dwindling and is now estimated at 1,200.

Spanish is the language of the country.

Voot, W., *The Population of Costa Rica and its Natural Resources*. Washington, D.C., 1946

CONSTITUTION AND GOVERNMENT. The constitution, promulgated on 7 Dec. 1871, has been modified very frequently, last in 1949. The legislative power is normally vested in a single chamber called the Legislative Assembly, which since 1962 consists of 57 deputies, 1 for every 25,214 inhabitants, elected for 4 years. The President is elected for 4 years; the candidate receiving the largest vote, provided it is over 40% of the total, is declared elected, but a second ballot is required if no candidate gets 40% of the total. By the election law of 18 Jan. 1946 all citizens who are 20 years of age are entitled to vote; married men and teachers, from the age of 18. Women over 21 were enfranchised in 1949. Elections are normally held on the first Sunday in February. Voting for President, Deputies and Municipal Councillors is secret and compulsory for all men under 70 years of age. Independent non-party candidates are barred from the ballot.

President: Dr José Figueres Ferrer, elected 12 Feb. 1970.
Vice-President: Dr Manuel Aquilar Bonilla.
Minister for Foreign Affairs: Lic. Gonzalo Facio.

Elections for Congress took place on 12 Feb. 1970; National Unification Party won 22, Liberation Party 32, others 3 seats.

The administration is normally carried on by 11 ministers, appointed by the President. The powers of the President are limited by the constitution, which leaves him the power to appoint and remove at will members of his cabinet. All other public appointments are made jointly in the names of the President and of the minister in charge of the department concerned.

National flag: Blue, white, red (horizontal).

National anthem: Noble patria, tu hermosa bandera (words by J. M. Zeledón, 1903; tune by M. M. Gutiérrez, 1851).

Zeledón, M. T., *Lecciones de Ciencia constitucional Constitución política de la República de Costa Rica.* San José, 1945

RELIGION. Roman Catholicism is the religion of the State, which contributes to its maintenance but controls the Church Patronage and insists on lay instruction in history, economics and similar subjects; there is entire religious liberty under the constitution, but religious appeals are forbidden in current political discussions. The Archbishop of Costa Rica has 4 bishops at Alajuela, Limón, San Isidro el General and Tilarán.

Protestants number about 40,000.

EDUCATION. Costa Rica has a very low illiteracy rate. Elementary instruction is compulsory and free; secondary education (since 1949) is also free. Elementary schools are provided and maintained by local school councils, while the national government pays the teachers, besides making subventions in aid of local funds. In 1969 there were 2,494 public primary schools with 9,855 teachers and administrative staff and 345,146 enrolled pupils; there were 99 public and private secondary schools with 64,252 pupils. The University of Costa Rica, founded in San José in 1843, has 584 professors in 13 faculties and 9,331 students. A medical school was opened in 1961. The budget for 1967 provides 171·9m. colones for public education. Since 1944 English has been taught in all secondary schools.

CINEMAS (1969). Cinemas numbered 132, with seating capacity of 90,000.

NEWSPAPERS (1969). There were 4 daily newspapers (including 1 English-language paper) all published in San José.

SOCIAL WELFARE. The labour code of 1943 provides considerable protection for the workers, while a system of social insurance against sickness covering 130,024 workers in 1965, old age and death covering 68,949, is gradually being extended throughout the country.

JUSTICE. Justice is administered by the Supreme Court, 4 appeal courts and the Court of Cassation. There are also subordinate courts in the separate provinces and local justices throughout the republic. Capital punishment cannot be inflicted.

FINANCE. Currency. A new par value of the *colón* came into effect on 1 Sept. 1961. At the same time the official market rate of 5·60 colones per US$ was abandoned, and all foreign payments are to be made at the rate of 6·625 colones = $1. At this time the IMF made available a credit of $15m., the US Treasury agreed to take up colones to a value of US$56m. and the World Bank agreed a loan of $8m.

The currency is chiefly notes. The Banco Central in 1951 printed and placed in circulation new notes for 5, 10, 20, 50, 100, 500 and 1,000 colones, replacing old notes previously issued by the Banco Nacional. Silver coins of 1 colon, 50 centimos and 25 centimos were in 1935 replaced by coins (2 and 1 colones and 50 and 25 centimos) made up of 3 parts copper and 1 part nickel, and given the same value as the subsidiary silver currency. There are copper coins (and chromium stainless steel coins) of 10 and 5 centimos.

Budget. The revenue and expenditure (in 1,000 colones) have been as follows ($1 = 6·63 colones) for calendar years:

	1965	1966	1967[1]	1968[1]	1969[1]	1970[1]
Revenue	473,588	659,000	635,100	680,300	945,706	1,262,952
Expenditure	476,216	659,000	635,100	680,300	889,426	1,262,952

[1] Estimate.

The income-tax law of 18 Sept. 1954 raised the maximum rate (for incomes of 500,000 colones and over) from 15 to 30%.

The public debt on 31 Dec. 1969 was 1,451·8m. colones. Debt service required 162·8m. colones in 1969.

DEFENCE. The army was abolished in 1948, and replaced by a Civil Guard reputed to be 1,200 strong. There has never been compulsory military service or training.

The republic has also 1 motor launch on the Atlantic coast and 1 on the Pacific coast for revenue purposes, a tug and smaller craft.

AGRICULTURE. Agriculture is the principal industry. The cultivated area is about 1m. acres; grass lands cover 1·8m. acres; forests and woodlands, 9,855,000 acres. There are thousands of square miles of public lands that have never been cleared, on which can be found quantities of rosewood, cedar, mahogany and other cabinet woods. Soil erosion is serious in some areas. The principal agricultural products are coffee and bananas. Coffee normally accounts for about half the country's foreign-exchange earnings. Cocoa, maize, sugar, tobacco, rice and potatoes are commonly cultivated. The distillation of spirits is a government monopoly.

Coffee production in 1967–68 was 1·7m. quintals (1·5m. in 1968–69).

Dairy-farming and cattle-raising are substantial pursuits. In 1970 cattle numbered 1·5m. and pigs 197,770.

Costa Rica is the seat of the Inter-American Institute of Agricultural Sciences, with headquarters at Turrialba.

MINING. Gold output is about 3,000 troy oz. per year. Salt production from sea water is about 10,000 tons annually. Haematite ore was discovered on the Nicoya Peninsula late in 1960 and sulphur near San Carlos in 1966. The United Nations have offered US$1m. towards a 3-year mining survey.

INDUSTRY. A Ministry of Industry was formed in 1961, but industry is still on a very small scale, though the Industrial Development and Protection Law of 1959 affords several facilities and advantages. Electricity, derived from water power in the highlands, is increasingly used as motive power. Output, 1965 was 592,933m. kwh. Total capacity in 1966 is 163,561 kw. An oil refinery and asphalt plant was completed on 1 June 1966.

Industrial production was valued at 1,267m. colones in 1965, compared with 771m. in 1958.

TOURISM. There was a total of 118,766 visitors in 1968.

LABOUR. As Costa Rica is still essentially an agricultural country, the organization of labour has made progress only in the larger centres of population, and even there it is not a strong movement. There are two main trade unions, *Rerum Novarum* (anti-Communist) and *Confederación General de Trabajadoros Costarricenses* (Communist). It is estimated that they have under 10,000 members each.

At the 1961 census the labour force totalled 412,406, 55% being agricultural; 11% manufacturing; 8% trade; 8% construction, transport and communications;

and 15% in government, finance and services. In 1963 there were 286 trade unions and 34 employers' organizations.

COMMERCE. The value of imports into and exports from Costa Rica in 5 years was as follows in US$ (6·63 colones = US$1):

	1965	1966	1967	1968	1969
Imports	178,173,000	178,568,000	190,697,930	213,941,661	245,137,529
Exports	112,347,000	138,745,000	143,780,037	170,821,290	189,706,699

The value (in US$1m.) of the principal imports in 1969 were: Manufactures, 97·1; machinery, including transport equipment, 68; chemicals, 41; foodstuffs, 21; fuel and mineral oils, 10·6.

Chief exports (in US$1m.) in 1969 were: Coffee, 55·8 (mostly to W. Germany and USA); bananas, 57·2m. (virtually all to USA); cocoa, 7; sugar, 7·4; manufactured goods and other products, 62·3.

Imports from US were valued at $85·5m. in 1969 and $80·7m. in 1968. Exports to US in 1969 were $88·7m; in 1968, $79·1m.

A new entity *Operadora Portuaria Costarricense* is planned to establish 3 'areas of international commerce' at the ports of Limón (Atlantic) and Puntarenas (Pacific) and the airport of El Coco on the Pan-American Highway near Alajuela.

Total trade between UK and Costa Rica (British Board of Trade returns, in £1,000 sterling):

	1966	1967	1968	1969	1970
Imports to UK	413	367	364	365	367
Exports from UK	2,611	3,722	2,656	5,748 }	4,745
Re-exports from UK	27	20	27	28 }	

SHIPPING. In 1968, 1,126 ships entered and cleared the ports of the republic (Puerto Limón, Puntarenas and Golfito); combined cargo, 1,647,022 metric tons. In 1958 the Costa Rican registry of foreign-owned ships was cancelled.

RAILWAYS. Two railway systems, totalling 427 miles (3 ft 6 in. gauge), connect San José with Limón, the Atlantic port (Costa Rica Railway Company), and San José with Puntarenas, the Pacific port (the state-owned Ferrocarril Eléctrico al Pacifico).

ROADS. About 3,250 km of all-weather motor roads are open. On the Costa Rica section of the Inter-American highway it is possible to motor to Panama during the dry season. A fairly good all-weather road leads into Nicaragua. Motor vehicles, 1969, numbered 74,160.

AVIATION. Passenger movement in and out of Costa Rica is almost entirely by air *via* the local company, LACSA, PANAM and TACA. LACSA links San José by daily services with all the more important towns. The international airport at El Coco was opened in June 1955; it can handle the most modern aircraft.

POST. A telephone service covering (1969) 50,093 subscribers operates in and between San José and 6 other provincial centres; it has been transferred to a government Instituto Costarricense de Electricidad, which is installing a nation-wide automatic system, and will eventually control all telecommunications.

The commercial wireless telegraph stations are operated by Cía Radiográfica Internacional de Costa Rica. The stations are located at Cartago, Limón, Puntarenas, Quepos and Golfito. The Government has 19 wireless telegraph stations in its local network. The principal or central station at San José also maintains international radio-telegraph circuits to Nicaragua, Honduras, San Salvador and Mexico. The Government has 202 telegraph offices and 88 official telephone stations. The official list of broadcasting stations shows 28 long-wave stations and 7 short-wave stations. Television was inaugurated in May 1960; there are 4 stations.

BANKING. By a law passed on 28 Jan. 1950 a Central Bank was established for the organization and direction of the national monetary system and of dealings in foreign exchange, the promotion of facilities for credit and the supervision of all banking operations in the country. The bank has a board of 7 directors appointed by the Government, including *ex officio* the Minister of Finance. On 31 Dec. 1969 it had foreign exchange of US$34·1m., compared with US$28·6m. in Dec. 1968; circulating media on 31 Dec. 1969 totalled 975·6m. colones.

In June 1948 the 3 small commercial banks were compulsorily nationalized; they held deposits of 1,005·3m. colones at 31 Aug. 1970 (962·1m. at 31 Dec. 1970).

The National Insurance Institute (Instituto Nacional de Seguros) is a Government organization, created in 1924, which has a monopoly of new insurance business.

WEIGHTS AND MEASURES. The metric system is legally established; but in the country districts the following old Spanish weights and measures are found: *libra* = 1·014 lb. avoirdupois; *arroba* = 25·35 lb. avoirdupois; *quintal* = 101·40 avoirdupois, and *fanega* = 11 Imperial bushels.

On 15 Jan. 1921 the republic adopted as its standard time that of the meridian 90° west of Greenwich, 6 hours behind GMT.

DIPLOMATIC REPRESENTATIVES

Costa Rica maintains diplomatic missions in:

Colombia	Honduras	Peru
Chile	Italy	Spain
China (Taiwan)	Kuwait	UK
Ecuador	Mexico	USA
El Salvador	Nicaragua	Uruguay
France	Panama	Vatican
Guatemala		

OF COSTA RICA IN GREAT BRITAIN (3 Zetland House, Marloes Road, W8)

Ambassador: Manuel Escalante Durán.
Minister-Counsellor: Gaston Fournier.

There are consular representatives at Birmingham and London.

OF GREAT BRITAIN IN COSTA RICA

Ambassador and Consul-General: I. M. Hurrell, MVO.
First Secretary: M. L. Creek (*Head of Chancery and Consul*).

There is also a consular office at Puerto Limón.

OF COSTA RICA IN THE USA (2112 S St. NW, Washington D.C., 20008)

Ambassador: Rafael Alberto Zuniga.
Minister-Counsellors: Rolando Ramirez (*Economic*), Rogelio Navas, Mrs M. V. de Perera. *First Secretary:* Ligia G. Haas.

OF THE USA IN COSTA RICA

Ambassador: Walter C. Ploeser.
Deputy Head of Mission: Ellwood M. Rabenold, Jr. *Heads of Sections:* Raymond E. González (*Political*); George T. Beck (*Commercial*); James E. Kerr, Jr (*Consular*); Richard W. Berg (*Administrative*). *Service Attaché:* Lieut.-Col. Daniel F. Resendes.

There is a consular agent at Puntarenas.

BOOKS OF REFERENCE

STATISTICAL INFORMATION. Official statistics are issued by the Director General de Estadística (Ministerio de Industria y Comercio, San José) as they become available. The compilation of statistics was started in 1861.

Biesanz, J. and M., *Costa Rican Life*. 3rd printing. New York, 1946
Fernández Guardia, L., *Historia de Costa Rica*. 2nd ed., 2 vols. San José, 1941
May, S., and others, *Costa Rica: A study in economic development*. New York, 1952
Trejos, Juan, *Geografía ilustrada de Costa Rica*. San José, 1948
Sandner, G., *Agrarkolonisation in Costa Rica*. Kiel, 1961

CUBA

República de Cuba

HISTORY. Cuba, except for the brief British occupancy in 1762–63, remained a Spanish possession from its discovery by Columbus in 1492 until 10 Dec. 1898, when the sovereignty was relinquished under the terms of the Treaty of Paris, which ended the struggle of the Cubans against Spanish rule. Cuba thus became an independent republic, but the United States stipulated under the 'Platt Amendment' (abrogated by Roosevelt in 1934) that Cuba must enter into no treaty relations with a foreign power, which might endanger its independence. A convention which assembled on 5 Nov. 1900 adopted the first constitution of the republic on 21 Feb. 1901.

The revolutionary movement against the Batista dictatorship, led by Dr Fidel Castro, started on 26 July 1953 (now a national holiday). It achieved power on 1 Jan. 1959 when Batista fled the country.

An invasion force of émigrés and adventurers landed in Cuba on 17 April 1961; the main body was defeated at the Bay of Pigs (Las Villas province) and mopped up by 20 April.

The US Navy blockaded Cuba from 22 Oct. to 22 Nov. 1962.

AREA AND POPULATION. The island of Cuba has an area of 44,206 sq. miles (114,524 sq. km); the Isle of Pines has 1,180 sq. miles, and other islands about 1,350 sq. miles. Estimated population in 1968 was 8·1m.

The area, population and density of population of the 6 provinces were as follows (1953 census, 1966 estimate):

Province	Area (sq. miles)	Population (28 Jun. 1953)	Population (Dec. 1966)	Population per sq. mile
Pinar del Río	5,211	448,422	588,000	106·3
Havana	3,173	1,538,803	2,088,000	642·0
Matanzas	3,259	395,780	463,000	146·0
Las Villas	8,264	1,030,162	1,235,000	118·0
Camagüey	10,169	618,256	826,000	77·4
Oriente	14,128	1,797,608	2,600,000	173·1
Total	44,206	5,829,029	7,800,000	167·9

Crude birth rate, 1964, 33·9; crude death rate (1962), 7 per 1,000; infant mortality (1962), 3 per 1,000.

The chief towns (with population, 1960) are: Havana, the capital, 787,765; Marianao, 229,576; Holguín, 226,779; Camagüey, 191,379; Santiago de Cuba, 166,384; Santa Clara, 142,176; Guantánamo, 124,685; Matanzas, 82,619; Cienfuegos, 99,530. Urban population is now (1965) 57·7% compared with 51·4% in 1953.

CONSTITUTION AND GOVERNMENT. The constitution has been suspended since Jan. 1959.

Since the last representative in Cuba of the King of Spain, Gen. Don Adolfo Jiménez Castellanos, handed over the island on 1 Jan. 1899 the following have been at the head of the administration:

	Took office		Took office
US Military Governors		Gen. Gerardo Machado y	
Maj.-Gen. John R. Brooke	1 Jan. 1899	Morales	20 May 1925
Maj.-Gen. Leonard Wood	23 Dec. 1899		dep. 12 Aug. 1933
		Dr Carlos Manuel de Cés-	
		pedes	12 Aug. 1933
			dep. 5 Sept. 1933
President of the Republic		Dr Ramón Grau San Martín	10 Sept. 1933
Tomas Estrada Palma	20 May 1902		res. 15 Jan. 1934
	res. 28 Sept. 1906	Col. Carlos Mendieta	Jan. 1934
			res. 12 Dec. 1935
		Dr José A. Barnet	12 Dec. 1935
		Dr Miguel Mariano Gómez y	
US Provisional Governors		Arias	20 May 1936
			impeached 23 Dec. 1936
Wlliiam Howard Taft	29 Sept. 1906	Dr Federico Laredo Bru	24 Dec. 1936
Charles Edward Magoon	13 Oct. 1906	Gen. Fulgencio Batista	10 Oct. 1940
		Dr Ramón Grau San Martín	10 Oct. 1944
		Dr Carlos Prío Socarrás	10 Oct. 1948
Presidents of the Republic			dep. 10 March 1952
Gen. José Miguel Gómez	28 Jan. 1909	Gen. Fulgencio Batista y	
Gen. Mario García Menocal	20 May 1913	Zaldívar	10 March 1952
Dr Alfredo Zayas y Alfonso	20 May 1921		abdicated 1 Jan. 1959

President: Dr Manuel Urrutia, assumed power on 1 Jan. 1959 after Gen. Batista had fled the country. He resigned on 17 July 1959 and Dr Osvaldo Dorticós Torrado was elected by the Cabinet to take his place.

Prime Minister and First Secretary of the Cuban Communist Party (PCC): Dr Fidel Castro Ruz.

Minister for Foreign Affairs: Dr Raúl Roa.

The President appoints the Cabinet, which consists of a Premier, the President's secretary and the heads of departments. There are 19 ministries and 13 government institutes and boards.

Dr Castro on 2 Dec. 1961 proclaimed 'a Marxist–Leninist programme adapted to the precise objective conditions existing in our country'. The provisional *Organizaciones Revolucionarias Integradas* (ORI) were established as an intermediate stage towards a single (communist) party, and gave way to the *Partido Unido de la Revolución Socialista* (PURS). This brought together the *Partido Socialista Popular, Movimiento de 26 Julio* and (Students') *Directorio Revolucionario*. The PURS in turn became (3 Oct. 1965) the *Partido Comunista de Cuba.* The Communist Party had been outlawed by Batista in 1954, but legally re-instated after the revolution.

National flag: 3 blue, 2 white stripes (horizontal); a white 5-pointed star in a red triangle at the hoist.

National anthem: Al combate corred bayameses (words and tune by P. Figueredo, 1868).

LOCAL GOVERNMENT. The country is divided into 6 provinces and 126 municipalities. A new plan was announced in Sept. 1963 for a political, administrative and economic division of the country into 44 regions. Local Government is the responsibility of the JUCEI (*Junta de Control, Ejecución e Inspección*).

RELIGION. There is no state Church, though Roman Catholics predominate. There is a bishop of the American Episcopal Church in Havana; there are large congregations of Methodists in Havana and in the provinces. Protestants numbered 265,000 in 1962; they have been organized as the Cuban Council of Evangelical Churches. Dr Castro has promised that the State will not interfere with the freedom of religion.

EDUCATION. Education is compulsory (between the ages of 6 and 14) and free, and now available everywhere. The 1953 census showed that 22·8% of all those over 10 years of age were illiterate. It is claimed that the Year of Education (1961), in which higher-education students went out to all parts of the country, reduced this to 3·9%. In 1964 illiteracy was officially declared to have been completely eliminated.

In 1969–70 the 3 universities had 30,708 students. Primary schools had 1,560,193 pupils; general secondary schools, 160,857 pupils; technical schools, 42,507 pupils; teachers' colleges, 24,442 students; other schools (*e.g.*, for fishermen), 17,862 pupils; adult education classes, 404,149 pupils. In 1962–63 a system of 'popular teachers' was introduced, who teach in primary schools while in training; they numbered 11,985 in March 1964. The 1965 education budget was $212·3m.

The Camilo Cienfuegos school city in the Sierra Maestra was designed for 12,000 boys and 8,000 girls by 1970 (1965: 4,000, total).

CINEMAS (1960). There are 454 cinemas with seating capacity of 402,000.

NEWSPAPERS (1965). The government-controlled press includes 3 morning and 1 evening newspapers in Havana; total circulation, 605,000.

HEALTH (1964). There were 4,855 posts for doctors, 154 hospitals with 47,861 beds. The 1965 health budget was $140·5m.

Free medical services are provided by the state policlinics, though some doctors still have private practices. All serious tropical diseases are effectively kept under control, and virtually all children under the age of 15 have been vaccinated against poliomyelitis.

JUSTICE. There is a Supreme Court in Havana and 7 courts of appeal (one in each provincial capital and one in Holguín). The provinces are divided into judicial districts, with courts for civil and criminal actions, with municipal courts for minor offences. The civil code guaranteed aliens the same property and personal rights as are enjoyed by nationals.

The 1959 Agrarian Reform Law and the Urban Reform Law passed on 14 Oct. 1960 have placed certain restrictions on both. Revolutionary Summary Tribunals will have wide powers.

FINANCE. **Currency.** The Cuban *peso* is equal to US$1, or to 0·8886 gramme of fine gold; accordingly, 1 troy oz. of fine gold = 35 pesos. This parity dates from the law of 7 Nov. 1914, which established that the monetary unit was a gold peso (equal to the US gold dollar) of 1·6718 grammes (1·5046 grammes fine) divided into 100 centavos. The old gold pesos and all US currency are no longer legal tender.

New copper–nickel coins of 40, 20, 5 and 1 cent are issued. Notes are for 100, 50, 20, 10, 5 and 1 peso.

Budget. Revenue and expenditure (in 1m. pesos) for calendar years balanced as follows: 1963, 2,903·6; 1964, 2,399; 1965, 2,536.

The 1965 expenditure included (in 1m. pesos): Agriculture, forestry and fishery, 367·9; industry, 194·4; commerce, 14·2; communications, 12·9; transport, 41·6; basic community services, 128·7; education, 219; central, provincial and local administration, 143·8; labour, 173·8; industries, 194·4.

During 1960 long-term loans at low interest were negotiated with the following countries (expressed in US$1m.): USSR, 100; China, 60; Czechoslovakia, 40; Rumania, 15; Hungary, 15; Poland, 12; German Democratic Republic, 10; Bulgaria, 5. The USSR is now subsidizing Cuba by permitting the accumulation in Soviet–Cuban trade of deficits which by 1965 exceeded US$600m.

DEFENCE. The chief of the armed forces is *Comandante* Fidel Castro, and his brother *Cdte*. Raúl Castro Ruz, Vice-Premier and Minister of Defence.

On 13 Nov. 1963 conscription was introduced for all men between the ages of 17 and 45 (3 years); women of the 17–35 age groups may volunteer (for 2 years).

Army. The strength was about 90,000 officers and men in 1970. Student, peasant and factory worker volunteers, both men and women, are being organized into armed militia groups, of a strength estimated at 200,000.

The Army is organized in 9 infantry brigades, 2 motorized brigades, 1 artillery brigade. It has 200 Russian-built tanks.

Navy. The Navy consists of 4 frigates, 2 escort vessels, 18 patrol vessels, 24 torpedo boats, 18 missile boats, 2 motor launches and 32 coast guard vessels. Its strength is 600 officers and 5,400 men. The USA is still in possession of the Guantánamo naval base, but the revolutionary government has refused to accept the nominal rent of $5,000 per annum.

Air Force. The Air Force has been extensively re-equipped with aircraft supplied by USSR and in 1970 had a strength of some 20,000 officers and men and 250 aircraft. Interceptor and ground-attack squadrons fly a total of about 130 MiG-21, MiG-19, MiG-17 and MiG-15 jet fighters. There is a squadron of Il-14 twin-engined transports; and Mi-4 helicopters, Zlin 226 piston-engined trainers and MiG-15UTI jet trainers. Many An-2M biplanes are operated by the Air Force, mainly on agricultural duties. Soviet-built surface-to-air ('Guideline') and coastal defence ('Samlet') missiles are in service.

AGRICULTURE. In May 1959 all land over 30 *caballerías* was nationalized and has since been turned into state farms. In Oct. 1963 private holdings were reduced to a maximum of 5 *caballerías* (approximately 166 acres). By 1960, 764 co-operative farms had been formed, and by late 1963 almost 70% of farm land was state-owned; the rest belongs to 200,000 small farmer-members in the National Association of Small Farmers.

In 1963 the total cultivated land included 432,461 hectares under the Credit and Services Co-operative, and 509 people's farms (3,820,112 hectares).

The staple products are tobacco and sugar, of which latter Cuba is the world's second largest producer; with its by-products it furnishes nearly 90% by value of the national exports. The 1970 crop was 8·5m. tons. There are 152 mills, including 40 of the largest, which were taken over from US interests, and which represent 39% of total capacity. Coffee, cocoa, cotton, maize, rice and potatoes are grown.

In 1964 production of important crops was (in 1,000 quintals): Sugar, 43,978 (1965, 60,500; 1966, 45,500); tobacco, 4,382; rice, 12,347; maize, 3,553; coffee, 3,203.

Tobacco is grown mainly in the Vuelta–Abajo district, near Pinar del Río. In 1964, 4,779 *caballerías* were planted. Coffee is grown chiefly in the province of Oriente.

Output of henequén fibre in 1964 was 233,919 tons. A fast-growing fibre, *kenaf*, originally from India, soft in texture, is replacing jute for sacking; the tobacco industry uses *majagua*, another local fibre, while a third fibre, *yarey*, from palms is also used. 138,000 tons of potatoes were produced in 1966. A nitrate plant has been built at Nuevitas and a large British-built urea plant at Cienfuegos. The principal fruits exported are pineapples, citrus fruit, tomatoes and pimentos. Pángola is an increasingly important forage crop (15,000 *caballerías* in 1960). A rice cultivation plan began in 1967 in the south of Havana province. Cultivation is highly mechanized and the area so far sown produces two crops a year. The aim is that Cuba should be self-supporting in rice by 1971.

After the devastation caused by hurricane Flora in Oct. 1963, citrus fruit production, 119,300 tons in 1964, was none the less 11·4% above 1963.

In 1962, 2,105 *caballerías* were allocated to cotton; cotton produced, 1964, was 2,653 tons against 13,000 tons in 1962.

In 1961 the livestock included 5·8m. head of cattle (6·4m. in 1963); 1·9m. hogs; 412,000 horses (1952); 194,000 sheep, 162,000 goats (1958).

FISHERIES. The fishing industry, still largely consisting of small, independent fishermen grouped into 32 co-operatives, landed over 100,000 tons in 1966. The state-owned deep sea fleet is being rapidly developed, however, and a plan to raise the 1967 total to 130,000 tons was running ahead of schedule.

FORESTRY. Cuba has extensive forest lands. These forests contain valuable cabinet woods, such as mahogany and cedar, besides dye-woods, fibres, gums, resins and oils. Cedar is used locally for cigar-boxes, and mahogany is exported. During the re-forestation campaign of 1959–60, 34,000 eucalyptus saplings were planted over 1,120 *caballerías*. Cedars, mahogany, *majagua*, teca, etc., are also being raised and planted out. Between 1960 and 1963 plantings included (in hectares): Pine, 9,947·81; eucalyptus, 52,699·43; *majagua preciosa*, 34,432·06; casuarina, 9,615·61.

MINING. Iron ore abounds, with deposits estimated at 3,500m. tons, of which 90% were held as reserves by American steel interests but are now controlled by the Cuban Mining Institute; output, 1958, 145,000; 1960, 15,000; 1961, 10,000 long tons. In 1961, 30,000 tons of steel bars were produced; steel production is to be increased to 500,000 tons by 1965 in connexion with the heavy-industry development near Nipe Bay (Oriente).

Output of refractory chromite suffers from Philippine competition; in 1962 only 22,000 long tons were mined, compared with 354,152 in 1943. Output of copper (1960) was 13,058 short tons; manganese ore (1963), 83,400 short tons; chromite (1963), 55,800 short tons. Other minerals are nickel (1957: 21,600 tons nickel content), cobalt, silica and barytes. Gold and silver are also worked; exports of gold, 1963, 61 fine oz.; of silver, including scrap, 1960, 121,415 fine oz. Cuba has a small output of petroleum (1956: 540,000 bbls from 53 wells); 4 refineries have started up. Salt output from the solar evaporation of sea water was 86,543 metric tons in 1964. Metal exports (in metric tons) in 1957 were: Copper ore, 79,514; chrome ore, 100,977; nickel oxide, 22,779; iron ore, 102,346.

All mineral resources were nationalized in 1960.

INDUSTRY. Industry has been largely nationalized and the state sector in 1967 controlled 982 factories, employing 123,000 workers and accounting for 90% of the industrial output.

Production in 1957 was: Rayon, 21·6m. lb.; cement, 644m. kg; wheat flour, 141m. lb.; naphtha and gasoline, 2·8m. bbls; fuel oil, 6·5m. bbls; kerosene and lubricants, 0·9m. bbls (kerosene, 1964, 179,021 tons); asphalt, 0·3m. bbls; gas oil, 3m. bbls; 156,966 tyres (1964: 450,800); 59,251 tubes; shoes, 15m. pairs (1963: 18·7m.); paint, 2·1m. gallons; absolute alcohol, 107m. litres; alcohol, 70m. litres; beer, 129m. litres; soft drinks, 576m. units; cigarettes, 611m. pkgs (1964: 16,015m.); fertilizers, 600m. lb. The value of output of light industries in 1963 was stated to be 1,432·6m. pesos.

ELECTRICITY (1962). Installed capacity was 429,143 kw.; this was to be increased to 1,240,843 kw. by 1966. Production in 1963 was 2,259m. kwh.

TRADE UNIONS. All trade unions are government-controlled.

COMMERCE. Official Cuban statistics of imports and exports (including bullion and specie) for calendar years (in 1,000 pesos; Cuban peso = US$1):

	1961	1962	1963	1964	1965 [1]
Imports (c.i.f.)	707,600	759,200	866,200	1,018,814	866,000
Exports (f.o.b.)	624,900	520,600	542,500	713,800	685,500

[1] No trade statistics available after 1965.

Cuba's principal exports are sugar, minerals and tobacco, which in 1964 were planned to furnish 85%, 6% and 5% respectively by value. The main imports from non-Communist countries are chemicals and engineering and electrical machinery and transport equipment.

The USA and most other Western Hemisphere countries, with the exception principally of Canada and Mexico, operate an economic boycott against Cuba. In Feb. 1970 Chile broke this boycott and agreed to supply US$11m. worth of agricultural produce to Cuba. In Oct. the amount was raised to US$35m. worth to be sold during 1970–71.

In 1961 annual trade exchanges were arranged with the following countries (US$1m., in each direction): USSR, 270; China, 117; Czechoslovakia, 30; German Democratic Republic, 25; Poland, 22; Romania, 11; Hungary, 10; Bulgaria, 7. Approximately 70% of Cuba's foreign trade is now with this group.

All foreign trade is channelled through state monopolies.

Total trade between Cuba and UK (British Board of Trade returns) in £1,000 sterling:

	1965	1966	1967	1968	1969	1970
Imports to UK	5,236	4,630	4,676	6,874	5,410	5,702
Exports from UK	14,778	7,737	8,369	12,318	13,053 }	20,559
Re-exports from UK	331	379	328	172	179 }	

SHIPPING. The coastline is 2,170 miles long and has 15 fine harbours. The merchant marine, in 1966, consisted of 40 sea-going vessels with a deadweight of over 300,000 tons.

RAILWAYS. There are 3,139 miles of public railway (mainly 4 ft 8½ in. gauge) owned by the National Railways (*Ferrocarriles Nacionales de Cuba*) formed on nationalization in 1960. In addition, the large sugar estates have 6,867 miles of lines connecting them with the main lines.

ROADS. There are 8,291 miles of highways open to traffic, including the Central Highway, traversing the island for 760 miles from Pinar del Río to Santiago. On 31 Dec. 1958 passenger automobiles numbered 143,828; hire cars, 29,710; coaches and buses, 4,306; lorries, 42,480; others, 12,987.

AVIATION. The state airline CUBANA operates all internal services, and from Havana to Mexico City and Prague. The other regular foreign services are Soviet, Czech and Spanish.

POST. There were (1938) 634 post and 358 telegraph offices and 150 radio and radio-telegraph stations (1940), of which 14 were operated by the Government. There are 3,545 miles of public and 8,902 miles of private telegraph wires. Cuba has 103 broadcasting stations and 2 television stations. Wireless receiving sets, 1958, numbered 900,000; television sets, 300,000. The national telephone system (1966) had 231,000 instruments (93% being automatic), of which 161,600 were in Havana.

BANKING. On 23 Dec. 1948 the president signed the law creating a central bank (with capital of $10m.) and (effective 30 Dec. 1951) a national currency system (with the peso alone being legal tender) replacing the dual system under which the peso and the dollar were both legal tender; the bank began operating on 27 April 1950; in Dec. 1957 it had $136m. in gold and $441m. in foreign exchange. Dollar reserves stood at $114m. in Jan. 1960. In 1959 exchange control and import licences on luxury and non-essential goods were introduced.

On 14 Oct. 1960 all banks were nationalized, except the Royal Bank of Canada and the Bank of Nova Scotia, which were bought out later. All banking is now carried out by the National Bank of Cuba, which has 6 regional offices and 25 agencies. In 1964, 1·6m. small savings accounts totalled $738m.

All insurance business was nationalized in Jan. 1964.

WEIGHTS AND MEASURES. The metric system of weights and measures is legally compulsory, but the American and old Spanish systems are much used. The sugar industry uses the Spanish long ton (1·03 metric tons) and short ton (0·92 metric ton). Cuba sugar sack = 329·59 lb. or 149·49 kg. Land is measured in *caballerías* (of 13·4 hectares or 33 acres).

DIPLOMATIC REPRESENTATIVES

Cuba maintains diplomatic relations with:

Albania	Greece	Pakistan
Algeria	Guinea	Philippines
Austria	Hungary	Poland
Belgium	India	Portugal
Bulgaria	Indonesia	Romania
Cambodia	Israel	Saudi Arabia
Canada	Italy	Spain
Ceylon	Japan	Switzerland
Chile	Korea (North)	Tanzania
China	Lebanon	Tunisia
Congo (Br.)	Luxembourg	Turkey
Cyprus	Mali	USSR
Czechoslovakia	Mexico	UAR
Denmark	Mongolia	UK
Finland	Morocco	Vatican
France	Netherlands	Vietnam (North)
Germany (East)	Norway	Yugoslavia

OF CUBA IN GREAT BRITAIN (57 Kensington Ct., W.8)

Ambassador: Srta Alba Antonia Griñán Núñez (accredited 22 Dec. 1965).
Commercial Counsellors: D. Arrana-Tremois, F. 1. Iglesias.
First Secretary: Firmin Rodriguez.

There are consular representatives in Belfast, Birmingham, Glasgow, Liverpool, London and Nottingham.

OF GREAT BRITAIN IN CUBA

Ambassador: A. Sykes, CMG, MC.
Counsellor: E. A. W. Bullock (*Head of Chancery*). *First Secretaries:* S. R. Airey, OBE (*Consul*); D. F. Ballantyne (*Commercial*); M. Cochran (*Labour*). *Service Attaché:* Lieut.-Col. R. J. Shackleton, MBE (resides in Mexico).

There are consular representatives at Camagüey, Havana and Santiago de Cuba.
The USA broke off diplomatic relations with Cuba on 3 Jan. 1961.

BOOKS OF REFERENCE

Anuario Estadístico de a República de Cuba. Havana, 1914, 1953, 1957 (these only)
Boletín Oficial, Ministerio de Comercio. Monthly
Estadística General: Comercio Exterior. Quarterly and Annual.—*Movimiento de Población.* Monthly and Annual. Havana
Ministry of Foreign Relations, *Profile of Cuba.* Havana, 1966
Anuario azucarero de Cuba. Havana, from 1937
Canet, G., and Raisz, E., *Atlas de Cuba.* Cambridge, Mass., 1949
Draper, T., *Castro's Revolution: Myths and Realities.* New York, 1962.—*Castroism: theory and practice.* New York, 1965
Goldenberg, B. *The Cuban Revolution and Latin America.* New York, 1965
Guerra y Sánchez, R., and others, *Historia de la Nación Cubana.* 10 vols. Havana, 1952
International Commission of Jurists, *Cuba and the Rule of Law.* Geneva, 1962
Julien, C., *La Révolution Cubaine.* Paris, 1961
Meyer, K. E., and Szulc, T., *The Cuban Invasion.* New York, 1962
Miller, W., *The Lost Plantation.* London, 1961
Mills, C. W., *Castro's Cuba.* London, 1961
Núñez Jiménez, A., *Geografia de Cuba.* Havana. 1961
Thomas, H., *Cuba: Or the Pursuit of Freedom.* London, 1971

CZECHOSLOVAKIA
Československá Socialistická Republika

HISTORY. The Czechoslovak State came into existence on 28 Oct. 1918, when the Czech *Národni výbor* (National Committee) took over the government of the Czech lands upon the dissolution of Austria–Hungary. Two days later the Slovak National Council manifested desire to unite politically with the Czechs. On 14 Nov. 1918 the first Czechoslovak National Assembly declared the Czechoslovak State to be a republic with T. G. Masaryk as President (1918–35).

The Treaty of St Germain-en-Laye (1919) recognized the Czechoslovak Republic, consisting of the Czech lands (Bohemia, Moravia, part of Silesia) and Slovakia. To these lands were added as a trust, the autonomous province of Subcarpathian Ruthenia.

This territory was broken up for the benefit of Germany, Poland and Hungary by the Munich agreement (29 Sept. 1938) between UK, France, Germany and Italy.

In March 1939 the German-sponsored Slovak government proclaimed Slovakia independent, and Germany incorporated the Czech lands into the Reich as the 'Protectorate of Bohemia and Moravia'. A government-in-exile, headed by Dr Beneš, was set up in London in July 1940.

Liberation by the Soviet Army and US Forces was completed by May 1945. Territories taken by Germans, Poles and Hungarians were restored to Czechoslovak sovereignty. Subcarpathian Ruthenia was transferred to the USSR.

Elections were held in May 1946, at which the Communist Party obtained about 38% of the votes.

A coalition government under a Communist Prime Minister, Klement Gottwald, remained in power until 20 Feb. 1948, when 12 of the non-Communist ministers resigned in protest against infiltration of Communists into the police.

In Feb. a predominantly Communist government was formed by Gottwald. In May elections resulted in an 89% majority for the government and President Beneš resigned.

In the first months of 1968 mounting pressure for liberalization culminated in the overthrow of the Stalinist President and Party Secretary, Antonín Novotný, and his associates. Under a new leadership the Communist Party introduced in April 1968 an 'Action Programme' of far-reaching political and economic reforms.

Soviet pressure to abandon this programme was exerted between May and Aug. at a number of talks with the Czechoslovak leadership (at Moscow, Prague, Cierna-nad-Tisou and Bratislava). Finally, Warsaw Pact forces (Soviet, Polish, Hungarian and Bulgarian) occupied Czechoslovakia on 21 Aug. The enforced Moscow agreement of 26 Aug. bound the Czechoslovak government to a policy of 'normalization' (*i.e.*, abandonment of most reforms) and to the stationing of Soviet forces on Czechoslovak soil. This situation was confirmed by the Czechoslovak–Soviet 'Status of Forces Agreement' of 16 Oct. In 1969 and 1970 Soviet pressure led to extensive changes in the Party and in the Federal and republican governments. In Oct. 1969 Czechoslovakia repudiated its condemnation of the Warsaw Pact invasion.

A Czechoslovak–Soviet 20-year Treaty of Friendship, Co-operation and Mutual Assistance was signed in May 1970.

CONSTITUTION AND GOVERNMENT. For details of previous constitutions, *see* THE STATESMAN'S YEAR-BOOK, 1968–69, pp. 927–28.

Since 1 Jan. 1969 Czechoslovakia has been a federal socialist republic consisting of two nations of equal rights and inalienable sovereignty: the Czech Socialist Republic (the Czech lands, previously Bohemia, Moravia and part of Silesia), and the Slovak Socialist Republic (Slovakia). Each Republic is governed by a National Council, which delegate to an overall Federal Assembly responsibility for state constitutional affairs, foreign affairs, defence, economic integration and certain important economic policy decisions. Centralized Federal responsibility was increased by a constitutional amendment of Dec. 1970 to include several further spheres of administration, mainly economic. The Federal Assembly consists of the Chamber of Nations, which has 75 Czech and 75 Slovak delegates elected by their respective National Councils, and the Chamber of the People, which has 200 deputies elected by national suffrage.

Under the previous constitution (1960), which remains in force where not specifically superseded, deputies were elected for 6 years. Minimum age of voters is 18, of deputies, 21 years. In 1968 more than one candidate was allowed to stand in each constituency. The last elections to the superseded National Assembly were held in 1964; elections to the new Federal Assembly have been postponed. As a result of purges during 1970, 26 delegates to the Chamber of the People and 49 to the Chamber of Nations were dismissed.

President of the Republic: Gen. Ludvík Svoboda (born 1896), elected on 30 March 1968, following the enforced resignation of President Novotný.

President of the Federal Assembly: Dalibor Haneš (replaced Alexander Dubček, Oct. 1969).

The *de facto* primary source of power is the Communist Party of Czechoslovakia, of which the Communist Party of Slovakia (*First Secretary:* Josef Lenárt) is a constituent part. Communists head the National Front, which incorporates the remaining political parties (Czechoslovak Socialist Party, People's Party, etc.) and the trade unions and youth organizations. Communist Party membership was 1,689,207 in 1967. In the course of extensive purges in 1970, 67,147 members were expelled, 259,670 had their membership cancelled and some further 150,000 resigned. In 1971 the Party had some 1·2m. members. The day after the Warsaw Pact occupation (21 Aug. 1968) the Communist Party met in a secret Congress and elected a new Central Committee and Presidium. This Congress was subsequently annulled. In Nov. 1968 a new Presidium was formed led by Alexander Dubček. This underwent a number of changes to make it acceptable to the USSR, and in April 1971 consisted of Gustáv Husák (*First Secretary*); Vasil Bilak; Peter Colotka (*Deputy Prime Minister*); Evžen Erban (*Chairman, National Front*); Antonín Kapek; Josef Kempný; Josef Korčák (*Deputy Prime Minister*); Josef Lenárt; Jan Piller (*Chairman, Central Council of Trade Unions*); Lubomír Štrougal (*Prime Minister*); Ludvík Svoboda.

In April 1971 members of the government not mentioned above included: (*Deputy Prime Ministers*) Jan Gregor; František Hamouz; Václav Hůla (*Chairman, State Planning Committee*); Karol Laco; Matej Lucan; Jindřich Zahradník; (other ministers) Andrej Barčák (*Foreign Trade*); Martin Dzúr (*Defence*); Radko Kaska (*Interior*); Drahomir Kolder (*Chairman, Czechoslovak Control Committee*); Ján Marko (*Foreign*); Rudolf Rohliček (*Finance*); Michal Stancel (*Labour*).

The Czech Prime Minister is Josef Korčák; the Slovak, Peter Colotka.

National flag: White and red (horizontal), with a blue triangle of full depth at the hoist, point to the fly.

National anthem: Kde domov můj (words by J. K. Tyl; tune by F. J. Škroup, 1834); combined with, Nad Tatru sa blyska (words by J. Matuška, 1844).

AREA AND POPULATION. The country is divided into 11 administrative regions (*kraj*), one of which is the capital, Prague (Praha). For former provinces *see* THE STATESMAN'S YEAR-BOOK, 1960, p. 925.

At the census of 1 March 1961 the population was 13,745,577. Estimate in Jan. 1968, 14,333,259 (4,468,210 in Slovakia; 7·3m. females), distributed as follows:

Region	Chief city	Area in sq. km	Population
Czech			
Prague	—	185	1,034,765
Středočeský	Prague (Praha)	11,298	1,273,051
Jihočeský	České Budějovice	11,349	655,414
Západočeský	Pilsen (Plzeň)	10,866	859,221
Severočeský	Ústi nad Labem	7,817	1,116,893
Východočeský	Hradec Králové	11,252	1,206,186
Jihomoravský	Brno	15,019	1,944,282
Severomoravský	Ostrava	11,066	1,775,217

Region	Chief city	Area in sq. km	Population
Slovak			
Západoslovenský	Bratislava	14,859	1,860,109
Středoslovenský	Banska Bystrica	17,970	1,384,312
Východoslovenský	Košice	16,179	1,215,789

The area of Czechoslovakia is 127,870 sq. km (49,362 sq. miles). Population density in 1968: 112 per sq. km.

National minorities have full political and cultural rights. In 1967 there were 563,000 Hungarians, 114,000 Germans, 72,000 Poles and 58,000 Ukrainians.

The population of the principal towns in 1968 was as follows (in 1,000):

Prague (Praha)	1,034	Ústi nad Labem	73	Děčin	42
Brno	335	Liberec	71	Nitra	41
Bratislava	281	Pardubice	68	Prešov	40
Ostrava	272	Hradec Králové	65	Žilina	39
Plzeň	144	Gottwaldov	63	Chomutov	39
Košice	117	Kladno	56	Jihlava	38
Olomouc	78	Most	55	Banská Bystrica	37
Havířov	78	Teplice	52	Trnava	36
Karviná	74	Opava	46	Prostějov	36
Čcské Budějovice	73	Karlovy Vary	46	Přerov	36

The German population of the border areas was transferred to Germany immediately after the war.

VITAL STATISTICS for calendar years:

	Live births	Marriages	Divorces	Deaths
1965	231,583	112,187	18,702	140,891
1966	222,501	115,654	20,244	141,918
1967	215,766	119,828	19,889	144,294

RELIGION. The majority of the population is Roman Catholic.

Churches are under state control, and clergymen's salaries are paid by the state. There is an Apostolic Administrator, and in 1967 there were 4 bishops (the remaining 8 dioceses were directed by Government-appointed capitulary vicars), 4,700 Roman Catholic priests (7,040 in 1948) and 3,200 Roman Catholic churches (10,473 in 1948).

Protestants were estimated (1962) at 1·2m., including 530,000 Reformed (360,000 Czech Brethren, 150,000 Reformed Church of Slovakia), 485,000 Lutherans (435,000 in Slovakia, 50,000 in Silesia), 10,000 Methodists, 10,000 Moravians, 10,000 Unity of Czech Brethren, 5,000 Baptists. In 1966 there were 15,000 Jews.

EDUCATION. In 1968–69 there were 8,067 kindergartens for children from 3 to 6 years of age, with 27,155 teachers and 371,073 pupils. All children receive free education from the ages of 6 to 15, where possible remaining at a single school for the whole 9 years. In 1968–69 there were 10,947 schools with 2,052,526 pupils and 98,399 teachers.

Subsequent education is of 3 types. First, 3 final years of secondary school (in 1967–68, 349 schools with 2,655 teachers and 98,918 pupils). Secondly, technical, teachers' training and other vocational schools (1967–68, 649 schools with 196,246 students). Thirdly, university level (100,193 full-time students, including 40,698 girls; and 34,059 part-time and correspondence students); university professors and readers number 3,631; other academic staff, 12,772. There are 35 institutions of higher education, with 98 faculties. These include the 4 old universities—the Charles University in Prague, founded 1348 (19,516 students); the Purkyně (formerly Masaryk) University in Brno, founded 1919 (6,150 students); the Comenius University in Bratislava, founded 1919 (12,939 students); the Palacký University in Olomouc, founded 1573 (5,591 students)—and 2 universities founded in and after 1959 and 12 technical universities or institutes. In 1970 political tests were re-introduced for teachers and students at all levels.

CINEMAS (1968). There were 3,570 cinemas.

NEWSPAPERS (1968). There were 28 daily newspapers, including 12 in Slovak. The Party daily *Rudé Právo* has a circulation of 100,000.

WELFARE. In 1967 Kčs. 6,600m. were spent on medical services and 9,601 on sick pay. In 1967 social insurance coverage was reorganized on an enterprise basis. There were, in 1968, 258 hospitals with a total of 114,199 beds, and 32,179 doctors and dentists.

JUSTICE. A new criminal code came into force on 1 Jan. 1962. The main emphasis in this and in the new criminal procedure law associated with it is on re-education rather than on punishment. Capital punishment is retained only as an extreme measure.

The emergency laws of 1969 have been incorporated into the criminal code.

Judges in local and district courts are elected by universal suffrage, those in regional courts by the regional local authority and the bench of the supreme court by the National Assembly.

FINANCE. Currency. The monetary unit in the Czechoslovak Republic is the *koruna* (Kčs.) *or* crown of 100 *haler*. Notes in circulation: Kčs. 3, 5, 10, 25, 50, 100. Coin: 3, 5, 10, 25, 50 halers, and Kčs. 1. The koruna is based on a gold content of 0·123426 gramme of pure gold and pegged on the rouble at Kčs. 1·80 = R.1. The International Monetary Fund did not approve this change of the par value, and Czechoslovak membership at 31 Dec. 1954. At the same date Czechoslovakia ceased to be a member of the International Bank. The official rates of exchange are £1 = Kčs. 17·30; US$1 = Kčs. 7·20; 1 Soviet rouble = Kčs. 8. Foreign tourists receive the equivalent of Kčs. 38·60 for £1.

Foreign exchange is a state monopoly and Czechoslovak currency may not be imported or exported.

Budget. Budgets for calendar years (in Kčs. 1m.)

	1964	1965	1966	1967	1968	1969
Revenue	130,414	116,203	152,905	142,522	144,800	156,200
Expenditure	130,318	116,138	152,905	142,522	144,800	156,200

Main items of the 1968 budget were (in Kčs. 1,000m.): Revenue: gross income levies, 47·9; turnover tax, 41·8; direct taxes, 17·8; other sources, 37·3. Expenditure: national economy, 64; culture, health and social services, 64·6; defence, 12·9; administration, 3·3.

DEFENCE. Defence is the responsibility of the Defence Council set up in Feb. 1969 and headed by the First Secretary of the Party. Army service lasts 2 years. There are 3 military districts.

The Army is organized in 15 divisions (4 tank, 1 airborne and 10 motorized divisions). The regular army had, in Dec. 1966, a total strength of about 175,000 men and 3,200 tanks, mainly T-54s with some T-55s.

The Air Force is organized as a tactical force, under overall army command, and has a strength of some 55,000 personnel and 500 combat aircraft. Service lasts 3 years. Six fighter regiments (each 3 squadrons of 12 aircraft) are equipped with 220 MiG-19 and -21 jets, and there are 4 regiments of 230 Su-7 and MiG-15 ground attack aircraft. Il-28s replaced in attack units have been converted for ECM duties. Transport units have Il-14 and Il-18 aircraft and Mil Mi-4 and Mi-8 helicopters. Training units are equipped with 2-seat MiG-21s and Czech-built aircraft, including L-29 Delfin jet advanced trainers, totalling 300 in all. Surface-to-air ('Guideline') missile units are operational.

The security forces and frontier guards are organized in regiments and brigades respectively; total strength, 40,000.

The Warsaw Pact invasion of Aug. 1968 brought an estimated 500,000 occupation troops into the country. By early 1970 this number had been reduced to 80,000 Soviet troops, the presence of which is legalized by the Czech–Soviet 'Status of Forces' Agreement of Oct. 1968.

In Feb. 1969 the government announced an increase in defence capacity, and Czechoslovakia resumed participation in Warsaw Pact meetings.

PLANNING. For details of the first three 5-year plans *see* THE STATESMAN'S YEAR-BOOK, 1964–65, p. 922. The fourth 5-year plan ran from 1966 to 1970. Between 1965 and 1968 there were a number of economic reforms which gave enterprise managers more autonomy, restricted central organs to long-range planning and gave freer play to the forces of the market. Since the Soviet intervention of Aug. 1968, however, the programme of economic innovations has been substantially vitiated, and the economy has reverted to a model closer to the traditional communist centrally planned type.

The fifth 5-year plan for 1971–76 envisaged an annual production increase of 5·2%.

AGRICULTURE. In 1968, 7·13m. hectares of land were classified as agricultural, of which 5·04m. hectares were arable. 6·38m. hectares belong to the 'socialist sector' (state and collective farms).

In 1968 there were 6,395 collective farms (10,816 in 1960) with 4,269,385 hectares under cultivation. Crop production in 1967 (in 1,000 metric tons): Wheat, 2,516; rye, 689; barley, 1,936; oats, 968; maize, 421; potatoes, 6,037; sugar-beet, 7,663.

Livestock. In Jan. 1968 the number of livestock was: Cattle, 4·44m. (including 1·92m. milch cows); horses, 166,000; pigs, 5·6m.; sheep, 770,000; poultry, 31·2m. In 1967 production of meat was 1,174,696 metric tons (live weight); milk, 4,204m. litres; butter, 82,181 tons; 3,218m. eggs.

FORESTRY. Czechoslovakia ranks among the most richly wooded countries in Europe, and the timber industry is important. Total forested area in 1968 was 4,452,951 hectares. The area re-afforested in 1967 was 55,217 hectares and the timber yield was 14·65m. cu. metres.

MINING. Mineral production includes both soft and hard coal (chief coalfields: Most, Chomutov, Kladno, Ostrava and Sokolov), iron, graphite and garnets, silver, copper and lead, rock-salt, aluminium and uranium. Production in 1968 (in metric tons): Iron ore, 1·57m.; coal, 26m.; lignite and brown coal, 68m.

INDUSTRY. Industrialization is well developed and antedates the Communist régime. All industry is nationalized.

Output in 1967 (in 1,000 metric tons): Pig-iron, 6,822; crude steel, 10,002; coke, 9,307; crude oil, 200; rolled-steel products, 7,111; cement, 6,460; paper, 584; sulphuric acid, 1,012; nitrogeneous fertilizers, 245; phosphate fertilizers, 274; sugar, 956,082; beer, 19·4m. hectolitres; cars, 111,700.

Textile production (in 1m. metres) in 1967: Cotton, 491·7; linen, 69·6; woollen, 46·4. Leather shoes, 52·4m. pairs.

Production of electricity in 1967: 38,622m. kwh.

There are 2 oil pipelines from the USSR, one to Bratislava and one to Zaluzi (near Most).

LABOUR. Number of workers in 1967: Industry, 2·6m.; agriculture, 1·2m.; building, 557,000; forestry, 106,000; supply, 48,000; retail trade and catering, 466,000; transport, 344,00; communications, 92,000; total, 6,798,000 (46·1% women) (5·28m. in the productive sector, 1·4m. in the non-productive sector).

Stringent labour disciplinary measures were introduced in 1969. Average monthly wage in 1967: Kčs. 1,534. A wage freeze of 1970 related increases to productivity and restricted them to 2·8%.

COMMERCE. Total trade (in Kčs. 1m.) for calendar years:

	1960	1965	1966	1967	1968	1969
Imports	13,072	19,242	19,699	19,296	22,155	23,718
Exports	13,892	19,357	19,764	20,622	21,638	23,900

In 1969 raw materials accounted for 46% of imports and 28% of exports, machinery and equipment 31% of imports and 49% of exports.

In 1969, 71% of foreign trade was with Communist countries. In Oct. 1969 a Soviet offer of economic aid over 5–6 years was accepted, including grants of hard currency and increased deliveries of raw materials. The Czech–Soviet trade agreement for 1971–74 envisages an increase of 43% in Czech exports and of 39% in imports. In 1969 Czechoslovakia imported from the USSR goods valued at Kčs. 7,957m. and exported to the USSR goods valued at Kčs. 8,144m.; followed by East Germany (imports, 2,305m.; exports, 2,294m.); Poland (imports, 1,434m.; exports, 1,691m.); Hungary (imports, 1,086m.; exports, 1,097m.).

Foreign trade is a state monopoly. From 1966 to 1969 trading corporations enjoyed a certain autonomy, but the organization of foreign trade has again been centralized. In 1969 it became official policy to reduce trade with the West 'to its essentials'. A trade and economic co-operation agreement for 1971–74 was signed with West Germany in Dec. 1970.

UK–Czechoslovak trade is conducted according to a 5-year agreement (1968–72). Arrangements for 1971 are the same as for 1970.

Total trade between UK and Czechoslovakia for calendar years (in £1,000 sterling, British Board of Trade returns):

	1965	1966	1967	1968	1969	1970
Imports to UK	17,398	19,517	20,501	23,096	21,508	22,774
Exports from UK	12,885	17,907	13,943	17,413	17,654 ⎱	20,376
Re-exports from UK	1,683	910	1,125	1,264	530 ⎰	

RAILWAYS. In 1968 the length of railway track was 13,317 km. Of this, 2,807 km was double-tracked and 2,389 km electrified. 607m. passengers and 228m. metric tons of freight were carried.

ROADS. In 1967 there were 73,057 km of motorways and first-class roads. In 1969 there were 699,960 passenger cars. In 1967 state road transport carried 1,717m. passengers and 230m. metric tons of freight.

SHIPPING. In 1967 'Czechoslovak Ocean Shipping' had 8 ocean-going vessels of together 80,556 gross tons, based on Szczecin. 834m. metric tons of cargo were carried. River freight transport within Czechoslovakia totalled 4·19m. metric tons.

AVIATION. Air transport is run by ČSA (Czechoslovak Airlines). The main airports are: Prague (Ruzyne), Brno (Cernovice), Bratislava (Vajnory), Olomouc (Holice), Kosice (Barca). In 1967, 1·39m. passengers and 22,453 metric tons of freight were flown. There are direct flights from Prague to some 50 cities, including most European capitals, Havana, Djakarta, Conakry and (from May 1970) New York and Montreal. BEA operates air traffic London–Prague, Air France Paris–Prague–Bucharest.

POST. Number of telephones in service on 1 Jan. 1969 was 1,789,373; 3·2m. people held wireless and 2·6m. TV licences. There are 5 television stations.

BANKING. In 1945 joint-stock banks were nationalized; in 1948 they were merged into 2 institutes: the Živnostenská Banka for Bohemia, Moravia and Silesia, and the Tatra Banka for Slovakia. These two and the post office savings bank were fused into the State Bank of Czechoslovakia (Československá Státní Banka) in 1950.

The Commercial Bank of Czechoslovakia (Československá Obchodní Banka, a.s.) was established in 1964 with a capital of Kčs. 500m.; it is jointly controlled by the State Bank of Czechoslovakia, the State Insurance Office, the Central

Co-operative Council, the 31 Czechoslovak foreign trade organizations and 13 industrial organizations in the export field. In 1965 it took over some of the functions of the State Bank, particularly in international banking and foreign-exchange operations.

DIPLOMATIC REPRESENTATIVES

Czechoslovakia maintains embassies in:

Afghánistán	Ghana	Norway
Albania	Greece	Pakistan
Algeria	Guinea	Poland
Argentina	Hungary	Ruanda
Belgium	Iceland	Romania
Brazil	India	Sierra Leone
Bolivia	Indonesia	Somali
Bulgaria	Iran	Sudan
Burma	Iraq	Sweden
Cambodia	Italy	Switzerland
Canada	Japan	Syria
Central African Republic	Jordan	Tanzania
Ceylon	Kenya	Togo
Chile	Korea (North)	Tunisia
China	Kuwait	Turkey
Congo (Br.)	Laos	Uganda
Congo (K.)	Lebanon	USSR
Cuba	Libya	UAR
Cyprus	Luxembourg	UK
Dahomey	Mali	USA
Denmark	Mexico	Uruguay
Ecuador	Mongolia	Vietnam (North)
Ethiopia	Morocco	Yemen
Finland	Netherlands	Yugoslavia
France	Nepál	Zambia
Germany (East)	Nigeria	

Czechoslovakia maintains legations in Austria and New Zealand and consulates-general in Australia, Colombia and Spain.

OF CZECHOSLOVAKIA IN GREAT BRITAIN (6–7 Kensington Palace Gdns, W8)

Ambassador: Dr Miloslav Růžek (accredited 27 Oct. 1966).
Counsellors: Vladimír Babáček (*Commercial*). *Military and Air Attaché:* Col. Bohumil Švejnoha. *First Secretaries:* Josef Konecký; Miroslaý Stoje.

OF GREAT BRITAIN IN CZECHOSLOVAKIA

Ambassador: Ronald S. Scrivener, CMG.
Counsellor: J. R. Rich. *First Secretaries:* C. G. Mays, J. R. Banks. *Consul:* A. White.
Service Attachés: Col. C. Scott (*Defence and Military*); Wing Cdr R. M. Sparkes (*Air*).

OF CZECHOSLOVAKIA IN THE USA (3900 Linnean Ave. NW, Washington, D.C., 20008)

Ambassador: Dr Ivan Rohat-Ilkiv.
Minister-Counsellor: Jaroslav Zantovsky.
Military and Air Attaché: Miroslav Dvorák. *Commercial Attaché:* Otakar Jakonbě.

OF THE USA IN CZECHOSLOVAKIA

Ambassador: M. Toon.
Deputy Head of Mission: A. J. Wortzel. *Heads of Sections:* S. G. Wise (*Political*); C. W. Schmidt (*Economic*); J. H. Madden (*Consular*); T. E. Russell. *Service Attachés:* Col. G. McCorkle (*Air*); Col. J. Cranford (*Army*).

BOOKS OF REFERENCE

The Constitution of the Czechoslovak Socialist Republic. [English ed.] Prague, 1960
Statistical Abstract. Prague, 1968
Statistická ročenka ČSSR. [Statistical Yearbook.] Prague, annual since 1958
Czechoslovak Foreign Trade. Prague, monthly
Statistika. Prague, Statistical Office, monthly since 1964
James, R. R., *The Czechoslovak Crisis,* London, 1969
Kavka, F., *An Outline of Czechoslovak History.* Prague, 1963
Littell, R. (ed.), *The Czech Black Book; prepared by the Institute of History of the Czechoslovak Academy of Sciences.* London, 1969
Procházka, J., *English–Czech and Czech–English Dictionary.* 16th ed. London, 1959
Schwartz, H., *Prague's 200 Days.* London, 1969
Suda, Z., *The Czechoslovak Socialist Republic.* Baltimore, 1969
Taborsky, E., *Communism in Czechoslovakia, 1948–60.* Princeton Univ. Press, 1961
Windsor, P., and Roberts, E. A. *Czechoslovakia, 1968.* London, 1969

DENMARK

Kongeriget Danmark

REIGNING KING. Frederik IX, born 11 March 1899; married 24 May 1935 to Princess Ingrid of Sweden, born 28 March 1910; *offspring:* Princess Margrethe, born 16 April 1940 (heir presumptive; married 10 June 1967 to Henri Count de Monpezat); Princess Benedikte, born 29 April 1944 (married 3 Feb. 1968 to Prince Richard of Sayn-Wittgenstein-Berleburg); Princess Anne-Marie, born 30 Aug. 1946 (married 18 Sept. 1964 to King Constantine of Greece). He succeeded to the throne on the death of his father, King Christian X, 20 April 1947.

Brother of the King. Prince Knud, born 27 July 1900; married 8 Sept. 1933 to Princess Caroline-Mathilde of Denmark, his cousin; *offspring:* Princess Elisabeth, born 8 May 1935; Prince Ingolf, since 1968 Count of Rosenborg, born 17 Feb. 1940; Prince Christian, born 22 Oct. 1942.

The crown of Denmark was elective from the earliest times. In 1448 after the death of the last male descendant of Swein Estridsen the Danish Diet elected to the throne Christian I, Count of Oldenburg, in whose family the royal dignity remained for more than 4 centuries, although the crown was not rendered hereditary by right till 1660. The direct male line of the house of Oldenburg became extinct with King Frederik VII on 15 Nov. 1863. In view of the death of the king, without direct heirs, the Great Powers signed a treaty at London on 8 May 1852, by the terms of which the succession to the crown of Denmark was made over to Prince Christian of Schleswig-Holstein-Sonderburg-Glücksburg, and to the direct male descendants of his union with the Princess Louise of Hesse-Cassel, niece of King Christian VIII of Denmark. In accordance with this treaty, a law concerning the succession to the Danish crown was adopted by the Diet, and obtained the royal sanction 31 July 1853. Linked to the constitution of 5 June 1953, a new law of succession, dated 27 March 1953, has come into force, which restricts the right of succession to the descendants of King Christian X and Queen Alexandrine, and admits the sovereign's daughters to the line of succession, ranking after the sovereign's sons.

King Frederik IX has a civil list of 6,028,690 kroner. Annuities to other members of the royal house amount to 1,690,703 kroner.

Subjoined is a list of the kings of Denmark, with the dates of their accession, from the time of election of Christian I of Oldenburg:

House of Oldenburg

Christian I	1448	Christian IV	1588	Frederik V	1746
Hans	1481	Frederik III	1648	Christian VII	1766
Christian II	1513	Christian V	1670	Frederik VI	1808
Frederik I	1523	Frederik IV	1699	Christian VIII	1839
Christian III	1534	Christian VI	1730	Frederik VII	1848
Frederik II	1559				

House of Schleswig-Holstein-Sonderburg-Glücksburg

Christian IX	1863	Christian X	1912	Frederik IX	1947
Frederik VIII	1906				

CONSTITUTION AND GOVERNMENT. The present constitution of Denmark is founded upon the 'Grundlov' (charter) of 5 June 1953.

The legislative power lies with the King and the *Folketing* (Diet) jointly. The executive power is vested in the King, who exercises his authority through the ministers. The judicial power is with the courts. The King must be a member of the Evangelical-Lutheran Church, the official Church of the State. The King cannot assume major international obligations without the consent of the *Folketing*. The *Folketing* consists of one chamber. All men and women of Danish nationality of more than 21 years of age and permanently resident in Denmark possess the franchise and are eligible for election to the *Folketing*, which is at present composed of 179 members; 135 members are elected by the method of proportional representation in 17 districts. In order to attain an equal representation of the different parties, 40 *tillægsmandater* (additional seats) are divided among such parties which have not obtained sufficient returns at the district elections. Two members are elected for the Faroe Islands and 2 for Greenland. The term of the legislature is 4 years, but a general election may be called at any time.

The *Folketing* must meet every year on the first Tuesday in October. Besides its legislative functions, it appoints every 6 years judges who, together with the ordinary members of the Supreme Court (*Højesteret*), form the *Rigsret*, a tribunal which can alone try parliamentary impeachments. The ministers have free access to the house, but can vote only if they are members.

Folketing, elected 23 Jan. 1968: 62 Social Democrats, 27 Radical Left, 34 Liberals, 37 Conservatives, 11 Socialist People's Party, 4 Left Socialists, 2 Faroe Islands and 2 Greenland representatives; total 179.

The executive (called the State Council (*Statsraadet*) when acting with the King presiding) is a coalition government, composed in Feb. 1968, as follows:

Prime Minister: Hilmer Baunsgaard (Radical).

Minister for Foreign Affairs: Poul Hartling (Lib.). *Labour:* Lauge Dahlgaard (Rad.). *Social Affairs:* Nathalie Lind (Lib.). *Housing:* Aage Hastrup (Cons.). *Interior:* H. C. Toft (Cons.). *Fisheries:* A. C. Normann (Rad.). *Defence:* Erik Ninn-Hansen (Cons.). *Agriculture:* Peter Larsen (Lib.). *Finance:* Poul Møller (Cons.). *Economic and Marketing Affairs:* P. Nyboe Andersen (Lib.). *Education:* Helge Larsen (Rad.). *Cultural Affairs:* K. Helveg Petersen (Rad.). *Ecclesiastical Affairs:* Arne Fog Pedersen (Lib.). *Trade:* Knud Thomsen (Cons.). *Justice:* K. Thestrup (Cons.). *Public Works:* Ove Guldberg (Lib.). *Greenland:* A. C. Normann (Rad.).

The ministers are individually and collectively responsible for their acts, and if impeached and found guilty, cannot be pardoned without the consent of the *Folketing*.

In 1948 a separate legislature (*Lagting*) and executive (*Landsstyre*) were established for the Faroe Islands, to deal with specified local matters.

The Constitution of 1953 gave Greenland equal status with the other parts of the Kingdom.

National flag: White cross on red (Dannebrog).

National anthems: Kong Kristian stod ved højen Mast (words by J. Ewald, 1778; tune by J. E. Hartmann, 1780) and Der er et yndigt land.

The Constitution of the Kingdom of Denmark Act and the Succession to the Throne Act. Copenhagen, 1953

LOCAL GOVERNMENT. For administrative purposes Denmark is divided into 277 municipalities (*primærkommuner*); each of them has a district council of between 5 and 31 members, headed by an elected mayor. Copenhagen forms a district by itself and is governed by a city council of 55 members, elected every 4 years, and an executive (*magistraten*), consisting of the chief burgomaster (*over-borgmesteren*), 5 burgomasters and 5 aldermen, appointed by the city council for 8 years. There are 14 counties (*amtskommuner*), each of which is administered by a county council (*amtsråd*) of between 13 and 31 members, headed by an elected mayor. All councils are elected directly by universal suffrage and proportional representation for 4-year terms.

The counties and Copenhagen are superintended by the ministry of interior affairs. The municipalities are superintended by 14 local supervision committees, headed by a governor (*amtmand*) who is a civil servant appointed by the King.

AREA AND POPULATION. According to the census held on 27 Sept. 1965 the area of Denmark proper was 43,069 sq. km (16,629 sq. miles) and the population 4,767,597. Estimate, 1 April 1970: 4,912,865.

Administrative divisions		Area (sq. km)	Population 1965	Population 1970	Population 1970 per sq. km
København (Copenhagen)	(city)	84	678,072	634,500	7,554
Frederiksberg	(borough)	9	110,847	102,751	11,714
Københavns	(county)	520	558,478	609,469	1,172
Frederiksborg	"	1,376	211,449	252,557	188
Roskilde	"	890	118,768	147,434	166
Vastsjællands	"	2,983	248,391	256,997	86
Storstrøms	"	3,396	252,498	251,815	74
Bornholms	"	588	48,744	47,405	81
Fyns	"	3,486	425,128	430,958	124
Sønderjyllands	"	3,929	230,903	237,270	60
Ribe	"	3,136	190,672	196,894	63
Vejle	"	2,992	293,906	304,358	102
Ringkøbing	"	4,849	231,002	240,014	49
Århus	"	4,571	498,291	525,167	115
Viborg	"	4,119	219,626	220,214	53
Nordjyllands	"	6,171	450,822	455,062	74
Total		43,069	4,767,597	4,912,865	114

The population is almost entirely Scandinavian; in 1960, of the inhabitants of Denmark proper, 97·8% were born in Denmark.

On 27 Sept. 1965 the population of the capital, Copenhagen (comprising Copenhagen, Frederiksberg and Gentofte municipalities), was 874,417 (including suburbs, 1,377,605); Aarhus, 117,748 (including suburbs, 187,342); Odense, 107,531 (including suburbs, 132,978); Aalborg, 85,632 (including suburbs, 99,815); Esbjerg, 55,882; Randers, 42,923; Horsens, 37,106.

VITAL STATISTICS for calendar years:

	Living births	Stillbirths	Marriages	Divorces	Deaths	Emigration	Immigration
1967	81,410	715	41,158	6,939	47,836	29,055	30,697
1968	74,543	636	39,457	7,572	47,290	30,067	26,655
1969	71,298	612	39,158	8,955	47,936	..	..

Illegitimate births: 1966, 10·2%; 1967, 11·1%; 1968, 11·1%; 1969, 11·3%.

RELIGION. The established religion is the Lutheran, which was introduced in 1536. The affairs of the national church are under the superintendance of 10 bishops, who have no political character. Complete religious toleration is extended to every sect, and no civil disabilities attach to Dissenters.

According to the census of 1921 there were 3,221,843 Protestants, 22,137 Roman Catholics (under a Vicar Apostolic resident in Copenhagen), 535 Greek Catholics, 5,947 Jews, 17,369 others or of no confession. There were 56 members of the Society of Friends in 1957.

Kjær, J. C., *History of the Church of Denmark*. Blair, Nebr., 1945

EDUCATION. Education has been compulsory since 1814. The compulsory school age is from 7 to 15. School leaving age will be increased to 16 years in 1972. There are no fees in public schools.

In the year 1969–70, 2,556 primary and lower secondary schools had 523,145 pupils in grades 1–7 and 170,794 pupils in grades 8–10 and employed 38,086 teachers. 108 upper secondary schools had 36,414 pupils and 3,863 teachers. The leaving examination from these schools (*Studentereksamen*) and the higher preparatory examination gives access to universities and institutions of higher education. Forms 8, 9 and 10 of the lower secondary schools are either voluntary non-examination forms or examination forms in the *réal* department terminating with the *Réal Examination*. About 10% of the total number of schools are private, and they are inspected either by the municipal authorities or by the State.

There are also 69 folk high schools, 30 agricultural schools and 32 home economics schools with a total enrolment of 14,780 pupils; 68 technical schools with 71,416 pupils receiving vocational training as apprentices or technicians; 162 commercial schools with a total enrolment of 43,229 pupils; 30 teacher-training colleges have a total enrolment of 12,183 students.

For higher education there are the University of Copenhagen, founded in 1479, with 21,907 students; the University of Aarhus, founded in 1928, with 9,666 students; the University of Odense (founded in 1964) with 908 students; the technical university (founded in 1829) with 2,947 students; engineering academies in Copenhagen and Aalborg with 6,057 students; the school of pharmacy with 593 students; 2 colleges of dentistry at Copenhagen and Aarhus with 1,291 students; a Royal Academy of fine arts with 1,374 students; a veterinary and agricultural college with 1,421 students; 2 high schools of economics, business administration and modern languages with 6,911 students; the Royal College of Education with 1,416 students; 2 academies of music with 628 students; a college of librarianship with 630 students.

CINEMAS (1970). There were 383 cinemas with a seating capacity of 140,788.

NEWSPAPERS (1969). There were 59 daily newspapers with a combined circulation of 1·78m. on weekdays; 10 of them (780,000) appeared in Copenhagen.

Kirkegaard, P., *The Public Libraries in Denmark*. Copenhagen, 1950; French ed., 1960
Nellermann, A., *Schools and education in Denmark*. Copenhagen, 1964
Skrubbeltrang, F., *The Danish Folk High Schools*. Copenhagen, 1947
Thorsen, S., *Newspapers in Denmark*. Copenhagen, 1953
Trane, E., *Education and Culture in Denmark*. Copenhagen, 1958

SOCIAL WELFARE. The main body of Danish social welfare legislation is consolidated in 10 acts concerning (1) health insurance, (2) disablement pensions, (3) old-age pensions, (4) widows pensions, (5) employment injuries insurance, (6) employment services and unemployment insurance, (7) social assistance including assistance to handicapped, (8) rehabilitation, (9) family allowances, and (10) child and juvenile guidance.

Health insurance, covering 95% of the population, provides free medical care and hospitalization, substantial subsidies for certain essential medicines together with some dental care and a funeral allowance. Wage-earners are granted daily sickness allowances, other can have limited daily sickness allowances. Hospitals are primarily municipal.

Disablement and old-age pensions cover the entire population. Old-age pension or folks pension is paid either as a minimum pension or as income-graded pension. Every person over 67 years is entitled to a minimum pension. Income-graded pension can be paid to single women over 62 years and to men and married women over 67 years. Minimum pensions amounted in 1968 to 2,760 kroner when both spouses are entitled, and 1,836 kroner to single persons. The income-graded pension is graded according to the income of the recipient. When both spouses are entitled to a pension it amounts to 12,204 kroner annually.

A single pensioner is entitled to roughly two-thirds of this amount. If the pensioner has other income exceeding certain limits, reductions are made, but not below the minimum pension. Pension rates are adjusted every year according to the cost-of-living index.

The disablement and widows pension schemes are nearly the same as that of the income-graded folks pension.

Employment injuries insurance provides for daily sickness allowances, disablement or survivors' pensions and funeral allowances. The scheme covers practically all employees.

Employment services are provided by regional public employment agencies. The insurance against unemployment provides daily allowances. The unemployment insurance funds have a membership of about 783,000.

The *Social Assistance Act* deals with the care of the aged (old people's homes), rehabilitation and training of cripples, the blind, etc. The social assistance provisions, moreover, cover cases of need which are not provided for by the insurance schemes.

The *Child and Juvenile Guidance Act* deals with the care of children, including placement of children and juveniles in foster homes or institutional care. Institutions for day-time care of children and some other benefits for children are provided for under this act.

Total social expenditure, including hospital and health services, amounted in the financial year 1968–69 to 6,468m. kroner.

Galenson, W., *The Danish System of Labour Relations*. Oxford, 1952
Halck, N., *Social Welfare in Denmark*. Copenhagen, 1961
Jensen, O., *Social Services in Denmark*. Copenhagen, 1961
Manniche, Peter, *Denmark: Living Democracy in Denmark*. Copenhagen, 1952

JUSTICE. The lowest courts of justice are organized in 105 tribunals (*underretter*), where minor cases are dealt with by a single judge. The tribunals at Copenhagen have 29 judges and Aarhus 8 and the other tribunals have 1 to 3. Cases of greater consequence are dealt with by the superior courts (*Landsretterne*); these courts are also courts of appeal for the above-named minor cases. Of superior courts there are two: *Østre Landsret* in Copenhagen with 33 judges, *Vestre Landsret* in Viborg with 20 judges. From these an appeal lies to the Supreme Court (*Højesteret*) in Copenhagen, composed of 15 judges. Judges under 70 years of age can be removed only by judicial sentence.

In 1968, 7,814 men and 633 women were convicted of crimes and delicts, fines not included. On 31 Dec. 1968, 1,721 men and 17 women were in the state prisons.

FINANCE. Currency. The monetary unit is the *krone* of 100 *øre*. In 1931 Denmark went off the gold standard, as established in 1873. For the present parity of the *krone see* p. 19; £1 = 17·95 *kroner*, US\$ = 7·5 *kroner*.

Small change: 5-kroner pieces of copper–nickel, 1-krone pieces of copper–nickel or copper–aluminium–nickel; 25-øre and 10-øre pieces of copper–nickel, and 5-øre, 2-øre and 1-øre pieces of copper–tin–zinc, pure aluminium or pure zinc.

Budget. The budget (*Finanslovforslag*) must be laid before the *Folketing* not later than 4 months before the beginning of a new fiscal year. The annual financial accounts (*Statsregnskab*) must be examined by 5 revisers, elected by the *Folketing*. Their report is submitted to the *Folketing*.

The following shows the actual revenue and expenditure for 2 fiscal years ending 31 March and the estimates for 3 years (in 1,000 kroner):

	1965–66	1966–67	1967–68	1968–69	1969–70
Current revenue	14,477,404	17,169,729	19,068,168	25,558,156	28,500,000
Current expenditure	13,145,503	15,488,984	18,279,304	24,002,384	28,000,000

Receipts and expenditures of special government funds and expenditures on public works are excluded.

The 1970–71 budget envisages revenue of 16,551m. kroner from income and property taxes and 15,149m. from consumer taxes (gross).
The central government debt on 31 March 1970 amounted to 3,579m. kroner.

DEFENCE. The Danish military defence is organized in accordance with the Defence Act of 1960. A new defence act, which came into force on 1 Jan. 1970, was passed in June 1969.

In accordance with the new act the Chief of Defence has full command of the three services: the Army, the Navy and the Air Force. The Chief of Defence, the Chief of Defence Staff and the Commanders-in-Chief of the Army, the Navy and the Air Force and part of their staffs, are integrated in the Defence Command.

The Minister of Defence is assisted by a Defence Council consisting of the Chief of Defence, the Chief of Defence Staff, the Chief of Danish Operational Forces, and the Commanders-in-Chief of the Army. the Navy and the Air Force.

The Constitution of 1849 declared it the duty of every fit man to contribute to the national defence, and this provision is still in force. According to a new Personnel Act which came into force on 1 Jan. 1970 the military personnel comprises officers, ncos and privates. Private personnel are provided by enlistment and by engagement of volunteers. At the age of 17 years the recruits are entered upon the conscription rolls, and between the age of 19 and 25 they receive their first military training over a period of 12 months. Afterwards conscripts may be recalled for refresher training or musters.

Army. The Army comprises field army commands and units and regional commands. After mobilization the field formations comprise 6 brigades and 1 battalion group with balanced supporting units and commands. Four of these brigades are manned in peacetime. Local defence reserve forces comprise 15 local defence battalions (infantry) and 15 local defence batteries (artillery). The men of the latest annual service groups form the troops of the line, while those of the previous years form the local defence, the reserve and the reserve for the Home Guard. Total strength, 26,000. The Army Home Guard consists of about 53,000 volunteers.

Navy. The Navy comprises the fleet and coast-defence. It includes 5 submarines, 6 frigates (4 for fishery protection), 8 minelayers, 4 corvettes, 16 torpedo boats, 9 seaward defence craft, 8 coastal minesweepers, 4 inshore minesweepers, 2 depot ships, 8 patrol craft, 2 oilers, 2 tenders and the royal yacht.

The construction programme includes a submarine being completed.

The coast defence includes several permanent fortifications. Naval personnel total 7,000 officers and men.

The Naval Home Guard consists of about 3,500 volunteers.

Air Force. The independent Royal Danish Air Force was formed on 1 Oct. 1950. Its operational units are controlled by a Tactical Air Command and are committed to NATO. They are supplemented by Training and Air Materiel Commands.

Total peacetime strength is about 10,000 personnel, with 105 combat aircraft. There are 3 fighter-bomber squadrons, of which 2 have F-100D/F Super Sabres and the other Swedish-built Saab-35XD Drakens, 2 all-weather fighter squadrons (F-104G Starfighters), 1 day interceptor squadron (Hunters), 1 reconnaissance squadron (RF-84F Thunderflashes, being replaced by Drakens), 1 transport squadron (C-54s and C-47s) and 1 search and rescue squadron (S-61 helicopters), plus training and general purpose units. Four air defence squadrons have Nike surface-to-air missiles; another 4 have Hawk surface-to-air missiles.

The Air Force Home Guard consists of about 11,500 volunteers.

PRODUCTION. In 1965, 14% of the population lived on agriculture, forestry and fishery, 26% on industries and handicrafts, 8% on construction, 12% on commerce, etc., 7% on transportation and communication, and 16% on administration, professional services, etc., while 13% received old-age pensions or had private means.

The following table sets forth the gross factor income (in 1m. kroner) by industrial origin in 3 calendar years:

	1967		1968		1969	
	Current prices	1955 prices	Current prices	1955 prices	Current prices	1955 prices
Agriculture	6,415	5,194	6,516	5,632	7,302	5,338
Forestry	112	101	109	120	103	116
Gardening, fur-farming, etc.	751	703	757	678	819	661
Fishing	398	372	508	465	552	417
Peat and lignite production	76	37	42	33	35	26
Total	7,722	6,407	7,931	6,828	8,811	6,558
Manufacturing industries	15,825	10,700	17,050	11,200	19,400	12,450
Handicrafts	7,725	3,850	8,275	3,900	9,050	4,075
Construction	8,025	4,185	8,330	4,025	9,945	4,495
Gas, electricity and water	1,534	1,170	1,881	1,452	2,470	1,950
Total	33,109	19,905	35,536	20,577	40,865	22,970
Wholesale and retail trade, etc.	11,600	7,725	12,100	7,850	13,250	8,400
Banking and insurance	2,703	1,325	2,649	1,370	3,000	1,500
Catering establishments	1,066	539	1,112	530	1,289	599
Cinemas, theatres, etc.	187	58	175	50	188	51
Total	15,253	9,647	16,036	9,800	17,727	10,550
Foreign shipping	1,699	1,301	1,946	1,392	2,142	1,490
Other transportation	6,399	3,512	6,915	3,633	7,280	3,736
Total	8,098	4,813	8,861	5,025	9,422	5,226
Use of dwellings	4,431	2,149	5,059	2,249	5,538	2,349
Professions	2,122	839	2,290	845	2,550	880
Domestic services	426	148	396	125	355	100
Government services	11,515	4,701	13,186	4,890	15,065	5,275
Gross factor income	82,676	48,609	89,296	50,339	100,333	53,908
Plus indirect taxes	10,935	—	13,199	—	15,461	—
Less subsidies	1,002	—	1,327	—	1,432	—
Gross domestic product at market prices	92,609	53,065	101,168	54,939	114,362	58,808

AGRICULTURE. The soil of Denmark is greatly subdivided. In 1969 the total number of farms was 146,211. There were 47,705 small holdings (0·55–10 hectares), 93,246 medium-size holdings (10–60 hectares) and 5,260 holdings with more than 60 hectares.

The number of agricultural workers has declined from 145,419 in July 1959 to 37,964 in June 1969, while the index of production increased from 90 in 1959 to 105 in 1968 (1963–64 = 100).

In June 1969 the cultivated area was utilized as follows (in 1,000 hectares): Grain, 1,704; peas and beans, 26; root crops, 310; other crops, 87; green fodder and grass, 828; fallow, 2; total cultivated area, 2,957.

	Area (1,000 hectares)			Production (in 1,000 metric tons)		
Chief crops	1967	1968	1969	1967	1968	1969
Wheat	90	97	98	421	464	429
Rye	38	38	38	118	131	126
Barley	1,170	1,254	1,305	4,382	5,047	5,255
Oats	243	218	205	904	863	765
Mixed grain	97	78	58	328	280	200
Potatoes	38	35	34	857	866	663
Root crops	319	302	277	16,945	16,496	11,827

Livestock, 27 June 1969: Horses, 41,706; cattle, 2,999,694; pigs, 8,022,222; sheep, 89,847; poultry, 18,421,260.

Production (in 1,000 metric tons) in 1969 (and 1968): Milk, 4,872 (5,122);

butter, 144 (159); cheese, 105 (109); beef, 258 (265); pork and bacon, 742 (772); eggs, 90 (86).

In June 1969 farm tractors numbered 174,000 and harvester-threshers 41,200.

FISHERIES. The total value of the fish caught was (in 1m. kroner), 1950, 156; 1955, 252; 1960, 376; 1965, 650; 1967, 598; 1968, 715; 1969, 745. The fishing fleet in 1969 consisted of 7,972 motor boats and 3,967 sailing boats.

MANUFACTURES. Although only very few industrial raw materials are produced within the country, considerable industries have been developed.

According to the census of manufacturing, 2 June 1958, there were 65,700 establishments employing altogether 616,100 persons. The following are some data for the most important industries in 1967. The table covers establishments with more than 5 wage-earners.

Branch of industry	Number of wage-earners	Value of production (1,000 kroner)	Value added (1,000 kroner)
Mining and quarrying	1,062	123,448	97,294
Food industry	36,447	11,119,055	2,469,069
Beverage industry	9,337	1,135,964	740,555
Tobacco factories	5,966	663,748	329,132
Textile industry	17,099	1,761,205	788,342
Footwear and clothing industry	20,490	1,603,856	750,328
Wood industry (except furniture)	8,758	814,042	392,122
Manufacturing of furniture	9,284	852,555	441,541
Paper industry	8,472	1,102,501	491,825
Graphic industry	16,611	2,001,872	1,364,146
Leather products (except footwear)	1,679	182,184	75,562
Rubber industry	2,810	255,149	133,544
Chemical industry	11,080	3,140,080	1,391,607
Oil and coal products	1,426	1,417,322	342,255
Stone, clay and glass industry	18,667	1,905,660	1,222,865
Metal works	5,637	974,758	334,154
Manufacture of metal products	22,921	2 262,067	1,178,713
Engine works, including iron foundries	31,622	3,522,273	1,816,170
Manufacture of electrical machines, etc.	20,311	2,191,627	1,121,062
Transportation equipment	26,967	2,573,845	1,192,896
Other manufacturing industries	10,863	1,253,987	701,240
Total	287,514	40,857,198	17,374,422

POWER. Owing to the concentration of power production, the number of generating power stations has declined from 371 in 1949–50 to 55 in 1965–66, while the net power production (in 1m. kwh.) has risen from 1,689 in 1949–50 to 7,606 in 1965–66.

TOURISM. In 1969, 10·8m. foreigners visited Denmark, spending some 1,952m. kroner.

Statistics of Industrial Production. Danmarks Statistik, Copenhagen (annually)
Economic Survey of Denmark. Economic Secretariat. Copenhagen (annually)
Agriculture in Denmark. Agricultural Council of Denmark. Copenhagen and London, 1967
Agricultural Statistics 1900–1965. Vol. I: *Agricultural Area and Harvest and Utilization of Fertilizers.* Danmarks Statistik. Copenhagen, 1968
Danish Industry in Facts and Figures. Federation of Danish Industries. Copenhagen, 1968
Industrial Exports . . . since 1953. 5 vols. Danmarks Statistik. Copenhagen, 1963–65
Energy Supply of Denmark, 1900–58 and *1948–65.* Danmarks Statistik. Copenhagen, 1959, 1967
Technical and Economic Changes in Danish Farming, 1917–57. Institute of Farm Management. Copenhagen, 1959
Nash, E. F., and Attwood, E. A., *The Agricultural Policies of Britain and Denmark.* London, 1961
Ravnholt, H., *The Danish Co-operative Movement.* Copenhagen, 1950
Skrubbeltrang, F., *Agricultural Development and Rural Reform in Denmark.* Rome, 1953

COMMERCE. The following table shows the value, in 1,000 kroner, of general imports and exports (excluding precious metal) for calendar years:

	1964	1965	1966	1967	1968	1969
Imports	18,016,709	19,423,264	20,653,693	21,866,749	24,191,887	28 494 468
Exports	14,385,050	15,702,048	16,589,861	17,263,945	19,378,795	22,197,341

Imports and exports (in 1,000 kroner) for calendar years:

Leading commodities	1968		1969	
	Imports	Exports	Imports	Exports
Live animals, meat, etc.	24,424	4,320,195	26,188	4,557,252
Dairy products, eggs	42,973	1,434,219	39,155	1,403,062
Fish and fish preparations	198,387	772,364	201,102	809,662
Cereals and cereal preparations	311,756	190,051	197,710	291,550
Sugar and sugar preparations	41,650	116,900	49,942	90,544
Coffee, tea, cocoa, etc.	439,068	26,280	509,330	24,191
Feeding stuff for animals	508,148	387,125	538,140	416,475
Wood, lumber and cork	538,408	102,898	668,382	111,394
Textile, fibres, yarns, fabrics, etc.	1,580,576	536,114	1,895,137	648,050
Fuels, lubricants, etc.	2,723,566	212,766	2,823,712	274,176
Pharmaceutical products	241,718	334,743	286,153	377,541
Fertilizers, etc.	441,640	94,363	488,258	115,945
Metals, manufactures of metals	2,501,239	684,096	3,365,490	783,843
Machinery, electrical equipment, etc.	4,177,156	3,683,255	5,075,185	4,564,164
Transport equipment	2,575,778	861,554	2,942,847	1,182,929

Distribution of Danish foreign trade (in 1,000 kroner) according to countries of origin and destination, for calendar years:

Countries	Imports			Exports		
	1967	1968	1969	1967	1968	1969
Belgium	550,433	587,666	808,761	275,819	338,038	290,884
Finland	579,277	674,260	796,245	351,712	394,582	490,083
France	858,156	1,029,898	1,206,895	482,963	527,964	611,598
Germany (West)	4,196,488	4,562,628	5,437,901	2,076,510[1]	2,395,804[1]	2,832,325[1]
Norway	976,524	1,023,832	1,182,989	1,268,810	1,425,493	1,532,507
Sweden	3,160,138	3,626,570	4,428,782	2,395,381	2,959,352	3,574,704
Switzerland	541,441	646,916	787,985	407,469	463,800	522,077
UK	3,034,103	3,293,926	3,916,922	3,998,261	4,079,728	4,362,113
USA	1,880,573	2,053,691	2,194,470	1,219,381	1,577,337	1,853,189
Allied forces in W. Germany	—	—	—	135,979	146,690	129,931

[1] Excluding Allied forces in W. Germany.

Total trade (British Board of Trade returns) between Denmark (without the Faroe Islands) and UK (in £1,000 sterling):

	1966	1967	1968	1969	1970
Imports to UK	206,109	217,438	239,062	245,104	275,038
Exports from UK	133,913	143,650	160,934	191,897 }	220,208
Re-exports from UK	2,417	2,786	2,525	3,872 }	

SHIPPING. On 31 Dec. 1969 the Danish merchant fleet consisted of 3,220 vessels (above 20 GRT) of 3,486,641 GRT.

In 1969, 56,500 vessels of 28m. net tons entered the Danish ports, unloading 36m. metric tons and loading 14m. metric tons of cargo; traffic by passenger ships and ferries is not included.

ROADS. Denmark proper had (1 Jan. 1967), 5,989 km of streets, 8,688 km of roads and 46,953 km of by-ways, excluding private roads. Motor vehicles registered at 31 Dec. 1969 comprised 1,010,320 passenger cars, 253,558 lorries, 12,797 taxicabs (including 3,110 for private hire), 4,713 buses and 49,980 motor cycles.

RAILWAYS. There were in 1970 railways of a total length of 2,989 km open for traffic. Of this total, 2,352 km belong to the State. The revenue for 1968–69 amounted to 469m. kroner from passenger transport (including bus traffic) and 434m. kroner from freight.

AVIATION. On 1 Oct. 1950 the 3 Scandinavian airlines, Det Danske Luftfartsselskab, ABA and DNL, combined in Scandinavian Airlines System. In 1968 SAS flew 89·9m. km and carried 4,220,500 passengers.

SAS inaugurated its transpolar routes Copenhagen–Los Angeles on 15 Nov. 1954 and Copenhagen–Tokyo on 25 Feb. 1957, and its trans-Asian express route Copenhagen–Bangkok–Singapore *via* Tashkent on 4 Nov. 1967.

POST. There were, in 1969, 1,498 post offices. On 31 Dec. 1968 the length of telephone circuits of private companies was 5,142,118 km. On 31 Dec. 1969 there were 1,124,340 telephone subscribers. Postal revenues, 1968–69, 1,190m. kroner; expenditure, 1,069m. kroner.

Wireless licences, 31 March 1969 numbered 235,732; television licences (also including a wireless set), 1,227,613.

BANKING. On 31 Dec. 1969 the accounts of the National Bank balanced at 15,816m. kroner. The assets included 666m. kroner in gold bullion. The liabilities included 5,816m. kroner note issue, 50m. kroner general capital fund and 180m. kroner reserve fund.

On 31 March 1969 there were 373 savings banks, with 4·92m. accounts and deposits of 15,611m. kroner.

On 31 Dec. 1969 there were 108 other banks for commercial, agricultural and industrial purposes; their deposits amounted to 31,893m. kroner; their advances to 29,644m. kroner.

WEIGHTS AND MEASURES. The use of the metric system of weights and measures has been obligatory in Denmark since 1 April 1912.

THE FAROE ISLANDS
Færøerne

Area, 1,399 sq. km (540 sq. miles); population (31 Dec. 1969), 38,527. The main industries are fishery and agriculture. Exports, mainly fresh, frozen and salted fish and dried cod, amounted to 182,154 kroner in 1969; imports to 234,491 kroner.

The parliament (*Lagting*), elected on 8 Nov. 1966, consists of 26 members: 7 Social Democrats, 6 Samband Party, 6 Folkeflok, 1 Progressive Party, 1 Home Rule Party, 5 Republicans.

From 1 Jan. 1968 the Faroe Islands were included in EFTA at their own request.

Total trade with UK (British Board of Trade returns, in £1,000 sterling):

	1965	1966	1967	1968	1969	1970
Imports to UK	700	769	805	1,383	1,014	1,221
Exports from UK	700	788	664	1,315	753 }	941
Re-exports from UK	49	56	43	57	56 }	

Williamson, K., *The Atlantic Islands: A Study of the Faroe Life and Scene.* London, 1958
Faroes in Figures. Thorshavn, annual, from 1956

GREENLAND
Grønland

Area, 2,175,600 sq. km (840,000 sq. miles), made up of 1,833,900 sq. km of ice cap and 341,700 sq. km of ice-free land. The population, 31 Dec. 1968, numbered 45,639; West Greenland, 41,884; East Greenland, 3,043; North Greenland (Thule), 712. Of the total, 7,261 were born outside Greenland.

On 5 June 1953 Greenland became an integral part of the Danish Realm with the same rights as other counties in Denmark and with a democratically elected council (*landsråd*).

A Danish–American agreement for the common defence of Greenland was signed on 27 April 1951.

Until the beginning of this century, the hunting of land and sea mammals, especially seals, was the main occupation of the population; now fishing is most important.

Some coal resources are still exploited, but it is planned to give up this production in 1972. A deposit of the valuable mineral cryolite is situated at Ivigtut. In 1948 deposits of lead and zinc were discovered in East Greenland. A Danish company 'Nordisk Mineselskab A/S' (The Northern Mining Company, Ltd) has been granted a concession for further exploitation, and utilization of the ore deposits found, some 1·2m. tons, began in 1956. However, production was discontinued in 1962. The interest of oil and mining companies in obtaining licences and concessions in and offshore Greenland has grown considerably during the last years, but still no concessions have been granted for exploitation, apart from the above mentioned.

Imports (c.i.f. Greenland) (in 1,000 kroner): 1965, 234,904; 1966, 269,133; 1967, 318,053; 1968, 358,056. Exports (f.o.b. Greenland) (in 1,000 kroner): 1965, 89,958; 1966, 102,704; 1967, 91,887; 1968, 87,576. Trade is mainly with Denmark.

Total trade with UK (British Board of Trade returns, in £1,000 sterling):

	1965	1966	1967	1968	1969	1970
Imports to UK	292	105	203	118	1	96
Exports from UK	121	175	74	257	974 ⎫	80
Re-exports from UK	3	—	—	—	— ⎭	

Greenland. R. Danish Ministry for Foreign Affairs. 3rd ed. Copenhagen, 1961
Meddelelser om Grønland. Ed. Kommissionen for videnskabelige undersøgelser i Grønland. Copenhagen, 1897 ff.
Birket-Smith, K. (ed.), *Grønlandsbogen.* 2 vols. Copenhagen, 1950
Bøggild, O. B., *The Mineralogy of Greenland.* Copenhagen, 1953
Boyd, L. A., and others, *The Coast of North-east Greenland.* New York, 1948
Williamson, G., *Changing Greenland.* London, 1953

DIPLOMATIC REPRESENTATIVES

Denmark maintains embassies in:

Afghánistán
Albania
Algeria
Argentina
Australia
Austria
Belgium
Bolivia
Brazil
Bulgaria
Burma
Cambodia
Canada
Ceylon
Chile
China
Colombia
Congo (K.)
Costa Rica
Cuba
Czechoslovakia
Dominican Republic
Ecuador
El Salvador
Ethiopia
Finland

France
Germany (West)
Ghana
Greece
Guatemala
Guinea
Haiti
Honduras
Hungary
Iceland
India
Indonesia
Iran
Iraq
Irish Republic
Israel
Italy
Ivory Coast
Japan
Jordan
Kenya
Korea (South)
Kuwait
Lebanon (also for Cyprus)
Liberia

Libya
Luxembourg
Malawi
Malaysia
Malta
Mexico
Mongolia
Morocco
Nepál
Netherlands
New Zealand
Nicaragua
Nigeria
Norway
Pakistan
Panama
Paraguay
Peru
Philippines
Poland
Portugal
Romania
Saudi Arabia
Senegal
Singapore
Spain

Sudan	Togo	USA
Sweden	Tunisia	Upper Volta
Switzerland	Turkey	Uruguay
Syria	Uganda	Venezuela
Tanzania	USSR	Yugoslavia
Thailand (legation for	UAR	Zambia
Laos and Sth. Vietnam)	UK	

OF DENMARK IN GREAT BRITAIN (29 Pont St., SW1)

Ambassador: Erling Kristiansen (accredited 20 May 1964).
Minister-Counsellors: Hans Kühne; Sven Aage Nielsen (*Economic and Consular*).
First Secretaries: Thomas Rechnagel; C. U. Haxthausen; C. Sode Mogensen. *Press and Cultural Counsellor:* Harry E. Agerbak. *Scientific Attaché:* Kristian Kristiansen. *Agricultural Counsellor:* Mogens Munch. *Commercial Counsellor:* N. E. Buch-Hansen. *Fisheries Attaché:* J. C. Bogstad. *Service Attaché:* HRH Lieut.-Col. Prince Georg of Denmark, CVO.

There are consular representatives at all important centres, including Aberdeen, Belfast, Birmingham, Bristol, Cardiff, Edinburgh, Glasgow, Hull, Liverpool, London, Manchester, Newcastle upon Tyne, Portsmouth and Southampton.

OF GREAT BRITAIN IN DENMARK

Ambassador: Andre Stark.
Counsellors: G. W. Marshall, MBE, BEM (*Commercial*), Kenneth R. C. Pridham (*Head of Chancery*).
First Secretaries: Miss M. W. Lloyd (*Information*); C. J. Hanbury (*Consul*); G. W. Hayward; D. Mellor (*Labour*); L. P. Hamilton (*Agriculture*).
Service Attaché: Cdr T. Firth (*Defence, Navy and Air*).

There are consular representatives at Aabenraa, Aalborg, Aarhus, Copenhagen, Esbjerg, Odense and at Thorshavn and Klaksvig (Faroe Islands).

OF DENMARK IN THE USA (3200 Whitehaven St., NW, Washington, D.C., 20008)

Ambassador: Torben Rønne.
Minister-Counsellors: Erik Hange *Economic*); Hans J. Christensen. *Secretaries:* K. O. Kapel; Ib. R. Andreasen. *Counsellors:* Anker K. A. Hansen (*Scientific*); Carlo Christensen (*Cultural*); F. K. Damgaard (*Agricultural*). *Service Attaché:* Capt. Bendt Hjorth Jensen.

OF THE USA IN DENMARK

Ambassador: Guildford Dudley, Jr.
Deputy Chief of Mission: Byron E. Blankinship (*Consul-General*). *Heads of Sections:* Emery P. Smith (*Political*); Wendell W. Woodbury (*Economic*); Robert A. Brown (*Commercial*); Raymond M. Bailey (*Consular*); Edward B. Fenstermacher (*Administrative*); Brooks McClure (*USIA*); Ernest E. Goodman (*Press*); William T. Crocker (*Culture*). *Service Attachés:* Capt. Harold E. Rice (*Defence and Navy*), Col. Robert F. Ingman (*Air*), Col. Orse Brewer, Jr (*Army*).

BOOKS OF REFERENCE

STATISTICAL INFORMATION. Danmarks Statistik (Frederiksholms Kanal 27, Copenhagen K.) was founded in 1849 and reorganized in 1966 as an independent institution; it is administratively placed under the Minister of Economic Affairs. *Chief:* N. V. Shak-Nielsen. Its main publications are: *Statistik Årbog* (Statistical Yearbook). From 1896: *Statistiske Efterretninger* (Statistical News). From 1909; *Statistiske Meddelelser* (Statistical Reports). From 1852; *Handelsstatistiske Meddelelser* (Reports on Foreign Trade). From 1910; *Statistiske Tabelværker* (Statistical Tables). From 1850; *Statistiske Undersøgelser* (Statistical Inquiries). From 1958.

Ministry of Foreign Affairs, *Danish Foreign Office Journal. Commercial and General Review.— Denmark.* 1961.—*Economic Survey of Denmark* (annual).—*Facts about Denmark.* 1959.— Hæstrup, J., *From Occupied to Ally: the Danish Resistance Movement.* 1963

Atlas over Danmark. R. Danish Geog. Society. Copenhagen, 1963
Bibliografi over Danmarks Offentlige Publikationer. Institut for International Udveksling, Copenhagen. Annual
Dania polyglotta. Annual Bibliography of Books . . . in foreign languages printed in Denmark. State Library, Copenhagen. Annual
Kongelig Dansk Hof og Statskalender. København. Annual
Brynildsen, F., *A Dictionary of the English and Dano-Norwegian Languages.* 2 vols. Copenhagen, 1902–07
Danstrup, J., *History of Denmark.* 2nd ed. Copenhagen, 1949
Frils, H. (ed.), *Scandinavia Between East and West.* Cornell Univ. Press, Ithaca, 1950
Gedde, K., *This is Denmark.* Copenhagen, 1948
Krabbe, L., *Histoire de Danemark.* Copenhagen and Paris, 1950
Lauring, P., *A History of Denmark.* Copenhagen, 1960
Nielsen, B. K., *Engelsk–Dansk Ordbog.* Copenhagen, 1964
Outze, B. (ed.), *Denmark During the German Occupation.* Copenhagen, 1946
Trap, J. P., *Kongeriget Danmark.* 5th ed. 11 vols. Copenhagen, 1953 ff.
Vinterberg, H., and Bodelsen, C. A., *Dansk-engelsk ordbog.* Copenhagen, 1966

NATIONAL LIBRARY. Det Kongelige Bibliotek, Copenhagen. *Librarian:* P. Birkelund.

DOMINICAN REPUBLIC
República Dominicana

HISTORY. On 5 Dec. 1492 Columbus discovered the island of Santo Domingo, which he called La Española; for a time it was called Hispaniola. The city of Santo Domingo, founded by his brother, Bartholomew, in 1496, is the oldest city in the Americas. The western third of the island—now the Republic of Haiti—was later occupied and colonized by the French, to whom the Spanish colony of Santo Domingo was also ceded in 1795. In 1808 the Dominican population, under the command of Gen. Juan Sánchez Ramirez, routed an important French military force commanded by Gen. Ferrand, at the famous battle of Palo Hincado. This battle was the beginning of the end for French rule in Santo Domingo and culminated in the successful siege of the capital. Eventually, with the aid of a British naval squadron, the French were forced to capitulate and the colony returned again to Spanish rule, from which it declared its independence in 1821. It was invaded and held by the Haitians from 1822 to 1844, when they were expelled, and the Dominican Republic was founded and a constitution adopted. Great Britain, in 1850, was the first country to recognize the Dominican Republic. The country was occupied by American Marines from 1916 until 1924. In 1936 the name of the capital city was changed from Santo Domingo to Ciudad Trujillo; and back again in 1961.

National flag: Blue, red; quartered by a white cross.
National anthem: Quisqueyanos valientes, alzemos (words by E. Prud'homme; tune by J. Reyes, 1883).

CONSTITUTION AND GOVERNMENT. A new constitution was promulgated on 28 Nov. 1966.

The President is elected for 4 years, by direct vote. In case of death, resignation or disability, he is succeeded by the Vice-president. There are 12 secretaries of state, a judicial adviser with secretary-of-state rank and 2 ministers without portfolio in charge of departments.

General elections, under a revised constitution at which women voted for the first time, were held on 16 May 1942; 2 women were elected to the chamber and 1 to the senate. Citizens are entitled to vote at the age of 18, or less when married.

Recent Presidents have been: Gen. Rafael Leonidas Trujillo Molina, 1930–38, 1942–52 (assassinated 30 May 1961); Héctor Bienvenido Trujillo Molina, 1952–60; Dr Joaquín Balaguer, 4 Aug. 1960–62; Lic. Rafael Bonnelly, 18 Jan. 1962; Professor Juan Bosch, 27 Feb.–25 Sept. 1963 (deposed); Dr Héctor García Godoy, 3 Sept. 1965–1 July 1966.

President: Joaquín Balaguer (elected 1966 and re-elected 1970).
Foreign Minister: Dr Jaime Manuel Fernandez.

The country's first free elections for nearly 40 years were held in Dec. 1962 when Juan Bosch was elected President with a clear majority, after which a new Constitution was approved on 29 April 1963. Bosch was overthrown by a military *coup d'état* in Sept. 1963 and the declared aim of the Constitutionalist side in the Civil War of April–Sept. 1965 was the restoration of Bosch as President and a return to the 1963 Constitution.

On 30 April 1965 USA landed a force of 23,000 Marines and Army, later assisted by Organization of American States contributions. The capital remained divided between these forces and various rival factions of nationals. A provisional government was eventually installed on 3 Sept. 1965.

Until elections on 1 June 1966 there was government by decree. The voting on this date was 754,409 votes for Dr Joaquín Balaguer (Reformist Party) against 517,784 for Juan Bosch (Revolutionary Party).

AREA AND POPULATION. The Dominican Republic occupies the eastern portion (about two-thirds) of the island of Hispaniola, Quisqueya or Santo Domingo, the western division forming the Republic of Haiti. It consists of the National District (containing the capital, Santo Domingo), and 25 provinces. Area is 48,442 sq. km (18,700 sq. miles) with 870 miles of coastline, 193 miles of frontier line with Haiti (marked out in 1936).

The populations of the 25 provinces (with density per sq. km) at the 1960 census were:

La Altagracia	141,797	(37·88)	Salcedo	93,625	(189·72)
Azua	102,457	(42·16)	Samaná	60,682	(61·38)
Bahoruco	71,156	(51·69)	Sánchez Ramírez	126,933	(108·09)
Barahona	108,923	(43·09)	San Cristóbal	338,712	(90·48)
Dajabón	55,911	(62·85)	San Juan	201,068	(56·46)
Duarte	217,889	(168·60)	San Pedro de Macorís	93,984	(80·62)
Espaillat	158,806	(162·98)	San Rafael	58,915	(32·95)
Independencia	38,022	(20·43)	Santiago	391,006	(125·66)
María Trinidad Sánchez	115,724	(88·32)	Santiago Rodríguez	54,563	(53·48)
Montecristi	81,189	(40·82)	El Seibo	156,136	(52·23)
Pedernales	12,067	(11·94)	Valverde	80,440	(138·70)
Peravia	144,875	(89·33)	La Vega	336,288	(97·71)
Puerto Plata	222,615	(110·35)			

Census population of 1964 was 3,451,700; estimate, 1969, 4,174,490.

Population of the principal municipalities (1969): National District (including Santo Domingo), 822,862; Santiago de los Caballeros, 351,656; San Cristóbal, 360,247; La Vega, 295.273; La Romana, 80,873; Azua, 102,407; Bahoruco, 66,223; Barahona, 102,481; Dajabón, 61,590; Duarte,213,920; Espaillat,141,356; Independencia, 35,208; María Trinidad Sánchez, 135,081; Montecristi, 74,966; Peravia, 134,860; Puerto Plata, 192,170; Salcedo, 93,669; Sánchez Ramírez, 145,276; Santiago Rodríguez, 48,367; El Seibo, 144,517; Valverde, 99,424.

The population is partly of Spanish descent, but is mainly composed of a mixed race of European and African blood. The 1950 census showed 600,994 whites, 245,032 Negroes, 1,289,285 of mixed blood and 561 of other races; 2,093,195 spoke Spanish, 25,405 French and 12,140 English. Tax-exempt land has been set aside for the settlement of European refugees, both Jewish and non-Jewish, who are guaranteed full civic rights.

RELIGION. The religion of the state is Roman Catholic; other forms of religion are permitted. There is a papal nuncio as well as an archbishop, known as the Primate of the Indies.

EDUCATION. Primary instruction (4,360 schools) is free and obligatory for children between 7 and 14 years of age; there are also secondary (53), normal, vocational and special schools, all of which (5,369 in 1962) were either wholly maintained by the state or state-aided; teachers numbered 11,249 and pupils

542,579. The campaign against adult illiteracy dates from 1941, but in 1964 about 65% of the population were still illiterate.

The University of Santo Domingo (founded 1538) had (1964) 11 schools with 5,503 students and 523 teachers.

CINEMAS (1966). Cinemas numbered 73, with seating capacity of 43,427.

NEWSPAPERS (1970). There were 7 daily newspapers.

WELFARE. In 1964, 78 towns had complete waterworks. There were, in 1962, 30 hospitals and Social Security clinics (with 1,385 beds) and 108 private clinics (with 1,776 beds).

JUSTICE. The judicial power resides in the Supreme Court of Justice, the courts of appeal, the courts of first instance, the communal courts and other tribunals created by special laws, such as the land courts. The Supreme Court consists of a president and 8 judges chosen by the Senate, and the procurator-general, appointed by the executive; it supervises the lower courts. Each province forms a judicial district, as does the *Distrito Nacional*, and each has its own procurator fiscal and court of first instance; these districts are subdivided, in all, into 72 municipalities and 18 municipal districts, each with one or more local justices. The death penalty was abolished in 1924, but is imposed in war-time for treason or espionage.

FINANCE. Currency. In Oct. 1947 the *peso oro*, equal to the USA dollar, was formally made the unit of currency, replacing the USA gold dollar, which had been the standard since 1 July 1897. On 31 July 1969 the Banco Central held gold and foreign exchange worth US$28m.

There are silver coins for 50, 25 and 10 centavos, a copper–nickel 5-centavo piece and a copper 1-centavo piece.

Budget. The receipts and disbursements for calendar years, in 1m. Dominican gold pesos (RD$), equal to the US$, were:

	1964	1965	1966	1967	1968[1]	1969[1]
Revenue	206·2	148·3	160·0	173·4	186·8	186·7
Expenditure	209·0	139·8	253·0	198·1	206·8	230·3

[1] Estimated.

Income tax, established in 1949, was replaced in 1950 by an identity-card tax, known as the 'cédula tax', but re-introduced in 1962.

DEFENCE. The armed forces are under the command of the President of the Republic, acting through the Secretary of State for the Armed Forces.

The total defence budget for 1966 is RD$36·1m.

Army. The Army has a strength of about 12,000 all ranks. It is organized in 4 infantry brigades, 1 artillery battalion and 1 anti-aircraft battalion, and has some light tanks and armoured cars.

Navy. The Navy includes 1 destroyer, 2 frigates, the Presidential Yacht (ex-frigate), 5 corvettes, 2 minesweepers, 3 patrol vessels, 3 landing craft, 3 coast-guard vessels, 3 motor launches, 3 oilers, 2 auxiliaries, 5 tugs. Personnel: 4,000 officers and men.

Air Force. The Air Force, with HQ at San Isidoro, has 2 operational squadrons, each with perhaps 20 first-line aircraft. One is equipped with F-51D Mustang piston-engined interceptors; the other with jet-powered Vampire Mk. 1 and Mk. 50 fighter-bombers and 7 B-26 piston-engined light bombers. There are also transport (C-45, C-46, etc.) and training units. Total strength is about 3,500 personnel and 110 aircraft.

AGRICULTURE. Agriculture is the chief source of wealth, sugar cultivation being the principal industry. Of the total area, 9,900 sq. miles are cultivable, and about 3,700 are under cultivation. 50% is under subsistence farming—small-holdings each of 15 *tareas* (2½ acres) or less.

Livestock in 1968: 804,000 cattle, 483,000 pigs, 25,000 sheep, 282,000 horses, mules and asses, 98,000 goats.

The largest sugar estates are in the south-eastern part of the republic. Sugar production, 1964, was 793,058 metric tons, of which 359,681 tons were sold to USA; 1965 production, 580,193 metric tons. Two companies (one American-owned, the other expropriated after the downfall of the Trujillo family) produce four-fifths of the total, but in all there are 16 sugar 'centrals'.

Coffee is exported mainly to USA. Output, 1968–69, 540,000 bags of 60 kg. Production of rice for home consumption and export is fostered; output, 1965, 144,000 metric tons. Cocoa is the second principal crop and covers 2m. *tareas* (340,000 acres); output in 1965, 40,000 metric tons. Other principal exports are leaf tobacco and molasses (279,846,080 litres in 1964). There are useful crops of maize (1965: 106,000 metric tons) and groundnuts (1965: 52,000 metric tons) for local consumption. Scientific growing of bananas (1965: 450,000 tons) and of tobacco (1965: 35,000 tons) is progressing.

MINING. The Aluminum Company of America sent its first shipment of bauxite for smelting, to Texas, on 13 Jan. 1959. Output in 1968 was 1,206,800 short tons. Silver and platinum have been found, and near Neiba there are several hills of rock salt (production 1967, 18,000 metric tons). Copper production (1969) 1,200 metric tons

INDUSTRY. In 1967, 1,230 industrial establishments employed 107,595 men and women, who earned RD$79·6m. Output was valued at RD$423·5m. Important manufactures are textiles, cement, glass bottles, paper and matches.

POWER. The electricity production capacity in 1968 was 192,597 kw.

COMMERCE. Total imports and exports in RD$1m. (equal to US$1m):

	1962	1963	1964	1965	1966	1968
Imports	160·3	192·4	91·7	160·8	174·7	180·0
Exports	174·1	179·4	125·5	136·7	156·2	165·0

Exports (in RD$1m.) in 1967 included: Sugar, 81·8; coffee, 17; fruit, 1·6; cacao, 11·6; tobacco, 10·3.

In 1967 the chief imports included (in RD$1m.): Machinery, 23·9; iron and steel, 11; foodstuffs, 34·3; petroleum and fuel oils, 12·9; paper products, 7·6; chemicals and pharmaceuticals, 17·9; silk products, 2·8; rubber products, 2·6.

In 1967 exports to USA were RD$133·1m. (1966: RD$119·2m.) and imports from USA were RD$90·1m. (1966: RD$74·2m.). The Netherlands, Canada, Italy, West Germany, Japan and Puerto Rico are also important trading partners.

Total trade between the Dominican Republic and UK (in £1,000 sterling, British Board of Trade returns):

	1966	1967	1968	1969	1970
Imports to UK	73	784	59	685	1,144
Exports from UK	2,184	2,168	2,621	2,835 }	3,552
Re-exports from UK	14	30	28	26 }	

SHIPPING. Santo Domingo is the leading port; Puerto Plata ranks next. In 1968, 1,631 vessels of 3,503,300 net tons entered the ports to discharge 4,731,000 tons of cargo.

ROADS. Three main trunk highways, with branches, extend from Santo Domingo eastward to Higuey (106 miles), northward to Santiago and Montecristi and Dajabón (204 miles) and westward to San Juan (128 miles) and Elías Piña on the Haitian border (161 miles). At Elías Piña the road joins the Haitian road to

Port-au-Prince. Total highway system in 1963 was 4,250 km first- and 2,000 km second-class roads; there were 647 bridges. Road transport is the chief means of travel. There were 32,103 motor vehicles in 1968.

RAILWAYS. There were, in 1963, 1,444 km of track, mainly on sugar estates. The Dominican Government Railway (220 km) closed in 1969.

AVIATION. The country is reached from the American continent and the Caribbean islands by 3 international airlines. Two local aviation companies provide interior services and connect Santo Domingo with San Juan in Puerto Rico, Curaçao, Aruba and Miami.

In 1961 internal traffic accounted for 4,145 passengers; external (in 1965) for 32,000.

POST. Number of post offices, 1960, 155; telephone or telegraph offices, 76; radio-telegraph offices, 36; telephone instruments (1969), 35,735, of which 25,441 in Santo Domingo. The telephone system is mainly operated by an American company. The telegraph has a total length of about 5,000 km, privately owned; they have been leased to All-America Cables, Inc., which also controls submarine cables connecting, in the north, Puerto Plata with Puerto Rico and New York, and in the south, Santo Domingo with Puerto Rico, Cuba and Curaçao.

There are 21 broadcasting stations in Santo Domingo, 13 in Santiago and 11 other towns; this includes the 2 government stations. There are 2 television stations, both in Santo Domingo.

BANKING. On 24 Oct. 1941 a law was passed for the creation of a Dominican commercial bank (government controlled) to be known as the Banco de Reservas de la República Dominicana, with a capital of RD$1m., now increased to RD$20m. This bank, starting with branches purchased from the National City Bank of New York, opened for business on 27 Oct. 1941 and now has 11 branches covering the country. It is authorized to perform all customary banking transactions. On 31 Oct. 1966 its assets and liabilities totalled RD$142,126,322. There are 4 foreign banks—the Royal Bank of Canada with 5 branches, the Bank of Nova Scotia, the First National City Bank of New York and the Chase Manhattan Bank. An agricultural and mortgage bank, with paid-up capital of RD$500,000, was established in 1945; in 1950 its capital was increased to RD$5m.; in 1952 steps were begun to raise it to cover a 5-year programme of agricultural expansion; it stood at RD$100m. in Nov. 1962.

In 1947 the Central Bank of the Dominican Republic was launched. Chief liability was note circulation, chiefly bank-notes of 1, 5 and 10 pesos (RD$104·5m. in 1966); total assets and liabilities were RD$215·8m. The net reserve of foreign exchange was US$32m. at 31 Aug. 1966.

A new Banco Popular Dominicano, with an authorized capital of RD$5m., opened in Jan. 1964.

WEIGHTS AND MEASURES. The metric system was nominally adopted on 1 Aug. 1913, but English and Spanish units have remained in common use in ordinary commercial transactions; on 17 Sept. 1954 a more drastic law requiring the decimal metric system was passed.

DIPLOMATIC REPRESENTATIVES

The Dominican Republic maintains embassies in:

Argentina	Chile	France
Austria	China (Taiwan)	Germany (West)
Belgium	Colombia	Guatemala
Brazil	Ecuador	Haiti
Canada	El Salvador	Israel

Italy	Panama	Uruguay
Japan	Peru	USA
Mexico	Spain	Vatican
Netherlands	Turkey	Venezuela
Nicaragua	UK	

The Dominican Republic maintains legations in:

Denmark	Lebanon	Portugal
Greece	Luxembourg	Sweden
Iran	Norway	Switzerland

OF THE DOMINICAN REPUBLIC IN GREAT BRITAIN
(62 Prince's Gate, SW7)

Ambassador: Porfirio Herrera Baéz (accredited 9 Feb. 1967); also Ambassador to Austria.

Military Attaché: (Vacant).

There are consular representatives at Belfast, Birmingham, Cardiff, Edinburgh, Glasgow, Grimsby, Liverpool, London, Manchester, Nottingham, Plymouth, and Southampton.

OF GREAT BRITAIN IN THE DOMINICAN REPUBLIC

Ambassador and Consul-General: L. Boas, OBE.
First Secretary: G. E. Cheeseman (*Consul*).

There are consular representatives in Puerto Plata and San Pedro de Macorís.

OF THE DOMINICAN REPUBLIC IN THE USA (1715–22nd St., NW, Washington, D.C., 20008).

Ambassador: Dr S. Salvador Ortiz.
Minister-Counsellor: Marco A. De Peña. *Counsellor:* Dario Suro (*Cultural*).
First Secretary: Emilia Mota. *Service Attaché:* Col. Renato Malagen-Montesano (*Air*).

OF THE USA IN THE DOMINICAN REPUBLIC

Ambassador: Francis E. Meloy, Jr.
Deputy Head of Mission: John J. Crowley, Jr. *Heads of Sections:* James C. Haahr (*Political*); Maurice F. W. Taylor (*Economic*); John F. Troy (*Commercial*); Joaquin A. Bazan, Jr (*Labour*); Allan F. McLean, Jr (*Consular*); Earl R. Michalka (*Administrative*); Alexander Fifer (*AID*). *Service Attachés:* Col. Joseph W. Weyrick (*Army*), Lieut.-Cdr Charles R. Carpenter (*Navy*), Lieut.-Col. Harry J. Koepp (*Air*).

There is a Consul at Santiago de los Caballeros and consular agents at La Romana and Manzanillo.

BOOKS OF REFERENCE

Anuario estadístico de la República Dominicana, 1944–45. Ciudad Trujillo. 1949. This has been succeeded by separate annual reports covering foreign trade, vital statistics, banking, insurance, housing and communications.
Dirección General de Estadística. *21 años de estadísticas dominicanas 1936–1956.* Ciudad Trujillo, 1957

ECUADOR
República del Ecuador

HISTORY. The Spaniards under Francisco Pizarro founded a colony after their victory at Cajamarca (16 Nov. 1532). Their rule was first challenged by the rising of 10 Aug. 1809. Marshal Sucre defeated the Spaniards at Pichincha in 1821, and in 1822 Bolívar persuaded the new republic to join the federation of Gran Colombia. The Presidency of Quito became the Republic of Ecuador by amicable secession 13 May 1830.

CONSTITUTION AND GOVERNMENT. Following a miltary *coup d'état* on 11 July 1963, the constitution of 1945 was suspended. The military junta was overthrown on 31 March 1966. President Yerovi appointed a civilian cabinet and civilian governors of provinces.

A Constituent Assembly was elected on 16 Oct. 1966. It elected Dr Arosemena Gómez as interim president and drafted a new constitution which was published on 25 May 1967. Elections for the Presidency and Congress were held on 2 June 1968.

On 22 June 1970 President José Maria Velasco Ibarra assumed dictatorial powers, following months of strife between student and security forces. He announced that the 1967 Constitution was abolished in favour of that drafted in 1946, which provided strong powers for executive government. President Ibarra said that he would retain supreme powers until the legal end of his term of office in 1972.

National flag: Yellow (2), blue (1), red (1), horizontal.

National anthem: Salve, on patria! (words by J. L. Mera; tune by A. Neumann, 1866).

The following is a list of the presidents and provisional executives since 1940, with the date on which they took office:

Carlos Alberto Arroyo del Rio, elected 12 Jan. 1940; resigned 30 May 1944.
Dr José María Velasco Ibarra, elected by Constituent Assembly, Aug. 1944; re-elected 11 Aug. 1946, but deposed 24 Aug. 1947.
Col. Carlos Mancheno, seized power 24 Aug. 1947; deposed 3 Sept. 1947.
Mariano Suárez Veintimilla (Vice-President), 3–15 Sept. 1947.
Carlos Julio Arosemena Tola (provisional) 15 Sept. 1947–31 Aug. 1948.
Galo Plaza Lasso, 1 Sept. 1948–31 Aug. 1952.

Dr José María Velasco Ibarra, 1 Sept. 1952–31 Aug. 1956.
Dr Camilo Ponce Enríquez, 1 Sept. 1956–31 Aug. 1960.
Dr José María Velasco Ibarra, 1 Sept. 1960–8 Nov. 1961 (withdrew).
Dr Carlos Julio Arosemena Monroy, 8 Nov. 1961–11 July 1963 (deposed).
Military Junta, 11 July 1963–31 March 1966.
Clemente Yerovi Indaburu, 31 March–16 Nov. 1966 (interim).
Dr Otto Arosemena Gómez. 17 Nov. 1966–1 Sept. 1968.
Dr José María Velasco Ibarra, 1 Sept. 1968–

Minister for Foreign Affairs: Lic. Rogelio Valdiviesco Eguiguren.

LOCAL GOVERNMENT. The country is divided politically into 20 provinces; 4 of them comprise the 'Región Oriental' and one the Archipelago of Galápagos, officially called 'Colón', situated in the Pacific Ocean about 600 miles to the west of Ecuador and comprising 15 islands. The provinces are administered by governors, appointed by the Government; their sub-divisions, or cantons, by political chiefs and elected cantonal councillors; and the parishes by political lieutenants. The Galápagos Archipelago is administered by the Ministry of National Defence.

AREA AND POPULATION. Ecuador is bounded on the north by Colombia, on the east and south by Peru, on the west by the Pacific Ocean. The frontier with Peru has long been a source of dispute between the two countries. The latest delimitation of it was in the treaty of Rio, 29 Jan. 1942, when, after being invaded by Peru, Ecuador ceded the latter over half her Amazonian territories. Ecuador unilaterally denounced this treaty in Sept. 1961. *See* map in THE STATESMAN'S YEAR-BOOK, 1942. No definite figure of the area of the country can yet be given, as a portion of the frontier has not been delimited. One estimate shows 455,454 sq. km, including the Archipelago of Colón (the Galápagos Islands) with 7,430 sq. km. The United Nations Statistical Office excludes the 'Región Oriental' and the Galápagos Islands and gives the settled portion of Ecuador as 270,670 sq. km (104,505 sq. miles).

Ecuador has 3 distinct zones: the *Sierra* or uplands of the Andes, consisting of high mountain ridges with valleys, with 2·57m. of the population and high-priced farming land; the *Costa*, the coastal plain between the Andes and the Pacific, with 2·02m., whose permanent plantations furnish bananas, cacao, coffee, sugar-cane and many other crops; the *Oriente*, the upper Amazon basin on the east, consisting of tropical jungles threaded by large rivers.

The population is predominantly of Amerindians, with small proportions of people of European or African descent. The official language is Spanish. The Amerindians of the highlands speak mainly the Quechua language; in the Oriental Region various tribes have languages of their own.

Ecuador's first census of population was taken on 29 Nov. 1950; it showed a total of 3,202,757 (1,594,803 males and 1,607,954 females). The census was hampered by strong opposition from the Indian villages. The working population was given as 1,236,590, of which two-thirds were agricultural. Estimated population in 1967, 5,585,400.

The population (estimate at 25 Nov. 1967) was distributed by provinces (capitals in brackets):

Provinces	Area (sq. km)	Population 1967
Azuay (Cuenca)	7,799	305,400
Bolívar (Guaranda)	3,216	165,100
Cañar (Azogues)	2,677	128,600
Carchi (Tulcán)	3,582	111,600
Chimborazo (Riobamba)	6,161	342,300
Cotopaxi (Latacunga)	4,614	223,600
El Oro (Machala)	7,451	208,700
Esmeraldas (Esmeraldas)	15,866	157,000
Guayas (Guayaquil)	21,259	1,238,800
Imbabura (Ibarra)	4,903	200,900
Loja (Loja)	28,900	343,300
Los Ríos (Babahoyo)	5,937	314,800
Manabí (Portoviejo)	18,963	743,200
Pichincha (Quito)	16,438	749,300
Tungurahua (Ambato)	3,204	245,600
Napo (Tena)		33,000
Pastaza (Puyo)		18,600
Morona-Santiago (Macas)	296,390	34,700
Zamora-Chinchipe (Zamora)		15,600
Galápagos Islands (San Cristobal)	7,844	3,100
Totals	455,454	5,585,400

There are 97 cantons, 169 urban parishes and 626 rural parishes. The chief towns (population estimate, 1966) are the capital, Quito (462,863), Guayaquil (680,209), Cuenca (71,484), Ríobamba (61,393), Ambato (89,541), Portoviejo (96,651).

Vital statistics for calendar years: Births, (1964), 219,137, (1965) 226,436, (1966) 220,930; deaths, (1964) 58,989, (1965) 60,202, (1966) 59,618,

RELIGION. The state recognizes no religion and grants freedom of worship to all. Civil registration of births, deaths and marriages is obligatory. Divorce is permitted. Illegitimate children have the same rights as legitimate ones with respect to education and inheritance.

The Catholic Church has 1 cardinal, 3 archbishops and 18 bishops. A modus vivendi was concluded with the Holy See on 24 July 1937, governing the relations between the Catholic Church and the state. Protestants numbered 19,200 in 1966.

EDUCATION. Primary education is free and in principle obligatory. Private schools, both primary and secondary, are under some state supervision. There were (1966–67) 6,714 primary schools with 800,507 pupils; 558 secondary schools with 131,569 pupils and 7 universities with 16,047 students. The 1950 census showed that 40% of those over 10 years of age were illiterate. A campaign against adult illiteracy was started in 1944. An intensive primary-school building-programme is in hand.

CINEMAS (1962). Cinemas numbered about 110 with total seating capacity of 22,000.

NEWSPAPERS (1968). There were 24 daily newspapers with an aggregate daily circulation of 195,000; 7 papers in Quito and Guayaquil have the bulk of the circulation.

SOCIAL WELFARE. From 1 May 1964 social benefits are extended to professional men, artisans and domestic workers; and to agricultural workers from 1 May 1965. The Ministry of Social Welfare and Labour was in 1967 divided into the Ministries of Social Welfare and of Public Health.

JUSTICE. The Supreme Court in Quito is the highest tribunal and consists of 5 justices and the Minister Fiscal. Of the 15 superior courts, 4 are composed of 6 judges and 11 of 3 judges each. There are numerous lower courts. The popular jury was abolished in 1928, and criminal cases are heard before a 'special jury' consisting of 1 judge and 3 members of the Ecuadorean bar, appointed annually by the superior courts. Capital punishment and all forms of torture are prohibited under the constitution, as are imprisonment for debt and contracts involving personal servitude or slavery. Substantial amendments expediting judicial procedure were introduced in 1936, and salaries for all judicial officials replaced remuneration by fees.

FINANCE. Currency. The monetary unit is the sucre, divided into 100 centavos. In circulation are a pure nickel 1-sucre and copper–nickel and copper–zinc 50-, 20-, 10- and 5-centavo pieces. The currency consists mainly of the notes of the Central Bank in denominations of 5, 10, 20, 50, 100, 500 and 1,000 sucres. In Aug. 1970 the US$1 stood at 25 sucres and the £ at 42·7 sucres in the official exchange.

Budget. Revenue and expenditure for calendar years, in 1m. sucres (18·18 sucres = US$1, official rate), balanced as follows: 1964, 3,033; 1965, 4,360; 1966, 2,791; 1967, 3,166; 1968, 4,944; 1969, 5,147

The division of the budget under main heads was, for 1968 (in 1m. sucres): Education, 788; defence, 411; interior, 137; social welfare, 25; foreign affairs, 46; finance, 73; public works, 560; commerce and industry, 22; planning board, 20; agriculture, 23.

The foreign debt on 31 Dec. 1967 was equal to US$163·7m.; internal debt, 4,516·6m. sucres on 30 Sept. 1967. On 11 Sept. 1970 the amount outstanding from the International Monetary Fund was US$18·25m.

DEFENCE. Military service is compulsory, with a 2-year period of conscription. The country is divided into 4 military zones, with headquarters at Quito, Guayaquil, Cuenca and Pastaza.

Army. The Army consists of 6 divisions and some small 'operation detachments'. There are 12 infantry battalions, 3 artillery groups, 3 mechanized squadrons (each with 17 light tanks obtained from USA in 1942), 2 sapper battalions, 2 anti-aircraft battalions, 3 signal companies and several independent infantry companies. A military academy for cadets and a war academy for officers are maintained at Quito.

Navy. The Navy consists of 4 frigates (comprising 2 British 'Hunt' class escort destroyers acquired in 1955, a US patrol frigate acquired in 1947 and a US destroyer escort transport acquired in 1967), 2 escort vessels, 2 gunboats, 6 patrol boats, 2 landing ships, 1 supply ship, 1 water carrier, 1 survey ship and 3 tugs. Naval personnel totals 4,000.

Air Force. The Air Force, formed with Italian assistance in 1920, was re-organized and re-equipped with US aircraft after Ecuador signed the Rio Pact of Mutual Defence in 1947. Current strength of about 3,500 personnel and 60 aircraft includes about 8 Meteor FR9 day reconnaissance fighters, 10 F-80C fighter-bombers, 5 Canberra 6 light bombers, one squadron of DC-6B and C-47 piston-engined transports, 3 HS-748 turboprop transports, T-28, T-33, T-34 and T-41A/D trainers, and various light aircraft.

PRODUCTION. Agriculture. Ecuador is divided into two agricultural zones: the coast and lower river valleys, where tropical farming is carried on in an average temperature of from 18° to 25° C.; and the Andean highlands with a temperate climate, adapted to grazing, dairying and the production of cereals, potatoes, pyrethrum and vegetables suitable to temperate climes. Some wheat has to be imported.

124,000 acres of rich virgin land in the Santo Domingo de los Colorados area has been set aside for settlement of smallholders.

Excepting the two agricultural zones and a few arid spots on the Pacific coast, Ecuador is a vast forest. Roughly estimated, 10,000 sq, miles on the Pacific slope extending from the sea to an altitude of 5,000 ft on the Andes, and the Amazon Basin below the same level containing 80,000 sq. miles, nearly all virgin forest, are rich in valuable timber, but much of it is still not commercially accessible.

The staple export products are bananas, cacao and coffee. These make up over 80% of her exports; the value of the bananas being some 58%. The production of wheat is increasing. Sugar is becoming important; some tea is being produced, mostly for export. Main crops, in metric tons:

	1965	1966		1965	1966
Cacao	51,570	56,000	Wheat	71,594	86,000
Coffee	71,952	91,000	Cotton	20,078	20,000
Rice	94,133	125,100	Bananas (stems)	100,108,750	89,569,200
Sugar	195,000	178,000	Maize	191,000	177,000

Livestock, estimated: Cattle 1·9m.; sheep, 1·2m.; pigs, 1·55m.

FISHERY. Fisheries and fish product exports were valued at US$6·3m. 1966; of these, shrimps comprised about half.

MINING. A few firms are engaged in stoping mineralized vein material for copper, gold, silver, lead and zinc. Production is small: that of gold continued to decline in 1966, but that of copper rose. Production of crude petroleum in 1966 was 108·8m. US gallons; production of refinery products was 243m. US gallons. New drilling along the coast has had some success, but Ecuador has to import some crude oil. Drilling near the river Putumayo started in 1967, and oil is reported to have been found in commercial quantities.

The country has some copper (142 short tons in 1965), iron and lead (125 short tons in 1965). There are coal deposits in the Biblián area, but their exploitation has so far proved uneconomic. Output of sea salt in 1966 was 35,000 metric tons.

INDUSTRY. The Industrial Development Law of 1965 has stimulated the establishment of new industries, including textiles, refrigerators, pharmaceuticals, tinned food, batteries etc. Cement output, 1966, from the country's 3 plants was 378,000 metric tons.

ELECTRICITY. In 1966, total working potential of hydraulic and thermal plants was 193,230 kw. Estimated output in 1965 was 570,000 kwh.

COMMERCE. Imports and exports for calendar years, in US$1m.:

	1964	1965	1966	1967	1968
Imports (c.i.f.).	153·4	155·0	171·9	165·9	103·4
Exports (f.o.b.).	161·4	174·8	186·9	166·0	176·8

Of the total exports in 1965 (and 1966) the largest items were: Bananas, $95·3m. ($106m.); coffee, $36·1m. ($32·1m.); cocoa, $20·5m. ($17·2m.). Other exports include sugar, castor-oil seed, pharmaceuticals, toquilla straw ('Panama') hats, balsa wood, rice, pyrethrum and fish products.

USA furnished 38% of imports in 1966 and took 53% of the exports.

Total trade between Ecuador and UK (in £1,000 sterling, British Board of Trade returns):

	1966	1967	1968	1969	1970
Imports to UK	242	240	447	399	588
Exports from UK	3,245	3,407	4,439	4,136 }	7,027
Re-exports from UK	25	55	41	18 }	

SHIPPING. Ecuador has 7 seaports, of which Guayaquil is the chief. The merchant navy comprises 31,128 tons of seagoing and 14,278 tons of river craft. In 1963 ships totalling 8·51m. GRT entered Ecuadorean ports, unloading 316,000 tons, and loading 1,219,000 tons.

There is river communication, improved by dredging, throughout the principal agricultural districts on the low ground to the west of the Cordillera by the rivers Guayas, Daule and Vinces (navigable for 200 miles by river steamers in the rainy season).

ROADS. There are 16,726 km of roads of all types in this mountainous country, but most are narrow and subject to landslides. A trunk highway through the coastal plain is under construction which will link Machala in the extreme south-west with Esmeraldas in the north-west and with Quito and the northern section of the Pan-American Highway. The paving of the main Quito–Santo Domingo–Guayaquil Highway was completed in 1966. Road construction has been accelerated during 1967.

In 1965 there were 17,500 passenger cars, 19,000 commercial vehicles and 3,500 buses.

RAILWAYS. A railway is open from Durán (opposite Guayaquil) to Quito (288 miles). The Quito–San Lorenzo railway was officially opened in Aug. 1957. The total length of the Ecuadorean State Railways in operation is over 990 km. Modernization of the Durán–Quito section was in progress in 1971.

AVIATION. The following international lines operate: Air France, Avianca, Braniff, Ecuatoriana de Aviación, KLM, Lufthansa, Area, LAN Chile, and Aerovías Peruanas. They connect Quito with Panama, Bogotá (Colombia), Guayaquil, New York and Europe. All the leading towns are connected by an almost daily service, but landing fields are small.

POST. Quito is connected by telegraph with Colombia and Peru, and by cable with the rest of the world. The main towns in the country are connected by radio-telephone. There are over 300 radio stations.

In 1965 there were 43,500 telephones in use, 18,000 in Quito and 15,000 in Guayaquil; all were operated by the Government; 98% were automatic. Television was inaugurated in 1960 in Guayaquil, in 1961 in Quito and in 1967 in Cuenca.

BANKING. The Central Bank of Ecuador, at Quito, with a capital of 20m. sucres, is modelled after the Federal Reserve Banks of US: through branches opened in 10 towns it now deals in mortgage bonds. On 24 Nov. 1967 the Central

Bank had gold and foreign-exchange reserves worth 957m. sucres. Banks must hold cash equal to 21% of sight, short-term and savings deposits.

All commercial banks must be affiliated to the Central Bank; the commercial banks, 31 Oct. 1967, had capital and reserves of 463m. sucres and total assets of 4,536m. sucres. In circulation, Feb. 1968, 3,188m. sucres.

The Bank of London and Montreal, Ltd, has branches in Quito and Guayaquil.

WEIGHTS AND MEASURES. By a law of 6 Dec. 1856 the metric system was made the legal standard but the Spanish measures are in general use. The quintal is equivalent to 101·4 lb.

The meridian of Quito has been adopted as the official time.

DIPLOMATIC REPRESENTATIVES

Ecuador maintains embassies in:

Argentina	Honduras	Poland
Belgium	Italy	Spain
Bolivia	Japan	Sweden
Brazil	Mexico	Switzerland
Chile	Netherlands	UAR
Colombia	Nicaragua	UK
El Salvador	Panama	USA
France	Paraguay	Uruguay
Germany (West)	Peru	Vatican
Guatemala		

OF ECUADOR IN GREAT BRITAIN (3 Hans Crescent, SW1)

Ambassador: Dr Antonio Parra Velasco.
Commercial Counsellor: Catulo Palau-Velasco. *Service Attaché:* Capt. Guillermo Jarrin, N.

There are consular representatives at Birmingham, Glasgow, Liverpool, London and Sheffield.

OF GREAT BRITAIN IN ECUADOR

Ambassador: G. N. Jackson, CMG, MBE.
First Secretaries: H. Lewty; J. Anderson (*Labour*). *Service Attaché:* Capt. F. G. Thatcher, RN (*Navy, Army and Air*, resident in Santiago de Chile).

There is a consular officer at Quito.

OF ECUADOR IN THE USA (2535–15th St., NW, Washington, D.C., 20009)

Ambassador: Carlos Mantilla Ortega.
Minister: Rodrigo Valdez. *First Secretary:* Gonzalo Paredes. *Service Attachés:* Col. Leopoldo Freire (*Army*), Capt. Octavio Jarrín S. (*Navy*), Col. Julio I. Espinosa (*Air.*).

OF THE USA IN ECUADOR

Ambassador: Edson O. Sessions.
Deputy Chief of Mission: John J. Crowley, Jr. *Heads of Sections:* Robert T. Follestad (*Political*); Joel W. Biller (*Economic*); David J. Dunford (*Commercial*); Everett L. Damron (*Consular*); Donald W. Barrett (*Administrative*); Robert J. Minges (*AID*).
Service Attachés: Col Harld J. Jacobs (*Army*), Lieut.-Col. John Sandoval (*Air*).

There is a Consul-General at Guayaquil.

BOOKS OF REFERENCE

Anurio de Legislación Ecuatoriana. Quito. Annual
Boletín del Banco Central. Quito
Boletín General de Estadística. Tri-monthly
Boletín Mensual del Ministerio de Obras Públicas. Monthly
Informes Ministeriales. Quito. Annual
Bibliografía Nacional, 1756–1941. Quito, 1942
Blanksten, G. I., Ecuador: Constitutions and Caudillos. Univ. of California Press, 1951
Buitrón, Aníbal, and Collier, Jr., J., The Awakening Valley: study of the Otavalo Indians. New York, 1950
Corporation of Foreign Bondholders. Annual Report. London
Hagen, V. W. von, Ecuador and the Galápagos Islands. Norman, Okla., 1949
Holdridge, L. R., and others, The Forests of Western and Central Ecuador. Washington, 1947
Linke, L., Ecuador, Country of Contrasts. R. Inst. of Int. Affairs, 3rd ed., 1959
Luna Yepes, J., Síntesis histórica y geográfica del Ecuador. Madrid, 1951

EL SALVADOR

República de El Salvador

HISTORY. In 1839 the Central American Federation, which had comprised the states of Guatemala, El Salvador, Honduras, Nicaragua and Costa Rica, was dissolved, and El Salvador declared itself formally an independent republic in 1841. There have since been a number of attempts to restore some looser form of Central American unity, the latest being the founding in 1951 of the Organization of Central American States (with Secretariat in San Salvador) and the Central American Common Market.

AREA AND POPULATION. El Salvador is the smallest and most densely populated of the Central American states. Its area (including 247 sq. km of inland lakes) is estimated at 21,393 sq. km (8,236 sq. miles), with population (census 1 May 1961) of 2,510,984 (estimate, 1 July 1968, 3,150,000). The capital is San Salvador (255,744 inhabitants in May 1961).

The republic is divided into 14 departments, each under an appointed governor. Their areas (in sq. km) and populations at 1 July 1966 were:

Department	Area	Population	Department	Area	Population
Ahuachapán	1,222·32	144,675	La Paz	1,201·85	159,782
Santa Ana	1,988·26	316,778	Cabañas	1,094·45	114,917
Sonsonate	1,189·28	200,517	San Vicente	1,206·69	134,765
Chalatenango	2,116·78	145,092	Usulután	1,974·84	251,938
La Libertad	1,661·65	244,672	San Miguel	2,166·98	280,236
San Salvador	871·42	561,382	Marazán	1,724·26	142,998
Cuscatlán	732·08	133,822	La Unión	1,995·25	184,814

Important towns (with population in May 1961) are: Santa Ana, 121,095; San Miguel, 82,974; Santa Tecla, 40,817; Zacatecoluca, 40,424; Ahuachapán, 40,359; San Vicente, 34,723; Sonsonate, 35,531; Usulután, 30,465; Cojutepeque, 18,347.

In 1966 births were 137,968 (45·4 per 1,000 population); deaths, 30,398 (10); infantile deaths, 8,497 (61·6 per 1,000 births); marriages, 9,966; divorces, 673.

There has been considerable emigration into nearby states. There are no tribal Indians. The language of the country is Spanish.

CONSTITUTION AND GOVERNMENT. The latest Constitution was enacted in Jan. 1962, slightly amending that of 1950. The Executive Power is vested in a President elected for a non-renewable term of 5 years, with Ministers and Under-Secretaries appointed by him. The Legislative power is an Assembly of 52 members elected by universal suffrage and proportional representation for a term of 2 years. The Judicial Power is vested in a Supreme Court, of a President and 8 Magistrates elected by the Legislative Assembly for renewable terms of 3 years; and subordinate courts.

President Lieut.-Col. José María Lemus, who was elected 4 March 1956 and assumed office 14 Sept., was deposed on 26 Oct. 1960 by a *Junta* of 3 soldiers and 3 civilians. This *Junta* was overthrown on 25 Jan. 1961, by a Directorio Cívico-Militar at first consisting of 2 soldiers and 3 civilians. A new Partido de Conciliación Nacional won all the seats of a new Assembly elected on 17 Dec. 1961. Its president, Dr Eusebio Cordón, was elected Provisional President of the Republic when it promulgated the new Constitution on 25 Jan. 1962. In Presidential elections on 29 April, Col. J. A. Rivera was returned without opposition and held office 1962–67. The elections of 13 March 1966 resulted in 31 Partido de Conciliación Nacional being elected against the opposition Partido Demócrata Cristiano (15) and various minor parties (6).

President: Fidel Sánchez Hermández, assumed office 1 July 1967 for 5 years.
Foreign Minister: Dr Alfredo Martínez Moreno.

National flag: Blue, white, blue (horizontal): the white stripe charged with the arms of the republic.

National anthem: Saludemos la patria orgullosos (words by J. J. Cañas; tune by J. Aberle).

RELIGION. The dominant religion is Roman Catholicism. Under the 1962 constitution churches are exempted from the property tax; the Catholic Church is recognized as a legal person, and other churches are entitled to secure similar recognition. There is an archbishop in San Salvador and bishops at Santa Ana, San Miguel, San Vicente, Santiago de María and Usulután. The Society of Friends had about 275 members in 1957.

EDUCATION. Education is free and obligatory, but there is a shortage of both schools and teachers. In 1929 the State took over control of all schools, public and private, but the provision that the teaching in government schools must be wholly secular was removed in 1945.

The census of 1961 showed that 52% of those 10 years of age or older were illiterate, but some headway has been made.

In 1966 there were 2,813 primary schools (state, municipal and private), with 453,987 pupils and 13,265 teachers. Secondary education was given at 255 high schools (38,849 pupils). The national university (in 1965) had 3,500 students.

CINEMAS (1965). Cinemas numbered 57.

NEWSPAPERS (1965). There are 4 daily newspapers in San Salvador and 1 each in Santa Ana and San Miguel.

SOCIAL WELFARE. A social-security law became effective 1 Jan. 1954, but applies only to limited groups of employees; employers are to pay 50% of whatever contribution is decided upon, employees 25% and the State 25%.

JUSTICE. Justice is administered by the Supreme Court of Justice, courts of first and second instance, besides minor tribunals. Magistrates of the Supreme Court and courts of second instance are elected by the Legislative Assembly for a renewable 3-year term.

An anti-Communist law, effective 29 Sept. 1962, has made the propagation of totalitarian or Communist doctrines an offence punishable by imprisonment; supplementary offences, contrary to democratic principles, are punished by prison terms of from 3 to 7 years.

FINANCE. Currency. The monetary unit is the *colón* of 100 centavos. Its exchange value since July 1934 had been kept at 40 cents US, and on 30 June 1942 the bank's gold stock was revalued, making it exactly equal to the exchange value of 40 cents. The country left the gold standard on 9 Oct. 1931. On 20 April 1961 exchange control was introduced to prevent the transfer of capital abroad. This control has since been extended to limit the length of credit on the import of consumer goods. The buying/selling rate for the £ is 6 and 6·06 colones respectively.

The colón is issued in denominations of 1, 2, 5, 10, 25 and 100 colones; 25 and 50 centavos (silver); 1, 5, 10 and 25 centavos (copper–nickel and copper–zinc).

Money in circulation (including sight deposits) was 304·3m. colones on 31 March 1967.

Budget. Revenue and expenditure for fiscal years ending 31 Dec., in 1,000 colones (2·5 colones = US$1):

	1964	1965	1966[1]	1967[1]	1968[1]	1969[1]
Revenue	210,448	224,542	232,000	234,236	234,233]	279,266
Expenditure	192,321	222,856	274,691	240,320	250,744	255,831

[1] Budget.

The 1966 budget proposed 22·2% for education, 13·6% for public works, 6·52% for agriculture, 12·2% for health and welfare, 10% for defence and security. Public revenue was to comprise: Import duties, 35·4%; export duties, 12·9%; income and capital taxes, 20·7%; excise duties, 26·5%.

External debt amounted to 213·7m. colones and internal debt to 47·6m. colones on 31 Dec. 1967. Foreign credits granted to the country since the end of the war include: Inter-American Development Bank, US$31·8m.; International Bank for Reconstruction and Development, $59m.; US Agencies, $42·9m.

DEFENCE. The Army is organized in 3 territorial divisions of 9 infantry, 1 artillery and 1 cavalry regiments. Total strength, 4,500 men. There are also the National Guard, the National Police and the Treasury Police.

In Oct. 1954 the US agreed to send a military mission to train the defence forces.

The Navy consists of 2 patrol boats and 3 other small craft.

The small Air Force, which came into being in the early 1920s, is equipped with aircraft supplied by the USA. They include 6 modernized Cavalier F-51D Mustang piston-engined fighter-bombers, a transport flight equipped with C-47s and a Canadair DC-4M, a single Fairchild Hiller FH-1100 light observation helicopter, and a few Beech T-34 and AT-34 and AT-11 piston-engined trainers.

AGRICULTURE. El Salvador is predominantly agricultural; 32·5% of its total area is used for crops and 30·2% for pasture. Area devoted to coffee is about 308,000 acres, almost entirely owned by nationals.

Rice is important for home consumption; other agricultural products are maize, cacao, tobacco, indigo, henequén and sugar (2·7m. quintals in 1966–67). A little rubber is exported.

Livestock estimate 1950 showed 114,556 horses, 35,435 mules; and in 1966: 1,288,050 cattle, 1,669,540 pigs, 215,000 sheep, 39,000 goats. Milk production in 1964 was estimated to be 233·4m. litres.

FORESTRY. In the national forests are found dye woods and such woods as mahogany, cedar and walnut. Balsam trees also abound; El Salvador is the world's principal source of this medicinal gum; exports, 1965, 144 metric tons.

MINING. The mineral output of the republic is now negligible, none being produced in 1964. Production of salt, 1964, 12 metric tons. An oil refinery has been built at Acajutla with a production of 14,000 bbls a day.

INDUSTRY. A steel rolling-mill was inaugurated on 29 July 1966, at Zacatecoluca. A 1961 industrial census showed 19,630 industrial establishments employing 85,655 people earning nearly 52m. colones; total product was valued in 1965 at 340m. colones; 17,120 commercial concerns had 43,483 employees earning 23m. colones. In 1964 the value (in 1,000 colones) of production in main industries was: Food and non-alcoholic drink, 29,257; alcoholic drinks, 21,931; textiles and clothing, 55,504; cement and its products, 10,918; sundry (including soap, vegetable oils, cigarettes, hemp, tanned goods and alcohol), 79,574; total, 197,184.

ELECTRICITY. El Salvador's biggest national enterprise, begun in 1950, is the construction of a 200-ft high dam across the (unnavigable) Lempa River, 35 miles north-east of San Salvador, designed to double the country's electric-power resources, from 31,000 to 78,000 kw. Consumption, 1965, was 158·5m. kwh.

LABOUR. A decree of Aug. 1950 permits the formation of trade unions except among agricultural workers and those engaged in seasonal work such as coffee-milling and sugar-refining; trade-union posts must be filled by natives, not foreigners.

COMMERCE. The imports (including parcels post) and exports have been as follows in calendar years in 1,000 colones (2·5 colones = US$):

	1964	1965	1966	1967	1968	1969
Imports	477,808	501,396	549,895	559,800	535,200	537,600
Exports	445,238	471,771	481,136	518,100	531,300	506,200

Of total exports, coffee furnishes about 20% by weight and 51% by value. The coffee is of the 'mild' variety; it is sold in bags of 46 kg, but trade statistics use a bag of 69 kg. Exports in 1966 were 97,000 metric tons (valued at 227m. colones), of which 45% went to Germany and 43% to USA. Cotton furnishes in value 20% of exports; in 1966, 51,000 metric tons (valued at 61m. colones) were exported, mostly to Japan. A US sugar quota recently granted was raised from 17,125 to 33,140 tons for the year 1966.

In 1965 US took 117·5m. colones of exports and furnished 156·4m. colones of the imports. The chief imports are normally wheat, flour, fuel-oil, cement, fertilizers, machinery, vehicles and iron and steel manufactures. The other Central American Republics, Germany, Japan, the Netherlands and the UK are also important trading partners.

Total trade between El Salvador and UK (British Board of Trade returns) for 5 years (in £1,000 sterling):

	1966	1967	1968	1969	1970
Imports to UK	96	219	243	172	340
Exports from UK	3,524	2,993	1,853	1,768 }	2,338
Re-exports from UK	21	10	15	12 }	

SHIPPING. The principal ports are La Unión, La Libertad and Acajutla, all on the Pacific. Passengers (and some freight) use the Guatemalan port of Puerto Barrios on the Atlantic, reaching El Salvador by rail or road.

RAILWAYS. A railway connects the port of Acajutla with Santa Ana, Sonsonate and San Salvador, the capital. It links San Salvador with the American-owned International Railways of Central America, which runs from the eastern to the western boundary of El Salvador, and extends into Guatemala City and Puerto Barrios on the north coast and on the Mexican border. Total length of railway open, about 459 miles, all of narrow gauge.

ROADS. There are 8,527 km of national roads in the republic, including 1,055 km of paved road; 3,256 km are usable all the year round and 4,215 only in the dry season. Motor vehicles registered, 1966, 54,106.

AVIATION. Air traffic is expanding and in 1965 there were 60 flights a week to other Central American capitals, Panama, Miami, Mexico and New Orleans. There is a modern airport at Ilopango, 5 miles from San Salvador, equipped to handle jet aeroplanes.

POST. The telephone and telegraph systems are government-owned; the radio-telephone systems are partly private, partly government-owned. Telephone instruments, 1966, 18,219. Two radio transmitting and receiving stations at San Salvador maintain communications with Latin America. El Salvador has, 1965, over 500,000 wireless receiving sets. In 1966, 2 television stations furnished 2 channels.

U

BANKING. There are 6 native commercial banks, including the Banco Salvadoreño (paid-up capital, 6m. colones). The Bank of London and Montreal and the First National City Bank of New York are the only foreign institutions. The Central Reserve Bank of El Salvador, constructed in 1934 out of the Banco Agrícola Comercial, was nationalized on 20 April 1961. Bank deposits, both term and sight, were 442·8m. colones in March 1967. Total gold and dollar reserves of the Banco Central on 30 June 1966 were 136·5m. colones compared with 150·7m. in June 1965. A stock exchange was officially inaugurated in Oct. 1962 with the declared intention of promoting investments in Central America; it began operations on 17 Aug. 1964 with a capital of 100,000 colones subscribed by 360 shareholders. Its activities have been limited.

WEIGHTS AND MEASURES. On 1 Jan. 1886 the metric system was made obligatory. But other units are still commonly in use, of which the principal are as follows: *Libra* = 1·014 lb. av.; *quintal* = 101·4 lb. av.; *arroba* = 25·35 lb. av.; *fanega* = 1·5745 bushels.

DIPLOMATIC REPRESENTATIVES

El Salvador maintains embassies in:

Argentina
Austria
Brazil
Chile
Colombia
Costa Rica
Dominican Republic (also Haiti)
Ecuador
France (also Belgium)
Germany (West) (also Denmark and Switzerland)
Guatemala
Honduras
Italy (also Israel)

Japan (also Taiwan)
Mexico
Nicaragua
Panama
Paraguay
Peru (also Bolivia)
Spain (also Morocco, UAR and Vatican)
UK (also Netherlands, Norway and Sweden)
USA (also Canada)
Uruguay
Venezuela

OF EL SALVADOR IN GREAT BRITAIN (9B Portland Place, W1)

Ambassador: Alfonso Quiñonez Meza.
Counsellor: Joaquin E. Medina.
First Secretary: Manuel Monterrosa.

There are consular representatives at Birmingham, Liverpool, London and Rochester.

OF GREAT BRITAIN IN EL SALVADOR

Ambassador and Consul-General: D. H. Clibbon, CMG.
First Secretaries: R. G. Farrar (*Head of Chancery and Consul*). *Service Attaché:* Wing Cdr. P. D. Thompson, DFC, DFM. (*Navy, Army and Air,* resident in Caracos).

There is a consular representative at La Libertad.

OF EL SALVADOR IN THE USA (2308 California St. NW, Washington, D.C., 20008)

Ambassador: Col. Julio A. Rivera.
Minister-Counsellors: Dr Juan Scaffini; José Arcadio Chavez (*Economic*). *First Secretary:* René Savavia. *Military and Air Attaché:* Col. Guillermo Segundo Martinez.

OF THE USA IN EL SALVADOR

Ambassador: William Garton Bowdler.
Deputy Head of Mission: Terrance G. Leonhardy. *Heads of Sections:* Eiler R.

Cook (*Political*); Richard B. Owen (*Economic*); Henry G. Krausse, Jr (*Consular*); Eladio Izquierdo (*Administrative*); Paul L. Oechsli (*AID*).
Service Attachés: Lieut.-Col. Robert L. Coxe (*Defence and Army*), Capt. Robert F. Lyons (*Navy*, resident in Mexico City), Col. John A. Carroll (*Air*, resident in Guatemala City).

BOOKS OF REFERENCE

STATISTICAL INFORMATION. The Dirección General de Estadística y Censos (Villa Fermina, Calle Arce, San Salvador) dates from 1937. *Director General:* Lieut.-Col. José Castro Meléndez. Its publications include *Anuario Estadístico.* Annual from 1911.—*Boletin Estadístico.* Quarterly.— *El Salvador en Gráficas.* Annual.—*Atlas Censal de El Salvador.* 1955 only.

Angel Gallardo, M., *Cuatro Constituciones Federales de Centro América y Las Constituciones Políticas de El Salvador.* San Salvador, 1945
Mestas, A., *El Salvador, país de lagos y volcanes.* Madrid, 1950
Vogt, W., *The Population of El Salvador and its Natural Resources.* Washington, D.C., 1946
Wallich, H. C. (ed.), *Public Finance in a Developing Country: El Salvador.* Harvard Univ. Press. 1951

EQUATORIAL GUINEA

República de Guinea Ecuatorial

HISTORY. The Republic of Equatorial Guinea became independent on 12 Oct. 1968 after having been a Spanish colony (Territorios Españoles del Golfo de Guinea) until 1959. From 1959 to 1963 the territory was made into two Spanish provinces with a status comparable to the metropolitan provinces. From 1964 to 1968 this Equatorial Region became an autonomous entity still retaining the status of two Spanish provinces, but with a certain amount of internal self-government. A cabinet of 8 African members headed by a President of the Government Council was responsible for internal affairs, defence and foreign affairs remaining reserved to a Spanish High Commissioner. Serious political disturbances in Rio Muni occurred in March–April 1969. This led to the partial withdrawal of the Spanish community since when UN agencies have supplied personnel to man hospitals, public utilities and ministries.

CONSTITUTION AND GOVERNMENT. Following the referendum of 11 Aug. and the elections of 22 and 29 Sept. 1968, Equatorial Guinea has become a sovereign state consisting of two provinces. The Republic is administered by a President who is chief of the armed forces and head of government.
The Assembly consists of 35 representatives (Fernando Poo, 12; Rio Muni, 19; Annobón, 2; Corisco, Elobey Grande, Elobey Chico, 2), elected by universal, direct and secret ballot. The President of the Republic and the Assembly are elected for a 5-year period. There is a cabinet of 9 ministers.

President and Minister of Defence and Foreign Affairs: Francisco Macias Nguema (Fang of Rio Muni).
Vice-President and Minister of Trade: Bubi of Fernando Poo.

AREA AND POPULATION. The total area is 28,051 sq. km (9,828 sq. miles). Total population, 245,989 (1960 census); 1968 estimate, 300,000.
The republic consists of 2 provinces: (1) the continental Rio Muni (26,017 sq. km including the adjacent islets of Corisco, Elobey Grande and Elobey Chico which cover 17 sq. km). The administrative and economic capital is Bata (3,548 inhabitants in 1960). Total population was 183,377, including 2,864 Europeans at the census of 1960; 1968 estimate, 220,000–230,000; (2) the island of Fernando Poo (2,034 sq. km including Annobón, 17 sq. km). The capital is Santa Isabel, which is also the capital of the Republic (19,869 inhabitants in 1960). Total population at the census of 1960 was 62,612 (including 1,415 for Annobón), including 4,220 Europeans; 1968 estimate about 70,000–80,000 with a significant increase of Nigerian plantation workers.

The majority of the Rio Muni population is Fang (Pámues in Spanish). Along the coast and in the islets are the Combes, the Bengas, the Bujebas, etc.

In Fernando Poo the aborigines are called Bubis. They are now a minority (perhaps 15,000). Other ethnic groups are the Fernandinos (descendants of English-speaking Creoles), the Fangs, coast people from Rio Muni and naturalized migrant workers from Nigeria, Cameroun and São Tomé. A fluctuating mass of plantation workers are about twice as numerous as the Equatorial Guineans. Annobón is peopled by descendants of slaves brought by the Portuguese; they still speak a Portuguese patois. Pidgin English is the lingua franca in Fernando Poo in spite of the official Spanish.

RELIGION. The population of Equatorial Guinea is nominally Roman Catholic (227,517 in 1966) with influential Protestant groups in Santa Isabel and Rio Muni.

EDUCATION. Elementary schools provide compulsory education up to 12 years and primary schools continue it to 14 years. There were in 1966, 147 elementary and 32 primary schools with 21,421 and 1,565 pupils respectively. There were 271 teachers (17 Europeans). Santa Isabel and Bata had a secondary school each, with together 31 teachers and 936 pupils. Santa Isabel had also an 'Escuela Superior provincial' with 100 students and a teacher-training school. Bata had a normal school and a technical secondary school. Less than 50 university students study abroad (mostly in Spain). In 1967 there were only about a dozen university graduates.

HEALTH. Equatorial Guinea has a fairly adequate health service with 2 large hospitals in Santa Isabel and Bata. With the exception of 3 African doctors in 1967, doctors come from Spain and other countries. A leper hospital exists in Micomeseng (200 beds with about 300 patients).

FINANCE. The budget for 1969–70 envisaged revenue of 712·5m. pesetas and expenditure of 1,139m.

DEFENCE. The *Guardia Nacional* consisted mainly of Fang soldiers with Spanish officers of the *Guardia Civil* seconded to it. Total strength about 1,000 Since 1969 all Spanish troops have been repatriated.

The Spanish navy usually maintained 1 frigate, 1 corvette and 1 survey ship on the station at Santa Isabel.

The Spanish air force had available the modern facilities of Santa Isabel and Bata airfields.

AGRICULTURE AND FORESTRY. The chief products are cocoa (56,400 hectares in 1966), coffee (12,000 hectares) and wood. In 1968 production was 33,192 metric tons of cocoa, most of it high-grade exported to Spain. Coffee, of mediocre quality, is chiefly a Fang product. Production (1968) 8,450 metric tons.

Wood is almost entirely exported from Rio Muni to Spain and Germany (337,438 metric tons to Spain in 1967). Plantations in the hinterland have been abandoned by their Spanish owners.

INDUSTRY. Fernando Poo has very few industries. Electricity production in 1967: Fernando Poo, 9·47m. kwh.; Rio Muni, 5·7m. kwh. Rio Muni has no industry except lumbering. In Fernando Poo a fish-processing industry is developing. Hopes based on the 4-year development plan (1964–68) have not materialized.

TRADE. In 1965 Equatorial Guinea exported 330,100 metric tons (value, 1,635·6m. pesetas; 1966, 1,817m.), of which 326,000 metric tons to Spain (value, 1,581·6m. pesetas). It imported 105,200 metric tons (value, 1,284·3m. pesetas; 1966, 1,278m.), of which 68,800 tons from Spain (value 750·1m. pesetas). Chief exports were: Cocoa, 720,514,700 pesetas; coffee, 348,730,200 pesetas; wood, 308,930,100 pesetas. Chief imports were rice (29,307,300 pesetas) and oil products (27,482,300 pesetas).

SHIPPING. Santa Isabel is the main port; 663 vessels entered and left in 1967. The other ports are San Carlos (bananas, cocoa) in Fernando Poo and Bata, Puerto Iradier and Rio Benito (wood) in Rio Muni. In 1966 in the 5 ports 141,600 metric tons were unloaded and 429,000 loaded.

ROADS. Fernando Poo has a good tarmac road network, but Rio Muni has few surfaced roads; the main artery is Rio Benito–Bata–Micomeseng–Ebebiyin.

AVIATION. An international airfield exists in Santa Isabel (28,029 passengers in 1967). Bata has more modest facilities (15,031 passengers in 1967). The line Madrid–Santa Isabel–Bata is subsidized by Spain. Links with Douala (from Santa Isabel) and Libreville (Gabon) exist.

POST. Estimated number of telephones (1969) 1,451.

BANKING. The Banco Central de Guinea Ecuatorial in Santa Isabel was established in 1969 with Spanish technical and financial assistance.

British Ambassador: (Vacant) (resident at Yaoundé).
US Ambassador: Lewis Hoffaker (resident in Yaoundé).

BOOKS OF REFERENCE

Atlas Histórico y Geográfico de Africa Española. Madrid, 1955
Plan de Desarrollo Económico de la Guinea Ecuatorial. Presidencia del Gobierno. Madrid, 1963
Resumén estadístico del Africa española, 1965–66. Madrid, 1967
Berman, S., *Spanish Guinea: an annotated bibliography.* Microfilm Service, Catholic University, Washington, D.C., 1961
Pélissier, R., *Les Territoires espagnols d'Afrique.* Paris, 1963.—*Los territorios españoles de Africa.* Madrid, 1964.—*Etudes Hispano–Guinéennes.* Paris, 1969

ETHIOPIA

HISTORY. The ancient empire of Ethiopia has its legendary origin in the meeting of King Solomon and the Queen of Sheba. Historically, the empire developed in the centuries before and after the birth of Christ, at Aksum in the north, as a result of Semitic immigration from South Arabia. The immigrants imposed their language and culture on a basic Hamitic stock. Ethiopia's subsequent history is one of sporadic expansion southwards and eastwards, checked from the 16th to early 19th centuries by devastating wars with Moslems and Gallas. Modern Ethiopia dates from the reign of the Emperor Theodore (1855–68).

Menelik II (1889–1913) defeated the Italians in 1896 and thereby safeguarded the empire's independence in the scramble for Africa. By successful campaigns in neighbouring kingdoms within Ethiopia (Jimma, Kaffa, Harar, etc.) he united the country under his rule and created the Empire as it is today.

In 1936 Ethiopia was conquered by the Italians, who were in turn defeated by the Allied forces in 1941 when the Emperor returned.

The former Italian colony of Eritrea, from 1941 under British military administration, was in accordance with a resolution of the General Assembly of the United Nations, dated 2 Dec. 1950, handed over to Ethiopia on 15 Sept. 1952. Eritrea thereby became an autonomous unit within the federation of Ethiopia and Eritrea, under the Ethiopian Crown. This federation became a unitary state on 14 Nov. 1962 when Eritrea was fully integrated with Ethiopia.

EMPEROR. Hailé Selassié I, born 23 July 1892; crowned King (Negus), on 7 Oct. 1928, proclaimed Emperor, after the death of the Empress Zauditu, on 2 April 1930, and crowned on 2 Nov. 1930. He married in 1911 Menen, who died on 15 Feb. 1962. There are a son and a daughter surviving. On 25 Jan. 1931 the eldest son, Asfa Wossen, was proclaimed Crown Prince and heir to the throne. He has one daughter by his first marriage and one son and 3 daughters by his second.

National flag: Green, yellow, red (horizontal).

National anthem: Ityopya hoy dass yiballish (tune by M. K. Nalbandian, 1925).

GOVERNMENT. The Empire is governed by a Council of Ministers, responsible to the Emperor, and a parliament consisting of a Senate and a Chamber of Deputies. The Chamber of Deputies consists of 250 members; the number of Senators must not exceed half the number of Deputies.

In 1955 a new constitution was promulgated. This provides for universal suffrage for men and women over 21 years old, for greater fiscal control by the Chamber and for a limited degree of ministerial responsibility to parliament. Elections were held in 1957, 1961, 1965 and 1969.

Prime Minister: Tsahafi Tizaz Aklilou Habte-Wold.

Foreign Minister: Ketema Yifru.

AREA AND POPULATION. The total area of the Empire is approximately 395,000 sq. miles or 1m. sq. km (Ethiopia 350,000, Eritrea, 45,000).

The official estimate of the population in 1967 was 22,667,400.

The most important race of Ethiopia, the Amhara, inhabit the central Ethiopian highlands. To the north of them are the Tigréans, akin to the Amhara and belonging to the same Christian church, but speaking a different, though related, language. Both these races are of mixed Hamitic and Semitic origin, and further mixed by inter-marriage with Galla and other races. The Gallas, some of whom are Christian, some Moslem and some pagan, comprise more than one-half of the entire population, and are a pastoral and agricultural people of Hamitic origin. Ogaden, Issa and other Somalis inhabit Harar province, the Somaliland plateau and the south-east. These and most of the Danakil are Moslem. There are also Sidamo, Nilotic and Nilo-Hamitic tribes in the south-west, and the Falashas (of Jewish religion) north of Lake Tana.

Addis Ababa, the capital, has 644,190 inhabitants, Asmara (capital of Eritrea), 178,537; Dire Dawa, 50,733; Harar, 42,771; Dessie, 40,619; Gondar, 30,734; Jimma, 30,580.

The country is divided into 14 provinces (*taqlai-gizat*), each under a Governor-General, under the administrative control of the Minister of the Interior. Each province is divided into about 7 sub-provinces (*awradja-gizat*) under a Governor, 87 in 1962. All revenues collected in the provinces are under the control of the Minister of Finance.

The most populous provinces are Hararge (3,341,700), Shoa (3,907,300), Wollo (3,119,700) and Tigre (2,307,300).

RELIGION. Since the conversion of the Amharas to Christianity in the 4th century they have retained their connexion with the Alexandrian Church through the Abuna, or Metropolitan who was always an Egyptian Copt, and who was appointed and consecrated by the Coptic Patriarch of Alexandria. Both the Egyptian and Ethiopian Coptic Churches are monophysite, rejecting the degrees of the Council of Chalcedon (A.D. 451) After the restoration of the Emperor relations between the Ethiopian and Egyptian churches were strained until the summer of 1948, when an agreement was reached which envisaged the appointment of an Ethiopian Archbishop, and in Jan. 1951 Abuna Basilios (who died in 1970) was elected Archbishop of Ethiopia. A further agreement in 1959 made the Ethiopian Church autocephalous, and Basilios assumed the rank of Patriarch, with seniority immediately after the Patriarch of Alexandria. The clergy is very numerous and the Church holds a considerable proportion of the land. Christianity is predominant in the following provinces in the north: Tigré,

Begemdir, Gojjam, Shoa. Wollo province in the north-east is half Christian, half Moslem. In the southern half of the country the provinces of Harar and Arussi have Moslem majorities, while all the other southern provinces have considerable Moslem minorities. In addition, the province of Gamu Gofa on the Kenya border and parts of Sidamo and Arussi have considerable pagan elements. Eritrea is half Moslem and half Christian. Each province now forms a diocese.

Islam is widely practised in the south and east of the Empire. Moslem minorities are found in Addis Ababa and in other commercial centres. The rite is mainly shafeitic. Harar is the most important Moslem centre. There are mosques and government schools for Moslems in most towns.

EDUCATION. In the academic year 1968–69 there were 2,013 primary, secondary and church schools providing education for about 618,000 pupils. Higher education is co-ordinated under the Hailé Selassié I University, chartered in 1961. The University College, the Engineering, Building and Theological Colleges are in Addis Ababa, Agricultural Colleges in Harar, Jimma and Ambo and the Public Health College in Gondar. The University of Asmara has 1,500 students. Altogether they provide tuition for about 4,000 students.

The main language of instruction from the secondary level upwards is English.

CINEMAS (1968). There were 9 cinemas in Addis Ababa and 6 in Asmara, with seating capacities of about 5,000 in each city, and about a dozen smaller cinemas in the provinces.

NEWSPAPERS. In Addis Ababa there is 1 English, 1 French and 1 Amharic dailies, and in Asmara 2 Italian dailies, 1 part-Tigrinya, part-Arabic, and 1 Amharic weekly. All the papers are government-controlled and have small circulations, varying between 1,000 and 12,000.

JUSTICE. The legal system is said to be based on the Justinian Code. A new penal code came into force in 1958. New criminal procedure, civil, commercial and maritime law codes have since been promulgated.

The extra-territorial rights formerly enjoyed by foreigners have been abolished, but any person accused in an Ethiopian court has the right to have his case transferred to the High Court, provided he asks for this before any evidence has been taken in the court of first instance. Under the Anglo-Ethiopian agreement of 1944 any British subject or British protected person whose case is before the High Court can insist on being heard by at least one judge with proven judicial experience in other lands.

Provincial and district courts have been established, and High Court judges visit the provincial courts on circuit. The Supreme Imperial Court at Addis Ababa is presided over by the Ethiopian Chief Justice.

FINANCE. Currency. The Ethiopian dollar, divided into 100 cents, is the unit of currency; it is based on 5·52 grains of fine gold. There are notes of $1, 5, 10, 20, 50, 100 and 500 denominations, and bronze 1-, 5-, 10- and 25-cent coins. Currency is issued by the National Bank, and, as at 31 March 1970, was notes, E$322·3m.; coins, E$54·6m. The note issue, under the Banking Proclamation of 1963, must be backed by gold and foreign securities in the international reserve fund to at least 25% of its value. At 31 March 1970, the fund stood at E$180·1m. The Ethiopian dollar = 40 cents US; E$6 = £1 sterling.

Budget. Revenue and expenditure estimates for financial years (ended 7 July) were as follows (in E$1m.):

	1965–66	1966–67	1967–68	1968–69	1969–70
Revenue	430·8	496·6	547·3	612·0	602·0
Expenditure	455·8	515·5	581·6	651·5	631·0

Of the estimated revenue in 1969–70, E$151·3m. is expected to come from customs duties and taxes, E$140·75m. from indirect taxes, E$105·6m. from direct taxes and E$88m. from external assistance. Of the expenditure, E$89·9m. is to be allocated to defence and E$79·8m. to education and culture. Capital expenditure will be E$129·7m. In 1969–70 the deficit is to be covered by external assistance E$147·3m. and domestic bank credit E$29m.

DEFENCE. Army. The Army, trained by British officers from 1947 to 1951, comprises 4 divisions, each nominally of three 3-battalion brigades, supporting arms and services. In addition, there is a mechanized brigade which includes 1 tank battalion and 2 APC battalions, a medium artillery battalion, 3 anti-aircraft batteries, 1 combat engineer battalion, an airborne infantry battalion and ancillary services. The total strength is about 40,000.

Israeli training teams are assisting in the training of both the Army and the police. An American military advisory and administrative group, established since 1954, is working down to divisional level. Ethiopian officers are trained at the Hailé Selassié I Military Academy, Harar, and at the Hailé Selassié I Military Training Centre, Holletta, near Addis Ababa.

Navy. The Imperial Navy, with headquarters at Addis Ababa, consists of a training ship (1,768 tons; *ex*-US seaplane tender), 5 patrol craft (*ex*-US coastguard motor boats) and 4 small landing craft. The Naval School is established at Massawa. Personnel, 225 officers and approximately 1,000 men. A small number of foreign, some retired British, officers are employed in executive positions and as advisers and training officers.

Air Force. The Imperial Air Force, trained originally by Swedish and American personnel, has its headquarters at Debre Zeit, near Addis Ababa. It comprises a training school and a central workshop, one bomber, one ground-attack, 2 dayfighter/ground-attack and one fighter/reconnaissance squadron, equipped with 4 Canberras, F-5s, F-86s, T-28s, Saab-17s and T-33s, and one transport squadron equipped with C-119s, C-54s, C-47s and Doves. Training aircraft include T-33 jet advanced trainers and piston-engined T-28s and Saab-91s. A few Agusta-Bell 204 and Alouette II and III helicopters are in service. Personnel, 330 officers and 1,790 men.

Police. In 1948 the regular police force of the capital and some provincial cities was amalgamated with the irregular territorial forces under the provincial governors-general. The total force now numbers about 32,000 officers and other ranks.

The frontier guard patrols the Somalia border, and commando police units are being employed to assist the Army and police in border patrols and anti-terrorist operations in Eritrea.

PLANNING. The second 5-year plan (1962–67) which envisaged a total expenditure of E$1,451m., including 376m. for industrial development, was claimed to have been fulfilled to 95%. The third 5-year plan (1969–73) involving a total expenditure of E$2,865m. (of which E$565m. for industry and E$624m. for transport and communications) hopes to achieve a growth rate of 6% per annum.

AGRICULTURE. Coffee is by far the most important source of rural income. Harari coffee (long berry Mocha) is cultivated in the east; Abyssinian coffee is produced in Kaffa and the surrounding provinces, much of it growing wild.

Teff (*Eragrastis abyssinica*) is the principal food grain, followed by barley, wheat, maize and durra. Pulses and oilseeds are imported for local consumption and export. Cane sugar is an important crop.

Livestock: 12·2m. sheep, 25m. cattle, 11·1m. goats; smaller numbers of donkeys, horses, mules and camels. Hides and skins and butter (ghee) are important for home consumption and export. Sheep, cattle and chickens (44·5m.) are the main providers of meat. The pig is little known. Seafishing is being developed at Massawa and Assab.

MINING. Ethiopia has little proved mineral wealth. Salt (202,035 tons in 1967–68) is produced mainly in Eritrea, while a placer goldmine is worked by the Government at Adola in the south. Gold production, in 1967–68, was 956,816 grammes. Small quantities of other minerals are produced. Deposits of potash salts in the Dankali salt plains in the north-east part of the country are now being worked.

American companies have been granted oil-exploration concessions in Ogaden and Eritrea respectively. A natural gas strike was made offshore near Massawa in Dec. 1969.

INDUSTRY. The most important products of the small but growing industries are cotton yarn and fabrics, cement, sugar, salt, cigarettes, canned foodstuffs, building materials, footwear and paint. Most industry is centred around Addis Ababa and Asmara.

A Russian state-owned oil refinery built at Assab came on stream in 1967 with a capacity of 600,000 tons of crude.

Installed electricity generating power of the Ethiopian Electric Light and Power Authority was 137 mW. in 1968. Production in 1967 totalled 294,493,000 kw.

COMMERCE. Coffee is by far the most important export, followed by pulses, oilseeds, hides, goat skins, sheep skins. Imports are textiles (mainly from Japan), vehicles, machinery, iron and steel goods, and petroleum products. Coffee exports, 1968, were 80,250 metric tons.

Imports and exports (in £1m. sterling) for 6 years (ending 9 Dec.):

	1964	1965	1966	1967	1968	1969
Imports	44·0	53·7	57·8	59·9	72·1	64·7
Exports	37·5	40·4	38·4	42·1	44·5	48·8

In 1969 the main supplying countries were: Italy (E$59·8m.), West Germany (E$55·6m.), Japan (E$42·1m.), USA (E$40m.), UK (E$39m.), France (E$19·8m.). The principal purchasing countries were: USA (E$125·2m.), West Germany (E$27m.), Italy (E$21m.), French Terr. of Afars and Issas (E$18·9m.), Saudi Arabia (E$17·2m.), Japan (E$14·1m.).

The chief items of import in 1969 were: Machinery and transport equipment (E$133·4m.), manufactured goods (E$86·5m.), mineral fuels and lubricants (E$28·2m.), chemical elements and compounds (E$43·5m.), meat and live animals (E$19·7m.). The main items of export were: Fruit and vegetables, fresh and frozen (E$28·7m.), coffee (E$174m.), hides and skins (E$29·2m.), oilseeds (E$27·3m.).

Total trade between Ethiopia and UK (British Board of Trade returns, in £1,000 sterling):

	1965	1966	1967	1968	1969	1970
Imports to UK	1,446	1,714	1,502	1,954	1,950	1,963
Exports from UK	4,275	4,472	3,928	5,120	4,813 }	4,834
Re-exports from UK	40	66	122	94	165	

ROADS. Loans totalling E$83·75m. have been made between 1951 and 1968 by the International Bank and the International Development Agency for 3 programmes for improving and extending the road system. A fourth programme began in 1968 and is being financed by E$190m. in foreign loans. The Imperial Highway Authority now maintains some 6,200 km of roads and is engaged in constructing another 850 km of all-weather roads. Chief motor roads: Massawa–Asmara–Sudan; Asmara–Dessie–Addis Ababa; Asmara–Gondar–Addis Ababa; Addis Ababa–Jimma; Addis Ababa–Lekemti; Addis Ababa–Nazareth; Dire-Dawa–Hargeisa; Dessie–Assab; Addis Ababa–Adola. Number of motor vehicles (1968): Cars, 34,430; lorries and trucks, 5,560; buses, 2,080; motor cycles, 1,670.

SHIPPING. A state shipping line was established in 1964. In Dec. 1969 it owned 5 cargo vessels and 2 tankers.

RAILWAYS. The Franco-Ethiopian Railway Co., owned by the 2 governments, operates the line from Djibouti to Addis Ababa. The line is of metre gauge, with a total length of 486½ miles. Trains run three times weekly in each direction, covering the distance in one night and one day. A branch line to Dilla (Sidamo province) is under construction. The railway carried 322,500 tons of freight and 384,800 passengers in 1968. The Northern Railway of Ethiopia from Massawa to Asmara and Agordat (191 miles, 95-cm gauge) is owned and operated by the Ethiopian Government. It carried 183,500 tons of freight and 310,000 passengers in 1967.

AVIATION. Ethiopian Air Lines, formed in 1946, operates through a management contract with Trans-World Air Lines; it provides services to Cairo, Athens, Frankfurt, Khartoum, Lagos, Accra, Rome, Nairobi, Entebbe, Dar es Salaam, Dijbouti, Aden, Beirut, Taiz, Karachi and Delhi, in addition to internal services. The following airlines operate through Asmara and Addis Ababa: Alitalia, East African Airways, Air India, Lufthansa, United Arab Airlines and Sudan Airways. Middle East Airlines, El Al and Air Djibouti operate through Addis Ababa only.

POST. The postal system serves 54 points in the Empire, mainly by air-mail. All the main centres are connected with Addis Ababa by telephone or radio telegraph. International telephone services are available at certain hours to most countries in Europe, North America and India. Number of telephones (1969), 36,034, of which 23,106 in Addis Ababa and 5,507 in Asmara. Television was introduced in Addis Ababa in Nov. 1964. There were 138 telex subscribers in 1969.

BANKING. The State Bank was renamed the National Bank of Ethiopia in Oct. 1963, when its commercial activities were transferred to the newly established Commercial Bank of Ethiopia. At the same time another new bank, the Investment Bank of Ethiopia, was set up with a capital of E$10m., of which the Government held the majority of shares. In Sept. 1965 it became the Ethiopian Investment Corporation, which is a substantial shareholder in a number of industrial and other ventures. The Investment Corporation has now been merged with the Development Bank of Ethiopia and the two are now known as 'The Agricultural and Industrial Development Bank, SC'

Two Italian banks have branches in Asmara; an Italian bank is represented in Addis Ababa. The Addis Ababa Bank Share Co. is connected with National & Grindlays Bank Ltd.

WEIGHTS AND MEASURES. The metric system of weights and measures is officially in use. Native weights and measures vary considerably in the various provinces; the principal ones are: *Frasilla* = approximately 37½ lb.; *gasha*, the principal unit of land measure, which is normally about 100 acres but can vary between 80 and 300 acres, depending on the quality of the land.

DIPLOMATIC REPRESENTATIVES

Ethiopia maintains embassies in:

Congo (K.)	Japan	Somalia
France	Jordan	Sudan
Germany (West)	Kenya	Sweden
Ghana	Liberia	Turkey
Greece	Mexico	USSR
Haiti	Morocco	UAR
India	Nigeria	UK
Israel	Saudi Arabia	USA
Italy	Senegal	Yugoslavia
Ivory Coast		

OF ETHIOPIA IN GREAT BRITAIN (17 Princes Gate, SW7)

Ambassador: Lieut.-Gen. Iyassu Mengesha.
Counsellor: Ato Engeda Abbebe.

OF GREAT BRITAIN IN ETHIOPIA

Ambassador: Alan Campbell, CMG.
Counsellor and Head of Chancery: R. B. Dorman.
Service Attachés: Lieut.-Col. R. M. Holman, MBE (*Defence, Navy and Army*);
Wing Cdr K. V. Metcalfe, DFC (*Air*). *First Secretaries:* R. C. Robinson, MBE
(*Commercial*); G. R. Sutherland (*Civil Air*, resident at Beirut).

There are Consuls at Addis Ababa and Asmara.

OF ETHIOPIA IN THE USA (2134 Kalorama Rd, NW,
Washington, D.C., 20008)

Ambassador: Dr Minasse Haile.
Service Attaché: Col. Taferi Bante.
First Secretaries: Ghebeyehou Mekbib; Berhanu Dinka.

OF THE USA IN ETHIOPIA

Ambassador: William O. Hall.
Deputy Head of Mission: R. L. Yost. *Heads of Sections:* Richard W. Petree
(*Political*); Ralph L. Lowry (*Consular*); Zachary P. Geaneas (*Administrative*).
Service Attachés: Col. John D. McClung, Jr (*Defence*), Col. Brian E. Gill, Jr
(*Army*).

There is a Consul-General at Asmara.

BOOKS OF REFERENCE

Handbook on Ethiopia. Univ. Press of Africa, 1969
Trade Directory of the Empire of Ethiopia. London, 1965
Clapham, C., *Haile Selassie's Government.* London, 1969
Doresse, J., *Ethiopia.* London, 1960
Lipsky, G. A. (ed.), *Ethiopia, its people, its society, its culture.* New Haven, Conn., 1962
Luther, E. W., *Ethiopia Today.* Stanford Univ. Press, 1958
Mosley, L., *Haile Selassie.* London, 1964
Rasmussen. *Welcome to Ethiopia.* Addis Ababa, 1967
Trevaskis, G. K. N., *Eritrea.* London, 1960
Ullendorf, E., *The Ethiopians.* 2nd ed. OUP, 1965

FINLAND
Suomen Tasavalta—Republiken Finland

HISTORY. Since the Middle Ages Finland was a part of the realm of Sweden.
In the 18th century parts of south-eastern Finland were conquered by Russia,
and the rest of the country was ceded to Russia by the peace treaty of Hamina in
1809. Finland became an autonomous grand-duchy which retained its previous
laws and institutions under its Grand Duke, the Emperor of Russia. After the
Russian revolution Finland declared itself independent on 6 Dec. 1917. The
country was freed from Russian troops in a war from Jan. to May 1918, in which,
simultaneously, domestic groups advocating a socialist system of government
were defeated.

On 30 Nov. 1939 Soviet troops invaded Finland, after Finland had rejected territorial concessions demanded by the USSR. These, however, had to be made in the peace treaty of 12 March 1940, amounting to 32,806 sq. km and including the Carelian Isthmus, Viipuri and the shores of Lake Ladoga.

When the German attack on the USSR was launched in June 1941 Finland again became involved in the war against the USSR. On 19 Sept. 1944 an armistice was signed in Moscow. Finland agreed to cede to Russia the Petsamo area in addition to cessions made in 1940 (total 42,934 sq. km) and to lease to Russia for 50 years the Porkkala headland to be used as a military base. Further, Finland undertook to pay 300m. gold dollars in reparations within 6 years (later extended to 8 years). The peace treaty was signed in Paris on 10 Feb. 1947. The payment of reparations was completed on 19 Sept. 1952. The military base of Porkkala was returned to Finland on 26 Jan. 1956.

An agreement of friendship, non-aggression and mutual assistance between Finland and the USSR was concluded in Moscow on 6 April 1948 for 10 years, extended on 19 Sept. 1955 to cover a period of 20 years and extended on 19 July 1970 for a further period of 20 years.

Treaty of Peace with Finland (10 Feb. 1947). Cmd. 7484

CONSTITUTION AND GOVERNMENT. Finland is a republic according to the Constitution of 17 July 1919.

Parliament consists of one chamber of 200 members chosen by direct and proportional election, in which all Finnish citizens (men or women) who have reached their 20th year have the vote. The country is divided into 15 electoral districts with a representation proportional to their population. Every citizen entitled to vote is eligible for Parliament, which is elected for 4 years, but can be dissolved sooner by the President.

The President is elected for 6 years by a college of 300 electors, elected by the votes of the citizens in the same way as the members of Parliament.

President of Finland: Dr Urho Kekkonen (elected 15 Feb. 1956, re-elected 15 Feb. 1962 and 15 Feb. 1968); he received 201 votes out of 300 in 1968.

Parliament elected on 15–16 March 1970: National Coalition, 37; Liberals, 8; Swedish Party, 12 (including 1 for Coalition of Åland); Centre, 36: Smallholders, 18; Social Democratic Party, 52; Democratic League, 36; Christian Federation, 1.

The following Council of State (Cabinet) was appointed by the President on 15 July 1970:

Prime Minister: Ahti Karjalainen (Centre).
Deputy Prime Minister and Labour: Veikko Helle (SDP).
Foreign Affairs: Väinö Leskinen (SDP). *Justice:* Erkki Tuominen (DL). *Interior:* Artturi Jämsén (Centre). *Defence:* Kristian Gestrin (Swedish). *Finance:* Carl Olof Tallgren (Swedish), Valto Käkelä (SDP). *Education:* Jaakko Itälä (Liberals), Meeri Kalavainen (SDP). *Agriculture:* Nestori Kaasalainen (Centre). *Traffic:* Veikko Saarto (DL). *Trade and Industry:* Arne Berner (Liberals), Kalervo Haapasalo (SDP). *Social Affairs:* Anna-Liisa Tiekso (DL), Katri-Helena Eskelinen (Centre). *Prime Minister's Office:* Olavi J. Mattila (Centre).

National flag: Blue cross on white.
National anthem: Maamme; Swedish: Vårt land (words by J. L. Runeberg, 1843; tune by F. Pacius, 1848).

Finnish and Swedish are the official languages of Finland.

LOCAL GOVERNMENT. For administrative purposes Finland is divided into 12 provinces (*lääni*, Sw.: *län*). The administration of each province is entrusted to a governor (*maaherra*, Sw.: *landshövding*) appointed by the President. He directs the activities of the provincial office (*lääninhallitus*, Sw.: *länsstyrelse*) and of local sheriffs (*nimismies*, Sw.: *länsman*). In 1970 the number of sheriff districts was 238.

The unit of local government is the commune. Main fields of communal activities are local planning, roads and harbours, sanitary services, education, health services and social aid. The communes raise taxes independent from state taxation. Three different kinds of communes are distinguished, of which two are urban (*kaupunki* and *kauppala*, Sw.: *stad* and *köping*) and one rural. In 1970 there were 518 communes, of which 78 belonged to the urban classes. In all communes communal councils are elected for terms of 4 years; all inhabitants (men and women) of the commune who have reached their 20th year are entitled to vote and eligible. The executive power is in each commune vested in a board which consists of members elected by the council and one or a few chief officials of the commune. Several communes often form an association for the administration of some common institution, *e.g.*, a hospital or a vocational school.

The autonomous county (*landskap*) of Åland has a county council (*landsting*) of one chamber, elected according to rules corresponding to those for parliamentary elections. In addition to its provincial governor it has a county board with executive power in matters within the field of the autonomy of the county.

Constitution Act and Parliament Act of Finland. Helsinki, 1959
The Finnish Parliament. Helsinki, 1957
Local Self-Government in Finland and the Finnish Municipal Law. Helsinki, 1960
Democracy in Finland. Studies in Politics and Government. Political Science Association. Helsinki 1960

AREA AND POPULATION. The area and the population of Finland on 31 Dec. 1969 (Swedish names in brackets):

Province	Area[1] (sq. km)	Population	Population per sq. km
Uusimaa (Nyland)	9,868	1,016,000	103·0
Turku-Pori (Åbo-Björneborg)	22,014	683,100	31·0
Ahvenanmaa (Åland)	1,481	21,600	14·6
Häme (Tavastehus)	17,715	639,700	36·1
Kymi (Kymmene)	10,736	348,400	32·5
Mikkeli (St Michel)	16,425	223,500	13·6
Pohjois-Karjala (Norra Karelen)	17,980	190,700	10·6
Kuopio	16,734	263,300	15·7
Keski-Suomi (Mellersta Finland)	15,764	247,100	15·7
Vaasa (Vasa)	26,119	435,200	16·7
Oulu (Uleåborg)	56,642	419,700	7·4
Lappi (Lappland)	93,997	218,700	2·3
Total	305,475	4,707,000	15·4

[1] Excluding inland water area which totals 31,557 sq. km.

The growth of the population, which was 421,500 in 1750, has been:

End of year	Urban	Rural	Total	Percentage urban
1800	46,600	786,100	832,700	5·6
1900	333,300	2,322,600	2,655,900	12·5
1950	1,302,400	2,727,400	4,029,800	32·3
1960	1,707,000	2,739,200	4,446,200	38·4
1969	2,365,600	2,341,400	4,707,000	50·3

The population on 31 Dec. 1960 by language primarily spoken: Finnish, 4,108,269 (92·4%); Swedish, 330,538 (7·4%); Russian, 2,752; Lapp, 1,312; other languages, 3,351.

The principal towns with estimated population, 31 Dec. 1969, are (Swedish names in brackets):

Helsinki (Helsingfors)—capital	533,960	Joensuu	36,121
(metropolitan area	804,256)	Imatra	35,074
Tampere (Tammerfors)	155,549	Kotka	34,244
(metropolitan area	217,311)	Kemi	29,682
Turku (Åbo)	154,707	Rovaniemi	29,273
(metropolitan area	220,340)	Hyvinkää (Hyvinge)	33,763
Espoo (Esbo)	93,041	Rauma (Raumo)	25,619
Lahti	89,349	Kouvola	25,698
Oulu (Uleåborg)	86,764	Mikkeli (St Michel)	25,327
Pori (Björneborg)	72,854	Varkaus	24,582
Jyväskylä	58,048	Kuusankoski	22,403
Kuopio	64,783	Riihimäki	22,844
Lappeenranta (Villmanstrand)	51,096	Karhula	22,039
Vaasa (Vasa)	49,583	Kokkola (Gamlakarleby)	22,729
Hämeenlinna (Tavastehus)	37,808	Seinäjoki	20,098

VITAL STATISTICS in calendar years:

	Living births	Of which illegitimate	Still-born	Marriages	Deaths (exclusive of still-born)	Emigration[1]
1967	77,289	3,908	825	41,273	43,790	951
1968	73,654	3,901	731	40,241	45,013	1,652
1969	68,111	..	624	40,744	46,036	2,007

[1] Excluding emigration to other Nordic countries.

In 1969 the rate per 1,000 was: Births, 14·5; infantile deaths (per 1,000 births), 13·9; marriages, 8·7; deaths, 9·8.

General Census of Population 1960. 13 vols. Helsinki, 1962–65
Vital Statistics. Annual, Helsinki

RELIGION. Liberty of conscience is guaranteed to members of all religions. National churches are the Lutheran National Church and the Greek Orthodox Church of Finland. The Lutheran Church is divided into 8 bishoprics (Turku being the archiepiscopal see), 72 provostships and 597 parishes. The Greek Orthodox Church is divided into 2 bishoprics (Kuopio being the archiepiscopal see) and 25 parishes, in addition to which there are 2 monasteries and convents.

Percentage of the total population at the end of 1968: Lutherans, 92·7; Greek Orthodox, 1·3; others, 0·7; not members of any religion, 5·3.

EDUCATION (1968–69). *Higher Education.* The institutions of academic education and the number of teachers and students are:

	Founded	Teachers	Students Total	Women
Universities				
Helsinki	1640[1]	1,730	23,011	12,327
Turku (Swedish)	1919	180	2,000	814
Turku (Finnish)	1922	649	6,278	3,441
Jyväskylä	1958[2]	236	3,588	2,074
Oulu	1958	449	3,453	1,396
Tampere	1966[3]	269	4,727	2,693
nstitute of Technology, Helsinki	1849	1,052	4,695	318
College of Veterinary Medicine, Helsinki	1946	46	159	64
Schools of Economics				
Helsinki (Finnish)	1911	120	2,651	1,218
Helsinki (Swedish)	1927	71	1,142	526
Turku (Swedish)	1927	61	364	146
Turku (Finnish)	1950	55	718	270
Vaasa	1968	31	150	91
Teachers' training colleges				
Helsinki	1947	37	275	158
Turku	1949	28	219	126
Jyräskylä	1934[4]	51	273	176
Oulu	1953[4]	26	161	104

[1] In Turku, moved to Helsinki in 1828.
[2] Previously teachers' training college since 1934.
[3] Previously College of Social Sciences in Helsinki since 1925.
[4] Previously included in data for the universities above.

Secondary Education (1968–69). There were 430 secondary schools with a curriculum of 8–9 years (aiming at later academic education) and 195 'middle' schools with a curriculum of 5–6 years (aiming at later higher vocational education). They had 16,193 teachers and 305,420 pupils, of which 169,689 were girls. In 11 training colleges for elementary school teachers there were 192 teachers and 1,267 students (of which 717 women). In 83 folk high schools there were 1,037 teachers and 8,016 pupils (5,837 females).

Elementary Education (1968–69). School attendance is compulsory between the ages of 7 and (usually) 16 years. For elementary education there were 553 schools in towns and 4,883 schools in other areas. The total number of teachers was 24,120 and the number of pupils 489,542.

Vocational Education (1968–69). Special institutions for vocational education in technical, commercial, agricultural, health service and other fields had a total of approximately 100,000 pupils.

CINEMAS. In Dec. 1969 there were 341 cinemas with a seating capacity of 104,584.

NEWSPAPERS. In 1969 the number of newspapers published more often than once a week was 118, of which 102 in Finnish, 15 in Swedish and 1 bilingual.

Gustafson, M., *Education in Finland*. Ministry for Foreign Affairs. Helsinki, 1967
Higher Education and Research in Finland. Ministry of Education. Helsinki, 1968
Niini, A., *Vocational Education*. National Board for Vocational Education. Helsinki, 1968

SOCIAL WELFARE. The National Pension Institute administers general systems of old age pensions (to all persons over 65 years of age and disabled younger persons) and of health insurance. An additional system of compulsory old age pensions paid for by the employers is in force and works through the Central Pension Security Institute. Systems for child welfare, care of vagrants, alcoholics and drug addicts and other public aid are administered by the communes and supervised by the National Social Board and the Ministry of Social Affairs and Health.

The total cost of social security amounted to 4,631m. marks in 1968. Out of this, 1,324m. (29%) was spent for health, 134m. (3%) for industrial accidents, 488m. (10%) for unemployment, 1,602m. (34%) for old age and disability, 638m. (14%) for family allowances and child welfare, 127m. (3%) for general welfare purposes, 187m. (4%) for war-disabled, etc., and 131m. (3%) as tax reductions for children. Out of the total expenditure 37% was financed by the State, 23% by local authorities, 31% by employers and 9% by the beneficiaries.

In 1969 there were 4,654 physicians, 2,619 dentists and 66,720 hospital beds.

Social Services in Finland: Social Welfare. Helsinki, 1969; *Social Insurance*. Helsinki, 1969; *Social Allowances*. Helsinki, 1969; *Labour Protection*. Helsinki, 1970
Social Security in the Nordic Countries 1966. Statistical Reports of the Nordic Countries, vol. 16. Copenhagen, 1970

JUSTICE. The lowest courts of justice are the municipal courts in towns and district courts in the country. Municipal courts are held by the burgomaster and at least 2 members of court, district court by judge and 5 jurors, the judge alone deciding, unless the jurors unanimously differ from him, when their decision prevails. From these courts an appeal lies to the courts of appeal (*Hovioikeus*) in Turku, Vaasa, Kuopio and Helsinki. The Supreme Court (*Korkein oikeus*) sits in Helsinki. Judges can be removed only by judicial sentence.

Two functionaries, the *Oikeuskansleri* or Chancellor of Justice, and the *Oikeusasiamies*, or Solicitor-General, exercise control over the administration of justice. The former acts also as counsel and public prosecutor for the Government; while the latter, who is appointed by the Parliament, exerts a general control over all courts of law and public administration.

In 1970 the prison population numbered 5,090 men and 112 women; the number of convictions in 1968 was 228,288, of which 167,334 were for minor offences with maximum penalty of fines or up to 6 months' imprisonment.

Merikoski, V., *Précis du droit public de la Finlande*. Helsinki, 1954

FINANCE. Currency. The unit of currency, starting 1 Jan. 1963, is the new *mark* of 100 *pennis*, equalling 100 old *marks*. The gold standard was suspended on 12 Oct. 1931. Aluminium bronze coins are 50, 20 and 10 *pennis*; copper coins, 5 and 1 *pennis*; aluminium coins, 1 *pennis*; silver, 1 *mark* pieces. Exchange rate from 31 Oct. 1970: 9·980 marks = £1; 4·176 marks = US$1.

Budget. Actual revenue and expenditure for the calendar years 1966–69, the ordinary budget for 1970 and the proposed budget for 1971 in 1m. marks:

	1966	1967	1968	1969	1970	1971
Revenue	7,413	7,897	9,513	10,786	10,298	10,957
Expenditure	7,167	8,058	9,785	10,210	10,297	10,956

Of the total revenue in 1969, 20% derived from direct taxes, 52% from indirect taxes and 5% from social-security contributions. Of the total expenditure in

1969, 16% went to education, 12% to social security, 7% to health, 12% to agriculture and forestry, 13% to transport and communications, 5% to defence and 14% to the public debt.

At the end of Dec. 1969 the foreign loans totalled 1,656m. marks, of which 1,594m. were long-term loans, 10m. promissory notes to international organizations and 51m. short-term loans. The internal loans amounted to 2,770m. marks, of which 2,317m. were consolidated debt and 453m. short-term loans. The cash deficit was 123m. marks. The total public debt was 4,426m. marks.

DEFENCE. The peace treaty of Paris, signed on 10 Feb. 1947, restricted the armed forces of Finland to a land Army, including frontier troops and anti-aircraft artillery, with a total strength of 34,400 personnel; a Navy with a personnel strength of 4,500 and a total tonnage of 10,000 tons; an Air Force, including any naval air arm, of 60 fighting aircraft, including reserves, with a total personnel strength of 3,000. Bombers with internal bomb-carrying facilities are expressly forbidden. Total strength of the trained reserve is about 700,000.

The military, naval and air clauses of the peace treaty are subject to modification by agreement between the Security Council of the United Nations and Finland.

The period of training is 240 to 330 days. Military training outside the Army, Navy and Air Force is forbidden.

Army. The Army consists of 1 armoured brigade, 6 infantry brigades, 4 artillery regiments. Total strength (1970), 34,000.

Navy. In 1970 the Navy comprised 2 frigates (*ex*-Soviet), a training ship (former British frigate), 2 corvettes, 2 minelayers, 15 fast patrol boats, 5 inshore minesweepers, 11 motor patrol boats, 4 coastguard patrol vessels, 9 transport craft, 8 icebreakers and a cable ship. Personnel, 2,000 officers and men.

Air Force. The Air Force has 3 operational groups, a military school of aviation and air force technical school, a depot, a transport squadron and a signal school. The combat units have received 38 MiG-21 day fighters and 4 MiG-21UTI two-seat trainers, supplementing an earlier squadron of Gnat light jet fighters. Other equipment includes Saab-91D Safir piston-engined primary trainers, Magister jet basic trainers, MiG-15UTI jet advanced trainers, DC-3 transport aircraft, Il-28 target tugs and some SM-1 (Polish-built Mi-1), Mi-4 and Agusta-Bell 204 helicopters. The Gnat squadron will be re-equipped with 12 Swedish-built Saab-35XS supersonic all-weather interceptors in 1974–75.

AGRICULTURE. Agriculture is one of the chief occupations of the people, although the cultivated area covers only 9% of the land. The arable area was divided in 1969 into 297,257 farms, and the distribution of this area by the size of the farms was: Less than 5 hectares cultivated, 108,796 farms; 5–20 hectares, 165,924 farms; 20–50 hectares, 20,625 farms; 50–100 hectares, 1,620 farms; over 100 hectares, 292 farms.

The principal crops (area in 1,000 hectares, yield in metric tons) were in 1969:

Crop	Area	Yield	Crop	Area	Yield
Rye	69·9	125.800	Oats	482·8	1,139,700
Barley	372·6	840.000	Potatoes	58·2	779.900
Wheat	203·5	481,400	Hay	927·6	2,922,800

The total area under cultivation in 1969 was 2,669,100 hectares. Creamery butter production in 1969 was 100,500 metric tons, and production of cheese was 34,900 metric tons.

Livestock (1970): Horses, 89,800; milch cows, 889,100; other cattle, 983,800; sheep, 188,600; pigs, 1,002,400; poultry, 8·6m.; reindeer, 184,600.

FORESTRY. The total forest land amounts to 21·87m. hectares. The productive forest land covers 16,909,000 hectares. The growing stock was valued at 1,410m. cu. metres in 1960–63 and the annual growth at 43m. cu. metres.

In 1969 there were exported: Round timber, 739,029 cu. metres; sawn wood, 959,144 standards; plywood and veneers, 614,076 cu. metres.

MINING AND MANUFACTURING. The most important mines are Outokumpu (copper, discovered in 1910) and Otanmäki (iron, discovered in 1953). In 1969 the metal content (in metric tons) of the output of copper concentrates was 33,135, of zinc concentrates 70,845, of nickel concentrates 3,626 and of iron concentrates and pellets 662,000.

The following data cover establishments with a total personnel of 5 or more in 1968:

Industry	Establishments	Personnel	Value of production Gross value (1m. marks)	Value added (1m. marks)
Metal mining	11	3,951	251	196
Other mining and quarrying	76	1,894	63	38
Food	1,485	46,667	5,789	1,110
Beverages	38	4,812	289	114
Tobacco	4	1,477	119	68
Textiles	259	27,969	849	397
Clothing, etc.	504	29,759	739	352
Wood	564	32,222	1,426	531
Furniture and fixtures	356	13,104	330	164
Pulp and paper	209	44,593	4,441	1,398
Printing and publishing	613	27,827	949	565
Leather	71	2,666	90	35
Rubber	80	5,322	175	103
Chemical products	185	16,110	1,279	567
Petroleum and coal products	18	1,549	610	194
Non-metallic mineral products	368	17,780	628	342
Basic metal industries	64	11,878	1,550	268
Metal products	394	23,789	732	394
Non-electrical machinery	419	41,613	1,454	787
Electrical machinery, etc.	145	17,560	790	328
Transport equipment	643	41,662	1,399	658
Other manufacturing	213	9,413	318	150
Electricity	370	15,571	1,432	734
Gas and steam	65	2,173	228	64
Water	53	1,219	97	80
Total	7,207	442,580	26,027	9,637

ELECTRICITY. The production of power is based mainly on water. The power production was (in 1m. kwh.) 8,605 in 1960; 17,834 in 1968 and 19,979 in 1969.

Economic Survey of Finland. Annual
Census of Agriculture 1959. Helsinki, 1962
Statistics of Agriculture. Annual
Industrial Statistics of Finland. Annual
Economic Review (Kansallis–Osake–Pankki). Quarterly
Knoellinger, C. E., *Labor in Finland.* Harvard Univ. Press, 1960
Westermarck, N., *Finnish Agriculture.* Helsinki, 1963

COMMERCE. Imports and exports for calendar years, in 1m. marks:

	1965	1966	1967	1968	1969
Imports	5,265·1	5,524·3	5,794·4	6,710·9	8.504·8
Exports	4,566·0	4,818·5	5,231·2	6,874·2	8,344·7

The trade with some principal import and export countries was (in 1,000 marks):

Country	Imports 1968	Imports 1969	Exports 1968	Exports 1969
Argentina	13,034	18,603	65,747	67,341
Belgium–Luxembourg	124,787	171.399	170,297	212,887
Brazil	75,821	107,732	46,974	36,917
China	29,276	30,853	48,377	23,927
Colombia	58,573	73,884	19,357	20,503
Denmark	210,625	261.542	249,925	329,596
France	250,955	303,837	275,024	352,699
Germany (East)	61,504	68,141	47,599	55,006
Germany (West)	1,023,486	1,380,970	723,544	831,075
Italy	159,601	195.252	206,986	239,071
Japan	106,665	172,610	19,211	29,986
Netherlands	208,545	271,046	316,274	362.211
Norway	150,842	234,395	180,223	205,029

Country	Imports		Exports	
	1967	1968	1967	1968
Poland	108,694	124,482	83,156	134,104
Sweden	961,262	1,289,485	720,139	1,104,229
Switzerland	175,398	208,920	78,377	124,691
USSR	1,123,598	1,089,285	1,055,978	1,165,178
UK	892,685	1,135,322	1,416,089	1,522,704
USA	303,751	434,356	405,006	500,301

Principal imports 1969 (in 1m. marks): Food and live animals, 704; crude materials, inedible, except fuels, 628; mineral fuels, lubricants, etc., 963; chemicals, 908, textile yarn, fabrics, etc., 528; iron and steel, 574, machinery apparatus and appliances, 1,673; transport equipment, 1,038.

Principal exports 1969 (in 1m. marks): Food and live animals, 279; wood shaped or simply worked, 831; wood pulp, 1,078; veneers, plywood, etc., and other wood manufactures, 480; paper and paper-board, 3,351; textiles including clothing, 421; machinery, apparatus and appliances, 807; transport equipment, 562.

Total trade between UK and Finland (in £1,000 sterling; British Board of Trade returns):

	1966	1967	1968	1969	1970
Imports to UK	122,858	129,767	160,686	173,608	195,005
Exports from UK	75,562	71,310	78,626	99,079 }	128,901
Re-exports from UK	1,365	1,298	1,276	2,285 }	

Finnish Foreign Trade Directory, 1969. Helsinki, 1968

SHIPPING. The total registered mercantile marine on 31 Dec. 1969 was 508 vessels of 1,242,300 gross tons. In 1969 the total number of vessels arriving in Finland from abroad was 17,296 and the goods discharged amounted to 18·4m. metric tons. The goods loaded for export from Finland ports amounted to 12m. metric tons.

The lakes, rivers and canals are navigable for about 6,600 km. Timber floating is important, and there are about 41,500 km of floatable inland waterways. In 1969, about 25,000 ships and 19,500 timber rafts passed through the canals.

On 27 Aug. 1963 the USSR leased to Finland the Russian part of the canal connecting Lake Saimaa with the Gulf of Finland. After extensive rebuilding the canal was opened for traffic in 1968. The Saimaa Canal and deepwater channels on Lake Saimaa (520 km) can be used by vessels with dimensions not larger than follows: length 78 metres, width 11 metres, draught 4·2 metres and height of mast 24·5 metres.

ROADS. In 1970 there were 39,870 km of highways and 32,109 km of other public roads. At the end of 1969 there were 643,057 registered cars, 45,210 lorries, 51,825 vans and 7,861 buses.

RAILWAYS. On 31 Dec. 1969 the total length of the railways was 5,722 km, of which all except 38 km was owned by the State. The gauge is 5 ft. In 1969 the number of passengers carried was 25·6m. and the amount of goods carried was 22·4m. metric tons. The total revenue in 1969 was 485m. marks and the total expenditure 600m. marks.

AVIATION. The scheduled traffic of Finnish airlines covered 17m. km in 1969. The number of passsengers was 1,035,280 and the number of passenger-km 587m. The air transport of freight and mail amounted to 13,452,000 metric ton-km.

TELECOMMUNICATIONS. In 1969 there were 4,754 post offices and 827 telegraph offices. The total length of telegraph wires was 287,917 km and that of telephone wires 5,323,192 km. The number of telephones (1969) was

1,089,700. All post and telegraph systems are administered by the State jointly with a large part of the telephone services. The total revenues from postal services were 259·1m. marks and from (wire and radio) telegraph services 24m. marks.

On 31 Dec. 1969 the number of wireless licences was 1,744,039 and that of television licences, 1,014,523.

BANKING. The Bank of Finland (founded in 1811) is owned by the State and under the guarantee and supervision of Parliament. It is the only bank of issue, and the limit of its right to issue notes is fixed to equal the value of its assets of gold and foreign holdings plus 500m. marks. Notes of 100, 50, 10, 5 and 1 marks are in circulation, and their total value at the end of 1969 was 1,298m. marks.

At the end of 1969 the deposits in banking institutions totalled 16,123m. marks and the loans granted by them 16,278m. marks. The most important groups of banking institutions were:

	Number of institutions	Number of offices	Deposits (1m. marks)	Loans (1m. marks)
Commercial banks	6	824	6,262	6,585
Savings banks	330	1,252	4,547	3,802
Post office savings bank	1	15[1]	1,637	1,049
Co-operative credit societies	465	1,224	3,198	3,228

[1] In addition: 2,882 post offices.

Bank of Finland Monthly Bulletin. Helsinki, from 1926
Unitas. Quarterly Review, issued by Nordiska Föreningsbanken. Helsinki, from 1929
Economic Review (issued quarterly by Kansallis–Osake–Pankki). Helsinki, from 1948

WEIGHTS AND MEASURES. The metric system of weights and measures was introduced in 1887 and is officially and universally employed.

DIPLOMATIC REPRESENTATIVES

Finland maintains embassies in:

Algeria (also for Libya and Tunisia)
Argentina (also for Chile, Paraguay and Uruguay)
Australia (also for New Zealand)
Austria (also for Vatican)
Belgium (also for Luxembourg)
Brazil
Bulgaria
Canada
China
Czechoslovakia (also Minister for Albania)
Denmark
Ethiopia (also for Kenya, Uganda and Zambia)
France
Hungary
India (also for Burma, Ceylon, Indonesia and Thailand)
Iraq
Israel
Italy (also for Cyprus and Malta)
Japan (also for Philippines)
Lebanon (also for Kuwait)
Mexico (also for Costa Rica, Cuba, El Salvador and Guatemala)
Netherlands (also for Irish Republic)
Nigeria (also for Cameroun, Ivory Coast, Senegal)
Norway (also for Iceland)
Peru (also for Bolivia, Colombia, Ecuador, Venezuela)
Poland
Romania
Spain (also for Morocco)
Sweden
Switzerland (also for Portugal)
Tanzania
Turkey (also for Afghánistán, Iran and Pakistan)
USSR (also for Mongolia)
UAR (also for Jordan, Sudan and Syria)
UK
USA
Yugoslavia (also for Greece)

Finland also maintains a legation in the Republic of South Africa and commercial representatives in East and West Germany.

OF FINLAND IN GREAT BRITAIN (66 Chester Sq., SW1)

Ambassador: Otso Uolevi Wartiovaara (accredited 15 Oct. 1968).
Counsellor: Göran Stenius. *First Secretary:* Esko Rajakoski. *Press Attaché:* Jaakko Bergquist.
Military, Air and Naval Attaché: Cdr. Kai Ruusuvuori.

There are consular representatives at Aberdeen, Belfast, Birmingham, Bradford, Bristol, Cardiff, Dover, Dundee, Edinburgh–Leith, Fowey, Glasgow, Great Yarmouth, Grimsby–Immingham, Hull, Leeds, Lerwick, Liverpool, London, Manchester, Newcastle upon Tyne, Nottingham, Preston, Rochester, St Helier, Sheffield, Southampton, Sunderland, Swansea and West Hartlepool.

OF GREAT BRITAIN IN FINLAND

Ambassador: W. B. J. Ledwidge, CMG.
Counsellor: R. Fox, OBE (*Commercial, Consul-General*).
Services Attachés: Lieut.-Col. J. W. Lloyd, MC (*Defence and Military*), Capt. H. M. Ellis, RN (*Navy*; resides at Moscow).
First Secretaries: A. C. Stuart (*Head of Chancery*); D. Stuart; D. A. Marston (*Information*); G. T. Burgess (*Commercial*); G. D. Cossar (*Labour*).

There are a Consul-General at Helsinki and Consuls at Hamina, Kotka, Oulu, Pori, Tampere, Turku and Vaasa.

OF FINLAND IN THE USA (1900–24th St. NW, Washington, D.C., 20008)

Ambassador: Olavi Munkki.
Counsellor: Niilo Pusa. *First Secretary:* Mauno Castrén. *Military, Naval and Air Attaché:* Col. Martti Frick.

OF THE USA IN FINLAND

Ambassador: Val Peterson.
Deputy Chief of Mission: James H. Lewis. *Heads of Sections:* John P. Owens (*Political*); David J. Dunford (*Economic*); Edward C. Howatt (*Commercial*); Gordon A. Cornell (*Consular*); Kenneth W. Linde (*Administrative*); Edmund R. Murphy (*USIA*). *Service Attachés:* Col. Wallace G. Matthews (*Defence and Air*), Col. George A. Rasula (*Army*), Cdr Roger F. Moury (*Navy*).

BOOKS OF REFERENCE

STATISTICAL INFORMATION. The Central Statistical Office (Tilastollinen päätoimisto, Swedish: Statistiska centralbyrån; address: P.O. Box 10 504, Helsinki 10) was founded in 1865 to replace earlier official statistical services dating from 1749 (in united Sweden–Finland). Statistics on foreign trade, agriculture, forestry, navigation, health and social welfare are produced by other state authorities. *Director:* Eino H. Laurila. Its publications include: *Statistical Yearbook of Finland* (from 1879) and *Bulletin of Statistics* (monthly, from 1924). A bibliography of all official statistics of Finland is published in Finnish, Swedish and English in each *Statistical Yearbook*.

Suomen valtiokalenteri (*State Calendar of Finland*; a Swedish version *Finlands statskalender* is published separately). Annual, Helsinki
Introduction to Finland (ed. G. Stenius). Ministry for Foreign Affairs. Helsinki, 1963 (with bibliography)
Alanne, V. S., *Finnish–English General Dictionary*. Helsinki, 1968
Facts about Finland. Helsinki, 1969
Finland: Creation and Construction. London, 1968
Finnish Foreign Policy: Studies in foreign politics. Political Science Association, Helsinki, 1963
Hall, W., *The Finns and their Country*. London, 1967
Jakobson, M., *Finnish Neutrality*. London, 1968
Jutikkala, E., and Pirinen, K., *A History of Finland*. New York, 1962
Platt, R. R. (ed.): *Finland and its Geography*. New York, 1955
Suomen Kartasto/Atlas of Finland/Atlas över Finland (ed. L. Aario). Finnish Geogr. Society, Helsinki, 1960
Suomi: Handbook of Finnish Geography. Finnish Geogr. Society, Helsinki, 1962
Törnudd, K., *The Electoral System of Finland*. London, 1969
Tuomikoski, A., and Slöör, A., *English–Finnish Dictionary*. Helsinki, 1964
Wuorinen, J. H., *A History of Finland*. Columbia Univ. Press, 1965

THE FRENCH COMMUNITY
La Communauté

The Constitution of the Fifth Republic 'offers to the oversea territories which manifest their will to adhere to it new institutions based on the common ideal of liberty, equality and fraternity and conceived with a view to their democratic evolution'. The territories were offered 3 solutions: they may keep their status; they may become overseas *départements*; they may become, singly or in groups, member states of the Community (Art. 76).

According to the amendment of the Constitution adopted on 4 June 1960, member-states of the Community may become independent and sovereign republics without ceasing to belong to the Community. The 12 African and Malagasy members availed themselves of this *loi constitutionnelle* and became independent by the transfer of 'common powers' (*compétences communes*).

The territorial structure of the Community and affiliated states is the following (March 1968):

I. FRENCH REPUBLIC

A. *Metropolitan Departments*

B. *Oversea Departments:*
 (i) Martinique
 (ii) Guadeloupe
 (iii) Réunion
 (iv) Guiana

C. *Overseas Territories:*
 (i) French Polynesia
 (ii) New Caledonia
 (iii) French Territory of the Afars and the Issas
 (iv) Comoro Archipelago
 (v) Saint-Pierre and Miquelon
 (vi) Southern and Antarctic Territories
 (vii) Wallis and Futuna Islands

II. MEMBER STATES

1. French Republic
2. Central African Republic
3. Republic of Congo
4. Republic of Gabon
5. Madagascar
6. Republic of Senegal
7. Republic of Chad

These countries have concluded formal 'Community participation agreements'.

III. 'Special relations' or 'special links' have been established by agreements between France and the other Franc zone countries and the following states:

1. Republic of Ivory Coast
2. Republic of Dahomey
3. Republic of Upper Volta
4. Islamic Republic of Mauritania
5. Republic of Niger
6. Federal Republic of Cameroun

IV. Co-operation in certain fields has been established by special agreements between France and the Republic of Mali.

V. Co-operation has been established between France and the Togo Republic by a convention signed on 10 July 1963.

VI. The states listed under II, 2–7, III, 1–3, 5 and 6, and V are members of the Organisation Commune Africaine et Malgache.

VII. Other regional organizations: (1) the Customs and Economic Union of Central Africa, comprising the Central African Republic, Congo, Gabon, Chad and Cameroun; the common external tariff, effective from 1 July 1962, does not apply to the countries listed under II and III; (2) the entente of Ivory Coast, Dahomey, Upper Volta, Niger; (3) the customs union of Senegal, Mali, Ivory Coast, Dahomey, Upper Volta, Niger and Mauritania; (4) the West-African monetary union of Senegal, Mauritania, Ivory Coast, Upper Volta, Niger, Dahomey and Togo.

VIII. Relations between France and Algeria (comprising the former Algerian and Sahara Departments) are governed by the Evian agreements of 19 March 1962 and subsequent agreements.

IX. The Anglo-French Condominium of the New Hebrides is administered according to the London Protocol of 6 Aug. 1914.

BOOKS OF REFERENCE

Blet, H., *Histoire de la colonisation français.* 3 vols. Paris, 1946–50
Brunschwig, H., *Mythes et réalités de l'impérialisme colonial français.* Paris, 1960
Ligot, M., *Les Accords de Coopération entre la France et les Etats Africains et Malgache d'expression française.* Paris, 1964
Nera, G., *La Communauté.* Paris, 1960

FRANCE

République Française

CONSTITUTION AND GOVERNMENT. The constitution of the Fifth Republic, superseding that of 1946, came into force on 4 Oct. 1958.

A referendum held in the French Republic and the oversea departments and territories on 28 Sept. 1958 approved the constitution drawn up by a committee which General de Gaulle had appointed in June. Apart from French Guinea, which voted over 90% against the constitution and for independence, the final result for metropolitan France, Algeria, the oversea departments and territories, and from French citizens living abroad or in trusteeship territories was as follows: Electorate, 45,840,642; voters, 36,893,979; valid votes, 36,486,251; Yes, 31,066,502; No, 5,419,749.

The Constitution consists of a preamble, dealing with the Rights of Man, and 92 articles. Emphasis is placed on the rôle of the President of the Republic. 'He sees that the Constitution is respected; he ensures, through his arbitration, the regular functioning of public powers as well as the continuity of the state. He is the guarantor of national independence' (Art. 5). He nominates and dismisses the Prime Minister and the other members of the government (Art. 8). He can dissolve the National Assembly after consultation with the Prime Minister and the presidents of the assemblies (Art. 12). He appoints to all military and civil offices of the Republic (Art. 13). 'When the institutions of the Republic, the independence of the Nation, the integrity of its territory or the fulfilment of its international commitments are threatened with immediate and grave danger, and when the regular functioning of constitutional public powers is interrupted, the President of the Republic takes the measures demanded by the circumstances, after official consultation with the Prime Minister, the presidents of the assemblies and the Constitutional Council' (Art. 16).

Under the revised article 6 of the constitution (6 Nov. 1962) the President of the Republic is now elected by direct universal suffrage. His term of office is 7 years.

'The government determines and conducts the policy of the nation' (Art. 20): 'the government may ask parliament for authority to take, by decrees and within a limited period, such measures as are normally within the province of the law' (Art. 38). Ministers must not be members of parliament (Art. 23). Votes of censure can only be carried by a majority of the members constituting the Assembly (Art. 49). The 2 ordinary sessions in autumn and spring are curtailed to a total of 5 months (Art. 28).

The 'Council of the Republic' has been re-named 'Senate'.

The 'Economic Council' has been re-named 'Economic and Social Council'.

The 'Constitutional Council' has to uphold the fairness of the elections and to act as a guardian of the constitution. It is composed of 9 members, 3 of whom are nominated by the President of the Republic, 3 by the President of the National

Assembly and 3 by the President of the Senate. In addition, past Presidents of the Republic are, by right, members of the Constitutional Council (Art. 56).

National flag: Blue, white, red (vertical).
National anthem: La Marseillaise (words and tune by C. Rouget de Lisle, 1792).

The Senate is composed of 283 members representing Metropolitan Departments, 7 Overseas Departments, 6 Oversea Territories, 6 Frenchmen residing outside France.

The elections for the National Assembly took place on 23 and 30 June 1968. State of parties: Union Democratique pour la République (Gaullists), 288; Democratic Centre (CPDM), 33; Federation of the Left (FGDS), 56; Communists, 34; Independent Republicans, 62; Independents, 10; Union of Democrats for the Republic (UDR), 292.

President of the Republic: Georges Pompidou; elected on 15 June 1969 having obtained, in the second ballot, 11,064,371 votes against 7,943,118 votes cast for Alain Poher.

The Cabinet, appointed on 25 Feb. 1971, is composed as follows:

Prime Minister: Jacques Chaban-Delmas.

Cultural Affairs: Jacques Duhamel. *National Defence:* Michel Debré. *Administrative Reforms:* Roger Frey. *Justice:* René Pléven. *Foreign Affairs:* Maurice Schumann. *Interior:* Raymond Marcellin. *Economy and Finance:* Valéry Giscard d'Estaing. *Education:* Olivier Guichard. *Planning and Territorial development:* André Bettencourt. *Industrial and Scientific Development:* François Ortoli. *Equipment and Housing:* Albin Chalandon. *Agriculture:* Michel Cointat. *Transport:* Jean Chamant. *War veterans:* Henri Duvillard. *Postal services and Telecommunications:* Robert Galley. *Overseas Departments and Territories:* Pierre Messmer. *Labour, Employment and Population:* Joseph Fontanet. *Health and Social Security:* Robert Boulin. *Relations with Parliament:* Jacques Chirac. *Nature Protection and Environment:* Robert Poujade.

LOCAL GOVERNMENT. For administrative purposes metropolitan France is divided into 95 departments. As from 1 Jan. 1947 the former colonies of Martinique, Guadeloupe, Réunion and Guyane have been given the status of overseas departments. On 10 July 1964 the departments of Seine and Seine-et-Oise were reorganized in 7 departments (Seine-et-Marne, Yvelines, Essonne, Haut-de Seine, Seine-Saint-Denis, Val-de-Marne, Val d'Oise).

The unit of local government is the *commune*, and size and population of which vary very much. There were, in 1968, in the 95 metropolitan departments, 37,708 communes. Most of them (33,315) had less than 1,500 inhabitants, and 24,007 had even less than 500; while 334 communes had more than 20,000 inhabitants. The local affairs of the commune are under a Municipal Council, composed of from 10 to 36 members, elected by universal suffrage, and by the *scrutin de liste* for 6 years by French citizens of 21 years or over after 6 months' residence.

Each Municipal Council elects a mayor, who is both the representative of the commune and the agent of the central government. He is the head of the local police and, with his assistants, acts under the orders of the prefect.

In Paris the Municipal Council is composed of 90 members. The 20 *arrondissements* into which the city is subdivided have been grouped in 9 sectors, each of which has its own mayor.

The next unit is the *canton* (3,209 in 1968), which is composed of an average of 12 communes, although some of the largest communes are, on the contrary, divided into several cantons.

The district, or *arrondissement* (322 in 1968), has an elected *conseil d'arrondissement*, with as many members as there were cantons, its chief function being to allot among the communes their respective parts in the direct taxes assigned to each *arrondissement* by the Council General.

Avril, P., *Le Régime politique de la Ve république.* Paris, 1964
Charnay, J.-P., *Le suffrage politique en France.* Paris, 1965
Fauvet, J., *Histoire du parti communiste français.* 2 vols. Paris, 1964–65

AREA AND POPULATION.

	Area	Census population		
Departments	(sq. km)	*March 1946*	*March 1962*	*March 1968*
Ain [1]	5,785	298,556	314,457	339,262
Aisne	7,428	453,411	512,920	526,346
Allier	7,382	373,481	380,221	386,533
Alpes-de-Haute-Provence	6,988	83,354	91,843	104,813
Alpes (Hautes-)	5,643	84,932	87,436	91,790
Alpes-Maritimes	4,298	453,073	618,265	722,070
Ardèche	5,556	254,598	248,516	256,927
Ardennes	5,253	245,335	300,247	309,380
Ariège	4,903	145,956	137,192	138,478
Aube	6,026	235,237	255,099	270,325
Aude	6,342	268,889	269,782	278,323
Aveyron	8,771	307,717	290,489	281,568
Belfort (Territoire de)	608	86,648	109,371	118,450
Bouches-du-Rhône	5,248	971,935	1,248,355	1,470,271
Calvados	5,693	400,026	480,757	519,695
Cantal	5,779	186,843	172,977	169,330
Charente	5,972	311,137	327,658	331,016
Charente-Maritime	7,232	416,187	470,897	483,622
Cher	7,304	286,070	293,514	304,601
Corrèze	5,888	254,574	237,926	237,858
Corse	8,722	267,873	275,465	269,831
Côte-d'Or	8,787	335,602	387,870	421,192
Côtes-du-Nord	7,218	526,955	501,923	506,102
Creuse	5,606	188,669	163,515	156,876
Dordogne	9,224	387,643	375,455	374,073
Doubs	5,260	298,255	384,881	426,363
Drôme	6,561	268,233	304,227	342,891
Essonne	1,811	294,482	479,446	674,157
Eure	6,037	315,902	361,943	383,385
Eure-et-Loir	5,940	258,110	277,546	302,207
Finistère	7,029	724,735	749,558	768,929
Gard	5,881	380,837	435,107	478,544
Garonne (Haute-)	6,367	512,260	594,633	690,712
Gers	6,291	190,431	182,264	181,577
Gironde	10,726	858,381	935,448	1,009,390
Hauts-de-Seine	175	992,859	1,381,805	1,461,619
Hérault	6,224	461,100	516,658	591,397
Ille-et-Vilaine	6,992	578,246	614,268	652,722
Indre	6,906	252,075	251,432	247,178
Indre-et-Loire	6,158	349,685	395,210	437,870
Isère [1]	7,904	542,573	678,041	768,450
Jura	5,055	216,386	225,682	233,547
Landes	9,364	248,397	260,479	277,381
Loir-et-Cher	6,422	242,419	250,741	267,896
Loire	4,799	631,591	696,348	722,383
Loire (Haute-)	5,001	228,076	211,036	208,337
Loire-Atlantique	6,980	665,064	803,372	861,452
Loiret	6,812	346,918	389,854	430,629
Lot	5,226	154,897	149,929	151,198
Lot-et-Garonne	5,385	265,449	275,028	290,592
Lozère	5,180	90,523	81,868	77,258
Maine-et-Loire	7,218	496,068	556,272	584,709
Manche	6,412	435,468	446,878	451,939
Marne	8,205	386,926	442,195	485,388
Marne (Haute-)	6,257	181,840	208,446	214,336
Mayenne	5,212	256,317	250,030	252,762
Meurthe-et-Moselle	5,280	528,805	678,078	705,413
Meuse	6,241	188,786	215,985	209,513
Morbihan	7,092	506,884	530,833	540,474
Moselle	6,253	622,145	919,412	971,314
Nièvre	6,888	248,559	245,921	247,702
Nord	5,774	1,917,452	2,293,112	2,417,899
Oise	5,887	396,724	481,289	540,988
Orne	6,144	273,181	280,549	288,524
Paris (Ville de)	105	2,725,374	2,790,091	2,590,771
Pas-de-Calais	6,752	1,168,545	1,366,282	1,397,159
Puy-de-Dôme	8,016	478,903	508,928	547,743
Pyrénées (Atlantiques)	7,712	415,795	466,036	508,734
Pyrénées (Hautes-)	4,534	201,954	211,433	225,730

[1] Population in 1946 and 1962 adjusted to area at 1 March 1968.

Departments	Area (sq. km)	Census population March 1946	March 1962	March 1968
Pyrénées-Orientales	4,144	228,776	1,22531	281,976
Rhin (Bas-)	4,793	673,281	770,150	827,367
Rhin (Haut-)	3,531	471,705	547,920	585,018
Rhône [1]	3,233	958,534	1,181,101	1,325,611
Saône (Haute-)	5,375	202,573	208,440	214,176
Saône-et-Loire	8,627	506,749	535,772	550,362
Sarthe	6,245	412,214	443,019	461,839
Savoie	6,188	235,965	266,678	288,921
Savoie (Haute-)	4,598	270,565	329,230	378.550
Seine	..	4,775,711	5,646,446	..
Seine-Maritime	6,342	846,131	1,035,844	1,113,977
Seine-et-Marne	5,931	407,137	524,486	604,340
Seine-et-Oise	..	1,414,910	2,298,932	..
Seine-Saint-Denis	236	730,361	1,083,724	1,251,792
Sèvres (Deux-)	6,054	312,756	321,118	326,462
Somme	6,277	441,368	488,169	512,113
Tarn	5,780	298,117	319,560	332,011
Tarn-et-Garonne	3,731	167,664	175,847	183,572
Val-de-Marne	244	672,037	974,980	1,121,340
Val-d'Oise	1,249	344,744	548,429	693,269
Var	6,023	370,688	469,557	555,926
Vaucluse	3,578	249,838	303,536	353,966
Vendée	7,016	393,787	408,928	421,250
Vienne	7,044	313,932	331,619	340,256
Vienne (Haute-)	5,555	336,313	332,514	341,589
Vosges	5,903	342,315	380,676	388.201
Yonne	7,461	266,014	269,826	283,376
Yvelines	2,271	430,764	686,902	853,386
Total	551,601 [2]	40,506,639 [3]	46,519,997	49,778,540

[1] Population in 1946 and 1962 adjusted to area at 1 March 1968.
[2] 212,919 sq. miles.
[3] Not including military, air and naval forces, crews of the commercial navy abroad and the personnel of the military government in Germany and Austria, numbering 312,105.

The figures include 2,664,060 foreigners in 1968.
The following table gives the area and census population of metropolitan France:

	Area (sq. km)	Domiciled population	Inhabitants per sq. km	Annual increase per 10,000
1801	537,699	27,349,003	51	—
1821	—	30,461,875	57	54
1841	—	34,230,178	64	58
1861	550,986	37,836,313	68	44
1866	—	38,067,064	69	36
1872	536,464	36,102,921	67	−88 [1]
1881	—	37,672,048	70	47
1891	—	38,342,948	71	18
1901	—	38,961,945	73	16
1911	—	39,604,992	70	16
1921	550,986	39,209,518	71	−10 [1]
1931	—	41,834,923	76	65
1946	—	40,506,639	74	−22 [1]
1954	—	42,777,174	78	67
1962	551,601	46,519,997	84	100
1968	—	49,778,540	90	101

[1] Decrease.

Estimated population on 1 Jan. 1970 was 50·5m. (24·6m. males and 25·9m. females).

VITAL STATISTICS for calendar years:

	Marriages	Divorces	Living births	Still-born	Deaths
1967	345,578	37,194	837,481	15,613	539,946
1968	356,615	36,063	832.847	14,906	550,492
1969	380,829	..	839,511	14,650	569,800

PRINCIPAL CONURBATIONS AND TOWNS (*agglomérations*) (census 1968):

	Con-urbation	Town		Con-urbation	Town
Paris	8,196,746	2,590,771	Angers	163,191	128,533
Lyon	1,074,823	527,800	Caen	152,332	110,262
Marseille	964,412	889,029	Limoges	148,119	132,935
Lille	881,439	190,546	Bethune	144,678	27,154
Bordeaux	555,152	266,662	Dunkerque	143,425	27,504
Toulouse	439,764	370,796	Avignon	139,134	86,096
Nantes	393,731	259,208	Amiens	136,713	117,888
Nice	392,635	322,442	Thionville	136,474	37,079
Rouen	369,793	120,471	Hagondange-Briey	134,154	10,567
Toulon	340,021	174,746	Denain	126,740	27,973
Strasbourg	334,668	249,396	Bruay-en-Artois	126,520	28,628
Grenoble	332,423	161,616	Nimes	124,854	123,292
St Etienne	331,414	213,468	Besançon	116,197	113,220
Lens	325,696	41,874	Montbéliard	114,670	23,908
Nancy	257,829	123,428	Troyes	114,209	74,898
Le Havre	247,374	199,509	Saint-Nazaire	110,897	63,289
Valenciennes	223,629	46,626	Pau	110,377	74,005
Cannes	213,397	67,152	Bayonne	110,163	42,743
Douai	205,432	49,187	Perpignan	106,927	102,191
Clermont-Ferrand	204,699	148,896	Lorient	98,655	66,444
Tours	201,556	128,120	Calais	94,316	74,624
Mulhouse	199,037	116,336	Boulogne-sur-Mer	93,103	49,276
Rennes	192,782	180,943	Angoulême	92,142	47,822
Dijon	183,989	145,357	Valence	92,111	62,358
Montpellier	171,467	161,910	Maubeuge	91,367	32,028
Brest	169,279	154,023	Aix-en-Provence	89,566	89,566
Reims	167,830	152,967	La Rochelle	87,532	73,347
Orléans	167,515	95,828	Forbach	85,375	23,120
Metz	166,354	107,537	Annecy	81,526	54,484
Le Mans	166,182	143,246	Béziers	80,492	80,492

Occupational structure (1968). Out of an economically active population of 20,002,240 persons, there are 3,133,400 engaged in fishing and agriculture; 241,240 in mining and quarrying; 2,091,740 in building and public works; 5,570,020 in other manufacturing industries; 856,000 in transportation; 3,367,000 in business, banking and insurance; 2,303,700 in services; 2,439,140 in public services, administration and armed forces.

Recensement de la population de 1968. Paris, Institut National de la Statistique et des Etudes Economiques, 1968
Demangeon, A., *La France économique et humaine.* Paris, 1946
Ormsby, H., *France, a regional and economic geography.* 2nd ed. London, 1950

RELIGION. No religion is officially recognized by the State. Under the law promulgated on 9 Dec. 1905, which separated Church and State, the adherents of all creeds are authorized to form associations for public worship (*associations culturelles*). The law of 2 Jan. 1907 provided that, failing *associations culturelles*, the buildings for public worship, together with their furniture, would continue at the disposition of the ministers of religion and the worshippers for the exercise of their religion; but in each case there was required an administrative act drawn up by the *préfet* as regards buildings belonging to the State or the departments, and by the *maire* as regards buildings belonging to the communes.

There are 17 archbishops and 68 bishops of the Roman Catholic Church, with 51,000 clergy of various grades. The Protestants of the Augsburg confession are, in their religious affairs, governed by a General Consistory, while the Reformed Church is under a Council of Administration, the seat of which is in Paris. In 1962 communicant Protestants numbered 722,453.

Schram, S. R., *Protestantism and Politics in France.* Alençon, 1954

EDUCATION. The primary, secondary and higher state schools constitute the 'Université de France'. The Supreme Council of 50 members has deliberative, administrative and judiciary functions, and a Consultative Committee advise respecting the working of the school system, but the inspectors-general are in direct communication with the Minister. For local education administration France is divided into 23 academic areas, each of which has an Academic Council whose members include a certain number elected by the professors or teachers. The Academic Council deals with all grades of education. Each is under a

Rector, and each is provided with academy inspectors, 1 for each department.

By decree of 6 Jan. 1959 the whole system of public instruction has been reorganized and the structure of the Ministry of National Education has consequently been modified. The educational stages are as follows:

1. Non-compulsory pre-school instruction for children aged 2–5, to be given in infant schools or infant classes attached to primary schools.

2. Compulsory elementary instruction for children aged 6–11, to be given in primary schools and certain classes of the *lycées classiques, modernes et techniques*. It consists of 3 courses: preparatory (1 year), elementary (2 years), intermediary (2 years). Physically or mentally handicapped children are cared for in special institutions or special classes of primary schools.

3. *Enseignement du Second Degre*, for pupils aged 13–18:

(*a*) *Enseignement du 1er cycle du Second Degre:* 4 years of study in the *Lycées classiques et modernes, Collèges d'Enseignement Secondaire* or *Collèges d'Enseignement Général*.

(*b*) *Enseignement du Second Cycle:*

Long, classique, moderne or *technique* provided by the *lycées* and leading to the *baccalauréat* or to the *baccalauréat de technicièn* after 3 years.

Court, professional courses of 3, 2 and 1 year are taught in the *Collèges d'enseignement technique,* or the specialized sections of the *lycées,* CES or CEG.

In addition students are also prepared for the *Sections de Techniciens Supérieurs* and the preparatory classes of the *Grandes Écoles*.

The names of the various types of schools have been changed as follows: *lycées* and *collèges; collèges techniques, écoles nationales professionnelles,* now *lycées classiques, modernes et techniques; centre d'apprentissage,* now *collège d'enseignement technique; cours complémentaire,* now *collège d'enseignement général*. Also additional establishments have been added: *collèges d'Enseignement Secondaire* (CES).

The following table shows the various types of schools, their numbers and the numbers of enrolled pupils:

	1968–69		1969–70	
Description	Schools	Pupils	Schools	Pupils
Infant and Elementary Schools:				
State	67,884	6,336,501	67,080	6,290,309
Private	9,475	1,049,868	9,253	1,043,289
Description	Boys	Girls	Boys	Girls
Collèges d'ens. général:				
State	310,518	348,364	302,663	331,656
Private	92,435	116,236	97,954	117,246
Collèges d'ens. secondaire:				
State	376,894	383,074	494,473	501,985
Lycées classiques, modernes et techniques:				
State	587,639	586,665	599,527	608,328
Private	219,686	241,088	233,350	251,513
Collèges d'ens. techniques:				
State	249,382	167,103	256,170	173,969
Private	52,139	126,895	50,654	121,858

Higher Instruction is supplied by the State in the universities and in special schools, and by private individuals in the free faculties and schools. The law of 12 July 1875 provided for higher education free of charge. This law was modified by that of 18 March 1880, which granted the state faculties the exclusive right to confer degrees. A degree of 28 Dec. 1885 created a general council of the faculties, and the creation of universities, each consisting of several faculties, was accomplished in 1897, in virtue of the law of 10 July 1896.

The faculties are of four kinds: 17 faculties of law (Paris, Aix, Bordeaux, Caen,

Clermont, Dijon, Grenoble, Lille, Lyon, Montpellier, Nancy, Nantes, Nice, Poitiers, Rennes, Strasbourg, Toulouse); 6 faculties of medicine (Paris, Amiens, Besançon, Montpellier, Nancy, Strasbourg); 4 faculties of pharmacy (Paris, Montpellier, Nancy, Strasbourg); 12 mixed faculties of medicine and pharmacy (Aix, Bordeaux, Clermont, Grenoble, Lille, Lyon, Nantes, Orléans, Reims, Rennes, Rouen, Toulouse); 23 faculties of science (Paris (2), Aix, Besançon, Bordeaux, Caen, Clermont, Dijon, Grenoble, Lille, Lyon, Montpellier, Nancy, Nantes, Nice, Orléans, Poitiers, Reims, Rennes (2), Rouen, Strasbourg, Toulouse); 21 faculties of letters (in the towns last named except for Reims). In addition, a certain number of university establishments (institutes and other centres attached to parent faculties) operate in some other major towns. As part of the implementation of the law of 12 Nov. 1968 imposing guide lines for higher education, all the activities of the universities and faculties are being progressively reorganized within the context of the universities, which will consist of Education and Research Units (UER) whose educational activities, research programmes and examinations are formulated in keeping with national regulations relating to national diplomas. A large number of these units have already been set up.

The following table shows the year of foundation and the total number of students of the universities in 1969–70:

Universities	Students	Universities	Students
Aix-Marseille (1409)	37,528	Nancy (1572)	20,311
Amiens (1964)	6,638	Nantes (1961)	15,988
Besançon (1485)	9,667	Nice (1965)	13,539
Bordeaux (1441)	33,262	Orléans (1961)	14,089
Caen (1432)	13,550	Paris (1150)	186,665
Clermont-Ferrand (1808)	13,855	Poitiers (1431)	11,088
Dijon (1722)	11,704	Reims (1961)	8,938
Grenoble (1339)	23,149	Rennes (1735)	24,129
Lille (1530)	31,081	Rouen (1964)	9,306
Limoges	5,382	Strasbourg (1567)	24,735
Lyon (1808)	38,558	Toulouse (1230)	35,423
Montpellier (1289)	27,901		

The following table shows the number of students in state institutions, by faculties or schools, for 3 years:

Students of	1967–68	1968–69	1969–70[1]
Law	114,382	126,696	131,628
Medicine	85,168	98,428	109,352
Science	116,053	123,347	117,368
Letters	171,168	196,144	208,515
Pharmacy	17,769	20,517	21,046
Technology	5,358	11,930	17,133
Others	—	10,234	11,444
Total	509,898	587,296	616,486

[1] Provisional

The other higher institutions under the Ministry of Public Instruction are the Collège de France (founded by Francis I in 1530), which has courses of study bearing on various subjects (literature and language, archæology, mathematical, natural science, psychology and social science, political economy, etc.); the Museum of Natural History, giving instruction in science and natural history; the École Pratique des Hautes Études (history and philology, mathematical and physico-chemical sciences, natural science, theology, economics and social science), having its seat at the Sorbonne; the École Normale Supérieure, which prepares teachers for secondary education and, since 1904, follows the curricula of the Sorbonne without special teachers of its own; the École des Chartes, which trains archivists and paleographers; the École des Langues Orientales vivantes; the École du Louvre, devoted to art and archaeology; the Bureau des Longitudes, the central meteorological bureau; the Observatoire de Paris; and the French Schools at Athens, Rome, Cairo and South-East Asia.

Outside Paris there are 12 observatories (Meudon, Besançon, Bordeaux, etc.). The observatory at Nice belongs to the University of Paris.

There are free faculties in Paris (the Catholic Institute of Paris comprising theology, law and advanced scientific and literary studies); Angers (theology, law, science, letters and agriculture); Lille (theology, law, medicine and pharmacy, science, letters, social science and politics); Lyon (theology, law, science and letters); Marseille (law); Toulouse (the Catholic Institute with theological, literary and scientific instruction).

Professional and Technical Instruction. The principal institutions of higher or technical instruction are: The Conservatoire des Arts et Métiers at Paris (with 20 evening courses on the applied sciences and social economy), the École Centrale des Arts et Manufactures (920 students in 1968–69), the École des Hautes Études Commerciales (901 students in 1967–68), 17 higher schools of commerce (5,994 pupils in 1967–68), under the Ministry of Public Instruction; the National Agronomic Institute at Paris, the veterinary school at Maisons-Alfort, Lyon and Toulouse, a school of forestry at Nancy, Écoles Nationales Supérieure gronomiques at Grignon, Rennes, Montpellier, Nancy and Toulouse, 98 schools of agriculture, etc., under the Ministry of Agriculture; the École Supérieure de Guerre, the École Polytechnique, the military school at Coët-quidan (formerly St Cyr), the École d'Artillerie at Fontainebleau, the École de Cavalerie at Saumur and other schools under the Ministry of War; the Naval School at Brest under the Ministry of Marine; the School of Mines at Paris, the School of Civil Engineering at Paris, the School of Mines at St Etienne and the Schools of Miners at Alès and Douai with other schools under the Ministry of Public Works; the École Nationale Supérieure des Beaux Arts, the École Nationale Supérieure des Arts Décoratifs and the Conservatoire de Musique et de Déclamation under the Department of Fine Arts, which is attached to the Ministry of Cultural Affairs. In the provinces there are national schools of fine arts, and schools of music, and several municipal schools, as well as free subventional schools, etc.

CINEMAS (1969). There were 4,678 cinemas with a seating capacity of 2,269,675

NEWSPAPERS (1969). There were 14 daily newspapers in Paris (*France-soir* having a circulation of 1·21m.) and 14 newspapers in the provinces with a circulation of more than 200,000 each and 7 with a circulation of between 100,000 and 200,000. The combined daily circulation of the 167 daily papers was 13·5m. in 1969.

HEALTH. At the end of 1969 there were 62,350 physicians, 16,858 pharmacists and (1967) 19,565 dentists practising. There were 1,870 public hospitals (444,615 (1966) beds), 113 public mental hospitals (98,875 (1967) beds), 1,935 private hospitals (73,740 beds) and 158 private mental homes (10,298 beds) at the end of 1968.

SOCIAL WELFARE. An order of 4 Oct. 1945 laid down the framework of a comprehensive plan of Social Security and created a single organization which superseded the various laws relating to social insurance, workmen's compensation, health insurance, family allowances, etc. All previous matters relating to Social Security are dealt with in the Social Security Code, 1956; this has been revised several times, and finally by orders laid down on 21 Aug. 1967, which were ratified on 31 July 1968. The Social Security general scheme covers all wage-earning workers in industry and commerce that are not covered by a special scheme of their own.

Contributions. All wage-earning workers or those of equivalent status are insured regardless of the amount or the nature of the salary or earnings. The funds for the general scheme are raised mainly from professional contributions, these being fixed within the limits of a ceiling (assessed at 18,000 francs per annum on 1 Jan. 1970) and calculated as a percentage of the salaries. The calculation of the contributions payable for family allowances, old age and industrial injuries relates only to this amount; on the other hand, the amount payable for sickness, maternity expenses, disability and death is calculated partly within the limit of the 'ceiling' and partly on the whole salary. These contributions are the responsibility of both employer and employee, except in the case of family allowances or industrial injuries, where they are the sole responsibility of the employer.

Self-employed Workers. From 17 Jan. 1948 allowances and old-age pensions were paid to self-employed workers by independent insurance funds set up within their own profession, trade or business. Schemes of compulsory insurance for sickness were instituted in 1961 for farmers and in 1966, with modifications in 1970, for other non-wage-earning workers.

Social Insurance. The orders laid down in Aug. 1967 ensure that the whole population can benefit from the Social Security Scheme; at present all elderly persons who have been engaged in the professions, as well as the surviving spouse, are entitled to claim an old-age benefit; 98% of the population, both working and retired, are covered by a compulsory scheme of insurance for sickness, the remaining 2% who are not covered by a compulsory insurance scheme have been able to participate in a voluntary scheme since 1967; the whole population benefit from the legislation regarding family allowances.

Sickness Insurance refunds the costs of treatment required by the insured, of the needs of his wife, of children under 16 and a half who are in his care and not earning, under 18 who are apprenticed, under 20 who are still studying or who cannot work on account of some chronic illness or infirmity, as well as relations, older or younger or of similar age living under the same roof who are engaged exclusively in domestic duties and in the education of at least 2 children under 14. The general principles relating to medical care consist of: a free choice by the patient of his doctor, his pharmaceutical chemist, his place of treatment, etc.; the medical practitioner is granted freedom of prescription. Reimbursement is not as a rule made in full; the insured person usually pays 25% of the legal rate except in cases of exemption. The insured who is recognized as medically unfit for work receives daily allowances equal to half of the wage which has been used to calculate the contributions, or to two-thirds of this if the person has 3 or more children. These allowances may be paid for 3 years, plus one additional year if the insured undergoes re-adaptation treatment or takes up fresh vocational training.

Maternity Insurance covers the costs of medical treatment relating to the pregnancy, confinement and lying-in period; the beneficiaries being the insured person or the spouse. Otherwise a daily allowance reckoned on the same basis as the sickness insurance is payable for a period of from 6 weeks before until 8 weeks after the confinement, on condition that all paid work is suspended for at least 6 weeks.

Insurance for Invalids is divided into 3 categories: (1) those who are capable of working; (2) those who cannot work; (3) those who, in addition, are in need of the help of another person. According to the category, the pension rate varies from 30 to 50% of the average salary for the last 10 years, with a minimum additional allowance for home help of 9,357·10 francs per year for the third category.

Old-age Pensions for workers were introduced in 1910 and revised in 1930, 1935 and 1941 and are now fixed by the Social Security Code. They are financed out of the contributions made to the Social Security organization by employers and employees. Insured persons over 65 years of age (or over 60 in the case of incapacity to work) are guaranteed a pension, the amount of which is determined by the number of years the person has been insured, by the age of the insured at the time of settlement, and by the average earnings during the last 10 years. In case of death, the annuity payable to one partner is paid to the surviving one.

Compulsory supplementary schemes ensure for those to whom they apply benefits additional to the old-age pensions.

Family Allowances. The system comprises: (a) Family allowances proper, equivalent to 22% of the basic monthly salary (394·5 francs in Paris) for 2 dependent children, 37% for the third and fourth child, and 33% for the fifth and each subsequent child; a supplement equivalent to 9% of the basic monthly salary for the second and each subsequent dependent child more than 10 years old and 16% for each dependent child over 15 years. (b) Single wage-earner allowance (when the wife does not work), according to the number of dependent children. (c) Housewife allowance (when an employer's or self-employed person's wife does not work), according to the number of dependent children. (d) Prenatal allowances paid in 3 instalments after medical examinations, the amount being equivalent to 22% of the basic monthly salary for 9 months. (e) Maternity allowances, equivalent to twice the basic monthly salary (under certain conditions relating to the mother's age and the interval of births).

Workmen's Compensation. The law passed by the National Assembly on 30 Oct 1946 supersedes the Act of 9 April 1898 and forms part of the Social Security Code. It is administered by the Social Security Organization. Employers are invited to take preventive measures. The application of these measures is supervised by consulting engineers (assessors) of the local funds dealing with sickness insurance, who may compel employers who do not respect these measures to make additional contributions; they may, in like manner, grant rebates to employers who have in operation suitable preventive measures. The injured person receives free treatment, the insurance fund reimburses the practitioners, hospitals and suppliers chosen freely by the injured. In cases of temporary disablement the daily payments are equal to half the total daily wage received by the injured. In case of permanent disablement the injured person receives a pension, the amount of which varies according to the degree of disablement and the salary received during the past 12 months.

A law promulgated on 11 Oct. 1946 has created a medical labour service of doctors who hold a diploma of 'industrial health specialists'. These doctors are entrusted with the control of hygiene and health matters in all industrial undertakings or groups of undertakings. In addition, it is the duty of this medical service to examine wage-earners when they are engaged, to carry out periodical medical examinations and to ensure the application of the existing rules relating to safety in work.

Unemployment Benefits vary according to circumstances (full or partial unemployment) and means test. Since 1926 unemployment benefits have been paid from public funds. Full unemployment benefit amounts to 7·75 francs per day for the head of the family and 3·05 francs for the spouse or a dependent person. After 3 months the payment is reduced to 7·05 francs.

A collective agreement signed on 31 Dec. 1958 between the national council of employers and certain trade unions has established a system of special allowances for unemployed workers in industry and trade. The costs are shared by employers (0·32%) and employees (0·08%) and the benefits amount to 35% of the wages for 12 months; to be extended for workers of old age and long employment. The system is administered by commissions composed of representatives of employers and employees in equal proportion. A similar agreement of 22 Feb. 1968 extends the system to partial unemployment.

Social Security in France. I.N.S.E.E., 1970
Questions de Sécurité Sociale. Paris, 1970

JUSTICE. The French judicial system has been reorganized by a number of ordinances and decrees dated 22 Dec. 1958.

Before this reform, the lowest courts were those of the Justices of Peace (*juges de paix*), 1 in each *canton*, who tried less important civil cases. The Tribunals of First Instance (*Tribunaux de Première Instance* or *Tribunaux Civils*), 1 in each *arrondissement*, dealt with more important civil cases and served as Tribunals of Appeal for the Justices of Peace, when their decisions were susceptible of appeal.

Since 2 March 1959, 467 *tribunaux d'instance* (10 in overseas departments), under a single judge each and with increased material and territorial jurisdiction, have replaced the cantonal justices of the peace; and 178 *tribunaux de grande instance* (6 in overseas departments) have taken the place of the 357 *tribunaux de première instance*.

The *tribunaux de grande instance* usually have a collegiate composition, however a law dated 10 July 1970 has allowed them to administer justice under a single judge in some civil cases.

All petty offences (*contraventions*) are disposed of in the Police Courts (*Tribunaux de Police*) presided over by the *Juge d'Instance*. The Correctional Courts pronounce upon all graver offences (*délits*), including cases involving imprisonment up to 5 years. They have no jury, and consist of 3 judges who administer both criminal and civil justice. In all cases of a *délit* or a *crime* the preliminary inquiry is made in secrecy by an examining magistrate (*juge d'instruction*), who either dismisses the case or sends it for trial before a court where a public prosecutor (*Procureur*) endeavours to prove the charge.

The Conciliation Boards (*Conseils des Prud'hommes*) composed of an equal number of employers and employees deal with small trade and industrial disputes. Commercial litigation goes to the Commercial Courts (*Tribunaux de Commerce*) composed of tradesmen and manufacturers elected for 2 years.

When the decisions of any of these Tribunals are susceptible of appeal, the cases go to the Courts of Appeal (*Cours d'Appel*). There are 31 Courts of Appeal (3 in overseas departments), composed each of a president and a variable number of members.

The Courts of Assizes (*Cours d'Assises*), composed each of a president, assisted by 2 other magistrates who are members of the Courts of Appeal, and by a jury of 9 people, sit in every *département*, when called upon to try very important criminal cases. The decisions of the Courts of Appeal and the Courts of Assizes are final; however, the Court of Cassation (*Cour de Cassation*) had discretion to verify if the law had been correctly interpreted and if the rules of procedure have been followed exactly. The Court of Cassation may annul any judgment, and the cases have to be tried again by a Court of Appeal or a Court of Assizes.

A State Security Court has been established by 2 laws dated 15 Jan. 1963. It is usually composed of 3 civilian judges, including the president, and 2 judges of general or field officer rank, and has jurisdiction to deal with subversion in peace-time.

The French penal institutions have been reorganized by the procedural code which came into force on 2 March 1959 and was modified by a law dated 17 July 1970. They consist of: (1) *maisons d'arrêt* and *de correction*, where persons awaiting trial as well as those condemned to short periods of imprisonment are kept; (2) central prisons (*maisons centrales*) for those sentenced to long imprisonment; (3) special establishments, namely (*a*) schools for young adults, (*b*) hostels for old and disabled offenders, (*c*) hospitals for the sick and psychopaths, (*d*) institutions for recidivists. Special attention is being paid to classified treatment and the rehabilitation and vocational re-education of prisoners, including work in open-air and semi-free establishments.

Juvenile delinquents go before special judges and courts; they are sent to public or private institutions of supervision and re-education.

The population at 1 Jan. 1970 of all penal establishments was 28,088 men and 938 women.

FINANCE. Currency. A new currency, the 'heavy franc' or '*nouveau franc*' (NF) worth 100 'light francs', was introduced on 1 Jan. 1960; since 1 Jan. 1963 it is called *franc* (F). £1 = 13·2 F; \$1 = 4·9 F.

Franc coins are issued for 1, 5, 10 and 20 centimes, $\frac{1}{2}$, 1, 5 and 10 francs; and bank-notes for 10, 50, 100 and 500 francs.

Budget. Budgets (in 1m. francs) for calendar years:

	1966	1967	1968	1969
Total revenue	108,431	117,139	125,684	149,374
Total expenditure[1]	107,274	122,901	134,753	148,575
of which Civil	85,990	99,903	109,127	121,759
Military	20,474	21,929	24,294	25,909

[1] Some expenditure has not been divided between civil and military expenditures.

The accounts of revenue and expenditure (in 1m. francs) are examined by a special administrative tribunal (*Cour des Comptes*), instituted in 1807.

Revenue	1966	1967	1968	1969
Taxes and monopolies	100,816	107,701	125,251	148,774
State industries	159	213	220	364
State domains	183	273	213	236
Total (including all others)	108,431	117,139	125,684	149,374
Civil expenditure				
Public debt	5,866	8,007	8,841	10,836
Supply services	33,189	36,072	41,634	47,583
President and Parliament	210	231	273	285
Economic state intervention	29,638	37,025	39,068	43,352
Total	68,903	81,335	89,816	102,056
Civil equipment and recon-struction	17,087	18,745	19,441	19,839
Total civil expenditure	85,990	100,080	109,257	121,895

The French public debt was as follows on 31 Dec. (in 1m. francs):

National Debt:	1966	1967	1968	1969
A. Funded debt—				
(a) *Interior:* Perpetual	554	554	554	554
Long, medium, short term	22,550	22,006	19,826	18,572
Treasury bonds	31,843	46,397	54,504	60,227
Liability towards issuing houses	8,877	8,603	8,818	8,339
(a) Total	63,824	77,560	83,702	87,702
(b) Foreign debt	3,457	3,303	3,145	3,359
B. Floating debt—				
(a) Interior	11,433	8,456	6,730	5,605
(b) Foreign	1,333	1,311	3,783	4,188
Posts and telecommunications	3,423	3,684	3,975	4,216
Total debt	83,470	94,314	101,335	105,070

Bloch-Lainé, F., *La Zone Franc*. Paris, 1956
Lattre, A. de, *Les Finances extérieures de la France, 1945–58*. Paris, 1959
Mérigot, J. G. and Coulbois, P., *Le Franc, 1938–50*. Paris, 1950

DEFENCE. The President of the Republic exercises command over the Armed Forces. He is assisted by the research organization of the High Council of Defence (*Conseil Supérieur de la Défense Nationale*) and two Committees (*Comité de Défense* and *Comité de Défense restreint*) which formulate directives. The Prime Minister is responsible for the national defence; he exercises his military responsibilities through the General Secretariat of National Defence (SGDN). Under the Prime Minister's authority, the *Comité d'Action Scientifique de Défense* co-ordinates research.

On 5 July 1969 the Army Ministry was replaced by the Ministry of State for National Defence which is responsible for the Army, Air Force and Navy. In addition to the powers of the Army Ministry, the Ministry of State prepares general directives for negotiations relating to defence. It has SGDN at its disposal for exercising these powers. It is assisted by the Departmental Assistant for Weapons, the Secretary-General for Administration, the Chief of Staff of the Armed Forces and the Chiefs of Staff of the 3 Armed Forces—Army, Navy and Air.

In 1962 the Armed Forces were reorganized in 3 groups: (1) nuclear strategic force; (2) operational forces; (3) home defence forces.

(1) The Nuclear Strategic Force (FNS), which is directly under the President's authority, will comprise three generations: at present, the Mirage IV and the 'A' bomb operated by the Air Force; as from 1971, ground-to-ground strategic ballistic missiles (SSBS); as from 1971, the nuclear submarine missile launcher (SNLE). Each of these weapons systems is intended to exist alongside the preceding one and to supplement it. The strategic nuclear weapons will be supplemented as from 1972 by a tactical nuclear weapons system.

(2) The Land, Sea and Air Forces consist of: (a) 5 mechanized divisions forming the land forces which comprise the First Army. Since 1 Aug. 1969 these have been placed under a single command (3 divisions in metropolitan France— 2 in West Germany); 1 division specializing in overseas operations; national reserves in metropolitan France; troops, chiefly marines, stationed overseas and organized in 3 commands in the departments and French overseas territories and 3 inter-service commands in the African states and Madagascar; (b) a naval force of 2 squadrons, comprising aircraft carriers, escorts and amphibious craft; (c) tactical aircraft (Mirage III), helicopters (Frelon), transports (Transall), etc.

(3) Organized in 7 defence zones, 7 military regions and 21 territorial divisions, with co-ordination of the civil and military authorities; also comprising all 3 services.

Army. The Army consists of regular officers and n.c.o.s, long-term n.c.o.s and soldiers, and conscripts serving 16 months.

The peace-time units comprise infantry, armoured troops and cavalry, artillery, engineering, signals, transport, matériel, naval infantry and artillery. In addition, there are the Foreign Legion, mountain and airborne troops and other specialized units.

On 1 Aug. 1970 the effective strength of the Army was 324,900 all ranks.

Higher military instruction is provided in 3 stages: the staff school (*École d'État-major*) for officers of formation staffs; the *École Supérieure de Guerre* for officers earmarked for the higher command; the *Institut des Hautes Études de Défense Nationale* where high-ranking officers and civilians study together the problems of national defence.

Light Army Aircraft. Formed in 1952, the *Aviation Légère de l'Armée de Terre* (ALAT) is a well-equipped force, with more than 600 light aeroplanes and nearly 300 helicopters for observation, reconnaissance, combat area transport, liaison and supply duties.

The *Gendarmerie* is an integral part of the Army but also co-operates with the civil administration in maintaining public order. Effective strength, 1970, 60,000.

Navy. The Navy is under the supreme direction of the Minister of Defence, being administered by the Chief and Deputy Chiefs of Naval Staff.

All naval aircraft and coastal defences are under the control of the Navy, and have been reorganized in 3 coast 'naval frontier' districts (with headquarters in Cherbourg, Brest and Toulon), in relation to the aircraft attached to the active fleet.

The French Navy is manned partly by conscription but mainly by voluntary enlistment. In 1970 the active personnel was 69,300 officers and men.

The following is a summary of the strength of the fleet at the periods shown:

					Completed at end of				
	1962	1963	1964	1965	1966	1967	1968	1969	1970
Aircraft carriers	4	3	4[1]	4[1]	4[1]	4[1]	4[1]	4[1]	4[1]
Submarines	22	21	21	19	21	23	21	21	20
Cruisers	3	4	3	3	3	2	2	2	2
Destroyers	18	18	18	18	20	17	17	17	17
Frigates	37	37	36	32	29	28	29	30	27

[1] Including 2 helicopter-carriers.

The principal surface ships of the French Navy are as follows:

Completed	Name	Standard displacement Tons	Armour Belt In.	Guns In.	Principal armament	Torpedo tubes	Shaft horse-power	Speed Knots
			Aircraft Carriers					
1963	Foch }	22,000	—	—	8 3·9 in.	—	126,000	32·0
1961	Clemenceau }							

The battlsehip *Richelieu* was relegated to an accommodation ship in 1960 and sold for scrap in 1968; and the battleship *Jean Bart* was similarly reduced in 1961 and condemned in 1968.

Completed	Name	Standard displacement Tons	Armour Belt In.	Guns In.	Principal armament	Torpedo tubes	Shaft horse-power	Speed Knots
			Cruiser Helicopter Carrier					
1963	Jeanne d'Arc	10,000	—	—	4 3·9-in.	—	40,000	26·5
1943	Arromanches	14,000	—	—	Small AA	—	40,000	24·0
			Cruisers					
1959	Colbert	9,080	—	—	16 5-in. AA [2]	—	86,000	32·0
1956	De Grasse [1]	10,238	4	5	12 5-in. AA	—	105,000	33·5

[1] Converted in 1966 for nuclear experiments.
[2] Being rearmed with twin missile launcher.

There are also 1 nuclear-powered ballistic missile submarine of 7,900 tons, 2 guided-missile frigates of 4,700 tons (destroyer-leader of escort-cruiser type), 17 destroyers of 2,750 tons, 27 escorts (frigates) of 1,290 to 1,750 tons, 19 diesel-powered submarines, 15 ocean minesweepers, 64 coastal minesweepers, 15 inshore minesweepers, 9 survey ships, 15 patrol vessels, 13 motor launches, 10 landing ships, 15 landing craft, 10 depot ships, 8 oilers, 16 transports, 4 sail training vessels and 50 other vessels.

Two more nuclear-powered ballistic-missile submarines, 3 large corvettes and 5 minehunters are under construction. Four conventional submarines, a helicopter carrier, 3 corvettes and 12 minecraft are projected.

The naval air arm, known usually as *Aéronavale*, has 3 squadrons of nationally designed Etendard IV-M transonic fighter-bombers, 1 squadron of Etendard IV-P reconnaissance fighters, 2 squadrons of US-built Crusader all-weather fighters, 3 squadrons of Alizé turboprop anti-submarine aircraft, 5 maritime reconnaissance squadrons with Atlantic and Neptune aircraft and 3 anti-submarine and assault squadrons with Super Frelon and Sikorsky HSS-1 helicopters. Strength is approximately 12,000 personnel and 350 aircraft, of which 200 are combat types.

Air Force. Formed as the *Service Aéronautique* in April 1910, the *Armeé de l'Air* is organized in 6 major commands. Its bases and installations were regrouped and modernized in 1967. The *Commandement des Forces Aériennes Stratégiques* (CFAS) commands the nuclear deterrent force. The *Commandement de la Force Aérienne Tactique* (FATAC) directs the tactical air forces, commands the air force reserve and is responsible for support of the ground forces. Under FATAC the 1st *Commandement Aérien Tactique* (1º CATAC) controls tactical air units based in eastern France; the 2nd *Commandement Aérien Tactique* (2º CATAC) controls the reserve forces. The *Commandement du Transport Aérien Militaire* (COTAM) is responsible for air transport operations and for the training and transport of airborne forces. The *Commandement Air des Forces de Défense Aérienne* (CAFDA) controls air defence forces. The *Commandement des Écoles de l'Armée de l'Air* (CEAA) is responsible for training the personnel for all branches of the Air Force. There is finally a *Commandement des Transmissions*, with responsibility for communications and electronic warfare.

The home-based French Air Force is divided territorially among 4 metropolitan air regions (Metz, Paris, Bordeaux, Aix-en-Provence); overseas, the air forces are integrated into the local joint-service commands. There are about 32 combat squadrons and the Air Force uses a total of 76 bases.

The strategic, tactical and air defence forces are equipped entirely with jet aircraft. The CFAS received a total of 62 Mirage IV supersonic nuclear bombers which are deployed in 3 wings (each with first-line strength of 3 squadrons of 4 aircraft) supported by 12 C-135F refuelling tanker transports. The 1º CATAC deploys 6 wings (15 squadrons, about 225 aircraft), consisting of Mirage III-C interceptor, III-E ground-attack and III-R reconnaissance fighters and F-100 Super Sabre interceptors. The air defence forces include 2 wings (4 squadrons) of Super Mystères, 1 wing (2 squadrons) of Mirage III-Cs and 1 wing (2 squadrons) of Vautour fighters. The COTAM is equipped with 4 wings of turboprop Transall C.160, Noratlas, Breguet Sahara and DC-6 transports, supplemented by 2 groups of C-47, DC-8, Caravelle, Nord 262, Fan Jet Falcon, Cessna 411 and M.S. 760 Paris aircraft. Other units are equipped with many different types of close-support aircraft, Broussard observation and general-purpose monoplanes, and 60 H-34 and 55 Alouette helicopters. Training aircraft include the Magister jet basic trainer and Mystère IVA, T-33 and Mirage III-B advanced trainers, with the first Anglo-French Jaguars scheduled to enter service in 1971. Also in production are the single-seat strike version of the Jaguar and the Mirage F.1 multi-mission fighter, for service from 1972.

Total aircraft in service in Jan. 1971, about 2,160, including 435 combat aircraft. Total personnel, about 104,000.

PLANNING. The post-war reconstruction and expansion of the French economy began under the guidance of the first 'Monnet plan' (1947–50), named after the then director of the planning office, Jean Monnet. This was followed by the second and third plans (1954–57, 1958–61), an intermediate plan for 1960 and 1961, and the fourth plan, 1962–65, and fifth plan, 1966–70. The preparation of the sixth plan (1971–75) is in progress.

Bauchet, P., *La Planification Française. Vingt Ans d'Experience.* Paris, 1966
Caire, G., *La Planification, Techniques et Problèmes.* Paris, 1967

AGRICULTURE. Of the total area of France (55·1m. hectares in 1969) 17·2m. are under cultivation, 13·9m. are pasture, 1·3m. are under vines, 13·7m. are forests and 7·7m. are uncultivated land.

The following table shows the area under the leading crops and the production for 4 years:

Crop	Area (1,000 hectares)				Produce (1,000 quintals)			
	1966	1967	1968	1969	1966	1967	1968	1969
Wheat	3,992	3,929	4,090	4,034	112,966	142,875	149,847	144,587
Rye	198	175	163	154	3,565	3,444	3,270	3,090
Barley	2,642	2,818	2,781	2,859	74,211	98,743	91,395	94,521
Oats	1,094	1,040	949	851	25,781	28,211	25,283	23,091
Potatoes	526	504	459	391	104,493	102,315	98.355	85,370
Industrial beet	295	313	404	399	128.893	127,687	175,568	175,248
Maize	961	1,013	1,022	1,184	43,311	41,394	53,790	57,227

Other crops in 1969 (figures for 1968 in brackets) include (in 1,000 quintals): Rice, 954 (848); tobacco, 439 (519); hops, 20 (17).

The annual production of wine and cider (in 1,000 hectolitres) appears as follows:

	Vineyards (1,000 hectares)	Wine produced	Wine import	Wine export	Cider produced
1938	1,513	60,332	16,257	1,032	34,601
1948	1,433	47,437	9,894	620	13,092
1958	1,315	47,735	19,862	1,266	27,440
1968	1,291	66,460	3,986	3,328	18,945
1969	1,208	51,290	6,105	3,642	13,709

The production of fruits (other than for cider making) and nuts for 1968 (figures for 1969 in brackets) is given in 1,000 quintals, as follows: Apples,

18,316 (18,313); pears, 4,407 (4,460); plums, 922 (1,098); peaches, 5,199 (6,149); apricots, 580 (1,322); cherries, 1,186 (1,351); nuts, 354 (324); grapes, 2,617 (3,051); chestnuts, 659 (611).

On 1 Oct. 1969 the numbers of farm animals (in 1,000) were (figures for 1968 in brackets): Horses, 763 (697); mules, 35 (33); asses, 36 (34); cattle, 22,093 (21,719); sheep, 9,506 (10,237); goats, 915 (925); pigs, 10,463 (10,622).

Silk culture, with government encouragement (*primes*), is carried on mainly in 15 departments—most extensively in Ardèche, Gard, Drôme, Hérault, Lozère and Vaucluse.

FISHERY (1969). There were 37,163 fishermen, and 13,491 sailing-boats, steamers and motor-boats. Catch (in 1,000 tons): Fresh fish, 428; salted cod, 43·6; crustaceans, 24·9; shell fish, 54·6; oysters, 59·6.

MINING. Principal minerals produced, in 1,000 metric tons:

	1967	1968	1969		1967	1968	1969
Coal	47,624	41,911	40,583	Potash salts	1,937	1.857	1,938
Lignite	2,931	3,221	2,950	Pig-iron	15,710	16,450	18,212
Iron ore	49,222	55,238	55,425	Crude steel	19,655	20,410	22,511
Bauxite	2,813	2,713	2,773	Aluminium	361	366	372

Output of petroleum in 1967, 2·83m.; 1968, 2·69m.; 1969, 2·5m. metric tons. The greater part came from the Parentis oilfield in the Landes. France has an important oil-refining industry, utilizing imported crude oil. Total yearly capacity at the end of 1969 was about 105·2m. metric tons. The principal plants are situated in Nord (production, in metric tons, 1969), 9m.; Basse Seine, 37·3m.; Atlantic, 11·3m.; Mediterranean, 26·4m., and Alsace, 8·1m.

There has been considerable development of the production of natural gas and sulphur in the region of Lacq in the foothills of the Pyrenees. Production of natural gas was 8,630m. cu. metres in 1968; 9,779m. in 1969.

MANUFACTURES. *Engineering Industry* (1969): 2·24m. vehicles (excluding small vehicles), 1,412,000 television sets, 2,836,000 radio sets, 68,200 agricultural tractors, 33·8m. tyres.

Chemical Industry (1969) (in 1,000 metric tons): Sulphuric acid, 3,527; caustic soda, 1,042; sulphur, 1,697; polystyrene, 117; polyvinyl, 369; polyethylene, 312; ammonia, 1,526; nitric acid, 591.

Textiles (1969) (in 1,000 metric tons): Woollen, 66; cotton, 193·7; linen (in 1,000 metres), 16·7; silk, 42·3; man-made fibres, yarns, 134·2; jute, 47.

Food (1969) (in 1,000 metric tons): Cheese, 722; chocolate, 86·6; biscuits, 239; sugar, 2,504; fish preparations, 90; jams and jellies, 77.

Construction (1969). Houses, 427,000; cement, 27·5m. tons.

See map in THE STATESMAN'S YEAR-BOOK, 1968–69, Industrial Redeployment.

ELECTRICITY. Production of electrical (and percentage of hydro-electric) power (in 1m. kwh.): 1965, 101,255 (46%); 1966, 105,938 (49%); 1967, 111,467 (40%); 1968, 117,741 (43%); 1969, 131,296 (40%).

TOURISM. In 1969 foreign visitors contributed about 5,090m. francs to the French economy.

TRADE UNIONS (1966). The most important trade unions are the Confédération Générale du Travail with a membership of 1m.; the Confédération Française des Travailleurs chrétiens (100,000); Confédération Française Démocratique du Travail with a membership of 500,000; the Confédération Générale du

Travail Force Ouvrière with a membership of approximately 400,000. All these figures are estimates, as the French conception of trade-union freedom does not permit the State to demand a list of members from the organizations, and each of the Confédérations tends to claim the highest figure plausible. On the other hand, the number of cards taken out does not necessarily correspond to the number of members, and must be adjusted according to the number of monthly stamps distributed.

Other smaller union organizations are Confédération Générale des Cadres, Confédération Autonome du Travail, Confédération Générale des Syndicats and Fédération de l'Education Nationale.

French Trade Unions: a Short History and Assessment. French Embassy, London
Trade Unions in France. French Embassy, London, 1967
Chardonnet, J., *L'Économie française.* 2 vols. Paris, 1958–59
Ehrmann, H. W., *Organized business in France.* Princeton Univ. Press, 1957
Jeanneney, J.-M., *Forces et faiblesses de l'économie française, 1945–59.* 2nd ed. Paris, 1959
Lorwin, V. R., *The French Labor Movement.* Harvard Univ. Press, 1955
Pilliet, G., *Inventaire économique de la France.* Annual from 1945. Paris

COMMERCE. Imports and exports, in 1m. francs for 6 calendar years were (including gold):

	1965	1966	1967	1968	1969	1970
Imports	51,059	58,672	61,251	69,029	90,023	106,190
Exports	44,633	53,837	56,198	62,723	77,759	99,640

The chief imports for home use and exports of home goods are to and from the following countries, in 1m. francs (including gold):

Countries	Imports 1969	Imports 1970	Exports 1969	Exports 1970
Franc area	8,434·4	9,691·2	8,970·0	11,302·5
UK	4,088·7	5,411·5	3,211·3	4,049·6
Germany (West)	20,061·9	23,440·7	15,897·2	20,490·2
Belgium–Luxembourg	10,241·1	11,920·3	8,385·2	10,929·4
Switzerland	2,798·2	2,836·0	3,513·6	4,700·5
Italy	9,020·9	9,806·6	8,063·1	11,107·3
USA	7,588·0	6,537·5	4,227·4	5,304·9
Brazil	681·3	912·9	338·3	443·8
Argentina	447·4	607·4	308·2	408·7
Australia and New Zealand	1,121·6	1,262·7	359·3	432·4
Canada	821·7	1,118·5	727·2	865·9
Sweden	1,808·6	2,176·9	1,153·9	1,433·2
Netherlands	5,701·4	6,265·6	4,562·8	5,598·5

Total trade between France and UK (in £1,000 sterling; British Board of Trade returns):

	1966	1967	1968	1969	1970
Imports to UK	212,338	255,021	311,928	324,448	368,243
Exports from UK	197,299	204,395	234,517	290,954 ⎫	339,229
Re-exports from UK	15,663	13,572	18,606	21,136 ⎭	

I.N.S.E.E., *Statistiques et indices du commerce extérieur.* Paris, 1964

SHIPPING. On 31 Dec. 1969 the French mercantile marine possessed 554 vessels of more than 100 tons, with a gross tonnage of 5·7m.

Shipping (excluding fishing vessels) in foreign trade in 1969: Entered, 70,355 vessels and disembarked 155·58m. tons of imports; cleared, 70,246 vessels and loaded 36,806,000 tons of exports.

In 1969 there were 7,500 km of navigable rivers, waterways and canals, with a total traffic of 110·21m. net tons.

ROADS. At the end of 1969 the French road system consisted of 787,702 km, namely 80,861 km of national roads (excluding 1,241 km of motorway), 286,600 km of departmental roads and about 419,000 km of local roads.

RAILWAYS. As from 1 Jan. 1938 all the independent railway companies were merged with the existing state railway system in a Société Nationale des Chemins de Fer Français, in which the State holds 51% of the shares.

The length of the railway lines, on 31 Dec. 1969, was 36,700 km, of which 9,029 km were electrified. The railways, in 1969 (and 1968), carried 610m. (579m.) passengers and 243m. (229m.) metric tons of goods. Railway receipts, 1968, 13,418m.; 1969, 15,078m.; expenses, 1968, 15,774m.; 1969, 17,049m.

The Paris transport network consisted in 1969 of 224 km of underground railway (Métro) and 1,732 km of bus routes. In 1969 it carried 1,177m. passengers on the Métro and 552m. by bus.

Lartilleux, H., *Géographie des chemins de fer français.* 2 vols. Paris, 1946–48
Peyret, H., *Histoire des chemins de fer en France.* Paris, 1949

AVIATION. Air France, UTA and Air Inter, the national airlines, had (31 Dec. 1970) a fleet of 157 aircraft, servicing Europe, North America, Central and South America, West and East Africa, Madagascar, the Near, Middle and Far East. There are local networks in the West Indies and Central America.

In 1969 Air France flew 1,242m. ton-km and 9,488m. passenger-km (5·66m passengers); UTA, 280m. ton-km and 1,778m. passenger-km (331,000 passengers); Air Inter, 95m. ton-km and 1·12m. passenger-km (2·28m. passengers).

POST. In 1968 the receipts on account of posts, telegraphs and telephones amounted to 10,940·4m. francs; 1969, 13,323·2m. francs.

On 1 Jan. 1970 the telephone system (government-owned) had 8,114,041 subscribers; the Paris region (including the Paris and Seine-et-Marne, Yvelines, Essonne, Hauts-de-Seine, Seine-Saint-Denis, Val-de-Marne and Val-d'Oise departments) accounted for 3,076,236.

On 31 Dec. 1966 wireless sets numbered 22m. and television sets, 7·5m. (10·1m., 1969).

BANKING. The Bank of France, founded in 1800, and placed under state control in 1806, has the monopoly (since 1848) of issuing bank-notes. The capital of the bank is fixed at 250m. francs. Note circulation on 31 Dec. 1968 was 74,650m. francs.

On 2 Dec. 1945 a law was passed to nationalize the Banque de France and the 4 principal deposit banks—Crédit Lyonnais, Société Générale, Comptoir National d'Escompte and the Banque Nationale pour le Commerce et l'Industrie (the 2 last-named amalgamated on 1 July 1966 as the Banque Nationale de Paris). It also instituted strict Government control over the activities of all other banks and established a new body, the National Credit Council, composed of 35 members appointed by the State, to check the flow of credit in France.

The 12 directors of the nationalized banks are appointed by the State as follows: 3 by the Minister of Finance from persons in commerce, industry or agriculture; 3 by the trade unions, 1 of whom is an employee of the bank; 3 by the Minister of Finance in virtue of their bank experience; 3 representing the Bank of France or other semi-public credit concerns.

The following are the principal banks: Crédit Foncier de France, founded in 1852 (mortgage bank); Crédit Lyonnais, founded in 1863; Société Générale, founded in 1864; Banque Nationale de Paris (nationalized deposit banks); Crédit Industriel et Commercial; Crédit Commercial de France (non-nationalized deposit banks); Banque de Paris et des Pays Bas, and Banque de l'Union Parisienne.

The ordinary savings banks number about 600. In addition, the state savings organization (*Caisse nationale d'épargne*) is administered by the post office on a giro system. On 31 Dec. 1969 ordinary savingsbanks had 60,442m. francs in deposits; the state saving banks had 33,888m. francs in deposits.

WEIGHTS AND MEASURES. The metric system is in general use.

DIPLOMATIC REPRESENTATIVES

France maintains embassies in:

Afghánistán	Greece	Norway
Albania	Guatemala	Pakistan
Algeria	Haiti	Panama
Argentina	Honduras	Paraguay
Australia	Hungary	Peru
Austria	Iceland	Philippines
Belgium	India	Poland
Bolivia	Indonesia	Portugal
Brazil	Iran	Romania
Bulgaria	Iraq	Rwanda
Burma	Irish Republic	Saudi Arabia
Burundi	Israel	Senegal
Cambodia	Italy	Sierra Leone
Cameroun	Ivory Coast	Somalia
Canada	Jamaica	South Africa, Republic of
Central African Republic	Japan	Spain
Ceylon	Jordan	Sudan
Chad	Kenya	Sweden
Chile	Korea	Switzerland
China	Laos	Syria
Colombia	Lebanon	Tanzania
Congo (Br.)	Liberia	Thailand
Congo (K.)	Libya	Trinidad
Costa Rica	Luxembourg	Togo
Cuba	Madagascar	Tunisia
Cyprus	Malaysia	Turkey
Czechoslovakia	Mali	Uganda
Dahomey	Malta	USSR
Denmark	Mauritania	UAR
Dominican Republic	Mexico	UK
Ecuador	Morocco	USA
El Salvador	Nepál	Upper Volta
Ethiopia	Netherlands	Uruguay
Finland	New Zealand	Vatican
Gabon	Nicaragua	Venezuela
Germany (West)	Niger	Yugoslavia
Ghana	Nigeria	Zambia

OF FRANCE IN GREAT BRITAIN (58 Knightsbridge, SW1)

Ambassador: Geoffroy de Courcel, GCVO, MC.

Minister: Jean-Paul Anglès.

Counsellors: René Ziller; Victor Garès (*Press*); Jean Gantier; Jean Lescêre; André Rigailland (*Commercial*); Eugène Taillart (*Shipping*); François Miquel (*Scientific*); Pierre de Boisdeffre (*Cultural*).

First Secretary: Jean-Louis Lucet.

Service Attachés: Col. Jean Chenet (*Army*), Rear-Adm. Paul Delahousse (*Navy*), Col. Pierre Bonnafont (*Air*).

Minister-Counsellors: Jean Wahl (*Commercial*); Jacques Dulière (*Financial*).

Commercial Attachés: Francis Loheac; Jean-Pierre Dutet; Guy Lombard (*Agriculture*).

There are consulates-general in Edinburgh, Glasgow, Liverpool, London. There are consulates at Belfast, Birmingham, Cardiff and Jersey.

OF GREAT BRITAIN IN FRANCE

Ambassador: Christopher Soames, PC, CBE.

Ministers: A. M. Palliser, CMG; J. S. Rooke, CMG, OBE (*Economic*); J. Galsworthy, CMG (*European Economic Affairs*).

Counsellors: G. W. Harding (*Information*); P. H. R. Marshall (*Head of Chancery*); J. A. Honeyford (*Administrative*); J. McAdam Clark, MC (*Consul-General*); P. H. Lawrence (*Commercial*); A. G. Wallis, DFC (*Labour*); P. Goodman (*Scientific*); R. Hibbert (*Defence, Supply, Civil Air*); D. M. D. Thomas (*Financial*); H. S. Colchester, CMG, OBE.

First Secretaries: H. J. H. Maud; M. K. O. Simpson-Orlebar; M. St. E. Burton; J. White; P. S. Fairweather; R. J. Alston; C. B. Shakespeare; G. T. S. Hinton; C. P. H. T. Isolani, MVO, OBE (*Information*); B. H. Wilcox, OBE (*Commercial*); G. E. Howe; Miss T. M. Cullis (*Consul*).

Service Attachés: Brig. I. M. Christie (*Army*), Air Cdre N. E. Hoad, CBE, AFC (*Defence and Air*), Capt. C. R. P. C. Branson (*Navy*).

Cultural Attaché: E. W. F. Tomlin, CBE.

There are Consuls-General in Bordeaux, Lyon, Marseille, Paris, Strasbourg, and Consuls in Le Havre, Lille and Nice.

OF FRANCE IN THE USA (2535 Belmont Rd. NW, Washington, D.C., 20008)

Ambassador: Charles Lucet.

Ministers: Jacques Leprette; Emmanuel de Margerie.

Counsellors: Gérard Gaussen; Jean-Pierre Cabouat; Jean Baubé; Yves Jacques; Jean Gory; André Baeyens; Jacques Jessel; Jean-Max Bouchaud; François Desbans; Miss Christiane Malitchenko; Guy Chaumet, Jean Bosson, Paul Gallepe (*Commercial*).

Service Attachés: Gen. Gustav Giraud (*Armed Forces and Air*); Brig.-Gen. René Pessey (*Army*), Rear-Adm. Nicolas-Maurice Houot (*Navy*).

OF THE USA IN FRANCE

Ambassador: Arthur K. Watson.

Deputy Chief of Mission: Perry A. Culley. *Heads of Sections:* Robert Anderson (*Political*); Robert A. Brand (*Economic*); Alexander J. Davit (*Commercial*); Leslie S. Brady (*USIA*).

Service Attachés: Maj.-Gen. Vernon A. Walters (*Defence and Army*), Capt. Peter P. Cummins (*Navy*), Col. George R. Guay (*Air*).

There are Consuls-General at Bordeaux, Lyon and Marseille, and Consuls at Strasbourg and Nice (also Consul to Monaco).

BOOKS OF REFERENCE

STATISTICAL INFORMATION. The Institut national de la Statistique et des Études économiques (29, Quai Branly, Paris 7e) is the central office of statistics. It was established by a law of 27 April 1946, which amalgamated the Service National des Statistiques (created in 1941 by merging the Direction de la Statistique générale de la France and the Service de la Démographie) with the Institut de Conjoncture (set up in 1938) and some statistical services of the Ministry of National Economy. The Institut comprises the following departments: Metropolitan statistics, Overseas statistics, Market research and economic studies, Documentation, Research statistics and economics.

The main publications of the Institute include:

Annuaire statistique de la France (from 1878)
Annuaire statistique des Territoires d'Outre-Mer (from 1959)
Tableaux de l'Economie Française (biennially, from 1956)
Documentation économique (bi-monthly)
Bulletin mensuel de statistique (monthly)
Données statistiques (trimestrial; formerly *Bulletin de statistique d'outre-mer*)
Economie et Statistique (monthly)
Tendances de la Conjoncture (monthly)

Bonneous, P. E., *L'Année Politique, Economique, Sociale et Diplomatique en France*. Paris, 1946 ff.
Pinchemel, P., *La France*. (2 vols.) Paris, 1969

OVERSEAS DEPARTMENTS
MARTINIQUE

Martinique has been in French possession since 1635, except during the Seven Years' War (1762–63) and the French Revolution and Empire (1794–1802, 1809–15) when it was under British occupation.

AREA AND POPULATION. Area, 1,090 sq. km (420 sq. miles), divided into 34 communes; population (census, 16 Oct. 1967), 320,030. Vital statistics (1966): Births, 10,074; deaths, 2,396.

The capital and chief commercial town is Fort-de-France (population, 99,051), with a landlocked harbour nearly 40 sq. km in extent.

GOVERNMENT. On 19 March 1946 the status of Martinique was changed to that of an overseas department. The department is under a prefect. An elected general council of 36 members votes the budget, and elective municipal councils administer the communes. Martinique is represented in the National Assembly by 3 deputies and in the Senate by 2 senators.

Prefect: Jean Terrade.

EDUCATION. In 1967 there were 3 *lycées* (1 for boys, 2,439 pupils; 1 for girls, 2,405 pupils; 1 technical, 1,474 pupils); 269 primary public schools, with 91,181 pupils; and 30 private schools (2,591 pupils). The *Institut Henri Vizioz* had 510 students of law, politics and economics.

JUSTICE. Justice is administered by 5 tribunals of the first instance, a superior court, a regional court of appeal (with jurisdiction over Guiana), a commercial court, a court of assizes and an administrative court.

FINANCE. The budget, 1965, balanced at 178m. francs. In addition, investment expenditures, aided by national subsidies, represented 100m. francs.

AGRICULTURE. Bananas, sugar and rum are the chief productions, followed by pineapples, food and vegetables. In 1969 there were 11,687 hectares under sugar-cane, 10,000 hectares under bananas, 350 hectares under pineapples and 1,100 hectares food-producing crops. In 1969 livestock numbered 37,000 cattle, 25,000 sheep, 30,000 pigs, 9,000 goats and 5,000 horses. There are 6 sugar works with distilleries attached, 28 agricultural distilleries producing rum and 3 factories for canning pineapples. In 1969 production of sugar was 31,571 metric tons; rum, 111,420 hectolitres.

COMMERCE. Trade in 1,000 metric tons and 1m. francs:

	1967		1968		1969	
	Quantity	Value	Quantity	Value	Quantity	Value
Imports	397·50	521·15	415·76	538·16	458·15	625·36
Exports	216·50	177·91	260·16	196·95	237·33	182·06

In 1969 the main items of import were foodstuffs; main items of export were sugar (20·76m. francs), bananas (98·6m. francs) and rum (24·8m. francs).

Total trade of the French West Indian Islands with UK (British Board of Trade returns, in £1,000 sterling):

	1966	1967	1968	1969	1970
Imports to UK	26	143	71	12	54
Exports from UK	633	591	824	773 ⎱	1,257
Re-exports from UK	2	8	4	8 ⎰	

The Chamber of Commerce and Industry administers the port, airport and industrial zone.

COMMUNICATIONS. The island is visited regularly by French and American steamers and by aircraft of Air France, PANAM and British West Indian Airways. In 1967, 1,244 vessels called at Martinique. In 1969, 170,432 passengers arrived and departed by air. There are 235 km of national roads, 560 km of district roads and 713 km of local roads.

There were, in 1962, 43 post offices and, in 1968, 13,149 telephones. Radiotelephone service to Europe is available.

BANKING. The Institut d'émission des départements d'outre-mer is the official bank of the department. The Caisse Centrale de Coopération économique is used by the Government in assisting the economic development of the department.

The Bank of Martinique with a capital of 5m. francs and a reserve fund of 2m. francs, the Crédit Martiniquais and a capital of 2·1m. francs, branches of the Banque Nationale de Paris and the Royal Bank of Canada are operating at Fort-de-France. There is also a post office savings bank.

British Consul: L. Devaux.
USA Consul: Robert S. Barrett, IV.

BOOKS OF REFERENCE

INFORMATION. Office départemental du Tourisme, Fort-de-France.
Annuaire statistique de la Martinique. Paris. (Latest issue, 1959–60)
Monographie de la Martinique. Préfecture, Martinique, 1964
Hannau, H. W., *Martinique.* Munich, 1966
Nicolas, M., *Guide Touristique de la Martinique.* 2nd ed. Martinique, 1969

See also under GUADELOUPE.

GUADELOUPE AND DEPENDENCIES

Guadeloupe has been a French possession since 1635; it was occupied by the British in 1759–63, 1794, 1810–16.

AREA AND POPULATION. Guadeloupe, situated in the Lesser Antilles, consists of 2 islands separated by a narrow channel, called Rivière Salée. That on the west is called Guadeloupe proper, the principal town of which is Basse-Terre, and that to the east Grande Terre; the chief town of Grande Terre is Pointe-à-Pitre. The 2 islands have a combined area of 1,780 sq. km (583 sq. miles). There are 5 dependencies, consisting of the smaller islands, Marie Galante (population, 15,867), Les Saintes (population, 3,269), Désirade (population, 1,559), St Barthélemy (population, 2,351) and St Martin (population, 5,061); the total area with these is 1,702 sq. km (657 sq. miles), and the total population (16 Oct. 1967) is 312,724. Les Saintes and St Barthélemy are still inhabited by the white descendants of the Normans and Bretons who came there 300 years ago. St Martin was occupied simultaneously by the French and the Dutch in 1648; by virtue of an agreement dated 23 March 1648, the island was divided, France receiving about two-thirds of the island, the capital of which is Marigot, a free port.

The seat of government is Basse-Terre (15,690 inhabitants). Pointe-à-Pitre (29,538 inhabitants) has a fine harbour.

GOVERNMENT. On 19 March 1946 the status of Guadeloupe was changed to that of an overseas department. The department is under a prefect and an elected general council of 36 members; it is represented in the National Assembly by 3 deputies, in the Senate by 2 senators and on the Economic and Social Council by 1 councillor.

Prefect: Pierre Brunon.

EDUCATION. In 1969 there were 3 *lycées* with 3,128 pupils, 4 *Collèges d'Enseignement Secondaire* (CES) with 4,343 pupils and 36 *Collèges d'Enseigne-ment Général* (CEG) and 5 *Collèges d'Enseignement Technique* (CET) with 3,206 pupils. Primary education was given in 312 public schools (68,964 pupils) and 25 private schools (5,152 pupils).

HEALTH. The medical services in 1969 included 8 public hospitals (2,580 beds), 16 private clinics (1,210 beds) and 39 dispensaries.

FINANCE. The budget for 1969 balanced at 362,849,695 francs.

AGRICULTURE. Chief products (1969) are bananas (130,000 metric tons), sugar (147,598 metric tons), rum (69,519 hectolitres), coffee, 1968 (250 metric tons), cocoa, 1968 (200 metric tons) and pineapples, 1968 (300 metric tons).

COMMERCE. Trade in 1,000 metric tons and 1m. francs:

	1967		1968		1969	
	Quantity	*Value*	*Quantity*	*Value*	*Quantity*	*Value*
Imports	420	492	400	505	405	547
Exports	305	160	318	188	271	176

There are Chambers of Commerce and Industry at Basse-Terre and Pointe-à-Pitre. There is a British consular agent at Pointe-à-Pitre.

COMMUNICATIONS. Guadeloupe is in direct communication with France by means of 4 steam navigation companies. Air France, British West Indian Airways, PANAM, Caribair and Air Antilles call at Guadeloupe. In 1967, 1,157 vessels of 2·41m. tons entered the department.

In 1966 there were 42 post offices, 7 wireless stations, 2,300 km of telephone circuits and (1969) 5,923 telephone subscribers. In 1970 there were 323 km of national roads, 507 km. of departmental roads and 866 km. of local roads.

BANKING. The Bank of Guadeloupe (founded 1851), with a capital of 2·4m. francs and reserve funds amounting to 1·44m. francs, advances loans chiefly for agricultural purposes. The Crédit Guadeloupéen has a capital of 5m. francs. The Banque Nationale de Paris has 3 and the Banque Antillaise has 2 branches in the department. The Royal Bank of Canada has a branch at Pointe-à-Pitre. The Caisse Centrale de Coopération économique is the official banking institution of the department, enjoying the privilege of issuing bank-notes. Silver coin has disappeared from circulation.

British Vice-Consul: W. G. A. Boyd.

BOOKS OF REFERENCE

INFORMATION. Office du Tourisme du département, Pointe-à-Pitre. *Director:* R. Fortuné.
Lasserre, G., *La Guadeloupe, étude géographique.* 2 vols. Bordeaux, 1961

LA RÉUNION

AREA AND POPULATION. Réunion (or Bourbon), about 569 miles east of Madagascar, has belonged to France since 1642. It has an area of 2,511·6 sq. km (968·5 sq. miles) and a population of 445,500 (31 July 1970). The chief towns are: St-Denis, the capital, with 85,992 inhabitants; St-Paul, 43,186; St-Pierre, 40,364; St-Louis, 26,740. Elected municipal councils administer the 24 communes.

GOVERNMENT. On 19 March 1946 the status of Réunion was changed to that of an overseas department. The department is under a prefect and an elected general council of 36 members. Réunion is represented in the National Assembly by 3 deputies, in the Senate by 2 senators, and in the Economic and Social Council by 2 councillors.

Prefect: Paul Cousseran.

EDUCATION. Réunion has 3 *lycées* with 2,740 pupils, 4 *Collèges d'Enseigne-ment Secondaire* (CES) with 6,909 pupils, 38 *Collèges d'Enseignement Général* (CEG) with 14,954 pupils and 6 *Collèges d'Enseignement Technique* (CET) with 1,802 pupils. Primary education is given in 356 public and 42 private schools. Teachers number 3,787 in the public and 325 in the private schools. The public schools were attended by 97,836 pupils; the private schools by 10,794 pupils. University courses are given in 3 high schools to 581 students by 54 teachers.

FINANCE. The budget for 1970 balanced at 11,448m. francs.

AGRICULTURE. The chief productions are sugar (35,000 hectares), rum, maize, manioc, vanilla, essences, tobacco and tea. The forests occupy about 51,200 hectares. The production of spirits (expressed as 100% alcohol) in 1968 amounted to 89,398 hectolitres of rum. The sugar production in 1969 was 259,891 metric tons.

Livestock (1969): 41,000 cattle, 75,000 swine, 17,600 sheep and goats.

COMMERCE. Trade in 1,000 metric tons had 1m. francs, CFA:

	1966		1967		1968		1969	
	Quantity	*Value*	*Quantity*	*Value*	*Quantity*	*Value*	*Quantity*	*Value*
Imports	441	25·8	473	28·7	492	31·1	552	38·0
Exports	247	9·7	238	9·0	353	11·4	241	11·8

The chief imports in 1969 were (in metric tons): Rice, 47,346; cotton goods, 486; cement, 141,898. Chief exports (1969): Sugar, 209,482 tons; rum, 46,742 hectolitres.

Total trade between Réunion and UK (British Board of Trade returns, in £1,000 sterling):

	1966	1967	1968	1969	1970
Imports to UK	34	69	260	46	57
Exports from UK	296	333	355	400 ⎱	539
Re-exports from UK	3	4	10	12 ⎰	

COMMUNICATIONS. There is telephone and telegraph connexion with Mauritius, Madagascar and metropolitan France. There are 50 post offices and a central telephone office; number of telephones (1968), 11,345.

There were, in 1966, 2,060 km of roads, 1,400 km of which are bitumenized.

Air France maintains a frequent air service. Three shipping lines serve the island. In 1967, 345 vessels (105 of them French) visited the island.

BANKING. The Institut d'émission des Départements d'Outre-mer has the right to issue bank-notes. Banks operating in Réunion are the Banque de la Réunion (Crédit Lyonnais), the Banque Nationale pour le Commerce et l'In-dustrie and the Caisse Régionale de Crédit Agricole Mutuel de la Réunion.

British Consul: R. Gaud.

BOOKS OF REFERENCE

Annuaire Statistique de la Réunion, 1958–60. Paris, 1961
Bulletin de l'Académie de la Réunion. Biennial
Bulletin de la Chambre d'Agriculture de la Réunion

GUIANA
Guyane Française

AREA AND POPULATION. Area about 91,000 sq. km (23,000 sq. miles), is situated on the north-east coast of South America, and population, including Inini, 44,392 (census 16 Oct. 1967), of whom 3,000 are tribal natives. Cayenne, the chief town, has a population of 24,581. These figures are exclusive of the floating population of miners, officials and troops.

From 1854 to 1938, Cayenne had a penal settlement for habitual criminals. The last convicts were, after 1945, sent back to France.

GOVERNMENT. On 19 March 1946 the status of Guiana was changed to that of an overseas department. It is administered by a prefect, has an elected council-general of 16 members and is represented in the National Assembly and the Senate by 1 deputy each. On 17 March 1969 the administration of Guiana was modified by dividing the territory into 2 *arrondissements* (Cayenne and Saint-Laurent du Maroni). The former territory of Inini (*see* THE STATESMAN'S YEAR-BOOK, 1969–70, p. 925) being divided between the 2 *arrondissements*. The number of communes was raised from 14 to 19.

Prefect: Jean Monfraix.

EDUCATION. Primary education has been free since 1889 in lay schools for the two sexes in the communes and many villages. In 1969 public primary schools had 750 teachers and 7,780 pupils, the *lycée* 97 teachers and 1,214 pupils; a technical school had 49 teachers and 756 pupils. Private schools had 89 teachers and 2,544 pupils.

JUSTICE. At Cayenne there are a court of first instance, and a superior court of appeal, with jurisdiction in other localities.

FINANCE. The budget for 1969 balanced at 61,256,396 francs.

AGRICULTURE. The country has immense forests (about 80,000 sq. km) rich in many kinds of timber. Only about 3,300 hectares are under cultivation. The crops consist of rice (20 tons in 1968), maize (85 tons), manioc (6,400 tons), bananas (2,500 tons), sugar-cane (3,047 tons) and pineapples (80 tons). The fishing of shrimps has been taken up by American companies.

Livestock, 1968: 2,300 cattle, 6,000 swine, 15 buffaloes, 400 sheep and 20,000 poultry.

COMMERCE. Trade in 1,000 metric tons and 1m. francs:

	1967		1968		1969	
	Quantity	*Value*	*Quantity*	*Value*	*Quantity*	*Value*
Imports	112·89	207·94	140·09	256·97	112 02	258 74
Exports	22·83	18·34	27·89	17·01	45·02	27·96

In 1969 France supplied 73·5% of imports; the next largest supplier was USA (9·5%).

The most important exports in 1969 were timber (14,621 metric tons; 3·3m. francs), shrimps (2,991 metric tons; 18·94m. francs).

Total trade between Guiana and UK, in £1,000 sterling (British Board of Trade returns):

	1966	1967	1968	1969	1970
Imports to UK	—	1	1	4	25
Exports from UK	102	193	256	224 }	2,549
Re-exports from UK	8	1	2	424 }	

COMMUNICATIONS. There are 3 ports: Cayenne, St-Laurent-du-Maroni and Kourou. Cayenne is visited regularly by ships of the Compagnie Générale Transatlantique and the Société Générale de Transports Maritimes. There is also steamboat communication between the capital and the other towns of the department. In 1968, 723 arrivals and departures of vessels were registered (passengers, 776; freight, 144,919 metric tons).

Three chief and some secondary roads connect the capital with most of the coastal area by motor-car services. There are 272 km of national and 462 km of departmental and communal roads. Connexions with the interior are made by waterways which, despite rapids, are navigable by local craft.

A telegraph system connects Cayenne with Macouria, Kourou, Sinnamary, Iracoubo and St-Laurent-du-Maroni. Number of telephones (1969), 4,058. There are wireless stations at Cayenne, Oyapoc, Régina, St-Laurent, Maripassoula, Saül, Camopi.

Air France calls at Cayenne four times a week, and Cruseiro do Sul twice a week; GAT airline services interior connexions. The airport at Cayenne-Rochambeau registered 7,499 arrivals and departures of aircraft in 1968.

BANKING. The Bank of Guiana had a capital of 2m. francs and reserve fund of 30,000 francs (as at 31 Dec. 1968). Loans totalled 68·1m. francs in Dec. 1969.

British Consul: Father Catty.

BOOKS OF REFERENCE

Abonnec, A., Hurault, J., Saban, R., *Bibliographie de la Guyane Française.* 2 vols. Paris, 1957
Henry, *Guyane Française, son histoire 1604–1946.* Cayenne
Hurault, J., *Guide du voyageur en Guyane.* Paris, 1949

OVERSEAS TERRITORIES
FRENCH POLYNESIA
Polynésie Française

GOVERNMENT. These islands, formerly called 'French Settlements in Oceania', scattered over a wide area in the eastern Pacific, opted in Nov. 1958 for the status of an Overseas Territory within the French Community. They are administered by a governor, a government council (over which the governor presides), consisting of 5 members elected by the assembly and a territorial assembly of 30 members elected every 5 years on the basis of universal suffrage. French Polynesia is represented in the National Assembly by 1 deputy, in the Senate by 1 senator and in the Economic and Social Council by 1 councillor.

Governor: Pierre Angeli

French Polynesia is administratively divided into the following *circonscriptions:*

1. The **Windward Islands** (Iles du Vent), comprising Tahiti with an area of about 1,042 sq. km and (census 1967) 61,519 inhabitants; Moorea with an area of 132 sq. km and 4,370 inhabitants; Makatea, 2,273 inhabitants; Maio, 206 inhabitants. The most important island is **Tahiti**; its chief town is Papeete with 22,278 inhabitants.

2. The **Leeward Islands** (Iles sous le Vent) (15,337 inhabitants), comprising Huahine, Raiatéa, Tahaa, Bora-Bora and Maupiti. The chief town is Uturoa (2,394 inhabitants) on Raiatéa.

The Windward and Leeward Islands together are called the Society Archipelago (Archipel de la Société).

3. The **Tuamotu group**, consisting of two parallel ranges of islands between 135° and 143° W. long. and 14° and 23° S. lat., east of the Society Archipelago, with a population of 6,664; chief centres, Rangiroa and Anaa. The **Gambier group** (of which Mangareva is the principal) have 30 sq. km of area; chief centre, Rikitea. The whole circonscription had 6,664 inhabitants in 1967.

4. The **Austral Islands**, of which Rurutu is the largest, Tubuai, Raivavae, Rimatara and, far to the south, Rapa, have together an area of 174 sq. km and 4,371 inhabitants.

5. The **Marquezas Islands**, with a total area of 1,274 sq. km and 5,147 inhabitants, the two largest islands being Nuku-Hiva and Hiva-Oa.

The total area is estimated at 4,000 sq. km (1,545 sq. miles); their population (census, 1967) was 98,378 (51,794 males, 46,584 females). The uninhabited island of Clipperton is under the authority of the Governor as Delegate of the French Government.

RELIGION. In 1962, 45,812 inhabitants were Protestants and 25,227 Roman Catholics.

EDUCATION. There were, in 1968, 162 primary schools (26,215 pupils), 17 secondary schools (4,018 pupils) and 2 technical schools (822 pupils).

FINANCE. The ordinary budget for 1967 balanced at 2,332m. francs CFP.

COMMERCE. Trade in 1,000 metric tons and 1m. francs du Pacifique (= 0·055 metropolitan francs):

	1967		1968		1969	
	Quantity	Value	Quantity	Value	Quantity	Value
Imports	311	10,229	352	15,619	285	10,367
Exports	18	1,169	20	1,031	21	1,303

Total trade between the French possessions in the Pacific and UK (British Board of Trade returns, in £1,000 sterling):

	1966	1967	1968	1969	1970
Imports to UK	8	31	13	4	8
Exports from UK	801	658	1,206	1,749 ⎫	2,583
Re-exports from UK	1	3	8	7 ⎭	

An important product is copra (coconut trees covering the coastal plains of the mountainous islands and the greater part of the low-lying islands), production (1969) 19,419 metric tons. Other produce for export are coffee, vanilla and mother-of-pearl, whereas tropical fruits, such as bananas, pineapples, oranges, etc., are grown only for local consumption. The phosphate deposits were exhausted in 1966.

Chief imports (by value) include metalwork, textiles, petrol, sugar and flour. Chief exports in 1967 were: Phosphates (1966) (200,113 metric tons, 246m. francs CP); copra (17,030 metric tons, 218m. francs CP); vanilla (58·9 metric tons, 72·3m. francs CP); mother-of-pearl (129·6 metric tons, 15·9m. francs CP). Tourism is very important, earning almost half as much as the visible exports. There were 23,574 tourists in 1967.

COMMUNICATIONS. Several shipping companies connect France, San Francisco, New Zealand and Australia with Papeete. Number of telephones (1969), 5,403.

Four international airlines connect Tahiti with Paris, Honolulu, USA, Mexico and New Zealand. There is also a regular air service between Tahiti and the Leeward Isles with occasional connexions to the other groups.

British Consul: (Vacant).

BOOKS OF REFERENCE

Journal Officiel des Etablissements Française de l'Océanie, and *Supplement containing Statistics of Commerce and Navigation.* Papeete

Andrews, E., *Comparative Dictionary of the Tahitian Language.* Chicago, 1944

Luke, Sir Harry, *The Islands of the South Pacific.* London, 1961

O'Reilly, P., and Reitman, E., *Bibliographie de Tahiti et de la Polynésie française.* Paris, 1967

O'Reilly, P., and Teissier, R., *Tahitiens. Répertoire bio-bibliographique de la Polynésie française.* Paris, 1963

NEW CALEDONIA AND DEPENDENCIES

Nouvelle Calédonie

AREA AND POPULATION. New Caledonia is situated between 20° 8' and 22° 25' S. lat., and 164° 15' and 162° 15' E. long. It has a total length exceeding 397 km and an average breadth of 50 km. Area, 19,103 sq. km (7,374 sq. miles). In 1969 the population was 100,580, including 32,120 Europeans (majority French), 47,110 Melanesians, 6,020 Vietnamese and Indonesians, 9,330 Polynesians and Wallisians. Noumea had 50,490 inhabitants.

GOVERNMENT. New Caledonia is administered by a governor, assisted by a government council of 5 which is elected by the Territorial Assembly. The Territorial Assembly is itself an elected body of 35 members. Nouméa, the capital, has a municipality; other centres of population are locally administered by municipal commissions.

High Commissioner for the Pacific Ocean and the New Hebrides and Governor of New Caledonia and Dependencies: Jean Risterucci.

The territory is represented in the National Assembly and the Senate by 1 deputy and 1 senator.

EDUCATION. In 1967, 25,756 children received instruction: 21,785 in primary schools, 2,749 in secondary schools and 1,123 in technical and vocational schools.

FINANCE. The ordinary budget for 1967 balanced at 2,114m. francs CFP, the extraordinary budget at 259m. francs CFP.

AGRICULTURE. Of the total area only about 6% is cultivable; about 1,600 sq. miles are pasture land; about the same area is cultivated or cultivable, and about 500 sq. miles contain forest; forest produce, 1967, 9,852 cu. metres. There are 4 forms of landownership: native reserves belonging to the local tribes, private estates, public land belonging to the New Caledonian territory and public land belonging to the metropolitan government. The chief agricultural products are coffee, copra, maize, fruits and vegetables. Livestock, 1966: 110,000 cattle, 3,700 sheep, 14,347 goats, 10,434 horses, 21,953 pigs.

MINING. The mineral resources are very great; nickel, chrome and iron abound; silver, gold, cobalt, lead and copper have been mined at different times; manganese is being mined now. The nickel deposits are of special value, being without arsenic. Production in 1967 (in 1,000 metric tons): Nickel ore, 3,800; iron ore, 203. About 294,270 hectares of mining land are owned, and 177,437 hectares have been granted for prospecting. In 1967 the furnaces produced 13,840 metric tons matte of nickel and 20,656 metric tons of nickel castings. Local industries are developing; there are a chlorine and oxygen plant, meat-preserving works, barking mills for coffee, and 5 furnaces melting nickel ore.

x

COMMERCE. Trade in 1,000 metric tons and 1m. francs[1]:

| | 1965 | | 1966 | | 1967 | |
	Quantity	Value	Quantity	Value	Quantity	Value
Imports	677	6,885	779	6,037	728	7,067
Exports	1,248	5,848	1,405	6,268	1,806	7,099

[1] The 'franc du Pacifique' equals 0·055 new francs.

In 1967, 53% of the imports came from, and 52% of the exports went to France and the Franc zone.

Chief imports in 1967 were (in 1,000 metric tons): Coal and coke, 322; petrol products, 215. Chief exports: Iron ore, 198; nickel matte, 16·6; ferro-nickel, 200; nickel ore, 1,508; copra, 1; coffee, 1.

COMMUNICATIONS. In 1967, 438 vessels entered Nouméa and unloaded 737,802 metric tons of goods and loaded 1,810,331 metric tons.

New Caledonia is connected by sea and air routes with France (the latter *via* Sydney–Singapore–Colombo–Athens), Australia (by Qantas Empire Airways), the New Hebrides, Wallis archipelago and Tahiti.

There were, in 1967, 5,080 km of roads, of which 1,500 km were of good quality. There were 50 post offices, 17,307 km of telephone lines, 3,000 km of telegraph lines and 6,004 telephones.

BANKING. There is a branch of the Banque de l'Indochine in Nouméa.

British Consul: (vacant).

Dependencies of New Caledonia:

1. The Isle of Pines, 30 miles to the south-east, with an area of 153 sq. km and a population of 925 (census 1963).

2. The Loyalty Islands, 60 miles east of New Caledonia, consisting of 3 large islands, Maré, Lifou and Uvéa, and many small islands with a total area of about 2,072 sq. km and a population of 13,459 natives and 158 Europeans (census 1963). The chief culture in the islands is that of coconuts: the chief export, copra.

3. The Huon Islands, 170 miles north-west of New Caledonia, a most barren group.

4. The Bélep Archipelago, about 7 miles north-east of New Caledonia.

5. Chesterfield Islands are on the 20° S. parallel, about 342 miles west of the northern headland of New Caledonia.

6. Walpole lies south-east of Maré (Loyalty Islands) and east of the Isle of Pines, about 93 miles from each of these islands.

BOOKS OF REFERENCE

Journal Officiel de la Nouvelle Calédonie et Dépendances
Notes sur l'économie de la Nouvelle-Calédonie

FRENCH TERRITORY OF THE AFARS
AND THE ISSAS

Territoire Français des Afars et des Issas

AREA AND POPULATION. The territory of the Afars and the Issas is situated in the Gulf of Aden between the Somali Republic and Ethiopia. The frontier starts from Loyada, on the coast, 20 km south-east of Djibouti, passes by Djalelo, the Degoueiné Mountains, crosses the Addis Ababa railway at Kilo-metre 110, 6 km to the north of Daouenlé, encloses the Gobaad Plain and Lake

Abbé, passes Mount Moussa Ali near Daddato, and terminates at Cape Doumeirah, opposite Perim, on the Straits of Bab el Mandeb.

The territory has an area of 23,000 sq. km (8,500 sq. miles). The population was estimated at 11 March 1967 at 125,050, including: Somalis, 58,240; Arabs, 8,285; Afars, 42,270; Europeans, 10,255; foreigners, 37,850. Djibouti, the seat of government, had 62,000 inhabitants.

GOVERNMENT. French Territory of the Afars and the Issas is administered by a Council of Government of 8 members. The council is elected by the Chamber of Deputies which is composed of 32 elected members. The Territory is represented in the National Assembly and the Senate by 1 deputy each. At a referendum held on 19 March 1967, 60% of the electorate voted for continued association with France rather than independence and the new statute for the territory came into being on 5 July 1967.

High Commissioner: Dominigre Ponchardier.
President of the Council of Government: Ali Aref Bourhan.

EDUCATION. In 1967 there were 118 public classes with 4,525 pupils and 40 private classes with 1,671 pupils for primary education. There were 1,177 pupils receiving a secondary education in high school, technical school and private secondary schools.

HEALTH. The medical services in 1968 included a hospital (650 beds), 8 dispensaries and 2 infirmaries.

FINANCE. Currency. A new currency, the Djibouti franc, was introduced on 17 March 1949. The currency is covered 100% by a US dollar fund. The Djibouti franc equals 0·026 new francs (*see* p. 19).

Budget. The ordinary budget for 1969 balanced at 2,227m. Djibouti francs.

DEFENCE. The army consists of 2 regiments and an artillery battalion (4,400 men); the navy has 2 minesweepers and some landing craft (150 men); the air force has 2 squadrons (550 men).

MINING. Minerals supposed to exist are gypsum, mica, amethyst and sulphur.

COMMERCE. The chief imports are cotton goods, sugar, cement, flour and benzene; the chief exports are hides, cattle and coffee (transit from Ethiopia). Special trade in 1,000 metric tons and 1m. Djibouti francs:

	1966		1967		1968	
	Quantity	*Value*	*Quantity*	*Value*	*Quantity*	*Value*
Imports	2·5	6,038	105·5	6,713	97·9	8,195
Exports	105·7	565	1·9	604	2·2	817

Trade with UK (British Board of Trade returns, in £1,000 sterling):

	1966	1967	1968	1969	1970
Imports to UK	38	57	207	108	29
Exports from UK	1,446	1,918	2,112	2,035 }	1,353
Re-exports from UK	10	—	12	8 }	

SHIPPING. In 1969 there entered at Djibouti 2,989 vessels, unloading 195,000 tons and loading 112,800 tons of merchandise.

ROAD TRAFFIC. In 1967 there were operating 5,000 passenger cars, 794 lorries, 356 motor cycles and 316 motorized bicycles.

RAILWAY. For the line Djibouti–Addis Ababa *see* p. 896. In 1968–69 the railway carried goods traffic of 189,965,905 ton-km.

POST. Number of telephones (1970), 1,500.

British Consul: A. E. Huttly.

BOOKS OF REFERENCE

Guide-Annuaire de la Côte Française des Somalis. Djibouti-Publicité, 1959
Poinsot, J.-P., *Djibouti et la Côte française des Somalis.* Paris, 1965
La Côte des Somalis. Paris, 1961

THE COMORO ARCHIPELAGO

Territoire des Comores

AREA AND POPULATION. The archipelago of the Comoro islands consist of the islands of Mayotte, Anjouan, Grande Comore and Mohéli. Area, about 2,170 sq. km (838 sq. miles): Grande Comore, 1,148; Anjouan, 424; Mayotte, 374; Mohéli, 290. Population (census 1966), 248,517 (Grande Comore, 126,205; Anjouan, 80,082; Mayotte, 31,930; Mohéli, 10,300); capital, Moroni (Grande Comore), population 11,515. Estimate (1970) 275,227 the majority of the inhabitants are Moslems, but there are about 2,000 Christians of French or Malagasy origin.

GOVERNMENT. On 22 Dec. 1961 the Comoro Archipelago was given a special statute which was amended on 3 Jan. 1968 to give greater internal autonomy. Mayotte was a colony since 1843; on 25 July 1912 the 3 other islands, hitherto protectorates, were also declared colonies. From 1914 to 1946 the whole archipelago was attached to the government-general of Madagascar. On 9 May 1946 it was granted administrative autonomy within the French Republic, and on 11 Dec. 1958 the Territorial Assembly decided to remain in the Republic.

The territory is governed by a council of ministers responsible to the chamber of deputies, whose 31 members are elected by universal suffrage.

The Comoro Archipelago is represented in the National Assembly by 2 deputies, in the Senate by 1 senator, and in the Economic and Social Council by 1 councillor.

High Commissioner: Jacques Mouradian.
President of the Council: Prince Said Ibrahim.

EDUCATION. In 1970, 325 elementary classes had 13,776 pupils, 3 secondary schools had 1,018 pupils.

FINANCE. The ordinary budget for 1970 balanced at 1,349m. francs CFA.

AGRICULTURE. The chief product was formerly sugar-cane, but now vanilla, copra, cacao, sisal, coffee, cloves and essential oils (citronella, ylang, lemon-grass) are the most important products.

COMMERCE. Imports in 1969 amounted to 37,097 metric tons (2,092m. francs CFA), exports to 13,125 metric tons (577·9m. francs CFA). Vanilla exports were (1968) 138 metric tons (349·5m. francs CFA); sisal, 218 tons (7·6m. francs CFA); copra, 5,266 tons (211·5m. francs CFA); ylang, 68 tons (340·1m. francs CFA); cloves, 87 tons (58·6m. francs CFA); jasmine, 0·4 ton (29·3m. francs CFA). Grande Comore has a fine forest and produces timber for building.

Trade with UK (in £1,000): Exports from UK, 1966, 16; 1967, 19; 1968, 16; 1969, 16; imports to UK, 1964–69, nil (British Board of Trade returns).

ST PIERRE AND MIQUELON
Territoire des Iles Saint-Pierre et Miquelon

The territory consists of a group of 8 small islands off the south coast of Newfoundland. Area of St Pierre group, 26 sq. km (10 sq. miles); population (census 12 June 1967), 4,614; area of Miquelon group, 216 sq. km (83·5 sq. miles); population, 621; total area, 242 sq. km (93·5 sq. miles), 5,235 inhabitants. Vital statistics (1970): Births 149; marriages, 24; deaths, 65.

The territory is represented in the National Assembly and the Senate by 1 deputy each.

Governor: J. J. Buggia.

The Governor is assisted by a privy council consisting of the service chiefs and 2 members appointed by the Minister of Overseas Territories. A general council of 14 elected members was set up by decree of 25 Oct. 1946. Chief town, St Pierre, is also the seat of the court of appeal and the see of the Apostolic Prefecture.

Primary instruction is free. There were, in 1969, 10 nursery and primary schools with 56 teachers and 1,284 pupils; 6 secondary schools (including 3 technical schools) with 44 teachers and 359 pupils.

The islands, being mostly barren rock, arc unsuited for agriculture. The chief industry is cod-fishing. The imports comprise textiles, salt, wines, coal, petrol, foodstuffs, meat; and the exports (in 1969), dried and salted fish (179 tons; 17m. francs CFA), frozen and smoked fish (1,813 tons; 252m. francs CFA) and fish meal (717 tons; 21m. francs CFA).

The ordinary budget for 1969 balanced at 655,044,030 francs CFA, the extraordinary budget at 193m. francs CFA.

Trade in metric tons and 1m. francs:

	1967		1968		1969	
	Quantity	*Value*	*Quantity*	*Value*	*Quantity*	*Value*
Imports	62,125	1,918	67,931	1,953	83,565	2,485
Exports	2,657	335	2,673	256	2,878	295

Total trade between St Pierre and Miquelon and UK (British Board of Trade returns, in £1,000 sterling):

	1966	1967	1968	1969	1970
Imports to UK	4	1	—	1	—
Exports from UK	46	57	53	72 }	84
Re-exports from UK	7	1	3	2 }	

St Pierre is in regular steam communication with North Sydney and Halifax, and is connected by radio-telecommunication with Europe and the American continent. There were 860 telephones in 1970. Air Saint-Pierre connects the territory with Sydney (Nova Scotia), and there are occasional flights to and from St John's (Newfoundland), Gander and New York.

British Consul-General: Sir Anthony Rouse KCMG, OBE (resident in New York).

BOOKS OF REFERENCE

De Curton, E., *Saint-Pierre et Miquelon.* Paris, 1944
De La Rüe, E. A., *Saint-Pierre et Miquelon.* Paris, 1963
Ribault, J. Y., *Histoire de Saint-Pierre et Miquelon: Des Origines à 1814.* St Pierre, 1962

SOUTHERN AND ANTARCTIC TERRITORIES

Terres Australes et Antarctiques Françaises

The Territory of the TAAF was created on 6 Aug. 1955. It comprises the islands of Saint Paul and Nouvelle Amsterdam, the Kerguelen and Crozet archipelagos, and Terre Adélie.

The Administrator is assisted by a consultative council which meets twice yearly in Paris; its members are nominated by the Government for 5 years and also a scientific council; its members are nominated by the Science Research Minister. The administration has its seat in Paris.

Administrator: Pierre Rolland.

There are 4 postal agencies; the TAAF has its own postage stamps.

The scientific stations of the TAAF which took an important part in the International Geophysical Year, 1956–58, have been made permanent; the staff of the French bases is renewed annually.

Kerguelen archipelago, situated 48–50° S. lat., 68–70° E. long., consists of 1 large and 300 small islands with a total area of 7,000 sq. km (2,700 sq. miles). It was discovered in 1772 by Yves de Kerguelen, but was effectively occupied by France only in 1949. Port-aux-Français has several scientific research stations (85 members). Reindeer, trout and sheep have been acclimatized.

Crozet archipelago, situated 46° S. lat., 50–52° E. long., consists of 5 larger and 15 tiny islands, with a total area of 300 sq. km (116 sq. miles); the western group includes Apostles, Pigs and Penguins islands; the eastern group, Possession and Eastern islands. The archipelago was discovered in 1772 by Nicolas Dufresne, whose mate, Crozet, annexed it for Louis XV. A meteorological and scientific station on Possession Island (15 members) was built in 1964.

Saint Paul, situated 38° S. lat., 77° E. long., has an area of 7 sq. km (2·7 sq. miles). It is uninhabited. It was perhaps discovered in 1559 by Portuguese sailors.

Nouvelle-Amsterdam, situated 37° S. lat., 70° E. long., with an area of 60 sq. km (25 sq. miles). It was discovered in 1522 by Magellan's companions, but first visited (together with Saint Paul) by a Dutch skipper. In 1950 an administrative office, research stations (30 members) and a hospital were established.

Terre Adélie comprises the antarctic continent between 136° and 142° E. long., south of 60° S. lat. It was discovered in 1840 by Dumont d'Urville. A research station (27 members) is situated at Base Dumont d'Urville, which is kept by the French Polar Expeditions.

BOOKS OF REFERENCE

T.A.A.F. Revue trimestrielle. Paris, 1957 ff.
Expéditions Polaires Françaises. Etudes et Rapports. Paris 1948–59

WALLIS AND FUTUNA

On 27 Dec. 1959 the inhabitants of these islands voted with an overwhelming majority in favour of exchanging their status from a protectorate to an oversea territory, which was granted by the French Parliament on 29 July 1961. The islands have, since 1842, been ruled by kings advised by a French Resident under the High Commissioner of New Caledonia.

The Wallis Archipelago, north-east of Fiji, has an area of 275 sq. km (106 sq. miles) and 5,380 inhabitants. The archipelago is in regular communication with Nouméa *via* Port Vila.

Futuna and Alofi, south of the Wallis Islands, have about 3,000 inhabitants.

ANGLO-FRENCH CONDOMINIUM

NEW HEBRIDES. *See* p. 161

MEMBER STATES OF THE COMMUNITY

CENTRAL AFRICAN REPUBLIC
République Centrafricaine

AREA AND POPULATION. The area of the Central African Republic covers 624,930 sq. km; its population in 1967 was 1,466,000. The capital is Bangui (150,000 inhabitants). In 1968 some 18,100 refugees from the Sudan and 1,700 from the Congo were living in the Central African Republic.

CONSTITUTION AND GOVERNMENT. The Central African Republic became independent on 13 Aug. 1960, after having been one of the 4 territories of French Equatorial Africa (under the name of Ubangi Shari) and from 1 Dec. 1958 a member state of the French Community. In Jan. 1959 the 4 republics formed an 'economic, technical and customs union'. The Republic was admitted to the UN on 20 Sept. 1960.

On 1 Jan. 1966 the army overthrew the government of President Dacko.

President of the Republic, Prime Minister and Minister of Defence: Gen. Jean Bedel Bokassa.
Foreign Minister: Jean Arthur Bandio.

FINANCE. The ordinary budget in 1966 envisaged revenue 7,953m. francs CFA (1967: 9,560m.), and expenditure 8,527m. francs CFA (1967: 10,400m.; 1968, 9,600m.).

DEFENCE. The army consists of an infantry battalion of about 1,000 men.

The air force has 1 C-47 transport, 10 Aermacchi AL.60C5 utility aircraft, 3 Broussard light communications aircraft and 1 Alouette II helicopter. It also maintains and operates the Dassault Falcon twin-jet presidential aircraft. Personnel total about 100.

PRODUCTION. A 4-year development plan (1967–70) provides for investment in industrial development of 5,600m. francs CFA. Production, 1967: Millet and sorghum, 40,000 metric tons; maize, 35,000 metric tons; groundnuts,

60,000 metric tons; coffee (1970), 12,359 metric tons; cotton (1970), 58,824 metric tons; diamonds (1970), 493,605 carats.

Cotton and coffee are the main export crops. A record of 48,000 metric tons of cotton was produced in 1967–68 and 38,000 metric tons in 1966–67.

TRADE. In 1970 imports were valued at 7,581m. francs CFA, exports at 7,695m. francs CFA. France accounted for 58% of imports and 52% of exports.

Trade of the Central African Republic with UK according to British Board of Trade returns, in £1,000 sterling:

	1965	1966	1967	1968	1969	1970
Imports to UK	509	729	377	318	585	444
Exports from UK	341	244	369	287	321 }	281
Re-exports from UK	—	—	1	—		

French High Representative: Jean Herly.
British Ambassador and Consul-General: A. J. Edden, CMG. *First Secretary:* A. B. Moore, MBE (both resident at Yaoundé).
Ambassador in USA: Michel Gallin-Douathe.
USA Ambassador: Geoffrey W. Lewis.

CONGO
République du Congo

AREA AND POPULATION. The area of the Congo Republic covers 331,850 sq. km; estimated population (1967), 900,000. The capital is Brazzaville (156,000 inhabitants, 1965).

CONSTITUTION AND GOVERNMENT. The Republic of the Congo became independent on 15 Aug. 1960, after having been one of the 4 territories of French Equatorial Africa (under the name of Middle Congo) and from 28 Nov. 1958 a member state of the French Community. In Jan. 1959 it formed an 'economic, technical and customs union' with the other 3 territories of the former government-general of French Equatorial Africa. The Republic was admitted to the UN on 20 Sept. 1960.

President of the Republic: Marien Ngouabi. *Vice-President:* Alfred Raoul.
Foreign Affairs: Auxence Ikonga.

FINANCE. The ordinary budget in 1964 balanced at 9,670m. francs CFA. Expenditure in 1967, 13,098m. (ordinary) and 1,613m. (investment).

DEFENCE. The army consists of an infantry and a paracommando battalion of 2,000 men.

The air force has a strength of about 200, with 1 C-47 transport, 3 Broussard communications aircraft and 1 Alouette II light helicopter.

FISHERIES. A factory, which will be collectively owned by 15,000 families, for smoking fish is (1969) under construction at Mossaka on the Congo River.

MINING. Production of lead was 13,700 short tons in 1965; gold (1963), 2,951 troy oz.

TRADE. In 1967 imports totalled 20,200m. francs CFA and exports 11,700m. Trade with UK (British Board of Trade returns, in £1,000 sterling):

	1965	1966	1967	1968	1969	1970
Imports to UK	3,667	2,341	3,124	2,961	1,609	1,782
Exports from UK	1,406	776	926	1,185	1,448 }	2,433
Re-exports from UK	8	4	11	2	8	

COMMUNICATIONS. A railway (516 km) and a telegraph line connect Brazzaville with Pointe-Noire. Brazzaville has an airport which in 1967 handled 4,239 metric tons of freight and 44,717 passengers arriving and departing. Pointe-Noire (76,000 inhabitants) is a considerable port, handling, in 1967, 1,090 ships and 2·5m. metric tons of freight. Telephones (1968) numbered 9,000, of which 5,191 in Brazzaville.

French High Representative: Maurice Delauney.
British Ambassador: (Vacant).

Diplomatic relations with USA were broken off on 13 Aug. 1965.

GABON
République Gabonaise

AREA AND POPULATION. The area of the Gabon Republic covers 267,000 sq. km; its population in 1970 was about 475,000, including about 12,000 Europeans. The capital is Libreville (73,000 inhabitants). A population census took place in 1970.

CONSTITUTION AND GOVERNMENT. The Gabonese Republic became independent on 17 Aug. 1960 after having been one of the 4 territories of French Equatorial Africa and, from 28 Nov. 1958, a member state of the French Community. In Jan. 1959 it formed an 'economic, technical and customs union' with the other 3 territories of the former government-general of French Equatorial Africa. The Republic was admitted to the UN on 20 Sept. 1960.

President of the Republic, Prime Minister and Minister of Defence: Albert-Bernard Bongo (on the death of Léon Mba on 28 Nov. 1967).
Foreign Minister: Jean Rémy Ayouné.

FINANCE. The ordinary budget for 1971 provided for expenditure of 16,700m. francs CFA, and the development expenditure, 7,800m.

DEFENCE. The army consists of 1 infantry battalion and 2 commando battalion companies, totalling 900 men.
The air force is reported to have one or two light communications aircraft, 3 Alouette helicopters and about 50 personnel.

PRODUCTION. 1967: Manganese ore, 1·1m. metric tons; oil, 3·4m. metric tons; uranium concentrates, 1,452 metric tons; natural gas, 17,423,000 cu. metres; gold, 29,157 troy oz.; timber (okoumé), 750,000 metric tons; 1962: cocoa, 3,800 metric tons; coffee, 1,200 metric tons.
The petroleum refinery in Port Gentil, a joint venture of the governments of the five members of the Central African Customs and Economic Union (UDEAC) and foreign petroleum companies, began trial operations in Oct. 1967. The refinery produced 4·6m. tons of crude oil in 1968 (1967, 3·5m.).

TRADE. In 1967 imports totalled 16,600m. francs CFA (1966: 16,400m.) and exports 29,700m. francs CFA (1966: 24,900m.). France, USA and Germany are Gabon's principal trading partners; the share of these countries in Gabon's exports has declined from 80% in 1966 to 66% in 1967, owing to the diversion of a substantial proportion of petroleum exports to other countries. These three countries continued to provide about 66% of Gabon's imports.
Trade with the UK (British Board of Trade returns, in £1,000 sterling):

	1965	1966	1967	1968	1969	1970
Imports to UK	1,332	915	2,641	2,506	1,681	1,152
Exports from UK	707	665	691	781	975 ⎱	
Re-exports from UK	3	4	7	23	30 ⎰	960

COMMUNICATIONS. Libreville and Port Gentil are the main ports. Together with Pointe-Noire (Congo), they received 1,531 vessels in 1963; merchandise unloaded was 176,400 tons; loaded, 1,319,000 tons. Telephones (1969), 4,300. Under a development plan (1966–70) 2,300m. francs CFA per annum are to be spent on road construction.

French High Representative: F. S. de Quirielle.
Ambassador to UK: Georges Rawiri (resident in Paris).
British Ambassador and Consul-General: A. J. Edden, CMG. *First Secretary:* A. B. Moore, MBE (both resident at Yaoundé).
Ambassador to USA: Leonard Antoine Badinga.
USA Ambassador: Richard Funkhouser.

Lasserre, G., *Libreville, la ville et sa région.* Paris, 1958
Thiery, Y. and Delarozière, R., *Carte ethnique du Gabon.* Paris, 1945

MADAGASCAR
République Malgache

HISTORY. Madagascar was discovered by the Portuguese, Diego Diaz, in 1500. On the return of Diaz to Portugal the King concluded that the island must be Madagascar, about which he had read in Marco Polo's 'Voyages'. Polo, however, had not been there, but believing his Arab informants, ascribed to an island what was really the kingdom of Mogadisho, on the east coast of Africa. Mispronouncing and mis-spelling the name, he coined the word Madagascar.

The last native sovereign in Madagascar, Queen Ranavalona III (born 1845, died 1917), succeeded in 1883. The French claimed a portion of the north-west coast as having been transferred to them by local chiefs, and hostilities were carried on in 1883–85 against the Merina, who refused to recognize the cession. In 1885 peace was made, Diégo-Suarez having been surrendered to France. By the agreement of 5 Aug. 1890 the protectorate of France over Madagascar was recognized by Great Britain; a French expedition was dispatched in May 1895 to enforce the claims of France and on 1 Oct. the Queen accepted the protectorate. In 1896 Diégo-Suarez and the islands of Nossi-Bé on the west coast (130 sq. miles) and Sainte-Marie on the east coast (64 sq. miles) were placed under the governor-general of Madagascar. By a law promulgated 6 Aug. 1896 the island and its dependencies were declared a French colony.

On 14 Oct. 1958 Madagascar was proclaimed a member state of the Community and on 26 June 1960 became an independent state within the Community. The Republic was admitted to the UN on 21 Sept. 1960.

AREA AND POPULATION. Madagascar is situated off the south-east coast of Africa, from which it is separated by the Moçambique Channel, the least distance between island and continent being 250 miles; its length is 980 miles; greatest breadth, 360 miles. The area is 594,180 sq. km (229,233 sq. miles). On 1 Jan. 1967 the population was 6,776,970, of whom 32,938 were French, 36,882 Comorians, 17,055 Indians, 9,203 Chinese and 4,728 other aliens.

There are 18 Malagasy ethnic groups, the more important being the Hova (1,744,685), the Betsimisáraka (997,551), the Bétsiléo (806,153), the Tsimihety (477,261), the Sakalava (381,753), the Antaisaka (355,639) and the Antandroy (370,473). Indians and Chinese carry on small retail trade.

Population of the provinces (1 Jan. 1968): Diégo-Suarez, 575,424; Fianarantsoa, 1,720,922; Majunga, 839,654; Tamatave, 1,096,235; Tananarive, 1·69m.; Tuléar, 1,086,721.

The populations of the chief towns were in 1970, the capital, Tananarive, 322,000; Tamatave, 50,500; Majunga, 43,500; Fianarantsoa, 39,500; Diégo-Suarez, 38,600; Tulear, 34,000.

Vital statistics, 1967: Births, 241,413; deaths, 82,815.

CONSTITUTION AND GOVERNMENT. The constitution of the republic was promulgated on 29 April 1959 and amended in June 1960. It provides for a national assembly of 107 and a senate of 52 members. The government consists of a president, 4 vice-presidents, ministers and secretaries of state.

President of the Republic and Chief of Armed Forces: Philibert Tsiranana.
Foreign Affairs: Jacques Rabemananjara.

The republic is divided into the 6 provinces of Fianarantsoa, Majunga, Tamatave, Diégo-Suarez, Tuléar and Tananarive. Each province is under the supervision of an administrator. The provinces are subdivided into prefectures, sub-prefectures, arrondissements and cantons. Each canton comprises a number of communes which correspond to the traditional *fokonolona.*

National flag: White (vertical), green and red (horizontal).
National anthem: Ry tanindrazanay malala ô!

Malagasy, which is a language of Malayo-Polynesian origin, is the official language together with French.

RELIGION. Since 1818 a large portion of the Merina and other ethnic groups in the central districts have been Christianized. Many of the missionary societies which worked in Madagascar have now established churches. The 2 largest religious bodies are Roman Catholics with 1·4m. members (5,000 churches) and Fiangonan'i Jesosy Kristy eto Madagascar (FJKM) with 1·03m. members and 5,161 churches. There are also other smaller Christian churches and 75 mosques The outlying tribes are still mostly animist.

EDUCATION. Education is compulsory from 6 to 14 years of age in the primary schools. In 1967–68 there were 602,844 pupils in public primary schools and 210,047 in private schools. The total number of primary schools was 4,606. There were 62 colleges of general education with 9,302 students and 12 *lycées* with a total of 13,314 students. There is a co-educational university at Tananarive with faculties of Law, Science and Letters. The total student body in 1968 was 3,779. In 1967–68 there were 16 technical colleges with 2,162 students and 3 technical *lycées* with 3,237 students.
There are also 4 agricultural schools at Nanisana, Ambatondrazaka, Marovoay and Ivoloina.

CINEMAS. There were, in 1969, 46 cinemas with a seating capacity of 21,000.

FINANCE. Currency. The monetary system is tied to that of France. The Malagasy Franc (FMG) = 0·02 French francs.

Budget. The local revenue is derived chiefly from direct taxation (including a poll tax and taxes on land, cattle and houses), from customs and other indirect taxes, from territorial lands, from posts and telegraphs, markets and miscellaneous sources. The chief branches of expenditure are general administration, public works, health services, education, the post office and the public debt. The general budget for 1971 provided for an expenditure of 35,500m. FMG. Capital expenditure will take 10,000m. FMG.

PLANNING. A 5-year development plan, 1964–68, provided for a total expenditure of 165,000m. francs, 31,000m. to be financed by foreign aid. Of the total, 51% was allocated to infrastructure and transportation, 23% to agriculture, 17% to industry and 9% to various social projects. A second plan is in the course of preparation.

DEFENCE. The army in 1968 had a strength of 4,000 organized in 2 mixed regiments, 1 engineer regiment and an artillery battery.
Created in 1961 and maintained with French Air Force assistance, the Malagasy Air Force has a few transport and communications aircraft, including 3 C-47, 3 Flamants, 7 Broussards, 1 Bell 47, 1 Alouette II and 2 Alouette III helicopters. Personnel total 400.

AGRICULTURE. The principal agricultural products in 1969 were (in 1,000 metric tons): Manioc, 3,626; rice, 40·4; cloves, 974 (tons); vanilla, 1,097 (tons); coffee, 49·6; groundnuts, 38·6; raffia, 5·2; bananas 10·7; beans, 3·4; sugar, 98·5; tobacco, 4·4; pepper, 3·5.

Cattle breeding and agriculture are the chief occupations. There were, in 1968, 9·5m. cattle, 560,000 pigs, 305,000 sheep, 410,000 goats and 14m. poultry.

FORESTRY. The forests contain many valuable woods, while gum, resins and plants for tanning, dyeing and medicinal purposes abound.

MINING (1967). Mining production (in metric tons) included: Mica (1968), 838; graphite (1968), 16,071; phosphates (1964), 2,020; chrome (1966), 2,383; ilmenite, 1,857; zircon, 209; beryl (industrial), 30; gold, 23 kg; garnet (industrial), 5.

INDUSTRY. Industry, hitherto confined mainly to the processing of agricultural products, is now extending to cover other fields. Thus in addition to rice milling, sugar making, distilling, oil-seed crushing, meat, fruit and vegetable canning, cigarette and chewing-tobacco production, soap and rope manufactures, cotton spinning and weaving, brewing, processing of cashew nuts, fruit juices and jams and meat canning, it now includes an oil refinery, a paper-mill, two vehicle assembly plants, plants for the assembly of batteries, transistor radio and television sets and bicycles, a plastics factory, two paint factories, metal furniture and window making, tyre-retreading and foam-rubber plants, an animal-feed factory, an iron-sheeting and nail-making plant, a metal packing plant, two undertakings producing aluminium ware, a chemical works and two biscuit and confectionery factories. A second cotton-mill will start production in 1970. A second cement factory is projected; the existing one produced 67,743 metric tons in 1968.

POWER. The consumption of electric power in 1968 amounted to 123·7m. kwh. (1966: 104·1m.).

COMMERCE. Trade in 1,000 metric tons and 1m. FMG:

	1967		1968		1969	
	Quantity	Value	Quantity	Value	Quantity	Value
Imports	624,010	35,885	435,953	42,024	928,254	46,199
Exports	489,402	25,711	561,507	28,608	592,214	29,154

In 1967 France supplied 64% in value of the imports; USA, 6·8%; West Germany, 5·4%; UK, 1·6%; France received 36·7% of the exports.

In 1969 the chief imports (in 1m. FMG) were: Metalware, 69,023; vehicles, 13,203; chemicals, 56,633; mineral products, 633,743; wines, 135,687; vegetables, 549; food, 25,882; animal products, 7,070. The chief exports in 1969 were: Foodstuffs, 94,697; textiles, 24,927; mineral products, 285,645; animals and animal products, 12,268.

Total trade between Malagasy Republic and UK (British Board of Trade returns, in £1,000 sterling):

	1966	1967	1968	1969	1970
Imports to UK	1,253	700	1,431	1,718	1,338
Exports from UK	658	582	1,047	945 }	923
Re-exports from UK	5	3	9	14 }	

SHIPPING. Tamatave, Majunga, Diégo-Suarez, Tuléar, Nossi-Bé and Manakara are the principal ports. In 1968, 5,237 vessels of 1,090,846 tons entered these ports.

RAILWAYS. Four railways are operating, namely: between Tananarive and Tamatave (373 km); between Tananarive and Antsirabe (noted for its thermal springs), 158 km; the branch line of the Tamatave railway, from Moramanga to Lake Alaotra (168 km) and the line from Fianarantsoa to the east coast (165 km). In 1968, 2·4m. passengers and 926,000 metric tons of cargo were transported; receipts amounted to 2,543·5m. francs.

ROADS. At the end of 1968 there were 40,000 km of roads suitable for motor traffic, of which 8,364 km are practicable all the year round. There is a motor-car service with a network of routes covering about 2,797 km. Motor vehicles registered at 1 Jan. 1969 included 40,544 passenger cars, 2,446 buses, 2,381 commercial vehicles, 27,538 lorries, 2,180 tractors and 4,549 motor cycles.

AVIATION. Air France and Air Madagascar connect Tananarive with Paris, Alitalia connects with Rome. Several weekly services operated by Air Madagascar connect the capital with the ports and the chief inland towns. The main airfields are at Ivato, Tamatave, Tuléar and Majunga. In 1968, 67,365 passengers, 2,446 metric tons of cargo and 82 metric tons of mail departed on international flights.

POST. There were in 1969, 460 post offices and agencies and 57 wireless telegraph stations. The telegraph line has a length of 17,400 km. There were 66,000 km of telephone line and 11,000 telephone subscribers. Direct telephone communications exist between Tananarive, Paris, Mauritius and Réunion. Wireless telegraph was established between Tananarive and Fianarantsoa on 12 Oct. 1962.

BANKING. The Banque Nationale Malagasy de Dévéloppement (BNM) created in 1963 to replace the Société Malgache d'Investissement et de Crédit is the national investment bank. The Banque de Madagascar et des Comores was formerly the bank of issue, but this privilege was, on 8 March 1962, transferred to a new national institute, the Institut d'Emission Malgache. The Banque de Madagascar et des Comores continues to serve as a bank of issue for the Comoro Islands and as a commercial bank there and in Madagascar where it has 14 offices and 2 sub-offices (in Tananarive). The other commercial banks are: Banque Malagasy d'Escompte et de Crédit (BAMES) (the Comptoir National d'Escompte de Paris holds 65% of its capital, the rest being owned by the Malagasy Government) with 9 offices throughout the island and 2 sub-offices in Tananarive; the Banque Nationale pour le Commerce et l'Industrie (BNCI) with 9 offices and 2 sub-offices (in Tananarive); the Banque Française pour le Commerce which has 1 office and 2 sub-offices in Tananarive and 1 office in Tamatave.

The savings bank had, at 31 Dec. 1969, 75,077 depositors.

DIPLOMATIC REPRESENTATIVES

The Malagasy Republic is also in diplomatic relations on ambassadorial level with:

Algeria	Israel	Mauritius	Sweden
Belgium	Italy	Netherlands	Switzerland
Canada	Japan	Norway	Taiwan
Germany (West)	Korea (South)	Pakistan	Turkey
Ghana	Luxembourg	Sierra Leone	Vatican
Greece			

French High Representative: Alain G. Plantey.
High Representative in France: Dr Albert Rakoto-Ratsimamanga.
Ambassador to UK: Alfred Rajaonarivelo.
British Ambassador: Timothy Crosthwait. *First Secretary:* S. E. Warder.
Ambassador to USA and Canada: Jules Razafimbahiny.
USA Ambassador: Anthony D. Marshall.
Indian Ambassador: Nugahalli Kesavan.

BOOKS OF REFERENCE

STATISTICAL INFORMATION. The Service de Statisque Générale in Tananarive published the *Bulletin mensuel de Madagascar* (from Oct. 1955); continuation of the trimestrial *Bulletin de statisque générale* (1949–54), the trimestrial *Revue de Madagascar*, the *Madagascar à travers ses provinces* (latest issue, 1953), the *Annuaire Statistique de Madagascar* (vol. 1, 1938–51, published 1953, the *Situation Economique au Janvier 1968*, and the *Statistiques du Commerce Exterieur de Madagascar*).

Bulletin de l'Académie Malgache (from 1902)
Deschamps, H., *Histoire de Madagascar.* Paris, 1960
Saron, G., *Madagascar et les Comores.* Paris, 1953
Stratton, A., *The great red island.* London, 1965
Thompson, V., and Adloff, R., *The Malagasy Republic.* Stanford Univ. Press, 1965

SENEGAL
République du Sénégal

AREA AND POPULATION. The Republic has a total area of 197,161 sq. km; the population in 1965 was about 3·5m. The capital is Dakar (population, 474,000). Kaolack (69,500), Thiès (69,000), Rufisque (48,300), Saint-Louis (47,900), Ziguinchor (29,000), Diourbel (28,500) and Louga are other important towns.

The principal autochthonous tribes are the Ouolofs (about 700,000, mostly Moslems), Bambaras, Mandingos, Peuls (Fulbés) and Toucouleurs. In 1967 some 57,000 refugees from Portuguese Guinea were living in Senegal.

The government has approved an extension of its territorial waters from 6 to 12 nautical miles and, by regulating fishing within a further 6 miles, intends to exercise its authority over a zone of 18 miles from its coast. This measure is intended to safeguard the supply of fish to the national fishing industry and the offshore area for petroleum research.

CONSTITUTION AND GOVERNMENT. The Republic of Senegal became independent on 20 Aug. 1960, after having been a French territory (1659 foundation of Saint-Louis, 1854–65 occupation of the hinterland), a member state of the French Community (from 25 Nov. 1958) and, from Jan. 1959 to 20 Aug. 1960, a partner (together with Sudan) of the Federation of Mali. The Republic was admitted to the UN on 29 Sept. 1960.

The Republic is administered by a government council of 15 ministers; it is divided into 12 'circles'. The national assembly consists of 60 members, elected by universal suffrage.

President of the Republic: Léopold Sédar Senghor.
Prime Minister, Minister of Defence and Armed Forces: Abdou Diouf
Foreign Affairs: Amodou Karim Gaye.

EDUCATION. Education is provided at 2 *lycées* (at Dakar and Saint-Louis), 6 modern colleges, 3 technical colleges, 3 training centres, 2 *écoles normales*, 3 *cours normaux* and 255 elementary schools. Total pupils in the elementary schools in 1964–65 was 206,431, including 26,000 attending 67 mission schools; in the secondary schools, 31,000 (of whom 3,400 attend 5 mission colleges); in the technical schools and courses, 7,000. The University in Dakar was established on 24 Feb. 1957, with faculties of law, science, the arts and a school of medicine and pharmacy; it had 3,826 students in 1967–68.

FINANCE. The ordinary budget for 1970–71 balanced at 39,000m. francs CFA.

DEFENCE. The army has a strength of 5,000, organized in 4 motorized infantry battalions of 5 companies each.

The Senegal air force, formed with French assistance, has 2 C-47 transports, 4 Broussard liaison aircraft, 2 Bell 47 and 2 Alouette II helicopters. Personnel total about 300.

PLANNING. A second development plan, covering 1965–69, was adopted on 1 July 1965. The plan provides for total investments of 118,000m. francs CFA, of which 72,000m. francs CFA will be in the public sector and 46,000m. francs CFA in the private sector. The bulk of public investments is to be financed from foreign sources (mainly France and the European Development Fund), and the Government will contribute 25,000m. francs CFA.

AGRICULTURE. The soil is generally sandy. Production (1965) in 1,000 metric tons: Millet, 599; maize, 27; rice, 120; groundnuts, 1,100. Livestock (1965): 2·24m. sheep and goats, 2·1m. cattle, 47,000 pigs, 101,000 asses, 3,000 camels and 175,000 horses.

INDUSTRY. Dakar has numerous industrial works. In 1965 the production of phosphate rock was 1,048,300 metric tons; cement, 181,000 metric tons, supplying nearly half the requirements of the former territories of French West Africa.

TRADE. Imports in 1967 amounted to 844,000 metric tons; exports to 1,458,000 metric tons (including Mali and Mauritania). The chief imports (1965) (in metric tons) were wheat (61,141), rice (179,221), sugar (66,072), petroleum products (164,408), textiles and machinery. The chief exports were groundnuts (216,845), groundnut oil (142,544), oil-cake (196,431), phosphates (99,900) and salt (6,144).

Imports in 1968 totalled 44,000m. francs CFA; exports, 37,000m.

Total trade with UK (British Board of Trade returns, in £1,000 sterling):

	1966	1967	1968	1969	1970
Imports to UK	1,266	1,243	1,575	1,783	2,109
Exports from UK	900	914	1,275	1,454 }	1,503
Re-exports from UK	79	12	10	80 }	

COMMUNICATIONS. There were, in 1956, 118 post offices. French cables connect Dakar with Brest, Casablanca and Conakry; English cables, with British West Africa; and a South American cable, with Pernambuco. Telephones in 1969 numbered 29,072, of which 20,991 were in Dakar.

There are 5 railway lines: Dakar–Kidira (continuing in Mali), Thiès–Saint-Louis (193 km), Guinguinéo–Kaolack (22 km), Louga–Linguère (129 km), and Diourbel–Touba (46 km). Total length, 1,304 km (metre-gauge).

In 1966, 4,434 vessels entered the port of Dakar. In 1967 aircraft disembarked and embarked 69,351 passengers and 4,475 metric tons of freight at Yoff (Dakar).

There is a river service on the Senegal from Saint-Louis to Podor (140 miles) open throughout the year, and to Kayes (924 km) open from July to October. The Senegal River is closed to foreign flags. The Saloum River is navigable as far as Kaolack, the Casamance River as far as Ziguinchor.

BANKING. Under an agreement with the Crédit Lyonnais a new commercial bank, the Union Sénégalaise de la Banque pour le Commerce et l'Industrie, was established in Sept. 1961; the Senegal government holds the larger part of its capital.

At 31 Dec. 1960 the savings banks had 35,360 depositors with 217,515,000 francs CFA to their credit.

French High Representative: J. Viau de Lagarde.
Ambassador to the UK: Henri-Louis Valantin. *Counsellor:* Ibrahim Thiam.
British Ambassador: J. G. Tahourdin, CMG. *First Secretary:* R. J. Langridge.
Ambassador to USA: Cheikh Ibrahima Fall.
USA Ambassador: Edward G. Clark.

Crowder, M., *Senegal: a study in French assimilation.* OUP, 1962

CHAD
République du Tchad

AREA AND POPULATION. The area of the Chad Republic covers 1,284,000 sq. km; its population in 1969 was estimated at 3·5m. The capital is Fort Lamy (132,500 inhabitants).

CONSTITUTION AND GOVERNMENT. The Republic of Chad became independent on 11 Aug. 1960, after having been one of the 4 territories of French Equatorial Africa and, from 28 Nov. 1958, a member state of the French Community. In Jan. 1959 it formed an 'economic and technical union' with the 3 other territories of the former government-general of French Equatorial Africa. The Republic was admitted to the UN on 20 Sept. 1960.

President of the Republic and of the Council: François Tombalbaye.
Minister of Foreign Affairs: Jacques Baroum.

FINANCE. The ordinary budget in 1970 provided for expenditure of 13,500m. francs CFA and receipts of 11,800m. francs CFA.

DEFENCE. The army consists of 2 infantry battalions and an engineer battalion, totalling 2,500 men.

The air force has a strength of about 200 officers and men, with 1 C-47 transport, 3 Broussard communications aircraft and 1 Alouette II light helicopter.

AGRICULTURE. Cotton and animal husbandry are the most important industries. The cotton crop in 1967–68 was 102,033 metric tons of unginned and 37,033 metric tons of ginned cotton. In 1965 cotton accounted for 91% of exports and provided work for 450,000 farmers. The European Development Fund of EEC agreed, in 1970, to grant 264m. francs CFA to help finance a cotton productivity programme during the 1971–72 season.

TRADE. In 1967 imports totalled 15,000m. francs CFA, exports 8,500m. France accounts for 30% of the imports and 40% of the exports.

Trade with UK (in £1,000 sterling, British Board of Trade returns):

	1965	1966	1967	1968	1969	1970
Imports to UK	1,076	384	54	293	66	143
Exports from UK	116	210	140	157	184 }	244
Re-exports from UK	—	1	—	5	7 }	

French High Representative: F. Wibaux.
British Ambassador and Consul-General: R. J. McM. Wilson, CMG. *First Secretary:* P. J. Barlow (both resident at Yaoundé).
Ambassador to USA: Lazare Massibe.
USA Ambassador: Terence A. Todman.

Le Gornec, J., *Histoire politique du Tchad de 1900 à 1962.* Paris, 1963

FORMER MEMBER STATES OF THE FRENCH UNION

IVORY COAST
République de Côte d'Ivoire

AREA AND POPULATION. Area, 322,463 sq. km; total population (1965), 3·84m., including 15,000 Europeans. The seat of administration and of the court of appeal is at Abidjan (population, 264,000 Africans, 18,000 Europeans); the office of agriculture, at Bingerville. Abidjan, Bouaké (population, 1964, 80,000) and Daloa (32,000) are important towns. There are 8 towns with populations of over 10,000 inhabitants and 12 with over 5,000 inhabitants. 43% of the population are below the age of 15; 10% above the age of 50.

The principal ethnical groups are the Agnis-Ashantis, Kroumen, Mandé, Baoulé, Dan-Gouro and Koua.

Of the total population, 23·5% are Moslems, 12·5% Christians and 65% animists.

CONSTITUTION AND GOVERNMENT. The Republic of Ivory Coast became independent on 7 Aug. 1960, after having been a territory of French West Africa from 1904. The Republic was admitted to the UN on 20 Sept. 1960.

The Republic is situated between Liberia and Ghana and has common frontiers with the Republics of Guinea, Mali and Upper Volta. France obtained rights on the coast in 1842, but did not actively and continuously occupy the territory till 1882. On 1 Jan. 1933 a portion of Upper Volta was added to the Ivory Coast, but on 1 Jan. 1948 the districts of Bobo-Dioulasso, Gaoua, Kondougou, Ouagadougou, Kaya, Tenkodogo and Dédougou were transferred to the reconstituted Upper Volta.

The Republic is administered by a government of 17 ministers. The legislative assembly has 85 members; all of them, elected on 27 Nov. 1960, belong to the Rassemblement Démocratique Africain. The Republic is administratively divided into 4 departments: North, West, Central, South-East.

President, Minister of Economy, Finance, Defence and Agriculture: Félix Houphouet-Boigny. (Re-elected for a third 5-year term in 1970.)

EDUCATION. There were, in 1964–65, 330,551 pupils in public primary schools, 94,700 in private primary schools, 20,229 in public secondary schools, 8,312 in private secondary schools and 2,704 in public technical schools. The university of Abidjan had 1,938 students in 1965.

JUSTICE. There are a court of first instance, 2 courts of second instance and a court of appeal.

WELFARE. In 1965 there were 5 hospitals and 59 medical stations, 58 maternity homes and 190 dispensaries, 6 leprosaries and a mental asylum, with together 8,500 beds; there were 162 doctors and 46 pharmacists.

FINANCE. The budget for 1969 balanced at 46,500m. francs CFA.

DEFENCE. The army consists of 3 infantry battalions and support units; total strength, 4,000.

The air force, formed in 1962, has 3 C-47 transports, 1 Falcon light jet transport, 4 Broussard, 1 Beech 18 and 1 Aero Commander 500 communications aircraft and 5 Alouette II/III helicopters. Personnel total 300.

PLANNING. A 4-year development plan, 1967–70, aims at increased agricultural diversification, greater emphasis on light industries, further improvements in communication and health facilities, improvements in education and a more balanced distribution of public investments.

AGRICULTURE. Production in 1964 included (in 1,000 metric tons): Yam, 1,859; manioc, 987; maize, 168; rice, 219; bananas, 140; 1963: millet, 55; 1960: palm oil, 16; cola nuts, 28. The cultivation of cotton is being developed; coconuts and a small quantity of rubber are collected. It was announced in 1968 that 100,000 tons of coffee would be destroyed. The measure was taken in order to facilitate a reduction of world coffee supply, in accordance with the International Coffee Agreement, and to alleviate the burden on the Government of stock financing. Ivory Coast is the third largest coffee producer in the world. The mahogany forests inland are worked.

Several factories produce palm-oil, fruit preserves and fruit juice.

Livestock, 1962: 300,000 cattle, 515,000 sheep, 600,000 goats, 92,000 pigs, 1,000 horses and 1,100 donkeys.

MINING. Diamond fields are being exploited; 202,424 carats in 1969. Manganese deposits yielded 127,050 metric tons in 1969 (175,916 in 1966).

TRADE. Exports in 1969 amounted to 118.000m. francs CFA; imports, 86,000m. francs CFA. In 1969 exports of timber furnished 35,000m.; coffee, 30,000m., and cocoa, 26,000m. Of the exports, 38% went to France, 65% to EEC and 14% to the USA. Of the imports, 55% came from France, 72% from EEC and 6% from the USA. Chief imports were metalwork, cement, wine, motor fuel and oils.

Total trade between the Ivory Coast and UK (British Board of Trade returns, in £1,000 sterling):

	1966	1967	1968	1969	1970
Imports to UK	4,503	4,517	7,683	10,107	9,637
Exports from UK	1,745	1,941	2,873	2,944 }	3,122
Re-exports from UK	15	16	28	46 }	

COMMUNICATIONS. From Abidjan a railway runs to Léraba (652 km) and thence through Upper Volta to Ouagadougou. Permanent roads total 32,620 km, of which 900 km are bitumenized. In 1964 there were 28,074 cars and 24,700 lorries and tractors. The main airport is at Abidjan-Port-Buet. In 1967 it handled 153,381 passengers and 5,597 tons of freight and 660 tons of mail.

The main ports are Abidjan, Sassandra and Tabou. In 1967, 2,605 vessels of 7,553,000 net tons entered Abidjan, loading and unloading 4,131,060 metric tons. The 4 main rivers, Comoé, Bandama, Sassandra and Cavally, are practically not navigable because of rapids and cataracts.

There were, in 1966, 125 post offices and (1969) 24,811 telephones.

BANKING. In 1960 the savings banks had 30,293 depositors with 290,611,000 francs CFA to their credit.

DIPLOMATIC REPRESENTATIVES

The Ivory Coast maintains embassies in:

Belgium	Ghana	Liberia	Tunisia
France	Israel	Nigeria	UK
Germany (West)	Italy	Switzerland	USA

Ambassador to France: Tanoe Akpagny.
French Ambassador: J. Raphael Leygues.
Ambassador to the UK: Honoré Mambé Polneau.
British Ambassador: P. Murray, CMG. *First Secretary:* P. H. C. Eyers, MVO.
Ambassador to USA: Timothée N'Guetta Ahoua.
USA Ambassador: John Frick Root.

STATISTICAL INFORMATION. Service de la Statistique, Abidjan. It publishes *Bulletin Statistique Mensuel* and (1958) *Inventoire Économique de la Côte d'Ivoire, 1947–56*

Panorama de la Côte d'Ivoire, 1960, ed. Direction de l'Information, Abidjan
Rapport sur l'évolution économique et sociale de la Côte d'Ivoire, 1960–64. Abidjan, 1965
Holas, B., *Industries et cultures en Côte d'Ivoire*. Abidjan, 1965

DAHOMEY
République du Dahomey

AREA AND POPULATION. The area is 112,600 sq. km, and the population, in 1965, 2·37m. The seat of government is Porto Novo (74,500 inhabitants); the chief port and business centre is Cotonou (111,000); other important towns are Abomey (42,100), Ouidah (19,600) and Parakou (16,300).

CONSTITUTION AND GOVERNMENT. The Republic of Dahomey became independent on 1 Aug. 1960, after having been a territory of French West Africa from 1904. The Republic was admitted to the UN on 20 Sept. 1960.

After being under military regimes for 2½ years a return to civilian rule was made on 17 July 1968.

President, Prime Minister, Minister of Interior and Defence: Dr Emile Derlin Zinsou.
Minister of Foreign Affairs: Dr Daouda Badorou.

EDUCATION. There were, in 1964–65, 77,800 pupils in public primary schools, 52,900 in private primary schools, 5,230 in public secondary schools, 6,064 in private secondary schools in 1969 and, in 1963–64, 1,050 in technical schools.

FINANCE. The ordinary budget for 1970 envisaged receipts of 8,349m. francs CFA and expenditures of 9,836m. francs CFA.

DEFENCE. The army consists of 2 infantry battalions and support units; strength, 2,100.
The air force has a strength of about 100 officers and men, 1 C-47 transport, 1 Aero Commander 500 and 2 Broussard communications aircraft.

PLANNING. The main objectives of the 5-year (1966–70) development plan are to foster rural development, mainly by increasing the output of export crops (oil palm, groundnuts, coconuts, cotton and coffee) and food crops (vegetables and rice), and to develop infrastructure and food processing. The earlier (1962–65) plan was over-ambitious and had to be abandoned.

AGRICULTURE. The population is mainly agricultural, growing maize (224,800 metric tons in 1968), millet (73,000 tons in 1964) and groundnuts (31,000 tons in 1964). In 1963 there were 346,000 cattle, 771,000 sheep and goats, 272,000 pigs, 3,000 horses, 1,000 donkeys. The forests contain oil palms, which have been profitably utilized. These furnish the chief exports—kernels and oil. Cotton cultivation has been successfully introduced in the north; coffee cultivation has given good results in the southern districts.

TRADE. Imports in 1969, 12,208m. francs CFA; exports, 5,508m. francs CFA. The principal imports in 1963 (in metric tons): Cement, 66,438; petroleum, 43,682; sugar, 8,070; rice, 4,304. The principal exports were: Palm-kernels (50,558), palm-oil (9,256), decorticated groundnuts (6,593).
Total trade between Dahomey and UK (British Board of Trade returns, in £1,000 sterling):

	1966	1967	1968	1969	1970
Imports to UK	70	23	199	267	536
Exports from UK	455	479	709	974 ⎫	1,265
Re-exports from UK	3	42	64	40 ⎭	

COMMUNICATIONS. There are 5,886 km of carriage roads, of which 594 km are bitumenized. The latter include the East Road from Savé to Malanville on the Niger (478 km) and the North-west Road from Tchaourou to Porga (452 km); other roads are Cotonou–Dassa-Zoumé–Savé (318 km), Cotonou to Anécho (109 km), Abomey to Ketou (121 km), Tchaourou to Djougou (134 km).
Railways (metre-gauge) connect Cotonou with Parakou (438 km); Pahou–Segboroué on Lake Aheme (34 km); Cotonou–Pobé (107 km).
There were, in 1956, 68 post offices and (1969) 4,800 telephones. A telegraph line connects Cotonou with Abomey, Togo, Niger and Senegal.
In 1967, 630 vessels of 1,662,000 net tons entered the port of Cotonou.
In 1967, 30,400 passengers and 940 metric tons of freight and 190 metric tons of mail were dealt with at Cotonou airport.

BANKING. In 1960 the savings banks had 30,436 depositors with 248,693,000 francs CFA to their credit.

French Ambassador: L. F. Delamare.
British Ambassador and Consul-General: F. Smitherman, MBE (resides at Lomé).
Ambassador to UK: Michel Ahouanmenou.
Ambassador to USA: Wilfred de Souza.
USA Ambassador: Matthew Looram, Jr.

Bulletin statistique du Dahomey. Porto-Novo. (Monthly)

UPPER VOLTA
République de Haute-Volta

AREA AND POPULATION. The Republic covers an area of 274,122 sq. km; population (1969) 5·33m., including 3,500 Europeans or assimilated. Ouagadougou, the capital (110,000 inhabitants, of whom 1,000 Europeans) and Bobo-Dioulasso (69,356 inhabitants, of whom 1,500 Europeans), are *communes de plein exercice.* The principal autochthonous tribe are the Mossi (about 2·5m.).

CONSTITUTION AND GOVERNMENT. The Republic of Upper Volta became independent on 5 Aug. 1960 and was admitted to the UN on 20 Sept. 1960.

A separate colony of Upper Volta was in 1919 carved out of the colony of Upper Senegal and Niger, which had been established in 1904. It was suppressed in 1932 and its territory divided between Ivory Coast, Sudan and Niger. On 4 Sept. 1947 the Territory of Upper Volta was re-established, comprising the area of the old colony of Upper Volta as at 5 Sept. 1932.

A new constitution was approved on 4 June 1970. Elections were held on 20 Dec. 1970 when the *Union démocratique voltaïque* gained 37 of the 57 seats.

President: Gen. Sangoulé Lamizana.
Prime Minister: Gérard Kango Ouedraogo.

EDUCATION. There were, in 1968, 97,929 pupils in 587 public elementary schools, 7,614 in 31 public secondary schools, 1,354 in 10 public technical schools.

FINANCE. The ordinary budget for 1968 balanced at 8,564m. francs CFA, that for 1968 at 8,564 francs CFA. Indirect taxes account for 58% of estimated total revenue.

DEFENCE. The army consists of 1 infantry battalion, 1 reconnaissance squadron, 1 paratroop company and support units; total strength, 1,750.

AGRICULTURE. Production, 1967 (in metric tons): Millet and sorghum (797,700), maize (137,000), rice (52,000); 1968: cotton (25,000). Rice and groundnuts are of increasing importance. Livestock (1964): 2,221,000 cattle, 3m. sheep and goats, 65,000 horses, 133,000 donkeys.

MINING. Deposits of manganese, gold (1964, 32,665 troy oz.; 1965, 34,468 troy oz.) and diamonds are being prospected.

TRADE. In 1968 imports totalled 10,119m. francs CFA and exports 5,290m. francs CFA. The principal exports were livestock, fish and decorticated groundnuts.

Trade with the UK (British Board of Trade returns, in £1,000 sterling):

	1966	1967	1968	1969	1970
Imports from UK	22	—	78	22	13
Exports from UK	49	37	27	73 }	51
Re-exports from UK	—	—	—	— }	

COMMUNICATIONS. Ouagadougou is the terminus of the Abidjan–Niger railway. Total freight handled in 1966 was 238,500 tons. The road system comprises 16,662 km, of which 5,989 km are all-weather roads. Ouagadougou and Bobo-Dioulasso are regularly served by French airlines and in 1967 dealt with 19,199 passengers and 540 metric tons of freight.

There were, in 1956, 40 post offices and (1969) 1,309 telephones.

BANKING. In 1968 the savings banks had 18,733 depositors with 777,606,000 francs CFA to their credit.

French Ambassador: R. Delaye.
Ambassador to UK: (Vacant).
British Ambassador: P. Murray, CMG. *First Secretary and Consul:* P. H. C. Eyers, MVO (both resident at Abidjan).
Ambassador to USA: Paul Rouamba.
USA Ambassador: W. E. Shaufele, Jr.

MAURITANIA
République Islamique de Mauritanie

AREA AND POPULATION. The Republic consists of the 12 districts of Assaba, Brakna, Gorgol, Guidimaka, Adrar, Western and Eastern Hodh, Inchiri, Lévrier Bay, Traza, Tiris–Zemmour and Tagant, with a total area of 1,030,700 sq. km. In 1969 the 12 districts will be divided into 7 administrative areas.

The population is estimated (1969) at 1·1m. Kaédi (10,000 inhabitants), Atar (4,200), Rosso (8,000) and Nonadibou (11,000) are the principal towns. Nouak-chott (20,000) is the capital.

CONSTITUTION AND GOVERNMENT. The Islamic Republic of Mauritania became independent on 28 Nov. 1960, after having been a French protectorate (1903) and colony (1920).

The Republic is administered by a government council of 12 ministers. The national assembly consists of 34 members, elected by universal suffrage.

President of the Republic, Prime Minister: Moktar ould Daddah.
Foreign Affairs: Hamdi ould Mouknass.

EDUCATION. There were, in 1968–69, 26,222 pupils in primary schools and 2,668 in secondary schools. There are 77 medical centres and 25 doctors.

FINANCE. The ordinary budget for 1969 balanced at 6,649m. francs CFA, the capital budget at 435m.; the ordinary budget for 1968 at 6,011m. and the capital budget at 286m.

DEFENCE. The army consists of 1 infantry battalion, 1 paracommando company and 3 motorized reconnaissance squadrons; total strength, 1,400.

The air force has 3 C-47 transports and 4 Broussard, 1 Cessna and 1 Aermacchi light aircraft. Personnel, 100.

AGRICULTURE. Chief products are cattle, gum, salt, niébé (a kind of haricot), béref (*citrullus vulgaris*), and dried and salted fish.

In 1968 there were 700,000 camels, 2·1m. cattle, 317,000 asses and horses, 7m. sheep and goats. Production (1967) of millet, 90,000 tons; dates, 13,000 tons; maize, 5,700 tons; rice, 400 tons. The 1968 harvest was exceptionally poor because of drought conditions. Rubber production (1967–68) 4,961 metric tons.

FISHERIES. Export of fish in 1967 (metric tons): Salted and dried, 5,093; fresh, 1,000; frozen, 5,826; lobster, 82.

MINING. Huge deposits of iron ore (Fort Gouraud) and copper (Akjoujt) are being exploited. Iron ore exports in 1968, 7·7m. tons.

TRADE. There is a chamber of commerce for Western Mauritania in Atar. In 1967 imports totalled 12,330m. francs CFA and exports 19,180m.

Total trade between Mauritania and UK (British Board of Trade returns, in £1,000 sterling):

	1966	1967	1968	1969	1970
Imports to UK	6,545	6,939	8,881	9,338	8,586
Exports from UK	67	267	543	1,720 ⎱	1,234
Re-exports from UK	1	3	5	138 ⎰	

There were, in 1968, 33 post offices and 1,318 telephones.

French Ambassador: Adrien Dafour.
British Ambassador: J. G. Tahourdin, CMG (resides in Dakar).

NIGER
République du Niger

AREA AND POPULATION. Area, 1,187,000 sq. km. The territory is divided into 7 *départements* with 33 *arrondissements*. Population (1968), 3·64m. Niamey is the capital (70,000 inhabitants). The population is composed chiefly of Hausa (1m.), Jerma and Sanghai (450,000) Peulh (300,000) and Tuareg (300,000). Precipitation determines the geographical division into a southern zone of agriculture, a central zone of pasturage and a desert-like northern zone. The country lacks water, with the exception of the western districts, which are watered by the Niger and its tributaries, and the southern zone, where there are a number of wells.

CONSTITUTION AND GOVERNMENT. The Republic of the Niger became independent on 3 Aug. 1960, after having been a territory of French West Africa from 1904 and was admitted to the UN on 20 Sept. 1960.

The Republic is administered by a government of 13 ministers. The national assembly consists of 60 members elected by universal suffrage.

President of the Republic: Diori Hamani.
Foreign Affairs: El Hadj. B. Courmo.

EDUCATION. There were, in 1968, 77,261 pupils in primary schools, 3,900 in secondary schools and 900 in a technical school.

FINANCE. The ordinary budget for 1969–70 balanced at 10,799m. francs CFA.

DEFENCE. The army consists of 4 infantry companies and an armoured-car squadron; total strength, 2,000.

The air force has 100 officers and men, 4 ex-*Luftwaffe* Noratlas transports, 1 C-47 transport and 3 Broussard light communications aircraft.

PLANNING. In Sept. 1965 the National Assembly approved an economic development plan, covering the period 1965–68. This plan followed a 3-year preparatory plan and was part of a 10-year economic programme (1965–74).

Compared with an initial estimate of 23,000m. francs CFA for the preparatory plan, investments under the 1965–68 plan totalled 43,000m. francs CFA. Some 4,000m. francs CFA was used for the development of water resources and 5,000m. francs CFA for the general improvement of agricultural production.

AGRICULTURE. The chief agricultural produce are millet, groundnuts (182,700 metric tons, 1967–68), beans and manioc and, in the river districts, cotton and rice. Gum arabic at Gouré, nearly all of which are exported to Nigeria. In 1963 there were 86,000 horses, 3·5m. cattle, 8m. sheep and goats, 300,000 asses, 350,000 camels.

MINING. Large uranium deposits have been discovered about 200 miles north of Agades. These deposits contain high-grade ore. Mining will be open-cast. A mining company is being formed with the Government of Niger and the French Atomic Energy Commission as shareholders. The construction of a uranium-ore concentrate plant was begun in 1968, with production starting in 1970. Salt and natron are produced at Manga and Agadez, tin ore in Aïr.

TRADE. Imports in 1967 were valued at 11,352m. francs CFA and exports at 6,301m. francs CFA.

Trade with the UK (British Board of Trade returns, in £1,000 sterling):

	1966	1967	1968	1969	1970
Imports to UK	1	12	6	19	107
Exports from UK	200	105	146	203 }	350
Re-exports from UK	—	1	1	1 }	

COMMUNICATIONS. Niamey and Zinder (13,300 inhabitants in 1955) are the termini of two trans-Sahara motor routes; the Hoggar–Aïr–Zinder road extends to Kano and Fort Lamy. The Republic is also a favourite resort of hunters of big game (lions, elephants, buffaloes, moufflons, oryx and addax).

There were, in 1966, 35 post offices and (1969) 3,073 telephones.

At Niamey airport 30,518 passengers and 2,870 metric tons of freight and mail were dealt with in 1967.

BANKING. In 1960 the savings banks had 4,717 depositors with 47,828,000 francs CFA to their credit.

French Ambassador: Michel Winterbert.
Ambassador to UK: Aboubacar Sidibé.
British Ambassador: P. Murray, CMG. *First Secretary:* P. H. C. Eyers, MVO (both resident at Abidjan).
Ambassador to USA: Georges M. Condat.
USA Ambassador: Roswell D. McClelland.

Boffardi, P., *La République du Niger*, Paris, 1960
Séré de Rivières, E., *Histoire du Niger*, Paris, 1965

CAMEROUN
République Fédérale du Cameroun

HISTORY. The former German colony of Kamerun was occupied by French and British troops in 1916. The greater portion of the territory (432,000 sq. km) was in 1919 placed under French administration, excluding the territory ceded to Germany in 1911, which reverted to French Equatorial Africa. The portion under French trusteeship was granted full internal autonomy on 1 Jan. 1959 and complete independence was proclaimed on 1 Jan. 1960.

The portion assigned to Great Britain (89,270 sq. km) consisted of 2 parts. A plebiscite held in Feb. 1961 in the northern part decided in favour of joining the Federation of Nigeria (145,265 votes) against joining the Cameroun Republic (97,654 votes). The Southern Cameroons held a plebiscite in Feb. 1961 and decided by 135,830 votes against some 30,000 to join the Cameroun Republic.

On 1 Oct. 1961 the former British trusteeship territory of Southern Cameroons and the Cameroun Republic combined in the Federal Republic of Cameroun.

AREA AND POPULATION. The total area of the Federal Republic is about 474,000 sq. km (East: 431,200; West: 42,900); its population is about 5·7m. Chief towns in the East: Yaoundé (population, 130,000); Douala (210,000), Nkongsamba (50,000), Edéa (15,000), Maroua (32,000), Ebolowa

(17,000), Garoua (20,000); in the West: Tiko (26,000), Kumba (50,000), Bamenda (40,000), Victoria (20,000), Buea, 1966 (9,000).

CONSTITUTION AND GOVERNMENT. The federal constitution provides for a President as chief of state and commander of the armed forces, who is elected for a 5-year term; a Vice-President; and a cabinet whose members must not be members of parliament.

The National Federal Assembly, elected by universal adult suffrage, consists of 40 representatives for East Cameroun and 10 for West Cameroun. The first federal elections took place on 26 April 1964.

The federal capital is Yaoundé.

National flag: Green, red, yellow, with 2 golden stars.

The two provinces of East Cameroun (formerly French), with Yaoundé as capital, and West Cameroun (formerly British), with Buea as capital, have their own assemblies (East: 100 members; West: 37 members) and cabinets; both premiers are appointed by the Federal President.

Federal President: Ahmadou Ahidjo.
Federal Vice-President: John Ngu Foncha.
Minister for Foreign Affairs: Simon Nko'o Etoungou.
Prime Minister of West Cameroun: S. T. Muna.
Prime Minister of East Cameroun: Simon-Pierre Tchoungui.

EDUCATION (1963). The Federation had 1,179 public primary schools with 3,507 teachers and 188,224 pupils (of whom 65,694 girls); 1,828 private primary schools with 5,781 teachers and 301,584 pupils (of whom 115,978 girls); 5,975 pupils in public secondary schools and 12,412 pupils in private secondary schools. The Federal University at Yaoundé, which opened in Nov. 1962, has 1,450 students in 3 faculties (Law and Economics, Humanities, Science).

FINANCE. Currency. The unit of currency is the franc CFA; the Nigerian £ ceased to be legal tender in West Cameroun on 31 May 1962.

Budget. The federal budget for 1969–70 balanced at 31,500m. francs CFA.

DEFENCE. The army consists of 4 infantry battalions and support units; total strength, 4,000.

The air force has 1 C-47 transport and 2 light aircraft. Personnel, about 300.

PRODUCTION. The Federation produced in 1965 (in 1,000 metric tons): Aluminium, 51 (1964: 52); gold, 1,454 (1964: 729) troy oz; cocoa (1968–69), 100; coffee (1968), 75; timber, 235; bananas (1967), 11·9; cotton, 45.

Livestock in the Federation (1962): 1·8m. cattle, 1m. sheep, 200,000 pigs.

TRADE. Imports and exports in 1,000 francs CFA were as follows:

	1964	1965	1966
Imports	28,593	32,997	32,308
Exports	30,037	29,276	32,417

In 1966, 53% of the imports came from France, 5% from US and 38% of exports went to France and 14% to US.

Trade with UK (British Board of Trade returns, in £1,000 sterling):

	1966	1967	1968	1969	1970
Imports to UK	2,620	1,477	2,447	2,247	2,081
Exports from UK	2,222	2,000	3,192	3,696 }	3,728
Re-exports from UK	148	167	361	295 }	

COMMUNICATIONS. Cameroun Railways (839 km) link Douala with Nkongsamba and Belabo, with branches M'Banga–Kumba and Makak–M'Balmayo. The extension northwards from Belabo to Ngaounderé is under construction. 3,381 vessels landed 559,000 tons and cleared 590,000 tons at Douala in 1967. In 1959: Victoria, entered 278 vessels of 581,727 tons; cleared 283 vessels of 577,590 tons; Tiko, entered 489 vessels of 590,907 tons; cleared 484 vessels of 579,336 tons.

There were (1957) 86 post offices and 6 postal agencies; telephone lines, 2,677 km; telephones (1969), 5,000; radio stations, 36.

In 1967, 35,505 passengers arrived at Yaoundé airport and 34,808 departed; 1,908 metric tons of freight were handled. At Douala airport, in 1967, 76,735 passengers arrived and 75,797 departed and 13,197 metric tons of freight was handled.

BANKING. At 31 Dec. 1960 savings banks had 22,248 depositors with 335m. francs CFA to their credit.

In Oct. 1967 Barclays Bank DCO in West Cameroun merged with the Banque Internationale pour le Commerce et l'Industrie du Cameroun.

French Ambassador: Jean-René Bénard.
Ambassador to UK: Lucas Zaa Nkweta.
British Ambassador and Consul-General: A. A. Golds, MVO. *First Secretary:* P. J. Barlow.
Ambassador to USA: Michel Koss Epangue.
USA Ambassador: Lewis Hoffacker.

BOOKS OF REFERENCE

STATISTICAL INFORMATION. The service de la Statistique Générale, at Douala, set up in 1945, publishes a monthly bulletin (from Nov. 1950)

Ardener, E. (and others), *Plantation and Village in the Cameroons: economic and social studies* OUP, 1960
Le Vine, V. T., *The Cameroons from Mandate to Independence.* California Univ. Press and CUP, 1965

MALI
République du Mal

AREA AND POPULATION. The frontiers of the former territory were readjusted in 1904, 1933, 1948 and 1954 (*see* THE STATESMAN'S YEAR-BOOK, 1959, p. 1011). The Republic now covers an area of 1,204,021 sq. km. with an estimated population of 4·7m. on 1 Jan. 1967. The most densely populated and richest of the 19 districts are those of San, Mopti, Sikasso, Koutiala, Bamako and Ségou. Bamako, the capital (population, 170,000), Mopti (32,400), Kayes (28,500), Ségou (28,100), Sikasso (21,800), Gao (15,400), San (14,900) and Tombouctou (9,000) are important towns.

CONSTITUTION AND GOVERNMENT. The Republic of Mali became independent on 22 Sept. 1960, after having been the territory of French Sudan and, from Jan. 1959 to 22 Sept. 1960, a partner (together with Senegal) of the Federation of Mali. The Republic was admitted to the UN on 29 Sept. 1960.

A National Liberation Committee assumed all political and administrative functions on 21 Nov. 1968.

Prime Minister: Moussa Traore. *Foreign Affairs:* Jean-Marie Koné.

EDUCATION. There were in 1966–67, 175,538 pupils in primary schools, 2,740 in secondary schools and 3,026 in technical schools.

FINANCE. Currency. On 5 May 1967 the Mali franc was devalued from MF 246·853 to MF 493·706 per US$. In Feb. 1967 Mali signed a monetary agreement with France whereby Mali re-entered the French franc zone which it had abandoned in 1962, and in March 1968 the Mali franc became convertible at the rate of MF 100 to 1 French franc.

Budget. The ordinary budget for 1967–68 provided for revenue of 21,200m. Mali francs and envisaged expenditure of 24,700m. Mali francs.

DEFENCE. The army consists of 3 infantry battalions; strength, 3,500.

The air force has received 5 MiG-15 jet fighters, 1 MiG-15 UTI trainer and 2 An-2 transports from USSR, Yak-12M liaison aircraft from Poland and 2 C-47 transports from USA.

PLANNING. A 4-year development plan (1961–65) envisages investments totalling 64,000m. francs CFA. Agriculture is being organized on collective lines as in Israel; its products are to be handled by state buying organizations. Public utilities industry and mining are to become state monopolies.

AGRICULTURE. Production of cotton increased from 5,900 tons (1959) to 34,390 tons (1966) with an area under cultivation of 68,000 hectares in 1964–65.

Production in 1965 included (in 1,000 metric tons) millet and sorghum (651), rice (130), maize (109), groundnuts (147). In 1965 there were 4·3m. head of cattle, 80,000 horses, 250,000 asses, 2·4m. sheep and goats and 100,000 camels.

Important irrigation schemes have been carried out in the Ségou and Mopti districts on the Niger River, of which the Sansanding Barrage is the centre; 50,000 hectares of cotton and rice lands are being irrigated.

TRADE. Imports in 1967 totalled 10,988m. Mali francs, exports, 4,074m. Chief imports are foodstuffs, automobiles, petrol, building material, sugar, salt, beer. Chief exports are groundnuts, karité, gum, dried fish and skins.

Trade with UK (British Board of Trade returns, in £1,000 sterling):

	1966	1967	1968	1969	1970
Imports to UK	85	—	26	231	318
Exports from UK	338	294	75	65 }	284
Re-exports from UK	—	—	3	0 }	

COMMUNICATIONS. Mali has a railway from Kayes to Koulikoro by way of Bamako, continuing the Dakar–Kayes line in the Senegal. An agreement was signed in May 1968 between Mali, Guinea and China to extend the railway from Kourrousa–Kankan in Guinea to Bamako. For about 7 months in the year small steamboats perform the service from Koulikoro to Tombouctou and Gao, and from Bamako to Kourroussa.

There are 12,080 km of roads, of which 7,500 km are usable in all seasons; they include 669 km of the metalled road Dakar–Niger (1,250 km). The navigable length of the Niger in Mali is 1,782 km and in 1966 carried 499,000 passengers and 254,030 metric tons of goods.

Air services connect the Republic with Paris, Dakar and Abidjan. The chief airport is at Bamako. In 1967 aircraft disembarked and embarked 48,282 passengers and 1,613 metric tons of freight and mail.

There were, in 1966, 116 post offices and (1969) 7,800 telephones.

Wireless telegraph connects Bamako with Paris.

BANKING. On 31 Dec. 1960 the savings banks had 13,972 depositors with 167m. francs CFA to their credit.

There are chambers of commerce in Bamako and Kayes.

French Ambassador: P. Pelen.
Ambassador to UK: Mady Diallo.
British Ambassador: J. G. Tahourdin, CMG.
Ambassador to USA: Seydon Traoré.
USA Ambassador: Robert O. Blake.

TOGO

République Togolaise

AREA AND POPULATION. Area, about 56,000 sq. km. The population of Togo in 1970 was 1,955,916. The capital is Lomé (population, 135,000, including 700 Europeans). Lomé, Anécho, Palimé, Bassari, Atakpamé, Sokodé and Tsévié are *communes de plein exercise.*

The southern part of Togo is peopled by tribes using several different languages, of which the principal are Ewe and Mina; these may be regarded as an offshoot of the Bantu peoples. The northern half contains, ethnologically, a totally different population descended largely from Hamitic tribes and speaking a fairly large number of different languages, of which Dagomba, Tim and Cabrais are the most important.

CONSTITUTION AND GOVERNMENT. The Republic of Togo became independent on 27 April 1960, after having been a German protectorate (1894–1914, subsequently divided between the French and the British), a mandate of the League of Nations (20 July 1922) and a trusteeship territory of the United Nations (14 Dec. 1946).

On 28 Oct. 1956 a plebiscite was held to determine the status of the territory. Out of 438,175 registered voters, 313,458 voted for an autonomous republic within the French Union and the end of the trusteeship system.

On 14 Nov. 1958 the general assembly of the United Nations accepted unanimously the French–Togolese proposal that the trusteeship should be abolished on the achievement of independence on 27 April 1960.

On 13 Jan. 1963 the President Sylvanus Olympio was murdered by n.c.o.s of the army. Nicolas Grunitzky, a former prime minister and Olympio's brother-in-law, was appointed President of the Republic and head of government. On 13 Jan. 1967 in a bloodless *coup* the army under Col. Etienne Eyadéma made President Grunitzky 'voluntarily withdraw'. On 14 April 1967 Col. Eyadéma assumed the offices of President and Defence Minister in a government of 4 officers and 8 civilians.

Administratively, Togo is divided into 19 districts: Lomé, Tsévié, Anécho, Atakpamé, Sokodé, Lama-Kara, Bassari, Mango, Dapango, Tabligbo, Akposso, Klouto, Nuatja, Bafilo, Niamtougou, Pagouda, Kandé, Sotouboua, Vogan.

RELIGION. In 1967 there were 449,890 Christians, of which 350,000 were Catholics and 99,890 Protestants. There were 134,760 Mohammedans.

EDUCATION. In 1968–69 there were 157,548 pupils in primary schools 13,126 pupils in secondary and technical schools.

FINANCE. The ordinary budget for 1971 balanced at 10,000m. francs CFA.

DEFENCE. The army consists of 1 infantry battalion of 1,000 men.

An air force, established with French assistance, has 1 C-47 transport, 2 Broussard light communications aircraft and 2 Alouette helicopters.

PLANNING. A first 5-year development plan (1966–70) was adopted by the National Assembly on 18 July 1965. The plan aims at an annual increase of 5·3% in the gross national product.

AGRICULTURE. Inland the country is hilly, rising to 3,600 ft, with streams and waterfalls. There are long stretches of forest and brushwood, while dry plains alternate with arable land. Maize, yams, cassava, plantains, groundnuts, etc., are cultivated; oil palms and dye-woods grow in the forests; but the main commerce is based on coffee, cocoa, palm-oil, palm-kernels, copra, ground-nuts, cotton, manioc. There are considerable plantations of oil and cocoa palms, coffee, cacao, kola, cassava and cotton.

Livestock (1967): Cattle, 170,000; sheep, 600,000; swine, 200,000; horses, 800; asses, 850; goats, 500,000.

MINING. A Mines Department was set up in 1953 after the discovery of very rich deposits of phosphate and bauxite; mining began in 1961. Output of phosphate rock (1,000 long tons): 1964, 801·4; 1965, 982; 1966, 1,111; 1968, 1,357. Other mineral deposits are limestone, estimated at 28m. tons; iron ore, estimated at 550m. tons with iron content varying between 40% and 55%, and 3 magnesian limestone deposits, estimated at about 170m. tons.

TRADE.

	1967		1968		1969	
	Metric tons	1m. francs	Metric tons	1m. francs	Metric tons	1m. francs
Imports	201,682	11,133	218,783	11,623	..	14,600
Exports	1,076,293	7,894	1,321,524	9,549	..	11,500

Exports in 1968 were (in metric tons): Cocoa, 14,340; cotton, 2,972; coffee, 10,221; palm-kernels, 12,876; palm-oil, 4·8; groundnuts (husked), 5,726; manioc flour, 47·3; manioc starch, 4,980; copra, 451; phosphate, 1,258,563. In 1967 phosphates constituted 94% of the total tonnage and 39% of the total value of exports; coffee and cocoa, 40% of the total value (75% in 1959).

Trade with UK (British Board of Trade returns, in £1,000 sterling):

	1966	1967	1968	1969	1970
Imports to UK	295	300	916	553	463
Exports from UK	904	1,155	1,544	3,149 }	3,395
Re-exports from UK	12	12	14	25 }	

COMMUNICATIONS. There were, in 1965, 4,644 km of roads, of which 155 km were paved. There are 3 railways connecting Lomé with Anécho, Palimé and Blitta; total, 443 km. There were (1967) 22 post offices and 12 postal agencies and (1969) 2,900 telephones. Togo is connected by telegraph and telephones with Ghana, Dahomey, Abidjan and Dakar, and by wireless telegraphy with Europe and America.

In 1967, 447 vessels landed 125,012 metric tons and cleared 53,802 metric tons at Lomé.

Air services connect Lomé with Paris, Dakar, Abijan, Douala, Accra, Lagos, Cotonou and Niamey. In 1967 aircraft disembarked 14,818 passengers, 500 metric tons of freight and 98 metric tons of mail.

BANKING. In Dec. 1966 the Crédit du Togo was reorganized as a national development bank, named Banque Nationale Togolaise, with a capital of 300m. francs CFA of which the government's share is 60%.

A savings bank was opened on 1 April 1953; at 31 Dec. 1965 it had deposits of 203·5m. francs CFA.

French Ambassador: Henri Langlais.
Ambassador to UK: (Vacant).
British Ambassador and Consul-General: F. Smitherman, MBE. *First Secretary:* D. W. R. Lewis (resides at Accra).
Ambassador to USA: Alexandre J. Ohin.
USA Ambassador: Dwight Dickinson.

Cornevin, R., *Histoire du Togo.* Paris, 1959

GERMANY

POST-WAR HISTORY. Since the unconditional surrender of the German armed forces on 8 May 1945 there has been no central authority whose writ runs in the whole of Germany. Consequently no peace treaty has been signed with a government representing the whole of Germany, and the country is virtually partitioned between West Germany (Federal Republic of Germany) and East Germany (German Democratic Republic).

By the Berlin Declaration of 5 June 1945 the governments of the USA, the UK, the USSR and France assumed supreme authority over Germany. Each of the 4 signatories was given a zone of occupation, in which the supreme power was to be exercised by the C.-in-C. in that zone (*see* map in THE STATESMAN'S YEAR-BOOK, 1947). Jointly these 4 Cs.-in-C. constituted the Allied Control Council in Berlin, which was to be competent in all 'matters affecting Germany as a whole'. The territory of Greater Berlin, divided into 4 sectors, was to be governed as an entity by the 4 occupying powers. The Allied Control Council, however, soon ceased to co-operate effectively and in March 1948 altogether ceased to function.

At the Potsdam Conference (17 July–2 Aug. 1945) the northern part of the Province of East Prussia, including its capital Königsberg (renamed Kaliningrad), was transferred to the Soviet Union, pending final ratification by a peace treaty; and it was agreed that, pending the final peace settlement, Poland should administer those parts of Germany lying east of a line running from the Baltic Sea immediately west of Swinemünde along the river Oder to its confluence with the Western Neisse and thence along the Western Neisse to the Czechoslovak frontier.

The agreements between the war-time allies concerning the occupation zones (12 Sept. 1944) and control of Germany (1 May 1945) were repudiated by the USSR on 27 Nov. 1958.

FEDERAL REPUBLIC OF GERMANY
Bundesrepublik Deutschland

The Federal Republic of Germany became a sovereign independent country on 5 May 1955. A member of EEC, the Council of Europe, Western European Union, NATO, the European Coal and Steel Community, Euratom, the European Monetary Agreement and the Agencies of the UN, the Federal Republic claims to speak and act on behalf of the whole German people.

In June 1948 the US, the UK and France agreed on a central government for the 3 western zones. An Occupation Statute, which came into force on 31 Sept. 1949, reduced the responsibilities of the occupation authorities. Formally, the Federal Republic of Germany came into existence on 21 Sept. 1949. The Petersberg Agreement of 22 Nov. 1949 freed the Federal Republic of numerous restrictions of the Occupation Statute. In 1951 the USA, the UK and France as well as other states terminated the state of war with Germany; the Soviet Union followed on 25 Jan. 1955. On 5 May 1955 the High Commissioners of the USA, the UK and France signed a proclamation revoking the Occupation Statute. On the same day, the Paris and London treaties, signed in Oct. 1954, came into force and established the sovereignty of the Federal Republic of Germany.

CONSTITUTION. The Constituent Assembly (known as the 'Parliamentary Council') met in Bonn on 1 Sept. 1948, and worked out a Basic Law which was approved by a two-thirds majority of the parliaments of the participating Länder and came into force on 23 May 1949.

The **Basic Law** (*Grundgesetz*) consists of a preamble and 146 articles. The first section deals with the basic rights which are legally binding for legislation, administration and jurisdiction.

The Federal Republic of Germany is a democratic and social federal state. The federal flag is black, red and golden. For the time being the Basic Law applies to the Länder Baden–Württemberg, Bavaria, Bremen, Greater Berlin (temporarily suspended), Hamburg, Hesse, Lower Saxony, North Rhine–Westphalia, Rhineland–Palatinate, Saarland and Schleswig–Holstein. The Basic Law decrees that the general rules of international law form part of the federal law. The constitutions of the Länder must conform to the principles of a republican, democratic and social state based on the rule of law. Executive power is vested in the Länder, unless the Basic Law prescribes or permits otherwise. Federal law supersedes Land law.

The organs of the Federal Republic are:

The Federal Diet (*Bundestag*), elected in universal, direct, free, equal and secret elections, for a term of 4 years.

The Federal Council (*Bundesrat*), consisting of members of the governments of the Länder. Each Land has at least 3 votes. Länder with more than 2m. inhabitants have 4, Länder with more than 6m. inhabitants have 5 votes.

The Federal President (*Bundespräsident*) is elected by the Federal Assembly for a term of 5 years and represents the Federal Republic in international relations. Re-election is admissible only once. The Federal Assembly (which meets only for the election of the Federal President) consists of the members of the Federal Diet and an equal number of members elected by the popular representative bodies of the Länder according to a particular system of semi-proportional representation.

The Federal Government consists of the Federal Chancellor, elected by the Federal Diet on the proposal of the Federal President, and the Federal Ministers, who are appointed and dismissed by the Federal President upon the proposal of the Federal Chancellor.

The Federal Republic has exclusive legislation on: (1) foreign affairs; (2) federal citizenship; (3) freedom of movement, passports, immigration and emigration, and extradition; (4) currency, money and coinage, weights and measures, and regulation of time and calendar; (5) customs, commercial and navigation agreements, traffic in goods and payments with foreign countries, including customs and frontier protection; (6) federal railways and air traffic; (7) post and telecommunications; (8) the legal status of persons in the employment of the Federation and of public law corporations under direct supervision of the Federal Government; (9) trade marks, copyright and publishing rights; (10) co-operation of the Federal Republic and the Länder in the criminal police and in matters concerning the protection of the constitution, the establishment of a Federal Office of Criminal Police, as well as the combating of international crime; (11) federal statistics.

For concurrent legislation in which the Länder have legislative rights if and as far as the Federal Republic does not exercise its legislative powers, *see* THE STATESMAN'S YEAR-BOOK, 1956, p. 1038.

Federal laws are passed by the Federal Diet and after their adoption submitted to the Federal Council, which has a limited veto. The Basic Law may be amended only upon the approval of two-thirds of the members of the Federal Diet and two-thirds of the votes of the Federal Council.

The foreign service, federal finance, railways, postal services, waterways and shipping are under direct federal administration.

In the field of finance the Federal Republic has exclusive legislation on customs and financial monopolies and concurrent legislation on: (1) excise taxes and taxes on transactions, in particular, taxes on real-estate acquisition, incremented value and on fire protection; (2) taxes on income, property, inheritance and donations; (3) real estate, industrial and trade taxes, with the exception of the determining of the tax rates.

Customs, the yield of monopolies, excise taxes with the exception of the beer tax, the transportation tax, the turnover tax and property dues serving non-

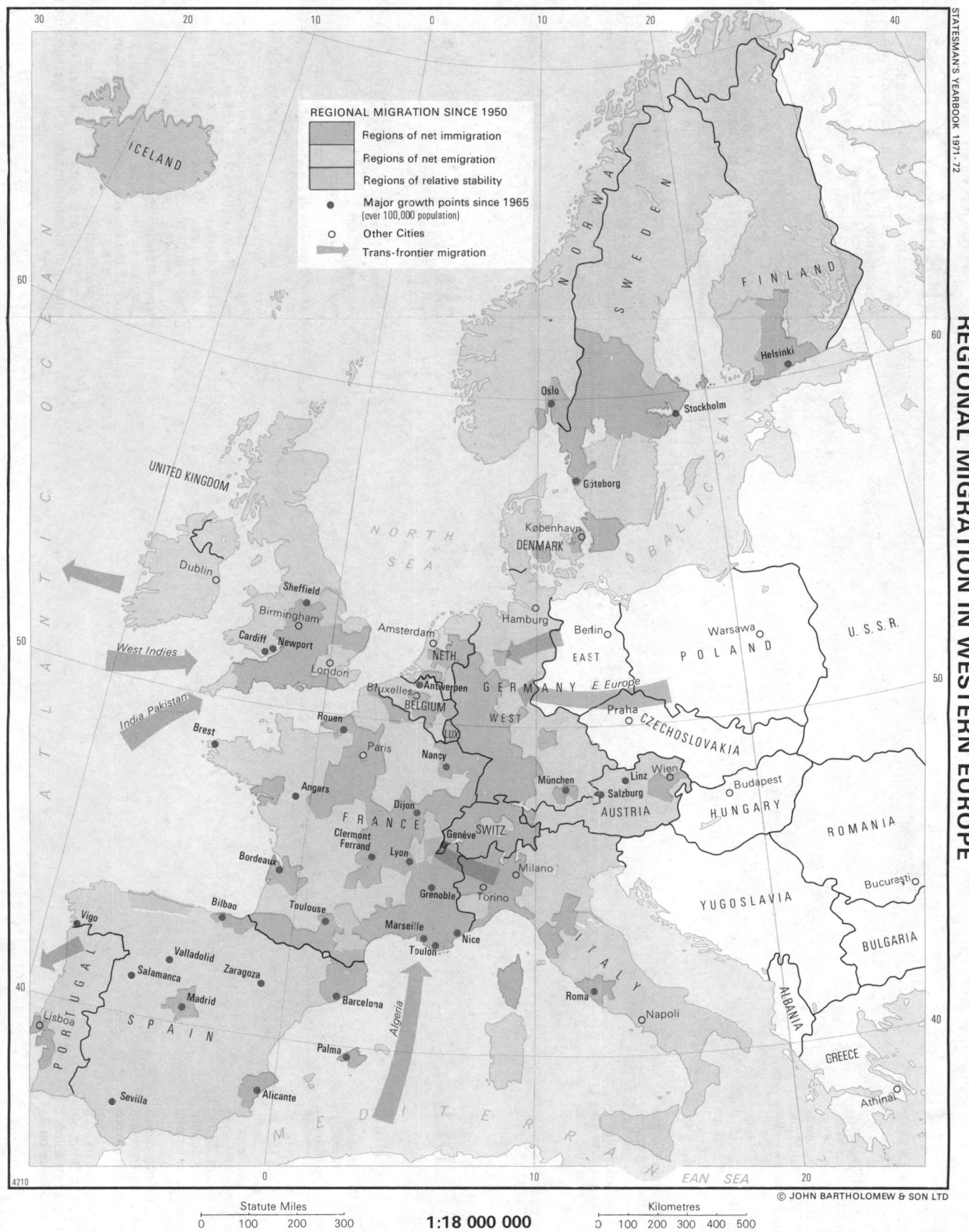

REGIONAL MIGRATION SINCE 1950

Regions of net immigration

Regions of net emigration

Regions of relative stability

● Major growth points since 1965
(over 100,000 population)

○ Other Cities

➡ Trans-frontier migration

REGIONAL MIGRATION IN WESTERN EUROPE

ICELAND

NORWAY

SWEDEN

FINLAND

Helsinki

Oslo

Stockholm

Göteborg

København

DENMARK

UNITED KINGDOM

Dublin

Sheffield

Birmingham

Cardiff   Newport

London

West Indies

India Pakistan

Brest

NORTH SEA

Amsterdam

Hamburg

NETH.

Bruxelles   Antwerpen

BELGIUM

LUX.

Rouen

Paris

Nancy

Berlin

EAST

GERMANY   E Europe

WEST

Praha

CZECHOSLOVAKIA

POLAND

Warsawa

U.S.S.R.

Angers

FRANCE

Dijon

Clermont
Ferrand   Lyon

Bordeaux

Toulouse

Grenoble

Genève   SWITZ.

München

Linz   Wien

Salzburg

AUSTRIA

Budapest

HUNGARY

ROMANIA

Bilbao

Vigo

Valladolid   Zaragoza

Salamanca

PORTUGAL

Madrid

SPAIN

Lisboa

Sevilla

Marseille   Nice

Toulon

Barcelona

Palma

Alicante

Algeria

Milano

Torino

ITALY

Roma

Napoli

YUGOSLAVIA

BULGARIA

ALBANIA

GREECE

Bucureşti

Athinai

MEDITERRANEAN SEA

BALTIC SEA

ATLANTIC OCEAN

Statute Miles
0   100   200   300

1:18 000 000

Kilometres
0   100   200   300   400   500

© JOHN BARTHOLOMEW & SON LTD

4210

GERMANY

POST-WAR HISTORY. Since the unconditional surrender of the German armed forces on 8 May 1945 there has been no central authority whose writ runs in the whole of Germany. Consequently no peace treaty has been signed with a government representing the whole of Germany, and the country is virtually partitioned between West Germany (Federal Republic of Germany) and East Germany (German Democratic Republic).

By the Berlin Declaration of 5 June 1945 the governments of the USA, the UK, the USSR and France assumed supreme authority over Germany. Each of the 4 signatories was given a zone of occupation, in which the supreme power was to be exercised by the C.-in-C. in that zone (*see* map in THE STATESMAN'S YEAR-BOOK, 1947). Jointly these 4 Cs.-in-C. constituted the Allied Control Council in Berlin, which was to be competent in all 'matters affecting Germany as a whole'. The territory of Greater Berlin, divided into 4 sectors, was to be governed as an entity by the 4 occupying powers. The Allied Control Council, however, soon ceased to co-operate effectively and in March 1948 altogether ceased to function.

At the Potsdam Conference (17 July–2 Aug. 1945) the northern part of the Province of East Prussia, including its capital Königsberg (renamed Kaliningrad), was transferred to the Soviet Union, pending final ratification by a peace treaty; and it was agreed that, pending the final peace settlement, Poland should administer those parts of Germany lying east of a line running from the Baltic Sea immediately west of Swinemünde along the river Oder to its confluence with the Western Neisse and thence along the Western Neisse to the Czechoslovak frontier.

The agreements between the war-time allies concerning the occupation zones (12 Sept. 1944) and control of Germany (1 May 1945) were repudiated by the USSR on 27 Nov. 1958.

FEDERAL REPUBLIC OF GERMANY
Bundesrepublik Deutschland

The Federal Republic of Germany became a sovereign independent country on 5 May 1955. A member of EEC, the Council of Europe, Western European Union, NATO, the European Coal and Steel Community, Euratom, the European Monetary Agreement and the Agencies of the UN, the Federal Republic claims to speak and act on behalf of the whole German people.

In June 1948 the US, the UK and France agreed on a central government for the 3 western zones. An Occupation Statute, which came into force on 31 Sept. 1949, reduced the responsibilities of the occupation authorities. Formally, the Federal Republic of Germany came into existence on 21 Sept. 1949. The Petersberg Agreement of 22 Nov. 1949 freed the Federal Republic of numerous restrictions of the Occupation Statute. In 1951 the USA, the UK and France as well as other states terminated the state of war with Germany; the Soviet Union followed on 25 Jan. 1955. On 5 May 1955 the High Commissioners of the USA, the UK and France signed a proclamation revoking the Occupation Statute. On the same day, the Paris and London treaties, signed in Oct. 1954, came into force and established the sovereignty of the Federal Republic of Germany.

CONSTITUTION. The Constituent Assembly (known as the 'Parliamentary Council') met in Bonn on 1 Sept. 1948, and worked out a Basic Law which was approved by a two-thirds majority of the parliaments of the participating Länder and came into force on 23 May 1949.

recurrent purposes accrue to the Federal Republic. The Federal Republic can, by federal law, claim part of the income and corporation taxes to cover its expenditures not covered by other revenues. Financial jurisdiction is uniformly regulated by federal legislation.

National flag: Black, red, golden (horizontal).
National anthem: Einigkeit und Recht und Freiheit (words by H. Hoffmann, 1841; tune by J. Haydn, 1797).

Hiscocks, R., *Democracy in Western Germany*. OUP, 1957
Mangoldt, H., *Das Bonner Grundgesetz (Kommentar)*. 2nd ed. Berlin, 1960
Maunz, Th., *Deutsches Staatsrecht*. 12th ed. Munich, 1963
Schäfer, H., *Der Bundesrat*. Cologne, 1955

GOVERNMENT. The *Federal Diet*, elected on 28 Sept. 1969, is composed of 496 members. In addition, there are 22 members for Berlin, who, however, have no vote.

State of the parties: Christian Democrats (CDU; CSU), 242 (1965: 245); Social Democrats (SPD), 224 (202); Free Democrats (FDP), 30 (49); other parties failed to obtain 5% of the votes or to elect a representative in a constituency, and therefore returned no members.

Bonn on the Rhine is the capital of the Federal Republic.

Federal President: Dr Gustav Heinemann (elected 5 March 1969, by 512 out of 1,036 votes).

The cabinet, a coalition of Social Democrats and Free Democrats, was formed on 21 Oct. 1969 as follows:

Chancellor: Willy Brandt (SPD).
Vice-Chancellor, Minister of Foreign Affairs: Walter Scheel (FDP).
Minister without Portfolio in the Chancellory: Prof. Horst Ehmke (SPD).
Interior: Hans-Dietrich Genscher (FDP).
Justice: Gerhard Jahn (SPD).
Finance: Alex Möller (SPD).
Economics: Prof. Karl Schiller (SPD).
Food, Agriculture and Forests: Josef Ertl (FDP).
Labour and Social Welfare: Walter Arendt (SPD).
Defence: Helmut Schmidt (SPD).
Transport, Posts and Telecommunications: Georg Leber (SPD).
Housing: Dr Lauritz Lauritzen (SPD).
Internal German Relations: Egon Franke (SPD).
Economic Co-operation: Dr Erhard Eppler (SPD).
Health: Frau Käte Strobel (SPD).
Education and Science: Hans Leussink (Ind.).

AREA AND POPULATION. On 23 April 1949 some minor frontier rectifications were carried out in favour of the Netherlands (68 sq. km), Belgium (18 sq. km), Luxembourg (6 sq. km) and France (7 sq. km), subject to a final peace settlement. Belgium (1956) and the Netherlands (1963) returned most of this territory to Germany.

Area and estimated population as at 31 Dec. 1969:

Länder	Area in sq. km	Male	Female	Total	Per sq. km
Schleswig–Holstein	15,676	1,229,300	1,327,900	2,557,200	163
Hamburg	753	843,600	973,500	1,817,100	2,413
Lower Saxony	47,408	3,395,100	3,705,400	7,100,400	150
Bremen	404	360,400	395,600	756,000	1,872
North Rhine–Westphalia	34,039	8,218,000	8,911,800	17,129,800	503
Hessen	21,111	2,607,200	2,815,400	5,422,600	257
Rhineland–Palatinate	19,831	1,746,500	1,924,800	3,671,300	185
Baden–Württemberg	35,750	4,296,800	4,612,900	8,909,700	249
Bavaria	70,550	5,022,400	5,546,900	10,568,900	150
Saarland	2,568	534,500	592,900	1,127,400	439
Berlin (West)	480	926,300	1,207,900	2,134,300	4,446
Federal Republic	248,574[1]	29,180,000	32,014,600	61,194,600	246

[1] 95,975 sq. miles.

VITAL STATISTICS for calendar years:

	Marriages	Live births	Of these illegitimate	Deaths	Divorces
1967	483,101	1,019,459	46,964	687,349	62,835
1968	444,050	969,825	46,209	734,048	65,264
1969[1]	446,582	903,458	45,497	744,360	..

[1] Preliminary.

The annual rate of the population increase (including migration) was 0·8% in 1966; 0·3% in 1967; 0·9% in 1968; 1·2% in 1969.

Crude birth rate was 14·8 per 1,000 population; marriage rate, 7·3; death rate, 12·2; infantile mortality, 2·3 per 100 live births.

Migrants from Eastern Germany to the Federal Republic, including West Berlin, totalled about 2,022,000 between 1955 and 1961. The East German Government tried to stop the outflow by erecting a brick wall along the border in Berlin on 13 Aug. 1961; despite the Berlin wall, the figures registered for persons moving from Eastern Germany and East Berlin into the Federal Republic were 21,500 in 1962, 47,100 in 1963, 39,300 in 1964, 29,500 in 1965, 24,300 in 1966, 20,700 in 1967, 18,600 in 1968 and 20,600 in 1969; most of them are older people with permission to emigrate. Migrants from the Federal Republic to Eastern Germany totalled about 279,000 between 1955 and 1961, 9,000 in 1962, 5,000 in 1963, 5,000 in 1964, 5,600 in 1965, 4,300 in 1966, 3,600 in 1967 and 2,900 in 1968.

The resident population of the principal towns was estimated as follows on 31 Dec. 1969:

Town	Land	Population	Town	Land	Population
Berlin (West)	Berlin (West)	2,134,256	Aachen	N. Rhine–Westph.	177,642
Hamburg	Hamburg	1,817.073	Mainz	Rhinel.–Pal.	176,720
Munich	Bavaria	1,326,331	Solingen	N. Rhine–Westph.	175,895
Cologne	N. Rhine–Westph.	866,308	Ludwigshafen	Rhinel.–Pal.	174.698
Essen	N. Rhine–Westph.	696,905	Bielefeld	N. Rhine–Westph.	169,347
Düsseldorf	N. Rhine–Westph.	680,806	Freiburg i.		
Frankfurt a.M.	Hessen	660,410	Breisgau	Baden–Württ.	165,960
Dortmund	N. Rhine–Westph.	648,883	Mönchen-		
Stuttgart	Baden–Württ.	628,412	gladbach	N. Rhine–Westph.	152,172
Bremen	Bremen	607,184	Bremerhaven	Bremen	148,793
Hannover	Lower Saxony	517,783	Darmstadt	Hessen	141,075
Nürnberg	Bavaria	477,108	Osnabrück	Lower Saxony	141,000
Duisburg.	N. Rhine–Westph.	457,891	Remscheid	N. Rhine–Westph.	137,374
Wuppertal	N. Rhine–Westph.	413,996	Oldenburg	Lower Saxony	131,434
Gelsenkirchen	N. Rhine–Westph.	348,620	Saarbrücken	Saarland	130,765
Bochum	N. Rhine–Westph.	346,886	Regensburg	Bavaria	128,083
Mannheim	Baden–Württ.	330,920	Recklinghausen	N. Rhine–Westph.	125,535
Bonn	N. Rhine–Westph.	299,376	Heidelberg	Baden–Württ.	121,929
Kiel	Schleswig–H.	269,106	Würzburg	Bavaria	120,317
Wiesbaden	Hessen	260,614	Offenbach a.M.	Hessen	118,754
Karlsruhe	Baden–Württ.	257,144	Salzgitter	Lower Saxony	118,020
Oberhausen	N. Rhine–Westph.	249,045	Neuss	N. Rhinc–Westph.	117,599
Lübeck	Schleswig–H.	242,191	Göttingen	Lower Saxony	115,227
Krefeld	N. Rhine–Westph.	227,754	Leverkusen	N. Rhine–Westph.	111,588
Brunswick	Lower Saxony	225,168	Bottrop	N. Rhine–Westph.	108,161
Augsburg	Bavaria	214,376	Koblenz	Rhinel.–Pal.	106,189
Kassel	Hessen	213,494	Trier	Rhinel.–Pal.	103,412
Münster (West.)	N. Rhine–Westph.	204,571	Wilhelmshaven	Lower Saxony	103,150
Hagen	N. Rhine–Westph.	201,721	Herne	N. Rhine–Westph.	100,798
Mülheim (Ruhr)	N. Rhine–Westph.	191,080	Rheydt	N. Rhine–Westph.	100,633

RELIGION. Of the population 51·1% are Protestants, 44·1% Roman Catholics and 0·04% Jews (census, 1961).

The German Evangelical Church is composed of 13 Lutheran Churches, 13 United (Lutheran and Reformed) Churches and 2 Reformed Churches. Its organs are the Synod, the Church Conference and the Council under the chairmanship of Dr Hermann Dietzfelbinger (elected 9 April 1967). There are also some 12 Free and Separated Churches, with together about 330,000 members in 1956. There were 547 members of the Society of Friends in 1957.

There are 5 Roman Catholic archbishops and 18 bishoprics, apart from the dioceses of Breslau and Ermland situated in the territories under Soviet and Polish administration. Chairman of the Bishops' Conference is Cardinal Frings,

Archbishop of Cologne. A concordat between Germany and the Holy See was signed on 20 July and ratified on 10 Sept. 1933.

The 'Old Catholics', who are in communion with the Church of England, numbered about 38,000 in 1956; they have a bishop at Bonn.

Kirchliches Jahrbuch für die Evangelische Kirche in Deutschland. Gütersloh, 1884 ff.
Taschenbuch der evangelischen Kirche in Deutschland. Stuttgart, 1962
Kirchliches Handbuch. Amtliches statistisches Jahrbuch der Katholischen Kirche Deutschlands. Vol. 24. Cologne, 1962
Luckey, G., *Free Churches in Germany.* Bad Nauheim, 1956

EDUCATION. *Schools providing general education* are primary schools (*Volksschulen*), special schools (*Sonderschulen*), intermediate schools (*Real-schulen*), high schools (*Gymnasien*) and 'new system' schools. Primary schools: Attendance is compulsory for all children having completed their 6th year of age. Compulsory education extends 9 years. After the first 4 (or 6) years at primary school children may attend postprimary schools (*Oberstufe*), intermediate schools high schools and other schools of general secondary education. The intermediate school comprises 6, the high school 9 years. The final high school certificate entitles the holder to enter any institution of higher education. There are also special schools for retarded, physically or mentally handicapped and socially maladjusted children.

In Oct. 1969 there were in the Federal Republic 23,035 primary schools with 180,373 teachers (103,642 female) and 6,112,060 pupils (3,000,621 girls); 2,192 special schools with 16,764 teachers (10,016 female) and 291,000 pupils (117,553 girls); 2,057 intermediate schools with 31,587 teachers (14,728 female) and 826,201 pupils (435,849 girls); 2,242 high schools with 65,942 teachers (20,730 female) and 1,357,399 pupils (590,476 girls).

Vocational education is provided in part-time, full-time and advanced full-time vocational schools (*Berufs-, Berufsfach-* and *Fachschulen*) and institutions for the training of technicians (*Technikerschulen*). Running parallel to the occupation, part-time vocational schools offer 6 to 12 hours per week of additional compulsory schooling. All young people who are apprentices, in some other employment or even unemployed have to attend them in general up to the age of 18 years or until the completion of the practical vocational training. Full-time vocational schools comprise courses of at least one year. They prepare for commercial and domestic occupations as well as specialized occupations in the field of handicrafts. Advanced full-time vocational schools are attended by pupils having completed their 18th year of age; courses vary from 6 months to 3 or more years.

In Nov. 1968 there were 1,799 part-time vocational schools with 24,964 teachers (7,260 female) and 1,754,765 pupils (773,338 girls); 2,544 full-time vocational schools with 9,157 teachers (5,032 female) and 204,111 pupils (125,351 girls); 1,160 advanced vocational schools with 6,125 teachers (2,463 female) and 86,223 pupils (39,927 girls); 748 full- and part-time vocational extension schools with 684 teachers (162 female) and 60,040 pupils (7,868 girls); 1,564 schools for public health occupations with 16,655 teachers (5,439 female) and 53,719 pupils (47,720 girls) and 286 (full-time and part-time) institutions for the training of technicians with 672 teachers (22 female) and 26,931 participants (1,350 female).

Colleges of engineering, architecture, electricity, agriculture, etc., offer highly qualified full-time technical and agricultural instruction. There were, in 1969, 147 colleges of engineering with 8,111 teachers (176 female) and 69,282 students (1,074 female).

Higher Education. Universities and equivalent institutions; teacher-training colleges and equivalent institutions which train teachers for primary schools, special schools, intermediate schools and schools providing vocational education; colleges of music, fine arts and the college for physical education in Cologne.

During the winter term 1969–70 there were 52 academic institutions of higher education with 335,577 students (82,267 female; 22,685 foreigners); they comprise

25 universities with 262,546 students (74,463 female); 9 technical universities with 63,908 students (6,025 female); 4 other institutions with university status with 7,337 students (1,606 female); 9 Roman Catholic theological colleges and 5 Protestant theological colleges with together 1,786 students (173 female).

In the winter term 1969–70 there were 99 teacher-training colleges and equivalent institutions (including institutions training teachers for needlework, domestic sciences, physical education, music and fine arts) with 67,865 students (43,090 female). Eight of these colleges and institutions with 9,995 students (5,897 female) are incorporated in universities and technical universities. (These students are counted twice.)

In the winter term 1969–70 there were 15 colleges of music, 10 colleges of fine arts, the college of film and television and the college for physical education with together 10,315 students (4,204 female; 1,391 foreigners).

CINEMAS (31 Dec. 1968). There were 4,060 cinemas with a seating capacity of 1,672,295 and 9 drive-in cinemas for 9,476 cars.

NEWSPAPERS (1969). There were 462 daily newspapers with a combined circulation of 23·5m.

HEALTH AND SOCIAL WELFARE. There were in 1968, 3,634 hospitals with 675,169 beds in the Federal Republic. In 1969 public assistance (including aid to tuberculars) and aid to war victims amounted to DM 3,325m. or DM 54·34 per head of population.[1]

---

[1] All subsequent statistics relate to the end of 1969 or the calendar year 1969.

SOCIAL SECURITY. *Social Health Insurance* (originally introduced in 1883). Compulsory insurants are in particular wage-earners and apprentices, salaried employees with a monthly income of up to DM 900 (from 1 Aug. 1969 up to DM 990 and from 1 Jan. 1970 up to DM 1,200), as well as the great majority of social-insurance pensioners. Insurants may voluntarily continue to insure when no longer liable to do so.

Benefits: Medical treatment, medicaments, hospital and nursing care, maternity benefits, death benefits for the insured and their families, sickness payments and out-patients' allowances.

Number of insurants, 29·1m. (1968), including compulsory insurants (16·7m.) and pensioners (7·4m.). Number of the cases of incapacity for work (1968), 15·2m. Total expenditure, DM 21,600m.

Accident Insurance (originally introduced in 1884). Insured are all persons in employment or service, apprentices and the greater part of the self-employed and the unpaid family workers.

Benefits in the case of industrial injuries and occupational diseases: Medical treatment and nursing care, sickness payments, pensions and other payments in cash and in kind, surviving dependants' pensions.

Number of insurants, 25·6m. (1968); number of current pensions, 1m.; total expenditure, DM 4,000m.

Workers' and Employees' Old-age Insurance Funds (originally introduced in 1889). Compulsory insurants are all wage-earners and self-employed craftsmen as well as all salaried employees with monthly salaries of up to DM 1,800, as from 1 Jan. 1968 all salaried employees irrespective of the level of their incomes, and certain liberal professions. Insurants may voluntarily continue to insure when no longer liable to do so or increase the insurance.

Benefits: Measures designed to maintain, improve and restore the earning capacity; pensions paid to persons incapable for work, old age and surviving dependants' pensions.

Number of pensions paid, 9·2m., of which pensions to insurants, 5·7m.; pensions to widows and widowers, 3·1m.; pensions to orphans, 0·4m. Total expenditure, DM 44,100m.

Miners' Pension Insurance Funds. Compulsory insurants are all persons employed in mining, excluding salaried employees functioning as employers. Insurants may voluntarily continue to insure when no longer liable to do so or increase the insurance.

Benefits: Measures designed to maintain, improve and restore the earning capacity; pensions paid to underground workers because of partial disability to work in mines, miners' pensions in the case of complete disability, miners' retirement benefits, surviving dependants' pensions.

Number of pensions paid (1968), 0·7m., of which pensions to insurants, 0·4m.; pensions to widows and widowers, 0·3m.; pensions to orphans, 0·04m. Total expenditure, DM 5,400m.

Farmers' Old-age Pension Funds; Unemployment Insurance and *Unemployment Relief* granted to unemployed persons who are not entitled to unemployment pay. Number of insured, 0·8m. (1968); number of current pensions, 0·3m. Total expenditure, DM 0·7m.

ASSISTANCE FOR WAR VICTIMS (war-disabled and surviving dependants of war victims).

Benefits: Medical treatment and nursing care, aid to war victims, disablement pensions, basic and equalization pensions paid to widows and orphans, parents' pensions, allowances for nursing care, compensation for occupational detriment, funeral allowances, lump-sum indemnification and indemnification paid upon marriage.

Persons (including those with permanent residence abroad) qualifying for pensions, 2·6m., of which disabled persons, 1·2m.; widows and widowers, 1·1m.; orphans, 0·1m.; parents, 0·2m. Total expenditure, DM 6,200m.

EQUALIZATION OF BURDENS (public relief and compensation payments). Eligible are expellees and persons who suffered damage because of the war or in connexion with the currency reform.

Benefits: Basic compensation, war-damage pensions, compensation for household equipment, accommodation assistance, currency-conversion compensation, compensation for holders of 'old savings', training grants, loans and other promotive measures.

Number of recipients of war damage pensions, 0·5m.; payments made (1 Sept. 1952–31 Dec. 1969) DM 69,600m., including basic compensation, DM 13,100m.; war damage pension, DM 24,300m.; accommodation assistance, DM 5,600m.; compensation for household equipment, DM 8,800m.

FAMILY ASSISTANCE. Persons are eligible for children's allowances from the family-allowance funds for the third and each subsequent child, provided they are not entitled to such payments as members of the public service or as recipients of social benefits. Persons with no more than 2 children receive allowances for the second child only, if the parents' annual income is less than DM 7,800.

ACCOMMODATION ALLOWANCES for tenants, owners of a homestead, a freehold flat or a small-holder's cottage.

PUBLIC WELFARE, AID TO WAR VICTIMS AND PUBLIC YOUTH WELFARE. *Public Welfare.* Public assistance or welfare (the latter from 1 June 1962) for needy persons, namely livelihood aid and aid in special situations (including aid to tuberculars) provided outside and inside institutions, homes and similar establishments.

Aid provided outside institutions, DM 1,328m.; aid provided inside institutions, DM 1,531m.

Aid to War Victims. Benefits for disabled persons and members of their families as well as for surviving dependants, namely vocational assistance, education allowances, supplementary livelihood aid; recovery, accommodation and special assistance. Total expenditure, DM 466m.

Public Youth Welfare. In particular, supervision of foster children, official guardianship, assistance with adoptions and affiliations, social assistance in juvenile courts, educational assistance and correctional education under a court order. Total expenditure, DM 1,141m.

Übersicht über die soziale Sicherung in Deutschland. Bundesministerium für Arbeit und Sozialordnung. 6th ed. Bonn, 1967

Tietz, G., *Zahlenwerk zur Sozialversicherung in der Bundesrepublik Deutschland* (and supplements). Berlin, 1963

Arbeits- und sozialstatistische Mitteilungen. Bundesminister für Arteit und Sozialordnung, Bonn (from 1950)

Öffentliche Sozialleistungen. Statistisches Bundesamt (from 1951)

Gesundheitswesen. Statistisches Bundesamt (from 1946)

JUSTICE. Justice is administered by the federal courts and by the courts of the Länder. In criminal procedures, civil cases and procedures of non-contentious jurisdiction the courts on the Land level are the local courts (*Amtsgerichte*), the regional courts (*Landgerichte*) and the courts of appeal (*Oberlandesgerichte*). On the federal level decisions regarding these matters are taken by the Federal Court (*Bundesgerichtshof*) at Karlsruhe. In labour law disputes the courts of the first and second instance are the labour courts and the Land labour courts and in the third instance, the Federal Labour Court (*Bundesarbeitsgericht*) at Kassel. Disputes about public law in matters of social security, unemployment insurance, maintenance of war victims and similar cases are dealt with in the first and second instances by the social courts and the Land social courts and in the third instance by the Federal Social Court (*Bundessozialgericht*) at Kassel. In most tax matters the finance courts of the Länder are competent and in the second instance, the Federal Finance Court (*Bundesfinanzhof*) at Munich. Other controversies of public law in non-constitutional matters are decided in the first and second instance by the administrative and the higher administrative courts (*Oberverwaltungsgerichte*) of the Länder, and in the third instance by the Federal Administrative Court (*Bundesverwaltungsgericht*) at Berlin.

For the inquiry into maritime accidents the admiralty courts (*Seeämter*) are competent on the Land level and in the second instance the Federal Admiralty Court (*Bundesoberseeamt*) at Hamburg.

The constitutional courts of the Länder decide on constitutional questions. The Federal Constitutional Court (*Bundesverfassungsgericht*) as the supreme German court decides such questions as loss of basic rights, unconstitutional character of political parties, validity of laws, charges against judges and complaints regarding violations of basic rights by the public force.

The death sentence is abolished. (It is retained in East Germany for espionage or sabotage and for treason.)

Manual of German Law. 2 vols. HMSO, 1950–52

FINANCE. Currency. Pursuant to the laws issued on the monetary reform by the military governors of the British, American, and French Zones, from 18 to 26 June 1948, the 'Reichmark' was replaced by the 'Deutsche Mark'. The RM notes circulated by the former Reichsbank were exchanged for DMs at the rate of 1 to 1 up to the amount of RM 60, and all amounts exceeding RM 600 as well as all bank and saving deposits at the ratio of RM 100 to DM 6·5. All RM liabilities, including securities, were depreciated at the ratio of 10 to 1.

On 31 July 1968 the circulation of coins in the Federal Republic amounted to DM 2,547m.; that of notes and coins to DM 34,095m.

The rate of exchange for DM (West) was fixed at 3·66 to the US$ from 26 Oct. 1969, and at 8·78 to the £ after the revaluation of DM in Oct. 1969.

Budget. The budget of the Federal Government shows the following figures (in DM 1m.) for calendar years:

	1967	1968	1969	1970[1]
Revenues				
Federal taxes and customs duties[2]	46,595	48,089	58,667	27,512
Share of Federal Government in joint taxes and trade tax levy[2]	16,232	17,937	19,829	58,888
Tax-like charges	1,307	1,496	1,625	1,442
From the European Orientation and Guarantee Fund	32	858	300	300
Others	2,735	2,871	3,083	2,617
Total revenue	66,901	71,251	83,204	90,459
Expenditures				
Defence and civil defence	20,641	17,511	20,165	20,025
Social security[4]	23,710	23,794	24,153	26,828
Agriculture and food	3,830	6,154	5,804	7,354
Transport and communications	5,420	5,620	6,430	6,925
Electricity, gas, water supply, industries and services	2,139	1,918	1,814	1,818
Education and science	2,136	2,315	2,524	3,222
Housing and settlements	1,360	1,676	1,346	1,516
All other expenditure[5]	16,492	17,084	19,327	21,628
Total expenditure	75,728	76,072	81,563	89,316
Balance of transitory means	−6	+154	+61	±0
Net financing balance	−8,833	−4,667	+1,702	+1,143
Financed from:				
Loans	11,299	8,634	7,927	3,747
Coinage[3]	153	183	163	165
Less:				
Redemption payments[6]	2,619	4,150	9,791	3,455
Addition to reserves	—	—	—	1,600

[1] Budget estimate.
[2] In 1970 redistribution of tax yield among central and local government pursuant to the laws on the fiscal reform.
[3] On a net basis.
[4] Excluding debt-register obligations to social insurance institutions, including restitution payments and promotion of wealth formation.
[5] Including interest and pensions.
[6] Including cover for deficits of previous years.

The total debt of the Federal Republic, the Equalization of Burdens Fund, ERP-Special Fund and the Länder was DM 82,971m., as at 31 Dec. 1969.

Debt Settlement. On 27 Feb. 1953 several agreements were signed in London settling Germany's external pre-war and post-war debts. These agreements entered into force on 16 Sept. 1953.

The claims arising from the post-war economic assistance given to Germany by the UK (£201·8m.), France ($15·79m.) and the USA ($3,014m.) were fixed at £150m., $11·84m. and $1,000m. respectively, of which only the claims of the USA bear interest at 2½%. Up to March 1961 the claims were paid off by regular and premature redemption as follows: Great Britain except for £67·5m., France except for $5,328,000 and the USA except for $787·37m. In April/May 1961 the *Deutsche Bundesbank* repaid on behalf of the Federal Republic the total claims of Great Britain and France and the amount of $587m. to the USA. The debt still outstanding on 30 Dec. 1966 (US$195·94m.) was also repaid by the Deutsche Bundesbank on behalf of the Federal Republic.

On 31 Dec. 1968 the London Debts Agreement of 27 Feb. 1953 was in force in a total of 56 foreign countries. 90% of all debts were claims of the USA, Great Britain, France and Switzerland.

Of the approximately DM 4,000m. of public pre-war debts, the sum of DM 1,705m. and of the approximately DM 2,200m. of private pre-war debts the amount of DM 253m. had still to be paid back on 31 Dec. 1968.

Inter-Allied Reparation Agency. Annual Report of the Secretary-General, from 1946
Stucken, R., *Deutsche Geld- und Kreditpolitik 1914–63*. Tübingen, 1964

DEFENCE. The Paris Treaties, which entered into force in May 1955, stipulated a contribution of the Federal Republic to western defence within the framework of NATO and the Western European Union. In Oct. 1968 the Federal Defence Force (*Bundeswehr*) had a total strength of 455,000 all ranks.

Army. In May 1970 the Army consisted of 12 armoured brigades, 16 armoured infantry brigades, 2 mountain brigades, 3 airborne brigades; total strength 326,674.

The principal combat unit is now the self-sufficient brigade of 3,100–4,500 men; each has infantry, armoured infantry, tanks, conventional artillery, anti-aircraft and anti-tank weapons, reconnaissance, signalling and supply units. The new armoured division consists of 3 brigades. Twelve battalions are equipped with American *Honest John* and 4 battalions with *Sergeant* surface-to-air missiles. The Army has 1,500 M, M-48 A2 Patton and 1,800 Leopard medium tanks, 7,000 armoured personnel carriers and 1,000 tank destroyers.

Territorial Defence. This special organization is being established in order to relieve the operational forces of tasks incompatible with combat mobility. Personnel, 1969, was 30,376.

Border Police. The Border Police is a special police force under Ministry of the Interior to protect the territory of the Federal Republic against illegal border crossings and other disturbances of public order which could threaten the security of the borders. The Border Police, established in 1951, numbered 30,000 men in 1968. There is also a police force (*Bereitschaftspolizei*) of 15,000 men.

Navy. At the end of 1970 the Navy had 12 submarines, 3 guided missile armed destroyers, 9 other destroyers, 8 frigates, 6 corvettes, 13 escort and support ships, 24 coastal minesweepers, 30 fast minesweepers, 21 inshore minesweepers, 40 torpedo boats, 2 minelayers (*ex*-landing ships), 24 landing craft, 39 auxiliaries and 28 service craft.

The new construction programme includes 4 large 'corvettes' (guided missile frigates), 12 submarines and 10 fast patrol boats (missile boats).

The Naval Air Arm has 2 wings (each 2 squadrons of 18 aircraft) of F-104G Starfighters and 1 wing of Breguet Atlantic maritime patrol bombers, supplemented by an anti-submarine helicopter wing. Albatross amphibians and Do 27 aircraft form an air-sea rescue wing.

Navy personnel, 1970, was 3,900 officers and 35,100 men.

Air Force. From Oct. 1970, the *Luftwaffe* has been re-organized into the following commands: German Air Force Tactical Command, German Air Force Support Command (including two German Air Force Regional Support Commands—North and South) and General Air Force Office. Its strength in May 1970 was 104,110 officers and men and about 820 combat aircraft. Combat units, including 18 fighter-bomber squadrons, 4 reconnaissance squadrons, 3 missile groups, and the air defence force of 4 interceptor squadrons, 24 batteries of Nike Hercules and 36 batteries of Hawk surface-to-air missiles, are assigned to NATO. There are 4 F-104G Starfighter interceptor squadrons, 10 F-104G fighter-bomber squadrons, 4 RF-104G reconnaissance squadrons (being re-equipped with RF-4E Phantoms) and 8 light attack/reconnaissance squadrons of Fiat G 91s. Three transport wings (each 2 squadrons of 18 aircraft) have mainly turboprop Transall C-160 and Noratlas aircraft; 4 helicopter squadrons operate UH-1D Iroquois. There are also VIP, support and light transport aircraft, and Piaggio P.149D and Do 27 training aircraft. Guided weapons in service include 2 wings of Pershing surface-to-surface missiles and 6 battalions of Nike-Hercules and 9 battalions of Hawk surface-to-air missiles.

A base was built in 1964 near Beja in Portugal, mainly for logistical purposes. All pilots are trained in USA.

Jahn, H. E., and Neher, K. (ed.), *Taschenbuch für Wehrfragen*. Bonn, 1966

AGRICULTURE. The agricultural area of Germany within the boundaries of 1937 comprised 28·5m. hectares, of which 14·7m. are now situated in the Federal Republic. In 1969 the arable land within the Federal Republic was 7,570,600 hectares; meadows and pastures, 5,661,000 hectares; gardens, vineyards, orchards, nurseries, 616,800.

The total number of agricultural holdings (with an agricultural area of 0·5 hectare or more) in the Federal Republic, and their classification by size, according to the agricultural area, were as follows (spring 1969):

	Total	0·5–5 hectares	5–20 hectares	20–100 hectares	Over 100 hectares
Schleswig–Holstein	51,032	14,431	13,908	22,077	616
Hamburg	2,942	2,089	559	270	6
Lower Saxony	212,558	89,617	75,039	46,973	929
Bremen	1,165	631	236	295	3
North Rhine–Westphalia	166,308	77,721	61,318	26,858	411
Hessen	119,619	68,884	42,335	8,215	185
Rhineland–Palatinate	130,378	77,812	45,186	7,323	57
Baden–Württemberg	264,632	157,441	94,528	12,498	165
Bavaria	375,008	139,322	196,638	38,585	463
Saarland	18,139	13,899	3,094	1,132	14
Berlin (West)	370	269	68	33	—
Federal Republic	1,342,133	642,116	532,909	164,259	2,849

There were a further 5·5m. households with a total area of less than 0·5 hectare used for horticultural, agricultural or forestry purposes (census, 6 June 1961).

Area (in 1,000 hectares) and yield (in 1,000 metric tons) of the main crops in the Federal Republic, were as follows:

	Area				Yield			
	1966	1967	1968	1969	1966	1967	1968	1969
Wheat	1,389	1,414	1,464	1,494	4,533	5,819	6,198	6,000
Rye	1,021	975	962	873	2,696	3,162	3,189	2,889
Barley	1,288	1,308	1,330	1,387	3,869	4,734	4,974	5,130
Oats	777	808	821	860	2,340	2,718	2,893	2,976
Potatoes	732	707	659	589	18,839	21,294	19,196	15,985
Sugar-beet	294	294	290	295	12,468	13,697	13,633	12,941

Wine must production (in 1m. hectolitres): 7·4 in 1960; 3·6 in 1961; 3·9 in 1962; 6 in 1963; 7·2 in 1964; 5 in 1965; 4·8 in 1966; 6·1 in 1967; 6 in 1968; 5·9 in 1969.

Livestock on 3 Dec. 1969 were as follows: Cattle, 14,285,900 (including 5,848,300 milch cows); horses, 254,000; sheep, 840,700; pigs, 19,323,000; goats, 60,300; poultry, 98,954,100.

FORESTRY. Forestry is an industry of great importance, conducted under the care of the State on scientific methods. The forest area of Germany within the boundaries of 1937 was 12·9m. hectares, of which 7m. are now in the Federal Republic. In 1968–69 cuttings amounted to 27m. cu. metres in the Federal Republic.

FISHERIES. In 1969 the yield of sea and coastal fishing in the Federal Republic was 641,700 metric tons, live weight, valued at DM 340·5m.

At the end of 1969 the number of vessels of the fishing fleet was 118 trawlers (124,449 gross tons), 34 luggers and 1,005 cutters.

MINING. The great bulk of the minerals in Germany is produced in North Rhine–Westphalia (for coal, iron and metal smelting-works), Central Germany (for brown coal), Lower Saxony (Salzgitter for iron ore; the Harz for metal ore). The chief oilfields are in Lower Saxony (Emsland).

The quantities of the principal minerals raised in the Federal Republic (until 1963 excluding Berlin) were as follows (in 1,000 metric tons):

Minerals	1964	1965	1966	1967	1968	1969
Coal	142,201	135,077	125,970	112,043	112,012	111,630
Lignite	110,945	101,906	98,088	96,766	101,515	107,424
Iron ore	11,613	10,847	9,467	8,553	7,714	7,451
Metal ore	2,119	2,097	2,133	2,155	2,151	1,453
Potash	20,588	22,209	21,483	19,850	20,187	20,310
Crude oil	7,673	7,884	7,868	7,927	7,982	7,876

The production of iron and steel in the Federal Republic was (in 1,000 metric tons):

	1964	1965	1966	1967	1968	1969
Pig-iron	27,182	26,990	25,413	27,366	30,305	33,764
Steel ingots and castings	37,339	36,821	35,316	36,744	41,159	45,316
Rolled products finished	24,954	24,836	24,244	24,922	28,697	32,247

INDUSTRY. In June 1970, 56,303 establishments (with 10 and more employees) in the Federal Republic employed 8,573,242 persons; of these 1,113,578 were employed in machine construction; 500,858 in textile industry; 1,092,206 in electrical engineering; 310,001 in mining; 592,992 in chemical industry.

The production of important industrial products in the Federal Republic was as follows:

Products	1966	1967	1968	1969
Electricity (1m. kwh.)	177,874	184,681	203,282	226,049
Aluminium (1,000 tons)	244	253	257	263
Petrol (1,000 tons)	11,372	11,774	12,774	13,148
Diesel oil (1,000 tons)	8,124	8,323	9,229	9,012
Potassium fertilizers, K_2O (1,000 tons)	2,291	2,131	2,220	2,283
Sulphuric acid, SO_3 (1,000 tons)[1]	3,130	3,084	3,436	3,658
Soda, Na_2CO_3 (1,000 tons)[1]	1,190	1,158	1,275	1,324
Cement (1,000 tons)[1]	34,738	31,711	33,443	35,079
Rayon:				
Staple fibre (1,000 tons)	202	178	190	185
Continuous rayon filament (1,000 tons)[1]	78	66	71	77
Cotton yarn (1,000 tons)[1]	281	251	255	252
Woollen yarn (1,000 tons)[1]	91	70	79	87
Passenger cars (1,000)[2]	2,830	2,296	2,862	3,313
Commercial cars and buses (1,000)	214	180	236	281
Bicycles (1,000)	1,029	1,131	1,461	1,614

[1] Including the quantities processed in the same factories.
[2] Including dual-purpose vehicles.

Industrie und Handwerk. Ed. Statistisches Bundesamt, Wiesbaden
Gutmann, G., and others, *Die Wirtschaftsverfassung der Bundesrepublik.* Stuttgart, 1964

LABOUR. The economically active persons (excluding the armed forces) totalled 26·17m. at the 1%-sample survey of the microcensus of April 1969. Of the total, 2,857,000 were self-employed, 1,942,000 unpaid family workers, 21·37m. employees; 2,577,000 were engaged in agriculture and forestry; 12,741,000 in power supply, mining, manufacturing and building; 4,564,000 in commerce and transport; 6,287,000 in other industries and services; 214,000 were unemployed.

In June 1970 foreign workers numbered 1,838,900, including 375,000 Italians, 229,400 Greeks, 328,000 Turks, 165,900 Spaniards, 389,000 Yugoslavs.

COMMERCE. The distribution of the imports and exports of the Federal Republic according to principal countries was as follows (in DM 1m.):

	Imports			Exports		
Country	1967	1968	1969	1967	1968	1969
Argentina	576·2	456·4	505·4	491·9	547·6	702·7
Australia	471·5	552·5	649·9	746·7	880·7	989·8
Austria	1,477·1	1,765·6	2.189·7	4,096·6	4,419·5	4,857·3
Belgium–Luxembourg	5,436·4	6,798·5	8.986·9	6,439·2	7,443·8	9,276·9
Brazil	824·4	894·7	1,117·0	760·6	912·1	991·8
Canada	946·6	1,124·5	1,239·7	926·5	1,106·4	1,259·3
Denmark	1,169·5	1,243·4	1,464·4	2,377·5	2,418·5	2,747·4
Finland	592·6	707·7	954·2	1,036·2	950·3	1,235·8
France	8,488·0	9,778·0	12.697·3	10,050·3	12,241·5	15,118·1
Greece	413·3	481·1	613·6	902·1	1,006·3	1,139·7
India	184·0	215·3	237·0	795·7	574·5	498·5
Iran	659·8	761·4	717·8	928·3	1,131·1	1,094·2
Italy	6,436·3	8,066·2	9,490·7	6,890·4	7,568·0	9.260·3
Japan	927·1	1,162·0	1,603·6	1,272·3	1,396·5	1,545·8
Libya	1,402·1	2,365·0	2.550·2	156·5	225·6	238·3
Netherlands	7,274·9	8,810·3	11.255·9	8,627·5	10,114·4	11.521·5
Norway	950·0	1,083·7	1,3·9·4	1,477·6	1,426·0	1,634·9
South Africa	1,045·2	982·4	1,207·6	1,251·4	1,418·6	1,633·6
Spain	712·5	850·3	1,050·8	1,765·6	1,689·9	2,020·4
Sweden	2,166·6	2,488·8	2,897·1	3,533·8	3,849·9	4,369·1
Switzerland	2,110·5	2,479·7	3,142·2	5,041·7	5,708·2	6.571·7
USSR	1,099·8	1,175·3	1,305·7	792·1	1,093·7	1,582·2
UK	2,931·9	3,406·9	3,912·6	3,472·0	4,027·9	4,591·1
USA	8,555·6	8,849·5	10.233·1	7,859·1	10,835·3	10.633·0

The main items of German imports in 1969 were foodstuffs ($4,947m.) and raw materials ($3,705m.); exports, finished manufactures ($19,534m.) and semi-finished manufactures ($5,415ın.)

Der Aussenhandel der Bundesrepublik Deutschland. Ed. Statistisches Bundesamt, Wiesbaden

Total trade between Federal Germany and UK, according to the British Board of Trade returns (in £1,000 sterling):

	1965	1966	1967	1968	1969	1970
Imports to UK	265,357	301,942	338,921	436,817	466,129	548,934
Exports from UK	254,985	253,436	246,700	323,267	366,498 ⎫	502,903
Re-exports from UK	30,371	35,576	30,042	39,416	47,485 ⎬	

SHIPPING. On 31 Dec. 1969 the West German mercantile marine comprised 2,732 ocean-going vessels of 7,478,800 BRT.

The inland-waterways fleet in the Federal Republic on 31 Dec. 1968 comprised 4·63m. tons. The length of the navigable rivers and canals in use was 4,353 km.

Sea-going ships (foreign trade only) in 1969 loaded 24,843,000 metric tons clearing and unloaded 95,539,000 metric tons entering in the ports of the Federal Republic. Inland waterways carried 233·8m. metric tons in 1969.

ROADS. On 1 Jan. 1970 the total length of classified roads in the Federal Republic was 162,344 km, including 4,110 km *autobahn*, 32,205 km highways, 65,358 km first-class and 60,671 km second-class country roads. Motor vehicles licensed in the Federal Republic on 1 July 1970 numbered 16,783,000 (including 228,600 motor cycles, 13,941,100 passenger cars, 1,119,300 trucks, 47,300 buses and 1,447,000 tractors).

Road casualties in 1969 totalled 472,387 injured and 16,646 killed.

RAILWAYS. The total operative length of railway line in the Federal Republic was 33,773 km (29,574 Federal Railways, 4,199 private railways) on 31 Dec. 1969; of these, 8,478 km were electrified. In 1969 the railways (including ships owned by the Federal Railways) carried 1,024m. passengers and 380m. metric tons of freight.

AVIATION. The Deutsche Lufthansa AG (set up on 6 Jan. 1953, as AG für Luftverkehrsbedarf and renamed on 6 Aug. 1954), with headquarters at Cologne, has capital of DM 400m. The Federal Republic owns 74·3%, Land North Rhine–Westphalia 2·2%, the Federal Railways 0·9%, Federal Post 1·8%, Kreditanstalt für Wiederaufbau 3% and private industry 17·8%.

Lufthansa operate internal, European, African, North and South Atlantic, Near and Far East routes. In 1969 the Lufthansa carried 5·87m. passengers, 150,709 tons of cargo and 28,001 tons of mail.

POST. The Federal Republic had, on 31 Dec. 1969, 25,995 post offices and agencies and 10,731 telecommunications offices. The total length of the telephone and telegraph network was 126,706 km lines with 209,619 km two-wire circuits and 427,056 km cables with 40,437,351 km pairs. Number of telephones, 12,456,000. Number of wireless licences, 19,368,260; of television licences, 15,909,146.

The postal bus services covered, in 1969, 185·1m. km and carried 366m. passengers.

The post office savings banks had, on 31 Dec. 1969, 15,426,422 depositors with DM 8,344·3m. to their credit.

In the financial year 1969 the postal revenues amounted to DM 13,439·4m. and the expenditure to DM 12,573m.

BANKING. On 14 Feb. 1948 the Bank of German Länder (Bank deutscher Länder) was established in Frankfurt as the central bank of issue for the Federal Republic and designated the exclusive agency for issuing notes and coins.

The Land Central Banks and the Berlin Central Bank were merged with the Bank deutscher Länder as from 1 Aug. 1957. The Bank deutscher Länder became the Deutsche Bundesbank.

The most important items of the balance sheets of the Deutsche Bundesbank in Frankfurt on 31 July 1970, were as follows (in DM 1m.):

Assets
Gold	14,701·7
Balances at foreign banks and money market investments abroad	18,308·2
Foreign notes, coins, bills and cheques	3,153·6
Loans to international institutions and consolidation loans	1,873·1
Domestic bills of exchange and advances against securities	16,484·0
Equalization claims[1]	6,254·8

Liabilities
Bank-notes in circulation	36,766·8
Deposits	28,211·6

[1] From the monetary reform.

WEIGHTS AND MEASURES. The metric system is in force.

DIPLOMATIC REPRESENTATIVES

The Federal Republic maintains embassies in:

Afghánistán
Argentina
Australia
Austria
Barbados
Belgium
Bolivia
Botswana
Brazil
Burma
Burundi
Cambodia
Cameroun
Canada
Central African Republic
Ceylon
Chad
Chile
Colombia
Congo (Br.)
Congo (K.)
Costa Rica
Cyprus
Dahomey
Denmark
Dominican Republic
Ecuador
El Salvador
Ethiopia
France
Gabon
Ghana
Greece
Guatemala
Haiti

Honduras
Iceland
India
Indonesia
Iran
Irish Republic
Israel
Italy
Ivory Coast
Jamaica
Japan
Jordan
Kenya
Korea (South)
Kuwait
Liberia
Libya
Luxembourg
Madagascar
Malaysia
Malawi
Mali
Malta
Mauritania
Mexico
Morocco
Nepál
New Zealand
Netherlands
Nicaragua
Niger
Nigeria
Norway
Pakistan
Panama

Paraguay
Peru
Philippines
Portugal
Romania
Rwanda
Saudi Arabia
Senegal
Sierra Leone
Somalia
South Africa, Republic of
Southern Yemen
Spain
Sweden
Switzerland
Tanzania
Thailand
Togo
Trinidad and Tobago
Tunisia
Turkey
Uganda
USSR
UK
USA
Upper Volta
Uruguay
Vatican
Venezuela
Vietnam (South)
Yemen
Yugoslavia
Zambia

OF THE FEDERAL GERMAN REPUBLIC IN GREAT BRITAIN
(21–23 Belgrave Sq., SW1)

Ambassador: Karl-Günther von Hase (accredited 11 Feb. 1970).
Minister: Dr Erwin Wickert. *Minister-Counsellors:* Dr Ernst Friedrich Jung (*Political*); Dr H. Naupert (*Economic*).
Counsellors: Dr B. Lohmeyer (*Cultural*); Dr C. Salander (*Scientific*); Dr H. Wentner (*Political*); Dr. W. Oxenius; Dr H. Schauer, CVO; Dr Th. Knatz (*Legal*); W. D. Freiberg. *First Secretaries:* H. Weder (*Economic*); Dr Kullak-Ublick (*Economic*); H. Schmelcher. *Service Attachés:* Col. K.-H. Böttger (*Army*), Brig.-Gen. R. Cescotti (*Defence and Air*), Capt. K.-T. Raeder (*Navy*).

There are German consulates at Edinburgh and Liverpool.

OF GREAT BRITAIN IN THE FEDERAL GERMAN REPUBLIC

Ambassador: Sir Roger Jackling, KCMG.
Ministers: F. Brooks Richards, CMG, DSC; D. D. Brown, CMG, MM (*Economic*).
Counsellors: C. J. Audland (*Head of Chancery*); D. W. Hennessy, OBE (*Administration*); P. J. E. Male, CMG, MC (*Information*); H. T. A. Overton (*Economic*); W. Steedman, CBE; J. L. Taylor (*Commercial*); E. C. M. Cullingford, CMG (*Labour*); A. L. Pope, CVO, OBE; W. E. G. Drury (*Scientific*); J. H. McEnery (*Defence Supply*). *First Secretaries:* R. J. O'Neil; A. H. Wyatt, W. D. Symington (*Information*); D. G. H. Brookfield, MBE; J. D. Campbell; D. A. S. Gladstone; T. G. Streeton; K. C. Wright; J. G. Jones, J. P. B. Simeon (*Commercial*); E. L. Bailey, MBE; P. L. Noble; Dr M. H. Proctor (*Scientific*); G. A. B. Lord (*Civil Air*); J. O. S. Wilde, DSC, K. G. Cumberbeach (*Defence Supply*); G. Brook.
Service Attachés: Brig. F. L. Clarkson, MBE (*Defence and Army*), Air Cdre C. G. Maughan, AFC (*Air*), Capt. J. M. H. Cox, RN (*Naval*).

There are British consular representatives at Berlin, Bremen, Düsseldorf, Frankfurt, Hamburg, Hanover, Munich and Stuttgart.

OF THE FEDERAL REPUBLIC IN THE USA (4645 Reservoir Rd, NW, Washington, D.C., 20007)

Ambassador: Dr Rolf Pauls.
Ministers: Dr Dirk Oncken; Dr Herbert A. Baron von Stackelberg.
Counsellors: Jobst W. Baron von Buddenbrock (*Cultural*); Helmut Middelmann (*Economic*); Carl Lahusen; Hartmut Schulze-Boysen; Heinz D. Herre; Dr Joseph J. Thomas (*Press*); Wolfgang Opfermann (*Scientific*); Dr Wilhelm H. Lampe (*Shipping and Aviation*); Dr Armin Freitag (*Economic*); Johann J. Blomeyer (*Legal*); Dr Renate Bärensprung; Dr Werner Handke (*Economic*); Hermann W. Bremer (*Labour*). *First Secretaries:* Dr Gert-Dietrich Wölki (*Agriculture*); Bernhard Wolf; Herbert Schmuck (*Shipping and Aviation*); Karl Richter; Rupert Dirnecker; Horst Holthoff; Dr Karl Treml (*Scientific*); Hans Helmut Freundt; Joachim Schönbeck (*Press*). *Service Attachés:* Rear-Adm. Herbert Trebesch (*Defence*), Col. Erich Rother (*Army*), Col. Georg Wroblewski (*Air*), Capt. Paul Brasack (*Navy*).

OF THE USA IN THE FEDERAL REPUBLIC

Ambassador: Kenneth Rush.
Deputy Chief of Mission: Russell Fessenden. *Heads of Sections:* Jonathan Dean (*Political*); Edwin G. Moline (*Economic*); Edmund F. Becker (*Commercial*); Norbert Krieg (*Consular*); Thomas Stern (*Administrative*); Gordon A. Ewing (*USIA*). *Service Attachés:* Col. Foster F. Flegeal (*Defence and Army*), Col. Selah H. Howell (*Air*), Capt. Robert D. Wood (*Navy*).

There are Consuls-General in Bremen, Düsseldorf, Frankfurt, Hamburg, Munich and Stuttgart.

BOOKS OF REFERENCE

STATISTICAL INFORMATION. The central statistical agency is the Statistisches Bundesamt 62 Wiesbaden, Gustav Stresemann Ring 11). *President:* Patrick Schmidt. Its publications include:

Statistisches Jahrbuch für die Bundesrepublik Deutschland (latest issue, 1970); *Statistisches Taschenbuch* (latest issue 1970; also in English and French); *Wirtschaft und Statistik* monthly, from 1949); *Das Arbeitsgebiet der Bundesstatistik* (from 1954; latest issue 1967; also in English: *Survey of German Federal Statistics*).

Documents on Germany under Occupation, 1945–54. Ed. B. Ruhm von Oppen. R. Inst. of Int. Affairs, 1955
Bluhm, G., *Die Oder-Neisse-Linie in der deutschen Aussenpolitik.* Freiburg, 1963
Dickinson, R. E., *The Regions of Germany.* London, 1945
Pounds, N. J. G., *The economic pattern of modern Germany.* 2nd ed. London, 1966
Trene, W., *Germany since 1848.* Bod Godesberg, 1969
Wiskemann, E., *Germany's Eastern Neighbours.* R. Inst. of Int. Affairs, 1956

NATIONAL LIBRARY. Deutsche Bibliothek, Untermainkai 14, Frankfurt (Main). *Director:* Professor Hanns Wilhelm Eppelsheimer.

THE LANDER

BADEN–WÜRTTEMBERG

CONSTITUTION. The Land Baden–Württemberg is a merger of the 3 Länder, Baden, Württemberg–Baden and Württemberg–Hohenzollern, which were formed in 1945. The merger was approved by a plebiscite held on 9 Dec. 1951, when 70% of the population of the 3 Länder voted in its favour.

The Diet, elected on 28 April 1968, consists of 60 Christian Democrats, 37 Social Democrats, 18 Free Democrats and 12 National Democrats.

The government is a coalition of Christian Democrats and Social Democrats, with Dr Hans Filbinger (CDU) as Prime Minister.

AREA AND POPULATION. Baden–Württemberg comprises 35,750 sq. km, with a population (at 31 Dec. 1968) of 8,713,900 (4,179,300 males, 4,534,600 females).

The Land is administratively divided into 4 areas (North Württemberg, North Baden, South Baden, South Württemberg–Hohenzollern), 9 urban and 63 rural districts, and numbers 3,378 communes. The capital is Stuttgart.

VITAL STATISTICS for calendar years:

	Live births	Marriages	Divorces	Deaths
1966	160,802	66,553	6,894	86,600
1967	155,617	64,226	7,165	87,276
1968	147,961	62,525	8,205	93,263

RELIGION. At the census of 6 June 1961, 48·9% of the population were Protestants and 46·8% Roman Catholics.

EDUCATION. In 1968 there were 3,876 primary schools with 25,621 teachers and 862,951 pupils; 383 special schools with 2,275 teachers and 38,009 pupils; 227 intermediate schools with 3,977 teachers and 116,485 pupils; 408 high schools with 8,719 teachers and 216,402 pupils; 9 Freie Waldorf schools with 286 teachers and 4,832 pupils; 469 part-time vocational schools with 3,459 teachers and 224,613 pupils; 663 full-time vocational schools with 2,011 teachers and 39,321 pupils; 181 advanced vocational schools with 768 teachers and 10,690 pupils; 203 schools for public health occupations with 2,500 teachers and 7,139 pupils. There were also 77 (full-time and part-time) institutions for the training of technicians with 4,285 participants and 17 colleges of engineering with 829 teachers and 8,805 students.

In the summer term 1969 there were 4 universities (Freiburg, 11,097 students; Heidelberg, 11,122; Tübingen, 11,776; Konstanz, 472); 2 technical universities (Karlsruhe, 6,055; Stuttgart, 6,663); the Agricultural College in Hohenheim (978); the Commercial College in Mannheim (4,305); 24 teacher-training colleges with 12,201 students; 6 colleges of music and 2 colleges of fine arts with together 2,197 students.

HEALTH. There were, in 1968, 688 hospitals with 98,359 beds.

SOCIAL WELFARE. In 1968 public assistance (including aid to tuberculars) and aid to war victims amounted to DM 310·9m. or DM 35·69 per head of population.

JUSTICE. There are a constitutional court (*Staatsgerichtshof*), 2 courts of appeal, 17 regional courts, 119 local courts, a Land labour court, 20 labour courts, a Land social court, 8 social courts, a finance court, a higher administrative court (*Verwaltungsgerichtshof*), 4 administrative courts.

LABOUR. The economically active persons totalled 3,953,000 at the 1%-sample survey of the microcensus of April 1968. Of the total, 448,000 were self-employed, 338,000 unpaid family workers, 3,166,000 employees; 445,000 were engaged in agriculture and forestry, 2,091,000 in power supply, mining, manufacturing and building, 562,000 in commerce and transport, 854,000 in other industries and services.

AGRICULTURE. Area and yield of the most important crops:

	Area (in 1,000 hectares)			Yield (in 1,000 metric tons)		
	1966	1967	1968	1966	1967	1968
Rye	28·5	25·9	22·6	79·5	75·5	67·2
Wheat	235·2	241·8	253·6	706·3	794·1	980·9
Barley	155·6	152·8	152·6	347·3	448·3	478·7
Oats	74·6	79·3	80·8	176·6	215·6	240·9
Potatoes	100·7	97·0	84·0	2,183·6	2,625·0	2,255·7
Sugar-beet	18·3	17·7	18·3	747·1	906·0	903·8

Livestock (4 Dec. 1968): Cattle, 1,902,000 (including 820,700 milch cows); horses, 30,700; pigs, 2,119,000; sheep, 126,200; goats, 30,000; poultry, 9,696,800.

INDUSTRY. In June 1969, 10,643 establishments (with 10 and more employees) employed 1,526,700 persons; of these, 270,500 were employed in machine construction; 151,300 in textile industry; 236,600 in electrical engineering; 145,700 in car building.

ROADS. On 1 Jan. 1969 there were 26,709 km of 'classified' roads, including 565 km of autobahn, 4,447 km of federal roads, 12,764 km of first-class and 8,933 km of second-class highways. Motor vehicles, at 1 July 1969, numbered 2,366,832, including 1,921,404 passenger cars, 5,324 buses, 131,581 lorries, 246,160 tractors and 46,741 motor cycles.

STATISTICAL INFORMATION. The Statistisches Landesamt (P.O.B. 898, Stuttgart) (*President:* Prof. Klaus Szameitat), publishes: *Statistische Monatshefte Baden–Württemberg; Jahrbücher für Statistik und Landeskunde von Baden–Württemberg; Statistik von Baden–Württemberg* (series); *Statistisches Handbuch Baden–Württemberg* (1955 and 1958); *Statistisches Taschenbuch* (1963, 1964, 1966 and 1968). *Die Stadt- und Landkreise Baden–Würtembergs in Wort und Zahl.*

Spreng, R., and others, *Die Verfassung des Landes Baden–Württemberg.* Stuttgart, 1954

BAVARIA
Bayern

CONSTITUTION. The Constituent Assembly, elected on 30 June 1946, passed a constitution on the lines of the democratic constitution of 1919, but with greater emphasis on state rights; this was agreed upon by the Christian Social Union and the Social Democrats.

The elections for the Diet, held on 20 Nov. 1966, had the following results: 110 Christian Social Union, 79 Social Democrats, 15 National Democrats. The cabinet of the Christian Social Union is headed by Minister President Dr Alfons Goppel (CSU).

AREA AND POPULATION. Bavaria has an area of 70,550 sq. km. The capital is Munich. There are 7 areas, 191 urban and rural districts and 7,067 communes. The population (31 Dec. 1968) numbered 10,405,600 (4,922,700 males, 5,482,895 females).

VITAL STATISTICS for calendar years:

	Live births	Marriages	Divorces	Deaths
1966	181,559	81,809	8,521	113,779
1967	176,362	79,342	9,320	116,521
1968	168,403	77,692	9,687	122,311

RELIGION. At the census of 6 June 1961 there were 71·3% Roman Catholics and 26·5% Protestants.

EDUCATION. In 1968 there were 5,540 primary schools with 32,653 teachers and 1,094,124 pupils; 244 special schools with 1,378 teachers and 26,947 pupils; 264 intermediate schools with 4,819 teachers and 107,378 pupils; 333 high schools with 10,910 teachers and 191,258 pupils; 2 Freie Waldorf schools with 79 teachers and 1,471 pupils; 382 part-time vocational schools with 4,374 teachers and 304,403 pupils; 236 full-time vocational schools with 1,193 teachers and 26,944 pupils; 286 advanced vocational schools with 1,445 teachers and 21,509 pupils; 170 schools for public health occupations with 2,004 teachers and 7,704 pupils. There were also 40 (full-time and part-time) institutions for the training of technicians with 4,537 participants, and 20 colleges of engineering with 775 teachers and 10,359 students.

In the winter term 1968–69 there were 4 universities (Erlangen–Nürnberg, 10,296 students; München, 27,127; Regensburg, 1,586; Würzburg, 8,640); the Technical University of München (8,512); 5 Roman Catholic theological colleges and 1 Protestant theological college with together 596 students. There were also 26 teacher-training colleges with 8,898 students (8 of the teacher-training colleges mentioned with 6,535 students are incorporated in universities; these students are counted twice); 1 college of music and 2 colleges of fine arts and 1 college of television and film 1,424 students.

HEALTH. There were, in 1968, 814 hospitals with 114,697 beds.

SOCIAL WELFARE. In 1968 public assistance (including aid to tuberculars) and aid to war victims amounted to DM 364·3m. or DM 35·02 per head of population.

JUSTICE. There are a constitutional court (*Verfassungsgerichtshof*), a supreme Land court (*Oberstes Landesgericht*), 3 courts of appeal, 21 regional courts, 167 local courts, a Land labour court, 11 labour courts, a Land social court, 7 social courts, 2 finance courts, a higher administrative court (*Verwaltungsgerichtshof*), 6 administrative courts.

LABOUR. The economically active persons totalled 4,771,000 at the 1%-sample survey of the microcensus of April 1968. Of the total, 637,800 were self-employed, 588,600 unpaid family workers, 3,544,600 employees; 794,000 were engaged in agriculture and forestry; 2,119,500 in power supply, mining, manufacturing and building; 786,000 in commerce and transport; 1,071,500 in other industries and services.

AGRICULTURE. Area and yield of the most important products:

	Area (1,000 hectares)			Yield (1,000 metric tons)		
	1966	*1967*	*1968*	*1966*	*1967*	*1968*
Wheat	475·6	486·0	499·2	1,538·7	1,909·7	2,062·4
Rye	170·9	151·3	145·9	385·2	402·7	437·0
Barley	390·7	386·1	384·0	1,061·4	1,342·6	1,371·5
Oats	164·4	173·8	174·6	423·7	550·0	566·0
Potatoes	251·0	251·7	237·9	6,121·5	7,256·8	6,760·1
Sugar-beet	53·3	52·5	55·1	2,270·1	2,528·5	2,801·1

Livestock (3 Dec. 1968): 4,267,900 cattle (including 1,990,800 milch and draught cows); 37,100 horses; 159,600 sheep; 19,100 goats; 3,861,200 pigs; 16,594,500 poultry.

INDUSTRY. In June 1969, 11,039 establishments (with 10 and more employees) employed 1,344,300 persons; of these, 246,100 were employed in electrical engineering; 181,300 in machine construction; 106,100 in textile industry; 106,300 in cloth manufacture.

ROADS. There were, on 1 Jan. 1969, 35,116 km of 'classified' roads including 932 km of autobahn, 7,188 km of federal roads, 13,506 km of first-class and 13,490 km of second-class highways. Number of motor vehicles, at 1 July 1969, was 2,887,987, including 2,199,214 passenger cars, 169,886 lorries, 6,511 buses, 447,878 tractors, 59,721 motor cycles.

STATISTICAL INFORMATION. The Bavarian Statistical Office (51, Neuhauser St., Munich 2) was founded in 1833. *President:* Dr Alban Haas. It publishes: *Statistisches Jahrbuch für Bayern* (1964). —*Statistisches Taschenbuch für Bayern* (1966.)—*Bayern in Zahlen.* Monthly (from Jan. 1947).— *Zeitschrift des Bayerischen Statistischen Landesamts.* July 1869–1943; 1948 ff.—*Beiträge zur Statistik Bayerns.* 1850 ff.—*Statistische Berichte (Informationsdienst).* 1951 ff.—*Schaubilderhefte.* 1951 ff.—*Bayerns Wirtschaft gestern und heute.* 1964 ff.—*Die kreisfreien Städte und Landkreise Bayerns in Zahlen.* 1965 ff.

Nawiasky, H., and Leusser, C., *Die Verfassung des Freisiaates Bayern vom 2. Dez. 1946.* Munich, 1948; supplement, by H. Nawiasky and H. Lechner, Munich, 1953

STATE LIBRARY. Bayerische Staatsbibliothek, Munich 22. *Director-General:* Dr Hans Striedl.

BERLIN

GOVERNMENT. Greater Berlin was under quadripartite Allied government (Kommandatura) until 1 July 1948, when the Soviet element withdrew. On 30 Nov. 1948, a separate Municipal Government was set up in the Soviet Sector (*see* p. 995).

AREA. The total area of Berlin is 883 sq. km, of which Western Berlin covers 480 sq. km and the Soviet Sector 403 sq. km. The *British Sector* includes the administrative districts of Tiergarten, Charlottenburg, Wilmersdorf and Spandau: the *American Sector* those of Kreuzberg, Neukölln, Tempelhof, Schöneberg, Zehlendorf and Steglitz; the *French Sector* covers the administrative districts of Wedding and Reinickendorf, and the *Soviet Sector*, those of Mitte, Friedrichshain, Prenzlauer Berg, Pankow, Weissensee, Lichtenberg, Treptow and Köpenick. The British, American and French sectors form an administrative unit, called Western Berlin.

On 13 Aug. 1961 the East German government completely severed all communications between West and East Berlin.

WEST BERLIN

CONSTITUTION AND GOVERNMENT. According to the constitution of 1 Sept. 1950, Berlin is simultaneously a *Land* of the Federal Republic (though not yet formally incorporated) and a city. It is governed by a House of Representatives (at least 200 members); the executive power is vested in a Senate, consisting of the Ruling Burgomaster, the deputy Burgomaster and not more than 16 senators.

In the municipal elections, held on 12 March 1967, the Social Democrats obtained 81 seats; the Christian Democrats, 47 seats; the Free Democrats, 9 seats. The government is a coalition of Social Democrats and Free Democrats.

Head of the Administration: Klaus Schütz (Social Democrat).

POPULATION. Estimated population, 31 Dec. 1968, 2,141,400 (922,800 males, 1,218,700 females). According to the census of 6 June 1961, 73·1% were Protestants and 11·4% Roman Catholics.

VITAL STATISTICS for calendar years:

	Live births	Marriages	Divorces	Deaths
1965	26,069	21,847	5,835	39,605
1966	26,084	21,830	5,608	39,405
1967	25,215	20,017	5,391	39,804
1968	23,500	19,038	6,020	41,645

EDUCATION. In 1968 there were 415 'new system' schools (including Freie Waldorf schools) with 8,295 teachers and 185,646 pupils; 56 special schools with 835 teachers and 11,486 pupils. In 1968 there were 50 part-time vocational schools with 302 teachers and 39,151 pupils; 30 full-time vocational schools with 357 teachers and 4,001 pupils; 38 advanced vocational schools with 257 teachers and 4,199 pupils; 83 schools for public health occupations with 1,118 teachers and 3,092 pupils. There were further 8 (full-time and part-time) institutions for the training of technicians with 1,690 participants, and 6 colleges of engineering with 324 teachers and 3,817 students.

In the winter term 1968–69 there were 1 university (14,812 students); 1 technical university (8,611); 1 Protestant theological college (207); 1 teacher-training college with 2,246 students; 1 college of music and 1 college of fine arts with together 1,043 students.

HEALTH. There were, in 1968, 146 hospitals with 32,217 beds.

SOCIAL WELFARE. In 1968 public assistance (including aid to tuberculars) and aid to war victims amounted to DM 230m. or DM 107·41 per head of population.

JUSTICE. There are a court of appeal (*Kammergericht*), a regional court, 9 local courts, a Land labour court, a labour court, a Land social court, a social court, a higher administrative court, an administrative court and a finance court.

LABOUR. The economically active persons totalled 966,000 at the 1%-sample of the microcensus of April 1968. Of the total, 74,000 were self-employed, 15,000 unpaid family workers, 877,000 employees; 5,000 were engaged in agriculture and forestry; 429,000 in power supply, manufacturing and building; 202,000 in commerce and transport; 330,000 in other industries and services.

AGRICULTURE. Agricultural area (1968), 14,156 hectares, including 2,234 hectares arable land and 11,739 hectares gardens, orchards, nurseries.

Livestock (4 Dec. 1968): Cattle, 2,100; pigs, 10,800; horses, 1,650; sheep, 1,100.

INDUSTRY. In June 1968, 2,110 establishments (with 10 and more employees) employed 260,000 persons; of these, 94,600 were employed in electrical engineering, 32,800 in machine construction, 20,900 in cloth manufacture, 15,000 in steel construction.

ROADS. There were, on 1 Jan. 1969, 114 km of 'classified' roads including 18 km of autobahn and 96 km of federal roads. On 1 July 1969, 434,800 motor vehicles were registered, including 390,300 passenger cars, 35,100 lorries, 5,100 motor cycles, 2,000 buses and 2,000 tractors.

MONEY. The legal tender of Berlin is the German Mark (DM), viz., the DM (East) in the Soviet Sector and the DM (West) in the Western Sectors. On 20 March 1949 when the DM (West) became the only legal tender of the Western Sectors, the Zentralbank of Berlin was established. Its functions were similar to those of the Zentralbanks of the Länder of the Federal Republic. The Berlin Central Bank was merged with the Bank deutscher Länder as from 1 Aug. 1957, when the latter became the Deutsche Bundesbank. The legal tender for the Western Sectors of Berlin is being issued by the Deutsche Bundesbank (formerly Bank deutscher Länder).

STATISTICAL INFORMATION. The Statistisches Landesamt, formerly Statistisches Amt der Stadt Berlin, was founded in 1862 (Berlin 31, Fehrbelliner Platz 1). *Director:* Dr Hanisch. It publishes: *Statistisches Jahrbuch* (from 1867); *Berliner Statistik* (monthly, from 1947).—*100 Jahre Berliner Statistik* (1962).

BREMEN
Freie Hansestadt Bremen

CONSTITUTION. Political power is vested in the House of Burgesses (*Bürgerschaft*), which appoints the executive, called the Senate.

The elections of 1 Oct. 1967 had the following result: 50 Social Democratic Party, 32 Christian Democratic Union, 10 Free Democratic Party, 8 National Democratic Party. The Senate is formed by a coalition of Social Democrats and Free Democrats; its president is Hans Koschnick (Social Democrat).

AREA AND POPULATION. The area of the Land, consisting of the towns and ports of Bremen and Bremerhaven, is 404 sq. km. Estimated population, 31 Dec. 1968, 754,200 (358,600 males, 395,600 females).

VITAL STATISTICS for calendar years:

	Live births	Marriages	Divorces	Deaths
1966	12,948	6,516	1,180	8,872
1967	12,308	6,339	1,352	8,832
1968	11,603	6,075	1,400	9,214

RELIGION. On 6 June 1961 (census) there were 84·1% Protestants and 9·9% Roman Catholics.

EDUCATION. In 1968 there were 169 'new system' (including Freie Waldorf) schools with 3,776 teachers and 89,254 pupils; 23 special schools with 310 teachers and 3,786 pupils; 20 part-time vocational schools with 516 teachers and 27,587 pupils; 13 full-time vocational schools with 61 teachers and 2,765 pupils; 9 advanced vocational schools with 138 teachers and 2,504 pupils; 13 schools for public health occupations with 181 teachers and 895 pupils. There were further 3 (full-time and part-time) institutions for the training of technicians with 387 participants and 1 college of engineering with 137 teachers and 1,319 students.

In the winter term 1968–69 there was 1 teacher-training college with 931 students.

HEALTH There were, in 1968, 20 hospitals with 8,137 beds.

SOCIAL WELFARE. In 1968 public assistance (including aid to tuberculars) and aid to war victims amounted to DM 55·8m. or DM 73·98 per head of population.

JUSTICE. There are a constitutional court (*Staatsgerichtshof*), a court of appeal, a regional court, 3 local courts, a Land labour court, 2 labour courts, a Land social court, a social court, a finance court, a higher administrative court, an administrative court.

Y

LABOUR. The economically active persons totalled 311,000 at the 1%-sample survey of the microcensus of April 1968. Of the total, 20,000 were self-employed, 4,000 unpaid family workers, 287,000 employees; 3,000 were engaged in agriculture and forestry, 126,000 in power supply, mining, manufacturing and building, 99,000 in commerce and transport, 83,000 in other industries and services.

AGRICULTURE. Agricultural area comprised (1968), 19,100 hectares; yield of grain crops, 6,600 metric tons; potatoes, 5,100 metric tons.

Livestock (3 Dec. 1968): 17,600 cattle (including 5,200 milch cows); 12,600 pigs; 400 sheep; 800 horses; 128,600 poultry.

FISHERIES. In 1967 the yield of sea and coastal fishing was 218,006 metric tons valued at DM 143·1m.

INDUSTRY. In June 1969, 446 establishments (10 and more employees) employed 96,986 persons; of these, 20,044 were employed in shipbuilding (except naval engineering); 8,614 in machine construction; 11,183 in electrical engineering; 7,731 in coffee processing.

ROADS. On 1 Jan. 1969 there were 213 km of 'classified' roads, including 33 km of autobahn, 73 km of federal roads, 59 km of first-class and 47 km of second-class highways. Registered motor vehicles on 1 July 1969 numbered 170,200, including 150,900 passenger cars, 15,300 trucks, 1,700 tractors, 500 buses and 1,800 motor cycles.

SHIPPING. Vessels entered in 1968, 12,581 of 27,764,000 net tons; cleared, 12,456 of 27,197,000 net tons. Sea traffic, 1968, incoming, 11,967,000 metric tons; outgoing, 7,019,000 metric tons.

STATISTICAL INFORMATION. The Statistisches Landesamt (An der Weide 14–16 (P.B. 909), 28 Bremen 1) was founded in 1850. *Director:* Reg.-Dir. Kuske. Its current publications include: *Statistische Mitteilungen aus Bremen* (from 1948).—*Monatliche Zwischenberichte* (1949–53); *Statistische Monatsberichte* (from 1954).—*Statistische Berichte* (from 1956).—*Statistisches Handbuch für das Land Freie Hansestadt Bremen* (*1950–1960*, 1961; *1960–1964*, 1967).

Beutin, L., *Bremen und Amerika*. Bremen, 1953

STATE LIBRARY, Bremer Staatsbibliothek, Breitenweg 27, 28 Bremen. *Director:* Dr Kluth.

HAMBURG
Freie und Hansestadt Hamburg

CONSTITUTION. The constitution of 1 July 1952 vests the supreme power in the House of Burgesses (*Bürgerschaft*) of 120 members. The executive is in the hands of the Senate, whose 13 members are elected by the Bürgerschaft.

The elections of 27 March 1966 had the following results: Social Democrats, 74; Christian Democrats, 38; Free Democrats, 8. The First Burgomaster is Professor Dr Herbert Weichmann (Soc.).

By a law of 13 April 1962 the territory has been divided into 7 administrative districts, each with a mayor and council.

AREA AND POPULATION. In 1938 the territory of the Free Hanse Town was reorganized by the amalgamation of the city and its 18 rural districts with 3 urban and 27 rural districts ceded by Prussia. Total area, 747 sq. km. Population (31 Dec. 1968), 1,822,837 (844,421 males, 978,416 females).

VITAL STATISTICS for calendar years:

	Live births	Marriages	Divorces	Deaths
1966	27,424	17,925	4,197	26,187
1967	26,167	17,161	4,129	25,645
1968	24,265	15,841	4,511	26,593

RELIGION. On 6 June 1961 (census) Evangelical Church and Free Churches 76·3%; Roman Catholic Church 7·4%.

EDUCATION. In 1969 there were 360 'new system' (including Freie Waldorf-Schule und Internationale Schule) schools with 7,607 teachers and 194,984 pupils; 71 special schools with 724 teachers and 9,290 pupils; 41 part-time vocational schools with 1,255 teachers and 47,520 pupils; 66 full-time vocational schools with 129 teachers and 8,361 pupils; 21 advanced vocational schools with 248 teachers and 3,793 pupils; 42 schools for public health occupations with 719 teachers and 2,083 pupils. There were further 5 (full-time and part-time) institutions for the training of technicians, with 596 participants and 8 colleges of engineering with 300 teachers and 3,499 students.

In the winter term 1968–69 there was 1 university with 19,529 students; 1 teacher-training college (which is incorporated in the university); 1 college of music and 1 college of fine arts with together 1,084 students.

HEALTH. There were, in 1968, 61 hospitals with 19,833 beds.

SOCIAL WELFARE. In 1968 public assistance (including aid to tuberculars) and aid to war victims amounted to DM 125·5m. or DM 68·83 per head of population.

JUSTICE. There is a constitutional court (*Verfassungsgericht*), a court of appeal, a regional court, 6 local courts, a Land labour court, a labour court, a Land social court, a social court, a finance court, a higher administrative court, an administrative court.

LABOUR. The economically active persons totalled 831,000 at the 1%-sample survey of the microcensus of April 1968. Of the total, 81,000 were self-employed, 21,000 unpaid family workers, 729,000 employees; 16,000 were engaged in agriculture and forestry, 305,000 in power supply, mining, manufacturing and building, 255,000 in commerce and transport, 255,000 in other industries and services.

AGRICULTURE. The agricultural area comprised 33,600 hectares in 1968. Yield, in metric tons, of cereals, 17,600; potatoes, 8,300.

Livestock (4 Dec. 1968): Cattle, 17,400 (including 5,500 milch cows); pigs, 17,500; horses, 2,300; sheep, 1,800; goats, 200; poultry, 238,400.

FISHERIES. In 1967 the yield of sea and coastal fishing was 48,881 metric tons valued at DM 34·7m.

INDUSTRY. In June 1969, 1,248 establishments (with 10 and more employees) employed 209,257 persons; of these, 24,980 were employed in electrical engineering; 27,722 in machine construction; 21,342 in shipbuilding (except naval engineering); 16,191 in chemical industry.

ROADS. On 1 Jan. 1969 there were 192 km of 'classified' roads including 35 km of autobahn, 157 km of federal roads. Number of motor vehicles (1 July 1969), 443,771, including 399,708 passenger cars, 35,504 lorries, 1,324 buses, 3,592 tractors, 6,643 motor cycles.

SHIPPING. Before the War, Hamburg was the third largest port in the world; it is still the biggest German port.

Vessels		1938	1958	1966	1967	1968
Entered:	Number	18,149	19,033	19,236	19,043	18,802
	Tonnage	20,567,311	27,454,640	36,616,000	35,977,000	37,073,215
Cleared:	Number	19,316	20,363	20,488	19,911	19,320
	Tonnage	20,547,148	27,579,914	36,543,000	35,715,000	36,820,828

STATISTICAL INFORMATION. The Statistisches Landesamt (Steckelhörn 12, Hamburg 11) was founded in 1866. Among its older publications, the *Statistik des Hamburger Staates* (91 vols., from 1867) is the most important. Current publications include: *Statistisches Jahrbuch für die Freie und Hansestadt Hamburg* (from 1925).—*Hamburg in Zahlen* (from 1947).—*Statistische Berichte,* formerly *Hamburger Statistische Informationen* (from Jan. 1954).—*Handel und Schiffahrt des Hafens Hamburg.* Annual, from 1845.

Studt-Olsen, B., *Hamburg, die Geschichte einer Stadt.* Hamburg, 1951

HESSEN

CONSTITUTION. The constitution was put into force by popular referendum on 1 Dec. 1946. The Diet, elected on 6 Nov. 1966, consists of 52 Social Democrats, 26 Christian Democrats, 10 Free Democrats and 8 National Democrats.

The Social Democrat cabinet is headed by Minister President Albert Osswald.

AREA AND POPULATION. The state of Hessen comprehends the areas of the former Prussian provinces Kurhessen and Nassau (excluding the exclaves belonging to Hesse and the rural counties of Oberwesterwald, Unterwesterwald, Unterlahn and St Goarshausen) and of the former Volksstaat Hessen, the provinces Starkenburg (including the parts of Rheinhessen east of the river Rhine) and Oberhessen. Hessen has an area of 21,110 sq. km. Its capital is Wiesbaden. There are 2 areas, 48 urban and rural districts and 2,665 communes. Estimated population, 31 Dec. 1968, was 5,333,200 (2,551,827 males, 2,781,373 females).

VITAL STATISTICS for calendar years:

	Live births	Marriages	Divorces	Deaths
1966	87,732	41,814	5,179	59,205
1967	86,016	40,850	5,590	58,770
1968	82,151	39,658	5,623	63,020

RELIGION. On 6 June 1961 (census) there were 63·4% Protestants and 32·1% Roman Catholics.

EDUCATION. In 1968 there were 2,258 primary schools with 15,286 teachers and 464,965 pupils; 141 special schools with 1,496 teachers and 21,470 pupils; 252 intermediate schools with 3,058 teachers and 76,996 pupils; 177 high schools with 6,370 teachers and 113,009 pupils; 3 Freie Waldorf schools with 98 teachers and 1,672 pupils; 112 part-time vocational schools with 2,115 teachers and 163,245 pupils; 240 full-time vocational schools with 1,068 teachers and 22,173 pupils; 74 advanced vocational schools with 431 teachers and 4,911 pupils; 137 schools for public health occupations with 1,973 teachers and 5,176 pupils. There were further 17 (full-time and part-time) institutions for the training of technicians with 1,432 participants, and 19 colleges of engineering with 524 teachers and 6,932 students.

In the winter term 1968–69 there were 3 universities (Frankfurt/Main, 15,122 students; Giessen, 7,260; Marburg, 8,407); 1 technical university in Darmstadt (6,608); 3 Roman Catholic theological colleges and 1 Protestant theological college with together 420 students. There were also 8 teacher-training colleges with 7,358 students (4 of them with 5,946 students are incorporated in the universities or the technical university; these students are counted twice); 1 college of music and 2 colleges of fine arts with together 531 students.

HEALTH. There were, in 1968, 342 hospitals with 61,822 beds.

SOCIAL WELFARE. In 1968 public assistance (including aid to tuberculars) and aid to war victims amounted to DM 284·6m. or DM 53·37 per head of population.

JUSTICE. There are a constitutional court (*Staatsgerichtshof*), a court of appeal, 9 regional courts, 58 local courts, a Land labour court, 12 labour courts, a Land social court, 7 social courts, a finance court, a higher administrative court (*Verwaltungsgerichtshof*), 4 administrative courts.

LABOUR. The economically active persons totalled 2,339,000 at the 1%-sample survey of the microcensus of April 1968. Of the total, 234,000 were self-employed, 168,000 unpaid family workers, 1,937,000 employees; 198,000 were engaged in agricultural and forestry, 1,155,000 in power supply, mining, manufacturing and building, 405,000 in commerce and transport, 581,000 in other industries and services.

AGRICULTURE. Area and yield of the most important crops:

| | Area (in 1,000 hectares) | | | Yield (in 1,000 metric tons) | | |
	1966	1967	1968	1966	1967	1968
Wheat	120·3	120·9	122·3	371·3	480·5	545·5
Rye	88·7	85·4	87·2	251·2	269·6	287·3
Barley	84·6	88·7	89·7	250·0	320·9	349·7
Oats	82·4	84·6	80·9	241·4	276·5	285·5
Potatoes	60·2	58·4	60·5	1,540·7	1,742·6	1,838·0
Sugar-beet	18·7	17·8	18·7	790·7	860·4	909·8

Livestock, 3 Dec. 1968: Cattle, 940,300 (including 379,600 milch cows); horses, 23,900; pigs, 1,428,700; sheep, 104,100; goats, 8,100; poultry, 6,333,300.

INDUSTRY. In June 1969, 4,934 establishments (with 10 and more employees) employed 713,007 persons; of these, 94,162 were employed in machine construction; 85,547 in chemical industry; 83,118 in electrical engineering; 71,227 in car building.

ROADS. On 1 Jan. 1969 the Land Hessen had 15,901 km of 'classified' roads, including 604 km of autobahn, 3,314 km of federal highways, 7,113 km of first-class highways and 4,870 km of second-class highways. Motor vehicles licensed on 1 July 1969 totalled 1,439,280, including 1,198,215 passenger cars, 3,493 buses, 87,770 trucks, 116,599 tractors and 25,399 motor cycles.

STATISTICAL INFORMATION. The Hessian Land Statistical Office (Rhein Str. 35, Wiesbaden) was established in Dec. 1945. *President:* Dr Willi Hüfner. Main publications: *Statistisches Handbuch für das Land Hessen* (1964).—*Statistisches Taschenbuch für das Land Hessen* (1961).—*Staat und Wirtschaft in Hessen* (Monthly).—*Hessische Bevölkerungs- und Wirtschaftskunde* (2nd ed., 1968).—*Die hessischen Landkreise und kreisfreien Städte* (3rd ed., 1967).—*Hessen im Wandel der letzten 100 Jahre* (1960).—*Hessen unter den Bundesländern* (1963).—*Die hessischen Gemeinden* (1966).—*Beiträge zur Statistik Hessens.—Statistische Berichte.—Hessische Gemeindestatistik 1960–61* (5 vols., 1963 ff.).

LOWER SAXONY
Niedersachsen

GOVERNMENT. The Land Niedersachsen was formed on 1 Nov. 1946 by merging the former Prussian province of Hanover and the *Länder* Brunswick, Oldenburg and Schaumburg-Lippe. The Diet, elected on 4 June 1967, consists of 66 Social Democrats, 63 Christian Democratic Union, 10 Free Democratic Party, 10 National Democratic Party.

The government is a coalition of the Social and Christian Democrats headed by Minister President Dr Georg Diederichs (Social Democrat).

AREA AND POPULATION. Lower Saxony (excluding the town of Bremerhaven, and the districts on the right bank of the Elbe in the Soviet Zone) comprises 47,411 sq. km, and is divided into 8 administrative districts, 60 rural districts, 15 towns and 4,142 communes; capital, Hanover.

Estimated population, on 31 Dec. 1968, was 7,039,169 (3,358,153 males, 3,681,016 females).

VITAL STATISTICS for calendar years:

	Live births	Marriages	Divorces	Deaths
1966	129,670	56,481	5,705	81,416
1967	126,711	56,148	5,920	79,975
1968	122,457	52,444	6,341	86,509

RELIGION. On 6 June 1961 (census) there were 76·9% Protestant and 18·8% Roman Catholics.

EDUCATION. In 1968 there were 3,838 primary schools with 24,333 teachers and 748,468 pupils; 209 special schools with 1,571 teachers and 28,994 pupils; 249 intermediate schools with 4.234 teachers and 116,362 pupils; 219 high schools with 6,802 teachers and 133,435 pupils; 187 part-time vocational schools with 2,596 teachers and 208,013 pupils; 283 full-time vocational schools with 1,034 teachers and 20,491 pupils; 146 advanced vocational schools with 728 teachers and 10,416 pupils; 262 schools for public health occupations with 6,204 pupils, There were also 39 (full-time and part-time) institutions for the training of technicians with 4,104 participants and 14 colleges of engineering with 365 teachers and 4,585 students.

In the winter term 1968–69 there were the University of Göttingen (10,192 students); 3 technical universities (Braunschweig, 5,182; Clausthal, 1,484; Hanover, 5,873); the medical college of Hanover (256), and the veterinary college in Hanover (814). There were also 10 teacher-training colleges with 8,906 students; 1 college of music and 1 college of fine arts with together 708 students.

HEALTH. There were, in 1968, 416 hospitals with 69,168 beds.

SOCIAL WELFARE. In 1968 public assistance (including aid to tuberculars) and aid to war victims amounted to DM 351m. or DM 50·05 per head of population.

JUSTICE. There are a constitutional court (*Staatsgerichtshof*), 3 courts of appeal, 11 regional courts, 132 local courts, a Land labour court, 15 labour courts, a Land social court, 8 social courts, a finance court, a higher administrative court (together with Schleswig–Holstein), 3 administrative courts.

LABOUR. The economically active persons totalled 2,924,000 at the 1%-sample survey of the microcensus of April 1968. Of the total, 354,000 were self-employed, 317,000 unpaid family workers, 2,254,000 employees; 458,000 were engaged in agriculture and forestry, 1,211,000 in power supply, mining, manufacturing and building, 546,000 in commerce and transport, 709,000 in other industries and services.

AGRICULTURE. Area and yield of the most important crops:

	Area (in 1,000 hectares)			Yield (in 1,000 metric tons)		
	1966	1967	1968	1966	1967	1968
Wheat	179·1	178·8	186·5	616·9	769·1	916·1
Rye	346·0	334·8	335·9	924·4	1,129·5	1,176·4
Barley	260·9	275·8	291·3	859·1	1,008·7	1,174·8
Oats	188·2	193·6	197·8	626·8	770·2	771·6
Potatoes	157·4	150·7	132·9	4,364·7	4,882·7	4,223·4
Sugar-beet	105·0	106·8	106·3	4,166·2	4,664·6	4,587·3

Livestock, 3 Dec. 1968: Cattle, 2,741,000 (including 1,044,300 milch cows); horses, 69,100; pigs, 4,986,600; sheep, 144,000; goats, 7,200; poultry, 26,914,700.

FISHERIES. In 1967 the yield of sea and coastal fishing was 192,705 metric tons valued at DM 106m.

INDUSTRY. In June 1969, 4,900 establishments (with 10 and more employees) employed 767,900 persons; of these, 84,600 were employed in machine construction; 120,600 in car building; 77,100 in electrical engineering; 33,500 in textile industry.

ROADS. At 1 Jan. 1969 there were in Lower Saxony 26,378 km of 'classified' roads, including 706 km of autobahn, 5,173 km of federal roads, 8,669 km of first-class and 11,830 km of second-class highways.

Number of motor vehicles, 1 July 1969, was 1,802,932, including 1,446,900 passenger cars, 117,509 lorries, 4,462 buses, 205,106 tractors, 28,955 motor cycles.

STATISTICAL INFORMATION. The 'Niedersächsisches Landesverwaltungsamt—Abteilung Statistik' (Auestr. 14, Hanover) fulfils the function of the 'Statistisches Landesamt für Niedersachsen'. *Head of Division:* Leitender Regierungsdirektor Dr Hans Kraus. Main publications are: *Statistisches Jahrbuch für Niedersachsen* (from 1950).—*Statistische Monatshefte für Niedersachsen* (from 1947).—*Statistik von Niedersachsen.*

LAND LIBRARY. Niedersächsische Staats- und Universitätsbibliothek, Göttingen. *Director:* Professor W. Grunwald.

NORTH RHINE–WESTPHALIA
Nordrhein–Westfalen

GOVERNMENT. The Land Nordrhein–Westfalen is governed by a coalition of Social Democrats and Free Democrats; Minister President, Heinz Kühn (SPD). The Diet, elected on 10 July 1966, consists of 99 Social Democrats, 86 Christian Democrats, 15 Free Democrats.

AREA AND POPULATION. The Land comprises 34,039 sq. km including the territories reincorporated from the Netherlands on 1 Aug. 1963. It is divided into 6 areas, 35 urban and 57 rural districts. Capital Düsseldorf. Population, 31 Dec. 1968, 16,950,515 (8,100,872 males, 8,849,643 females).

VITAL STATISTICS for calendar years:

	Live births	Marriages	Divorces	Deaths
1966	294,493	136,125	15,522	188,676
1967	286,001	142,295	17,301	187,880
1968	269,761	117,589	16,542	202,229

RELIGION. On 6 June 1961 (census) there were 42·8% Protestants and 52·1% Roman Catholics.

EDUCATION. In 1968 there were 5,800 primary schools with 43,059 teachers and 1,595,782 pupils; 620 special schools with 4,377 teachers and 88,192 pupils; 477 intermediate schools with 7,486 teachers and 220,202 pupils; 591 high schools with 15,819 teachers and 367,231 pupils; 4 Freie Waldorf schools with 102 teachers and 1,742 pupils; 357 part-time vocational schools with 6,542 teachers and 507,140 pupils; 620 full-time vocational schools with 2,521 teachers and 56,344 pupils; 253 advanced vocational schools with 1,273 teachers and 18.607 pupils; 603 schools for public health occupations with 6,745 teachers and 19,066 pupils. There were also 64 (full-time and part-time) institutions for the training of technicians with 7,868 participants, and 42 colleges of engineering with 1,708 teachers and 17,362 students.

In the winter term 1968–69 there were 5 universities (Bochum, 7,394 students; Bonn, 14,502; Düsseldorf, 1,185; Cologne, 18,431; Münster, 17,310); the Technical University of Aachen (9,595); 1 Roman Catholic and 2 Protestant theological colleges with together 589 students. There were also 15 teacher-training colleges with 18,771 students; 3 colleges of music, 1 college of fine arts and the college for physical education in Cologne with together 2,467students.

HEALTH. There were, in 1968, 744 hospitals with 190,983 beds.

SOCIAL WELFARE. In 1968 public assistance (including aid to tuberculars) and aid to war victims amounted to DM 1,055m. or DM 62·24 per head of population.

JUSTICE. There are a constitutional court (*Verfassungsgerichtshof*), 3 courts of appeal, 19 regional courts, 168 local courts, 2 Land labour courts, 29 labour courts, a Land social court, 8 social courts, 2 finance courts, a higher administrative court, 7 administrative courts.

LABOUR. The economically active persons totalled 6,841,000 at the 1%-sample survey of the microcensus of April 1968. Of the total, 674,000 were self-employed, 294,000 unpaid family workers, 5,873,000 employees; 327,000 were engaged in agriculture and forestry, 3,706,000 in power supply, mining, manufacturing and building, 1·24m. in commerce and transport, 1,568,000 in other industries and services.

AGRICULTURE. Area and yield of the most important crops:

	Area (in 1,000 hectares)			Yield (in 1,000 metric tons)		
	1966	1967	1968	1966	1967	1968
Wheat	167·2	168·4	172·2	523·0	730·6	761·6
Rye	242·0	234·2	233·3	666·4	840·3	775·6
Barley	189·6	201·5	207·8	625·0	812·6	847·0
Oats	95·2	99·5	99·3	291·0	338·1	353·2
Potatoes	74·0	67·9	65·8	1,948·1	2,109·2	1,983·4
Sugar-beet	64·2	66·4	58·3	2,823·3	3,267·8	2,825·6

Livestock, 3 Dec. 1968: Cattle, 1,933,078 (including 787,623 milch cows); pigs, 3,758,105; sheep, 135,726; goats, 5,988; horses, 60,163; poultry, 20,360,934.

INDUSTRY. In June 1969, 15,783 establishments (with 10 and more employees) employed 2,609,966 persons; of these, 248,854 were employed in mining; 337,004 in machine construction; 232,575 in iron and steel production; 215,839 in chemical industry; 189,514 in electrical engineering; 159,071 in textile industry.

Output and/or production in 1,000 metric tons, 1968: Hard coal, 100,751; lignite, 87,871; pig-iron, 21,160; raw steel ingots, 29,139; rolled steel, 19,232; castings (iron, steel and malleable castings), 1,953; cement, 12,132; fireproof products, 902; sulphuric acid (including production of cokeries), 2,001; thomas meal, 200; staple fibres and rayon, 90; metalworking machines, 116; equipment for smelting works and rolling mills, 88; machines for mining industry, 158; cranes and hoisting machinery, 47; installation implements, 31; cables and electric lines, 266; springs of all kinds, 139; chains of all kinds, 91; locks and fittings, 182; spun yarns, 235; electric power, 101,913m. kwh.; gas (including cokery-gas of industry), 14,191m. cu. metres. Of the total population, 15·3% were engaged in industry.

ROADS. There were (1 Jan. 1968) 27,666 km of 'classified' roads, including 787 km of autobahn, 5,675 km of federal roads, 12,212 km of first-class and 8,992 km of second-class highways. Number of motor vehicles, 1 July 1969, 3,908,600, including 3,382,500 passenger cars, 278,500 lorries, 10,900 buses, 179,800 tractors and 56,900 motor cycles.

STATISTICAL INFORMATION. The Statistisches Landesamt (Ludwig-Beck-St. 23, Düsseldorf) was founded in 1946, by amalgamating the provincial statistical offices of Rhineland and Westphalia. *President:* Dr E. Schon. The Landesamt publishes: *Statistisches Jahrbuch Nordrhein–Westfalen.* From 1949.—*Statistische Rundschau für das Land Nordrhein–Westfalen.* Monthly from Jan. 1949.—*Statistisches Taschenbuch Nordrhein–Westfalen.* From 1955.

LAND LIBRARY. Landes- und Stadtbibliothek, Grabbeplatz 7, Düsseldorf. *Director:* Dr E. Galley.

RHINELAND–PALATINATE
Rheinland–Pfalz

CONSTITUTION. The constitution of the Land Rheinland–Pfalz was approved by the Consultative Assembly on 25 April 1947 and by referendum on 18 May 1947, when 579,002 voted for and 514,338 against its acceptance.

The elections of 23 April 1967 returned 49 Christian Democrats, 39 Social Democrats, 8 Free Democrats, 4 National Democrats.

The cabinet is a coalition of Christian Democrats and Free Democrats, headed by Dr Helmut Kohl (Christian Democrat).

AREA AND POPULATION. Rheinland–Pfalz comprises 19,837 sq. km. Capital Mainz. Population (at 31 Dec. 1968), 3,644,500 (1,728,700 males, 1,915,800 females).

VITAL STATISTICS for calendar years:

	Live births	Marriages	Divorces	Deaths
1966	64,249	26,844	2,736	40,758
1967	61,090	27,875	3,114	41,041
1968	58,533	25,695	3,346	44,219

RELIGION. On 6 June 1961 (census) there were 41·9% Protestants and 56·2% Roman Catholics.

EDUCATION. In 1968 there were 2,615 primary schools with 12,625 teachers and 409,234 pupils; 112 special schools with 664 teachers and 10,202 pupils; 74 intermediate schools with 1,133 teachers and 30,712 pupils; 128 high schools with 3,673 teachers and 90,561 pupils; 82 part-time vocational schools with 1,556 teachers and 118,844 pupils; 168 full-time vocational schools with 480 teachers and 12,535 pupils; 62 advanced vocational schools with 276 teachers and 4,049 pupils; 107 schools for public health occupations with 885 teachers and 3,144 pupils. There were also 16 (full-time and part-time) institutions for the training of technicians with 1,082 participants and 10 colleges of engineering with 227 teachers and 2,603 students.

In the winter term 1968–69 there were the University of Mainz (10,883 students) and the Roman Catholic theological college in Trier (270). There were also 6 teacher-training colleges with 4,204 students.

HEALTH. There were, in 1968, 229 hospitals with 41,892 beds.

SOCIAL WELFARE. In 1968 public assistance (including aid to tuberculars) and aid to war victims amounted to DM 149m. or DM 40·80 per head of population.

JUSTICE. There are a constitutional court (*Verfassungsgerichtshof*), 2 courts of appeal, 8 regional courts, 61 local courts, a Land labour court, 4 labour courts, a Land social court, 3 social courts, a finance court, a higher administrative court, 2 administrative courts.

LABOUR. The economically active persons totalled 1,561,000 at the 1%-sample survey of the microcensus of April 1968. Of the total, 218,000 were self-employed, 210,000 unpaid family workers, 1,134,000 employees; 274,000 were engaged in agriculture and forestry, 661,000 in power supply, mining, manu-facturing and building, 255,000 in commerce and transport, 371,000 in other industries and services.

AGRICULTURE. Area and yield of the most important products:

	Area (1,000 hectares)			Yield (1,000 metric tons)		
	1966	1967	1968	1966	1967	1968
Wheat	116·5	121·5	130·7	376·9	506·2	487·2
Rye	63·2	58·9	52·4	178·0	196·3	163·2
Barley	88·1	88·3	90·7	256·9	327·1	316·6
Oats	65·0	66·8	70·4	184·7	218·4	216·0
Potatoes	60·9	54·5	55·0	1,565·0	1,627·0	1,498·9
Sugar-beet	19·6	18·7	19·5	985·0	959·1	1,066·6
Wine (1,000 hectolitres)	48·1	48·7	49·2	3,457·1	4,544·2	4,339·1
Tobacco	1·0	1·1	1·1	3·3	3·0	3·1

Livestock (3 Dec. 1968): Cattle, 755,300 (including 293,800 milch cows); horses, 19,500; sheep, 47,300; goats, 2,100; pigs, 786,900; poultry, 5,069,100.

INDUSTRY. In June 1969, 2,998 establishments (with 10 and more employees) employed 382,500 persons; of these 69,500 were employed in chemical industry; 36,900 in production of leather goods and footwear; 44,300 in machine construction; 25,300 in processing stones and earthenware.

ROADS. There were (1 Jan. 1969) 18,047 km of 'classified' roads, including 184 km of autobahn, 3,396 km of federal roads, 6,792 km of first-class and 7,675 of second-class highways. Number of motor vehicles, 1 July 1969, was 948,055, including 744,575 passenger cars, 63,133 lorries, 2,447 buses, 119,189 tractors and 18,711 motor cycles.

STATISTICAL INFORMATION. The Statistisches Landesamt (Mainzer St., 15–16, Bad Ems) was established in 1946. *President:* Dr Nellessen. Its publications include: *Statistisches Jahrbuch für Rheinland–Pfalz* (from 1948); *Statistische Monatshefte Rheinland–Pfalz* (from 1948); *Statistik von Rheinland–Pfalz* (from 1947) 200 vols. to date; *Rheinland–Pfalz im Spiegel der Statistik* (1968).

Klöpper, R., and Körber, J., *Rheinland–Pfalz in seiner Gliederung nach zentralörtlichen Bereichen.* Remagen, 1957

Süsterhenn, A., and Schäfer, H., *Verfassung von Rheinland–Pfalz: Kommentar.* Koblenz, 1950

SAARLAND

HISTORY. In 1919 the Saar territory was placed under the control of the League of Nations. Following a plebiscite, the territory reverted to Germany in 1935. In 1945 the territory became part of the French Zone of occupation, and was in 1947 accorded an international status inside an economic union with France. In pursuance of the German–French agreement signed in Luxembourg on 27 Oct. 1956 the territory returned to Germany on 1 Jan. 1957. Its reintegration with Germany was completed by 5 July 1959.

CONSTITUTION. Saarland now ranks as a *Land* of the Federal German Republic and is represented in the Federal Diet by 8 members. The constitution passed on 15 Dec. 1947 is being revised.

The Saar Diet, elected on 27 June 1965, is composed as follows: 24 Christian Democrats, 21 Social Democrats, 4 Saarland Democrats Party, 1 Saarland Peoples Party/Christian Peoples Party (SVP/CVP).

Saarland is governed by a coalition of Christian Democrats and Saarland Democrats. Minister President, Dr Franz Josef Röder (Chr. Dem.).

AREA AND POPULATION. Saarland has an area of 2,568 sq. km. Estimated population, 31 Dec. 1968, 1,128,902 (535,709 males, 593,500 females). The capital is Saarbrücken.

VITAL STATISTICS for calendar years:

	Live births	Marriages	Divorces	Deaths
1966	19,455	7,885	571	11,685
1967	18,620	8,373	644	12,045
1968	17,358	7,573	566	12,875

RELIGION. On 6 June 1961 (census) 73·3% of the population were Roman Catholics and 24·9% were Protestants.

EDUCATION. In 1968 there were 565 primary schools with 3,975 teachers and 133,217 pupils; 47 special schools with 314 teachers and 5,498 pupils; 15 intermediate schools with 375 teachers and 9,747 pupils; 46 high schools with 1,224 teachers and 29,455 pupils; 43 part-time vocational schools with 583 teachers and 38,685 pupils; 73 full-time vocational schools with 291 teachers and 5,805 pupils; 24 vocational extension schools with 33 teachers and 3,230 pupils; 11 advanced vocational schools with 52 teachers and 880 pupils; 35 schools for public health occupations with 543 teachers and 1,413 pupils. There were also

7 (full-time and part-time) institutions for the training of technicians with 345 participants, and 2 colleges of engineering with 89 teachers and 905 students.

In the winter term 1968–69 there was the University of Saarbrücken with 7,687 students; (1967–68) 3 teacher-training colleges with 1,105 students (1 of them with 163 students is incorporated in the university; these students are counted twice); (1968–69) 1 college of music with 193 students.

HEALTH. There were in 1968, 49 hospitals with 12,167 beds.

SOCIAL WELFARE. In 1968 public assistance (including aid to tuberculars) and aid to war victims amounted to DM 56·5m. or DM 50·07 per head of population.

JUSTICE. There are a constitutional court (*Verfassungsgerichtshof*), a court of appeal, a regional court, 16 local courts, a Land labour court, 3 labour courts, a Land social court, a social court, a finance court, a higher administrative court, an administrative court.

LABOUR. The economically active persons totalled 395,000 at the 1%-sample survey of the microcensus of April 1968. Of the total, 36,000 were self-employed, 15,000 unpaid family workers, 344,000 employees; 15,000 were engaged in agriculture and forestry, 209,000 in power supply, mining, manufacturing and building, 78,000 in commerce and transport, 93,000 in other industries and services.

AGRICULTURE AND FORESTRY. The cultivated area occupies 133,300 hectares or slightly more than half the total area; the forest area comprises nearly 32% of the total.

Area and yield of the most important crops:

	Area (1,000 hectares)			Yield 1,000 metric tons)		
	1966	*1967*	*1968*	*1966*	*1967*	*1968*
Wheat	12·7	12·4	12·1	37·8	43·7	39·5
Rye	8·0	8·4	7·9	22·7	27·1	23·5
Barley	7·5	7·6	8·8	19·4	24·7	25·7
Oats	8·5	8·7	8·9	21·5	25·4	25·8
Potatoes	8·2	8·2	8·0	191·9	241·3	222·2
Sugar-beet	0·1	0·1	0·1	4·3	5·1	2·6

Livestock, 4 Dec. 1968: Cattle, 74,400 (including 30,600 milch cows); pigs, 81,700; sheep, 9,200; goats, 1,100; horses, 2,100; poultry, 972,900.

INDUSTRY. In June 1969, 656 establishments (with 10 and more employees) employed 156,600 persons; of these, 28,000 were engaged in coalmining, 37,500 in iron and steel production, 11,600 in machine construction, 10,800 in steel construction. In 1968 the coalmines produced 11·3m. metric tons of coal. Five iron foundries had 15 blast furnaces working and produced 3·8m. metric tons of pig-iron and 4·6m. metric tons of crude steel.

ROADS. At 1 Jan. 1969 there were 1,983 km of 'classified' roads, including 33 km of autobahn, 522 km of federal roads, 708 km of first-class and 719 km of second-class highways. Number of motor vehicles, 1 July 1969, 246,000, including 209,300 passenger cars, 18,000 lorries, 1,000 buses, 9,800 tractors and 7,900 motor cycles.

STATISTICAL INFORMATION. The Statistical Office of the Saar (Saarbrücken 1, Hardenberg-strasse 3) was established on 1 April 1938. As from 1 June 1935, it was an independent agency; its predecessor, 1920–35, was the Statistical Office of the Government Commission of the Saar. *Chief:* Direktor Dr Götz. The most important publications are: *Statistisches Handbuch für das Saarland*, from 1950.—*Statistisches Taschenbuch für das Saarland*, from 1959.—*Saarländische Bevölkerungs- und Wirtschaftszahlen.* Quarterly, from 1949.—*Saarland in Zahlen* (special issues).—*Einzelschriften zur Statistik des Saarlandes*, from 1950.

Fischer, P., *Die Saar zwischen Deutschland und Frankreich.* Frankfurt, 1959
Freymond, J., *Le Conflit sarrois, 1945–55.* Brussels, 1959. [*The Saar Conflict.* New York, 1960]
Schmidt, R. H., *Saarpolitik 1945–57.* 3 vols. Berlin, 1959–62

SCHLESWIG–HOLSTEIN

GOVERNMENT. The elections of 23 April 1967 gave the Christian Democratic Union 34, the Free Democratic Party 4, the Social Democratic Party 30, the National Democratic Party 4 and the South Schleswig Association 1 seat. Minister President, Dr Helmut Lemke (Christian Democrat).

AREA AND POPULATION. The area of Schleswig–Holstein is 15,658 sq. km; it is divided into 4 urban and 17 rural districts and 1,378 communes. The capital is Kiel. The population (estimate, 31 Dec. 1968) numbered 2,528,700 (1,213,100 males, 1,315,600 females).

VITAL STATISTICS for calendar years:

	Live births	Marriages	Divorces	Deaths
1966	45,930	20,750	2,617	29,811
1967	45,351	20,245	2,935	29,556
1968	43,833	19,845	3,030	32,159

RELIGION. On 6 June 1961 (census) there were 88·2% Protestants and 5·6% Roman Catholics.

EDUCATION. In 1968 there were 1,227 primary schools with 7,122 teachers and 223,884 pupils; 111 special schools with 665 teachers and 12,381 pupils, 116 intermediate schools with 1,836 teachers and 42,278 pupils, 75 high schools with 2,477 teachers and 47,011 pupils, 1 Freie Waldorf school with 25 teachers and 441 pupils; 57 part-time vocational schools with 1,057 teachers and 78,067 pupils, 82 full-time vocational schools with 152 teachers and 4,391 pupils, 70 advanced vocational schools with 359 teachers and 4,269 pupils; 53 schools for public health occupations with 650 teachers and 2,007 pupils. There were also 2 (full-time and part-time) institutions for the training of technicians with 634 participants, and 8 colleges of engineering with 207 teachers and 2,817 students.

In the winter term 1968–69 the University of Kiel had 7,476 students. There were also (1968–69) 2 teacher-training colleges and 1 teacher-training course on rehabilitation with together 2,131 students.

HEALTH. There were, in 1968, 125 hospitals with 25,894 beds.

SOCIAL WELFARE. In 1968 public assistance (including aid to tuberculars) and aid to war victims amounted to DM 131m. or DM 55·21 per head of population.

JUSTICE. There are a court of appeal, 4 regional courts, 60 local courts, a Land labour court, 9 labour courts, a Land social court, 4 social courts, a finance court, an administrative court.

LABOUR. The economically active persons totalled 979,000 at the 1%-sample survey of the microcensus of April 1968. Of the total, 115,000 were self-employed, 65,000 unpaid family workers, 799,000 employees; 118,000 were engaged in agriculture and forestry, 375,000 in power supply, mining, manufacturing and building, 208,000 in commerce and transport, 278,000 in other industries and services.

AGRICULTURE. Area and yield of the most important crops:

	Area (1,000 hectares)			Yield 1,000 metric tons		
	1966	1967	1968	1966	1967	1968
Wheat	80·7	83·1	85·8	270·0	350·2	398·9
Rye	70·4	72·8	74·1	184·7	209·8	249·8
Barley	109·5	106·1	103·7	344·6	372·1	404·0
Oats	98·2	100·6	107·5	332·6	360·6	430·4
Potatoes	18·9	17·6	13·9	459·3	515·0	395·9
Sugar-beet	14·5	14·3	13·8	521·1	532·7	534·6

Livestock, 3 Dec. 1968: 16,000 horses, 1·41m. cattle (including 519,000 milch cows), 1,668,000 pigs, 100,000 sheep, 800 goats, 5,154,000 poultry.

FISHERIES. In 1968 the yield of sea and coastal fishing was 97,800 metric tons valued at DM 58·3m.

INDUSTRY. In June 1969, 1,575 establishments (with 10 and more employees) employed 182,800 persons; of these, 21,100 were employed in shipbuilding (except naval engineering); 25,800 in machine construction; 25,800 in food and kindred industry; 16,900 in electrical engineering.

ROADS. There were (1 Jan. 1969) 8,864 km of 'classified' roads including 67 km of autobahn, 2,009 km of federal roads, 3,579 km of first-class and 3,209 km of second-class highways. Number of motor vehicles, 1 July 1969, was 636,127, including 515,512 passenger cars, 45,178 lorries, 1,558 buses, 65,667 tractors, 8,212 motor cycles.

KIEL CANAL. The Kiel Canal, 98·7 km (51 miles) long, is on Schleswig–Holstein territory. In 1938, 53,530 vessels of 22·6m. net tons passed through it; in 1958, 67,738[1] vessels of 33·5m. net tons; in 1964, 82,792[1] vessels of 44·6m. net tons; in 1965, 85,019[1] vessels of 43·4m. net tons; in 1966, 82,827[1] vessels of 43·4m. net tons; in 1967, 80,330[1] vessels of 41·4m. net tons; in 1968, 80,204[1] vessels of 42m. net tons.

STATISTICAL INFORMATION. Statistical Office (Mühlenweg 166, Kiel); *Director:* W. Laskowski. Publications: *Statistisches Taschenbuch Schleswig–Holstein*, from 1954; *Statistisches Jahrbuch Schleswig–Holstein*, from 1951.—*Statistische Monatshefte Schleswig–Holstein*, from 1949.— *Statistische Berichte*, from 1947.—*Beiträge zur historischen Statistik Schleswig–Holstein*, from 1967.

Baxter, R. R., *The Law of international waterways.* Harvard University Press, 1964
Brandt, O., *Grundriss der Geschichte Schleswig–Holsteins.* 5th ed. Kiel, 1957
Handbuch für Schleswig–Holstein. 14th ed. Kiel, 1968

LAND LIBRARY. Schleswig–Holsteinische Landesbibliothek, Kiel, Schloss. *Director:* Dr Olaf Klose.

---

[1] Plus, 1958, 2,873; 1964, 4,042; 1965, 4,626; 1966, 5,366; 1967, 5,501; 1968, 5,836 small sporting craft without indication of their net register tons, which were included in the figures relating to the previous years.

GERMAN DEMOCRATIC REPUBLIC
Deutsche Demokratische Republik

CONSTITUTION AND GOVERNMENT. Upon the establishment of the Federal Republic of Germany, the People's Council of the Soviet-occupied zone, appointed in 1948, was converted into a provisional People's Chamber.

On 7 Oct. 1949 the provisional People's Chamber enacted a constitution of the 'German Democratic Republic'. The republic is, however, not recognized by Britain and most other non-Communist nations.

In July 1952 the 5 Länder of Mecklenburg, Saxony-Anhalt, Brandenburg, Saxony and Thuringia were replaced by 14 districts (*Bezirke*).

A new 'socialist constitution' was approved by a referendum on 6 April 1968, when 94·54% of the electorate voted for the constitution; it came into force on 8–9 April, 1968. The People's Chamber, of 500 deputies, is declared to be 'the supreme organ of state power'; it elects the Council of State, the Council of Ministers, the National Defence Council and the judges of the Supreme Court.

COUNCIL OF STATE. After the death of President Wilhelm Pieck (7 Sept. 1960), the People's Chamber on 12 Sept. 1960 abolished the office of president and elected instead a council of state. This consists of a chairman, 6 deputy chairmen, 16 members and a secretary. The Council is authorized to issue decrees and decisions with the force of law and to interpret existing laws. The Chairman of the Council of State represents the GDR in international law. *Chairman:* Walter Ulbricht.

On 20 Sept. 1961 the People's Chamber passed a 'law for the defence of the GDR'; the chairman is authorized to declare a 'state of defence' to put the law into operation.

At the elections held on 2 July 1967, the list of the National Front received 99·93% of the valid votes.

The cabinet was, in Dec. 1970, composed as follows:

Prime Minister: Willi Stoph (Socialist Unity Party).

Deputy Prime Ministers: Alfred Neumann, Alexander Abusch, Kurt Fichtner, Wolfgang Rauchfuss, Gerhard Schürer, Gerhard Weiss, Herbert Weiz, Manfred Flegel, Max Sefrin, Werner Titel, Kurt Wünsche.

Members of the Presidium of the Council of Ministers: All members of the cabinet and Siegfried Böhme, Georg Ewald, Walter Halbritter and 8 other Ministers.

National flag: Black, red, golden (horizontal); in the centre, on both sides, the coat of arms showing a hammer and compass with a wreath of grain entwined with a black, red and golden ribbon.

National hymn: Auferstanden aus Ruinen (words by Johannes R. Becher, tune by Hanns Eisler).

East Berlin ('Democratic Berlin') is the capital of the German Democratic Republic. *Head of the Administration:* Herbert Fechner.

AREA AND POPULATION. Area and population (31 Dec. 1969):

Districts	Area in sq. km	Male	Female	Total	Per sq. km
Rostock	7,074	403,581	452,643	856,224	121
Schwerin	8,672	279,246	318,795	598,041	69
Neubrandenburg	10,792	302,766	336,816	639,582	59
Potsdam	12,568	523,747	609,884	1,133,631	90
Frankfurt/O	7,185	316,063	361,056	677,119	94
Cottbus	8,262	399,900	457,453	857,353	104
Magdeburg	11,525	609,842	710,746	1,320,588	115
Halle	8,771	896,811	1,034,079	1,930,890	220
Erfurt	7,348	581,167	674,655	1,255,822	171
Gera	4,004	339,819	397,929	737,748	184
Suhl	3,856	258,452	294,435	552,887	143
Dresden	6,738	846,346	1,030,785	1,877,131	279
Leipzig	4,966	677,495	818,937	1,496,432	301
Karl-Marx-Stadt[1]	6,009	933,718	1,123,482	2,057,200	342
Berlin (East)	403	482,620	601,236	1,083,856	2,690
German Democratic Republic	108,173[2]	7,851,573	9,222,931	17,074,504	158

[1] Formerly Chemnitz.   [2] 41,722 sq. miles.

The population was steadily decreasing from its peak at the end of 1947 with 19,102,000 to 17,003,655 in 1964, but has been rising since.

An agreement proclaiming the Oder–Neisse line the permanent frontier between Germany and Poland was concluded between the German Democratic Republic and Poland on 6 July 1950. A protocol on the delimitation of the frontier was signed on 27 Jan. 1951.

Resident population of the principal towns as at 31 Dec. 1969:

Leipzig	585,803	Magdeburg	269,690	Zwickau	127,395
Dresden	501,184	Halle	259,957	Gera	111,398
Karl-Marx-Stadt (Chemnitz)	298,543	Rostock	195,144	Potsdam	110,750
		Erfurt	194,547		

VITAL STATISTICS:

	Marriages	Live births	Deaths	Divorces
1967	117,146	252,817	227,068	28,303
1968	119,676	245,143	242,473	28,721
1969	125,233	239,256	243,368	28,908

Crude birth rate per 1,000 population was 16·5 in 1965; 15·7 in 1966; 14·8 in 1967; 14·3 in 1968; 14 in 1969[1]; marriage rate, 7·6 in 1965; 7·1 in 1966; 6·9 in 1967; 7 in 1968; 7.3 in 1969; death rate, 13·5 in 1965; 13·2 in 1966; 13·3 in 1967; 14·2 in 1968; 14.3 in 1969; infantile mortality per 100 live births 2·5 in 1965; 2·3 in 1966; 2·1 in 1967; 2 in 1968 and 1969.

[1] Preliminary.

RELIGION. According to the census of 1950, 80·5% of the population were Protestants and 11% were Roman Catholics; the 1964 census gave 59·4% Protestants and 8·1% Roman Catholics.

EDUCATION. There are 2 types of schools: (a) the Polytechnical High Schools, with 10 grades (the former elementary and middle schools), numbering (1969) 6,923 with 2,485,367 pupils; (b) the Extended Polytechnical High Schools, with 12 grades, numbering (1969) 304 with 51,923 pupils.

In addition there were (1969) 1,153 vocational schools (*Berufsschulen*) with 14,956 teachers and 456,631 pupils and (1969) 188 technical schools with 151,000 pupils. There were also 54 universities and other high schools with (1962) 4,275 professors, 6,780 assistants and (1969) 122,790 full-time students, including 41,661 women.

CINEMAS (1969). There were 864 cinemas with a seating capacity of 319,710.

NEWSPAPERS (1966). There were 40 daily newspapers with a combined circulation of 6·2m.

HEALTH. In 1969, 641 hospitals had 192,026 beds. There were 444 policlinics each with at least 5 special branches. There were 25,943 physicians and 7,058 dentists.

SOCIAL WELFARE. In Dec. 1969 there were 63,412 recipients of welfare benefits. Expenditure for social welfare was M 118,328,000 in 1963.

FINANCE. Currency. The circulating Reichsmark notes were in June 1948 exchanged for 'Deutsche Mark' (East), renamed 'Mark of the German Bank of Issue' (MDN) from 1 Aug. 1964. The circulation of notes and coins at 31 Dec. 1969 was M 7,045 m. Since 1 Nov. 1953 the DM (East) currency has been based on gold, the gold content of the DM (East) being fixed at 0·399902 gramme. This fixation (which would mean a relation of £1 = M 6·22, $1 = M 2·22) has not been recognized by the International Monetary Fund.

Budget. The budget of the German Democratic Republic was as follows (in M 1m.) for calendar years:

	1964	1965	1966	1967	1968	1969
Revenue	56,885	56,361	61,329	59,542	60,183	65,761
Expenditure	56,317	55,759	60,831	59,026	59,505	65,004

Of the 1969 expenditures, 26,235m. was earmarked for health and social services, education and *Kultur* and 5,800m. for defence.

FISHERIES. Total catch (1969) 309,931 metric tons. Inland catch was 13,567 metric tons, of which 9,457 tons was carp. The fishing fleet in 1966 had 72,406 GRT.

DEFENCE. On 18 Jan. 1956 the Diet passed laws for the establishment of a 'national people's army' and a defence ministry. A 12-member defence council, under the chairmanship of W. Ulbricht, First Secretary of the Central Committee, was set up on 10 Feb. 1960.

The 'law for the defence of the GDR', of 20 Sept. 1960, makes military service (in case of emergency) and civil defence compulsory for all citizens.

Conscription for men between 18 and 25 years was introduced on 24 Jan. 1962 (18 months' service in the army, 2 years in the navy and air force).

Army. The Army, set up on 1 March 1956, is organized in 2 army corps, including 2 armoured divisions and 4 motorized infantry divisions. They are armed with 1,800 tanks (mostly Soviet T-54 and T-55), 300 self-propelled guns and ground-to-air 'Guideline' missiles. The Border Police was incorporated in the Army in Sept. 1961. The total strength is 85,000 all ranks.

Police. The police force (*Volkspolizei*) numbered 20,000 security and 70,000 border troops. There are also 250,000 militiamen organized in combat groups. The militia receive military instruction by the People's Police.

Navy. The 'People's Navy' includes 4 escorts, 12 missile boats, 16 minesweepers, 67 torpedo-boats, 24 inshore minesweepers, 26 patrol vessels, 5 coastal minesweepers, 60 coastguard boats, 18 landing craft, 7 oilers, 20 auxiliary ships and 10 tugs. Personnel (1970), 16,000 all ranks.

Air Force. The *ex*-'air-police', set up in Nov. 1950, had in 1970 a strength of about 21,000 officers and men and 275 combat aircraft. Two fighter divisions consist each of 3 or 4 wings (each with nominal 3 squadrons of 16 aircraft), equipped mainly with MiG-21 supersonic day and all-weather interceptors and Su-7 supersonic ground attack fighters. These types replaced earlier MiG-19 and MiG-17 fighters, some of which remain in service. Other units include a wing of Mi-1 and Mi-4 helicopters, a wing of Il-14, An-2, An-14, An-24 and 1 or 2 Tu-124 jet transports and a Flight Training Division with Yak-18, Trener, L-29 Delfin, MiG-15UTI and MiG-21UTI training aircraft. 'Guideline' surface-to-air missile units are operational.

Twenty Soviet divisions of about 258,000 men with about 1,000 heavy tanks and 6,000 armoured vehicles are stationed in the German Democratic Republic, chiefly along the Polish border.

AGRICULTURE AND FORESTRY. In 1969 the arable land was 4,636,370 hectares; meadows and pastures 1,461,285 hectares; forests, 2,946,826 hectares. Since 1945, the estates of Junkers, war criminals and leading Nazis have been sequestrated; 3·1m. hectares have been distributed among farmers. In 1969 there were 9,836 collective farms of 5·41m. hectares, 527 state farms of 434,035 hectares.

The yield of the main crops in 1969 was as follows (in 1,000 metric tons): Wheat, 1,987; rye, 1,544; barley, 2,067; oats, 841; potatoes, 8,832; sugarbeet, 4,856.

Livestock (in 1,000) on 31 Dec. 1969: Cattle, 5,171 (including 2,166·9 milch cows); pigs, 9,237; sheep, 1,696·1; goats, 157·9; horses, 144·7; poultry, 42,565.

The Ministry of Agriculture was abolished on 8 Feb. 1963 and replaced by an Agricultural Council.

MINING. In the production of lignite, the German Democratic Republic takes first place in world output. Rare metals, such as uranium, cobalt, bismuth, arsenic and antimony, are being exploited in the western Erzgebirge and eastern Thuringia. Annual output of silver, about 4·8m. troy oz.

The principal minerals raised are as follows (in 1,000 metric tons):

	1967	1968	1969		1967	1968	1969
Coal	1,789	1,579	2,346	Copper ore	1,268	. .	. .
Lignite	242,027	247,027	254,533	Potash	2,206	2,293	2,346
Iron Ore	1,680	1,414	899				

INDUSTRY. Industry produced about 60% of the national income in 1969; the nationally owned and co-operative undertakings were responsible for 82·6% of the gross national product and the semi-state enterprises for 11·4%. The percentage of privately owned enterprises was 29·3 in 1950 and 6·1 in 1969.

There were, at 31 Dec. 1969, 12,255 industrial establishments employing 2,818,756 employees, including 3,416 private firms with 79,549 employees.

Production of iron and steel (in 1,000 metric tons):

	1964	1965	1966	1967	1968	1969
Crude steel	3,851·7	3,890·0	4,084·5	4,243·2	4,695·4	4,823·8
Pig-iron	2,259·9	2,338·0	2,447·7	2,525·0	2,332·9	2,098·3
Rolled steel	2,900·3	2,986·3	3,051·0	3,075·2	3,156·0	3,181·9

Leading chemical products in 1969 were (in 1,000 metric tons): Nitrogen fertilizers, 391; synthetic rubber, 114; sulphuric acid, 1,104; calcined soda, 606; caustic soda, 394; ammonia, 593; other industrial products: cement, 7,410; cotton fabrics, 237m. sq. metres; leather shoes, 33·7m. pairs.

The 340-km pipeline from Schwedt on the Oder to Leuna near Halle was completed in Jan. 1967; it carries Soviet oil direct to the industrial centre of East Germany. Total pipeline length within GDR (1969) 649 km.

POWER. Generation of electric power (in 1m. kwh.): 1950, 19,466; 1960, 40,305; 1962, 45,063; 1964, 51,032; 1965, 53,611; 1966, 56,866; 1967, 59,686; 1968, 63,230; 1969, 65,463.

W. F. Stolper, *The Structure of the East German Economy.* Harvard Univ. Press, 1960

COMMERCE. The distribution of trade with the main groups of countries was as follows (in 1m. Valuta-Mark; 4·20 Valuta-Marks = US$1):

	Socialist countries		West Germany		Other countries		Total	
	Import	Export	Import	Export	Import	Export	Import	Export
1967	10,056·0	10,915·8	1,288·5	1,249·0	2,426·4	1,350·4	13,770·9	14,515·2
1968	10,743·7	12,194·9	1,227·3	1,409·9	2,293·2	2,318·0	14,249·8	15,922·8
1969	12,498·4	12,741·5	1,953·9	1,535·2	2,786·8	3,166·3	17,237·1	17,443·0

In 1969 goods valued at 7,326m. Valuta-Mark came from, and 6,961·7m. went to, the USSR.

Total trade between the German Democratic Republic and UK (British Board of Trade returns, in £1,000 sterling):

	1965	1966	1967	1968	1969	1970
Imports to UK	12,102	13,538	12,088	17,556	14,620	16,082
Exports from UK	8,064	15,913	13,587	11,643	12,131 }	
Re-exports from UK	220	511	3,469	809	624 }	16,901

ROADS. There were, in 1969, 45,737 km of classified roads. Road traffic amounted to 10,749m. ton-km of goods and 16,332m. passenger-km (by buses). Motor vehicles included 1,039,229 passenger cars, 209,783 lorries, 2·79m. motor cycles.

RAILWAYS. There were, in 1969, 14,909 km of railway line, of which 1,285 km were electrified. Traffic amounted to 39,445m. ton-km of goods and 17,610m. passenger-km.

SHIPPING. The port of Rostock is being reconstructed and enlarged so as to absorb the whole sea-going traffic of the German Democratic Republic and the Czechoslovak hinterland. Sea-going traffic in 1969 was 5,026 vessels of 10·87m. BRT. In 1969 navigable inland waterways had a length of 2,519 km; they handled 1,834m. ton-km of goods. The state-owned merchant fleet had, in 1969, 169 vessels of 878,130 BRT.

AVIATION. The Lufthansa of the GDR was in Aug. 1963 taken over by Interflug. It had (1969) 33 aircraft, mostly Ilyushin 14, and operates services between East Berlin and Prague, Warsaw, Budapest, Bucharest, Moscow, Sofia, Belgrade, Tirana, Cairo and Kiev. Passengers carried (1969), 809,500; freight, 15,878 metric tons.

POST. In 1969 there were 11,869 post offices and agencies and 918,793 telephone subscribers. Number of wireless licences, 5·98m.; television licences, 4·34m.

BANKING. The 'German Bank of Issue' in Berlin, set up in June 1948, is the central institute for the 'Emissions- and Girobanken' established in April 1947 in the 5 Länder of the Soviet Zone. Savings, as at 31 Dec. 1969, totalled 48,049m. M.

DIPLOMATIC REPRESENTATIVES

The German Democratic Republic maintains embassies in:

Albania	Cuba	Poland
Algeria	Czechoslovakia	Romania
Bulgaria	Guinea	Somalia
Cambodia	Hungary	Sudan
Central African Republic	Iraq	Syria
Ceylon	Korea (North)	USSR
China	Maldives, Republic of	Vietnam (North)
Congo (Br.)	Mongolia	Yugoslavia

and has commercial representatives in 33 other countries.

BOOKS OF REFERENCE

STATISTICAL INFORMATION. The central statistical agency is the Staatliche Zentralverwaltung für Statistik (Hans-Beimler-Str. 70–72, 102, Berlin).
  The Zentralverwaltung publishes: *Statistisches Jahrbuch der Deutschen Demokratischen Republik* from 1956).—*Statistisches Taschenbuch der DDR* (annual, from 1959; also Arabic, English, French, Russian, Spanish, Swedish editions).—*Statistische Praxis* (monthly, from 1946).
  Jahrbuch der Deutschen Demokratischen Republik, ed. Institut für Zeitgeschichte (latest issue 1961).

Childs, D., *East Germany*. London, 1969
Hornsby, L. (ed.), *Profile of East Germany*. London, 1966

NATIONAL LIBRARY. Deutsche Bücherei, Leipzig C.1. *Director:* Helmut Rötzsch.—Deutsche Staatsbibliothek, Berlin. *Director:* Professor H. Kunze.

GREECE

Vasileion tis Ellados

HISTORY. Greece gained her independence from Turkey in 1821–29, and by the Protocol of London, of 3 Feb. 1830, was declared a kingdom, under the guarantee of Great Britain, France and Russia. For details of the subsequent history to 1947 *see* THE STATESMAN'S YEAR-BOOK, 1957, pp. 1069–70.

National flag: Blue and white, horizontal; with white cross in top-left corner.
  National anthem: Se gnorizo apo tin kopsi (words by Dionysios Solomos, 1824; tune by N. Mantzaros, 1828).

REIGNING KING. Constantine II, born 2 June 1940, married 18 Sept. 1964 Princess Anne-Marie, daughter of King Frederik IX of Denmark (born 30 Aug. 1946); succeeded his father Paul I on 6 March 1964. *Offspring:* Princess Alexia, born 10 July 1965; Crown Prince Paul, born 20 May 1967; Prince Nicolaos, born 1 Oct. 1969.
  The King's privy purse provides for £202,000 per annum.

Mother of the King: Queen Frederika, born 18 April 1917, daughter of Duke Ernest Augustus of Brunswick; married Prince Paul on 9 Jan. 1938.

Sisters of the King: Princess Sophia, born 2 Nov. 1938, married Prince Juan Carlos of Spain on 14 May 1962; Princess Irene, born 11 May 1942.

Greek Rulers

Othon (Prince Otto of Bavia) 18 Jan. 1833–23 Oct. 1862 (dethroned).
Georgios I (Prince William of Denmark) 1863–18 March 1913 (assassinated).
Constantine I, 18 March 1913–11 June 1917 (expelled), 19 Dec. 1920–27 Sept. 1922 (abdicated).
Alexander, 11 June 1917–25 Oct. 1920.

Georgios II, 27 Sept. 1922–19 Dec. 1923 (expelled), 25 Nov. 1935–30 Dec. 1944, 1 Sept 1946–1 April 1947.
Republic, 13 April 1924–3 Nov. 1935.
Regency, 30 Dec. 1944–1 Sept. 1946.
Paulos I, 1 April 1947–6 March 1964.
Constantine II, 6th March 1964–.

GOVERNMENT AND CONSTITUTION. On 22 Dec. 1951, Parliament ratified a new Constitution, which came into force on 1 Jan. 1952, amending the Constitution of 1911.

A revolution took place on 21 April 1967, 'to avert the danger of a communist threat against the nation'. A National Government was formed, which suspended certain articles of the 1952 Constitution and took over all constitutional and legislative powers.

Following the unsuccessful counter-coup on 13 Dec. 1967, King Constantine went abroad. The exercising of the King's duties was entrusted to Lieut.-Gen. G. Zoetakis, who acts as Regent in the name of the King.

A committee of legal experts, under the Chairmanship of the former President of the Council of State, worked out a draft constitution. This was submitted to a referendum on 29 Sept. 1968, in which, out of a total of 5,048,981 votes, 4,638,543 approved and 392,923 rejected the constitution; 1,467,304 voters abstained.

Three new institutions are introduced by the draft Constitution: (a) The National Council which will advise the King on important decisions including the dissolution of Parliament. (b) The Constitutional Court which, *inter alia*, will examine the statutes and aims of parties, prior to their being granted recognition. (c) The National Educational Council, which will ensure the exclusion of education from politics.

In July 1970 the government was composed as follows:

Prime Minister, Minister of National Defence, National Education and Foreign Affairs: George Papadopoulos.

Deputy Premier and Minister of Interior: Stylianos Pattakos. *Deputy Prime Minister and Minister of Interior:* Stylianos Pattakos. *Co-ordination:* Nickolas Makarezos; *Alternate:* Emmanouel Fthenakis. *Justice:* Angelos Tsoukalas. *Finance:* Adamantios Androutsopoulos. *Commerce:* Spyridon Zappas. *Industry:* Constantine Kypraios. *Public Works:* Constantine Panadimitriou. *Communications:* George Vallis. *Agriculture:* John Papavlachopoulos. *Social Service:* George Douvalopoulos. *Mercantile Marine:* John Cholevas. *Labour:* Paul Manolopoulos. *Public Order:* Panayiotis Tzevelekos. *Northern Greece:* Loukas Patras. *Ministers without Portfolio:* Loukas Patras, Nicholas Ephessios. *Alternate Minister to the Prime Minister's Office:* John Agathangelou. *Alternate Minister for National Education:* Nikitas Sioris.

AREA AND POPULATION. The total area is 131,944 sq. km (50,942 sq. miles), of which the islands account for 24,761 sq. km (9,560 sq. miles).

Athens is the capital; population of Greater Athens, in 1961, 1,852,709.

The population of the country was 8,388,553 according to the census of 19 March 1961. Estimate, mid-1966, 8·61m.

The following table shows the prefectures (Nomoi) and their population:

Nomos	Area in sq. km	Population 1961	Capital	Population 1961
Central Greece and Euboea	24,475	970,949		
Aetolia and Acarnania	5,447	237,738	Missolonghi	11,266
Attica (without Athens)	2,496	150,054	Athens	1,852,709
Boeotia	3,211	114,256	Levadeia	12,609
Euboea	3,908	166,097	Chalcis	24,745
Evrytania	2,045	39,716	Karpenissi	3,523
Phthiotis	4,368	160,035	Lamia	21,509
Phokis	2,121	47,842	Amphissa	6,076

Nomos	Area in sq. km	Population 1961	Capital	Population 1961
Peloponnessos	21,439	1,096,390		
Argolis	2,214	90,145	Nauplion	8,918
Arcadia	4,419	135,042	Tripolis	18,500
Akhaïa	3,209	239,206	Patras	95,364
Elia	2,681	188,861	Pyrgos	20,558
Korinthia	2,289	112,505	Korinthos	15,892
Lakonia	3,636	118,661	Sparte	10,412
Messenia	2,991	211,970	Calamata	38,211
Ionian Islands	2,307	212,573		
Zakynthos	406	35,509	Zante	9,506
Kerkyra	641	101,770	Kerkyra	26,991
Kefallenia	935	46,314	Argostolion	7,322
Lefkas	325	28,980	Levkas	6,552
Epirus	9,203	352,604		
Arta	1,612	82,630	Arta	16,399
Thesprotia	1,515	52,125	Hegoumenitsa	3,235
Yannina	4,990	155,326	Yannina	34,997
Preveza	1,086	62,523	Preveza	11,172
Thessaly	13,904	689,927		
Karditsa	2,576	152,543	Karditsa	23,708
Larissa	5,354	230,769	Larisa	55,391
Magnessia	2,636	163,834	Volos	49,221
Trikkala	3,338	142,781	Trikkala	27,876
Macedonia	34,203	1,896,112		
Grevena	2,338	43,484	..	..
Drama	3,468	121,006	Drama	32,195
Imathia	1,699	114,515	Verria	25,765
Thessaloniki	3,560	544,394	Thessaloniki	250,920
Kavala	2,109	140,751	Kavala	44,517
Kastoria	1,685	47,487	Kastoria	10,162
Kilkis	2,597	102,812	Kilkis	10,963
Kozani	3,562	152,809	Kozani	21,537
Pella	2,506	133,224	Edessa	15,534
Pieria	1,548	97,697	Katerini	28,046
Serres	3,987	248,041	Serres	40,063
Florina	1,863	67,356	Florina	11,933
Khalkidiki	2,945	79,849	Polyghyros	3,541
Mount Athos	336	2,687	Karyai	429
Thrace	8,578	356,555		
Evros	4,242	157,760	Alexandroupolis	18,712
Xanthi	1,793	89,594	Xanthi	26,377
Rodopi	2,543	109,201	Komotini	28,335
Aegean Islands	9,071	477,476		
Cyclades	2,572	99,959	Hermoupolis	14,402
Lesvos	2,154	140,251	Mitylini	25,758
Samos	778	52,022	Limin Vatheos	5,469
Khios	904	62,223	Khios	24,053
Dodecanese	2,663	123,021	Rhodes	27,393
Crete	8,331	483,258		
Iraklion	2,641	208,374	Heraklion	63,458
Lassithi	1,818	73,880	Aghios Nikolaos	3,709
Rethymnon	1,496	69,943	Rethymnon	14,999
Canea	2,376	131,061	Canea	38,467

In 1961 cities (*i.e.*, communes of more than 10,000 inhabitants, including Greater Athens) had 3,628,105 inhabitants (43%), towns (*i.e.*, communes with between 2,000 and 9,999 inhabitants), 1,085,856 (13%), villages and rural communities (under 2,000 inhabitants), 3,647,592 (44%).

Mount Athos, the easternmost of the three prongs of the peninsula of Chalcidice, is a self-governing community composed of 20 monasteries. (*See* THE STATESMAN'S YEAR-BOOK, 1945, p. 983.) For centuries the peninsula has been administered by a Council of 4 members and an Assembly of 20 members, 1 deputy from each monastery. The Greek Government on 10 Sept. 1926 recognized this autonomous form of government; Articles 109–112 of the Constitution of 1927 gave legal sanction to the Charter of Mount Athos, drawn up by representatives of the 20 monasteries on 20 May 1924. Article 103 of the 1952 Constitution confirms the special status of Mount Athos.

VITAL STATISTICS (1968): 162,839 live births; 2,434 stillbirths; 1,620 illegitimate births; 81,706 marriages; 71,975 deaths; 5,611 infantile deaths; 42,730 emigrants.

RELIGION. According to the census of 1961, there were 8,118,000 adherents of the Greek Orthodox Church, 35,000 Roman and Greek Catholics, 10,200 Armenians including 9,450 Monophysites, 15,000 Protestants, 8,000 Jehovah's Witnesses, 108,000 Moslems (300 mosques) and 5,800 Hebrews.

The Greek Orthodox Church is under an archbishop and 67 metropolitans, 1 archbishop and 8 metropolitans in Crete, and 4 metropolitans in the Dodecanese. The Roman Catholics have 3 archbishops (in Naxos and Corfu and, not recognized by the State, in Athens) and 2 bishops. The Exarchs of the Greek Catholics and the Armenians are not recognized by the State.

Complete religious freedom is recognized by the Constitution of 1952, but proselytizing from, and interference with, the Greek Orthodox Church is forbidden.

EDUCATION. Elementary education is provided in primary schools for 6 years, starting at $5\frac{1}{2}$ years of age and since 1963 free at all levels.

In Dec. 1969 there were 9,805 public day primary schools with 989,534 pupils; private day primary schools had 43,367 pupils; 431 evening primary state schools 11,742 pupils. Primary school teachers numbered 27,857. 2,194 nursery schools had 55,513 children and 2,334 teachers. Secondary education is provided in public gymnasia for a further 6 years. It is divided into 2 three-year periods. At the end of the first 3 years, the pupils choose between the classical and practical streams of education, the former laying emphasis on classics and the latter on mathematics and science. In Dec. 1969 there were 739 gymnasia with 366,440 pupils and 12,163 teachers. There were also 197 private gymnasia with 45,711 pupils and 3,564 teachers. There were 49 public technical and vocational schools with 15,535 pupils and 255 private with 65,770 pupils.

In 1965–66 there were 2 universities, at Athens (408 professors, 17,180 students) and Thessaloniki (278 professors, 17,814 students), the Athens polytechnic (62 professors, 3,267 students), a high school of commerce (22 professors, 4,779 students) and political science (17 professors, 4,621 students), 2 industrial colleges at Piraeus and Thessaloniki (together 45 professors, 5,428 students), an agricultural college at Athens (56 professors, 891 students). A new university at Patras opened in 1966–67 (40 professors, 144 students).

There are 14 teacher-training colleges with 223 professors, 2,857 students.

Illiteracy in the age groups of 10 years and over was 17% in 1961 (8% among men).

The Greek language consists of 2 branches, *katharevousa*, a conscious revival of classical Greek, used for official purposes and in newspapers, and *demotiki*, the spoken language.

CINEMAS (1965). There were 1,400 cinemas.

NEWSPAPERS (1968). The 9 daily newspapers published in Athens have a combined monthly circulation of 14m. There are also 79 provincial dailies.

HEALTH (1969). There were 901 hospitals and sanatoria with a total of 57,743 beds. There were 13,760 doctors and 3,934 dentists.

FINANCE. Currency. On 11 Nov. 1944 the Greek currency was stabilized at 1 'new' drachma equalling 50,000m. 'old' drachmai. Further readjustments took place in 1946, 1949 and 1953. A 'new issue' of notes and coins was put into circulation on 1 May 1954, 1 new drachma equalling 1,000 old drachmai (72 drachmai = £1; 30 drachmai = US$1). The 'new issue' comprises notes of 50, 100, 500 and 1,000 drachmai and metal coins of 1, 2, 5, 10 and 20 drachmai and 5, 10, 20 and 50 lepta.

Budget. The revenue and expenditure for calendar years were as follows (in 1m. drachmai):

	1964	1965	1966	1967[1]	1968[1]	1969[1]	1970[1]
Revenue	29,506	32,798	38,685	45,630	44,300	51,100	57,500
Expenditure	29,825	33,923	39,039	45,630	42,800	48,600	53,800

[1] Estimates.

Debt. The International Financial Commission was established in Feb. 1898 to control revenue and its disbursal in covering the public debt (from the monopolies of salt, matches etc., receipt stamps, import duties, etc.). This Commission was at first composed of 5 members, but since the end of the Second World War consists only of the representatives of Great Britain and France. The financial and economic agreement between the British and Greek governments of 24 Jan. 1946 provides for negotiations with the view to the termination of the International Financial Commission. By the Franco-Greek agreement of 14 Dec. 1965 the French Government agreed to the termination of the International Financial Commission as soon as possible.

Settlements of the pre-war foreign debts were reached with USA (Oct. 1962), UK (July 1964), France (Dec. 1965) and Sweden (April 1966).

On 22 July 1964 all outstanding economic differences with Czechoslovakia were settled by a payment to Greece of US$200,000.

On 9 July 1964, 12 agreements with Bulgaria were signed. Bulgaria is to pay US$7m. in war reparations, part of which is to be paid in goods or to be offset against flood control of the river Arda. The minimum annual payment has been fixed at US$600,000.

On 2 Sept. 1966 Romania agreed to pay within 4 years £1·25m. in merchandise as a compensation for Greek property nationalized in Romania, and to waive all claims for real property in Greece, valued at £535,000.

On 27 April 1963 Greece and Hungary settled economic matters from the First World War and those arising after the Second World War. Hungary paid Greece the amount of US$200,000. By agreement reached on 21 Nov. 1963, between Greece and Poland, Poland paid Greece US$230,000. By agreement reached on 26 Sept. 1966 between Greece and the UAR, the UAR will pay Greece 65% of the value of every nationalized or expropriated property item belonging to Greek nationals in Egypt; £E15·5m. is the minimum amount to be received by Greece.

DEFENCE. In Aug. 1950 the Ministries of War, Marine and Military Aviation were fused into a single Ministry of National Defence. The General Staff of National Defence is directly responsible to the Minister on general defence questions, besides the special staffs for Army, Navy and Air Force. Defence expenditure in 1967 was 6,955m. drachmai.

Army. Military service is compulsory and universal. Liability begins in the 21st year and lasts up to the 50th. The normal term of service in the active Army is 24 months for all arms, followed by 19 years in the first reserve of the active Army and 10 years in the second. The normal annual contingent of recruits in peace-time is about 50,000. Every 3 months a quarter of the current year's contingent is called up for service.

Since 1945, the organization and establishment of the Army units have been adapted to British models. In Feb. 1952 an American Mission took over from a British Military Mission the training of the Army.

The Army consists of 11 infantry and 1 armoured division and a commando brigade, with a total strength of 118,000 men.

Navy. The Royal Hellenic Navy includes 2 submarines, 8 fleet destroyers, 4 frigates (destroyer escorts), 5 escort minesweepers (corvettes), 2 minelayers, 7 patrol vessels, 14 coastal minesweepers, 7 torpedo boats, a repair ship, 10 landing ships, 14 landing craft, 2 depot ships, a salvage vessel, 7 oilers, 3 lighthouse tenders, 6 water carriers and 14 fleet tugs. Personnel (1970): 1,620 officers and 16,180 ratings (called up for 18 months, or enlisted).

Air Force. The Royal Hellenic Air Force has a strength of about 23,000 officers and men and some 270 operational aircraft, consisting of 2 squadrons of F-104G Starfighters, 4 squadrons F-84F Thunderstreak fighter-bombers (some to be re-equipped with F-5s), 3 squadrons of F-5 fighters, 1 squadron of F-102A Delta

Dagger all-weather interceptors, 1 squadron of RF-84F Thunderflash reconnaissance fighters and 1 squadron of HU-16B Albatross ASW amphibians.
There are also transport, training and helicopter units, and anti-aircraft units
equipped with Nike-Ajax, Nike-Hercules and Hawk surface-to-air missiles. Seven
of the tactical combat squadrons and 1 transport squadron are assigned to
NATO.

The RHAF is organized into Tactical, Training and Materiel Commands.
Training of pilots and ground staff is done in Greece and abroad.

PRODUCTION. Greek economy was completely ruined as the result of the
occupation of the country by the Italians, Germans and Bulgarians from 1941 to
1944.

Of the economically active population in 1961, 53·4% were engaged in agriculture, 13·7% in mining and industry, 7·2% in commerce, 4·6% in building and
construction and 4·1% in transport and communications.

AGRICULTURE. Of the total area only 32% is cultivable, but it supports
50% of the whole population. The total area under cultivation in 1965 was
3,685,053 hectares, forest area was 2,512,418 hectares (445,715 of which is
privately owned).

Among products cultivated in Greece are wheat (about 1m. hectares), which
covers the needs of the Greek people, fodder and export crops, such as cotton
and tobacco, also citrus fruits, grapes, olives, vegetables, apples, peaches, apricots,
etc. Cattle breeding does not cover the requirements, and Greece imports meat
and dairy products.

There are about 53,000 two-axle tractors, 30,000 single-axle tractors, 4,500
harvesters.

A big problem of Greek agriculture is the small area under irrigation (600,000
hectares). Efforts are being made to increase this area.

Yield (1,000 metric tons) of the chief crops:

Crop	1964	1965	1966	1967	1968	1969
Wheat	2,088	2,072	2,020	1,848	1,515	1,752
Maize	249	248	275	379	375	428
Barley	242	338	563	839	487	529
Oats	139	150	167	165	105	119
Rice (paddy)	107	104	80	912	108	103
Potatoes	544	517	531	721	648	718
Vegetables	1,111	1,140	1,242	..	..	..
Cotton	225	228	260	264	210	300
Tobacco	134	126	104	102	78	70
Must	359	406	..	458	478	504
Sultanas	73	96	90	57	96	78
Currants	90	81	93	90	91	92
Grapes	153	188	157	152	184	182
Citrus	556	570	642	305	426	580
Olive oil	135	204	180	194	154	150
Olives	36	65	73	52	45	47

Tobacco normally furnishes, by value, 28% of Greece's total exports (87,740
tons, worth US$137m. in 1967). The harvested area was 132,000 hectares in 1965.

Olives are abundant, about 500,000 hectares being under cultivation.

Rice is cultivated in Macedonia, the Peloponnese, Epirus and Central Greece.
Successful experiments have been made in growing rice on alkaline land previously regarded as unfit for cultivation. The main kinds of cheese produced are
sliced cheese in brine (commercially known as Fetta) and hard cheese, such as
Kefalotyri.

Livestock (in 1,000), 1965: 1,046 cattle, 38 buffaloes, 558 pigs, 7,819 sheep,
3,895 goats, 294 horses, 213 mules, 441 asses, 21,783 poultry.

FISHERIES. In 1966, 15,531 fishermen were active. 53 metric tons of sponges
were produced in 1966.

MINING. Greece produces a variety of ores and minerals, including iron (average content 44–52%; annual production about 300,000 tons), iron-pyrites (104,000 metric tons in 1965), emery (7,600 metric tons in 1967), bauxite (1·5m. metric tons in 1967), zinc, lead (14,800 short tons in 1965), silver (238,000 troy oz. in 1967), manganese (73,600 metric tons in 1965), chromite (42,400 metric tons in 1965), antimony, nickel, magnesite ore, baryte (131,361 metric tons in 1965), gold (4,823 troy oz. in 1960), sulphur (225,000 metric tons in 1964), ochre, bitumen, marble (white and coloured) and various other earths, chiefly from the Laurium district, Thessaly, Euboea and the Aegean islands. There is no coal, only lignite of indifferent quality (5,000,000 metric tons in 1967). Oil was struck in 1963 by British Petroleum at Kleisoura in west central Greece.

INDUSTRY. The main products are canned vegetables and fruit, fruit juice, beer, wine, alcoholic beverages, cigarettes, textiles, yarn, leather, shoes, synthetic timber, paper, plastics, rubber products, chemical acids, pigments, pharmaceutical products, cosmetics, soap, disinfectants, fertilizers, glassware, porcelain sanitary items, wire and power coils and household instruments.

Production in 1967 (in 1,000 metric tons): Cement, 3,450; fertilizers, 700; steel and steel products, 600; aluminium, 75.

ELECTRICITY. Total installed capacity of the Public Power Corporation was 1·6m. kw as at 31 Dec. 1967. Total net production in 1967 was 6,655m. kwh. (5,013m. thermal, 1,642m. hydraulic).

TOURISM. Tourism earned US$149·5m. in 1969, with a total 1,205,889 tourist arrivals (752,695 from Europe and 444,785 from North America).

TRADE UNIONS. The status of trade unions in Greece is regulated by the Associations Act 1914. Trade-union liberties are guaranteed under the Constitution, and the right to strike is subject to the Settlement of Collective Labour Disputes Act of 21 Nov. 1935, which, while not making strikes illegal, introduced the principle of compulsory arbitration.

The national body of trade unions in Greece is the Greek General Confederation of Labour.

Pepelasis, A. A., and Yotopoulos, P. A., *Surplus Labor in Greek Agriculture, 1953–60.* Athens, 1962

COMMERCE. Foreign trade (in 1m. drachmai) for 6 calendar years was:

	1962	1963	1964	1965	1966	1967
Imports	21,038	24,129	26,552	34,012	36,685	35,588
Exports	7,503	8,703	9,257	9,833	12,179	14,856

Imports, 1967, totalled 8,891,994 metric tons (1966: 8,725,794); exports, 3,953,754 metric tons (1966: 3,586,424).

The trade was distributed, by principal countries, as follows (in 1m. drachmai):

Countries	Imports from			Exports to		
	1965	1966	1967	1965	1966	1967
Austria	614	688	643	145	135	136
Belgium–Luxembourg	1,236	1,305	1,271	103	253	436
Bulgaria	539	400	244	228	557	278
Czechoslovakia	325	461	404	253	288	348
Finland	412	375	367	75	62	61
France	2,885	2,581	2,836	515	723	1,367
Germany, West	5,866	6,335	6,732	2,238	2,415	2,343
Italy	3,094	3,680	3,683	501	603	1,477
Japan	1,172	1,419	957	232	70	275
Netherlands	995	1,216	1,299	303	328	375
Sweden	1,129	1,220	1,081	102	97	130
Switzerland	638	586	650	112	80	172
USSR	1,096	1,142	1,125	807	849	915
UK	3,106	3,601	3,266	760	707	743
USA	3,381	3,935	3,003	936	1,279	1,953
Yugoslavia	721	733	907	400	631	809

In 1967 the Soviet bloc took 18% of all Greek exports, the USSR accounting for 6·1%.

Leading exports by weight (in metric tons):

	1963	1964	1965	1966	1967
Fruits, fresh, dried, preserved	300,266	307,011	384,962	385,464	407,349
Vegetables	46,453	61,579	70,067	47,703	83,069
Beverages and tobacco	95,508	97,661	121,020	130,744	147,156
Natural abrasives	49,344	127,761	206,747	192,742	120,707
Other crude minerals	277,155	330,913	360,178	367,016	416,027
Non-ferrous ores	1,174,087	1,128,420	1,235,713	1,245,208	1,187,259

Leading exports by value (in 1,000 drachmai):

	1964	1965	1966	1967	1968
Fruits	1,707,948	1,889,800	2,338,398	2,359,461	2,355,514
Beverages and tobacco	3,673,841	3,716,769	3,585,051	3,561,940	4,347,370
Cotton	952,482	960,116	614,161	833,872	1,252,178

The largest buyers of tobacco were, in 1965 and 1966, West Germany and USA; in 1967 USA (23,653 tons) and West Germany (21,517 tons).

Total trade (in £1,000 sterling) between Greece and UK was (British Board of Trade returns):

	1965	1966	1967	1968	1969	1970
Imports to UK	11,161	11,347	12,153	11,782	16,626	19,604
Exports from UK	30,641	35,208	33,154	39,903	57,943 }	57,239
Re-exports from UK	460	566	655	833	1,006 }	

SHIPPING. In 1970 the merchant navy comprised 1,878 vessels of 8,198,975 GRT. Greek-owned ships under foreign flags totalled 1,069 with an aggregate tonnage of 14,556,971.

There is a canal (opened 9 Nov. 1893) across the Isthmus of Corinth (about 4 miles).

There is (since 1925) in the town and port of Thessaloniki a free zone, covering today a land area of 536 sq. km. In the same port there was established in 1923 and operating since 1929 a Yugoslav free zone with 94 sq. km total area of land and seaway. In 1923 there was created a free zone in the town of Piraeus, covering a land area of 181·5 sq. km.

ROADS. There were, in 1965, 38,942 km of roads, of which 8,016 were national and 30,926 provincial roads. Number of motor vehicles in Dec. 1966: 122,479 passenger cars, 72,382 goods vehicles, 8,980 buses.

RAILWAYS. Total length of the Greek railway system in 1940 was 2,679 km, of which 1,325 km belonged to the State Railways (SEK) and 1,354 to various private companies, the most important being the Piraeus–Athens–Peloponnese Company (SPAP).

During the war the railways suffered great losses, especially during the departure of German troops, who systematically destroyed all the railway installations and equipment. Only 670 km were left fit for use after the liberation in 1944. The railway system is now fully restored (2,573 km in 1969), and all lines are state-owned except Hellenic Electric Railways Co. Ltd (27 km).

AVIATION. Olympic Airways connects Athens with all important cities of the country, Europe, the Middle East and USA. Thirty-four foreign companies connect Athens with the principal cities of the world. The principal airport is at Athens. In 1967, 38,343 aircraft arrived, carrying 1,405,899 passengers, 13,170 tons of freight and 3,370 tons of mail.

POST. In 1967 telephone and telegraph lines had a length of 36,553 km; there were 11,495 telegraph offices, 1,637 post offices and, in 1969, 761,550 telephones.

The agreement under which Cable and Wireless, Ltd, were responsible for Greek telegraph communications since 1866 was terminated by the Greek Government in Jan. 1956, effective at the end of 1956.

In 1967 there were about 1·38m. registered radio receivers.

BANKING. The Bank of Greece (Trapeza tis Ellados) is the bank of issue. On 31 Dec. 1967 bank-notes in circulation amounted to 33,249m. drachmai.

In 1953 the National Bank of Greece and the Bank of Athens were amalgamated; in 1957 its name was changed to National Bank of Greece (Ethniki Trapeza tis Ellados). Gold and foreign exchange reserves at 31 Dec. 1967 stood at 8,760m. drachmai.

The National Investment Bank for industrial development was set up in Dec. 1963; of its capital of 180m. drachmai, the National Bank provided 60%.

Other important banks are the Ionian and Popular Bank of Greece, the Commercial Bank of Greece, the National Mortgage Bank, the Hellenic Industrial Development Bank, the Investment Bank, the Commercial Credit Bank and the General Bank of Greece.

Post office savings bank deposits amounted to 42,901m. drachmai, to the credit of 37,990 depositors at 31 Dec. 1965.

WEIGHTS AND MEASURES. The metric system was made obligatory in 1959; the use of other systems is prohibited. The Gregorian calendar was adopted in Feb. 1923.

DIPLOMATIC REPRESENTATIVES

Greece maintains embassies in:

Algeria
Argentina (also for Chile, Paraguay, Uruguay)
Australia (also for New Zealand)
Austria
Belgium (also for Luxembourg)
Brazil
Bulgaria
Canada
Congo (K.)
Cyprus
Czechoslovakia
Denmark (also for Iceland and Norway)
Ethiopia
France
Germany (West)
Hungary
India (also for Ceylon, Indonesia, Malaysia, Nepál, Thailand)
Iran (also for Afghánistán and Pakistan)
Italy
Japan (also for China, Korea and the Philippines)
Jordan

Kenya
Lebanon (also for Iraq)
Libya
Mexico
Morocco
Netherlands
Poland
Portugal
Romania
Saudi Arabia
South Africa, Republic of
Spain
Sudan
Sweden (also for Finland)
Switzerland
Syria
Tunisia
Turkey
USSR
UAR
UK
USA
Yugoslavia

Greece also maintains a representative in Israel.

OF GREECE IN GREAT BRITAIN (51 Upper Brook St., W1)

Ambassador: John A. Sorocos (accredited 14 Nov. 1969).

Counsellors: E. Lagakos, M. Cosmetatos (*Special Adviser*), E. Antonopoulos (*Consul-General*), C. A. Roussen (*Press and Information*), A. Zafeiropoulos (*Commercial*); N. Diamantopoulous. *Service Attaché:* Capt. N. Stathakis, RHN.

There are consular officers of Greece at Belfast, Birmingham, Bradford, Bristol, Cardiff, Edinburgh, Falmouth, Glasgow, Hull, Immingham, Leeds, Liverpool, London, Newcastle upon Tyne, Plymouth, Portsmouth, Southampton.

OF GREAT BRITAIN IN GREECE

Ambassador: Sir Michael Stewart, KCMG, OBE (accredited 26 July 1967).
Counsellers: J. E. Powell-Jones (*Consul-General*); S. Y. Dawbarn (*Commercial*).
First Secretaries: P. L. O'Keeffe (*Head of Chancery*); J. D. M. Blyth; A. G. K.
Butler (*Information:* R. Burns (*Labour*). *Service Attachés:* Brig. H. J. Baxter, OBE,
GM (*Defence and Army*), Capt. L. C, Darling, OBE, RN (*Navy and Air*).

There are consular officers at Athens, Corfu, Rhodes, Samos and Thessaloniki.

OF GREECE IN THE USA (2221 Massachusetts Ave. NW, Washington, D.C.,
20008)

Ambassador: Vassilios Vitsaxis.
Minister: Costa P. Caranicas (*Economic*). *Counsellors:* Michael Mazarakis;
Stephanos Th. Hourmouziades (*Commercial*). *First Secretary:* Michael Dountas.
Service Attachés: Brig.-Gen. Odysseus E. Tsiliopoulos (*Army*), Capt. Demetrios
Evgenides, RHN (*Navy*), Col. Panaviotis J. Skoutelis, RHAF (*Air*).

OF THE USA IN GREECE

Ambassador: Henry Tasca.
Deputy Chief of Mission: Robert M. Brandin. *Heads of Sections:* Archer
K. Blood (*Political*); Frank P. Butler (*Economic*); Max E. Hodge (*Commercial*);
Peter J. Peterson (*Consular*); Martin F. March (*Administrative*); William A.
Acton (*AID*); Abraham M. Sirkin (*USIA*). *Service Attachés:* Col. Selwyn P.
Rogers, Jr, (*Army*), Capt. Earl E. Luehman (*Navy*), Col. James R. French (*Air*).

There is a Consul-General at Thessaloniki.

BOOKS OF REFERENCE

STATISTICAL INFORMATION. The General Statistical Service of Greece is an independent department under the supervision of the Ministry of Co-ordination (9 Piraeus St. Athens). Its
publications include: *Statistical Year book* (latest issue, 1957). *Bulletin mensuel de statistique.*
*Recensements de la population. Recensement de l'agriculture. Bulletins mensuels et annuels du
commerce spécial de la Grèce avec les pays étrangers. Recensement de l'industrie.*

Forster, E. S., *A short history of modern Greece.* 3rd ed. London, 1958
Kayser, B., *Géographie humaine de la Grèce.* Paris, Presses Universitaires, 1964
Kousoulas, D. G., *Revolution and defeat: the story of the Greek Communist Party.* OUP, 1965
Kykkotis, I., *English–Modern Greek and Modern Greek–English Dictionary.* 3rd ed. London,
1957
Munkman, C. A., *American Aid to Greece.* New York, 1958
Noel-Baker, F., *The Land and People of Greece.* 2nd ed. London, 1961
Phillipson, A., *Die griechischen Landschaften: eine Landeskunde.* 4 vols. Frankfurt, 1951–59
Spring, J. T., *The Oxford Dictionary of Modern Greek.* 2 vols. OUP, 1966–67
Xydis S. G. *Greece and the Great Powers, 1944–47.* Thessaloniki, 1963

GUATEMALA
República de Guatemala

HISTORY. From 1524 to 1821 Guatemala was a Spanish captaincy-general,
comprising the whole of Central America. It became independent in 1821 and
formed part of the Confederation of Central America from 1823 to 1839, when
Rafael Carrera dissolved the Confederation.

CONSTITUTION AND GOVERNMENT. Following the revolution of
June 1954 the Constitution of 1945 was replaced in Aug. 1954 by a 'Political
Statute'. On 1 March 1956 a new Constitution came into force. This Constitution was in 1963 replaced by a Fundamental Charter of Government. A new
constitution was promulgated on 15 Sept. 1965 with effect from 6 May 1966.

President of the Republic: Col. Carlos Arana Osorio, elected by Congress for a 4-year term beginning 1 July 1970. *Vice-President:* Lic. Eduardo Cáceres Lenhoff.

Minister of Foreign Affairs: Dr Roberto Herrera Ibargüen.

The administration is carried on, under the President, by the new Cabinet; the Council of State of 14 members from the 3 branches of Government; the municipalities; the University of San Carlos; agriculture; commerce; industry; banking; labour. Mayors of municipalities, with their councils, are appointed by the Head of Government.

National flag: Blue, white, blue (vertical).

National anthem: ¡Guatemala! feliz (words by J. J. Palma; tune by R. Alvarez).

AREA AND POPULATION. The area is 108,889 sq. km (42,042 sq. miles). In March 1936 Guatemala, El Salvador and Honduras agreed to accept the peak of Mount Montecristo as the common boundary point.

The population was 5·4m. in 1970. About 45% are 'pure Indians, of 21 different groups descended from the Maya-Quiché tribe; most of the remainder are mixed Indian and Spanish (*ladinos*); and these supply the ruling classes. Density of population, 1968, 44 per sq. km.

Vital statistics, 1968: Births, 211,779; deaths, 79,421; marriages, 17,606; infant deaths, 19,468. Crude birth rate, 1967, 45·5 per 1,000 population; crude death rate, 16·6; crude marriage rate, 3·6.

Guatemala is administratively divided into 22 departments, each with a governor appointed by the Head of Government. Population, 1970:

Departments	Population	Departments	Population
Alta Verapaz	316,422	Petén	34,308
Baja Verapaz	121,461	Quezaltenango	337,712
Chimaltenango	204,963	Quiché	310,983
Chiquimula	192,217	Retalhuleu	145,685
El Progreso	82,998	Sacatepéquez	100,484
Escuintla	340,920	San Marcos	417,246
Guatemala	1,033,117	Santa Rosa	203,463
Huehuetenango	368,309	Sololá	131,435
Izabal	154,251	Suchitepéquez	227,237
Jalapa	126,872	Totonicapán	176,280
Jutiapa	264,536	Zacapa	123,360

The capital is Guatemala City with 768,987 inhabitants (1970), almost all *ladinos*. Other towns are Quezatenango (54,487), Puerto Barrios (29,435), Mazaltenango (23,932), Antigua (17,270), Zacapa (14,324) and Cobán (12,048).

RELIGION. Roman Catholicism is the prevailing faith; but all other creeds have complete liberty of worship. Guatemala has an archbishopric.

EDUCATION. In 1969 there were 4,735 primary schools with 12,594 teachers and an attendance of 474,919 pupils; these figures include private schools. There are 360 secondary and other schools having 5,005 teachers and an attendance of 63,175 pupils; the autonomous University of San Carlos de Borromeo, founded in 1678, was reopened in 1910 with 7 faculties and schools and there are 3 new universities. Total university enrolment (1969) approximately 13,000. All education is in theory free, but owing to a grave shortage of state schools private schools flourish. The 1964 census showed that 63% of those 10 years of age and older were illiterate.

CINEMAS (1970). Cinemas numbered over 107.

NEWSPAPERS (1970). There are 8 daily newspapers.

SOCIAL WELFARE. A comprehensive system of social security was outlined in a law of 30 Oct. 1946. Medical personnel, 1968, included about 1,250 doctors and 275 dentists for the whole republic. There were 50 public hospitals and about 100 dispensaries.

JUSTICE. Justice is administered in a Supreme Court, 6 appeal courts and 28 courts of first instance. Supreme Court and appeal court judges are appointed by the Head of Government. Judges of first instance are appointed by the supreme court.

All holders of public office have to show on entering office, and again on leaving, a full account of their private property and income.

FINANCE. Currency. The gold *quetzal* was established 7 May 1925 equal to 60 old Guatemala paper pesos, with a gold content equal to that of the US$. The exchange rate has remained at $1 since 1926. Gold coins have been withdrawn from circulation. New coins of 25, 10, 5 and 1 centavos were issued by the Banco de Guatemala on 16 Sept. 1965; they are of a lower value than the previous ones. There are also paper notes of 100, 20, 10, 5, 1 and ½ quetzales (50 centavos).

Budget. The estimates of ordinary revenue and expenditure balanced as follows, in quetzales (1 quetzal = US$): 1967, 190·6m.; 1968, 178m.; 1969, 198m.; 1971, 221·4m. Income tax was introduced for the first time in 1963; revenue from this was Q.16m. in 1968.

The national debt was Q.182m. in 1968, including Q.78m. of external debt.

DEFENCE. Military service (2 years) is compulsory, but not universal, between the ages of 18 and 50 (from 18 to 30 in the special reserves), and conscripts may be called upon for work in communications, reforestation and agriculture. The Army numbers between 7,000 and 8,000, organized in 6 infantry battalions and some motorized units with a few Sherman tanks. The Policía Nacional has between 2,000 and 3,000.

There is a small Air Force with a squadron of F-51D Mustang piston-engined fighter-bombers, a squadron of B-26 Invader light bombers, a squadron of C-47 transports and T-33 jet and T-6 piston-engined training units. Total strength is about 1,000 personnel and 40 aircraft.

A Naval force was formed in 1959. In 1970 it comprised 1 gunboat, 4 very small patrol craft and 1 rescue boat.

The President of the Republic is chief of the armed forces.

PRODUCTION. The Cordilleras divide Guatemala into two unequal drainage areas, of which the Atlantic is much the greater. The Pacific slope, though comparatively narrow, is exceptionally well watered and fertile between the altitudes of 1,000 and 5,000 ft, and is the most densely settled part of republic. The Atlantic slope is sparsely populated, and has little of commercial importance beyond the chicle and timber-cutting of the Petén, coffee cultivation of Cobán region and banana-raising of the Motagua Valley and Lake Izabal district.

PLANNING. A 5-year development plan (1971–75) is aimed at increasing the value of exports, improving the collection of revenues from taxation and making the best use of foreign credits (Q.453m. in the period) to bring about a cumulative annual growth rate of 7·8% in the GDP by 1975.

AGRICULTURE. The soil in general is exceedingly fertile and agriculture is the most important industry. But soil erosion is serious and a single week of heavy rains suffices to cause flooding of fields and much crop destruction.

On 17 June 1952 an 'Agrarian Reform Law' was enacted providing for the expropriation (with eventual compensation) of those parts of landed estates which were not under cultivation. The US Government in 1953 protested against the expropriation of 234,000 acres belonging to the United Fruit Company. Under the new government the expropriation was halted and the 'Agrarian Reform Law' was superseded by a 'Statute' early in 1956, which provided small holdings to several thousand peasant farmers. This distribution of land continues, now under the provisions of the 'Agrarian Transformation Law' of 1962. In 1966, 24 state farms and 17 farms owned by banks were transformed into co-operatives.

The principal crop is coffee; there are about 12,000 coffee plantations with 138m. coffee trees on about 338,000 acres, but 80% of the crop comes from 1,500 large coffee farms employing 426,000 workers. Coffee exports in 1968 were valued at Q.74m. mainly to USA and Germany.

Bananas are still an important export crop, but exports have at times been seriously reduced, partly by labour troubles and by hurricanes. Exports 1968 were worth Q.5,091,000.

Cotton has become the second most important export and in 1968 were valued at Q.41m. Other important exports (1967) were sugar, Q.8·8m.; beef, Q.8m. Guatemala is, after Mexico, the largest producer of chicle gum (used for chewing-gum manufacture in USA). Rubber development schemes are under way, assisted by US funds. Tobacco output (all for home consumption) is about 5m. lb. grown on 8,300 acres. Guatemala is one of the largest sources of essential oils (citronella and lemon grass); exports in 1968 were valued at Q.1,657,184. Cattle-grounds (*potreros*) occupy about 758,000 acres; and in 1966 the Ministry of Economy authorized formation of a national reserve herd of 4,000 head. It is calculated that there are some 1·4m. head of cattle (mostly beef) in the country.

FORESTRY. The forest area has an extent of 17,784,000 acres. The department of Petén is rich in mahogany and other woods.

FISHERIES. The 1968 catch of fish and shrimps was 2·1m. lb. Exports were about Q.1m.

MINING. Mineral production is limited to zinc and lead concentrates; exports (1967) Q.2·7m. In 1965 a subsidiary of International Nickel Co. of Canada was granted a 40-year concession to extract and process nickel ore in Northern Guatemala. Eventual production will be 50m. lb. a year.

POWER. 411m. kwh. of electricity were generated in 1968. A new thermo-electric plant of 14,000 kw. capacity was inaugurated at Escuintla in Sept. 1965 and another of 13,000 kw. at Los Esclavos on 24 Sept. 1966.

INDUSTRY. The principal industries are food and beverages, tobacco, chemicals, hides and skins, textiles, garments and non-metallic minerals. New industries include electrical goods, glass, plastic sheet and metal furniture.

TRADE UNIONS. Trade unions are small; they were organized in 1950 in a Left-wing national federation, the Guatemalan Autonomous Labor Federation (FLAG) and a federation of farm workers (CNCG). In 1954 the trade unions were ordered to reorganize: there are now 2 main federations—the Autonomous Trade Union Federation (FAS) and the National Trade Union Council (Consejo Sindical Nacional).

COMMERCE. Values in Q.1,000 (1 quetzal = US$1) were:

	1963	1964	1965	1966	1967	1968
Imports (c.i.f.)	165,500	202,100	229,300	206,858	247,290	247,383
Exports (f.o.b.)	154,000	164,400	185,800	226,120	197,934	222,231

Value (in Q.1,000) of principal imports, 1968: Raw materials and intermediate products, 95,240; consumer goods, 78,780; machinery, tools and equipment, 48,700; petroleum products, 15,600; building materials, 14,040. Chief exports are coffee (US$74·6m. in 1968), cotton ($41m.), bananas, beef, essential oils, timber, chicle and shrimps. The main trading partners are USA and West Germany, and the partners of the Central American Common Market (*see* p. 51).

Total trade between Guatemala and UK for 6 years (in £1,000 sterling, British Board of Trade returns):

	1965	1966	1967	1968	1969	1970
Imports to UK	684	642	762	1,047	799	859
Exports from UK	2,915	3,632	3,045	4,019	3,505 ⎫	4,150
Re-exports from UK	17	29	19	44	40 ⎭	

SHIPPING. The chief ports on the Atlantic coast are Puerto Barrios and Santo Tomás de Castilla; on the Pacific coast, San José and Champerico. Total tonnage handled was, 1968, 1·3m. tons.

RAILWAYS. The principal railway system is the government-owned (since 1968) Ferrocarriles de Guatemala. All railways are of 3 ft gauge. Total length of all lines is about 500 miles. Passengers carried, 1966, numbered 1,647,000, and freight carried, 694,000 short tons. The bridge across the Suchiate River between Mexico and Guatemala in 1942 linked the railways of North and Central America, though differences in gauge make it necessary to change trains at Ayutla.

ROADS. There are about 12,000 km of roads, of which 2,000 are paved. There is a trunk highway from coast to coast *via* Guatemala City. There are 2 trunk highways from the Mexican to the Salvadorean frontier: the Pacific Highway serving the fertile coastal plain and the Pan-American Highway running through the highlands and Guatemala City. Motor vehicles number about 54,000.

AVIATION. The government-owned airline, Aviateca, furnishes both domestic and international services; 6 other airlines handle international traffic. In 1968 air cargo amounted to 4·6m. kg; number of passengers, 160,562.

POST. The Government own and operate the telegraph and telephone services; there are about 35,000 telephone instruments. There are some 70 broadcasting stations. Radio receiving sets in use, 1969, numbered about 250,000. There are 3 commercial television stations.

BANKING. By an Act effective 4 Feb. 1946 the Central Bank of Guatemala (founded in 1926 as a mixed central and commercial bank) was superseded by a new institution, the Banco de Guatemala, to operate solely as a central bank. Savings and term deposits at commercial banks were Q.129m. at the end of 1968. Total currency circulation (backed by a gold reserve fixed by law at a minimum of 40%) on 31 Dec. 1969 was Q.176m.; gold stocks were Q.27·27m., mostly deposited with the US Federal Reserve and unchanged since Dec. 1947; total net international reserves amounted to Q.18·7m. on 31 Dec. 1969. In July 1965 the country's quota with the IMF was increased from US$15m. to 25m. Exchange control was imposed in Oct. 1962.

There are 11 banks, including the Banco de Guatemala, Instituto Nacional de Fomento de la Producción, which grants loans to stimulate production, the Banco Nacional Agrario, set up in Oct. 1953, to make loans to the peasants who have received land under the Agrarian Reform law, its counterpart for small industries (Banco de los Trabajadores) set up in Jan. 1966 with initial capital of US$1·3m., a branch of the Bank of London and Montreal Ltd and a branch of the Bank of America.

WEIGHTS AND MEASURES. The metric system has been officially adopted, but is little used in local commerce.

Libra of 16 oz.	= 1·014 lb.	*League*	= 3 miles
Arroba of 25 libras	= 25·35 lb.	*Vara*	= 32 in.
Quintal of 4 arrobas	= 101·40 lb.	*Manzana*	= 10,00 varas sq.
Tonelada of 20 quintals	= 18·10 cwt	*Caballeria* of 64 man-	
Fanega	= 1½ Imp. bushels	zanas	= 110 acres

DIPLOMATIC REPRESENTATIVES

Guatemala maintains embassies in:

Argentina	China (Taiwan)	El Salvador
Benelux	Colombia	France
Bolivia	Costa Rica	Germany (West)
Brazil	Dominican Republic	Haiti
Chile	Ecuador	Honduras

Italy	Paraguay	USA
Israel	Peru	Uruguay
Mexico	Spain	Vatican
Nicaragua	Switzerland	Venezuela
Panama		

Guatemala broke off diplomatic relations with the UK on 31 July 1963. Britain retains a consulate in Guatemala City.

OF GUATEMALA IN THE USA (2220 R St. NW, Washington, D.C., 20008)

Ambassador: Dr Francisco Linares Aranda.
Minister-Counsellor: Enrique Secaira. *First Secretary:* Lionel E. Asensio.
Armed Forces Attaché: Col. Kjell E. Langerud.

OF THE USA IN GUATEMALA

Ambassador: Nathaniel Davis.
Deputy Chief of Mission: John T. Dreyfuss. *Heads of Sections:* Lawrence A. Pezzullo (*Political*); S. Moray Bell (*Economic*); John D. Perkins (*Commercial*); Roy J. Apel (*Consular*); James A. Dibrell (*Administrative*); Marvin Weissen (*AID*).
Service Attachés: Lieut.-Col. James B. Sampson (*Air*), Col. Frank P. Connelly, Jr (*Defence and Army*), Capt. Richard A. Gibson (*Navy*).

BOOKS OF REFERENCE

The official gazette is called *El Guatemalteco.*

Adler, J. H., and others, *Public Finance and Economic Development in Guatemala.* Stamford Univ. Press, 1952
Banco de Guatemala, *Memoria annual y Estudio económico*
Bianchi, W. J., *Belize.* New York, 1959
Bloomfield, L. M., *The British Honduras–Guatemala Dispute.* Toronto, 1953
Holleran, M. P., *Church and State in Guatemala.* New York, 1949
Humphreys, R. A., *The Diplomatic History of British Honduras 1638–1901.* London, 1961
Male, P. J. E., *Economic and Commercial Conditions in Guatemala.* HMSO, 1956
Mendoza, J. L., *Britain and her Treaties on Belize.* Guatemala, 1946
Morton, F., *Xelahuh.* London, 1959
Rosenthal, M., *Guatemala.* New York, 1961
Whetton, N. L., *Guatemala: the land and the people.* Yale Univ. Press, 1961

NATIONAL LIBRARY. Biblioteca Nacional, 5a Avenida and 8a Calle, Zone 1, Guatemala City.

GUINEA
République de Guinée

AREA AND POPULATION. The republic lies on the west coast between Portuguese Guinea and Sierra Leone.

The area is 245,857 sq. km (95,000 sq. miles), and the estimated population in 1968 was 3·8m. In 1964 Conakry, the capital, had approximately 120,000 inhabitants; Kankan, 29,100; Kindia, 25,000; Siguiri, 12,700; Labé, 12,500, and N'Zérékoré, 8,600 inhabitants.

The most important ethnic groups are the Peuls (1·02m.), Malinké (600,000), Soussou (325,000) and Kissi (160,000).

CONSTITUTION AND GOVERNMENT. The independent republic of Guinea was proclaimed on 2 Oct. 1958, after the territory of French Guinea had decided at the referendum of 28 Sept. to leave the French Community. The constitution provides for the limitation or renunciation of sovereignty in favour of African unity. This principle found expression in the agreements with Ghana (Nov. 1958) and Ghana–Mali (Dec. 1960).

Co-operation with France in economic and cultural matters was established by a convention signed on 22 May 1963.

The official language is French.

National flag: Red, gold, green (vertical).

The constitution of 12 Nov. 1958 declared Guinea 'a democratic, secular and social republic'. The President of the republic is elected for a 7-year term and can be re-elected.

President and Prime Minister: Sékou Touré (elected Jan. 1961, re-elected Jan. 1968). After the deposition of Dr Nkrumah in Ghana (*see* p. 408), President Sékou Touré on 2 March 1966 declared him to be the joint head of state of Guinea.

Foreign Affairs: El Hadj Diallo Saifoulaye.

Elections for the National Assembly, held on 1 Jan. 1968, returned the 75 members (including 16 women) from the single official list of the Parti Démocratique de Guinée.

EDUCATION. There were, in 1963–64, 188,717 pupils in elementary schools and 6,678 in technical and secondary schools.

In Aug. 1961 the French Roman Catholic Archbishop was expelled because of his objection to the take-over of private schools. Only African priests are permitted to function.

HEALTH. The medical service maintains 6 hospitals and 32 dispensaries.

FINANCE. Currency. The monetary unit is the Guinea franc, divided into 100 *centiemes* and on a par with the franc CFA. The issue consists of notes of 10,000, 5,000, 1,000, 500, 100 and 50 francs, and coins of 25, 10 and 5 francs.

Budget. The budget for 1969–70 balanced at 24,386m. Guinea francs.

DEFENCE. The army of 5,000 men has been equipped with Soviet, Czech and Chinese weapons, armoured cars and artillery.

An air force is being formes with Soviet assistance; it is reported to be equipped with 8 MiG-17 jet-fighters, 2 Il-18 turboprop transports and 4 Il-14 piston-engined transports, all Russian built.

AGRICULTURE. The chief products are rice, palm-nuts, bananas, coffee, pineapples, orange juice, groundnuts, millet. Coffee is grown in forest districts. There are experimental fruit gardens at Camayenne near Conakry, Kindia and Dalaba, 2 stations for rice selection (Kankan, Koba) and an experimental quinine station at Sérédou. Fouta Djallon contains cattle in abundance. In 1961 there were 1·5m. cattle, and in 1959, 546,756 sheep and goats.

Agricultural production (in 1,000 metric tons), (1959) manioc, 330; (1962) rice, 319; (1965) bananas, 87; (1965) coffee, 13·5.

MINING. Diamonds are found in the Macenta district (72,000 carats in 1965). Bauxite exists in the Los islands, the Boké district and the Kindia–Telimélé district; output, 1968, 2,118,000 metric tons. Production of iron ore in the Kaloum peninsula was 716,000 metric tons in 1965.

POWER. Production of electrical energy was 10·6m. kwh. in 1955.

COMMERCE. In 1963 imports totalled 11,355m. Guinea francs; exports, 13,820m. Guinea francs. Of the imports, 34% came from USSR, 26% from France, 11% from West Germany, 10% from UK. Alumina forms about 60% of the exports.

Total trade between Guinea and the UK (in £1,000 sterling, British Board of Trade returns):

	1966	1967	1968	1969	1970
Imports to UK	796	185	1	28	1,041
Exports from UK	885	388	664	1,137 }	1,258
Re-exports from UK	17	7	6	91 }	

SHIPPING. In 1960, 807 vessels called at Conakry.

RAIL AND ROAD. A railway connects Conakry with Kankan (662 km) and this is to be extended to Bamako in Mali, by Chinese engineers. A line 150 km long linking bauxite deposits at Sangaredi with Port Kamsar is nearing completion. There are 3,500 km of all-weather roads and 7,000 km of dry-season roads.

AVIATION. There are airports at Conakry and Kankan; in 1957, 2,040 aircraft disembarked and embarked 36,526 passengers and 1,049 tons of freight and mail in Conakry.

POST. The territory is connected by cable with France and Pernambuco; also with Freetown, Monrovia and other places. There is a wireless station at Conakry affording communication with all territories of West Africa. Telephones, 1967, numbered about 6,400.

BANKING. The Banque de la République de Guinée, with a capital of 500m. francs, is controlled by a governor with ministerial rank. It is the sole bank of issue.

In Jan. 1962 all insurance companies and the Banque de l'Afrique Occidentale, the only private bank in Conakry, were nationalized.

OF GUINEA IN GREAT BRITAIN

Ambassador: Fadiala Keita, accredited 26 Nov 1969 (resides in Washington, D.C.).

OF GREAT BRITAIN IN GUINEA

Ambassador: J. G. Tahourdin, CMG (resides in Dakar).

OF GUINEA IN THE USA (2112 Leroy Pl. NW,
Washington, D.C., 20008).

Ambassador: Fadiala Keita.

OF THE USA IN GUINEA

Ambassador: Albert W. Sherer, Jr. *Deputy Chief of Mission:* Donald R. Norland.

Bulletin statistique et économique de la Guinée. Monthly. Conakry
Taylor, F. W., *A Fulani–English Dictionary.* Oxford, 1932

HAITI
République d'Haiti

HISTORY. Haiti occupies the western third of the large island of Hispaniola which was discovered by Christopher Columbus in 1492. The Spanish colony was ceded to France in 1697 and became her most prosperous colony. After the extirpation of the Indians by the Spaniards (by 1533) large numbers of African slaves were imported whose descendants now populate the country. The slaves obtained their liberation following the French Revolution, but subsequently Napoleon sent his brother-in-law, Gen. Leclerc, to restore French authority and re-impose slavery. Toussaint Louverture, the leader of the slaves who had been appointed a French general and governor, was kidnapped and sent to France, where he died in gaol. However, the reckless courage of the Negro troops and the ravages of yellow fever forced the French to evacuate the island and surrender to the blockading British squadron.

The country declared its independence on 1 Jan. 1804, and its successful leader, Gen. Jean-Jacques Dessalines, proclaimed himself Emperor of the newly-named Haiti. After the assassination of Dessalines (1806) a separate régime was set up in the north under Henri Christophe, a Negro general who in 1811 had himself proclaimed King Henry. In the south and west a republic was constituted, with the mulatto Alexander Pétion as its first President. Pétion died in 1818 and was succeeded by Jean-Pierre Boyer, under whom the country became re-united after Henry had committed suicide in 1820. From 1822 to 1844 Haiti and the eastern part of the island (later the Dominican Republic) were united. After one more monarchical interlude, under the Emperor Faustin (1847–59), Haiti has been a republic. From 1915 to 1934 Haiti was under United States occupation.

AREA AND POPULATION. The area is 27,750 sq. km (10,700 sq. miles), of which about three-quarters is mountainous. The population was estimated in 1968 to be about 4·7m. (highest density in Central America), of which 85% are living in rural areas. Infant deaths per 1,000 live births in 1964 were estimated at 171·6.

The country is divided into 9 *Départements*: the original Nord-Ouest, Artibonite, Nord, Ouest, Sud; plus (1962) Nord Est, Centre, Sud Est and Grande Anse; these latter 5 have not yet been delineated. The Ile de la Gonave, some 40 miles long, lies in the main gulf of the same name. Among other islands is La Tortue, off the north peninsula. The majority of the population are Negroes, with an important minority of mulattoes and only about 2,000 white residents, almost all foreign. The capital, Port-au-Prince (Ouest) has an estimated population of 250,000; Cap Haitien (Nord), 30,000; Les Cayes (Sud), 14,000; Gonaives (Artibonite), 14,000, and Jérémie (Sud), 12,000; Port de Paix (Nord-Ouest), 6,500. Less than 15% of the population lives in the towns.

Haiti is the only French-speaking republic in the Americas. The standard French of government, parliament and the press is understood by the small literate minority, but the great majority of the people speak only the dialect known as Créole.

CONSTITUTION AND GOVERNMENT. The 1950 constitution, under which Dr François Duvalier was elected president on 22 Oct. 1957, provided that no president was immediately re-eligible. The new constitution later in 1957 did not forbid re-election.

A single-chamber legislature of 58 deputies elected for a 6-year term was established in April 1961.

In 1964 the constitution was again rewritten and Dr Duvalier named Life President (22 June); the deputies were made capable of indefinite re-election.

President of the Republic: In April 1961 elections were held for the Legislative Chamber, and afterwards it was announced that Dr Duvalier had been re-elected President for a further 6 years (on 22 June 1964 extended to 'life'), although the next presidential election was not due until 1963 and there had been neither nominations nor campaign. (For the series of *coups d'état* in 1956–57, *see* THE STATESMAN'S YEAR-BOOK, 1960, p. 1085.)

National flag: Black, red (vertical); in the centre, the coat of arms on a white square.

National anthem: 'La Dessalinienne': Pour le pays, pour les ancêtres (words by J. Lhérisson; tune by N. Geffrard, 1903).

RELIGION. Since the Concordat of 1860, the official religion is Roman Catholicism, under an archbishop with 5 suffragan bishops. The clergy are mostly French and French-Canadians, with some 160 Haitians. Other Christian churches number perhaps 350,000 members, or 10% of the population. The folk religion is Voodoo.

EDUCATION. The school system is modelled after that of France, with the country divided into 36 inspectors' districts (32 rural and 4 urban). The law calls for free and compulsory elementary education in the French language.

In 1965 urban primary schools reported 3,782 teachers and 143,144 pupils; 802 rural schools, including schools for farming, 2,286 teachers and 131,238 pupils; in 1959, 16 national *lycées*, 32 private secondary schools, 27 professional schools had a total of 9,856 pupils. Agricultural and industrial education was provided for 4,177 students (401 teachers), secondary education for 8,850 students (498 teachers). Higher education (free) is offered at the Faculties of Medicine, Law and Dentistry; in addition, there are the National Schools of Agriculture, Pharmacy, Obstetrics, Ethnology, Surveying, Teachers' and Polytechnic, all of which constitute the State University of Haiti with, in 1961, 1,500 students and 211 professors. There are some schools maintained by the Catholic teaching orders and a small group under Protestant direction. A school of Higher International Studies was founded in Oct. 1958. The founding of a school of Higher Studies in Physics and Chemistry was approved by law in 1959.

A United Nations investigation (1949) found about 85% of the population illiterate, with only one-fifth or one-sixth of the children attending school. A law was passed in Sept. 1958 providing for a 5-year campaign to eliminate illiteracy. In 1959, 14,781 children and adults were attending the 334 educational centres maintained by the Ministries of Education and of Labour.

CINEMAS (1964). There were 18 cinemas and 2 drive-in cinemas with a combined seating capacity of about 10,000.

NEWSPAPERS (1970). There were 6 daily newspapers in Port-au-Prince and 1 weekly newspaper in Cap Haitien with a combined circulation not exceeding 17,000.

HEALTH. There were, in 1965, 302 doctors in practice, 11 hospitals, 12 outpatient clinics, 155 rural clinics and 17 sanatoria. The hospitals total 2,571 beds, of which 134 were in private clinics.

JUSTICE. Judges, both of the lower courts and the court of appeal, are appointed by the President. The legal system is basically French.

Police. The Police number about 600 in Port-au-Prince, and 2,250 over the rest of the country.

FINANCE. Currency. The unit of currency is the *gourde*, which is equivalent to 20 cents US currency; on 9 April 1954 the IMF accepted this as the official par value. It stood at 13·99 to £1 in March 1964. The total currency in circulation on 31 March 1965 was 72·5m. gourdes in notes, and 8m. gourdes in coins. There are copper–nickel coins for 50, 20, 10 and 5 centimes and copper–zinc–nickel coins of 10 and 5 centimes. The amount of US currency in circulation is not known, due to the fact that it is used freely with the local currency.

Budget. Revenue and expenditure (fiscal year ending 30 Sept.) in US$1m. (5 gourdes = US$1), balanced as follows: 1962–63, 28·8; 1963–64, 30·9; 1964–65, 28·6; 1965–66, 28·2; 1966–67, 28·14; 1967–68, 28·04.

The major part of the revenue is derived from customs duties and export taxes. A revised income tax, on individuals and companies, became effective 1 Oct. 1961.

Proposed expenditures for the year 1965–66 (in US$1m.) were: Interior and defence, 7; health, 3·2; education, 3; debt service, 2·4. The chief sources of revenue are customs duties (12) and sales and excise taxes (9·4).

The total public debt is approximately US$75m., of which $41m. is owed abroad.

For 1964–65 the International Monetary Fund's US$4m. stand-by credit was renewed from the previous year. US aid from 1946 to 1963 was some $100m.

DEFENCE. La Force Armée d'Haiti (FAd'H) totals 390 officers and 4,500 men. The President is C.-in-C. and appoints the officers. The Army of about 100 officers and 1,000 men are armed mainly with light infantry weapons, but have a few pieces of light artillery and 9 light tanks. The Presidential Guard is a superior unit of about 15 officers and 250 men.

The Air Force of about 30 officers and 140 men has a number of vintage aircraft including about 6 F-51D Mustang piston-engined fighter-bombers and 3 DC-3s with which an internal air service is maintained.

The Coastguard of about 40 officers and 250 men has 8 patrol vessels of 47 to 650 tons, not all of which are operational.

The President directly commands an additional para-military civilian militia (VSN: *Volontaires de la Sécurité Nationale*) of perhaps 10,000, an active reserve of armed government partisans (including women) and nominal military training and organization.

AGRICULTURE. Only one-third of the country is arable and most people own the tiny plots they farm; the resulting pressure of population is the main cause of rural poverty. Number of farms is estimated at 560,000.

The occupations of Haiti are nine-tenths agricultural, carried on in 7 large plains, from 200,000 to 25,000 acres, and in 15 smaller plains down to 2,000 acres. Irrigation is used in some areas. A dam forming part of the project was finished in 1956. Haiti's most important product is coffee of good quality, classified as 'mild', and grown by peasants. Production in 1964–65 totalled 375,000 bags (of 60 kg). Second most important crop is sisal (1962–63: 16,000 tons). The cultivation of bananas (brought to Haiti in 1515) is decreasing and exports have almost ceased. Cotton also decreased, but new types are being tried. Rice is being developed, especially in the Artibonite Valley. Output of four main crops in 1968 (metric tons) was: Coffee, 29,000; sugar, 51,000; cocoa, 2,000; tobacco, 1,000.

Rum and other spirits are distilled. Essential oils from lime, vetiver, neroli and amyris are becoming important. Cattle and horse breeding are encouraged.

MINING. Haiti may possess undeveloped mineral resources of gold, silver, mirogoane, antimony, sulphur, coal, nickel, gypsum and porphyry. Three foreign companies are engaged in exploitation and exploration for bauxite (359,192 metric tons in 1967), copper (2,350 metric tons in 1967), lignite and manganese.

INDUSTRY. There are 2 textile-mills producing cheap denim with a total of 550 looms and 14,000 spindles. One mill, with 450 looms and 12,000 spindles, has been operating for many years; the other was completed in 1955. A soap factory, which was opened in 1954, produces approximately 5,000 cases of 250 11-oz. bars per month and a second factory has recently been opened with approximately the same production. A cement factory located near the capital produces approximately 50,000–60,000 tons per year. There are also a pharmaceutical plant, a tannery, a plastics plant, 4 aerated-water plants, a paint-works and a flour-mill located in and near Port-au-Prince. The 1960 survey of larger industrial enterprises reported 422 units, employing 10,221, mainly in the conversion of agricultural products.

TOURISM. The tourist trade in 1968 earned some $3·9m., and 51,156 (43,842 in 1967) tourists visited Haiti.

ELECTRICITY. Consumption in 1963 was: Port au Prince, 62·7m. kw.; Cap Haitien, 3·1m. kw.

LABOUR. Trade unions were recognized in Feb. 1946; in 1954, 56 unions were registered, with an estimated membership of 7,000. In 1964 there were 48, and the Government exercises a strong influence over them. In 1960 the agricultural work force was said to have risen to 2m.; the industrial force had dropped slightly to 63,100.

COMMERCE. Imports and exports for fiscal years ending 30 Sept. (in US$1m.):

	1961	1962	1963	1964	1965	1966
Imports	35·0	44·8	26·3	40·7	36·3	36·0
Exports	32·0	40·8	27·4	40·4	36·2	38·3

Chief exports from Haiti during the period 1 Oct. 1963–30 Sept. 1964 were (in US$1m.) as follows: Coffee, 19·4; sisal, 3·7; sugar, 2·5; bauxite, copper, handi-crafts and essential oils are also normally significant.

Of total imports in 1964, USA supplied 58·7%, UK 4·5% and W. Germany 4·2%; of exports, the main destinations were: USA 50·4%, W. Germany 4·7% and UK 0·3%.

The leading imports are cotton manufactured goods, foodstuffs, machinery, mineral oils and vehicles.

Total trade between Haiti and UK in £1,000 sterling (British Board of Trade returns):

	1965	1966	1967	1968	1969	1970
Imports to UK	34	272	141	178	178	144
Exports from UK	542	557	490	682	812 }	976
Re-exports from UK	24	28	25	7	4 }	

SHIPPING. American and Dutch lines connect Haiti with New York, Pana-ma and Florida, and others (French, German, Japanese and Dutch) with Europe and the Far East. In 1964, 615 steam and water vessels entered and cleared Haitian ports; 76 of them were British.

ROADS. Total length of roads is some 3,000 km, little of which is practicable in ordinary motors. In 1964 there were about 5,100 passenger and 1,800 com-mercial vehicles.

RAILWAYS. The 'National Railroad of Haiti' no longer runs from Port-au-Prince to Verrettes. Plain of the Cul-de-Sac Railway (121 km) operates 2 lines.

AVIATION. There are air services to the US, Jamaica, Dominican Republic and Puerto Rico. An airport capable of handling jets was opened at Port-au-Prince in Jan. 1965. The Air Force runs an airline connecting Port-au-Prince with other towns in Haiti.

POST. The principal towns are connected by the government telegraph system, with 4,780 km of wire, 50 main offices and 86 sub-offices. Cables run from Port-au-Prince to Cuba, and from the Mole St Nicholas to Santiago de Cuba, Port-au-Prince, Cap Haitien, Puerto Plata (Dominican Republic) and to New York and South America. There are 133 post offices.

The state telephone service has 6 automatic telephone exchanges, but has not been in effective working order for some time. Work on the new telephone system was suspended in 1957. Instruments, 1968, number 4,335, of which 86% are automatic.

BANKING. The Banque Nationale de la République d'Haiti, owned by the State, was established 21 Oct. 1910 with a capital of US$5m., and has a mono-poly of the note issue. Note issue is limited to three times the bank's paid-up capital. US dollars may be included in the minimum required reserves. Reserves totalled US$0·1m. gold and 1·6m. foreign exchange in Nov. 1966. The Royal Bank of Canada has a branch at Port-au-Prince.

WEIGHTS AND MEASURES. The metric system is officially accepted.

DIPLOMATIC REPRESENTATIVES

Haiti maintains embassies in:

Argentina	Dahomey	Ivory Coast	Peru
Belgium	El Salvador	Japan	Senegal
Brazil	France	Liberia	Spain
Canada	Germany (West)	Mali	UK
Chile	Guatemala	Mexico	USA
Colombia	Italy	Panama	Vatican

OF HAITI IN GREAT BRITAIN (22 Hans Rd., SW3)
First Secretary and Consul-General: Delorme Méhu (*Chargé d'Affaires a.i.*).
There is an honorary consul in Liverpool.

OF GREAT BRITAIN IN HAITI (residence at Kingston, Jamaica)
Ambassador: E. N. Larmour, CMG.
Counsellor: R. Blaikley. *First Secretaries:* W. H. Fullerton; E. M. Smith
(*Commercial*); T. L. Laister, OBE (*Information*).

OF HAITI IN THE USA (4400–17th St. NW. Washington, D.C., 20011)
Ambassador: Arthur Bonhomme. *Minister Counsellor:* Jean Targete. *First
Secretaries:* Fritz Dominique, Mrs Serge Bazelais. *Service Attaché:* Col. Nerva
Staco.

OF THE USA IN HAITI
Ambassador: Clinton E. Knox.
Deputy Chief of Mission: John R. Burke. *Heads of Sections:* Richard A. Cleve-
land (*Political*); David R. Raynolds (*Economic*); T. Cummings (*Consular*); G.
Levesque (*Administrative*).
Service Attachés: Lieut.-Col. E. Roy (*Army*), Col. Roy D. Wathen (*Air*, resi-
dent in Caracas).

BOOKS OF REFERENCE
The official gazette is *Le Moniteur.*

Revue Agricole d'Haiti. From 1946. Quarterly
Bellegarde, D., *Histoire du Peuple Haïtien.* Port-au-Prince, 1953
De Young, M., *Man and Land in the Haitian Economy.* Univ. of Florida Press, 1958
Institut Haïtien de Statistique, *Guide Économique de la République d'Haiti*
Rodman, S., *Haiti, the Black Republic.* New York, 1954
Simmonds, S., *Economic and Commercial Conditions in Hayti.* HMSO, 1956
Talleyrand and Talleyrand. *Digest of the Laws of Haiti.* Port-au-Prince, 1964
Turnier, A. *Les Etats-Unis et le Marché Haïtien.* Washington D.C., 1955

NATIONAL LIBRARY. Bibliothèque Nationale, Rue du Centre. Port-au-Prince. *Librarian:*
Mme Max Adolphe.

HONDURAS
República de Honduras

CONSTITUTION AND GOVERNMENT. In 1838 Honduras declared
itself an independent sovereign state, free from the Federation of Central
America, of which it had formed a part.
Legislative power is vested in a single chamber, the Congress of Deputies consisting of 58 members, chosen for 6 years by popular vote, in the ratio of 1 per
30,000 inhabitants. It meets for 100 days (may be extended to 150 days) on
21 Nov. each year. A Permanent Commission of 5 members sits while Congress
is not in session for the transaction of routine or emergency business. The
President of the Republic is elected by popular vote for 6 years, holding office
from 21 Dec. All men and women over 18 are entitled to vote.
Elections for a Constituent Assembly, held on 16 Feb. 1965, returned 35
members of the Partido Nacional (328,412 votes) and 29 members of the Partido
Liberal (267,808 votes).
On 3 Oct. 1963 the Liberal President Dr Villeda Morales, whose term was due
to expire in Dec., was overthrown by the armed forces, and the former Commander in Chief appointed an administrative cabinet. A return to constitutional
government was made on 5 June 1965.

President: Gen. Oswaldo López Arellano (installed 5 June 1965).
Foreign Minister: Dr Tiburcio Carias Castillo.

National flag: Blue, white, blue (horizontal; 5 blue stars arranged saltire-wise in the middle).
National anthem: Tu bandera es un lampo de cielo (words by A. C. Coello; tune by C. Hartling).

AREA AND POPULATION. Area (as revised July 1953) is 112,088 sq. km (43,227 sq. miles), with a population, census of 18 June 1950 (revised 1961) of 1,884,765 (16·7 per sq. km or 43 per sq. mile); estimate, 1969, 2·49m.

The boundary with Nicaragua from Teoteacinte to the Atlantic coast was fixed on 5 Aug. 1961 by a commission appointed by the Organization of American States.

The capital of Honduras is Tegucigalpa, with (1969) a population of 218,510. The next most important town is San Pedro Sula, 96,341. The main ports are Amapala (3,568) on the Pacific, and, on the Atlantic, La Ceiba (35,222), Puerto Cortés (22,296) and Tela (14,176). The port of entry for the Bay Islands is Roatán.

The republic is divided into 18 departments with their populations: Gracias a Dios (15,100), La Paz (71,200), Valle (99,100), Yoro (167,500), Olancho (138,300) Atlántida (127,500), Islas de la Bahía (9,800), Colón (58,200), Cortés (281,500), El Paraíso (134,800), Santa Bárbara (207,500), Francisco Morazán (406,800), Copán (161,800), Choluteca (200,600), Comayagua (130,100), Intibucá (89,300), Lempira (135,400) and Ocotepeque (60,400).

Aboriginal tribes number over 35,000, principally Miskito, Payas and Xicaques Indians and Zambos, each speaking a different language. The Spanish-speaking inhabitants are chiefly *mestizos*, Indians with an admixture of Spanish blood. Gracias a Dios is still practically unexplored and is inhabited by pure native races who speak little or no Spanish.

In 1963 there were 93,649 live births and 19,510 deaths. Crude birth rate was 46·3 per 1,000 population; crude death rate, 9·6; marriage rate, 3·2; infant mortality rate, 47 per 1,000 births.

RELIGION. Roman Catholicism is the prevailing religion, but the constitution guarantees freedom to all creeds, and the State does not contribute to the support of any. Protestants number about 36,000. The Society of Friends had, in 1957, about 900 members.

EDUCATION. Instruction is free, compulsory (from 7 to 15 years of age) and secular. In 1966 the 4,120 primary schools had 330,779 children (11,339 teachers); the 96 secondary, normal and technical schools had 26,527 pupils (1,950 teachers); 7 university faculties had 2,572 students (182 teachers) at Tegucigalpa offering law, medicine, pharmacy, economics (2), engineering and dentistry. Preparatory institutions in Tegucigalpa and San Pedro Sula offer courses in nursing, journalism, public administration, business administration, and auditing and accounting.

Probably only 68% of school-age children attend classes. The illiteracy rate was 42% of those 10 years of age and older in 1969.

CINEMAS (1963). Cinemas numbered about 40 with seating capacity of some 36,000.

NEWSPAPERS (1969). There were 4 daily and 3 weekly newspapers published in the capital; and in the provinces, 2 daily and 6 weekly.

JUSTICE. The judicial power resides in the Supreme Court, with 7 judges elected by the National Congress for 6 years; there are 6 appeal courts, and departmental and local judges.

FINANCE. Currency. By a decree of 9 March 1931 the gold *lempira* (named after a native chief) is the monetary unit; its value is that of 0·836 gramme of gold, 900 fine, or 50 cents US currency. It is backed by a reserve fund of US deposits and securities; the fund stood at $29m. on 31 July 1965, against a total note circulation of Lps.46·3m. and coin of Lps.4·9m. Silver coins of 1 *lempira*, 50 and 20 centavos; copper–nickel, 10 and 5 centavos; copper–zinc–tin, 2 centavos and 1 centavo are in circulation. The value of the silver *lempira* was legally fixed in 1931 to 50 cents US. There are also 1, 5,10, 20 and 100 *lempira* notes in circulation.

Rate of exchange, Aug. 1968: 2 *lempiras* = US$1, 4·8 *lempiras* = £1.

Budget. The fiscal and calendar years have coincided since 1 Jan. 1957. Recent budgets (in 1m. lempiras) balance as follows: 1963, 110·2; 1964, 112·2; 1965, 127·9; 1966, 144·3; 1967, 169·9m.; 1968, 196·1m.; 1969, 215·7m.

The largest sources of income anticipated (1969) were (in 1m. lempiras): Import duties, 53·5; income tax, 39·2; sales and consumption taxes, 36·9. The Ministries in receipt of revenue are (1969): National defence, 14·5; education, 41·2; communications and public works, 58·3; national resources, 14·6; health, 9·5.

Total internal debt stood at the end of Dec. 1968 at 66·78m. lempiras, and net reserves of foreign currency at 30 June 1969 at 61·15m. lempiras.

A tripartite treaty of economic association was signed with El Salvador and Guatemala on 6 Feb. 1960.

DEFENCE. Army. Every citizen is liable to serve in the Army from the age of 18 to 55. Service in the active Army is for 8 months and in the reserves from the age of 32 to 55. Foreigners are exempt from service. Under the terms of the Washington Central American Conventions of 1923 the size of the regular Army is fixed at 2,500 men, including the National Guard, organized in 23 companies of infantry and 1 battery of artillery.

Navy. A frigate was in 1962 converted for mercantile use. The coastguard consists of 3 cutters.

Air Force. The equipment, all of US origin, includes a small number of F-86K all-weather jet fighters and Corsair piston-engined fighter-bombers, 1 C-54 and 4 C-47 transports, T-33 and T-6 trainers, light aircraft and helicopters. Total strength about 1,200 personnel and 35 aircraft.

AGRICULTURE. Honduras is essentially an agricultural country whose main exports are bananas, coffee, timber, dairy and beef cattle, and minerals. The chief products (agricultural year 1965–66, in 100-lb. bags) were: Coffee (771,365), cotton (239,424), maize (1,885,300), beans (1,083,930), rice, in shell (598,680), sugar-cane (14,732,390). Cattle and hogs exports, 1965–66, 131,447 head; pop corn, 1,029,070 lb., tobacco, 105,010 lb. In 1968 banana exports were US$87m. (1967: US$83·5m.).

FORESTRY. Honduras has an abundance of hard- and softwoods. Large stands of mahogany and other hardwoods—granadino, guayacán, walnut and rosewood—grow in the north-eastern part of the country, in the interior valleys, and near the southern coast. Stands of pine occur almost everywhere in the interior, but are severely damaged by bark beetle. 1967 exports (in cu. metres) mainly to USA, El Salvador, Jamaica, Venezuela, UK and W. Germany, were: Pinewood (11,837), cedar (166), mahogany and ebony (2,095) and granadino (54). In 1965 timber exports were 332,377 cu. metres worth 24·31m. lempiras.

FISHERIES. Shrimp exports from the Atlantic coast had exceeded 2m. lb. in 1966 and were processed in several plants.

MINING. The mineral resources of Honduras are gold, silver, copper, lead, zinc, iron, antimony, some of them being found in almost every department, but only silver (1967: 349,991 troy oz.), lead (1967: 22·4m. lb.) and zinc (1967: 21,483 metric tons) are usually mined. The principal mines are American-owned. Exports, 1965, were: Silver, valued at 6,246,856 lempiras (4,291 metric tons); gold, in bars or concentrates (225,591 lempiras; 2,803 troy oz.), lead (971,340 lempiras; 12,543 kg) and other metals.

Foreign concessionaries must employ Honduran citizens up to one-half of their labour force and may not import Negroes or persons of the yellow races. Concessions may not be sold. A United Nations Development Programme is carrying out a 2-year mineral studies project in 4,000 sq. miles of the north-western area.

INDUSTRY. A good quality of Panama hat is manufactured in the departments of Copán and Santa Bárbara, along with many other articles of domestic use. Clothing factories have been established in Tegucigalpa and San Pedro Sula. There are some oil-driven electric power-plants. An important hydro-electric scheme is being built at Río Lindo, the first phase being complete, with the opening of the 100m.-kwh. plant at Cañaveral, to serve the central and Costa Norte regions.

LABOUR. The organization of trade unions was begun in 1954 with the assistance of ORIT (Inter-American Regional Organization) sponsored by the USA trade unions. In 1969 they had about 37,000 members. A 'Charter of Labour' was granted in Feb. 1955 and an advanced Labour Code and Social Security Bill passed into law in May 1959. The application of these measures is not yet complete.

A Ministry of 'Labour, Social Assistance and the Middle Class' was created in 1955; the last four words of its title were expunged in 1957.

COMMERCE. Imports and exports (including re-exports) for fiscal years in lempiras (the lempira = 50 cents US):

	1963	1964	1965	1966	1967
Imports	190,161,371	203,267,866	243,875,193	298,100,942	329,524,049
Exports	164,274,776	185,019,652	251,965,262	288,262,769	311,829,142

Percentages of trade with main countries was:

	1965 Imports	1965 Exports	1966 Imports	1966 Exports	1967 Imports	1967 Exports
USA	46·9	57·6	49·8	55·8	48·0	44·8
Germany (West)	5·7	10·9	5·4	15·6	5·4	22·0
Japan	5·4	3·9	3·6	2·5	4·5	2·8
UK	3·1	0·4	3·0	—	2·8	0·3
Canada	0·9	0·4	0·6	—	0·8	—
El Salvador	10·1	10·3	11·0	7·4	12·1	7·3

Total trade between Honduras and UK (in £1,000 sterling) was (according to British Board of Trade returns) as follows:

	1966	1967	1968	1969	1970
Imports to UK	296	228	342	347	260
Exports from UK	1,028	936	1,148	1,282 }	1,506
Re-exports from UK	4	8	11	11 }	

ROADS. Honduras is connected with Guatemala, El Salvador and Nicaragua by the Pan-American Highway; a western highway to connect with Guatemala and El Salvador is under construction. Tegucigalpa, the capital, is connected with both the Caribbean Sea and the Pacific Ocean. Roads in 1969 were 5,185 km (500 paved). Motor vehicles, 1 Aug. 1962, included 11,606 cars, 5,893 lorries and buses.

RAILWAYS. Only 3 railways exist; they are confined to the north coastal region and are used mainly for transportation of bananas. Tegucigalpa, the capital, is not served by any railway, and there are no international railway connexions. The total railways operating at Dec. 1969 were 1,028 km.

SHIPPING. The German Hamburg–Amerika Line has a fortnightly service to Puerto Cortés, on the Caribbean. In 1966 the IBRD granted a loan of US$4·8m. for improvements at this port.

In 1966 the flag of Honduras was flown by 43 ships of 69,816 tons.

AVIATION. Over a large part of the country the aeroplane is the normal means of transport for both passengers and freight. There are 34 unpretentious local airports and 1 large international one, at Tegucigalpa; fares are reasonable, distances short and the planes are treated as casually as buses.

A second international airport at La Mesa, San Pedro Sula, was opened on 28 Feb. 1965.

POST. The Government at June 1956 operated 2,824 km of telephone lines and 8,465 km of telegraph lines. Number of government telephones in use, 1968, 10,162; telephone offices, 48; number of telegraph offices, 228; combined telephone and telegraph offices, 107. Fruit, railway and mining companies own 1,105 km of telephone lines and 1,726 instruments. There are 369 post offices and agencies, 25 government and 38 private and 103 commercial broadcasting stations; wireless sets in use, 1959, about 140,000. Commercial television began with a station in Tegucigalpa in Sept. 1959. In July 1969 there were estimated to be 25,000 receivers in use.

BANKING. The power to issue notes was taken over from the 2 private banks —Banco de Honduras and Banco Atlántida—by the new government bank, Banco Central de Honduras, which was inaugurated on 1 July 1950 with a capital of US$250,000. All private bank-notes have been withdrawn. The Banco Central has restored complete freedom in foreign-exchange transactions, controlled since 1934. Another government bank, the National Development Bank, founded in 1950 with a capital of $750,000, grants long-term loans to coffee planters and 'supervised credits' to the poorer farmers; and a Banco de los Trabajadores was set up in 1966 with a capital of 500,000 lempiras.

The Bank of London and Montreal operates in Tegucigalpa, La Ceiba and San Pedro Sula. The Central American Bank of Economic Integration opened in Tegucigalpa on 30 May 1961.

WEIGHTS AND MEASURES. The metric system has been legal since 1 April 1897, but English pounds and yards and the old Spanish system are still in use: 1 *vara* = 32 in.; 1 *manzana* (10,000 sq. *varas*) = 700 sq. metres; 1 *arroba* = 25 lb.; 1 *quintal* = 100 lb.; 1 *tonelada* = 2,000 lb.

DIPLOMATIC REPRESENTATIVES

Honduras maintains embassies in:

Argentina	Germany (West)	Peru
Brazil	Guatemala	Spain
Chile	Israel	UK
Colombia	Italy	USA
Dominican Republic	Netherlands	Vatican
Ecuador	Panama	Venezuela
France		

OF HONDURAS IN GREAT BRITAIN (48 George St., W1)

Chargé d'Affaires: Roman Humberto España Nini.

There are consular representatives at Birmingham and London.

OF GREAT BRITAIN IN HONDURAS

Ambassador and Consul-General: L. P. F. L'Estrange, OBE.

First Secretaries: K. H. Jones, MBE (*Consul*). *Naval and Air Attaché:* Wing Cdr P. D. Thompson, DFC, DFM (resident in Caracas).

There is a consular representative at Tegucigalpa.

OF HONDURAS IN THE USA (4715–16th St. NW,
Washington, D.C., 20011)

Ambassador: Roberto Galvez Barnes.
Counsellor: Armijo Radillo (*Economic*). *First Secretary:* Armando Alvarez Martinez. *Military Attaché:* Col. Alonso Flores Guerra.

OF THE USA IN HONDURAS

Ambassador: Hewson Anthony Ryan.
Deputy Chief of Mission: Jean M. Wilkowski. *Heads of Sections:* Edward M. Rowell (*Political*); Albert L. Zucca (*Economic*); Richard C. Graham (*Commercial*); John L. DeOmellas (*Labour*); Allan F. McLean, Jr (*Consular*); Elmer C. Pitman (*Administrative*); Walter G. Storreman (*AID*). *Service Attachés:* Col. Roman J. Lutz (*Army*), Col. John A. Carroll (*Defence and Air*).

There is a Consul at San Pedro Sula and a consular agent at La Ceiba.

BOOKS OF REFERENCE

The *Anuario Estadístico* (latest issue, *Comercio Exterior de Honduras*, 1967) is published by the Dirección de Estadísticas y Censos, Tegucigalpa. *Director:* Carlos Raudeles.

Banco Central de Honduras: *Monthly Bulletin*
Checchi, V. (and others), *Honduras, a Problem in Economic Development*. New York, 1959
Rubio Melhado, A., *Geografía General de la Republica de Honduras*. Tegucigalpa, 1953
Stokes, W. S., *Honduras: an area study in government*. Madison, Wisc., 1950

HUNGARY
Magyar Népköztársaság

HISTORY. Hungary first became an independent kingdom in 1001. For events in Hungary since 1918 *see* THE STATESMAN'S YEAR-BOOK, 1945, pp. 1006–7, and 1957, p. 1096.

On 23 Oct. 1956 an anti-Stalinist revolution broke out, and the newly formed coalition government of Imre Nagy on 1 Nov. withdrew from the Warsaw Pact and asked the United Nations to protect Hungarian neutrality. János Kádár, one of Nagy's ministers, formed a counter-government on 3 Nov. and asked the Soviet Government for support. Russian troops suppressed the revolution and abducted Nagy and his Ministers, who were later secretly executed.

The United Nations has passed several resolutions condemning the Soviet intervention.

On 7 Sept. 1967 the Soviet–Hungarian treaty of friendship (first signed in 1948) was renewed for a further 20 years.

CONSTITUTION AND GOVERNMENT. On 1 Feb. 1946 the National Assembly proclaimed the Hungarian Republic.

A new constitution of a 'republic of workers and working peasants' was adopted on 18 Aug. 1949. Supreme power is vested in Parliament. Parliament elects a Presidential Council, which exercises the functions of Parliament between sessions. It can dissolve government bodies and annul legislation if they 'infringe the constitution or are detrimental to the interests of the working people' and is collectively the titular Head of State (usually represented by its chairman).

National minorities have equal rights, education in their own tongue and the right to develop their national culture.

National flag: Red, white and green (horizontal).
National anthem: God bless the Hungarians—Isten áldd a Magyart (words by Ferenc Kölcsey, tune by Ferenc Erkel).

Chairman of the Presidential Council: Pál Losonczi, appointed on 14 April 1967. *Deputy Chairmen:* Sándor Gáspár and Ödön Kisházi. *Secretary:* Lajos Cseterki.

In 1949 the Hungarian Working People's Party (Communists), the Small-holders' Party, the National Peasant Party, the Trade Union Federation, the Association of Working Peasants, the Democratic Women's Association and the Federation of Working Youth were merged in the Hungarian People's Independence Front. In 1954 a new comprehensive organization was formed, the People's Patriotic Front. The Communist Youth Association (Kisz) had 800,000 members in 1970.

The Communist Party was reorganized after the 1956 revolution and changed its name to 'Hungarian Socialist Workers' Party'. It had 662,397 members in 1970. Supreme *de facto* power is in the hands of the Party's Politburo, composed in March 1971 of: János Kádar, *First Secretary of the Central Committee*; György Aczel; Antal Apró; Valéria Benke; Béla Biszku; Lajos Fehér; Jenő Fock; Sándor Gáspár; Gyula Kállai; Zoltan Komocsin; Dezső Nemes; Károlyi Nemeth; Rezső Nyers.

The Government was in March 1971 composed as follows: *Prime Minister:* Jenö Fock. *Deputy Prime Ministers:* Miklós Ajtai, Antal Apró, Lajos Fehér Mátyás Timár. *Finance:* Péter Vályi. *Foreign Affairs:* Dr János Péter. *Chairman, National Planning Office:* Imre Párdi. *Speaker, National Assembly:* Gyula Kállai. *Interior:* András Benkei. *Culture:* Pál Ilku. *Defence:* Gen. Lajos Czinege. *Foreign Trade:* József Biró. *Justice:* Mihály Korom.

At the elections held on 19 March 1967, 7,131,151 votes were cast (*i.e.*, 98·8% of the electorate). All candidates stood on behalf of the People's Patriotic Front. Parliament consists of 349 deputies, elected for a 4-year term by all citizens over 18 years. The latest elections were held in March 1971.

Since 1967 more than one candidate has been permitted to stand in each constituency. In 1967 unofficial candidates stood in 9 constituencies, but were all defeated. In Oct. 1970 voters gained the right to make direct nominations of candidates, though all candidates must support the Patriotic Front platform.

LOCAL GOVERNMENT. Hungary is administratively divided into 19 counties (*megyék*) and 5 county boroughs (large towns with county status), which are subdivided into districts, towns and boroughs. Councils for the 3 latter are elected for 4-year terms, and in turn elect Executive Committees to carry on day-to-day administration and the members of the county councils. In the March 1971 elections councillors were elected for only 2 years so that local elections should no longer coincide with general elections.

AREA AND POPULATION. The peace treaty of 10 Feb. 1947 restored the frontiers as of 1 Jan. 1938. The area of Hungary is 93,030 sq. km (35,911 sq. miles). The official language is Hungarian (Magyar), a member of the Finno-Ugrian group.

At the census of 1 Jan. 1970 the population was 10,314,152 (4,991,000 males and 5,323,000 females).

45% of the population is urban (19% in Budapest). Population density, 111 per sq. km. Birth rate, 1969, 15 per 1,000; growth rate, 3%; expectation of life: males, 67; females, 72. In 1970, 1·25m. Hungarians lived abroad.

Vital statistics, 1969: Births, 154,319; marriages, 95,615; divorces, 21,100; deaths, 116,647; infant mortality, 35·8 per 1,000 live births.

Area (in sq. km) and population (in 1,000) of counties, county boroughs and county towns:

Counties (1 Jan. 1970)	Area	Population	Chief town	Population
Baranya	4,388	279	Pécs	145
Bács-Kiskun	8,362	573	Kecskemét	77
Békés	5,669	447	Békéscsaba	55
Borsod-Abaúj-Zemplén	7,024	608	Miskolc	173
Csongrád	4,150	323	Hódmezővásárhely	53
Fejér	4,374	389	Székesfehérvár	72
Győr-Sopron	4,012	405	Győr	87
Hajdú-Bihar	5,765	375	Debrecen	155
Heves	3,638	348	Eger	45
Komárom	2,250	302	Tatabánya	65

Counties (1 Jan. 1970)	Area	Population	Chief town	Population
Nógrád	2,544	241	Salgótarján	37
Pest	6,393	870	Budapest	1,940
Somogy	6,083	363	Kaposvár	54
Szabolcs-Szatmár	5,936	592	Nyíregyháza	71
Szolnok	5,571	450	Szolnok	61
Tolna	3,609	259	Szekszárd	24
Vas	3,340	281	Szombathely	65
Veszprém	5,187	409	Veszprém	35
Zala	3,284	267	Zalaegerszeg	39

County boroughs (1 Jan. 1970)	Area	Population	County boroughs (1 Jan. 1970)	Area	Population
Budapest (capital)	525	1,940	Pécs	145	146
Miskolc	223	173	Szeged	112	119
Debrecen	446	155			

National minorities in 1970 (in 1,000): Germans, 220; Slovaks, 100; Croats and Serbs, 100; Romanians, 25.

RELIGION. All religions have equal standing. Each church receives state subsidies totalling in all some 80m. forints per annum, of which half goes to the Roman Catholic Church.

State approval is required for all ecclesiastical appointments, transfers and dismissals and all clergy have to take an oath of allegiance to the State. The State has the right to appoint its own nominees for all vacant bishoprics which are not filled within 90 days; and to fill church posts of lower rank which have not been filled by the bishops within 60 days.

In 1964 by an agreement with the Vatican the Pope appointed an archbishop and 5 bishops, who took the oath of allegiance to the State. By a further agreement of 23 Jan. 1969 the hierarchy was increased to 2 archbishops (Kalocsa, Eger), 3 bishops, 5 apostolic administrators and 2 auxiliaries.

Estimates (1956) of Church membership: Roman Catholics, 6·2m.; Reformed, 2m.; Lutherans, 433,000; Orthodox, 273,000; Baptists, 35,000; Seventh-Day Adventists, 14,000; Methodists, 2,500; Jews, 80,000.

EDUCATION. Education is free and compulsory from 6 to 16. 'General' schooling ends at 14; secondary schooling is available at general, technical, apprentices' or continuation schools.

In 1969–70 there were 3,385 kindergartens with 11,682 teachers and 213,115 pupils; 5,626 general schools with 62,834 teachers and 1,177,887 pupils; 555 secondary schools with 13,222 teachers and 337,126 pupils; 395 continuation schools with 12,387 pupils.

There are 4 universities proper (Budapest, Pécs, Szeged, Debrecen), and 14 specialized universities (6 technical, 4 medical, 3 arts, 1 economics). At these and at 20 other institutions of higher education there were, in 1969–70, 78,889 students and 9,413 teachers. There were 13 teacher-training colleges with 4,151 students and 351 teachers, 37 technical colleges with 11,413 students and 951 teachers and 2 vocational colleges with 2,761 students and 138 teachers. Reforms were introduced in Feb. 1969 to give more autonomy to higher institutes of learning.

CINEMAS (1969). There were 3,981 cinemas; attendance totalled 82·3m. Forty-one full-length feature films were made in 1969.

NEWSPAPERS. In 1969 there were 29 dailies and 445 other periodicals. The Party daily is Népszabadság ('People's Freedom') (circulation 740,000 weekdays, 790,000 Sundays).

LIBRARIES. There are 5,439 public, 4,056 trade union and 1,624 research and professional libraries.

SOCIAL WELFARE. Medical treatment is free. Patients bear 15% of the cost of medicines. Sickness benefit is 75% of wages, old age pensions (at 60 for men, 55 for women) 60–70%. In 1969, 27m. forints were paid out in social insurance benefits.

Family allowances (per month) are 300 forints for a second child, 510 forints for a third and 680 forints for a fourth.

In 1969 there were 22,692 doctors and dentists and 83,600 hospital beds.

JUSTICE. The administration of justice is the responsibility of the Procurator-General, who is elected by Parliament for a term of 6 years. Civil and criminal cases fall under the jurisdiction of the district courts, county courts and the Supreme Court in Budapest. Criminal proceedings are dealt with by district courts through 3-member councils and by county courts and the Supreme Court in 5-member councils.

District Courts act only as courts of first instance; county courts as either courts of first instance or of appeal. The Supreme Court acts normally as an appeal court, but may act as a court of first instance in cases submitted to it by the Public Prosecutor. All courts, when acting as courts of first instance, consist of 1 professional judge and 2 people's assessors, and, as courts of appeal, of 3 professional judges. Local government Executive Committees may try petty offences.

District or county judges and assessors are elected by the district or county councils, all members of the Supreme Court by Parliament.

There are also military courts of the first instance. Military cases of the second instance go before the Supreme Court.

Judges are appointed for life, subject to removal for disciplinary reasons.

FINANCE. Currency. A decree of 26 July 1946 instituted a new monetary unit, the *forint* subdivided into 100 *fillér*. The official rate of exchange is 28·2 forints to the £ sterling, 11·74 forints = US$1, 13 forints = 1 rouble. Tourist rate: 71·93 forints = £1 sterling, 30 forints = US$1.

Budget. The budget for calendar years was as follows (in 1,000m. forints):

	1965	1966	1967	1968	1969	1970	1971[1]
Revenue	97·98	95·51	104·75	137·282	154·219	168·395	193·061
Expenditure	97·81	95·41	104·70	138·768	155·929	175·285	195·226

[1] Estimates.

The continuing deficit is a result of 'new economic mechanism': prior investment commitments are no longer met from enterprise profits.

Hungary's bonded debt to the UK is estimated at £19m., some of it in default since 1931. Settlement talks between Hungary and the UK culminated in an offer on 19 Nov. 1967. In Jan. 1970 an agreement was signed with the USA providing for the settlement of pre-war Hungarian commercial debts.

DEFENCE. The 1947 Treaty authorized Hungary to have an army up to a strength of 65,000 personnel, and an air force of 90 aircraft, of which not more than 70 may be combat types, with a personnel strength of 5,000.

Army. Hungary is divided into 4 army districts: Budapest, Debrecen, Kiskunfélegyháza, Pécs. The strength of the Army is 95,000 men. It is organized in 1 tank and 5 motorized divisions, with about 700 T-54 and T-55 tanks. Active military service begins at the age of 18 and lasts 2 years and in some specialist branches 3 years.

Navy. In 1969 it was officially stated by the Hungarian Embassy in London that there were no longer any fighting ships in Hungary since the small fleet had been dispersed. In 1970 it was stated that there were no plans to enter new vessels into service.

Air Force. The Air Force is an integral part of the Army, with a strength of about 7,000 officers and men and 140 first-line aircraft, in 2 fighter divisions. The interceptor division has 3 regiments of MiG-21 and MiG-17 fighters. Su-7 fighter-bombers are replacing MiG-17s in the other division. Transport units are equipped with An-2, Il-14 and Li-2 (DC-3) aircraft. Other types in service include Mi-4 helicopters and L-29 Delfin and MiG-15UTI trainers. 'Guideline' surface-to-air missiles are also operational.

The security police (BKH) was reformed after the revolution of 1956 and now comes under the Ministry of the Interior.

The Militia has been taken over by the ordinary police and the Workers' Militia, a para-military organization armed with automatic weapons. Its strength in 1966 was about 35,000.

Three Soviet divisions are stationed in Hungary.

PLANNING. For details of past plans *see* previous issues of THE STATESMAN'S YEAR-BOOK. A 'New Economic Mechanism' came into effect on 1 Jan. 1968. It restricts central direction to overall policies, replaces direct by financial control and gives local managers more initiative. Some 20% of prices are now free; the remainder are fixed or subsidized. The fourth 5-year plan (1971–75) gives priority to power production and the chemical, aluminium and motor industries. Industrial production is scheduled to rise by 32%, agricultural production by 15%, national income by 30%, of which 75% is earmarked for investment.

AGRICULTURE. The large private holdings which characterized pre-war agriculture were broken up by the Communist government and distributed as individual smallholdings. After 1950 this policy was superseded by collectivization. A land law of 1968 permits collectives to own land, and guarantees individuals' rights to private plots. Collectives meet in a National Council of Agricultural Co-operatives.

In 1969 the agricultural area was (in 1,000 hectares) 8,383, of which 5,053 were arable, 1,284 meadows and pastures, 233 vineyards and 318 gardens.

In 1969 there were 2,678 collective farms with 5·9m. hectares of land (including 741,000 hectares of household plots) and 192 state farms with 1m. hectares. There were 546,000 hectares of private farm land. The irrigated area was 221,000 hectares; 67,000 tractors were in use.

Production statistics (in 1,000 metric tons):

Crops	1967	1968	1969	Crops	1967	1968	1969
Wheat	2,718	2,828	3,579[1]	Maize	3,521	3,764	4,732
Rye	225	238	234	Potatoes	1,507	1,335	1,590
Barley	934	904	907	Sugar-beet	3,354	3,471	3,300
Oats	86	68	80	Turnips	1,086	1,251	1,359

[1] Includes fodder wheat. 524,000 tons of fodder wheat were produced in 1968

Livestock in 1969 was (in 1,000 head) as follows: Cattle, 2,006; pigs, 5,334; poultry, 26,618; sheep, 3,277; horses, 249.

Livestock products (1969): Eggs, 2,640m.; milk, 1,845m. litres; wool, 10,830 metric tons; animals for slaughter, 1·35m. metric tons; butter, 21,300 metric tons.

The north shore of Lake Balaton and the Tokaj area are important wine-producing districts. Wine production in 1969 was 560m. litres.

FORESTRY. The area under forest in 1969 was 1,463,000 hectares. 22,000 hectares were afforested and 4·56m. cu. metres of timber were cut.

FISHERIES. Hungary retains important fishery preserves in the Danube and Tisza rivers and in Lake Balaton. Catch in 1969: 20,000 metric tons.

MINING. Coal and bauxite are mined, and there is some iron ore. Oil and natural gas have been found in the Szeged basin and in Zala county.

INDUSTRY. For a summary of the successive stages of nationalization from 1946 to 1952, *see* THE STATESMAN'S YEAR-BOOK, 1954, p. 1115.

Production statistics (in 1,000 metric tons):

	1965	1966	1967	1968	1969
Coal	31,437	30,348	27,029	27,213	26,500[1]
Iron ore	762	747	715	638	681
Pig-iron	1,581	1,633	1,657	1,638	1,753
Crude steel	2,520	2,648	2,739	2,903	3,032
Steel ingots and castings	781	1,743	1,784	1,983	2,020
Bauxite	1,478	1,428	1,649	1,959	1,935

[1] Including 3m. tons of lignite and 19·4m. tons of brown coal.

	1965	1966	1967	1968	1969
Aluminium	58	60	62	63	64
Alumina	267	288	328	381	408
Crude oil	1,802	1,705	1,686	1,807	1,754
Natural gas (1m. cu. metres)	..	1,553	2,045	2,691	3,235
Electricity (1m. kwh.)	11,177	11,856	12,475	13,155	14,069
Cement	2,383	2,601	2,656	2,801	2,565
Nitrogenous fertilizers	724	816	917	1,196	1,464
Superphosphates	615	711	824	846	917
Sulphuric acid	378	393	424	446	454
Sugar	428	436	432	389	417
Cotton cloth (1m. sq. metres)	306	308	329	330	311
Woollen (1m. sq. metres)	30	32	41	40	35
Silk and rayon (1m. sq. metres)	35	37	39	46	54
Flax and hemp (1m. sq. metres)	41	43	46	31	29
Leather footwear (1m. pairs)	26	27	30	33	33

An 800-Mw. nuclear power station is being built with Soviet help to begin producing in 1975.

PIPELINE. 2,266 km in 1969, for oil and natural gas, 3·7m. metric tons were supplied. The 'Friendship II' pipeline from the Ukraine supplies all crude oil, 92% of diesel and 89% of fuel oil imported.

LABOUR. In 1969 there were 4·99m. wage-earners (41% women) distributed as follows: Industry, 34%; agriculture 30%; education, health, administration, 16%; commerce, 8%; transport, 6%; building, 6%. A new labour code came into force on 1 Jan. 1968. It contains regulations in line with the 'New Economic Mechanism', abolishing many of the restrictions on the termination of employment and the obligation of the State to fix wages. Trade unions play an increased role. A 44-hour week is being selectively introduced and applied to some 2m. workers in 1970. The average monthly wage in 1970 was 2,032 forints. Trade union membership was 3·43m. in 1971.

COMMERCE. Hungary is heavily dependent on foreign trade, which even under the 'New Economic Mechanism' remains basically under state control. Trade for calendar years (in 1m. forints):

	1960	1965	1966	1967	1968	1969
Imports	10,260	17,849	18,379	20,841	21,163	22,631
Exports	11,455	17,721	18,705	19,971	21,004	24,462

In 1969, 68% of Hungary's trade was with communist countries (35% with USSR).

All exports and imports require licensing by the Ministry of Foreign Trade, and and mainly handled by 29 specialized foreign-trade agencies. From 1 Jan. 1968 hard currency has been available through the National Bank for enterprises trading with the west. Since 1968 also some 90 industrial and agricultural enterprises have been permitted to trade directly with foreign customers.

On 28 Feb. 1968 an Anglo-Hungarian trade agreement was signed for the period 1968–72 to develop mutual trade.

Total trade between Hungary and UK according to British Board of Trade returns (in £1,000 sterling):

	1966	1967	1968	1969	1970
Imports to UK	7,304	9,593	9,971	9,408	10,629
Exports from UK	10,120	12,216	12,429	12,744 }	18,995
Re-exports from UK	357	224	252	579 }	

SHIPPING. The Hungarian Danube–Sea Navigation Co. (Mahart) had in 1964, 12 sea-going vessels of together 9,300 gross tons; 290,000 tons of cargo were carried in 1967. Navigable waterways have a length of 1,688 km; 3·2m. tons of cargo and 3·1m. passengers were carried in 1969.

z

ROADS. In 1969 there were 29,405 km of road, including 6,026 km of first- and second-class motor roads. In 1968 passenger cars numbered 163,000. 130m. metric tons of freight and 422m. passengers were transported by road.

RAILWAYS. Construction length of public lines, 8,768 km, of which 781 km are electrified. In 1969, 35% of trains were still hauled by steam. 111m. metric tons of freight and 547m. passengers were carried.

AVIATION. Hungarian Air Lines (Malév) operate from Ferihegy airport, 16 km from Budapest. There is an internal line to Debrecen. In 1969, 318,085 passengers were carried. Malév operates flights to Austria, Belgium, France, West Germany, Greece, Italy, Scandinavia, UAR, UK and European communist capitals. Western airlines with flights to Budapest include BEA, Air France, SABENA and KLM.

POST. Number of post offices (1969), 2,433; number of telephones, 684,389. Wireless licences, 2,531,400; television licences, 1,595,600. Hungary, Czechoslovakia, Poland, USSR and East Germany are linked in the Intervision system. There are 2 central radio stations and a television station.

BANKING. All banking activities are controlled by the National Bank of Hungary, including the post office savings bank. (Deposits in 1967: 24,800m. forints.) The National Bank is the main authority over foreign-exchange transactions: it controls security deposits, issues hard currency to enterprises trading abroad and authorizes the acceptance of foreign credits. In 1967 it set up a Credit Policy Council to administer a new credit, tax and profit allocation system for enterprises. Since 1 Jan. 1968 banks have been permitted to give unlimited credit to enterprises judged efficient.

The National Credit Institute of Co-operatives handles all credit transactions for farmers, artisans and co-operatives.

WEIGHTS AND MEASURES. The metric system of weights and measures is in use. For land measure a cadastral yoke (1 acre = 0·7033 cadastral yoke) is used.

DIPLOMATIC REPRESENTATIVES

Hungary maintains embassies in:

Afghánistán	Finland	Netherlands
Albania	France	Nigeria
Algeria	Germany (East)	Norway
Argentina	Ghana	Peru
Austria	Greece	Poland
Belgium	Guinea	Romania
Bolivia	India	Sweden
Bulgaria	Indonesia	Switzerland
Burma	Iran	Syria
Cambodia	Iraq	Tanzania
Canada	Italy	USSR
Ceylon	Japan	UAR
Chile	Jordan	UK
China	Kenya	USA
Congo (K.)	Korea (North)	Uruguay
Cuba	Kuwait	Venezuela
Czechoslovakia	Laos	Vietnam (North)
Denmark	Mongolia	Yemen
Ethiopia	Morocco	Yugoslavia

Hungary maintains legations in Brazil and Sudan.

Hungary is also in diplomatic relations with:

Central African	Ecuador	Nepál
Republic	Equatorial Guinea	Pakistan
Ceylon	Iceland	Sierra Leone
Colombia	Lebanon	Singapore
Congo (Br.)	Malaysia	Togo
Costa Rica	Mali	Tunisia
Cyprus	Malta	Uganda
Dahomey	Mauritania	Zambia

OF HUNGARY IN GREAT BRITAIN (35 Eaton Place, SWI)

Ambassador: Dr Vencel Hàzi.
Counsellors: Lászlo Ujházy (*Commercial*); György Varsányi. *Military and Air Attaché:* Col. G. Paszka. *First Secretaries:* Géza Meszlényi; Pál Csillag (*Press*); András Halász (*Cultural*).

OF GREAT BRITAIN IN HUNGARY

Ambassador: D. S. L. Dodson, CMG, MC.
First Secretaries: O. R. Blair (*Head of Chancery*); P. D. R. Davies; J. Reeve (*Commercial*); C. R. Hewer (*Cultural*); Miss A. M. Wood (*Consul and Visa Officer*). *Service Attachés:* Lieut.-Col. M. H. Burge (*Defence and Military*); Wing Cdr J. H. Rogers, AFC (*Air*).

There is a consular representative in Budapest.

OF HUNGARY IN THE USA (2437–15th St. NW, Washington, D.C., 20009)

Ambassador: János Nagy.
Counsellor: József Molnar (*Commercial*). *First Secretary:* Dr Sandor Vargar. *Military and Air Attaché:* Lieut.-Col. Imre Mozsik.

OF THE USA IN HUNGARY

Ambassador: Alfred Puhan.
Deputy Chief of Mission: F. Meehan. *Heads of Sections:* Ross P. Titu, (*Political*); H. E. Wilgis (*Economic*); C. G. Scerback (*Press and Cultural*); W. H. Shephard (*Consular*). *Service Attachés:* Col. W. O. Peake (*Army*), Lieut.-Col. R. P. von Romberg (*Air*).

BOOKS OF REFERENCE

Statisztikai Évkönyv. Budapest, annual; occasional editions in English (latest, 1970)
Statistical Pocket Book of Hungary (in English). Budapest, from 1962
Hungarian Review. Budapest, monthly
Hungary 66 (67 etc.). Budapest, annual from 1966
Erdei, F. (ed.), *Information Hungary.* London, 1968
Friss, I. (ed.), *Reform of the Economic Mechanism in Hungary.* Budapest, 1969
Halász, Z. (ed.), *Hungary: geography, history, political and social system* [etc.]. Budapest, 1963
Kovrig, B., *The Hungarian People's Republic.* Baltimore, 1970
Macartney, C. A., *Hungary: a short history.* London, 1962
Orzágh, L., *Magyar-Angol Szótár.* Budapest, 1968.—*Angol-Magyar Szótár.* Budapest, 1968
Pécsi, M., and Sárfalvi, B., *The Geography of Hungary.* Budapest, 1964

ICELAND

Lýðveldið Ísland

HISTORY. The first settlers came to Iceland in 874. Between 930 and 1264 Iceland was an independent republic, but by the 'Old Treaty' of 1263 the country recognized the rule of the King of Norway. In 1381 Iceland, together with Norway, came under the rule of the Danish kings, but when Norway was separated from Denmark in 1814, Iceland remained under the rule of Denmark. Since 1 Dec. 1918 it has been acknowledged as a sovereign state. It was united with Denmark only through the common sovereign until it was proclaimed an independent republic on 17 June 1944.

CONSTITUTION AND GOVERNMENT. On 24 May 1944 the people of Iceland decided in a referendum to sever all ties with the Danish Crown. The voters were asked whether they were in favour of the abrogation of the Union Act, and whether they approved of the bill for a republican constitution: 70,725 voters were for severance of all political ties with Denmark and only 370 against it; 69,048 were in favour of the republican constitution, 1,042 against it and 2,505 votes were invalid. On 17 June 1944 the republic was formally proclaimed, and as the republic's first president the Alþingi elected Sveinn Björnsson for a 1-year term (re-elected 1945 and 1949; died 25 Jan. 1952). The President is now elected for a 4-year term.

President of the Republic of Iceland: Kristján Eldjárn (elected 30 June 1968, with 67,544 out of 102,972 valid votes, inaugurated 1 Aug. 1968).

National flag: Red cross, with white borders, on blue.
National anthem: Ó Guð vors lands (words by M. Jochumsson, 1874; tune by S. Sveinbjørnsson).

The official language is Icelandic (*íslenzka*).

The *Alþingi* (Parliament) is divided into two Houses, the Upper House and the Lower House. The former is composed of one-third of the members elected by the whole Alþingi in common sitting. The remaining two-thirds of the members form the Lower House. The members of the Althing receive payment for their services, besides travelling expenses.

The budget bills must be laid before the two Houses in joint session, but all other bills can be introduced in either of the Houses. If the Houses do not agree, they assemble in a common sitting and the final decision is given by a majority of two-thirds of the voters, with the exception of budget bills, where a simple majority is sufficient. The ministers have free access to both Houses, but can vote only in the House of which they are members.

The electoral law enacted in 1959 provides for an Alþingi of 60 members. Of these, 49 are elected in 8 constituencies by proportional representation; the remaining 11 are apportioned to the parties according to their total vote.

At the elections held on 11 June 1967 the following parties were returned: Independence Party, 23; Progressives, 18; Labour Union (Communists), 10; Social Democrats, 9.

The executive power is exercised under the President by the Cabinet. The coalition Cabinet, as constituted in Oct., 1970, is composed as follows:

Prime Minister and Manufacturing Industries: Jóhann Hafstein (Ind. Party).
Justice and Church: Andur Anduns (Ind. Party).
Fisheries and Health and Social Welfare: Eggert Þorsteinnson (Soc. Dem.).
Foreign and Social Affairs: Emil Jónsson (Soc. Dem.).
Finance: Magnús Jónsson (Ind. Party).
Education and Commerce: Gylfi Þ. Gíslason (Soc. Dem.).
Agriculture and Communications: Ingólfur Jónsson (Ind. Party).

The ministers are responsible for their acts. They can be impeached by the Alþingi, and in that case their cause will be decided by the *Landsdómur*, a special tribunal for parliamentary impeachments.

LOCAL ADMINISTRATION. For administrative purposes Iceland is divided into 16 provinces (*syslur*), each under a chief executive (*syslumaður*). Each province forms one or two municipal districts with a council superintending the 213 rural municipalities. There are also 14 urban municipalities with a town council, independent of the provinces, and forming by themselves administrative districts co-ordinate with the provinces. The municipal councils are elected direct by universal suffrage (men and women over 20 years of age), in urban municipalities by proportional representation, but in rural municipalities by simple majority.

AREA AND POPULATION. Iceland is a large island in the North Atlantic, close to the Arctic Circle, and comprises an area of about 103,000 sq. km (39,758 sq. miles), with its extreme northern point (the Rifstangi) lying in 66° 32′ N. lat., and its most southerly point (Dyrhólaey, Portland) in 63° 24′ N. lat., not including the islands north and south of the land; if these are included, the country extends from 67° 10′ N. (the Kolbeinsey) to 63° 19′ N. (Geirfuglasker, one of the Westman Islands). It stretches from 13° 30′ (the Gerpir) to 24° 32′ W. long. (Látrabjarg). The skerry *Hvalbakur* (The Whaleback) lies 13° 16′ W. long.

The 25 constituencies of the country are now grouped in 7 districts.

District	Inhabited land (sq. km)	Mountain pasture (sq. km)	Waste-land (sq. km)	Total area (sq. km)	Population (1 Dec. 1969)
Reykjanes area	1,266	716	—	1,982	118,798
West	5,011	3,415	275	8,711	13,282
Western Peninsula	4,130	3,698	1,652	9,470	10,138
Northland West	4,867	5,278	2,948	13,093	10,000
Northland East	9,890	6,727	5,751	22,368	22,113
East				(21,991	11,274
South	16,921	17,929	12,555	(25,214	17,887
Iceland	42,085	37,553	23,181	102,819	203,442

In 1969, 32,502 were domiciled in rural districts and 170,940 in towns and villages (of over 300 inhabitants). The population is almost entirely Icelandic. In 1964 foreigners numbered 2,758; of these 1,173 were Danish, 443 USA, 402 German and 233 Norwegian nationals.

The capital, Reykjavík, had on 1 Dec. 1969, a population of 81,476, other towns are Akranes, 4,245; Akureyri, 10,567; Hafnarfjörður, 9,538; Húsavik, 1,988; Ísafjörður, 2,678; Keflavík, 5,533; Kópavogur, 10,991; Neskaupstaður, 1,527; Ólafsfjörður, 1,092; Sauðarkrókur, 1,507; Seyðisfjörður, 905; Siglufjörður, 2,248; Vestmannaeyjar, 5,074.

VITAL STATISTICS for calendar years:

	Living births	Still-born	Marriages	Divorces	Deaths	Infant deaths
1966	4,692 [1]	58 [1]	1,551	192 [1]	1,391	64
1967	4,404 [1]	50	1,700	184	1,385 [1]	59 [1]
1968	4,227 [1]	52	1,687	210	1,387	59
1969	4,200	47	1,722	263	1,450	49

[1] Revised.

RELIGION. The national church, and the only one endowed by the State, is Evangelical Lutheran. But there is complete religious liberty, and no civil disabilities are attached to those not of the national religion. The affairs of the national church are under the superintendence of a bishop. In 1964, 2,104 persons (1·1%) were Dissenters and 1,999 persons (1·1%) did not belong to any religious community.

EDUCATION. There is a university in Reykjavík, inaugurated on 17 June 1911, with an enrolment of about 1,500 students. In 1968–69 there were 5 grammar schools (2,200 pupils), 128 general secondary schools (13,500 pupils), 10 vocational schools of home economics for women (380 pupils), one training school for primary and secondary school teachers (820 pupils) and 2 other teachers' training colleges (40 pupils), 2 agricultural and 1 horticultural school (125 pupils), 5 schools of navigation (410 pupils), 2 commercial high schools (620 pupils), 18 part-time vocational training schools for apprentices in trade (about 2,750 pupils), 1 technological college (150 pupils), 3 schools for training of nurses, midwives, etc. (320 pupils). There are also many part-time schools of cultural activities, such as 23 schools of music, 3 schools of art and crafts, 3 schools of dance and drama and 2 schools of athletics. There are also some courses on various subjects for adults and continuation schools for young people. Elementary instruction is compulsory for children from 7 to 15 years.

CINEMAS (1968). There were 25 cinemas with a seating capacity of 12,600.

NEWSPAPERS (1969). There are 5 daily newspapers, all in Reykjavík, with a combined circulation of about 85,000.

SOCIAL WELFARE. In 1946 there was enacted a new national insurance scheme, covering the whole nation, and operative from 1947. It falls into two main classes of activities, health service (including health protection and medical treatment and the care of sick persons) and income insurance (securing for the insured persons a living wage when they are no longer able to earn their bread themselves, as, for instance, owing to old-age, disablement, sickness, accident or want of support). The health service division, however, is only partially operative.

JUSTICE. The lower courts of justice are those of the provincial magistrates (sýslumenn) and town judges (bæjarfógetar). From these there is an appeal to the Supreme Court (hæstiréttur) in Reykjavík, which has 5 judges.

FINANCE. Currency. The Icelandic monetary unit is the króna, pl. krónur. After several devaluations (1960, 1961, 1967, 1968) the US$1 = kr. 88; £1 = kr. 210). Note circulation, 31 Dec. 1969, was 1,226·2m. kr.

Budget. Current revenue and expenditure for calendar years (in 1,000 kr.):

	1965	1966	1967	1968[1,2]	1969	1970
Revenue	3,690,226	4,677,787	4,646,000	6,195,296	7,096,482	8,396,973
Expenditure	3,413,479	3,899,193	4,265,000	6,120,431	7,000,607	8,187,384

[1] Estimates.   [2] Not comparable with former years.

Main items of the Treasury accounts for 1969 in (1,000 kr.):

Revenue		Expenditure	
Direct taxes	1,514,994	Presidency	4.221
Indirect taxes	5,068,708	Althing	51,553
Profit from government enterprises	801,757	Cabinet	3,169
		Justice and ecclesiastical affairs	662,418
		Education	1,232,955
		Social affairs	2,495,316
		Commerce	501,510
		Foreign affairs	135,428
		Fisheries, agriculture and power	990,624
		Finance	446,336
		Communications and industry	1,047,389

The public debt of Iceland was on 31 Dec. 1969, 3,062·9m. kr., of which the foreign debt amounted to 512·6m. kr. and the internal debt to 2,550·3m. kr.

DEFENCE. Iceland possesses neither an army nor a navy. Under the North Atlantic Treaty, US army, navy and air forces are stationed in Iceland as the Iceland Defence Force.

Five armed fishery protection vessels are maintained by the Coast Guard.

AGRICULTURE. Of the total area of Iceland, about six-sevenths is unproductive, but only about 0·5% is under cultivation, which is confined to hay, potatoes and turnips. In 1968 the total hay crop from cultivated and uncultivated land was 307,707 metric tons; the crop of potatoes, 5,600 metric tons, and of turnips, 500 metric tons. At the end of 1968 the livestock was as follows: Horses, 34,671; cattle, 52,274 (including 36,001 milch cows); sheep, 820,166; pigs, 4,148; poultry, 153,735.

FISHERIES. Fishing vessels in Dec. 1967 numbered 773 with a gross tonnage of 80,226. Total catch in 1968, 599,296 tons; 1969, 685,853 tons.

The Icelandic Government on 30 June 1958 issued a decree according to which the fishery limits off Iceland were, effective 1 Sept. 1958, extended from 4 to 12 nautical miles. On 11 March 1961 Great Britain withdrew her objection to the 12-mile limit around Iceland, but was permitted to fish in certain areas of the outer 6 miles of the limit until 11 March 1964. The base-lines from which the limit is calculated have been modified in favour of Iceland.

ELECTRICITY. The installed capacity of power plants at the end of 1969 totalled 354,500 kw. (333,200 in public-owned plants), of which 247,100 kw. comprised hydro-electric plants. Total energy production in public-owned plants in 1969 amounted to 903m. kwh.; in privately-owned plants, 10m. kwh.

COMMERCE. Total value of imports and exports in 1,000 kr.:

	1964	1965	1966	1967	1968	1969
Imports	5,635,993	5,901,034	6,852,621	7,116,231	8,246,177	10,855,863
Exports	4,775,949	5,558,800	6,046,951	4,299,368	5,097,724	9,466,368

Leading exports (in 1,000 kg and 1,000 kr.):

	1968		1969	
	Quantity	Value	Quantity	Value
Salted fish	29,279·5	728,647	31,024·6	999,349
Frozen fish	61,705·8	1,554,267	77,111·2	3,121,039
Stockfish	3,545·9	172,247	7,983·2	412,624
Herring (cured, frozen, salted)	47,625·5	715,332	59,393·7	646,874
Herring oil	26,829·4	145,600	28,990·4	239,747
Herring meal	35,726·3	249,749	31,443·9	375,197

Leading imports (in 1,000 metric tons and 1,000 kr.):

	1968		1969	
	Quantity	Value	Quantity	Value
Ships (number)	34	245,582	1	46,975
Fuel oil	444,929·6	623,565	342.025·1	680,045
Cereals	12,809·0	115,977	13,419·5	169,751
Animal feed	57,811·7	304,433	55,065·7	381,118
Gasoline	56,188·4	110,850	52,436·0	149,759
Wood (1,000 cu. ft)	1,516·9	191,289	804·1	100,861
Motor vehicles (number)	2,814	274,561	1,159	129,038
Fishing nets	522·2	99,817	586·6	156,132

Value of trade with principal countries for 3 years (in 1,000 kr.):

	1967		1968		1969	
	Imports (c.i.f.)	Exports (f.o.b.)	Imports (c.i.f.)	Exports (f.o.b.)	Imports (c.i.f.)	Exports (f.o.b.)
Austria	14,514	222	15,652	352	23.725	5,128
Belgium	139,631	44,174	196,687	9,629	173.603	33,094
Brazil	84,255	31,064	94,824	64,243	168.986	171,908
Canada	17,306	20,504	13,852	1,190	26.588	2,648
Czechoslovakia	95,832	48,018	107,512	42,325	132.280	55,678
Denmark	636,072	220,515	833,285	160,484	1,032,820	538,090
Faroe Islands	664	31,314	2,321	64,828	896	101,695
Finland	153,326	155,365	214,494	188,212	290,110	230,417
France	94,239	57,927	172,922	21,222	211,111	86,105
Germany (East)	143,974	53,953	40,418	10,473	55,113	7,615
Germany (West)	917,749	274,928	1,309,903	416,147	1,818,718	813,780
Greece	331	36,680	564	66,946	783	99,946
Hungary	7,422	104	6,170	3,369	95.165	9,520
India	7,162	—	5,784	—	14.995	—
Irish Republic	3,957	13,400	4,659	7,059	3,450	18,604
Israel	11,141	979	15,259	8,862	28.296	482
Italy	106,608	128,686	120,828	239,856	208.282	319,967
Japan	266,598	1,247	278,590	5,556	281.320	10,441
Netherlands	451,931	125,528	515,133	65,618	568,797	219,853
Netherlands West Indies	82,682	—	93,594	—	—	—
Nigeria	195	76,479	429	63,682	191	209.887
Norway	604,708	63,250	617,034	75,425	699.284	172.781
Poland	95,423	101,155	124,942	150,378	179,749	168,220

	1967		1968		1969	
	Imports (c.i.f.)	Exports (f.o.b.)	Imports (c.i.f.)	Exports (f.o.b.)	Imports (c.i.f.)	Exports (f.o.b.)
Portugal	12,180	188,661	12,338	270,926	35,822	412,501
Spain	65,403	14,017	57,084	136,691	66,267	105,709
Sweden	469,638	358,373	463,277	464,509	528,001	589,032
Switzerland	65,403	14,017	157,857	27,937	452,216	103,450
USSR	452,558	506,616	653,906	520,462	870,129	839,986
UK	949,862	896,254	1,079,788	644,237	1,378,416	1,323,926
USA	1,095,289	650,619	903,409	1,280,698	934,351	2,614,465

Total trade (British Board of Trade returns) between Iceland and UK (in £1,000 sterling):

	1966	1967	1968	1969	1970
Imports to UK	8,719	8,578	5,158	6,774	8,951
Exports from UK	7,400	7,040	6,730	5,891 }	9,284
Re-exports from UK	176	212	147	174 }	

SHIPPING. The mercantile marine of Iceland consisted, in Dec. 1969, of 20 steam vessels (13,853 gross tons) and 826 motor vessels (135,904 gross tons).

ROADS. There are no railways in Iceland. Iceland possesses between 9,000–10,000 km of high roads, whereof the greater part has been made carriageable. Motor vehicles registered at the end of 1969 numbered 43,854, of which 37,859 were passenger cars and 5,717 trucks; there were also 278 motor cycles. On 26 May 1968 Iceland changed from left-hand to right-hand traffic.

AVIATION. One large and some small companies maintain regular services between Reykjavík and various places in Iceland (1969: 107,032 passengers, 455 metric tons of mail; 3,283 metric tons of freight). The chief company maintains regular services between Iceland and the UK and Europe. Another Icelandic company provides regular air service between the Scandinavian countries, Luxembourg, Amsterdam and the UK on the one hand and New York on the other hand. In 1969 the two companies carried in scheduled foreign flights 248,359 passengers, 593 metric tons of mail and 2,108 metric tons of freight.

POST. At the end of 1969 the number of post offices was 229 and telephone and telegraph offices 187, number of telephone subscribers 54,943, number of holders of wireless licences about 51,000 and television licences 36,000.

BANKING. By Act of 29 March 1961 the Central Bank of Iceland was established, which took over the central bank function up to that date exercised by the *Landsbanki Íslands* (owned entirely by the State). Other banks are: *Búnaðarbanki Íslands* (the Rural Bank of Iceland), a state bank, founded in 1930; *Útvegsbanki Íslands* (the Fishing Trade Bank), founded in 1930 as a joint-stock bank, which in 1957 became a state bank; *Iðnaðarbanki Íslands* (Industrial Bank), a joint-stock bank, established 1953, part of the shares being owned by the Government; *Verzlunarbanki Íslands*, established in 1961; *Samvinnubanki Íslands* (Co-operative Bank), established in 1963. On 31 Aug. 1970 the accounts of the Central Bank balanced at 11,057·3m. kr.

At the end of 1969 there were 53 savings banks with deposits amounting to 1,936m. kr.

WEIGHTS AND MEASURES. The metric system of weights and measures is obligatory.

DIPLOMATIC REPRESENTATIVES

Iceland maintains embassies in:

Belgium
Denmark (also for Irish Republic and Turkey)
France (also for Luxembourg and Yugoslavia)

Germany (West) (also for Greece, Iran, Japan and Switzerland)
Norway (also for Czechoslovakia, Israel, Italy and Poland)
Sweden (also fo Austria and Finland)

USSR (also for Bulgaria, Hungary and Romania)
UK (also for the Netherlands, Portugal and Spain)

USA (also for Argentina, Brazil, Canada, Cuba and Mexico)

OF ICELAND IN GREAT BRITAIN (1 Eaton Terrace, SW1)

Ambassador: Guðmunur Í. Guðmundsson, KBE (accredited 3 Nov. 1965).
Counsellor: Eiríkur Benedikz.

There are consular representatives in Aberdeen, Bristol, Dover, Edinburgh, Fleetwood, Glasgow, Grimsby, Hull, Lerwick, Liverpool, Manchester and Newcastle upon Tyne.

OF GREAT BRITAIN IN ICELAND

Ambassador and Consul-General: John McKenzie, CMG, MBE.
First Secretary: D. H. Fowler, MBE.

There are also consular representatives at Akureyri and Ísafjörður.

OF ICELAND IN THE USA (2022 Connecticut Ave. NW.
Washington, D.C., 20008)

Ambassador: (Vacant).
Counsellor: Hörður Helgason.

OF THE USA IN ICELAND

Ambassador: Luther I. Replogle. *Deputy Head of Mission:* Theodore A. Tremblay.

BOOKS OF REFERENCE

STATISTICAL INFORMATION. The Icelandic Statistical Office, Hagstofa Islands (Reykjavík was founded in 1914. *Director:* Klemens Tryggvason. Its main publications are

Hagskýrslur Islands. Statistique de l'Islande (from 1912)
Hagtíðindi (Statistical Journal) (from 1916)
Statistical Bulletin. Issued quarterly by the National Bank of Iceland and the Statistical Bureau of Iceland (from 1931 to 1962, monthly)

Heilbrigðisskýrslur. Public Health in Iceland (latest issue for 1956; published 1959)
Briem, Helgi P., *Iceland and the Icelanders.* Maplewood, 1945
Cleasby, R., *An Icelandic–English Dictionary.* 2nd ed. Oxford, 1957
Foss, H. (ed.), *Directory of Iceland.* Annual. Reykjavík, 1907–40, 1948 ff.
Hansson, Ólafur, *Facts about Iceland.* Reykjavík, 1951
Hermannsson, Halldór, *Islandica*—An annual relating to Iceland and the Fiske Icelandic Collection in Cornell University Library. Ithaca (from 1908)
Hood, J. C. F., *Icelandic Church Saga.* London, 1946
Leaf, H., *Iceland Yesterday and Today.* London, 1949
Þorðarson, Björn, *Iceland: Past and Present.* 2nd ed. Oxford, 1945
Þorðarson, Matthias, *The Althing, Iceland's Thousand-Year-Old Parliament, 930–1930.* Reykjavík, 1930
Þorsteinsson, Þorsteinn, *Iceland, 1946: A Handbook published on the 60th Anniversary of the National Bank of Iceland.* 4th ed. Reykjavík, 1946
Trial, G. T., *History of Education in Iceland.* Cambridge, 1945
Zoëga, G. T., *Íslensk-ensk (and Ensk-íslensk) orðabók.* 3rd ed. 2 vols. Reykjavík, 1932–51

NATIONAL LIBRARY. Landsbókasafnið, Reykjavík. *Librarian:* Dr Finnbogi Gudmundsson.

REPUBLIC OF INDONESIA
Republik Indonesia

GOVERNMENT AND CONSTITUTION. Indonesia is a sovereign, independent republic which was proclaimed by Dr Sukarno and Dr Hatta on 17 Aug. 1945. In the 16th century Portuguese traders in quest of spices settled in some of the islands, but were ejected by the British, who in turn were ousted by the Dutch (1595). From 1602 the Netherlands East India Company conquered the Netherlands East Indies, and ruled them until the dissolution of the company in 1798. Thereafter the Netherlands Government ruled the colony from 1816 to 1945.

Complete and unconditional sovereignty was transferred to the Republic of the United States of Indonesia on 27 Dec. 1949, except for the western part of New Guinea, the status of which was to be determined through negotiations between Indonesia and the Netherlands within one year after the transfer of sovereignty. A union was created to regulate the relationship between the two countries. A settlement of the New Guinea (West Irian) question was, however, delayed until 15 Aug. 1962, when, through the good offices of the United Nations, an agreement was concluded for the transfer of the territory to Indonesia on 1 May 1963. In Feb. 1956 Indonesia abrogated the union and in Aug. 1956 repudiated Indonesia's debt to the Netherlands.

During 1950 the federal system which had sprung up in 1946-48 (see THE STATESMAN'S YEAR-BOOK, 1950, p. 1233) was abolished, and Indonesia was again made a unitary state. The provisional constitution was passed by the Provisional House of Representatives on 14 and came into force on 17 Aug. 1950. On 5 July 1959 by Presidential decree, the Constitution of 1945 was reinstated and the Constituent Assembly dissolved.

On 12 Jan. 1960 President Sukarno issued a decree enabling him to control the political parties, with the power (on the recommendation of the Supreme Court) to dissolve them. He also set up a mass organization, the National Front, and a supreme State body called the People's Consultative Assembly.

On 6 March 1960 the President prorogued Parliament to be reorganized on the basis of the 1945 constitution. Local administrations nominated 130 members representing political parties and 153 members representing functional groups, who formed the new 'Mutual Co-operation House of Representatives'.

A communist attempt to overthrow the government in Sept./Oct. 1965 was suppressed by the army. Some 80,000 communists are said to have been killed, and the communists killed 6 generals and several officials of the armed forces. The Communist Party was banned on 12 March 1967.

The 3-year 'confrontation' with Malaysia ended on 11 Aug. 1966, when an agreement was signed in Jakarta, terminating hostilities and re-establishing diplomatic relations.

On 11–12 March 1966 the military commanders under the leadership of Lieut.-Gen. Suharto took over the executive power while leaving President Sukarno as the head of State. The Communist Party was at once outlawed and the National Front was dissolved in Oct. 1966. On 22 Feb. 1967 Sukarno handed over all his powers to Gen. Suharto.

President, Prime Minister and Minister of Defence: Gen. Suharto, elected by the Provisional People's Consultative Congress and sworn in on 27 March 1968 and formed a new cabinet on 6 June with the following membership:

General elections are to be held on 5 July 1971.

Home Affairs: Lieut.-Gen. Amir Machmud. *Foreign Affairs:* Adam Malik. *Justice:* Professor Umar Seno Adji. *Information:* Air Vice-Marshal Budiardjo. *Finance:* Dr Ali Wardhana. *Commerce:* Professor Sumitro Djojohadikusumo. *Agriculture:* Professor Thojib Hadiwidjaja. *Industry:* Maj.-Gen. Mohammad Jusuf. *Mining:* Professor Sumantri Brodjonegroro. *Health:* Professor G. A. Siwabessi. *Religious Affairs:* K. H. Muhammad Dachlan. *Labour:* Vice-Admiral Mursalin. *Resettlement and Co-operatives:* Lieut.-Gen. Sarbini.

National flag: Red, white (horizontal).
National anthem: Indonesia Raya (tune by Wage Rudolf Supratman, 1928).

Feith, H., *The Decline of Constitutional Democracy in Indonesia.* Cornell Univ. Press, 1962
Schiller, A. A., *The Formation of Federal Indonesia, 1945–49.* The Hague, 1955
Palmier, L. H., *Indonesia and the Dutch.* OUP, 1961

AREA AND POPULATION. Indonesia, covering a total area of 1·9m. sq. km (575,450 sq. miles), consists of the islands of Sumatra, Java and Madura, Sulawesi (Celebes), Kalimantan (Borneo), Nusa Tenggara (Lesser Sundas),

Maluku (Moluccas), West Irian (the western half of New Guinea) and some 3,000 smaller islands and islets. The capital is Djakarta with a population of approximately 4·75m. Indonesia has a tropical climate with two monsoons; the dry (June–Sept.) and the wet (Oct.–April).

The total population in 1961 (census) was 97,085,348, distributed as follows: Java and Madura, 63m.; Sumatra, 15·7m.; Sulawesi, 7m.; Nusa Tenggara, 6·5m.; Kalimantan, 4m. The population of West Irian was in 1962 estimated at about 700,000.

Estimated population, 1969, was 118m., of whom 74m. lived in Java and 19·7m. in Sumatra.

Indonesia is divided into the following provinces (capitals in brackets): Atjeh (Banda Atjeh, formerly Kutaradja), North Sumatra (Medan), West Sumatra (Padang), Riau (Pakan Baru), Djambi (Telanaipura, formerly Djambi), South Sumatra (Palembang), West Java (Bandung), Central Java (Semarang), East Java (Surabaya), West Kalimantan (Pontianak), South Kalimantan (Bandjarmasin), East Kalimantan (Samarinda), Central Kalimantan (Palangka Raja, formerly Pahandut), North Sulawesi (Menado), South Sulawesi (Makassar), Bali (Singaradja), West Nusa Tenggara (Mataram), East Nusa Tenggara (Kupang), Maluku (Ambon), West Irian (Djajapura, formerly Sukarnapura).

In Dec. 1957 Dutch citizens in Indonesia numbered about 60,000. On 5 Dec. the Indonesian Government ordered the expulsion, by stages, of all unemployed Dutch nationals. Dutch citizens in 1962 numbered under 10,000.

The principal ethnic groups are the Atjinese, Bataks and Minangkabaus in Sumatra, the Javanese and Sundanese in Java, the Madurese in Madura, the Balinese in Bali, the Sasaks in Lombok, the Menadonese and Buginese in Sulawesi, the Dayaks in Borneo and the Ambonese in the Moluccas.

Bahasa Indonesia is the official language of the Republic.

RELIGION. Religious liberty is granted to all denominations. The majority of the Indonesians are Moslems. There are nearly 3m. Christians; their main strength is in Central and East Java, North Sulawesi, East Nusa Tengarra and the Moluccas. There are also about a million Buddhists, probably for the greater part Chinese. Hinduism flourishes on the island of Bali.

There are 30 Protestant bodies affiliated with the National Council of Churches in Indonesia, with about 4,000 congregations, 3,000 Indonesian ministers, 100 foreign missionaries and 2·2m. adherents.

The Roman Catholic Church had 1,129,000 members in 1962.

EDUCATION. The following table shows the number of schools, teachers and students:

Schools	Number	Teachers	Students
Primary schools (1960–61).	37,376	205,860	8,552,475
Secondary schools (1959–60)	6,742	57,953	731,262
Universities and Academies (1958–59)	299	4,316	41,000

English is the first foreign language taught in schools.

Higher education is given at the University of Indonesia at Djakarta and Bogor (9,038 students in 1956), the University of Gadjah Mada at Jogjakarta (11,772 students), Airlangga University at Surabaya, Malang and Bali (6,789 students), Andalas University (1956) at Bukittinggi, Pajakumbuh, Padang and Batusangkar (1,001 students), Hasanuddin University (1956) at Makassar and Tondano (1,224 students), Padjadjaran University (1958) at Bandung (4,720 students), the University of North Sumatra at Medan (2,000 students), and the Institute of Technology at Bandung (3,000 students), the State Institute of Islam (1960) at Jogjakarta, the Sriwidjaja University (1960) at Palembang and Tandjungkarang, the Lambung Mangkurat University (1960) at Bandjarmasin, the University of Sjah Kuala at Banda Atjeh, the University of Diponegoro at Semarang, the University of North and Central Sulawesi at Menado, the Institute of Technology at Surabaja and the new universities of Riau (at Pakanbaru), Maluku (at Ambon), East Nusa Tenggara (at Kupang), West Nusa Tenggara (at

Mataram), and Tjenderawasih (at Djajapura), Mulawarman (at Samarinda), Brawidjaja (at Malang), Pantjasila (at Djakarta) and Bung Karno (at Surakarta) universities. In 1961 a separate Department of Higher Education and Science was set up.

In 1963, 18% of the population were illiterate. On 1 Jan, 1965 the country was declared free from illiteracy in the age-groups 13 to 45.

CINEMAS (1962). There were 1,011 cinemas with a seating capacity of 470,000.

NEWSPAPERS (1970). There were 11 leading Indonesian daily newspapers with an estimated circulation of 329,000.

JUSTICE. The judicial organization is under the direction of the Minister of Justice. There are courts of first instance, high courts of appeal in the larger towns and a supreme court of justice for the whole of Indonesia in the capital.

In civil law the population is divided into three main groups: Indonesians, Europeans and foreign Orientals, to whom different law systems are applicable. When, however, people from different groups are involved, a system of so-called 'inter-gentile' law is applied.

The present criminal law, which has been in force since 1918, is codified and is based on European penal law. This law is equally applicable to all groups of the population. For private and commercial law, however, there are various systems applicable for the various groups of the population. For the Indonesians, a system of private and agrarian law is applicable; this is called Adat Law, and is mainly uncodified. For the other groups the prevailing private and commercial law system is codified in the Private Law Act (1847) and the Commercial Law Act (1847). These Acts have their origins in the French *Code Civile* and *Code du Commerce* through the similar Dutch codifications. These Acts are entirely applicable to Europeans, whereas to foreign Orientals they are applicable with some exceptions, mainly in the fields of family law and inheritance.

FINANCE. **Currency.** The monetary unit is the *rupiah* (abbreviated Rp.), divided into 100 *sen*. There are bank-notes of 1, $2\frac{1}{2}$, 5, 10, 25, 50 and 100 rupiahs and aluminium coins of 1, 5, 10, 25 and cupro-nickel coins of 50 sen.

On 24 Aug. 1959 the currency denominations were reduced to a tenth of their nominal value. Further devaluations took effect on 14 Dec. 1965, when a new *rupiah* worth 1,000 old rupiahs was introduced, and on 22 Dec. 1965, when the *rupiah* for imports and exports was revalued at Rp. 10,000 = US$1.

Special bank-notes—called 'Irian Barat rupiah'—were issued on 1 May 1963 for the province of West Irian.

Budget. The budget, for calendar years, was as follows (in Rp. 1m.):

	1960	1961	1962	1963	1964	1965
Gross revenue	50,300	62,200	74,000	162,100	283,300	923,400
Gross expenditure	57,100	88,500	122,100	285,400	682,000	2,244,100

Energetic measures to carry into effect a rehabilitation and stabilization programme have been taken in hand, effective from Sept. 1966 to be implemented by the end of 1969. The programme envisages the decrease and ultimate elimination of the inflation, the balancing of imports and exports, the restoration of the production capacity of the country (including transport) and the encouragement of capital inflow.

DEFENCE. The Indonesian Armed Forces were formally set up on 5 Oct. 1945. On 11 Oct. 1967 the Army, Navy, Air Force and Police were unified under the Ministry of Defence and Security. Their commanders no longer hold cabinet rank. There is an emergency compulsory service.

Army. There are 16 territorial units, including artillery, engineers and technical services. Total strength in 1971 was 275,000.

Navy. The Navy, in 1970, included 6 submarines, 1 cruiser, 8 destroyers, 12 frigates, 6 fleet minesweepers, 21 torpedo boats, 18 coastal gunboats, 18 patrol vessels, 10 coastal minesweepers, 75 small patrol craft and motor launches, 8 landing ships, 10 landing craft, 2 training ships, 2 surveying vessels, 4 oilers, 4 transports, 3 depot ships, 5 tugs, 8 auxiliaries and 2 tenders. The naval air arm has Gannet anti-submarine aircraft.

Naval personnel totalled 25,000 officers and ratings, including air arm, and 14,000 men of the marine commando corps.

Air Force. The Air Force has about 200 operational first-line aircraft, most of the combat types being of Russian design. There are 4 fighter squadrons, equipped with about 80 MiG-21, MiG-19 and MiG-17 jet aircraft and piston-engined Mustangs, 2 medium bomber squadrons of Tu-16 aircraft carrying long-range anti-shipping missiles, 1 squadron of B-26 Invader piston-engined bombers, 2 transport squadrons equipped respectively with turboprop An-12 and C-130B Hercules and piston-engined Il-14 and C-47 aircraft, 1 maritime patrol squadron with Catalina and Albatross amphibians and an assortment of other aircraft in transport, helicopter and training units, including a small number of Mi-6 heavy transport helicopters. A high proportion of the Soviet-built fixed-wing aircraft are believed to be currently inactive. Soviet-built 'Guideline' surface-to-air missiles are operational. Total personnel, about 20,000.

PLANNING. On 15 Aug. 1960 the National Planning Council produced the draft of the First National Overall Development Plan, which the Consultative Assembly subsequently ratified. The Plan aims at establishing 'Indonesian socialism', the first stage of which was completed by Dec. 1968. Rp. 240,000m. were spent on investment programmes during these 8 years. A further 5-year Development Plan was announced in 1969.

AGRICULTURE. Indonesian agriculture is divided between estate and small-holders cultivation.

Production in 1965 included (in metric tons): Rice, 9,688,000; corn, 2·4m.; sugar 1·2m.; tea, 43,000 from estates and 45,000 from smallholders; coffee, 12,000 from estates and 93,000 from smallholders; rubber, 172,860 from estates and 510,000 from smallholders; tobacco, 10,000 from estates and 90,000 from smallholders.

Livestock, 1961 (1,000 head): Cattle, 5,715; buffaloes, 2,792; horses, 692; sheep and goats, 10,623; pigs, 2,180.

Salt is a government monopoly; production in 1961, 300,000 short tons.

FORESTRY. The forest area is 902,808 sq. km. Production, 1965, in 1,000 cu. metres: Lumber, 525; firewood, 621; charcoal, 26.

FISHERIES. In 1966 the catch of sea fisheries was 700,000 metric tons; inland fisheries, 500,000 metric tons.

MINING. The tin mines of Bangka, Billiton and Riouw are worked by the Government. In 1967 their total yield was 13,597 metric tons. Output in 1965 of bauxite was 700,000 metric tons; coal, 390,000 metric tons; manganese (1963), 15,390 metric tons; nickel, 78,700 metric tons.

Oil plays an important part in Indonesian economy, being a major source of revenue and providing employment for some 50,000. Indonesia is the principal producer of petroleum in the Far East, production coming from Sumatra, Kalimantan (Indonesian Borneo) and Java, where Anglo-Dutch and US interests operate. The 1965 output of crude oil was 27·8m. cu. metres. Indonesian refinery capacity was about 15m. tons per annum at the end of 1959.

On 1 Nov. 1960 the Government announced a new regulation providing that all mineral oil and gas exploitation must be exclusively in the hands of Indonesian Government mining companies. Mining rights held by oil and gas companies issued before the new regulation will continue.

From 28 Aug. 1961 Anglo-Dutch and American oil companies have been operating as government contractors, the Government receiving 60% (formerly 50%) of the profits.

INDUSTRY. At the beginning of Dec. 1957 the trade unions expropriated all Dutch-owned banks, trading firms, hotels, etc., which were then placed under government control. On 3 Dec. 1958 parliament passed a bill for the nationalization of all Dutch-owned businesses.

In Nov. 1963 all business enterprises owned 'wholly or partly by Malaysian nationals or Indonesian nationals domiciled in Malaysia' were sequestrated by presidential decree.

There are shipyards at Djakarta, Surabaya, Semarang and Amboina. There are many textile factories (total production in 1965, 394m. metres), large paper factories, match factories (1965: 11,123 metric tons), automobile and bicycle assembly works, large construction works, tyre factories, glass factories, a caustic soda and other chemical factories. A cement factory produced 389,500 metric tons in 1965.

POWER. All gas and electricity undertakings were nationalized by presidential degree of 3 Oct. 1953, retroactive from 23 Dec. 1952. Three large-scale hydroelectric plants are under construction on the Djatiluhur and Brantas rivers in Java and on the Asahan River in Sumatra.

TOURISM. In 1968 about 40,000 tourists visited Indonesia (1966, 15,000; 1967, 25,000).

TRADE UNIONS. The largest group of trade unions in Indonesia is the Serekat Organasasi Karjawan Seluruh Indonesia (SOKSI), the Central Council of All Indonesia Trade Unions, with a membership of 2·6m., to which 28 national unions and 832 local unions are affiliated. The second largest is the Kongres Buruh Seluruh Indonesia (KBSI), the All Indonesia Trades Union Congress, with a membership of nearly 400,000. To the KBSI 25 national unions and 54 local unions are affiliated. Besides the set here are the HISSBI (Federation of Indonesian Trade Unions), with a membership of 180, 203, and the KBKI (Indonesian Democratic Labour Organization), with a membership of 94,477. In addition, there are also trade-union centres which are closely connected with the Islamic Parties, viz., Serikat Buruh Islam Indonesia, with a membership of 275,000; the Sarekat Buruh Muslimin Indonesia, with a membership of 11,950, and the Gerakan Organisasi Buruh Sjarekat Islam Indonesia, with a membership of 1,347.

Allen, G. C., and Donnithorne, A. G., *Western Enterprise in Indonesia and Malaya*. New York, 1956.
Hall, C. J. J. van, and Koppel, C. van de (ed.). *De Landbouw in den Indischen Archipel*. 4 vols The Hague, 1946–49
Higgins, B., *Indonesia's Economic Stabilization and Development*. New York, 1957

COMMERCE. Imports and exports (including oil) in Rp. 1m.

	1957	1958 [3]	1959 [3]	1960 [4]	1961 [4]	1962 [4]
Imports [1]	9,098	5,900	5,227	25,839	35,732	29,133
Exports [2]	11,052	8,612	9,943	37,823	35,266	30,676

[1] f.o.b. excluding postal parcels, passengers' goods, ships chandlery, gold and silver.
[2] c.i.f. excluding postal parcels, passengers' goods, gold and silver.
[3] Figures based on an exchange rate of £1 = Rp. 31·30.
[4] Figures based on an exchange rate of £1 = Rp. 145·45.

The main export items (in 1,000 metric tons) in 1961 were: Rubber, 677; petroleum, 15,453; copra, 397; tin ore, 25; tobacco, 17; palm-oil and kernels, 150; tea, 36; coffee, 65.

Total trade between UK and Indonesia (British Board of Trade returns) in £1,000 sterling:

	1965	1966	1967	1968	1969	1970
Imports to UK	3,932	5,046	4,941	7,663	6,599	7,273
Exports from UK	9,010	3,692	5,744	5,903	8,793 }	11,840
Re-exports from UK	84	63	85	140	86 }	

SHIPPING. The national shipping company Pelajaran Nasional Indonesia (PELNI) had in 1961 a fleet of 271 vessels, maintains interinsular communications. The Djakarta Lloyd maintains regular services between Djakarta, Amsterdam, Hamburg and London.

In 1961 the principal ports had a turnover of 5,491,000 metric tons of imports and 17,847,000 metric tons of exports.

ROADS. In 1960 Indonesia had 81,000 km of roads. Motor vehicles, as of 1 Jan. 1960, totalled 92,463 passenger cars, 72,359 trucks, 14,837 buses and 131,860 motor cycles.

RAILWAYS. In 1969 the state-controlled railway company operated 7,282 km; total receipis were Rp. 7,113m.

AVIATION. The Government and KLM in 1949 set up 'Garuda Indonesian Airways' as a mixed enterprise on a 50–50 capital basis under KLM management. The agreement was to last until 1960. In 1954, however, the Government bought up the shares held by KLM for 15m. guilders and nationalized GIA; and in Jan. 1958, the Government unilaterally terminated the contracts with the technical assistants provided by KLM. GIA maintains a direct service between Djakarta and Manila, Bangkok, Hong Kong, Toyko and Amsterdam.

POST. In 1954 the postal and telegraph services of Indonesia included 727 post offices, 1,146 rural postal agencies, 515 telegraph offices, and 66 fixed coast and 12 aeronautical radio stations. There were 722 telegraph offices and 37 fixed, 3 coast and 4 aeronautical radio stations of other government services and private companies. The government telegraph lines extended over 4,573 miles, the government telegraph cables over 252 miles; the government telephone aerial lines over 16,921 miles, the government telephone cables over 1,479 miles. Number of telephones (1967), 164,373.

Radio Republik Indonesia, under the Department of Information, operates 26 stations. There were, in 1961, 785,010 registered receivers. Television was introduced in the Tijakarta area in 1962.

In 1961 total postal receipts were Rp. 1,122,364,000, of which Rp. 832,815,000 came from Java and Madura.

BANKING. The Bank Indonesia, formerly the Java Bank, established in 1828, was made the central bank of Indonesia on 1 July 1953. It had an original capital of Rp. 25m.; a reserve fund of Rp. 18m. and a special reserve of Rp. 84m. Owing to the continuous overvaluation of the rupiah and the increased demand of foreign currency, the international reserves fell from US$259·9m. at the end of 1959 to US$8·6m. at the end of 1965.

Bank Negara Indonesia is a state bank and is designed to act as a source of credit for reconstruction purposes. The Bank Pembangunan Indonesia accords long-term credits for agricultural, industrial and mining projects. The Bank Koperasi Tani & Nelajan extends credits to co-operative societies and smaller business men.

There are 7 major commercial banks and 10 foreign banks; the latter include the Chartered Bank, the Hongkong and Shanghai Banking Corporation, the Bank of America, the First National City Bank and the Bank of Tokio.

In Aug. 1964, 37,808 co-operative societies had a combined membership of 6·8m.

The post office savings bank had, in Dec. 1961, deposits of Rp. 804·08m. to the credit of 2·26m. accounts.

WEIGHTS AND MEASURES. The metric system of weights and measures was officially introduced in Feb. 1923, and came into full operation on 1 Jan. 1938.

The following are the old weights and measures: *Pikol* = 136·16 lb. avoirdupois; *Katti* = 1·36 lb. avoirdupois; *Bau* = 1·7536 acres; *Square Pal* = 227 hectares = 561·16 acres; *Tjengkal* = 4 yd; *Pal* (Java) = 1,506 metres; *Pal* (Sumatra) = 1,852 metres.

DIPLOMATIC REPRESENTATIVES

Indonesia maintains embassies in:

Afghánistán	Germany (West)	Romania
Algeria	Ghana	Saudi Arabia
Argentina	Guinea	Singapore
Australia	Hungary	Sweden
Austria	India	Switzerland
Belgium	Iran	Syria
Brazil	Iraq	Tanzania
Bulgaria	Italy	Thailand
Burma	Japan	Tunisia
Cambodia	Malaysia	Turkey
Canada	Mexico	USSR
Ceylon	Morocco	UAR
Czechoslovakia	Netherlands	UK
Cuba	Pakistan	USA
Ethiopia	Philippines	Vietnam (North)
France	Poland	Yugoslavia

Indonesia maintains legations in Jordan and the Vatican.

OF INDONESIA IN GREAT BRITAIN
(38 Grosvenor Sq., W.1)

Ambassador: Roesmin Nurjadin.
Minister-Counsellor: M. Buntarian. *First Secretary:* Samsi Abdullah.
Services Attachés: Col. Sunaryo (*Air*), Col. Edi Sugardo (*Army*), Cdre Achmod Dipo (*Navy*).

OF GREAT BRITAIN IN INDONESIA

Ambassador: Willis Ide Combs, CMG.
Counsellor: M. P. Preston (*Consul-General*).
Service Attachés: Col. M. P. F. Jones, CBE, DSO (*Defence and Army*), Wing Cdr C. T. K. Cody (*Air*), Cdr G. A. Plumer (*Navy*).
First Secretaries: A. K. Mason (*Head of Chancery*); I. A. Carpenter (*Information*); D. J. Brown, MBE (*Commercial*); J. Von M. Lister; E. W. Cook, D. H. M. Allen (*Labour*, resident at Singapore).

There are also Consuls at Medan and Surabaya.

OF INDONESIA IN THE USA (2020 Massachusetts Ave. NW., Washington, D.C., 20036)

Ambassador: Soedjatmoko.
Minister: Abdul Moeis. *Minister-Counsellor:* R.M. S. J. Haditirto (*Commercial*). *Counsellor:* Ali Alatas. *First Secretaries:* Achmad Dahlan Ibrahim (*Economic*); Widaja Suriadiradja. *Service Attachés:* Brig.-Gen. Mohamad Soesilo Soedarman (*Army*), Cmdre. Soekardjo (*Navy*), Col. Soemadji (*Air*).

OF THE USA IN INDONESIA

Ambassador: Francis J. Galbraith.
Heads of Sections: Lewis M. Purnell (*Political*); Peter A. Seip (*Economic*); Alphonse F. La Porta (*Consular*); Frederick B. Cook (*Administrative*).

Service Attachés: Col. John S. Sandiland (*Defence and Army*), Lieut.-Col. John A. Minnich, Jr (*Air*), Col. Charles W. Tuma (*Navy*).

There are Consuls at Medan and Surabaya.

BOOKS OF REFERENCE

Bemmelen, R. W. van, *Geology of Indonesia.* 2 vols. The Hague, 1949
Echols, J. M., and Shadily, H., *An Indonesian–English Dictionary.* 2nd ed. Cornell Univ. Press, 1963
Fischer, L., *The Story of Indonesia.* London, 1959
Grant B., *Indonesia.* Melbourne Univ. Press, 1964
Helsdingen, W. H. van, and Hoogenberk, H. (ed.), *Mission Interrupted; the Dutch in the East Indies . . . in the 20th century.* Amsterdam, 1946
Hindley, D., *The Communist Party of Indonesia, 1951–63.* California Univ. Press and CUP, 1965
Kroef, J. M. van der, *Indonesian Social Evolution.* Amsterdam, 1958.—*The Communist Party of Indonesia.* Univ. of Br. Columbia Press, 1965
Lewis, R., *Indonesia—Troubled Paradise.* London, 1962
McVey, R. T. (ed.), *Indonesia.* New Haven, 1963
Paauw, D. S., *Financing Economic Development: the Indonesian case.* Glencoe, Ill., 1960
Palmier, L. H., *Social Status and Power in Java.* Athlone Press, London, 1960
Schrieke, B., *Indonesian Sociological Studies.* The Hague, 1955
Taylor, A. M., *Indonesian Independence and the United Nations.* Cornell Univ. Press, 1960
Verhoeff, H. G., *Netherlands New Guinea.* The Hague, 1958

IRAN
Keshvaré Shahanshahiyé Irân

REIGNING KING (SHAH). Mohammad Reza Pahlavi (born 26 Oct. 1919) was sworn before the Majles on 18 Sept. 1941 on the abdication of his father Reza Shah Pahlavi (died 26 July 1944), who after the overthrow of the Qajar dynasty had been elected shah on 13 Dec. 1925. After the dissolution of two former marriages, the Shah on 21 Dec. 1959 married Farah Diba, daughter of an army officer. *Offspring:* Prince Reza Pahlavi, born 31 Oct. 1960 (*Heir apparent*); Princess Farahnaz, born 12 March 1962; Prince Ali Reza Pahlavi, born 28 April 1966; Princess Leila, born 27 March 1970. The Shah crowned himself and the Queen on 26 Oct. 1967.

Minister of the Court: Amir Asadullah Alam.

AREA AND POPULATION. Iran has an area of about 1,621,860 sq. km (620,000 sq. miles), but a vast portion is desert, and the average density is only 13 inhabitants to the sq. km.

According to the results of the census taken in Oct. 1966, the population of Iran is 25,781,090. Population of Tehrán, the capital (1970) 3·15m.

The principal cities and their population are: Abadan, 270,726; Ahwaz, 206,265; Tabriz, 468,459; Esfahán, 575,001; Meshed, 417,171; Rasht, 141,756; Hamadán, 161,944; Qum, 133,941; Rezáyeh, 110,419; Qazvin, 103,791; Ardabil, 83,548; Kermán, 118,344; Khorramshahr, 95,100; Yezd, 150,531; Arák, 72,087; Dizful, 105,381; Káshán, 81,651; Zanján, 82,530.

CONSTITUTION AND GOVERNMENT. In Jan. 1906 the Shah, up to then an absolute ruler, gave his consent to the establishment of a National Assembly, or 'Majles', which drew up a constitution, which received the Shah's approval on 30 Dec. 1906. The Constitution also provided for the establishment of a Senate, but this body was constituted only in Feb. 1950; 30 of its 60 members are nominated by the Shah, while the other 30 are elected. As the result of constitutional amendments approved in 1949 and 1957 the number of Majles deputies has been increased from the original 136 to 200 and the term of each Majles has been extended from 2 to 4 years; the Shah has the right to dissolve either or both houses of parliament and to return to the Majles finance bills for further consideration. All other legislation approved by parliament the Shah is obliged to sign and promulgate as law.

A programme of social reform designed by the Shah was approved on 26 Jan. 1963 in a nation-wide referendum by 5,598,711 votes against 4,115.

In Jan. 1971 the Cabinet was composed as follows:

Prime Minister: Amir Abbas Hoveyda. *Assistant Prime Ministers:* Nasir Assar; Lieut.-Gen. Nematollah Nasiri; Lieut.-Gen. Mohamed Behrooz; Yadollah Shahbazi; Dr Hussein Tadayyon. Maj.-Gen. Parviz Khosrovani. *Interior:* Hassan Zahedi. *Development and Housing:* Kuros Amuzegar. *Economy:* Hushang Ansari. *Education:* Mrs Farrokhra Parsa. *Culture and Arts:* Mehrdad Pahlbod. *Finance:* Dr Jamshid Amouzegar. *Foreign Affairs:* Ardeshir Zahedi. *Food and Consumer Goods:* Gen. Assadollah Sani'i. *Health:* Dr Manouchehr Shahqoli. *Information:* Javad Mansur. *Labour:* Abdul Majid Majidi. *Land Reform and Farm Co-operatives:* Dr Abdol-Azim Valian. *Natural Resources:* Nasser Golsorkhi. *Posts:* Fatullah Sutudeh. *Roads:* Hassan Shalchian. *Science and Higher Education:* Hossein Kazemzadeh. *War:* Gen. Reza Azimi. *Water and Power:* Mansur Rauhani. *Ministers of State:* Dr Mahmoud Kashfian; Dr Hadi Hedayati; Manuchehr Gordarzi. *Deputy Prime Minister for Economic Affairs:* Safi Asfia.

The country is divided into 14 *ustán* (administrative provinces), 6 governor-generalships, 145 governorships and 454 districts. The provinces are divided into *shahrestán* (counties), each under a *farmándár* (governor). The *shahrestáns* are subdivided into *bakhsh* (districts) under a *bakhshdár* and *dehistán* (group of villages) under a *dehdár*. Each village has a *kadkhodá* (headman). All these officials, with the exception of the village headmen, are appointed, directly or indirectly, by the central government.

The 14 *ustáns* are as follows:

The central province; capital Tehrán; population, 2,979,081. Khorásán; capital Meshed; population, 2,497,381. Esfáhán; capital Esfáhán; population, 1·7m. Eastern Azerbáiján; capital Tabriz; population, 2·6m. Western Azerbáiján; capital Rezáyeh; population, 1m. Khuzistán; capital Ahwáz; population, 1·6m. Mázándárán; capital Sári; population, 1·8m. Fárs; capital Shiráz; population, 1·5m. Gilán; capital Resht; population 1·7m. Kermán; capital Kermán; population, 773,669. Kermánsháhán; capital Kermánsháh; population, 776,409. Ports and Islands of the Sea of Oman; capital Bándár Abbás; population, 605,387. Báluchestán and Sistán; capital Záhedán; population, 454,996. Kurdestán; capital Sánándáj; population, 624,256.

The governor-generalships are named as follows: Hámádán, Lurestán, Semnán, Chár-Máhál and Bákhtiári, Ilám, and Kohkilueh and Boyer-Ahmedi.

On 3 Nov. 1955 Iran joined the Baghdad pact between Turkey, Iraq, Pakistan and Great Britain; now, without Iraq, known as CENTO (*see* p. 45).

National flag: Green, white, red (horizontal).

National anthem: Shahanshah é ma zendeh bad (words by Prince Afsar, tune by Da'ud Najmi Moghaddam).

RELIGION. The official religion is the Shia branch of Islam, known as the *Ithna-'Ashariyya*, which recognizes 12 Imáms or spiritual successors of the Prophet Mohammad. Of the total population, 850,000 are of the Sunnî sect, 10,000 are Parsîs (Zartushti), 40,000 Jews, 50,000 Armenians, 20,000 Nestorians and 8,500 Protestants.

The Shia Moslems reject the *Sunna* or tradition, as distinct from the actual text of the Koran, both of which are recognized by the Sunnî Moslems. The power of the clergy has diminished, as the result of the increased power of the central government. The highest authority is the leading *ayatullah*, at present *ayatullah* Hakim.

All mosques and shrines have some endowments (*ouqáf*, sing. *vaqf*), now devoted to charitable and educational institutions and administered by the Ministry of Education. The shrines of some favourite saints are richly endowed and own extensive property.

The Gregorian National Armenians form 2 dioceses, each under a bishop, the one residing at Tabriz and the other at Esfahán. There are also a few thousand Roman Catholic Armenians, who have a bishop of their own rite at Esfahán, the bishop of the Latin rite residing at Rezayeh (Urmia). There is an Anglican bishop residing at Esfahán.

EDUCATION. A law providing for the gradual establishment of compulsory primary education was passed in July 1943. In 1960 schooling was available for two-thirds of the children of school age. The literate population is estimated at 40%.

The influence of the French educational system has been prominent. As in France, education is highly centralized. The curricula for primary and secondary schools are drawn up by the Ministry of Education.

The great majority of primary and secondary schools are state schools. Grants are made to private schools. Elementary education in state schools and university education are free; small fees are charged for state-run secondary schools. Textbooks are issued free of charge to pupils in the first 4 grades of elementary schools.

In 1967 there were 15,429 primary and 1,867 secondary schools with 2,575,667 and 674,058 pupils respectively. In addition, technical and vocational schools had 16,273 pupils and a teachers' training college had 6,693 students.

Higher education is provided by universities and technical colleges. In 1966, 28,982 students were attending institutes of higher education. Tehrán University (with 11 constituent faculties) is the largest in Iran; it maintains a secondary teachers' training college and a midwifery school. There are also universities at Shiráz (letters, agriculture, science, medicine), Tabriz (letters, agriculture, science, medicine, pharmacy), Rezayeh (agriculture), Esfahán (letters, pharmacy, medicine), Meshed (medicine, letters, theology) and Ahwáz (agriculture, science, medicine). There are in Tehrán an Institute of Technology for the training of teachers of vocational subjects at secondary-school level; a Polytechnic with institutes of mechanical, textile and electrical engineering and building construction; and the National University, a private institution for fee-paying students. The National Iranian Oil Company maintains an institute of technology at Abadán. The Central Treaty Organization in 1959 set up an institute of nuclear science in Tehrán (which has now been handed over to Iran), and in 1961 opened an agricultural machinery and soil conservation training centre at Karaj near Tehrán, and in 1960 a vocational training centre south of Tehrán.

CINEMAS (1966). There were 94 cinemas in Tehrán.

NEWSPAPERS There are numerous daily papers in Tehrán and other cities. Their circulation is relatively small, *Ettela'át* and *Kayhán* leading with about 65,000 each. Two English-language and a French-language daily appear in Tehrán.

HEALTH. The Ministry of Health controls the health of the country through the Department of Public Health, which has achieved some remarkable results in the fight against malaria; large areas along the Caspian and the Persian Gulf and in Azerbáiján are now free from malaria. Opium addiction has been greatly reduced, and the cultivation of the poppy has been practically eradicated. Programmes to combat tuberculosis, smallpox, trachoma, venereal diseases, etc., have been introduced.

In 1967, about 27,000 hospital beds (half of them in Tehrán) were available. Medical personnel included 5,024 physicians and surgeons, 810 dentists, 2,702 pharmacists and 2,000 nurses. Numerous hospitals, health centres, dispensaries and maternal and child health clinics and 14 schools of nursing have been set up.

JUSTICE. The judicial system is modelled on that of France. There are justices of the peace in villages and small towns, higher courts in the large towns, police magistrates in all important places, courts of appeal in Tehrán,

Tabriz, Shiráz, Kermánsháh, Esfahán, Meshed, Kermán and Ahwáz, and a court of cassation, or supreme court, in Tehrán. The courts are supervised by the Ministry of Justice. New civil, criminal and commercial codes based on French and Swiss codes were introduced in the early 1930s.

WELFARE. A system of social security benefits covering accident, sickness, retirement, death, marriage, maternity and childbirth and free medical attention and hospitalization for insured contributors and their families is embodied in the Workers' Social Insurance Law, 1960. This law provides for the insurance under the scheme of all workers in receipt of wages or salaries, but is at present being applied to some 250,000 workers employed mainly in industrial and mining establishments employing 10 or more workers. It also provides for the compulsory payment by employers of family allowances to workers with 2 or more children.

FINANCE. Currency. The Iranian unit of currency is the *rial* sub-divided into 100 *dinars*.

Notes in circulation are of denominations of 20, 50, 100, 200, 500 and 1,000 rials. Coins in circulation are bronze–aluminium and copper, 50 dinar; silver alloy, 1, 2, 5 and 10 rials, and nickel–copper, 1, 2 and 5 rials. There are also gold *pahlavi* and $\frac{1}{2}$ *pahlavi* pieces containing 7·322382 and 3·661191 grammes of gold respectively which do not constitute part of monetary circulation, but have a market value as any other commodity.

The basis of the note cover was revised by the Monetary and Banking Law of 1960, under which at least 40% of the total note issue must be covered by gold and foreign currencies, including Iranian Government subscriptions to the IMF, IBRD, etc.

Government control of foreign exchange was introduced on 1 March 1936. The official parity of the rial is 75·75 rials = US$1. This parity is used only in calculating the value of the gold and foreign exchange held as reserve for the note cover. The effective rates for all authorized foreign-exchange payments are: Buying, £1 sterling = 180·50 rials, US$1 = 76·5 rials; selling, £1 = 185·30 rials, $1 = 75·50 rials.

Budget. Budget estimates for years ending 20 March (in 1m. rials):

	1963–64	1964–65	1965–66	1967–68	1968–69	1969–70
Revenue	56,941	52,145	140,953	175,000	217,232	330,300
Expenditure	59,151	55,148	144,444	176,600	217,232	330,300

The main items of estimated revenue in the budget for 1968–69 are (in 1m. rials): Direct taxation, 12,750; indirect taxation, 34,505; treasury share of oil revenues, 15,762,000. Main items of estimated expenditure (in 1m. rials): Education, 42,018; defence, 36,743; police and gendarmerie, 9,691; health, 5,779.

The estimated budget for the fourth 5-year development plan which began in 1968 is more than $11,000m., the major portion of which will be covered by oil revenue.

DEFENCE. Army. The Army consists of about 200,000 men organized in 7 infantry divisions, 1 independent armoured brigade, 1 armoured division and auxiliary units. Two years' military service is compulsory. Gendarmerie strength is about 25,000. Its function is internal security in rural areas. A US Military Mission is attached in an advisory capacity to the Army and another to the Gendarmerie.

Navy. The Navy comprises 1 destroyer, 5 frigates, 5 corvettes, 4 coastal mine-sweepers, 2 inshore minesweepers, 4 patrol boats, 2 dispatch boats, 3 landing craft, 1 repair ship, 9 motor launches, 9 coastguard cutters, the Imperial yacht, 2 oilers, 1 water carrier, 1 tender and 2 tugs.

A British destroyer (*ex*-HMS *Sluys*) was sold to Iran in 1966 and modernized in 1969, and 4 Vosper Mark 5 frigates were built in Britain in 1967–70.

Air Force. In Aug. 1955 the Air Force became a separate and independent arm. In 1970 it comprised 4 wings, including tactical wings with 5 squadrons (each 16 aircraft) of F-5 fighter-bombers, 2 interceptor squadrons of F-4D Phantoms and 1 of F-86F Sabre fighters, a reconnaissance squadron of RT-33s (to be re-equipped with RF-5s) and a transport wing with 56 C-130EH Hercules turboprop transports, some C-47s (being replaced by 12 F-27 Friendships) and smaller types. Aircraft on order include 2 squadrons of F-4E Phantom fighters. There are also strong helicopter units equipped with 3-engined Super Frelons, single-engined JetRangers and other types with 22 Italian-built CH-47C Chinooks on order. The Air Force has a total strength of some 17,000 officers and men, and 180 jet combat aircraft. Missiles in service include Rapier and Tigercat surface-to-air weapons.

PRODUCTION. Iran's chief natural products are oil, wool, cotton, silk, fruit, nuts, cereals, vegetables, gum, timber, oil seeds, copper and other metalliferous ores, coal, cattle, sheep and goats. Its principal manufactured or processed products are textiles, carpets, skins, casings, vegetable oil, soap, metal products, plastic products, furniture, beet sugar, tea, tobacco and cigarettes, wine, vodka, soft drinks, caviar, footwear, petroleum products, glass products, tiles, bricks, cement, leather and leather goods, dairy products and manufactured foodstuffs, and printed matter.

DEVELOPMENT. The fourth development plan 1968–73 envisages an expenditure of 610,000m. rials, of which 480,000m. rials is to be allocated to individual projects. Of this amount about 13% is to be allotted to agriculture, 16% to communications, 20% to mining and industry, 19% to waters and power, 8% to education and 4% to telecommunications.

AGRICULTURE. Reliable statistics of production are not available. It is estimated, however, that out of 163·6m. hectares of land area only 16,857,000 are crop land (including 10,300 hectares fallow), 27·8m. hectares are forests and ranges and 32·7m. hectares are potentially cultivable waste.

Tractors in use numbered 12,000 in 1965–66.

Crop returns for 1967–68 (in 1,000 metric tons): Wheat, 4,618; barley, 1,034; rice, 940; cotton, 338; sugar-beet, 2,857; tea, 59.

Wool comes principally from Khorásán, Kermánsháh, Mázandarán and Azerbáiján. The most popular carpets are manufactured in the environs of Tabriz, Kermán, Arák, Káshán, Esfahán, Shiráz and Hamadán. Esfahán is the traditional textile manufacturing centre, but in recent years important textile mills, particularly cotton, have been built in other towns, including Tehrán. Exports of carpets were valued at 1,930·6m. rials in 1960–61.

Rice is grown largely on the Caspian shores.

Tobacco is grown along the shores of the Caspian. It is purchased by the Tobacco Monopoly and manufactured in the government factory at Tehrán. Production in 1967 was 22,136 tons.

Opium, until 1955, was an important export commodity in Iran. On 7 Oct. 1955 an Act was approved by Parliament to prohibit the cultivation and usage of opium. The government has been contemplating reintroducing poppy cultivation on a limited scale and under rigid state control in an effort to fight narcotic trafficking and addiction.

Livestock (1964): 26m. sheep, 14m. goats, 5·5m. cattle; (1960) 2m. asses, 600,000 horses, 234,000 camels.

LAND REFORM. Before the enactment of the 1962 land reform law most of the more than 50,000 villages in Iran were owned by absentee landlords. Several earlier land reform laws presented to the Majlis by the government had remained ineffective, and the only large-scale distribution of land to smallholders was that of the Crown property, which the Shah began in 1951. However, as a result of the implementation of the 1962 land reform law, all the large estates coming under the land reform law have been purchased from the landlords by the government and distributed among the farmers. Up to 1968 more than 3m. farm families comprising some 14m. farmers have become the owners of the land they till.

FISHERIES. The Caspian Fisheries Co. (Shilát) is a government monopoly. Its catch in 1966 was 2,650 tons, including 207 tons of caviare.

MINING. Iran has substantial mineral deposits relatively undeveloped. Production figures for 1966–67 (in 1,000 tons): Iron ore, 3; copper, 11, lead, 88; chromite, 104; coal, 285; salt, 245.

INDUSTRY. Apart from the oil industry, the industries employing most workers are textiles, sugar refining, flour-milling, fruit processing, tea, furniture, printing, leather, matches, glass, building materials and light metal goods. A number of automobile assembly plants have been set up in recent years employing several thousand workers. A steel-mill, a machine-tool factory, a tractor plant and a huge petrochemical complex are also going into production.

OIL. The exploitation of Iran's large oil resources was undertaken by the Anglo-Persian (later Anglo-Iranian) Oil Company, which held a concession for a considerable area of southern Iran, built a large refinery and produced the following quantities of crude oil (in long tons): 1946, 19,189,551; 1948, 24,871,058; 1950, 31,750,147; 1951 (Jan.–Oct.), 16,176,000.

This concession was terminated as a result of the nationalization of the Iranian oil industry in 1951. The ensuing dispute (*see* THE STATESMAN'S YEAR-BOOK, 1954, p. 1294) led to the cessation of oil exports in June 1951, and of the company's operations in Iran in Oct. 1951. The dispute was finally settled on 5 Aug. 1954, and on 29 Oct. 1954, the date when the Shah signed it, an agreement came into force between the Iranian Government and the National Iranian Oil Company, on the one hand, and 17 international oil companies, on the other; of these, the British Petroleum Co. Ltd. holds 40% of the shares. These companies came to be known collectively as the Consortium.

The agreement is for 25 years with provision for three 5-year extensions, at the option of the Consortium under specific terms and conditions. Two operating companies—Iraanse Aardolie Exploratie en Producte Maatschappij (Iranian Oil Exploration and Producing Company) NV and Iraanse Aardolie Raffinage Maatschappij (Iranian Oil Refining Company) NV—were formed by Consortium member companies and they received the necessary rights and powers from Iran to be solely responsible respectively for exploration and production in a defined area in South Iran and for the operation of the Refinery of Abadan. While the National Iranian Oil Company, the shares of which are held by the Iranian Government, is the owner of the fixed assets of the oil industry in South Iran, the Operating Companies have the unrestricted use of them. The two Operating Companies do not sell the oil; their function is solely to produce and refine it. So-called Trading Companies, subsidiaries representing Consortium members, deal individually and independently of each other with the buying and selling in Iran of oil for export.

The National Iranian Oil Company was united in Jan. 1955 with the Iran Oil Company, whose object is the exploration and production of oil throughout Iran except in regions subject to special agreements. The National Iranian Oil Company operates the Naft-i-Shah oilfield and the Kermánsháh refinery in West Iran and is solely responsible for the distribution and marketing of oil in Iran. The net effect of the financial aspects of the sale of oil by the National Iranian Oil Company to the Trading Companies for export is to bring about an equal sharing between Iran and each Trading Company of the profits arising in Iran from the Trading Companies operations.

Total income to Iran from Trading and Operating Companies for 1960, £101·9m.; 1961, £103·9m.; 1962, £115·4m.; 1963, £135m.

Crude oil production figures since the Consortium began operations in Oct. 1954 have been (in metric tons):1958, 40·4m.; 1959, 53·6m.; 1960, 50·1m.; 1961, 56·3m.; 1962, 64·5m.; 1963, 66m.; 1964, 84m.; 1965, 92m.; 1966, 106m.; 1967, 121m.; 1968, 133m.; 1969, 153m.; 1970, 172m.

The Iran Pan American Oil Company and the Société Irano-Italienne des Pétroles both struck oil offshore in the Persian Gulf in 1961. The National Iranian Oil Company have also reached oil at several wells at Alborz, near Qum.

LABOUR. Legislation regulating conditions of employment in certain industrial undertakings was first introduced in 1949. The subsequent adoption of certain international minimum standards led to the enactment of the Labour Act of 1959, which establishes basic provisions dealing with hours of work; holidays with pay; the payment of wages, salaries and overtime; the formation, registration and activities of employers' and workers' organizations; employment contracts and collective agreements; the settlement of disputes; industrial safety, health and welfare; and labour inspection. Regulations concerning safety, health and welfare in industrial premises, conciliation procedure and the settlement of disputes, the formation, registration and activities of trade unions, the duties and powers of labour inspectors have since been promulgated. The employment of foreigners is controlled by regulations promulgated in 1960. Responsibility for the enforcement of the Labour Act, 1959, and supporting legislation is entrusted to provincial and district departments of labour.

According to a survey of manpower undertaken in 1958, the country's non-agricultural work force numbered about 1·37m., of whom nearly 70,000 were women and about 33,000 were under 13 years of age. Just over half (718,000) were engaged in crafts, production process and related occupations, while 18% were employed in sales and related occupations.

COMMERCE. The quantity (in metric tons) and value (in 1,000 rials) of the imports and exports (excluding oil exports and duty-free imports) were as follows for fiscal years 21 March–20 March:

| | Imports | | Exports | |
	Weight	Value	Weight	Value
1963–64	1,355,410	39,281,857	595,800	9,616,550
1964–65	2,311,903	56,788,998	72,454,246	11,485,088
1965–66	2,275,286	66,517,286	89,324,464	13,982,662

Value is assessed for imports on the basis of official rate plus certificate rate; for exports on the basis of declared price.

The following tables show the value (in 1,000 rials) and the weight (in metric tons) of the chief imports into and exports from Iran during the year ending 20 March 1966. The value of imports (c.i.f.) is on the basis of £1 = 214·20 rials and exports on the basis of (f.o.b.) of declared price:

Imports	Weight	Value	Exports	Weight	Value
Sugar	354,124	2,013,599	Raw cotton	105,558	3,757,805
Chemicals and phar-			Wool and animal		
maceuticals	104,262	5,387,273	hair	2,919	201,305
Iron and ironware	725,730	8,415,566	Hides and skins	11,534	760,059
Machinery	114,355	14,111,438	Fresh and dried fruit	75,838	1,721,274
Electrical machinery	31,270	4,100,619	Carpets	15,184	3,401,602
Passenger cars	13,887	1,386,015	Metallic ores	344,202	806,539
Paper, cardboard,			Gum tragacanth	4,088	286,459
etc.	81,676	1,584,139			

Distribution of trade in the year ending 20 March 1966 (1,000 rials):

	Imports	Exports (excluding oil)	Exports (including oil)
Belgium	1,649,157	278,083	3,945,403
France	3,178,843	588,668	6,854,168
Germany (West)	13,811,179	1,932,158	3,515,159
India	1,072,637	148,915	4,251,488
Italy	3,165,060	480,102	3,842,809
Japan	5,467,886	295,292	18,584,489
Netherlands	2,082,872	382,454	8,187,209
Switzerland	1,446,787	475,233	517,669
USSR	1,267,691	1,306,337	1,307,426
UK	8,773,511	1,097,862	13,753,505
USA	11,833,115	1,488,543	4,931,360

Total trade between Iran and UK (British Board of Trade returns) in £1,000 sterling:

	1966	1967	1968	1969	1970
Imports to UK	38,241	136,668	90,705	73,768	76,054
Exports from UK	39,047	42,765	60,225	70,844 }	66,335
Re-exports from UK	562	523	808	783 }	

SHIPPING. During the year ended 21 March 1961, 15,096 vessels of 48,284,725 tons entered at ports on the Persian Gulf, and 116 vessels totalling 32,238 tons entered ports on the Caspian Sea.

Navigation on the Lake of Rezáyeh, from Sharaf-Kháneh to Kolmankháneh, is served by some 5 tugs and 9 barges for the transport of goods and passengers. The service runs twice a week. On the river Karun likewise, from Khorramshahr to Ahwáz, an irregular service for cargo only both ways is run by the Iran Transport Co. and the Karun Navigation Co., and some local firms run daily trips by motor boat, for passengers and merchandise. By changing into lighter-draught boats at Ahwáz both can be taken up to Shallili near Shushtar.

ROADS. In 1965 there were 4,907 km of completely surfaced roads and 504 km of roads in the process of surfacing. First- and second-class (graded, all weather) roads total 20,000 km and third-class roads 14,140 km.

In 1967 passenger cars and taxis numbered 169,374; commercial vehicles, 57,735.

RAILWAYS. The Iranian State Railways have a total length of 3,480 km, distributed as follows: Tehrán–Bandar Sháh, 464; Tehrán–Bandar Sháhpoor, 928; Ahwáz–Khorramshahr, 121; Tehrán–Tabriz, 734; Garmsar–Meshed, 813; Qum–Káshán, 98; Tabriz–Julfa, 145; Soofian–Sharaf Kháneh, 52; Záhedán–Mirjáveh, 92; oil company railways, 165; Tehrán–Shahr Rey, 8; Bandar Sháh–Gorgán, 36. The further section from Káshán to Yazd is under construction.

AVIATION. The principal airlines which link Tehrán with Europe and the Middle East are Air France, BOAC, Ariana, Iraqi Airways, Alitalia, PANAM, Swissair, LIA, KLM, PIA, SAS, Qantas, SABENA, El Al, Lufthansa, Aeroflot and Middle East Air Lines. BOAC, Qantas, Lufthansa, PANAM and Air France also connect Tehrán with the Far East. Aryana (Afghánistán) Airline connects Tehrán with Lebanon, Syria and Afghánistán. BOAC, KLM and SAS operate services to Abadán and Iran National Airlines Corporation, registered on 29 March 1962, has monopoly rights on all internal flights and also operates in the Persian Gulf; in 1965 it inaugurated European services. The Iranian Government owns 51% of its shares.

On 11 Aug. 1964 an agreement was signed in Tehran between the Iranian and Soviet authorities for services by the two national airlines between Tehran and Moscow with connexions to Europe and the Far East.

POST. Postal, telegraph and telephone services are administered by the Iranian Ministry of Posts, Telegraphs and Telephones.

The Indo-European Telegraph Company relinquished its lines in Iran in 1931, while the telephone system was nationalized in 1952. There is wireless-telegraph communication between Tehrán and Tabriz, Meshed, Kermánsháh, Kermán, Khorramshahr, Bushehr, Yazd, Shiráz and Lingeh and a wireless-telephone link between Tehrán and Tabriz. Tehrán is also in wireless communication with Europe and is linked by wireless telephone with Baghdad, London, Berne and New York. In 1966 the number of telephones was 207,530, of which some 101,500 were in Tehrán. Wireless sets numbered over 1m. in 1962.

BANKING. The following banks are established in Iran: (1) Bank Markazi (Central Bank), which was officially established in 1961 under the Monetary and Banking Law of May 1960 to implement the monetary and credit policy of the country. The Central Bank took over from the Bank Melli many of its functions, including the issue of bank-notes.

The liabilities and assets of the Bank Markazi on 22 Sept. 1965 were as follows (in rials): Liabilities: notes in circulation, 28,320m.; capital, 3,600m.; sight deposits, 14,380,782,533; total liabilities, 73,680,341,197. Assets: gold, 9,357,750,340; subscription to the International Monetary Fund, 1,325,624,997; subscription to international agencies, 645,693,001; Government obligations secured by Crown jewels, 16,990,931,660; total assets, 73,680,341,197.

(2) Bank Melli Iran, founded in 1927, continues to be the leading commercial bank with branches all over the country. The National Savings Bank, founded in 1939, is a branch of the Bank Melli. (3) Bank Keshavarzi Iran (Agricultural Bank), formerly a section of the Bank Melli Iran, was made a separate establishment in 1933. It has a nominal capital of 1,500m. rials and has branches at the principal agricultural centres in Iran. The bank gives assistance for the agricultural development of the country.

(4) The Bank Sepah, founded in 1926, deals principally in inland exchange and manages army accounts; paid-up capital, 400m. rials. (5) Bank Rahni Iran (Mortgage Bank), founded in 1939, has an authorized capital of 720m. rials and fulfils the functions of a building society. (6) Bank Tows'eh Sanati va Madani (Industrial and Mining Development Bank), founded in 1959 under the 7-year plan with a paid-up capital of 400m. rials and with the object of assisting the modernization and development of Iran's industries. (7) The Foreign Trade Bank of Iran, with a capital of 275m. rials, of which 51% belong to the Bank Melli, 24% to American and 12½% each to German and Italian banks. (8) Bank Sakhtemani (Building Bank) was formed with an authorized capital of 150m. rials with the object of building and selling houses to the poorer classes. (9) Bank Omran (Development Bank) was founded in 1953 with a nominal capital of 15m. rials to finance farmers and peasants who come into possession of land by virtue of the distribution of Crown lands. (10) Sherkat Sahami Bimeh Iran (The Iran Insurance Co.), in 1954 inaugurated a banking department.

In addition, there are 19 privately owned banks.

The Russo-Iran Bank is the oldest foreign bank operating in Iran; it finances Soviet–Iranian trade. An Irano-French bank (Bank Etabarate) opened in 1958. The Irano-British Bank, the Bank of Iran and the Middle East, the Mercantile Bank of Iran and Holland, and the Bank of Iran and Japan opened in 1959.

The British Bank of Iran and the Middle East, formerly the Imperial Bank of Iran, founded in 1899, withdrew from Iran in 1952.

Most banks are now authorized to deal in foreign exchange.

WEIGHTS AND MEASURES. By a law passed on 8 Jan. 1933, the official weights and meaures are those of the metric system.

The Iranian year is a solar year running from 21 March to 20 March; the Hejra year 1347 corresponds to the Christian year 21 March 1968–20 March 1969.

DIPLOMATIC REPRESENTATIVES

Iran maintains embassies in:

Afghánistán	Kuwait
Algeria	Morocco
Argentina (also for Chile)	Netherlands
Austria	Pakistan
Belgium	Poland (also legation for Romania)
Brazil (also for Venezuela)	Saudi Arabia
Canada	Spain
Czechoslovakia	Sweden
Denmark	Switzerland
Ethiopia	Syria
France (also for Portugal)	Tunisia
Germany (West)	Turkey
Greece	USSR
India (also legation for Thailand)	UAR
Indonesia	UK
Iraq	USA (also for Dominican Republic
Italy	and Mexico)
Japan (also for Taiwan)	Vatican
Jordan	Yugoslavia

OF IRAN IN GREAT BRITAIN (16 Princes Gate, SW7)

Ambassador: A. Khosrow Afshar, KCMG, (accredited 6 Nov. 1969).
Minister-Counsellors: Mostafa Elm; Dr Ahmad Minai. *Counsellors:* Nasser
Majd; Khosrow Gharai; Kazen Shiva; Djamchid Tavallali.
First Secretaries: Morteza Mortezaie; Abdol Ali Jahaubin. *Military
Attaché:* Col. H. Reshard.

OF GREAT BRITAIN IN IRAN

Ambassador: Sir Denis Wright, KCMG.
Counsellors: D. F. Murray; J. C. Cloake *(Commercial).*
Service Attachés: Col. F. J. T. Durie, MBE *(Defence and Military),* Group
Capt. P. D. Thorne, OBE, AFC *(Air),* Capt. C. R. A. O'Brien, RN *(Navy).*
First Secretaries: J. S. Champion, OBE *(Head of Chancery);* B. G. Cartledge
(Commercial); W. J. Dawson, OBE; M. C. S. Weston; R. T. Eland *(Information);*
A. J. Breeze; D. M. Edwards, DSC *(Consul);* J. W. H. O'Regan, OBE
(Development); G. R. Sutherland *(Civil Air,* resides in Beirut).

There is a Consul at Khorramshahr.

OF IRAN IN THE USA (3005 Massachusetts Ave. NW,
Washington, D.C., 20008)

Ambassador: Amir-Aslan Afshar.
Ministers: Kiyoomars Vazeen; Dr Jahangir Amuzegar *(Economic).*
Counsellors: Mahmud Hatef; Hoochang Manoochehrian, Enayattollah Sha-
poorian *(Financial);* Dr Fereidoon Nasseri *(Economic);* Dr Ahmad Hodjati
(Commercial); Kambig Yazdan-Panah *(Press). Service Attaché:* Col. Vali Allah
Dana.

OF THE USA IN IRAN

Ambassador: Douglas MacArthur, II.
Deputy Chief of Mission: Douglas G. Heck. *Heads of Sections:* John A.
Armitage *(Political);* Robert H. Harlan *(Economic);* David Post *(Commercial);*
James M. Ealum *(Consular);* John V. Hedberg, *(Administrative);* Edward F.
Tennant *(AID).*
Service Attachés: Col. John E. Wilson *(Army),* Cdr George B. Bird, Jr.
(Navy), Col. Duncan E. Duvall *(Air).*

There are consular representatives at Esfahán, Khorramshahr, Meshed and
Tabriz.

BOOKS OF REFERENCE

STATISTICAL INFORMATION. The principal statistical agencies of the Government are: (1) De-
partment of Census, Civil Registration, and Statistics (Ministry of the Interior). *Director-General:*
Sayyed Mehdi Hesabi. Publications on demographical statistics, in Persian. (2) Publicity and
Information Department of the Seven-year Plan Organization. *Director:* Dr Mohammed Ali
Rashti. Publications on industry, labour, agriculture, in English and Persian. (3) Statistical and
Economic Research Department of the Bank Melli Iran. Publishes *Monthly Bulletin,* in English
and Persian. (4) Customs Department (Ministry of Finance), publishes monthly and annual
reports, in French and Persian. (5) and (6) Ministry of Labour and Ministry of Industry and
Mines, publish statistical year-books.

H.M. The Shah, *Mission for my country.* 1961.—*The White Revolution.* 1967 [both in Persian]
Adli, Abolfazi, *Aussenhandel und Aussenwirtschaftspolitik des Iran.* Berlin, 1960
Arberry, A. J. (ed.), *The Cambridge History of Iran.* 8 vols. CUP, 1968 ff.
Avery, P., *Modern Iran.* New York, 1965
Benedick, R. E., *Industrial finance in Iran.* Harvard Univ. Press, 1964
Bobek, H., *Iran.* Frankfurt, 1962
Farahmand, S., *Der Wirtschaftsaufbau des Iran.* Basel, 1965
Haim, S., *Shorter Persian–English Dictionary.* Tehran, 1958
Handley-Taylor, G., *Bibliography of Iran.* London, 1964; latest ed., 1968
Lambton, A. K. S., *Landlord and Peasant in Persia.* OUP, 1953.—*Persian Vocabulary.* CUP, 1954
Lenczowski, George, *Russia and the West in Iran.* Cornell Univ., 1948; supplement, 1954
Malek-Mahdavi, Ahmed, *Le Parlement Iranien.* Univ. of Neuchâtel, 1954
Steinglass, F. J., *A Comprehensive Persian–English Dictionary.* 2nd ed. London, 1930
Ward, P., *Touring Iran.* London, 1971
Wilber, D. N., *Iran past and present.* 6th ed. Princeton Univ. Press, 1967
Zakhoder, B. N. (ed.), *Sovremennyi Iran.* Moscow, 1957

IRAQ

al Jumhouriya al 'Iraqia

CONSTITUTION AND GOVERNMENT. On 14 July 1958 the Republic of Iraq was declared by a group of Army officers, after an armed *coup d'état* in which the reigning King Faisal II and his uncle, the ex-Regent the Emir Abdul Ilah, and the Prime Minister, Nuri al Said, lost their lives. For the next 4 years the country was under the control of Gen. Qasim, who was executed on 9 Feb. 1963, following a *coup d'état* by the Army and Air Force on the previous day.

The republican régime terminated the adherence of Iraq to the Arab Federation (*see* THE STATESMAN'S YEAR-BOOK, 1958, p. 806).

The provisional constitution on 4 May 1964 declares Iraq to be an 'Arab, Islamic, independent and sovereign republic' based on democracy and socialism; complete Arab unity is the aim. The National Council for the Revolutionary Command, which took office on 8 Feb. 1963, following the overthrow of Gen. Qasim, affirmed its adherence to the spirit of the 14 July Revolution. It abolished the Sovereignty Council, which had exercised the functions of the Presidency since 1958, and appointed a new President and Cabinet. It reached agreement with Kuwait on the question of Kuwaiti sovereignty, which Gen. Qasim had disputed, but failed to find a peaceful solution to the 2-year-old Kurdish revolt. Increasing domination of the government by Ba'ath Party members and consequent estrangement from Egypt led to a military *coup-d'état* on 18 Nov. 1963. In April 1966 Field Marshal Abdul Salam Muhammad Arif, who came to power in Feb. 1963, and survived the revolution of Nov. 1963, was killed in a helicopter crash. His brother, Abdul Rahman Muhammad Arif, was elected President by the National Defence Council.

A cease-fire in Kurdistan was proclaimed on 10 Feb. 1964, but fighting was resumed in April 1965. In June 1966 the Government announced a peace plan which the Kurds accepted in principle. In March 1970 the Revolutionary Command Council announced a complete and constitutional settlement of the Kurdish issue.

On 16 Oct. 1964 an agreement was signed with the United Arab Republic to establish a 'joint political leadership' charged with achieving full constitutional union within 2 years, since increased to 5 or more years. In June 1967 the two countries agreed to the complete elimination of customs duties.

The following cabinet was formed on 30 July 1968:

President: Maj.-Gen. Ahmed Hassan Bakr.

Defence: Gen. Harden Abdul Ghaffar. *Interior:* Saleh Mahdi Ammash. *Foreign Affairs:* Abdul Karim al Shaikhaly. *Finance:* Amin Abdul Karim. *Justice:* Aziz Shareif. *Education:* Dr Ahmed Abdul Sattar Juwari. *Labour and Social Affairs:* Anwar Abdul Kader. *Health:* Dr Izzat Mustapha. *Culture and Information:* Hamid Al-Jibouri. *Communications:* Adnan Ayub Sabri. *Agriculture:* Salah Umar Al-Ali. *Planning:* Jawad Hashem. *Economy:* Fakhri Yassin Kaddouri. *Industry:* Maj.-Gen Khaled Makki alHashini. *Rural and Municipal Affairs:* Ghaeb Mawloud Monkhless. *Development of the North:* Mohsen Dizayi. *Arab Unity Affairs:* Abdullah al Khobeir.

AREA AND POPULATION. The country has an area of 438,446 sq. km (169,240 sq. miles) and a population (census 14 Oct. 1965) of 8,261,527 (4,205,201 males, 4,056,326 females). Estimated population (1968) 8,765,915. The capital is Baghdad.

Each *muhafasa* is administered by a Muhafis, and is subdivided into *qadhas* (under Qaimaqams) and *nahiyahs* (under Mudirs). The following are the area (in sq. km) and population (census 14 Oct. 1965) for each *muhafasa*:

Amara	17,945	346,663	Kut	14,814	335,495
Arbil	15,315	360,285	Mosul	50,881	954,157
Baghdad	19,922	2,124,323	Nasiriyah [1]	14,452	500,033
Basra	18,022	673,623	Ramadi [2]	137,969	319,289
Diyala	15,742	400,049	Sulaimaniya	11,993	408,220
Diwaniya	83,343	548,830	Half of Neutral		
Hilla	6,889	448,023	Zone	3,522	..
Karbela	7,170	339,696			
Kirkuk	19,543	462,027	Iraquis abroad	924	40,818

[1] Formerly Muntafiq. [2] Formerly Dulaim.

Vital statistics, registered in 1967: Births, 160,743; deaths, 34,250; infant mortality, 2,598.

The largest towns are Baghdad, Basra, Mosul, Kirkuk and Najaf.

On 25 Nov. 1933 the Council of the League of Nations fixed the boundary between Iraq and Syria, including the whole of the Jebel Sinjar in Iraq.

RELIGION. In 1957 there were 6,057,493 Moslems, 206,206 Christians, 4,906 Jews, 55,885 Yazidis, 11,825 Sabians and some 3,645 others.

EDUCATION. Primary and secondary education is free but not compulsory. Primary school age is 6–12. Secondary education is for 6 years, of which the first 3 are termed intermediate. The medium of instruction is Arabic; Kurdish is used in primary schools in some northern districts. The figures for the school year 1968–69 are as follows: Government and private primary schools, 5,137 with 1,017,050 pupils and 47,058 teachers.

There were, in 1966–67, 689 government and private secondary schools with 243,435 pupils and 7,948 teachers. Thirty-six vocational schools had 8,632 students; 56 primary teachers' training schools had 13,303 students.

There are 5 universities in Iraq; in 1964 Baghdad University had about 21,000 students; Al-Hikma University, which opened in 1962, had 436. Baghdad University has branches at Basra and Mosul. Total students at universities and the 10 other institutions of higher education in 1966–67 was 34,926 and 1,619 teachers.

CINEMAS (1966). There were 25 cinemas in Baghdad, with a seating capacity of 24,000.

NEWSPAPERS (1966). In Baghdad there are 8 daily newspapers (one of which is in English) and one in Basra.

HEALTH. In 1967 there were 1,905 doctors; 147 hospitals with 15,542 beds.

JUSTICE. The courts are established throughout the country as follows: For civil matters: the court of cassation in Baghdad; 5 courts of appeal at Baghdad, Basra, Hilla, Mosul and Kirkuk; 14 courts of first instance with unlimited powers and 44 courts of first instance with limited powers, all being courts of single judges. In addition, 6 peace courts have peace court jurisdiction only. Tribal law was abolished in Aug. 1958.

For *Shara'* (religious) matters: the Sunni and Shia benches of revision in Baghdad; Shara' courts at all places where there are civil courts, constituted in some places of specially appointed Qadhis (religious judges) and in other places of the judges of the civil courts. For criminal matters: the court of cassation; 6 sessions courts (2 being presided over by the judge of the local court of first instance and 4 being identical with the courts of appeal). Magistrates' courts at all places where there are civil courts, constituted of civil judges exercising magisterial powers of the first and second class. There are also a number of third-class magistrates courts, powers for this purpose being granted to municipal councils and a number of administrative officials. Some administrative officials are granted the powers of a peace judge to deal with cases of debts due from cultivators.

Special religious courts for non-Catholic Christians at Baghdad, Basra and Mosul deal with matters of personal status, such as divorce, separation and maintenance between husband and wife.

The prison population at the end of 1968 was 7,147 men and 80 women, including persons on remand and in the reformatory school.

Police. In 1967 the police force consisted of 18,538 officers and men. Of these, 7,485 belonged to the Mobile Force.

FINANCE. Currency. The monetary unit is the *Iraqi dinar* (I.D.) = 1,000 *fils* = 10 *riyals* = 20 *dirhams* = £1·17. Silver alloy coins for 100 and 50 fils (*Dirham*) and 25 fils are in circulation, and other coins for 10, 5 and 1 fils. Notes are for $\frac{1}{4}$, $\frac{1}{2}$ and 1 dinar, and for 5 and 10 dinars. The total currency in circulation in Sept. 1967 amounted to 144·4m. dinars. The currency was formerly controlled by an Iraqi Currency Board sitting in London, but was taken over by the National Bank of Iraq on 1 July 1949, which in 1956 was re-named the Central Bank of Iraq.

Budget. Revenue and expenditure (in 1,000 Iraqi dinars) for fiscal years ending 31 March:

	1965–66	1966–67	1967–68 [1]	1968–69 [1]	1969–70 [1]
Revenue	179,131	158,648	218,000	292,000	379,000
Expenditure	186,656	192,428	495,000	373,000	379,000

[1] Estimates.

The above figures relate to the ordinary state budget; development expenditure is financed through a separate budget. Until the 1959–60 budget, 70% of the Iraqi government's share of oil revenues was allocated to development, the remainder going to the ordinary state budget. In 1959, however, the proportions were altered and the amount assigned to development was to be not less than 50% (1967–68: 158m. dinars).

Oil revenues account for over half, customs and excise for about a third of the total revenue. Defence and security take about two-fifths, education about a quarter of the expenditure.

The public debt was 166·7m. dinars on 31 Dec. 1968.

DEFENCE. Military training is compulsory for all men when they reach the age of 18. This consists of 2 years' service with the colours and 18 years on the reserve. However, a man may volunteer for service in the army or change his conscript service into voluntary service. In such circumstances voluntary service is for 2 years, and he may extend it by periods of 2 years until he reaches the age of 45. The 2-year compulsory service can be extended in a national emergency. Many technicians and technically qualified reserve officers serve up to 4 or 5 years.

Army. The strength of the Iraqi Army is about 70,000, organized into 2 infantry divisions, 2 mountain divisions, 1 armoured division and Ministry of Defence troops. The infantry divisions are organized on the lines of British infantry divisions, while the mountain division differs only in armament and its use of pack animals in addition to mechanical transport. The armoured division consists of 2 armoured and 1 infantry brigades. Ministry of Defence troops include an infantry brigade, 2 regiments of heavy anti-aircraft artillery and 2 Republican Guards battalions. Three-quarters of all equipment is of Russian origin, including T-34 and T-54/55 tanks.

Training establishments include a staff college and a military college for cadets.

Navy. The navy comprises 12 *ex*-Soviet torpedo boats, 3 *ex*-Soviet submarine chasers, 4 training craft, 4 river gunboats, 8 harbour patrol boats, 4 despatch launches, a lighthouse tender, the *ex*-royal yacht and a tug.

Air Force. Except for squadrons of Hunter jet fighter-bombers and Wessex helicopters acquired from Britain and Alouette III helicopters from France, the combat and transport squadrons are equipped primarily with aircraft of Soviet design, including 8 Tu-16 medium bombers, 10 Il-28 light bombers, 50 Su-7 fighter-bombers, 60 MiG-21 interceptors, MiG-17d night fighters and MiG-17c day interceptor and ground attack fighters, Mi-4 helicopters, and An-12 and An-2 transports. A few Il-14s, Herons and Doves are used in a transport–communications role, while Hunter and Jet Provost aircraft are employed with Soviet MiG-15UTI trainers and other types in the Air Force College and operational conversion unit. Total strength is about 7,500 personnel and 225 combat aircraft. Soviet 'Guideline' surface-to-air missiles are operational.

PLANNING. The second 5-year economic plan 1965–70 envisaged total investments of I.D.640·7m., of which 27·1% was allocated to agriculture, 29·2% to industry, 17·2% to transport and communications, 21·5% to housing. Oil revenues were to provide 385m., foreign loans 80m.

Iraq is a land of great potentialities. The soil of the country is rich, but there are vast areas which can be cultivated only if irrigated by canals or pumps. The Irrigation Ministry operates several canal systems, new dams have been completed and other irrigation works are under construction.

AGRICULTURE. An Agrarian Reform Law, issued in Sept. 1958, limits land ownership to 1,000 *dunums* for flow-irrigated land and to 2,000 *dunums* for rain-irrigated land.

In 1957–58, 16m. *mesharas*, were planted, 13m. lay fallow, 2m. were uncultivable, 595,000 were orchards and vineyards, 18,000 were pasture and 45,000 woodland. About 13m. *mesharas* were irrigated.

The chief winter crops (1967) are wheat, 1,371,000 metric tons, and barley, 931,000 metric tons. The chief summer crop is rice (1968: 325,000 tons). The date crop is important (average yearly production, 350,000 tons), the country furnishing about 80% of the world's trade in dates (exports, 1968, 254,795 tons); the chief producing area is the totally irrigated riverain belt of the Shatt-el-Arab. Wool is also an important export (1968: 3,325 tons). In 1968, 4,156 tons of cotton were exported.

Livestock (1969): Cattle, 167,923; buffaloes, 224,622; sheep, 11,040,205; goats, 1,845,488; horses, 122,189; asses, 542,414; mules, 71,705; camels, 201,839.

FORESTRY. Up to 1969, 614,953 *dunums* have been demarcated and surveyed in Arbil, Mosul and Sulaimaniya Liwas.

INDUSTRY. Industrial and constructional establishments in 1967 numbered 27,670, employing a total of 215,380 persons. Constructional establishments employed the largest number of workers, 59,138. Other large employers were the brick industry, water and electricity services, date packing, the textile industry, cigarette factories, oil refining and the cement industry. Iraq is still relatively under-developed industrially, but work has begun on 13 new industrial plants which are being established with Soviet equipment and technical assistance. A light-industries company was formed in 1960 to foster smaller industries.

On 14 July 1964 all banks, insurance companies and 32 of the largest industrial and commercial companies were nationalized. The nationalized industries comprise cement, asbestos, cigarettes, spinning and weaving, steel, paper, leather tanning, flour-mills and trading companies. Small firms in these fields were left in the private sector, except for cement, asbestos and cigarettes, which will be entirely in the public sector. The owners of the nationalized companies are to be compensated for the value of their shares with state bonds maturing in 15 years and bearing 3% interest.

OIL. The greater part of Iraq's oil production comes from the Iraq Petroleum Company's field at Kirkuk (found in 1927). This company, an international group, has constructed pipelines to the Mediterranean, including one to Banias on the Syrian coast, with a throughput of about 35m. tons in 1960. The Mosul Petroleum Co. Ltd holds a concession for oil covering Iraqi territory west of the Tigris and north of the 33rd parallel of latitude. Oil was found at Ain Zalah, north-west of Mosul, and the company has laid a pipeline from there to Baiji. The Basra Petroleum Company have been granted a concession for oil covering the southernmost part of Iraq (the old Basra vilayet). High-grade quality oil has been found here, and production started in Dec. 1951. Production at the oilfield of Rumaila started in Dec. 1954; its pipeline is linked to the Zubair–Fao system. An oilfield near Khanaqin, in the area known as the Transferred Territories near the Iranian frontier, was, until Nov. 1958, operated by the Khanaqin Oil Company, a subsidiary of the British Petroleum Company, and is now being operated by the Iraqi Government. There is a pipeline to a refinery near Khanaqin. Oil for consumption in Iraq is refined by the government oil refineries administration (GORA) and is distributed and marketed in Iraq at cheap prices by the Ministry of Oil and Minerals.

Under an agreement dated 3 Feb. 1952 between the Government and the Iraq, Basra and Mosul Petroleum Companies, the Government receives 50% of the profits before the deduction of foreign taxes, and in any case not less than I.D.25m. in 1955 and thereafter, from which date onward the minimum rate of oil-production will be 30m. tons annually. On 11 Dec. 1961, on the severance of the negotiations with the oil companies, the Iraqi Government enacted a law defining the areas in which the Iraq Petroleum Company and its associates may carry out operations. The defined areas total less than ½% of the concessions.

The total crude petroleum exported by foreign oil companies was (in 1,000 long tons) 66,590 in 1966, 58,937 in 1967, 72,609 in 1968, 69,969 in 1969. Revenue received by the Iraqi Government from oil amounted to I.D. 140·8m. in 1966; I.D.131·7m. in 1967; I.D.174m. in 1968; I.D.170m. in 1969.

An oil refinery (annual output, 1m. tons) at Daura near Baghdad, and a bitumen refinery (annual output 60,000 tons) at Gayyarah in the Mosul district both started production in 1955 under the direction of the GORA. The Daura refinery has a capacity of 70,000 bbls per annum. A lubricating oil plant (annual output, 36,000 tons) had been added to the Daura refinery and started production in May 1957. A new refinery with a capacity of 1·3m. tons is planned at Basra.

COMMERCE. Imports and exports for 5 calendar years were as follows (in 1,000 Iraqi dinars):

	1963	1964	1965	1966	1967	1968
Imports	114,027	147,448	162,608	176,092	151,243	144,165
Local exports	19,689	15,291	18,119	23,238	20,664	23,029
Transit	1,254	1,666	1,730	5,884	11,150	20,492

Movements of gold bullion and currency are excluded from the above table. Import values are c.i.f. plus landing charges, and include all goods cleared for home consumption whether subsequently re-exported or not. Exports do not include shipments of oil or re-exports, and are valued f.o.b.

Principal imports (value in 1,000 dinars):

	1967		1968	
	Quantity	Value	Quantity	Value
Cotton textiles (1,000 sq. metres)	53,116	5,219	49,859	4,937
Sugar (tons)	328,858	7,657	250,837	6,098
Tyres and tubes (tons)	5,566	2,562	3,797	1,664
Sheets and plates of iron or steel (tons)	35,519	1,977	37,330	2,116
Tea (tons)	17,335	4,431	25,140	6,098
Electrical generators and motors (tons)	1,994	1,017	2,089	948
Motor vehicles (no.)	5,576	6,868	4,374	4,922
Artificial textiles (1,000 sq. metres)	50,750	5,158	59,058	6,077
Paper and cardboard (tons)	29,384	2,602	37,451	3,223
Timber (tons)	57,033	2,572	..	..
Radios and TV sets and parts (tons)	1,556	2,352	1,332	1,450
Refrigerators (tons)	2,865	1,562	2,141	991
Internal combustion engines (tons)	7,183	4,660	4,471	3,492
Tubes and pipes of iron and cast iron (tons)	34,019	2,456	..	..

The distribution of trade was as follows (in 1,000 dinars):

Imports	1967	1968	Imports	1967	1968
Belgium	4,085	4,864	USA	13,891	5,988
Ceylon	3,841	4,078			
Czechoslovakia	2,410	2,595	Exports		
Germany (West)	15,520	10,403	China	1,903	1,933
India	2,892	5,856	Germany (West)	753	
Italy	7,860	7,441	India	998	1,065
Japan	9,234	12,972	Lebanon	226	2,851
Netherlands	3,792	1,896	Saudi Arabia	2,100	2,585
Sweden	3,941	4,265	USSR	1,084	1,482
USSR	1,242	12,550	UK	550	297
UK	19,421	10,403	USA	1,092	817

The total trade between Iraq and UK according to the British Board of Trade returns, was as follows for 5 years (in £1,000 sterling):

	1966	1967	1968	1969	1970
Imports to UK	65,554	24,068	28,023	31,119	18,729
Exports from UK	25,835	16,686	15,615	21,332 ⎫	23,774
Re-exports from UK	438	592	316	571 ⎭	

SHIPPING. In 1967, 1,011 vessels of 13·5m. NRT entered the Port of Basra.

RAILWAYS. The Iraqi state railway system consists of a metre-gauge line from Basra, at the head of the Persian Gulf, to Baghdad, 669·2 km. At Baghdad the line crosses the river Tigris by a combined road and rail bridge and then extends through Juloula (Qaraghan), which is 147·8 km from Baghdad on to Kirkuk 321·8 km, thence to the terminal station of Arbil 104·9 km. Khanaqin on the Iraqi–Iranian frontier is served by a branch line from Juloula (27·9 km). There is also a standard gauge (4 ft 8½ in.) line from Baghdad to Tel-Kotchek (528 km) on the Syrian frontier, following the right bank of the Tigris *via* Mosul; it links with the Syrian railway system at Tel-Kotchek, thus establishing a through service from the Persian Gulf to Turkey, Egypt and Europe. The total length of track open in 1969 was 2,352 km.

A standard-gauge Baghdad–Basra line was completed in 1968. This mostly runs parallel to the metre-gauge route, which it will eventually replace.

ROADS. About 4,550 miles of roads and tracks have been developed for vehicular traffic. The main surfaced roads are: (1) the road north from Baghdad *via* Kirkuk, Arbil and Mosul to a point near the Turkish frontier at Zakho, with branches from Kirkuk to the Kurdish province of Sulaimaniya, from Arbil to the Iranian frontier, and from Mosul to Sinjar; (2) about 350 miles of the main road west from Baghdad to the Jordan frontier; (3) the road east of Baghdad, which connects the road system of Iran near Khanaqin; and (4) the road south from Baghdad to Hilla and the holy city of Kerbela.

Vehicles registered in 1967 included 42,292 passenger cars, 18,373 taxis, 30,054 lorries, 9,100 buses.

AVIATION. Baghdad and Basra airports are served by BOAC, Lufthansa, Alitalia, Swissair, KLM, Middle East Air Lines, PIA, Iraqi Airways, Iranian Airways, Air Liban, United Arab Airlines and Aeroflot. In 1968 there arrived by air 101,565 passengers; 80,542 passengers left Iraqi airports.

POST. In 1966 there were 328 post and telegraph offices. Wireless telegraph services exist with UK, USA, UAR, Lebanon and Saudi Arabia, and wireless telephone services with UK, USA, Italy, UAR and USSR. Telephones, 1 Jan. 1969, were estimated at 113,388, of which 63,018 were in Baghdad.

BANKING. The British Bank of the Middle East and the Eastern Bank and all other banks were nationalized on 14 July 1964.

In 1941 the Rafidain Bank, financed by the Iraqi Government, was instituted to carry out normal banking transactions with head office in Baghdad and branches in the chief towns and abroad, including London. In addition, there are

4 government banks which are authorized to issue loans to companies and individuals: the Industrial Bank, the Agricultural Bank, the Estate Bank, the Assisting Bank and the Mortgage Bank.

In March 1969 post office savings amounted to 5,257,211 dinars held by 141,960 depositors.

WEIGHTS AND MEASURES. The metric system is gradually being introduced and is mandatory for linear measures, but native weights and measures are still met with, the principal ones being: *Hogga* = 2·8 lb.; *man* = 56 lb.; *wazna* = 224 lb.; *tughar* = 4,480 lb.; *dhar* = 29·38 in. (27 in. in Aleppo); *meshara* or *donum* = 0·62 acre or 4 hectares.

DIPLOMATIC REPRESENTATIVES

Iraq maintains embassies in:

Afghánistán	Italy	Spain
Austria	Japan	Sudan
Belgium	Jordan	Sweden
China	Kuwait	Switzerland
Czechoslovakia	Lebanon	Syria
France	Libya	Tunisia
Ghana	Morocco	Turkey
Greece	Netherlands	USSR
India	Nigeria	UAR
Indonesia	Pakistan	UK
Iran	Saudi Arabia	

Iraq is also in diplomatic relations with:

Albania	Germany (East)	Portugal
Bulgaria	Guinea	Romania
Ceylon	Hungary	Thailand
Denmark	Mexico	Venezuela
Ethiopia	Norway	Yugoslavia
Finland	Poland	

Iraq broke off diplomatic relations with USA on 7 June 1967. Belgium serves as protective power.

OF IRAQ IN GREAT BRITAIN
(21 Queen's Gate, SW7)

Ambassador: Kadhim Muhsin al-Khalaf.

Counsellors: Adid Ahmad Nafi; Ahmed Abdul Wahid. *First Secretaries:* A.-K. Al-Mudaris; Hisham Al-Khudhairy; K. R. Jawdat.

OF GREAT BRITAIN IN IRAQ

Ambassador: H. G. Balfour Paul, CMG.

Counsellors: D. F. Hawley, MBE (*Commercial*); P. McKearney (*Consul-General and Head of Chancery*). *First Secretaries:* J. D. Perris; J. H. Symons; E. A. McNaught; R. L. Morris, OBE (*Labour*); G. R. Sutherland. *Service Attachés:* Col. J. R. D. Sharpe (*Defence and Military*), Wing Cdr H. Harrison, AFC (*Air*).

BOOKS OF REFERENCE

STATISTICAL INFORMATION. The Central Statistical Organization, Ministry of Planning, Baghdad (*President:* Dr Salah Al-Shaikhly) publishes an annual *Statistical Abstract* (latest issue 1967) and a *Quarterly Bulletin of Statistics*. Foreign Trade statistics are published annually by the Ministry of Planning.

Arfa, H., *The Kurds.* OUP, 1966
Langley, K. M., *The Industrialization of Iraq.* Harvard Univ. Press, 1961
Longrigg, S., and Stoakes, F., *Iraq.* London, 1959
Wirth, E., *Agrargeographie des Irak.* Hamburg, 1962

IRISH REPUBLIC

Éire

HISTORY. In April 1916 an insurrection against British rule took place and a republic was proclaimed. The armed struggle was renewed in 1919 and continued until 1921. The independence of Ireland was reaffirmed in Jan. 1919 by the National Parliament (*Dáil Éireann*), elected in Dec. 1918.

In 1920 an Act was passed by the British Parliament, under which separate Parliaments were set up for 'Southern Ireland' (26 counties) and 'Northern Ireland' (6 counties). The Unionists of the 6 counties accepted this scheme, and a Northern Parliament was duly elected on 24 May 1921. The rest of Ireland, however, ignored the Act.

On 6 Dec. 1921 a treaty was signed between Great Britain and Ireland by which Ireland accepted dominion status subject to the right of Northern Ireland to opt out. This right was exercised, and the border between *Saorstát Éireann* (26 counties) and Northern Ireland (6 counties) was fixed in Dec. 1925 as the outcome of an agreement between Great Britain, the Irish Free State and Northern Ireland. The agreement was ratified by the three parliaments.

Subsequently the constitutional links between *Saorstát Éireann* and the UK was gradually removed by the *Dáil*. The remaining formal association with the British Commonwealth by virtue of the External Relations Act, 1936, was severed when the Republic of Ireland Act, 1948, came into operation on 18 April 1949.

National flag: Green, white, orange (vertical).

National anthem: The Soldier's Song (words by P. Kearney; music by P. Heaney).

CONSTITUTION AND GOVERNMENT. The Irish Republic is a sovereign independent, democratic republic. Its parliament exercises jurisdiction in 26 of the 32 counties of Ireland.

The first constitution of the Irish Free State came into operation on 6 Dec. 1922. Certain provisions which were regarded as contrary to the national sentiments were gradually removed by successive amendments, with the result that at the end of 1936 the text differed considerably from the original document. On 14 June 1937 a new constitution was approved by Parliament (*Dáil Éireann*) and enacted by a plebiscite on 1 July 1937. This constitution came into operation on 29 Dec. 1937. Under it the name Ireland (Éire) was restored.

The constitution provides that, pending the reintegration of the national territory, the laws enacted by the Parliament established by the constitution shall have the same area and extent of application as those of the Irish Free State.

The *Oireachtas* or National Parliament consists of the President and two Houses, viz., a House of Representatives, called *Dáil Éireann*, and a Senate, called *Seanad Éireann*, consisting of 60 members. The *Dáil*, consisting of 144 members, is elected by adult suffrage. Of the 60 members of the Senate, 11 are nominated by the *Taoiseach* (Prime Minister), 6 are elected by the universities and the remaining 43 are elected from 5 panels of candidates establishments on a vocational basis, representing the following public services and interests: (1) national language and culture, literature, art, education and such professional interests as may be defined by law for the purpose of this panel; (2) agricultural and allied interests, and fisheries: (3) labour, whether organized or unorganized; (4) industry and commerce, including banking, finance, accountancy, engineering and architecture; (5) public administration and social services, including voluntary social activities. The electing body is a college of about 900 members, comprising members of the *Dáil*, Senate, county boroughs and county councils.

A maximum period of 90 days is afforded to the Senate for the consideration or amendment of Bills sent to that House by the *Dáil*, but the Senate has no power to veto legislative proposals.

No amendment of the constitution can be effected except with the approval of the people given at a referendum.

Irish is the first official language; English is recognized as a second official language.

For further details of the Constitution *see* THE STATESMAN'S YEAR-BOOK, 1952, pp. 1123–24.

President: Éamon de Valéra (installed on 25 June 1966 for second term). The President holds office for 7 years.

Former Presidents: Dr Douglas Hyde (1938–45); Seán T. O Ceallaigh (1945–59; 2 terms).

A general election were held on 18 June 1969: Fianna Fáil, 75 (1965 election, 72); Fine Gael, 50 (47); Labour Party, 18 (22); Independents, 1 (2).

There are no formal party divisions in the Senate.

The Fianna Fáil Government consistsof the following members:

Taoiseach (Prime Minister): Seán Ó Loinsigh (John Lynch).
Tánaiste (Deputy Prime Minister) and Minister for Health: Erskine H. Childers.
External Affairs: An Dr Pádraig Ó hIrighile (Dr Patrick J. Hillery).
Transport and Power: Brian Ó Luineacháin (Brian Lenihan).
Labour and Social Welfare: Seosamh Ó Braonáin (Joseph Brennan).
Finance and the Gaeltacht: Seoirse Ó Colla (George Colley).
Lands: Seán Ó Flannagáin (John Flanagan)
Education: Pádraig Ó Fachtna (Patrick Faulkner).
Agriculture and Fisheries: Séamus Mac Giobúin (James Gibbons).
Industry and Commerce: Pádraig Ó Leathlobhair (Patrick Lalor).
Justice: Deasún Ó Máille (Desmond O'Malley).
Defence: Diarmaid Ó Cróinín (Jeremiah Cronin)
Local Government: Riobárd Ó Maoildhia (Robert Molloy).
Posts and Telegraphs: Gearóid Ó Coileáin (Gerard Collins).
Attorney-General (not in the Cabinet): Colm Condún, AS (Colm Condon, SC).

LOCAL GOVERNMENT. There are 27 administrative counties and 4 county boroughs governed by councils which are elected quinquennially. The county councils administer county affairs generally, can hold property, levy rates and borrow money. The county borough council possesses, with certain exceptions, the powers of a county council.

The administrative counties include the urban county districts, which are urban areas that have been constituted sanitary districts. Each such district is governed by an elected council that administers the Acts relating to sanitary services, housing, urban roads, etc., and is the sole rating authority within its area. There are 56 urban sanitary districts and 28 towns constituted under the Towns Improvement (Ireland) Act, 1854, which are not urban sanitary districts. These towns have elected town commissioners who exercise certain minor powers.

The county and county borough councils, the urban district councils and other elective bodies have a system of government which combines an elected council with a manager. The manager for a county is, by virtue of his office, the manager for every elective body in the county. These councils have certain specified functions, including the making of a rate, raising loans and making bye-laws. All functions formerly exercised by the councils other than those now specifically reserved by law are exercised by the manager, a paid official, who has control over all officers, and whose removal from office is, like theirs, subject to the sanction of the central authority.

Elected members of local authorities are not paid, but provision is made for payment of travelling expenses and subsistence allowances.

Elections to county and county borough councils, urban district councils and town commissioners are held according to the principle of proportional representation by means of the single transferable vote. A person of full age is entitled to be registered once as a local-government elector for a local authority at the place of ordinary residence on a qualifying date or in respect of lands or premises occupied as owner or tenant during a qualifying period. Women are eligible for election as members of all local-government bodies in the same manner and on the same conditions as men.

A central body called the Local Appointments Commission is charged with the duty of selecting suitable persons to be appointed by local authorities to chief executive offices, professional offices and other prescribed offices. Where a prescribed office is not being filled by promotion, the local authority must request the Commissioners to recommend to them a suitable person. The Commissioners normally select persons for appointment by the machinery of selection boards.

A scheme of combined purchasing has been established in order to enable local authorities to obtain commodities of standard quality at the lowest possible price. Official contractors are appointed annually by the Minister for Local Government on the recommendation of an Advisory Committee.

AREA AND POPULATION.

Counties and county boroughs	Area in sq. miles[1]	Census population, 1966		
		Males	Females	Total
Province of Leinster				
Carlow	346	17,320	16,273	33,593
Dublin County[2]	356	375,692	419,355	795,047
Dublin City[3]	45	267,070	301,702	568,772
Conurbation	..	39,541	41,840	81,381
Dun Laoghaire Borough[3]	7	23,159	28,613	51,772
Conurbation	..	16,080	16,962	33,042
Kildare	654	34,829	31,575	66,404
Kilkenny	796	31,390	29,073	60,463
Laoighis	664	23,622	20,973	44,595
Longford	403	15,245	13,744	28,989
Louth	317	34,664	34,855	69,519
Meath	903	34,877	32,446	67,323
Offaly	771	27,007	24,710	51,717
Westmeath	680	27,101	25,799	52,900
Wexford	908	42,270	41,167	83,437
Wicklow	782	30,231	30,197	60,428
Total of Leinster	**7,580**	**694,248**	**720,167**	**1,414,415**
Province of Munster				
Clare	1,231	38,667	34,930	73,597
Cork County[2]	2,880	170,010	169,693	339,703
Cork City[3]	14	58,122	64,024	122,146
Conurbation	..	1,629	1,508	3,137
Kerry	1,815	58,674	54,111	112,785
Limerick County[2]	1,037	69,135	68,222	137,357
Limerick City[3]	7	26,747	29,165	55,912
Conurbation	..	993	1,177	2,170
Tipperary	1,643	63,416	59,396	122,812
Waterford County[2]	709	36,466	36,614	73,080
Waterford City[4]	4	14,140	15,702	29,842
Total of Munster	**9,315**	**436,368**	**422,966**	**859,334**
Province of Connacht				
Galway	2,293	77,696	70,644	148,340
Leitrim	589	16,444	14,128	30,572
Mayo	2,084	59,829	55,718	115,547
Roscommon	951	29,782	26,446	56,228
Sligo	694	26,346	24,917	51,263
Total of Connacht	**6,611**	**210,097**	**191,853**	**401,950**
Province of Ulster (part of)				
Cavan	730	28,803	25,219	54,022
Donegal	1,865	55,606	52,943	108,549
Monaghan	499	23,910	21,822	45,732
Total of Ulster (part of)	**3,094**	**108,319**	**99,984**	**208,303**
Total	**26,600[5]**	**1,449,032**	**1,434,970**	**2,884,002**

[1] Exclusive of certain rivers, lakes and tideways.   [2] Including the city.
[3] Population within legally defined boundary.   [4] Has no suburbs or environs.
[5] 68,893 sq. km.

The population has declined since 1841, when the 26 counties had 6,528,799 inhabitants; there were 3,221,823 in 1901; 3,096,000 in 1921; 2,968,420 in 1936; 2,955,107 in 1946; 2,898,264 in 1956; 2,818,341 in 1961; thereafter it has again increased.

VITAL STATISTICS for 4 calendar years:

	Births	Marriages	Deaths		Births	Marriages	Deaths
1966	62,215	16,849	35,113	1968	61,004	18,993	33,157
1967	61,307	17,788	31,400	1969	62,911	19,863	33,734

Passenger movements by sea were, in 1969, outward, 969,576, inward, 956,830.

RELIGION. According to the census of population taken in 1961 the principal religious professions were as follows:

	Leinster	Munster	Connacht	Ulster (part of)	Total
Roman Catholics	1,246,904	826,618	411,312	188,639	2,673,473
Church of Ireland	64,367	17,743	6,653	15,253	104,016
Presbyterians	5,936	753	459	11,805	18,953
Methodists	3,875	1,484	264	1,053	6,676
Other denominations	11,067	2,605	777	774	15,223

EDUCATION. ELEMENTARY. Elementary education is free and is given in 4,260 national schools. The average daily enrolment of pupils in 1968–69 was 497,128; the percentage average daily attendance 89·4; the number of teachers of all classes 14,732 in 1967–68. There are 6 state-aided training colleges. The estimated state expenditure on elementary education for 1970–71 is £25,258,000, excluding the cost of administration.

Pre-fabricated classroom buildings have been provided for a considerable number of larger urban primary schools in which there was a current shortage of accommodation. It is intended where feasible to close 1-teacher and 2-teacher schools and to convey the pupils to larger schools by state-aided transport services.

SECONDARY. The secondary schools are under private control and are conducted in many cases by religious orders; all schools receiving grants from the state are open to inspection by inspectors of the Department of Education. The number of recognized secondary schools during the school year 1969–70 was 601, and the number of pupils in attendance was 145,024. Total state expenditure for 1969–70 is £19,626,000.

Grants for the provision of modern language teaching equipment in 430 secondary schools have been sanctioned under a scheme introduced in 1964. The experimental schools television service, comprising programmes in physics, chemistry and mathematics for senior and junior pupils is being continued, and 480 schools have received grants for the purchase of television sets.

CONTINUATION AND TECHNICAL. Vocational schools provide courses of continuation and technical education, apprentice training, courses of technician training and courses leading to professional qualifications (e.g., architecture, engineering, accountancy). These schools and temporary centres are controlled by the local Vocational Education Committees, and are maintained partly by the rates and partly by state grants. The estimated state expenditure for 1970–71 is £10·32m., excluding the cost of administration, and the expenditure from the local rates, £1,663,564.

COMPREHENSIVE SCHOOLS which are established and financed by the State combine academic and technical subjects in one broad curriculum so that each pupil may be offered an education structured to his needs, abilities and interests. Pupils are prepared for the State examinations and for entrance to universities and institutes of further education. To date, 4 comprehensive schools have been built. The estimated State expenditure on these schools for 1970–71, including building and running costs, is £685,000.

AGRICULTURAL. Full-time instruction in agriculture is provided for all sections of the farming community. There are 3 state agricultural colleges for young men, administered by the Department of Agriculture and Fisheries, and 7 private state-aided agricultural colleges, at each of which a 1-year course in agriculture is given. Scholarships tenable at these colleges, all of which are residential, are awarded by the County Committees of Agriculture. These Committees provide a comprehensive agricultural advisory service and also conduct winter classes in agriculture and horticulture at local centres. A more comprehensive course is provided in winter farm schools, which are intended, in general, for persons of not less than 17 years of age who are engaged in farming. Second-year courses in agriculture are provided at 3 of the private colleges.

HORTICULTURAL. Courses of training in horticulture are provided at the National Botanic Gardens, Dublin, and at Warrenstown Agricultural College, conducted by the Salesian Fathers. A similar course for girls is also provided by the Irish-countrywomen's Association in Co. Louth.

POULTRY-KEEPING AND FARM HOME MANAGEMENT. Advanced 3-year residential courses are provided at the Munster Institute, Cork, for young women who wish to qualify for teaching and advisory posts in poultry-keeping and dairying and in farm home management. The farm home management course includes instruction in poultry-keeping, butter and cheese-making, general farming and home management. A 1-year non-residential course of instruction for the training of young men and women as technicians in poultry husbandry is also provided at the Munster Institute (which is administered by the Department of Agriculture and Fisheries).

RURAL DOMESTIC ECONOMY AND RURAL SCIENCE. A year course for young women in poultry-keeping, dairying and rural domestic economy is given at 6 private residential schools of rural domestic economy, 2 private residential schools of rural domestic science and Gurteen Agricultural College. The County Committees of Agriculture award scholarships tenable at these institutions. Classes in poultry-keeping and farm home management are also conducted by the County Committees at local centres. Rural science (including practical gardening and surveying) is taught in some 100 day vocational schools throughout the country.

A scheme of farm apprenticeship is operated by the Farm Apprenticeship Board, which represents various agricultural interests. The scheme provides for up to 4 years' practical training on well-managed commercial farms.

HIGHER EDUCATION IN AGRICULTURE, HORTICULTURE, DAIRY SCIENCE AND VETERINARY SCIENCE. Higher education in general agriculture and horticulture, leading to University degrees, is provided by University College, Dublin, and in dairy science by University College, Cork. Dublin University (Trinity College) also confers degrees in agriculture. Training in veterinary medicine and surgery, leading to University degrees, is provided at the Veterinary College, Ballsbridge, Dublin, by University College, Dublin, and Trinity College.

UNIVERSITY EDUCATION is provided by the National University of Ireland, founded in Dublin in 1908, and by the University of Dublin (Trinity College), founded in 1592. The National University comprises 3 constituent colleges—University College, Dublin, University College, Cork, and University College, Galway—and a 'recognized' college, St Patrick's College, Maynooth, Co. Kildare. St Patrick's College is a national seminary for Catholic priests and a pontifical university with the power to confer degrees up to doctoral level in philosophy, theology and canon law. It now admits lay students (men and women) to the courses in arts, celtic studies, science and education which it provides as a recognized college of the National University.

Proposals are under consideration for the re-organization of university education in Ireland. It is envisaged that University College, Dublin, and Trinity College, Dublin, will become complementary institutions in a new University of Dublin, and that University College, Cork, and University College, Galway, will be constituted as separate independent universities.

Legislation is proposed to provide for the establisement of a Higher Education Authority to deal with the financial and organizational problems of higher education generally in Ireland. Pending its establishment on a statutory basis the Authority has been set up on an *ad hoc* basis to advise the Minister. Statistics for the academic year 1968–69:

Universities	Academic Staff	Full-time Students
University College, Dublin	649	7,611
University College, Cork	331	2,918
University College, Galway	169	2,393
Trinity College, Dublin	294	3,996
St Patrick's College, Maynooth	53	779

CINEMAS (1961). There were 183 cinemas, with a seating capacity of about 152,000.

NEWSPAPERS (1969). There are 7 daily newspapers (all in English) with a combined circulation of 702,432; 5 of them are published in Dublin (circulation, 609,947).

SOCIAL WELFARE. Social-welfare services concerned primarily with income maintenance are under the general control of the Minister for Social Welfare. The services administered by the Department of Social Welfare are divided into Insurance and Assistance schemes.

Insurance Services. Non-manual employees earning up to £1,200 a year and all manual employees irrespective of their earnings are compulsorily insured from age 16 to 70 years and pay weekly contributions. (The insured population is approximately 795,000.) Subject to appropriate statutory conditions (but without regard to the recipients' means) the following insurance benefits are available: Disability benefit, invalidity benefit, unemployment benefit, widow's pension, orphan's allowance, marriage benefit, maternity benefit, treatment benefit, retirement pension payable at 65, old-age pension payable at the age of 70 and a death grant. The cost of these benefits is borne by a Social Insurance Fund, which is maintained on a tripartite basis by (approximately equal) contributions from employers and employees, supplemented by a state grant sufficient to keep the Fund in equilibrium.

The insurance services also provide for payment of benefits in respect of injury, disablement or death, as well as medical care resulting from an occupational accident or disease. These benefits are available to employees, irrespective of age, other than non-manual workers earning over £1,200 a year, and are paid from an Occupational Injuries Fund which is financed by employers' contributions.

Assistance Services. Children's allowances are payable without a means test in respect of each child under 16 years of age normally residing with the claimant. The following Assistance services are subject to means and, sometimes, residence tests: Non-contributory widows' and orphans' pensions to the survivors of persons whose lack of insurance (or inadequate insurance record) precludes payment of contributory pensions; deserted wife's allowance to women under 70 years of age who have been deserted by their husbands; old age pensions payable at age 70 to persons not entitled to insurance pensions; blind pensions (under the same general conditions as apply to old age pensions) payable at age 21; old age (care) allowance to persons age 70 or over who are so incapacitated as to require full time care and attention which is provided by a female relative; unemployment assistance payable during unemployment to persons not entitled to receive unemployment benefit. A person unable to provide the necessaries of life for himself is eligible for public assistance; failing assistance in an institution, such a person must be given home assistance, generally in the form of a cash payment on a weekly basis, but, in particular cases, in kind.

HEALTH SERVICES. Persons in the lower income group (those who are unable to provide medical services from their own resources, and their dependants) are entitled to free general medical practitioner attention, including any medicines or appliances that may be necessary, free hospital and specialist treatment, free maternity care and infant-welfare services, free dental, ophthalmic and aural treatment and appliances, and free mental-hospital treatment. Persons in the middle income group (*i.e.*, those outside the lower income group in the categories made up of insured workers, persons whose yearly means are less than £1,200, farmers with a rateable valuation of £60 or less, and dependants of such persons) are entitled to hospital (including mental hospital) treatment at a charge not exceeding 10*s.* a day, specialist treatment (with a small charge for out-patients) and free maternity care and infant-welfare services. Hospital treatment for tuberculosis and certain other infectious diseases is provided free of charge to all classes of the community. All diabetics are eligible for a free supply of drugs and other necessary medicines, etc. Pupils of national (elementary) schools are provided with a free school health-examination service and are also eligible for free hospital and specialist treatment and free dental, ophthalmic and aural services for defects discovered at school health examinations. A free child-welfare clinic service for children under 6 years of age is available in many urban areas. All these services are provided by local health authorities under the direction and control of the Minister for Health. The local health authorities are generally the County Councils, but the Dublin, Cork, Limerick and Waterford health authorities provide the services in both the city and county areas in each case.

JUSTICE. The Constitution provides that justice shall be administered in public in Courts established by law by Judges appointed by the President on the advice of the Government. The jurisdiction and organization of the Courts are dealt with in the Courts (Establishment and Constitution Act, 1961) and the Courts (Supplemental Provisions) Acts, 1961–68. These Courts consist of Courts of First Instance and a Court of Final Appeal, called the Supreme Court. The Courts of First Instance are the High Court with full original jurisdiction and the Circuit and the District Courts with local and limited jurisdiction. A Judge may not be removed from office except for stated misbehaviour or incapacity and then only on resolutions passed by both Houses of the *Oireachtas*. Judges of the Supreme, High and Circuit Courts are appointed from among practising barristers. Judges of the District Court (called District Justices) may be appointed from among practising barristers or practising solicitors.

The Supreme Court, which consists of the Chief Justice (who is *ex officio* an additional Judge of the High Court) and 4 ordinary judges, has appellate jurisdiction from all decisions of the High Court. The President may, after consultation with the Council of State, refer a Bill, which has been passed by both Houses of the *Oireachtas* (other than a money bill and certain other bills), to the Supreme Court for a decision on the question as to whether such Bill or any provision thereof is or are repugnant to the Constitution.

The High Court, which consists of a President (who is *ex officio* an additional Judge of the Supreme Court) and 6 ordinary judges, has full original jurisdiction in and power to determine all matters and questions, whether of law or fact, civil or criminal. In all cases in which questions arise touching the validity of any law having regard to the provisions of the Constitution, the High Court alone exercises original jurisdiction. The High Court on Circuit acts as an appeal court from the Circuit Court.

The Court of Criminal Appeal consists of the Chief Justice or an ordinary Judge of the Supreme Court, together with either 2 ordinary judges of the High Court or the President and one ordinary judge of the High Court. It deals with appeals by persons convicted on indictment where the appellant obtains a certificate from the trial judge that the case is a fit one for appeal, or, in case such certificate is refused, where the court itself, on appeal from such refusal, grants leave to appeal. The decision of the Court of Criminal Appeal is final, unless that court or the Attorney-General certifies that the decision involves a point of law of exceptional public importance, so that an appeal should be taken to the Supreme Court.

The High Court exercising criminal jurisdiction is known as the Central Criminal Court. It consists of a Judge or judges of the High Court, nominated by the President of the High Court. The Court sits in Dublin and tries criminal cases which are outside the jurisdiction of the Circuit Court or which may be sent forward to it for trial from the Circuit Court on the application of the Attorney-General or the accused person.

The country is divided into a number of circuits for the purposes of the Circuit Court. The President of the Circuit Court is *ex officio* an additional judge of the High Court. The jurisdiction of the court in civil proceedings is limited to £600 in contract and tort, £1,000 in actions founded on hire-purchase and credit-sale agreements, £2,000 in equity and £5,000 in probate and administration, save by consent of the parties, in which event the jurisdiction is unlimited. In criminal matters it has jurisdiction in all cases except murder, treason, piracy and allied offences. The Circuit Court acts as an appeal court from the District Court.

The District Court has a summary jurisdiction in a large number of criminal cases where the offence is not of a serious nature. In civil matters the Court has jurisdiction in contract and tort (except slander, libel, criminal conversation, seduction, slander of title, malicious prosecution and false imprisonment) where the claim does not exceed £50; in proceedings founded on hire-purchase and credit-sale agreements, the jurisdiction is £100.

All criminal cases, except those of a minor nature, are tried by a judge and a jury of 12. Juries are also used in very many civil cases. In a criminal case the jury must be unanimous in reaching a verdict, but in a civil case the agreement of 9 members is sufficient.

FINANCE. Currency. The unit of currency is the Irish *pound*, equivalent to US$2.40 and the £ sterling. The Central Bank has the sole right of issuing legal-tender notes; token coinage is issued by the Minister for Finance through the Bank. Decimal currency was adopted in 1971.

The volume of the legal-tender note issue was £143,671,514 on 31 March 1970. Total notes and coins in circulation in March 1970 amounted to £151,338,544.

Budget. Receipts and expenditures (in £1m.) for fiscal years ending 31 March:

Receipts	1969–70 Actual	1970–71 Estimated
Customs duties	87·7	89·6
Excise duties	87·9	98·1
Income tax and sur-tax	93·3	107·2
Corporation profits tax, etc.	14·9	18·1
Stamp duties	7·5	6·0
Estate, etc., duties	7·7	8·3
Motor vehicle duties	13·4	14·8
Post Office	27·4	28·3
Turnover tax	20·4	43·0
Wholesale tax	20·2	23·4
Total (including other items)	411·0	474·9

Current expenditure	Provisional	Estimated
Debt service	88·8	101·6
Agriculture, etc.	73·9	82·1
Education	52·9	59·6
Transport	14·4	15·5
Post Office	19·9	21·8
Defence	14·4	14·3
Justice (including Police)	11·8	12·6
Social Welfare	59·2	69·4
Health	32·1	37·4
Superannuation	12·1	14·5
Industry	9·2	10·8
Total (including other items)	411·5	474·9

Capital expenditure amounted to 114·6m. in 1969–70, and the estimate for 1970–71 is 126·9m.

On 31 March 1970 the liabilities totalled £1,009m. The assets were: Electricity scheme, £55·8m.; local loans fund, £224·2m.; purchase of creameries, £1·4m.; turf development, £20·9m.; national loan sinking funds, £68·2m.; shares in companies established under state auspices, £73·2m.; exchequer balance, £700,000; other assets, £111·8m.; total, £576·2m.

DEFENCE. Under the direction of the President, and subject to the provisions of the Defence Act, 1954, the military command of the Defence Forces is exercisable by the Government through the Minister for Defence. To aid and counsel the Minister for Defence on all matters in relation to the business of the Department of Defence on which he may consult it, there is a Council of Defence consisting of the Parliamentary Secretary to the Minister, the Secretary of the Department of Defence, the Chief of Staff, the Adjutant-General and the Quartermaster-General. Establishments provide at present for a Permanent Defence Force of approximately 13,000 all ranks including the Air Corps and the Naval Service. The Defence Estimates for the year ending 31 March 1971 provide for approximately 24,200 all ranks of the Reserve Defence Force. Recruitment is on a voluntary basis. Minimum term of enlistment for the Army is 3 years in the Permanent Defence Force, or 3 years in the Permanent Defence Force and 9 years in the Reserve Defence Force. For the Naval Service, enlistment is for 4 years in the Permanent Force or 6 years in the Permanent Defence Force and 6 years in the Reserve Defence Force.

The Naval Service had 3 old corvettes and 2 tenders. Two new fishery protection vessels were projected but in 1970 3 coastal minesweepers were purchased from Britain.

The Air Corps is for defence and training purposes. Equipment includes a small number of Chipmunk, Provost, Vampire and Dove trainers, and 3 Alouette III helicopters. The strength of the Corps is approximately 500 all ranks. The Defence Estimates for the year ending 31 March 1971 provide for an expenditure of £14,308,000.

Since April 1964 an Irish Contingent has formed part of the UN Force in Cyprus. Irish officers have served also with the UN in the Lebanon, New Guinea and, from Sept. 1965 to March 1966, with the UN India–Pakistan Observation Mission. Irish officers are at present serving with the UN Truce Supervision Organization in the Middle East.

AGRICULTURE. General distribution of surface (in acres) in 1969: Crops and pasture, 11,902,200; other land, including grazed mountain, 5,121,500; total, 17,023,700.

Area (statute acres) under principal crops, with estimated yield (in tons), calculated from sample returns covering approximately 60% of the country.

Crops	Area 1967	1968	1969	Produce 1967	1968	1969
Wheat	188,800	223,600	203,600	293,300	405,800	357,100
Oats	237,900	218,300	189,500	288,900	281,000	247,500
Barley	451,200	454,000	490,200	666,000	740,500	775,600
Rye	1,400	800	800	1,000	600	700
Potatoes	159,600	146,500	136,300	1,720,100	1,598,600	1,429,700
Turnips	108,800	107,700	99,200	2,366,400	2,408,700	1,975,700
Mangels	30,100	29,500	27,200	746,900	769,400	661,200
Sugar-beet	63,900	64,100	61,500	941,100	1,075,800	902,400
Hay	2,047,600	2,084,900	2,192,000	4,573,600	4,823,300	5,213,300

Agricultural output for the year 1969 was valued at £311,812,000.

Livestock at 1 June 1969: Cattle, 5·69m.; sheep, 4,006,200; pigs, 1,115,500; horses, 124,900; poultry, 10,334,600.

FORESTRY. The total area of state forests was 509,930 acres in 1969.

FISHERIES. The number of vessels and men engaged in fishing in 1969 were 855 motor, 1,056 boats propelled by outboard engines, sails and oars; men

5,631. The quantities and values of fish landed during 1969 were: Demersal fish, 314,470 cwt, value £1,253,835; pelagic fish. 760,452 cwt, value £851,117; shell-fish, value £890,458. Total value, £2,995,550.

INDUSTRY. The census of industrial production for 1968 gives the following details of the values (in £) of gross and net output for the principal manufacturing industries. The figures for net output are those of gross output minus cost of materials, including fuel, light and power.

	Gross output	Net output
Tobacco	62,587,754	6,565,158
Creamery butter, cheese, condensed milk, chocolate crumb, ice-cream and other edible milk products	78,852,654	13,102,976
Grain milling and animal feeding stuffs	49,444.827	9,737,952
Bacon factories	45,563,544	7,547,893
Assembly construction and repair of mechanically propelled road and land vehicles	44,976,758	12,900,231
Manufacture and refining of sugar and manufacture of cocoa, chocolate and sugar confectionery	31,452,333	9,511,951
Bread, biscuit and flour confectionery	30,164,301	12,787,669
Slaughtering, preparation and preserving of meat other than by bacon factories	54,854,162	5,593,860
Brewing[1]	23,160,171	17,017,036
Metal trades (excluding machinery and transport equipment)	39,566,410	17,166,952
Woollen and worsted (excluding clothing)	23,621,418	10,322,931
Printing, publishing and allied trades	24,607,018	16,010,672
Manufacture of paper and paper products	21,190,824	8,866,012
Manufacture of electrical machinery, apparatus and appliances	36,653,068	16,385,396
Hosiery	22,045,145	10,928,957
Boot and shoe (wholesale factories)	12,194,347	6,323,332
Clothing (wholesale factories), women's and girls' readymade clothing (other than hosiery)	15,165,666	7,453,358
Structural clay products, asbestos goods, plaster, gypsum and concrete products, slate, dressed stone and cement	22,807,454	12,313,189
Linen and cotton spinning, weaving and manufactures	11,444,970	4,411,919
Fertilizers	18,307,638	5,890,762
Jute, canvas, rayon, nylon, cordage and miscellaneous textiles	13,916,433	5,970,539
Oils, paints, inks and polishes	10,031,429	3,418,634
Fellmongery, tanning and dressing of leather	8,346,039	2,651,864
Clothing (wholesale factories), men's and boys' readymade suits, overcoats, hats and caps	9,513,836	4,417,436
Manufacture and assembly of machinery except electrical	9,262,217	4,337,415
Manufactures of wood and cork except furniture	11,306,264	5,021,370
Canning of fruit and vegetables and manufacture of preserves, jams, jellies, etc.	14,035,575	5,309,110
Manufacture of furniture and fixtures: brushes and brooms	8,881,707	4,488,119
Chemicals and drugs	19,481,387	12,407,260
Glass and glassware, pottery, china and earthenware	6,903,725	4,741,528
Aerated and mineral waters	5,773,509	3,474,322
Clothing (wholesale factories) shirtmaking	4,487,348	1,827,273
Margarine, compound cooking fats and butter blending	4,010,333	1,398,612
Manufacture of railroad equipment	2,367,396	1,962,142
Malting	3,087,468	1,124,990
Ship- and boatbuilding and repairing	5,698,065	1,303,105
Soaps, detergents and candles	3,800,691	2,054,626
Manufacture of made-up textile goods except apparel	3,386,938	952,623
Miscellaneous food preparations including canning and preserving of fish	4,540,572	1,598,185
Distilling	3,027,613	2,010,513
Assembly, construction and repair of vehicles other than mechanically propelled road and land vehicles	3,509,286	1,921,149
Clothing (wholesale factories) miscellaneous articles of apparal	1,894,322	912,018
Manufacture of leather and leather substitutes, except footwear and other wearing apparel	1,478,037	781,541
Total (including all other manufacturing industries)	888,062,133	305,502,090

[1] Excluding excise duty £21,499,270.

TOURISM. Estimated number of visits by foreigners (including cross-border movement) in 1969 was 15,484,000; they spent an estimated £78·1m.

LABOUR. The Department of Labour is responsible for the administration of legislation concerning: (i) the safety, health and welfare mainly of industrial workers, and those employed in mining and quarrying; (ii) conditions of employment and holidays with pay in the non-agricultural sectors; (iii) national manpower service; (iv) industrial training (through *An Chomhairle Oiliúna*—the Industrial Training Authority); (v) redundancy payments and resettlement allowances; (vi) industrial relations; and (vii) trade unions.

An Industrial Training Authority was established by the Minister for Labour under the Industrial Training Act, 1967, to assist in the improvement of industrial training; under the programme of the Authority, apprentice recruitment and training has been expanded, facilities have been provided in industrial training centres for the training and re-training of adult workers, industries have been designated for training purposes under the Act, and a levy-grant scheme for the stimulation of training by industry itself has been initiated.

The Redundancy Payments Act, 1967, provides for financial compensation to workers who lose their employment as a result of redundancy. In general, non-manual workers earning up to £1,200 a year and all manual workers, with a minimum of 4 years' service (to be reduced to 2 years in the near future) with their employers, are entitled to benefit under the Act.

The Resettlement Allowances Scheme, administered by the Department of Labour, provides financial assistance for unemployed workers who wish to take up employment away from their home areas. Grants and allowances are payable towards the costs involved for the workers in transferring dependants and household effects to the new employment areas.

The National Manpower Service is responsible for the development of job placement and post-school guidance work throughout the country and for the collection and dissemination of information on manpower.

Labour and Employment. The total labour force at mid-April 1969 was 1,127,000 and there were 58,000 persons out of work.

The number of registered trade unions in 1968 was 95, with a total membership of 368,000. Of this membership, some 209,000 were concentrated in 6 general unions catering for both white-collar and manual workers. Of the balance, 77,000 were in 43 manual workers' unions and 82,000 in unions catering for distributive, office, professional and service workers.

COMMERCE. Value of imports and exports of merchandise (excluding bullion and specie and goods transhipped under bond) for calendar years (in £):

	1965	1966	1967	1968	1969
Imports	371,846,473	372,566,792	392,259,635	496,092,551	589,753,079
Exports	214,909,715	236,357,478	276,458,771	323,411,204	358,531,438
Re-exports	5,901,771	7,965,544	8,627,243	9,064,044	12,909,160

The values of the chief imports and domestic exports are shown in the following table (in £):

	Imports		Exports	
	1968	1969	1968	1969
Live animals and food	69,219,059	69,826,607	164,303,579	171,109,214
Raw materials	36,516,737	38,447,979	21,766,742	32,000,895
Mineral fuels and lubricants	40,928,967	44,612,552	3,503,986	5,020,978
Chemicals	47,925,847	53,010,591	12,568,171	17,346,296
Manufactured goods	103,805,925	127,094,378	43,125,382	46,066,637
Machinery and transport equipment	119,782,343	171,298,740	19,493,637	20,473,828
Manufactured articles	37,353,269	46,685,249	32,019,798	39,421,812

Distribution of trade, by principal countries of origin in the case of imports and destination in the case of exports (in £):

	Imports		Domestic Exports	
Country	1968	1969	1968	1969
Argentina	2,439,876	2,660,702	353,731	314,433
Australia	4,093,620	3,712,013	1,554,077	2,197,331
Belgium and Luxembourg	6,883,605	7,636,981	5,157,617	5,097,338
Brazil	1,983,561	1,791,504	106,327	204,896
Canada	9,428,500	9,000,189	4,063,416	4,436,758
Ceylon	1,058,657	1,250,716	296,369	298,837

Country	Imports		Domestic Exports	
	1968	1969	1968	1969
Denmark	4,312,018	5,097,625	517,289	434,561
Finland	6,938,439	7,969,066	181,580	240,928
France	15,079,349	16,773,922	9,902,062	13,176,698
German (East)	927,759	462,047	63,787	73,740
Germany (West)	36,284,040	43,367,308	7,949,009	10,569,197
Ghana	2,116,143	3,172,977	83,693	145,140
Great Britain	233,186,057	285,455,129	185,316,627	189,643,259
Hong Kong	1,173,614	1,687,858	388,709	632,342
India	3,884,621	3,893,368	66,432	37,723
Iran	2,834,307	5,382,448	70,089	113,941
Iraq	7,667,087	2,999,029	51,951	45,376
Israel	2,066,256	1,809,627	157,063	168,060
Italy	7,635,584	9,952,186	1,656,724	4,679,889
Japan	4,834,079	6,124,350	2,068,042	2,294,954
Malaysia	1,086,652	953,479	337,918	309,874
Morocco	3,037,013	2,453,750	799,889	695,270
Netherlands	14,689,842	14,207,374	4,432,477	7,105,325
New Zealand	1,688,721	2,224,768	183,512	256,096
Northern Ireland	20,095,619	24,582,726	41,128,944	46,689,601
Norway	2,985,500	2,519,708	458,754	612,556
Pakistan	1,396,768	1,425,715	19,682	62,615
Poland	4,967,517	5,456,671	548,708	1,131,263
Saudi Arabia	3,213,040	4,891,705	165,453	120,360
South Africa, Rep. of	2,423,655	2,378,930	754,684	996,962
Spain	2,714,675	3,880,159	846,735	3,426,117
Sweden	8,946,082	10,396,889	1,559,043	2,423,348
Switzerland	3,829,276	5,799,257	907,569	1,810,288
USSR	2,753,952	1,785,271	307,647	224,281
USA	36,619,303	52,509,292	31,878,481	38,060,327
Venezuela	235	5	1,170,102	1,586,643

An Anglo-Irish free-trade agreement to remove progressively all duties between July 1966 and July 1975 was signed in London on 14 Dec. 1965.

Trade with UK (British Board of Trade returns) in £1,000 sterling:

	1966	1967	1968	1969	1970
Imports to UK	186,142	223,644	268,719	293,635	341,255
Exports from UK	179,042	186,489	260,914	316,549 }	381,209
Re-exports from UK	10,319	10,105	12,003	13,097 }	

SHIPPING. The principal ports are Cork (and its sub-ports), Drogheda, Dublin, Dundalk, Dun Laoghaire, Galway, Limerick, Rosslare and Waterford. The total number of vessels with cargo or in ballast in the foreign trade which arrived at ports in the country during 1969 was 14,613 of 20,255,339 NRT; of these, 2,025 of 2,098,443 NRT, were Irish registered vessels.

INLAND WATERWAYS. There are 309 miles open for navigation including the Grand Canal (156 miles), the Shannon navigation (123 miles) and the Barrow navigation (30 miles). The traffic carried is nil.

ROADS. At 31 March 1969 there were 53,060 miles of public roads, consisting of 9,348 miles of main trunk and link roads, 42,686 miles of county roads and 526 miles of county borough and urban roads.

Number of licensed motor vehicles in 1969: Private cars, 353,961; public-service vehicles, 5,986; commercial goods vehicles, 45,838; agricultural tractors, 60,133; motor cycles, 41,474.

The total number of miles run by road motor passenger vehicles of the omnibus type during 1969 was 54,022,421. Passengers carried numbered 285,254,044 and the gross receipts from passengers were £11,985,906.

RAILWAYS. The total route length of railway open for traffic at 31 March 1970 was 1,332 route miles, all 5 ft 3 in. gauge.

Córas Iompair Éireann, the national transport undertaking, operates all rail services in the State.

Railway statistics for years ending 31 March	1968	1969
Passengers (no.)	8,889,565	9,548,722
Miles run by coaching trains	4,341,067	4,508,948
Merchandise and mineral traffic conveyed (tons)	2,861,236	3,153,644
Livestock conveyed (no.)	369,155	313,396
Miles run by freight trains	3,197,466	3,183,619
Receipts (£)	10,194,542[1]	11,363,217[1]
Expenditure (£)	12,379,879[1]	13,506,172[1]

[1] Including docks, harbours and wharves.

AVIATION. During the year ended 31 March 1970 Aer Lingus–Irish International Airlines carried 1,207,755 passengers, 70,554,000 lb. of cargo and 3·9m. lb. of mail on its European services and 256,769 passengers, 19·7m. lb. of cargo and 489,067 lb. of mail on its transatlantic services.

POST (1970). Number of post offices, 2,200; telegraph offices, 1,363; telephone subscribers, 291,478; public telephones, 3,462; telephone exchanges, 1,083.

Radio and television broadcasting is operated by Radio Telefís Éireann, a statutory public body appointed by the Minister for Posts and Telegraphs under the Broadcasting Authority Acts. In July 1970 there were 434,680 holders of receiving licences (radio and television) and 145,314 holders of receiving licences (wireless only).

BANKING. The Central Bank, which was established as from 1 Feb. 1943, in accordance with the Central Bank Act, 1942, replaced the Currency Commission, which was set up under the Currency Act, 1927, and had been responsible *inter alia* for the regulation of the note issue. In addition to the powers and functions of the Currency Commission the Central Bank has the power of receiving deposits from banks and public authorities, of rediscounting Exchequer bills and bills of exchange, of making advances to banks against such bills or against Government securities, of fixing and publishing rates of interest for rediscounting bills, of buying and selling certain Government securities and securities of any international bank or financial institution formed wholly or mainly by governments. The Bank also collects and publishes information relating to monetary and credit problems. The capital of the Bank is £40,000, of which £24,000 has been paid up and is held by the Minister for Finance.

The Board of Directors of the Central Bank consists of a Governor, appointed by the President of the Republic on the advice of the Government, and 8 directors, all appointed by the Minister for Finance, 5 direct and 3 from a panel selected by the Associated Banks (the term applied to the 8 shareholding banks associated with the former Currency Commission).

The aggregate withdrawals of Bank of England notes through the Central Bank and the Commercial Banks for repatriation during 9 months ended 31 Dec. 1969 amounted to £40,826,230.

There are 8 commercial banks associated with the Central Bank: The Bank of Ireland, the Hibernian Bank, the Munster and Leinster Bank, the Provincial Bank of Ireland, the Royal Bank of Ireland, the Ulster Bank, the Northern Bank and the National Bank of Ireland.

In the December quarter of 1969 the commercial banks had total liabilities and assets balancing at £1,070,399,000, including £955,175,000 current deposit and other accounts, £510·9m. loans and advances, £160m. government investments and £54·5m. certificates of deposit with the Central Bank.

The post office savings bank has approximately 1,653,000 accounts and the amount due at 31 Dec. 1969 was £120·8m. The trustee savings banks had deposits of £30m. at 30 May 1970.

DIPLOMATIC REPRESENTATIVES

The Irish Republic maintains embassies in:

Argentina	Canada	Germany (West)
Australia	Denmark	India
Belgium	France	Italy

Netherlands | Spain | UK
Nigeria | Sweden | USA
Portugal | Switzerland | Vatican

OF THE IRISH REPUBLIC IN GREAT BRITAIN
(17 Grosvenor Place, SW1)

Ambassador: Dr Donal O'Sullivan (accredited 16 Feb. 1970).
Minister: Kevin Rush. *Counsellors:* C. Howard (*Press and Information*); H. G. Foster (*Economic*); J. C. Holloway (*Economic*). *First Secretary:* D. Hurley.

OF GREAT BRITAIN IN THE IRISH REPUBLIC
Ambassador: John Howard Peck, CMG.
Counsellor: J. T. Williams (*Head of Chancery*). *Military Attaché:* Brig. F. G. MacMullen, DSO. *First Secretaries:* G. Miles, OBE (*Commercial*); P. J. C. Evans (*Information*).

OF THE IRISH REPUBLIC IN THE USA (2234 Massachusetts Ave, NW, Washington, D.C., 20008)
Ambassador: W. Warnock.
Counsellors: Dr S. O'hEideáin; Robert Cullen (*Agriculture*). *First Secretaries:* James Kirwan (*Press*); John Carbery.

OF THE USA IN THE IRISH REPUBLIC
Ambassador: John D. J. Moore.
Deputy Chief of Mission: Roger A. Sorenson.
Heads of Sections: Roger A. Sorensen (*Economic*); Virgil P. Randolph (*Political*); Eugene T. Ransom (*Agricultural*); Corlos M. Yordan (*Administration*); Kiyonao Okami (*Consular*). *Defence and Army Attaché:* Col. Joseph O'Connor.

BOOKS OF REFERENCE

STATISTICAL INFORMATION. The Central Statistics Office (Earlsford Terrace, Dublin, 2) was established in June 1949, and is attached to the Department of the Taoiseach; *Director:* T. P. Linehan, B.E., B.Sc.

The Central Statistics Office took over the work carried out since 1922 by the Statistics Branch, Department of Industry and Commerce, which in turn had continued the statistical work carried out by the Department of Agriculture and Technical Instruction (since 1900) and by the Irish Department of the Ministry of Labour, London (since 1919). Vital statistics from 1864, annual agricultural statistics prior to 1900 and decennial census of population were compiled by the Registrar-General for Ireland. The population censuses were carried out in 1926, 1936 and 1946 by the Statistics Branch of the Department of Industry and Commerce and are now the responsibility of the Central Statistics Office, which has also, as from July 1950, taken over from the Registrar-General the compilation of Vital Statistics. The Statistics Act 1926 confers wide powers for the collection, compilation and publication of statistics. Other Acts under which statistics are collected are Workmen's Compensation Act, Merchant Shipping Act, Customs Consolidation Act and Road Transport Act.

Principal publications of the Central Statistics Office are *National Income and Expenditure* (annually), *Statistical Abstract* (annually), *Census of Population Reports, Census of Industrial Production Reports, Trade and Shipping Statistics* (annually and monthly), *Trend of Employment and Unemployment* (annually), *Reports on Vital Statistics* (annually), *Irish Statistical Bulletin* (quarterly).

Facts about Ireland. Dublin, Department of External Affairs, 1968
Chubb, B., *A Source Book of Irish Government.* Dublin, Institute of Public Administration, 1964
Curtis, E., *A History of Ireland.* London, Methuen 1961
Delaney, V. T. H., *The Administration of Justice in Ireland.* Dublin, Institute of Public Administration, 1962
Eager, A. R., *Guide to Irish Bibliographical Materials.* London, 1964
Encyclopaedia of Ireland. Dublin, 1968
Freeman, T. W., *Ireland: A General and Regional Geography.* 2nd ed. London, 1965
Hayden and Moonan, *A Short History of the Irish People.* 2 vols. Dublin, 1960
Johnston, T. J., and others, *A History of the Church of Ireland.* Dublin, 1953
Kelly, J. M., *Fundamental Rights in the Irish Law and Constitution.* Dublin, 1966
McDunphy, Michael, *The President of Ireland: His Powers, Functions and Duties.* Dublin, 1945
McElligott, T. J., *Education in Ireland.* Dublin, Institute of Public Administration, 1966
MacLiammoir, Micheál, and Smith, Edwin, *Ireland.* London, 1966
MacManus, F. (ed.), *The Years of the Great Test, 1926–1939.* Cork, 1967
Nevill W. E., *Geology and Ireland.* Dublin, 1963
O'Donnell, J. D., *How Ireland is Governed.* Dublin, Institute of Public Administration, 1965
O'Mahony, David, *The Irish Economy.* Cork University Press, 1966
O'Neill's Commercial Who's Who and Industrial Directory of Ireland. 18th ed. Dublin, 1963
Thom's Directory of Ireland. 3 vols. (Dublin, Professional, Commercial). Dublin, 1960–67

ISRAEL

Medinat Israel—State of Israel

In 1967, following some years of uneasy peace, events in the Middle East came to a head. Local clashes on the Israeli-Syrian border were followed by Egyptian mass concentration of forces on the borders of Israel. The UN emergency force was expelled and a blockade of shipping to Israel was imposed by Egypt in the Red Sea. Israel struck out at Egypt on land and in the air on 5–6 June 1967. Jordan joined in the conflict which spread to the Syrian borders. By 11 June, when the United Nations' appeal for a cease-fire was generally accepted, the Israelis had occupied the Gaza Strip and the Sinai peninsula as far as the Suez Canal in the UAR, West Jordan as far as the Jordan valley and the heights east of the Sea of Galilee, including the town of Quneitra in Syria.

The following statements and statistics refer generally to the situation existing before the war.

CONSTITUTION AND GOVERNMENT. Israel is an independent sovereign republic, established by proclamation on 14 May 1948. For the history of the British Mandate, *see* THE STATESMAN'S YEAR-BOOK, 1920–49, under PALESTINE.

In 1950 the Knesset (*Parliament*), which in 1949 had passed the Transition Law dealing in general terms with the powers of the Knesset, President and Cabinet, resolved to enact from time to time fundamental laws, which eventually, taken together, would form the Constitution. The first of these fundamental laws, dealing with the Knesset, Israel Lands and the President, were passed in 1958, 1960 and 1964 respectively.

National flag: White with 2 horizontal blue stripes, the blue Shield of David in the centre.

National anthem: Hatikvah (The Hope). Words by N. N. Imber (1878); adopted as the Jewish National Anthem by the first Zionist Congress (1897).

The Knesset, a one-chamber parliament, consists of 120 members. It is elected for a 4-year term by secret ballot and universal direct suffrage. The system of election is by proportional representation. In April 1971 the Knesset was composed as follows: 'Labour Alignment', consisting of the Labour Party (a merger of Mapai, Abduth Ha'avoda and Rafi) and left wing Mapam, 56; Gush Herut-Liberalim or Gahal, 26; National Religious Party, 12; Alignment-affiliated Arab list, 4; Independent Liberals, 4; Agudat Israel, 4; New Communist list, 3; State list, 4; Israel Communist Party, 1; Haolam Hazeh-New Force, 2. The President is elected by the Knesset by secret ballot by a simple majority; his term of office is 5 years. He may be re-elected once.

President of the State: Zalman Shazar, elected on 21 May 1963 (re-elected 26 March 1968), after the death (on 23 April) of President Izhak Ben-Zvi, by 67 to 33 votes and 7 abstentions.

The reshuffled coalition government was, in April 1971, composed as follows:

Prime Minister: Mrs Golda Meir.

Deputy Prime Minister, Education and Culture: Yigal Allon (Labour). *Foreign Affairs:* Abba Eban (Labour). *Defence:* Moshe Dayan (Labour). *Finance, Trade and Industry:* Pinhas Sapir (Labour). *Agriculture:* Hayim Gvati (Labour). *Labour:* Yosef Almogi (Labour). *Justice:* Yaacov S. Shapira (Labour). *Housing:* Zeev Sharef (Labour). *Police:* Shlomo Hillel (Labour). *Transport and Communications:* Shimon Peres (Labour). *Social Welfare:* Michael Hazani (NRP). *Religions:* Zerah Warhaftig (NRP). *Tourism:* Moshe Kol (Ind. Liberal).

Without Portfolio: Israel Galili (Labour). *Interior:* Yoseph Burg. *Absorption of Immigration:* Natan Peled (Mapam). *Health:* Victor Shemtov (Mapam).

LOCAL GOVERNMENT. Local authorities are of three kinds, namely, municipal corporations, local councils and regional councils. Their status, powers and duties are prescribed by statute. Regional councils are local authorities set up in agricultural areas and include all the agricultural settlements in the area under their jurisdiction. All local authorities exercise their authority mainly by means of bye-laws approved by the Minister of the Interior. Their revenue is derived from rates and a surcharge on income tax. Local authorities are elected for a 4-year term of office.

There are 27 municipalities (2 Arab), 116 local councils (44 Arab and Druze) and 47 regional councils (1 Arab) comprising 686 villages.

AREA AND POPULATION. The area of Israel, within the boundaries defined by the 1949 armistice agreements with Egypt, Jordan, the Lebanon and Syria, is 20,700 sq. km (7,993 sq. miles), with a population (1 Jan. 1971) of 2,999,000, of whom 2,560,000 were Jews, 326,000 Moslems, 76,000 Christians and 36,000 Druzes. The area within the cease fire lines is 89,359 sq. km (34,493 sq. miles). Population of areas which came under Israeli administration as a result of the 6-day war was approximately 1m. Judaea and Samaria (West Bank), 600,000. Gaza Strip, 365,000. Northern Sinai, 33,000 and a few thousand on the Golan Heights.

Crude birth rate per 1,000 population of Jewish population (1969), 23·4; non-Jewish, 46·4; crude death rate, Jewish, 7·2; non-Jewish, 5·9; infantile mortality rate per 1,000 live births, Jewish, 19; non-Jewish, 40·3.

On 23 Jan. 1950 the Knesset proclaimed Jerusalem the capital of the state. Population of the main towns (1 Jan. 1971): Tel-Aviv/Jaffa, 382,900; Jerusalem, 283,100; Haifa, 214,500; Ramat Gan, 112,600; Holon, 84,700; Petach Tikva, 80,000; Bat-Yam, 76,600; Beersheba, 74,500; Bnei Brak, 66,700; Netanya, 62,500.

The official languages are Hebrew and Arabic.

IMMIGRATION. The following table shows the numbers of Jewish immigrants entering Palestine (Israel), including persons entering as travellers who subsequently registered as immigrants. For a year-by-year breakdown, *see* THE STATESMAN'S YEAR-BOOK, 1951, p. 1167.

1919–32	84,093	1940–47	92,563	1952–61	334,000
1933–39	218,099	1948–51	702,779	1962–69	299,424

During the period 1948–67, 45·4% of the immigrants came from Europe, America and Oceania, and 54·6% from Asia and Africa.

The Jewish Agency for Palestine, which, in accordance with Article IV of the Palestine Mandate, played a leading role in laying the political, economic and social foundations on which the State of Israel was established, continues to be instrumental in organizing immigration.

RELIGION. Religious affairs are under the supervision of a special Ministry, with departments for the Christian and Moslem communities. The religious affairs of each community remain under the full control of the ecclesiastical authorities concerned: in the case of the Jews, the Sephardic and Ashkenasic Chief Rabbis, in the case of the Christians, the heads of the various communities, and in the case of the Moslems, the Qadis. The Druzes were officially recognized in 1957 as an autonomous religious community.

The Jewish Sabbath and Holy Days are observed as days of rest in the public services. Full provision is, however, made for the free exercise of other faiths, and for the observance by their adherents of their respective days of rest and Holy Days.

A A

The General Assembly of the United Nations proposed, in its resolution of 29 Nov. 1947, the establishment of an international regime for the Jerusalem area. Following the war of June 1967 the State of Israel, in spite of repeated protests by the UN, undertook the responsibility for all Holy Sites and places of worship of all faiths in Jerusalem and the areas under military administration.

EDUCATION. The school system is under the direction of the Ministry of Education and Culture, and comprises kindergarten, primary, secondary and technical schools.

A law passed by the Knesset on 12 Sept. 1949 provides for free and compulsory primary education from 5 to 14 years of age. Youths in the age groups 14–18, who have not completed their primary schooling, must attend special classes.

The State Education Law of 12 Aug. 1953 established a unified state-controlled elementary school system with a provision for special religious schools. The standard curriculum for all elementary schools is issued by the Ministry with a possibility of adding supplementary subjects comprising not more than 25% of the total syllabus. Many schools in towns are private, a number are maintained by municipalities and some are administered by teachers' co-operative or trustees.

Statistics relating to schools under government supervision, 1969–70:

Type of School	Schools	Teachers	Pupils
Hebrew Education—Total	*5,317*	*45,214*	*727,194*
Kindergartens	3,235	3,672	107,668
Primary schools	1,235	22,673	375,534
Schools for handicapped children	156	1,645	13,002
Schools for working youth	128	408	5,818
Post-primary schools—Total	*544*	*12,371*	*129,436*
Secondary	192	..	58,479
Secondary evening	14	..	1,323
Continuation classes	104	..	8,508
Vocational	258	..	49,556
Agricultural	30	..	7,641
Preparatory classes for teachers	13	..	3,929
Teachers' training colleges	40	1,034	5,083
Arab Education—Total	*257*	*2,890*	*82,745*
Kindergartens	177	316	10,357
Primary schools	207	2,483	65,784
Schools for handicapped children	4	19	107
Schools for working youth	8	22	248
Post-primary schools—Total	*35*	*286*	*5,092*
Secondary schools	18	..	3,820
Vocational schools	16	..	882
Agricultural schools	1	..	390
Teachers' training colleges	1	34	370

There are also a number of private schools maintained by religious foundations—Jewish, Christian and Moslem—and also by private societies.

The Hebrew University of Jerusalem, founded in 1925, comprises faculties of the humanities, social sciences, law, science, medicine and agriculture. In 1971 it had a teaching staff of 1,500 and 15,000 students.

The Technion in Haifa had, in 1971, 18 faculties and departments with over 1,000 teachers and 20,525 students. The Weizmann Institute of Science in Rehovoth is engaged in research in chemistry, physics and biology; founded in 1949, it had a staff of 1,100 in 1967.

In 1971 the Tel Aviv University had 6 faculties, some 1,500 teachers and 11,000 students. The religious Bar-Ilan University at Ramat Gan, opened in 1965, had, in 1969, 4 faculties (Jewish studies, natural sciences, social sciences, philology), 630 teachers and 5,000 students. There are university colleges at Haifa and Beersheba.

CINEMAS (1970). There were 275 cinemas with a seating capacity of 190,000.

NEWSPAPERS (1969). There were 23 daily newspapers, including 13 in Hebrew, 2 in Arabic, 1 each in Yiddish, German, English, French, Hungarian, Polish, Bulgarian, Romanian, with a total circulation of over 500,000.

SOCIAL WELFARE. In 1971 Israel had 142 hospitals with 22,866 beds. The 'Malben' organization cares for sick, aged or handicapped immigrants. The Women's International Zionist Organization has a number of children's homes, crèches and kindergartens as well as vocational schools and training institutions for nurses.

The National Insurance Law, which took effect in April 1954, provides for old-age pensions, survivors' insurance, work-injury insurance, maternity insurance and family allowances. In 1971 there were plans for unemployment insurance.

JUSTICE. LAW. Under the Law and Administration Ordinance, 5708/1948, the first law passed by the Provisional Council of State, the law of Israel is the law which was obtaining in Palestine on 14 May 1948 in so far as it is not in conflict with that Ordinance or any other law passed by the Israel legislature and with such modifications as result from the establishment of the State and its authorities.

Capital punishment was abolished in 1954, except for support given to the Nazis and for high treason.

The law of Palestine was derived from three main sources, namely, Ottoman law, English law (Common Law and Equity) and the law enacted by the Palestine legislature, which to a great extent was modelled on English law. The Ottoman law in its turn was derived from three main sources, namely, Moslem law which had survived in the Ottoman Empire, French law adapted by the Ottomans and the personal law of the non-Moslem communities.

CIVIL COURTS. Municipal courts, established in certain municipal areas, have criminal jurisdiction over offences against municipal regulations and bye-laws and certain specified offences committed within a municipal area.

Magistrates courts, established in each district and sub-district, have limited jurisdiction in both civil and criminal matters.

District courts, sitting at Jerusalem, Tel-Aviv and Haifa, have jurisdiction, as courts of first instance, in all civil matters not within the jurisdiction of magistrates courts, and in all criminal matters, and as appellate courts from magistrates courts and municipal courts.

The Supreme Court has jurisdiction as a court of first instance (sitting as a High Court of Justice dealing mainly with administrative matters) and as an appellate court from the district courts (sitting as a Court of Civil or of Criminal Appeal).

In addition, there are various tribunals for special classes of cases, such as the Rents Tribunals and the Tribunals for the Prevention of Profiteering and Speculation. Settlement Officers deal with disputes with regard to the ownership or possession of land in settlement areas constituted under the Land (Settlement of Title) Ordinance.

RELIGIOUS COURTS. The rabbinical courts of the Jewish community have exclusive jurisdiction in matters of marriage and divorce, alimony and confirmation of wills of members of their community other than foreigners, concurrent jurisdiction with the civil courts in such matters of members of their community who are foreigners if they consent to the jurisdiction, and concurrent jurisdiction with the civil courts in all other matters of personal status of all members of their community, whether foreigners or not, with the consent of all parties to the action, save that such courts may not grant a decree of dissolution of marriage to a foreign subject.

The courts of the several recognized Christian communities have a similar jurisdiction over members of their respective communities.

The Moslem religious courts have exclusive jurisdiction in all matters of personal status over Moslems who are not foreigners, and over Moslems who are foreigners, if under the law of their nationality they are subject in such matters to the jurisdiction of Moslem religious courts.

Where any action of personal status involves persons of different religious communities, the President of the Supreme Court will decide which court shall have jurisdiction, and whenever a question arises as to whether or not a case is one of personal status within the exclusive jurisdiction of a religious court, the matter must be referred to a special tribunal composed of 2 judges of the Supreme Court and the president of the highest court of the religious community concerned in Israel.

FINANCE. Currency. The unit of currency is the Israeli £ (I£), divided into 100 *agorot* (up to 31 Dec. 1959; 1,000 *prutah*). There are coins of I£$\frac{1}{2}$ and I£1 as well as of 1 *agora*, 5, 10 and 25 *agorot* and bank-notes of I£1, 5, 10, 50 and 100; Currency in circulation (in I£1m.) on 31 Dec. 1969 was 1,207·1.

Budget. The budget year runs from 1 April to 31 March. The main items of the 1970–1971 budget are as follows (in I£m.):

Revenue:		Expenditure:	
Taxes on income and pro-		Economic purposes	1,498
perty	2,648	Social services	1,988
Taxes on expenditure	2,433	Administration and security	4,420
Taxes on transactions:		Debt repayments, circulat-	
licences and fees	162	ing capital, etc.	2,002
Other local revenues	865		
	———		
Ordinary Revenue	6,108		
Revenue from counterpart			
funds, loans and collec-			
tions for the development			
budget, payment of loans			
and special expenditures	2,333		
Foreign loans and transfers	1,025		
	———		———
Total	9,910	Total	9,910

The main items of expenditure (in I£1m.) are: Security, 4,097; education, 628; communications, 325; agriculture and water, 153; industry, 256; health, 234; social welfare, 212; housing, 632.

Income tax is levied progressively up to a maximum of 62·5%. A Defence Levy of 10% on income tax paid was introduced during the 6-day war.

DEFENCE. The Defence Service Law of 8 Sept. 1949, as amended, provides a compulsory 30-month conscription (extended to 36 months in 1968) for men between the ages of 18 and 26 and a 2-year conscription for men in the age-group of 27–29 years. Unmarried women aged 18–26 serve 20 months. The compulsory military service includes a period of agricultural training. After their term of military service, men and childless women are on the reserves until the ages of 55 and 34 years respectively. In addition, all are liable to 1 day's service per month. Officers and n.c.o.s are liable to an additional 1 week's service per year.

Men over 49 years are exempted from service in the reserves, but may volunteer for civil defence. Women exempted from service in the armed forces on religious grounds are to be employed in agricultural work, service in new immigrants' centres or service in other institutions.

Army. The regular army has a strength of 61,500, organized in 4 brigades and an armoured division. The reserve army of about 200,000 men is organized in 26 brigades.

The highest army rank is that of Lieut.-General (*Rav Alouf*), and the Chief-of-Staff, who is the C.-in-C., holds that rank. A divisional commander is a Brigadier (*Tat Alouf*), and a brigade commander a Colonel (*Alouf Mishne*).

Navy. The Navy includes 3 submarines (acquired from Britain), 2 destroyers, a patrol vessel, 9 torpedo boats, 12 missile boats, 8 motor-launches and 10 landing craft. The former Nautical School in Haifa has been reorganized as a Naval Officers' School in Acre.

Air Force. The Air Force has a personnel strength of about 8,000, with 300 first-line aircraft. All first-line combat aircraft are jets, mostly of French and US manufacture. Three squadrons received a total of 72 Mirage III supersonic multi-mission fighters (some armed with Matra R. 530 missiles); and 50 F-4E Phantom fighters, 6 RF-4E reconnaissance fighters and 70 A-4 Skyhawk light bombers have been acquired from the USA with more F-AEs and A-4s to follow. Two fighter-bomber squadrons are equipped with Mystère IVAs, and 1 interceptor squadron has supersonic Super Mystères. There are also a reconnaissance attack squadron of twin-jet Vautours, 2 transport squadrons of Noratlas, C-47 and locally modified 'swing-tail' Stratocruiser aircraft, 2 helicopter squadrons of CH-53, Super Frelon, S-58, Agusta-Bell 205 and Alouette aircraft, and training units, the last-named having locally-built Magister jet trainers, which can also be used in a light ground-attack role. Hawk surface-to-air missiles are in service.

AGRICULTURE. In the coastal plain (Sharon, Emek Hefer and the Shephelah) mixed farming, poultry raising, citriculture and vineyards are the main agricultural activities. The Emek (the Valley of Jezreel) is the main agricultural centre of Israel. Mixed farming is to be found throughout the valleys; the subtropical Beisan and Jordan plainlands are also centres of banana plantations and fish breeding. In Galilee mixed farming, olive and tobacco plantations prevail. The Hills of Ephraim are a vineyard centre; many parts of the hill country are under afforestation. In the northern Negev farming has been aided by the Yarkon–Negev water pipeline. This has become part of the overall project of the 'National Water Carrier', which is to take water from the Sea of Galilee (Lake Kinnereth) to the south. The plan includes a number of regional projects such as the Lake Kinnereth–Negev pipeline which came into operation in 1964; it has an annual capacity of 320m. cu. metres.

A land-utilization survey has graded the country as follows: 3,392,000 dunams under dry farming and 3,938,000 dunams under irrigation suitable for all types of cultivation, 697,000 dunams under dry farming and 1,339,000 dunams under irrigation suitable for plantations, 8·49m. dunams suitable for pasture, 882,000 dunams suitable for afforestation, 470,000 dunams unfit for any type of cultivation.

The area under cultivation (in 1,000 acres) in 1969–70 was 1,058, of which 428 were under irrigation. Of the total cultivated area 695 acres were under field crops, 92 under vegetables, potatoes and melons, 213 under citrus and orchards, 13 under fish ponds and 41 under miscellaneous crops.

Industrial crops, such as cotton and sugar beet, have successfully been introduced. In 1966 the area under cotton totalled 220,000 dunams and under sugar beet 50,000.

Livestock (1966) included 209,000 cattle, (1970) 333,000 sheep and goats, 26,000 draught animals, 7m. laying hens.

Characteristic types of rural settlement are, among others, the following: (1) The *Kibbutz* and *Kvutza* (communal collective settlement), where all property and earnings are collectively owned and work is collectively organized. (2) The *Moshav Ovdim* (workers' co-operative smallholders' settlement) which is founded on the principles of mutual aid and equality of opportunity between the members, all farms being equal in size; hired labour is prohibited. (3) The *Moshav Shitufi* (co-operative settlement), which is based on collective ownership and economy as in the *Kibbutz*, but with each family having its own house and being responsible for its own domestic services. (4) The *Moshav* (smallholders' settlement), which resembles the *moshav ovdim* but lacks the latter's rigid ideological basis; hired labour, for instance, is permitted. (5) The *Moshava* (village), in which land and property are privately owned and every resident is responsible for his own well-being. In 1967, of the 801 rural settlements in Israel, 232 were kibbutzim (population, 82,000), 343 moshvei ovdim and other smallholder settlements (121,000), 22 moshavim shitufiim (4,900), 60 moshavot and other villages based on private marketing (50,000), 99 Arab villages (181,000, not including 32,500 Bedouin); the rest were temporary settlements and educational institutions.

MINING. The most valuable natural resources of the country are the potash, bromine and other salt deposits of the Dead Sea, which are exploited by the Dead Sea Works, Ltd. Geological research and exploration of the natural resources in the Negev are undertaken by the Israel Mining Corporation. Copper is being worked at Timna near Eilat. Potash production in 1970–71 was 1,000,000 tons.

Oil was first discovered in Sept. 1955 at Heletz in the Negev. Thirty-eight oil-wells were in operation in 1969 with output of 115,000 tons. Natural gas is being exploited at Rosh Zohar, near the Dead Sea; output in 1969 equalled 127,000 tons of fuel oil.

INDUSTRY. A wide range of products is manufactured, processed or finished in the country, including chemicals, metal products, textiles, tyres, diamonds, paper, plastics, leather goods, glass and ceramics, building materials, precision instruments, tobacco, foodstuffs, electric goods, including refrigerators and radios.

A law for the encouragement of capital investment, passed on 29 March 1950, grants substantial privileges to foreign investors. An Investment Centre was established in May 1950, and had by early-1971 approved investments totalling I£1,000m.

POWER. Electric-power consumption amounted during 1968–69 to 4,714m. kwh., of which 34% were used for industrial purposes and 24% for irrigation.

LABOUR. The General Federation of Labour (Histadrut) founded in 1920, had, in 1967, about 1m. members (including 40,000 Arabs); including workers' families, this membership represents 60% of the Jewish population. Several trades unions of lesser importance also exist.

Histadrut participates in over 70% of Israeli agriculture and 23% of industrial production; it runs the Kupat Holim (workers' health service) and has large interests in banking, insurance, retail business, construction and building.

In 1969 the average daily number of registered unemployed was 2,395.

COMMERCE. External trade, in US$1,000, for calendar years:

	1963	1964	1965	1966	1967	1968	1969
Imports	661,370	837,509	837,477	832,588	754,640	1,081,000	1,318,000
Exports	336,400	332,235	429,147	503,282	558,343	640,200	723,983

In 1968, of the imports 80% came from US, UK and the EEC; of the exports 25% went to the EEC, 12% to UK, 22% to US, 13% to Africa and 5% to Asia.

The main exportable commodities are citrus fruit and by-products, fruit-juices, textiles, wines and liquor, sweets, polished diamonds (1,445,969 carats, valued at US$193m. in 1967), chemicals, motor cars, tyres, textiles, electrical goods, flowers. Exports of citrus fruit in 1969 amounted to US$96·6m.

Total trade with UK (British Board of Trade returns, in £1,000 sterling):

	1966	1967	1968	1969	1970
Imports to UK	26,533	32,309	43,832	39,304	45,079
Exports from UK	51,921	49,205	87,036	101,086 ⎱	96,157
Re-exports from UK	1,240	994	1,106	1,697 ⎰	

SHIPPING. Israel has 3 commercial ports, Haifa, Ashdod and Eilat. The deep-water port at Ashdod came into use at the end of 1965, when the ports of Tel-Aviv and Jaffa were closed for freight services. An Israel Ports Authority began to operate in 1962. In 1966 2,310 ships anchored in Israeli ports; 4·6m. tons of freight (not including fuel) were handled. The Israeli merchant fleet consisted at 1 Jan. 1969 of 114 vessels, totalling 1·7m. GRT.

RAILWAYS. Internal communications are provided by 477 km of main railway lines and 285 km of branch lines (1969). The 30-km line Beersheba–Dimona was extended to Oran and from Mamshit to Tzefa in 1970. In 1969, 5m. passengers and 3m. tons of freight were carried by rail.

ROADS (1969). There were 4,037 km of paved roads maintained by the Government.

Registered motor vehicles in 1969 included 3,200 buses and 112,000 private cars.

AVIATION. Air communications are centred in the airport of Lod, near Tel-Aviv. In 1968, 7,370 planes touched Israeli airports on international flights, carrying 537,100 passengers and 12,495 metric tons of freight. The Israeli airline El Al maintains regular flights to London, Paris, Rome, Amsterdam, Brussels, Athens, Vienna, New York, Zürich, Munich, Nicosia, Istanbul, Tehran, Johannesburg, Nairobi, Frankfurt and Copenhagen. In 1968–69 El Al carried 489,716 passengers.

POST. The Ministry of Posts controls the postal, telegraph and telephone service. In 1969 there were 460 post offices and postal agencies, 34 mobile post offices and 380,000 telephones.

The broadcasting station in Jerusalem is called Kol Israel (Voice of Israel); it is controlled by the Broadcasting Authority, established in 1965. Wireless licences in 1969 numbered approximately 600,000 and television licences 72,000.

BANKING. On 24 Aug. 1954 the Knesset passed the Bank of Israel Law, establishing a state-owned central bank. The Bank of Israel started operations on 1 Dec. 1954; it is the bank of issue and sole banker of the Government. Other principal banks are Bank Leumi le Israel BM, the Israel Discount Bank, Barclays Bank DCO and the Workers' Bank, Ltd. Assets and liabilities in the 28 commercial banks and the 18 Co-operative Credit Societies operating in Israel totalled I£4,819m. at 31 July 1969.

WEIGHTS AND MEASURES. The metric system is in general use. The (metrical) *dunam* = 1,000 sq. metres (about 0·25 acre).

The Jewish year 5728 corresponds to 5 Oct. 1967–22 Sept. 1968; 5729 to 23 Sept. 1968–12 Sept. 1969.

DIPLOMATIC REPRESENTATIVES

Israel maintains embassies in:

Argentina	Denmark	Korea (South)
Australia	Dominican Republic	Laos
Austria	Ecuador	Liberia
Belgium	El Salvador	Luxembourg
Bolivia	Ethiopia	Madagascar
Brazil	Finland	Malawi
Burma	France	Mali
Burundi	Gabon	Malta
Cambodia	Germany (West)	Mexico
Cameroun	Ghana	Nepál
Canada	Guatemala	Netherlands
Chad	Guinea	New Zealand
Chile	Haiti	Nicaragua
Central African Republic	Honduras	Niger
Colombia	Iceland	Nigeria
Congo (Br.)	Italy	Norway
Congo (K.)	Ivory Coast	Panama
Costa Rica	Jamaica	Paraguay
Cyprus	Japan	Peru
Dahomey	Kenya	Philippines

Romania	Tanzania	USA
Rwanda	Thailand	Upper Volta
Senegal	Togo	Uruguay
Sierra Leone	Trinidad	Venezuela
Sweden	Uganda	Zambia
Switzerland	UK	

Israel maintains legations in Cuba, Greece, Republic of South Africa and Turkey.

OF ISRAEL IN GREAT BRITAIN (2 Palace Green, W8

Ambassador: Michael Comay

Ministers: Eytan Ruppin; Joshua Jaffe (*Economic*). *Counsellors:* R. M. Sivan; Ami Shachori (*Agriculture*); Ovadia Shragai (*Commercial*); Ari Avnerre (*Information*); Ephraim Tari; Yehuda Taggar; R. Amir (*Scientific*); Aharon Megged (*Cultural*); Moshe Nathaniel (*Economic*). *First Secretaries:* Haim Gomma; Moshe Arad (*Press*); Zvi Barlev. *Defence Attaché:* Maj.-Gen. Shmuell Eyal.

OF GREAT BRITAIN IN ISRAEL

Ambassador: E. J. W. Barnes, MBE.

Counsellors: P. M. Foster; P. H. Moberly. *Service Attachés:* Col. P. G. Howard-Harwood (*Army*), Cdr G. M. A. James (*Navy*; resident in Ankara), Group Capt. A. D. Boyle (*Defence and Air*). *First Secretaries:* W. J. M. Speirs; J. D. Garner (*Commercial*); J. C. Church, MBE (*Information*); P. G. Wallis; Miss O. Goodinson (*Consul*); T. Spence (*Labour*).

There are Consuls-General at Jerusalem and Tel-Aviv, and a Consul at Haifa.

OF ISRAEL IN THE USA (1621–22nd St. NW, Washington, D.C., 20008)

Ambassador: Yitzhak Rabin.

Ministers: Shlomo Argov; Zvi Brosh (*Press*); Shimon Alexandroni (*Economic*). *Minister-Counsellor:* Nir Baruch. *Counsellors:* Moshe Raviv; Meir Avidan; Johanan Bein, Moshe Meirav (*Economic*); Shaul Ben Haim (*Press*); Asher Naim; Yehuda Avner. *First Secretaries:* Yosef Ben-Aharon; Yehoshua Simon. *Defence Attaché:* Maj.-Gen. Eliahu Zeira.

There are Consuls-General in Atlanta, Chicago, Houston, Los Angeles, New York, Philadelphia and San Francisco.

OF THE USA IN ISRAEL

Ambassador: Walworth Barbour.

Deputy Chief of Mission: J. Owen Zurhellen, Jr. *Heads of Sections:* Heywood H. Stackhouse (*Political*); Richard C. Breithut (*Economic*); Margaret L. Plunkett (*Labour*); Clifton P. English (*Consular*); John M. Curry (*Administrative*).

Service Attachés: Col. James W. Marsio (*Defence and Air*), Col. William R. Healey (*Army*), Cdr James P. Neyland (*Navy*).

BOOKS OF REFERENCE

STATISTICAL INFORMATION. There is a Central Bureau of Statistics and Economic Research at the Prime Minister's Office, Jerusalem. It publishes monthly bulletins of economic statistics, social statistics, foreign trade statistics and an English summary.

Government Yearbook. Government Printer, Jerusalem. 1951 ff. (latest issue, 1970, 71)
Facts about Israel 1969. Government Printer, Jerusalem
Statistical Abstract of Israel. Government Printer, Jerusalem (from 1949/50)
Israel Yearbook. Tel-Aviv, 1948–49 ff.
Statistical Bulletin of Israel. 1949 ff.
Reshumoth (Official Gazette)
Middle East Record, ed. Y. Oron. London, 1960 ff.
Laws of the State of Israel. Authorized translation. Government Printer, Jerusalem, 1958 ff.
Alkalay, R., *The Complete English–Hebrew Dictionary.* 4 vols. Tel-Aviv, 1959–61
Atlas of Israel. London, 1970

Badi, J., *The Government of the State of Israel*. New York, 1963
Ben-Gurion, D., *Ben-Gurion looks back*. London, 1965.—*The Jews in their land*. London, 1966
Bentwich, J. S., *Education in Israel*. London, 1965
Bentwich, N., *The New–Old Land of Israel*. London, 1960
Comay, J., *Israel*. London and New York, 1969
Churchill, R. S. and W. S., *The six-day war*. London, 1967
Crossman, R., *Nation Reborn*. London, 1960
Dagan, P. (ed.), *Who's Who in Israel*. Tel Aviv, 1962
Drabkin-Darin, H., *The Other Society*. London, 1962
Eigenstadt, S. N., *Israel Society*. London, 1969
Elston, D. R., *Israel—the Making of a Nation*. London, 1963
Horowitz, D., *The Economics of Israel*. New York and Oxford, 1967
Hyamson, A. M., *Palestine under Mandate, 1920–48*. London, 1951
Laqueur, W. (ed.), *The Israel–Arab Reader*. London 1970
Lissak, M., *Social Mobility in Israel Society*. Jerusalem, 1969
Malkosh, N., *Co-operation in Israel*. Tel-Aviv, 1959
Orni, E., and Efrat, E., *Geography of Israel*. Jerusalem and London, 1966
Sykes, C., *Crossroads to Israel*. London, 1965
Weizmann, C., *Trial and Error*. London, 1949
Who's Who in Israel. Tel-Aviv, 1965

NATIONAL LIBRARY. The Jewish National and University Library, Jerusalem. *Director:* Dr. C. Worman.

ITALY

Repubblica Italiana

CONSTITUTION AND GOVERNMENT. On 10 June 1946 Italy became a republic on the announcement by the Court of Cassation that a majority of the voters at the referendum held on 2 June had voted for a republic. The final figures, announced on 18 June, showed: For a republic, 12,718,641 (54·3% of the valid votes cast, which numbered 23,437,143); for the retention of the monarchy, 10,718,502 (45·7%); invalid and contested, 1,509,735. Total 24,946,878, or 89·1% of the registered electors, who numbered 28,005,449. For the results of the polling in the 13 leading cities, *see* THE STATESMAN'S YEAR-BOOK, 1951, p. 1175. Voting was compulsory, open to both men and women 21 years of age or older, including members of the Civil Service and the Armed Forces; former active Fascists and a few other categories were excluded.

On 18 June the then Provisional Government without specifically proclaiming the republic, issued an 'Order of the Day' decreeing that all court verdicts should in future be handed down 'in the name of the Italian people', that the *Gazzetta Ufficiale del Regno d'Italia* should be re-named *Gazzetta Ufficiale della Repubblica Italiana*, that all references to the monarchy should be deleted from legal and government statements and that the shield of the House of Savoy should be removed from the Italian flag.

Thus ended the reign of the House of Savoy, whose kings had ruled over Piedmont for 9 centuries and as Kings of Italy since 18 Feb. 1861. (For fuller account of the House of Savoy, *see* THE STATESMAN'S YEAR-BOOK, 1946, p. 1021.) The Crown Prince Umberto, son of King Vittorio Emanuele III, became Lieut.-Gen. (*i.e.*, Regent) of the kingdom on 5 June 1944. Following the abdication and retirement to Egypt of his father on 9 May 1946, Umberto was declared King Umberto II; his reign lasted to 13 June, when he left the country. King Victor Emmanuel III died in Alexandria on 28 Dec. 1947.

The new constitution was passed by the constituent assembly by 453 votes to 62 on 22 Dec. 1947; it came into force on 1 Jan. 1948. The constitution consists of 139 articles and 18 transitional clauses. Its main dispositions are as follows:

Italy is described as 'a democratic republic founded on work'. Parliament consists of the Chamber of Deputies and the Senate. The Chamber is elected for 5 years by universal and direct suffrage; 1 deputy, who must be 25 years or over, for 80,000 inhabitants. The Senate is elected for 6 years on a regional basis; each Region having at least 6 senators, 1 for 200,000 inhabitants; the Valle d'Aosta is represented by 1 senator only. The President of the Republic can nominate

5 senators for life from eminent men in the social, scientific, artistic and literary spheres. On the expiry of his term of office, the President of the Republic becomes a senator by right and for life, unless he declines.

The President of the Republic is elected in a joint session of Chamber and Senate, to which are added 3 delegates from each Regional Council (1 from the Valle d'Aosta). A two-thirds majority is required for the election, but after a third indecisive scrutiny the absolute majority of votes is sufficient. The President must be 50 years or over; his term lasts for 7 years. The President of the Senate acts as his deputy. The President can dissolve the chambers of parliament, except during the last 6 months of his term of office.

The Cabinet can be forced to resign only on a motivated motion of censure; the defeat of a government bill does not involve the resignation of the Government.

A Constitutional Court, consisting of 15 judges who are appointed, 5 each, by the President of the Republic, Parliament (in joint session) and the highest law and administrative courts, has rights similar to those of the Supreme Court of the USA. It can decide on the constitutionality of laws and decrees, define the powers of the State and Regions, judge conflicts between the State and Regions and between the Regions, and try the President of the Republic and the Ministers. The court was set up in Dec. 1955.

The re-organization of the Fascist Party is forbidden. Direct male descendants of King Victor Emmanuel are excluded from all public offices, have no right to vote or to be elected, and are banned from Italian territory; their estates are forfeit to the State. Titles of nobility are no longer recognized, but those existing before 28 Oct. 1922 are retained as part of the name.

National flag: Green, white, red (vertical).
National anthem: Fratelli d'Italia (words by G. Mameli; tune by M. Novaro, 1847).

The peace treaty was signed in Paris on 10 Feb. 1947, and ratified on 15 Sept. 1947. Italy ceded to France 4 frontier districts on the Little St Bernard Pass, the Mont-Cenis Plateau, the Mont-Thabor and Chaberton areas, and the upper valleys of the Tinée, Vésubie and Roya (*see* map in THE STATESMAN'S YEAR-BOOK, 1948); to Yugoslavia, nearly the whole of the province of Venezia Giulia, the commune of Zara and the island of Pelagosa; to Greece, the Dodecanese; to Albania, the island of Saseno; to China the Italian concession at Tientsin. Italy also gave up her former colonies.

Under the peace treaty Italy was to pay reparations to the following states: Greece, $105m.; Yugoslavia, $125m.; USSR, $100m.; Ethiopia, $25m.; Albania, $5m. By 30 Nov. 1967 the whole debt had been paid.

Head of State: On 28 Dec. 1964 Chamber and Senate in joint session elected by an absolute majority (646 votes out of 937 votes cast) Giuseppe Saragat (Social Democrat; born 19 Sept. 1898) President of the Republic.

Former Presidents of the Republic: Luigi Einaudi (1948–55); Giovanni Gronchi (1955–62); Antonio Segni (1962–64).

General elections for the Senate and Chamber of Deputies took place on 19 May 1968.

Senate. At 30 June 1970: Christian Democrats, 137; Communists, 76; Socialists, 46; Italian Social Movement, 13; Liberals, 16; Party of Proletarian Unity, 14; other groups, 20. Total: 322.

Chamber. At 30 June 1970: Christian Democrats, 265; Communists, 167; Socialists, 91; Italian Social Movement, 24; Liberals, 31; Party of Proletarian Unity, 23; other groups, 29. Total: 630.

The Cabinet, a 4 party coalition, as constituted in 6 Aug. 1970:

Prime Minister: Emilio Colombo (DC).
Deputy Prime Minister: Francesco De Martino (PSI). *Foreign Affairs:* Aldo Moro (DC). *Interior:* Franco Restivo (DC). *Justice:* Oronzo Reale (PRI). *Budget:* Antonio Giolitti (PSI). *Finance:* Luigi Preti (PSU). *Treasury:* Mario Ferrari Aggradi (DC). *Defence:* Mario Tanassi (PSU). *Education:* Riccardo Misasi (DC). *Public Works:* Salvatore Lauricella (PSI). *Agriculture:* Lorenzo Natali (DC). *Transport and Civil Aviation:* Italo Viglianesi (PSI). *Posts and Telegraphs:* Giacinto Bosco (DC). *Industry and Commerce:* Silvio Gava (DC). *Labour and Social Security:* Carlo Donat Cattin (DC). *Foreign Trade:* Mario Zagari (PSI). *Merchant Navy:* Salvatore Mannironi (DC). *State-subsidized Industries:* Flaminio Piccoli (DC). *Public Health:* Luigi Mariotti (PSI). *Tourism and Recreation:* Gian Matteo Matteotti (PSU). *Without portfolio:* Emilio Taviani (DC), Engenio Gatto (DC), Remo Gaspari (DC), Camillo Ripamonti (DC), Carlo Russo (DC), Giuseppe Lupis (PSU).

Ten Years of Italian Democracy, 1946–56. Presidency of the Council of Ministers, Rome, 1956
Adams, J. C., and Barile, P., *The Government of Republican Italy.* Boston, Mass, 1961
Cross, E. (ed.), *La Constitution Italienne de 1948.* Paris, 1950
Ruini, M., and others, *La Nuova Costituzione Italiana.* Rome, 1947
Vedovato, G., *Il Trattato di Pace con l'Italia.* Rome, 1947

REGIONAL ADMINISTRATION. Italy is administratively divided into regions, provinces (*province*) and municipalities (*comuni*). The division into 20 autonomous regions (*regioni*), as envisaged in the 1948 constitution, has been completed.

Art. 116 of the constitution provided for the establishment of 5 autonomous regions with special statute (*regioni autonome con statuto speciale*). All these 5 regions have been organized. These special regions have their own parliaments (*consiglio regionale*) and governments (*giunta regionale e presidente*) with certain legislative and administrative functions adapted to the circumstances of each region. A government commissioner is in charge for the co-ordination between regional and national activities.

I. *Sicily* (Sicilia), established on 15 May 1946, comprises the islands of Sicily, the Lipari and Egadi groups, Ustica and Pantelleria, divided into 9 provinces; capital, Palermo. The regional elections on 11 June 1967 returned 36 Christian Democrats, 5 Liberals, 1 Monarchist, 7 Social Movement, 10 Socialists, 19 Communists, 3 Party of Proletarian Unity, 4 Republicans, 5 others. The regional government is a coalition of Christian Democrats and Socialists, headed by Dr Mario Fasino (Christian Democrat).

D. Dolci, *Inchiesta a Palermo.* Turin, 1954. (*To feed the hungry.* London, 1959.)
Orsini di Camerota, P. d'A., *Sicilia Regione.* Rome, 1951
Petrullo, V., *Contemporary Sicily.* Hamilton, N.Y., 1951
Torneo, F., *Gli incentivi per la industrializzazione della Sicilia.* Caltanissetta, 1964

II. *Sardinia* (Sardegna), established on 26 Feb. 1948, comprises Sardinia and the surrounding small islands, divided into 3 provinces; capital, Cagliari. The regional elections on 15 June 1969 returned 36 Christian Democrats, 3 Liberals, 2 Monarchists, 2 Social Movement, 9 Socialists, 15 Communists, 3 Sardinian Action Party, 3 Party of Proletarian Unity, 1 other. The regional government is a coalition of Christian Democrats and Socialists, headed by Dr Lucio Albis (Christian Democrat).

SVIMEZ, *Aspetti sociali e culturali dello sviluppo economico della Sardegna.* 2nd ed. Rome, 1960

III. *Aosta*, established on 26 Feb. 1948, comprises the valley of Aosta which is inhabited for the major part by a French-speaking population; capital, Aosta. The regional elections of 21 April 1968 returned 6 members of the Unione Valdotain, 13 Christian Democrats, 7 Communists, 4 Socialists and 5 others. The regional government is a coalition of the Unione Valdotain, Socialists and Communists, headed by Cesare Bionaz (Christian Democrat).

IV. *Trentino–Alto Adige* (South Tirol), established on 26 Feb. 1948, comprises the portion of Tirol south of the Brenner pass which Austria ceded to Italy in 1919. The Paris agreement signed by the Austrian and Italian foreign ministers in 1946 provided for the autonomy of the population of Alto Adige (South Tirol).

The population of Alto Adige comprises about 222,000 German-speaking, 110,000 Italian-speaking and 9,500 Ladin-speaking inhabitants; the Italian-speaking population live mainly in the towns of Bozen, Brixen and Meran. The German-speaking inhabitants are assured of equality of rights and safeguard of their ethnical character, in the fields of culture and economics, including the parity of the German and Italian languages.

The autonomous region consists of the 2 provinces of Bolzano and Trento, each of which has a semi-autonomous status. The regional parliament meets alternately for 2 years in Trent, the capital of the Trentino, and for 2 years in Bozen, the capital of Alto Adige, with an Italian-speaking and a German-speaking chairman also alternating.

The regional elections on 17 Nov. 1968 returned (*a*) in Trentino, 16 Christian Democrats, 2 Trentino Tirolese, 1 Liberal, 4 Socialists, 2 Communists, 1 other; (*b*) in South Tirol, 16 South Tirol People's Party, 4 Christian Democrats, 1 Social Movement, 2 Socialists, 1 Communist, 1 Liberal, 1 other. The provincial government of Bolzano is a coalition of the South Tirol People's Party and the Christian Democrats, headed by Dr Giorgio Grigolli (Christian Democrat).

Toscano, M., *Storia diplomatica della questione dell'Alto Adige.* Bari, 1967

V. *Friuli-Venezia Giulia*, established on 31 Jan. 1963; capital, Trieste. The region comprises the provinces of Gorizia, Udine and Trieste. The regional elections of 26 May 1968 returned 29 Christian Democrats, 12 Communists, 6 Socialists, 3 Party of Proletarian Unity, 3 Liberals, 3 Social Movement, 3 Movimento friulano, 2 others. The regional government is a coalition of Christian Democrats and Socialists, headed by Alfredo Berzanti (Christian Democrat).

The other 15 autonomous regions with ordinary statute (*regioni autonome con statuto ordinario*) have been established with regional elections on 7 June 1970. The results returned:

Piedmonte: 20 Christian Democrats, 13 Communists, 5 Socialists, 4 Liberals, 4 Party of Unitarian Socialists, 2 Social Movement, 2 others.

Lombardia: 36 Christian Democrats, 19 Communists, 9 Socialists, 4 Liberals, 5 Party of Unitarian Socialists, 3 Social Movement, 4 others.

Veneto: 28 Christian Democrats, 9 Communists, 5 Socialists, 2 Liberals, 3 Party of Unitarian Socialists, 1 Social Movement, 2 others.

Liguria: 14 Christian Democrats, 13 Communists, 4 Socialists, 3 Liberals, 3 Party of Unitarian Socialists, 1 Social Movement, 2 others.

Emilia-Romagna: 14 Christian Democrats, 24 Communists, 3 Socialists, 1 Liberal, 3 Party of Unitarian Socialists, 1 Social Movement, 4 others.

Toscana: 17 Christian Democrats, 23 Communists, 3 Socialists, 1 Liberal, 3 Party of Unitarian Socialists, 1 Social Movement, 2 others.

Umbria: 9 Christian Democrats, 13 Communists, 3 Socialists, 1 Party of Unitarian Socialists, 2 Social Movement, 2 others.

Marche: 17 Christian Democrats, 14 Communists, 3 Socialists, 1 Liberal, 2 Party of Unitarian Socialists, 1 Social Movement, 2 others.

Lazio: 18 Christian Democrats, 13 Communists, 4 Socialists, 3 Liberals, 3 Party of Unitarian Socialists, 5 Social Movement, 4 others.

Abruzzi: 20 Christian Democrats, 10 Communists, 3 Socialists, 1 Liberal, 2 Party of Unitarian Socialists, 2 Social Movement, 2 others.

Molise: 16 Christian Democrats, 5 Communists, 3 Socialists, 2 Liberals, 2 Party of Unitarian Socialists, 1 Social Movement, 1 other.

Campania: 25 Christian Democrats, 13 Communists, 7 Socialists, 2 Liberals, 4 Party of Unitarian Socialists, 5 Social Movement, 4 others.

Puglia: 22 Christian Democrats, 14 Communists, 5 Socialists, 1 Liberal, 2 Party of Unitarian Socialists, 4 Social Movement, 2 others.

Basilicata: 14 Christian Democrats, 7 Communists, 4 Socialists, 1 Liberal, 2 Party of Unitarian Socialists, 1 Social Movement, 1 other.

Calabria: 17 Christian Democrats, 10 Communists, 6 Socialists, 1 Liberal, 2 Party of Unitarian Socialists, 2 Social Movement, 2 others.

AREA AND POPULATION. The population (present in actual boundaries) at successive censuses were as follows:

31 Dec. 1871	27,577,640	21 April 1931	40,582,043
31 Dec. 1881	29,277,927	21 April 1936	42,302,680
10 Feb. 1901	33,370,138	4 Nov. 1951	47,158,738
10 June 1911	35,694,582	15 Oct. 1961	50,623,569[1]
1 Dec. 1921	37,403,956	1 June 1970[2]	54,418,831[1]

[1] Resident population.   Estimate.

The following table gives area and population of the Regions (census of 4 Nov. 1951 and of 15 Oct. 1961):

Regions	Area in sq. km (1961)	Resident pop. census, 1951	Resident pop. census, 1961	Density per sq. km (1961)
Piedmont	25,399·21	3,518,177	3,914,250	154
Valle d'Aosta	3,262·26	94,140	100,959	31
Liguria	5,415·05	1,566,961	1,735,349	320
Lombardy	23,803·91	6,566,154	7,406,152	311
Trentino-Alto Adige	13,613·09	728,604	785,967	58
Veneto	18,376·96	3,918,059	3,846,562	209
Friuli–Venezia Giulia	7,851·00	1,226,121	1,204,298	153
Emilia-Romagna	22,123·34	3,544,340	3,666,680	166
Marches	9,692·00	1,364,090	1,347,489	139
Tuscany	22,990·06	3,158,811	3,286,160	143
Umbria	8,456·04	803,918	794,745	94
Latium	17,203·13	3,340,798	3,958,957	230
Campania	13,594·92	4,346,264	4,760,759	350
Abruzzi and Molise	15,232·01	1,684,030	1,564,318	103
Apulia	19,346·90	3,220,485	3,421,217	177
Basilicata	9,987·63	627,586	644,297	65
Calabria	15,080·25	2,044,287	2,045,047	136
Sicily	25,707·85	4,486,749	4,721,001	184
Sardinia	24,089·34	1,276,023	1,419,362	59
Total	301,224·95	47,515,537	50,623,569	168

VITAL STATISTICS for calendar years:

		Living Births				Deaths excl. of
	Marriages	Legitimate	Illegitimate mate	Total	Still-born	still-born
1967	380,178	929,724	19,048	948,772	17,346	510,122
1968	374,097	911,158	19,014	930,172	16,282	532,571
1969	385,044	..	..	934,278	15,208	536,924

Emigrants to non-European countries, by sea and air: 1966, 77,141; 1967, 62,567; 1968, 57,251. Since 1960 nearly nine-tenths of these emigrants have gone to Canada, USA and Australia.

Communes of more than 100,000 inhabitants, with population resident on 31 Dec. 1969:

Roma (Rome)	2,731,397	Cagliari	223,002	Bergamo	125,310
Milano (Milan)	1,701,612	Taranto	219,484	Pescara	116,723
Napoli (Naples)	1,276,824	Brescia	206,379	Rimini	116,678
Torino (Turin)	1,177,039	Livorno (Leghorn)	173,839	Vicenza	112,734
Genova (Genoa)	841,841	Parma	172,341	Ancona	109,422
Palermo	659,177	Modena	167,310	Monza	107,823
Bologna	490,675	Reggio di C.	166,022	Sassari	107,308
Firenze (Florence)	459,058	Ferrara	156,207	Terni	106,062
Catania	412,721	Salerno	150,657	Siracusa	
Venezia (Venice)	367,631	Foggia	139,981	(Syracuse)	104,862
Bari	352,425	Prato	139,972	Bolzano	104,699
Trieste	278,370	Ravenna	131,279	Forlì	104,175
Messina	272,312	La Spezia	128,652	Piacenza	104,092
Verona	258,559	Reggio nell'E.	127,269	Pisa	103,011
Padova (Padua)	226,244	Perugia	126,887		

RELIGION. The treaty between the Holy See and Italy, of 11 Feb. 1929, confirmed by article 7 of the constitution of the Republic, lays down that the Catholic Apostolic Roman Religion is the only religion of the State. Other creeds are permitted, provided they do not profess principles, or follow rites, contrary to public order or moral behaviour.

The appointment of archbishops and of bishops is made by the Holy See; but the Holy See submits to the Italian Government the name of the person to be appointed in order to obtain an assurance that the latter will not raise objections of a political nature.

Catholic religious teaching is given in elementary and intermediate schools. Marriages celebrated before a Catholic priest are automatically transferred to the civil register. Marriages celebrated by clergy of other denominations must be made valid before a registrar. In 1969 there were 280 dioceses with 27,422 parishes and 42,704 priests. There were 193,317 members (165,902 women) of the 20,382 religious houses.

In 1962 there were about 100,000 Protestants and about 50,000 Jews.

Annuario Cattolica d'Italia, a cura del CNEC. 14th ed. 1969–70, Rome, 1970
Burgalassi, S., *La Sociologia della Religione in Italia dalle origini al 1967.* Rome, 1967

EDUCATION. Education is compulsory from 6 to 14 years of age. An optional pre-school education is given to the children between 3 and 5 years in the preparatory schools (nnrsery and kindergarten schools). Illiteracy of males over 6 years was 6·6% in 1961, of females 10%.

Compulsory education can be classified as primary education (5-year course) and junior secondary education (3-year course).

Senior secondary education is subdivided in classical (*ginnasio* and classical *liceo*), scientific (scientific *liceo*) and technical education: agricultural, industrial, commercial, technical, nautical institutes, institutes for surveyors, institutes for girls (5-year course) and teacher-training institutes (4-year course).

University education is given in Universities and in University Higher Institutes (4, 5, 6 years, according to degree course).

Statistics for the academic year 1969–70:

Elementary schools	No.	Teachers	Pupils
Kindergarten	21,610	39.888	1,407,542
Public elementary schools	36,347	210,550	4,452,540
Private elementary schools	} 2,914	13,256	344,053
Private elementary recognized schools (*parificate*)			

Government secondary schools	No.	Teachers	Males	Females	Total
Junior secondary schools	8,755	..	—	—	2,064,762
Classical lyceum	722	14,272	101.333	103,441	204,774
Lyceum for science	597	14,031	143,582	76,634	220,216
Teachers' schools	152	} 18,394	—	25,666	25,666
Teachers' institutes	637		27,092	182,256	209,348
Technical and professional institutes	1,864	21,807	137,483	94,882	232,365
Agricultural institutes	71		14,537	1,020	15,557
Industrial institutes	473		236,224	5,129	241,353
Nautical institutes	40		12,591	282	12,873
Commercial institutes	683		117,654	111,302	228,956
Surveyors' institutes	365	} 49,961	113,487	2,897	116,384
Technical institute for tourism	13		738	1,700	2,438
Managerial institutes	87		1,859	9,786	11,645
Technical girls' schools	88		—	13,815	13,815
Artistic studies	123	2,347	..	..	21,625
Language schools	5	1,138	..	..	1,984

The elementary and secondary schools in Alto Adige are divided according to the mother-tongues of the pupils. In 1969–70, 26,994 elementary and 12,329 secondary children were taught in German, 12,872 elementary and 5,537 secondary children in Italian.

Universities and higher institutes	Date of foundation	Students[1]	Teachers[1]	Universities and higher institutes	Date of foundation	Students[1]	Teachers[1]
Ancona	1965	1,231	36	Palermo	1805	23,507	477
Bari	1924	26,749	540	Parma	1502	9,677	388
Bologna	1200	25,992	400	Pavia	1390	7,110	933
Cagliari	1626	13,019	236	Perugia	1276	11,850	392
Camerino	1727	1,231	52	Pescara	1965	4,243	33
Cassino	1968	872	19	Piacenza	1924	349	23
Catania	1434	20,760	309	Pisa	1338	15.792	383
Chieti	1965	978	30	Roma	1303	57,058	2,520
Feltre (Belluno)	1969	193	..	Reggio di C.	1968	267	14
Ferrara	1391	2,885	196	Salerno	1944	7,227	90
Firenze	1924	17,389	1,034	Sassari	1677	2,092	81
Genova	1243	16.849	668	Siena	1300	3,582	170
L'Aquila	1956	4,625	87	Teramo	1965	832	43
Lecce	1959	4,869	81	Torino	1404	21,806	932
Macerata	1290	972	49	Trento	1965	4,369	32
Messina	1549	18,134	397	Trieste	1924	7,800	290
Milano	1924	44,390	1,328	Udine	1969	863	5
Modena	1678	4,081	232	Urbino	1564	5,255	179
Napoli	1224	54,957	1,462	Venezia	1868	5,803	86
Padova	1222	19,060	1,108	Verona	1969	6,009	54

[1] 1969–70.

The total of students in 1969–70 was 474,727.

CINEMAS (1969). There were 9,770 cinemas with a seating capacity of about 5m.

NEWSPAPERS (1969). There were 70 daily newspapers with a combined circulation of 2·54m. copies; of the papers, 12 are published in Rome and 7 in Milan. One daily each is published in German, Slovene and English.

SOCIAL WELFARE. The main public welfare acts include the establishment of a *Patronato Scolastico* for the benefit of children in primary schools (22 Jan. 1925) and of the national institution for the protection of maternity and infancy (*Opera Nazionale per la protezione della Maternità e dell'Infanzia*; 10 Dec. 1925). On 3 June 1937 there was set up in every commune an assistance body (*Ente Communale di Assistenza*) to dispense charity to the needy, out of funds provided partly by the assets of the provinces, communes and other public and private *Enti* and partly by special taxation.

In the calendar year 1969 government expenditure (*Conti di competenza*) on social welfare amounted to 777,364m. lire.

JUSTICE. Italy has 1 court of cassation, in Rome, and is divided for the administration of justice into 23 appeal court districts (and 3 detached sections), subdivided into 159 tribunal districts, and these again into *mandamenti* each with its own magistracy (*Pretura*), 899 in all. There are also 85 first degree assize courts and 26 assize courts of appeal. For civil business, besides the magistracy above mentioned, *Conciliatori* have jurisdiction in petty plaints.

On 31 Dec. 1969 there were 584 establishments for imprisonment before trial with 20,943 male and 1,163 female prisoners), 76 penal establishments (with 7,743 male and 234 female prisoners) and 36 establishments for preventive measures of safety (with 2,093 male and 219 female prisoners).

FINANCE. Currency. The standard coin is the *lira*. From 30 March 1960 the gold standard was formally established as equal to 0·00142187 gramme of gold per lira.

State metal coins are of 5, 10, 20, 50, 100 and 500 lire. There are also in circulation State notes of 500 and bank-notes of 1,000, 5,000, 10,000, 50,000 and 100,000 lire; they are neither convertible into gold as foreign moneys nor exportable abroad, nor importable from abroad into Italy (except for certain specified small amounts).

Circulation of money at 31 May 1970: State coins and notes, 205,800m. lire; bank-notes, 5,722,100m. lire.

In Aug. 1970 the rate of exchange was 627·69 lire per US$1 and 1,498·2 lire per £1 sterling.

Budget. Total revenue and expenditure for fiscal years, in 1m. lire:

	Revenue	Expenditure		Revenue	Expenditure
1965	7,724,189	8,463,789	1968	11,120,180	11,840.607
1966	9,542,841	9,516,539	1969	12,378,900	13,953.330
1967	9,473,324	10,322,091	1970[1]	12,152,000	14,019,000

[1] Initial estimates.

In the revenue for 1969 turnover and other business taxes accounted for 3,272 056m. lire, customs duties and indirect taxes for 2,305,562m. lire.

The public debt at 30 June 1970 totalled 8,390,548m. lire, including consolidated debt of 42,218m. lire and the floating debt 3,760,545m. lire.

DEFENCE. Most of the restrictions imposed upon Italy in Part IV of the peace treaty signed on 10 Feb. 1947 were repudiated by the signatories on 21 Dec. 1951, only the USSR objecting.

Head of the armed forces is the Defence Chief of Staff. In 1947 the ministries of war, navy and air were merged into the ministry of defence. The technical and scientific council for defence directs all research activities.

National service lasts 15 months in the Army and Air Force, and 24 months in the Navy.

Army. The Army is divided into the expeditionary force and the national defence force. It is composed of 5 infantry divisions, 2 armoured divisions (with M-47 and M-60 tanks), 5 Alpini brigades, 4 infantry brigades, 1 parachute brigade, 1 cavalry brigade (with M-47 tanks), 1 rocket brigade, 4 surface-to-air missile battalions and various special and support units. Total strength, 313,100.

Navy. Particulars of the principal surface ships in the Italian Navy:

Com-pleted	Name	Standard displace-ment Tons	Armour Belt In.	Big guns In.	Principal armament	Tor-pedo tubes	Shaft horse-power	Speed Knots
					Cruisers			
1969	Vittorio Veneto	7,500	—	—	8 3-in.; twin 'Terrier'; 9 helicopters	6	73,000	32
1964 1964	Andrea Doria[1] Caio Duilio[1] }	6,000	—	—	8 3-in.; twin 'Terrier'; 4 helicopters	6	70,000	31
1937	Giuseppe Garibaldi	9,802	4½	4	4 5·3-in.; 8 3-in.; twin 'Terrier'	—	85,000	30

[1] Rated as guided-missile escort cruisers.
[2] Converted into a guided-missile cruiser in 1957–62.

Summary of the Italian Navy: 10 submarines, 4 guided-missile cruisers, 2 guided-missile destroyers, 2 large destroyers (*ex*-light cruisers converted), 4 destroyers, 13 frigates, 21 corvettes, 4 ocean minesweepers, 37 coastal minesweepers, 20 inshore minesweepers, 8 motor torpedo-boats, 7 motor gunboats, 6 landing support gunboats, 3 landing ships, 1 survey ship, 1 salvage ship, 5 transports, 2 training ships, 2 oilers, 19 water carriers, 2 netlayers, 27 auxiliaries, 47 landing craft (motor transports) and 25 tugs. The ban imposed by the Peace Treaty having expired, Italy re-introduced submarines in 1953. The nucleus of the submarine flotilla comprised 4 new coastal boats resurrected from the laid-up wartime fleet and 5 large submarines transferred from the US Navy.

Two guided-missile destroyers, 5 missile boats and a nuclear-powered fast fleet replenishment ship are under construction or projected.

The coastline of the peninsula is divided into zones, with headquarters at Spezia, Naples, Taranto and Ancona; all are under the jurisdiction of flag officers with the status of C.-in-C. The admirals commanding on the coasts of Sardinia and Sicily do not rank as C.-in-C. Other localities of strategic importance under naval administration are Brindisi, where there is an admiral commanding, and Genoa, Leghorn, Augusta and Venice, each of which is under a senior naval officer.

The personnel of the Navy in 1970 numbered 41,000 officers and ratings.

Air Force. With an operational history dating back to 1911, the Air Force has been built up since 1951 largely with US assistance. It is divided into 3 air regions, with HQ at Rome, Milan and Bari.

Italy's air contribution to NATO forces includes 3 air brigades (each of 3 squadrons of 12–18 aircraft) of F-104G Starfighter and F-84F Thunderstreak fighter-bombers and one air brigade (2 squadrons) of RF-84F Thunderflash reconnaissance-fighters. There are also a brigade (3 squadrons) of F-86K and F-104G interceptors for home defence, 3 squadrons of G.91 tactical fighters, 3 squadrons of S2F Tracker anti-submarine aircraft, 3 squadrons of C-119 transport aircraft and various squadrons of training aircraft, air/sea rescue aircraft and helicopters. The F-84F aircraft are being replaced by Fiat G.91Ys, the F-86Ks by F-104S Starfighters, 1 squadron of C-119s by C-130E Hercules, and the S2Fs by Breguet Atlantics. The air-defence fighter units are supplemented by a brigade of Nike surface-to-air missiles. Strength is about 60,000 officers and men and 400 combat aircraft.

AGRICULTURE. The area of Italy on 30 June 1969 comprised 301,251 sq. km, of which 273,752 sq. km was agricultural and forest land and 27,499 sq. km was unproductive; the former was mainly distributed as follows (in 1,000 hectares): Cereals, 5,923; leguminous plants, 800; garden produce, 573; vines, 1,142; olive trees, 944; woods, 6,152; forage and pasture, 10,325; vines grown among other crops, 1,630; olive trees grown among other crops, 1,295.

At the first general census of agriculture (15 April 1961) agricultural holdings numbered 4,310,134 and covered 26,016,195 hectares. 3,529,556 owners (81·9%) farmed directly 14,250,860 hectares (54·8%); 295,157 owners (6·9%) worked with hired labour on 7,380,751 hectares (28·4%); 336,876 share-croppers (7·8%) tilled 3,199,103 hectares (12·3%); the remaining 148,545 holdings (3·4%) of 1,185,481 hectares (4·5%) were operated in other ways.

Under the land reform laws of 1950, about 800,000 hectares have been acquired for allocation to peasants; by 30 June 1962 more than 634,000 hectares had been allocated to 113,901 families.

According to the labour force survey in April 1970 persons engaged in agriculture numbered 3·75m. (2,618,000 males and 1,137,000 females).

In 1969, 584,214 farm tractors were being used.

The production of the principal crops (in 1,000 metric quintals) in 1969: Wheat, 95,366; barley, 2,919; oats, 4,911; rye, 707; maize, 45,058; sugar-beet, 105,215; potatoes, 39,693; tomatoes, 36,700; rice, 8,615; olive oil, 4,713; hemp, 21; oranges, 14,329; tangerines, 2,739; lemons, 7,780; other citrus fruit, 451.

Production of wine, 1969, 71·32m. hectolitres; of tobacco, 79,404 tons.

In 1969 consumption of chemical fertilizers in Italy was as follows (in 1,000 tons): Perphosphate, 1,112·6; deposed slags, 113·1; sulphurate of ammonium, 524·2; calciocianamide $\frac{20}{21}$, 82·3; nitrate of ammonia, 447·5; nitrate of calcium $\frac{15}{16}$, 272·1; potash salts, 121·3; potassic salts, 0·7.

Livestock estimated in 1969: Cattle, 10·1m.; pigs, 7·3m.; sheep and goats, 9,251,000; horses, 310,000; donkeys, 306,000; mules, 204,000.

Facca, V., and Martella, T., *Esami operativi della produttività in agricoltura.* Bologna, 1959
Problemi d'agricoltura meridionale. Naples, Cassa per il Mezzogiorno, 1953
Merlini, G., *Le regioni agrarie in Italia.* Bologna, 1948

FISHERY. The Italian fishing fleet comprised in 1969, 19,463 motor boats (223,256 gross tons) and 27,580 sailing vessels (35,925 gross tons). The catch in 1969 was 241,202 metric tons.

MINING. The Italian mining industry is most developed in Sicily (Caltanissetta), in Tuscany (Arezzo, Florence and Grosseto), in Sardinia (Cagliari, Sassari and Iglesias), in Lombardy (particularly near Bergamo and Brescia) and in Piedmont.

Italy's fuel and mineral resources are wholly inadequate. Only sulphur and mercury outputs yield a substantial surplus for exports. In 1969 outputs, in metric tons, of coal and similar fuels was 2,235,895; cast-iron ingots, 7,780,521; raw steel, 16,428,135; rolled iron, 13,353,547.

Production of metals and minerals (in metric tons) was as follows:

	1964	1965	1966	1967	1968	1969
Iron pyrites	1,395,347	1,401,395	1,304,912	1,410,308	1,406,452	1,474,688
Iron ore	875,638	784,694	827,880	736,902	708,291	763.648
Manganese	47,803	47,810	44,099	47,850	50,821	52.966
Lead	50,914	54,481	58,317	60,905	58,641	60.626
Zinc	225,604	225,075	228,764	259,543	313,692	294.221
Crude sulphur	678,497	649,073	590,788	500,991	541,098	413,468
Bauxite	247,300	244,393	255,486	241,402	216,197	228,149
Mercury	1,965	1,976	1,846	1,657	1,838	1,680
Lead	37,912	45,420	53,768	60,499	57,554	62,325
Zinc	73,013	80,898	77,229	87,993	112,274	130,321
Aluminium	115,595	128,505	127,790	127,778	142,348	144,559

OIL. The Sicilian district of Ragusa, Gela and Fontanarossa is rapidly developing into one of the largest European oilfields. Production in 1969 amounted to 1,519,914 metric tons, of which 1,387,077 came from Sicily.

INDUSTRY. The textile industry is the largest and most important. In the cotton industry, 945 factories had, in Dec. 1969, 4·36m. spindles and 79,837 looms. Silk culture, while flourishing most extensively in Lombardy, Piedmont and Venezia, is carried on all over Italy. The silk industry, Dec. 1969, had 844,671 spindles and 25,113 looms; output of raw silk in 1969, 499 metric tons. The production of artificial and synthetic fibre (including staple fibre and waste) in 1969 was 432,475 metric tons in 32 factories with 777,878 spindles. The woollen industry had, in 1969, 811 combing and spinning factories with 2,683 combers, 640,932 carding spindles and 1,048,666 combing spindles; woollen weaving was done in 248 factories with 11,226 looms. Output, 1969 (in metric tons): Pure cotton yarns, 194,120; pure cotton fabrics, 108,744; jute yarns, 29,381; pure wool yarns, 59,608.

The chemical industry produced, in 1969 (in metric tons): Sulphuric acid (at 50 Be), 5,366,584; mineral superphosphate, 1,414,056; sugar, 1,273,732.

Production of motor cars was 1,595,951 in 1969 (1,663,648 in 1968). 630,076 were exported in 1969.

Confederazione Generale ded' Industria Italiana: *L'industiria italiana alla metà del secolo XX*. Rome, 1953.—*Annuario 1954*. Rome, 1954

ELECTRICITY. Italy has greatly developed her water-power resources. In 1969 the total power generated was 110,447m. kwh., of which 42,001m. kwh. were generated by hydro-electric plants.

TOURISM. In 1969, 31·2m. foreigners visited Italy; they included 6·1m. German, 4·4m. Swiss, 4·3m. French, 3·1m. Yugoslav, 3m. Austrian, 1·7m. USA, 1·6m. British and 1·4m. Dutch citizens. They spent about 1,020,000m. lire.

LABOUR. The census of industry and commerce, of 15 Oct. 1961, recorded 1,907,513 firms employing 9,427,419 workers. Mining employed 103,847 workers; food and tobacco manufacture, 432,968; textile industries, 592,131; clothing, shoes, skins and leather industries, 576,699; engineering, 1,134,297; metallurgy, 191,689; chemical, rubber and paper industries, 358,746; building, 825,302; transport and communications, 747,003; commerce, 2,392,650; banking and insurance, 219,450; electricity, gas and water works, 107,581.

As at April 1970, 18·9m. persons were employed, 538,000 unemployed.

TRADE UNIONS. Membership of the 4 main groups in 1961 : Confederazione Generale Italiana del Lavoro (Communist-dominated), 3,673,430; Confederazione Italiana Sindacati Lavoratori (Catholic), 2,425,262; Unione Italiana del Lavoro, 1,547,491; Confederazione Italiana Sindacati Nazionali Lavoratori, 1,015,988.

COMMERCE. The territory covered by foreign trade statistics includes Italy, the Republic of San Marino, but excludes freeport zones, the Vatican City, the municipalities of Livigno and Campione.

The following table shows the value of Italy's foreign trade (in 1m. lire), excluding gold and legal-tender money:

	1964	1965	1966	1967	1968	1969
Imports	4,532,793	4,611,432	5,367,949	6,141,642	6,428,712	7,781,079
Exports	3,724,016	4,499,754	5,024,020	5,440,855	6,365,969	7,330,813

The following table shows trade by countries in 1m. lire:

Countries	Imports into Italy from			Exports from Italy to		
	1967	1968	1969	1967	1968	1969
Argentina	191,959	140,688	168,802	45,527	47,546	69,717
Australia	84,610	73,257	86,056	45,278	52,056	47,326
Austria	127,298	122,117	144,426	116,258	108,563	117,068
Belgium–Luxembourg	180,005	200,829	276,568	241,707	264,400	286,499
France	654,781	728,211	966,594	657,577	801,229	1,060,922
Germany (West)	1,060,431	1,148,422	1,459,509	959,748	1,189,252	1,441,134
Japan	42,707	53,301	73,898	33,204	42,096	51,144
Netherlands	229,332	249,811	308,764	249,245	295,081	326,115
Switzerland	142,221	156,135	185,946	259,299	285,780	328,174
USSR	172,032	179,784	154,415	78,172	109,783	179,400
UK	270,952	272,814	312,400	262,962	281,165	263,744
USA	664,996	748,414	881,890	539,826	681,240	795,509
Yugoslavia	144,177	127,113	146,307	144,084	179,853	215,364

In 1969 the main imports were maize, wood, greasy wool, metal scrap, pitcoal, petroleum, raw oils, meat, paper, rolled iron and steel, copper and alloys, mechanical and electric equipment, motor vehicles. The main exports were fruit and vegetables, fabrics, footwear and other clothing articles, rolled iron and steel, machinery, motor vehicles, plastic materials and petroleum by-products.

Italy's imports normally exceed her exports, leaving an adverse balance to be made up, if possible, by receipts from shipping, tourists' expenditures and remittances from Italians abroad. Her balance of trade (in 1,000m. lire) has been estimated as follows:

	Goods and services			Income from investments and work, balance	Net balance
	Export	Import	Balance		
1966	6,878	6,072	+ 806	+271	+1,077
1967	7,442	6,919	+ 523	+249	+ 772
1968	8,509	7,389	+1,120	+301	+1,421
1969	9,742	8,926	+ 816	+390	+1,206

Remittances from Italians abroad (in US$1m.): 1950, 72; 1955, 80; 1960, 214; 1967, 347; 1968, 401; 1969, 426.

Total trade between Italy and UK (British Board of Trade returns, in £1,000 sterling):

	1966	1967	1968	1969	1970
Imports to UK	166,154	195,070	235,815	222,920	249,176
Exports from UK	127,999	140,268	160,405	190,994 }	239,663
Re-exports from UK	19,959	17,3 21	17,495	18,667 }	

SHIPPING. The mercantile marine at 31 Dec. 1969 consisted of 4,014 vessels of 7,139,577 gross tons; of these 3,971 were steam- or motor-driven (7,138,621 gross tons), and 43 sailing vessels (956 gross tons).

In 1969, 222,269,000 tons of cargo were unloaded, and 71,849,000 tons of cargo were loaded in Italian ports.

In 1967 navigable waterways had a length of 1,989 km (852 km of which were canals).

RAILWAYS. Railway history in Italy begins in 1839, with a line between Naples and Portici (8 km). Length of railways (31 Dec. 1969), 20,335 km, including 16,014 km of state railways, of which 7,916 had not yet been electrified. In 1969 the state railways carried 314,275,000 passengers and 55·26m. metric tons of goods.

ROADS. Italy's roads totalled (31 Dec. 1969) 285,138 km, of which 41,730 km were state roads, 91,844 km provincial roads, 148,090 km communal roads. Motor vehicles, Dec. 1969: Cars, 9,028,400; buses, 29,135; lorries, 785,210; motor cycles, light vans, etc., 3,711,965.

The Mont Blanc tunnel road (11·6 km) from Entreves to Les Pelerins (France) was opened on 16 July 1965.

AVIATION. The Italian airline Alitalia (with a capital of 50,000m. lire, of which 91·2% is owned by the State) operates flights to every part of the world. Airports include 19 international, 29 national and 73 club airports. Domestic and international traffic in 1969 registered 6,730,877 passengers arrived and 6,731,562 departed, while freight and mail (excluding luggage) amounted to 104,259 metric tons unloaded and 146,302 metric tons loaded.

POST. On 31 Dec. 1969 there were 13,071 post offices; telegraph lines had a length of 21,455 km; there were 11,076 telegraph offices. The maritime radio-telegraph service had 19 coast stations. On 31 Dec. 1969 the telephone service had 8,530,751 apparatus; radio licences numbered 2,196,785; television and radio licences, 9,016,236.

BANKING. According to the law of 6 May 1926 there is only one bank of issue, the Banca d'Italia. Its gold reserve amounted to 1,863,707m. lire in June 1970; the foreign credit reserves of the Exchange Bureau (*Ufficio Italiano Cambi*) amounted to 523,600m. at the same date.

Since 1936, all credit institutions have been under the control of a state organ, named 'Inspectorate of Credit'; the Bank of Italy has been converted into a 'public institution', whose capital is held exclusively by corporate bodies of a public nature. Other credit institutions, totalling 1,232, are classified as: (1) 6 chartered banks (Banco di Napoli, Banco di Sicilia, Banca Nazionale del Lavoro, Monte dei Paschi di Siena, Istituto di S. Paolo di Torino, Banco di Sardegna); (2) 3 banks of national interest (Banca Commerciale Italiana in Milan, Credito Italiano in Genoa and Banco di Roma); (3) banks and credit concerns in general, including 172 joint-stock banks and 199 co-operative banks; (4) 90 savings banks and Monti di pegno (institutions granting loans against personal chattels as security), and (5) 762 Casse rurali e agrarie (agricultural banks, established as co-operative institutions with unlimited liability of associates).

At the end of 1969 there were 345 credit institutes handling 97% of all deposits and current accounts, with capital and reserves of 1,013,883m. lire.

On 31 May 1970 the post office savings banks had deposits and current accounts of 6,112,713m. lire; ordinary credit institutions, 35,273,365m. lire.

Insurance. By a decree of 29 April 1923 life-assurance business is carried on only by the National Insurance Institute and by other institutions, national and foreign, authorized by the Government. At 31 Dec. 1969 the insurances vested in the *Istituto Nazionale delle Assicurazioni* amounted to 2,357,340m. lire, including the decuple of life annuities.

Associazione Bancaria Italiana, *La legge bancaria*. 6th ed. Rome, 1964

WEIGHTS AND MEASURES. The metric system is in general use.

DIPLOMATIC REPRESENTATIVES

Italy maintains embassies in:

Afghánistán
Albania
Algeria
Argentina
Australia
Austria
Belgium
Bolivia
Brazil
Bulgaria
Burma
Cameroun (also for Central African
 Republic, Chad, Congo (Br.) and
 Gabon)
Canada
Ceylon (also for Maldives)
Chile
Colombia
Congo (K.)
Costa Rica
Cuba
Cyprus
Czechoslovakia
Denmark
Dominican Republic
Ecuador
El Salvador (also for Jamaica)
Ethiopia
Finland
France
Germany (West)
Ghana
Greece
Guatemala
Guinea (also for Mali)
Haiti
Honduras
Hungary
India (also for Nepál)
Indonesia
Iran
Iraq
Irish Republic
Israel
Ivory Coast (also for Dahomey, Niger,
 Togo, Upper Volta)
Japan
Jordan
Kenya
Korea (South)
Kuwait

Lebanon
Liberia (also for Sierra Leone)
Libya
Luxembourg
Madagascar
Malaysia
Malta
Mexico
Morocco
Netherlands
New Zealand
Nicaragua
Nigeria
Norway (also for Iceland)
Pakistan
Panama
Paraguay
Peru
Philippines
Poland
Portugal
Romania
Saudi Arabia
Senegal (also for Mauritania,
 Gambia)
Singapore
Somalia
South Africa, Republic of (also for
 Lesotho, Swaziland)
Spain
Sudan (also for Southern Yemen)
Sweden
Switzerland
Syria
Tanzania
Thailand (also for Laos)
Tunisia
Turkey
Uganda (also for Burundi, Ruanda)
USSR
UAR
UK
USA
Uruguay
Vatican
Venezuela (also for Trinidad and
 Tobago)
Vietnam (South) (also for Cambodia)
Yemen
Yugoslavia
Zambia (also for Botswana, Malawi)

OF ITALY IN GREAT BRITAIN (14 Three Kings Yard, W1)
Ambassador: Raimondo Manzini, GCVO.
Ministers: Pasquale Ricciulli, KCVO, CMG; Enzo Malgeri, CVO (*Commercial*).
Service Attachés: Capt. Corrado Vittori (*Defence and Navy*), Col. Stelio
Nardini (*Air*), Col. Mario Bucalossi, MVO (*Army*).

Counsellors: Ugo Barzini; Sergio Berlinguer, MVO (*Press*); Francesco Pulcini (*Labour*); Vittorio Amedeo Farinelli, Paolo Galli.
First Secretaries: Sergio Berlinguer; Italo Di Muccio (*Commercial*).

There are consular representatives at Bedford, Belfast, Birmingham, Cardiff, Edinburgh, Glasgow, Manchester and Nottingham.

OF GREAT BRITAIN IN ITALY

Ambassador: Sir Patrick Hancock, KCMG.
Minister: R. W. Selby, CMG.
Counsellors: P. A. Rhodes (*Head of Chancery*); C. W. Wallace (*Commercial*); A. A. W. Landymore (*Agricultural*); K. Kenney, OBE (*Labour*); I. C. Alexander, OBE (*Information*).
Service Attachés: Col. G. D. Gill, MBE (*Army*), Group Capt. R. G. Churcher, DSO, MVO, DFC (*Air*), Capt. J. J. Phillips (*Navy*).
First Secretaries: G. E. Fitzherbert; E. A. F. Seaman; J. A. Shorten; D. A. McAlindon (*Economic*); Miss M. B. Lewis (*Consul*); S. A. Shepherd, A. A. C. Nash, MBE (*Commercial*); M. W. Ponsonby, CBE; T. C. Wood.

There are consular representatives at Bari, Cagliari, Florence, Genoa, Messina, Milan, Naples, Palermo, Rome, Trieste, Turin and Venice.

OF ITALY IN THE USA (1601 Fuller St. NW, Washington, D.C., 20009)

Ambassador: Egidio Ortona.
Ministers: Giulio Terruzzi; Umberto La Rocca; Alberto Rossi (*Commercial*).
Counsellors: Piero Ferraboschi; Giorgio Vecchi; Bartolomeo Attolico (*Press*); Giorgio Reitano (*Commercial*); Enrico Capobianco (*Labour*). *First Secretaries:* Antonio Catalano di Melilli; Fabio Migliorini. *Service Attachés:* Maj.-Gen. Carlo Tommasi (*Air*), Capt. Claudio Boido (*Navy*), Col. Salvatore Pontieri (*Army*).

OF THE USA IN ITALY

Ambassador: Graham Anderson Martin.
Deputy Chief of Mission: Wells Stabler. *Heads of Sections:* Robert E. Barbour (*Political*); Louis C. Boochever (*Economic*); Thomas D. Bowie (*Labour*); John L. Kuhn (*Consular*); Henry C. Boudreau (*Administrative*). *Service Attachés:* Capt. George W. Cogswell (*Defence and Navy*), Col. J. R. Castelli (*Air*), Col. James D. Clavio (*Army*).

There are Consuls-General at Genoa, Milan, Naples, Palermo, Rome and Consuls at Florence, Trieste and Turin.

BOOKS OF REFERENCE

STATISTICAL INFORMATION. The Istituto Centrale di Statistica (16 Via Cesare Balbo 00100 Rome) was set up by law of 9 July 1926 as the central institute in charge of census and all statistical information. *President:* Professor Giuseppe de Meo. *Directors-General:* Dr Salvatore Marino and Dr Luigi Pinto. Its publications include:

Annuario statistico italiano. 1970
Compendio statistico italiano. 1970
Bollettino mensile di statistica. Monthly, from 1950
Annuario di statistiche demografiche. 1967
Annuario di statistica agraria. 1969
Statistica della navigazione marittima. 1968
Annuario statistico del commercio interno. 1969
Statistica annuale del commercio con l'estero. 1968
Statistica mensile del commercio con l'estero. Monthly
Annuario di statistiche del lavoro e dell'emigrazione. 1970

Annuario di statistiche provinciali. 1970
Censimento generale dell'agricoltura, 1961. 7 vols, 1961–69
Censimento generale della popolazione, 1961. 10 vols, 1961–69
Censimento generale dell'industria e del commercio, 1961. 7 vols., 1961–69
Sommario di statistiche storiche dell'Italia, 1861–1965
Il valore della lira dal 1861 al 1965. 1967
Indagine statistica sullo sviluppo del reddito nazionale dal 1861 al 1956. 1957
Produttività e distribuzione del reddito in Italia, 1951–63. 1965
Studi statistici sulla finanza pubblica. 1966
Sviluppo della popolazione italiana dal 1861 al 1961. 1966
Redditi e produttività in Italia, 1951–66. 1967

Italy. Documents and Notes. Servizi delle Informazioni, Rome. 1952 ff.
Italian Books and Periodicals. Bimonthly from 1958
Banco di Roma, *Review of the Economic Conditions in Italy* (in English). Bimonthly, 1947 ff.
Credito Italiano, *The Italian Economic Situation.* Bimonthly. Milan, from June 1961 (in Italian), from June 1962 (in English)
Compendio Economico Italiano. Rome, Unione Italiana delle Camere di Commercio. Annually, from 1954
Almagià, R., *L'Italia.* 2 vols. Turin, 1959
Carone, G., *Il Turismo nell'economia internazionale.* Milan, 1959
Clough, S. B., *The economic history of modern Italy.* Columbia Univ. Press, 1964
Danielli, G., *Atlanie Fisico Economico d'Italia.* Milan, 1950
Di Vittorio, G. (ed.), *I sindacali in Italia.* Bari, 1955
Grindrod, M., *The Rebuilding of Italy, 1945–55.* R. Inst. of Int. Affairs, 1955
Hildebrand, G. H., *Growth and structure in the economy of modern Italy.* Harvard Univ. Press, 1965
Kogan, N., *A political history of postwar Italy.* London, 1966
Lutz, V., *Italy: a study in economic development.* R. Inst. of Int. Affairs, 1962
SVIMEZ, *Un secolo di statistiche italiane: Nord e Sud, 1861–1961.* Rome, 1962
Zanetti, G., and Filippi, E., *Finanza e sviluppo della grande industria in Italia.* 2 vols. Milan, 1967

NATIONAL LIBRARY. Biblioteca Nazionale Centrale Vittorio Emanuele II Via Collegio Romano 27, Rome. *Director:* Dr Emidio Cerulli.

JAPAN

Nippon (*or* Nihon)

HISTORY. The house of Yamato, from about 500 B.C. the rulers of one of several kingdoms, in about A.D. 200 united the nation; the present imperial family are their direct descendants. From 1186 until 1867 successive families of Shoguns exercised the temporal power. In 1867 the Emperor Meiji recovered the imperial power after the abdication on 14 Oct, 1867 of the fifteenth and last Tokugawa Shogun Keiki (in different pronunciation: Yoshinobu). In 1871 the feudal system (Hōken Seido) was abolished; this was the beginning of the rapid westernization.

At San Francisco on 8 Sept. 1951 a Treaty of Peace was signed by Japan and representatives of 48 countries. For details *see* THE STATESMAN'S YEAR-BOOK, 1953, p. 1169. On 26 Oct. 1951 the Japanese Diet ratified the Treaty by 307 votes to 47 votes with 112 abstentions. On the same day the Diet ratified a Security Treaty with the US by 289 votes to 71 votes with 106 abstentions. The treaty provided for the stationing of American troops in Japan until Japan was able to undertake her own defence.

The peace treaty came into force on 28 April 1952, when Japan regained her sovereignty.

EMPEROR. The Emperor bears the title of Nihon-koku Tennō ('Emperor of Japan'). Hirohito, born in Tōkyō, 29 April 1901; succeeded his father, Yoshihito, 25 Dec. 1926; married 26 Jan. 1924, to Princess Nagako, born 6 March 1903. Living sons: (1) Prince Akihito (Tsugunomiya), born 23 Dec. 1933; formally installed as Crown Prince on 10 Nov. 1952; married to Miss Michiko Shoda (born 20 Oct. 1934), 10 April 1959. *Offspring:* Prince Naruhito (Hironomiya), born 23 Feb. 1960; Prince Fumihito (Ayanomiya), born 30 Nov. 1965. (2) Prince Masahito (Hitachinomiya), born 28 Nov. 1935; married to Miss Hanako Tsugaru, 30 Sept. 1964.

By the Imperial House Law of 11 Feb. 1889, revised on 16 Jan. 1947, the succession to the throne was fixed upon the male descendants.

CONSTITUTION AND GOVERNMENT. Japan's Government is based upon the Constitution of 1947 which superseded the Meiji Constitution of 1889. In it the Japanese people pledge themselves to uphold the ideas of democracy and peace. The Emperor is the symbol of the States and of the unity of the people. Sovereign power rests with the people. The Emperor has no powers related to government. Japan renounces war as a sovereign right and the threat or the use of force as a means of settling disputes with other nations. Fundamental human rights are guaranteed.

National flag: White, with a red sun (without rays).
National anthem: Kimi ga yo wa (words 9th century, tune by Hiromori Hayashi, 1881).

Legislative power rests with the Diet, which consists of the House of Representatives (of 486 members), elected by men and women over 20 years of age for a 4-year term, and the House of Councillors of 250 members (100 elected at large and 150 from prefectural districts), one-half of its members being elected every 3 years. The Lower House controls the budget and approves treaties with foreign powers.

The former House of Peers is replaced by the House of Councillors, whose members, like those of the House of Representatives, are elected as representatives of all the people. The House of Representatives has pre-eminence over the House of Councillors.

After the elections of 7 July 1968 the House of Councillors consists of 137 Liberal-Democrats, 73 Socialists, 24 Komeito, 10 Democratic Socialists, 7 Independents, 5 Communists.

After the elections of 27 Dec. 1969 the House of Representatives was composed as follows: Liberal-Democratic Party, 300; Socialist Party, 90; Democratic Socialist Party, 32; Komeito, 47; Communists, 14; Independents, 3.

Executive power is vested in the Cabinet, which is collectively responsible to the Diet. Prime Ministers must be civilians.

The Cabinet, as constituted on 17 Feb. 1971, is composed as follows:

Prime Minister: Eisaku Sato.

Justice: Koshiro Ueki. *Foreign Affairs:* Kiichi Aichi. *Finance:* Takeo Fukuda. *Education:* Michita Sakata. *Health and Welfare:* Tsunco Uchida. *Agriculture and Forestry:* Todao Kuraishi. *Trade and Industry:* Kiichi Miyazawa. *Transport:* Tomisabaro Hashimoto. *Post and Telecommunications:* Ichitaro Ide. *Labour:* Masakatsu Nohara. *Construction:* Ryntaro Nemoto. *Home Affairs:* Daisuke Akita. *Ministers of State:* Masuo Araki; Ichiro Sato; Shinichi Nishida; Shigeru Hori (*Cabinet Secretary*); Sadanori Yamanaka (*Prime Minister's Office*); Yasuhiro Nakasone (*Defence*); Ichiro Sato (*Economic Planning*); Masami Takatsuji.

LOCAL GOVERNMENT. The country is divided into 46 prefectures (*Todōfuken*), including Tōkyō-to (the capital), Ōsaka-fu and Kyōto-fu, Hokkai-dō, and 42 *Ken*. Each *Todōfuken* has its governor (*Chiji*) elected by the voters in the area. The prefectural government of Tōkyō-to is also responsible for the urban part (formerly Tōkyō-shi) of the prefecture. Each prefecture, city, town and village has a representative assembly elected by the same franchise as in parliamentary elections.

Administratively there are (as of Oct. 1965), 46 prefectures; 575 rural districts (*Gun*), 560 cities, 1,998 towns and 819 villages.

New legislation, which came into effect on 1 July 1954, has given the central government complete control of the police throughout the country.

JAPAN 1103

AREA AND POPULATION. Japan, as constituted after the Second World War, has total area of 369,662 sq. km (142,726·5 sq. miles). The 4 main islands are Honshū (mainland), Kyūshū, Hokkaidō and Shikoku.

On 26 June 1968 the USA retroceded to Japan the Bonin and Volcano Islands groups (*see* THE STATESMAN'S YEAR-BOOK, 1968–69, pp. 781–83).

Census population, 1 Oct 1965, was 98,281,955, with density of 265·9 per sq. km (48·3m. males, 50m. females). Foreigners registered, June 1966, were 667,072, of whom 584,560 were Koreans, 49,413 Chinese, 15,699 Americans, 2,279 British, 1,856 Germans, 1,372 Canadians.

Japanese overseas, March 1966, 1·21m.; of these, 595,053 lived in Brazil, 464,332 in USA, 29,157 in Canada, 19,200 in Argentina, 8,100 in Bolivia.

Census population (preliminary), 1970, 104·65m.

The leading cities, with census population, 1 Oct. 1965 (in 1,000), are:

Akita	217	Kawaguchi	249	Otaru	197
Amagasaki	501	Kawasaki	855	Sakai	466
Aomori	224	Kitakyushu	1,042	Sapporo	821
Asahikawa	245	Kōbe	1,217	Sasebo	247
Chiba	332	Kochi	218	Sendai	481
Fukuoka	750	Koriyama	223	Shimizu	219
Fukuyama	205	Kumamoto	407	Shimonoseki	254
Funabashi	224	Kurashiki	275	Shizuoka	368
Gifu	358	Kure	225	Takamatsu	258
Hachioji	208	Kyōto	1,365	Tokushima	213
Hakodate	252	Matsuyama	283	Tōkyō	8,893
Hamamatsu	393	Nagano	269	Toyama	256
Higashiosaka	443	Nagasaki	405	Toyohashi	239
Himeji	368	Nagoya	1,935	Toyonaka	292
Hiroshima	504	Niigata	356	Urawa	221
Ichikawa	208	Nishinomiya	337	Utsunomia	266
Ichinomiya	204	Oita	226	Wakayama	329
Iwaki	334	Okayama	292	Yokkaichi	219
Kagoshima	328	Omiya	216	Yokohama	1,789
Kanazawa	336	Osaka	3,156	Yokosuka	317

VITAL STATISTICS (in 1,000) for calendar years:

	1960	1961	1962	1963	1964	1965	1966	1967	1968
Births	1.606	1,586	1,616	1,657	1,715	1,822	1,359	1,935	1,870
Deaths	707	695	710	671	673	700	670	675	686

Crude birth rate of Japanese nationals in present area, 1968, was 18·6 per 1,000 population (1947: 34·3); crude death rate, 6·8; crude marriage rate, 9·5; infant mortality rate per 1,000 live births, 15·3.

RELIGION. There has normally been religious freedom, but Shintō (literally, The Way of the Gods) was given the status of *quasi*-state-religion in the 1930s; in 1945 the Allied Supreme Command ordered the Government to discontinue state support of Shintō. State subsidies have ceased for all religions, and all religious teachings are forbidden in public schools.

In 1966 Shintoism claimed 79·5m. adherents, Buddhism 78·77m.; these figures obviously overlap. Christians numbered 735,000, of whom two-thirds are Protestants.

EDUCATION. Education is compulsory and free between the ages of 6 and 15. All institutions are co-educational. On 1 May 1969 there were 35,432 kindergartens and elementary schools with 423,587 teachers and 10,954,238 pupils; 11,278 junior high schools with 227,405 teachers and 4,865,206 pupils; 4,817 senior high schools with 200,806 teachers and 4,337,905 pupils; 473 junior colleges with 15,445 teachers and 263,362 pupils.

There were also 407 special schools for handicapped children (11,429 teachers, 50,183 pupils).

Japan has 7 main state universities, formerly known as the Imperial Universities: Tōkyō University (1877); Kyōto University (1897); Tōhoku University, Sendai (1907); Kyūshū University, Fukuoka (1910); Hokkaidō

University, Sapporo (1918); Osaka University (1931), and Nagoya University (1939). In addition, there are various other state and municipal as well as private universities of high standing, such as Keio (founded in 1859), Waseda, Rikkyo, Hosei, Meiji universities, and several women's universities, among which Tōkyō and Ochanomizu are most notable. There are 439 colleges and universities with (1969) 1,396,464 students and 77,787 teachers.

CINEMAS (1966). Cinemas numbered 4,828, with an annual attendance of 346m. (1960: 1,014m.).

NEWSPAPERS (1968). Daily newspapers numbered 118 with aggregate circulation of 49·7m., including 4 major English-language newspapers.

The Japanese Press. Tokyo, annual from 1949

SOCIAL WELFARE. Hospitals in 1969 numbered 7,817 with 1,033,139 beds. Physicians, in 1966, numbered 110,759; dentists, 36,022.

There are in force various types of social security schemes, such as health insurance, unemployment insurance and old-age pensions. The total population come under one or more of these schemes.

In 1963, 1,033 welfare officers were employed. In 1970 some 1·4m. persons received some form of regular public assistance.

JUSTICE. The Supreme Court is composed of the Chief Justice and 14 other judges. The Chief Justice is appointed by the Emperor, the other judges by the Cabinet. Every 10 years a justice must submit himself to the electorate. All justices and judges of the lower courts serve until they are 70 years of age.

Below the Supreme Court are 8 regional higher courts, district courts (*Chihō-saibansho*) in each prefecture (4 in Hokkaidō) and the local courts.

The Supreme Court is authorized to declare unconstitutional any act of the Legislature or the Executive which violates the constitution.

FINANCE. Currency. Coins of 1, 5, 10, 50, 100 and 1,000 *yen* are in circulation as well as the notes of the Bank of Japan, of 1, 5, 10, 50, 100, 500, 1,000, 5,000 and 10,000 *yen*; the notes of 1, 5, 10, 50 and 100 *yen* being gradually replaced by coins of the same denomination.

In Dec. 1967 the currency circulation consisted of 3,411,599m. yen Bank of Japan notes and 190,606m. yen subsidiary coins.

On 25 April 1949 an official rate of 360 yen per US$ was established for all permitted foreign-trade and exchange transactions. After the devaluation of the £ sterling in Sept. 1970 the exchange rate is 864 yen to the £ and 356 yen to the US$.

Budget. Ordinary revenue and expenditure for fiscal years ending 31 March balanced as follows, in 1m. yen: 1965–66, 3,744,725; 1966–67, 4,314,270; 1967–68, 5,203,437; 1968–69, 5,818,598.

Of the proposed revenue in 1968–69 (in 1m. yen), 4,697,852 is to come from taxes and stamps, 640,000 from public bonds. Main items of expenditure: Local government, 1,092,337; public works, 1,065,962; social security, 815,661; education and science, 702,448; defence, 422,075.

The national debt in Sept. 1966 was 2,188,900m. yen.

On 30 Sept. 1959 Japan's external debt consisted of £53,156,461 in sterling bonds, $85,395,100 in dollar bonds and 115,727,000 francs in French franc bonds.

LOCAL. The estimated 1965–66 budgets of the prefectures and other local authorities forecast a total revenue of 4,649,518m. yen, to be made up partly by local taxes on land, houses, occupations, and partly by government grants and local loans; and a total expenditure of 4,536,623m.

Ministry of Finance, *An outline of Japanese tax.* Tokyo, 1962

DEFENCE. On 1 July 1954 legislation brought the ground, naval and air services under a Joint Staff Council which comes under the Director-General of the Defence Agency, who is a Cabinet Minister.

The Japan–USA security treaty of April 1952 gave the USA the right to maintain armed forces and bases in Japan. Under the Japan–USA mutual defence assistance pact of Sept. 1954 the USA supplies almost the entire equipment of the Japanese forces. The treaty of mutual co-operation and security, signed on 19 Jan. 1960, put the two countries on a footing of equality.

Army. The 'Ground Self-Defence Force' had in Jan. 1970 an authorized strength of 169,000 uniformed personnel, plus a reserve of 30,000 men. The Army is organized in 5 armies, 12 infantry divisions, 1 mechanized division, 1 airborne brigade, artillery, engineer and signal brigades.

The Northern Army, stationed in Hokkaidō, consists of 4 divisions (1 of which is mechanized), an artillery brigade (including 1 Hawk anti-aircraft missile battalion), a tank group and an engineering group. The Western Army stationed in Kyūshū, consists of 2 divisions. The North-Eastern Army (2 divisions), the Eastern Army (2 divisions), the Central Army (3 divisions) and an independent parachute brigade are stationed in Honshū. The infantry division establishment is approximately 9,000 with 4 infantry regiments or 7,000 (lower establishment) with 3 infantry regiments. Each infantry division has an artillery unit, an anti-tank unit, a tank battalion and an engineering battalion in addition to administrative units.

Navy. The 'Maritime Self-Defence Force' comprises 10 submarines, a guided-missile destroyer completed in 1965, 27 destroyers, 13 frigates, 2 minelayers, 34 coastal minesweepers, 20 patrol vessels, 6 minesweeping boats, 10 motor torpedo-boats, 27 motor launches, 4 landing ships, 6 landing craft, 3 depot ships, 2 oilers, 9 tugs and 100 auxiliaries. Personnel in 1970 numbered 42,590 officers and ratings.

Eight submarines, 10 destroyers, 8 destroyer escorts, a training ship, 4 coastal minesweepers and 27 other vessels are being built or projected.

The Navy has a strong air arm, including 58 S2F and 60 P2V anti-submarine patrol bombers, 65 trainers, 43 helicopters and 11 other aircraft.

The 'Maritime Safety Agency' (Coast Guard) controls 10 large patrol vessels, 22 medium patrol vessels, 57 small patrol vessels, 211 patrol craft, 26 survey ships and 26 navigation supply vessels. Personnel in 1970 numbered 11,073 officers and men.

Air Force. An 'Air Self-Defence Force' was inaugurated on 1 July 1954. In 1970 its equipment included 7 squadrons (each 24 aircraft) of F-104J Starfighters, 8 squadrons of F-86F Sabre day fighters, 1 squadron of RF-86F reconnaissance fighters and 2 squadrons of C-46 transports, some of which are equipped with special electronic systems for ECM duties. Many of the F-104Js and the RF-86Fs will be replaced by F-4EJ and RF-4EJ Phantoms respectively in 1973–75, and the C-46s by NAMC C-1 twin-turbofan transports. Four NAMC YS-11 turboprop transports were acquired in 1965–66 and have since been supplemented by further aircraft of this type. About 12 S-62 helicopters and MU-2S twin-turboprop aircraft (17 being delivered) do search, rescue and general duties. Training units use piston-engined T-34 Mentor basic trainers, Fuji T-1 jet intermediate trainers and T-33 jet advanced trainers, with the supersonic Mitsubishi T-2 scheduled for service from 1974. Several Nike-Ajax and 2 Hawk surface-to-air missile battalions are in service. Total strength is about 1,065 aircraft and 40,000 officers and men.

PLANNING. The National Income Doubling Plan 1961–70 was replaced by the Economic and Social Development Programme, 1967–1972, which has been superseded by the Plan for Social and Economic Development 1970–76. The Plan envisages an annual growth rate of 10·5%.

AGRICULTURE. Farm population, 1969, was 8·99m. (1950: 37·8m.). Arable land is estimated at 5,401,000 hectares, or 16% of the land area; 3·3m. hectares are in rice, 2,093,000 hectares in field crops and 304,000 hectares in trees. About 315,250 hectares are devoted to industrial crops, chiefly mulberry trees (for silkworm rearing), tea, tobacco, flax and pyrethrum. The forest and field area is about 25m. hectares.

In 1964, 5,269,000 agricultural tractors and threshers were in use.

For post-war land reform, see THE STATESMAN'S YEAR-BOOK, 1955, p. 1179. Holdings average 2 acres (0·8 hectare); only 5% are more than 10 acres.

Rice is Japan's greatest crop, occupying 55% of the cultivated area. Much marginal land is used at a severe cost in labour and fertilizer. The entire crop is consumed plus imports (where possible) of another 15 or 20%. Output of rice (in 1m. tons) was 12·81 in 1963, 12·48 in 1964, 12·41 in 1965, 12·75 in 1966.

Output in 1,000 metric tons (1965) of barley was 915·9; of wheat, 318·1, and of soybeans, 229·7. Sweet potatoes for several decades have mitigated the effects of rice famines; yield, in 1965, was 4,955,000 tons. Sugar production covers only 14% of the country's requirements; about 1·5m. tons have to be imported annually, half of it from Taiwan and Australia.

Fruit production, 1965 (in 1,000 metric tons): Peaches, 228·7; pears, 360·2; apples, 1,320; grapes, 224·7; persimmons, 346·4, and mandarins, 1,317.

Livestock (Feb. 1968): 3·16m. cattle (including 1·49m. milch cows), 216,000 horses, 5·54m. pigs, 83,000 sheep, 223,000 goats, 165·82m. chickens. Milk output is increasing—in 1967, 3·57m. metric tons of milk.

Takekazu Ogura, *Agricultural development in modern Japan*. Tokyo, 1967

FORESTRY. Forests and grasslands cover about 61m. acres (67% of the whole land area), with an estimated timber stand of 1,890·3m. cu. metres. In 1967, 73·96m. cu. metres of industrial timber were felled.

FISHERIES. Before the War, Japanese catch represented one-half to two-thirds of the world's total fishing; in 1965 it was 13·2%. The catch in 1965 was 6·9m. metric tons, excluding deep-sea fishing and whaling. Japan is the leading whaling nation. Output of whale-oil, 1965–66, 85,326 metric tons from 21,429 whales caught.

MINING. Ore production in metric tons, 1965, of copper, 106,369; lead, 56,345; aluminium (1964), 263,800; manganese, 311,849; iron, 1,118,726; zinc, 226,521; tungsten, 586; asbestos, 14,399; antimony, 122; coal (1964), 50·9m.; cadmium (1964), 1,215; chromite, 39,946; molybdenum, 531; gold, 8·1; silver, 282·8.

Output of crude petroleum, 1965, was 786,932 kilolitres, almost entirely from oilfields on the island of Honshū, but 72m. kilolitres of crude oil had to be imported. Output of natural gas, 1965, 1·79m. cu. metres.

INDUSTRY. Japan's industrial equipment, Dec. 1966, numbered 595,000 plants of all sizes, employing 10·3m. production workers.

Since 1920 there has been a shift from light to heavy industries. The production of electrical appliances and electronic machinery has made great strides: television sets (1966: 5·65m.), transistor sets (1966: 25·3m.), cameras (1966: 2·8m.), computing machines, automation equipment are produced in increasing quantities. The chemical industry ranks third in production value after textiles and iron and steel. Production, 1966, included (in metric tons) 2·65m. ammonium sulphate, 1·29m. calcium superphosphate, 6·03m. sulphuric acid, 1·44m. caustic soda.

Output (1967), in 1,000 metric tons, of pig-iron was 40,095; crude steel, 62,154; hot rolled steel (1966), 38,956.

In 1966 paper production was 8·2m. tons and pulp production, 5·69m. tons.

Japan's textile industry before the War had 13m. cotton-yarn spindles. After the War she resumed with 2·78m. spindles; in 1964, 8·42m. spindles were operating. Output of cotton yarn, 1966, 505,642 metric tons, and of cotton cloth, 2,913m. sq. metres.

In wool, Japan aims at wool exports sufficient to pay for the imports of raw wool. Output, 1966, 164,327 metric tons of woollen yarns and 345·4m. sq. metres of woollen fabrics.

The rayon industry (the world's largest in 1936) was heavily stripped during the War, only about 30% surviving. Output, 1966, of rayon fabrics, 382·77m. sq. metres; rayon staple fabrics, 934·71m. sq. metres; synthetic fibre fabrics, 1,443·1m. sq. metres; silk fabrics, 175·09m. sq. metres.

Since 1955 Japan has led the world in shipbuilding. In 1966, 6,685,000 gross tons were launched, of which 3,993,000 were exported; the figures for 1967 were 7,497,000 and 4·56m. respectively.

POWER. As of March 1965, generating facilities were capable of an output of 41m. kw.; electricity produced in 1966 was 215,276m. kwh. The maximum output of the 10 largest thermo-electric plants ranges from 530,000 to 1,256,000 kw.; that of the 9 largest hydro-electric plants from 127,000 to 380,000 kw.

TOURISM. In 1969, 608,744 foreigners visited Japan, while the number of Japanese travelling abroad totalled 712,000; 300,390 visitors came from USA, 30,124 from UK. Japanese tourist payments showed a deficit of US$93m.

LABOUR. Total labour force, 1969 was, 50·98m., of which 8·9m. were in agriculture and forestry, 470,000 in fishing, 240,000 in mining, 3·71m. in construction, 13·45m. in manufacturing, 11·33m. in commerce and finance, 3·38m. in transport and other public utilities, 7·22m. in services (including the professions) and 1·56m. in government work.

In June 1966 there were 10·4m. workers organized in 53,985 unions. The largest federation is the 'General Council of Japanese Trade Unions' (Sōhyō) with 4·25m. members. The 'Japanese Confederation of Labour' (Domei Kaigi) was formed in Dec. 1963 as a merger of the 'Trade Union Congress' (Zenrō), the 'Federation of Trade Unions' (Sodomei) and the 'National Council of Government and Public Workers' Union' (Zen Kanko), total membership, 1·73m. The 'Federation of Independent Unions' (Churitsu Roren) was formed in Jan. 1962 by 18 unions; membership, about 1·02m.

In Oct. 1966, 360,000 (0·7%) were unemployed.

Year Book of Labour Statistics, 1961. Ministry of Labour, Tokyo, 1962
Ayusawa, I. F., *A history of labor in modern Japan.* Honolulu, 1967.—*Organized Labour in Japan.*
2 vols. Tokyo, 1962

COMMERCE. Trade, excluding bullion and specie (in US$1,000; US$1 = 360 yen, 1,000 yen = US$2·77):

	1962	1963	1964	1965	1966	1967
Imports	5,637	6,736	7,938	8,169	9,523	11,663
Exports	4,916	5,452	6,673	8,452	9,776	10,442

Distribution of trade by countries (customs clearance basis), in US$1m.:

	Exports			Imports		
	1964	1965	1966	1964	1965	1966
Hong Kong	292·0	287·9	369·9	28·9	35·3	47·1
Singapore	114·2	124·0	142·8	26·7	32·7	30·3
Malaysia	59·2	74·6	89·4	256·1	262·5	307·1
Taiwan	137·9	217·9	255·4	140·9	157·3	147·4
Thailand	213·3	219·1	300·8	130·6	130·8	153·2
Philippines	190·8	204·3	278·3	224·3	253·7	325·0

		Exports			Imports	
	1964	1965	1966	1964	1965	1966
Indonesia	121·1	204·7	118·6	128·3	148·8	175·5
India	189·4	203·6	166·8	179·6	139·0	205·9
Pakistan	80·5	103·9	99·5	31·1	26·5	30·5
Iran	46·8	58·4	71·9	202·4	246·9	362·2
UK	197·8	205·1	225·5	185·3	162·6	214·4
Netherlands	72·7	118·9	145·1	58·8	43·4	60·5
Germany (West)	149·0	215·0	246·6	249·5	222·8	236·9
Canada	166·2	214·4	255·8	378·7	356·8	451·3
USA	1,841·6	2,479·2	2,969·5	2,336·0	2,366·1	2,657·7
Australia	233·9	341·1	297·7	581·8	552·1	679·6
Korea (South)	108·8	180·3	335·2	41·7	41·3	71·7
South Africa	116·2	137·5	127·0	153·7	120·3	133·4
Liberia	193·8	371·4	322·9	21·6	17·3	17·0
China	152·7	245·0	315·2	157·7	224·7	306·2
USSR	181·8	168·4	214·0	226·7	240·2	300·4

Principal items in 1967, with value in US$1m. were:

Imports, c.i.f.		Exports, f.o.b.	
Wheat	307·6	Rubber	88·7
Sugar	122·1	Fish	243·4
Wool	364·8	Cotton fabrics	248·1
Raw cotton	442·8	Iron and steel products	1,272·4
Iron and steel scrap	311·7	Textile machines	106·3
Coal	400·8	Vessels	982·5
Crude oil and petroleum		Sewing machines	96·7
products	1,798·1	Chinaware	95·1

Total trade between Japan and UK for calendar years in £1,000 sterling (British Board of Trade returns):

	1966	1967	1968	1969	1970
Imports to UK	77,113	91,048	115,184	104,453	134,414
Exports from UK	65,041	82,779	94,922	124,678 }	147,841
Re-exports from UK	3,924	4,667	3,487	3,947	

SHIPPING. In Oct. 1967 the merchant fleet consisted of 7,000 vessels (over 100 gross tons) of 16,883,000 gross tons; there were 129 ships for passenger transport (76,000 gross tons), 3,251 cargo ships (6,453,000 gross tons) and 1,566 oil tankers (3,642,000 gross tons).

ROADS. The total length of roads (excluding urban and other local roads) was 148,561 km in 1965; the 'national' roads extend 28,048 km, of which 14,434 km were paved; prefectural roads covered 120,513 km (16,246 km paved). Motor vehicles, in 1966, numbered 7,746,500, including 2·83m. passenger cars and 4·8m. commercial vehicles.

RAILWAYS. The first railway was completed in 1872, between Tōkyō and Yokohama (29 km). Total length of railways, March. 1969, was 27,855 km, of which the national railways had 20,827 km (5,418 km electrified) and private railways, 7,128 km (5,875 km electrified). In 1966 the national railways carried 6,868m. passengers (private, 9,075m.) and 199m. tons of freight (private, 52m.).

AVIATION. The principal airlines are Japan Airlines and All Nippon Airways. Japan Airlines, founded in 1953, operate international services from Tōkyō to the United States, Europe, the Middle East and Southeast Asia, including flights to London over the North Pole and to Moscow by way of Siberia. In 1965 Japanese companies carried 5·17m. passengers in domestic services and 436,000 passengers in international services.

POST. The telephone services, operated by a public corporation, on 1 Jan. 1969 had 20·53m. instruments.

In Dec. 1966 wireless subscribers numbered 21·38m., television subscribers 19m. Sound broadcasting started in 1925, television in 1953, regular colour television in 1960.

BANKING. The modern banking system dates from 1872. The Nippon Ginko (Bank of Japan) was founded in 1882. The Bank of Japan has undertaken to finance the Government and the banks; its function is similar to that of a Central Bank in other countries. The Bank undertakes the actual management of Treasury funds and foreign exchange control.

The total gold and foreign currency holdings of the Government and the Bank of Japan in Nov. 1966 stood at US$2,044m.

The Yokohama Specie Bank (specializing in foreign exchange) became the Bank of Tōkyō in Aug. 1954. There were 87 banks with total assets of 31,325,000m. yen in Sept. 1966.

The post office savings bank is modelled upon the British; deposits amounted to 3,088,902m. yen at 20 Dec. 1966.

Fourteen foreign banks operate branches in Japan: Bank of Indo-China, Hongkong & Shanghai Banking Corporation, Chartered Bank of India, Australia and China, Bank of India, Mercantile Bank of India, Bank of Korea, Bank of China, Algemene Bank Nederland NV, National Handelsbank NV, Bank of America, National City Bank of New York, Chase Manhattan Bank, Bangkok Bank and American Express Co.

Schiffer, H. F., *The modern Japanese banking system.* New York, 1962

WEIGHTS AND MEASURES. The metric system was made obligatory by a law passed in March 1921, and the period of grace for its compulsory use ended on 1 April 1966.

DIPLOMATIC REPRESENTATIVES

Japan maintains embassies in:

Afghánistán	Germany (West)	Paraguay
Argentina	Ghana	Peru
Australia	Greece	Philippines
Austria	Hungary	Poland
Belgium	India	Portugal
Bolivia	Indonesia	Saudi Arabia
Brazil	Iran	Senegal
Burma	Iraq	Spain
Cambodia	Israel	Sudan
Canada	Italy	Sweden
Ceylon	Kuwait	Switzerland
Chile	Laos	Thailand
China (Taiwan)	Lebanon	Turkey
Colombia	Madagascar	USSR
Congo	Malaysia	UAR
Cuba	Mexico	UK
Czechoslovakia	Morocco	USA
Denmark	Nepál	Uruguay
Dominican Republic	Netherlands	Vatican
Ecuador	New Zealand	Venezuela
Ethiopia	Nigeria	Vietnam (South)
Finland	Norway	Yugoslavia
France	Pakistan	

Japan maintains legations in:

Bulgaria	Honduras	Luxembourg
Costa Rica	Iceland	Nicaragua
El Salvador	Irish Republic	Panama
Guatemala	Jordan	Romania
Haiti	Libya	Tunisia

OF JAPAN IN GREAT BRITAIN (44–46 Grosvenor St., W1)

Ambassador: Morio Yukawa (accredited 11 July 1968).
Minister: Tsutomu Wada
Counsellor: Toshihiko Nishiwaki (*Commercial*); Hidezo Hara (*Financial*).
First Secretaries: Kenichi Yanagi (*Political*); Akira Matsuura (*Agriculture*);
Firoshi Sawano (*Finance*); Naomichi Tsukahara (*Finance*); Yoshio Hatano;
Hideaki Sagara (*Transport*); Masanao Akai; Yoshio Ide (*Scientific*); Kaji Saka
(*Political*); Tadashi Mano (*Transport*); Hiroshi Kawasaki (*Commercial*);
Toshihiko Kubota (*Consul*); Taizo Watanabe (*Press and Information*);
Toshiyuki Hiraga (*Labour*); Hidero Maki (*Agriculture*); Capt. Keizo Ohashi
(*Defence*); Tetsuya Endo (*Economic*); Takehiro Togo (*Political*).

OF GREAT BRITAIN IN JAPAN

Ambassador: Sir John Pilcher, KCMG.
Minister: D. R. Ashe, CMG.
Counsellors: H. A. H. Cortazzi (*Commercial*); J. R. Greenwood (*Information*);
R. A. H. Duke, OBE (*Cultural*); Dr C. R. S. Manders, CBE (*Scientific*); J. G.
Morley, CBE. *First Secretaries:* B. Hitch (*Head of Chancery*); J. S. Whitehead
(*Commercial*); B. Thorne; P. H. D. Wetton; A. F. R. Harvey (*Commercial*); R.
J. Newton (*Scientific*); H. T. Tompkins (*Consul*); R. P. Whitehead; D. Hardwick,
MBE; Dr V. C. Bickley, MBE (*Cultural*); E. P. Hotchen (*Atomic Energy*); W. L.
Ward. *Service Attachés:* Capt. J. B. Robotham, RN (*Naval and Air*), Col. P. H.
Hislop (*Defence and Army*).

There is a Consul-General at Osaka, Consuls at Tōkyō and Yokohama and
Honorary Consuls at Kitakyusha (Moji) and Nagoya.

OF JAPAN IN THE USA (2520 Massachusetts Ave. NW,
Washington, D.C. 20008)

Ambassador: Nobuhiko Ushiba
Ministers: Bunroku Yoshino; Haruo Nakajima. *Counsellors:* Hironori Ito;
Kiyoaki Kikuchi (*Economic*); Hideo Yoshizaki (*Commercial*); Keijiro Tanaka
(*Financial*); Mizno Kuroda (*Information*).
First Secretaries: Akitane Kiuchi; Shinichiro Asao; Terno Matsushita;
Kenjiro Sase; Sho Watanabe; Mikio Morikawa (*Labour*); Manabu Akatsu
(*Economic Planning*); Hiroshi Ohki (*Economic*); Tsutomu Hirabayashi (*Com-
mercial*); Hiroyo Sano (*Agriculture*); Toyoichiro Nakada (*Transport*); Kiichi
Wantanabe (*Financial*); Takashi Ishikawa (*Scientific*).
Defence Attachés: Col Kozaburo Kawazu; Capt. Fumiro Shimizu; Col.
Hiroshi Doi.

OF THE USA IN JAPAN

Ambassador: Armin H. Meyer.
Deputy Chief of Mission: David L. Osborn. *Heads of Sections:* Richard A.
Ericson, Jr (*Political*); Herman H. Barger (*Economic*); Richard Garnitz (*Com-
mercial*); Thomas H. Murfin (*Consular*); Robert E. Peck (*Administrative*).
Service Attachés: Capt. Lawrence A. Kurtz (*Defence and Navy*), Lieut.-Col.
Andrew J. Roach (*Army*), Col. Richard G. Leech (*Air*).

There are Consuls-General at Tōkyō, Yokohama, Osaka and Kōbe and
Consuls at Fukuoka, Naha (Okinawa) and Sapporo.

BOOKS OF REFERENCE

Statistics Bureau of the Prime Minister's Office: *Statistical Year-Book* (from 1949).—*Statistical
Abstract* (from 1950).—*Statistical Handbook* (1967).—*Monthly Bulletin* (from April 1950)
Economic Planning Agency: *Economic Survey* (annual), *Economic Statistics* (monthly), *Economic
Indicators* (monthly)
Ministry of International Trade: *Foreign Trade of Japan* (annual)
Ministry of Foreign Affairs: *Statistical Survey of Economy of Japan, 1966*

Japan Times Year Book. (*I. Year Book of Japan. II. Who's Who in Japan. III. Business Directory of Japan.*) Tokyo, first issue 1933
Treaty of Peace with Japan. (Cmd. 8392.) HMSO, 1951; (Cmd. 8601.) HMSO, 1952
Ackerman, E. A., *Japan's Natural Resources.* Univ. of Chicago Press, 1953
Allen, G. C., *Short Economic History of Modern Japan.* London, 1946.—*Japan's Economic Recovery.* R. Inst. of Int. Affairs, 1957.—*Japan's Economic Expansion.* OUP, 1965
Asahi Newsprinting Co. *This is Japan.* Tokyo, annual from 1954
Bisson, T. A., *Zaibatsu Dissolution in Japan.* CUP, 1954
Brown, D. M., *Nationalism in Japan.* Univ. of California Press, 1955
Colegrove, K., *The Constitutional Development of Japan.* Evanston, Ill., 1951
Dening, Sir E., *Japan.* London, 1960
Dore, R. P., *Land Reform in Japan.* R. Inst. of Int. Affairs, 1959
Gerr, Stanley, *A Gazetteer of Japanese Place-Names.* Cambridge, Mass., 1942
Japan Travel Bureau, *Japan, the Official Guide.* Tokyo, 1961
Jones, F. C., *Japan's New Order in East Asia, 1937–45.* OUP, 1954
Kenkyusha's *New Japanese–English [and English–Japanese] Dictionary.* 2 vols. New ed. Cambridge, Mass., and Berkeley, Cal., 1960
Kennedy, M. D., *A History of Japan.* London, 1963
McNelly, T., *Contemporary Government of Japan.* London, 1964
Miyazaki, S., *The Japanese Dictionary explained in English.* Tokyo, 1950
New Japan. Mainichi Newspapers, Tokyo, annual, from 1948
Nihon Keizai Shimbun, *Industrial Review of Japan.* Tokyo, annual, from 1956
Nippon: a charted survey of Japan. Tsuneta Yano Memorial Society. 12th ed. Tokyo, 1967
Quigley, H. S., and Turner, J. E., *The New Japan.* Univ. or Minnesota Press, 1956
Sansom, G. B., *The Western World and Japan.* New York, 1950.—*A History of Japan.* 3 vols. London, 1958–64
Schwind, M., *Das iapanische Inselreich.* 3 vols. Berlin, 1967 ff.
Simpson, C., *Picture of Japan.* Melbourne, 1958
Storry, G. R., *Japan.* OUP, 1965
Takekazu Ogura (ed.), *Agricultural Development in Modern Japan.* Tokyo, 1963
Trewartha, G. T., *Japan: A Physical, Cultural and Regional Geography.* Madison, Wisconsin, and London, 1945
Yabuki, K. (ed.), *Japan Bibliographic Annual.* 2 vols. Tokyo, annual

THE HASHEMITE KINGDOM OF JORDAN

Al Mamlaka al Urduniya al Hashemiyah

The official statistics given for the calendar year 1967 include estimates for the West Bank and East Jerusalem, at present under Israeli occupation, but the figures for 1968 and 1969 relate only to that part of Jordan under the direct control of the Jordanian Government.

CONSTITUTION AND GOVERNMENT. The Kingdom is a constitutional monarchy headed by His Majesty King Hussein, GCVO, eldest son of King Talal, who, being incapacitated by mental illness, was deposed by Parliament on 11 Aug. 1952. The King was born 14 Nov. 1935, and married Princess Dina Abdul Hamid on 19 April 1955 (divorced 1957) and Toni Avril Gardiner (Muna al Hussein) on 25 May 1961. Offspring: Princess Alia, born 13 Feb. 1956: Prince Abdulla, born 30 Jan. 1962: Prince Faisal, born 11 Oct. 1963: Princesses Zein and Aisha, born 23 April 1968. *Crown Prince* (appointed 1 April 1965): Prince Hassan, younger brother of the King.

By a treaty, signed in London on 22 March 1946, Great Britain recognized Transjordan as a sovereign independent state. A new Anglo-Transjordan treaty was signed in Amman on 15 March 1948. The treaty was to remain in force for 20 years, but by mutual consent was terminated on 13 March 1957.

The Arab Federation between the Kingdoms of Iraq and Jordan, which was concluded on 14 Feb. 1958, lapsed after the revolution in Iraq of 14 July 1958, and was officially terminated by royal decree on 1 Aug. 1958.

On 25 May 1946 the Amir Abdullah assumed the title of King, and when the treaty was ratified on 17 June 1946 the name of the territory was changed to that of 'The Hashemite Kingdom of Jordan'. The legislature consists of a lower house of 60 members elected by manhood suffrage (30 from East Jordan and 30 from West Jordan), and a senate of 30 members nominated by the King. Elections took place on 16 April 1967.

The constitution passed on 7 Nov. 1951 provides that the Cabinet is responsible to Parliament.

The cabinet, at April 1970, is composed as follows:

Prime Minister: Bahjat al Talhouni.
Deputy Prime Minister and Minister for Foreign Affairs: Abdul Munem al Rifai.
Deputy Prime Minister and Minister of Defence: Ahmad Touqan. *Qadi al Qudat and Minister of Wakfs, Islamic Affairs and Shrines:* Abdullah Ghosheh. *Minister of National Economy:* Dr Sami Judeh. *Minister of Finance:* Ya'coub Mu'ammar. *Minister of Reconstruction and Development and Transport:* Dr Subhi Amin Amr. *Minister of Culture, Information, Tourism and Antiquities:* Salah Abu Zeid. *Minister of Education:* Dhougan al Hindawi. *Minister of Agriculture:* Sami Ayoub. *Minister of the Interior (Municipal and Rural Affairs):* Musa Abul Ragheb. *Minister of Health:* Maj.-Gen. A. Salam al Majali. *Minister of Public Works:* Maj.-Gen. Raschid Areiqat. *Minister of Social Affairs and Labour:* Emile al Ghori. *Minister of Communications:* Bwhan Kamal. *Minister of Justice:* Dr Jamal Nasser.

National flag: Black, white, green (horizontal); a red triangle near the hoist, with a white 7-pointed star on it.

The official language of the country is Arabic.

AREA AND POPULATION. The part of Palestine remaining to the Arabs under the armistice with Israel 3 April 1949, with the exception of the Gaza strip, was in Dec. 1949 placed under Jordan rule and formally incorporated in Jordan on 24 April 1950; for the frontier lines *see* MAP in THE STATESMAN'S YEAR-BOOK, 1951. On 10 Aug. 1965 a treaty with Saudi Arabia provided for an exchange of about 6,000–7,000 sq. km in order to facilitate the development of the port of Aqaba.

Area, 97,740 sq. km (37,730 sq. miles): census population (18 Nov. 1961), 1,706,226; estimate, 1969, 2·2m. In 1961, 805,450 lived in West Jordan (5,650 sq. km) and 834,589 in East Jordan (84,535 sq. km), including some 550,000 refugees from Palestine but excluding some 53,000 nomads. About 63,000 Jordanians live abroad. Density of population per sq. km, 51 in East Jordan, 143 in West Jordan.

The country is divided into the Desert Area and 10 districts, viz., Ajlun, Amman, Balqa, Karak, Ma'an, Zarka, Jerusalem, Hebron and Jenin. The last 3 named districts are known collectively as the West Bank, which, since the hostilities of June 1967, has been occupied by Israel.

The largest towns, with estimated population, 1967: Amman, the capital, 330,220; Zerqa, 121,300; Jerusalem, 66,000; Irbid, 63,000; Nablus, 61,000; Hebron, 43,000; Jenin, 20,000.

In 1966 registered births numbered 94,299; deaths, 10,116; marriages, 15,870; divorces, 2,124.

EDUCATION (1968). Government schools, 935; private schools, 156; UNRWA schools, 112. Number of pupils, 287,396 (including 112,704 girls); number of teachers, 7,923. Budget provision for education in 1969 was JD.5,536,080. The University of Jordan, inaugurated on 15 Dec. 1962 had 2,207 students (including 537 girls) and 159 teachers.

Five teacher-training colleges had 545 male and 282 female students. Two agricultural schools had 17 teachers and 293 students; 5 industry schools had 71 teachers and 970 pupils. There was 1 school for the handicapped with 4 teachers and 28 students and 3 nursing, midwifery and childcare schools with 15 teachers and 227 students. One social service school had 4 teachers and 59 students.

CINEMAS (1968). Cinemas numbered 32 with a total attendance of 5m.

NEWSPAPERS (1968). There were 2 daily, 3 weekly and 1 monthly papers.

HEALTH (1968). There were 571 physicians, 78 dentists and 31 hospitals with 1,636 beds.

FINANCE. Currency. On 1 July 1950 Jordan began to issue its own currency, the Jordan *dinar*, divided into 1,000 *fils*. The Jordan dinar equals £1·15. Jordan is a member of the sterling area. The following banknotes and coins are in circulation: 50, 10, 5 dinars, 1 dinar, 500 fils (notes), 250, 100, 50, 25, 20 fils (cupro-nickel), 10, 5, 1 fils (bronze). Circulation on 31 Dec. 1967 was JD.53m.

Budget. The budget estimates for the calendar year 1970 provide for expenditure of JD.88m. and revenue of JD.84m.

DEFENCE. Army. The Army is organized in 2 infantry divisions, each consisting of up to 9 infantry brigades and 2 armoured brigades. In addition there is an independent infantry brigade group which includes 1 armoured car regiment. Total strength is about 53,000 men.

Navy. The Coastal Guard or Sea Force flotilla consists of 8 armed motor launches based at Aqaba.

Air Force. The Air Force has 2 operational squadrons of Hunter fighter-bombers, and has acquired from the USA a total of 36 F-104A Starfighters to equip 2 supersonic interceptor squadrons. Total strength is about 2,000 officers and men.

AGRICULTURE. The country east of the Hejaz Railway line is largely desert; north-western Jordan is potentially of agricultural value but entirely dependent on the rainfall. The resources are agricultural and pastoral products; hillsides are being terraced, fruit-trees planted, irrigation has started. In 1967 the area under wheat was estimated at 2,259,800 dunums, yielding 196,100 tons; under barley at 583,900 dunums, yielding 63,400 tons. 1,928 tractors were in use.

MINING. Phosphate rock production in 1967 was 1,082,338 tons. Potash is found in the Dead Sea, and a concession for exploiting it was granted to Arab Potash Co., Ltd. Oil prospecting in the southern area is being undertaken by the government in association with INA of Yugoslavia. No oil was produced in 1967.

TOURISM. In 1968, 375,432 foreigners visited Jordan, including 3,155 American and 13,139 British; they contributed an estimated JD.4·6m.

COMMERCE. Imports in 1968 were valued at JD.59,491,700 and exports and re-exports at JD.14,262,539. The main supplying countries were (in JD.1m.) the UK (7·15), USA (6·37), West Germany (5·99), Lebanon (4·33), Japan (2·89), Syria (2·87), Saudi Arabia (2·17).

Total trade with UK (in £1,000 sterling), according to British Board of Trade returns:

	1966	1967	1968	1969	1970
Imports to UK	439	130	70	202	217
Exports from UK	8,963	7,021	8,105	16,410	12,266
Re-exports from UK	82	208	164	62	

ROADS. Asphalt roads connect Amman with all the chief towns in the country. Unmetalled roads have been constructed, making motor traffic possible from Amman to most other areas. The road from Amman to Ma'an and Aqaba (394 km) has branches to Karak, Tafileh, Shobak and Wadi Musa (Petra). The town of Jerash is joined by a good road to Amman. The normal asphalted route from Amman to Deraa (in Syria) and thence to Damascus is through Jerash. The oasis of Azraq may be reached by motor car from Mafraq, Zarka or Amman. Total length of metalled roads, 2,116 km. Motor vehicles in 1967 included 10,651 private passenger cars and taxis, 4,380 goods vehicles and 968 buses.

RAILWAYS. The Hejaz Railway runs from Nassib to Ma'an and Naqb Ishtar. Communication between Aqaba and the railhead at Naqb Ishtar is by road only. In Dec. 1963 the governments of Saudi Arabia, Syria and Jordan awarded to a British consortium a contract to rebuild the line from Ma'an to Mecca and Medina and by Dec. 1969 bridges and earthworks on the whole line had been completed.

SHIPPING (1968). The port of Aqaba was touched by 275 vessels, handling 856,164 tons; 25 vessels, loading and unloading 39,207 tons, were British.

AVIATION (1967). The Royal Jordanian Airlines (ALIA) maintains services from Amman to Athens, Beirut, Cairo, Dhahran, Doha, Kuwait, Jidda, Nicosia, Benghazi, Rome, Paris and London. Alitalia, KLM, Middle East Airways, United Arab Airlines, Saudi Arabian, Iraqi, Kuwaiti and Cyprus Airways also operate in Jordan.

POST (1968). There were 24,931 (14,207 in Amman) telephones.

BANKING. The Central Bank of Jordan started operations on 1 Oct. 1964, taking over the sterling assets and the commitments of the Jordan Currency Board.

DIPLOMATIC REPRESENTATIVES

Jordan maintains embassies in:

Algeria	Iran	Pakistan	USSR
Chile	Iraq	Saudi Arabia	UAR
China (Taiwan)	Italy	Spain	UK
Denmark	Kuwait	Sudan	USA
France	Lebanon	Syria	Yugoslavia
Germany (West)	Libya	Tunisia	
India	Morocco	Turkey	

OF JORDAN IN GREAT BRITAIN (6 Upper Phillimore Gdns, W8)

Ambassador: Zaid Al Rifa'i (accredited 15 Dec. 1970).
Counsellor: Nabih N. Nimr. *Military, Naval and Air Attaché:* Brig. Rakan Inad Jazi. *First Secretary:* Musa Keilani.

OF GREAT BRITAIN IN JORDAN

Ambassador: John F. S. Phillips, CMG.
Counsellor: B. L. Strachan. *Service Attachés:* Col. R. N. Harrison, OBE (*Defence, Army and Navy*), Wing Cdr D. L. F. Thornton (*Air*). *First Secretaries:* C. D. Lush (*Consul and Head of Chancery*); J. A. Speares; A. W. B. Strachan (*Development*); A. V. E. Gray (*Commercial*); R. L. Morris, OBE (*Labour*, resides in Beirut); G. R. Sunderland (*Civil Air*, resides in Beirut).

OF JORDAN IN THE USA (2319 Wyoming Ave. NW, Washington, D.C., 2008)

Ambassador: Sherif Abdul Hamid Sharaf.
Counsellor: Dr Nasir Batayneh.

OF THE USA IN JORDAN

Ambassador: Harrison M. Symmes.
Deputy Chief of Mission: Harry I. Odell. *Heads of Sections:* Morris Draper (*Political*); Arthur C. Bauman (*Economic*); David E. Zweifel (*Consular*); T. J. Figura (*Administrative*); Arthur M. Handly (*AID*). *Service Attaché:* Col. Gerard E. Cosgrove.

BOOKS OF REFERENCE

The Department of Statistics, Ministry of National Economy, publishes a *Statistical Yearbook* (in Arabic and English), latest issue 1968, and a *Statistical Guide*, latest issue 1965.—*External Trade Statistics*, 1968.—*National Accounts and Input–Output Analysis, 1959–65*, 1967.

The Constitution of the Hashemite Kingdom of Jordan. Amman, 1952
The Jordanian Seven Year Plan. Development Board. Amman, 1966
Dearden, A., *Jordan.* London, 1958
Glubb, J. B., *The Story of the Arab Legion.* London, 1948—*A Soldier with the Arabs.* London, 1957
Kirkbride, A. S., *A Crackle of Thorns.* London, 1956
Morris, J., *The Hashemite Kings.* London, 1959
Seton, C. R. W., *Legislation of Transjordan, 1918–30.* London, 1931. [Continued by the Government of Jordan as an annual publication: *Jordan Legislation.* Amman, 1932 ff.]

KOREA

Han Kook

HISTORY. Korea was united in a single kingdom under the Silla dynasty from 668. China, which claimed a vague suzerainty over Korea, recognized Korea's independence in 1895. Korea concluded trade agreements with the USA, Great Britain, Germany (1883), Italy and Russia (1884). After the Russo-Japanese war of 1904–5 Korea was virtually a Japanese protectorate until it was formally annexed by Japan on 22 Aug. 1910, thus ending the rule of the Yi dynasty which had begun in 1392.

Following the collapse of Japan in 1945, American and Russian forces entered Korea to enforce the surrender of the Japanese troops there, dividing the country for mutual military convenience into two portions separated by the 38th parallel of latitude. Negotiations between the American and Russians regarding the future of Korea broke down in May 1946.

On 25 June 1950 the North Korean forces crossed the 38th parallel and invaded South Korea. The same day, the Security Council of the United Nations asked all member states to render assistance to the Republic of Korea. When the UN forces had reached the Manchurian border Chinese troops entered the war on the side of the North Koreans on 26 Nov. 1950 and penetrated deep into the south. By the beginning of April 1951, however, the UN forces had regained the 38th parallel.

On 23 June 1951 Y. A. Malik, President of the Security Council, suggested a cease-fire, and on 10 July representatives of Gen. Ridgway met representatives of the North Koreans and of the Chinese Volunteer Army. An agreement was signed on 27 July 1953.

For the contributions of member-nations of the United Nations to the war, *see* THE STATESMAN'S YEAR-BOOK, 1954, p. 1195, and 1956, p. 1180.

On 9 Aug. 1953 the USA and Korea signed a mutual defence pact and on 28 Nov. 1956 a treaty of friendship, commerce and navigation.

AREA AND POPULATION. After a transfer of some frontier districts by the United Nations command on 12 Aug. 1954 the area of South Korea is now 38,452 sq. miles (98,431 sq. km).

The census population was 31·46m. on 1 Oct. 1970. The population of the largest cities was as follows: Seoul, the capital, 5,509,993, and Pusan, 1,878,785.

South Korea includes 9 provinces and the cities of Seoul and Pusan, which have provincial status.

GOVERNMENT. The first general election was held, under United Nations observation, on 10 May 1948. The National Assembly adopted a constitution on 17 July, elected Dr Syngman Rhee President of the Republic on 20 July and proclaimed the Republic of Korea on 15 Aug., when US military government ended.

President Syngman Rhee was re-elected on 5 Aug. 1952, 15 May 1956 and 15 March 1960, but was forced to resign and leave the country at the end of April 1960. The National Assembly on 15 June 1960 amended the constitution, changing the presidential-government system to a cabinet system, with the president as the symbolic head of state. A joint session of both Houses of Parliament on 12 Aug. 1960 elected the Democratic leader, Posun Yun, president.

The elections held on 29 July 1960 gave the Democratic Party 31 out of 58 seats in the House of Councillors and 181 out of 233 seats in the National Assembly.

The democratically elected government of Dr Myum Chang was overthrown by a military revolution on 16 May 1961. The National Assembly was dissolved and political parties were banned. The rule of the 'Supreme Council for National Reconstruction' under Gen. Chung Hee Park ended on 15 Oct. 1963 with his election as President of the Republic.

A new constitution was approved by a referendum on 17 Dec. 1962. On 14 Sept. 1969, the National Assembly passed a constitutional amendment bill, and the revision of the constitution was approved by a referendum on 17 Oct. 1970. The principle contents of the constitutional revision bill were that the number of members of the National Assembly shall be determined by law and shall not be more than 250 persons and the President may be elected for a maximum of 3 consecutive terms. The elections held on 26 Nov. 1963 and on 8 June 1967 gave Gen. Park's Democratic Republic Party a large majority.

President of the Republic: Chung Hee Park (re-elected 3 May 1967).
Premier: Paik Too Chin. *Foreign Minister:* Kyu Ha Choi.

RELIGION. Basically the religions of Korea have been Animism, Buddhism (introduced A.D. 372) and Confucianism, which was the official faith from 1392 to 1910. Catholic converts from China introduced Christianity in the 18th century, but the ban on Roman Catholics was not lifted until 1882. Estimated Christian population in 1967 was 2·88m. (one-third Presbyterians, one-sixth each Roman Catholics and Methodists).

EDUCATION. In 1968 Korea had 5,548,577 pupils enrolled in 5,418 elementary schools, 1,013,494 pupils in 1,420 middle schools and 470,000 pupils in 840 high schools (including 425 vocational schools).

For higher education there were, in 1968, 13 national universities, 14 private universities, 58 colleges and 22 junior colleges; 703 technical schools had 123,659 students.

The Korean language belongs to the Ural–Altaic group, is polysyllabic, agglutinative and highly developed syntactically. The modern Korean alphabet of 10 vowels and 14 consonants forms a script known as Hangul.

NEWSPAPERS (1969). There were 44 daily papers, including 8 national dailies and 2 English papers appearing in Seoul.

HEALTH. Korea had, at the end of 1967, 12,269 physicians, 1,843 dentists and 5,912 midwives. There are 5,281 hospitals.

FINANCE. Currency. On 14 June 1949 a presidential decree established a dual rate of exchange for the *won*, one of 450 *won* = US$1 for government transactions and another of 900 *won* = $1 for all other transactions. Severe inflation followed until on 17 Feb. 1953 President Rhee abolished the *won*, substituting a new unit, the *hwan*, equal to 100 *won*. The *hwan* depreciated from 60 in Feb. 1953 to 1,300 to US$1 in April 1961. On 10 June 1962 the *hwan* was revalued at the rate of 10 *hwan* = 1 *won*. The exchange rate is determined daily by the Foreign Exchange Bank of Korea; it is about 311·6 *won* = US$1.

Total money supply, in Dec. 1969, was 217,900m. *won*, of which 106,000m. was in deposits and 111,000m. in circulation.

Budget. The 1971 budget envisaged expenditure of 523,200m. *won* and revenue at 510,700m. *won*, of which 27% was for defence.

DEFENCE. Army. The army, in 1969 had 550,000 men in 19 divisions, including 10 armoured battalions equipped with M-47 and M-48 tanks, 80 artillery battalions. Two infantry divisions and engineer units (50,000 men) are serving in South Vietnam.

Navy. The navy comprises 3 destroyers, 3 destroyer escorts, 4 frigates, 6 fast transports (*ex*-destroyer escorts), 11 escort vessels, 6 patrol vessels, 11 coastal minesweepers, 20 landing ships, 1 repair ship, 5 supply ships, 4 oilers and 2 tugs. Personnel in 1970: 16,600 officers and men.

Air Force. The air force has a total strength of 23,000 men and about 200 combat aircraft in 10 first-line squadrons. These include 18 F-4D Phantoms, 55 F-5 tactical fighters, 20 F-86D all-weather interceptors, 100 F-86F fighter-bombers, 10 RF-86F reconnaissance aircraft. There are also Commando and Skymaster transports, a few Chickasaw and Iroquois helicopters and T-28 and T-33 trainers.

PLANNING. The 5-year plan 1962–66 aimed at achieving a self-sufficient agricultural economy on which two-thirds of the population is dependent; manufactured goods of the light industries showed a particularly significant increase. The actual annual growth rate was 8·5%.

The second 5-year plan (1967–71) envisages an annual growth rate of 11·7%; emphasis is placed on industrial development, such as petro-chemical plants, iron and steel plants, machinery manufacturing plants and more oil refineries.

AGRICULTURE. The arable land in South Korea comprises 22·4m. acres, of which nearly 5m. acres are cultivated.

The chief crops are rice (1969: 4·09m. metric tons), barley, wheat, beans, grain of all kinds and tobacco.

Output of tobacco manufactures, a government monopoly, was 113,700 metric tons in 1967.

Raising of livestock, once a flourishing industry, has barely survived as a by-product of agriculture. But the Government and the UN are aiding its revival. In 1967 cattle numbered 1·24m.; hogs, 1·3m.; poultry, 17·3m.

FISHERIES. The catch in 1969 was 862,800 metric tons. Whale fishing is carried on off the coast.

MINING. Korea, in 1961, had 448 mining companies and in 1969 employed 113,000 people. Mineral deposits are mostly small, with the exception of tungsten; the Sangdong mine is one of the world's largest deposits of tungsten. Korea's output, 1969, included (in 1,000 metric tons): Anthracite coal, 9,039; iron ore, 734; tungsten concentrate, 733,847 short tons; kaolin, 52; limestone, 7,530; copper ore, 15·6; lead ore, 24; zinc concentrate, 40; gold refined, 1,445 kg; silver refined, 19,584 kg.

INDUSTRY. Manufacturing industry, which (Dec. 1969) employed 1·22m. persons, is concentrated primarily in the production of light consumer goods for domestic consumption and export.

Output of principal products in 1969 (in metric tons): Cotton yarn, 64,712; raw silk, 2,074·5; worsted yarn, 5,136; cotton cloth, 186·1m. sq. ft; rayon and nylon cloth, 131m. sq. ft; woollen cloth, 11·4m. sq. ft; newsprint, 84,195; plastic products, 57,889; paint, 12,946; fertilizers, 664,400; cement, 4·83m.

POWER. Consumption of electric power, 1966, was 3,885·8m. kwh.; generating capacity was 4,913·1m. kwh.

COMMERCE. In 1969 the total exports were equal to US$622·5m. (1968: 455·4m.), while imports (including 'aid goods') were US$1,836·6m. (1968: 1,462·9m.).

Total trade between Korea and UK (in £1,000 sterling, British Board of Trade returns):

	1966	1967	1968	1969	1970
Imports to UK	1,705	2,645	2,656	4,099	6,239
Exports from UK	971	2,325	6,169	12,042 }	11,393
Re-exports from UK	4	16	13	109 }	

SHIPPING. In 1969 there were registered 2,285 vessels of 837,300 tons.

RAILWAYS. In 1969, 5,379 km of railways were in operation.

ROADS. In 1969 there were 634 949 km of roads. Motor vehicles totalled 106,994, including 40,134 trucks, 14,237 buses, 50,299 passenger cars.

POST. Post offices total 1,822; telephones (all government-owned) were 489,912 in 1969. Korea introduced television in May 1956. Wireless licences numbered 3,922,800 in Dec. 1969.

BANKING. State-run banks include the Bank of Korea, the Korean Construction Bank, the Medium Industry Bank, the Citizen's National Bank, the Foreign Exchange Bank, the National Agricultural Co-operatives Federation, Federation of Fisheries Co-operatives serve as banking and credit institutions for farmers and fishermen, Trust Bank of Korea, the Korea Housing Bank, Korea Development Finance Corporation.

There are 6 commercial banks: the Bank of Seoul Ltd, the Cho Heung Bank Ltd, the Commercial Bank of Korea, the First City Bank of Korea, the Hamil Bank Ltd, the Talgu Bank Ltd. The Bank of Korea is the central bank and the only note-issuing bank, the authorized purchaser of domestically produced gold. All foreign exchange is held by the Foreign Exchange Bank. At the end of 1969 the bank had issued a total of 129,900m. won and held US$549·5m.

DIPLOMATIC REPRESENTATIVES

Korea maintains embassies in:

Argentina (also for Bolivia and Paraguay)
Australia (also for New Zealand)
Austria
Belgium
Brazil (also for Colombia, Ecuador, Peru, Venezuela)
Canada
Chile
China
Ethiopia
France (also for Cameroun, Gabon, Congo (K.), Luxembourg, Malagache, Netherlands, Portugal, Senegal, Spain)
Germany (West)
Iran
Italy (also for Greece)
Ivory Coast (also for Dahomey, Liberia, Niger, Sierra Leone, Togo, Upper Volta)

Japan
Kenya
Malaysia
Mexico (also for Costa Rica, Dominica, El Salvador, Guatemala, Honduras, Jamaica, Nicaragua, Panama)
Morocco
Philippines
Sweden (also for Denmark, Iceland and Norway)
Switzerland (also for Vatican)
Thailand
Tunisia
Turkey (also for Jordan and Saudi Arabia)
Uganda
UK (also for Gambia and Malta)
USA
Uruguay
Vietnam (South)

OF KOREA IN GREAT BRITAIN (36 Cadogan Sq., SWI)

Ambassador: Ei Whan Pai (accredited 12 Dec. 1967).
Ministers: Keun Park, Keun Sup Chang. *Military, Naval and Air Attaché:* Col. Sang Sup Rim. *Counsellor:* Jae Won Rae (*Commercial*).

OF GREAT BRITAIN IN KOREA

Ambassador and Consul-General: N. C. C. Trench, CMG.
First Secretary: D. G. Reid (*Commercial*). *Service Attachés:* Brig. A. B. Taggart, MC (*Defence and Army*), Capt. A. J. Abraham, RN (resides at Tōkyō).

OF KOREA IN THE USA (2320 Massachusetts Ave. NW,
Washington, D.C., 20008)

Ambassador: Dong Jo Kim.

Ministers: Sang Jin Chyun, Sang Ho Lee, Ha Koo Yeon, Yoon Ho Kim.
Counsellors: Chan Yoon, Doug Whie Kim, Kwang Soo Choi, Hong Tae Choi,
Sung Kwoo Kim. *Service Attachés:* Maj.-Gen. Pil Sang Kim (*Army*), Cdre
Chang Kuk Park (*Navy*), Col. Chong In Ma (*Air*).

OF THE USA IN KOREA

Ambassador: William J. Porter.

Deputy Chief of Mission: L. Wade Lathram. *Heads of Sections:* Thomas M.
Judd (*Political*); Nicholas S. Lakos (*Economic*); Robert P. Gallagher (*Commercial*); Alice W. Clements (*Consular*); Powhatan W. Baber (*Administrative*);
Howard E. Houston (*AID*).

Service Attachés: Col. Donald E. Cowan (*Army*), Lieut.-Col. John E. Clewes
(*Navy*), Lieut.-Col. Gordon F. Ware (*Air*).

BOOKS OF REFERENCE

Korea: An annotated bibliography. 3 vols. Washington, Library of Congress, 1950
Hand Book of Korea. New York, 1958
Korea: Its Land, People and Culture of All Ages. Seoul, 1960
UNESCO Korean Survey. Seoul, 1960
Guide to Geographical Names in Korea (Chosen). United States Board of Geographical Names.
Major Economic Indicators, 1958–69. Seoul, 1970
    Washington, 1945
Kyung Cho Chung, *Korea Tomorrow.* New York, 1956
Lew, H. J., *New Life Korean–English, English–Korean Dictionary.* 2 vols. Seoul, 1947–50
Marcus, R. (ed.), *Korean Studies Guide.* Univ. of California Press, 1954
Martin, S. F. (ed.), *A Korean–English Dictionary.* Yale Univ. Press, 1968
Osgood, C., *The Koreans and their Culture.* New York, 1951
Thomas, R. C. W., *The War in Korea, 1950–53.* Aldershot, 1954

NORTH KOREA

Chosun Minchu-chui Inmin Konghwa-guk

HISTORY. In northern Korea the Russians, arriving on 8 Aug. 1945, one
month ahead of the Americans, who landed 8 Sept., established a Communist-led
'Provisional Government'. The newly created Korean Communist Party
merged in 1946 with the New National Party into the Korean Workers' Party.
In July 1946 the KWP, with the remaining pro-Communist groups and non-party
people, formed the United Democratic Patriotic Front. On 25 Aug. 1948 the
Communists organized elections for a Supreme People's Assembly, both in
Soviet-occupied North Korea (212 deputies) and in US-occupied South Korea
(360 deputies, of whom a certain number went to the North and took their seats).
The USSR established diplomatic relations in 1948 and withdrew its armed
forces.

AREA AND POPULATION. The area of North Korea is 47,225 sq. miles
(122,370 sq. km). Population in 1970, 13·9m. Rate of population increase, 2·2%
per annum. The capital is Pyongyang, with 1·5m. inhabitants.

The country is divided into 11 administrative units: two cities (Pyongyang and
Kaesong) and 9 provinces (capitals in brackets): South Pyongan (Wonsan),
North Pyongan (Sinuiji), Jagang (Kanggye), South Hwanghai (Haijoo), North
Hwanghai (Sariwon), Kangwon (Choonchun), South Hamkyung (Hamheung),
North Hamkyung (Chungjin), Ryanggang (Hyesan). The leading ports are
Chungjin (200,000 inhabitants) and Heungnam, near Hamheung (150,000).

CONSTITUTION AND GOVERNMENT. The political structure is based upon the Constitution of 1948 as amended in 1954 and 1955, which provides for a Supreme People's Assembly elected by universal suffrage. Elections were held in 1948, 1957 and 1962.

In practice the country is ruled by the Korean Workers' (*i.e.*, Communist) Party which elects a Central Committee which in turn appoints a Politburo. In March 1971 this was composed of: Marshal Kim Il-Sung, *General Secretary of the Party, Prime Minister* since 1948, *Supreme Commander of the Armed Forces*; Vice-Marshal Choi Yong Kun, *Chairman of the Presidium of the Supreme People's Assembly* (*i.e.*, titular Head of State); Kim Il, *Deputy Prime Minister*; Pak Sung Chul, *Deputy Prime Minister*; Gen. Choe Hyon, *Minister of National Defence*; Kim Yong Ju; O Jin Yu; Kim Dong Gyu; So Chol; Kim Jung Rin; Han Ik Su. There are also 4 'alternate members'.

Ministers not in the Politburo include Ho Dam (*Foreign Minister*); Kye Ung Tae (*Foreign Trade*); Choe Yun Su (*Finance*); Kim Su Duk (*Education*); and Chong Jun Taek (*Deputy Prime Minister*).

LOCAL GOVERNMENT is administered by People's Assemblies at city, province and *ri* (town, workers' or rural commune) level. The latest elections were in March 1970.

In 1965 the Party had 1·61m. members.

There is also the Religious Chongu Party and various organizations combined in a Fatherland Front.

EDUCATION. In April 1967 a new 9-year system of free compulsory technical education was introduced (4 years primary education starting at the age of 8, followed by 5 years secondary). It is intended to extend the course eventually to 11 years by providing 128 new advanced technical colleges catering for 227,000 students.

In 1970–71, 9,260 schools of all grades were attended by 3·2m. pupils, including 214,000 students in 569 institutes of higher education, two-thirds of whom were studying technical and engineering subjects. Kindergartens and crèches looked after 1·32m. infants.

There are 3 universities—Kim Il Sung University, Kim Chaek Technical University, Pyongyang Medical School—and an Academy of Sciences (founded 1952).

In 1970 Kim Il Sung University had some 10,000 students.

NEWSPAPERS. The Government-Party newspaper is *Nodong* (or *Rodong*) *Sinmun* (Labour News).

JUSTICE. The judiciary consists of the Supreme Court, whose judges are elected by the Assembly for 3 years; provincial courts; and city or county people's courts. The prosecutor-general, appointed by the Assembly, has supervisory powers over the judiciary and the administration; the Supreme Court controls the judicial administration.

FINANCE. Currency. The monetary unit is the *won*, divided into 100 *jun*. Official rate of exchange: US$1 = 1·2 *won*. This 'new' *won* was adopted in Feb. 1959.

Budget (in 1m. *won*) for calendar years:

	1964	1965[1]	1966	1967	1968	1969	1970[1]
Revenue	3,435	3,700	3,670	3,960	5,215	..	..
Expenditure	3,435	3,700	3,570	3,960	..	5,200	6,200

[1] Estimates.

31% of 1969 expenditure was on defence. Average monthly income was 70 *won* in 1970.

DEFENCE. Military service is compulsory at the age of 17 and lasts 3–4 years.

Army. In 1968 the army was believed to number about 345,000 men, organized in 1 armoured and 18 infantry divisions, with 800 Soviet tanks; it has about 300 Guideline surface-to-air missiles.

Navy. The navy comprises 2 *ex*-Soviet submarines, 2 coastal escorts, 10 fleet minesweepers, 11 motor gunboats, 20 submarine chasers, 42 torpedo boats, 24 minesweeping boats, 30 auxiliaries and 100 armed junks. Personnel in 1970: 9,000 officers and men.

Air Force. With Chinese and Soviet assistance, the air force has been increased to a total of approximately 525 combat aircraft and 35,000 personnel. Equipment is believed to include about 90 supersonic MiG-21 interceptors, 20 MiG-19s, 350 MiG-17s, 60 Il-28 twin-jet light bombers, and a variety of transport and training aircraft and helicopters.

PLANNING. Past plans: 3-year plan, 1954–56, rehabilitated the country after the Korean War (1950–53); 5-year plan, 1957–61; 7-year plan, originally intended for 1961–67, but extended in 1966 to 1970. It was officially acknowledged that this plan was retarded by the burden of military expenditure.

The present, 6-year, plan runs from 1971 to 1976. It aims at a steady introduction of technical innovations and the expansion of consumer industries by local, small-scale plant. Priority is given to the power, mining, metallurgical and chemical industries. An electronics industry is being developed. Industrial output is expected to grow by 14% per annum. Plan targets for 1976: Electricity, 30,000m. kwh.; (in metric tons) coal, 50m.; pig-iron, 3·5m.; steel, 3·8m.; rolled steel, 3m.; chemical fertilizers, 2·8m., and total grain, 7m. (3·5m. rice).

AGRICULTURE. 20% of the land is cultivable; the rest is mountains and forests. Intensive water and soil conservancy is practised. In 1946 all Japanese-owned and landowners' property above 5 *jungbo* (1 *jungbo* = 1 hectare = 2·5 acres) was distributed among some 724,500 landless peasants and smallholders.

Full-scale collectivization was begun in 1954 and completed in 1958, when there were 13,309 'co-operatives' averaging 130 *jungbo*. In 1958 these were merged into 3,843 larger units (*ri*), averaging 500 *jungbo*, modelled on the Chinese communes. Co-operatives farm 90% of the cultivated land. Livestock farming is mainly carried on by large state farms

Some 3m. *jungbo* are under cultivation, of which 1m. *jungbo* have regular irrigation. There are 8,000 km of irrigation canals. The 6-year plan (1971–76) aims to extend irrigation so as to make possible 2 rice harvests a year. There were, in 1968, 55,000 tractors (in 15-h.p. units) and 49,000 trailing farm machinery. The technical revolution in agriculture (nearly 95% of ploughing, etc., is mechanized) considerably increased the yield of grain (sown on 2·3m. *jungbo* of land); this amounted to some 7·5m. tons in 1968 (mainly rice).

Livestock, 1964: 699,000 cattle, 1·5m. pigs, 161,000 sheep. 700m. eggs are produced a year.

FORESTRY. From 1966 to 1970 a 5-year plan was implemented to preserve existing forests and plant new ones.

FISHERY. The catch was 745,400 tons in 1965. There are about 3,000 modern motor and sailing fishing craft. In 1967 a development plan was started to equip the deep-sea fleet with factory and refrigerator ships, and to provide more cold storage at fishing ports.

MINING. North Korea is rich in minerals (coal, iron, lead, zinc, copper, tungsten, nickel, manganese and graphite) and has important metallurgical works. Oilwells went into production in 1957. Coalmines are being enlarged and modernized. There are large open-cast workings at Yonghung. 27·5m. metric tons of coal were mined in 1970 and 6m. metric tons of iron ore extracted in 1966.

INDUSTRY. Industries were intensively developed by the Japanese, notably cotton spinning, hydro-electric power, cotton, silk and rayon weaving, and chemical fertilizers. Production (in metric tons) in 1970: Chemical fertilizers, 1·5m.; cement, 4m.; steel, 2·2m.; textiles, 400m. sq. metres.

POWER. In 1966 a thermal power station was completed at Unbong with a capacity of 400 megawatts. Others are under construction at Pyongyang (500 megawatts) and Pukchang (600 megawatts). Output in 1970 was 12,600m. kwh. Hydro-electric potential exceeds 8m. kw.

COMMERCE. Foreign trade is almost exclusively with communist countries. A trade and aid agreement for 1967–70 with the USSR promoted a large expansion of trade. A trade agreement with China was signed in March 1970. Total trade with non-communist countries, mainly with Japan, amounted to US$90m. in 1969. The chief exports are metal ores and products.

Exports to the USSR in 1969 (and 1968) were worth 113·9m. (108·8m.) roubles; imports from the USSR, 181·4m. (155m.) roubles.

Total trade between North Korea and UK (British Board of Trade returns, in £1,000 sterling):

	1965	1966	1967	1968	1969	1970
Imports to UK	27	194	527	687	442	602
Exports from UK	39	17	28	154	302	157

RAILWAYS. Extensive railway construction was carried out under the Japanese occupation. Because these lines served strategic purposes, however, and because of the separation of North and South Korea, not all of them were suitable for inclusion in the present railway network. The two trunk-lines Pyongyang–Sinuiji and Pyongyang–Myongchon are both electrified. The 'Wonra' line runs from Wonsan to Rajin and has an electrified intermediate section from Myongchon to Chongjin. Lines are under construction from Sepo to Inchon and from Kanggye *via* Hyesan to Musan. The Hyesan–Samsok section opened to traffic in 1971. In 1966 there were some 10,000 km of track, about 30% electrified. A further 850 km were electrified during the 7-year plan (terminated 1970). In 1969, 55% of trains were hauled by electricity and 30·6m. metric tons were transported.

ROADS. Motor transport is very important, as about one-third of the inhabited places are without railway communications. Roads are bad and mostly unpaved; statistics about their length, etc., are lacking. In 1961 lorries and coaches transported 17·7m. tons of freight.

SHIPPING. There are excellent and important seaports, predominantly on the east coast (Japan Sea). However, west coast ports (Yellow Sea) also play their role, and Nampo, the port of Pyongyang, has been dredged and expanded. Pyongyang is connected to Nampo by railway and river. The 7-year plan (extended to 10 years) raised the shipping tonnage to some 36,500 GRT.

The biggest navigable river is the Yalu, 698 km up to the Hyesan district.

AVIATION. There are weekly flights to Moscow and Peking. Domestic lines: Pyongyang–Hamheung–Chongjin.

RADIO. In 1961 there were 600,000 radio receivers. The Pyongyang Central Broadcasting Station was rebuilt about 1955.

DIPLOMATIC RELATIONS. North Korea maintains embassies in Albania, China, East Germany, Sweden, USSR and North Vietnam, and is in diplomatic relations with all other communist countries, Algeria, Ceylon, Guinea, Iraq, Mali, Mauritania and UAR.

BOOKS OF REFERENCE

Baik Bong, *Kim Il Sung: biography*. 3 vols. New York, 1969–70
Facts About Korea. Pyongyang, 1961
Outline of Korean Geography. Pyongyang, 1957
Koreya: Sever i Yug. Moscow, 1965
Kim Il Sung, *Selected Works*. 2 vols. Pyongyang, 1965
Koh, B. C., *The Foreign Policy of North Korea*. New York, 1969
Paige, G. D., *The Korean People's Democratic Republic*. Stanford, Cal., Hoover Institution, 1966
Rudolph, P., *North Korea's Political and Economic Structure*. New York, 1959
Scalapino, R. A. (ed.), *North Korea Today*. New York, 1963

KUWAIT

Dowlat al Kuwait

HISTORY. The independent and sovereign of State Kuwait is situated on the north-western coast of the Arabian Gulf. The ruling dynasty was founded by Shaikh Sabah al-Owel, who ruled from 1756 to 1772. In 1899 the then ruler Shaikh Mubarak concluded a treaty with Great Britain wherein, in return for the assurance of British protection, he undertook not to alienate any of his territory without the agreement of Her Majesty's Government. In 1914 the British Government recognized Kuwait as an independent government under British protection. On 19 June 1961 an agreement reaffirmed the independence and sovereignty of Kuwait and recognized the government of Kuwait's responsibility for the conduct of internal and external affairs; the agreement of 1899 was terminated and Her Majesty's Government expressed their readiness to assist the government of Kuwait should they request such assistance.

Ruler: HH Shaikh Sabah as-Salim as-Sabah, the 12th Amir of Kuwait, succeeded on 24 Nov. 1965 on the death of his brother. *Crown Prince:* Shaikh Jabir al-Ahmad al-Jabir as-Sabah (appointed on 31 May 1966).

Flag (adopted on 1 Jan. 1962): A horizontal rectangle, whose length is twice its breadth. It is divided into green, white and red horizontal stripes of equal size, and contains a black trapezoid whose longer base is against the flagstaff and is equivalent in length to the breadth of the flag, whose shorter base is equivalent in length to the breadth of the white division and whose height is a quarter of the length of the flag.

AREA AND POPULATION. Area, about 9,375 sq. miles (24,280 sq. km); the total population at the census of 1969 was 733,000, of which 315,190 were non-Kuwaitis.

The country is divided into 3 governorates, Kuwait (the capital), Ahmadi and Hawali.

The Neutral Zone (3,560 sq. miles, 5,700 sq. km), jointly owned and administered by Kuwait and Saudi Arabia from 1922 to 1966, was partitioned between the two countries in May 1966, but the exploitation of the oil and other natural resources will continue to be shared.

CONSTITUTION AND GOVERNMENT. Elections for a National Assembly of 50 members were held on 23 Jan. 1971. Ten seats were won by the Arab Nationalist Movement.

The official language is Arabic; English is used as the second language.

Prime Minister: Shaikh Jabir al-Ahmad as-Sabah (appointed 30 Nov. 1965). *Foreign Affairs:* Shaikh Sabah al-Ahmad as-Sabah. *Finance and Oil:* Abdul Rahman al-Atiqi.

EDUCATION. In 1968–69 there were 120,550 pupils in government schools and 20,401 pupils in private schools. The University of Kuwait had 1,320 students in 1968.

HEALTH. Medical services are free to all residents. There are altogether 12 hospitals with over 3,381 beds in the State, including 3 tuberculosis sanatoria, 2 mental hospitals and over 150 clinics. The Ministry of Health employs 575 physicians and 63 dentists.

FINANCE. Currency. The Kuwait *dinar* of 1,000 fils replaced the Indian external rupee on 1 April 1961; KD 1 = £1·17. Coins in circulation are 1, 5, 10, 20, 50 and 100 fils. The amount of currency in circulation in 1967 was KD 62m.

Budget. The financial year runs 1 April–31 March. In 1970–71 revenue, KD 319·4m.; expenditure, 319·4m.; in 1969–70 revenue, KD 302·5m.; expenditure, KD 234·5m. In 1966–67 oil accounted for KD 232·6m. of the revenue (1965–66: 217·6m.); KD 217·2m. (1965–66: 204·1m.) derived from the Kuwait Oil Company.

The Kuwait Fund for Arab Economic Development, founded in 1961 with a capital of KD 50m., was increased to KD 200m. on 25 June 1966. By the middle of 1967, Algeria, Jordan, Lebanon, Morocco, Sudan, Tunisia and UAR had been granted loans, totalling over KD 170m. In Aug. 1967 Kuwait contributed nearly half of the KD 140m. aid extended by Kuwait, Libya and Saudi Arabia to Jordan, Syria and the UAR.

DEFENCE. Kuwait maintains a small, well-equipped and mobile army.

The first operational air-force unit consisted of 4 Hunter ground-attack fighters and 2 Hunter 2-seat fighter-trainers. It has been followed by a squadron of 12 British-built Lightning F.53 supersonic fighters and 2 Lightning T.55 2-seat trainers. Other equipment includes 2 Caribou twin-engined STOL transports, 6 BAC 167 Strikemaster armed jet trainers, 6 armed Jet Provost trainers, 6 Agusta-Bell 204B and 4 Agusta-Bell JetRanger helicopters.

INDUSTRY. Oil. Kuwait oil comes mainly from the Burgan oilfields, the residential and administrative centre for oil operations being at Ahmadi. Oil reserves in Kuwait and its share of the neutral zone were estimated at 10,400m. tons in Dec. 1968. The field is developed by the Kuwait Oil Co., a joint British–American company. Production of crude oil began in 1946; in 1967 it totalled 912·1m. bbls, and in 1968, 956·6m. bbls. Pipelines connect the oilfields to the port of Mina al Ahmadi, near the village of Fahahil, which has 2 deep-water piers capable of handling up to 5 super-tankers simultaneously. The refinery at Mina al Ahmadi has been expanded to process 190,000 bbls of crude oil per stream day but over 80% of the production from the fields is exported as crude oil. Revenue from oil operations is being utilized for large-scale developments works, including power stations, schools, medical facilities and the supply of fresh water to Kuwait town. On 3 Dec. 1951 an agreement was concluded which gave the Government an equal share of the company's profits.

In 1968 there were 249 industrial establishments (excluding oil) employing 9,042 people with a total capital investment of KD 78·76m.

In 1948 a concession was granted by the Amir to the American Independent Oil Company to exploit oil in the Kuwait Neutral Zone which Kuwait shares with Saudi Arabia. The Saudi Arabian portion is exploited by the Getty Oil Co. Oil was discovered in March 1953; exports of commercial quantities began at the end of the year. Total oil production of the American Independent Oil Company in 1968 was 15·3m. bbls in Kuwait and the Neutral Zone.

In May 1958 a Japanese company was granted offshore oil rights in the Neutral Zone, in return for 57% of the profits. Twelve wells were drilled in 1960 and drilling continues. The first commercial shipment of oil to Japan was made on 25 March 1961. Production in 1968 was 55·2m. bbls.

The Royal Dutch-Shell group was granted a concession to exploit oil in the offshore area of Kuwait itself in Nov. 1960. The concession agreement, in the name of the Kuwait Shell Petroleum Development Co. Ltd, was signed on 15 Jan. 1961.

On 3 May 1967 the Kuwait National Petroleum Co. and the Spanish state company Hispanoil were granted a 33-year concession covering 10,000 sq. km, on a 51–49% partnership basis.

COMMERCE. The port of Kuwait formerly served mainly as an entrepôt for goods for the interior, for the export of skins and wool, and for pearl fishing. Entropôt trade continues but, with the development of the oil industry, is declining in importance. Pearl fishing is now on a small scale. Dhows and launches of traditional construction are still built.

Trade in calendar years, in Kuwaiti dinars:

	1960	1964	1965	1966	1967	1968
Imports	86,393,732	115,079,762	134,698,006	165,287,735	..	21,832,257
Exports[1]	8,291,261	11,832,893	14,139,281	13,648,929	15,294,875	20,858,169

[1] Excluding oil.

In 1968 the main imports were (in 1m. Kuwaiti dinars): Machinery and transport equipment, 76·2; food, 35·2; manufactured goods, 83·4. The main suppliers were (in 1m. Kuwaiti dinars): USA, 37·3; UK, 27·9; Japan, 27·9; West Germany, 20·8.

The manufacture or import of alcoholic drinks is prohibited.

Total trade with UK, in £1,000 sterling (British Board of Trade returns):

	1966	1967	1968	1969	1970
Imports to UK[1]	92,663	73,570	151,436	171,982	165,397
Exports from UK	25,789	25,145	28,659	40,888 }	36,224
Re-exports from UK	219	166	482	630 }	

[1] Including oil.

COMMUNICATIONS. Ships of 27 lines make regular calls at Kuwait. BOAC, Kuwait Airways, Iraqi Airways, Iranian Airways, United Arab Airlines, Middle East Airlines, Saudi Arabian Airways, Lebanese International Airways, Air Liban, Air India, Lufthansa, Japanese Airlines, TWA, PIA, KLM and Gulf Aviation operate scheduled air services. Wireless communication was taken over by the Kuwait Government in 1956, internal postal services in Feb. 1958 and external postal services in 1959. There are about 15,000 telephones in Kuwait, 6,550 in Hawali and about 3,000 in Ahmadi. There are a broadcasting and a television station .

BANKING. Five banks operate in Kuwait: the British Bank of the Middle East, the Kuwait National Bank, the Commercial Bank of Kuwait Ltd, the Gulf Bank of Kuwait and the Ahlly Bank.

WEIGHTS AND MEASURES. The metric system was adopted in 1962.

DIPLOMATIC RELATIONS. Kuwait maintains diplomatic relations with:

Algeria	India	Netherlands	Taiwan
Belgium	Iran	Norway	Thailand
Bulgaria	Iraq	Pakistan	Tunisia
China	Italy	Poland	Turkey
Czechoslovakia	Japan	Romania	USSR
Denmark	Jordan	Saudi Arabia	UAR
France	Lebanon	Somalia	UK
Germany (West)	Libya	Spain	USA
Greece	Malaysia	Sudan	Venezuela
Guinea	Mali	Switzerland	Yugoslavia
Hungary	Morocco	Syria	

Ambassador to the UK: Ahmad Al-Nakib (accredited 25 March 1971). *Counsellor:* Mohammed Khalaf.

British Ambassador: A. J. Wilton, CMG, MC. *Counsellor:* A. C. Goodison; *First Secetaries:* C. T. McGurk (*Commercial*); H. Halliwell (*Consul*); S. Muir. *Chargé d'Affaires a.i in USA:* Nouri A. Shuaib. *USA Ambassador:* John Patrick Walsh.

Kuwait Economy 1968–69. Kuwait Government Press, 1970
Dickson, H. R. P., *Kuwait and her Neighbours.* London, 1956
Freeth, Z., *Kuwait Was My Home.* London, 1955
Shiber, S. G., *The Kuwait urbanization.* Kuwait Government Press, 1964
Kuwait today: a welfare state. Nairobi, 1963

LAOS

HISTORY. The Kingdom of Laos, once called Lanxang (the Land of a Million Elephants), was founded in the 14th century. With its capital at what was later called Luang Prabang, the kingdom has always depended on the maintenance of good relations with its more powerful neighbours Thailand, Burma and Vietnam. In 1563 the King moved the capital south to Vientiane, and in the beginning of the 18th century Lanxang broke into two separate kingdoms, centred on Luang Prabang and Vientiane and an independent principality called Champassac. In 1827 the 3 countries accepted Thai suzerainty.

In 1893 Laos became a French protectorate and in 1907 acquired its present frontiers. In 1945 French authority was suppressed by the Japanese. When the Japanese withdrew in 1945 an independence movement known as Lao Issara (Free Laos) set up a government under Prince Phetsarath, the Viceroy of Luang Prabang. This government collapsed with the return of the French in 1946 and the leaders of the movement fled to Thailand.

Under a new Constitution of 1947 Laos became a constitutional monarchy under the Luang Prabang dynasty, and in 1949 became an independent sovereign state within the French Union. Most of the Lao Issara leaders returned to Laos but a few remained in dissidence under Prince Souphannouvong, who allied himself with the Vietminh and subsequently formed the 'Pathet Lao' (Lao State) rebel movement.

In April 1953 the Vietminh, aided by the Pathet Lao, invaded Laos, threatening the royal capital of Luang Prabang. An agreement on the cessation of hostilities was, however, reached at the Geneva Conference in July 1954 which provided for the military and political integration of the Pathet Lao with the rest of Laos, the withdrawal from Laos of foreign forces, except for certain French instructors and garrisons, the concentration of the forces of the Pathet Lao in the provinces of Phong Saly and Sam Neua and the setting up of an International Commission for Supervision and Control in Laos (ICC) (its members provided by Canada, India (Chairman) and Poland) to supervise the carrying out of the agreement.

Lengthy negotiations between Prince Souvanna Phouma, the Prime Minister, and Prince Souphanouvong led to the formation on 19 Nov. 1957 of a Government of National Union in which Prince Souphanouvong and another Pathet Lao Minister were included. The success of the NLHS in the supplementary elections held in May 1958 (less than a third of the votes but more than half the seats) inspired the formation of the Committee for Defence of National Interests (CDIN). With CDIN support a new government was formed in Aug. 1958 with Phoui Sananikone as Prime Minister. This government included no NLHS members, but 4 CDIN members who were not members of the Assembly.

In the summer of 1959 the breakdown of the government of National Union, the failure to integrate the Pathet Lao forces and the arrest of NLHS leaders led to further Pathet Lao guerilla activity. Under pressure from the army, led by Gen. Phoumi Nosavan, Phoui Sananikone resigned office at the end of Dec. 1959. There followed a period of army rule under a caretaker government, until a right-wing government headed by Prince Somsanith was formed in June 1960.

On the night of 8–9 Aug. 1960 the Second Paratroop Battalion led by Capt. Kong Le took Vientiane. This *coup* led to the return to power of Prince Souvanna Phouma, committed to neutralism and conciliation with the Pathet Lao. A right-wing counter-attack led by Gen. Phoumi Nosavan in Dec. 1960, however, forced Prince Souvanna Phouma to flee the country, and a new government was set up by Prince Boun Oum of Champassak, the Southern rightist leader.

In April 1961 a joint appeal by the Soviet and British Governments (as cochairmen of the 1954 Geneva Conference) led to a cease fire, the return of the International Control Commission (adjourned *sine die* in 1958) to Laos and the convening at Geneva on 16 May 1961 of a 14 nations conference to secure the neutrality of Laos. After prolonged negotiations between the Three Princes (Souvanna Phouma, Boun Oum and Souphannouvong) a government of National Union was formed on 23 June 1962 under Prince Souvanna Phouma. On 23 July 1962 an agreement was signed by all 14 nations attending the Geneva Conference providing for the withdrawal of foreign troops and international guarantees of Laotian neutrality.

On 1 April 1963 Quinim Pholsena, the left-wing neutralist Foreign Minister, was assassinated. Hostilities broke out once more and the NLHS Ministers (including Prince Souphannouvong) left Vientiane. A right-wing *coup* took place on 19 April 1964, but after a short period of house arrest Prince Souvanna Phouma carried on as Prime Minister. The government was reshuffled, leaving the Pathet Lao ministers in their previous posts but nominating others to act for them temporarily. An abortive right-ring *coup* in Feb. 1965 resulted in the departure of Gen. Phoumi Nosavan, the right-wing Deputy Prime Minister, to Thailand.

Elections on a limited franchise, boycotted by the Pathet Lao, were held in July 1965. The results gave approximately equal numbers of seats to the neutralists under Prince Souvanna Phouma; a new party of young officials formed by Sisouk Na Champassak, the Minister of Finance; and the southern right-wing group led by Prince Boun Oum. The National Assembly passed a vote of confidence in Prince Souvanna Phouma and his government of National Union. However, in Sept. 1966, the National Assembly precipitated its own dissolution by rejecting the government's budget proposals.

On 21 Oct. 1966 aircraft from Savannakhet, in southern Laos, bombed military installations in Vientiane. The Savannakhet air base was later retaken, and the instigator of the action, Gen. Thao Ma, Commander-in-Chief of the Air Force, fled to Thailand. Meanwhile on 17 Oct. Gen. Kong Le left the headquarters of the Neutralist Army in Vang Vieng for Thailand. He has never returned to Laos and is now in France. In March 1967 he was replaced as Commander-in-Chief of the Neutralist Army by Col. Somphet.

Elections, on a full franchise, for the Laotian National Assembly were again held on 1 Jan. 1967. The NLHS again refused to participate, but about 80% of the registered electorate voted and an assembly which supported the government of Prince Souvanna Phouma was returned to power. In June 1967 the Prime Minister appointed 4 new Secretaries of State.

Since 1967 the North Vietnamese have steadily escalated their military activities in Laos. In Jan. 1968 they captured the Government enclave at Nam Bac in Northern Laos and in early 1968 they took the important military post of Na Khang in the north-east of Xieng Khouang Province; as a riposte the Government captured the town of Xieng Khouang from the Communists, but this did not prevent the North Vietnamese from overwhelming the Neutralists at Muong Soui in June. However, the NVA overextended themselves, for in Sept. 1969 the forces of Maj.-Gen. Vang Pao, Meo Commander of 2 Military Region in the north-east, unexpectedly stormed across the Plain of Jars, destroying large quantities of Communist military equipment and recovering a wide area that had not been under Government control for 5 years. The NVA recaptured the Plain of Jars and Muong Soui in Feb. 1970, and in March–April occupied and destroyed Vang Pao's guerrilla base at Sam Thong to the south-west of the Plain. In Oct. Vang Pao struck out into the high ground to the west of the Plain, and reoccupied Muong Soui on 9 Oct.

With the closure of the Cambodian port of Kompong Som (Sihanoukville) in March 1970 to Communist supply ships, NVA military pressure in southern Laos rapidly built up as the Communists sought to secure their supply lines through Laos into South Vietnam and Cambodia. The provincial capitals of Attopeu and Saravane fell to the Communists in April and June, and there was heavy fighting around Government positions on the eastern edge of the Bolovens Plateau.

In June Tiao Souk Vongsak, titular Secretary of State for Public Works and Transport and Prince Souphanouvong's special emissary, arrived in Vientiane from Sam Neua to discuss with the Prime Minister the modalities of a conference to be held between the two sides at Khang Khay to negotiate a peaceful settlement. By the end of the year, however, no agreement had been reached on the security arrangements for the talks. Meanwhile, in Dec. 1970 there were rumours of an abortive right-wing officers' plot in Savannakhet.

National flag: Red background in the centre of which is a 3-headed white elephant, standing on a pedestal with 5 steps, surmounted by a 7-tiered white parasol.

National anthem: Peng Sat Lao (Hymn of the Lao People).

GOVERNMENT. Laos is a constitutional monarchy. The national sovereignty rests wholly with the people. The King exercises this sovereignty in accordance with the Constitution which came into force on 11 May 1947. The Laotian throne is inherited by the Crown Prince, or by the male descendants of the reigning dynasty. The King exercises his powers through Ministers, nominated by himself, after they have received the confidence of the National Assembly. He appoints the Prime Minister, who then forms his government which he must submit for the approval of the National Assembly. The National Assembly is composed of members elected by universal suffrage every 5 years.

The National Assembly passes all laws which are then referred to the King's Council, before being submitted to His Majesty to receive the Royal Assent.

THE KING: His Majesty Savang Vatthana, succeeded to the throne on 29 Oct. 1959 on the death of his father, King Sisavang Vong.

Prime Minister and Foreign Affairs: HH Prince Souvanna Phouma.

Deputy Prime Minister and Minister of Education: Phagna Leuam Insisienmay.

Deputy Prime Minister and Minister of Planning and the Economy: HH Prince Souphanouvong (absent from Vientiane).

PROVINCIAL ADMINISTRATION. Laos is divided into 16 provinces, and the Province Chief (Chao Khoueng) is responsible for carrying out orders from higher authority and for the application of laws and regulations as well as for the general administration of the Province (Khoueng).

AREA AND POPULATION. Laos is a land-locked country of about 91,000 sq. miles (235,700 sq. km) bordered on the north by China, the east by North and South Vietnam, the south by Cambodia and the west by Thailand and Burma. Apart from the Mekong River plains along the border of Thailand, the country is mountainous, particularly in the north, and in places densely forested. The climate is of a tropical monsoon type with a wet season from May to Oct. and a dry one from Nov. to April. Most of northern Laos receives about 40–80 in. of rainfall annually, while parts of the Bolovens Plateau in southern Laos have over 150 in.

There has been no complete census in Laos, but estimates place the population at about 2·7m. The most heavily populated areas are the Mekong River plains by the Thailand border. Otherwise, the population is sparse and scattered, particularly in the northern provinces, and the eastern part of the country has been depopulated by war. The majority of the population is officially divided into 4 groups: about 40% Lao-Lum (Valley-Lao), 16% Lao-Tai (tribal

Tai); 34% Lao-Theung (Lao of the mountain sides); and 9% Lao-Soung (Lao of the mountain tops), who comprise the Meo and Yao. Other minorities include Vietnamese, Chinese, Europeans, Indians and Pakistanis.

The Lao-Lum and Lao-Tai belong to the Lao branch of the Tai peoples, who migrated into South-East Asia at the time of the Mongol invasion of South China. The valley Lao are Buddhists, following the Hinayana (Theravada) form. The Lao-Tai, who live mainly in northern Laos, are mostly patrilineal, believing in ancestral deities. The majority of the Lao-Theung—a diverse group consisting of many tribes—are animists.

The Meo and Yao live in northern Laos. Far greater numbers live in both North Vietnam and China, having migrated over the last century. Their religions have strong Confucian and animistic features but some are Christians.

Compared with other parts of Asia, Laos has few towns. The administrative capital and largest town is Vientiane, with a population of about 150,000. Other important towns are Luang Prabang, the royal capital (about 22,000), Pakse (about 35,000) in the extreme south, and Savannakhet (about 36,000).

LANGUAGE. Lao is the official language of the country, but French is also widely used in the various administrative departments. Pali or Nang Xu Tham, a Sanskrit language of Hindu origins, is generally used by the priests.

EDUCATION. At the close of the 1968–69 school year there were 2,995 elementary schools and 79 private schools in operation (200,000 pupils approx.); 16 colleges, 4 *lycées* and 3 technical schools provided secondary education for approximately 7,000 pupils.

There are 6 teachers' training colleges, one school of Medicine, one Institute of Law and Administration and an advanced school of Pali.

JUSTICE. The King is the final arbiter of justice. There are magistrates' courts, courts of first instance, 3 courts of appeal and a court of annulment.

FINANCE. Currency. The Laotian National Bank is responsible for the issue of currency. The unit of currency is the Kip (K.). In Jan. 1970 the official rate of exchange was K.234 = US$1, K.564 = £1. There is also a free rate of exchange (approx. K.500 = US$$1; K.1,200 = £1), for all non-official transactions.

Budget. The budget for the Laotian fiscal year 1970–71 (ended 30 June) was estimated as follows: Revenue K.9,048m.; expenditure K.18,248m., of which the military budget appropriates K.8,869m. The deficit is made up by foreign aid in the form of donations to a Foreign Exchange Operations Fund (Stabilization Fund). The fund is administered by agreement between the Laotian Government and the donor countries who are the USA, UK, Australia, France and Japan, and maintains the free market value of the kip.

DEFENCE. Army. A state of war has existed ever since the departure of the French administration in 1954 except for two brief periods. The right-wing and neutralist army are equipped entirely with US Army equipment mostly of Second World War vintage. The Pathet Lao and dissident neutralist army uses Communist equipment including a few PT76 light tanks. In 1969 the right-wing forces numbered about 55,000, the neutralist forces about 10,000 and the Pathet Lao and dissident neutralists about 50,000 (including North Vietnamese specialists and cadres). In addition, it is estimated that there are 48,000 North Vietnamese regular troops in Laos. The right-wing has also a small and dwindling river flotilla manned by the army and used mainly for transportation.

Navy. It is officially stated that river squadrons formed since 1968 total 42 craft of 6 different types.

Air Force. A small air force, equipped with about 60 T-28D piston-engined trainers, fitted with guns and rockets for ground-support duties, some AC-47 ground-attack aircraft, 10 C-47 transports (some converted to carry bombs), helicopters, observation and light communications aircraft. Operations by the left-wing forces are handicapped by having no air arm or air support.

PLANNING. There is a development plan for the period 1969–74 comprising about 12 large projects costing some £40m. and some 80 lesser projects costing just under £10m. About half the the funds for the large projects have been promised in external aid. The large projects include the Nam Ngum Dam, a bridge across the Mekong and development of the infrastructure. The other projects, particularly the project for the integrated agricultural development of the Vientiane Plain, emphasize development of the productive sector, particularly agriculture.

AGRICULTURE. The chief products are rice (average annual production about 570,000 tons), maize (average production 30,000 tons), tobacco (4,000 tons), cotton (2,200 tons), citrus fruits, sticklac, benjohn tea and in the Boloven plateau coffee (3,700 tons), potatoes, cardamon and cinchara. Opium is produced and is estimated to be worth upwards of US$2m. per year to producers. Cattle, buffalo and pigs are numerous.

FORESTRY. The forests in the north produce valuable woods, teak in particular; the logs are floated southwards on the Mekong. Elephants are trained in forest work.

MINING. Various minerals are found, but only tin is mined at present, and only at 2 mines (1968 production, 1,173 metric tons of 50% concentrate). There are extremely rich deposits of high-quality iron ore in Xieng Knouang province.

INDUSTRY. Industry is limited to rubber sandals, cigarettes, matches, soft drinks, plastic bags, saw-mills, rice-mills, weaving, pottery, distilleries, ice, bricks, etc.

POWER. Only a few towns in Laos have an electricity service. A power plant with a capacity of 2,200 kw. is installed at Vientiane, but there are only small thermo-electric plants in other towns. Laos has, however, co-operated in the international programme for the development of the Lower Mekong River since its establishment in 1957 under the aegis of ECAFE. Two projects in Thailand have now been completed and 4 are in the construction stage, including 3 in Laos. The major project is the Nam Ngum project for electric power and irrigation situated about 45 miles north of Vientiane. A dam is to be constructed with an ultimate installed capacity of 135,000 kw. with first priority for a 30,000-kw. generator and transmission line to Vientiane and North-east Thailand. Work on the dam was started in Feb. 1967 and is due for completion in 1971. Besides this there is the Lower Sedone project for a dam and power plant about 30 km north of Pakse. Power is to be generated from 2 units of 720 kw. each and the project will be completed in 1970. The other project is the Nam Dong, an electric power project located about 9 km south of Luang Prabang. Power is to be generated from 2 units of 345 kw. in the first stage with an additional unit of 345 kw. envisaged for the final stage.

COMMERCE. In 1968 imports amounted to K.12,843m. (plus K.19,310m. of gold) and exports (excluding gold) to K.1,638m. In 1968 the main imports were agricultural products, petroleum products and transport vehicles. The main exports were green coffee, timber and tin. The chief supply countries were Thailand, USA, Japan and Indonesia.

Total trade with UK (British Board of Trade returns, in £1,000 sterling):

	1965	1966	1967	1968	1969	1970
Imports to UK	2	—	1	—	2	3
Exports from UK	578	666	454	607	585	313
Re-exports from UK	1	2	3	4	4	

SHIPPING. The river Mekong and its tributaries are an important means of transport, but rapids, waterfalls and narrow channels often impede navigation and make transhipments necessary.

ROADS. In 1969 there were 2,156 km of all-weather, asphalted or permanent roads and 4,119 km of non-all-weather roads though few of the roads are usable by normal traffic during the 6 wet months of the year. Road improvements, however, are being undertaken with US aid funds.

RAILWAY. There is no railway in Laos, but the Thai railway system extends to Nongkhai, on the Thai bank of the Mekong, which is connected by ferry with Thadeua about 12 miles east of Vietniane.

AVIATION. Royal Air Lao and Lao Airlines provide scheduled domestic air services linking major towns in Laos. Royal Air Lao, Air Vietnam and Lao Airlines maintain services between Vientiane and Saigon; Royal Air Lao and Thai Airways between Vientiane and Bangkok; Lao Airlines betwwen Vietiane and Phnom Penh, and Royal Air Lao between Vientiane and Hong Kong. Aeroflot has begun a weekly service to Hanoi calling at Vientiane.

TELECOMMUNICATIONS. The British Government has provided a radio network for Laos (with contributions of equipment from the USA, Australia and West Germany) and a team of technical experts to advise on and assist in the running of the system. The main station in Vientiane became operational on 6 Aug. 1968.

In 1969 there were 1,081 telephones in Laos. A telephone link with Bangkok was opened in 1967, and telephonic communication was established with most parts of the world in 1968.

DIPLOMATIC REPRESENTATIVES

Laotian ambassadors are resident in:

Cambodia	Japan	USSR	USA
France	Thailand	UK	Vietnam (South)
India			

Laotian ambassadors are accredited to, but not resident in:

Australia	Hungary	Nepál	Romania
Belgium	Iran	New Zealand	Spain
Bulgaria	Israel	Netherlands	Sweden
Burma	Italy	Pakistan	Switzerland
Ceylon	Malaysia	Philippines	Turkey
Czechoslovakia	Mongolia	Poland	Yugoslavia

A Laotian minister is accredited to, but not resident in, Denmark.
Chargés d'Affaires are resident in Australia, China and Germany (West).

OF LAOS IN GREAT BRITAIN (5 Palace Green, W8)

Ambassador: HRH Prince Khammao (accredited 13 Dec. 1967).
First Secretary: Vannavong Panya.

OF GREAT BRITAIN IN LAOS

Ambassador and Consul-General: John O. Lloyd, CBE.
First Secretaries: C. Wilson (*Head of Chancery*); D. R. Gallwey; J. G. Wallace (*Aid*). *Defence, Military and Air Attaché:* Col. D. H. Thursby-Pelham.

OF LAOS IN THE USA (2222 S St. NW, Washington, D.C., 20008)

Ambassador: (Vacant).
Counsellor: Lane Pathammavong, *Chargé d'Affaires a.i.*

OF THE USA IN LAOS

Ambassador: G. McMurtrie Godley.
Deputy Chief of Mission: Monteagle Stearns. *Head of Sections:* Charles Rushing (*Political*); Charles A. Mann (*Economic*); Norman C. Barnes (*USIS*); Reed P. Robinson (*Administrative*). *Service Attachés:* Lieut.-Col. J. A. Frye (*Army*), Capt. L. C. Miles (*Navy*), Col. Hayden C. Curry (*Air*).

BOOKS OF REFERENCE

La Constitution du Laos. Notes et Etudes. 1957
International Conference on the Settlement of the Laotian Question. Geneva, 12th May 1961–23rd July 1962 (Cmnd. 1828). HMSO, 1962
Declaration and Protocol on the Neutrality of Laos. Geneva, 23rd July 1962 (Cmnd. 2025). HMSO, 1963
White Book on the Violations of the Geneva Accords of 1962 by the Government of North Vietnam. Ministry of Foreign Affairs, Vientiane, 1968
Berval, Rene De and others, *Kingdom of Laos.* Saigon, 1959
Champassak, Sisouk Na, *Storm over Laos. A Contemporary History.* New York, 1961
Dommen, Arthur J., *Conflict in Laos.* New York, 1965
Halpern, Joel M., *Economy and Society of Laos: brief survey.* Yale University Press, 1964.—
Government, Politics and Social Structure in Laos. Yale University Press, 1964
Toye, H., *Laos: Buffer State or Battleground.* OUP, 1968

LEBANON
al-Jumhouriya al-Lubnaniya

HISTORY. After 20 years' French mandatory régime, the Lebanon was proclaimed independent at Beirut on 26 Nov. 1941. On 27 Dec. 1943 an agreement was signed between representatives of the French National Committee of Liberation and of Lebanon, by which most of the powers and capacities exercised hitherto by France were transferred as from 1 Jan. 1944 to the Lebanese Government. The evacuation of foreign troops was completed in Dec. 1946.

In early May 1958 the opposition to President Chamoun, consisting principally (though not entirely) of Moslem pro-Nasserist elements, rose in insurrection; and for 5 months the Moslem quarters of Beirut, Tripoli, Sidon and the northern Bekaa were in insurgent hands. On 15 July the USA Government acceded to President Chamoun's request and landed a considerable force of army and marines who re-established the authority of the government.

In the subsequent presidential elections, Gen. Fouad Chehab replaced President Chamoun and a return to normality enabled US forces to be withdrawn.

In 1964 Charles Helou succeeded President Chehab. His term of office ends in 1970.

In 1967, on the outbreak of hostilities with Israel, the Lebanese Government withdrew their ambassadors from Washington and London and requested the US and British governments to withdraw their representatives in Beirut. Relations at ambassadorial level were resumed later that year. In April 1969 the Government headed by Rashid Karamé resigned after disturbances in Beirut and other cities had resulted in fatal casualties in clashes between demonstrators and security forces. Policy differences concerning the presence of armed Palestinian resistance units on Lebanese territory obstructed the formation of a new government, and the issue led to fighting between fedayeen and the Lebanese Army in Oct. 1969. As a result of UAR mediation, a secret agreement between the Palestinian Armed Struggle Command and the Lebanese Commander-in-Chief was signed in Cairo on 1 Nov. 1969. Despite the improved atmosphere in internal politics which resulted, a government could not be formed until 25 Nov. 1969.

AREA AND POPULATION. The Lebanon is a mountainous country about 135 miles long and varying between 20 and 35 miles wide, bounded on the north and east by Syria, on the west by the Mediterranean and on the south by Israel. Between the two parallel mountain ranges of Lebanon and Anti-Lebanon lies the fertile Bekaa Valley. About one-half of the country lies at an altitude of over 3,000 ft.

The area of Lebanon is estimated at 10,400 sq. km (3,400 sq. miles) and the population at 2,179,000 (1967). The principal towns, with estimated population, are: Beirut (the capital), 600,000; Tripoli, 150,000; Zahlé, 40,000; Saida (Sidon), 22,000; Tyre, 12,000.

Vital statistics, 1968: Births, 76,850; deaths, 11,993; marriages, 15,478; divorces (1968), 1,048.

The official language is Arabic. French and, increasingly, English are widely spoken in official and commercial circles.

CONSTITUTION AND GOVERNMENT. Lebanon is an independent republic and a member of the United Nations and the Arab League. The first constitution was established under the French Mandate on 23 May 1926. It has since been amended in 1927, 1929, 1943 (twice) and 1947. It is a written constitution based on the classical separation of powers, with a President, a single chamber elected by universal adult suffrage, and an independent judiciary. The Executive consists of the President and a Prime Minister and Cabinet appointed by him. The system is, however, adapted to the peculiar communal balance on which Lebanese political life depends. This is done by the electoral law which allocates deputies according to the confessional distribution of the population, and by a series of constitutional conventions whereby, *e.g.*, the President is always a Maronite Christian, the Prime Minister a Sunni Moslem and the Speaker of the Chamber a Shia Moslem. There is no highly developed party system.

President of the Republic: Soliman Frangié (elected on 17 Aug. 1970 by 50 to 49 votes).

The government, appointed in Oct. 1970, is composed as follows:

Prime Minister and Interior: Saeb Salam.
Deputy Prime Minister, Defence and Finance: Dr Elias Saba. *Justice and PTT:* Jamil Kebbé. *Public Works:* Henri Eddé. *Foreign Affairs:* Khalil Abou Hamas. *National Economy and Tourism:* Soeb Jaroudi. *Planning:* Hassan Moucharafié. *Social Affairs:* Mounir Hamdane. *Education:* Negib Abou-Haydor. *Water Resources:* Jaafar Charafeddine. *Public Health:* Emilo Bitar. *Information:* Henri Torbey.

National flag: Red, white, red (horizontal), with a green cedar on the white stripe.
National anthem: Kullu na lil watan lil 'ula lil' alam (words by Rashid Nachleh, tune by Mitri El-Murr).

RELIGION. About half the population are Christians, who have been indigenous since the earliest time of Christianity. There were in 1958, 792,000 Christians, of whom 424,000 were Maronites, 150,000 Greek Orthodox, 69,000 Armenians, 91,000 Greek and Roman Catholics, 14,500 Armenian Catholics, 14,000 Protestants. Moslems numbered 536,000, of whom 286,000 were Sunnis and 250,000 Shiites. There were also 88,000 Druzes and 6,600 Jews.

EDUCATION. Government schools in 1967 comprised 1,257 primary and secondary schools. There were also 1,298 private primary and secondary schools. There are also 5 teachers' training colleges and 4 universities, namely the Lebanese (State) University, the American university, the French university of St Joseph (founded in 1875) and the Arab University, a branch of Alexandria University. The French Government runs the École Supérieure de Lettres and the Centre d'Études Mathématiques.

The Lebanese Academy of Fine Arts includes schools of architecture, art, music, political and social science.

CINEMAS (1964). There were over 100 cinemas with a seating capacity of about 50,000.

NEWSPAPERS (1969). There were about 30 daily newspapers in Arabic, 3 in French, 1 in English and 4 in Armenian, with a total circulation of 200,000.

HEALTH. In 1965 there were 1,430 physicians and (1964) 7,649 hospital beds.

FINANCE. Currency. The Lebanese pound, divided into 100 piastres, is issued by the Banque du Liban, which commenced operations on 1 April 1964. The official rate of exchange is £Leb.8·62 = £1 sterling, but this in practice is used only for the calculation of ad-valorem customs duties on Lebanese imports and for import statistics. For other purposes the free market is used; the rate of the £ sterling on 25 Nov. 1970 was £Leb.7·72 = £1; the US$ rate was £Leb.3·22 = $1.

On 31 Dec. 1969 the note circulation was £Leb.930m., the gold cover being 85%.

Budget. The general budget for 1970 provides for a total expenditure of £Leb.736·5m. (660·5m. in 1968), the main items being: Public works, 106·6 (73·3); defence, 171·8 (160); education 123·7 (112·1); public health, 23·6 (22); agriculture, 20 (15·2); foreign affairs, 25·8 (25·1); hydro-electric resources, 26·6 (17·7). In addition, there are special budgets covering 4 semi-autonomous, self-financing public agencies with a total expenditure of £Leb.93m.

DEFENCE. Army. The Army strength is about 12,000, the gendarmerie about 4,000, the police force about 600 and the security force about 250 men. Army and gendarmerie use British, American and French equipment.

Navy. The Navy consisted in 1970 of 1 patrol vessel, 3 coastal motor launches, 1 fishery protection vessel and 1 landing craft. Personnel about 200 men.

Air Force. The Air Force has about 600 men and 45 aircraft, including a squadron of Mirage III-EL supersonic fighters, 2 Mirage III-BL two-seat trainers, 10 Hunter jet fighter-bombers, 1 Dove light transport, 10 Alouette II and III helicopters, and Chipmunk primary and Super Magister and Vampire jet trainers.

AGRICULTURE. Lebanon is essentially an agricultural country, although owing to its physical character only about 38% of the total area of the country is at present cultivated. The forests of the past have been denuded by exploitation and the unrestricted grazing of goats, and only about 80,000 hectares of indifferent timber remain, and soil erosion is considerable.

The estimated yield (in 1,000 metric tons) of the main crops in 1969 was as follows: Oranges, 162; apples, 100; grapes, 110; potatoes, 63; lemons, 62; sugarbeet, 94; olives, 60; bananas, 23.

Livestock (estimated, 1968): Goats, 357,310; sheep, 199,540; cattle, 86,379 (including 45,132 dairy cows); camels, 433; hogs, 13,611; horses, 2,944; donkeys, 28,310; mules, 3,504; egg-laying hens, 3·04m.; broilers, 13·5m.

MINING. Iron ore exists but is difficult to work. Other minerals known to exist are iron pyrites, copper, bituminous shales, asphalt, phosphates, ceramic clays and glass sand; but the available information is of doubtful value.

INDUSTRY. Manufacturing industry is still small but has doubled in the last 10 years. At the end of 1968 the total capital invested was estimated at £Leb.1,068m. and the total number of employees, 68,460. The most important sectors invested in 1965 (in £Leb.1m.) were: Food and drink, 150; textiles, 80; tobacco, 76; foundries, 48; cement, bricks, etc., 48; petroleum, 45; chemicals, 30.

There are 2 oil refineries in Lebanon, one at Tripoli, the property of the Iraq Petroleum Company, which there refines oil brought by pipeline from Iraq, and the other at Sidon, the property of the Mediterranean Refining Company, which there refines oil brought from Saudi Arabia by a pipeline owned by the Trans-Arabian Pipeline Company. The section of this pipeline running across Syria was damaged in May 1970 and has since been closed because of a dispute between Tapline and the Syrian Government. At the end of 1970 the Sidon refinery was refining oil shipped by tanker from Tripoli. The production of these refineries, which in 1969 was estimated to be 1,777,700 tons, is sufficient to meet the country's requirements of refined fuel.

COMMERCE. Foreign as well as local wholesale and retail trade is the principal source of income in Lebanon and provides about 30% of the total. Because of the protectionist policies followed in some neighbouring countries, this sector has been declining, the sectors to gain being those of banking, real estate, government and services (especially tourism, US$ 11Bm, 1968).

In 1969 imports totalled 3,059,801 tons, valued at £Lcb.1,639m. (excluding gold, coins, stamps and bank-notes); exports totalled 1,147,471 tons, valued at £Leb.525,084,095 (excluding gold, coins, stamps and bank-notes). Of the imports, 10·8% came from West Germany, 10·4% from USA, 8% from Italy, 7·8% from France, 7·2% from UK and 6% from Syria. Of the exports, 19·7% went to Saudi Arabia, 10·4% to Kuwait, 9% to Syria, 6·9% to Jordan, 6·3% to Iraq, 4·4% to Libya, 4·2% to USA, 3·8% to UK, 2·5% to Italy and 2% to France.

Total trade with UK (British Board of Trade returns, in £1,000 sterling):

	1966	1967	1968	1969	1970
Imports to UK	2,602	3,125	4,229	3,995	3,124
Exports from UK	16,417	13,080	20,192	20,874 ⎱	23,013
Re-exports from UK	467	541	765	508 ⎰	

Customs duties are usually imposed on an *ad valorem* basis: the receipts are the Lebanese Government's main source of income; estimated yield in 1970, £Leb.190m. The considerable adverse balance of trade is offset by invisible receipts, including foreign capital investment in Lebanese real estate, remittances from émigrés and receipts from tourism and international arbitrage operations.

Receipts from tourism was £Leb.388m. in 1969.

SHIPPING. Beirut is by far the largest and busiest port. In 1969, 3,126 vessels (total tonnage 4,361,512) were handled. Activity in the port of Tripoli is growing due to increased movements in goods and petroleum. The small port of Sidon in the south, near to the closed Lebanese–Israeli frontier, is at present of little importance.

In 1966, the Lebanese flag was flown by 149 ships of 745,019 tons.

RAILWAYS. There are 3 railway lines in Lebanon, all operated by the Office des Chemins de Fer de l'Etat Libanais (CFL): (1) Nakoura–Beirut–Tripoli (standard gauge); the Nakoura–Sidon section has been idle since the establishment of Israel; (2) a narrow-gauge line running from Beirut to Riyak in the Bekaa Valley and thence to Damascus, Syria; (3) a standard-gauge line from Tripoli to Homs and Aleppo in Syria, providing access to Ankara and Istanbul. From Homs a branch of the CFL line extends south and re-enters Lebanon, terminating at Riyak.

The railway system is operated at a considerable annual loss, attributable largely to unrestricted competition from road transport. 72,600 passengers and 659,800 tons of goods were carried in 1969.

ROADS. The main roads in Lebanon are good. The surface is normally of asphalt and they are normally well maintained. In Dec. 1968 there were 570 km of international roads, 1,420 km of main roads and 4,310 km of secondary and local roads, all asphalted. The main arterial routes are the north–south coastal road and the west–east trunk road (Beirut to Damascus).

Passenger transport outside the town of Beirut is provided by a great number of small private companies running cheap and regular bus services and long-distance taxi services. Most goods traffic is hauled by road.

At 31 Dec. 1969 there were 129,674 cars and taxis, 1,763 buses and 14,473 commercial vehicles.

AVIATION. Beirut International Airport is used by many international airlines which connect Lebanon with most countries in the world. Extensive local services cover the Middle East, Persian Gulf and Europe. There are 2 national airlines, Middle East Airlines/Air Liban and Trans-Mediterranean Airways. In 1969, 40,053 flights passed through Beirut international airport, carrying a total of 1,571,726 passengers (1968: 1,513,000) and 47,636 tons of freight (1968: 46,215).

POST. There is an automatic telephone system in Beirut, Tripoli and Sidon which is being extended to other towns and villages. There are no telegraph, postal or telephone communications with Israel. Number of telephones (1969), 150,370.

The state radio transmits in Arabic, French and English. There are 2 commercial television stations, transmitting in Arabic, French and English.

BANKING. Beirut is an important international financial centre, and there were 78 banks registered with the central bank at 31 Dec. 1969, including 2 British banks, the British Bank of the Middle East and the Eastern Bank.

WEIGHTS AND MEASURES. The use of the metric system is legal and obligatory throughout the whole of the country. In outlying districts the former weights and measures may still be in use. They are: 1 *okiya* = 0·47 lb.; 6 *okiyas* = 1 *oke* = 2·82 lb.; 2 *okes* = 1 *rottol* = 5·64 lb.; 200 *okes* = 1 *kantar*.

DIPLOMATIC REPRESENTATIVES

The Lebanon maintains embassies in:

Argentina	Greece	Mexico	Switzerland
Australia	India	Morocco	Tunisia
Austria	Indonesia	Nigeria	Turkey
Belgium	Iran	Pakistan	USSR
Brazil	Iraq	Poland	UAR
Canada	Italy	Romania	UK
Colombia	Japan	Saudi Arabia	USA
Cuba	Jordan	Somalia	Vatican
Cyprus	Kuwait	Spain	Venezuela
Czechoslovakia	Libya	Sudan	Yugoslavia
France			

The Lebanon also maintains legations in Ghana and Liberia.

OF THE LEBANON IN GREAT BRITAIN (21 Kensington Palace Gdns, W8)

Ambassador: Nadim Dimechkié (accredited 18 July 1966).
Counsellor: Khalil Makkawi. *Service Attaché:* Col. Tufic Jalbout.

There are consular representatives at London and Manchester.

OF GREAT BRITAIN IN THE LEBANON

Ambassador: A. J. Edden, CMG.
Counsellors: E. F. Given, CMG; Sir Hugh Parry, CBE (*Deputy Head of Middle East Development Division*). *First Secretaries:* A. J. Sindall; N. M. Darbyshire, OBE; N. G. S. Beckett (*Commercial*); J. R. Clube; P. Joy, OBE (*Information*); J. A. Bryan (*Consul*); M. S. Buckmaster (*Information*); R. J. Morris, OBE

(Labour); G. R. Sunderland *(Civil Aviation)*. *Military and Defence Attaché:*
Lieut.-Col. S. A. R. Cawston.

OF THE LEBANON IN THE USA (2560-28th St., Washington, DC., 20008)

Ambassador: Najati Kabbani.
Counsellors: Assas Moukaddem *(Tourism)*; Walid R. Naja *(Economic)*; Miss
Afifa M. Dirani *(Cultural)*. *Armed Forces Attaché:* Brig. Shawki Golmieh.

OF THE USA IN THE LEBANON

Ambassador: William B. Buffum.
Deputy Chief of Mission: Robert Bigelow Houghton. *Heads of Sections:*
Curtis F. Jones *(Political)*; Norman K. Pratt *(Economic)*; Joe Lill *(Commercial)*;
J. P. Condon *(Labour)*; William D. Morgan *(Consular)*; Eugene Champagne, Jr
(Administrative).

Books of Reference

STATISTICAL INFORMATION. Import and export figures are produced by the Conseil Supérieur
des Douanes. The Service de Statistique Générale (M. A. G. Ayad, *Chef du Service*) publishes a
quarterly bulletin (in French and Arabic) covering a wide range of subjects, including foreign trade
production statistics and estimates of the national income.

Binder, L. (ed.), *Politics in Lebanon*. New York, 1966
Cowan, J. M., *Dictionary of Modern Arabic*. Wiesbaden, 1961
Hitti, P. K., *A short history of Lebanon*. London, 1965
Naccache, G., *Les Partis libanais en 1959*. Beirut, 1959
Rizk, C., *Le Régime politique libanais*. Paris, 1966
Salibi, K. S., *Modern History of Lebanon*. London, 1965
Ward P., *Touring Lebanon*. London, 1971

NATIONAL LIBRARY. Dar el Kuttub, Parliament Sq., Beirut.

LIBERIA

HISTORY. The Republic of Liberia had its origin in the efforts of several
American philanthropic societies to establish freed American slaves in a colony
on the West African coast. In 1822 a settlement was formed near the spot where
Monrovia now stands. On 26 July 1847 the state was constituted as the Free and
Independent Republic of Liberia. The new state was first recognized by Great
Britain and France, and ultimately by other powers.

CONSTITUTION AND GOVERNMENT. The constitution of the Re-
public is modelled on that of the US. The executive power is vested in a President
and Cabinet, and the legislative power in a legislature of 2 Houses, the Senate
(18 members) and the House of Representatives (52 members). The President is
elected for 8 years in the first instance, the House of Representatives for 4 and
the Senate for 6 years.

President of Liberia: William V. S. Tubman (elected on 6 May 1943; re-elected
in 1951, 1955, 1959, 1963 and 1967).
Vice-President: William Richard Tolbert, Jr.

The President may be re-elected for any number of subsequent 4-year terms.
He must be a citizen of over 25 years' residence and have unencumbered real
estate to the value of $2,500. Electors must be of Negro blood and owners of
land. By the end of 1945, legislation was passed granting manhood suffrage to
the tribes in the hinterland who are now represented in the legislature. In 1947
the franchise was extended to women.
The official language is English.

National flag: Six red and 5 white horizontal stripes alternating. In the upper
corner, nearest the staff, is a square of blue covering a depth of 5 stripes. In the
centre of this blue field is a 5-pointed white star.

National anthem: All hail, Liberia, hail! (words by President Warner; tune by O. Luca, 1860).

On 22 Dec. 1950 an agreement of assistance and co-operation was signed in Washington whereby a development programme is implemented under control of a joint American–Liberian Commission. In 1963 the US Agency for International Development announced loans for the construction of a hydro-electric project ($24·3m.), schools ($1·7m.) and hospitals ($4·7m.); the Federal Republic of Germany made a loan for road construction ($8·2m.).

AREA AND POPULATION. Liberia has about 350 miles of coastline, extending from Sierra Leone, on the west, to the Ivory Coast, on the east, and it stretches inland to a distance, in some places, of about 200 miles. The boundaries were determined by the Anglo-Liberian agreement of 1885 and the Franco-Liberian agreements of 1892 and 1907–10. In 1911 the territory of Kanran-Lahun was transferred to Sierra Leone in exchange for a strip on the south side of Morro River, which now is the boundary.

The total area is about 43,000 sq. miles (111,000 sq. km). A census taken in 1962 gave the total population as 1,016,000 (estimated population in 1967, 1,098,985). The indigenous natives belong in the main to 6 principal stocks: (1) The Mandingos (Muhammedan), (2) the Gissi, (3) the Gola, (4) the Kpelle, (5) the Kru and (6) the Greboes. The other principal tribes are: Vai, Mendi, Belle, Dey, Manoh, Geo, Bassa, Buzzi, Gbandi, Krahn and Geh.

Monrovia, the capital, has an estimated population of 100,000 and is administered as a commonwealth district by a Municipal Board appointed by the President. It is one of the 9 ports of entry along the 350 miles of coast, the others being Robertsport (Cape Mount), Marshall (Junk), Buchanan (Grand Bassa), River Cess, Greenville (Sinoe), Sasstown, Grand Cess and Harper (Cape Palmas). Other towns are Kolahun, Voinjama, Bomi Hills, Zorzor, Kakata, Nimba, Suakoko, Gbarnga, Ganta, Sanniquellie, Saklape and Tappita.

The country was in 1964 divided into 9 counties and 4 territories.

RELIGION. The main denominations represented in Liberia are Methodist, Baptist, Episcopalian, African Methodist, Pentecostal, Seventh Day Adventist, Lutheran and Roman Catholic, working through missionaries and mission schools.

EDUCATION. Schools are classified as: (1) Public schools, maintained and run by the Government; (2) Mission schools, supported by foreign Missions and subsidized by the Government, and operated by qualified Missionaries and Liberian teachers; (3) Private schools, maintained by endowments and subsidized by the Government; (4) Tribal schools, maintained by tribal authorities.

By the end of 1964 there were said to be 893 schools with 2,983 teachers and 85,800 pupils. In 1967, 320 US Peace Corps Volunteers were teaching in schools throughout the country.

JUSTICE. Justice is administered by a supreme court of 5 judges, circuit courts and lower courts. A new Liberian code of laws has been published (5 vols. to 1961).

FINANCE. Currency. The money in circulation is US currency since 3 Nov. 1942, but there is a Liberian coinage in silver and copper. Official accounts are kept in dollars and cents. The Liberian coins are as follows: Silver, $1, 50-, 25-, 10- and 5-cent pieces; alloy, 2- and 1-cent pieces.

British currency ceased to be legal tender after the end of 1943, and on 1 Jan. 1944 the Liberian dollar was raised to parity with the US$.

Budget. The budgets for fiscal years ended 30 Sept. and calender years from 1968, were as follows (in US$1,000):

	1964–65	1965–66	1966–67	1968	1969
Revenue	46,050	44,190	47,932	51,400	58,000
Expenditure	48,062	46,840	50,432	55,900	60,100

DEFENCE. For defence every citizen from 16 to 45 years of age capable of bearing arms is liable to serve. The establishment organized on a militia basis numbers 4,000, divided into 10 infantry regiments. There is in addition an enlisted frontier force, the Liberian National Guard, of 93 officers and 2,200 men. An American Military Mission to train these forces arrived in Sept. 1951.

The small naval service or coastguard comprises 2 motor gunboats, 2 patrol vessels, the presidential yacht, and a number of landing craft for transport and general utility. Personnel about 200 officers and men.

On 31 March 1942 an agreement was signed between the USA and Liberia by which the US were given the right to construct, control, operate and defend airports in Liberia for the duration of the war. On 8 June 1943 a further mutual aid agreement was concluded with the US, which extended lend-lease aid to Liberia for the purpose of defence and enabled it to increase its Armed Forces.

AGRICULTURE. The soil is productive, but due to excessive rainfall (from 160 to 180 in. per year), there are large swamp areas. Rice, cassava, coffee and sugar-cane are cultivated. Rice production is inadequate for local needs, but strenuous efforts are being made to increase production by the substitution of swamp rice for hill rice cultivation. Sugar-cane is grown for manufacture of locally consumed rum. Coffee production is considerable (exports, 1967, 9·2m. lb.). Concessions have been given to foreign firms for timber production.

FORESTRY. Many forest products are gathered for export, of which palm-kernels (exports, 1967, 29·4m. lb.) is the most important. The Firestone Plantation Co. have large rubber plantations, employing about 35,000 men. Their concession comprises about 1m. acres and expires in the year 2025. About 100,000 acres have been planted. Independent producers have a further 65,000 acres planted.

The B. F. Goodrich Co. was, on 9 July 1954, granted an 80-year concession to produce rubber; part of the 12,300 acres planted came into production in 1963. Rubber exports, in 1967, 136·7m. lb.

MINING. Mineral resources have not been completely surveyed. However, the Liberia Mining Co. at Bomi Hills, the National Iron Ore Co. near the Mano River, the Liberian American–Swedish Mineral Co. in the Nimba Mountains and the Liberian–German Mining Co. (DELIMCO) at Bong Hills are exploiting their iron-ore concession areas. Iron ore exports amounted to 17·2m. long tons in 1967. Gold and diamonds are found on a small scale.

A pelletizing and washing plant was inaugurated in 1968 for the American–Swedish Minerals Co. near the port of Buchanan. Another pelletizing plant is being constructed by the Bong Mining Co.

INDUSTRY. There are a number of small factories (brick and tile, soap, nails, mattresses, shoes, plastics, paint, oxygen, acetylene, tyre retreading, a brewery and soft drinks).

COMMERCE. Foreign trade for 5 calendar years was as follows (in $):

	1964	1965	1966	1967	1968
Imports	117,360,766	104,543,045	113,664,416	125,173,811	108,500,000
Exports	142,756,094	135,414,557	150,458,592	158,767,668	169,000,000

The principal exports in 1968 were: Rubber, $25·5m.; iron ore, and concentrates, $118·3m. The principal imports in 1968 were machinery and transport equipment ($27·1m.) and manufactured goods ($22·2m.). Main suppliers in 1968 were: USA ($43·4m.), UK ($13·3m.), West Germany ($10·1m.), Japan ($8·6m.).

According to British Board of Trade returns, the value of the trade between UK and Liberia was as follows (in £1,000 sterling):

	1966	1967	1968	1969	1970
Imports to UK	7,152	8,282	8,341	8,693	11,972
Exports from UK	3,085	5,156	14,056	13,655 ⎱	13,628
Re-exports from UK	352	284	424	219 ⎰	

The figures for exports from the UK include the value of shipping transferred to the Liberian flag; the genuine exports are considerably lower.

Liberia was placed in the American account area in 1952.

SHIPPING. In 1966, 440 main-line ships entered Monrovia.

The Liberian merchant navy, in 1966, consisted of 1,436 ships of 20,603,301 GRT. The Liberian Government requires only a modest registration fee and an almost nominal annual charge and maintains no control over the operation of ships flying the Liberian flag.

Constructed under the auspices of the USA Government under lend-lease terms, the port of Monrovia, a free port, was opened on 26 July 1948.

A modern port for the shipment of iron-ore from the mines at Nimba has been built at Lower Buchanan, capable of accommodating vessels up to 45,000 tons.

The river St Paul is navigable for a distance of 25 miles from its mouth for small craft of shallow draught. The Cavalla River is navigable for 50 miles.

RAILWAY. A railway (for freight only) was built in 1951, connecting Monrovia with the Bomi Hills iron-ore mines about 40 miles distant; this has been extended to the National Iron Ore Co. area. A line from Nimba to Lower Buchanan (170 miles) was completed in 1963 and another line from Bong to Monrovia was completed in 1965.

ROADS. There are over 1,200 miles of state roads, suitable for motor traffic, as well as roads on private plantations. The principal highway connects Monrovia with the road system of Guinea, with branches leading into the Eastern and Western areas of Liberia. The latter branch reaches the Sierra Leone border and joins the Sierra Leone road system. A bridge over the St Paul River carries road and rail traffic to the iron-ore mines at Bomi Hills.

In the interior, communication is maintained by tracks, all goods being carried by native porters, but secondary roads are being constructed by native chiefs with state assistance, and transportation by vehicle is becoming increasingly common.

AVIATION. The airport for Liberia is Roberts Airport (38 miles from Monrovia). The James Spriggs Payne Airfield, 5 miles from Monrovia, can be used by light aircraft only. Air services are maintained by PANAM, Ghana Airways, Nigeria Airways, UTA, Middle East Airlines, Air Mali, Air Afrique, SAS, KLM, Swissair, Liberian National Airlines and Air Guinée.

POST. There is cable communication (French) with Europe and America *via* Dakar, and a wireless station is maintained by the Government at Monrovia. There is a telephone service (3,600 telephones, 1969), in Monrovia, which is gradually being extended over the whole country.

There are wireless stations at Monrovia, Bassa, Harper, Kolahun, Cape Mount and Sinoe. The wireless stations at Harbel and Gedetarbo, near Cape Palmas, have since 1928 been operated as a public utility by the US–Liberia Radio Corporation, a subsidiary of Firestone Plantations Co.

Postal agencies have been organized throughout the interior.

A commercial broadcasting station opened in Dec. 1959 and a television service on 1 Jan. 1964.

BANKING. The Bank of Monrovia, Inc., previously owned by the Firestone Plantation Co., was taken over by the First National City Bank of New York on 15 Sept. 1955.

Tha Bank of Liberia, Inc., was founded on 28 July 1955. An Italian bank, Tradevco, started business in 1955. The International Trust Co. of Liberia opened a commercial banking department at the end of 1960. The Commercial Bank of Liberia and a branch of the Chase Manhattan Bank opened in 1961. The Union National Bank (Liberia) Inc., opened in 1962.

WEIGHTS AND MEASURES. Weights and measures are the same as in Great Britain and US.

DIPLOMATIC REPRESENTATIVES

Liberia maintains embassies in:

Belgium	Israel	Sweden
Cameroon	Italy	Togo
Ethiopia	Ivory Coast	UAR
France	Japan	UK
Germany (West)	Netherlands	USA
Ghana	Nigeria	Yugoslavia
Guinea	Sierra Leone	
Haiti	Spain	

Liberia also maintains legations in Lebanon and at the Vatican.

OF LIBERIA IN GREAT BRITAIN (21 Princes Gate, SW7)

Ambassador: J. Dudley Lawrence (accredited 16 Oct. 1964).
Counsellors: R. Burlington King; C. William Birch (*Consul-General*).

There are consular representatives at Cardiff, Glasgow, Hull, Liverpool, London and Manchester.

OF GREAT BRITAIN IN LIBERIA

Ambassador and Consul-General: M. J. Moyniham, MC.
First Secretary: R. G. Osborn (*Head of Chancery and Consul*).

OF LIBERIA IN THE USA (5201–16th St. NW, Washington, D.C., 20011)

Ambassador: S. Edward Peal.
Counsellors: James B. Freeman; A. Benjamin Wordsworth (*Commercial*).
First Secretary: Urias Nelson.

OF THE USA IN LIBERIA

Ambassador: Samuel Z. Westerfield, Jr.

Deputy Chief of Mission: John M. Howison. *Heads of Sections:* John Linehan (*Political*); Frank M. Tucker (*Economic*); Edwin J. Rankin (*Commercial*); Leonard F. Willems (*Consular*); Schubert E. Smith (*Administrative*); *Naval and Air Attaché:* Cdr C. P. Moore.

BOOKS OF REFERENCE

Clower, R. W. (ed.), *Growth without development: an economic survey of Liberia.* Evanston, North-western Univ. Press, 1966
Cole, H. B. (ed.), *The Liberian Year Book.* Monrovia, 1962
Fraenkel, M., *Tribe and Class in Monrovia.* OUP, 1964
McLaughlin, R. U., *Foreign investment and development in Liberia.* New York, 1966
Richardson, N. R., *Liberia's Past and Present.* London, 1959
Welch, G., *The Jet Lighthouse.* London, 1960

LIBYAN ARAB REPUBLIC
Aljumhuria Al-Arabia Allibya

HISTORY. Tripoli fell under Turkish domination in the 16th century, and though in 1711 the Arab population secured some measure of independence, the country was in 1835 proclaimed a Turkish vilayet. In Sept. 1911 Italy occupied Tripoli and on 19 Oct. 1912, by the Treaty of Ouchy, Turkey recognized the sovereignty of Italy in Tripoli.

After the expulsion of the Germans and Italians in 1942 and 1943, Tripolitania and Cyrenaica were placed under British, and the Fezzan under French, military administration. Britain recognized the Amir Mohammed Idris Al-Senussi as Amir of Cyrenaica in June 1949.

A treaty of friendship and alliance between the UK and Libya, together with military and financial agreements, was signed at Benghazi on 29 July 1953; and an agreement governing the use of bases in Libya by the US forces was signed at Benghazi on 9 Sept. 1954.

A Franco-Libyan treaty providing for the evacuation of French forces from the Fezzan was signed on 10 Aug. 1955.

Libya became an independent, sovereign, federal kingdom under the Amir of Cyrenaica, **Mohammed Idris Al-Senussi,** as King of the United Kingdom of Libya, on 24 Dec. 1951, when the British Residents in Tripolitania and Cyrenaica and the French Resident in the Fezzan transferred their remaining powers to the federal government of Libya, in pursuance of decisions passed by the United Nations in 1949 and 1950. The King is married to his cousin Fatima and to Aliyah Lamlun. In Nov. 1956 the King announced the appointment of HRH Prince Al Hassan Rida as Crown Prince unless he himself should have an heir.

On 1 Sept. 1969 King Idris was deposed. The first government of the Libyan Arab Republic was announced on 8 Sept. with Dr Mahmoud Soliman al Magh-rabi as Prime Minister. A new cabinet was announced on 16 Jan. 1970.

National flag: Red, black, green (horizontal), with a white crescent and star in the centre.

CONSTITUTION. Until 1963 Libya was a federal state, each of the 3 provinces, Tripolitania, Cyrenaica and Fezzan, being administered by a governor assisted by an executive and legislative council. In April 1963, however, comprehensive unity was proclaimed and the federal system (together with the governors and the executive and legislative councils) abolished. The country is divided into 10 divisions, each administered by a commissioner (*muhafidh*).

Arabic is the official language. Tripoli and Benghazi form the dual capital, but it is planned to establish a single capital at Beida.

Prime Minister and Minister of Defence: Col. Moamer al Kadhafi.
Foreign Affairs: Salah Bousseir.

AREA AND POPULATION. The area is estimated at 1,759,540 sq. km (679,358 sq. miles). The population, according to the census of 1964, was 1,564,364. Estimate, 1968, 1·8m.

According to an arrangement with France (12 Sept. 1919), the western frontier extends in a curve from west of Ghadames to south of Tummo, including Ghat. According to the agreement with France of 7 Jan. 1935, the southern frontier runs along a line between Tummo and a cross-point indicated by 24° E. long. from Greenwich and 18° 45' N. lat. Further frontier agreements with France were signed on 10 Aug. 1955 and 26 Dec. 1956. In 1926 Egypt ceded the oasis of Jarabub to Italy, in exchange for a rectification of the frontier near Sollum. The eastern boundary follows in general the 25° parallel E. long. (*See* map in THE STATESMAN'S YEAR-BOOK, 1952.)

The country is administratively divided into the following 10 divisions (with population in brackets): Tripoli (376,177), Benghazi (279,665), Sebha 46,700),

Western Mountain (181,334), Zawia (189,032), Homs (137,205), Misurata (145,468), Derna (84,001), Green Mountain (87,803), Ubari (32,014).

The 2 most important towns are Tripoli (245,000 inhabitants) and Benghazi (140,000).

RELIGION. Islam is declared the State religion, but the right of others to practise their religions is provided for.

EDUCATION. Pupils spend 6 years in elementary schools, 3 in preparatory and 3 in secondary. In 1960–61 there were 197,208 pupils in Tripolitania, 46,525 in Cyrenaica and 11,230 in Fezzan. The Libyan University had, in 1961, 702 undergraduates studying arts and teaching, commerce and economics, and science. In 1960 Libyan university students abroad numbered 279 (135 in Egypt, 54 in the UK, 26 in USA, 24 in Italy, 17 in Turkey, the remainder in western Europe).

There are several schools, mainly in Tripoli, providing British, French, Italian, American and Dutch curricula, mainly on elementary and intermediate levels and chiefly for the non-Libyan communities.

JUSTICE. The Civil, Commercial and Criminal codes are based mainly on the Egyptian model. Matters of personal status of family or succession matters affecting Moslems are dealt with in special courts according to the Moslem law. All other matters, civil, commercial and criminal, are tried in the ordinary courts, which have jurisdiction over everyone.

There are civil and penal courts in Tripoli and Benghazi, with subsidiary courts at Misurata and Derna; courts of assize in Tripoli and Benghazi, and courts of appeal in Tripoli and Benghazi. The Supreme Court consists of a president and judges appointed by the King.

FINANCE. Currency. The Libyan pound, which is equivalent to £1·15 sterling, is divided into 1,000 millièmes.

Budget. The budget for the fiscal year ending 31 March 1970 balanced at £L426·3m. Estimated revenue included £L353m. from petroleum.

DEFENCE. Army. The Army, of 14,000 men, is organized in 2 armoured, 5 infantry, 1 anti-aircraft artillery battalion and 2 artillery battalions.

Navy. Two inshore minesweepers were acquired from Great Britain in 1963. A minvessel was built in Great Britain in 1965–66. There are also a maintenance repair craft purchased from Great Britain in 1966 and 9 coastguard patrol boats. Three fast patrol boats of the gas-turbine Vosper MTB type and a logistic support ship (Vosper-Thornycroft) were completed in Britain in 1968. A fast frigate was launched by Vosper-Thornycroft in 1969.

Air Force. The creation of an air force began in 1959 with the acquisition of 2 Egyptian-built Gomhouria primary trainers. Equipment in 1970 comprised 7 F-5A and 2 F-5B supersonic combat and training aircraft, 6 T-33A jet trainers, 6 C-130E Hercules and 10 C-47 transports and about 15 Bell 47, Alouette II and JetRanger helicopters. In 1971, delivery began of 30 Mirage III-E fighter-bombers, 50 Mirage 5 fighters, 20 Mirage III-B two-seat trainers and a Dassault Falcon equipped with Mirage avionics and controls for pilot training.

PLANNING. A new development plan was published in 1970.

AGRICULTURE. Tripolitania has 3 zones from the coast inland—the Mediterranean, the sub-desert and the desert. The first, which covers an area of about 17,231 sq. miles, is the only one properly suited for agriculture, and may be further subdivided into: (1) the oases along the coast, the richest in North Africa, in which thrive the date palm, the olive, the orange, the peanut and the potato; (2) the steppe district, suitable for cereals (barley and wheat) and pasture;

it has olive, almond, vine, orange and mulberry trees and ricinus plants; (3) the dunes, which are being gradually afforested with acacia, robinia, poplar and pine; (4) the Jebel (the mountain district, Tarhuna, Garian, Nalut-Yefren), in which thrive the olive, the fig, the vine and other fruit trees, and which on the east slopes down to the sea with the fertile hills of Msellata. Of some 25m. acres of productive land in Tripolitania, nearly 20m. are used for grazing and about 1m. for static farming. The sub-desert zone produces the alfa plant. The desert zone and the Fezzan contain some fertile oases, such as those of Ghadames, Ghat, Socna, Sebha, Brak.

Cyrenaica has about 10m. acres of potentially productive land, most of which, however, is suitable only for grazing. Certain areas, chief of which is the plateau known as the Barce Plain (about 1,000 ft above sea-level), are suitable for dry farming; in addition, grapes, olives and dates are grown. With improved irrigation, production, particularly of vegetables, could be increased, but stock raising and dry farming will remain of primary importance. About 143,000 acres are used for settled farming; about 272,000 acres are covered by natural forests. The National Agricultural Settlement Authority plans to reclaim 6,000 hectares each year for agriculture.

In the Fezzan there are about 6,700 acres of irrigated gardens and about 297,000 acres are planted with date palms.

The average annual cereal production of the whole of Libya is about 110,000 tons. Olive trees number about 3·4m. and productive date-palm trees about 3m. Livestock: 931,000 sheep, 1,236,000 goats, 93,500 camels.

INDUSTRY. Amongst the more important industries of Tripolitania and Cyrenaica are sponge fishing, tunny fishing, tobacco growing and processing, dyeing and weaving of local wool and imported cotton yarn, and olive oil. Tripolitania also produces bricks, salt, leather and esparto grass for papermaking. Home industries of both territories include the making of matting, carpets, leather articles and fabrics embroidered with gold and silver.

The preliminary results of the first industrial census (1965) show that there are 622 manufacturing establishments with 5 or more employees, employing a total of 11,106 workers; production in 1964 exceeded £24m. Fifteen establishments employed 100 or more persons and 22 between 50 and 99 persons. On 21 Sept. 1969 a decree laid down that all business concerns should be 100% Libyan-owned, but oil companies and banks were excluded.

OIL. In 1968, 41 companies were working concession areas; the most important discoveries so far made are: (i) Zelten, about 200 miles south from Benghazi and 100 miles from the nearest point on the coast; discovered by Esso (the local subsidiary of the Standard Oil Company of New Jersey) in April 1959. Exports from this field began at the end of 1961, the oil being piped to the port of Marsa Bregha. (ii) Dahra, roughly midway between Tripoli and Benghazi and about 90 miles from the coast, discovered in 1958–59; a pipeline to Ras El Sidr was completed in 1962. (iii) Beida, about 140 miles from the coast and just east of the Tripolitanian/Cyrenaican border, discovered by Caltex in 1959. (iv) Other discoveries, either non-commercial or not yet evaluated, have been made by Mobiloil of Canada, Shell, Gulf, CPTL. British Petroleum has also discovered oil in commercial quantities in southern Cyrenaica some 400 miles from the coast, connected to the Tobruk terminal by pipeline. Occidental Oil Co. have made 2 high-yield strikes and are planning the construction of a pipeline and terminal at Zueitina.

In 1968 production averaged 2·6m. bbls per day with total annual production of 949m. bbls. Exports in 1965 were 58·48m. tons; 1966, 72·24m. tons; 1967, 83·5m. tons.

Oil companies imported about £14·13m. worth of equipment in 1966, and employ about 12,600 staff.

MINING. Annual production of minerals (in metric tons): Cement, 200,000; gypsum, 14·4m.; salt, 16,000.

POWER. Production of electric power in 1957 was 50,667,897 kwh. in Tripolitania and 23,643,768 kwh. in Cyrenaica.

COMMERCE. Total imports into Libya in 1968 were valued at £L228m. (c.i.f.) and exports at £L668m. (f.o.b.), mostly crude oil.

Total trade between Libya and UK (British Board of Trade returns, in £1,000 sterling):

	1966	1967	1968	1969	1970
Imports to UK	60,701	66,389	156,949	151,557	166,876
Exports from UK	28,844	22,514	34,195	42,465 ⎫	24,346
Re-exports from UK	520	569	572	685 ⎭	

ROADS. Good motor roads connect Tripoli through Zuara with Tunis, and through Homs and Misurata with Benghazi and thence with Tobruk and Alexandria. Other roads go to Tagiura, Garian, Yefren and Nalut. A new road connects Sebha with the main coastal road.

Surface communication between Benghazi and Tripoli is by twice-weekly bus service, and between Benghazi and Alexandria by weekly bus service to Sollum and thence by rail. Communication between Benghazi, Barce, Derna and Tobruk is by frequent bus services.

AVIATION. Benghazi and Tripoli are both served by international airlines, including BEA and BOAC, linking them with each other and Athens, Cairo, Geneva, Rome, Malta, Tunis, Nairobi, West Africa and London.

A national airline, the Kingdom of Libya Airlines (KLA), was inaugurated on 30 Sept. 1965. Apart from internal flights KLA operate to Athens, Geneva, London, Rome, Beirut, Cairo, Paris, Malta and Tunis.

POST. Tripoli is connected by telegraph cable with Malta and by telephone lines with Bengardane (Tunis). There are overseas wireless-telegraph stations at Benghazi and Tripoli, and radio-telephone services connect Libya with the UK and most countries of western Europe. A submarine cable from Tripoli to Italy became operative in 1968. In 1962 some 20,000 telephones and 15,000 wireless sets were in use.

BANKING. A National Bank of Libya was established in 1955; it was renamed Bank of Libya in 1963. As at 31 March 1965, its assets amounted to £L77·8m. and currency in circulation to £L27·8m.

The National Agricultural Bank has offices in Tripoli and Benghazi.

There are branches of Barclays Bank DCO in Tripoli, Misurata, Homs, Benghazi, Tobruk and Derna. The Bank of North Africa, the Banco di Roma and the Nahda Bank have branches in Tripoli and Benghazi; the Banco d'Italia, Sahara Bank, Banco di Napoli, the Société de Banque and the Commercial Bank have branches in Tripoli and the Société de Banque in Sebha; the Arab Bank has branches in Benghazi and Tripoli.

WEIGHTS AND MEASURES. Although the metric system has been officially adopted, the following weights and measures are still used: *oke* = 1·282 kg; *kantar* = 40 *okes* = 51·28 kg; *draa* = 46 cm; *handaza* = 68 cm.

DIPLOMATIC REPRESENTATIVES

Libya maintains embassies in:

Algeria	Iraq	Poland	USSR
Belgium	Italy	Saudi Arabia	UAR
Chad	Jordan	Spain	UK
France	Lebanon	Syria	USA
Germany (West)	Morocco	Tunisia	Yugoslavia
Ghana	Nigeria	Turkey	

Libya maintains a legation in Niger.

OF LIBYA IN GREAT BRITAIN (58 Prince's Gate, SW7)
Ambassador: (Vacant).
Counsellor: Ismail S. Ismail.
Cultural Attaché: Mohamed O. Barundi. *First Secretaries:* S. S. Feituri;
M. Mannaa; Abdul R. Shennib.

OF GREAT BRITAIN IN LIBYA
Ambassador: J. P. Tripp, CMG.
Counsellor : M. P. V. Hannam (*Commercial*).
First Secretaries: D. K. Haskell; D. J. Pugh (*Consul*).

OF LIBYA IN THE USA (2344 Massachusetts Ave, NW,
Washington, D.C., 20008)
Minister: Abdalla Suwesi (*Chargé d'Affaires, a.i.*).

OF THE USA IN LIBYA
Ambassador: Joseph Palmer, II.
Deputy Chief of Mission: Harold G. Josif. *Heads of Sections:* Holsey G.
Handyside (*Political*); John E. Cunningham (*Economic*); Thomas T. Turqman
(*Commercial*); Robert A. Deitschman (*Administrative*).

BOOKS OF REFERENCE

The Economic Development of Libya. International Bank, 1960
Assan, G., *La Libia e il mondo arabo.* Rome, 1959
Khadduri, M., *Modern Libya.* Johns Hopkins Press, 1963

LIECHTENSTEIN

HISTORY. The Principality of Liechtenstein, situated between the Austrian
province of Vorarlberg and the Swiss cantons of St Gallen and Graubünden, is a
sovereign state whose history dates back to 3 May 1342, when Count Hartmann I
became ruler of the county of Vaduz. Additions were later made to the count's
domains, and by 1434 the territory reached its present boundaries. It consists of
the two former counties of Schellenberg and Vaduz (until 1806 immediate fiefs of
the Roman Empire). The former in 1699 and the latter in 1712 came into the
possession of the house of Liechtenstein and, by diploma of 23 Jan. 1719,
granted by the Emperor Charles VI, the two counties were constituted as the
Principality of Liechtenstein.

REIGNING PRINCE. Francis Joseph II, born 16 Aug. 1906; succeeded his
great uncle, 25 July 1938; married on 7 March 1943 to Countess Gina von
Wilczek; there are 4 sons, Princes Hans Adam (*heir apparent*, born 14 Feb.
1945; married on 30 July 1967 to Countess Marie Kinsky), Philip Erasmus,
Nikolaus Ferdinand and Franz Josef Wenzel, and one daughter, Princess Nora
Elisabeth. The monarchy is hereditary in the male line.

National flag: Blue, red, with golden crown in the blue stripe.
National anthem: Oben am jungen Rhein (words by H. H. Jauch, 1850; tune,
'God save the Queen').

AREA AND POPULATION. Area, 160 sq. km (61·8 sq. miles); population,
of Alemannic race (census 1960), 16,628; estimate, 1969, 27,758. In 1960 there
were 15,352 Catholics, 1,124 Protestants, 4 Christian Catholics, 37 Jews and
111 others. In 1969 there were 420 births and 168 deaths.

CONSTITUTION AND GOVERNMENT. The constitution, adopted on 5 Oct. 1921, provides for a Diet of 15 members elected for 4 years by direct vote on the basis of universal suffrage and proportional representation. The capital and seat of government is Vaduz (population, 1968, 4,067), and there are 10 more villages all connected by modern roads. Since Feb. 1921 Liechtenstein has had the Swiss currency, and since Jan. 1924 has been united with Switzerland in a customs union. Switzerland has also since 1919 represented the Principality diplomatically.

At the elections for the Diet, on 1 Feb. 1970, the Patriotic Union Party obtained 8 seats, the opposition Progressive Citizens' Party 7 seats.

Head of Government: Dr Alfred Hilbe.

EDUCATION (19)70. In 14 primary and 5 secondary schools there were 3,302 pupils and 157 teachers (101 men and 56 women).

JUSTICE. The principality has a High Court and its own penal and civil code.

Police. The principality has no army. Police force, 27, auxiliary police, 29.

FINANCE. Budget estimates for 1971: Revenue, 54,091,200 Swiss francs; expenditure, 43,227,525 Swiss francs. Public debt on 31 Dec. 1970, 1·5m. Swiss francs.

PRODUCTION AND INDUSTRY. The country has a great variety of light industries (textiles, ceramics, steel screws, precision instruments, canned food, pharmaceutical products, heating appliances, etc.).

Liechtenstein has during the past 30 years changed from a predominantly agricultural country to a highly industrialized country. The farming population has gone down from 70% in 1930 to only 5·5% in 1970. The rapid change-over has led to the immigration of foreign workers (Austrians, Germans, Italians, Spaniards). Industrial undertakings in 1969 employed 4,874 workers earning 70m. Swiss francs.

Electricity produced in 1970 was 44,928,200 kwh.

AGRICULTURE. The rearing of cattle, for which the fine alpine pastures are well suited, is highly developed. On 21 April 1967 there were 6,144 cattle, 105 horses, 1,116 sheep, 103 goats, 4,315 pigs, 3,451 rabbits and 14,554 chickens.

TOURISM. In 1969, 66,109 foreign visitors stayed in Liechtenstein, spending an estimated 16m. Swiss francs.

TRADE. Exports of home produce in 1969 amounted to 280,270,312 Swiss francs. 50·2% went to EFTA countries and 33·9% to EEC countries. The biggest customer is Switzerland (99·4m.).

Total trade with UK is included with Switzerland from 1968.

COMMUNICATIONS. On 3 April 1943 a canal for irrigating the valley, 26 km in length, was opened. In Dec. 1947 a tunnel, 740 metres long and connecting the Rhine and Samina valleys, was opened. The 11½ miles of main line railway passing through the country is operated by Austrian Federal Railways.

In 1968 there were 7,903 telephones, 4,519 wireless sets and 2,491 television sets. The post and telegraphs are administered by Switzerland.

USA Consul-General: George R. Irminger (resident in Zürich).

BOOKS OF REFERENCE

STATISTICAL INFORMATION. Press and Information Service, Vaduz. *Chief:* Walter Kranz.

Rechenschaftsberischt der fürstlichen liechtensteinischen Regierung. Vaduz. Annual, from 1922
Jahrbücher der Historischen Vereins. Vaduz. Annual since 1900
Batliner, E. H., *Das Geld- und Kreditwesen des Fürstentums Liechtenstein.* Winterthur, 1959
d'Havrincourt, H., *Liechtenstein.* Lausanne, 1964
Greene, B., *Liechtenstein, Valley of Peace.* Vaduz, 1967
Kranz, W., *Principality of Liechtenstein—Documentary Handbook.* Vaduz, 1969
Steger, G., *Fürst und Landtag nach Liechtensteinischem Recht.* Vaduz, 1950

LUXEMBOURG

Grand-Duché de Luxembourg

REIGNING GRAND DUKE. Jean, born 5 Jan. 1921, son of Grand Duchess Charlotte and the late Prince Felix of Bourbon-Parma; succeeded 12 Nov. 1964 on the abdication of his mother; married to Princess Joséphine-Charlotte of Belgium, 9 April 1953. *Offspring:* Princess Marie Astrid, born 17 Feb. 1954; Prince Henri, *heir apparent*, born 16 April 1955; Prince Jean and Princess Margareta, born 15 May 1957; Prince Guillaume, born 1 May 1963.

The civil list is fixed at 300,000 gold francs per annum, to be reconsidered at the beginning of each reign.

On 28 Sept. 1919 a referendum was taken in Luxembourg to decide on the political and economic future of the country. The voting resulted as follows: For the reigning Grand Duchess, 66,811; for the continuance of the Nassau-Braganza dynasty under another Grand Duchess, 1,286; for another dynasty, 889; for a republic, 16,885; for an economic union with France, 60,133; for an economic union with Belgium, 22,242. But France refused in favour of Belgium, and on 22 Dec. 1921 the Chamber of the Grand Duchy passed a Bill for the economic union between Belgium and Luxembourg. The agreement, which is for 50 years, provides for the disappearance of the customs barrier between the two countries and the use of Belgian, in addition to Luxembourg, currency as legal tender in the Grand Duchy. It came into force on 1 May 1922.

The Grand Duchy was under German occupation from 10 May 1940 to 10 Sept. 1944. The Grand Duchess Charlotte and the Government carried on an independent administration in London. Civil government was restored in Oct. 1944.

National flag: Red, white, blue (horizontal).
National anthem: Ons Hemecht (words by M. Lentz, 1859; tune by J. A. Zinnen).

AREA AND POPULATION. Luxembourg has an area of 2,586 sq. km (999 sq. miles), and a population (31 Dec. 1969) of 338,500. The capital, Luxembourg, had 77,463 inhabitants; Esch-Alzette, the centre of the mining district, 27,330; Differdange, 17,770; Dudelange, 14,480, and Petange, 11,840.

Vital statistics (1969): 4,503 births, 4,193 deaths, 2,221 marriages.

CONSTITUTION AND GOVERNMENT. The Grand Duchy of Luxembourg is a constitutional monarchy, the hereditary sovereignty being in the Nassau family. The constitution of 17 Oct. 1868 was revised in 1919, 1948 and 1956. The revision of 1948 has abolished the 'perpetually neutral' status of the country and introduced the concepts of right to work, social security, health services, freedom of trade and industry, and recognition of trade unions. The revision of 1956 provides for the devolution of executive, legislative and judicial powers to international institutions.

The national language is Luxemburgish; French, German and English are widely used.

The country forms 4 electoral districts. An elector must be a citizen (male or female) of Luxembourg and have completed 21 years of age; to be eligible for election the citizen must have completed 25 years of age.

The Chamber of Deputies consists of 21 Christian Social, 18 Socialists, 11 Democrats and 6 Communists (elections of 15 Dec. 1968). Members are elected for 5 years; they receive a salary and a travelling allowance.

The head of the state takes part in the legislative power, exercises the executive power and has a certain part in the judicial power. The constitution leaves to the sovereign the right to organize the Government, which consists of a Minister of State, who is President of the Government, and of at least 3 Ministers.

The Cabinet was, in Feb. 1969, composed as follows:

Minister of State, President of the Government, Treasury: Pierre Werner (Christian Socialist).

Vice-President, Interior and Justice: Eugène Schaus (Lib.). *Foreign Affairs; Civil Service and Sport:* Gaston Thorn (Lib.). *National Economy, Middle Classes, Tourism, Transport and Energy:* Marcel Mart (Lib.). *National Education, Labour and Social Security:* Jean Dupong (Christian Socialist). *Agriculture and Public Works:* Jean-Pierre Buchler (Christian Socialist). *Family, Youth, Social Solidarity, Public Health and Cultural Affairs:* Madeleine Frieden-Kinnen (Christian Socialist).

Besides the Cabinet there is a Council of State. It deliberates on proposed laws and Bills, on amendments that might be proposed; it also gives administrative decisions and expresses its opinion regarding any other question referred to it by the Grand Duke or the Government. The Council of State is composed of 21 members chosen for life by the sovereign, who also chooses a president from among them each year.

RELIGION. The population is Catholic, save (31 Dec. 1960) 2,951 Protestants, 643 Jews, 1,090 belonging to other denominations and 13,697 without religion (or having given no indication on this subject). The Protestant Church is organized on an inter-denominational basis.

EDUCATION (1969–70). Education is compulsory for all children between the ages of 6 and 15. The primary schools had 1,597 teachers (822 women) and 36,035 pupils (17,995 girls); 3 state middle schools had 1,135 (423 girls); 1 private middle school had 127 girls; 8 state grammar schools had 7,359 pupils (2,585 girls); 6 private grammar schools had 1,330 girls.

Technical and vocational schools: 17 state schools had 6,469 pupils; 16 private schools had 1,613 pupils (1,387 girls). Two institutes of agriculture had together with 1 institute of viticulture 295 pupils (108 girls). One teachers' training college had 155 students (83 girls). There also are 9 music schools.

CINEMAS (1965). There were 48 cinemas with a seating capacity of 22,831.

NEWSPAPERS (1969). There were 7 daily newspapers with an aggregate circulation of 140,000.

FINANCE. Currency. On 14 Oct. 1944 the Luxembourg franc was fixed at par value with the Belgian franc. Notes of the Belgian National Bank are legal tender in Luxembourg.

Budget. Revenue and expenditure (including extraordinary) for years ending 30 April (in 1m. francs):

	1966	1967	1968	1969	1970[1]	1971[1]
Revenue	9,931·3	9,975·8	10,904·2	11,948·5	11,592·6	13,468·4
Expenditure	9,950·2	10,125·1	11,040·5	11,661·5	11,911·2	13,455·2

[1] Estimates.

Consolidated debt at 31 Dec. 1969 amounted to 10,036·3m. francs (long-term) and 4,240m. francs (short-term).

DEFENCE. A law passed by parliament on 29 June 1967 abolished compulsory service and instituted a battalion-size army of volunteers enlisted for 3 years. The defence estimates for 1970 amounted to 402·78m. francs.

Luxembourg is an original member of NATO.

AGRICULTURE. Agriculture is carried on by about 16,000 of the population; 135,699 hectares were under cultivation in 1969. The principal crops are oats, potatoes and wheat.

Livestock (May 1969): 1,358 horses, 191,375 cattle, 90,351 pigs, 4,167 sheep.

MINING. The mining and metallurgical industries are the most important. In 1969 production (in metric tons) of iron ore was 6,310,574; of pig-iron, 4,872,274; of steel, 5,520,965.

The number of blast furnaces in 1969 was 25, that of steelworks, 8; number of workers in the mining and metallurgical industries, 22,603.

ELECTRICITY. Power production was 2,120m. kwh. in 1969.

COMMERCE. By treaty of 5 Sept. 1944, signed in London, and the treaty of 14 March 1947, signed in The Hague, the Grand Duchy, together with Belgium and the Netherlands, became a party to the Benelux Customs Union, which came into force on 1 Jan. 1948. For further particulars *see* pp. 764 and 1183.

Total trade between Luxembourg and UK (British Board of Trade returns), in £1,000 sterling:

	1965	1966	1967	1968	1969	1970
Imports to UK	1,678	3,143	3,237	5,352	4,657	4,306
Exports from UK	1,342	1,176	1,104	1,732	2,020 ⎱	5,653
Re-exports from UK	139	320	148	222	673 ⎰	

ROADS. In 1969 there were 2,831 km of state roads and 2,118 km of local roads. Motor vehicles registered in Luxembourg on 1 Jan. 1970 included 84,816 passenger cars, 11,376 trucks, 560 buses, 9,844 tractors, 3,992 motor cycles.

RAILWAYS. In 1970 there were 281 km of railway (standard gauge).

POST. In 1967 the telephone system had 2,100 km of telegraph and telephone line and (1970) 102,172 telephones, 99 post offices and 514 telegraph offices.

BANKING. On 31 Dec. 1969 there were 256,467 depositors in the State Savings Bank, with a total of 9,445,425,835 francs to their credit.

DIPLOMATIC REPRESENTATIVES

Luxembourg maintains embassies in:

Belgium	Netherlands	USA (also for Canada
France	Switzerland	and Mexico)
Germany (West)	USSR (also for Poland)	Vatican
Italy	UK (also for Iceland)	

In virtue of an agreement of 6/7 Jan. 1880, revised on 24 March 1964, the Netherlands diplomatic agencies represent Luxembourg in 53 other countries.

OF LUXEMBOURG IN GREAT BRITAIN (27 Wilton Crescent, SW1)

Ambassador: André J. Clasen, GCVO (accredited as ambassador, 27 Oct. 1955).
Secretary: Paul Helminger.

OF GREAT BRITAIN IN LUXEMBOURG

Ambassador and Consul-General: J. C. A. Roper, CMG, MC.
First Secretary: T. E. J. Mound (*Consul*).
Resident in Brussels: *Counsellor:* G. F. Hiller, CMG, DSO (*Commercial*).
Defence Attaché: Brig. A. L. Hulton, MBE. *First Secretary:* J. S. Vigors (*Labour*).

OF LUXEMBOURG IN THE USA (2210 Massachusetts Ave. NW,
Washington, D.C., 20008)
Ambassador: Jean Wagner.

OF THE USA IN LUXEMBOURG
Ambassador: Kingdom Gould, Jr.
Deputy Chief of Mission: Marshall H. Noble. *Heads of Sections:* Merwin W.
Peake (*Political*); Stephen Lande (*Economic*); Gus P. Peleuses (*Administrative*).

BOOKS OF REFERENCE

STATISTICAL INFORMATION. The Service Central de la Statistique was founded in 1900 and
reorganized in 1962 (19, Avenue de la Porte Neuve, Luxembourg-City). *Director:* Georges Als.
Main publications: *Bulletin du Statec.—Annuaire statistique.—Cahiers économiques.*
Bulletin de Documentation. Government Information Service. From 1945 (monthly)
Luxembourg 963–1963. Le livre du millénaire. Luxembourg, 1963
Tausend Jahre Luxemburg. Luxembourg, 1963
Cooper-Pritchard, A. H., *History of the Grand-Duchy of Luxembourg.* Luxembourg, 1950
Majerus, P., *Le Luxembourg indépendant.* Luxembourg, 1948.—*L'État Luxembourgeois.* Luxem-
bourg, 1948
Petit, J., *Luxemburg, plateforme internationale.* Luxembourg, 1960
Weber, P., *Histoire du Grand-Duché de Luxembourg.* Brussels, 1949.—*Histoire de l'économie
luxembourgeoise.* Luxembourg, 1950
ARCHIVES OF THE STATE. Luxembourg-City. *Director:* Paul Spang.
NATIONAL LIBRARY. Luxembourg-City, 14a Boulevard Royal. *Director:* Prof. Dr Joseph
Goedert.

REPUBLIC OF MALDIVES

The Republic of Maldives, 400 miles to the south-west of Ceylon, consists of some
2,000 low-lying coral islands (only 220 inhabited), grouped into 12 clearly defined
clusters of atolls but divided into 19 for administrative purposes. Area 115 sq.
miles (298 sq. km). Population (census 1963), 96,432. Capital Malé (10,875
inhabitants; 5,779 males, 5,096 females). The people are all Moslems, and Islam
is reflected in the constitution and the judicial system. The islands are covered
with coconut palms and yield millet and fruit as well as coconut produce.
The official language is Maldivian, which is akin to Elu or old Sinhalese.

President: Ibrahim Nasır.
British Ambassador: The British High Commissioner to Ceylon.

The islands were under British protection from 1887 to mid-1965. They
now enjoy complete independence under the agreement signed in Colombo
on 26 July 1965. The Republic of Maldives became a republic on 11 Nov.
1968.
The 1965 agreement confirmed the agreement of 1956, which allowed the
British Government to reactivate the wartime air staging post on Gan island in
Addu Atoll, the southernmost of the group (8,235 inhabitants). There is another
airstrip at Hulele in the Malé atoll, some 300 miles from Gan.
In 1960 the British Government made a gift of £100,000 to the Maldivian
government and a further £750,000 to be spent over a period of five or more
years for development projects in the Republic. These projects have included
the establishment of a hospital, a small inter-atoll dispensary ship, expansion of
the fishing industry and shipping. In 1969 a further sum of £500,000 was made
available for expenditure on additional development projects.
The Maldivian economy is based on the fishing industry. Dried bonito
('Maldive fish') is the main export commodity. Exports and imports balanced at
about Rs 9·5m. in 1964. There is no direct taxation.

Bell, H. C. P., *History, Archaeology and Epigraphy of the Maldive Islands.* Ceylon Govt. Press
Colombo, 1940

MEXICO

Estados Unidos Mexicanos

HISTORY. Mexico's history falls into four epochs: the era of the Indian empires (before 1521), the Spanish colonial phase (1521–1810), the period of national formation (1810–1910), which includes the war of independence (1810–21) and the long presidency of Porfirio Díaz (1876–80, 1884–1911), and the present period which began with the social revolution of 1910–21 and is regarded by Mexicans as the period of social and national consolidation.

CONSTITUTION AND GOVERNMENT. A new constitution, amending the constitution of 1857, was promulgated on 5 Feb. 1917, and amended frequently from 1929 to 1953. Mexico is a federal republic, divided into 29 states, each of which has the right to manage its own local affairs. Citizenship, including the right of suffrage, is vested in all nationals who are 18 years old and have 'an honourable means of livelihood'; women were given equal citizenship and suffrage with men in 1952–53. Thumbprints are taken of registered voters.

Congress consists of a Chamber of Deputies elected for 3 years by universal suffrage, and a Senate of 60 members, 2 for each state and the federal district, elected for 6 years. Since 1964 additional 'party deputies' have also been elected to the Chamber according to a system of partial proportional representation. There are (1970) 213 seats, of which the 3 small opposition parties hold 35. Senators and deputies are ineligible for re-election until another term has elapsed. Congress sits from 1 Sept. to 31 Dec. During the recess there is a permanent committee consisting of 14 senators and 15 representatives appointed by the respective Houses.

The President is elected by direct popular vote in a general election, and holds office for 6 years. He can never be re-elected. If the office falls vacant during the first 2 years a general election must be held; if after the first 2 years, then Congress elects a successor who completes the term. The administration is carried on under the direction of the President and a cabinet formed by the secretaries of 15 ministries, the Attorney-General and the heads of 3 departments.

The names of the presidents from 1920 are as follows:

Gen. Alvaro Obregón, 1 Dec. 1920–30 Nov. 1924

Gen. Plutarco Elías Calles, 1 Dec. 1924–30 Nov. 1928.

Emilio Portes Gil (Provisional),[1] 1 Dec. 1928–4 Feb. 1930.

Pascual Ortiz Rubio, 5 Feb. 1930–3 Sept. 1932.[2]

Gen. Abelardo L. Rodríguez, 4 Sept. 1932–30 Nov. 1934.

Gen. Lázaro Cárdenas, 1 Dec. 1934–30 Nov. 1940.

Gen. Manuel Ávila Camacho, 1 Dec. 1940–30 Nov. 1946.

Miguel Alemán Valdés, 1 Dec. 1946–30 Nov. 1952.

Adolfo Ruiz Cortines, 1 Dec. 1952–30 Nov. 1958.

Adolfo Lopez Mateos, 1 Dec. 1958–30 Nov. 1964.

Gustavo Diaz Ordaz, 1 Dec. 1964–30 Nov. 1970.

[1] Took office after the assassination on 17 July 1928, of Gen. Obregón, the President-elect.
[2] Resigned.

President: Luis Echeverría Alvarez (born in 1922), formerly Minister of the Interior, elected 5 July 1970 to serve for 6 years. He polled 11,923,755 votes out of the total of 14,027,816 (assumed office on 1 Dec. 1970).

Minister for Foreign Affairs: Emilio O. Rabasa.

National flag: Green, white, red (vertical); the national coat of arms on white.

National anthem: Mexicanos, al grito de guerra (words by F. González Bocanegra; tune by Jaime Nunó, 1854).

LOCAL GOVERNMENT. Mexico is divided into 29 states, 1 federal district (comprising México City and 12 surrounding villages) and 2 territories, Quintana Roo and Baja California Sur. Each state has its own constitution, government, taxes and laws, and its governor, legislature and judicial officers popularly elected. Inter-state customs duties are not permitted. The President appoints the governors of the territories and the chief of the federal district.

AREA AND POPULATION. Mexico comprises 1,967,183 sq. km (761,530 sq. miles), excluding inland waters and uninhabited islands (5,363 sq. km) off-shore. The language is Spanish.

Census results for 1960 and 1970 are shown in the following table (capitals of states and territories in brackets):

States and territories	Area (sq. km)	Census 1960	Census (Prelim.) 1970	Approx. density per sq. km 1960
Aguascalientes (Aguascalientes)	5,589	243,363	334,936	56·54
Baja California (Mexicali)	70,113	520,165	856,773	14·89
Baja California, T.S.	73,677	81,594	123,786	1·44
Campeche (Campeche)	56,114	168,219	250,391	4·26
Coahuila (Saltillo)	151,571	907,734	1,140,989	8·08
Colima (Colima)	5,455	164,450	240,235	43·63
Chiapas (Tuxtla Gutiérrez)	73,887	1,210,870	1,578,180	21·06
Chihuahua (Chihuahua)	247,087	1,226,793	1,730,012	7·39
Distrito Federal (México City)	1,499	4,870,876	7,005,855	4,953·30
Durango (Durango)	119,648	760,836	919,381	8·02
Guanajuato (Guanajuato)	30,589	1,735,490	2,285,249	76·04
Guerrero (Chilpancingo)	63,794	1,186,716	1,573,098	25·39
Hidalgo (Pachuca)	20,987	994,598	1,156,177	61·08
Jalisco (Guadalajara)	80,137	2,443,261	3,322,750	41·73
México (Toluca)	21,461	1,897,851	3,797,861	130·61
Michoacán (Morelia)	59,864	1,851,876	2,341,556	40·96
Morelos (Cuernavaca)	4,941	386,264	620,392	120·83
Nayarit (Tepic)	27,621	389,929	547,992	20·82
Nuevo León (Monterrey)	64,555	1,078,848	1,653,808	25·99
Oaxaca (Oaxaca)	95,364	1,727,266	2,011,946	22·75
Puebla (Puebla)	33,919	1,973,837	2,483,770	75·91
Querétaro (Querétaro)	11,769	355,045	464,226	39·68
Quintana Roo (Terr.) (Chetumal)	42,030	50,169	91,044	1·90
San Luis Potosí (San Luis Potosí)	62,848	1,048,297	1,257,028	22·85
Sinaloa (Culiacán)	58,092	838,404	1,273,228	20·40
Sonora (Hermosillo)	184,934	783,378	1,092,458	6·75
Tabasco (Villa Hermosa)	24,661	496,340	766,346	28·02
Tamaulipas (Ciudad Victoria)	79,829	1,024,182	1,438,350	18·63
Tlaxcala (Tlaxcala)	3,914	346,699	418,334	116·00
Veracruz (Jalapa)	72,815	2,727,899	3,813,613	49·84
Yucatán (Mérida)	43,379	614,699	774,011	18·83
Zacatecas (Zacatecas)	75,040	817,831	949,663	14·42
Total	1,967,183[1]	34,923,129	48,313,438	24·81

[1] Excludes islands (5,363 sq. km).

At the census of 28 Jan. 1970, 23,873,207 were males and 24,440,231 females. Urban population, 1960, was 17,705,118 (50·7%) and rural population 17,218,011 (49·3%); economically active were 11,332,016 (32·4%). Of the 3,030,254 Indians, 1,104,955 spoke only their native language. There were 31 different language groups, and 21 minor linguistic divisions. Foreign-born, 1950, numbered 182,707, including 106,315 born abroad.

The chief cities, with population (in 1,000), at census, 1970 are: México City (capital), 7,006 (and another 1·2m. outside the area of the Federal District but within the Valley of Mexico); Guadalajara, 1,196·2; Monterrey, 830·3; Netzahn-alcoyott, 571; León, 454; Ciudad Juárez, 436; Mexicali, 390·4; Nancalpan, 373·6; Tlalnepankla, 373; Chihuahua, 363·8; Culiacán, 358·8; Tijuana, 335·1; Puebla, 321·9; San Luiz Potosí, 274·3; Torreón, 257; Mérida 253·8; Veracruz, 242·3; Acapulco, 234·8; Tolnea, 230·1; Aguascalientes, 222·1; Ecataple, 220·9; Morelia, 209·5; Hermosillo, 206·6; Tampico, 196·1; Durango, 192·9; Saltillo, 191·8; Matamoros, 182·9; Irapuato, 175·9; Mazatlan, 171·8; Cuernavaca, 159·5; Nuevo Laredo, 150·9.

Movement of population for 3 years:

	Marriages	Births	Deaths	Immigration	Emigration
1966	307,992	1,954,340	424,141	1,732,355	1,454,992
1967	314,268	1,981,363	420,298	1,903,511	1,595,274
1968	347,120	2,058,251	331,347	2,260,000	1,834,473

Crude birth rate, 1968, was 43·5 per 1,000 population; crude death rate, 9·6 (26·1 in 1932); infant mortality rate, 64·2 per 1,000 live births (139·3 in 1933); crude marriage rate, 7 per 1,000 population; divorces, 25,623.

For the regulations governing immigration, *see* THE STATESMAN'S YEAR-BOOK, 1951, p. 1234. An Immigration Tax law came into effect 1 Jan. 1951. The net immigration in 1968 included: 938 USA subjects; 502 Spaniards; 27 Cubans; 122 Germans; 49 Italians; 25 Japanese; 53 British; 57 French.

RELIGION. The prevailing religion is the Roman Catholic (33·7m. members at the census of 1960, about 97% of the total population); with 10 archbishops, 38 bishops, but by the constitution of 1857, the Church was separated from the State, and the constitution of 1917 provided strict regulation of this and all other religions. No ecclesiastical body may acquire landed property, and since 1917 the property of the Church has been held to belong to the State. In the 1920s the Government suppressed the political influence of the priesthood and temporarily (1929–31) closed the churches. An understanding between State and Church was, however, reached, and all churches eschewing public affairs flourish freely. Protestant churches had about 600,000 members in 1962. At the 1960 census 100,750 Jews and 137,208 members of other religions were also numbered.

EDUCATION. Primary education is free and compulsory (up to 15 years of age), and secular. Clergy are forbidden to establish primary schools. All private schools must conform to government standards. Military drill is compulsory for boys of 18 years. In the federal district and in the territories education is controlled by the national government; elsewhere by the state authorities.

In 1968–69 there were:

	Schools	Teachers	Pupils
Kindergarten	3,038	11,612	419,036
Primary	43,820	182,851	8,619,462
Secondary	4,099	70,551	997,685
Pre-university	506	16,387	189,201
Teacher training	291	3,547	33,834
Professional	316	19,879	188,001

There are 105 institutions teaching at higher education level in Mexico with the status of a university. The most important university is the Universidad Nacional Autónoma de México (UNAM) in México City which, with its associated universities and schools, has 96,050 pupils and 7,701 teachers. UNAM was founded in 1552, reorganized in 1910, and granted full autonomy in 1920. Other universities of particular importance in México City are El Colegio de México, a small, independent university concentrating on research in the humanities and social sciences, the Instituto Politecnico Nacional, specializing in applied science, and the Universidad Iberoamericana, a private university. Outside México City the more notable universities are, in Monterrey, the Universidad de Nuevo Leon and the Instituto Tecnólügico de Estudios Superiores de Monterrey; in Guadalajara, the Universidad de Guadalajara and the Universidad Autónoma de Guadalajara; and in Xalapa, the Universidad Veracruzana.

CINEMAS (1968). Cinemas numbered 1,836 with annual attendance of 251·2m.

NEWSPAPERS (1970). There were 195 dailies with an aggregate circulation of nearly 5m.; 17 in México City have about half of the total circulation.

Kneller, G. F., *The Education of the Mexican Nation*. New York, 1951

HEALTH. In 1967 Mexico had 21,293 physicians (1 to 1,519 population); in 1967 there were 807 state and private internship hospitals and 1,761 state and private externship hospitals, with together about 100,000 beds.

JUSTICE. Magistrates are appointed by Congress for 6 years; but the judges of the Supreme Court can be removed only on impeachment. The courts include the Supreme Court with 21 magistrates, 6 circuit courts with 3 judges each, 6 unitary and 47 district courts with one judge each. The penal code of 1 Jan. 1930 abolished the death penalty, except for the Army, and set up a commission of alienists and other specialists, in place of the courts, to deal with criminal cases (for federal offences); each state appoints its own local magistrates also.

Mexican civil law has the legal remedy known as *amparo*, which gives any injured person whose constitutional rights have, in his opinion, been infringed, right to immediate access to the courts and full remedy, combining the swiftness of the Anglo-Saxon writ of *habeas corpus* and the breadth of remedy available through the injunction.

FINANCE. Currency. The monetary unit is the *peso* divided into 100 *centavos*.
There are coins for 1 peso and 50, 20, 10 and 5 centavos; notes for 10,000, 5,000, 1,000, 500, 100, 50, 20, 10, 5 and 1 pesos.
Rate of exchange, Jan. 1971: 12·49 pesos = US$1; 29·9 pesos = £1.

Budget. Ordinary receipts and expenditure in 1m. pesos for calendar years:

	1965	1966	1967	1968	1969	1970
Revenue	17,200	20,132	22,108	24,221	26,512	28,134
Expenditure	17,855	20,132	22,108	24,221	26,512	28,134

In 1970, 7,947m. pesos was spent on education, 1,797m. on defence and 1,804m. on debt service.
The 1970 budgetary total balanced at 72,229m. pesos including the budgets of 20 autonomous agencies whose estimates balance at 44,095m. pesos.
The powers of federal, state and municipal authorities to contract debt are circumscribed by the constitution.
The national debt on 31 Dec. 1967 was 42,732m. pesos, of which 10% was external debt.

DEFENCE. Supreme command is vested in the President, exercised through the Ministries of Defence (for Army and Air Force) and Marine.

Army. The country is divided into 35 zones in which both the regular army and volunteer corps are trained. The Army, in 1965, had 50 battalions of infantry, 2 infantry brigades, 21 regiments of cavalry, 1 mechanized cavalry regiment, 2 regiments of artillery and 2 coastal batteries. Peace-time strength is 51,000. Military education is provided for officers, at the National Military School, the Application Centre for Army Officers and the Staff College, as well as in other specialized schools. To combat illiteracy in the Army, schools have been established in every regular and volunteer group.

Navy. The Navy consists of 8 frigates (including 4 former US destroyer escort transports), 20 escort minesweepers, 2 patrol vessels, 8 patrol boats, 1 transport, 2 oilers and a survey ship, formerly the presidential yacht. In 1962, 20 fleet minesweepers were aquired from the USA, but they are used as escorts. There are 4 naval districts on the Atlantic and 4 on the Pacific coast. Naval personnel in 1970 totalled 12,300 officers and men including marines. There are 7 companies of marines on active duty, with 1 regiment (3 companies) in reserve, formed by military service conscripts.

Air Force. The Air Force has a strength of about 5,000 officers and men, and 160 aircraft. These include 15 T-33A dual-purpose jet-trainer fighter-bombers, C-118A, C-54, C-47 and LASA-60 transports, 30 T-28A and 45 T-6 armed piston-engined trainers and some light helicopters.

AGRICULTURE. Grains occupy 68% of the cultivated land, with about 53% given to maize and about 9% to wheat. Irrigation is needed, 43% of the land having less than 500 mm. of rain a year. The arable land is approximately 24m. hectares, of which half is devoted to the chief crops: maize, wheat, beans, cotton, coffee, sorghum, sugar and rice. In 1964, 52,000 tractors were said to be in use.
In 1967 the area irrigated was 3·2m. hectares. The irrigated districts were equal in 1967–68 to 18% of the cultivated land and provided two-thirds of the agricultural production. Not until there are 17m. acres under irrigation, it is estimated, will Mexico be self-supporting; about 20·3m. acres in all might eventually be brought under cultivation. Soil-conservation work has been started; it includes teaching contour ploughing, terracing, crop rotation, transplanting of the maguey and reafforestation.

Livestock (1967): Cattle, 37·7m.; sheep, 6·7m.; hogs, 14·5m.; horses, 5·2m.; goats, 13·2m.; mules, 2m.; donkeys, 3·6m.; poultry, 95m.

Production of hides reached 3·96m. in 1968; production of meat, 593,124 tons.

Mexico's basic food crop is maize, and a rapid expansion of this crop is one of the chief aims of Mexican agricultural policy, balanced by the demand for 'cash crops' for export, such as cotton, sugar, garbanzos (chick peas), bananas, winter vegetables and coffee. Local production of nitrogen fertilizers in 1968 was 190,000 tons, and of phosphatic, 92,800 tons.

Principal products in metric tons for 1967 were: Maize, 9·49m. (1968: 9·36m.); rice, 454,580; sugar-cane, 28m.; wheat, 1·89m.; coffee, 171,000; beans, 1·04m.; tomatoes, 602,000; oranges, 892,440; bananas, 551,040. Nine-tenths of the coffee is available for export. Sugar output since 1946 has left surpluses for export; sugar crop in 1964–65 was 1·98m. tons; in 1965–66, 2·18m.

The Yucatán peninsula produces about 50% of the world's supply of sisal (known locally as henequén); plantations are almost wholly Mexican-owned and the crop was handled exclusively by the state of Yucatán until 20 June 1955, since when the principal industries were grouped together in the private enterprise Cordemex, S.A., which exercised a virtual monopoly. In April 1964 these interests were purchased by the central government and are now controlled by a state board. The industry has since suffered from over-production and, in the face of competition from Brazilian, African and synthetic products, a decline in the world price for the fibre. The 1964 sisal crop amounted to 160,200 metric tons of fibre.

Tobacco, 1968, 62,000 metric tons. Banana production started in 1895 in the state of Tabasco, reaching a peak in 1937, when 14,752,424 stems were exported; exports, 1960, 0·6m. stems. The cotton production, 1968, was 1,552,000 metric tons. Wool output, 1963, 3,679 metric tons; 1964, 3,845.

FORESTRY. Timber lands are estimated to extend over 95m. acres (about 60m. of commercial importance), containing pine, spruce, cedar, mahogany, logwood and rosewood. Reckless lumbering has destroyed the timber stands on many watersheds, resulting in spring floods and lowered water supplies in summer. In 1951 federal edicts had halted all timber-cutting in 22 states, regardless of concessions; but they have been resumed under strict supervision. There are 14 forest reserves (nearly 800,000 hectares) and 47 national park forests of 750,000 hectares. In 1966 wood products amounted to 3,438,592 cu. metres; others in metric tons (1968): chicle, 1,349; pitch, 5,551; resins, 43,819; turpentine, 1,479; fibres, 7,882; vegetable waxes, 2,418; tan-barks, 258.

FISHERY. Coastal fishing is important. The catch in 1968 was 240,060 metric tons, of which 194,428 was edible, the remainder for industry. In 1967 the industry employed 45,618 men.

MINING. Mining is the principal industry in Mexico, but practically 97% of the 31,000 mining properties are foreign-owned. Of the annual output (from 189 active mines and 127 metallurgical plants), measured in pesos, probably less than 10% is Mexican-owned. The discovery of uranium and similar deposits in the states of Chihuahua, Durango, Sonora and Querétaro was announced in Jan. 1959.

Output of silver in 1960 was 21·2% of world production. Silver output (in metric tons) was 1,245 in 1968; 1,190 in 1967. Exports, 1968, of bar and refined silver, 1·16m. kg. About half the production in minted, including a 'token' coin (1949) weighing 1 troy oz. Gold output: 1968, 5,504 kg.; 1967, 5,141 kg.

Mexico has large coal resources, including high-grade coking coal at Sabinas in Coahuila; output fluctuates, but reached 2·01m. metric tons in 1965 and 2·1m. in 1966. 13,965m. cu. metres of natural gas were produced in 1965 and 14,985m. in 1966. There are large undeveloped reserves of iron ore; the new Peña Colorado field in Colima State seems to be promising. Output, 1968 (in metric tons): Pig-iron, 1,972,470; steel ingots, 3·27m.

Quantities of mineral products (in metric tons) for 6 calendar years:

Metals	1963	1964	1965	1966	1967	1968
Copper	55,861	52,506	69,162	74,396	56,012	61,110
Lead	189,987	174,824	170,092	182,071	163,907	174,169
Zinc	239,818	235,603	224,878	219,180	241,215	240,021
Antimony	4,826	4,788	4,467	4,478	3,738	3,464
Graphite	29,993	30,337	40,414	38,752	40,690	52,694
Quicksilver	562	433	662	761	..	593
Arsenic	9,486	11,169	10,128	11,894	14,968	10,248
Bismuth	427	472	484	454	504	525
Cadmium	724	748	725	812	1,246	1,194
Tin	1,072	1,226	511	802	588	528
Tungsten	20	5	110	86	188	266
Manganese	54,341	64,089	58,810	31,099	30,799	26,706
Barytes	256,594	334,044	368,342	291,584	223,280	246,539
Sulphur	1,553,462	1,733,041	1,581,268	1,701,060	1,891,155	1,684,948
Cement	3,762,072	4,463,686	4,303,593	4,907,214	5,486,125	6,096,938
Fluorite	481,619	642,872	735,381	726,397	785,114	926,000

Mine production of minerals, 1961 (gold, silver and iron included) was valued at 2,595·4m. pesos.

OIL. The chief Mexican oilfields (with proved reserves in 1962 of 2,764m. bbls and 353·8m. cu. metres of natural gas) are grouped in 3 widely separated regions. The international companies which discovered and developed them were expropriated by government decree, 18 March 1938. The only foreign concession left —Mexican Gulf Oil—was purchased by the Government in Dec. 1950. The industry is now controlled by Pemex (Petróleos Mexicanos). Pemex is exploiting mainly the rich Poza Rica field (discovered in 1938) and the nearby fields in Escolín and Mecatepec. In 1961, 7 new oil areas were announced. Crude petroleum output (30m. cu metres in the peak year, 1921) was 21·2m. in 1968; 20·2m. in 1967. The petroleum fields have 20 plants and 14 refineries, employing 64,800 men; Mexican refineries handled 115·8m. bbls in 1960. Areas bearing, 1966, were 146, with 96 productive oilwells and 48 gas. Mexico is obliged to export crude oil and fuel oil (for which prices are relatively low) and import kerosene and petrol at higher prices; imports, 1960, were 1,020,456 metric tons and exports, 2,255,614. Output of crude in 1969 was 23·73m. cu. metres and natural gas production (1968) 16·34m. cu. metres.

INDUSTRY. The industrial census of 1965 showed 135,188 manufacturing establishments with invested capital of 92·3m. pesos; 1,343,510 production workers were employed. In 1970 the economically active population was 15,891,139.

POWER. In 1968 the 2,194 electric generating plants had installed capacity of 6·1m. kw.; consumption, including imports, was 22·92m. kwh.

TOURISM. Tourism is the largest single source of dollar income and in 1967 1,788,003 tourists visited Mexico spending US$918m.

Freithaler, W. O., *Mexico's Foreign Trade and Ecomomic Development*. Baltimore, 1966
Gill, T., *Land Hunger in Mexico*. Washington, 1951
Mosk, S. A., *Industrial Revolution in Mexico*. Berkeley, Cal., 1950
Powell, J. R., *The Mexican Petroleum Industry*. Univ. of California Press, 1956
Reina, J. G., *Minería y Riqueza Minera de México*. México City, 1944
Tannenbaum, F., *Mexico: The struggle for peace and bread*. New York, 1950
Whetton, N. L., *Rural Mexico*. Chicago, 1948

COMMERCE. Trade for calendar years in 1m. pesos:

	1963	1964	1965	1966	1967	1968
Imports	15,496	18,662	19,495	20,065	21,823	24,501
Exports	11,504	12,492	13,609	14,534	13,798	15,673

Export figures for metals and for certain foreign-owned agricultural products are heavily undervalued to reduce export taxes.

Of total imports (1m. pesos) in 1967, 13,742 (62%) came from USA, 1,645 from West Germany, 942 from Japan, 915 from France, 846 from UK and

453 from Canada. Leading imports were oil, motor vehicles and parts, maize, wool, machinery and parts, fertilizers and paper.

Of total exports (1m. pesos) in 1967, 7,743 went to USA, 858 to Japan, 581 to France, 570 to Switzerland, 261 to West Germany and 124 to UK. The main visible exports in 1967 were cotton, coffee, sugar, shrimps, maize, zinc, petroleum, sulphur, salt and lead (all above US$25m.).

Total trade between UK and Mexico, in £1,000 sterling (according to British Board of Trade returns):

	1966	1967	1968	1969	1970
Imports to UK	12,313	11,495	18,034	14,525	6,343
Exports from UK	20,198	26,406	31,721	29,170	34,170
Re-exports from UK	439	529	497	760	

SHIPPING. Mexico has 49 ocean ports, of which the most important are Veracruz, Coatzacoalcos, Acapulco and Tampico. Merchant shipping loaded 17·8m. tons and unloaded 10·3m. tons in 1967. Passengers embarked, 122,585; landed, 123,169.

ROADS. Total length, 31 Dec. 1966, 65,995 km, of which 60,329 km are hard-surfaced highroads and 7,666 km local roads.

Motor vehicles registered at 31 Dec. 1968 included 999,910 passenger cars, 29,407 buses, 465,815 trucks and 87,476 motor cycles.

RAILWAYS. In 1937 the main railway lines were nationalized. In June 1946 the Government purchased the British-owned Mexican Railway Company for US$8·6m. 38,759,000 passengers and 45·4m. metric tons of freight were carried in 1967. Standard-gauge railway tracks, 23,826 km. The 173-km Viborillas–Villa de Reyes cut-off was opened by the National Railways in 1970, shortening the the distance between México City and the US border, at Nuevo Laredo, by 69 km.

AVIATION. Mexico has an excellent air service. Each of the larger states has a local airline which links them with main airports, which, in turn, furnish services to US, Central and South America and Europe. Thirty companies in 1968 maintained international services, of these 2 were Mexican. Domestic flights are handled by 60 companies. In 1969 commercial aircraft carried 3·9m. passengers and some 110,431 tons of mail and freight.

POST. On 31 Dec. 1966 the federal, state and private telegraph and telephone system had 3,051 offices and 256,660 km of telegraph lines and 4·9m. km of telephone line. Telephones in use, 1 Jan. 1969, 1,074,943; public companies operated all except 8,228 instruments; 83·8% were automatic; the Federal District had 626,877 instruments.

In 1969 there were 547 broadcasting stations: receiving sets were 13m. Television stations numbered 63; there were about 2·55m. receiving sets.

BANKING. The Bank of Mexico, established 1 Sept. 1925, is the central bank of issue; it is modelled on the Federal Reserve system, with large powers to 'manage' the currency. The Government holds 51% of the capital stock.

On 31 Jan. 1964 metallic monetary reserves (gold, silver and foreign exchange forming the required 25% reserve against notes and other demand liabilities) were 2,000m. pesos; 'authorized' holdings of securities, 4,064·3m. pesos; note circulation (outside the Bank of Mexico) was 9,472·7m. pesos. On 31 Aug. 1966 gold and dollar reserves totalled $566·5m. Total supply of money, 28 Feb. 1967, was 31,300m. pesos, divided between currency (9,880m.) and bank deposits (13,700m.).

WEIGHTS AND MEASURES. The metric system was introduced in 1896, and its sole use is enjoined by law of 14 Dec. 1928.

DIPLOMATIC REPRESENTATIVES

Mexico maintains embassies in:

Argentina
Austria
Belgium (also for Luxembourg)
Bolivia
Brazil
Canada
Chile
Colombia
Costa Rica
Cuba
Czechoslovakia
Denmark
Dominican Republic
Ecuador
El Salvador
Ethiopia
Finland
France
Germany (West)
Greece
Guatemala
Haiti
Honduras
India (also for Afghánistán and Ceylon)
Indonesia

Israel
Italy
Jamaica
Japan
Lebanon
Netherlands
Nicaragua
Norway
Panama
Paraguay
Peru
Philippines
Poland
Portugal
Sweden
Switzerland
Turkey
USSR
UAR (and Saudi Arabia)
UK
USA
Uruguay
Venezuela
Yugoslavia (also for Greece)

Diplomatic relations exist with:

Ghana
Guinea
Guyana
Korea
Morocco
Pakistan
Senegal

Syria
Taiwan
Trinidad
Tunisia
Vietnam (South)
Government in Exile of Republican
Spain

OF MEXICO IN GREAT BRITAIN (8 Halkin St., SW1)

Ambassador: Vicente Sánchez Gavito.
Minister: Antonio Gonzalez de Leon.

There are consular representatives at Hull and London.

OF GREAT BRITAIN IN MEXICO

Ambassador: C. P. Hope, CMG, TD.
Counsellors: D. I. Dunnett, CMG, OBE; R. A. C. Du Vivier, MBE (*Cultural*).
Defence Attaché: Lieut.-Col. R. J. Shackleton, MBE.
First Secretaries: J. L. Y. Sanders (*Head of Chancery*); A. C. Catchpole; A. White (*Commercial*).

There are also consular posts at Acapulco, Guadalajara, Mazatlán, Mérida, Monterrey, Pachuca, Tampico, Tapachula, Veracruz.

OF MEXICO IN THE USA (2829–16th St. NW,
Washington, D.C., 20009)

Ambassador: Dr José Juan de Olloqui.
Ministers: Julián Sáenz Hinojosa; Alberto Becerra-Sierra; Juan António Merigo-Aza

Counsellors: Mrs Concha Romero James (*Cultural*); Romeo Domínguez. *Service Attachés:* Maj.-Gen. Roberto Salido Beltran (*Army and Air*); Vice-Adm. Miguel Manzarraga (*Navy*).

OF THE USA IN MEXICO

Ambassador: Robert H. McBride.
Deputy Chief of Mission: Jack B. Kubisch. *Heads of Sections:* H. Freeman Matthews, Jr (*Political*); Thomas R. Favell (*Economic*); Henry L. Pitts (*Commercial*); Margaret Hussman (*Consular*); Ralph J. Ribble (*Administrative*).
Service Attachés: Brig.-Gen. Jefferson J. Irvin (*Army*), Col. William E. Moelich (*Air*), Capt. Richard H. Gibson (*Navy*).

There are Consuls-General at Ciudad Juárez, Guadalajara, Monterrey, Tijuana and Hermosillo, and Consuls at Matamoros, Mazatlan, Mérida, Mexicali, Nogales, Nuevo Laredo, Piedras Negras, Tampico and Veracruz.

BOOKS OF REFERENCE

Anuario Estadístico de los Estados Unidos Mexicanos. Annual (latest issue 1965)
Revista de Estadística (Monthly); *Revista de Economía* (Monthly)
Compendio Estadístico. Direction General de Estadística. Mexico, 1962
Banco de México S.A., Annual report (latest, 42nd, 1964)
Banco Nacional de Comercio Exterior. *Comercio Exterior*, monthly.—*Mexico 1964.* Annual (in Spanish or English)
Bermúdez, A. J., *The Mexican National Petroleum Industry.* Stanford Univ. Press, 1963
Bulletin of the International Commission of Jurists, No. 24, Dec. 1965: *Mexico, constitutional changes in the electoral system*
Cline, H. F., *Mexico: Revolution to Evolution, 1940–60.* R. Inst. of Int. Affairs, 1962
Ker, A. M., *Mexican Government Publications: A Guide, 1821–1936.* Washington, 1940
Nacional Financiera S.A. *Informe Anual,* 1964
Parkes, H. B., *A History of Mexico.* Rev. ed. Boston, 1950
Peña, M. T. de la, *El Pueblo y su Tierra.* Mexico City, 1964
Vernon, R., *The Dilemma of Mexico's Development: the roles of the private and public sectors.* Harvard Univ. Press, 1963

MONACO

HISTORY. Monaco is a small Principality on the Mediterranean, surrounded by the French Department of Alpes Maritimes except on the side towards the sea. From 1297 it belonged to the house of Grimaldi. In 1731 it passed into the female line, Louise Hippolyte, daughter of Antoine I, heiress of Monaco, marrying Jacques de Goyon Matignon, Count of Torigni, who took the name and arms of Grimaldi. The Principality was placed under the protection of the Kingdom of Sardinia by the Treaty of Vienna, 1815, and under that of France in 1861. Prince Albert I (reigned 1889–1922) acquired fame as an oceanographer; and his son Louis II (1922–49) was instrumental in establishing the International Hydrographic Bureau.

National flag: Red and white (horizontal).

REIGNING PRINCE. Rainier III, born 31 May 1923, son of Princess Charlotte, Duchess of Valentinois, daughter of Prince Louis II, born 30 Sept. 1898 (married 19 March 1920 to Prince Pierre, Comte de Polignac, who had taken the name Grimaldi, from whom she was divorced 18 Feb. 1933). Prince Rainier succeeded his grandfather Louis II, who died on 9 May 1949. He married on 19 April 1956 Miss Grace Kelly, a citizen of the USA. *Issue:* Princess Caroline Louise Marguerite, born 23 Jan. 1957; Prince Albert Alexandre Louis Pierre, born 14 March 1958 (*heir apparent*); Princess Stephanie Marie Elisabeth, born 1 Feb. 1965.

AREA AND POPULATION. The area is 149 hectares or 368 acres. Population (1968), 23,035. The official language is French.

CONSTITUTION AND GOVERNMENT. Prince Rainier III on 28 Jan. 1959 suspended the Constitution of 5 Jan. 1911, thereby dissolving the National Council and the Communal Council. On 28 March 1962 the National Council (18 members) and the Communal Council (16 members) were re-established as elected bodies. Elections took place on 24 Feb. 1963.

On 17 Dec. 1962 a new constitution was promulgated. It maintains the hereditary monarchy, though Prince Rainier renounces the principle of divine right. The supreme tribunal becomes the custodian of fundamental liberties, and guarantees are given for the right of association, trade union freedom and the right to strike. It provides for votes for women and the abolition of the death penalty. The constitution can be modified only with the approval of the elected National Council.

The territory of the Principality is divided into three sections—Monaco-Ville, La Condamine and Monte Carlo—which are administered by a municipal body, elected by vote. Women were given the vote in 1945.

Monegasque relations with France were based on a convention of neighbourhood and administrative assistance of 1951. This was terminated by France on 11 Oct. 1962, but has been replaced by several new conventions signed on 18 May 1963.

RELIGION. There has been since 1887 a Roman Catholic bishop, directly dependent on the Holy See.

JUSTICE. The Code Louis, adopted in 1919, is based upon the French codes. There is a Court of First Instance as well as a Juge de Paix's Court. A semi-military police force has taken the place of the 'guard of honour' and troops formerly maintained.

FINANCE. The budget (in 1,000 francs) was as follows:

	1965	1966	1967	1968	1969
Revenue	119,182	126,108	131,692	155,409	161,804
Expenditure	117,804	125,571	131,270	155,407	160,664

PLANNING. The territory of Monaco is being increased by more than 20% by projects to reclaim land from the sea Most of this new land will be used for industrial development, the rest to improve tourist facilities.

COMMUNICATIONS. The harbour has an area of 47 acres, depth at the entrance 90 ft, and alongside the quay 24 ft at least. The 1·6m. km of main line passing through the country is operated by French National Railways (SNCF). Telephones numbered 14,015 in 1969. Monaco issues its own postage-stamps.

British Consul-General (resident in Nice): D. G. Crichton.
Consul-General for Monaco in London: I. S. Ivanovic.
USA Consul (resident in Nice): Joseph Williams.

BOOKS OF REFERENCE

Journal de Monaco. Bulletin Officiel. 1858 ff.
Handley-Taylor, G., *Bibliography of Monaco.* London, 1968
La Gorce, P. M. de, *Monaco.* Lausanne, 1969

MONGOLIAN PEOPLE'S REPUBLIC

Bügd Nayramdakh Mongol Ard Uls

HISTORY. Outer Mongolia was a Chinese province from 1691 to 1911, an autonomous state under Russian protection from 1912 to 1919 and again a Chinese province from 1919 to 1921. On 31 March 1921 a Provisional People's Government was established which declared the independence of Mongolia and on 5 Nov. 1921 signed a treaty with Soviet Russia annulling all previous unequal treaties and establishing friendly relations. On 26 Nov. 1924 the Government proclaimed the country the Mongolian People's Republic.

On 5 Jan. 1946 China recognized the independence of Outer Mongolia after a plebiscite in Mongolia (20 Oct. 1945) had resulted in an overwhelming vote for independence. A Sino-Soviet treaty of 14 Feb. 1950 guaranteed this independence.

Relations with the USSR were based on treaties of friendship and mutual aid (27 Feb. 1946), trade (17 Dec. 1957), economic and technical assistance (9 Sept. 1960), now replaced by a 20-year treaty of friendship, co-operation and mutual assistance (15 Jan. 1966).

Relations with China were based on treaties of economic and cultural co-operation (4 Oct. 1952), economic and technical and (29 Aug. 1956), friendship and mutual aid (31 May 1960), commerce (26 April 1961 and 18 March 1963) and a border agreement (26 Dec. 1962). Sino-Mongolian relations have deteriorated since the estrangement between China and USSR.

On 28 Oct. 1961 Mongolia was admitted to the United Nations.

CONSTITUTION AND GOVERNMENT. According to the fourth constitution (1960) power is vested in the *People's Great Khural*, elected for 3 years by universal suffrage of voters over 18 years of age, on the basis of 1 deputy for every 2,500 of the population. It elects from its number 9 members of the Presidium, which carries on current state affairs.

Mongolia is a single-party state. The Mongolian People's Revolutionary (*i.e.*, Communist) Party had 48,570 members and candidates in 1966; the youth organization over 90,000 in 1970.

The last general election took place on 23 June 1969; 293 members were elected on a single list. 69 of the deputies are workers, 144 are members of state and collective farms, and 65 are described as officials and members of the intelligentsia.

National flag: Red–sky-blue–red (vertical), with a golden 5-pointed star and under it the golden *soyombo* emblem on the red stripe nearest to the flag-pole.

Titular head of state is Jamsrangiyn Sambuu, *Chairman of the Presidium of the Khural. Prime Minister and First Secretary of the Party:* Yumjagiyn Tsedenbal. The other 5 members of the Politburo of the Party, which is *de facto* the highest policy-making body, are: S. Luvsan, *First Deputy Prime Minister*; N. Jagvaral, *Deputy Prime Minister*; D. Maydar, *Chairman, State Construction Council and Deputy Prime Minister*; D. Molomjamts; Ts. Dügersüren. Ministers not in the Politburo include: *Chairman, State Planning Commission and Deputy Prime Minister:* B. Rinchin Peljee; *Minister of Defence:* Col.-Gen. B. Dorj; *Minister of Public Security:* Maj.-Gen. B. Jambalsüren; *Foreign Minister:* (vacant since Sept. 1970); *Minister of Foreign Trade:* Yë. Ochir.

AREA AND POPULATION. Area, 1,565,000 sq. km (604,095 sq. miles); population (1970), 1·2m. (50% male, 1965; 39% urban, 1969). Density, 0·7 per sq. km. Birth rate (1968), 42 per 1,000; death rate (1968), 9 per 1,000. Rate of increase, 3·9%. The population is predominantly made up of Mongolian peoples (75% Khalkha). There is a Turkic Kazakh minority (4·3% of the population). The official language is Mongolian.

The Republic is administratively divided into 2 cities (Ulan Bator, the capital, population, 254,000 in 1969, and Darkhan, population, 10,000 in 1967), and 18 provinces (*aimag*). Local government is administered by People's Deputies' Khurals. The provinces are subdivided into districts (*somon*).

RELIGION. Buddhist Lamaism was the prevalent form of religion. The church was suppressed in the 1930s, and only one monastery of 110 lamas exists today, at Ulan Bator.

EDUCATION. Schooling begins at the age of 8. There are 4-year, 7- or 8-year and 10-year schools. 4-year schooling is universal. Efforts are now being made to extend 7- or 8-year schooling to the whole country. In 1970 there were 32,000 children in kindergartens, 227,600 pupils in 504 'general' schools and 11,240 in technical schools in Mongolia and abroad. There is a state university (founded 1942) at Ulan Bator (40 professors, 240 lecturers and 2,500 students in 1967), and other institutes of higher learning (teacher training, medicine, agriculture, economics, etc.) under the supervision of an Academy of Sciences (founded 1953; reorganized, 1961). In 1970 there were 8,289 students in institutes of higher learning, and some 3,000 students a year are sent to study in the USSR and Eastern Europe.

In 1946 the Mongolian alphabet was replaced by one based on Russian, but now enjoys a limited revival.

CINEMAS. There were 14 cinemas in 1966.

NEWSPAPER (1967). The Party daily paper *Ünen* ('Truth') is the only national daily newspaper; it has a circulation of 107,500.

HEALTH AND WELFARE. There were, in 1966, 1,554 doctors and 10,200 hospital beds. There were 69 hospitals, 38 clinics and 692 other medical stations. Old-age and disablement pensions vary from 125 to 800 *tugriks* per month.

FINANCE. Currency. 100 *möngö* = 1 *tugrik*. Official exchange rates: £1 = 9·65 *tugriks*; US$1 = 4 *tugriks*; 1 rouble = 4 *tugriks*. Tourists receive a 50% exchange premium on hard-currency notes.

Budget (in 1m. *tugrik*):

	1960	1965	1968	1969	1970[1]
Revenue	1,067	1,482	1,785	1,860	1,920
Expenditure	981	1,476	1,770	1,043	1,913

[1] Estimates.

In 1969–70 it was planned to invest 2,360m. *tugriks* on the national economy and social and cultural measures. In 1969, 132m. *tugriks* were spent on defence. Estimates for 1970: 149m. *tugriks*. Mongolia receives economic aid from the USSR and other communist countries. (In the 5-year plan period 1966–70, 710m. roubles, of which 660m. were from the USSR, and technical aid from the UN.)

DEFENCE. Military service is 2 years. The army was estimated to number 17,500 in 1967, but has certainly increased in size since. It is equipped with Soviet weapons and includes some mechanized units (T-34 medium tanks). The air force is engaged primarily in running civil air services. It has 500 men and about 35 aircraft (6 MiG-15 fighter-bombers as well as 20 Il-14, Li-2 and An-2 transports and trainers). There is a para-military security force of about 15,000 men. A Civil Defence force was set up in 1970. There are large Soviet forces in the country.

PLANNING. Mongolia has had for centuries a traditional nomadic pastoral economy, which the government aims to transform into an 'agricultural–industrial economy'. For earlier plans *see* previous issues of THE STATEMAN'S YEAR-BOOK. The fourth 5-year plan (1966–1970) fell short in many of its targets, especially in animal husbandry, which suffered from severe spring frosts in 1968. The current plan aims to re-instate and develop livestock farming, and develop light and medium processing, building materials industries and electric power production.

AGRICULTURE. The Mongols are mainly herdsmen, and in 1965 had 2·4m. horses, 684,500 camels, 2·1m. cattle, 13·8m. sheep and 4·8m. goats. Pastures occupy 84% of the total area, forests 10·5%. In 1967 there were 309 collective farms, 45 state farms and 44 machine and breeding stations. All cultivated land and 80% of livestock belong to collective or state farms. Collective farms had a membership of 655,000 in 1968. Farms cover vast areas and average 100,000 head of livestock.

Collectivization was carried through at the end of the 1950s. In the 1960s a start was made with a virgin lands campaign to grow grain.

The sown area in 1967 was 481,500 hectares, 86·4% sown to grain, 11·7% to fodder and 1·9% to vegetables. The 1967 crop was 357,000 metric tons of grain. 1968 and 1969 were bad years and figures have not been published. Retrospective estimates: 180,000 and 80,000 metric tons. 1966 production (in 1,000 metric tons): Meat, 158; milk, 216; wool, 24. In 1965, 8,200 tractors and 2,029 combine-harvesters were in use.

FORESTRY. Forests, chiefly larch, cedar, fir and birch, occupy about 160,000 sq. km. In 1963, 469,900 cu. metres of timber were cut.

MINING. There are some goldmines and other mineral deposits of un-ascertained value. Wolfram and fluorspar are exported to the USSR. There are major coalmines near Ulan Bator and Darkhan. Coal production in 1969 was 1·44m. metric tons. Oil is produced in the eastern Gobi desert at Dzüünbayan; production, 1965, 39,500 metric tons.

INDUSTRY. Industry is small in scale and local in character. The main industrial centre is Ulan Bator; others are being built at Darkhan and Choy-balsan where power stations were completed with Soviet help in 1970 and 1971. 1965 production figures: Electricity, 296·2m. kwh. (1967); washed wool, 7,900 tons; leather footwear, 1·4m. pairs; processed sheep and goat skins, 1,002,800 sq. metres; woollen textiles, 739,000 sq. metres; fluorspar, 49,000 tons. Power stations are at Ulan Bator, Choybalsan, Tolgoyt, Sükh Bator and Darkhan. Trade union membership was 171,000 in 1966, and the industrial and building labour force was some 59,000. There is a serious labour shortage.

COMMERCE. Foreign trade is a state monopoly. Mongolia has been a member of Comecon since 1962. The main exports are live cattle and horses, wool and hair, meat, grain, hides and skins, furs, non-ferrous and precious metal ores, and butter. 99% of Mongolia's foreign trade is with communist countries (80% with USSR). In 1970 trade with China was less than 3m. roubles (*cf.* 24m. roubles in 1961). There is a chronic trade deficit. Just over half the imports are consumer goods and just under half are machinery and industrial raw materials. Switzerland is Mongolia's most regular non-communist trading partner, and there is a trade agreement with Japan valued at US$1m. per annum.

Mongolia exported no goods to the UK in 1969 (1970: £2,000) and imported from the UK goods valued at £13,000 (1970: nil) (British Board of Trade returns). Exports to USSR in 1968 (and 1969): 47·8m. (47·5m.) roubles; imports: 174·5m. (176·6m.) roubles.

RAILWAYS. The Trans-Mongolian Railway (1,427 km in 1966) connects Ulan Bator with the Soviet Union and China. The Moscow–Ulan Bator–Peking express runs each way once a week. There are spur lines to the coalmines at Nalaykha and Sharin Gol. A separate line connects Choybalsan in the east with Borzya on the Trans-Siberian railway. 6m. passengers and 3·26m. tons of freight were carried in 1967.

ROADS. There are macadam and concrete roads in and around Ulan Bator and a macadam road runs north towards the USSR for about 80 km. Truck services run throughout the country where there are no surfaced roads. 33·3m. passengers and 9·7m. tons of freight were carried in 1967.

SHIPPING. There is a steamer service on the Selenge River and a tug and barge service on Khövsgöl Lake. 200,000 passengers were carried in 1967.

AVIATION. The air service between Irkutsk and Ulan Bator links with the Moscow service; it is operated by the Mongolian airline. Soviet airlines (Aeroflot) operate a flight to Moscow, weekly in winter and twice weekly in summer.

POST. There were, in 1964, 370 post offices, 25 telegraph offices and 31 telephone exchanges in the country. Number of telephones (1969), 16,220.
There are wireless stations at Ulan Bator and Olgiy. In 1964 there were 64,000 radio listening posts and 60,000 radio receivers. Television broadcasting began in 1967. There are some 2,000 receivers.

WEIGHTS AND MEASURES. The metric system is in use, but traditional units are still found.

Ambassador in London: Sodnomdorjiin Dambadarjaa.
British Ambassador: Roland Carter.

There are 13 other diplomatic missions in Ulan Bator, including, since 1966, a peripatetic French ambassador (M. Georges Perruche), and Mongolia is in diplomatic relations with some 25 other countries (not including the USA).

BOOKS OF REFERENCE

The Central Statistical Office: *Economic Statistics of the MPR for 40 Years*. 1961.—*40 Years of the MPR Revolution*. 1961

Statistikiyn Emkhetgel [Statistical Yearbook, in Mongolian]. Ulan Bator, 1960 ff.
Istoriya Mongol'skoi Narodnoi Respubliki. 2nd ed. Moscow, 1967
Bawden, C. R., *The Modern History of Mongolia*. London, 1968
Boberg, F., *Mongolian–English, English–Mongolian Dictionary*. 3 vols. Stockholm, 1954–55
Gungaadash, B., *Mongoliia Segodnia: priroda, lindi, khoziaistvo* [trans. from Mongolian]. Moscow, 1969
Haltod, M. (ed.), *Mongolian–English Dictionary*. Berkeley, Cal., 1961
Lattimore, O., *Nationalism and Revolution in Mongolia*. Leiden, 1955.—*Nomads and Commissars*. OUP, 1965
Rupen, R. A. *Mongols of the Twentieth Century*. Indiana U.P., 1964
Sandag, S., *The Mongolian People's Struggle for National Independence*. Ulan Bator, 1966
Sanders, A. J. K. *The People's Republic of Mongolia: a general reference guide*. OUP, 1968

MOROCCO
al-Mamlaka al-Maghrebia

HISTORY. From 1912 to 1956 Morocco was divided into a French protectorate (established by the treaty of Fez concluded between France and the Sultan on 30 March 1912), a Spanish protectorate (established by the Franco-Spanish convention of 27 Nov. 1912) and the international zone of Tangier (set up by France, Spain and Great Britain on 18 Dec. 1923).
On 2 March 1956 France and the Sultan terminated the treaty of Fez; on 7 April 1956 Spain relinquished her protectorate, and on 29 Oct. 1956 France, Spain, Great Britain, Italy, USA, Belgium, the Netherlands, Sweden and Portugal abolished the international status of the Tangier Zone.

REIGNING KING. Hassan II, born on 9 July 1929, succeeded on 3 March 1961, on the death of his father Mohammed V, who reigned 1927–61. The royal style was changed from 'His Sherifian Majesty the Sultan' to 'His Majesty the King' on 18 Aug. 1957. *Heir apparent:* Crown prince Sidi Mohammed, born 21 Aug. 1963.

The King holds supreme civil and religious authority; the latter in his capacity of Emir-el-Muminin or Commander of the Faithful. He resides usually at Rabat, but occasionally in one of the other traditional capitals, Fez (founded in 808), Marrakesh (founded in 1062), Meknès and Tangier (which has become his summer capital).

GOVERNMENT AND CONSTITUTION. The constitution was approved by referendum on 7 Dec. 1962 (3,919,737 for, 113,199 against, 72,722 void) and was promulgated on 14 Dec. 1962. In July 1970 a modification of the 1962 constitution was approved by referendum. The Kingdom of Morocco is a constitutional monarchy with a legislature of a single chamber composed of 240 deputies Deputies for 150 seats are elected by indirect vote through an electoral college representing the town councils, the regional assemblies, the chambers of commerce, industry and agriculture, and the trade unions. Deputies for the remaining 90 seats are by general election. The King, as sovereign head of State, appoints the Prime Minister and other Ministers, has the right to dissolve Parliament and approves legislation.

National flag: Red, with a green 5-pointed star in the centre.

Elections were held on 21 and 28 Aug. 1970.

Director of the Royal Cabinet: Driss Slaoui. *Minister representative of HM King:* Hadj Ahmed Balafrej. *Minister of the Royal House:* Mohamed Maameri Zouaoui. *Prime Minister:* Dr Ahmed Laraki. *Minister of State:* S. A. Moulay Hassan Ben Driss. *Minister of Justice:* Ahmed Ben Bouchta. *Minister of Foreign Affairs:* Dr Youseff Bel Abbas.

The country is administratively divided into 19 provinces and 2 urban prefectures. The provinces are: Rabat, Meknès, Fez, Taza, Oujda, Al-Homina, Nador, Ouarzazate, Marrakesh, Agadir, Khouribga, Settat, Al Jadida, Ksar-es-Souk, Beni-Mellal, Safi, Tangier, Tetuan, Tarfaya. The prefectures are: Casablanca and Rabat-Salé.

AREA AND POPULATION. As the south-eastern boundaries of Morocco have not been delimited, no exact figure can be given, but the total area is officially given as 500,000 sq. km (166,000 sq. miles). On 30 June 1969 the former Spanish province of Ifni was returned to Morocco, see THE STATESMAN'S YEAR-BOOK, 1969–70, p. 1322.

The population at the census of June 1961 totalled 11,598,070, of whom 3·4m. were urban and 8·2m. rural; foreigners numbered 400,000. Estimate, 1 March 1969, 15·03m., including 170,000 foreigners.

The principal towns (and their Moslem population) are Casablanca (1,177,000), Rabat (261,450), Marrakesh (264,300), Fez (249,000), Meknès (205,000), Oujda (149,300), Tangier (166,290), Kenitra (99,380), Safi (99,870), Tetuan (117,000). The capital is Rabat.

The official language is Arabic; French and Spanish are considered subsidiary languages.

RELIGION. Islam is the established state religion. The majority of the Moroccans are Sunni Moslems of the Malekite school. The French and Spanish settlers are Roman Catholics under the Archbishop of Rabat. The once large Jewish population is diminishing (180,000 in 1961).

EDUCATION. In 1959 a standardization of the various school systems (French, Spanish, Israeli, Moslem, etc.) was begun. Education has been made compulsory from the age of 7 to 13.

In 1969, 1·14m. children were enrolled in state primary schools and 293,193 in state secondary schools.

The language of instruction in primary schools is Arabic during the first 2 years, and half-Arabic and half-French during the following 3 years; in secondary schools lessons are in French.

The University at Rabat had 8,000 students in 1964. A new university was opened in Fez in Nov. 1961. The Qarawin Islamic University has over 4,000 students. Total of university students (1969) 12,970.

CINEMAS (1962). There are about 160 cinemas with a seating capacity of 90,000.

JUSTICE. A uniform legal system is being organized, based mainly on French and Islamic law codes and French legal procedure. The judiciary consists of a Supreme Court, courts of appeal, regional tribunals and magistrates' courts.

FINANCE. Currency. In Oct. 1959, a national currency was introduced. Its unit is the *dirham* (abbreviated DH), equalling 100 French Moroccan francs (1 French franc = 1·025 DH; US$1 = 5·01 DH; £1 = 10·135 DH. Notes: 5, 10, 50, 100 DH; coins: 0·02, 0·05, 0·10, 0·20, 0·50, 1 DH. The exchange rate in 1969 was: US$1 = 5 DH; £1 sterling = 12·12 DH. At the end of 1963 the total circulation of money was 1,291m. DH.

Budget. The ordinary budget for 1971 envisaged revenue of 4,432m. DH (4,006m. in 1970). The main items of revenue in 1967 were (in 1m. DH): Direct taxation, 531; customs, 438·5; indirect taxation, 559·5; monopolies and exploitations, 259·9. The public debt in 1967 amounted to 264·6m. DH.

DEFENCE. Army. The Army consists of volunteers, numbering 45,000 officers and men, organized in 2 motorized brigades, 1 armoured brigade, 1 light security brigade, 1 paratroop brigade and 12 infantry battalions. Its equipment is of French, American and (since 1962) Soviet origin.

Navy. The Navy includes 1 frigate, 2 patrol vessels, 1 seaward patrol craft and 1 landing craft acquired from France.

Air Force. The Air Force, formed in Nov. 1956, received from the Soviet Union 16 MiG-17 fighter-bombers, 2 MiG-15UTI jet trainers and 2 Il-28 light bombers. The MiGs are now in storage, and equipment in current use is mainly of US and West European origin. It includes 12 F-5A supersonic flghter-bombers, T 28 and T-6 armed piston-engined trainers, 24 Magister jet basic trainers, Agusta-Bell 205 and Alouette helicopters, and C-119 and C-47 transport aircraft. Personnel strength is about 3,000.

PLANNING. A 3-year plan (1965–67) gave priority to agriculture, tourism and professional training at a total expenditure of 711m. dirhams. A 5-year plan (1968–72) envisages a total expenditure of 1,010m. dirhams. The stated aims are the same as for the first plan, but in addition priority will be given to provide for the development of industry as a means of providing employment for a growing population.

AGRICULTURE. Agriculture is by far the most important industry, on which 70% of the population exists. The principal crops are cereals, especially wheat and barley; beans, chickpeas, fenugreek and other legumens; canary seed; cumin and coriander; linseed; olives; almonds and other fruits, especially citrus. The almost universal wild palmetto is put to various uses, including the manufacture of *crin végétal*. The trees include cork (*covering* 310,000 hectares; production in 1963, 35,043 metric tons), cedar, arar, argon, oak and various conifers. Wine production, 1964, 2·6m. hectolitres. Tizra wood is exported for tanning purposes. Production of esparto grass, 1963, was 110,000 metric tons. Stock-raising is an important industry. Citrus exportation and marketing was nationalized in 1965.

In 1964, out of a total area of 41,649,000 hectares, 23,728,000 hectares were under cultivation, including 4,743,000 of arable land, 580,000 of vine and olive plantations, 7·8m. of pastures, 2·8m. of esparto grass and 5,325,000 of forests. Effective irrigation affects 59,000 hectares.

Production (in 1,000 metric tons) in 1969: Winter wheat, 1,130; summer wheat, 339; oranges, 618.

Livestock (1963, in 1,000 heads): Camels, 200; horses, 542; asses, 1,125; cattle, 2,900; pigs, 48; sheep, 15,000; goats, 7,400.

MINING. The principal mineral exploited is phosphate, the output of which (under a state monopoly) was 12·29m. metric tons in 1969. Other important minerals (in 1,000 metric tons) are: Coal (482), crude petrol (738 bbls of 42 gallons); iron ore (742), lead (116·9), cobalt (14·66), zinc (82·76); manganese, 197·75; silver, 773,000 troy oz.

FISHING. The coasts abound in fish. The chief fishing centres are Agadir, Safi, Essaouira and Casablanca. In 1965 there were 3,400 fishing vessels of 22,000 tons. Catch (in metric tons) in 1969: 169,366 sardines, 13,951 mackerel. Catch in 1964: 4,938 tunny, 2,671 anchovy, 18,808 fresh fish, 799 shellfish.

POWER. The power-plants produced 1,693·1m. kwh. in 1969.

TOURISM. In 1969, 716,367 foreign visitors came to Morocco.

COMMERCE. Imports and exports were (in 1m. dirhams):

	1965	1966	1967	1968	1969
Imports	2,291·5	2,400	2,620	..	2,844
Exports	2,176·2	2,168	2,146	..	2,455

Imports and exports were (in 1,000 tons):

	1965	1966	1967	1968	1969
Imports	3,322·3	3,311	3,756	..	..
Exports	13,173·9	12,416	12,636	..	..

Main imports, 1969, consumer goods and industrial products. Main exports, 1969, citrus fruit, phosphates and minerals.

In 1968 588,409 metric tons of citrus fruits were exported (490,713 of which were oranges). France imported 243,026 metric tons (182,106 metric tons were oranges).

A royal proclamation of 30 Aug. 1959 abrogated the former economic status of Tangier and integrated the zone in the kingdom. However, Tangier was declared a free port from 1 Jan. 1962; and commercial transactions within the free zone were further liberalized by decree of 8 Nov. 1965.

Total trade between Morocco and UK in £1,000 sterling (British Board of Trade returns):

	1965	1966	1967	1968	1969	1970
Imports to UK	11,389	11,248	12,297	13,809	15,690	16,250
Exports from UK	4,491	5,115	6,855	9,386	12,617⎫	12,609
Re-exports from UK	170	125	140	261	263⎭	

SHIPPING. In 1960, 19,015 vessels of 26,613,000 net tons entered and cleared the ports of Morocco. The merchant navy had 31 ocean-going vessels of 56,223 tons on 1 Oct. 1965.

In 1966 the Moroccan ports handled 15·38m. tons of maritime traffic, of which Casablanca dealt with 10·74m.

RAILWAYS. In 1969 there were 1,756 km of railways, of which 760 km were electrified. The principal standard-gauge lines are from Casablanca eastward to the Algerian border, forming part of the continuous rail line to Tunis; Casablanca to Marrakesh with 2 important branches, one eastward from a point slightly north of Settat (Sidi el Aïdi) to Oued Zem tapping the Khouribga phosphate mines, the other westward from Ben Guerir to the port of Safi passing about midway through the phosphate district of Youssoufia (formerly Louis Gentil); the line Oujda-Bou Arfa, serving the manganese mines of Bou Arfa and the coalmines of Jerada.

In 1969 Moroccan railways carried 3·5m. passengers and 16m. tons of goods.

ROADS. In 1969 there were 24,757 km of paved roads out of a total of 23,700 km of surfaced roads. At the end of 1969 there were in use 79,253 private cars.

AVIATION. There are 19 airfields, of which Casablanca–Arfa and Casablanca–Nouaceur are the most important. Total international air services in 1966 comprised 565,314 passengers arrived and departed; 5,640 metric tons of freight and 1,006 tons of mail handled.

POST. Communication with Europe is maintained by cables between Casablanca and Brest, Tangier–Casablanca–Le Havre, Tangier–Gibraltar, Tangier–Cádiz, Larache–Cádiz via Algeciras.

Telephone subscribers totalled 160,326 at the end of 1969; of these, 43,513 were in Casablanca, 26,180 in Rabat and 10,937 in Tangier.

Broadcasting is done in Arabic, Berber, French, Spanish and English from Rabat and Tangier; television in Arabic and French began in 1962.

BANKING. The bank of issue is the Banque du Maroc in Rabat. Other important institutions are the Banque Marocaine du Commerce Extérieur (Casablanca), the Banque Nationale pour le Développement Economique (Rabat) and the Caisse de prêts immobiliers (Casablanca). There are 23 other banks in Casablanca, 3 in Tangier and 1 each in Tetouan, Fez, Kenitra, Meknès, Oujda and Rabat.

The gold and foreign-exchange reserves of the Banque du Maroc amounted to US$110m. at the end of 1963 and US$62m. at the end of 1964.

WEIGHTS AND MEASURES. The metric system of weights and measures is the sole legal system.

DIPLOMATIC REPRESENTATIVES

Morocco maintains embassies in:

Algeria	Japan	Senegal
Argentina	Jordan	Spain
Belgium	Kuwait	Sweden
Brazil	Lebanon	Switzerland
China	Libya	Syria
France	Mali	Tunisia
Germany (West)	Mauritania	Turkey
Ghana	Nigeria	USSR
India	Norway	UAR
Iran	Pakistan	UK
Iraq	Poland	USA
Italy	Portugal	Yugoslavia
Ivory Coast	Saudi Arabia	

OF MOROCCO IN GREAT BRITAIN (49 Queen's Gate Gdns, SW7)

Ambassador: (Vacant).

Minister-Counsellor: Aissa Benchekroun. *First Secretary:* Mustapha Mzabi. *Military, Naval and Air Attaché:* Comm. Mustapha Jabrane. *Commercial Attaché:* Mohamed Fenzar.

OF GREAT BRITAIN IN MOROCCO

Ambassador: T. G. Shaw, CMG.

First Secretaries: A. E. Saunders (*Head of Chancery, Consul*); E. H. Noble, MBE (*Commercial*); A. C. Wells (*Labour*). *Service Attaché:* Lieut.-Col. P. J. L. Wickes.

There are also consular representatives at Casablanca, Larache and Tangier.

OF MOROCCO IN THE USA (1601 21st St. NW, Washington, D.C., 20009)

Ambassador: (Vacant).

Counsellors: Abdeslam Tadlaoui (*Economic*); A. Bekkali (*Press*). *Service Attaché:* Lieut.-Col. Abdeslam Bouziane.

OF THE USA IN MOROCCO

Ambassador: Henry J. Tasca.

Deputy Chief of Mission: Dwight Dickinson. *Heads of Sections:* H. Earle Russell, Jr (*Political*); Edward A. Dow (*Economic*); M. Hollis Kannenberg (*Administrative*); Philip Birnbaum (*AID*). *Service Attachés:* Capt. Charles G. Strum (*Defence and Navy*), Col. Gordon A. Schraeder (*Army*), Col. Benjamin C. Kenyon (*Air*).

There are Consuls-General at Tangier and Casablanca.

BOOKS OF REFERENCE

STATISTICAL INFORMATION. The Service Central des Statistiques (BP 178, Rabat) was set up in 1942. Its publications include: *Annuaire de Statistique Générale* (latest issue, 1952).—*La Conjoncture Économique Marocaine* (monthly; with annual synthesis).—*Résultats du Recensement général de la population de 1951–52.*—*Bulletin économique et social du Maroc* (trimestral).

Bulletin Official (in Arabic and French). Rabat. Weekly
Ashford, D. E., *Political Change in Morocco*. Princeton University Press, 1961
Barber, N., *Survey of North Africa*, 2nd ed. OUP, 1962.—*Morocco*. London, 1965
Decroux, P., *Les sociétés au Maroc*. Paris, 1950
D'Étienne, J., and others, *L'évolution sociale du Maroc*. Paris, 1950
Drague, G., *Esquisse d'histoire religieuse du Maroc*. Paris, 1951
Joly, F., and others, *Géographie du Maroc*. Paris, 1949
Landau, R., *Moroccan Drama 1900–55*. San Francisco, 1956.—*Morocco Independent under Mohammed V*. London, 1961.—*Hassan II, King of Morocco*. London, 1962.—*The Moroccans Yesterday and Today*. London, 1963
Mercier, H., *Dictionnaire arabe-français*. Rabat, 1951
Miège, J.-L., *Morocco*. New York, 1953
Rivière, P. L., *Précis de Législation marocaine*. New ed. in collaboration with G. Catteriz. 2 vols. Caen, 1942–46
Sonnier, E., *Code des eaux du Maroc*. Rabat, 1954

NATIONAL LIBRARY. Bibliothèque Générale et Archives, Rabat.

NEPÁL

HISTORY. From 1846 to 1951 Nepál was virtually ruled by the Ráná family, a member of which always held the office of prime minister, the succession being determined by special rules. The last Ráná prime minister (and, until 18 Feb. 1951, Supreme C.-in-C.) was HH Máhárája Mohan Shumsher Jung Bahádur Ráná, who resigned in Nov. 1951.

RULING KING. The sovereign is HM Mahárájádhirája **Mahendra Bir Bikram Sháh Deva**, born on 11 June 1920, who succeeded his father Tribhuvan Bir Bikram Sháh Deva on 14 March 1955. HRH Prince Birendra Bir Bikram Sháh Deva is the heir apparent.

CONSTITUTION AND GOVERNMENT. On 18 Feb. 1951 the King proclaimed a constitutional monarchy, and on 16 Dec. 1962 a new constitution of the 'Constitutional Monarchical Hindu State'. The village and town *panchayat*, recognized as the basic units of democracy, elect the district *panchayat*, these elect the zonal *panchayat*, and these finally the 90 members of the national *panchayat*. In addition, 19 representatives of professional organizations and university graduates, and royal nominees not exceeding 15% of the elected members, will be included in the national *panchayat*. The executive power is vested in the King, who appoints a council of ministers from the national *panchayat*. A state council will advise the King and proclaim the successor or, if the heir is a minor, a regency council. Art. 81 empowers the King to declare a state of emergency and to suspend the constitution.

On 25 Aug. 1963 the King formed a 31-member National Guidance Council under his chairmanship.

Relations with the UK are regulated by the treaty of peace and friendship signed on 29 Oct. 1950, which supersedes the treaties of 1792, 1815 and 1923. Diplomatic relations with the USA were established in 1947.

For relations with Tibet, *see* p. 816.

National anthem: 'May glory crown our illustrious sovereign' (1952).

AREA AND POPULATION. Nepál, situated between 26° 20′ and 30° 10′ N. lat. and between 80° 15′ and 88° 15′ E. long., is bounded on the north by Tibet, on the east by Sikkim and West Bengal, on the south and west by Bihar and Uttar Pradesh. On 5 Oct. 1961 a treaty was signed in Peking, according to which the Chinese–Nepalese boundary line 'runs generally south-eastwards along the mountain ridge, passing through Cho Oyu mountain, Pumoli mountain, Mount Chomo Lungma (the Chinese name for Everest) and Lhotse Too Makalu mountain'. Nepál gained about 300 sq. miles of territory. Area about 54,600 sq. miles (141,400 sq. km); population (estimate, 1964), 9·5m.

In 1966 about 7,000 refugees from Tibet were living in Nepál.

Capital, Káthmándu, 75 miles from the Indian frontier; population about 195,260, and of the surrounding valley 415,000, including Pátan with a population of 135,230, and Bhádgáon with 84,240.

The aboriginal stock is Mongolian with a considerable admixture of Hindu blood from India. They were originally divided into numerous hill clans and petty principalities, one of which, Gorkha or Gurkha, became predominant in 1559 and has since given its name to men from all parts of Nepál. The 15 semi-independent feudal chieftainships were integrated into the kingdom on 10 April 1961.

The country is administratively divided into 14 zones and 75 development districts.

RELIGION. Sanátan or Pauranic, *i.e.*, traditional or ancient Hinduism, and Buddhism are the religions of the bulk of the people. Christian missions are admitted, but conversion is forbidden. The royal family is Hindu.

EDUCATION. In 1964 there were 5,001 primary schools, 645 secondary schools, 31 colleges and the Tribhuvan University (founded 1960).

About 12% of the population are literate. The national language is Nepáli.

JUSTICE. The Supreme Court Act, 1956, established a uniform judicial system, culminating in a supreme court of a Chief Justice and no more than 6 judges. Special courts to deal with minor offences may be established at the discretion of the Government.

FINANCE. Currency. The Nepalese rupee is 171 grains in weight, as compared with the Indian rupee, which weighs 180 grains. The rate of exchange is

135 Nepalese rupees for 100 Indian rupees. 100 Nepalese pice = 1 Nepalese rupee. Coins of all denominations are minted. The Rástra Bank also issues notes of 1, 5, 10 and 100 rupees.

Budget. The general budget for the fiscal year 1970–71 envisages total expenditure of NRs 973m., of which development expenditure amounts to NRs 633m. Current revenues are estimated at NRs. 494m. The deficit is to be financed by foreign aid (NRs 402m.) and domestic loans (NRs 30m.). The main sources of foreign aid are: India, NRs 150m.; USA, NRs 67m.; Mainland China, NRs 65m.; UK, NRs 17m.; USSR, NRs 3·5m.; others, 25·8m.

DEFENCE. The army consists of about 20,000 men, mainly infantry, all of whom are regulars. It is being modernized with the aid of Britain and USA. British equipment delivered to date includes 1 Skyvan and 3 Twin Pioneer transport aircraft.

PLANNING. The third plan of 5 years, ran from 1965 to 1970. Its cost is estimated at NRs 2,500m., of which 500m. is expected to come from foreign aid and 1,250m. from external loans. Priority was given to transport, communications, power, agriculture, irrigation, training of technicians and schools.

AGRICULTURE. Nepál has valuable forests in the southern part of the country. In the northern part, on the slopes of the Himálayas, there grow large quantities of medicinal herbs which find a world-wide market. Of the total area, nearly one-third (11·2m. acres) is under forest; 5·4m. acres is covered by perpetual snow; 9·6m. acres is under paddy, 2·9m. maize and millet, 0·8m. wheat.

Livestock: Cattle, 7m., including 2·1m. cows and 1·2m. buffaloes; sheep and goats, 1·75m.; hogs, 140,000; poultry, 14m.

INDUSTRY. New industries, such as jute- and sugar-mills, match, leather and shoe factories, and chemical works have been established. The third economic plan envisages a 60,000-kw. capacity from hydro-electric plants.

TRADE. The principal articles of export are food grains, jute, timber, oilseeds, ghee (clarified butter), potatoes, medicinal herbs, hides and skins, cattle. The chief imports are textiles, cigarettes, salt, petrol and kerosene, sugar, machinery, medicines, boots and shoes, paper, cement, iron and steel, tea. The trade is mostly financed by the Nepál Bank, Ltd (established in 1937) and the Rástra Bank of Nepál (established in 1956).

Total trade between Nepál and UK (British Board of Trade returns, in £1,000 sterling):

	1965	1966	1967	1968	1969	1970
Imports to UK	22	66	101	499	702	857
Exports from UK	163	310	364	452	526	} 1,767
Re-exports from UK	5	3	3	24	37	

RAILWAYS (2 ft 6 in. gauge) connect Raxaul with Amlekganj (30 miles) and Jayanagar on the North Eastern Indian Railway with Janakpur and thence with Bijulpura (33 miles).

ROADS. With the co-operation of India and the USA 900 miles of motorable roads are being constructed, including the East–West Highway through southern Nepál. A road from the Tibetan border to Káthmándu is being built with Chinese aid.

There are about 500 miles of motorable roads. A ropeway for the carriage of goods covers the 14 miles from Dhursing above Bhimphedi into the Káthmándu valley. A road connects Káthmándu with the railhead at Amlekhganj (80 miles).

AVIATION. The Royal Nepal Airline Corporation has linked Káthmándu, the capital, with 11 districts of Nepál; and 23 more airfields are under construction. The Royal Nepalese Airline Corporation has services between Káthmándu and Calcutta, Patna, New Delhi and Dacca.

POST. Káthmándu is connected by telephone with Birganj and Raxaul (North Eastern Indian Railway) on the southern frontier with Bihar; and with the eastern part of the Terai foothills; an extension to the western districts is being completed. Number of telephones (1969) 5,400, of which 5,000 in Káthmándu. Under an agreement with India and the USA, a network of 56 wireless stations is being established in Nepál, with further stations in Calcutta and New Dehli. Radio Nepál at Káthmándu broadcasts in Nepáli and English. Wireless telecommunication was inaugurated on 1 Oct. 1964.

All post, telephone and telegraph services have been taken over from India. The Indian, originally English, post office, established in 1816, closed on 13 April 1965.

DIPLOMATIC REPRESENTATIVES

Nepál maintains embassies in:

Burma	Israel	UAR
China	Japan	UK
France	Pakistan	USA
Germany (West)	Thailand	
India	USSR	

Nepál maintains diplomatic relations with:

Afghánistán	Ethiopia	Netherlands
Algeria	France	New Zealand
Argentina	Greece	Philippines
Australia	Hungary	Poland
Austria	Indonesia	Romania
Belgium	Iran	Spain
Bulgaria	Iraq	Sudan
Canada	Jordan	Sweden
Ceylon	Laos	Switzerland
Chile	Lebanon	Turkey
Czechoslovakia	Malaysia	Yugoslavia
Denmark	Mongolia	

OF NEPÁL IN GREAT BRITAIN (12a Kensington Palace Gdns, W8)

Ambassador: Upendra Bahadur Basnyat (accredited 5 Nov. 1969).
First Secretary: Ishwari Raj Pandey. *Military Attaché:* Lieut.-Col. Samudra Bahadur Thapa.

OF GREAT BRITAIN IN NEPÁL

Ambassador: T. J. O'Brien, MC.
First Secretaries: W. D. Wilson, OBE, MC (*Consul*); D. A. Spain (*Information*). *Defence and Military Attaché:* Lieut.-Col. D. F. Neill, OBE, MC.

OF NEPÁL IN THE USA (2131 Leroy Pl. NW, Washington, D.C., 20008)

Ambassador: Kul Shekhar Sharma.
First Secretary: Bishwa Pradhan. *Military Attaché:* Lieut.-Col. Hikmat B. Bisht.

OF THE USA IN NEPÁL

Ambassador: Miss Carol C. Laise.
Deputy Chief of Mission: Davis Eugene Boster. *Heads of Sections:* Thomas S. Brooks (*Political*); Henry E. Mattox (*Economic*); Bruce K. Deakin

(*Administrative*); William C. Ide (*AID*). *Service Attachés:* Col. Edwin H. Moot, Jr (*Air*), Capt. Jerome L. Wolf (*Navy*) both resident at New Delhi, and Col. William T. Stites (*Defence and Army*).

BOOKS OF REFERENCE

STATISTICAL INFORMATION. A Department of Statistics was set up in Káthmándu in 1950.

Hagen, T., *Nepal*. Bern, 1961
Karan, P. P., and Jenkins, W. M., *Nepal: a cultural and physical geography*. Univ. of Kentucky Press, 1960
Mihaly, E. B., *Foreign aid and politics in Nepal*. OUP, 1965
Regmi, D. R., *Modern Nepal*. Calcutta, 1961

THE NETHERLANDS
Koninkrijk der Nederlanden

REIGNING QUEEN. **Juliana Louise Emma Marie Wilhelmina**, born 30 April 1909, daughter of Queen Wilhelmina (born 31 Aug. 1880, died 28 Nov. 1962) and Prince Henry of Mecklenburg-Schwerin (born April 1876, died 3 July 1934); succeeded to the throne on the abdication of her mother, 4 Sept. 1948, and was enthroned on 6 Sept.; married to Prince Bernhard Leopold Frederick Everhard Julius Coert Karel Godfried Pieter of Lippe-Biesterfeld (born 29 June 1911) on 7 Jan. 1937. *Offspring:* Princess Beatrix Wilhelmina Armgard, born 31 Jan. 1938 (*heir presumptive*), married to Claus von Amsberg on 10 March 1966 (*sons:* Prince Willem-Alexander, born 27 April 1967; Prince Johan Friso, born 25 Sept. 1968; Prince Constantijn, born 11 Oct. 1969); Princess Irene Emma Elisabeth, born 5 Aug. 1939, married to Prince Charles Hugues de Bourbon-Parma on 29 April 1964 (*son:* Prince Carlos Javier Bernardo, born 27 Jan. 1970); Princess Margriet Francisca, born in Ottawa, 19 Jan. 1943, married to Pieter van Vollenhoven on 10 Jan. 1967 (*son:* Prince Maurits, born 17 April 1968; Prince Bernhard, born 25 Dec. 1969); Princess Maria Christina, born 18 Feb. 1947.

The Queen's civil list was in Nov. 1968 fixed at 4·75m. guilders.

The founder of the dynasty was William of Orange (1533–84), who, as the German count of Nassau, inherited vast possessions in the Netherlands and the Princedom of Orange in France. He was the initiator of the struggle for independence from Spain (1568–1648); in the Republic of the United Netherlands he and his successors became the 'first servants of the Republic' with the title of 'Stadhouder' (governor). In 1689 William III acceded to the throne of England, becoming joint sovereign with Mary II, his wife. William III died in 1702 without issue, and after a stadhouderless period a member of the Frisian branch of Orange-Nassau was nominated hereditary stadhouder in 1747; but his successor, Willem V, had to take refuge in England, in 1795, at the invasion of the French Army. In Nov. 1813 the United Provinces were freed from French domination. The Congress of Vienna joined the Belgian provinces, the 'Austrian Netherlands' before the French Revolution, to the Northern Netherlands. The son of the former stadhouder Willem V was proclaimed King of the Netherlands at The Hague on 16 March 1815 as Willem I. The union was dissolved by the Belgian revolution of 1830, and the treaty of London, 19 April 1839, constituted Belgium an independent kingdom.

Netherlands Sovereigns

Willem I	1815–40 (died 1843)	Wilhelmina	1890–1948 (died 1962)
Willem II	1840–1849	Juliana	1948–
Willem III	1849–1890		

The Hague is the seat of the Court, Government and Parliament.

National flag: Red, white, blue (horizontal).

National anthem: Wilhelmus van Nassouen (words by Philip Marnix van St Aldegonde, *c.* 1570).

CONSTITUTION AND GOVERNMENT.

According to the Constitution of the Kingdom of the Netherlands, the Kingdom consists of the Netherlands, Surinam and the Netherlands Antilles. Their relations are regulated by the 'Statute' for the Kingdom, which came into force on 29 Dec. 1954. Each part enjoys full autonomy; they are united, on a footing of equality, for mutual assistance and the protection of their common interests.

The first Constitution of the Netherlands after its restoration as a Sovereign State was promulgated in 1814. It was revised in 1815 (after the addition of the Belgian provinces, and the assumption by the Sovereign of the title of King), 1840 (after the secession of the Belgian province), 1848, 1884, 1887, 1917, 1922, 1938, 1946, 1948, 1953, 1956 and 1963.

The Netherlands is a constitutional and hereditary monarchy. The royal succession is in the direct male line in the order of primogeniture; in default of male heirs, the female line ascends the throne. The Sovereign comes of age on reaching his 18th year. During his minority the royal power is vested in a Regent—designated by law—and in some cases in the Council of State.

The central executive power of the State rests with the Crown, while the central legislative power is vested in the Crown and Parliament (the *Staten-Generaal*), consisting of 2 Chambers. After the 1956 revision of the Constitution the Upper or First Chamber is composed of 75 members, elected by the members of the Provincial States, and the Second Chamber consists of 150 deputies, who are elected directly. Members of the States-General must be Netherlands subjects and 25 years of age or over; they may be men or women. They receive an allowance.

First Chamber (as constituted in 1969): Catholics, 24; Labour Party, 20; Party for Freedom and Democracy, 8; Christian Historicals, 8; Anti-Revolutionaries, 7; Pacifist Socialist Party, 3; Farmers Party, 3; Communists, 1; Radicals, 1.

Second Chamber (elected on 16 Feb. 1967): Catholics, 39; Labour Party, 37; Party for Freedom and Democracy, 17; Anti-Revolutionaries, 15; Christian Historicals, 12; Democracy, 1966, 7; Communists, 5; Pacifist Socialist Party, 4; Farmers Party, 3; Political Calvinists, 3; Radicals, 3; 2nd Farmers Party (Harmsen), 3; Reformed Political Union, 1; Independents, 1.

The revised Constitution of 1917 has introduced an electoral system based on universal suffrage and proportional representation. Under its provisions, members of the Second Chamber are directly elected by citizens of both sexes who are Netherlands subjects not under 21 years (since 1965). Criminals, lunatics and certain others are disqualified; for certain crimes and misdemeanours there may be temporary disqualification.

The members of the Second Chamber are elected for 4 years, and retire in a body, whereas the First Chamber is elected for 6 years, and every 3 years one-half retires by rotation. The Sovereign has the power to dissolve both Chambers of Parliament, or one of them, subject to the condition that new elections take place within 40 days, and the new House or Houses be convoked within 3 months.

The Sovereign and the Second Chamber may propose Bills; the First Chamber can only approve or reject them without inserting amendments. The meetings of both Chambers are public, though each of them may by a majority vote decide on a secret session. It is a fixed custom, that Ministers and Secretaries of State, on their own initiative or upon invitation of the Parliament, attend the sessions to defend their policy, their budget, their proposals of Bills, etc., when these are in discussion. A Minister or Secretary of State, however, cannot be a member of Parliament at the same time.

The Constitution can be revised only by a Bill declaring that there is reason for introducing such revision and containing the proposed alterations. The passing of this Bill is followed by a dissolution of both Chambers and a second

C C

confirmation by the new States-General by two-thirds of the votes. Unless it is expressly stated, all laws concern only the realm in Europe, and not the overseas parts of the kingdom. Every act of the Sovereign has to be covered by a responsible Minister.

The Ministry, appointed 5 April 1967, is composed as follows:

Prime Minister and Minister for General Affairs: P. J. S. de Jong, DSC (Cath.).
First Deputy Prime Minister and Finance: Dr H. J. Witteveen (Freedom & Democracy).
Second Deputy Prime Minister and Transport and Waterways: J. A. Bakker (Anti-Rev.).
Foreign Affairs: J. M. A. H. Luns, GCMG (Cath.). *Aid for developing countries:* B. J. Udink (Christian Hist.). *Justice:* C. H. F. Polak (Freedom & Democracy). *Home Affairs:* H. K. J. Beernink (Christian Hist.). *Education and Sciences:* Dr G. H. Veringa (Cath.). *Defence:* Lieut.-Gen. W. den Toom (Freedom & Democracy). *Housing and Building:* W. F. Schut (Anti-Rev.). *Economic Affairs:* R. J. Nelissen (Cath.). *Agriculture and Fisheries:* P. J. Lardinois (Cath.). *Social Affairs and Health:* B. Roolvink (Anti-Rev.). *Culture, Recreation and Social Welfare:* Miss Dr M. A. M. Klompé (Cath.). *Minister plenipotentiary for Surinam:* Dr J. D. V. Polanen. *Minister plenipotentiary for the Netherlands Antilles:* Dr E. Jonckheer.

There are also 11 Secretaries of State.

The Council of State (*Raad van State*), appointed and presided over by the Sovereign, is composed of a deputy chairman and not more than 16 members. It can be consulted on all legislative matters. Decisions of the Crown in administrative disputes are prepared by a special committee of the Council.

LOCAL GOVERNMENT. The kingdom is divided in 11 provinces and 873 municipalities. Each province has its own representative body, the Provincial States. The members are elected for 4 years, directly from the Netherlands inhabitants of the province who are 21 years of age. The electoral register is the same as for the Second Chamber. The members retire in a body and are subject to re-election. The number of members varies according to the population of the province, from 83 for South Holland to 43 for Zeeland. The Provincial States are entitled to issue ordinances concerning the welfare of the province, and to raise taxes pursuant to legal provisions. The provincial budgets and the provincial ordinances and resolutions relating to provincial property, loans, taxes, etc., must be approved by the Crown. The members of the Provincial States elect the First Chamber of the States-General. They meet twice a year, as a rule in public. A permanent commission composed of 6 of their members, called the 'Deputy States', is charged with the executive power and, if required, with the enforcement of the law in the province. Deputy as well as Provincial States are presided over by a Commissioner of the Sovereign, who in the former assembly has a deciding vote, but attends the latter in only a deliberative capacity. He is the chief magistrate in the province. The Commissioner and the members of the Deputy States receive an allowance.

Each municipality forms a Corporation with its own interests and rights, subject to the general law, and is governed by a Municipal Council, directly elected for 4 years, by the electorate registered for the Provincial States, provided they are residents of the municipality. All Netherlands inhabitants 21 years of age are eligible, the number of members varying from 7 to 45, according to the population. The Municipal Council has the right to issue bye-laws concerning the communal welfare. The Council may levy taxes pursuant to legal provisions; these ordinances must be approved by the Crown. All bye-laws may be vetoed by the Crown. The Municipal Budget and resolutions to alienate municipal property require the approbation of the Deputy States of the province. The Council meets in public as often as may be necessary, and is presided over by a Burgomaster, appointed by the Sovereign. The day-to-day administration is carried out by the Burgomaster and 2–7 Aldermen (*wethouders*), elected by and from the Council; this body is also charged with the enforcement of the law. The Burgomaster may suspend the execution of a resolution of the Council for 30 days, but is bound to notify the Deputy States of the province. In maintaining public order, the Burgomaster acts as the chief of police. The Burgomaster and Aldermen receive allowances.

AREA AND POPULATION. Growth of census population:

1829	2,613,298	1889	4,511,415	1930	7,935,565
1849	3,056,879	1909	5,858,175	1947	9,625,499
1869	3,579,529	1920	6,865,314	1960	11,461,964

Area, density and estimated population on 31 Dec. 1959 and 1969:

	Land area (in sq. km)	Population		Density per sq. km
Province	1969	1959	1969	1969
Groningen	2,301·64	474,657	517,305	225
Friesland	3,381·09	478.206	521,751	154
Drenthe	2,647·45	311,196	366,590	138
Overijssel	3,806·32	799,024	920,882	242
Gelderland	5,014·11	1,270,173	1,505,760	300
Utrecht	1,327·90	673,601	801,285	603
Noord-Holland	2,662·42	2,054,509	2,244,456	843
Zuid-Holland	2,831·45	2,697,894	2,968,670	1,048
Zeeland	1,748·19	283,721	305,754	175
Noord-Brabant	4,922·50	1,484,671	1,787,783	363
Limburg	2,171·54	882,386	998,570	460
Zuidelijke IJsselmeerpolders [1]	964·22	805	14,925	15
Central Register of population [2]	—	6,411	3,890	—
Total	33,778·83	11,417,254	12,957,621	384

[1] The Zuidelijke IJsselmeerpolders (drained in 1957) are part of the former Zuiderzee, now called IJsselmeer; they have not yet been incorporated in any province.
[2] The Central Register of population includes persons who are residents of the Netherlands but who have no fixed residence in any particular municipality (living in caravans and houseboats, population on inland vessels, etc.).

Of the total population on 31 Dec. 1969, 6,465,081 were males, 6,492,540 females.

The total area of the Netherlands up to the low water line (*i.e.*, sea-level at low tide) is 40,892·84 sq. km (15,784·64 sq. miles), of which 33,778·8 sq. km (13,042 sq. miles) is land area.

On 14 June 1918 a law was passed concerning the reclamation of the Zuiderzee. The work was begun in 1920; the following sections have been completed: 1. The Noordholland–Wieringen Barrage (2·5 km), 1924; 2. The Wieringermeer Polder (208 sq. km), 1930 (inundated by the Germans in 1945, but drained again in the same year); 3. The Wieringen–Friesland Barrage (30 km), 1932; 4. The Noordoost Polder (467 sq. km), 1942; 5. Oost Flevoland (536 sq. km), 1957; 6. Zuidelijk Flevoland (550 sq. km), 1967.

The polder Markerwaard (400 sq. km) is being reclaimed. A portion of what used to be the Zuiderzee behind the barrage will remain a fresh-water lake: IJsselmeer (1,250 sq. km). The 'Delta-project', scheduled to be completed in about 1980, comprises the building of enclosure dams in the estuaries between the islands in the south-western part of the country, excluding the sea-entrances to the ports of Rotterdam and Antwerp; it will also create fresh-water reservoirs. *See* map in THE STATESMAN'S YEAR-BOOK, 1959.

VITAL STATISTICS for calendar years:

	Live births		Still births	Marriages	Divorces	Deaths	Net migration
	Total	Illegitimate					
1967	238,678	4,953	2,916	115,115	7,464	99,792	−11,508
1968	237,112	4,819	2,699	117,534	8,146	104,989	+ 6,007
1969	247,588	5.378	2,752	117,497	9,080	107,615	+20,183

Population of principal municipalities on 1 Jan. 1970:

Alkmaar	52,091	's-Gravenhage	550,613	Rheden	48,713
Almelo	58,941	Groningen	168,843	Ridderkerk	41,899
Alphen a/d Rijn	33,430	Haarlem	172,235	Roermond	35,850
Amersfoort	78,189	Haarlemmermeer	58,966	Roosendaal	45,935
Amstelveen	69,167	Hardenberg	26,011	Rotterdam	686,586
Amsterdam	831,463	Heemskerk	28,152	Rijswijk (Z.-H.)	50,172
Apeldoorn	123,628	Heemstede	26,507	Schiedam	83,049
Arnhem	132,531	Heerenveen	31,434	Sittard	33,887
Assen	38,956	Heerlen	75,147	Smallingerland	38,627
Barneveld	30,046	Den Helder	60,612	Sneek	26,244
Bergen op Zoom	39,051	Hellendoorn	29,410	Soerst	35,713
Beverwijk	41,357	Helmond	57,889	Stadskanaal	32,829
De Bilt	29,153	Hengelo (O.)	69,618	Tilburg	152,589
Breda	121,209	's-Hertogenbosch	81,574	Utrecht	278,966
Brunssum	25,783	Hilversum	99,792	Veenendaal	29,637
Bussum	41,787	Hoogeveen	37,485	Veldhoven	27,307
Capelle a/d Yssel	25,766	Hougezand-		Velsen	67,580
Delft	83,698	Sappemeer	30,189	Venlo	62,694
Deventer	65,319	Kampen	28,902	Venray	26,056
Doetinchem	31,097	Katwijk	36,236	Vlaardingen	79,085
Dordrecht	88,699	Kerkrade	48,150	Vlissingen	40,197
Ede (Gld.)	71,952	Leeuwarden	88,668	Voorburg	45,011
Eindhoven	188,631	Leiden	101,221	Wageningen	26,572
Emmen	79,707	Leidgehandam	29,265	Wassenaar	27,235
Enschede	139,245	Maassluis	25,870	Weert	35,190
Epe	27,515	Maastricht	93,927	Winterswijk	26,230
Ermelo	37,198	Middelburg	30,211	Zaandam	63,535
Geldrop	26,909	Noordoostpolder	31,929	Zeist	55,619
Geleen	36,121	Nijmegen	148,790	Zutphen	27,610
Goes	25,822	Oosterhout	31,826	Zwolle	76,167
Gorinchen	26,380	Oss	40,085	Zwijndrecht	31,761
Gouda	45,990	Renkum	33,619		

Urban agglomerations as at 1 Jan. 1970: Amsterdam, 1,040,395; Rotterdam, 1,061,253; The Hague, 719,426; Utrecht, 445,078; Eindhoven, 334,954; Heerlen-Kerkrade, 263,850; Arnhem, 270,473; Haarlem, 238,608; Enschede-Hengelo, 229,958; Groningen, 201,397; Tilburg, 202,733; Nijmegen, 203,028; Geleen-Sittard, 166,016; s'Hertogenbosch, 167,023; Dordrecht, 168,742; Leiden, 162,549; Breda, 147,462; Maastricht, 143,460; Velsen-Beverwijk, 137,089; Zaandam, 126,955; Hilversum, 115,322.

RELIGION. Entire liberty of conscience is granted to the members of all denominations. The royal family belong to the Dutch Reformed Church.

The number of adherents of the Churches according to the census of 1960 was: Dutch Reformed Church, 3,240,481; Reformed Churches, 1,068,600; Roman Catholics, 4,634,478; other creeds, 416,170; no religion, 2,102,235.

The government of the Reformed Church is Presbyterian. On 1 Jan. 1970 the Dutch Reformed Church had 1 synod, 11 provincial districts, 54 classes, 147 districts and 1,901 parishes. Their clergy numbered 2,000. The Roman Catholic Church had, Jan. 1970, 1 archbishop (of Utrecht), 7 bishops and 1,845 parishes and rectorships. The Old Catholics had (end of 1968) 1 archbishop (Utrecht), 2 bishops and 29 parishes. The Jews had, in 1970, 46 communities.

EDUCATION. Statistics for the scholastic year 1968–69:

	Full-time			Part-time [1]		
		Pupils			Pupils	
	Schools	Total	Female	Schools	Total	Female
Nursery schools	5,959	488,819	238,134	—	—	—
Primary schools	8,125	1,438,831	703,932	—	—	—
Special schools	754	70,428	24,707	—	—	—
Secondary general schools	1,812	555,380	266,024	18	6,438	1,250
Secondary vocational schools: Junior—						
Technical	381	153,193	556	605	101,825	451
Agricultural	202	15,760	378	80	1,770	220
Domestic science	605	110,598	110,480	1	5,455	5,320
Other	93	20,291	7,504	—	—	—

[1] Including apprenticeship schemes.

	Full-time			Part-time[1]		
	School	Pupils		School	Pupils	
		Total	Female		Total	Female
Senior—						
Technical	98	26,501	428	161	10,873	208
Agricultural	60	5,179	258	—	—	—
Domestic science	273	25,370	25,350	1	1,289	1,267
Teachers' training (nursery schools)	50	8,266	8,266	1	3,380	3,380
Other	72	7,245	2,718	177	21,881	7,121
Third level non-university training:						
Technical	64	18,282	1,214	58	5,436	1,005
Agricultural	13	2,139	87	—	—	—
Arts	44	6,817	3,046	20	3,538	1,200
Teachers' training (primary schools)	98	24,313	9,931	—	—	—
Teachers' training (sec. general schools)	12	5,244	2,397	9	12,639	4,369
Teachers' training (sec. vocational schools)	54	4,991	4,899	31	8,053	396
Other	39	1,917	444	36	5,248	3,072

[1] Including apprenticeship schemes.

Full-time: 1968–69

		Pupils	
	Schools	Total	Female
University education:		84,776	15,769
Humanities		14,888	5,820
Social sciences		28,727	5,301
Natural sciences	13	10,754	1,343
Technical sciences		13,568	237
Medical sciences		13,313	2,523
Agricultural sciences		3,508	545

CINEMAS (1970). There were 452 cinemas with a seating capacity of 221,626.

NEWSPAPERS (1970). There were 77 daily newspapers with a total circulation of over 3·9m.

JUSTICE. Justice is administered by the High Court of the Netherlands (Court of Cassation), by 5 courts of justice (Courts of Appeal), by 19 district courts and by 62 cantonal courts; trial by jury is unknown. The Cantonal Court, which deals with minor offences, is formed by a single judge; the more serious cases are tried by the district courts, formed as a rule by 3 judges (in some cases one judge is sufficient); the courts of appeal are constituted of 3 and the High Court of 5 judges. All judges are appointed for life by the Sovereign (the judges of the High Court from a list prepared by the Second Chamber of the States-General). They can be removed only by a decision of the High Court.

Juvenile courts were set up in 1922. The juvenile court is formed by a single judge specially appointed to try children's civil cases, at the same time charged with the administration of justice for criminal actions committed by young persons who are between 12 and 18 (in special cases up to 21) years old, unless imprisonment of 6 months or more ought to be inflicted; such cases are tried by 3 judges.

Number of persons convicted (tax offenders excluded):

Major offences	1966	1967	1968	Minor offences	1967	1968	1969
Males	34,607	36,197	37,960	Males	912,602	969,790	917,166
Females	4,395	4,820	4,923	Females	73,008	84,900	80,425

In addition, prosecution was evaded by paying a fine to the police in 847,892 cases in 1966, 801,607 in 1967, 855 375 in 1968, 797,880 in 1969.

Police. There are both State and Municipal Police. The State Police, about 4,800 men strong, serves 786, and the Municipal Police, about 13,600 men strong, serves 123 municipalities. The State Police includes ordinary as well as water, mounted and motor police. The State Police Corps is under the jurisdiction of the Police Department of the Ministry of Justice, which also includes the National Criminal Investigation Office, which deals with serious crimes throughout the country, and the International Criminal Investigation Office, which informs foreign countries of international crimes.

FINANCE. Currency. The monetary unit is the *gulden* (guilder, florin) of 100 cents. The official rate of exchange is US$1 = 3·62 guilders since 6 March 1961 and £1 = 8·69 guilders from 20 Nov. 1967.

Legal tender are bank-notes, currency notes of 2½ guilders, silver 2½-guilder pieces, silver 1-guilder pieces, nickel 25-cent pieces, nickel 10-cent pieces, bronze 5-cent pieces and bronze 1-cent pieces. Note circulation, 17 Aug. 1970, 9,289m. guilders, and on 29 Dec. 1969, 9,399m.

Budget. The revenue and expenditure of the central government (ordinary and extraordinary) were, in 1m. guilders, for calendar years:

	1964[3]	1965[3]	1966[3]	1967[3]	1968[4]	1969[4]	1970[5]
Revenue[1]	13,287	15,842	17,032	18,902	21,253	24,249	27,222
Expenditure[2]	14,566	17,139	19,036	21,035	24,753	27,277	29,397

[1] Without the revenue of loans.
[2] Including the deficit of the agricultural equilization fund.
[3] Accounts.   [4] Preliminary accounts.   [5] Estimates.

The revenue and expenditure of the Fund for Central Government roads (established in 1965) have been incorporated in the general budget.

The national debt, in 1m. guilders, was on 31 Dec.:

	1964	1965	1966	1967	1968	1969
Internal funded debt	14,407	15,015	16,104	18,028	19,784	21,254
„ floating „	5,969	6,613	7,118	7,704	8,665	9,390
External funded „	419	367	345	345	108	108
Total	20,795	21,995	23,567	26,077	28,557	30,752

DEFENCE. The Netherlands are bordered on the south by Belgium, on the east by Germany. On both sides the country is quite level and has no natural defences, except the barriers of some large rivers, running east to west and south to north. The country has an excellent roadnet and a vast railway system, enabling rapid movement. The west part of the country is densely populated.

Army. Service is partly voluntary and partly compulsory; the voluntary enlistments bear a small proportion to the compulsory of a total peace strength of 80,000. 29,000 are regular personnel; they comprise officers, n.c.o.s and technical specialists, *i.e.*, young men, who serve for a period of 4–6 years and receive specific military and civilian-trade training, leading to official civilian certificates. The Army also employs 14,000 civilians. The legal period of active service for the national servicemen is 22–24 months; the actual service obligations are 16 months for enlisted personnel and 18 months for reserve officers and n.c.o.s. The balance may be spent at will as 'short leave'. After the obligatory period the conscript personnel are sent on long leave, but remain—until the age of 35 (n.c.o.s 40, officers 45)—liable to call-up for refresher exercises or in the event of a mobilization.

The Netherlands have assigned to NATO the 1st Netherlands Army Corps, consisting of standing and mobilizable units. The standing part of the Corps comprises 2 armoured brigades, 4 armoured infantry brigades and 40% of the corps troops (headquarters, combat and service support units); the brigades and the division-type headquarters may be organized into 2 mechanized divisions, 1st and 4th Division. Part of this force is stationed in West Germany. The peacetime strength of the standing brigades amounts to 85% of the wartime authorized strength. The mobilizable units are tank battalions (600 Centurions partly being replaced by Leopards), armoured infantry battalions, heavy (175 mm) and medium (155 mm and 105 mm) artillery battalions (mainly self-propelled), armoured engineer units, armoured reconnaisance units, armoured tank-destroyer units and helicopter squadrons.

The National Command forces consist of training centres and schools, logistical units and staffs. In event of mobilization, territorial brigades with support and logistical units are called up in the 3 Army Territories. Territorial units are also maintained in Surinam. Some units in the Netherlands are earmarked for assignment to the United Nations as peace-keeping forces. A group of officers is permanently attached to the UN Truce Supervision Organization force in the Middle East. For civil defence purposes there are a number of military (mobilizable) fire-fighting, rescue and medical battalions. In time of war these units turn to the command of the National Commander of the Civil Defence.

Navy. The Royal Netherlands Navy has its main base in the Netherlands at Den Helder and a secondary base in the Netherlands Antilles at Willemstad, Curaçao.

Principal surface ships of the Royal Netherlands Navy:

Com-pleted	Name	Standard dis-placement (tons)	Principal armament	Shaft horse-power	Max. speed (knots)
1953[1]	De Zeven Provincien (guided-missile cruiser)	9,850	4–15, 2 cm; 6–57 mm; 4–40 mm; twin 'Terrier' SAM launcher	} 85,000	32
1953	De Ruyter (light cruiser)	9,529	8–15, 2 cm; 8–57 mm; 8–40 mm		

[1] Converted to guided missile cruiser in 1962–64.

The aircraft carrier *Karel Doorman* was sold to Argentina in 1968 and re-named *25 de Mayo*.

There are also 6 submarines, 12 destroyers, 6 frigates, 6 corvettes, 3 escorts (*ex*-ocean minesweepers), 3 mine countermeasures support ships (*ex*-ocean minesweepers), 5 patrol vessels, 2 survey ships, 39 coastal minesweepers, 2 coastal minehunters, 16 inshore minesweepers, 5 diving vessels, 5 small survey craft and 37 auxiliary ships.

On 1 Jan. 1970 naval personnel totalled 20,200 officers and men, including the Royal Marine Corps.

The naval air service maintains 1 squadron Lockheed Neptunes (SP-2H), 1 squadron Breguet Atlantics, 2 squadrons Grumman Trackers (S-2A), 1 squadron Wasp helicopters, 1 squadron utility helicopters (Agusta-Bell UH-1 and Sikorsky UH-34J), 2 squadrons for training purposes equipped with Beechcraft TC-45J and Fokker S-11.

Naval estimates (in 1m. guilders): 1968, 776; 1969, 824; 1970, 936.

Air Force. The Royal Netherlands Air Force was established 1 July 1913. Its current strength is approximately 22,300 personnel and it has a first-line combat force of 8 squadrons of aircraft and 18 squadrons of surface-to-air missiles. Two F-104G Starfighter interceptor squadrons are operated by Air Defence Command, which also controls a USAF squadron of F-4E Phantom II tactical fighter-bombers based in the Netherlands. Tactical Air Command has 2 squadrons of F-104G Starfighter and 3 of NF-5 fighter-bombers, and 1 reconnaissance squadron of RF-104G aircraft. The 75 single-seat NF-5A and 30 two-seat NF-5B aircraft were built in Canada.

There are 8 Nike-Hercules surface-to-air missile (high-altitude) squadrons and 12 Hawk surface-to-air missile (low-altitude) squadrons; 2 of the latter were deactivated in 1970, under economic measures which also reduced from 18 to 12 the number of operational Starfighters in each squadron.

In addition the RNLAF comprises 1 transport squadron (Fokker Friendship) and 3 observation and communication squadrons of light aircraft and Alouette III helicopters. The observation and communication squadrons are under the operational command of the Army.

Training is undertaken jointly with the Belgian Air Force.

Air Force estimates (in 1m. guilders): 1968, 786; 1969, 827·6.

AGRICULTURE. The net area of all holdings[1] was divided as follows (in hectares):

	1965	1966	1967	1968	1969
Field crops	801,943	773,532	751,920	742,506	720,498
Grass	1,337,151	1,349,325	1,361,536	1,359,698	1,364,378
Market gardening	102,633	103,556	105,400	103,163	102,319
Land for flower bulbs	11,464	11,533	10,886	11,694	12,214
Flower cultivation	1,933	1,933	2,153	2,400	2,476
Nurseries	3,448	3,494	3,560	3,617	3,748
Fallow land	7,288	11,575	10,604	8,385	9,335
Total	2,265,860	2,254,948	2,246,059	2,231,463	2,214,968
Plantations with undercropping	*9,892*	*7,790*	*6,814*	*5,157*	*4,314*
Total agricultural area	2,255,968	2,247,158	2,239,245	2,226,306	2,210,654

[1] Excluding non-agrarian holdings of less than 1 hectare.

The net areas[1] under special crops were as follows (in hectares):

Products	1968	1969	Products	1968	1969
Autumn wheat	89,340	86,086	Colza	6,726	6,170
Spring wheat	64,156	69,308	Flax	10,391	8,940
Rye	75,013	62,188	Agricultural seeds	11,028	9,899
Autumn barley	7,069	4,655	Potatoes, edible[2]	90,167	82,911
Spring barley	100,178	94,686	Potatoes, industrial[3]	58,830	62,401
Oats	75,780	82,511	Sugar-beets	103,550	102,868
Peas	11,096	12.087	Fodder-beets	11,585	10,529

[1] Excluding non-agrarian holdings of less than 1 hectare.
[2] Including early and seed potatoes.
[3] Including seed potatoes.

The yield of the more important products, in metric tons, was as follows:

Crop	Average 1940–49	Average 1950–58	1967[1]	1968[1]	1969[1]
Wheat	322,003	348,464	738,587	678,971	677,181
Rye	439,055	454,992	239,077	239,081	206,532
Barley	145,892	258,049	446,679	389,478	389,393
Oats	315,642	464,041	365,425	317,998	321,655
Field beans	15,799	5,693	866	443	269
Peas	65,460	93,664	48,386	35,757	40,095
Colza	24,763	18,358	15,186	18,009	12,192
Flax, fibre	82,906	138,165	58.200	59,249	50,152
Potatoes, edible[2]	2,861,793	2,745,505	3,207,099	3,014,474	2,727,001
Potatoes, industrial	1,242,326	1,003,994	1,632,297	2,030,834	1,976,911
Sugar-beet	1,667,711	2,935,881	5,073,697	5,127,676	5,001,966
Fodder-beet	..	..	1,120,314	963,496	853,967

[1] Excluding non-agrarian holdings of less than 1 hectare.
[2] Including early potatoes.

Livestock, May 1969: 4,276,522 cattle, 4,755,159 pigs; 57,196 horses (3 years old and over, for agricultural purposes), 554,463 sheep, 50m. poultry.

In 1969 the production of butter, under state control, amounted to 110,296 metric tons; that of cheese, under state control, to 259,695 metric tons. Export value of arable crops amounted to 3,379m. guilders; animal produce, 4,128m. guilders, and horticultural produce, 2,146 guilders.

FISHERIES. The total produce of fish landed from the North Sea in 1968 was valued at 167,327,000 guilders; the total weight amounted to 140,300 tons. In 1968 the herring fishery had a value of 18,141,500 guilders and a weight of 16,957 tons. The quantity of oysters produced in 1968 amounted to 802 tons (5,496,000 guilders).

MINING. Coalmining will be stopped completely. On 1 Jan. 1970 only 3 mines in private ownership were still being operated.

The daily average of workers was 15,800 in 1969 (of whom 10,000 worked underground).

Production of coal in 1,000 metric tons: 1938, 13.488: 1948, 11,032; 1958, 11,880; 1966, 10,052; 1967, 8,065; 1968, 6,663; 1969, 5,564.

The production of crude petroleum (in 1,000 metric tons) amounted in 1943 (first year) to 0·2; 1953, 820; 1967, 2,265; 1968, 2,147; 1969, 2,020.

There are saltmines at Hengelo and Delfzijl; production (in 1,000 metric tons), 1950, 412·6; 1960, 1,096; 1967, 1,926; 1968, 2,414; 1969, 2,668.

POWER. The total production of electrical energy (in 1m. kwh.) amounted in 1938 to 3,688; 1958, 13,854; 1967, 30,056; 1968, 33,619; 1969, 37,144. The total net production of manufactured gas amounted in 1950 to 11,004 tcal; 1955, 14,332; 1960, 16,760; 1967, 11,079; 1968, 10,385; 1969, 8,919. Production of natural gas in 1950, 8 cu. metres; 1955, 139; 1960, 384; 1967, 6,989; 1968, 14,056; 1969, 21,848.

INDUSTRY. Numbers employed (in 1,000) and turnover (in 1m. guilders) in manufacturing enterprises with 10 workers and more, excluding building and public utilities:

Class of industry	Numbers employed		Turnover	
	1968	1969	1968	1969
Earthenware, glass, lime and stoneware	48·4	48·4	2,230	2,252
Cutting and polishing of diamonds and other precious stones	0·5	0·3	34	33
Graphic industry	49·3	50·6	1,813	1,969
Chemical industry	86·8	99·2	10,649	11,533
Manufacture of goods of wood and straw	46·1	47·5	1,961	1,915
Clothing	64·9	61·6	1,969	2,636
Cleaning	13·1	12·5	234	233
Leather and rubber industry	35·3	32·9	1,436	1,419
Mining and quarrying	36·0	23·6	1,572	1,763
Metal industry	417·3	444·6	18,962	21,250
Paper industry	33·7	32·5	2,138	2,146
Textile industry	89·7	87·8	4,173	4,427
Manufacture of foodstuffs	159·4	159·2	20,049	20,867
Total	1,080·5	1,094·9	67,221	71,842

COMMERCE. On 5 Sept. 1944 and 14 March 1947 the Netherlands signed agreements with Belgium and Luxembourg for the establishment of a customs union. On 1 Jan. 1948 this union came into force and the existing customs tariffs of the Belgium–Luxembourg Economic Union and of the Netherlands were superseded by the joint Benelux Customs Union Tariff. It applies to imports into the 3 countries from outside sources, and exempts from customs duties all imports into each of the 3 countries from the other two. The Benelux tariff has 991 items and 2,400 separate specifications.

Returns of special imports and special exports (including parcel post and diamond trade, excluding unrefined and partly-worked gold, gold coins and coins in current circulation made of other metal) for calendar years (in 1,000 guilders):

	Imports	Exports		Imports	Exports
1939	1,559,667	1,005,875	1966	24,023,829	29,443,247
1949	5,331,569	3,851,126	1967	30,180,971	26,379,942
1959	14,968,454	13,702,927	1968	33,638,489	30,196,863
1965	27,009,829	23,143,934	1969	39,796,801	36,073,739

Value of the trade (including parcel post and diamond trade, excluding unrefined and partly-worked gold, gold coins and coins in current circulation made of other metal) with leading countries (in 1,000 guilders):

	Imports			Exports		
Country	1967	1968	1969	1967	1968	1969
Belgium–Luxembourg	5,566,847	6,046,405	7,044,932	3,885,919	4,318,791	5,030,209
France	1,920,006	2,182,987	3,087,994	2,422,813	3,179,680	4,166,649
Germany (West)	7,669,895	8,875,612	10,618,121	6,885,462	8,393,423	10,712,460
Indonesia	354,508	215,874	188,768	165,808	135,476	163,540
Italy	1,299,371	1,523,801	1,801,564	1,296,436	1,450,752	1,781,343
Kuwait	506,692	696,455	581,099	39,668	39,868	42,834
Sweden	705,627	786,439	926,820	760,630	835,661	911,320
UK	1,673,756	1,843,947	2,262,424	2,329,589	2,579,339	2,750,022
USA	3,207,836	3,671,244	3,861,601	1,241,437	1,578,987	1,623,243
Venezuela	134,759	96,592	96,502	87,590	85,531	98,147

Total trade between the Netherlands and UK (in £1,000 sterling) for calendar years (British Board of Trade returns):

	1966	1967	1968	1969	1970
Imports to UK	291,139	328,674	393,002	409,140	459,102
Exports from UK	196,315	193,666	242,176	278,929 ⎫	377,767
Re-exports from UK	10,826	11,935	13,282	16,052 ⎭	

SEA-GOING SHIPPING. Survey of the Netherlands mercantile marine as at 1 Jan. (capacity in 1,000 GRT):

Ships under Netherlands flag (including Netherlands Antilles and Surinam)	1969		1970	
	Number	Capacity	Number	Capacity
Passenger ships[1]	22	259	17	219
Freighters (500 GRT and over)	371	2,435	375	2,400
Freighters (under 500 GRT)	769	323	655	277
Tankers	118	1,976	118	1,937
Total	1,280	4,833	1,165	4,833

[1] With accommodation for 13 or more cabin passengers.

In 1969, 44,257 sea-going ships of 208·53m. gross tons entered Netherlands ports (1968, 44,249 ships of 187·04m. gross tons).

Total goods traffic by sea-going ships in 1969 (with 1968 figures in brackets), in 1m. metric tons, amounted to 171·3 (150·8) unloaded of which, 79·2 (64) were imports, 33 (29·7) stored in bonded warehouses and 59·1 (57) transit, and 47·3 (40·4) loaded, of which 23·7 (18·2) were exports, 7·7 (5·9) were released from bonded warehouses and 15·9 (16·3) transit, excluding bunker fuel. The total seaborne freight traffic at Rotterdam was 176·1m. (153·4m.) and at Amsterdam 19·1m. (17·4m.) metric tons.

The number of containers at Rotterdam in 1969 was: unloaded from ships, 103,327, of which 37,797 from North America, and 92,778 loaded into ships, of which 17,540 to North America.

INLAND SHIPPING. The total length of navigable rivers and canals is 5,707 km, of which about 2,434 km is for ships with a capacity of 1,000 and more metric tons. On 1 Jan. 1970 the Netherlands inland fleet (with carrying capacity in 1,000 metric tons) was composed as follows:

Class of tonnage	Number	Capacity	Class of tonnage	Number	Capacity
21–99 tons	6,820	380	1,000–1,499 tons	820	1,044
100–199 tons	4,292	580	1,500 tons and over	458	928
200–399 tons	3,984	1,178			
400–599 tons	2,155	1,073		20,334	6,605
600–999 tons	1,805	1,422			

In 1969, 237m. (1968: 242m.) metric tons of goods were transported on rivers and canals, of which 146·5m. (147·4m.) in international traffic. Goods transport on the Rhine (Lobith) amounted to 45·2m. (48·4m.) metric tons downstream and 63·6m. (61·5m.) upstream.

RAILWAYS. All railways are run by the mixed company 'N.V. Nederlandsche Spoorwegen'. Length of line in 1970 was 3,148 km, of which 1,646 km were electrified. The last steam train was abolished in Jan. 1958. Passengers carried (1969), 179·8m.; goods transported, 26·3m. metric tons.

ROADS. In 1970 the length of the Netherlands network of surfaced inter-urban roads was 47,777 km. Buses transported in 1969, 687m. passengers, of whom 295m. in local traffic. Number of private cars (1969), 2·3m.

AVIATION. The Royal Dutch Airlines (KLM) was founded on 7 Oct. 1919. The company has a paid-up capital of 311m. guilders (1 March 1970). Revenue traffic, 1969–70: Passengers, 2·5m.; freight, 114·9m kg; mail, 3·8m. kg.

TELECOMMUNICATIONS. On 1 Jan. 1970 there were 2,001,000 telephone connexions and 3·1m. apparatus.

Wireless receiving sets totalled 2,809,000 on 1 Jan. 1970; in addition, 279,000 families have radio-redistribution. Television sets totalled 2·94m., but holders of television licences may, in addition, have wireless receiving sets.

BANKING. The Netherlands Bank, founded as a private institution, was nationalized on 1 Aug. 1948, the shareholders receiving, for a share of 1,000 guilders, a security of 2,000 guilders on the 2½% National Debt. Since 1863 the bank has the sole right of issuing bank-notes. The bank does the same business as other banks, but with more guarantees. The capital amounts to 20m. guilders.

In the year 1969 the state post office savings bank had deposits of 1,673m. guilders and withdrawals of 1,543m. guilders. Private savings banks: Deposits, 7,360m. guilders; withdrawals, 6,894m. guilders.

WEIGHTS AND MEASURES. The metric system of weights and measures was adopted in the Netherlands in 1820.

DIPLOMATIC REPRESENTATIVES

The Netherlands maintains embassies in:

Afghánistán	Guatemala	Norway
Algeria	Guinea	Pakistan
Argentina	Guyana	Panama
Australia	Haiti	Paraguay
Austria	Honduras	Peru
Barbados	Hungary	Philippines
Belgium	Iceland	Poland
Bolivia	India	Portugal
Botswana	Indonesia	Romania
Brazil	Iran	Rwanda
Bulgaria	Iraq	Saudi Arabia
Burma	Irish Republic	Senegal
Burundi	Israel	Sierra Leone
Cambodia	Italy	Singapore
Cameroun	Ivory Coast	Somalia
Canada	Jamaica	South Africa, Republic of
Central African Republic	Japan	Spain
Ceylon	Jordan	Sudan
Chad	Kenya	Swaziland
Chile	Korea (South)	Sweden
China	Kuwait	Switzerland
Colombia	Laos	Syria
Congo (K.)	Lebanon	Tanzania
Congo (Br.)	Lesotho	Thailand
Costa Rica	Liberia	Togo
Cuba	Libya	Trinidad
Cyprus	Luxembourg	Tunisia
Czechoslovakia	Madagascar	Turkey
Dahomey	Malawi	Uganda
Denmark	Malaysia	USSR
Dominican Republic	Mali	UAR
Ecuador	Malta	UK
El Salvador	Mauritania	USA
Ethiopia	Mauritius	Upper Volta
Finland	Mexico	Uruguay
France	Morocco	Vatican
Gabon	Nepál	Venezuela
Gambia	New Zealand	Vietnam (South)
Germany (West)	Nicaragua	Yugoslavia
Ghana	Niger	Zambia
Greece	Nigeria	

OF THE NETHERLANDS IN GREAT BRITAIN (38 Hyde Park Gate, SW7)
Ambassador: Baron W. J. G. Gevers (accredited 24 Feb. 1971).
Ministers: Jhr J. L. R. Huydecoper; P. C. Witte (*Economic*). *Counsellors:* P. A. van Buuren; A. U. W. van Werven (*Consular Section*); J. B. Braaksma, CBE (*Cultural*); D. J. van Wijnen (*Press*) C. H. A. Plug (*Commercial*).
First Secretary: Count L. de Merchant et d'Ansembourg; Jhr R. de Beaufort, MVO (*Consul*). *Service Attaché:* Capt. F. de Blocq van Kuffeler (*Naval*), Col. Y. J. Beek (*Air*), Col.C. A. de Regt (*Army*). *Agricultural Attaché:* Drs W. G. F. van Oosten.

There are consular representatives at Belfast, Birmingham, Cardiff, Dundee, Edinburgh, Glasgow, Harwich, Hull, Liverpool, Manchester, Newcastle upon Tyne, Portsmouth, Southampton, Sunderland and other places.

OF GREAT BRITAIN IN THE NETHERLANDS
Ambassador: Sir Edward Tomkins, KCMG, CVO.
Counsellors: R. S. Faber (*Head of Chancery*); G. L. Pearson, MC (*Commercial*).
First Secretaries: R. N. Gardner; T. S. Trout, MBE (*Information*); T. E. Martin (*Commercial*). *State Attachés:* Capt. R. D. Franklin, RN (*Defence and Navy and Military*), Group Capt. E. F. Pippet, OBE (*Air*), Lieut.-Col. K. G. Wesley (*Military*).

There are Consuls-General at Amsterdam and Rotterdam.

OF THE NETHERLANDS IN THE USA (4200 Linnean Ave, NW, Washington, D.C., 20008)
Ambassador: Baron Rijnhard B. van Lynden.
Ministers: H. C. Maclaine Pont; C. W. J. Jonckheer; F. Kupers (*Economic*). *Counsellors:* J. E. Schaap (*Press and Cultural*); N. Van Dijl; Jhr E. S. B. T. Beelaerts van Blokland; S. C. van Nispen (*Commercial*); Jan Grooters (*Financial*); W. Lak (*Shipping*). *First Secretaries:* W. Roosdorp; A. G. O. Smit; H. E. Th. E. Mathon; Miss Ch. Y. Henny; H. C. van Vierssen (*Scientific*). *Service Attachés:* Rear-Adm. E. H. van Rees (*Navy*), Col. S. D. Catalani (*Army*), Col. A. J. Marinus (*Air*). *Agricultural Attaché:* G. W. J. Pieters.

OF THE USA IN THE NETHERLANDS
Ambassador: John W. Middendorf.
Deputy Chief of Mission: John A. Bovey. *Heads of Sections:* Oliver B. Bongard (*Economic*); Thomas Dunnigan (*Political*); Patricia G. van Delden (*Public Relations*); John Sinozich (*Administrative*). *Service Attachés:* Col. James B. Gregorie (*Army*), Capt. Joseph A. Grace (*Navy*), Col. Ned Thomas (*Air*).

There are Consuls-General at Amsterdam and Rotterdam.

BOOKS OF REFERENCE

STATISTICAL INFORMATION. The 'Centraal Bureau voor de Statistiek' at The Hague, is the official Netherlands statistical service. *Director-General of Statistics:* Dr J. Ch. W. Verstege.
The Bureau was founded in 1899. Prior to that year, statistical publications were compiled by the 'Centrale commissie voor de statistiek', the 'Vereniging voor staathuishoudkunde en statistiek' and various government departments. These activities have gradually been taken over and co-ordinated by the Central Bureau, which now compiles practically all government statistics. Its current publications include:

Jaarcijfers voor Nederland (*Statistical Year Book*). From 1923/24 (preceded by *Jaarcijfers voor het Koninkrijk der Nederlanden, 1898–1922*); latest issue, 1967–68
Statistisch zakboek (*Pocket Year Book*). From 1899/1924 (1 vol.); latest issue 1970
Maandschrift van het CBS (*Monthly Bulletin*). From 1906
Maandstatistiek van de buitenlandse handel (*monthly statistical bulletin of foreign trade*). From 1917
Naionale Rekeningen (*National Accounts*), from 1948–50; latest issue 1969
Uitkomsten van de Bedrijfstelling 1963 (*Results of the Census of Industries, 1963*)
Uitkomsten van de 13e Algemene volkstelling, 31 mei 1960 (*Results of the Thirteenth Census, Population and Housing, 31 May, 1960*)
Statistische en econometrische onderzoekingen (*Statistical and Econometric Studies*). From 1946
Statistical Studies. From 1953

BENELUX INFORMATION. See p. 763.

OTHER OFFICAL PUBLICATIONS

Central Economic Plan. Centraal Plan-bureau, The Hague (Dutch text), annually, from 1946
Digest of the Kingdom of the Netherlands. 5 vols. Ministry of Foreign Affairs. The Hague, 1967
Economic Information on the Netherlands. Ministry of Economic Affairs. The Hague, 1963
Netherlands. Organization for Economic Co-operation and Development. Paris, annual from 1964

Staatsalmanak voor het Koninkrijk der Nederlanden. Annual. The Hague, from 1814
Staatsblad van het Koninkrijk der Nederlanden. The Hague, from 1814
Staatscourant (State Gazette). The Hague, from 1813
Atlas van Nederland. Government Printing Office, The Hague, from 1963 ff.
Memoranda on the Condition of the Netherlands State Finances. Ministry of Finance. The Hague, from 1906.
Guide to the Establishing of Industrial Operations in the Netherlands. Ministry of Economic Affairs. The Hague, 1969
Holland as a Trade Partner. Netherlands Government Economic Information Service. The Hague, 1969
Agriculture in the Netherlands. Ministry of Agriculture and Fisheries. The Hague, 1968
Nederlandsche Bank. Annual Report, from 1865
Nederlandsche, De, Economic in 1973. Central Plan Bureau, The Hague 1970

NON-OFFICIAL PUBLICATIONS

Amsterdam-Rotterdam Bank, *Economic Quarterly Review,* from 1965
Cassell's Dutch-English, English-Dutch Dictionary. London, 1952
Jansonius, H., *Groot Nederlands-Engels Woordenboek.* 2 vols. Leiden, 1950–51; suppl. 1959
Lingsma, J. S., *Holland and the Delta Plan.* Rotterman/The Hague, 1964
Miller, C., *Basic Data on the Economy of the Netherlands.* Washington, 1970
Pyttersen's Nederlandse Almanak. Zaltbommel, annual, from 1899
Holland Herald. Amsterdam. from 1967
Commerce and Industry in the Netherlands. Amsterdam-Rotterdam Bank, Amsterdam, 1969
Hints to Businessmen Visiting the Netherlands. London, 1969

NATIONAL LIBRARY. De Koninklijke Bibliotheek, Lange Voorhour 34, The Hague. *Director:* Dr C. Reedijk.

OVERSEAS PARTS OF THE KINGDOM

For the constitutional position of the overseas parts of the Kingdom of the Netherlands, according to the Constitution of 29 Dec. 1954, *see* p. 1175.

SURINAM

HISTORY. At the peace of Breda (1667) between Great Britain and the United Netherlands, Surinam was assigned to the Netherlands in exchange for the colony of New Netherland in North America, and this was confirmed by the treaty of Westminster of Feb. 1674. Since then Surinam has been twice in British possession, 1799–1802 (when it was restored to the Batavian Republic at the peace of Amiens) and 1804–16, when it was returned to the Kingdom of the Netherlands according to the convention of London of 13 Aug. 1814, confirmed at the peace of Paris of 20 Nov. 1815.

AREA AND POPULATION. Surinam is situated on the north coast of South America and bounded on the north by the Atlantic Ocean, on the east by the Marowijne River, which separates it from French Guiana, on the west by the Corantijn River, which separates it from Guyana, and on the south by forests and savannas, which separate it from Brazil.

Area, 181,455 sq. km (70,087 sq. miles). Estimated population (1970), 400,000, including 33,000 Bush Negroes and 8,000 aboriginal Indians. The capital, Paramaribo, has about 150,000 inhabitants.

Birth-rate 46 per 1,000, death-rate 9 per 1,000.

The official language is Dutch. English is widely spoken next to Hindi, Javanese and Chinese as inter-group communication. A vernacular, called 'Sranan Tongo' or 'Surinamese', is used as a lingua franca.

GOVERNMENT. The Government consists of the Governor and the Council of Ministers. The Governor is the representative of the sovereign and the constitutional head of the Government. He is assisted by an Advisory Council of 6 members.

Governor: Dr J. H. E. Ferrier.

There is a council of 13 ministers who are responsible to the Legislative Council (*Staten van Suriname*). The Legislative Council (39 members) is elected for a 4-year period by universal adult suffrage. Seven political parties are represented in the Legislative Council.

Minister-President and Minister of General Affairs: Dr. J. Sedney.

Surinam is divided into 9 districts: Paramaribo (urban district), Commewijne, Coronie, Marowijne, Nickerie, Saramacca, Suriname, Brokopondo and Para.

RELIGION. There is entire religious liberty. At the end of 1964 the various religious bodies were: Reformed and Lutheran, 16,675; Moravian Brethren, 54,392; Roman Catholics, 71,166; Moslems, 63,809; Hindus, 87,575; Confucians, 147; others, 3,680.

EDUCATION. At the end of 1968 there were 488 schools, including kindergarten, with a total of 122,217 pupils and 3,721 teachers. There are also a University with schools of medicine and law, a technical school and 2 teachers' training colleges.

Schooling is compulsory from 6 to 12 years of age. Primary education is free and is undertaken by the Government in public schools and by the Roman Catholic and Protestant Missions in denominational schools.

CINEMAS (1970). There are 20 cinemas with a seating capacity of 18,000.

NEWSPAPERS (1970). There are 6 daily newspapers and 1 weekly with a combined circulation of over 30,000.

JUSTICE. There is a court of justice, whose members are nominated by the Sovereign. There are 3 cantonal courts.

WELFARE. The Government subsidizes orphanages and other religious or philanthropical institutions, and maintains an almshouse and institutions for delinquent boys and girls. There are 11 modern hospitals in the country, 4 of which are operated by missions, 2 by a private company, 1 by the military forces and 4 by the Government.

FINANCE. Currency. Surinam florin notes ranging from 5 to 1,000 Surinam florins are legal tender. Currency notes of 1·00 and 2·50 guilders are issued by the Government. US$1 = 1·87 Surinam florins; £1 sterling = Sfl4·50 and 1 Netherlands florin = Sfl0·52.

Budget. The expenditures and local revenues (derived from import, export and excise duties, taxes on houses and estates, personal imports and some indirect taxes) are as follows (in 1,000 Surinam guilders):

	1964	1965	1966	1967[1]	1968[1]	1969[1]
Revenues	104,400	110,754	122,200	115,754	134,671	164,200
Expenditures	101,200	108,038	123,500	128,750	137,216	167,200

[1] Provisional figures.

Outstanding loans in 1968: Local, 22·9m.; foreign, 102·2m. Surinam guilders. Public debt as at 31 March 1968, 125·2m. Surinam guilders.

SURINAM 1189

DEFENCE. Armed forces of the Kingdom of the Netherlands stationed in Surinam consist mainly of infantry with support units. Personnel are recruited also on a voluntary basis.

AGRICULTURE. Agriculture is restricted to the alluvial coastal zone; cultivated area in 1968, 47,248 hectares. The staple food crop is rice; 35,273 hectares of paddy were planted in 1968, chiefly in the Nickerie, Commewijne, Saramacca and Coronie districts.

Principal products (in 1,000 units) in 1968:

Sugar-cane (kg)	203,413	Maize on cob (kg)	625	Oranges (pieces)	45,386
Cocoa (kg)	78	Bananas (kg)	44,998	Grapefruit (pieces)	11,913
Coffee (kg)	359	Rum 50% (litres)	1,678	Tubers (kg)	2,085
Paddy (kg)	115,626	Molasses (kg)	8,318	Coconuts (pieces)	8,170

Livestock, 1968: 45,600 head of cattle, 8,100 sheep and goats, 9,900 pigs, 400 horses, mules and donkeys, 466,900 poultry.

FORESTRY. Surinam has great timber resources. Production 1968 included 125 metric tons of balata, 1,316 cu. metres of sleepers, 4,300 staple metres of fuel wood, 128,000 pieces of hewn squared timber, 28,400 cu. metres of plywood and particle board, chiefly from the Suriname and Marowijne districts.

FISHERY. The catch in 1968 amounted to 6,886 metric tons.

MINERALS. Bauxite is the most important mineral; it is being mined in the Suriname and Marowijne districts. Fresh deposits have been found in the western areas. The ore is exported mainly to USA, but partly processed locally into alumina and aluminium. Production in 1968: Bauxite, 5,660,000 metric tons; gold, 146 kg; alumina, 813,200 metric tons; aluminium, 43,200 metric tons.

INDUSTRY. There are 3 large bauxite plants, 1 alumina and 1 aluminium smelting plants, sugar- and rice-mills, 2 paint factories, a fruit-juice plant, a shrimp freezing plant, a plywood factory, timber-mills, a milk pasteurization plant, a butter and margarine factory and a considerable number of various medium and small industries.

COMMERCE. Imports and exports in calendar years (in 1,000 Surinam guilders):

	1963	1964	1965	1966	1967	1968
Imports	110,200	152,100	179,700	168,800	193,800	188,900
Exports	86,200	90,100	110,700	171,900	201,000	218,500

Principal exports in 1968 (value in 1,000 Surinam guilders): Rice, 9,923; oranges, 432; grapefruit, 235; coffee, 393; balata, 248; bauxite, 77,268; alumina, 76,454; aluminium, 34,199; timber, 7,750.

Principal imports in 1968 (value in 1,000 Surinam guilders): Fuels and lubricants, 17,800; foodstuffs, beverages and tobacco, 19,100; construction material, 12,500; material for other industries, 55,300; textile yarn and fabrics, 6,900; furnishing, household goods, lighting commodities, 7,700; investment goods, 42,200; passenger cars and motor cycles, 5,300.

Total trade with UK (in £1,000 sterling, British Board of Trade returns):

	1966	1967	1968	1969	1970
Imports to UK	211	189	239	410	78
Exports from UK	1,854	2,116	2,578	2,671 }	3,135
Re-exports from UK	19	16	28	27 }	

SHIPPING. The Royal Netherlands Steamship Co. plies between Amsterdam, Rotterdam, Antwerp, Hamburg and Paramaribo, and New York, Baltimore, New Orleans and Paramaribo. Regular sailings are made to Georgetown, Ciudad Bolívar and most Caribbean ports. The Surinam Navigation Co. maintains services from Paramaribo to Georgetown and Cayenne, and once a month to the Caribbean area. A French and an Italian company maintain passenger services to Europe. The Alcoa Steamship Co. has a fortnightly service to New York, Baltimore, Mobile and New Orleans; a Japanese line sails once a month from Hong Kong and Yokohama to Paramaribo; the Boomerang Line maintains a monthly freight and passenger service between Surinam and Australia. In 1968, 1,837 vessels totalling 5·78m. GRT entered and 1,834 of 5·75m. GRT cleared Paramaribo.

ROADS. There are 1,335 km of main roads. Two of them lead from Paramaribo to the bauxite centres of Smalkalden (29 km) and Paranam (30 km) and to the airport of Zanderij (49 km). Another main road runs across the districts of Saramacca (71 km) and Coronie (68 km), a fourth across the Commewijne district (41 km) and a fifth in the Marowijne district, from the bauxite centre Moengo to Albina (45 km).

The 'East–West connexion' is almost completed, linking the Corantijn and the Marowijne rivers (375 km).

In 1968 there were 38,090 registered motor vehicles in Surinam, including 10,871 passenger cars, 2,020 trucks, 484 buses, 21,603 powered bicycles and 2,632 motor cycles and scooters.

RAILWAY. There is one single-track railway, running from Onverwacht to Bronsweg (86 km); part of the track, from Paramaribo to Onverwacht (34 km) has been removed.

AVIATION. Regular air services are maintained by KLM, PANAM, VIASA, Air France and Empressa de Transportes Aerovias Brasil. The international airfield at Zanderij is capable of handling all types of planes.

Surinam Airways Ltd provides daily services between all major districts and maintains also a charter service.

In 1968, 2,498 aircraft landed at Zanderij airport with 21,624 incoming and 23,710 outgoing passengers, 542 tons of incoming and 213 tons of outgoing mail and freight.

POST. Automatic telephone service links most of the districts in the interior. In 1969 there were about 11,000 telephones. Wireless telephone connects Surinam with the Netherlands, USA, Curaçao, Guyana, French Guiana and Trinidad. There are 5 broadcasting and 1 television stations.

BANKING. The Central Bank of Surinam is a bankers' bank and also a bank of issue; the Surinaamsche Bank, the Hollandsche Bank Unie and the O.R.G. Verruurt's Banking Corporation Ltd, are commercial banks; the Surinam People's Credit Bank operates under the auspices of the Government; Surinaamse Postspaarbank (postal savings bank), Surinaamse Hypotheekbank NV (mortgage bank); Surinaamse Investerings Mij. NV (investment bank); Agentschap van de Maatschappij tot financiering van het Nationaal Herstel NV (long-term investments); National Development Bank.

British Honorary Vice-Consul: P. Sheppard.
USA Consul-General: Donald A. Johnston.

BOOKS OF REFERENCE

STATISTICAL INFORMATION. The General Bureau of Statistics in Paramaribo was established on 1 Jan. 1947. Its publications comprise trade statistics, *Surinam in Figures* (including, from 1953, the former *Handelsstatistiek*) and *Statistische Berichten*.

Economische Voorlichting Suriname. Ministry of Trade and Industry, Paramaribo
Annual Report of the Central Bank of Surinam

THE NETHERLANDS ANTILLES

De Nederlandse Antillen

The Netherlands Antilles are an integral part of the Netherlands and comprises two groups of islands, viz. the Leeward Islands, Curaçao, Aruba and Bonaire, and the Windward Islands, St. Maarten, St Eustatius and Saba. The Leeward Islands are situated 40–70 miles north of the Venezuelan coast between 12° and 13° N. lat. and 68° and 71° W. long. The Windward group lies east of Puerto Rico.

AREA AND POPULATION. The total area is 1,011 sq. km (390 sq. miles) and the population was 216,355 on 31 Dec. 1968.

Benedenwinds group	Sq. km	Popula-tion	Bovendewinds group	Sq. km	Popula-tion
Curaçao	472	141,393	St Maarten (St Martin)[1]	34	5,547
Aruba	190	59,231	St Eustatius	21	1,335
Bonaire	281	7,844	Saba	13	1,005

[1] The southern part belongs to the Netherlands Antilles, the northern to France.

In 1968, 4,946 births, 1,082 deaths, (1967) 1,217 marriages and (1967) 224 divorces were registered.

GOVERNMENT. Since Dec. 1954, the Netherlands Antilles have been fully autonomous in internal affairs, and constitutionally equal with the Netherlands and Surinam. The Sovereign of the Kingdom of the Netherlands is Head of the Government of the Netherlands Antilles and is represented by a Governor.

The executive power in internal affairs rests with the Governor and the Council of Ministers, who together form the government. The Ministers are responsible to the unicameral legislature (*Staten*). This consists of 22 members (12 from Curaçao, 8 from Aruba, 1 from Bonaire, 1 from the Windward Islands) and is elected by general suffrage.

The executive power in external affairs is vested in the Council of Ministers of the Kingdom, in which the Antilles is represented by a Minister Plenipotentiary with full voting powers.

In 1951 the Netherlands Antilles Islands Regulation provided for self-government of each of the 4 insular communities Aruba, Bonaire, Curaçao and the Windward Islands. The autonomous powers of the insular communities are divided between the Island Council (elected by general suffrage), the Executive Council and the Lieut.-Governor (*Gezaghebber*), who is responsible for maintaining public peace and order.

Governor: Dr B. M. Leito.
Prime Minister: E. O. Petronia.

Dutch is the official language. Spanish and English are also spoken. In addition a 'lingua franca', *Papiamento*, has evolved out of Spanish, Dutch and some other languages.

RELIGION. In 1960, 82% of the population were Roman Catholics, 8% were Protestants.

EDUCATION (1969). Schools numbered 277, with 69,272 pupils and 2,193 teachers.

CINEMAS (1966). Curaçao and Aruba had 13 cinemas with a seating capacity of 11,000. There is a drive-in cinema for 500 cars in Curaçao and for 350 cars at Aruba.

HEALTH. In 1968 there were 79 physicians, 51 specialists, 30 dentists and 20 pharmacists. In 1968, 7 hospitals had 1,311 beds.

FINANCE. The central budget for 1968 envisaged 69,252,924 guilders revenue and 69,206,226 guilders expenditure.

The public debt was 122,095,711 guilders as at 31 Dec. 1968.

The official rate of exchange is £1 = 4·61 (buying) and 4·39 (selling) Netherlands Antilles guilders.

ECONOMY. The economy of the Netherlands Antilles is almost entirely based on the refining of oil imported from Venezuela to Curaçao and Aruba. About 25% (Curaçao) and 30% (Aruba) of the gainfully occupied are working at the refineries or their shipping establishments. On account of the activities of the oil companies (affiliated to the Royal Dutch/Shell and the Standard Oil of New Jersey), the prosperity on Curaçao and Aruba is good in comparison with the other islands.

About 100,000 tons of calcium phosphate are annually mined in Curaçao.

In Aruba there are some petrochemical factories; Curaçao has a paint factory, 2 cigarette factories, a brewery and some smaller industries. The Texas Instruments Co. has established an electronic factory. Almost all products needed for consumption and production are imported, as the rocky soil permits little agriculture and local fishing is insufficient for home consumption. The tourist industry is being developed.

Bonaire has a textile factory. St Maarten has a rum factory and fishing is important. St Eustatius and Saba are of less economic importance.

TOURISM. In 1969, 180,909 foreign tourists visited the Netherlands Antilles.

TRADE (1968). Total imports amounted to 1,259,000 guilders; total exports to 1·13m. guilders, of which oil and oil products accounted for 965,000 guilders.

Total trade between the Netherlands Antilles and UK in £1,000 sterling (British Board of Trade returns):

	1966	1967	1968	1969	1970
Imports to UK	16,318	16,158	16,760	13,062	13,137
Exports from UK	4,581	5,042	5,903	6,448 ⎱	8,260
Re-exports from UK	64	96	125	126 ⎰	

The Free-Zones Ordinance of 1956 has established free zones in the ports of Curaçao and Aruba.

SHIPPING (1968). There entered the port of Curaçao, 5,221 vessels of 43·7m. gross tons; Aruba, 2,813 vessels of 39·3m. gross tons.

ROADS. In 1968 the Netherlands Antilles had 1,183 km of surfaced highway distributed as follows: Curaçao, 541; Aruba, 380; Bonaire, 209; St. Maarten, 53. Number of motor vehicles (31 Dec. 1968): 21,870 in Curaçao, 9,877 in Aruba.

POST. Number of telephones, 1 Jan. 1969, 24,920.

British Consul: R. F. Storm.
USA Consul-General: H. M. Lofton (*Curaçao*).

BOOKS OF REFERENCE

STATISTICAL INFORMATION. Statistical publications (on population, trade, cost of living, etc., are obtainable on request from the Statistics and Planning Bureau, Willemstad, Curaçao) *Statistisch Jaarboek 1969* (text in Dutch, English and Spanish).

De West Indische Gids. The Hague. Monthly from 1919
Braam, H. L., *Hoe ons land geregeerd wordt.* Willemstad, 1959
Hartog, J., *Aruba.* Oranjestad, 1953.—*Bonaire.* Oranjestad, 1958.—*Curaçao.* Oranjestad, 1961
Nordlohne, E., *De Economisch-geographische Structuur der Benedenwindse Eilanden.* Rotterdam, 1951
Poll, W. van de, *De Nederlandse Antillen.* The Hague, 1950
Walle, J. van de, *De Nederlandse Antillen.* Willemstad, 1954
Westerman, J. H., *Overzicht van de geologische en mijnbouwkundige kennis der Nederlandse Antillen.* Amsterdam, 1949
Curaçao Trade Industry Directory. 6th ed. 1966–67

NICARAGUA
República de Nicaragua

HISTORY. Active colonization of the Pacific coast was undertaken by Spaniards from Panama, beginning in 1523. After links with other Central American territories, and Mexico, Nicaragua became completely independent in 1838, but subject to a prolonged feud between the 'Liberals' of León and the 'Conservatives' of Granada. Mosquitia remained an autonomous kingdom on the Atlantic coast, under British protection until 1860.

On 5 Aug. 1914 the Bryan–Chamorro treaty between Nicaragua and the United States was signed, under which the US in return for $3m. acquired a permanent option for a canal route through Nicaragua and a 99-year option for a naval base in the Bay of Fonseca on the Pacific coast and Corn Island on the Atlantic coast. It was ratified by Nicaragua on 7 April 1916 and by the US on 22 June 1916. US Marines finally left in 1933.

CONSTITUTION AND GOVERNMENT. Since 1963 the President of the Republic, 3 Vice-Presidents, 16 Senators, 42 deputies and members of local councils are directly elected for a term of 4 years. A secret ballot has been introduced. The franchise extends to all men and women over 21 and to those over 18 who can read or write or are married as well as to those under 18 who have a 'bachelor's', *i.e.*, school-leaver's, degree. Deputies are elected on a national list, senators in 4 electoral districts. Seats in Congress (the Senate and the Chamber of Deputies) are awarded by a modified system of proportional representation which secures not less than one-third of the seats to the minority parties. In addition, ex-presidents of the Republic are life senators and the presidential candidate who is runner up in the elections is a senator for the succeeding term. The supervision of the elections is in the hands of the Supreme Electoral Tribunal and subordinate tribunals which rank as a fourth 'power' of the state '*el poder electoral*' together with the Executive, Legislative and Judicial powers.

Under the constitution the President of the Republic and members of his family 'to the fourth degree of consanguinity and affinity' are debarred from the Presidency for the succeeding presidential term, though not thereafter.

President: Gen. Anastasio Somoza Debayle, elected 5 Feb. 1967, for the term beginning 1 May 1967.

Minister for Foreign Affairs: Dr Lorenzo Guerrero.

Ministers, who are heads of departments, are chosen by the President and cannot be members of Congress.

The republic is divided into 16 'departments' and 1 *comarca* (district), each of which is under a political head (appointed by the President), who has supervision of finance, education and other matters. The departments have 123 *municipios*, headed by a mayor (*alcalde*). The Mosquito Reserve now forms part of the departments of Zelaya and Río San Juan.

National flag: Blue, white, blue (horizontal); with the coat of arms on the white stripe.

National anthem: Salve a ti Nicaragua (words by S. Ibarra Mayorga, 1937).

AREA AND POPULATION. Area estimated at 148,000 sq. km (57,143 sq. miles) or 139,000 sq. km (54,296 sq. miles) if the lakes are excluded. The coastline runs 336 miles on the Atlantic and 219 miles on the Pacific. Population estimate at the end of 1969 was 1·78m.

Nicaragua is the largest in area and most thinly populated of the Central American republics. Crude birth rate, 1960, 43·24 per 1,000 population; crude death rate, 8·57; infantile mortality rate, 70·21 per 1,000 live births; crude marriage rate, 6·99 per 1,000 population.

About 80% of the inhabitants live in the area between the great lakes and the Pacific. The two areas differ greatly in many respects, and there is little communication between them, the journey by trail and river being slow and difficult though progress is being made.

The people of the western half of the republic are principally of mixed Spanish and Indian extraction, some of pure Spanish descent and many Indians. The population of the eastern half is composed mainly of Mosquito and other Indians and Zambos, and Negroes from Jamaica and other islands of the Caribbean. The main ethnic groups in 1963 were: Mestizo, 71%; white, 14%; Negro, 8%; Indio, 4%.

Nicaragua is administratively divided into the following 16 departments and 1 territory, with population as on 30 June 1963:

Boaco	71,905	Jinotega	74,818	Nueva Segovia	45,323
Carazo	66,028	León	148,595	Río San Juan	15,333
Chinandega	125,476	Madriz	49,966	Rivas	63,924
Chontales	75,547	Managua	317,641	Zelaya	89,023
Estelí	68,046	Masaya	76,433		
Granada	65,706	Matagalpa	170,263	Cabo Gracias a Dios	1,456

Of the 123 *municipios*, 98 have from 2,000 to 50,000 inhabitants. The capital is Managua, situated on the lake of the same name, 180 ft above sea level, with (1967) 300,000 inhabitants; Bluefields, 17,706; Chinandega, 36,885; Granada, 40,200; Jinotepe, 15,957; León, 61,649; Masaya 34,127; Matagalpa, 61,383; Diriamba, 24,177; Boaco, 20,428; Juigalpa, 18,259; Estelí, 26,764.

RELIGION. The prevailing form of religion is Roman Catholic, but religious liberty is guaranteed by the Constitution. The republic constitutes 1 archbishopric (seat at Managua) and 6 bishoprics (León, Granada, Estelí, Matagalpa, Juigalpa and Puerto Cabezas). Protestants, established principally on the Atlantic coast, numbered 54,100 in 1966.

EDUCATION. There were (1959–60) 2,082 elementary schools, of which 1,967 were state and 115 private, with a total (1962–63) of 172,419 pupils; and 102 secondary schools, 68 of which were private, with 12,267 pupils. Illiterate persons, of all ages, number 63·7% of the population. The National University at León has faculties of medicine, law, pharmacy, dentistry, engineering (at Managua) and economics. It had 1,621 students in 1963–64. An AID loan of US$700,000 (1964) is for an expansion of capacity so that the annual intake can increase from the present 550, to 1,500 by 1971.

A Roman Catholic university was founded in Managua in 1961, and has faculties of engineering, public administration and law; 531 students.

CINEMAS. Cinemas numbered over 100 in 1965 and seated over 60,000.

NEWSPAPERS. There are 7 daily newspapers (5 in Managua and 2 in León), with a total circulation of about 75,000.

SOCIAL WELFARE. From 26 May 1963 a minimum daily wage of 6 córdobas was introduced nationally. Workers in towns of over 20,000 inhabitants receive 40% more; agricultural workers receive additional food allowances and house loans.

JUSTICE. The judicial power is vested in a Supreme Court of Justice at Managua, 5 chambers of second instance (León, Masaya, Granada, Matagalpa and Bluefields) and 153 judges of inferior tribunals.

FINANCE. Currency. The monetary unit is the *córdoba* (C$), divided into 100 *centavos*. Its exchange parity with gold is managed by the Central Bank of Nicaragua and the Government. No gold or silver coins are minted. On 31 Dec. 1964 total money supply was 460m. córdobas. Gold coins provided by law (1912) were 10, 5 and 2½ córdobas, but have never been struck. National banknotes form the greater part of the currency, in denominations from 1,000 córdobas to 1 córdoba. Silver coins struck, but now out of circulation, are 50, 25 and 10 centavos; copper–nickel and copper–zinc coins, 50, 25, 10 and 5 centavos; copper coin, 1 centavo.

Rate of exchange, Feb. 1970: 7 córdobas = US$1; 16·75 córdobas = £1.

Budget. Revenue and expenditure for fiscal years, ending 30 June (from 1965, calendar years), in 1m. córdobas (C$1 = 14·2857 US cents):

	1965²	1966¹	1967¹	1968¹	1969¹	1970¹
Revenue	447·4	583·7	673·5	661·2	659	686·2
Expenditure	465·4	583·7	673·5	661·2	659	686·2

¹ Estimates.   ² Last 6 months.

The 1967 budget included C$42·5m. for the Ministry of Finance and Public Credit, 119·2m. for education, 165·8m. for development and public works, 72·4m. for defence and 61·3m. for health. On 1 July 1964 a special budget, balanced at C$207·6m., was announced, to cover the 6-month period to 31 Dec. 1964. From then the calendar year was followed.

The practice of borrowing heavily from the National Bank resulted in a debt of 28·25m. córdobas, which, 1950, was funded for 25 years.

Of Nicaragua's external debt, the sterling bonds were finally redeemed in 1958. The external debt at the end of 1965 was equal to US$55·3m.; the internal debt at 31 Dec. 1964 was 124·3m. córdobas.

A Social Security scheme became operative in 1958 for the Managua area and was extended to the City of León in 1964.

DEFENCE. The National Guard (which functions as police force and army) numbers 560 officers and some 4,850 other ranks, besides 4,000 in the trained reserve. Period of enlistment, 3 years, but military service may be made compulsory at any time. There is a military academy.

Some small coastguard boats patrol the east and west coast to prevent smuggling.

Formed in June 1938 as the Nicaraguan Army Air Force, the air force has been semi-independent since 1947. Its combat units have re-equipped with 6 T-33 armed jet trainers, 6 B-26 light piston-engined bombers and 6 T-28 armed piston-engined trainers. Other equipment includes a few C-47 transports, T-6 piston-engined trainers and smaller communications aircraft. Approximate strength is 1,500 personnel and 60 aircraft.

PRODUCTION. Of the total land area (about 36·1m. acres), about 17·5m. acres are under timber, 0·9m. acres are used for grazing and 2·1m. acres are arable. In 1964, 58·9% of the population were estimated to live in rural areas. The unit of area used locally is the *manzana* (= 1·73 acres). A survey in 1954 showed that of the arable only 1,044,000 acres were actively cultivated, 500,000 in annual crops such as cotton and rice and the remainder in perennial crops such as coffee and sugar-cane, or in two harvests a year in the cases of maize, sorghum and beans. Five-sevenths of the working population are in agriculture. A Natural Resources Law came into operation on 17 April 1958, and a new Agrarian Reform Institute came into being on 1 July 1964.

AGRICULTURE. Agriculture is the principal source of national wealth, finding work for 65% of the labour force, and furnishing, 1961, 37% of the gross national product of C$2,294,424,000. There are big plans to increase its efficiency by means of irrigation schemes depending on the Tipitapa and Tuma rivers. The principal production of the eastern part of the republic was formerly bananas, but the exports in 1961 were only 62,766 stems. An American company, in 1961, laid out banana plantations on the west coast on new soil which should be free of the Panama disease. The Chinandega crop was valued at C$20m. in 1963–64; it suffered heavy storm damage in Feb. 1965, which destroyed 50% of the trees. Cotton production in 1962–63 was 1·5m. quintals, of which approximately 700,000 quintals was exported, value US$26m. Production was 419,000 bales in

1963–64 and 541,000 in 1964–65. There are 19 gins, of which 16 are operating. Plantains, oranges, pineapples, sweet potatoes and yucca are raised for home consumption.

The products of the western half are much more varied, the most important being cotton, coffee, now under the aegis of the new *Instituto del Café*, sugar-cane, cocoa, maize, sesame and beans. A firm has been organized to produce soluble banana, cocoa and coffee powder, principally for export. Sugar-cane output, 1963–64, was 1·1m. tons. The first shipments of a Havana-type tobacco were made in 1964 from a farm controlled by the *Instituto de Fomento Nacional*. A USA company bought the entire crop, valued at C$1·2m.

Rice is grown (500,561 quintals in 1962–63) and wheat in León and the hilly Jinotega district, while tobacco is cultivated round Masaya. Sesame seed is the country's only oilseed of importance, but it is ninth after coffee, gold, cotton, meat, sugar, powdered coffee, cotton seed and copper as an export; the 1963–64 crop was 102,000 quintals. An experimental planting of castor seed was made in May 1957. The coffee crop (from 155,000 acres) was 375,000 quintals in 1965 (360,687 in 1964). There are 67 processing plants. Some other 1963–64 crops (in quintals) were: Maize, 3·1m.; beans, 0·7m.; sorghum, 0·9m. With the exception of plantains and yucca or cassava, the greater part of the food supply of the eastern section is imported from the US. The western half of the country produces much of its own food, but is seriously dependent upon weather conditions. There are about 1·8m. head of cattle. A modern meat-packing plant was established in 1955; slaughterings were 151,522 in 1961, rising to 200,000 in 1965. There are 350,000 pigs. Beef exports in 1963 were valued at US$8·4m., third only to coffee and cotton. A big programme for the improving of the quality of the cattle was jointly introduced in 1965 by the National Development Institute and the National Bank of Nicaragua.

FISHERY. On the Atlantic coast fisheries are an important subsistence activity. Over 6m. lb. of shrimps were exported in 1967 and were processed in 3 plants at Schooner Cay, El Bluff and Corn Island. The fishing limit off the coast has been defined as 200 nautical miles. Within that limit, fishing is subject to the provisions of the Natural Resources Exploration Law.

FORESTRY. Timber production has been declining, though the forests, which cover 10m. acres and 4 distinct zones, contain mahogany and cedar, which were formerly largely exported, three varieties of rosewoods, guayacán (*lignum vitae*) and dyewoods. In 1968–69 exploitation of these vast areas of timber with a potential production of 300,000 tons per annum was begun.

MINING. Production of gold in 1964 was 211,900 fine oz.; of silver, 332,370 troy oz.; exports in 1963 being valued at US$7·11m. Copper (20,262,417 lb. in 1964); there is no iron or coalmining. Large deposits of tungsten in Nueva Segovia were announced in 1961. Exploration for petroleum began off the Pacific and Atlantic coasts in 1965. A petroleum refinery handling 5,000 bbls a day is functioning at Managua. A new mining law was enacted in March 1965 to replace the mining code of 1906.

INDUSTRY. Chief local industries are matches, cigarettes, beer, soap, leather, plastics, metal products, flour, cement (1·6m. sacks of 94 lb. in 1964), cotton and silk, strong and soft drinks, soluble coffee, dairy products, meat, plywood, cosmetics, detergents and paints. In 1964 almost 100 new enterprises received tax incentive authorization under the law.

POWER. In 1964, 71 diesel and 11 hydro-electric power units produced 155·9m. kwh. Construction work on the Río Tuma hydro-electric scheme, designed to augment the supply to Managua and west-coast districts, continues; the first unit of 25,000 kw. began on 27 March 1965.

LABOUR. In 1960 there were some 477,338 persons gainfully employed; of these: agriculture, 64%; manufacturing, construction, mining and power, 16·7%;

services, transport and commerce, 19·3%. There were fully six times as many males as females 'economically active'.

COMMERCE. The foreign trade of Nicaragua, in US$1m., was as follows in calendar years:

	1961	1962	1963	1964	1965	1966	1967
Imports	74·4	98·2	110·7	109·8	136·7	152·0	204
Exports	68·4	90·2	106·8	125·5	143·0	141·2	146

The main imports in 1964 (in US$1m.) were: Manufactured goods, 28·1; machinery and vehicles, 41·2; chemicals, 23·7; foodstuffs, 12·1. These were supplied largely by USA, Germany, Japan, UK and Guatemala. Imports from the ODECA countries were almost double those of 1963.

In 1964 the main exports (in US$1m.) were: Cotton, 58·1; coffee, 21·1; meat, 6·1; timber, 2·1; sugar, 5·7; soluble coffee, 3·8; bananas, 2·1. The coffee export quota for 1965–66 is 489,000 bags (of 60 kg).

Total trade between Nicaragua and UK (British Board of Trade returns) in £1,000 sterling:

	1965	1966	1967	1968	1969	1970
Imports to UK	1,357	563	697	1,216	996	821
Exports from UK	2,106	1,790	2,895	2,127	2,939 ⎱	2,724
Re-exports from UK	5	5	10	3	14 ⎰	

SHIPPING. The Pacific ports are Corinto (the largest), San Juan del Sur and Puerto Somoza through which pass most of the external trade. The chief eastern ports are El Bluff (for Bluefields) and Puerto Cabezas. The merchant marine consists solely of the Mamenic Line with 4 vessels owned and 5 chartered. In 1960, 1,034 ships entered and 1,015 left Nicaraguan ports.

ROADS. 800·1 km are paved, out of a total of 6,124 km. The whole 368·5 km of the Nicaraguan section of the Pan-American Highway is now (1970) paved. The all-weather Roosevelt Highway linking Managua with the river port Rama was completed in 1968, to provide the first overland link with the Atlantic coast. There are paved roads to San Juan del Sur, Puerto Somoza and Corinto. Motor vehicles, 1964, were 14,383 passenger cars, 5,050 trucks, 570 buses and 3,610 motor cycles.

RAILWAYS. The Pacific Railroad of Nicaragua, owned and operated by the Government, has a total length of 348 km. all single-track, and connects Corinto, Chinandega, León, Managua, Masaya and Granada. Passengers carried (1969), 756,000; freight, 136,000 metric tons.

AVIATION. LANICA, the Nicaraguan airline, 77% national and 23% Pan-American owned, has 3 flights a week to Miami and to Bluefields, Puerto Cabezas and the mining towns of Siuna and Bonanza. PANAM and TACA (Transportes Aéreos Centroamericanos), a US-owned line registered in El Salvador, have daily services to Panama, Mexico, the other central Americans countries and USA. Craft Airlines, a new airline, has begun daily service between Managua, Nicaragua, and San José, Costa Rica. In 1963, 61,588 passengers entered and left, and air freight was nearly 3m. kg in either direction.

Las Mercedes airport, Managua, is being extended to accommodate jet aircraft, with the help of a 1963 A.I.D. loan of US$950,000.

POST. There are (1962) 7,474 km of (government-owned) telegraph wire and 221 offices; also 6,284 km of telephone wire and 208 telephone stations serving (1969) 23,484 instruments, 75% automatic and all government-operated. There are 233 post offices, and good service between the chief towns of the western section; service into the interior is carried by air-mail. All American Cable Co. connects with New York and has a powerful station at San Juan del Sur.

The Tropical Radio Telegraph Company maintains a powerful station at

Managua, and branch stations at Bluefields and Puerto Cabezas. The Government operates the National Radio with 47 broadcasting stations: there are 31 commercial stations and some 70 others. Number of wireless sets in 1963 was 80,000. There is a television station at Managua.

BANKING. The National Bank of Nicaragua at Managua, founded in 1912, owned by the Government since 1924 was completely reorganized in May 1940. On 1 March 1962 its capital was increased to C$130m. and a new law gave it increased responsibilities as a development bank. The Central Bank of Nicaragua came into operation on 1 Jan. 1961 as an autonomous bank of issue, absorbing the issue department of the National Bank. The total gold and foreign-exchange reserve of the Central Bank was, as of 31 Dec. 1964, US$41·3m.

A new exchange law came into force on 1 March 1963 under which the free convertibility of the Nicaraguan córdoba was decreed. A new import law effective also as from 1 March 1963 waived the formality of issuing import permits for consular purposes. The standard 3 classifications still remain in force, namely essential goods, less essential goods and non-essential or luxury goods. The Foreign Investment Law of 26 Feb. 1955 guarantees the repatriation of capital and profits of foreign investments.

A new Workers' Bank (*Banco Obrero y Campesino*) was established by law of 2 May 1966; the State provides C$5m. over 5 years towards the initial capital. In 1967 a savings and loan company, *Centroamericana de Ahorro y Préstamo*, opened in Managua.

Two private commercial banks opened in Managua in 1953, the Banco Nicaragüense SA and the Banco de América SA, with paid-up capital of C$15m. and $C14·5m. respectively. There is a branch of the Bank of London & Montreal Ltd in Managua, and the Bank of America National Trust and Savings Association opened a branch there in 1964. The legal minimum cash holding for commercial banks with the Central Bank is 28% for all accounts.

WEIGHTS AND MEASURES. Since 1893 the metric system of weights and measures has been recommended.

DIPLOMATIC REPRESENTATIVES

Nicaragua maintains embassies in:

Argentina	Ecuador	Honduras	Spain
Brazil	El Salvador	Italy	UK
Chile	France	Mexico	USA
China (Taiwan)	Germany (West)	Panama	Vatican
Colombia	Guatemala	Peru	Venezuela
Costa Rica			

Nicaragua maintains legations in Belgium, Japan, Malta and Paraguay.

OF NICARAGUA IN GREAT BRITAIN (8 Gloucester Road, SW7)
Ambassador: (Vacant).

There are consular representatives at Birmingham, Glasgow and London.

OF GREAT BRITAIN IN NICARAGUA
Ambassador and Consul-General: G. M. Warr, CBE.
First Secretaries: F. B. Sedgwick-Jell (*Head of Chancery and Consul*); M. Cochran (*Labour*, resides in Mexico City).
Service Attaché: Wing Cdr P. D. Thompson, (resides at Caracas).

OF NICARAGUA IN THE USA (1627 New Hampshire Ave. NW, Washington, D.C., 20009)

Ambassador: Dr Guillermo Sevilla-Sacasa.
Minister-Counsellors: Dr Alvaro Rizo Castellón; Dr Gustavo Escoto Goenaga (*Economic*). *First Secretary:* Juan Rafael Asensio. *Service Attaché:* Col. Julio Gutierrez Rivera.

OF THE USA IN NICARAGUA

Ambassador: Kennedy M. Crockett.
Deputy Chief of Mission: Malcolm R. Barneby. *Heads of Sections:* Robert T.
Shaw (*Political*); John J. St. John (*Economic*); John P. Crawford (*Commercial*);
Mario Calvani (*Consular*); Douglass Bjorn (*Administrative*); Rognar L. Arnesen
(*AID*). *Service Attaché:* Lieut.-Col. William A. Watt.

BOOKS OF REFERENCE

Dirección General Estadística y Censos, *Boletín de Estadística* (irregular intervals); and *Censos de Población y Vivienda . . . 1963.* 1964
Memoria de la Recaudación General de Aduanas (Customs statistics). Annual
Boletín de la Superintendencia de Bancos. Banco Central, Managua
Terán, F., and J. Incer. *Geografía de Nicaragua.* Managua, 1964
NATIONAL LIBRARY. Biblioteca Nacional, Managua, D.N.

NORWAY
Kongeriket Norge

HISTORY. By the Treaty of 14 Jan. 1814 Norway was ceded to the King of
Sweden by the King of Denmark, but the Norwegian people declared themselves
independent and elected Prince Christian Frederik of Denmark as their king.
The foreign Powers refused to recognize this election, and on 14 Aug. a convention proclaimed the independence of Norway in a personal union with
Sweden. This was followed on 4 Nov. by the election of Karl XIII (II) as King
of Norway. Norway declared this union dissolved, 7 June 1905, and Sweden
agreed to the repeal of the union on 26 Oct. 1905. The throne was offered to a
prince of the reigning house of Sweden, who declined. After a plebiscite, Prince
Carl of Denmark was formally elected King on 18 Nov. 1905, and took the name
of Haakon VII.

Norwegian Sovereigns

Inge Baardssøn	1204	Erik of Pomerania	1389
Haakon Haakonssøn	1217	Kristofer af Bavaria	1442
Magnus Lagabøter	1263	Karl Knutsson	1449
Eirik Magnussøn	1280	Same Sovereigns as in Denmark	1450 1814
Haakon V Magnussøn	1299	Christian Frederik	1814
Magnus Eriksson	1319	Same Sovereigns as in Sweden	1814–1905
Haakon VI Magnussøn	1355	Haakon VII	1905
Olav Haakonssøn	1381	Olav V	1957
Margreta	1388		

REIGNING KING. Olav V, born 2 July 1903, married on 21 March 1929 to
Princess Märtha of Sweden (born 28 March 1901, died 5 April 1954), daughter
of the late Prince Carl (son of King Oscar II). He succeeded on the death of
his father, King Haakon VII, on 21 Sept. 1957. *Offspring:* Princess Ragnhild
Alexandra, born 9 June 1930 (married, 1953, Hr. Erling Lorentzen); Princess
Astrid Maud Ingeborg, born 12 Feb. 1932 (married, 12 Jan. 1961, Hr. Johan
Martin Ferner); Crown Prince Harald, born 21 Feb. 1937, married, 29 Aug.
1968, Sonja Haraldsen.

CONSTITUTION AND GOVERNMENT. Norway is a constitutional
and hereditary monarchy. The royal succession is in direct male line in the order
of primogeniture. In default of male heirs the King may propose a successor to
the Storting, but this assembly has the right to nominate another, if it does not
agree with the proposal.

The constitution, voted by the constituent assembly at Eidsvoll on 17 May
1814 and modified at various times, vests the legislative power of the realm in the

Storting (Parliament). The royal veto may be exercised twice; but if the same Bill passes three Stortings formed by separate and subsequent elections it becomes the law of the land without the assent of the sovereign. The King has the command of the land, sea and air forces, and makes all appointments.

Since June 1938 all branches of the Government service, including the state church, are open to women.

National flag: A blue cross with white borders on red.
National anthem: Ja, vi elsker dette landet (words by B. Bjørnson, 1865; tune by R. Nordraak, 1865).

The Storting assembles every year. The meetings take place *suo jure*, and not by any writ from the King or the executive. They begin on the first weekday in October each year, and their duration is not limited. Every Norwegian subject of 20 years of age (provided that he resides and has resided for 5 years in the country) is entitled to vote, unless he is disqualified for a special cause. Women are, since 1913, entitled to vote under the same conditions as men. The mode of election is direct and the method of election is proportional. The country is divided into 20 districts, each electing from 4 to 13 representatives.

At the elections for the Storting held on 7–8 Sept. 1969 the following parties were elected: Labour, 74; Conservative, 29; Centre Party, 20; Christian Popular, 14, and Liberal, 13.

The Storting, when assembled, divides itself by election into the *Lagting* and the *Odelsting*. The former is composed of one-fourth of the members of the Storting, and the other of the remaining three-fourths. Each Ting (the Storting, the Odelsting and the Lagting) nominates its own president. Most questions are decided by the Storting, but questions relating to legislation must be considered and decided by the Odelsting and the Lagting separately. Only when the Odelsting and the Lagting disagree, the Bill has to be considered by the Storting in plenary sitting, and a new law can then only be decided by a majority of two-thirds of the voters. The same majority is required for alterations of the Constitution, which can only be decided by the Storting in plenary sitting. The Storting elects 5 delegates, whose duty it is to revise the public accounts. The Lagting and the ordinary members of the Supreme Court of Justice (the *Høyesterett*) form a High Court of the Realm (the *Riksrett*) for the trial of ministers, members of the *Høyesterett* and members of the Storting. The impeachment before the *Riksrett* can only be decided by the Odelsting.

The executive is represented by the King, who exercises his authority through the Cabinet or Council of State (*Statsråd*), composed of a Prime Minister (*Statsminister*) and 14 ministers (*Statsråder*). The ministers are entitled to be present in the Storting and to take part in the discussions, but without a vote.

The Cabinet was in April 1971 composed as follows:

Prime Minister: Trygve Bratteli.
Foreign Affairs: Andreas Cappelen. *Finance:* Ragnar Christiansen. *Defence:* Alv Jakob Fostervoll. *Ecclesiastical Affairs and Education:* Bjartmar Gjerde. *Fisheries:* Knut Hoem. *Industries:* Finn Lied. *Transport and Communications:* Reiulf Steen. *Wages and Prices:* Olav Gjærevoll. *Social Affairs:* Odd Højdahl. *Family and Consumer Affairs:* Inger Louise Valle. *Municipal Affairs and Labour:* Oddvar Nordli. *Agriculture:* Torstein Treholt. *Commerce and Shipping:* Per Kleppe. *Justice:* Oddvar Berrefjord.

The official languages are Bokmål (or Riksmål) and Nynorsk (or Landsmål).

LOCAL GOVERNMENT. For the purposes of administration the country is divided into 20 counties (*fylker*), in each of which the central government is represented by a county governor (*fylkesmannen*). In addition, there are 47 urban districts (*by-kommuner*) and 402 rural districts (*herredskommuner*), each of which usually corresponds in size to a parish (*prestegjeld*). The districts are administered by district councils (*kommunestyre*), whose membership may vary between

13 and 85 councillors, and by a committee (*formannskap*) which is elected by and from the members of the council. The council is four times the size of the committee. The council elects a chairman and a vice-chairman from among its members. Councillors are elected in accordance with rules which are in most cases identical with the rules governing election to Parliament.

Each of the 18 counties forms a county district (*fylkeskommune*), while the remaining 2, Oslo and Bergen, each comprise an urban district. The supreme authority in a county district is the county council (*fylkesting*). Every district council elects its district representatives in the proportion of one to every 6,000 inhabitants, though no one district may elect more than one-third of the total number of representatives in the county council. In a county district the county committee (*fylkesutvalg*) occupies a position corresponding to that of the committee (*formannskap*) in the primary districts. The county committee is elected by and from among the members of the county council. The number of county committee members is one-fourth of the membership of the county council, but must be at least 7 and not more than 11. The county council elects from among the members of the county committee a county sheriff (*fylkesordfører*) and a deputy sheriff.

AREA AND POPULATION.

Fylker	Area (sq. km)	Census population 1 Nov. 1960	Population 1 Jan. 1970	Pop. per sq. km 1970
Oslo (city)	453·28	475,562	487,363	1,129·9
Akershus	4,908·56	233,747	312,235	68·0
Østfold	4,179·73	202,641	218,505	56·3
Hedmark	27,343·96	177,195	178,557	6·8
Oppland	25,312·71	166,109	171,855	7·1
Buskerud	14,933·22	168,328	196,315	14·1
Vestfold	2,213·94	174,362	173,401	81·1
Telemark	15,315·32	149,828	156,917	11·1
Aust-Agder	9,211·71	77,061	80,178	9·3
Vest-Agder	7,280·33	108,876	123,048	18·0
Rogaland	9,140·57	238,662	266,271	31·2
Hordaland	15,581·30	225,296	255,225	17·2
Bergen (city)	49·64	115,689	115,738	2,393·2
Sogn og Fjordane	18,566·00	99,844	101,064	5·7
Møre og Romsdal	15,075·81	213,027	223,378	15·2
Sør-Trøndelag	18,918·76	211,648	232,147	12·8
Nord-Trøndelag	22,463·35	116,635	118,150	5·6
Nordland	38,327·01	237,193	243,179	6·7
Troms	25,953·90	127,549	136,563	5·4
Finnmark	48,618·96	71,982	76,379	1·6
Total	323,878·06[1]	3,591,234	3,866,468	12·6

[1] 125,247 sq. miles.

In 1970, 2,217,626 persons lived in rural municipalities and 1,648,842 in towns.

Conjugal condition of the domiciled population over 15 years of age, 1960: Unmarried: 407,217 males, 350,938 females; married: 833,562 males, 834,225 females; widowed or divorced: 72,562 males, 164,577 females.

Population of the principal towns at 1 Jan. 1969:

Oslo	487,363	Ålesund	39,351	Bodø	28,530
Trondheim	126,190	Tromsø	38,094	Haugesund	27,391
Bergen	115,738	Sandefjord	31,752	Halden	26,694
Stavanger	81,741	Porsgrunn	31,587	Gjøvik	25,176
Kristiansund	56,119	Sandnes	30,015	Moss	24,571
Drammen	49,250	Fredrikstad	29,870	Lillehammer	20,492
Skien	45,396	Ringerike	28,923	Steinkjer	20,191

VITAL STATISTICS for calendar years:

	Marriages	Divorces	Births[2]	Still-born	Illegitimate	Deaths
1966	27,680	2,672	67,061	812	3,335	36,010
1967	29,154	2,876	66,779	735	3,428	36,216
1968	29,441	3,058	67,350	756	3,770	37,200[1]

[1] Provisional figures.　　　　[2] Excluding still-born.

RELIGION. There is complete freedom of religion, the Evangelical Lutheran Church, however, being the national church, endowed by the State. Its clergy are nominated by the King. All other religions are tolerated. Ecclesiastically Norway is divided into 10 *Bispedømmer* (bishoprics), 91 *Prostier* (provostships or archdeaconries) and 586 *Prestegjeld* (clerical districts). In 1960 there were 134,551 dissenters. The Roman Catholics are under a Bishop at Oslo, a Vicar Apostolic at Trondheim and an Apostolic Prefect at Tromsø.

EDUCATION. In Norway the children normally start their school attendance the year they complete 7. Some children (1·6%) start when they are 6. Norway has now 7 years compulsory school, but from 1959 a compulsory 9 years compulsory school has been under gradual introduction, as the municipalities from that year were authorized to extend the school attendance by 2 years by introducing an 'upper stage' in primary schools. According to the 1969 Act on Primary Schools, the 9 years compulsory schooling will have been completed by 1974–75.

On 1 Oct. 1969 the number of Primary Schools and pupils were as follow:

(*a*) Rural municipalities: 2,561, primary schools, lower stage, 241,575 pupils; 363, primary schools, upper stage, 76,769 pupils; 284, continuation schools, 11,333 pupils. (*b*) Urban municipalities: 530, primary schools, lower stage, 146,727 pupils; 130, primary schools, upper stage, 52,492 pupils; 50, continuation schools, 3,331 pupils.

On 1 Oct. 1969 the number of secondary general schools, lower stage, was 272 with 83,804 pupils.

In 1968–69, 6,126 students attended Folk High Schools and 82,111 Vocational Schools (of 8,049 attended Teachers Training Colleges).

There are in Norway 4 universities and 6 institutions equivalent to universities. In the autumn 1969 the total number of students was 27,469. The University of Oslo, founded in 1811, had in 1969, 15,507 students. The University of Bergen, founded in 1948, had in 1969, 4,968 students. The University of Trondheim consists for the time being, of the State Institute of Technology, founded in 1910, and the State College for Teachers, founded in 1925. At each of them the number of students was in the autumn 1969, 3,516 and 1,213 respectively. The University of Tromsø was established in 1968. Regular students have not, however, yet started. The State College of Business Administration and Economics had in 1969, 814 students, the State College of Agriculture, 460 students, the Independent Theological College, 457 students, the State Veterinary College, 211 students, the State College of Sport, 191 students, and the State College of Architecture, 142 students.

In 1969–70, 3,389 Norwegians were studying at foreign universities.

CINEMAS (1966). There were 592 cinemas with a seating capacity of 163,800.

NEWSPAPERS (1969). There were 82 daily newspapers with a combined circulation of 1,495,772; of these, 10 with a combined circulation of 531,096 appear in Oslo.

SOCIAL WELFARE. In 1969 a total of 6,533m. kroner were paid under different social insurance schemes, amounting to 12·3% of the net national income.

The National Insurance Act of 17 June 1966, which came into force on 1 Jan. 1967, replaces the schemes relating to old age pensions, disability benefits, widows' and mothers' pensions, survivors' benefit for children and rehabilitation aid. Schemes relating to health insurance, unemployment insurance and occupational injury insurance came into force on 1 Jan. 1971.

The following conspectus gives a survey of the schemes established by law. Many municipalities grant additional benefits to old-age and disablement pensions.

Type of scheme	Introduced[1]	Scope	Principal benefits in 1970
Unemployment insurance	1939 (1970)	Nearly all wage-earners	Daily allowance during unemployment kr. 7 to 44 per day; contributions to training and retraining, removal expenses, wage subsidies in the case of relief work
Health insurance	1911 (1969)	All residents, benefits in kind; wage-earners, also cash sickness benefit	Hospital expenses; about ¾ of doctors' fees; kr. 7 to 44 per day cash sickness benefit
National insurance:	1967		
Old-age pensions[2]	1937	All persons above 70 years of age	Basic pensions: Single, kr. 6,800; couples, kr. 10,200 per annum; supplementary pensions based on previous contributions; various allowances
Rehabilitation benefits[2]	1961	Persons unfit for work because of disablement	Training; hospitalization; rehabilitation allowances; grants and loans
Disablement pension[2]	1961	Persons, between 18 and 70 years of age, disabled by 50% or more, unfit for rehabilitation	Full disability pension equals old-age pension; additional benefits for persons with special needs.
Death grants	1967	All residents	20% of basic amount (kr. 6,800); 45% if deceased left a widow or children
Survivors' benefits[2]	1965	All residents	Full pension = kr. 6,800 per annum + 55% of the supplementary pension due to the deceased, transitional benefits, assistance benefits and educational allowances
Children's pension[2]	1958	Under 18 years, after loss of one or both parents	40% of basic amount (kr. 6,800) for first child, 25% for each additional child. If both parents are dead, full survivors' pension for first, 40% for second, 25% third, etc., child
Benefits for unmarried mothers[2]	1965	All unmarried mothers	Maternity grant kr. 2,516, transitional allowance, full amount kr. 6,800 per annum assistance benefits and educational allowances
Additional allowances to national insurance pensions	1969	Certain groups of pensioners on basic rates	Full additional allowance, kr. 510
Compensation supplement to national insurance pensions	1970	Certain groups of pensioners	Compensation supplement kr. 500
Occupational injuries insurance, combining:	1960	All employed persons, school children and students; self-employed on a voluntary basis	Pensions according to disablement and insured income. Maximum kr. 18,000 per annum with additional children's allowances, widows' and orphans' pensions; sickness benefit, cash in kind
Industrial workers	1970 1895		
Seamen	1915		
Fishermen	1909		
Military personnel	1953		
Family allowances	1946 1969	All families with children under 16	Kr. 500 for the first child, kr. 1,500 for the second, kr. 2,000 for the third, kr. 2,200 for the fourth and kr. 2,400 for the fifth and each additional child
War pensions	1946 1970	War victims, 1939–45	Pensions up to kr. 37,800 per annum with additional allowances, widows' and orphans' pensions
Special pensions schemes:		Persons with at least:[3]	Maximum old-age pensions for couples:
Seamen	1948 (1967)	150 months' service (360 „ „)	Kr. 15,144[4] per annum (officers) „ 10,812[4] „ „ (others)
Forestry workers	1952 1969	750 premium weeks (1,500 „ „)	„ 9,000 „ „
Fishermen	1958 1969	750 „ „ (1,500 „ „)	„ 9,900 „ „

[1] Date of latest revision in brackets.
[2] Transferred to national insurance scheme and revised in 1967.
[3] Requirements for maximum pensions in brackets.
[4] Supplement for service during war not included.

Provisions have been laid down for the integration of more than one benefit, pension, etc., so as to limit the total amount.

JUSTICE. The judicature in Norway is common to both civil and criminal cases. The same judges, who are state officials, preside over both kinds of cases. The participation of lay assessors and jurors, summoned for each case, varies according to the civil or criminal nature of the case.

The ordinary Court of First Instance (*Herreds- og byrett*) is presided over by a judge who in criminal cases is, and in civil cases may be, assisted by 2 lay assessors, chosen by ballot from a panel elected by the district council. In criminal matters the Court of First Instance is generally competent in cases where the maximum penalty incurred is 5 years imprisonment. Altogether there are 104 Courts of First Instance. There is a Conciliation Council (*Forliksråd*) for each community, consisting of 3 men or women, elected by the district council, before which, as a general rule, civil cases must first be brought for mediation.

The Court of Second Instance (*Lagmannsrett*) is presided over by a judge, together with 2 other judges. In civil matters they may be assisted by lay assessors, ordinarily 4 but in some cases 2, chosen and elected in the same way as mentioned above. In criminal cases the lay element is a jury composed of 10 jurors. This court is a court of appeal in both civil and criminal cases. In addition, as a court of first instance, it takes cognizance of all criminal cases (other than those coming under the *Riksrett*—the court for impeachments) which do not come under the competence of the Court of First Instance. The kingdom is divided into 5 districts (*Lagdømmer*) for the purpose of the Courts of Second Instance.

The Supreme Court (*Høyesterett*) is the ultimate court of appeal. In criminal cases the competence of the court, however, is limited to the complaints against the application of laws, the measuring out of the penalty and the trial of the case of the subordinate courts. The Supreme Court consists of a president and 17 judges. In each single case the court consists of 5 judges.

All serious offences are prosecuted by the State. The public prosecution is led by a general prosecutor (*riksadvokat*) and there are 15 district prosecutors (*statsadvokater*). Counsel for the defence is, generally, paid by the State.

There are 4 central penal and correctional institutions for delinquents: inmates (1 July 1970), 378 males and 12 females. There are also 40 local prisons in which were detained (1 July 1970) 1,167 males and 7 females.

FINANCE. Currency. By a treaty signed 16 Oct. 1875 Norway adopted the same monetary system as Sweden and Denmark. The Norwegian *krone*, of 100 *øre*, is of the value of 1*s.* at par, or about 17 kroner to £1 sterling. National bank-notes of 10, 50, 100, 500 and 1,000 kroner are legal means of payment. On 27 Sept. 1931 the gold standard exchange clause was suspended and there was placed an embargo on gold.

On 30 June 1970 the nominal value of the coin in circulation was 304m. kroner; notes in circulation, 6,794m. kroner.

Budget. Current revenue and expenditure for years ending 31 Dec. (in 1,000 kroner):

	1965	1966	1967	1968	1969	1970[1]
Revenue	10,224,764	11,321,470	12,636,392	13,528,414	15,307,417	16,589,727
Expenditure	10,023,047	10,828,522	12,184,625	13,723,414	15,443,945	17,939,727

[1] Estimates.

National debt[1] for years ending 31 Dec. (in 1,000 kroner):

1950 (30 June)	4,704,960	1964	10,877,300	1967	13,792,429
1955 (30 June)	6,347,473	1965	11,447,600	1968	14,720,500
1960 (30 June)	9,299,900	1966	12,142,920	1969	15,824,100

[1] At the rate of par on foreign loans; including treasury bills (in 1m. kroner) amounting to 84 in 1950; 131 in 1955; 37 in 1960; 36 in 1962; 10 in 1963; 4 in 1964; nil in 1965 and 1966; 2 in 1967 and 1968, and nil in 1969.

DEFENCE. Service is universal and compulsory, liability in peace-time commencing at the age of 20 and continuing till the age of 44. The training period in the Army is 12 months, in the Navy and Air Force, 15 months.

Army. The Army is organized in 5 regional commands, comprising all land forces. The regional commands again are divided into a number of land defence districts. Major units are organized mainly in Regimental Combat Teams. Peace establishment includes 1 RCT, a number of independent units and supporting elements as well as training units. Total peace-time strength, 21,000.

Navy. The Navy is organized in 5 regional commands, and consists of the coastal batteries and the following naval units: 15 coastal submarines, 5 frigates, 2 patrol vessels, 10 coastal minesweepers, 26 torpedo boats, 20 fast gunboats, 4 coastal minelayers, 1 mineplanter, 1 training ship, 2 depot ships, the royal yacht *Norge* and 6 fishery protection vessels.

Total personnel (1970), 5,200 officers and ratings.

Air Force. The Royal Norwegian Air Force is organized in 2 regional commands. It operates 6 squadrons of F-5 supersonic fighter-bombers (including 1 squadron equiped with RF-5A reconnaissance fighters), 1 squadron of F-104G Starfighters, 1 maritime patrol squadron of P-3B Orions, 1 squadron of C-130H Hercules transports, and a number of UH-1B Iroquois helicopter, communications, rescue and training units, as well as 4 Nike surface-to-air missile batteries and several light anti-aircraft artillery units. Ten Westland Sea King helicopters were ordered in 1970, primarily for search and rescue duties. Total strength is approximately 9,000 officers and men.

Home Guard. The Home Guard is organized in small units equipped and trained for special tasks in their home area. Compulsory service after basic training is 50 hours a year. The total strength is approximately 70,000.

PRODUCTION. The following table sets forth the estimated value of net production, at factor cost, by industries, in 1m. kroner:

	1963	1964	1965	1966	1967	1968	1969[1]
Agriculture	1,486	1,543	1,654	1,706	1,828	2,212	2,147
Forestry	883	971	1,083	971	988	850	853
Fishing	373	459	733	916	726	554	576
Whaling	18	70	81	49	27	3	−2
Mining and quarrying	346	365	427	505	539	580	692
Manufacturing	9,281	10,290	11,451	12,456	13,306	14,342	15,779
Construction	2,831	2,930	3,218	3,755	4,357	4,353	4,774
Electricity, gas and water	666	728	759	802	951	1,106	972
Trade	4,584	4,890	5,399	5,648	5,923	6,272	6,760
Financial institutions	938	1,062	1,153	1,231	1,510	1,687	1,892
Commercial buildings	1,122	1,204	1,303	1,396	1,545	1,765	1,899
Water transport	2,303	2,723	2,934	3,038	3,625	3,880	3,528
Other transport	1,868	2,028	2,206	2,445	2,742	2,959	3,247
Government services	1,700	1,888	2,084	2,263	2,579	2,787	3,075
Community, business and personal service	4,115	4,633	5,216	5,806	6,664	7,446	8,454
Net production at factor cost	32,516	35,784	39,701	42,987	47,320	50,796	54,646
+ Indirect taxes	5,603	6,263	7,102	7,883	8,644	9,148	10,379
− Subsidies	1,847	1,746	2,276	2,394	2,604	2,875	3,486
Net production at market price	36,272	40,301	44,527	48,476	53,360	57,069	61,539

[1] Provisional

The distribution of the population according to professions in 1960, showed 546,770 (15·2%) dependent on agriculture, forestry and gardening; 1,247,086 (34·7%) on mining, manufacturing, building, etc.; 370,735 (10·3%) on commerce; 366,994 (10·2%) on transportation; 141,400 (3·9%) on fishery, sealing and whaling; 473,590 (13·2%) on public administration, liberal professions and services.

AGRICULTURE. Norway is a barren and mountainous country. The arable soil is found in comparatively narrow strips, gathered in deep and narrow valleys and around fiords and lakes. Large, continuous tracts fit for cultivation do not exist. Of the total area, 75·7% is unproductive, 21% productive forest and 3·3% under cultivation and other used soils.

Principal crops	Area (hectares)			Produce (metric tons)		
	1967	1968	1969	1967	1968	1969
Wheat	3.293	4,806	3,827	10,583	16,365	11,111
Rye	707	1,256	1,350	2,319	4,224	4,170
Barley	178,648	175,917	184,698	485,459	621,255	485,614
Oats	45,044	49,938	54,128	122,836	175,612	139,718
Mixed corn	829	740	490	2,319	2,569	1,184
Potatoes	40,138	38,052	32,641	806,766	912,327	720,646
Hay	460,988	459,202	445,511	2,749,029	2,873,184	2,518,257

Livestock, 20 June 1969: 40,630 horses, 991,856 cattle (436,314 milch cows), 1,841,133 sheep, 91,168 goats, 621,483 pigs, 5,250.593 poultry.

Fur production in 1968–69 was as follows (1969–70 estimates in brackets): Silver fox, 600 (1,300); blue fox, 133,000 (155,000); mink, 2·53m. (2·24m.).

FORESTRY. The forests are one of the chief natural sources of wealth. The total area covered with forests is estimated at 83,300 sq. km, of which 64,800 sq. km is productive forest. 81% of the productive forest area consisted of conifers and 19% of broadleaves. Forests in public ownership cover 8,970 sq. km of productive forests and 5,820 sq. km of unproductive forests. Besides the home consumption of timber and fuel wood, the essential part of the cut is consumed as raw material in the paper industry. The annual natural increase is about 13·2m. cu. metres. In 1968–69, 6·9m. cu. metres were cut for production of pulp and other industrial wood products. In 1969 the export of timber produce was 15% of the total exports.

FISHERIES. The number of persons in 1968 engaged in cod fisheries was 19,251; in winter herring fisheries, 5,200; the total number of persons engaged in the fisheries was 47,797, of whom 12,413 had another chief occupation. The number of fishing vessels with motor was 36,286 in 1968; of these, 27,148 were open boats.

The value of sea fisheries in kroner in 1969 was: Cod, 328m.; mackerel, 219m.; coal-fish (saithe), 59m.; haddock, 62m.; herring, 165m.; dogfish, 16m.; deep-water prawn, 30m. The catch totalled in 1969, 2·2m. metric tons, valued at 1,053m. kroner.

Whale oil and sperm oil (in 1,000 bbls): 131 in 1966, 109 in 1967, 36 in 1968, 6 in 1969. Total value of oil and by-products was, in 1966, 79m.; 1967, 55m.; 1968, 22m., 1969, 3m. kroner.

The Norwegian fishery limit is 12 miles from 1 Sept 1961, for the coast east of Lindesnes from 1 July 1967.

MANUFACTURES. Industry is chiefly based on raw materials produced within the country (wood, fish, etc.) and on water power, of which the country possesses a large amount. The pulp and paper industry, the canning industry and the chemical and basic metal industries are the most important export manufactures. In the following table are given figures for industrial establishments in 1968, excluding one-man shops. Electrical plants, construction and building industry are not included. The values are given in 1,000 kroner.

Industries	Establish-ments	Number of Salaried staff	Wage earners	Gross value of produc-tion	Value added by manu-facture
Coalmining	1	134	567	26,774	23,916
Metal-mining	20	799	3,642	382,971	310,637
Stone-quarrying	376	216	1,636	176,196	155,668
Other non-metallic mining and quarrying	97	124	1,022	92,724	84,525
Food industries	3,492	8,735	34,420	7,863,838	1,475,341
Beverages	99	1,013	3,327	737,706	581,406
Tobacco	11	642	897	531,129	448,144
Textiles	382	2,846	12,493	1,101,983	576,986
Clothing, etc.	1,150	3,243	17,378	1,332,677	666,813
Wood	1,894	2,011	13,274	1 540 708	675,569
Furniture and fixtures	1,594	1,527	11,884	1,221,494	613,603
Pulp and paper	261	4,090	19,106	3,411,928	1,144,216
Printing and publishing	1,184	7,700	21,716	2,036,725	1,217,340

Industries	Establish-ments	Number of Salaried staff	Wage earners	Gross value of produc-tion	Value added by manu-facture
Leather	112	238	1,162	114,453	55,653
Rubber	138	816	3,561	300,280	185,992
Chemical	409	7,199	14,717	3,426,409	1,455,026
Manufacture of products of petroleum and coal	45	561	1,197	1,005,050	245,448
Non-metallic mineral pro-ducts	710	2,376	10,502	1,163,186	704,610
Basic metal industries	155	5,747	20,758	4,572,281	1,726,427
Metal products	1,162	6,166	21,535	2,187,921	1,231,502
Machinery	911	4,162	12,788	1,503,269	824,867
Electrical machinery, etc.	356	6,299	12,093	1,768,215	930,978
Transport equipment	2,542	10,601	46,957	4,788,462	2,296,938
Total (all included)	17,696	78,882	293,437	42,013,206	18,038,198

MINING. Production and value of the chief concentrates, metals and alloys were:

	1967		1968	
Concentrates and minerals	Metric tons	1,000 kroner	Metric tons	1,000 kroner
Copper concentrates	32,869	47,790	38,505	56,899
Pyrites	636,863	68,835	692,585	76,560
Iron ore and titaniferous con-centrates	3,803,296	210,786	4,105,759	16,958
Zinc and lead concentrates	30,732	16,529	29,934	..
Molybdenum concentrates	487	7,225	399	..
Metals and alloys				
Copper	20,302[1]	..	23,583[1]	..
Nickel	28,159	..	32,172	..
Aluminium	360,983[1]	1,184.962	468,299[1]	1,542,013
Ferro-alloys	595,612	493.224	714,228	573,529
Semi-finished steel	631,528[2]	432,456	655,278[2]	498,236
Pig-iron	636,834	..	674,079	..
Zinc	54,801[1]	..	60,110[1]	..
Lead and tin	644[3]	..	566[3]	..

[1] Primary, for sale and own use.   [2] For sale and own use.   [3] Secondary.

ELECTRICITY. Norway is a large producer of hydro-electric energy. The potential total hydro-electric power, for a whole year at regulated minimum water flow and by 82% efficiency, is estimated at 15m. kw. or about 131,000m. kwh. annually. About 60% of the water power suitable for development consists of waterfalls with a height of at least 900 ft.

By the end of 1968, 6·24m. kw. (about 42%) of the available water power had been developed for production of electricity At the same time the capacity of the installations for production of thermo-electric energy amounted to only 141,000 kw. As at 31 Dec. 1968 the total capacity of generators (of hydro-electric plants) was 14m. kva.

In 1968 the total production of electricity amounted to 59,701m. kwh., of which 99·8% was produced by hydro-electric plants.

Most of the electricity is used for industrial purposes, especially by the chemical and basic metal industries for production of nitrate of calcium and other nitrogen products, carbide, ferrosilicon and other ferro-alloys, aluminium and zinc. The paper and pulp industries are also big consumers of electricity.

Bjerve, P. J., *Planning in Norway 1947–1956*. Amsterdam, 1959
Bourneuf, A., *Norway, the Planned Revival*. Cambridge, Mass., 1958
Galenson, W., *Labor in Norway*. Cambridge, Mass., and London, 1949
Leiserson, M. W., *Wages and Economic Control in Norway, 1945–57*. Harvard Univ. Press, 1959

COMMERCE. Total imports and exports in calendar years (in 1,000 kroner):

	1964	1965	1966	1967	1968	1969
Imports	14,169,000	15,787,000	17,169,000	19,627,000	19,331,000	21,011,000
Exports	9,219,000	10,309,000	11,168,000	12,411,000	13,841,000	15,741,000

Trade according to countries was as follows (in 1,000 kroner):

| | 1968 | | 1969 | |
Countries	Imports	Exports	Imports	Exports
Argentina	56,745	77,978	60,094	63,824
Australia and New Zealand	92,804	103,196	94,804	125,560
Belgium and Luxembourg	428,505	234,631	529,855	314,786
Brazil	185,037	135,810	230,720	124,463
anada	821,453	90,965	800,551	87,952
Czechoslovakia	80,732	51,768	87,645	51,850
Denmark	1,314,411	977,260	1,373,820	1,144,544
Finland	325,919	246,863	378,206	393,575
France	650,709	341,648	792,504	504,616
Germany (West)	2,673,119	1,816,238	3,136,828	2,287,826
India	21,816	47,325	21,043	65,378
Italy	397,947	29,674	442,646	413,571
Netherlands	615,856	396,866	753,890	483,137
Poland	137,300	84,232	107,523	117,773
Portugal	76,914	67,776	92,771	70,670
Spain	136,929	140,113	138,231	151,557
Sweden	3,711,008	2,098,494	3,988,299	2,456,995
Switzerland	342,441	154,173	437,627	190,574
UK	2,390,161	2,665,616	2,792,072	2,713,457
USA	1,472,875	1,140,347	1,655,140	1,080,455
USSR	193,870	135,898	161,455	109,351

Principal items of import in 1969 (in 1,000 kroner): Machinery, transport equipment, etc., 7,196,026; base metals and manufactures thereof, 2,390,814; fuel oil, etc., 1,539,286; textiles, 1,824,155; chemicals, 895,605.

Principal items of export in 1969 (in 1,000 kroner): Pulp and papers, 1,869,888; edible animal products, 1,245,828; base metals and manufactures thereof, 4,470,750; machinery and transport equipment, 3,796,806.

Total trade between Norway and UK (British Board of Trade returns, in £1,000 sterling):

	1966	1967	1968	1969	1970
Imports to UK	119,663	127,357	162,176	179.656	198,637
Exports from UK	106,892	126,954	124,529	140,781 }	173,834
Re-exports from UK	2,570	2,700	2,889	3,872 }	

SHIPPING. The total registered mercantile marine on 1 Jan. 1970 was 2,199 vessels, 18·42m. gross tons (steam and motor vessels above 100 gross tons). These figures do not include fishing and catching boats, floating whaling factories, tugs, salvage vessels, ice-breakers and similar special types of vessel, totalling 758 vessels of 256,000 gross tons.

| Vessels in foreign trade 1969 | With cargoes | | In ballast | | Total | |
	No.	Net tons	No.	Net tons	No.	Net tons
Entered:						
Norwegian	6,578	6,917,504	2,403	2,750,562	8,981	9,668,066
Foreign	6,213	7,971,794	4,194	9,914,095	10,407	17,885,889
Total entered	12,791	14,889,298	6,597	12,664,657	19,388	27,553,955
Cleared:						
Norwegian	7,523	7,848,037	1,475	1,823,125	8,998	9,671,162
Foreign	7,790	13,006,749	2,620	4,853,745	10,410	17,860,494
Total cleared	15,313	20,854,786	4,095	6,676,870	19,408	27,531,656

Goods (in 1,000 metric tons) discharged, 17,543; loaded, 36,833, of which 21,543 was Swedish iron ore shipped from Narvik.

ROADS. On 1 Jan. 1970 the length of the public roads (including roads in towns) was 71,101 km. Of these, 53,341 km were main roads; 11,485 km had some kind of paving, mostly bituminous treatment, 7,682 km were oil-gravel roads, the rest being gravel-surfaced.

Number of registered motor vehicles (31 Dec. 1969) was 1,061,711, including 699,683 passenger cars (including taxis), 65,331 lorries, 73,587 vans, 7,304 buses, 3,574 special vehicles, 172,576 motor cycles and mopeds. The scheduled bus and lorry services in 1968 drove 3,600m. passenger-km and 187m. net ton-km.

RAILWAYS. The length of state railways on 31 Dec. 1969 was 4,242 km; of private companies, 52 km. On 2,269 km of state and 16 km of private railways elecrtic power is installed. Total receipts of the state railways and road traffic in 1969 were 790m. kroner; total expenses (excluding interest on capital), 902m. kroner. The state railways carried 29·7m. metric tons of freight (of which 20·2m. was iron ore on the Ofoten railway) and 29·1m. passengers.

AVIATION. Det Norske Luftfartselskap (DNL) started its post-war activities on 1 April 1946. On 1 Aug. 1946 DNL, together with DDL (Danish Airlines) and ABA/SILA (Swedish Airlines), formed the 'Scandinavian Airlines System'— SAS. The 3 companies remained independent units, but all services were co-ordinated. In 1951 a new agreement was signed (retroactive from 1 Oct. 1950) according to which the 3 national companies became holding partners in a new organization which took over the entire operational system. Denmark and Nor-way hold each two-sevenths and Sweden three-sevenths of the capital, but they have joint responsibility towards third parties.

In the autumn of 1969 SAS had a fleet of 68 planes (including 54 jet planes). Length of route network, about 208,000 km.

Norwegian scheduled air services:

	1,000 km flown	Passengers carried	1,000 passenger-km	Post, luggage, freight and passengers (1,000 ton-km)	
				Total	Of which post
1967	32,304	1,798,163	1,440,495	169,364	7,321
1968	35,997	1,960,976	1,608,000	199,000	8,000
1969	37,553	2,194,952	1,737,000	224,000	8,000

TELECOMMUNICATIONS. Number of telephones in 1970 was 1,090,662 (28 per 100 of population). Receipts, 974·1m. kroner; expenses, 865·2m. kroner (interest on capital included).

BANKING. The Norges Bank is a joint-stock bank; in 1949 the state acquired all the shares hitherto privately owned. The bank is governed by laws enacted by the State, and its directors are elected by the Storting, except the president and vice-president of the head office, who are nominated by the King. It is the only bank of issue.

At the end of 1969 there were 46 private joint-stock banks. Their total amount of capital and funds was 1,566m. kroner (capital 494m., funds 772m.). Deposits amounted to 14,282m. kroner, of which 4,480m. kroner were at call and notice, and 9,802m. kroner on time.

The number of savings banks at the end of 1969 was 509. The total amount of the funds of the savings banks amounted to 691m. kroner, and total deposits 15,071m. kroner, of which 2,280m. kroner were at call and notice and 12,791m. kroner on time.

WEIGHTS AND MEASURES. The metric system of weights and measures has been obligatory since 1875.

SVALBARD

An archipelago situated between 10° and 35° E. long. and between 74° and 81° N. lat. Total area, 62,000 sq. km (24,000 sq. miles).

The main islands of the archipelago are Spitsbergen (formerly called Vestspits-bergen), Nordaustlandet, Edgeøya, Barentsøya, Prins Karls Forland, Bjørnøya, Hopen, Kong Karls Land, Kvitøya, and many small islands. The arctic climate is tempered by mild winds from the Atlantic.

The archipelago was probably discovered by Norsemen in 1194 and redis-covered by the Dutch navigator Barents in 1596. In the 17th century the very lucrative whale-hunting caused rival Dutch, British and Danish–Norwegian claims to sovereignty and quarrels about the hunting-places. But when in the

18th century the whale-hunting ended, the question of the sovereignty of Svalbard lost its actuality; it was again raised in the 20th century, owing to the discovery and exploitation of coalfields. By a treaty, signed on 9 Feb. 1920 in Paris, Norway's sovereignty over the archipelago was recognized. On 14 Aug. 1925 the archipelago was officially incorporated in Norway.

Coal is the principal product. Of the 3 Norwegian and 3 Soviet mining camps, only 1 Norwegian and 2 Soviet camps are operating. In 1969–70, 2,900 persons (980 in Norwegian and 1,920 in Soviet establishments) wintered in Svalbard. In 1969, 394,114 metric tons of coal were exported from the Norwegian and 449,035 metric tons from the Soviet mines.

Norwegian and foreign companies have been prospecting for oil. So far only one deep drilling has been made: insignificant amounts of gas were found.

The following Norwegian stations are in operation in Svalbard: 3 meteorological and coast radio stations (Bjørnøya, since 1920; Hopen, since 1945, and Isfjord Radio, since 1934); 1 telemetry station furnishing the European Space Research Organization (ESRO) with satellite data (Ny-Ålesund, since 1967); 1 permanent research station (Ny-Ålesund, since 1968).

Norsk Polarinstitutt, Skrifter. Oslo, from 1948 (under different titles from 1922)
Svalbard-Spitsbergen. Bergen, 1961
Orvin, A. K., 'Twenty-five Years of Norwegian Sovereignty in Svalbard 1925–1950' (in *The Polar Record, 1951*)

JAN MAYEN

This bleak, desolate and mountainous island of volcanic origin is situated 71° N. lat. and 8° 30′ W. long., 300 miles NNE of Iceland. The total area is 380 sq. km (147 sq. miles). Beerenberg, its highest peak, reaches a height of 2,277 metres. Volcanic activity, which has been dormant, possibly for centuries, or even millennia, was reactivated in Sept. 1970.

The island was possibly discovered by Henry Hudson in 1608, and it was first named Hudson's Tutches (Touches). It was again and again rediscovered and renamed. Its present name derives from the Dutch whaling captain Jan Jacobsz May, who indisputably discovered the island in 1614. It was uninhabited, but occasionally visited by seal hunters and trappers, until 1921 when Norway established a radio and meteorological station. On 8 May 1929 Jan Mayen was officially proclaimed as incorporated in the Kingdom of Norway. Its relation to Norway was finally settled by law of 27 Feb. 1930. A LORAN station (1959), a landing strip for aircraft (1963); and a CONSOL station (1968) have been built.

BOUVET ISLAND
Bouvetøya

This uninhabited island, situated 54° 26′ S. lat. and 3° 24′ E. long., was discovered in 1739 by a French naval officer, Jean Baptiste Lozier Bouvet, but no flag was hoisted till, in 1825, Capt. Norris raised the Union Jack. In 1928 Great Britain waived its claim to the island in favour of Norway, which in Dec. 1927 had occupied it. A law of 27 Feb. 1930 declared Bouvetøya a Norwegian dependency. The area is 58 sq. km (22 sq. miles).

PETER I ISLAND
Peter I øy

This uninhabited island, situated 68° 48′ S. lat. and 90° 35′ W. long., was sighted in 1821 by the Russian explorer, Admiral von Bellingshausen. The first landing was made in 1929 by a Norwegian expedition which hoisted the Norwegian flag. On 1 May 1931 Peter I Island was placed under Norwegian sovereignty, and on 24 March 1933 it was incorporated in Norway as a dependency. The area is 249 sq. km (96 sq. miles).

QUEEN MAUD LAND
Dronning Maud Land

On 14 Jan. 1939 the Norwegian Cabinet placed that part of the Antarctic Continent from the border of Falkland Islands dependencies in the west to the border of the Australian Antarctic Dependency in the east (between 20° W. and 45° E.) under Norwegian sovereignty. The territory had been explored only by Norwegians and hitherto been ownerless. Since 1949 expeditions from various countries have explored the area. In 1957 Dronning Maud Land was given the status of a Norwegian dependency.

DIPLOMATIC REPRESENTATIVES

Norway maintains embassies in:

Argentina (also for Paraguay and Uruguay)
Australia (also for New Zealand)
Austria
Belgium (also for Luxembourg)
Brazil
Canada
Chile (also for Peru)
China
Czechoslovakia (also for Romania)
Denmark
Finland
France
Germany (West)
Greece
Hungary
Iceland
India (also for Burma and Ceylon)
Indonesia
Iran (also for Pakistan and Afghánistán)
Israel (also for Cyprus)
Italy (also for Greece and Malta)
Ivory Coast (also for Niger, Liberia, Guinea and Senegal),
Japan (also for Korea)
Kenya (also for Uganda, Tanzania, Zambia, Malawi and Madagascar)

Mexico (also for Costa Rica, Cuba, El Salvador, Guatemala, Honduras, Nicaragua)
Morocco (also for Algeria, Tunisia and Libya)
Netherlands
Nigeria (also for Cameroun and Ghana)
Philippines
Poland
Portugal
Singapore
Spain
Sweden
Switzerland
Thailand (also for Malaysia)
Turkey (also for Kuwait and Iraq)
USSR (also for Mongolia)
UAR (also for Lebanon, Ethiopia, Sudan and Jordan)
UK (also for Irish Republic)
USA
Venezuela (also for Colombia, Ecuador and Panama)
Yugoslavia (also for Bulgaria)

OF NORWAY IN GREAT BRITAIN (25 Belgrave Sq., SW1)

Ambassador: Paul Koht (accredited 22 Oct. 1968).

Counsellors: Tore Bøgh; Svein Haaland (*Consul-General*), Kaare Daehlen; Herman Pedersen (*Press and Information*); Semund Remoy (*Fisheries*); Per Smith-Kielland (*Commercial*). *Cultural Attache:* Hans Aanestad. *First Secretaries:* John Grieg; Helge Vindenes; Lars Tangeraas. *Defence Attaché:* Capt. Ole Andreas Aslaksrud.

There are consular representatives at Belfast, Birmingham, Bradford, Bristol, Cardiff, Edinburgh, Glasgow, Hull, Jersey, Kirkwall, Lerwick, Liverpool, Leith–Edinburgh, Manchester, Middlesbrough, Milford Haven, Newcastle upon Tyne, Southampton, Sunderland, Swansea.

OF GREAT BRITAIN IN NORWAY

Ambassador: T. F. Brenchley, CMG.

Counsellors: G. A. Crossley (*Commercial*); Dr M. H. Proctor (*Scientific*, resides in Stockholm).

First Secretaries: T. Quinlan (*Commercial*); R. S. Young; G. D. Cossar (*Labour*, resident in Stockholm).

Service Attachés: Wing Cdr N. E. Bowen (*Defence, Army and Air*), Cdr E. J. Leatherby (*Navy*).

There are consular representatives at Ålesund, Bergen, Kristiansund, Narvik, Oslo, Stavanger, Tønsberg, Tromsø and Trondheim.

OF NORWAY IN THE USA (3401 Massachusetts Ave. NW, Washington, D.C., 20007)

Ambassador: Arne Gunneng.

Councillors: Günnar Harum; Knut Sverre; Frode E. T. Nilsen (*Shipping*); Georg Krane (*Press*). *First Secretaries:* Odvar Mosnesset; Klaus Nergaard. *Defence, Military and Air Attaché:* Maj.-Gen. Arne G. Lund. *Naval Attaché:* Capt. Rolf Henningsen.

OF THE USA IN NORWAY

Ambassador: Philip K. Crowe.

Deputy Chief of Mission: John Ausland. *Heads of Sections:* Robert T. Hennemeyer (*Political*); Lucian L. Rocke, Jr (*Economic*); Marion E. Anderson (*Commercial*); Theodore Sellin (*Labour*); Joseph R. Yodzis (*Administrative*). *Service Attachés:* Col. John D. Kinser (*Army*), Capt. Robert O. Coulthard, Jr (*Navy*), Col. Leslie H. Armin (*Air*).

BOOKS OF REFERENCE

STATISTICAL INFORMATION. The Central Bureau of Statistics, Statistisk Sentralbyrå (Dronningensgate 16, Oslo 1), was founded in 1876 as an independent state institution. *Director:* Petter Jakob Bjerve. The earliest census of population was taken in 1769. The Sentralbyrå publishes the series *Norges Offisielle Statistikk*, Norway's official statistics (from 1828), and *Social Economic Studies* (from 1954). The main publications are:

Statistisk Årbok for Norge (annual, from 1880; from 1952 with English explanations)
Økonomisk Utsyn (annual, from 1935; with English summary from 1952)
Historisk Statistikk 1968 (historical statistics; bilingual Norwegian–English)
Statistisk Månedshefte (monthly, from 1880; with English index)

Norges Statskalender. From 1816; annual from 1877

NON-OFFICIAL PUBLICATIONS

The Norway Year Book. 7th ed. Oslo, 1967
Facts about Norway. Ed. by Aftenposten. 11th ed. Oslo, 1970
Bank of Norway, *Economic Bulletin.* Quarterly, from 1925 (under the present title from 1966)
Norway: Directory of industries and exports. Ed. Norges Industriforbund and Norges Exportråd. 3rd ed. 1969–70. Oslo, 1969
Norwegian Commercial Banks: Financial Review. Monthly
Norge: Land og folk [with English summary]; *Geografisk leksikon; Atlas.* 4 vols. Oslo, 1963
Bjorge, J. H. B., *Engelsk–amerikansk–norsk ordbok.* Oslo, 1959
Bugge, A., and Steen, S., *Norsk Kulturhistorie.* 5 vols. Oslo, 1938–42
Christensen, Chr. A. R., *Norway, a Democratic Kingdom 1905–1955. Fifty years of progress.* Oslo 1955
Derry, Thomas K., *A Short History of Norway.* London, 1957
Gleditsch, Th., *Engelsk–norsk ordbok.* 2nd ed. Oslo, 1948
Grønland, E., *Norway in English. Books on Norway . . . 1742–1959.* Oslo, 1961
Haugen, E., *Norwegian–English Dictionary.* Oslo, 1965
Holtedahl, O. (ed.), *Geology of Norway.* Oslo. 1960
Hove, O., *The System of Education.* Oslo, 1968
Knudsen, O., *Norway.* Oslo, 1965
Larsen, K., *A History of Norway.* New York, 1948
Nielsen, K., and Nesheim, A., *Lapp Dictionary: Lapp–English–Norwegian.* 5 vols. Oslo, 1963
Paine, R., *Coast Lapp Society.* 2 vols. Tromsø, 1957–65
Stagg, F. N., *The Heart of Norway.* London, 1953.—*North Norway.* London, 1952.—*East Norway and its Frontier.* London, 1956.—*West Norway and its Fjords.* London, 1954.—*South Norway.* London, 1958
Vorren, Ø. (ed.), *Norway North of 65.* Oslo, 1960
NATIONAL LIBRARY. The University Library, Drammensveien 42b, Oslo. *Director:* Gerhard F. W. Munthe.

OMAN

Sultanat Oman

The Sultanate of Oman is an independent sovereign state, situated in south-east Arabia. It was known as the Sultanate of Muscat and Oman until 1970. Its seaboard is nearly 1,000 miles long and extends from the Ras al Khaimah Shaikdom near Tibat on the east side of the Musandum Peninsula to Ras Dharbat Ali, which marks the boundary between Oman and the territory of the People's Republic of South Yemen. A small strip of the coast on the east side of the Musandum Peninsula from Dibah to Khor Kalba is administered by 2 shaikhs of Trucial Oman, independent of the Sultan. The sultanate extends inland to the borders of the Rub' al Khali ('Empty Quarter'). Physically Oman consists of three divisions—a coastal plain, a range of hills and a plateau. The coastal plain varies in width from 10 miles near Suwaiq to practically nothing in the vicinity of Matrah and Muscat towns, where the hills descend abruptly into the sea. The mountain range reaches its greatest height (of over 9,000 ft) in the Jebel Akdhar region. The hills are for the most part barren, but in the high area round Jebel Akdhar they are green and there is considerable cultivation. The plateau has an average height of 1,000 ft. With the exception of oases there is little or no cultivation. North-west of Muscat the coastal plain, known as the Batinah, is fertile and prosperous. The date gardens extend for over 150 miles. The Batinah dates are famous for their flavour; they ripen in the first half of July, well before the Basra dates. The coastline between the capital, Muscat, and the province of Dhofar is barren. The fertile province of Dhofar lies on the south-eastern coast of Arabia. Sugar-cane is grown and cattle are raised. Its principal town is Salalah on the coast, while Murbat is the port.

In the valleys of the interior, as well as on the Batinah, date cultivation has reached a high level, and there are possibilities of agricultural development were the water supply more certain. The average annual crop of dates is 6,000 tons, most of which is exported to India. Camels are bred in large numbers by the inland tribes. There are no industries of any importance.

AREA AND POPULATION. The area has been estimated at about 82,000 sq. miles (212,000 sq. km) and the population at 750,000, chiefly Arabs; of these, some 40,000 live in Dhofar. The town of Muscat is the capital (population, 6,000). Formerly of some commercial importance, it has now lost most of its trade to the adjacent town of Matrah (population, 14,000), which is the starting point for the trade routes into the interior. The population of both towns consists of pure Arabs, Indians, Pakistanis and Negroes; numerous merchants are Khojas (from Sind and Kutch) and Hindus (mostly from Gujarat and Bombay). Other ports are Sohar, Khaburah and Sur; none, however, affords shelter from bad weather.

The port of Gwadur and a small tract of country on the Balúchistán coast of the Gulf of Oman were handed over to Pakistan on 8 Sept. 1958.

The **Kuria Muria** islands were ceded to the United Kingdom in 1854 by the Sultan of Muscat and Oman for the purpose of a cable station. On 30 Nov. 1967 the islands were retroceded to the Sultan of Muscat and Oman, in accordance with the wishes of the population.

Ruler: The present Sultan is Qabus bin Said (born Dec. 1940). He took over from his father Said bin Taimur, on 24 July 1970 in a Palace *coup.*

National flag: Red.

The Treaty of Friendship, Commerce and Navigation between Britain and the Sultan, signed on 20 Dec. 1951, reaffirmed the close ties which have existed between the British Government and the Sultanate of Oman for over a century and a half.

FINANCE. Currency. The *Rial Saidi* which is equal to £1 sterling was introduced into the Sultanate on 7 May 1970. It is divided into *baizas*. There are notes of 100, 250 and 500 baiza and 1, 5 and 10 Rial Saidi and coins of 2, 5, 10, 20, 50 and 100 baiza.

Budget. Annual revenue from customs duties is about £1m. For oil revenues *see* below.

DEFENCE. The air force, formed in 1959, has 12 BAC 167 Strikemaster light jet attack aircraft, 3 Caribou, 6 Skyvans and 3 Beaver light transports, and 10 helicopters for security duties.

The army is of approximately brigade strength.

DEVELOPMENT. Several public buildings have been completed or are in the course of construction including a post office, a secretariat, a girls' school, flats for government staff and hospitals at Rui and Taua'am. The fresh water pipeline from Sib to Muscat (over 33 miles) has been completed. Work on the construction of a new port at Muttrah has been started and a survey for 242 miles of road to Sohar along the Batinah coast and to Nizwa in the interior is being undertaken. The Sultan has put forward some of his own plans for future development which include agricultural expansion, water resources throughout the country to be surveyed and developed, a survey of the radio and television requirements of the country to be carried out, a public transport system to be established and roads improved.

OIL. In 1937 a 75-year oil concession was granted to Petroleum Development (Oman) Ltd (a subsidiary of I.P.C.). A concession covering Dhofar was granted in 1953 to Dhofar Cities Service Petroleum Corporation; this was transferred to MECOM, who abandoned it in 1967. In 1969 the Dhofar concession was taken up by P.D. (O.) Ltd.

In 1964 Petroleum Development (Oman) Ltd (now a subsidiary of Royal Dutch Shell, C.F.P. and Partex) announced that drilling had proved sufficient reserves to go into commercial production. The export of crude oil started in 1967, at a forecast initial rate of 7m. tons per annum; by the end of 1969 the rate was 350,000 bbls per day, equivalent to 17m. tons in a full year. The route is by a pipeline through the Sumail gap to the terminal at Mina al Fahl a few miles west of Muscat town. The P.D.O. concession covers Oman and its territorial waters; a German group, including Wintershall, has the Gulf of Oman off-shore concession and begun drilling off the coast near Sohar.

COMMERCE. Trade is mainly with UK, India, Pakistan and the Persian Gulf States. In the calendar year 1969 imports amounted to £5,619,167 (1968: £4,044,761), excluding duty-free imports for government and oil company use. The overall import figure would be about £12m. Chief imports were rice, wheat flour, sugar, cement, vehicles and accessories, cigarettes, coffee, cotton piece-goods and building materials. The main countries exporting to Oman in 1969 were UK, India, Pakistan, Australia, Singapore and Thailand.

Exports, excluding oil, consist of dates, dried limes, dried fish, tobacco leaf and frankincense, valued at about £800,000 annually.

Trade with UK (British Board of Trade returns, in £1,000 sterling):

	1965	1966	1967	1968	1969	1970
Imports to UK	9	16	1,075	11,086	10,368	7,813
Exports from UK	2,178	3,071	2,313	2,781	5,280 }	7,791
Re-exports from UK	26	56	35	114	67 }	

SHIPPING. In 1969, 182 ships called at Muscat and 46 at Mina al Fahal. In addition, 218 tankers called at Mina al Fahl and took on 119·2m. bbls of crude oil.

ROADS. The road Muscat–Matrah continues as a motorable track for 260 miles up the coast to Khor Fakkan *via* Kalba at the far end of the Batinah. Hajar,

Boshar and Qariyat are also connected by motorable tracks with Matrah. Cars run frequently between Muscat and the towns in the Batinah, *via* Shinas and the Wadi al Khor to Sharjah, and up various *wadis* to the interior.

AVIATION. Gulf Aviation run a 4 times a week service from Bahrain to Muscat *via* Doha, and Dubai. The airport at Bait al Falaj is 5 miles from Muscat.

POST. A Sultanate post office operates in Muscat. Cable and Wireless, Ltd maintain a telegraph office at Muscat and an automatic telephone system which includes Matrah (240 telephones) and Saeh-el-Maleh, the oil company terminal. Telephone and telex connexions with Bahrain serves to establish communication with other parts of the world.

WEIGHTS AND MEASURES. The weights in use are 1 *kiyas* = the weight of 6 dollars of 5·9375 oz.; 24 kiyas = 1 Muscat *maund*; 10 maunds = 1 *farásala*; 200 maunds = 1 *bahár*. Rice is sold by the bag; other cereals by the following measures: 40 *palis* = 1 *ferrah*; 20 ferrah = 1 *khandi*.

British Consul-General: D. G. Crawford.
Indian Consul-General: M. L. Suri.
USA Consul: Lee F. Dinsmore (resident in Dhahran).

There are also West German and Netherlands Consuls-General, resident in Kuwait and Baghdad respectively.

Phillips, W., *Unknown Oman*. London, 1967.—*Oman: a history*. London, 1968
Thesiger, W., *Arabian Sands*. London, 1959

PANAMA
República de Panamá

HISTORY. A revolution, inspired by the USA, led to the separation of Panama from the United States of Colombia and the declaration of its independence on 3 Nov. 1903. The *de facto* Government was on 13 Nov. recognized by the USA, and soon afterwards by the other Powers. In 1914 Colombia agreed to recognize the independence of Panama. This treaty was ratified by the USA and Colombia in 1921, and on 8 May 1924 diplomatic relations between Colombia and Panama were established.

For the treaties regulating the relations between Panama and the United States see p. 1210.

CONSTITUTION AND GOVERNMENT. The new constitution of 1 March 1946 continued the existing provisions for a National Assembly of 42 members. The deputies' mandate was for 4 years. The Assembly met annually on 1 Oct. The term of the President of the Republic, elected by direct vote, was 4 years, and he was not eligible for the two succeeding terms. Women had equal rights with men.

There were normally 2 vice-presidents, elected every 4 years by direct popular vote, and a cabinet of 7 ministers nominated by the President, who might attend and address the legislature but could not vote. The Comptroller General was elected by the National Assembly for 4 years.

On 11 October 1968, however, the newly elected President, Dr Arnulfo Arias, was deposed after only 11 days in office, in a 'coup' conducted by the National Guard. The National Assembly was suspended and a provisional government set up consisting of a two-man military Junta and a civilian cabinet. In Dec. 1969 the military members of the Junta resigned and were replaced by civilians.

Commander-in-Chief of the National Guard: Brig.-Gen. Omar Torrijos.
President of the Junta: Demetrio Lakas.
Member of the Junta: Arturo Sucre.
Minister for Foreign Affairs: Juan Antonio Tack.

The official language is Spanish.

National flag: Rectangle of 4 quarters: white with blue star, blue, white with red star, red.

National anthem: Alcanzamos por fin la victoria (words by J. de la Ossa; tune by Santos Jorge, 1903).

AREA AND POPULATION. Extreme length is about 480 miles; breadth between 37 and 110 miles; coastline, 426 miles on the Atlantic and 767 on the Pacific; total area (excluding the Canal Zone) is 29,201 sq. miles (75,650 sq. km); population according to the census of 10 May 1970 was 1,414,737 (preliminary figures). No recent figures are available of the racial composition of the population; the 1940 census gave 12% white, 14·5% Negro, 72% mixed and 1·5% other races. There are approximately 10,000 British subjects, chiefly coloured people from the West Indies.

The capital is Panama City, on the Pacific coast; population, census 1970, 412,000. There are 9 provinces (with populations, 1970) as follows (the capitals in brackets): Bocas del Toro (Bocas del Toro), 41,700; Chiriquí (David), 232,600; Coclé (Penonomé), 117,600; Colón (Colón), 134,500; Los Santos (Las Tablas), 71,100; Herrera (Chitré), 73,100; Darién (La Palma), 25,200; Panama (Panama City), 568,900; Veraguas (Santiago), 150,200. The port of Colón on the Atlantic coast had 65,600. Smaller ports on the Pacific are Aguadulce, Pedregal, Montijo, Puerto Mutis and Puerto Armuelles; on the Atlantic, Bocas del Toro, Almirante, Portobello, Mandinga and Permé.

Birth rate, 1968, was 38·7 per 1,000 population; death rate, 7·2; marriage rate, 18·8; infantile death rate, 41·2 per 1,000 live births. The figures exclude the tribal Indians.

RELIGION. The 1950 census showed that 95% of the population was Roman Catholic and 5% Protestant. There is freedom of religious worship and separation of Church and State. Clergymen may teach in the schools but may not hold public office.

EDUCATION. Elementary education is compulsory for all children from 7 to 15 years of age, with an estimated 221,692 students in schools throughout the Republic in 1968; 1,455 official primary schools had 208,817 pupils and 64 private ones, 12,875; 45 official secondary schools had 42,147 pupils, and 145 private ones, 27,199. The University of Panama at Panama City, inaugurated on 7 Oct. 1935, had a total enrolment (1968) of 8,946 students in the schools of law, science and other professional subjects; the university was granted autonomy on 28 Sept. 1946. Up to the academic year 1956–57 the university was a centre of evening studies (except for the faculty of medicine); since 1956–57 all faculties hold day classes as well. A new site, called University City, on the outskirts of Panama City was inaugurated in June 1950. The Catholic university Sta. Maria La Antigua, inaugurated on 27 May 1965, had 444 students in 1968.

The 1960 census showed that 14% of the population over 10 years old were illiterate, excluding the tribal Indians (compared with 28·3% in 1950).

CINEMAS. There were, in Dec. 1969, 82 cinemas, of which 40 were in the district of Panama. All films must have Spanish subtitles.

NEWSPAPERS. Of the 4 daily newspapers published in the capital, 1 has both morning and afternoon editions and 2 have separate English editions. There is also an English weekly with a Spanish supplement, catering for the large British West Indian community in Panama.

JUSTICE. The death penalty does not exist. The Supreme Court consists of 9 justices appointed by the executive with the approval of the National Assembly, one every 2 years to serve 18 years.

FINANCE. Currency. The monetary unit is the *balboa*, which is of the same size and fineness as the US silver dollar but is maintained equivalent to the gold dollar. Other coins whose metallic content is required by law to correspond exactly to that of similar US coins are the half-balboa (equal to 50 cents US); the quarter and tenth of a balboa piece; a cupro-nickel coin of 5 cents, and a copper coin of 1 cent. US coinage is also legal tender. Volume of the currency has not been disclosed since 31 Dec. 1950, when it stood at 1·5m.; 5·1m. balboas of Panamanian coin had been minted up to 31 Dec. 1963. The only paper currency used is that of the USA.

Budget. The budget for calendar years since 1967 balanced as follows (in balboas; 1 balboa = US$1): 1967, 114·9m.; 1968, 130m.; 1969, 130m.; 1970, 162·7m.

The revenue includes the rent paid by the US Government for the Canal (US$1·93m. per annum); other transactions with the Canal Zone accounted for US$133·4m. in 1968. Panamanian citizens working in the Canal Zone are now subject to taxation by Panama.

The funded internal debt on 31 Dec. 1968 amounted to 97,862,500 balboas, and the external debt to 70,833,400 balboas.

DEFENCE. The Republic has no Army or Navy to support, but there are 2 coastguard patrol vessels, and compulsory military service may be imposed in case of need. The National Police Force has an authorized strength of 4,700 officers and men.

AGRICULTURE. Of the whole area (1961 census), only 23·9% is developed, 4·3% is cultivated, 10·6% is natural or artificial pasture land and 9% is fallow. Of the remainder only a small part is cultivated, though the land is rich in resources. About 60% of the country's food requirements are imported. In Jan. 1953 the Institute for Economic Development, a semi-governmental organization, was formed with large powers, *e.g.*, to buy up leading crops at fixed prices and to loan machinery to farmers. Of the land under cultivation, 18% is owned and 59% is usufructuary. The most important export product is bananas, grown by an affiliate of the United Fruit Company and shipped to the USA. Exports, 1968, 17·4m. stems. Most important food crop, for home consumption, is rice, grown on 80% of the farms, Panama's *per capita* consumption is very high. Output of rough rice from 128,600 hectares, was 3,594,000 quintals in 1968–69. Other products are maize (100,300 hectares, yielding 1·85m. quintals in 1968–69), cocoa, abacá fibres, abacá seeds, coffee and coconuts. Beer, whisky, rum, 'seco', anice and gin are produced. Coffee is grown in the province of Chiriquí, near the Costa Rican frontier; total production in 1968–69 was 99,300 quintals, and small amounts were exported to West Germany and USA. The country has great timber resources, notably mahogany. According to the livestock estimate of July 1968 there were 1,118,600 cattle, 173,800 pigs and 3,002,400 poultry. Hides are among minor articles of export.

ENERGY. Production of electric energy, 1968, amounted to 484,618 Mw (Panama City and Colón). Gas production was 696,960 cu. ft.

INDUSTRY. Local industries include cigarettes, clothing, food processing, shoes, soap, cement factories; foreign firms are being encouraged to establish industries, and a petrol refinery is operating in Colón. In 1968 a United Nations mineral survey team discovered what may prove to be valuable copper deposits in the Colón province.

TOURISM. In 1967, 132,166 foreigners (excluding passengers in transit) visited Panama, spending an estimated 18·8m. balboas.

COMMERCE. The imports and exports (including re-exports), for 6 calendar years are as follows (in 1,000 balboas; 1 balboa = US$1):

	Imports	Exports		Imports	Exports
1963	162,776	48,561	1966	214,530	79,744
1964	165,390	60,988	1967	229,273	86,355
1965	189,620	70,169	1968	243,460	95,334

The USA have the right to import into the Canal Zone supplies of all descriptions required for canal construction, maintenance and protection and for the use of their employees, free of all taxes.

The huge adverse trade balance is mainly with the USA and is due to the heavy import of consumer goods for sale to the Canal Zone employees and to the big transient population. In 1968 the USA furnished 38·4% of Panama's imports and took 76·6% of her exports. The UK was the sixth largest supplier.

A Free Zone has been constructed at Colón for the storage, processing or sale of goods in transit; a number of US manufacturers and a British firm have leased warehouses and begun operations.

Chief exports (virtually all to the USA) in 1968 (in 1,000 balboas or dollars) were: Bananas, 53,046; fresh shrimps, 9,727; cacao, 232; coffee, 561; sugar (cane and beet), 4,623; fishmeal, 954; petroleum products, 18,857.

Chief imports, 1968, were valued (in 1m. balboas f.o.b.): Fuel, minerals and similar, . . ; food, 19·9; chemicals, 23·9; manufactured goods, 55·9; machinery and transport material, 58·5.

Total trade between Panama (including Canal Zone) and UK (British Board of Trade returns, in £1,000 sterling):

	1966	1967	1968	1969	1970
Imports to UK	1,786	2,070	2,451	2,699	1,839
Exports from UK [1]	5,443	6,544	5,999	7,575 }	8,765
Re-exports from UK	89	123	114	171 }	

[1] Including new ships built for foreign owners and registered in Panama.

SHIPPING. Ships under Panamanian registry on 31 Dec. 1968 numbered 1,884 of 5,037,822 tons; most of these ships elect Panamanian registry because fees are low and labour laws lenient. All the international maritime traffic for Colón and Panama runs through the Canal Zone ports of Cristóbal and Balboa; Almirante is used for both the provincial and international trade.

RAILWAYS. The Panama Railroad (owned by the Panama Canal Company), which connects Ancón on the Pacific with Cristóbal on the Atlantic, is the principal railway. It is 47·61 miles long and lies entirely within the Canal Zone territory. As most vessels unload their cargo at Cristóbal (Colón), on the Atlantic side, the greater portion of the merchandise destined for Panama City is brought overland by the Panama Railroad. Between David and La Concepción there is a line 18 miles long, which has now been extended to the port of Puerto Armuelles. From Almirante and Guabito (property of the United Fruit Company), a third railway runs to Suretka on the Costa Rican border (51 miles).

The Chiriqui National Railroad operates 169 km with a terminus at Armuelles.

ROADS. Panama had on 31 Dec. 1968, 6,720·5 km of roads. The road from Panama City westward to the cities of David and Concepción, with several branches, is part of the Pan-American Highway. From Concepción it continues towards the frontier to link up with the Costa Rican road system. Construction of the last 26 miles of the 300-mile road was completed in June 1967; it was aided by an Export-Import Bank loan of US$3·5m. granted in Sept. 1964. A concrete highway, maintained by the USA, connects Panama City and Colón.

On 31 Dec. 1968 registered motor vehicles, private and commercial, numbered 53,433; this excludes vehicles owned by Government departments, and in the Canal Zone.

AVIATION. Commercial aviation has developed rapidly. PANAM, Braniff Airways, KLM and other international companies operate at Tocumen Airport (17 miles from Panama City), which takes jets. The Compañía Panameña de Aviación (COPA) and (RAPSA) provide a local service between Panama City and the provincial towns, and internationally, to other points in Central America. In 1968 a total of 377,972 passengers arrived by air, of whom 201,818 were in transit.

POST. There are telegraph cables from Panama to North America and Central and South American ports, and from Colón to the USA and Europe. There is also inter-continental communication by satellite. There are 50 licensed commercial broadcasting stations, nearly all operated by private companies, one of which functions in the Canal Zone. There are 3 television stations, one of them run by the US Army in the Canal Zone. Number of telephones in Dec. 1968 was 53,020 in Panama City and 6,847 in Colón.

BANKING. The National Bank of Panama (not a central bank) on 31 March 1968 had (in balboas or dollars) capital of 7·3m., reserves of 1·4m., current deposits of 73·1m. and loans, net outstanding, of 49·3m. In 1956 the National Bank took over the 4 provincial banks formerly operated by the Institute of Economic Development. The First National City Bank and the Chase Manhattan Bank of New York have branches in Panama City and Balboa (CZ), Colón and David, the latter also in Chitré. The Bank of London and Montreal opened a branch in Panama City in June 1966. Other foreign-owned banks include the Bank of America, as well as Colombian, French and Spanish banks.

WEIGHTS AND MEASURES. English weights and measures are in general use; those of the metric system are also used.

DIPLOMATIC REPRESENTATIVES

Panama maintains embassies in:

Argentina	France	Nicaragua
Bolivia	Germany (West)	Peru
Brazil	Guatemala	Spain
Colombia	Haiti	UAR
Costa Rica	Honduras	UK
Chile	Italy	USA
China (Taiwan)	Jamaica	Uruguay
Ecuador	Japan	Vatican
El Salvador	Mexico	Venezuela

Diplomatic relations also exist with:

Austria	Lebanon	Sweden
Belgium	Netherlands	Switzerland
Denmark	Norway	Turkey
Greece	Paraguay	Yugoslavia
Israel	Poland	

OF PANAMA IN GREAT BRITAIN (23 Billiter St., EC3)

Ambassador: Dr Jorge E. Reyes Medina.

There are consular representatives at Birmingham, Glasgow, Liverpool, London and Newcastle upon Tyne.

OF GREAT BRITAIN IN PANAMA

Ambassador: Dugald Malcolm, CMG, CVO, TD.
First Secretary: C. D. Sanderson (*Head of Chancery and Consul*).
Defence Attaché: Cdr F. Bromilow, RN (resides at Lima).

There is also a Consul at Colón.

OF PANAMA IN THE USA (2601–29th St. NW, Washington, D.C., 20008)

Ambassador: Lic. José A. de la Ossa.

Minister-Counsellor: Lic. Henry Kourany. *Secretaries:* Lic. Lawrence Chewning; Lic. Marina Mayo. *Labour Attaché:* George Fisher.

OF THE USA IN PANAMA

Ambassador: Robert M. Sayre.

Deputy Chief of Mission: Herbert B. Thompson. *Heads of Sections:* Sam Moskowitz (*Political*); Louis Mark (*Economic*); John Mullin (*Commercial*); George Huey (*Consul*); Francis P. McCormick (*Administrative*); Alexander Firfer (*AID*).

BOOKS OF REFERENCE

STATISTICAL INFORMATION. The Comptroller-General of the Republic (Contraloria General de la República, Calle 35 y Avenida 6, Panama City) publishes an annual report and other statistical publications.

Fiscal Survey of Panamá. Johns Hopkins Press, 1964
Biesanz, J. M., and *The People of Panama.* Columbia Univ. Press, 1955
Castillero, Ernesto J., *Historia de Panamá.* 5th ed. Panama City, 1965
Howarth, D., *The Golden Isthmus.* London, 1966
Larsen, H. and M., *The forests of Panama.* London, 1964
Susto, J. A., *An Introduction to Panamanian Bibliography* (Publications of the National Library, No. 4). Panama, 1946

NATIONAL LIBRARY. Biblioteca Nacional, Departamento de Información. Calle 22, Panama.

THE PANAMA CANAL AND THE CANAL ZONE

On 18 Nov. 1903 a treaty between the USA and the Republic of Panama was signed making it possible for the US to build and operate a canal connecting the Atlantic and Pacific oceans through the Isthmus of Panama. The treaty granted the US in perpetuity the use, occupation and control of a Canal Zone, approximately 10 miles wide, in which the US would possess full sovereign rights 'to the entire exclusion of the exercise by the Republic of Panama of any such sovereign rights, power or authority'. In return the US guaranteed the independence of the Republic and agreed to pay the Republic $10m. and an annuity of $250,000. The US purchased the French rights and properties—the French had been labouring from 1879 to 1899 in an effort to build the Canal—for $40m. and in addition, paid private landholders within what would be the Canal Zone a mutually agreeable price for their properties.

The treaty of 1936 increased the annuity to $430,000 and, as desired by Panama, withdrew the guarantee of independence. In 1955 the annuity was increased to $1·93m., and the Panama Canal Company turned over to the Republic the Panama City railroad yards and other properties valued at $22m. At the end of 1962 the US completed the construction of a high-level bridge over the Pacific entrance of the Canal, and the flags of Panama and the US were flown jointly over areas of the Canal Zone under civilian authority.

Governor of the Canal Zone and President of the Panama Canal Company: Maj.-Gen. W. P. Leber, US Army.
Lieut.-Governor and Vice-President: Col. Richard S. Hartline, US Army.

The Canal Zone Government is responsible for such governmental functions as police and fire protection, postal service, and schools and hospital services (such as the Gorgas hospital, greatly enlarged in 1964). The Panama Canal

Company is concerned primarily with the actual operation of the Canal. The Panama Canal has not increased tolls since 1914 and has operated at a minimal net margin averaging about $4m. per year, after paying its own expenses as well as reimbursing the US Treasury for the net cost of the Canal Zone Government and paying interest on the $490m. net investment of the US Government in the Canal enterprise.

The area of the Canal Zone, including land and water, is 647·29 sq miles (1,676·3 sq. km). The water area of the zone, including the water area within the 3-mile limit from the Atlantic and Pacific ends, is 274·97 sq. miles.

The total civilian and military population of the Canal Zone (July 1970) was 50,344, of whom 39,084 are US citizens. The total full-time force employed by the Panama Canal Company and the Canal Zone Government on 30 June 1970 numbered 4,193 US citizens and 11,731 others, mostly Panamanian citizens.

There are 144·4 miles of improved streets and highways in the zone, exclusive of those within Armed Forces reservations. Motor vehicles number over 18,000.

The Canal was opened to commerce on 15 Aug. 1914. It is 85 ft above sea-level. It is 51·2 statute miles in length from deep water in the Caribbean Sea to deep water in the Pacific ocean, and 36 miles from shore to shore. The channel ranges in bottom-width from 300 to 1,000 ft; the widening of Gaillard Cut to a minimum width of 500 ft was completed in 1969. The average time of a vessel in Canal waters is 15 hours, 8 of which are in transit through the Canal proper. A map showing the Panama, Suez and Kiel canals on the same scale will be found in THE STATESMAN'S YEAR-BOOK, 1959.

Particulars of the ocean-going commercial traffic through the canal are given as follows (vessels of 300 tons Panama Canal net and 500 displacement tons and over; cargo in long tons):

Fiscal year ending 30 June	North-bound (Pacific to Atlantic)		South-bound (Atlantic to Pacific)		Total		Tolls levied (in $)
	Vessels	Cargo	Vessels	Cargo	Vessels	Cargo	
1967	6,140	32,201,920	6,272	53,991,510	12,412	86,193,430	76,768,605
1968	6,588	35,190,046	6,611	61,360,119	13,199	96,550,165	83,907,063
1969	6,610	36,640,325	6,536	64,732,419	13,146	101,372,744	87,423,430
1970	6,664	40,595,595	6,994	73,661,665	13,658	114,257,260	94,654,468

In the fiscal year ending 30 June 1970, of the 13,658 toll-paying ships which passed through the canal 1,601 were Liberian; 1,591 British; 1,520 US; 1,323 Norwegian; 1,178 Japanese; 1,108 West German; 799 Panamanian; 568 Greek; 493 Netherlands; 462 Swedish, and 434 Danish.

Books of Reference

STATISTICAL INFORMATION. The Panama Canal Information Office, Balboa Heights, Canal Zone. *Information Officer:* Frank A. Baldwin.

Annual Reports on the Panama Canal, by the Governor of the Canal Zone
Rules and Regulations Governing Navigation of the Panama Canal. Balboa Heights, CZ *or* Washington, DC
Baxter, R. R., *The Law of international waterways.* Harvard Univ. Press, 1964
Du Val, M. P., *Cadiz to Cathay: the diplomatic struggle for the Panama Canal.* 2nd ed. Stanford Univ. Press, 1947.—*And the Mountains will Move: the building of the Panama Canal.* Stanford Univ. Press, 1947
Mack, Gerstle, *The Land Divided.* New York, 1944

PARAGUAY
República del Paraguay

HISTORY. The Republic of Paraguay gained its independence from Spain on 14 May 1811. In 1814 Dr José Gaspar Rodríguez de Francia was elected dictator, and in 1816 perpetual dictator (el Supremo), by the National Assembly. He died 20 Sept. 1840. In 1844 a new constitution was adopted, under which Carlos Antonio López (first elected in 1842, died 10 Sept. 1862) and his son, Francisco Solano López, ruled until 1870. During the devastating war against

Brazil, Argentina and Uruguay (1865–70) Paraguay lost probably 500,000 men. Argentina, in Aug. 1942, and Brazil, in May 1943, voided the reparations which Paraguay had never paid. Further severe losses were incurred during the war with Bolivia (1932–35) over territorial claims in the Chaco. A peace treaty by which Paraguay obtained most of the area her troops had conquered was signed in July 1938.

CONSTITUTION AND GOVERNMENT. A new constitution replacing that of 1940 was drawn up by a Constituent Convention in which all legally recognized political parties were represented and was signed into law on 25 Aug. 1967. It provides for a two-chamber parliament consisting of a 30-seat Senate and a 60-seat Chamber of Deputies. Two-thirds of the seats in each Chamber are allocated to the majority party and the remaining one-third shared among the minority parties in proportion to the votes cast. Voting is compulsory for all citizens over 18. The President, who has wide emergency powers, is elected for 5 years and can be re-elected for a further term. He appoints the Cabinet and during parliamentary recess can govern by decree through the Council of State, the members of which are representatives of the Government, the armed forces and other bodies.

The first elections under the new constitution were held on 11 Feb. 1968. The Senate consists of 20 Colorados, 9 Radicals and 1 Liberal; the Chamber of Deputies, of 40 Colorados, 16 Radicals, 3 Liberals and 1 Febrerista.

President: Gen. Alfredo Stroessner, Commander-in-Chief, elected 11 July 1954 to complete the presidential period of his predecessor; assumed office 15 Aug. He was re-elected as 'Colorado' candidate in 1958, 1963 and 1968.

The following is a list of past presidents since 1940, with the date on which each took office:

Gen. Higinio Morínigo, 7 Sept. 1940 (resigned).
Dr Juan Manuel Frutos, 3 June 1948.[1]
Dr J. Natalicio González, 15 Aug. 1948 (deposed).
Gen. Raimundo Rolón, 30 Jan. 1949.

Dr Felipe Molas López, 26 Feb. 1949[1] (resigned).
Dr Federico Chávez, 16 July 1950 (resigned).
Tomás Tomero Pereira, 4 May 1954.

[1] Provisional, *i.e.*, following a *coup d'état*.

The President has a cabinet of 11 ministers.

National flag: Red, white, blue (horizontal); the white stripe charged with the arms of the republic on the obverse, and, on the reverse, with a lion and the inscription *Paz y Justicia*—the only flag in the world with different obverse and reverse.

National anthem: ¡Paraguayos, república o muerte! (words by F. Acuña de Figueroa; tune by F. Dupey).

The country is divided into 2 sections: the 'Oriental', east of Paraguay River, and the 'Occidental', west of the same river. The Oriental section is divided into 13 departments, subdivided into 133 *partidos*. The more important departments are supervised by a *Delegado* appointed by and directly responsible to the central government. Municipalities are administered by elected municipal councils. The Occidental section, or Chaco, is under military government and divided into 3 departments (with 4 *partidos*).

AREA AND POPULATION. The area of the Oriental section is officially estimated at 159,827 sq. km (61,705 sq. miles) and the Occidental section at 246,925 sq. km (95,337 sq. miles), making the total area of the republic 406,752 sq. km (157,042 sq. miles).

The population at the census taken in 1970 was 2,395,614. The capital, Asunción, had 437,136 inhabitants.

The 16 departments and principal towns had the following populations at the time of the 1970 census:

Concepción	110,555	San Ignació	18,408
Concepción	52,826	Santa Rosa	17,120
Horqueta	29,090	Paraguarí	228,192
San Pedro	127,767	Ybycuí	28,006
San Pedro	26,797	Carapeguá	27,991
San Estanislao	25,737	Yaguarón	17,860
De la Cordillera	199,621	Alto Paraná	67,497
Pirebebuy	23,869	Hernandarias	43,883
Arroyos y Esteros	19,935	Central	256,458
Caacupé	21,732	Lambaré	21,506
Caraguatay	18,895	Luque	35,790
Guaira	132,772	Itá	26,913
Villarrica	38,052	Capiatá	23,994
Caaguazú	226,657	San Lorenzo	20,458
Coronel Oviedo	59,307	Ñeembucú	69,639
Caaguazú	73,583	Pilar	15,324
San José	15,293	Amambay	67,917
Caazapá	105,578	Pedro Juan Caballero	52,005
Caazapá	23,349	Presidente Hayes	42,141
Yuty	23,788	Villa Hayes	34 648
Itapuá	201,670	Boquerón	47,033
Encarnación	47,333	Mcal. Estigarribia	36,788
San Pedro del Paraná	29,255	Olimpo	4,940
Misiones	74,023		

Number of births, 1968, was 57,882; deaths 14,120 (of which about 2,500 for children less than 1 year old).

The population is overwhelmingly *mestizo* (mixed Spanish and Guarani Indian) forming a homogeneous stock. There are some 40,000 unassimilated Indians of other tribal origin, in the Chaco and the forests of eastern Paraguay. There are some small traces of Negro descent. About half the population speak only Guaraní; some 4% speak only Spanish; the rest are bilingual.

Mennonites who arrived in 3 groups (1927, 1930 and 1947) are settled in the Chaco and Oriental Paraguay and were estimated in 1969 to number 13,000, of whom 2,000 came from Canada and 11,000 from Germany. The Japanese colonists in the Oriental section, who first came in 1935, were reckoned to number 7,000 in 1969. Under an agreement signed with Japan in 1959 up to 85,000 Japanese were to be admitted over 30 years. An agreement with Korea was signed in 1966.

RELIGION. Religious liberty is guaranteed by the 1967 constitution. Article 6 thereof recognizes Roman Catholicism as the official religion of the country. The same article disposes that relations between Paraguay and the Holy See shall be regulated by concordats or other bilateral agreements, but no such agreements have yet been negotiated.

The Roman Catholic Church is organized into the Archdiocese of Asunción, 3 other dioceses (San Juan Bautista de las Misiones, Concepción and Villarrica); 4 Prelatures (Coronel Oviedo, Encarnación, Alto Paraná and Caacupé); and 2 Vicariates Apostolic (Chaco and Pilcomayo). The bishops meet in a Conference of Paraguayan Bishops. Only civil marriages are legally valid. There are numerous non-Catholic communities, the largest of whom are the Mennonites. There is a small Anglican church in Asunción, with missions in the Chaco, which comes under the jurisdiction of a Bishop of the South American Missionary Society resident at Salta in the northern Argentine.

EDUCATION. Education is free and nominally compulsory, but schools are not everywhere available, and the system has been extensively revised to provide, *inter alia*, primary education for adults. Illiteracy is estimated at 32%. In 1968 there were 2,748 government primary schools and 253 private schools, with about 400,000 pupils and 12,729 teachers; 437 secondary schools had 45,000 pupils. The National University in Asunción had, in 1969, approximately 5,500 students and 637 professors. In 1968 the Catholic University and associated colleges had 2,000 students. Many university students attend on a part-time basis.

D D

CINEMAS (1968). Cinemas numbered 45 in Asunción. The larger country towns usually have an outdoor cinema.

NEWSPAPERS (1969). There are 5 daily newspapers, 4 based on Asunción and one provincial, with an aggregate circulation of about 80,000. Some of the political opposition papers have been suspended by the government.

JUSTICE. The highest court is the Supreme Court with 5 members. There are special Chambers of Appeal for civil and commercial cases, and criminal cases. Judges of first instance deal with civil, commercial and criminal cases in 6 departments. Minor cases are dealt with by Justices of the Peace.

The Attorney-General represents the State in all jurisdictions, with representatives in each judicial department and in every jurisdiction. In matters of revenue, taxes, etc., the State is represented by the Abogado del Tesoro.

FINANCE. Currency. The *guaraní* was established on 5 Oct. 1943 equal to 100 old paper pesos. Total monetary circulation was Gs.5,773m. in July 1967; of this, notes were Gs.2,671m. and the remainder money at sight.

Rate of exchange, Sept. 1969: 126 guaraníes = US$1; 295–305 guaraníes = £1.

Budget. Revenue and expenditure, in Gs.1m. for calendar years:

	1964	1965	1966[1]	1967[1]	1968[1]	1969
Revenue	4,496·0	5,459·3	5,542·3	7,744·7	8,973	9,994
Expenditure	4,090·3	4,492·7	6,030·3	8,587·0	9,889	10,441

[1] Estimate.

The 1970 budget provided Gs.7,662m. for current and 2,780m. for capital expenditure: National defence, 1,748m.; public works, 1,650m., and education, 1,147m.; taxes on imports and exports, 1,861m.; exchange surcharge, 1,023m.; excise, 2,501.

Total external debt outstanding at the end of June 1968, including undisbursed sums (which amounted to US$41m.), was US$111m.

DEFENCE. The army, navy and air forces are separate services under a single command. The President of the Republic is the active Commander-in-Chief. The armed forces total about 13,500 officers and men. Of these, the Army account for about 11,000 (75% conscripts), the Navy about 1,700 (25% conscripts) and the Air Force about 800 (25% conscripts). There are also about 6,500 armed police (75% conscripts). Military service is compulsory between the ages of 18 and 20 but there are many exemptions.

The main units of the Army are: a Presidential Escort Regiment, 5 infantry regiments, a Cavalry Division with 4 regiments, an Artillery Division and an Engineer Command with 5 battalions.

The Navy consists of 5 armoured river gunboats (2 of 636 tons built in Italy and 3 *ex*-Argentine minesweepers), 3 river patrol boats and a training ship (*ex*-tug).

The Air Force came into being in the early thirties as a combat service, but now has only transport and training formations. These are equipped with US aircraft of wartime origin, including a number of C-54 4-engined and C-47 twin-engined transports and T-6 Texan armed basic trainers. HQ and flying school are at Campo Grande, Asunción.

PRODUCTION. In 1968 the gross domestic product was estimated at about US$528m., of which 33·6% originated in agriculture, livestock and forestry; 15·6% in manufacturing and mining; 3% in construction, and 47·8% in trade, services, etc. The labour force was estimated at about 690,000, of whom 54·2% were engaged in agriculture, livestock and forestry, and 13·7% in manufacturing and mining.

AGRICULTURE. It is estimated that agriculture absorbs some 2m. hectares, as against 14m. for grasslands and 24m. for woodlands. Small holdings predominate: 89% are of less than 10 hectares.

Area (in hectares) and yield (in metric tons) of the main agricultural products in 1967–68:

	Area	Yield		Area	Yield
Cotton	27,600	30,000	Castor beans	5,380	7,000
Rice	8,040	18,500	Citrus	31,400	27,500
Sugar-cane	20,640	702,000	Tobacco	16,660	20,000
Maize	180,000	180,000	Wheat	19,850	25,000
Manioc	100,260	1,504,000	Soybeans	8,440	13,500
Beans and peas	30,000	18,400	Peanuts	22,500	18,000

Wheat, soybean, cotton, sugar, tobacco, coffee are increasing in importance, as are also essential oils and oilseeds. *Yerba maté*, or strongly flavoured Paraguayan tea, continues to be produced but is declining in importance.

The principal sources of finance for agricultural development are USAID and Interamerican Development Bank loans and, for the wheat programme, suppliers' or other credits administered by the National Development Bank.

Livestock. In 1968 Paraguay had about 5·6m. cattle, 600,000 horses, 625,000 pigs and 415,000 sheep. Jerked beef, corned beef and other animal products are exported. Exports of meat products in 1968 were 17,800 metric tons. In 1968 production of fresh meat was 97,720 metric tons; of preserved meat, 15,000 metric tons; slaughtered livestock was 484,161 for local consumption and 170,135 for 'industrialization'. Paraguay produces and exports salted and dry cattle hides.

FORESTRY. In the Oriental section there are huge reserves of hardwoods and cedars that have scarcely been exploited. Palms, tung and other trees are exploited for their oils. The Japanese are experimenting with mulberries for silk growing. Pines and firs have been introduced under a United Nations project. In the Chaco the accessible Quebracho forests have nearly been worked out but plans are being made to open up new areas. In 1968 production of quebracho extract, from which tannin is made, was 17,428 metric tons.

MINING. Iron, manganese and other minerals have been reported but have not been shown to be commercially exploitable. There are large deposits of limestone, and also salt, kaolin and apetite. *Pennzoil Paraguay* started in 1969 to prospect for oil and natural gas in the northern Chaco.

INDUSTRY. There are 3 main meat-packing plants and other factories producing vegetable oils. A textile industry in Pilar and Asunción meets a large part of local needs. As a result of government restrictions on the export of logs the sawmilling and woodworking industry has recently been expanding. A cement works at Valle-mi, with a capacity of 7,000 bags a day, was inaugurated in Jan. 1970. The oil refinery at Villa Elisa, which has been in operation since 1966, has a production of about 3,500 bbls a day. There are some flour-mills and small match, pharmaceutical, soap, cigarette, footwear, furniture and building materials industries.

ELECTRICITY. The Acaray hydro-electric plant, with a first stage capacity of 45,000 kw., went into operation at the end of 1968 but so far supplies only the Asunción area.

TOURISM. Visitors numbered 111,643 in 1969, 67,793 in 1968.

LABOUR. Trade unionists number about 25,000 (Confederación Paraguaya del Trabajo and Confederación Cristiana de Trabajadores).

A contributory national insurance scheme for all salary and wage earners except civil servants, domestic servants (from 1 Jan. 1967) and railway employees went into effect 1 Jan. 1951.

COMMERCE. Imports and exports since 1963 (in US$1m.):

	1963	1964	1965	1966	1967	1968
Imports	32·6	33·7	44·0	49·5	51·9	72·7
Exports	40·2	49·7	57·3	49·4	50·8	47·5

Chief exports in 1968 included (in US$1m.): Meat products, 13·5; timber, 7·99; oils, 6·1; tobacco, 4·5; cotton, 1·4; quebracho extract, 2; palmitos, 2; coffee, 1·9.

Of the imports in 1968 (principally foodstuffs, vehicles and machinery, chemicals, fuels and textiles; in US$1m.) 15·1 came from USA, 12 from Argentina, 8·9 from W. Germany and 3·8 from the UK. Of the exports, Argentina took 12·7; USA, 11·5; UK, 5·8; W. Germany, 1·9.

The trade between Paraguay and UK (British Board of Trade returns) in £1,000 sterling was as follows:

	1965	1966	1967	1968	1969	1970
Imports to UK	1,910	1,592	2,287	2,721	2,122	2,271
Exports from UK	1,289	1,272	1,259	2,029	2,412 }	2,210
Re-exports from UK	15	23	14	14	38 }	

The import licence and official exchange-market system was abolished on 12 Aug. 1957.

SHIPPING. In flood the Paraguay River, which divides the country into two distinct parts, is navigable for 12-ft-draft vessels as far as Concepción, 180 miles north of Asunción, and for smaller vessels for a further distance of 600 miles northward. Drought conditions often restrict navigation to lighter traffic. The Paraná River is navigable by large boats from Corrientes up to Puerto Aguirre, at the mouth of the Yguazú River. Boats of a few hundred tons capacity navigate the tributary rivers.

Asunción, the chief port, is 950 miles from the sea. In June 1945 the Government formed—after a break of 80 years—a national merchant marine which operates in the river Plate basin, connecting with Argentine, Uruguayan and Brazilian ports. The cargo fleet includes 25 vessels of 300–1,000 tons, 3 tankers of 1,100–1,700 tons, 2 passenger river boats and 1 ocean-going freighter of 713 tons.

RAILWAYS. The President Carlos Antonio López (formerly Paraguay Central) Railway runs from Asunción to Encarnación, on the Río Alto Paraná, with a length of 274 miles (4 ft 8½ in.). The railway was sold to the Paraguayan Government for £200,000 in Oct. 1961. There is a through train service from Asunción to Buenos Aires twice a week.

ROADS. In 1968 there were 6,258 km of roads, of which 638 were paved, 1,025 of gravel and 4,595 of earth. The principal paved roads are Ronte No. 2/7 running from Asunción to the bridge over the Parana at Puerto Presidente Stroessner, and thence down to the ocean at Paranaguá; and Ronte No. 1 to Encarnación in the south. The other main arteries (unpaved) are the road from Coronel Oviedo, on the Asunción–Puerto Presidente Stroessner road, to Pedro Juan Caballero in the north, and the trans-Chaco road which starts from the ferry across the Paraguay River north of Asunción and ends near Nueva Asunción on the Bolivian border. Unpaved roads are closed when it rains. In the Argentine, a paved road starts from Clorinda, opposite Asunción, and provides good communication with Buenos Aires. Motor vehicles, 1967, numbered 18,058, of which 8,433 were motor cars; 1,937 buses; 4,520 pick-ups and 3,186 lorries.

AVIATION. International services are furnished by 8 airlines (domestic and foreign). Internal routes are operated by military aircraft and some small private lines.

POST. The national telegraph (137 offices) connects Asunción with Corrientes and Posadas in the Argentine Republic, and thus with the outside world; new direct links have been opened with Germany, USA, Bolivia and Chile. In addition, 34 stations are operated by the President Carlos Antonio López Railway; total, 2,070 miles. Three companies (12 stations) offer radio-telegraph and telex services to several countries. The telephone system has been under government control since 5 Oct. 1945; a new government agency, the National Telephone Administration, took over the telecommunication services in July 1947. Telephone lines, 1949, 5,225 miles; instruments, 1968, 16,048, of which 14,918 were in Asunción and were automatic. There are one state and 7 commercial radio stations in Asunción and one in each of 8 main provincial centres, and a television station in Asunción.

BANKING. The Banco Central del Paraguay opened 1 July 1952 to take over the central banking functions previously assigned to the National Bank of Paraguay, which had opened in March 1943 and been reorganized as the Banco del Paraguay in Sept. 1944 with a monetary, a banking and a mortgage department. The Banco del Paraguay closed in Nov. 1961 and has been replaced, with the aid of a US loan of US$3m., by the Banco Nacional de Fomento; the latter's authorized capital was increased on 13 June 1966 by Gs.600m. to 2,100m.

The Banco Central on 31 Nov. 1969 had gold amounting to US$82,000 and foreign exchange equal to US$5·5m. exclusive of IMF holdings.

The Banco Nacional de Fomento, Bank of London and South America, Ltd, Banco Exterior do Brasil, First National City Bank of New York, Banco de Asunción, Banco Exterior SA, Banco Paraguayo de Comercio, Banco Holandés Unido, Bank of America all have agencies in Asunción and branches in some main towns. From 1 Sept. 1966 their legal cash requirements in local currency must be 42% of total deposits (previously 39%).

WEIGHTS AND MEASURES. The metric system was officially adopted on 1 Jan. 1901.

DIPLOMATIC REPRESENTATIVES

Paraguay maintains embassies in:

Argentina	Germany (West) (also	Peru
Belgium	Minister for Denmark,	Spain
Brazil	Norway and Sweden)	UK
Bolivia	Guatemala	USA
Chile	Italy	Uruguay
Colombia	Japan	Vatican
Ecuador	Mexico	Venezuela
France		

Paraguay has legations in Costa Rica, El Salvador, Netherlands.

OF PARAGUAY IN GREAT BRITAIN (51 Cornwall Gdns, SW7)

Ambassador: Lic. Numa A. Mallorquin (accredited 5 Dec. 1969).
Counsellor: Ignacio A. Pane. *First Secretary:* Jorge Antonio Colman.

There is a consulate-general in London and a consulate in Liverpool.

OF GREAT BRITAIN IN PARAGUAY

Ambassador and Consul-General: B. C. MacDermot, CBE, MVO.
First Secretary: A. G. L. Turner (*Head of Chancery and Consul*).
Service Attaché (resident at Buenos Aires): Col. G. W. Croker, MBE, MC (*Defence, Naval, Military and Air*).

OF PARAGUAY IN THE USA (2400 Massachusetts Ave. NW, Washington, D.C., 20008)

Ambassador: Dr Roque Jacinto Avila.

Counsellors: Dr Luis González Arias; Dr Gilberto Caniza; Dr Julio Cesar Gutierrez. *First Secretary:* Dr Marcos Martinez-Mendieta. *Service Attachés:* Vice-Adm. Benito Pereira Saguier (*Naval*); Col. René F. Zotti (*Military and Air*).

OF THE USA IN PARAGUAY

Ambassador: J. Raymond Ylitalo.

Deputy Chief of Mission: Roger C. Brewin. *Heads of Sections:* Adrian A. Basora (*Political*); Daniel N. Arzac, Jr (*Economic*); Garett G. Sweany (*Consular*); George R. Jennings (*Administrative*); Peter M. Cody (*AID*). *Service Attachés:* Lieut.-Col. Ross W. Winne, Jr (*Army*), Capt. Raymond E. Ford (*Navy*, resident at Buenos Aires), Col. Gordon M. Johnson (*Air*, resident at Buenos Aires).

BOOKS OF REFERENCE

Gaceta Oficial, published by Imprenta Nacional, Estrella y Estero Bellaco, Asunción
Anuario Daumas. Asunción
Anuario Estadistico de la Republica del Paraguay. Asunción. Annual
Report of the Council of the Corporation of Foreign Bondholders. Annual. London
Pendle, G., *Paraguay, a riverside nation.* R. Inst. of Int. Affairs, 3rd ed., 1967
Raine, P., *Paraguay.* New Brunswick, N.J, 1956

NATIONAL LIBRARY. Biblioteca Nacional, Sarmiento, Asunción.

PERSIAN GULF STATES

The Persian Gulf States include the British protected states of Bahrain, Qatar and the Trucial States. They are in special treaty relations with Great Britain dating mainly from the 19th century, by which H.M. Government is responsible for the conduct of their foreign relations. This responsibility is exercised through H.M. Political Resident in the Persian Gulf, who has his headquarters in Bahrain and, subordinate to him, Political Agents in Bahrain, Doha (Qatar), Dubai and Abu Dhabi (Trucial States). *See* MAP in THE STATESMAN'S YEAR-BOOK, 1956. Until 19 June 1961 Kuwait was also in similar treaty relations (*see* p. 1123).

On 27 Feb. 1968 the rulers of Bahrain, Qatar and the 7 Trucial States decided to form a union when British forces withdraw from the Gulf in 1971.

British Political Resident: G. G. Arthur, CMG.
Deputy Political Resident: P. R. H. Wright.

Persian Gulf Gazette. Ed. British Political Resident. London and Bahrain, 1953 ff.
Persian Gulf Pilot. Ed. Admiralty. 10th ed. London, 1955
Al-Baharna, H. M., *The Legal Status of the Arabian Gulf States.* Manchester, 1968
Berreby, J. J., *Le Golfe persique.* Paris, 1959
Hay, Sir Rupert, *The Persian Gulf States.* Washington, D.C., 1959
Kelly, J. B., *Eastern Arabian Frontiers.* London, 1964
Marlowe, J., *The Persian Gulf in the 20th century.* London, 1962

BAHRAIN

Area and Population. The Bahrain islands form an archipelago in the Persian Gulf, between the Qatar peninsula and the mainland of Saudi Arabia. The total area is about 400 sq. miles (598·3 sq. km). Bahrain ('Two Seas'), largest island, is 30 miles long and 10 miles wide. Muharraq, to the north-east, 4 miles long and 1 mile wide, is connected with Bahrain by a causeway, nearly 1·5 miles long, carrying a motor road. Other islands are Sitra, to the east, 3 miles long and 1 mile wide; Umm An-Nasaan, to the west, 3½ miles by 2½ miles; Jidda, also to the west, 1 mile by ½ mile, the Hawar group off Qatar and several islets, some uninhabited. From Sitra oil pipelines and a causeway carrying a road extend out to sea for 3 miles to a deep-water anchorage. The islands are low lying, the highest ground being a hill in the centre of Bahrain, 450 ft high.

The population in 1969 was estimated at 200,000. The majority of the people are Moslem Arabs. There is an Indian community, a number of Pakistanis and Persians, and about 3,000 Europeans, including the staff of the Bahrain Petroleum Company.

Manama, the capital of the state and the commercial centre, is situated at the northern end of the largest island and extends for 1½ miles along the shore. It has a population of 79,098 (1965 census). Electricity from the government power-stations in Manama supplies light and power in Manama, Muharraq (41,143), Hidd (5,230), and Rifa'a (9,403) and the villages. Water is obtained from artesian wells, and there is a piped supply in Manama, Muharraq, Rifa'a and most villages.

Reigning Shaikh: The ruling family, the Al Khalifah, an Arab dynasty, who have been in power since 1782. The present ruler, HH Shaikh Isa bin Sulman Al-Khalifa (born 1933) succeeded on 2 Nov. 1961 and who is also President of the Council of State. *Heir and Head of Defence:* Shaikh Hamed bin Isa Al-Khalifa.

Flag: Scarlet, with white serrated border on hoist.

Government. Bahrain is administered by a Council of State, which was formed in Jan. 1970 and given complete executive powers by the Ruler of Bahrain. *Head of Foreign Affairs:* Sheikh Mohamed bin Mubarak Al-Khalifa. *Head of Finance:* Sayyed Mahmud Al-Alawi.

Education. There were, in 1969, 107 schools for boys and girls with 2,312 teachers and 47,666 pupils. Three boys' secondary schools have a commercial studies section. There is a boys' technical school, at intermediate and secondary level, with 361 pupils. In addition there are 7 private schools. The Men's Teacher Training College (established 1966) and the Woman's Teacher Training College (established 1967) give 2-year courses. Approximately 263 Bahrainis have graduated from universities abroad. The Gulf Institute of Higher Technical Studies opened in Bahrain in Sept. 1968.

Health. There is a free medical service for all residents of Bahrain. There are 11 government hospitals with 930 beds, an American mission hospital and 2 oil company hospitals.

Finance. *Currency.* The Bahrain *dinar* equals 17s. 6d. and is divided into 1,000 *fils*. The Bahrain currency board issues notes of 10, 5, 1, ½ and ¼ *dinars* and 100 *fils*, and coins of 500, 100, 50, 25, 10, 5 and 1 *fils*.

Budget. The revenue of the state is derived from oil royalties and from customs duties, which are 10% *ad valorem* for luxury goods and 5% for essential goods. The exceptions are liquor (50%) and tobacco (15%). Total revenues in 1964, BD 7·8m.; 1965, BD 9m.; 1966, BD 9·5m; 1967, BD 11·2m.; 1968, BD 12·5m.; 1969, BD 14·8m.

On 2 Jan. 1958 Manama was declared a free transit port and the former 2% transit duty was abolished, but storage charges are levied.

Production. In 1932 oil was discovered. Operations are being conducted by the Bahrain Petroleum Company, registered in Canada but owned by US interests, under a concession granted by the Shaikh. Production of oil in 1969 was 27·77m. US bbls. A large oil refinery on Bahrain Island, besides treating crude oil produced locally, also processes oil from Saudi Arabia, transported by pipeline. Refinery throughput in 1969 was 83·31m. US bbls.

Under the terms of the agreement signed between Bahrain and Saudi Arabia in 1958, Bahrain will receive 25% of the profits on any oil produced in the Abu Saafa area of sea between Bahrain and Saudi Arabia. Aramco, which is responsible for the development of this field, began production in 1966.

Bahrain is being developed as a major manfacturing state, the first important enterprise being the Aluminium Bahrain Smelter, which will be operated by a company whose share holders include the Bahrain Government and British, Swedish, West German and US interests. The aluminium operation will be the largest non-oil industry in the Middle East. Ancillary industries being developed around aluminium smelting include the production of aluminium powder and paste. Other projects at present under consideration include the manufacture of magnesium, the further development of marine industries and the expansion of Bahrain's tourist potential.

In addition to the traditional minor industries such as boat-building, weaving, pottery, etc., other modern industries have developed, which include the manufacture of building materials, soft drinks, drinking straws, paper bags, woollen garments, plastic and other consumer goods. There is also an important fishing industry and a fairly large farming community. The most important crops are dates and vegetables, and there is also dairy and poultry farming.

The pearling industry for which Bahrain used to be famous has considerably declined. Only about 10 boats visit the pearl banks each year, as compared with the 600–1,000 that were employed 30 years ago.

Bahrain's traditional position as the entrepôt of the Southern Gulf has been supplemented by the development of Mina Sulman—the new modern harbour—as a free transit and industrial area. Local and international companies have developed industries in this area, which is also used as a storage centre for firms selling elsewhere in the Gulf. The facilities offered by Mina Sulman include engineering and ship repairing yards; the Kanoo slipway is probably the largest between Rotterdam and Hong Kong.

Commerce. In 1969 imports totalled BD 57,939,000; exports and re-exports, BD 19,874,000. Chief imports were (in BD 1,000): Household goods, 6,057; machinery, 5,121; wearing apparel, 4,757; hardware and cutlery, 3.393.

Exports and re-exports (in BD 1,000) went to Saudi Arabia, 9,924; Qatar, 2,309; Kuwait, 1,733; Dubai, 1,257; Abu Dhabi, 977; Iran, 658.

Import of arms and ammunition and telecommunication equipment is subject to special permission; the sale of alcoholic liquor is restricted and the import of cultured pearls is forbidden.

Total trade between Bahrain and UK, in £1,000 sterling (British Board of Trade returns):

	1966	1967	1968	1969	1970
Imports to UK	5,636	2,868	1,914	2,072	1,554
Exports from UK	7,636	8,403	10,648	12,454	24,340
Re-exports from UK	442	150	256	314	

Communications. Steamships of several lines and BOAC aircraft make regular calls. The airport, situated at Muharraq, can take the largest aircraft. Gulf Aviation, Middle East Airlines, Pakistan International Airways, Qantas, Kuwait Airways, Air India International and Saudi Arabian Airlines also operate to and from Bahrain. Bahrain International Airport is the Arabian Gulf's main air communication centre. It is at present being expanded, the runway is being extended to 12,000 ft and a new terminal building constructed to meet the demands of the Jumbojets that will start using Bahrain as a main stopping point on the routes between the Far East and Australia and Europe and the Middle East. There were, in 1967, 8,094 telephones, not counting 1,959 telephones on the oil company exchange. There is a state-operated radio station.

Banking. Banking facilities are provided by the Bank of Bahrain and branches of the Eastern Bank, the British Bank of the Middle East, the Arab Bank, Habib Bank (Overseas), United Bank, First National City Bank and the Rafidain Bank.

Weights and Measures. British and US standard weights and measures are understood. The following local weights are in use: 1 tola = 180 grains = 11·641 grammes; 39 tolas = 1 ratl (lb.) = 0·454 kg; 4 ratls = 1 Ruba' (4 lb.) = 1·816 kg; 14 Ruba'as = 1 Maund (56 lb.) = 54·424 kg.

British Political Agent: A. J. D. Stirling.

STATISTICAL INFORMATION. Department of Information, P.O. Box 253, Manama. *Director of Information:* Mohamad Jaber Ansari.

Belgrave, Sir Charles, *Personal Column*. London, 1960
Belgrave, J. H. D., *Welcome to Bahrain*. 5th ed. Manama, 1965
Tweedy, M., *Bahrain and the Persian Gulf*. Ipswich, 1952

QATAR

Area and Population. This state, which includes the whole of the Qatar peninsula, extends on the landward side from Khor al Odeid to the boundaries of the Saudi Arabian province of Hasa. Area, about 4,247 sq. miles (11,000 sq. km); population estimate in 1970 about 130,000, including a number of migrant labourers from neighbouring states. The relations of the ruler of Qatar with the British Government are regulated by a treaty of 3 Nov. 1916.

The capital is Doha (population, 100,000), which is the main port and where there are branches of the Eastern Bank, the British Bank of the Middle East, the Ottoman Bank, the Arab Bank, The Intra Bank and headquarters of the Qatar National Bank. Other towns are Dukhan, the centre of oil production, and Umm Said, oil-terminal of Qatar.

Ruler: HH Shaikh Ahmad, son of Ali bin Abdullah Al Thani, KBE, succeeded on his father's abdication on 24 Oct. 1960. *Heir apparent, Deputy Ruler and Prime Minister:* Shaikh Khalifa bin Hamad Al-Thani.

Flag: Maroon, with white serrated border on hoist.

Education. There were, in 1969–70, 10,209 boys at 47 schools with 557 teachers; 38 girls' schools had 7,115 pupils and 375 teachers.

Health. There are 5 hospitals (including one for women and one for gynaecology and obstetrics) with a total of 621 beds.

Finance. *Currency.* The Indian external rupee was withdrawn in June 1966 and replaced temporarily by the Saudi riyal. In Sept. 1966 the new Qatar/Dubai currency was introduced (one riyal being equivalent to 1s. 9d. since the devaluation of the £ in Nov. 1967).

Budget. The revenue from oil operations is the principal source of income; it has enabled the Government to institute an extensive development programme.

Defence. The Qatar Public Security Forces received 3 Whirlwind 3 helicopters in 1968 and subsequently ordered from UK 6 Hunter jet fighter-bombers and Tigercat surface-to-air missile systems.

Production. There are 4 oil companies operating in Qatar, the Qatar Petroleum Co. (a subsidiary of the Iraq Petroleum Co.), Qatar Oil Co. Japan, S.E. Asia Oil and Gas Co. and the Shell Co. of Qatar (a subsidiary of Royal Dutch Shell). The Q.P.C. concession now covers part of the land surface from which the Company is producing at the rate of about 9m. tons a year. The Shell Co. concession covers part of the offshore seabed, from which production began in 1964. Qatar Oil Co. (Japan) was granted an 8,900-sq. km offshore concession in March 1969. The terminal of Halul Island was completed in March 1966; from it about 7m. tons of oil were exported in 1969.

Trade. Total trade between Qatar and UK, in £1,000 sterling (British Board of Trade returns):

	1966	1967	1968	1969	1970
Imports to UK	16,849	4,283	24,349	24,743	30,581
Exports from UK	3,292	3,688	7,153	5,815 ⎫	7,430
Re-exports from UK	23	21	43	32 ⎭	

Communications. Ships of several lines used to call at Umm Said; with the completion in 1969 of the new Doha port, it has become the main port of Qatar.

The Gulf Aviation Co., Ltd, operates daily services from Bahrain; BOAC, Middle East and 9 other airlines operate regular international flights from Doha airport.

Telephone and radio-telephone services connect Qatar with Europe and America; there were 10,926 telephones in Dec. 1970.

Banking. Banking facilities are provided by the Qatar National Bank (established 1965), and branches of the Eastern Bank, the British Bank of the Middle East, the Ottoman Bank, First National City Bank, Bank Sodirat Iran and the Arab Bank. The Intra Bank reopened in March 1968 for limited banking transactions.

British Political Agent (in Doha): E. F. Henderson.

THE TRUCIAL STATES

From Sha'am, 35 miles south-west of Ras Musan dam, for nearly 400 miles to Khor al Odeid at the south-eastern end of the peninsula of Qatar, the coast, formerly known as the Pirate Coast, of the Persian Gulf (together with 50 miles of the coast of the Gulf of Oman) belongs to the rulers of the 7 Trucial States. In 1820 these rulers, after committing acts of hostility against the East India Company, signed a treaty prescribing peace with the British Government and perpetual abstention from plunder and piracy (specifically including the slave trade) by land and sea. This treaty was followed by further agreements providing for the suppression of the slave trade and by a series of other engagements, of which the most important are the Perpetual Maritime Truce (May 1853) and the Exclusive Agreement (March 1892). Under the latter, the shaikhs, on behalf of themselves, their heirs and successors, undertook that they would on no account enter into any agreement or correspondence with any power other than the British Government, receive foreign agents, or cede, sell or give for occupation any part of their territory save to the British Government.

Area and Population. The area of these states is approximately 32,300 sq. miles (83,660 sq. km). The total population at census (1968), 180,200, of whom about one-tenth are nomads. The formerly independent small state of Kalba on the Gulf of Oman was merged with Sharjah in 1952.

The largest and most important town on the Trucial Coast is Dubai (about 60,000 inhabitants). Abu Dhabi has a population in excess of 50,000 and has expanded rapidly since the State became an important oil producer. Traditionally the inhabitants of the Coast have depended for their livelihood on trading, fishing and pearling. In recent years there has been a drift towards the towns, and the oil industry, particularly in Abu Dhabi, has become the major employer.

Government. The Trucial States Council, composed of the rulers of the 7 Trucial States, meets regularly to promote interstate co-operation. It is responsible, *inter alia*, for the administration of the Trucial States Development Fund, to which the wealthier gulf states contribute as well as other countries, including the UK. The fund finances a large-scale development programme.

The rulers of the Trucial States are:

Abu Dhabi	Shaikh Zaid bin Sultan al Nahayan	Succeeded 1966
Dubai	Shaikh Rashid bin Said al Maktoum	„ 1958
Sharjah	Shaikh Khalid bin Mohammed al Qasimi	„ 1965
Ajman	Shaikh Rashid bin Humaid al Naimi	„ 1928
Umm al Qaiwain	Shaikh Ahmad bin Rashid al Mu'alla, MBE	„ 1929
Ras al Khaimah	Shaikh Saqr bin Mohammed al Qasimi	„ 1948
Fujairah	Shaikh Mohammed bin Hamad al Sharqi	Recognized 1952

Education. Primary-intermediate education for boys is available in all the Trucial states, and for girls in Dubai (4 schools), Sharjah, Ras al Khaimah and Abu

Dhabi; a limited secondary education for boys, in Dubai (8 schools), Abu Dhabi, Sharjah and Ras al Khaimah and for girls in Sharjah. There are 5 boys' schools in Sharjah; 6 boys' and 5 girls' schools in Ras al Khaimah, 1 boys' and 1 girls' school in Fujairah; and 1 boys' school in Ajman. The education system is the same as that followed in Kuwait, and many of the teachers in the Trucial States are supplied by the Kuwait, Qatar, UAR, Jordan and Bahrain education departments. The oil companies in Abu Dhabi operate apprentice training schools. A vocational training centre is under construction.

There are trade schools in Sharjah, Dubai and Ras al Khaimah; they are administered and financed by the Trucial States Development Office.

Health. There are several hospitals in Dubai, including a 400-bed hospital now under construction, in Ras al Khaimah and in Sharjah and clinics have been built in Sharjah and other towns. A tuberculosis sanatorium is to be constructed by the State of Kuwait in Sharjah. The health services are run by the Government of Dubai, the Trucial States Council, the State of Kuwait and the Iranian Red Lion and Sun Society.

Agriculture. The fertile Buraimi Oasis is largely in Abu Dhabi territory, but owing to lack of water and good soil there is little agriculture in the rest of the Trucial States. However, since the establishment of an agricultural trials station and an agricultural school in Ras al Khaimah the number of gardens under cultivation has more than doubled and there have been remarkable increases in the variety of crops and the length of the agricultural season. In 1970 a herd of dairy cattle was imported for the agricultural trials station.

Finance. *Currency.* Dubai and the Northern Trucial States use the Qatar/Dubai riyal. Abu Dhabi adopted the Bahrain dinar.

Budget. Revenue is principally derived from customs dues on imports and oil-concession payments. Accurate estimates of the States' income are difficult to make but Dubai's income in 1970 is believed to have been about £4m. and may rise with increasing oil revenue to about £15m. by 1972. The 5 smallest states have incomes of less than £1m. per annum.

Defence. Formation of an air wing in Abu Dhabi, to support land forces, began in 1968 with the purchase of 2 Britten-Norman Islander light STOL transports and 4 Agusta-Bell JetRanger light helicopters. Four larger Caribou STOL transports have since been delivered and are being followed by 10 Hunter fighters and reconnaissance fighters and 2 Hunter 2-seat trainers. Initial personnel are mostly British.

Planning. Public projects under construction include the 15-berth Port Rashid Harbour, the £4m. airport terminal building and the £6m. Rashid Hospital. A municipal sewerage scheme is under way and a police headquarters is planned. Further developments are expected to include reclamation of part of the sea front, improvement of the creek unloading facilities and a traffic tunnel or additional bridge over the creek. In Sharjah, Mina Khalid is now operational and ships are using the new jetty, while improvement of the creek entrance and additional wharfage are now being undertaken. There are plans for a cement works and a flour-mill in Dubai in the near future.

Oil. In 1962 oil was shipped for the first time from Das Island in Abu Dhabi territory by Abu Dhabi Marine Areas Ltd (owned two-thirds by British Petroleum and one-third by Compagnie Française des Pétroles). The Abu Dhabi Petroleum Company (a subsidiary of the Iraq Petroleum Co.), who hold the land concession in Abu Dhabi, started to ship oil in Dec. 1963. Oil production in the Dubai offshore concession started in Sept. 1969. The concession is operated by Continental Oil Co.'s subsidiary Dubai Petroleum Co., on behalf of Dubai Marine Areas which is owned half by CFP and half by Hispanoil, and Texaco and Dubai Sun Oil Co. Other concessions in the Northern Trucial States are held by Dubai Petroleum Co. (Dubai Onshore), Buttes Gas & Oil Co. (Sharjah West Coast Offshore), Occidental Petroleum Co. (Ajman On and Offshore and Umm al Qaiwain Offshore), Union Oil/Southern Natural Gas (Ras al Khaimah Offshore), Shell Hydrocarbons (Sharjah Onshore West Coast, Umm al Qaiwain and Ras al Khaimah Onshore), and Shell Minerals (Sharjah East Coast On and Offshore and Fujairah On and Offshore). Drilling was planned at several sites in the area during 1970–71. In 1967 a land concession in Abu Dhabi was awarded to a group consisting of Phillips Petroleum Co., Ammoil and AGIP, and an offshore concession was awarded to the Abu Dhabi Oil Co. Ltd consisting of Maruzen Oil, Daiko Oil and Nippon Mining (all of Japan). In 1968 and 1970 land concessions were awarded in Abu Dhabi to 5 companies from Mitsubishi group of Japan known as Middle East Oil Co. (Japan) Ltd. In June 1970 a consortium composed of Pan Ocean Oil Corporation, Syracuse Oils Ltd, Wington Enterprises Ltd were awarded an offshore concession in Abu Dhabi.

Commerce. Imports in 1965, excluding Abu Dhabi, amounted to about £17·4m.; exports and re-exports to £2·6m. The UK was the principal supplier (£3m.), followed by Japan (£2·4m.) and India (£1·7m.).

Total trade between the Trucial States (excluding Abu Dhabi) and UK, in £1,000 sterling (British Board of Trade returns):

	1966	1967	1968	1969	1970
Imports to UK	3,199	6,660	36,739	13,632	13,378
Exports from UK	2,804	5,282	8,968	13,258 }	13,748
Re-exports from UK	90	57	110	270 }	

Total trade between Abu Dhabi and UK, in £1,000 sterling (British Board of Trade returns):

	1967	1968	1969	1970
Imports to UK	15,900	14,500	16,600	18,730
Exports from UK	6,755	9,600	14,900 }	10,802
Re-exports from UK	169	58	106 }	

Shipping. British and European shipping lines call at Dubai (30–40 vessels a month) and Abu Dhabi.

Aviation. Dubai, Sharjah and Abu Dhabi have civil airports. Gulf Aviation, Ltd, operate services from Bahrain, Kuwait and London. Regular services are operated by BOAC between London, Abu Dhabi, Dubai, Bombay and Karachi; by Middle East Airlines between Beirut, Doha, Abu Dhabi and Dubai, by Iranair to Dubai; by Pakistan International Airways and Kuwait Airlines to Dubai; by Syrian Arab Airlines to Dubai; by Saudi Arabian Airlines to Dubai; by Royal Jordanian Airlines to Abu Dhabi and by Air India to Dubai and Abu Dhabi.

Posts and Telecommunications. The Dubai State Telephone Co. has carried out an expansion scheme to increase the number of lines available to 5,500. In Sharjah a new telephone company has been formed and the other Northern Trucial States are now linked by telephone. The new Cable and Wireless Station at Jebel Ali in the State of Dubai links the system with the international communications network.

All the Trucial States have their own post offices and issue their own stamps. The British Post Office is responsible for their representation in the Universal Postal Union.

Banking. The British Bank of the Middle East has branches in Dubai, Abu Dhabi, Sharjah, Khor Fakkan and Ras al Khaimah; the Eastern Bank has branches in Dubai, Sharjah, Abu Dhabi and Al Ain; the National & Grindlays Bank (Ottoman Branch) has branches in Abu Dhabi and Al Ain. The Arab Bank has branches in Al Ain, Ras al Khaimah, Sharjah, Abu Dhabi and Dubai; the First National City Bank of New York has branches in Dubai and Abu Dhabi;

the Habib Bank of Pakistan have branches in Dubai and Sharjah and the United Bank Ltd of Pakistan branches in Dubai, Sharjah, Abu Dhabi and Al Ain. There is also the National Bank of Dubai, formed in 1963, which has a branch in Abu Dhabi and Umm al Qaiwain, and the Bank of Oman Ltd, formed in 1967, which has a branch in Al Ain. The Commercial Bank opened in Dubai in 1969. The Bank Sadarat of Iran has branches in Abu Dhabi, Dubai, Fujairah and Ras al Khaimah. The National Bank of Abu Dhabi, formed in 1967, has its head office in Abu Dhabi and a branch office in Al Ain.

British Political Agent (in Abu Dhabi): C. J. Treadwell.
British Political Agent (in Dubai): J. L. Walker, MBE.

Fenelon, K. G., *The Trucial States: a brief economic survey.* Beirut, 1967

PERU

República del Perú

HISTORY. The Republic of Peru, formerly the most important of the Spanish vice-royalties in South America, declared its independence on 28 July 1821; but it was not till after a war, protracted till 1824, that the country gained its actual freedom.

CONSTITUTION AND GOVERNMENT. On 3 Oct. 1968 a military junta overthrew the government of President Fernando Belaúnde Terry and installed Gen. Juan Velasco Alvarado as President of a 'Revolutionary Government' with a cabinet composed entirely of officers of the armed services. Gen. Velasco retired from active army service in Jan. 1969, having reached retiring age, but remained in office as President. Congress has been suspended and rule is by Decree Law.

The Government have stated that the existing Constitution will be revised before fresh elections are held.

At present the Constitution provides for a Legislature consisting of a Senate (45 members) and a Chamber of Deputies (140 members) and an Executive formed of the President of the Republic and a Council of Ministers appointed by him. Elections are to be held every 6 years with the President and Congress elected at the same time, by separate ballots. All literate Peruvians (native-born or naturalized) over the age of 21 are eligible to vote; in 1968 the number of registered voters was 275,6,588, including 1m. in Lima province. Voting is compulsory; women were fully enfranchised in 1955.

Augusto Bernardino Leguia, 4 July 1919–24 Aug. 1930.[1]
Gen. Manuel Ponce (Acting), 24 Aug. 1930–28 Aug. 1930.[2]
Col. Luis M. Sánchez Cerro (Acting), 28 Aug. 1930–1 March 1931.[2]
Ricardo Leoncio Elias (Acting), 1 March 1931–5 March 1931.[2]
Col. Gustavo A. Jiménez (Acting), 5 March 1931–10 March 1931.[2]
David Samanez Ocampo (Acting), 10 March 1931–8 Dec. 1931.
Gen. Luis M. Sánchez Cerro (Constitutional), 8 Dec. 1931–30 April 1933.[3]
Gen. Oscar Raimundo Benavides, 30 April 1933–8 Dec. 1939.

Dr Manuel Prado y Ugarteche, 8 Dec. 1939–28 July 1945.
Dr José Luis Bustamante y Rivero, 28 July 1945–27 Oct. 1948.[1]
Gen. Manuel A. Odría (Acting), 27 Oct. 1948–1 June 1950.[2]
Gen. Zenón Noriega, 1 June 1950–28 July 1950.
Gen. Manuel A. Odría, 28 July 1950–28 July 1956.
Dr Manuel Prado y Ugarteche, 28 July 1956–July 1962.
Gen. Ricardo Pérez Godoy, 18 July 1962–3 March 1963.[1]
Gen. Nicolás Lindley López, 3 March–28 July 1963.
Fernando Belaúnde Terry, 28 July 1963–3 Oct. 1968.[1]

[1] Deposed.   [2] Resigned.   [3] Assassinated.

President: Gen. Juan Velasco Alvarado.
Prime Minister: Gen. Ernesto Montagne Sánchez.
Minister of Foreign Affairs: Gen. Edgardo Mercado Jarrín.

As of 30 June 1965 the 23 departments are divided into 148 provinces (plus the constitutional province of Callao) and 1,662 districts; the province of Callao has some of the functions of a department. Each department is administered by a prefect, and each province by a sub-prefect. The first municipal elections for 40 years were held in Dec. 1963.

National flag: Red, white, red (vertical).

National anthem: Somos Libres, seámos lo siempre (words by J. de la Torre Ugarte; tune by J. B. Alcedo, 1821).

AREA AND POPULATION. A report dated 30 Jan. 1959, by the Military Institute of Geography, calculated the total area of Peru to be 1,285,215 sq. km (496,093 sq. miles).

The long-standing dispute with Chile over the provinces of Tacna and Arica (*see* THE STATESMAN'S YEAR-BOOK, 1928, p. 1198) reached an amicable settlement on 3 June 1929 at Lima, Tacna going to Peru and Arica to Chile. For an account of the settlement of other boundary disputes, *see* THE STATESMAN'S YEAR-BOOK, 1948, p. 1173. A map of the boundary with Ecuador is to be found in THE STATESMAN'S YEAR-BOOK, 1942.

The census taken on 2 July 1961 gave the population as 10,420,375, including an estimated 100,830 nomadic jungle Indians. The estimate for 1970 was: 13,586,000, based on an annual population growth rate of 3·1%. At the time of the 1961 census the population was distributed as follows: northern zone, 29·8%; central zone, 39·6%; southern zone, 23·9%; jungle area or eastern zone, 6·7%. The language is Spanish, but the Indian population speak either Quechua or Aymará.

Foreign residents registered in March 1966 included: Japanese, 11,729; Chinese, 8,704; Italian, 7,178; USA, 7,050; Spanish, 6,691; German, 3,318; Chilean, 2,875; British, 2,622 (1970: about 3,561); Swiss, 1,370; French, 1,336; grand total (other nationals included): 68,447.

The census population (2 July 1961, preliminary) of Lima was 1,715,971 (estimate 1966: 1,883,700); Callao City, 161,286 (279,500); Arequipa, 156,657 (167,080); Cuzco, 78,289 (95,660); Trujillo, 99,808 (129,470); Chiclayo, 86,904 (127,040); Chimbote, 63,970 (81,760); Iquitos, 55,695 (67,920); Huancayo, 46,015 (80,570); Ica (61,360); Sullana (39,540); Piura (92,670); Tacna (34,850); Talara (34,230).

In 1960 there were registered 376,356 births, 114,605 deaths and 43,549 marriages.

The area of the 23 departments and the constitutional province of Callao are given below with the population, according to the official census (revised) of 1940 and that of 2 July 1961 approved by decree of 1964. The department of Pasco, created in Nov. 1944 from the department of Junín, is shown with its present area and 1959 estimate. The area of the department of Puno includes the Peruvian zone of Lake Titicaca, 4,996·28 sq. km. The chief towns are shown in brackets:

	Area (sq. km) 1959	Population 2 July 1961 (census)	1970 (June estimate)	Pop. per sq. km 1961
Departments				
Amazonas (Chachapoyas)	41,297·1	129,003	176,200	2·85
Ancash (Huaraz)	36,308·3	605,548	744,700	16·20
Apurímac (Abancay)	20,654·6	303,648	330,400	16·36
Arequipa (Arequipa)	63,527·6	407,163	518,300	6·47
Ayacucho (Ayacucho)	45,503·1	430,289	476,100	9·85
Cajamarca (Cajamarca)	35,417·8	786,599	1,009,600	21·15
Callao (Callao)[1]	73·8	219,420	335,400	2,901·46
Cuzco (Cuzco)	84,140·9	648,168	759,000	7·30
Huancavelico (Huancavelica)	22,870·9	315,730	367,100	13·07
Huánuco (Huánuco)	35,314·6	355,003	438,800	10·24
Ica (Ica)	21,251·4	261,126	362,700	11·48
Junín (Huancayo)[2]	32,354·4	548,662	708,100	15·64
La Libertad (Trujillo)	23,241·3	609,105	784,900	25·29

[1] With Province.
[2] Present area and 1958 population shown but the population for 1940 is that of the larger area (22,814 sq. miles) from which Pasco was carved in 1944.

	Area	Population 2 July	1970	Pop. per
Departments	(sq. km) 1959	1961 (census)	(June estimate)	sq. km 1961
Lambayeque (Chiclayo)	16,585·9	353,657	485,500	20·93
Lima (Lima)	33,894·9	2,093,435	3,155,800	68·42
Loreto (Iquitos)	478,336·2	411,340	560,130	0·69
Madre de Dios (Maldonado)	78,402·7	25,269	34,000	0·19
Moquegua (Moquegua)	16,174·7	53,260	68,800	3·60
Pasco (Cerro de Pasco)	21,854·1	150,575	193,000	5·79
Piura (Piura)	33,067·1	692,414	922,300	21·68
Puno (Puno)	72,382·4	727,309	849,000	10·20
San Martín (Moyobamba)	53,063·6	170,456	229,400	3·06
Tacna (Tacna)	14,766·6	67,800	93,900	4·68
Tumbes (Tumbes)	4,731·5	57,378	84,000	21·10
Total	1,285,215·6	10,420,357	13,586,000	8·06

RELIGION. Religious liberty exists, but the Roman Catholic religion is protected by the state, and since 1929 only Roman Catholic religious instruction is permitted in schools, state or private. In 1956 there were 4 Roman Catholic archbishops (the archdiocese of Lima, dating from 1545, takes precedence), 12 bishops, 4 vicars-general, 2 apostolic prefects, 1,662 priests, 605 cloistered monks and 3,182 members of religious orders.

Protestants numbered 128,000 in 1966.

All marriages must be civil, regardless of religion and preceded by medical examination; there are liberal divorce regulations, including divorce for 'absence without just cause for more than 2 years', and by mutual consent. Divorcees may remarry immediately. A law of 1936 emphasizes that the religious obligations of marriage are fully recognized.

EDUCATION. Elementary education is compulsory and free for both sexes between the ages of 7 and 16; secondary education is also free. But schools, despite substantial increases, are still too few. The system is highly centralized; all teaching appointments are made by the Minister of Education for the public schools; for the private schools he supervises plant and equipment and limits fees but does not appoint teachers.

In 1966 there were public, private and state-supervised elementary schools, including kindergartens, with 49,523 teachers and 2,206,000 pupils; 612 secondary schools, with 12,476 teachers and 356,500 students. Training in 401 public technical schools is also free; in 1966 they had 5,984 teachers and 76,900 pupils. The 'normal' schools had 948 teachers and 19,200 pupils. Education centres for adult illiterates had 3,226 teachers and 96,132 students. There are also 29 schools for teachers.

Higher education is provided at the central university in Lima, called 'Universidad Nacional Mayor de San Marcos', founded by Charles V in 1551. Students in 1962 numbered 14,000; teachers, 1,200. There are other state universities at Arequipa (founded in 1827), Cuzco, Trujillo, Ayacucho (Universidad de Huamanga), Puno, Iquitos, Huancayo (Universidad del Centro) and some Catholic universities. The state maintains the National Engineering University and the Agrarian University of La Molina. In Lima there are also 4 universities described as private. In 1966 the total number of university students was 64,400.

CINEMAS (1966). Cinemas numbered some 230, of which 124 in the Lima area; total seating capacity, 243,000.

NEWSPAPERS. There are numerous daily newspapers; the main Lima dailies are *La Prensa*, *El Comercio* and *Expreso*.

SOCIAL WELFARE. There were, in 1966, 289 hospitals (28,564 beds), of which 140 were private, 95 administered by the state and 54 by public welfare organizations. At 31 Aug. 1966 there were 5,061 doctors in Peru, being 1 to every 800 people in Lima, against 1 to every 18,000 in the provinces.

JUSTICE. The Peruvian judicial system is a pyramid at the base of which are the justices of the peace who decide minor criminal cases and civil cases involving small sums of money. The apex is the Supreme Court with 17 members; in between are the judges of first instance, who usually sit in the provincial capitals, and the superior courts of which there are 18.

The Revolutionary Government decreed in Dec. 1969 that all judges, except justices of the peace, will in future be elected by the National Council of Justice, composed of representatives of the Executive, the Legislature, the Judiciary, the National Federation of the College of Lawyers and 2 of the university law faculties. Justices of the peace will be appointed, as before, by the superior courts.

FINANCE. Currency. The monetary unit is the *sol*. It was devalued by 40% in Sept. 1967 and in Sept. 1969 stood at the free market rate of 103·4 to the £ and 43·5 to the US$. In May 1970 exchange control was imposed on the small free exchange market. Foreign residents were exempted from a number of the regulations but Peruvian citizens were required to repatriate overseas bank deposits and declare all foreign assets. The official exchange rate is S/.103·44 to the £ and S/.43·38 to the US$ for normal transactions. The certificate exchange rate is S/.38·70 to the US$.

Coins include the new 10- and 5-sol pieces (copper 75%; nickel 25%), the sol and half sol (copper 30%; zinc 70%), the 20, 10 and 5 centavos (copper–zinc); the 2- and 1-centavo pieces (zinc) have been discontinued. Peru has a paper currency issued by the Banco Central de la Reserva in denominations of 1,000, 500, 200, 100, 50, 10 and 5 soles. Money in circulation at 30 June 1970 was S/.22,470m.

Budget. On a cash-flow basis (*i.e.*, development loans considered as receipts and debt service included in payments) the revenue and expenditure for calendar years were as follows (in 1m. soles):

	1966	1967[1]	1968[2]	1969[2]	1970
Revenue	21,494	28,222	30,745	32,300	42,715
Expenditure	25,979	33,183	30,745	32,300	44,877

[1] Budget year 15 months ending 31 March 1968. [2] Estimates.

In the 1970 budget proposed expenditure includes (in 1m. soles): Defence, 7,463; finance, 8,296; interior including police, 4,848; education, 8,794; health, 2,871; transport and communications, 3,208; agriculture, 3,115; energy and mines, 1,290.

The external debt rose from US$311m. in 1964 to 847m. in 1969.

DEFENCE. The national budget for 1970 included the following estimates: War, S/.3,447m.; Air, S/.1,967m.; Navy, S/.2,048m.

Army. While military service is compulsory youths are only conscripted to fill the annual quota. The term of service is 2 years and all males of 20–25 years of age are liable. The country is divided into 5 military regions.

The Army comprises approximately 35,000 all ranks, of which some 3,000 are regular officers. There are 7 light infantry divisions, 1 jungle infantry division, 1 armoured division, 1 armoured group, 1 cavalry division and 1 special forces division which includes parachute and commando battalions. There is an air element of 4 Helio Courier 395 communications aircraft. Equipment consists of approximately 150 tanks (AMX13 and Sherman) over 50 light armoured fighting vehicles and 105-mm./155-mm. field artillery.

The section of the national police force with a para-military role is known as the *Guardia Civil* and comprises approximately 21,000 personnel.

Navy. The Peruvian Navy consists of 4 submarines completed in USA in 1954–55; 2 cruisers, *Almirante Grau* (ex-*Newfoundland*) and *Coronel Bolognesi* (ex-*Ceylon*), acquired from Great Britain in 1959–60; 2 destroyers acquired from USA during 1960–61; 3 destroyer escorts; 2 corvettes (*ex*-fleet minesweepers) acquired from USA in 1960–61; 6 coastal patrol boats (built in Britain in 1964–65); 2 coastal minesweepers; 4 landing ships; 3 patrol launches (acquired in 1960 from Italy); 7 river gunboats; 3 transports; 5 oilers, and 2 tugs. Two Daring Class destroyers were purchased from Britain in 1969. They are undergoing refit and are due to be operational in mid-1971.

All naval training takes place in the Callao area at various schools. The main naval base and dockyard are also in Callao. Smaller bases are at Iquitos on the Amazon, and at San Lorenzo. Naval personnel in 1970 totalled 7,680 officers and men.

Air Force. The Air Force is under the direction of the Minister for Air, who is also C-in-C. Command is exercised through base and unit commanders.

The operational force consists of 3 combat groups. No. 6 Group has 2 squadrons of Canberra jet-bombers and 1 of Mirage 5-P jet fighters. No. 7 Group has 1 squadron of B-26C Invader piston-engined bombers. No. 11 Group has 1 squadron of F-86F and T-33A jet combat aircraft and 1 squadron of Hunter F.4 fighters. Other aircraft in service include 9 medium transports (C-54 and C-118), 42 light transports (C-46, C-47, Twin Otter, Beaver and Catalina), 13 helicopters, 100 training aircraft (T-33, T-37, Mirage, Cessna 172) and a small number of miscellaneous types for photographic and communications duties. There are military airfields at Talara, Chiclayo, Piura, Pisco, Lima (2) and Iquitos, with another under construction at La Joya. In addition there is a seaplane base at Iquitos. All officers and pilots are trained at the Air Academy at Lima (Las Palmas). The approximate strength of the Peruvian Air Force is 7,000 personnel and 240 aircraft. On order are 16 Buffalo twin-turboprop transports, 8 Twin Otters and 2 C-130 Hercules aircraft.

PLANNING. Peru has had a National Planning Institute since 1963. The plans it has published are of an indicative nature. The plan for the year 1970 has as its targets substantial increases in public and private investment, a growth rate in GNP of 7% and equilibrium in the balance of payments. The Institute is drawing up a comprehensive plan for economic and social development in the years 1971–75.

AGRICULTURE. There are 4 zones: the coast strip, with an average width of 80 miles; the Sierra or Uplands, formed by the coast range of mountains and the Andes proper; the Montaña or high wooded region which lies on the eastern slopes of the Andes, and the jungle in the Amazon Basin, known as the Selva. Land under cultivation, 1967, was about 2·75m. hectares. There are 4 fertilizer factories, near Callao and in Cuzco.

Peru is a substantial importer of foodstuffs, chiefly wheat (681,000 metric tons, 1969), but also fats and oil, meat and dairy products, which use up over 25% of the available foreign exchange.

Nearly half of the population is dependent on agriculture, which accounted for 15% of the GDP in 1969. Peru's third land reform law, that of June 1969, is the most comprehensive. It provides for the large sugar estates in the north of Peru to be turned into co-operatives. Maximum permitted sizes for other types of land holding are stipulated for the various regions of the country. These range from 150 acres for irrigated land on the coast to an area capable of supporting 5,000 sheep for pasture land in the Sierra. These sizes may be increased if certain efficiency criteria are met. Holdings too small to be economically viable are to be consolidated into co-operative units. The chief agricultural productions of Peru are, in the order named: Cotton, sugar, wool, hides, skins, coffee and rice.

Production in 1968 (in metric tons): Cotton, 87,320; exports of ginned cotton, (1969) 88,453; sugar, 748,132; exports (1969), 317,558; coffee, 57,330; exports (1969), 42,867; cocoa, 2,150; wheat, 148,000; rice, 288,198.

Wild rubber gathered in 1965, 2,258 metric tons; cultivated, 170 metric tons. Coca exports in 1968 (leaf), 277 metric tons.

Output of cattle hides, 1965, 624,140; sheepskins, 1,989,524; goatskins, 1,149,721. Export of hides and skins, 1964, 2,139 metric tons. Output of sheep wool in 1964 was 11,000 metric tons. Alpaca and llama wool and vicuña hair, 4,186 metric tons; exports, 1964, were sheep wool, unwashed, 3,432·2 metric tons; llama, alpaca and vicuña wool, 3,869·6 metric tons.

Peru suffers from periodically severe droughts particularly in the northern zone; losses were estimated at 1,000m. soles in 1968.

Livestock (1965). 4·28m. llamas, alpacas, etc., 925,380 horses and mules, 3·6m. cattle, 15·2m. sheep, 3·95m. goats, 1·99m. swine, 27·8m. poultry.

FISHERIES. Peru is the world's largest exporter of fishmeal and produces around 45% of the world's total fishmeal supplies or nearly 2m. tons a year. Fishmeal production dominates the Peruvian fishing industry and there are 120 fishmeal plants employing 3,000 workers spread among the 23 ports of the 1,400-mile Peruvian coastline. Over 30% of the capacity is in Chimbote. There are approximately 1,300 fishing boats employing 20,000 fulltime fishermen. There are about 7 active canning plants, 4 freezing plants and 1 whale reducing plant. In 1969 fishmeal production was 1,610,800 tons, compared with 1968 figures of 1,922 metric tons.

The principal fishing industry exports, in metric tons:

	1965	1966	1967	1968	1969
Fishmeal	1,259,997	1,302,014	1,560,900	2,053,205	1,655,570
Fish oil	111,238	87,389	195,968	323,580	141,070
Frozen	11,703	14,103	16,321	13,578	16,084
Canned	11,293	13,431	3,445	3,328	2,753
Total	1,394,231	1,416,937	1,776,634	2,393,691	1,815,477

MINING. Mineral exports accounted for about 55% of foreign trade earnings in 1969; copper alone accounted for 27%. Lead, copper, iron, silver, zinc and petroleum are the chief minerals exploited. Mineral exports in 1969 were valued at US$476m. and amounted to (in metric tons) 6,844,700 made up as follows: copper, 200,500; silver, 1,100; lead, 156,200; zinc, 310,800; iron, 5,847,200; petroleum and derivatives, 325,700. Crude petroleum output in 1969 was 26·3m. bbls. Mine production (in metric tons, 1968) of copper, 206,550; lead, 155,480; zinc, 303,790; antimony, 122; tungsten, 647; bismuth, 790; molybdenum, 730; cadmium, 241; mercury, 99; tin, 75; manganese (1966), 850; silver (troy oz.), 36m.; gold, 1,101,000 grammes. Diamonds were discovered during 1966 in the department of Cuzco (Canchis). Iron deposits are large; production (62% Fe), 1968, 9m. long tons. Excellent coal deposits, with an ash content of from 5 to 7%, lie near by; output, 1966, 68,345 metric tons. Nepheline was discovered in Puno department in 1962. More anthracite was discovered in Alta Chicama, La Libertad department, in 1966 and mine concessions totalled 11,688.

Oil deposits have been discovered and are now being exploited on the Continental Shelf. On 9 Oct. 1968 the Revolutionary Government announced the expropriation of the International Petroleum Company's oilfield at La Brea y Pariñas and refinery at Talara. Mine concessions, 1968, numbered 1,028. The State is now the largest producer.

In Sept. 1969 a law was introduced to force the major mining companies to work their hitherto unexploited concessions or lose them. In April 1970 a new Guiding Law to the Mining Industry was published which introduced a new tax structure for the industry and stated that as a matter of policy the State would undertake the marketing and refining of minerals.

The government-controlled guano deposits on Huanillos, Punta Lobos and other islands are important; the 1966 production was 55,505 metric tons.

Production of domestic and industrial salt in 1966 was 173,148 metric tons.

INDUSTRY. The Industrial Promotion Law, 1959, has succeeded in encouraging local enterprises. The manufacturing industry has been the fastest growing sector of the economy in recent years. The average compounded annual growth rate for the period 1960–69 was 7·4% per annum. In 1969 it was estimated that the manufacturing industries accounted for 20% of the GNP. In July 1970 a new Law of Industry was promulgated. This classifies industries according to national priorities and defines certain basic industries which it will be in the interests of the economy for the State to control. It also provides for worker participation in industrial companies to the extent that they will share both in the profits and ultimately, through the creation of an industrial community, own 50% of all companies. In future foreign owned companies must either become Peruvianized or operate under a special contract with the Government, which will enable them to recover their investment and reasonable profits, but eventually for the enterprise to pass to the hands of the Peruvian Government. In the motor vehicle industry approximately 17,000 units were assembled in 1969 by 13 different plants. The Government in an attempt to rationalize the industry, has stipulated that as from 1 Jan. 1971 there will only be 5 plants assembling automobiles. The aim of the Government is progressively to increase the proportion of nationally produced vehicle parts and components.

Peru's first iron and steel mill came into production at Chimbote in April 1958. Products include pig-iron, blooms, billets, largets, round and round-deformed bars, wire rod, black and galvanized sheets and galvanized roofing sheets. Refractories are manufactured at Lima.

The Government has a monopoly in the import and/or local manufacture and sale of guano, salt, alcohol and explosives. The monopoly in matches was abandoned in 1954 and that in tobacco in June 1955.

LABOUR. Only about 3,298,000 male inhabitants were considered to be economically active in 1968. The female labour force, which has grown significantly over the last few years, now numbers 970,000. The total economically active population of 4·27m. represents about 31·8% of the country's population and is roughly distributed as follows: agriculture, stock-raising and fishing, 2·25m.; miscellaneous services, 600,000; manufacturing industry, 550,000; construction, 150,000; transportation, 130,000; mining, 90,000; other activities, 450,000.

ELECTRICITY. In 1968 the production of electric energy was 4,880m. kw. The installed capacity in 1968 increased by 10·08% in comparison with the previous year to reach 1,669·6m. kw.

TOURISM. Tourism ranks as seventh among dollar earning industries. In 1968, 113,532 foreigners visited Peru, spending about US$28m.

TRADE UNIONS. Trade unions have about 2m. members (approximately 1·5m. in peasant organizations and 0·5m. in industrial). The major trade union organization is the *Confederación de Trabajadores del Perú*, which was reconstituted in 1956 after being in abeyance for some years. In 1962 a beginning was made with minimum wage agreements for various coastal cities and certain central and southern provinces.

COMMERCE. The value of trade has been as follows (in US$1m.):

	1965	1966	1967	1968	1969
Imports	729·4	816·9	818·9	629·8	600
Exports	667·3	764·4	757·0	866·1	865

On 2 May 1961 Peru ratified the Montevideo treaty and thereby became one of the members of the Latin American Free Trade Area (LAFTA).

On 26 May 1969 Peru signed the Cartagena Agreement between Bolivia, Colombia, Chile and Ecuador establishing the Andean Group, the aim of which is to accelerate the process of economic integration and development on a subregional basis within the ambit of LAFTA. Venezuela has until 1971 to join.

In 1969 the principal imports were: Machinery and appliances (25%); foodstuffs, beverages and tobacco (22%); metals and manufactures (8%); chemicals and allied products (14%); wood, pulp and paper (5%); textiles (4%); fuel, lubricants and other non-metallic minerals (4%); rubber, plastics, etc. (4%); miscellaneous (4%).

The principal exports were: Minerals and metals (54%); fishmeal (26%); cotton (8%); sugar (5%); coffee (3%); wool (1%); petroleum (1%); miscellaneous (2%).

The major suppliers were (in S/.1m.):

	Imports from		Exports to			Imports from		Exports to	
	1968	1969	1968	1969		1968	1969	1968	1969
USA	9,182	7,196	13,166	11,560	Argentine	2,850	2,404	486	592
Germany (West)	3,090	2,642	3,550	4,051	UK	1,328	1,020	786	1,047
Japan	1,725	1,673	4,965	5,413	Italy	1,002	636	775	877

Principal exports have been (in US$1m.):

	1965	1966		1965	1966
Copper	121·3	186·2	Zinc (metal content)	35·8	..
Iron (ore)	47·0	53·4	Cotton	87·5	85·4
Lead (metal content)	32·9	..	Fish and fish products	186·5	206·5
Petroleum	9·3	..	Sugar	37·5	..
Silver (metal content)	39·1	..	Coffee	29·0	..

Total trade between Peru and UK in £1,000 sterling (British Board of Trade returns):

	1966	1967	1968	1969	1970
Imports to UK	9,757	7,697	11,622	13,903	15,197
Exports from UK	11,883	12,356	11,541	11,569 ⎱	9,905
Re-exports from UK	128	98	93	227 ⎰	

SHIPPING. In 1966, 6,900 vessels of 26,602,270 tons entered, and 6,871 of 26,610,772 tons cleared the ports. Since 1928 the coasting trade has been largely reserved for Peruvian-owned vessels with Peruvian crews; in 1960 it handled 2,246,000 metric tons, valued at 1,665m. soles.

ROADS. There were at 30 June 1966, 45,549 km, of which 17,114 km were made up and 4,547 km asphalted. Work on the Carretera Marginal de la Selva (South American Marginal Forest Highway) started in 1965; the 5,600 km road between the Colombian–Venezuelan border and Sta. Cruz, Bolivia, of which the Peruvian portion consists of 394 km already existing, 503 km now under construction and 1,565 km outstanding, to make a sectional total of some 2,460 km.

On 30 June 1966 there were 315,629 licensed road vehicles, including private cars, 178,152; lorries, 95,402; buses, 12,351; motorized cycles and tricycles, 29,724.

RAILWAYS. In 1967 the total working length of the railways was 2,880 km, including 389 km state-owned. The Peruvian Corporation owned 1,546 km.

AVIATION. Air services connect Lima and the capitals of every South American republic. The first Peruvian international line, Aerolíneas Peruanas SA, began operating with 3 planes on 3 June 1957.

POST. An earth satellite ground communication station at Lurin connects Peru through Intelsat. III to the US and Europe. In 1967 there were 1,179 post offices, 316 telegraph and radio-telegraph offices. Length of telegraph lines was 26,121 km. The privately owned telephone system (1969) had 165,121 instruments, of which 102,328 were in Lima, and the system is being considerably extended; radio-telephone circuits connect Lima with distant towns. Three submarine telegraph cables connect Peru and Chile, and one connects Peru and the republics to the north. There are 153 broadcasting stations, of which 29 are in Lima. Wireless receiving sets, about 2m. There are 7 television stations in Lima, 16 in the provinces and 45 relay stations.

BANKING. The Government bank of issue is the Banco Central de la Reserva del Perú, which was established in 1922. A new charter for the bank was promulgated in Aug. 1968; this, *inter alia*, raised the bank's authorized capital from 50m. to 10m. soles and extended the bank's authority with regard to the organization of the commercial banking system and the regulation of foreign-exchange operations. In July 1970 the Central Bank's gold and foreign-exchange holdings stood at US$311m.

Banks, domestic and foreign, are supervised by the Superintendent of Banks. There were, in Nov. 1967, 30 domestic banks and 5 foreign—1 British, 1 Canadian, 2 American and 1 Japanese. Legislation of Aug. 1968 provides that two-thirds of the issued share capital of commercial banks must be held by Peruvian nationals or foreigners resident in Peru for not less than 5 years. At 15 Oct. 1968 advances in Peruvian currency stood at 17,138m. soles and deposits at 19,427m. soles.

WEIGHTS AND MEASURES. The metric system of weights and measures was established by law in 1869, and since 1916 has come into general use.

DIPLOMATIC REPRESENTATIVES

Peru maintains embassies in:

Australia	Finland	Norway
Argentina	France	Panama
Austria	Germany (West)	Paraguay
Belgium	Guatemala	Portugal
Bolivia	Haiti	Romania
Brazil	Honduras	Spain
Bulgaria	Hungary	Sweden
Canada	India	Switzerland
Chile	Israel	USSR
Colombia	Italy	UAR
Costa Rica	Jamaica	UK
Czechoslovakia	Japan	USA
Denmark	Mexico	Uruguay
Dominican Republic	Morocco	Vatican
Ecuador	Netherlands	Venezuela
El Salvador	Nicaragua	Yugoslavia

Peru has missions to the Latin American Free Trade Area, the EEC, the United Nations (New York), FAO, Unesco, International Organizations at Geneva and the Organization of American States, and has representatives accredited to Barbados, China (Taiwan), Greece, the Lebanon, Luxembourg, Norway, the Order of Malta, Poland, Korea (South), Thailand, Trinidad and Tobago.

OF PERU IN GREAT BRITAIN (52 Sloane St., S2)

Ambassador: Adhemar Montagne (accredited 1 April 1969).
Counsellor: Walter Stubbs.
Service Attaché: Rear-Adm. Guillermo de las Casas (*Navy*).

There are consular representatives at Belfast, Birmingham, Glasgow, Hull, Liverpool and London.

OF GREAT BRITAIN IN PERU

Ambassador: H. T. Morgan, CMG.
Counsellor: Stafford Campbell, OBE (*Head of Chancery*). *First Secretary:* J. G. Macdonald, MBE (*Commercial*).
Defence, Military and Air Attaché: Group Capt. G. D. Fuller. *Naval Attaché:* Cdr. F. Bromilow, RN.

There are Consuls at Lima, Iquitos and Arequipa, and Vice-Consuls at Callao and Mollendo.

OF PERU IN THE USA (1320–16th St. NW, Washington, D.C., 20036)

Ambassador: Dr Fernando Berckemeyer Pazos.
Minister-Counsellors: Luis Marchand; Alfredo Valencia (*Commercial*); Alfonso Espinoza (*Cultural*). *Counsellor:* Igor Velásquez. *First Secretary:* Alicia Pérez.
Service Attachés: Gen. Enrique López (*Army*), Rear-Adm. Fernando Elias (*Navy*), Maj.-Gen. Daniel Peña Mariategui (*Air*).

OF THE USA IN PERU

Ambassador: T. G. Belcher.
Deputy Chief of Mission: Edward W. Clark (*Consul-General*). *Heads of Sections:* Ramond Gonzalez (*Political*); George Bennsky (*Economic*); David Post (*Commercial*); Arthur Purcell (*Labour*); Willard B. Devlin (*Consular*); Weikko A. Forsten (*Administrative*); George Greko (*AID*).
Service Attachés: Col. William C. Sibert (*Army*), Capt. A. McEwan (*Navy*), Lieut.-Col. F. Christman (*Air*).

There is a Consul at Piura.

BOOKS OF REFERENCE

The official gazette is *El Peruano*, Lima.

Anuario Estadístico del Perú. Annual.—*Boletín de Estadística Peruana*. Quarterly.—*Demarcación Política del Perú*. (Dirección Nacional de Estadística), Lima
Censo Nacional Población, 1940. 9 vols. Lima, 1947–49
Estadística del Comercio Exterior (*Superintendencia de Aduanas*). Lima
Banco Central de Reserva. Monthly Bulletin.—*Renta Nacional del Perú*. Annual, Lima
   Ministerio de Fomento Lima publishes separate annual statistics on the mining and petroleum industries and on general industry; the wool textile and cotton textile industries, the Peruvian Chamber of Commerce and the National Agrarian Society furnish annual studies.

Bourricaud, F., *Pouvoir et Société dans le Pérou contemporain*. Paris, 1965
Hemming, J., *The Conquest of the Incas*. London, 1970
Kanto, H., *The ideology and program of the Peruvian Aprista movement*. Univ. of California Press, 1953
Marrett, Sir R., *Peru*. London, 1969
Mejía Baca, J., and Tauro, A., *Diccionário Enciclopédico del Perú*. 3 vols. 1966
Owens, R. J., *Peru*. OUP, 1964
Pike, *A modern history of Peru*. London, 1967
Vargas, Padre, *Historia General del Perú*. Lima, 1967

NATIONAL LIBRARY. Avenida Abancay, Lima. *Director:* Guillermo Lohmann Villena.

REPUBLIC OF THE PHILIPPINES
República de Filipinas—Republika ñg Pilipinas

HISTORY. The Philippines was discovered by Magellan in 1521 and conquered by Spain in 1565. Following the Spanish–American war, the islands were ceded to the USA on 10 Dec. 1898, after the Filipinos had tried in vain to establish an independent republic in 1896.

The Republic of the Philippines came into existence on 4 July 1946, by agreement with the US Government embodied in an Act of Congress signed by President Roosevelt on 24 March 1934, accepted by the Philippine Legislature on 1 May 1934 and ratified at a plebiscite on 14 May 1935. This Act established a 10-year transitional period, designated as that of the Philippine Commonwealth, at the end of which complete independence was automatically effective.

CONSTITUTION AND GOVERNMENT. The republic is governed by a constitution adopted on 14 May 1935 and amended in 1940 and 1946. The President and Vice-President are elected for 4 years; both may be re-elected for another term. The President is assisted by 11 departmental secretaries in charge of Foreign Affairs; Finance; Justice; National Defence; Health; Education; Public Works and Communications; Labour; Commerce and Industry; Agriculture and Natural Resources; General Services; by 6 other officials of cabinet rank, namely the Executive Secretary, the Budget Commissioner, the Chairman of the National Economic Council, the Press Secretary, the Administrator of Economic Co-ordination, the Commissioner of National Integration; and 12 officials invited to cabinet meetings.

President: Ferdinand E. Marcos (Nationalist), elected for a second term of 4 years on 11 Nov. 1969, obtained 3,759,479 votes in the election against 1,372,641 cast for Senator Sergio Osmena, Jr (Liberal).

Vice-President: Fernando Lopez.

Congress consists of a Senate of 24 members and a House of Representatives of 104 members. All male and female citizens 21 years of age or older who can read or write Spanish, English or a native dialect and who meet certain residential qualifications are entitled to vote. Registered voters at the 1961 local elections numbered 9·6m.

The constitution vests in the republic all ownership of the country's natural resources, which, apart from public agricultural land, may not be alienated. An agreement with the USA signed on 4 July 1946, ratified by plebiscite on 11 March 1948 and expiring in 1974, admits American interests or companies to the exploitation of any resources and public-utility business open to Filipinos. Concessions and leases are limited to 25 years, renewable for another 25 years; maximum area of agricultural public land which any corporation may acquire or lease is 1,024 hectares (2,529 acres) and not more than 2,000 hectares (4,940 acres) if used for grazing purposes.

National flag: Blue and red (horizontal), with a white canton charged with a gold sun (with 8 rays) and 3 gold stars.

National hymn: 'Tierra adorado', 'Land of the morning', lyric in English by M. A. Sane and C. Osias, in Spanish by Jisé Palma (1899), tune by Julian Felipe (1898); 'Pambansang Awit ñg Pilipinas', Tagalog lyric by the Institute of National Language, music by Julian Felipe.

LOCAL GOVERNMENT. The country is administratively divided into 67 provinces, 59 chartered cities, 1,423 municipalities and 21 municipal districts. Each province elects its executive, consisting of a governor, and 3 members of the provincial board. The municipalities are public corporations, each composed of a number of *barrios;* the elected municipal mayor is the executive official. The mayors of the chartered cities are elective.

AREA AND POPULATION. The Philippines is situated between 21° 20′ and 4° 30′ N. lat. and between 110° 55′ and 126° 36′ E. long. It is composed of 7,107 islands and islets, 2,870 of which are named. Approximate land area, 115,600 sq. miles (299,400 sq. km). The 12 most important islands with their areas (in sq. miles) are: Luzon, 41,845; Mindanao, 36,381; Samar, 5,184; Negros, 5,278; Palawan, 5,751; Panay, 4,749; Mindoro, 3,995; Leyte, 3,090; Cebu, 1,964; Bohol, 1,589; Masbate, 1,562; Catanduanes, 583.

The total population at the census of 6 May 1970 was 37,008,419 (provisional). The population of Manila, the capital, in 1970, was 1,582,000. The new capital, Quezon City, just north-east of Manila, had a population of 585,100. Other cities, with their population in May 1970, are: Iloilo on Panay, 213,000; Cebu on Cebu, 351,000; Zamboanga on Mindanao, 188,300; Davao on Mindanao, 315,300; Basilan on Basilan Island, 222,000; Bacolod on Negros, 165,600; San Carlos, 174,000; Pasay, 183,500.

On 7 June 1940 the President of the Philippines approved a law, effective 4 July 1946, making a new language based on Tagalog (a Malayan dialect) the official national language of the republic. About 10,689,200 people speak English and about 558,650 Spanish; for government and commercial purposes these two languages are commonly used. Some 70 native languages are spoken in the Philippines, of which 9 are of major importance; they belong to the Malayo-Polynesian family.

RELIGION. In 1967 there were 24,176,989 Roman Catholics; in 1960, 1,414,431 Aglipayans, 1,317,475 Moslems, 785,399 Protestants, 270,104 members of the Iglesia ni Kristo, 39,631 Buddhists and 574,549 others.

The Roman Catholics are organized in 10 archbishoprics, 43 bishoprics, 12 prelatures nullius, 4 apostolic vicariates, 4 apostolic prefectures and 1,633 parishes. The Philippine Independent Church, founded in 1902, and comprising about 5% of the population, denies the spiritual authority of the Roman Pontiff. It is divided into two groups, one of which has accepted ordinations by the Episcopalian Church.

EDUCATION. Education is free in the primary schools and is completely co-educational. In all schools English is the main medium of instruction, although the Filipino language is also taught. The vernaculars are used as the medium of instruction in the lower primary grades, and Spanish is one of the possible subjects in all high schools and obligatory in all colleges. In 1960, of the persons 10 years old and over, 72% were literate.

In 1967–68, 6,579,349 attended elementary, 452,771 secondary and 8,830 collegiate schools. In 1967–68, 287,111 pupils attended private elementary schools, 812,906 secondary, 539,378 collegiate. The University of the Philippines (founded in 1908) had 21,776 students in 1966–67.

NEWSPAPERS (1967). There were 770 newspapers and magazines with a circulation of 206m.; 18 of them are dailies, of which the 6 largest are published in English.

SOCIAL WELFARE. The government programme includes the purchase and subdivision of big landed estates for resale on easy instalment plans to tenants, the opening of virgin lands and settlement of landless families, the granting of bank loans to such families for seeds and the building of homes, the opening of rural roads and rural schools, the setting up of travelling medical clinics and the distribution of relief goods, including food, clothing and medicine, to families who have been displaced due to the depredations of the communist outlaws.

JUSTICE. The judiciary is headed by the Supreme Court, with a chief justice and 10 associate justices; it can declare a law or treaty unconstitutional by the concurrent votes of 8 justices. There is a court of appeal, headed by a presiding justice, with 17 associate justices. There are 16 judicial districts subdivided into 212 branches, each with a presiding judge of first instance. Every city has a city court and every municipality has one municipal judge. In addition, the juvenile and domestic relations court in Manila has exclusive jurisdiction to try all cases involving minors and matrimonial disputes.

There are also 3 agencies of the Government which have been denominated as 'courts', namely, the Court of Tax Appeals, the Court of Industrial Relations and the Court of Agrarian Relations, which perform judicial as well as quasi-judicial functions.

All members of the judiciary are appointed by the President with the consent of the Commission on Appointments.

FINANCE. Currency. The republic is on a free foreign-exchange market with the peso equivalent to about 26 cents US. Total money supply, Dec. 1966, was P.3,371·3m., of which P.1,543·4m. was currency in circulation and P.1,287·9m. were demand deposits. The peso contains 20 grammes of silver, 0·800 fine. The coins used are: Peso, one-half peso, peseta (20 centavos), media peseta (10 centavos), all in silver of 0·750 fine; 5 centavo in cupro-nickel, and 1 centavo in copper–tin–zinc. Central Bank notes are of 5, 10, 20 and 50 centavos denominations. Treasury certificates and Central Bank notes are issued in 1, 2, 5, 10, 20, 50, 100 pesos denominations.

Budget. The revenues and expenditures of the central government for fiscal years (ending 30 June) were, in 1m. Philippine pesos as follows:

	1965–66	1966–67[1]	1967–68[1]	1968–69[1]	1969–70[1]
Revenue	2,148	2,371	2,830	3,156	3,502
Expenditure	2,228	2,354	2,764	3,013	3,197

[1] Estimates.

Taxation furnished P.1,523m. of the revenue for 1964–65, P.1,799m. for 1965–66, P.1,945m. for 1966–67 and P.2,199m. for 1967–68.

Expenditure (1967–68) included (in 1m. pesos): National defence and police, 382; education, health and welfare, 1,016; general administration, 308; economic development, 826; public debt, 156.

As of 31 Dec. 1966 the total internal public debt outstanding of the national and local governments, including those of the government corporations, stood at P.3,520m., while the external public debt amounted to US$501m., of which US$260m. was short-term obligations.

DEFENCE. On 14 March 1947 the Philippine and US Governments signed a 99-year military-base arrangement. The USA was granted the use of a series of army, navy and air bases, with the right to use a number of others on mutual agreement. On 21 March a second agreement provided for a US Military Advisory Group as well as military assistance. A treaty of mutual assistance was signed in Washington on 30 Aug. 1951; the instruments of ratification were exchanged in Manila on 27 Aug. 1952. The Philippines is also a signatory of the S.E. Asia Collective Defence Treaty (*see* pp. 44–46).

The Chief of Staff of the Armed Forces has overall command over the Army, Air Force, Navy and Constabulary.

Army. The Army consists of 18,000 officers and men in the active force. It is organized in 1 combat-ready division and 4 training divisions, equipped with M-24 and M-41 tanks.

Navy. The Navy includes 7 escort vessels, 3 command ships, 2 coastal minesweepers, 7 patrol vessels, 24 patrol boats, 4 hydrofoils, 6 landing ships, 10 auxiliary vessels, all *ex*-USA, and 24 coastguard vessels. Naval personnel in 1970 totalled 8,000 officers and men.

Air Force. The Air Force has a strength of some 9,000 officers and men, with 188 aircraft, and has been built up with US assistance to meet its commitments to SEATO. Its fighter-bomber wing is equipped with 1 squadron of supersonic F-5s and 2 squadrons of F-86F Sabre jets, and there is a squadron of F-86D Sabre all-weather fighters. There are also transport, observation, air/sea rescue and training units, flying aircraft of US design, including 36 Japanese-built Mentor primary trainers (received as war reparations).

Police. Public order is maintained partly through the Philippine constabulary and partly through the local police forces. The constabulary now forms part of the Armed Forces.

AGRICULTURE. Of the total area of 29,741,290 hectares, 8,257,556 hectares are commercial forests; 4,102,021 hectares non-commercial forests; 11,210,050 hectares cultivated land; 662,447 hectares mangrove and marshes, 2,033,917 hectares brush land and 3,475,299 hectares open land.

About 98·4% of the total cultivated area is owned by Filipinos; the average size of the farm is 3·21 hectares. The principal products are unhusked rice (palay), Manila hemp (abaca), copra, sugar-cane, maize and tobacco. In Oct. 1966, 6·29m. persons were employed in agriculture (57·5% of the working population).

In 1968 production (in metric tons) was: Rough rice, 4·56m.; copra, 1·54m.; desiccated coconut, 56,300; sugar (muscovado), 1·66m.; molasses, 502,900; abaca fibre, 103,400.

Minor crops are fruits, nuts, root crops, vegetables, onions, beans, coffee, cacao, peanuts, ramie, rubber, maguey and kapok.

Livestock, estimated in 1968: 4,173,000 carabaos (water buffaloes), 1,643,800 cattle, 281,700 horses, 6,090,200 hogs, 623,500 goats; (1967) 1,750 sheep and 70·4m. poultry.

FORESTRY. The forests (covering 44·3% of the area, with an estimated stand of 416,400,000m. bd ft) furnish cabinet and construction timber, gums and resins, vegetable oils, rattan and bamboo, tan and dye barks and dye woods. About 97·5% of this belongs to the Government. In 1967, 3,637,199,000 bd ft of timber and 48,479,000 bd ft of sawn lumber was exported.

FISHERIES. Fish production from all sources was 937,684 metric tons and was valued at P.361,938,000 in 1968.

MINING. Mineral production in 1968–69 (in metric tons): Lead, 56; zinc, 2,824; copper, 117,973; manganese, 57,542; chromite, 463,618; iron, 1·47m.; coal, 61,540; salt, 161,606; molybdenum, 33; gypsum, 29,298; gold, 546,315 fine oz.; silver, 1·5m.; fine oz.; quicksilver, 3,505 flasks (of 76 lb.). Other minerals include cement, rock asphalt, sand and gravel.

INDUSTRY. Manufacturing is largely carried on in homes (chiefly embroidery, buntal hats, woven cloths, mats and pottery), but the number of factories has been fast increasing. In 1963 there were 17 coconut-oil mills, 102 cigar and cigarette factories, 8,215 rice-mills, 928 shoe factories, 25 sugar centrals, 6 cement plants and 17 hydro-electric plants. The non-agricultural labour force in Oct. 1966 was 4,646,000 out of a total of 10,936,000 employed.

ELECTRICITY. In 1968 the Manila Electric Company produced 3,853m. kwh. (3,431m. in 1967).

COMMERCE. The values of imports and exports for calendar years are stated as follows in 1m. pesos:

	1963	1964	1965	1966	1967	1968
Imports	2,487·1	3,106·7	3,236	3,398	4,125	4,470
Exports	2,812·6	3,046·4	3,100	3,423	3,477	3,752

The principal exports in 1968 were (in P.1m.): Copra, 530; sugar (centrifugal), 503; logs, lumber and timber, 892; abaca fibres, 48; coconut oil, 314; copper concentrates, 296; desiccated coconut, 120.

Main imports in 1968 (in P.1m.): Machinery, 894; mineral fuels and lubricants, 378; cereals, 162; dairy products, 148; transport equipment, 479; base metals, 428: electrical machinery and appliances, 254.

Owing to the commercializing of agriculture for export, foodstuffs have to be imported, representing normally from 15 to 20% of all imports, chiefly meat and fish products and wheat and dairy products from USA.

For over a half-century the foreign trade has been chiefly with the USA. The trade relationship of the two countries is governed by the Philippine Trade Act of 1946 as amended. American goods entering the Philippines now pay a tariff duty of 90% of the regular duty on other foreign goods to 31 Dec. 1973, and 100% from 1 Jan. 1974.

Philippine products entering the USA paid 10% of the US tariff in 1959–61, and pay 20% in 1962–64, 40% in 1965–67, 60% in 1968–70, 80% in 1971–73 and 100% from 1 Jan, 1974.

The Philippines exported to the USA goods valued at $437·1m. in 1968 and imported from the Philippines goods valued at $1,533·5m.

Total trade between the Philippines and UK (British Board of Trade returns, in £1,000 sterling):

	1965	1966	1967	1968	1969	1970
Imports to UK	3,806	3,089	5,113	3,689	4,333	7,480
Exports from UK	13,468	16,465	19,353	22,343	27,911 }	25,087
Re-exports from UK	99	246	206	101	258 }	

SHIPPING. In 1966, 2,303 vessels of 10,483,576 net tons entered and 2,323 vessels of 10,568,555 net tons cleared all ports. Of the vessels entering, 376 (2·1m. tons) were American, 395 (2·05m. tons) Norwegian, 446 (2·47m. tons) British and 1,086 (3·86m. tons) Filipino.

ROADS. In 1967 highways extended 56,180 km. In 1965 there were registered 303,300 motor vehicles of all types.

RAILWAYS. Railway tracks (1966), 1,026 km in Luzon. In 1964–65, 8,234,792 passengers and 918,973 metric tons of freight were carried by rail.

AVIATION. The Philippine Air Lines, Inc., with a capital of P.6m., in 1968 carried 2,298,196 passengers, 47·7m. lb. of cargo and 2·2m. lb. of mail.

POST. In 1965 there were in operation 1,414 post offices and 978 telecommunication stations. There were (1968) 207,593 telephones, of which 123,740 were in Manila; the Government operated 28,706 and private companies 178,887.

Licensed radio stations in 1964 numbered 5,153, including 904 ship stations and 145 aircraft stations.

BANKING. In 1966 there were 343 branches of commercial banks, 7 of them being overseas branches. Total deposits of the commercial banks in June 1967 were P.5,188·9m. In June 1967 the post office savings bank held deposits of P.60·4m.

Under a law passed 15 June 1948 the Central Bank of the Philippines was created to have sole control of the credit and monetary supply, independent of the Treasury. It has a capital of P.10m. furnished solely by the Government. Its total assets, as of 31 Dec. 1966, were P.3,373·3m.

DIPLOMATIC REPRESENTATIVES

The Philippines maintains embassies in:

Argentina	Finland	Korea (South)	Switzerland
Australia	France	Laos	Taiwan
Austria	Germany (West)	Malaysia	Thailand
Belgium	Greece	Mexico	Turkey
Brazil	India	Netherlands	UAR
Burma	Indonesia	Norway	UK
Cambodia	Iran	Pakistan	USA
Ceylon	Israel	Portugal	Vatican
Chile	Italy	Spain	Vietnam (South)
Denmark	Japan	Sweden	

OF THE PHILIPPINES IN GREAT BRITAIN (9A Palace Green, W8)

Ambassador: Jaime Zobel de Ayala. *Minister-Counsellors:* Tiburcio C. Baja; Rodolfo H. Severino.

Armed Forces Attaché: Col. Pedro L. Los Banos.

OF GREAT BRITAIN IN THE PHILIPPINES

Ambassador: J. N. O. Curle, CMG, CVO.
Counsellors: R. W. H. du Boulay; Henry F. Bartlett, OBE (*Commercial*).
First Secretary: P. R. Spendlove (*Head of Chancery*).
Naval, Military and Air Attaché: Wing Cdr R. A. Nosh.

There are consular representatives at Bacolod, Cebu, Iloilo and Manila.

OF THE PHILIPPINES IN THE USA (1617 Massachusetts Ave. NW, Washington, D.C., 20036)

Ambassador: Ernesto V. Lagdameo.
Deputy Chief of Mission: Dr José F. Imperial. *Ministers:* Pablo R. Suarez; Ernesto C. Pineda. *Counsellor:* Abelardo L. Valencia *(Press)*. *First Secretary:* Gerdenio G. Manuel. *Armed Forces Attaché:* Capt. Gregorio Lim.

OF THE USA IN THE PHILIPPINES

Ambassador: Henry A. Byroade.
Deputy Chief of Mission: Richard B. Finn. *Heads of Sections:* Francis Underhill *(Political)*; William E. Knight II *(Economic)*; George A. Ellsworth *(Commercial)*; Anthony S. Luchek *(Labour)*; Wilbur Chase, Jr *(Consular)*; Eldon B. Smith *(Administrative)*; Wesley C. Haraldson *(AID)*.
Service Attachés: Col. Alfred K. Patterson. *(Defence and Air)*, Col. Hartwin R. Peterson *(Army)*.

There is consular service at Cebu.

BOOKS OF REFERENCE

Republic of the Philippine Government Manual, 1950. Manila, 1950.
The Philippines: a Handbook of Information. Manila, 1955
Gazetteer of the Philippine Islands. United States Department of Commerce. Washington, 1945
Barton, R. F., *The Kalingas.* Chicago, 1949
Bernstein, D., *The Philippine Story.* New York, 1947
Chapman, A., *Philippine Nationalism.* New York, 1950
Forbes, W. C., *The Philippine Islands.* 3 vols. Rev. Cambridge, Mass., 1945
Golay, F. H. *The Philippines: Public Policy and National Economic Development.* Cornell Univ., Press, 1961
Hainsworth, R. G., and Moyer, R. T., *Agricultural Geography of the Philippine Islands.* Washington, 1945
Kurihara, K. K., *Labor in the Philippine Economy.* Stanford University Press, 1945
Meyer, M. W., *A diplomatic history of the Philippine Republic.* Univ. of Hawaii Press, 1965
Mills, L. A., *The New World of Southeast Asia.* University of Minnesota Press, 1949
Zafra, U. A., *Philippine Economic Handbook.* Silver Spring, Md., 1960

POLAND

Polska Rzeczpospolita Ludowa

HISTORY. In 1966 Poland celebrated its millennium, but modern Polish history begins with the partitions of the once-powerful kingdom between Russia, Austria and Prussia in 1772, 1793 and 1795. After the creation by Napoleon I of a semi-independent Grand Duchy of Warsaw, the country was again partitioned at the Congress of Vienna in 1815 between Russia (Congress Poland), Austria and Prussia (Grand Duchy of Posen), and the free city of Cracow.

The Polish revolution of 1830–31 caused the suppression of the 1815 constitution and made 'Congress Poland' virtually a Russian province. The revolution of 1846–48 led to the incorporation of Cracow in Austria, the abolition of the Grand Duchy of Posen and further repression in 'Congress Poland', which was intensified after the revolution of 1863–64.

During the First World War Russian Poland was occupied by the Austro-German forces. On 10 Nov. 1918 independence was proclaimed by Joseph Piłsudski, the founder of the Polish Legions during the war. On 28 June 1919 the Treaty of Versailles recognized the independence of Poland.

On 1 Sept. 1939 Germany invaded Poland, on 17 Sept. 1939 Russian troops entered eastern Poland, and on 29 Sept. 1939 the fourth partition of Poland took place. After the German attack on Russia, the Germans occupied the whole of Poland. War casualties and victims of German terror amounted to 6–7m. people. By March 1945 the country had been liberated by the Russians.

In July 1944 the USSR recognized the Polish Committee of National Liberation (*Polski Komitet Wyzwolenia Narodowego*) established in Lublin as an executive organ of the National Council of the Homeland (*Krajowa Rada Narodowa*). The Committee was transformed into the Provisional Government in Dec. 1944, and on 28 June 1945, supplemented by members of the Polish Government in London (which had been recognized by the UK and USA), it was re-established— in Moscow— as the Polish Provisional Government of National Unity and on 6 July recognized as such by the UK and USA.

Elections were held on 19 Jan. 1947. Of the 12·7m. votes cast, 11·24m. were recognized as valid, and 9m. were given for the Communist-dominated 'Democratic Bloc'.

In 1948 the Socialist and Communist parties merged into the Polish United Workers' Party. In 1949 the Peasants' Party and the Polish Peasants' Party merged into the United Peasants' Party. All parties form part of the Communist-controlled National Unity Front.

Relations between Poland and West Germany were normalized by a treaty of 7 Dec. 1970, by which West Germany recognized as permanent and inviolable Poland's western boundary as laid down by the Potsdam Conference on 2 Aug. 1945 (the 'Oder–Neisse line').

CONSTITUTION AND GOVERNMENT. The present Constitution was adopted on 22 July 1952.

After riots in Poznań in June 1956 nationalist anti-Stalinist elements gained control of the Communist Party in 1956, under the leadership of Władysław Gomułka, who had spent several years in prison for 'Titoist deviation'. Following student unrest in March 1968, the goverment carried out purges of Party and military personnel, intellectuals and 'Zionists'.

In Dec. 1970 strikes and riots broke out in the ports of Gdańsk, Szczecin and Gdynia in protest against steep rises in food prices. Despite savage repression the situation deteriorated and led to the resignation of Gomułka (ostensibly for reasons of health) and a number of other ministers and members of the Politburo. He was replaced by Edward Gierek (born 1913), formerly provincial Party secretary in Katowice, Silesia. The price increases were cancelled on 1 March 1971, a step made possible by credits from the USSR.

The titular head of state is the Chairman of the Council of State, Józef Cyrankiewicz (formerly Prime Minister; replaced Marian Spychalski on 23 Dec. 1970).

Supreme *de facto* power is in the hands of the Pollburo of the Polish United Workers' Party, in March 1971 composed as follows: Edward Gierek, *First Secretary of the Central Committee*; Mieczysław Moczar; Piotr Jaroszewicz, *Chairman of the Council of Ministers* (*Prime Minister*); Stefan Olszowski; Edward Babiuch; Jan Szydtak; Józef Cyrankiewicz; Stefan Jędrychowski, *Foreign Minister*; Władysław Kruczek, *Chairman, Central Council of Trade Unions*; Józef Tejchma. Candidate members: Mieczysław Jagielski, *Deputy Prime Minister*; Henryk Jabloński; Gen. Wojciech Jaruzielski *Minister of Defence*; Józef Kempa. Ministers not in the Politburo include: Janusz Burakiewicz (*Foreign Trade*); Franciszek Szlachcicz (*Interior*); Józef Trendota (*Finance*).

In 1969 the Polish United Workers' Party had 2,203,600 members; the United Peasants' Party, 399,500, and the Democratic Party, 86,500.

The authority of the Polish People's Republic is vested in the Sejm, which is elected for 4 years by all citizens over 18. The Sejm elects a Council of State, composed of a Chairman, the Secretary and 14 members, including 4 vice-chairmen. It also elects the Council of Ministers. Local administration is carried out by People's Councils, elected for 4 years in provinces, districts, boroughs, towns and villages.

Elections for the Sejm took place on 1 June 1969. The electorate numbered 21,148,879; of these 18,982,316 (97·61%) voted; the single list of the National Unity Front received 99·22% of the votes. The 460 seats are distributed as follows: 255 United Workers' Party, 117 United Peasants' Party, 39 Democratic Party,

49 independents, including 14 Catholic representatives. The Sejm has 62 women deputies.

National flag: White, red (horizontal).
National anthem: Jeszcze Polska nie zginęła (words by J. Wybicki, 1797; tune by M. Ogiński, 1796).

AREA AND POPULATION. The republic comprises an area of 312,700 sq. km (120,633 sq. miles), and a population (census, 6 Dec. 1960) of 29,776,000 (14·4m. males; 14m. urban). Estimate, 1 Jan. 1970, 32·67m. (15·88m. males; 16·83m. urban); density 105 per sq. km.

Poland is administratively divided into 17 'voivodships' or provinces (*wojewodztwo*, plural *wojewodztwa*) and 5 cities of province status. These are subdivided into 322 rural and 74 urban districts. The capital is Warsaw (Warszawa).

Area (in sq. km) and population (in 1,000) on 1 Jan. 1970:

Province	Area	Population	Province	Area	Population
Warsaw City	446	1,289	Gdańsk (Danzig)	10,939	1,416
Warsaw	29,333	2,560	Koszalin	17,974	790
Bydgoszcz	20,800	1,915	Szczecin (Stettin)	12,677	896
Poznań City	220	462	Zielona Góra	14,514	883
Poznań	27,705	2,188	Wrocław City (Breslau)	225	517
Łódź City	212	753	Wrocław	18,827	1,994
Łódź	17,153	1,690	Opole	9,509	1,046
Kielce	19,408	1,910	Katowice	9,515	3,645
Lublin	24,876	1,956	Kraków City (Cracow)	230	577
Białystok	23,148	1,191	Kraków	15,350	2,200
Olsztyn	21,023	985	Rzeszów	18,646	1,763

Population (in 1,000) of the largest towns (Dec. 1969):

Warsaw	1,284	Bydgoszcz	279	Radom	154
Łódź	751	Lublin	238	Chorzów	151
Kraków (Cracow)	571	Zabrze	200	Sosnowiec	144
Wrocław (Breslau)	514	Bytom	187	Ruda Śląska	141
Poznań	460	Częstochowa	186	Wałbrzych	126
Gdańsk (Danzig)	370	Gdynia	182	Toruń	126
Szczecin (Stettin)	335	Gliwice	168	Kielce	121
Katowice	296	Białystok	163	Bielsko-Biała	103

Rate (per 1,000 persons) of live births, in 1968 (and 1969), was 16·2 (16·3); of deaths, 7·6 (8·1); marriages, 8 (8·3); divorces, 0·91 (0); infantile mortality, 33·4 (34·4).

The rate of natural growth is declining: 8·2 per 1,000 in 1969 (*cf.* 19·5 in 1955). Expectation of life in 1966 was 66·8 years for males, 72·8 years for females. In 1970, 40% of the population was under 25.

National minorities in Dec. 1963 numbered 453,000, including 180,000 Ukrainians, 165,000 Byelorussians, 31,000 Jews, 21,000 Slovaks and 10,000 Lithuanians.

In 1969, 10·33m. Poles lived abroad (6·5m. in USA, 1·4m. in USSR, 145,000 in UK).

RELIGION. 95% of the population is Roman Catholic. Church–State relations are regulated by agreements of 14 April 1950 and 8 Dec. 1956. The Church has a university (Lublin), 48 seminaries and 16,000 'catechism posts'. It has the right to publish and propagate the faith. Relations worsened in 1966, when Church and State held counter-celebrations of the Polish millennium.

The archbishop of Warsaw and Gniezno is the primate of Poland (since 1948, Stefan Cardinal Wyszyński). The Vatican considers the archbishoprics of Lwów and Vilnius (incorporated in the USSR in 1940) as still being under Polish jurisdiction. There are 5 archbishoprics, 25 dioceses and 6,333 parishes. In 1967 there were 69 bishops, 17,931 priests, 3,281 monks, 28,054 nuns and 12,395 churches and chapels.

In 1967 the Vatican made the 4 bishops in the (formerly German) western territories apostolic administrators and created the archbishop of Kraków a second cardinal.

The Polish Orthodox Church, which broke away from Moscow after the Russian Revolution and received canonical status under the Patriarchate of Constantinople, in 1948 returned to Moscow obedience and was granted autocephaly. In Sept. 1967 it claimed 527,000 members in 2 dioceses with 215 parishes, under a Metropolitan.

Protestants are estimated at 140,000, including 100,909 Lutherans, 15,000 Methodists and Baptists, and 5,000 Reformed. There are also 21,870 Old Catholics in 41 parishes with headquarters at Płock and 56,646 'Polish Catholics'.

The number of Jews, who in 1939 constituted 10% of the population (about 3·5m.), is now estimated at 31,000. At least 3m. perished under the Nazi occupation.

EDUCATION. Basic education from 7 to 15 is free and compulsory. Optional free secondary education is then available in technical-vocational or general schools. In 1969–70 there were: Kindergartens, 8,757 with 512,000 pupils and 23,715 teachers; primary schools, 26,379 with 5,443,100 pupils and 210,138 teachers; secondary schools, 860 with 309,700 pupils and 15,475 teachers; schools for the handicapped, 532 with 82,500 pupils; primary schools for adults, 401 with 47,400 pupils and 667 teachers; secondary schools for adults (including correspondence courses), 311 with 136,300 pupils and 1,392 teachers; vocational schools, 9,142 with 1,605,000 pupils and 62,222 teachers, and 84 institutions of higher education (9 universities, 18 polytechnics, 7 agricultural schools, 6 schools of economics, 9 teachers' training colleges, 10 medical academies, 5 schools of physical training, 16 academies of arts, 2 naval colleges and 2 theological academies) with 322,100 students (including 117,000 part-time and correspondence students) and 2,866 professors, 3,625 readers and 21,671 lecturers and assistants. After student demonstrations in 1968 the Government took measures to strengthen its control of higher education.

CINEMAS AND THEATRES. In 1969 there were 3,506 cinemas, 92 theatre and 37 concert halls.

NEWSPAPERS (1969). There are 54 papers of which *Trybuna Ludu* (People's Tribune) is the Party organ (circulation 205,000).

SOCIAL WELFARE. In 1969 there were 677 hospitals with 201,400 beds, 68 tuberculosis sanatoria with 19,036 beds, 5,268 dispensaries and 2,556 health centres. There were 47,328 doctors and 13,095 dentists.

JUSTICE. The legal system was reorganized in 1950. A new penal code was adopted in 1969. Espionage and treason carry the severest penalties and severer punishment is provided for 'serious crimes'. For minor crimes there is more provision for probation sentences and fines. Previous jurisprudence was based on a penal code of 1932 supplemented by the Concise Penal Code of 1946.

There exist the following courts: The Supreme Court; voivodship, district and special courts. Judges and lay assessors are elected. The State Council elects the judges of the Supreme Court for a term of 5 years, and appoints the Prosecutor-General. The office of the Prosecutor-General is separate from the judiciary.

Lawyers belong to 'legal collectives'; private practice has been abolished.

399,678 crimes were reported in 1969, including 416 cases of homicide, 203,805 of larceny and 2,651 of 'speculation'.

FINANCE. Currency. The currency unit is the *złoty*, divided into 100 *groszy* From 30 Oct. 1950 to 31 Dec. 1960 the zloty equalled the Soviet rouble, but with the revaluation of the rouble on 1 Jan. 1961, the basic relation changed to 1 rouble = 4·44 zlotys and, for non-trade transactions within the Soviet bloc, to 1 rouble = 1·5 zlotys. The currency consists of notes of 5, 10, 20, 50, 100, 500 and, since 1 June 1966, 1,000 zlotys; and of coins of 1 grosz, 2, 5, 10, 20 and 50 groszy and 1, 2, 5 and 10 zlotys. The official rate of exchange is £1 sterling = 9·60 zlotys, US$1 = 4 zlotys. Tourist rates; £1 = 57·46 zlotys, US$1 = 24 zlotys.

Budget. Budget in 1m. zlotys, for calendar years:

	1964	1965	1966	1967	1968	1969
Revenue	283,300	299,900	326,700	326,700	329,700	357,600
Expenditure	273,800	288,900	318,300	326,400	326,200	351,000

Main items of 1969 revenue (in 1m. zlotys): Sales tax and profits tax from non-trading state enterprises, 209,600; profits tax from other state enterprises, 61,100; social insurance contributions, 19,800; personal taxes, 23,500; taxes from the private economic sector (mainly agriculture), 10,800.

Main items of 1969 expenditure (in 1m. zlotys): State enterprises, 185,500; social security, 16,500; education, 68,200; defence, 33,000; administration,17,600.

Polish debts to UK have been fully repaid. Poland does not accept liability for the £495,000 debts of Danzig.

DEFENCE. Poland is divided into 3 military districts: Warsaw (the eastern half of Poland); Pomerania (Baltic coast, part of central Poland; headquarters at Bydgoszcz); Silesia (Silesia and southern Poland; headquarters at Wrocław).

The armed forces are on Soviet lines and divided into army (2 years' service), air force (3 years), navy (3 years), anti-aircraft, rocket and radio-technological units (3 years) and internal security forces (27 months). In 1965 the security forces were taken away from the Ministry of Internal Affairs and placed under the Defence Ministry.

The military age extends from the 19th to the 50th year. The strength of the armed forces is estimated at 275,000, plus 45,000 security and frontier forces both of which include armoured brigades.

Army. The Army consists of 5 armoured, 9 motorized and 1 airborne divisions. Total strength, 185,000. Tanks (mostly T-54) number 3,000.

Navy. The Navy comprises 6 submarines, 3 destroyers, 24 fleet minesweepers, 8 patrol vessels, 12 missile craft, 38 patrol boats, 20 torpedo boats, 4 coastal craft, 16 landing ships, 10 landing craft, 2 training ships, 27 minesweeping boats, 1 survey ship, 5 oilers and 5 auxiliaries. It has 50 naval aircraft (mostly MiG-17). Personnel in 1970 totalled 20,000 officers and men.

Air Force. The Air Force has a strength of some 70,000 officers and men and 750 first-line jet aircraft of Soviet design. Six interceptor and fighter-bomber divisions each comprise 3 wings (of 2 or 3 squadrons each) of MiG-21, MiG-19 and MiG-17 fighters. A bomber division (2 wings) has about 40 Il-28 twin-jet light bombers, but its role is likely to be taken over by the several ground-attack wings operating Sukhoi Su-7B and MiG-17 fighters. Another fighter division (2 wings) supports the Navy. There are also transport, helicopter and training units. Soviet 'Guideline' surface-to-air missiles are operational.

Some 30,000 Soviet troops (2 divisions, 1 armoured) were stationed in Poland in 1969.

PRODUCTION. Before 1940 Poland was a predominantly agricultural country, but by 1969 only 33% of the population made a living by agriculture. In the mid-1960s some steps were taken towards decentralizing the economy: funds were made available to enterprises proportional to labour inputs, and profits are maximized at a planned output level. Major investments are decided upon and supervised by the Government. Industrial undertakings employing over 50 workers are under the control of Central Industrial Boards. Workers participate in the management of industrial undertakings through 'workers' self-management councils' (*konferencje samorządu robotniczego*), of which there were 8,751 in 1969 with 243,619 members.

PLANNING. The 5-year plan for 1959–65 reached its targets in industry, but fell short in agriculture and consumer goods.

The 5-year plan 1966–70 had the following targets: Electricity, 66–67,000m. kwh.; natural gas, 123,600m. cu. metres; coal, 126 128m.; oil, 600,000;

steel, 11m.; pig-siron, 7m. The crisis of Dec. 1973 (*see* p. 1251) has caused a revision of the targets and priorities of the current 5-year plan (1971–75).

AGRICULTURE AND FORESTRY. In 1969 there were 19·6m. hectares of agricultural land, of which 16·4m. were in private hands, 0·3m. in co-operatives, 2·8m. in state farms. Private holdings average 5 hectares, and may not exceed 50 hectares. 15·2m. hectares were arable, 0·2m. orchards, 2·5m. meadows, 1·7m. pasture lands; 8m. hectares were forests (82% coniferous). 124,800 hectares were afforested in 1969, and 18m. cu. metres of timber gained.

Collectivization has been abandoned; there were only 1,106 co-operatives in 1968. A new approach is being tried with 'agricultural circles' (34,500 with 2·4m. members in 1969). In 1969 there were 6,110 state farms.

Farmers, on retiring, are encouraged to turn over their private plots to state farms in exchange for a pension.

	Area (1,000 hectares)			Yield (1,000 metric tons)		
Crops	*1965*	*1968*	*1969*	*1965*	*1968*	*1969*
Wheat	1,660	1,844	1,965	3,422	4,670	4,700
Rye	4,494	4,263	4,174	8,289	8,520	8,200
Barley	1,349	628	759	1,468	1,494	1,900
Oats	1,349	1,395	1,367	2,541	2,891	3,100
Potatoes	2,803	2,720	2,719	43,263	50,817	44,900
Sugar-beet	476	414	409	12,314	14,800	11,300

Livestock (1969): 11·1m. cattle (6·3m. cows), 14·4m. pigs, 3·3m. sheep, 2·6m. horses, 85·5m. poultry. Milk production in 1968 was 14,400m. litres.

Tractors in use in 1969: 227,900 (in 15-h.p. units).

FISHERIES. In 1969 the fishing fleet numbered 708 vessels totalling 237,200 GRT. The catch was 386,600 metric tons.

In 1966 Poland joined the Fisheries Convention of 1964, extending the fishing limits from 3 to 12 miles.

INDUSTRY. Production in 1969 (and 1968) (in 1,000 metric tons): Coke, 16,200 (15,700); pig-iron, 7,028 (6,840); crude steel, 11,291 (11,007); rolled steel, 7,655 (7,327); cement, 11,830 (11,595); sulphuric acid (100%), 1,516 (1,314); nitrogenous fertilizers, 938 (759); phosphoric fertilizers, 534 (474); aluminium, 96·8 (93·5); electrolytic copper, 54·7 (43·6); lead, 50·7 (48·7); zinc, 208 (203); crude oil, 439 (475); salt, 2,817 (2,634); sugar, 1,551 (1,665); electricity, 60,100m. kwh. (55,500m.); natural gas, 3,920m. cu. metres (2,556m.). In 1969, 59 ships were built and 50,200 passenger cars.

Output of light industry in 1969 (and 1968): Cotton fabrics, 846m. metres (835); woollen fabrics, 98·1m. metres (93·9); silk fabrics, 152m. metres (145); linen and hemp fabrics, 121m. metres (116); leather shoes, 68·4m. pairs (63·2); soap, 83,600 metric tons (86,800); paper, 702,000 metric tons (681,000).

MINING. Poland is a leading copper producer with reserves of some 10m. metric tons. There are also iron ore, lead and zinc. Coal reserves are estimated at 71,000m. metric tons. Production in 1969 (in 1,000 metric tons): Coal, 135,000; brown coal, 30,900; copper ore, 4,385; iron ore, 2,821; zinc–lead ores, 3,221.

LABOUR. Atypically in Communist Eastern Europe, there is serious unemployment, largely the result of a 'population explosion' in the early 1950s.

Total number employed in 1969: 9·9m., of which 205,000 were in private industry. Industrial workers numbered 4,212,000; building workers, 1,086,000. Total number of women employed: 3,865,500. Trade unions had a membership of 9·3m. in 1968 (including 3·4m. women). Monthly wage: legal minimum, 1,000 zlotys; average earnings (1969), 2,382 zlotys.

COMMERCE. Trade statistics for calendar years (in 1m. zlotys):

	1960	1965	1967	1968	1969
Imports	5,980	9,361	10,579	11,412	12,839
Exports	5,302	8,911	10,106	11,431	12,566

Main imports in 1969 (in metric tons): Iron ore, 11·6m.; petroleum and products, 8·9m.; fertilizers, 3·8m.; wheat, 1m.; coking coal, 1m.; motor vehicles, 19,500 units.

Main export in 1969: Coal, 26·4m. metric tons; lignite, 4·3m. metric tons; coke, 2·3m. metric tons; ships, 421,000 dead-weight tons; cement, 58,000 metric tons.

65% of Poland's trade is with Communist countries. UK is Poland's fourth largest trade partner after USSR, East Germany and Czechoslovakia.

A Soviet–Polish trade agreement for 1971–75 was signed on 29 Dec. 1970. Soviet credits have been available to enable the government to keep prices down. Soviet exports are to include raw materials, chemicals, food and machinery; Polish, machinery, ships and consumer goods.

Total trade between Poland and UK for 5 years (according to British Board of Trade returns) was (in £1,000 sterling):

	1966	1967	1968	1969	1970
Imports to UK	53,617	56,100	60,469	57,001	63,025
Exports from UK	35,320	48,207	44,018	54,175 ⎫	59,695
Re-exports from UK	1,129	527	617	894 ⎭	

An Anglo-Polish trade agreement of Dec. 1967 increased export quotas and liberalized imports of consumer goods and textiles. Quotas for 1971 were established after Ango-Polish talks.'

SHIPPING. The principal ports are Gdynia, Gdańsk (Danzig) and Szczecin (Stettin). The merchant marine is grouped into Polish Ocean Lines, based on Gdynia and operating regular liner services, and Polish Steamship Lines, based on Szczecin and operating tramp services. There are 6,855 km of inland waterways.

In 1969 the merchant marine had 250 vessels totalling 1,261,193 GRT (including 29 vessels over 10,000 tons). There are regular lines to London, Hull, Taku Bar, Shanghai, North Vietnam and some African and Latin American countries.

Total shipping entering Polish ports in 1969 was 11,010 vessels of 14·6m. NRT.

Freight traffic in 1969 was 16·6m. metric tons.

ROADS. In 1969 Poland had 128,339 km of hard-surfaced roads. Number of motor vehicles: Passenger cars, 374,560 (of which 345,222 private); lorries, 226,461 (17,753 private); motor cycles, 1,686,853 (1,674,321 private).

In 1969 state and co-operative road transport carried 1,281m. passengers and 797m. metric tons of freight.

RAILWAYS. The length of the standard gauge railway system was (1969) 23,205 km (3,477 km electrified); of narrow gauge, 3,396 km. In 1969 the railways carried 373·7m. tons of freight and 104·8m. passengers.

AVIATION. In 1969 the state airline 'Lot' had 38 aircraft, operated 15 internal routes and flew services to 22 countries. 856,200 passengers were flown and 16,060 metric tons of freight.

PIPELINE. In 1969 there were 900 km of oil pipeline delivering 13·64m. metric tons of oil.

POST. In 1969 there were 7,498 post offices and 1,650,896 telephone subscribers, including 506,600 private persons.

Wireless licences in 1969 numbered 5·65m.; television licences, 3·83m. There are 19 television broadcasting stations and 2 channels.

BANKING. The banking system was reorganized in 1948. The National Bank of Poland (established 1945) is the central bank, has exclusive authority to issue currency, is charged with control of money and credit, and has responsibility for financial implementation of the national economic plan. Since its merger with the former Investment Bank in 1 Jan. 1970 it exercises centralized control over investment financing.

The Agricultural Bank (Bank Rolny) has exclusive responsibility for direct financing of rural areas through both short-term and investment loans. It operates through a comprehensive network of branch offices and communal co-operative banks. The General Savings Bank (Powszechna Kasa Oszczędności) exercises central control over savings activities, transfers and checking trans-actions, including activities of workers' co-operative banks.

In addition to the National Bank of Poland, other authorized foreign-exchange banks are: Bank for the National Economy, the Polish Welfare Bank (Bank Polska Kasa Opieki SA) and the Commercial Bank of Warsaw (Bank Handlowy w Warszawie SA).

Deposits in savings institutions amounted to 120,794m. zlotys on 31 Dec. 1969.

WEIGHTS AND MEASURES. The metric system is in general use.

DIPLOMATIC REPRESENTATIVES

Poland maintains embassies in:

Afghánistán	Korea (North)
Albania	Lebanon
Argentina	Libya
Austria	Mali
Belgium (also Minister for Luxembourg)	Mexico (also Minister for Colombia, Costa Rica, Dominican Republic, Ecuador, El Salvador, Haiti, Honduras, Nicaragua, Panama)
Bolivia	
Brazil	
Bulgaria	Mongolia
Burma	Morocco
Cambodia	Nepál
Canada	Netherlands
Ceylon	Nigeria
Chile	Norway
China	Pakistan
Cuba	Romania
Cyprus	Sierra Leone
Czechoslovakia	Singapore
Denmark	Sudan
Finland	Sweden
France	Switzerland
Germany (East)	Syria
Ghana	Tanzania
Greece	Tunisia
Guinea	Turkey
Hungary	USSR
India	UAR
Indonesia	UK
Iran	USA
Iraq	Venezuela
Italy	Vietnam (North)
Japan	Yugoslavia
Jordan	

Poland maintains a legation in Uruguay. Poland also recognizes the 'Provisional Revolutionary Government' of South Vietnam.

OF POLAND IN GREAT BRITAIN (47 Portland Place, W1)

Ambassador: Marian Dobrosielski (accredited 22 Oct. 1969).
Counsellors: Janusz Zabłocki; Włodzimierz Wiśniewski (*Commercial*); Paweł Cieslar (*Press*). *First Secretaries:* Dr Antoni Knychala; Narcyz Grzechowiak; Juliusz Bialy.
Military, Air and Naval Attaché: Col. Witold Lokuciewski.

There are a Consul-General in London and a Consul in Glasgow.

OF GREAT BRITAIN IN POLAND

Ambassador: J. N. Henderson, CMG.
Counsellors: A. B. Horn (*Head of Chancery*); H. T. Kennedy, OBE (*Commercial*).
Service Attachés: (Vacant) (*Defence and Air*), Lieut.-Col. D. J. Lear (*Navy and Army*).
First Secretaries: Miss M. K. Dean (*Consul*); M. E. Pike; Dr R. K. Rowntree; K. E. L. Barton.

OF POLAND IN THE USA (2640–16th St. NW, Washington, D.C., 20009)

Ambassador: Jerzy Michalowski.
Counsellors: Zdzisław Szewczyk; Czesław Makowski; Zbigniew Bidziński (*Economic*); Jerzy M. Pietowski (*Commercial*). *First Secretaries:* Dr Stanisław Pawlak; Andrzej K. Konopacki (*Press*); Waldemar Wawrzyniak; Henryk Walenda (*Press*). *Service Attaché:* Col. Bronisław Jabłoński.

OF THE USA IN POLAND

Ambassador: Walter J. Stoessel, Jr.
Deputy Chief of Mission: Walter E. Jenkins. *Heads of Sections:* N. G. Andrews (*Political*); I Shiffman (*Economic*); Stephen A. Dobrenchuk (*Consular*); J. Leaken (*Administrative*).
Service Attaché: Col. George P. Welch.

There is a Consul at Poznań.

BOOKS OF REFERENCE

STATISTICAL INFORMATION. The Central Statistical Office, Warsaw (Wawelska 1–3), publishes *Statistical News* (Aug. 1945–49; restarted Sept. 1956, bimonthly); *Statistical Studies and Works* (from 1950); *Statistics of Poland* (20 vols. 1946–51; restarted 1957 as *Biuletyn statystyczny*, monthly); *Rocznik statystyczny* (annual); *Concise Statistical Year Book of Poland.*

Bibliographie sur la Pologne. 2nd ed. Warsaw, 1963
Constitution of the Polish People's Republic. Warsaw, 1964
Twenty Years of the Polish People's Republic. Warsaw. 1964
Beneš, V. L., and Pounds, N. G. J., *Poland.* London, 1970
Bethell, N., *Gomułka: his Poland and his Communism.* London, 1969
Bromke, A., *Poland's Politics.* Harvard U.P., 1967
Bulas, K., and others, *English–Polish and Polish–English Dictionary.* 2 vols. The Hague, 1959–61
Ehrlich, S., and others, *Social and Political Transformations in Poland.* Warsaw, 1964
Gieysztor, A., and others, *History of Poland.* Warsaw, 1969
Halecki, O., *A History of Poland.* 2nd ed. London, 1956.—(ed.), *Poland.* New York, 1957
Horak, S., *Poland's International Affairs, 1919–60.* Indiana U.P., 1964
Karpiński, A., *Twenty Years of Poland's Economic Development.* Warsaw, 1964
Morrison, J. F., *The Polish People's Republic.* Baltimore, 1968
Roos, H., *A History of Modern Poland.* London, 1966
Starr, R. F., *Poland 1944–62.* Louisiana U.P., 1962
Syrop, K., *Poland: between hammer and anvil.* London, 1968

NATIONAL LIBRARY. Biblioteka Narodowa, Rakowiecka 6, Warsaw.

PORTUGAL
República Portuguesa

CONSTITUTION AND GOVERNMENT. Portugal has been an independent state since the 12th century; until 1910 it was a monarchy. The last King was Manuel II of the house of Braganza-Coburg, born 15 Nov. 1889, died 2 July 1932. On 5 Oct. 1910 the republic was proclaimed with Dr Teófilo Braga as the provisional president (5 Oct. 1910 to 24 Aug. 1911). Thereafter there were duly elected presidents, as follows:

Dr Manuel de Arriaga, 24 Aug. 1911–29 May 1915.[1]
Dr Joaquim Teófilo Braga, 29 May 1915–5 Oct. 1915.
Dr Bernardino Luís Machado Guimarães, 5 Oct. 1915–11 Dec. 1917.[2]
Dr Sidonio Bernardino Cardoso da Silva Pais, 11 Dec. 1917–14 Dec. 1918.[3]
Adm. João de Canto e Castro Silva Antunes, 16 Dec. 1918–5 Oct. 1919
Dr António José de Almeida, 5 Oct. 1919–5 Oct. 1923.

Manuel Teixeira Gomes, 5 Oct. 1923–11 Dec. 1925.[1]
Dr Bernardino Luís Machado Guimarães, 11 Dec. 1925–1 June 1926.[1]
Provisional government, 1 June–29 Nov. 1926.
Marshal António Oscar Fragoso Carmona, 29 Nov. 1926–18 April 1951.
Marshal Francisco Higino Craveiro Lopes, 22 July 1951–9 Aug. 1958.

[1] Resigned. [2] Deposed. [3] Assassinated.

President of the Republic: Rear-Adm. Américo de Deus Rodrigues Tomás; born 19 Nov. 1894 (elected 22 July 1958; assumed office 9 Aug. 1958; re-elected 9 Aug. 1965).

National flag: Green, red (vertical).
National anthem: A Portuguesa (words by Lopes de Mendonça, 1890; tune by Alfredo Keil).

On 19 March 1933 the present constitution, which declares that the Portuguese state is a unitary and corporative republic, was adopted by plebiscite. The latest amendment to the constitution was passed on 29 Aug. 1959. The president is to be elected for 7 years by an electoral college, constituted of members of the National Assembly and the Corporative Chamber, with representatives of municipalities and oversea legislative councils.

The National Assembly (one chamber) of 130 Deputies is elected for 4 years by direct suffrage. Angola and Moçambique are represented by 7 deputies each, India by 3, Cape Verde by 2, Guinea, S. Tomé and Principe, Macao, Timor by 1 each.

At the elections in Nov. 1965 only government candidates stood for re-election.

A State Council composed of the Prime Minister, the Presidents of the National Assembly, the Corporative Chamber and the Supreme Court, the Public Prosecutor and 10 other members assists the President of the Republic. A Corporative Chamber functions alongside the National Assembly.

The Cabinet was on 6 Dec. 1970 composed as follows:

Prime Minister: Dr Marcello José das Neves Alves Caetano.
Foreign Affairs: Dr Rui Manuel de Maedeiros d'Espiney Patricio.
Defence: Gen. Horácio José de Sá Viana Rebelo.
Interior: Dr António Manuel Gonçalves Rapazote.
Justice: Dr Mário Júlio Brito de Almeida Costa.
Finance: Dr João Augusto Dias Rosas.
Army: Gen. Horácio José de Sá Viana Rebelo.
Marine: Cdr Manuel Pereira Crespo.
Public Works: Rui Alves da Silva Sanches.
Overseas Provinces: Dr Joaquim Moreira da Silva Cunha.
Education: Dr José Veiga Simão.
Communications: Rui Alves da Silva Sanches.

National Economy: Dr João Augusto Dias Rosas.
Corporation and Social Security, Health and Welfare: Dr Baltasar Leite Rebelo de Seusa.

AREA AND POPULATION.

	Area (sq. km)	Population 1960 (census)	1969 (estimate)	Per sq. km 1969
Continent	88,500	8,292,975	8,978,800	101·5
Islands	3,141	596,417	603,800	192·2
Portugal (total)	91,641[1]	8,889,392	9,582,600	104·6
Districts:				
Aveiro	2,708	524,592	585,900	216·4
Beja	10,240	276,895	274,700	26·8
Braga	2,730	596,768	667,700	244·6
Bragança	6,545	233,441	247,000	37·7
Castelo Branco	6,704	316,536	321,700	48·0
Coimbra	3,956	433,656	445,900	112·7
Évora	7,393	219,916	226,400	30·6
Faro	5,072	314,841	315,300	62·2
Guarda	5,496	282,606	270,300	49·2
Leiria	3,516	404,500	429,000	122·0
Lisboa	2,762	1,382,959	1,590,700	575·9
Portalegre	5,889	188,482	184,000	31·3
Porto	2,282	1,193,368	1,375,200	602·6
Santarém	6,689	461,707	481,800	72·0
Setúbal	5,152	377,186	442,100	85·8
Viana do Castelo	2,108	277,748	287,000	136·1
Vila Real	4,239	325,358	343,600	81·1
Viseu	5,019	482,416	490,500	97·7
Islands:				
Angra do Heroísmo	710	96,174	104,800	147·6
Funchal	797	268,937	268,700	337·1
Horta	780	49,382	44,300	56·8
Ponta Delgada	854	181,924	186,000	217·8

[1] 34,861 sq. miles.

In 1960 the population consisted of 4,254,416 males and 4,634,976 females, or 109 females to every 100 males.

The Azores islands are divided into 3 widely separated groups, with clear channels between, São Miguel together with Santa Maria being in the most easterly. About 100 miles north-west of them lies the central cluster of Terceira, Graciosa, São Jorge, Pico and Faial. Still another 150 miles to the north-west are Flores and Corvo, the latter being the most isolated and primitive of the islands. São Miguel, Terceira and Pico are the largest, the first measuring 41 miles in length and 9 in breadth, and containing over half the total population of the archipelago. For political and administrative purposes they are divided into 3 districts, each sending its representatives to the Chamber at Lisbon. The capitals of the 3 districts are the chief seaports, Ponta Delgada on São Miguel Island, Horta on Faial Island and Angra do Heroísmo on Terceira Island.

VITAL STATISTICS for calendar years:

	Births	Still-births	Marriages	Divorces	Deaths	Emigrants
1967	202,061	6,407	78,864	722	95,816	92,502
1968	194,962	5,769	76,553	743	94,661	80,452
1969	189,739	5,838	79,180	501	101,088	70,165

In 1969 the births included 98,054 (1968: 101,125) boys and 91,685 (93,837) girls; the deaths, 51,611 (48,315) males and 49,477 (46,346) females.

At the census of 15 Dec. 1960 the population of Lisbon was 802,230 (metropolitan area, 1,034,141); Oporto, 303,424 (metropolitan area, 693,170); Vila Nova de Gaia, 45,739; Coimbra, 46,313; Setúbal, 44,435; Braga, 40,977; Amadora, 36,331; Matosinhos, 37,694; Almada, 30,688; Barreiro, 30,399; Évora, 24,144; Guimarães, 23,229; Covilhã, 23,091; Moscavide, 22,065; Faro, 18,909.

In 1969, 2,537 emigrants went to Brazil and 13,111 to USA.

RELIGION. The predominant faith is the Roman Catholic, but there is freedom of worship, both in public and private, with the exception of creeds incompatible with morals and the life and physical integrity of the people.

On 7 May 1940 a Concordat and a Missionary Agreement with the Vatican were signed. The Concordat recognizes the lawful existence of the Catholic Church and the exercise of its spiritual mission according to the Canon Law. Religious marriages, duly notified to the Registrar's Office, are recognized, and divorce is forbidden to parties married by the Church. Church property which had come into the possession of the State is restored, except that used for public services or classified as immovable property of public interest, or national monuments.

The Missionary Agreement regulates religious activities in the Overseas Provinces. Since the 16th century, Portugal has had the privilege of the Roman Catholic jurisdiction in the Orient (Padroado), which had by 1950 been reduced to Portuguese India and part of India; agreements of 18 July 1950 and 25 Sept. 1953 adapted the Concordat to the changed political situation in India.

Portuguese territory is divided into 6 ecclesiastical provinces, with their sees at Lisbon, Braga, Évora, Goa (India), Luanda (Angola) and Lourenço Marques (Moçambique). The Archbishop of Lisbon (Patriarch since 1716 and Cardinal since 1737) has suffragans in Guarda, Leiria and Portalegre-Castelo Branco on the continent; Angra do Heroísmo and Funchal in the adjacent islands, and Cape Verde in Africa. The Archbishop of Braga (Primate of the Iberian Peninsula) has as suffragans: Aveiro, Bragança, Coimbra, Lamego, Oporto, Vila Real and Viseu. The Archbishop of Évora has 2 suffragans: Beja and Faro.

By the concordat of 1940 the metropolitan sees of Luanda (Angola) and Lourenço Marques (Moçambique) were created. The former has as suffragans, besides the see of S. Tomé, the 7 new dioceses of Nova Lisboa, Silva Porto, Sá da Bandeira, Malange, Luso, Carmona–S. Salvador and Benguela; the second has as suffragans the 8 new dioceses of Beira, Inhambane, Nampula, Quelimane, Porto Amélia, Tete, Vila Cabral and Vila Pery. The Archbishop of Goa and Damão (who also holds the titles of Archbishop of Cranganor, Primate of the East and Patriarch of Eastern India) has jurisdiction over the diocese of Goa. The privilege of the Far East is constituted by the suffragan sees of Macao, with the vicariates of Shiu-Hing, Singapore and Malacca, and Dili (Timor). The province of Guinea is an Apostolic Prefecture.

EDUCATION. According to the latest statistics, 70% of the population over 7 years could read and write. Compulsory education has been in force since 1911. In 1968–69 there were 16,401 public primary schools with 912,298 pupils and 27,232 teachers. Private elementary schools numbered 730 with 49,240 pupils and 2,034 teachers. Secondary preparatory schools numbered 1,079 with 73,285 pupils. Secondary instruction is supplied in two types of schools: in the *liceus* and other grammar schools, and in schools of technical instruction. In 1968–69 there were 49 *liceus* and 408 institutions of *liceu* standard, with 143,970 pupils, and 369 professional and technical secondary schools, with 149,855 pupils. For higher education there are 3 universities: at Lisbon (founded in 1911), Coimbra (founded 1290) and Oporto (founded 1911). In 1968–69 the number of students at the universities was 28,662; and the Technical University at Lisbon (founded in 1930) had 7,449 students. There are also a military and a naval school, art schools in Lisbon and Oporto (1,789 students) and 7 colleges of music (130 students).

CINEMAS (1969). There were 484 cinemas with a seating capacity of 275,215.

NEWSPAPERS (1969). There were 32 daily newspapers with a combined circulation of 261,614; 10 of these, with a combined circulation of 184,679, appeared in Lisbon.

JUSTICE. Portuguese law distinguishes civil (including commercial) and penal, labour, administrative and fiscal law, each branch having its lower courts, courts of appeal and the Supreme Court.

The republic is divided for civil and penal cases into 171 *comarcas*; in every comarca there is a lower court. In the comarca of Lisbon there are 33 lower courts (16 for criminal procedure and 17 for civil or commercial cases); in the comarca of Oporto there are 17 lower courts (8 for criminal and 9 for civil or commercial cases); at Braga, Setúbal, Guimarães, Santarém, Leiria, Aveiro, Viseu, Almada, Feira, Anadia, Cascais and Funchal there are 2 courts; at Coimbra there are 3 courts. There are 3 courts of appeal (Tribunal de Relação) at Lisbon, Coimbra and Oporto, and a Supreme Court in Lisbon (Supremo Tribunal de Justiça). There are also 33 municipal courts, which are lower courts, similar to those of the comarcas; their jurisdiction is, however, limited.

Capital punishment is abolished, except, in the case of war, by court martial. The prison population as at 31 Dec. 1969 was 8,180.

FINANCE. Currency. The unit of currency is the *escudo* of 100 *centavos*, which contains 0·66567 gramme of fine gold. It was stabilized on 9 June 1931, and the paper currency re-linked to gold when the notes of the Bank of Portugal became payable in gold or its equivalent in foreign currency. When Great Britain devalued the £ in Nov. 1967, Portugal fixed the value at 76·71 escudos = £1 sterling. 1,000 escudos is called a *conto*.

At present there are silver coins of 50, 20, 10 and 5 escudos; 5 and 2½ escudos (nickel and copper); Alpaca coins of 1 and ½ escudo (50 centavos), and bronze coins of 1 and ½ escudo and 20 and 10 centavos. The 20- and 10-centavo coins, issued in 1943, were made of an alloy of 95% copper, 3% zinc and 2% tin.

Budget. Revenue and expenditure for calendar years (in 1,000 centos):

	1965	1966	1967	1968	1969	1970 [1]
Revenue	18,157	19,736	23,461	25,768	28,724	28,799
Expenditure	18,055	19,621	23,359	25,193	27,435	28,794

[1] Estimates.

Main items of estimated revenue and expenditure (in 1,000 escudos):

Revenue	1968	1969	Expenditure	1968	1969
Direct taxes	6,267,597	7,330,827	Public debt	2,427,988	2,181,301
Indirect taxes	8,816,767	9,889,273	Presidency, legislative		
Industries under special tax regime	1,231,863	1,466,187	bodies and pensions	1,478,895	1,550,320
			Finance	779,213	920,031
Yields of various services	1,126,562	1,241,546	Interior	686,585	788,534
			Justice	245,867	245,781
State domain and industries and participation in profits	1,176,343	1,227,881	Army	1,261,327	1,332,116
			Navy	1,013,983	1,072,070
			Foreign affairs	280,037	295,475
Yield of capital shares, etc.	266,892	265,934	Public works	720,929	885,939
			Overseas Provinces	95,960	96,761
Reimbursements, etc.	1,384,679	1,400,874	Education	1,652,482	2,086,168
Consignment of receipts	1,557,147	1,808,761	Economy	482,534	655,639
			Communications	1,668,914	1,803,787
			Corporations and Social Security	84,885	89,156
			Health	1,007,718	1,104,666
Total ordinary	21,827,840	24,631,283	Total ordinary	13,887,317	15,107,744
Extraordinary	3,939,924	4,093,097	Extraordinary	11,305,955	12,326,867

On 31 Dec. 1968 the public debt was as follows: Consolidated debt: 4% (1940) (centenários), 1,278,714 contos; 3½% (1941), 416,403 contos; 3% (1942), 2,806,728 contos; 2¾% (1943), 986,537 contos; public debt certificates 4%), 6·48m. contos. The internal redeemable debt was as follows: Titles, 5,075,968 contos; Caixa Geral de Depósitos, 94,017 contos. External redeemable debt: 8,362,001 contos.

DEFENCE. Continental Portugal is divided into 5 military regions with headquarters at Oporto, Tomar, Évora and Lisbon and the territorial military command of Algarve.

Insular Portugal comprises the territorial military commands of Madeira and the Azores.

Overseas Portugal comprises the military regions of Angola and Moçambique, and the territorial military commands of Cape Verde, S. Tomé and Príncipe, Portuguese Guinea, Macao and Timor.

Every Portuguese citizen in good physical condition is subject to compulsory military service from the age of 20 to 45 years.

Pre-military training is entrusted to the *Mocidade Portuguesa* (Portuguese Youth Movement), the *Colégio Militar* and the *Instituto Técnico e Profissional dos Pupilos do Exército*, with particular emphasis on physical and moral training of youths aged from 7 to 21 years.

Army. The permanent effectives of the Army in Continental and Insular Portugal consist of 16 regiments of infantry, 3 independent battalions of infantry, 7 battalions of *caçadores*, 5 regiments of field artillery, 2 regiments of heavy artillery, 1 regiment of coastal artillery, 1 regiment of AA artillery, 2 mixed batteries of coastal and AA artillery, 2 independent battalions of AA artillery, 1 independent coastal battery; 5 regiments of cavalry, 2 armoured regiments, 1 regiment of engineers, 1 battalion of engineers, 1 battalion of telegraphists, 1 signal regiment, 1 signal battalion, 1 railway battalion, 1 medical regiment, 2 quartermaster battalions, 1 transport battalion, 1 ordnance company. Effective strength (1970), 177,000 all ranks.

The permanent effectives of the army in Overseas Portugal consist of 3 regiments of infantry, 6 battalions of *caçadores*, 15 independent companies of *caçadores*, 5 battalions of field artillery, 5 independent batteries of field artillery, 1 battalion of motorized cavalry, 5 independent squadrons of motorized cavalry, 2 battalions of engineers, 1 signal battalion and several quartermaster units.

In 1970 the Republican Guard (*Guarda Nacional Republicana*) consisted of 9,760 all ranks, the Police (*Polícia de Legurança Pública*) of 13,700 all ranks and the Fiscal Guard (*Guarda Fiscal*) of 5,662 all ranks. The *Legião Portuguesa* and Civil Defence force numbered 90,000 volunteers.

Navy. The Navy comprises 4 submarines, 13 frigates, 1 corvette, 4 ocean mine-sweepers, 1 minesweeping trawler, 14 patrol vessels, 12 coastal minesweepers, 44 patrol launches, 1 sail training ship, 4 surveying vessels, 4 landing craft, 1 fleet oiler, 1 lighthouse tender, 2 depot ships, 5 large, 58 small landing craft, and 2 support ships. The navy personnel in 1970 totalled 1,650 officers and 16,050 men including marines.

Air Force. Formed in 1912, the Air Force has been independent since 1952, when it was combined with the naval air service and given equal status with the Army and Navy. In 1970 it had a strength of about 17,500 officers and men, with some 750 aircraft. It contributes 1 maritime reconnaissance squadron to NATO.

Portugal is divided into 3 air regions, with headquarters in Lisbon, Luanda and Lourenço Marques.

In 1970 the Air Force comprised 1 interceptor squadron (F-86F Sabre jets), 1 fighter-bomber squadron (F-84G), 1 light-strike squadron (G-91Rs), 1 bombing squadron of obsolescent PV-2 Harpoon piston-engined aircraft, 1 ASW reconnaissance squadron (P2V-5 Neptune), a military air transport service (Noratlas, C-47, C-54 and DC-6) and a number of light attack and counter-insurgency units equipped with armed T-6 aircraft and Alouette III and Puma helicopters. Other aircraft in service include Chipmunk, T-6 and Do 27 piston-engined trainers and liaison aircraft, T-37C jet trainers and T-33 jet advanced trainers, and two Boeing 707 long-range jet transports.

There is a paratroop regiment of 4,000, which comes under Air Force command.

DEVELOPMENT. During the first 6-year plan (1953–58), 16·5m. contos were invested (11·6m. in metropolitan Portugal, 4·9m. in the overseas provinces). The second 6-year plan (1959–64) envisaged investments of 31m. contos (22m. in metropolitan Portugal, 9m. overseas). The interim plan 1965–67 envisaged expenditures of 34·78m. contos in metropolitan Portugal and 14·4m. contos overseas. The third 6-year plan (1968–73) envisages investments of 122m. contos in metropolitan Portugal and 46·5m. in the overseas provinces. The main items in metropolitan Portugal are industry (30·85m.), transport and communications (27·1m.), energy (17·9m.), agriculture and forestry (14·6m.) and tourism (11·85m.).

AGRICULTURE. The following figures show the area (in hectares) and yield (in metric tons) of the chief crops:

	1967		1968		1969	
Crop	Area	Yield	Area	Yield	Area	Yield
Wheat	586,128	637,210	614,130	747,474	563,203	451,932
Maize	436,462	576,840	433,891	547,916	426,861	552,592
Oats	226,190	110,770	223,866	129,424	206,540	79,354
Barley	106,734	73,497	135,045	93,590	119,416	54,382
Rye	238,929	174,837	239,194	199,179	235,769	167,279
Rice	32,268	146,035	32,929	149,023	37,559	175,807
French beans	373,444	54,554	379,800	50,111	381,819	50,616
Potatoes	116,682	1,295,693	105,168	1,083,106	106,671	1,126,382

Wine production, 1969, 8,081,241 hectolitres, and olive oil, 1969, 790,493 hectolitres. In 1955, 228,996 hectolitres of port wine were exported; 1960, 211,560; 1966, 314,035; 1967, 303,324; 1968, 337,986; 1969, 359,675.

Livestock. In 1955 Portugal (continental and islands) possessed 73,782 horses, 127,354 mules, 236,961 asses, 1,065,056 oxen, 3·64m. sheep, 738,338 goats and 1,516,131 pigs.

FORESTRY. The forest area covers 3·2m. hectares, of which 1·41m. are pine, 758,000 cork oak, 704,000 other oak, 75,000 chestnut, 155,000 eucalyptus and 135,000 other species.

Portugal surpasses the rest of the world in the production of cork (1967, 139,222; 1968, 200,552; 1969, 163,490 metric tons). Most of it is exported crude; exports of cork and cork products totalled 142,432 metric tons in 1967; 139,208 in 1968; 152,070 in 1969. Production of resin (in metric tons) was 88,953 in 1966; 91,369 in 1967; 91,954 in 1968; 44,238 in 1969, more than two-thirds are exported. Exports of turpentine (in metric tons) were 12,299 in 1967; 14,014 in 1968; 5,691 in 1969.

FISHERIES. The fishing industry is of importance. At 31 July 1969 there were 38,186 men and boys employed, with 10,588 boats. The sardine catch, 1969, was 64,133 metric tons, valued at 362,989 contos; 1968, 79,645 metric tons valued at 326,989 contos; 1967, 114,817 metric tons, 381,313 contos; 1966, 124,950 metric tons, 449,599 contos. Exports of tinned sardines (in metric tons) amounted to 55,288 in 1964, 61,170 in 1965, 54,835 in 1966, 52,016 in 1967. The most important centres of the sardine industry are at Matosinhos, Setúbal, Portimão and Olhão.

As from 1 Sept. 1966 the zone of fishing rights has been extended from 6 to 12 miles.

MINING. Portugal possesses considerable mineral wealth. Production in metric tons:

	1967	1968	1969		1967	1968	1969
Coal	481,333	427,534	424,425	Cement	1,821,431	1,861,298	2,034,761
Cupriferous pyrites	528,022	561,286	531,125	Wolframite	1,872	2,399	2,289
Copper (precipitated)	93	88	107	Hematite	55,655	59,415	39,837
Tin ores	935	970	710	Magnetite	87,339	87,639	67,428
Kaolin	37,209	41,948	44,830	Manganese	9,832	9,665	6,928
Gold (refined)	0·573	0·541	0·508	Lead con-			
Beryl	14	128	29	centrates	16	259	51

ELECTRICITY. Total production of electrical power in 1969 was 6,837·9m. kwh. (1968: 6,214·9m. kwh.); the installed capacity totalled 2,540,596 kva. (1968: 2,538,090), of which 1,781,738 kva. (1968: 1,781,496) were hydro-electric. New power plants were inaugurated in 1951 (Castelo do Bode, Venda Nova, Belver), 1953 (Salamonde), 1954 (Cabrill), 1955 (Caniçada and Bouçá), 1958 (Picote), 1960 (Miranda), 1964 (Bemposta) and 1965 (Tàvora).

TOURISM. Tourism is of increasing importance for the invisible balance of payments. In 1968, 2·5m. visitors (1969: 2·8m.) spent about 5,786m. escudos (1969: 4,792m.); they included in 1969, 339,474 British and 304,100 USA citizens.

TRADE UNIONS. The organization of trade unions is based on the Labour Charter (*Estatuto do Trabalho Nacional*), implemented by the decree no. 23 : 050 of 23 Sept. 1933. 325 unions (*sindicatos nacionais*) had in 1969 a membership of 1,410,840 (1,098,034 men; 312,806 women).

COMMERCE. Imports for consumption and exports (exclusive of coin and bullion and re-exports) for calendar years, in 1,000 escudos:

	1964	1965	1966	1967	1968	1969
Imports	22,377,339	26,552,743	29,406,445	30,452,613	33,857,829	37,261,721
Exports	14,830,706	16,572,654	17,811,700	20,166,184	21,916,557	24,525,997

The principal articles of imports and exports (in 1,000 escudos):

Imports	1967	1968	1969	Exports	1967	1968	1969
Dried cod	494,345	175,573	231,872	Sardines	914,504	850,785	688,197
Wheat	633,225	436,710	610,043	Cork	1,507,589	1,563,767	1,641,095
Tobacco, unmanu-				Wine	1,479,002	1,691,404	1,727,884
factured	181,714	236,134	192,309	Olive oil	192,159	201,881	215,938
Oil seeds	947,686	778,800	938,674	Resin	346,177	342,177	435,129
Coffee	243,806	262,119	282,038	Turpentine	48,502	61,477	42,679
Sugar	642,336	641,433	582,145	Pyrites	86,142	97,755	84,400
Hides	198,240	205,387	192,890	Wolfram	135,016	160,131	168,809
Ammonium				Pit-props	12,131	10,776	6,741
sulphate	158	201	229	Pulpwood	438,831	769,460	1,114,721
Iron and steel:				Fuel and gas			
Ingots	1,308,323	1,309,244	1,649,422	oils	210,536	185,913	191,426
Manufactured	513,896	539,200	483,394	Rubber tyres			
Coal, etc.	394,456	310,575	401,451	and tubes	180,320	148,994	146,359
Cotton, raw	1,343,942	1,713,240	1,791,187				
Dyes	60,524	75,627	93,476				
Motor vehicles	1,768,136	1,941,179	2,445,770				
Petroleum and							
shale oil, crude	1,167,205	1,245,161	1,502,101				
Fuel and gas oil	452,013	600,058	484,975				

The distribution of the imports and exports (in 1,000 escudos):

From or to	Imports from			Exports to		
	1967	1968	1969	1967	1968	1969
Angola	2,524,292	3,165,738	3,512,246	2,668,976	2,916,518	3,187,791
Belgium	848,405	850,778	1,103,707	377,948	416,276	428,520
France	2,091,697	2,347,807	2,675,251	936,807	1,006,611	1,278,364
Great Britain	4,164,407	4,409,706	5,167,787	4,329,696	4,611,371	5,157,771
Italy	1,763,100	1,998,738	2,128,230	494,018	489,826	635,917
Moçambique	1,600,753	1,901,322	1,757,840	1,729,269	1,984,548	2,191,914
Netherlands	906,392	855,492	1,017,901	473,865	475,179	498,247
Spain	1,360,796	1,407,297	1,596,872	359,639	343,858	423,076
USA	2,094,031	2,468,916	1,813,697	2,026,949	2,309,169	2,314,260
West Germany	4,590,672	5,289,683	5,861,194	1,073,623	1,257,724	1,569,738

Total trade (in £1,000 sterling) between Portugal (excluding the Azores and Madeira) and UK (British Board of Trade returns):

	1965	1966	1967	1968	1969	1970
Imports to UK	40,939	46,593	55,679	73,786	75,907	85,630
Exports from UK	39,545	46,062	46,895	58,698	74,850 }	86,776
Re-exports from UK	466	687	642	1,031	1,298 }	

Trade (in £1,000 sterling) between the Azores and UK (British Board of Trade returns):

	1965	1966	1967	1968	1969	1970
Imports to UK	232	102	184	178	426	227
Exports from UK	258	313	296	412	302 }	557
Re-exports from UK	3	4	5	15	11 }	

Trade (in £1,000 sterling) between Madeira and UK (British Board of Trade returns):

	1965	1966	1967	1968	1969	1970
Imports to UK	268	254	242	285	336	516
Exports from UK	818	817	844	733	905 ⎱	1,307
Re-exports from UK	15	6	7	7	8 ⎰	

SHIPPING. In 1969, 16,283 vessels of 55,517,414 tons entered the ports (continental and islands). Of those entering 7,518 (15,888,235 tons) were Portuguese, 688 (6,899,933 tons) British and 777 (1,610,474 tons) Spanish. On 31 Dec. 1969 the merchant marine consisted of 141 transport vessels of 687,045 tons.

RAILWAYS. A decree of 9 May 1951, based on the law of 7 Sept. 1945, merged all leases and concessions in a single concession for all Portuguese railways, granted to the *Companhia dos Caminhos de Ferro Portugueses*, except the Estoril railway (Lisbon–Cascais), of 26 km length. In 1969 total railway length was 3,617 km. (5 ft 6 in. and metre gauges). In 1969, 144,655,000 passengers were carried and 3,518,548 tons of merchandise transported.

ROADS (1969). There were 29,932 km of road. There were registered in continental Portugal in 1969, 662,203 motor vehicles, including 55,449 motor cycles and 36,770 tractors; not counting vehicles used by the armed forces.

AVIATION. Regular services connect Lisbon with Brussels, Johannesburg, New York, Madrid, Paris, London, Frankfurt, Rio de Janeiro and the overseas provinces. These lines in 1969 carried 890,351 passengers and 9,542 metric tons of freight. The Azores are served by airlines between S. Miguel, Sta Maria and Terceira, carrying, in 1966, 35,072 passengers and 176 metric tons of freight.

POST (1969). The length of telegraph lines was 170,082 km; number of offices, 1,719. The state owned 1,180,628 km of telephone line and the *Telefones de Lisboa e Porto* owned 1,112,076 km of lines. Number of telephones was 698,075, of which 217,177 were government-owned.

Cable and Wireless, Ltd, operate in Portugal (Carcavelos), the Azores, Madeira and Cape Verde Islands, connecting Portugal with Great Britain, North and South America, and West and South Africa.

BANKING. The one bank of issue for the mainland of the country and adjacent islands is the Bank of Portugal, founded 19 Nov. 1846. By decree of 29 June 1962, its constitution was modified and its privileges were prolonged until 30 June 1991. The capital of the bank was fixed at 200m. escudos. The bank is the treasury of the State, and its reserve must be not less than 50% of the total amount of its notes in circulation and other sight liabilities. Not less than 25% of the amount of the notes in circulation and other sight liabilities must be represented by gold (coin or bullion). The bank issues notes of 1,000, 500, 100, 50 and 20 escudos. Its gold and foreign exchange reserves were 25,410m. escudos on 31 July 1970. The notes in circulation amounted to 31,315m. escudos.

The National Development Bank began operations on 4 Jan. 1960. Of its total capital of 1,000m. escudos, 650m. have been subscribed by the Government and 75m. by the Bank of Angola.

There are 24 banks registered on the mainland and 1 in the islands, with cash in hand on 31 Dec. 1969, 25,764m. escudos; bills, 62,407m. escudos; deposits, 109,606m. escudos. The deposits in the savings banks and general deposit bank (state) amounted to 26,744m. escudos.

WEIGHTS AND MEASURES. The metric system of weights and measures is the legal standard.

DIPLOMATIC REPRESENTATIVES

Portugal maintains embassies in:

Argentina	Germany (West)	Norway
Australia	Greece	Pakistan
Austria	Guatemala	Panama
Belgium	Iceland	Peru
Bolivia	Iran	Philippines
Brazil	Irish Republic	South Africa, Republic of
Canada	Italy	Spain
Ceylon	Japan	Sweden
Chile	Lebanon	Switzerland
Colombia	Luxembourg	Thailand
Costa Rica	Malawi	Turkey
Cuba	Malta	UK
Denmark	Mexico	USA
Ecuador	Morocco	Uruguay
Finland	Netherlands	Vatican
France	Nicaragua	Venezuela

OF PORTUGAL IN GREAT BRITAIN (11 Belgrave Sq., SW1)

Ambassador: António Leite de Faria (accredited 18 Dec. 1968).
Counsellors: Luis Soares de Oliveira, MVO; Luis de Oliveria Nunes (*Consul-General*); António Rato Potier, MVO (*Press*). *Service Attachés:* Lieut.-Col. Renato Fernando Marquis Pinto (*Military and Air*), Cdr José Baptista Pinheiro de Azevedo (*Navy*). *Commercial Attaché:* Dr Alexandre Rey Colaço de Castro Freire.

There are consular representatives at Aberdeen, Barrow-in-Furness, Belfast, Birmingham, Bristol, Cardiff, Dartmouth, Dover, Dundee, Leith–Edinburgh, Falmouth, Glasgow, Hull, Leeds, Liverpool, London, Londonderry, Manchester, Middlesbrough, Newcastle upon Tyne, Plymouth, Saint-Hélier, Southampton and Swansea.

OF GREAT BRITAIN IN PORTUGAL

Ambassador: D. F. Muirhead, CMG, CVO.
Counsellor: G. E. Hall.
First Secretaries: S. F. St. C. Duncan (*Head of Chancery*); A. G. Battle (*Consul-General*); S. J. Aspden, MBE (*Commercial*).
Service Attachés: Lieut.-Col. M. F. Robert Bullock (*Defence and Military*), Cdr D. L. G. James, RN (*Navy and Air*).

There are consular representatives at Lisbon, Oporto, Vila Real de Santo Antonio, Ponta Delgada (Azores), Funchal (Madeira).

OF PORTUGAL IN THE USA (2125 Kalorama Rd. NW, Washington, D.C., 20008)

Ambassador: Vasco Vieira Garin.
Counsellors: Antonio Cabrita Matias; Albino Cabral Pessoa (*Financial*); Manuel Bramão (*Commercial*). *Service Attachés:* Cdr V. A. Martins Rodrigues (*Navy*), Col. Manuel Leitão P. Marques (*Military and Air*).

OF THE USA IN PORTUGAL

Ambassador: Ridgway Knight.
Deputy Chief of Mission: (Vacant). *Heads of Sections:* Alf E. Bergesen (*Political*); Herbert E. Weiner (*Economic*); John C. Amott (*Commercial*); Frank Tumminia (*Consular*); Norman H. Grady (*Administrative*). *Service

Attachés: Col. LeRoy Nigra (*Defence and Air*), Col. Stanley Blum (*Army*), Capt. John H. Howard (*Navy*).

There are consular representatives at Oporto, Ponta Delgada (Azores) and Funchal (Madeira).

BOOKS OF REFERENCE

STATISTICAL INFORMATION. The Instituto Nacional de Estatística (Avenida Dr António José de Almeida, Lisbon) was set up in 1935 in succession to the Direcção-Geral de Estatística. The Centro de Estudos Económicos and the Centro de Estudos Demográficos were affiliated to the Instituto in 1944. *Director:* Amaro Duarte Guerreiro. The main publications are:

Anuário Estatístico. Annuaire statistique. Annual, from 1875
Estatísticas do Comércio Externo. 2 vols. Annual from 1967 (replacing *Comércio Externo,* 1936–66, and *Estatística Comercial,* 1927–1937)
Censo da População de Portugal. 1864 ff. Decennial (latest ed. 1960)
Estatística da Organização Corporativa. 1938–49; Organização Corporativa e Previdência Social. 1950 ff.
Estatísticas Financeiras. 1947 ff. Annual (replacing *Situação Bancária,* 1919–46)
Estatística Agrícola. Statistique Agricole. 1943–64; replaced by *Estatísticas Agrícolas e Alimentares.* From 1965. Annual
Estatística Industrial. Statistique Industrielle. 1943 ff. Annual
Estatísticas Demográficas. From 1967 (replacing *Anuário Demográfico,* 1929–66)
Boletin Mensal do Instituto Nacional de Estatística. Monthly since 1929
Centro de Estudos Económicos. Revista. 1945 ff.
Centro de Estudos Demográficos. Revista. 1945 ff.
Estatísticas das Contribuições e Impostos. Annual from 1967 (replacing *Anuário Estatístico das Contribuições e Impostos,* 1936–66)
Estatísticas da Educação. 1940 ff.
Estatísticas Judiciária. 1936 ff.
Estatísticas das Sociedades. 1939 ff.
Estatísticas do Turismo. 1969 ff.
Estatísticas do Energia. 1969 ff.

Azevedo, Gonzaga de, *História de Portugal.* 6 vols. Lisbon, 1935–44
Bradão, O., *Assistência Social.* 2 vols. Lisbon, 1949
Brazão, E., *The Anglo-Portuguese Alliance.* London, 1957
Cortezão, J., *Descobrimentos Portugueses.* Lisbon, 1959
Eça, V. da Cunha d', *The Portuguese Economic Development Drive.* Lisbon, 1951
Ferreira, D., *Corporativismo.* Lisbon, 1955
Ferreira, J. A., *Dicionário inglês–português.* 2 vols. Porto, 1948
Guerreiro, A. D. (ed.), *Bibliografia sobre a economia portuguesa, 1948–62.* 14 vols. Lisbon, 1958–68
Higgins, M. H., and Winton, C. F. S. de, *Survey of Education in Portugal.* London, 1942
Livermore, H. V., *A New History of Portugal.* CUP, 1966
Nunes, A. Sedas, *Situação e Problemas do Corporativismo.* Lisbon, 1954
Pattee, R., *Portugal and the Portuguese World.* London, 1958
Pereira, A. M., *Organização política e administrativa de Portugal.* Oporto, 1949
Ribeiro, Orlando, *Portugal, o Mediterrâneo e o Atlântico: estudo geográfico.* 2nd ed. Lisbon, 1963
Salazar, A. de O., *Doctrine and Action: Internal and Foreign Policy of the New Portugal, 1928–39.* London, 1939.—*Discursos, 1928–58.* 5 vols. 5th ed. Coimbra, 1958.—*Política Portuguesa.* Santiago de Chile, 1952
Stanislawski, D., *The Individuality of Portugal: a study in historical-political geography.* Univ. of Texas Press, 1959
Taylor, J. L., *Portuguese-English Dictionary.* London, 1959

NATIONAL LIBRARY. Biblioteca Nacional, Campo Grande, Lisbon. *Director:* Dr Manuel do Santos Estevens.

OVERSEAS TERRITORIES

By law no. 2.048 of 11 June 1951 the status of the Portuguese overseas possessions was changed from 'colonies' to 'overseas territories'. Each one has a Governor and enjoys financial and administrative autonomy. Their budgets are under approval of the Minister for the Overseas Territories. They are not allowed to contract public loans in foreign countries.

On 6 Sept. 1961 all Africans were given full Portuguese citizenship, thereby achieving the same status as the inhabitants of Portuguese India and the other provinces.

All customs duties between Portugal and the overseas provinces were abolished with effect from 1 Jan. 1964.

Area (in sq. km) and population (1960 census):

Africa	Area	Population	Asia and Oceania	Area	Population
Cape Verde Islands	4,033	201,549	In India	4,194	625,831
Guinea	36,125	521,336	China: Macao, etc.	16	169,299
S. Tomé and Principe Islands	964	64,263	Total, Asia	4,210	795,130
Angola	1,246,700	4,830,449			
Moçambique	784,961	6,603,653	Timor	14,925	517,079
Total, Africa	2,072,783	12,221,250	Total, Overseas territories	2,091,918	13,533,459

Total trade of the Portuguese Overseas Territories with UK, in £1,000 sterling (British Board of Trade returns):

	Exports to UK			Imports from UK		
	1968	1969	1970	1968	1969	1970
West Africa (excl. Angola)	4	5	11	544	747	1,171
Angola	1,806	3,639	8,920	11,047	11,101	13,819
Moçambique	5,190	4,019	5,859	10,977	11,597	13,131
Macao	40	104	16	21	29	21
Timor	—	—	—	51	25	58

Atlas de Portugal Ultramarino. Lisbon: Ministério das Colónias. 1948
Anuário Estatístico, II: Ultramar. Annuaire statistique, II: Outre-mer. Lisbon, 1961 ff (1950–60 under the title *Anuário Estatístico do Ultramar*)
Boletin da Agência Geral do Ultramar. Lisbon. Monthly
Documentação ultramarina portuguesa. Centro de Estudos Históricos Ultramarinos. Lisbon, 1960
Andrade, A. A., *O Tradicional Anti-Racismo da Acção Civilizadora Portuguesa* (in Portuguese and English). Lisbon, 1953
Bahia dos Santos, F., *Unidade c cooperação entre a metrópole e o ultramar.* Lisbon, 1953
Boxer, C. R., *Race relations in the Portuguese empire.* OUP, 1963
Caetano, M., *Tradições, Princípios e Métodos da Colonização Portuguesa* (in Portuguese, French and English). Lisbon, 1951
Cunha, S., *O Sistema Português de Política Indigena.* Lisbon, 1953
Duffy, J., *Portuguese Africa.* Harvard Univ. Press, 1959.—*Portugal in Africa.* Harmondsworth, 1962
Freyre, G., *The Portuguese and the tropics.* Lisbon, 1961
Galvão, H., and Selvagem, C., *Império Ultramarino Português.* 4 vols. Lisbon, 1950–53
Nogueira, F., *The United Nations and Portugal.* London, 1963
Oliveira, J. da Costa, *Aplicação de capitais nas províncias ultramarinas.* Lisbon, 1961
Pattee, R., *Portugal na Africa contemporânea.* Coimbra, 1959

CAPE VERDE ISLANDS

The Cape Verde Islands were discovered in 1460 by Diogo Gomes, the first settlers arriving in 1462. In 1587 its administration was unified under a governor. The territory consists of 10 islands and 5 islets which are administered by a Governor, whose seat is at Praia, the capital. The islands are divided into 2 groups, named Barlavento (windward) and Sotavento (leeward), the prevailing wind being north-east. The former is constituted by the islands of São Vicente, Santo Antão, São Nicolau, Santa Luzia, Sal and Boa Vista, and the small islands named Branco and Raso. The latter is constituted by the islands of Santiago, Maio, Fogo and Brava, and the small islands named Rei and Rombo. São Vicente is an oiling station which supplies all navigation to South America. The total area is 4,033 sq. km (1,557 sq. miles). The population (census of 15 Dec. 1960) was 201,549. There were, in 1968–69, 233 primary schools (26,990 pupils), 6 secondary schools (2,718 pupils), 5 technical schools (485 pupils) and a church school (75 pupils).

The chief products are bananas, salt, tunny, coffee, nuts and pozzolana. The coffee is of excellent quality; exports in 1969 were 13 metric tons. In 1969 there were 24,518 goats, 13,893 cattle, 9,187 pigs and 5,455 asses. The revenue in 1968 was 258,619,000 escudos and expenditure was 232,863,000 escudos; public debt, 746,436,000 escudos. Imports, in 1969, 418,801 contos (special commerce); exports, 44,606 contos (special commerce).

In 1969, 5,330 steamers entered the ports of the province; total shipping, 7,253,645 net tons. There were 874 km of roads in 1968. There is an airport at Ilha do Sal.

There are British and American consular representatives at São Vicente.

Governor: Brig.-Gen. Antonio Lopes dos Santos.

Anuário Estatístico de Cabo Verde. Praia. Annual
Cabo Verde. Agência-Geral do Ultramar. Lisbon, 1961

PORTUGUESE GUINEA

Portuguese Guinea, on the coast of Guinea, was discovered in 1446 by Nuno Tristão. It became a separate colony in 1879. It is bounded by the limits fixed by the convention of 12 May 1886 with France, and is bounded by Senegal in the north and by Guinea in the east and south. It includes the adjacent archipelago of Bijagoz, with the island of Bolama. The capital is, since 1942, Bissau. Area is 36,125 sq. km (13,948 sq. miles); population (census, 1960), 521,336. There were, in 1966–67, 151 primary schools with 7,233 pupils; 1 technical school with 658 pupils and a secondary school with 446 pupils.

Chief products are rice, palm-oil, groundnuts, coconuts, timber, hides, seeds, wax. The revenue in 1968 was 333,131, the expenditure 305,555 and the public debt 270,275 contos. Imports in 1968, 506,657 contos; exports, 87,474 contos (special commerce). The chief port is Bissau. Other ports are Bolama and Cacheu. In 1968, 128 vessels of 186,428 net tons entered the ports of the province. There are (1967) 3,165 km of roads and (1969) 1,344 telephones.

Governor: Gen. António Sebastião Ribeiro Spínola.
British Consul-General: A. G. Battle (resident at Lisbon).

Anuário da Guiné Portuguesa. Bissau (latest issue, 1956–58)
Relatório e Mapas do Movimento Comercial e Marítimo da Guiné. Bolama. Annual
Guiné. Agência-Geral do Ultramar. Lisbon, 1961
Mota, T. de, *Guiné Portuguesa.* Lisbon, 1954

SÃO TOMÉ E PRINCIPE

The islands of S. Tomé and Principe, which are about 125 miles off the coast of Africa, in the Gulf of Guinea, were discovered in 1471 by Pedro Escobar and João Gomes, and since 1522 constitute a province under a Governor. The province also includes the islands of Pedras Tinhosas and Rolas; the fort of St Jean Baptiste d'Ajudá on the coast was annexed by the Dahomey republic on 1 Aug. 1961. Area of the islands 964 sq. km (372 sq. miles). According to the census of 1960 the population of the islands was 64,263. There were, in 1968–69, 43 primary schools with 8,281 pupils, a secondary preparatory school with 453 pupils, a technical school with 127 pupils and a secondary school with 544 pupils. The chief commercial products are cacao, copra, coconut, coffee, palm-oil and cinchona. In 1969 there were 1,027 goats, 2,159 sheep, 3,283 pigs and 3,060 cattle.

In 1968 revenue was 156,973 contos and expenditure 134,175 contos; public debt, 381,158 contos. Imports (1969), 224,856 contos; exports, 247,199 contos.

There were 284 km of roads in 1967. In 1967, 879 vessels of 650,206 net tons entered the ports. There were, in 1967, 2 wireless stations, 243 km of telephone lines and a telephone exchange (with 474 instruments).

Governor: Lieut.-Col. António da Silva Sebastião.

S. Tomé e Príncipe. Agência-Geral do Ultramar, 1964

ANGOLA

Angola, with a coastline of over 1,000 miles, is separated from the Congo (Br.) by the boundaries assigned by the convention of 12 May 1886; from the Congo (K.) by those fixed by the convention of 22 July 1927; from Rhodesia in accordance with the convention of 11 June 1891, and from South West Africa in accordance with that of 30 Dec. 1886. The Congo region was discovered by the Portuguese in 1482, and the first settlers arrived there in 1491. Luanda was founded in 1575. It was taken by the Dutch in 1641 and occupied by them until 1648. The area is 1,246,700 sq. km (481,351 sq. miles). By a decree of 20 Oct. 1954 it is divided into 13 districts. The important towns are S. Paulo de Luanda (capital), Benguela, Moçâmedes, Lobito, Sá da Bandeira, Malange and Huambo (Nova Lisboa) the future capital. The population numbers about 5m., of whom 300,000 are white.

For primary education there were (1967–68) 3,326 primary schools with 296,269 pupils; 58 secondary schools with 20,723 pupils; 77 professional technical schools with 19,945 pupils; 4 teachers' training schools with 172 students; 9 high schools (989 pupils); an art school (598 pupils); 6 church schools (619 pupils).

There were, in 1968, 33 cinemas with a seating capacity of 26,743.

In 1968 the revenue was 8,071,098 contos and the expenditure 7,648,849 contos. The public debt was 5,549,123 contos.

Livestock, 1969: 2,171,144 cattle, 161,197 sheep, 759,276 goats, 319,578 pigs. The principal crops are coffee, maize, sugar, palm-oil and palm kernels. Other products are cotton, wheat, tobacco, cocoa, sisal and wax. The country possesses valuable diamond deposits. Production of diamonds during 1968 totalled 1·67m. carats (1969: 2·02m.). Production (1969) of iron ore, 5,477,657 metric tons; crude petroleum, 2,457,512 metric tons; salt, 80,181 metric tons.

Imports, 1969, 9,261m. (1968: 8,710m.) escudos; exports, 9,387m. (1968: 7,788m.) escudos. The chief imports are textiles, transport equipment, foodstuffs, pig-iron and steel; chief exports are coffee (182,944 tons in 1969), diamonds, sisal, iron ore, fish, maize, crude oil, palm-oil. Coffee exports were valued at 3,237m. escudos in 1969.

The Portuguese National Navigation Company has most of the carrying trade to and from Europe. The length of railways open for traffic in 1969 was 3,159 km. The Benguela Railway runs from Lobito through the Congo (K.) and Rhodesia, ending at Beira in Moçambique. A further extension goes through Rhodesia, as far as Mafeking, and from thence to Komati Port, in the Republic of South Africa, where it connects with the Lourenço Marques Railway. The total length of railway, from Lobito to Lourenço Marques, is 5,638 km. In 1969 Angola's railways carried 1,691,000 passengers and 7,433,000 metric tons of freight.

There were, in 1969, 72,291 km of roads.

Angola is connected by cable with east, west and south African telegraph systems. There were, in 1969, 1,808 km of telegraph lines, 59 telephone stations (with 24,836 instruments), 174 telegraph stations and 33 wireless stations.

In 1969, 5,337 vessels of 11,699,905 net tons entered Angolan ports.

Regular air service is maintained by the Divisão de Transportes Aéreos from Luanda to: (South) Moçâmedes *via* Lobito and Sá da Bandeira, with connexions to Porto Alexandre and Lucira; (east) Vila Luso *via* Cela, Nova Lisboa and Silva Porto; (north) Pointe Noire (Congo) *via* Cabinda; and to Léopoldville (Congo); (east) Portugália *via* Malange and Henrique de Carvalho; (south) Vila Pereira d'Eça *via* Nova Lisboa, Sá da Bandeira and Rocadas; Windhoek *via* Sá da Bandeira.

Governor-General: Lieut.-Col. Rebocho Vaz.
British Consul-General (Luanda): R. W. Ford.
USA Consul (Luanda): Richard St. F. Post.

Anuário Estatístico de Angola. Luanda, from 1897
How to invest in Angola. Luanda, 1963
Araújo, A. Correia de, *Aspectos do desenvolvimento económico e social de Angola.* Lisbon, 1964

EE

Bahia dos Santos, F., *Angola.* Lisbon, 1954
Dias, G. de Sousa, *Os portugueses em Angola.* Lisbon, 1959
Egerton, F. C. C., *Angola in Perspective.* London, 1957
Sharman, T. C., *Economic and Commercial Conditions in Portuguese West Africa.* HMSO, 1954

MOÇAMBIQUE

Moçambique was discovered by Vasco da Gama's fleet on 1 March 1498, and was first colonized in 1505. The frontier with British Central and South Africa was fixed between Great Britain and Portugal in June 1891. The border with Tanganyika, according to agreements of 1886 and 1890, runs from Cape Delgado at 10° 40′ S. lat. till it meets the courses of the Rovuma, which it follows to the point of its confluence with the 'Msinje, the boundary thence to Lake Nyasa being the parallel of latitude of this point. The Treaty of Versailles, 1919, allotted to Portugal the original Portuguese territory south of the Rovuma, known as the 'Kionga Triangle' (formerly part of German East Africa).

Moçambique, with an area of 784,961 sq. km (303,070 sq. miles) is administered by the state, since 19 July 1942, when the state took over the territory of Manica and Sofala, which was incorporated as a fourth district of the province, with Beira as its capital. The Companhia de Moçambique was then wound up on the expiration of its charter. Lourenço Marques is the capital of the province. As established by decree of 20 Oct. 1954, the province is divided into 9 districts: Lourenço Marques, Gaza, Inhambane, Manica and Sofala, Tete, Zambézia, Moçambique, Cabo Delgado, Niassa.

There is a government council composed of officials and elected representatives of the commercial, industrial and agricultural classes, and also an executive council. The population, according to the census of 1960, was 6,663,653. In 1967–68 there were 3,691 primary schools with 485,055 pupils; 46 secondary schools with 9,514 pupils (1966–67); 10 normal schools with 974 pupils; 25 professional technical schools with 14,093 pupils; 9 high schools with 904 pupils; 6 church schools with 594 pupils; 7 art schools with 444 pupils.

There were, in 1968, 23 cinemas with a seating capacity of 17,100.

In 1968 the revenue was 7,534,784 contos, expenditure 7,220,696 contos and public debt 3,793,171 contos.

The chief agricultural exports in 1968 were (in metric tons): Sugar, 131,812; cotton, 38,887; copra, 96,776; sisal, 25,142; cashew nuts, 132,146; tea, 14,070. Mining products in 1968: Gold, 0·2 kg; beryl, 95 metric tons; bauxite, 3,274 metric tons; coal, 314,408 metric tons.

Livestock 1968: 1,223,846 cattle, 475,021 goats, 102,982 sheep, 124,190 pigs, 17,042 asses.

Imports, 1968, amounted to 6,740,137 contos; exports, 4,420,172 contos.

The principal ports are: Lourenço Marques (1,920 vessels of 9,940,716 net tons handled in 1968), Beira (1,265 vessels of 4,899,958 net tons), Moçambique (115 vessels of 340,576 net tons) and Nacala 268 vessels of 860,399 net tons).

There were, in 1968, 3,589 km of railway and (1969) 37,085 km of road, of which 11,305 km are main roads. Motor vehicles, in 1968, included 64,222 passenger cars, 14,876 lorries and buses and 3,614 motor cycles.

The Delagoa Bay Railway has a length of 64 miles in Portuguese territory and is continued for 290 miles to Pretoria. The Beira Railway has a length of 200 miles in the territory formerly administered by the Moçambique Co., and links up at the frontier with the Rhodesian Railway system. The Trans-Zambézia Railway, 175 miles in length, from Dondo, on the Beira Junction Railway, to Murraça, on the southern bank of the Zambezi, was opened for traffic on 1 July 1922. On the northern bank of the Zambezi, the Central Africa Railway (61 miles long, of which 45 miles are in Portuguese territory) connects at Port Herald with the Shiré Highlands Railway. With the opening of the Lower Zambezi Bridge on 14 Jan. 1935 (3,677 metres, one of the longest bridges in the world), these 3 railways give a continuous connexion between Malawi and the port of Beira.

Regular air service is maintained between Lourenço Marques, Johannesburg and Durban; and between Beira, Salisbury and Blantyre.

Beira is connected by telegraph with Salisbury in Rhodesia, and Lourenço Marques with the Transvaal system. Quelimane has telegraphic communication with Chiromo. In 1969 there were 72,825 km of telegraph line, 25 wireless stations, 108 telephone stations and 224 telegraph stations; length of telephone lines, 72,821 km, including 55,616 km of conductor wires in cable; number of telephones (1969), 24,300.

Barclays Bank DCO has branches in Beira and Lourenço Marques.

Note circulation, Dec. 1969, was 1,851,000 contos. The metric system is used.

Governor-General: Eng⁰ Eduardo de Arantes e Oliveira.
British Consul-General (Lourenço Marques): P. A. Wilde. There is also a Consul at Beira.
USA Consul-General (Lourenço Marques): John G. Gossett.

Anuário Estatístico da Provincia de Moçambique. Lourenço Marques
Moçambique. Documentário trimestral. Lourenço Marques (since 1935)
Guia economico de Moçambique. Lourenço Marques, 1952
Principal legislação aplicável aos indigenas da Provincia de Moçambique. Lourenço Marques
Boléo, O., *Moçambique.* Lisbon, 1961
Marjay, F. P., *Mozambique.* Lisbon, 1963
Ribeiro, S., *Anário de Moçambique.* Lourenço Marques. (First issue, 1908)
Galvão, H., and Selvagem, C., *Moçambique.* Lisboa, 1953

MACAO

Macao, in China, situated on a peninsula of the same name at the mouth of the Canton River, which came into possession of the Portuguese in 1557, forms with the 2 small adjacent islands of Taipa and Colôane a province, divided into 2 wards, each having its own administrator. The boundaries have not yet been definitely agreed upon; at present Portugal holds the territory in virtue of the treaty with China of 1 Dec. 1887. The area of the province is 16 sq. km (6 sq. miles). The population, according to the census of 1960, is 169,299 (7,974 Portuguese, 160,764 Chinese, 561 others); the steady influx of Chinese refugees is creating serious social and economic difficulties, while Chinese communists cause sporadic political unrest.

Revenue in 1968 was 293,963 contos, expenditure 283,121 contos and public debt 143,323 contos.

Education (1967/68) is provided at 33 secondary schools (7,040 pupils), 113 elementary schools (25,836 pupils), 16 technical schools (1,570 pupils), 4 professional schools (288 pupils), 3 church schools (46 pupils) and an art school (90 pupils).

The trade, mostly transit, is handled by Chinese merchants. Imports, in 1969, 1,710,441 contos; exports, 1,072,625 contos. The province has 693 km of telephone line (5,259 instruments in 1969). It is served by a Portuguese and various British and Dutch steamship lines. In 1969, 13,970 vessels of 4,319,277 gross tons entered the port.

Governor: Dr José Manuel Nobre de Carvalho.
British Consul (resides at Hong Kong): J. K. Blackwell, CBE.

Anuário Estatístico de Macau. Macao
Brazão, E., *Macau.* Lisbon, 1957

TIMOR

Portuguese Timor has been under Portuguese administration since 1586. It consists of the eastern portion of the island of that name in the Malay Archipelago, with the territory of Ambeno and the neighbouring islands of Pulo Cambing and Pulo Jako, a total area of 14,925 sq. km. By treaty of April 1859, ratified 18 Aug. 1860, the island was divided between Portugal and Holland; by convention of 1 Oct. 1904, ratified in 1908, the boundaries were straightened and settled. The territory, formerly administratively joined to Macao, was in 1896 (confirmed in 1926) made an independent province. Population in 1960, 517,079. There were (1966–67) 2 secondary schools with 833 pupils, 174 primary schools with 20,534 pupils, 1 technical school with 14 pupils, 1 church school with 46 pupils and a normal school with 83 pupils.

In 1968 the revenue was 134,169 contos, expenditure 148,561 contos and public debt 25,983 contos. Imports (1969), 183,504 contos; exports, 61,518 contos. Chief exports are coffee, copra, rubber and wax.

Livestock, 1969: 67,035 (1968: 56,797) cattle; 38,920 (1968: 40,003) sheep; 204,274 (1968: 215,810) goats; 202,849 (1968: 213,991) pigs; 123,955 (1968: 120,800) buffaloes; 106,772 (1968: 104,854) horses.

The port is Dili, the capital (population, 10,753). In 1969, 52 ships of 61,558 net tons entered and cleared. In 1968 there were 2,000 km of roads, telephone lines (1969) of 4,222 km, 58 telephone stations (638 instruments) and 4 wireless stations at Dili.

Governor: Brig.-Gen. José Nogueira Valente Pires.
British Consul (resides at Djakarta)*:* M. P. Preston.

Felgas, H. E., *Timor Português*. Lisbon, 1956
Oliveira, Luna de, *Timor na História de Portugal*. 3 vols. Lisbon, 1949–52
Exploration of Portuguese Timor. *Report of Allied Mining Corporation to Asia Investment Company, Ltd.* Victoria, Hong Kong, 1937
Martinho, José S., *Timor Quatro séculos de colonização portuguesa*. Porto, 1943

Portuguese India (Estado da India) was under Portuguese rule 1505–1961. It consisted of Goa, containing the capital, Goa, together with the islands of Angediva, São Jorge and Morcegos, on the Malabar coast; Damão, with the territories of Dadrá and Nagar-Haveli, on the Gulf of Cambia; and Diu, with the continental territories of Gogola and Simbor, on the coast of Gujerat.

In violation of the United Nations charter, Indian troops invaded Goa, Damão and Diu without declaration of war on 18–19 Dec. 1961 and forcibly incorporated the Portuguese territory in the Indian Union (*see* p. 383).

Correia, G., *História da Colonização Portuguesa na India*. 5 vols. Lisbon, 1948–54

ROMANIA
Republica Socialistă România

HISTORY. For the history and constitution of Romania from 1859 to 1947, *see* THE STATESMAN'S YEAR-BOOK, 1947, pp. 1187–89. On 30 Dec. 1947 King Michael abdicated under Communist pressure and parliament proclaimed the 'People's Republic'.

CONSTITUTION AND GOVERNMENT. The present Constitution was adopted on 21 Aug. 1965 and supersedes those of 13 April 1948 and 24 Sept. 1952. Under it Romania becomes a 'Socialist' (as opposed to 'People's') Republic. The leading role of the Communist Party is reaffirmed. The Grand National Assembly of 465 is elected for 4 years. It holds short sessions twice a year, and between sessions delegates its legislative rights to the State Council (the President, head of state; 4 Vice-presidents, 1 secretary and 22 members). By a law of Nov. 1969 the policy of ministries is shaped by deliberative collegiate bodies of which the minister is the chairman. All citizens of 18 and over have the right to vote and electoral law provides for the nomination of 'one or more' candidates in each constituency. The National Council of the Socialist Unity Front functions as a consultative body on home and foreign affairs. It has a central and local councils in which workers, peasants, professional bodies, ethnic minorities and the Communist Party are represented. It replaces the Popular Democratic Front which was a coalition formed in 1948 of the Romanian

Workers' Party (a merger of the Communist and Social Democratic Parties), the Ploughmen's Front (a pro-Communist Peasant Party), the National Popular Party and the Hungarian Popular Union.

Elections were held on 30 Nov. 1952, 3 Feb. 1957, 5 March 1961, 7 March 1965 and 2 March 1969.

At the 1969 elections 99·96% of the electorate voted and 99·75% of the votes were for candidates on the single list of the Socialist Unity Front.

In 1965 the Romanian Workers' Party was renamed the Romanian Communist Party. The Party Congress elects the General Secretary, and its Central Committee elects the Executive Committee (22 full and 11 alternate members), the Permanent Presidium (8 members) and the Secretariat (General Secretary and 7 secretaries). The Party had over 1,924,000 members in 1969.

President of the State Council: Nicolae Ceauşescu, succeeded Chivu Stoica in Dec. 1967. *Vice-Presidents:* Emil Bodnaraş, Manea Mănescu, Ştefan Péterfi, Vasile Vîlcu.

Permanent Presidium of the Communist Party: Nicolae Ceauşescu (*General Secretary*); Ion Gheorghe Maurer, *Chairman of the Council of Ministers:* Army-Gen. Emil Bodnaraş; Paul Niculescu-Mizil; Gheorghe Pană; Gheorghe Rădulescu; Virgil Trofin; Ilie Verdeţ.

Council of Ministers (March 1971). *Chairman:* Ion Gheorghe Maurer. *First Vice-Chairman:* Ilie Verdeţ. *Vice-Chairman:* Janos Fazekaş; Gheorghe Rădulescu; Leonte Răutu; Iosif Banc; Emil Drăgănescu; Mihai Marinescu; Ion Pǎţan. *Interior:* Cornel Onescu; *Foreign Affairs:* Corneliu Mănescu; *Armed Forces:* Col.-Gen. Ion Ioniţǎ; *Foreign Trade:* Cornel Burticǎ; *Finance:* Florea Dumitrescu; *Justice:* Teodor Vasiliu; *Chairman, State Planning Commission:* Maxim Berghianu. *Chairman, State Security Council:* Ion Stănescu.

Since the mid-1960s Romania has been taking an increasingly independent stand in foreign affairs, and denounced the Soviet intervention in Czechoslovakia in 1968. In July 1970 Romania signed a treaty of friendship, cooperation and mutual assistance with the USSR. A previous such treaty had expired in 1968.

National flag: Blue, yellow, red (vertical), with the coat of arms of the republic in the middle.

National anthem: Te slăvim Românie, pămînt strămoşesc (We praise thee, fatherland Romania).

AREA AND POPULATION. The area of Romania is 237,500 sq. km (91,699 sq. miles). Pre-war Romania had an area of 113,918 sq. miles. Population figures at censuses: 1930, 18,025,884 (of whom 14,208,729 lived within the boundaries of present-day Romania); 1948, 15,872,624 (48·3% male); 1966 19,103,163 (49% male, 37·6% urban).

On 1 Jan. 1970 the population was 20·14m. (49% male, 42% urban), density per sq. km, 84·3. Vital statistics, 1969 (per 1,000 population): Live births, 23·3; deaths, 10·1; marriages, 7; divorces, 0·4; stillborn (per 1,000 live births), 1·5; infant mortality (per 1,000 live births), 54·9; average expectation of life, 68·51 years; population growth rate, 1·5% in 1969.

Administratively, Romania is divided into 39 districts and 2,706 communes. The capital is Bucharest (Bucureşti).

District	Area in sq. km	Population 1970	Capital	Population 1970
Alba	6,231	391,686	Alba Iulia	27,547
Arad	7,654	492,439	Arad	137,194
Argeş	6,801	568,854	Piteşti	74,237
Bacău	6,603	648,596	Bacău	91,045
Bihor	7,535	606,969	Oradea	137,662
Bistriţa-Năsăud	5,305	281,335	Bistriţa	27,832
Botoşani	4,965	475,240	Botoşani	40,387

District	Area in sq. km	Population 1970	Capital	Population 1970
Braşov	5,351	473,812	Braşov	182,105
Brăila	4,770	361,476	Brăila	151,650
Buzău	6,072	504,942	Buzău	71,300
Caraş-Severin	8,514	366,338	Reşiţa	67,980
Cluj	6,650	666,355	Cluj	202,715
Constanţa	7,055	513,293	Constanţa	172,464
Covasna	3,705	184,407	Sf. Gheorghe	24,975
Dîmboviţa	3,738	455,083	Tîrgovişte	33,359
Dolj	7,403	724,159	Craiova	175,454
Galaţi	4,425	525,135	Galaţi	179,189
Gorj	5,641	317,045	Tg. Jiu	42,935
Harghita	6,610	295,386	Miercurea-Ciue	18,034
Hunedoara	7,016	504,640	Deva	38,579
Ialomiţa	6,211	381,682	Slobozia	14,988
Iaşi	5,469	677,537	Iaşi	183,776
Ilfov	8,225	797,303	Bucureşti	1,475,050
Maramureş	6,215	458,142	Baia Mare	76,855
Mehedinţi	4,900	317,629	Turnu Severin	54,619
Mureş	6,696	592,427	Tg. Mureş	98,201
Neamţ	5,890	508,623	Piatra Neamţ	53,630
Oltenia	5,517	498,863	Slatina	24,872
Prahova	4,694	752,684	Ploieşti	162,937
Satu Mare	4,405	373,933	Satu Mare	78,812
Sălaj	3,850	267,943	Zalău	17,169
Sibiu	5,422	440,581	Sibiu	120,118
Suceava	8,555	616,021	Suceava	44,941
Teleorman	5,872	539,605	Alexandria	24,131
Timiş	8,678	636,186	Timişoara	192,616
Tulcea	8,430	250,049	Tulcea	41,981
Vaslui	5,300	459,816	Vaslui	22,739
Vîlcea	5,705	390,036	Rîmnicu-Vîlcea	34,668
Vrancea	4,817	371,755	Focşani	39,629

The 1966 census listed the following ethnic groups (in 1,000): Romanians, 16,746; Hungarians, 1,620; Germans, 383.

The official language is Romanian.

RELIGION. Churches are organized and function in accordance with art. 30 of the Constitution. Churches administer their own affairs and run seminaries for the training of priests. Expenses and salaries are paid by the State. There are 14 Churches, all under the control of the 'Department of Cults'. The largest is the Romanian Orthodox Church, which claimed 13·67m. members in 1950. It is autocephalous, but retains dogmatic unity with the Eastern Orthodox Church. It is administered by the consultative Holy Synod and National Ecclesiastical Assembly and the executive National Ecclesiastical Council and Patriarchal Administration. It is organized into 12 dioceses grouped into 5 metropolitan bishoprics (Hungaro-Wallachia; Moldavia-Suceava; Transylvania; Oltenia; Banat), and headed by Patriarch Justinian Marina (since May 1948). There are some 11,800 churches, 2 theological colleges and 6 'schools of cantors', as we ll as seminaries.

The Uniate (Greek Catholic) Church severed its connexion with the Vatican (formed 1698) to rejoin the Romanian Orthodox in 1948.

Other churches: Serbs have a Serbian Orthodox Vicariate at Timişoara. There is a Roman Catholic archbishopric of Bucharest–Iaşi and a bishopric of Alba Iulia. There were 820 priests and 254 monks in 1958. The Church has not secured approval for a Statute and has no hierarchical ties with the Vatican.

Calvinists (780,000; mainly Hungarian) have bishoprics at Cluj and Oradea; Lutherans (250,000, mainly Germans) a bishopric at Sibiu and Unitarians a bishopric at Cluj. These sects share a Protestant seminary at Cluj.

Baptists (814 communities), Adventists (587), Evangelicals (165) and Pentecostals (447) have formed a federation.

The 3 main Jewish communities (110,000 members) have formed a federation under a Chief Rabbi with 300 rabbis and some 300 synagogues.

Moslems have a Muftiate at Constanţa.

EDUCATION. General education is free and compulsory and lasts 10 years (from 6 to 15). Secondary education is then available in general, technical or vocational schools, or (since 1968) in lycées combining both types of education.

In 1969–70 education at all levels (including evening classes) comprised 10,032 kindergartens with 18,275 teachers and 428,480 children; 15,500 general education schools with 149,604 teachers and 3,323,601 pupils; 217 specialized-curriculum schools with 5,780 teachers and 108,988 pupils; 322 technical schools with 2,585 teachers and 44,903 pupils; 410 vocational schools with 11,527 teachers and 202,048 pupils. There are 1,722 general and 265 secondary schools for ethnic minorities, with over 240,000 pupils.

There are universities at Iaşi (founded 1860), Bucharest (1864), Cluj (1919), Timişoara (1962) and Craiova (1965). There are 49 institutes of higher education, 14 teacher-training colleges, 15 institutes of technology, 5 schools of medicine 5 schools of agriculture and 1 of economics. Student population in 1969–70: 151,705.

The Academy, with seat at Bucharest, has 2 branches at Iaşi and Cluj, 2 research centres at Timişoara and Tîrgu Mureş, an observatory and 15 research institutes. The National Council for Scientific Research co-ordinates research.

Spelling reforms were introduced in 1954 and 1965.

CINEMAS. There were, in 1969, 6,316 cinemas.

NEWSPAPERS. There were, in 1969, 51 daily newspapers, including 10 in minority languages. The party newspaper is *Scînteia*.

WELFARE. In 1969 there were 163,983 hospital beds and 29,471 doctors.

JUSTICE. Justice is administered by the Supreme Court, the 39 district courts and lower courts. People's assessors (elected for 4 years) participate in all court trials, collaborating with the judges. The Procurator-General exercises 'supreme supervisory power to ensure the observance of the law' by all authorities, central and local, and all citizens. The Procurator's Office and its organs are independent of any organs of justice or administration, and only responsible to the Grand National Assembly (which appoints the Procurator-General for 4 years) and, between its sessions, to the State Council. Since 1968 the Ministry of the Interior has been responsible only for 'ordinary' police work. State security is the responsibility of a new, separate State Security Council. A new penal code came into force on 1 Jan. 1969. It is based on 'the rule of law' and is aimed at preventing illegal trials. The death penalty is retained for 'specially serious offences' (treason, some classes of murder, theft of state property having serious consequences).

FINANCE. Currency. The monetary unit is the *leu*, pl. *lei* (of 100 *bani*). On 1 Feb. 1954 the gold content of the leu was changed to 0·148112 gramme of fine gold. Exchange rates: £1 = 14·4 lei; US$1 = 6 lei; 1 rouble = 6·67 lei. Tourist rates: £1 = 43·2 lei; US$1 = 18 lei; 1 rouble = 8·30 lei.

Bank-notes of 1, 3, 5, 10, 25 and 100 lei are issued by the National Bank, and there are coins of 5, 10, 15 and 25 bani and 1 and 3 lei.

Budget. Revenue and expenditure (in 1m. lei) for calendar years:

	1964	1965	1966	1967	1968	1969
Revenue	92,454	96,871	108,867	129,307	138,757	146,957
Expenditure	87,084	92,998	105,372	124,321	131,920	142,805

In lei, 1969 revenue included 45m. from state enterprises, 38m. from sales tax, 10m. from direct taxes and 8m. from social insurance contributions. Expenditures: 98m. on the economy, 34m. social and cultural, 6m. defence.

The revenues of local councils yielded 21·2m. lei in 1969.

Romania's external debts consist of pre-war obligations and those stipulated in the peace treaty. Total UK claims in 1961 amounted to over £100m., including some £20m. of bonded debt. A financial agreement of 1960 provided for payment by Romania of £1·25m. in settlement of British claims arising out of the peace treaty, to be completed by 31 Jan. 1967. Negotiations for a settlement were resumed in 1966.

DEFENCE. Defence is the responsibility of the Defence Council, which is controlled by the Council of State and headed by President Ceauşescu.

Army. Service is 16 months. Strength in 1969 was reported to be some 150,000 men plus 50,000 in para-military forces (frontier troops, internal-security troops, militia, military firemen).

Units of the Ministry of the Armed Forces are under one of the 3 military regions of Iaşi, Bucharest and Cluj. There are 3 army corps, each made up of 3 infantry divisions and supporting tank, artillery, engineer and reconnaissance elements. There are also 2 mountain divisions at Tîrgu Mureş and Sinaia, 2 tank divisions at Bucharest and Lipova, 2 motorized divisions and an independent artillery division at Tecuci. The AA artillery consists of 14 regiments. There are 2,000 T-34, T-54 and T-55 tanks. A Territorial Defence Force was set up in 1970.

Navy. In 1970 there were 4 missile boats, 8 torpedo boats, 3 patrol vessels, 4 minesweepers, 22 inshore minesweepers, 2 training ships and 30 service craft. Headquarters of the Danube flotilla and main river port is Brăila. The naval school is in Constanţa. Personnel in 1970 totalled 5,000 officers and men. Service is 2 years.

Air Force. Service is 2 years. The Air Force numbers some 15,000 men, with 275 combat aircraft. These are organized into 2 light bomber/reconnaissance squadrons (each with 12 aircraft) with Il-28s, 9 interceptor squadrons with MiG-19 and MiG-21 fighters and 9 ground-support squadrons with MiG-15 and MiG-17 fighters. There are also 150 training aircraft, 10 transports and 10 helicopters. 'Guideline' surface-to-air missiles are operational, and short-range surface-to-surface missiles have been displayed, but may not have warheads.

PLANNING. Economic policy is implemented by the State Planning Commission. There have been three 5-year plans (1951–56, 1956–60, 1966–70) and one 6-year (1960–65). The fourth 5-year plan (1971–75) envisages an annual industrial growth rate of 8·5–9·5% to expand industry by 50–57%, and an expansion of agriculture by 28–31%. Industries scheduled for particular development: machine-building, iron and steel, non-ferrous metals, chemicals and electric power. Guidelines for the development of the economy up to 1980 have also been drawn up. Output of main products:

Product	1950	1960	1965	1966	1967	1968	1969
Crude oil (1,000 metric tons)	5,047	11,500	12,571	12.825	13,206	13,285	13,246
Electric energy (1m. kwh.)	2,113	7,650	17,215	20,805	24,769	27,828	31,509
Pig-iron (1,000 metric tons)	320	1,014	2,019	2,198	2,456	2,992	3,477
Steel (1,000 metric tons)	555	1,806	3,425	3,670	4,088	4,751	5,540
Coal (1,000 metric tons)	3,893	8,163	12,095	13,451	15,019	17,020	19,152
Methane gas (1,000 cu. metres)	2,057	6,707	13,038	14,252	16,036	17,226	19,066
Wheat (1,000 metric tons)	2,219	3,450	5,937	5,065	5,820	4,848	4,349
Maize (1,000 metric tons)	2,101	5,530	5,877	8,022	6,858	7,105	7,676
Sugar-beet (1,000 metric tons)	633	3,399	3,275	4,368	3,830	3,936	3,783

Other product figures are given below.

Economic reforms were introduced in 1967 to give enterprises 'functional autonomy'.

AGRICULTURE. Utilization of the land in 1969 (in 1,000 hectares): Arable, 9,771; meadows and pasture, 4,423; vineyards and fruit trees, 773.

Production in 1969 (in 1,000 metric tons): Wheat, 4,349; barley, 544; maize, 7,676; potatoes, 2,165; sunflower seed, 747.

Livestock in 1970: 686,000 horses, 5m. cattle, 5·6m. pigs, 13·8m. sheep and 53·6m. poultry.

In 1969 there were 4,655 collective farms, with 9m. hectares of land (7·3m. arable). State farms numbered 359 (731 in 1966), with 2·1m. hectares of land, of which 1·67m. hectares were arable. There were 296 machine and tractor stations with 71,964 tractors, 45,480 mechanical seeders and 36,440 mechanical harvesters. Total number of tractors, 101,906. The socialist sector comprises 90·8% of the agricultural land. The National Union of Agricultural Co-operatives promotes self-management in collective farms, and gives guidance on planning and marketing. In 1967 the state-farm system was reorganized and specialized farms (2,800 by 1969) were set up under state agricultural enterprises; farm managers have full autonomy over production. In 1969 there were 632,500 hectares of irrigated land.

FORESTRY. Total forest area is 6·32m. hectares. In 1969 the output of sawn timber was 5·3m. cu. metres (2·7m. coniferous). In 1969, 55,614 hectares were afforested.

MINING. The principal minerals are oil and natural gas, salt, brown coal, lignite, iron and copper ores, bauxite, chromium, manganese and uranium. The oilfields are in the Prahova, Băcau, Gorj, Crişana and Argeş districts. Refining capacity (13m. tons per annum) exceeds production of crude oil and efforts are being made to expand it; some crude is imported. Salt is mined in the lower Carpathians and in Transylvania; production in 1969 was 2·7m. metric tons.

1969 (and 1968) output (in 1,000 metric tons): Iron ore, 2,990 (2,747); crude oil, 13,246 (13,285); coal, 15,152 (17,020).

INDUSTRY. Output of main products in 1969 (and 1968) (in 1,000 metric tons): Pig-iron, 3,477 (2,992); steel, 5,540 (4,751); steel tubes, 756 (706); metallurgical coke, 939 (1,133); rolled steel, 3,816 (3,393); chemical fertilizers, 720 (603); washing soda, 595 (471); caustic soda, 312 (276); paper, 398 (380); cement, 7,515 (7,026); sugar, 491 (384); edible oils, 268 (268); butter, 31 (29). Fabrics (in 1m. sq. metres): Cotton, 410 (377); woollens, 56 (52); silk, 43 (38). Light industry (in 1,000 units): Radio sets, 428 (388); TV sets, 221 (161); bicycles, 211 (190); sewing machines, 86 (83); footwear, 63m. pairs (61); washing machines, 174 (109); refrigerators, 147 (148).

ELECTRICITY. The second 10-year power plan (1966–75) envisages an output of electric power of 55,000–60,000m. kwh. by 1975. Installed electric power in 1969: 6,432,000 kw. Output: 31,509m. kwh. A joint Romanian-Yugoslav hydro-electric power plant is being built on the Danube at the 'Iron Gates'; yearly output is to be 5,000m. kwh. Atomic power stations are being built.

LABOUR. The labour force in 1969 was 4·96m., of whom 2m. worked in industry; 94% of the labour force is employed in the 'socialist sector'. The minimum monthly wage is 800 lei.

COMMERCE. Between 1949 and 1959 some 80% of external trade was with communist countries, but since 1960 this proportion has dropped, e.g., to 55% in 1969 (30% with USSR).

In 1969 exports totalled 9,798m. lei and imports 10,442m. lei.

Principal exports in 1969 were (in 1,000 metric tons): Oil (crude and products), 5,065; cement, 1,182; agricultural products, 2,881; timber, 1·9m. cu. metres; tractors, 11,372 units; oilfield equipment, 263m. lei; equipment for cement mills, 22·9m. lei; equipment for chemical factories, 43·5m. lei; equipment for refineries, 18·8m. lei; shipbuilding, 213m. lei. Principal imports (in 1,000 metric tons): Iron ore, 5,389; industrial coke, 2,096; rolled ferrous metals, 1,343; electrical equipment, 294m. lei; electric motors, 45,451; motor cars, 16,500; television sets, 25,500; and industrial and agricultural equipment.

In 1969 (and 1968) the main export trade (in 1m. lei) went to: USSR, 2,729 (2,734); Czechoslovakia, 844 (677); East Germany, 728 (463); West Germany, 724 (634); Italy, 625 (454); Poland, 368 (352); UK, 294 (337). In 1969 (and 1968) the main import trade (in 1m. lei) came from: USSR, 2,789 (2,562); West Germany, 1,027 (1,031); Czechoslovakia, 652 (603); Italy, 625 (614); East Germany, 617 (549); UK, 611 (603); France, 564 (484).

Total trade between Romania and UK for calendar years (British Board of Trade returns) in £1,000 sterling:

	1966	1967	1968	1969	1970
Imports to UK	15,131	25,657	25,839	24,970	23,188
Exports from UK	10,344	9,891	31,149	28,637⎱	29,077
Re-exports from UK	331	210	909	423⎰	

In 1968 the Romanian and UK Governments signed a trade arrangement to run until the end of Sept. 1973. It did not introduce major changes in the structure of trade, but looks forward to a steady expansion. By an agreement in 1969 the number of Romanian exports subject to quota restrictions in UK was reduced to 15%. A trade agreement for 1966–70 between Romania and USSR provided for a trade exchange of 3,800m. roubles. Romania delivered machinery, ships, oil products and textiles, and import machinery, cars, coal and metals.

Under decentralization measures which came into force on 1 Jan. 1971 all foreign trade is handled by industrial agencies under the overall supervision of the Ministry of Foreign Trade. Joint production schemes with Western firms have been set up.

SHIPPING. The main ports are Constanţa on the Black Sea and Brăila and Galaţi on the Danube. The largest shipyard is at Galaţi.

In 1966 the mercantile marine (NAVROM) had 44 ocean-going ships of 289,000 deadweight tons. By 1970 the fleet was planned to expand to 70 ships totalling 600,000 tons. In 1969 sea-going transport carried 5·04m. tons of freight; river transport, 3m. tons.

RAILWAYS. Length of track (4 ft 8½ in. gauge) in 1969 was 10,337 km; (narrow-gauge), 633 km. Freight carried, 155m. tons; passengers, 306m.

ROADS. There were in 1969, 12,158 km of national roads, of which 8,322 km were modernized. Freight carried, 216m. tons; passengers, 307m.

AVIATION. TAROM (Transporturi Aeriene Române), the state airline, operates all internal services, and also services to Berlin, Prague, Vienna, Moscow, Athens, Cairo, Tel-Aviv, Rome, Paris, London, Belgrade, Budapest, Sofia, Warsaw, Amsterdam, Istanbul, Beirut, Brussels, Copenhagen, Cologne, Frankfurt, Düsseldorf and Zürich. Bucharest is also served by BEA, from London; SABENA, from Brussels; Aeroflot, from Moscow and Sofia; Air France, from Paris; Interflug, from East Berlin; ČSA, from Prague; MALEV, from Budapest; Austrian Air Lines, from Vienna; Lot, KLM, TABSO, El Al, Alitalia, Lufthansa, JAT and Swissair.

Bucharest's airports are at Băneasa (most international flights; 3 miles from the city centre) and Otopeni (12 miles) Air transport in 1969 carried 680,000 passengers and 18,000 tons of freight.

POST. Number of telephone subscribers, in 1969, 593,000. Radio receiving sets, in 1969, 3·05m.; television sets, 1·3m. There are 41 broadcasting stations and 83 television stations.

BANKING. In 1948 most banks were dissolved and the National Bank of Romania (founded 1880, nationalized 1946) was made the State Bank under the Minister of Finance. Half its profits are allotted to the State budget. There are also a Bank of Investments, a Foreign Trade Bank, an Agricultural Bank and the Savings Bank, all state-owned.

WEIGHTS AND MEASURES. The metric system for weights and measures was introduced in 1881. The Gregorian calendar was adopted in 1919.

DIPLOMATIC REPRESENTATIVES

Romania maintains embassies in:

Afghánistán	Germany (West)	Norway
Albania	Ghana	Pakistan
Algeria	Greece	Peru
Argentina	Guinea	Poland
Australia	Hungary	Rwanda
Austria	Iceland	Senegal
Belgium	India	Sierra Leone
Bolivia	Indonesia	Singapore
Bulgaria	Iran	Somalia
Burma	Iraq	South Yemen
Burundi	Israel	Sudan
Cambodia	Italy	Sweden
Canada	Ivory Coast	Switzerland
Central African Republic	Japan	Syria
Ceylon	Jordan	Tanzania
Chile	Kenya	Tunisia
China	Korea (North)	Turkey
Colombia	Kuwait	Uganda
Congo (Br.)	Laos	USSR
Congo (K.)	Lebanon	UAR
Costa Rica	Luxembourg	UK
Cuba	Madagascar	USA
Cyprus	Malaysia	Upper Volta
Czechoslovakia	Mali	Uruguay
Dahomey	Malta	Venezuela
Denmark	Mauritania	Vietnam (North)
Ecuador	Mongolia	Yemen
Ethiopia	Morocco	Yugoslavia
Finland	Nepál	Zambia
France	Netherlands	
Germany (East)	Nigeria	

Romania maintains a legation in Brazil; and consular and commercial relations with Spain. Romania also recognizes the National Liberation Front in South Vietnam as the 'Republic of South Vietnam'.

OF ROMANIA IN GREAT BRITAIN (4 Palace Green, W8)

Ambassador: Vasile Pungan (accredited 9 April 1966).
Counsellor: C. Rădulescu (*Commercial*). *First Secretaries:* Stefan Năstăsescu; Gh. Gustea. *Service Attaché:* Lieut.-Col. D. Badea.

OF GREAT BRITAIN IN ROMANIA

Ambassasor: D. S. Laskey, CMG, CVO.
Counsellor (*Commercial*): R. M. Russell. *First Secretaries:* P. Yarnold; A. A. Rowell. *Service Attachés:* Lieut.-Col. C. U. Blascheck, MC (*Defence, Navy and Army*); Wing Cdr J. H. Rogers, AFC (*Air*).

OF ROMANIA IN THE USA (1607–23rd St. NW, Washington, D.C., 20008)

Ambassador: Corneliu Bogdan.
Counsellors: Octavian Neda; D. Butnaru; G. Ionita. *First Secretaries:* Mircea Mitsan; Miron Sava (*Consular*). *Service Attaché:* Col. Dumitru Apostol.

OF THE USA IN ROMANIA

Ambassador: Leonard C. Meeker.
Deputy Chief of Mission: Harry G. Barnes, Jr. *Heads of Sections:* Daniel Lee McCarthy (*Economic*); Jai K. Katzen (*Consular*); Daniel J. Hafrey (*Press*); Adolph W. Jones (*Administrative*). *Service Attachés:* Col. James C. Jeffries (*Army*), Col. William Wildman (*Air*).

BOOKS OF REFERENCE

Atlas Geografic Republica Socialistă România. Bucharest, 1965
Anuarul Statistic al R.S.R. Statistical Pocket Book of the Socialist Republic of Romania. Bucharest, both annual
Buletin Statistic Trimestrial (with Russian and French translations). Bucharest
Ceaușescu, N., *Romania: achievements and prospects.* Bucharest, 1969.—*Romania on the Way of Completing Socialist Construction.* 3 vols. Bucharest, 1968–69.—*Romania on the Way of Completing the Many-sided Developed Socialist Society.* Bucharest, 1970
Dicționar Enciclopedic Român. Bucharest, 1962–66
Revista de Statistică. Bucharest, monthly
Economic and Commercial Guide to Romania. Bucharest, annual since 1969
Fischer-Galati, S. A., *Rumania: a bibliographical guide.* Library of Congress, 1963.—*The New Rumania.* Mass. Inst. of Technology, 1968.—*The Socialist Republic of Rumania.* Baltimore, 1969
Ionescu, G., *Communism in Rumania, 1944–62.* OUP, 1964.—*The Reluctant Ally.* London, 1965
Latham, P., *Romania: a complete guide.* London, 1968
Montias, J. M., *Economic Development in Communist Rumania.* Mass. Inst. of Technology, 1968
Morariu, T., and others, *The Geography of Rumania.* 2nd ed Bucharest,. 1969
Dictionarul Limbii Romine Moderne. Academy of SRR. Bucharest, 1958
Levițchi, L., *Dictionar Român-Englez.* 2nd ed. Bucharest, 1965
Sădeanu, F. (ed.), *Dictionar Englez-Romin.* Bucharest, 1958

RWANDA

HISTORY. From the 16th century to 1959 the Tutsi kingdom of Rwanda shared the history of Burundi (*see* pp. 790–91). In 1959 an uprising of the Hutu destroyed the Tutsi feudal hierarchy and led to the departure of the Mwami Kigeri V. Elections and a referendum under the auspices of the United Nations in Sept. 1961 resulted in an overwhelming majority for the republican party, the Parmehutu (Parti du Mouvement de l'Emancipation du Bahutu), and the rejection of the institution of the Mwami. The republic proclaimed by the Parmehutu on 28 Jan. 1961 was recognized by the Belgian administration (but not by the United Nations) in Oct. 1961. Internal self-government was granted on 1 Jan. 1962, and by decision of the General Assembly of the UN the Republic of Rwanda became independent on 1 July 1962. An agreement, signed with Burundi under United Nations auspices at Addis Ababa in April 1962, provided for a monetary and customs union. These and other common organizations came to an end by 1 Oct. 1964.

AREA AND POPULATION. Rwanda lies between lat. 1° and 3° S. and long. 29° and 31° E., with an area of 26,330 sq. km (10,166 sq. miles). The Nile–Congo mountain divide (about 9,000 ft) and the Kirunga volcanoes (Mt. Karisimbi, 14,825 ft), rising steeply from Lake Kivu in the west, slope down first to a hilly central plateau (7,000–5,000 ft) and farther eastwards to a complex of marshy lakes in the upper reaches of the Kagera River. Rwanda is bounded in the south by Burundi, in the west by Lake Kivu and the Congo, in the north by Uganda and in the east by Tanganyika.

The population, the densest in Africa outside the Nile delta, probably about 3·3m. There are 3 ethnic groups, the Tutsi (Nilotic), the Hutu (Bantu) and a few Twa (pygmoid). The Tutsi, traditionally the ruling caste and about 15% of the population, have greatly diminished in number since the troubles of 1959–61, as a result of which over 140,000 took refuge in neighbouring territories. In Jan. 1964 several thousand Tutsi were massacred by the Hutu, and an exodus of 12,000 more Tutsi followed. The Tutsi now form only 9% of the total population. There are some 1,200 Europeans and 750 Asians.

Kigali, the capital, has a population of some 7,000, including about 250 Europeans and 75 Asians. Nyanza (between Kigali and Butare) is the seat of the High Court. Other centres are Gisenyi and Cyangugu on Lake Kivu, and Gitarama.

GOVERNMENT. Rwanda is a republic with an executive President as Head of State, assisted by a Council of 12 Ministers. The National Assembly consists of 47 members elected by universal suffrage for 4 years. The administrative divisions are 10 prefectures (Kigali, Kibungo, Byumba, Ruhengeri, Gisenyi, Kibuye, Gitarama, Gikongoro, Butare, Cyangugu) and 144 communes.

President of the Republic and Prime Minister: Gregoire Kayibanda (elected 26 Oct. 1961; re-elected 3 Oct. 1965 and 28 Sept. 1969).

On 3 Oct. 1965 the Parmehutu party won all seats in the National Assembly.

Flag: Three equal vertical panels of red, yellow and green (left to right), the letter 'R' in black superimposed on the centre panel.

RELIGION. The population is predominantly Roman Catholic; there is an archbishop (Kabgayi) and 3 bishops. The Ruanda Mission of the Church Missionary Society have 4 stations.

EDUCATION. In 1965 there were 352,406 children attending primary schools. There were 25 secondary schools of various types with a total of 7,800 pupils; but only 135 completed the full 6-year course. The National University, opened at Butare in 1963, had over 300 students in 1969.

The local language is Kinyarwanda, a Bantu language. French is also an official language, and Kiswahili is spoken in the commercial centres.

FINANCE. Currency. On 12 April 1966 the Rwanda franc was devalued. The previous official rate of Rwanda francs 140 = £1 and the free rate of about Rwanda francs 330 = £1 were abolished and a single official rate of Rwanda francs 280 = £1 substituted; since Nov. 1967 the rate is 240 francs to the £.

Budget. There has been a budget deficit since 1954. The budget for 1967 envisaged revenue of 1,360,000m. and expenditure of 1,500,000m. Rwanda francs.

DEFENCE. The national army has a strength of nearly 2,500 all ranks, including a Belgian cadre.

AGRICULTURE. Subsistence agriculture accounts for most of the gross national product. Staple food crops are beans, cassava, maize, sweet potatoes, peas, groundnuts and sorghum. The climate is the same as that of Burundi; the annual rainfall varies from under 40 in. in the north-east to 60 in. in the west and over 70 in. in the extreme north-west.

The main cash crop is *aravica* coffee as in Burundi; the 1967 crop was about 11,000 tons. Tea production has begun on a pilot plot.

On 30 July 1964 the Rwanda Industrial Produce Bureau was established, which will be responsible for organizing and controlling the quality of Rwandese agricultural exports, notably coffee.

Long-horned Ankole cattle, 682,000 head in 1967, play an important traditional role. Efforts are being made to improve their present negligible economic value. There are over 370,000 goats and some 147,000 sheep.

INDUSTRY. There is no general industrial development apart from mining. About 2,000 tons of cassiterite are exported each year. There are 4 hydro-electric installations and a large modern brewery. Methane gas is abundant under Lake Kivu.

COMMERCE. Trade between Rwanda and UK (British Board of Trade returns, in £1,000 sterling):

	1966	*1967*	*1968*	*1969*	*1970*
Imports to UK	44	112	274	373	974
Exports from UK	203	129	315	328 ⎫	261
Re-exports from UK	1	2	2	1 ⎭	

COMMUNICATIONS. There are about (1968) 1,500 miles of main and 2,200 miles of secondary roads. Some of the main roads are metalled. There are road links with Burundi, Uganda, Tanzania and the Congo. There were in 1967 2,122 cars and 1,243 trucks. Because of the strained political relations with Burundi nearly all goods traffic passes through Kampala and Mombasa.

Shipping on Lake Kivu in 1967 amounted 70,000 metric tons. Kigali has an international airport, with services to Bujumbura, Bukavu *via* Kamembe, Entebbe, Goma, Lubumbashi, Athens and Brussels.

BANKING. On 5 Aug. 1967 a Development Bank was created with a capital of 50m. Rwanda francs, of which 27·5m. can be held only by the government or public bodies. There are 4 other banks in Rwanda.

Ambassador in Brussels: Augustin Munyaneza (also accredited to Britain, the Netherlands and the Vatican).
British Ambassador: R. M. K. Slater, CMG (resides at Kampala).
Ambassador in USA: Fidèle Nkundabagenzi (also accredited to Canada).
USA Ambassador: Leo G. Cyr.
Belgian Ambassador: Herman Dehennin.

BOOKS OF REFERENCE

Hance, W. A., *African Economic Development.* London, 1967
Lacroix, B., *Le Rwanda.* Montreal, 1966
Northumb, D., *Un Humanisme Africain.* Brussels, 1965

SAN MARINO
Repubblica di San Marino

On 22 March 1862 San Marino concluded a treaty of friendship and good neighbourhood, including a *de facto* customs union with the kingdom of Italy, preserving the independence of the ancient republic, although completely surrounded by Italian territory. The treaty was renewed on 27 March 1872, 28 June 1897 and 31 March 1939, with 7 amendments in 1942–68. The republic has extradition treaties with Great Britain, Belgium, France, the Netherlands and USA.

National flag: Sky-blue and white (horizontal).

The frontier line is 38·6 km in length, area is 61·19 sq. km (24·1 sq. miles) and the population (31 July 1968), 18,360; some 20,000 citizens live abroad.

The legislative power is vested in the Great and General Council of 60 members elected every 5 years by popular vote, 2 of whom are appointed every 6 months to act as regents (*Capitani reggenti*).

The elections held on 13 Sept. 1964 gave 29 seats to the Christian Democrats, 10 to the Democratic Socialists (the government coalition), 14 to the Communists, 6 to the left-wing Socialists and 1 to the Movement for Statutory Liberties (opposition).

Women were given the vote in 1960, but cannot be elected.

The regents exercise executive power together with the Congress of State (*Congresso di Stato*), which comprises 10 departments, and through Commissions on social welfare, public works, etc. Law is administered by a Commissioner for civil and commercial cases and a Commissioner for criminal cases (acting with a penal judge), from whom appeals can be made to a civil appeals judge and a criminal appeals judge respectively. The highest legal authority is, in certain cases, the *Consiglio dei XII.*

There are 14 infant schools, 17 elementary schools, a secondary school and a grammar school, the diplomas of which are recognized by Italian universities. Civil marriage was instituted in Sept. 1953.

The budget (ordinary and extraordinary) for the financial year ending 31 March 1970 balanced at 7,391,051,365 lire.

The militia consists, in case of necessity, of all able-bodied citizens between the ages of 16 and 55, with certain exceptions (teachers and students, etc.). The chief exports are wine, textiles, tiles, varnishes, ceramics and the building stone quarried on Mount Titano. Italian and Vatican City currency is in general use, but the republic issues its own postage stamps.

In 1968, 2,152,972 tourists visited San Marino.

San Marino is connected with Rimini by a bus service and, in summer, by helicopters. There were 2,397 telephones in 1970.

British Consul-General (resides at Florence): S. H. Hebblethwaite, CMG
USA Consul-General (resides at Florence): William J. Barnsdale.
Consul-General in London: Charles Forte.
Acting Consul-General in Washington: Gaspar Morell.

BOOKS OF REFERENCE

INFORMATION. Segreteria di State per gli Affari Esteri; Ente Governativo per il Turismo.

Garbeletto, A., *Evoluzione storica della costituzione di S. Marino.* Milan, 1956
Rossi, G., *San Marino.* San Marino, 1954

SAUDI ARABIA

al-Mamlaka al-'Arabiya as-Sa'udiya

HISTORY. Saudi Arabia was founded by Abdul-Aziz ibn Abdur-Rahman al-Faisal Al Sa'ud, GCB, GCIE (born about 1880; died 9 Nov. 1953), who had been proclaimed King of the Hejaz on 8 Jan. 1926 and had in 1927 changed his title of Sultan of Nejd and its dependencies to that of king, thus becoming 'King of the Hejaz and of Nejd and its Dependencies'. On 20 May 1927 a treaty was signed at Jidda between Great Britain and Ibn Sa'ud, by which the former recognized the complete independence of the dominions of the latter. The name of the State was changed to 'The Saudi Arabian Kingdom' by decree of 23 Sept. 1932.

In Nov. 1937 a general agreement between Saudi Arabia and the Yemen concerning the settlement of disputes was ratified, and an agreement regarding the delimitation of the frontiers was negotiated. In March 1953 the treaty of Taif, first signed with the Yemen in May 1934, was extended for 20 lunar years.

In 1942 Saudi Arabia and the British Government, acting on behalf of the Shaikh of Kuwait, signed agreements for friendship and neighbourly relations, for the extradition of offenders and for the regulation of trade between Saudi Arabia and Kuwait.

In Aug. 1962 Saudi Arabia and Jordan agreed on measures of co-operation in the military, political and economic fields.

GOVERNMENT AND CONSTITUTION. The Kingdom has been welded together from Hejaz, Nejd, Asir and Al-Hassa. Riyadh is the political capital and Mecca the religious capital.

In May 1958 a 'Cabinet system' was instituted under which, from 1962, effective power devolved upon the President of the Council of Ministers.

The religious law of Islam is the common law of the land, and is administered by religious courts, at the head of which is a chief judge, who is responsible for the Department of Sharia (legal) Affairs. The constitution also provides for the setting up of certain advisory councils, comprising a consultative Legislative Assembly in Mecca, municipal councils in each of the towns of Mecca, Medina and Jidda, and village and tribal councils throughout the provinces. The members of these councils consist of chief officials and of notables nominated or approved of by the King.

Reigning King. **Faisal ibn Abdul-Aziz,** GBE, born 1905; succeeded on 2 Nov. 1964, when the Council of Ministers and the Consultative Assembly deposed King Saud, his brother. *Crown Prince:* Prince Khaled ibn Abdul-Aziz, Deputy Minister, younger brother of the King (appointed 29 March 1965).

Royal flag: Green, with white crossed swords and the text 'There is no God but God and Mohammed is his prophet' in white Arabic characters.

National flag: Green, with one sword and same text as royal flag in white Arabic characters.

AREA AND POPULATION. The total area of Saudi Arabia is estimated to be 927,000 sq. miles (2·4m. sq. km).

The population of the Hejaz is about 2m.; Mecca is said to have 250,000; Jidda, 300,000; Medina, 60,000, and Taif, 30,000. The chief port is Jidda on the Red Sea; ports of less importance are Yenbo, Gizan, El Wejh, Rabigh, Lith and Kunfida. Taif, about 3,800 ft above sea-level and some 50 miles from Mecca, is a summer resort.

The population of Nejd is 3m.–4m. The largest towns are: Riyadh, the capital (about 300,000), Buraida (70,000), Anaiza (25,000–30,000), Hail, Jauf and Sakaka. The total population is about 6m.

Slavery was declared illegal in Nov. 1962.

EDUCATION. Administration is in educational districts (23 in 1969). Schooling is in three stages, elementary, intermediate, and secondary which is to prepare older pupils for college. Education is free in all these stages; monthly scholarships are paid to students in higher education. Girls' education is separate. In 1969–70 there were 1,472 elementary schools with 342,600 pupils. In 1968 there were 150 intermediate schools with 30,716 pupils and 44 secondary schools with 10,783 students. There are also adult literacy schools, special schools, commercial, agricultural and industrial schools including the Royal Vocational Institute in Riyadh which can take 8,000 students on two daily shifts. There were 34 teacher-training schools in 1968.

The University of Riyadh (founded 1957) has faculties of arts, science, pharmacy, commerce, agriculture, engineering, education and medicine. The Islamic University at Medina was founded in 1961. The National King 'Abdal-Aziz' University in Jiddah opened in 1967 as a school of economics and business administration, and is to have three more faculties and a girls' college.

WELFARE. The Ministry of Health is responsible for 10 administrative districts, serving both Saudi citizens and pilgrims. In 1968 there were 49 hospitals, 63,000 beds, 180 clinics and 270 health units. The Jiddah Quarantine Centre, designed by WHO and primarily for pilgrims, can take 2,400 patients. In 1970 there were 3 nursing schools and 3 sanitation training institutes. There is a strict system of health controls for visiting pilgrims and strict supervision of sanitation and water supply.

FINANCE. Currency. The legal monetary unit is the *rial*, a silver coin containing 0·34 oz. fine (4·5 *rials* = US$1). There are silver coins for ¼, ½ and 1 *rial*, and a nickel *qurush*, 20 of which (or 11 for certain official payments including Customs duties) equal 1 *rial*. For higher denominations the Saudi gold guinea is the official currency, although now seldom seen; most have been withdrawn because of skilful replicas circulating on the market. The genuine Saudi sovereign has a fixed rate of 40 rials (not quite £4).

In 1960 the Saudi Arabian Monetary Agency announced the issue of a paper rial to replace the 'pilgrims' receipts'; the paper rial is divided into 20 *qurush* (instead of 22) and backed 100% by gold or transferable currencies; the gold rial will cease to be legal tender. The gold cover of the currency was raised to 50% in Sept. 1961.

Budget. The fiscal year runs from 15 Oct. to 14 Oct. The budget for 1970–71 balanced at SR6,380m., that for 1966–67 at SR5,025m., that for 1967–68 at SR4,937m.; that for 1968–69 at SR5,530m., and that for 1969–70 at SR5,966m. Receipts from the oil companies account for 80% of revenue; since Jan. 1950 Saudi Arabia has had a 50/50 share in oil profits.

The main items of expenditure in 1969–70 were (in SR1m.): Education, 587·4; labour training and social services, 100·4; health, 168·2; agriculture and irrigation, 382·3 (including 300 for special projects).

DEFENCE. In 1937 a Ministry of Defence and a training school for officers were established. British Military and Civil Air Missions helped in training the Army and civil aviation from 1947 to 1941. The United States now maintains a Military Mission (with an Air Force element). Personnel are now trained in Saudi Arabia and the UK.

The Air Force began as a small army support unit in 1932 and has been built up considerably with British and US assistance since 1946.

Complete re-equipment began in 1966 when orders were placed in Britain for 34 Lightning F.53 supersonic fighters, 6 Lightning T.55 two-seat fighter trainers and 25 BAC 167 armed strike and training aircraft, with associated radar and American-designed Hawk surface-to-air missiles. As interim equipment, a total of 7 Lightning F.52 fighters and Lightning T.54 trainers, 4 Hunter F.6 fighters, 2 Hunter T.66 two-seat trainers and Thunderbird surface-to-air missiles were acquired from Britain. Two JetStar VIP jet transports, some Agusta-Bell 205 and 206 helicopters, and about 12 Cessna T-41A piston-engined trainers have been bought. Other current equipment includes a squadron of F-86F Sabre fighters, T-33A jet advanced trainers, T-34 Mentor and T-28 basic trainers, and C-130 Hercules and C-123 Provider transports of US design; and Chipmunk primary trainers from the UK. The main bases are at Riyadh and Jidda.

AGRICULTURE. The Saudi Arabian Agricultural Bank in Riyadh had (1970) capital of SR30m. Most of the loans granted were for agricultural equipment or for drilling or deepening wells. SR300m. has been allocated to major projects of desert reclamation, including irrigation schemes, land preparation and sowing, drainage and control of surface water, control of moving sands and distribution of undeveloped land to farmers. A full survey of water resources is in progress; there are 3 sea-water desalination plants working and 4 others proposed.

Medina produces excellent dates in abundance; Taif and other oases in the mountains and valleys produce honey and a fair variety of fruit: while Beduin products are hides, wool, charcoal and clarified butter. The products of Nejd are dates, wheat, barley, coffee, limes, henna, pearls, hides, wool, oil, clarified butter (*saman* or *ghi*) and abaas (Arab cloaks), besides camels, horses, donkeys and sheep.

OIL. The geologic–geographical mapping of Saudi Arabia was completed in 1961 under the joint sponsorship of the Saudi Arabian and US governments.

Oil operations are chiefly carried out by the Arabian American Oil Co. (Aramco) owned by US interests. Other American interests have secured a concession of Saudi Arabia's oil rights in the Kuwait/Saudi Arabia Neutral Zone. Here first shipments began in 1954. In 1958 a Japanese concern obtained concessions for both the Saudi and Kuwait half-shares in the Neutral Zone offshore. Crude oil production was 146,000 bbls daily in 1946 and 3m. bbls daily in 1970.

The operating centre is at Dhahran, and the principal oilfield at Abqaiq; the next most important producers are in Ain Dar and the Dammam oilfield, where the original discovery of oil was made in 1938. Several other oilfields, notably the great Ghawar field south of Ain Dar and the offshore wells of Safaniya, are being developed. Of the 1948 concession area, Aramco had by March 1963 retained only 105,000 sq. miles, *i.e.*, about 20%.

Some crude oil is refined in a large refinery at Ras Tanura (11m. tons in 1960), and some is transported by pipeline to Bahrain Island, for refining there. Crude oil is also shipped from the Persian Gulf. In addition, some 15m. long tons of crude oil is annually transported along the Trans-Arabian Pipeline system (TAPline). This 1,068-mile long pipeline connects the oilfields to a Mediterranean oil port at Saida; it came into operation at the end of 1950.

The government-established General Petroleum and Mineral Organization (Petromin) works to set up new oil- and mineral-related industries, and to co-ordinate national interest in oil production. Petromin handles exploration and concession agreements and is active in drilling, distribution and marketing. It has 75% interest in a new refinery at Jiddah and is building another at Riyadh.

COMMERCE. Exports amounted to the equivalent of US $508m. in 1966–67. The US was the main supplier, accounting for 23% of the total. Other major supplying countries were the UK (8%), Italy (8%), Lebanon (7%), Japan (7%) and West Germany (6%). Foodstuffs accounted for 30% and machinery, electrical appliances and transport items for another 30%.

Total trade with UK (British Board of Trade returns, in £1,000 sterling):

	1965	1966	1967	1968	1969	1970
Imports to UK	28,104	39,681	62,542	68,718	86,796	104,231
Exports from UK	12,563	20,299	15,856	46,648	56,161 }	35,249
Re-exports from UK	228	598	311	382	808 }	

SHIPPING. The ports of Dammam on the Persian Gulf and Jidda on the Red Sea have deep-water piers.

ROADS. There are asphalted roads from Jidda to Mecca, to Medina, to Taif and to Riyadh. There is also a track from Mecca eastward through Riyadh to Uqair and Dhahran on the Persian Gulf, a distance of 829 miles, which is used for motor transport. Motor cars can travel between Riyadh and Kuwait, Riyadh and Hail, Jauf and the northern frontier towns, Jidda and Hail, and between Jidda and Jizan and Sabya.

RAILWAYS. A railway from Riyadh to Dammam on the Persian Gulf *via* Dhahran and the oilfields Abqaiq, Ithmaniya (near Hofuf) and Haradh was completed in Oct. 1951. That section of the Hejaz Railway which is in Saudi Arabian territory is not now in working order, but the Damascus–Medina section is being re-constructed by a British firm.

AVIATION. Saudi Arabian Air Lines, a government-owned company managed by Trans-World Airlines, operates regular internal air services, and services to Cairo and other North African countries, to Beirut and to London, as well as special flights for pilgrims. The pilots are mainly Americans, with a grow-ing number of Saudi Arabian co-pilots. The main airports are at Jidda, Dhahran and Riyadh.

TELECOMMUNICATIONS. Jidda, Mecca and Taif are linked by tele-phone, Jidda and Cairo by radio-telephone. An international radio-telephone station at Riyadh was opened in 1956. Number of telephones (1969), about 44,000. Number of post offices (1970) about 400.

BANKING. Branches of the Algemene Bank Nederland NV, the Banque de l'Indochine, the British Bank of the Middle East, the Arab Bank (of Jerusalem), the Banque de Caire, the National Bank of Pakistan and the Banque du Liban et d'Outremer conduct banking business in Jidda. The Banque de l'Indochine, the British Bank of the Middle East, the Algemene Bank Nederland, the Banque de Caire and the Arab Bank have branches in Al Khobar and Dammam; the last two banks have also branches in Riyadh. The locally-controlled National Commercial Bank has branches in Jidda, Mecca, Taif, Medina, Riyadh, Al Khobar and Dammam.

DIPLOMATIC REPRESENTATIVES

The following have embassies at Jidda:

Afghánistán	Indonesia	Libya	Thailand
Belgium	Iran	Mali	Tunisia
China (Taiwan)	Iraq	Morocco	Turkey
Ethiopia	Italy	Pakistan	UAR
France	Jordan	Sudan	UK
Greece	Kuwait	Sweden	USA
India	Lebanon	Syria	

The Netherlands has a legation.

OF SAUDI ARABIA IN GREAT BRITAIN
(27 Eaton Place, SW1)

Ambassador: Shaikh Abdulrahman Al-Helaissi, GCVO.
Counsellors: Salem Azzam, CVO; Mohamed Nouri Ibrahim, CVO. H. St. J. B. Armitage; *Commercial Counsellor:* Ibrahim Malaikah, CVO. *Defence Attaché:* Col. Abdulla I. Al-Saheal.

OF GREAT BRITAIN IN SAUDI ARABIA
Ambassador: W. Morris, CMG.
Counsellor: I. S. Winchester. *First Secretaries:* H. R. Leach; H. St. J. B. Armitage, OBE; D. A. Hamley (*Commercial*); G. R. Sunderland (*Civil Air*, resides at Beirut). *Service Attachés:* Col. W. G. Neilson (*Defence and Military*), Group Capt. W. J. Ives (*Air*).

There is a Consul at Jidda.

OF SAUDI ARABIA IN THE USA (1520-18th Street, NW,
Washington, D.C., 20036)
Ambassador: Shaikh Ibrahim Al-Sowayel.
Minister: Muhammed J. Nadir.
Service Attaché: Col. Mohamed A. Al-Sheikh (*Army and Navy*).

OF THE USA IN SAUDI ARABIA
Ambassador: Nicholas G. Thatcher.
Deputy Chief of Mission: William A. Stoltzfus. *Heads of Sections:* Francois M. Dickman (*Political*); C. Melvin Sonne, Jr (*Economic*); David M. Ransom (*Consular*); William Kelley (*Administrative*). *Service Attaché:* Lieut.-Col. Ralph R. Vaught (*Defence and Air*).

There is a Consul-General at Dhahran.

BOOKS OF REFERENCE

Annual Report, 1380 A.H. Sauri Arabian Monetary Agency, Jidda, 1962
Aramco Handbook (English and Arabic), 1960
Dickson, H. R. P., *The Arab of the Desert.* London, 1949
Doughty, C. M., *Travels in Arabia Deserta.* 2 vols. New definitive edition. London, 1936
El Wassie, A., *Education in Saudi Arabia.* London, 1970
Howarth, D., *The Desert King: Ibn Saud and his Arabia.* New York, 1964
Ingrams, H., *Arabia and the Isles.* 2nd ed. London, 1952
Lewis, B., *Handbook of Diplomatic and Political Arabic.* London, 1947
Meulen, D. van der, *The Wells of Ibn Sa'ud.* London, 1957
Philby, H. St. J. B., *Arabian Jubilee.* London, 1952.—*Sa'udi Arabia.* London 1955
Twitchell, K. S., and Jurji, F. J., *Saudi Arabia: With an account of the development of its natural resources.* 2nd ed. Princeton, 1953

SOMALI DEMOCRATIC REPUBLIC
Al-Jumhouriya As-Somaliya Al-Domocradia

The Somali Republic came into being on 1 July 1960 as a result of the merger of the British Somaliland Protectorate, which became independent on 26 June 1960, and the Italian Trusteeship Territory of Somalia. For the previous history of these territories see THE STATESMAN'S YEAR-BOOK, 1960, pp. 337 and 1367.

AREA AND POPULATION. The Somali Republic has a total area of about 700,000 sq. km (270,000 sq. miles) with an estimated population of 2·73m. Mogadiscio is the capital (population, 100,000). Other towns: Hargeisa (50,000), Kisimayu (30,000), Berbera (20,000).

Negotiations are going on to settle a long-standing territorial dispute with Kenya.

CONSTITUTION AND GOVERNMENT. The constitution of the Somali Republic was established under the Italian trusteeship during 1960. It was provisionally adopted on 1 July 1960 by the two regions by means of an Act of Union and approved by a national referendum in June 1961. The Somali armed forces took over supreme power in the country from the civilian Government on 21 Oct. 1969. The Parliament was dismissed, the constitution suspended and Supreme Court dissolved.

A Supreme Revolutionary Council was formed which took over the responsibility of Legislature, Executive and Judiciary. Fourteen civilian Secretaries of State responsible for Government Ministries were appointed by the Revolutionary Council.

The Supreme Court was re-established with new Judges by the Revolutionary Council.

The Somali Democratic Republic is administratively divided into 8 regions, Migiurtinia, Hiran, Mudugh, Benadir, Upper Giuba, Lower Giuba, North Western Province (consisting of Hargeisa, Berbera and Borama districts) and North-Eastern Province (consisting of Burao, Erigavo and Las Anod).

The national language is Somali. Arabic, Italian and English are all official languages of the Government, and all 3 are extensively spoken.

RELIGION. The population is about entirely Sunni Moslems. There are very few Roman Catholics, mainly in the capital.

EDUCATION. Statistics 1966–67:

	No.	Pupils	Teachers
Government schools			
Elementary	211	21,050	738
Intermediate	40	7,532	341
Secondary	13	1,836	143
Teacher training	3	382	43
Private schools			
Pre-elementary	7	349	9
Elementary	17	2,370	88
Intermediate	5	767	63
Secondary	2	251	15

HEALTH. There are 67 physicians and 15 hospitals with about 3,200 beds.

FINANCE. Currency. The currency is the Somali shilling, divided into 100 cents (17·143 Somali shillings = £1 sterling). The Somali Republic did not devalue its currency after the devaluation of the pound. The money is issued in notes of 1, 5, 10, 20 and 100 shillings and coins of 1, 5, 10, 50 cents and 1 shilling, Currency in circulation about Som.Sh.60m.

Budget. The budget for 1971 envisaged Som.Sh.306·3m. expenditure (1970: 300m.) and Som.Sh.316·3m. revenue (1970: 307·9m.).¦ Indirect taxation accounts for more than 80% of the revenue. The deficit is expected to be covered by foreign assistance.

DEFENCE. Army. The army is being built up to about 10,000 by Soviet military and technical advisers; the police numbers about 4,000, the finance guards about 400 and the local Illaloes (rural police) about 2,500.

Air Force. Formed with a nucleus of aircraft taken over from the former Italian Air Corps of Somalia, in 1960, the Air Corps was built up with Soviet aid. Current equipment includes a small number of MiG-21 and MiG-15 jet-fighters and obsolescent F-51D Mustang piston-engined fighter-bombers and small transport and training units.

DEVELOPMENT. A 5-year development plan (1963–67) envisaged capital expenditure of Som.Sh.1,400m., to be vested mainly in transport and communications (29%), agriculture (18%) and industry (16%). Owing to shortage of skilled manpower only about 20% of the plan has been implemented. In 1970 a new development plan was under preparation.

AGRICULTURE. Somalia is essentially a pastural country, and about 80% of the inhabitants depend on livestock-rearing (cattle, sheep, goats and camels). In Southern Somalia, especially along the Shebeli and Giuba rivers, there are Somali and Italian plantations with a cultivated area of some 90,000 hectares. There is an estimated annual output (1,000 quintals) of sugar from sugar-cane, 110; bananas, 900; durra, 650; maize, 465. Fresh fruit and oil seeds are grown in increasing quantities. There are an estimated 140,000 acres under cultivation in the North-Western Province, where the main crop is sorghum.

INDUSTRY. There are a number of small meat and fish canneries, a small leather tanning industry, oil seed and fresh fruit processing plants, a small shoe and leather-works industry, weaving of coloured cloth for local use and some woodwork, milk.

MINING. Deposits of iron are in the south and gypsum in the north are known to exist. Beryl and columbite are also found in the north. None are commercially exploited. Several firms hold exploration and drilling licences for oil. Uranium is found in Juiba region.

TRADE. In 1961 imports were estimated at £10m. and exports at £7m. The chief exports are fresh fruit, livestock, hides and skins. The adverse balance of trade is offset by foreign-aid receipts and remittances from Somalis living abroad.

Total trade between the Somali Republic and UK (British Board of Trade returns, in £1,000 sterling):

	1965	1966	1967	1968	1969	1970
Imports to UK	20	121	133	105	88	72
Exports from UK	935	646	697	999	985 ⎫	1,224
Re-exports from UK	16	12	28	9	21 ⎭	

Customs duties are very high and are usually imposed on an *ad-valorem* basis.

ROADS. Somalia has no developed transport system. Internal freight and passenger transport is almost entirely by means of road haulage. There are 2 asphalt roads from the capital northwards and southwards (600 km). Other roads are generally passable in dry weather. There are no railways. In 1964 there were 4,200 passenger cars and 6,300 commercial vehicles, including buses.

POST. There is a manual telephone system in several towns, but Mogadiscio has an automatic system; number of telephones (1969), about 4,800. The state radio stations transmit in Somali, Arabic, English and Italian from Mogadiscio, Hargeisa, Anhazic, Swahili, Koti.

AVIATION. There is a commercial national airline, Somali Airlines. Mogadiscio airport is used by Alitalia, United Arab Airlines, Aden Airways and East African Airlines. Through Nairobi to the south and Aden to north there are reasonable connexions for travelling to any part of the world.

BANKING. The Banco di Roma, Napoli, National & Grindlays Bank and Banco di Portsaid have all more than one branch each in the country. The Somali National Bank and the Somali Development Bank are both state-owned.

WEIGHTS AND MEASURES. The metric system is used in six provinces and the Imperial system in two; the latter is gradually disappearing.

DIPLOMATIC REPRESENTATIVES. The Somali Republic maintains embassies in:

Belgium	Kenya	USSR
Ethiopia	Saudi Arabia	UAR
France	Southern Yemen	UK
Germany (West)	Sudan	USA
Italy	Tanzania	Zambia

OF SOMALIA IN GREAT BRITAIN (60 Portland Place, W1)
Ambassador: Ahmed Haji Dualeh.
Counsellors: Ibrahim Haji Musa; Mohamud Haji Nur. *First Secretary:* Mohamed Osman Omer.

OF GREAT BRITAIN IN SOMALIA
Ambassador: J. Bourn.
First Secretary and Consul: D. G. Barr.

OF SOMALIA IN USA (1875 Connecticut Ave. NW, Washington, D.C. 20009)
Ambassador: Dr Adbullahi Ahmed Addou.
First Secretary: Ibrahim Mohamed Egal.

OF USA IN SOMALIA
Ambassador: Fred L. Hadsel.
Deputy Chief of Mission: Alfred P. Dennis. *Heads of Section:* John W. MacDonald, Jr (*Political*), George T. Colman, Jr (*Economic*), Daly C. Lavergne (*AID*). *Service Attaché:* Lieut. Col. William F. Ames.

BOOKS OF REFERENCE

Directory of Somalia. London, 1968
D'Antonio, M., *Italia e Somalia: Dieci anni di collaborazione.* Rome 1962.—*La Costituzione Somala* Rome, 1962.
Drysdale, J., *The Somali Dispute.* London, 1964
Karp, M., *The Economics of Trusteeship in Somalia.* Boston Univ. Press, 1960
Lewis, I. M., *A Pastoral Democracy.* London, 1962.—*The Modern History of Somaliland.* London, 1965
Lytton, The Earl of, *The Stolen Desert.* London, 1966
Touval, S., *Somali Nationalism.* Harvard Univ. Press and OUP, 1963

REPUBLIC OF SOUTH AFRICA

Republiek van Suid-Afrika

CONSTITUTION AND GOVERNMENT. The Republic of South Africa Constitution Act 1961 established with effect from 31 May 1961, the Republic, consisting of the 4 provinces—the Cape of Good Hope, Natal, the Transvaal and the Orange Free State—which until then comprised the Union of South Africa.

On 5 Oct. 1960 a referendum was held among the white voters (1,800,426 on roll) to decide whether the Union should become a republic. Of the 1,634,240 votes polled, 850,458 were in favour of a republican constitution, 775,878 against it; 7,904 votes were invalid. The voting was as follows: Transvaal, 406,632 for, 325,041 against; Cape Province, 271,418 for, 269,784 against; Orange Free State, 110,171 for, 33,438 against; Natal, 42,299 for, 135,598 against South West Africa, 19,938 for, 12,017 against.

The head of the Republic is the State President, who is elected for a 7-year term by an electoral college consisting of the members of the Senate and the House of Assembly at a meeting specially convened for the purpose.

Legislative power is vested in a Parliament consisting of the State President, a Senate and a House of Assembly. The State President has power to summon, prorogue and dissolve Parliament, either both Houses simultaneously or the House of Assembly alone. He may also dissolve the Senate at any time within 120 days of any dissolution of the House of Assembly or the expiry of the term of office of a provincial council. A session of Parliament must be held once at least in every year.

The Senate consists of 54 members, 11 being nominated by the State President-in-Council (2 for each of the Provinces, 2 for South West Africa and 1 for the Coloured voters in the Cape Province) and 43 being elected (14 in the Transvaal, 11 in the Cape Province, 8 in Natal, 8 in the Orange Free State, 2 in South West Africa). A senator must be a white South African citizen, at least 30 years of age, qualified as a voter in one of the provinces and resident for 5 years within the Republic. Senators hold their seats for 5 years, subject to a prior dissolution of the Senate.

At least one of the 2 senators nominated by the State President from each province should be thoroughly acquainted with the interests of the Coloured population. Similarly, one of the senators nominated from South West Africa should be selected mainly for his thorough acquaintance with the reasonable wants and wishes of the Coloured races of the Territory.

The House of Assembly consists of 166 members chosen in electoral divisions as follows: Cape of Good Hope, 54; Natal, 18; Transvaal, 73; Orange Free State, 15; South West Africa, 6.

A member of the House of Assembly must be a white South African citizen, qualified as a voter and resident for 5 years within the Republic. Every House of Assembly continues for 5 years unless sooner dissolved.

Only the House of Assembly can originate money bills, but may not pass a bill for taxation or appropriation unless it has been recommended by the State President during the session. Restrictions are placed on the amendment of money bills by the Senate. Provision is made respecting disagreements between the Houses and the State President's assent to bills.

A member of one House cannot be elected to the other, but a minister and a deputy minister may sit and speak, but not vote, in the House of which he is not a member. To hold an office of profit under the State (with certain exceptions) is a disqualification for membership of either House, as are also insolvency, crime and insanity. Pretoria is the seat of government, and Cape Town is the seat of legislature.

The state of the parties in the House of Assembly after the elections of 30 Oct. 1969 is as follows: National Party, 127; United Party, 38; Progressive Party, 1.

In the Senate, for which elections were held on 26 Nov. 1965, the National Party has 41 members and the United Party 13.

The Executive Council (National Party) was, in May 1970, composed as follows:

State President: J. J. Fouché (elected 19 Feb., installed 10 April, 1968).

Prime Minister: B. J. Vorster.

Transport: B. J. Schoeman. *Finance:* Dr N. Diederichs. *Agriculture:* D. C. H. Uys. *Defence:* P. W. Botha. *Tourism, Sport and Recreation, Indian Affairs:* F. W. Waring. *Foreign Affairs:* Dr H. Muller. *Labour and Interior:* M. Viljoen. *Bantu Administration and Development and Bantu Education:* M. C. Botha. *Justice and Prisons:* P. C. Pelser. *Mines and Health:* Dr C. de Wet. *Posts and Telegraphs:* M. C. van Rensburg. *Community Development and Public Works:* B. Coetzee. *Economic Affairs and Police:* S. L. Muller. *Water Affairs and Forestry:* S. P. Botha. *Information, Social Welfare and Pensions, Immigration:* Dr C. P. Mulder. *National Education:* Senator J. van der Spuy. *Planning and Coloured Affairs:* J. J. Loots.

The following are Deputy Ministers, who do not have Cabinet rank and are not members of the Executive Council: *Transport:* H. E. Martins. *Bantu Administration:* Dr P. G. J. Koornhof. *Finance and Economic Affairs:* A. H. du Plessis. *Agriculture:* H. Schoeman. *Bantu Development:* Theo Gerdener. *Social Welfare, Pensions and Coloured Affairs:* Dr S. W. van der Merwe.

The Prime Minister receives an annual salary of R13,000 and a reimbursive allowance of R4,500; a member of the Cabinet an annual salary of R10,000 and a reimbursive allowance of R1,500; and a Deputy Minister an annual allowance of R8,000, a reimbursive allowance of R2,000 plus R1,740 in lieu of an official residence.

The English and Afrikaans languages are both official, subject to amendments carried by a two-thirds majority in joint session of both Houses of Parliament.

National flag: Orange, white, blue (horizontal), with the flags of the Orange Free State, the South African Republic and the Union Jack superimposed on the white stripe.

National anthem: Die Stem van Suid-Afrika (words by C. J. Langenhoven, 1918; tune by M. L. de Villiers, 1921).

PROVINCIAL ADMINISTRATION. In each province there is an Administrator appointed by the State President-in-Council for 5 years, and a provincial council elected for 5 years, each council electing an executive committee of 4 (either members or not of the council), the Administrator acting as chairman. Members of the provincial council are elected on the same system as members of Parliament. The provincial committees and councils have authority to deal with local matters, of which provincial finance, education (primary and secondary, other than higher education and technical education), hospitals, roads and bridges, townships, horse and other racing, and game and fish preservation are the most important. In 1953 the administration and control of Bantu education was transferred from the provincial councils to the central government. All ordinances passed by a provincial council are subject to the veto of the State President-in-Council.

BANTU ADMINISTRATION. In 1951 the Natives Representative Council was abolished and the Bantu Authorities Act enacted to provide a system of Bantu tribal, regional and territorial authorities. These were given administrative, executive and judicial functions and limited legislative powers. In 1959 the main ethnic groups received legislative recognition by the passing of the Promotion of Bantu Self-Government Act, which provided *inter alia* for the 8 main Bantu groups to develop into self-governing national units, with a Commissioner-General for each of the 5 main ethnic units representing the Government and guiding the people towards greater development.

The territorial authorities were also given the power to pass enactments instead of bye-laws, while special provision was made for the transfer to territorial authorities of certain rights and obligations in respect of land at present held by the State President in his capacity as Trustee of the South African Native Trust.

As the Act envisages eventual political autonomy for each of the various national units and as representation in the highest European governing bodies is regarded as a retarding factor, the representation by Europeans in Parliament and the Cape Provincial Council was abolished with effect from 30 June 1960.

The Coloured Peoples Representative Council consists of 40 elected and 20 nominated members. Elections took place in Sept. 1969 and Tom Swartz, leader of the Federal Party, was appointed Chairman of the Council by the State President.

In 1961 the ex-chief of the Umvoti Mission reserve, Albert Luthuli was awarded the Nobel Peace Prize for his advocacy of peaceful means in the achievement of Bantu aspirations.

The Transkei territory allotted to the Xhosa nation has an area of 16,675 sq. miles and a population of about 1·5m. (half of the total Xhosa population). At the election for its first Legislative Assembly in Nov. 1963, Paramount Chief Victor Poto was supported by 30 and Chief (now Paramount Chief) Kaizer Matanzima by 15 of the elected members then returned, but at the subsequent secret ballot of the total membership (109) of the Legislative Assembly in Dec. 1963, Chief Kaizer Matanzima received a majority of their votes cast and therefore became Chief Minister in terms of the Transkei Constitution Act. In the second general election in 1968 the ruling Transkei National Independence Party headed by Paramount Chief Matanzima won 28 of the 45 seats, the Democratic party 14 and independents 3. Of the 64 chiefs in the Assembly all but 8 support Matanzima. The ruling party supports the policy of separate development.

Partial self government was also granted to the Ciskei, Ovamboland and Tswanaland during 1968 followed in 1969 by Lebowa (North Sotho), Vendaland and Machangana (Shanganaland).

Following the completion in 1966 at a cost of R114m. of the first 5-year plan for the development of the Bantu homelands, a second 5-year plan estimated to cost R490m. was announced. The amount will be spent as follows (in R1m.): Physical development, 162·6; education, 163·6; economic development, 39·4; grants to Bantu authorities, 6·6; social development, 59; settlement of Bantu, 3·4; reimbursement of Bantu (moved for agricultural purposes), 3·2; supply roads, 2·4; land purchase—capital requirements, 50 (for the purchase of 1,625,000 acres of land).

Rhoodie, N. J., and Venter, H. J. *Apartheid: A socio-historical exposition of the origin and development of the apartheid idea.* Cape Town, 1959

AREA AND POPULATION. The total area of the Republic is 471,445[1] sq. miles (1,221,042 sq. km), divided between the provinces as follows: Cape of Good Hope, 278,380 (721,004); Natal, 33,578 (86,967); Transvaal, 109,621 (283,918); Orange Free State, 49,866 (129,153).

On 25 Dec. 1947 the Union formally took possession of Prince Edward Island and, on 30 Dec., of Marion Island, about 1,200 miles south-east of Cape Town.

[1] Excludes Walvis Bay (434 sq. miles), which is an integral part of the Cape Province but is administered under Act No. 24 of 1922 by South West Africa.

The census taken in 1904 in each of the four colonies was the first simultaneous census taken in South Africa. In 1911 the first Union census was taken.

	All races			Whites		Non-Whites	
	Total	Whites	Non-Whites	Males	Females	Males	Females
1904	5,174,827	1,117,234	4,057,593	635,317	481,917	2,046,370	2,011,223
1911	5,972,757	1,276,319	4,696,438	685,206	591,113	2,383,879	2,312,559
1921	6,927,403	1,521,343	5,406,060	783,006	738,337	2,753,188	2,652,872
1936	9,587,863	2,003,334	7,584,529	1,017,557	985,777	3,818,211	3,766,318
1946	11,415,925	2,372,044	9,043,881	1,194,201	1,177,843	4,610,862	4,433,019
1951	12,671,452	2,641,689	10,029,763	1,322,754	1,318,935	5,109,331	4,920,432
1960	16,002,797	3,088,492	12,914,305	1,539,103	1,549,389	6,504,390	6,409,915
1970[1]	21,282,000	3,779,000	17,503,000	..	..	..	..

[1] Census, May 1970.

Of the non-White population in 1970, 14,893,000 were Bantu, 614,000 Asiatic and 1,996,000 Coloured. The numerically leading Bantu nations are the Xhosa (3·9m.), Zulu (3·8m.), Tswana (1·7m.), Bapedi (1·6m.), Sotho (1·4m.).

In 1960 Afrikaans was the home language of 1·79m. Whites, English of 1·15m. Whites. Of the 12·7m. Bantu about 50% can read and write, and 2·4m. (80%) of Bantu children of school-going age were attending school in 1969.

The projection for 1970 (and 2000) envisages a population of 20m. (40m.) of whom 3·8m. (6·5m.) will be White, 2m. (5m.) Coloured and 13·6m. (26m.) Bantu.

VITAL STATISTICS for calendar years:

	Whites					Asiatics and Coloureds		
	Births	Deaths	Marriages	Immi-grants	Emigrants	Births	Deaths	Marriages
1966	79,195	30,116	35,493	41,920	9,888	100,858	30,995	15,787
1967	81,625	32,015	..	38,937	10,737	97,243	32,527	..
1968	81,525	36,664	..	40,548	10,589	98,262	32,781	..

Immigrants in 1969 numbered 35,993.

From 1 Jan. 1924 registration of Bantu vital events in rural areas was abolished, but made compulsory in all urban areas. Compulsory registration in rural areas was re-introduced from 1 July 1952, but is still incomplete.

Principal cities (excluding suburbs) according to the latest statistics (1968) are:

Town	Whites	Bantu	Coloureds	Asiatics	Total
Johannesburg	476,712	773,415	76,331	38,065	1,364,523
Durban	184,692	203,855	30,680	263,683	682,910
Cape Town	200,090	80,840	337,210	7,600	625,740
Pretoria	261,000	202,432	13,605	14,840	492,577
Port Elizabeth	118,845	151,127	106,143	5,112	381,227
Germiston	65,200	126,700	2,265	2,855	197,020
Bloemfontein	63,200	75,300	7,700	—	146,200
Springs	48,102	91,894	1,945	1,236	143,177
Welkom	39,000	34,000	362	—	73,362
East London	51,570	72,813	10,444	1,930	136,757
Benoni	45,000	84,308	—	6,510	135,818
Pietermaritzburg	45,930	33,980	6,013	26,770	112,693
Roodepoort-Maraisburg	62,500	51,000	1,550	1,750	116,800
Carletonville	23,000	80,000	400	100	103,500
Krugersdorp	35,300	62,200	2,300	725	100,525
Kimberley	30,000	45,000	20,000	1,200	96,200
Vereeniging	35,495	45,383	1,410	1,259	83,547
Brakpan	34,500	29,000	448	29	63,977
Boksburg	44,000	54,000	10,000	850	108,850

Bruwer, J. P., *Die Bantoe van Suid-Afrika*. Johannesburg, 1958
Millin, Sarah G., *The People of South Africa*. London, 1951
Patterson, Sheila, *Colour and Culture in South Africa*. London, 1953
Ritter, E. A., *Shaka Zulu*. London, 1955
Saron, G., and Hotz, L. *The Jews in South Africa*. London, 1955
Schapera, I., *The Bantu-speaking Tribes of South Africa*. Cape Town, 1953

RELIGION. A sample tabulation of the 1960 census results as regards religious denominations shows the following: *Whites:* Nederduits Gereformeerde Kerk, 1,326,344; Gereformeerde Kerk, 101,470; Nederduits Hervormde Kerk, 190,342;

Anglicans, 389,859; Presbyterians, 110,873; Congregationalists, 16,656; Methodists, 269,825; Lutherans, 33,631; Roman Catholics, 192,799; Apostolics, 107,700; other Christians, 166,098; Jews, 116,066; others, 66,829. *Non-Whites:* Afrikaans Churches, 1,011,399; Anglicans, 1,021,655; Presbyterians, 212,476; Congregationalists, 272,713; Methodists, 1,433,051; Lutherans, 612,670; Roman Catholics, 890,729; Apostolics, 375,175; Bantu Churches, 2,188,303; other Christians, 654,868; Mohammedans, 191,746; Hindus, 310,839; others and unspecified, 3,718,548.

EDUCATION. *Higher Education.* There are 11 universities in the Republic: (1) The University of Cape Town. (2) The University of Natal, Durban and Pietermaritzburg. (3) The University of the Orange Free State at Bloemfontein. (4) Potchefstroom University for Christian Higher Education, Potchefstroom. (5) The University of Pretoria. (6) Rhodes University, Grahamstown, C.P. (7) The University of Stellenbosch. (8) The University of the Witwatersrand, Johannesburg. (9) The University of South Africa, with its seat in Pretoria, which conducts a Division of External Studies by means of correspondence and vacation courses; it is also an examining body. (10) The University of Port Elizabeth. (11) Rand Afrikaans University, Johannesburg.

The University College of Fort Hare, the University College of the North near Pietersburg and the University College of Zululand near Empangeni, Natal, are operated by the Department of Bantu Education and provide education at university level for the Bantu, the University College of the Western Cape, Kasselsvlei, offers university facilities to the Coloured population and is administered by the Department of Coloured Affairs; while the University College for Indians at Durban falls under the Department of Indian Affairs.

The following statistics refer to 1967:

University	Professors	Lecturers Full-time	Part-time	Students
Cape Town	73	292	469	6,712
Natal	72	366	122	5,522
Orange Free State	44	107	94	3,066
Potchefstroom	55	120	59	2,964
Pretoria	120	339	222	10,636
Rhodes	33	133	117	1,776
Stellenbosch	120	357	579	6,631
Witwatersrand	76	394	262	8,208
South Africa	56	270	19	21,886 [1]
Rand Afrikaans	—	—	—	—
Port Elizabeth	27	55	22	581
Fort Hare	26	69		451 [a]
North	13	60	—	611 [a]
Zululand	12	48	—	368 [2]
West Cape	12	28	6	640 [2]
Salisbury Island (Durban)	13	123		—

[1] 1970.   [2] 1968

Technical and Vocational Education. The Government is responsible for all vocational education, except agricultural schools, which fall under the jurisdiction of the provincial education departments. The Department of Education, Arts and Science administers technical colleges, schools of industries and technical, housecraft and commercial high schools for Whites. It is also responsible for the education and training of White blind, deaf, epileptic and deviate children, who are sent to schools of industries or reformatory schools.

The Department of Coloured Affairs has taken over all schools of this nature for Coloureds from the Department of Education, Arts and Science.

In 1967, 15 technical colleges for Whites had 892 teachers and 10,022 students; 15 for Coloureds had 163 teachers and 3,395 students; one for Asiatics had 98 teachers and 1,141 students. In addition there are 9 vocational schools for Coloureds. Provision is made for vocational education for the Bantu at 6 technical schools and 24 industrial or trade schools; total enrolment at these institutions was nearly 3,000 in 1966. Twelve schools for the blind, the deaf, epileptics and cerebral palsy had 1,321 white pupils.

State and State-aided Education other than Higher Education. Primary and secondary public education for Whites falls under the Provincial Administrations. In terms of the National Education Policy Act, 1967, the Minister of Education, Arts and Science may, after consultation with the Provincial Administrators and the National Advisory Education Council, determine general educational policy within the framework of the Act. Bantu education is the responsibility of the Department of Bantu Education, while education for Coloureds and Indians is controlled by the Departments of Coloured Affairs and Indian Affairs respectively.

Public schools in 1968: 2,821 for Whites with (1966) 66,400 teachers and 822,482 pupils; in 1967: 1,832 for Coloureds with 14,273 teachers and 453,338 pupils; in 1968: 358 for Indians with (1967) 5,736 teachers and 155,961 pupils; 9,551 for Bantu (in the Republic) with (1967) 30,335 teachers and 2,397,152 pupils. (Bantu teachers include those in teacher-training schools, technical and private schools.)

Private Schools. To a certain extent the activities of private schools are controlled by government regulations. Their pupils generally sit for the state schools' examinations. These schools make provision for kindergarten, elementary and preparatory, general primary, secondary and commercial education.

In 1966, 221 private schools for Whites had 2,424 teachers and 50,266 pupils; in 1967, 29 for Coloureds had 158 teachers and 4,494 pupils; 4 for Asiatics had 491 pupils; 492 for Bantu in the Republic had 1,942 teachers and 82,393 pupils; 53 in Transkei had 6,087 pupils.

Teacher-training colleges in 1966: 16 for Whites had 737 teachers and 9,734 students; in 1967, 2 for Coloureds had 127 teachers and 1,887 students; 2 for Asians had 66 teachers and 855 students; 23 for Bantu in the Republic had 4,332 students and 7 in Transkei had 1,099 students.

NEWSPAPERS (1968). There are 6 Afrikaans and 14 English daily newspapers with a combined circulation of about 1,003,295, of which 810,232 are English.

HEALTH. In 1968 there were 10,021 medical practitioners and 1,468 dentists; in 1969, 765 hospitals had 39,064 beds for Whites and 99,869 for non-Whites.

SOCIAL WELFARE. Social Security. In 1967 social pensions (old-age, blind persons, disability grants, maintenance for children, war veterans) were paid to 143,274 White and 455,861 non-White beneficiaries; the total provision amounted to R92·49m. in 1968.

Welfare Services. South Africa is not a welfare state, yet provides many services for the community. Welfare work on behalf of the Government is done by the Departments of Social Welfare and Pensions, Coloured Affairs, Indian Affairs, and Bantu Administration and Development. There are also a great number of voluntary welfare societies which undertake a variety of welfare services.

The Department of Social Welfare and Pensions formulates the broad policy and takes care of the co-ordination of the various welfare services. The National Council for Welfare, a statutory body set up under the National Welfare Act of 1965, among others, is used by the Government for the execution of this policy. Four specialized commissions serve under the National Council. These are: the Commission for Social Work, the Commission for Family Life, the Commission for Welfare Planning and the Commission for Welfare Organizations. The Department also provides such personal services as pensions and allowances, and practical assistance to individuals or families who may have social problems, neglected and uncared-for children, juvenile delinquents, adults needing special guidance and alcoholics.

Voluntary Welfare Societies. These organizations supply supplementary services to those provided by the Government. Voluntary welfare organizations must register at the Department of Social Welfare and Pensions under the National Welfare Act of 1965. There are more than 2,000 registered welfare organizations;

they have organized themselves into national and provincial councils so as to co-ordinate their activities. Funds for these voluntary services are raised mainly by public subscription; however, the Department of Social Welfare and Pensions subsidizes many of the voluntary welfare organizations.

In the past the State, with the assistance of local authorities, voluntary welfare agencies and church organizations, provided welfare services for the Bantu, the voluntary agencies being controlled by White committees. However, this situation is gradually changing as more Bantu are taking an interest in welfare work. The various Bantu nations are being encouraged and assisted to form their own voluntary agencies and so to provide, as far as possible, welfare services for their own people. As far as is practicable, the institutions required for the care of the aged and the disabled and for needy children are sited in the homelands, and are staffed by Bantu.

Child and Family Welfare. Welfare or professional officers employed by the State are responsible for the implementation and administration of the Children's Act (amended and consolidated in 1960). This Act makes provision for the prevention and treatment of neglected and maladjusted children, with the full integration of the services of voluntary child and family welfare organizations. Children's institutions, mainly established and controlled by private organizations, are subsidized by the State, as are crèches, community centres and other projects in aid of child and family welfare.

General. Apart from retreats managed by private organizations for the voluntary treatment of inebriates, the State has a retreat for female alcoholics and retreats and rehabilitation centres for male alcoholics and won't works. The inmates in the latter institutions are committed there by the courts and are under compulsory detention for at least 12 months.

JUSTICE. The common law of the Republic is the Roman–Dutch law—that is, the uncodified law of Holland as it was at the date of the cession of the Cape in 1806. The law of England as such is not recognized as authoritative, though by statute the principles of English law relating to evidence and to mercantile matters, e.g., companies, patents, trademarks, insolvency and the like, have been introduced. In shipping and insurance, English law is followed in the Cape Province, and it has also largely influenced civil and criminal procedure throughout the Republic. In all other matters, family relations, property, succession, contract, etc., Roman–Dutch law rules, English decisions being valued only so far as they agree therewith

The Supreme Court of South Africa is constituted as follows. (i) The Appellate Division, consisting of the Chief Justice and 7 Judges of Appeal, is the highest court and its decisions are binding on all courts. It has no original jurisdiction, but is purely a Court of Appeal. (ii) The Provincial Divisions: In each province there is a provincial division of the Supreme Court, while in the Cape there are two such divisions possessing both original and appellate jurisdiction. (iii) The Local Divisions: There is a local division each in the Cape, the Transvaal and Natal exercising the same original jurisdiction within limited areas as the provincial divisions. The division in the Cape has appellate jurisdiction within its area of jurisdiction.

The judges hold office till they attain the age of 70 years. No judge can be removed from office except by the State President upon an address from both Houses of Parliament on the ground of misbehaviour or incapacity. The circuit system is fully developed.

The Bantu appeal courts and 3 Bantu divorce courts have jurisdiction to some extent concurrent with and in certain respects exclusive of that of the Supreme Court in cases in which Bantu are parties.

Each province is further divided into districts with a magistrate's court having a prescribed civil and criminal jurisdiction. From this court there is an appeal to the provincial and the Cape local divisions of the Supreme Court, and thence to the appellate division. Magistrates' convictions carrying sentences above a prescribed limit are subject to automatic review by a judge. In addition, several regional divisions consisting of a number of districts have been constituted. Convictions of such courts are not subject to automatic review by a judge.

Courts of Bantu affairs commissioners have been constituted in defined areas to hear all civil cases and matters between Bantu and Bantu only. An appeal lies to the Bantu appeal court, whose decision is final, unless the court consents to an appeal to the apellate division of the Supreme Court on a point stated by the court itself. Bantu affairs commissioners have concurrent criminal jurisdiction with magistrates' courts in respect of certain offences committed by Bantu, while a limited civil and criminal jurisdiction is conferred upon the Bantu chief or headman over his own tribe.

Persons of all races convicted, all courts, 1966–67: 431,099, including 44,218 White and 234,205 Bantu males and 2,631 White and 27,482 Bantu females.

The death penalty may be imposed for murder, rape, armed robbery, treason and sabotage.

Police. In 1967 the police force consisted of 1,361 White officers and 5,721 n.c.o.s, 278 Coloured n.c.o.s, 2,071 Bantu n.c.o.s and 127 Indian n.c.o.s. There were 9,452 White, 1,095 Coloured, 511 Indian and 10,806 Bantu constables.

FINANCE. Currency. The Decimal Coinage Act, 1959, introduced the decimal system, the units being the *rand* (abbreviated as R) and the *cent* (abbreviated as c). The rand/cent coinage system came into operation on 14 Feb. 1961. The decimal coins are: *Gold coins.* 2 rand; 1 rand. *Silver coins.* 50 cents; 20 cents; 10 cents; 5 cents. *Bronze coins.* 2 cents; 1 cent.

Budget. The financial relations between the central government and the provinces are being investigated by a commission of enquiry.

Prior to 1913–14 the expenditure of the 4 provinces was entirely met from grants by the Union Government. Since then various Financial Relations Acts have been passed defining the conditions upon which subsidies shall be granted to the provinces, assigning and transferring to them certain revenues and limiting their powers of taxation.

Ordinary revenue and expenditure of the central government (excluding Railways and Harbours Administration) in R1,000:

	1965–66	1966–67	1967–68	1968–69	1969–70	1970–71[2]
Revenue	1,152,633	1,285,196	1,490,569	1,565,730	1,812,404	1,992,376
Expenditure [1]	1,083,349	1,252,121	1,421,168	1,472,900	1,627,158	1,885,400

[1] Excluding subsidies.   [2] Estimates.

Details of ordinary revenue and expenditure of the central government for years ended 31 March (in R1,000):

Revenue	1969–70	1970–71	Expenditure [1]	1969–70	1970–71
Customs	178,004	196,000	Bantu administration	72.227	90,657
Excise	312.269	340,220	and development		
Income tax	936,418	1,039,000	Bantu education	15,015	15,072
Licences, stamp duties			Foreign affairs	6,958	8.250
and fees	91.527	82,630	Defence	271,506	257.100
Interest	86,947	98,960	Public debt	166,666	168.911
			Provincial administra-		
			tions	297.992	362,653
			Education	50,749	71,727
			Social welfare and pen-		
			sions	130.441	149,252
			Public health	63.213	77,522
			Police	85,442	94.288
			Indian affairs	22,363	26.428
			Coloured development	63,407	72,990

[1] Estimates.

Public debt on 30 Jan. 1969, R4,810·5m., of which R113m. was foreign debt; internal debt, R4,711·8m.

DEFENCE. The South African Defence Force comprises a Permanent Force, a Citizen Force and a Commando organization. The Permanent Force consists of professional soldiers, airmen and seamen who are responsible for the administration and training of the whole Defence Force in peace-time, but who are gradually absorbed into the Citizen Force in time of war. The Permanent Force and the Citizen Force consist of Army, Air Force and Naval components; the Commando organization is an army and air organization.

Every citizen between the ages of 17 and 65 is liable to undergo training and to render personal service in time of war. Those between the ages of 16 and 25 are liable to undergo a compulsory course of peace training. Peace-time training in Commando organizations extends over a period of 16 years' intermittent training. Training in the Citizen Force takes the form of 1 year of continuous training, followed by 9 years during which training takes place at regular intervals.

Aliens have become liable for military service after 5 years' residence by Act of Parliament, 1967.

Most of the officers and many of the other ranks serving in the Citizen Force and Commando organization are volunteers. The number of citizens who are compulsorily posted to the Citizen Force and Commando organization is accordingly influenced by the number of volunteers accepted for service, the man-power needs and the international situation.

The S.A. Defence Force and the Cadet Corps are administered by the Commandant-General, SADF, the Army, Air and Naval Chiefs of Staff, the Adjutant-General, the Quartermaster-General and the Surgeon-General. The Secretary for Defence is the Permanent Head of the department as well as the Accounting Officer.

Army. South Africa is divided into 11 territorial Commands: Western Province, Eastern Province, Natal, Orange Free State, Western Transvaal, Northern Transvaal, Witwatersrand, North West Cape, South West Africa, South Western Districts and Walvisbaai Commands. Within the various Commands are training units and full-time force units, of which members of the Permanent Force form the permanent staff. Courses of various types are held also at the S.A. Military College. Total strength, 5,700 regulars and 60,000 Citizen Force.

Navy. The South African Navy, with its headquarters at Simonstown, is administered by the Naval Chief of Staff, who holds the rank of Rear-Admiral. The Navy includes 3 new French-built submarines, 3 British-built anti-submarine frigates, 2 destroyers (*Jan van Riebeck*, ex-HMS *Wessex*, and *Simon van der Stel*, ex-HMS *Whelp*), 1 fast anti-submarine frigate (*Vrystaat*, ex-HMS *Wrangler*), 2 training frigates, 1 ocean minesweeper, 10 coastal minesweepers, 1 survey ship (ex-frigate), 1 boom defence vessel, 6 seaward defence boats and a fleet replenishment ship. Naval personnel in 1970 totalled 3,440 officers and ratings.

The facilities of the base at Simonstown are available for use by the Royal Navy and ships serving with the Royal Navy and by navies or allies of the United Kingdom in any war in which the United Kingdom is involved.

Air Force. Units of the South African Air Force are organised in Strike, Transport, Maritime, Light Aircraft and Maintenance Commands. In 1970 there were 1 squadron of Mirage III-CZ and 1 squadron of Mirage III-EZ multi-purpose supersonic fighters, 1 squadron of Sabre 6 fighter-bombers (probably to be replaced by Mirage III-EZs), 1 squadron of Canberra light jet bombers, 1 squadron of Buccaneer strike-reconnaissance aircraft, and 1 squadron of Shackleton maritime patrol aircraft. Other equipment includes Transall C-160 and C-130B Hercules turboprop transports, DC-4, C-47 and Piaggio P.166 piston-engined transports, some of which are used also for coastal patrol, Super Frelon, SA.330 Puma, Alouette II/III and Wasp helicopters, and large numbers of locally-built Impala (Macchi M.B.326M) basic jet trainers which are capable of carrying armament for light attack duties. Advanced training is done at the S.A. Air Force College.

AGRICULTURE. The number of farms owned by Whites in 1963 was 104,681, with an area of 104·51m. morgen (1 morgen = 2·11 acres) and an estimated selling value (in 1962) of R3,703·1m.

South African farmers produced mainly the following crops for the years indicated:

Product	Year ends	1967	1966–67[1]	1967–68
Maize (200 lb.)	30 April	109,000,000	8,087	57,700,000
Kaffircorn (200 lb.)	„	10,270,000	670	2,300,000
Wheat (200 lb.)	31 Oct.	11,600,000	873	12,000,000
Barley (150 lb.)	„	610,000	..	..
Oats (150 lb.)	„	2,460,000	..	..
Rye (150 lb.)	„	135,000	..	..
Sugar-cane (2,000 lb.)	30 April	..	..	..
Sugar produced (2,000 lb.)	„	838,439	1,400	1,006
Tobacco (1m. lb.)	„	..	60	74

[1] In 1,000 tons.

In addition there were produced in 1967–68, 1·66m. tons of groundnuts, 1,112,000 tons of sunflower seed, 578,000 tons of deciduous fruit and 682m. tons of citrus fruit.

LIVESTOCK, in 1,000 (1966): 10,446 cattle; 40,307 sheep; 5,674 goats (1964); 1,164 pigs (1964); 11,811 poultry; 1960: 472 horses; 57 mules; 377 donkeys.

In 1968, 1,952,710 tons of cattle and 4,785,449 tons of sheep and goats were slaughtered.

The annual production of butter is about 100m. lb.; tinned milk, 100m. lb.; milk powder, 30m. lb.; cheese, 40m. lb.

Wool exported in 1969–70 amounted to 261·4m. lb. valued at R96·2m.

Cotton-growing is now undertaken by many farmers, the plant being found a better drought resistant than either tobacco or maize.

IRRIGATION. The government activities in respect of the control and utilization of water are governed by the Water Act, 1956, which is administered by the Department of Water Affairs. The Department's expenditure on revenue account during 1970–71 amounted to R17,457,000.

The Orange River Project, launched in 1966, will take about 30 years to complete. It is to embrace 3 major dams on the Orange River, 9 smaller dams or weirs, a 51½-mile tunnel, 20 hydro-electric power stations and a system of canals. The first of the major dams—the Hendrik Verwoerd Dam—is being built 5 miles upstream from Norvalspont.

VITICULTURE. About 5,000 farmers in the western Cape Province cultivate some 300m. vines on 380,000 morgen. The annual production of wine is about 42m. bulk gallons, while 6m. gallons are distilled. In 1967 more than 1m. gallons of South African sherry were shipped to the UK.

FORESTRY. The forested surface occupies about 2·9m. acres, of which 0·6m. acres are indigenous trees and 2·3m. acres exotic trees (fir, gum, wattle). The annual output of timber is about 250m. cu. ft.

FISHING. The catch of off-shore whaling in 1967 was 2,698 whales. Whaling is conducted off the Natal coast.

In 1967, 1·8m. metric tons of fish were landed, including (in 1966) 181,471 short tons of pilchards. 6,145 fishing boats, including 1,599 motor boats, were engaged.

MANUFACTURES. The manufacturing industry's contribution to the gross domestic product is 21·7%—nearly twice as much as the share of the mining industry. The gross value of output of all private industries rose from about R892m. in 1946–47 to just over R4,044m. in 1966. The number of private factories increased during the same period from 11,413 to 21,969, while the total industrial labour force increased from 488,992 (White and non-White) to 1,030,500 in industry, excluding mining, in 1968.

Wages paid to workers in manufacturing industry in 1966 were R1,024,966,000. The gross sales of the principal groups of industries were (in R1,000) in 1967: Food, beverages and tobacco, 1,277,269; textiles, 301,041; wood, furniture, 194,275; paper, printing, 273,293; chemicals, 273,293; non-metal mineral products, 226,487; basic metal, 422,526; metal products, 548,551; machinery and transport equipment, 824,336.

Census of wholesale, retail, catering, accommodation, business services and automotive industry:

	Whole-sale 1960–61	Retail 1960–61	Catering services 1958–59	Accommo-dation 1958–59	Busi-ness services 1958–59	Auto-motive industry 1960–61
Establishments (no.)	5,486	36,330	2,164	12,156	392	4,724
Working proprietors (no.)	1,714	38,505	2,630	2,119	263	3,226
(i) White	1,332	23,130	2,532	2,119	256	3,056
(ii) Non-white	382	177,371	98	—	7	170
Paid employees (no.	122,124	76,286	13,599	47,164	5,930	65,842
(i) White	53,426	71,085	2,996	7,153	2,772	29,346
(ii) Non-white	68,698	104,873	10,929	40,011	3,158	36,496
Salaries and wages (R1,000)	127,524	134,873	5,882	19,255	5,637	58,938
Stocks (R1,000):						
Opening	348,258	274,241	2,266	3,737	—	
Closing	393,954	290,239	2,388	4,193	—	80,509
Total sales (R1,000)	2,095,107	1,500,861	..	105,751[1]	16,906[1]	..
Total expenses (R1,000)	314,440	289,302	12,785	45,136	14,451	127,270
Net profit (R1,000)	81,733	78,767	3,633	6,287	2,455	13,487

[1] Represents total trading revenue and not only sales.

The wholesale and retail trade excludes the motor trade, which is now regarded as a separate economic sector. The retail trade also excludes provision dealers (café) which are now regarded as catering services. The automotive industry covers the motor trade and other motor-industry establishments, including manufacturers and assemblers.

MINING. Total value of the mineral production sales (in R1,000):

	1965	1966	1967	1968	1969
Asbestos	25,209	28,698	26,469	31,714	30,966
Chrome ore	6,976	7,716	7,682	8,913	..
Coal	81,366	81,461	77,600	97,283	97,062
Copper	40,480	92,160	97,723	99,427	..
Diamonds	49,601	42,900	59,000	71,599	77,000
Gold	766,549	776,000	763,325	777,532	783,801
Iron ore	17,661	19,262	26,918	24,898	29,356
Iron pyrites	2,713	3,213	3,607	3,968	..
Lime and limestone	11,368	11,924	12,913	13,610	..
Magnesite	725	746	690	564	564
Manganese ore	17,823	24,174	23,872	23,559	24,000
Silver	2,903	2,937	3,507	5,000	..
Tin	4,305	4,285	3,921	4,078	..
Vermiculite	1,527	1,461	1,555	1,714	..
Uranium oxide	..	..	..	..	..
Total, incl. items no named	1,152,907	1,248,800	1,279,297	..	..

Mineral production in 1968: Gold, 31,086,000 fine oz., about 81% of the free world's production; silver, 3,198,000 fine oz.; iron ore, 7,959,000 tons; iron pyrites, 648,000 tons; magnetic, 65·9m. tons; copper, 146,600 tons; manganese ore, 2,675,000 tons; chrome ore, 1,271,000 tons; coal, 56,934,000 tons; asbestos, 260,500 tons; diamonds, 7,433,300 carats; uranium oxide, 7,746,000 lb.; phosphates, 1·73m. tons.

In 1967 the number of persons engaged in mining totalled 574,841 (including 61,600 Whites). Of these 396,300 (including 31,971 Whites) were engaged in goldmining.

The Mineral Resources of the Union of South Africa, with a Summary of the Mineral Resources of South West Africa. Geological Survey, Department of Mines. 4th ed. Pretoria, 1959
Minerals. A quarterly report of production and sales. Department of Mines Pretoria, from 1936

ELECTRICITY. The total capacity of the power plants controlled by the Electricity Supply Commission was, at the end of 1967, about 7,000 Mw. Power sold in 1968 was 40,944m. kwh.

TRADE UNIONS. In 1967 there were 172 trade unions with a total membership of 360,176 Whites and 123,935 Coloureds and Asians.

The total revenue of trade unions in 1964–65 was R3,857,545; their total assets were valued at R10,624,661.

Although there is no legal provision for Bantu trade unions, there is no legal prohibition of trade unions by Bantu workers for the purpose of private negotiation with employers. However, the vast majority of Bantu workers have not shown much interest in trade unionism.

The Wage Board inquires into the wage levels of numerous categories of workers, particularly the Bantu, and it fixes minimum levels of pay. Special machinery exists under the Bantu Labour (Settlement of Disputes) Act to safeguard the interests of Bantu workers. This Act provides for the establishment by Bantu workers of local labour committees which are linked with regional committees. The latter committees are in contact with the Central Bantu Labour Council and should disputes arise between these councils and the Industrial Councils, the matter would go to the Wage Board for a final and binding decision.

Doxey, G. V., *The Industrial Colour Bar in South Africa.* OUP, 1961
Horrell, M., *South African trade unionism.* Johannesburg, 1961
Walker, I. D., and Weinbren, B., *2000 casualties: a history of the trade unions and the labour movement in the Union of South Africa.* Johannesburg, 1961

COMMERCE. Up to 31 Dec. 1954, the statistical territory 'Union of South Africa' in trade statistics comprehended the trade of the political territory of the Union of South Africa and the High Commission Territories of Basutoland, Swaziland and Bechuanaland Protectorate.

As from 1 Jan. 1955 it includes, in addition, the territory of South West Africa.

The total value of the imports and exports, exclusive of specie and gold bullion, was as follows (in Rand):

	Imports	Exports		Imports	Exports
1963	1,202,856,167	915,761,774	1966	1,642,700,000	1,202,500,000
1964	1,539,932,687	1,042,067,611	1967	1,921,000,000	1,362,000,000
1965	1,752,500,000	1,056,300,000	1968	1,871,000,000	1,430,700,000

The principal articles of import and export (in R1m.) were:

Imports	1967	1968	Exports	1967	1968
Food and live animals	89·2	70·5	Food and live animals	317·3	374·4
Crude materials	131·7	111·4	Wool	106·6	..
Mineral fuel (including			Machinery	75·3	91·0
petroleum)	111·3	123·0	Chemicals	46·1	52·2
Chemicals	158·0	156·0	Diamonds (rough and		
Manufactured goods	406·4	378·0	uncut)	116·6	140·6
Machinery and transport			Diamonds (cut and po-		
equipment	804·4	826·4	lished	39·1	49·7
			Metal and metal manu-		
			factures	231·7	..

The distribution of imports (including government stores) into and exports (South African produce) from South Africa was as follows (in R1m.):

	Imports		Exports	
Country	1966	1967	1966	1967
Belgium	18·6	23·6	62·1	58·9
France	41·2	53·8	33·3	30·8
Germany (West)	176·1	231·7	64·5	80·9
Italy	51·4	70·8	43·6	49·4
Japan	90·3	116·0	84·5	174·9
Netherlands	41·5	54·3	19·6	22·5
UK	449·2	497·1	409·3	410·3
USA	291·5	322·6	133·9	107·3

Trade with UK (in £1,000 sterling; British Board of Trade returns):

	1966	1967	1968	1969	1970
Imports to UK	191,408	219,567	271,729	302,222	258,266
Exports from UK	242,880	257,640	260,881	285,797 ⎫	332,896
Re-exports from UK	3,804	3,841	3,997	5,083 ⎭	

RAILWAYS. Railway history in South Africa begins in 1860 with the line Durban–Point. With the formation of the Union in 1910, the state-owned lines in the 4 provinces (7,577 miles) were amalgamated into one state undertaking, which also took over the control of the harbours—the South African Railways and Harbours Administration.

Government-owned lines operated by the administration at 31 March 1969 totalled 13,726 miles, of which 2,512 miles were electrified. Passenger journeys, 1969, 515·8m.; goods traffic (1968), 118·3m. tons.

ROADS. The railway administration operated road motor services over a route mileage of 31,793 at 31 March 1968; during that year 10·98m. passengers were conveyed and 3·77m. tons of goods were carried.

There were at 31 March 1967, 6,668 miles of national roads, of which 5,583 miles were tarred. In addition, there were 200,000 miles of provincial roads.

Motor vehicles in operation in 1968 included 1,415,000 passenger cars, 373,000 commercial vehicles, 29,000 buses and 112,000 motor cycles.

SHIPPING. The 4 main ports are Durban, Cape Town, Port Elizabeth and East London. Smaller ports are Mossel Bay, Simonstown, Port Nolloth, Walvisbay and Lüderitz. During 1967 a total of 17,649 commercial vessels, whaling boats and fishing boats entered these ports, which handled 41·7m. tons of cargo.

AVIATION. Civil aviation in South Africa is controlled by the Department of Transport, which administers the following state-owned airports: Jan Smuts Airport, Johannesburg; D. F. Malan Airport, Cape Town; Louis Botha Airport, Durban; J. B. M. Hertzog Airport, Bloemfontein; J. G. Strydom Airport, Windhoek; Ben Schoeman Airport, East London; H. F. Verwoerd Airport, Port Elizabeth; B. J. Vorster Airport, Kimberley. At 13 other airports the Department provides air navigation services.

South African Airways, as the national air carrier, operate scheduled international air services within Africa and to Europe, South America, the USA and Australia. Twenty-one other lines also operate scheduled international air services; they include BOAC, PANAM, KLM, SAS, TAP, Swiss Air, Olympic, El-Al, Qantas, Alitalia, SABENA, Lufthansa, DETA, Central African Airways, Rhodesian Air Services, East African Airways, LUXAIR, Lesotho Airways, Swazi Air, Air Malawi, Air Madagaskar. Trek Airways operate international non-scheduled flights.

South African Airways, Commercial Air Services Ltd, Suidwes Lugdiens and Namakwaland-lugdiens operate scheduled air services within South Africa.

During 1968 South African Airways carried 1,055,381 passengers and 25·84m. tons of freight and mail.

POST. On 31 March 1967 there were in South Africa (excluding South West Africa) 3,379 post and telegraph offices. In 1966–67 post office turnover amounted to R732m.

In 1967 the international telex switchboard enabled telex subscribers in South Africa to communicate with telex subscribers in 84 countries. Some 3,650 tele-printers were in use. There were 140 automatic telephone exchanges, 14,528 trunk (long-distance) lines in operation in 1967.

There were, in 1967, 1,179,811 telephone stations and 16,609 public call offices, excluding those owned by the Durban Corporation.

The South African Broadcasting Corporation had, in 1967, 1,588,739 listeners' licences.

BANKING. Statistics of the South African Reserve Bank,[1] May 1969, are as follows (in R1m.):

Liabilities		Assets	
Notes in circulation	432·3	Gold coin and bullion	908·6
Deposits:		Foreign assets	187·1
Bankers	216·0	Domestic Bills discounted	7·2
Government and others	488·0	Loans and advances	93·1

[1] In Dec. 1920, under the South African Currency and Banking Act, 1920, a Central Reserve Bank was established at Pretoria. It commenced operations in June 1921, and began to issue notes in April 1922. The bank has branches in Johannesburg, Cape Town, Durban, Port Elizabeth, East London, Bloemfontein, Pietermaritzburg and Windhoek.

Ratio of legal reserve to liabilities to the public was 80% on 31 May 1968.

The number of depositors in the post office savings bank at the end of March 1968 was 1,710,659, and the amount standing to their credit R134,544,229.

WEIGHTS AND MEASURES. The Weights and Measures Act, 1922, which came into effect on 1 April 1923, established standard weights and measures throughout the Union and embodied the principle of optional use of the metric system, subject to certain provisions. The Act was amended in 1933 and 1940, repealed and consolidated in 1958, and again amended by the Weights and Measures Amendment Act, 1960. South Africa is in the process of changing to the metric system.

Regulations (consolidated and revised in 1962) prescribe the manner and frequency of assizing of trade weighing and measuring instruments, as well as controlling the sale of goods and fixing standard quantities for commodities in general use. Official steps have been taken to facilitate the gradual introduction of metric weights and measures.

DIPLOMATIC REPRESENTATIVES

The Republic of South Africa maintains embassies in:

Argentina (also for Chile and Paraguay)	Chile	Paraguay
	France	Portugal
Australia	Germany (West)	Spain
Austria	Greece	Switzerland
Belgium	Italy	UK
Bolivia	Luxembourg	USA
Canada	Netherlands	Uruguay

The Republic of South Africa maintains legations in Brazil, Finland, Malawi and Sweden (also for Finland).

OF SOUTH AFRICA IN GREAT BRITAIN (South Africa House, Trafalgar Sq., WC2)

Ambassador: Dr H. G. Luttig (accredited 3 May 1967).
Minister: P. R. Killen. *Counsellors:* D. S. Franklin; G. du T. Roux; Paul Theron (*Commercial*); Dr D. O. Rhoodie (*Information*). *Armed Forces Attaché:* Rear Adm. M. R. Terry-Lloyd, SM. *First Secretaries:* P. H. Viljoen; P. A. Grobbelaar; P. C. Schoeman.

OF GREAT BRITAIN IN SOUTH AFRICA

Ambassador: Sir Arthur Snelling, KCMG, KCVO.
Minister: S. J. Cross, CMG. *Counsellors:* M. H. Morgan (*Head of Chancery*); A. H. Reed (*Economic*). *First Secretaries:* D. V. Morris; Miss M. E. E. Buchanan (*Economic*); M. S. Berthoud; R. W. Chisholm. *Cultural Attaché:* D. E. Frean, OBE.

Service Attachés: Air Cdre E. W. Wright, CBE, DFC, DFM (*Defence and Air*), Col. W. P. Lunn-Rockcliffe, DSO, MC (*Army*), Cdre T. E. Fanshawe, DSC (*Navy*).

There are Consuls-General at Cape Town, Durban and Johannesburg, and a Consul at Port Elizabeth.

OF SOUTH AFRICA IN THE USA (3051 Massachusetts Ave. NW, Washington, D.C., 20008)

Ambassador: H. L. T. Taswell.

Minister: D. P. Olivier. *Counsellors:* W. G. Lubbe (*Economic*); Dr G. van Drimmelin; W. J. Le Roux (*Information*); L. G. R. Hyman; Dr R. G. Shuttleworth (*Scientific*); John Kincaid. *Armed Forces Attaché:* Brig. H. J. P. Burger, SM, DFC, AM.

There are Consuls-General in New Orleans, New York and San Francisco.

OF THE USA IN SOUTH AFRICA

Ambassador: John G. Hurd.

Deputy Chief of Mission: Robert P. Smith. *Heads of Sections:* Bruce B. Cheever (*Political*); Enoch S. Duncan (*Economic*); Charles A. Lemmo (*Administrative*). *Service Attachés:* Col. Carroll B. Markel (*Defence and Air*), Col. Fred E. Wagoner, Jr (*Army*), Cdr James C. Burnett (*Navy*).

There are Consuls-General at Cape Town, Durban and Johannesburg and a Consul at Port Elizabeth.

BOOKS OF REFERENCE

STATISTICAL INFORMATION. The Bureau (formerly Office) of Census and Statistics (Schoeman St., Pretoria), established on 1 April 1917 as a division of the Department of the Interior and now directly under the Minister of Economic Affairs, is based mainly on the Consolidated Census Act, No. 76, of 1957, and the Consolidated Statistics Act, No. 73, of 1957. Main publications:

Official Year Book of the Union of South Africa and of Basutoland, Bechuanaland Protectorate and Swaziland. From 1918 (preceded by the *Statistical Year Book, 1913–17*). Latest issue No. 30 (1960)
Union Statistics for 50 Years: Jubilee Issue, 1910–60 (1960)
Statistical Year Book. From 1964
Statistics of Production: Industrial. Annual, from 1915/16 (but suspended from 1929/30 to 1931/32 and from 1938 to 1942)
Statistics of Production: Agricultural. Annual, from 1917/18 (but suspended from 1920/30 to 1931/32 and from 1939 to 1946)
Monthly Bulletin of Statistics (from 1922)
Population Census, 1960. (Various special reports in course of publication)
South African Reserve Bank, *Quarterly Bulletin of Statistics*
State of South Africa, Year Book 1970
Official South African Municipal Year Book 1967–68

The Customs and Excise Office, Pretoria, publishes *Monthly Abstract of Trade Statistics* (from 1946) and *Trade and Shipping of the Union of South Africa* (annually, 1910–55); *Foreign Trade Statistics* (annually, from 1956)

Bate, H. M., *South Africa without prejudice.* London, 1956
Bosman, D. B., *Tweetalige Woordeboek.* 2 vols. Cape Town, 1946–49
Cole, M., *South Africa.* London, 1961
Hepple, A., *Verwoerd.* Harmondsworth, 1967
Kruger, D. W., *The Making of a Nation.* Johannesburg, 1969
Marquard, L., *The Story of South Africa.* 3rd ed. London, 1964
Metrowich, F. R., *Africa in the Sixties.* Pretoria, 1970
Muller, C. F. J., *500 Years of South African History.* Pretoria, 1969
Reeve, A. (Bishop of Johannesburg), *Agony of South Africa.* London, 1960
Talbot, A. M. and W. J., *Atlas of the Union of South Africa.* Pretoria, Govt. Printer, 1960
Walker, E. A., *History of Southern Africa.* London, 1957
Wellington, J. H., *Southern Africa, a geographical guide.* 2 vols. CUP, 1955
The Oxford History of South Africa. 3 vols. OUP, 1969

PROVINCE OF THE CAPE OF GOOD HOPE

Kaaprovinsie

HISTORY. The colony of the Cape of Good Hope was founded by the Dutch in the year 1652. Britain took possession of it from 1795 to 1803 and again in 1806, and it was formally ceded to Great Britain by the Convention of London, 13 Aug. 1814. Letters patent issued in 1850 declared that in the colony there should be a Parliament which should consist of the Governor, a Legislative Council and a House of Assembly. On 31 May 1910 the colony was merged in the Union of South Africa, thereafter forming an original province of the Union.

ADMINISTRATION. At the provincial council election in March 1965 the following parties were returned: Nationalists, 40; United Party, 12; Progressive Party, 2.

Cape Town is the seat of the provincial administration.

Administrator: V. H. Vosloo.

The province is divided into 135 magisterial districts, and the province proper, but exclusive of the Transkeian territories (with the exception of the districts of Mount Currie and Matatiele, where there are also divisional council divisions), into 92 divisional council divisions. Each division has a council of at least 6 members (14 in the Cape Division) elected quinquennially by the owners or occupiers of immovable property. The duties devolving upon divisional councils include the construction and maintenance of roads and bridges, local rating, vehicle taxation (except motor vehicles) and preservation of public health.

There are 170 municipalities, each governed by a mayor and councillors. Municipal elections are held triennially. There are also 78 village management boards and 11 local boards.

AREA AND POPULATION. The following table gives the population of the Cape of Good Hope[1] (area 278,380 sq. miles) at the last census:

	All races			Whites		Non-Whites	
	Total	*Males*	*Females*	*Males*	*Females*	*Males*	*Females*
1921	2,781,542	1,347,791	1,433,751	329,367	321,268	1,018,424	1,112,483
1936	3,527,865	1,663,169	1,864,796	396,058	394,993	1,267,011	1,469,803
1946	4,051,424	1,924,334	2,127,090	433,849	436,300	1,490,485	1,690,790
1951	4,426,726	2,110,674	2,316,052	463,917	471,168	1,646,757	1,844,884
1960	5,362,853	2,554,521	2,808,332	494,612	508,595	2,059,909	2,299,737

[1] Excluding Walvis Bay (434 sq. miles).

Estimate,1968, 6·34m.

Of the non-White population in 1960, 18,477 were Asiatics, 3,011,080 were Bantu and 1,330,089 Coloureds. The great majority are engaged in agricultural or domestic employments.

Chief towns, with White population (1967): Uitenhage, 21,300; Paarl, 16,000; Worcester, 12,500; Stellenbosch, 13,900; Grahamstown, 11,800.

VITAL STATISTICS for calendar years:

	Whites			Asiatics and Coloureds		
	Births	*Deaths*	*Marriages*	*Births*	*Deaths*	*Marriages*
1960	22,738	9,505	8,760	64,950[1]	21,185	9,635
1961	23,448[1]	9,641	8,510	66,597[1]	21,649	9,175
1962	23,160[1]	10,088[1]	..	69,185[1]	21,616[1]	..

[1] Preliminary.

RELIGION. Sample tabulation, 1960 census. *Whites:* Nederduits Gereformeerde Kerk, 532,343; Gereformeerde Kerk, 12,153; Nederduits Hervormde

Kerk, 8,033; Anglicans, 146,870; Presbyterians, 30,899; Congregationalists, 8,824; Methodists, 79,098; Lutherans, 11,244; Roman Catholics, 58,514; Apostolics, 21,979; other Christians, 46,141; Jews, 32,389; others, 14,720. *Non-Whites*[1]*:* Afrikaans Churches, 497,603; Anglicans, 503,650; Presbyterians, 105,125; Congregationalists, 218,296; Methodists, 748,100; Lutherans, 108,278; Roman Catholics, 229,862; Apostolics, 92,206; Bantu Churches, 478,594; other Christians, 196,795; Mohammedans, 89,082; Hindus, 4,852; others, 1,067,070.

[1] Excludes 20,133 Bantu omitted from sample.

EDUCATION. Higher and vocational education is under the control of the Department of Education, Arts and Science, Pretoria. Primary and secondary education and the training of primary teachers are controlled by the Provincial Administration in respect of White pupils and by the Department of Bantu Education in respect of Bantu pupils. Coloured education has been transferred to the Department of Coloured Affairs from 1 Jan. 1964.

There are 114 school districts, each under a school board, consisting of both elected (by the ratepayers) and nominated members (by the Provincial Administration and the local authorities). Education is compulsory for all White children. Except for a few schools, primary and secondary education is free to the end of the calendar year in which the age of 19 years is attained.

Whites (1968). There were 1,041 government and aided schools and 7 teacher-training colleges with 10,020 teachers and 218,998 pupils; 93 private schools with 1,628 teachers and 18,829 pupils.

Coloureds (1968). There were 1,661 government and aided schools with 12,228 teachers and 399,528 pupils; 10 teacher-training schools with 1,632 students; 21 private schools with 115 teachers and 3,374 pupils; 3 vocational schools with 1,498 pupils.

Bantu (1968). There were 1,634 public and private schools and teacher-training colleges with 4,568 teachers and 269,679 pupils.

Asians (1968). Two state schools with 14 teachers and 200 pupils. Two private schools with 5 teachers and 37 pupils.

FINANCE. In 1969–70 revenue amounted to R85,915 and expenditure to R216,273.

AGRICULTURE. Viticulture in the Republic is almost exclusively confined to the Cape Province, but practically all other forms of agricultural and pastoral activity are pursued.

INDUSTRY The province has brick, tile and pottery works, saw-mills, engineering works, foundries, grain-mills, distilleries and wineries, clothing factories, furniture, boot and shoe factories, etc.

MINING For mineral production, *see* p. 1292.

BOOKS OF REFERENCE

Official Guide. Cape Town, 1953
Du Toit, P. S., *Onderwys in Kaapland, 1652–1939.* Pretoria, 1940
Kilpin, R., *The Parliament of the Cape.* London, 1939
Marais, J. S., *The Cape Coloured People, 1652–1937.* London, 1939

PROVINCE OF NATAL

HISTORY. Natal was annexed to Cape Colony in 1844, placed under separate government in 1845, and on 15 July 1856 established as a separate colony. By this charter partially representative institutions were established, and in 1893 the colony obtained responsible government. The province of Zululand was annexed to Natal on 30 Dec. 1897. The districts of Vryheid, Utrecht and part of Wakkerstroom, formerly belonging to the Transvaal, were annexed in Jan. 1903. On 31 May 1910 the colony was merged in the Union of South Africa as an original province of the Union.

ADMINISTRATION. At the provincial council elections in March 1965 there were returned: United Party, 16; Nationalists, 8; independent, 1.

The seat of provincial government in Natal is Pietermaritzburg.

Administrator: W. Havemann.

AREA AND POPULATION. The province (including Zululand, 10,375 sq. miles) has an area of 33,578 sq. miles, with a seaboard of about 360 miles. The climate is sub-tropical on the coast and somewhat colder inland. It is well suited to White persons. The province is divided into 45 magisterial districts.

The returns of the total population at the census were:

	Total	All races		Whites		Non-Whites	
		Males	*Females*	*Males*	*Females*	*Males*	*Females*
1921	1,429,398	707,600	721,798	70,506	66,381	637,094	655,417
1936	1,946,468	944,220	1,002,248	95,157	95,392	849,063	906,856
1946	2,202,392	1,073,510	1,128,882	117,425	119,272	956,085	1,009,600
1951	2,415,318	1,182,931	1,232,387	136,300	137,940	1,046,631	1,094,447
1960	2,979,920	1,445,030	1,534,890	167,853	172,382	1,277,177	1,362,508

Of the non-White population in 1960, 394,854 were Asiatics, 45,253 Coloureds and 2,199,578 Bantu.

VITAL STATISTICS for calendar years:

	Whites			Asiatics and Coloureds		
	Births	*Deaths*	*Marriages*	*Births*	*Deaths*	*Marriages*
1960	7,365	3,234	2,732	15,889[1]	3,435	3,615
1961	7,301[1]	3,412	2,803	19,234[1]	3,509	3,617
1962	7,622[1]	3,561[1]	..	18,575[1]	3,728	..

[1] Preliminary.

RELIGION. Sample tabulation, 1960 census. *Whites:* Nederduits Gereformeerde Kerk, 64,052; Gereformeerde Kerk, 2,895; Nederduitse Hervormde Kerk, 5,319; Anglicans, 94,349; Presbyterians, 25,852; Congregationalists, 4,652; Methodists, 53,283; Lutherans, 7,226; Roman Catholics, 35,747; Apostolics, 9,827; other Christians, 18,973; Jews, 6,266; others, 11,794. *Non-Whites:* Afrikaans Churches, 25,411; Anglicans, 128,400; Presbyterians, 35,013; Congregationalists, 16,267; Methodists, 173,088; Lutherans, 122,052; Roman Catholics, 270,744; Apostolics, 25,229; Bantu Churches, 495,747; other Christians, 95,828; Mohammedans, 59,957; Hindus, 282,797; others, 909,152.

EDUCATION. The Natal Provincial Administration controls primary and secondary education for Whites. Higher technical and vocational education for all races is provided by the central government. *See also* pp. 1297–98.

Whites (1968). There were 268 government and aided schools with 4,625 teachers and 87,564 pupils; 3 teacher-training colleges with 897 students; 16 private schools with 1,894 pupils.

Coloureds (1968). There were 57 government and aided schools with 628 teachers and 19,553 pupils; 1 teacher-training college with 48 students; 1 private school with 1 teacher and 19 pupils; 1 vocational school with 302 pupils.

Bantu (1967). There were 1,935 schools with 7,613 teachers and 429,502 pupils.

Asians (1968). There were 293 government and aided schools with 4,791 teachers and 134,277 pupils; 2 private schools with 850 pupils; 1 teacher-training school with 41 teachers and 612 students.

FINANCE. In 1969–70 revenue amounted to R45·7m. and expenditure to R86·9m.

AGRICULTURE. Sugar and citrus growing are of major importance. On the coast and in Zululand there are vast plantations of sugar-cane (about 800,000 acres), producing, in 1967, 15,547,000 tons. Cereals of all kinds (especially maize), fruits, vegetables, the *Acacia molissima* (the bark of which is much used for tanning purposes) and other crops are produced. Large areas are being afforested.

INDUSTRY. Natal is highly industrialized. Metallurgical, chemical, paper, rayon and food-processing plants include iron and steel foundries, petrol, refineries, pulp-mills, explosives and fertilizer plants, milk- and meat-canning factories.

MINING. The province is rich in mineral wealth, particularly coal. For figures of mineral production, *see* p. 1303.

BOOKS OF REFERENCE

Town and Regional Planning Commission, Natal: *The Tugela Basin* (1952), *Towards a Plan for the Tugela Basin* (1960), *The Population and Labour Resources of Natal* (1960)

Cullingvorsh's *Natal Almanac*. Annual. Durban
Doke, C. M., and Vilakazi, B. W., *Zulu–English Dictionary*. Johannesburg, 1948
Fair, T. J. D., *Natal Regional Survey*. 3 vols. OUP, 1955
Kuper, H., *Indian People in Natal*. Natal Univ. Press, 1960
Tatlow, A. H., *Natal Province: Descriptive Guide and Official Handbook*. Durham and London. Annual

PROVINCE OF THE TRANSVAAL

HISTORY. The Transvaal was one of the territories colonized by the Boers who left the Cape Colony during the Great Trek in 1831 and following years. In 1852, by the Sand River Treaty, Great Britain recognized the independence of the Transvaal, which, in 1853, took the name of the South African Republic. In 1877 the Republic was annexed by Great Britain, but the Boers took up arms towards the end of 1880. In 1881 peace was made and self-government, subject to British suzerainty and certain stipulated restrictions, was restored to the Boers. The London Convention of 1884 removed the suzerainty and a number of these restrictions but reserved to Great Britain the right of approval of the Transvaal's foreign relations, excepting with regard to the Orange Free State. In 1886 gold was discovered on the Witwatersrand, and this discovery, together with the great influx of foreigners which it occasioned, gave rise to many grave problems. Eventually, in 1899, war broke out between Great Britain and the Transvaal. Peace was concluded on 31 May 1902, the Transvaal and the Orange Free State both losing their independence. The Transvaal was governed as a crown colony until 12 Jan. 1907, when responsible government came into force. On 31 May 1910 the Transvaal became one of the four provinces of the Union.

ADMINISTRATION. At the provincial council election in March 1965 there were returned: National Party, 51; United Party, 17.

The seat of provincial government is at Pretoria, which is also the administrative capital of the Republic of South Africa.

Administrator: S. G. J. van Niekerk.

AREA AND POPULATION. The area of the province is 109,621 sq. miles, divided into 53 districts. The following table shows the population at each of the last censuses:

		All races		Whites		Non-Whites	
	Total	Males	Females	Males	Females	Males	Females
1921	2,087,636	1,159,430	928,206	285,185	259,788	874,245	668,418
1936	3,341,470	1,846,576	1,494,894	424,470	396,286	1,422,108	1,098,608
1946	4,283,038	2,374,323	1,908,715	541,053	522,068	1,833,270	1,386,647
1951	4,812,838	2,619,314	2,193,524	737,194	731,111	2,575,119	2,230,053
1960	6,273,477	3,312,313	2,961,164	737,194	731,111	2,575,119	2,230,053

Of the non-White population in 1960, 4,633,378 were Bantu, 63,787 Asiatics and 108,007 Coloureds.

Important towns of the province are listed on p. 1286.

VITAL STATISTICS for calendar years:

		Whites			Asiatics and Coloureds		
	Births	Deaths	Marriages	Births		Deaths	Marriages
1960	38,983	11,786	14,565	5,290[1]	5,290[1]	1,887	990
1961	39,725[1]	11,658	14,555	6,194[1]	6,194[1]	1,900	941
1962	40,199[1]	12,600[1]	..	6,530[1]	6,330[1]	2,042[1]	..

[1] Preliminary.

RELIGION. Sample tabulation, 1960 census. *Whites:* Nederduits Gereformeerde Kerk, 539,491; Gereformeerde Kerk, 72,404; Nederduits Hervormde Kerk, 167,693; Anglicans, 137,207; Presbyterians, 50,196; Congregationalists, 3,071; Methodists, 123,218; Lutherans, 13,880; Roman Catholics, 91,235; Apostolics, 67,550; other Christians, 90,504; Jews, 74,221; others, 37,635. *Non-Whites:* Afrikaans Churches, 278,006; Anglicans, 309,047; Presbyterians, 50,924; Congregationalists, 29,839; Methodists, 318,424; Lutherans, 365,836; Roman Catholics, 270,493; Apostolics, 179,739; Bantu Churches, 1,030,853; other Christians, 310,162; Mohammedans, 42,707; Hindus, 23,190; others, 1,595,952.

EDUCATION. All education for Whites except that of university and vocational type is under the provincial authority. The province has been divided for the purposes of local control and management into 21 school districts. Instruction in government schools, both primary and secondary, is free. The medium of instruction is the home language of the pupil. The teaching of the other language begins at the earliest stage at which it is appropriate on educational grounds. Both languages are taught as examination subjects to every pupil above the fifth standard.

Whites (1968). There were 886 public schools with 15,735 teachers and 383,651 pupils; 4 teacher-training colleges with 6,024 students; 95 private schools with 1,300 teachers and 28,734 pupils.

Coloureds (1968). There were 66 state and state-aided schools with 1,086 teachers and 32,550 pupils; 1 teacher-training college with 267 students; 4 private schools with 724 pupils; 1 vocational school with 412 pupils.

Asians (1968). There were 63 public schools with 891 teachers and 21,990 pupils; 1 teacher-training college with (in 1967) 25 teachers and 243 students.

Bantu (1967). There were 2,072 public and private schools with 16,749 teachers and 943,023 pupils.

FINANCE. In 1969–70 revenue amounted to R145,356,000 and expenditure to R254,016,000.

AGRICULTURE. The province is in the main a stock-raising country, though there are considerable areas well adapted for agriculture, including the growing of tropical crops.

INDUSTRY. The province has iron and brass foundries and engineering works, grain-mills, breweries, brick, tile and pottery works, tobacco, soap and candle factories, coach and wagon works, clothing factories, etc.

MINING. For mineral production, *see* p. 1303. Gold output in 1967 was 19,591,000 oz. worth R492,978,000.

BOOKS OF REFERENCE

Transvaal Official Guide. Cape Town, 1955
Eliovson, E., *Johannesburg, the Fabulous City.* Cape Town, 1956
Symonds, F. A., *The Johannesburg Story.* London, 1953

PROVINCE OF THE ORANGE FREE STATE

Oranje-Vrystaat

HISTORY. The Orange River was first crossed by Europeans in the middle of the 18th century. Between 1810 and 1820, settlements were made in the southern parts of the Orange Free State, and the Great Trek greatly increased the number of settlers during and after 1836. In 1848 Sir Harry Smith proclaimed the whole territory between the Orange and Vaal rivers as a British possession called the 'Orange River sovereignty'. However, in 1854, by the Convention of Bloemfontein, British sovereignty was withdrawn and the independence of the country was recognized.

During the first 5 years of its existence the Orange Free State was much harassed by incessant raids by the Basutos. These were at length conquered, but, owing to the intervention of the British Government, the treaty of Aliwal North incorporated only a part of the territory of the Basutos in the Orange Free State.

On account of the treaty with the South African Republic, the Orange Free State took a prominent part in the South African War (1899–1902) and was annexed on 28 May 1900 as the Orange River Colony. Crown colony government continued until 1907, when responsible government was introduced. On 31 March 1910 the Orange River Colony was merged in the Union of South Africa as the province of the Orange Free State.

ADMINISTRATION. At the provincial council election in March 1965 there were returned 25 Nationalists.

The seat of provincial government is at Bloemfontein. There are 68 municipalities and 8 village boards of management.

Administrator: G. F. van L. Froneman.

AREA AND POPULATION. The area of the province is 49,866 sq. miles; it is divided into 45 districts. The census population has varied as follows:

		All races			Whites		Non-Whites	
	Total	Males	Females	Males	Females	Males	Females
1921	628,827	321,373	307,454	97,948	90,900	223,425	216,554
1936	772,060	381,903	390,157	101,872	99,106	280,031	291,051
1946	879,071	432,896	446,175	101,874	100,203	331,022	345,972
1951	1,016,570	519,166	497,404	115,637	112,015	403,529	385,389
1960	1,386,547	731,629	654,918	139,444	137,301	592,185	517,617

Of the non-White population in 1960, 1,083,886 were Bantu, 25,909 Coloureds and 7 Asiatics.

VITAL STATISTICS for calendar years:

	Whites			Asiatics and Coloured		
	Births	Deaths	Marriages	Births	Deaths	Marriages
1960	7,214	2,264	2,381	701	473	180
1961	7,136[1]	2,297	2,314	781[1]	467	126
1962	7,088[1]	2,441[1]	..	858[1]	527[1]	..

[1] Preliminary.

RELIGION. Sample tabulation, 1960 census. *Whites:* Nederduits Gereformeerde Kerk, 190,458; Gereformeerde Kerk, 14,018; Nederduits Hervormde Kerk, 9,297; Anglicans, 11,433; Presbyterians, 3,926; Congregationalists, 109; Methodists, 14,226; Lutherans, 1,281; Roman Catholics, 7,303; Apostolics, 8,344; other Christians, 10,480; Jews, 3,190; others, 2,680. *Non-Whites:* Afrikaans Churches, 210,379; Anglicans, 80,554; Presbyterians, 21,414; Congregationalists, 8,309; Methodists, 193,439; Lutherans, 16,504; Roman Catholics, 119,629; Apostolics, 78,001; Bantu Churches, 183,109; other Christians, 52,083; others, 146,374.

EDUCATION. Higher and vocational education is under the control of the central Education Department, while primary and secondary education and the training of primary teachers in respect of Whites are controlled and financed by the provincial administration. The province is divided into 24 school districts, for each of which there is a school board elected by the school committees in the district.

Education is free in all public schools up to the university matriculation standard, but certain schools are allowed to charge fees. Attendance is compulsory for Whites between the ages of 7 and 16, but exemption may be granted in special cases. The home language of the pupil is the medium of instruction.

Whites (1968). There were 265 government and aided schools and 1 teacher-training college with 69,284 pupils; 11 private schools with 1,325 pupils; total number of teachers, 3,710.

Coloureds (1968). There were 41 government and aided schools with 231 teachers and 6,512 pupils.

Bantu (1967). There were 1,404 schools with 4,067 teachers and 246,842 pupils.

FINANCE. In 1968–69 revenue amounted to R18·02m. and expenditure to R51·56m.

AGRICULTURE. The province consists of undulating plains, affording excellent grazing and wide tracts for agricultural purposes. The rainfall is moderate. The country was mainly devoted to stock-farming, but now a rapidly increasing quantity of grain is being raised, especially in the eastern districts.

INDUSTRY. The more important manufacturing industries in the province are the oil-from-coal factory at Sasolburg; fertilizer, agricultural implement, blanket and woollen products, clothing, hosiery, cement and pharmaceutical factories, grain-mills and brick, tile and pottery works.

MINING. For mineral statistics, *see* p. 1303. The production of the goldfields in the province has increased tremendously since 1951, when the output was 18,545 oz. valued at £230,186. The output in 1961 was 7,235,647 oz. valued at R181,320,401.

Orange Free State Official Guide. Cape Town, 1956
Orange Free State Bulletin. 1961 ff.

SOUTH WEST AFRICA
Suidwes-Afrika

HISTORY. The territory (excluding Walvis Bay and certain islands) was proclaimed a German protectorate in 1884, but was surrendered to the Forces of the Union of South Africa on 9 July 1915 at Khorab. The administration was vested in the Government of the Union of South Africa by mandate of the League of Nations dated 17 Dec. 1920. In 1921 the Governor-General delegated certain of his functions to the Administrator of the Territory, who assisted by an Advisory Council and, from 1925, by an Executive Committee and the Legislative Assembly.

On 18 July 1966 the International Court of Justice decided, by the President's casting vote, that Ethiopia and Liberia had no legal right in applying for a decision on the international status of South West Africa.

ADMINISTRATION. The South West Africa Affairs Amendment Act, 1949, abolished the Advisory Council and the nominated members of the Legislative Assembly. All 18 members of the Assembly are now elected by the registered voters of the Territory. The election held on 20 April 1970 returned 18 Nationalists.

The Territory is represented in the South African House of Assembly by 6 members elected by the registered voters of the Territory, and in the Senate by 4 Senators, of which number 2 are elected by the members of the Legislative Assembly and the representatives of the Territory in the House of Assembly, and 2 nominated by the President of the Republic. One of the nominated Senators is selected mainly on the ground of his acquaintance with the conditions of the coloured races of South West Africa.

On 13 Oct. 1966 the security and apartheid laws of the Republic of South Africa were extended to South West Africa, retrospective to 1950. On 2 Oct. 1968 the South African government announced the formation of a 42-member Legislative Council for Ovamboland.

The seat of the administration is Windhoek. The country is divided into 22 districts controlled by magistrates.

Administrator: J. G. H.van der Wath.

AREA AND POPULATION. The total area of the Territory, including the Caprivi-Zipfel, is 317,836 sq. miles (823,145 sq. km); this figure includes that of Walvis Bay, administered by South West Africa, 434 sq. miles (1,124 sq. km).

The country is bounded on the north by Portuguese West Africa (Angola) and Zambia, on the west by the Atlantic Ocean, on the south and southern portion of the eastern boundary by the Cape Province, and on the remainder of the eastern boundary by Botswana and Zambia. There are 3 main regions: the Namib, an extremely arid and desolate desert region stretching along the entire coastline to a width of between 80 to 130 km. The major portion of the Namib receives an annual rainfall of less than 50 mm. per annum; the Central Plateau is the region lying to the east of the Namib. It varies in altitude between 1,000 and 2,000 metres and offers a diversified landscape of rugged mountains, rocky outcrops, sand-filled valleys and plains. It covers approximately 50% of the total area; the Kalahari covers the eastern, north-eastern and northern areas of South West Africa. The dominant feature of this region is its thick cover of terrestrial sands and limestones and its near-total lack of surface water.

The rainfall increases steadily from less than 50 mm. in the west and southwest up to 600 mm. in the Caprivi Strip.

The Kunene River and the Okavango, which form portions of the northern border of the country, the Zambesi, which forms the eastern boundary of the Caprivi-Zipfel, the Kwando or Mashi, which flows through the Caprivi-Zipfel from the north between the Okavango and the Zambesi, and the Orange River in the south, are the only permanently running streams. But there is a system of great, sandy, dry river-beds throughout the country, in which water can generally be obtained by sinking shallow wells. In the Grootfontein area there are large supplies of underground water, but except for a few springs, mostly hot, there is no surface water in the country.

On 13 Oct. 1964 and 29 Jan. 1969 the Republic of South Africa and Portugal signed agreements on the common use of the Kunene River.

Owing to the difficulty of satisfactorily controlling that part of the Caprivi-

Zipfel, east of the line running due south from Beacon 22, situated west of the Kwando (or Mashi) River, the control of this area was in Aug. 1939 transferred to the Union Department of Native Affairs.

The population at the census 1960 and 1970 was:

	1960	1970
Ovambos	239,363	340,000
Whites	73,464	90,000
Damaras	44,353	64,000
Hereros	35,354	43,000
Namas	34,806	33,000
Kavangos	27,871	50,000
East Caprivians	15,840	25,000
Coloureds	12,708	28,000
Basters	11,257	16,000
Bushmen	11,762	21,000
Tswana and others	9,992	17,000
Kaokolanders	9,234	18,000
	526,004	749,000

The population grew at a rate of 3·7% per annum between 1960 and 1970.

The Ovambos are a Bantu race and are both agriculturists and owners of stock. They still possess tribal organization to its full extent.

The Hereros are a pastoral people who formerly owned enormous herds of cattle. Wars with Namas and Germans destroyed their tribal organization. Under the Union and Republic administration, reserves have been set apart and they have considerably increased in numbers and in animal wealth.

The Bergdamaras or Damara are also of Bantu origin. They were alternatively the slaves of the Hereros and the Namas, whose language they now speak, in pre-European days.

The Namas consist of 2 distinct sections: one, the Hamitic, whose remnants are found in the central portions of the country, being of pure native extraction, is thought to have migrated from the region of the Central African lakes in prehistoric times; the other, the Khoisan, is composed of tribes whose members are descended from persons born in the Cape a couple of centuries ago with an admixture of European and Nama blood.

The Bushmen are among the oldest inhabitants of southern Africa.

In the centre of the country just south of the Windhoek district is the Rehoboth Gebiet, occupied by a race known as the Basters, who are of mixed Nama–European descent and whose ordinary language is Afrikaans.

A commission of inquiry, appointed by the South African Government, in 1964 recommended the establishment of 'homeland areas' for the non-White groups. All these areas should be governed by legislative councils, headed by executive committees; franchise should be granted to males and females over 18 years who qualify for citizenship in their respective homelands.

On 17 Oct. 1968 and 22 Oct. 1970 respectively the first sessions of the Legislative Councils of Ovambo (42 members) and Kavango (30 members) were opened.

EDUCATION (1970). *Whites.* There were 81 schools, 1,141 teachers and 22,355 pupils.

Coloureds. There were 56 schools with together 406 teachers and 12,270 pupils.

Bantu. There were 424 schools with 2,243 teachers and 95,302 pupils.

HEALTH (1970). There are 156 hospitals and clinics, of which 117 serve the indigenous and Coloured population groups, 22 served all population groups and 17 the White population group. The ratio of beds per population was 8·87 per 1,000 and the ratio of doctors to population was 1 per 4,100 inhabitants (excluding the Eastern Caprivi). Nursing staff numbered 1,846.

FINANCE. The revenue and expenditure (in R1,000) were:

	1964–65	1965–66	1966–67	1967–68	1968–69
Revenue	54,016	71,816	79,389	88,466	88,948
Expenditure	63,607	69,925	70,181	79,431	85,825

AGRICULTURE. South West Africa is essentially a stock-raising country, the scarcity of water and poor rainfall rendering agriculture, except in the northern and north-eastern portions, almost impossible. Generally speaking, the southern half is suited for the raising of small stock, while the central and northern portions are better fitted for cattle. Livestock (1969): 2·8m. cattle, 5·2m. sheep, 1·8m. goats, 75,308 (1967) horses, mules and donkeys. In 1969, 244,174 head of cattle and 283,024 head of small stock were exported.

In 1968–69, 31·4m. lb. of butter and 161,779 lb. of factory cheese were manufactured.

The production of karakul pelts is of increasing importance. In 1969, 3,739,200 pelts, worth R22,210,848, were exported.

FISHING. The total catch in 1969 was 954,082 short tons.

MINING. Mineral export/sales amounted to R139,381,475 in 1969. Diamonds, which constitute the principal production, are mainly recovered from alluvial terraces on a 60-mile stretch along the coastline from the Orange River mouth northward.

COMMERCE. The statistics concerning the external trade of South West Africa are included in those of the Republic of South Africa.

The bulk of the direct imports into the country is landed at Walvis Bay.

Total trade between South West Africa and UK, in £1,000 sterling (British Board of Trade returns):

	1965	1966	1967	1968	1969	1970
Imports to UK	18,912	24,103	21,344	24,464	26,429	26,052
Exports from UK	2,087	1,457	2,129	1,383	1,615 ⎫	1,883
Re-exports from UK	10	28	6	95	24 ⎭	

RAILWAYS. The South West Africa system connects with the main system of the South African Railways at De Aar. The total length of the line inside South West Africa is 1,645 miles of 3 ft 6 in. gauge.

ROADS. In 1969 there were 5,723 miles of main roads, 2,162 miles of secondary roads, 12,283 miles of district roads and 15,940 proclaimed farm roads. 1,388 miles of these roads were tarred. In the same year there were 70,500 registered motor vehicles.

SHIPPING. In 1969–70 Walvis Bay harbour handled 1,441,089 tons of cargo.

AVIATION. The Territory is served by regular air services of South African Airways. In 1969–70, 62,448 passengers and 885 tons of freight were conveyed between South Africa and South West Africa.

POST. At 31 March 1970 there were 94 post offices and postal agencies, and 1m219 private bag services distributed by rail or road transport.

There were 11,860 circuit miles of trunk lines, 76,565 miles of carrier circuits, 96,333 miles of telegraph circuits and 26,410 miles of farm telephone lines; 73 telegraph offices, 122 telephone exchanges, 31,677 telephones. There are 13 post-office and 1,091 licensed radio stations in operation.

In 1970, 47,061 wireless licences were issued.

A post office savings bank was established in 1916. The number of accounts open at 31 March 1966 was 40,529 with a credit of R3,625,261. Savings certificates of a value of R200 are also issued. The balance due to holders as at 31 March 1966 amounted to R314,400.

BANKING. Barclays Bank DCO, Volkskas Bank, Standard Bank, Netherlands Bank, Trust Bank and South African Reserve Bank have branches in the Territory.

BOOKS OF REFERENCE

The Territory of South West Africa. (In *Official Year Book of the Republic of South Africa*
Department of Foreign Affairs. *South West Africa Survey 1967*
Department of Mines: *Quarterly Information Circulars: Industrial Minerals*
Wipplinger, O., *The Storage of Water in Sand.* Windhoek, 1959

SOUTHERN YEMEN

Between August and October 1967 the 17 sultanates of the Federation of South
Arabia (*see* MAP in the STATESMAN'S YEAR-BOOK, 1965–66) were overrun by the
forces of the National Liberation Front (NLF). The rulers were deposed,
resigned or fled. At the same time the rival organization of FLOSY (Front for the
Liberation of Occupied South Yemen) fought a civil war against NLF and
harassed the British forces and civilians in Aden. In November the UAR withdrew its support from FLOSY, and with the backing of the army the NLF took
over throughout the country.

The last British troops left Aden on 29 Nov., and on 30 Nov. the Southern
Yemen People's Republic was proclaimed. A bloodless *coup d'état* occurred on
24 June 1969 when President Qahtan Muhammad as-Shaabi was deposed.

Chairman of Presidential Council: Salem Rubayyi.
Prime Minister: Mohammed Ali Haithem.
Foreign Affairs: Ali Salem al Beidh.

AREA AND POPULATION. Southern Yemen covers an area of approximately 61,890 sq. miles (160,300 sq. km). The population is estimated at about
1·5m. The capital is Madinet al-Shaab (formerly Al Ittahad). The main towns
are Aden (population, 250,000), Shaikh Othman (30,000), Mukalla (25,00) and
Little Aden (9,500).

The island of **Kamaran** in the Red Sea (area 70 sq. miles) was in British occupation
from 1915 to 1967, when the inhabitants opted in favour of remaining with the
Southern Yemen Republic.

The island of **Perim** was first occupied by the French in 1738. In 1799 the
British took formal possession but evacuated the island the same year. It was
re-occupied by the British in Jan. 1851 and was later used as a coaling station.
In Nov. 1967 the inhabitants opted in favour of remaining with the Southern
Yemen Republic.

EDUCATION. There were in the Federation and the Protectorate 314 primary schools, 38 intermediate and secondary schools, and 5 teacher-training
centres, run by the government, as well as 16 primary and 22 intermediate and
secondary schools, aided as well as non-aided.

CINEMAS (1965). There are 14 cinemas in Aden with a seating capacity of
about 13,000.

FINANCE. Currency. The currency is the South Arabian dinar (SA£), divided
into 1,000 *fils*, on parity with the £ sterling. Coins: 50, 25, 5, 1 *fils*; notes: 5 and
1 dinar, 500 and 250 fils.

Budget. The budget of the Federation (in £ sterling) for financial years ending
31 March was as follows:

	1963–64	1964–65	1965–66	1966–67[1]	1968–69[1]
Revenue	8,596,637	10,563,998	13,834,732	18,675,725	11,000,000
Expenditure	8,238,981	10,779,377	13,840,452	18,967,184	18,000,000

[1] Estimates.

DEFENCE. Until South Yemen became independent, Britain was responsible for financing, training and equipping the army.

Army. The army, about 11,000 strong, is being reconstructed with Soviet aid. All British officers were dismissed in Feb. 1968.

Navy. The navy comprise 3 inshore minesweepers given by Britain and 15 small patrol boats built in Britain.

Air Force. Formed in 1967, the air force received as initial equipment 4 Jet Provost armed trainers, 4 C-47 transports (1 since lost), 6 Beaver light communications aircraft and 6 Sioux (Bell 47) light helicopters. Four BAC 167 Strikemaster light attack aircraft have since been delivered. Additional aircraft have been requested from the USSR and about 12 MiG-17 jet fighter-bombers have been received.

AGRICULTURE. Agriculture is the main occupation of the people. This is largely of a subsistence nature, sorghum, sesame and millet being the chief crops, and wheat and barley widely grown at the higher elevations. Of increasing importance, however, are the cash crops which have been developed since the Second World War, by far the most important of which is the Abyan long-staple cotton, now the country's major export.

Owing to paucity of rainfall, cultivation is largely confined to fertile valleys and flood plains on silt, built up and irrigated in the traditional manner. These traditional methods are being augmented and replaced by the use of modern earth-moving machinery and pumps. Irrigation schemes with permanent installations are in progress.

COMMERCE. The trade of Aden is mainly transhipment and entrepôt, the port serving as a centre of distribution to and from neighbouring territories. Transit trade is mainly in cotton piece-goods, grains, coffee, hides and skins, and cheap consumer goods.

Total imports 1965, £107,539,374 (by sea, £104,415,644; by land, £1,522,120; by air, £166,001; by post, £1,435,609). Total exports and re-exports 1965, including ships' stores and bunker fuel, £66,748,668 (by sea, £64,876,796; by land, £1,849,082; by air, £22,790).

In 1966 imports totalled £102m.; exports and re-exports, £67·92m.

Total trade (in £1,000 sterling) between Aden (State and Protectorate) and UK (British Board of Trade returns):

	1965	1966	1967	1968	1969	1970
Imports to UK	13,485	13,825	10,611	6,811	14,619	9,626
Exports from UK	13,911	13,175	9,347	8,147	6,650 ⎫	4,987
Re-exports from UK	234	269	279	49	104 ⎭	

SHIPPING. Because of its favourable geographical position and its efficient service to ships, Aden used to be one of the busiest oil-bunkering ports in the world, handling some 550 ships a month.

ROADS. Aden has 140 miles of roads of which 127 are asphalted. Registered motor vehicles in 1965 numbered 16,789.

AVIATION. Twelve airlines used to operate scheduled services: Aden Airways, Air-India, Alitalia, BOAC, East African Airways Corporation, Ethiopian Airlines, Ghana Airlines, Middle East Airlines, United Arab Airlines, Saudi Arabian Airlines, Sudan Airways, Yemen Airlines.

Aden Airways ceased operations in June 1967.

POST. There were 17 post offices in the Federation and 9 in the Protectorate. There were 13 postal agencies in the Protectorate and one each at Perim and Kamaran. The automatic telephone system provided service to about 9,410 subscribers in 1970.

F F

Radio telephone services were available with London (with extensions to Europe and America), Kenya (with extensions to Tanzania and Uganda), Bombay, French Territory of Afars and Issas, Bahrain and Addis Ababa.

BANKING. The following banks used to operate in Aden: The National Grindlays Bank, Ltd, the Eastern Bank, Ltd, the British Bank of the Middle East, Cowasjee Dinshaw & Brothers, the Bank of India, Ltd, the Chartered Bank, Ltd, the Habib Bank, Ltd, the Arab Bank, Ltd, and a savings bank operated by the Post Office.

British Ambassador: A. R. H. Kellos, CMG.
Ambassador in Britain: Fadhle Ahmed Sallami.

BOOKS OF REFERENCE

Hickinbotham, Sir Tom, *Aden.* London, 1959
Thesiger, W., *Arabian Sands.* London, 1959

SPAIN
Estado Español

GOVERNMENT AND CONSTITUTION. The Spanish State was established by Gen. Franco on 1 Oct. 1936. For a short account of the Civil War in Spain, 17 July 1936 to 1 April 1939, *see* THE STATESMAN'S YEAR-BOOK, 1939, pp. 1325-6. On 30 Jan. 1938 the first civil government was proclaimed, with Gen. Franco, possessing dictatorial powers, at its head. It was, on 30 Oct. 1969, reconstituted as follows:

Leader (Caudillo) of Spain, Chief of the State, C.-in-C. of the Armed Forces, Prime Minister and Head of the National Movement: Gen. Francisco Franco Bahamonde (born 4 Dec. 1892).

Vice-President of Government and Under-Secretary of the Presidency: Vice-Adm. Luis Carrero Blanco.

Foreign Affairs: Gregorio López Bravo de Costro.
Justice: Antonio Maria Oriol y Urquijo.
Army: Gen. Juan Castañón de Mena.
Navy: Adm. Adolfo Baturone Colombo.
Finance: Alberto Monreal Luque.
Interior: Tomás Garicano Goñi.
Public Works: Gonzalo Fernandez de la Mora.
Education and Science: José Luis Villar Palasi.
Industry: José Maria López de Letona y Núñez del Pino.
Agriculture: Tomás Allende y García-Baxter.
Air: Gen. Julio Salvador y Diaz-Benjumú.
Labour: Licinio de la Fuentes y de la Fluentes.
Commerce: Enrique Fontana Codina.
Information and Tourism: Alfredo Sanchez Bella.
Housing: Vicente Mortes Alfonso.

Without portfolio: Laureano López Rodó (*Economic and Social Development Plan*), Torcuato Fernandez Mirand (*Secretary-General of the Movement*), Enrique Garcia del Ramal Cellalbo (*Sindicatos*).

On 31 March 1947 Gen. Franco announced that Spain is to become a monarchy, with a regency council and himself as the head of state. In July 1969, Prince Don Juan Carlos de Borbon was sworn in as successor to the Head of State and bears the title of HRH Prince of Spain until such time as he becomes King. On 6 July 1947 the 'Law of Succession' was approved by a referendum; out of a total of 17,178,812 electors, 14,145,163 voted for, and 722,656 against it; 351,744 votes were invalid.

National flag: Red, yellow, red (horizontal).
National anthem: Marcha grandera.

On 19 April 1937 the various political groups in the Nationalist Movement
were united by Gen. Franco into one single political party, under the title *Falange
Española Tradicionalista y de las Juntas de Ofensiva Nacional Sindicalistas*, comprising the *falange española* created on 29 Oct. 1933 by José Antonio Primo de
Rivera, eldest son of the general who was Dictator of Spain from 1923 to 1930,
and the traditionalists.

The constitutional regulations contained in the Law of the Cortes, the Succession Act, the Fuero of the Spaniards, the Fuero of Labour, etc. (*see* THE
STATESMAN'S YEAR-BOOK, 1966–67, pp. 1425 f.) were consolidated and partly
modified by the 'Organic Law of the Spanish State' (*La Ley Orgánica del Estado
Español*), unanimously approved by the Cortes on 22 Nov. 1966 and ratified by a
national referendum on 14 Dec. 1966.

The Organic Law distinguishes the executive powers of the Head of State
(*Jefe del Estado*) and those of a Premier (*Presidente del Gobierno*), who is to be
chosen by the Head of State from a list of 3 names submitted by the Council of
the Realm; the Premier's term of office will be 5 years, though he may be removed
earlier by the Head of State on the proposal of the Council of the Realm but not
by the Cortes.

'The Head of the State directs the government apparatus (*gobernación*) of the
Kingdom by means of the Council of Ministers. . . . In the absence or illness of
the Chief of State, his functions will be assumed by the Heir to the Throne if over
30 years of age, or by the Council of Regency.'

The Council of the Realm consists of 16 members, 10 of them elected by the
Cortes; the President of the Cortes is its chairman.

The National Council consists of 1 elected councillor for each province, 40
councillors appointed by the Head of State, 12 councillors elected by the Cortes
to represent 'basic structures of the nation' (family, local corporations, trade
unions), 6 councillors appointed by the Prime Minister and a secretary-general
appointed by the Head of State.

The Cortes are composed of the members of the Government; the national
councillors; the presidents of the supreme court of justice, of the council of the
realm, of the supreme military tribunal, of the court of exchequer and of the
national economic council; 150 representatives of the trade unions; representatives of the municipalities and provincial councils elected by their respective
corporations; 100 deputies (2 from each province) elected by the heads of
families (men or women); and some 30 representatives of the universities, learned
and professional societies, chambers of commerce, etc.

Religious liberty is proclaimed as having State-guaranteed protection by
means of a legal guardianship which at the same time safeguards morals
and the public order. Trade unions are no longer subject to control by the
Falange; there will be *sindicatos* of business-owners, technicians or workers,
respectively.

LOCAL GOVERNMENT. The provinces are constituted by the association of
municipalities (9,202 in 1960). All municipalities are autonomous in their respective spheres, and at their heads stands the *Ayuntamiento*. The municipal
councils are elected by the heads of family. The *Alcalde* or Mayor is appointed
by the Minister of the Interior in municipalities of over 10,000 inhabitants, and
elsewhere by the Civil Governors. The *Diputaciones Provinciales* have entire
jurisdiction over their own province and are their sole administrators. Each
island of the Canaries has a corporation known as *Cabildo Insular*, to rule their
special interests; the Balearic Islands have the same provincial administration as
the mainland. Each province of Spain has its own Assembly, the *Diputación
Provincial*.

The reconstruction of devastated regions is under the care of the *Instituto de la
Vivienda* and by the *Banco de Crédito a la Reconstrucción*, whose duty is to grant

and administer loans approved for reconstructing buildings, and the *Banco de Crédito Agrícola* and *Banco de Crédito Industrial* with regard to industries, agriculture, commerce and mining, and merchant vessels.

AREA AND POPULATION. Continental Spain has an area of 492,592 sq. km, and including the Balearic and Canary Islands 504,879 sq. km (194,883 sq. miles). Estimated population in 1968 was 32,411,407.

The growth of the population has been as follows:

Census year	Population	Rate of annual increase	Census year	Population	Rate of annual increase
1860	15,655,467	0·34	1940	25,877,971	0·98
1910	19,927,150	0·72	1950	27,976,755	0·81
1920	21,303,162	0·69	1960	30,903,137	0·88
1930	23,563,867	1·06			

Area and registered population of the provinces, as at 31 Dec. 1960:

Province	Area (sq. km)	Population	Per sq. km	Province	Area (sq. km)	Population	Per sq. km
Alava	3,047	138,934	45·6	Madrid	8,002	2,606,524	325·7
Albacete	14,862	370,976	25·0	Málaga	7,285	775,167	106·4
Alicante	5,863	711,942	121·4	Murcia	11,317	800,463	70·1
Almería	8,774	360,777	41·1	Navarra	10,421	402,042	38·6
Avila	8,048	238,372	29·6	Orense	6,979	451,474	64·7
Badajoz	21,657	834,370	38·5	Oviedo	10,895	989,344	90·8
Baleares	5,014	443,327	88·4	Palencia	8,019	231,977	28·9
Barcelona	7,733	2,877,966	372·2	Palmas (Las)	4,065	453,793	111·6
Burgos	14,328	380,791	26·6	Pontevedra	3,330	680,229	204·3
Cáceres	19,945	544,407	27·3	Salamanca	12,336	405,729	32·9
Cádiz	7,385	818,847	110·9	Santa Cruz de Tenerife	3,208	490,655	152·9
Castellón	6,679	339,229	50·8	Santander	5,289	432,132	81·7
Ciudad-Real	19,749	583,948	29·6	Segovia	6,949	195,602	28·2
Córdoba	13,718	798,437	58·2	Sevilla	14,010	1,234,435	88·1
Coruña (La)	7,903	991,729	125·5	Soria	10,301	147,052	14·3
Cuenca	17,062	315,433	18·5	Tarragona	6,283	362,679	57·7
Gerona	5,886	351,369	59·7	Teruel	14,797	215,183	14·5
Granada	12,531	769,408	61·4	Toledo	15,345	521,637	34·0
Guadalajara	12,190	183,545	15·0	Valencia	10,763	1,429,708	132·8
Guipúzcoa	1,997	478,337	239·5	Valladolid	8,345	363,106	43·5
Huelva	10,085	399,934	39·6	Vizcaya	2,224	754,383	339·2
Huesca	15,680	233,543	14·9	Zamora	10,572	301,129	28·5
Jaén	13,492	736,391	54·6	Zaragoza	17,132	656,772	38·3
León	14,070	584,594	38·8				
Lérida	12,066	333,765	27·7				
Logroño	5,034	229,852	45·6				
Lugo	9,881	479,530	48·5	Total	503,545	30,430,698	60·4

In 1960 there were 14,763,388 males and 15,667,310 females.

By decree of 21 Sept. 1927 the islands which form the Canary Archipelago were divided into 2 provinces, under the name of their respective capitals: Santa Cruz de Tenerife and Las Palmas de Gran Canaria. The province of Santa Cruz de Tenerife is constituted by the islands of Tenerife, Palma, Gomera and Hierro, and that of Las Palmas by Gran Canaria, Lanzarote and Fuerteventura, with the small barren islands of Alegranza, Roque del Este, Roque del Oeste, Graciosa, Montaña Clara and Lobos. The area of the islands is 7,273 sq. km; population (1 Jan. 1959), 908,718.

Places under Spanish sovereignty in Morocco are: Alhucemas, Ceuta, Chafarinas, Melilla and Peñón de Vélez.

The following were the registered populations of the principal towns at 31 Dec. 1968:

Town	Population	Town	Population	Town	Population
Albacete	84,074	Badajoz	103,557	Cádiz	137,925
Alcoy	60,889	Badalona	150,143	Cartagena	147,353
Algeciras	76,746	Baracaldo	113,253	Castellón	87,206
Alicante	162,944	Barcelona	1,759,148	Ceuta	70,092
Almería	105,413	Bilbao	400,505	Córdoba	231,641
Avilés	76,318	Burgos	107,744	Cornellá	66,323

Town	Popu-lation	Town	Popu-lation	Town	Popu-lation
Elche	105,623	Lorca	62,896	San Sebastián	161,944
El Ferrol	87,351	Lugo	70,043	Sta Coloma de	
Gijón	152,784	Madrid	3,030,689	Grammanet	91,162
Granada	170,127	Málaga	350,977	Sta Cruz de Tenerife	180,666
Hospitalet	216,435	Manresa	62,670	Santander	143,130
Huelva	94,897	Mataró	68,465	Santiago de Com-	
Jaén	74,522	Melilla	77,877	postela	67,675
Jérez de la Frontera	150,124	Mieres	69,044	Sevilla	622,145
La Coruña	194,967	Orense	74,389	Tarragona	69,921
La Laguna	71,067	Oviedo	142,769	Tarrasa	130,549
Langreo	71,304	Palma de Mallorca	208,127	Valencia	624,227
Las Palmas	263,328	Pamplona	137,372	Valladolid	211,795
León	101,949	Pontevedra	65,532	Vigo	191,816
Lérida	82,319	Sabadell	149,887	Vitoria	123,921
Linares	61,935	Salamanca	120,265	Zaragoza	439,451
Logroño	79,050	San Fernando	63,674		

VITAL STATISTICS for calendar years:

	Marriages	Births	Deaths	Immigrants[1]	Emigrants[1]
1967	232,914	672,039	274,021	18,597	19,258
1968	231,546	659,677	277,652	15,969	19,405
1969 [2]	238,102	657,449	297,126	13,736	20,045

[1] Transoceanic movements by sea.   Provisional figures.

RELIGION. Catholicism is again established as the religion of the State. Religious bodies have recovered their legal status; confiscated property has been returned; allowances to clergy are again paid by the State; divorce is suppressed; cemeteries are brought back to ecclesiastical jurisdiction. There are 10 metropolitan sees and 64 suffragan sees, the chief being Toledo, where the Primate resides.

A concordat was signed in Rome on 27 Aug. 1953 to replace the concordat of 1851, which the Republic had denounced in 1931.

There are about 26,000 Protestants, with 200 churches and chapels, outside which no public ceremonies are permitted. There is no liberty for propaganda, and the circulation of Holy Scripture, except in annotated Roman Catholic editions, is forbidden. Several churches were closed in 1958 and 1959. The British and Foreign Bible Society was, on 10 March 1963, allowed to resume its activities.

The first synagogue since the expulsion of the Jews in 1492 was opened in Madrid on 2 Oct. 1959. The number of Jews is estimated at about 1,000.

EDUCATION. Spain is divided into 12 educational districts, with the universities as centres. Primary education is compulsory and free. The *Frente de Juventudes* (Youth Front) was created by law of 6 Dec. 1940; it comprises 3 sections (educational, labour, rural) and had, in 1958, 1,494,413 members. There is also the University Militia for army training under conscription.

In 1967–68 there were 118,786 primary schools attended by 4,179,000 pupils, with 22,800 teachers, including (in 1964–65) 9,775 private schools (10,042 teachers, 358,528 pupils) and 15,853 church schools (16,371 teachers, 686,068 pupils). Secondary education is conducted in 3,748 middle schools, with 59,900 teachers and 1,089,100 pupils. For higher education, there are 96 centres with 150,000 pupils and 9,906 teachers. There are 13 universities, attended (1965–66) by 125,771 students, with 3,078 teachers. The universities are at Barcelona, Granada, Madrid, Murcia, Oviedo, Salamanca, Santiago, Sevilla, Valencia, Valladolid, Zaragoza, Pamplona and La Laguna (Canaries). There is, besides, a medical and science faculty at Cádiz in connexion with the University of Deville.

In 1960, 3,158,850 persons over 10 years of age (14·24%) could not read or write. A literacy test for all Spaniards born after 31 Dec. 1946 was introduced in 1963, to be able to vote, occupy administrative posts or obtain government contracts.

CINEMAS (1969). There were 8,314 cinemas with a seating capacity of 4,925,000.

NEWSPAPERS (1969). There appeared 198 daily newspapers with a total daily circulation of about 5·2m. copies. Thirteen of them were published in Madrid and 10 in Barcelona; all must be printed in Castilian.

JUSTICE. Justice is administered by *Tribunales* and *Juzgados* (Tribunals and Courts), which conjointly form the *Poder Judicial* (Judicial Power). Judges and magistrates cannot be removed, suspended or transferred except as set forth by law.

The Judicature is composed of the *Tribunal Supremo* (Supreme High Court); 15 *Audiencias Territoriales* (Division High Courts); 50 *Audiencias Provinciales* (Provincial High Courts); 579 *Juzgados de Primera Instancia* (Courts of First Instance), and 9,203 *Juzgados Municipales, Comarcales y de paz* (District Court, or Court of Lowest Jurisdiction held by Justices of the Peace).

The *Tribunal Supremo* consists of a President (appointed by the Government) and various judges distributed among 6 chambers: 1 for trying civil matters, 3 for administrative purposes, 1 for criminal trials and 1 for social matters. The *Tribunal Supremo* has disciplinary faculties; is court of cassation in civil criminal trials; for administrative purposes decides in first and second instance disputes arising between private individuals and the State, and in social matters resolves in the last instance all cases involving over 100,000 pesetas.

The *Audiencias Territoriales* have power to try in second instance sentences passed by judges in civil matters.

The *Audiencias Provinciales* try and pass sentence in first instance on all cases filed for delinquency. The jury system is in operation except for military trials.

The *Juzgados Municipales* try small civil cases and petty offences. The *Juzgados Comarcales* deal with the same charges, but their jurisdiction embraces larger districts.

Military cases are tried by the *Tribunal Supremo de Justicia Militar*.

The prison population was, on 31 Dec. 1968, 12,176, including 593 women.

Police. The Minister of the Interior (*Gobernación*) controls the armed police, the secret police and the para-military *Guardia Civil*.

SOCIAL WELFARE. Schemes of wide social range include the Labour Charter (*Fuero del Trabajo*) of 9 March 1938, for a better distribution and remuneration of the working classes, with uninterrupted Sunday and feast-day wages. The law of Family Subsidy (*Subsidio Familiar*), which came into force on 1 March 1939, makes all working people contribute 1% of their earnings, plus an additional 6% from the employers, in a system of social insurance which entitles all families with from 2 to 12 children under 14 years of age to a proportional monthly allowance ranging from 60 to 4,500 pesetas, with an additional 3,000 pesetas for each child in excess of 12 (2 Sept. 1955). Married workers receive an additional bonus. Since 1949, old age pensions and health and maternity insurances have been added; workers contribute 1% and employers 5%. A decree of 22 Feb. 1941 established state loans on marriage to help large families, and the institution known as *Auxilio Social*, the funds of which are derived among other channels from a fortnightly public collection throughout the country, for supplying food and clothing to needy persons and the maintenance of nurseries and infirmaries. A national health insurance for all workers is now also in operation.

By a law dated 27 Feb. 1908 the *Instituto Nacional de Previsión* was founded for the purpose of granting old age pensions and administering a system of social insurance. The family-allowance and health-insurance schemes, described above, have been incorporated in the *Instituto*. In 1966, 2,032m. pesetas were paid out in family subsidies to 3,861,600 persons; 1,415·m. pesetas were paid out in sickness benefits; 6,792m. pesetas for old age pensions, and 3,340·4m. pesetas in injury benefits.

FINANCE. Currency. The *peseta* of 100 *céntimos* had the nominal value of a pre-war franc, 9½*d.*, or 25·22 pesetas to the £ sterling. The exchange value of the pesetas in Oct. 1970 was 166 = £1; 70 = US$1.

Bank-notes of 1,000, 500, 100, 50, 25, 5 and 1 peseta and coins of 5 and 10 *céntimos* (aluminium, tin and copper), 1 *peseta* (copper and aluminium), 5, 25, 50 *pesetas* (nickel and copper) and 100 *pesetas* (silver) are in circulation. In Oct. 1968 the circulation of bank-notes was 209,196m. pesetas and of coins, 9,736m. pesetas.

Budget. Revenue and expenditure in 1m. pesetas:

	1962/63	*1964/65*	*1966*	*1967*	*1968*	*1969*
Revenue	86,855	120,844	185,282	213,420	237,800	271,795
Expenditure	86,788	120,966	185,071	213,161	237,800	271,795

The budget for 1968 is made up as follows (in 1m. pesetas):

Revenue		*Expenditure*	
Direct taxes	61,740	Chief of State	25
Indirect taxes	140,450	Regency Council	2
Loans, etc.	19,293	Cortes	96
Financial transactions	5,621	National Council	603
Transfer of investments	6,391	Court of Accounts	8,223
		Public Debt	18,922
		Pensions	44
		National fund	5,353
		Presidency of the Government	8,457
		Ministry of Foreign Affairs	2,098
		„ Justice	6,075
		„ War	21,141
		„ Marine	6,852
		„ Interior	22,834
		„ Public Works	35,428
		„ Education	24,706
		„ Labour	4,316
		„ Industry	1,824
		„ Agriculture	11,103
		„ Air	9,104
		„ Commerce	7,908
		„ Information and Tourism	2,727
		„ Housing	9,418
		„ Finance	2,289
		Other charges	28,252

The total state debt (including credits to foreign countries) on 1 Jan. 1967 was 222,292·3m. pesetas, of which 10,179·1m. pesetas were Treasury bonds.

DEFENCE. On 26 Sept. 1953 the US and Spain signed three agreements covering the construction and use of military facilities in Spain by the US, economic assistance, and military and item assistance. These agreements were renewed for another 5 years on 26 Sept. 1963. The American naval and air base at Rota (near Cádiz) is connected by pipelines with the American bomber bases at Morón de la Frontera (near Seville), Torrejón (near Madrid) and Zaragoza.

A further agreement was signed on 6 Aug. 1970 replacing the one signed in 1953 which was due to expire on 26 Sept 1970 having been extended for 18 months in 1969. The agreement will expire in 1975 but could be extended for a further period of 5 years.

Length of service is 16 months in the army, 24 months in the navy and 18 months in the air force.

Army. The Army was reorganized by a decree published on 24 July 1939 to be constituted by 8 army corps in the Peninsula and 2 in Morocco, in addition to the 2 *Comandancias Generales* in the Balearic and Canary Islands as heretofore. A decree of 30 Aug. 1939 created the High General Staff of the Army as the highest military authority.

On 1 Jan. 1944 a slight reorganization was made by withdrawing from the 2nd Región Militar the eastern provinces of Granada, Málaga and Almería, which were to form the 9th Región Militar. After this reorganization there were 8 army corps attached to the 8 original military regions; 1 Región Militar, the 9th, with 1 division only and the Capitanías Generales on the Balearic and Canary Islands as heretofore.

The army corps are as follows: I, Madrid, 2 divisions; II, Sevilla, 2 divisions; III, Valencia, 2 divisions; IV, Barcelona, 2 divisions; V, Zaragoza, 2 divisions; VI, Burgos, 2 divisions; VII, Valladolid, 2 divisions; VIII, La Coruña, 2 divisions; 9th Región Militar, 1 division. There are also 1 armoured division with M-47 and M-48 tanks, 2 mechanized infantry divisions, 2 mountain divisions, 1 cavalry brigade, 1 parachute brigade and 1 battalion with surface-to-air missiles.

Army personnel is about 500 generals, 40,000 officers and 180,000 other ranks.

In Africa the army corps are as follows: IX (Ceuta), 2 divisions; X (Melilla), 2 divisions. Total strength in Africa, about 32,000 men.

Navy. Particulars of the principal ships:

Completed	Name	Standard displacement Tons	Armour Belt In.	Turrets In.	Principal armament	Shaft horsepower	Speed Knots
			Helicopter Carrier				
1943	Dedalo	11,000	—	—	16 40-mm. A.A.	100,000	32

A former US aircraft carrier, converted and transferred to Spain in 1966–67.

			Cruiser				
1936	Canarias	10,670	2	1	8 8-in.; 8 4·7-in. A.A.	90.000	33

The anti-aircraft cruiser *Méndez Núñez* was stricken from the list in 1963 and the cruisers *Almirante Cervera*, *Galicia* and *Miguel de Cervantes* in 1964–66.

There are 4 submarines, 4 midget submarines, 19 destroyers, 6 frigates, 6 corvettes, 6 frigate minelayers, 13 minesweepers, 12 coastal minesweepers, 2 patrol vessels, 3 torpedo boats, 17 motor launches, 10 coastguard patrol vessels, 1 training ship, 5 survey ships, 5 patrol craft, a river patrol boat, 8 landing ships, 3 landing craft, 4 oilers, 3 transports, 2 tenders, a boom defence vessel and 14 tugs.

Ships under construction include 5 frigates of USA design and 2 submarines of French design,

Shipbuilding is mainly carried on at the dockyards at El Ferrol and Cartagena, Cádiz having a smaller share in it.

There are naval wireless telegraphic stations at Cádiz, Barcelona, Mahón, Pontevedra. Cartagena and E. Ferrol.

Barcelona, Bilbao, Seville and Cádiz are the chief naval yards.

In 1970 naval personnel totalled 51,200 officers and ratings, including marines.

Air Force. The Air Force is organized as an independent service, dating from 1939. It comprises air regions (with HQ at Madrid, Seville and Zaragoza), an overseas air zone (Canary Islands) and a separate Air Defence Command which controls interceptor squadrons (including USAF elements) and the control and warning radar network and Tactical and Transport Commands. Strength is 32.600 personnel and more than 200 combat aircraft.

The *Aviación Táctica* has 2 fighter-bomber squadrons of Spanish-built Northrop SF-5s, 2 light bomber squadrons equipped with obsolete Spanish-built Heinkel He 111 bombers, 2 squadrons of HA-200D Saeta light attack jet aircraft of Spanish design and manufacture, and 1 aero-naval co-operation wing with 3 P-3B Orion and about 7 HU-16B Albatross anti-submarine aircraft. A further 25 HA-220 light attack aircraft, evolved from the HA-200, are being built for counter-insurgency operations. Air Defence Command has 1 squadron of Mirage III-Es, 3 squadrons of F-86F Sabres and 1 squadron of F-104G Starfighters. Further Sabre squadrons will be re-equipped with Mirages and F-4C Phantoms, as will the F-104G squadron. Two transport wings operate a total of more than 100 C-130 Hercules, C-54s, C-47s, Caribou and Spanish-built CASA Azors.

American-built T-34 and T-6 piston-engined aircraft are used for basic training, together with HA-200 Saeta twin-jet training aircraft. American-built T-33A and F-86F jet aircraft and 2-seat versions of operational types are used as advanced trainers.

PRODUCTION. A 4-year development plan, 1963–67, envisaged a total investment of 355,000m. pesetas. The second development plan, 1968–71, provides 552,700m. pesetas, of which 466,900m. represent real investment and 85,800m. loans.

The economically active population numbered 12,520,100 at the end of 1968 (38·5% of the total population). Of these, 3·9m. were occupied in agriculture and fishing, 3·25m. in manufactures, 1·29m. in trade, 2·15m. in public and personal services.

AGRICULTURE. Spain is mainly an agricultural country. In 1967 the total value of agricultural produce was 222m. pesetas; of livestock, 152·6m.; of forestry, 17·3m. Land under cultivation in 1967 (in 1,000 hectares) included: Cereals, 7,286; vegetables, 875; potatoes, 754. In 1969, 240,000 tractors and 30,000 harvesters were in use.

Principal crops	Area (in 1,000 hectares)				Yield (in 1,000 metric tons)			
	1966	1967	1968	1969	1966	1967	1968	1969
Wheat	4,194	4,296	3,977	3,744	4,876	5,650	5,312	4,691
Barley	1,362	1,525	1,940	2,164	2,006	2,576	3,441	3,855
Oats	469	491	515	498	418	492	539	533
Rye	387	400	371	333	357	336	355	348
Rice	58	60	61	66	385	366	362	404
Maize	456	484	528	525	1,162	1,195	1,473	1,577
Potatoes	376	380	383	386	4,423	4,508	4,546	4,717
Sugar beet	148	175	180	194	4,055	4,282	4,620	5,079
Tomatoes	52	52	52	55	1,323	1,253	1,310	1,407

In 1967, 1,584,000 hectares were under vines; in 1967 production of wine was 2·47m. hectolitres. The area of onions in 1967 was 33,000 hectares, yielding 843,000 tons. Production of oranges and manderines in 1969 was 2,111,000 tons. other products are esparto (41,477 tons in 1964), flax, hemp and pulse. Spain has important industries connected with the preparation of wine and fruits. Silk culture is carried on in Murcia, Alicante and other provinces; 27 tons were produced in 1969. Spain produced in 1968, 8,951 tons of honey and 500 tons of beeswax. Beer factories produced 10·8m. hectolitres in 1969.

Tobacco crop in 1969 was 25,000 tons; sugar-cane (1968), 407,000 tons.

Livestock. The number of farm animals in 1969 was estimated as follows (in 1,000): Horses, 304; mules, 606; asses, 421; cows, 4,215; sheep, 17,024; goats, 2,529; pigs, 7,488.

FISHERIES. The most important catches are those of sardines, tunny fish and cod. The total catch amounted in 1968 to 1,184,500 tons, representing a value of 21,611·3m. pesetas. In the tinned fish industry there were, in 1969, 674 factories, producing 80,897 tons. The Spanish fishing fleet in 1968 consisted of 13,522 vessels of 604,687 tons.

MINING. Spain is rich in minerals. The production of the more important minerals in 1969 were as follows (in 1,000 metric tons):

Anthracite	2,767	Iron ore	5,200	Tin ore (1968)	2
Coal	8,817	Lead ore	104	Zinc ore	149
Lignite	2,736	Manganese ore	23	Wolfram ore (1968)	1·4
Copper blister	37·6	Potash	4,065	Silver	55
Copper refined	76·02	Sulphur	38·5	Gold (1965)	276 kg

In June 1964 oil was struck about 40 miles north of the city of Burgos.

In 1964, 332,200 workers were employed in the mining and metallurgical industries. In 1965 the total value of the mining production was 21,998m. pesetas; of metallurgical production, in 1966, 108,732m. pesetas. In 1967 Spain produced 2·69m. tons of pig-iron and 4·33m. tons of steel ingots and castings. A uranium plant to supply the material for nuclear energy was inaugurated at Andujar in Andalusia in Feb. 1960.

INDUSTRY. The manufacture of cotton and woollen goods is important, principally in Catalonia. In 1966 there were 4,732 textile factories in operation, with 53,669 looms and 2,378,000 spindles, employing 209,850 workmen. Production, in 1,000 metric tons (1967): Silk yarn, 42; wool yarn, 33; cotton (yarn, 103·7; fabrics, 101·8), rayon fabrics, 20·91. 280 paper-mills produced in 1969, 581,234 tons of writing, printing, packing and cigarette paper. The production of cork in 1966 was 58,400 tons. The production of cement reached 13,117,000 tons in 1967.

Spanish shipyards launched 343,117 BRT in 1966. In 1967, 531,227 motor vehicles were built, including 275,017 passenger cars.

POWER. Electric power-stations in 1968 had a total installed capacity of 14m. kw., of which 8·5m. was hydro-electric. The total output (1969) amounted to 51,488m. kwh. Gas production in 1969 was 714m. cu. metres.

TOURISM. In 1968, 21·7m. foreigners visited Spain, spending 91,749m. pesetas.

LABOUR. The economic policy is centred on vertical syndicates (trade unions) created under the Charter of Labour on 8 Aug. 1939, replacing the former local and provincial syndicates. The law of 23 June 1941 classified these syndicates into 26 branches of production, each working within its own respective economic sphere, without interrupting their unity or formation. The individual is replaced by the producing concern as a whole, made up of the capitalists, managers, experts and all those rendering some sort of labour, whether intellectual or manual. The vertical syndicate is invested with authority and hierarchy. The appointments are made from top to bottom. At the top stands the National Delegate of Syndicates, who is responsible for his conduct to the Minister who appoints him. Production, wages, prices and the distribution of domestic and foreign merchandise are controlled, and legislation has been adopted requiring government permission for the establishment of new industries.

The daily minimum wage of workers is 96 pesetas (from 1 Oct. 1967).

COMMERCE. Foreign trade of Spain (Peninsula, Baleares, Canaries, Ceuta, Melilla) (in 1m. pesetas):

	1965	1966	1967	1968	1969
Imports	181,128	215,444	211,828	246,547	296,306
Exports	57,989	75,213	84,659	111,244	133,012

In 1969 the most important items of import were (in 1m. pesetas): Manufactures, 164,821; animal and vegetable oils and fats, 53,565; food, drink and tobacco, 38,685; mineral fuels and lubricants, 37,065. The main items of exports were: Manufactured goods, 74,319; food, drink, tobacco, 42,480.

In 1969 the main supplying countries were (in 1m. pesetas): USA, 50,956; West Germany, 39,634; France, 30,067; UK, 22,481; Italy, 17,711. The main receiving countries were (in 1m. pesetas): USA, 19,957; West Germany, 14,291; France, 12,836; UK, 11,962; Italy, 6,880.

Of the 66·84m. litres of sherry exported in 1969, 36·9m. went to the UK. In 1969, 86·71m. litres of wine were exported.

Total trade between Spain and UK, in £1,000 sterling (British Board of Trade returns):

	1965	1966	1967	1968	1969	1970
Imports to UK	57,430	61,774	73,593	98,616	98,774	108,490
Exports from UK	84,122	99,295	90,165	96,340	115,254 }	123,169
Re-exports from UK	1,871	2,260	2,309	2,411	3,403 }	

In Dec. 1948 special exchange rates were established to facilitate Spanish exports to the sterling and dollar countries, Belgium, Denmark, Netherlands, Portugal, Sweden and Switzerland.

SHIPPING. The merchant navy in 1969 contained 2,754 vessels of a gross tonnage of 2,919,000.

In 1968, 96,286 (1967: 93,810) ships entered Spanish ports, carrying 1,926,300 (1967: 1,854,000) passengers and discharging 73,459,000 (1967: 64m.) tons of cargo; 95,871 (1967: 93,683) ships cleared, carrying 1,985,800 (1967: 1,813,000) passengers and loading 48,697,000 (1967: 35·7m.) tons of cargo.

ROADS. In 1965 the total length of highways and roads in Spain was 138,670 km, of which 55,336 km were macadamized. Number of motor cars was 3,969,000 in 1969.

RAILWAYS. The total length of the railways in 1969 was 17,458 km, of which two-thirds are of 5ft 6in. gauge. There are 3,811 km of lines electrified. On 1 Feb. 1941 the Spanish railways, of broad gauge only, passed into state owner- ship; they are under a board known as the *Red Nacional de Ferrocarriles Españoles* (RENFE). The gauge of the principal Spanish railways has, for strategic reasons, been kept different from that of France; passengers therefore must change trains at the frontier stations except by certain trains having variable gauge axles. Number of passengers carried in 1969 by government-owned lines was 158·9m.; freight carried was 29·54m. tons. A 10-year modernization plan (1964–73) is to cost 62,000m. pesetas.

AVIATION. The most important Spanish airline is 'Iberia'; it maintains a regular service with Tangier, Morocco, the Balearic and Canary Islands, Lisbon, Switzerland, London, Buenos Aires, Venezuela, Cuba, Canada and USA. There are 37 civilian and 7 military airports.

In 1969, 209,772 aircraft entered Spain, carrying 8·6m. passengers and 62,727 metric tons of merchandise; 8·73m. passengers and 70,949 metric tons of merchandise left Spain by air.

POST. The receipts of the post office in 1969, were 4,787m. pesetas; expenses, 5,100m. pesetas. There were 13,145 post offices and 4,093,000 telephones, nearly all privately operated.

The length of telegraph lines in 1969 was 41,236 km; number of telegraph offices, 10,918; receipts, 992m. pesetas; expenses, 1,707m. pesetas.

The 'Compañía Nacional de Telegrafía sin Hilos' holds the government con- cession for the public service with ships, and between the Peninsula and the Canary Islands, and the international service with England, Italy, France, Switzerland and America, as well as various special press services. The National Radio Service 'Redera' operates a broadcasting station at Arganda, 15 miles from Madrid.

The overseas radio telegraph circuits are operated in Spain mainly by Trans- radio Española, SA. Under an agreement with Cable and Wireless, Ltd, London, Transradio Española lease and operate the Bilbao end of the Bilbao–Great Britain cable and the Barcelona end of the Barcelona–Marseilles cable.

In 1968 there were 292 radio stations and 3 television stations.

BANKING. On 1 Jan. 1922 the Bank of Spain came under the Bank Ordinance Law, according to which the Government participate in its net profits.

In 1963 the Banco Central set up the Banco de Fomento (capital, 225m. pesetas) for long-term financing; the new bank is to absorb the Banco Central's investment company (Hispana de Inversiones), after which its capital is to be increased by 75m.

On 30 Dec. 1967 the gold holdings of the Bank of Spain amounted to 4,701·6m. pesetas (paper). A decree of 11 July 1941 established the voluntary nationalization of foreign banks in Spain, and the transference and amalgamation of the business of national banks.

Gold reserves at 30 Dec. 1967 consisted of: Revalued gold of Bank of Spain, 3,185·2m. pesetas (paper); authorized gold acquisition, 180·8m. pesetas; treasury gold, 1,335·5m. pesetas (paper); current accounts of institute of foreign exchange, 62,422m. pesetas; gold in current accounts, 16,455m. pesetas.

Savings bank deposits (Popular Savings Banks) in Spain, 31 Dec. 1967, amounted to 251,849m. pesetas. Post office savings banks opened on 12 March

1916. Deposits, 31 Dec. 1967, amounted to 23,574m. pesetas; private banks saving deposits, 311,486m. pesetas.

By a decree of 20 Nov. 1941 the post office savings bank opens an account with an initial entry of 1 peseta for every Spanish child born.

WEIGHTS AND MEASURES. On 1 Jan. 1859 the metric system of weights and measures was introduced, but the old weights and measures are still largely used. They are: The *quintal* = 220·4 lb. avoirdupois; the *libra* = 1·014 lb. avoirdupois; the *arroba*, for wine = 3½ Imperial gallons; for oil = 2¾ Imperial gallons; the *square vara* = 1·09 vara = 1 yard; the *fanega* = 1½ Imperial bushels.

DIPLOMATIC REPRESENTATIVES

Spain maintains embassies in:

Algeria	Jordan
Argentina	Lebanon (also for Kuwait)
Austria	Liberia (also for Ivory Coast, Niger,
Belgium (also for Luxembourg)	Sierra Leone, Upper Volta)
Bolivia	Libya
Brazil	Mauritania (also for Mali)
Cambodia	Morocco
Cameroun (also for Central Afr. Rep.)	Netherlands
Canada	Nicaragua
Chile	Nigeria (also for Dahomey, Toga)
Colombia	Norway (also legation for Iceland)
Congo (K.)	Pakistan
Costa Rica	Panama
Cuba	Paraguay
Denmark	Peru
Dominican Republic	Philippines
Ecuador	Portugal
El Salvador	Senegal (also for Gambia, Guinea)
Ethopia (also for Madagascar)	South Africa, Republic of
Finland	Sweden
France	Switzerland
Gabon	Syria
Germany (West)	Taiwan
Greece	Thailand (also for Vietnam)
Guatemala	Tunisia
Haiti	Turkey (also legation for Afghánistán)
Honduras	UAR (also legation for Sudan)
India (also for Ceylon)	UK
Iran	USA
Iraq	Uruguay
Irish Republic	Vatican
Italy	Venezuela
Japan (also for Korea, South)	

OF SPAIN IN GREAT BRITAIN (24 Belgrave Sq., SW1)

Ambassador: The Marqués de Santa Cruz (accredited 8 May 1958).

Ministers: The Marqués de Espinardo; Ernesto Barnach-Calbo; Luis Villalba. *Minister-Counsellor:* Manuel G. Acebo. *Service Attachés:* Lieut.-Col. Juan Cano Hevia (*Army*), Capt. Salvador Moreno (*Navy*), Lieut.-Col. Enrique Tapias (*Air*). *Counsellors:* The Conde de Campo Rey (*Consuler*); The Marqués de los Arcos; Francisco José Mayans (*Information*). *First Secretaries:* Juan Lugo-Roigi; Gil Armangne; Miguel Angel Garcia-Mina; Antonio de Oyarzabal; Fernando Schwartz y Giren.

There are consuls at Liverpool and Southampton, and consular agents in 21 towns.

OF GREAT BRITAIN IN SPAIN
Ambassador: Sir John Russell, GCVO, CMG.
Minister: T. W. Keeble. *Counsellors:* M. H. M. Reid (*Commercial*); *First Secretaries:* Lord N. Gordon Lennox, MVO (*Head of Chancery*); A. W. D. Eves (*Commercial*); K. G. MacInnes (*Information*); J. R. Curtis; J. R. C. McGlashan; Miss A. M. Wood (*Consul*).
Service Attachés: Brig. W. Hine-Haycock (*Defence and Army*), Wing Cdr J. A. G. Slesser (*Air*), Cdr J. F. Webb, DSC (*Navy*).
Cultural Attaché: N. N. Tett, OBE.

There are consular representatives at Algeciras, Barcelona, Bilbao, Cádiz, Cartagena, Granada, Jérez de la Frontera, La Coruña, La Línea, Málaga, Palma, San Sebastian, Seville, Valencia, Vigo and Santa Cruz (Tenerife).

OF SPAIN IN THE USA (2700–15th St. NW, Washington, D.C., 20009)
Ambassador: Jaime Arguelles.
Minister-Counsellor: Aurelio Valls. *Ministers:* The Conde de San Román (*Economic*); Antonio Gill-Casares. *Counsellors:* The Visconde de Priego; Pedro Ortiz Armengol; José A. Lopez de Letona (*Information*); Joaquin Gutierrez Cano (*Financial*).
First Secretaries: Carlos Fernandez Espeso; Felipe de la Morena y Calvet; Tomás Chávarri y del Rivero; Jaime de Ojeda. *Service Attachés:* Lieut.-Col. Jesús Ruiz Molina (*Military*), Col. Juan José Sanchez Cabal (*Air*), Capt. Teodoro de Leste (*Navy*).

OF THE USA IN SPAIN
Ambassador: Robert C. Hill.
Deputy Chief of Mission: Joseph J. Montllor. *Heads of Sections:* Philip Axelrod (*Political*); Frank D. Taylor (*Economic*); Wayland B. Waters (*Commercial*); Daniel W. Montenegro (*Labour*); Margaret Hussman (*Consular*); Arch K. Jean (*Administrative*).
Service Attachés: Col. Cecil K. Charbonneau (*Army*), Cdr Willard C. Doe (*Navy*), Col. Edward J. Fox (*Air*).

There are consuls-general at Barcelona and Seville, and consuls at Bilbao and Valencia.

BOOKS OF REFERENCE

STATISTICAL INFORMATION. The Instituto Nacional de Estadistica (Ferraz 41, Madrid) combines the administrative work of a government department attached to the Presidency of the Government with a centre of statistical studies. *Director-General:* Alberto Cerrolaza Asenjo. Its publications include: *Anuario Estadístico de España.* Annual (latest vol., 1966). *Edición manual* (latest vol., 1967).—*Reseñas estadísticos provinciales.*—*Nomenclator de las ciudades, villas lugares, aldeas, y demás entidades de población de España.* 6 vols. Madrid, 1963.—*Censo de Población de España.* Madrid, 1960.—*Diccionario Corográfico de España.* 4 vols. Madrid, 1948.—*Boletín de Estadística.* Madrid. (No. 1, Jan.–March 1939; monthly from 1948).—*Estadística española.* *Revista trimestral* (from 1959)

Aguilar (ed.), *Nuevo Atlas de España.* Madrid, 1961
Altamira y Crevea, R., *A History of Spain.* New York and London, 1950
Anuario del Mercado Español. Madrid, 1965
Enciclopedia Universal Ilustrada. 70 vols., 10 appendices, 10 supplements. Madrid
Garcia Venero, M., *Historia del Nacionalismo Vasco, 1793–1936.* Madrid, 1945
Hills, G., *Franco: the man and his nation.* London, 1967
Lafuente, M., and Valera, J., *Historia General de España.* New ed. 25 vols. Barcelona, 1925
López Oliván, J., *Repertorio Diplomático Español.* [*Collection of treaties, 1125–1935.*] Madrid, 1944
Madariaga, S. de, *Spain.* London, 1942
Peers, E. A. (ed.), *Spain: a companion to Spanish studies.* 5th ed. London, 1956
Vicens Vives, J., *Historia económica de España.* 5 vols. Barcelona, 1959

NATIONAL LIBRARY. Biblioteca Nacional, Madrid. *Director:* Cesareo Goicoechea.

PROVINCE IN AFRICA

In Jan. 1958 the territory of 'Spanish West Africa' was divided into the provinces of Ifni and Spanish Sahara; both were under the jurisdiction of the commanding officer of the Canary Islands. The former colony of *Equatorial Guinea* became the independent Republic of Equatorial Guinea on 12 Oct. 1968 and the province of Ifni was returned to Morocco on 30 June 1969.

Trade of the Spanish territories with UK (British Board of Trade returns in £1,000 sterling):

	Imports to UK			Exports from UK		
	1968	1969	1970	1968	1969	1970
Canary Islands	18,148	16,225	18,034	16,297	15,715	19,526
North Africa	9	4	—	315	500	498

The establishment of new foreign enterprises of any kind in the territories of Spanish West Africa has been prohibited by a presidential order of 27 Nov. 1950. Foreign enterprises already established may continue their activities, but without extending the scope or increasing the capital. Foreign oil companies, however, have been authorized to prospect in the province of Sahara; no oil had been struck by the end of 1968 and oil prospecting has been discontinued.

The **Province of Spanish Sahara** consists of 2 districts: Sekia El Hamra (82,000 sq. km) and Rio de Oro (184,000 sq. km). Area 266,000 sq. km (102,680 sq. miles). The population consists of some 10,000 Spanish civilians, about 15,000 Spanish soldiers and perhaps 30,000–50,000 nomadic Saharans. The capital is El Aaiún (population, 4,000–5,000). The strip between 27° 40′ N. and Wad Draa was ceded by Spain to Morocco on 10 April 1958. Strong pressure was brought, in 1970, by Morocco, Mauritania and Algeria for a referendum to be conducted by Spain in the province.

In 1968 there were 73 primary schools with 2,446 pupils and 2 secondary schools with 776 pupils.

Rich phosphate deposits were discovered in 1963 and port facilities were inaugurated in 1967 at Villa Cisneros and Playa de El Aaiún (20 km from the capital).

Internal revenue is negligible; expenditure, 1969, 250m. pesetas. Imports, 1968, 210·35m. pesetas; exports are negligible.

Governor-General: Gen. José María Pérez de Lema y Tejero.

BOOKS OF REFERENCE

Atlas Histórico y Geográfico de África Española. Madrid, 1955
Resumén estadístico del África aspañola, 1965–66. Madrid, 1967
Caro Baroja, J., *Estudios saharianos.* Madrid, 1955
Hernández-Pacheco, E., and others, *El Sahara español.* Madrid, 1949
Pélissier, R., *Les Territoires espagnols d'Afrique.* Paris, 1963.—*Los territorios españoles de Africa.* Madrid, 1964
Rumeu de Armas, A., *España en el Africa Atlántica.* 2 vols. Madrid, 1956–57

THE DEMOCRATIC REPUBLIC OF THE SUDAN

Jamhuryat es-Sudan Al Democratia

CONSTITUTION AND GOVERNMENT. The Sudan was proclaimed a sovereign independent republic on 1 Jan. 1956. On 19 Dec. 1955 the Sudanese parliament passed unanimously a declaration that a fully independent state should be set up forthwith, and that a Council of State of 5 should temporarily assume the duties of Head of State. The Co-domini, the UK and Egypt, gave their assent on 31 Dec. 1955.

For the history of the Condominium and the steps leading to independence, see THE STATESMAN'S YEAR-BOOK, 1955, pp. 340–41.

National flag: Black, white, red (horizontal) with green triangle at the masthead.

On 17 Nov. 1958 the Army took over the government. The Council of State and the cabinet were dismissed, parliament and all political parties were declared dissolved, and the provisional constitution was suspended. The supreme authority was vested in the Supreme Council of the Armed Forces under Lieut.-Gen. Ibrahim Abboud.

On 25 Oct. 1964 President Abboud dissolved the Supreme Council and dismissed the Cabinet. On 30 Oct. President Abboud appointed a civilian Cabinet with Ser al-Khatm Khalifa as Prime Minister.

On 15 Nov. 1964 President Abboud resigned as chief of state and supreme commander. In conformity with the provisional constitution of 1956 a 5-member Council of Sovereignty replaced the presidency.

On 8 July 1965 the Constituent Assembly elected Ismail El-Azhari as President of the Supreme Council. Following a crisis in the coalition Cabinet the Prime Minister, Mohammed Ahmed Mahgoub resigned on 23 April 1969. The Government was taken over by a 10-man Revolutionary Council on 25 May 1969 under the Chairmanship of Col. Jaafar M. al Nemery.

Prime Minister: Babikr Awadalla.
Deputy Prime Minister and Minister of Justice: Sayed Babiker Awadalla.
Foreign Affairs: Sayed Farouk Abu Eisa.

On 9 Dec. 1965 the Constituent Assembly proscribed the Communist Party.

LOCAL GOVERNMENT. The Sudan is divided into 9 provinces and 84 local government areas. In each province there is a province administration set up under the Provincial Administration Act, 1960, and in each local government area there is a local government authority set up under the Local Government Act, 1951.

A Province Administration is composed of the commissioner, the province council and the province authority. The commissioner is the chairman of the province authority and the head of all government officials in the province. The province council, warranted by the Council of Ministers, may be composed of ex-officio members, members elected by and from local government authority panels and members appointed by the Government. A province council has competence to pass the province budget and has supervisory powers over local government authorities. The province authority is composed of the head representatives of the various central government ministries in the province. Its main functions is the execution of the province council decisions. A local government authority is either a local government council warranted by the Council of Ministers (59 areas) or a government official (25 areas). A local government council is two-thirds elected by residents in the area and one-third appointed by the Minister.

AREA AND POPULATION. The Sudan covers an area of 967,500 sq. miles (2·5m. sq. km). The Eritrea–Sudan frontier and the frontier with the Chad and Central African Republics have been delimited and demarcated, as also has the greater part of the frontier with Ethiopia.

The population according to the 1955–56 census was 10,262,674. The estimate for 1968 was 14·77m.

The population consists mainly (two-thirds to four-fifths) of Moslem Arabs, and Nubians in the north and Nilotic and Negro tribes in the south.

Area (in sq. miles) and population of provinces (Jan. 1961 estimate), with inhabitants of provincial capitals (Jan. 1964 estimate) were as follows:

Province	Area	Population	Capital	Inhabitants
Bahr El Ghazal	82,530	1,157,016	Wau	11,000
Blue Nile	54,880	2,397,528	Wad Medani	57,000
Darfur	191,650	1,538,712	El Fasher	30,000
Equatoria	76,495	1,049,664	Juba	15,000
Kassala	131,528	1,097,376	Kassala	49,000
Khartoum	8,097	584,472	Khartoum	135,000
Kordofan	146,930	2,051,616	El Obeid	60,000
Northern	184,200	1,013,880	El Dammer	7,000
Upper Nile	91,190	1,037,736	Malakal	11,000

The capital is Khartoum. Other important cities are: Omdurman (154,000), Khartoum North (53,000), Port Sudan (57,000), Atbara (45,000), Kosti (30,000).

RELIGION. The population of the 6 northern provinces is almost entirely Moslem (Sunni), the majority of the 3 southern provinces is pagan. There are small Christian communities, with 2 Coptic Bishops, a Greek Orthodox metropolitan, an Anglican bishop and assistant bishop, 4 Roman Catholic bishops and Greek Evangelical, Evangelical and Maronite congregations. In 1962 Protestants numbered about 95,000. Some of the foreign missionaries were expelled from the southern provinces in March 1964.

EDUCATION (1964–65). Private kindergartens had 2,210 pupils; government elementary schools, 315,189 boys and 151,684 girls; private elementary schools, 6,025 boys and 5,475 girls; government intermediate schools, 34,304 boys and 6,777 girls; private intermediate schools, 20,917 boys and 6,366 girls; government secondary schools, 13,506 boys and 2,449 girls; private secondary schools, 7,640 boys and 1,577 girls. Higher technical training was given to 839 boys and 68 girls, higher vocational training to 230 boys; teachers' training colleges had 1,733 male and 577 female students. Khartoum University had over 5,098 students in 1969–70.

HEALTH. In 1970 the Ministry of Health maintains 93 hospitals, 1,766 dispensaries and dressing stations, 73 health centres (with together 12,085 beds) and 1,108 doctors.

JUSTICE. The judiciary is a separate and independent department of state directly and solely responsible to the Supreme Council of State. The general administrative supervision and control of the judiciary is vested in the Chief Justice.

Civil Justice is administered by the courts constituted under the Civil Justice Ordinance, namely the High Court of Justice—consisting of the Court of Appeal and Judges of the High Court, sitting as courts of original jurisdiction—and Province Courts—consisting of the Courts of Province and District Judges. The law administered is 'justice, equity and good conscience' in all cases where there is no special enactment. Procedure is governed by the Civil Justice Ordinance.

Justice in personal matters for the Moslem population is administered by the Mohammedan law courts, which form the Sharia Divisions of the Court of Appeal, High Courts and Kadis Courts; President of the Sharia Division is the Grand Kadi. The religious law of Islam is administered by these courts in the matters of inheritance, marriage, divorce, family relationship and charitable trusts.

Criminal Justice is administered by the courts constituted under the Code of Criminal Procedure, namely Major Courts, Minor Courts and Magistrates' Courts. Serious crimes are tried by Major Courts, which are composed of a President and 2 members and have the power to pass the death sentence. Major Courts are, as a rule, presided over by a Judge of the High Court appointed to a Provincial Circuit or a Province Judge. There is a right of appeal to the Chief Justice against any decision or order of a Major Court, and all its findings and sentences are subject to confirmation by him.

The President of the Supreme Council of the Armed Forces has power to commute a capital sentence. The Chief Justice has power to remit any case subject to confirmation by him to the Court of Criminal Appeal composed of the Chief Justice and 2 Magistrates of the first class, one of whom has to be a Judge of the High Court.

Lesser crimes are tried by Minor Courts consisting of 3 Magistrates and presided over by a Second Class Magistrate, and by Magistrates' Courts consisting of a single Magistrate or a bench of lay magistrates. In Provinces in which circuits of the High Court exist the High Court Judge, in other cases the Province Judge, exercises an appellate jurisdiction and a general supervision over these courts. The greater part of the criminal law is codified in the Sudan Penal Code.

Local Courts, constituted under the Native Courts Ordinance, 1932, and the Chiefs Courts Ordinance, 1931, administer civil and criminal justice in accordance with the native custom and deal with offences against specific ordinances; they work to some extent parallel with the state courts. Appeals lie to members of the state judiciary and *ex-officio* magistrates, and local courts are subject to supervision by them.

Juvenile Offences are dealt with by the 2 juvenile delinquent courts, constituted under the Code of Criminal Procedure, at Wad Medani and Omdurman.

All legislative enactments, ordinances and regulations (previously printed in 4 vols.) have been reprinted (in 11 vols.) in English. A committee is undertaking its translation into Arabic.

FINANCE. Currency. The monetary unit is the Sudanese pound (£S) divided into 100 piastres and 1,000 milliemes. Sudanese bank-notes of £S10, £S5, £S1, 50 and 25 piastres and Sudanese coins of P. 10, 5, 2; m/ms 10, 5, 2, 1 are in circulation. Currency in circulation at 29 Feb. 1968 totalled £S44·5m.

Budget. Revenue and expenditure in Sudanese pounds for financial years ending 30 June:

	1966–67	1967–68[1]	1968–69[1]	1969–70[1]	1970–71[1]
Revenue	87,867,961	91,866,077	113,500,000	142,000,000	158,000,000
Expenditure	83,267,506	85,659,317	100,000,000	..	113,000,000

[1] Estimates.

The chief sources of revenue in 1965–66 were indirect taxation from custom duties on imports and royalties on exports (£S34,680,440) and profits on trading concerns, railways, shares on cotton schemes (£S15,114,270). The main items of expenditure were education (£S6,462,830), public works (£S3,883,666), health (£S4,833,160), communications (£S6,469,786), agriculture (£S4,195,376) and defence (£S14,129,602).

The total external debt of the country at the end of 1964 was £S44,751,000.

DEFENCE. The Army is organized in 13 infantry battalions, 1 armoured regiment and 2 artillery regiments. The equipment used to be British, but is being replaced by German guns, rifles and cars. Total strength, 26,500.

A Navy was established in 1962 with a nucleus of 4 patrol boats built in Yugoslavia. Since then 2 more patrol boats, 2 landing craft, an oiler, a water carrier and a survey ship have been acquired from Yugoslavia.

The Air Force is being built up with Soviet assistance. About 16 MiG-21 supersonic fighters are reported to have been delivered in 1970, as initial equipment for 2 combat squadrons, with small numbers of An-12 and An-24 turboprop transports. Earlier equipment in service includes about 13 armed Jet Provost trainers, 3 piston-engined Provost trainers, 2 C-47s, 3 Pembroke light transports, 3 Fokker Troopship transports and 8 Swiss-built Turbo-Porter light STOL transports.

PLANNING. The 10-year plan 1961/62–1970/71 envisaged a total expenditure on social and economic development of £S287·3m. A draft 5-year plan for 1970–75 is under discussion and envisages government expenditure of £S200m. and investment by the private sector of £S170m.

AGRICULTURE. In the Sudan, a predominantly agricultural country, cotton is by far the most important cash crop on which the Sudan depends for earning foreign currency. The two types of cotton grown in the Sudan are: (a) long staple sakellaridis and sakel types (derivatives of sakellaridis), grown in Gezira, White Nile, Abdel Magid and private pump schemes; (b) short staple, mainly American types, in Equatoria and Nuba Mountains, generally by rain cultivation. Total production of all types in 1964–65 was 797,205 bales.

Cotton production	Area (in feddâns)			Crop (in kantars)[1]		
	1962–63	*1963–64*	*1964–65*	*1962–63*	*1963–64*	*1964–65*
(a) *Egyptian Types*						
Sudan Gezira Board	483,701	508,478	508,228	1,862,776	1,163,987	1,798,318
Abdel Magid (WNSB)	10,040	10,040	12,282	26,368	21,385	33,101
White Nile Scheme Board	10,074	11,020	14,005	42,538	42,096	65,569
Private Scheme and Sagias	208,088	200,399	211,833	987,605	655,920	832,231
Gash Delta	21,204	4,943	586	10,058	2,202	—
Melut Scheme	—	2,860	2,695	—	4,947	4,249
(b) *American Types*						
American, irrigated (pumps)	8,098	7,649	7,753	29,504	26,147	29,424
American (flood)	8,822	17,832	84,511	9,855	13,515	114,834
American, rain grown	315,905	286,220	225,679	394,923	260,763	248,402
Total	1,065,932	1,049,441	1,067,572	3,363,627	2,190,962	3,125,928

[1] Of 315 rotls seed cotton.

Other products of the Sudan include groundnuts, sesame, dates, hides and skins, melonseeds, oil-cakes, dura, pulses, seed oil, castor seed, camels, cattle and sheep.

The Rural Water Supplies and Soil Conservation Board, set up in Oct. 1944, was in May 1956 replaced by the Land Use and Rural Water Development Board and an executive department.

Livestock (1970): Cattle, 12·3m.; sheep, 10·3m.; goats, 7·2m.

FORESTRY. The forests of the Sudan, their extent and dominant species are approximately as follows: (1) desert, 728,800 sq. km; (2) semi-desert, 491,000 sq. km (*Acacia Tortilis, Maerua crassifolia*); (3) woodland savannah: (a) low rain, 691,000 sq. km (*Acacia melifera, Acacia seyal, Acacia senegal, cambretum*), (b) high rain, 347,000 sq. km (*Anogeissus, Khaya, Isoberlinia*); (4) flood region, 246,000 sq. km (*Papyrus*); (5) montane vegetation, 6,000 sq. km (*Podocarpus, Olea*).

The types 2 and 3 (a) are the only local sources of fuel (firewood and charcoal). More than 20m. cu. metres of firewood are consumed annually.

The average annual production of sawn timber is 1m. cu. ft, which constitutes about 50% of the Sudan requirements of sawn timber and includes all the sleeper requirements of Sudan Railways and the Sudan Gezira Board. Different tree species of softwood are used for afforestation to produce the future demand of the Sudan of softwood. In 1962 nearly 13,000 acres were afforested.

Gum arabic, mainly hashab gum from *Acacia senegal*, is the sole forest produce exported from the Sudan on a major scale. About 50,000 tons (95% of the total world supply) are exported annually, fetching about £S6m. It ranks as the second cash crop to cotton. The bulk of gum production originates from Kordofan, Darfur, Kassala and Blue Nile Provinces.

A forest research and education institute has been established by the Sudan Government in co-operation with the United Nations Special Fund.

MINING. The following minerals are known to exist in the Sudan: gold, graphite, sulphur, chromite (20,500 metric tons in 1965), iron-ore, manganese-ore, copper-ore, zinc-ore, fluorspar, natron, gypsum and anhydrite, magnesite, asbestos, talc, halite, kaolin, white mica, coal, diatomite (kiesel guhr), limestone and dolomite, pumice, lead-ore, wollastonite, black sands, vermiculite pyrites.

Gold is being exploited on a small scale at Deweishat (south of Wadi Halfa) and at Birkateib (in Kassala Province); alluvial gold is occasionally exploited in Southern Fung and Equatoria. Total gold production in 1963, 900 troy oz.

Iron-ore has been smelted in the past, on a very limited scale and by primitive methods, in the Eastern and Southern Provinces. Iron-ore mining in the northern Red Sea hills started in 1965, and some 30,000 tons were exported to Europe in the first year.

Copper at Hofrat en Nahas was mined in the 19th century; the mine has been leased to foreign interests for exploitation. A few thousand tons of medium-grade manganese-ore have been shipped annually since 1956. Mining and processing of white mica, as an industry, is beginning to be established. Vermiculites, mined near Sinkat in Kassala Province, is beginning to find its way into foreign markets. Salt pans at Port Sudan supply the whole needs of the country, and considerable quantities of salt are exported annually; output, 1962, 57,870 metric tons. Mining of chromite from the Ingessena Hills, southern Blue Nile Province, commenced in 1962. Quartz and marble for glass and tile manufacture is being quarried in the Red Sea Hills. Marble is quarried for cement manufacture in Atbara (Northern Province) and Rabak on the White Nile.

An asbestos deposit in Qala El Nahal in Kassala province is being examined by a foreign concern.

COMMERCE. Total trade for calendar years, in £S:

	1965	1966	1967	1968	1969
Imports[1]	72,288,651	77,456,697	74,329,149	89,709,233	92,475,767
Exports	67,138,552	69,782,135	74,058,873	80,834,368	85,624,389
Re-exports	817,682	947,016	550,422	315,144	572,118

[1] Including government imports.

Principal items of imports and exports in 1969 (quantities in metric tons, value in £S1,000):

	Quantity	Values
Imports:		
Cotton fabrics	11,424	9,462
Sugar	80,184	2,898
Motor fuel	105,880	1,454
Motor vehicles (number)	4,229	8,586
Piece-goods, art, textiles	3,487	1,892
Tea	10,009	2,101
Wheat flour	50,688	1,125
Timber (cu. metres)	...	...
Coffee	3,892	453
Cigarettes and tobacco	543	980
Machinery		11,582
Fertilizers	68,209	1,588
Exports:		
Cotton, ginned	171,990	49,448
Gum arabic	48,781	8,668
Sesame	112,602	8,017
Groundnuts	82,141	5,990
Dura	1,780	43
Cottonseed	65,067	1,489
Animal feeding stuff	206,599	4,180
Vegetable oils (not processed)	13,510	949

Principal sources of import into the Sudan in 1967 (in £S1m.): UK (22), India (10·6), US (8·7). Principal countries of export from the Sudan: Italy (11·8), India (9·1), Germany (11·8).

Trade with UK (in £1,000 sterling), British Board of Trade returns:

	1966	1967	1968	1969	1970
Imports to UK	4,918	6,552	7,538	7,310	7,624
Exports from UK	16,312	17,373	19,230	21,558	18,181
Re-exports from UK	114	211	96	191	

RAILWAYS. The main railway lines run from Khartoum to El Obeid *via* Wad Medani, Sennar Junction, Kosti and El Rahad (701 km); El Rahad to Nyala *via* Abu Zabad, Babanousa and Ed-Daein (698 km); Sennar Junction to Kassala *via* Gedaref (455 km) and to Roseires *via* Singa (220 km); Kassala to Port Sudan *via* Haiya Junction and Sinkat (550 km); Khartoum to Wadi Halfa *via* Shendi, El Dammer, Atbara, Berber and Abu Hamad Junction (924 km); Abu Hamad to Karima (248 km); Atbara to Haiya Junction (271 km); Babanousa to Wau (444 km). The main flow of exports and imports is to and from Port Sudan *via* Atbara and Kassala. The total length of line open for traffic was 4,752 km as at 31 July 1969. The gauge is 3 ft. 6 in.

SHIPPING. Supplementing the railways are regular river steamer services of the Sudan Railways, between Karima and Dongola, 319 km; from Khartoum to Kosti, 319 km; from Kosti to Juba, 1,436 km, and from Kosti to Gambeila, 1,069 km. Port Sudan is the country's only seaport; it is equipped with 13 berths.

ROADS. Roads in Northern Sudan, other than town roads, are only cleared tracks mostly impassable directly after rain. In Upper Nile Province motor traffic is limited mostly to the months Jan.–May. In Equatoria and Bahr El Ghazal Provinces there are a number of good gravelled roads with permanent bridges which can be used all the year round, though minor roads become impassable after rain.

Notes on Motoring in the Sudan is obtainable from the Under Secretary, Ministry of Interior, Khartoum, or the Sudan Embassy in London, to whom application should be made for permission to motor through the Sudan.

AVIATION. Sudan Airways is a government-owned airline, with its headquarters in Khartoum, operating domestic and international services. The latter include services to Asmara, Addis Ababa, Aden, Jiddah, Cairo, Athens, Rome, Frankfurt, London, Beirut, Nairobi and Entebbe. In 1964 Sudan Airways carried 104,824 passengers and 1,541,857 kg of mail and freight.

POST AND TELECOMMUNICATIONS (1965). There are 129 permanent post and telegraph offices, 23 travelling post and telegraph offices, 1 branch office and 167 agencies. There are 27 wireless telegraph and 99 radio-telephone stations, 130 telephone exchanges (36 of them automatic) and 340 telephone call boxes; number of telephones in 1969 was 44,508 (27,469 in Khartoum). There are 2 transmitting stations and 10 radio-beacon stations.

BANKING. The Bank of Sudan opened in Feb. 1960 with an authorized capital of £S1·5m. as the central bank of the country; it has the sole right to issue currency. Its foreign reserves stood at £S23·4m. as at 29 Feb. 1968. All foreign banks were nationalized in 1970.

The post office savings bank had 114,902 depositors each with an average balance of £S56 as at Dec. 1963.

DIPLOMATIC REPRESENTATIVES

The Sudan maintains embassies in:

Algeria
Belgium
Chad (also for Central African Republic)
Congo (K.) (also for Congo (Br.) and Gabon
Ethiopia
France (also for Netherlands, Spain and Switzerland)
Germany (East)
Greece
Ghana (also for Liberia, Mali, Guinea, Senegal, Sierra Leone and Upper Volta)
India (also for Ceylon)
Iraq (also for Turkey and Jordan)
Italy (also for Albania and Austria)

Kenya
Kuwait
Lebanon (also for Syria)
Nigeria (also for Dahomey, Cameroun and Niger)
Pakistan (also for China)
Saudi Arabia (also for Yemen)
Somalia
Tanzania
Uganda
USSR (also for Czechoslovakia, Bulgaria, Hungary, Poland and Romania)
UAR (also for Libya, Morocco and Tunisia)
UK
Yugoslavia (also for Cyprus)

Diplomatic relations with the USA were broken off on 7 June 1967.

Ambassador in London: Sayed Abidin Ismail (accredited 24 March 1970)
Ambassador in Khartoum: R. G. A. Etherington-Smith, CMG.

BOOKS OF REFERENCE

Sudan Almanac. Khartoum (annual)
Trade Directory of the Republic of the Sudan; with Who's Who in the Sudan. 8th ed. London, 1966
Barbour, K. M., *The Republic of the Sudan.* London, 1967
Duncan, J. S. B., *The Sudan's Path to Independence.* London, 1957
Fabunni, L. A., *The Sudan in Anglo-Egyptian Relations.* London and New York, 1960
Fawzi, Saad Ed-Din, *The Labour Movement in the Sudan, 1946–55.* R. Inst. of Int. Affairs, 1957
Gaitskell, A., *Gezira.* London, 1959
Henderson, K. D. D., *The Sudan Republic.* London, 1965
Hill, R., *Sudan transport: a history of railway, marine and river services.* OUP, 1965
Holt, P. M., *A modern history of the Sudan.* New York, 1961
Jackson, H. C., *Behind the Modern Sudan.* London, 1956
Lebon, J. H. G., *Land use in Sudan.* Bude, 1965
Macmichael, Sir H. A., *The Anglo-Egyptian Sudan.* London, 1954
Said, Beshir M., *The Sudan.* London, 1965
Tothill, J. D., *Agriculture in the Sudan.* OUP, 1952
Trimingham, J. S., *Islam in the Sudan.* London, 1949

SWEDEN
Konungariket Sverige

REIGNING KING. **Gustaf VI Adolf,** born 11 Nov. 1882, succeeded on the death of his father, King Gustaf V, 29 Oct. 1950. Married: (1) 15 June 1905 to Princess Margaret Victoria, born 15 Jan. 1882, died 1 May 1920, daughter of Prince Arthur, Duke of Connaught; (2) 3 Nov. 1923, to Lady Louise Mountbatten, born 13 July 1889, daughter of Prince Louis of Battenberg, afterwards 1st Marquess of Milford Haven, died 7 March 1965.

Children of the King. (1) Prince Gustaf Adolf, born 22 April 1906, died 26 Jan. 1947; married, 20 Oct. 1932, to Princess Sibylla, born 18 Jan. 1908, daughter of Duke Karl Eduard of Saxe-Coburg-Gotha; issue: Princess Margaretha, born 31 Oct. 1934, married 30 June 1964 to Mr John Ambler; Princess Birgitta, born 19 Jan. 1937, married 25 May 1961 (civil marriage) and 30 May 1961 (religious ceremony) to Johann Georg, Prince of Hohenzollern; Princess Désirée, born 2 June 1938, married 5 June 1964 to Baron Niclas Silfverschiöld; Princess Christina, born 3 Aug. 1943; Prince Carl Gustaf, Duke of Jämtland, *heir apparent,* born 30 April 1946; (2) Princess Ingrid, born 28 March 1910; married 24 May 1935, to Frederik, Crown Prince of Denmark (King Frederik IX); (3) Prince Bertil, Duke of Halland, born 28 Feb. 1912.

The royal family of Sweden have a civil list of 3·4m. kronor; this does not include the maintenance of the royal palaces.

The following is a list of the kings and queens of Sweden, with the dates of their accession from the accession of the House of Vasa:

House of Vasa		*House of Pfalz-Zwei-brücken* (contd.)		*House of Bernadotte*	
Gustaf I	1523	Carl XII	1697	Carl XIV Johan	1818
Eric XIV	1560	Ulrica Eleonora	1718	Oscar I	1844
Johan III	1568			Carl XV	1859
Sigismund	1592	*House of Hesse*		Oscar II	1872
Carl IX	1600	Fredrik I	1720	Gustaf V	1907
Gustaf II Adolf	1611			Gustaf VI Adolf	1950
Christina	1632				
		House of Holstein-Gottorp			
House of Pfalz-Zwei-brücken		Adolf Fredrik	1751		
		Gustaf III	1771		
Carl X Gustaf	1654	Gustaf IV Adolf	1792		
Carl XI	1660	Carl XIII	1809		

CONSTITUTION AND GOVERNMENT. The fundamental laws of the kingdom are: 1, the Constitution (*Regeringsformen*) of 6 June 1809 (modified in 1969); 2, the Parliament Act (*Riksdagsordningen*) of 22 June 1866 (modified in 1909, 1921, 1949 and 1969; 3, the law of Royal Succession of 26 Sept. 1810, and 4, the law on the Freedom of the Press of 5 April 1949 (replacing the Press Act of 1812). The King must be a member of the Lutheran Church.

Parliamentary government was finally established in 1917. Beginning 1971, the Diet (*Riksdag*) consists of one chamber. (A two-chamber Diet worked until the end of 1970.) The new unicameral Diet consists of 350 members directly elected by universal suffrage, for a period of 3 years. Every man and woman over 19 years of age and not under wardship have the right to vote and to stand for election.

The manner of election to the Diet is proportional. The country is divided into 28 constituencies. In these constituencies 310 members are elected. The remaining 40 seats constitute a nation-wide pool intended to give absolute proportionality to parties that receive at least 4% of the votes. A party receiving less than 4% of the votes in the country is, however, entitled to participate in the distribution of seats in a constituency, if it has obtained at least 12% of the votes cast there.

A state subsidy is given to all political parties which have obtained at least one seat in the Diet at the last election. The subvention (24·5m. kr. in 1970–71) is distributed in the ratio of 70,000 kr. per seat. Furthermore a municipal subsidy may be decided by the commune councils and the county councils. The subsidy is distributed in a fixed ratio per seat in the council.

The Diet, elected 20 Sept. 1970, has 163 Social Democrats, 58 Liberals, 41 Conservatives, 71 Centre Party and 17 Communists.

The executive power is in the hands of the King, who acts on the advice of a Council of State, the head of which is the Prime Minister.

The Social Democrat Cabinet, appointed on 14 Oct. 1969, was composed as follows in Oct. 1970.

Prime Minister: Olof Palme.

Foreign Affairs: Torsten Nilsson. *Justice:* Lennart Geijer. *Defence:* Sven Andersson. *Social Affairs:* Sven Aspling. *Communications:* Bengt Norling. *Finance:* Gunnar Sträng. *Education:* Ingvar Carlsson. *Agriculture:* Ingemund Bengtsson. *Commerce:* Kjell Olof Feldt. *Industry:* Krister Wickman. *Interior and Health:* Eric Holmqvist. *Civil Service:* Svante Lundkvist. *Without Portfolio:* Sven-Eric Nilsson, Mrs Alva Myrdal, Mrs Camilla Odhnoff, Sven Moberg, Bertil Löfberg, Carl Lidbom.

All the members of the Council of State are reponsible for the acts of the Government.

Public administration in Sweden is characterized by a unique degree of functional decentralization. The Ministries are not really administrative agencies. They prepare bills for the *Riksdag*, issue general directives and make higher appointments, but, as a rule, do not take individual administrative decisions. The routine administrative work is attended to by the central boards (*centrala ämbetsverk*). Each board's sphere of activity depends partly on its organization which is decided by the appropriations granted by the Riksdag. The King-in-Council often asks the boards' opinion on proposed measures, but is not bound to follow their advice.

National flag: Yellow cross on blue.

National anthem: Du gamla, du fria, du fjällhöga nord (words by R. Dybeck, 1844; folk-tune).

The official language is Swedish. The capital is Stockholm.

LOCAL GOVERNMENT. For administrative purposes Sweden is divided into 24

SWEDEN 1341

counties (*län*), in each of which the central government is represented by a governor (*landshövding*), who is nominated by the King.

Local government is based on the municipal laws of 18 Dec. 1953 and, for the capital, of 1 March 1957; and the levying of local taxes on a special law. According to the municipal laws Sweden is divided into communes in which all men and women over 19 years of age, and not under wardship, are entitled to elect the commune or town council. These councils are named *Kommunfullmäktige*. The earlier distinction between rural districts, boroughs and towns was abolished in 1971. Ecclesiastical affairs in all parishes with more than 1,000 inhabitants are dealt with by church councils (*Kyrkofullmäktige*); smaller parishes may make the same arrangement. The number of communes has, since 1952, been reduced from 2,500 to 464 and is estimated that the number will be 270 in Jan. 1974. Each county, except Gotland, which consists of only one commune, has a county council (*Landsting*) elected by men and women who enjoy municipal suffrage. The *Landstings* chiefly administer the health service and regional vocational schools. All elections are conducted on the proportional system.

Swedish Public Administration at Work. Stockholm, 1955
The Swedish Civil Service. Ministry of Finance, Stockholm, 1967
Andrén, N., *Modern Swedish Government.* 2nd ed. Stockholm, 1968
Håstad, E., *The Parliament of Sweden.* London, 1957
Heckscher, G., *Pluralist Democracy, the Swedish Experience.* Stockholm, 1949

AREA AND POPULATION. The first census took place in 1749, and it was repeated at first every third year, and, after 1775, every fifth year. Since 1860 a general census has been taken every 10 years and, in addition, in 1935, 1945 and 1965.

Latest census figures: 1940, 6,371,432 (annual increase since 1935: 0·38%); 1945, 6,673,749 (0·94% since 1940); 1950, 7,041,829 (1·10% since 1945); 1960, 7,495,316 (0·64% since 1950); 1965, 7,766,424 (1·04% since 1960).

Counties (Län)	Land area: sq. km	Census population 1 Nov. 1965	Estimated population 31 Dec. 1969	Pop. per sq. km 1969
Stockholm (city)[1]	186	787,315	747,490	4,019
Stockholm (county)[1]	7,529	591,247	712,324	95
Uppsala	5,252	183,699	201,882	38
Södermanland	6,245	240,511	247,703	40
Östergötland	10,058	365,789	375,947	37
Jönköping	10,589	295,808	305,045	29
Kronoberg	8,503	164,186	166,105	20
Kalmar	11,571	235,383	242,150	21
Gotland	3,140	53,751	54,004	17
Blekinge	2,909	149,148	152,702	52
Kristianstad	6,115	261,611	265,772	43
Malmöhus	4,792	667,174	707,323	148
Halland	4,755	180,023	194,266	41
Göteborg and Bohus	5,130	665,427	699,395	136
Älvsborg	11,571	390,158	400,995	35
Skaraborg	7,801	254,618	255,964	33
Värmland	17,606	287,194	284,930	16
Örebro	8,650	267,991	275,243	32
Västmanland	6,493	249,183	260,869	40
Kopparberg	28,350	282,136	279,138	10
Gävleborg	18,191	292,584	293,377	16
Västernorrland	24,123	277,328	274,104	11
Jämtland	47,508	131,049	126,158	3
Västerbotten	55,428	233,427	233,971	4
Norrbotten	98,911	259,484	256,750	3
Total	411,406 [2]	7,766,424	8,013,696	19

[1] From Jan. 1968 Stockholm city and Stockholm county have been united in Stockholm county.
[2] 158,845 sq. miles.

On 31 Dec. 1969 there were 4,000,092 males and 4,013,604 females.

On 1 July 1970 aliens employed in Sweden numbered 218,649. Of these, 107,494 were Finns, 20,013 Yugoslavs, 18,876 Danes, 14,606 Germans, 13,858 Norwegians, 7,550 Greeks, 4,804 Italians and 3,389 Austrians.

VITAL STATISTICS for calendar years:

	Total living births	Of which illegitimate	Still-born	Marriages	Divorces	Deaths exclusive of still-born
1967	121,360	18,323	1,157	56,561	10,722	79,783
1968	113,193	17,891	1,026	52,534	11,011	82,613
1969	107,314	..	..	47,949	..	83,256

Immigration: 1966, 46,970; 1967, 29,989; 1968, 36,038; 1969, 63,919. Emigration: 1966, 19,730; 1967, 19,979; 1968, 23,211; 1969, 20,172.

In 1860 the town population numbered 435,000 (11% of the total population) and on 31 Dec. 1965, 4,177,212 (54%); including other densely populated areas, the urbanized population in 1965 was 77·4%.

Towns over 20,000 inhabitants on 31 Dec. 1969:

Alingsås	20,053	Kristianstad	42,819	Östersund	26,982
Avesta	28,545	Kristinehamm	22,018	Piteå	32,635
Boden	24,727	Köping	21,887	Ronneby	29,607
Borås	71,227	Landskrona	33,898	Sandviken	26,687
Borlänge	29,793	Lidingö	36,334	Skellefteå	61,895
Eskilstuna	67,536	Lidköping	34,871	Skövde	29,147
Falun	34,550	Linköping	80,767	Södertälje	58,873
Gävle	72,987	Luleå	57,838	Solna	56,607
Göteborg	446,875	Ludvika	21,689	Stockholm	747,490
Halmstad	46,515	Lund	54,410	Sundbyberg	27,666
Hälsingborg	82,137	Malmö	258,311	Sundsvall	63,939
Härnösänd	27,032	Mölndal	33,296	Trelleborg	36,021
Jönköping	55,372	Motala	29,203	Trollhättan	43,566
Kalmar	38,912	Nacka	26,865	Uddevalla	36,453
Karlshamm	31,610	Norrköping	95,851	Umeå	54,536
Karskoga	38,981	Nybro	22,149	Uppsala	101,696
Karlskrona	36,326	Nyköping	32,205	Vänerborg	20,280
Karlstad	54,072	Nässjö	20,268	Västerås	113,389
Katrineholm	21,790	Örebro	90,930	Västervik	23,830
Kiruna	28,942	Oskarshamm	25,177	Växjö	35,994

Befolkningsförändringer (*Population Changes*). Annual. National Central Bureau of Statistics, Stockholm.
Historisk statistik för Sverige. I: Befolkning (*Population*), *1720–1967.* 2nd ed. Stockholm, 1969

RELIGION. The overwhelming majority of the population belong to the Evangelical Lutheran Church, which is the established national church. There were 13 bishoprics (Uppsala being the metropolitan see) and 2,566 parishes at the beginning of 1970. The clergy are chiefly supported from the parishes and the proceeds of the Church lands. The nonconformists mostly still adhere to the National Church. The largest denominations, on 1 Jan. 1969, were: Swedish Missionary Society, 86,918; Pentecost Movement, 90,000; Evangelical National Missionary Society, 28,222; Salvation Army, 36,721; Swedish Baptist Church, 26,717; Alliance Missionary Society, 13,811; Methodists, 9,095; Örebro Missionary Society, 19,292. There were also about 50,000 Roman Catholics (under a Bishop resident at Stockholm), about 20,000 Orthodox Catholics and about 13,000 Jews.

Parliament and Convocation (*Kyrkomötet*) decided in 1958 to admit women to ordination as priests.

EDUCATION. The kingdom has 5 state universities, at Uppsala (founded in 1477) with 18,692 students, Lund (founded in 1668), with 18,628 students, Göteborg (founded as private university in 1889; state university in 1954) with 14,419 students, Stockholm (founded as private university in 1877; state university in 1960) with 23,580 students and Umeå (founded in 1963) with 6,640 students in the autumn of 1969. In 1967–68 there were established 4 affiliated universities: in Örebo, 1,470 students, in Växjö, 1,217, in Karlstad, 1,106 and in Linköping, 1,395 students in autumn 1968. There is also in Stockholm a state faculty of medicine (founded in 1810), with 2,608 students and a dental college with 546 students. In Stockholm and Göteborg there are also academies of commerce, with 2,922 students. The institute of technology in Lund (founded in 1961) had 2,373 students. The institute of technology in Stockholm had 5,326; that in Göteborg, 4,092 and the institute of agriculture in Uppsala, 698 students.

The college of veterinary medicine had 321; the pharmaceutical institute (higher course), 443; the college of forestry, 258; 2 institutes of gymnastics, 455; 3 institutes of physiotherapy, 499; the teachers' university colleges in Stockholm, Malmö, Göteborg, Uppsala, Linköping and Umeå, 1,940; and the schools of social work and public administration in Stockholm, Göteborg, Lund, Umeå and Örebro, 3,695 students. The journalist's university colleges in Stockholm and Göteborg had 463 students. At the academy of art school and the college of music in Stockholm there were 773 pupils.

In 1969–70 there were 630,000 pupils in primary education (grade 1–6 in comprehensive schools and all grades in public primary schools). Secondary education at the lower level (grades 7–9 in comprehensive schools and all remaining grades in older secondary schools) comprised 317,200 pupils. In secondary education, the higher stage, there were 227,800 pupils (full-time courses). Part-time courses in vocational schools had 92,000 pupils. People's colleges had 12,800 pupils. There are also teacher-training colleges, military, navigation, agricultural and other special schools; besides institutions and schools for the deaf, blind and mentally deficient.

CINEMAS (1969). There were 1,483 cinemas.

NEWSPAPERS (1969). There were 148 daily newspapers with a total circulation of 4·42m.

Educational policy and planning, Sweden. OECD, Paris, 1967
Higher Education in Sweden, A Guide for Foreign Students. Stockholm, 1969
Orring, J., *Schools in Sweden: A Survey of Primary, Middle and Secondary Education.* Stockholm, 1969
Ottervik, G., and others, *Libraries and Archives in Sweden.* Stockholm, 1954
Paulston, R. G., *Educational Change in Sweden: Planning and accepting the comprehensive school reforms.* New York, 1968
Pers, A. Y., *The Swedish Press.* Stockholm, 1963
Stahre, S.-A., *Adult Education in Sweden.* Stockholm, 1966

JUSTICE. The administration of justice is entirely independent of the Government. The *Justitiekansler,* or Chancellor of Justice (a royal appointment) and the *Justitieombudsmän* (Judical Commissioners appointed by the Diet), exercise a control over the administration. In 1968 a reform was carried through which meant that the offices of the former *Justitieombudsman* (Ombudsman for civil affairs) and the *Militieombudsman* (Ombudsman for military affairs) were turned into one sole institution with 3 Ombudsmen, each styled *Justitieombudsman.* They exert a general supervision over all courts of law, the civil service, military laws and the military services. In 1969 they received altogether 3,128 cases; of these, 393 were instituted on their own initiative and 2,735 on complaints. They dismissed 747 cases, investigated 1,527 without taking direct action, offered criticisms in 557 cases, instituted 5 prosecutions and made 7 proposals to government.

Hackensack, S. (trans.), *The Swedish Code of Judical Procedure.* New York, 1968
Justitieombudsmännens ämbetsberättelse avgiven till Riksdagen år 1969. Stockholm, 1969
Rowat, D. C., *The Ombudsman: Citizen's Defender.* London, 1965

The *Riksåklagaren* (a royal appointment) is the chief public prosecutor.

The kingdom has a Supreme Court of Judicature and is divided into 6 high-court districts and 135 district-court divisions.

These district courts (or courts of first instance) deal with both civil and criminal cases. More serious criminal cases are generally tried by a judge and a jury (*nämnd*) of 7–9 members; in minor criminal cases the jury is reduced to 3; petty cases are tried by the judge alone. In larger towns civil cases are tried as a rule by 3 to 4 judges or in minor cases by 1 judge. In rural districts and small towns civil cases are tried in the same way as criminal cases.

In trials by jury the judge decides the case except when the whole jury—or at least 7 members if the jury consists of more than 7—differs from him, when the decision of the jury prevails.

Persons of poor or moderate means may be provided with the services of lawyers in civil and criminal proceedings from special state-aided legal aid centres, and may also be granted costs for their proceedings. Moreover, the community may bear the cost of free legal advice to poor persons by private lawyers in cases not brought before a court.

There were 73 penal and correctional institutions for delinquents, with 4,746 male and 119 female inmates on 31 Dec. 1969. Besides, there were 23 institutions with 929 places for children and juveniles in need of care owing to viciousness, maladjustment or delinquency.

SOCIAL WELFARE. The social security schemes are greatly expanding. Supported by a referendum, the Diet in 1958 and 1959 decided that the national pensions should be increased successively until 1968 and supplementary pensions paid from 1963. These pensions are of invariable value. In 1969 the Diet decided that as from 1 July 1969 an increment to the basic pension was to be paid to persons without supplementary pensions, and this amount is to be successively increased in a 10-year period. The basic and supplementary pensions consist of old-age and family pensions, as well as pensions paid to the disabled. The financing of the supplementary system is based on the current-cost method.

The most important social welfare schemes are described in the conspectus below.

Type of scheme	Intro-duced	Scope	Principal benefits
Sickness insurance (compulsory—current law, 1962)	1955	All residents	Hospital fees, about 75% of doctors' fees, district physicians and doctors in hospitals charge the insured person only 7 kr. for full medical treatment, some reimbursement of cost of transportation as well as costs of physiotherapy, convalescent care, etc., medicines at reduced prices or free of charge. During sickness daily allowance of 6–52 kr. plus children's supplement (1–3 kr. a day). There is generally no maximum benefit period.
Employment injury insurance (compulsory—current law, 1956)	1918	All employed persons	Medical treatment, medicine and medical appliances, hospital care, sickness benefit 6–52 kr. plus children's supplement 1–3 kr. a day (first 90 days covered by sickness insurance), disability annuities, funeral benefit and survivor's pensions.
Unemployment insurance (current law, 1956)	1934	Members of recognized unemployment insurance societies (about 60% of all employees)	Up to 50 kr. per day plus 2 kr. for each child.
Basic pensions (current law, 1962)			
Old-age	1913	All citizens	Payable from the age of 67 or, at a reduced rate, from the age of 63. 9,728 kr. per annum for married couples, 6,144 kr. for others (including the special increment of 768 kr. and 384 kr. respectively for those without supplementary pension); about half of them receive municipal housing supplement.
Disability	1913	All citizens	Payable before the age of 67. Full pension: the same amount as concerning old-age pension (*see above*).

In addition to old-age pension and disablement pension children's supplement is paid (up to 1,600 kr. for each child).

Type of Scheme	Intro-duced	Scope	Principal benefits
Basic pensions (current law, 1962) *contd.*			
Survivors	1948	All citizens	Widow's pension is payable before the age of 67. The pension is 6,144 kr. (including the special increment of 384 kr.) but less for those who have become widows before the age of 50 and have no child below 16. Many of them receive municipal housing supplements. Child pension is payable before the age of 16. The pension amounts to 1,600 kr. (fatherless or mother-less) and 2,240 kr. (orphans).
Supplementary pensions (current law, 1962)			
Old-age	1960	All gainfully occu-pied persons	Payable from the same age as the basic pension (*see above*). The pension is in principle 60% of the insured person's average annual earnings during the best 15 years except an amount corresponding to the basic pension and subject to a ceiling.
Disability	1959	All gainfully occu-pied persons	Payable before the age of 67. Full pension corresponds in principle to supplementary old-age pension.
Survivors	1959	All gainfully occu-pied persons	Payable to widow and children, before the age of 19, of a deceased person as a certain percentage of the deceased's supplementary pen-sion.
Maternity insurance (com-pulsory—current law, 1962)	1955	All child-bearing women	Maternity hospital fee and cost of transportation. 1,080 kr. (1,620 for twins, etc.). Employed women may receive 1–46 kr. a day up to 180 days.
Children's allowances	1948	All children below 16	900 kr. per annum.
		Children at school 16–18	75 kr. per month during school-courses.

Total social expenditure, including also hygiene, care of the sick and social assistance, amounted to 20,218m. kr. in 1967, representing 20·4% of the national income.

Modern Trends in Swedish Pension Systems. Stockholm, 1968
Socialnytt (Official Journal of the National Board of Health and Welfare). Stockholm, from 1968
Die Sozialgesetzgebung in Schweden. Stockholm, 1963
Social Benefits in Sweden. Stockholm, 1968
Fleisher, W., *Sweden—the Welfare State.* New York, 1956
Michanek, E., *For and against the Welfare State: Swedish experiences.* Stockholm, 1964
Persson, K., *Social Welfare in Sweden.* Stockholm, 1959
Rosenthal, A.-H., *The Social Programs of Sweden, A Search for Security in a Free Society.* Min-neapolis, 1967
Sterner, P., *Services for the Handicapped.* Stockholm, 1969

FINANCE. Currency. The Swedish *krona*, of 100 *öre*, averaged in 1968 of the value of approximately 12·38 kr. to the £ sterling and 5·17 kr. to the US$.

Gold coins do not exist as a currency. National bank-notes for 5, 10, 50, 100, 1,000 and 10,000 kr. are legal means of payment, and the bank is formally bound to exchange them for gold on presentation, but the obligation to re-demption is suspended.

Budget. Revenue and expenditure of the ordinary budget for fiscal years ending 30 June (in 1,000 kr.):

	Revenue	Expenditure		Revenue	Expenditure
1965–66	28,014,920	26,915,832	1968–69	34,836,101	35,047,522
1966–67	30,440,702	30,751,660	1969 70	38 887,114	38,595,722
1967–68	32,101,424	32,971,012	1970 71[1]	43,949,313	40,795,070

[1] Estimates.

The actual revenue and expenditure (current accounts) for the financial year 1 July 1969 to 30 June 1970 was as follows (in 1,000 kr.):

Current Revenue:

Income and property taxes	17,047,625
Death duty and other stamp-duties	623,450
Motor-car duty	3,752,014
Special employers' fee	698,058
Customs duties	1,045,960
Purchase tax	7,134,192
Excise on spirits, tobacco, etc.	5,267,202
Civil service fees, etc.	914,214
Miscellaneous	632,211

Net receipts from state capital funds:

State enterprises:

Posts, Telecommunications	162,941
Hydro-electric power	277,922
Forests	12,000
Railways	40,668
Defence factories	16,172
Civil aviation	15,050
Real estate funds	155,320
Interest on state-owned shares	19,371
Interest on outstanding loans	732,536
Other funds	140,206
Shares in the profits of Bank of Sweden	200,000

Current Expenditure:

Royal household	7,615
Justice	1,616,605
Foreign affairs	503,765
Defence	5,605,581
Social welfare	11,830,672
Communications	2,498,680
Finance	2,508,058
Religion and education	6,931,190
Agriculture	852,405
Commerce	185,430
Interior and health	2,241,995
Pensions, etc.	737,252
Expenses for the Diet, etc.	70,673
Unforeseen expenses	2,762

Expenditure on state funds:

National debt (interest, etc.)	1,679,259
Depreciation of new capital investment	1,108,113
Appropriation for covering capital losses	1,000

Net capital investments (in 1,000 kr.): 1965–66, 1,432, 578; 1966–67, 1,256,584; 1967–68, 1,903,771; 1968–69, 2,364,029; 1969–70, 3,933,746.

Revenue and expenditure of state business enterprises (in 1m. kr.):

	Revenue	Expenditure		Revenue	Expenditure
Forest Service 1968	443·3	433·0	Post Office, 1968–69	2,010·3	1,990·3
Power Administration, 1969	1,166·2	848·4	Telecommunications, 1968–69	2,619·0	2,490·8
Railways, 1968–69	2,389·3	2,383·6			

On 31 Dec. 1969 the national debt amounted to 32,943m. kr.

Riksrevisionsverkets [National Accounting and Audit Bureau] *årsbok.* Annual. Stockholm, from 1929–30
Riksgäldskontoret [National Debt Office] *årsbok.* Annual. Stockholm, from 1920
Taxes in Sweden. Stockholm, 1966
The Swedish Budget. Ministry of Finance, from 1962/63

DEFENCE. A Supreme Commander is, under the King, in command of the three services. He is assisted by the Defence Staff under a chief of staff.

The military forces are recruited on the principle of national service, supplemented by voluntarily enlisted personnel who form the permanent cadres for training purposes.

Liability to service commences at the age of 18, and lasts till the end of the 47th year. From 1966 the period of training is 330–643 days, depending on the service and the conscripts' particular duties. Training is performed in a first period of 251–450 days at a training centre, and later on in 5 periods of 15–32 days each in combat units. Some conscripts receive additional training of about 10 months to become officers in the reserve.

In 1966 a new territorial organization was introduced, consisting of 6 military commands (each under a general officer commanding) which took over some of the tasks previously dealt with by the naval and air-area commands.

Army. The C.-in-C. of the Royal Swedish Army has at his disposal the Army Staff under a chief of staff.

The peace-time Army consists for training purposes of 15 infantry, 3 cavalry, 8 armour, 7 artillery, 6 AA, 3 engineer, 3 signal and 4 Army Service Corps units, most of which are called 'regiments' (*regementen*), each usually consisting of several battalions.

The Army is organized and equipped with regard to the varying geographical and climatic conditions of the country. The Home Guard (*Hemvärnet*) raised during the War continues to be in force.

Sweden's ground forces can be said to consist of a standing Army which for the most part is on indefinite leave, but which on short notice can be ready for action. One of the basic principles of the Swedish system of mobilization is the local recruitment of as many units as possible. Efforts are also made to decentralize as much as possible the storage of equipment and supplies.

The active personnel of the Army comprises about 12,000 officers, warrant officers and n.c.o.s.

Navy. There are 3 Naval Bases: those of the southern, eastern and western coast.

The Navy has one cruiser *Göta Lejon*, completed in 1947, with a displacement of 8,200 tons, belt armour of 5 in., 7 6-in. guns, 6 21-in. torpedo tubes, 100,000 shaft h.p. and a speed of 33 knots.

There are 24 submarines, 8 destroyers, 7 anti-submarine frigates, 1 minelayer, 18 coastal minesweepers, 17 inshore minesweepers, 42 torpedo boats, 1 submarine depot ship, 31 patrol launches, 10 mining tenders, 8 tenders, 12 surveying vessels, 4 ice-breakers, 2 oilers, 1 communication ship, 1 salvage vessel, 23 landing craft, 2 sail training ships, 1 supply ship and 3 water carriers.

The coast artillery defence areas are those of the Stockholm archipelago, Blekinge, Gothenburg, Gotland and Norrland. There are 5 coastal artillery regiments. The active personnel of the navy and coast artillery in 1970 totalled about 16,000 officers and men including conscripts.

Air Force. The C.-in-C. of the Royal Swedish Air Force has at his disposal the Air Staff under a chief of staff. Directly subordinate to the C.-in-C. of the Air Force are also the Inspectors of Air Base Control and Reporting Services, and of Flying Safety. Technical matters are managed by the Air Materiel Department (formerly Air Force Board) which is the Air Force section of the Materiel Administration of the Swedish Armed Forces.

The combat units consist of 9 fighter-interceptor and 4 ground-attack wings (*flottiljer*), each with 2–3 squadrons of 12–15 aircraft, together with 5 reconnaissance squadrons (*divisioner*). Total peace-time strength of the combat units is 37 squadrons with about 650 first-line aircraft.

Standard night- and all-weather-fighters are the Swedish-built Saab J32B Lansen (3 squadrons) and J35 Draken (18 squadrons). The 4 ground-attack wings (10 squadrons) are equipped with A32 Lansen aircraft, which are to be replaced progressively with Saab AJ37 Viggens from 1971. There are also reconnaissance versions of the Draken and Lansen (Saab S35 and S32), and transport and helicopter formations. Six Bloodhound surface-to-air missile squadrons are operational. Some ground-attack squadrons have the Sk60B/C versions of the Saab-105 twin-jet light multi-purpose aircraft. The Sk60A version is the Air Force's standard advanced trainer (with attack capability), to which pupils progress after initial training on piston-engined Sk50 Safirs (to be replaced with Scottish Aviation Bulldogs). Other trainers in service include the Sk16 (T-6), and Sk35C Draken.

The active personnel consists of about 2,500 officers and warrant officers, 300 n.c.o.s and technicians and 6,500 civilians (technicians, meteorologists, etc.).

AGRICULTURE. According to the farm register which is revised annually the following data was provided in 1969. The number of farms in cultivation, of more than 2 hectares of arable land, was 162,155; of these there were 119,315 of 2–20 hectares; 40,383 of 20–100 hectares; 2,457 of above 100 hectares. Of the total land area of Sweden (41,140,600 hectares), 3,034,652 hectares (except kitchen gardens and fruit gardens) were arable land, 141,698 hectares cultivated pastures and 22,794,000 hectares forests.

Chief crops	Area (1,000 hectares)[1]			Produce (1,000 metric tons)		
	1967	1968	1969	1967	1968	1969
Wheat	256·4	249·8	267·0	1,130	1,073	916
Rye	62·0	69·8	72·8	195	209	182
Barley	572·2	599·8	639·2	1,564	1,776	1,575
Oats	488·5	518·9	513·3	1,396	1,584	1,129
Mixed grain	102·9	95·5	83·7	259	262	177
Peas and vetches	6·9	2·3	2·4	..	..	..
Potatoes	68·1	68·6	64·8	1,399	1,486	931
Sugar-beet	39·6	42·0	40·3	1,798	1,982	1,469
Fodder-roots	4·9	..	..	..	..	..
Tame hay	911·1	850·0	815·5	3,885	3,556	2,825
Oil seed	97·9	111·8	107·4	252	267	211

[1] Figures refer to holdings of over 2 hectares of arable land.

Area of rotation meadows for pasture was (in 1,000 hectares): 1967, 239; 1968, 237; 1969, 222.

Total dairy production of milk (in 1,000 metric tons): 1967, 3,318; 1968, 3,308; 1969, 3,139. Butter production in the same years was (in 1,000 metric tons): 65, 66, 63; and cheese, 60, 59, 58.

Livestock, 1969: Cattle, 2,043,835; sheep, 342,405; pigs, 2,065,125.

Number of farm tractors in 1967, 174,067.

The number of pelts produced in 1969 was as follows: Silver fox and its varieties, 300; blue fox and white fox, 8,000; mink, 1·5m.

FORESTRY. Nearly 23·5m. hectares or 55% of the total land area are covered with forests. The total amount of standing timber is estimated at 2,300m. cu. metres with bark; 85% of this volume consists of coniferous wood (pine and spruce). Half of the forest area is privately owned, the other half is equally divided between public authorities (Crown, Church, communities. etc.) and joint-stock companies. The total cut in 1969 was 54m. cu. metres solid volume (without bark); of these 22m. were coniferous timber, 28m. pulpwood, 3m. fuel wood. In 1967 and in 1968 the total cut was 55 and 50m. cu. metres respectively.

In 1969 there were over 1,000 saw-mills with 5 or more workers, the total production of which—representing some 90% of the country's total production —amounted to 11m. cu. metres sawn and planed wood, including box-boards. The production of the 100 pulp-mills in Sweden in 1969 amounted to 7·4m. metric tons pulp (dry weight). There was an export of approximately 2·78m. cu. metres of roundwood; exports of sawn coniferous wood amounted to 6·8m. cu. metres, of plywood (including blockboards) to 4,500 metric tons and of pulp 3·8m. metric tons.

FISHERIES. In 1969 the total value of the catches of the sea fisheries was estimated at 204m. kr.; of this sum, 145m. kr. came from Göteborg, Bohus and Halland.

MINING. Sweden is one of the leading exporters of iron ore. The largest deposits are found north of the polar circle in the area of Kiruna and Gällivare–Malmberget. The ore is exported via the Norwegian port of Narvik and the Swedish port of Luleå. There are also important resources of iron ore in southern Sweden (Bergslagen). The most important fields are Grängesberg and Stråssa and the ores are shipped via the port of Oxelösund. Some of the southern deposits have, in contrast to the fields in North Sweden, a low phosphorus content.

There are also some deposits of copper, lead and zinc ores especially in the Boliden area in the north of Sweden. These ores are often found together with pyrites. Non-ferrous ores, except zinc ores, are used in the Swedish metal industry and barely satisfy domestic needs.

The total production of iron ores amounted to 33·2m. tons in 1969 and exports to 30·8m. tons. The production of copper ore was 112,200 tons, of lead ore 107,800 tons, of zinc ore 160,700 tons, of manganese ore 8,800 tons, of coal 21,700 tons.

There are also deposits of raw materials for aluminium not worked at present. In southern Sweden there are big resources of alum shale, containing oil and uranium.

MANUFACTURING. The most important sector of Swedish manufacturing is the production of metals, metal products, machinery and transport equipment, covering almost half of the total value added by manufacturing. Production of high-quality steel is an old Swedish speciality. A large part of this production is exported. The production of ordinary steel is also steadily increasing but is still short of domestic demand. The total production of steel amounted to 5m. tons in 1968, 26% of which was high-quality steel. There is also a corresponding production of other metals (aluminium, lead and copper) and rolled semi-manufactured goods of these metals.

These basic metal industries are an important basis for the production of more developed metal products, machinery and equipment, which are to a large extent sold on the world market, *i.e.*, hand tools, mining drills, ball-bearings, turbines, pneumatic machinery, refrigerating equipment, machinery for pulp and paper industries, etc., sewing machines, machine tools, office machinery, high-voltage electric machinery, telephone equipment, cars and trucks, ships and aeroplanes.

Another important manufacturing sector is based on Sweden's forest resources. This sector includes saw-mills, plywood factories, joinery industries, pulp- and paper-mills, wallboard and particle board factories, accounting for about 15% of the total value of manufacturing.

A fast increasing sector is the chemical industry, especially the petro-chemical branch. Minerals industries include production of building materials, decorative arts products of glass and china.

Industry groups	No. of establishments 1967	No. of establishments 1968	Average no. of wage-earners 1967	Average no. of wage-earners 1968	Sales value of production (gross) in 1m. kr. 1967	Sales value of production (gross) in 1m. kr. 1968
Mining and quarrying	*246*	*224*	*11,650*	*10,961*	*1,566*	*1,645*
Coalmining	..	..	..	..	..	..
Metal-ore mining	77	69	9,194	8,777	1,379	1,462
Other mining	169	155	2,456	2,184	187	183
Manufacturing	*13,965*	*13,864*	*648,941*	*636,321*	*78,601*	*82,988*
Manufacture of food, beverages and tobacco	1,879	1,831	55,444	55,081	14,396	14,954
Textile, wearing apparel and leather industries	1,763	1,717	74,262	69,168	5,063	5,020
Manufacture of wood products, including furniture	2,613	2,589	62,889	64,397	5,660	6,108
Manufacture of paper and paper products, printing and publishing	1,272	1,252	77,466	75,051	9,948	10,341
Manufacture of chemicals and chemical, petroleum, coal, rubber and plastic products	800	802	38,792	39,552	6,461	7,362
Manufacture of non-metallic mineral products, except products of petroleum and coal	994	992	33,910	32,495	2,933	3,017
Basic metal industries	212	212	48,050	47,758	6,947	7,564
Manufacture of fabricated metal products, machinery and equipment	4,226	4,268	252,633	247,789	26,759	28,187
Other manufacturing industries	206	201	5,395	5,030	434	434
Electricity, gas and water	*1,538[1]*	*1,490[1]*	*13,098*	*12,696*	*5,071*	*5,667*
Electricity, gas and steam	1,346	1,325	11,714	11,329	4,792	5,313
Water works and supply	192	165	1,384	1,367	279	354

[1] Number of power stations.

ELECTRIC ENERGY. Sweden is rich in water power resources. The total electric energy production in 1969 was 58,076m. kwh. About 72% of this energy was produced in hydro-electric plants. All the economically harnessable water-power resources will soon have been developed and the new plants in the 1970s will probably be based on thermal power, mainly nuclear.

Arbetsmarknadsstatistik (*Labour Market Statistics*). National Labour Market Board, Stockholm, from 1963
Bolin, B., *Labour Legislation in Sweden*. Stockholm, 1963
Johansson, Ö. *The gross domestic product of Sweden and its composition 1861–1955*. Stockholm, 1967
Jordbruksekonomiska meddelanden (Journal of Agricultural Economics, published monthly by the National Agricultural Marketing Board). Stockholm, from 1939
Meddelanden från Konjunkturinstitutet. Series A (1938–59, discontinued) and B (from 1939); both with summaries in English. Stockholm
The Swedish Economy. The Secretariat for Economic Planning of the Ministry of Finance and National Institute of Economic Research. Stockholm, from 1960
The Swedish Economy, 1966–70, and the general outlook for the seventies. Ministry of Finance. Stockholm, 1966
Historisk statistik för Sverige, II (Climate, land surveying, agriculture, forestry, fisheries). Stockholm, 1959
Modern Swedish Labour Market Policy. Stockholm, 1966
The 500 Largest Companies in Sweden. Stockholm, from 1968

COMMERCE. The imports and exports of Sweden, unwrought gold and coin not included, have been as follows (in 1m. kr.):

	1963	1964	1965	1966	1967	1968	1969
Imports	17,552	19,946	22,644	23,704	24,319	26,516	30,571
Exports	16,568	19,014	20,541	22,071	23,422	25,553	29,459

Imports and exports by products (in 1m. kr.):

	Imports		Exports	
Product	1968	1969	1968	1969
Food and live animals	2,551	2,729	601	726
Cereals and cereal preparations	156	150	202	241
Fruits and vegetables	827	909	46	43
Coffee, tea, cocoa, spices	598	612	18	21
Feeding stuff for animals	262	256	5	4
Beverages and tobacco	373	356	9	13
Crude materials. inedible, except fuels	1,561	1,768	5,533	6,124
Hides, skins and fur skins, undressed	94	114	162	170
Crude rubber, including synthetic	155	183	16	16
Wood, lumber and cork	138	146	1,667	1,856
Pulp and waste paper	5	13	2,243	2,453
Textile fibres and waste	173	178	81	81
Crude fertilizers and minerals	267	266	56	63
Metalliferous ores and metal scrap	412	553	1,254	1,406
Mineral fuels and lubricants	3,258	3,210	333	297
Coal, coke and briquettes	255	256	5	13
Petroleum and petroleum products	2,923	2,824	288	246
Chemicals	2,425	2,712	1,024	1,213
Manufactured goods	5,754	6,979	7,199	8,423
Paper, paper board and manufactures thereof	256	312	2,378	2,706
Textile yarn and fabrics	1,492	1,696	385	465
Non-metallic mineral manufactures	446	525	210	241
Iron and steel	1,209	1,673	2,257	2,620
Non-ferrous metals	1,163	1,346	685	837
Manufactures of metals	621	757	766	966
Machinery and transport equipment	7,420	8,925	9,425	10,946
Machinery other than electric	3,367	3,952	4,463	4,977
Electric machinery, apparatus and appliances	1,882	2,370	1,700	7,961
Transport equipment	2,171	2,602	3,262	4,008
Miscellaneous manufactured articles	3,019	3,711	1,244	1,549

Principal import and export countries (in 1m. kr.):

	Imports from		Exports to	
	1968	1969	1968	1969
Belgium–Luxembourg	752	976	782	975
Denmark	1,908	2,339	2,420	2,937
Finland	887	1,403	1,200	1,617
France	1,193	1,310	1,189	1,532
Germany (West)	4,959	5,808	2,959	3,460
Italy	961	1,003	800	924

	Imports from		Exports to	
	1968	1969	1968	1969
Netherlands	1,215	1,318	1,176	1,312
Norway	1,542	1,795	2,669	2,920
Switzerland	687	787	610	802
USSR	553	676	423	575
UK	3,595	4,219	3,784	3,840
USA	2,453	2,623	1,973	1,847

Total trade between Sweden and UK (British Board of Trade returns, in £1,000 sterling):

	1966	1967	1968	1969	1970
Imports to UK	217,057	247,464	314,415	332,805	371,047
Exports from UK	229,867	218,927	256,422	294,766 ⎱	364,065
Re-exports from UK	6,209	5,939	6,598	6,446 ⎰	

Utrikeshandel (Foreign Trade). National Central Bureau of Statistics, Stockholm. Annually, from 1911

Utrikeshandel, kvartalsstatistik (Foreign Trade, Quarterly Bulletin). National Central Bureau of Statistics, Stockholm, from 1961

Utrikeshandel, månadsstatistik (Foreign Trade, Monthly Bulletin). National Central Bureau of Statistics, Stockholm, from 1913

SHIPPING. The Swedish mercantile marine consisted on 1 Jan. 1970 of 795 vessels of 4·75m. gross tons (only vessels of at least 100 gross tons, and excluding fishing vessels and tugs). Stockholm and Göteborg, with together 383 vessels of 3·6m. gross tons in Jan. 1970 are the two largest ports.

Vessels entered from and cleared for foreign countries, exclusive of passenger liners and ferries, with cargoes and in ballast, in 1969, as follows (only vessels of at least 20 net tons included): With cargoes, 41,967 of 35·6m. net tons; in ballast, 21,056 of 23·9m. net tons.

ROADS. On 1 Jan. 1970 there were 98,050 km of public roads, of which 26,318 km were surfaced. Motor vehicles on 31 Dec. 1969 included 2,193,634 passenger cars, 156,181 buses and lorries and 42,948 heavy motor cycles.

AVIATION. Commercial air traffic is maintained in (1) Sweden and other parts of the world by Scandinavian Airlines System (SAS), of which AB Aerotransport (ABA = Swedish Air Lines) is the Swedish partner (DDL = Danish Air Lines and DNL = Norwegian Air Lines being the other two); (2) only within Sweden by Linjeflyg AB. Scandinavian Airlines System have a joint paid-up capital of about Sw. kronor 596·5m. Capitalization of ABA, Sw. kronor 220m., of which 50% is owned by the Government and 50% by private enterprises. Capitalization of Linjeflyg, Sw. kronor 11·1m., of which 50% is owned by SAS and 50% by ABA.

In scheduled air traffic during 1969 the total number of km flown was 49·05m.; passenger-km, 2,184m.; goods, 97,176,000 ton-km; mail, 12·8m. ton-km. These figures represent the Swedish share of the SAS traffic (Swedish domestic and three-sevenths of international traffic) and the Linjeflyg traffic.

RAILWAYS. At the end of 1969 the total length of railways was 12,543 km, of which 11,884 km belonged to the State; 7,520 km were electrified. In 1969 the number of passengers on the railways was 64m.; weight of goods, including Lapland ore, 68m. metric tons.

POST. The length of telegraph circuits in Jan. 1969 was 1,014,000 km. The circuits of the telephone had a length of 18,033,000 km. Early in 1970 there were 4,283,279 instruments employed in the telephone service.

Number of combined radio and television reception fees paid on 30 June 1970 was 2,481,110; radio reception fees paid, 388,670.

The overseas radio-telegraph and radio-telephone services are conducted by the Swedish Telecommunications Administration.

The number of post offices at the end of 1969 was 2,681. For receipts of the post and telecommunication services see the section on FINANCE.

BANKING. The Riksbank, or National Bank of Sweden, belongs entirely to the State and is managed by directors elected for 3 years by the Diet, except the chairman, who is designated by the King. The bank is under the guarantee of the Diet, its capital and reserve capital are fixed by its constitution. The note circulation is fixed at 13,500m. kr. Since 1904, only the Riksbank has the right to issue notes. On 31 Dec. 1969 its note circulation amounted to 10,963m. kr.; its combined gold and net foreign-exchange holdings (including surplus value of gold) totalled 2,888m. kr.

There are 16 commercial banks. On 31 Dec. 1969 their total deposits (including savings accounts but excluding interest) amounted to 41,050m. kr.; domestic bills and loans to 33,521m. kr.

The savings-banks statistics (exclusive of post office) are as follows, at the end of the year:

	1964	1965	1966	1967	1968	1969
Accounts, 1,000 [1]	7,401	7,635	7,939	8,218	8,475	8,982
Deposits, 1m. kr. [1]	20,531	22,263	24,511	27,259	29,685	30,779
Capital and reserve funds, 1m. kr.	807	858	906	960	1,017	1,017

[1] Including interest.

At the end of 1969 the post office savings bank had 5·5m. depositors and 8,829m. kr. of deposits, including interest.

Sveriges Riksbank, årsbok. Annual. Stockholm, from 1908
Skandinaviska Banken. Quarterly Review (in English). Stockholm, from 1920
Göteborgs Bank, *Economic Survey,* from 1950

WEIGHTS AND MEASURES. The metric system is obligatory.

DIPLOMATIC REPRESENTATIVES

Sweden maintains embassies in:

Algeria (also for Mali)
Argentina (also for Paraguay)
Australia
Austria
Belgium (also for Luxembourg)
Brazil
Bulgaria
Canada
Chile
China (also for Cambodia and North Vietnam)
Colombia (also for Ecuador and Panama)
Congo (K.) (also for Congo (Br.) Cameroun, Equatorial Guinea and Gabon)
Czechoslovakia
Denmark
Ethiopia (also for Madagascar)
Finland
France
Germany (West)
Greece
Guatemala (also for Costa Rica, Honduras, Nicaragua and El Salvador)
Hungary
Iceland
India (also for Ceylon and Nepál)
Indonesia (also for Philippines)
Iran (also for Afghánistán)
Iraq (also for Kuwait)
Irish Republic
Israel
Italy (also for Malta)
Japan (also for Korea)
Kenya (also for Uganda)
Lebanon (also for Cyprus, Jordan, Saudi Arabia and Syria)
Liberia (also for Guinea, Ivory Coast and Sierra Leone)
Mexico (also for Cuba)
Morocco (also for Gambia and Senegal)
Netherlands
New Zealand
Nigeria (also for Dahomey, Ghana, Niger and Upper Volta)
Norway
Pakistan
Peru (also for Bolivia)
Poland
Portugal
Romania
Spain
Switzerland

Tanzania
Thailand (also for Burma, Laos, South Vietnam, Malaysia and Singapore)
Tunisia (also for Libya)
Turkey
USSR (also for Mongolia)
UAR (also for Somalia and Sudan)
UK
USA
Uruguay
Venezuela (also for Dominican Republic and Trinidad)
Yugoslavia (also for Albania)
Zambia (also for Malawi)

Sweden also maintains a legation in the Republic of South Africa (also for Botswana and Lesotho).

OF SWEDEN IN GREAT BRITAIN (23 North Row, W1)

Ambassador: Leif Axel Lorentz Belfrage, GBE.
Minister: E. G. Fagrell. *Counsellors:* K. A. Fältheim (*Commercial*); O. A. Ternström (*Press*). *Service Attachés:* Col. E. Å. Hultin (*Army*), Capt. S. L. Ahrén (*Navy*), Lieut.-Col. L. H. Sonesson (*Air*). *First Secretary:* G. R. Ekholm. *Labour Attaché:* B. E. Carlson. *Press Attaché:* K. G. Holm.

There are consular representatives at Aberdeen, Belfast, Birmingham, Bradford, Bristol, Cardiff, Dundee, Edinburgh, Glasgow, Hartlepool, Hull, Leeds, Liverpool, Manchester, Newcastle upon Tyne, Plymouth, Portsmouth, Sheffield, Southampton and other places.

OF GREAT BRITAIN IN SWEDEN

Ambassador: Sir Archibald Ross, KCMG.
Counsellors: P. M. Hutchinson (*Head of Chancery*); J. I. McGhie (*Commercial*). *First Secretaries:* J. P. Davies; O. G. Griffiths, OBE, MVO (*Commercial*); J. K. B. Davenport; J. C. Longbotham, MBE (*Economic*); G. D. Cossar (*Labour*); Allan Kerfoot (*Commercial*); E. W. Bird. *Cultural Attaché:* A. D. Thomas, OBE.
Service Attachés: Group Capt. B. Brownlow, OBE, AFC (*Defence and Air*); Lieut.-Col. D. G. Raschen, OBE (*Army*); Cdr J. R. Symonds-Taylor, RN (*Navy*).

There are consular representatives at Gävle, Göteborg, Hälsingborg, Luleå, Malmö, Norrköping, Stockholm and Sundsvall.

OF SWEDEN IN THE USA (2249 R St. NW, Washington, D.C., 20008)

Ambassador: Hubert de Besche.
Minister: L. Leifland. *Counsellors:* G. F. Bundy (*Commercial*); S. Frychius (*Press*). *First Secretaries:* R. N. G. Fremlin; J. D. Wingstrand; L. G. Karlström; T. A. J. Bengtsson. *Service Attachés:* Col. G. C. M. Lundström (*Air*), Cdr L. Lindgren (*Navy*), Col. C. G, Ståhl (*Army*). *Scientific Attaché:* R. G. I. Andreasson. *Labour Attaché:* I. Norén. *Cultural Attaché:* Ingrid H. Arvidsson.

There are consular representatives at Anchorage, Atlanta, Baltimore, Boston, Chicago, Cleveland, Dallas, Detroit, Honolulu, Houston, Jamestown (N.Y.), Kansas City, Los Angeles, Milwaukee, Minneapolis, New Orleans, New York, Norfolk, Omaha, Philadelphia, Portland (Oregon), San Francisco, Seattle, St Louis and other places.

OF THE USA IN SWEDEN

Ambassador: Dr Jerome H. Holland.
Deputy Chief of Mission: John C. Guthrie, Jr. *Heads of Sections:* Edelen M. Fogarty (*Economic*); C. Arthur Borg (*Political*); Merle E. Arp (*Consular*); John V. Hedberg (*Administrative*). *Service Attachés:* Lieut.-Col. Charles S. Johnson, Jr (*Army*), Capt. Robert A. Norin (*Navy*), Col. Paul B. Munroe, Jr (*Air*).

BOOKS OF REFERENCE

STATISTICAL INFORMATION. The National Central Bureau of Statistics (Statistiska Central-byrån, Fack, S-10250 Stockholm 27) was founded in 1858, in succession to the Kungl. Tabell-kommissionen, which had been set up in 1756. *Director-General:* Dr Ingvar Ohlsson. Its publications include:

Statistisk årsbok för Sverige (Statistical Abstract of Sweden). From 1914
Historisk statistik för Sverige (Historical Statistics of Sweden). 1955 ff. (4 vols. to date)
Sveriges officiella statistik (Official Statistics of Sweden). From 1911. (With summaries in French; from 1952 in English)
Årsbok för Sveriges kommuner. From 1918
Allmän månadsstatistik (Monthly Digest of Swedish Statistics). From 1963
Statistisk tidskrift (Statistical Review). 1860–1913; new series 1952–62; 3rd series from 1963
Statistiska meddelanden (Statistical Reports). From 1963

Ahlmann, H. W. (ed.), *Sverige, Land och Folk.* 3 vols. Stockholm, 1967
Ander, F., *The Building of Modern Sweden.* Rock Island, 1958
Andersson, I., *A History of Sweden.* Stockholm, 1962
Andersson, I., and others, *Introduction to Sweden.* 5th ed. Stockholm, 1961
Atlas över Sverige. Stockholm, 1953 ff. [publ. in separate parts dealing with population, economics, etc.]
Documentation on Sweden. Stockholm, 1968
Documents of Swedish Foreign Policy, 1968. Stockholm, 1969
Facts about Sweden. 13th ed. Stockholm, 1969
Fleisher, F., *The New Sweden.* New York, 1967
Guesde, J. M., *La Suède d'hier et d'aujourd'hui.* Stockholm, 1957
Gullberg, I. E., *Swedish–English Dictionary of technical terms.—Svensk-Engelsk Fackordbok.* Stockholm, 1964
Heilborn, A., *Travel, study and research in Sweden.* 6th ed. Stockholm, 1965
Nobel, The Man and His Prizes. Published by the Nobel Foundation. Stockholm, 1950
Nordic Council, *Yearbook of Nordic Statistics.* From 1962 (in English and one Nordic Language)
Scott, G. W., *The Swedes: a jigsaw puzzle.* London, 1967
Svensk-engelsk ordbok. Stockholm, 1968
Sveriges statskalender. Published by Vetenskapsakademien. Annual, from 1813

NATIONAL LIBRARY. Kungliga Biblioteket, Stockholm. *Director:* Dr Uno Willers.

SWITZERLAND
Schweiz—Suisse—Svizzera

HISTORY. On 1 Aug. 1291 the men of Uri, Schwyz and Unterwalden entered into a defensive league. In 1353 the league included 8 members and in 1513, 13. Various territories were acquired either by single cantons or by several in common, and in 1648 the league became formally independent of the Holy Roman Empire, but no addition was made to the number of cantons till 1798. In that year, under the influence of France, the unified Helvetic Republic was formed. This failed to satisfy the Swiss, and in 1803 Napoleon Bonaparte, in the Act of Mediation, gave a new constitution, and out of the lands formerly allied or subject increased the number of cantons to 19. In 1815 the perpetual neutrality of Switzerland and the inviolability of her territory were guaranteed by Austria, France, Great Britain, Portugal, Prussia, Russia, Spain and Sweden, and the Federal Pact, which included 3 new cantons, was accepted by the Congress of Vienna. In 1848 a new constitution was passed without foreign interference. The 22 cantons set up a Federal Government (consisting of a Federal Parliament and a Federal Council) and a Federal Tribunal. This constitution, in turn, was on 29 May 1874 superseded by the present constitution.

CONSTITUTION AND GOVERNMENT. Switzerland is a republic. The highest authority is vested in the electorate, *i.e.*, all male Swiss citizens of over 20. This electorate—besides electing its representatives to the Parliament—has the voting power on amendments to, or on the revision of, the constitution. It also takes decisions on laws and international treaties if requested by 30,000 voters or 8 cantons (facultative referendum), and it has the right of initiating constitutional amendments, the support required for such demands being 50,000 voters (popular initiative).

The Federal Government is supreme in matters of peace, war and treaties; it regulates the army, the railway, telecommunication systems, the coining of money, the issue and repayment of bank-notes and the weights and measures of the republic. It also legislates on matters of copyright, bankruptcy, patents, sanitary police in dangerous epidemics, and it may create and subsidize, besides the Polytechnic School at Zürich and at Lausanne, 2 federal universities and other educational institutions. There has also been entrusted to it the authority to decide concerning public works for the whole or great part of Switzerland, such as those relating to rivers, forests and the construction of national highways and railways. By referendum of 13 Nov. 1898 it is also the authority in the entire spheres of common law. In 1957 the Federation was empowered to legislate on atomic energy matters and in 1961 on the construction of pipelines of petroleum and gas.

National flag: A white cross on red.
National anthem: Trittst im Morgenrot daher (words by Leonard Widmer, 1808–68; tune by Alberik Zwyssig, 1808–54); adopted by the Federal Council in 1962.

The legislative authority is vested in a parliament of 2 chambers, a *Ständerat*, or Council of States, and a *Nationalrat*, or National Council.

The *Ständerat* is composed of 44 members, chosen and paid by the 22 cantons of the Confederation, 2 for each canton. The mode of their election and the term of membership depend entirely on the canton. Three of the cantons are politically divided—Basel into Stadt and Land, Appenzell into Ausser-Rhoden and Inner-Rhoden, and Unterwalden into Obwalden and Nidwalden. Each of these 'half-cantons' sends one member to the State Council.

The *Nationalrat*—after the referendum taken on 4 Nov. 1962—consists of 200 National Councillors, directly elected for 4 years, in proportion to the population of the cantons, with the proviso that each canton or half-canton is represented by at least one member. The members are paid from federal funds at the rate of 70 francs for each day during the session.

In 1967 the 200 members were distributed among the cantons[1] as follows:

Zürich (Zurich)	35	Schaffhausen (Schaffhouse)	2
Bern (Berne)	33	Appenzell—Outer- and Inner-Rhoden	3
Luzern (Lucerne)	9	St Gallen (St Gall)	13
Uri	1	Graubünden (Grisons)	5
Schwyz	3	Aargau (Argovie)	13
Unterwalden—Upper and Lower	2	Thurgau (Thurgovie)	6
Glarus (Glaris)	2	Ticino (Tessin)	7
Zug (Zoug)	2	Vaud (Waadt)	16
Fribourg (Freiburg)	6	Valais (Wallis)	7
Solothurn (Soleure)	7	Neuchâtel (Neuenburg)	5
Basel (Bâle)—town and country	13	Genève (Genf)	10

[1] The name of the canton is given in German, French or Italian, according to the language most spoken in it, and alternative names are given in brackets.

At the elections held on 29 Oct. 1967 the following parties were returned to the National Council: Social Democrats, 50; Radicals, 49; Catholic Conservatives, 45; Peasant Party, 21; Independents, 16; Democrats and Protestant Party, 6; Liberals, 6; Communists, 5; others, 2.

Council of States (1968): Catholic Conservatives, 18; Radicals, 14; Socialists, 2; Peasant Party, 3; Independents, 1; Liberals, 3; Democrats and Protestant Party, 3.

A general election takes place by ballot every 4 years. Every citizen of the republic who has entered on his 20th year is entitled to a vote, and any voter, not a clergyman, may be elected a deputy. Laws passed by both chambers may be submitted to direct popular vote, when 30,000 citizens or 8 cantons demand it; the vote can be only 'Yes' or 'No'. This principle, called the *referendum*, is frequently acted on.

Women's suffrage, although advocated by the Federal Council and the Federal Assembly, was on 1 Feb. 1959 rejected, but in a subsequent *referendum*, held on 7 Feb. 1971, women's suffrage was carried.

The chief executive authority is deputed to the *Bundesrat*, or Federal Council, consisting of 7 members, elected from 7 different cantons for 4 years by the *Vereinigte Bundesversammlung*, i.e., joint session of both chambers. The members of this council must not hold any other office in the Confederation or cantons, nor engage in any calling or business. In the Federal Parliament legislation may be introduced either by a member, or by either House, or by the Federal Council (but not by the people). Every citizen who has a vote for the National Council is eligible for becoming a member of the executive.

The President of the Federal Council (called President of the Confederation) and the Vice-President are the first magistrates of the Confederation. Both are elected by the Federal Assembly for one calendar year and are not immediately re-eligible to the same offices. The Vice-President, however, may be, and usually is, elected to succeed the outgoing President.

President of the Confederation for 1971: Rudolf Gnägi (Bern), born 1917.

Vice-President of the Federal Council for 1971: Nello Celio (Ticino), born 1914.

The 7 members of the Federal Council—each of whom has a salary of 110,000 francs per annum, while the President has 122,000 francs—act as ministers, or chiefs of the 7 administrative departments of the republic. The city of Berne is the seat of the Federal Council and the central administrative authorities.

The Federal Council is composed as follows (from 1 July 1968):

Foreign Affairs: Pierre Graber (Vaud), Social Democrat.
Interior: Hanspeter Tschudi (Basel), Social Democrat.
Justice and Police: Ludwig von Moos (Obwalden), Catholic Conservative.
Military: Rudolf Gnägi (Bern), Peasant and Middle Class Party.
Finance: Nello Celio (Ticino), Radical.
Agriculture and Industry: Ernst Brugger (Zürich), Radical.
Transport, Communications and Energy: Roger Bonvin (Valais), Catholic Conservative.

LOCAL GOVERNMENT. Each of the cantons and demi-cantons is sovereign, so far as its independence and legislative powers are not restricted by the federal constitution; all cantonal governments, though different in organization (membership varies from 5 to 11, and terms of office from 1 to 5 years), are based on the principle of sovereignty of the people.

In all cantons a body chosen by universal suffrage, usually called *der Grosse Rat*, or *Kantonsrat*, exercises the functions of a parliament. In all the cantonal constitutions, however, except those of the cantons which have a *Landsgemeinde*, the referendum has a place. By this principle, where it is most fully developed, as in Zürich, all laws and concordats, or agreements with other cantons, and the chief matters of finance, as well as all revisions of the constitution, must be submitted to the popular vote. In Appenzell, Glarus and Unterwalden the people exercise their powers direct in the *Landsgemeinde*, i.e., the assembly in the open air of all male citizens of full age. In all the cantons the *popular initiative* for constitutional affairs, as well as for legislation, has been introduced, except in Lucerne, where the *initiative* exists only for constitutional affairs. In most cantons there are districts (*Amtsbezirke*) consisting of a number of communes grouped together, each district having a Prefect (*Regierungsstatthalter*) representing the cantonal government. In the larger communes, for local affairs, there is an Assembly (legislative) and a Council (executive) with a president, maire or syndic, and not less than 4 other members. In the smaller communes there is a council only, with its proper officials.

In 1959 the cantons of Vaud and Neuchâtel, in 1960 the canton of Geneva, in 1966 the canton of Basel-Stadt, in 1968 the canton of Basel-Land, in 1969 the cantons of Ticino, Fribourg and in 1970 the cantons of Valais (Wallis) and Luzern adopted women's suffrage in cantonal and communal affairs.

Basler Handelskammer, *La neutralité suisse*, 1962
Bonjour, E., *Swiss Neutrality*. London, 1946
Huber, H., *How Switzerland is Governed*. Zürich, 1947
Hughes, C., *The Federal Constitution of Switzerland*. *Translation and Commentary*. Oxford, 1954
Hughes, C. J., *The Parliament of Switzerland*. Hansard Society, 1962
Marx, Dr Paul, *Systematisches Register zu den geltenden Staatsverträgen der schweizerischen Eidgenossenschaft und der Kantone mit dem Auslande*. Zürich, 1918. *Appendix*, 1934
Rappard, W. E., *La Constitution fédérale de la Suisse*. Zürich, 1948.—*Collective Security in Swiss Experience*. London, 1948
Ruck, Erwin, *Schweizerisches Staatsrecht*. Zürich, 1933
Silbernagel-Caloyanni, Alfred, *Suisse: Organisation Politique, Administrative et Judiciaire de la Conféderation Helvétique et de Chaque Canton*. Paris, 1936

AREA AND POPULATION. Area and population, according to the census held on 1 Dec. 1950 and the census held on 1 Dec. 1960, are shown in the following table. The cantons are given in the official order and the year of the entrance of each into the league or confederation is stated:

Canton	Area (sq. km)	Census population 1 Dec. 1950	Census population 1 Dec. 1960	Pop. per sq. km, 1960
Zürich (Zurich) (1351)	1,729	777,002	952,304	551
Bern (Berne) (1353)	6,887	801,943	889,523	129
Luzern (Lucerne) (1332)	1,494	223,249	253,446	170
Uri (1291)	1,075	28,556	32,021	30
Schwyz (1291)	908	71,082	78,048	86
Obwalden (Obwald) (1291)	492	22,125	23,135	47
Nidwalden (Nidwald) (1291)	274	19,389	22,188	81
Glarus (Glaris) (1352)	684	37,663	40,148	59
Zug (Zoug) (1352)	239	42,239	52,489	220
Fribourg (Freiburg) (1481)	1,670	158,695	159,194	95
Solothurn (Soleure) (1481)	791	170,508	200,816	254
Basel-Stadt (Bâle-V.) (1501)	37	196,498	225,588	6,081
Basel-Land (Bâle-C.) (1501)	428	107,549	148,282	346
Schaffhausen (Schaffhouse) (1501)	298	57,515	65,981	221
Appenzell A.-Rh. (Rh.-Ext.) (1513)	243	47,938	48,920	202
Appenzell I.-Rh. (Rh.-Int) (1513)	172	13,427	12,943	75
St Gallen (St Gall) (1803)	2,016	309,106	339,489	168
Graubünden (Grisons) (1803)	7,109	137,100	147,458	21
Aargau (Argovie) (1803)	1,404	300,782	360,940	257
Thurgau (Thurgovie) (1803)	1,006	149,738	166,420	165
Ticino (Tessin) (1803)	2,811	175,055	195,566	70
Vaud (Waadt) (1803)	3,211	377,585	429,512	134
Valais (Wallis) (1815)	5,231	159,178	177,783	34
Neuchâtel (Neuenburg) (1815)	797	128,152	147,633	185
Genève (Genf) (1815)	282	202,918	259,234	919
Total	**41,288[1]**	**4,714,992**	**5,429,061**	**131**

[1] 15,941 sq. miles.

The German language is spoken by the majority of inhabitants in 19 of the 25 cantons (French names given in brackets), the French in 5 (Fribourg, Vaud, Valais, Neuchâtel and Genève, for which the German names are given in brackets), the Italian in one (Ticino). In 1960, 69·3% spoke German, 18·9% French, 9·5% Italian, 0·9% Romansch and 1·4% other languages; counting only Swiss nationals, the percentages were 74·4, 20·2, 4·1, 1 and 0·3. On 8 July 1937 Romansch was made the fourth national language; it is spoken mostly in Graubünden.

At the end of 1969 the population figures of the principal towns (and their '*agglomérations*' or conurbations) were as follows: Zürich, 427,600 (674,400); Basel, 213,400 (370,000); Geneva, 171,900 (314,900); Bern, 166.200 (260,600); Lausanne, 138,700 (217,700); Winterthur, 93,600 (106,000); St Gallen, 79,000; Luzern, 73,100 (150,900); Biel, 67,000 (91,600); La Chaux-de-Fonds, 43,000.

The number of foreigners resident in Switzerland in 1960 was 584,739. The number of Swiss resident outside Switzerland on 31 Dec. 1969 was 163,814: in France, 32,768; West Germany, 22,445; USA, 18,641; Italy, 12,801; Canada, 10,498; UK, 8,560; Argentina, 4,176; Austria, 4,174; Brazil, 3,916.

VITAL STATISTICS for calendar years:

| | Live births | | | | | |
	Total	Illegitimate	Marriages	Divorces	Still births	Deaths
1967	107,417	4,141	45,269	5,198	1,070	55,142
1968	105,130	4,034	45,711	5,599	1,068	57,374
1969	102,520	3,871	46,886	..	962	58,002

The excess of emigrants over remigrants was: 1962, 988; 1963. 1,533; 1964, 3,075; 1965, 3,716; 1966, 4,338; 1967, 4,145; 1968, 3,065; 1969, 3,276.

Historisch-Biographisches Lexikon der Schweiz. 7 vols. Neuenburg, 1919–34. (Also in French)
Früh, J., Geographie der Schweiz. 3 vols. St Gallen, 1930–38
Jacot, A., Neues schweizerisches Orts-Lexikon mit Verkehrs-Karte. Lucerne, 1949
Leeman, Walter, Landeskunde der Schweiz. Zürich, 1939
Mayer, Kurt B., The Population of Switzerland. New York and London, 1952

RELIGION. There is complete and absolute liberty of conscience and of creed. No one is bound to pay taxes specially appropriated to defraying the expenses of a creed to which he does not belong. No bishoprics can be created on Swiss territory without the approbation of the Confederation. The Society of Jesus and its affiliated societies cannot be received in any part of Switzerland; all functions clerical and scholastic are forbidden to its members, and the interdiction can be extended to any other religious order whose action is dangerous to the State, or interferes with the religious peace. The foundation of new convents or religious orders is forbidden.

According to the census of 1 Dec. 1960 Protestants numbered 2,861,522 (52·7% of the population); Roman Catholics, 2,463,214 (45·4%); Old Catholics, 29,754 (0·5%) and Jews, 19,984 (0·4%). In 1960 Protestants were in a majority in 10 of the cantons and Catholics in 12. Of the more populous cantons, Zürich, Bern, Vaud, Neuchâtel and Basel (town and land) were mainly Protestant, while Luzern, Fribourg, Ticino, Valais and the Forest Cantons are mainly Catholic. The Roman Catholics are under 6 bishops, viz., of Basel (resident at Solothurn), Chur, St Gallen, Lugano, Lausanne–Geneva–Fribourg (resident at Fribourg) and Sitten (Sion), all of them immediately subject to the Holy See. The Old Catholics have a theological faculty at the university of Bern.

Lampert, U., Kirche und Staat in der Schweiz. 2 vols. Freiburg, 1937

EDUCATION. Education is administered by the cantons. Before the year 1848 most of the cantons had organized a system of primary schools, and since that year elementary education has steadily advanced. In 1874 it was made obligatory for the whole country (the school age varying in the different cantons) and placed under the civil authority. In some cantons the cost falls almost entirely on the communes, in others it is divided between the canton and communes. In all the cantons primary instruction is free.

In most cantons there are also secondary schools for youths of from 12 to 15, gymnasia, higher schools for girls, teachers' seminaries, commercial and administrative schools, trade schools, art schools, technical schools, schools for the instruction of girls in domestic economy and other subjects, agricultural schools, schools for horticulture, for viticulture, for arboriculture and for dairy management. There are also institutions for the blind, the deaf and dumb and feeble-minded.

There are 7 universities in Switzerland. These universities are organized on the model of those of Germany, governed by a rector and a senate, and divided into 4 faculties of theology, jurisprudence, philosophy and medicine. In 1969–70 the Federal Institute of Technology at Zürich (founded in 1855) had 421 teachers and 5,829 matriculated students; the Federal Institute of Technology at Lausanne, independent of the university since 1946, had 1,346 students; the St Gall School of Economics and Social Sciences, founded in 1899, had 126 teachers and 1,479 matriculated students.

University statistics in the winter of 1968–69:

	Theology	Law	Economics and Social Sciences	Medicine	Arts and science	Total	Teaching staff
Basel (1460	131	425	411	1,182	1,834	4,013	356
Zürich (1523 & 1833)	192	1,095	917	1,982	3,737	7,923	660
Bern (1528 & 1834)	92	617	700	1,338	2,079	4,826	404
Genève (1559[1] & 1873[2])	41	582	1,013	903	1,398	5,384	555
Lausanne (1537[1] & 1890[2])	57	322	976	825	946	3,321	280
Fribourg (1889)	325	270	559	419	1,428	3,001	191
Neuchâtel (1866[1] & 1909)	50	89	353	76	654	1,340	135

[1] Founded as an academy.　　　　　　[2] Reorganized as a university.

These numbers are exclusive of 'visitors', but inclusive of women students.

CINEMAS (1969). There were 595 cinemas with a seating capacity of 217,742.

NEWSPAPERS (1970). The number of daily newspapers was estimated to be 110 with a combined circulation of 2·5m.

SOCIAL INSURANCE. The Federal Insurance Law against illness and accident, of 13 June 1911, entitles all Swiss citizens to insurance against illness; foreigners may be admitted to the benefits. Compulsory insurance against illness does not exist as yet, but cantons and communities are entitled to declare insurance obligatory for certain classes or to establish public benefit (sick fund) associations, and to make employers responsible for the payment of the premiums of their employees. In 1968 the 857 societies insuring against illness had 5,824,000 members.

Unemployment insurance is based upon the federal law of 22 June 1951, which lays down the rules on which public or private insurance organizations have to work, and fixes the subsidies paid by the Federation to these organizations. In a number of cantons unemployment insurance is compulsory for all wage-earners with low incomes; in other cantons the regulation is left to the communes. At 30 Sept. 1969 there existed 157 public and private unemployment insurance organizations with a total membership of 543,676.

Insurance against accident is compulsory for all officials, employees and workmen of all the factories, trades, etc., which are under the federal liability law. The Swiss Accident Insurance Institution commenced operations on 1 April 1918.

On 6 July 1947 a federal law was accepted by a referendum, providing compulsory old age and widows and widowers insurance for the whole population, as from 1 Jan. 1948. In 1968 the number of normal pensioners was 827,530, the number of interim pensioners, 181,102. On 1 Jan. 1960 the old-age insurance scheme was extended to cover invalidity. In 1968, 72,434 invalids received a regular annuity and 43,872 invalids an interim annuity.

JUSTICE. The Federal Tribunal (*Bundes-Gericht*), which sits at Lausanne, consists of 26–28 members, with 11–13 supplementary judges, appointed by the Federal Assembly for 6 years and eligible for re-election; the President and Vice-President serve for 2 years and cannot be re-elected. The President has a salary of 100,000 francs a year, and the other members 90,000 francs. The Tribunal has original and final jurisdiction in suits between the Confederation and cantons; between cantons and cantons; between the Confederation or cantons and corporations or individuals, the value in dispute being not less than 8,000 francs; between parties who refer their case to it, the value in dispute being at least 20,000 francs; in such suits as the constitution or legislation of cantons places within its authority; and in many classes of railway suits. It is a court of appeal against decisions of other federal authorities, and of cantonal authorities applying federal laws. The Tribunal also tries persons accused of treason or other offences against the Confederation. For this purpose it is divided into 4 chambers: Chamber of Accusation, Criminal Chamber (*Cour d'Assises*), Federal Penal

Court and Court of Cassation. The jurors who serve in the Assize Courts are elected by the people, and are paid 70 francs a day when serving.

On 3 July 1938 the Swiss electorate accepted a new federal penal code, to take the place of the separate cantonal penal codes. The new code, which abolished capital punishment, came into force on 1 Jan. 1942.

By federal law of 5 Oct. 1950 several articles of the penal code concerning crime against the independence of the state have been amended with a view to reinforcing the security of the state.

Thormann, P., and Overbeck, A. (ed.), *Das Schweizerische Strafgesetzbuch*. Zürich, 1939
Williams, Ivy, *The Swiss Civil Code*. English version. Oxford, 1925

FINANCE. Currency. The *franc* of 100 *Rappen* or *centimes* is the monetary unit. By law of 17 Dec. 1952, which came into force on 20 April 1953, the value of the franc was fixed at 0·20322 gramme of fine gold. The legal gold coins are 20- and 10-franc pieces; cupro-nickel coins are 5, 2, 1 and ½ franc, 20, 10 and 5 centimes; bronze, 2 and 1 centime.

On 31 Dec. 1969 the coin in circulation (of nominal value of 1,000 francs) was as follows: 516,133,000 silver coins of 740,578; 1,293,984 nickel and cupro-nickel coins of 549,261 and 218,332 bronze coins of 2,822; total, 2,028,349 coins of 1,293,661.

Budget. Revenue and expenditure of the Confederation, in 1,000 francs, for calendar years:

	1965	1966	1967	1968	1969	1970[1]
Revenue	4,951,755	5,687,653	5,717,857	6,603,540	7,108,445	7,571,047
Expenditure	4,920,315	5,682,935	5,873,831	6,446,745	7,080,838	7,594,210

[1] Estimates.

The budget estimates, in 1,000 francs, for 1970:

Revenue		Expenditure	
General administration	8,180	General administration	85,573
Departments:		Departments:	
Political	6,765	Political	285,744
Interior	46,355	Interior	2,920,151
Justice and Police	38,649	Justice and Police	202,402
Military	28,000	Military	1,815,643
Finance and Customs	7,047,091	Finance and Customs	1,236,224
Commerce, Industry and Agriculture	321,957	Commerce, Industry and Agriculture	864,927
Transport, Communications and Energy	74,050	Transport, Communications and Energy	183,545

The consolidated debt of the Confederation on 1 Jan. 1970 amounted to 5,223,650 francs. The floating debt was 81·8m. francs.

Schweizerisches Finanz-Jahrbuch. Bern. Annual. From 1899

DEFENCE. There are fortifications in all entrances to the Alps and on the important passes crossing the Alps and the Jura. Large-scale destructions of bridges, tunnels and defiles are prepared for an emergency.

Switzerland depends for defence upon a *national militia*. Service in this force is compulsory and universal, with few exemptions except for physical disability. Those excused or rejected pay certain taxes in lieu. Liability extends from the 20th to the end of the 50th year for soldiers and of the 55th year for officers. The first 12 years are spent in the first line, called the *Auszug*, or *Élite*, the next 10 in the *Landwehr* and 8 in the *Landsturm*. The unarmed *Hilfsdienst* comprises all other males between 20 and 50 whose services can be made available for noncombatant duties of any description.

The initial training of the Swiss militia soldier is carried out in recruits' schools, and the periods are 118 days for infantry, engineers, artillery, etc., and 132 days for cavalry. The subsequent trainings, called 'repetition courses', are 20 days annually; but after going through 8 courses further attendance is excused for all under the rank of sergeant. The *Landwehr* men are called up for training courses of 13 days every 2 years, and the *Landsturm* men have to undergo a refresher course of 13 days.

The army is divided into 3 armoured divisions, 3 infantry divisions, 3 frontier divisions, 3 mountain divisions, 18 horse cavalry squadrons and into frontier-, fortress- and territorial brigades, organized in 4 army corps.

The administration of the Swiss Army is partly in the hands of the Cantonal authorities, who can promote officers up to the rank of captain. But the Federal Government is concerned with all general questions and makes all the higher appointments.

In peace-time the Swiss Army has no general; only in time of war the Federal Assembly in joint session of both Houses appoints a general.

The Swiss infantry are armed with the Swiss automatic rifle and with machine-guns, bazookas and mortars. The field artillery is armed with a Q.F. shielded 10·5 Bofors and field howitzers of 10·5 cm calibre. The heavy artillery is armed with guns of 10·5 cm and howitzers of 15 cm calibre. The armoured troops are equipped with the light French AMX, the British Centurion and a modern Swiss tank.

The Air Force consists of 3 regiments, made up of 21 first-line squadrons with 375 aircraft. The fighter squadrons are equipped with Mirage IIIS supersonic interceptor/ground-attack (2 squadrons), Mirage IIIRS fighter/reconnaissance (1 squadron), Venom ground-attack (13 squadrons) and Hunter interceptor (5 squadrons) aircraft. Bloodhound surface-to-air missile batteries are operational. Training aircraft are Pilatus P-2 and P-3, Harvard and Vampire; there are also a number of communications and transport aircraft and helicopters. Personnel numbers 5,000 regulars, 5,000 conscripts and 40,000 reservists.

There are 10 patrol boats on Lake Constance.

Ernst, A., *Die Ordnung des militärischen Oberbefehls.* Basel, 1948

AGRICULTURE. Of the total area of the country of 4,128,790 hectares, about 1,007,710 hectares (24·4%) are unproductive. Of the productive area of 3,121,090 hectares, 980,650 hectares are wooded. The agricultural area, in 1969, consisted of 260,400 hectares arable land (including vineyards), 106,751 hectares artificial meadows, 693,371 hectares permanent meadow and 1,079,630 hectares pasture land. In 1969 there were 149,306 farms with a total area of 1,079,599 hectares. The gross value of agricultural products was estimated at 3,652m. in 1965, 3,953m. in 1966, 4,224m. in 1967, 4,195m. in 1968,

In 1969, 175,315 hectares were plated with cereals, of which 98,841 hectares were wheat; rye, 11,328; barley, 31,256; potatoes, 31,528; sugar-beet, 8,520; vegetables, 6,993; tobacco, 728. Production, 1968 (in 1,000 metric tons): Wheat, 338; rye, 58; barley, 111; potatoes, 1,098; sugar-beet, 453; tobacco, 2. Milk production (in 1m. quintals): 1955, 28·3; 1960, 31·1; 1965, 31·2; 1967, 32·7; 1968, 33·2; 1969, 32·1.

The fruit production (in 1,000 metric tons) in 1968 was: Apples, 270; pears, 194; cherries, 50; plums, 48; apricots, 11; nuts, 7.

Wine is produced in 18 of the cantons. In 1968 Swiss vineyards (11,900 hectares) yielded 1.034,216 hectolitres of wine, valued at 200,484,000 francs.

Livestock, 1969: 52,650 horses, 291,000 sheep, 74,707 goats (1966), 1,907,400 cattle (including 901,000 cows), 1,752,000 pigs, 6·3m. poultry.

FORESTRY. Of the forest area of 960,905 hectares, 49,334 were owned by the Federation or the cantons, 630,050 by communes and 281,521 by private persons or companies in 1967. The utilization of timber, in 1966 was 3,520,552 cu. metres, of which 264,200 in state-owned, 2,398,556 in communal and 857,796 in private forests.

MINING. There are 2 salt-mining districts; that in Bex (Vaud) belongs to the canton, but is worked by a private company, and those at Schweizerhalle,

Rheinfelden and Ryburg are worked by a joint-stock company formed by the cantons interested. The output of salt of all kinds in 1969 was 266,592 metric tons. At Sargans (St Gallen) and Herznach (Aargau) iron ore and manganese ore were mined; output (in 1,000 metric tons) 1960, 125; 1965, 113. Since 1966 the mine of Gonzen (at Sargans) and since 1967 Herznach are closed.

INDUSTRIES. The chief food producing industries, based on Swiss agriculture, are the manufacture of cheese, butter, sugar and meat. The production in 1969 was (in tons): Cheese, 84,600; butter, 32,100; sugar, 56,609; meat, 319,575. There are 61 breweries, producing in 1969, 4·65m. hectolitres of beer. Tobacco products in 1969: Cigars, 746m.; cigarettes, 24,177m.

Among the other industries, the manufacture of textiles, wearing apparel and footwear, chemicals and pharmaceutical products, bricks, glass and cement, the manufacture of basic iron and steel and of other metal products, the production of machinery (including electrical machinery and scientific and optical instruments) and watch and clock making are the most important. In 1969 there were 12,208 factories with 882,414 workers. Of these 63,332 were working in textile industries, 66,213 in the manufacture of textile goods and footwear, 61,507 in chemical works, 28,837 in the manufacture of clay products, glass and glass products, cement and cement products, 121,103 in manufacture of metal products, 264,867 in the manufacture of machinery and 76,649 in watch and clock making and in the manufacture of jewellery.

Production in 1968 was: Cotton yarn pure and mixed, 37,205 metric tons; woven cotton fabrics pure and mixed, 160·7m. metres, rayon and acetate filament yarn, 11,417 metric tons; rayon and acetate staple, 5,525 metric tons; footwear, 15m. pairs; cement, 4,534,444 metric tons; raw aluminium, 77,060 metric tons; chocolate, 58,287 metric tons. 48,844,000 watches and clocks were exported.

POWER. In 1969 Switzerland had electrical power-plants with a capacity of 28m. kw., of which 1·52m. kw. were in thermo-electric plants. The total production of energy amounted to 29,666m. kwh. in 1968–69 (Oct.–Sept.); 28,145m. kwh. were generated by hydro-electric plants. Gas is manufactured in 45 gasworks. The production, in 1969, was 380m. cu. metres; coke production amounted to 279,024 metric tons, and tar production to 14,055 metric tons.

TOURISM. Tourism is an important industry. In 1969, 3,389,000 Swiss and 6,259,000 foreigners (including 537,173 British) visited Swiss holiday resorts. The tourist trade earned 1,745m. francs in 1968 and 1,860m. francs in 1969.

LABOUR. According to the general economic census of 1965 the total working population amounted to about 2·9m., of which 9% were active in agriculture and forestry, 51% in manufacture and construction and 40% in services. In all non-agricultural sectors there were 248,605 establishments (including 594 being shut down) with 2,368,264 occupied persons, divided in 195,467 occupants and 2,172,797 employees. The number of apprentices among them was 137,056 (40,722 commercial, 96,334 industrial).

The main groups show the following numbers of gainfully occupied persons: Agriculture and forestry, 252,392; food processing, 128,140; textiles, 166,451, chemical industry, 57,703; metalwork, 191,783; engineering, 301,424; watch-making, 76,443; construction, 321,476; wholesale trade, 107,824; retail trade, 211,016; banking and insurance, 62,847; transport and postal services, 149,480; catering, 151,923.

In 1969 the foreign labour force with permit of temporary residence was 659,229 in Aug. and 630,194 in April 1970. Of the number recorded in Aug. 398,929 were Italians, 57,199 Germans, 95,696 Spaniards, 19,865 Austrians and 36,842 Frenchmen. 152,195 were construction workers, 124,711 metal-workers and mechanics, 100,973 housekeepers, cooks and waiters and 16,045 agricultural and forestry workers.

The Swiss Federation of Trade Unions had, in 1969, a membership of 434,806. Other organizations of employees had about 462,000 members.

COMMERCE. The special commerce, excluding gold (bullion and coins) and silver (coins), was (in 1m. Swiss francs) as follows:

	1964	1965	1966	1967	1968	1969
Imports	15,541	15,929	17,005	17,786	19,924	22,734
Exports	11,462	12,861	14,204	15,165	17,349	20,009

The following table, in 1m. francs, shows the distribution of the special trade of Switzerland among the principal countries:

Countries	Imports from				Exports to			
	1960	1967	1968	1969	1960	1967	1968	1969
W. Germany	2,840·7	5,102·0	5,737·0	6,643·0	1,492·6	2,024·2	2,463·3	3,034·8
France	1,211·7	2,453·8	2,521·4	2,353·4	543·9	1,383·1	1,496·2	1,717·8
Italy	1,012·7	1,751·0	1,936·9	2,200·6	670·6	1,303·4	1,512·7	1,753·3
Belgium–Luxembourg	424·0	630·1	667·1	392·7	287·5	380·0	418·6	468·6
Netherlands	401·0	651·4	691·6	818·5	333·5	444·8	444·9	512·7
EEC	5,890·1	10,588·3	11,554·0	13,208·2	3,328·1	5,535·5	6,335·7	7,487·2
Austria	209·4	625·1	731·6	956·6	259·6	777·1	842·6	1,004·8
UK	573·3	1,374·0	1,422·1	1,833·4	471·7	1,130·8	1,291·2	1,382·7
Portugal	20·1	60·7	249·1	85·6	93·2	172·8	366·9	218·0
Denmark	84·5	257·4	67·6	296·2	148·6	330·8	183·4	427·3
Norway	38·6	75·7	98·5	118·0	89·6	191·8	189·1	251·7
Sweden	174·5	468·8	548·4	689·7	233·2	508·8	595·9	641·1
Finland	23·9	72·1	86·0	127·7	85·5	166·9	168·5	206·6
EFTA	1,100·4	2,933·8	3,203·3	4,107·1	1,295·9	3,279·0	3,637·6	4,132·2
Other European countries[2]	383·6	692·9	731·9	915·3	663·1	1,316·1	1,450·1	1,801·6
Libya	0·1	70·2	86·2	163·0	2·4	21·1	53·7	58·5
Nigeria	43·7	63·9	60·7	55·1	15·5	27·2	24·7	38·6
South Africa	23·1	33·8	42·8	38·2	94·2	188·3	226·6	256·8
Rhodesia	20·9[1]	17·0	15·0	15·6	7·7[1]	8·4	10·9	6·6
UAR	30·0	29·8	27·4	25·5	58·7	35·1	26·6	62·4
China	37·8	74·9	68·8	78·1	34·9	91·7	83·8	62·3
Hong Kong	5·0	63·2	70·8	102·8	110·1	225·0	259·9	346·9
India	25·8	55·8	56·2	65·5	104·7	95·8	118·3	93·5
Iran	21·9	43·1	34·2	42·9	48·8	93·4	113·9	112·3
Israel	25·4	58·4	59·9	74·4	35·2	95·5	127·6	154·7
Japan	115·8	278·5	304·3	403·7	127·5	370·6	460·4	538·1
Lebanon	1·3	5·8	7·1	11·3	26·2	53·1	68·1	61·7
Pakistan	3·5	6·1	9·8	14·0	37·5	62·7	58·8	74·1
Singapore	3·2	0·8	1·3	2·8	45·3	59·2	60·4	75·9
Argentina	67·3	122·0	86·4	113·3	93·1	105·4	162·7	184·1
Brazil	47·9	71·6	92·7	117·9	109·1	163·7	249·2	247·8
Canada	171·4	142·3	150·7	182·1	142·2	245·4	256·4	304·0
Cuba	18·5	21·9	11·3	5·9	10·4	2·5	4·1	40·8
Mexico	40·7	48·1	79·9	42·0	95·8	160·1	191·2	211·2
USA	1,095·6	1,488·3	1,736·7	1,922·4	806·9	1,554·7	1,779·8	1,883·9
Venezuela	6·2	7·0	6·6	8·0	95·0	92·4	108·0	110·3
Australia and Oceania	28·1	57·3	43·3	62·5	153·5	243·7	249·1	279·3

[1] Including USSR, Turkey and Cyprus.
[2] Including Zambia and Malawi.

Custom receipts (in 1,000 francs): 1966, 1,903,906; 1967, 2,066,923; 1968, 2,231,170; 1969, 2,273,800.

Total trade between Switzerland (including Liechtenstein from 1968) and UK (in £1,000 sterling) for calendar years (British Board of Trade returns):

	1966	1967	1968	1969	1970
Imports to UK	98,169	119,398	150,765	174,462	198,839
Exports from UK	105,149	110,552	125,089	167,716	} 209,298
Re-exports from UK	6,094	6,338	11,428	16,025	

Federal Customs Office, *Statistique mensuelle du commerce extérieur de la Suise.* From 1925.—
Statistique annuelle du commerce extérieur de la Suise. 2 vols. From 1840.—*Rapport annuel de
la statistique du commerce Suisse.* From 1889
Handbuch der schweizerischen Volkswirtschaft. 2 vols. Bern, 1955

RAILWAYS. Railway history in Switzerland begins in 1847. In 1969 the
length of the Swiss federal railways was 2,913 km, of which 2,897 km were electrified. The operating receipts amounted to 1,719,413,000 francs; operating
expenses, 1,352,389,000 francs. Traffic was 43·3m. metric tons and 231·15m.
passengers.

ROADS. There are 17,856 km of main roads, including 469 km of 'national
roads' for motor cars only. There is a postal autobus service, which, in 1966,
carried 35,256,000 passengers. Motor vehicles, as of 30 Sept. 1969, numbered
2,039,236, including 1,146,033 private cars, 237,584 trucks, 624,353 motor cycles,
4,921 buses and 26,345 agricultural tractors and special cars.

SHIPPING. A merchant marine was created by a decree of the Swiss Government dated 9 April 1941, the place of registry of its vessels being Basel. On
31 Dec. 1969 it consisted of 31 vessels with a total of 202,292 GRT. In 1969,
7,707,255 metric tons of goods entered and 309,353 metric tons left the port of
Basel.

AVIATION. In 1969 civil aviation on domestic and international routes
carried 6,343,479 passengers, 200,098 metric tons of mail, freight and luggage,
and flew 123,966,000 km.

The air transport organization Swissair (founded in 1931) in 1970 flew 1,149m.
ton-km, carrying 3,927,864 passengers. Swissair is a mixed enterprise with a
capital of originally 14m. francs, raised to 218·75m. in 1967. Its fleet consisted of
39 aircraft on 31 Dec. 1970.

POST. In 1969 there were in Switzerland 4,102 post offices. There were
2,685,800 telephones, all integrated in one dial system.

Wireless communication is furnished by 3 main medium-wave stations and one
short-wave station. There are 3 television studios and 86 transmitters. All
stations are operated by the Federal Post, Telephone and Telegraph (PTT)
services. Radio-telegraph circuits are operated by Radio Suisse SA, radio-
telephone circuits by the PTT. Radio licences, 1969, 1,800,341; television
licences, 1,144,154.

The total expenditure of the PTT in 1969 was 2,527m. francs, the total gross
receipts 2,572m. francs.

BANKING. The National Bank, with headquarters divided between Bern and
Zürich, opened on 20 June 1907. It has the exclusive right to issue bank-notes.
On 31 Dec. 1968 the condition of the bank was as follows (in 1m. francs): Gold,
11,434·5; foreign exchange, 5,792·9; discounts and advances, 1,008·5; securities,
170·2; notes in circulation, 12,518·4; deposits, 6,914·8.

In 1968 there were 1,609 banking institutions with total assets of 140,544m.
Swiss francs. They included 28 cantonal banks (36,427m. francs), 5 big banks
(74,248m.), 97 mortgage banks (10,409m.), 64 other local banks (5,240m.),
113 savings banks (5,477m.), 1,136 mutual credit banks (3,418m.) and 165 others
(10,211m.).

On 31 Dec. 1968 the total amount of savings deposits in Swiss banks was
33,675m. francs, with 9m. depositors.

National Bank: Bulletin mensuel.—Das schweizerische Bankwesen. Yearly. From 1920

WEIGHTS AND MEASURES. The metric system of weights and measures
was made compulsory by the federal law on 3 July 1875 and since 1 Jan. 1887
only metric units have been legal. By the federal law of 24 June 1909 the international electric units were also adopted.

DIPLOMATIC REPRESENTATIVES

Switzerland maintains embassies in:

Afghánistán	Greece	Nicaragua
Algeria	Guatemala	Niger
Argentina	Guinea	Nigeria
Australia	Haiti	Norway
Austria	Honduras	Pakistan
Belgium	Hungary	Panama
Bolivia	Iceland	Paraguay
Botswana	India	Peru
Brazil	Indonesia	Philippines
Bulgaria	Iran	Poland
Burma	Iraq	Portugal
Burundi	Irish Republic	Romania
Cambodia	Israel	Rwanda
Cameroun	Italy	Saudi Arabia
Canada	Ivory Coast	Senegal
Central African Republic	Jamaica	Sierra Leone
Ceylon	Japan	Singapore
Chad	Jordan	South Africa, Republic of
Chile	Kenya	Spain
China	Korea (South)	Sudan
Colombia	Kuwait	Sweden
Congo (Br.)	Laos	Syria
Congo (K.)	Lebanon	Tanzania
Costa Rica	Lesotho	Thailand
Cuba	Liberia	Togo
Cyprus	Libya	Trinidad
Czechoslovakia	Luxembourg	Tunisia
Dahomey	Malagasy Republic	Turkey
Denmark	Malawi	Uganda
Dominican Republic	Malaysia	USSR
Ecuador	Mali	UAR
El Salvador	Malta	UK
Ethiopia	Mauritania	USA
Finland	Mexico	Upper Volta
France	Mongolia	Uruguay
Gabon	Morocco	Venezuela
Gambia	Nepál	Yugoslavia
Germany (West)	Netherlands	Zambia
Ghana	New Zealand	

OF SWITZERLAND IN GREAT BRITAIN (77–81 Gloucester Place, W1)

Ambassador: Albert Weitnauer (accredited 26 Feb. 1971).
Counsellor: J. A. Iselin. *Military and Air Attaché:* Col. Helmut von Fritschig.
First Secretaries: Charles Bruggmann, Franz Muheim, Franz Birrer

There is a consular representative at Manchester.

OF GREAT BRITAIN IN SWITZERLAND

Ambassador: E. A. Midgley, CMG, MBE.
Counsellors: G. G. Brown, CMG; G. V. Britten, CBE (*Head of Chancery*).
Defence Attaché: Col. J. I. G. Capadose. *First Secretary:* H. R. W. Whatham.

There are Consuls-General at Geneva and Zürich; a Consul at Basel and a Vice-Consul at Montreux.

OF SWITZERLAND IN THE USA (2900 Cathedral Ave. NW, Washington, D.C., 20008)

Ambassador: Felix Schnyder.
Minister: Bernard Turrettini. *Counsellors:* Robert Lempen; Auguste Geiser (*Economic*); Hans Muller (*Cultural*). *First Secretaries:* Peter Dietschi; Ernest Andres. *Armed Forces Attaché:* Col. Karl Erny.

There are Consuls-General at Chicago, Los Angeles, New Orleans, New York and San Francisco; Consuls at Atlanta, Boston, Cleveland, Houston, Philadelphia, St Louis and Seattle.

OF THE USA IN SWITZERLAND

Ambassador: Shelby C. Davies.
Deputy Chief of Mission: Richard D. Vine. *Heads of Sections:* Herman T. Skofield (*Political*); Robert C. Huffmann (*Economic*); F. Pierce Olson (*Commercial*); Colette M. Meyer (*Consular*); James N. Leaken (*Administrative*). *Service Attachés:* Col. William Y. Pennington (*Army*), Col. Burton C. Andrus (*Air*).

There is a Consul-General at Zürich.

BOOKS OF REFERENCE

STATISTICAL INFORMATION. The Bureau féderal de statistique (15 Hallwyl St, Bern) was established in 1860. *Director:* J.-J. Senglet. Its principal publications are:

Annuaire statistique de la Suisse. Bâle. From 1891
Statistique de la Suisse. From 1930
Contributions à la Statistique Suisse. From 1930
Bibliographie Suisse de statistique et d'économie politique. Annual, from 1937

Swiss Confederation

Annuaire; Budget; Message du Budget; Compte d'Etat (annual) *Feuille Fédérale; Recueil des Lois fédérales* (weekly)
Recueil systématique des lois et ordonnances, 1848–1947 (in German, French and Italian). Bern, 1951
Sammlung der Bundes- und Kantonsverfassungen (in German, French and Italian). Bern, 1937

Federal Department of Economics

La vie économique (and supplements). Monthly. From 1928
Législation sociale de la Suisse. Annual, from 1928

Behrendt, R. F. (ed.), *Strukturwandlugen der schweizerischen Wirtschaft und Gesellschaft.* Bern, 1962
Bonjour, E., Offler, H. S., and Potter, G. R., *A Short History of Switzerland.* Oxford, 1952
Dürrenmatt, P., *Schweizer Geschichte.* Zürich, 1963.—*Schweiz.* Zurich, 1962.—*Wir Schweizer und der totale Krieg.* Zürich, 1960
Imhof, E. (ed.), *Atlas der Schweiz.* Bern, 1965 ff.
Meyer, Alice, *Anpassung oder Widerstand. Die Schweiz zur Zeit des Nationalsozialismus.*
Tschäni, H., *Profil der Schweiz.* Zürich, 1967
Unser Schweizer Standpunkt 1914, 1939, 1964. Bern, 1964
Handbuch der schweizerischen Volkswirtschaft. Bern, 1955
Who's Who in Switzerland. Ed. H. and E. Girsberger. Zürich, 1952

NATIONAL LIBRARY. Bibliothèque Nationale Suisse, 15 Hallwyl St, Bern, *Director:* F. G. Maier.

SYRIA

al-Jamhouriya al Arabia as-Souriya

HISTORY. For the history of Syria from 1920 to 1946 *see* THE STATESMAN'S YEAR-BOOK, 1957, pp. 1408 f. For the union with Egypt concluded on 1 Feb. 1958, *see* THE STATESMAN'S YEAR-BOOK, 1961, pp. 1527 ff. On 28 Sept. 1961 a national revolution broke out, and on 5 Oct. President Nasser acknowledged the dissolution of the union. Syria was re-admitted to the United Nations (13 Oct.) and the Arab League.

GOVERNMENT. On 8 March 1963 a National Council of Revolution seized power, probably in collusion with the revolutionary junta in Iraq and President Nasser of Egypt.

On 23 Feb. 1966 the government of President Gen. Al-Hafiz was overthrown by the 'Provisional National Leadership' of the Baath Party. They appointed Dr Nureddin al-Atassi as head of state and Dr Yussif Zeayen as prime minister.

Lieut.-Gen. Hafez al Assad seized power on 13 Nov. 1970 and formed a cabinet on 21 Nov. A provisional Constitution was published and on 16 Feb. 1971 a People's Council of 173 members was nominated by presidential decree. Lieut.-Gen. Assad was sworn in as President on 14 March 1971.

President: Lieut.-Gen. Hafez al Assad.
Foreign Affairs: Mahmoud Ayoubi.

AREA AND POPULATION. Syria is bounded by the Mediterranean and the Lebanese Republic on the west, by Israel and Jordan on the south, by Iraq on the east and by Turkey on the north. The frontier between Syria and Turkey (Nisibim-Jeziret ibn Omar) was settled by the Franco-Turkish agreement of 22 June 1929.

The administrative districts of Syria consist of the *mohafazets* of Damascus, Hama, Homs, Dera'a, Aleppo, Lattakia, Deir-ez-Zor, Sweida, Hassakeh, Raqqa, Idlib, Kunaitra and Tartous.

The area of Syria is 185,680 sq. km (71,772 sq. miles), of which 35,000 sq. km have been surveyed. The census of 20 Sept. 1960 gave a total population of 4,565,121, showing about 10% less than the estimates. Estimate (1968) 5·7m. The principal towns, with population in 1960, are: Damascus, 557,252; Aleppo, 425,467; Homs, 137,217; Hama, 97,390; Lattakia, 67,604; Deir-ez-Zor, 42,036.

Arabic is the official language.

RELIGION. The population is composed mainly of Moslems, of whom there were 3,286,243 in 1954. The majority are Sunni Moslems (2,702,531); there were also 15,193 Shiites and 38,106 Ismailis. The Druzes number 117,804 and the Alawites, 409,514. Christians number 489,731, of whom 172,873 are Greek Orthodox, 57,344 Greek Catholics, 111,648 Armenian Orthodox, 52,758 Syrian Orthodox, 19,889 Armenian Catholics, 14,393 Protestants, 17,010 Maronites, 20,013 Syrian Catholics, 6,880 5,570 Chaldeans, Latins, 11,348 Nestorians and 5 Assyrians. There are also 31,899 Jews and 3,095 Yezides.

EDUCATION. The Syrian University was founded in 1924, although the faculties of law and of medicine had omoted previously. In 1968 the University of Damascus comprised 12 faculties and the University of Aleppo comprised 6 faculties. Students 1968 numbered 32,509 in these 2 institutions, with a teaching staff of 479.

In 1968, 4,881 primary schools had 21,228 teachers and 767,895 pupils; 641 secondary schools, 8,509 teachers and 214,516 pupils; vocational schools, 641 teachers and 5,764 pupils; teacher-training colleges, 522 teachers and 6,277 students.

NEWSPAPERS (1964). There are 2 national daily newspapers in Damascus; local dailies appear in Hama, Homs, Aleppo and Lattakia.

HEALTH. In 1968 there were 1,787 physicians and 4,887 beds in government hospitals.

FINANCE. Currency. The monetary unit is the Syrian £, divided into 100 piastres. The official rate of exchange, which is only applied to transactions with distributing oil companies and for calculating import statistics, is £Syr.10·75 to £ sterling and £Syr.2·19 to US$1.

In March 1968 total currency in circulation amounted to £Syr.1,278m.

Budget. The ordinary budget for the calendar year 1970 balanced at £Syr.2,780m., for 1969 at £Syr.2,200m.

G G

A 5-year development plan for 1960/61–1964/65 incorporated many of the features in the 7-year expenditure development project of 1955 and the 10-year plan of 1958 (*see* THE STATESMAN'S YEAR-BOOK, 1958, p. 1426, and 1961, p. 1541). The total expenditure in the second 5-year plan was estimated at £Syr.4,955m. About 13·1% of the total cost was to be spent on Euphrates project, 6·2% on irrigation and land reclamation, 8·8% on agriculture, 8% on industry and mining, 12·4% on power and fuel, 18% on transport and communications, 25·8% on public utilities, 7·7% on services, etc.

DEFENCE. The post of Commander-in-Chief of the Army and the Armed Forces, abolished on 12 Sept. 1965, was re-established on 23 Feb. 1966.

On 4 Nov. 1966 a defence agreement was signed with the United Arab Republic, providing for a joint defence council and a joint military command (to be assigned to the UAR chief of staff).

On 28 April 1964 Syria abrogated the military union pact with Iraq.

Army. The Army is composed of about 75,000 trained men, the gendarmerie of 5,000, the Bedouin Control Force of about 1,000 and the civil police of 1,800. Equipment and technical advisers are being supplied increasingly by the USSR including (in 1970) 150 T-34 and 700 T-54/55s medium tanks.

Navy. The Navy includes 2 minesweepers, 3 patrol vessels, 6 missile boats and 17 torpedo boats.

Air Force. The Air Force has been re-equipped with Soviet assistance following its losses in the June 1967 war. It is believed to have about 10,000 personnel and up to 200 first-line jet combat aircraft, made up of 90 MiG-21 supersonic interceptors, 40 Su-7 supersonic fighter-bombers and 70 MiG-17 and MiG-15 fighter-bombers. Training units have Russian Yak-18 and Yak-11 piston-engined primary and intermediate trainers. There are also transport and helicopter units.

AGRICULTURE. Syria is essentially an agricultural country, the bulk of the population being engaged in the cultivation of the soil and in cattle breeding. In 1967 the cultivated area was 3,337,914 hectares, of which 538,003 are irrigated; in 1967, 891,000 hectares were under wheat and 631,000 hectares under barley. The total cultivable area is 8·63m. hectares, including 450,299 hectares of forest and 5,390,242 hectares of pasture.

The Agrarian Reform Law of 1958, as modified by 1963, allows proprietors a maximum of 15–50 hectares of irrigated land and 80 hectares of uncultivated land, taking into account irrigation possibilities, rainfall, size of families, etc.

Yield of principal crops, 1968 (in 1,000 metric tons): Wheat, 600; barley, 512; olives, 112; tobacco, 8·5; lentils, 48·3; millet, 37·4; sugar-beet. 166.

Area under cotton, 1968, 288,400 hectares; crop, ginned, 126,513 metric tons.

Livestock, 1968: 4,847,000 sheep, 779,000 goats, 6,400 camels, 63,000 horses, 273,000 cattle, 235,000 asses, 65,000 mules.

MINING. Syria is poorer in minerals than in other resources, but this may be due to insufficient exploration. Search for petroleum in the Lattakia and Deir ez Zor regions continues. A branch of the Iraq Petroleum Company's oil pipeline from Kirkuk crosses Syria between Makaleb in the east and Nahr el Kebir valley in the west. The Iraq Petroleum Company has constructed a new pipeline from Kirkuk to the small fishing port of Banias (south of Lattakia), which came into use in April 1952; the Trans-Arabian Pipeline Company's line to Sidon crosses southern Syria. Another pipeline is being constructed from the Karachouk oilfield *via* Homs to the port of Tartous.

On 8 Dec. 1955 the Syrian Parliament ratified a Supplemental Convention concluded with the Iraq Petroleum Company. By the terms of the Convention, Syria will receive an annual payment of approximately £6·5m. sterling as transit dues and a sum of £8·5m. in settlement of claims for back payment. Oil has been discovered in the Jezirah region. A dispute with the Iraq Petroleum Company concerning an increase in pipeline royalties was settled in March 1967.

There are indications of phosphates, lead, copper, antimony, nickel, chrome; gypsum is widely distributed. Manganese ore was mined before 1914. Sodium chloride and bitumen deposits are being worked. There is abundance of good calcareous building stone and basalt. Deposits of natural gas have been discovered in the Jezirah.

INDUSTRY. The most important industries are flour, oils, soap, cement, tanning, tobacco, textiles, knitwear, glassware, spinning, sugar, margarine, hosiery, footwear and brassware. Limited nationalization of certain basic industries was decreed in March 1963. On 3 Jan. 1965, 22 companies were completely nationalized, the owners of 61 companies were allowed to keep a quarter share and those of 24 companies to retain a tenth of their property.

Industrial production in 1968 included (in 1,000 metric tons): Cement, 91·7; sugar, 83; cotton yarn, 17; vegetable oil, 22·9; woollen fabrics, 1,440; manufactured tobacco, 4; salt, 29·7; cottoncake, 94. In addition, 1·9m. pairs of shoes were manufactured and 8,979 refrigerators assembled.

COMMERCE. In April 1965 a state trading company (SIMEX) was set up to handle the nationalized imports and exports.

Trade in calendar years in £Syr.1m. was as follows:

	1963	1964	1965	1966	1967	1968
Imports	896·0	898	812	1,103	1,099	1,193
Exports	720·9	673	644	661	591	673

In 1967 both imports and exports of Syria declined and the trade deficit improved slightly. Imports fell by 9%, to £Syr.1,009m., and exports dropped by 11%, to £Syr.591m. The trade deficit, at £Syr.418m., was £Syr.24m. smaller than in 1966.

Total trade of Syria with UK (British Board of Trade returns, in £1,000 sterling):

	1965	1966	1967	1968	1969	1970
Imports to UK	2,138	1,037	479	494	1,235	489
Exports from UK	6,106	6,938	5,237	4,995	7,128 ⎫	5,995
Re-exports from UK	65	66	45	26	55 ⎭	

An agreement providing for a customs and economic union between Syria and Jordan was signed in Damascus on 5 Aug. 1956; a similar agreement with Egypt, on 3 Sept. 1957.

SHIPPING. Following the separation of Syria from the common customs union with the Lebanon in March 1950, Syria has made improvements at Lattakia Port and issued regulations providing for the transit through that port of much of Syria's imports and the bulk of her exports. The amount of cargo discharged there in 1968 was 14,349,632 NRT and the amount loaded 14,287,758 NRT. A deep water harbour at Lattakia is being built by a Yugoslav firm. Tartous remains a fishing port and Banias is used as an oil terminal and loading port by the Iraq Petroleum Co., Ltd.

RAILWAYS. In Syria the following railways are open (in addition to those listed under LEBANON (p. 1125): Standard gauge from Aleppo to Meidan-Ekbes (Turkish frontier), 72 miles; Aleppo to Tel-Kotchek (Iraq frontier), 325 miles; narrow gauge from Damascus to El Hammé, 120 miles; Damascus to Dera'a (Jordan frontier) 80 miles. Two lines have recently been constructed: a standard gauge from Akari to Tartous, 42 km, and from Aleppo to Tabka, 148 km, which is part of the Al-Jezirah to Lattakia line.

ROADS. In 1968 there were 6,936 km of asphalted roads, 1,184 km of paved non-asphalted road and 1,184 km of levelled roads. The first-class roads are capable of carrying all types of modern motor transport and are usable all the year round, while the second-class roads are usable during the dry season only, *i.e.*, for about 9 months. The Nairn Transport Company operate a trans-desert pullman motor coach service between Damascus and Baghdad. The motor vehicles registered at the end of 1968 totalled 49,998, including 6,102 motor cycles, 1,557 buses, 27,999 cars and 8,926 goods vehicles.

POST. An automatic telephone system has been installed in Damascus, Aleppo, Homs, Hama and Lattakia. Number of telephones (1970), 103,687; of these nearly, 46,604 were in Damascus and 22,479 in Aleppo.

BANKING. The Central Bank has the sole right of issuing currency. Other banks were nationalized in March 1963, namely, the Omaya Bank and its subsidiary, the Popular Mortgage Bank; the Orient Arab Bank; the Bank of Syria and Overseas; the Agricultural Bank; the Arab World Bank.

WEIGHTS AND MEASURES. A decree dated 22 Aug. 1935 makes the use of the metric system legal and obligatory throughout the whole of the country. In outlying districts the former weights and measures may still be in use. They are: 1 *okiya* = 0·47 lb.; 6 *okiyas* = 1 *oke* = 2·82 lb.; 2 *okes* = 1 *rottol* = 5·64 lb.; 200 *okes* = 1 *kantar*.

DIPLOMATIC REPRESENTATIVES

Syria maintains embassies in:

Albania	Finland	Korea (North)	Spain
Algeria	France	Kuwait	Sudan
Argentina	Germany (East)	Libya	Switzerland
Austria	Germany (West)	Luxembourg	Tanzania
Belgium	Greece	Mauritania	Tunisia
Brazil	Guinea	Morocco	Turkey
Bulgaria	Hungary	Netherlands	USSR
Chile	India	Nigeria	UAR
China	Indonesia	Pakistan	Vatican
Colombia	Iran	Poland	Venezuela
Cuba	Iraq	Romania	Yemen
Cyprus	Italy	Saudi Arabia	Yugoslavia
Czechoslovakia	Jordan	Somalia	

Diplomatic relations with the UK and USA were broken off on 6 June 1967.

BOOKS OF REFERENCE

STATISTICAL INFORMATION. In 1948 a Department of Statistics was established in the Ministry of National Economy, Damascus. It publishes a monthly summary and an annual Statistical Abstract (in Arabic and English).

Census of Population 1960. 15 vols. Ministry of Planning, Damascus, 1961–65
The Economic Development of Syria. International Bank Report. Baltimore, 1955
Asfour, E. Y., *Syria: development and monetary policy.* Harvard Univ. Press, 1959
Barthélemy, A., *Dictionnaire arabe-français. Dialectes de Syrie.* 4 vols. Paris, 1935–50
Hourani, A. H., *Syria and Lebanon.* 2nd ed. R. Inst. of Int. Affairs, 1954
Ziadeh, N. A., *Syria and Lebanon.* New York, 1957

THAILAND

Prades Thai, or Muang-Thai

On 24 June 1939 the President of the Council of Ministers issued a declaration that the name of the country, hitherto known as Siam, should henceforward be Thailand, and of the people and nationality, Thai.

REIGNING KING. **Bhumibol Adulyadej,** born 5 Dec. 1927, younger brother of King Ananda Mahidol, who died on 9 June 1946. King Bhumibol married on

28 April 1950 Princess Sirikit, and was crowned 5 May 1950. Children: Princess Ubol Ratana (born 5 April 1951), Prince Vajiralongkorn (born 28 July 1952), Princess Sirindhorn (born 2 April 1955), Princess Chulabhorn (born 4 July 1957).

AREA AND POPULATION. The area of Thailand is 514,000 sq. km (198,250 sq. miles).

The census taken on 25 April 1960 gave a population of 26,257,916 (13,154,149 males, 13,103,767 females), of whom 8,271,302 lived in the Central region, 8,991,543 in the North-east region, 3,271,965 in the South region, 5,723,106 in the North region. Of the 1960 population, 1·6% were Chinese. Estimate, 1967, 32m.

Bangkok is the capital (metropolitan population 1960, 2·3m.; city population (31 May 1968), 2·04m.). Other important towns are Thonburi (540,300) and Chiengmai (66,000).

CONSTITUTION AND GOVERNMENT. Until 24 June 1932 Siam was an absolute monarchy. On that date a *coup d'état* was effected and a Provisional Constitution Act was promulgated on 27 June. This was replaced by the constitution of 10 Dec. 1932, which in turn was superseded by new constitutions on 10 May 1946 and 23 March 1949, decreed by the leaders of successive *coups d'état* in 1947, 1951, 1957 and 1958.

An interim constitution was decreed on 28 Jan. 1959. It provided for the appointment by the Government of a constituent assembly of 240 members to draft a permanent constitution; this was promulgated in June 1968. According to this, the sovereign power emanates from the Thai people and is exercised by the King through Parliament, the Council of Ministers and the courts of law. The rights and freedoms of the people in religious belief, properties, speech, writing, publication, education and peaceful assembly are recognized and guaranteed. Parliament is to be composed of a Senate and a House of Representatives. Senators are appointed by the King; their number shall be equal to three-fourths of the total membership in the House of Representatives, who are elected on the basis of one member per 150,000 population in each province. Membership in the Senate lasts 6 years and that in the House of Representatives 4 years. The King appoints the Prime Minister and 15–30 other Ministers of State, who may not be members of either House and who must be collectively responsible to Parliament.

The first general election for the members of the House of Representatives under the new constitution was held on 10 Feb. 1969. There were 219 seats and the Government-support-party, the Saha Pracha Thai (United Thai People) gained 75 seats, the Prachatipat (Democrats) 57, Independents 72 and other minor parties 15.

On 11 March 1969 the King appointed Field Marshal Thanom Kittikachorn as prime minister and minister of defence.

Minister for Foreign Affairs: Dr Thanat Khoman.

National flag: Red, white, blue, white, red (horizontal, the blue band being twice as wide as the white or red ones).

LOCAL GOVERNMENT. For purposes of administration Thailand is divided into 71 provinces (*changwads*), each under the control of a *changwad* governor. The *changwads* are subdivided into 509 districts (*amphurs*) and 27 sub-districts (*king amphurs*), 5,036 communes (*tambons*) and 44,606 villages (*moobans*). Local legislative and executive bodies with limited powers are being established with functions, procedure and method of election closely modelled on those of the central Assembly.

RELIGION. The prevailing religion is Buddhism. In 1960 there were 24,563,523 Buddhists, 1,025,569 Moslems, 150,053 Christians, 461,317 Confucianists, 3,483 Hindus, 35,238 others and 13,979 professing no religion.

EDUCATION. Primary education is compulsory for children between the ages of 7–14 and free in local and municipal schools. In 1964 there were 58 kindergartens with 628 teachers and 13,083 pupils; 24,603 primary schools with 104,342 teachers and 3,932,474 pupils; 444 secondary schools with 9,301 teachers and 159,136 pupils; 35 teachers' training colleges with 1,932 teachers and 15,342 students. In 1968 there were 8 universities: Chulalongkorn University (1917), Thammasat University (1934), Universities of Medical Science, Agriculture and Fine Arts; all in Bangkok; Chiengmai University (1964), the University of the North-East in Khon Kan (1966), and Prince of Songkhla University (1968) in the South. There were also 201 vocational schools with together 5,261 teachers and 44,839 students.

The literacy of the population 10 years of age and over was 70·8% in 1960 (53·7% in 1947).

CINEMAS (1965). There were 385 cinemas with a seating capacity of 131,134.

NEWSPAPERS. There are 18 daily newspapers in Bangkok, including 2 in English and 4 in Chinese, with a combined circulation of 300,000. There are 37 weekly papers in the provinces.

HEALTH. In 1965 there were 205 general hospitals, including 10 mental hospitals, with together 23,776 beds. There were also 157 health centres and 94 private maternity clinics. In 1965 there were 4,323 physicians, 414 dentists and 1,294 pharmacists.

JUSTICE. The judicial power is exercised in the name of the King, by (a) courts of first instance, (b) the court of appeal (Uthorn) and (c) the Supreme Court (Dika). The King appoints, transfers and dismisses judges, who are independent in conducting trials and giving judgement in accordance with the law.

Courts of first instance are subdivided into 20 magistrates' courts (Kwaeng) with limited civil and minor criminal jurisdiction; 85 provincial courts (Changwad) with unlimited civil and criminal jurisdiction; the criminal and civil courts with exclusive jurisdiction in Bangkok and Thonburi; the central juvenile court for persons under 18 years of age in Bangkok and Thonburi.

The court of appeal exercises appellate jurisdiction in civil and criminal cases from all courts of first instance. From it appeals lie to Dika Court on any point of law and, in certain cases, on questions of fact.

The Supreme Court is the supreme tribunal of the land. Besides its normal appellate jurisdiction in civil and criminal matters, it has semi-original jurisdiction over general election petitions. The decisions of Dika Court are final. Every person has the right to present a petition to the Government who will deal with all matters of grievance.

FINANCE. Currency. The unit of currency is the baht, formerly called in English the tical, which is divided into 100 santung. Silver coins have gone out of circulation. Only nickel, copper, tin and bronze coins are now minted, in denominations of 1 baht, 50, 25, 10 and 5 satang. Currency notes, first issued in 1902, now comprise 5, 10, 20, 100 baht notes.

In May 1970 the total amount of coins in circulation was 655m. baht and 12,949m. baht of notes.

The currency law is based on the Currency Act of Aug., B.E. 2501 (1958). The 1971 rate of exchange is about 50·4 baht to £1 and 21 baht to US$1.

Budget. Revenue and expenditure in 1m. baht (fiscal years, Oct.–Sept.):

Budget(actual)	1964–65[2]	1965–66[2]	1966–67[2]	1967–68[2]	1968–69[1]	1969–70[1]
Revenue	10,570	12,524	13,321	16,259	17,529	19,020
Expenditure[1]	8,890	15,050	17,940	21,130	23,324	27,299

[1] Includes both current and capital expenditure.　　　　[2] Estimates.

Ordinary expenditures in 1970 (in 1m. baht) provided 4,903 for defence; 6,182 for general administration; 8,185 for economic services, 6,956 for social services.

Revenue in 1969–70 derived from taxes and duties, 17,094; sales and charges, 375; government enterprises, 569.

In April 1970 the national internal debt was 19,065·6m. baht, of which long-term debt amounted to 17,426·3m. External debt in Feb. 1970 totalled 6,241·2m. baht, including US$122·1m. and DM 96·7m.

DEFENCE. Under the Ministry of Defence Organization Act of 1960 the Ministry of Defence has assumed the Supreme Command and the control of the Army, Navy and Air Force with the advice of the Defence Council headed by the Minister of Defence. The National Defence College, the Armed Forces Staff College and the Military Preparatory School serve the education of officers. Each service has its own C.-in-C., service council, schools of arms and Command and General Staff College.

Under the Military Service Act of 1954 every able-bodied man between the ages of 21 and 30 is liable to serve 2 years with the colours; 7 years in the first reserve; 10 years in the second reserve; 6 years in the third reserve.

Army. The Army is organized in 3 infantry divisions and 1 separate regimental combat team. Peace-time strength is 110,000.

Navy. In 1970 the Navy included 1 destroyer escort, 4 frigates, 1 armoured gunboat, 1 escort minesweeper, 1 survey ship, 2 coastal minelayers, 4 coastal minesweepers, 18 patrol vessels, 10 patrol boats, 6 landing ships, 8 landing craft, 2 transports, 4 oilers, 2 water carriers and 2 tugs. Naval personnel totalled 2,000 officers and 13,000 men. The Marine Corps numbered 400 officers and 6,000 men. There is a Royal Naval Academy at Paknam.

There is a small naval air arm, equipped with obsolete piston-engined Firefly reconnaissance-fighters and Helldiver bombers.

At the mouth of the Chao Praya River are the Paknam forts. The naval dockyard has been reconstructed; a large new graving dock is under consideration.

Air Force. The Royal Thai Air Force has been reorganized with the assistance of a US Military Air Advisory Group. It has 6 combat wings (each 1–3 squadrons of 16 aircraft), equipped with single squadrons of F-5A/B and F-86F and F-86L Sabre jet fighter-bombers and 6 squadrons of T-28D and T-6 armed piston-engined aircraft (being supplemented by 16 OV-10C Broncos) for security duties. There are also RT-33A jet reconnaissance aircraft, transport units equipped with HS 748, C-123 Provider, Caribou, C-54, C-47 and C-45 aircraft, training units with Chipmunk primary, T-6 and T-37 intermediate and T-33A advanced trainers, and helicopters for assault and rescue duties. First-line strength is about 120 aircraft. Total strength is about 20,000 officers and men and 250 aircraft.

PRODUCTION. A National Economic Council, responsible for planning, was set up by parliament in 1950. This was in 1959 replaced by a new office of the National Economic Development Board.

According to the 1960 census, 82·3% of the economically active population 11 years of age and over (13,772,104 persons) were engaged in agriculture, forestry, hunting and fishing, and 3·4% in manufacturing.

AGRICULTURE. The chief produce of the country is rice, which forms the national food and the staple article of export. The area under paddy is about 18m. acres. With the completion of the Chao Phya dam located near Chai-nat in 1957 the irrigable area in the Central Plain had by 1962 been extended to about 8,409,000 Rai (3,363,600 acres). Additional projects now under construction will bring the irrigable lands to the total of about 11,605,900 Rai (4,642,360 acres). Tank irrigation projects which were designed to ensure water supply for upland crop cultivation, especially in the north-eastern part, irrigate 325,418 Rai (130,167 acres).

Output of the major crops in 1968 was (in 1,000 metric tons): Paddy, 10,772·1; maize, 1,000; sugar-cane, 5,682; coconuts, 1,250; groundnuts, 195; cotton, 89; kenaf, 280; tobacco, 90; sesame, 19; castor beans, 45.

Livestock, 1966 (in 1,000 heads): Elephants, 11; horses, 175; buffaloes, 6,878; cattle, 5,167; swine, 4,045; fowl, 45,112.

FORESTRY. About 60% of the land area of Thailand is under forest. In the north, mixed deciduous forests with teak (*Tectona grandis, Linn.*), growing in mixture with several other species, predominate. In the north-eastern section hardwood of the *Dipterocarpus* species, especially *Shorea obtusa* and *Pentacme Siamensis, Kurz* exist in most parts. In all other regions of the country tropical evergreen forests are found, with the well-known timber of commerce, Yang (*Dipterocarpus alatus, Roxb* and *Dipterocarpus* spp.) as the outstanding crops. Most of the teak timber exploited in northern Thailand is floated down to Bangkok. Some of them, however, are exported through the Salween into Burma.

About one-third of the teak-forest area is being exploited by the Forest Industry Organization, and the remaining two-thirds is to be worked by timber company lessees and other private enterprises.

Output of main foresty products in 1969 was (in 1,000 cu. metres): Teak, 364·5; yang, 537·4; other woods, 1,912·1; firewood, 1,604; charcoal, 562.

Rubber production (in 1,000 metric tons), 1955, 133·3; 1960, 170·8; 1964, 211; 1965, 217; 1966, 220; 1967, 219; 1968, 259.

FISHERY. In 1968 the catch of sea fish was 1·28m. metric tons and of freshwater fish, 92,000 metric tons.

MINING. The mineral resources are extensive and varied, including cassiterite (tin ore), wolfram, scheelite, antimony, coal, copper, gold, iron, lead, manganese, molybdenum, rubies, sapphires, silver, zinc and zircons. By far the most important are tin and wolfram. Ore output in 1969 (in metric tons): Tin, 28,793; wolfram, 1,267; lead, 4,230; antimony, 1,807; manganese, 29,936; iron, 477,393; fluorite, 297,560; gypsum, 92,033; lignite, 347,811.

INDUSTRY. Production of manufactured goods in 1969 included 2·4m. metric tons of cement, 318,120 metric tons of sugar, 44·9m. gunny bags, 29,101 metric tons of paper, 14,419 metric tons of tobacco, 3·6m. kilolitres of petroleum products.

TOURISM. In 1967 about 328,000 foreigners visited Thailand, spending an estimated 710m. baht, excluding an estimated 216m. baht spent by USA military personnel.

TRADE UNIONS. The Thai National Trade Union Congress is a member of the International Confederation of Free Trade Unions.

COMMERCE. The foreign trade (in 1m. baht) was as follows:

	1964	1965	1966	1967	1968	1969
Imports (c.i.f.)	14,253·4	15,433	18,504	22,188	24,103	26,248
Exports (f.o.b.)	12,339·2	12,941	14,099	14,166	13,679	14,792

Distribution of trade by countries in 1968 (in 1m. baht):

	Imports (c.i.f.)	Exports (f.o.b.)		Imports (c.i.f.)	Exports (f.o.b.)
Japan	8,274	2,874	UK	1.673	435
Hong Kong	428	921	West Germany	2,021	621
Indonesia	178	181	Netherlands	456	967
Malaysia	204	1,038	Italy	592	191
Singapore	282	1,181	France	400	129
USA	4,512	1,789	Taiwan	579	515

In 1968 the main items of imports were (in 1m. baht): Motor vehicles, 1,871 (1966); iron and steel, 1,303; industrial machinery, 1,526 (1966); petroleum products, 1,992; electric machinery, 402.

In 1968 exports of rice were 1·07m. metric tons (3,775m. baht); rubber, 252,220 metric tons (1,816m. baht); maize, 1·48m. metric tons (1,556m. baht); tin, 24,017 metric tons (1,510m. baht); teak, 29,446 cu. metres (169m. baht); jute and kenaf, 289,478 metric tons (674m. baht); tapioca products, (888,854 metric tons (772m. baht).

Total trade between Thailand and UK (British Board of Trade returns) in £1,000 sterling:

	1966	1967	1968	1969	1970
Imports to UK	5,643	5,363	5,889	5,705	5,509
Exports from UK	21,147	22,060	28,060	30,758 }	32,112
Re-exports from UK	136	209	225	218 }	

SHIPPING. In 1964, 1,317 vessels of 4,583,522 NRT entered and 1,903 of 4,738,335 NRT cleared the port of Bangkok.

The port of Bangkok, about 30 km from the mouth of the Chao Phya River, is capable of berthing ocean-going vessels of 10,000 gross tons and 28 ft draught. Bangkok is now a port of entry for Laos, and goods arriving in transit are sent up by rail to Nong Khai and ferried across the river Mekhong to Vientiane.

In 1965 there were 3 Thai steamship companies: Thai Navigation Co. Ltd (4 vessels); Thai Maritime Navigation Co. Ltd (3 vessels); Thai Lines Ltd (10 vessels). There are also 31 foreign steamship lines serving the port.

RAILWAYS. In 1969 there were 3,765 km of state railways open to traffic.

The nothern line runs from Bangkok to Chieng Mai (741 km), the extreme northern terminus. The southern line (990 km) runs from Bangkok down the Peninsula to the frontier station of Padang Besar, where it connects with the Malayan railway from Penang, and to Singapore. Another line (214 km) branching off from Haad Yai on the southern line runs along the east coast of the peninsula to Su-gnai Kolok, where it connects with the Malayan railway line. There are branch lines (totalling 190 km) to Song Khla, Nakon-Sithamrat, Kan Tang and Tha-Kanon. The extensions of the north-eastern line (264 km) from Nakhon Ratsima (Korat) to Nong Khai (360 km) and from Kaeng Koi to Buayai (250 km) have been completed. The Nakhon Ratsima–Ubol line (311 km) has been completed as far as Ubol Rat Thani. The eastern line (255 km) runs from Makkasan to Aran Pradet on the Cambodian frontier. The northern and southern railway systems are linked by a railway bridge over the Menam Chao Phya, and both systems terminate in Bangkok. All state railways are under one management. Gross receipts of the state railways in 1968–69 were 903·3m. baht and expenditure of 843·2m. baht.

ROADS. In 1968 the length of highways open to traffic was 9,878 km, of which 5,706 km were concrete or asphalt-surfaced. In addition there were 2,793 km of provincial highways. Motor vehicles registered in 1965 included 67,261 passenger cars, 17,638 buses, 58,098 lorries, 105,379 motor cycles.

AVIATION. Thai Airways Co. Ltd (TAC), established in 1947, is the sole Thai air transport enterprise, with authorized capital of 300m. baht. The Company operates 11 domestic routes and 3 international routes. On 24 Aug 1959 Thai Airways and the Scandinavian Airlines System set up a new company, Thai International Airways, to operate the international air services from Thailand.

During 1967 there were 22 foreign scheduled airlines operating through Bangkok: Air France, Air India, Air Vietnam, Alitalia, BOAC, Civil Air Transport, Cathay Pacific Airways Ltd, Garuda Indonesian Airways, Japan Air Lines Co. Ltd, KLM, Lufthansa, Malayan Airways Ltd, PANAM, Philippine Air Lines, Qantas Empire Airways Ltd, Royal Air Lao, SAS, Swissair, Union of Burma Airways, United Arab Airlines, Cie de Transports Aériens Intercontinentaux, Trans-World Airlines.

POST. In 1965 there were 276 post offices proper, 414 licensed and Amphur post offices and 447 railway-station post offices. Length of telegraph lines was

17,489 km. There were, in 1969, 114,419 telephones, of which 87,422 were in Bangkok.

In 1959, 51 wireless stations were dealing with inland traffic; 1 high-power transmitting station on telefunken system at Laksi and 1 receiving station at Nondhaburi serve foreign traffic.

BANKING. In 1942 the Bank of Thailand was established under the Bank of Thailand Act, B.E. 2485 (1942) and began operations on 10 Dec. 1942, with the functions of a central bank. The Bank was organized on similar lines to the Bank of England, having its banking activities entirely separate from the management of the note issue. The Bank also took over the note issue previously performed by the Treasury Department of the Ministry of Finance. Although the entire capital is owned by the Government, the Bank is an independent body. Its gold and foreign-exchange reserves, at the end of May 1967, amounted to US$880·91m.

In Jan. 1966 the Agricultural Bank and the Provincial Bank merged in the Krung Thai Bank (capital 105m. baht, of which 80% is owned by the government).

Banks incorporated under Thai law include the Bangkok Bank Ltd, the Bangkok Bank of Commerce Ltd, the Bank of Asia for Industry & Commerce Ltd, the Bank of Ayudhya Ltd, Bangkok Metropolitan Bank Ltd, the Laem Thong Bank Ltd, the Siam City Bank Ltd, the Siam Commercial Bank Ltd, Thai Development Bank Ltd, the Thai Farmers Bank Ltd, Thai Danu Bank Ltd, the Thai Military Bank Ltd, the Union Bank of Bangkok Ltd and the Wang Lee Chan Bank Ltd. Foreign banks include the Chartered Bank, the Hongkong and Shanghai Banking Corporation, the Indian Overseas Bank Ltd, the Mercantile Bank Ltd, Banque de l'Indochine, Sze Hai Tong Bank Ltd, Bank of Canton Ltd, Bank of China Ltd, the National Handelbank N.V., Bank of America, N.T. & S.A., the Mitsui Bank Ltd and the Bank of Tokyo Ltd.

The commercial Thai banks had, in 1968, 535 branches in Thailand and 11 abroad; only Mae Hongson province has no commercial bank services. The deposits held by commercial banks in March 1968 amounted to 20,753·5m. baht.

The Government Savings Bank, which was established as an independent organization in 1947, originated in 1913 when the Government Savings Office was established.

WEIGHTS AND MEASURES. The metric system was made compulsory by a law promulgated on 17 Dec. 1923. The actual weights and measures prescribed by law are: Units of weight: 1 *standard picul* = 60 kg; 1 *standard catty* ($\frac{1}{100}$ picul) = 600 grammes; 1 *standard carat* = 20 centigrammes. Units of length: 1 *sen* = 40 metres; 1 *wah* ($\frac{1}{20}$ sen) = 2 metres; 1 *sauk* ($\frac{1}{4}$ wah) = 0·05 metre; 1 *keup* ($\frac{1}{2}$ sawk) = 0·25 metre. Units of square measure: 1 *rai* (1 sq. sen) = 1,600 sq. metres; 1 *ngan* ($\frac{1}{4}$ rai) = 400 sq. metres; 1 *sq. wah* ($\frac{1}{100}$ ngan) = 4 sq. metres. Units of capacity: 1 *standard kwien* = 2,000 litres; 1 *standard ban* ($\frac{1}{2}$ kwien) = 1,000 litres; 1 *standard sat* ($\frac{1}{50}$ ban) = 20 litres; 1 *standard tanan* ($\frac{1}{20}$ sat) = 1 litre.

Legislation passed in 1940 provided that the calendar year shall coincide with the Christian year, and that the year of the Buddhist era 2484 shall begin on 1 Jan. 1941. (The New Year's Day was previously 1 April.) The years B.E. 2512–2513 therefore correspond to A.D. 1969 and 1970.

DIPLOMATIC REPRESENTATIVES

Thailand maintains embassies in:

Argentina	Canada
Australia	Ceylon
Austria	China
Belgium	Denmark
Brazil	Ethiopia
Burma	France

Germany (West)
India
Indonesia
Iran
Italy (also for Greece and Israel)
Japan
Korea (South)
Laos
Malaysia
Nepál
Netherlands
New Zealand
Nigeria

Pakistan
Philippines
Saudi Arabia
Singapore
Spain
Sweden
Switzerland
USSR
UAR
UK
USA
Vietnam (South)

OF THAILAND IN GREAT BRITAIN (30 Queen's Gate, SW7)

Ambassador: Konthi Suphamongkhon (accredited 21 May 1970).
Counsellors: Phan Wannamethee; Sngat Srivanig; Pandit Bunyapana. *First Secretary:* Sawat Nana. *Service Attachés:* Col. Chaloei Sanguansak (*Army*), Capt. Chinda Chai-Udom (*Navy*), Group Capt. Bundit Chotichanapibal (*Air*).

There are consular representatives at Birmingham, Cardiff, Glasgow, Hull and Liverpool.

OF GREAT BRITAIN IN THAILAND

Ambassador: Sir Arthur de la Mare, KCMG.
Counsellors: G. S. Littlejohn Cook; G. McD. Wilson (*Civil Air*).
First Secretaries: P. Scanlon (*Information*); C. W. Squire (*Head of Chancery*); D. Montgomery (*Commercial*); M. H. Wrigley; J. C. Edwards (*Economic*); W. Boyes (*Consul*); J. D. Maher. *Service Attachés:* Col. W. V. B. Smith, MBE, MC (*Defence and Army*), Wing Cdr. P. A. Knapton, DFC (*Air*), Cdr J. M. Walkey (*Navy*).

OF THAILAND IN THE USA (2300 Kalorama Rd. NW, Washington, D.C., 20008)

Ambassador: Sunthorn Hongladarom.
Counsellor: Lieut.-Gen. Fong Pramualrat (*Educational*). *First Secretaries:* Wichian Watanakum; Sakol Vanabriksha. *Public Relations Attaché:* Siri Tembuñklart. *Service Attachés:* Col. Pamoto Thavornchan (*Army*), Capt. Tada Ditbanjong (*Navy*), Group Capt. Surayuto Niwaenhthi (*Air*).

There are consular representatives in Chicago, Detroit, El Paso, Honolulu, Kansas City, Los Angeles, Miami and Philadelphia.

OF THE USA IN THAILAND

Ambassador: Leonard Unger.
Deputy Chief of Mission: George S. Newman. *Heads of Sections:* William C. Hamilton (*Political*); J. Robert Fluker (*Economic*); Konrad Bekker (*Commercial*); John L. Hagan (*Consular*); Maurice E. Trout (*Administrative*); Howard L. Parsons (*AID*).
Service Attachés: Col. Robert J. Rankin (*Defence and Air*), Col. Fred A. Barringer (*Army*), Capt. Lee C. Miles (*Navy*).

There are Consuls at Chiengmai, Songkhla and Udorn.

BOOKS OF REFERENCE

Thailand Statistical Yearbook 1966. National Statistical Office, Bangkok
Thailand Official Yearbook 1968. Government Printer, Bangkok
Varin, Manit (ed.), *Thailand at a Glance.* 4th ed. Thailand Information Service, London, 1969
Bibliography of materials about Thailand in western languages. Chulalongkorn University, Bangkok, 1960
Blanchard, W., and others, *Thailand, its people, its society, its culture.* New Haven, Conn., 1958

Chamni Phimphisan (ed.), *The Siam Directory*. Bangkok, 1967
Chu, V., *Thailand Today*. New York, 1968
Exell, F. K., *The land and people of Thailand*. London, 1960
Haas, M. R., *Thai–English student's dictionary*. OUP, 1966
Insor, D., *Thailand: a political, social and economic analysis*. London, 1963
Kirkup, J., *Bangkok*. London, 1968
Muscat, R. J., *Development strategy in Thailand: a case study of economic modernization*. London, 1966
Perara, W. (ed.), *Thailand Year Book, 1966–67*. Bangkok, 1966
Phloyphrom, P., *Modern Standard Thai–English Dictionary*. Bangkok, 1958
Riggs, F. W., *Thailand: the modernization of a bureaucratic policy*. Honolulu, 1966
Silcock, T. H. (ed.), *Thailand: social and economic studies*. Canberra, 1967

TUNISIA

Al-Djoumhouria Attunusia

CONSTITUTION AND GOVERNMENT. Tunisia is a sovereign independent republic. The monarchy was abolished by the Constituent Assembly on 25 July 1957. The National Assembly was elected on 8 Nov. 1959 when all 90 seats were won by the Neo-Destour Socialist party.

The constitution of the republic was promulgated on 1 June 1959. The President and the National Assembly are elected simultaneously by direct universal suffrage for a period of 5 years. The President cannot be re-elected more than 3 times consecutively. An amendment to the constitution in 1969 gives the Prime Minister power to act as President in case of a sudden vacancy of the Presidency.

President of the Republic and Head of Government: Habib Bourguiba (elected 25 July 1957, re-elected 8 Nov. 1959, 8 Nov. 1964 and 2 Nov. 1969).

The Ministry consists of 15 Ministers and 6 Secretaries of State.

Prime Minister: Hedi Nouira.
Foreign Affairs: Mohamed Masmoudi. *Defence:* Hassib Ben Ammar.

By decree of 21 July 1959 the country was divided into 13 *gouvernorats*, each subdivided into *délégations, communes* and *cheikhats*.
The official language is Arabic.

Flag: Red with a white circle in the middle, on which is a 5-pointed red star encircled by a red crescent.

AREA AND POPULATION. The boundaries are on the north and east the Mediterranean Sea, on the west Algeria and on the south Libya. The area is about 164,150 sq. km (63,362 sq. miles), including that portion of the Sahara which is to the east of the Djerid, extending towards Ghadamès.

At the census of 3 May 1966 there were 4,457,862 inhabitants (2,267,915 males and 2,189,947 females). Estimate (1969) 4·73m.

The estimated populations of the *gouvernorats* were as follows as at 3 May 1966 (in 1,000): Tunis and suburbs (789), Bizerta (325), Béja (317), Jendouba (253), Le Kef (307), Kassérine (210), Gafsa (315), Médénine (237), Gabès (204), Sfax (424), Kairouan (277), Sousse (511), Nabeul (317).

Tunis, the capital, had, on 3 May 1966, 642,384 inhabitants; Sfax, 249,991; Bizerta, 95,023; Sousse, 82,666; Kairouan, a holy city of the Moslems, 82,299; Gabès, 76,356; Béja, 72,034; Djerba, 65,533; Médénine, 39,218; Hammam-Lif, 22,161.

VITAL STATISTICS (1967). Births, 187,329; deaths, 49,203; marriages, 28,193.

RELIGION. The constitution recognizes Islam as the state religion. There are about 20,000 Roman Catholics, under the Archbishop of Carthage. The Greek Church, the French Protestants and the English Church are also represented.

EDUCATION. All education was in 1956 made dependent on the Ministry of National Education. The 208 independent koranic schools have been nationalized and the distinction between religious and public schools has been abolished. All education is free from primary schools to university. A teachers' training college (*école normale supérieure*) was established in 1955. There are also a high school of law, a centre of economic studies, a school of engineering, 1 medical school, a faculty of agriculture and an institute of business administration.

In 1970–71 primary schools had 964,206 pupils; secondary, technical and vocational schools had 183,928 pupils; higher education mainly at the University of Tunis had 14,050 students.

CINEMAS (1968). There were 108 cinemas with a seating capacity of 41,895.

NEWSPAPERS. There are 2 Arabic and 2 French daily newspapers.

SOCIAL WELFARE. In 1967 there were 82 hospitals (14,406 beds). The registered medical personnel in Tunisia comprised 656 doctors (297 Tunisians and 359 foreigners), 137 pharmacists, 57 dentists and 48 veterinaries. A system of social security was set up in 1950 (amended 1963, 1964 and 1970).

JUSTICE. The Government has abolished the multiple jurisdictions of religious (shara'ic and rabbinic) tribunals. These have been integrated into the civil courts so as to form a single three-level jurisdiction (courts of primary jurisdiction, courts of appeal and the High Court).

A Personal Status Code was promulgated on 13 Aug. 1956 and applied to Tunisians from 1 Jan. 1957. This raised the status of women, made divorce subject to a court decision, abolished polygamy and decreed a minimum marriage age.

FINANCE. Currency. On 1 Nov. 1958 a new currency, the *dinar*, divided into 1,000 *millimes*, was established. The *dinar* equals £0·80; US$1 = 520 *millimes*. The Central Bank of Tunisia is the note-issuing agency. Note circulation, 31 Dec. 1967, was 55·27m. *dinars*.

The issue consists of coins of 1, 2, 10, 20, 50 and 100 *millimes*, and notes of 500 *millimes*, 1 *dinar*, 5 and 10 *dinars*.

Budget (in 1,000 dinars). Ordinary receipts and expenditure for calendar years balanced as follows: 1964, 68,300; 1965, 86,000. Budget estimates, 1966, revenue, 100,500; expenditure, 135,500. The budget for 1967 balanced at 108,100; 1968, 124,000; 1969, 130,000; 1970, 146,500; 1971, 154,000.

At 31 Dec. 1960 the public debt amounted to 77,023,900 dinars. The Kuwait Fund for Arab Economic Development granted Tunisia 3 loans, totalling KD 10·6m.

DEFENCE. A Tunisian National Army was created in 1956. It consisted in 1969 of about 17,000 officers and men. Selective military service is 1 year. Officer-cadets are being trained in France. Defence expenditure in 1966 was 4·3m. dinars.

The army consists of 7 infantry battalions, 1 mixed squadron (including M.41 tanks) and 1 artillery group.

The navy consists of 1 corvette, 3 patrol vessels, 10 patrol boats and a tug.

The air force has a single squadron of 12 F-86 jet fighters, 14 Saab-91D Safir primary trainers, delivered by Sweden in 1960–61, 12 T-6 Texan advanced trainers, supplied by France in 1963, 8 Italian-built M.B. 326 armed jet trainers, of which delivery began in 1965, 12 French-built Alouette II/III helicopters and 3 Flamant light transports.

PLANNING. A 4-year development plan, 1956–68, was approved by parliament 28 May 1965. It envisaged an annual average rate of growth of 6·5% and investments amounting to 455m. dinars, of which 280m. was to be financed by domestic savings and the rest by foreign aid.

AGRICULTURE. Tunisia may be divided into 5 districts—the north, characterized by its mountainous formation, having large and fertile valleys (*e.g.*, the valley of the Medjerdah and the plains of Mornag, Mateur and Béja); the northeast, with the peninsula of Cap Bon, the soil being specially suited for the cultivation of oranges, lemons and tangerines; the Sahel, where olive trees abound; the centre, the region of high table lands and pastures, and the desert of the south, famous for its oases and gardens, where dates grow in profusion.

The chief industry is agriculture, and large estates predominate. Of the total area of 15,583,000 hectares, about 9m. hectares are productive, including 2m. under cereals, 3·6m. used as pasturage, 900,000 forests and 1·3m. uncultivated.

Products		1964	1965	1966	1967	1968	1969
Corn		350	420	415	400	..	..
Wheat		71	100	44	50	48	38
Barley		130	180	110	70	..	80
Oats		10	..	..	..	..	..
Maize	(in 1,000	5	..	..	..	..	..
Olive oil	metric tons)	89	96	53	22	56	27
Oranges and		60	62	52 ⎫	110		80
Lemons[1]		14	14	14 ⎭		73	
Dates[1]		42	54	42	41	36	27
Olives[2]		985	954	605	920	..	..
Grapes		26	24	20	20	..	..
Wine (in 1,000 hectolitres)		1,830	1,850	1,265	924	985	847

[1] Crop year 1961–62, etc.
[2] In 1,000 caffis (1 caffis = 420–50 kg).

Other products are apricots, pears, apples, peaches, plums, figs, pomegranates, almonds, shaddocks, pistachios, esparto grass, henna and cork. Agricultural tractors numbered 18,360 in 1966.

Livestock in 1967 (in 1,000): Horses, 90; asses, 200; mules, 70; cattle. 569: sheep, 4,350; goats, 585; camels, 214; pigs, 3.

FISHING. In 1967, 7,000 boats with 20,000 men were engaged in fishing. In 1969 the catch amounted to 36,000 metric tons.

In Oct. 1962 territorial waters were extended from 3 to 6 miles and fishing limits to 12 miles offshore.

MINING. Mineral production (in 1,000 metric tons) in 1969 (and 1968): Phosphate, 2,600 (3,442); iron ore, 950 (1,020); lead ore, 38 (24); zinc ore, 17 (7).

Processed minerals (in 1,000 metric tons) in 1966 (and 1965): Simple superphosphates, 32·9 (28); triple superphosphates, 271·3 (292); hyperphosphates, 73·1 (120·6); lead, 14 (14·2); antimony lead, 1·3 (1·3); oil products, 715·3 (63·9).

INDUSTRY. Major modern plants include a sugar refinery in Béja (47,000 metric tons in 1965), a cellulose plant in Kassérine (19,033 metric tons in 1968), a petroleum refinery in Bizerta and a steel plant at Menzel Bourguiba which in 1966 turned out 92,000 tons of pig-iron, 25,000 tons of steel and 30,000 tons of finished products. There is a marble work plant and a tyre factory at Mégrine.

TOURISM. In 1969, 373,000 tourists visited Tunisia, not counting ship's passengers in transit.

POWER. The electricity, gas and water services, formerly run by a French company, were nationalized on 26 Nov. 1959 and are now run by the Société Tunisienne d'Electricité et du Gaz.

Electrical energy generated was 677·7m. kwh. in 1968, of which 444·4m. was produced by STEG.

TRADE UNIONS. The Union Générale des Travailleurs Tunisiens was placed under government control in Aug. 1965. There are 4 other unions.

COMMERCE. The customs union with France was repealed on 5 Sept. 1959. The imports and exports for calendar years (in 1,000 dinars) were as follows:

	1963	1964	1965	1966	1967	1968	1969
Imports	93,662	110,845	129,062	131,224	137,087	110,484	134,563
Exports	52,922	57,304	62,916	73,690	78,360	82,831	86,960

In 1969 imports totalled 1·78m. metric tons; exports totalled 4·99m. metric tons. Exports to France in 1969 totalled 23·2m. dinars, and imports from France, 45·5m. dinars. Imports from USA were valued at 21·5m. dinars in 1969 (20·9m. in 1965).

In 1969 exports of iron ore totalled 567,000 metric tons; lime phosphates, 1·8m.; hyperphosphates, 69,500.

Total trade between Tunisia and UK (British Board of Trade returns, in £1,000 sterling) was:

	1966	1967	1968	1969	1970
Imports to UK	3,953	2,334	3,733	2,835	2,487
Exports from UK	2,724	1,720	2,691	3,488 ⎱	4,306
Re-exports from UK	8	34	6	32 ⎰	

SHIPPING. The main port is Tunis, and its outer port is Tunis-Goulette. These two ports and Sfax, Sousse and Bizerta are directly accessible to ocean-going vessels. The port of La Skhirra, in the south, is used for the shipping of Algerian and Tunisian oil.

In 1966 (and 1967) 4,037 (5,147) ships of 6,436,800 (12,102,000) tons entered Tunisian ports.

ROADS. In 1964 there were 15,692 km of roads, of which 6,713 km were main roads.

Number of motor vehicles, 31 Dec. 1967, included 56,602 private cars, 32,346 commercial cars, 10,008 motor cycles and 18,645 tractors.

RAILWAYS. In 1968 there were 2,298 km of railways, owned by the state Société Nationale des Chemins de Fer Tunisiens. Traffic in 1969 was 14·5m. passengers and 5·9m. metric tons of freight.

AVIATION. The national airline is 'Tunis-Air'. The main airport is at Tunis-Carthage. In 1967, 215,200 passengers arrived and 221,100 departed.

POST. There were, in 1969, 61,923 telephones, of which 22,871 were in Tunis. There were, in 1966, 381 post offices, and a wireless transmitting station. Wireless sets in use at 31 Dec. 1967 were 240,000. Television began in 1966 and in 1967 there were 33,000 sets.

BANKING. In 1966 there were 14 banks operating in Tunisia, including 3 French and 1 British banks. Bank deposits amounted to 169·2m. dinars at 31 Dec. 1968.

WEIGHTS AND MEASURES. The metric system of weights and measures has almost entirely taken the place of those of Tunisia, but corn is still sold in *kaffis* and *wibas*. The *kfiz* (of 16 *wiba*, each of 12 *sa*') = 16 bushels. The *ounce* = 31·487 grammes; the multiples of the ounce are the various denominations of the *R'lal*, which contains from 16 to 42 oz.

The principal measure of length is the *pik*: the *pik Arbi* for linen = 0·5392 yd; the *pik Turki* for silk = 0·7058 yd; the *pik Andoulsi* for cloth = 0·7094 yd.

DIPLOMATIC REPRESENTATIVES

Tunisia maintains embassies in:

Algeria	Germany (West)	Netherlands	Turkey
Austria	Italy	Poland	USSR
Belgium	Ivory Coast	Saudi Arabia	UAR
Bulgaria	Jordan	Senegal	UK
Canada	Kuwait	Spain	USA
Congo (K.)	Lebanon	Sweden	Yugoslavia
Czechoslovakia	Libya	Switzerland	
France	Morocco	Syria	

OF TUNISIA IN GREAT BRITAIN (29 Princes Gate, SW7)
Ambassador: Ismail Khelil.
Secretaries: Mustapha Mizouni; Hamid Zaouche; Mustapha Zardi.

OF GREAT BRITAIN IN TUNISIA
Ambassador and Consul-General: A. R. K. Mackenzie, CBE.
First Secretary and Consul: J. B. Wright.
There is also a Vice-Consul at Sfax.

OF TUNISIA IN THE USA (2408 Massachusetts Ave. NW,
Washington, DC., 20008)
Ambassador: Slaheddine El Goulli.
Minister: Ahmed Ghézal. *First Secretary:* Ahmed Badra.

OF THE USA IN TUNISIA
Ambassador: John A. Calhoun.
Deputy Chief of Mission: (Vacant). *Heads of Sections:* Francis J. Jeton
(*Political*); Robert Sherwood (*Economic*); Stephen M. Block (*Labour*); Frederick
H. Hassett (*Consular*); Richard T. Salazar (*Administrative*). *Army Attaché:* Col.
Stephen G. Martin.

BOOKS OF REFERENCE

STATISTICAL INFORMATION. The Service Tunisien de la Statistique (Dar-el-Bey, Tunis) was
set up on 13 March 1947. Its main publications are: *Annuaire statistique de la Tunisie* (latest issue,
1967).—*Bulletin du Service Tunisien des Statistiques* (trimestrial, with monthly suppl.).

Tournal Officiel de la République Tunisienne (in Arabic and French)
Junisie, 1953. (*L'Encyclopedie d'outre-mer.*) Paris, 1953
Bannour, A. (ed.), *Economic Yearbook of Tunisia.* 2nd ed. Tunis, 1966
Garas F., *Bourguiba et la Naissance d'une Nation.* Paris, 1956
Ling, D. L., *Tunisia: From Protectorate to Republic.* Indiana Univ. Press, 1967
Rudebeck, L., *The Tunisian Experience: Party and People.* London, 1970
Rossi, P., *Bourguiba's Tunisia.* Tunis, 1967
Sylvester, A., *Tunisia.* London, 1969
Tlatli, S. E., *Tunisie Nouvelle: Problèmes et Perspectives.* Tunis, 1957
Vibert, J., *Tableau de l'Économie Tunisienne.* Tunis, 1955

TURKEY
Türkiye Cumhuriyeti

HISTORY. The Turkish War of Independence (1919–22), following the dis-
integration of the Ottoman Empire, was led and won by Mustafa Kemal (Atatürk)
on behalf of the Grand National Assembly which first met in Ankara on 23 April
1920. On 20 Jan. 1921 the Grand National Assembly voted a constitution which
declared that all sovereignty belonged to the people and vested all power, both
executive and legislative, in the Grand National Assembly. The name 'Ottoman
Empire' was later replaced by 'Turkey'. On 1 Nov. 1922 the Grand National
Assembly abolished the office of Sultan and Turkey became a republic on 29
Oct. 1923.

On 27 May 1960 the Turkish Army, directed by a National Unity Committee
under the leadership of Gen. Cemal Gürsel, overthrew the government of the
Democratic Party. The Grand National Assembly was dissolved and party
activities were suspended. Party activities were legally resumed on 12 Jan. 1961.

CONSTITUTION AND GOVERNMENT. The constitution of 9 July 1961
has consolidated the modernizing reforms: the abolition of the Caliphate and of
old-style religious education (1924), the prohibition of oriental headgear (1925),
the suppression of the dervish orders (1925), the introduction of the Western

civil code, ending polygamy (1926), the substitution of the Latin for the Arabic alphabet (1928), the abolition of old-style titles (1934) and the prohibition of clerical garb (1934). Religious courts were abolished in 1924, Islam ceased to be the official state religion in 1928, women were given the franchise and western-style surnames were adopted in 1934.

Legislative power is vested in the Grand National Assembly, executive power in the President of the Republic and the Council of Ministers, judicial power in independent courts. The President of the Republic is elected by the National Assembly and the Senate in joint session for a 7-year term; he is not re-eligible.

Turkish men and women are entitled to vote at the age of 21 and to become deputies at the age of 30. Secret ballot was introduced by law on 10 July 1948.

Elections held on 12 Oct. 1969 resulted in the following composition of the National Assembly: Justice Party, 259; Republican People's Party, 144; Reliance Party, 15; Union Party, 8; New Turkey Party, 6; Nation Party, 6; Turkish Labour Party, 2; National Action Party (formed from former Republican Peasants Nation Party), 1; Independents, 9. Total, 450.

The Senate (150 members elected by direct vote, 15 nominated by the President of the Republic, and 18 life senators, formerly members of the National Unity Committee) is composed of: Justice Party, 93; Republican People's Party, 34; Reliance Party, 9; Nation Party, Turkish Labour Party, National Action Party, New Turkey Party, 1 each; Independents, 8, and vacant, 2.

National flag: A white crescent and star on red.
National anthem: Korkma! Sönmez bu şafaklarda yüzen al sancak (words by Mehmed Akif Ersoy; tune by Zeki Güngör; adopted 12 March 1921).

Past Presidents of the Republic: Mustafa Kemal Atatürk (29 Oct. 1923–10 Nov. 1938), İsmet İnönü (11 Nov. 1938–21 May 1950), Celâl Bayar (22 May 1950–27 May 1960), Cemal Gürsel (26 Oct. 1961–27 March 1966).

President of the Republic: Cevdet Sunay (elected 28 March 1966) by 461 out of 532 votes).

The Cabinet of a coalition of 3 parties was in March 1971 constituted as follows:

Prime Minister: Nihat Erim.
Ministers of State: Sadi Koçaş, Atillâ Karaosmanoğlu, Mehmet Özgüneş. *Justice:* İsmail Arar. *National Defence:* Ferit Melen. *Interior:* Hamdi Ömeroğlu. *Foreign Affairs:* Osman Olcay. *Finance:* Sait Naci Ergin. *National Education:* Şinasi Orel. *Public Works:* Cahit Karakaş. *External Economic Relations:* Özer Derbil. *Health and Social Welfare:* Prof. Türkân Akyol. *Customs and Monopolies:* Haydar Özalp. *Agriculture:* Orhan Dikmen. *Communications:* Halûk Arık. *Labour:* Atillâ Sar. *Industry and Commerce:* Ayhan Çilingiroğlu. *Power and Natural Resources:* İhsan Topaloğlu. *Tourism:* Erol Yılmaz Akçal. *Reconstruction and Housing:* Selâhattin Babüroğlu. *Rural Affairs:* Cevdet Aykan. *Forestry:* Prof. Selâhattin İnal. *Youth and Sports:* Sezai Ergun.

LOCAL GOVERNMENT. The constitution of 1921 provided for the administrative division of the country into *İl*, province (now 67 in number), divided into *İlçe* (district), sub-divided in their turn into *Bucak* (township or commune). At the head of each İl is a Vali representing the Government. Each İl has its own elective council.

The İlçe is regarded as a mere grouping of Bucaks for certain purposes of general administration. The Bucak or commune is an autonomous entity and possesses an elective council charged with the administration of such matters as are not reserved to the State.

According to the municipal law passed in 1930, Turkish women have the right to be electors and to be elected at municipal elections.

AREA AND POPULATION. The Treaty of Peace between the Allied Powers and Turkey, which was signed at Lausanne on 24 July 1923, defined the

European frontier of the new Turkey and to some extent her Asiatic frontiers. This treaty was ratified by the Grand National Assembly in Ankara on 23 Aug. 1923 and entered into force 6 Aug. 1924.

The Treaty of Lausanne and the conventions attached to it provided for the demilitarization of zones adjoining the European frontier, the Dardanelles and the Bosphorus, subject to the right to maintain a garrison at İstanbul, for the demilitarization of İmroz, Bozcaada (Tenedos) and Tavşan Islands, as well as the islands in the Sea of Marmora with one exception and for a special administrative regime in İmroz and Bozcaada.

On 10 July 1936 a new Straits Convention was signed at Montreux (ratified on 9 Nov. 1936) to take the place of the 1923 Convention, whereby Turkey obtained the right of re-militarizing the zone of the Straits, and this area was re-occupied by Turkish troops on 21 July 1936. The International Commission of the Straits ceased to function on 30 Sept. 1936.

By an agreement between the Turkish and French Governments concluded at Ankara on 23 June 1939, the Sanjak of Alexandretta (the Hatay) was incorporated in the Turkish Republic.

The territorial waters were on 25 Aug. 1964 extended from 3 to 6 nautical miles.

The area of Turkey (including lakes) is 780,576 sq. km (301,302 sq. miles). Area in Europe (Trakya), 23,721 sq. km; population, 1965, 2,655,768. Area in Asia (Anadolu), 756,855 sq. km; population, 1965, 28,735,653.

The census population of Turkey is given as follows:

	Males	Females	Total	Increase %
1927	6,563,879	7,084,391	13,648,270	—
1935	7,936,770	8,221,248	16,158,018	21·2
1940	8,898,912	8,922,038	17,820,950	17·3
1945	9,446,580	9,343,594	18,790,174	10·5
1950	10,527,085	10,420,103	20,947,188	22·9
1955	12,233,421	11,831,342	24,064,763	29·7
1960	14,163,888	13,590,932	27,754,820	28·9
1965	15,996,964	15,394,457	31,391,421	13·1
1970[1]	..	..	35,666,549	26·0

[1] Provisional

The population of the İls, at the census of 24 Oct. 1965, was as follows:

Adana	902,712	Erzincan	258,586	Maraş	438,423
Adıyaman	267,288	Erzurum	628,001	Mardin	397,880
Afyonkarahisar	502,248	Eskişehir	415,101	Muğla	334,973
Ağrı	246,961	Gaziantep	511,026	Muş	198,716
Amasya	285,729	Giresun	428,015	Nevşehir	203,316
Ankara	1,644,302	Gümüşane	262,731	Niğde	362,444
Antalya	486,910	Hakkâri	83,937	Ordu	543,863
Artvin	210,065	Hatay	506,154	Rize	281,099
Aydın	524,918	İçel	511,273	Sakarya	404,078
Balıkesir	708,342	Isparta	266,240	Samsun	755,946
Bilecik	139,041	İstanbul	2,293,823	Siirt	264,832
Bingöl	150,521	İzmir	1,234,667	Sinop	266,069
Bitlis	154,069	Kars	606,313	Sivas	705,186
Bolu	383,939	Kastamonu	441,638	Tekirdağ	287,381
Burdur	194,950	Kayseri	536,206	Tokat	495,352
Bursa	755,504	Kırklareli	258,386	Trabzon	595,782
Çanakkale	350,317	Kırşehir	196,836	Tunceli	154,175
Çankırı	250,706	Kocaeli	335,518	Urfa	450,798
Çorum	485,567	Konya	1,122,622	Uşak	190,536
Denizli	463,369	Kütahya	398,081	Van	266,840
Diyarbakır	475,916	Malatya	452,624	Yozgat	437,883
Edirne	303,234	Manisa	748,545	Zonguldak	650,191
Elâzığ	322,727				

The population of towns of over 50,000 inhabitants was as follows in 1965:

İstanbul	2,247,630[1]	Sivas	108,300	Urfa	100,231[1]
Ankara	2,208,791[1]	Samsun	107,500	Antalya	71,800
İzmir	520,686[1]	Erzurum	105,300	Manisa	69,700
Adana	351,655[1]	Malatya	104,400	Balıkesir	69,300
Bursa	211,600	Diyarbakir	138,657[1]	Trabzon	65,500
Eskişehir	173,900	Kocaeli	89,600	Maraş	105,206[1]
Gaziantep	255,881[1]	İçel	86,700	Denizli	64,300
Konya	157,900	Sakarya	86,100	Antakya	57,900
Kayseri	126,700	Elâzığ	78,600		

[1] Census, 1970.

The population of Turkey according to 'mother tongue' (1965 census) comprises 28,317,579 Turks, 2,180,721 Kurds, 365,971 Arabs, 57,337 Circassians, 48,143 Greeks, 32,484 Armenians, 32,334 Georgians, 23,715 Lazes and 9,124 Spanish-speaking Jews.

RELIGION. Freedom of religion is guaranteed by the constitution. Although Islam is no longer the official state religion of Turkey, Moslems form 98·92% of the population. The administration of the Moslem religious organizations is in charge of the Presidency of Religious Affairs, attached to the Prime Minister's office. Under the imperial system the non-Moslem communities were recognized as organized communities or *millets*, the heads of which exercised spiritual as well as civil functions; their authority is now purely ecclesiastical. The Turkish Republic is a secular state.

İstanbul is the seat of the Œcumenical Patriarch, who is the head of the Orthodox Church in Turkey. The Armenian Church (Gregorian) is ruled by a Patriarch in İstanbul who is subordinate to the Katholikos of Etchmiadzin, the spiritual head of all Armenians. The Armenian Apostolic Church is ruled by the Patriarch of Cilicia. The Chaldeans (Nestorian Uniats) have a Bishop at Mardin. The Syrian Uniats have a See of Mardin and Amida, but it is united with their Patriarchate of Antioch (residence, Damascus). Greek Uniats (Byzantine Rite) have as their Ordinary in İstanbul, the Titular Bishop of Gratianopolis. The Latins have an Apostolic Delegate in İstanbul and an Archbishop in İzmir, but their Patriarch of İstanbul is titular and non-resident. There is a Grand Rabbi (Hahambaşı) in İstanbul for the Jews, who are nearly all Sephardim.

At the 1965 census there were in Turkey 31,391,421 Moslems, 73,725 Orthodox, 69,526 Gregorians, 25,833 Roman Catholics, 22,983 Protestants, 14,758 other Christians (unspecified), 18,267 Jews, 14,661 adherents of other religions, 1,212 without religion and 602 undeclared or unknown.

A law passed in Dec. 1934 forbids the wearing of clerical garb except in places of worship and during divine service. The 1961 constitution forbids the political exploitation of religion or any impairment of the secular character of the republic.

In lieu of religious formulae, all citizens take oaths on their honour.

EDUCATION. Elementary education is compulsory and co-educational and, in state schools, free. All children from 7 to 12 are to receive primary instruction, which may be given in state schools, schools maintained by communities, or private schools, or, subject to certain tests, at home. The state schools are under the direct control of the Ministry of Education. They include primary schools, secondary or middle schools, and *lycées* or secondary schools of a superior kind. There are also training schools for male and female teachers and technical schools. There are 2 universities in İstanbul, 3 in Ankara (including the Middle East Technical University designed to meet the technical needs of the whole Middle East), the Aegean University in İzmir, Atatürk University in Erzurum (opened in Nov. 1957) and the Black Sea Technical University in Trabzon. The important non-Moslem communities in İstanbul maintain their own schools, which, like all 'private' schools, are subject to the supervision of the Ministry of Education.

Literacy of the population of 6 years and over was 10·6% in 1927, 19·2% in 1935, 29% in 1945, 40·9% in 1955, 39·5% in 1960, 48·7% in 1965, 49% in 1970.

Religious instruction in schools, hitherto prohibited, was made optional in elementary and middle schools in May 1948. There are many training schools for Moslem clergy as well as a Faculty of Theology in Ankara.

Statistics for 1969–70	Number	Teachers	Students
Primary schools (state and private)	37,177	114,990	4,907.090
Middle schools (state and private)	1,648	20.439	735.601
Lycées (state and private)	454	8.384	227,205
Professional and technical schools	885	13,867	226,330
Teachers' training colleges[1]	10	515	4,785
Colleges of higher education (state and private)[1]	70	3,935	67,883
Universities	..	9,642	152,287
Minority schools (nursery, primary and secondary)	108	1,122	12,007

[1] 1968–69.

On 1 Nov. 1928 the Grand National Assembly voted a law for the adoption of Latin characters as from 1 Dec. 1928. The publication of books in Arabic characters was forbidden after 1 Jan. 1929.

CINEMAS (1960). There were about 800 cinemas.

NEWSPAPERS (1965). Of the 338 daily newspapers in the Turkish language 24 appear in İstanbul and 22 in Ankara. There are also 2 dailies published in Greek, 1 in French, 2 in Armenian and 1 in English.

HEALTH. Public health is the responsibility of the Ministry of Health and Social Welfare, established in 1920; social insurance for workers comes under the Workers' Insurance Institution attached to the Ministry of Labour. A law promulgated in 1961 and being implemented from 1963 provides for the nationalization of the health services within 15 years. In 1969, 1·21m. workers and employees were covered by social insurance, including free medical care.

In 1969 there were about 12,389 doctors and over 77,700 beds in some 686 hospitals.

The counterpart of the Red Cross in Turkey is the Red Crescent Society founded in 1877.

JUSTICE. The unified legal system consists of: (1) justices of the peace (single judges with limited but summary penal and civil jurisdiction): (2) courts of first instance (single judges, dealing with cases outside the jurisdiction of (3) and (4)); (3) central criminal courts (a president and 2 judges, dealing with cases where the crime is punishable by imprisonment over 5 years); (4) commercial courts (3 judges).

The Court of Cassation sits at Ankara.

The Council of State is the highest administration tribunal; it consists of 5 chambers. Its 31 judges are nominated from among high-ranking personalities in politics, economy, law, the army, etc. The Military Court of Cassation in Ankara is the highest military tribunal.

The Constitutional Court, set up under the 1961 constitution, can review and annul legislation and try the President of the Republic, Ministers and senior judges. It consists of 15 regular and 5 alternate members.

The Civil Code and the Code of Obligations have been adapted from the corresponding Swiss codes. The Penal Code is largely based upon the Italian Penal Code, and the Code of Civil Procedure closely resembles that of the Canton of Neuchâtel. The Commercial Code is based on the German.

FINANCE. Currency. The Turkish *Lira* (TL) is divided into 100 *kuruş* (*piastres*). Coins in general circulation are of the following values: 5, 10 and 25 *kuruş*; 1 and 2½ *Lira*. Bank-notes in circulation are as follows: 5, 10, 20, 50, 100, 500 and 1,000 *Lira*.

The value of the Turkish Lira is 36 to £1 and 15 to US$1. The Turkish Lira was devalued by 66·6% on 10 Aug. 1970.

Budget. Estimates of revenue and expenditure (in TL1,000) for financial years 1 March–28/29 Feb.:

	1965–66	*1966–67*	*1967–68*	*1968–69*[1]	*1969–70*[1]
Revenue	14,021,419	15,583,000	18,601,321	20,712,211	24,497,364
Expenditure	14,421,419	16,475,702	18,322,015	21,612,211	25,696,976

[1] Estimates.

The revenue and expenditure estimates for the financial year ending 28 Feb. 1970 are as follows (in TL1,000):

Revenue

Taxes		Taxes	
Income and wealth	6,950,000	Others including stamp duties	1,468,000
Production	⎫	State property and income from	
Services	⎪	state enterprises	403,300
Customs	⎬ 12,831,242	Miscellaneous and fines	728,822
Monopolies	⎪	Savings bonds and other sources	2,116,000
Consumption	⎭		

Expenditure	Normal appropriation	Investments	Transfers
Senate	14,555	—	316
National Assembly	59,520	3,016	1,884
Presidency of the Republic	4,298	187	40
Court of Accounts	19,848	5,000	140
Constitutional Court	2,834	—	17
Prime Ministry	113,012	41,024	21,292
State Planning Organization	14,749	50,000	30,027
The Supreme Council	14,274	—	100
State Statistics Institute	20,333	4,000	190
Religious Affairs	194,485	85	191
Cadastre and Registration	99,982	42,370	200
Justice	431,019	1,200	1,329
Defence	4,177,790	92,882	90,992
Interior	134,807	1,800	119,497
Security	380,422	20,505	2,035
Gendarmerie	484,490	2,591	6,356
Foreign Affairs	139,151	2,615	42,048
Finance	738,740	1,000	11,055,484
Education	2,433,547	184,085	52,413
Public Works	22,718	1,552,653	35,636
Commerce	37,799	—	1,407
Health	847,469	34,600	30,055
Customs and Monopolies	50,208	4,696	997
Agriculture	472,252	416,827	61,934
Meteorological Department	41,076	3,159	1,743
Communications	13,835	2,210	616
Labour	18,496	1,115	16,927
Industry	14,910	248,383	2,330
Tourism and Information	42,775	6,200	10,975
Reconstruction	40,456	186,094	55,068
Land redistribution and resettlement	46,244	8,000	12,243

The excess of expenditure over revenue is to be met through internal loans and administrative savings during the financial year.

At 31 Dec. 1968 the public debt (excluding interest) totalled TL33,651m., consisting of TL18,260m. internal and TL15,391m. external debts, of which US$1,344m. are repayable in foreign currency.

DEFENCE. Several bills for the reorganization of the armed forces were passed in June 1949 by the Grand National Assembly. One of these placed all organizations connected with national defence under the authority of the Minister of National Defence. Another created a Supreme Council of National Security, under the chairmanship of the Prime Minister, with the object of co-ordinating the resources of the country in case of war. Besides the Minister of National Defence and the Chief of the General Staff, the heads of economic Ministries are members of this council.

Military service in Army, Air Force and Navy is 18 months for officers and 20 months for other ranks. Men are called up when they reach the age of 20. The average number of men liable to be called up is 175,000 every year. The strength of the forces is about 514,000 officers and men. The total number that could be mobilized is estimated at over 2m.

Army. The land forces contain 13 infantry divisions (1 mechanized), 1 armoured division and 4 armoured brigades (M-48 tanks), 1 armoured cavalry brigade, 3 mechanized infantry brigades, 2 parachute battalions. The units are largely equipped with 10·5 cm, 15·5 cm and 20·3 cm howitzer guns. Ground forces have been assigned to the South-Eastern Command of NATO, of which İzmir is the headquarters. Total strength, 514,000; trained reservists, 450,000.

Navy. The Navy includes 10 submarines, 10 destroyers, 1 minelayer, 9 escort minesweepers, 6 coastal escorts, 6 coastal minelayers, 13 coastal minesweepers, 6 patrol vessels, 11 torpedo boats, 3 inshore minesweepers, 30 coastal craft, 2 repair ships, a large training ship (ex-yacht), a submarine rescue ship, 4 oilers, 6 boom defence vessels and 1 tender. The battle cruiser Yavus, formerly the German Goeben, launched in 1911, displacing 22,734 tons, and armed with ten 11-in. guns was decommissioned in 1960.

The naval bases are at Gölcük in the Gulf of İzmit, at İskenderun and at İzmir.

Personnel strength in 1970 was 2,795 officers and 33,920 men.

Air Force. The Air Force is under the control of the General Staff and, operationally, under 6 ATAF. It is organized in 3 tactical air forces. The 1st TAF has 6 squadrons (each 20–25 aircraft) of F-100C Super Sabres, 2 squadrons of F-104G Starfighters, 2 squadrons of F-5s and 1 squadron of RF-84F Thunderflash reconnaissance aircraft. The 3rd TAF has 6 fighter-bomber squadrons, 4 flying F-100Cs and 2 flying F-5s, and 1 squadron of F-84 reconnaissance aircraft. The Turkish 2nd TAF forms an Air Defence Command, with 1 squadron of *ex*-USAF Convair F-102A supersonic interceptors, 1 squadron of F-5s, 2 squadrons of F-86E Sabre day interceptors, and 4 squadrons of Sabre all-weather interceptors, of which 2 are equipped with F-86Ds and 2 with F-86Ks, plus Nike-Ajax and Nike-Hercules surface-to-air missile batteries. The transport units are equipped with C-130 Hercules, C-54, C-47 and C-45 aircraft. Training types include T-33A and supersonic T-38A Talon advanced trainers, Harvard intermediate and T-34 Mentor primary trainers. Personnel strength is about 50,000, with 500 combat aircraft.

DEVELOPMENT. The first 5-year development plan, 1963–67, provided for investments of TL68,000m. (at 1965 prices); TL64,000m. were invested, the gross national product increasing at the rate of 6·7% per annum. The external financing amounted to US$1,350m.

The second 5-year plan (1968–72) sets out to achieve an annual growth of 7%; external financing amounting to US$1,716m.

AGRICULTURE. The number of people engaged in agriculture in 1967 was 9,903,000.

In 1966, of the total land area of 78,058,000 hectares, 15,454,000 were under field crops, 27,995,000 were meadows and pastures, 888,000 were fruit and vegetable gardens and orchards, 830,000 were vineyards, 666,000 were olive groves, 10,584,000 were forests, 8,546,000 were fallow and 13,095,000 were unproductive.

The soil for the most part is very fertile; the principal products are cotton, tobacco, cereals (especially wheat), figs, silk, olives and olive oil, dried fruits, liquorice root, nuts, almonds, mohair, skins and hides, furs, wool, gums, canary seed, linseed and sesame. The principal tobacco districts are Samsun, Bafra, Çarsamba, İzmit and İzmir. Two-thirds of the exports of leaf tobacco goes to the USA. The principal centre for silk production is Bursa. The production of olive oil, mainly confined to the İls of Aydın and Balıkesir, is very important (155,000 metric tons in 1966). Sugar production (refined) in 1967 was 663,000 metric tons. Agricultural production (in metric tons) in 1967 included 3·5m. grapes, 232,000 figs, 465,000 oranges and lemons, 71,000 hazelnuts, 640,000 apples, 50,000 mandarins, 495,000 olives, 103,000 peaches, 550,000 onions, 1·76m. potatoes.

Turkey produced 3,900 metric tons of flax fibre and 7,000 tons of hemp fibre in 1967.

Cotton production in 1967 was 360,000 metric tons (1966: 382,000 tons).

Agricultural tractors numbered 65,103 in 1966.

Area (in 1,000 hectares) and yield (in 1,000 metric tons) of principal crops:

	1964		1966	1967	1968
	Area	Yield	Yield	Yield	Yield
Wheat	7,870	8,400	9,715	10,150	9,520
Barley	2,750	3,200	3,850	3,800	3,560
Oats	410	550	560	510	..
Maize	680	1,000	1,000	1,050	..
Rye	700	735	875	980	900
Rice	35	100	150	140	..
Tobacco	272	194	164	164	..

On 7 June 1945 the Grand National Assembly passed the Land Reform Bill under which large tracts of agricultural land are being distributed to peasants without land or with insufficient for their subsistence.

Livestock, 1964, 32,654,000 sheep, 15·5m. ordinary goats, 5,563,000 Angora goats, 13·2m. cattle (1966: 13·77m.), 1,918,000 asses, 216,000 mules, 1·2m. horses, 262,000 buffaloes, 46,000 camels.

In 1965 Turkey produced 50,000 metric tons of wool (1967: 44,000) and 12,000 tons of mohair.

FORESTRY. On 8 Feb. 1937 a new forest law was voted, providing for state control of all forests, including those under private ownership. It contains measures for planting, protection against fire, marauders and insects, and lays down penalties for infringements of its clauses. The most wooded İls are Kastamonu, Aydın, Bursa, Bolu, Trabzon, Konya and Balıkesir. Of the forest land, 10,417,560 hectares belonged to the State in 1951. In 1967 the value of forest products was TL1,497m.

FISHING. On 25 Aug. 1964 Turkey extended her waters in which she has exclusive fishing rights to 12 nautical miles.

MINING. The Turkish provinces, especially those in Asia, are reported rich in minerals. Turkey is one of the four principal producers of chrome in the world.

Production of principal minerals (in 1,000 metric tons) was:

	1963	1964	1965	1966	1967
Coal (S and P)	6,796·9	7,141	7,006	4,889 (S)	7,457
Lignite (S and P)	4,852·0	5,767	6,296	5,910 (S)	6,451
Chrome (S and P)	282·5	411	582	502	614
Sulphur (S)	14·9	22	22	25	..
Manganese (P)	20·0	23	28	40	..
Iron ore (S and P)	748·2	876	1,545	1,026	1,485
Copper ore (S)	698·7	773	..	1,270	..
Copper (Blister) (S)	24·8	25	26	27	25
Antimony (P)	33·4	16	..	3	2
Borates (S and P)	107·9	99	171	228	229
Petroleum (S and P)	744·9	886	1,472	2,041	2,728

(S) State; (P) Private enterprise.

Production of bauxite started in 1966 with 32,000 tons.

Of the Government organizations producing these ores, Zonguldak coal mines operates under the Turkish State Coal Exploitation; while the copper mines at Murgul and Ergani, the Eastern chromite mines, Keçiborlu sulphur, Emet colemanite, Küre pyrite and cupriferous pyrite, Keban argentiferous lead mines operate under the Etibank.

Oil is being produced in Garzan and Raman by the Turkish Petroleum Company. Under the oil law of 14 Oct. 1954 private companies can explore and produce oil. Three private companies (2 of them foreign) produced 1,737,000 tons in 1967. The 3 refineries refined 5·5m. tons of crude oil in 1967. The oil pipeline Batman–İskenderun (494 km) was opened on 4 Jan. 1967.

INDUSTRY. Production in 1967 included: 700m. metres of cotton fabrics, 27m. metres of woollen fabrics, 127,000 tons of cotton yarns, 24,000 tons of woollen yarns; 4·25m. metric tons of cement, 109,000 metric tons of paper. Industrial plants number about 30,000.

In 1967 Turkey produced 847,000 tons of pig-iron, 996,000 tons of steel ingots, 266,000 tons of sheets and pipes and 1·36m. tons of coke. There are steel works at Karabük, Ereğli and İskenderun.

POWER. The potential hydro-electric power in Turkey is estimated at 56,000m. kwh. In 1967 the electrical power plants (hydro-electric or thermal) had a total installed capacity of 2,001m. kw. and produced 6,178m. kwh.

TOURISM. A tourist industry is developing. The number of foreign tourists was 481,000 (provisional) in 1969.

LABOUR AND SOCIAL SECURITY. On 27 June 1945 a Ministry of Labour was set up, superseding the Department of Labour under the control of the Ministry of Economic Affairs. According to the strikes and lock-outs law, which came into effect on 24 Aug. 1963, strikes and lockouts may be declared only after due effort has been made to negotiate and after the local authorities as well as the Ministry of Labour have been informed.

Conditions of work are regulated by the Labour Act of 12 Aug. 1967, which covers all places of work, employing more than 3 persons, outside agriculture. Children under 16 must not be employed for more than 8 hours a day, and employment should not impede school attendance. The Act provides for annual paid holidays of 12–24 working days and regulates overtime payment.

Free public employment exchanges began to operate, under the general control of the Ministry of Labour, in 1946.

In 1967 Turkey's labour force numbered 13·74m., of which 72·3% were engaged in agriculture and 10·4% in manufacturing industries.

The trade-union movement began in 1947. There are 4 national confederations (including Türk-İş and Disk) and 6 federations.

COMMERCE. Imports and exports (in TL1m.) for calendar years:

	1964	1965	1966	1967[1]	1968	1969
Imports	4,878	5,193	6,465	684·7	4,934	8,010
Exports	3,697	4,174	4,415	522·7	4,468	5,367

[1] In US$1m.

In metric tons, exports totalled 2,130,998 in 1963; 2,619,108 in 1964; 2,661,108 in 1965; 2,564,000 in 1966; 2,022,300 in 1967. Imports, 5,457,483 in 1963; 4,818,353 in 1964; 4,993,113 in 1965; 5,318,700 in 1966; 4,958,400 in 1967.

Imports from the principal countries were as follows (in TL1m.):

Country	1963	1964	1965	1966	1967	1968
Belgium–Luxembourg	88·6	77·9	69·6	98·1	108·0	122·1
Czechoslovakia	127·0	76·1	77·2	103·6	119·2	111·9
France	308·3	187·6	193·9	393·4	246·2	245·1
Germany (West)	939·9	728·3	762·4	1,023·2	1,213·6	1,413·4
Italy	315·1	290·0	331·9	488·5	454·2	609·3
Japan	144·2	62·2	85·1	142·6	146·4	106·7
Netherlands	120·4	118·2	121·4	143·7	138·3	169·7
Sweden	102·2	84·2	63·5	94·0	95·1	..
Switzerland	76·7	84·4	112·4	168·4	175·2	208·6
UK	693·7	506·1	502·6	714·9	798·9	894·0
USA	1,904·6	1,403·3	1,458·6	1,567·0	1,114·4	1,095·2

Exports to the principal countries were as follows (in TL1m.):

Country	1963	1964	1965	1966	1967	1968
Belgium–Luxembourg	98·3	132·6	207·1	238·5	145·0	148·2
Czechoslovakia	87·1	63·9	98·4	96·4	95·6	123·7
France	144·9	224·4	177·4	221·2	260·2	196·3
Germany (West)	556·7	588·7	649·4	687·0	758·0	777·7
Italy	390·6	258·7	269·6	286·0	326·1	217·3
Lebanon	166·0	159·0	189·6	159·3	165·7	..
Sweden	34·0	35·2	45·8	45·8	61·7	..
Switzerland	189·9	211·5	126·4	176·8	243·8	240·9
UK	423·9	401·1	371·1	420·9	308·2	305·5
USA	448·0	656·8	735·8	722·1	836·4	652·9

Imports and exports of chief commodities (in TL1m.):

Imports	1965	1966	1967	Exports	1965	1966	1967
Machinery	1,501·9	2,043·0	2,050·2	Tobacco	812·4	962·3	1,062·0
Iron and steel	537·8	603·0	419·4	Fruits	932·5	873·8	1,173·2
Oil, etc.	515·1	495·0	481·5	Cotton	924·0	1,156·5	1,187·6
Transport	402·1	676·0	537·3	Minerals	265·4	431·1	329·4
Fabrics and yarns	341·6	369·0	379·8	Cereals	37·3	..	14·3
Chemicals	538·2	597·6	674·1				

Total trade between Turkey and UK (British Board of Trade returns) in £1,000 sterling:

	1966	1967	1968	1969	1970
Imports to UK	17,371	13,545	16,819	15,658	15,609
Exports from UK	23,593	29,240	34,149	33.890 ⎫	35,932
Re-exports from UK	740	800	678	1,091 ⎭	

SHIPPING. In 1968 Turkish Maritime Lines had a gross tonnage of 391,536, of which 35 vessels were cargo and tankers, and 20 were passenger liners. The main ports in order of tonnage capacity are: İstanbul, İzmir, Samsun, Mersin, İskenderun and Trabzon.

Ports built or extended since 1950 are İskenderun, Ereğli, Trabzon, Samsun, Mersin, Zonguldak, Giresun, Hopa, Antalya and Bandirma. New facilities have been provided at Haydarpaşa, Salıpazari, Hopa, Yarımca and İzmir.

ROADS. Turkey had, in 1967, 58,792 km of national highways, of which 15,100 were hard surfaced. In 1969 there were registered 294,500 motor vehicles, including 137,000 passenger cars.

RAILWAYS. The total length of railway lines in 1970 was 7,985 km, all state-owned; 28 km are electrified. In 1969 Turkish railways carried 5,520m. ton-km.

AVIATION. The State Airways Administration, formed in 1938, has been converted into the mixed company Turkish Airlines (Türk Havayolları Anonim Ortaklığı); BOAC became a partner in July 1957. It conducts foreign services to Athens, Beirut, Brussels, Amsterdam, Munich, Rome, Frankfurt, Vienna, Belgrade, Nicosia and Tel-Aviv. In 1968 Turkish Airlines carried 770,232 passengers, 1·08m. kg of mail and 14·1m. kg of freight. İstanbul or Ankara are connected with all the principal countries by 27 national airlines.

POST. In 1963 there were 248,450 km of telephone lines. Number of post and telegraph offices, 3,441. Number of telephones in 1969 was 451,769.

In 1970 there were 3,125,981 licensed (and over 1m. unlicensed) wireless sets.

BANKING. The Turkish banking system is composed of the Central Bank of the Republic of Turkey (Merkez Bankası) and 45 other banks. Thirteen (including the Central Bank) are established by special laws.

The 13 banks established by special laws carry out specialized banking activities beside their general banking transactions. Five of them are state economic enterprises whose capital is owned wholly by the State. They include Ziraat Bankası (rural credits, capital: TL1,500m.), Sümerbank (textiles, etc., capital: TL1,500m.), Etibank (mining, energy, capital: TL500m.), İller Bankası (urban works, capital: TL1,200m.), İstanbul Emniyet Sandığı (savings bank). Six of them are joint-stock companies; the majority of their share capital is owned by the public sector. They include: the Emlâk Kredi Bankası (housing, capital: TL1,000m.), Denizcilik Bankası (shipping, capital: TL1,500m.), Türkiye Vakıflar Bankası (investments of pious foundations, funds, capital: TL50m.), Türkiye Halk Bankası (small business, capital: TL50m.); Türkiye Öğretmenler Bankası (teachers' housing, capital: TL30m.), T. C. Turizm Bankası (tourism, capital: TL300m.).

The development banks are: Devlet Yatırım Bankası (investment credits to state economic enterprises, capital: TL1,000m.), Türkiye Sınaî Kalkınma Bankası (investment credit to the private sector, capital: TL50m.), Sınaî Yatırım ve Kredi Bankası (industrial medium-term credit, capital: TL40m.).

Of the 31 commercial banks, 5 are foreign banks established in Turkey, and one is a bank whose capital is shared by a foreign bank.

The total deposits with banks at 31 Dec. 1968 amounted to TL26,969m., and total credits to TL26,584m., excluding the State Investment Bank.

WEIGHTS AND MEASURES. The metric system came into force on 1 Jan.

1934. On 24 May 1928 the Grand National Assembly made European numerals obligatory as from 1 June 1929.

On 1 March 1917 the Gregorian calendar was introduced into Turkey, to be used side by side with the Hegira calendar, while as from 26 Dec. 1925 it was decided finally to adopt the Gregorian calendar alone, the Turkish civil year 1342 becoming 1926.

DIPLOMATIC REPRESENTATIVES

Turkey maintains embassies in:

Afghánistán	Hungary	Portugal
Albania	India	Romania
Algeria	Indonesia	Saudi Arabia
Argentina	Iran	Senegal
Australia	Iraq	Spain
Austria	Italy	Sudan
Belgium	Japan	Sweden
Brazil	Jordan	Switzerland
Bulgaria	Kenya	Syria
Canada	Korea (South)	Taiwan
Chile	Kuwait	Thailand
Cyprus	Lebanon	Tunisia
Czechoslovakia	Libya	USSR
Denmark	Mexico	UAR
Ethiopia	Morocco	UK
Finland	Netherlands	USA
France	Nigeria	Vatican
Germany (West)	Norway	Venezuela
Ghana	Pakistan	Yugoslavia
Greece	Poland	

Turkey maintains a legation in Israel.

OF TURKEY IN GREAT BRITAIN (43 Belgrave Sq., SW1)

Ambassador: Zeki Kuneralp (accredited 30 Oct. 1969).
Counsellors: Sadi Akarcalıoğlu, Yalçin Tuğ; Galib Balkar; Celil Vayisoğlu (*Commercial*); Hayrettin Dzansoy (*Financial*); Nejat Sönmez (*Press*). *Service Attachés:* Brig.-Gen. Hasan Sağlam (*Armed Forces*); Col. Selahattin Dayicioğlu (*Army*); Capt. Hasan Sarioğlu (*Navy*); Wing Cdr Yüksel Aykut (*Air*).

There are Honorary Consuls at Birmingham and Cardiff, and a Consul-General in London.

OF GREAT BRITAIN IN TURKEY

Ambassador: Sir Roderick Sarell, KCMG.
Counsellors: R. Walker (*Commercial*); J. C. Edmonds. *First Secretaries:* Miss A. E. Stoddart; J. Dodds; M. C. A. Large, MBE (*Information*); R. S. Edlin; P. J. Kirchner, MBE (*Consul*); B. V. White (*Commercial*). *Service Attachés:* Brig. D. S. Sole, OBE (*Defence and Army*), Cdr G. M. A. James, RN (*Navy*), Wing Cdr F. C. P. Elliott (*Air*).

There is a Consul-General at İstanbul, a Consul at İzmir and a Vice-Consul at İskenderun.

OF TURKEY IN THE USA (1606–23rd St. NW, Washington, D.C., 20008)

Ambassador: Melih Esenbel.
Counsellors: Necdet Tezel; Mehmet Akmansu, Zeki Toker, Şinasi Arık (*Financial*); İzzet Zincir; Sabahattin Dumer, Emin Boysan (*Commercial*); Zeyyad Gören (*Press*). *First Secretaries:* Reşat Arım. *Service Attachés:* Brig.-Gen. Cevat Duman (*Senior Army*), Col. Emin Şifa (*Air*), Capt. Şerafettin Batbay (*Navy*).

OF THE USA IN TURKEY
Ambassador: William J. Handley.
Deputy Chief of Mission: David C. Cuthell. *Heads of Sections:* David C.
Cuthell *(Political)*; Robert B. Hill *(Economic)*; Norman W. Getsinger *(Commercial)*; E. Paul Taylor *(Consular)*; Neil Muhonen *(Administrative)*. *Service Attachés:* Col. William H. Dunham, III *(Army)*, Capt. Oliver S. Burnette *(Navy)*, Col. Sidney S. Hirshberg *(Air)*.

There are Consuls-General at İstanbul and İzmir and a Consul at Adana.

BOOKS OF REFERENCE

STATISTICAL INFORMATION. The State Institute of Statistics in Ankara consists of a research bureau and 10 sections dealing with agriculture, education, foreign trade, etc. It published an *Annuaire Statistique/İstatistik Yıllığı* (1928–53) and *Aylık İstatistik Bülteni*, Monthly Bulletin of Statistics.

Constitution of the Turkish Republic. Engl, trans., Ankara, 1961
Resmî Gazete, Official Gazette. Ankara
Konjonktür. Ministry of Commerce (three times a year, from 1940)
Banque Centrale de la République de Turquie. *Bulletin Mensuel* (from Jan. 1953)
Bulletins of the Chambers of Commerce of İstanbul and İzmir
Cenani, Rasim, *Foreign Capital Investments in Turkey.* 2nd ed. İstanbul, 1958
ENAT (Economic News about Turkey.) İstanbul, from Dec. 1967
Eren, Nuri, *Turkey Today—and Tomorrow.* London, 1964
Herschlag, *Turkey: The challenge of growth.* Leiden, 1968
Iz, Fahir, and Hony, H. C., *A Turkish–English English–Turkish Dictionary.* 2 vols. 2nd ed. OUP, 1957
Karpat, Kemal H., *Turkey's Politics: The transition to a multi-party system.* Princeton Univ. Press, 1959
Kılıç, A., *Turkey and the World.* Washington, 1959
Kinross (Lord), *Atatürk.* London, 1964
Koray, Enver, *Türkiye Tarih Yayınları Bibliografyası 1729–1950 [Bibliography of Historical Works on Turkey].* Ankara, 1952
Lewis, B., *The Emergence of Modern Turkey.* OUP, 1961
Lewis, G., *Turkey.* 3rd ed. London, 1965
Mango, A., *Turkey.* London and New York, 1968
Robinson, D. R., *The First Turkish Republic.* Harvard Univ. Press and OUP, 1964
Williams, G., *Turkey: a traveller's guide and history.* London, 1967

STATE LIBRARY. Millî Kütüphane Müdürlüğü, Ankara. *Director-General:* Müjgân Cumbul.

UNION OF SOVIET SOCIALIST REPUBLICS

Soyuz Sovyetskikh Sotsialisticheskikh Respublik

POST-REVOLUTION HISTORY. Up to 12 March 1917 the territory now forming the USSR (together with that of Finland, Poland and certain tracts ceded in 1918 to Turkey, but less the territories then forming part of the German, Austro-Hungarian and Japanese empires—East Prussia, Eastern Galicia, Transcarpathia, Bukovina, South Sakhalin and Kurile Islands—which were acquired during and after the Second World War) was constituted as the Russian Empire. It was governed as an autocracy under the Tsar, with the aid of Ministers responsible to himself and a State Duma with limited legislative powers, elected by provincial assemblies chosen by indirect elections on a restricted franchise.

On 12 March 1917 a revolution broke out. The Duma parties, the same day, set up a Provisional Committee of the State Duma, while the factory workmen and the insurgent garrison of Petrograd elected a Council (Soviet) of Workers' and Soldiers' Deputies. Soviets were also elected by the workmen in other towns, in the Army and Navy and, as time went on, by the peasantry. On 15 March 1917 the Tsar abdicated, and the Provisional Committee, by agreement with the Petrograd Soviet, appointed a Provisional Government and, on 14 Sept., proclaimed a republic. However, a political struggle went on between the supporters of the Provisional Government—the Mensheviks and the Socialist-Revolutionaries—and the Bolsheviks, who advocated the assumption of power by the Soviets. When they had won majorities in the Soviets of the principal cities and of the armed forces on several fronts, the Bolsheviks organized an insurrection through a Military-Revolutionary Committee of the Petrograd Soviet. On 7 Nov. 1917 the Committee arrested the Provisional Government and transferred power to the second All-Russian Congress of Soviets. This elected a new government, the Council of People's Commissars, headed by Lenin.

On 31 Jan. 1918 the third All Russian Congress of Soviets issued a Declaration of Rights of the Toiling and Exploited Masses, which proclaimed Russia a Republic of Soviets of Workers', Soldiers' and Peasants' Deputies; and on 10 July 1918 the fifth Congress adopted a Constitution for the Russian Socialist Federal Soviet Republic. In the course of the civil war other Soviet Republics were set up in the Ukraine, Belorussia and Transcaucasia. These first entered into treaty relations with the RSFSR and then, in 1922, joined with it in a closely integrated Union.

CONSTITUTION. Constituent Republics. The Union of Soviet Socialist Republics was formed by the union of the RSFSR, the Ukrainian Soviet Socialist Republic, the Belorussian Soviet Socialist Republic and the Transcaucasian Soviet Socialist Republic; the Treaty of Union was adopted by the first Soviet Congress of the USSR on 30 Dec. 1922. In May 1925 the Uzbek and Turkmen Autonomous Soviet Socialist Republics and in Dec. 1929 the Tadzhik Autonomous Soviet Socialist Republic were declared constituent members of the USSR, becoming Union Republics.

At the 8th Congress of the Soviets, on 5 Dec. 1936, a new constitution of the USSR was adopted. The Transcaucasian Republic was split up into the Armenian Soviet Socialist Republic, the Azerbaijan Soviet Socialist Republic and the Georgian Soviet Socialist Republic, each of which became constituent republics of the Union. At the same time the Kazakh Soviet Socialist Republic and the Kirghiz Soviet Socialist Republic, previously autonomous republics within the RSFSR, were proclaimed constituent republics of the USSR.

In Sept. 1939 Soviet troops occupied eastern Poland as far as the 'Curzon line', which in 1919 had been drawn on ethnographical grounds as the eastern frontier of Poland, and incorporated it into the Ukrainian and Belorussian Soviet Socialist Republics. In Feb. 1951 some districts of the Drogobych Region of the Ukraine and the Lublin Voivodship of Poland were exchanged.

On 31 March 1940 territory ceded by Finland was joined to that of the Autonomous Soviet Socialist Republic of Karelia to form the Karelo-Finnish Soviet Socialist Republic, which was admitted into the Union as the 12th Union Republic. On the 16 July 1956 the Supreme Soviet of the USSR adopted a law altering the status of the Karelo-Finnish Republic from that of a Union (constituent) Republic of the USSR to that of an Autonomous (Karelian) Republic within the RSFSR.

On 2 Aug. 1940 the Moldavian Soviet Socialist Republic was constituted as the 13th Union Republic. It comprised the former Moldavian Autonomous Soviet Socialist Republic and Bessarabia (44,290 sq. km, ceded by Rumania on 28 June 1940), except for the districts of Khotin, Akerman and Ismail, which, together with Northern Bukovina (10,440 sq. km), were incorporated in the Ukrainian Soviet Republic. The Soviet–Rumanian frontier thus constituted was confirmed by the peace treaty with Rumania, signed on 10 Feb. 1947. On 29 June 1945 Ruthenia (Sub-Carpathian Russia, 12,742 sq. km) was by treaty with Czechoslovakia embodied in the Ukrainian Soviet Socialist Republic.

On 3 Aug. 1940 Estonia, Latvia and Lithuania were incorporated in the Soviet Union as the 14th, 15th and 16th Union Republics. The change in the status of the Karelo-Finnish Republic has reduced the number of Union Republics to 15.

After the defeat of Germany it was agreed by the governments of the UK, the USA and the USSR (by the Potsdam declaration) that part of East Prussia should be embodied in the USSR. The area (11,655 sq. km), which includes the towns of Königsberg (renamed Kaliningrad), Tilsit (renamed Sovietsk) and Insterburg (renamed Chernyakhovsk), was joined to the Russian Soviet Federal Socialist Republic by decree of 7 April 1946.

By the peace treaty with Finland, signed on 10 Feb. 1947, the province of Petsamo (Pechenga), ceded to Finland on 14 Oct. 1920 and 12 March 1946, was returned to the Soviet Union. On 19 Sept. 1955 the Soviet Union renounced its treaty rights to the naval base of Porkkala-Udd and on 26 Jan. 1956 completed the withdrawal of the forces from Finnish territory.

In 1945, after the defeat of Japan, the southern half of Sakhalin (36,000 sq. km) and the Kurile Islands (10,200 sq. km) were, by agreement with the Allies, incorporated in the USSR.[1]

[1] However, Japan asks for the return of the Etorofu and Kunashiri Islands as not belonging to the Kurile Islands proper. The Soviet Government informed Japan on 27 Jan. 1960 that the Habomai Islands and Shikotan would be handed back to Japan on the withdrawal of the American troops from Japan.

GOVERNMENT. The Soviet Union is a socialist state of workers and peasants, the political units of which are the Soviets of Working People's Deputies. All central and local authority is vested in these Soviets.

The economic foundation of the USSR is the socialist system of economy and the socialist ownership of the means of production. There are two forms of socialist property: (1) state property (property of the whole people); (2) co-operative and collective farm (*Kolhoz*) property (property of individual collective farms and property of co-operative associations). The land, mineral deposits, waters, forests, mills, factories, mines, railways, water and air transport, banks, means of communication, large state-organized agricultural enterprises, such as state farms (*Sovhozy*), machine-repair stations and the like, as well as municipal enterprises and the principal dwelling-house properties in the cities and industrial localities, are state property, but the land occupied by collective farmers is secured to them in perpetuity so long as they use it in accordance with the laws of the country. The members of the *Kolhozy* may have small plots of land attached to their dwellings for their own use. Peasants unwilling to enter a Kolhoz may retain their individual farms, but they are not allowed to employ hired labour. The right of personal property of citizens in their income from work and in their savings, in their dwelling-houses and auxiliary household economy, their domestic furniture and utensils and objects of personal use and comfort, as well as the right of inheritance of personal property of citizens, are protected by law. The constitution recognizes the right of all citizens to work, rest, leisure, education and maintenance in old age, sickness or incapacity, without distinction of sex, race or nationality, and lays down that any direct or indirect restriction of the rights of, or conversely, the establishment of direct or indirect privileges for, citizens on account of their race or nationality, as well as the advocacy of racial or national exclusiveness or hatred and contempt, is punishable by law. The franchise is enjoyed by all citizens of the USSR, including members of the Armed Forces, who have reached the age of 18, irrespective of sex, with the exception of the insane and of persons convicted by court of law to sentences including deprivation of rights. Candidates for election to the Supreme Soviet of the USSR must be 23 years of age, and to the Supreme Soviets of the Union Republics and Autonomous Republics 21; for all regional and other local authorities the minimum age for candidates is 18. A member of any Soviet may be recalled by a decision of a majority of his or her electors if he or she fails to give satisfaction (law on procedure for this, 30 Oct. 1959).

The USSR consists of 15 Union Republics, each inhabited by a major nationality which gives its name to the Republic. These are divided into 113 territories and regions, and these again into 2,993 districts and 1,935 towns and 3,569 urban settlements (1 Jan. 1971). Within the districts there are 40,820 rural districts (usually each including a number of villages). The territories and regions also include a number of smaller nationalities, forming their own self-governing units—20 Autonomous Republics, 8 Autonomous Regions and 10 National Areas.

The highest legislative organ is the Supreme Soviet of the USSR. It consists of 2 chambers with equal legislative rights, elected for a term of 4 years: the Soviet of the Union and the Soviet of Nationalities.

The Soviet of the Union is elected by the citizens of the USSR on the basis of 1 deputy for every 300,000 of the population. The Chamber elected on 14 June 1970 consists of 767 members (*Chairman*, A. P. Shitikov).

The Soviet of Nationalities is elected by the citizens of the USSR, voting by Union and Autonomous Republics, Autonomous Regions and National Areas on the basis of 32 (from June 1966) deputies from each Union Republic, 11 deputies from each Autonomous Republic, 5 deputies from each Autonomous Region and 1 deputy from each National Area. The Chamber elected on 14 June 1970 consists of 750 members (*Chairman*, Y. S. Nasriddinova).

Each chamber has 12 standing committees: planning and budget; industry; transport and communications; building; agriculture; health and social welfare; education, science and culture; trade and services; draft legislation; foreign affairs; youth affairs; natural environment.

The highest executive and administrative organ is the Council of Ministers (called People's Commissars before 16 March 1946); they are appointed by the Supreme Soviet.

The Presidium of the Supreme Soviet of the USSR is elected at a joint session of both chambers of the Supreme Soviet and consists of the chairman, 15 vice-chairmen (one from each of the Union republics), 20 members and the secretary. It acts as the supreme state authority between sessions of the Supreme Soviet and is accountable to the latter for all its activities.

Deputies are elected by the voters on the basis of universal, equal and direct suffrage by secret ballot. The only legal political party is the Communist Party; non-members are classed as non-party citizens. Candidates up to the present have been selected at a preliminary 'constituency electoral consultation' (selection conference), to which organizations which have put forward nominations send delegates, who discuss the various nominees. As a consequence, so far, a single candidate has been arrived at in each constituency, whose name has appeared on the ballot paper, to be struck out or approved by a cross as the voter desires. This procedure, however, is not laid down by the constitution, and may be altered. At the election held on 14 June 1970, 153,172,213 electors voted. The Supreme Soviet elected on that day consists of 1,096 Communist and 421 non-party deputies; 463 were women, 481 manual workers in industry and state farms, and 282 collective farmers.

On 1 Feb. 1944 each of the constituent republics of the Union was given the right to have separate Commissariats (now Ministries) for Defence and Foreign Affairs. After the death of Stalin, 5 March 1953, a number of Ministries comprising different branches of trade, engineering, transport and electricity were merged into single Ministries. In 1957 the number of Ministries in the central government was reduced from 52 to 19, and in Dec. 1959 to 15; but in Oct. 1964 it was again increased to 47, in Aug. 1966 to 48 and in 1968 to 56.

The Council of Ministers, in July 1970, included 11 vice-chairmen, the Premiers of the 15 Union Republics, the head of the Central Statistical Department, the chairmen of 7 commissions of the Presidium of the Council of Ministers (4 of them vice-chairmen of the Council), of the Committee for People's Control, State Planning Committee, the Agricultural Technique Organization and of 7 other State Committees; 57 Ministers; and the chairman of the State Bank.

Soon after the adoption of the 1936 constitution all the constituent republics of the Union held their Soviet congresses, at which they adopted their own constitutions based in all essentials on the constitution of the Union, but adapted where necessary to national and local requirements. Article 14 of the constitution reserves to the central government the spheres of war and peace, diplomatic relations, defence, foreign trade, state security, economic planning, education, criminal and civil codes, etc. The right of the constituent republics to withdraw from the Union is expressly recognized.

The 20 Autonomous Republics include 16 in the RSFSR, 1 in Azerbaijan, 2 in Georgia and 1 in Uzbekistan. Five Autonomous Regions are in the RSFSR,

1 each in Georgia, Azerbaijan and Tadzhikistan; all 10 National Areas are in the RSFSR.

The Autonomous Republics are governed by their own Supreme Soviet and Council of Ministers: the regions and territories, districts, towns and rural areas have their own Soviets, elected for a term of 2 years. In March 1969, 2,070,539 members were elected, 923,313 of them (44·6%) women, 1,138,907 (55%) non-Party and 1,331,454 (64·3%) industrial workers and collective farmers.

In Nov. 1970 there were over 44,000 rural and urban Soviets with 1·5m. deputies, 1·7m. voluntary co-opted members participating in their standing committees and 43,000 women were chairmen or secretaries of Soviets.

State flag: Red, with sickle and hammer in gold in the upper corner near the staff, and above them a 5-pointed star bordered in gold.

National anthem: Soyuz nerushimy respublik svobodnykh (words by S. Mikhalkov and El-Registan; music by A. V. Alexandrov; 1944).

The Presidium of the Supreme Soviet may, within the framework of the constitution, issue edicts (*ukaz*) interpreting existing legislation or amending it, subject to ratification subsequently by the Supreme Soviet.

Legislation by decree and executive authority is vested in the Council of Ministers. The Council of Ministers is responsible to the Supreme Soviet of the USSR and in the intervals between sessions to the Presidium of the Supreme Soviet.

President of the Presidium of the Supreme Soviet of the USSR: Nikolai Viktorovich Podgorny (Aug. 1966).

Secretary of the Presidium: M. P. Georgadze.

Chairman of the Council of Ministers: Alexei Nikolayevich Kosygin (Oct. 1964).

First Vice-Chairman: K. T. Mazurov, D. S. Polyansky.

Minister of Defence: Marshal A. A. Grechko. *Minister of Foreign Trade:* N. S. Patolichev. *Minister for Foreign Affairs:* A. A. Gromyko.

Yezhegodnik BSE. Moscow (annual)
Denison, A., and Kirichenko, M., *Soviet State Law.* Moscow, 1960
Hazard, J. N., *The Soviet System of Government.* Univ. of Chicago Press, 1957
Meyer, A. G., *The Soviet political system: an interpretation.* New York, 1965

COMMUNIST PARTY. According to the rules adopted by the 22nd Congress of the Party on 31 Oct, 1961, the Communist Party of the Soviet Union 'unites, on a voluntary basis, the more advanced, politically more conscious section of the working class, collective-farm peasantry and intelligentsia of the USSR', whose principal objects are to build a Communist society by means of gradual transition from Socialism to Communism, to raise the material and cultural level of the people, to organize the defence of the country and to strengthen ties with the workers of other countries.

The Party is built on the territorial-industrial principle. The supreme organ is the Party Congress. Ordinary congresses are convened not less than once in 4 years. The Congress elects a Central Committee which meets at least every 6 months, carries on the work of the Party between congresses, and guides the work of central Soviet and public organizations through Party groups within them.

The Central Committee forms a Political Bureau to direct the work of the Central Committee between plenary meetings, a Secretariat to direct current work and a Commission of Party Control to consider appeals against decisions about expulsion. Similar rules hold for the Regional, Territorial and Republican Party organizations.

Over 370,000 primary Party organizations exist in mills, factories, state machine and tractor stations and other economic establishments, in collective farms, units of the Soviet Army and Navy, in villages, offices, educational establishments, etc., where there are at least 3 Party members. On 1 March 1971 over 40% of the members were industrial workers, 15% were collective farmers and 45% office and professional workers. 21% were women.

The Central Committee elected by the 24th Congress in April 1971 consisted of 245 members and 155 candidate members.

In March 1968 the Political Bureau of the Central Committee consisted of the following members: L. I. Brezhnyov, V. V. Grishin, A. P. Kirilenko, A. N. Kosygin, K. T. Mazurov, A. Y. Pelshe, N. V. Podgorny, D. S. Polyansky, M. A. Suslov, D. A. Kunayev, V. V. Shcherbitsky F, T. Kulakov, P. E. Shelest, A. N. Shelepin, G. I. Voronov; and the following alternate members: Y. V. Andropov; P. N. Demichev, P. M. Masherov, V. P. Mzhavanadze, S. R. Rashidov, D. F. Ustinov.

Secretariat: L. I. Brezhnyov (*First Secretary*); P. N. Demichev; I. V. Kapitonov; K. F. Katushev; A. P. Kirilenko; F. D. Kulakov; B. N. Ponomaryov; M. S. Solomentsev; M. A. Suslov.

Chairman of the Commission of Party Control: A. Y. Pelshe.

Vice-Chairman: Z. T. Serdyuk.

In April 1971 the Communist Party had 14·5m. members. Membership of the Young Communist League was 28m.

The Communist International (the Comintern), founded on the initiative of the Russian Communist Party in 1919, was dissolved on 15 May 1943. In Oct. 1947 a Communist Information Bureau (Cominform) was set up in Belgrade to serve the Communist parties of Bulgaria, Czechoslovakia, France, Hungary, Italy, Poland, Rumania, USSR and Yugoslavia. On 28 June 1948 Yugoslavia was expelled from the Cominform and the bureau was transferred to Bucharest. The Cominform was on 17 April 1956 declared dissolved.

Hammond, T. T. (ed.), *Soviet Foreign Relations and World Communism.* Princeton and OUP, 1965
Hunt, R. N. C., *Books on Communism* in [English]. London, 1960
Kassof, A., *The Soviet Youth Program.* Harvard and OUP, 1965
Schapiro, L., *The Communist Party of the Soviet Union.* New York, 1960.—*The government and politics of the Soviet Union.* New York, 1965
History of the Communist Party of the Soviet Union (English ed.). Moscow, 1960; rev. Russian ed., Moscow, 1965

AREA AND POPULATION. The total area of the Soviet Union in April, 1956 was 22·4m. sq. km (8·65m. sq. miles). The census population on 15 Jan. 1959 was 208·8m. (94m. males and 114·8m. females; 99·8m. urban, 109m. rural). Estimated population on 1 Jan. 1960 was 212·3m. (95·9m. males, 116·4m. females; 103·7m. urban, 108·6 rural); 1966, 232m. (125m. urban, 107m. rural); on 1 July 1967, 235·5m. (108·1m. males, 127·4m. females; 129·1m. urban, 106·4m. rural). The census population on 15 Jan. 1970 was 241·7m. (111·3m. males, 130·4m. females; 136m. urban, 105·7 rural). The increase of 36m. in urban population between 1959 and 1970 was due to a natural increase of 19·6m., an influx of over 16m. from the countryside and the transformation of rural areas with a population of 5m. into urban areas. The natural increase in the rural areas exceeded 18m., but for the reasons stated the net rural population declined by 3m.

Regions, towns, streets, factories, schools, etc., named after Stalin were renamed in Nov. 1961 when Stalin's body was removed from the Lenin–Stalin tomb in Red Square in Moscow. Similarly, in Jan. 1962 towns bearing the names of Molotov, Voroshilov, Kaganovich and Malenkov were renamed.

The areas (in 1,000 sq. km) and census population (in 1m., in Jan. 1970) of the constituent republics are as follows (capitals in brackets):

Constituent Republics	Area	Population	Constituent Republics	Area	Population
RSFSR (Moscow)	17,075	130·1	Lithuania (Vilnius)	64	3·1
Ukraine (Kiev)	601	47·1	Kirgizia (Frunze)	198	2·9
Kazakhstan (Alma-Ata)	2,756	12·9	Tadzhikistan (Dushanbe)	143	2·9
Uzbekistan (Tashkent)	409	12·0	Latvia (Riga)	64	2·4
Belorussia (Minsk)	208	9·0	Armenia (Yerevan)	30	2·5
Georgia (Tbilisi)	70	4·7	Turkmenistan (Ashkhabad)	468	2·2
Azerbaijan (Baku)	87	5·1			
Moldavia (Kishinev)	34	3·6	Estonia (Tallin)	45	1·4

Nationalities. The most numerous nationalities at the 1959 census were: 114·1m. Russians, 37·3m. Ukrainians, 7m. Belorussians, 6m. Uzbeks, 5m. Tatars, 3·6m. Kazakhs, 2·9m. Azerbaijanians, 2·8m. Armenians, 2·7m. Georgians, 2·3m.

Lithuanians, 2·3m. Jews, 2·2m. Moldavians, 1·6m. Germans, 1·5m. Chuvashes, 1·4m. Latvians, 1·4m. Tadzhiks, 1·4m. Poles, 1·3m. Mordovians, 1m. Turkmenians, 989,000 Bashkirs, 989,000 Estonians, 969,000 Kirgiz. The great majority (in each case 84–99%) indicated the language of their nationality as their native tongue; exceptions were the Bashkirs (62%), Poles (46%) and Jews (21%).

Estimated losses of population in the Second World War, 20m., of which 7m. were military losses.

The following tables show the growth of the population in Russia:

1897 (Russian Empire)	126,900,000	1939 (census)	170,600,000
1913 (Russian Empire)	170,900,000	1959 (census)	208,826,000
1913 (present frontiers)	159,200,000	1970 (census)	241,748,000

The following was the population on 15 Jan. 1970 of the larger towns (in 1,000):

Aktyubinsk	150	Kishinev	357	Petropavlovsk (North	
Alma-Ata	730	Klaipeda	140	Kazakhstan)	173
Andizhan	188	Kokand	133	Petrozavodsk	185
Angarsk	204	Kolomna	136	Podolsk	169
Anjero-Sudjensk	106	Kommunarsk	123	Poltava	220
Arkhangelsk	343	Komsomolsk-on-Amur	218	Prokopyevsk	275
Armavir	146	Kopeisk	150	Riga	733
Ashkhabad	253	Kostroma	223	Rostov-on-Don	789
Astrakhan	411	Kovrov	123	Rubtsovsk	145
Baku	1,261	Kramatorsk	151	Ryazan	351
Barnaul	439	Krasnodar	465	Rybinsk	218
Belovo	108	Krasnoyarsk	648	Samarkand	267
Berezniki	145	Kremenchug	148	Saransk	190
Biisk	186	Krivoi Rog	573	Saratov	758
Blagoveshchensk	128	Kuibyshev	1,047	Semipalatinsk	236
Bobruisk	138	Kurgan	244	Serov	100
Bryansk	318	Kursk	284	Serpukhov	124
Cheboksary	216	Kustanai	123	Sevastopol	229
Chelyabinsk	874	Kutaisi	161	Shakhty	205
Cherepovetz	189	Leninakan	164	Simferopol	250
Chernigov	159	Leningrad	3,950	Smolensk	211
Chernovtzy	187	Leninsk-Kuznetski	128	Sochi	224
Chimkent	247	Lipetsk	290	Stavropol	198
Chita	244	Lvov	553	Sterlitamak	185
Djambul	188	Lyubertsy	139	Sumy	159
Dneprodzerzhinsk	227	Magnitogorsk	364	Sverdlovsk	1,026
Dnepropetrovsk	863	Mahachkala	186	Syzran	174
Donetsk	879	Makeyevka	393	Taganrog	254
Dushanbe	374	Melitopol	137	Tallin	363
Dzerzhinsk (Gorky re		Miass	132	Tambov	229
gion)	223	Minsk	916	Tashkent	1,385
Elektrostal	123	Mogilev	202	Tbilisi	889
Engels	130	Moscow	7,061	Temirtau	167
Frunze	431	Murmansk	309	Togliatti	251
Gomel	272	Mytishchi	119	Tomsk	339
Gorlovka	335	Nalchik	146	Tselinograd	180
Gorky	1,170	Namangan	175	Tula	462
Grozny	341	Nikolayev	331	Tyumen	269
Habarovsk	437	Nizhni Tagil	378	Ufa	773
Irkutsk	451	Norilsk	136	Ulan-Ude	254
Ivanovo	419	Novocherkassk	162	Ulyanovsk	351
Izhevsk	422	Novokuznetsk	499	Uralsk	134
Kadievka	137	Novomoskovsk	134	Ussuriisk	128
Kalinin	345	Novorossiisk	133	Ust-Kamenogorsk	230
Kaliningrad	297	Novoshakhtinsk	102	Vladimir	234
Kaluga	211	Novosibirsk	1,161	Vladivostok	442
Kamensk-Uralski	169	Odessa	822	Vilnius	372
Karaganda	522	Omsk	821	Vinnitsa	211
Kaunas	306	Ordzhonikidze		Vitebsk	231
Kazan	869	(Vladikavkaz)	236	Volgograd	818
Kemerovo	385	Orehovo-Zuyevo	120	Vologda	178
Kertch	128	Orenburg	345	Vorashilovgrad	282
Kherson	261	Orsk	225	Voronezh	660
Kharkov	1,223	Oryol	232	Yaroslavl	517
Kiev	1,632	Pavlodar	187	Yerevan	767
Kirov	332	Penza	374	Yoshkar-Ola	166
Kirovabad		Perm	850	Zaporozhye	658
(Azerbaidjan)	190	Pervouralsk	117	Zhdanov	417
Kirovograd	189	Petropavlovsk-		Zhitomir	161
Kiselyovsk	126	Kamchatski	154	Zlatoust	181

Balzac, Vasyutin and Felgin, *Economic Geography of the USSR*. London, 1951
Baransky, N. N., *Economic Geography of the USSR*. Moscow, 1956 (in English)
Cole, J. P., and German, F. C., *A Geography of the USSR*. London, 1961
Leimbach, W., *Die Sowjet-Union*. Stuttgart, 1950
Narodnoye Hoziaistvo SSSR v 1969. Moscow, 1970
The Oxford Regional Atlas of the USSR. Clarendon Press, Oxford, 1956
Yezhegodnik B.S.E., 1970

RELIGION. With the Revolution the Orthodox Church lost its position as the dominant religion and all religions were placed on an equal footing. Article 124 of the 1936 constitution of the USSR reads as follows: 'With the aim of ensuring freedom of conscience for the citizens, the Church in the USSR is separated from the State and the school from the Church, and freedom of religious worship and anti-religious propaganda is permitted to all citizens.'

By decree of 23 Jan. 1918 the Orthodox Church was disestablished; its property, together with that of all other denominations, was nationalized. The congregations themselves have to maintain their churches and clergy, regardless of confession or denomination, and may organize a minimum of 20 persons, which may request and receive the use of a church building, free of charge, except for maintenance, insurance, land taxes, etc. About two-thirds of all the churches have been closed. Religious instruction may be given in private, but otherwise only in church classes. The income of religious communities is not subject to taxation.

Relations between the religious communities of all creeds and the Government are maintained through a Council for Religious Affairs (*Chairman*, V. A. Kuroyedov).

The Russian Orthodox Church, represented by the Patriarchate of Moscow, had, in 1967, 30m. regular worshippers. There are still many Old Believers, whose schism from the Orthodox Church dates from the 17th century. The Russian Church is headed by the Patriarch of Moscow and All Russia, assisted by the Holy Synod, which has 6 members—the Patriarch himself and the Metropolitans of Krutitsy (Moscow), Leningrad and Kiev *ex officio*, and 3 bishops alternating for 6 months in order of seniority from the 3 regions forming the Moscow Patriarchate. In 1967 there were 20,000 places of worship (54,000 before the Revolution). Religious instruction in classes for persons under 18 is forbidden. The Patriarchate of Moscow maintains jurisdiction over a few parishes of Russian Orthodox abroad, at Tehran, Jerusalem, East Germany, France (1 archbishop), England, North and South America (2 bishops).

After the Russian Orthodox Church the next Christian community in importance are the Armenians; their Catholicos (Patriarch), whose seat is at Etchmiadzin, is head of all the Armenian (Gregorian) communities throughout the world.

The Georgian Church has its own organization under a Catholicos (Patriarch).

Protestantism is represented chiefly by the Evangelical Christian Baptists, with over 512,000 baptized adult members and some 5,000 churches: the Lutheran (350,000 in Estonia, 600,000 in Latvia) are concentrated mainly in the Baltic States, the Reformed in the Transcarpathian Region of the Ukraine (70,000).

The Roman Catholics are most numerous in Lithuania and the western Ukraine. There are only 4 bishops now in office. In 1946 some 3·5m. Uniates in the USSR withdrew their allegiance to Rome and came under the jurisdiction of the Orthodox Patriarchate in Moscow.

The Moslems, mainly Sunnis, are divided into 4 administrative regions; 3 of them (Central Asia, European Russia and Siberia, Northern Caucasus) headed by a Mufti; the largest (Transcaucasia, with its centre at Baku) by a Shaikh-ul-Islam.

The Armenian-Gregorian and the Roman Catholic churches and the Moslems of Central Asia maintain theological colleges.

There are various Jewish communities, the chief being in Moscow and Kiev. The Central Buddhist Council of the USSR is headed by a Lama with communities in Buryatia, Tuva, Kalmykia and in the national (minority) areas of the Chita and Irkutsk regions.

Bordeaux, M., *Opium of the People. The Christian Religion in the USSR*. London, 1965.—*Religious Ferment in Russia*. London, 1968
Braham, R. L., *Jews in the Communist World; a bibliography, 1945–1960*. New York, 1961
Conquest, R. (ed.), *Religion in the USSR*. London, 1968
Curtiss, J. S., *The Russian Church and the Soviet State, 1917–50*. New York, 1953
Fejtö, F., *Les Juifs et l'antisémitisme dans les pays communistes*. Paris, 1960
Fletcher, W. C., *A study in survival: the church in Russia 1927–43*. New York, 1965
Goldberg, B. Z., *The Jewish Problem in the Soviet Union*. New York, 1961
Kolarz, W., *Religion in the Soviet Union*. London, 1961
Leneman. L., *La Tragédie des Juifs en URSS*. Bruges, 1959
Novosti Press Agency (ed.), *Soviet Jews: Fact and Fiction*. Moscow, 1970
Struve, N., *Les Chrétiens en URSS*. Paris, 1963

EDUCATION. Education is free and compulsory from 7 to 15/16. Co-education was reintroduced in all schools on 1 Sept. 1954. There are 3 types of schools—those with a 4-year, an 8-year and an 11-year curriculum; the school-leaving age had been raised to 17 in all large towns and industrial settlements by the end of 1955. Under a law of 24 Dec. 1958 general polytechnical education is to last 8 years (*i.e.*, until the age of 15 or 16) and thereafter is to be combined for 2 years with work in production (except for the specially artistically gifted who go to art schools). Instruction is given in more than 100 languages.

In 1969–70 there were 197,000 primary and secondary schools. Pupils in primary, secondary, technical, etc., schools numbered 49·4m. (7,557,000 of them in the 16–18 age-groups) and the teachers 2·6m. There were 16,971 schools providing a 10-year secondary education for 4m. workers and peasants who had already begun earning their living.

At the end of 1940 labour reserve schools (both vocational and industrial) were organized, admitting applicants from 14 to 17 years of age. From 1959 onwards these and other technical schools were reorganized as town and rural professional and technical schools. Between 1940 and 1970 they trained 22m. skilled workers. In 1969 about 1·5m. graduated from such schools, including 411,000 for agriculture; another 681,000 agricultural mechanics were trained in state and collective farms. Over 5,190 vocational training schools existed in 1970.

In 1969, 7·8m. children of from 3 to 7 years of age attended 80,700 kindergartens. Children in boarding schools numbered 800,000 in 1970.

In 1970 there were 4,196 technical colleges with 4·3m. students, and 800 universities, institutes and other places of higher education, with 4·5m. students (including 2·4m. taking correspondence or evening courses).

Among the university towns are: Moscow, Leningrad, Kharkov, Odessa, Tartu, Kazan, Saratov, Tomsk, Kiev, Sverdlovsk, Tbilisi, Alma-Ata, Tashkent, Minsk, Gorky and Vladivostok. On 1 Jan. 1970 there were 833,400 scientific workers in places of higher education, research institutes and Academies of Sciences.

The Academy of Sciences of the USSR has 637 members and corresponding members. Total learned institutions under the USSR Academy of Sciences number 229, with 34,441 scientific staff. Fourteen of the Union Republics have their own Academies of Sciences, with scientific staff numbering over 35,650. On 1 Jan. 1970 there were 99,532 post-graduate students.

An Academy of Pedagogical Sciences had 17 research institutes with 1,238 staff.

In Jan. 1970 there were employed in the national economy 6·5m. specialists with a completed higher education and 9·6m. with a completed secondary technical education.

In Jan. 1970 about 78·6m. people were studying at schools, colleges and training or correspondence courses.

CINEMAS (1970). There were 146,400 permanent and 10,500 mobile cinemas.

NEWSPAPERS. In 1969, 9,024 newspapers with a total circulation of 135m. copies were published in 57 languages of the USSR.

Central Statistical Administration, *Land of Soviets over 50 Years* (in Russian). Moscow, 1967
Bereday, G. Z. F. (ed.), *The Changing Soviet School*. Boston, Mass, 1960
King, B., *Russia Goes to School: A Guide to Soviet Education*. London, 1948
Korol, A. G., *Soviet Research and Development: its organization. personnel and funds*. Cambridge, Mass., 1965
Matthews, W. K., *Languages of the USSR*. London, 1951
Myuller, V. K., and Boyanus, S. K., *English–Russian (and Russian–English) Dictionary*. 2 vols. Moscow, 1931–35
Shore, M. J., *Soviet Education, its psychology and philosophy*. New York, 1947

HEALTH. All health services are free of charge; but private practice exists. Health is administered by the Ministry of Health of the USSR, which supervises the work of the Health Ministries of the Union Republics and the Autonomous Republics.

In 1944 an Academy of Medical Sciences was formed; it has under its direct control 34 research institutes. In all, there were, in 1966, 368 medical research institutions. Smallpox and malaria have been virtually eliminated.

In 1969–70, 98 institutes and medical faculties had a total of 309,000 students taking a 6-year course.

In 1970 there were 26,384 civil hospitals with 2,567,000 beds. Children's nurseries accommodated 5·57m. babies in permanent crèches and 4·5m. in seasonal summer establishments. 592,000 doctors (excluding dentists) were in the health service. All confinements in towns and 75% in the country were in hospital.

There were 38,000 clinics and dispensaries, of which 7,500 were attached to factories.

The death rate in the USSR in 1969 was 8·1 per 1,000, and the birth rate 17 per 1,000. Infant death rate was 26 (per 1,000 live births) in 1969, compared with 273 in 1913, 184 in 1940 and 81 in 1950.

Social insurance is administered by the trade unions, through social insurance councils elected in places of work and social insurance sub-committees of factory committees: about 5m. volunteers are engaged in this work. 9·7m. people were sent to sanatoria or rest homes by the unions in 1969. There were over 40m. pensioners in 1969. 12m. collective farmers were receiving state-aided pensions in 1969.

Total number of sanatoria in 1969 was 2,235, with 427,000 beds; in addition, there were 1,783 'one-night' or 'one-day' sanatoria, with 106,000 beds. There were 845 rest homes with 224,000 beds.

State expenditure (in 1m. new roubles) on health services proper, 1958, 4,100; 1960, 4,800; 1966, 7,100; 1967, 7,451; 1968, 8,100; 1969, 8,600.

Between 1950 and 1969, 39,035,000 apartments (in towns) and houses (in rural areas) were built. In 1970, 2·3m. apartments and houses were built.

Bogolepova, L. S., *Health Education in the USSR*. Moscow, 1952
Field, M. G., *Doctor and patient in Soviet Russia*. Harvard Univ. Press, 1957
Sosnovy, T., *The Housing Problem in the Soviet Union*. New York, 1951
Vinogradov, N. A., *Public Health in the Soviet Union*. Moscow, 1950

JUSTICE. The basis of the judiciary system is the same throughout the Soviet Union, but the constituent republics have the right to introduce modifications and to make their own rules for the application of the code of laws. The Supreme Court of the USSR is the chief court and supervising organ for all constituent republics and is elected by the Supreme Soviet of the USSR for 5 years. Supreme Courts of the Union and Autonomous Republics are elected by the Supreme Soviets of these republics, and Territorial, Regional and Area Courts by the respective Soviets, each for a term of 5 years.

Court proceedings are conducted in the local language with full interpreting facilities as required. All cases are heard in public, unless otherwise provided for by law, and the accused is guaranteed the right of defence.

Laws establishing common principles of criminal legislation, criminal responsibility for state and military crimes, judicial and criminal procedure and military tribunals were adopted by the Supreme Soviet on 25 Dec. 1958 for the courts both of the USSR and the constituent Republics.

The Law Courts are divided into People's Courts and higher courts. The People's Courts consist of the People's Judge and 2 Assessors, and their function is to examine, as the first instance, most of the civil and criminal cases, except the more important ones, some of which are tried at the Regional Court, and those of the highest importance at the Supreme Court. The Regional Courts supervise the activities of the People's Courts and also act as Courts of Appeal from the decisions of the People's Court. Special chambers of the higher courts deal with offences committed in the Army and the public transport services.

People's Judges and rota-lists of Assessors are elected directly by the citizens of each constituency : judges for 5 years, assessors for 2; they must be over 25 years of age. Should a judge be found not to perform his duties conscientiously and in accordance with the mandate of the people, he may be recalled by his electors.

The People's Assessors are called upon for duty for 2 weeks in a year. The People's Assessors for the Regional Court must have had at least 2 years' experience in public or trade-union work. The list of Assessors for the Supreme Court is drawn up by the Supreme Soviet of the republic.

The Labour Session of the People's Court supervises the regulations relating to the working conditions and the protection of labour and gives decisions on conflicts arising between managements and employees, or the violation of regulations.

Disputes between State institutions must be referred to an arbitration commission. Disputes between Soviet State institutions and foreign business firms may be referred by agreement to a Foreign Trade Arbitration Commission of the All-Union Chamber of Commerce.

The Procurator-General of the USSR is appointed for 7 years by the Supreme Soviet. All procurators of the republics, autonomous republics and autonomous regions are appointed by the Procurator-General of the USSR for a term of 5 years. The procurators supervise the correct application of the law by all state organs, and have special responsibility for the observance of the law in places of detention. The procurators of the Union republics are subordinate to the Procurator-General of the USSR, whose duty it is to see that acts of all institutions of the USSR are legal, that the law is correctly interpreted and uniformly applied; he has to participate in important cases in the capacity of State Prosecutor.

Capital punishment was abolished on 26 May 1947, but was restored on 12 Jan. 1950 for treason, espionage and sabotage, on 7 May 1954 for certain categories of murder, in Dec. 1958 for terrorism and banditry, on 7 May 1961 for embezzlement of public property, counterfeiting and attack on prison warders and, in particular circumstances, for attacks on the police and public order volunteers and for rape (15 Feb. 1962) and for accepting bribes (20 Feb. 1962).

In view of criminal abuses, extending over many years, discovered in the security system, the powers of administrative trial and exile previously vested in the security authorities (M.V.D.) were abolished in 1953; accelerated procedures for trial on charges of high treason, espionage, wrecking, etc., by the Supreme Court were abolished in 1955; and extensive powers of protection of persons under arrest or serving prison terms were vested in the Procurator-General's Office (1955). Supervisory commissions, composed of representatives of trade unions, youth organizations and local authorities, were set up in 1956 to inspect places of detention.

Further reforms of the civil and criminal codes were decreed on 25 Dec. 1958. Thereby the age of criminal responsibility has been raised from 14 to 16 years; deportation, banishment and deprivation of citizenship have been abolished; a presumption of innocence is not accepted, but the burden of proof of guilt has been placed upon the prosecutor; secret trials and the charge of 'enemy of the people' have been abolished.

Babb, H. W., and Hazard, J. N., *Soviet Legal Philosophy.* Harvard Univ. Press, 1951
Berman, H. J., *Soviet criminal law and procedure.* Harvard Univ. Press, 1966

David, R., and Hazard, J. N., *Le Droit Soviétique*. 2 vols. Paris, 1954
Feifer, G., *Justice in Moscow*. New York, 1964
Gsovski, V., *Soviet Civil Law*. 2 vols. Ann Arbor, 1948-49
Schlesinger, R., *Soviet Legal Theory*. London, 1945

FINANCE. Currency. As from 1 Jan. 1961 the gold content of the rouble was raised from 0·222 168 to 0·987 412 gramme. The official exchange rates are 90 kopeks = US$1, and (from Nov. 1967) 2·16 roubles = £1.

The gold holdings of the USSR were, in Dec. 1955, estimated at about 200m. fine oz. (US$7,000m.), or about 20% of the world total of monetary gold.

The currency in circulation is: (1) State Bank notes in denominations of 10, 25, 50 and 100 roubles; (2) Treasury notes in denominations of 1, 3 and 5 roubles; (3) cupro-nickel coins in denominations of 10, 15, 20 and 50 kopeks and 1 rouble; (4) cupro-zinc coins in denominations of 1, 2, 3 and 5 kopeks.

Budget. Revenue and expenditure in 1m. new roubles for calendar years:

	1965	1966	1967	1968	1969	1970
Revenue	102,305	106,297	117,161	130,800	140,033	153,900
Expenditure	101,621	105,577	115,242	128,500	138,531	152,300

The 1970 budget allotted 71·4m. roubles to the national economy, 17·9m. to defence and 56m. to social and cultural services.

The social insurance budget, which is controlled by the Central Council for Trade Unions and its affiliated bodies, was fixed at 17,290m. roubles for 1970 and 18,489 roubles in 1971.

The national income was assessed (in 1,000m. roubles) at 137 in 1959, 147·9 in 1960, 157·9 in 1961, 166·9 in 1962, 173·7 in 1963, 189·4 in 1964, 200·7 in 1965, 218 in 1966, 225 in 1967, 244 in 1968, 261·7 in 1969.

Income tax was abolished on 1 Oct. 1961 for earnings up to 60 roubles per month and reduced for earnings between 61 and 70 roubles; in Dec. 1967 further cuts of 25% were made for earnings from 61 to 80 roubles.

Davies, R. W., *The Development of the Soviet Budgetary System*. CUP, 1958

Investments and Credits. Capital investment (1969) was 63,400m. roubles. This total included 55,800m. by State and co-operative enterprises, 5,900m. by collective farms and 1,700m. by individuals (on housing). Taking 1913 as 100, the physical volume of industrial production within the present territory of the USSR was 769 in 1940 and 8,440 in 1969.

The debts contracted by the tsarist régime, *i.e.*, before 1917, have been repudiated by the Soviet Government.

After the Second World War the USSR has become one of the biggest creditor countries in the world. Between 1955 and Jan. 1969 economic aid in the form of 2% or 2½% loans to be repaid, as a rule, over 12 years has been advanced for 1,593 industrial and agricultural enterprises in Socialist countries and 680 enterprises in under-developed countries; the latter including loans (in 1m. old roubles): India, 2,500m.; Egypt, 2,300m.; Iraq, 550m.; Afghánistán, 480m.; Indonesia, 443m.; Argentina, 400m.; Ethiopia, 400m.; Guinea, 140m.; Cuba, US$100m.

Berliner, J. S., *Soviet Economic Aid in Underdeveloped Countries*. New York, 1958

DEFENCE. On 26 Feb. 1946 the control of the Soviet Armed Forces was unified under a single Ministry of the Armed Forces. On 25 Feb. 1950 the Defence Ministry was divided into a War Ministry and a Navy Ministry; on 15 March 1953 a single Ministry of Defence was reconstituted.

In 1955 the Air Defence Command and in 1960 the Strategic Rocket Forces were established as the 4th and 5th 'branches' of the armed forces beside the army, navy and air force.

The direction of Party and political work in the Armed Forces is exercised by the Central Committee of the Communist Party of the Soviet Union through the chief political directorate of the Ministry of Defence. The chiefs of the political departments of military commands, fleets and armies must be Party members of 5 years' standing and the chiefs of political departments of divisions and regiments Party members of 3 years' standing. Nearly 90% of the officers are members of the Communist Party or Young Communist League.

Military service begins at the age of 19 (or 18 for graduates of secondary schools). Active service lasts 2 years for privates in the Army and M.V.D. troops, 3 years for n.c.o.s in the Army and M.V.D. troops and for privates and n.c.o.s in the Air Force, 4 years for privates and n.c.o.s in the Coastal Defence, 5 years for ratings in the Navy. Reserve service lasts up to the ages of 35, 45 or 50 years according to fitness, family status and other considerations. Conscientious objection is treated as a criminal offence. Students in places of higher education are freed from military service, but receive military instruction.

In Jan. 1960 Prime Minister Khrushchov quoted the following figures of the armed forces of the Soviet Union: 1927, 586,000; 1937, 1,433,000; 1941, 4,207,000; May 1945, 11,365,000; 1948, 2,874,000; 1955, 5,763,000; 1959, 3,623,000; 1960, 2,423,000. The reduction, according to Khrushchov, was mainly due to the switch-over to rocket and nuclear weapons.

The estimated expenditure on defence (in 1m. new roubles) for 1961 was 9,255; 1962, 13,410; 1963, 13,300; 1966, 13,400; 1967, 14,500; 1968, 16,700; 1969, 17,702; 1970 (estimate), 17,900.

Eastern Security Treaty. On 14 May 1955 the USSR, Albania, Bulgaria, Czechoslovakia, the German Democratic Republic, Hungary, Poland and Rumania signed in Warsaw a 20-year treaty of friendship and collaboration, after the USSR had (on 7 May) annulled the 20-year treaties of alliance with the UK (1942) and France (1944).

The main provisions of the treaty are as follows:

ARTICLE 4. In case of armed aggression in Europe against one or several States party to the pact by a State or group of States, each State member of the pact . . . will afford to the State or States which are the object of such aggression immediate assistance . . . with all means which appear necessary, including the use of armed force. . . . These measures will cease as soon as the Security Council takes measures necessary for establishing and preserving international peace and security.

ARTICLE 5. The contracting Powers agree to set up a joint command of their armed forces to be allotted by agreement between the Powers, at the disposal of this command and used on the basis of jointly established principles. They will also take over agreed measures necessary to strengthen their defences.

ARTICLE 9. The present treaty is open to other States, irrespective of their social or Government regime, who declare their readiness to abide by the terms of the treaty in order to safeguard peace and security of the peoples.

ARTICLE 11. In the event of a system of collective security being set up in Europe and a pact to this effect being signed—to which each each party to this treaty will direct its efforts—the present treaty will lapse from the day such a collective security treaty comes into force.

The USA Secretary of Defence in 1963 estimated the armed forces of the Warsaw pact countries to total 4·5m., including 3·3m. Russians, compared with 5m. NATO forces.

Marshal Grechko was from July 1960 to April 1967 C.-in-C. of the united Armed Forces, with headquarters in Moscow. He was succeeded by Marshal I. I. Yakubovsky in 1967.

In 1962 Albania was no longer invited to the Warsaw Pact meetings, without being formally expelled.

Two (or 3) Soviet divisions are stationed in Poland, 22 divisions in East Germany, 2 divisions and 2 air divisions in Hungary.

Army. The Army was, in 1970, thought to consist of about 157 divisions, of which some 100 are of combat readiness, numbering about 2m. men.

The mechanized and tank divisions are equiped with the T34 medium tank, mounting an 85-mm gun, and with the Stalin III heavy tank, mounting a 122-mm gun. The T34 and T54 are being replaced by the T62 medium tank mounting a 115-mm gun. Rocket units are stated to be 'the main force' of the Army.

In addition to the Soviet Army, there are some 350,000 security and border troops.

Navy. There are 5 shipyards in and near Leningrad; Black Sea yards are at Nikolaiev and Sevastopol, new shipyards are at Molotovsk in the White Sea region and at Komsomolsk on the Amur.

The completion of a through canal system between the Baltic and White Seas and the opening of regular traffic *via* the North-East Passage (during the ice-free season) have enabled the Soviet Government to transfer tonnage between the Baltic and Far East.

The principal surface ships of the Soviet Navy are as follows:

Completed	Name	Standard displacement Tons	Armour Belt In.	Armour Guns In.	Principal armament	Shaft horsepower	Speed Knots
					Helicopter Carriers		
1968	Leningrad	} 15,000	5	4	{ 3 twin missile launchers; 2 twin 57-mm AA guns	} 130,000	34
1967	Moskva						
					Cruisers		
1958	Admiral Senyavin						
1957	Mikhail Kutuzov						
1956	Dimitri Pojarski						
1956	Oktyabrskaya Revolutsiya (ex-Molotovsk)						
1956	Admiral Lazarev						
1955	Alexandr Suvorov	} 15,450	5	4	12 5·9-in.; 12 3·9-in.	130,000	34
1954	Admiral Ushakov						
1954	Dzerzhinski[1]						
1953	Alexandr Nevski						
1953	Murmansk						
1953	Zhdanov						
1953	Sverdlov						
1951	Zheleznyakov	} 11,500			12 6-in.; 8 4-in.	113,000	35
1950	Komsomolets						
1944	Slava (ex-Molotov)	} 8,800	3	4	9 7·1-in.; 8 4-in. AA	110,000	35
1938	Kirov						

[1] *Dzerzhinski* has only nine 6-in. guns—3 triple turrets, 'x' turret having been replaced by a win guided missile launcher.

There are also 75 nuclear-powered submarines, 320 conventional submarines, 9 light cruisers (guided missile armed destroyer leaders), 100 destroyers, 100 escorts, 275 coastal escorts, 300 minesweepers, 125 missile patrol boats, 300 motor torpedo-boats, 100 amphibious ships, 130 amphibious craft, and thousands of support ships, auxiliaries and service craft.

The Minister of Defence stated that the main force of the navy consisted of submarines, primarily nuclear-powered and armed with nuclear rockets.

Estimated number of personnel (1970), 50,000 officers and 450,000 men.

Air Force. The Soviet Air Force was believed to consist, in 1970, of over 500,000 officers and men, nearly 10,000 first-line aircraft and a large number of second-line, transport and training aircraft. To supplement an increasing number of long-range rocket missiles (1,300 ICBM, 700 MRBM/IRBM), the DA strategic bomber force is estimated to have still 90 Tupolev Tu-95 ('Bear')[1] 4-turboprop bombers, 90 Myasishchev Mya-4 4-jet bombers and flight-refuelling tankers ('Bison') and 700 Tupolev Tu-16 ('Badger') and supersonic Tupolev Tu-22

[1] For convenience Soviet aircraft and missiles are usually referred to by invented English names in non-Soviet military writings.

('Blinder') twin-jet bombers. All 4 types are used also by the Naval Air Force for long-range maritime reconnaissance; the Tu-16, Tu-95 and Tu-22 can carry air-to-surface guided self-propelled missiles and all 4 types have provision for flight refuelling.

The FA tactical air forces, under local army command in the field, have an estimated total of 3,750 ground attack and reconnaissance aircraft, including twin-jet Yakovlev Yak-28 ('Brewer') multi-purpose combat aircraft, single-jet Sukhoi Su-7B ('Fitter') and MiG-21 ('Fishbed') fighter-bombers and diminishing numbers of older types such as the twin-jet MiG-19 ('Farmer') and single-jet MiG-17 ('Fresco'). The PVO defence command has an estimated total of 3,400 jet interceptors, consisting primarily of MiG-21, MiG-19, Sukhoi Su-9 ('Fishpot') and Yak-28P ('Firebar') fighters. The twin-jet Tu-28 ('Fiddler') fighter, armed with long-range missiles and carrying powerful search radar, and the Sukhoi Su-11 ('Flagon') twin-jet all-weather fighter have re-equipped some squadrons. The Mach 3 MiG-23 ('Foxbat') may also be entering service. Early warning and fighter-control duties are performed by radar-carrying adaptations of the Tu-114 turboprop transport ('Moss'). Very large numbers of surface-to-air guided missiles are operational, including the 'Guild', 'Guideline', 'Goa' and 'Ganef', the long-range 'Griffon' and the 'Galosh' which is deployed around Moscow and is claimed to have anti-missile capability. The more modern 'Gainful' missile system, for defence against low-flying aircraft, may be expected in service in the early 1970s.

Soviet Air Force transport squadrons have an estimated total of 1,500 aircraft, consisting primarily of An-12 ('Cub') 4-turboprop transports and piston-engined Il-14s ('Crates'), with a few very large An-22s ('Cock'), a variety of older and smaller types and many helicopters, including the turbine-powered Mi-6, Mi-8 and Mi-10 flying crane. Training aircraft include the piston-engined Yak-18 primary trainer, the Czech-built L-29 Delfin jet basic trainer and versions of operational types such as the MiG-21, MiG-15, Su-7, Yak-28 and Tu-22.

Naval Air Force. Under the control of the various naval commands, *i.e.*, Baltic, Black Sea and Pacific, the Naval Air Force has an estimated 400 land-based maritime patrol bombers and many flying-boats. Primary offensive aircraft are the Tu-16 ('Badger') twin-jet bomber, able to carry long-range air-to-surface missiles, the supersonic twin-jet Tu-22 ('Blinder') reconnaissance bomber and the Beriev M-12 ('Mail') maritime patrol amphibian. Tu-95 ('Bear') and Mya-sishchev ('Bison') 4-engined bombers, as well as the Tu-16, are used for long-range over-water reconnaissance. Anti-submarine helicopters, notably the Ka-25 ('Hormone'), are carried by some naval vessels, including 2 helicopter carriers.

Berman, H. J., and Kerner, M. (ed.), *Soviet Military Law and Administration*. 2 vols. Harvard Univ. Press, 1955
Kilmarx, R. A., *A History of Soviet Air Power*. London, 1962
O'Ballance, E., *The Red Army*. London, 1964
Saunders, M. G. (ed.), *The Soviet Navy*. London, 1958

PLANNING. Planning is based on public ownership in industry and trade, and on mixed public and collective (co-operative) ownership in agriculture. The first plan drawn up by Gosplan (the State Planning Commission) was the 'Goelro' drawn up in 1920. This was to be the basis for the economic development of the country and for the construction of a system of electrical power plants with an aggregate capacity of 1·75m. kw., in the course of 15 years. By 1927–28 the capacity of the electrical stations in operation was already 1,792,000 kw. with an output of 5,160m. kwh.

In 1925 Gosplan started to draw up annual plans for the national economy, and in 1927–29 undertook to draw up the first 5-year plan, which was to have run from 1 Oct. 1928 to 30 Sept. 1933. It was considered completed in Dec. 1932, when 93·7% of the planned industrial output for the 5 years had been carried out. Stress was laid on the development of the heavy industries, particularly in the outlying areas rich in natural resources and inhabited by the national minorities.

The second 5-year plan ran from 1933 to 1937. It aimed at strengthening the defensive capacity of the Soviet Union, and more stress was laid than in the first 5-year plan on increasing the output and improving the quality of consumer goods. About one-half of the total investments in new heavy industrial constructions was allocated to the eastern areas. By the end of 1937 the plan for large-scale industry was overfulfilled by 4%, but the target for the light industries and consumer goods was not reached.

The third 5-year plan, 1938–42, envisaged an average annual increase in output of 13·5%, but that of the means of production was to be 15·2% and the means of consumption 11%; stress was to be laid on war industry. During the first 3½ years, industrial output was increasing annually by an average of 13%. In the Urals, the Volga area, Siberia and Central Asia industrial output increased during 1938–40 by about 50%. One of the richest grain-growing areas of the Soviet Union was created in the eastern part of the country. Capital construction amounted in value to a total of 130,000m. roubles; more than one-third fell to the eastern areas. The plan was interrupted in June 1941, when Hitler attacked the USSR. The whole of the national economy was switched to help the war effort, and whole industries were shifted from the western areas to the east.

For details of the fourth 5-year plan, 1946–50, see THE STATESMAN'S YEAR-BOOK, 1952, pp. 1424 f. The 1950 target of the gross output of industry was exceeded by 2%.

On 10 Oct. 1952 the 19th Congress of the Communist Party issued directives for the fifth 5-year plan, 1951–55; for details see THE STATESMAN'S YEAR-BOOK, 1953, pp. 1435–36. During Sept. and Oct. 1953 the Government issued a number of decrees to stimulate the development of agriculture, the output of consumer goods and the expansion of the home trade. For details of these decrees, see THE STATESMAN'S YEAR-BOOK, 1955, pp. 1448–50.

The directive for the sixth 5-year plan, 1956–60, was adopted by the 20th Congress of the Communist Party on 25 Feb. 1956; for details see THE STATESMAN'S YEAR-BOOK, 1958, p. 1472.

In May 1955 Gosplan was reorganized to consist of 2 state commissions for long-term planning (Gosplan) and for current planning (Goseconomcommissya); at the same time a committee was set up to improve the application to industry of advance science and technology (Gostekhnika).

Between 1954 and 1956 considerable changes were made in planning methods. In March 1954 collective farms were given greater authority over planning their own output, only the quantities required by the State in fixed deliveries being determined beforehand, and voluntary sales by contract. In 1955 they were authorized to make changes in their statutes, which had followed a fixed model since 1935. In 1955–57 over 15,000 industrial establishments in various basic industries, previously controlled by the Union Government, and later a number of entire light industries were turned over to the Constituent (Union) Republics. By 1962 they controlled from 95 to 100% of all industrial output.

In 1957 a comprehensive plan for decentralization of management of industry was initiated. Industrial establishments responsible for about 71% of all Soviet industrial output were turned over to Economic Councils set up in 104 (in 1963: 47) economic administrative areas. These in 1962 controlled 73% of all industrial production. The Ministeries previously responsible for the industries concerned were either abolished or transformed into purely planning and supervisory bodies. The State Committee for current planning was abolished, and Gosplan was given wider powers.

In consequence of this change a 7-year plan for 1959–65 was adopted by the 21st Congress of the Communist Party in Feb. 1959. Industrial output was to increase by 80%; it was in fact, in 1965, 84% above that of 1959. Capital investments would roughly equal the total for 1917–58: special attention was to be given to mechanization of agriculture and arduous industrial labour, automation and new technological processes, and housing. Diesel or electric traction of railway freight was to rise to 85%. Real incomes were to rise 40%, the 7-hour day (6 hours for miners) became general in 1960 and the 40-hour week in 1961, and introduction of the 35-hour week (30 hours for miners) began in 1964.

In Oct. 1965 the regional and Republic Economic Councils were abolished and also 28 Ministries for various branches of industry (17 Union-Republican, *i.e.*, corresponding to similar Ministries in the Union Republics, and 11 all-Union).

A 20-year plan was adopted by the 22nd Congress of the Communist Party on 31 Oct. 1961. Compared with 1960, by 1980 the output is to be increased as follows: Electric power, ninefold; steel, fourfold; oil, fivefold; coal, double; machinery, tenfold; fertilizers, ninefold; cement, fivefold; textiles, treble; leather footwear, double; grain, double; milk, treble; meat, fourfold. Two new iron and steel centres are to be developed in Kazakhstan and in Kursk region. A single deepwater system is to link the main inland waterways in the European USSR. Some rivers in northern Asia are to be diverted south for irrigation purposes. A 6-hour day for a 6-day week or 35 hours for a 5-day week were to be achieved by 1970. Housing, water, gas, heating, public urban transport and school meals were to be free by 1980. These and cognate measures are to provide 'the material and technical basis of communism'.

The 23rd Congress of the Communist Party in April 1966 adopted 'directives' for a 5-year plan for 1966–70. Under these, power output is to reach 830,000–850,000m. kwh., oil 345–355m. tons, coal 665–675m. tons, steel 124–129m. tons, mineral fertilizers 62–65m. tons, machine-tools 220,000–230,000, cars 700,00–800,000, tractors 600,000–625,000, paper 5–5·3m. tons, cement 100–105m. tons, fabrics 9·5–9·8m. sq metres, leather footwear 610–630m. pairs, meat 5·9–6·2m. tons, butter 1·2m. tons, sugar 9·8–10m. tons. The average annual output of grain was to increase 30 % over 1964–65. 7,000 km of new railway line, 63,000 km of new motor roads and 35–40 new airports are to be built; marine tonnage was to be increased by 50%.

On 14 Feb. 1971, outlines of a 9th Five-Year Plan (1971–75) were published. They provided for an increase in electric power output to at least 1,000,000m. kwh., oil to 480–500m. tons; gas, 300,000m. cu. metres; steel, 142–150m. tons; coal, 685–695m. tons; mineral fertilisers, 90m. tons; tractors, 575,000; passenger cars, over 1m., and lorries, 750,000. A new feature is that, while output of these and other means of production is to increase by 41–45%, output of consumption goods is to grow by 44–48%. Grain output is to rise to an average over the 5 years of at least 195m. tons; raw cotton, 7–7·2m. tons; meat, 14·3m. tons; milk, 92·3m. tons. Average wages are to increase by 20–22%, incomes of collective farmers 30–35%, and the average of real incomes by about 30%. 3,000–3,750 miles of new railway tracks are to be built and 3,750–4,400 miles electrified, with 17,000 miles of new oil pipelines, and 40% more cargo carried by sea. 565–575m. sq. metres of new housing (about 16m. flats and homes) are to be built.

By mid-1970, 42,000 industrial plants had been transferred to the new system of decentralized cost-accounting: they produced 92 % of total output of Soviet industry and 93 % of its total profit.

The National Economy of the USSR in 1968. (Statistical annual in Russian.) Moscow, 1969
23rd Congress of the CPSU. Moscow, 1966 (in English)
Bernard, P. J., *Planning in the Soviet Union.* Oxford, 1966
Bor, M., *Aims and Methods of Soviet Planning.* London, 1967
Dobb, M., *Soviet Economic Development since 1917.* London, 1966

Council for Mutual Economic Aid

(SEV: Soviet Ekonomicheskoy Vzaimopomoshchi), known in the West as COMECON, was founded in Moscow on 25 Jan. 1949, 'to strengthen the economic collaboration of the socialist countries and to co-ordinate their economic development on the basis of equal rights of all member states by organizing the exchange of economic and technical experience and rendering mutual aid'. Founding members were Albania, Bulgaria, Czechoslovakia, Hungary, Poland, Rumania and USSR. The German Democratic Republic was admitted in 1950, Mongolia in 1962; Albania left COMECON in Oct. 1961. Yugoslavia, Cuba, North Korea and North Vietnam are represented by observers.

The Council is the supreme body; its recommendations must be unanimous and can be put into effect only by inter-governmental agreements. The Executive Committee, set up in June 1962, is composed of permanent delegates from each member country; its functions are the co-ordination of national economic development plans, investments and policy on trade with, and payments to, capitalist countries and supervision of collaboration on scientific and technical research. The Executive Committee has a Planning Bureau (set up in 1962) and Standing Committees (first created in 1956, numbering 17 in 1962). A joint Bank for Economic Co-operation was established on 1 Jan. 1964 with a capital of 300m. convertible roubles. An International Investment Bank began operations in Moscow on 1 Jan. 1971. Since 1945, 1,590 industrial enterprises have been erected by the USSR in the Socialist countries.

The Secretariat is in Moscow; *Secretary-General:* N. V. Fadeyev (USSR).

AGRICULTURE. The Soviet Union, up to about 1928 predominantly agricultural in character, has become an industrial–agricultural country. Of the gross social product, industry and transport accounted for 42·1% in 1913 and 79% in 1968; agriculture for 57·9% in 1913 and 15·3% in 1968. Of the total state land fund of 2,227·5m. hectares, agricultural land in use in 1969 amounted to 546m., state forests and state reserves to 1,122m. hectares.

The total area under cultivation (including single-owner peasant farms, state farms and collective farms) was (in the same territory) 118·2m. hectares in 1913, 129·7m. in 1933, 223·5m. in 1962, 222·9m. in 1966, 223·3m. in 1969.

Collective farms on 1 Nov. 1969 possessed 360·1m. hectares, of which 110·8m. were under crops of various kinds; state farms and other state agricultural undertakings possessed 684·3m. hectares, of which 110·1m. were under crops; manual and clerical workers held 3·2m. hectares as allotments.

In Nov. 1969 the Third Congress of collective farmers adopted a new model resolution, considerably enlarged the planning powers of collective farms and made payments to their members a priority.

Since 1969 conferences of collective farms have elected 2,346 district collective farm councils with 75,000 members, to study and co-ordinate local experience in methods and finance.

Produce marketed (after consumption by collective farmers) was, in 1m. metric tons, for the present area of the USSR:

	1966	1967	1968	1969		1966	1967	1968	1969
Grain	82·0	63·2	75·2	62·9	Meat[2] and fats	7·8	8·4	8·7	8·8
Raw cotton[1]	6·0	6·0	6·0	5·7	Milk and milk				
Sugar-beet	69·7	81·6	84·2	65·3	products	42·1	44·7	46·4	46·0
Potatoes	15·6	18·0	18·3	17·3	Eggs (1,000m.)	15·2	16·9	18·1	19·5
Vegetables	10·2	12·0	11·4	11·6					

| [1] Seed-cotton unginned. | [2] Slaughter weight. |

Since 1954 grain crops have been measured in 'barn crop' (*i.e.*, net quantities delivered to barns) and not in 'gross harvest' or 'biological yield' (*i.e.*, calculated as growing crops) as previously. Average annual crops (in 1m. tons): 1909–13, 72·5; 1946–50, 64·8; 1951–55, 88·5; 1956–60, 121·5; 1961–65, 130·3; 1966–69, 162·8. Other produce (in 1m. tons) in 1969: Raw cotton, 5·7; sunflower, 6·4; meat (slaughter weight), 11·8; milk, 81·5; sugar-beet, 71·2; 37,000m. eggs.

In Dec. 1963 collective farms comprised 99·7% of all peasant holdings. In 1969 they produced 53% of all marketed grain, cotton 78%, sugar-beet 91%, potatoes 29%, vegetables 37%, meat 44%, milk 54%, eggs 24%.

Between 1953 and 1 Jan. 1970 the number of collective farms was reduced, mainly by amalgamation and partly by transformation into state farms, from 93,300 to 34,700, their cultivated area falling from 132m. hectares to 100·3m. The number of state farms rose in the same period from 4,857 to 14,310, their cultivated area from 15·2m. hectares to 92·5m. Over 5,300 state farms had been transferred to a decentralized cost-accounting basis by the end of 1970.

State purchases in 1968 (in 1m. tons; 1969 figures in brackets): Grain, 69 (55·5); sugar-beet, 84·2 (65·3); cotton, 6 (5·7); milk, 44 (43·4).

By 1961, in the collective farms 99% of the ploughing of the areas under grain, cotton and sugar-beet and 97–98% of the sowing under these crops (57% under potatoes) were mechanized; 95% of their areas under grain and 56% under sugar-beet were harvested by combines.

Rural electrical stations in 1940 had a capacity of 265,000 kw.; in 1968, 4·9m. kw. 99·7% of collective farms and 99% of state farms were using electric power in 1969. In 1969 agriculture consumed 33,260m. kwh. of electric power.

Investments in agriculture in 1969 were 8,500m. roubles by the State and 5,900m. by collective farms.

In 1913 the total of irrigated land was 4m. hectares; in 1953, 11m.; in 1969, 10·5m. The total of land drained was 8·4m. hectares in 1956 and 9·5m. in 1969.

In 1913, 188,000 tons of mineral fertilizers were used; in 1950, 5·3m. tons, and in 1969, 38·9m. On 1 Jan. 1970 there were 4·1m. tractors (calculated on 15 h.p. basis), 605,000 grain combine harvesters and 1,153,000 lorries in the countryside; under the 5-year plan (1966–70) agriculture is to receive 1·7m. tractors and 550,000 grain combines.

Livestock. Livestock (1 Jan. 1970), in 1m. heads: Cattle, 95·2 (including 40·5 milch cows); pigs, 56; sheep and goats, 135·8. Since 1957 the enumeration of livestock is being made on 1 Jan. instead of 1 Oct., *i.e.*, after the winter sales and slaughtering for the market.

Percentage of farm production in 1969:

	All grain	Cotton	Sugar-beet	Pota-toes	Vege-tables	Meat	Milk	Eggs	Wool
State	43	22	9	13	35	31	27	31	40
Collective	55	78	91	20	26	34	36	13	39
Private[1]	2	0	0	67	39	35	37	56	21

[1] *I.e.*, household plots of collective farmers.

FORESTRY. On the 747m. hectares of forest land of the USSR, a large portion is administered and worked by the State, and the other, about 39m. hectares in extent, is granted for use to the peasantry free of charge.

The largest forest areas are 515m. hectares in the Asiatic part of the USSR, 51·4m. along the northern seaboard, 25·4m. in the Urals and 17·95m. in the north-west.

On 24 Oct. 1948 a plan was published for planting crop-protecting forest belts, introducing crop rotation with grasses and building of ponds and water reservoirs in the steppe and forest-steppe areas of the European part of the USSR. By the middle of 1952 some 2·6m. hectares had been planted with shelter-belt trees and 13,500 ponds and reservoirs had been built. The planting of the shelter belts in the Kamyshin–Volgograd and Byelgorod–Don areas has in the main been completed. A Volga forest belt has been planted along 1,200 km of railway.

Belov, F., *The History of a Soviet Collective Farm*. New York, 1956
Jasny, N., *The Socialized Agriculture of the USSR: Plans and Performance*. Stanford Univ. Press, 1949
Vasiliev, P., and Kozlovsky, V., *Forest Wealth of the USSR* (in Russian). Moscow, 1959

PRODUCTION. The organization of industry in the USSR is based on state ownership and control, administered by a separate Ministry for each large industry.

Under the successive 5-year plans, large-scale modern industrial works have been constructed, namely: 1st, over 1,500; 2nd, 4,500; 3rd (up to June 1941), 3,000; war-time, 3,500 (apart from reconstruction of destroyed plants); 4th, 6,200; 5th, 3,200; 6th (1956–58), 2,700; 7-year plan (1959–65), 5,470; 8th (1966–70) nearly 1900.

MINING. Miners are trained in 6 mining, 3 oil and 1 peat institutes, the mining faculties of 17 higher educational establishments, oil faculties of 2 industrial institutes and a peat faculty at the Belorussian Polytechnical Institute.

The Soviet Union is rich in minerals. Soviet scientists claim that it contains 58% of the world's coal deposits, 58·7% of its oil, 41% of its iron ore, 76·7% of its apatite, 25% of all timber land, 88% of its manganese, 54% of its potassium salts and nearly one-third of its phosphates.

Estimated output (in metric tons) in 1962: Copper, 634,900; zinc, 399,000; lead, 363,000; tungsten, 10,500; antimony, 5,980; silver, 27m. fine oz. Output in 1963: Baryte, 199,500; magnesium, 31,745; aluminium, 961,400; manganese ore (1964), 7·1m.; graphite, 54,000; bauxite, 4·3m.; asbestos, 1·3m.; phosphate rock, 3·7m. (plus 7·4m. apatite); chromite, 1·23m.; gold, 12·5m. fine oz.; molybdenum, 12·5m. lb.; cadmium (1956), 160.

Output of iron and steel in the USSR (in 1m. tons):

	Pig-iron	Ingot steel	Rolled steel		Pig-iron	Ingot steel	Rolled steel
1913	4·2	4·2	3·5	1955	33·3	45·3	35·3
1928–29	4·0	4·8	3·9	1960	46·8	65·3	50·9
1932	6·2	5·9	4·4	1965	66·2	91·0	61·7
1940	14·9	18·3	13·1	1967	74·8	102·0	70 6
1946	10·0	13·4	9·6	1968	78·8	106·5	74 1
1950	19·2	27·3	20·9	1969	81·6	110·0	76 3

Coal production (in 1m. metric tons) was 29·1 in 1913, 64·4 in 1932, 165·9 in 1940, 261·1 in 1950, 513 in 1960, 595 in 1967, 594 in 1968, 608 in 1969.

The main centre of the atomic industry is at Ust-Kamenogorsk in the Altai mountains. Uranium deposits are being worked near Taboshar (south-east of Tashkent), Adizhan (in the Tynya-Muyan Mountains), Slyudianka (near Lake Baikal), on the Kolyma River and in Southern Armenia.

Output of natural gas reached 181,000m. cu. metres in 1969; oil, 328m. tons.

OIL. In the 1930s practically all Soviet oil came from the Caucasian fields, of which the Baku fields yielded 75–80% and the Grozny and Maikop fields between them 15%. Since then, the distribution has considerably changed. The Ural–Volga area, the 'Second Baku', has 4 large centres in operation, at Samarska Luka (Kuibyshev), Tuimazy (Bashkiria), Ishimbaev (Bashkiria) and Perm. A large new oilfield has been developed in the Trans-Volga area of the Saratov region. The USSR is now the second-largest oil-producer in the world after the USA (see pp. xxiii f.).

The total length of pipeline on 1 Jan. 1939 was 4,212 km, divided as follows: Baku–Batumi, 1,717 km; Grozny–Mahach-Kala, 150 km; Grozny–Armavir–Tuapse, 618 km; Armavir–Trudovaya, 488 km; Guriev–Orsk, 845 km, and other, 394 km. One pipeline (1,700 km) was completed in 1955, connecting Tuimazy in Bashkiria with the refineries of Omsk. In 1957 the Almetyevsk–Gorky pipeline (580 km) and 479 km of the Stavropol–Moscow pipeline were completed. At the end of 1969 there were 36,900 km of pipeline, through which (in 1969) were conveyed 324m. tons of oil.

The construction of the 'Druzhba' pipeline of about 4,600 km from the oilfields near Kuibyshev to Poland and the German Democratic Republic (northern branch) and to Czechoslovakia and Hungary (southern branch)—separating in Belorussia—begun in 1960, was completed in 1965.

In 1969 the USSR exported 90·8m. metric tons of crude oil and oil products.

INDUSTRY. Output of some heavy industries was as follows:

Industry	1913	1940	1950	1960	1968	1969
Iron ore (1m. tons)	9·2	29·9	39·7	106·2	176·6	186·1
Oil (1m. tons)	9·2	31·1	37·9	148·0	309·2	328·3
Electric power (1,000m. kwh.)	1·9	48·3	91·2	292·0	638·7	689·1
Mineral fertilizers (1m. tons)	0·07	3·0	5·5	13·8	43·5	45·9
Machine tools (1,000)	1·5	58·4	70·6	154·0	200·8	205·3
Steam and gas turbines (1,000 kw.)	5·9	972·0	2,381·0	9,200·0	15,752·0	15,004·0
Oil industry equipment (1,000 tons)	—	15·5	47·9	92·8	125·1	123·0
Oil locomotives (1,000)	—	5·0	125·0	1,303·0	1,500·0	1,464·0
Electric locomotives (1,000)	—	9·0	102·0	396·0	305·0	296·0
Lorries and buses (1,000)	—	136·0	294·4	385·0	520·5	550·1
Tractors (1,000)	—	31·6	108·8	238·5	423·4	441·7
Looms (1,000)	4·6	1·8	8·7	16·4	17·6	17·3
Excavators (no.)	—	274·0	3,540·0	12,290·0	26,953·0	29,338·0
Timber (hauled, 1m. cu. metres)[1]	27·2	117·9	161·0	261·5	289·9	286·3
Cement (1m. tons)	1·8	5·7	10·2	45·5	87·5	89·7

[1] Excluding collective farm production.

The process of industrial mechanization and the installation of automatic remote control is being pushed ahead. About 90% of Soviet pig-iron and 87% of the steel is produced in fully automatic furnaces. All hydro-electric plants (in terms of capacity) are fully automatic. Coal production in open-cast mines has been completely mechanized; hydraulic mining is coming into general use. Coal-cutting and underground haulage had been over 99% mechanized by the end of 1962 (loading on inclined seams 56%); peat-cutting, 100%, and loading, nearly 80%; timber-cutting, 98%; haulage to loading centres, 93%, and despatch, 97%.

Output in some consumer industries was as follows:

Industry	1913	1940	1950	1960	1968	1969
Cotton fabrics (1m. metres)	2,672·0	3,954·0	3,899·0	4,800[1]	6,116[1]	6,208[1]
Woollen fabrics (1m. metres)	103·0	119·7	155·5	439[1]	585[1]	618[1]
Silk fabrics (1m. metres)	42·6	77·3	129·7	675[1]	950[1]	1,026[1]
Leather footwear (1m. pairs)	60·0	211·0	203·4	419	598	636
Clocks and watches (1m.)	0·7	2·8	7·6	26	36	38
Radio and television sets (1,000)	—	161·0	1,083·0	5,900	12,700	13,861
Bicycles and mopeds (1,000)	4·9	255·0	649·3	2,800	4,303	4,372
Paper (1,000 tons)	269·0	812·0	1,193·0	2,334	3,955	4,046
Meat (abattoirs) (1,000 tons)[2]	1,042·0	1,501·0	1,556·0	4,400	6,601	6,483
Dairy butter (1,000 tons)[2]	104·0	226·0	336·0	737	1,044	954
Granulated sugar (1,000 tons)	1,363·0	2,165·0	2,523·0	6,360	10,767	10.347
Soap, 40% fat-content (1,000 tons)	168·0	700·0	816·0	1,474	1,674	1,608
Canned foods (1,000m. tins)	116·0	1,113·0	1,113·0	4,864	9,548	9,660

[1] Recorded in sq. metres.
[2] Excluding collective farm and other home production, home-killed meat, etc.

Since 1945 the cotton industry has expanded, especially in the Urals, Central Asia and Siberia. Large mills have been built at Kamyshin, Kherson, Barnaul, Engels, Alma-Ata, Chernigov and Frunze.

In 1969 the eastern regions (Urals, Siberia, Far East and Central Asian Republics) accounted for 51% of the coal output, 34% of the oil, 37% of the pig-iron, 40% of the steel and 40% of electric power.

New industrial enterprises that went into production in 1970 included power station at Vladivostok, Grodno, in Estonia, Morman region, Stavropol territory and elsewhere; coalmines at Sahalin and in Lvov, Voroshilovgrad, Dnepropetrovsk and other regions; steel plants at Novo-Lipetsk, Chelyabinsk, Karaganda; chemical works at Mogilev, Novogorod, Rustavi, Djambul; textile factories at Chernovtsy, Orenburg, Dubossary; mechanized dairies at Omsk and Zheleznovodsk. In 1969 the total length of long-distance gas pipelines reached 63,200 km. Construction of a 530-km natural gas pipeline from Doliny (Ukraine) to Bratislava (Czechoslovakia) and reconstruction of a line to Poland began in 1965.

A natural-gas pipeline from Gazli, near Khiva, to Voskresensk, near Moscow (2,750 km), with a capacity of 10,500m. cu. metres per annum, began operating in Oct. 1967.

ELECTRICITY. Many hydro-electrical power stations are being constructed. The Irkutsk station (4,500m. kwh. output per annum) is in operation; Bratsk (4·5m. kw. capacity) was completed in 1967. Krasnoyarsk (6m. kw. capacity) and Sayano-Shushenskaya (in eastern Siberia) are under construction; the 10th turbine at Krasnoyarsk raised its capacity to 5m. kw. in 1970.

The Kremenchug power station (625,000 kw. capacity) was completed in Nov. 1960, rendering the Dnieper navigable for large vessels from Kanev to the Black Sea (over 800 km). Two power-stations in Central Asia are under construction: at Nurek on the Amu-Darya (2·7m. kw.) and at Toktogul in the Syr-Darya basin (1·2m. kw.).

Total installed capacity of electrical plants in 1938 was 8·7m. kw. and 153·8m. kw. in 1969. Industry consumes about 70% of the total electricity. Over 35,000 small rural power stations have been closed in recent years owing to supply from State stations becoming available, but there are still 65,000 operating in the countryside.

An atom-driven power station, with a capacity of 5,000 kw., was put into operation at Obninsk (Kaluga region) on 27 June 1954; the Novo-Voronezh station (210,000 kw.) began operating in Dec. 1964, and at Beloyarsk (1m. kw.) in 1965. Total capacity of atom-driven power stations was over 900,000 kw. in Jan. 1965. Other such stations are being built at Kirovsk in the north; Novy Uzen, on the Caspian; Bilibino, Shevchenkovo and elsewhere.

The 5-year plan (1966–70) envisaged the construction of several dozen thermal stations (mostly 300,000 kw. units) and the completion of hydro-electric stations with a total capacity of about 64–66m. kw.

The integrated power grid of European USSR had a capacity of 80m. kw. in 1968. A Central Siberian grid (20m. kw.) is being set up.

A unified power grid ('Mir') with all the Socialist countries of eastern Europe was built up between 1962 and 1967. The USSR exported 1,800m. kwh. of electric power over this grid in 1967.

Granick, D., *Management of the Industrial Firm in the USSR.* Columbia Univ. Press, 1954
Hassmann, H., *Oil in the Soviet Union.* Princeton Univ. Press, 1953
Schwartz, H., *Russia's Postwar Economy.* 2nd ed. New York, 1954
Shimkin, D. B., *Minerals, a Key to Soviet Power.* Harvard Univ. Press, 1953

TRADE UNIONS AND LABOUR. Trade unions are organized on an industrial basis, all workers, whether manual or brain, in every branch of a given industry being eligible for membership of the same union.

Since 1933 the trade unions have carried out the functions of the former Labour Commissariat; they control and supervise the application of labour laws, introduce new labour laws for approval by the Government and administer social insurance and factory inspection. Social insurance is non-contributory. The All-Union Congress has met at irregular intervals; the 14th Congress met in 1968.

In 1944 there were 176 unions. This number was reduced by amalgamation of unions to 22 in 1958, but increased to 25 in 1968; membership in 1970, 93m. (including wage-earners in collective farms). Contributions range from 0·5 to 1% of wages.

Chairman, Central Council of Trade Unions: A. N. Shelepin.

The number of industrial and clerical workers engaged in the whole national economy of the Soviet Union was 87·9m. in 1969. The 7-hour day (6 hours for miners underground and other heavy trades) was generally in operation by the end of 1960. The average working week in 1969 was 39·4 hours and the working day in industry 6·93 hours. The 5-day week (without reduction of total working hours) was introduced in 1967.

New 'Fundamentals of Labour Legislation', intended to codify and extend labour laws adopted in the last 40 years, were adopted by the Supreme Soviet in July 1970. They lay down, *inter alia*, the right to receive wages irrespective of the income of the enterprise concerned, the right to free vocational and advanced technical training; the right to form trade unions without state registration; the right of trade unions to participate in and supervise management and planning, labour legislation, safety regulation and housing, fixing of working conditions and wages, etc.

The Trade Union Situation in the USSR. International Labour Office, 1960
Chapman, J. G., *Real Wages in Soviet Russia since 1928.* Harvard Univ. Press, 1963
Pacherstnik, A., *La Législation du travail en URSS.* Paris, 1947
Swianiewicz, S., *Forced Labour and Economic Development.* OUP, 1965

COMMERCE. Retail home trade takes three forms—state, co-operative and the free market, *i.e.*, sales by individual collective-farm members and by the collective farms of their surplus products, after having fulfilled their statutory deliveries and made their regular allocations to their members.

In 1970 the consumer co-operative societies had a membership of 59m. and did over 29% of the retail trade of the USSR. They were organized in 16,500 societies, employing 2·7m. workers, with 299,000 rural shops, 70,900 catering establishments, 15,000 bakeries and 460 canneries. Their central union is affiliated to the International Co-operative Alliance. Retail trade by the State and co-operatives totalled 144·4m. roubles in 1969; by collective farm markets (agricultural produce), 4·1m. roubles.

Foreign trade is organized as a state monopoly. Importation and exportation of goods are effected under licences issued by the Ministry for Foreign Trade and its respective departments in pursuance of a plan annually sanctioned by the Government. The right of purchasing goods for importation, and that of selling Soviet exports abroad, is vested in Trade Delegations and representatives of the appropriate state corporations in foreign countries.

There are 29 state import and export organizations, including chartering and tourist corporations (one, Vostokintorg, dealing with Mongolia, Sinkiang and Afghánistán). The Central Union of Consumers' Societies (Centrosoyuz) is also authorized to conduct foreign trade operations.

For foreign trade up to 1938 see THE STATESMAN'S YEAR-BOOK, 1951, p. 1465. The Central Statistical Department of the USSR estimates that, in comparable prices, the volume of foreign trade in 1938 was less than one-third that of 1913, but was in 1969, 5·3 times as large as in 1913. Exports in 1969 were valued at 10,490m. roubles (6,914m. to the Socialist countries), and imports at 9,294m. roubles (6,026m. from the Socialist countries).

Russia's imports of fuel and raw materials, between 1913 and 1969, declined from 50·8 to 24·6%, of machinery and equipment increased from 16·6 to 37·5%; imports of manufactured consumer goods increased from 10·3 to 19%.

Main items of exports in 1969:

Oil (1 m. tons)	63·9	Vegetable oil (1,000 tons)	696·0
Coal (1m. tons)	23·3	Tractors (1,000)	30·7
Iron ore (1m. tons)	33·1	Lorries (1,000)	31·5
Iron and rolled metal (1m. tons)	11·2	Motor cars (1,000)	73·8
Paper (1,000 tons)	429·3	Clocks and watches (1,000)	9,400·0
Cotton (1,000 tons)	455·0		

Total trade between the USSR and UK in £1,000 sterling for calendar years (British Board of Trade returns):

	1966	1967	1968	1969	1970
Imports to UK	125,471	123,459	158,085	197,155	
Exports from UK	49,708	63,250	102,878	96,401	
Re-exports from UK	656	956	1,853	757	

Kawan, L., *Nouvelle orientation du commerce extérieur soviétique*. Brussels, 1958

RAILWAYS. The length of railways in Jan. 1970 was 134,600 km (1913: 58,500). By the end of 1969, 105,800 km of main-line railways had changed to electric and diesel traction, and 96% of railway freights went by these means. In 1969, 66% of all goods traffic and 50% of passenger transport went by rail (in 1913, 57% and 91% respectively). The Moscow–Donetz, Leningrad–Leninakan and Moscow–Baikal lines have been electrified.

There are 43 main railway systems which may be grouped as follows:

In the west: Estonian (1,388 km), Latvian (3,100 km) and Lithuanian (2,100 km), Kalinin (2,064 km, Moscow–Orsha and Moscow–Zilupe, centre at Smolensk), Belorussian (5,800 km), October (Moscow–Leningrad, centre Leningrad, 3,857 km), Lvov (south-western Ukraine, 4,257 km), South-western (centre Kiev–western Ukraine and southern Belorussia, 3,888 km), Moscow–Kiev (centre Kaluga–western Russia, eastern Belorussia, north-Ukraine, western 3,821 km).

In the north: Northern (Moscow and north European Russia, centre Yaroslavl, 3,750 km), Pechora (centre Kotlas: north-eastern European Russia, 1,953 km), Kirov (Murmansk–Petrozavodsk–Volhovstroi, centre Petrozavodsk, 3,587 km).

H H

In the European south: Moscow–Kursk–Donbass (centre Moscow, 3027 km), Southern (centre Kharkov: eastern Ukraine, south-eastern Russia, 3,304 km), South-Eastern (centre Voronezh: Ukraine–Urals, Rostov–Penza regions, 2,579 km), Odessa (south-eastern Ukraine–south-western Moldavia, centre Odessa, 3,839 km), Moldavian (Kishinev, 1,200 km), Stalin (centre Dnepropetrovsk, links this heavy-industry area with the Black Sea coast, 3,298 km), North Caucasus (centre Rostov-on-Don, 3,391 km), Ordzhonikidze (links northern Caucasus Autonomous Republics with Caspian coast, centre Ordzhonikidze, 1,708 km). Donetz (centre Donetsk, served the Donetz coalfield, 2,862 km). The entire route from Leningrad to Simferopol (Crimea) was electrified during 1970.

In eastern European Russia: Moscow–Ryazan (centre Moscow, 2,089 km), Kazan (centre Kazan, links Volga with Urals, 2,783 km), Gorky (Moscow–Ryazan–north-eastern Russia, centre Gorky, 1,543 km), Ufa (links Bashkir and Tartar Republics and northern Volga regions, centre Ufa, 1,866 km), Kuibyshev (centre Kuibyshev, links Volga regions with Urals, 2,012 km), Volga (centre Saratov, links it with Volgograd and Astrakhan, 3,149 km).

In the Urals and western Asia: Sverdlovsk (centre Sverdlovsk, links northern Urals with western Siberia, 4,000 km), South Urals (centre Chelyabinsk, links eastern regions of Russia in Europe with northern Kazakhstan, 2,875 km), Orenburg (centre Orenburg, links southern Urals with Siberia, 3,150 km), Omsk (centre Omsk, links western Siberia with northern Kazakhstan and Altai, 2,050 km), Tomsk (centre Novosibirsk, links western Siberia, Kemerovo coalfield and Altai, 3,039 km).

In south-western Asia: Transcaucasian (centre Tbilisi, links Black Sea coast with Yerevan, 1,887 km), Azerbaidjan (centre Baku, 1,650 km).

In Central Asia: Tashkent (centre Tashkent, links Tadjik, Uzbek, Kirgiz and Kazakh republics with Orenburg, 2,420 km), Ashkhabad (centre Ashkhabad, links Caspian coast and Turkmen Republic with Uzbekistan, 2,647 km), Kazakh (centre Alma-Ata, 9,000 km). The 334-km Guriev–Astrakhan railway, across the Caspian desert, began operating on 1 Jan. 1971, shortening the route from Central Asia to the Caucasus by nearly 700 km.

In central and eastern Siberia: Krasnoyarsk (centre Krasnoyarsk, a part of Trans-Siberian line but with new branches serving the Khakass and Tuva republics, 1,279 km), East Siberia (centre Irkutsk, serves Irkutsk region and Buryat Republic with link to Mongolian People's Republic, 1,696 km), Transbaikal (centre Chita, part of Trans-Siberian line but serving Buryatia and linked with China and Mongolia, 3,320 km). The Abakan–Taishet line, connecting the South-Siberian and main Trans-Siberian lines and linking the Bratsk and Kuznetzk industrial areas (640 km), began operating in 1964 with electric traction.

A line from Khrebtovaya, on the Taishet–Zena railway in East Siberia, to Ust-Ilimskaya on the Angara (215 km) has been opened, as the first section of a new North Siberian main line.

In the Far East: Far Eastern (centre Habarovsk, serves Maritime regions, 1,712 km), Amur (centre Blagoveshchensk, part of Trans-Siberian line, serves the Amur valley, 2,468 km), South Sahalin (centre Yuzhno-Sahalinsk, 752 km).

SHIPPING. In 1967 the Soviet mercantile marine comprised 1,350 vessels of 11m. tons deadweight, of which 80% were built between 1957 and 1966. By the end of 1970 the tonnage was 12m. tons.

Freights carried were: In 1913 (present frontiers), 15·1m. tons; in 1940, 31·2m. tons; in 1950, 33·7m. tons, and in 1969, 148·7m. tons; 34·6m. passengers were carried. The Soviet share in world marine tonnage was 2% in 1960 and 6·5% in 1967.

The North Sea route affords convenient communication between the European USSR and the Far East along the Soviet coast, for the produce of the basins of the Obi, Yenissei, Lena and Kolyma rivers.

The length of navigable rivers and canals in exploitation was (1969) 144,800 km, of which the length of floatable rivers is 81,800 km. There are several thousand miles of canals and other artificial waterways; among them the Baltic and

White Sea Canal (235 km), the Moscow–Volga Canal (130 km). Goods turnover on inland waterways was 28,900m. ton-km in 1913, 35,900m. in 1940, 45,900m. in 1950 and 160,000m. in 1969; freight carried rose from 35·1m. tons in 1913 to 332·7m. tons in 1969.

The Volga–Don Shipping Canal was opened for traffic in 1952. The Volga–Don waterway from Volgograd to Rostov is 540 km long, of which the Volga–Don canal comprises 101 km. The canal has transformed the section of the river from Kalach, where the Don is joined by the Volga–Don canal, to Rostov into a deep-water highway suitable for big Volga shipping. The canal links the White, Baltic, Caspian, Azov and Black Seas into a single water transport system. In Oct. 1964 the 2,430-km Baltic–Volga waterway, linking Klaipeda on the Baltic to Kahovka at the mouth of the Dnieper and suitable for 5,000-ton vessels, was begun. Reconstruction of the 18th-century Mariinsky canal system in north-west Russia was completed, providing a through waterway from Leningrad to Rybinsk (on the Upper Volga) and cutting the passage of freight from 18 to 2½ days.

In 1962 a canal was completed across the Kara-Kum desert in southern Turkmenistan (replacing an earlier project for a more costly scheme across the north of the republic). The canal, from Bussag on the river Amu-Darya to Archnan, north-west of Ashkhabad, through the Murgab oasis, 820 km long, supplies water to an area exceeding 200,000 hectares, suitable for cotton, fruit, vineyards and livestock. An extension to the Caspian (500 km) is under construction.

An irrigation canal system (250 miles), bringing water from Kahovka on the Dnieper to North Crimea, is nearing completion. Work on diverting water from the Pechora and Vychegda rivers (flowing into the White Sea) south to the Volga is in progress. Work has begun on a 300-mile canal which will supply water from the Irtysh to Karaganda in Central Kazakhstan, irrigating over 150,000 acres; the first 37 miles were opened in 1965 and another 45 miles in Dec. 1967.

ROADS. By 1941 there were over 1·5m. km of constructed roads, of which 143,000 km were suitable for motor traffic. The total length of motor roads in 1969 was 483,200 km. Road freights by lorry amounted to 859m. tons in 1940 and 13,392m. tons in 1969. Passengers carried were 590m. in 1940 and 24,669m. in 1969. In 1969, 15,445 inter-urban bus routes had a total length of 1,910,700 km.

AVIATION. In 1970 total length of internal airlines in the USSR was approximately 691,000 km; 75m. passengers were carried. The Central Asian Airways in some instances provide the only means of communication across the desert and mountainous regions of the local republics. An 8,500-km air service was opened in Feb. 1941 between Moscow and Anadyr (Eastern Siberia), through Archangel, Igarka, Khatanga, Tiksi Bay and Cape Schmidt, i.e., along the entire course of the Northern Sea Route. There are also other Arctic airlines, e.g., Igarka–Gulf of Kozhevnikov; Igarka–Dickson Island; Yakutsk–Tiksi Bay; Yakutsk–Viluisk; Yakutsk–Verkhoiansk.

Direct air services are maintained throughout the year between Moscow and the capitals of all Soviet republics as well as London, New York, Montreal, Tokyo, Delhi, Rangoon, Belgrade, Peking, Pyongyang, Ulan Bator, Kabul, Tirana, Paris, Warsaw, Prague, Budapest, Bucharest, Sofia, Vienna, Berlin, Helsinki, Stockholm, Copenhagen, Djakarta and Dakar.

Soviet air services reach 57 countries, and 20 foreign lines have regular services to the USSR, including BEA, KLM, SAS, Air France, Sabena, Air India, PANAM.

Hunter, H., *Soviet transportation policy*. Harvard Univ. Press, 1957

POST. In 1969 the number of post, telegraph and telephone offices was 80,000 and of telephones 9·9m.

The international radio-telecommunications services are operated by the Ministry of Communications of the USSR. The Great Northern Telegraph Co., Ltd, of Denmark, operate cables connecting Denmark with Leningrad, whence connexion is made by means of a trans-Siberian landline with Vladivostok. From the latter place the Great Northern Telegraph Co. owns cables connecting with Japan, China and Hong Kong. Direct radio and telephone communication with India is provided for in an agreement concluded in 1955.

At the end of 1969 there were 1,089 television and rediffusion centres, and 30·8m. television sets.

BANKING. The State Bank began operations on 16 Nov. 1921. By an edict of 7 April 1959 a number of specialized banks for planned long-term investments, which had existed since 1932, were abolished. The State Bank, in addition to short-term credits, effects long-term investments in agriculture and in individual rural house-building. The Bank for Financing Capital Investments (*Stroibank*) covers industry, transport, urban housing schemes and public utilities and individual house-building in towns.

Deposits in 77,700 savings banks were over 38,000m. new roubles to the credit of 73m. depositors at 1 Jan. 1970.

WEIGHTS AND MEASURES. The metric system has been in use since 1 Jan. 1927. The Gregorian Calendar was adopted as from 14 Feb. 1918.

DIPLOMATIC REPRESENTATIVES

The USSR maintains embassies in:

Afghánistán	Finland	Norway
Albania	France	Pakistan
Argentina	Germany (East)	Poland
Australia	Germany (West)	Romania
Austria	Greece	Rwanda
Belgium	Hungary	Senegal
Bolivia	Iceland	Sudan
Bulgaria	India	Sweden
Burma	Indonesia	Switzerland
Cameroun	Iran	Tanzania
Canada	Israel	Thailand
Central African Republic	Italy	Tunisia
Chad	Korea (North)	Turkey
Chile	Lebanon	UAR
China	Libya	UK
Congo (Br.)	Luxembourg	USA
Cuba	Mexico	Uruguay
Cyprus	Mongolia	Vietnam (North)
Czechoslovakia	Morocco	Yemen
Dahomey	Nepál	Yugoslavia
Denmark	Netherlands	
Ethiopia	New Zealand	

The USSR also has diplomatic relations with, but no diplomatic representatives in:

Costa Rica	Guatemala	Saudi Arabia
Dominican Republic	Nicaragua	Somalia
Ecuador		

OF THE USSR IN GREAT BRITAIN (13 Kensington
Palace Gdns, W8)

Ambassador: Mikhail Nikolayevich Smirnovsky (accredited 10 Feb. 1966).
Trade Representative: Boris S. Gordeev. *Minister-Counsellor:* Ivan I. Ippolitov.
Counsellors: S. G. Voronin; D. P. Mussin; V. D. Konuzin; V. V. Karyagin;
A. P. Chuev; N. I. Efimov; Ivan A. Gavva; Y. N. Voronin.
Service Attachés: Col. Yuri A. Chelpanov (*Army*), Rear-Adm. Boris D. Yashin
(*Navy*), Col. Vladimir P. Konobeev (*Air*). *First Secretaries:* Ivan P. Azarov;
Vladimir I. Kiryushin; Ivan F. Kovalenko; Georgi V. Shevchenko; I. A. Shish-
kin; Anatolii G. Strelnikov; A. I. Borisenko.

OF GREAT BRITAIN IN THE USSR

Ambassador: Sir Duncan Wilson, KCMG.
Minister: R. H. G. Edmonds, CMG, MBE.
Counsellors: N. E. Cox (*Commercial*); K. B. A. Scott (*Head of Chancery*);
T. Garrett (*Scientific*); G. L. Scullard, OBE (*Administration*). *First Secretaries:*
E. J. Field (*Cultural*); A. Barwood-Smith (*Scientific*); M. B. Nicholson; D. J. E.
Ratford (*Commercial*); Dr R. R. B. Baxendire. *Service Attachés:* Air Cdre
R. P. Harding, CBE (*Defence and Air*), Capt. H. M. Ellis, RN (*Navy*), Brig.
H. L. B. Salman (*Army*).

OF THE USSR IN THE USA (1125–16th St., NW,
Washington, D.C., 20036)

Ambassador: Anatoly F. Dobrynin.
Minister-Counsellor: Yuly M. Vorontsov. *Counsellors:* Boris A. Solomatin;
Vladimir P. Pletnev; Viktor A. Osipov; Yuli M. Vorontsov; Viktor G. Kom-
plektov; Sergei A. Shevchenko (*Commercial*); Georgi I. Isatchenko (*Information*);
Valentin M. Kamenev, Alexei N. Stepunin (*Cultural*); Valeri A. Racheyev
(*Scientific*). *First Secretaries:* Valerian V. Mikhailov; Vladimir I. Tchernyshev;
Yakov K. Bukashev; Igor A. Rogachev; Igor D. Bubnov; Stanislav P. Tarasov;
Igor S. Khramtsov; Leonid V. Sabelnikov (*Commercial*); Alexander L. Makarov;
Vladimir I. Bogchev (*Information*). *Service Attachés:* Maj.-Gen. Mikhail I.
Stolnik (*Army*), Col. V. I. Pereverzev (*Air*), Capt. Nikolai I. Roshchin (*Navy*).

OF THE USA IN THE USSR

Ambassador: Jacob Beam.
Deputy Chief of Mission: Boris H. Klosson, *Heads of Sections:* David E. Klein
(*Political*); Ralph E. Lindstrom (*Economic*); Samuel E. Fry, Jr (*Consular*); Yale
W. Richmond (*Cultural*); J. Harlan Southerland (*Administrative*).
Service Attachés: Col. William P. Schneider (*Air*), Col. William F. Scott
(*Army*), Capt. Franklin G. Babbitt (*Navy*).

BOOKS OF REFERENCE

OFFICIAL PUBLICATIONS

Narodnoye Hozyaistvo SSSR (National Economy of the USSR). Statistical Summary. 1969
SSSR v Tsifrakh. Central Statistical Department, 1967
Pravda [Truth]. Daily organ of the Central Committee of the Communist Party
Izvestia [News]. Daily organ of the Presidium of the Supreme Soviet of the USSR
Viedomosti Verkhovnovo Sovieta. Bulletin of the Supreme Soviet of the USSR, in the languages
   of the 16 republics
Sovietskaia Torgovlia. Thrice-weekly publication of the Ministry of Trade of the USSR
Planovoye Khoziaistvo. Monthly. Moscow
Voprosy Torgovli. A monthly journal published by the Ministry of Trade of the USSR
Vneshnaya Torgovlya. Published by the Ministry for Foreign Trade. Monthly. Moscow
Trud. The daily organ of the All-Union Central Council of Trade Unions
Professionalnye Soyuzy. A trade union monthly. Moscow
Kommunist. A fortnightly organ of the Communist Party of the Soviet Union
Finansy i Khoziaistvo. A weekly publication of the Ministry for Finance
Sotsialistitcheskoye Zemledelie. A daily publication of the Ministry of Agriculture
Soviet Foreign Policy during the Patriotic War; Documents and Materials, 2 vols (translated by
   A. Rothstein). London, 1946–47

History of the USSR. Published by the Soviet Academy of Sciences. 3 vols. Moscow, 1948–57. (In Russian.) German edition, *Geschichte der Völker der Sowjetunion.* Basle, 1945
Bolshaya Sovietskaya Entsiklopedia. 65 vols. Moscow 1926–47; 2nd ed., 51 vols. Moscow, 1949–58; annual supplement (*Yezhegodnik*)
Soviet Union. A monthly pictorial. Moscow. (In English)
Soviet Import–Export Dictionary (in Russian, with English, etc., terms). Moscow, 1952
Velikaia Otechestvennaya Voina Sovetskogo Soyuza. Moscow, 1965

OTHER PUBLICATIONS

Soviet Studies; a Quarterly Review. Ed. J. Miller and R. J. A. Schlesinger. Oxford, 1949 ff.
The Current Digest of the Soviet Press. Published by Joint Committee on Slavic Studies. Weekly. Washington, D.C.
Arakin, Vygodskaya, Ilyina, *Anglo-russkii slovar.* 4th ed. Moscow, 1962
Beloff, M., *The Foreign Policy of Soviet Russia, 1929–41.* 2 vols. 1947–49.—*Soviet Policy in the Far East.* Oxford, 1953.—*Soviet Policy in Asia, 1944–52.* Oxford, 1953
Carr, E. H., *The Bolshevik Revolution.* 8 vols. London, 1950–64
Coates, W. P., and Coates, Zelda K., *A History of Anglo-Soviet Relations.* 2 vols. London, 1944–58
Degras, J. (compiler), *Soviet Documents on Foreign Policy, 1917–41.* 3 vols. London, 1948–52
Deutscher, K., *Trotsky.* 3 vols. OUP, 1954 ff.
Fitzsimmons, T., and others, *USSR; Its People, Its Society, Its Culture.* New Haven, 1960
Horecky, P. L. (ed.), *Russia and the Soviet Union: a bibliographical guide to western-language publications.* Univ. of Chicago Press, 1965
Lenin, V. L., *Collected Works* (in progress: 40 vols. published 1960–69). London
Maynard, J., *Russia in Flux.* London, 1941.—*The Russian Peasant: and Other Studies.* London, 1942.—*Russia in Flux* (abridged ed. of the two foregoing books). New York, 1948
Moore, Harriet L., *Soviet Far Eastern Policy, 1931–45.* Princeton and Oxford, 1946
Pares, Sir B., *A History of Russia.* London, 1962
Preobrazhensky, A. G., *Etymological Dictionary of the Russian Language.* Columbia Univ. Press, 1951
Rothstein, A., *A History of the USSR.* 2nd ed. London, 1951
Schlesinger, R., *The Spirit of Post-war Russia. Soviet Ideology, 1917–46.* London, 1947.—*Changing Attitude in Soviet Russia: The Family.* London, 1949
Slusser, R. M., and Triska, J. F., *A Calendar of Soviet Treaties, 1917–57.* Stanford Univ. Press, 1959
Smirnitzky, A. I. (ed.) *Rusko–angliiskii slovar.* 4th ed. Moscow, 1959
Stalin, J. V., *Collected Works.* 13 vols. London, 1952–55
Utechin, S. V. (ed.), *Everyman's Concise Encyclopaedia of Russia.* London, 1961
Vernadsky, G., *A History of Russia.* 4th ed. Yale Univ. Press, 1954

RUSSIAN SOVIET FEDERAL SOCIALIST REPUBLIC (RSFSR)

Rossiskaya Sovietskaya Federativnaya Sotsialisticheskaya Respublika

The RSFSR adopted its present constitution at the 17th Extraordinary All-Russian Congress of Soviets in Jan. 1937. Since then slight alterations have been introduced in the constitution from time to time.

President, Presidium of the Supreme Soviet: M. A. Yasnov.
Chairman, Council of Ministers: G. I. Voronov.
Foreign Minister: A. Rodionov.

A special bureau of the Central Committee of the Communist Party of the USSR has been set up for the RSFSR.
The RSFSR consists of:

(1) *Territories:* Altai, Khabarovsk, Krasnodar, Krasnoyarsk, Primorye, Stavropol.

(2) *Regions:* Amur, Archangel, Astrakhan, Belgorod, Briansk, Chelyabinsk, Chita, Gorki, Irkutsk, Ivanovo, Kaluga, Kalinin, Kaliningrad, Kamchatka, Kemerovo, Kirov, Kostroma, Kuibyshev, Kurgan, Kursk, Leningrad, Lipetsk, Magadan, Moscow, Murmansk, Novgorod, Novosibirsk, Omsk, Orel, Orenburg, Penza, Perm, Pskov, Rostov, Ryazan, Sakhalin, Saratov, Smolensk, Volgograd, Sverdlovsk, Tambov, Tomsk, Tula, Tyumen, Ulyanovsk, Vladimir, Vologda, Voronezh, Yaroslavl.

(3) *Autonomous Soviet Socialist Republics:* Bashkir, Buryat, Checheno-Ingush, Chuvash, Daghestan, Kabardino-Balkar, Kalmyk, Karelian, Komi, Mari, Mordovian, North Ossetia, Tatar, Tuva, Udmurt, Yakut.

(4) *Autonomous Regions:* Adygei, Karachayevo-Cherkess, Gorno-Altai, Jewish, Khakass.

(5) *National Areas:* Aginsky Buryat, Chukot, Evenki, Khanty-Mansi, Komi-Permyak, Koryak, Nenetz, Taimyr (Dolgano-Nenetz), Ust-Ordynsky Buryat, Yamalo-Nenetz.

The Supreme Soviet, elected in March 1967, consisted of 884 deputies (1 per 150,000 population); 594 were Communists and 299 women.

On 16 March 1969, 1,092,775 deputies were elected to local authorities; 498,315 (46·5%) were women, 609,118 (55·7%) non-Party and 669,545 (61·3%) industrial workers and collective farmers.

AREA AND POPULATION. The RSFSR occupies over 76% of the total area of the USSR stretching from the Far North to the Black Sea in the south and from the Far East to Kaliningrad in the west. Four-fifths of its population in Jan. 1968 were Russians, the rest being 38 national minorities such as the Tartars, Jews, Mordovians, Chuvashis, Bashkirs, Poles, Germans, Udmurts, Buryats, Mari, Yakuts and Ossetians. The 2 principal cities are Moscow, the capital, with a population (est. Jan. 1970) of 7·06m. (without suburbs, 6,942,000), and Leningrad, the second capital, 3·95m. (without suburbs, 3,518,000). Among other important large towns are Gorki, Rostov-on-Don, Volgograd, Sverdlovsk, Novosibirsk, Chelyabinsk, Kazan, Omsk and Kuibyshev.

The RSFSR has a variety of climates (ranging from arctic to sub-tropical) and of geographical conditions (tundra, forest lands, steppes and rich agricultural soil). It also contains great mineral resources: iron ore in the Urals, the Kerch Peninsula and Siberia; coal in the Kuznetz Basin, Eastern Siberia, Urals and the sub-Moscow Basin; oil in the Urals, Azov–Black Sea area and Bashkiria. It also has abundant deposits of gold, platinum, copper, zinc, lead, tin and rare metals.

The RSFSR produces about 70% of the total industrial and agricultural output of the Soviet Union. Industrial and office workers averaged 53·3m. in 1969.

EDUCATION. In 1969–70 there were 25·8m. pupils in 108,491 primary 7-year and secondary schools, technical schools and other secondary educational establishments; 2,655,800 students in 454 higher educational establishments (including correspondence students) and 2,556,800 students in 2,403 technical colleges of all kinds (including correspondence students). There were 4·03m. children attending 50,704 kindergartens. There were, on 1 Jan. 1970, 603,236 scientific staff in 2,527 learned and scientific institutions (about 70% of the total for the USSR).

In 1957 a Siberian branch of the Academy of Sciences was organized, in charge of all scientific research institutions from the Urals to the Pacific.

There is an Academy of Municipal Economy (with 4 research institutions and a staff of 427).

Newspapers. In 1969 there were 4,704 newspapers, 4,413 of them in Russian, with a circulation of 89,986,000 and 87,747,000 respectively.

HEALTH. Doctors at the end of 1969 numbered 363,900, and hospital beds 1·42m. (133,400 in 1913 and 482,000 in 1940); 1·57m. infants in crèches.

FINANCE. Revenue and expenditure balanced as follows (in 1m. new roubles): 1961, 25,488; 1962, 26,412; 1963, 27,862; 1964, 29,293; 1965, 31,635; 1966, 33,162; 1967, 27,696; 1968, 28,737; 1969, 32,193.

Annual planned investments in the national economy rose from 14,762m. roubles in 1956 to 37,305m. in 1969.

COMMUNICATIONS. Length of railways on 1 Jan. 1970, was 77,350 km, inland waterways 123,800 km, hard-surface motor roads 209,100 km.

BASHKIRIAN AUTONOMOUS SOVIET SOCIALIST REPUBLIC

Area 143,600 sq. km (55,430 sq. miles), population (census 1970) 3,819,000. Capital, Ufa. Bashkiria was annexed to Russia in 1557. It was constituted as an Autonomous Soviet Republic on 23 March 1919. 247 deputies were elected on 12 March 1967, 82 of them women.

There are expanding chemical, coal, steel, electrical engineering, timber and paper industries. There were 635 collective farms and 106 state farms in 1969. Bashkiria is the second largest oil producer in USSR.

In 1969 there were over 5,000 schools with 922,600 pupils. There is a state university and a branch of the USSR Academy of Sciences. There were 60,100 students in technical colleges and 41,400 receiving higher education.

In Jan. 1969 there were 3,460 doctors and 31,710 hospital beds.

BURIAT AUTONOMOUS SOVIET SOCIALIST REPUBLIC

The Buriat Republic, situated to the south of the Yakut Republic, adopted the Soviet system on 1 March 1920. This area was penetrated by the Russians in the 17th century and finally annexed from China by the treaties of Nerchinsk (1689) and Kyakhta (1727).

The area is 351,300 sq. km (135,650 sq. miles). The population (census 1970) was 812,000. Capital, Ulan-Udé. The name of the Republic was changed from 'Buriat-Mongol' on 7 July 1958.

127 deputies were elected on 12 March 1967, 42 of them women.

The main industries are coal, timber, building materials, fisheries, sheep and cattle farming. In 1969 there were 58 state and 78 collective farms. Two-thirds of the collective farms have been electrified. Gold, molybdenum and wolfram are mined.

In 1969 there were over 700 schools with 203,900 pupils, 16 technical colleges with 20,900 students and 2 higher educational institutions with 19,800 students.

At the end of 1967 there were 1,467 doctors and 8,541 hospital beds.

CHECHENO-INGUSH AUTONOMOUS SOVIET SOCIALIST REPUBLIC

Area, 19,300 sq. km (7,350 sq. miles); population (census 1970), 1,065,000. Capital, Grozny. After 70 years of almost continuous fighting, the Chechens and Ingushes were conquered by Russia in the late 1850s. In 1918 each nationality separately established its 'National Soviet' within the Terek Autonomous Republic, and in 1920 (after the Civil War) were constituted areas within the Mountain Republic. The Chechens separated out as an Autonomous Region on 30 Nov. 1922 and the Ingushes on 7 July 1924. In Jan. 1934 the two regions were united, and on 5 Dec. 1936 constituted as an Autonomous Republic. This was dissoved in 1944, but reconstituted on 9 Jan. 1957: 232,000 Chechens and Ingushes returned to their homes in the next 2 years.

149 deputies were elected on 12 March 1967, 64 of them women.

The Republic has one of the major Soviet oilfields: also a number of large engineering works, chemical factories, building materials works and food canneries. There is an expanding timber, woodworking and furniture industry. In 1969 there were 52 state and 51 collective farms.

There were, in 1969, 464 schools with 273,300 pupils, 10 technical colleges with 14,700 students and 2 places of higher education with 13,200 students.

In 1969 there were 1,970 doctors and 4,440 hospital beds.

CHUVASH AUTONOMOUS SOVIET SOCIALIST REPUBLIC

Area, 18,300 sq. km (7,064 sq. miles); population (census 1970), 1,224,000. Capital, Cheboksary. The territory was annexed by Russia in the middle of the 16th century. On 24 June 1920 it was constituted as an Autonomous Region, and on 21 April 1925 as an Autonomous Republic.

149 deputies were elected on 12 March 1959, 54 of them women.

Like most of the Autonomous Republics, Chuvashia before 1914 was a region of primitive agriculture, with a certain development of the timber industry. Today it has several big railway repair works, an expanding electrical and other engineering industry, building materials, chemicals, textiles and food industries; timber felling and haulage are largely mechanized. There are 321 collective farms and 46 state farms. Grain crops account for nearly two-thirds of all sowings and fodder crops for nearly a quarter. Fruit and wine-growing are a developing branch of agriculture.

In 1969 there were 865 schools attended by 287,800 children, 22 technical colleges with 21,200 students and 3 places of higher education with 11,900 students.

There were 1,917 doctors and 11,275 hospital beds.

DAGESTAN AUTONOMOUS SOVIET SOCIALIST REPUBLIC

Area, 50,300 sq. km (19,416 sq. miles); population (census 1970), 1,429,000. Capital, Mahachkala. Over 30 nationalities inhabit this republic apart from Russians; the most numerous are the Avartsy, Dargintsy, Lezginy, Kumyki, Laki, Tabasaranly and Azerbaidjanis. Annexed from Persia in 1723, Dagestan was constituted an Autonomous Republic on 20 Jan. 1921.

178 deputies were elected on 12 March 1967, 75 of them women.

There are large engineering, oil, chemical, woodworking, textile, food and other light industries. Agriculture is very varied, ranging from wheat to grapes, with sheep farming and cattle breeding; in 1969 there were 387 collective farms and 151 state farms. A chain of power stations is under construction in the Sulak River (total capacity 2·5m. kw.).

In 1969 there were 1,665 schools with 384,000 pupils, 26 technical colleges with 22,600 students and 4 higher educational establishments with 19,900 students; and a branch of the USSR Academy of Sciences. Doctors numbered 1,400 and hospital beds 7,000.

On 14 May 1970 an earthquake rendered 35,668 families homeless, destroyed school buildings and hospitals. By 1 Nov. considerable progress had been made in rehousing and classes were restarted in 170 new and repaired schools.

KABARDINO-BALKAR AUTONOMOUS SOVIET SOCIALIST REPUBLIC

Area, 12,500 sq. km (4,825 sq. miles); population (census 1970), 589,000. Capital, Nalchik. Kabarda was annexed to Russia in 1557. The Republic was constituted on 5 Dec. 1936.

138 deputies were elected on 12 March 1967, 56 of them women.

Main industries are ore-mining, timber, engineering, coal, food processing, timber and light industries, building materials. Grain, livestock breeding, dairy farming and wine-growing are the principal branches of agriculture. There were, in 1969, 34 state and 75 collective farms.

In 1969 there were 320 schools with 138,500 pupils, 8,800 students in technical colleges and 8,800 students receiving higher education; over 1,000 doctors and 4,735 hospital beds.

KALMYK AUTONOMOUS SOVIET SOCIALIST REPUBLIC

The Kalmyks migrated from western China to Russia (Nogai Steppe) in the early 17th century. The territory was constituted an Autonomous Region on 4 Nov. 1920, and an Autonomous Republic on 22 Oct. 1935; this was dissolved in 1943. On 9 Jan. 1957 it was reconstituted as an Autonomous Region and on 29 July 1958 as an Autonomous Republic once more.

116 deputies were elected on 12 March 1967, 44 of them women.

Area, 75,900 sq. km (29,300 sq. miles); population (census 1970), 268,000. Capital, Elista (50,000).

Main industries are fishing, canning and building materials. Cattle breeding and irrigated farming (mainly fodder crops) are the principal branches of agriculture. In 1969 there were 63 state and 27 collective farms.

In 1969 there were 66,800 pupils in 242 schools, 5,300 students in technical colleges and 1,500 at a pedagogical institute; 468 doctors and 2,960 hospital beds.

KARELIAN AUTONOMOUS SOVIET SOCIALIST REPUBLIC

Before 1917, Karelia (then known as the Olonetz Province) was noted chiefly as a place of exile for political and other prisoners.

After the November Revolution of 1917, Karelia formed part of the RSFSR. In June 1920 a Karelian Labour Commune was formed and in July 1923 this was transformed into the Karelian Autonomous Soviet Socialist Republic (one of the autonomous republics of the RSFSR). On 31 March 1940, after the Soviet–Finnish war, practically all the territory (with the exception of a small section in the neighbourhood of the Leningrad area) which had been ceded by Finland to the USSR was added to Karelia and the Karelian Autonomous Republic was transformed into the Karelo-Finnish Soviet Socialist Republic as the 12th republic of the USSR. In 1946, however, the southern part of the Republic, including its whole seaboard and the town of Viipuri (Vyborg) and Keksholm, was attached to the RSFSR. In 1956 the status of the Republic was changed (*see* p. 1394).

Karelia is chiefly noted for its wealth of timber, some 70% of its territory being forest land. It is also rich in other natural resources, having large deposits of diabase, spar, quartz, marble, mica, granite, zinc, lead, silver, copper, molybdenum, tin, baryta, iron ore, etc. Karelia takes first place in the USSR for the production of mica. It has 43,643 lakes, which, as well as its rivers, are rich in fish.

Area and Population. The Karelian Autonomous Republic, capital Petrozavodsk, covers an area of 172,400 sq. km, with a population of 714,000 (census 1970).

133 deputies were elected on 12 March 1967, 42 of them women.

Education. In 1969 there were 150,600 pupils in 747 schools. There were 10,300 students in 3 places of higher education and 15,500 in 10 technical colleges.

There are in Petrozavodsk a university (2,499 students in 1961), 2 other higher institutes and a teachers' training college. A branch of the Academy of Sciences was set up in 1949.

Health. There were 1,723 doctors in 1967, and 9,240 hospital beds.

Agriculture. There were 13 collective farms and 56 state farms in 1969. Livestock on 1 Jan. 1970 included 83,000 cattle, 37,000 pigs, 68,000 sheep and goats.

Industry. The Republic has some 25 large-scale enterprises, such as timber-mills, paper-cellulose works, mica, chemical plants, electrical stations and furniture factories. Output, 1969: Timber, 16m. cu. metres; paper and cellulose, 1,162,000 tons; power, 2,577m. kwh; canned fish. 8·3m. tins.

The construction of the White Sea–Baltic Canal had a powerful influence on the economic development of Karelia. A new refrigerating plant, household goods factories and a radio relay system began operating in 1967.

Communications. A railway between Petrozavodsk and Suoyarvi connects the capital and the Murmansk Railway with the main railway line Sortavala–Vyborg. A railway line was also laid between Kandalaksha and Kuolayarvi. Length of track, 1,600 km.

KOMI AUTONOMOUS SOVIET SOCIALIST REPUBLIC

Area, 415,900 sq. km (160,540 sq. miles); population (census 1970), 965,000. Capital, Syktyvkar (125,000). Annexed by the princes of Moscow in the 14th century and occupied by British and American forces in 1918–19, the territory was constituted as an Autonomous Region on 22 Aug. 1921 and as an Autonomous Republic on 5 Dec. 1936.

150 deputies were elected on 12 March 1967, 49 of them women.

There are large coal, oil, timber, gas, asphalt and building materials industries; light industry is expanding. Livestock breeding (including dairy farming) is the main branch of agriculture. There were 39 state and 25 collective farms in 1969.

In 1969 there were 215,300 children in 789 schools, 5,000 students receiving higher education, 17,100 students in 13 technical colleges; and a branch of the Academy of Sciences.

There were 2,344 doctors and 13,507 hospital beds.

MARI AUTONOMOUS SOVIET SOCIALIST REPUBLIC

Area, 23,200 sq. km (8,955 sq. miles); population (census 1970), 685,000. Capital, Yoshkar-Ola. The Mari people were annexed to Russia, with other people of the Kazan Tartar Khanate, when the latter was overthrown in 1552. On 25 Nov. 1920 the territory was constituted as an Autonomous Region, and on 5 Dec. 1936 as an Autonomous Republic.

113 deputies were elected on 12 March 1967, 36 of them women.

There are over 300 modern factories. The main industries are metalworking, timber, paper, woodworking and food processing. There are 170 collective farms and 28 state farms. Over 69% of cultivated land is under grain, but flax, potatoes, fruit and vegetables are also expanding branches of agriculture, as is also livestock farming.

Estimated reserves of the Pechora coalfield are 262,000m. tons.

In 1969 there were 714 schools with 162,500 pupils, 12 technical colleges and institutes with 9,900 students and 2 higher educational establishments with 11,100 students; also 1,188 doctors and 7,500 hospital beds.

MORDOVIAN AUTONOMOUS SOVIET SOCIALIST REPUBLIC

Area, 26,200 sq. km (10,110 sq. miles); population (census 1970), 1·03m. Capital, Saransk. By the 13th century the Mordovian tribes had been subjugated by the Russian princes of Ryazan and Nizhni-Novgorod. In 1928 the territory was constituted as a Mordovian Area within the Middle-Volga Territory, on 10 Jan.

1930 as an Autonomous Region and on 20 Dec. 1934 as an Autonomous Republic.

138 deputies were elected on 12 March 1967, 49 of them women.

The Republic has a wide range of industries: Electrical, timber, cable, building materials, furniture, textile, leather and other light industries. Agriculture is devoted chiefly to grain, sugar-beet, sheep and dairy farming. In 1967 there were 46 state and 330 collective farms.

There were 249,100 children at school, 15,100 students in technical colleges and 18,900 at the state university and institutes, in 1969. There were 1,400 doctors and 8,115 hospital beds.

NORTH OSSETIAN AUTONOMOUS SOVIET SOCIALIST REPUBLIC

Area, 8,000 sq. km (3,088 sq. miles); population (census 1970), 553,000. Capital, Ordzhonikidze (formerly Vladikavkaz). The Ossetians, known to antiquity as Alani (who were also called by their immediate neighbours 'Ossi' or 'Yassi'), were annexed to Russia after the latter's treaty of Kuchuk-Kainardji with Turkey, and in 1784 the key fortress of Vladikavkaz was founded on their territory (given the name of Terek region in 1861). On 4 March 1918 the latter was proclaimed an Autonomous Soviet Republic, and after the Civil War this territory with others was set up as the Mountain Autonomous Republic (20 Jan. 1921), with North Ossetia as the Ossetian (Vladikavkaz) Area within it. On 7 July 1924 the latter was constituted as an Autonomous Region and on 5 Dec. 1936 as an Autonomous Republic.

128 deputies were elected on 12 March 1967, 43 of them women.

The main industries are non-ferrous metals (mining and metallurgy), maize-processing (at the Beslan Works, the largest in Europe), timber and woodworking, textiles, building materials, distilleries and food processing. There is also a prosperous and varied agriculture. In 1969 there were 20 state and 43 collective farms.

There were in 1969, 115,400 children in 276 schools, 15,600 students in technical colleges and 19,900 students in 4 higher educational establishments (pedagogical, agriculture, medical and mining-metallurgical institutes). There were over 2,000 doctors and 5,000 hospital beds in 1969.

TARTAR AUTONOMOUS SOVIET SOCIALIST REPUBLIC

Area, 68,000 sq. km (26,250 sq. miles); population (census 1970), 3,131,000. Capital, Kazan. From the 10th to the 13th centuries this was the territory of the flourishing Volga-Kama Bulgar State; conquered by the Mongols, it became the seat of the Kazan (Tartar) Khans when the Mongol Empire broke up in the 15th century, and in 1552 was conquered again by Russia. On 27 May 1920 it was constituted as an Autonomous Republic.

207 deputies were elected on 12 March 1967, 73 of them women.

The Republic has highly developed engineering, oil and chemical industries, while timber, building materials, textiles, clothing and food industries are also expanding. In 1969, 625 collective and 140 state farms served a total area under crops of 3·9m. hectares.

In 1969 there were 3,492 schools with 720,400 pupils, 39 technical colleges with 45,900 students and 12 higher educational establishments with 61,000 students (including a state university). There is a branch of the USSR Academy of Sciences and a total of 39 scientific research institutions.

Doctors at the end of 1969 numbered 4,500 and hospital beds 25,500.

TUVA AUTONOMOUS SOVIET SOCIALIST REPUBLIC

Area, 170,500 s, km (65,810 sq. miles); population (census 1970), 231,000. Capital, Kizyl (52,000). Tuva was incorporated in the USSR as an autonomous region on 13 Oct. 1944 and elevated to an Autonomous Republic on 10 Oct. 1961. It is situated to the north-west of Mongolia, between 50° and 53° N. lat. and between 90° and 100° E. long. It is bounded to the east, west and north by Siberia, and to the south by the Republic of Mongolia. The Tuvans are a Turki people, formerly ruled by hereditary or elective tribal chiefs. (For the earlier history of the former Tannu-Tuva Republic, see THE STATESMAN'S YEAR-BOOK, 1946, p. 798.)

110 deputies were elected to its Supreme Soviet on 12 March 1967, 30 of them women.

Tuva is well-watered and has much good pastoral land; 47 hydro-electric stations have been set into operation. The Tuvans are mainly herdsmen and cattle farmers, but, in 1969, 352,000 hectares were under crops. There are deposits of gold, cobalt and asbestos. The main exports are hair, hides and wool, and the imports manufactured goods and iron. There are 28 collective farms and 26 state farms. Mining, woodworking, garment, leather, food and other industries are rapidly developing.

In 1969 there were 194 schools with 56,500 pupils; 5 technical colleges with 3,570 students, and an Institute of Linguistics, Literature and History with 1,468 students; 11 newspapers (2 in Russian). There were 498 doctors and 3,190 hospital beds.

A Soviet steamer-service along the river Yenisei maintains communication with Minussinsk, in Central Siberia. Internal transport is chiefly by lorry and motor coach. There is an air service from Kizyl to Krasnoyarsk.

UDMURT AUTONOMOUS SOVIET SOCIALIST REPUBLIC

Area, 42,100 sq. km (16,250 sq. miles); population (census 1970), 1,417,000. Capital, Izhevsk. The Udmurts (formerly known as 'Votyaks') were annexed by the Russians in the 15th and 16th centuries. On 4 Nov. 1920 the Votyak Autonomous Region was constituted (the name was changed to Udmurt—used by the people themselves—in 1932), and on 28 Dec. 1934 it was raised to the status of an Autonomous Republic.

178 deputies were elected on 12 March 1967, 58 of them women.

Heavy industry includes the manufacture of locomotives, machine tools and other engineering products, timber and building materials. There are also light industries—clothing, leather, furniture, food, etc.

There were 67 state and 284 collective farms in 1969.

In 1969 there were 513 schools with 326,300 pupils, 20 technical colleges with 19,500 students and 5 places of higher education with 20,900 students.

There were 3,000 doctors and 14,500 hospital beds on 1 Jan. 1969.

YAKUT AUTONOMOUS SOVIET SOCIALIST REPUBLIC

The area is 3,103,000 sq. km (1,197,760 sq. miles); population (census, 1970), 664,000. Capital, Yakutsk (108,000). The Yakuts were subjugated by the Russians in the 17th century. The territory was constituted an Autonomous Republic on 27 April 1922.

201 deputies were elected on 12 March 1967, 64 of them women.

The principal industries are mining (gold, tin, mica, coal) and livestock-breeding. The Soviet Trust Soyuz-Zoloto and a number of individual prospectors are working the fields. Silver- and lead-bearing ores and coal are worked; large diamond fields have been opened up. Timber and food industries are developing. There were 24 collective farms in 1968 with an area under grain of 70,000 hectares, and 58 state farms. Trapping and breeding of fur-bearing animals (sable, squirrel, silver fox, etc.) are an important source of income A severe climate and lack of railways are serious obstacles to the economic development of the republic. There are, however, 10,000 km of roads and internal airlines totalling 10,000 km. There is an air service between Irkutsk and Yakutsk.

In 1969 there were 737 schools with 164,800 pupils; 70 were secondary schools. There are 18 technical colleges with 11,000 students, a state university and a pedagogical institute with 6,400 students and a branch of the Academy of Sciences with 15 research institutes and 539 scientific staff.

There were 1,640 doctors and 10,675 hospital beds.

ADYGEI AUTONOMOUS REGION

Part of Krasnodar Territory. Area 7,600 sq. km (2,934 sq. miles); population (census 1970), 386,000. Centre, Maikop (111,000). Established 27 July 1922.

Chief industries are timber, woodworking, food processing; but engineering is rapidly expanding. Cattle breeding predominates in agriculture. There are 41 collective and 22 state farms.

In 1969 there were 264 schools with 79,400 pupils, 6 technical colleges with 5,800 students and a pedagogical institute with 3,800 students. Regional news-papers are in Adygei and Russian. There are 3,380 hospital beds.

GORNO-ALTAI AUTONOMOUS REGION

Part of Altai Territory. Area, 92,600 sq. km (35,740 sq. miles); population (census 1970), 168,000. Capital, Gorno-Altaisk (34,000). Established 1 June 1922 as Oirot Autonomous Region; renamed 7 Jan. 1948.

Chief industries are gold, mercury and brown coal mining, timber chemicals and dairying. Cattle breeding predominates: pasturages and hay meadows cover over 1m. hectares, but 130,000 hectares are under crops. There are 29 collective and 26 state farms.

There are 239 primary and secondary schools with 40,400 pupils; technical colleges have 2,500 students and 1,500 students are receiving higher education. There are 188 doctors, 32 hospitals and 173 crèches and kindergartens (6,100 children).

JEWISH AUTONOMOUS REGION

Part of Habarovsk Territory. Area, 36,000 sq. km (13,895 sq. miles); population (census 1970), 173,000 (Russians, 128,000; Ukrainians, 14,000; Jews, 15,000). Capital, Birobidjan (56,000). Established as Jewish National District in 1928, became an autonomous region 7 May 1934.

Chief industries are non-ferrous metallurgy, building materials, timber, engineering, textiles, paper and food processing. There are 50 factories, 123,800 hectares under crops, 66,700 cattle and 38,500 pigs. There were 22 state farms and 2 collective farms in 1968.

In 1967 there were 38,500 schoolchildren; students in technical colleges numbered 4,665. There are a Yiddish national theatre, a Yiddish weekly paper and a Yiddish broadcasting service. Doctors number 181.

KARACHAYEVO-CHERKESS AUTONOMOUS REGION

Part of Stavropol Territory. Area, 14,100 sq. km (5,442 sq. miles); population (census 1970), 345,000. Capital, Cherkessk (67,000). A Karachai Autonomous Region was established on 26 April 1926 (out of a previously united Kara-chayevo–Cherkess Autonomous Region created in 1922), and dissolved in 1943. A Cherkess Autonomous Region was established on 30 April 1928. The present Autonomous Region was re-established on 9 Jan. 1957.

Ore-mining, engineering, chemical and woodworking industries have been built up since 1917. There are 70 large factories, and a copper works and sugar factory are under construction. A large irrigation scheme, Kuban–Kalaussi, is being developed, to irrigate 200,000 hectares. Livestock breeding and grain growing predominate in agriculture; crop area is 198,800 hectares.

There are 84,400 pupils in 205 schools, 6 technical colleges with 2,100 students and 2 institutes with 1,700 students; 469 doctors and 2,565 hospital beds.

KHAKASS AUTONOMOUS REGION

Part of Krasnoyarsk Territory. Area, 61,900 sq. km (23,855 sq. miles); population (census 1970), 446,000. Capital, Abakan (90,000). Established 20 Oct. 1930.

Coal- and ore-mining, timber and woodworking industries have been highly developed since 1917. The region is linked by rail with the Trans-Siberian line. Large textile and sugar factories are being built.

In 1969 about 636,000 hectares were under crops. Livestock breeding, dairy and vegetable farming are developed. There are 42 state farms and 14 collective farms.

There are 107,000 pupils in 387 schools, 7 technical colleges with 8,700 students and a pedagogical institute with 3,500 students; 598 doctors and 5,000 hospital beds. A Khakass alphabet was created after the Revolution.

BOOKS OF REFERENCE

Armstrong, T., *Russian settlement in the north.* CUP, 1965
Dallin, D. J., *The Rise of Russia in Asia.* New York, 1949.—*Soviet Russia and the Far East*, London 1949
Kolarz, W., *The Peoples of the Soviet Far East.* London, 1954
Leprince-Ringuet, F., *L'Avenir de l'Asie russe.* Paris, 1951
Mikhailov, N. L., *Sibir.* Moscow, 1955
Thiel, E., *The Soviet Far East.* London, 1957
Wallace, H., *Soviet Asia Mission.* London, 1947
Yezhegodnik, B. S. E., *1969.* Moscow, 1968

UKRAINE
Ukrainska Radyanska Sotsialistichna Respublika

The Ukrainian Soviet Socialist Republic was proclaimed on 27 Dec. 1917 and was finally established in Dec. 1919. In Dec. 1920 it concluded a military and economic alliance with the Russian Soviet Federal Socialist Republic and on 6 July 1923 formed, together with the other Soviet Socialist Republics, the Union of Soviet Socialist Republics. On 1 Nov. 1939 Western Ukrain (about 88,000 sq. km) was incorporated in the Ukrainian SSR. On 2 Aug. 1940 Northern Bukovina (about 6,000 sq. km) ceded to the USSR by Rumania 28 June 1940, and the Khotin, Akkerman and Izmail provinces of Bessarabia were included in the Ukrainian SSR, and on 29 June 1945 Ruthenia (sub-Carpathian Russia), about

1430   UNION OF SOVIET SOCIALIST REPUBLICS

7,000 sq. km, was also incorporated. From the new territories 2 new regions (provinces) were formed, Chernovitz and Izmail.

The Ukrainian Soviet Socialist Republic consists of the following regions: Cherkassy, Chernigov, Chernovtzy, Crimea (transferred from the RSFSR on 19 Feb. 1954), Dniepropetrovsk, Donetsk, Ivan Franko, Khmelnitsky (formerly Kamenetz-Podolsk), Kharkov, Kherson, Kiev, Kirovograd, Lugansk, Lvov, Nikolaiev, Odessa, Poltava, Rovno, Sumy, Ternopol, Vinnitza, Volhynia, Zakarpatskaya (Transcarpathia), Zaporozhye, Zhitomir.

The Supreme Soviet, elected in 1967, consists of 469 deputies (1 per 90,000 population); 319 are Communists and 160 women.

At elections to regional, district, urban and rural Soviets (16 March 1969), out of 425,374 deputies returned, 179,602 (42·2%) were women, 223,584 (52·6%) non-Party and 305,454 (71·8%) industrial workers and collective farmers.

President, Presidium of the Supreme Soviet: A. P. Lyashko (June 1969).
Chairman, Council of Ministers: V. V. Shcherbitsky.
Foreign Minister: D. Z. Belokolos.
First Secretary, Communist Party: P. E. Shelest.

AREA AND POPULATION. In 1938 the Ukrainian SSR covered an area of 445,000 sq. km (171,770 sq. miles); it now covers 603,700 sq. km (231,990 sq. miles).

The population in Jan. 1959 was 41,869,000 (77% Ukrainians, 17% Russians, 2% Jews). Census population, 15 Jan. 1970, 47,136,000.

The principal towns are the capital Kiev, Kharkov, Donetsk, Odessa, Dniepropetrovsk, Lvov, Zaporozhye and Krivoi Rog.

Several Christian Churches have their adherents in the Ukraine, the chief being the Orthodox Greek Church and the Catholic Church. The Western Ukraine Uniate Church, which in 1596 had been forced by the Poles to establish unity with the Roman Church, severed this connexion in March 1946 and joined the Orthodox Church. There are also some Protestants as well as Jews and others.

EDUCATION. In 1969–70 the number of pupils in 31,048 primary, secondary and special schools was 8·48m.; 138 higher educational establishments had 804,100 students, and 757 technical colleges 789,600 students; 1·06m. children were attending 12,481 kindergartens; 3,700 crèches accommodated 443,000 infants.

The Ukrainian Academy of Sciences was established in 1919; in 1969 it had 71 institutions with 9,816 scientific staff. There is an academy of building and architecture. Total scientific staff in 740 learned institutions numbered 122,754 in 1969.

Newspapers (1969). Out of 2,647 newspapers, 2,149 were in Ukrainian, with a circulation of 19,575,000 and 13·7m. respectively.

HEALTH. Doctors numbered 125,900 in 1969, and hospital beds, 494,900.

FINANCE. Budget estimates (in 1m. new roubles), 1962, 7,616; 1963, 7,887; 1964, 8,292; 1965, 9,283; 1966, 9,871; 1967, 9,900; 1968, 10,296; 1969, 10,446.

AGRICULTURE. The Ukraine contains some of the richest land in the USSR. It raises wheat, buckwheat, beet, sunflower, cotton, flax, tobacco, soya, hops, the rubber plant kok-sagyz, fruit and vegetables, and in 1969 provided nearly a quarter of the grain production in the USSR and 58% of the sugar-beet. Nine-tenths of the grain exported from Russia came from the Ukraine. The area under cultivation was 27·9m. hectares in 1913, 27m. in 1939 before the new territories were added, and 33·1m. in 1969.

Output (in 1m. tons) in 1969 (1913 figures in brackets): Wheat, 16·6 (8); maize, 8·2 (0·87); other grains, 11·7 (14·3); sugar-beet, 41·6 (9·3); sunflower seed, 3·1 (0·07); flax, 0·11 (0·004); potatoes, 17·9 (8·5); meat and fats, 2·7 (1·1); milk, 18·3 (4·7); wool, 0·025 (0·015); 8,603m. eggs (3,005m.).

On 1 Jan. 1970 there were 20·3m. cattle, 17·3m. pigs, 8·3m. sheep, 377,000 goats. In 1949 silver-fox breeding farms were started.

On 1 Jan. 1970 there were 1,543 state farms and 9,416 collective farms.

Irrigation networks supplied 838,000 hectares of land; 1·5m. hectares were drained.

INDUSTRY. Coal in the Donetz field (25,900 sq. km stretching from Donetsk to Rostov), estimated to contain 60% of the bituminous and anthracite-coal reserves of the Union, yielded, in 1961, 186·1m. metric tons—about 36% of the Union production. Large new seams have been found near Novo-Moskovsk (Dniepropetrovsk region), Kharkov, Lugansk (beyond the Don) and on the left bank of the Dnieper. Within the present frontiers of the Ukraine, coal output was 22·8m. tons in 1913, 83·8m. tons in 1940, 78m. tons in 1950 and 204·4m. tons in 1969.

Combining coal from the Donetz field with the iron-ore from the mines in Krivoi Rog has made possible the development of a large ferrous metallurgical industry in the Ukraine. Output of iron ore was 6·9m. tons in 1913, 18·9m. tons in 1940 and 99·2m. tons in 1968.

Manganese is also available at Nikopol.

Pig-iron output was 2·9m. tons in 1913, 9·6m. tons in 1940, 9·2m. tons in 1950 and 39·3m. tons in 1969. Steel output (in the present frontiers) was 2·4m. tons in 1913, 8·9m. in 1940, 8·4m. in 1950 and 45·9m. in 1969.

The Ukraine also contains oil, rich deposits of salt and various important chemicals. Oil output was 1m. tons in 1913 (in present frontiers), 353,000 tons in 1940 and 13·4m. tons in 1969; with 55·4m. cu. metres of natural gas.

The Ukraine has highly developed chemical and machine-construction industries producing one-fifth of the total output of machinery and chemicals in the Soviet Union. 142,000 tractors and 1,374 main-line diesel locomotives were produced in 1969; with 29,053 machine tools.

In Northern Bukovina there are deposits of gypsum, oil, alabaster, brown coal and timber. Output of mineral fertilizers were 36,000 tons in 1913 and 9·9m. tons in 1969; cement output increased in the same years from 269,000 to 16·9m. tons (in present frontiers in both cases). Paper output in 1969 was 186,500 tons (1913: 26,900).

Consumer goods and food industries are important. Output of cotton fabrics was (in present frontiers) 4·7m. metres in 1913, 13·8m. in 1940, 20·6m. in 1950 and 242m. in 1969. Granulated sugar output in the same years was 1·1m. tons, 1·6m. tons, 1·8m. tons and 6·4m. tons. Leather footwear manufactured in 1940 totalled 40·8m. pairs; 1969, 134m.

The number of industrial and office workers at the end of 1950 was 6·9m., and the average in 1969, 15·7m. There were 954,000 specialists with a higher education.

During the first 5-year plan (1929–32) the Dnieper power-station was built; destroyed during the War, it was restored during the fourth plan (1946–50). Another large hydro-electric station at Kahovka began operations during the fifth plan (1951–55). Power output (in 1,000m. kwh.) increased as follows: 1913, 0·5; 1940, 12·4; 1950, 14·7; 1969, 128·2.

COMMUNICATIONS. The total length of railways of the Ukrainian SSR in 1969 was 22,100 km, and the navigable rivers, 4,800 km. Length of hard-surface motor roads was 85,500 km.

Airlines connect Kiev, Lvov, Chernovtsy and Odessa with Crimean and Caucasian spas, Kiev with Tbilisi, Odessa with Riga and Donetsk.

BOOKS OF REFERENCE

Allen, W. E. D., *The Ukraine: A History*. London, 1940
Andrusyshen, C. H. (ed.), *Ukrainian–English Dictionary*. Toronto, 1955
Brégy, Pierre, and Obolensky, Prince S., *The Ukraine: A Russian Land*. London, 1940
Chamberlin, W. H., *The Ukraine*. New York, 1945
Chirovsky, N. L., *The Ukrainian Economy*. New York, Paris, Toronto, 1965
Doroshenko, D., *History of the Ukraine*. 2nd ed. Edmonton (Alberta), 1941

Holubnychy, V., *The Industrial Output of the Ukraine, 1913–56*. Munich, 1957
Hrushevsky, M., *A History of the Ukraine*. New Haven, 1941
Manning, C. A., *Twentieth-century Ukraine*. New York, 1951
Mirchuk, L. (ed.), *Ukraine and its People*. London, 1949
Soviet Ukraine. (English ed.) Ukrainian Soviet Encyclopaedia, 1970

BELORUSSIA

Belaruskaya Sovietskaya Sotsialistychnaya Respublika

The Belorussian Soviet Socialist Republic was set up on 1 Jan. 1919. It forms one of the constituent republics of the USSR.

Belorussia is situated along the Western Dvina and Dnieper; it is hilly, with a general slope towards the south. It contains large tracts of marsh land, particularly to the south-west, and valuable forest land wooded with oak, elm, maple and white beech.

The Supreme Soviet, elected in 1967, consists of 421 deputies (1 per 20,000 population): 292 are Communists and 153 women.

At elections to regional, district, urban and rural Soviets (16 March 1969), of 81,808 deputies returned, 35,900 (43·9%) were women, 45,876 (56·1%) non-Party and 50,383 (61·6%) industrial workers and collective farmers.

> *President, Presidium of the Supreme Soviet:* S. O. Pritytsky.
> *Chairman, Council of Ministers:* T. Y. Kiselyov.
> *Foreign Minister:* A. E. Gurinovich.
> *First Secretary, Communist Party:* P. M. Masherov.

AREA AND POPULATION. The area is 207,600 sq. km (80,134 sq. miles). The capital is Minsk. Other important towns are Gomel, Vitebsk, Mogilev, Bobruisk, Grodno and Brest. On 2 Nov. 1939 western Belorussia was incorporated with an area of over 108,000 sq. km and a population of 4·8m. About 81% of this population are Belorussians, 8% Russians, 7% Poles, 2% Ukrainians and 2% Jews. Census population, 15 Jan. 1970, 9m.

Belorussia now comprises the following regions: Brest, Gomel, Grodno, Mogilev, Minsk, Vitebsk.

EDUCATION. In 1969–70 there were 137,300 students in 28 places of higher education and 144,400 students in 131 technical colleges. There were 20,631 scientific personnel in 185 institutions, and 201,000 specialists with a higher education employed in the national economy. The Belorussian Academy of Sciences controlled 31 learned institutions with 3,068 scientific staff. The number of children in primary, secondary and special schools was 489,000 in 1914–15, and 1·85m. in 1969–70. 188,700 children were attending 1,944 kindergartens in Jan. 1970.

Newspapers (1969). Of 180 newspapers 134 were published in Belorussian, with a circulation of 3·8m. and 1·46m. respectively.

HEALTH. In 1969 there were 22,400 doctors (900 in 1913, within present frontiers), 90,600 hospital beds (6,400 in 1913) and 28,900 cots in crèches, with another 42,400 in crèche-sections of kindergartens.

FINANCE. Budget estimates (in 1m. new roubles), 1962, 1,345; 1963, 1,474; 1964, 1,532; 1965, 1,661; 1966, 1,842; 1967, 2,067; 1968, 2,211; 1969, 2,499.

AGRICULTURE. The area under cultivation (in hectares) was 4·5m. in 1913, 5·2m. in 1940 and 6·1m. in 1969. There were 5·07m. cattle, 3,651,000 pigs and 639,000 sheep on 1 Jan. 1970.

Output of main agricultural products (1,000 tons) in 1969 (1913 figures in brackets): Flax, 116 (33); sugar-beet, 905 (0); potatoes, 13,531 (4,024); meat, 678 (219); milk, 5,204 (1,429); wool, 1·2 (2·3); 1,512m. eggs (413m.).

Agriculturally, Belorussia may be divided into three main sections: Northern: growing flax, fodder, grasses and breeding cattle for meat and dairy produce; Central: potato growing and pig breeding; Southern: good natural pasture land, hemp cultivation and cattle breeding for meat and dairy produce.

At the end of 1969 there were 2,349 collective farms and 738 state farms. About 1·64m. hectares of marsh land had been drained for agricultural use, 520,000 of these for crops. This land has been found to be as rich as the soil of the Black Earth zone, and yields good harvests of grain, fodder, potatoes, koksagyz and other crops.

In Jan. 1970 there were 139,100 tractors and 21,500 grain combine harvesters.

INDUSTRY. Industry in this republic was almost completely destroyed during the years 1941–45. By 1956, aggregate industrial output was three times what it had been in 1940. Plants producing tip-lorries, machine-tools and agricultural machinery are prominent.

The republic also contains timber works; a match factory in Borisov; building materials, machine, pre-fabricated house construction, glass-blowing and other factories; canneries, creameries and other food industries; chemical, textiles, artificial-silk, flax-spinning and leather works.

The automobile and tractor industry produced 79,500 tractors and 29,400 lorries in 1969. Cement output, 33,000 tons in 1913, was 1,917,000 tons in 1969. Leather footwear output, 9·8m. pairs in 1940, was 35·6m. pairs in 1969. Linen fabrics, 13,000 metres in 1913, 59·2m. in 1969; woollens, 37,000 metres in 1913, 24·1 in 1969.

Particular attention has been paid to the development of the peat industry with a view to making Belorussia as far as possible self-supporting in fuel, and in 1939 local peat provided 67·5% of her total requirements of fuel. Total output in 1969 was 31m. tons (excluding collective farm output).

There are also rich deposits of rock salt. In 1951 the first sugar refinery in Belorussia was opened in Grodno; sugar output in 1969 was 166,800 tons.

Output of electricity in 1969 was 12,934m. kwh. (508m. in 1940). New power-plants have been built in Baranovichi, Grodno, Molodechno and Lida.

The number of industrial and office workers at the end of 1969 was 2·2m. and 201,000 specialists with a higher education in the national economy.

COMMUNICATIONS. There are 5,410 km of railways, 65,100 km of motor roads (24,000 km hard-surface) and 3,900 km of navigable waterways.

BOOKS OF REFERENCE

Kovalevski, G. T., and Rakov, Y. G. (ed.), *Belorusskaya SSR, an outline of her economic geography.* Minsk, 1953
Vakar, N. P., *Belorussia.* Harvard Univ. Press, 1956.—*A Bibliographical Guide to Belorussia.* Harvard Univ. Press, 1956

AZERBAIJAN
Azarbaijchan Soviet Sotsialistik Respublikasy

The 'Mussavat' (Nationalist) party, which dominated the National Council or Constituent Assembly of the Tartars, declared the independence of Azerbaijan on 28 May 1918, with a capital, first at Ganja (Elizavetpol) and later at Baku. On 28 April 1920 Azerbaijan was proclaimed a Soviet Socialist Republic. With Georgia and Armenia it formed the Transcaucasian Soviet Federal Socialist Republic. In 1936 it assumed the status of one of the Union (constituent) republics of the USSR.

The Supreme Soviet, elected in 1967, consists of 380 deputies (1 per 10,000 population); 269 are Communists and 110 women.

At elections to the Nagorno-Karabagh regional Soviet and the district, urban and rural Soviets (16 March 1969), of 44,561 deputies returned, 19,732 (44·3%) were women, 24,767 (55·6%) non-Party and 30,584 (68·6%) industrial workers and collective farmers.

President, Presidium of the Supreme Soviet: K. A. Halilov.
Chairman, Council of Ministers: A. I. Ibrahimov.
First Secretary, Communist Party: G. A. Aliev.

AREA AND POPULATION. Azerbaijan covers an area of 86,600 sq km (33,430 sq. miles) and has a population (Jan. 1970) of 5,111,000. Its capital is Baku. Other important towns are Kirovabad and Sumgait. Nahichevan is the capital of the Autonomous Republic of the same name.

Azerbaijan includes the Nahichevan Autonomous Republic and the Nagorno-Karabagh Autonomous Region. Situated in the eastern area of Transcaucasia, it is protected by mountains in the west and north and washed by the Caspian Sea in the south and east. Its climate is inclined to drought.

About two-thirds of the population are Azerbaijan Tiurks. Other nationalities are Russians (14%), Armenians (12%) and Georgians (2·7%).

EDUCATION. In 1969–70 there were 1·39m. pupils in 5,449 elementary and secondary schools and 84,300 children attending 1,213 kindergartens. There were 78 technical colleges with 68,900 students, 12 higher educational institutions, including a state university at Baku, with 99,200 students (including correspondence students).

The Azerbaijan Academy of Sciences has 30 research institutions with 3,553, research workers. There are 130 learned and scientific institutions, with 16,594 research workers in all.

Newspapers (1969). There were 121 newspapers, 95 of them in the Azerbaijani language, with a circulation of 2m. and 1·6m. respectively.

HEALTH. In 1969 there were 12,400 doctors and 46,400 hospital beds. There were also 268 maternity and infant welfare centres and 300 permanent crèches for 11,100 children, with 13,000 cots in crèche-sections of kindergartens.

FINANCE (in 1m. new roubles). Estimate, 1961, 670; 1962, 706; 1963, 761; 1964, 820; 1965, 931; 1966, 994; 1967, 1,008; 1968, 1,105; 1969, 1,228

AGRICULTURE. The chief agricultural products are grain, cotton, rice, vine, fruit, vegetables, tobacco and silk. The Mexican rubber plant *grayule* has been acclimatized. A new kind of high-yielding winter wheat has been produced for use in mountainous parts of the republic.

Livestock on 1 Jan. 1970: Cattle, 1·56m.; pigs, 90,000; sheep, 3·8m.

Output of main agricultural products (1,000 tons) in 1969 (1913 figures in brackets): Wheat, 395 (315); maize, 23 (4); cotton, 299 (4); potatoes, 113 (38); tea, 9·3 (0); meat, 93 (40); milk, 425 (203); wool, 7 (4·1); grapes, 272; fruit, 52; 356m. eggs (94m.).

Azerbaijan has become an important cotton-growing and sub-tropical base. About 70% of cultivated land is irrigated. On the irrigated land crops of Egyptian and Sea-Island cotton are obtained. Here, too, rice and lucerne are cultivated, and in the mountain valleys there are also orchards, vineyards and silk cultures.

In the south along the coast of the Caspian, where the climate is more moist, there are tea plantations, and citrous fruits and other sub-tropical plants are grown.

In 1941 a scientific research institute for sub-tropical research was opened to develop the culture of sub-tropical plants in Azerbaijan and other parts of Transcaucasia. A forestry research institute was opened in 1949.

There were at the end of 1969, 999 collective farms, 398 state farms, 47,300 tractors and 4,100 grain combine harvesters.

INDUSTRY. The Republic is rich in natural resources: oil, iron, aluminium, copper, lead, zinc, precious metals, sulphur pyrites, limestone and salt. Iron and steel and aluminium works have been built at Sumgait.

The most important industry is the oil industry, especially in the Baku region. The output of oil was 7·7m. tons in 1913, 22·2m. tons in 1940 and 20·4m. tons in 1969. The largest producing area lies along the western shore of the Caspian Sea, north and south of Baku, where the largest refineries are located. Other wells lie west of Baku, and some have been drilled in the Caspian itself, off the Apsheron Peninsula. Baku is connected by a double pipeline with Batum on the Black Sea. All the oilfields have been electrified and are connected with Baku.

Azerbaijan has also copper, chemical, cement and building material, food, timber, salt, textiles and fishing industries. 728,500 tons of steel were produced in 1969. 1·3m. tons of cement, 123m. metres of cotton fabrics, 10·3m. pairs of leather footwear, 16·2m. metres of silk fabrics.

In addition to Baku, among the important industrial centres are Kirovabad, Nukha, Stepanakert, Nahichevan, Lenkoran.

In 1969 electric power output was 11·7m. kwh. Output of gas, which began in 1928 with 176m. cu. metres, was 4,938m. in 1969. Pipelines from Karadag to Baku and Sumgait supply gas fuel for all oil-cracking factories and most engineering works.

Synthetic rubber works (Sumgait), tyre works and a worsted combine (Baku) and a large textile combine (Mingechaur) have been built.

The number of industrial and office workers in 1969 (average for year) was 1·23m., and specialists with a higher education employed in the national economy numbered 115,000.

COMMUNICATIONS. Railway lines, apart from narrow gauge, 1,800 km. The first electrical railway (42 km) in the USSR was constructed in Azerbaijan in 1924; in 1949, 27 km was added, and the line now runs Baku–Surakhany–Sabunchi–Buzovny–Baku. The capital is also linked by rail with Tbilisi, Yerevan, Derbent, Julfa and Astara. There were, in 1969, 20,900 km of motor roads (12,700 km hard-surface) and 500 km of inland waterways.

NAHICHEVAN AUTONOMOUS SOVIET SOCIALIST REPUBLIC

Area 5,500 sq. km (2,120 sq. miles), population (census 1970), 202,000. Capital, Nahichevan (33,000). This territory, on the borders of Turkey and Iran, forms part of the Azerbaijan SSR although separated from it by the territory of Soviet Armenia. Its population, mainly Azerbaijanis, had a chequered history for 1,500 years under the ancient Persians, Arabs, Seljuk Turks, Mongols, Ottoman Turks and modern Persians before being annexed by Russia in 1828. On 9 Feb. 1924 it was constituted as an Autonomous Republic within Azerbaijan. Its Supreme Soviet, elected 17 March 1967, has 80 members, 34 of them women.

The Republic has silk, clothing, cotton, canning, meat-packing and other factories. Nearly 70% of the people are engaged in agriculture, of which the main branches are cotton and tobacco growing. Fruit and grapes are also produced in increasing quantity. There are 68 collective and 12 state farms.

In 1969 there were 211 primary, 8-year and 11-year schools with 60,300 pupils. There were 1,200 pupils in 2 technical colleges.

Doctors numbered 250, and hospital beds, 1,900.

NAGORNO-KARABAGH AUTONOMOUS REGION

Populated by Armenians and Azerbaijanis, a separate khanate in the 18th century, it was established on 7 July 1923 as an autonomous region within Azerbaijan. Area, 4,400 sq. km (1,700 sq. miles); population (census 1970), 149,000. Capital, Stepanakert (30,000).

Main industries are silk, wine, dairying and building materials. Crop area is 95,000 hectares; cotton, grapes and winter wheat are grown.

In 1969 there were 219 8-, 10- and 11-year schools and 16 schools for working youth, with over 43,000 pupils. There are a medical school, a teachers' training college and 2 agricultural schools with a total of 2,300 students; 235 doctors and 1,525 hospital beds.

BOOKS OF REFERENCE

Baddeley, J. F., *The Rugged Flanks of Caucasus.* 2 vols. Oxford, 1941
Tutaeff, D., *The Soviet Caucasus.* London, 1942

GEORGIA

Sakartvelos Sabchota Sotsialisturi Respublica

The independence of the Georgian Social Democratic Republic was declared at Tiflis on 26 May 1918 by the National Council, elected by the National Assembly of Georgia on 22 Nov. 1917. The independence of Georgia was recognized by the Soviet Union on 7 May 1920. On 12 Feb. 1921 a rising broke out in Mingrelia, Abhazia and Adjaria, and Soviet troops invaded the country, which, on 25 Feb. 1921, was proclaimed the Georgian Soviet Socialist Republic. At the first Trans-caucasian Soviet Congress, 15 Dec. 1922, Georgia, together with Armenia and Azerbaijan, united to form the Transcaucasian Soviet Federal Socialist Republic, and a federal constitution was adopted and published 10 Jan. 1923. In 1936 the Georgian Soviet Socialist Republic became one of the constituent republics of the USSR and, like other republics of the Union, adopted a new constitution.

The Georgian Soviet Socialist Republic includes the Abhazian ASSR, the Adjarian ASSR and the South Ossetian Autonomous Region.

The Supreme Soviet, elected in 1967, consists of 400 deputies (1 per 10,000 population); 125 are women.

At elections to the district, rural and urban Soviets, and that of the South Ossetian region (16 March 1969), of 48,749 deputies returned 22,098 (45·3%) were women, 26,680 (54·7%) non-Party and 31,929 (65·5%) industrial workers and collective farmers.

President, Presidium of the Supreme Soviet: G. S. Dzotsenidze.
Chairman, Council of Ministers: G. D. Djavakhishvili.
First Secretary, Communist Party: V. P. Mzhavanadze.

AREA AND POPULATION. Georgia occupies the whole of the western part of Transcaucasia and covers an area of 69,700 sq. km (26,900 sq. miles). Its population on 15 Jan. 1970 was 4·69m. The capital is Tbilisi (Tiflis). Other important towns are Kutaisi, Batoumi (101,000), Sukhumi (102,000), Rustavi (102,000), Poti (42,500), Gori (33,100).

Protected from the north by the Caucasian mountains, and receiving in the west the warm, moist winds from the Black Sea, into which most of its rivers flow, Georgia is outstanding for its fine, warm climate and its natural wealth, variety and beauty. It has the highest snow-capped peaks of the Caucasian mountains. Georgia contains valuable sulphur and other medicinal springs. Georgians, an ancient highly cultured people, form 64% of the population; Armenians, 11%; Russians, 10%; Azerbaijanis, 4%.

EDUCATION. In 1969–70 there were 1,016,000 pupils in 4,585 primary and secondary schools, 50,600 in 94 technical colleges and 90,100 students in 18 higher educational institutions. Tbilisi University has 15,000 students. In 1951, 8-year school attendance was made compulsory in all rural areas; in towns, 11 years' education is usual. In Abastumani there is an astro-physical observatory. In 1936 a branch of the Academy of Sciences of the USSR was formed in Tbilisi, and in Feb. 1941 a Georgian Academy of Sciences was opened, which in 1969 had

40 institutions with scientific staff totalling 4,075. There were in all 188 research institutions with 18,621 scientific staffs.

In 1969, 95,500 children were attending 1,345 kindergartens.

Newspapers (1969). Out of 145 newspapers, 126 were in Georgian, with a circulation of 2,809,000 and 2,376,000 respectively.

HEALTH. There were 17,400 doctors and 42,300 hospital beds in 1969. Permanent crèches had 12,600 cots, with 6,600 cots in crèche-sections of kindergartens.

FINANCE (in 1m. new roubles). Budget estimates, 1962, 749; 1963, 804; 1964, 837; 1965, 945; 1966, 994; 1967, 980; 1968, 1,018; 1969, 1,154.

AGRICULTURE. There are 3 main agricultural areas: (1) The moist subtropical area along the Black Sea coast, where are cultivated tea, citrus fruits (lemons, oranges, mandarins, etc.), the tung tree (which yields special industrial oils), eucalyptus, bamboo, high-quality tobacco; (2) Imeretia (the Kutais region). where the chief cultures are grapes and silk, and (3) Kakhetia, along the Alazani (a tributary of the Kura River), famed for its orchards and wines. Land (in hectares) under cultivation was 748,000 in 1913, 896,000 in 1940, 778,000 in 1961, 747,000 in 1969.

Output of main agricultural products (1,000 tons) in 1969 (1913 figures in brackets): Wheat, 204 (158); maize, 327 (184); sugar-beet, 100 (0); fruit, 321; grapes, 475; tea in leaf, 232; meat, 100 (49); wool, 4·7 (3·4); milk, 494 (222); silk, 402; 358m. eggs (119m.); wine, 5·3m. decalitres.

In 1969 there were 1,354 collective farms working over 77% of all agricultural land, 210 state farms working nearly 23% of such land. In the Colchis area 115,000 hectares of extremely rich land have been reclaimed. There are 331,000 hectares of irrigated land. 129,000 hectares of marshland have been drained. Tractors numbered 32,100; grain combines, 1,600.

Livestock on 1 Jan. 1970: Cattle, 1·4m.; pigs, 589,000; sheep, 1,688,000.

Georgia is rich in forest lands where fine varieties of timber are grown. Area covered by forests, 2·4m. hectares.

INDUSTRY. The most important mining industry of Georgia is the exploitation of the manganese deposits, the richest of which lie in the Chiatura region, where 3m. tons of ore were produced in 1965. Manganese deposits in Georgia are calculated at 250m. tons, distributed over an area of 140 sq. km. The most important coal seams are at Tkvarcheli (deposits estimated at 250m. tons) and Tkibuli (deposits of 80m. tons). Other important minerals are baryta, the best in the USSR, fire-resisting and other clays, diatomite shale, oil, agate, marble, cement, alabaster, iron and other ores, building stone, arsenic, molybdenum, tungsten and mercury. In 1941 a goldfield was discovered. Output of coal in 1969 was 2·3m. tons (625,000 in 1940).

Since the Second World War the Transcaucasian Metallurgical Plant has been built at Rustavi (near Tbilisi) and a motor works at Kutaisi. There are modern factories for processing green tea-leaves, creameries and breweries; Georgia has also textile and silk industries.

In 1969, 802,000 tons of pig-iron, 1·38m. tons of steel, 1,035,000 tons of rolled metal were produced; also 1·38m. tons of cement, 492,000 tons of mineral fertilizer, 60·2m. metres of cotton fabrics, 31·4m. metres of silk fabrics, 13·5m. pairs of leather footwear and 27,000 tons of granulated sugar.

Georgia's fast flowing rivers form an abundant source of energy. The most powerful electric station in Transcaucasia is in Georgia on the river Kura, the Zemo-Avachal hydro-electric station of 36,000 h.p. Power output in 1969 was 8,334m. kwh. (742m. in 1940).

There were 1·38m. industrial and office workers in 1969, and 166,000 specialists with a higher education in the national economy.

COMMUNICATIONS. Length of railways in 1968 was 1,420 km. The trunk line leading from Batum through Tbilisi to Baku on the Caspian Sea has several narrow-gauge branches on Georgian territory to the coalmines of Tkibuli, to the port of Poti, to the manganese mines of Chiaturi, to the mineral springs of Borjom and the health resort Bakuriani, to the towns Signakh and Telavi, in Kakhetia, and to the Armenian frontier, across the coalmine district of Alaverdi. The last branch divides in Armenia, going on the one side to Tabriz in Iran, and on the other to Erzerum in Anatolia. A railway line from Akhal-Senaki along the Black Sea coast, through Sukhum to Tuapse, was completed in 1946. Over two-thirds of the lines are electrified. In 1969 there were 20,700 km of motor roads, 16,100 km of them hard-surfaced.

The Tbilisi airport has been reconstructed and is now used for scheduled jet aircraft (TU-104) services.

ABHAZIAN AUTONOMOUS SOVIET SOCIALIST REPUBLIC

Area, 8,600 km (3,320 sq. miles); population (census 1970), 487,000. Capital, Sukhumi, 102,000. This area, the ancient Colchis, included Greek colonies from the 6th century B.C. onwards. From the 2nd century B.C. onwards, it was a prey to many invaders—Romans, Byzantines, Arabs, Ottoman Turks—before accepting a Russian protectorate in 1810. However, from the 4th century A.D. a West Georgian kingdom was established by the Lazi princes in the territory (known to the Romans as 'Lazica') and by the 8th century the prevailing language was Georgian and the name Abhazia. On 4 March 1921 a congress of local Soviets proclaimed it a Soviet Republic, and its status as an Autonomous Republic, within Georgia, was confirmed on 17 April 1930.

130 deputies were elected on 19 March 1967, 44 of them women.

The Abhazian coast (along the Black Sea) possesses a famous chain of health resorts—Gagra, Sukhumi, Akhali-Antoni, Gulripsha and Gudauta—sheltered by thickly forested mountains.

The republic has coal, electric power, building materials and light industries. In 1969 there were 135 collective farms and 21 state farms; main crops are tobacco, tea, grapes, oranges, tangerines and lemons.

Livestock, 1 Jan. 1970: 142,000 cattle, 63,000 pigs, 40,000 sheep and goats, and 14,000 horses.

108,400 pupils were attending 460 schools in 1969–70. There were 7 technical colleges with 2,700 students; 8,100 students were receiving higher education (including correspondence courses).

Doctors numbered 1,100 and hospital beds 2,600; cots in crèches, 2,300.

ADJARIAN AUTONOMOUS SOVIET SOCIALIST REPUBLIC

Area, 3,000 sq. km (1,160 sq. miles); population (census 1970), 310,000. Capital, Batumi 101,000. After a history similar to that of Abhazia, it fell under Turkish rule in the 17th century, and was annexed to Russia (rejoining Georgia) after the Berlin Treaty of 1878. On 16 June 1921 the territory was constituted as an Autonomous Republic within the Georgian SSR.

90 deputies were elected on 19 March 1967, 26 of them women.

The republic specializes in sub-tropical agricultural products. These include tea, mandarines and lemons, grapes, bamboo, eucalyptus, etc. Livestock breeding for meat and milk is expanding. In 1969 there were 167 collective farms and 18 state farms.

There are shipyards at Batumi, modern oil-refining plant (the pipeline from the Baku oilfields ends at Batumi), food-processing and canning factories, clothing, building materials, drug factories, etc.

Health resorts are Kobuleti, Tsihis-Dari, Batumi on the coast and Beshumi in the hills. The sub-tropical climate and flora, and the combination of mountains and sea, make this republic (like Abhazia) a favourite holiday country.

In 1969 there were 426 schools with 66,700 pupils, several technical colleges with 3,900 students, a pedagogical institute and several research institutions. 2,700 students were receiving a higher education.

There were 900 doctors and 2,100 hospital beds in 1960.

SOUTH OSSETIAN AUTONOMOUS REGION

This area was populated by Ossetians from across the Caucasus (North Ossetia), driven out by the Mongols in the 13th century. The region was set up within the Georgian SSR on 20 April 1922. Area, 3,900 sq. km (1,505 sq. miles); population (census 1970), 100,000. Capital, Tskhinvali (30,000).

Main industries are mining, timber, electrical engineering and building materials. Crop area, chiefly grains, was 24,600 hectares in 1969; other pursuits are sheep-farming (71,600 sheep and goats) and vine-growing.

There are a pedagogical institute (2,496 students) and several technical colleges (599 students). In 1969 there were 25,600 pupils in elementary and secondary schools. Hospital beds in 1960 numbered 875; cots in crèches, 225.

Books of Reference

Avalishvill, Zourab, *The Independence of Georgia in International Politics, 1918–21*. London, 1940
Gvesiani, G. G., and Klopotovsky, B. A., *Gruzinskaya SSR*. Moscow, 1955
Lang, D. M., *A modern history of Georgia*. London, 1962
Tutaeff, D., *The Soviet Caucasus*. London, 1942

ARMENIA
Haikakan Sovetakan Sotsialistakan Respublika

On 29 Nov. 1920 Armenia was proclaimed a Soviet Socialist Republic. The Armenian Soviet Government, with the Russian Soviet Government, was a party to the Treaty of Kars (March 1921), which confirmed the Turkish possession of the former Government of Kars and of the Surmali District of the Government of Yerevan. From 1922 to 1936 it formed part of the Transcaucasian Soviet Federal Socialist Republic. In 1936 Armenia was proclaimed a constituent republic of the USSR.

The Supreme Soviet, elected in 1967, consists of 310 deputies (1 per 5,000 population); 101 are women.

At elections to the district, urban and rural Soviets (16 March 1969), of 25,273 deputies returned 10,898 (43·1%) were women, 13,515 (53·5%) non-Party and 17,022 (67·4%) industrial workers and collective farmers.

President, Presidium of the Supreme Soviet: N. H. Harutiunyan.
Chairman, Council of Ministers: B. A. Muradyan.
First Secretary, Communist Party: A. E. Kochinyan.

AREA AND POPULATION. Armenia covers an area of 29,800 sq. km (11,490 sq. miles). It is bounded in the north by Georgia, in the east by Azerbaijan and in the south and east by Turkey and Iran. It is a very mountainous country with but little forest land, has many turbulent rivers and a highly fertile soil, but subject to drought. In Jan. 1970 the population was 2,493,000. About 88% of the population are Armenians, the rest are Georgians, Russians (3%), Kurds (1·5%), Azerbaijanians (6%), Persians and Jews. The capital is Yerevan. Other large towns are Leninakan and Kirovakan.

EDUCATION. In 1969–70 there were 635,000 pupils in 1,503 primary, secondary and special schools; 60 technical colleges with 45,300 students; 12 higher educational institutions with 53,400 students (including correspondence students). Erevan houses the Armenian Academy of Sciences, 43 scientific institutes, a medical institute and other technical colleges, and a state university. 33 learned institutions with 2,246 scientific staff are under the Academy of Sciences; scientific workers totalled 12,000 in 120 institutions in 1970.

In 1969 there were 854 kindergartens with 71,000 children.

Newspapers (1969). Out of 96 newspapers 84 appeared in Armenian, with a circulation of 1,057,000 and 976,000 respectively.

HEALTH. In 1970 there were 7,100 doctors and 20,400 hospital beds; 1,400 cots in crèches, with another 16,700 in the crèche-sections of kindergartens.

FINANCE. Budget estimates (in 1m. new roubles), 1961, 367; 1962, 398; 1963, 461; 1964, 533; 1965, 604; 1966, 683; 1967, 639; 1968, 684; 1969, 824.

AGRICULTURE. The chief agricultural area is the valley of the Arax and the area around Yerevan. Here there are considerable cotton plantations as well as orchards and vineries. Sub-tropical plants, such as almonds and figs, are also grown. Olive groves and pomegranate plantations occupy large areas; experiments are being made to naturalize cork oak. In the mountainous areas the chief pursuit is livestock raising. In 1913 the total cultivated area of Armenia amounted to 346,000 hectares; in 1940, 434,000; in 1961, 411,000; in 1964, 415,000; in 1968, 403,000; in 1969, 398,000.

Output of main agricultural products (1,000 tons) in 1969 (1913 figures in brackets): Wheat 116 (110); sugar-beet, 96 (0); potatoes, 191 (47); fruit, 70; grapes, 195; meat, 52 (19); milk, 351 (129); wool, 3·4 (2·3); and 205m. eggs (54m.).

Area of irrigated land in Armenia in 1969 was 244,000 hectares.

There were, in 1970, 490 collective farms, and these together with the 253 state farms tilled 99·9% of the total cultivated area. Livestock on 1 Jan. 1970 included 94,000 pigs, 670,000 cattle and 1,959,000 sheep. All the state farms and collective farms had been electrified by the end of 1960. There were 19,300 tractors and 1,600 grain and cotton combines in 1970.

INDUSTRY. Armenia contains large deposits of copper, zinc, aluminium, molybdenum and other metals. It is also rich in marble, granite, cement and other building materials. The mining of these minerals is becoming more and more important. Among other industries are the chemical, producing chiefly synthetic rubber and fertilizers, and the extraction and processing of building materials such as cement, pumice-stone, tuffs, marble, volcanic basalt and fireproof clay, ginning- and textile-mills, carpet weaving, food, including winemaking, fruit, meat-canning and creameries. Machine-tool and electrical engineering works have also been established. Among the industrial centres are Yerevan, Leninakan, Alaverdi, Kafan, Kirovakan, Daval, Megri and Oktemberyan. Output of electricity in 1969 was 5,408m. kwh. A chain ('cascade') of 8 hydro-electric stations on the river Razdan, as it falls about 3,300 ft from the mountain lake Sevan to its junction with the Arax, has been completed.

In 1969 there were produced 670,000 tons of cement, 156,000 tons of mineral fertilizers, 97·2m. metres of cotton fabrics, 11·19m. metres of silk fabrics, 10m. pairs of leather footwear, 9,200 tons of granulated sugar and 3·9m. decalitres of wine (excluding collective farm output).

There were 805,000 industrial and office workers and 72,000 specialists with a higher education working in the national economy.

COMMUNICATIONS. Length of railways in 1969, 560 km; motor roads, 8,300 km (hard surface, 5,300); airlines, 570 km.

BOOKS OF REFERENCE

Baghdasargan, A. B. (ed.) *Atlas Armyanskoy SSR*. Moscow, 1961
Kouyoumdjian, M. G., *A Comprehensive Dictionary Armenian–English, English–Armenian*. Cairo, 1951–61
Kurkjian, V., *A History of Armenia*. New York, 1958
Missakian, J., *A Searchlight on the Armenian Question, 1878–1950*. Boston, Mass., 1950
Shaginyan, M., *A Journey Through Soviet Armenia*. Moscow (English ed., 1954)

MOLDAVIAN SOVIET SOCIALIST REPUBLIC

Respublika Sovietike Sochialiste Moldovenyaske

The Moldavian Soviet Socialist Republic, capital Kishinev, was formed by the union of part of the former Moldavian Autonomous Soviet Socialist Republic (organized 12 Oct. 1924), formerly included in the Ukrainian Soviet Socialist Republic, and the areas of Bessarabia (ceded by Rumania to the USSR, 28 June 1940) with a mainly Moldavian population. As from 2 Aug. 1940 the MSSR includes the following regions of the former Moldavian Autonomous Soviet Socialist Republic: Grigoriopol, Dubossarsk, Kamensk, Rybnitz, Slobedzeisk and Tiraspol, and the following districts of Bessarabia: Beltsk, Bender, Kagulsk, Kishinev, Orgeev and Sorok. The republic, however, is divided not into regions but into 32 rural districts, 20 towns and 33 urban settlements.

The Supreme Soviet, elected in 1967, consists of 315 deputies (1 per 10,000 population); 119 are women.

At elections to the district, urban and rural Soviets (16 March 1969), of 33,120 deputies returned, 15,949 (48·2%) were women, 17,470 (52·7%) non-Party and 22,422 (67·7%) industrial workers and collective farmers.

President, Presidium of the Supreme Soviet: K. F. I. Ilyashenko.
Chairman, Council of Ministers: P. A. Paskar.
First Secretary, Communist Party: I. I. Bodyul.

AREA AND POPULATION. The area is 33,700 sq. km (13,000 sq. miles). In Jan. 1970 the population was 3·6m., of whom 65% are Moldavians. Others include Ukrainians (15%), Russians (10%), Jews (3·3%), Bulgarians (2%). Apart from Kishinev, larger towns are Tiraspol (106,000) Beltsy (102,000) and Bendery.

EDUCATION. In 1969 there were 795,000 pupils in 2,245 primary, secondary and special schools, 49,700 students in 48 technical colleges and 45,500 students in 8 higher educational institutions including the state university. A Moldavian Academy of Sciences was established in 1961: it has 19 research institutions and a staff of 726. In all, there are 61 learned institutions with 5,504 scientific staff. In 1969 there were 76,600 children attending 802 kindergartens.

Newspapers (1969). There were 122 newspapers, of which 53 were in the Moldavian language, with a circulation of 1,491,000 and 1,052,000 respectively.

HEALTH. Moldavia has 800 medical centres, many district hospitals, a state medical institute and 9 medical schools with over 2,500 students. Doctors in 1969 numbered 7,100; hospital beds, 34,700; 5,300 cots in crèches, with 22,000 in crèche-sections of kindergartens.

FINANCE. Budget estimates (in 1m. new roubles), 1961, 329; 1962, 352; 1963, 393; 1964, 435; 1965, 513; 1966, 576; 1967, 600; 1968, 626; 1969, 681.

AGRICULTURE. On 1 Jan. 1970 there were 490 collective farms and 130 state farms. All ploughing and sowing is mechanized. Livestock included

(1 Jan. 1970) 809,000 cattle, 1,181,000 pigs and 1,344,000 sheep. There were 62,400 tractors and 3,600 combine harvesters.

Output of main agricultural products (1,000 tons) in 1969 (1913 figures in brackets): Wheat, 827 (526); maize, 1,302 (639); sugar-beet, 2,668 (15); sunflower seeds, 339 (9); potatoes, 353 (119); vegetables, 517; fruit, 770; grapes, 978; meat, 169 (53); milk, 759 (210); wool, 3·3 (3); 514m. eggs (275m.).

Bessarabia has an equable climate and very fertile soil. It contains nearly one-third of the vineyards of the USSR. Bessarabia is also rich in fish in the south: sturgeon, mackerel, brill.

INDUSTRY. There are canning plants, wine-making plants, woodworking and metallurgical factories, a factory of ferro-concrete building materials, and footwear and textile plants. Moldavia takes third place in the USSR in the production of wine, tobacco and food-canning. Power output in 1969 was 7,028m. kwh. Production in 1969 included 13·5m. metres of silk fabrics, 10·1m. pairs of leather footwear, 337,400 tons of granulated sugar, 917m. tins of preserves and 24·1m. decalitres of wine. Meat and dairy produce are rapidly expanding food industries.

There are lignite, phosphorites, gypsum and valuable building materials.

In 1969 there were 893,000 industrial and office workers and 66,000 specialists with a higher education working in the national economy.

COMMUNICATIONS. Length of railways, 1,040 km. There is direct air communication with Leningrad, Moscow, Kiev, Lvov and across the Black Sea. There are 10,200 km of motor roads (6,800 hard surface), and 700 km of inland waterways.

Zlatova, Y., and Kotelnikov, V., *Across Moldavia* [English ed.]. Moscow, 1959

ESTONIA
Eesti Nõukogude Sotsialistlik Vabariik

The workers' and soldiers' Soviets in Estonia took over power on 8 Nov. 1917, were overthrown by the German occupying forces in March 1918, and were restored to power as the Germans withdrew in Nov. 1918, establishing the 'Estland Labour Commune'. It was overthrown with the assistance of British naval forces in May 1919, and a democratic republic proclaimed.

The secret protocol of the Soviet–German agreement of 23 Aug. 1939 assigned Estonia to the Soviet sphere of interest. An ultimatum (16 June 1940) led to the formation of a government acceptable to the USSR, which applied for Estonia's admission to the Soviet Union; this was effected by decree of the Supreme Soviet on 6 Aug. The incorporation has been accorded *de facto* recognition by the British Government, but not by the US Government, which continues to recognize an Estonian consul-general in New York.

The Supreme Soviet, elected in 1967, consists of 178 deputies (1 per 10,000 population); 62 are women, 116 Communists.

At elections to district, urban and rural Soviets (16 March 1969), out of 11,293 deputies returned, 5,379 (47·6%) were women, 6,860 (60·7%) non-Party and 6,961 (61·6%) industrial workers and collective farmers.

President, Presidium of the Supreme Soviet: A. P. Vader.
Chairman, Council of Ministers: V. I. Klauson.
First Secretary, Communist Party: I. G. Kebin.

AREA AND POPULATION. Area, 45,100 sq. km (17,410 sq. miles); population, 1,357,000 (Jan. 1970). 74·6% are Estonians, 20·1% Russians, 1·4% Finns. The capital is Tallinn. Other large towns are Tartu (87,000), Parnu, Narva. There are 15 districts, 33 towns and 24 urban settlements.

EDUCATION. Estonia has retained an 11-year school curriculum, when it was reduced to 10 years elsewhere in the USSR. In 1969–70 pupils in 883 primary, secondary and special schools numbered 211,000. There were 22,500 students in 6 higher educational establishments, including Tartu (Dorpat) University, founded in 1632, and 24,500 students in 37 technical colleges.

The Estonian Academy of Sciences, founded in 1946, has 15 institutions with 723 scientific staff; in all, 4,523 scientists are working in 75 institutions.

In 1969 there were 40,000 children attending 542 kindergartens.

Newspapers (1969). There were 43 newspapers, 31 of them in Estonian, with a circulation of 1,005,000 and 884,000 respectively.

HEALTH. In 1969 there were 4,300 doctors and 14,900 hospital beds; 5,100 cots in crèches, with another 10,000 in crèche-sections of kindergartens.

FINANCE. Budget estimates (in 1m. new roubles), 1962, 341; 1963, 351; 1964, 374; 1965, 405; 1966, 431; 1967, 455; 1968, 474; 1969, 548.

AGRICULTURE. Agriculture and dairy farming are the chief occupations. Area under cultivation was 697,000 hectares in 1913, 918,000 hectares in 1940 and 784,000 hectares in 1969. There were 348 agricultural and 26 fishery collectives and 171 state farms in 1969, using 25,000 tractors and 3,000 grain combines. 97% of state farms and 70% of collective farms were receiving electric power.

On 1 Jan. 1970 there were 666,000 head of cattle, 157,000 sheep, 610,000 pigs and 3·3m. poultry.

Output of main agricultural products (1,000 tons) in 1969 (1913 figures in brackets): Potatoes, 1,272 (689); grains, 842 (428); vegetables, 123; meat (slaughter weight), 128 (60); milk, 1,018 (415); wool, 0·4 (0·7); 319m. eggs (67m.).

INDUSTRY. Some 22% of the territory is covered by forests which provide good material for its sawmills, furniture, match and pulp industries, as well as wood fuel. Since the end of the war, 80,000 hectares have been afforested. Over 809,000 hectares of marsh land had been reclaimed by 1969.

Estonia has rich high-quality shale deposits (particularly in the north-east) which are estimated at 3,700m. tons. Shale output was 1·9m. tons in 1940 and 17·5m. in 1969. Gas output (from shale and coal) increased in the same years from 1·7m. cu. metres to 581m. A factory for the production of gas from shale and a pipeline (208 km long) from Kohtla-Järve supplies shale gas to Leningrad and Tallinn. Estonian factories are now turning out agricultural and peat-digging machines, complex control and measuring instruments. The 'Volta' factory in Tallinn produces electric motors.

In the neighbourhood of Tallinn, phosphorites have been found, and in 1947 a plant for refining and for the production of superphosphates was started. Estonia also contains valuable peat deposits, and some of her electrical stations work on peat. A hydro-electric station was erected in 1955 on the Narva. There are 350 rural electric stations. Output of mineral fertilizers in 1969 was 1,033,000 tons; cement, 953,800 tons; paper, 104,200 tons; electric power, 9,878m. kwh.; cotton fabrics, 216m. metres; linen fabrics, 8·7m. metres; leather footwear, 6·7m. pairs; sawn timber, 832,000 cu. metres.

In 1969 there were 603,000 industrial and office workers and 41,000 specialists with a higher education engaged in the national economy.

COMMUNICATIONS. Length of main railways 1,290 km, of secondary lines 730 km. Estonia has 20 ports, but Tallinn handles four-fifths of the total sea-going transport. Inland waterways total 500 km; motor roads 23,200 km (hard surface, 18,000 km). Airlines link Tallinn with Moscow, Leningrad, Riga and the Estonian islands.

BOOKS OF REFERENCE

Druzhinin, V., *Soviet Estonia*. Moscow, 1953 (in English)
Estonia. Basic facts on geography, history and economy. Stockholm, 1948
Jackson, J. H., *Estonia*. London, 1948
Kareda, E., *Estonia in the Soviet Grip*. London, 1949
Pranspill, A., *Estonian Athology*. Milford, Conn., 1957
Silvet, J., *Inglise–eesti sõnaraamat*. Vadstena, 1949
Varetz, E. F. and Tarmisto, V. Y., *Estonia*. Moscow, 1967 (in Russian)
Woods, E. G., *The Baltic Region: A Study in Physical and Human Geography*. London, 1945

LATVIA

Latvijas Padomju Socialistiska Republika

In the part of Latvia unoccupied by the Germans, the Bolsheviks won 72% of the votes in the Constituent Assembly elections (Nov. 1917). Soviet power was proclaimed in Dec. 1917, but was overthrown when the Germans occupied all Latvia (Feb. 1918). Restored when they withdrew (Dec. 1918), it was overthrown once more by combined British naval and German military forces (May–Dec. 1919), and a democratic government set up.

The secret protocol of the Soviet–German agreement of 23 Aug. 1939 assigned Latvia to the Soviet sphere of interest. An ultimatum (16 June 1940) led to the formation of a government acceptable to the USSR, which applied for Latvia's admission to the Soviet Union on 22 July; this was effected by decree of the Supreme Soviet on 5 Aug. The incorporation has been accorded *de facto* recognition by the British Government, but not by the US Government, which continues to recognize the *Chargé d'Affaires*, Dr Anatol Dinbergs, in Washington D.C.

The Supreme Soviet, elected in 1967, consists of 310 deputies (1 per 10,000 population); 101 are women.

At elections to district, urban and rural Soviets (16 March 1969), of 23,905 deputies returned, 11,314 (47·3%) were women, 13,350 (55·8%) non-Party and 15,169 (63·5%) industrial workers and collective farmers.

President, Presidium of the Supreme Soviet: V. P. Ruben.
Chairman, Council of Ministers: Y. Y. Ruben.
First Secretary, Communist Party: A. E. Voss.

AREA AND POPULATION. Latvia has a total area of 63,700 sq. km (25,590 sq. miles). Population, Jan. 1970, 2·4m., of whom 62% are Letts and 27% Russians. There are 26 districts, 56 towns and 35 urban settlements.

The chief town is Riga (the capital); other principal towns are Liepāja (Libau), Daugavpils (Dvinsk) (101,000), Jelgava (Mitau) and Ventspils (Windau).

The Latvian Lutheran Church numbered 600,000 members in 1956.

EDUCATION. In 1969–70 there were 1,246 primary, continuation and secondary schools, with a total of 353,000 pupils: 50,300 children attended 650 kindergartens. Ten places of higher education had 40,400 students, 55 technical colleges had 39,300 students; there were also 21 music and art schools, 3 teachers' training colleges and an agricultural academy. In 1946 an Academy of Sciences was opened which in 1969 had 16 research institutes and a staff of 1,424 scientific workers; there were in all 8,618 scientific workers in 121 research institutions.

Newspapers (1969). There were 85 newspapers (54 in Lettish), with a circulation of 1·25m. and 920,000 respectively.

HEALTH. There were 8,300 doctors, 27,500 hospital beds and 5,200 cots in crèches in 1969, with 13,400 cots in crèche-sections of kindergartens.

FINANCE. Budget estimates (in 1m. new roubles), 1961, 476; 1962, 497; 1963, 525; 1964, 553; 1965, 563; 1966, 614; 1967, 655; 1968, 691; 1969, 771.

AGRICULTURE. Latvia is now no longer mainly an agricultural country. The urban population, 35% of the total in 1939, was 62% in Jan. 1970.

Latvian forest lands, state and private (1,727,000 hectares), produced in 1937–38, 3,439,256 cu. metres of timber; 1969 output, 6·02m. cu. metres.

Area under cultivation was 1·4m. hectares in 1913, 2m. in 1940, 1·5m. in 1969. 1,043,000 hectares of marshland have been drained.

Cattle breeding and dairy farming are the chief agricultural occupations. Oats, barley, rye, potatoes and flax are the main crops.

After the establishment of the Soviet regime about 960,000 hectares were distributed among the landless peasants or those with very small holdings. In 1969 there were 205 state farms and 696 collective farms. In 1970 there were 43,200 tractors and 5,700 grain combine harvesters. By 1 Jan. 1964, all state farms and collective farms were using electric power.

Livestock (1 Jan. 1970): Cattle, 1,144,000 (1939: 1·3m.); sheep, 319,000 (1939: 1·5m.); pigs, 966,000 (1939: 891,500).

Output of main agricultural products (1,000 tons) in 1969 (1913 figures in brackets): Sugar-beet, 159 (0); potatoes, 1,881 (645); all grains, 1,202 (880); vegetables, 219; fruit, 42; meat and fats, 199 (122); milk, 1,745 (673); wool, 0·7 (1·4); 446m. eggs (136m.).

INDUSTRY. Latvia is the main producer of electric railway passenger cars and long-distance telephone exchanges in the USSR, fourth in output of paper and woollen goods, fifth of sawn timber, sixth of mineral fertilizers.

Industrial output in 1969 included 442,600 tons of steel, 305,000 tons of rolled metal, 820,800 tons of cement, 60m. sq. metres of cotton fabrics, 15m. sq. metres of linen fabrics, 12·2m. pairs of leather footwear; 152,200 tons of granulated sugar; woollens, 13·3m. metres; silks, 10·1m. metres; fish catch, 413,000 tons (1940: 12,400 tons). Electric power output was 2,452m. kwh.; radio sets, 1·68m.; paper, 141,500 tons.

The peat deposits extend over 645,000 hectares or about 10% of the total area, and it is estimated that the total deposits of peat are 3,000–4,000m. tons; output, 1966, 1·7m. tons. There are also gypsum deposits; amber is frequently found in the coastal districts.

In 1969 industrial and office workers numbered 1,012,000; 68,000 specialists with a higher education were employed in the national economy.

COMMUNICATIONS. In 1969 the length of railways was 2,640 km, and motor roads, 24,100 km (hard surface, 10,600 km). Riga is the largest port in the Baltic after Leningrad.

BOOKS OF REFERENCE

Latvian Academy of Sciences, *Istoria Latviiskoi SSR*. Riga, 1952–58
Central Statistical Department, Latvian Branch, *Latviiskaya SSR v Tsifrakh*. Riga, 1962
Bilmanis, A., *A History of Latvia*. Princeton Univ. Press, 1951
Roze, B. and K., *Latviska–angliska Vārdnicā*. Göppingen, 1948
Skujenicks, M., *Atlas Statistique de la Lettonie*. Riga, 1938
Spekke, A., *History of Latvia*. Stockholm, 1951
Turkina, E., *Angliski–Latviska Vārdnicā*. Riga, 1948

LITHUANIA
Lietuvas Taryu Socialistine Respublika

In 1914–15 the German army occupied the whole of Lithuania. On its withdrawal (Dec. 1918) Soviets were elected in all towns and a Soviet republic was proclaimed. In the summer of 1919 it was overthrown by Polish, German and nationalist Lithuanian forces, and a democratic republic established.

The secret protocol of the Soviet–German frontier treaty of 28 Sept. 1939 assigned the greater part of Lithuania to the Soviet sphere of influence. In Oct. 1939 the province and city of Vilnius (in Polish occupation 1920–39) were ceded by the USSR. An ultimatum (16 June 1940) led to the formation of a government acceptable to the USSR. A 'people's diet', elected on 14–15 July, applied for Lithuania's admission to the Soviet Union on 22 July, which was effected by decree of the Supreme Soviet on 3 Aug. and included also those parts of Lithuania which had been reserved for inclusion in Germany. This incorporation has been accorded *de facto* recognition by the British Government, but not by the US Government, which continues to recognize a Lithuanian *Chargé d'Affaires* in Washington, D.C.

The Supreme Soviet, elected in 1967, consists of 290 deputies (1 per 15,000 population); 94 are women.

At elections to district, urban and rural Soviets (16 March 1969), of 29,557 deputies returned, 13,043 (44·1%) were women, 16,689 (56·5%) non-Party and 18,623 (63%) industrial workers and collective farmers.

President, Presidium of the Supreme Soviet: M. Y. Shumauskas.
Chairman, Council of Ministers: J. A. Maniusis.
First Secretary, Communist Party: A. Y. Snechkus.

AREA AND POPULATION. The total area of Lithuania is 65,200 sq. km (25,170 sq. miles) and the population (Jan. 1970) 3·1m., of whom 79% were Lithuanians, 8·5% Russians and 8·5% Poles. The capital is Vilnius (Vilna). Other large towns are Káunas (Kovno), Klaipéda (Memel), Šauliai and Panevéžys There are 44 rural districts, 92 towns and 23 urban settlements.

In 1956, the Lithuanian Lutheran Church had 215,000 members; Roman Catholics, including those in Estonia and Latvia, numbered 2·5m.

EDUCATION. In 1969–70 there were 573,000 pupils in 3,955 primary, secondary and special schools. The University of Vytautas the Great, at Káunas, was opened on 16 Feb. 1922. On 15 Jan. 1940 certain faculties were transferred to Vilnius as an independent institution to form the University of Vilnius There were 12 higher educational institutions with 55,700 students: in 81 technical colleges of all kinds there were 64,700 students. The Lithuanian Academy of Sciences, founded in 1941, had 12 institutions with a total scientific staff of 1,036; there were 106 scientific institutions with 8,270 research personnel. 57,300 children in 1969 were attending 697 kindergartens.

Newspapers (1969). Of 91 newspapers, 73 were in Lithuanian, with a circulation of 2,028,000 and 1,808,000 respectively.

HEALTH. In 1969 there were 8,300 doctors, 31,400 hospital beds and 4,700 cots in crèches, with 12,200 in crèche-sections of kindergartens.

FINANCE. Budget estimates (in 1m. new roubles), 1961, 546; 1962, 580; 1963, 630; 1964, 693; 1965, 765; 1966, 839; 1967, 932; 1968, 1,022; 1969, 1,112.

AGRICULTURE. Lithuania before 1940 was a mainly agricultural country, but has since been considerably industrialized. The urban population was 23% of the total in 1937 and 50% in Jan. 1970. The resources of the country consist of timber and agricultural produce. Of the total area, 49·1% is arable land, 22·2% meadow and pasture land, 16·3% forests and 12·4% unproductive lands.

Area under cultivation in 1913 was 1·9m.; in 1938, 2·7m.; in 1969, 2·3m. hectares. By 1969 over 1,509,000 hectares of swamps had been drained.

Output of main agricultural products (1,000 tons) in 1969 (1913 figures in brackets): All grains, 2,187 (1,449); sugar-beet, 473 (0); flax, 11 (17); potatoes, 2,926 (1,375); vegetables, 322; fruit, 65; meat and fats, 367 (159); milk, 2,465 (832); wool, 0·3 (1·5); 674m. eggs (264m.).

By 1970 all collective and state farms had an average of 500 hectares of drained land, raising grain yields from 1·8 tons per hectare in 1966 to 2·8 in 1970.

On 1 Jan. 1970 there were 1,714,000 cattle, 2·1m. pigs, 152,000 sheep and 7,000 goats.

Forests cover 1,554,000 hectares; 70% of the forests consist of conifers, mostly pines. Peat reserves total 4,000m. cu. metres.

Between 1940 and 1947 about 575,500 hectares (about 1·4m. acres) were distributed among the landless and poor peasant farmers. In 1969 there were 67,700 tractors and 8,500 grain combines serving 1,455 collective farms and 308 state farms. Over 90% of collective farms and all state farms received electric power in 1963.

INDUSTRY. Heavy engineering, shipbuilding and building material industries are developing. Industrial output included, in 1969, 880,000 tons of cement, 30·2m. metres of cotton fabrics, 10·3m. pairs of leather footwear, 135,400 tons of granulated sugar, 19·6m. metres of linens, 10m. metres of woollens, 1·36m. cu. metres of sawn timber and 95,800 tons of paper; electric power, 7,028m. kwh.

In 1969 there were 1·13m. industrial and office workers and 70,000 specialists with a higher education employed in the national economy.

COMMUNICATIONS. Length of railways, 2,000 km. Vilnius has one of the largest airports of the USSR. There are 33,900 km of motor roads (13,900 km hard surface) and 600 km of inland waterways.

BOOKS OF REFERENCE

Jurgéla, C. R., *History of the Lithuanian Nation*. New York, 1948
Metelsky, G., *Lithuania, land of the Niemen*. Moscow, 1959
Peteraitis, V., *Lithuanian–English Dictionary*. 2 vols. Chicago, 1960

SOVIET CENTRAL ASIA

Soviet Central Asia embraces the Kazakh Soviet Socialist Republic, the Uzbek Soviet Socialist Republic, the Turkmen Soviet Socialist Republic, the Tadzhik Soviet Socialist Republic and the Kirghiz Soviet Socialist Republic.

Turkestan (by which name part of this territory was then known) was conquered by the Russians in the 1860s. In 1866 Tashkent was occupied and in 1868 Samarkand, and subsequently further territory was conquered and united with Russian Turkestan. In the 1870s Bokhara was subjugated, the emir, by the agreement of 1873, recognizing the suzerainty of Russia. In the same year Khiva became a vassal state to Russia. Until 1917 Russian Central Asia was divided politically into the Khanate of Khiva, the Emirate of Bokhara and the Governor-Generalship of Turkestan.

In the summer of 1919 the authority of the Soviet Government became definitely established in these regions. The Khan of Khiva was deposed in Feb. 1920, and a People's Soviet Republic was set up, the medieval name of Khorezm being revived. In Aug. 1920 the Emir of Bokhara suffered the same fate, and a similar regime was set up in Bokhara. The former Governor-Generalship of Turkestan was constituted an Autonomous Soviet Socialist Republic within the RSFSR on 11 April 1921.

In the autumn of 1924 the Soviets of the Turkestan, Bokhara and Khiva republics decided to redistribute the territories of these republics on a nationality basis; at the same time Bokhara and Khiva became Socialist Republics. The redistribution was completed in May 1925, when the new states of Uzbekistan, Turkmenistan and Tadzhikistan and several autonomous regions were established. The remaining districts of Turkestan populated by Kazakhs were united with Kazakhstan. Kirghizia, until then part of the RSFSR, was established as a Union Republic in 1936.

BOOKS OF REFERENCE

Nove, A. and Newth, J. A., *The Soviet Middle East*. London, 1967
Vaidyanathy, R., *The formation of the Soviet Central Asian Republics*. New Delhi, 1967
Wheeler, G., *The Modern History of Soviet Central Asia*. London, 1964
Yuldashev, M. (ed.), *Oktiabrskaya Sotsialisticheskaya Revolutsia i Grajdanskaya Voina v Turkestane*. Tashkent, 1957
Zevelyov, A. (ed.), *Za Sovetski Turkestan*. Tashkent, 1963

KAZAKHSTAN

Kazak Soviettik Sotzialistik Respublikasy

On 26 Aug. 1920 Uralsk, Turgai, Akmolinsk and Semipalatinsk provinces formed the Kazakh Soviet Socialist Republic within the RSFSR. It was made a constituent republic of the USSR on 5 Dec. 1936. To this republic were added the parts of the former Governorship of Turkestan inhabited by a majority of Kazakhs. It consists of the following regions: Aktyubinsk, Alma-Ata, Chimkent, Dzhambul, East Kazakhstan, Guryev, Karaganda, Kokchetav, Kustanai, Tselinograd, Kzyl-Orda, North Kazakhstan, Pavlodar, Semipalatinsk, Taldy-Kurgan, Turgai, Uralsk. The capital is Alma-Ata, formerly Verny.

Kazakhstan is bounded on the west by the Caspian Sea and the RSFSR, on the east by China, on the north by the RSFSR and on the south by Uzbekistan and Kirghizia.

The Supreme Soviet, elected in 1967, consists of 476 deputies (1 per 20,000 population); 160 are women.

At elections to the regional, district, urban and rural Soviets (16 March 1969), out of 109,160 deputies returned, 47,184 (43·2%) were women, 62,457 (57·2%) non-Party and 66,706 (61·1%) industrial workers and collective farmers.

President, Presidium of the Supreme Soviet: S. B. Niyazbekov.
Chairman, Council of Ministers: B. A. Ashimov.
First Secretary, Communist Party: D. A. Kunayev.

AREA AND POPULATION. The area of the republic is 2,715,100 sq. km (1,048,030 sq. miles). It is the next in size to the RSFSR, is far larger than all the other Central Asian Soviet Republics combined and stretches nearly 3,000 km from west to east and over 1,500 km from north to south. Population (Jan. 1970), 12·85m., of whom 51% live in urban areas. The Kazakhs form nearly 30%, and Russians and Ukrainians together about 51% (owing to the industrialization of the country since 1941 and the opening of virgin lands since 1945). The population includes over 100 nationalities.

The capital is Alma-Ata; other large towns are Karaganda, Semipalatinsk, Chimkent and Petropavlovsk. In all there are 77 towns, 173 urban settlements and 181 rural districts.

EDUCATION. Nearly the whole population is literate. In 1969–70 there were 3,154,000 pupils at 10,154 elementary and secondary schools; 187 technical colleges with 209,700 students, 43 higher educational institutions with 195,700 students, and 163 research institutes with 25,319 scientific personnel. The Kazakh Academy of Sciences, founded in 1945, had, in 1969, 35 institutions, the scientific staff of which numbered 3,001. 379,800 children were attending 4,991 kindergartens.

Newspapers (1969). Of 354 newspapers, 127 were in the Kazakh language, with a circulation of 4,056,000 and 1·4m. respectively.

HEALTH. In 1969 there were 27,200 doctors and 146,100 hospital beds; cots in crèches, 47,100, with 116,500 in crèche-sections of kindergartens.

FINANCE. The budget (in 1m. new roubles) balanced as follows: 1963, 3,566; 1964, 3,913; 1965, 3,981; 1966, 3,990; 1967, 3,984; 1968, 4,240; 1969, 4,561.

AGRICULTURE. Kazakh agriculture has changed from primarily nomad cattle breeding to production of grain, cotton and other industrial crops. In 1969 the crop area was 32m. hectares—over 14% of the total cultivated area of the USSR (1913, 4·2m.; 1940, 6·8m.).

1,209,000 hectares of land have an irrigation network.

The 'Ukrainka' winter wheat has been transformed into a spring wheat suitable for cultivation in Kazakhstan. Tobacco, rubber plants and mustard are also cultivated. Kazakhstan has rich orchards and vineyards; 18,000 hectares were under vines and 91,000 under orchards in 1969. Between 1954 and 1959, over 23m. hectares of virgin and long fallow land were opened up, 544 new state grain farms being organized for the purpose. Grain deliveries to the state were 10·5m. tons in 1960; 7·5m. in 1961; 8·2m. in 1962; 4·8m. in 1963; 15·4m. in 1964; 2·4m. in 1965; 17m. in 1966; 8·2m. in 1967; 11·7m. in 1968; 11m. in 1969.

Kazakhstan is noted for its livestock, particularly its sheep, from which excellent quality wool is obtained. The Akharomerino is a newly developed crossbreed of merino sheep and the wild Akhar mountain ram. Livestock on 1 Jan. 1970 included 7·2m. cattle, 29·7m. sheep, 547,000 goats and 1,617,000 pigs.

There were, in 1969, 452 collective farms and 1,593 state farms with 481,900 tractors and 95,200 grain combine harvesters. There were 5,293 rural power stations of 307,800 kwh. capacity.

Output of main agricultural products (1m. tons) in 1969 (1913 figures in brackets): All grains, 21·6 (2·2); cotton, 0·9 (0·015); sugar-beet, 2·3 (0); potatoes, 2·1 (0·18); vegetables, 0·7; meat, 0·8 (0·44); milk, 3·7 (11·80); 1,480m. eggs (233m.); wool, 0·8 (0·04).

INDUSTRY. Kazakhstan is extremely rich in mineral resources. Coal and tungsten in Karaganda (in the centre), oil along the river Emba (in the west), copper, lead and zinc—Kazakhstan contains about one-half of the total deposits of these three metals contained in the USSR—Iceland spar (in the south), nickel and chromium in the Kustanai and Semipalatinsk regions, molybdenum and other minerals. In 1943 big deposits of manganese were found in Eastern Kazakhstan; new coal seams were also discovered there. In South Kazakhstan new copper and bauxite deposits have been found.

Coal, oil, non-ferrous metallurgy, heavy engineering and chemical industries have brought Kazakhstan to the third place among the industrial republics of the USSR.

Coal output in 1969 was 57·5m. tons; oil output, 10·1m. tons; steel, 1,325,000 tons; rolled metal, 1,786,000 tons; cement, 4,774,000 tons; mineral fertilizers, 1,124,000 tons; cotton fabrics, 57·3m. metres; leather footwear, 25·8m. pairs; woollen fabrics, 5m. metres; granulated sugar, 177,000 tons. The Leninogorsk and Chimkent lead plants, the Balkhash, Irtysh and Karaskpai copper-smelting works and others supply the country with nonferrous metals. A meat-packing plant has been built in Semipalatinsk, a fish cannery in Guryev, a chemical plant in Aktyubinsk and a superphosphate plant in Dzhambul; 34 new industrial plants began operating in 1969. The oil industry in Emba and Aktyubinsk yields high-quality aviation oil. Iron ore output in 1968 was 16·5m. tons.

Aviation plays an important part in agriculture. About 1m. hectares have in recent years been treated from the air (destruction of pests, surface feeding of sugar-beet plantations, pollination of orchards, etc.).

Among recent enterprises are a champagne combine in Alma-Ata, a canning works for tinned milk in Pavlodar, meat-packing plants in Tselinograd, Aktiubinsk and Pavlodar, a tea-packing factory in Alma-Ata.

Electric power output in 1969 was 30,982m. kwh.

There were, in 1969, 4·55m. (average for year) industrial and office workers in the national economy and 242,000 specialists with a higher education.

RAILWAYS. A 430-km railway line between the settlements of Mointi and Chu in Kazakhstan to complete the Transkazakh trunk line, connecting Petropavlovsk, Akmolinsk, Karaganda and Balkhash, was opened in 1953. The new line links the Transkazakh trunk line with the Turkestan–Siberian railway carrying Karaganda coal to South Kazakhstan. The Akmolinsk–Pavlodar railway (438 km), a section of the South Siberian line, was opened in Dec. 1953. Other lines in operation are Dzhambul–Chalaktan, Akmolinsk–Kartaly, Uralsk–Iletsk, Guriev–Kandagach. In 1969 the total length of railways in operation was 13,400 km. Over 600 km of narrow-gauge line and 700 km. of broad-gauge line were built in the virgin lands area in 1951–57.

ROADS. In 1969 there were 108,900 km of motor roads (37,200 km hard surface).

INLAND WATERWAYS. 6,200 km. A 500-km canal to bring water from the Irtysh at Yermak, below Pavlodar, along the Shiderta, Tuzda and Nura rivers to the new industrial centre of Karaganda was begun in 1960. It is to irrigate in all 60,000 hectares and provide water for a number of new industrial towns.

BOOKS OF REFERENCE

Central Statistical Dept. of Kazakh SSR., *Narodnoye Hoziaistvo Kazakhstana.* Alma-Ata,1968
Alampiev, P., *Soviet Kazakhstan.* Moscow, 1958.—*Where Economic Inequality is no More.* Moscow, 1959
Grauman, J., and others, *The Kazakhs under Changing Russian Regimes.* Washington, 1951
Lias, G., *Kazak Exodus.* London, 1956

TURKMENISTAN
Tiurkmenostan Soviet Sotsialistik Respublikasy

The Turkmen Soviet Socialit Republic was formed on 27 Oct. 1924 and covers the territory of the former Trans-Caspian Region of Turkestan, the Charjiui vilayet of Bokhara and a part of Khiva situated on the right bank of the Oxus. In May 1925 the Turkmen Republic entered the Soviet Union as one of its constituent republics. It is bounded on the north by the Autonomous Kara-Kalpak Republic, a constituent of Uzbekistan, by Iran and Afghánistán on the south, by the Uzbek Republic on the east and the Caspian Sea on the west.

The Supreme Soviet, elected in 1967, consists of 285 deputies (1 per 5,000 population); 100 are women.

At elections to regional, district, urban and rural Soviets (16 March 1969), of 18,481 deputies returned, 7,763 (42%) were women, 10,473 (56·7%) non-Party and 12,363 (66·9%) industrial workers and collective farmers.

President, Presidium of the Supreme Soviet: A. M. Klychev.
Chairman, Council of Ministers: O. N. Orazmuhamedov.
First Secretary, Communist Party: M. Gapurov.

AREA AND POPULATION. The principal Turkmen tribes are the Tekkés of Merv and the Tekkés of the Attok, the Ersaris, Yomuds and Goklans. All speak closely related varieties of a Turkoman language (of the south-western group of Turk languages); many are Sunni Mohammedans. The country passed under Russian control in 1881, after the fall of the Turkoman stronghold of Gök-Tépé. Over 60% of the population are Turkmenians, most of whom were nomads before the First World War. Over 17% are Russians living mostly in urban areas, and 8·3% Uzbeks. There are also Kazakhs, Tartars, Ukrainians, Armenians and others.

The area of Turkmenistan is 488,100 sq. km (186,400 sq. miles), and its population in Jan. 1970 was 2,158,000.

There are 3 regions: Maruy, Chardzhou and Tashauz, comprising 34 rural districts, 15 towns and 67 urban settlements.

The capital is Ashkhabad (Poltoratsk); other large towns are Chardzhou, Maruy (Merv), Krasnovodsk and Nebit-Dag.

EDUCATION. In 1969–70 there were 1,653 primary and secondary schools with 536,000 pupils, 5 higher educational institutions with 29,200 students, 29 technical colleges with 28,100 students, and 11 music and art schools. The Turkmen Academy of Sciences directs the work of 16 learned institutions with a staff of 650 scientists; there were 56 research institutions in all, with 3,483 research workers, in 1965. A Turkmenian State University was opened in 1951: in 1961 it had 4,180 students.

In 1969, 51,900 children were attending 749 kindergartens.

Newspapers (1969). Of 49 newspapers, 32 were in the Turkmen language, with a circulation of 660,000 and 483,000 respectively.

HEALTH. In 1969 there were 4,600 doctors, 21,700 hospital beds and 9,700 cots in crèches, with 13,400 in crèche-sections of kindergartens.

FINANCE. Budget estimates (in 1m. new roubles), 1961, 363; 1962, 379; 1963, 416; 1964, 422; 1965, 462; 1966, 481; 1967, 520; 1968, 545; 1969, 600.

AGRICULTURE. The main occupation of the people is agriculture, based on irrigation. Turkmenistan produces cotton, wool, Astrakhan fur, etc. It is also famous for its carpets, and produces a special breed of Turkoman horses and the famous Karakul sheep.

There were 330 collective farms and 51 state farms in 1969, with 41,800 tractors and 1,000 grain combines. There were 608 rural power stations.

A considerable area is under Egyptian cotton, and from it has been evolved an original Soviet long-fibred cotton.

The main grain grown is maize. Sericulture, fruit and vegetable growing are also important; dates, olives, figs, sesame and other southern plants are grown. There is fishing in the Caspian. 560,000 hectares were under cultivation in 1969 (1913, 318,000; 1940, 411,000). Wine production in 1969 was 121,700 hectolitres.

Geological researches have revealed extensive zones of subterranean waters in the Kara-Kum Desert, and wells and water reservoirs have been and are being constructed, irrigating over 900,000 hectares.

Livestock on 1 Jan. 1970: Cattle, 433,000; pigs, 49,000; sheep, 3,775,000; goats, 183,000.

Output of main agricultural products (1,000 tons) in 1969 (1913 figures in brackets): Wheat, 36 (113); cotton, 692 (69); vegetables, 141; grapes, 7; fruit, 8; meat, 47 (58); milk, 170 (63); wool, 12·2 (9·7); 95m. eggs (18m.).

INDUSTRY. Turkmenistan is rich in minerals, such as ozocerite, oil, coal, sulphur and salt. Industry is being developed, and there are now chemical, tailoring, textile, light, food, agricultural implements, cement and other factories, oil refineries, as well as ore-mining.

In the Kara-Kum Desert deposits of magnesium, minerals and coal were discovered, as well as some 50 new saltmines. Here a new oil town, Nebit-Dag, has sprung up. On the Kara-Bogaz bay a sulphate industry has been developed. Industrial output in 1969 included 13·7m. tons of oil, 308,300 tons of cement, 20·5m. metres of cotton fabrics, 1·9m. pairs of leather footwear. Electric power output was 1,738m. kwh. (in 1940: 83·5m.). 7,535m. cu. metres of natural gas were produced.

In 1969 there were 459,000 industrial and office workers in the national economy; specialists with a higher education numbered 38,000.

COMMUNICATIONS. Length of motor roads 8,700 km (4,300 km hard surface). Motor communication exists between Ashkhabad and Meshed (Iran).

Length of railways, 2,110 km. The line Chardzhou–Kungrad crosses the Chardzhou and Tashauz regions of Turkmenia and runs across Uzbekistan. Another line connects Chardzhou and Urgench. Inland waterways, 1,300 km.

Airlines connect Leninsk and Tashauz, and Ashkhabad and remote areas in the west, north and east.

Freikin, Z. G., *Turkmenskaya SSR*. Moscow, 1954

UZBEKISTAN
Ozbekiston Soviet Sotsialistik Respublikasy

In Oct. 1917 the Tashkent Soviet assumed authority, and in the following years established its power throughout Turkestan. The semi-independent Khanates of Khiva and Bokhara were first (1920) transformed into 'People's Republics', then (1923–24) into Soviet Socialist Republics and finally merged in the Uzbek SSR and other republics.

The Uzbek Soviet Socialist Republic was formed on 5 Dec. 1924 from lands formerly included in Turkestan. It includes a large part of the Samarkand region, the southern part of the Syr Darya, Western Ferghana, the western plains of Bukhara, the Kara-Kalpak ASSR and the Uzbek regions of Khorezm. In May 1925 Uzbekistan, by the decision of the Congress of Soviets of the USSR, was accepted as one of the constituent republics in the Soviet Union.

Uzbekistan is bordered on the north by the Kazakh Soviet Socialist Republic, on the east by the Kirghiz Soviet Socialist Republic and the Tadzhik Soviet Socialist Republic, on the south by Afghánistán and on the west by the Turkmen Soviet Socialist Republic.

The Supreme Soviet, elected in 1967, consists of 458 deputies (1 per 15,000 population); 141 are women.

At elections to the regional, district, urban and rural Soviets (16 March 1969), of 82,175 deputies returned, 36,727 (44·7%) were women, 44,056 (53·6%) non-Party and 54,530 (66·4%) industrial workers and collective farmers.

President, Presidium of the Supreme Soviet: Nazar Matchanov.
Chairman, Council of Ministers: Rakhmankul Kurbanov.
First Secretary, Communist Party: S. R. Rashidov.

AREA AND POPULATION. The Uzbeks, who form 62% of the population, were the ruling race in Central Asia, until the arrival of the Russians during the third quarter of the 19th century. The several native states over which Uzbek dynasties formerly ruled were founded in the 15th century upon the ruins of Tamerlane's empire. The Uzbek speak Jagatai Turk, which is related to Osmanli and Azerbaijan Turk; many are Sunni Mohammedans. Russians number 13·5%, other Central Asians 11·8%, Tatars 5·5%.

The area of Uzbekistan is 449,600 sq. km (173,546 sq. miles). The population in Jan. 1970 was 11·96m. (36% urban). The country comprises the following regions: Andijan, Bukhara, Ferghana, Kashkadar, Khorezm, Namangan, Samarkand, Surkhan-Darya, Syr-Darya (formed 16 Feb. 1963), Tashkent and the Autonomous Soviet Republic of Kara-Kalpakia. The capital of the Republic is Tashkent; other large towns are Samarkand, Andizhan, Namangan.

On 19 Sept. 1963 the Supreme Soviet of the USSR confirmed decisions of the Supreme Soviets of Kazakhstan and Uzbekistan, transferring over 40,000 sq. km from the former to the latter to ensure more efficient use of the Hungry Steppe.

EDUCATION. In 1969–70 there were 9,291 elementary and secondary schools with 3,154,000 pupils, 38 higher educational establishments with 231,900 students and 159 technical colleges with 155,600 students. Uzbekistan has an Academy of Sciences and 146 research institutes with 24,079 scientific staff, 3,275 of them in

30 institutions of the Uzbek Academy of Sciences. There are universities and medical schools in Tashkent and Samarkand. In 1969, 230,200 children were attending 2,606 kindergartens.

The Uzbek Arabic script was in 1929 replaced by the Latin alphabet which in 1940 was superseded by one of the Cyrillic alphabet.

Newspapers (1969). There were 135 newspapers in the Uzbek and Kara-Kalpak languages out of a total of 235, with a circulation of 2,427,000 and 3·4m. respectively.

HEALTH. In 1969 there were 22,700 doctors and 119,100 hospital beds; cots in permanent crèches, 39,600, with 63,500 in crèche-sections of kindergartens.

FINANCE. Budget estimates (in 1m. new roubles), 1962, 1,240; 1963, 1,364; 1964, 1,599; 1965, 1,841; 1966, 1,951; 1967, 2,225; 1968, 2,344; 1969, 2,616.

AGRICULTURE. Uzbekistan is a land of intensive farming, based on artificial irrigation. It is the chief cotton-growing area in the USSR and the third in the world. About 2·7m. hectares of collective and state farmland have irrigation networks; 2·6m. are in full use.

In 1939 the Ferghana Canal (270 km) was built. During 1940, among the irrigation canals completed were: the North Ferghana Canal (165 km), and Andreev South Ferghana Canal (108 km) and the first section of the Tashkent Canal (63 km). A canal from the Amu-Darya to Bokhara across the Kzil-Kum and Ust-Urt deserts (180 km) was completed in 1965. A 200-km canal joining the river Zeravshan with the Kashka Darya at the village of Paruz was completed in Aug. 1955; it is part of the Iski–Angara Canal. The first section (93 km) of a canal irrigating the southern 'Hungry Steppe' was opened in 1960; 500,000 hectares of this desert were under cultivation in 1967.

Agriculture flourishes, particularly in the well-watered, warm, rich oases areas, such as the Ferghana valley, Zeravshan, Tashkent and Khorezm, where cotton, fruit, silk and rice are cultivated. In the higher-lying plains grain is grown; the wide desert and semi-desert area of Western Uzbekistan is mainly given to pasture land and the breeding of the Karakul sheep; there is a Karakul institute at Samarkand.

Orchards occupied 146,000 hectares and vineyards 55,000 hectares in 1969. The Central Asian Branch of the Scientific Research Institute of Viticulture in Tashkent has produced now frost resistant grapes by crossing the wild Amur grape with Central Asian and European types. In 1969 there were 1,049 collective farms and 354 state farms, with 204,100 tractors and 7,000 grain combines. Ploughing, cotton-sowing and cultivation are completely mechanized.

Uzbekistan provides 67% of the total cotton, 50% of the total rice and 60% of the total lucerne grown in the USSR. The area under crops was 2,189,000 hectares in 1913, 3,036,000 hectares in 1940 and 3·5m. hectares in 1969.

Livestock on 1 Jan. 1970: 2·89m. cattle, 6·9m. sheep, 410,000 goats and 271,000 pigs.

Output of main agricultural products (1,000 tons) in 1969 (1913 figures in brackets): Wheat, 385 (513); maize, 66 (39); cotton, 3,861 (517); potatoes, 170 (46); fruit, 168; grapes, 139; meat, 200 (89); milk, 1,276 (231); wool, 20 (5·3); 734m. eggs (87m.).

Afforestation over an area of 50,000 hectares has been carried out to protect the Bokhara and Karakul oases from the advancing Kzyl-Kum sands and to stop the sand-drifts in a number of districts of Central Ferghana.

Fish abound in the mouth of the Amu-Darya.

INDUSTRY. Of its mineral resources, in addition to oil and coal, copper and building materials and ozocerite deposits are now also exploited. New very rich coal deposits were discovered in 1944 and 1947 near Tashkent.

There are nearly 1,600 factories and mills. They include a factory of agricultural machinery (in Tashkent), a cement factory, a sulphur-mine, an oxygen factory, a paper-mill, a leather factory, textile-mills, clothing factories, iron and steel works, the Chirchik electro-chemical plant, a superphosphate plant in Kokand and oil refineries, coalmines, etc. Output in 1969 included 4·2m. tons of coal, 383,000 tons of steel, 1·8m. tons of oil, 2,899,500 tons of cement, 3·5m. tons of mineral fertilizers, 214m. metres of cotton fabrics, 48·7m. metres of silk fabrics, 17·8m. pairs of leather footwear, 731,000 hectolitres of wine (apart from collective farm output). Gold is being worked at Murantau, Chadak and Kochbulak.

There are some 800 electrical power stations in the republic. Power output in 1969 was 15,776m. kwh. (481m. kwh. in 1940). Two natural-gas pipelines (Djaikak–Tashkent, Ferghana–Kokand) and a third from Bukhara to the Urals are operating. Natural gas output (1969) was 30,769m. cu. metres.

In 1969 there were 2·6m. industrial and office workers in the national economy and 216,000 specialists with a higher education.

COMMUNICATIONS. The total length of railway in 1969 was 2,870 km. Branches lead to Karshe-Kitab, Kerki-Termez, Jalal-Abad, Namangan, Andijan and other centres. In 1947–55 a new line was built from Chardzhou to Kungrad.

The Great Uzbek Highway was completed in April 1941. Total length of motor roads in 1969 was 29,500 km (hard surface, 20,600 km). Inland waterways, 1,200 km.

An airline, serving all of Central Asia, is most developed in Uzbekistan.

Istoria Uzbekskoi SSSR. 2 vols. Tashkent, 1955–57
Pobeda Oktiabrskoi Revolutsii v Uzbekistane. Vol. I. Tashkent, 1963

KARA-KALPAK AUTONOMOUS SOVIET SOCIALIST REPUBLIC

Area, 165,600 sq. km (63,920 sq. miles); population (Jan. 1970), 702,000. Capital, Nukus (74,000). The Karakalpaks are first mentioned in written records in the 16th century as tributary to Bokhara, and later to the Kazakh Khanate. In the second half of the 19th century, as a result of the Russian conquest of Central Asia, they came under Russian rule. On 11 May 1925 the territory was constituted within the then Kazakh Autonomous Republic (of the Russian Federation) as an Autonomous Region. On 20 March 1932 it became an Autonomous Republic within the Russian Federation, and on 5 Dec. 1936 it became part of the Uzbek SSR.

164 deputies were elected on 12 March 1967, of whom 56 are women.

Its manufactures are in the field of light industry—bricks, leather goods, furniture, canning, wine. Output of cotton in 1969 was 222,000 tons (in 1913: 8,000 tons). There were 4,217 tractors. Cattle numbered 249,000 and sheep 420,000. There were 42 collective and 52 state farms.

In 1969 there were 173,000 pupils in 605 schools; there are also a pedagogical institute and teachers' training college with 8,400 students and a national research institute with 5,500 students.

There were 800 doctors and 7,000 hospital beds.

TADZHIKISTAN
Respublikai Sovieth Sotsialistii Tojikiston

The Tadzhik Soviet Socialist Republic was formed from those regions of Bokhara and Turkestan where the population consisted mainly of Tadzhiks. It was admitted as a constituent republic of the Soviet Union on 5 Dec. 1929.

Tadzhikistan is situated between 39° 40′ and 36° 40′ N. lat. and 67° 20′ and 75° E. long., north of the Oxus (Amu-Darya). On the west and north it is bordered by Uzbekistan and by the Kirghiz Soviet Socialist Republic; on the east by Chinese Turkestan and on the south by Afghánistán. It consists of 40 rural districts, 18 towns and 43 urban settlements, and includes the Gorno-Badakhshan Autonomous Region. Its highest mountains are Communism Peak (7,495 metres) and Lenin Peak (7,127 metres). Even the lowest valleys in the Pamirs are not below 3,500 metres above sea-level. The huge mountain glaciers are the source of many rapid rivers—the tributaries of the Amu-Darya, which flows from east to west along the southern border of Tadzhikistan. A Leninabad region, about one-sixth of the Republic's territory, has been formed.

The Supreme Soviet, elected in 1967, consists of 315 deputies (1 per 5,000 population); 104 are women.

At elections to the district, urban and rural Soviets and the regional Soviet of Gorno-Badakhshan (16 March 1969), out of 20,455 deputies returned, 9,000 (44%) were women, 11,006 (53·8%) non-Party and 13,708 (67%) industrial workers and collective farmers.

President, Presidium of the Supreme Soviet: Makhmadullo Kholov.
Chairman, Council of Ministers: Abdulahad Kakharov.
First Secretary, Communist Party: D. Rasulov.

AREA AND POPULATION. About 53% of the population are Tadzhiks. They speak an Iranian dialect, little different from Persian, and they are considered to be the descendants of the original Aryan population of Turkestan. Unlike the Persians, the Tadzhiks are mostly Sunnis. Of the rest, 23% are Uzbeks living in the north-west of the Republic. Russians and Ukrainians number 14·7%.

The area of the territory is 143,100 sq. km (55,240 sq. miles). Population (Jan. 1970), 2·9m. The capital is Dushanbe. Other large towns are Leninabad (103,000), Kurgan-Tyube, Kulyab.

EDUCATION. In 1969–70 there were 3,063 primary and secondary schools with 740,000 pupils, 7 higher educational institutions with 42,600 students and 36 technical colleges with 34,000 students; the Tadzhik state university had 4,350 students. In 1969, 44,500 children were attending 419 kindergartens. In 1951 an Academy of Sciences was established; it has 16 institutions, the scientific staff of which numbers 963; there are 60 research institutions in all, with 4,725 scientific personnel. The Pamir research station is the highest altitude meteorological observatory in the world.

In 1940 a new alphabet based on Russian was introduced.

Newspapers (1969). 62 newspapers had a total circulation of 835,000. Of these, 51 with 564,000 circulation, were in Tadzhik.

HEALTH. There are 120 hospitals as well as maternity homes, clinics and special institutes to combat tropical diseases. There were 4,600 doctors in 1969 and 27,700 hospital beds; 5,400 cots in crèches, with 14,100 in crèche-sections of kindergartens.

FINANCE. Budget estimates (in 1m. new roubles), 1962, 360; 1963, 389; 1964, 435; 1965, 491; 1966, 531; 1967, 539; 1968, 581; 1969 661.

AGRICULTURE. The occupations of the population are mainly farming, horticulture and cattle breeding. Area under crops in 1969 was 720,000 hectares (1913, 494,000 hectares; 1940, 807,000). Wine production, 1969, was 331,900 hectolitres.

There are 43,000 km of irrigation canals: the irrigation networks cover about 510,000 hectares of land.

Tadzhikistan grows many varieties of fruit, including apricots, figs, olives, pomegranates, a local variety of lemons and oranges, and in the south sugar-cane has been grown. Even on the highest mountain plateaux of the Pamirs, the roof of the world, the biological station of Tadzhikistan (3,860 metres above sea-level) has succeeded in raising crops of 60 varieties of barley, 10 varieties of oats, 4 of wheat, as well as vegetables. Eucalyptus and geranium are grown for the perfumery industry. Jute, rice and millet are also grown.

Tadzhikistan contains rich pasture lands, and cattle breeding is a very important branch of its agriculture. Livestock on 1 Jan. 1970: 973,000 cattle, 2,073,000 sheep, 424,000 goats and 62,000 pigs.

The Gissar sheep is famous for its meat and fat in the south; the Karakul sheep is widely bred for its wool.

There were 302 collective farms (208 with electric power) and 68 state farms in 1969; with 35,100 tractors and 1,200 combine harvesters.

Output of main agricultural products (1,000 tons) in 1969 (1913 figures in brackets): Wheat, 113 (133); maize, 5 (2); cotton, 626 (32); potatoes, 48 (10); vegetables, 163; fruit, 98; grapes, 17; meat, 57 (48); milk, 260 (102); wool, 4·7 (2·1); 114m. eggs (20m.).

INDUSTRY. The original small-scale handicraft industries have been replaced by big industrial enterprises, including mining, engineering, food, textile, clothing and silk factories.

There are rich deposits of brown coal, lead, zinc and oil (in the north of the Republic), rare elements, such as uranium, radium, arsenic and bismuth. Asbestos, mica, corundum and emery, lapis lazuli, potassium salts, sulphur and other minerals have been found in other parts of the Republic. Of 270 known deposits, 60 are being exploited.

Industrial output in 1969 included: 818,000 tons of coal, 155,000 tons of oil, 790,000 tons of cement, 98·6m. metres of cotton fabrics, 44·3m. metres of silk fabrics; leather footwear, 5·4m. pairs.

There are 80 big electrical stations. The hydro-electric Varzob station began to work in 1954, that at Kairak-Kum on the Syr Darya River was completed in 1957 and 2 more at Murgab in 1964. Output in 1969 was 2,995m. kwh. (in 1940: 62m. kwh.).

Construction of an electro-chemical combine, the largest in the USSR, has begun in the Yavan steppe in south Tadjikistan, and of a 3·2m. kw. power station in the upper reaches of the Vakhsh River.

In 1969 there were 553,000 industrial and office workers in the national economy, and 40,000 specialists with a higher education.

ROADS. There are 13,200 km of motor roads. Of these, 7,400 km are hard surface, including the Osh–Khorog (700 km), Yasui–Bazar–Charm (107 km) and Dushanbe–Khorog in the Pamirs (557 km) roads.

RAILWAYS. A railway line between Termez and Dushanbe (258 km) connects the Republic with the railway system of the USSR. The mountainous nature of the Republic makes ordinary railway construction difficult; accordingly 345 km of narrow gauge railways have been constructed (Kurgan–Tyube–Piandzh and Dushanbe–Kurgan–Tyube, connecting Dushanbe with the cotton-growing Vakhsh valley and are particularly important).

SHIPPING. A steamship line on the Amu-Darya runs between Termez, Sarava and Jilikulam on the river Vakhsh (200 km).

AVIATION. Dushanbe is connected by air with Moscow, Tashkent, Baku and the regional and district centres of the Republic.

GORNO-BADAKHSHAN
AUTONOMOUS REGION

Comprising the Pamir massif along the borders of Afghánistán and China, the region was set up on 2 Jan. 1925. Area, 63,700 sq. km (24,590 sq. miles); population (est. Jan. 1970), 98,000 (83% Tadjiks, 11% Kirghiz). Capital, Khorog (12,000).

There were 26,400 pupils in 285 schools in 1968.

Mining industries are developed (gold, rock-crystal, mica, coal, salt). Wheat, fruit and fodder crops are grown and cattle and sheep are bred in the western parts. In 1969 there were 62,900 cattle, 221,000 sheep and goats.

In 1965 there were 47 collective farms and 1 state (livestock) farm.

BOOKS OF REFERENCE

Chumichev, D. A., *Tadzhikskaya SSR.* Moscow, 1954
Academy of Science of Tadzhikistan, *Istoria Tadzhikskogo Naroda.* 3 vols. Moscow, 1963–65
Luknitsky, P., *Soviet Tajkistan* [In English]. Moscow, 1954

KIRGHIZIA
Kyrgyz Sovietik Sotsialistik Respublikasy

After the establishment of the Soviet regime in Russia, Kirghizia was part of Soviet Turkestan, which itself became an Autonomous Soviet Socialist Republic within the RSFSR in April 1921. In 1924, when Central Asia was reorganized territorially on a national basis, Kirghizia was separated from Turkestan and formed into an autonomous region within the RSFSR. On 1 Feb. 1926 the Government of the RSFSR transformed Kirghizia into an Autonomous Soviet Socialist Republic within the RSFSR and finally in Dec. 1936 Kirghizia was proclaimed one of the constituent Soviet Socialist Republics of the USSR.

The Supreme Soviet, elected in 1967, consists of 339 deputies (1 per 5,000 population); 120 are women.

At elections to the regional, district, urban and rural Soviets (16 March 1969), of the 23,853 deputies returned, 10,409 (43·6%) were women, 13,006 (54·5%) non-Party and 16,055 (67·3%) industrial workers and collective farmers.

President, Presidium of the Supreme Soviet: Turabay Kulatov.
Chairman, Council of Ministers: A. S. Suyumbayev.
First Secretary, Communist Party: T. U. Usubaliev.

AREA AND POPULATION. The territory of Kirghizia covers 198,500 sq. km (76,460 sq. miles), and its population in Jan. 1970 was 2·9m. The republic comprises 3 regions: Osh, Issyk-Kul and Naryn. There are 15 towns and 33 urban settlements. Its capital is Frunze (formerly Pishpek). Other large towns are Osh (120,000), Przhevalsk, Kyzyl-Kia, Tokmak.

Kirghizia is situated on the Tian-Shan mountains and bordered on the east by China, on the west by Kazakhstan and Uzbekistan, on the north by Kazakhstan and in the south by Tadzhikistan. The Kirghizians are of Turkic origin and form 40% of the population; the rest are Russians (30%), Ukrainians (6·6%), Uzbeks (10·6%) and others.

EDUCATION. Kirghizia had 1,884 primary, continuation (8-year) and secondary schools with 751,000 pupils in 1969–70; 61,900 children attended 709 kindergartens. There were also 9 higher educational institutions with 46,200 students, 36 technical and teachers' training colleges with 40,500 students, as well as music and art schools. The Kirghizian Academy of Sciences was established in 1954. In 1969 there were 50 research institutes, 18 of them, with 1,097 scientific staff, under the Kirghiz Academy of Sciences; the other 33 have scientist staffs of 5,486. A university was opened in 1951. In Sept. 1940 a new alphabet, based on Russian, was introduced.

Newspapers (1968). Of 89 newspapers with 846,000 circulation, 47 with 527,000 circulation are in the Kirghiz language.

HEALTH. In 1969 there were 6,100 doctors and 30,300 hospital beds; cots in crèches, 10,500, with 16,100 in crèche-sections of kindergartens.

FINANCE. Budget estimates (in 1m. roubles), 1961, 396; 1962, 422; 1963, 454; 1964, 474; 1965, 531; 1966, 581; 1967, 600; 1968, 641; 1969, 709.

AGRICULTURE. Kirghizia is famed for its livestock breeding. On 1 Jan. 1970 there were 907,000 cattle, 207,000 pigs, 9m. sheep and 219,000 goats. Yaks are bred as meat and dairy cattle, and graze on high altitudes unsuitable for other cattle. Crossed with domestic cattle, hybrids are produced much heavier than ordinary Kirghiz cattle and giving twice the yield of milk. The Kirghizian horse is famed for its endurance, but it is of small stature; it has in recent years been crossed with Don, Arab and other breeds.

In 1969 there were 247 collective and 102 state farms. Area under crops (1969), 1·25m. hectares (1913, 640,000 hectares; 1940, 1,056,000). There were 40,100 tractors and 3,400 grain combine harvesters in 1969; nearly all collective and state farms received electric power.

Kirghizia raises wheat sufficient for its own use and other grains and fodder, particularly lucerne; also sugar-beet, hemp, kenaf, kendyr, tobacco, medicinal plants and rice. Sericulture, orchards, vineries, vegetables and apiary are also important branches of Kirghiz agriculture. Agriculture is highly mechanized; over two-thirds of the area under crops is worked by tractors. In 1969 irrigation networks in collective and state farms covered 870,800 hectares; practically all were in use. A canal in the western Tien-Shan ranges and a reservoir in the Urto-Tokoi mountains are being constructed.

The health resorts of Jety-Oguz (7,200 ft high) and Jalal-Abad are famous for their mild alpine climate and mineral springs.

Output of main agricultural products (1,000 tons) in 1969 (1913 figures in brackets): Wheat, 505 (250); maize, 112 (37); cotton, 140 (28); sugar-beet, 1,620 (0); potatoes, 256 (19); vegetables, 196; fruit, 43; grapes, 25; meat, 130 (39); milk, 502 (91); wool, 24·5 (4·7); 245m. eggs (19m.).

INDUSTRY. Kirghizia contains about 500 large modern industrial enterprises, including sugar refineries, tanneries, cotton and wool-cleansing works, flour-mills, a tobacco factory, food, timber, textile, engineering, metallurgical, oil and mining enterprises.

The output of coal in 1969 was 3·6m. tons; oil, 286,000 tons; cotton fabrics, 1·9m. metres; leather footwear, 7·6m. pairs; granulated sugar, 163,200 tons; silk fabrics, 7·9m. metres.

Hydro-electric power stations are being built in the Central Tien-Shans and the cotton-growing districts in the Osh Region, the Chui valley and on the shore of Lake Issy-Kul. Power output (1969) was 3,519m. kwh.

There were, in 1969, 751,000 industrial and office workers in the national economy, and 56,000 specialists with a higher education.

COMMUNICATIONS. In the north a railway runs from Lugovaya through Frunze to Rybachi on Lake Issy-Kul. Towns in the southern valleys are linked by short lines with the Ursatyevskaya–Andizhan railway in Uzbekistan. Total length of railway lines is 370 km. Most of the traffic is by road; there were 19,500 km of motor roads (10,900 hard surface) in 1969. A road tunnel through the Tien Shan mountains at an altitude of 9,600 ft, connecting Frunze and Osh, is being constructed. Inland waterways, 600 km. Airlines link Frunze with Moscow and Tashkent.

Istoria Kirgizii. Frunze, 1956
Ryazantsev, S. N., *Kirghizia.* Moscow, 1951

UNITED ARAB REPUBLIC

al-Jumhuria al-Arabia al-Muttahida

HISTORY. On 1 Feb. 1958 President Nasser of Egypt and President Kuwatly of Syria proclaimed in Cairo the union of their countries, under one head of state, with a common legislature, a unified army and one flag.

On 8 March the Kingdom of Yemen federated with the United Arab Republic under the name of the United Arab States.

On 26–28 Sept. 1961 Syria broke away and resumed its independence. President Nasser accepted the situation on 29 Sept.

On 26 Dec. 1961 Egypt also declared the union with Yemen terminated; but in Nov. 1962 concluded a defence pact with the republican régime.

On 13 Aug. 1964 the UAR, Iraq, Kuwait, Jordan and Syria signed a document forming an Arab Common Market, which aims at the free movement of the currency and products of the member countries. The market was to come into being on 1 Jan. 1965, but this has not taken place.

CONSTITUTION AND GOVERNMENT. The constitution proclaimed by President Nasser on 25 March 1964 is to remain in force until the permanent constitution, to be drawn up by the National Assembly, has been ratified by a plebiscite.

The constitution defines the UAR as 'a democratic socialist state' and the Egyptian people as 'part of the Arab nation'; with Islam as a state religion and Arabic as the official language. The national economy is directed by the state; the 3 sectors of state, co-operative and private ownership are supervised and controlled by the people. 'Freedom of belief is absolute; freedom of the press, printing and publication is guaranteed within the limits of the law'. Public education is free at all stages.

The National Assembly is elected by universal suffrage and has 360 members; the President of the Republic may appoint up to 10 additional members. The President of the Republic is nominated by the National Assembly and confirmed by plebiscite for a 6-year term. He is the supreme commander of the armed forces and presides over the defence council.

President of the Republic: Anwar Sadat (sworn in on 17 Oct. 1970).

The cabinet appointed on 18 Nov. 1970 includes 32 Ministers.

Prime Minister: Dr Mahmoud Fawzi. *Vice-Premier and Minister of Production, Commerce, Industry, Petroleum and Mineral Resources:* Dr Aziz Sidky. *Vice-Premier and Minister of Agriculture and Agrarian Reform:* Shyed Marei. *Vice-Premier and Foreign Minister:* Dr Mahmoud Riad. *Vice-Premier and Minister of the Interior and Public Services:* Sharawy Mohammed Gomma.

The constitution is supplemented by the Charter of 21 May 1962, which sketches the principles and aims of the regime since the overthrow of the monarchy on 23 July 1952; and by the Statute of the Arab Socialist Union of 7 Dec. 1962. This organization has been created as 'the socialist vanguard' for safeguarding and furthering the 'socialist revolution' on all levels of local, district and national administration.

National flag: Red, white, black (horizontal), with 2 green 5-pointed stars in the white stripe.

AREA AND POPULATION. The total area of Egypt is about 386,198 sq. miles (1m. sq. km), but the cultivated and settled area, that is, the Nile valley, delta and oases, covers only about 13,500 sq. miles (35,500 sq. km). Canals, roads, date plantations, etc., cover 1,900 sq. miles; 2,850 sq. miles constitute the surface of the Nile, marshes and lakes. Egypt is divided into two districts— 'Wagh-el-Bahari', Lower Egypt, and 'El-Saïd', Upper Egypt.

In accordance with the armistice concluded with Israel on 24 Feb. 1949 the Egyptian Forces hold a coastal strip in south-west Palestine, covering an area of 258 sq. km and including the town of Gaza and the railway junction of Rafah.

The following table gives the area of the settled land surface, and the results of the census taken in 1960:

Governorates[1]	Area in sq. km	1960 census (in 1,000)		
		Males	*Females*	*Total*
Cairo	214·2	1,714	1,635	3,349
Alexandria	289·5	770	746	1,516
Suez	306·9	106	98	204
Port Said	828·8	125	120	245
Ismailia	397·4	144	140	285
Damietta	599·2	198	190	388
Behera (Damanhûr)	4,592·5	833	852	1,685
Gharbîya (Tanta)	1,994·5	855	860	1,715
Daqahlîya (Mansûra)	3,462·1	1,013	1,002	2,015
Sharqîya (Zagazig)	4,701·5	914	906	1,820
Menûfîya (Shibin-el-Kôm)	1,514·2	676	672	1,348
Qalyûbîya (Benha)	943·6	503	485	988
Kafr el Sheikh	3,492·4	483	490	973
Gîza	1,078·5	673	663	1,336
Beni Suef	1,312·8	423	437	860
Faiyûm	1,792·1	416	423	839
Minya	2,273·9	785	775	1,560
Asyût	1,553·0	677	653	1,330
Sohag	1,540·2	787	792	1,579
Qena	1,810·7	674	677	1,351
Aswân	882·2	189	197	386
Red Sea	—	16	10	26
New Valley	—	17	17	34
Matruh	—	50	53	103
Sinai	—	27	23	50
Total (excluding deserts)	35,500	13,068	12,916	25,984

[1] Capitals in brackets, where different from the name of the governorate.

The density of population is 732 per sq. km. The nomadic population of about 78,000 is not included in the above table.

The principal towns, with their populations (in 1,000), according to census of 1960, are: Cairo, 3,346; Alexandria, 1,513; Port Said, 244; Gîza, 250; Tanta, 184; Mahalla el Kubra, 178; Suez, 203; Mansûra, 152; Damanhûr, 126; Zagazig, 124; Asyût, 122; Ismailia, 111; Faiyûm, 102; Imbaba, 136; Minya, 94; Beni Suef, 79; Damietta, 72; Sohag, 62; Shibîn el-Kôm, 55; Aswan, 48; Qena, 58.

Estimated population in 1967 was 30,907,000 (Census, 1966, 30,075,858).

VITAL STATISTICS for 1963: Births, 1,178,000; deaths, 428,000.

Crude birth rate (1963), 42·1 per 1,000 population; crude death rate, 15·3; infantile mortality rate, 118; marriage rate, 19·3; divorce rate, 4·2.

RELIGION. In 1947 the population (excluding Nomads) consisted of 17,397,946 Moslems (91·46%); 1,186,353 Orthodox Copts; 86,918 Protestant Copts; 72,764 Roman Catholic Copts; 89,062 other Orthodox; 50,200 other Roman Catholics; 16,338 other Protestants; 1,547 other and unknown. By 1968 nearly all Jews had left the country.

There are in Egypt large numbers of native Christians connected with the various Oriental Churches; of these, the largest and most influential are the Copts, who adopted Christianity in the 1st century. Their head is the Coptic

Patriarch. There are 25 metropolitans and bishops in Egypt; 4 metropolitans for Ethiopia, Jerusalem, Khartoum and Omdurman, and 12 bishops in Ethiopia. Priests must be married before ordination, but celibacy is imposed on monks and high dignitaries. The Copts use the Diocletian (or Martyrs') calendar, which begins in A.D. 284.

EDUCATION. Education was made compulsory for all children between the ages of 6 and 12 in 1933; primary education (6 years) was made free in 1944, secondary and technical education in 1950. Compulsory education is provided in primary schools (6 years).

Statistics for state and private schools in the school year 1968–69: Primary schools, 7,816 with 3,550,119 pupils; preparatory schools, 1,308 with 798,208 pupils; secondary schools, 575 with 524,937 pupils.

Teachers' training colleges in 1964–65 numbered 71 with 41,259 students, including 17,732 women. In 1965 the Ministry of Education delegated 4,032 teachers to Arab League countries and 1,141 to other countries.

There are 4 universities in Egypt. Cairo University, founded in 1908 as a private institution and taken over by the Government in 1925, had, in 1968–69, 43,076 students; Alexandria University, founded by the Government in 1942, had 33,404 students; the Ein Shams University, founded by the Government in Cairo in 1950, had 37,217 students; Asyût University, opened in 1957, had 10, 530 students.

The principal seat of Koranic learning is the Mosque and University of Al-Azhar at Cairo, founded in the year 361 of the Hegira (A.D. 972). The University had, in 1968–69, 18,748 students, including (1964–65) 318 women, first admitted in Oct. 1962.

CINEMAS (1955). There were 355 cinemas with a seating capacity of 343,000.

NEWSPAPERS. On 23 May 1960 all newspapers were nationalized.

HEALTH. In 1966 there were about 6,000 doctors and 66,862 state hospital beds and (in 1965) 8,580 private hospital beds.

JUSTICE. The national courts, established in 1883, consist of 165 summary tribunals and of 14 judicial delegations, each presided over by a single judge, with civil jurisdiction in matters up to £E250 in value, and criminal jurisdiction in offences punishable by fine or by imprisonment up to 3 years (*i.e.*, police offences and misdemeanours), except in cases relating to the trafficking in narcotics, where the period rises up to perpetual hard labour and a fine not exceeding £E10,000. There are also 19 central tribunals, each of the chambers of which is also (since 1959) presided over by a single judge; and 5 courts of appeal each consisting of 3 judges. Civil cases not within the competence of the summary tribunals are heard in first instance by the central tribunals, with an appeal to one of the courts of appeal. The central tribunals also hear civil and criminal appeals from the summary tribunals. Serious crimes, trafficking in narcotics and Press offences are tried at the central tribunals by 3 judges of the court of appeal sitting as an assize court, assizes being held monthly.

In 1931 a court of cassation above the courts of appeal was set up. It is composed of a president, 4 deputy presidents and 36 judges and divided into 3 chambers, one for criminal, one for civil and commercial and one for personal law.

There is also an administrative court, created in 1946 at the Conseil d'Etat; it is composed of 3 judges, or of 5 in cases when the validity of administrative regulations is contested.

All religious courts, Moslem as well as non-Moslem, were abolished by decree of 21 Sept. 1955, effective from Jan. 1956.

FINANCE. Currency. By decree of 18 Oct. 1916 (20 Zi-El-Higga 1934), the monetary unit of Egypt is the gold Egyptian pound of 100 piastres of 1,000 millièmes. Coins in circulation are 20, 10, 5, 2 piastres (silver); 2, 1 piastre, 5 millièmes, 1 millième (bronze). Gold coins are no longer in circulation. Silver coin is legal tender only up to £E2, and bronze coins up to 10 piastres. The Treasury issues 5- and 10-piastre currency notes.

In 1953 the weights of the 20-, 10- and 5-piastre coins were reduced by 50% and their silver content from 833⅓ per mille to 625 per mille.

Bank-notes are issued by the National Bank in denominations of 5, 10, 25 and 50 piastres, £E1, 5 and 10.

Budget. Ordinary revenue and expenditure for fiscal years ending 30 June, in £E1,000:

	1965–66	1966–67	1967–68	1968–69	1969–70[1]
Revenue	1,205,000	1,309,200	1,176,000	..	1,661,855
Expenditures	1,206,018	1,316,225	1,217,000	..	1,661,855

[1] Estimates.

DEFENCE. The total strength of the defence forces is about 230,000. There is also a national guard of about 130,000.

Army. Service in the Army is compulsory for all male citizens at the age of 18. The Army comprises 2 armoured divisions, 4 mechanized infantry divisions, a parachute brigade of 3 battalions and 12 artillery regiments. Its tank strength is about 1,200. Total strength is about 180,000 men.

Navy. There are 16 submarines, 8 destroyers, 4 escorts, 2 corvettes (ex-fleet minesweepers), 4 fleet minesweepers, 2 inshore minesweepers, 45 torpedo-boats, 20 missile boats, 8 submarine chasers, 2 rocket assault ships, 20 landing-craft and some fleet tugs. Naval personnel in 1970: 14,000 officers and men.

Air Force. The Air Force is equipped largely with aircraft supplied by the USSR and Czechoslovakia and has a strength of about 15,000 personnel and 525 combat and transport aircraft. The Tu-16 twin-jet long-range bombers destroyed in the June 1967 war have been replaced by similar aircraft bearing UAR insignia but believed to be flown by Soviet crews. The main strike force consists of about 90 Su-7B supersonic fighter-bombers and 30 Il-28 twin-jet bombers. Other fighter divisions are equipped with an estimated 150 MiG-21s, 100 MiG-19s, 50 MiG-17s and 25 MiG-15s, operating in conjunction with many 'Guideline' and 'Goa' missile batteries. The 'Goa' missiles are Soviet-operated, as are many MiG-21 fighters of the latest 'Fishbed-J' type. Transport units have an estimated 20 turboprop An-12 heavy freighters, 30 Il-14 twin-engined transports, a few An-24s and about 75 Mi-4, Mi-6 and Mi-8 helicopters. Training units are equipped with Yak-11 and Yak-18 piston-engined trainers, locally-built Hispano HA-200 and Czech-built L-29 Delfin jet trainers and two-seat versions of the Su-7, MiG-15 and MiG-21.

PLANNING. A 'permanent council of national production' was established in 1952.

The 5-year development plan 1960–65 envisages an average annual investment by the public and private sectors of £E315m.

In 1961–62 a number of sweeping socialist measures were carried out, which contributed largely to the Syrian defection in Sept. 1961. In addition to the nationalization of banks, insurance companies, etc. (see below under BANKING), about 1,000 private businessmen had their property confiscated by Jan. 1962. In 1963 complete nationalization was enforced of all cotton exporting and ginning firms, pharmaceutical factories and some 400 other companies in which the state had previously held a half-share. Share owners were compensated by government bonds redeemable over 15 years at 4% interest.

AGRICULTURE. Rain seldom falls in Upper Egypt, and only at irregular intervals in Cairo, where the average for the year is no more than 1·2 in. At Alexandria the average is 8 in.

The cultivated area of Egypt proper was estimated in 1964 at 10,346,000 feddâns (1 feddân = 1·038 acres), and of this 4,728,000 feddâns were under winter crops, 3,874,000 under summer crops and 1,577,000 under Nile crops.

The following table shows the number of owners and their holdings (both in 1,000) in 1964:

	Owners		Area	
Size in feddâns[1]	Number	%	Feddâns	%
Under 5	2,965	94·3	3,353	54·8
5–10	61	2·0	527	8·6
10–20	29	0·9	815	13·3
20–50	6	0·2	392	6·4
50–100	4	0·1	421	6·9
Total	3,143	100·0	6,122	100·0

[1] 1 feddân = 1·038 acres

The Agricultural Reform Decree of Sept. 1952 limits agricultural ownership to 200 feddâns, reduced to 100 feddâns in July 1961. Foreigners were debarred in 1963 from owning any land. Holdings in excess of this limit will be redistributed; compensation, equivalent to 10 times the rental value of the land, will take the form of 3% (from 1958: 1½%) bonds redeemable within 30 years (from 1958: 40 years). All national waqfs are to be dissolved.

Irrigation occupies a predominant place in the economic development of the country. The Aswân reservoir can now hold up to 5,500m. cu. metres of water, and the Gebel Aulia reservoir, completed in 1937, holds 2,000m. cu. metres. Barrages have been erected at Esna, Nag' Hammâdi, Asyût and Zifta, and at the bifurcation of the Nile below Cairo. Nag' Hammâdi barrage, completed in 1930, ensures full basin supplies even in low flood to Girga province, and will facilitate perennial irrigation when basin lands are converted. Asyût barrage, having been remodelled, will meet the greater demands of the area it now commands. The Esna barrage now secures basin irrigation to lands in Qena province. New barrages (Mohamed Ali barrages) have been completed at the bifurcation of the Nile below Cairo to replace the existing structures which, built in 1861, are now unable to meet the conditions following the increase in summer supplies, the reclamation of large areas of waste lands and the earlier watering of food crops.

On 8 Nov. 1959 the United Arab Republic and Sudan concluded agreements on the sharing of the Nile waters (after construction of the Aswân High Dam), and trade, payments and Customs dues. The agreement provides that from the time the High Dam starts to store water (15 May 1964) Sudan will be entitled to 18,500m. cu metres of the total annual flow, instead of 4,000m., and Egypt to 55,500m., compared with the present 48,000m. Egypt is to pay £E13m. to meet the cost of providing new homes and lands for between 60,000 and 70,000 Sudanese living in Wadi Halfa and other areas which will be inundated by the waters.

The area and production of raw cotton for crop years ending 31 Aug. were:

	Area in 1,000 feddâns	Crop in 1,000 qantârs		Area in 1,000 feddâns	Crop in 1,000 qantârs
1958	1,905	9,925	1962	1,657	8,479
1959	1,760	10,175	1963	1,627	8,334
1961	1,986	6,344	1964	1,611	9,117

In 1964 the area and yield (both in 1,000) of wheat were, 1,295 feddâns and 9,993 ardebs; barley, 121 feddâns and 1,179 ardebs; beans, 408 feddâns and 2,359 ardebs; lentils, 79 feddâns and 328 ardebs; onions, 48 feddâns and 14,378 qantârs; maize, 320 feddâns and 13,814 ardebs; millet, 443 feddâns and 5,285 ardebs; groundnuts, 50 feddâns and 614 ardebs; sugar-cane, 134 feddâns and 114,484 quantârs.

The area under rice averaged 772,000 acres in 1959–63 and was 1·25m. acres in 1964; rice crop (in 1m. metric tons); 1·7 in 1962, 1·5 in 1963, 2·2m. in 1964.

Livestock, 1958: 45,000 horses, 950,000 donkeys, 11,000 mules, 1·39m. cows, 1,395,000 buffaloes, 1,259,000 sheep, 723,000 goats, 157,000 camels and 17,000 pigs.

I I

FISHERIES. The catch of the Egyptian sea, Nile and lake fisheries in 1957 amounted to 102,600 metric tons. In 1952 there were 48,947 men and 16,347 boys engaged in fishing and 11,739 boats used for fishing.

MINING. Production (in metric tons, except for gold, which is in ounces):

	1966	1967	1968		1966	1967	1968
Lead and zinc	55	1.143	1.329	Iron ore	440,000	423,000	447,000
Phosphate rock	661,000	683,000	1,441,000	Salt, marine	627,000	584,000	622.000

Petroleum in commercial quantities was first discovered at Gemsah in 1908. Production is now obtained from fields at Ras Gharib, Asl, Sudr, Ghardaka, Ras Matarma, Firan, Balaim and Abu Kodis. Operations are carried on by Anglo-Egyptian Oilfields. A US company is jointly concerned in production in the Asl and Sudr fields.

In Sept. 1963 oil concessions were granted to Phillips Petroleum (37,500 sq. miles between Rosetta and the Libyan frontier) and Ente Nazionale Idrocarburi (in the Delta and along the Gulf of Suez); in Oct. 1963 the American International Oil Co. received a 30-year concession to explore 28,000 sq. miles south of Cairo and west of the Nile.

There are 4 oil refineries, at Suez (2), Mostorod and Alexandria. Crude oil production (in 1,000 cu. metres) was 2,613 in 1952; 3,485 in 1958; 4,155 in 1961; 5,138 in 1962; 6,162 in 1963; 6,500 in 1964.

INDUSTRY. The census of industrial production (1966) showed 875,000 persons engaged in 4,000 industrial establishments employing 10 or more persons. Total value of industrial production in 1963 was £E952·6m.

Production in 1962 of pig-iron was 99,770 metric tons; of steel ingots and castings, 149,655 metric tons.

Electricity generated in 1964 was 5,444m. kw.

TOURISM. In 1964, 497,382 foreigners (1965: 542,000), including 66,353 (63,000) Americans, visited Egypt.

LABOUR. A comprehensive labour code was issued in April 1959. It applies to all categories of workers, including agricultural workers, encourages the formation of trade unions, organizes conciliation and arbitration procedures (strikes and lock-outs being forbidden) and provides for an 8-hour working day and paid holidays.

In 1959 a Labour Stability and Social Insurance Code revised the legislation of 1955 and set up a Social Insurance Institution with regional and local branch offices. It covers employment injuries, old age, invalidity benefits.

Trade unions were first recognized in 1942. In 1952 the acts concerning trade unions, individual contracts, and conciliation and arbitration were recast. Employment exchanges and unemployment statistics were introduced in 1953. Social insurance was enacted in 1955.

COMMERCE. Imports and exports for fiscal years (in £E1,000):

	1961–62	1962–63	1963–64	1964–64	1965–66	1966–67
Imports	271,257	344,266	414,415	405,875	463,500	376,500
Exports	150,987	197,818	234,377	263,132	256,500	261,300

In 1965 the principal imports were (in £E1m.): Agricultural products, 69; chemicals, 45; mining and quarrying machinery, 37; metal products, 43; transportation equipment, 33. Principal exports in 1966–67: Raw cotton, 127·6; rice, 26·9; petroleum, 4·5.

Exports of cotton (in 1,000 qantârs) during the marketing period 1963–64 (1 Sept.–25 March) to principal export markets: USSR, 853; India, 363; West Germany, 300; Czechoslovakia, 285; Japan, 249; China, 247; Italy, 191; France, 131; Poland, 100; UK, 89; East Germany, 59.

Raw cotton accounted for 67·6% of the total agricultural exports in 1958 (72% in 1959). The main buyers in 1959 were: USSR, 24·2% (1958, 26·8%); Czechoslovakia, 12·7% (12·1%); China, 10·2% (11·2%); India, 6·4% (3·8%); East Germany, 5·7% (3·7%); West Germany, 5·4% (0·6%). In 1959, the Soviet bloc countries took 63·7% of the cotton exports, Western Europe, 5·4% and USA, 0·6%.

Total trade between the UAR and UK (in £1,000 sterling) for calendar years (British Board of Trade returns):

	1966	1967	1968	1969	1970
Imports to UK	8,673	7,341	10,314	9,302	10,852
Exports from UK	18,002	10,926	12,177	15,036	18,724
Re-exports from UK	583	170	263	493	

SHIPPING. The Egyptian merchant navy in 1966 consisted of 37 steamers of 291,000 tons and 2 sailing ships of 930 tons each.

In 1959, excluding warships and vessels requisitioned by the military authorities, 38,998 steamers of 249,217 NRT entered at, and 38,993 steamers of 249,073 NRT departed from, all the Egyptian ports.

Suez Canal. The Suez Canal was opened for navigation on 17 Nov. 1869. By the convention of Constantinople of 29 Oct. 1888 the canal is open to vessels of all nations and is free from blockade, except in time of war, but the UAR Government does not allow Israeli ships to use the canal. It is 101 miles long (excluding 7 miles of approach channels to the harbours), connecting the Mediterranean with the Red Sea. Its minimum width is 197 ft at a depth of 33 ft, and its depth permits the passage of vessels up to 38 ft draught; this was to have been widened and deepened with the help of a Kuwait loan, so as to enable the Canal to take tankers of 110,000 tons by 1972.

On 26 July 1956 President Nasser proclaimed the nationalization of the Suez Canal Company, the concession of which was to expire on 17 Nov. 1968. The shareholders of the Suez Canal Company received £28m. compensation; the final instalment was paid in Jan. 1963. The Company, now the Suez Financial Company, continues as an investment trust.

On 22 Dec. 1959 the World Bank granted the United Arab Republic a loan of US$56·5m. for the deepening, widening and general improvement of the Canal and Port Said harbour. The interest of the loan is 6%; amortization will extend over 15 years.

The number and net tonnage of vessels that have passed through the Suez Canal (including warships), and the transit receipts (in £Elm.), have been as follows:

	No. of transits	Suez net tonnage	Receipts		No. of transits	Suez net tonnage	Receipts
1961	18,148	187,059,000	52	1964	19,943	227,991,000	78
1962	18,518	197,837,000	54	1965	20,289	246,817,000	86
1963	19,146	210,498,000	71	1966	21,250	274,466,000	..

Vessels passing through the Suez Canal in 1965 included 3,693 British, 2,273 Liberian, 2,110 Norwegian, 1,331 Greek, 1,307 Italian, 1,186 French, 1,216 USSR, 967 USA, 944 German, 931 Dutch, 600 Panamanian, 493 Swedish, 458 Danish, 139 UAR.

The number of passengers who went through the canal was, in 1952, 571,416; 1955, 520,774; 1956 (Jan.–Oct.), 319,798; 1957 (April–Dec.), 188,361; 1958, 342,404; 1961, 323,000; 1962, 270,000; 1963, 298,000; 1964, 270,000; 1965, 286,000.

The total rates payable by all ships were raised as from 29 June 1964 so as to provide an extra $3·45m. revenue.

During the war with Israel in June 1967 the UAR blocked the Canal, which has since been unusable.

Lauterpacht, E. (ed.), *The Suez Canal Settlement, 1956–59*. London, 1960
Baxter, R. R., *The Law of International Waterways*. Harvard Univ. Press, 1964
Marlow, J., *The Making of the Suez Canal*. London, 1964

RAILWAYS. In 1969 there were 4,510 km of state railways. The state railways have a gauge of 4 ft 8½ in. inside rails, except that to the Western Oases, which is 2 ft 5½ in.

In 1968 the railways ran 5,512m. passenger-km and 3,000m. ton-km.

ROADS. Egypt had 22,142 km of macadamized surface roads in 1969. Motor vehicles, as at 31 Dec. 1959: 57,296 private cars, 10,143 taxis, 16,225 trucks, 3,894 buses.

AVIATION. There are 5 international aerodromes: Cairo, Alexandria, Luxor, Aswan and Mersa Matruh. The national airline 'The United Arab Airlines' has a fleet of 20 aircraft. The UAA operates scheduled flights connecting Cairo with Athens, Rome, Frankfurt, Geneva, Zürich, London, Khartoum, Asmara, Aden, Jeddah, Doha, Dharan, Kuwait, Beirut, Jerusalem, Baghdad and Tripoli. In addition, the United Arab Airlines operates scheduled flights on a widespread domestic network connecting Cairo with Port Said, Mersa Matruh, Assiout, Luxor, Aswân.

In 1966 United Arab Airlines flew 733m. passenger-km and 6·96m. ton-km.

POST. The telephone service was taken over by the Egyptian Government in April 1918. In 1958–59 the state telegraphs had a length of 15,381 km of wire, and telephones, 1,076,159 km. There were, in 1963, 1,319 government and 1,378 private post offices. Number of telephones in 1969, 365,000. Number of wireless licences in 1964, 864,000.

The internal telecommunications system is owned and operated by the Telecommunications Organization. Government landlines connect with those of the Gaza sector and the Sudan.

BANKING. On 18 Aug. 1960 a Central Bank of Egypt was established by decree. It manages the note issue, the Government's banking operations and the control of commercial banks. At the same date the National Bank founded in 1898 ceased to be the central bank and became a purely commercial bank. The position of the bank in June 1967 was (in £E1m.): Foreign assets and gold, 37·6; government securities and treasury bills, 40·5; notes issued, 441; advances and bills discounted, 270·6; clearing and other accounts, 35·4. Liabilities, government deposits, 4·5; bankers' deposits, 124·5; other deposits, 153·1; clearing and other accounts, 118·7.

In 1901 a post office savings bank was opened; on 31 Dec. 1959 the total deposits amounted to £E38·6m.

Commercial banks in Egypt numbered 27 in Dec. 1959, including 16 Egyptian joint-stock companies (of which by far the most important are Bank Misr and Bank of Alexandria), the rest being branches of foreign banks. On 15 Jan. 1957 all English and French banks and insurance companies were nationalized. All banks and insurance companies must now be limited-liability companies with a paid-up capital of not less than £E500,000 for banks and £E100,000 for insurance companies; all shareholders, directors and managers must be Egyptian nationals.

The Bank el Goumhouria subsequently took over the Ottoman Bank and the Ionian Bank; the Bank of Cairo took control of the Crédit Lyonnais and the Comptoir National d'Escompte de Paris; the Bank of Alexandria was established to take over the 40 branches of Barclays Bank DCO, and the Banque de l'Union Commerciale took over the Crédit d'Orient.

Other banks in Egypt include the Crédit Foncier Egyptien (founded in 1880) and the Land Bank of Egypt (1905), both for mortgage lending, the Crédit Agricole et Cooperarif (1931), the Crédit Hypothécaire d'Egypte (1932) and the Industrial Bank (1949). The National Bank and the Bank Misr were nationalized on 11 Feb. 1960.

WEIGHTS AND MEASURES. In 1951 the metric system was made official with the exception of the feddân and its subdivisions.

CAPACITY. *Kadah* = 1/96th ardeb = 3·63 pints. *Rob* = 4 kadahs = 1·815 gallons. *Keila* = 8 kadahs = 3·63 gallons. *Ardeb* = 96 kadahs = 43·555 gallons, or 5·44439 bu., or 198 cu. decimetres.

WEIGHTS. *Rotl* = 144 dirhems = 0·9905 lb. *Oke* = 400 dirhems = 2·75137 lb. *Qantâr* or 100 rotls or 36 okes = 99·0493 lb. 1 *Qantâr* of unginned cotton = 315 lb. 1 *Qantâr* of ginned cotton = 99·05 lb. The approximate weight of the ardeb is as follows: Wheat, 150 kg; beans, 155 kg; barley, 120 kg; maize, 140 kg; cotton seed, 121 kg.

SURFACE. *Feddân*, the unit of measure for land = 4,200·8 sq. metres = 7,468·148 sq. pics = 1·03805 acres. 1 sq. pic = 6·0547 sq. ft = 0·5625 sq. metre.

DIPLOMATIC REPRESENTATIVES

The United Arab Republic maintains embassies in:

Afghánistán	Cyprus	Liberia	Somalia
Albania	Czechoslovakia	Libya	Spain
Algeria	Denmark	Malaysia	Sudan
Argentina	Ecuador	Mali	Sweden
Australia	Ethiopia	Mexico	Switzerland
Austria	Finland	Morocco	Syria
Belgium	France	Netherlands	Tanzania
Bolivia	Ghana	Nigeria	Thailand
Brazil	Greece	Norway	Togo
Bulgaria	Guinea	Pakistan	Tunisia
Burma	Hungary	Panama	Turkey
Cambodia	India	Peru	USSR
Cameroun	Indonesia	Philippines	Uruguay
Canada	Iran	Poland	Vatican
Ceylon	Iraq	Romania	Venezuela
Chile	Italy	Saudi Arabia	Yemen
China	Japan	Senegal	Yugoslavia
Colombia	Kuwait	Sierra Leone	
Cuba	Lebanon	Singapore	

Diplomatic relations with USA were severed on 6 June 1967.

OF THE UAR IN GREAT BRITAIN (26 South St., W1)

Ambassador: (Vacant).
Minister: M. Samir Ahmed. *Counsellors:* Dr Hussain Fawzi (*Cultural*); Omran Lel-Shafei; Ahmed Fawzi Mohamed Mahboub (*Consul*). *First Secretaries:* Mustafa Khaled Hamdi (*Commercial*); Dr Kawal Hagras.

OF GREAT BRITAIN IN THE UAR

Ambassador: Sir Richard Beaumont, KCMG, OBE.
Counsellors: D. L. L. Stewart, CMG; G. L. Simmons, MVO (*Commercial*). *First Secretaries:* M. I. Goulding (*Head of Chancery*); M. R. Postgate (*Information*); M. W. Marshall; M. J. Wilmhurst (*Commercial*); P. J. Monk.

BOOKS OF REFERENCE

STATISTICAL INFORMATION. The Department of Statistics and Census (15, Sharia Mansour, Cairo) was formed in 1905. *Chief:* Under-Secretary of State for Statistical Affairs, Dr Hasan M. Husein. Previously, various government departments had their own statistical sections. Estimates of population were made in 1800, 1821 and 1846; the first census took place in 1873. Among the publications of the Department are the following: *Annuaire Statistique* (Arabic and French). *Annual Return of Shipping* (Arabic and English). *Monthly Summary, and Annual Statement of Foreign Trade* (Arabic and English). *Monthly Bulletin of Agriculture and Economic Statistics* (Arabic and English). *Vital Statistics* (Arabic and English). *Statistical Pocket Year-Book* (Arabic and English).

The UAR Year Book, 1963
The Egyptian Almanac. Annual
Le Mondain Egyptien (*Who's Who*). Cairo. Annual
Connell, J., *The Most Important Country.* London, 1957
Elias, E. A., *Modern Dictionary English–Arabic.* 5th ed. Cairo, 1946
Hansen, B., and Marzouk, G. A., *Development and economic policy in the UAR.* Amsterdam, 1965
Issawi, C., *Egypt in Revolution: an economic analysis.* OUP, 1963
O'Brien, P., *The revolution in Egypt's economic system, 1952–65.* OUP, 1966
Saab, G. S., *The Egyptian Agrarian Reform, 1952–62.* OUP, 1967
Vatikiotos, P. J., *The Modern History of Egypt.* London, 1969

URUGUAY

República Oriental del Uruguay

HISTORY. The Republic of Uruguay, formerly a part of the Spanish Vice-royalty of Río de la Plata and subsequently a province of Brazil, declared its independence 25 Aug. 1825 which was recognized by the treaty between Argentina and Brazil signed at Rio de Janeiro 27 Aug. 1828. The first constitution was adopted 18 July 1830.

CONSTITUTION AND GOVERNMENT. Since 1900 Uruguay has been unique in her constitutional innovations, all designed to protect her from the emergence of a dictatorship. The favourite device of the group known as the 'Batllistas' (a *Colorado* faction) which, until defeated at the 1958 elections, held the majority for over 90 years, has been the collegiate system of government, in which the two largest political parties were represented.

One such pattern lasted from 1917 to 1933, when it was abolished by a dictator who re-established the system of an individual President. Until 1951 Presidents were elected every 4 years and they selected their own Cabinet Ministers (*see* list of Presidents in THE STATESMAN'S YEAR-BOOK, 1956, p. 1493). In 1951, on the initiative of the 'Batllistas', the Constitution was amended: the individual presidency was abolished and the executive power vested in a National Council of Government of 9 members (6 from the majority and 3 from the minority parties).

As a result of a referendum held in conjunction with the elections on 27 Nov. 1966, which gave the Colorado party a majority, Uruguay returned to the presidential system. The President appoints a council of 11 Ministers; the Vice-President presides over the Senate and the General Assembly when this takes place.

President: Jorge Pacheco Areco (assumed office on 6 Dec. 1967 on the death of President Oscar Gestido).

Minister for Foreign Affairs: Jorge Peirano Facio.

Parliament consists of 2 Houses, the Senate composed of 31 members and the Chamber of Representatives composed of 99 members. The President, Vice-President and members of both Houses are elected for a 5-year term. All people of 18 years or over at the election date are entitled to vote.

The electorate in 1966 numbered 1·2m.; women constituted 42%.

The Colorado party favours 'statism' and social-welfare legislation. Most banking and all forms of insurance are government monopolies, as are also the railways and all the public utilities except one company in Montevideo. The Government controls cement, fuel, petroleum and alcohol, including the manufacture of *caña*, a cheap rum-like drink which is the national beverage.

National flag: A white field with 4 horizontal azure blue stripes; a golden sun in splendour with 16 rays, alternately straight and wavy, in a white canton.

National anthem: Orientales, la patria ó la tumba (words by Francisco Acuña de Figueroa; music by Francisco José Deballi).

AREA AND POPULATION. The area is 186,926 sq. km (72,172 sq. miles). The following table shows the area and the population of the 19 departments (capitals in brackets) at the census of 16 Oct. 1963:

Departments	Area, sq. km	Population	Pop. per sq. km
Artigas (Artigas)	11,378	63,589	5·6
Canelones (Canelones)	4,752	201,359	42·4
Cerro-Largo (Melo)	14,929	110,339	7·3
Colonia (Colonia)	5,682	135,038	23·8
Durazno (Durazno)	14,315	99,063	6·9
Flores (Trinidad)	4,519	35,565	7·9
Florida (Florida)	12,107	106,284	8·8
Lavalleja (Minas)	12,485	115,852	9·3
Maldonado (Maldonado)	4,111	67,933	16·5
Montevideo (Montevideo City)	664	836,165	1,259·3
Paysandú (Paysandú)	13,252	92,417	7·0
Río Negro (Fray Bentos)	8,471	51,954	6·1
Rivera (Rivera)	9,829	91,740	9·3
Rocha (Rocha)	11,089	86,334	7·8
Salto (Salto)	12,603	108,030	8·6
San José (San José)	6,963	96,848	13·9
Soriano (Mercedes)	9,223	99,927	10·8
Tacuarembó (Tacuarembó)	21,015	119,658	5·7
Treinta y Tres (Treinta y Tres)	9,539	72,063	7·5
Total	186,926	2,590,158	13·9

Estimated population in 1967 was 2·78m. In 1964 Montevideo (the capital) had an estimated population of 1·2m.; Paysandú, 60,000; Salto, 60,000; Rivera, 40,000.

Crude birth rate, 1957, 20 per 1,000 population and crude death rate, 7·91 (both unofficial calculations). Crude marriage rate, 1957, 7·6; infant mortality rate, 46·6 per 1,000 live births (65·7 in 1955). Births in 1960, 60,163; deaths, 23,026; marriages, 19,725.

The 387 immigrants in 1967 were reported as: from Spain, 144; US, 58; Argentina, 47; Italy, 21; Germany, 20; others, 97.

The language of the country is Spanish.

RELIGION. State and Church are separated, and there is complete religious liberty. The religion professed by the majority of the inhabitants is Roman Catholic. The archbishopric of Montevideo has 9 suffragan bishops in Salto, Melo, Florida, Minas, San José, Canelones, Tacuarembó, Mercedes and Maldonado.

Protestants numbered about 10,500 in 1957.

EDUCATION. Primary education is obligatory; both primary and superior education are free.

In 1968 there were 1,939 primary public schools with 318,624 pupils and 10,193 teachers; in 1968, 249 secondary schools had 189,204 pupils. There are also evening courses for adults. Illiteracy is now confined largely to the older age groups.

The University of the Republic at Montevideo, inaugurated in 1849, has about 16,200 students; tuition is free to both native-born and foreign students; there are 10 faculties. There are 43 normal schools for males and females, and a college of arts and trades with about 26,909 students. There are also many religious seminaries throughout the Republic with a considerable number of pupils, a school for the blind, 2 for the deaf and dumb and a school of domestic science.

Hospital beds, 1960, numbered 14,157; physicians numbered 2,812.

CINEMAS (1962). Cinemas numbered 212 with seating capacity of 117,700.

NEWSPAPERS (1970). There were 8 daily newspapers in Montevideo with aggregate daily circulation of about 210,000; most of the 25–30 provincial newspapers appear bi-weekly.

JUSTICE. The Supreme Court consists of 5 judges elected by the 2 Chambers sitting as a National Assembly. The President is chosen annually by the members of the court from among themselves. This court has original jurisdiction in constitutional, international and admiralty cases, and hears appeals from the appellate courts, of which there are 4, each with 3 judges. In Montevideo there are also 8 courts for ordinary civil cases, 3 for government (*Juzgado de Hacienda*), as well as criminal and correctional courts. Each departmental capital has a departmental court; each of the 224 judicial divisions has a justice of peace court. In Sept. 1907 the death penalty was abolished, replaced by penal servitude for a period of 30–40 years.

FINANCE. Currency. There is no gold in circulation, but the monetary standard is gold, the theoretical gold coin being the *peso oro*, gold content of which was fixed, Dec. 1964, at 0·05924 gramme. It is equal to 100 *centésimos*. The actual circulating medium consists of paper notes issued by the Bank of the Republic in denominations of 10,000, 5,000, 1,000, 500, 100, 50 *pesos*. There are also aluminium–bronze coins of 10, 5, 1, *pesos* and copper–nickel coins of 50 and 20 *pesos*.

In 1971, there were UR$250 to the US$; UR$598 = £1.

Budget. The receipts and expenditure of the national accounts as approved by the National Council of Government (UR$1m.):

	1964	1965	1966	1967 [1]	1968	1969 [1]
Revenue	3,467·8	5,451·5	12,314·9	18,700	45,983	46,383
Expenditure	4,646·1	8,125·2	15,377·7	22,200	50,088	52,288

[1] Estimates.

The 1965 budget was approved on 24 Feb. 1967. Now covering a 5-year period it is presented during the year following election of each new government; differences in actual annual income and expenditure and amendments to the budget (including new taxes) must be approved by Parliament each year-end; these usually come forward in June or July each year.

Expenditures in 1964 (in 1m. pesos) included 135·6 for education and welfare, 369·4 for defence, 331·8 for health, 280·4 for interior, 149·3 for finance and 41·9 for public works administration. Actual expenditure on works is separately financed from specific revenues (*e.g.* fuel tax). A law inaugurating income tax came into operation on 1 July 1961.

Public debt outstanding on 31 March 1970 was 14,756m. pesos. Total gold reserves of the Banco Central on 31 May 1970 was US$76m.

DEFENCE. Army. The Army is composed of the active army and its reserves. The active army is formed of volunteers, who contract for 1 year or 2 years service. There are 2 armoured regiments, 6 regiments of cavalry, 4 of artillery, 4 of infantry, 4 battalions of engineers. Peace-time strength 9,000 men.

The reserve is formed by elements who, for some reason or other, retire from the active army, and by citizens who are trained every year in accordance with the law of compulsory military instruction. It is reckoned that about 120,000 men could be mobilized in case of war.

Navy. The Navy consists of 2 destroyer escorts, 1 training frigate, 1 escort (*ex*-fleet minesweeper), 2 patrol vessels, 1 survey ship, 1 salvage vessel, 1 rescue launch, 1 oiler and 1 tug. Personnel in 1970: 440 officers and 2,300 ratings.

There is a small naval air service, with 3 bases on the river Plate estuary.

Air Force. Organized with US aid, the Air Force has about 75 aircraft, including 1 fighter-bomber squadron with 6 F-80C Shooting Stars and 6 AT-33 armed jet trainers, 2 transport squadrons with 13 C-47s and a photographic Beechcraft T-11, a search and rescue squadron with 4 H-23F light helicopters and 3 Piper L-21As, and a number of Cessna U-17A/182 and T-6 aircraft for liaison duties. Basic training type is the T-6.

AGRICULTURE. Uruguay is primarily a pastoral country. Of the total land area of 46m. acres some 41m. are devoted to farming, of which 90% to livestock and 10% to crops. Some large *estancias* have been divided up into family farms; rural landlordism is much less than elsewhere. Uruguay is said to be the only Latin American country in which agricultural workers have the protection of a minimum-wage law. Animals and animal products constitute 71% of the exports. The 1966 census reported on 79,101 farms of all kinds, totalling 16·5m. hectares.

In July 1961 the Government finally approved a US$7m. loan from the IRBD for a Livestock Improvement Plan which is being carried out on some 600 farms in conjunction with their own Agricultural Development Plan costing some UR$80m. The latest IRBD loan of US$12·7m. was agreed in Oct. 1965. There are 8·8m. cattle, 21·7m. sheep, 498,097 horses, 383,357 pigs and 10,461 goats.

Wool exports for the year 1 Oct. 1967 to 30 Sept. 1968 were 174,763 bales and of these the UK took 50,105. Exports, 1966, of sheepskins were 2,221 metric tons; cattle hides, 10,820 metric tons.

Agricultural products are raised chiefly in the departments of Paysandú, Río Negro, Colonia, San José, Soriano and Florida. The average farm is about 250 acres. The principal crops and their estimated yield (in metric tons) in 3 crop years were as follows:

| | Area (hectares) | | | Yield (metric tons | | |
	1967–68	1968–69	1969–70	1967–68	1968–69	1969–70
Wheat	22,060	535,200	336,250	143,776	469,790	403,185
Linseed	51,250	81,680	111,990	26,838	56,458	81,225
Oats	54,150	89,200	74,800	32,954	73,155	59,745
Barley	29,800	39,560	39,360	13,520	48,058	41,088
Rye	880	2,530	7,540	490	1,735	4,462
Maize	161,700	175,800	182,800	69,165	128,829	139,205
Sunflower	108,970	90,750	97,070	48,558	65,515	64,905
Groundnuts	2,564	3,180	3,153	1,193	2,527	2,448
Rice	30,747	34,340	37,490	104,456	134,496	142,296
Cotton	1,173	615	813	678	516	513

Uruguay is self-sufficient in rice, with usually a small surplus for export. Three sugar refineries handle cane and (mainly) beet, their total production being approximately 70,000 metric tons, and approaching self-sufficiency.

Wine is produced chiefly in the departments of Montevideo, Canelones and Colonia, about enough for domestic consumption. The country has some 6m. fruit trees, principally peaches, oranges, tangerines and pears.

INDUSTRY. In 1960 there were 34,427 registered enterprises with 284,600 employees. These cover basic activities such as meat packing, lumbering, oil refining, cement manufacture and also many branches of light industry, including one rolling mill for steel and one for aluminium, light engineering and electrical, chemical and textile production. There are 555 textile mills, but with the exception of half a dozen large plants, these are on the whole small. Total capital invested in industry is UR$340·2m.: there are some 147,500 cotton, woollen and rayon spindles, 1,300 looms for woollen fabric and 1,000 looms for cotton rayon goods.

A number of public works programmes are under consideration, including the Carrasco and internal airport modernization, port of Montevideo modernization and bridges and/or ferry boats to link with Argentina across the river Uruguay; in addition to contracts issued for Highways 5 and 26 with IBRD loans.

The Commission for Investment and Economic Development (CIDE) published its 10-year development plan (1965–74) in Oct. 1965. It consists of 3 plans, plus specific projects, of which some overlap the 3 plan periods. The 3-year public works programme includes on-going projects, and the *Plan Agropecuario* (agriculture and livestock) is in full execution. The overall plan aims at a gross national product growth rate of 5·2% per annum. The plan has been costed at UR$53,000m. at 1963 prices (UR$14 = US$1). It is envisaged that 95% of the required finance will be obtained from internal resources.

LABOUR. Trade unions number about 150,000 members. About 1,036,000 (40%) of the population are classed as gainfully occupied.

POWER. The supply of electricity for light, power and traction has been a State monopoly since 1897. In Jan. 1949 the first hydro-electric plant at the site of the dam of Rincón del Bonete was completed with an installed capacity of 128 megawatts. Another plant at Rincón de Baygorria on the Río Negro came into operation in 1960, with a capacity of 108 megawatts. Power output in 1969 was 1,912m. kwh. An extension of the ANCAP refining plant, opened at Montevideo on 6 Dec. 1961, gives a capacity of 7,500 cu. metres daily of high-octane petrol and high-grade gas for domestic and industrial use.

TOURISM. In 1968, 604,189 tourists and 31,455 motor cars entered the country.

COMMERCE. The Latin American Free Trade Association came into being as a result of a conference in Montevideo in 1961 (*see* p. 48). The foreign trade (officially stated in US$, with the figure for imports based on the clearance permits granted and that for exports on export licences utilized) was as follows (in US$1,000):

	1963	1964	1965	1966	1967	1968	1969
Imports	176·9	198·4	150·5	162·2	171·4	159·3	197·3
Exports	165·2	178·9	191·2	185·8	158·8	179·2	200·3

Of the imports in 1969 (and 1968) (in US$1m.) USA furnished 26·7 (36); Brazil, 26·4 (15); West Germany, 21·7 (14·6); Argentina, 20·8 (15·5); UK, 12·1 (7·3); and Kuwait, 11·7 (13·2); of the exports U.K. took 27 (37·9); Italy, 21 (12·7); West Germany, 20·2 (11·7); Spain, 16·1 (12·1); Netherlands, 14·2 (10·5); USA, 13·2 (21·7); Brazil, 10·6 (7·5).

Principal imports and exports (in US$1,000):

Imports	1968	1969	Exports	1968	1969
Raw materials	69,221	77,816	Meat and meat products	60,291	62,083
Machinery and accessories	13,086	31,798	Wool	52,461	42,716
Motor vehicles	6,266	24,006	Spun, woven goods, etc.	31,349	31,054
Fuel and lubricants	28,955	24,941	Leather and hides	16,463	23,884

Total trade between Uruguay and UK (British Board of Trade returns) in £1,000 sterling:

	1966	1967	1968	1969	1970
Imports to UK	13,687	17,511	13,119	12,918	8,556
Exports from UK	3,347	3,248	4,709	4,745 }	
Re-exports from UK	86	113	133	106 }	6,401

SHIPPING. On 31 Dec. 1969 the 10 merchant vessels and 3 tankers under the Uruguayan flag had a gross registered tonnage of 100,860. In 1969, 1,144 ocean-going vessels of 5·3m. net tons entered Montevideo. River transport (1,270 km) is extensive; its main importance being to link Montevideo with Paysandú and Salto.

ROADS. The main highways, linking Montevideo with the interior, have a total length of 7,820 km, of which about 5,000 km are paved. Other roads, unpaved, are about 33,800 km. Considerable improvements, financed both internally and by international loans, have been carried out in the last few years.

Registered motor vehicles, 31 Dec. 1960, are estimated at 76,469 passenger cars and 50,545 trucks and buses; all figures are rapidly increasing.

RAILWAYS. The 4 principal railway systems, embracing 2,398 km, were all built by British capital amounting to £14,513,000. The Uruguayan Government in 1948 bought these railways for £7·15m., assuming control in that year. The East Coast Railway (125·5 km) and 3 minor lines were already controlled by the State under a separate administration. In Oct. 1952 the railways were brought under a single administration and a 'caretaker' Directorate is planning repairs and modernization. The total railway system open for traffic is 2,975 km of standard gauge. In 1969 it carried 8·6m. passengers, 2·03m. tons of freight. The revenue in 1963 was estimated at UR$103m.

AVIATION. Carrasco, 22·5 km from Montevideo, is the most important airport. American, Argentine, Brazilian, Chilean, Dutch, French, German, Italian, Scandinavian and Paraguayan airlines ply to and from Uruguay. The state-operated civil airline PLUNA runs services in the interior of the country and to Brazil, Paraguay and Argentine.

POST. The telegraph lines in operation have a total length of 12,083 km. The telephone system in Montevideo is controlled by the State; small companies operate in the interior. Telephone instruments, 1969, numbered 205,174. There are 1,277 post offices. Uruguay has 54 long-wave and 17 short-wave broadcasting stations. There are about 1m. wireless sets and 200,000 television receivers. There are 4 television stations. The State itself operates one of the most powerful sound broadcasting stations in South America. Four cable companies connect Montevideo with the US and Europe.

BANKING. The Bank of the Republic (founded 1896), whose president and directors are appointed by the Government, has a paid-up capital of UR$1,191m The Banco Central was inaugurated on 16 May 1967. On 31 Dec. 1966 foreign exchange was oversold by US$48m.; note circulation on 31 May 1969 was UR$42,318m.

A state-owned National Insurance Bank (Banco de Seguros del Estado) has a monopoly of new insurance business of all kinds. The Bank re-insures much of its business in London.

Of the 36 banks in Uruguay the Bank of London and South America (British) has a main office and 10 branch agencies.

WEIGHTS AND MEASURES. The metric system was adopted in 1862.

DIPLOMATIC REPRESENTATIVES

Uruguay maintains embassies in:

Argentina	Czechoslovakia	Israel	Spain
Belgium	Ecuador	Italy	USSR
Bolivia	El Salvador	Mexico	UK
Brazil	Germany (West)	Netherlands	USA
Canada	France	Panama	Vatican
Chile	Guatemala	Paraguay	Venezuela
Colombia	Hungary	Peru	Yugoslavia

Uruguay maintains legations in:

Australia	Finland	Japan	Sweden
Austria	Greece	Lebanon	Switzerland
Costa Rica	Guatemala	Norway	UAR
Denmark	Haiti	Portugal	

OF URUGUAY IN GREAT BRITAIN (48 Lennox Gdns, SW1)

Ambassador: Jorge Barreiro.
Counsellor: Carlos Alberto Ghiringhelli.

There are consular representatives at Cardiff, Glasgow, Liverpool, London, Manchester, Southampton and Swansea.

OF GREAT BRITAIN IN URUGUAY

Ambassador: G. H. S. Jackson, CMG.
First Secretaries: J. P. I. Hennessey, OBE (*Head of Chancery and Consul*); D. R. Collard (*Commercial*). *Service Attachés* (resident at Buenos Aires): Col. G. W. Croker, MBE, MC (*Defence and Army*), Capt. J. Hood, RN (*Navy*), Group Capt. J. F. C. Melrose, DFC (*Air*).

OF URUGUAY IN THE USA (2362 Massachusetts Ave. NW, Washington, D.C., 20008)
Ambassador: Dr Héctor Luisi, OBE.
Minister: Alfredo J. Platas. *Service Attachés:* Gen. Juan A. Decillis (*Army*), Capt. Eduardo A. Laffitte (*Navy*), Col. Atilio Bonelli (*Air*), *Cultural Attaché:* Román Fresnedo Airi.

OF THE USA IN URUGUAY

Ambassador: Charles W. Adair, Jr.
Deputy Chief of Mission: Frank Ortiz. *Heads of Sections:* James L. Tull (*Political*); William E. Knepper (*Economic and Commercial*); Robert S. Gershenson (*Administrative*).
Services Attachés: Col. John S. Komp (*Army*), Col. James W. Smith (*Defence and Navy*), Lieut.-Col. James Keenan (*Air*).

BOOKS OF REFERENCE

The official gazette is the *Diario Oficial*
Statistical Reports of the Government. Montevideo. Annual and biennial
Anales de Instruccion Primaria. Montevideo. Quarterly
Alisky, M., *Uruguay: a contemporary survey.* New York, 1969
Arcas, J. A., *Historia del siglo XX uruguayo, 1897–1943.* Montevideo, 1950
Brannon, R. H., *The Agricultural Development of Uruguay.* New York, 1968
De Carlos, M., *La escuela púplica uruguaya.* Montevideo, 1949
Fernández Saldaña José M., *Diccionario Uruguayo de Biografías.* Montevideo, 1945
Fitzgibbon, R. H., *Uruguay, portrait of a democracy.* New Brunswick, NJ, 1954; London, 1956
Montañés, M. T., *Desarrollo de la agricultura en el Uruguay.* Montevideo, 1948
Pendle, G., *Uruguay.* 3rd ed. R. Inst. of Int. Affairs, 1963
Salgado, José, *Historia de la Republica O. del Uruguay.* 8 vols. Montevideo, 1943

NATIONAL LIBRARY. Biblioteca Nacional del Uruguay, Guayabo 1793, Montevideo. *Director:* Dionisio Trillo Pays. It publishes *Anuario Bibliográfico Uruguayo.*

VATICAN CITY STATE
Stato della Città del Vaticano

HISTORY. For many centuries the Popes bore temporal sway over a territory stretching across mid-Italy from sea to sea and comprising some 17,000 sq. miles, with a population finally of over 3m. In 1859–60 and 1870 the Papal States were incorporated with the Italian Kingdom. Although, by an Italian law dated 13 May 1871, there was guaranteed to His Holiness and his successors for ever, besides the use of the Vatican and Lateran palaces and the villa of Castel Gandolfo, a yearly income of 3,225,000 lire, this allowance remained unclaimed and unpaid until 11 Feb. 1929, when the 'Roman question' was settled by three treaties between the Italian Government and the Vatican: (1) A Political Treaty, which recognized the full and independent sovereignty of the Holy See in the city of the Vatican; (2) a Concordat, to regulate the condition of religion and of the Church in Italy; and (3) a Financial Convention, in accordance with which the Holy See received 750m. lire in cash and 1,000m. lire in Italian 5% state bonds. This sum was to be a definitive settlement of all the financial claims of the Holy See against Italy in consequence of the loss of its temporal power in 1870. The treaty and concordat were ratified on 7 June 1929. The treaty has been embodied in the Constitution of the Italian Republic of 1947.

AREA AND POPULATION. The area of the Vatican City is 44 hectares (108·7 acres). It includes the Piazza di San Pietro (St Peter's Square), which is to remain normally open to the public and subject to the powers of the Italian police. It has its own railway station (opened Nov. 1932), postal facilities, coins and radio. Twelve buildings in and outside Rome enjoy extra-territorial rights, including the Basilicas of St John Lateran, St Mary Major, St Paul without the Walls and the Pope's summer villa at Castel Gandolfo. On 8 Oct. 1951 extra-territorial rights were also granted to a new Vatican radio station on Italian soil. The Vatican City has about 1,000 inhabitants.

Supreme Pontiff: Paul VI (Giovanni Battista Montini), born at Concesio near Brescia, 26 Sept. 1897; Secretariat of State 1923–54; Archbishop of Milan 1954–63; elected Pope 21 June 1963; coronation 30 June 1963.

Secretary of State: Cardinal Jean Villot (appointed 5 May 1969).

The Pope exercises the sovereignty and has absolute legislative, executive and judicial powers. The judicial power is delegated to a tribunal in the first instance, to the Sacred Roman Rota in appeal and to the Supreme Tribunal of the Signature in final appeal.

The Pope is elected by the College of Cardinals, meeting in secret conclave. The election is by scrutiny and requires a two-third majority.

From the accession of Clement VII in 1523 all Popes have been Italians.

Name and family	Election	Name and family	Election
Benedict XIV (*Lambertini*)	1740	Pius IX (*Mastai-Ferretti*)	1846
Clement XIII (*Rezzonico*)	1758	Leo XIII (*Pecci*)	1878
Clement XIV (*Ganganelli*)	1769	Pius X (*Sarto*)	1903
Pius VI (*Braschi*)	1775	Benedict XV (*della Chiesa*)	1914
Pius VII (*Chiaramonti*)	1800	Pius XI (*Ratti*)	1922
Leo XII (*della Genga*)	1823	Pius XII (*Pacelli*)	1939
Pius VIII (*Castiglioni*)	1829	John XXIII (*Roncalli*)	1958
Gregory XVI (*Cappellari*)	1831	Paul VI (*Montini*)	1963

The Roman Pontiff (in orders a Bishop, but in jurisdiction held to be by divine right the centre of all Catholic unity, and consequently Pastor and Teacher of all Christians) has for advisers and coadjutors the Sacred College of Cardinals, consisting in Dec. 1970 of 7 Cardinal-Bishops, 104 Cardinal-Priests and 15 Cardinal-Deacons. (These terms have only historical significance, all present Cardinals having been consecrated Bishops.) In 1586 Sixtus V fixed their number at 70, but John XXIII raised it to 87 and Paul VI to 134. The Cardinals, who are under 80 years, compose the various Sacred Congregations, govern the Church while the Apostolic See is vacant and elect the new Pope.

In April 1971 the College of Cardinals comprised 123 members, namely 37 Italians, 11 Frenchmen, 9 Americans, 6 Spaniards, 5 Germans, 4 Brazilians, 4 Canadians, 3 British, 2 Belgians, 2 Dutch, 2 Filipinos, 2 Indians, 1 Irish, 2 Mexicans, 2 Poles, 2 Portuguese, and 1 Algerian, Argentinian, Armenian, Australian, Austrian, Bolivian, Sinhalese, Chinese (Taiwan), Chilean, Colombian, Congolese (K.), Ecuadorian, Egyptian, Guatemalan, Hungarian, Indonesian, Korean (South), Lebanese, Malagasy, New Zealander, Peruvian, South African, Swiss, Tanzanian, Ukrainian, Upper Voltan, Uruguayan, Venezuelan, Yugoslav.

There are 40 cardinals at the Curia, of whom 28 are Italian.

In addition to the College of Cardinals, the Pope has created a 'Synod of Bishops'. This is to consist of the Patriarchs and certain Metropolitans of the Catholic Church of Oriental Rite, of elected representatives of the national episcopal conferences and religious orders of the world, and of the Cardinals in charge of the Roman Congregations. The Synod is to meet as and when decided by the Pope; its first session was held in the autumn of 1967, with about 190 bishops invited. An extraordinary session was held in Oct. 1969.

The central administration of the Roman Catholic Church is carried on by a number of permanent committees called Sacred Congregations, each composed of a number of Cardinals and 7 diocesan bishops (both appointed for 5-year periods), with Consultors and Officials. Besides the Secretariat of State and the Council for Public Affairs of the Church (which deals with external relations) there are now 10 Sacred Congregations, viz.: Doctrine, Oriental Churches, Bishops, Discipline of the Sacraments, Clergy, Religious, Catholic Education and Evangelization of the Peoples, Causes of the Saints and Divine Worship. There are also 3 Secretariats: for Christian Unity, Non-Christians and Non-Believers; a Prefecture of Economic Affairs, a Prefecture of the Pontifical Household and a Statistical Office. Furthermore, the Roman Curia contains 3 tribunals, the Apostolic Penitentiary, the Supreme Tribunal of the Apostolic Signature and the Sacred Roman Rota; and, lastly, various offices, as the Apostolic Chancery, the Apostolic Chamber, etc. The Pontifical Academy of Sciences was revived by Pius XI in 1936 with 70 members.

More than 2,500 Roman Catholic prelates and 99 observer-delegates from 27 other Christian Churches attended the Second Vatican Council which met 11 Oct. 1962 and 8 Dec. 1965. Sixteen Constitutions and Decrees were approved at the Council, and 7 commissions were set up to implement these decisions.

In its diplomatic relations with foreign countries the Holy See is represented by the Council for Public Affairs of the Church. The Pope is, however, pledged to perpetual neutrality in political disputes between governments and to abstention from international congresses called to cope with them, unless his mediation is specifically requested by both parties to a dispute.

The Holy See maintains diplomatic relations with:

Austria	Germany (West)	Lesotho	San Marino
Belgium	India	Liberia	Senegal
Burundi	Indonesia	Luxembourg	Spain
Cameroun	Iran	Madagascar	Switzerland
Canada	Iraq	Malawi	Syria
Central African	Irish Republic	Malta	Tanzania
Republic	Italy	Mauritius	Thailand
China (Taiwan)	Ivory Coast	Monaco	Turkey
Congo (K.)	Japan	Netherlands	Uganda
Ethiopia	Kenya	Pakistan	UAR
Finland	Korea (South)	Philippines	UK
France	Kuwait	Portugal	Yugoslavia
Gabon	Lebanon	Rwanda	Zambia

and all Latin-American republics except Guyana and Mexico.

In 1930 the issue of Papal coinage was resumed, after a lapse of 60 years. In virtue of a special convention between the Vatican City and the Italian Government (last renewed in 1962), each state allows the currency of the other to circulate in its territory. The Vatican City has, however, given an undertaking that the total value of its coins issued in ordinary years will not exceed 100m. lire, 200m. lire in years of 'Sede vacante' or holy years, or 300m. in the year of the opening of a Council.

Envoy and Minister to the Holy See: D. J. C. Crawley, CMG, CVO. *First Secretary:* A. G. L. Turner. *Attaché:* J. P. Blackledge.

Apostolic Delegate[1] for Great Britain, Bermuda and Gibraltar: Mgr Domenico Enrici, Titular Archbishop of Ancusa.

[1] An apostolic delegate is a representative of the Holy See without diplomatic status or privileges.

BOOKS OF REFERENCE

Acta Apostolicæ Sedis Romanæ. Rome
Annuario Pontificio. Rome. Annual
L'Attività della Santa Sede. Rome. Annual
The Catholic Directory. London. Annual
Codex Juris Canonici. Latest ed., 1948
Atlas Missionum. Vatican City, 1958
Bilan du Monde: Encyclopédie catholique du monde chrétien. Tournai, 1964
Cardinale, Mgr. Igino, *Le Saint-Siège et la diplomatie.* Paris and Rome, 1962
Hales, E. E., *The Catholic Church and the Modern World.* London, 1958.
Kerr, W. S., *A Handbook on the Papacy.* London, 1950
Nichols, P., *The Politics of the Vatican.* London, 1968
Purdy, W., *The Church on the Move.* London, 1966

VENEZUELA
Republica de Venezuela

CONSTITUTION AND GOVERNMENT. The constitution of 1958 provides for popular election for a term of 5 years of a President, a National Congress, and State and Municipal legislative assemblies, and guarantees the freedom of labour, industry and commerce. Aliens are assured of treatment equal to that extended to nationals.

Congress consists of a Senate and a Chamber of Deputies. At least 2 Senators are elected for each State and for the Federal District. Senators must be Venezuelans by birth and over 30 years of age. Deputies must be native Venzuelans over 21 years of age; there is 1 for every 50,000 inhabitants. The territories, on reaching the population fixed by law, also elect deputies. Voting (by proportional representation) is compulsory for men and women over 18. Owing to the high rate of illiteracy, voting is by coloured ballot cards.

The President must be a Venezuelan by birth and over 30 years of age; he has a qualified power of veto.

The following is a list of presidents since 1941:

	Took Office		Took Office
Gen. Isaias Medina Angarita	6 May 1941	Col. Marcos Pérez Jiménez.	3 Dec. 1952 [1]
Rómulo Betancourt	20 Oct. 1945	Rear-Adm. Wolfgang Lar-	
Rómulo Gallegos	15 Feb. 1948	razábal Ugueto	23 Jan. 1958 [2,3]
Lieut.-Col. Carlos Delgado		Dr Edgard Sanabria	14 Nov. 1958 [3]
Chalbaud	24 Nov. 1948 [4]	Rómulo Betancourt	13 Feb. 1959
Dr G. Suárez Flamerich	27 Nov. 1950 [2]	Raul Leoni	11 March 1964

[1] Deposed.   [2] Resigned.   [3] Provisional.   [4] Assassinated 13 Nov. 1950.

President: Dr Rafael Caldera, elected 1 Dec. 1968 with 1,082,941 out of 3,723,000 votes, assumed office on 11 March 1969.

Presidential and general elections, held on 1 Dec. 1968, resulted in the leader of the Christian Social party (Copei) being elected as President of the Republic although *Acción Democrática* party remains the largest single party in Congress.

Foreign Minister: Dr. Aristides Calvani

The city of Caracas is the capital. The 20 states, autonomous and politically equal, have each a legislative assembly and an elected governor. The states are divided into 156 districts and 613 municipalities. There are also 2 federal territories with 7 departments, and a federal district with 2 departments and 2 parishes. Each district has a municipal council, and each municipio a communal junta. The federal district and the 2 territories are administered by the President of the Republic.

National flag: Yellow, blue with 7 yellow stars in a semi-circle, red (horizontal).

National anthem: Gloria al bravo pueblo (1811; words by Vicente Salias, tune by Juan Landaeta).

AREA AND POPULATION. The official estimate of the area is 912,050 sq. km (352,143 sq. miles); the frontiers with Colombia, Brazil and Guyana extend for 2,972 miles. Over half the population live in the valleys of Caracas and Valencia (once the capital). There are 20 states, 2 territories, the federal district and the federal dependencies (*i.e.*, 72 islands in the Antilles); further states may be created from the territories. Bolívar, the largest state, has an area of 91,868 sq. miles; the other states are far smaller. The federal district embraces 745 sq. miles.

The language of the country is Spanish.

Population according to the census (revised of 26 Feb. 1961):

State	Capital	Pop.	State	Capital	Pop.
Anzoátegui	Barcelona	382,002	Portuguesa	Guanare	203,707
Apure	San Fernando	117,577	Sucre	Cumaná	401,992
Aragua	Maracay	313,274	Táchira	San Cristóbal	399,163
Barinas	Barinas	139,271	Trujillo	Trujillo	326,634
Bolívar	Ciudad Bolívar	213,543	Yaracuy	San Felipe	175,291
Carabobo	Valencia	381,636	Zulia	Maracaibo	919,863
Cojedes	San Carlos	72,652	Ter. Amazonas	Puerto Ayacucho	11,757
Falcón	Coro	340,450	Ter. Delta Ama-		
Guárico	San Juan	244,966	curo	Tucupita	33,979
Lara	Barquisimeto	489,140	Federal District	Caracas	1,257,515
Mérida	Mérida	270,668	Federal Depen-		
Miranda	Los Teques	492,349	dencies	—	861
Monagas	Maturín	246,217			
Nueva Esparta	La Asunción	89,492		Total	7,523,999

The 1961 census excluded tribal Indians estimated at 31,800, of whom 20,000 are in Ter. Amazonas and 4,000 in Zulia.

In March 1968 the total population was estimated at 9·6m. Of the working population of 2·9m. more than 87,000 were between 10 and 14 years and 337,000 were between 15 and 19 years.

The 1964 population of Caracas was 1m. (metropolitan area, estimate, 1968, 2m.); Maracaibo, 457,416; Barquisimeto (sugar district), 234,703; Maracay, 142,192; Valencia, 204,273; San Cristóbal, 129,159; Cumaná, 110,201.

Vital statistics, 1962: 334,678 births, 39,541 marriages, 52,841 deaths.

RELIGION. The Roman Catholic is the prevailing religion, but there is toleration of all others. There are 4 archbishops, 1 at Caracas, who is Primate of Venezuela, 2 at Mérida and 1 at Ciudad Bolívar. There are 19 bishops. In the state primary schools instruction is given only to those children whose parents expressly request it. Protestants number about 20,000.

EDUCATION. Elementary instruction is free and, from the age of 7 to the completion of the primary grade, compulsory. In 1962–63 Venezuela had 12,599 primary schools, of which 997 were private, with 37,187 teachers and a total enrolment of 1,346,751 pupils; there were 669 secondary and technical schools, of which 367 were private, with a total of 197,454 pupils. For superior education (1961–62) there are the University of Los Andes at Mérida (2,921 students), the Central University in Caracas (300 years old, rebuilt and modernized in 1944) with 16,740 students, the University of Zulia at Maracaibo (3,607 students), the University of Carabobo (1,610 students), the University of Oriente (607 students) and the Instituto Pedagógico (1,992 students). The first 3 universities were granted autonomy on 28 Sept. 1946. Bs.535m. from the yearly national revenue was assigned to the national universities in 1966. A Workers' University in Caracas was set up by law in 1947. Two private universities in Caracas (Universidad Católica 'Andrés Bello', 2,377 students and Universidad Santa María, (1,280 students) were authorized by the Government in 1953. The census of 1950 showed that 48·7% of those 10 years of age and older were unable to read and write; this figure was (1965) less than 20%.

CINEMAS (1961). There were 660 cinemas.

NEWSPAPERS (1968). There were 23 daily newspapers and 75 weeklies out of a total of 354 periodicals. In 1961 Caracas had 9 daily and 14 weekly newspapers with a total circulation of about 445,000.

JUSTICE. The Supreme Court, which operates in Divisions, each with 5 members, is elected by Congress for 5 years. The country is divided into 17 legal districts. They select their own President and Vice-President. The Federal Procurator-General is appointed for 5 years. There are lower federal courts.

Each state has a Supreme Court with 3 members, a superior court, or superior tribunal, courts of first instance, district courts and municipal courts. In the territories there are civil and military judges of first instance, and also judges in the municipios. Finally, there is an income-tax claims tribunal.

FINANCE. Currency. The official monetary unit is the *bolívar*. As a result of exchange reforms of Jan. 1964 the selling rate to the public was changed to Bs.4·50 = US$1. The selling rate applicable to iron and petroleum companies is Bs.4·40 = US$1. Cocoa and coffee exporters may sell exchange to the Central Bank at Bs.4·485. Importers of wheat and powdered milk are eligible for subsidies amounting to the difference between the previous selling rate of Bs.3·35 and the current sellers' Bs.4·50=US$1. The exchange rate of the devalued £ sterling is Bs.10·75; 4·48 Bs. to US$.

The bolívar is divided into 100 *céntimos*. Gold coins, 100 (*pachanos*), 20 and 10 bolívars have been minted but are no longer in circulation; silver coins are 5 (*fuerte*), 2, 1 bolívars; nickel, 50 (*real*), 25 (*medio*) and 12·5 *céntimos* (*locha*), copper-nickel, 5 *céntimos* (*puya*).

The bank-notes in circulation are 500, 100, 50, 20 and 10 bolívars. The circulation of foreign bank-notes is forbidden.

Budget. The revenue and expenditure for calendar years were, in 1m. bolívars, as follows:

	1964 [1]	1965 [2]	1966	1967	1968 [2]	1969 [2]
Revenue	7,209	7,273	7.951	8,625	8,965	9,280
Expenditure	7,078	7,020	7,852	8,186	8,965	9,280

[1] Revised estimates. [2] Estimates.

The oil industry contributes about 70% of ordinary revenue in the form of royalties and income-tax, the government share of oil companies' profit amounts to about 66%.

The 1968 estimates include receipts of 5,792m. bolívars from the oil industry, and expenditures of 304m. for public debt repayments and 3,273m. for investments. Expenditure (in 1m. bolívars) in 1968 comprised: Health and social welfare, 766; education, 1,219; transport, 306; defence, 889; justice and police, 230; public works, 1,801; foreign relations, 73; agriculture, 615; mines, 179.

The 1961 Constitution provides for a Central Government contribution to the State Governments on a scale rising by 1966 to 15% of its ordinary revenue; in 1965 it totalled Bs.1,025m. (14·5%). In 1965 the autonomous Government Institutes received Bs.904m.

The public debt on 31 May 1968 was Bs.3,007m.

DEFENCE. In 1958 a Joint Staff Organization was established under the Minister of Defence for the closer integration of defence policy and administration of the three Services and the National Guard.

Army. All Venezuelans on reaching 18 years of age are liable for 2 years in the Armed Forces. They can opt for the Air Force or the Navy instead of the Army, but their allocation is finally dependent upon current requirements. The Army's established strength of approximately 18,000 all ranks furnishes a cavalry regiment, 12 infantry battalions, 2 tank squadrons and supporting engineering, anti-aircraft and supply services. There is a military academy for cadets, a school for staff studies and other technical training schools. Women can also be conscripted, as nurses, clerks, etc.

Navy. Strength includes 1 submarine, 3 large destroyers built in Great Britain in 1953–56, 6 light destroyers built in Italy in 1956–57, 10 patrol vessels, 4 landing ships, a repair ship, 3 survey ships, 12 coastguard vessels, 4 light transports and 3 tugs. Eleven coastguard vessels are operated by the National Guard. There is a naval academy for the training of officer cadets and in addition a school of staff studies and various technical training schools. Personnel in 1970: 3,500 officers and men and 4,000 Marine Corps.

Air Force. Formed in 1920, the Air Force of some 9,000 officers and men is a small, but well-equipped service with a total of about 200 aircraft. There are 5 fighter squadrons, equipped with about 20 F-86F day fighter-bombers and 47 F-86K all-weather fighters, and 3 squadrons of jet-powered Canberra bombers. Some obsolescent Venom and Vampire fighters also remain in service. A helicopter force consists of Bell 47s, H-19s, UH-1Ds and Alouette IIIs. Transport units are equipped with C-123 Providers in 2 squadrons and a number of C-47 aircraft. Communications aircraft are Beechcraft Queen Airs and other types. T-6 Texans, T-34 Mentors and Jet Provosts are used for training. A battalion of paratroops comes within Air Force responsibility. There is a staff college and a cadet academy.

National Guard, a volunteer force of some 10,000 under the Ministry of Defence, is broadly responsible for internal security. It includes customs and forestry duties among its tasks.

PRODUCTION. Within the last 30 years Venezuela has been transformed from a largely agricultural country to a leading producer of oil. Since 1960 the government has encouraged the diversification of the economy by industrialization to avoid over-dependence upon oil. In 1964 the gross national product amounted to Bs.32,104m. (at 1960 prices), principal items being: Oil and natural gas production, 21%; manufactures, 17·6%; agriculture, 6·5%; commerce, 15·6%; services, 26·5%; construction, 10·9%; transport and communications, 4%. The cost of living has remained fairly stable for a number of years.

AGRICULTURE. Venezuela is divided into 3 distinct zones—the agricultural, the pastoral and the forest zone. In the first are grown coffee, cocoa, sugar-cane, maize, rice, wheat (grown in the Andes), tobacco, cotton, beans, sisal, etc.; the second affords grazing for more than 6m. cattle and numerous horses; and in the third, which covers a very large portion of the country, tropical products, such as caoutchouc, balatá (a gum resembling rubber), tonka beans, dividivi, copaiba, vanilla, growing wild, are worked by the inhabitants. The 1950 census showed 40% of the population engaged in agriculture; the 1955 livestock estimate showed 6·23m. cattle; 1964; 756,367 hogs. Area under cultivation is 5,530,898 acres.

Production in metric tons in 1965: Beans, 16,177; beef, 194,107; cocoa, 54,388; yuca, 301,423; coffee, 54,388; maize, 521,000; potatoes, 135,390; rice, 199,900; sesame (1967), 32,377; sugar (1967), 330,000; bananas, 2,064,645 stems.

The coffee plantations number 62,673, covering 543,400 acres with 135m. bushes. The Venezuelan cocoa, from 13,000 plantations, is considered to be of high quality; it is grown chiefly in the states of Sucre and Miranda. The sugar industry has 6 government and 20 privately owned mills.

Under the Agrarian Reform Law of 1960, the Instituto Agrario Nacional establishes agricultural colonies where farmers are settled on smallholdings. Since the Agrarian Reform Act of early 1960 to the end of 1966, 119,384 families received about 6·5m. acres of land. In 1966 two-thirds of the rural population had a *per capita* annual income of less than Bs.800. The ultimate envisaged is 300,000 farmers possessing 74m. acres. There were some 12,700 tractors in use in 1960.

FORESTRY. Resources have been barely tapped; 600 species of wood have been identified. Output of timber, two-thirds being soft wood (in cu. metres): 1965, 438,525; 1966, 452,181.

FISHERIES. The total catch for 1965 consisted of 97,148 tons of fresh-water and 7,372 tons of salt-water fish.

OIL. Venezuela is the largest petroleum exporting country in the world and the third largest producer; production began in 1917 with 18,000 cu. metres; for latest statistics *see* p. xxiii. The oil-producing region around Maracaibo, covering some 30,000 sq. miles, produces about three-quarters of Venezuelan petroleum.

Proved reserves were stated in 1965 to be 17,000m. bbls, at over 3·3m. bbls production per day. A bituminous belt north of the Orinoco River is estimated to contain a further 20,000m. bbls.

Powerful foreign oil groups own all the concessions; Venezuelan capital (the CVP) is beginning, starting in July 1961, to enter the industry. Major producers are 3: Creole (Standard Oil of New Jersey), with 40% of total production; Shell de Venezuela, 25%, and Mene Grande (Gulf Oil), 13%. Nineteen companies are active. The government-owned CVP began drilling in the Mata–Acema region between Anzoátegui and Monagas at the end of 1964 and has a small refinery at Morón. Natural gas is produced during normal operations, the proportion utilized rising from 30% (1957) to 55·4% (1961). In June 1956 the dredging of a channel in the Maracaibo basin was completed, enabling ocean-going vessels to use the port of Maracaibo. 4·21m. hectares are under concession, and 10,350 wells in production.

MINING. There are important goldmines in the region south-east of Bolívar State, and new deposits have been discovered near El Callao (1959) and Sosa Méndez (1961) in the Guayana region. Output, 1968, amounted to 640 kg. Imports of 7,000 kg per annum are necessary for industrial purposes. Diamond output, from Amazonas territory, was 114,000 carats in 1968. Manganese deposits, estimated at several million tons, were discovered in 1954. Phosphate-rock deposits (yielding from 64 to 82% tricalcium phosphate) are found in the state of Falcón; reserves of 15m. tons of high-quality rock have been established. The state of Sucre has large sulphur deposits. Coal is worked in the states of Táchira, Aragua and Anzoátegui, production in 1968 being 32,000 tons. An important nickel deposit (at Loma de Hierro near Tejerías) is estimated to equal 600,000 tons of pure nickel. Saltmines are now worked by the Government on the Araya peninsula; output, 1962, 144,799 metric tons. Asbestos and copper pyrite are being exploited.

Iron ore is exploited in Bolívar State by the Orinoco Mining Co. and Iron Mines of Venezuela, subsidiaries respectively of the US Steel Corp. and the Bethlehem Steel Co. Proven reserves at the end of 1963 were 1,513m. metric tons. National output of iron ore, 1968,16·2m. metric tons.

A largely state-run petrochemical complex is being developed at Morón and in the state of Zulia, and private investmene in this and the chemical industry is being encouraged.

INDUSTRY. Venezuela is not yet highly industrialized, but the government are encouraging the establishment of local industries both by offering financial assistance and by establishing and equipping factories, which are then leased out to manufacturers. The development of local industries is fostered either in the form of high import duties or by the virtual elimination of imports through licensing restrictions. In 1960–64 the State Development Corporation (CVF) advanced credit and authorized financial decrees amounting to Bs.1,178m.

Electric power is being expanded rapidly. National production: 1966, 8,770 kwh. On completion of the first stage of the Guri dam project in 1967 there will be an additional 1·75m. kw. hydro-electric power available.

A government steel works is being developed in Puerto Ordaz, with an annual capacity of 600,000 tons of finished products; production began at the end of 1961. This is planned to be the centre of a heavy industry complex in Guayana.

Well-established industries include food processing, textiles, shoes, chemicals (195,140 tons in 1966, of which 240,236 tons is fertilizers), wood, finished metal goods and assembly of cars and trucks.

LABOUR. The first trade unions were those of the workers in the oilfields (36,897 in all) formed in 1935. Members of trade unions and peasant leagues now number 1·8m. The important Venezuelan Workers' Confederation has 600,000 members in 14 industrial and 21 regional federations and a peasant membership of 700,000. By 1963 over 500,000 workers were covered by long-term collective agreements.

Ministry of Development figures reported 2,735,000 people 'economically active' in 1961. These were (in 1,000): Agriculture, 739; services, 572; manufactures, 295; commerce and finance, 304; building, 128; transport, 106, extractive, including oil, 47; public utilities, 25; unemployed, 328.

In mid-1964 the Instituto Nacional de Cooperación Educativa estimated that about 90,000 enter the labour market each year, but there are new openings only for about 35,000. In 1966 the total labour force was rated at 2·93m., of whom 8·1% were unemployed.

TOURISM. 54,175 tourists brought in Bs.94m. in foreign exchange in 1965.

COMMERCE. The International Monetary Fund carries the values of Venezuela's exports and imports in the following convenient form (in 1m. bolívars):

	1961	1962	1963	1964	1965	1966
Exports	8,084	8,689	8,807	11,946	12,255	11,942
Whereof oil	7,441	8,025	8,154	10,982	11,229	11,038
Imports	3,522	3,871	3,685	4,898	5,590	5,121
By oil companies	157	264	233	265	270	198

The principal foreign imports in 1966 came, by value in US$1m., from USA, 613·6; West Germany, 118·1; UK, 66·3; Canada, 64·4; Japan, 63·5; Italy, 63. The value of main exports in 1966 was, in US$1m.: Petroleum, 2,508; iron ore, 144; coffee, 14.

Total trade between UK and Venezuela (according to British Board of Trade returns, in £1,000 sterling):

	1966	1967	1968	1969	1970
Imports to UK	58,151	68,290	73,068	56,653	50.825
Exports from UK	23,496	21,372	32,341	31,035	33,706
Re-exports from UK	388	290	498	620	

SHIPPING. Foreign vessels are not permitted to engage in the coasting trade, except by special concessions or by contract with the Government. La Guaira, Maracaibo, Puerto Cabello, Puerto Ordaz and Guanta are the chief ports. In Dec. 1963 the merchant fleet—with a total of 100 ships of 100 tons and over—had an aggregate gross tonnage of 363,337; this included 14 tankers of 216,734 gross tons.

The principal navigable rivers are the Orinoco and its tributaries Apure and Arauca, from San Fernando to Tucupita through Ciudad Bolívar, Puerto Ordaz and San Félix; San Juan from Carípito to the Gulf of Paria; and Esculante in Lake Maracaibo.

ROADS. There were, 1963, 28,198 km of road fit for traffic the year round; of these 13,220 km are paved, 10,130 km are gravel. There are 200 km of high-speed 4-lane motorway type. The motorway system runs from Caracas to Puerto Cabello via Valencia and will shortly be linked direct with one from La Guaira to Caracas. Venezuela has received two World Bank loans for US$45m. and 30m. in connexion with this programme, for improvements of the express-ways in Caracas and for 2 roads in the South West of the country. Motor vehicles, 1963, totalled 286,600 passenger cars and taxis; 101,922 delivery vans and trucks; 6,423 buses and coaches. The 1,678-metre Angostura bridge linking the Orinoco cities of Ciudad Bolívar and Soledad was opened in Jan. 1967.

RAILWAYS. The state-run railways consist of 175 km of standard gauge. There are also 300 km used by the two US-owned iron-mining companies. Railway passengers, 1963, 371,373; goods carried, 1963, 174,201 metric tons; omnibus, taxi and coach passengers, 1963, 256,027,577.

AVIATION. The chief Venezuelan airlines are LAV (Líneas Aéreas Venezolanas), a government-owned concern, and AVENSA (Aerovías Venezolanas). Both operate numerous internal services. VIASA operates international routes in conjunction with KLM. There are also 3 specialist air freight companies. In all there are over 100 commercial aircraft in operation. In addition to Venezuelan international services, a number of US and Latin American and European lines operate services to Venezuela. BOAC operates twice-weekly flights between London and Caracas.

POST. The telegraph system had a network, 1955, of 22,349 km with 437 telegraph offices. It is supplemented by wireless telegraphy, with 72 stations, and by wireless telephony. There are telephone systems in the principal towns (nationalized in 1954). There were 345,704 instruments in 1969, of which 97·7% were in automatic systems; 226,010 were in Caracas. The telephone network is to be extended by 100,000 additional lines over the next 3 years. An international telex service operates in the Caracas metropolitan zone. There is a submarine telephone link with USA.

There are 77 radio stations at Caracas, Maracaibo, Maracay and other towns. There are 3 television stations in Caracas, of which 2 cover, with relays, most of the country. In Oct. 1963 a new station with transmitter located in Valencia but relaying programmes to Caracas began operations.

BANKING. In Oct. 1939 a Central Bank was established, with a capital of 10m. bolívars (one-half by the Government and one-half by the public) to regulate the currency and to act as fiscal agent for the Government. This was opened on 1 Jan. 1941 with a gold stock equal to US$29m., which rose to US$503m. in Oct. 1956. On 31 Aug. 1963 the Central Bank had notes in circulation of 1,446m. bolívars; deposits were 779m. bolívars. In mid-Jan. 1968 its gold and foreign reserve totalled US$939m.

On 30 Sept. 1966 money in circulation was Bs.4,087m. (compared with Bs.4,134m. at the end of 1965).

Before 1939 the Bank of Venezuela, with (now) a capital of 105m. bolívars, was the sole depository of government funds and controlled the circulation of the currency. There are 36 commercial banks, of which 32 are Venezuelan (including the Banco Nacional de Descuento, with an authorized capital of 120m. bolívars), Banco Unión (100m.), Banco Mercantil y Agrícola (60m.), Banco Venezolano de Crédito (42m.), Banco de Maracaibo (40m.); and 4 are foreign (1 Canadian, 1 American, 1 Dutch and 1 French–Italian). Banco Obrero, with capital and reserves of 1,038m. bolívars, and Banco Agrícola y Pecuario (176m.) are important instruments of official policy. On 1 June 1965 the British Bank of London and South America merged with the Venezuelan Banco de La Guaira under the name of Banco La Guaira Internacional.

WEIGHTS AND MEASURES. Decrees of 1873 and 1917 introduced the metric system.

DIPLOMATIC REPRESENTATIVES

Venezuela maintains embassies in:

Argentina	France	Mexico	Sweden
Belgium	Germany (West)	Netherlands	Switzerland
Bolivia	Guatemala	Nicaragua	Trinidad
Brazil	Guyana	Panama	Turkey
Canada	Haiti	Paraguay	USSR
Chile	Iran	Peru	UK
Colombia	Israel	Poland	USA
Costa Rica	Italy	Portugal	Uruguay
Denmark	Kuwait	Saudi Arabia	Vatican
El Salvador	Lebanon	Spain	Yugoslavia

Venezuela maintains legations in:

Austria	Honduras	Japan	Norway
Ethiopia	India	Luxembourg	Taiwan
Finland			

OF VENEZUELA IN GREAT BRITAIN (3 Hans Crescent, SW1)

Ambassador: Dr Carlos Pérez de la Cova (accredited 18 Dec. 1970).
Minister: Dr Manuel Villanueva. *Minister-Counsellor:* Dr Hernán González Vale (*Consular*). *Counsellors:* Dr Pedro Liscano-Lobo (*Economic*); Dr Ramon Delgado. *Service Attachés:* Col. P. J. Tejera Marquez (*Army*), Col. Federico Schael (*Air*). *First Secretary:* Dr Alejandro Tinoco.

There are consular representatives at Birmingham, Cardiff, Liverpool and London.

OF GREAT BRITAIN IN VENEZUELA

Ambassador: Sir Donald Hopson, KCMG, DSO, MC, TD.
Counsellors: T. C. Barker (*Head of Chancery*); I. F. S. Vincent, CMG, MBE (*Commercial*). *First Secretaries:* M. Alan-Smith (*Commercial*); T. Pidgeon; M. J. F. Duncan (*Information*); D. M. Jones (*Labour*). *Service Attachés:* Wing Cdr P. D. Thompson, DFC, DFM (*Defence and Air*), Cdr D. L. J. Corner (*Naval and Military*).

There are Vice-Consuls at El Cardón, Maracaibo, Puerto La Cruz and Valencia.

OF VENEZUELA IN THE USA (2445 Massachusetts Ave. NW, Washington, D.C., 20008)

Ambassador: Dr. Julio Sosa-Rodriguez.
Minister-Counsellors: Dr Carlos Pérez de la Cova (*Chargé d'Affaires ad interim, and Economic*); Enrique Tarchetti. *First Secretary:* Dario Bander. *Service Attachés:* Gen. Marco Antonio Morín (*Army*), Rear-Adm. Miguel Benatuil (*Navy*), Gen. Roosevelt Adrianca Galvis (*Air*).

OF THE USA IN VENEZUELA

Ambassador: Robert McClintock.
Deputy Chief of Mission: Frank T. Devine. *Heads of Sections:* Edward T. Walters (*Political*); Henri A. Weismann (*Economic*); John J. Eddy (*Commercial*); John L. Ohmans (*Labour*); Charles G. Sommer (*Consular*); Seymour Levenson (*Administrative*); David S. Arroyo (*AID*). *Service Attachés:* Col. Roy D. Wathen (*Defence and Air*), Col. John J. Morgan (*Army*), Capt. Neil S. Weary (*Navy and Naval Air Force*).

There are Consuls at Maracaibo and Puerto La Cruz.

BOOKS OF REFERENCE

STATISTICAL INFORMATION. The following are some of the principal publications:

Dirección General de Estadística, Ministerio de Fomento, *Boletín Mensual de Estadística.*—*Octavo Censo General de Población* (26 Nov. 1950)
    Banco Central, *Memoria Anual* and *Boletin Mensual*
    Ministerio de Sanidad y Asistencia Social, Dirrección de Salud Pública, *Anuario de Epidemiología y Asistencia Social*

Buitrón, A., *Causas y Efectos del Exodo Rural en Venezuela.*—*Efectos Economicos y Sociales de las Inmigraciones en Venezuala.*—*Las Inmigraciones en Venezuela.* Pan American Union, Washington, D.C., 1956
Lieuwen, E., *Venezuela.* 2nd ed. OUP, 1965
Luzardo, R., *Venezuela Business and Finances.* Englewood Cliffs, N.J., 1957
Martz, J. D., *Acción Democratica . . . in Venezuela.* Princeton Univ. Press, 1966
Morón, G., *A History of Venezuela* (ed. J. Street). London, 1964
Perales, P., *Manual de Geografía Económica de Venezuela.* Caracas, 1955
Ward, E., *The New El Dorado, Venezuela.* London, 1957.

VIETNAM

HISTORY. The recorded history of Vietnam can be traced to Tonkin (now known as the northern part of Vietnam) at the beginning of the Christian era. Conquered by the Chinese (Han dynasty) in A.D. 111, the kingdom of Nam-Viet, as it was then called, broke free of Chinese domination in 939, though at many subsequent periods it again became a nominal vassal of the Chinese emperors.

By the end of the 15th century the Vietnamese had conquered most of the kingdom of Champa (in Annam, now known as the central part of Vietnam) and by the end of the 18th had acquired Cochin-China (now known as the southern part of Vietnam), formerly Cambodian territory.

French interest in Vietnam started in the late 16th century with the arrival of French and Portuguese missionaries. The most notable of these was Alexander of Rhodes, who, in the following century, romanized Vietnamese writing. At the end of the 18th century a French bishop and several soldiers of fortune helped to establish the Emperor Gia-Long (with whom Louis XVI had signed a treaty in 1787) as ruler of a unified Vietnam, known then as the Empire of Annam.

An expedition sent by Napoleon III in 1858 to avenge the death of some French missionaries led in 1862 to the cession to France of part of Cochin-China, and thence, by a series of treaties between 1874 and 1884, to the establishment of French protectorates over Tonkin and Annam, and to the formation of the French colony of Cochin-China. By a Sino-French treaty of 1885 the Empire of Annam (including Tonkin) ceased to be tributary to China. Cambodia had become a French protectorate in 1863, and in 1899, after the extension of French protection to Laos in 1893, the Indo-Chinese Union was proclaimed.

In 1940 Vietnam was occupied by the Japanese and used as a military base for the invasion of Malaya. During the occupation there was considerable underground activity among nationalist, revolutionary and Communist organizations. In 1941 a nominally nationalist coalition of such organizations, known as the Vietminh League, was founded by the Communists.

On 9 March 1945 the Japanese interned the French authorities and proclaimed the 'independence' of Indo-China. In Aug. 1945 they allowed the Vietminh movement to seize power, dethrone Bao Dai, the Emperor of Annam, and establish a republic known as Vietnam, including Tonkin, Annam and Cochin-China, with Hanoi as capital. In Sept. 1945 the French re-established themselves in Cochin-China and on 6 March 1946, after a cease-fire in the sporadic fighting between the French forces and the Vietminh had been arranged, a preliminary convention was signed in Hanoi between the French High Commissioner and President Ho-Chi-Minh by which France recognized 'the Democratic Republic of Vietnam' as a 'Free State within the Indo-Chinese Federation'. Subsequent conferences convened in the same year at Dalat and Fontainebleau to draft a definitive agreement broke down chiefly over the question of whether or not Cochin-China should be included in the new republic. On 19 Dec. 1946 Vietminh forces made a surprise attack on Hanoi, the signal for hostilities which were to last for nearly 8 years.

An agreement signed by the Emperor Bao Dai on behalf of Vietnam on 8 March 1949 recognized the independence of Vietnam within the French Union, and certain sovereign powers were forthwith transferred to Vietnam. Others remained partly under French control until Sept. 1954. The remainder connected with services in which Cambodia, France, Laos and Vietnam had a common interest were regulated by the Pau conventions of Dec. 1950. These conventions were abrogated by the Paris agreements of 29 Dec. 1954, which completed the transfer of sovereignty to Vietnam. Supreme authority in the military field remained with the French until the departure of the last French C.-in-C. in April 1956. Treaties of independence and association were initialled by representatives of the French and Vietnamese governments on 4 June 1954.

An agreement on the cessation of hostilities in Vietnam was reached on 20 July 1954 at the Geneva conference. The agreement was signed on behalf of the

C.-in-C. of the French Union Forces in Indo-China and on behalf of the C.-in-C. of the People's Army of Vietnam. The Government of Vietnam did not sign the agreement.

Important articles of the agreement were: (i) The withdrawal within 300 days, by stages, of the forces of both parties to regroupment zones on either side of a provisional military demarcation line (this line divides Vietnam at about 17° N.); (ii) pending general elections designed to bring about the unification of Vietnam, the conduct of civil administration in each zone to be in the hands of the party regrouped in that zone; (iii) until the expiry of the 300 days civilians to be permitted and helped to move to and live in the zone of their choice; (iv) a ban on the introduction of fresh troops, military personnel, arms and munitions, and on the establishment of new foreign military bases in either zone; (v) a ban on the adherence of either zone to any military alliance. An international commission composed of representatives of Canada, India and Poland is responsible for the control and supervision of the application of the provisions of the agreement.

The final declaration of the Geneva conference (21 July 1954) declared that the general elections should take place in July 1956. The elections did not take place, and Vietnam remains in effect divided into two separate countries—the northern and southern zones.

Documents relating to British involvement in the Indo-China conflict, 1945–65. Cmnd. 2834. HMSO, 1965
Fall, B., *Le Viet-Minh*. Paris, 1960
Fishel, W. R. (ed.), *Problems of Freedom: South Vietnam since independence*. New York, 1962
Lancaster, D., *The Emancipation of French Indo-China*. OUP, 1961

SOUTHERN ZONE

Viet Nam Cong Hoa—Republic of Vietnam

AREA AND POPULATION. The zone comprises most of the 18 southern provinces of the central part of Vietnam and the 27 provinces of the southern part of Vietnam. It has an area of 171,665 sq. km (66,263 sq miles). The population was estimated in 1965 at 15·1m., including some 677,000 highlanders and 454,000 Cambodians, Chinese and French. As a consequence of the Geneva agreement over 800,000 refugees from the northern zone have migrated to the south. The chief towns are Saigon, the capital (1966 population of Saigon–Cholon, 2m.), Da Nang (1966: 144,300) and Hué (1962: 103,500). The population is concentrated in the fertile plain of the Mekong Delta in the southern part and in the lowland region of the central part. The highland region of the central part is sparsely populated by primitive people radically distinct from the Vietnamese, such as the Bahnar, Rhadé, Jarai, etc.

CONSTITUTION AND GOVERNMENT. On 23 Oct. 1955 a referendum showed a majority of 98% in favour of the deposition of the Emperor Bao Dai and the elevation of Ngo-dinh-Diem to Chief of State. His first act, on 26 Oct., was to declare Vietnam a Republic of which he became the President.

On 26 Oct. 1956 a new Constitution was promulgated under which executive power is vested in the President and legislative power in a single chamber National Assembly. Both are elected by universal suffrage and secret ballot.

On 19 Oct. 1961 the President declared a state of emergency and the National Assembly conferred upon the President full powers 'to protect national security and to mobilize all manpower resources'. In 1963 these powers were used by the President and his Roman Catholic family and entourage to launch a ruthless persecution of Buddhists and other opponents of the Diem dictatorship. On 1 Nov. 1963 their régime was overthrown by the Army. President Diem and his brother were shot, and the Revolutionary Military Council took over the government. The junta, headed by Maj.-Gen. Duong Van Minh, was on 30 Jan. 1964 ousted by another group of generals, led by Gen. Nguyen Khanh and the commander of the Saigon army corps, Gen. Tran Thien Khiem.

The National Assembly, elected on 27 Sept. 1963, was dissolved by the Military Revolutionary Council on 1 Nov. A council of notables, appointed on 19 Dec., was dissolved on 30 Jan. 1964.

On 26 Oct. 1964 the Military Revolutionary Council resigned and civilian rule was restored, but on 27 Jan. 1965 Gen. Nguyen Khanh again seized power. He was superseded as commander-in-chief by Maj.-Gen. Tran Van Minh on 21 Feb. On 20 June 1965 the army again took over control of the government in the form of a National Leadership Council, a 'Directory', with Maj.-Gen. Nguyen van Thieu as head and Air Vice-Marshal Nguyen cao Ky as prime minister. In June 1966, 10 civilians were co-opted into the Directory, and on 11 Sept. 1966 nation-wide elections were held for a National Constituent Assembly. Its 117 deputies drafted a constitution and agreed upon elections for President, Vice-President, Senate and House of Representatives. The presidential and senatorial elections were held on 3 Sept. and those for the lower house on 22 Oct. 1967. The estimated poll on 3 Sept. was 83%.

President of the Republic: Gen. Nguyen van Thieu. *Vice-President:* Gen. Nguyen cao Ky.
Prime Minister: Nguyen van Loc. *Foreign Minister:* Dr Tran van Do.
Defence Minister: Lieut.-Gen. Nguyen van Vy.

RELIGION. Taoism in all its manifestations—ancestor worship, the worship of spirits and the worship of Vietnamese national heroes—is the real religion of the country. Buddhism is widespread, and in 1956 there were just over a million Catholics in the southern zone. Caodaism, a religious synthesis based on Christianity, Buddhism and Confucianism, and founded in 1926, had about 1·5m. followers at the end of 1954. The Hoa Hao sect, with about a million believers, is associated with Buddhism. The political and military power of the Caodaist and Hoa Hao sects and of the non-religious Binh Xuyen sect was broken by the Government in 1955 and 1956.

EDUCATION. On 31 Aug. 1965 there were the following schools in the southern zone: 5,762 private and public primary schools (1,563,756 pupils and 27,218 teachers), 156 state secondary schools (123,271 pupils and 2,453 teachers) and 442 private and semi-private secondary schools (205,958 pupils and 7,622 teachers). The Universities at Saigon, Hué and Dalat with 17 faculties, had 24,122 students, of whom about 6,000 were female.

The official language is Vietnamese; French is still the main language of higher education, and English is gaining ground, especially in medical teaching.

NEWSPAPERS. There are 24 vernacular, 3 English, 2 French and 8 Chinese dailies.

JUSTICE. Mixed Franco-Vietnamese courts were abolished on 16 Sept. 1954, when complete sovereignty in the judicial field was transferred to the Vietnamese Government.

FINANCE. Currency. The official parity of the piastre was fixed at 80 to the US$ on 19 June 1966. A surcharge of VN$38 per US$1, which makes the effective rate VN$118 = US$1, is applicable to almost all transactions.

Budget. The budget for 1966 forecasts expenditure of VN$55,000m. and receipts of VN$38,000m. The 1967 budget envisaged revenue of VN$58,000m. (28,000m. Vietnam resources, 30,000m. American aid) and expenditure of VN$75,000m.

The foreign debt in May 1967 amounted to VN$5,747m.

DEFENCE. Army. South Vietnam maintained in 1969 an Army of about 370,000 regulars, including infantry, armour, artillery, an airborne brigade, engineer, signals and administrative units. All formations and units are commanded entirely by Vietnamese officers who are trained at the officers' schools at Dalat and Thu Duc. There are also 2 auxiliary forces, the Regional Forces, formerly the Civil Guard (141,000) and the Popular Forces, formerly the Self-Defence Corps and Combatant Youth (paper strength, 140,000). The Army and auxiliary forces are being trained under the supervision of a US military Aid Assistance Command.

Navy. The Navy includes 7 escort vessels, 7 patrol vessels, 3 coastal minesweepers, 22 gunboats, 25 landing ships, 119 landing craft, 1 training ship, 12 minesweeping launches, 200 river assault craft, 3 oilers, 2 supply vessels, 500 auxiliary gunboats (motorized junks), a water carrier and other small craft. Personnel, including 5 battalions of the Marine Brigade, in 1970, was 29,000 officers and men.

Air Force. The Air Force was reorganized as an independent service in 1955 and has since received considerable US assistance. Its combat units are deployed in 5 air divisions, each with an average of 4 squadrons of attack and liaison aircraft and helicopters. Main attack force comprises 5 squadrons of A-37B jet light attack aircraft, 3 squadrons of A-1 Skyraider piston-engined aircraft and 1 squadron of supersonic F-5 fighter-bombers. Transport units are equipped with C-119s and C-47s. Other C-47s are equipped as gunships and for reconnaissance and ECM duties. Cessna O-1 Bird Dog, Beaver and U-17 Skywagon aircraft are used for liaison, forward air control and psychological warfare duties. A large helicopter force operates 11 squadrons (more than 250 aircraft) of CH-47 Chinook, UH-1 and H-34 aircraft. Initial pilot training is on T-41D aircraft, followed by basic and advanced training in USA. Personnel, about 37,000, with 700 aircraft. Very large USAF and US Army air forces as well as squadrons of the RAAF are also based on South Vietnam, together with US surface-to-air missile units.

AGRICULTURE. Rice and rubber are the two most important products. In 1965, 2·4m. hectares yielded 4·82m. metric tons of paddy; in 1966, 480,000 hectares produced 46,438 metric tons of rubber. Tea (1965 production, 5,905 metric tons from 9,685 hectares), coffee (1965: 3,530 tons from 10,785 hectares) and tobacco (1965: 7,575 tons from 8,540 hectares) are grown in the high plateaux, which also produce cinnamon, vegetable dyes, bamboo, excellent timber, raw silk and vegetables. Other products are maize (1965: 43,820 tons from 36,180 hectares), sugar-cane (1965: 1,092,850 tons from 34,000 hectares), groundnuts and copra. Cattle rearing is of some importance, though dairy farming is little developed. Pigs and poultry abound.

FISHERIES. Fishing is an important occupation. Fresh and dried fish and fish sauce form major ingredients of the local diet. Vietnam had, in 1967, 12,240 motorized and 46,240 non-motorized fishing craft.

MINING. The known mineral resources are limited to a small coal-bearing region at Nong-Son (near Da Nang), which, however, was completely abandoned in 1965; 19,810 metric tons of charcoal were produced in 1966; a goldmine at Bong-Mieu, peat beds and scattered deposits of molybdenum which are in the early stages of exploitation. There are also important phosphate deposits on the Paracel Islands.

INDUSTRY. There is little heavy industry in South Vietnam, but an industrial estate is being developed near Da Nang. Most industry is concentrated in the Saigon–Cholon area and comprises rice-milling, brewing, distilling, ice-making, cotton spinning and weaving, the manufacture of gunny bags, cement, paper and tyres, the assembly of radios, motor scooters, sewing-machines and bicycles, the manufacture of mineral water, tobacco products and matches, the production of oxygen, acetylene and carbonic acid gases, and the processing of duck feathers. There are also small factories making soap, paint, ball-point pens, pencils, articles in plastic, ceramic tiles, aluminium hollow-ware, dry-cell batteries, fruit and fish conserves, etc.

The following are some figures of production in 1966: Beer, 116·8m. litres; soft drinks, 80·5m. litres; rice alcohol, 9·2m. litres; ice, 231,588 metric tons; matches, 74·26m. boxes; acetylene gas, 2·1m. cu. metres; carbonic dioxide, 122 tons.

The textile industry is under intensive development with the active help of Nationalist Chinese technicians and some American investment. A total of 110,000 spindles and 18,784 looms had been installed by mid-1964.

Production of the existing jute-bag mill was 991,000 bags in 1966; plans for a second mill to be built with Italian capital have been postponed. Between them these two factories should cover Vietnam's total estimated needs of some 9m. rice and sugar bags a year.

Seven paper-mills in Saigon and one in Bien-Hoa were in production in 1967. A glass plant, with a capacity of about 50 tons a day, covers local requirements of simpler kinds of glassware but is working at only 60% capacity (13,514 tons in 1966). Two cement factories and a particle board factory have been built; a urea fertilizer plant is under construction (with Japanese war reparations aid). A plywood factory is planned.

In 1967 sugar was processed in 3 large sugar mills and a number of small artisan mills. The Hiep-Hoa Sugar Co. of Vietnam are government owned. The Vinh-Phu Sugar Co. is privately owned and refines imported raw and domestic brown sugar. The sugar production is insufficient to meet local requirements and there are plans for 3 new sugar mills to help meet the increasing demand for sugar. In 1966 sugar produced was 75,340 tons of refined sugar and 24,430 tons of brown sugar.

During 1965, 33 rice-mills were operating in the Saigon–Cholon area.

POWER. In 1966 total power produced was 601·6m. kwh. thermal electricity. Work on the construction of a hydro-electric project at Da-Nhim has been abandoned until the security situation permits its resumption.

Under economic agreements with France, 3 thermal stations totalling 54,000 kw. are to be built at Nha-be, near Saigon, at the Nong-Son coalmines, and at Da-Nang (Tourane).

COMMERCE. In 1965 imports amounted to US$12,506m. and exports to US$1,250m. Although USA aid continues to finance some categories of goods, the majority of commercial imports are now financed by Vietnam's abundant foreign-exchange reserve.

Total trade between South Vietnam and UK (British Board of Trade returns, in £1,000 sterling):

	1965	1966	1967	1968	1969	1970
Imports to UK	2,248	1,498	1,038	794	615	446
Exports from UK	1,910	4,861	3,916	3,609	4,372 }	4,382
Re-exports from UK	6	11	47	9	19 }	

ROADS. In 1964 there were 20,027 km of roads in the southern zone. Of these, 5,495 km were asphalted and 3,655 km roughly metalled. The remainder can be used by private cars only during the dry 6 months of the year. The best roads are in the south, the hill country of the centre being badly served.

RAILWAYS. The railways in working order in 1969 were Phu Cat–Song Pha, Da Nang–Hué and Cholon–Saigon–Long Khanh.

SHIPPING. The major ports are Saigon and Da Nang. During 1966, 2,265 ships took 5·93m. metric tons of goods into Saigon and 2,967 ships took 1·02m. metric tons of goods out; 1,015 ships took 2·17m. tons into Da Nang and 1,015 ships took 17,000 tons out of Da Nang.

In 1961 there were 4,762 km of navigable waterways, of which just over 2,000 were more than 2·5 metres deep and 50 metres wide.

AVIATION. In 1966 domestic air traffic carried 659,724 arriving and 655,324 departing passengers, unloading 5,525 tons of freight and loading 7,845 tons. International air traffic carried 427,025 arriving and 349,361 departing passengers, unloading 79,573 tons of freight and loading 30,957 tons.

POST. Of the 23,160 telephones in use in Jan. 1966, 19,273 were in Saigon–Cholon.

BANKING. On 31 Dec. 1954 the quadripartite Institut d'Emission ceased operations and a new Vietnamese National Bank became responsible for the issue of currency. Apart from the National Bank and its commercial subsidiary, the Crédit Commercial, there are 21 banks or bank-agencies at Saigon, including the Banque française pour le commerce, Banque française de l'Asie, Banque nationale de Paris, Bank of America, the Chase-Manhattan Bank, the Hongkong and Shanghai Bank, and the Chartered Bank.

DIPLOMATIC REPRESENTATIVES

Vietnam maintains embassies in:

Australia	Korea	New Zealand	Tunisia
Belgium	Laos	Norway	Turkey
Germany (West)	Luxembourg	Philippines	UK
Italy	Malaysia	Senegal	USA
Ivory Coast	Morocco	Sweden	
Japan	Netherlands	Thailand	

OF VIETNAM IN GREAT BRITAIN (12 Victoria Rd, W8)

Ambassador: Lê Ngoc Chân (accredited 2 May 1967).
Counsellor: Than Trong-Nghia.
First Secretary: De Thieu Liet.

OF GREAT BRITAIN IN VIETNAM

Ambassador: J. O. Moreton, CMG, MC.

Counsellor: C. M. James (*Consul-General*). *First Secretaries:* D. K. Middleton (*Head of Chancery*); M. J. Thompson; N. F. J. Mercer. *Service Attachés:* Col. J. L. Waddy, OBE (*Defence and Army*), Group Capt. M. J. E. Swiney, OBE (*Air*).

OF VIETNAM IN THE USA (2251 R St. NW, Washington, D.C., 20008)

Ambassador: Bui Diem.

Counsellors: Nguyen Dinh Hoa; Nguyen Hoan (*Economic*). *First Secretary:* Truong Duu Dien. *Armed Forces Attaché:* Col. Nguyen Linh Chieu.

OF THE USA IN VIETNAM

Ambassador: Ellsworth Bunker. *Deputy Ambassador:* Samuel D. Berger.

Heads of Sections: Galen L. Store (*Political*); James H. Ennis (*Economic*); Robert A. Bishton (*Consular*); Roger C. Abraham (*Administrative*); D. G. MacDonald (*AID*); B. Zorthian (*Information*).

NORTHERN ZONE
Viet-Nam Dan-Chu Cong-Hoa
Democratic Republic of Vietnam

AREA AND POPULATION. The zone comprises 25 provinces in all and 2 centrally-administered cities, Hanoi and Haiphong. It includes the 4 northern provinces of Central Vietnam and the 5 and 3 provinces respectively of the 2 Autonomous Regions, Viet-Bac (50,180 sq. km., 330,000 inhabitants) and Tay-Bac (26,000 sq. km, 800,000 inhabitants); area 158,800 sq. km. At the census of 1 March 1960 the total population was 15,916,955 (7,687,814 males, 8,229,141 females); 48% male; 9·6% urban; estimate, 1968, 18·8m. The capital, Hanoi, had 643,576 inhabitants (with suburbs, 850,000), and Haiphong, the next town in size and the port of the region, 369,248. The population is crowded into the Red River delta and coastal plain and reaches densities of up to 1,500 per sq. km. Average density, 102 per sq. km.

Vital statistics: Death rate (1964), 6 per 1,000; infant mortality (1968), 28 per 1,000; growth rate (1966), 3·6% per annum.

About 88% of the population are Vietnamese (Kinh), concentrated in the delta and the plains. There are also over 60 minority groups thinly spread in the extensive mountainous regions which constitute four-fifths of North Vietnam's territory. The largest minorities are the Tays (525,000) and Nungs (335,000), north-east of the Red River, and the Muongs (450,000), south of it. Thais (435,000) are spread widely in the west and straddle the frontier with Laos; the Mees (400,000) dwell mainly in small pockets of territory at an elevation of 3,000 ft or higher. There are also about 300,000 Chinese, chiefly in Hanoi and Haiphong.

CONSTITUTION AND GOVERNMENT. The present, second, Constitution dates from 1960 (the first was promulgated in 1946). It consists of a preamble and 112 articles grouped into 12 chapters. It states that North Vietnam is a 'people's democratic state based on the alliance between the workers and peasants and led by the working class', and that the 'DRV is advancing step by step from people's democracy to socialism' and aims at 'the peaceful re-unification of all Vietnam'.

The National Assembly is elected every 4 years and meets twice a year. It has a permanent executive body in its Standing Committee. All citizens may vote at 18 and be elected to office at 21. Rural constituencies contain 50,000 electors, urban 10,000–30,000. The President of the Republic is elected by the National Assembly, and the Great Council consists of the Premier, Vice-Premiers and other Ministers.

Elections to the National Assembly of North Vietnam were last held in April 1964. There are 368 deputies, 63 of whom represent national minorities and including 62 women.

Local government authorities are the people's councils, which appoint executive committees. A special form of autonomous administration has been established in the regions inhabited by the ethnic minorities.

President: Ton Duc Thang (succeeded Ho Chi Minh who died 3 Sept. 1969).
Vice-President: Nguyen Luong Bang.

Standing Committee of the National Assembly Chairman: Truong Chinh; *Secretary-General:* Ton Quang Phiat.

All political power stems from the communist Worker's Party of Vietnam (Dang Lao Dong), founded in 1930; it had 800,000 members in 1968. In April 1970 the Politburo consisted of 10 full and 2 alternate members: Le Duan (*First Secretary*); Truong Chinh (*President of the National Assembly*); Pham Van Dong (*Prime Minister*); Pham Hung; Vo Nguyen Giap (*Minister of Defence*); Le Duc Tho; Nguyen Chi Than; Nguyen Duy Trinh (*Foreign Minister*); Le Thanh Nghi; Hoang Van Hoan; (candidates) Tran Quoc Hoan (*Minister of Public Security*) and Van Tien Dung.

There are 2 puppet parties, the Democratic (founded 1944) and the Socialist (1946), which are unified with the trade and youth unions in the Fatherland Front.

National flag: Red, with a 5-pointed golden star in the centre.
National anthem: 'Tien quan ca' ('The troops are advancing')

RELIGION. Buddhism is the prevalent religion. In 1966 there were officially estimated to be 800,000 Roman Catholics.

EDUCATION. Primary education consists of a 10-year course divided into 3 levels of 4, 3 and 3 years respectively. In 1966–67 there were 10,987 schools.

In 1964–65 there were 149,000 children in kindergartens, 780,300 in infant schools, 2,666,000 in primary schools, 35,600 pupils in 28 technical schools and 27,000 students in 16 institutes of higher education. There were 90,000 teachers. Total literacy was claimed in 1970.

At Hanoi University (founded 1918) and 35 other institutes of higher education there were 72,000 students in 1970. A polytechnical university, donated by the USSR, was completed in Hanoi in 1965. In 1967 there were 2,100 Vietnamese studying in the USSR.

CINEMAS. There were 41 cinemas in 1961. Since 1959 some 20 films have been made.

NEWSPAPERS (1968). The official organ of the Workers' Party, *Nhan Dan* ('The People') has a circulation of 100,000. There are 126 other newspapers and periodicals, including 3 dailies.

JUSTICE. There are the Supreme People's Court, local people's courts and military courts. The president of the Supreme Court is responsible to the National Assembly, as is the Procurator-General, who heads the Supreme People's Office of Supervision and Control.

HEALTH. In 1965 there were over 2,000 doctors and 480 hospitals.

FINANCE. Currency. The monetary unit is the *dong* = 100 *sau*. There are coins of 1, 2 and 5 *sau*, and notes of 1, 2, 5 and 10 *dong*. Official rates of exchange: £1 sterling = 9 *dong*; US$1 = 3·5 *dong*; 100 *dong* = 30·6 roubles.

Budget. The budget for 1962 balanced at 1,725,152,000 *dong*. The expenditure was earmarked as follows: 62·5% for economic construction, 20% for defence and administration, 11·2% for social and cultural affairs. An estimated US$350m. were spent on defence in 1967.

For foreign aid *see* COMMERCE (p. 1493).

DEFENCE. Army. Estimated strength in 1969, 447,000, of whom at least 85,000 were serving in South Vietnam. The army is organized in 13 infantry divisions and includes about 400 armoured vehicles and 6,000 anti-aircraft guns.

Navy. In 1970 the Navy comprised 3 patrol vessels, 15 torpedo boats, 28 motor gunboats, 4 minesweeping boats, 30 patrol craft, 24 landing craft and 10 service craft. Personnel numbered 270 officers and 2,730 men.

Air Force. The Air Force, built up with Soviet and Chinese assistance, has 1 squadron of Il-28 twin-jet tactical bombers, about 50 MiG-21 supersonic fighters, 60 MiG-17 jet fighter-bombers, about 40 helicopters, including 12 large Mi-6s, and transport, liaison and training aircraft. Fighter pilots are trained in the USSR. 'Guideline' surface-to-air missiles are operational in large numbers. Personnel, about 4,500 with 225 aircraft.

PLANNING. Long-term forward planning envisages the creation of local industry geared to agriculture manned by surplus peasant labour as a first step towards the development of a heavy industrial base. Following a 3-year plan (1958–60), the first 5-year plan ran from 1961 to 1965. Planning since has been on a year-to-year basis.

Considerable success was claimed in fulfilling the plan for 1970 which gave priority to the development of industry, but departed from precedent in stepping up agricultural and consumer goods production. The 1971 plan aims at a massive increase in rice production and extension of irrigation.

AGRICULTURE. In 1966 there were 28,000 agricultural co-operatives, each comprising 200–400 households; in 1964 there were 59 state farms. 4·66m. metric tons of rice were produced in 1965 (4·3m. in 1964). Other crops include sugar-cane, maize, sweet potatoes and cotton. The cultivated area in 1962 was 3m. hectares, of which 2·4m. were under rice; in 1964, 2·4m. hectares were irrigated. A considerable quantity of raw silk is produced and woven locally.

Livestock. Cattle (1963), 2·23m., (1964), 2·32m.; pigs (1962), 4·24m.

FORESTRY. 50% of the area is forested; 10·95m. cu. metres of timber were produced in 1964.

FISHERIES. Fishing is carried out, especially in Along Bay, which is rich in prawns and crayfish. Total catch in 1960 was 151,000 metric tons.

MINING. North Vietnam is rich in coal (anthracite, lignite and hard coal). The open-cast anthracite mines near Along Bay produced 3·4m. tons in 1964. There are deposits of iron ore, manganese, titanium, chromite, bauxite and a little gold. Chromite production in 1962 was 35,000 tons. Reserves of apatite are some of the biggest in the world: production in 1963, 740,000 tons, plus 50,000 tons of phosphates. Annual salt production is about 130,000 tons.

INDUSTRY. Next to mining, food processing and textiles are the most important industries; there is also some machine building. Older industries include cement, cotton and silk manufacture. Under the 1970 plan the coal, electricity, timber, machine-building, textile and paper industries were expanded. It was announced in 1971 that the policy of dispersing industry to remote areas was being ended. Local industries and handicrafts account for 50% of production.

Production in 1964 (in 1,000 metric tons): Coal, 3,410; steel, 50; cement, 595; paper, 19·4; sugar, 26·7; mineral fertilizers, 177; cotton fabrics, 105·2m. metres; irrigation pumps, 2,064 units. In 1967 trade unions had 1·1m. members, 95% of the non-agricultural labour force.

POWER. In 1964, 548·7m. kwh. of electricity were produced (442m. kwh. in 1963). A power plant at Wong Bi (capacity, 24,000 kw.) is being constructed with Soviet aid.

COMMERCE. In 1965, 85% of trade was with Communist countries. Imports, 162m. roubles; exports 88m. roubles. Other trade partners are Japan, Cambodia and France. North Vietnamese imports from USSR in 1969 totalled 170·4m. roubles; exports to USSR, 15·2m. roubles. China, in Sept. 1969 and again in May 1970, and the USSR, in Oct., 1969 and in Oct. 1970, both signed agreements pledging free economic and military aid. Sweden is to give £16m. of aid during 1970–73.

Trade between North Vietnam and UK (British Board of Trade returns, in £1,000 sterling):

	1965	1966	1967	1968	1969	1970
Imports to UK	119	91	75	51	85	74
Exports from UK	70	33	67	103	66 }	54
Re-exports from UK	2	4	—	3	1 }	

ROADS. In 1952 there were about 13,500 km of roads. Many roads and bridges were destroyed during hostilities, but by 1963, 6,560 km are said to have been restored with Chinese help.

RAILWAYS. Railways reported to be in working order (1969) were Hanoi–Haiphong ((104 km), Hanoi–Muc Quan (162 km), Hanoi–Thanh Hoa (167 km), Hanoi–Laokay (296 km) and Dong Anh–Thai Nguyen (completed to serve the projected steel works at Thai Nguyen—51 km).

SHIPPING. The principal port is Haiphong, which can handle ships of 10,000 tons. It is regularly visited by Polish vessels. In 1953 there were 830 km of navigable waterways open to ships of less than 2 metres draught at high water, and 530 km at low.

The total volume of traffic by rail, road, river and sea in 1962 was stated to have been 2,463m. ton-km of freight and 1,372m. passenger km.

AVIATION. Scheduled flights are operated by the Chinese airline between Peking and Gia Lam (the airport of Hanoi) twice a week. The Vietnamese operate internal services to Vinh and Dong Hoi (near the demarcation line) and to Dien Bien Phu.

POST. Postal and telegraphic communications between the northern zone and China were officially opened on 1 Jan. 1955; and international mail for the UK is now carried by this route. In 1965 there was one radio set per 61 inhabitants.

BANKING. The bank of issue is the National Bank of Vietnam (founded in 1951). Its director is a member of the Great Council.

DIPLOMATIC REPRESENTATION. The following countries maintain embassies at Hanoi:

Albania	Czechoslovakia	Korea (North)	USSR
Algeria	Germany (East)	Laos	UAR
Bulgaria	Guinea	Mali	Yugoslavia
China	Hungary	Poland	
Cuba	Indonesia	Romania	

Diplomatic relations exist also with Ceylon, Congo (Br.), Ghana, Iraq, Mauritania, Mongolia, South Yemen, Sweden, Syria and Tanzania.

French interests are attended to by a Delegate-General. The UK, India and Burma are represented at Hanoi by consulates-general.

British Consul-General: J. M. Lindzius, OBE.

Vietnam Today. Hanoi, 1965
Buttinger, J., *Vietnam: a political history.* London, 1969
Cameron, J., *Witness.* London, 1966
Dang Lao Dong, *Third National Congress of the Viet-Nam Workers' Party* [in English]. 4 vols. Hanoi, 1960
Fall, B. B., *The Two Viet-Nams: a political and military analysis.* 3rd ed. New York, 1966.—*Viet-Nam Witness.* London, 1966
Gettleman, M. E. (ed.), *Vietnam.* Harmondsworth, 1966
Giap, Vo Nguyen, *Big Victory, Great Task.* London, 1968
Hammer, E., *Vietnam Yesterday and Today.* New York, 1966
Ho Chi Minh, *On Revolution: selected writings, 1920–66.* London, 1967
Honey, P. J., *Communism in North Vietnam.* London, 1965
Le Van Hung, *Vietnamese–English Dictionary.* Paris, 1955
Salisbury, H. E., *Behind the Lines—Hanoi.* London, 1967
V'etnam: spravochnik. Moscow, 1969

YEMEN

al Jamhuriya al Arabiya al Yamaniya

On the death of the Iman Ahmad on 18 Sept. 1962, army officers seized power on 26–27 Sept., declared his son, Saif Al-Islam Al-Badr (Imam Mansur Billah Muhammad), deposed and proclaimed a republic. The republican régime was supported by Egyptian troops, whereas the royalist tribes received aid from Saudi Arabia.

On 24 Aug. 1965 President Nasser and King Faisal signed an agreement according to which the two powers are to support a plebiscite to determine the future of the Yemen; a conference of republican and royalist delegates met at Haradh on 23 Nov. 1965, but no plebiscite was agreed upon. At a meeting of the Arab heads of state in Aug. 1967 the President and the King agreed upon disengaging themselves from the civil war in Yemen. At the time there were still about 50,000 Egyptian troops in the country, holding San'a, Ta'iz, Hodeida and the plains, whereas the mountains are in the hands of the royalist tribes. By the end of 1967 the Egyptians had withdrawn.

CONSTITUTION AND GOVERNMENT. On 31 Oct. 1962, 13 April 1963, 17 April 1964, 9 May 1965 the revolutionary council issued 'interim' constitutions and on 28 Dec. 1970 a first permanent constitution was announced with provision for a Council of 179 members (20 members would be chosen by the President and the remainder by general franchise).

Prime Minister and Foreign Affairs: Muhsin al Aini.

National flag: Red, 5 white 5-pointed stars, white scimitar in the centre.

AREA AND POPULATION. The area is about 75,000 sq. miles (195,000 sq. km), with a population of 4·5m. (official estimate, 1953). The capital is Ta'iz with a population of about 30,000.

The most important towns are the port of Hodeida (population, 30,000), San'a (altitude 7,200 ft) and Ta'iz (altitude 4,600 ft); other towns are Ibb (6,275 ft), Yerim (8,600 ft), Dhamar (7,650 ft) and the ports of Mokha and Loheiya.

There are between 0·5m. and 1m. Yemenis abroad, principally on the Red Sea and Persian Gulf coasts.

In the north the boundary between the Yemen and Saudi Arabia has been defined by the Treaty of Taif concluded in June 1934. This frontier starts from the sea at a point some 5 or 10 miles north of Maidi and runs due east inland until it reaches the hills some 30 miles from the coast, whence it runs northwards for approximately 50 miles so as to leave the Sa'da Basin within the Yemen. Thence it runs in an easterly and south-easterly direction until it reaches the desert area near Nejran.

The British and Yemeni governments in 1934 concluded a treaty of friendship whereby Britain recognized the Imam as King of the Yemen. In 1951 they agreed on the exchange of diplomatic representatives.

FINANCE. Currency. The currency is the silver *riyal* of 40 *bugshahs* (approximately £0·33).

Budget. The budget for 1967–68 balanced at 50,948,500 rials (1966–67: 47,408,600 rials); estimated revenue, 29,343,500 rials; estimated expenditure, 50,948,500 rials, the balance being achieved by foreign aid.

DEFENCE. Air Force. Built up with Egyptian, Soviet and Czech aid, the air force has about 12 MiG-17 jet fighters, 12 Il-28 light jet bombers, Il-14 and C-47 transports, Mi-4 helicopters and Yak-11 armed trainers.

PRODUCTION. Wherever water-supply allows, and in general throughout the south-western part of the country, millet (*dhurra*) is grown as a subsistence crop. The traditional cultivation of coffee (no longer exported through Mokha) continues, but is giving place to that of *qat* (*cathula edulis*), a narcotic shrub. Cotton is grown in the Tihama, the coastal belt, round Bait al Faqih and Zabid (seat of a medieval university). Fruit is plentiful, especially fine grapes from the San'a district.

In Nov. 1955 an oil and mineral concession for 30 years was granted to an American group, the Yemen Development Corporation. The concession extends over an area of 40,000 sq. miles. No oil has yet been found.

Russian, Chinese and USA economic aid has been provided. The Chinese have built a road from Hodeida to San'a; the Russians have built a new port near

kk

Hodeida. The Americans are building a metalled road from Mokha to Ta'iz and San'a, and installing a water-supply for Ta'iz.

COMMERCE. Trade with the UK (British Board of Trade returns, in £1,000 sterling):

	1966	1967	1968	1969	1970
Imports to UK	26	15	8	29	325
Exports from UK	24	133	315	663 ⎫	
Re-exports from UK	4	—	2	7 ⎭	1,887

DIPLOMATIC REPRESENTATIVES

Before the revolution Yemen maintained legations in:

Czechoslovakia	Italy	Saudi Arabia	UAR
Ethiopia	Jordan	Somalia	UK
Germany (West)	Lebanon	USSR	USA
Iraq			

British Ambassador: W. Morris, CMG (resides in Jedda). The USA closed its embassy on 7 June 1967.

BOOKS OF REFERENCE

Heyworth-Dunne, G. E., *Al-Yemen. Social, Political and Economic Survey.* Cairo, 1952
Ingrams, H., *The Yemen.* London, 1963
Macro, E., *Yemen and the Western World, 1571–1964.* London, 1967

YUGOSLAVIA

Socijalistička Federativna Republika Jugoslavija—
Socialist Federal Republic of Yugoslavia

On 29 Nov. 1945 Yugoslavia was proclaimed a republic. On 8 March 1947 King Peter II and the other members of the Karageorgevitch dynasty were deprived of their nationality and their property was confiscated.

The peace treaty with Italy, signed in Paris on 10 Feb. 1947, stipulated the cession to Yugoslavia of the greater part of the Italian province of Venezia Giulia, the commune of Zara and the island of Pelagosa and the adjacent islets (*see* p. 1082).

CONSTITUTION AND GOVERNMENT. The Constitution passed on 31 Jan. 1946 declared that the Federal Republic is composed of the 6 republics: Serbia, Croatia, Slovenia, Bosnia and Herzegovina, Macedonia and Montenegro.

On 13 Jan. 1953 a new Constitution (Fundamental Law) confirmed the management of all public affairs by the workers and their representatives (which was introduced in 1950) as the basis of the entire social, economic and political system of Yugoslavia.

The Constitution promulgated on 7 April 1963 changed the name of the country into the Socialist Federal Republic of Yugoslavia, composed of the socialist republics of Bosnia and Herzegovina, Crna Gora (Montenegro), Croatia, Macedonia, Serbia and Slovenia (*i.e.*, now ranking in alphabetical order).

According to the new Constitution, the working people are the sole holder of power and the only factor taking decisions on social affairs. Social self-government is exercised by the representative bodies of communes, districts, autonomous provinces, republics and the Federation. The rights to self-government and distribution of income proclaimed in 1953 are now extended to the employed in public services as well. The former Council of Producers, in which only the workers and employees engaged in economic production were represented, has been replaced by Councils of Working Communities representing the working people employed in every field of social activity. These representative bodies are the supreme organs of authority and social self-government in each territorial community. They consist of delegates of citizens (political councils) and of delegates of working people (councils of working communities).

Every citizen over the age of 18 has the suffrage. The maximum working week is 42 hours. Religion is free.

All the means of production as well as mineral and other natural resources are social property. The exceptions are peasants' holding (up to the maximum of 10 hectares of arable land) and handicrafts. Citizens may be owners of houses and dwellings for their personal and family needs.

National flag: Blue, white, red (horizontal); with a red 5-pointed star in the middle.

The Federal Assembly is the supreme organ of government and social self-government of the Federation. It has 5 chambers (Federal, Economic, Education and Culture, Social Welfare and Health, Organizational-Political Chamber); every chamber has 120 deputies. The Federal Chamber comprises also 70 members delegated by the 6 republics (10 from each) and 2 autonomous provinces (5 from each); they sit as a Chamber of Nationalities to safeguard the rights and equality of peoples and republics.

Elections were held on 9 and 23 April 1967 (replacing one-half of the deputies) for the Federal Assembly (670 members) and the assemblies of the 6 socialist republics (2,260 members), 2 autonomous provinces (620 members) and communes (40,279 members).

The members of all assemblies are being elected for a 4-year term. Every second year, one-half of each assembly is renewed. No person can be elected twice successively as a member of the same chamber or of the Federal Executive Council. The President of the Republic can be re-elected for a second 4-year term; this restriction does not apply to Josip Broz-Tito. Federal and republic officials cannot hold the same post longer than 4 years except when the assembly approves it.

The Federal Assembly at a joint meeting of all Chambers elects the President of the Republic, and the president and 6 vice-presidents of the Federal Assembly. The functions of the President of the Republic are separated from those of the President of the Federal Executive Council.

The President and the members of the Federal Executive Council are elected by the Federal Chamber from among its deputies. The Federal Executive Council is the political executive organ of the Federal Assembly. It comprises the President, 2 vice-presidents and 14 members.

President of the Republic: Josip Broz-Tito (elected 14 Jan. 1953; re-elected 30 Jan. 1954, 19 April 1958, 30 June 1963 and 17 May 1967).

President of the Federal Assembly: Milentije Popović (elected 16 May 1967).
Chairman of the Federal Executive Council: Mitja Ribičič. *Vice-Chairman:* Alexander Grličkov; Dr Vikola Miljanic; Mišo Pavićević.
State Secretary for Foreign Affairs (Acting): *Mirko Tepavac. State Secretary for National Defence:* Nikola Ljubičić. *Federal Secretary for Home Affairs:* Radovan Stijačić. *Federal Secretary for Finance:* Janko Smole. *Federal Secretary for Foreign Trade:* Hadic Muhamed. *Federal Secretary for Economy:* Borivoje Jelić.

In addition to the 2 State Secretariats, there are 4 Federal Secretariats, 4 Federal Administrations and 5 Federal Councils.

Chairmen of the Republic Executive Councils: Bosnia and Hercegovina: Dragutin Kosovac; Montenegro: Žarko Bulajić; Croatia: Dragutin Haranija; Macedonia: Ksente Bogoev; Slovenia: Stane Kavčić; Serbia: Milenko Bojanić;

The Communist League of Yugoslavia had 1,146,084 members in Dec. 1968. As of Mar. 1969 its Presidency had 15 members, with President Tito as President of the League.

AREA AND POPULATION. According to the census taken 31 March 1961 the area and population of Yugoslavia are shown as follows:

Federal units	Area in sq. km	Population	Pop. per sq. km
Bosnia and Hercegovina	51,129	3,277,948	64·1
Montenegro	13,812	471,894	34·2
Croatia	56,538	4,159,696	73·6
Macedonia	25,713	1,406,003	54·7
Slovenia	20,251	1,591,523	78·6
Serbia with Vojvodina and Kosovo	88,361	7,642,227[1]	86·5
Total	255,804[2]	18,549,291[3]	72·5

[1] Serbia proper, 4,823,274; Vojvodina, 1,854,965; Kosovo, 963,988.
[2] 98,725 sq. miles.
[3] Estimate, 30 June 1970, 20,529,000; 1969, 20,351,000.

The population of the principal towns and their conurbations (census, 31 March 1961) are as follows:

	Town	Conurbation		Town	Conurbation
Serbia			*Croatia* (contd.)		
Beograd (capital)	598,346	843,209	Osijek	73,125	118,572
Niš	84,741	144,650	Karlovac	40,180	68,322
Kragujevac	52,792	91,213	Pula	37,403	58,999
Leskovac	34,396	68,029	*Slovenia*		
Vojvodina			Ljubljana (capital)	157,412	206,289
Novi Sad (capital)	110,877	162,075	Maribor	85,144	152,939
Subotica	75,036	122,076	Kranj	21,477	47,779
Zrenjanin	55,578	92,676	*Bosnia and Hercego-*		
Pančevo	46,679	93,744	*vina*		
Sombor	37,760	96,191	Sarajevo (capital)	175,424	198,914
Kikinda	34,059	68,562	Tuzla	53,008	83,439
Vršac	31,620	47,433	Banja Luka	51,158	131,681
Senta	25,062	31,089	Mostar	48,738	72,452
Bečej	24,963	44,585	*Macedonia*		
Kosovo			Skopje (capital)	171,893	270,299
Priština (capital)	38,593	87,322	Bitolj	49,001	54,982
Croatia			Prilep	39,611	49,276
Zagreb (capital)	457,499	821,651	*Montenegro*		
Rijeka-Sušak	100,898	127,029	Titograd (formerly		
Split	93,386	132,873	Podgorica) (capital)	30,657	72,219

The working population at the 1961 census was (in 1,000) 8,340; broken down as follows: Agriculture and forestry, 4,748; industry and mining, 1,138; building, 318; government and administration, 182; crafts, 379; commerce, 310; transport 250.

VITAL STATISTICS for calendar years:

	Live births	Still-born	Deaths	Infantile deaths	Marriages	Divorces
1967	389,640	3,887	174,060	27,193	169,282	20,840
1968	383,202	3,592	174,868	22,280	170,470	20,987
1969	381,772	3,366	186,668	21,499	173,607	19,507
1970	361,944	2,586	189,750	20,095	185,981	20,244

Three closely allied languages are recognized in the Yugoslav state: Serbo-Croat, Macedonian and Slovene. Serbo-Croat serves as the *lingua franca* of the state, Serb being printed in Cyrillic, and Croat in Latin characters. Macedonian is printed in the same Cyrillic characters as Serb (the Cyrillic alphabets used for Bulgarian, Russian, Ukrainian and Byelo-Russian are each slightly different from this), while Slovene is written exclusively in Latin characters.

RELIGION. On the basis of the constitution of Yugoslavia and the basic law on the legal status of religious communities, the religious communities are detached from the State and are free to perform religious affairs and religious rights. All religious communities, recognized by law, enjoy the same rights.

As the results of the historical development of the Yugoslav people, nowadays in Yugoslavia there are more than 30 religious communities. The 1953 percentage of the denominations was as follows: Orthodox, 41·2%; Roman Catholic, 31·7%; Moslems, 12·3%; Protestants, 0·9%; without religion, 12·6%. Accordingly, the greatest number of believers belong to the Orthodox Pravoslav churches, the Serbian Orthodox Church and the Macedonian Orthodox Church, then the Roman Catholic Church and the Moslem Religious Community.

The Serbian Orthodox Church with the Patriarch Mgr. Gherman with its seat in Belgrade has 20 bishoprics within the country and 4 abroad, 3 in US and Canada and 1 in Hungary. The Serbian Orthodox Church numbers about 2,000 priests.

The Macedonian Orthodox Church with the Archbishop of Ohrid and Macedonia with Mgr. Dositej as its head in Skopje, has four bishoprics in the country and one abroad (American–Canadian–Australian). The Macedonian Orthodox Church numbers about 300 priests.

The Roman Catholic Church is divided into two provinces: Zagreb with 4 suffragan sees, and Sarajevo with 2 suffragan sees. In addition, the Roman Catholic Church has 4 archbishoprics, 10 independent bishoprics directly connected with the Vatican and 3 Apostolic Administrators. There is a National Conference of Bishops with Archbishop, the cardinal of Zagreb, Mgr Franja Šeper as its head. The Roman Catholic Church has about 4,000 priests.

Diplomatic relations between Yugoslavia and the Vatican were broken off in 1952. However, with the protocol on talks between the Representatives of the Holy See and the government, on 25 June 1966 in Belgrade, the relations have been re-established on the basis of acknowledgment of the constitution and the basic law on the legal status of religious communities.

The Moslem Religious Union has 4 republic Superiorates in Sarajevo, Skopje, Titograd and Priština. The highest authority is the supreme synod of the Islamic Religious Community, which elects the Reis-ul-Ulema and the Supreme Islamic Superiorate. Its head is Mgr F. Kemura. The Moslem religious community has about 2,000 priests.

The Protestant churches covering 4 independent Lutheran Churches, numbering about 150,000 believers, the Reformed Christian Church, numbering about 60,000 believers, include also several much smaller churches of Baptists, Methodists, Adventists, Nazarenes, etc., numbering together about 100,000 believers. The Protestant churches have about 450 priests.

Also there are independent Old Catholic Churches with Synodal Council at Zagreb.

The Jewish religious community has about 35 communities making up a common league of Jewish Communities with its seat in Belgrade.

EDUCATION (1968–69). Elementary schools (4-year course and complementary schools (6- and 8-year courses), 14,048 with 113,908 teachers and 2,875,075 pupils; senior secondary schools, 411 with 9,683 teachers and 183,360 pupils; teachers' training colleges, 56 with 1,333 teachers and 27,233 students; technical schools, 791 with 14,606 teachers and 452,519 students; schools for adults, 575 with 3,002 teachers and 61,238 pupils.

For higher and specialized education there were 247 faculties, academies and high schools with 15,950 professors and instructors and 239,701 students.

The national minorities have been provided with elementary, secondary and teachers' training schools of their own, namely: Albanian (1,015, 27, 74), Magyar (221, 8, 48), Bulgarian (87, 1, 0), Czech (12, 1, 0), Slovak (32, 1, 1), Italian (29, 5, 2), Romanian (28, 1, 1), Turkish (56, 3, 5), Ruthenian (7, 0, 1).

CINEMAS (1969). There were 1,645 cinemas with a seating capacity of 541,993.

JUSTICE. There are county tribunals, district courts, the supreme court of the Autonomous Province of Vojvodina, supreme courts of the constituent republics and the supreme court of the Socialist Federal Republic of Yugoslavia. In county tribunals and district courts the judicial functions are exercised by professional judges and by lay assessors constituted into collegia. There are no assessors at the supreme courts.

All judges are elected by the social-political communities in their jurisdiction. The judges exercise their functions in accordance with the legal provisions enacted since the liberation of the country.

FINANCE. Currency. On 26 July 1965 the value of 1 *dinar*, divided into 100 *para*, was fixed at 0·710937 milligrammes of fine gold instead of 2·96224 milligrammes. On 24 Jan 1971 the dinar was devalued. The official exchange rate was established at 36 *dinars* to £ and 15 *dinars* to the US $.

A new *dinar*, equivalent of 100 old dinars, was introduced on 1 Jan. 1966.

The National Bank issues coins of 0·05, 0·1, 0·2, 0·5 and 1 new dinar, and notes of 5, 10, 50 and 100 new dinars. Coins and notes in old dinars are still in circulation.

Circulation of notes and coins, as of 31 Dec. 1968, was 9,584m. new dinars.

Budget. Revenue and expenditure for calendar years (in 1m. new dinars):

	1963	1964	1965[1]	1966[1]	1967	1968
Revenue	11,167	13,234	18,724	19,427	18,563[1]	20,429
Expenditure	10,994	12,674	18,802	19,133	18,426	20,167

[1] The figures from 1965 are not comparable with earlier ones due to the change-over of the financing from the system of budget expenditures to the system of resource distribution for the territorial communities.

The revenue, 1969 (and 1968), was composed of 10,752m. (10,829) dinars in the federal budget, 4,300m. (3,830) dinars in the states budgets and 6,802m. (5,771) dinars in other budgets.

Main items of distributed resources in 1969 (in 1m. new dinars): Defence, 6,277; education, 561; government, 4,530; contributions to territorial communities, 1,777; investments in economy, 934.

In 1949–50 the US Export-Import Bank granted loans amounting to $55m. at 3½% interest; the International Bank for Reconstruction and Development granted loans amounting to $60m. A British loan of £16·5m. granted in 1950 is to be repaid in 1962–67 at 3% interest. In 1955 the USSR advanced credits to the value of US$54m. and granted a loan of US$30m. at 2% interest.

Yugoslavia in 1960 resumed partial service on the sterling loans of 1909 and 1936; final settlement will be negotiated in 1967.

DEFENCE. Army. The Yugoslav Army comprises 8 army corps, of 13 infantry, 3 armoured and 6 mountain divisions. Peace-time strength, 220,000.

Navy. The Navy comprises 5 submarines, 3 destroyers, 2 small frigates, 100 torpedo boats, 1 minelayer, 3 patrol vessels, 4 coastal minesweepers, 17 patrol boats, 20 inshore minesweepers, 14 river minesweepers, 10 landing craft, a training ship, a salvage vessel, a yacht, a despatch vessel, 2 transports, 5 oilers and 6 tugs. Personnel in 1970: 27,000 officers and ratings.

Air Force. The Air Force has about 400 first-line aircraft and is organized in 2 Air Corps, with HQ at Zagreb and Zemun. There are 2 divisions of Russian-built MiG-21 (2 squadrons), MiG-19, Canadian-built Sabre Mk. 2 and 4 and F-86E Sabre jet interceptors, 2 ground-attack divisions of F-84 Thunderjet fighter-bombers (some being replaced by locally-built Jastreb light jet attack aircraft), locally-built Kraguj piston-engined light attack aircraft, and 2 squadrons of RT-33A jet reconnaissance aircraft. Transport units fly Russian Il-14 and American-built C-47 twin-engined aircraft and 4 ex-airline DC-6Bs. Apart from T-33A jet advanced trainers, training types are of national design, including the Galeb jet basic trainer. A number of Whirlwind and Mi-4 helicopters are in service. 'Guideline' surface-to-air missiles have been supplied by the USSR. Personnel numbers 20,000.

PLANNING. A 5-year plan of economic development was adopted on 6 July 1966, for 1966–70. Industrial production was to increase annually by 9–10%, and that of agriculture by 4·6%. A Danube–Tisa canal system is under construction. A 5-year plan for 1971–75 is being prepared.

AGRICULTURE. Yugoslavia, with a total area of 25,580,400 hectares, had a cultivated area of 10·2m. hectares in 1967. A law of 22 May 1953 limits private land holdings to 10 hectares and provides for expropriation of larger estates. Compensation of 30,000–100,000 dinars a hectare of expropriated land is to be paid over a period of 20 years.

Area (in hectares) and yield (in 1,000 metric rons) in 1969: Maize, 2·4m. (78); wheat, 2m. (4,880); barley, 0·3m. (299); rye, 0·12m. (135); tobacco, 53,896 (46); hemp, 16,450 (83); sunflower, 218,829 (390); potatoes, 330,000 (3,144).

Livestock, 15 Jan. 1970: 1·1m. horses, 5m. cattle, 8·9m. sheep, 5m. pigs.

The 1969 yield of fruit was as follows (in 1,000 metric tons): Apples, 485; pears, 111; grapes, 1,499; plums, 1,290; olives, 7; walnuts, 39; 7·1m. hectolitres of wine and 381,000 metric tons of sugar-beet were produced.

There were, on 31 Dec. 1969, 1,278 peasant co-operatives with (1968) 775,135 members, using 12,347 tractors and 1,927 threshing machines.

FORESTRY. The forest areas of Yugoslavia consist largely of beech, oak and fir. The timber cut in 1968 was 5m. cu. metres.

FISHERIES. In 1969 the landings of fish were 44,060 metric tons (salt-water, 27,100; freshwater, 16,960). The number of fishing craft was 193 motor vessels (7,190 GRT) and 2,141 sailing and rowing vessels.

MINING. Yugoslavia has considerable mineral resources, including coal (chiefly brown coal), iron, copper ore, gold, lead, chrome, antimony and cement. The most important iron mines are at Vareš and Ljubija in Bosnia, and there are also considerable siderite and limonite iron ores between Prijedor, Sanski Most and Topusko. Copper ore is exploited chiefly at Bor (Serbia). The principal lead mines are at Trepča and Mežice. Chrome mines are in southern Serbia (Kosovo) and Macedonia (Skopje, Kumanovo). There are 2 antimony mines in western Serbia (Podrinje).

Mining output, in 1,000 metric tons, in 1968 (and 1969): Coal, 835 (861); lignite, 25,897 (26,815); coke, 1,236 (1,226); bauxite, 2,072 (2,127); mercury, 0·5 (0·5); salt, 138 (146); manganese ore, 14 (12); iron ore, 2,720 (2,721); copper ore, 7,002 (8,715); lead and zinc ore, 2,693 (2,928); chrome ore, 4 (4); antimony ore, 109 (93); crude petroleum, 2,494 (2,699); pyrite concentrates, 274 (272); magnesite, 400 (477). In 1969, gold output was 2,615 kg; silver, 107,500 kg.

INDUSTRY. The majority of industries are situated in the north-west part of the country. Employees in nationalized industries numbered 1,356,386 in 1968, 1,398,404 in 1969.

Industrial output (in 1,000 metric tons) in 1968 (and 1969): Pig-iron, 1,201 (1,198); steel, 1,924 (2,047); cement, 3,765 (3,964); sulphuric acid, 589 (696); nitric acid, 340 (488); fertilizers, 1,645 (1,789); iron castings, 259 (306); steel castings, 32·1 (39·3). Fabrics (in 1m. sq. metres): Corron, 401 (415); woollen, 49 (49); rayon, 31 (30); hemp, 11·6 (19·9).

ELECTRICITY. Generation of electricity in 1968 (and 1967) was 20,641m. kwh. (18,702m.), of which 11,768m. kwh. (10,655m.) was hydro-electric.

TOURISM. In 1969, 4,746,000 (1968: 3,887,430) tourists visited Yugoslavia, spending an estimated 7,292·4m. (6,131m.) new dinars.

COMMERCE. Foreign trade, in 1m. new dinars, for calendar years:

	1965	1966	1967	1968	1970
Imports	16,099·4	19,692·9	21,341·7	22,460·2	26,672·1
Exports	13,643·8	15,251·0	15,645·8	15,796·3	18,730·9

Imports to Yugoslavia, 1969, in 1m. new dinars, from: West Germany, 4,858·9; Italy, 3,996·3; USSR, 2,102·3; Czechoslovakia, 1,498·3; USA, 1,155·;8 UK, 1,492·3. Exports from Yugoslavia, 1969, in 1m. new dinars, to: USSR, 2,580·1; Italy, 2,837; West Germany, 2,023·7; East Germany, 550·3; Czechoslovakia, 784·9.

The main imports (by value) in 1969 were (in 1m. new dinars): Machinery and metal products, 8,298; chemicals, 3,118; textiles, 2,962; iron and steel, 1,915; electro industry, 1,750. The main exports: Timber, 1,569; non-ferrous metals, 2,543; animals and animal produce, 2,220; machinery and metal products, 2,050.

Total trade between Yugoslavia and UK, in £1,000 sterling (British Board of Trade returns):

	1966	1967	1968	1969	1970
Imports to UK	13,298	15,670	23,535	24,799	21,725
Exports from UK	26,907	22,877	24,504	31,251 }	45,608
Re-exports from UK	447	229	488	528 }	

SHIPPING. In 1969 Yugoslavia possessed a total of 365 (1940: 210) vessels of 1·43m. (1940: 374,391) gross tons.

In 1969 vessels of 27m. net tons entered the ports of Yugoslavia.

In 1968 Yugoslavia had 1,262 river craft. The length of the navigable rivers amounted to 1,844 km, that of canals to 191 km. There are 2 navigable lakes: Skadarsko (391 sq. km, of which 243 in Yugoslavia) and Ohridsko (348 sq. km, of which 230 in Yugoslavia).

RAILWAYS. In 1969 Yugoslavia had 10,956 km (1930: 9,647) of railway, carrying 163,216m. passengers, 70,198m. metric tons of freight.

ROADS (1969). There were 21,744 km of asphalted roads and 42,304 km of macadamized roads. There were 562,509 passenger motor cars and 121,662 trucks and buses.

AVIATION. The national airline, Jugoslovenski Aero Transport (Adria-aviopromet, Pan-adria and Aviogenex) in 1969 flew on its home services, 5,823,000 km and carried 424,542 passengers and 975,000 ton-km of freight; international services (without Pan-adria), 16·3m. km, 645,436 passengers and 7·4 ton-km of freight. The chief airfields are Belgrade, Zagreb, Ljubljana, Sarajevo, Skopje, Dubrovnik, Split, Titograd Pula and Zadar.

POST (1969). There were 3,288 post offices, 622,939 telephone subscribers; 8 large and 73 small broadcasting stations. Number of wireless licences the end of 1969, was 3,220,000.

BANKING. All banking was nationalized immediately after the War, with the banks passing completely into the hands of the State. The main bank of the country is the National Bank. At 31 Dec. 1969 total credits for working assets amounted to 62,108m. new dinars. Savings deposits totalled 12,927m. new dinars at that date.

WEIGHTS AND MEASURES. The metric weights and measures have been in use since 1883. The *wagon* of 10 metric tons is used as a unit of measure for coal, roots and corn. The Gregorian calendar was adopted in 1919.

DIPLOMATIC REPRESENTATIVES

Yugoslavia maintains embassies in:

Afghánistán	Ghana	Pakistan
Algeria	Greece	Peru
Argentine	Guiana	Poland
Australia	Guinea	Romania
Austria	Hungary	Senegal
Belgium	India	Somalia
Bolivia	Indonesia	Southern Yemen
Brazil	Iran	Sudan
Bulgaria	Iraq	Sweden
Burma	Italy	Switzerland
Burundi	Japan	Syria
Cambodia	Kenya	Tanzania
Cameroun	Kuwait	Togo
Canada	Laos	Tunisia
Ceylon	Lebanon	Turkey
Chile	Liberia	Uganda
China	Libya	USSR
Cuba	Mali	UAR
Cyprus	Mauritania	UK
Czechoslovakia	Malta	USA
Denmark	Mexico	Uruguay
Ethiopia	Mongolia	Vatican
Finland	Morocco	Venezuela
France	Netherlands	Zambia
Germany (East)	Nigeria	
Germany (West)	Norway	

Yugoslavia also maintains legations in:

Albania	Ivory Coast	Paraguay
Congo (K.)	Jamaica	Thailand
Costa Rica	Jordan	Yemen
Ecuador	Luxembourg	Vietnam
Honduras	Nepál	
Iceland	Panama	

OF YUGOSLAVIA IN GREAT BRITAIN (25 Kensington Gore, SW7)

Ambassador: Dobrivoje Vidlć.
Minister: Vojislav DAIC. *Counsellors:* Svetozar Marković (*Economic*); Milan Lupán (*Press and Cultural Affairs*). *Defence Attaché:* Col. Svetozar Oro.

OF GREAT BRITAIN IN YUGOSLAVIA

Ambassador: Sir Terence Garvey, KCMG.
Counsellors: W. Bentley; P. McKearney (*Commercial*).
First Secretaries: T. J. Clark (*Information*); K. H. M. Duke; D. M. Harrison (*First Secretary and Consul*); G. C. Gullan (*Commercial*); D. A. Garton. *Service Attachés:* Col. C. M. Moir, OBE (*Defence and Army*), Wing Cdr D. O. Luke (*Navy and Air*).

There are consular representatives at Zagreb (C.G.), Belgrade and Split.

OF YUGOSLAVIA IN THE USA (2410 California St. NW, Washington, D.C., 20008)

Ambassador: Bogdan Crnobrnja.
Minister: Mirko Bruner. *Counsellors:* Cvijeto Job (*Press and Culture*); Dušan Ljubojevic (*Consular and Legal*). *First Secretaries:* Živko Knežević, Miss Mira Jovanovic. *Service Attaché:* Col. Jovan D. Kokot (*Army, Navy* and *Air*).

OF THE USA IN YUGOSLAVIA

Ambassador: William Leonhart.
Deputy Chief of Mission: Thomas O. Enders. *Heads of Sections:* Robert C.
Mudd (*Political*); Raymond J. Albright (*Economic and Commercial*); Robert I.
Miller (*Consular*).
Service Attachés: Col. Leland B. Fair (*Army*), Cdr Robert T. Frankenfield
(*Navy*), Lieut.–Col. Jason J. Carlisle (Air).

There is a Consul-General at Zagreb.

BOOKS OF REFERENCE

STATISTICAL INFORMATION. The Federal Institute for Statistics (Kneza Miloša 20, Belgrade)
was founded in Dec. 1944 and constituted in Jan. 1948; it was reorganized as the Federal Statistical
Institute in May 1951. *Director:* Ibrahim Latifić. It publishes: *Index* (from April 1952, with
English and French translations); *Statistički Biltea* (1950 ff., with English or French translations);
Statistical Yearbook (from 1954, with English, Russian and French translations); *Statistics of
Foreign Trade of the SFR Yugoslavia* (annual, from 1946; half-yearly, from 1951); *Statistical
Pocket-book* (from 1955; in 5 eds.: Yugoslav, English, French, Russian, German).

The Constitution of the SFR of Yugoslavia. Belgrade, 1963
Auty, P., *Yugoslavia.* New York, 1965
Bogadek, F. A., *English–Croatian, Croatian–English Dictionary.* London, 1950
Clissold, S., *A short history of Yugoslavia.* CUP, 1966
Dedijer, V., *Tito speaks.* London, 1953
Djordjević, J., *La Yougoslavie, démocratie socialiste.* Paris, 1959
Hoffman, G. W., and Neal, F. W., *Yugoslavia and the New Communism.* New York, 1962
Kotnik, J., *Slovensko–angleški slovar.* 4th ed. Ljubljana, 1959
Maclean, F., *Disputed Barricade: The Life and times of Josip Broz-Tito.* London, 1957
Mellen, M., and Winston, V. H., *The Coal Resources of Yugoslavia.* New York, 1956
Ristić, Simić, Popović: *An English–Serbocroatian Dictionary.* 2 vols. Belgrade, 1956
Skerlj, R., *English-Slovene Dictionary.* 4th ed. Ljubljana, 1957

NATIONAL LIBRARY. Narodna biblioteka, 56 Knez Mihailova, Belgrade. *Director:* Svetislav
Djurić.

INDEX

INDEX

1507

LL

Tobacco, product of:
— Fiji, 519
— France, 922
— Germany, 991
— Ghana, 412
— Greece, 1005, 1007
— Guatemala, 1012
— Haiti, 1019
— Honduras, 1023
— India, 348
— — Gujarat, 359
— — Mysore, 369
— — Orissa, 372
— Indonesia, 1043–44
— Iran, 1051
— Israel, 1083
— Italy, 1095
— Japan, 1106
— Korea, South, 1117
— Laos, 1130
— Libya, 1144
— Madagascar, 946
— Malawi, 477
— Mauritius, 510
— Mexico, 1156
— Nicaragua, 1196
— Nigeria, 432
— Oman, 1214
— Paraguay, 1225–26
— Philippines, 1247
— Réunion, 931
— Rhodesia, 525–26
— Ryukyu Is., 720
— S. Africa, 1302
— Spain, 1327–28
— Swaziland, 513
— Switzerland, 1361
— Syria, 1368
— Tanzania, 473
— Thailand, 1373
— Turkey, 1388, 1390
— Uganda, 464, 473
— USA, 565–66, 572
— — Connecticut, 605
— — Florida, 610
— — Georgia, 612
— — Indiana, 622
— — Kentucky, 628
— — Maryland, 636
— — Massachusetts, 638
— — North Carolina, 667
— — Pacific Is. (USA), 720
— — Pennsylvania, 680
— — Puerto Rico, 712
— — South Carolina, 685
— — Tennessee, 689
— — Virginia, 699
— — Wisconsin, 707
— USSR, Abhazia, 1438
— — Azerbaijan, 1434
— — Georgia, 1437
— — Kazakhstan, 1449
— — Kirghizia, 1458
— — Moldavia, 1442
— — Nahichevan, 1435
— — Ukraine, 1430
— Venezuela, 1480
— Vietnam, 1488
— Yugoslavia, 1501
— Zambia, 486
— Zanzibar, 452
Tobago (W. Indies), 462
Tobruk (Libya), 1144–45
Tocumen (Pan.), 1219
Togliatti (USSR), 1399
Togo, 907, 961–62
Tokaj (Hungary), 1030
Tokat (Turkey), 1384
Tokelau Is. (NZ), 323–24
Tokmak (USSR), 1457

Toktogul (USSR), 1413
Tokushima (Japan), 1103
Tōkyō (Japan), 15, 1102–04, 1108–10
Tolbuhin (Bulg.), 787
Toledo (Ohio), 543, 671
Toledo (Spain), 1322–23
Tolgoyt (Mongolia), 1164
Tolima (Colom.), 829, 832
Tolna (Hungary), 1028
Tolnea (Mex.), 1153
Toluca (Mex.), 1153
Tomar (Port.), 1262
Tombouctou (Mali), 959
Tomsk (USSR), 1399, 1401, 1416, 1420
Tonawanda (N.Y.), 664
Tondano (Indon.), 1041
Tonga (Pacific), 515–17
Tongareva (Cook Is.), 324
Tongatapu (Tonga), 515
Tongoa (New Hebr.), 161
Tongsa (Bhután), 768
Tønsberg (Norway), 1212
Toowoomba (Queensld.), 235, 285
Topeka (Kans.), 543, 625–26
Topusko (Yug.), 1501
Torbay (UK), 70
Torkham (Afghán.), 728–29
Toro (Uganda), 463
Toronto (Ont.), 179, 190, 214–15
Torrance (Calif.), 543, 598
Torrejon (Spain), 1325
Torreón (Mex.), 1153
Torres Is. (Pacific), 156
Torrington (Conn.), 604
Torrington (Wyo.), 709
Tortola (Br. Virgin Is.), 167
Toruń (Poland), 1252
Toscana (Italy), 1090
Tosk, see Vlorë
Totonicapán (Guat.), 1010
Touba (Senegal), 949
Toulon (France), 912, 920
Toulouse (France), 912, 914–15
Tournai (Belgium), 760
Tours (France), 912
Tower Hamlets (UK), 72
Tower Hill (Vic.), 278
Townsville (Queensld.), 235, 285
Toyama (Japan), 1103
Toyohashi (Japan), 1103
Toyonaka (Japan), 1103
Trabzon (Turkey), 1384–85, 1389, 1391
Trail (B.C.), 225
Trakya (Turkey), 1384
Transcona (Man.), 217
Transjordan, see Jordan
Transkei (Cape), 1295, 1298
Transvaal (S. Afr.), 1293, 1295, 1299, 1301
Transylvania (Romania), 1276, 1279, 1311–13
Traralgon (Vic.), 279
Traun (Austria), 752
Travancore-Cochin (India), 334, 352–53
Traza (Mauritania), 955
Treasury (Br. Solomon Is.), 160
Treinta-y-Tres (Urug.), 1469
Trelawny (Jamaica), 455
Trelew (Argen.), 750
Trelleborg (Sweden), 1342
Trengganu (Malaya), 415, 418–19
Trent (Italy), 1090
Trentino (Italy), 1089–91
Trento (Italy), 1090, 1093
Trenton (N.J.), 543, 658
Trepča (Yug.), 1501
Triangle (Rhodesia), 525
Trier (Germ.), 966, 991
Trieste (Italy), 13, 1090–91, 1093, 1100
Trikkala (Greece), 1002
Trincomalee (Ceylon), 401, 405